E. **Comparability:** Enables users to identify and explain similarities and differences between two (or more) items of information. Includes *Consistency*: Conformity of information from period to period.

F. **Constraints:** Limits to help identify useful accounting information. Includes (1) *Benefits Greater Than Costs*: Benefits obtained by users of information must be greater than costs of providing information, and (2) *Materiality*: Monetary impact of the information must be large enough to make a difference in decision making (*quantitative constraint*).

V. ACCOUNTING ASSUMPTIONS AND CONVENTIONS

A. **Entity:** Information is recorded and reported about each separate economic entity (company).

B. **Continuity (Going Concern):** Company is assumed to continue future operations, unless substantial contrary evidence exists.

C. **Period of Time:** Information is reported in a company's financial statements at least on an annual basis.

D. **Historical Cost:** Generally, exchange price is retained in the accounting records as the value of an item until it is consumed, sold, or liquidated and removed from records.

E. **Monetary Unit:** National currency of company is used as stable unit of measure in preparing financial reports.

F. **Realization:** Process of converting noncash resources into cash or rights to cash.

G. **Recognition:** Process of formally recording and reporting an item in a company's financial statements.

H. **Accrual Accounting:** Process of relating financial effects of trans nts, and circumstances having cash consequences to the period in which they occu n the cash receipt or payment occurs.

I. **Prudence (Conservatism):** Process of ensuring, to ev s and risks related to a company are reflected in its accounting i

VI. GENERALLY ACCEPTED ACCOUNTING PRINC (GAAP)

A. **Definition:** Guidelines, procedures, and practices that a company is required to use in recording and reporting the accounting information in its audited financial statements.

B. **Sources:** (in descending order of importance)
1. Pronouncements of authoritative bodies (FASB, APB, CAP, SEC); e.g., FASB *Statements of Financial Accounting Standards and Interpretations*, APB *Opinions*, and CAP (AICPA) *Accounting Research Bulletins* (and SEC *Regulation S-X* and *Financial Reporting Releases* for companies that file with the SEC).
2. Pronouncements of bodies of expert accountants that have been exposed for public comment; e.g., FASB *Technical Bulletins*, AICPA *Industry Audit and Accounting Guides*, and AICPA *Statements of Position*.
3. Pronouncements of bodies of expert accountants that have not been exposed for public comment; e.g., FASB EITF *Consensus Positions* and AICPA *Practice Bulletins*.
4. Widely accepted practices and pronouncements representing prevalent practice in a particular industry or applications to specific circumstances, e.g., AICPA *Accounting Interpretations*, FASB *Q's and A's*, and AICPA *Accounting Trends and Techniques*.
5. Other accounting literature; e.g., FASB *Statements of Financial Accounting Concepts*, APB *Statements*, AICPA *Issue Papers*, AICPA *Technical Practice Aids*, and accounting texts and articles.

(Continued on inside back cover)

NINTH EDITION
INTERMEDIATE ACCOUNTING

LOREN A. NIKOLAI

**ERNST & YOUNG PROFESSOR, SCHOOL OF ACCOUNTANCY,
UNIVERSITY OF MISSOURI-COLUMBIA**

JOHN D. BAZLEY

**PROFESSOR, SCHOOL OF ACCOUNTANCY,
UNIVERSITY OF DENVER**

Australia · Canada · Mexico · Singapore · Spain · United Kingdom · United States

Intermediate Accounting, 9e

Loren A. Nikolai and John D. Bazley

Editor-in-Chief:
Jack W. Calhoun

Team Leader:
Melissa S. Acuña

Acquisitions Editor:
Sharon Oblinger

Developmental Editor:
Erin McGraw

Marketing Manager:
Keith Chassé

Production Editor:
Amy A. Brooks

Manufacturing Coordinator:
Doug Wilke

Compositor:
Techbooks

Printer:
Quebecor World Taunton
Taunton, MA

Design Project Manager:
Bethany Casey

Internal Designer:
Michael H. Stratton and Bethany Casey

Cover Designer:
Bethany Casey

Cover Image:
Photodisk, Inc.

Library of Congress Cataloging-in-Publication Data
Nikolai, Loren A.
Intermediate accounting / Loren A. Nikolai,
John D. Bazley. — 9th ed.
p. cm.
Includes index.
ISBN 0-324-30412-9
1. Accounting. I. Bazley, John D. II. Title.

HF5635 .N6924 2004
657'.044—dc21   2002030496
ISBN: 0-324-30412-9

ABOUT THE AUTHORS

LOREN A. NIKOLAI

Loren Nikolai is the Ernst & Young Professor and Director of Masters Programs in the School of Accountancy at the University of Missouri-Columbia (MU). He received his B.A. and M.B.A. from St. Cloud State University, and his Ph.D. from the University of Minnesota. Professor Nikolai has taught at the University of Wisconsin at Platteville and at the University of North Carolina at Chapel Hill. Professor Nikolai is the recipient of the University of Missouri system-wide 1999 Presidential Award for Outstanding Teaching, the MU Alumni Association 1996 Faculty Award, the MU College of Business and Public Administration 1994 Accounting Professor of the Year Award, the Missouri Society of CPAs 1993 Outstanding Accounting Educator of the Year Award, the MU 1992 Kemper Fellowship for Teaching Excellence, the MU College of Business and Public Administration 1991 Faculty Member of the Year Award, the St. Cloud State University 1990 Distinguished Alumni Award, and the Federation of Schools of Accountancy 1989 Faculty Award of Merit, as well as the corecipient of the 1997 Holstein Creativity Award. He holds a CPA certificate in the state of Missouri and previously worked for the 3M Company. Professor Nikolai is a coauthor of *Accounting Information for Business Decisions*, Second Edition textbook (South-Western).

Professor Nikolai has published numerous articles in *The Accounting Review*, *Journal of Accounting Research*, *The Accounting Educator's Journal*, *Journal of Accounting Education*, *The CPA Journal*, *Management Accounting*, *Policy Analysis*, *Academy of Management Journal*, *Journal of Business Research*, and other professional journals. He was also lead author of a monograph published by the National Association of Accountants. Professor Nikolai is a member of the American Accounting Association, the American Institute of Certified Public Accountants (AICPA), and the Missouri Society of CPAs (MSCPA). He has served on the AICPA's Accounting and Auditing Practice Analysis Task Force Panel and the Accounting Careers Subcommittee; he has also served on the MSCPA's Relations with Educators, Accounting Careers, and Accounting and Auditing Committees. Professor Nikolai has chaired or served on numerous Federation of Schools of Accountancy (FSA) and American Accounting Association (AAA) committees, was AAA Director of Education for 1985–1987, and was President of the FSA for 1994. Professor Nikolai is married and has two adult children and three grandsons. His family has three cats, and he is an avid basketball player and weight lifter.

JOHN D. BAZLEY

John D. Bazley, Ph.D., CPA, is Professor of Accountancy in the School of Accountancy of the Daniels College of Business at the University of Denver, where he has received the University 1990 Distinguished Teaching Award, the Vernon Loomis Award for Excellence in Advising, the Alumni Award for Faculty Excellence, the Jerome Kesselman Endowment Award for Excellence in Research, and the 1995 Cecil Puckett Award of the Daniels College of Business. Professor Bazley earned a B.A. from the University of Bristol in England and an M.S. and Ph.D. from the University of Minnesota. He has taught at the University of North Carolina at Chapel Hill and holds a CPA certificate in the state of Colorado. He has taught national professional development classes for a major CPA firm and was consultant for another CPA firm. Professor Bazley is a coauthor of *Accounting Information for Business Decisions*, Second Edition textbook (South-Western).

Professor Bazley has published articles in professional journals, including *The Accounting Review, Management Accounting, Accounting Horizons, Practical Accountant, Academy of Management Journal, The Journal of Managerial Issues, The International Journal of Accounting,* and the *Journal of Accounting Education.* He is also a coauthor of a monograph on environmental accounting published by the National Association of Accountants. Professor Bazley has served on numerous committees of the Federation of Schools of Accountancy, including chair of the Student Lyceum Committee; the American Accounting Association; and the Colorado Society of CPAs, including the Continuing Professional Education Board. He is a member of the American Institute of Certified Public Accountants, the Colorado Society of CPAs, and the American Accounting Association. Professor Bazley is married and has two children, who especially enjoy their three cats and two dogs. He enjoys skiing, playing golf, car racing, and listening to jazz.

PREFACE

Known for its balanced coverage of both concepts and procedures, *Intermediate Accounting* gives students an unparalleled look at financial accounting information and its increasingly varied uses in the world today. This timely ninth edition skillfully imparts essential knowledge and skills through compelling real-world financial statements and research cases—all in a student-friendly format. The "hands-on" approach vividly helps students make the connection between classroom exercises and business-world procedures. *Intermediate Accounting*, Ninth Edition's up-to-date content and carefully designed pedagogy make it the most effective book in relating the current intermediate accounting body of knowledge. In addition, the ancillary package accompanying *Intermediate Accounting* is extensive. Both students and instructors will benefit from the range of carefully developed supplemental materials.

From Internet assignments, to ethical dilemmas, to financial statements from real companies, *Intermediate Accounting* gives students a strong foundation on which to build an understanding of, and appreciation for, today's accounting needs and practices.

Intermediate Accounting, Ninth Edition consists of five parts containing 22 chapters, as follows:

Part 1   Financial Reporting: Concepts, Financial Statements, and Related Disclosures
(Chapters 1–5)

Part 2   Financial Reporting: Asset Measurement and Income Determination
(Chapters 6–11)

Part 3   Financial Reporting: Valuation of Liabilities and Investments
(Chapters 12–14)

Part 4   Financial Reporting: Stockholders' Equity
(Chapters 15–16)

Part 5   Financial Reporting: Special Topics
(Chapters 17–22)

MAJOR CONTENT FEATURES

Each chapter features essential content and helpful pedagogy that bring accounting principles and procedures into the students' realm of experience and understanding. Moving beyond teaching just technical skills, *Intermediate Accounting* makes even the most complex procedures accessible to students without sacrificing depth of coverage.

1. *ENVIRONMENT OF ACCOUNTING.* Chapter 1 takes students on an exploration of the current environment of financial reporting. An explanation of capital markets (Exhibit 1-1), external users' decision making, and the hierarchy of generally accepted accounting principles (Exhibit 1-4) are all discussed. Students will also find a discussion of the various organizations that influence GAAP and their interrelationship (Exhibit 1-8).

2. *FASB CONCEPTUAL FRAMEWORK.* Students are introduced to the "conceptual framework" in Chapter 2. This discussion involves an identification and explanation of the objectives of financial reporting (Exhibit 2-3) and the qualitative characteristics of useful accounting information (Exhibit 2-5). The chapter also includes an explanation of the interrelationship between financial reports,

types of useful information, and external decision making (Exhibit 2-4), as well as a framework of financial accounting theory and practice (Exhibit 2-6). A quick review of the concepts underlying financial accounting is provided in the *Conceptual Reference Guide*, located inside the front and back covers of the book.

3. *ASSETS AND LIABILITY CONCEPTS, DEFINITIONS, AND MEASUREMENT.* Because the FASB defines revenues and expenses in terms of changes in assets and liabilities, students need a clear understanding of asset and liability concepts and definitions as well as alternative measurement approaches (e.g., current cost, current market value). We introduce the topics in Chapter 3. We reinforce and expand the concept and definition of liabilities later in Chapter 12, which is the first of two chapters on liabilities.

4. *REVENUE AND EXPENSE RECOGNITION.* Students get a thorough understanding of the importance of the income statement in Chapter 4, as well as the related conceptual and practical issues. We introduce the concept of capital maintenance and contrast this concept to the transactional approach to measuring income, including the concept of *comprehensive income*. We identify conceptual reporting guidelines and revenue and discuss expense recognition criteria. We give a brief exposure to the alternative revenue recognition methods in Chapter 4 and a complete discussion in Chapter 17.

5. *PROCEDURAL DISCUSSION.* For each topic, students will find a clear and concise discussion of the related generally accepted accounting principles. We enhance the discussion with a thorough explanation and illustration of the corresponding practices and procedures.

6. *CONCEPTUAL DISCUSSION.* Supported by the FASB conceptual framework introduced in Chapter 2, in later chapters we relate the discussion of specific topics to the objectives of financial reporting, qualitative characteristics of accounting information, and conceptual reporting guidelines, and to the concepts of liquidity, financial flexibility, risk, operating capability, and return on investment. Where there are significant conceptual issues concerning an accounting principle, we provide an objective discussion of the alternative views. Icons are included in the margins to identify these discussions. This integrated discussion of accounting theory is not at the expense of sound, procedural pedagogy, and we emphasize a balanced presentation of concepts to practice.

7. *ACTUAL FINANCIAL REPORTING.* We include excerpts from the actual annual reports of many companies to illustrate the proper disclosure for various topics and help students appreciate the immediate relevance of classroom work to real-world accounting practice. Appendix A contains the financial reporting section of the 2001 annual report of The Coca-Cola Company.

8. *TIMELY COVERAGE OF ETHICS.* In response to the need for students to be more aware of ethical issues in the accounting environment, we provide a complete section on this topic in Chapter 1. Through the use of cases dealing with ethical dilemmas, found throughout the text, students can think through problems they may encounter on the job.

9. *ESSENTIAL CREATIVE AND CRITICAL THINKING COVERAGE.* Due to the increased emphasis on enhancing students' abilities to think creatively and critically in the accounting environment, we include a section on these topics in Chapter 1. Clearly marked creative and/or critical thinking cases appear at the ends of chapters.

10. *COMPREHENSIVE INTERNATIONAL COVERAGE.* Due to the increased "globalization" of business, most chapters include a brief discussion of the differences between U.S. GAAP and international accounting principles for the chapter topics. We designate international topic discussions with an icon.

11. *CONCEPTUAL AND ANALYTICAL ICONS.* To increase students' awareness of conceptual issues, you will find a large "conceptual icon" in the margin beside each section discussing the concepts related to a particular topic. You will also find a large "analysis" icon in the margin beside each section discussing analytical issues related to a particular topic. For the same reason, we have used a smaller

"conceptual icon" and a smaller "analysis icon" in the margin beside conceptual and analytical issues imbedded in the technical discussions of various topics.

MAJOR PEDAGOGICAL FEATURES

Intermediate Accounting's carefully designed pedagogy engages students while it conveys essential skills, procedures, and practices. With more illustrations, flowcharts, and exhibits than ever before, the ninth edition attains an unparalleled level of pedagogical effectiveness. Some of the major pedagogical features of the chapters are:

1. *CLEAR OBJECTIVES.* Objectives at the beginning of each chapter prepare students for what they will be learning. We list each objective in the margin beside the topical coverage to reinforce students' learning.
2. *AN EMPHASIS ON IMPORTANT ELEMENTS.* We present key terms, concepts, definitions, and official statements in **boldface**. To illustrate their importance, we show particularly important information in *italics*. Frequent use of illustrations of journal entries, supporting schedules, and financial statements clarifies concepts or procedures. Margin notes help students cross-reference information with discussions in other chapters.
3. *ILLUSTRATIVE FLOWCHARTS AND DIAGRAMS.* The use of flowcharts and diagrams helps students visualize the concepts and procedures. For instance, Chapter 9 includes a flowchart for similar productive asset exchanges (Exhibit 9-2), Chapter 16 includes a flowchart for earnings per share (Exhibit 16-4), and Chapter 20 includes a diagram for classifying leases (Exhibit 20-3).
4. *CLARIFYING COMPUTATIONAL STEPS.* Because complex computations can be hard for students to master, we reduce many computational procedures to a series of steps outlined in list format. For instance, Exhibit 7-13 includes a series of steps for dollar-value LIFO calculations. Similar lists of steps for the gross profit inventory method, retail inventory method, and dollar-value LIFO retail method appear in Chapter 8. We include other computational steps where appropriate throughout the rest of the book.
5. *HELPFUL SUMMARY EXHIBITS.* Summary exhibits throughout the text help students pull together and understand what they have learned so far. For instance, Exhibit 4-13 summarizes corporate earnings and cash flow topics, Exhibit 20-2 summarizes the criteria and classifications for leases, and Exhibit 22-8 summarizes the impacts on financial statements of the methods used for accounting changes and errors.
6. *BACK-TO-BACK COVERAGE OF LONG-TERM LIABILITIES AND INVESTMENTS.* Due to the reciprocal nature of accounting for certain liabilities and assets (i.e., bonds payable and investments in held-to-maturity bonds, notes payable and notes receivable), we present these topics in back-to-back coverage in Chapters 13 and 14. This facilitates the students' understanding of these complex issues.
7. *FLEXIBILITY IN COVERAGE.* Since instructors have different ways of teaching, certain chapters are written to allow flexibility in reading assignments. For example, some instructors may prefer acceleration of the coverage of Chapter 17 on revenue recognition to correspond with the discussion of the income statement in Chapter 4. Others may prefer an earlier assignment of Chapter 21 on the statement of cash flows because of the importance of this financial statement.
8. *COMPREHENSIVE CHAPTER SUMMARIES.* Each chapter ends with a summary of the key points for each major topic. These summaries provide students with a quick review of the important topical issues.

MAJOR CHANGES

Since the first edition, *Intermediate Accounting* has been praised for its ability to convey to students a desire to further explore the dynamics of accounting. Now with this ninth edition, the pedagogy is further refined, the content is updated to reflect several significant changes in accounting principles, and the book's overall user-friendliness is enhanced. The major changes are:

1. *UP-TO-DATE FASB COVERAGE.* We have included detailed coverage of the latest FASB statements through **FASB Statement No. 147.** As new statements are issued, we will provide timely updates at our Web site, http://nikolai.swcollege.com.

2. *IASC CONCEPTUAL FRAMEWORK.* Because of the continuing globalization of companies, we added a discussion of the International Accounting Standards Board's *Framework for the Preparation and Presentation of Financial Statements.* This Framework provides the conceptual underpinning for the international accounting standards that we discuss in later chapters.

3. *INTERNATIONAL ACCOUNTING STANDARDS.* We modified the discussion of international accounting standards in many chapters to expand the discussion and bring it up to date. We reduced the discussion of accounting principles in specific countries because of the increasing harmonization of international standards.

4. *RESULTS OF DISCONTINUED OPERATIONS.* We modified the discussion related to reporting the results from the discontinuance of a component of a company in accordance with **FASB Statements No. 144** and **146.** This discussion includes the accounting for a component that is considered "held for sale." The discussion also includes illustrations of what is and is not a sale of a component.

5. *EXTINGUISHMENT OF DEBT.* We modified the discussion of reporting a gain or loss on the extinguishment of debt in accordance with **FASB Statement No. 145.** In Chapters 4 and 13, we explain that a company reports this type of gain or loss in its income from continuing operations and not as an extraordinary item. We also modified the discussion of gains and losses on troubled-debt restructurings in a similar manner.

6. *TRANSFERS OF RECEIVABLES.* The discussion in Chapter 6 of pledging, assigning, and factoring of receivables incorporates the new requirements of **FASB Statement No. 140.**

7. *INVENTORIES.* We added Exhibit 8-15 to help students understand the relationships among the inventory topics (e.g., inventory systems, costing methods, and LCM) discussed in Chapters 7 and 8.

8. *ASSET RETIREMENT OBLIGATIONS.* We added a new section to Chapter 9 that deals with accounting for asset retirement obligations (e.g., recording a liability for a power plant when the plant is acquired) in accordance with **FASB Statement No. 143.**

9. *IMPAIRMENT OF NONCURRENT ASSETS.* We updated the discussion of the impairment of property, plant, and equipment in Chapter 10 (and of intangibles with a finite life in Chapter 11) in accordance with **FASB Statement No. 144.**

10. *INTANGIBLES.* We completely revised Chapter 11 (and modified the discussion in Chapter 3) to incorporate the new accounting principles for intangibles set out in **FASB Statement No. 142.** The discussion includes an explanation of accounting for intangible assets with finite useful lives, intangible assets with indefinite lives, and goodwill. In Chapter 14, we also modified the discussion of accounting for investments under the equity method because of the elimination of goodwill amortization.

11. *PROPOSED GAAP.* In Chapter 13, we added a section at the end of the chapter dealing with two Exposure Drafts. If adopted, the Exposure Drafts would change the accounting for the issuance of convertible bonds and the accounting for certain guarantees.

12. *STOCK OPTIONS.* In Chapter 17, we expanded the discussion of the intrinsic value method of accounting for stock option plans by providing an example for when the option price is less than the market price at the date of grant.

13. *ACCOUNTING FOR CHANGES IN PRICES.* We moved the appendix to Chapter 17 dealing with the concepts and procedures underlying the alternative methods of accounting for changing prices and created a new Appendix E at the end of the book. This adjustment shortens Chapter 17 and provides a free-standing discussion of this topic.

14. *DEFERRED INCOME TAXES.* In Chapter 18, we added Exhibits 18-6 and 18-8. Exhibit 18-6 clarifies the relationship between an asset's book value and the related deferred tax liability. Exhibit 18-8 clarifies the relationship between a liability's book value and the related deferred tax asset.

15. *PENSIONS WORKSHEET.* In Chapter 19, we added a worksheet for students to use to compute a company's pension expense and the related journal entry. The worksheet also provides students with information about a company's projected benefit obligation and plan asset amounts for disclosures in the notes to the company's financial statements.

16. *PRESENT VALUE.* We updated Appendix D for the impact of **FASB Statement of Financial Accounting Concepts No. 7.** This Statement of Concepts provides a framework for using future cash flows as the basis for determining the value of various assets and liabilities.

17. *TECHNICAL DISCUSSION.* We thoroughly reviewed the discussion and examples of technical procedures and have modified them where necessary to clarify the explanations.

18. *READABILITY.* To improve the book's user-friendliness, much of the discussion is in the active voice. Where appropriate, we have shortened sentences and simplified wording without changing the content or meaning of any discussion.

END-OF-CHAPTER FEATURES

1. *ABUNDANT END-OF-CHAPTER ASSIGNMENTS.* The text's extensive end-of-chapter materials allow students to test their understanding, as well as discover where they may need improvement. Questions primarily address key concepts and terms in the chapter. Cases focus on the various conceptual and reporting issues within the chapter. Each Exercise reinforces a chapter topic at a relatively elementary level. The Problems either consolidate a number of chapter topics or focus on a comprehensive analysis of a single topic. After Chapter 1, each chapter contains ten multiple-choice items (and selected cases, exercises, and problems) based on past Uniform CPA Examination questions. The book features a boldfaced title beside each case, exercise, and problem number to indicate the subject content.

2. *CLASSIFICATION OF CASES.* In accordance with the Accounting Education Change Commission recommendations about improving certain skills of students, we present cases at the end of each chapter in three sections. The Communication section includes cases designed to help students improve their written communication skills. The Creative and Critical Thinking section includes cases designed to help students improve their thinking skills. Where applicable, a Research section helps students develop their researching GAAP skills.

3. *ETHICS CASES.* We include cases dealing with ethical and financial reporting issues in each chapter. Students should develop solutions from financial reporting and ethical perspectives.

4. *ANALYSIS OF COCA-COLA'S FINANCIAL STATEMENTS.* To give students insight into real-world financial reporting, several cases require students to review selected portions of the Coca-Cola Company's annual report (in Appendix A). These cases enhance critical-thinking skills as they require students to answer user-oriented and financial reporting questions related to the chapter topics.

5. *RESEARCHING GAAP.* "Researching GAAP" cases, found in most chapters, help students become more familiar with how to find generally accepted accounting principles that are applicable to a given topic. We designed the cases to be used with the *FASB Current Text* or *Original Pronouncements*.

6. *USER-ORIENTED HOMEWORK.* For selected exercises and problems, you will find questions that require students to develop answers from a user-oriented perspective.

7. *INTERNET ASSIGNMENTS.* The Internet homework assignments at the end of each chapter encourage students to make full use of information that can be found on the Web. These assignments require students to answer questions based on a company's most current financial statements located on South-Western College

Publishing's Web site or in the SEC's EDGAR system. In many cases, students must analyze the disclosures from an external user's perspective.

8. *REVISION OF HOMEWORK ASSIGNMENTS.* In addition to the cases and user-oriented questions, we have changed the numbers and solutions in over 50 percent of the previous homework assignments. We have also changed the company names in selected homework items.

A COMPLETE TEACHING AND LEARNING PACKAGE

Intermediate Accounting's ancillary package is comprised of a comprehensive set of teaching and learning tools that are as carefully developed as the book itself. From print-based supplements to electronic study aids, you're sure to find top-quality support in this package.

1. *STUDY GUIDE*

   With a list of objectives, a synopsis of each chapter, self-evaluation exercises, and a set of post-tests with accompanying answers, this essential guide reinforces student understanding. The enhancement of selected topics will enrich students' learning experience and assist them in studying the material. The *Study Guide* now includes check figures of key answers to all text exercises and problems. Prepared by Natalie Krawitz, Vice-President of Finance, University of Missouri-Columbia; Theodora Arthur, Harry C. Winfrey CPA Firm; and Loren A. Nikolai, University of Missouri-Columbia.

2. *WORKING PAPERS*

   This two-volume set contains pre-set-up forms for the problem assignments. This saves students time as they complete each problem.

3. *EXCEL™ TEMPLATES*

   The main text contains selected problems that are to be solved using these templates. Each template assignment is designated by an icon. The solutions are available free to all students at our website http://nikolai.swcollege.com. To access the templates, students should go to the text site, click on Student Resources, and choose the Excel Template needed.

4. *WEB SITE*

   This helpful Internet site provides resources to both students and instructors. For the student, it contains links to the resources needed to answer the Internet assignments in the text, the *PowerPoint™ Presentation* slides, interactive quizzing which reviews key points in each chapter, Excel™ Templates, and links to many accounting-related resources. For instructors, the *Solutions Manual*, *Instructor's Manual*, and *Excel™* template solutions are provided. There is a "Communicate with the Authors" link for sending e-mail. As needed, the authors will post updates to this site to keep adopters informed of the latest FASB pronouncements.

5. *XTRA! CD-ROM FOR INTERMEDIATE ACCOUNTING*

   This CD-ROM provides students with *alternative study materials* such as demonstration problems, quizzing, and alternative problems with solutions so that students can test their understanding of the content presented in the text. Packaged free with each new text, students receive an access code so that they can receive Xtra! reinforcement in intermediate accounting.

For the instructor, the supplements include:

1. *SOLUTIONS MANUAL*

   This two-volume manual includes: a suggested solution for each question, case, multiple-choice item, exercise, and problem; all supporting calculations; and helpful notes to the instructor concerning any difficult areas within each problem. It also includes a content analysis of the exercises and problems in each chapter, as well as a sample syllabus and a list of assignments appropriate for group activities. Prepared by Loren Nikolai and John Bazley.

2. *INSTRUCTOR'S MANUAL*

   For each chapter you'll find a list of objectives, synopsis, lecture outline, instructional notes, and content analysis of exercises and problems by topic. Appendix D provides compound interest tables for convenient reference. Illustrative teaching transparency masters consisting of selected exhibits from the text can be easily made into overheads for use in lecture presentations. Check figures of key answers to all text exercises and problems are also provided. Prepared by Loren Nikolai and John Bazley.

3. *TEST BANK*

   With examination materials covering each chapter, this updated two-volume *Test Bank* includes approximately 2,100 multiple-choice, essay, and short-answer problems and solutions.

4. *COMPUTERIZED TEST BANK*

   Containing the same questions as the printed *Test Bank*, the computerized test bank is available on the Instructor's Resource CD-ROM for the IBM PC or compatible. The electronic format makes it easy for you to edit questions and customize your own exams.

5. *TRANSPARENCIES*

   This two-volume set of acetates (set in large, bold type) for all problems and exercises adds an important visualization element to classroom presentations and discussions.

6. *POWERPOINT™ PRESENTATIONS*

   Available on the Instructor's Resource CD-ROM and for download on the text support site, these colorful and detailed slides enhance lectures and class discussion. *PowerPoint™* viewer software is included with the files. *MS-Windows®* is required.

7. *INSTRUCTOR'S RESOURCE CD-ROM*

   The Instructor's Resource CD-ROM contains electronic files for all the resources an instructor needs to teach from this text. It includes the computerized test bank in ExamView format; the ExamView testing software; the Microsoft Word and Word Perfect files for the printed Instructor's Manual, printed Test Bank, and Solutions Manual; and the PowerPoint Presentations.

8. *WEBTUTOR® ON WEBCT™ OR BLACKBOARD®*

   Available on both platforms, this rich course management product is a specially designed extension of the classroom experience that enlivens the course by leveraging the power of the Internet with comprehensive educational content. Instructors or students can use these resources along with those on the Product Web Site to supplement the classroom experience. Use this effective resource as an integrated solution for your distance learning or web-enhanced course! This powerful, turnkey solution provides the following content customized for this edition:

- *Annotated Spreadsheets*—Excel spreadsheet templates with annotated steps help walk students through some of the most difficult problems.
- *Quiz Bowl*—Students can review chapter content using this on-line game, which is similar to Jeopardy!®.
- *Annotated Problem Solutions*—Solutions to select text problems are presented in Excel spreadsheets with notations that explain each step in reaching the solution.
- *Interactive Quizzes*—Multiple choice, true/false, and sentence completion questions test student knowledge of the chapter content and provide immediate feedback on the accuracy of the response. These quizzes help students pinpoint areas in which they need more study.
- *Alternate Problems with Solutions*—Additional practice for students. Problems and exercises that are very similar to those found in the end of chapter. Solutions are provided to help students understand the steps they need to take in order to solve problems in the text.
- *Key terms quizzing*—Students can use this quizzing tool to test themselves on key terms found in the text.
- *Rama Review of Introductory Accounting Principles*—Professors often find that the most basic rules and information that students learned in the introductory accounting course have long been forgotten when the students arrive in Intermediate Accounting. From the same authors that created the *Rama Intermediate Tutorial* comes the *Rama Review of Introductory Accounting Principles*. This tool is a way for students to review the basic introductory accounting concepts that they may have forgotten over the summer. Like the Intermediate Tutorial, it explains the concept and then uses problem demonstrations to illustrate the concept and its application. Review questions and exercises reinforce the review.
- *Rama Intermediate Tutorial*—A great reviewing tool for students, the *Rama Intermediate Tutorial* provides a variety of materials to help reinforce concepts that students learn in class and supplement the explanations given in the text. The *Tutorial* explains some of the difficult and basic Intermediate accounting concepts and then uses problem demonstrations to illustrate those concepts and their application. Review questions and interactive quizzing is also available through this tool.
- *Accounting Calculators*—A few of the calculators that students will need in order to solve end of chapter material are provided. Present value calculator is an example.
- *Spanish Dictionary*—To aid Spanish-speaking students, a Spanish dictionary of key financial accounting terms is provided.

ADDITIONAL INTERMEDIATE ACCOUNTING RESOURCES

Listed below are additional intermediate accounting resources that are offered by South-Western and may be helpful in discussion and practice for your students. Please talk to your local South-Western representative if you are interested in any of these products.

1. *PRACTICE CASES*

- *Sharkey Incorporated*—This case study allows the students to assume the role of a financial consultant for Sharkey, Inc. for a two-year term. The goal of the case study is for the student to maximize both earnings per share and return on assets.
- *Foxcor Manufacturing Company*—This comprehensive practice case pulls together the concepts learned in the first half of the intermediate accounting course. The case also draws upon theory and concepts learned in foundation

accounting courses. After completing this case, students will be able to read and interpret the financial statements and understand how individual journal entries support a set of financial statements and related footnote disclosures.

2. *ACCOUNTING AND AUDITING RESEARCH: A PRACTICAL GUIDE, FIFTH EDITION*

This is the only step-by-step guide that provides methodology for conducting practical accounting research. In addition, the book offers up-to-date references to the primary sources of authoritative accounting literature, including electronic databases, and contains a special section on the Internet as a research tool. Written by Thomas Weirich, Central Michigan University, and Alan Reintstein, Wayne State University.

3. *ACCOUNTING ETHICS IN THE POST—ENRON AGE, FIRST EDITION*

With the Enron/Andersen debacle, ethics is becoming an increasingly important (and interesting) part of accounting education. Ethics coverage is also required by the AACSB for accreditation purposes. Most texts include some limited ethics coverage, but many instructors would like to include more. This timely supplement contains ethics cases based on real situations in the business world. Examples include cases tied to Enron, Global Crossing, and Boston Chicken. Identifying ethical dilemmas and projecting their resolution will allow students to develop essential skills for success in their future careers. In each section of the textbook, the problems will be labeled according to subject matter (i.e. bad debt expense, revenue recognition.) This allows the instructor to select problems consistent with the needs of the course. Written by Iris Stuart, of California State University-Fullerton, and Bruce Stuart.

4. *INSIDE LOOK: ANALYSIS FROM ALL ANGLES*

Accounting is in the news *and* the classroom with access to this new Web site from South-Western. The *Access Card* allows the instructor and the student to utilize information related to the Enron, Andersen, and other "names in the news" that involve accounting-related concerns. Well-known, popular news sources provide the background for the selected current events. Teaching tools are available to the instructor to implement class discussions, while analysis and questions are available to the student to utilize in many accounting discipline areas. This site is intended to help instructors teach and students to learn about critical current issues and understand them in the context of their accounting studies. For a Demo, go to: http://insidelook.swcollege.com.

5. *INFOTRAC®COLLEGE EDITION*

With this resource, your students can receive anytime, anywhere on-line access to a database of full-text articles from hundreds of popular and scholarly periodicals, such as *Newsweek, Fortune, Entrepreneur, Journal of Accountancy*, and *Nation's Business*, among others. Students can use its fast and easy search tools to find relevant news and analytical information among the tens of thousands of articles in the databases, which is update daily and goes back as far as four years, all at a single web site. InfoTrac® is a great way to expose students to online research techniques, with the security that the content is academically based and reliable. For more information, visit http://www.swcollege.com/infotrac.html.

6. *THOMSON ANALYITICS*

Thomson Analytics is the premier web-based analytics tool for accessing the industry's leading collection of authoritative content. By combining trusted source data, flexible searching, instant charting, and built-in analytical capabilities, Thomson Analytics not only gives students the data—it provides the tools that give it meaning!

ACKNOWLEDGMENTS

We wish to express appreciation to users of the earlier editions who provided meaningful comments and constructive criticism. We are grateful to Professors Martin Mellman, CUNY-Baruch; Larry Sallee, Winona State University; Scott Summers, Brigham Young University; James C. Buckley, Mesa State College; Norman A. Sunderman, Angelo State University; Peggy Dwyer, University of Central Florida; Tom W. Schmidt, University of Tennessee at Martin (retired); Robin Roberts, University of Central Florida; Kenneth R. Lambert, University of Memphis; Emil J. Hensler, Jr., Seton Hall University (retired); James P. Dunigan, University of Wisconsin-Stevens Point (retired); Sandra D. Byrd, Southwest Missouri State University; Rita J. Hopewell; T. J. Atwood, University of Illinois; Ben Hsien Bao, Hong Kong Polytechnic University; Judy Wenzel, Gustavus Adolphus College; John Sweeney, Washington State University; Brad Jordan, University of Kentucky; Ray Brooks, Oregon State University; Doug Cloud, Pepperdine University-Mallibu and Raymond C. Dockweiler (retired), Inder Khurana, Earl Wilson, Billie Cunningham, Sun Kim, and Joe Silvoso (deceased), University of Missouri-Columbia for their reactions to selected topics. Special thanks go to Donald Green, Scott I. Jerris, San Francisco State University; Paula Kock; Walter Parker, Central Connecticut State University (retired); Norma Powell, University of Massachusetts at Lowell; and Daryl G. Krause, CPA, for their contributions of homework. We also wish to thank our graduate and undergraduate students, including Jenny Reed, Verna Hazelrigg (deceased), Beth Adair, JoAnne Leuders, Stephen Underhill, Devra Niemann, Teresa Hickam, Cherie Wadlin, Trish Nikolai, Lori Thompson, Lisa Klempert, Lori Hamilton, Terry Phillips, Theresa Spaedy, Kyle Newell, Carrie Hammond, Cassi Costner, Emily Kliethermes, Nathan Troup, and Herman Eckerle. We are sincerely indebted to our typists, Anita Blanchar, Karen Staggs, and Mary Meyer, whose quality work and perseverance enabled us to complete the manuscript in a timely and orderly fashion. Appreciation is also extended to the Accounting/Tax Team at South-Western.

We are grateful to our respective Schools of Accountancy and to the American Institute of Certified Public Accountants, the Financial Accounting Standards Board, and the Institute of Certified Management Accountants of the Institute of Management Accountants for granting us permission to quote from their respective pronouncements and use their examination questions and unofficial answers. We are also grateful to our wives, children, and friends, who provided us with considerable moral support and understanding during the entire manuscript production process.

The authors wish to express their appreciation to those who served as reviewers and who provided insightful comments and valuable suggestions in the planning and writing of this textbook:

Cheryl L. Fulkerson
University of Texas, San Antonio

David J. Harr
George Mason University

Penny Hanes, MBA, CPA
Mercyhurst College

Richard C. Brooks
West Virginia University

Richard S. Sathe
University of St. Thomas

Jefferson Jones
Auburn University

Jeff Ritter
Associate Professor of Business Administration
St. Norbert College

Loren A. Nikolai
John D. Bazley

BRIEF CONTENTS

PART 1
Financial Reporting: Concepts, Financial Statements, and Related Disclosures

1 The Environment of Financial Reporting 2
2 Financial Reporting: Its Conceptual Framework 26
3 The Balance Sheet and the Statement of Changes in Stockholders' Equity 55
4 The Income Statement and Statement of Cash Flows 102
5 Additional Aspects of Financial Reporting and Financial Analysis 173

PART 2
Financial Reporting: Asset Measurement and Income Determination

6 Cash and Receivables 232
7 Inventories: Cost Measurement and Flow Assumptions 283
8 Inventories: Special Valuation Issues 332
9 Property, Plant, and Equipment: Acquisition and Disposal 372
10 Depreciation and Depletion 415
11 Intangibles 456

PART 3
Financial Reporting: Valuation of Liabilities and Investments

12 Current Liabilities and Contingencies 498
13 Long-Term Liabilities and Receivables 544
14 Investments 604

PART 4
Financial Reporting: Stockholders' Equity

15 Contributed Capital 660
16 Earnings Per Share and Retained Earnings 718

PART 5
Financial Reporting: Special Topics

17 Income Recognition and Measurement of Net Assets 778
18 Accounting for Income Taxes 829
19 Accounting for Postemployment Benefits 881
20 Accounting for Leases 944
21 The Statement of Cash Flows 1000
22 Accounting Changes and Errors 1065

APPENDIX A
The Coca-Cola Company 2001 Annual Report: Financial Section A1

APPENDIX B
List of Official Pronouncements of the AICPA and FASB B1

APPENDIX C
Review of the Accounting Process C1

APPENDIX D
Compound Interest D1

APPENDIX E
Accounting for Changes in Prices E2

INDEX I1

CONTENTS

PART 1
Financial Reporting: Concepts, Financial Statements, and Related Disclosures

1 The Environment of Financial Reporting   **2**

ACCOUNTING INFORMATION: USERS, USES, AND GAAP. External and Internal Users. Financial and Managerial Accounting Information Systems. Financial Reporting. Generally Accepted Accounting Principles. THE ESTABLISHMENT OF ACCOUNTING STANDARDS. Committee on Accounting Procedure (CAP). Accounting Principles Board (APB). Financial Accounting Standards Board (FASB). Other Organizations Currently Influencing Generally Accepted Accounting Principles. ETHICS IN THE ACCOUNTING ENVIRONMENT. CREATIVE AND CRITICAL THINKING IN THE ACCOUNTING ENVIRONMENT.

2 Financial Reporting: Its Conceptual Framework   **26**

FASB CONCEPTUAL FRAMEWORK. OBJECTIVES OF FINANCIAL REPORTING. Information Useful in Decision Making. Information Useful to External Users in Assessing Future Cash Receipts. Information Useful in Assessing Company Cash Flows. Information About Economic Resources and Claims to These Resources. Information About Comprehensive Income and Its Components. Information About Cash Flows. Other Issues. TYPES OF USEFUL INFORMATION. Return on Investment. Risk. Financial Flexibility. Liquidity. Operating Capability. QUALITATIVE CHARACTERISTICS OF USEFUL ACCOUNTING INFORMATION. Hierarchy of Qualitative Characteristics. Understandability. Decision Usefulness. Relevance. Reliability. Comparability and Consistency. Constraints to the Hierarchy. ACCOUNTING ASSUMPTIONS AND CONVENTIONS. Entity. Continuity. Period of Time. Historical Cost. Monetary Unit. Realization and Recognition. Matching and Accrual Accounting. Conservatism. GAAP AND FINANCIAL STATEMENTS. Balance Sheet. Income State-ment. Statement of Cash Flows. Statement of Changes in Equity. Model of Business Reporting. IASB Framework. OVERVIEW.

3 The Balance Sheet and the Statement of Changes in Stockholders' Equity   55

INTERRELATIONSHIP OF FINANCIAL STATEMENTS. PURPOSES OF THE BALANCE SHEET. Liquidity, Financial Flexibility, and Operating Capability. Capital and Capital Maintenance. RECOGNITION IN THE BALANCE SHEET. ELEMENTS OF THE BALANCE SHEET. Assets. Liabilities. Stockholders' Equity. MEASUREMENT OF THE ELEMENTS OF THE BALANCE SHEET. Historical Cost. Current Cost. Current Market Value. Net Realizable Value. Present Value. Valuations on Today's Balance Sheet. Limitations of the Balance Sheet. REPORTING CLASSIFICATIONS ON THE BALANCE SHEET. Current Assets. Current Liabilities. Working Capital. Long-Term Investments. Property, Plant, and Equipment. Intangible Assets. Other Assets. Long-Term Liabilities. Other Liabilities. Conceptual Guidelines for Reporting Assets and Liabilities. Stockholders' Equity. Contributed Capital. Capital Stock and Additional Paid-In Capital. Retained Earnings. Accumulated Other Comprehensive Income. Miscellaneous Items. STATEMENT OF CHANGES IN STOCKHOLDERS' EQUITY. OTHER DISCLOSURE ISSUES. Summary of Accounting Policies. Fair Value and Risk of Financial Instruments. Contingent Liabilities and Assets. Subsequent Events. Related Party Transactions. Comparative Financial Statements. Auditor's Report. SEC Integrated

Disclosures. Miscellaneous Disclosures. International Accounting Differences. REPORT-
ING TECHNIQUES. Statement Format (Balance Sheet). Combined Amounts. Rounding.
Notes, Supporting Schedules, and Parenthetical Notations. ILLUSTRATIVE STATE-
MENTS.

4   The Income Statement and Statement of Cash Flows   **102**

CONCEPTS OF INCOME. Capital Maintenance Concept. Transactional Approach.
CONCEPTUAL REPORTING GUIDELINES. General Conceptual Guidelines. Specific
Conceptual Guidelines. User Group Conceptual Guidelines. ELEMENTS OF THE
INCOME STATEMENT. Revenues. Expenses. Gains and Losses. INCOME STATE-
MENT CONTENT. All-Inclusive versus Current Operating. Condensed Income
Statements. INCOME STATEMENT: INCOME FROM CONTINUING OPERA-
TIONS. Sales Revenue (Net). Cost of Goods Sold. Operating Expenses. Other Items.
Income Tax Expense Related to Continuing Operations. Single-Step and Multiple-Step
Formats. Alternative Income Captions. INCOME STATEMENT: RESULTS FROM
DISCONTINUED OPERATIONS. Operating Income (or Loss). Gain or Loss on Sale.
Disclosure. INCOME STATEMENT: EXTRAORDINARY ITEMS. INCOME STATE-
MENT: EFFECTS OF ACCOUNTING CHANGES. Change in Accounting Principle.
Change in Accounting Estimate. INCOME STATEMENT: EARNINGS PER SHARE.
INCOME STATEMENT: RELATED ISSUES. Summary of Selected Financial Information.
Limitations of the Income Statement. International Accounting Differences. STATEMENT
OF RETAINED EARNINGS. Prior Period Adjustments. Net Income and Dividends.
Combined Statements. COMPREHENSIVE INCOME. Conceptual Evaluation. STATE-
MENT OF CASH FLOWS. Conceptual Overview and Uses of the Statement of Cash
Flows. Reporting Guidelines and Practices. SUMMARY OF DISCLOSURES.

5   Additional Aspects of Financial Reporting and Financial Analysis   **173**

MARKET EFFICIENCY. AUDITOR'S REPORT (OPINION). AUDIT COMMITTEE
AND MANAGEMENT'S REPORT. MANAGEMENT'S DISCUSSION AND ANALY-
SIS. SEGMENT REPORTING. Reporting on Operating Segments. Conceptual
Evaluation. INTERIM FINANCIAL REPORTS. Revenues. Expenses. Income Taxes.
Extraordinary Items, Discontinued Operations, and Cumulative Effects. Earnings per
Share. Preparation and Disclosure of Summarized Interim Financial Data. SEC RE-
PORTS. INTERNATIONAL ACCOUNTING DIFFERENCES. INTRACOMPANY
COMPARISONS. INTERCOMPANY COMPARISONS. PERCENTAGE ANALYSES.
Horizontal Analysis. Vertical Analysis. RATIO ANALYSIS. Stockholder Profitability
Ratios. Company Profitability Ratios. Liquidity Ratios. Activity Ratios. Stability Ratios.
Cash Flow Ratios.

PART 2
Financial Reporting: Asset Measurement and Income Determination

6   Cash and Receivables   **232**

CASH. Cash and Cash Equivalents. Cash Management. Petty Cash. BANK RECON-
CILIATION. Causes of the Difference. Procedures for Preparing a Bank Reconciliation.
Illustration. SPECIAL TOPICS INVOLVING CASH. Electronic Funds Transfer Systems.
Compensating Balances. RECEIVABLES. REVENUE RECOGNITION AND VALUA-
TION OF TRADE RECEIVABLES. Normal Revenue Recognition. Right of Return.
Valuation Issues. ACCOUNTS RECEIVABLE. Cash (Sales) Discounts. Sales Returns
and Allowances. VALUATION OF ACCOUNTS RECEIVABLE FOR UNCOLLECTIBLE
ACCOUNTS. Estimated Bad Debts Method. Percentage of Sales (or Net Credit Sales).
Percentage of Outstanding Accounts Receivable. Aging of Accounts Receivable. Writing
Off Uncollectible Accounts. Collection of an Account Previously Written Off. Direct
Write-Off Method. GENERATING IMMEDIATE CASH FROM ACCOUNTS RE-
CEIVABLE. Pledging of Accounts Receivable. Assignment of Accounts Receivable.
Factoring (Sale) of Accounts Receivable. Disclosure of Financing Agreements of Accounts

Receivable. NOTES RECEIVABLE. Short-Term Interest-Bearing Notes Receivable. Short-Term Non-Interest-Bearing Notes Receivable. Notes Receivable Discounted. FINANCIAL STATEMENT DISCLOSURES OF RECEIVABLES.

7   Inventories: Cost Measurement and Flow Assumptions   283

CLASSIFICATIONS OF INVENTORY. Raw Materials Inventory. Goods in Process Inventory. Finished Goods Inventory. Inventories of Service Companies. ALTERNATIVE INVENTORY SYSTEMS. Perpetual Inventory System. Periodic Inventory System. ITEMS TO BE INCLUDED IN INVENTORY QUANTITIES. DETERMINATION OF INVENTORY COSTS. Manufacturing Overhead Costs. Standard Costs. Variable Costing. Purchases Discounts. COST FLOW ASSUMPTIONS. Specific Identification. First-In, First-Out (FIFO). Average Cost. Last-In, First-Out (LIFO). Comparison of Inventory Cost Flow Assumptions. CONCEPTUAL EVALUATION OF INVENTORY COST FLOW ASSUMPTIONS. Income Measurement. Income Tax Effects. Liquidation of LIFO Layers. Income Manipulation. Inventory Valuation. Average Cost. Management's Selection of an Inventory Cost Flow Assumption. DOLLAR-VALUE LIFO. Determination of Cost Index. Inventory Pools. ADDITIONAL LIFO CONSIDERATIONS. LIFO Valuation Adjustment. Interim Statements Using LIFO. Change to or from LIFO. International Accounting Differences. DISCLOSURE OF INVENTORY VALUES AND METHODS.

8   Inventories: Special Valuation Issues   332

LOWER OF COST OR MARKET. Application of Lower of Cost or Market Method. Conceptual Evaluation of the Ceiling and Floor. Approaches to Implementing Lower of Cost or Market Rule. Recording the Reduction of Inventory to Market. Lower of Cost or Market and Interim Financial Statements. CONCEPTUAL EVALUATION OF LOWER OF COST OR MARKET. International Accounting Differences. PURCHASE OBLIGATIONS AND PRODUCT FINANCING ARRANGEMENTS. VALUATION ABOVE COST. GROSS PROFIT METHOD. Conceptual Evaluation of the Gross Profit Method. RETAIL INVENTORY METHOD. Retail Inventory Method Terminology. Application of the Retail Inventory Method. Additional Cost and Retail Adjustments. CONCEPTUAL EVALUATION OF THE RETAIL INVENTORY METHOD. DOLLAR-VALUE LIFO RETAIL METHOD. EFFECTS OF INVENTORY ERRORS. SUMMARY OF INVENTORY ISSUES.

9   Property, Plant, and Equipment: Acquisition and Disposal   372

CHARACTERISTICS OF PROPERTY, PLANT, AND EQUIPMENT. Evaluation of Use of Historical Cost. ACQUISITION OF PROPERTY, PLANT, AND EQUIPMENT. Determination of Cost. Lump-Sum Purchase. Deferred Payments. Issuance of Securities. Assets Acquired by Donation. Start-up Costs. International Accounting Differences. ASSETS ACQUIRED BY EXCHANGE OF OTHER ASSETS. Exchanges of Dissimilar Productive Assets. Exchanges of Similar Productive Assets. Summary of Productive Asset Exchanges. SELF-CONSTRUCTION. Interest During Construction. International Accounting Differences. Fixed Overhead Costs. Income on Self-Construction. Development Stage Companies. COSTS SUBSEQUENT TO ACQUISITION. Additions. Improvements and Replacements. Rearrangement and Moving. Repairs and Maintenance. DISPOSAL OF PROPERTY, PLANT, AND EQUIPMENT. Asset Retirement Obligations. DISCLOSURE OF PROPERTY, PLANT, AND EQUIPMENT.

10   Depreciation and Depletion   415

FACTORS INVOLVED IN DEPRECIATION. Asset Cost. Service Life. Residual Value. METHODS OF COST ALLOCATION. Activity Methods. Time-Based Methods. RECORDING DEPRECIATION. CONCEPTUAL EVALUATION OF DEPRECIATION METHODS. DISCLOSURE OF DEPRECIATION. International Accounting Differences. ADDITIONAL DEPRECIATION METHODS. Group Depreciation. Composite Depreciation. Retirement and Replacement Methods. Inventory Systems.

DEPRECIATION FOR PARTIAL PERIODS. Compute Depreciation to the Nearest Whole Month. Compute Depreciation to the Nearest Whole Year. Compute One-Half Year's Depreciation on All Assets Purchased or Sold During the Year. IMPAIRMENT OF NONCURRENT ASSETS. Conceptual Evaluation of Asset Impairment. International Accounting Differences. DEPRECIATION AND INCOME TAXES. MACRS Principles. Illustration of MACRS. CHANGES AND CORRECTIONS OF DEPRECIATION. DEPLETION.

11 Intangibles   **456**

ACCOUNTING FOR INTANGIBLES. Cost of Intangibles. Amortization or Impairment of Intangible Assets. RESEARCH AND DEVELOPMENT COSTS. Conceptual Evaluation of Accounting for Research and Development Costs. International Accounting Differences. IDENTIFIABLE INTANGIBLE ASSETS. Patents. Copyrights. Franchises. Computer Software Costs. Internal-Use Software. Leases and Leasehold Improvements. Trademarks and Tradenames. Deferred Charges. Organization Costs. UNIDENTIFIABLE INTANGIBLES. Internally Developed Goodwill. Purchased Goodwill. Recording the Acquisition. Impairment of Goodwill. Negative Goodwill. DISCLOSURE OF INTANGIBLES ASSETS. CONCEPTUAL EVALUATION OF ACCOUNTING FOR INTANGIBLES. International Accounting Differences. Estimating the Value of Goodwill. Steps Used in Estimating the Value of Goodwill. Other Methods of Estimating Goodwill.

PART 3
Financial Reporting: Valuation of Liabilities and Investments

12 Current Liabilities and Contingencies   **498**

CONCEPTUAL OVERVIEW OF LIABILITIES. NATURE AND DEFINITION OF CURRENT LIABILITIES. Classification and the Operating Cycle or Year. Liquidity, Financial Flexibility, and Current Liabilities. Classification of Current Liabilities. VALUATION OF CURRENT LIABILITIES. CURRENT LIABILITIES HAVING A CONTRACTUAL AMOUNT. Trade Accounts Payable. Notes Payable. Currently Maturing Portion of Long-Term Debt. Dividends Payable. Advances and Refundable Deposits. Accrued Liabilities. Unearned Items. CURRENT LIABILITIES WHOSE AMOUNTS DEPEND ON OPERATIONS. Sales and Use Taxes. Liabilities Related to Payrolls. Income Taxes Payable. Bonus Obligations. CURRENT LIABILITIES REQUIRING AMOUNTS TO BE ESTIMATED. Property Taxes. Warranty Obligations. Premium and Coupon Obligations. CONTINGENCIES. Accrual of Loss Contingencies. Disclosure of Loss Contingencies in the Notes to the Financial Statements. Disclosure of Gain Contingencies in the Notes to the Financial Statements. Executory Contracts. Illustrations of Contingency Disclosures. International Accounting Differences. OTHER LIABILITY CLASSIFICATION ISSUES. Short-Term Debt Expected to be Refinanced. Classification of Obligations That Are Callable by the Creditor. FINANCIAL STATE-MENT PRESENTATION OF CURRENT LIABILITIES.

13 Long-Term Liabilities and Receivables   **544**

REASONS FOR ISSUANCE OF LONG-TERM LIABILITIES. BONDS PAYABLE. Characteristics of Bonds. Bond Selling Prices. RECORDING THE ISSUANCE OF BONDS. Bonds Issued Between Interest Payment Dates. AMORTIZING DISCOUNTS AND PREMIUMS. Straight-Line Method. Effective Interest Method. Bond Issue Costs. Accruing Bond Interest. Zero Coupon Bonds. International Accounting Differences. EXTINGUISHMENT OF LIABILITIES. Bonds Retired at Maturity. Bonds Retired Prior to Maturity. BONDS WITH EQUITY CHARACTERISTICS. Bonds Issued with Detachable Stock Warrants. Convertible Bonds. LONG-TERM NOTES PAYABLE. Notes Payable Issued for Cash. Notes Payable Exchanged for Cash and Rights or Privileges. Notes Payable Exchanged for Property, Goods, or Services. Disclosure of Long-Term Liabilities. LONG-TERM NOTES RECEIVABLE. Loan Fees. Impairment of a Loan. Future Developments. ACCOUNTING BY THE DEBTOR. Modification of

Terms. Equity or Asset Exchange. Equity or Asset Exchange Combined with a Modification of Terms. Disclosure of Restructuring Agreements. ACCOUNTING BY THE CREDITOR. Equity or Asset Exchange. Modification of Terms. Equity or Asset Exchange Combined with Modification of Terms. CONCEPTUAL EVALUATION OF ACCOUNTING FOR TROUBLED DEBT RESTRUCTURINGS. RECORDING THE ISSUANCE AND INTEREST EXPENSE OF SERIAL BONDS. EARLY REDEMPTION OF SERIAL BONDS.

14   Investments   **604**

INVESTMENTS: CLASSIFICATION AND VALUATION. INVESTMENTS IN DEBT AND EQUITY TRADING SECURITIES. INVESTMENTS IN AVAILABLE-FOR-SALE DEBT AND EQUITY SECURITIES. Recording Initial Cost. Recording Interest and Dividend Revenue. Recognition of Unrealized Holding Gains and Losses. Realized Gains and Losses on Sales of Available-for-Sale Securities. INVESTMENTS IN HELD-TO-MATURITY DEBT SECURITIES. Recording Initial Cost. Recognition and Amortization of Bond Premiums and Discounts. Amortization for Bonds Acquired Between Interest Dates. Sale of Investment in Bonds before Maturity. TRANSFERS AND IMPAIR-MENTS. Transfers of Investments Between Categories. Impairments. DISCLOSURES. Financial Statement Classification. FASB STATEMENT NO. 115: A CONCEPTUAL EVALUATION. Fair Value Is Required for Certain Investments. Fair Value Is Not Required for Certain Liabilities. Reporting of Unrealized Gains and Losses. Classification of Securities Is Based on Management Intent. International Accounting Differences. EQUITY METHOD. Accounting Procedures. Financial Statement Disclosures. Special Issues. International Accounting Differences. ADDITIONAL ISSUES FOR INVEST-MENTS. Nonmarketable Securities. Stock Dividends and Splits. Stock Warrants. Convertible Bonds. Cash Surrender Value of Life Insurance. Investments in Funds. FAIR VALUE HEDGE. CASH FLOW HEDGE.

PART 4
Financial Reporting: Stockholders' Equity

15   Contributed Capital   **660**

CORPORATE FORM OF ORGANIZATION. Types of Corporations. Formation of a Corporation. CORPORATE CAPITAL STRUCTURE. Capital Stock and Stockholders' Rights. Basic Terminology. Legal Capital. Additional Paid-In Capital. Stockholders' Equity. ISSUANCE OF CAPITAL STOCK. Authorization. Issuance for Cash. Stock Issuance Costs. Stock Subscriptions. Subscription Defaults. Combined Sales of Stock. Nonmonetary Issuance of Stock. Stock Splits. Stock Rights to Current Stockholders. NONCOMPENSATORY STOCK OPTION PLANS. COMPENSATORY STOCK OPTION PLANS. Conceptual Overview and Historical Perspective. Measurement of Fair Value. Recognition of Compensation Expense. Intrinsic Value Method for Compensatory Stock Option Plans. Additional Disclosures. Conceptual Evaluation. PREFERRED STOCK CHARACTERISTICS. Preference as to Dividends. Cumulative Preferred Stock. Participating Preferred Stock. Convertible Preferred Stock. Preferred Stock with Stock Warrants (Rights). Callable Preferred Stock. Redeemable Preferred Stock. Preference in Liquidation. Voting Rights. Disclosures. CONTRIBUTED CAPITAL SECTION. TREASURY STOCK (CAPITAL STOCK REACQUISITION). Cost Method. Par Value Method. Balance Sheet Presentation. Acquisition at Greater Than Market Value. Donated Treasury Stock. Retirement of Treasury Stock. Conceptual Overview of Treasury Stock.

16   Earnings Per Share and Retained Earnings   **718**

EARNINGS AND EARNINGS PER SHARE. CONCEPTUAL OVERVIEW AND USES OF EARNINGS PER SHARE INFORMATION. BASIC EARNINGS PER SHARE. Numerator Calculations. Denominator Calculations. Components of Earnings Per Share. Example of Basic Earnings Per Share. DILUTED EARNINGS PER SHARE. Stock Options and Warrants. Convertible Securities. Computation of Tentative and Final

Diluted Earnings Per Share. ADDITIONAL CONSIDERATIONS. Conversion Ratios. Contingent Issuances. Additional Disclosures. International Accounting Differences. EPS DISCLOSURE ILLUSTRATION. CONTENT OF RETAINED EARNINGS. DIVIDENDS. Cash Dividends. Property Dividends. Scrip Dividends. Stock Dividends. Liquidating Dividends. PRIOR PERIOD ADJUSTMENTS (RESTATEMENTS). APPROPRIATIONS (RESTRICTIONS) OF RETAINED EARNINGS. STATEMENT OF RETAINED EARNINGS. Illustration of Retained Earnings Statement. Accumulated Other Comprehensive Income. MISCELLANEOUS CHANGES IN STOCKHOLDERS' EQUITY. STATEMENT OF CHANGES IN STOCKHOLDERS' EQUITY. International Accounting Differences.

PART 5
Financial Reporting: Special Topics

17 Income Recognition and Measurement of Net Assets   778

OVERVIEW OF REVENUE RECOGNITION ALTERNATIVES. EXAMPLES OF REVENUE RECOGNITION ALTERNATIVES. Example 1: Revenue Recognition at Time of Sale. Example 2: Revenue Recognition During Production. Example 3: Revenue Recognition at Time of Cash Receipt. Summary of Revenue Recognition Alternatives. CONCEPTUAL ISSUES. ALTERNATIVE REVENUE RECOGNITION METHODS. REVENUE RECOGNITION PRIOR TO THE PERIOD OF SALE. Long-Term Construction Contracts. Percentage-of-Completion Method. Completed-Contract Method. Illustration of the Two Methods. Losses on Long-Term Construction Contracts. Additional Considerations in Accounting for Long-Term Construction Contracts. Long-Term Service Contracts. Proportional Performance Method. REVENUE RECOGNITION AFTER THE PERIOD OF SALE. Installment Method. Example of the Installment Method. Additional Considerations for the Installment Method. Cost Recovery Method. Comparison of the Installment and Cost Recovery Methods. REVENUE RECOGNITION DELAYED UNTIL A FUTURE EVENT OCCURS. Deposit Method. ADDITIONAL REVENUE RECOGNITION ISSUES. Software Revenue Recognition. Franchises. Real Estate Sales. Retail Land Sales. Consignment Sales. SAB No. 101. International Accounting Differences. SUMMARY OF ALTERNATIVE REVENUE RECOGNITION METHODS.

18 Accounting for Income Taxes   829

OVERVIEW AND DEFINITIONS. Causes of Differences. Definitions. INTERPERIOD INCOME TAX ALLOCATION: BASIC ISSUES. Permanent Differences. Temporary Differences. INTERPERIOD INCOME TAX ALLOCATION: CONCEPTUAL ISSUES. Deferred Tax Liability. Deferred Tax Asset. Measurement. INTERPERIOD INCOME TAX ALLOCATION: RECORDING AND REPORTING OF CURRENT AND DEFERRED TAXES. Basic Entries. Example 1: Deferred Tax Liability—Single Temporary Difference. Example 2: Deferred Tax Liability—Single Temporary Difference and Multiple Rates. Example 3: Deferred Tax Asset—Single Temporary Difference. Example 4: Deferred Tax Asset and Valuation Allowance. Example 5: Permanent and Temporary Differences. OPERATING LOSS CARRYBACKS AND CARRYFORWARDS. Conceptual Issues. Generally Accepted Accounting Principles. COMPREHENSIVE ILLUSTRATION. INTRAPERIOD INCOME TAX ALLOCATION. FINANCIAL STATEMENT PRESENTATION AND DISCLOSURES. Balance Sheet Presentation. Financial Statement Disclosures. MISCELLANEOUS ISSUES. Change in Income Tax Laws or Rates. Investment Tax Credit. Alternative Minimum Tax and Other Tax Credits. International Accounting Differences. ILLUSTRATIVE DISCLOSURES. ALLOCATION VERSUS NONALLOCATION. COMPREHENSIVE VERSUS PARTIAL ALLOCATION. ALTERNATIVE ALLOCATION METHODS.

19 Accounting for Postemployment Benefits   881

CHARACTERISTICS OF PENSION PLANS. HISTORICAL PERSPECTIVE OF PENSION PLANS. ACCOUNTING PRINCIPLES FOR DEFINED BENEFIT PENSION

PLANS. Key Terms Related to Pension Plans. Pension Expense. Pension Liabilities and Assets. Measurement Methods. Disclosures. EXAMPLES OF ACCOUNTING FOR PENSIONS. Example 1: Pension Expense Equal to Pension Funding. Example 2: Pension Expense Greater Than Pension Funding. Example 3: Pension Expense Less Than Pension Funding, and Expected Return on Plan Assets Different from Both Actual Return and Discount Rate. Example 4: Pension Expense Including Amortization of Unrecognized Prior Service Cost. Example 5: Calculation of Amortization of Unrecognized Prior Service Cost. Example 6: Pension Expense Including Net Gain or Loss (to Extent Recognized). Example 7: Recognition of Additional Pension Liability. Example 8: Disclosures. Pension Worksheet. Summary of Issues Related to Pensions. CONCEPTUAL ISSUES RELATED TO DEFINED BENEFIT PENSION PLANS. Pension Expense. Pension Liabilities. Balance Sheet Presentation of Pension Plan Assets. ADDITIONAL ASPECTS OF PENSION ACCOUNTING. Transition Requirements. Vested Benefits. Accounting for Defined Contribution Plans. Disclosures by Funding Agencies. Employee Retirement Income Security Act of 1974. Pension Plan Settlements and Curtailments. Termination Benefits Paid to Employees. Multi-Employer Plans. International Accounting Differences. OTHER POSTEMPLOYMENT BENEFITS. Similarities to and Differences from Pensions. Accounting Principles. OPEB Expense. OPEB Liability or Asset. Differences from Accounting for Pensions. ILLUSTRATION OF ACCOUNTING FOR OPEBS. CONCEPTUAL EVALUATION OF ACCOUNTING FOR OPEBS. Relevance and Reliability. Differences in Funding. Transition Liability. Attribution Period. Interaction with Deferred Income Taxes. Minimum Liability. Impacts of the Adoption of *FASB Statement No. 106.* Service Cost. Interest on Projected Benefit Obligation. Expected Return on Plan Assets. Amortization of Unrecognized Prior Service Cost. Pension Expense and Liability.

20   Accounting for Leases   944

ADVANTAGES OF LEASING. Advantages of Leasing from Lessee's Viewpoint. Advantages of Leasing from Lessor's Viewpoint. KEY TERMS RELATED TO LEASING. CLASSIFICATION OF PERSONAL PROPERTY LEASES. ACCOUNTING AND REPORTING BY A LESSEE. Operating Lease (Lessee). Capital Lease (Lessee). Illustrations of Lessee's Capital Lease Method. Other Lessee Capitalization Issues. Disclosure Requirements of the Lessee. ACCOUNTING AND REPORTING BY A LESSOR. Operating Lease (Lessor). Direct Financing Leases (Lessor). Initial Direct Costs Involved in a Direct Financing Lease. Sales-Type Leases (Lessor). Initial Direct Costs Involved in a Sales-Type Lease. Unguaranteed and Guaranteed Residual Values. Disclosure Requirements for the Lessor. SUMMARY OF ACCOUNTING BY LESSEE AND LESSOR. ADDITIONAL LEASE ISSUES. Conceptual Evaluation of Accounting for Leases. International Accounting Differences. LEASE ISSUES RELATED TO REAL ESTATE. Lease of Land Only. Lease of Both Land and Buildings That Transfers Title or Contains a Bargain Purchase Option. Lease of Land and Buildings That Does Not Transfer Title or Contain a Bargain Purchase Option. Lease Involving Equipment as Well as Real Estate. SALE-LEASEBACK ISSUES. Lessor's Accounting Issues. Lessee's Accounting Issues. Leveraged Leases. CHANGES IN LEASE PROVISIONS. Review of Estimated Unguaranteed Residual Value. Impact of Renewal of Lease on Guarantee of Residual Value. Changes to Sales-Type or Direct Financing Lease Prior to Lease Term Expiration That Change the Lease to an Operating Lease. Renewal or Extension of Sales-Type or Direct Financing Lease Resulting in a New Lease That Qualifies as a Sales-Type Lease.

21   The Statement of Cash Flows   1000

CONCEPTUAL OVERVIEW AND REPORTING GUIDELINES. Reporting Guidelines and Practices. Illustration. CASH INFLOWS AND OUTFLOWS. Inflows of Cash. Outflows of Cash. Classifications of Cash Flows. NET CASH FLOW FROM OPERATING ACTIVITIES. Direct Method. Indirect Method. PROCEDURES FOR PREPARATION OF STATEMENT. Visual Inspection Method of Analysis. Simple Example (Visual Inspection Method). Worksheet Method of Analysis. Steps in Preparation (Worksheet Method). Comprehensive Example (Worksheet Method). SPECIAL TOPICS.

Sale of Depreciable Assets. Interest Paid and Income Taxes Paid. Flexibility in Reporting. Partial Cash Investing and Financing Activities. Temporary and Long-Term Investments. Cash Dividends Declared. Financial Institutions. Effects of Exchange Rates. Cash Flow Per Share. International Accounting Differences. OPERATING CASH FLOWS. Operating Cash Inflows. Operating Cash Outflows. Diagram of Operating Cash Flows. PROCEDURES FOR STATEMENT PREPARATION. Visual Inspection Method. Worksheet Method. EXAMPLE: WORKSHEET AND DIRECT METHOD.

22 Accounting Changes and Errors   **1065**

TYPES OF ACCOUNTING CHANGES. METHODS OF DISCLOSING AN ACCOUNTING CHANGE. ACCOUNTING FOR A CHANGE IN ACCOUNTING PRINCIPLE. Cumulative Effect Method. Prior Period Restatement Method. Transition Methods Required by the FASB. ACCOUNTING FOR A CHANGE IN AN ESTIMATE. ADDITIONAL ISSUES. A Change in Principle Distinguished from a Change in an Estimate. Preferability of the New Accounting Principle. Accounting Changes in Interim Financial Statements. CONCEPTUAL EVALUATION OF ACCOUNTING FOR A CHANGE IN ACCOUNTING PRINCIPLE AND A CHANGE IN ESTIMATE. Prior Period Restatement. Cumulative Effect Adjustment. Prospective Adjustment. ACCOUNTING FOR A CHANGE IN A REPORTING ENTITY. ACCOUNTING FOR A CORRECTION OF AN ERROR. Error Analysis. Error Correction. International Accounting Differences. SUMMARY OF METHODS FOR ACCOUNTING CHANGES AND ERRORS.

APPENDIX A
The Coca-Cola Company 2001 Annual Report: Financial Section   **A2**

APPENDIX B
List of Official Pronouncements of the AICPA and FASB   **B1**

APPENDIX C
Review of the Accounting Process   **C1**

THE ACCOUNTING SYSTEM. Accounting Equation. Transactions, Events, and Supporting Documents. Accounts. Financial Statements. THE ACCOUNTING CYCLE. Recording in the General Journal (Step 1). Posting to the Ledger (Step 2). Preparation of Adjusting Entries (Step 3). Preparation of the Financial Statements (Step 4). Preparation of Closing Entries (Step 5). REVERSING ENTRIES. THE WORKSHEET. SUBSIDIARY LEDGERS. SPECIAL JOURNALS. Sales Journal. Purchases Journal. Cash Receipts Journal. Cash Payments Journal. General Journal. Voucher System. COMPUTER SOFTWARE. CASH-BASIS ACCOUNTING.

APPENDIX D
Compound Interest   **D1**

SIMPLE INTEREST AND COMPOUND INTEREST. FUTURE VALUE OF A SINGLE SUM AT COMPOUND INTEREST. The Idea. Formula Approach. Table Approach. Summary and Illustration. PRESENT VALUE OF A SINGLE SUM. The Idea. Shortcut Approaches. Summary and Illustration. MEASUREMENTS INVOLVING AN ANNUITY. FUTURE VALUE OF AN ORDINARY ANNUITY. Shortcut Approaches. Summary and Illustration. FUTURE VALUE OF AN ANNUITY DUE. Solution Approach. PRESENT VALUE OF AN ANNUITY. PRESENT VALUE OF AN ORDINARY ANNUITY. Solving by Determining the Present Value of a Series of Single Sums. Shortcut Approaches. Summary and Illustration. PRESENT VALUE OF AN ANNUITY DUE. Shortcut Approaches. Another Application. PRESENT VALUE OF A DEFERRED ORDINARY ANNUITY. Another Application. SUMMARY OF PRESENT AND FUTURE VALUE CALCULATIONS. CONCEPTUAL EVALUATION OF PRESENT VALUE TECHNIQUES IN FINANCIAL REPORTING.

APPENDIX E
Accounting for Changes in Prices   E2

CURRENT VALUE AND THE GENERAL PRICE LEVEL. Current Value. General Price Level. Four Alternative Concepts. THREE ALTERNATIVES TO HISTORICAL COST. Current Cost Financial Statements. Historical Cost/Constant Purchasing Power Financial Statements. Current Cost/Constant Purchasing Power Financial Statements. ADDITIONAL MEASUREMENT ISSUES. Measurement of Current Cost. Adjustment of Historical Dollars. Purchasing-Power Gain or Loss on Net Monetary Items. CONCEPTUAL ISSUES RELATING TO ALTERNATIVES TO HISTORICAL COST. Capital Maintenance Concept (Income Statement). Balance Sheet. Reliability. Understandability. Costs and Benefits. Current Cost and Operating Savings. Current Cost versus Partial Adjustments. Current Exit Values. DISCLOSURES. Conceptual Evaluation of the Elimination of the Required Disclosures. International Accounting Differences.

INDEX   I1

PART 1

Financial Reporting: Concepts, Financial Statements, and Related Disclosures

Chapter 1   The Environment of Financial Reporting

Chapter 2   Financial Reporting: Its Conceptual Framework

Chapter 3   The Balance Sheet and the Statement of Changes in Stockholders' Equity

Chapter 4   The Income Statement and Statement of Cash Flows

Chapter 5   Additional Aspects of Financial Reporting and Financial Analysis

objectives

1 Understand capital markets and decision making.

2 Know what is included in financial reporting.

3 Explain generally accepted accounting principles (GAAP) and the sources of GAAP.

4 Identify the types of pronouncements issued by the FASB.

5 Understand how the Financial Accounting Standards Board (FASB) operates.

6 Describe the relationship between the Securities and Exchange Commission (SEC) and the FASB.

7 Use ethical models for decision making about ethical dilemmas.

8 Understand creative and critical thinking

CHAPTER 1

The Environment of Financial Reporting

Accounting may be described as the process of identifying, measuring, recording, and communicating economic information to permit informed judgments and decisions by users of information.[1] It is also called the "language of business." In the United States economy, most published accounting information is about different types of companies (primarily corporations). Companies engage in many transactions and generate large amounts of data. Since people can absorb only limited amounts of information,[2] accounting systems are designed to report that data in a concise, understandable format. In this sense, accounting may be viewed as the link between a company's economic activities and decision makers.

In this chapter we review the uses of accounting information and who uses it, the development of principles for the accumulation and communication of accounting information, and the ethical frameworks within which these accounting principles are applied.

ACCOUNTING INFORMATION: USERS, USES, AND GAAP

The U.S. economy is a free-market economy in which the decisions of many buyers and sellers influence the demand for and supply of products and services offered by companies. Individuals acting within this economy have limited resources to consume or to invest, whereas typically companies need large amounts of capital for their operations. Companies may obtain this capital from the issuance of capital stock (equity) and bonds (debt), from other borrowings, or from resources generated by their operations. The exchange of capital by investors for the stocks and bonds of companies occurs in **capital markets,** as we show in Exhibit 1-1. There are organized capital markets, such as the New York Stock Exchange (NYSE), the American Stock Exchange (AMEX), and the Nasdaq Stock Market, Inc. (NASDAQ), in which the capital stock and bonds of many corporations are purchased and sold daily. These corporations are called *publicly held* (or publicly traded) companies. These markets sometimes are referred to as *secondary markets* because the sales and purchases are among the investors themselves. That is, the corporation that initially issued the capital stock or bonds is not involved in the exchange.

---

1. Committee to Prepare a Statement of Basic Accounting Theory, *A Statement of Basic Accounting Theory* (Evanston, Ill.: AAA, 1966), p. 1.
2. See, for example, Robert Libby, *Accounting and Human Information Processing: Theory and Applications* (Englewood Cliffs, N.J.: Prentice-Hall, 1981) and Ahmed Riahi-Belkaoui, *Human Information Processing in Accounting* (New York: Quorum Books, 1989).

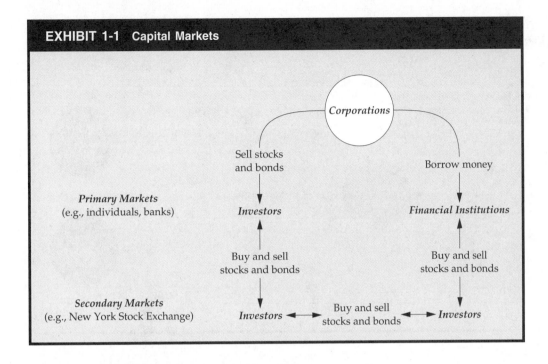

EXHIBIT 1-1   Capital Markets

There also are more loosely organized capital markets in which fewer exchanges occur. For instance, companies may borrow from lending institutions, or corporations may issue new capital stock or bonds, either through "public offerings" or through "private placements." Public offerings involve the advertising and sale to many investors (i.e., the general public). Private placements involve the advertising and sale to a few private institutions such as insurance companies and pension funds, or to employees. These markets sometimes are called *primary markets* because the exchange is directly between a corporation and the investors. Whether investors or lending institutions are involved in primary or secondary markets, they are interested in earning dividends and interest, and in a safe return of their resources. Investors in publicly traded securities participate in the increase (or decrease) in the market price of the capital stock and bonds. These investors are concerned with the efficient allocation of their scarce resources to achieve these objectives. Accounting information is useful in making decisions for this allocation process within these capital markets. It is useful for other purposes as well.

External and Internal Users

The decision makers or users of accounting information can be divided into two major categories, external users and internal users, as we show in Exhibit 1-2. These two user groups have somewhat dissimilar information needs because of their different relationships to the company providing the economic information. **External users are actual or potential investors (stockholders and bondholders); creditors, such as suppliers and lending institutions; and other users,** such as employees, financial analysts, advisers, brokers, underwriters, stock exchanges, taxing and regulatory authorities, labor unions, and the general public. (Note that bondholders are "creditors" by contract and legal definition, but are considered "investors" as this term is commonly used.) Investors have a direct relationship with the company, and their capital market information needs revolve around three basic decisions:

1 Understand capital markets and decision making.

1. *Buy*. A potential investor decides to purchase a particular security (e.g., a stock or bond) on the basis of communicated accounting information.
2. *Hold*. An actual investor decides to retain a particular security on the basis of communicated accounting information.

EXHIBIT 1-2   Accounting Information: Economic Activities and Decision Making

3. *Sell.* An actual investor decides to dispose of a particular security on the basis of communicated accounting information.

Creditors, such as suppliers and lending institutions, also have a direct relationship with companies. While creditors do not purchase securities, they make similar decisions that require accounting information. The decisions in this case are to extend credit, to maintain the credit relationship, or not to extend credit. Other users employ accounting information in their decision making. For instance, stock exchanges use accounting information for listings, cancellations, and rule-making decisions. Labor unions use accounting information in negotiating wage agreements. Financial analysts use accounting information for making investment and credit recommendations.

Investment and credit decisions should be continuously reevaluated. A timely communication of information to external decision makers is very important. The publication of financial statements (e.g., in "hard copy" or on a company's web site) is a primary method by which relevant information is communicated. Studies have shown, however, that decision makers also use other reporting sources to satisfy their information needs.[3]

This area of study, known as efficient capital markets research, is discussed in Chapter 5.

Internal users are the company managers who are responsible for the planning and control of operations on a day-by-day and a long-term basis. In contrast to external users, who mainly use financial statement information in their decision processes, internal users may request any type of information that the accounting system is capable of providing to assist them in making decisions on internal operations. For example, internal users may request information relating specifically to the purchase of new equipment or the addition of a new product.

---

3. In addition to the use of published financial statements, accounting information may be communicated to external users by other methods, such as reports filed with the Securities and Exchange Commission (discussed later), news releases, and management forecasts. Evidence from capital markets research studies tends to show that security prices fully reflect all *publicly* available information. For a more detailed discussion, see T. R. Dyckman and D. Morse, *Efficient Capital Markets and Accounting: A Critical Analysis,* 2nd ed. (Englewood Cliffs, N.J.: Prentice-Hall, 1986), R. L. Watts and J. R. Zimmerman, *Positive Accounting Theory* (Englewood Cliffs, N.J.: Prentice Hall, 1986), or W. H. Beaver, *Financial Reporting: An Accounting Revolution,* 3rd ed. (Upper Saddle River, N.J.: Prentice Hall, 1998).

Financial and Managerial Accounting Information Systems

Two major branches of accounting are used to meet the specialized needs of external and internal users. **Financial accounting is the information accumulation, processing, and communication system designed to satisfy the investment and credit decision-making information needs of external users.** Financial accounting information is communicated (reported) through published financial statements and must follow the pronouncements of several policy-making groups. **Managerial accounting is the information accumulation, processing, and communication system designed to meet the decision-making information needs of internal users.** Managerial accounting information is communicated via internal company reports and is not subject to the policy standards applied to externally communicated information. It is restricted by the usefulness of the information provided for a specific decision and the cost of providing that information. Financial and managerial accounting thus have somewhat different objectives, as they provide information with which to make different decisions. Exhibit 1-3 summarizes some of the more important differences.

EXHIBIT 1-3 Comparison of Financial and Managerial Accounting

	Financial Accounting	Managerial Accounting
1. Source of authority	Generally accepted accounting principles (GAAP)	Internal needs
2. Time frame of reported information	Primarily historical	Present and future
3. Scope	Mainly total company	Individual departments, divisions, and total company
4. Type of information	Primarily quantitative	Qualitative as well as quantitative
5. Statement format	Prescribed by GAAP; oriented toward investment and credit decisions	Determined by company; focused upon specific decisions being made
6. Decision focus	External	Internal

The company's accountants prepare both the financial accounting and the managerial accounting reports, and the information comes from the same information system. The differences lie in the selection and presentation of the communicated information. This book focuses on financial accounting and its usefulness in investors', creditors', and other users' decision making. We generally do not discuss the selection of managerial accounting information. On the other hand, the rules of a game influence how the game is played. The management of a company often is evaluated based on "performance criteria" (e.g., net income, rate of return) that are a function of accounting measures used in financial accounting reports. Thus, the financial accounting system may influence the managerial accounting system, or vice versa.

In other words, the amounts reported or methods used for financial accounting may influence management decisions, or the management of a company (perhaps in its own self-interest) may use the managerial accounting system to influence financial reporting. In this regard, the term *agency theory* describes the relationship between the manager (the "agent") and the stockholder (the "principal"). The theory suggests that agents do not always act in the best interests of the principals. For example, managers might make a decision that increases their compensation while reducing the wealth of the company, and therefore the wealth of the stockholders. Research suggests that an effective way to align the interests of the agent and the principal is to base the manager's compensation on the performance of the company. Examples include the payment of bonuses that are a percentage of the company's income, and the awarding of stock options. In later chapters we discuss the effects on financial reporting that result from the occurrence, or the potential for occurrence, of agency theory relationships.

Bonuses and stock options are discussed in Chapters 12 and 15.

Financial Reporting

Financial reporting is the process of communicating financial accounting information about a company to external users. A company may report its financial accounting information in several ways, and one important way is through its *annual report*. The financial reporting section of a company's annual report includes the company's financial statements and the notes to the financial statements. Companies present at least three major financial statements: (1) the *balance sheet* (or statement of financial position), which summarizes a company's financial position at a given date, (2) the *income statement*, which summarizes the results of a company's income-producing activities for a period of time, and (3) the *statement of cash flows*, which summarizes a company's cash inflows and cash outflows for a period of time. Many companies include the *statement of changes in stockholders' equity*, which summarizes the changes in each item of stockholders' equity for a period of time, as a fourth major financial statement.[4]

The Coca-Cola Company's annual report is included in Appendix A at the end of this book.

The *notes* to the financial statements include discussions that further explain items shown in the financial statements. Many of these notes also include supporting schedules of computations (some companies include the statement of changes in stockholders' equity here). The information in the notes is essential to understanding a company's activities. Most financial statements and accompanying notes presented to external users are *audited* by an independent certified public accountant (CPA). As we discuss in Chapters 3 and 5, after completion of the audit, the CPA expresses an opinion as to the fairness, in accordance with *generally accepted accounting principles*, of the financial statements and accompanying notes. These financial statements and notes (and supporting schedules) to the financial statements as they relate to financial reporting are the subject of this book.

2 Know what is included in financial reporting.

Generally Accepted Accounting Principles

The information communicated to external users in financial reporting is based on standards that establish generally accepted accounting principles (GAAP). **Generally accepted accounting principles are the guidelines, procedures, and practices that a company is required to use in recording and reporting the accounting information in its audited financial statements.** GAAP define accepted accounting practices at a particular time and provide a standard by which to report financial results. They are like laws and are the rules that must be followed in financial reporting.

The evolution of GAAP took place over many years and involved several accounting policy-making bodies, including the Financial Accounting Standards Board (FASB), Accounting Principles Board (APB), American Institute of Certified Public Accountants (AICPA), and Securities and Exchange Commission (SEC). Unfortunately, there is no single document that includes all the accounting standards. [There are electronic databases such as the FASB *Financial Accounting Research System (FARS)* that include most accounting standards.] Nonetheless, an accountant must be able to determine if a particular procedure for handling a transaction is acceptable under GAAP. Accountants therefore must know the sources of generally accepted accounting principles and must know how to find authoritative sources to aid in recording and reporting a particular

---

4.   Some companies include a *statement of comprehensive income* as another major financial statement. We discuss this statement in Chapter 4.

EXHIBIT 1-4   Hierarchy of Sources of GAAP

Categories	Authoritative Sources (Pronouncements)
A. Pronouncements of authoritative bodies (FASB, APB, CAP, SEC)	FASB *Statements of Financial Accounting Standards* and *Interpretations*, APB *Opinions*, and CAP (AICPA) *Accounting Research Bulletins* (as well as SEC *Regulation S-X* and *Financial Reporting Releases* for companies that file with the SEC)
B. Pronouncements of bodies of expert accountants that have been exposed for public comment*	FASB *Technical Bulletins*, AICPA *Industry Audit* and *Accounting Guides*, and AICPA *Statements of Position*
C. Pronouncements of bodies of expert accountants that have not been exposed for public comment*	FASB Emerging Issues Task Force *Consensus Positions* and AICPA *Practice Bulletins*
D. Widely accepted practices and pronouncements representing prevalent practice in a particular industry or applications to specific circumstances	AICPA *Accounting Interpretations*, FASB *Q's and A's*, and AICPA *Accounting Trends and Techniques*
E. Other accounting literature	For instance, FASB *Statements of Financial Accounting Concepts*, APB *Statements*, AICPA *Issue Papers*, AICPA *Technical Practice Aids*, and accounting texts and articles

*"Exposed for public comment" means that accountants and external users (the "public") have an opportunity to make suggestions (comment) on proposed pronouncements. Pronouncements in Categories B and C must also be "cleared" by an authoritative body from Category A, which means that the authoritative body does not object to the pronouncement.

transaction. Throughout this book we discuss GAAP for various transactions, events, and circumstances. However, to aid in researching the sources of generally accepted accounting principles, Exhibit 1-4 provides a "hierarchy" of five categories of GAAP and the authoritative sources applicable to each category for companies.[5]

These categories are listed in descending order of importance, with Category A as the most important. Accountants must follow the GAAP established by the pronouncements applicable to this category unless, in unusual circumstances, they result in misleading financial statements. In these circumstances or in situations where the accounting for a transaction or event is not specified by a pronouncement in Category A, then pronouncements in Categories B through D may be used to identify GAAP. Generally, pronouncements in Category B take precedence over those in Category C which, in turn, take precedence over those in Category D. When none of the pronouncements in Categories A through D is applicable, then the accountant may consider other accounting literature (Category E). We discuss each of the policy-making bodies and related pronouncements in the sections that follow.

3 Explain generally accepted accounting principles (GAAP) and the sources of GAAP.

THE ESTABLISHMENT OF ACCOUNTING STANDARDS

Even though accounting records dating back thousands of years have been discovered in various parts of the world, there was little organized effort to develop accounting standards in the United States prior to the 1930s. One of the most important initial

---

5. See *AICPA Professional Standards*, Volume 1 (New York: AICPA, 2002), sec. 411.05–.10, for more discussion. Note that a hierarchy of GAAP for state and local governments also exists.

attempts to develop standards began shortly after the onset of the Great Depression in 1929 with a series of meetings in the early 1930s between representatives of the New York Stock Exchange and the American Institute of Accountants (later to become the American Institute of Certified Public Accountants). The goal was to discuss accounting and reporting issues involving the interests of investors, the New York Stock Exchange, and accountants.

These concepts are discussed in Chapters 3 and 5.

The result of these meetings was a form of the auditor's opinion similar to the one used today. Specifically, the concepts of *fairness* and *consistency* in the application of accounting principles were introduced into the auditor's opinion. Fairness, in this regard, means that the accounting methods and procedures adopted by a company comply with traditional and conventional practice and that they adequately portray the economic reality of the company. Since these meetings, several groups have been responsible for the establishment of generally accepted accounting principles in the private sector of the United States. Exhibit 1-5 shows a "time-line" of the establishment of GAAP (Category A of Exhibit 1-4) in the private sector.

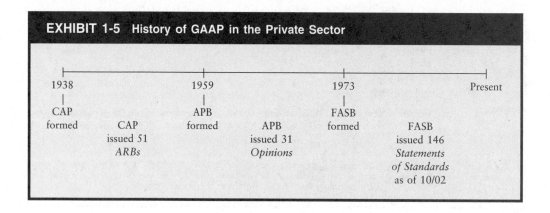

EXHIBIT 1-5   History of GAAP in the Private Sector

1938		1959		1973		Present
CAP formed		APB formed		FASB formed		
	CAP issued 51 ARBs		APB issued 31 Opinions		FASB issued 146 Statements of Standards as of 10/02	

Committee on Accounting Procedure (CAP)

In 1938 the AICPA formed the **Committee on Accounting Procedure (CAP)**. This group was responsible for issuing pronouncements to narrow the differences in accounting procedures and practice. Its conclusions were published as **Accounting Research Bulletins (ARBs)**. However, because at that time the AICPA did not have the authority to require compliance, the CAP could not enforce its pronouncements, and their application was optional. By 1953 the CAP had issued 42 *Accounting Research Bulletins*, and it then reviewed these pronouncements and codified them into **Accounting Research Bulletin No. 43**. The CAP issued eight more *Accounting Research Bulletins*, ending with No. 51 before it was replaced by the Accounting Principles Board in 1959. All *Accounting Research Bulletins* now are sources of generally accepted accounting principles unless specifically superseded or amended by other authoritative bodies.

Accounting Principles Board (APB)

After World War II the process of formulating accounting principles was increasingly criticized and wider representation in rule making was sought. In 1959 the AICPA formed the **Accounting Principles Board (APB)** as an attempt to (1) alleviate this criticism and (2) create a policy-making body whose rules would be binding on companies rather than optional. The APB comprised 17 to 21 members, selected primarily from the accounting profession. Representatives from industry, the government, and academia also served on the Board. The pronouncements of the APB were termed **Opinions of the Accounting Principles Board,** and 31 of these Opinions were issued. *APB Opinions* are sources of generally accepted accounting principles unless specifically amended or rescinded. Some of these Opinions were based upon *Accounting Research Studies.*

However, the conclusions drawn in these studies were solely the opinion of the individuals commissioned by the APB to write them. In several cases the APB either did not act upon the recommendations or came to different conclusions.

The members of the APB were volunteers whose employers allowed them time to serve on the Board. But by the late 1960s, criticism again arose concerning the development of accounting principles. This criticism centered on three factors:

1. *Independence.* The members of the APB were part-time volunteers whose major responsibilities were to the business, governmental, or academic organizations employing them.
2. *Representation.* The public accounting firms and the AICPA were too closely associated with the development of accounting standards.
3. *Response time.* Emerging problems were not solved quickly enough by the part-time members of the APB.

The AICPA reacted to those criticisms by appointing a committee to evaluate the method of formulating accounting principles. This committee, called the Wheat Committee after its chairman Francis Wheat, recommended that the APB be abolished and that a new full-time body be established with even wider representation.

Financial Accounting Standards Board (FASB)

The AICPA adopted the recommendations of the Wheat Committee. The APB was phased out and replaced in 1973 by the **Financial Accounting Standards Board (FASB)**. Exhibit 1-6 illustrates the current structure of the FASB.

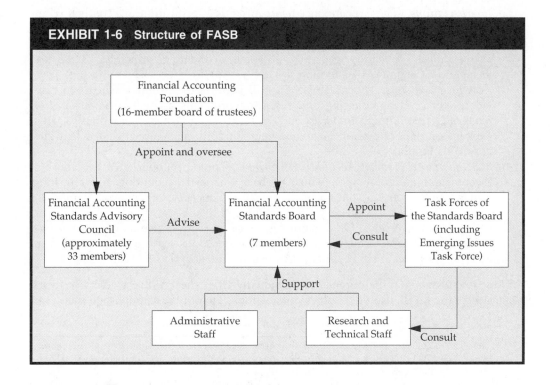

EXHIBIT 1-6 Structure of FASB

ORGANIZATION The Financial Accounting Foundation is the parent organization of the FASB. It is governed by a 16-member Board of Trustees appointed from the memberships of nine organizations (the AICPA, Financial Executives International, Institute of Management Accountants, Association for Investment Management and Research, American Accounting Association, Securities Industry Association, Government Finance

Officers Association, Comptrollers and Treasurers, and National Association of State Auditors) interested in the formulation of accounting principles.[6] The primary responsibilities of the Financial Accounting Foundation are to provide general oversight to its operations and appoint the members of the Financial Accounting Standards Advisory Council (FASAC) and the FASB. The FASAC consists of about 33 influential members. It is responsible for advising the FASB about major policy issues, the priority of topics, the selection of task forces, the suitability of tentative decisions, and other matters.

There are seven members of the FASB. Appointees to the FASB are full-time, fully paid members with no other organizational ties and are selected to represent a wide cross-section of interests. Each Board member is required to have a knowledge of accounting, finance, and business; high intelligence, integrity, and discipline; and a concern for the public interest regarding financial reporting. Currently, the FASB includes five members who are CPAs and who have been in public practice and two members from other areas related to accounting (e.g., academia and industry). The FASB is responsible for identifying financial accounting issues, conducting research to address these issues, and resolving them. The FASB is supported by a research and technical staff that performs numerous functions such as researching issues, communicating with constituents, and drafting preliminary findings. The administrative staff assists the FASB by handling library, publications, personnel, and other activities.[7]

4 Identify the types of pronouncements issued by the FASB.

The FASB issues several types of pronouncements:

1. *Statements of Financial Accounting Standards.* These pronouncements establish generally accepted accounting principles. They are releases indicating the methods and procedures required on specific accounting issues and are included in Category A of Exhibit 1-4.
2. *Interpretations.* These pronouncements provide clarification of conflicting or unclear issues relating to previously issued *FASB Statements of Financial Accounting Standards, APB Opinions,* or *Accounting Research Bulletins.* Interpretations also establish or clarify generally accepted accounting principles. They are included in Category A of Exhibit 1-4.
3. *Technical Bulletins.* The staff of the FASB issues these pronouncements to provide guidance on accounting and reporting problems related to *Statements of Financial Accounting Standards* or *Interpretations.* The guidance may clarify, explain, or elaborate upon an underlying standard. They are included in Category B of Exhibit 1-4.
4. *Statements of Financial Accounting Concepts.* These pronouncements establish a theoretical foundation upon which to base financial accounting and reporting standards. They are the output of the FASB's "Conceptual Framework" project.[8] They are included in Category E of Exhibit 1-4.

The Conceptual Framework project is discussed in Chapter 2.

5. *Other Pronouncements.* On a major topic, the FASB staff also may issue a *Guide for Implementation,* which is in the form of questions and answers (referred to as *FASB Q's and A's*). These are included in Category D of Exhibit 1-4.

These documents may be purchased individually from the FASB. As a service to its constituency, the FASB also offers other publications. Two of these, published each year

---

6. The Financial Accounting Foundation also is the parent organization of the *Governmental Accounting Standards Board* (GASB), which establishes accounting principles for state and local governmental entities. We briefly discuss the GASB later in the chapter.
7. For a more detailed look at the FASB's operations, see P. B. Miller, R. J. Redding, and P. R. Bahnson, *The FASB: The People, the Process, and the Politics,* 4th ed. (Boston: The McGraw-Hill Companies, Inc., 1998).
8. The similarity in the titles *Statement of Financial Accounting Concepts* and *Statement of Financial Accounting Standards* makes an abbreviated reference to each potentially ambiguous. To avoid confusion, throughout this book a reference to **FASB Statement No. __** in the body of the text will always refer to a statement of *standards,* while a full reference will be presented for each statement of *concepts.*

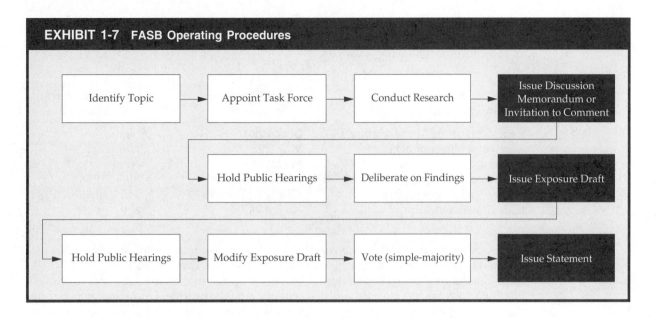

EXHIBIT 1-7 FASB Operating Procedures

Identify Topic → Appoint Task Force → Conduct Research → Issue Discussion Memorandum or Invitation to Comment

Hold Public Hearings → Deliberate on Findings → Issue Exposure Draft

Hold Public Hearings → Modify Exposure Draft → Vote (simple-majority) → Issue Statement

as part of the FASB's Accounting Standards series, are useful references for accountants. One two-volume set, entitled *Original Pronouncements*, includes all of the first four types of pronouncements as of its date of publication. Another two-volume set, entitled *Current Text* (*General Standards* and *Industry Standards*), is a topical integration of currently effective accounting and reporting standards as of its date of publication. These documents are also available on the *FARS* electronic database.

OPERATING PROCEDURES Before issuing a statement of concepts or standards, the FASB generally completes a multistage process as outlined in Exhibit 1-7, although the sequence and number of steps may vary. Initially, a topic or project is identified and placed on the FASB's agenda. This topic may be the result of suggestions from the FASAC, the accounting profession, industry, or other interested parties. On major issues a Task Force may be appointed to advise and consult with the FASB's Research and Technical Staff on such matters as the scope of the project and the nature and extent of additional research. The Staff conducts any research specifically related to the project.

5 Understand how the Financial Accounting Standards Board (FASB) operates.

Then the FASB usually publishes a Discussion Memorandum or Invitation to Comment (which outlines the research related to the issues) and sets a public comment period. During this period, the FASB may hold public hearings similar to those conducted by Congress. The intent is to receive information from and views of interested individuals and organizations on the issues. Many parties submit written comments ("position papers") or make oral presentations. These parties include representatives of CPA firms and interested corporations, security analysts, members of professional accounting associations, and academics. After deliberating on the views expressed and the information collected, the FASB issues an Exposure Draft of the proposed Statement. Interested parties generally have 30 to 90 days to provide written comments of reaction. On major issues, the FASB may hold more public hearings. Sometimes, the FASB conducts "field tests" of the proposed standards with selected companies to evaluate implementation issues. A modified draft is prepared, if necessary, and brought to the FASB for a final vote. After a *simple-majority* (i.e., 4 to 3) vote is attained, the *Statement* is issued.

The time involved to complete each of the steps varies depending on the complexity of the topic. For some complex topics the time frame involves several years; for other, less complex topics only a few months are needed. For instance, the FASB deliberated on basic conceptual and practical issues involving the statement of cash flows for more than ten years. The Board issued a Discussion Memorandum in 1980, but then deferred consideration of cash flows reporting until it dealt with related theoretical issues in its Conceptual Framework project. In 1985 the FASB reactivated the topic. It held public hearings and received over 450 comment letters in response to its Exposure Draft. *FASB Statement No. 95*, entitled "Statement of Cash Flows," was issued in November 1987, as shown in the following summary.

Step in Procedures	FASB Statement No. 95	FASB Statement No. 102
Issue *Discussion Memorandum*	Dec. 1980	None
Receive public comments	May 1981	None
Appoint Task Force	May 1985	None
Issue *Exposure Draft*	July 1986	Nov. 1988
Receive public comments	Through Mar. 1987	Through Jan. 1989
Issue *Statement*	Nov. 1987	Feb. 1989

On the other hand, *FASB Statement No. 102*, which amended *FASB Statement No. 95* for banks, brokers and dealers in securities, and similar companies, was issued within three months after the related Exposure Draft was issued. In this case the FASB concluded that it could reach an informed decision without a public hearing. During the public comment period it did receive 69 comment letters, which were used in the deliberation process.

SOCIOPOLITICAL ENVIRONMENT   As Exhibit 1-7 and the related discussion show, the operating procedures of the FASB are designed so that accounting standards are developed in an efficient manner, with due process, and in a public forum. The intent is to consider all related research on a particular topic, as well as the views of all interested parties, before coming to a logical conclusion concerning the appropriate accounting standard for the topic.

An inexperienced viewer of the FASB operating procedures might think that accounting standards are always "ideal" because they are the result of "rational policy making," where there are clearly defined objectives, an integrated body of theory, and known consequences of the actions. Yet this may not always be the case, because accounting is part of a broader social system. Often, objectives are not clear, research results are conflicting, and only "best guesses" can be made of the future consequences of current standards because "in no instance involving complex social [e.g., accounting] issues has anyone demonstrated . . . that a particular [accounting] policy decision was 'right' in the sense of coming closer than another decision to specified objectives."[9]

A former member of the Accounting Principles Board argues that "the setting of accounting standards is as much a product of political action as of flawless logic. . . ."[10] He feels that since accounting standard setting is a social decision that places restrictions on behavior, the affected parties must accept these decisions. To achieve "acceptable decisions" it is only natural for the affected parties to attempt to influence the decisions. Since the FASB holds public hearings and open meetings, it is relatively easy for various external user groups (e.g., investors and creditors) and other interested groups (e.g., affected corporations and CPA firms), which often hold conflicting views, to attempt to influence the FASB to develop new standards, continue existing standards, or change existing standards in their own best interests. For instance, the FASB recently decided that a new accounting standard for "stock options" was desirable, but it could not get support from external user groups. Therefore, it decided to allow companies to use either the new standard or the existing standard. Because the FASB has such a wide constituency and focuses on general purpose financial reporting, it often must establish accounting standards that are the result of *compromise*. Compromise is inevitable as the FASB responds to the "globalization" of industry. In this regard, the FASB has been working with the International Accounting Standards Committee (discussed later) and the accounting rule-making bodies of other countries to "harmonize" accounting

---

9. D. L. Gerboth, "'Muddling Through' with the APB," *Journal of Accountancy* (May 1972), p. 43.
10. C. T. Horngren, "The Marketing of Accounting Standards," *Journal of Accountancy* (October 1973), p. 61.

standards among different countries. As Dennis Beresford (former Chair of the FASB) states: "Different countries have different domestic concerns that are reflected in the way they think about financial reporting. None of the viewpoints are more 'right' than one another, just different. Compromises are an inevitable part of harmonization."[11]

In regard to U.S. standards, for a given topic each FASB member will have certain issues of high priority and others of lower priority. In the FASB's deliberation process each Board member will attempt to persuade the other members to accept the important issues and to drop the less important ones. This negotiation is necessary to reach a consensus so that a majority vote may be attained on the topic.[12] Whenever a compromise is reached, some in the FASB's constituency may be unhappy because they perceive that the new GAAP is somehow "unfair" to them. This dissatisfaction was especially true in cases prior to January 1, 1991, where only a simple majority (4 to 3 vote) was necessary to issue a standard. In such a situation, many in the constituency found fault with the conclusions reached by the FASB. They criticized the FASB for failing to listen to constituents, moving too quickly on topics, not giving sufficient consideration to cost/benefit issues, creating logically inconsistent rules, and establishing complex standards that are too difficult to implement.

The Financial Accounting Foundation, in its general oversight role of the FASB, has implemented procedures to overcome these criticisms. These procedures include use of an oversight committee to monitor the FASB's standard-setting process, periodic Financial Accounting Foundation and FASB discussions, stronger input by the FASAC on agenda determination and task force use, and additional publication and field testing of preliminary views. Between 1991 and 2002, as a way to minimize compromise at least a 5 to 2 vote by the FASB was required to issue a standard. Compromise is not necessarily bad; in fact, it can be beneficial. Compromise, however, can slow down the deliberation process. To make the process more efficient, effective in April 2002, a 4 to 3 vote (simple-majority) by the FASB is required to issue a new standard.

In a democratic society, "only politically responsible institutions have the right to command others to obey their rules."[13] Accounting standards are not unchangeable. The FASB fulfills its responsibility by (1) establishing standards that are the most acceptable, given the various affected constituencies, and (2) continually monitoring the consequences of its actions so that revised standards can be issued where appropriate. As Dennis Beresford (former Chair of the FASB) points out, the FASB carries out its public responsibility in an environment characterized by subtlety, complexity, and an absence of clear-cut answers. The FASB works hard to develop accounting standards that can be defended in terms of facts and circumstances, logic, and the fairness of the process that produces them.[14] Reinforcing this fairness idea in testimony before a Senate committee, Edmund Jenkins (then Chair of the FASB) stated that the notion of neutrality is a fundamental element of the FASB's standard-setting process. The Board must be objective in its decision making to ensure the neutrality of the information resulting from its standards, because information that is not neutral loses credibility and value.[15]

Other Organizations Currently Influencing Generally Accepted Accounting Principles

In addition to the policy-making bodies discussed in the previous section, several other organizations have had an impact on the development of generally accepted accounting principles during the past several decades.

---

11. D. R. Beresford, "Notes from the Chairman," *FASB Status Report No. 282*, (November 18, 1996), p. 2.
12. For additional discussion of the FASB's political process, see Miller, Redding, and Bahnson, *op. cit.*, chap. 1.
13. D. L. Gerboth, "Research, Intuition, and Politics in Accounting Inquiry," *The Accounting Review*, (July 1973), p. 481.
14. D. R. Beresford and R. V. Riper, "The Not-So-Mysterious Ways of the FASB," *Journal of Accountancy* (February 1992), p. 83.
15. E. L. Jenkins, "FASB Chairman Testifies on Business Combinations Accounting," *FASB Status Report No. 207-C.* (March 24, 2000), p. 2.

SECURITIES AND EXCHANGE COMMISSION (SEC)   The SEC was created to administer various securities acts under powers provided by Congress in the Securities Act of 1933 and the Securities Exchange Act of 1934. Under these Acts, **the SEC has the legal authority to prescribe accounting principles and reporting practices for all companies issuing publicly traded securities.** While this authority has seldom been used, from time to time the SEC has exerted pressure on the CAP, the APB, and the FASB. It has been especially interested in narrowing areas of difference in accounting practice and in increasing disclosures.

The 1933 Act requires each company offering securities for sale to the public in the primary and secondary markets to file a registration statement and to provide each investor with a proxy statement prior to each stockholders' meeting. The 1934 Act established extensive reporting requirements to aid in full disclosure. Among the most commonly required reports are:

Form S-1. A registration statement.

Form 10-K. An annual report.

Form 10-Q. A quarterly report of operations.

Form 8-K. A report used to describe any significant events that may affect the company.

Proxy Statement. A report used when management requests the right to vote through proxies for shareholders at stockholders' meetings.

Companies are required to file these forms electronically with the SEC, and these forms are located in the SEC's Electronic Data Gathering Analysis and Retrieval System (commonly known as EDGAR on the Internet (www.sec.gov/edgar.shtml).

These disclosures are further discussed in Chapters 3 and 5.

The SEC establishes accounting principles with respect to the information contained within the preceding reports and issues reporting guidelines in the form of its *Regulation S-X*, its *Financial Reporting Releases*, and its *Staff Accounting Bulletins* for companies that file with the SEC. In some instances the SEC has required the disclosure of information not typically found in published financial reports.

The impact of the SEC generally has been through its informal approval of *APB Opinions* and *FASB Statements* before their issuance. While the SEC has the authority to decide what constitutes "generally accepted accounting principles," in many cases it has exercised this authority through persuasion rather than edict. Evidence of the SEC's position can be found where it endorsed the concept of "substantial authoritative support" by asserting that "principles, standards, and practices promulgated by the FASB in its *Statements* and *Interpretations* will be considered by the Commission as having substantial authoritative support, and those contrary to such FASB promulgations will be considered to have no such support."[16] The result of this position has been to *allow accounting principles to be formulated in the private sector* rather than by the government.

6 Describe the relationship between the Securities and Exchange Commission (SEC) and the FASB.

However, the SEC has been criticized for not exercising its responsibility, and there is no assurance that the position will remain in effect. In fact, during 1978 the SEC refused to support **FASB Statement No. 19** requiring the use of the successful-efforts method in the oil and gas industry, and the FASB reacted by suspending the effective date of this release. Then, in the late 1980s the House Energy and Commerce Committee's Oversight and Investigations Subcommittee, chaired by Congressman John Dingell, was critical of the SEC for its alleged failure to monitor the detection of fraud and to establish an "early warning" system for identifying potential business failures. Although these hearings did not result in changes involving the establishment of generally accepted accounting principles, they did have an impact on *auditing* standards. Furthermore, the SEC pressured the FASB to adopt a standard requiring the use of market

---

16. "Codification of Financial Reporting Policies," *SEC Accounting Rules* (Chicago: Commerce Clearing House, 2002), sec. 101. This Codification contains the accounting principles and reporting guidelines issued prior to 1982 in the SEC's *Accounting Series Releases*. In 1982 the name was changed to *Financial Reporting Releases* to better reflect the nature of the documents.

values by companies for reporting certain types of investments, and the Board issued **FASB Statement No. 115** in response to this pressure.

AMERICAN INSTITUTE OF CERTIFIED PUBLIC ACCOUNTANTS (AICPA) The AICPA dates back to 1887 and is the professional organization for all certified public accountants in the United States. To be a member of the AICPA, an individual must have passed the Uniform CPA Examination, possess a CPA certificate, agree to abide by its bylaws and Code of Professional Ethics, and have 150 hours of higher education. The primary purpose of the AICPA is to provide the necessary technical support to assure that CPAs serve the public interest in performing quality professional services.

To fulfill this purpose, the AICPA publishes numerous documents that, in certain circumstances, may be considered as sources of generally accepted accounting principles, as listed in Exhibit 1-4. *Industry Audit Guides* and *Industry Accounting Guides* (Category B of Exhibit 1-4) are publications designed to assist independent auditors in examining and reporting on financial statements of various types of entities in specialized industries (e.g., banking). *Statements of Position* (Category B of Exhibit 1-4) are publications intended to influence the development of financial accounting principles that best serve the public interest. *Practice Bulletins* (Category C of Exhibit 1-4) are publications that provide guidance on specific technical issues.

During the tenure of the Accounting Principles Board, the AICPA issued numerous *AICPA Accounting Interpretations* to provide timely guidance on accounting issues without the formal procedures necessary for an APB Opinion. These Interpretations (Category D of Exhibit 1-4) are still sources of generally accepted accounting principles unless specifically rescinded or amended. The AICPA also annually publishes *Accounting Trends and Techniques* (Category D of Exhibit 1-4), which provides a study of the latest accounting practices and trends, as identified from a survey of 600 published annual reports. Reference may be made to this publication to identify a consensus about generally accepted accounting principles for a particular issue or methods of disclosure. In this book we often cite disclosure information from *Accounting Trends and Techniques* that applies to a specific accounting practice. Finally, the AICPA develops *Issue Papers* (Category E of Exhibit 1-4) to help the FASB identify accounting areas that need to be addressed and clarified.

FASB EMERGING ISSUES TASK FORCE (EITF) The EITF was established in 1984 as a response by the FASB to criticisms that the Board did not always provide timely guidance on new accounting issues. Members of the EITF meet every six weeks; they include technical experts from all the major CPA firms and representatives from smaller CPA firms and from industry. These individuals are knowledgeable in accounting and financial reporting and are in positions to be aware of emerging problems. The Chief Accountant of the SEC also participates in EITF meetings. The primary objectives of the EITF are (1) to identify significant emerging accounting issues (i.e., unique transactions and accounting problems) that it feels the FASB should address and (2) to develop *consensus positions* on the implementation issues involving the application of standards. As shown in Category C of Exhibit 1-4, in some cases these consensus positions may be viewed as the "best available guidance" on generally accepted accounting principles, particularly as they relate to new accounting issues. The FASB publishes a summary of the proceedings of the EITF in a loose-leaf service and in an annual bound version entitled *EITF Abstracts*. The summary is also available electronically on the *FARS* database.

COST ACCOUNTING STANDARDS BOARD (CASB) The CASB was established in 1970 as an agency of the U.S. Congress. It ceased to exist in 1980 when Congress failed to vote funds for its continuance, but was reinstated in 1988. The CASB is responsible only for negotiated federal contracts and subcontracts exceeding $500,000 and has issued several *Cost Accounting Standards* in this regard. Since internal cost accounting procedures often impact on externally reported financial information, these cost accounting standards occasionally influence external reporting. In the past, consideration has been given to replacing the FASB with a governmental board like the CASB. Although this change has not been implemented, the possibility of additional governmental involvement in the formulation of accounting principles should not be discounted.

INTERNAL REVENUE SERVICE (IRS)   The IRS administers the provisions of the Internal Revenue Code enacted by Congress. Federal income tax laws have had a significant impact upon financial reporting practices since they were first enacted in 1913. Although the Internal Revenue Code generally does not affect financial accounting practice directly, managers often prefer to lessen its impact upon the accounting systems within their companies. The result in many cases has been the adoption of those accounting methods and procedures that result in the lowest taxable income, without regard for what is proper from the standpoint of financial accounting theory and practice.

The impact of the Internal Revenue Code on financial accounting for income taxes is discussed in Chapter 18.

You should understand that accounting for income tax purposes and accounting for financial reporting purposes *are* and *should be* different. The goal of financial accounting is to provide information to financial statement users so that they may make decisions. The goal of income tax accounting is to legally minimize or postpone the payment of income taxes. Frequently the goals of financial reporting and income tax reporting come into conflict. For this reason, in this book we are concerned with determining the proper *financial* accounting recording and reporting procedures. What is, or should be, proper under the Internal Revenue Code is an entirely different question, which we only discuss when it has an impact on financial accounting and reporting.

AMERICAN ACCOUNTING ASSOCIATION (AAA)   The AAA is an organization composed primarily of academics and practicing accountants. The mission of the AAA is to foster world-wide excellence in the creation, dissemination, and application of accounting knowledge and skills. Its goals are to encourage excellence in accounting research and accounting instruction, and to contribute to excellence in accounting practice. These goals are primarily implemented through various meetings; the AAA's journals—*The Accounting Review, Issues in Accounting Education*, and *Accounting Horizons;* and the work of various committees such as the AAA Financial Accounting Standards Committee (FAS). The FAS responds to various documents of the FASB relating to proposed statements of concepts and standards. The AAA has no official stature in the development of financial accounting practice, so its impact is through education and persuasion rather than through formal pronouncements. However, its members have served on the APB, FAF, and the FASB, and have appeared before the FASB in its hearings on particular issues.

INTERNATIONAL ACCOUNTING STANDARDS BOARD (IASB)   Companies are becoming increasingly international in scope by selling and buying products and services as well as establishing operations in other countries. This globalization of business activity has led to increased information in a company's financial statements about its international operations. Investors and creditors in international markets, in turn, prefer that the information they use for investment and credit decisions be consistently prepared within countries and be internationally comparable from company to company across countries. The IASC International Accounting Standards Committee (IASC) Foundation is the parent organization of the International Accounting Standards Board (IASB). The objectives of the Foundation are to: (1) develop high quality, understandable, and enforceable global accounting standards that lead to useful, comparable financial reporting to help users in the world's capital markets make informed economic decisions, (2) promote the use and rigorous application of these standards, and (3) bring national accounting standards into agreement with international accounting standards.

The operating structure of the IASC Foundation consists of (1) a group of *Trustees* which is responsible for fundraising, appointing IASB members, and overseeing the effectiveness of the IASB, (2) the *IASB*, which issues *International Accounting Standards* and includes 12 full-time members (and 2 part-time members) from various countries, (3) an *International Financial Reporting Interpretations Committee* to interpret the application of the Standards, and (4) a *Standards Advisory Council* to give advice to the IASB on priorities and views of organizations on major standard setting projects. The operating procedure of the IASB is somewhat similar to that of the FASB and includes study of the topic, issuance of an Exposure Draft, evaluation of comments, and consideration of a revised draft. If approved by at least eight members of the IASB, the revised draft becomes an *International Accounting Standard*. To date, the IASB has issued 41 Standards.

There are, however, important differences between the environments in which the FASB and the IASB operate. The FASB operates as a private standard-setting organization, and the emphasis for establishing accounting standards in the United States is on the usefulness of accounting information to investors and creditors. On the other hand, in many other countries the emphasis in financial reporting is on meeting legal (e.g., tax) requirements, so that standard setting has evolved as a governmental rather than a private function. A role of the IASB, then, is to consolidate many countries' accounting regulations into international standards. In this regard, in response to an appeal from the International Organization of Securities Commissions, the IASB has developed a set of "core standards" that comprise a comprehensive set of accounting principles for the financial statements of companies making "crossborder" offerings of their securities. As a result, the European Commission requires that listed European companies must use international accounting standards by 2005. Although there are areas of difference, financial statements prepared according to U.S. generally accepted accounting principles usually will comply with international accounting standards. Furthermore, as we noted earlier, the FASB and IASB are working together to harmonize accounting standards. However, financial statements prepared according to international accounting standards may *not* comply with U.S. GAAP. In later chapters, where U.S. accounting principles differ from international principles, we will discuss those differences briefly as they relate to the topics being covered.

GOVERNMENTAL ACCOUNTING STANDARDS BOARD (GASB) The GASB was established in 1984 and operates under the auspices of the Financial Accounting Foundation. The GASB operates in a manner similar to the FASB. It consists of a full-time chair and six other members, plus a supporting staff. The GASB's responsibility is to establish financial accounting standards for certain state and local governmental entities. Its impact on accounting principles for the private sector is minimal.

G4 + 1 The G4 + 1 is a group of accounting standard setting boards which has as its objective to influence the development and harmonization of high quality accounting standards which will improve the usefulness of information provided to international capital markets participants. Members of the G4 + 1 include the standard setters for the US, UK, Australia, Canada, and New Zealand. The IASC participates as an observer. The members of the G4 + 1 discuss new ideas and approaches to financial reporting issues, and pool their resources to support joint research efforts. The G4 + 1 group does not issue accounting standards.

PROFESSIONAL ASSOCIATIONS There are also several professional organizations that play an important role in the accounting standard-setting process. The **Financial Executives International (FEI)** consists primarily of high-level financial executives (such as financial vice-presidents, treasurers, and controllers) of major corporations. The FEI publishes a monthly journal called the *Financial Executive* and has sponsored research projects dealing with financial reporting issues. Membership in the **Institute of Management Accountants (IMA)** is open to anyone, although its primary focus is on management accounting and financial management issues. The IMA publishes a monthly journal called *Strategic Finance*, which includes articles involving strategies in accounting, finance, and information management. Members of the **Association for Investment Management and Research (AIMR)** are financial analysts who use accounting information in various investment management and security analysis decisions. The AIMR publishes the *Financial Analysts Journal*, and its members participate in FASB research studies that deal with the impact of proposed accounting standards on users of financial accounting information. As we noted earlier, each of these organizations is also a member of the Financial Accounting Foundation and provides input to the FASB through its operations, as well as through position papers and oral presentations in the public hearings process.

EXHIBIT 1-8   Participants in the Development of GAAP

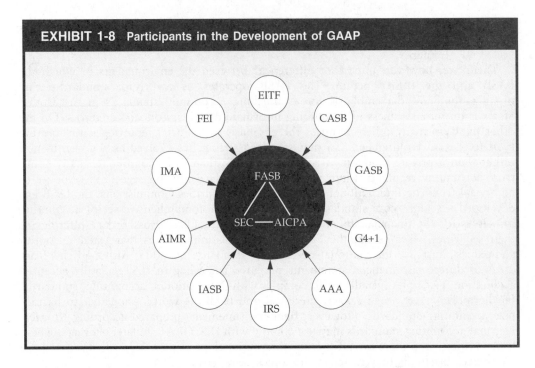

RELATIONSHIP OF ORGANIZATIONS IN CURRENT STANDARD-SETTING ENVIRONMENT   As we discussed earlier, accounting standards are set in a sociopolitical environment. Currently there are three major organizations in the private and public sector that develop GAAP for companies: the FASB, the AICPA, and the SEC. To a lesser extent, the other organizations we discussed in this section also are influential in the standard-setting process. We illustrate the relationship of the various participants in this process in Exhibit 1-8.

ETHICS IN THE ACCOUNTING ENVIRONMENT

In recent years there have been an increasing number of news reports about unethical behavior on the part of companies or individuals acting in their own self-interest without regard to the impact on society. These unethical actions include, for instance, polluting lakes and streams, illegal shipments of weapons to foreign countries, savings and loan scandals, selling products that are hazardous to users' health, overcharging on government contracts, false advertising, and "insider trading" activities. All of these unethical behaviors have a common theme: increased profits at the expense of some aspect of society. While these unethical actions often are sensational and capture the national headlines, there are also many situations of a smaller scale in which accountants face ethical dilemmas.

Earlier we mentioned that accountants who record and report financial information must follow generally accepted accounting principles, and that auditors must express an opinion as to the fairness (in accordance with GAAP) of the financial statements. Among other things, the financial statements of a company communicate how well the employees of the company at the department, division, and corporate levels have performed in operating the company. The results reported in the audited financial statements are likely to have an impact on the company's ability to sell stock or borrow money, as well as on employees' compensation and promotion opportunities. Consequently, these employees have a vested interest in portraying their performances in the best light and may pressure accountants to do so. We also mentioned that in the FASB's public hearings and open meetings various parties attempt to influence the Board in their own self-interest. These are but a few examples of situations in which accountants may be faced with *ethical dilemmas* (*ethical conflicts*), situations in which an accountant must make a decision about what is the "right" (ethical) action to take in a given set of circumstances. With the realization that accounting is a service activity that plays an important role in society, professional accounting organizations have established "codes of ethics" for their members. One of these applies to members of the AICPA.[17]

Members of the AICPA recognize that they assume an obligation of self-discipline above and beyond the requirements of laws and regulations. To help guide members in public practice, industry, government, and education in performing their responsibilities, the AICPA adopted the **Code of Professional Conduct (CPC)**. The CPC includes six *Principles* that express the basic tenets of ethical and professional conduct and call for an unswerving commitment to honorable behavior, even at the sacrifice of personal advantage. Exhibit 1-9 summarizes these Principles.[18]

EXHIBIT 1-9 Principles of the AICPA Code of Professional Conduct

   I. *Responsibilities*: In carrying out their responsibilities as professionals, members should exercise sensitive professional and moral judgments in all their activities.

  II. *The Public Interest*: Members should accept the obligation to act in a way that will serve the public interest, honor the public trust, and demonstrate commitment to professionalism.

 III. *Integrity*: To maintain and broaden public confidence, members should perform all professional responsibilities with the highest sense of integrity.

 IV. *Objectivity and Independence*: A member should maintain objectivity and be free from conflicts of interest in discharging professional responsibilities. A member in public practice should be independent in fact and appearance when providing auditing and other attestation services.

  V. *Due Care*: A member should observe the profession's technical and ethical standards, strive continually to improve competence and the quality of services, and discharge professional responsibility to the best of the member's ability.

 VI. *Scope and Nature of Services*: A member in public practice should observe the Principles of the CPC in determining the scope and nature of services to be provided.

While this code of ethics establishes guidelines for accountants in performing their responsibilities, it does not provide a structured approach for "moral reasoning" in ethical dilemmas. Ethical behavior may be different from legally acceptable behavior. What is legal may still be unethical in certain circumstances. Ethicists have developed alternative "models" to help individuals make sound moral judgments and guide their behavior when faced with ethical dilemmas involving various stakeholders. In the business environment of a company, the *stakeholders* may include past, current, and potential investors; creditors; employees; suppliers; competing companies; local, state, and federal governments; and citizens in the local, regional, national, and even international communities.

According to Velasquez, a noted ethicist, there are three basic approaches to moral reasoning. Each of these approaches uses a different set of moral standards in distinguishing between right and wrong. These approaches include (1) the *utilitarian* model, which evaluates actions based on the extent to which they result in the "greatest good for the greatest number," (2) the *rights* model, which embraces actions that protect individual moral rights, and (3) the *justice* model, which emphasizes a fair distribution of benefits and burdens. In determining whether an action is ethical or which of several alternative behaviors is the most ethical, Velasquez suggests that no single set of moral standards is sufficient. Instead, he proposes a several-step process that combines all three types of moral standards. This process includes (1) gathering the facts (e.g., who are the "stakeholders," what are my responsibilities); (2) asking whether the action is acceptable according to three ethical criteria: (a) utility: does the action optimize the satisfactions of all stakeholders? (b) rights: does the action respect the rights of all

7 Use ethical models for decision making about ethical dilemmas.

---

17. For the code of ethics of the IMA, another professional accounting organization, see *Ethical Standards,* IMA: www.imanet.org.

18. *AICPA Code of Professional Conduct*, AICPA: www.aicpa.org.

individuals? and (c) justice: is the action fair and just?; (3) considering whether there are any "overwhelming factors," such as conflicts between criteria that may justify disregarding one or more of the ethical criteria; and (4) deciding whether the action is ethical (or what ethical action to take) based on an evaluation of the applicable ethical criteria.[19]

Accountants are noted to have high ethical standards.[20] Acting in an ethically appropriate manner is not always easy; sometimes it is very difficult. However, because of the important role of accounting in society, every accountant must have high moral standards and strive to behave at the highest ethical level.

CREATIVE AND CRITICAL THINKING IN THE ACCOUNTING ENVIRONMENT

The business environment in which accountants work is constantly changing and becoming more complex. New products and services are continually introduced, and existing products are modified. Production techniques are changing, as are the channels of distribution and the approaches to promoting these products. There is an explosion of information technology as computers are networked, satellites allow global audiovisual communication, fax machines, the Internet, and electronic mail enable nearly instantaneous information transmittal, and cellular phones link customers and suppliers. Globalization is occurring, with more and more companies becoming international in their operating activities by buying, producing, and selling products in foreign countries. Government regulations are increasing, as more concern is given to such issues as worker safety and environmental impacts.

In response to these changes, companies are becoming more innovative in the ways they manage their businesses, how they finance their activities, what they invest in to expand their operating capabilities, and what approaches they use in their credit and collection processes. They are restructuring their organizations and operations to increase efficiency, and are more sensitive to changing technology and product obsolescence. They are more creative in the ways they structure their executive and employee compensation packages. Accounting systems that are designed to accumulate, process, and communicate information for decision making in this changing environment must change to satisfy the needs of users. Accounting principles must evolve to reflect this changing environment. Accountants responsible for establishing, modifying, operating, monitoring, and evaluating these systems, as well as for establishing and applying accounting principles, must be both *creative* thinkers and *critical* thinkers.

Research in psychology has found that each side of the brain deals with a different type of thinking. The right side focuses on creative thinking, involving visualizing and developing ideas. The left side focuses on critical thinking, involving analyzing and evaluating ideas. All individuals think creatively and critically, but the degree to which each side of the brain is used differs among individuals. However, through practice, it is possible for individuals to increase their ability to think creatively and critically.

8 Understand creative and critical thinking.

Different aspects of creative thinking and critical thinking have been studied and discussed for many years and in numerous areas. Here, we discuss briefly what role these concepts play in financial accounting. There are many ways creative thinking and critical thinking are defined, in part because they are not mutually exclusive and the differences between the two types of thinking are not clear-cut. For our purposes, **creative thinking is the process of finding new relationships (ideas) among items of information that potentially can be used to solve a problem.** Creative thinking involves constructively using imagination and insight to see issues in a different light. Terms that are used to describe a creative thinker include insightful, intuitive, imaginative,

19. M. Velasquez, *Business Ethics: Concepts and Cases*, 4th ed. (Englewood Cliffs, N.J.: Prentice Hall, 1998), ch. 2.
20. "The CPA Span of Influence Study," Research Study for AICPA by Peter W. Hart Research Associates (March 16, 2000).

sensitive, flexible, original, adaptable, and tolerant of ambiguity.[21] In contrast, **critical thinking is the process of testing these new relationships (ideas) to determine how well they will work.** Critical thinking involves using inductive or deductive reasoning to analyze an issue logically. Terms that are used to describe a critical thinker include objective, independent, analytical, logical, rational, able to synthesize, consistent, and organized.[22]

In financial accounting, accountants tend to be "problem solvers." When an accounting issue or problem arises, the accountant is responsible for its resolution. Several steps have been identified in the problem-solving process, as we show in Exhibit 1-10. These steps include (1) recognizing a problem, (2) identifying alternative solutions, (3) evaluating the alternatives, (4) selecting a solution from among the alternatives, and (5) implementing the solution. Creative thinking and critical thinking both play a role in each step of the problem-solving process. However, creative thinking is probably most critical in the *identification* of alternative solutions, while critical thinking is most critical in the *evaluation* of the alternative solutions.

The degree of complexity may differ from one problem to another. Problems can range from structured problems to unstructured problems. For *structured* problems, virtually complete information is known about the alternatives (in fact, there may be only one alternative) so that identifying, evaluating, selecting, and implementing an alternative is straightforward. At the other extreme are *unstructured* problems where even the basic issue may not be readily apparent, the alternative solutions are unclear once the problem is identified, and there is a lack of information about the alternatives, so that the identification, evaluation, selection, and implementation process is much more complex. Between these extremes is the *partially structured* problem, where either the alternative solutions are unclear or there is a lack of information about the alternative solutions.

At the policy-making level the FASB deals with complex unstructured problems. The Board members engage in higher-order creative thinking and critical thinking in their problem-solving processes involving the *establishment* of generally accepted accounting principles. In this book we discuss the major issues faced by the FASB in setting standards. However, our primary focus is on the *application* of generally accepted accounting principles in the recording and reporting of various topics. These topics may be general (e.g., income measurement) or specific (e.g., inventory). For each topic, we identify GAAP, discuss the related conceptual issues, and explain the recording and reporting procedures.

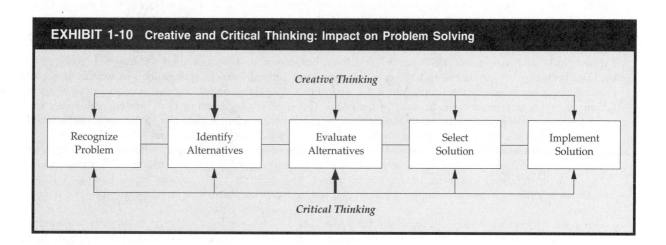

EXHIBIT 1-10   Creative and Critical Thinking: Impact on Problem Solving

Creative Thinking

Recognize Problem → Identify Alternatives → Evaluate Alternatives → Select Solution → Implement Solution

Critical Thinking

---

21. For a more extensive discussion of creative thinking, see S. F. Isaksen, K. Dorval, and D. Treffinger, *Creative Approaches to Problem Solving*, 2nd ed. (Williamsville, NY: Creative Problem Solving Group-Buffalo, 2000).

22. For a more extensive discussion of critical thinking, see J. Chaffee, *Thinking Critically*, 6th ed. (New York: Houghton Mifflin Company, 2000).

In the exercises and problems at the end of each chapter, we focus primarily on assignments intended to help you reinforce your understanding of the topical material. We do so by requiring you to prepare solutions to issues related to the chapter topics. These assignments generally involve structured problems for which there are only one or two correct solutions, so that the steps of identification, evaluation, and selection of alternatives in the problem-solving process are reduced or omitted. This approach does not mean that your creative thinking and critical thinking processes are not at work, however. In solving these assignments, you are practicing both creative and critical thinking, but at a lower level. It is important to master the understanding of basic recording and reporting issues in financial accounting before moving to more complex accounting issues that involve less structured problems and entail higher-level creative and critical thinking.

As a step in helping you develop your higher-level creative and critical thinking skills, there are also cases at the end of each chapter. These cases may require you to explain your understanding of interrelated concepts and practices. They may also require you to determine solutions to issues to which specific generally accepted accounting principles do not apply directly. These cases may deal with accounting issues that are emerging because of changes in the business environment discussed earlier. They may focus on topics that are too "industry specific" to be included in the chapter material. In these latter situations, the cases will require you to "research GAAP" in documents such as the FASB's *Current Text* or *Original Pronouncements* (or FARS) and, in so doing, stimulate your higher-level creative and critical thinking as you complete the problem-solving process. If your instructor does not assign these cases, you may still want to analyze them as a way of practicing creative and critical thinking. Your ability to think creatively and critically will be very important in your future accounting and business (as well as personal) activities.

SUMMARY

At the beginning of the chapter, we identified several objectives you would accomplish after reading the chapter. The objectives are listed below, each followed by a brief summary of the key points in the chapter discussion.

1. **Understand capital markets and decision making.** Capital markets are organized exchanges such as the NYSE, AMEX, and NASDAQ, where the capital stock and bonds of publicly held corporations are purchased and sold. Investors make buy-hold-sell decisions in regard to securities traded on these capital markets based on accounting information.

2. **Know what is included in financial reporting.** Financial reporting involves communicating financial accounting information about a company to external users. An important way to do so is in a company's annual report. In its annual report, a company includes at least three financial statements—a balance sheet, income statement, and statement of cash flows—and may include a statement of changes in stockholders' equity. It also includes notes to the financial statements.

3. **Explain GAAP and its sources.** GAAP are the guidelines, procedures, and practices that a company is required to use in recording and reporting the accounting information in its audited financial statements. The sources of GAAP included pronouncements by the FASB, APB, CAP, and SEC in five categories of descending order of importance.

4. **Identify the types of pronouncements issued by the FASB.** The FASB issues several types of pronouncements including *Statements of Financial Accounting Standards, Interpretations, Technical Bulletins, Statements of Financial Accounting Concepts,* and other pronouncements, such as *Guides for Implementation* and *FASB Q's and A's.*

5. **Understand how the FASB operates.** The FASB is a seven-member board. Before issuing a statement of concepts or standards, the FASB goes through several steps which include conducting research and issuing a Discussion Memorandum or Invitation to Comment, holding public hearing and deliberating on findings before issuing an Exposure Draft, holding more public hearings, modifying its tentative conclusions, voting (simple-majority), and issuing the Statement.

6. **Describe the relationship between the SEC and the FASB.** The SEC has the legal authority to prescribe accounting principles and practices for all publicly traded companies. It, however, endorsed the workings of the FASB by stating that the standards set by the FASB will be considered by the SEC to have substantial authoritative support.

7. **Use ethical models for decision making about ethical dilemmas.** Models for ethical decision making include the *utilitarian* model, the *rights* model, and the *justice* model. In using these models, one several-step approach includes (1) gathering the facts; (2) asking whether the action is acceptable according to utility, rights, and justice ethical criteria; (3) considering any "overwhelming factors"; and (4) deciding whether the action is ethical.

8. **Understand creative and critical thinking.** Creative thinking is the process of finding new relationships (ideas) among items of information that potentially can be used to solve a problem. Critical thinking is the process of testing these

new relationships (ideas) to determine how well they will work. In problem solving, creative thinking is most important in the *identification* of alternative solutions, while critical thinking is most important in the *evaluation* of the alternative solutions.

QUESTIONS

Q1-1 Distinguish between primary markets and secondary markets.

Q1-2 Distinguish between the categories of users of financial statements. Why might their decision-making needs be different?

Q1-3 Compare and contrast financial and managerial accounting.

Q1-4 What is financial reporting and what is the primary way a company's financial information is reported?

Q1-5 What are the three major financial statements of a company and what do they summarize? What is the fourth major financial statement that many companies present, and what does it summarize?

Q1-6 What are generally accepted accounting principles? List the four accounting bodies that have established generally accepted accounting principles.

Q1-7 How many "categories" are in the hierarchy of generally accepted accounting principles? List the pronouncements that are included in Category A.

Q1-8 What are (were) the CAP, APB, and FASB? What documents that constitute generally accepted accounting principles have been issued by each of these organizations?

Q1-9 Briefly discuss the procedures followed by the FASB for issuing a statement of concepts or standards.

Q1-10 List and briefly discuss the types of pronouncements issued by the FASB.

Q1-11 List several organizations other than the FASB that have had an impact on the development of generally accepted accounting principles.

Q1-12 What is the IASB and how does it operate?

Q1-13 List several professional organizations that play an important role in the accounting standard-setting process.

Q1-14 What is the *Code of Professional Conduct* and what are the six areas covered in the Principles of this code?

Q1-15 List the steps a person should follow to determine whether an action is ethical.

Q1-16 What is creative thinking? How would you describe a creative thinker?

Q1-17 What is critical thinking? How would you describe a critical thinker?

CASES

COMMUNICATION

C1-1 Pronouncements

Several accounting groups have issued various pronouncements establishing or related to generally accepted accounting principles. The following is a list of six pronouncements, as well as a list of statements describing each pronouncement.

A. Statements of Financial Accounting Standards
B. Opinions
C. Technical Bulletins
D. Statements of Financial Accounting Concepts
E. Interpretations
F. Accounting Research Bulletins

_____ 1. Pronouncements that provide clarification of conflicting or unclear issues relating to previously issued FASB *Statements of Standards*, APB *Opinions*, or *Accounting Research Bulletins*.

_____ 2. Issued by the FASB to provide guidance on accounting and reporting problems related to *Statements of Standards* or *Interpretations*.

_____ 3. Pronouncements of the APB that constitute generally accepted accounting principles unless specifically amended or rescinded, many of which were based on *Accounting Research Studies*.

_____ 4. Issued by the FASB as a series establishing a theoretical foundation upon which to base financial accounting and reporting standards.

_____ 5. Pronouncements of the Committee on Accounting Procedure (CAP) that constitute generally accepted accounting principles unless superseded or amended by other authoritative bodies.

_____ 6. Pronouncements issued by the FASB that establish generally accepted accounting principles and indicate the methods and procedures required on specific accounting issues.

Required Place the appropriate letter (A–F) identifying each pronouncement on the line in front of the statement describing the pronouncement.

C1-2 Organizations

Certain organizations have been influential in the establishment of accounting principles. The following is a list of abbreviations for several of these organizations, as well as a list of statements describing the organizations.

A. IRS   G. CASB
B. APB   H. FASB
C. CAP   I. AAA
D. IASB   J. GASB
E. SEC   K. AICPA
F. FASAC   L. EITF

_____ 1. First organization in United States to be given authority to issue pronouncements on accounting procedures and practice. Issued *Accounting Research Bulletins*.

_____ 2. Establishes cost accounting standards for United States government contracts.

_____ 3. Administers the provisions of the Internal Revenue Code.

_____ 4. Helps establish internationally comparable accounting principles.

_____ 5. Establishes accounting standards for state and local governmental entities.

_____ 6. Establishes generally accepted accounting principles in the private sector of the United States.

_____ 7. Organization of academics and practicing accountants.

_____ 8. Responsible for advising the FASB about technical areas, task forces, and other matters.

_____ 9. Established 31 *Opinions*, many of which still constitute generally accepted accounting principles.

_____ 10. Has legal authority to prescribe accounting principles and reporting practices for all companies issuing publicly traded securities.

_____ 11. Professional organization for all CPAs in the United States.

_____ 12. Develops consensus positions on the implementation issues involving the application of standards.

Required Place the appropriate letter (A–L) for each organization in front of the statement describing the organization. In addition, write out the full name of the organization.

C1-3 Establishment of GAAP

Since the late 1930s, three organizations have been primarily responsible for the establishment of generally accepted accounting principles in the private sector of the United States.

Required Write a brief report that identifies the three organizations and provides a brief chronological history of each, including the pronouncements issued that still constitute generally accepted accounting principles.

C1-4 Accounting Principles

At the completion of the Darby Department Store audit, the president asks about the meaning of the phrase "in conformity with generally accepted accounting principles" that appears in your audit report on the management's financial statements. He observes that the meaning of the phrase must include more than what he thinks of as "principles."

Required

1. Explain the meaning of the term "accounting principles" as used in the audit report. (Do not discuss in this part the significance of "generally accepted.")

2. The president wants to know how you determine whether or not an accounting principle is generally accepted. Discuss the sources of evidence for determining whether an accounting principle has substantial authoritative support. Do not merely list the titles of publications. *(AICPA adapted)*

C1-5 Standard Setting

When the Accounting Principles Board was founded in 1959, it planned to establish financial accounting standards using empirical research and logical reasoning only; the role of political action was little recognized at that time. Today, there is wide acceptance of the view that political action is as much an ingredient of the standard-setting process as is research evidence. Considerable political and social influence is wielded by user groups—those parties who are most interested in or affected by accounting standards.

Two basic premises of the Financial Accounting Standards Board (FASB) are (1) that it should be responsive to the needs and viewpoints of the entire economic community, and (2) that it should operate in full view of the public, affording interested parties ample opportunity to make their views known. The extensive procedural steps employed by the FASB in the standard-setting process support these premises.

Required Write a brief report that describes why financial accounting standards inspire or encourage political action and social involvement during the standard-setting process. *(CMA adapted)*

C1-6 Organization of the FASB

The FASB is organized to establish generally accepted accounting principles. It is assisted by various groups and operates under a set of procedures.

Required Prepare a short written report that summarizes the structure, types of pronouncements, and operating procedures of the FASB.

C1-7 GAAP and the AICPA

The American Institute of Certified Public Accountants (AICPA) has been in existence for many years to help CPAs provide high-quality professional services. Among other activities, in certain circumstances the AICPA establishes or provides guidance on generally accepted accounting principles (GAAP).

Required Summarize the GAAP-related documents that the AICPA publishes.

C1-8 Code of Professional Conduct

In a few years, you may become a member of the AICPA and be subject to its Code of Professional Conduct (CPC).

Required Identify and briefly discuss the first five principles of the CPC. Provide examples that illustrate each principle.

CREATIVE AND CRITICAL THINKING

C1-9 GAAP Hierarchy

A friend of yours says, "I understand there are 'rules' for financial reporting. But what are these rules, where can a person find them, and which ones are more important?"

Required Prepare an answer for your friend.

C1-10 Lobbying the FASB

One of your friends remarks, "I understand that before voting on a Statement of Standards the FASB allows written comments and oral presentations in which interested parties can lobby for a particular ruling. Do you think this is a good idea?"

Required Prepare a written response that discusses the advantages and disadvantages of the FASB's allowing interested parties to provide input to its deliberative process.

C1-11 Ethical Responsibilities

Each person in one of your accounting classes is required to write a report on an accounting topic. Included in the report must be a discussion from a specific library book. When you go to the library, you find that the only copy of the book is "missing." While sitting at a study desk, you overhear one of your classmates say that he has "misfiled" the book in the library so he can use it again later without having to wait for other students to finish using it.

Required Discuss the steps you would take to address this ethical dilemma. It is not necessary to state what ethical action you would take, but be prepared to discuss your reasoning for each step.

C1-12 Ethical Responsibilities

You and a friend are in the same accounting class. During the first test, you observe that your friend cheated by copying one of her answers from another student (who was unaware of the copying). When the exams are returned, your grade is a B, while your friend's grade is an A.

Required Discuss the steps you would take to address this ethical dilemma. It is not necessary to state what ethical action you would take, but be prepared to discuss your reasoning for each step.

INTERNET ASSIGNMENTS

Go to the Nikolai and Bazley **Intermediate Accounting** web site (http://Nikolai.swcollege.com). Click on Student Resources and internet homework assignments. Then click on the appropriate hot link (icon) for each organization's web site, find the relevant information, and answer the following questions.

I1-1   Go to the FASB web site.

   Required What are the names of the seven FASB board members? Who is chairman? What are their qualifications for serving on the FASB? Do their qualifications make you feel confident that the FASB will make the "right" decisions? Why or why not?

I1-2   Go to the SEC web site.

   Required What is the SEC, and what is the purpose of the laws and rules that govern the securities industry? How is the SEC organized, and what types of professionals work for the SEC? What is the overall responsibility of the Division of Corporation Finance?

I1-3   Go to the AICPA web site. Clik on About the AICPA.

   Required In regard to Section 53: Article (Principle) II (The Public Interest) of the AICPA's Code of Professional Conduct, how is the "public interest" defined? Who are included in the accounting profession's "public"? How do members of the accounting profession deal with conflicting pressures in discharging their professional responsibilities? Do you agree this is the proper approach? Why or why not?

objectives

1 Explain the FASB conceptual framework.

2 Understand the relationship among the objectives of financial reporting.

3 Identify the general objective of financial reporting.

4 Describe the three specific objectives of financial reporting.

5 Discuss the types of useful information for investment and credit decision making.

6 Explain the qualities of useful accounting information.

7 Understand the accounting assumptions and conventions that influence GAAP.

8 Define the elements of financial statements.

CHAPTER 2

Financial Reporting: Its Conceptual Framework

As we saw in Chapter 1, accounting standards were developed in the United States by the Committee on Accounting Procedure (CAP) and the Accounting Principles Board (APB) prior to the inception of the Financial Accounting Standards Board (FASB). Neither the CAP nor the APB attempted to develop a broad, normative conceptual framework of accounting theory. The APB did issue **APB Statement No. 4,** "Basic Concepts and Accounting Principles Underlying Financial Statements of Business Enterprises." However, this document described current practice rather than what *should* be appropriate accounting. Although the CAP and APB gave some consideration to theoretical accounting concepts in the establishment of accounting standards, generally this was limited to the concepts related to the particular accounting issue at hand. This led, at times, to the development of accounting principles that were inconsistently applied from one issue to another. In this chapter we discuss a conceptual framework of accounting theory. This framework includes the objectives of financial reporting, the types of useful accounting information, the qualitative characteristics of accounting information, and accounting assumptions and conventions, as well as a brief review of generally accepted accounting principles and financial statements.

FASB CONCEPTUAL FRAMEWORK

1 Explain the FASB conceptual framework.

Since its formation, the FASB has been given two charges. First, it is to develop a conceptual framework of accounting theory. Second, it is to establish standards (generally accepted accounting principles) for financial accounting practice. The intent is to develop **a theoretical foundation of interrelated objectives and concepts that leads to the establishment of consistent financial accounting standards.** In other words, the conceptual framework should provide a logical structure and direction to financial accounting and reporting. This conceptual framework is expected to (1) guide the FASB in establishing accounting standards, (2) provide a frame of reference for resolving accounting questions in situations where a standard does not exist, (3) determine the bounds for judgment in the preparation of financial statements, (4) increase users' understanding of and confidence in financial reporting, and (5) enhance comparability (discussed later). The FASB expects that the conceptual framework will serve the public by encouraging companies to provide financial (and related) information that is useful in efficiently allocating scarce economic resources in capital and other markets.[1]

---

1. This discussion is based on a background paper, "The Conceptual Framework Project," Financial Accounting Standards Board (Stamford, Conn., 1980).

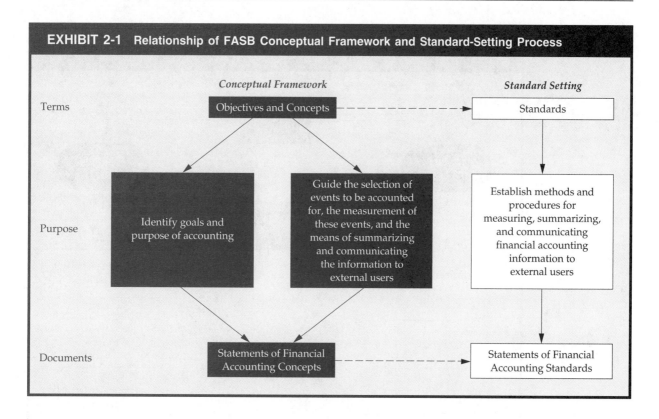

EXHIBIT 2-1 Relationship of FASB Conceptual Framework and Standard-Setting Process

Exhibit 2-1 shows the relationship among the objectives, concepts, and standards, their purposes, and the documents issued by the FASB. The outputs of the conceptual framework are *Statements of Financial Accounting Concepts*. The conceptual framework is nearly complete and seven Statements of Concepts have been issued. The outputs of the standard-setting process are *Statements of Financial Accounting Standards*: to date 146 have been issued. The numerous "statements of standards" are required to identify the preferable accounting practice from among the various alternatives that arise in response to the constantly changing, dynamic business environment. As much as possible, the FASB gives due consideration to the output of its conceptual framework in establishing these standards.

Because of the enormity of the task, the FASB divided its conceptual framework activities into several projects. Exhibit 2-2 shows these projects. The first project dealt with identifying the objectives of financial reporting. This project resulted in the issuance of **FASB Statement of Financial Accounting Concepts No. 1,** "Objectives of Financial Reporting by Business Enterprises." This document established the focus of the remaining projects, which are divided into two groups (accounting and reporting). The Qualitative Characteristics Project linked together the accounting and reporting projects, as illustrated by the dashed lines in Exhibit 2-2. It also resulted in the issuance of **FASB Statement of Financial Accounting Concepts No. 2,** entitled "Qualitative Characteristics of Accounting Information."

The accounting projects are concerned with defining the accounting elements (e.g., assets, liabilities, revenues, expenses) and identifying which elements should be reported, when they should be reported (recognized), and how they should be measured.[2] The reporting projects are concerned with how the elements of financial reports are "displayed." Issues of concern include general questions such as what information

---

2. For a discussion of these and other issues, see L. T. Johnson and R. K. Storey, "Recognition in Financial Statements: Underlying Concepts and Practical Conventions," *Research Report* (Stamford, Conn.: FASB, 1982).

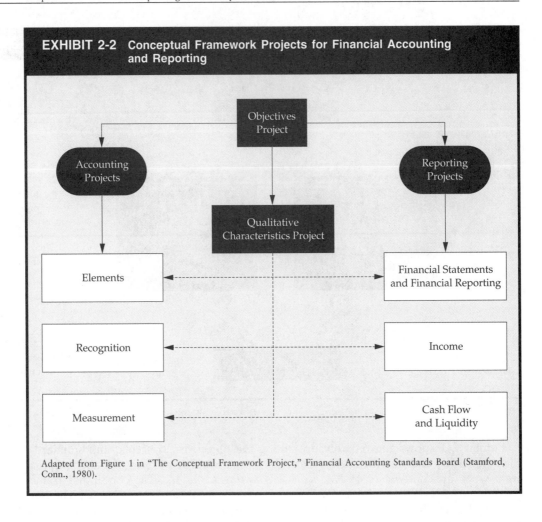

EXHIBIT 2-2   Conceptual Framework Projects for Financial Accounting and Reporting

Objectives Project

Accounting Projects

Reporting Projects

Qualitative Characteristics Project

Elements

Recognition

Measurement

Financial Statements and Financial Reporting

Income

Cash Flow and Liquidity

Adapted from Figure 1 in "The Conceptual Framework Project," Financial Accounting Standards Board (Stamford, Conn., 1980).

The Statements of Concepts dealing with the elements, recognition and measurement, and reporting of income and cash flows are discussed in Chapters 3 and 4.

should be provided, who should be required to provide the information, and where the information should be presented. Also included are more specific questions about income and its components, as well as cash flow and its components.

The FASB has issued several Statements of Concepts that deal with one or more of these accounting and reporting projects. **FASB Statement of Financial Accounting Concepts No. 3** was issued in 1980. However, this Statement of Concepts was replaced in 1986 by **FASB Statement of Financial Accounting Concepts No. 6,** "Elements of Financial Statements." **FASB Statement of Financial Accounting Concepts No. 5,** "Recognition and Measurement in Financial Statements of Business Enterprises," was issued in 1984.[3] **FASB Statement of Financial Accounting Concepts No. 7,** "Using Cash Flow Information and Present Value in Accounting Measurements," was issued in 2000. An Exposure Draft, *FASB Proposed Statement of Financial Accounting Concepts,* "Reporting Income, Cash Flows, and Financial Position of Business Enterprises," has been issued regarding the reporting projects. In addition, several working documents dealing with both accounting and reporting issues were published that may eventually lead to the issuance of other statements of financial accounting concepts.

We discuss the first two Statements of Concepts, dealing with the objectives of financial reporting and the qualitative characteristics of accounting information, as well as parts of the Exposure Draft dealing with types of useful information, in this chapter.

---

3. **FASB Statement of Financial Accounting Concepts No. 4,** entitled "Objectives of Financial Reporting by Nonbusiness Organizations," has also been issued but is not discussed in this book.

OBJECTIVES OF FINANCIAL REPORTING

In its first concepts statement, the FASB observed that the objectives of financial reporting are those of *general-purpose* external reporting by companies. That is, the objectives relate to a *variety* of *external* users (as opposed to specific internal users, such as management) who do not have the authority to prescribe the financial information they desire from a particular company and therefore must use the information that the management of the company communicates to them.[4]

2 Understand the relationship among the objectives of financial reporting.

The FASB identified several objectives of financial reporting. These objectives proceed from the more general to the more specific. Exhibit 2-3 shows these objectives and we discuss them in the following sections.[5]

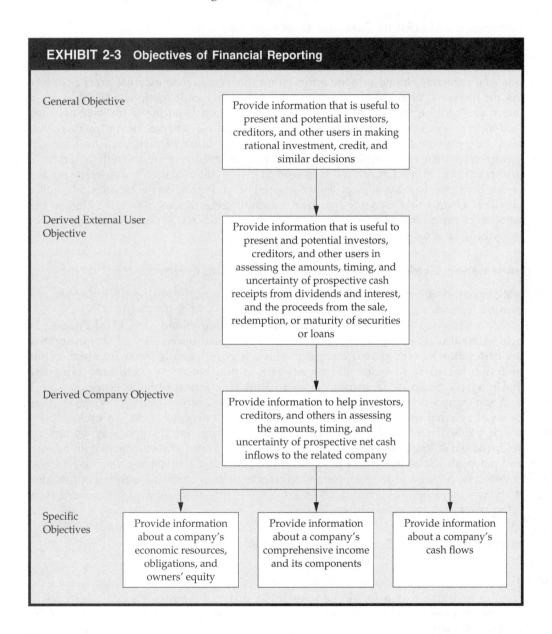

EXHIBIT 2-3 Objectives of Financial Reporting

General Objective

Provide information that is useful to present and potential investors, creditors, and other users in making rational investment, credit, and similar decisions

Derived External User Objective

Provide information that is useful to present and potential investors, creditors, and other users in assessing the amounts, timing, and uncertainty of prospective cash receipts from dividends and interest, and the proceeds from the sale, redemption, or maturity of securities or loans

Derived Company Objective

Provide information to help investors, creditors, and others in assessing the amounts, timing, and uncertainty of prospective net cash inflows to the related company

Specific Objectives

Provide information about a company's economic resources, obligations, and owners' equity

Provide information about a company's comprehensive income and its components

Provide information about a company's cash flows

---

4. "Objectives of Financial Reporting by Business Enterprises," *FASB Statement of Financial Accounting Concepts No. 1* (Stamford, Conn.: FASB, 1978), par. 28.

5. The discussion in this section primarily is a summary of that presented by the FASB in its "Objectives of Financial Reporting by Business Enterprises."

Information Useful in Decision Making

3 Identify the general objective of financial reporting.

The top of Exhibit 2-3 shows the most general objective. This objective states that **financial reporting should provide useful information for present and potential investors, creditors, and other external users in making their investment, credit, and similar decisions.** Investors include both equity security holders (stockholders) and debt security holders (bondholders). Creditors include suppliers, customers and employees with claims, individual lenders, and lending institutions. Other external users include brokers, lawyers, security analysts, and regulatory agencies. These external users are expected to have a reasonable understanding of business and economic activities and be willing to study carefully the information in order to comprehend the financial information.

Information Useful to External Users in Assessing Future Cash Receipts

The second objective shown in Exhibit 2-3 relates to external users' needs. It states that **financial reporting should provide information that is useful to external users in assessing the amounts, timing, and uncertainty of prospective cash receipts.** This objective is important because individuals and institutions make cash outflows for investing and lending activities primarily to increase their cash inflows. Whether or not they are successful depends on the extent to which they receive a return of cash, goods, or services greater than their investment or loan. That is, they must receive not only a return *of* investment, but also a return *on* investment relative to the risk involved. Investment and credit decisions involve choices between present and prospective future cash flows. Financial information is needed to help establish expectations about the timing and amount of prospective cash receipts (e.g., dividends, interest, proceeds from resale, or repayment) and assess the risk involved.

Information Useful in Assessing Company Cash Flows

Since investors invest in and creditors lend to a particular company, their current and prospective cash receipts are affected by the cash flows of the company. Thus, a third objective shown in Exhibit 2-3 is that **financial reporting should provide information to help external users in assessing the amounts, timing, and uncertainty of the prospective net cash inflows to the related company.** This objective logically flows from the second objective, because a company also invests cash in noncash resources to earn more cash and receive a return *on* its investment in addition to a return *of* its investment.

A company's activities regarding its investments are more complex, however, than those of external users. The company completes an "operating cycle" or cycles during which goods or services are acquired, their value is increased, the goods or services are sold, and the selling price is collected. Within this operating cycle numerous cash receipts and payments are collected and paid, in no precise order. The company's ability to generate net cash inflows (i.e., cash inflows greater than cash outflows) affects both its ability to pay dividends and interest and the market prices of its securities, which, in turn, affect investors' and creditors' cash flows.

Information About Economic Resources and Claims to These Resources

4 Describe the three specific objectives of financial reporting.

The most specific objectives in Exhibit 2-3 are those in the bottom tier, which indicate the types of information that should be provided in financial reports. **A specific objective of financial reporting is to provide information about a company's economic resources, obligations, and owners' equity.** This information is useful to external users for four reasons: (a) to identify the company's financial strengths and weaknesses and to assess its liquidity, (b) to provide a basis for evaluating information about the company's performance during a given period, (c) to provide direct indications of the cash flow potentials of some resources and the cash needed to satisfy obligations, and (d) to indicate the potential cash flows that are the joint result of combining various resources in the company's operations.

Information About Comprehensive Income and Its Components

Another specific objective of financial reporting is to provide information about a company's financial performance during a specified period in order to help external users form expectations about its future performance. The *primary* focus of financial reporting about a company's performance is information concerning the company's *comprehensive income* and its components. Information about comprehensive income is useful to external users in (a) evaluating management's performance, (b) estimating the company's "earning power," or other amounts perceived as being representative of long-term income-producing ability, (c) predicting future income, and (d) assessing the risk of investing in or lending to the company.

Comprehensive income is discussed in Chapter 4.

The measurement of comprehensive income should relate (i.e., match) the costs (sacrifices) of operations to the benefits from operations. The measurement should also include the benefits and costs of other nonoperating transactions, events, and circumstances. This is accomplished through the use of **accrual accounting,** whereby the financial effects of a company's transactions, events, and circumstances having cash consequences are related to the period in which they occur rather than to when the cash receipt or cash payment takes place.[6]

Information About Cash Flows

Although information about comprehensive income is a significant concern of external users, **another specific objective of financial reporting is to provide information about a company's cash flows.** Cash flow information shows how a company obtains and spends cash in regard to operations, investments, borrowings, and capital transactions, including cash dividends and other distributions of company resources to owners. External users use cash (or cash and cash equivalents) flow information about a company (a) to help understand its operations, (b) to evaluate its financing and investing activities, (c) to assess its liquidity, and (d) to interpret the comprehensive income information provided.

Other Issues

The FASB raised two other important issues in *FASB Statement of Concepts No. 1.* First, **financial reporting should provide information about how the management of a company has discharged its stewardship responsibility** to owners (stockholders) for use of the company resources entrusted to it. The management is responsible to the owners for the custody and safekeeping of the resources, their efficient and profitable use, and their protection against unfavorable economic impacts, technological developments, and social changes.

Second, **financial statements and other means of financial reporting should include explanations and interpretations by management to help external users understand the financial information provided.** This is known as **full disclosure.** Since a company's management knows more about the company's activities than "outsiders," the usefulness of financial information can be enhanced by, for instance, (a) explanations of certain transactions, events, and circumstances, (b) interpretations of the effects on the financial results of dividing continuous operations into accounting periods, and (c) explanations of underlying assumptions or methods used and any related significant uncertainties.

Management's discussion and analysis is discussed in Chapter 5.

The FASB established the qualitative characteristics (e.g., relevance, reliability) that accounting information should possess in order to be included in financial reports in *FASB Statement of Concepts No. 2,* and we include them in the next section of this chapter. The FASB includes definitions of the elements (e.g., assets, liabilities, revenues, and expenses) of financial statements in *FASB Statement of Concepts No. 6,* and we include them later in this chapter.

Financial statement elements are discussed in Chapters 3 and 4.

---

6. *FASB Statement of Concepts No. 1* originally used the term "earnings" instead of "comprehensive income." This latter term was substituted in *FASB Statement of Concepts No. 5* because comprehensive income encompasses more components. We discuss this issue more fully in Chapter 4.

The establishment of the objectives of financial reporting was the FASB's first step in developing its conceptual framework for financial accounting and reporting. The FASB intends that the objectives within this framework will act as guidelines for providing financial information for investment and credit decisions, thus facilitating the efficient operation of the capital markets and promoting the efficient allocation of scarce resources.

TYPES OF USEFUL INFORMATION

5 Discuss the types of useful information for investment and credit decision making.

The general objective of financial reporting is to provide information that is useful in investment and credit decision making. On a more specific level, a company's financial reports should provide information to help external users assess the amounts, timing, and uncertainty about the future net cash inflows of the company. The FASB has identified five types of information, explained in this section, as being useful in meeting this specific objective. Exhibit 2-4 shows the interrelationship of this useful information with financial reports and external decision making.

Return on Investment

Return on investment provides a measure of overall company performance. Shareholders (stockholders) invest capital for a share of the equity (stockholders' equity) of a company. These investors are concerned with a return *on* capital. Before a company can provide a return on capital, its capital must be maintained or recovered (i.e., first there must be a return *of* capital to the company). Once a company's capital is maintained, the return *on* capital (i.e., comprehensive income) may be distributed to investors or may be retained by the company for reinvestment.

Risk

Risk is the uncertainty or unpredictability of the future results of a company. The greater the range within which future results are likely to fall, the greater the risk associated with an investment in or extension of credit to the company. Risk is caused by numerous factors including, for example, high rates of technological change, uncertainty about

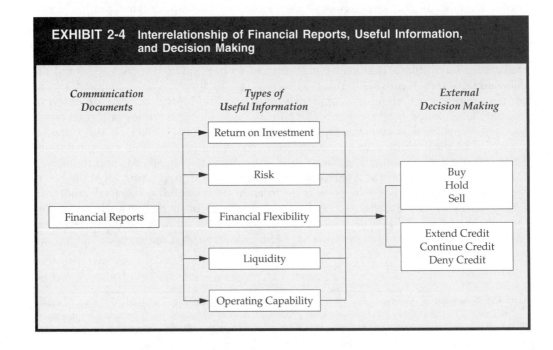

EXHIBIT 2-4   **Interrelationship of Financial Reports, Useful Information, and Decision Making**

demand, exposure to the effects of price changes, and political changes in the United States and other countries. In general, the greater the risk associated with an investment in a particular company, the higher the rate of return expected by investors (or the higher the rate of interest charged by creditors).

Financial Flexibility

Financial flexibility is the ability of a company to take effective actions to change the amounts and timing of cash flows. Financial flexibility is important because it enables a company to respond to unexpected needs and opportunities. Financial flexibility comes from the ability of a company to (a) adapt operations to increase net operating cash inflows, (b) raise new capital through, for instance, the sale of debt or stock securities at short notice, and (c) obtain cash by selling assets without disrupting ongoing operations. Financial flexibility affects risk as well as cash flows. It reduces the risk of failure in the event of a shortage in net cash flows from operations.

Liquidity

Liquidity is the term used to describe how quickly an asset can be converted into cash or a liability paid. Liquidity reflects an asset's or liability's nearness to cash. For operating assets, liquidity relates to the timing of cash flows in the normal course of business. For nonoperating assets, liquidity refers to marketability. The liquidity of a company is an indication of its ability to meet its obligations when they come due. Liquidity is positively related to financial flexibility but negatively related to both risk and return on investment. A more liquid company is likely to have a superior ability to adapt to unexpected needs and opportunities, as well as a lower risk of failure. On the other hand, liquid assets often offer lower rates of return than nonliquid assets.

Operating Capability

Operating capability refers to the ability of a company to maintain a given physical level of operations. This level of operations may be indicated by the quantity of goods or services (e.g., inventory) of a specified quality produced in a given period or by the physical capacity of the fixed assets (e.g., property, plant, and equipment). Information about operating capability is helpful in understanding a company's past performance and in predicting future changes in its volume of activities. Operating capability may be affected by changes in methods of operations, changes in product lines, and the timing of the replacement of the service potential used up in operations.[7]

QUALITATIVE CHARACTERISTICS OF USEFUL ACCOUNTING INFORMATION

In the previous sections we discussed the types of information that are helpful in investment and credit decision making. But what are the characteristics of useful information? The purpose of *FASB Statement of Financial Accounting Concepts No. 2* is to specify the qualitative characteristics or "ingredients" that accounting information should possess in order to be most useful.[8] These characteristics should be considered when choosing among accounting alternatives, because these qualities distinguish more useful from less useful information.

---

7. "Reporting Income, Cash Flows, and Financial Position of Business Enterprises," *FASB Proposed Statement of Financial Accounting Concepts* (Stamford, Conn.: FASB, 1981), par. 7–33.

8. The discussion in this section primarily is a summary of that presented in "Qualitative Characteristics of Accounting Information," *FASB Statement of Financial Accounting Concepts No. 2* (Stamford, Conn.: FASB, 1980).

Each accounting alternative, however, may possess more of one quality and less of another. Although considerable agreement exists about the qualitative characteristics that "good" accounting information should possess, no mathematical "model" or "equation" can determine which information has the "best" combination of qualitative characteristics for decision-making purposes. Furthermore, the FASB strives to meet the needs of all users through *general-purpose* financial statements. This does not reduce the importance of using the qualitative characteristics to establish common accounting standards. The qualitative criteria are helpful to the FASB in establishing "minimum" and "maximum" limits of useful accounting information so that it can develop logical accounting standards consistent with these "limits."

Hierarchy of Qualitative Characteristics

6 Explain the qualities of useful accounting information.

Exhibit 2-5 shows a hierarchy of the qualitative characteristics of accounting information. This section presents an overview of the hierarchy, after which we define and discuss the components in detail. The hierarchy is bounded by *two constraints*: (1) in order to justify providing the accounting information, **the benefits must be greater than the costs;** and (2) **the dollar amount of the information must be material** (i.e., large enough to make a difference in decision making). The hierarchy is not designed to assign priorities among the qualitative characteristics in all circumstances. To be useful, **accounting information must have each of the qualitative characteristics to a minimum degree.**

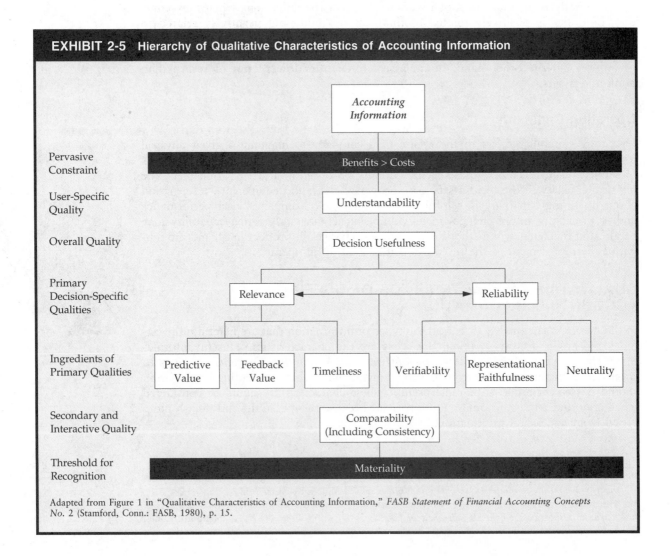

EXHIBIT 2-5   Hierarchy of Qualitative Characteristics of Accounting Information

Adapted from Figure 1 in "Qualitative Characteristics of Accounting Information," *FASB Statement of Financial Accounting Concepts No. 2* (Stamford, Conn.: FASB, 1980), p. 15.

However, different situations may require tradeoffs, whereby the level of one quality is sacrificed for an increase in that of another quality.

Understandability

Accounting information should be **understandable to users who have a reasonable knowledge of business and economic activities and who are willing to study the information with reasonable diligence.** *Understandability* serves as a "link" between the decision makers and the accounting information. Since the FASB establishes standards for general-purpose financial statements, it is concerned with the understandability of accounting information to *broad classes* of decision makers.

Decision Usefulness

Decision usefulness is the *overall* qualitative characteristic to be used in judging the quality of accounting information. Whether or not information is useful depends on the decision to be made, the way in which it is made, the information already available, and the decision maker's ability to process the information. Since the FASB establishes standards for broad classes of users, however, it must consider the quality of decision usefulness in a broad context. For purposes of evaluation, this overall quality can be separated into the primary qualities of relevance and reliability.

Relevance

Accounting information is relevant if it can make a difference in a decision by helping users predict the outcomes of past, present, and future events or confirm or correct prior expectations. In this context, an "event" is a happening that is significant to a company (e.g., the purchase of a building), and an outcome is the effect or result of an event or series of events (e.g., cash flows generated by use of the building). To be relevant, accounting information need not be expressed as a prediction. Information about the current status of a company's resources or obligations or about its past performance commonly is used as a basis for expectations. To be relevant, accounting information should have either predictive or feedback value, or both. In addition, it should be timely.

PREDICTIVE VALUE AND FEEDBACK VALUE   Accounting information has **predictive value** when it helps decision makers forecast more accurately the outcome of past or present events. Accounting information has **feedback value** when it enables decision makers to confirm or correct prior expectations. Often, information has both predictive value and feedback value because knowledge about the previous actions of a company (i.e., feedback) generally will improve a decision maker's ability to predict the results of similar future actions. An example is an interim income statement, which provides feedback about income to date and serves as a basis for forecasting the annual income.

TIMELINESS   Accounting information is **timely** when it is available to decision makers before it loses its ability to influence decisions. Timeliness is an ingredient of relevance. If information is not available when it is needed, it lacks relevance and is of little or no use. Timeliness alone cannot make information relevant, but a lack of timeliness reduces its potential relevance. However, a gain in relevance resulting from increased timeliness may involve a sacrifice of other desirable qualitative characteristics (e.g., reliability). The SEC has defined timeliness, requiring that each company under its jurisdiction file a Form 10-K annual report within 60 days of its fiscal year-end and a Form 10-Q quarterly report within 35 days of the end of each quarter effective in 2004.

Reliability

Accounting information is most useful when it is reliable as well as relevant. **Reliable information is reasonably free from error and bias, and faithfully represents what it is**

intended to represent. That is, to be reliable, information must be verifiable, neutral, and possess representational faithfulness. Reliability does not necessarily imply certainty or precision. For instance, estimates may be reliable. Reliability has different degrees, and what is an acceptable degree of reliability will depend on the circumstances.

VERIFIABILITY   Accounting information is **verifiable** (sometimes called **objective**) when measurers (i.e., accountants) can form a consensus (agree) that the selected method has been used without error or bias—that is, the measurement results can be duplicated. Verification is useful in reducing *measurer bias*, because by using the same method to repeat measurements, both unintentional and intentional errors are reduced.

Audit reports are discussed in Chapters 3 and 5.

Verification is a primary concern of auditing. The **Certified Public Accountant (CPA)** is an independent professional who reviews (audits) the published financial statements of a company. The performance of this duty is termed the **attest function.** It involves a review of a sample of a company's transactions during a reporting period to provide assurance that the recording and reporting of the financial information shown can be duplicated substantially by an independent measurer. As a result of the review, the CPA issues an auditor's report. Verification does not, however, ensure the appropriateness of the accounting methods used. That quality of accounting information is representational faithfulness.

REPRESENTATIONAL FAITHFULNESS   Accounting information has **representational faithfulness** when there is a relationship between the reported accounting measurements or descriptions and the economic resources, the obligations, and the transactions and events causing changes in these items. Social scientists define this concept as "validity." For instance, a company may record an item leased on a long-term basis from another entity as an economic resource even though it does not own the item. This recording increases the representational faithfulness of the reported economic resources available to the company. Having a high degree of representational faithfulness is useful in reducing *measurement bias*. Having representational faithfulness in one decision-making context, however, does not mean that accounting information will be relevant for other decisions. For instance, the current value of an economic resource that a company expects to replace in the near future would be useful information, but it might not be useful if the company has no intention of replacing it.

NEUTRALITY   Accounting information is **neutral** when there is an absence of bias intended to attain a predetermined result or to influence behavior in a *particular* direction. Neutrality does not mean that accounting information has no purpose or does not influence human behavior. The purpose of providing accounting information is to serve a variety of different users with diverse interests. Furthermore, accounting information is intended to be useful in decision making, thereby influencing the decision makers' behavior, but not in a predetermined direction. Neutrality also implies *completeness* of information. An omission of information can lead to bias if it is intended to induce or inhibit a particular behavior.

Comparability and Consistency

A secondary qualitative characteristic of accounting information is comparability (including consistency). Information about a company is more useful if it can be compared with similar information from other companies (this is referred to as *intercompany* comparison) or with similar information from past periods within the company (*intracompany* comparison). Comparability is not considered a primary quality of useful information, like relevance and reliability, because it must involve more than one item of information. It is an *interactive quality* of the relationship between two or more items of information. **Comparability of accounting information enables users to identify and explain similarities and differences between two or more sets of economic facts.**

Closely linked to comparability is consistency. **Consistency means conformity from period to period, with accounting policies and procedures remaining unchanged.** Consistency, like comparability, is a quality of the relationship between numbers rather than a quality of the numbers themselves. Consistency is an important condition in enhancing comparability across periods. Without consistency, it would be difficult for a user to determine whether differences in results were caused by economic differences or simply by differences in accounting methods. On the other hand, a change in accounting method is sometimes desirable. Economic situations may change, or more preferable new accounting methods may evolve. A company must make some sacrifice in consistency at certain times in order to improve the usefulness of its accounting information.

Constraints to the Hierarchy

Two constraints to the hierarchy of qualitative characteristics help to identify further what accounting information should be disclosed in financial reports. The first is a benefit/cost constraint; the second is a threshold-for-recognition, or materiality, constraint.

BENEFITS GREATER THAN COSTS Accounting information is a commodity. Unless the benefits expected to be received from a commodity exceed its costs, the commodity will not be sought after. The costs of providing financial information fall initially on the preparer (the company) and then are passed on to consumers (external users). These costs include the cost of collecting, processing, auditing, and communicating the information, as well as those associated with losing a competitive advantage by disclosing the information. The benefits are enjoyed by a diverse group of investors and creditors, by customers (because they are assured a steady supply of goods and services), and by the preparer itself (for use in internal decision making). To be reported, accounting information not only must be relevant and reliable but it also must satisfy the benefit/cost constraint. That is, the FASB must have reasonable assurance that the costs of implementing a standard will not exceed the benefits.

MATERIALITY The second constraint, that of materiality, is really a *quantitative* "threshold" constraint linked very closely to the qualitative characteristic of relevance. **Materiality refers to the magnitude of an omission or misstatement of accounting information that, considering the circumstances, makes it likely that the judgment of a reasonable person relying on the information would have been influenced by the omission or misstatement.** Materiality and relevance are both defined in terms of the influences that affect a decision maker, but the two terms can be distinguished. A company may make a decision to disclose certain information because users have a need for that information (it is relevant) *and* because the amount is large enough to make a difference (it is material). Alternatively, a decision not to disclose certain information may be made because the user has no need for the information (it is not relevant) *or* because the amount is too small to make a difference (it is not material).

The FASB did not set overall quantitative guidelines for materiality in the *Statements of Concepts*. It felt that materiality involves judgment, and that no general standards could be set that took into account all the elements of sound human judgment. Materiality judgments should be concerned with thresholds of recognition. Is an item large enough to pass over the threshold that separates material from immaterial items? To answer that question, the FASB suggested that a company give consideration to (1) the *nature* of the item (i.e., items considered too small to be significant when they result from routine transactions might be material if they arose from abnormal circumstances), and (2) the *relative size* rather than absolute size of an item (i.e., a $10,000 error in inventory of a large company may be insignificant while a similar $10,000 error by a small company may be material). The FASB observed that quantitative guidelines have been and will continue to be set for specific accounting issues where appropriate.

In regard to the relative size of a misstatement, many companies establish a percentage threshold; for instance, 5% of net income for the income statement and 5% of total assets for the balance sheet. Thus, if the misstatement of an amount is less than 5% of net income it is not considered material for the income statement. External users have expressed concern that some companies are using a percentage threshold as an "absolute" cutoff without considering the qualitative factors of the information, such as the surrounding circumstances or the "total mix" of information. In response, several groups (the SEC, the AICPA, and the Big Five Audit Materiality Task Force) have provided guidance in assessing the materiality of a misstated item for a company. These include, for instance, whether the misstatement (1) has an effect on trends (particularly trends in profitability), (2) masks a change in earnings (and earnings per share), (3) is currently immaterial but may have a material impact in future periods because of a cumulative effect, (4) changes a loss into net income (or vice versa), (5) misrepresents the company's compliance with loan agreements, (6) relates to a segment of the company that is of particular importance to the company's long-run profitability, and (7) has the effect of increasing management's compensation.[9] Thus, companies may use a quantitative threshold as an initial step in assessing materiality, but need to consider qualitative factors in making the final judgment on the materiality of an item.

ACCOUNTING ASSUMPTIONS AND CONVENTIONS

7 Understand the accounting assumptions and conventions that influence GAAP.

To this point we have identified the objectives of financial reporting, the types of useful information for investment and credit decision making, and the qualitative characteristics of useful accounting information. Consideration of these factors is necessary to establish accounting standards. In addition, certain accounting assumptions and conventions have had an important impact upon the development of generally accepted accounting principles. Exhibit 2-6 is useful in understanding the relationship among the objectives, types of useful information, qualitative characteristics, accounting assumptions and conventions, generally accepted accounting principles, financial reports, and elements of financial statements. We discuss the accounting assumptions and conventions listed in Exhibit 2-6 in this section. We will discuss others later in the book as they apply to specific accounting standards.

Entity

Most of the economic activity in the United States can be directly or indirectly attributed to business enterprises, termed **economic entities.** These entities vary in size from small, one-owner companies such as hair salons or restaurants, to partnerships such as law or accounting firms, and to large multinational corporations such as the **ExxonMobil Corporation.** Financial accounting is concerned with the economic activity of each of these entities, regardless of its size, and involves recording and reporting its transactions and events. A transaction involves the transfer of something of value between the entity and another party. In certain instances the financial records of related but separate legal entities may be *consolidated* (combined) to report more realistically the resources, obligations, and operating results of the overall economic entity.

Because the entity assumption distinguishes each organization from its owners, each separate entity prepares its own financial records and reports. The personal transactions of the owners are kept separate from those of the business enterprise. Throughout this book we refer to a business enterprise as a *company* (and when the discussion applies to a type of company, we use the specific type of entity, e.g., *corporation*).

Continuity

The **continuity assumption** is also known as the **going-concern assumption.** This assumption is that the company will continue to operate in the near future, unless substantial evidence to the contrary exists. Obviously not all companies are successful, and failures do occur. However, the continuity assumption is valid in most cases and is necessary for

---

9. For a more extensive discussion, see "Materiality," *SEC Staff Accounting Bulletin No. 99* (Washington, DC: Securities and Exchange Commission, August 12, 1999), "Audit Risk and Materiality in Conducting an Audit," *AICPA Professional Standards,* Volume 1 (New York: AICPA, 2002), sec. 312, and "Materiality in a Financial Statement Audit: Considering Qualitative Factors when Evaluating Audit Findings," Big Five Audit Materiality Task Force (August, 1998: available at www.aicpa.org).

EXHIBIT 2-6 Framework of Financial Accounting Theory and Practice

Framework	*Content*
Objectives	1. Provide information useful to external users in assessing amounts, timing, and uncertainty of a company's cash flows. 2. Provide information about a company's economic resources, obligations, and owners' equity. 3. Provide information about a company's comprehensive income and its components. 4. Provide information about a company's cash flows. 5. Provide information about the stewardship responsibility of a company's management. 6. Provide full disclosure to help external users understand the preceding information.
Types of Useful Information	1. Return on investment. 2. Risk. 3. Financial flexibility. 4. Liquidity. 5. Operating capability.
Qualitative Characteristics of Useful Accounting Information	1. Decision usefulness. 2. Relevance (predictive value, feedback value, timeliness). 3. Reliability (verifiability, neutrality, and representational faithfulness). 4. Comparability (including consistency). 5. Benefits greater than costs, materiality.
Accounting Assumptions and Conventions	1. Entity. 2. Continuity (going concern). 3. Period of time. 4. Historical cost. 5. Monetary unit. 6. Realization and recognition. 7. Matching and accrual. 8. Conservatism (prudence).
Generally Accepted Accounting Principles	1. Guidelines, procedures, and practices required by a company to record and report its accounting information in audited financial statements. 2. Sources of GAAP are financial accounting standards established in pronouncements of FASB, APB, AICPA, and SEC, and in other accounting literature (see Exhibit 1-4).
Financial Reports	1. Balance sheet. 2. Income statement. 3. Statement of cash flows. 4. Statement of changes in stockholders' equity. 5. Notes to financial statements. 6. Supplementary and other information.
Elements of Financial Statements	1. Assets, liabilities, and equity. 2. Revenues, expenses, gains, and losses. 3. Operating, investing, and financing cash flows. 4. Investments by and distributions to owners.

many of the accounting procedures used. For example, if a company is not regarded as a going concern, the company should not depreciate its fixed assets over their expected useful lives nor should the company record its inventory at its cost, because the receipt of future economic benefits from these items is uncertain.

Nevertheless, the continuity assumption does not imply permanence. It simply indicates that the economic entity will operate long enough to carry out its existing commitments. If a company appears to be on the verge of going bankrupt, it must discard the continuity assumption. The company then reports its financial statements on a liquidation basis, with all assets and liabilities valued at the amounts estimated to be collected or paid when they are sold or liquidated.

Period of Time

The profit or loss earned by a company cannot be determined accurately until it ceases to function. At that time the total lifetime profit or loss may be determined by comparing the cash on hand after liquidating the business plus any cash distributions to the owners during the period of operations with the amount invested by the owners during the company's lifetime. Obviously, financial statement users need more current information to evaluate a company's profitability. Companies primarily use a year as the reporting period. In accordance with the **period-of-time assumption,** a company prepares financial statements at the end of each year and includes them in its annual report. Furthermore the annual reporting period (called the **accounting period** or **fiscal year**) is used for reports issued to government regulators such as the Internal Revenue Service (IRS) and the Securities and Exchange Commission (SEC).

The adjusting entry process is reviewed in Appendix C.

The period-of-time assumption is the basis for the adjusting entry process in accounting because, if companies did not prepare financial statements on a yearly (or shorter time) basis, there would be no reason to determine the time frame affected by particular transactions. Historically most companies adopted the calendar year as the accounting period. However, many companies now choose a fiscal year that more closely approximates their annual *business cycle.* (The yearly period from lowest sales through highest sales and back to lowest sales is known as a business cycle.) For example, consider Exhibit 2-7, which illustrates the annual sales pattern for Company G. Notice that peak sales occur each year in January, while the lowest sales volume occurs in June. Such a sales pattern might be representative of a company that sells ski equipment. If Company G were to report on a calendar-year basis, the financial reports would be prepared at about the time of peak yearly sales (i.e., the midpoint of the business cycle). Alternatively, a fiscal year that ended on June 30 would incorporate a single complete annual business cycle. Many large retail chains have a fiscal year-end that follows the peak Christmas selling season. For example, Wal Mart's year-end is January 31, which is after most of the returns and allowances related to those sales have occurred. Fiscal-year reports incorporating an annual business cycle contain information that is more easily comparable to past and future periods because annual sales patterns are not broken by the reporting period.

In addition to annual reports, publicly traded companies issue financial statements for interim (quarterly) periods. These interim periods are considered integral parts of the annual period, and interim reports disclose summary information to provide investors with more timely information.

EXHIBIT 2-7   Company G Annual Business Cycle

Historical Cost

The economic activities and resources of a company initially are measured by the exchange price of a transaction at the time the transaction occurs. Usually the exchange price (the **historical cost**) is retained in the accounting records as the value of an item until the item is consumed, sold, or liquidated and removed from the records. That is, a company usually delays recording gains and losses resulting from value changes of assets (or liabilities) until another exchange occurs. The rationale behind the use of historical cost (as opposed to other valuation methods such as current market value or appraisal value) is that it is reliable, and that source documents usually are available to substantiate the recorded amount. Also, historical cost provides evidence that an independent buyer and seller were in agreement on the value of an exchanged good or service at the time of the transaction and thus has the qualities of representational faithfulness, neutrality, and verifiability.

One of the most frequently heard criticisms of accounting comes from those who would prefer alternative valuation methods that they believe would report information more relevant for user decisions. Accountants do understand that historical cost information may not always be completely *relevant* for all decisions, but it does have a significant degree of *reliability*. In certain cases accountants use valuation methods other than historical cost to report the *fair value* of selected items in the financial statements when these methods provide more relevant information and possess an acceptable degree of reliability. Generally, however, it is felt that the measurement problems inherent in alternative valuation methods are greater than those of historical cost. That is, reliability often takes precedence over relevance. The FASB, however, understands the significance of this relevance/reliability tradeoff and encourages companies to disclose *supplemental* current value information in their annual reports. Also, you should understand that the recognition by a company of changes in values of its assets and liabilities would require that the company include these value changes in its comprehensive income for the period.

Valuation methods are discussed in Chapter 3.

Supplemental current value information is discussed in Appendix E.

Monetary Unit

Since the time when gold and other precious metals were accepted in exchange for goods and services, thereby replacing the barter system, there has been a unit of exchange. This unit of exchange is different for almost every nation, but accountants generally have adopted the national currency of the reporting company as the unit of measure in preparing financial statements.

In using the dollar or any other currency as the unit of measure, accountants traditionally have assumed that it is a stable measuring unit. Prior to the FASB, accounting policy-making bodies had taken the position that fluctuations in the value of the dollar were not a serious enough problem to have an adverse effect upon the comparability of accounting information and thus did not warrant any adjustment in the monetary unit assumption.

In today's world the assumption that the dollar or any other national currency is a stable measure over time is not necessarily valid. Consider the building you are now in. If you were to measure its width in feet and inches today, next year, and five years from now, an accurate physical measurement would yield the same results each time. In contrast, consider the monetary value of the same building. Real estate prices have changed (increased or decreased) during the past several years and undoubtedly will continue to vary, resulting in changing monetary measures of value even though the physical capacity remains the same.

There are two primary reasons for changes in reported values over time:

1. The real value of the item in question may change in relation to the real value of all other goods and services in the economy.
2. The purchasing power of the measuring unit (in this case the dollar) may change.

Currently the dollar is considered to be a stable monetary unit for preparing a company's financial statements. As we mentioned earlier, however, to enhance comparability the

FASB encourages companies to make supplemental disclosures relating to the impacts of changing prices.

Realization and Recognition

Recognition criteria are discussed in Chapters 3 and 4.

Realization means the process of converting noncash resources and rights into cash or rights to cash. **Recognition** means the process of formally recording and reporting an item in the financial statements of a company. A recognized item is depicted in both words and numbers, with the amount included in the financial statement totals. The FASB has identified four fundamental recognition criteria. To be recognized, an item must (1) meet the definition of an element, (2) be measurable, (3) be relevant, and (4) be reliable. In regard to revenues, two other factors provide guidance for revenue recognition. Revenues should be recognized when (1) realization has taken place, and (2) they have been earned. These factors provide acceptable assurance of the existence and amounts of revenues.

It is an accounting convention to recognize revenue at the time of sale because usually this is when realization occurs (i.e., cash or receivables are obtained) and the earning process is substantially complete. Actually, revenue is earned by a company throughout the *earning process* as economic utility is added to goods. This process includes acquisition, production and/or distribution, sales, and the collection and payment of cash. Revenue could be recognized at one or more points in this process. In this regard, the FASB suggests that revenues are considered to be earned when a company has substantially completed what it must do to be entitled to the benefits (i.e., assets) generated by the revenues. Usually, this is the point of sale.[10]

Revenue recognition is discussed in Chapters 4 and 17.

Occasionally a company may advance (accrue) or delay (defer) the recognition of revenue in the earning process in order to depict more accurately the nature of its operations. Thus, a company may not recognize (record) revenue at the same time as realization. Revenue might be recognized (1) during production, (2) at the end of production, or (3) after the sale. In the case of certain long-term construction contracts extending over more than one accounting period, a company usually recognizes revenue during production to better depict economic reality by the use of the **percentage-of-completion** method. Similarly, revenue usually is recognized for certain long-term service contracts by use of the **proportional performance** method. These methods allocate the revenues of each contract to each period, based on an estimate of the percentage completed during the period.

A company might recognize revenue at the completion of production if there is a fixed selling price and there is no limit on the amount that can be sold. This situation might be the case for certain valuable minerals or for farm products sold on the futures market. Finally, revenue may be recognized after the sale if the ultimate collectibility of the revenue is highly uncertain. This situation might arise, for instance, in the case of real estate land sales where a very small down payment is required and the payment terms extend over many years. In situations of high uncertainty about collections, a company uses either the installment or the cost-recovery method to recognize revenue. Under the **installment** method, a portion of each receipt is recognized as revenue. Under the **cost-recovery** method, no revenue is recognized until the cost of the product has been recovered.

Matching and Accrual Accounting

Earlier, **accrual accounting** was defined as the process of relating the financial effects of transactions, events, and circumstances having cash consequences to the period in which they occur rather than to when the cash receipt or payment occurs. The **matching** principle is linked closely to accrual accounting and to revenue recognition.

---

10. "Recognition and Measurement in Financial Statements of Business Enterprises," *FASB Statement of Financial Accounting Concepts No. 5* (Stamford, Conn.: FASB, 1984), par. 63 and 83.

The matching principle states that to determine the income of a company for an accounting period, the company computes the total expenses involved in obtaining the revenues of the period and relates these total expenses to (matches them against) the total revenues recorded in the period. Thus, some expenses are advanced (accrued) or delayed (deferred) in a manner similar to revenues. The intent is to match the sacrifices against the benefits (i.e., the efforts against the accomplishments) in the appropriate accounting period.

A company recognizes and matches expenses against revenues on the basis of three principles: (1) association of cause and effect, (2) systematic and rational allocation, and (3) immediate recognition. Expenses recorded as a result of associating cause and effect include sales commissions and the **product costs** included in cost of goods sold. Expenses recorded on the basis of systematic and rational allocation include depreciation of property and equipment and amortization of intangibles. Immediate recognition is appropriate for **period costs**—those expenses related to a period of time, such as administrative salaries.[11]

Some smaller companies do not use accrual accounting and matching. Instead they use **cash basis** accounting for simplicity. In cash basis accounting, a company computes its income for an accounting period by subtracting the cash payments from the cash receipts from operations. While this method may be convenient to use, it can lead to incorrect evaluations of a company's operating results because the receipt and payment of cash may occur much earlier or later than the sale of goods or the providing of services to customers (benefits) and the related costs (sacrifices). Because cash basis accounting does not attempt to match expenses against revenues, it is not a generally accepted accounting principle.

Accruals and deferrals are discussed and illustrated in Appendix C.

Expense and loss recognition are discussed in Chapter 4.

Conservatism

The convention of **conservatism** states, in effect, that when alternative accounting valuations are equally possible, the accountant should select the one that is least likely to overstate assets and income in the current period. Over the years conservatism gained prominence because of the optimism of management and the tendency, during the first three decades of the twentieth century, to overstate assets and net income on financial statements. Recently, conservatism has been criticized for being "anticonservative" in the years following the conservative act. That is, a deliberate understatement of an asset with a corresponding loss and understatement of income in one year will result in an overstatement of income in a later year when the asset is sold because of the greater difference between the selling price and recorded value of the asset. Furthermore, conservatism can conflict with qualitative characteristics such as neutrality. For instance, conservative financial statements may be unfair to present stockholders and biased in favor of prospective stockholders because the net valuation of the company does not include some future expectations. This factor may be reflected in a relatively lower current market price of the company's common stock. These criticisms notwithstanding, conservatism has played an important role in the establishment of certain generally accepted accounting principles.

The FASB has attempted to modify the convention of conservatism so that it is more synonymous with **prudence**. That is, conservatism should be a prudent reaction to uncertainty so as to ensure, to the extent possible, that the uncertainties and risks inherent in business situations are adequately considered. These uncertainties and risks should be reflected in accounting information to improve its predictive value and neutrality. Prudent reporting based on a healthy skepticism promotes integrity and best serves the various users of financial reports.[12]

---

11. "Elements of Financial Statements," *FASB Statement of Financial Accounting Concepts* No. 6 (Stamford, Conn.: FASB, 1985), par. 146–149.

12. *FASB Statement of Financial Accounting Concepts* No. 2, *op. cit.*, par. 95–97.

GAAP AND FINANCIAL STATEMENTS

Components of this model are discussed in Chapters 3, 4, and 22.

As we noted in Chapter 1, generally accepted accounting principles (GAAP) are the guidelines, procedures, and practices that a company is required to use in recording and reporting its accounting information in its audited financial statements. In its *Conceptual Framework*, the FASB has identified various sources from which investors, creditors, and other users might obtain information useful in decision making. Exhibit 2-8 shows this model of financial reporting.

Conceptually the FASB identified the four specific financial statements listed in Exhibit 2-8. In practice companies prepare at least three major financial statements: (1) the balance sheet (statement of financial position), (2) the income statement, and (3) the statement of cash flows. Many companies also prepare a statement of changes in equity as a major financial statement (or in a note to the financial statements).[13] In this section we discuss briefly these financial statements and the elements of the financial statements. **The elements of each financial statement are the broad classes of items comprising it.** In other words, they are the "building blocks" with which each financial statement is prepared.[14] We discuss the financial statements and their elements in more depth in later chapters.

8 Define the elements of financial statements.

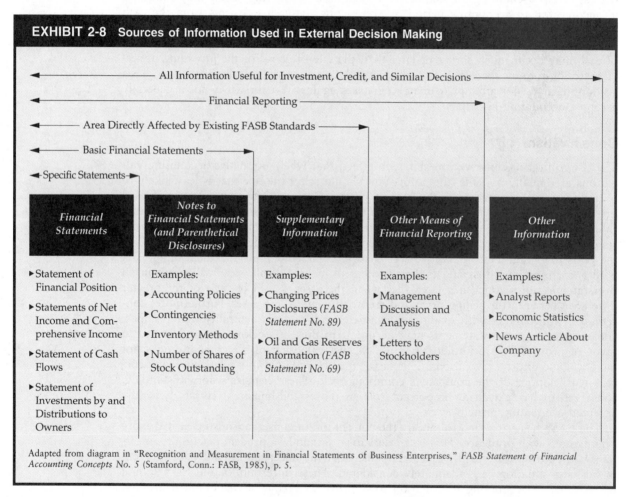

EXHIBIT 2-8   Sources of Information Used in External Decision Making

Adapted from diagram in "Recognition and Measurement in Financial Statements of Business Enterprises," *FASB Statement of Financial Accounting Concepts No. 5* (Stamford, Conn.: FASB, 1985), p. 5.

---

13. Each company also must report its comprehensive income and may choose to do so on its income statement, a statement of comprehensive income, or on its statement of changes in stockholders' equity. We will discuss these alternatives in Chapter 4.

14. The discussion in this section primarily is a summary of that presented in "Elements of Financial Statements of Business Enterprises," *FASB Statement of Financial Accounting Concept No. 6* (Stamford, Conn.: FASB, 1985) and "Statement of Cash Flows," *FASB Statement of Financial Accounting Standards No. 95* (Stamford, Conn.: FASB, 1987).

Balance Sheet

A **balance sheet** (or statement of financial position) is a financial statement that summarizes the financial position of a company on a particular date (usually the end of the accounting period). The financial position of a company includes its economic resources, economic obligations, and equity, and their relationships to each other. There are three elements of a balance sheet:

1. **Assets:** Assets are the probable future economic benefits obtained and controlled by a company as a result of past transactions or events.

2. **Liabilities:** Liabilities are the probable future sacrifices of economic benefits arising from present obligations of a company to transfer assets or provide services in the future as a result of past transactions or events.

3. **Equity:** Equity is the owners' residual interest in the assets of a company that remains after deducting its liabilities.

In other words, the assets of a company are its economic resources, and the liabilities are its economic obligations. The equity of a corporation is referred to as stockholders' equity because the owners are the stockholders.

Income Statement

An **income statement** is a financial statement that summarizes the results of a company's operations (i.e., net income) for a period of time (generally a one-year or one-quarter accounting period). A company's operations (sometimes called the earning process) include its purchasing, producing, selling, delivering, servicing, and administrating activities. There are four elements of an income statement:

1. **Revenues:** Revenues are inflows or other enhancements of assets of a company or settlement of its liabilities (or a combination of both) during a period from delivering or producing goods, rendering services, or other activities that are the company's ongoing major or central operations. Revenues increase the equity of a company.

2. **Expenses:** Expenses are outflows or other using up of assets of a company or incurrences of liabilities (or a combination of both) during a period from delivering or producing goods, rendering services, or carrying out other activities that are the company's ongoing major or central operations. Expenses decrease the equity of a company.

3. **Gains:** Gains are increases in the equity of a company from peripheral or incidental transactions and from all other transactions and other events and circumstances affecting the company during a period, except those that result from revenues or investments by owners.

4. **Losses:** Losses are decreases in the equity of a company from peripheral or incidental transactions and from all other transactions and other events and circumstances affecting the company during a period, except those that result from expenses or distributions to owners.

Revenues may be thought of as measures of the accomplishments of a company during its accounting period, while expenses are measures of the efforts to achieve the revenues. Gains are similar to revenues and losses are similar to expenses, except that revenues and expenses relate to a company's primary operations, while gains and losses relate to its secondary activities.

Statement of Cash Flows

A **statement of cash flows** is a financial statement that summarizes the cash inflows and outflows of a company for a period of time (generally one year or one quarter). There are three elements of a statement of cash flows:

1. **Operating Cash Flows:**   Operating cash flows are the inflows and outflows of cash from acquiring, selling, and delivering goods for sale, as well as providing services.

2. **Investing Cash Flows:**   Investing cash flows are the inflows and outflows of cash from acquiring and selling investments, property, plant, and equipment, and intangibles, as well as from lending money and collecting on loans.

3. **Financing Cash Flows:**   Financing cash flows are the inflows and outflows of cash from obtaining resources from owners and paying them dividends, as well as obtaining and repaying resources from creditors on long-term credit.

In addition to these three elements, the statement of cash flows reconciles the amount of cash a company reports on its balance sheets at the beginning and end of the accounting period.

Statement of Changes in Equity

A **statement of changes in equity** summarizes the changes in a company's equity for a period of time (generally one year or one quarter). For a corporation, the statement is called the statement of changes in stockholders' equity. There are two elements in a statement of changes in equity:

1. **Investments by Owners:**   Investments by owners are increases in the equity of a company resulting from transfers of something valuable (usually cash) to the company from other entities in order to obtain or increase ownership interests.

2. **Distributions to Owners:**   Distributions to owners are decreases in the equity of a company caused by transferring assets, rendering services, or incurring liabilities to owners.

In addition to these elements, the statement of changes in equity also reconciles the amounts of the equity items a company reports on its beginning and ending balance sheets for such items as net income and other comprehensive income.

Model of Business Reporting

The AICPA Special Committee on Financial Reporting issued a report that addressed concerns about the relevance and usefulness of reporting by companies. In conjunction with this report, the committee developed a comprehensive model of *business reporting*—the information that a company provides to help users with capital allocation decisions about the company. The model was designed to help focus attention on a broader, integrated range of information than that addressed in the FASB's conceptual framework, so as to provide the foundation for future improvement in business reporting. The model includes ten items within five categories of information. These categories are designed to fit the decision processes of users to make projections, value companies, or assess the likelihood of loan repayments. The framework of the model is as follows:

1. *Financial and nonfinancial data* including (a) financial statements and related disclosures and (b) high-level operating data and performance measurements that a company's management uses to manage the business.

2. *Management's analysis of the financial and nonfinancial data*, including (a) reasons for changes in the financial, operating, and performance-related data and (b) the identity and past effect of key trends.

3. *Forward-looking information*, including (a) the assessment of opportunities and risks, including those resulting from key trends, (b) management's plans, including critical success factors, and (c) a comparison of actual business performance to previously disclosed opportunities, risk, and management's plans.

4. *Information about management and shareholders*, including (a) directors, management, compensation, and major shareholders and (b) transactions and relationships among related parties.

5. *Background about the company*, including (a) broad objectives and strategies, (b) scope and description of the company's business and properties, and (c) the impact of industry structure on the company.

The model is responsive to users' needs, but includes practical constraints to balance the costs and benefits of reporting. Since the AICPA committee is not a standard-setting body, the model is a recommendation to standard setters who have an interest in improving the cost-effective quality of business reporting.[15]

Components of this model are discussed in Chapters 3, 4, and 5.

IASB FRAMEWORK

The Board of the International Accounting Standards Board (IASB) has issued a **Framework for the Preparation and Presentation of Financial Statements** that is similar, in many respects, to the FASB Conceptual Framework.

The IASB Framework states that the objective of financial statements is to provide information about the financial position, performance, and changes in financial position of a company that is useful to a wide range of users in making economic decisions. The Framework has two underlying assumptions; that a company is a going concern and uses accrual accounting. It identifies four qualitative characteristics of financial statements—understandability, relevance (including materiality), reliability (including faithful presentation, substance over form, neutrality, prudence, and completeness), and comparability. Three constraints on relevant and reliable information are identified; they include timeliness, balance between benefit and cost, and balance between the qualitative characteristics. The Framework calls for financial statements that present a true and fair view of the company and a fair presentation of the company's activities.

The IASB Framework identifies and defines the elements of a statement of financial position (i.e., assets, liabilities, and equity) and a statement of performance (i.e., income and expenses). It also discusses conceptual issues dealing with the recognition of the elements of financial statements, measurement of the elements, and concepts of capital and capital maintenance.

The IASB Framework is designed (1) to help the Board in developing future International Accounting Standards and reviewing existing Standards and (2) to promote the harmonization of regulations, accounting standards, and accounting procedures regarding the preparation of financial statements.[16]

OVERVIEW

We discuss the financial statements and their elements, as they fit into the FASB's model of financial reporting and the AICPA's model of business reporting, in depth in the later chapters of this book. In addition, we discuss supplementary schedules and notes to the financial statements, along with various recognition and measurement

---

15. "Improving Business Reporting—A Customer Focus," *AICPA Special Committee on Financial Reporting* (New York: AICPA, 1994), pp. 2–9.

16. For a more complete discussion, go to the IASC's web site, www.iasc.org.uk.

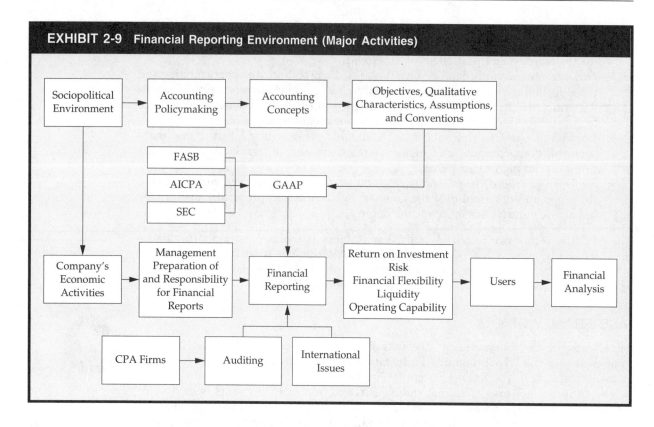

EXHIBIT 2-9   Financial Reporting Environment (Major Activities)

issues. As you read the discussions, it may be helpful for you to place them in the context of the *FASB Conceptual Framework* as we summarized in Exhibit 2-6, as well as the financial reporting environment as we summarize in Exhibit 2-9. If it would be helpful to review the recording and reporting procedures that comprise an accounting system, you should refer to Appendix C at the end of this book.

SUMMARY

At the beginning of the chapter, we identified several objectives you would accomplish after reading the chapter. The objectives are listed below, each followed by a brief summary of the key points in the chapter discussion.

1. **Explain the FASB conceptual framework.** The FASB conceptual framework is a theoretical foundation of interrelated objectives and concepts that leads to the establishment of consistent financial accounting standards. It provides a logical structure and direction to financial accounting and reporting.

2. **Understand the relationship among the objectives of financial reporting.** The FASB conceptual framework consists of four levels of objectives that proceed from the more general to the more specific. The top level is the general objective of financial reporting, the next level is the derived external user objective, the third level is the derived company objective, and the final level includes the specific objectives.

3. **Identify the general objective of financial reporting.** The general objective states that financial reporting should provide useful information for present and potential investors, creditors, and other external users in making their investment, credit, and similar decisions.

4. **Describe the three specific objectives of financial reporting.** The three specific objectives are to provide information about a company's: (1) economic resources, obligations, and owners' equity; (2) comprehensive income and its components; and (3) cash flows.

5. **Discuss the types of useful information for investment and credit decision making.** For investment and credit decision making, a company's financial reports should provide useful information about its return on investment, risk, financial flexibility, liquidity, and operating capability.

6. **Explain the qualities of useful accounting information.** Accounting information should be understandable and have decision usefulness. The two primary decision-specific qualities are relevance and reliability. To be relevant, accounting information must have predictive value, feedback value, and timeliness. To be reliable, it must have verifiability, representational faithfulness, and neutrality. In addition, accounting information should be comparable and consistent. Two constraints in preparing and reporting accounting information are that the benefits must be greater than the costs of preparing the information and that the information must be material.

7. **Understand the accounting assumptions and conventions that influence GAAP.** Certain assumptions and conventions play an important role in the development of GAAP. These include the entity, continuity (going-concern), accounting period, historical cost, monetary unit, realization and recognition, accrual accounting and matching, and conservatism (prudence) assumptions and conventions.

8. **Define the elements of financial statements.** The elements of each financial statement are the broad classes of items comprising it. For a balance sheet, the elements are assets, liabilities, and equity. For an income statement, they are revenues, expenses, gains, and losses. For a statement of cash flows, they are operating, investing, and financing cash flows. For a statement of changes in equity, they are investments by and distributions to owners.

QUESTIONS

Q2-1 What is the "conceptual framework" of the FASB? What are the titles of the *Statements of Concepts* issued by the FASB?

Q2-2 What is the most general objective of financial reporting? Who are investors and creditors?

Q2-3 What is the "derived external user objective" and why is it important?

Q2-4 What is the "derived company objective" and what types of information about a company should be reported to satisfy this objective?

Q2-5 List the reasons why external users use information about a company's (a) economic resources and claims to these resources, (b) comprehensive income and its components, and (c) cash flows.

Q2-6 Define (a) return on investment, (b) risk, (c) financial flexibility, (d) liquidity, and (e) operating capability.

Q2-7 What is the overall qualitative characteristic of useful accounting information and what are its two primary qualities?

Q2-8 What is relevant accounting information? Identify and define the ingredients of relevant accounting information.

Q2-9 What is reliable accounting information? Identify and define the ingredients of reliable accounting information.

Q2-10 Identify the secondary quality of useful accounting information. Why is this important and how does it relate to consistency?

Q2-11 What is materiality and how does it relate to relevance?

Q2-12 What is the continuity assumption and why is it important in financial accounting?

Q2-13 What is the period-of-time assumption and why is it important in financial accounting?

Q2-14 Discuss the relationship between historical cost and reliability.

Q2-15 What is realization? What is recognition? What two factors provide guidance for revenue recognition? Why is revenue usually recognized at the time of sale?

Q2-16 What is accrual accounting and how does it relate to the matching principle?

Q2-17 List the three principles for matching expenses against revenues.

Q2-18 What is conservatism and how might it conflict with neutrality?

Q2-19 Define a balance sheet and list its three elements.

Q2-20 Define an income statement and list its four elements.

Q2-21 Define a statement of cash flows and list its three elements.

Q2-22 Define a statement of changes in equity and list its two elements.

Q2-23 For the IASB Framework, list the objective of financial statements and identify the underlying assumptions, qualitative characteristics, and constraints.

CASES

C O M M U N I C A T I O N

C2-1   Qualitative Characteristics

In *FASB Statement of Concepts No. 2*, several qualitative characteristics of useful accounting information were identified. The following is a list of these qualities as well as a list of statements describing the qualities.

A. Comparability   H. Verifiability
B. Decision usefulness   I. Neutrality
C. Relevance   J. Representational
D. Reliability   faithfulness
E. Predictive value   K. Consistency
F. Feedback value   L. Materiality
G. Timeliness

_____   1.   Ability of measurers to form a consensus that the selected accounting method has been used without error or bias.
_____   2.   Making information available to decision makers before it loses its capacity to influence decisions.
_____   3.   Capacity to make a difference in a decision.
_____   4.   Overall qualitative characteristic.
_____   5.   Absence of bias intended to influence behavior in a particular direction.
_____   6.   Reasonably free from error and bias.
_____   7.   Helps decision makers forecast correctly.
_____   8.   Validity.
_____   9.   Interactive quality; helps identify and explain similarities and differences.
_____   10.   Quantitative "threshold" constraint.
_____   11.   Conformity from period to period.
_____   12.   Helps decision makers confirm or correct prior expectations.

Required Place the appropriate letter identifying each quality on the line in front of the statement describing the quality.

C2-2   Accounting Assumptions and Conventions

Certain accounting assumptions and conventions have had an important impact on the development of generally accepted accounting principles. The following is a list of these assumptions and conventions as well as a list of statements describing certain accounting practices.

A. Entity   E. Monetary unit
B. Continuity   F. Realization
C. Period of time   G. Matching
D. Historical cost   H. Conservatism

_____   1.   The business, rather than its owners, is the reporting unit.
_____   2.   Depreciation costs are expensed in the periods of use rather than at the time the asset is acquired.

_____   3.   Accounting measurements are reported in dollars.
_____   4.   The year is the normal reporting unit.
_____   5.   In the absence of evidence to the contrary, the business will operate long enough to carry out its existing commitments.
_____   6.   Revenue is usually recognized at the time of sale.
_____   7.   Exchange price is retained in the accounting records.
_____   8.   An accounting alternative is selected that is least likely to overstate assets and income.

Required Select the accounting assumption or convention that justifies each accounting practice and place the appropriate letter on the line preceding the statement.

C2-3   Objectives of Financial Reporting

The FASB has identified several objectives of financial reporting. These objectives proceed from the more general to the more specific and are intended to act as guidelines for providing accounting information in financial reports.

Required Starting with the most general objective, prepare a written report that identifies and briefly explains the objectives of financial reporting.

C2-4   Qualities of Useful Accounting Information

A friend of yours, who is not an accounting major, is concerned about the "usefulness" of accounting information. The friend states: "I have watched you prepare many financial statements in completing your homework assignments. But how do you determine whether the information in these financial statements is useful? What are the characteristics or qualities of useful accounting information?"

Required Prepare a written response for your friend that identifies and explains the qualitative characteristics of useful accounting information.

C2-5   Cost and Expense Recognition

An accountant must be familiar with the concepts involved in determining earnings of a company. The amount of earnings reported for a company is dependent on the proper recognition, in general, of revenue and expense for a given time period. In some situations costs are recognized as expenses at the time of product sale; in other situations guidelines have been developed for recognizing costs as expenses or losses by other criteria.

Required

1. Explain the rationale for recognizing costs as expenses at the time of product sale.
2. What is the rationale underlying the appropriateness of treating costs as expenses of a period instead of assigning the costs to an asset? Explain.
3. Some expenses are assigned to specific accounting periods on the basis of systematic and rational allocation of asset cost. Explain the underlying rationale for recognizing expenses on this basis. *(AICPA adapted)*

C2-6 Characteristics of Useful Information

Financial accounting and reporting provide information that is used in decision making regarding the allocation of resources. In **Statement of Financial Accounting Concepts No. 1,** "Objectives of Financial Reporting by Business Enterprises," the FASB defined the following basic objectives of financial reporting:

Financial reporting should provide understandable information to present and potential users:

- That is useful in making rational decisions.
- That facilitates assessing the amounts, timing, and uncertainty related to the company's cash flows.
- About the company's economic resources, its claims to those resources, and the changes in its resources and obligations occurring from earnings and other operating activities.

The qualitative characteristics of useful accounting information were identified in the FASB's **Statement of Financial Accounting Concepts No. 2,** "Qualitative Characteristics of Accounting Information." These characteristics distinguish better information (more useful) from inferior information (less useful).

Required

1. For the primary quality relevance,
   a. define relevance
   b. explain the meaning and importance of each of the three ingredients of relevance

2. For the primary quality reliability,
   a. define reliability
   b. explain the meaning and importance of each of the three ingredients of reliability
3. Explain the concepts of
   a. comparability
   b. consistency
   c. materiality *(CMA adapted)*

C2-7 Objectives, Users, and Stewardship

The owners of CSC Inc., a privately held company, are considering a public offering of the company's common stock as a means of acquiring additional funds. Prior to making a decision about a public offering, the owners had a lengthy conversation with John Duncan, CSC's chief financial officer. Duncan informed the owners of the reporting requirements of the Securities and Exchange Commission, including the necessity for audited financial statements. At the request of the owners, Duncan also discussed the objectives of financial reporting, the sophistication of users of financial information, and the stewardship responsibilities of management, all of which are addressed in **Statement of Financial Accounting Concepts No. 1,** "Objectives of Financial Reporting by Business Enterprises."

Required

1. Discuss the primary objectives of financial reporting.
2. Describe the level of sophistication that can be expected of the users of financial information.
3. Explain the stewardship responsibilities of management. *(CMA adapted)*

C2-8 Segment Reporting

The FASB requires that a company organized in different "operating segments" disclose the revenues, profits, and assets of each of its major operating segments.

Required Prepare a short memo that briefly explains what types of useful information for investment decision making is provided by requiring these disclosures.

CREATIVE AND CRITICAL THINKING

C2-9 Relevance versus Reliability

You are listening to two accounting majors, both of whom are seniors. They are debating the merits of having relevant versus reliable accounting information for external decision making. One student states: "In my decision making, if given a choice between relevant and reliable accounting information, I would prefer to have relevant information." The other student replies: "Nonsense! If you cannot rely on the information, then of what use is it?"

Required Based on your knowledge of the FASB's conceptual framework, define the qualitative characteristics of relevance and reliability. Include definitions of the ingredients of each. Which do you think is more important?

C2-10 Inconsistent Statements on Accounting Principles

The following two statements have been taken directly or with some modification from the accounting literature. Each of them is either taken out of context, involves circular reasoning, and/or contains one or more fallacies, half-truths, erroneous comments, conclusions, or inconsistencies (internally or with generally accepted principles or practices).

Statement 1 Accounting is a service activity. Its function is to provide quantitative financial information that is intended to be useful in making economic decisions about and for economic entities. Thus the accounting function might be viewed primarily as being a tool or device for providing quantitative financial information to management to facilitate decision making.

Statement 2 Financial statements that were developed in accordance with generally accepted accounting principles, which apply the conservatism convention, can be free from bias (or can give a presentation that is fair with respect to continuing and prospective stockholders as well as to retiring stockholders).

Required Evaluate each of the preceding numbered statements as follows:

1. List the fallacies, half-truths, circular reasoning, erroneous comments or conclusions, and/or inconsistencies.
2. Explain by what authority and/or on what basis each item listed in (1) can be considered to be fallacious, circular, inconsistent, a half-truth, or an erroneous comment or conclusion. If the statement or a portion of it is merely out of context, indicate the context(s) in which the statement would be correct. (AICPA adapted)

C2-11 Accounting Entity

The concept of the accounting entity often is considered to be the most fundamental of accounting concepts, one that pervades all of accounting.

Required

1. a. What is an accounting entity? Explain.
   b. Explain why the accounting entity concept is so fundamental that it pervades all of accounting.
2. For each of the following indicate whether the accounting concept of entity is applicable; discuss and give illustrations.
   a. A unit created by or under law
   b. The product-line operating segment of an enterprise
   c. A combination of legal units and/or product-line operating segments
   d. All of the activities of an owner or a group of owners
   e. An industry
   f. The economy of the United States (AICPA adapted)

C2-12 Timing of Revenue Recognition

Revenue usually is recognized at the point of sale. Under special circumstances, however, bases other than the point of sale are used for the timing of revenue recognition.

Required

1. Why is the point of sale usually used as the basis for the timing of revenue recognition?
2. Disregarding the special circumstances when bases other than the point of sale are used, discuss the merits of each of the following objections to the sales basis of revenue recognition:
   a. It is too conservative because revenue is earned throughout the entire process of production.
   b. It is not conservative enough because accounts receivable do not represent disposable funds; sales returns and allowances may be made; and collection and bad debt expenses may be incurred in a later period.

3. Revenue may also be recognized (a) during production and (b) when cash is received. For each of these two bases of timing revenue recognition, give an example of the circumstances in which it is properly used and discuss the accounting merits of its use in lieu of the sales basis. (AICPA adapted)

C2-13 Accruals and Deferrals

Generally accepted accounting principles require the use of accruals and deferrals in the determination of income.

Required

1. How does accrual accounting affect the determination of income? Include in your discussion what constitutes an accrual and a deferral, and give appropriate examples of each.
2. Contrast accrual accounting with cash accounting. (AICPA adapted)

C2-14 Revenue Recognition

The following are brief descriptions of several companies in different lines of business.

A. Company A is a construction company. It has recently signed a contract to build a highway over a 3-year period. A down payment was collected; the remaining collections will occur periodically over the construction period based upon the degree of completion.
B. Company B is a retailer. It makes sales on a daily basis for cash and on credit cards.
C. Company C is a health spa. It has recently signed contracts with numerous individuals to use its facilities over a 2-year period. The contract price was collected in advance.
D. Company D is a land development company. It has recently begun developing a "retirement community" and has sold lots to senior citizens. The sales contract requires a small down payment and periodic payments until completion of the roads and a clubhouse, after which the remainder of the purchase price is due. Prior to this point, a purchaser may cancel the contract and receive a refund of all payments.

Required Describe when revenue should be recognized by each company. If revenue should not be recognized at the time of sale, indicate what method should be used to recognize the revenue. Justify your decision.

C2-15 Violations of Assumptions and Conventions

The following are accounting procedures and practices used by several companies.

A. As soon as it purchases inventory, Sokolich Company records the purchase price as cost of goods sold to simplify its accounting procedures.
B. At the end of each year Sloan Company records and reports its economic resources based on appraisal values.
C. Ebert Company prepares financial statements only every two years to reduce its costs of preparing the statements.

D. Guthrie Company sells on account and records revenue at that time, even though it knows that collection is highly uncertain and very significant efforts have to be made to collect the accounts.

E. Because of inflation, Cross Company adjusts its financial statements each year to show the current purchasing power for all items.

F. David Thomas combines his personal transactions and business transactions when he prepares his company's financial statements so that he can tell how well he is doing on an "overall" basis.

G. At the end of each year Vann Company reports its economic resources on a liquidation basis even though it is likely to operate in the future.

Required Identify what accounting assumption, principle, or convention each procedure or practice violates, and indicate what should be done to rectify the violation.

C2-16   Conceptual Framework

The Financial Accounting Standards Board has developed a conceptual framework for financial accounting and reporting. The FASB has issued 7 **Statements of Financial Accounting Concepts.** These statements set forth objectives and fundamentals that will be the basis for developing financial accounting and reporting standards. The objectives identify the goals and purposes of financial reporting. The fundamentals are the underlying concepts of financial accounting concepts that guide the selection of transactions, events, and circumstances to be accounted for; their recognition and measurement; and the means of summarizing and communicating them to interested parties.

The purpose of **Statement of Financial Accounting Concepts No. 2,** "Qualitative Characteristics of Accounting Information," is to examine the characteristics that make accounting information useful. The characteristics or qualities of information discussed in *Concepts No. 2* are the ingredients that make information useful and are the qualities to be sought when accounting choices are made.

Required

1. Identify and discuss the benefits which can be expected to be derived from the FASB's conceptual framework study.

2. What is the most important quality for accounting information as identified in **Statement of Financial Accounting Concepts No. 2?** Explain why it is the most important.

3. **Statement of Financial Accounting Concepts No. 2** describes a number of key characteristics or qualities for accounting information. Briefly discuss the importance of understandability, relevance, and reliability for financial reporting purposes. *(CMA adapted)*

C2-17   Ethics and Income Reporting

You have been hired as an "accounting consultant" by Watson Company to evaluate its financial reporting policies. Watson is a small corporation with a few stockholders owning stock that is not publicly traded. In a discussion with you, Chris Watson, the company president, says "For the Watson Company's annual income statement, it is our policy to always record and report revenues when we collect the cash and to record and report expenses when we pay the cash. I like this approach and I think our stockholders and creditors do too. This policy results in income that is reliable and conservative, which is the way accounting should be. Besides, it is easy to keep track of our income. All I need are the receipts and payments recorded in the company's checkbook."

Required From financial reporting and ethical perspectives, how would you reply to Chris?

MULTIPLE CHOICE

Select the best answer for each of the following.

M2-1 Accruing net losses on noncancelable purchase commitments for inventory is an example of the accounting concept of

  a. Conservatism   c. Consistency
  b. Realization   d. Materiality

M2-2 The information provided by financial reporting pertains to

  a. Individual companies, rather than to industries or the economy as a whole or to members of society as consumers.

  b. Individual companies and industries, rather than to the economy as a whole or to members of society as consumers.

  c. Individual companies and the economy as a whole, rather than to industries or to members of society as consumers.

  d. Individual companies, industries, and the economy as a whole, rather than to members of society as consumers.

M2-3 According to **Statement of Financial Accounting Concepts No. 2,** an interim earnings report is expected to have which of the following?

	Predictive value	Feedback value
a.	No	No
b.	Yes	Yes
c.	Yes	No
d.	No	Yes

M2-4 A patent, purchased in 2001 and being amortized over a ten-year life, was determined to be worthless in 2004. The write-off of the asset in 2004 is an example of which of the following principles?

a. Associating cause and effect
b. Immediate recognition
c. Systematic and rational allocation
d. Objectivity

M2-5 An accrued expense is an expense

a. Incurred but not paid
b. Incurred and paid
c. Paid but not incurred
d. Not reasonably estimable

M2-6 Which of the following accounting concepts states that an accounting transaction should be supported by sufficient evidence to allow two or more qualified individuals to arrive at essentially similar measures and conclusions?

a. Matching
b. Verifiability
c. Periodicity
d. Stable monetary unit

M2-7 Which of the following is considered a pervasive constraint by **Statement of Financial Accounting Concepts No. 2?**

a. Benefits/costs
b. Conservatism
c. Timeliness
d. Verifiability

M2-8 The valuation of a promise to receive cash in the future at present value on the financial statements of a company is valid because of the accounting concept of

a. Entity
b. Materiality
c. Going concern
d. Neutrality

M2-9 Under **Statements of Financial Accounting Concepts,** which of the following relates to both relevance and reliability?

a. Timeliness
b. Neutrality
c. Feedback value
d. Consistency

M2-10 Under **Statement of Financial Accounting Concepts No. 6,** which of the following, in the most precise sense, means the process of converting noncash resources and rights into cash or claims to cash?

a. Allocation
b. Recordation
c. Recognition
d. Realization

(AICPA adapted)

INTERNET ASSIGNMENTS

Go to the Nikolai and Bazley **Intermediate Accounting** web site. (http://Nikolai.swcollege.com). Click on Student Resources and internet homework assignments. Then click on the appropriate hot link (icon) for each organization's web site, find the relevant information, and answer the following questions.

I2-1   Go to the FASB web site.

Required What is the mission of the FASB? How does the FASB act to accomplish its mission? What are concepts useful for, and what does the conceptual framework help establish?

I2-2   Go to the IASC web site. Click on Standards, then click on The IASC Framework.

What is the IASB Framework? How does it assist the IASB? Who else might it assist? Is the Framework an International Accounting Standard and does it define standards for a particular measurement or disclosure issue?

CHAPTER 3

The Balance Sheet and the Statement of Changes in Stockholders' Equity

objectives

1 Understand the purposes of the balance sheet.

2 Define the elements of a balance sheet.

3 Explain how to measure the elements of a balance sheet.

4 Classify the assets of a balance sheet.

5 Classify the liabilities of a balance sheet.

6 Report the stockholders' equity of a balance sheet.

7 Prepare a statement of changes in stockholders' equity

8 Understand the other disclosure issues for a balance sheet.

9 Describe the SEC integrated disclosures.

10 Explain the reporting techniques used in an annual report.

FASB Statement of Concepts No. 5 recommends that a full set of financial statements for an accounting period should show a company's (1) financial position at the end of the period, (2) net income for the period, (3) comprehensive income for the period, (4) cash flows for the period, and (5) investments by and distributions to owners for the period.[1] Currently, companies present at least three major financial statements and numerous supporting schedules as the "full set" of financial statements in their **annual reports**. The three major financial statements are (1) the balance sheet or statement of financial position, which summarizes the company's financial position at one point in time in the accounting period, (2) the income statement, which summarizes the results of the company's income-producing activities for the accounting period, and (3) the statement of cash flows, which summarizes the cash inflows and cash outflows of the company for the accounting period. Many companies include a statement of changes in stockholders' equity, which summarizes the changes in each item of stockholders' equity for the accounting period, as a fourth major financial statement.[2] A company also provides explanatory notes in its annual report to supplement these financial statements.

In this chapter, we focus primarily on the balance sheet, the statement of changes in stockholders' equity, and the accompanying notes. The balance sheet is the first financial statement we discuss because the FASB defines revenues and expenses in terms of changes in assets and liabilities. Thus, you need a thorough understanding of the nature and measurement of assets and liabilities to understand net income and its components. Furthermore, the chapters of this book in general follow a balance sheet framework. Consequently an understanding of its purpose, content, format, and preparation is helpful for understanding the more complex issues discussed later. The statement of changes in stockholders' equity helps to explain the changes that occurred in each stockholders' equity item on a company's balance sheet from the beginning to the end of the accounting period. We also discuss this statement in this chapter as it relates to the balance sheet. The discussion focuses on the corporation, the major business entity in the United States.

The income statement and statement of cash flows are discussed in Chapter 4.

---

1. "Recognition and Measurement in Financial Statements of Business Enterprises," *FASB Statement of Financial Accounting Concepts No. 5* (Stamford, Conn.: FASB, 1984), par. 13.
2. Some companies include a statement of comprehensive income as another major financial statement. We discuss this statement in Chapter 4.

INTERRELATIONSHIP OF FINANCIAL STATEMENTS

Exhibit 3-1 illustrates the interrelationship of the information contained in the major financial statements of a company. The solid lines indicate the major flows of interrelated financial accounting information among the financial statements as a result of transactions and events during the period. For instance, the company may consume assets from the beginning balance sheet (i.e., the ending balance sheet from the previous period) in an income-producing activity or it may sell them as a source of cash. The related financial accounting information will affect the company's income statement and statement of cash flows, respectively. Both the information relating to the income-producing activities in the income statement and the information pertaining to the cash inflows and cash outflows reported in the company's statement of cash flows will affect the accounting information reported in the ending balance sheet. The dashed line indicates a secondary flow of the interrelated information; that is, the income-producing activities that the company reports on its income statement also provide a net source of cash from operating activities. We further explore the relationships among the balance sheet, income statement, and statement of cash flows in the remaining sections of this chapter and in the subsequent chapters of this book.

PURPOSES OF THE BALANCE SHEET

One objective of financial reporting for a company is to help investors, creditors, and others in assessing the amounts, timing, and uncertainty of the prospective net cash inflows of the company. To meet this objective, the FASB suggested that a company should provide certain types of accounting information in its financial statements. A specific objective of a company's financial statements is to provide information about its economic resources, obligations, and owners' equity. This information is reported on a balance sheet. **A balance sheet summarizes the *financial position* of a company at a particular date.** A balance sheet also may be called a **statement of financial position.** The financial position of a company includes its economic resources (i.e., assets), economic obligations (i.e., liabilities), and equity, and their relationships to each other at a moment in time. A corporate balance sheet, then, discloses the assets, liabilities, stockholders' equity, and related information of the corporation on a specific date. The statement reports a corporation's *resource structure* (i.e., major classes and amounts of assets) and its *financial structure* (i.e., major classes and amounts of liabilities and

1 Understand the purposes of the balance sheet.

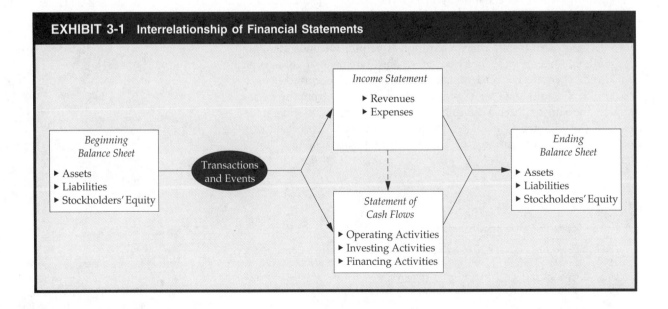

EXHIBIT 3-1   Interrelationship of Financial Statements

Income Statement
▸ Revenues
▸ Expenses

Beginning Balance Sheet
▸ Assets
▸ Liabilities
▸ Stockholders' Equity

Transactions and Events

Statement of Cash Flows
▸ Operating Activities
▸ Investing Activities
▸ Financing Activities

Ending Balance Sheet
▸ Assets
▸ Liabilities
▸ Stockholders' Equity

equity). Its name evolved because the balance sheet is a detailed summary of the basic accounting equation (which must always remain in balance):

Assets = Liabilities + Stockholders' Equity

The balance sheet does not attempt to show the fair value of a company. Together with other financial statements and other information, however, it should provide information that is useful to external users who desire to make their own estimates of the company's fair value. More specifically, a company's balance sheet is intended to help external users (1) assess the company's liquidity, financial flexibility, and operating capability and (2) evaluate information about its income-producing performance during the period.

Liquidity, Financial Flexibility, and Operating Capability

The term *liquidity* is used to describe how quickly an asset can be converted into cash or a liability paid. That is, liquidity refers to the "nearness to cash" of a company's economic resources and obligations. Information about liquidity is important in evaluating the *timing* of cash flows in the near future. Information about short-term cash inflows is useful because these cash inflows are part of total cash inflows. Furthermore, a company needs short-term cash inflows to take advantage of new investment opportunities and to meet its short-term obligations. Liquidity is also one aspect of a company's financial flexibility.

Liquidity, financial flexibility, and operating capability are discussed in Chapter 2.

Financial flexibility refers to the ability of a company to use its financial resources to adapt to change. Adaptation may be thought of as being "offensive" or "defensive." Offensive adaptation is necessary to take advantage of an unexpected new investment opportunity, while defensive adaptation is required to survive a reduction in cash flows from operating activities. Financial flexibility comes from a quick access to the cash generated from more "liquid" economic resources. But liquidity is only part of financial flexibility. A company's financial flexibility stems from its ability to generate sufficient net cash inflows from operations, from additional capital contributed by investors or long-term creditors, or from liquidating long-term economic resources without disrupting continuing operations. Information about a company's financial flexibility is important to external users in assessing the uncertainty of the company's future cash flows.

Operating capability refers to the ability of a company to maintain a given physical level of operations. This level may be indicated by the quantity of goods or services produced in a given period (i.e., inventory) or by the physical capacity of the operating assets (i.e., property, plant, and equipment) used to produce the goods or services. Information about a company's operating capability may be helpful to external users in understanding its performance and predicting future changes in its volume of activity and related cash flows.[3]

Capital and Capital Maintenance

A company's balance sheet provides a basis for evaluating its income-producing performance during a period. Therefore, a company's capital is important. **The capital (or *net assets*) of a company is the economic resources (assets) less economic obligations (liabilities), or owners' equity.** For a corporation, the stockholders' equity is the capital. This capital is used by the management of the corporation in fulfilling its responsibilities to the corporate stockholders. When a stockholder invests in a corporation, the stockholder is interested in a return *of* investment as well as a return *on* investment. To provide for a return of investment, the stockholders' equity (capital) of the corporation

---

3. *Ibid.*, par. 24, 26, and 27 and "Reporting Income, Cash Flows, and Financial Position of Business Enterprises," *FASB Proposed Statement of Financial Accounting Concepts* (Stamford, Conn.: FASB, 1981), par. 25-32.

must be maintained; this is referred to as **capital maintenance.** Once this capital is maintained, any income of the corporation is an increase in stockholders' equity and is the basis for providing a return *on* investment to stockholders. Dividends are a return on investment, as is market price appreciation on the stock. Many investors prefer market price appreciation to dividends. Information about a corporation's capital is important in assessing the adequacy of the corporation's profitability and its ability to provide a return on investment.

Capital maintenance and income are discussed in Chapter 4.

Another way of looking at Exhibit 3-1 is to think in terms of capital and capital maintenance. You can think of the beginning balance sheet as presenting the capital of the corporation at the beginning of the accounting period. The income statement and the statement of cash flows disclose the results of management's activities to use, maintain, and increase the capital during the accounting period. The ending balance sheet reports the capital at the end of the accounting period. But before it can be determined whether capital is maintained or a corporation has earned income, the initial (beginning) and subsequent (ending) capital must be determined.

Capital can be thought of in terms of (1) financial capital or (2) physical capital. **Financial capital is the monetary value of the net assets** contributed by stockholders and the value of the increase in net assets resulting from earnings retained by the corporation (cumulative income in excess of cumulative dividends). **Physical capital is a quantitative measure of the physical productive capacity** (e.g., square feet of factory space) of the corporation to provide goods or services, and it is related to the concept of operating capability that we discussed in the previous section.[4] The difference between financial capital and physical capital is important in considering whether and when capital is maintained and income is earned (Chapter 4). The difference is not as important for reporting the capital at a point in time because accounting information primarily is expressed in dollars. Thus, a dollar value must be attached to the physical capital before it is reported on a balance sheet. We discuss the alternative ways of measuring the net assets (capital) of a corporation later in the chapter.

RECOGNITION IN THE BALANCE SHEET

A company may disclose an item of information related to its financial position in its balance sheet, in a supporting schedule, or as part of the notes accompanying the financial statements. Recall from Chapter 2 that **recognition is the process of formally recording and reporting an element in the financial statements.** It includes depiction of an element in both words and numbers, with the amount included in the totals. Generally, the most useful (i.e., the best combination of relevance and reliability) information about assets, liabilities, and equity should be recognized and reported in the main body of the balance sheet. There are four fundamental recognition criteria. To be recognized, an item (and information about it) must meet the definition of an element and be measurable, relevant, and reliable.[5] Thus, to meet the objectives of a company's balance sheet—to provide relevant and reliable information to assess its liquidity, financial flexibility, and operating capability and to evaluate its income-producing performance during the period—the company must determine what, how, and where to disclose the "elements" of the balance sheet. That is, the company must complete a three-stage process:

1. Identification of what items meet the definitions of the elements
2. Measurement (valuation) of the elements
3. Reporting (classification) of the elements

---

4. For a further discussion, see "Conceptual Framework for Financial Accounting and Reporting: Elements of Financial Statements and Their Measurement," *FASB Discussion Memorandum* (Stamford, Conn.: FASB, 1976), ch. 6.
5. "Recognition and Measurement in Financial Statements of Business Enterprises," *FASB Statement of Financial Accounting Concepts No. 5, op. cit.,* par. 58–64.

ELEMENTS OF THE BALANCE SHEET

In order for a company to report an item of information on its balance sheet, the item must meet the definition of an element. **The elements of the balance sheet are the broad classes of items comprising it.** They are the building blocks with which the balance sheet is prepared. The elements of financial statements are defined in **FASB Statement of Concepts No. 6.** We define and discuss each of the elements of a corporate balance sheet—assets, liabilities, and stockholders' equity—in the following sections.[6]

2 Define the elements of a balance sheet.

Assets

> **Assets are probable future economic benefits obtained or controlled by a company as a result of past transactions or events.**

Assets are the economic resources used to carry out a company's economic activities of consumption, production, and exchange. The primary attribute of all assets is *service potential*, the capacity to provide services or benefits to the company that uses them. To be considered an asset, an economic resource must have three characteristics:

1. The resource must be able to contribute directly or indirectly to the company's future net cash inflows. This service potential may exist because the asset is expected to be exchanged for something else of value to the company (e.g., accounts receivable), to be used in producing goods (e.g., factory) or services, to increase the value of other assets (e.g., patent), or to be used to settle its liabilities (e.g., cash).
2. The company must be able to obtain the future benefit and control others' access to it. Control means that the company can deny or regulate the ability of others to use the asset.
3. The transaction or event giving the company the right to or control over the benefit must have occurred. That is, a company has no asset for a particular future benefit if the transaction or event giving it access to or control over the benefit has yet to occur. As a corollary, once an asset is acquired by a company, it continues to be an asset until it is exchanged or used up or until some other event destroys the future benefit or removes the company's ability to obtain or control it.

Assets may be natural or man-made, tangible or intangible, and either exchangeable or useful only in the company's activities. Furthermore, they may be acquired by purchase, production, stockholder investments, discovery, or other nonreciprocal (one-way) transfers.

Liabilities

> **Liabilities are probable future sacrifices of economic benefits arising from present obligations of a company to transfer assets or provide services to other entities in the future as a result of past transactions or events.**

An obligation of a company must have three characteristics to be considered a liability:

1. It must involve a responsibility to another entity or entities that will be settled by a sacrifice involving the transfer of assets, provision of services, or other use of assets at a specified or determinable date, on occurrence of a specified event, or on demand. The specific identity of the "creditor" need not be known with certainty for a liability to exist, as long as a future transfer or use of assets to settle the liability is *probable*.

---

6. The discussion of the elements in the following sections is a summary of that presented in "Elements of Financial Statements of Business Enterprises," FASB *Statement of Financial Accounting Concepts No. 6* (Stamford, Conn.: FASB, 1985).

2. The responsibility must obligate the company in such a way that it has little or no discretion to avoid the future sacrifice. Although most liabilities involve legal rights and duties, some are the result of equitable (ethical or moral) obligations or constructive (inferred from the facts) obligations. Thus, the company must be bound by a legal, equitable, or constructive responsibility to transfer assets or provide services to one or more other entities.

3. The transaction or other event obligating the company must have occurred. Once a liability has been incurred, it continues to be a liability until the company settles it or another event discharges it or removes it from the company's responsibility.

Liabilities arise primarily from deferring payment for goods or services received and from borrowing funds. Other liabilities result from collecting economic resources in advance of providing goods or services to customers. Liabilities also arise from selling products subject to warranties, from regulations imposed by governmental units, and from nonreciprocal transfers to owners or other entities.

Stockholders' Equity

Equity is the residual interest in the assets of a company that remains after deducting its liabilities.

The equity of a company is equal to its net assets (assets minus liabilities). Equity stems from ownership rights, and therefore it is the ownership interest. Since a company generally is not obligated to transfer assets to its owners, owners' equity ranks after liabilities as a claim to or interest in the assets and thus is a residual interest. For a corporation, stockholders' equity represents the interest of the stockholders, who bear the ultimate risks and uncertainties involved in the company's operations and activities and who obtain the resulting rewards. It is created by stockholders' investments of economic resources and subsequently is modified by additional investments, net income, distributions to owners, and other changes in assets and liabilities. Stockholders' equity may not exist apart from the corporate assets and liabilities, since it is a residual interest.

MEASUREMENT OF THE ELEMENTS OF THE BALANCE SHEET

3 Explain how to measure the elements of a balance sheet.

In order for a company to report an element on its balance sheet, the element must be reliably measured (valued) in monetary terms. The FASB has identified five alternatives for measuring elements. We show these alternative valuation methods in Exhibit 3-2 and discuss them in the following sections. Later in the chapter, when we discuss specific assets and liabilities, we identify the applicable valuation method. We do not include stockholders' equity in Exhibit 3-2 because it may not exist apart from assets or liabilities. That is, the measurement of assets and liabilities (i.e., net assets) will determine the dollar amount of stockholders' equity. To conserve space, we focus the discussion on the measurement of assets, but our comments generally are equally applicable to liabilities.

Historical Cost

The historical cost of an asset is the exchange price in the transaction in which the asset was acquired. The historical cost is measured by the cash paid for the asset or, in the case of a noncash exchange, by the estimated cash equivalent of the noncash asset or liability exchanged. After acquisition, the historical cost of an asset may be reduced due to the recognition of depreciation, amortization, impairment, or other adjustments.

Current Cost

Current cost methods are discussed in Appendix E.

The current cost of an asset is the amount of cash (or equivalent) that would be required on the date of the balance sheet to obtain the same asset. The "same asset" may be an identical asset or one with equivalent productive capacity. Alternative methods for

EXHIBIT 3-2 Measurement of Assets and Liabilities		
Alternative	Assets	Liabilities
1. Historical cost/historical proceeds	Initially, the amount of cash (or its equivalent) paid to acquire an asset (historical cost); subsequent to acquisition, the historical amount may be adjusted for depreciation, amortization, or other adjustments.	Initially, the amount of cash (or its equivalent) received when an obligation was incurred (historical proceeds); subsequent to incurrence, the historical amount may be adjusted for amortization.
2. Current cost/current proceeds	Amount of cash (or its equivalent) that would have to be paid if the same asset were acquired currently.	Amount of cash (or its equivalent) that would be obtained if the same obligation were incurred currently.
3. Current market value	Amount of cash (or its equivalent) that could be obtained currently by selling the asset in orderly liquidation.	Amount of cash (or its equivalent) that would be required currently to eliminate the liability.
4. Net realizable value	Amount of cash (or its equivalent) into which the asset is expected to be converted in due course of business less direct costs necessary to make that conversion.	Amount of cash (or its equivalent) expected to be paid to eliminate the liability in due course of business.
5. Present value	Present value of future cash inflows into which the asset is expected to be converted in due course of business less present value of future cash outflows necessary to obtain those inflows.	Present value of future cash outflows to eliminate the liability in due course of business.

Source: Adapted from "Conceptual Framework for Financial Accounting and Reporting: Elements of Financial Statements and Their Measurement," *FASB Discussion Memorandum* (Stamford, Conn.: FASB, 1976), p. 193 and "Recognition and Measurement in Financial Statements of Business Enterprises," *FASB Statement of Financial Accounting Concepts* No. 5 (Stamford, Conn.: FASB, 1984), p. 23.

obtaining the current cost include quoted market prices, the use of specific price indexes, and appraisals. Current cost is an *input value* and is sometimes referred to as *current replacement cost*.

Current Market Value

The current market value of an asset is the amount of cash (or equivalent) that could be obtained on the date of the balance sheet by selling the asset, in its present condition, in an orderly liquidation. An orderly liquidation means the asset is disposed of in a systematic and organized fashion. A current market value would be determined by obtaining a quoted market price for the sale of an asset of similar kind and condition. The term current market value is potentially confusing, because current cost and current market value are both "market values." Therefore, sometimes current market value is referred to as *current exit value*.

Net Realizable Value

The net realizable value of an asset is the amount of cash (or equivalent) into which the asset is expected to be converted in the ordinary operations of the company, less

any expected conversion costs (e.g., completion, disposal, or collection costs). Net realizable value differs from current exit value by being based upon expected *future* sales proceeds of the asset (perhaps in a different form) rather than upon the *current* disposal value of an asset in its existing form. Net realizable value is sometimes referred to as *expected exit value*.

Present Value

Discounting and the computation of present value are discussed in Appendix D.

The present value of an asset is the net amount of discounted future cash inflows less the discounted future cash outflows relating to the asset. Each future cash flow may be a single amount; in this case, the amount is referred to as an *estimated* cash flow. Or, each future cash flow may involve a range of possible amounts. In this case, a "weighted average" amount is determined and is referred to as an *expected* cash flow. When the estimated cash flows are used to determine present value, they are similar to those used to determine net realizable value; the difference between the two alternatives is that under the present value approach the time value of money (i.e., interest) is considered.[7]

Valuations on Today's Balance Sheet

The valuation method primarily used in a company's balance sheet is historical cost. In general, each asset and liability of the company is recorded at the exchange price of the transaction in which the asset is obtained or the liability is incurred. Usually the company then reports this exchange price in its balance sheet until another exchange has taken place. Certain assets such as property, plant, and equipment are measured and reported at their exchange price (historical cost) adjusted for depreciation. Historical cost is used extensively as a valuation method because it is based on transactions and provides information that has a high degree of *reliability*. It has been criticized, however, because some users of financial statements argue that historical cost is not as *relevant* as the amounts reported under some alternative valuation methods. That is, historical cost may not represent the amount of future cash inflows (or outflows) that the company is likely to obtain (or pay) for the asset (or liability).

The FASB sometimes requires a company to report an asset or liability at its **fair value**. Depending on the circumstances, by fair value the FASB may mean current cost, current exit value, net realizable value, or present value. For instance, a company uses current cost for valuing certain "inventories," current exit value for "marketable securities," net realizable value for "receivables," and present value for "bonds payable." We identify the valuation method used for each type of asset and liability in the next section and we discuss these methods more fully in later chapters. As increased emphasis is placed upon reporting information concerning a company's liquidity, financial flexibility, and operating capability, it is likely that the FASB will require valuation methods other than historical cost on balance sheets (or related notes). The extent of the use of other valuation methods will depend, among other considerations, on the tradeoff between relevance and reliability. It is possible the FASB may develop GAAP in which "financial" assets and liabilities are valued at fair value while "non-financial" assets and liabilities are valued at historical cost.

Limitations of the Balance Sheet

In addition to the criticism that the use of historical costs for valuing assets and liabilities does not help users assess the likely amounts of future cash flows relating to these items, there are other limitations of the balance sheet. First, a company's

---

7. *FASB Statement of Financial Accounting Concepts No. 5, op. cit.*, par. 67, and "Conceptual Framework for Financial Accounting and Reporting: Elements of Financial Statements and Their Measurement," *FASB Discussion Memorandum, op. cit.*, pp. 196–206, and "Using Cash Flow Information and Present Value in Accounting Measurements," *FASB Statement of Financial Accounting Concepts No. 7* (Norwalk, Conn.: FASB, 2000) p. 1.

balance sheet does not include all of its economic resources and economic obligations. For instance, "human resources" or "intellectual capital" such as high-quality management or highly creative employees are not included as assets, primarily because of the difficulty of reliably measuring their values. Or, possible legal obligations for air or water pollution may not be reported as liabilities, again due to measurement problems. Second, many of the amounts that a company reports are based on estimates, which are subject to change. As we discuss in the next section, estimates are involved in the determination of amounts for items such as uncollectible accounts and depreciation, as well as warranty and pension liabilities. Finally, in periods of inflation the amounts listed on a company's balance sheet do not show the "purchasing power" of its assets and liabilities. The FASB is aware of these limitations and in certain instances, as we discuss later in the chapter, requires companies to disclose additional information in the notes to the financial statements to help users in their decision making.

REPORTING CLASSIFICATIONS ON THE BALANCE SHEET

A company's accounting system processes vast amounts of data. When the company prepares the financial statements, it simplifies, condenses, and classifies that data. The classifications are designed to help analysis by grouping items with essentially similar characteristics. The intent is to improve the predictive value, and hence the usefulness, of the financial information for assessing the amounts, timing, and uncertainty of future cash flows.[8] **The arrangement of each company's balance sheet items and subtotals should be designed to be useful to its various external user groups.** But there must be flexibility in classifications to ensure such usefulness, due to differences in companies, industries, and economic conditions. Nonetheless a general classification scheme may be presented that captures the majority of items reported by most companies.

A corporation usually divides its balance sheet into three sections, and groups the items reported within each section in some informative manner. A representative classification would be:

1. *Assets*
    a. Current assets
    b. Long-term investments
    c. Property, plant, and equipment
    d. Intangible assets
    e. Other assets
2. *Liabilities*
    a. Current liabilities
    b. Long-term liabilities
    c. Other liabilities
3. *Stockholders' equity*
    a. Contributed capital
        (1) Capital stock
        (2) Additional paid-in capital
    b. Retained earnings
    c. Accumulated other comprehensive income

4 Classify the assets of a balance sheet.

We discuss each of these groupings in the following sections. A comprehensive illustration of a balance sheet at December 31, 2004 for the Caron Manufacturing Company is shown in Exhibit 3-4 on pages 66 and 67. For selected items, we show illustrations of disclosures of actual companies in related exhibits. Appendix A includes The Coca-Cola Company's balance sheet at December 31, 2001.

---

8. *Ibid., FASB Statement of Financial Accounting Concepts No. 5,* par. 20–22.

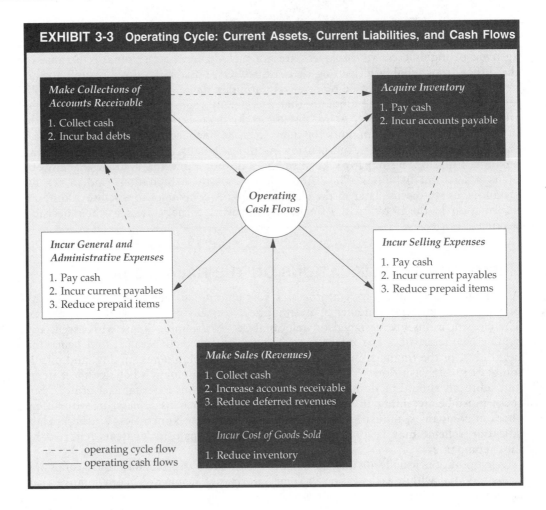

EXHIBIT 3-3 Operating Cycle: Current Assets, Current Liabilities, and Cash Flows

Current Assets

Current assets are cash and other assets that are expected to be converted into cash, sold, or consumed within one year or the normal operating cycle, whichever is longer. An *operating cycle* is the average time taken by a company to spend cash for inventory, process and sell the inventory, and collect the receivables, converting them back into cash. We show an example of a company's operating cycle in Exhibit 3-3. Note the relationship between current assets, current liabilities (discussed in the next section), and operating cash flows. Most companies have operating cycles of a year or less. A few, such as construction, lumber, distillery, and tobacco companies, have operating cycles that are longer than one year. In that case the longer time period should be used to determine the current assets.[9]

A company's current assets may include five items: (1) cash (and cash equivalents), (2) temporary investments in marketable securities, (3) receivables, (4) inventories, and (5) prepaid items. (Companies may use different titles than the ones we use here.) These items usually are presented in the current asset section in the order of their liquidity, as we show in Exhibit 3-4 on pages 66 & 67.

Cash includes cash on hand and readily available in checking and savings accounts. Many companies also include "cash equivalents" with cash. *Cash equivalents* are risk-free securities, such as money market funds and treasury bills that will mature in three

Operating cash flows are discussed in Chapters 2 and 4.

---

9. "Restatement and Revision of Accounting Research Bulletins," *Accounting Research and Terminology Bulletins, Final Edition, No. 43* (New York: AICPA, 1961), ch. 3, sec. A, par. 4 and 5.

months or less from the date acquired by the holder. **Temporary investments in marketable securities** include debt and equity securities that are classified as "trading securities" and "available-for-sale securities" and that management intends to convert into cash within one year or the normal operating cycle (whichever is longer). Also included are "derivative financial instruments" such as options to buy stock. Alternative titles include *short-term marketable securities* and *short-term investments*. They are listed at their market (fair) value (current market value). **Receivables** include accounts receivable and notes receivable with short-term maturity dates. They are listed at their estimated collectible amounts (net realizable values).

Marketable securities are discussed in Chapter 14.

Inventories include goods held for resale in the normal course of business plus, in the case of a manufacturing company, raw materials (items to be converted into finished goods) and goods in process (partially completed goods) inventories. They are listed at their historical cost or market value (current cost), whichever is lower. The inventory costing method (LIFO, FIFO, average cost) is disclosed parenthetically or in the related notes. To reduce the detail on its balance sheet, a company might show a total inventory amount in current assets and include a schedule of the components in the notes to the financial statements. This procedure is used by Johnson & Johnson, as shown in Exhibit 3-5 on page 68. **Prepaid items** such as insurance, rent, office supplies, and taxes will not be converted into cash but will be consumed. Conceptually, prepaid items should not be classified as current assets in the sense that they do not directly enter into the operating cycle. However, they are included as current assets because had they not been paid in advance, cash would have been paid out within the cycle. Furthermore, even though a two-year prepayment of insurance would extend over more than an annual operating cycle, the payment is usually classified as a current asset on the basis of a lack of materiality. Prepaid items are listed at the historical cost of the remaining amounts.

Current Liabilities

We discuss current liabilities next because of their close relation to current assets. **Current liabilities are those obligations whose liquidation is expected to require the use of existing current assets, or the creation of other current liabilities within one year or the normal operating cycle, whichever is longer.** Several types of liabilities should be included as current liabilities:

1. Obligations for items (goods or services) that have entered into the operating cycle. These include, for instance, accounts payable and salaries payable.
2. Advance collections for the future delivery of goods or performance of service—for instance, obligations under short-term derivative financial instruments (such as options to sell stock) as well as unearned rent and unearned ticket sales. These latter items sometimes are referred to as short-term deferred (unearned) revenues.
3. Other obligations that will be paid within one year or the operating cycle, such as short-term notes payable, interest payable, dividends payable, income taxes payable, the estimated liability for short-term product warranties, and the portions of long-term liabilities that mature during this period.[10]

These obligations are listed on the balance sheet at the amount owed (historical proceeds) or estimated to be owed. Exhibit 3-4 shows the current liabilities section of the Caron Manufacturing Company.

An obligation that is due within the next accounting period but which will be refinanced by issuing new long-term liabilities is not classified as a current liability. This obligation is not a current liability, because it will not require the use of current assets to satisfy the debt.

---

10. *Ibid.*, par. 7.

EXHIBIT 3-4   Balance Sheet

CARON MANUFACTURING COMPANY

Balance Sheet
December 31, 2004

Assets

Current Assets
Cash		$ 14,300
Temporary investments in available for sale securities		19,700
Accounts receivable	$ 68,200	
Less: Allowance for doubtful accounts	(3,200)	65,000
Inventories		
Raw materials	$ 32,000	
Goods in process	49,500	
Finished goods	66,100	147,600
Prepaid items		
Insurance	$ 4,800	
Office supplies	2,200	7,000

Total current assets	$253,600

Long-Term Investments
Investment in held-to-maturity bonds	$ 17,000	
Fund to retire long-term bonds payable	17,400	
Total long-term investments		34,400

Property, Plant, and Equipment

	Cost	Accumulated Depreciation	Book Value
Land	$ 36,000	—	$ 36,000
Buildings	428,000	$207,000	221,000
Equipment	192,000	63,700	128,300
Totals	$656,000	$270,700	$385,300

Total property, plant, and equipment	385,300

Intangible Assets
Trademarks	$ 12,600	
Patents (net)	16,900	
Total intangible assets		29,500

Total Assets	$702,800

Working Capital

The working capital of a company is the financial resources utilized during its operating cycle. **Working capital is the excess of current assets over current liabilities.** Although a company seldom computes its working capital on the balance sheet, it is often used by creditors and others as an indicator of the short-run liquidity of the company. Often external users use a slightly different computation, the **current ratio** (current assets divided by current liabilities), for the same purpose. Users must be careful when using working capital information in the current ratio because the liquidity *composition* of the working capital components (particularly current assets) is very important. The FASB has suggested several general guidelines for more homogeneous classifications of assets to help external users assess the nature, amounts, and liquidity of available resources. One classification alternative might be to separate the current assets into two groups. The first group would include the *liquid* assets of cash and temporary investments in marketable securities that are immediately convertible into cash. The second

EXHIBIT 3-4 Continued

Liabilities

Current Liabilities
Accounts payable	$ 87,100	
Salaries payable	3,300	
Income taxes payable	27,400	
Advances from customers	19,600	
Current portion of mortgage payable	8,400	
Total current liabilities		$145,800

Long-Term Liabilities
Bonds payable (10%, due 2017)	$ 90,000		
Less: Unamortized bond discount	(8,200)	$ 81,800	
Mortgage payable (12%, due 2005–2009)		52,600	
Accrued pension cost		34,700	
Total long-term liabilities			169,100

Other Liabilities
Deferred income taxes		14,300
Total Liabilities		$329,200

Stockholders' Equity

Contributed Capital (see Exhibit 3-8)
Common stock, $5 par (20,000 shares authorized, 14,300 shares issued and outstanding)	$ 71,500	
Additional paid-in capital on common stock	173,900	
Total contributed capital		$245,400
Retained Earnings (see Exhibit 3-8)		116,200

Accumulated Other Comprehensive Income
Unrealized increase in value of available-for-sale securities (see Exhibit 3-8)		12,000
Total Stockholders' Equity		$373,600
Total Liabilities and Stockholders' Equity		$702,800

group would be comprised of *separable assets*, those assets that can be separated from the company and converted into cash but with some time lag and conversion costs. These would include such items as receivables and inventories.[11] Users can develop alternative groupings of current assets and current liabilities, as well as other ratios for assessing liquidity and financial flexibility.

Long-Term Investments

Companies make investments for a variety of reasons. They may be interested in appreciation of the investment (the company expects the market value of the investment to increase), in income from interest or dividends, in exercising control over certain other

---

11. For a further discussion, see "Reporting Funds Flows, Liquidity, and Financial Flexibility," *FASB Discussion Memorandum* (Stamford, Conn.: FASB, 1980), ch. 8 and 9.

EXHIBIT 3-5   Inventory Disclosures

JOHNSON & JOHNSON

At December 30, 2001 and December 30, 2000	2001	2000
(in millions)		
Current assets (in part):		
Inventories (Notes 1 and 2)	$2,992	$2,905

NOTES TO CONSOLIDATED FINANCIAL STATEMENTS (in part):

2 Inventories

At the end of 2001 and 2000, inventories comprised of:

	2001	2000
Raw materials and supplies	$ 842	$ 718
Goods in process	605	480
Finished goods	1,545	1,707
	$2,992	$2,905

Q U E S T I O N S

Ⓠ What is the percentage of each type of inventory for 2001? for 2000? Ⓠ What might you be concerned (or optimistic) about in regard to the changes in the percentages?

---

companies, as in the case of a subsidiary or a major supplier, and in using the investment for specific future purposes such as the acquisition of property, plant, and equipment for expansion. Whether or not the investment is readily marketable, **if management expects to hold the item for more than one year or the operating cycle, whichever is longer, it is classified as a long-term (noncurrent) investment.**

Long-term investments include holdings of available-for-sale debt and equity securities that management does not intend to convert into cash within one year or the normal operating cycle (if longer than a year). Long-term investments also include investments in debt securities (e.g., bonds) expected to be held to maturity, noncurrent notes receivable from unaffiliated companies, long-term advances to unconsolidated affiliated companies, and financial instruments (such as options to buy stock) that are noncurrent. Investments in property and equipment being held for future operations, such as land being held for a future building site, also are included. Special funds established to retire bonds payable or preferred stock (often called sinking funds) or to acquire future facilities are included as long-term investments. Finally, miscellaneous investments, including the cash surrender value of life insurance policies, should be listed in this section of the balance sheet. Investments are listed at their market (fair) value, historical cost, book value, or present value, depending on the type of investment. The method of valuation for each long-term investment should be disclosed either parenthetically or in the notes to the financial statements. Exhibit 3-4 illustrates the long-term investments section of Caron Manufacturing Company.

Property, Plant, and Equipment

The property, plant, and equipment section of a company's balance sheet includes the tangible assets used in its operations. Often these are called *fixed assets* because of their relative permanency in the company's operations. A merchandising company sometimes will title this section Property and Equipment because it does not have manufacturing (plant) facilities. Assets that have a physical existence, such as land, buildings, equipment, machinery, furniture, and natural resources are listed in this category. Except for land, all the fixed assets are depreciable or depletable (in the case of natural resources). Land is listed at its historical cost, while the remaining fixed assets are listed at their book values (historical cost less accumulated depreciation or depletion). A *contra-asset* account, such as accumulated depreciation, usually is used to reduce fixed assets (except natural resources) to their book values while still disclosing historical cost. The method of depreciating the fixed assets is disclosed in the notes to the financial statements. In the case where the earning power of a fixed asset has been impaired, it is reported at a reduced market (fair) value. Exhibit 3-4 illustrates the property, plant, and equipment section of Caron Manufacturing Company. Some companies show a total amount of property, plant, and equipment on their balance sheets and a breakdown in the related notes. This procedure is used by Campbell Soup Company for its plant assets, as we show in Exhibit 3-6.

Certain long-term lease contracts relating to leased property, plant, and equipment also are included in this section. Long-term leases of assets are a popular way for a lessee to acquire the rights to the use of the assets without a large cash down payment. In the case of a *capital lease*, one that contains many of the characteristics of a purchase, both the assets and the liabilities sections of the lessee's balance sheet are affected. Since the lease allows the lessee company relatively unrestricted rights to the use of the asset for an extended period, the rights represent economic resources to the company, even though the asset is not legally owned. A capital lease initially is recorded by the lessee as an asset, Leased Equipment Under Capital Lease, at the present value of the future lease payments. It is amortized in a manner similar to other legally owned assets of the company. The book value of the leased asset is reported in the property, plant, and equipment section. Similarly, since the capital lease

Accounting for leases is discussed in Chapter 20.

EXHIBIT 3-6 Plant Assets

CAMPBELL SOUP COMPANY

	July 29, 2001	July 30, 2000
(in millions)		
Assets (in part):		
Plant assets, net of depreciation (Note 13)	$1,637	$1,644

NOTES TO CONSOLIDATED FINANCIAL STATEMENTS (in part):

13 Plant Assets (in part):

	2001	2000
Land	$ 50	$ 43
Buildings	840	808
Machinery and equipment	2,354	2,283
Projects in progress	133	162
	3,377	3,296
Accumulated depreciation	(1,740)	(1,652)
	$1,637	$1,644

Q U E S T I O N S

Q What percentage of the total cost is "projects in progress" on July 30, 2000 and July 29, 2001? **Q** What might this indicate?

payments are noncancelable over an extended number of years, these payments are a long-term liability of the lessee company. The obligation in regard to a capital lease also is recorded initially at the present value of the future lease payments and subsequently reduced by the amount of each lease payment (after adjustment for interest). As we discuss later, the capital lease liability is reported in the long-term liabilities section of the balance sheet.

Intangible Assets

Accounting for intangible assets is discussed in Chapter 11.

Intangible assets are those noncurrent economic resources that are used in the operations of the business but have no physical existence. They generally derive their value from the rights held by the company for their use. A company may have three categories of intangible assets: (1) intangible assets with finite useful lives, (2) intangible assets with indefinite lives, and (3) goodwill. Intangible assets with finite useful lives (such as patents, franchises, and computer software costs) are amortized over their useful lives and reported on the balance sheet at their book values (historical cost less accumulated amortization). The accumulated amortization of these intangibles is disclosed in the notes to the financial statements. Intangible assets with indefinite useful lives (such as copyrights and trademarks) are not amortized, but are reviewed for impairment annually. Impairment arises when the earning power of an intangible asset has been reduced to the point where its fair value is less than its historical cost. These intangible assets are reported on the balance sheet at their historical cost or, if impaired, at their lower fair value. Goodwill, another type of intangible asset, is not amortized but is also reviewed for impairment annually. Goodwill is also reported on the balance sheet at its historical cost or, if impaired, at its lower fair value. Many companies have valuable "intangible assets," such as their human resources and intellectual capital (employees), but these resources are not reported on the balance sheet because of the difficulty in reliably measuring their value. Exhibit 3-4 illustrates the intangibles section of Caron Manufacturing Company.

Other Assets

Finally an "Other Assets" section occasionally is used to report miscellaneous assets that may not be readily classified within one of the previous sections. This section sometimes is referred to as *deferred charges*. Examples of items that have been classified in this section include long-term prepayments (such as for rent or insurance), deferred tax assets, prepaid pension costs, bond issue costs, assets of a component of the company that is being discontinued, advances to officers, idle fixed assets, cash from customers' security deposits on returnable containers, assets leased to others, and assets temporarily restricted by foreign countries. Classification within this section should be made judiciously. Many items that are listed in this section might be classified correctly in one of the previous sections.

Long-Term Liabilities

5 Classify the liabilities of a balance sheet.

Long-term liabilities are those obligations that are not expected to require the use of current assets or *not* expected to create current liabilities within one year or the normal operating cycle (whichever is longer). Long-term liabilities may be called **noncurrent liabilities.** Many of these obligations may be outstanding for several years. Items such as long-term notes payable, obligations under capital lease contracts, mortgages payable, obligations under noncurrent financial instruments (e.g., options to sell stock), estimated liabilities from long-term warranties, accrued pension cost (i.e., obligation for future pension payments), and bonds payable are included in this category.

As a means of financing its activities, a corporation may issue long-term bonds (sometimes called debentures). A bond entails a written promise to repay a specific amount (its *face value*) at some future maturity date. Nearly all bonds also pay a specified interest rate (either semiannually or annually) that may vary from company to company.

Many bonds sell in a bond market similar to that of a stock market. Frequently a corporation may issue a bond at more or less than its face value. This occurs when the bond pays a stated interest rate greater or less than the yield rate investors can earn elsewhere on a similar security, consequently making it more or less valuable.

When a bond is issued for more than its face value, it is sold at a *premium*; when it is issued for less, it is sold at a *discount*. At the time of sale the Bonds Payable account is recorded at the face value of the bond, and an adjunct account called Premium on Bonds Payable (or a *contra* account called Discount on Bonds Payable) is used to record the amount by which the selling price is greater than (less than) the face value. Subsequently, each period this premium (or discount) is amortized as an adjustment to interest expense (generally by use of a present value approach), and at the maturity date only the face value of the bonds payable remains. Whenever a balance sheet is prepared, the remaining premium is added to (or the discount is subtracted from) the face value of the bonds payable to determine the book value. Most long-term liabilities are reported at present value, but some are listed at cost. Any applicable interest rates, maturity values, and other provisions are disclosed parenthetically on the balance sheet or in the notes to the financial statements. Exhibit 3-4 illustrates the long-term liabilities section of Caron Manufacturing Company. Some companies show a total amount of long-term liabilities on their balance sheets and a schedule of the individual amounts in the related notes. This procedure is used by Kimberly-Clark for its long-term debt, as we show in Exhibit 3-7.

Other Liabilities

A final section sometimes is used to report miscellaneous liabilities. This section might include such items as deferred tax liabilities, obligations of a component of the company that is being discontinued, and long-term advances from customers. As in the case of other assets, this category should be used judiciously.

Conceptual Guidelines for Reporting Assets and Liabilities

In the previous sections we discussed the typical classifications of assets and liabilities in a balance sheet. A company, however, should classify its assets and liabilities in the most informative manner for its external user groups. In addition to the "liquid" and "separable" subclassifications of current assets we discussed earlier, the FASB has suggested several guidelines for developing *homogeneous classes* of assets and liabilities. These guidelines include:

1. Reporting assets according to their type or expected function in the central operations or other activities of the company. For example, assets held for resale (inventory) should be reported separately from assets held for use in production (property, plant, and equipment).
2. Reporting as separate items assets and liabilities that affect the financial flexibility of the company differently; for example, assets used in operations, assets held for investment, and assets subject to restrictions (such as leased equipment).
3. Reporting assets and liabilities according to the measurement method used to value the items; for example, assets and liabilities measured at net realizable value versus those measured at current cost.

These general guidelines are intended to result in asset and liability classifications that help users assess the nature, amounts, and liquidity of available resources, including the intentions of management regarding their functional use, and the amounts and timing of obligations that require liquid resources for settlement.

The AICPA Special Committee on Financial Reporting extends these guidelines by suggesting that companies distinguish between "core" and "non-core" assets and liabilities. Core assets and liabilities result from a company's usual and recurring activities, transactions, and events. Conversely, non-core assets result from unusual or nonrecurring activities, transactions, or events. For instance, non-core assets might include

EXHIBIT 3-7   Long-Term Debt

KIMBERLY-CLARK CORPORATION

Liabilities and Stockholders' Equity (in part):

	December 31	
	2001	2000
(in millions)		
Long-term Debt	$2,424.0	$2,000.6

NOTES TO CONSOLIDATED FINANCIAL STATEMENTS (in part):

Note 5. Debt (in part)

Long-term debt is composed of the following:

	Weighted-Average Interest Rate	Maturities	December 31	
			2001	2000
Commercial paper to be refinanced –	–	$ 400.0 $	–	
Notes and debentures	7.1%	2002–2028	1,469.8	1,652.8
Industrial development revenue bonds	4.7%	2002–2034	413.4	414.1
Bank loans and other financings in various currencies	8.6%	2002–2025	278.5	211.2
Total long-term debt			2,561.7	2,278.1
Less current portion			137.7	277.5
Long-term portion			$2,424.0	$2,000.6

At December 31, 2001, $400 million of short-term commercial paper was classified as long-term debt because on February 8, 2002, the Corporation issued $400 million of 5⅝% Notes due February 15, 2012 and used the proceeds to retire commercial paper.

Fair value of total long-term debt was $2,639.5 million and $2,295.9 million at December 31, 2001 and 2000, respectively. Scheduled maturities of long-term debt for the next five years are $71.8 million in 2003, $116.7 million in 2004, $60.3 million in 2005 and $6.1 million in 2006.

At December 31, 2001, the Corporation had $1.475 billion of syndicated revolving credit facilities. These facilities, unused at December 31, 2001, permit borrowing at competitive interest rates and are available for general corporate purposes, including backup for commercial paper borrowings. The Corporation pays commitment fees on the unused portion but may cancel the facilities without penalty at any time prior to their expiration. Of these facilities, $737.5 million expires in October 2002 and the balance expires in November 2006.

At December 31, 2001 and 2000, the weighted-average interest rate for commercial paper was 1.9 percent and 6.5 percent, respectively.

Q U E S T I O N S

ⓠ What information regarding cash flows is available in the note but is not available in the balance sheet?

ⓠ Compute the approximate interest expense on the total long-term debt for the year ended December 31, 2001.

a receivable related to an unusually large sale of inventory that is not expected to recur in the foreseeable future. Non-core liabilities might include those related to a discontinued component.[12]

---

12. "Reporting Income, Cash Flows, and Financial Position of Business Enterprises," *FASB Proposed Statement of Financial Accounting Concepts, op. cit.*, par. 50, 51, and 170, and "Improving Business Reporting—A Customer Focus," *AICPA Special Committee on Financial Reporting* (New York: AICPA, 1994), App. II, pp. 138–139.

Stockholders' Equity

Stockholders' equity is the residual interest of the stockholders in the assets of the corporation. A company may be organized in three different ways: as a sole proprietorship, a partnership, or a corporation.

A sole proprietorship is a single-owner company. Because this is typically a small company where the owner acts as manager and has direct access to the accounting records, separate accounts typically are not used for the owner's investment and retained earnings. Normally the total owner's equity is summarized in a single *capital* account.

A partnership involves two or more persons who have agreed to combine their capital and efforts in the operations of a company. The partnership generally has a *partnership agreement*, a legal document that includes the investment requirements, allocation of income, and withdrawal provisions for each partner. Separate capital accounts are used for each partner to summarize the partner's equity.

The corporation is the most complex business organization. Usually there is *absentee* ownership, where the stockholders are external to the corporate management activities. To protect these absentee owners, numerous state laws have been established, many of which relate to the accounting for stockholders' equity. Stockholders' equity consists of three components: (1) contributed capital, (2) retained earnings, and (3) accumulated other comprehensive income.

6 Report the stockholders' equity of a balance sheet.

Contributed Capital

The owners of a corporation hold shares of stock in that corporation. A stockholder may acquire shares directly from the corporation or by purchasing them on the stock market from another investor. The corporation's balance sheet is affected only in the first situation. Most state laws protecting stockholders and creditors entail the establishment of a certain amount of legal capital. **Legal capital is the minimum amount of stockholders' equity that the corporation may not distribute as dividends;** it is one element of the total amount of contributed capital. The accounting for contributed capital relates as much to following these legal requirements as it does to providing significant financial information. Contributed capital frequently is separated into two components, capital stock (relating to the legal capital) and additional paid-in capital.

Protection of the interests of stockholders and creditors is discussed in Chapter 15.

Capital Stock and Additional Paid-In Capital

Corporations may issue two types of capital stock, preferred stock and common stock. **Preferred stock** has different ownership features (which some investors consider more attractive) from common stock, including preference to a specified dividend, if one is paid. **Common stock** carries the right to vote at the annual stockholders' meeting and to share in residual profits. The corporate charter includes the number of shares that a corporation is legally authorized to issue, as well as the types and characteristics of its capital stock. Common stock is the most prevalent type of capital stock. Each of these types of stock typically sells on a stock market, which establishes its *market value* per share.

Based upon state laws, a corporation may issue (1) par value, (2) stated value, or (3) no-par (no stated value) capital stock. Legally, capital stock may be required to carry a par value or a stated value. Par value or stated value refers to a specific dollar amount per share that is printed on the stock certificate.[13] Often this par value is a very small amount, say $1 or $5 per share, because states generally do not allow a corporation to issue stock at less than par. The par value of a share of stock has no direct relationship to the share's market value. Nonetheless, the legal (par) value must be accounted for separately.

When a corporation issues par value capital stock (common or preferred), it must allocate the proceeds (market price) between a capital stock account for the par value

---

13. There are certain legal differences between par value and stated value. We discuss these in Chapter 15. Since the accounting for stated value stock generally is identical to that for par value stock, our remaining discussion focuses on par value stock.

and another contributed capital account for the difference between the par and the market value. This latter account has a title such as Additional Paid-in Capital, Paid-in Capital in Excess of Par, or Premium on Common (or Preferred) Stock. For instance, if a corporation sold 100 shares of its $5 par common stock for $30 per share, the journal entry to record the transaction is as follows (the number of shares issued in the transaction is also recorded):

Cash	3,000	
Common Stock, $5 par		500
Additional Paid-in Capital on Common Stock		2,500

Many states allow corporations to issue no-par capital stock. When a corporation issues no-par capital stock, the amount of the proceeds from the sale usually is the legal capital, and the corporation records the entire amount in the capital stock account. Due to various other stock transactions, it is possible for a corporation issuing no-par stock to have certain additional paid-in capital accounts.

A corporation sometimes will repurchase its own capital stock. When it does, the number of shares outstanding is reduced. The corporation usually records the *cost* of the reacquisition in a contra stockholders' equity account entitled **Treasury Stock.** This account has a debit balance and the corporation deducts the amount from the total of contributed capital, retained earnings, and accumulated other comprehensive income to determine its total stockholders' equity.

Regardless of whether a corporation issues par or no-par stock, the corporation lists the balances in the Preferred Stock, Common Stock, and Additional Paid-in Capital accounts separately on its balance sheet and sums the amounts to determine the total amount of its contributed capital. The par value or stated value per share, as well as the number of shares authorized, issued, and outstanding, should be disclosed either parenthetically in the contributed capital section or in the notes to the financial statements. Exhibit 3-4 illustrates the contributed capital section of Caron Manufacturing Company.

Retained Earnings

Retained earnings is the total amount of corporate net income that has not been distributed to stockholders as dividends. A corporation may retain the assets generated from this net income for use in its daily operations, to maintain its productive facilities, or for growth. In any event, a retained earnings balance has no relationship to the funds that are available for cash dividends. The resources generated by net income are invested in all assets. The Retained Earnings account balance is an addition in stockholders' equity. A negative (debit) retained earnings balance (due to cumulative net losses and dividends exceeding cumulative net income), called a *deficit*, is subtracted in stockholders' equity.

Sometimes a company *restricts* or *appropriates* a portion of retained earnings to indicate that it cannot be reduced by the distribution of dividends. This may occur as a result of a legal or contractual requirement. Usually, such a restriction is disclosed in the notes to the financial statements.

Accumulated Other Comprehensive Income

As we discuss in Chapter 4, a company is required to report its total comprehensive income for the accounting period. Comprehensive income includes both net income and "other comprehensive income." Other comprehensive income (loss) might include four items: (1) unrealized increases (gains) or decreases (losses) in the market (fair) value of investments in available-for-sale securities, (2) translation adjustments from converting the financial statements of a company's foreign operations into U.S. dollars, (3) certain gains and losses on "derivative" financial instruments, and (4) certain pension liability adjustments.

A corporation includes its total net income earned to date in its retained earnings amount reported in stockholders' equity. The corporation includes its other comprehensive income (or loss) accumulated to date in its **accumulated other comprehensive income (or loss)** amount reported in stockholders' equity. If a corporation has more than one item of other comprehensive income, it has a choice. It may report the amount of accumulated other comprehensive income for each item in stockholders' equity. Or, it may report the total amount of accumulated other comprehensive income for all the items in stockholders' equity. If the corporation uses this approach, it must disclose the amounts for each of the items in the notes to its financial statements.[14]

General Motors Corporation uses the first approach. In the stockholders' equity section of its December 31, 2001 balance sheet, General Motors reported an accumulated other comprehensive loss of $12,295 million, consisting of four items as follows:

Accumulated foreign currency translation adjustments	$ (2,919)
Net unrealized loss on derivatives	(307)
Net unrealized gains on securities	512
Minimum pension liability adjustment	(9,581)
Accumulated other comprehensive loss	$(12,295)

The Caron Manufacturing Company has one item of accumulated other comprehensive income, as we show in Exhibit 3-4. Unless a corporation has miscellaneous items of equity (discussed next), it adds the totals for contributed capital, retained earnings, and accumulated other comprehensive income to determine the total stockholders' equity.

Miscellaneous Items

In rare instances a company may increase its assets without a corresponding outflow of assets, increase in liabilities, recognition of income, or issuance of capital stock. For instance, a company may receive donated assets from a governmental unit or it may discover previously unrecorded assets. In either case, when the company recognizes the asset's fair value it also increases stockholders' equity. These items are listed separately in stockholders' equity.

STATEMENT OF CHANGES IN STOCKHOLDERS' EQUITY

7 Prepare a statement of changes in stockholders' equity.

When a corporation issues financial statements, it must disclose the changes in its stockholders' equity accounts. This disclosure may be in a financial statement, a supporting schedule, or a note to the financial statements.[15] This reporting is consistent with the FASB's suggestion that a full set of financial statements should show, among other information, investments by and distributions to owners during the period. The intent is to help report on the changes in a company's financial structure to aid in assessing its financial flexibility.

FASB **Statement of Concepts No. 6** defines investments by owners and distributions to owners, as follows:

> **Investments by owners are increases in the equity of a company resulting from transfers of something valuable to the company from other entities in order to obtain or increase ownership interests.**
>
> **Distributions to owners are decreases in the equity of a company caused by transferring assets, rendering services, or incurring liabilities to owners.**

Assets are the economic resources most commonly received from investments by owners, but the items received may include services or the conversion of liabilities of the

---

14. "Reporting Comprehensive Income," *FASB Statement of Financial Accounting Standards No. 130* (Norwalk, Conn.: FASB, 1997), par. 17 and 26.

15. "Omnibus Opinion—1967," *APB Opinion No. 12* (New York: AICPA, 1967), par. 10.

EXHIBIT 3-8   Statement of Changes in Stockholders' Equity

SCHEDULE A
CARON MANUFACTURING COMPANY

Statement of Changes in Stockholders' Equity
For Year Ended December 31, 2004

	Common Stock, $5 par	Additional Paid-in Capital	Retained Earnings	Accumulated Other Comprehensive Income	Total
Balance, January 1, 2004	$65,000	$143,400	$ 64,900	$10,000	$283,300
Unrealized increase in value of available-for-sale securities				2,000	2,000
Net income			62,500		62,500
Cash dividends paid			(11,200)		(11,200)
Common stock issued	6,500	30,500			37,000
Balance, December 31, 2004	$71,500	$173,900	$116,200	$12,000	$373,600

---

company. Through investments by owners, a company obtains the resources it needs to begin or expand operations, to retire liabilities, or for other business purposes. Distributions by a company to its owners decrease its net assets and decrease or terminate ownership interests of those who receive them.[16]

The statement of changes in stockholders' equity is also discussed in Chapter 16.

To disclose investments by and distributions to owners, many companies will combine the retained earnings changes normally contained in a retained earnings statement and the changes in accumulated other comprehensive income with the other capital account changes in a statement of changes in stockholders' equity. Exhibit 3-8 illustrates this statement. Note that the totals of the columns in this exhibit are the same as those shown in the stockholders' equity section of Exhibit 3-4.

OTHER DISCLOSURE ISSUES

8 Understand the other disclosure issues for a balance sheet.

All the relevant financial information about a company's activities cannot be reported directly in the body of the financial statements because some items do not meet the recognition criteria we discussed earlier in the chapter. As indicated throughout the balance sheet discussion, a company may make many disclosures in the notes accompanying its financial statements. We discuss other significant disclosure issues here.

Summary of Accounting Policies

To understand the content of a company's financial statements, an external user needs to know the accounting policies, practices, and methods used by the company. For this reason, generally accepted accounting principles require the disclosure of certain information in the annual report presented to external users.

APB Opinion No. 22 requires that a company include a description of all significant accounting policies as an integral part of its financial statements. The disclosure should include principles relating to revenue recognition and asset allocation, particularly when these principles and methods involve (1) a selection from existing acceptable alternatives, (2) principles and methods peculiar to the industry in which

---

16. *FASB Statement of Financial Accounting Concepts No. 6, op. cit.*, par. 66–69.

EXHIBIT 3-9 Summary of Accounting Policies

BLACK & DECKER CORPORATION

Notes to Consolidated Financial Statements (in part)

Note 1: Summary of Accounting Policies (in part):

Principles of Consolidation: The Consolidated Financial Statements include the accounts of the Corporation and its subsidiaries. Intercompany transactions have been eliminated.

Inventories: Inventories are stated at the lower of cost or market. The cost of United States inventories is based primarily on the last-in, first-out (LIFO) method; all other inventories are based on the first-in, first-out (FIFO) method.

Property and Depreciation: Property, plant, and equipment is stated at cost. Depreciation is computed generally on the straight-line method for financial reporting purposes.

Q U E S T I O N S

Q Why is it important to disclose the method of computing the cost of inventories?
Q Why is it important to disclose the depreciation method? **Q** If the company used accelerated depreciation for financial reporting purposes, how would the income statement and balance sheet be affected?

---

the company operates, and (3) unusual or innovative applications of generally accepted accounting principles. Examples cited include, among others, those policies related to the basis for consolidation, depreciation methods, amortization of intangibles, inventory pricing, recognition of profits on long-term contracts, and revenue recognition from franchise and leasing operations. Although allowing for flexibility, the disclosure is particularly useful when made in a separate *Summary of Significant Accounting Policies* preceding the notes to the financial statements or as the initial note.[17] This summary (in part) for the Black & Decker Corporation is illustrated in Exhibit 3-9.

A complete summary is included in the Coca-Cola Company financial statements in Appendix A.

Fair Value and Risk of Financial Instruments

Some companies, many of which are banks and brokerage firms, deal in financial instruments. These *financial instruments* include such items as notes payable and receivable, contracts for loan commitments, collateralized mortgages, interest rate swaps, and put and call options on stocks. In recent years, both the types and uses of financial instruments have increased to the point where the FASB has addressed the reporting and disclosure of their fair values and risk. **FASB Statement No. 107** requires a company to disclose the fair value of all its financial instruments (both assets and liabilities), whether recognized or not on its balance sheet. The *Statement* also requires a company to disclose all significant concentrations of credit risk due to its financial instruments. A company typically makes these disclosures in the notes to its financial statements. **FASB Statement No. 133** requires a company to recognize all *derivative financial instruments* as either assets or liabilities on its balance sheet, and to measure these items at fair value. A derivative financial instrument is, for example, an option to buy stock where the value of the option depends on the price of the stock. The fair value is the amount at which the instrument could be purchased or sold in a current transaction between willing parties (i.e., current market value). The *Statement* also requires a company to disclose information such as the

Disclosures about fair values and risks of financial instruments are discussed in Chapter 12 and the Appendix to Chapter 14.

---

17. "Disclosure of Accounting Policies," *APB Opinion No. 22* (New York: AICPA, 1972), par. 8, 12, 13, and 15.

types of derivative instruments it holds, its objectives in holding the instruments, and its strategies for achieving these objectives. The description must indicate the company's risk management policy in regard to each type of instrument. The intent of these disclosures is to improve the reporting of a company's *risk, liquidity, and financial flexibility.*[18]

Contingent Liabilities and Assets

Loss and gain contingencies are discussed in Chapter 12.

Certain conditions, situations, or circumstances exist for a company on its balance sheet date that involve uncertainty as to possible losses or gains that the company may incur if some future event(s) occurs or fails to occur. These are known as **loss contingencies** or **gain contingencies** and may need to be included directly in the company's financial statements by establishing related accounts through a journal entry, or disclosed in a note accompanying the financial statements.[19]

A company accrues (reports a loss and a liability or a reduction of an asset) an estimated loss (or expense) from a loss contingency if (1) it is *probable* that a liability has been incurred (or an asset impaired) and (2) the amount of the loss can be *reasonably estimated*. Examples of this type of loss contingency include product warranties and uncollectible accounts receivable. If either of these conditions is *not* met—that is, if there is only a reasonable possibility that the loss may have been incurred or if the amount of the loss cannot be reasonably estimated—the company discloses the loss contingency in the notes to its financial statements.

The following diagram illustrates the alternative ways of accounting for loss contingencies:

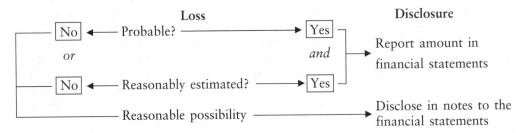

Examples of a loss contingency that are disclosed in the notes to the financial statements include guarantees of the debts of others and pending litigation against the company, where either the outcome of the litigation or the amount of possible loss is uncertain. An illustration of this type of contingency for **Boise Corporation** is shown in Exhibit 3-10. Gain contingencies are not reported in a company's financial statements and, if disclosed in a note, should be carefully explained to avoid misleading implications as to the likelihood of future revenues or gains.[20]

Subsequent Events

A company usually does not issue its annual report for several weeks or months after the end of the accounting period, due to the time needed for adjusting and closing the books and auditing the financial statements. During this time it is possible for significant business events and transactions to occur which, if not disclosed in the company's annual report, would cause this report to be misleading. Subsequent events are discussed more fully in an auditing book; they are briefly summarized here.

---

18. "Disclosures About Fair Value of Financial Instruments," *FASB Statement of Financial Accounting Standards No. 107* (Norwalk, Conn.: FASB, 1991) and "Accounting for Derivative Instruments and Hedging Activities," *FASB Statement of Financial Accounting Standards No. 133* (Norwalk, Conn.: FASB, 1998).

19. "Accounting for Contingencies," *FASB Statement of Financial Accounting Standards No. 5* (Stamford, Conn.: FASB, 1975), par. 1.

20. *Ibid.*, par. 8–17.

A subsequent event is one that occurs between the balance sheet date and the date of issuance of the annual report, as we illustrate in the following time diagram:

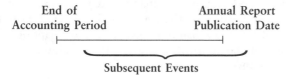

End of
Accounting Period

Annual Report
Publication Date

Subsequent Events

If a subsequent event occurs that (1) provides additional evidence concerning conditions that *existed* on the balance sheet date and (2) significantly affects the estimate(s) used in the preparation of the company's financial statements, the company must make an adjustment to the financial statements. For instance, if a company obtains additional information indicating that a major customer's account receivable is unlikely to be collected, it makes an adjustment to the allowance for doubtful accounts and the bad debt expense.

When a subsequent event occurs that provides evidence concerning conditions that did *not* exist on the company's balance sheet date, but instead occurred after that date, the company does *not* adjust its financial statements. Instead, the information is disclosed in a note, pro forma ("as if") statement, or an explanatory paragraph in the audit report, depending upon the materiality of the financial impact. Examples of these events include a fire or flood loss, a litigation settlement, and the sale of a bond or stock issue after the balance sheet date.[21]

Related Party Transactions

Transactions between related parties frequently occur in the normal course of business. Related parties of a company include affiliated entities such as subsidiaries, trusts for the benefit of employees, its management, and its principal owners or immediate families.

EXHIBIT 3-10 Contingency

BOISE CORPORATION

Notes to Financial Statements (in part)

17. Legal Proceedings, Commitments and Contingencies (in part)

In March 2000, EPA Regions VI and X issued Boise a combined Notice of Violation (NOV) alleging violations of air emission permits and the New Source Review/Prevention of Significant Deterioration program. In March 2001, the EPA issued a second NOV, supplementing the original notice. The NOV alleges violations at seven of our plywood plants and one particleboard plant for the period 1979 through 1998. No civil or criminal actions have been filed with regard to these allegations. The NOV, however, sets forth EPA's authority to seek, among other things, penalties of up to $27,500 per day for each violation. We believe federal statutes of limitation would limit any penalties assessed to a five-year period. We are negotiating with the EPA to resolve these allegations. We have had several meetings and exchanged correspondence regarding a resolution of the issues raised by the NOV. Settlements by other companies in the wood products industry that have received similar NOVs have involved the payment of penalties and agreements to install emission control equipment and undertake supplemental environmental projects. The effect of this NOV on our financial position or results of operations is unknown at this time.

Q U E S T I O N

What possible impact might the NOV have on Boise's future financial position or results of operations?

Relationships between related parties may enable one of the parties to exercise influence over the other so that it is given preferential treatment. To provide sufficient information for external users to understand a company's financial statements, **FASB Statement No. 57** requires certain disclosures by the company. For related party transactions these include (1) the nature of the relationship involved, (2) a description of the transactions, (3) the dollar amounts of the transactions, and (4) any amounts due to or from the related parties on the balance sheet date.[22]

Comparative Financial Statements

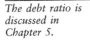

The debt ratio is discussed in Chapter 5.

Exhibits 3-4 and 3-8 show the ending balance sheet and the statement of changes in stockholders' equity of the Caron Manufacturing Company for one year. Many external users are interested in comparing the current financial statements with those of the previous year. Furthermore, many times *trend* information about a company will reveal useful insights about its past performance and future success. For this reason nearly all companies present **comparative financial statements** for the current and preceding accounting periods. Additionally, in a supplemental schedule most companies will present a summary of key accounting information for, say, the past 5 to 10 years. For instance, some companies report their **debt ratio** (total liabilities ÷ total assets) to help external users (creditors and stockholders) assess the risk of their investment in the company. The **Coca-Cola Company** presents comparative financial statements, as well as a supplemental schedule for eleven years, as shown in Appendix A.

Auditor's Report

The auditor's report is discussed in Chapter 5.

Many major financial decisions by investors, bankers, other creditors, and other users are based upon the financial information presented in a company's financial statements and related notes. These financial statements are the responsibility of the company's management. In order to help ensure a fair presentation of corporate financial resources, obligations, and activities, the financial statements and accompanying notes presented to external users by companies are audited by an independent certified public accountant. In an audit the certified public accountant is responsible for making an examination of a company's accounting system, records, and reports *in accordance with generally accepted auditing standards*. Based on this examination, the auditor expresses an *opinion* as to the *fairness in accordance with generally accepted accounting principles* of the company's financial statements and accompanying notes. Although this opinion is *not* itself part of the financial statements, it is an extremely important item of information, and one on which external users place much significance.

SEC Integrated Disclosures

The contents of a Form 10-K annual report are discussed in Chapter 5.

As we noted in Chapter 1, the Securities and Exchange Commission has the legal authority to prescribe accounting principles and reporting practices for all regulated companies. Each year, within 60 days of its fiscal year-end, a regulated company must file a *Form 10-K* annual report with the SEC. This report must be filed electronically according to the EDGAR requirements. Each company's chief executive and chief financial officer both must "certify" that the company's annual report within the Form 10-K (or interim report within the company's Form 10-Q) is both complete and accurate. The SEC has also developed an "integrated" set of disclosure requirements that enable a company to satisfy certain Form 10-K disclosure requirements by referring to its stockholders' annual report, provided the latter report includes certain items. Since many regulated companies now include these items in their annual reports, we briefly summarize the items as follows. For a more detailed discussion, see *Regulation S-X* of the SEC.

---

22. "Related Party Transactions," *FASB Statement of Financial Accounting Standards No. 57* (Stamford, Conn.: FASB, 1982), par. 2.

COMPARATIVE FINANCIAL STATEMENTS As we discussed in the previous section, most companies present comparative financial statements for at least two years. The SEC requires comparative balance sheets for *two* years and comparative income statements and statements of cash flows for *three* years.

9 Describe the SEC integrated disclosures.

SELECTED FINANCIAL DATA As we discussed in the previous section, most companies present a summary of important accounting information for several years. The SEC requires *specific* disclosures for a *five-year period*. These include net sales or operating revenues, income (loss) from continuing operations and related earnings per share, total assets, long-term obligations and redeemable stock, and cash dividends declared per share. The SEC encourages the inclusion of other information that will help users understand and highlight trends.

MANAGEMENT'S DISCUSSION AND ANALYSIS Management must include a discussion and analysis (MD&A) of the company's financial condition, changes in financial condition, and results of operations. The intent is to give investors the opportunity to look at the company from management's perspective. Management is asked to discuss the dynamics of the company's business and to analyze the financial statements. The discussion is intended to provide information that does not clearly appear in the financial statements but is useful in evaluating cash flows from operations and from outside sources. The major items covered should include, for instance, specific information about short-term and long-term liquidity and capital resources, a narrative discussion of the impact of inflation on sales and on income from continuing operations, explanations of material changes in financial statement items between years, and known events and uncertainties expected to impact future operations. Other kinds of "forward-looking" information (e.g., trends) are required as well.

The content of MD&A is discussed in Chapter 5.

COMMON STOCK MARKET PRICES AND DIVIDENDS Several disclosures must be made. These include the principal trading markets for the company's common stock, the high and low market prices for each quarter in the last two years, the approximate number of stockholders, the dividends paid in the last two years, and any dividend restrictions.

Miscellaneous Disclosures

In addition to the disclosures discussed throughout this chapter, a company must make numerous other disclosures to provide adequate information concerning its activities. These include information about such items as the company's stock option, pension, and insurance plans, long-term lease and purchase commitments, bond indenture provisions, notes receivable, and notes payable provisions. We discuss specific disclosure requirements as we address each topic in the remaining chapters.

International Accounting Differences

One of the objectives of the IASB is to ensure, to the extent possible, that a company's published financial statements comply with international accounting standards. The financial statements required by the IASB are similar to those in the U.S. They include a balance sheet, statement of changes in equity, income statement, and statement of cash flows, as well as related notes and other explanatory materials. However, International Accounting Standards do not *require* a particular format; the appropriate format depends on the type of company.

A company may classify its assets on the balance sheet into noncurrent assets and current assets, with noncurrent assets presented first. Noncurrent assets include property, plant, and equipment, as well as other items (investments, long-term receivables, intangibles). These classifications are similar to those in the United States. Current assets are also similar to those under U.S. GAAP.

The ordering of the liabilities and owners' equity sections is usually different than under U.S. GAAP, with "capital and reserves" listed first. The capital and reserves section includes issued capital, reserves, and accumulated profits (losses). The issued capital includes share capital and share premium. A company is required to disclose the par value, as well as the number of shares authorized, issued and fully paid, and issued but not fully paid. It must also disclose dividends that have been proposed but not formally approved for payment. Reserves may result from revaluations of properties and investments, as well as currency translation differences. A company must also provide a description of the nature and purpose of each reserve.

Noncurrent liabilities are usually listed next and include items such as interest-bearing borrowings, deferred income, deferred taxes, and retirement benefit obligations. Deferred income may include government grants, which are a form of financial assistance to a company for compliance with certain conditions. On the other hand, some government grants for the construction of assets are treated as a reduction in the book value of the asset. Current liabilities are listed last and are similar to those under U.S. GAAP. As with U.S. GAAP, a company is not required to separate its assets and liabilities into current and noncurrent classifications; it decides on the disclosures based on their usefulness.

A company's statement of changes in equity includes the changes in share capital and share premium, as well as any changes in the company's reserves due to, for instance, a surplus on the revaluation of properties or a deficit on the revaluation of investments. A company must also disclose any changes in accumulated profits (losses) due to changes in accounting policies, corrections of fundamental errors, net income, and dividends.

In the notes to its financial statements, a company is required to disclose items similar to those required under U.S. GAAP. These disclosures include its accounting policies, narrative descriptions of financial statement items, and contingencies. For revaluations, they also include the measurement basis used. Furthermore, companies in "hyperinflationary" economies (e.g., the cumulative inflation rate over three years exceeds 100 percent) are required to prepare general price-level-adjusted financial statements. In the following chapters, we briefly discuss the major differences between international and U.S. accounting standards as they apply to specific assets, liabilities, and income.[23]

REPORTING TECHNIQUES

10 Explain the reporting techniques used in an annual report.

Companies use numerous reporting techniques in the presentation of their annual reports. We discuss the major ones relating to the financial statement presentations next.

Statement Format (Balance Sheet)

The format that a company uses for its balance sheet depends upon its size, the industry in which it operates, certain regulatory requirements, and tradition. Three basic formats are generally used: the report form, the account form, and the financial position form.

Most companies use the **report form.** Here the balance sheet is shown in a vertical format. The asset accounts are listed first, and the liability and stockholders' equity accounts are listed in sequential order directly below the assets. In contrast, the **account form** of the balance sheet is organized in a horizontal fashion, with the asset accounts listed on the left-hand side and liabilities and stockholders' equity accounts on the right-hand side. This is the format used in Exhibit 3-4. In the seldom-used **financial position form,** current assets and current liabilities are listed vertically first to derive the working capital. The remaining assets are added and the remaining liabilities deducted to derive the residual stockholders' equity. Of 600 companies surveyed, the report form, account form, and financial position form are used by 502, 97, and 1 respectively.[24]

Combined Amounts

To reduce the size of a company's financial statements, it may combine certain related amounts. For instance, a company may list a single amount for property and equipment

---

23. For a more complete discussion, see Carrie Bloomer (editor), *The IASC—U.S. Comparison Project: A Report on the Similarities and Defferences between IASC Standards and U.S. GAAP,* 2nd ed. (Norwalk, Conn.: FASB, 1999).

24. *Accounting Trends and Techniques,* (New York: AICPA, 2001), p. 129.

on the face of its balance sheet and then itemize the amounts applicable to land, buildings, and equipment in a note to the financial statements. Frequently the amounts for inventories are similarly combined and itemized, as illustrated in Exhibit 3-5 for Johnson & Johnson. Generally, it is *not* proper to offset asset and liability accounts. For instance, the amount in a special Bond Sinking Fund account to retire long-term bonds would not be offset against the Bonds Payable account balance. In a few circumstances, a *right of offset* exists whereby a debtor (Company A) has a legal right to discharge all or some of the liability owed to another party (Company B) by applying an amount that the other party (Company B) owes to the debtor (i.e., a receivable of Company A) against the liability.[25] For instance, when a bank loans money to a company in exchange for the company's accounts receivable that are assigned to the bank, the company would offset the assigned accounts receivable on its balance sheet against the liability owed to the bank.

Right of offset is discussed in Chapter 6.

Rounding

In Exhibits 3-3 and 3-8 the amounts presented for each account, subtotal and total, were rounded to the nearest hundred dollars. Rounding is usually done to increase readability and to reduce the likelihood that readers will attach more precision to the numbers than is warranted. In fact, many major companies round to the nearest million dollars. In the Coca-Cola Company financial statements the amounts have been rounded as indicated.

Notes, Supporting Schedules, and Parenthetical Notations

Additional information not included in the accounts reported on a company's financial statements is disclosed in a note, supporting schedule, or parenthetical notation.

The **notes** (sometimes called *footnotes*) accompanying the financial statements are extremely useful ways of presenting additional information. Generally accepted accounting principles *require* that a company disclose certain information (for instance, contingent liabilities that are reasonably possible) in the notes to the financial statements, while sound accounting practice mandates additional note disclosures when they add to the completeness of the annual report. Notes usually contain narrative discussion, additional monetary amounts, and sometimes supplemental schedules.

We illustrated several notes of actual companies earlier in this chapter. We discuss required and suggested disclosures in notes throughout this text as they apply to specific topics. Because notes must communicate technical accounting information in a narrative format, several practices would improve their clarity and readability. In the preparation and writing of financial reporting notes, the accountant should (a) specify what data are to be disclosed, (b) outline the desired format of the note, (c) construct and use short sentences in the note, (d) use terminology understandable to the external user, and (e) be concise but complete.

Supporting schedules may be freestanding or part of the notes. A supporting schedule may complement an entire financial statement (such as the retained earnings statement) or may explain a summary amount on a specific financial statement (such as an itemization of inventories). We discuss and illustrate supporting schedules throughout the text.

Parenthetical notations following specific accounts are used to explain such items as the method of valuation (e.g., cost, lower of cost or market) or of determining the ending inventory (e.g., average cost), or to cross-reference certain related asset and liability accounts (e.g., bond sinking fund and bonds payable).

---

25. For the criteria to be met for a right of offset to exist, see "Offsetting of Amounts Related to Certain Contracts," *FASB Interpretation No. 39* (Norwalk, Conn.: FASB, 1992), par. 5 and "Offsetting of Amounts Related to Certain Repurchase and Reverse Repurchase Agreements," *FASB Interpretation No. 41* (Norwalk, Conn.: FASB, 1994), par. 3.

ILLUSTRATIVE STATEMENTS

The actual financial statements and accompanying notes of the Coca-Cola Company for the year ended December 31, 2001 are shown in Appendix A. Although you may not understand all of these items at this point, pay particular attention to each statement's format and content and, in particular, to the notes accompanying the reports. Your understanding will increase as you study this book.

SUMMARY

At the beginning of the chapter, we identified several objectives you would accomplish after reading the chapter. The objectives are listed below, each followed by a brief summary of the key points in the chapter discussion.

1. **Understand the purposes of the balance sheet.** A balance sheet summarizes the *financial position* of a corporation on a specific date by reporting on its assets, liabilities, and stockholders' equity. The balance sheet reports a corporation's *resource structure* and its *financial structure.*

2. **Define the elements of a balance sheet.** The elements of a balance sheet are the broad classes of items comprising it. The elements include assets, liabilities, and stockholders' equity. Briefly, assets are a corporation's economic resources, liabilities are its present obligations, and stockholders' equity is the residual interest in the assets.

3. **Explain how to measure the elements of a balance sheet.** There are five alternatives for measuring the elements (assets and liabilities) of a balance sheet. These include: (1) historical cost/historical proceeds (2) current cost/current proceeds, (3) current market value, (4) net realizable value, and (5) present value. Alternatives (2) through (4) are ways of measuring the fair value of an element. Each of these alternatives is used under specific circumstances for measuring certain assets and liabilities.

4. **Classify the assets of a balance sheet.** The assets of a balance sheet may be classified into five groups: (1) current assets, (2) long-term investments, (3) property, plant, and equipment, (4) intangible assets, and (5) other assets.

5. **Classify the liabilities of a balance sheet.** The liabilities of a balance sheet may be classified into three groups: (1) current liabilities, (2) long-term liabilities, and (3) other liabilities.

6. **Report the stockholders' equity of a balance sheet.** The stockholders' equity of a balance sheet consists of contributed capital (capital stock and additional paid-in capital), retained earnings, and accumulated other comprehensive income.

7. **Prepare a statement of changes in stockholders' equity.** A statement of changes in stockholders' equity starts with the beginning balances of capital stock, additional paid-in capital, retained earnings, and accumulated other comprehensive income. It then reconciles these beginning balances to the ending balances by showing the changes (and reasons for the changes) in each of these items.

8. **Understand the other disclosure issues for a balance sheet.** To help users understand the elements of its balance sheet (and other financial statements), a company also discloses useful information in the notes to the financial statements. This information includes a summary of the company's accounting policies, the fair value and risk of its financial instruments, any contingent liabilities and assets, any subsequent events, and any related party transactions. The company also includes comparative financial statements, all of which must be audited.

9. **Describe the SEC integrated disclosures.** A company can satisfy certain SEC 10-K disclosure requirements by including an "integrated" set of disclosures in its annual report. The company must include comparative financial statements, selected financial information for a five-year period, a management's discussion and analysis (MD&A), and common stock market prices and dividends.

10. **Explain the reporting techniques used in an annual report.** A company may use various reporting techniques in its annual report. It may use a *report form*, *account form*, or *financial position form* of balance sheet. It may combine amounts of certain elements, and may round the reported numbers. It may provide additional information in the notes to the financial statements, supporting schedules, or parenthetical notations.

QUESTIONS

Q3-1 What are the major financial statements of a company and what do they summarize?

Q3-2 What does a company's financial position include?

Q3-3 What are two purposes of a company's balance sheet?

Q3-4 Define liquidity, financial flexibility, and operating capability.

Q3-5 What is financial capital? Why is capital maintenance important?

Q3-6 What does "recognition" mean in accounting?

Q3-7 Define an asset. What are the three characteristics of an asset?

Q3-8 Define a liability. What are the three characteristics of a liability?

Q3-9 What is stockholders' equity?

Q3-10 Identify the five alternatives for measuring (valuing) assets. Which valuation method is usually used in a company's balance sheet?

Q3-11 List the major sections (and the components of each section) of a company's balance sheet.

Q3-12 How are current assets defined and what are the major items that may be included in current assets? How are current liabilities defined? Give three examples of such liabilities.

Q3-13 Define a company's operating cycle. How does working capital relate to this cycle? How is working capital computed?

Q3-14 What items are classified as (a) long-term investments, (b) property, plant, and equipment, and (c) intangible assets?

Q3-15 What items are classified as (a) long-term liabilities and (b) other liabilities?

Q3-16 What is a bond? Give an illustration of how bonds payable would be disclosed on a company's balance sheet.

Q3-17 Define (a) capital stock, (b) additional paid-in capital in excess of par, (c) treasury stock, (d) retained earnings, (e) deficit, and (f) accumulated other comprehensive income.

Q3-18 What are investments by owners? Distributions to owners? In what statement do many companies report these items?

Q3-19 What accounting policies are disclosed in the notes accompanying a company's financial statements? Why is this disclosure important?

Q3-20 Give several examples of financial instruments and identify the required *disclosures* for a company's financial instruments.

Q3-21 What is a loss contingency? What criteria have to be met for a company to accrue a contingent liability? If these criteria are not met, how does a company disclose a contingent liability?

Q3-22 Why is it necessary for a company to disclose subsequent events? What kinds of subsequent events are disclosed by an adjustment to the company's financial statements and what kinds are disclosed in a note?

Q3-23 What must a company disclose for related party transactions?

Q3-24 Why are comparative financial statements important?

Q3-25 What is an audit and why is the auditor's report an important item of information?

Q3-26 Briefly describe the SEC "integrated" disclosures that most regulated companies include in their annual reports.

Q3-27 Briefly list the format of a company's balance sheet under international accounting standards.

Q3-28 What is the difference between the report form and the account form of the balance sheet?

Q3-29 What alternative methods are used to disclose additional information not included in the accounts reported on a company's financial statements? Give examples of the types of information disclosed by each method.

Q3-30 What factors should be considered when an accountant prepares and writes financial reporting notes?

CASES

C O M M U N I C A T I O N

C3-1 Alternative Valuation Methods

A friend of yours who had a bookkeeping course in high school and who is currently a business major says, "I thought that assets were always reported at their historical cost on a company's balance sheet. Recently, however, I heard several accounting majors discussing 'alternative valuation methods' for measuring the value of assets. I know that historical cost is the exchange price paid for an asset, so I cannot understand how there can be any other 'value' for the asset."

Required Write a short memo that identifies and briefly explains the valuation methods (other than historical cost) that a company could use to measure the value of an asset. For each valuation method, include in your discussion examples of assets whose values are often reported based on the use of that method.

C3-2 Contingencies and Subsequent Events

The bookkeeper of a company you are auditing states, "Our balance sheet is dated December 31, the end of our accounting period. I don't understand contingent liabilities and subsequent events. Furthermore, I see no reason for disclosing these items on the company's balance sheet because they deal with events that might occur or have occurred *after* the balance sheet date."

Required Write a short report to the bookkeeper that explains contingent liabilities and subsequent events, as well as the importance of their disclosure on the company's balance sheet.

C3-3   Securities and Exchange Commission Disclosures

The Securities and Exchange Commission (SEC) has encouraged managements of public companies to disclose more information in the shareholders' annual report. As a consequence, a significant amount of the information required in the SEC's Form 10-K now appears in published annual reports.

At the same time, the SEC has made the annual financial reporting process simpler and more efficient by approving an integrated disclosure system.

Required

1. Identify the major classes of information that must be included in both the annual report to shareholders and Form 10-K filed with the SEC.
2. The integrated disclosure system is intended to simplify the annual reporting process with the SEC by expanding the ability to incorporate by reference.
   a. Define what is meant by *incorporating by reference* and identify the documents that are involved when incorporating by reference.
   b. Explain how the integrated disclosure system reduces managements' efforts in filing annual reports with the SEC.
   c. Explain the SEC's principal reasons for making the changes in the annual reporting process.
   d. Identify and explain potential problems the integrated disclosure system could have on the annual reporting process from the aspect of users of financial information. (*CMA adapted*)

C3-4   Asset Valuation

It is the end of 2004 and you are an accountant for the Stone Company. During 2004, sales of the company's products slumped and the company's earnings are expected to be much less than those of 2003. The president comes to you with an idea. He says, "Our company's property, plant, and equipment cost $300,000, and that is the amount we usually report on our balance sheet. However, I just had these assets appraised by an independent appraiser, and she says they are worth $400,000. I think that the company should report the property, plant, and equipment at this amount on its December 31, 2004 balance sheet, and should report the $100,000 increase in value as a gain on the 2004 income statement. If we use this approach, it will show how much our company is really worth and increase our earnings. This will make our stockholders happy. What do you think?"

Required Prepare a written response to the president.

C R E A T I V E   A N D   C R I T I C A L   T H I N K I N G

C3-5   Valuation of Assets and Stock

A friend has come to you for advice. He states that he owns several shares of stock in a corporation. He has examined the most recent balance sheet of the corporation and has found that the common stock issued and outstanding totals 40,000 shares, and the market price per share is $25 on the balance sheet date. He is sure that the balance sheet must be in error because, in his words, "the total assets are $1,100,000 and this current value should be the same as the $1,000,000 total value of the outstanding common stock."

Required Explain to your friend how the "values" of the various assets of the corporation typically are measured and reported on its balance sheet, and how the "value" of the $1,100,000 total assets is determined. Continue the discussion by explaining to your friend why the "values" of the assets and the stock are not the same.

C3-6   Valuation of Assets

Valuation of assets is an important topic in accounting theory. Suggested valuation methods include the following:

   Historical cost (past purchase price)
   Historical cost adjusted to reflect general price-level changes

   Discounted cash flow (future exchange price)
   Market price (current selling price)
   Replacement cost (current purchase price)

Required

1. Why is the valuation of assets a significant issue?
2. Explain the basic theory underlying each of the valuation methods cited, including the effect on earnings. Do not discuss advantages and disadvantages of each method. (*AICPA adapted*)

C3-7   Analyzing Coca-Cola's Accounting Policies

A company must include a summary of its accounting policies in the notes to its financial statements. The Coca-Cola Company includes this summary as the first of its notes to the consolidated financial statements shown in Appendix A.

Required

1. Explain what is required to be disclosed about the accounting policies of a company.
2. Review the Coca-Cola Company's note on its accounting policies and answer the following questions:
   a. What accounts do the consolidated financial statements include?

b. What items are classified as cash equivalents?

c. How are inventories valued, and generally what inventory costing method(s) is used?

d. How are property, plant, and equipment stated, and what depreciation method is used?

e. How are trademarks and other intangible assets stated, and what was the accumulated amortization at December 31, 2001?

f. How does the company account for production costs of print, radio, and television advertisements? What was the amount of advertising costs included in prepaid expenses and other assets and noncurrent other assets as of December 31, 2001?

C3-8   Ethics and Accounts Receivable Adjustment

It is February 16, 2005 and you are auditing the Davenport Corporation's financial statements for 2004 (which will be issued in March, 2005). You read in the newspaper that Travis Corporation, a major customer of Davenport, is in financial difficulty. Included in Davenport's accounts receivable is $50,000 (a material amount) owed to it by Travis. You approach Jim Davenport, president, with this information and suggest that a reduction of accounts receivable and recognition of a loss for 2004 might be appropriate. Jim replies, "Why should we make an adjustment? Ted Travis, the president of Travis Corporation, is a friend of mine; he will find a way to pay

us, one way or another. Furthermore, this occurred in 2005, so let's wait and see what happens; we can always make an adjustment later this year. Our 2004 income and year-end working capital are not that high; our creditors and stockholders wouldn't stand for lower amounts than they already are."

Required From financial reporting and ethical perspectives, prepare a response to Jim Davenport regarding this issue.

C3-9   Ethics and Note Due from President

You are the accountant for Spaedy Company and are preparing the financial statements for 2004. Near the end of 2004, Spaedy Company loaned its president $100,000 (a material amount) because she was having financial difficulties. The note was properly recorded as a note receivable by Spaedy Company. You are unsure of how to classify this note on the 2004 ending balance sheet and ask the president when the note is due. She replies, "We never really set a due date; I might repay it in 2005 or maybe in a couple of years when I get more financially secure. It would be best to classify this note as a current asset in the usual manner because that will increase our working capital and current ratio, which will make our creditors and stockholders happy."

Required From financial reporting and ethical perspectives, what do you think of the president's suggestion?

R E S E A R C H

C3-10   Researching GAAP

You are the assistant accountant for Tyler Corporation. It is mid-January, 2005 and you are helping to prepare the Tyler Corporation's balance sheet for December 31, 2004. Tyler will publish this balance sheet on March 1, 2005, after the auditors have completed their work. Tyler has a $100,000 note payable that was issued in 2003 and that is due March 6, 2005. On January 5, 2005, Tyler sold 2,000 shares of its $10 par common stock for $80,000. Its intent is to use these proceeds (plus $20,000

cash it already has on hand) to repay the note payable on March 6. The head accountant says "I'm not sure how to classify the $100,000 note payable on the December 31, 2004 balance sheet. Check this out for me."

Required Research the related generally accepted accounting principles and prepare a short memo to the head accountant that explains how Tyler Corporation should report the $100,000 note payable on its December 31, 2004 balance sheet.

MULTIPLE CHOICE

Select the best answer for each of the following.

M3-1 *APB Opinion No. 22*, "Disclosure of Accounting Policies"

a. Requires a description of every accounting policy followed by a reporting entity

b. Provides a specific listing of all types of accounting policies that must be disclosed

c. Requires disclosure of the format for the statement of cash flows

d. Requires a description of all significant accounting policies to be included as an integral part of the financial statements

M3-2 Which of the following contingencies should generally be accrued on the balance sheet when the occurrence of the contingent event is reasonably possible and its amount can be reasonably estimated?

	Gain Contingency	Loss Contingency
a.	Yes	Yes
b.	Yes	No
c.	No	Yes
d.	No	No

M3-3 A donated fixed asset (from a governmental unit) for which the fair value has been determined should be recorded as a debit to fixed assets and a credit to

a. Unrealized capital   c. Deferred income
b. Retained earnings   d. Other income

M3-4 On October 2, 2002, a company borrowed cash and signed a 3-year interest-bearing note on which both the principal and interest are payable on October 2, 2005. At December 31, 2004 the accrued interest should

a. Be reported on the balance sheet as a current liability
b. Be reported on the balance sheet as a noncurrent liability
c. Be reported on the balance sheet as part of long-term notes payable
d. Not be reported on the balance sheet as a liability

M3-5 Financial statements that are expressed assuming a stable monetary unit are

a. General-price-level financial statements
b. Historical-dollar financial statements
c. Current-value financial statements
d. Fair-value financial statements

M3-6 Rent revenue collected one month in advance should be accounted for as

a. Revenue in the month collected

b. A current liability
c. A separate item in stockholders' equity
d. An accrued liability

M3-7 Which of the following should be disclosed in the Summary of Significant Accounting Policies?

a. Rent expense amount
b. Maturity dates of long-term debt
c. Methods of amortizing intangibles
d. Composition of plant assets

M3-8 A company receives an advance payment for special-order goods to be manufactured and delivered within six months. The advance payment should be reported on the company's balance sheet as a

a. Deferred charge
b. Contra-asset account
c. Current liability
d. Noncurrent liability

M3-9 The FASB has identified five alternatives for measuring balance sheet elements. Which of the following alternatives may be used?

	Net Realizable Value	Present Value
a.	No	No
b.	No	Yes
c.	Yes	No
d.	Yes	Yes

M3-10 The balance sheet provides information about each of the following items, except

a. Operating capability of entity
b. Results of entity's operations
c. Entity's liquidity
d. Financial flexibility of entity

(AICPA adapted)

EXERCISES

E3-1   *Current Assets*   Listed here are certain accounts of the Jenkins Company at the end of 2004:

Account	Debit (Credit)
Land	$12,000
Prepaid insurance	1,530
Cash on hand	1,120
Notes receivable (due 2007)	4,300
Cash in bank	5,400
Allowance for doubtful accounts	(1,100)
Marketable securities (short-term)	3,380
Accumulated depreciation	(8,700)
Accounts receivable	15,600
Office supplies	970
Buildings	27,200
Inventory	19,700

Required Prepare the current asset section of Jenkins' balance sheet.

E3-2 *Plant and Equipment* Your analysis of the fixed asset accounts at the end of 2004 for the Moen Corporation reveals the following information:

1. The company owns two tracts of land. The first, which cost $18,000, is being held as a future building site. It has a current market value of $20,000. The second, which cost $19,000, was purchased 10 years ago. On this site were built the current office and factory buildings. The land has a current market value of $56,000.
2. The company owns two buildings. The office building and the factory building were both built 10 years ago at a cost of $50,000 and $120,000, respectively. At that time each was expected to have a life of 30 years, and a residual value of 10% of original cost. They are being depreciated on a straight-line basis.
3. The company owns factory machinery with a total cost of $51,000 and accumulated depreciation of $35,300. Included in factory machinery is one machine that cost $7,000 and has accumulated depreciation of $4,200. This machine is being held for resale and is not being used in operations.
4. The company owns office equipment that cost $14,500 and has a book value of $6,300. It owns office furniture that cost $17,900 and has a book value of $11,400.

Required Prepare the property, plant, and equipment section of Moen's 2004 ending balance sheet.

E3-3 *Stockholders' Equity* The following are several accounts of the Graf Corporation at the end of 2004:

Account	Credit Balance
Common stock, $10 par	$ 47,100
Bonds payable (due 2011)	126,000
Premium on preferred stock	39,600
Retained earnings	209,000
Premium on bonds payable	12,300
Unearned rent	4,800
Preferred stock, $100 par	65,400
Premium on common stock	53,900
Unfunded accrued pension cost	18,400
Treasury stock (cost)	(7,600) debit
Accumulated other comprehensive income	8,200

Required Prepare the stockholders' equity section of Graf's 2004 ending balance sheet.

E3-4 *Classifications on Balance Sheet* A balance sheet may contain the following major sections:

A. Current assets	G. Long-term liabilities
B. Long-term investments	H. Other liabilities
C. Property, plant, and equipment	I. Contributed capital
D. Intangible assets	J. Retained earnings
E. Other assets	K. Accumulated other comprehensive income
F. Current liabilities	

Required The following is a list of fifteen accounts. Using the letters A through K, indicate in which section of the balance sheet each account would most likely be classified. Place a check mark (√) beside each item that is a contra account. If an account cannot be classified in any of the preceding sections, indicate with an X and explain.

_____ 1. Temporary investments in marketable securities
_____ 2. Discount on bonds payable (bonds due in 5 years)
_____ 3. Additional paid-in capital on common stock
_____ 4. Accounts receivable
_____ 5. Notes payable (due in 5 years)
_____ 6. Patents (net)
_____ 7. Unrealized decrease in value of available-for-sale securities

_____ 8. Preferred stock
_____ 9. Unearned rent (to be earned within next 6 months)
_____ 10. Accrued pension cost
_____ 11. Trademarks
_____ 12. Deficit
_____ 13. Salaries payable
_____ 14. Land
_____ 15. Investment in Ace Company preferred stock (to be held for 3 years)

E3-5   *Classifications on Balance Sheet*   The balance sheet contains the following major sections:

A. Current assets
B. Long-term investments
C. Property, plant, and equipment
D. Intangible assets
E. Other assets
F. Current liabilities

G. Long-term liabilities
H. Other liabilities
I. Contributed capital
J. Retained earnings
K. Accumulated other comprehensive income

Required   The following is a list of several accounts. Using the letters A through K, indicate in which section of the balance sheet each of the accounts would be classified. Place a check mark (√) beside each item that is a contra account. If an account cannot be classified in any of the preceding sections, indicate with an X and explain.

_____ 1. Cash
_____ 2. Bonds payable (due in 8 years)
_____ 3. Machinery
_____ 4. Deficit
_____ 5. Unexpired insurance
_____ 6. Franchise (net)
_____ 7. Fund to retire preferred stock
_____ 8. Current portion of mortgage payable
_____ 9. Accumulated depreciation
_____ 10. Copyrights
_____ 11. Investment in held-to-maturity bonds

_____ 12. Allowance for doubtful accounts
_____ 13. Notes receivable (due in 3 years)
_____ 14. Property taxes payable
_____ 15. Deferred taxes payable
_____ 16. Premium on preferred stock
_____ 17. Premium on bonds payable (due in 8 years)
_____ 18. Goods in process
_____ 19. Common stock, $1 par
_____ 20. Land
_____ 21. Treasury stock (at cost)
_____ 22. Unrealized increase in value of available-for-sale securities

E3-6   *Balance Sheet*   The balance sheet accounts and amounts of the Baggett Company as of December 31, 2004 are shown in random order as follows:

Account	Debit (Credit)	Account	Debit (Credit)
Income taxes payable	$ (3,800)	Premium on preferred stock	$ (7,900)
Prepaid items	1,800	Allowance for doubtful accounts	(1,600)
Premium on common stock	(9,300)	Bonds payable (due 2014)	(23,000)
Land	12,200	Buildings	57,400
Notes payable (due 2007)	(6,000)	Sinking fund to retire bonds payable	5,000
Notes receivable (due 2006)	16,400	Advances from customers (long-term)	(2,600)
Accounts receivable	12,600	Cash	4,300
Premium on bonds payable	(1,400)	Accumulated depreciation: equipment	(9,700)
Accounts payable	(13,100)	Retained earnings	(18,300)
Inventory	7,400	Preferred stock, $100 par	(18,600)
Accumulated depreciation: buildings	(21,000)	Wages payable	(1,400)
Patents (net)	4,600	Common stock, $10 par	(12,700)
Equipment	28,700		

Required

1. Prepare a December 31, 2004 balance sheet for the Baggett Company.
2. Compute the debt ratio.

E3-7   *Balance Sheet*   The December 31, 2004 balance sheet accounts of the Hitt Company are shown here in alphabetical order:

Accounts payable	$ 22,400	Current taxes payable	$ 10,400
Accounts receivable	21,500	Discount on bonds payable	6,900
Accumulated depreciation: buildings	53,000	Equipment	72,400
Accumulated depreciation: equipment	35,100	Inventory	37,200
Additional paid-in capital on common stock	24,000	Land	30,000
		Marketable securities (short-term)	6,100
Additional paid-in capital on preferred stock	11,500	Patents (net)	9,800
		Preferred stock, $100 par	21,000
Allowance for doubtful accounts	800	Retained earnings	46,200
Bonds payable (due 2018)	77,000	Salaries payable	2,000
Buildings	144,000	Trademarks	3,700
Cash	2,900	Unrealized increase in value of	
Common stock, $10 par	30,000	marketable securities	1,100

Required

1. Prepare the December 31, 2004 balance sheet of the Hitt Company.
2. Compute the working capital and the current ratio.

E3-8   ***Balance Sheet Calculations***   The balance sheet information at the end of 2004 and 2005 for the Dawson
Company is as follows:

	2004	2005
Current assets	$ (a)	$25,000
Long-term liabilities	(b)	34,900
Total contributed capital	(c)	(g)
Long-term investments	19,200	(h)
Retained earnings	50,000	60,000
Total liabilities	(d)	(i)
Intangible assets	10,400	9,200
Current liabilities	14,500	12,300
Capital stock, $5 par	(e)	20,000
Total assets	142,200	(j)
Additional paid-in capital	15,000	(k)
Property, plant, and equipment (net)	85,700	92,800
Accumulated other comprehensive income	6,900	7,000
Total stockholders' equity	(f)	(l)

Additional information: The company did not issue any common stock during 2005.

Required Fill in the blanks labeled (a) through (l). All the necessary information is provided. (*Hint*: It is not
necessary to calculate your answers in alphabetical order.)

E3-9   ***Balance Sheet Calculations***   The balance sheet information of the Fermer Company at the end of 2004 and
@   2005 is as follows:

	2004	2005
Total stockholders' equity	$ (1)	$100,700
Accumulated other comprehensive income	4,800	5,000
Current liabilities	(2)	9,800
Intangible assets	12,600	12,000
Property, plant, and equipment (net)	(3)	87,500
Current assets	19,100	(8)
Total contributed capital	51,000	(9)
Long-term liabilities	(4)	30,200
Retained earnings	40,900	(10)
Total assets	(5)	(11)
Common stock, $10 par	(6)	(12)
Working capital	9,900	10,200
Additional paid-in capital	(7)	36,000
Long-term investments	23,700	(13)
Total liabilities	38,100	(14)

Additional information: At the end of 2004, additional paid-in capital is twice the amount of capital stock.
In 2005, the company issued (sold) 100 shares of common stock.

Required Fill in the blanks numbered (1) through (14). All the necessary information is provided. (*Hint*: It
is not necessary to calculate your answers in numerical order.)

E3-10   *Correction of Balance Sheet*   On December 31, 2004, the Stevens Company bookkeeper prepared the following erroneously classified balance sheet:

STEVENS COMPANY
Balance Sheet
For Year Ended December 31, 2004

Current Assets		Current Liabilities	
Inventory	$ 6,000	Accounts payable	$9,900
Accounts receivable	5,900	Allowance for doubtful accounts	800
Cash	2,300	Salaries payable	1,500
Treasury stock (at cost)	3,300	Taxes payable	2,500
Long-Term Investments		Long-Term Liabilities	
Temporary investments in marketable		Bonds payable (due 2011)	11,000
securities	3,200	Unearned rent (for 3 months)	900
Investment in held-to-maturity bonds	10,000		
Plant and Equipment			
Land	8,100		
Office supplies	800	Owners' Equity	
Buildings and equipment	35,600	Retained earnings	24,200
Intangibles		Accumulated depreciation on buildings	
Patents (net)	5,000	and equipment	9,200
Prepaid insurance (for 6 months)	1,200	Premium on common stock	10,400
Discount on bonds payable	1,000	Common stock, $10 par	12,000
Total Assets	$82,400	Total Credits	$82,400

Required You determine that the account balances listed on the balance sheet are correct but, in certain cases, incorrectly classified. Prepare a properly classified balance sheet for the Stevens Company as of December 31, 2004.

E3-11   *Changes in Stockholders' Equity*   On January 1, 2004 the Powder Company listed the following stockholders' equity section of its balance sheet:

Contributed Capital	
Preferred stock, $100 par	$ 92,800
Common stock, $5 par	37,400
Additional paid-in capital on preferred stock	21,500
Additional paid-in capital on common stock	58,700
Total contributed capital	$210,400
Retained Earnings	185,700
Total Stockholders' Equity	$396,100

During 2004 the following transactions and events occurred and were properly recorded:

1. The company issued 1,800 shares of common stock at $13 per share.
2. The company issued 340 shares of preferred stock at $130 per share.
3. The company earned net income of $38,950.
4. The company paid a $7 per share dividend on the preferred stock and a $1 per share dividend on the common stock outstanding at the end of 2004.

Required Prepare a statement of changes in stockholders' equity of the Powder Company for 2004. (Include retained earnings.)

E3-12   *Changes in Stockholders' Equity*   On January 1, 2004 the Osborne Company reported the following alphabetical list of stockholders' equity items:

Additional paid-in capital on common stock	$170,000
Additional paid-in capital on preferred stock	12,000
Common stock, $2 par	80,000
Preferred stock, $100 par	60,000
Retained earnings	209,000

During 2004, the company sold 3,000 shares of common stock for $10 per share and 500 shares of preferred stock for $125 per share. It also earned income of $99,000 and paid dividends of $8 per share on the preferred stock and $1.50 per share on the common stock outstanding at the end of 2004.

Required Prepare a statement of changes in stockholders' equity of the Osborne Company for 2004. (Include retained earnings.)

PROBLEMS

P3-1　*Classifications on Balance Sheet*　The current balance sheet of Day Company contains the following major sections:

A. Current assets
B. Long-term investments
C. Property, plant, and equipment
D. Intangible assets
E. Other assets
F. Current liabilities

G. Long-term liabilities
H. Other liabilities
I. Contributed capital
J. Retained earnings
K. Accumulated other comprehensive income

The following is a list of 37 accounts. Using the letters A through K, indicate in which section each account would most likely be classified. Place a check mark (√) beside each item that is a contra account. If an account cannot be classified in any of the preceding sections, indicate with an X and explain.

_____ 1. Patents (net)
_____ 2. Income taxes payable
_____ 3. Notes receivable (due in 5 months)
_____ 4. Unearned rent (for 10 months)
_____ 5. Discount on bonds payable (long-term bonds)
_____ 6. Data processing center
_____ 7. Furniture
_____ 8. Land held for future expansion
_____ 9. Timberland (net)
_____ 10. Treasury stock, at cost
_____ 11. Advances to sales personnel
_____ 12. Idle machinery
_____ 13. Deferred taxes payable
_____ 14. Raw materials
_____ 15. Investment in held-to-maturity bonds
_____ 16. Pollution control facilities
_____ 17. Cash from security deposits of customers on returnable containers
_____ 18. Donated capital for industrial parkbuilding site from Toma City
_____ 19. Trademarks

_____ 20. Finished goods
_____ 21. Cash dividends payable
_____ 22. Bond sinking fund
_____ 23. Temporary investments
_____ 24. Retained earnings
_____ 25. Advances to affiliated company (long-term)
_____ 26. Cash surrender value of life insurance
_____ 27. Leased equipment under capital lease
_____ 28. Additional paid-in capital on preferred stock
_____ 29. Interest receivable (due in 5 months)
_____ 30. Office supplies
_____ 31. Accrued pension cost
_____ 32. Obligation under capital lease contract
_____ 33. Investment in 8-year certificates of deposit
_____ 34. Unearned ticket sales
_____ 35. Estimated warranty (6-months) obligations
_____ 36. Unrealized decrease in value of available-for-sale securities
_____ 37. Cash

P3-2　*Balance Sheet without Amounts*　The following is an alphabetical list of the accounts of the Oliver Manufacturing Company as of December 31, 2004:

Accounts payable
Accounts receivable

Accrued pension cost
Accumulated depreciation: buildings

Accumulated depreciation: equipment	Interest revenue
Accumulated depreciation: machinery	Investment in available-for-sale securities
Additional paid-in capital on common stock	Land
Additional paid-in capital on preferred stock	Land for future plant site
Administrative expenses	Loss on sale of equipment
Allowance for doubtful accounts	Machinery
Bond sinking fund	Mortgage payable (20 equal annual payments)
Bonds payable (due 2016)	Notes payable (short-term)
Buildings	Notes receivable (short-term)
Cash in bank	Office supplies
Cash on hand	Patents (net)
Cash surrender value of life insurance	Preferred stock
Common stock	Premium on bonds payable
Cost of goods sold	Prepaid insurance
Deferred taxes payable	Raw materials
Dividends payable	Retained earnings
Equipment	Salaries payable
Estimated warranty (1-year) obligations	Sales
Finished goods	Sales discounts taken
General expenses	Sales returns
Goods in process	Selling expenses
Income tax expense	Temporary investments in marketable securities
Income taxes payable	Trademarks
Interest expense	Treasury stock, at cost
Interest payable	Unearned rent
Interest receivable	Unrealized increase in value of available-for-sale securities

Required Prepare a balance sheet (without amounts) in proper format for the Oliver Manufacturing Company.

P3-3   **Balance Sheet**   The following is an alphabetical list of the December 31, 2004 balance sheet accounts and amounts for the Green Manufacturing Company:

Accounts payable	$20,900	Interest payable	$ 500
Accounts receivable	15,300	Investment in available-for-sale	
Accrued pension cost	13,300	stock	16,400
Accumulated depreciation: buildings	32,400	Land	17,000
Accumulated depreciation: machinery		Machinery and equipment	57,800
and equipment	30,000	Marketable securities (short-term)	8,400
Allowance for doubtful accounts	1,000	Notes payable (short-term)	5,000
Bond sinking fund	7,700	Patents (net)	8,600
Bonds payable (due 2018)	29,000	Preferred stock, $100 par	30,000
Buildings	92,500	Premium on common stock	16,300
Cash	7,200	Premium on preferred stock	7,000
Common stock, $10 par	44,100	Prepaid insurance	2,600
Deferred taxes payable	2,800	Raw materials	10,100
Discount on bonds payable	2,500	Retained earnings	28,100
Dividends payable	5,600	Unearned rent	5,000
Finished goods	23,800	Unrealized increase in value of available-	
Goods in process	14,700	for-sale stock	2,000
Income taxes payable	8,900	Wages payable	2,700

Required Prepare a properly classified balance sheet for the Green Manufacturing Company on December 31, 2004. List the additional parenthetical or note disclosures (if any) that should be made for each item. Compute the working capital and the current ratio.

P3-4 *Balance Sheet* The following is a list (in random order) of the December 31, 2004 balance sheet accounts of the Midwest Company:

Additional paid-in capital on preferred stock	$ 1,600	Accounts payable	$16,500
Accounts receivable	13,800	Prepaid insurance	900
Dividends payable	1,800	Discount on bonds payable	2,000
Buildings	50,000	Common stock, $10 par	15,000
Bonds payable (due 2010)	29,000	Equipment	29,000
Retained earnings	25,800	Allowance for doubtful accounts	700
Office supplies	1,900	Preferred stock, $50 par	10,000
Current income taxes payable	4,200	Accumulated depreciation: buildings	12,400
Accumulated depreciation: equipment	8,300	Current interest payable	2,900
Patents (net)	2,400	Investment in held-to-maturity bonds	9,000
Notes payable (due January 1, 2007)	17,000	Cash	8,200
Inventory	24,400	Treasury stock (at cost)	1,500
Additional paid-in capital on common stock	7,700	Accrued wages	3,700
Sinking fund for bond retirement	4,000	Land	9,500

Required Prepare a properly classified balance sheet for the Midwest Company on December 31, 2004.

P3-5 *Balance Sheet from Adjusted Trial Balance* The following is the alphabetical adjusted trial balance of the Meadows Company on December 31, 2004:

	Debits	Credits
Accounts payable		$ 9,800
Accounts receivable	$ 18,000	
Accrued payables		6,500
Accumulated depreciation		44,000
Additional paid-in capital		50,600
Cash	7,900	
Common stock, $5 par		29,600
Cost of goods sold	175,500	
Current portion of long-term debt		6,200
Deferred taxes payable		12,500
Dividends distributed	7,000	
General expenses	27,560	
Income tax expense	12,340	
Income taxes payable		7,500
Interest expense	4,300	
Inventories	32,000	
Investment in held-to-maturity bonds	36,000	
Long-term debt		56,300
Long-term receivables	38,600	
Marketable securities (short-term)	10,100	
Patents (net)	13,000	
Prepaid insurance	5,000	
Property, plant, and equipment	148,000	
Retained earnings, 1/1/04		64,800
Sales		278,000
Sales returns	8,000	
Selling expenses	21,500	
Unrealized decrease in value of available-for-sale securities	1,000	
	$565,800	$565,800

Required Prepare the December 31, 2004 balance sheet of the Meadows Company. Compute the debt ratio.

P3-6   **Balance Sheet and Notes**   Listed here in random order are the balance sheet accounts and related ending balances of the Eubanks Company as of December 31, 2004:

Income taxes payable	$ 24,700	Temporary investments	$19,100
Cash surrender value of life insurance	8,900	Bonds payable	80,000
Preferred stock	40,000	Additional paid-in capital on common stock	30,300
Premium on bonds payable	4,800	Inventories	98,500
Cash	11,600	Accounts receivable	32,300
Property, plant, and equipment (net)	229,300	Patents (net)	18,200
Accounts payable	58,000	Investment in bonds	25,000
Common stock	62,800	Additional paid-in capital on preferred stock	23,400
Retained earnings	123,400	Miscellaneous current payables	6,200
Land held for building site	19,500	Estimated liability for product warranties	7,300
Allowance for doubtful accounts	1,500		

Additional information:

1. The company uses control accounts for inventories and property, plant, and equipment and lists the latter at its book value.
2. The straight-line method is used to depreciate buildings, machinery, and equipment, based upon their cost and estimated residual values and lives. A breakdown of property, plant, and equipment shows the following: land at a cost of $32,000, buildings at a cost of $182,400 and a book value of $120,200, machinery at a cost of $63,900 and related accumulated depreciation of $18,600, and equipment (40% depreciated) at a cost of $53,000.
3. Patents are amortized on a straight-line basis directly to the patent account.
4. Inventories are listed at the lower of cost or market value using an average cost. The inventories include raw materials $22,200, goods in process $34,700, and finished goods $41,600.
5. Common stock has a $10 par value per share, 12,000 shares are authorized, 6,280 shares have been issued.
6. Preferred stock has a $100 par value per share, 1,000 shares are authorized, 400 shares have been issued.
7. The investment in bonds is carried at the original cost, which is the face value, and is being held to maturity.
8. Temporary investments in marketable securities were purchased at year-end.
9. The bonds payable mature on December 31, 2009.
10. The company attaches a one-year warranty on all the products it sells.

Required

1. Prepare the December 31, 2004 balance sheet of the Eubanks Company (including appropriate parenthetical notations).
2. Prepare notes to accompany the balance sheet that itemize company accounting policies, inventories, and property, plant, and equipment.
3. Compute the current ratio. Which current assets would you classify as *liquid* and which as *separable* according to the FASB's conceptual guidelines? Why might these classifications be useful?

P3-7   **Comprehensive: Balance Sheet, Schedules, and Notes**   The following is an alphabetical listing of the balance sheet accounts and account balances of the Blazer Company on December 31, 2004:

Accounts payable	$ 44,200	Income taxes payable	$ 19,700
Accounts receivable	37,100	Inventory	85,300
Accumulated depreciation	109,300	Investment in affiliate	30,000
Additional paid-in capital on common stock	20,000	Long-term liabilities (book value)	91,000
Additional paid-in capital on preferred stock	3,200	Miscellaneous current payables	6,800
Allowance for doubtful accounts	1,600	Notes receivable	17,000
Bond sinking fund	12,500	Preferred stock	32,000
Cash	13,800	Property and equipment	296,700
Common stock	80,000	Retained earnings	84,600

Additional information:

1. The company uses a control account for property and equipment, accumulated depreciation, and for long-term liabilities. The latter account is listed at its book value.
2. The straight-line method is used to depreciate property and equipment based upon cost, estimated residual value, and estimated life. The costs of the assets in this account are: land $29,500, buildings $164,600, store fixtures $72,600, and office equipment $30,000.
3. The accumulated depreciation breakdown is as follows: buildings $54,600, store fixtures $37,400, and office equipment $17,300.

4. The long-term debt includes 12%, $36,000 face value bonds that mature on December 31, 2009 and have an unamortized bond discount of $1,000; 11%, $48,000 face value bonds that mature on December 31, 2013, have a premium on bonds payable of $1,800, and whose retirement is being funded by a bond sinking fund; and a 13% note payable that has a face value of $6,200 and matures on January 1, 2007.

5. The noninterest-bearing note receivable matures on June 1, 2005.

6. Inventory is listed at lower of cost or market; cost is determined on the basis of average cost.

7. The investment in affiliate is carried at cost. The company has guaranteed the interest on 12%, $50,000, 15-year bonds issued by this affiliate, the Jay Company.

8. Common stock has a $10 par value per share, 10,000 shares are authorized, and 1,000 shares were issued during 2004 at a price of $13 per share, resulting in 8,000 shares issued at year-end.

9. Preferred stock has a $50 par value per share, 2,000 shares are authorized, and 140 shares were issued during 2004 at a price of $55 per share, resulting in 640 shares issued at year-end.

10. On January 15, 2005, before the December 31, 2004 balance sheet was issued, a building with a cost of $20,000 and a book value of $7,000 was totally destroyed. Insurance proceeds will amount to only $5,000.

11. Net income and dividends paid during the year were $50,500 and $21,000, respectively.

Required

1. Prepare the December 31, 2004 balance sheet (including appropriate parenthetical notations) of the Blazer Company.

2. Prepare a statement of changes in stockholders' equity for 2004. (*Hint*: Work back from the *ending* account balances.)

3. Prepare notes that itemize the balance sheet control accounts and those necessary to disclose any company accounting policies, contingent liabilities, and subsequent events.

4. Compute the debt ratio at the end of 2004. What is your evaluation of this ratio if it was 39% at the end of 2003?

P3-8 *Corrections to Balance Sheet* The Cable Company prepared the following balance sheet:

CABLE COMPANY
Balance Sheet For Year Ended December 31, 2004

Working capital	$ 22,800	Noncurrent liabilities	$ 62,000
Other assets	152,000	Stockholders' equity	112,800
Total	$174,800	Total	$174,800

Your analysis of these accounts reveals the following information:

1. Working capital consists of:

Land	$ 12,000
Accounts due from customers	18,000
Accounts due to suppliers	(22,700)
Inventories, including office supplies of $3,500	35,500
Income taxes owed	(16,400)
Wages owed	(3,600)
Note owed to bank (due December 31, 2006)	(17,000)
Securities held as a temporary investment	17,000
	$ 22,800

2. Other assets include:

Cash	$ 12,300
Prepaid insurance	2,400
Buildings and equipment	100,000
Discount on bonds payable	3,000
Investment in available-for-sale stock	29,000
Treasury stock (at cost)	5,300
	$152,000

3. Noncurrent liabilities consist of:

Bonds payable (due 2014)	$ 33,000
Allowance for doubtful accounts	1,400
Premium on preferred stock	2,600
Common stock, $5 par	25,000
	$ 62,000

4. Stockholders' equity includes:

Accumulated depreciation: buildings and equipment	$ 40,000
Preferred stock, $100 par	12,000
Premium on common stock	15,600
Retained earnings	40,000
Accrued pension cost	6,500
Unrealized decrease in value of available-for-sale securities	(1,300)
	$112,800

Required Based on your analysis, prepare a properly classified December 31, 2004 balance sheet for the Cable Company.

P3-9   **Corrections to Balance Sheet**   The Brandt Company presents the following December 31, 2004 balance sheet:

BRANDT COMPANY
Sheet of Balances
For Year Ended December 31, 2004

Current assets	$ 44,300	Current liabilities	$ 66,600
Long-term investments	13,600	Long-term liabilities	24,100
Property and equipment	123,500	Contributed capital	17,000
Intangible assets	7,700	Unrealized capital	22,500
Other assets	13,600	Retained earnings	72,500
Total assets	$202,700	Total equities	$202,700

The following information is also available:

1. Current assets include cash $3,800, accounts receivable $18,500, notes receivable (maturity date July 1, 2006) $10,000, and land $12,000.
2. Long-term investments include a $4,600 investment in available-for-sale securities that is expected to be sold in 2005 and a $9,000 investment in Dray Company bonds that are expected to be held until their December 31, 2013 maturity date.
3. Property and equipment include buildings costing $63,400, inventory costing $30,500, and equipment costing $29,600.
4. Intangible assets include patents that cost $8,200 and on which $2,300 amortization has accumulated, and treasury stock that cost $1,800.
5. Other assets include prepaid insurance (which expires on November 30, 2005) $2,900, sinking fund for bond retirement $7,000, and trademarks that cost $3,700 and are not impaired.
6. Current liabilities include accounts payable $19,400, bonds payable (maturity date December 31, 2015) $40,000, and accrued income taxes payable $7,200.
7. Long-term liabilities include accrued wages $4,100 and mortgage payable (which is due in five equal annual payments starting December 31, 2005) $20,000.
8. Contributed capital includes common stock ($5 par) $11,000 and preferred stock ($100 par) $6,000.
9. Unrealized capital includes premium on bonds payable $4,300, premium on preferred stock $2,400, premium on common stock $14,700, and unrealized increase in value of securities available for sale $1,100.
10. Retained earnings includes unrestricted retained earnings, $37,800, allowance for doubtful accounts $700, and accumulated depreciation on buildings and equipment of $21,000 and $13,000, respectively.

Required Based on the preceding information, prepare a properly classified December 31, 2004 balance sheet for the Brandt Company.

See WebTutor for annotated problem solution.

P3-10 **Balance Sheet Calculations** The balance sheet information of the John Company at the end of 2004 and
@   2005 is as follows:

	2004	2005
Long-term liabilities	$ (a)	$ 33,100
Accumulated other comprehensive income	8,000	8,900
Working capital	17,900	19,800
Intangible assets	19,100	18,600
Common stock, $10 par	(b)	(i)
Total stockholders' equity	(c)	179,000
Accumulated depreciation	(37,500)	(48,600)
Total liabilities	51,900	(j)
Current assets	(d)	39,800
Retained earnings	83,300	(k)
Total contributed capital	66,700	(l)
Total assets	(e)	(m)
Additional paid-in capital	(f)	(n)
Long-term investments	40,100	(o)
Current liabilities	(g)	(p)
Property, plant, and equipment	(h)	180,000

Additional information: At the end of 2004, (a) the amount of long-term liabilities is twice the amount of current liabilities, and (b) there are 2,900 shares of common stock outstanding. During 2005 the company (a) issued 100 shares of common stock for $25 per share, (b) earned net income of $20,600, and (c) paid dividends of $1 per share on the common stock outstanding at year-end.

Required Fill in the blanks lettered (a) through (p). All of the necessary information is provided. (*Hint:* It is not necessary to calculate your answers in alphabetical order.)

P3-11   *Erroneous Balance Sheet*   The Cutler Corporation prepared the following balance sheet:

CUTLER CORPORATION
Balance Report For Year Ended December 31, 2004

Current Assets			Current Liabilities		
Cash		$ 6,300	Accounts payable		$ 13,000
Accounts receivable		15,900	Accumulated depreciation: buildings		17,100
Inventory, at higher of cost or market			Wages payable		3,000
(cost $27,200)		28,000	Additional paid-in capital		
Long-Term Investments			on common stock		23,200
Treasury stock (at cost)		1,400	Long-Term Liabilities		
Investment in D Company bonds			Bonds payable	$46,000	
(at book value)		7,300	Less: Sinking fund to retire		
Marketable securities,			bonds	(6,000)	40,000
short-term at market value		10,000	Preferred stock, $50 par		15,000
Property, Plant, and Equipment			Premium on preferred stock		5,100
Land		11,300	Accumulated depreciation: equipment		7,000
Patents	$8,000		Current taxes payable		9,600
Less: Accumulated amortization	(2,800)	5,200	Owners' Equity:		
Buildings		40,800	Common stock, $2 par		8,000
Equipment		19,000	Unrealized gain on write-up		
Intangibles			of marketable securities		
Trademarks		5,700	to market value		1,300
Other Assets			Unrealized gain on write-up		
Cash surrender value of life insurance		5,000	of inventory to market value		800
Discount on bonds payable		3,900	Retained earnings		16,000
Total Assets		$159,800	Allowance for doubtful accounts		700
			Total Equities		$159,800

Required

1. Identify the errors made in the Cutler balance sheet.
2. Prepare a corrected, properly classified balance sheet.

P3-12   *Complex Balance Sheet*   Presented below is the unaudited balance sheet as of December 31, 2004, prepared by the bookkeeper of Zues Manufacturing Corporation.

ZUES MANUFACTURING CORPORATION
Balance Sheet For the Year Ended December 31, 2004

Assets		Liabilities & Stockholders' Equity	
Cash	$ 225,000	Accounts payable	$ 133,800
Accounts receivable (net)	345,700	Mortgage payable	900,000
Inventories	560,000	Notes payable	500,000
Prepaid income taxes	40,000	Lawsuit liability	80,000
Investments	57,700	Income taxes payable	61,200
Land	450,000	Deferred tax liability	28,000
Building	1,750,000	Accumulated depreciation	420,000
Machinery and equipment	1,964,000	Total Liabilities	$2,123,000
Goodwill	37,000		
Total Assets	$5,429,400	Common stock, $50 par; 40,000	
		shares issued	2,231,000
		Retained earnings	1,075,400
		Total Stockholders' Equity	$3,306,400
		Total Liabilities and	
		Stockholders' Equity	$5,429,400

Your firm has been engaged to perform an audit, during which the following data are found:

1. Checks totaling $14,000 in payment of accounts payable were mailed on December 31, 2004 but were not recorded until 2005. Late in December 2004, the bank returned a customer's $2,000 check, marked "NSF," but no entry was made. Cash includes $100,000 restricted for building purposes.
2. Included in accounts receivable is a $30,000 note due on December 31, 2007 from Zues' president.
3. During 2004, Zues purchased 500 shares of common stock of a major corporation that supplies Zues with raw materials. Total cost of this stock was $51,300, and market value on December 31, 2004 was $47,000. The decline in market value is considered temporary. Zues plans to hold these shares indefinitely.
4. Treasury stock was recorded at cost when Zues purchased 200 of its own shares for $32 per share in May 2004. This amount is included in investments.
5. On December 31, 2004, Zues borrowed $500,000 from a bank in exchange for a 10% note payable, maturing December 31, 2009. Equal principal payments are due December 31 of each year, beginning in 2005. This note is collateralized by a $250,000 tract of land acquired as a potential future building site, which is included in land.
6. The mortgage payable requires $50,000 principal payments, plus interest, at the end of each month. Payments were made on January 31 and February 28, 2005. The balance of this mortgage was due June 30, 2005. On March 1, 2005, prior to issuance of the audited financial statements, Zues consummated a noncancelable agreement with the lender to refinance this mortgage. The new terms require $100,000 annual principal payments, plus interest, on February 28 of each year, beginning in 2006. The final payment is due February 28, 2013.
7. The lawsuit liability will be paid in 2005.
8. Of the total deferred tax liability, $5,000 is considered a current liability.
9. The current income tax expense reported in Zues' 2004 income statement was $61,200.
10. The company was authorized to issue 100,000 shares of $50 par value common stock.

Required Prepare a corrected classified balance sheet as of December 31, 2004. This financial statement should include a proper heading, format, and necessary descriptions. (*AICPA adapted*)

P3-13   ***Changes in Stockholders' Equity***   On January 1, 2004 the Knox Company showed the following alphabetical list of stockholders' equity balances:

Additional paid-in capital on common stock	$130,000
Additional paid-in capital on preferred stock	6,000
Common stock, $10 par	100,000
Preferred stock, $100 par	50,000
Retained earnings	224,000

During 2004 the following events occurred and were properly recorded by the company:

1. The company purchased an investment in available-for-sale securities. At year-end the market value of the securities had increased by $9,000.
2. The company issued 2,000 shares of common stock for $25 per share.
3. The company issued 110 shares of preferred stock for $116 per share.
4. The company reacqquired 400 shares of its common stock as treasury stock at a cost of $26 per share. (*Hint*: Record the reacquisition cost in a Treasury Stock account.)
5. The company earned net income of $57,000.
6. The company paid a $7 per share dividend on the preferred stock and a $1.25 per share dividend on the common stock outstanding at the end of 2004 (treasury stock is not entitled to dividends).

Required Prepare a statement of changes in stockholders' equity for 2004. (Include retained earnings.)

P3-14   ***Analyzing Coca-Cola's Balance Sheet Disclosures***   Review the financial statements and related notes of the Coca-Cola Company in Appendix A.

Required Answer the following questions. (*Note*: You do not need to make any calculations. All answers may be found in the financial report.) Indicate on what page of the annual report you located the answer.

1. What was the amount of the current assets on December 31, 2001?
2. What was the amount in the allowance for doubtful accounts on December 31, 2001?
3. What is the par value of the company's common stock? How many shares had been issued at the end of 2001?
4. What was the total amount of inventories on December 31, 2001? What were the principal categories of inventory on this date?
5. What was the long-term debt on December 31, 2001? Of this total, how much was for the $5\frac{3}{4}$%, U.S. dollar notes due 2011?

6. What was the allowance for depreciation on December 31, 2001? What method does the company use to depreciate its property, plant, and equipment?
7. What was the amount of accounts payable and accrued expenses on December 31, 2001? How much was for accrued marketing expenses?
8. What inventory costing method was used for most inventories in 2001?
9. What was the reinvested (retained) earnings on December 31, 2001?
10. What was the total property, plant, and equipment before and after allowance for depreciation on December 31, 2001?
11. What were the total assets on December 31, 2001?
12. What were the current liabilities on December 31, 2001?
13. What were the number of shares and cost of the treasury stock held by the company on December 31, 2001?
14. What was the amount of marketable securities on December 31, 2001? What was the net change in unrealized gain (loss) on securities during 2001?
15. How much was the company contingently liable for guarantees of indebtedness owed by third parties on December 31, 2001?

INTERNET ASSIGNMENTS

Go to the Nikolai and Bazley **Intermediate Accounting** web site (http://Nikolai.swcollege.com). Click on Student Resources and internet homework assignments. Then click on the appropriate hot link (icon) for each company's web site, find the relevant accounting information, and answer the following questions.

I3-1   Go to the Eastman Kodak web site.

Required What are the company's current assets for each of the two most recent years? Current liabilities? Compute the company's working capital and current ratio for each of the two most recent years. What is your evaluation of the change in the company's liquidity? Are there any items of current assets or current liabilities that you might not include in a liquidity ratio?

I3-2   Go to the General Mills web site.

Required How many shares of treasury stock did the company hold at the end of each of the two most recent years? What was the cost? What was the company's debt ratio at the end of each of the two years? What is your evaluation of the change in the risk of an investment in the company?

objectives

1 Understand the concepts of income.

2 Explain the conceptual guidelines for reporting income.

3 Define the elements of an income statement.

4 Describe the major components of an income statement.

5 Compute income from continuing operations.

6 Report results from discontinued operations.

7 Identify extraordinary items.

8 Prepare a statement of retained earnings.

9 Report comprehensive income.

10 Explain the statement of cash flows.

11 Classify cash flows as operating, investing, or financing.

CHAPTER

4

The Income Statement and Statement of Cash Flows

The **income statement** summarizes the results of a company's operations for the accounting period. This statement is alternatively referred to as a *statement of income, statement of earnings,* or *statement of operations.* Many users consider it to be the most important financial statement in a company's annual report. Supporting the balance sheet and income statement is a schedule entitled the *statement of retained earnings* (or simply the *retained earnings statement*), which serves as the link between the two statements. The operations of a company encompass routine ongoing activities, as well as activities that are infrequent or unusual. In addition, a company may divest itself of a major component of its operations, report extraordinary items, make changes in accounting principles, and make adjustments to prior periods' financial statements. We discuss the disclosure of each of these items in this chapter as it relates to the presentation of the income statement or the statement of retained earnings. We also discuss the alternative ways a company may report its comprehensive income in its financial statements. We also introduce the **statement of cash flows** in this chapter because of the relationship of operating, investing, and financing cash flows to different sections of the income statement and balance sheet.

CONCEPTS OF INCOME

The income statement is an important financial statement for several reasons. The growth of large-scale corporations has resulted in absentee ownership, in which management operates the corporation, but it is owned by a diverse set of stockholders. Accounting fulfills a **stewardship** function. The capital invested in the corporation by stockholders and the corporation's income both are reported so that stockholders may evaluate management's operating effectiveness in maintaining and increasing capital. The *past* income of a corporation is considered to be a useful indicator in predicting future earnings and net cash flows.[1] In turn, this is useful in **predicting cash flows** for *current* and *future* dividend payments by the corporation, as well as its stock price—important considerations of current and potential investors. Similarly, short- and long-term creditors have found that an analysis of corporate income provides useful information about the corporation's ability to generate cash from operations that can be used to pay interest charges and operating obligations.

1 Understand the concepts of income.

While corporate income information is useful to a variety of user groups, accountants and economists have long debated what "income"

---

1. C. A. Finger, "The Ability of Earnings to Predict Future Earnings and Cash Flow," *Journal of Accounting Research* 32 (Autumn 1994), pp. 210–223; P. M. Dechow, S. P. Kothari, and R. L. Watts, "The Relation between Earnings and Cash Flows," *Journal of Accounting and Economics* 25(2) (May 1998), pp. 133–168.

is and how it should be measured. One *concept* of income is that of capital maintenance; a useful way to *measure* income is by using the transactional approach.

Capital Maintenance Concept

The capital maintenance concept focuses upon the capital, or net assets (assets minus liabilities), of the corporation. Under this concept, corporate income for a period of time is the amount that may be paid to stockholders during that period and still enable the corporation to be as well off at the end of the period as it was at the beginning.[2] In other words, **capital must be maintained before a corporation earns income on that capital.** Although capital may be thought of as financial capital or physical capital, the FASB uses a financial capital maintenance concept. Application of this concept requires a comparison of the beginning and ending capital (that is, the net assets) after adjusting for any additional investments or disinvestments during the period. The resulting difference is the corporate income. Given this definition, accountants and economists probably would agree on the total income that a corporation earned over its entire lifetime. This lifetime income would be computed by comparing the total proceeds received from the liquidation of the net assets at the end of the life with the capital invested at the beginning of the life, adjusted for any additional investments or withdrawals. Here there is certainty regarding the value of the net assets at the two points in time.

The capital maintenance concept was also discussed in Chapter 3.

However, **income information is needed on a more timely basis** (for example, on an annual basis) and there is more uncertainty about the value of the net assets that have not been liquidated at the end of such a shorter time period. For a shorter time period the values of a company's assets and liabilities at the beginning and end of the period may be measured in several ways. For a particular corporation these might include use of (1) the historical cost, (2) the current cost, (3) the current market value, (4) the net realizable value, or (5) the present value of future cash flows. Once the values of the assets and liabilities at the two points in time are measured using one of these methods, corporate income can be computed as the difference between the beginning and ending net assets (after any adjustments for additional investments or disinvestments). Many accountants and economists have advocated a particular valuation concept and methodology.[3] (A thorough discussion of the conceptual merits of these alternatives is an appropriate topic for an accounting theory book.)

We provide a brief example of the capital maintenance approach to determining corporate income here, using the historical cost method of valuing net assets. Assume that a corporation has net assets of $50,000 at the beginning and $90,000 at the end of the year, and that no additional investments or withdrawals were made. Based upon a comparison of the ending and the beginning net assets, the corporation could pay out $40,000 to stockholders and still be as well off at year-end. This $40,000 is the corporate income for the year, using the capital maintenance concept *based on historical costs.* To illustrate further, assume that a corporation has beginning net assets of $45,000 and ending net assets of $80,000. An additional capital investment of $10,000 was made by stockholders during the year. The total income of the corporation for the year is $25,000 computed as follows:

Ending net assets	$80,000
Less: Additional investment	(10,000)
Ending net assets excluding additional investments	$70,000
Less: Beginning net assets	(45,000)
Total income for the year	$25,000

2. S. S. Alexander, "Income Measurement in a Dynamic Economy," *Five Monographs on Business Income* (New York: AICPA Study Group on Business Income, 1950), p. 15.

3. See, for instance, E. O. Edwards and P. W. Bell, *The Theory and Measurement of Business Income* (Berkeley: University of California Press, 1970).

Unfortunately, in either of the two examples, **the corporation's total income is not very useful to various user groups.** The total income includes all amounts affecting net assets, whether they relate to usual or unusual, to extraordinary or ordinary events. But the total income is just that, a total. **The total income does not show a breakdown that identifies the causal relationships and operating activities** of the corporation that may be of interest to a specific user group. This specific information is shown under the transactional approach to income measurement.

Transactional Approach

As we noted in Chapter 2, an objective of financial reporting is to provide information that is useful to investors, creditors, and other external user groups to evaluate the amounts, timing, and uncertainty of the future net cash inflows for a particular company. A derived specific objective is to **provide information about a company's comprehensive income and its components.** That is, user groups are interested not only in a company's total income, but also in the resources obtained from and the resources given up for ongoing operations, discontinued operations, and unusual and/or infrequent activities. Accountants are also concerned with developing reliable (verifiable) evidence of the company's income-producing and other business activities reported in its financial statements.

As a result, a transactional approach to income measurement has evolved. Generally, **in the transactional approach, a company records its net assets at their historical cost, and it does not record changes in the assets and liabilities unless a transaction, event, or circumstance has occurred that provides reliable evidence of a change in value.** The transactional approach uses the accrual basis of accounting. **In accrual accounting a company records the financial impacts of transactions and other events and circumstances in the periods during which they occur rather than only in the periods in which it receives or pays cash.** In the transactional approach certain changes in values of the specific assets or liabilities are associated with the earning activities and are included in the company's income.

The transactional approach to income measurement is used in accounting today. It is consistent with the traditional capital maintenance concept because the income represents the difference between the beginning and ending adjusted net assets on an historical cost basis. However, **the accrual-based transactional approach to income measurement** is more informative because **it relates (matches) the accomplishments and the efforts** so that the reported income measures the performance of a company's earnings activities.[4] The FASB has developed the concept of **comprehensive income** as follows:

> Comprehensive income is the change in equity of a company during a period from transactions, other events, and circumstances relating to nonowner sources. It includes all changes in equity during a period except those resulting from investments by owners and distributions to owners.[5]

The intent of the FASB is (1) to develop a concept of income broad enough to include changes in value not traditionally reported in net income under the transactional approach, and (2) to allow for flexibility as to where certain components of income are reported in the financial statements. We discuss the reporting of a company's comprehensive income later in the chapter. First, we focus on its primary component, net income.

In the accrual-based transactional approach, a corporation's net income for an accounting period currently is measured as follows:

Net Income = Revenues − Expenses + Gains − Losses

---

4. "Objectives of Financial Reporting by Business Enterprises," *FASB Statement of Financial Accounting Concepts No. 1* (Stamford, Conn.: FASB, 1978), par. 45.
5. "Elements of Financial Statements," *FASB Statement of Financial Accounting Concepts No. 6* (Stamford, Conn.: FASB, 1985), par. 70.

The FASB has defined the various elements (revenues, expenses, gains, and losses) comprising net income. We discuss these definitions and their relationships later in the chapter and throughout the book as they relate to specific situations. The definitions are intended to distinguish, but not to draw a fine line, between the elements of net income. The identification of what elements to include in the determination of net income, when these should be included (recognized), and the measurement of each element depends on the definitions. Accounting rules and conventions (generally accepted accounting principles) also play a role in determining net income. Before we look at the definitions and generally accepted accounting principles, it is important to have an understanding of the concepts underlying the reporting of net income.

CONCEPTUAL REPORTING GUIDELINES

By following the transactional approach to income measurement, the FASB is concerned with how a company reports net income and its components. In particular, the FASB is interested in improving the reporting of income statement information relating to return on investment, risk, financial flexibility, and operating capability. **Return on investment is a measure of overall company performance.** Stockholders (investors) invest capital to obtain a return *on* capital. Before a company can provide a return on investment, its capital must be maintained. **Risk is the uncertainty or unpredictability of the future results of a company.** The greater the range and time frame within which future results are likely to fall, the greater the risk associated with an investment in or extension of credit to the company. Generally, the greater the risk, the higher the rate of return expected. **Financial flexibility is the ability of a company to adapt to unexpected needs and opportunities.** Financial flexibility stems from, among other qualities, the ability to adapt operations to increase net operating cash flows and the ability to sell assets without disrupting operations. **Operating capability refers to a company's ability to maintain a given physical level of operations.** This level of operations may be indicated by the quantity of goods or services (e.g., inventory) produced in a given period or by the physical capacity of the fixed assets (e.g., property, plant, and equipment). The reporting of income statement information should also guard against "earnings management" by the managers of a company. Earnings management occurs when managers enter into transactions or select from alternative generally accepted accounting principles for the purpose of artificially influencing reported net income (by changing revenues/gains or expenses/losses).

Return on investment, risk, financial flexibility, and operating capability were discussed in Chapter 2.

General Conceptual Guidelines

In regard to providing information about the preceding items, the FASB suggests that a company's income statement can be improved by:

2 Explain the conceptual guidelines for reporting income.

1. Providing information about its operating performance separately from other aspects of its performance.
2. Presenting the results of particular significant activities or events that predict the amounts, timing, and uncertainty of its future income and cash flows.
3. Providing information useful for assessing the return on investment.
4. Providing feedback that enables users to assess their previous predictions of income and its components.
5. Providing information to help assess the cost of maintaining its operating capability.
6. Presenting information about how effectively management has discharged its stewardship responsibility regarding the company's resources.

To accomplish these goals, the FASB has established general concepts to guide decisions about reporting information on (or related to) the income statement. It suggests that **the components of net income may be more important than the total amount.** A company should report a component of net income separately if it is important for the assessment of some aspect of future income. This guide implies the separate reporting of income from ongoing central operations, discontinued operations, and one or more components relating to peripheral activities, unusual activities, and other events and circumstances affecting the company. The guide also indicates that it is desirable to report information about operating segments.

Specific Conceptual Guidelines

More specific guidelines may aid in decisions about how to report revenues, expenses, gains, and losses. We summarize these guidelines as follows:

1. Those items that are judged to be unusual in amount based on past experience should be reported separately.
2. Revenues, expenses, gains, and losses that are affected in different ways by changes in economic conditions should be distinguished from one another. For instance, changes in revenues are the joint result of changes in sales volume and selling prices. Information about both types of changes is helpful in assessing future operating results.
3. Sufficient detail should be given to aid in understanding the primary relationships among revenues, expenses, gains, and losses. In particular, it is helpful to report separately (a) expenses that vary with volume of activity or with various components of income, (b) expenses that are discretionary, and (c) expenses that are stable over time or depend upon other factors, such as the level of interest rates or the rate of taxation.
4. When the measurements of revenues, expenses, gains, or losses are subject to different levels of reliability, they should be reported separately.
5. Items whose amounts must be known for the calculation of summary indicators (e.g., rate of return) should be reported separately.[6]

These guidelines are intended to provide assistance for decisions about the grouping of items to show the components of net income and the elements that should be reported separately. The benefits of any additional information should, of course, be weighed against the costs of providing the information.

User Group Conceptual Guidelines

The AICPA Special Committee on Financial Reporting suggests similar general and specific guidelines for the reporting of a company's income. Based on input from external user groups, the Committee developed a "model" for business reporting. In this model, the Committee recommends that a company report separately the effects on earnings from its "core" and "non-core" activities. Core activities are usual and recurring activities, transactions, or events, and continuing operations, excluding interest. Conversely, non-core activities, transactions, or events are unusual or nonrecurring.

Under this approach a company's income statement would present two categories of earnings: (1) core earnings, and (2) non-core earnings and financing costs. The core earnings category would include income (or loss) from core activities and recurring nonoperating gains and losses. The non-core earnings and financing costs category would include nonrecurring income (or loss) from such items as discontinued operations, unusually large nonrecurring transactions, the effects of a rare natural disaster, unique transactions, the effects of changes in accounting principles, and interest income and expense. The Committee also recommends increasing the amount of detail on the income statement. This includes, for instance, dividing operating expenses into categories such as fixed and variable, controllable and noncontrollable,

---

6. "Reporting Income, Cash Flows, and Financial Position of Business Enterprises," *FASB Proposed Statement of Financial Accounting Concepts* (Stamford, Conn.: FASB, 1981), par. 34 and 46–48.

or discretionary and nondiscretionary, as well as providing more detail about the components and cost of goods sold.

In addition to the annual income statement disclosures, the Committee recommends improved interim reporting, as well as reporting disaggregated information on an operating segment basis. In regard to quarterly reporting, the Committee recommends that fourth-quarter results be shown separately within the annual report so that year-end adjustments can be reviewed for continuity and additional insight. Disaggregated information should be improved by aligning more closely what is reported in a company's annual report with what is reported internally to the company's management and board of directors.[7]

These recommendations were made to enhance the predictive and feedback value of the information reported in a company's income statement and the related notes. The intent is to help external users to better identify the opportunities and risks of investments in or credit extensions to the company. Although the Committee is not a standard-setting body, the FASB has implemented some of its recommendations in regard to the reporting of operating segment information (which we discuss in Chapter 5). The FASB is considering other recommendations of the Committee in its deliberations about required future disclosures.

ELEMENTS OF THE INCOME STATEMENT

The elements of the income statement are the broad classes of items comprising the statement. They are the "building blocks" with which the income statement is prepared. Each of the four elements—revenues, expenses, gains, and losses—is defined in **FASB Statement of Concepts No. 6.**

3 Define the elements of an income statement.

Revenues

> Revenues are inflows of (or increases in) assets of a company or settlement of its liabilities (or a combination of both) during a period from delivering or producing goods, rendering services, or other activities that are the company's ongoing major or central operations.

Revenues represent actual or expected cash inflows (or the equivalent) that occur as a result of the company's ongoing primary operating activities. Revenues are a measurement of the *accomplishments* of the operating activities during the accounting period. It is important to remember that revenues are a component of equity. The transactions that result in revenues are of various types, depending on the kinds of operations involved and the way revenues are recognized.[8]

REVENUE RECOGNITION   Recognition is the process of formally recording and reporting an item in a company's financial statements. To be recognized, an item must meet the definition of an element and be reliably measurable in monetary terms. Recognition involves the depiction of an item in both words and numbers, with the amount included in the totals of the financial statements. Most revenues are the joint result of many operating activities of a company and are "earned" gradually and continually as a result of this entire set of activities. These activities may be described as a company's earning process. **The earning process includes purchasing, producing, selling, delivering, administering, and collecting and paying cash.** Although revenues are defined in conjunction with this entire earnings (operating) process, **revenues generally are recognized when two criteria are met: (1) realization has taken place, and (2) they have been earned.** These criteria provide an

7. "Improving Business Reporting—A Customer Focus," *AICPA Special Committee on Financial Reporting* (New York: AICPA, 1994), Appendix II, pp. 137–140.

8. The discussion in this section is a summary of that presented by the FASB in *FASB Statement of Financial Accounting Concepts No. 6, op. cit*; "Recognition and Measurement in Financial Statements of Business Enterprises," *FASB Statement of Financial Accounting Concepts No. 5* (Stamford, Conn.: FASB, 1984).

acceptable level of assurance (i.e., reliability) of the existence and amounts of revenues. Sometimes one and sometimes the other criterion is the more important, but both must be satisfied to a reasonable degree for revenue to be recognized.

Concerning the first criterion, *realization* **means the process of converting noncash resources into cash or rights to cash.** Realization encompasses two terms: (1) realized and (2) realizable. *Realized* refers to the actual exchange of noncash resources into cash or near cash (e.g., receivables). *Realizable* refers to the situation where noncash resources are readily convertible into known amounts of cash or claims to cash. "Readily convertible" noncash resources (e.g., gold, wheat) have interchangeable units and can be sold at quoted prices on an active market. In regard to the second criterion, **revenues are *earned* when the earning process is complete, or essentially complete.** This occurs when the company has accomplished what it must do in order to be entitled to the benefits (e.g., assets) represented by the revenues.

A company usually recognizes revenue at the time goods are sold or services are rendered. Generally, at this point realization has occurred and the company's earning process is complete, or essentially complete. Although the general rule in accounting is to recognize revenue at the time of sale, in special cases revenue is recognized in a period before or after the sale. This is done to reflect more accurately the nature of a company's operations (i.e., to increase the predictive value and representational faithfulness of the accounting information). These *exceptional* cases arise because:

1. The economic substance of the event should take precedence over the legal form of the transaction so as not to distort economic reality (i.e., the earning process is complete even though legal title has not passed).
2. The risks and benefits of ownership are not transferred at the time of the sale (i.e., the earning process is not complete).
3. There is great uncertainty about the collectibility of the receivable involved in a sale (i.e., realization has not occurred).

The alternative methods for recognizing revenue in a period other than the period of sale include (1) the **percentage-of-completion method,** used for certain long-term construction contracts; (2) the **proportional-performance method,** used for certain long-term service contracts; (3) the **installment method,** used when the collectibility of the receivable is very uncertain; and (4) the **cost-recovery method,** used when the collectibility of the receivable is extremely uncertain. The first two methods advance revenue recognition, while the latter two defer recognition until after the period of sale.[9]

Revenue recognition methods are discussed in Chapter 17.

The points of usual revenue recognition, advanced recognition, and deferred recognition, as they relate to the earning process, are shown in the following diagram:

Revenue Recognition Alternatives		Advanced Recognition	Usual Recognition	Deferred Recognition
Earning Process	Purchase of Raw Materials	Production Activities	Sales on Account	Cash Receipt

Although the preceding diagram is helpful in identifying the alternative revenue recognition methods, a recent study indicated that the overstatement of revenue (i.e.,

---

9. See also L. T. Johnson and R. K. Storey, "Recognition in Financial Statements: Underlying Concepts and Practical Conventions," *Research Report* (Stamford, Conn.: FASB, 1982); H. J. Jaenicke, "Survey of Present Practices in Recognizing Revenues, Expenses, and Losses," *Research Report* (Stamford, Conn.: FASB, 1981).

recognizing revenue too soon) is involved in over half of the financial reporting frauds in the United States. Hence, the FASB and SEC continue to examine the generally accepted accounting prinicples related to revenue recognition. For instance, the SEC issued *SEC Staff Accounting Bulletin No. 101* that provides additional guidance on "early" revenue recognition issues related to items such as sales agreements between companies, shipments to third-party warehouses, "layaway" programs, and nonrefundable up-front fees.[10]

Expenses

Expenses are outflows of (or decreases in) assets of a company or incurrences of liabilities (or a combination of both) during a period from delivering or producing goods, rendering services, or carrying out other activities that are the company's ongoing major or central operations.

Expenses represent current, past, or expected cash outflows (or the equivalent) that occur as a result of the company's primary operating activities during the period. Expenses are a measurement of the *efforts* or *sacrifices* made in the operating activities. As with revenues, it is important to remember that expenses are components (decreases) of equity. The transactions and events that cause expenses are of many types, depending on the kinds of operations involved and the way expenses are recognized.

EXPENSE RECOGNITION To determine the income related to a company's primary operations during the accounting period, **the expenses (efforts) are recognized and matched against the revenues (benefits).** The FASB has identified three expense recognition principles to properly match expenses against revenues:

1. *Association of Cause and Effect.* Some costs are recognized as expenses on the basis of a presumed direct association with specific revenues.

Some transactions result simultaneously in both a revenue and an expense. The revenue and expense are directly related to each other, so that the expense is recognized at the same time as the revenue. Examples include costs of products sold, transportation costs for delivery of goods to customers, and sales commissions.

2. *Systematic and Rational Allocation.* Some costs are recognized as expenses in a particular accounting period on the basis of a systematic and rational allocation among the periods in which benefits are provided.

Many assets provide benefits for several periods. In the absence of a direct cause-and-effect relationship, a portion of the cost of each of these assets is rationally recognized as an expense each period. The allocation system should be based upon the pattern of benefits anticipated and should appear reasonable to an unbiased observer. Examples include depreciation of fixed assets, amortization of intangible assets, and the allocation of prepaid costs.

3. *Immediate Recognition.* Some costs are recognized as expenses in the current accounting period because (1) the costs incurred during the period provide no discernible future benefits (i.e., they do not result in assets), or (2) the allocation of costs among accounting periods or due to cause-and-effect relationships does not serve a useful purpose.

Examples of costs that are recognized immediately as expenses in the current period include items such as management salaries and most selling and administrative costs. Sometimes it is difficult to determine whether a cost should be recorded as an expense

---

10. "Revenue Recognition in Financial Statements," *SEC Staff Accounting Bulletin No. 101*, (Washington, D.C.: U.S. Government, 1999).

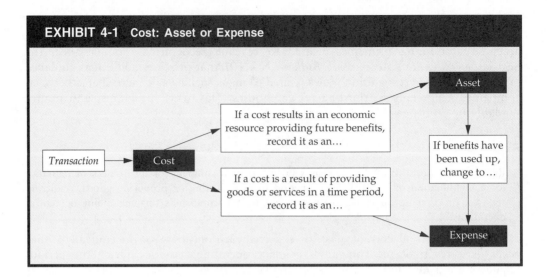

EXHIBIT 4-1   Cost: Asset or Expense

or as an asset, and, if it is recorded as an asset, when the expense recognition should occur. Exhibit 4-1 is helpful in understanding the relationships among the terms cost, asset, and expense.

Gains and Losses

Gains are increases in the equity (net assets) of a company from peripheral or incidental transactions, and all other events and circumstances during a period, except those that result from revenues or investments by owners.

Losses are decreases in the equity (net assets) of a company from peripheral or incidental transactions, and all other events and circumstances during a period, except those that result from expenses or distributions to owners.

Gains and losses, like revenues and expenses, are components of equity. Revenues and gains are similar, and expenses and losses are similar, but several differences are important in communicating information about a company's performance. First, while revenues and expenses relate to a company's major operating activities, **gains and losses are identified with peripheral or incidental activities or with the effects of other events and circumstances,** many of which are beyond its control. Second, revenues and expenses are reported as "gross" amounts, which are matched against each other to determine earnings. **Gains and losses are reported "net"**—either because two or more measures are offset against each other or because they involve only a single increase or decrease in an asset or liability, without an offsetting or related decrease or increase in some other asset or liability. A third difference between revenues and gains relates to realization. In the case of revenues, these generally are recognized when realized; that is, when noncash goods or services are exchanged for cash or near cash. Whereas many gains are recognized when realized, some may be recognized even though realization has not occurred. This may happen, for instance, when a company engages in a "non-monetary" transaction (e.g., an exchange of land for equipment) where the earning process is complete.

Although the definitions of revenues, expenses, gains, and losses give broad guidance, they do not distinguish precisely between revenues and gains and between expenses and losses. The distinction depends to a significant degree on the nature of the company, its operations, and its other activities. Items that are revenues (expenses) for one company may be gains (losses) for another. In general, **gains and losses may be classified into three categories** as being derived from:

1. Exchange transactions
2. The holding of resources or obligations while their values change
3. Nonreciprocal (i.e., "one-way") transfers between a company and nonowners

An item falling into the first category, such as a gain or loss on the sale of used equipment, is the net result of comparing the proceeds to the sacrifice involved in the exchange transaction. Examples of gains or losses resulting from value changes include those from the writing down of inventory from cost to market; from a change in the market price of trading securities held by financial institutions; from a change in value of certain derivative financial instruments; from an impairment of property, plant, or equipment or intangibles; and from a change in a foreign exchange rate between the time of a credit transaction and the related cash flow. Finally, gains or losses from nonreciprocal transfers include those due to lawsuits, assessments of fines or damages by a court, or natural catastrophes such as earthquakes or fires.

The revenues, expenses, gains, and losses, as defined here, are classified and measured in accordance with generally accepted accounting principles. The results of the major operating activities, as well as peripheral activities, are reported on the income statement.

INCOME STATEMENT CONTENT

Although the *form* of the income statement may differ from company to company, its *content* is relatively standard. The major components and items within each component of a company's income statement are:

4 Describe the major components of an income statement.

1. Income from continuing operations
   a. Sales revenue (net)
   b. Cost of goods sold
   c. Operating expenses
   d. Other items
   e. Income tax expense related to continuing operations
2. Results from discontinued operations
   a. Income (loss) from operations of discontinued components (net of income taxes)
   b. Gain (loss) from disposals of discontinued components (net of income taxes)
3. Extraordinary items (net of income taxes)
4. Cumulative effects of changes in accounting principles (net of income taxes)
5. Net income
6. Earnings per share

Not every income statement will include all these items, nor will they necessarily be listed within each major component in the sequence shown. We discuss each in the following sections of this chapter. Exhibit 4-2 shows a comprehensive illustration of the Banner Corporation income statement. Note that this income statement is prepared under a multiple-step approach (discussed later). Supporting schedules for this income statement are illustrated in related exhibits.

The Coca-Cola Company's 2001 income statement is shown in Appendix A at the end of this book.

All-Inclusive versus Current Operating

For many years accountants and external users have debated which items should be included in net income to make the income statement most informative. Some advocated the **current operating performance** concept. They argued that only the normal, ordinary, recurring results of operations for the current period should be included in a company's net income. Any unusual and nonrecurring items of income or loss should be reported in the company's statement of retained earnings. The reasoning was that investors are interested primarily in continuing operating income and that the disclosure of additional information would unnecessarily "clutter" the income statement. Others advocated the **all-inclusive** concept. Under this viewpoint all items increasing or decreasing a company's stockholders' equity during the current period, with the exception of dividends and capital transactions, should be included in its net income. Here it was argued that unusual and nonrecurring income or loss items are part of the earnings history of a company, and their omission from the income statement might cause them to be overlooked. With the issuance

EXHIBIT 4-2   Multiple-Step Income Statement

BANNER CORPORATION

Income Statement
For Year Ended December 31, 2004

Sales revenue		$150,000
Less: Sales returns and allowances	$ 4,000	
Sales discounts taken	2,300	(6,300)
Net sales		$143,700
Cost of goods sold (Exhibit 4-3)		(86,000)
Gross profit		$ 57,700
Operating expenses		
Selling expenses (Exhibit 4-5)	$10,200	
General and administrative expenses (Exhibit 4-5)	16,000	
Depreciation expense (Exhibit 4-5)	7,800	
Total operating expenses		(34,000)
Operating income		$ 23,700
Other items		
Interest revenue	$ 1,800	
Dividend revenue	600	
Loss on sale of equipment	(4,000)	
Interest expense	(2,100)	(3,700)
Pretax income from continuing operations		$ 20,000
Income tax expense		(6,000)
Income from continuing operations		$ 14,000
Results from discontinued operations		
Income from operations of discontinued component A		
(net of $1,950 income taxes)	$ 4,550	
Loss on disposal of component A		
(net of $3,150 income tax credit)	(7,350)	(2,800)
Income before extraordinary items		$ 11,200
Extraordinary loss from explosion (net of $750 income tax credit)		(1,750)
Cumulative effect on prior years' income of change in depreciation		
method (net of $600 income taxes)		1,400
Net Income		$ 10,850

Components of Income	Earnings per Common Share (5,000 shares)
Income from continuing operations	$2.80
Results from discontinued operations	(0.56)
Extraordinary loss from explosion	(0.35)
Cumulative effect on prior years' income of change in depreciation method	0.28
Net income	$2.17

of **APB Opinion No. 9** the all-inclusive concept gained prominence. In this *Opinion* it was concluded that net income should include all items of profit or loss during the period, with the exception of certain material prior period adjustments that should be included as adjustments of the opening retained earnings balance. **APB Opinions No. 20 and 30 and FASB Statement No. 144** require disclosure on the income statement of the cumulative effects of changes in accounting principles, extraordinary items, and results from discontinued operations. With the issuance of these *Opinions*, the all-inclusive concept became even more prominent. Finally, **FASB Statement No. 16** narrowed the interpretation of prior period adjustments so that the all-inclusive content of the income statement currently is as shown in the preceding outline.

Although the FASB subscribes to the all-inclusive concept of net income, it requires that a company exclude a few "gains" and "losses" from net income. As we noted earlier, in *FASB Statement of Concepts No. 5*, the Board suggested that a full set of financial statements should show, among other items, (1) net income for the period and (2) comprehensive income for the period.[11] These gains and losses are reported in a company's other comprehensive income, as we discuss later.

Condensed Income Statements

For full disclosure, the financial statements of a company should disclose all information important enough to influence the judgment of informed external users. However, disclosures may be made in several ways. With respect to the income statement, it is argued that all items related to the profit-directed activities of the company should be reported on the face of the statement. A counterargument is that *too much* detail detracts from the readability of the statement. Most companies take a compromise position and present a condensed income statement. Here only the major important items are reported directly on the income statement, frequently in an aggregated amount, while supporting schedules and note disclosures supplement this information. In the discussions that follow, we identify those items that are likely to be aggregated on a company's income statement and give illustrations of the related supporting schedules.

INCOME STATEMENT: INCOME FROM CONTINUING OPERATIONS

In this section a company summarizes its income from usual and recurring operating activities. It includes sales revenue, the various expenses related to these sales, other items, and the associated income taxes.

5 Compute income from continuing operations.

Sales Revenue (Net)

Sales revenue includes the gross charges to customers for the goods and services provided during the period. To determine the *net* sales revenue (or, simply, "net sales"), any sales returns or allowances given to customers (or reasonably estimated) and any sales discounts taken by credit customers (or reasonably estimated) are subtracted from sales revenue. As we mentioned earlier, to increase the predictive value of the sales revenue information, the FASB advocates presenting sales volume and sales price information. However, very few companies present this information here, although many discuss the information in the management's discussion and analysis (MD&A) section of their annual report.

Cost of Goods Sold

The cost of goods sold is the cost of the inventory items sold to customers during the period. In the case of a *perpetual* inventory system, a company records this amount at the time of each sale and shows the total amount in the Cost of Goods Sold account. The company reports this amount as the cost of goods sold on its income statement. When a company uses a *periodic* inventory system, it does not reduce its inventory at the time of the sale. Consequently, the company must calculate its cost of goods sold amount on the basis of a physical inventory taken at the end of the period. Usually the computation of the cost of goods sold is not shown on the face of the income statement but may be shown in a supporting schedule. The calculation of cost of goods sold will depend on whether the company is a merchandising company or a manufacturing company. In the case of a merchandising company, net purchases are added to

The items included in Cost of Goods Sold are discussed in Chapter 7.

---

11. *FASB Statement of Financial Accounting Concepts No. 5, op. cit.*, par. 13.

EXHIBIT 4-3   Cost of Goods Sold: Merchandising Company

BANNER CORPORATION

Schedule 1: Cost of Goods Sold
For Year Ended December 31, 2004

Inventory, January 1, 2004		$ 41,000
Purchases	$80,300	
Freight-in	5,500	
Cost of purchases	$85,800	
Less: Purchases returns	(2,800)	
Net purchases		83,000
Cost of goods available for sale		$124,000
Less: Inventory, December 31, 2004		(38,000)
Cost of goods sold		$ 86,000

its beginning inventory. Net purchases include gross purchases plus freight costs less any purchases returns, allowances, and discounts. Theoretically, such costs as receiving, storing, and insurance during transport also should be included in purchases. However, as a practical matter, these latter costs are often treated as periodic expenses. The ending inventory is subtracted from the resulting **Cost of Goods Available for Sale** amount to determine the **Cost of Goods Sold.** The Banner Corporation uses a periodic inventory system; Exhibit 4-3 shows its cost of goods sold schedule.

In the case of a company that manufactures instead of purchases its inventory, a **Cost of Goods Manufactured** amount replaces net purchases. The factory cost incurred during the period is computed by adding (1) the cost of **raw materials** used in the production process, (2) the cost of **direct labor** used to convert raw materials into partially or fully completed inventory, and (3) the cost of the other factory items (referred to as **factory overhead**), such as factory utilities and depreciation, supervision, maintenance, and supplies. This total current factory cost is added to the beginning goods in process inventory (partially completed inventory from the previous period), from which the ending goods in process inventory is subtracted to determine the cost of goods manufactured. The cost of goods sold is computed by adding the cost of goods manufactured to the beginning finished goods inventory and subtracting the ending finished goods inventory. Exhibit 4-4 shows the Banner Corporation's cost of goods sold schedule, assuming that it is a manufacturing company. The cost of goods sold is subtracted from net sales to determine gross profit, as shown earlier in Exhibit 4-2.

Operating Expenses

Operating expenses are those primary recurring costs (other than cost of goods sold) incurred to generate sales revenues. These expenses typically are classified according to *functional categories*. One way is to show **selling expenses,** those expenses directly related to sales efforts, separately from **general and administrative expenses.** Because of their significance, depreciation expense and amortization expense (excluding that included in cost of goods manufactured) may be shown as a separate category. Research and development expense[12] may also be shown as a separate category. Frequently, aggregate

---

12. Research and development expense is the cost incurred in the planned search for new knowledge and the translation of that knowledge into a plan or design for a new product or process or for a significant improvement to an existing product or process.

EXHIBIT 4-4 Cost of Goods Sold: Manufacturing Company

BANNER CORPORATION

Schedule 1: Cost of Goods Sold
For Year Ended December 31, 2004

Raw materials used		$ 35,000
Direct labor		29,000
Factory overhead		
Depreciation of factory items	$5,100	
Heat, light, and power	4,000	
Indirect factory labor	7,300	
Repairs and maintenance	3,400	
Miscellaneous factory expense	1,200	21,000
Current manufacturing costs		$ 85,000
Add: Goods in process, January 1, 2004		27,000
Less: Goods in process, December 31, 2004		(29,000)
Cost of goods manufactured		$ 83,000
Add: Finished goods inventory, January 1, 2004		41,000
Cost of goods available for sale		$124,000
Less: Finished goods inventory, December 31, 2004		(38,000)
Cost of goods sold		$ 86,000

---

amounts are listed on the income statement for selling, general and administrative, and depreciation expense. When this occurs, a supporting schedule that identifies the amounts of the individual expenses contained in each major classification may be included. Exhibit 4-5 shows this supporting schedule for Banner Corporation.

Research and development costs are discussed in Chapter 11.

An alternative to classifying expenses by functions is to classify them according to how they vary with the volume of the main activities of the company. Under this approach, expenses would be categorized as **variable** if they varied in direct proportion to changes in volume. Expenses would be categorized as **fixed** if their amount was not affected by changes in volume during the accounting period. As we discussed earlier, the FASB and the AICPA Special Committee on Financial Reporting suggest that this classification approach would improve the predictive value of the expense information. Although many companies classify their costs as fixed and variable for internal (management) reports, virtually all continue to classify them by functions on their external financial statements. The total of the operating expenses is subtracted from the gross profit to determine the operating income, as shown earlier in Exhibit 4-2.

Other Items

Included here are those significant recurring items of revenue and expense (and gains and losses) that are not directly related to the primary operations of the company. Examples include dividend revenue, interest revenue and expense, gains or losses from changes in values of certain derivative financial instruments, and items such as rent, storage, and service revenues (for a manufacturing or merchandising company). Also included in this section are (1) material gains and losses resulting from sales of assets that are *not* considered to be "components" (as we will discuss in the results of discontinued operations section later in this chapter), and (2) material but "nonextraordinary" gains and losses that result from events that are *either* unusual in nature *or* infrequent in occurrence, such as the loss from the write-down of obsolete inventories; the gain or loss from the disposal of property; the loss from the impairment of property, plant, and equipment; the loss from the impairment of intangibles (including goodwill); and the gain or

---

EXHIBIT 4-5 Operating Expenses

BANNER CORPORATION

Schedule 2: Operating Expenses
For Year Ended December 31, 2004

Selling Expenses

Delivery expense	$ 1,800
Advertising expense	3,300
Sales salaries expense	4,100
Sales supplies expense	700
Miscellaneous selling expenses	300
Total selling expenses	$10,200

General and Administrative Expenses

Administrative salaries	$ 6,900
Office salaries	3,700
Taxes and insurance expenses	2,200
Bad debts expense	1,500
Office supplies expense	700
Miscellaneous expenses	1,000
Total general and administrative expenses	$16,000

Depreciation Expense

Office equipment	$ 3,300
Store equipment	4,500
Total depreciation expense	$ 7,800

---

loss from the extinguishment of debt. As shown in Exhibit 4-2, a loss on the sale of equipment is included in this section of the Banner Corporation's income statement because the sale is considered to be an infrequent but not unusual event. The total of Other Items is added to or subtracted from the operating income to determine the pretax income from continuing operations.

Income Tax Expense Related to Continuing Operations

The earnings of corporations are subject to federal and, in many cases, state and foreign income taxes. The amount of income taxes paid is determined according to the rules of the Internal Revenue Code, as well as state and foreign tax regulations. Income taxes are a significant expense on a corporation's income statement that is presented in its annual report. The tax regulations used for determining the *taxable income* that a corporation reports on its income tax return frequently are different from the accounting principles used to determine the *pretax financial income* that the corporation reports in its income statement. Additionally, pretax financial income consists of several major components. Because of these differences, two types of tax allocation are necessary.

Interperiod tax allocation involves allocating a corporation's income tax obligation as an expense to various accounting periods because of temporary (timing) differences between its taxable income and pretax financial income. Generally, interperiod tax allocation requires that (1) the annual income tax *expense* for financial reporting be based

Interperiod and intraperiod tax allocation are discussed in Chapter 18.

on pretax *financial* income and prior period adjustments (and items of other comprehensive income, if any), (2) that the *current* income tax obligation (*liability*) be based on *taxable* income, and (3) that the *deferred* income tax *liability* (or asset) be based on the *temporary* differences.[13] Once the total income tax expense for the period is determined, intraperiod (or *within*-the-period) tax allocation is necessary.

Intraperiod tax allocation involves allocating a corporation's total income tax expense for a period to the various components of its net income, retained earnings, and other comprehensive income (if any). That is, a portion of the income tax expense is *matched* against (1) the income from continuing operations, (2) the income (loss) from the operations of a discontinued component, (3) the gain (loss) from the disposal of a discontinued component, (4) the extraordinary items, (5) the cumulative effect of any change in accounting principle, (6) any prior period adjustments, and (7) any items of other comprehensive income. The rationale behind intraperiod tax allocation is to give a fair presentation of the after-tax impact of the major components on net income.

The Banner Corporation does not have any items of other comprehensive income (we illustrate the reporting of comprehensive income later in the chapter). Hence, the portion of the total income tax expense applicable to each segment of the Banner Corporation's income statement and statement of retained earnings is calculated in Exhibit 4-6. (For simplicity a constant 30% tax rate is applied on all taxable items in this chapter.) As we show in Exhibit 4-2, the portion of the income tax expense applicable to continuing operations is listed as a separate "line item" and is subtracted from pretax income from continuing operations to determine income from continuing operations. However, the results from discontinued operations, each extraordinary item, the cumulative effect of a change in accounting principle, and any prior period adjustments are shown *net* of the income tax effect. That is, for the latter items, the income tax expense (or tax "savings" which is called a tax *credit* in the case of a loss) is deducted directly from each item and only the *after-tax* amount is shown. However, it is sound

---

EXHIBIT 4-6 Intraperiod Tax Allocation

BANNER CORPORATION

Schedule of Income Tax Expense (Intraperiod Allocation)
For Year Ended December 31, 2004

Component (Pretax)	Pretax Amount	×	Income Tax Rate	=	Income Tax Expense (Credit)
Income from continuing operations	$20,000	×	0.30	=	$6,000
Income from operations of discontinued component A	6,500	×	0.30	=	1,950
Loss on disposal of component A	(10,500)	×	0.30	=	(3,150)
Extraordinary loss from explosion	(2,500)	×	0.30	=	(750)
Cumulative effect of change in accounting principle on prior years' income	2,000	×	0.30	=	600
Prior period adjustment	5,000	×	0.30	=	1,500
Total income tax expense					$6,150

---

13. "Accounting for Income Taxes," *FASB Statement of Financial Accounting Standards No. 109* (Norwalk, Conn.: FASB, 1992), par. 8.

accounting practice to disclose the amount of the tax impact on these items, either parenthetically or in a note to the financial statements.

Single-Step and Multiple-Step Formats

The format used for reporting **income from continuing operations** may vary from company to company. Many variations of two basic formats, *single-step* and *multiple-step*, are used in actual practice. **Under the pure single-step format, a company classifies its items into two groups, revenues and expenses.** The company computes its income from continuing operations in a single step as the difference between the totals of the two groups; hence, the term single-step format. A variation in this format involves the income tax expense applicable to continuing operations. Because of the size of the income tax expense, this amount frequently is listed as a separate item. In this case a subtotal entitled pretax income from continuing operations is computed; from that the associated income tax expense is deducted to determine income from continuing operations. The single-step format has been advocated because of its simplicity and flexibility, and because the limited number of subclassifications does not attribute more importance to certain items of revenue and expense than may be warranted. Although it is still a fairly common form of income statement, the number of companies using it is decreasing. Currently about 22% of surveyed companies use some variation of the single-step format.[14] Exhibit 4-7 illustrates this format. Note that the lower portion (after income from continuing operations) of Exhibit 4-7 is the same as the lower portion of Exhibit 4-2, which illustrated the multiple-step format.

Some accountants argue that the simplicity of the single-step format detracts from the usefulness of the income statement to external users. The FASB suggests that components of a financial statement often reflect more homogeneous classes of items than the whole statement. Furthermore, the individual items, subtotals, or other parts of a financial statement may be more useful than the aggregate amounts for external decision making. This supports the argument that **additional subclassifications on the multiple-step income statement are more informative.** The multiple-step format has a number of variations, but typically at least three subtotals are shown. Initially the cost of goods sold amount is deducted from net sales to determine the **gross profit or gross margin on sales.** The operating expenses are then deducted from (that is, matched against) gross profit to show **operating income,** the major portion of income from continuing operations. The other revenues, expenses, gains, and losses, those important but nonoperating items that do not relate to the primary activities of the company, are then summarized in the next section called "Other Items." The net total of this section is added to (or deducted from) operating income to determine pretax income from continuing operations, which is reduced by the related income tax expense to determine **income from continuing operations.**

Two criticisms may be raised against the multiple-step format. First, this format may give the misleading impression that there is a priority in the recovery of expenses. However, *all* expenses must be recovered in order to earn income. Second, disagreement, particularly across different industries, as to which items of revenue and expense should be classified as operating (or primary) and nonoperating can lead to different classification methods and result in noncomparable income statement formats. Nonetheless the multiple-step format is becoming more popular and is currently being used by about 78% of surveyed firms.

Alternative Income Captions

In the preceding discussion of both single-step and multiple-step formats, we referred to the total of the initial section on the income statement as Income from Continuing

---

14. *Accounting Trends and Techniques* (New York: AICPA, 2001), p. 289.

EXHIBIT 4-7 Single-Step Income Statement

BANNER CORPORATION

Income Statement
For Year Ended December 31, 2004

Revenues		
Sales revenue (net of $2,300 discounts and $4,000 returns and allowances)	$143,700	
Interest revenue	1,800	
Dividend revenue	600	
Total revenues		$146,100
Expenses		
Cost of goods sold (Exhibit 4-3)	$ 86,000	
Selling expenses (Exhibit 4-5)	10,200	
General and administrative expenses (Exhibit 4-5)	16,000	
Depreciation expense (Exhibit 4-5)	7,800	
Loss on sale of equipment	4,000	
Interest expense	2,100	
Income tax expense	6,000	
Total expenses		(132,100)
Income from continuing operations		$ 14,000
Results from discontinued operations		
Income from operations of discontinued component A (net of $1,950 income taxes)	$ 4,550	
Loss on disposal of component A (net of $3,150 income tax credit)	(7,350)	(2,800)
Income before extraordinary items		$ 11,200
Extraordinary loss from explosion (net of $750 income tax credit)		(1,750)
Cumulative effect on prior years' income of change in depreciation method (net of $600 income taxes)		1,400
Net Income		$ 10,850

Components of Income	Earnings per Common Share (5,000 shares)
Income from continuing operations	$2.80
Results from discontinued operations	(0.56)
Extraordinary loss from explosion	(0.35)
Cumulative effect on prior years' income of change in depreciation method	0.28
Net income	$2.17

Operations. This caption presumes that the company is reporting results from discontinued operations, extraordinary items, and cumulative effects of changes in accounting principles. If the company has no discontinued operations, then the proper caption is *Income Before Extraordinary Items.* If the company has no extraordinary items, then the caption *Income Before Cumulative Effects of Changes in Accounting Principles* should be used. Finally, if none of the latter three items appears on the income statement, then the total of the initial section should be labeled *Net Income.* At this point it may be useful to go back and review the upper portion of Exhibit 4-2, through Income from Continuing Operations.

INCOME STATEMENT: RESULTS FROM DISCONTINUED OPERATIONS

6 Report results from discontinued operations.

A company may decide to "discontinue" some of its operations and sell a component of these operations. This component may contain long-lived assets (e.g., property, plant, and equipment) as well as liabilities (e.g., bonds payable.) Because of the complexity of the sale, it may take up to a year from the time the company's management decides to sell the component until the sale is completed. **FASB Statement No. 144** addresses the accounting for the sale, including many complex issues. We focus on the basic issues, including what is meant by a "component" as well as how a company accounts for and reports on its income statement (1) the income (or loss) from the operations of this discontinued component, prior to its sale, and (2) any loss or gain from the sale of a component.

A component of a company involves operations and cash flows that can be clearly distinguished, operationally and for financial reporting purposes, from the rest of the company. A component of a company may be, for instance, a subsidiary, an operating segment (e.g., division), or an asset group.

A company's income statement information is intended to be useful for predicting the amounts, timing, and uncertainty of its earnings, as well as to enable users to assess the company's operating capability and return on investment. To enhance the usefulness of a company's income statement, it is important for the company to report separately the results of its continuing, routine, and typical operations, and also to highlight the material aspects involving the sale of a discontinued component. A company reports information about a discontinued component in a section of the income statement called *results from discontinued operations* when: (1) the operations and cash flows of the component have been eliminated, and (2) the company will have no significant continuing involvement in the operations of the component after the disposal.

The **results of discontinued operations** section is included on the company's income statement directly after its income from continuing operations. The results from discontinued operations section includes (1) the operating income (loss) of the discontinued component, and (2) the gain (loss) from its sale,[15] as we discuss in detail later. We show this section below (using assumed amounts):

Income from continuing operations		$93,000
Results of discontinued operations		
Income from operations of discontinued		
Division X (net of $2,880 income taxes)	$ 6,720	
Loss on sale of Division X (net of $6,000 income		
tax credit)	(14,000)	(7,280)
Net Income		$85,720

Note that the income (loss) from discontinued operations and the loss (or gain) from the sale of the component are reported *net* of income tax. That is, the related income taxes are deducted directly from each item, and only the after-tax amount is included in the computation of net income. Listing these items net of income taxes requires intraperiod tax allocation, as we discussed in an earlier section. If the company also had extraordinary items (or a cumulative effect of an accounting change), the caption "Net income" would be titled "Income before extraordinary items." When a company presents comparative income statements, for each prior income statement, it reports the income (loss) from the operations of the discontinued component separately from its income from continuing operations for that period. Exhibit 4-2 illustrates the results from

---

15. A company may elect to combine the two amounts and disclose the gain (loss) from the sale in the notes to its financial statements. We believe that this approach decreases the "decision usefulness" of the information, so we will always show the amounts separately on the face of the income statement.

EXHIBIT 4-8 Discontinued Operations

MARATHON OIL CORPORATION

CONSOLIDATED STATEMENT OF INCOME (in part)

(In millions)	2001	2000
Income from continuing operations	$1,318	$420
Discontinued operations		
Income (loss) from discontinued operations	(169)	(9)
Loss on disposition of United States Steel Corporation	(984)	—

NOTES 1 AND 2 (in part)

... on December 31, 2001, Marathon disposed of its steel business through a tax-free distribution of the common stock of its wholly owned subsidiary United States Steel Corporation ... to holders of Steel Stock in exchange for all outstanding shares of Steel Stock on a one-for-one basis (the Separation).

Marathon has accounted for the business of United States Steel as a discontinued operation. ... The results of operations of United States Steel ... have been classified as discontinued operations for all periods presented in the Statement of Income and are summarized as follows:

(In millions)	2001	2000
Revenues and other income	$6,375	$6,132
Cost and expenses	6,755	6,010
Income (loss) from operations	(380)	122
Net interest and other financial costs	101	105
Income (loss) before income taxes	(481)	17
Provision (credit) for estimated income taxes	(312)	26
Net income (loss)	$ (169)	$ (9)

The computation of the loss on disposition of United States Steel on December 31, 2001 was as follows:

(In millions)	
Market value of Steel Stock (89,197,740 shares of stock issued and outstanding at $18.11 per share)	$1,615
Less:	
Net investment in United States Steel	2,564
Costs associated with the Separation, net of tax	35
Loss on disposition of United States Steel	$ (984)

Q U E S T I O N S

Ⓠ What types of businesses did Marathon Oil dispose of? Ⓠ What was the *pretax* loss from discontinued operations of the component for 2001? Ⓠ How was the loss on disposition determined? Ⓠ How much income would you use to compute the company's return on total assets (income ÷ average total assets)?

---

discontinued operations of the Banner Corporation (the tax amounts are taken from Exhibit 4-6). Exhibit 4-8 shows the disclosure by Marathon Oil Corporation of the results of its discontinued operations. *Accounting Trends and Techniques* indicates that 10% of surveyed companies reported results of discontinued operations.[16]

Any material gain or loss resulting from a transaction identified as *not* being the sale of a component is reported as a separate item of income from continuing operations.

---

16. *Accounting Trends and Techniques, op. cit.*, p. 386.

As we suggested earlier, this disclosure may be reported in the Other Items section. Frequently, companies refer to these as "restructuring" gains or losses. This type of gain or loss is *not* shown net of income taxes. **FASB Statement No. 146,** "Accounting for Costs Associated with Exit or Disposal Activities," also requires a company to recognize costs, such as employee severance costs, associated with a restructuring, discontinued operation, or other exit activity when they are incurred. We do not discuss these costs here.

A company must distinguish the sale of a component from the sale of other assets, as well as from other activities related to the evolution of the company's business, such as the phasing out of a product line, the shifting of service activities, or the changing of its manufacturing process. Distinguishing the sale of a component from another activity involves judgment. *FASB Statement No. 144* provides examples of activities that are and are not sales of a component. These include:

1. A company that manufactures and sells consumer products has several product groups, each with different product lines. For this company, a product group is the lowest level at which the operations and cash flows can be clearly distinguished from the rest of the company. Therefore, each product group is a component of the company. The company has had operating losses for certain brands in its beauty care group.
   A. *Sale of a component.* The company decides to exit the beauty care business and sells the product group. This is a sale of a component and any operating income (loss) and any gain (loss) on the sale of the beauty care business are reported in the company's results of discontinued operations.
   B. *Not a sale of a component.* The company decides to stay in the beauty care business but to sell the brands that are generating operating losses. This is *not* a sale of a component because the brands are only part of a product group. Any operating income (loss) and any gain (loss) on the sale of the brands are reported in the company's income from continuing operations.
2. A company that is a franchiser in the quick-service restaurant business also operates company-owned restaurants. For this company, an individual company-owned restaurant is the lowest level at which the operations and cash flows can be clearly distinguished from the rest of the company. Therefore, each company-owned restaurant is a component of the company. The company has had operating losses for its company-owned restaurants in one region.
   A. *Sale of a component.* The company sells the company-owned restaurants in that region to another company. This is a sale of a component, and any operating income (loss) and any gain (loss) on the sale of the restaurants are reported in the company's results of discontinued operations.
   B. *Not a sale of a component.* The company decides to sell the company-owned restaurants in that region to an existing franchisee. This is *not* a sale of a component because the company will receive franchise fees and have significant continuing involvement in the operations of the restaurants. Any operating income (loss) and any gain (loss) on the sale of the company-owned restaurants are reported in its income from continuing operations.
3. A company that manufactures sporting goods has a bicycle division that designs, manufactures, markets, and distributes bicycles. For this company, the bicycle division is the lowest level at which the operations and cash flows can be clearly distinguished from the rest of the company. Therefore, the bicycle division is a component of the company. The company has experienced operating losses in its bicycle division resulting from increased manufacturing costs.
   A. *Sale of a component.* The company decides to exit the bicycle business and sells the division. This is a sale of a component, and any operating income (loss) and any gain (loss) on the sale of the bicycle division are reported in the company's results of discontinued operations.
   B. *Not a sale of a component.* The company decides to remain in the bicycle business but outsources the manufacturing operations and sells the related manufacturing facility. This is *not* a sale of a component because the manufacturing facility is only part of the bicycle division. Any operating income (loss) of the

bicycle division and any gain (loss) on the sale of the manufacturing facility are reported in the company's income from continuing operations.[17]

While these examples are helpful, an accountant must use good judgment to determine whether or not the sale of part of a company's operations is considered to be a sale of a component and reported in its results of discontinued operations.

Operating Income (or Loss)

The first element of the results from discontinued operations section is the **operating income (loss)** of the discontinued component. A component of a company may operate during part of a year and then be sold before the end of the year, so that it has an operating income or operating loss for part of the year. It would be inappropriate to include this income or loss as part of income from continuing operations because the component has been discontinued (sold.) Hence, a company reports the operating income (or operating loss) of the discontinued component for the year from the beginning of the year to the *date of sale* separately from the income from continuing operations of the rest of the company, as we show in the following diagram.

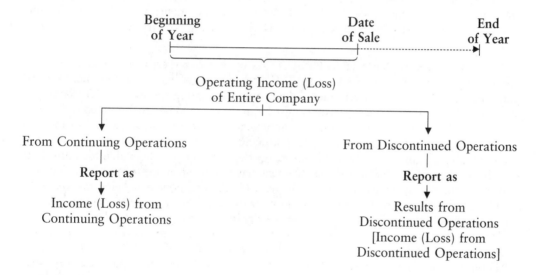

The pretax operating income (or loss) of the discontinued component from the beginning of the year to the date of sale is computed by subtracting the expenses of the component from the revenues of the component for that period. The related income taxes are deducted to determine the after-tax operating income (or loss.)

Gain or Loss on Sale

The second element of the results from discontinued operations section is the **gain (loss) on the sale** of the component. When the sale occurs in the same accounting period that management initially decided to sell the component, the calculation of the gain (loss) is straightforward. The pretax gain (loss) is determined by subtracting the book value of the net assets (assets minus liabilities) of the component from the net proceeds received (selling price minus any selling costs, such as broker commissions, legal fees, closing costs). This is similar to the accounting treatment for the sale of a single asset. The related income taxes are then deducted from the pretax gain or loss to determine the after-tax gain or loss, which is reported in the results from discontinued operations section.

---

17. "Accounting for the Impairment or Disposal of Long-Lived Assets," *FASB Statement of Financial Accounting Standards No. 144* (Norwalk, Conn: FASB, 2001), par. A25–A28.

To illustrate, suppose that on September 30, 2004, Duvall Company sells Division C (a component of its operations) for $102,000 and incurs $2,000 of legal fees and closing costs. At the time of the sale, the book values of Division C's assets and liabilities are $150,000 and $80,000, respectively. Duvall Company is subject to a 30% income tax rate. Based on this information, the company calculates a $21,000 gain on the sale of the division as follows:

Net cash received ($102,000 − $2,000)		$100,000
Book value of net assets of Division C:		
Assets	$150,000	
Liabilities	(80,000)	
Net book value		(70,000)
Pretax gain		$ 30,000
Income taxes (30%)		(9,000)
After-tax gain		$ 21,000

Duvall Company reports the $21,000 gain on the sale of Division C in the results from discontinued operations section of its 2004 income statement, as well as the income (loss) from the operations of discontinued Division C for January through September, 2004.

SALE IN A LATER ACCOUNTING PERIOD   As we noted earlier, it may take some time for a company to plan and make a sale of a component of its operations. Because this time frame may extend over more than one accounting period, *FASB Statement No. 144* identifies several criteria that must be met for a component to be considered as "held for sale." A company classifies a component as *held for sale* at the end of the current accounting period when *all* of the following criteria are met: (1) management has committed to a plan to sell the component, (2) the component is available for immediate sale in its present condition, (3) management has begun an active program to locate a buyer, (4) the sale is probable within one year, (5) the component is being marketed for sale at a price that is reasonable in relation to the component's current fair value, and (6) it is unlikely that management will make significant changes to the plan.

When a company classifies a component as held for sale, it records and reports the component at the lower of (1) its book value (book value of assets minus book value of liabilities) or (2) its fair value less any costs to sell. If the fair value (less any costs to sell) is less than the book value, the company records a loss and adjusts the book values of the *assets* of the component. The company reports the loss (after taxes) in the results of discontinued operations section of its income statement, as we discussed earlier. It reports the assets and the liabilities in the respective asset and liability sections of its ending balance sheet, as we discussed in Chapter 3.

To illustrate, suppose that Elmo Company classifies Division M (a component of its operations) as "held for sale" at the end of 2004. Elmo Company expects to sell Division M in 2005 and estimates that the fair value of Division M is $200,000. For simplicity, we assume that any selling costs are immaterial. At the end of 2004, the book value of Division M is $240,000 (consisting of assets with a book value of $330,000 and liabilities with a book value of $90,000.) The company is subject to a 30% income tax rate. Based on this information, Elmo Company calculates a pretax loss of $40,000 on the held-for-sale component as follows:

Fair value of Division M		$200,000
Book value of net assets of Division M:		
Assets	$330,000	
Liabilities	(90,000)	
Net book value		(240,000)
Pretax loss		$(40,000)

To record the loss and decrease the assets, Elmo Company records the following journal entry at the end of 2004:

Loss on Write-Down of Held-For-Sale Division M (pretax)   40,000
    Assets of Division M   40,000

Elmo Company reports a $28,000 loss [$40,000 pretax loss − $12,000 income tax credit ($40,000 × 30%)] in the results from discontinued operations section of its 2004 income statement, along with the income (loss) from the operations of held-for-sale Division M for all of 2004. Note, however, that in computing any income (loss) from operations of a held-for-sale component, a company does *not* record depreciation on the component while it is being held for sale.[18] Elmo Company reports $290,000 of assets ($330,000 − $40,000) and $90,000 of liabilities for Division M on its December 31, 2004 balance sheet and identifies these as being held-for-sale.

After a company writes down a held-for-sale component to its fair value, there may be subsequent changes (increases or decreases) in this fair value. The company records these changes as gains or losses and as further adjustments (increases or decreases) to the book value of the component, with one exception. The company cannot increase the book value of the component to an amount higher than the component's book value before it was classified as held for sale. These adjustments are made primarily when the company prepares interim financial statements, as we discuss in Chapter 5. The company combines these quarterly gains (losses) and reports only one net gain (loss) in its annual financial statements. Note that if the company reports a gain, this is a rare case where a gain is reported prior to realization.

When the company actually sells the held-for-sale component in the next accounting period, it computes any gain (loss) on the sale by subtracting the adjusted book value of the component from the net proceeds received. (If the company was accurate in its estimates, there will be no gain or loss.) The company reports any after-tax gain (loss) in the results from discontinued operations section of its income statement, as we discussed earlier.

Disclosures

FASB Statement No. 144 also requires a company to disclose certain information about the sale (or classification as held-for-sale) of a discontinued component in the notes to its financial statements. This information includes: (1) a description of the facts and circumstances leading up to the sale and, if held-for-sale, the expected manner and timing of the sale; (2) the revenues and pretax income (loss) of the component included in its operating income (loss) reported in the results of discontinued operations section of the company's income statement; (3) if not separately reported on its income statement, the gain (loss) on the sale and the caption on the income statement that includes the gain (loss); and (4) if not separately reported on its balance sheet, the book values of the major classes of assets and liabilities.[19]

INCOME STATEMENT: EXTRAORDINARY ITEMS

For some companies **extraordinary items** may occur that result in material gains or losses. **APB Opinion No. 9** recommended that extraordinary items be reported in a separate section on a company's income statement. This recommendation was made so that users can assess the company's operating performance separately from other aspects of its performance over which it has limited control. Unfortunately the criteria to be used in identifying an extraordinary item were not well defined, resulting in considerable variations in judgment. As a result the APB further addressed extraordinary items in

7 Identify extraordinary items.

---

18. *Ibid.*, par. 34.
19. *Ibid.*, par. 47.

APB Opinion No. 30. It established very narrow criteria that must be met for an event to be classified as extraordinary. **An extraordinary item is an event or a transaction that is unusual in nature *and* infrequent in occurrence.** *Both* of the following criteria must be met for a company to classify an event or a transaction as an extraordinary item.[20]

a. **Unusual nature**—the underlying event or transaction possesses a high degree of abnormality and is of a type clearly unrelated to, or only incidentally related to, the ordinary and typical activities of the company, taking into account the environment in which the company operates.

b. **Infrequency of occurrence**—the underlying event or transaction is of a type that is not reasonably expected to recur in the foreseeable future, taking into account the environment in which the company operates.

In discussing the **unusual nature** criterion, the APB suggested that **the environment in which a company operates is a primary consideration.** This environment includes such factors as the characteristics of the industry in which the company operates, its geographical location(s), and the nature and extent of government regulation. An event may be unusual in nature for one company but not for another because of differences in their respective environments. Similarly, the determination of whether an event is **infrequent** in occurrence should consider the operating environment of the company. An event might be considered infrequent for one company and frequent for another because of different probabilities of recurrence within each respective operating environment.

To illustrate, a loss from an explosion in an office building of a company may be classified as extraordinary, while a loss from an explosion in a munitions factory may *not* be considered extraordinary because the nature of the event is not unusual. Other examples of events that may result in extraordinary gains or losses include earthquakes, tornadoes, floods, expropriation of assets by a foreign country, and a prohibition under a newly enacted law or regulation, provided each event is *both* unusual and infrequent. One other item is required to be reported as an extraordinary item. As prescribed in **FASB Statement No. 141,** in the rare situation where a company purchases another company and pays less than the fair value of the net assets of the other company, it reports the difference (sometimes called "negative goodwill") as an extraordinary gain.

Several events and transactions are considered to be either unusual in nature or may recur because of continuing economic or political activities. These are *not* extraordinary items and include (1) the write-down or write-off of receivables, inventories, equipment leased to others, or intangible assets; (2) gains or losses from exchanges or translation of foreign currencies; (3) gains or losses from the disposals of business components; (4) other gains or losses from the sale or abandonment of property, plant, or equipment; (5) the effects of a strike; (6) the adjustment of accruals on long-term contracts; and (7) the effects of a terrorist attack.[21]

In order to clarify further the distinction between extraordinary and nonextraordinary items, the following illustrations were presented in a separate pronouncement. **Events or transactions are reported as extraordinary items** when they meet both criteria, as in the following cases:

1. A large portion of a tobacco manufacturer's crops is destroyed by a hailstorm. Severe damage from hailstorms in the locality where the manufacturer grows tobacco is rare.

Goodwill is discussed in Chapter 11.

---

20. "Reporting the Results of Operations," *APB Opinion No. 30* (New York: AICPA, 1973), par. 20.

21. *Ibid.,* par. 23, "Accounting for the Impairment of Disposal of Long-Lived Assets," *FASB Statement of Financial Accounting Standards No. 144* (Norwalk, Conn.: FASB, 2001), par. 43; "Accounting for the Impact of the Terrorist Attacks of September 11, 2001," *FASB Emerging Issues Task Force Issue 01-10* (Norwalk, Conn: FASB, 2001), par. 6. The Emerging Issues Task Force concluded that companies should report all the losses that were directly related to the September 11, 2001, terrorist attacks in income from continuing operations. The primary reason for this decision was that it would be very difficult for a company to separate these losses from those related to its normal operations, and to measure the amounts.

2. A steel-fabricating company sells the only land it owns. The land was acquired 10 years ago for future expansion, but shortly thereafter the company abandoned all plans for expansion and held the land for appreciation.

3. A company sells an investment in a block of common stock of a publicly traded firm. The block of shares, which represents less than 10% of the publicly held firm, is the only security investment the company has ever owned.

4. An earthquake destroys one of the oil refineries owned by a large multinational oil company.

Events or transactions are *not* reported as extraordinary items when they do not meet both criteria, as in these examples:

1. A citrus grower's Florida crop is damaged by frost. Frost damage is normally experienced every three to four years. The criterion of infrequency of occurrence, taking into account the environment in which the company operates, is not met because the history of losses caused by frost damage provides evidence that such damage may be expected to recur in the foreseeable future.

2. A company that operates a chain of warehouses sells the excess land surrounding one of its warehouses. When the company buys property to establish a new warehouse, it usually buys more land than it expects to use for the warehouse with the expectation that the land will appreciate in value. In the past five years there have been two instances in which the company sold such excess land. The criterion of infrequency of occurrence is not met because past experience indicates that such sales may be expected to recur in the foreseeable future.

3. A large diversified company sells a block of shares from a portfolio of securities that it acquired for investment purposes. This is the first sale from its portfolio of securities. Because the company owns several securities for investment purposes, it should be concluded that sales of such securities are related to its ordinary and typical activities in the environment in which it operates, thus the criterion of unusual nature is not met.

4. A textile manufacturer with only one plant moves to another location. It has not relocated a plant in 20 years and has no plans to do so in the foreseeable future. Notwithstanding the infrequency of occurrence of the event as it relates to this particular company, moving from one location to another is an occurrence that is a consequence of customary and continuing business activities. Therefore the criterion of unusual nature is not met.[22]

As in the case of discontinued operations, good judgment must be exercised in determining whether an item is extraordinary.

Material extraordinary gains or losses are reported (net of income taxes) on a company's income statement below the results from discontinued operations (if any). Materiality of the gain or loss should be assessed in relation to income before extraordinary items, to trends in this income, or by other appropriate criteria. Assuming no cumulative effects of a change in accounting principle (discussed in the next section), the suggested format is as follows (using assumed amounts):

Income before extraordinary items	$87,000
Extraordinary gain . . . (net of $4,800 income taxes, Note D)	11,200
Net income	$98,200

If a company has more than one extraordinary item, *individual* extraordinary gains and losses should be disclosed in the income statement or in the notes to the financial statements. The income taxes applicable to the extraordinary items should be disclosed on the face of the income statement, although disclosure in the notes is acceptable. Either

---

22. *Accounting Interpretations of APB Opinion No. 30* (New York: AICPA, 1973).

EXHIBIT 4-9 Extraordinary Items

EXXONMOBIL CORPORATION

CONSOLIDATED STATEMENTS OF INCOME (in part)

Years Ended December 31 (in millions of dollars)	2000
(millions of dollars)	
Income before extraordinary item and cumulative effect of accounting change	$15,990
Extraordinary gain from required asset divestitures, net of income tax	1,730
Net income	$17,720

NOTES TO CONSOLIDATED FINANCIAL STATEMENTS (in part)

2. Extraordinary Item and Accounting Change (in part)
Net income for 2000 included a net after-tax gain of $1,730 million (net of $308 million of income taxes), or $0.49 per common share—assuming dilution, from asset divestments that were required as a condition of the regulatory approval of the Merger. The net after-tax gain on required divestments was reported as an extraordinary item according to accounting requirements...

Q U E S T I O N S

Q Why did ExxonMobil have an extraordinary gain in 2000? **Q** What was the *pretax* amount of the extraordinary gain? **Q** What activities did the company engage in that resulted in the extraordinary gain?

of these disclosure techniques requires intraperiod tax allocation. The Extraordinary Item section of the Banner Corporation income statement is shown earlier in Exhibit 4-2 (the related income taxes were taken from Exhibit 4-6). **ExxonMobil** reported an extraordinary item in 2000, as we show in Exhibit 4-9.

The APB also addressed the disclosure of material gains and losses from events that are *either* unusual in nature *or* infrequent in occurrence, *but not both*. The examples cited earlier as events that are not extraordinary in nature generally would fall into this category. The APB required that a company reports material unusual or infrequent gains or losses as a separate component of income from continuing operations. We suggest including these items in the Other Items section, as we illustrated earlier. Because these items are a component of income from continuing operations, for which a related income tax expense is computed, unusual or infrequent gains or losses are *not* shown net of income taxes. The following diagram illustrates where to report gains and losses on a company's income statement:

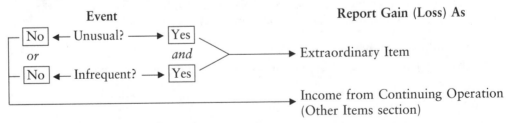

While the interpretation of what is unusual and infrequent still requires professional judgment, it was the intent of the APB to reduce the number of extraordinary items. As a result of the issuance of *APB Opinion No. 30*, very few companies now report extraordinary items.[23]

---

23. Prior to 2003, companies were required to report material gains or losses from the extinguishment of debt as extraordinary items. *FASB Statement No. 145* prohibits this classification.

INCOME STATEMENT: EFFECTS OF ACCOUNTING CHANGES

Occasionally a company makes an accounting change. Accounting changes may be classified into four categories: (1) a change in an accounting principle, (2) a change in an accounting estimate, (3) a correction of an error, and (4) a change in the reporting entity. We briefly discuss a voluntary change in an accounting principle and a change in an accounting estimate here because each has an impact upon a company's income statement.

Accounting changes are discussed in Chapter 22.

Change in Accounting Principle

In *APB Opinion No. 20* the APB stated that **a change in accounting principle occurs when a company adopts a generally accepted accounting principle different from the one it has been using in its financial reporting.** Here the term "accounting principle" includes not only principles, but also accounting practices and the methods of application.[24] The consistent use of accounting principles from year to year improves intracompany comparability. Consequently, there is a presumption that once a company adopts an accounting principle, it continues to use that principle for similar transactions. However, consistency does not preclude a change in accounting principle when this change results in more informative financial statements. A company must justify a voluntary change in accounting principle. Examples of changes in principles include (1) a change in the method of inventory costing, such as from first-in, first-out (FIFO) to average cost; and (2) a change in the depreciation *method* for previously recorded assets, such as a switch from double-declining balance to straight-line depreciation.

In most instances, for a change in accounting principle, a company reports the cumulative effect on *prior* years' earnings in its net income for the *year in which it makes the change.* That is, the related existing asset or liability account balance at the *beginning* of the current year is recalculated. The *new* balance is determined under the assumption that the new accounting principle was applied during prior years. The account is debited or credited to bring its balance to the required amount, and the offsetting credit or debit is the cumulative effect of the change in accounting principle on *prior* years' earnings and is included in net income. **This cumulative effect (net of the related income tax effect) is reported directly after any extraordinary items and directly preceding net income.** For instance, suppose a company acquired certain equipment in 2000 and was depreciating it using the double-declining-balance method. At the beginning of 2004, it decides to change to the straight-line method for this equipment. To make this change, the company calculates its total depreciation *to date* under the straight-line method. It records the difference in total depreciation between the two methods as a *decrease* in the Accumulated Depreciation account balance at the beginning of 2004. If the company had actually used the straight-line method in the prior years, the lesser depreciation expense in each of those years would also result in increased earnings in those years. The company records the *cumulative* increase in the prior earnings as an *increase* to a "Cumulative Effect" account and reports this amount (net of income taxes) on its 2004 income statement. Exhibit 4-3 illustrates this disclosure for the Banner Corporation.

A company then applies the new accounting principle during the current year. It discloses the effect of adopting the new principle on income before extraordinary items, net income, and earnings per share for the *current* year in a note to its financial statements.[25] This note includes an explanation and justification for the adoption of the new accounting principle. In our example the company would disclose the effect on net income caused by the difference in depreciation expense for 2004 that resulted from using the straight-line method rather than the double-declining-balance method in such a note. Changes in accounting principles that have a material effect on income are relatively rare.

Some changes in accounting principles are accounted for differently, as explained in Chapter 22.

---

24. "Accounting Changes," *APB Opinion No. 20* (New York: AICPA, 1971), par. 7.
25. In addition, the pro forma effects of the retroactive application of the accounting principle are disclosed on the face of the income statement, as we discuss in Chapter 22.

Change in Accounting Estimate

Because companies present financial statements on a periodic basis, accounting estimates are necessary, and changes in these estimates frequently occur. Examples include changes in estimates of uncollectible receivables, inventory obsolescence, service lives and residual values of depreciable or depletable assets, and warranty costs. These changes may arise as a result of new events, as additional experience is acquired, or as more information is obtained. Note that they are *not* corrections of errors (which are prior period adjustments, discussed later), but instead are changes due to additional facts not known at the time the original estimate was made. **When a company changes an accounting estimate, it accounts for the change in the current year, and in future years if the change affects both.** For instance, suppose that in 2004, due to new information, a company determines that a machine it owns has a remaining life of five years instead of its original estimate of eight years. The company bases the depreciation on the machine in 2004 and future years on the shorter five-year life. As a result, the company reports a higher depreciation expense on its current and future income statements. No restatement of prior years' financial statements is made. However, in the year of the change in estimate a company includes a note to its financial statements that shows the effect of the change on that year's income before extraordinary items, net income, and earnings per share. This note is included not only for a material change in estimate that affects several future years but also for a material change that affects only the current year.[26] Thus, in this example, the company discloses the effect on each of these income items due to the increase in depreciation expense in a note to its 2004 financial statements.

INCOME STATEMENT: EARNINGS PER SHARE

Net income frequently is referred to as the "bottom line" on a company's income statement because it is the sum of income from continuing operations, the results from discontinued operations, extraordinary items, and the cumulative effect of a change in accounting principle. Actually the term "bottom line" is a misnomer because **earnings per share information must be reported on a company's income statement, and this disclosure usually is shown directly below the net income.**

Earnings per share is an important ratio in financial analysis. It is often used to predict future earnings and dividends and is compared to the market price at which a stock currently is selling to determine the relative attractiveness of that stock. Earnings per share refers only to common stock. **In its simplest form, earnings per share is computed by dividing the net income by the number of common shares outstanding throughout the entire year.** Frequently companies refer to this as "basic earnings per share." However, many companies have preferred stock outstanding, which has first priority to dividends. They may also have some shares of common stock outstanding for only a portion of the year. Other companies have complex capital structures that include securities such as convertible preferred stock, convertible bonds, and stock options that may be converted into shares of common stock. The conversion of these securities to common stock would have an impact on the denominator (and in certain cases the numerator) of the earnings per share ratio. Therefore, companies with complex capital structures are required to disclose additional earnings per share information (called "diluted earnings per share"), as we discuss in Chapter 16.

All companies are required to report the earnings per share amounts relating to income from continuing operations and net income on their income statements. It is also required that earnings per share amounts for the results from discontinued operations, extraordinary items, and the cumulative effect of any change in accounting principle be reported on the income statement (or in a note to the financial statements).[27] We suggest the presentation of an earnings per share schedule that shows

---

26. *APB Opinion No. 20, op. cit.,* par. 33.
27. "Earnings per Share," *FASB Statement of Financial Accounting Standards No. 128* (Norwalk, Conn.: FASB, 1997), par. 37.

the per share amounts (after tax) associated with each of the major components of net income and culminates in the per share amount related to net income. The schedule also should disclose the number of common shares used in the calculations. The format of this schedule is shown here (using assumed amounts and ignoring diluted earnings per share):

Net income $49,600

Components of Income	Earnings per Common Share (10,000 common shares)
Income from continuing operations	$4.05
Results from discontinued operations	(0.63)
Extraordinary gain	0.84
Cumulative effect of change in accounting principle	0.70
Net income	$4.96

A similar schedule is shown on the Banner Corporation income statement in Exhibit 4-2. The earnings per share disclosure of Whirlpool Corporation is shown in Exhibit 4-10.

INCOME STATEMENT: RELATED ISSUES

There are several other important issues related to the items that a company reports on its income statement.

Summary of Selected Financial Information

As we discussed in Chapter 3 most companies present a summary of key financial information for a 5- to 10-year period in their annual report to help external users evaluate their performance. Frequently, ratios are included in this summary that either link income statement items or show a relationship between the income statement and balance sheet items. For instance, a company might report its *profit margin* (net income ÷ net sales) to show its efficiency in controlling expenses in relation to sales. It might report the *return on stockholders' equity* (net income ÷ average stockholders' equity) as a measure of the return provided to owners. The Coca-Cola Company presents an 11-year summary of selected financial data, as shown in Appendix A of this book.

The profit margin and return on stockholders' equity ratios are discussed in Chapter 5.

Limitations of the Income Statement

The income statement has several limitations. First, many of the expenses that are matched against revenues are based on an allocation of historical cost (e.g., depreciation expense) instead of "current value." It is argued that the amount of net income under this approach does not adequately distinguish between a return *of* capital and a return *on* capital. Second, many of the expenses (e.g., bad debts, warranties, and depreciation) are based on estimates that are subject to change and are less reliable. Third, in some cases companies may have too much leeway in selecting an accounting method (e.g., LIFO or FIFO for cost of goods sold), which leads to a lack of comparability across companies. Fourth, adherence to rigid accounting rules (e.g., recognizing revenue at the point of sale, expensing research and development costs when incurred) may lead to a distorted picture of a company's earnings activities. Fifth, the use of different formats (e.g., single-step versus multiple-step) by companies in the same industry may hide differences in operating results. Finally, the use of "functional" classifications (e.g., selling and administration) for operating expenses instead of "activity" classifications (fixed, variable) may not provide sufficient information for predicting future cash

EXHIBIT 4-10   Earnings Per Share

WHIRLPOOL CORPORATION

CONSOLIDATED STATEMENTS OF EARNINGS (in part):

(In millions of dollars, except per share data) Year Ended December 31	2001	2000	1999
Earnings from continuing operations	34	367	347
Loss from discontinued operations, net of tax	(21)	—	—
Cumulative effect of change in accounting principle, net of tax	8	—	—
Net earnings	$21	$367	$347
Per share of common stock			
Basic earnings from continuing operations	$0.51	$5.24	$4.61
Loss from discontinued operations, net of tax	(0.32)	—	—
Cumulative effect of change in accounting principle, net of tax	0.12	—	—
Basic net earnings	$0.31	$5.24	$4.61
Diluted earnings from continuing operations	$0.50	$5.20	$4.56
Loss from discontinued operations, net of tax	(0.31)	—	—
Cumulative effect of change in accounting principle, net of tax	0.12	—	—
Diluted net earnings	$0.31	$5.20	$4.56
Dividends	$1.36	$1.36	$1.36
Weighted-average shares outstanding (millions)			
Basic	66.7	70.2	75.2
Diluted	68.0	70.6	76.0

Q U E S T I O N S

Q How did the income or loss from discontinued operations affect basic earnings per share in 2001? **Q** How did the cumulative effect of the accounting change affect basic earnings per share in 2001? **Q** What do you think about the trend in earnings per share from 1999 through 2001? What were the primary causes?

outflows. The FASB is aware of these limitations and either requires or encourages companies to disclose additional information in the notes or supplemental schedules to their financial statements to help users in their decision making.

International Accounting Differences

International Accounting Standards require a company to use accrual accounting under the historical cost framework, considering economic substance instead of legal form. Therefore, U.S. and international accounting standards related to income are similar. In addition, much of a company's income statement content is similar in that international accounting standards require disclosure of revenues, operating expenses, finance costs, tax expense, income (loss) from ordinary activities, results of discontinued operations, extraordinary items, net income (loss), and earnings per share. A company is also required to disclose a form of comprehensive income. However, because it is difficult to obtain agreement on uniform international accounting standards, many of these standards allow a choice of alternative accounting treatments, thus leading to a lack of comparability. The IASB, in collaboration with several national accounting rule-making bodies, is working to eliminate these alternative treatments, which should bring IASB standards closer to U.S. standards.[28]

Currently, several differences exist between U.S. and international accounting standards. We discuss selected differences in later chapters as they relate to specific topics; we identify a few briefly here. For instance, under international accounting standards, a company may use either the percentage-of-completion or completed-contract method for long-term contracts, while U.S. standards specify the conditions for use of each method. Under international standards, a company may make adjustments to depreciation and cost of goods sold to reflect the effects of changing prices. Furthermore, as we discussed in Chapter 3, a company in a hyperinflationary economy is required to restate all revenues and expenses to reflect the general purchasing power and to include any purchasing power gain or loss on net monetary items in net income. The accounting for research and development costs may also differ between U.S. and international accounting standards. As we noted in Chapter 3, some foreign countries provide government grants to companies for compliance with certain conditions. When a company reports these grants as deferred income on its balance sheet, it recognizes them as income in later periods on a systematic and rational basis and includes the income as other income on its income statement. When it treats them as a reduction in the book value of an asset, it recognizes them in later periods on the income statement as a reduction in depreciation expense.

STATEMENT OF RETAINED EARNINGS

Retained earnings is the link between a corporation's balance sheet and its income statement. Retained earnings is the total amount of corporate earnings that has not been returned to stockholders as dividends and is a major component of stockholders' equity. Although *not* a required financial statement, whenever a corporation issues an income statement and a balance sheet, it may include a schedule that reconciles the beginning retained earnings balance with the ending retained earnings balance. This schedule is referred to as the **statement of retained earnings.** Because the all-inclusive concept of net income is used in the income statement presentation, generally the retained earnings statement includes only the addition of net income to and the deduction of dividends from the beginning retained earnings balance. If a corporation has any prior period adjustments, these are also included in the retained earnings statement. The suggested format for the statement is as follows (using assumed amounts):

8 Prepare a statement of retained earnings.

Beginning retained earnings	$59,200
Plus (minus): Prior period adjustment (net of $2,400 income taxes)	5,600
Adjusted beginning retained earnings	$64,800
Plus (minus): Net income (loss)	22,300
	$87,100
Minus: Dividends (specifically identified, including per share amounts)	(9,400)
Ending retained earnings	$77,700

Prior Period Adjustments

FASB Statement No. 16 addressed the issue of prior period adjustments. Before its issuance, there was no agreement on how to report certain items that are in some way related to previous operations. In the *Statement* the FASB concluded that the correction

---

28. See K. Cearns, "Reporting Financial Performance: A Proposed Approach," *Special Report* (Norwalk, Conn.: FASB), 1999.

of a material error in the financial statements of a prior period must be accounted for and reported as a prior period adjustment.[29]

A company occasionally may make an error in the financial statements of one accounting period that is not discovered until a later period. The error may be due to a mathematical mistake, the incorrect use of existing facts, an oversight, the use of an accounting principle that is not generally accepted, or fraud. The correction of a material error is accounted for as a prior period adjustment to the beginning retained earnings balance in the period that the accounts are corrected. The asset or liability account in error at the beginning of the period is corrected, and the offsetting debit or credit amount is made directly to the retained earnings account. For instance, suppose that during 2004 a company found it inadvertently had not recorded depreciation expense on a building in 2003. Thus, in 2003 its depreciation expense was too low, accumulated depreciation was too low, and net income (which was closed to retained earnings) was too high. The correction in 2004 includes a debit to retained earnings and a credit to accumulated depreciation for the amount of the misstated depreciation. Any related impact upon income taxes also is recorded. The company describes and reports the prior period adjustment (net of income taxes) as a decrease in the beginning retained earnings on its statement of retained earnings. As a result, the adjusted beginning retained earnings balance is the amount that retained earnings *would have been* if the error had not been made. Corrections of material errors are relatively rare. The prior period adjustment for the Banner Corporation due to an error in counting the 2003 ending inventory is shown in Exhibit 4-11 (using assumed amounts).

EXHIBIT 4-11   Statement of Retained Earnings

BANNER CORPORATION

Statement of Retained Earnings
For Year Ended December 31, 2004

Retained earnings, January 1, 2004	$68,150
Add: Prior period adjustment, correction of understatement of 2003 ending inventory (net of $1,500 income taxes)	3,500
Adjusted retained earnings, January 1, 2004	$71,650
Add: Net income	10,850
	$82,500
Less: Cash dividends, $0.50 per share	(2,500)
Retained earnings, December 31, 2004	$80,000

Net Income and Dividends

The two most common components of the statement of retained earnings are net income (loss) and dividends. The net income (loss) amount from the income statement is added to (subtracted from) adjusted beginning retained earnings. All dividends declared during the accounting period, including cash dividends on preferred stock and

---

29. "Prior Period Adjustments," *FASB Statement of Financial Accounting Standards No. 16* (Stamford, Conn.: FASB, 1977), par. 11, as amended by "Accounting for Income Taxes," *FASB Statement of Financial Accounting Standards No. 109* (Norwalk, Conn.: FASB, 1992), par. 288(n). This *Statement* did not affect the reporting of a few other rare items as prior period adjustments in accordance with the requirements set out in previous *Opinions* and *Statements*. We discuss these in Chapter 22.

common stock, as well as any stock dividends (dividends involving the distribution of the company's own stock), are subtracted to determine the ending retained earnings balance. Typically, the cash dividends per share are disclosed parenthetically on the statement. Exhibit 4-11 shows the net income and dividend components for the Banner Corporation.

Combined Statements

The statement of retained earnings may be issued as a separate schedule or included either in a schedule that summarizes the changes in stockholders' equity or as a supporting schedule on the income statement directly below net income. Companies are required to disclose separately the changes in all the stockholders' equity accounts. When these disclosures are made in the statement of changes in stockholders' equity, the statement of retained earnings usually is included as part of this statement. Either a separate retained earnings statement or inclusion of the reconciliation in the statement of changes in stockholders' equity is recommended. We do not recommend reconciling the beginning and ending balances of the retained earnings account directly on the income statement because this would add unnecessary additional information to an already-complex financial statement and might confuse users about the amount of income reported by a company.

COMPREHENSIVE INCOME

Earlier in the chapter we noted that the FASB has developed the concept of comprehensive income, and that it generally adheres to the all-inclusive concept of net income. Over the years, however, a number of items of comprehensive income have emerged that bypass the income statement. Generally, the *total* of these items has been reported as a component of stockholders' equity, while the *change* in them has been disclosed in the notes to the financial statements. Some users of financial statements have expressed concern that the changes in these items are "hidden" so that it is difficult to assess the timing and size of a company's future cash flows as they relate to such issues as its risk, financial flexibility, and operating capability.

9 Report comprehensive income.

In response to these users' concerns, the FASB requires companies to report their comprehensive income (or loss) for the accounting period. **A company's comprehensive income consists of two parts: net income and other comprehensive income.** Currently, there are four items of a company's other comprehensive income: (1) any unrealized increase (gain) or decrease (loss) in the market (fair) value of its investments in available-for-sale securities, (2) any change in the excess of its additional pension liability over unrecognized prior service cost, (3) certain gains and losses on "derivative" financial instruments, and (4) any translation adjustment from converting the financial statements of its foreign operations into U.S. dollars. (We discuss the first three items later in the book; the last item is discussed in an advanced accounting book.) If a company has no items of other comprehensive income, then it does not have to report comprehensive income.

The FASB allows for flexibility in which financial statement comprehensive income (or loss) is disclosed. A company may report its comprehensive income under three alternatives:

1. On the face of its income statement
2. In a separate statement of comprehensive income
3. In its statement of changes in stockholders' equity

Whichever financial statement a company uses to report its comprehensive income, the company must display that statement as a *major* financial statement in its annual report. In reporting its comprehensive income, a company must add its other comprehensive income to its net income. The other comprehensive income items may be reported at their gross amounts or net of tax. If each item is reported at its gross amount, then the total pretax amount of other comprehensive income must be reduced by the related income tax expense, and the amount of tax applicable to each item must be reported in the notes to the financial statements. A company is not required to report earnings per share on its comprehensive income.[30]

To illustrate the alternative reporting formats, assume that at the beginning of 2004 the Sara Company's stockholders' equity was as follows: common stock ($10 par, 7,000 shares), $70,000; additional paid-in capital, $50,000; and retained earnings, $80,000. During 2004, the company had revenues of $60,000 and expenses of $40,000, and the income tax rate was 30%. It also issued 2000 shares of its $10 par common stock for $38,000 and paid dividends of $5,000. During 2004, the company invested $21,000 in available-for-sale securities, and at the end of the year the securities have a market value of $26,000 which it reports on its ending 2004 balance sheet. So the company records a $5,000 unrealized increase in the value of these securities.[31] The company shows its other comprehensive income net of tax.

If Sara Company reports its comprehensive income on the income statement (alternative 1), its condensed statement of income and comprehensive income for 2004 would appear as follows:

Statement of Income and Comprehensive Income

Revenues	$60,000
Expenses	(40,000)
Income before income taxes	$20,000
Income tax expense	(6,000)
Net income	$14,000
Other comprehensive income:	
Unrealized increase in value of available-for-sale securities (net of $1,500 income taxes)	3,500
Comprehensive income	$17,500

If Sara Company reports its comprehensive income on a separate statement of comprehensive income (alternative 2), its income statement for 2004 would show net income of $14,000. Its statement of comprehensive income for 2004 would appear as follows:

Statement of Comprehensive Income

Net income	$14,000
Other comprehensive income	
Unrealized increase in value of available-for-sale securities (net of $1,500 income taxes)	3,500
Comprehensive income	$17,500

If Sara Company reports its comprehensive income on its statement of changes in stockholders' equity (alternative 3), its income statement for 2004 would show net income of $14,000. Its statement of changes in stockholders' equity for 2004 would appear as follows:

---

30. "Reporting Comprehensive Income," *FASB Statement of Financial Accounting Standards No. 130* (Norwalk, Conn.: FASB, 1997), par. 15–25.

31. If the company sold some of these securities during the year and recorded a realized gain or loss on these securities, then it would record and report a "reclassification adjustment" as part of its other comprehensive income. We discuss this adjustment in Chapter 14.

Statement of Changes in Stockholders' Equity

	Comprehensive Income	Common Stock, $10 par	Additional Paid-in Capital	Retained Earnings	Accumulated Other Comprehensive Income	Total
Balances, January 1, 2004		$70,000	$50,000	$80,000	$0	$200,000
Comprehensive income						
Net income	$14,000			14,000		14,000
Other comprehensive income						
Unrealized increase in value of available-for-sale securities (net of $1,500 income taxes)	3,500				3,500	3,500
Comprehensive income	$17,500					
Cash dividends paid				(5,000)		(5,000)
Common stock issued		20,000	18,000			38,000
Balances, December 31, 2004		$90,000	$68,000	$89,000	$3,500	$250,500

Regardless of which financial statement Sara Company uses to report its comprehensive income, it would report the $3,500 *total* unrealized increase in the value of its investments in available-for-sale securities as accumulated other comprehensive income in the stockholders' equity section of its December 31, 2004 balance sheet, as we discussed in Chapter 3. Currently, about 81% of surveyed companies report their comprehensive income in the statement of changes in stockholders' equity, while 13% report it in a separate statement of comprehensive income and only 6% report it on a statement of income and comprehensive income.[32]

We show the relationship of a company's comprehensive income (or loss) components and its "flow" into the company's balance sheet accounts in the following diagram:

Beginning Retained Earnings   +(−) Net Income (Loss)   − Dividends = Ending Retained Earnings

Beginning Accumulated Other   +(−) Other Comprehensive   = Ending Accumulated Other
Comprehensive Income (Loss)   Income (Loss)   Comprehensive Income (Loss)
                     Comprehensive Income (Loss)

General Motors Corporation reports its comprehensive income in its statement of stockholders' equity. For 2001, it reported net income of $601 million and reported an other comprehensive loss of $10,329 million. The other comprehensive loss included a $417 million loss from foreign currency translation adjustments, a $307 million loss on derivatives, $69 million unrealized losses on securities, and a $9,536 million loss on its minimum pension liability adjustment.

Conceptual Evaluation

In the *Exposure Draft* for *FASB Statement No. 130*, the Board planned to require companies to report comprehensive income in one or two statements of financial performance (i.e., types of "income statements"), and to report a per share amount for comprehensive income. Many companies and users of these statements objected to the FASB's approach for several reasons. First, they argued that reporting both net income

---

32. *Accounting Trends and Techniques* (New York: AICPA, 2001), p. 401.

and comprehensive income on one income statement would result in reduced *under-standability*—that users would not be able to determine which measure is appropriate for investment and credit decisions or capital resource allocation. Second, they argued that the items of other comprehensive income are not "performance related" and it would not be *relevant* to include them on an income statement. Third, some argued that comprehensive income would be volatile from period to period and that this volatility would be related to market forces beyond the control of a company's management. Finally, they argued that requiring the reporting of a per share amount for comprehensive income would be confusing and lead to a lack of *comparability*, because some analysts would quote earnings per share while other analysts would quote comprehensive income per share. The FASB responded to these criticisms by allowing flexibility in reporting comprehensive income and by not requiring the reporting of the related per share amount. Because of this flexibility, many companies report their comprehensive income in their statement of changes in stockholders' equity and display this statement as a major financial statement in their annual reports.

STATEMENT OF CASH FLOWS

10 Explain the statement of cash flows.

Traditionally, every company prepared an income statement for its accounting period and a balance sheet at the end of the period. The income statement reported the profitability of its operating activities while the balance sheet reported its ending financial position. Many external users asked questions about a company's "funds" flows, such as how were funds from operations generated? How was expansion financed? How was long-term debt retired? What happened to the proceeds from the issuance of capital stock? These questions could not be answered directly from the income statement or the balance sheet information. The APB realized that a gap existed in the reporting of a company's financial activities, and *APB Opinion No. 19* was issued in 1971. This *Opinion* required that a company prepare a statement of changes in financial position along with its balance sheet and income statement. The *Opinion* permitted companies flexibility in their choice of the definition of funds, classifications, and formats of the statement. Over the years, external users expressed concern that diversity in the focus of the statement, differences in the definitions of funds from operating activities, variations in classifications of funds flows, and differences in formats of the statement caused a lack of comparability across companies. They also recognized the importance of information about a company's *cash* flows.

As a result, **FASB Statement No. 95**, entitled "Statement of Cash Flows," was issued. This *Statement* requires that **a company present a statement of cash flows for the accounting period along with its income statement and balance sheet.** The primary purpose of a statement of cash flows is to provide relevant information about a company's cash receipts and cash payments during an accounting period. Therefore, the statement of cash flows provides information about the cash effects of a company's operating, investing, and financing activities during an accounting period. Because this statement is related to the other financial statements and is an integral part of a company's annual report, we briefly discuss it next.

The preparation of the statement of cash flows is discussed in Chapter 21.

Conceptual Overview and Uses of the Statement of Cash Flows

In Chapter 2 we noted that one of the specific objectives of financial reporting is to provide information about a company's cash flows. The statement of cash flows is useful in meeting this objective. Furthermore, external users are interested in information to assess a company's **liquidity** (the nearness to cash of its assets and liabilities), **financial flexibility** (its ability to take effective actions to alter the amount and timing of future cash flows so the company can respond to unexpected needs and opportunities), and **operating capability** (its ability to maintain a given physical level of operations). The statement of cash flows also is useful in meeting these information needs. When used with a company's other financial statements, **the statement of cash flows helps external users assess:**

1. The company's ability to generate positive future cash flows
2. The company's ability to meet its obligations and pay dividends
3. The company's need for external financing
4. The reasons for differences between the company's net income and associated cash receipts and payments
5. Both the cash and noncash aspects of the company's investing and financing transactions during the accounting period[33]

Reporting Guidelines and Practices

To aid external users in making the preceding assessments, *FASB Statement No. 95* requires that **a statement of cash flows must report on a company's cash inflows, cash outflows, and net change in cash from its operating, investing, and financing activities during the accounting period, in a manner that reconciles the beginning and ending cash balances.** This reconciliation causes the statement of cash flows to **articulate** with the balance sheet.

A company's *operating activities* include all the transactions and other events related to its earning process, such as those involved in acquiring, producing, selling, and delivering goods for sale, as well as providing services. *Investing activities* include transactions involving acquiring and selling property, plant, and equipment; acquiring and selling long-term investments; and lending money and collecting on the loans. *Financing activities* include transactions involved in obtaining resources from owners and providing them with a return on, and of, their investment, as well as obtaining resources from creditors and repaying the amounts borrowed.

These activities generate cash flows (inflows and outflows) that can be categorized according to each activity as follows:

This categorization is used in the statement of cash flows.

The statement of cash flows of a company includes three major sections: (1) net cash flow from operating activities, (2) cash flows from investing activities, and (3) cash flows from financing activities.[34] The **Net Cash Flow from Operating Activities** section reports the cash flows from the operating activities of the company. The most common way to prepare this section is called the *indirect method*.[35] Under this method, net income is listed first and then adjustments (additions or subtractions) are made to net income:

11 Classify cash flows as operating, investing, or financing.

1. To eliminate certain amounts, such as depreciation expense, that were included in net income but that did not involve a cash inflow or cash outflow for operating activities

---

33. "Statement of Cash Flows," *FASB Statement of Financial Accounting Standards No. 95* (Stamford, Conn.: FASB, 1987), par. 3–6.

34. Transactions involving investing and financing activities that *do not* affect cash receipts or cash payments also are included in a separate schedule accompanying the statement of cash flows. We discuss this schedule in Chapter 21.

35. According to *Accounting Trends and Techniques* (New York: AICPA, 2001, p. 505), over 98% of surveyed companies use the indirect method.

2. To include any changes in the current assets (other than cash) and current liabilities involved in the company's operating cycle that affected cash flows differently than net income

These adjustments are made to convert the net income to the net cash provided by (or used in) operating activities. The indirect method has the advantage of showing the "quality" of income by providing information about differences between income flows and operating cash flows.

The **Cash Flows from Investing Activities** section includes all the cash inflows and outflows involved in the investing activities transactions of the company. The most common cash inflows from and cash outflows for investing activities are:

1. Receipts from selling property, plant, and equipment
2. Receipts from selling investments in stocks and debt securities (e.g., bonds)
3. Payments for purchases of property, plant, and equipment
4. Payments for investments in stocks and debt securities

Similarly, the **Cash Flows from Financing Activities** section includes all the cash inflows and cash outflows involved in the financing activities transactions of the company. The most common cash inflows from and cash outflows for financing activities are:

1. Receipts from the issuance of debt securities (e.g., bonds, mortgages, notes)
2. Receipts from the issuance of stocks
3. Payments of dividends
4. Payments to retire debt securities
5. Payments to reacquire stock (i.e., treasury stock)

To complete the statement of cash flows, the cash inflows and outflows within each section are subtotaled, the subtotals are summed to determine the net increase (or decrease) in cash of the company during the accounting period, and the net change in cash is added to or subtracted from the beginning cash balance to reconcile to the ending cash balance reported on the company's year-end balance sheet.[36]

Exhibit 4-12 shows the statement of cash flows of the Trevor Corporation for 2004 (using the *indirect* method for operating activities). The statement of cash flows of the Coca-Cola Company, as presented in its 2001 annual report, is shown in Appendix A. Note in Exhibit 4-12 that the Trevor Corporation provided a net cash inflow of $70,400 from its *operating activities* in 2004. This amount was determined by adjusting the $59,600 net income for several differences between its income flows and cash flows. For instance, depreciation expense of $16,500 was "added back" to net income because it had been deducted as an expense on the income statement but there was no cash outflow. On the other hand, the $1,800 increase in accounts receivable was subtracted because this increase resulted from credit sales, which increased sales revenue (and net income) on the income statement, but provided no cash inflow at the time of the sale. The other adjustments to net income were made for similar reasons, as we discuss more fully in Chapter 21.

The net cash used for *investing activities* was $78,900. The cash outflows were for the purchase of a building and for an investment in bonds. The cash inflow was from the sale of land. The net cash provided by *financing activities* was $16,600. The cash outflows were for the payment of dividends and a mortgage. The cash inflow was from the issuance of common stock.

The $8,100 net increase in cash was determined by adding the $70,400 net cash provided by operating activities and the $16,600 net cash provided by financing activities, and subtracting the $78,900 net cash used for investing activities. The $8,100 net

---

36. As we noted in Chapter 3, a company may report cash and cash equivalents on its balance sheet. In this case, the reconciliation on the statement of cash flows is to the ending cash and cash equivalents.

EXHIBIT 4-12   Statement of Cash Flows

TREVOR CORPORATION

Statement of Cash Flows
For Year Ended December 31, 2004

Net Cash Flow From Operating Activities

Net income	$ 59,600	
Adjustments for differences between income flows and cash flows from operating activities:		
Add: Depreciation expense	16,500	
Amortization expense	2,000	
Bond discount amortization	1,100	
Decrease in prepaid items	400	
Increase in salaries payable	700	
Increase in income taxes payable	2,200	
Increase in deferred income taxes	900	
Less: Increase in accounts receivable (net)	(1,800)	
Increase in inventories	(7,300)	
Decrease in accounts payable	(2,600)	
Decrease in advances from customers	(1,300)	
Net cash provided by operating activities		$70,400

Cash Flows From Investing Activities

Payment for purchase of building	$(73,900)	
Payment for investment in bonds	(10,000)	
Proceeds from sale of land	5,000	
Net cash used for investing activities		(78,900)

Cash Flows From Financing Activities

Payment of dividends	$(12,400)	
Payment of mortgage	(14,000)	
Proceeds from issuance of common stock	43,000	
Net cash provided by financing activities		16,600
Net Increase in Cash		$ 8,100
Cash, January 1, 2004		17,200
Cash, December 31, 2004		$25,300

increase in cash was added to the $17,200 cash balance on January 1, 2004 to reconcile to the $25,300 cash balance on December 31, 2004.

The other way to report cash flows from operating activities is the *direct method*. In *FASB Statement No. 95*, the FASB encourages use of the direct method. This method has the advantage of separating operating cash inflows from operating cash outflows, which may be useful in estimating future cash flows. Under the direct method, a company's operating cash inflows are listed first. The operating cash outflows are then deducted from the operating cash inflows to determine the net cash provided by (or used in) operating activities. The most common cash inflows from and cash outflows for operating activities are as follows:

The direct and indirect methods are discussed in Chapter 21.

Operating Cash Inflows
1. Collections from customers
2. Interest and dividends collected

Operating Cash Outflows
1. Payments to suppliers and employees
2. Payments of interest
3. Payments of income taxes

If the Trevor Corporation used the direct method *instead* of the indirect method, the operating cash flows section of Exhibit 4-12 would be as follows:

Cash Flows From Operating Activities
 Cash Inflows:

Collections from customers	$248,100	
Interest and dividends collected	3,800	
Cash inflows from operating activities		$251,900
Cash Outflows:		
Payments to suppliers and employees	$(143,600)	
Payments of interest	(17,200)	
Payments of income taxes	(20,700)	
Cash outflows for operating activities		(181,500)
Net cash provided by operating activities		$ 70,400

Note that the $70,400 reported as the net cash provided by operating activities is the same under the direct and indirect methods, only the approach to determining the amount is different. The remainder of the statement of cash flows is the same under either method. You should use the *indirect* method for all homework, unless indicated otherwise.

SUMMARY OF DISCLOSURES

In this chapter we have discussed the conceptual issues and disclosure requirements of numerous complex items concerning corporate earnings and cash flows. Exhibit 4-13 presents a brief summary of the most important pronouncements, the conceptual criteria, and the disclosure requirements for material items. You should review the specific related pronouncements for a complete technical discussion of each topic.

EXHIBIT 4-13 Summary of GAAP for Comprehensive Income and Cash Flows

Item	Pronouncement	Criteria	Disclosure
Income from continuing operations	*APB Opinion No. 30*	Revenues and expenses related to usual and recurring operating activities	Upper portion of income statement. Multiple- or single-step format.
Nonextraordinary gains or losses	*APB Opinion No. 30*	Either unusual in nature or infrequent in occurrence but not both	In income from continuing operations (Other Items) on income statement.
Results from discontinued operations	*FASB Statement No. 144*	Sale of a component of a company	On income statement, directly below income from continuing operations. Include (1) gain or loss on sale, and (2) income or loss from operations of discontinued component. Show both net of income taxes.

EXHIBIT 4-13 (Continued)

Item	Pronouncement	Criteria	Disclosure
Extraordinary gains or losses	*APB Opinions No. 9 and 30; FASB Statements No. 4 and 145*	Unusual in nature *and* infrequent in occurrence	On income statement, directly below results from discontinued operations. Show net of income taxes.
Cumulative effect of change in accounting principle	*APB Opinion No. 20*	Adoption of a generally accepted accounting principle different from one previously used	On income statement, directly below extraordinary items. Show net of income taxes.
Change in accounting estimate	*APB Opinion No. 20*	Modification of accounting estimate due to occurrence of new events, additional experience, or more information	Note to financial statements showing effect of the change on income before extraordinary items, net income, and earnings per share.
Earnings per share	*APB Opinions No. 20 and 30; FASB Statement No. 128*	Net income and components divided by number of common shares outstanding	On income statement, directly below net income. Show earnings per share related to net income and each major component of net income.
Prior period adjustments	*APB Opinions No. 9 and 20; FASB Statements No. 16 and 109*	Correction of a material error in financial statements of a prior period	On statement of retained earnings as adjustment to beginning retained earnings. Show net of income taxes.
Comprehensive income	*FASB Statement No. 130*	Net income plus other comprehensive income	On income statement, statement of comprehensive income, or statement of changes in stockholders' equity
Operating cash flows	*FASB Statement No. 95*	Cash flows related to earning process	First section on statement of cash flows.
Investing cash flows	*FASB Statement No. 95*	Cash flows from lending activities, and from buying and selling noncurrent assets	Second section on statement of cash flows.
Financing cash flows	*FASB Statement No. 95*	Cash flows from issuing and reacquiring debt and equity securities, and for paying dividends	Third section on statement of cash flows.

SUMMARY

At the beginning of the chapter, we identified several objectives you would accomplish after reading the chapter. The objectives are listed below, each followed by a brief summary of the key points in the chapter discussion.

1. **Understand the concepts of income.** Under the capital maintenance concept of income, a corporation's capital (net assets) must be maintained before the corporation earns income on that capital. But the corporation's total income

is not very useful in evaluating its operating activities. To improve the usefulness of its income information, a corporation uses accrual accounting, under the transactional approach, to match its accomplishments with its efforts in order to provide information about the corporation's comprehensive income and its components.

2. **Explain the conceptual guidelines for reporting income.** Some general guidelines are to provide information about a company's operating performance that is useful in (1) predicting future income and cash flows, (2) assessing the return on the investment, (3) providing feedback to assess previous predictions, (4) assessing the cost of maintaining its operating capability, and (5) evaluating management's stewardship.

3. **Define the elements of an income statement.** The elements of an income statement are the broad classes of items comprising it. The elements include revenues, expenses, gains, and losses. Briefly, revenues result from sales of goods or services, while expenses result from providing the goods or services. Gains (losses) are increases (decreases) in a company's equity from other events and circumstances.

4. **Describe the major components of an income statement.** The major components of an income statement are: (1) income from continuing operations, (2) results from discontinued operations, (3) extraordinary items, (4) cumulative effects of changes in accounting principles, (5) net income, and (6) earnings per share.

5. **Compute income from continuing operations.** Income from continuing operations starts with net sales. Cost of goods sold is deducted from net sales to determine gross profit. Total operating expenses (consisting of selling expenses and general and administrative expenses) are deducted from gross profit to determine operating income. The total of any other items is added to (or deducted from) operating income to determine pretax income from continuing operations, from which income tax expense is deducted to determine income from continuing operations.

6. **Compute results from discontinued operations.** The results of discontinued operations consists of the sum of two items: (1) the income from operations of the discontinued component during the accounting period, and (2) the gain (or loss) from the disposal of the component. These items are reported net of taxes.

7. **Identify extraordinary items.** An extraordinary item is an event or a transaction that is both unusual in nature and infrequent in occurrence. Briefly, unusual in nature refers to a high degree of abnormality, while infrequent in occurrence refers to an expectation that the event or transaction will not recur in the foreseeable future.

8. **Prepare a statement of retained earnings.** A statement of retained earnings starts with the beginning balance in retained earnings. Any prior period adjustment (net of taxes) is added or subtracted to determine the adjusted beginning retained earnings. Net income is then added and dividends are subtracted to determine the ending balance in retained earnings.

9. **Report comprehensive income.** A company's comprehensive income is the sum of its net income and other comprehensive income [e.g., unrealized increase (decrease) in market value of its investments in available-for-sale securities]. A company may report its comprehensive income on the face of its income statement, in a separate statement of comprehensive income, or in its statement of changes in stockholders' equity.

10. **Explain the statement of cash flows.** A company's statement of cash flows reports on its cash inflows, cash outflows, and net change in cash from its operating, investing, and financing activities during the accounting period, in a manner that reconciles the beginning and ending cash balances. Its purpose is to help users assess a company's liquidity, financial flexibility, and operating capability.

11. **Classify cash flows as operating, investing, or financing.** A company's operating cash flows result from all the transactions and other events related to its earning process. Its investing cash flows are the cash inflows and outflows resulting from its investing activities (e.g., purchasing equipment). Its financing cash flows are the cash inflows and outflows resulting from its financing activities (e.g., issuing bonds).

QUESTIONS

Q4-1   Define income under the "capital maintenance" concept. Identify the alternative ways of measuring capital under this concept.

Q4-2   Briefly discuss the transactional approach to income measurement. Explain its relationship (if any) to the capital maintenance concept of income.

Q4-3   Define comprehensive income. What was the intent of the FASB in developing this conceptual definition?

Q4-4   Discuss (a) return on investment, (b) risk, (c) financial flexibility, and (d) operating capability.

Q4-5   List the specific conceptual guidelines suggested by the FASB for reporting (presenting) revenues, expenses, gains, and losses.

Q4-6   Define revenues. What operating activities are likely to result in revenues?

Q4-7   What two criteria must ordinarily be met for revenues to be recognized? When does a company usually recognize revenue?

Q4-8   Why might revenue be recognized at a time other than the sale? What are the alternative revenue recognition methods and for what might they be used?

Q4-9   Define expenses. Of what are expenses a measurement?

Q4-10   What are three principles for recognizing the expenses to be matched against revenues? Give examples of expenses that would be recognized under each principle.

Q4-11   Define gains and losses. Give examples of three different types of gains and losses.

Q4-12   What items are included in a company's "income from continuing operations"? How are these categorized if the company uses (a) a single-step format, or (b) a multiple-step format?

Q4-13   Discuss the difference between the "current operating performance" and the "all-inclusive" concepts of net income. Which concept is currently used?

Q4-14   What elements are listed as Other Items on a company's income statement?

Q4-15   What is intraperiod tax allocation and why is it necessary? How is the income tax expense related to each major component of income disclosed on the income statement?

Q4-16   What items are included in a company's results from discontinued operations? For this purpose, how is a "component" defined?

Q4-17   How is an extraordinary item defined? Explain the two criteria that must be met to classify an event as extraordinary. Give two examples of gains or losses from extraordinary items.

Q4-18   How are gains or losses that are either unusual or infrequent reported on a company's income statement?

Q4-19   What is a change in accounting principle and how is it reported on a company's income statement?

Q4-20   Why do changes in accounting estimates arise? Give examples of a change in accounting estimate and indicate how such a change should be accounted for.

Q4-21   Where is earnings per share disclosed in a company's financial statements? What components of earnings per share should be disclosed?

Q4-22   Briefly list several differences between international and U.S. accounting standards in regard to a company's income statement.

Q4-23   What items are included in a company's statement of retained earnings?

Q4-24   What are the possible causes of an error in a company's financial statements? How is the correction of a material error accounted for and how is the correction reported on the financial statements?

Q4-25   What is included in a company's comprehensive income? Currently, what are the four items of a company's other comprehensive income?

Q4-26   Where does a company report its comprehensive income?

Q4-27   What is a statement of cash flows? What are the three major sections of the statement?

Q4-28   When used with a company's other financial statements, what does the statement of cash flows help external users assess?

Q4-29   What are the three types of activities that a statement of cash flows reports on for a company? Provide examples of transactions for each type of activity.

Q4-30   Under the indirect method, how is the net cash provided by operating activities determined in a company's statement of cash flows?

Q4-31   Under the direct method, what are the most common cash inflows from and the most common cash outflows for operating activities in a company's statement of cash flows?

CASES

COMMUNICATION

C4-1   Revenue Recognition

A friend of yours who is not an accounting major states, "I always thought that a company recognizes revenues at the time of sale. Recently, however, I heard that there are specific criteria for revenue recognition and that included in the criteria is something about realization (whatever that means). Furthermore, I also heard that revenue may be recognized before or after the sale. Please explain revenue recognition to me."

Required Prepare a written response for your friend. Include an explanation of the revenue recognition criteria

and realization. Also include a discussion of the reasons for, and alternative methods of, recognizing revenue in a period other than the period of sale.

C4-2   Expense Recognition

The FASB states that expenses are recognized according to three principles to properly match expenses against revenues.

Required Write a concise report that identifies the three principles, briefly explains each, and provide examples of expenses that would be recognized under each principle.

C4-3   Cost, Expense, and Loss

You were requested to personally deliver your auditor's report to the board of directors of Sebal Manufacturing Corporation and answer questions posed about the financial statements. While reading the statements, one director asked, "What are the precise meanings of the terms 'cost,' 'expense,' and 'loss'? These terms seem sometimes to identify similar items and other times dissimilar items."

Required

1. Explain the meanings of the terms (a) "cost," (b) "expense," and (c) "loss" as used for financial reporting in conformity with generally accepted accounting principles. In your explanation discuss the distinguishing characteristics of the terms and their similarities and interrelationships.
2. Classify each of the following items as a cost, expense, loss, or other category, and explain how the classification of each item may change:
   a. Cost of goods sold
   b. Bad debts expense
   c. Depreciation expense for plant machinery
   d. Spoiled goods
3. The terms "period cost" and "product cost" are sometimes used to describe certain items in financial statements. Define these terms and distinguish between them. To what types of items does each apply? (*AICPA adapted*)

C4-4   Results of Discontinued Operations

FASB Statement No. 144 dealt with, among other issues, reporting the results of discontinued operations. In the *Statement*, a section of the income statement was created and several terms were defined, including "component."

Required Identify the elements of a company's results of discontinued operations section of its income statement. Define the previously listed term and explain how the elements of the section are computed if the company sells a component in the same accounting period that its management decided to sell the component.

C4-5   Extraordinary Items

APB Opinion No. 30 establishes two narrow criteria that must be met in order for an event or transaction to be classified as an extraordinary item.

Required

1. Identify and explain each criterion.
2. Develop examples of events that might be extraordinary to one company but not extraordinary to another, such as:
   a. An earthquake
   b. A flood
   c. A tornado
   d. A severe frost
   Justify your reasoning.
3. Explain how the following are reported on a company's income statement:

   a. An extraordinary item
   b. An event or transaction that does not meet both criteria

C4-6   Extraordinary Items

Morgan Company grows various crops and then processes them for sale to retailers. In the latter part of this year, Morgan had a large portion of its crops destroyed by a hail storm. Morgan has incurred substantial costs in raising the crops destroyed by the hail storm. Severe damage from hail storms in the locality where the crops are grown is rare.

Required

1. Where should Morgan report the effects of the hail storm in its income statement? Why?
2. How does the classification in the income statement of an extraordinary item differ from that of an operating item? Why? Do not discuss earnings per share requirements. (*AICPA adapted*)

C4-7   Nonrecurring Items

Lynn Company sells a component of its business in the middle of the year. On the date of sale, the net proceeds received were less than the aggregate book value of the component's net assets. The component was operating at a loss from the beginning of the year.

In addition, Lynn had one of its manufacturing plants destroyed by an earthquake during the year. The loss is properly reported as an extraordinary item.

Required

1. Explain how Lynn should report discontinued operations of a component of its business on its income statement for this year. Do not discuss earnings per share requirements.
2. What are the criteria for classification as an extraordinary item?
3. Explain how Lynn should report the extraordinary loss from the earthquake on its income statement for this year.

Do not discuss earnings per share requirements. (*AICPA adapted*)

C4-8   Statement of Cash Flows

The president of a company, which is being audited for the first time, is concerned about all the unnecessary financial information the company is being required to disclose, and says, "We have always prepared only a balance sheet and an income statement. Surely these are enough. The only information anyone is interested in is how much we earned and what we have left. Now I am told we must prepare a statement of cash flows. What is this statement, what information does it provide, what are the major sections of the statement, and what is included in each section (under the indirect method)?"

Required Prepare a written response that answers the president's questions.

CREATIVE AND CRITICAL THINKING

C4-9 Capital Maintenance

At the beginning of 1992 the Hill family organized the Hill Corporation and issued 8,000 shares of stock to family members for $20 per share. During 1995 it issued an additional 1,600 shares of stock for $25 per share to family members. The 9,600 shares were held by the family until the corporation was liquidated at the end of 2004. At that time the corporate assets were sold for $600,000 and the $50,000 of corporate liabilities were paid off. The remainder was returned to stockholders. During the 13 years of operation the corporation had a volatile operating life. It started out slowly but then increased its activities in later years. It had operated in several industry segments, being quite successful in some, not so successful in others. It had survived a major earthquake, but not without incurring significant losses. The corporation paid out dividends of $100,000 during its lifetime.

You are a member of the Hill family who has just inherited a sizable fortune from one of your relatives. Although you were quite young during the operating life of the Hill Corporation, you are considering establishing and investing in a new corporation that operates in some of the same lines of business, provided that the corporation would be profitable. You have just received your undergraduate accounting degree and upon investigation find that, with the exception of the preceding information, all the corporate accounting records were destroyed in a recent fire. You have been told that these records were sketchy at best, but that a capital maintenance approach to income measurement might yield some useful information.

Required Compute the lifetime income of the Hill Corporation and comment upon what additional information you would desire before making your investment decision.

C4-10 Accrual Accounting

Generally accepted accounting principles require the use of accruals and deferrals in the determination of income.

Required

1. Explain how accrual accounting affects the determination of a company's income. Include in your discussion what constitutes an accrual and a deferral, and give appropriate examples of each.
2. Contrast accrual accounting with cash accounting. (*AICPA adapted*)

C4-11 Ethics and Sale of Operating Component

It is the end of 2004, and, as an accountant for Newell Company, you are preparing its 2004 financial statements. On December 29, 2004, the management of Newell decided to sell one of its major divisions, subject to some legal work that is expected to be completed during the first week in April 2005 (after the 2004 financial statements have been issued). During 2004, the division earned a small operating income that is just enough for the company to report "record earnings" for the year. However, the estimated fair value of the division at the end of 2004 is less than its net book value, so that management anticipates the component will be sold at a loss.

The president of Newell stops by your office and says to you, "You have been doing a fine job. Keep up the good work, because you are heading for a promotion in early 2006. Once we report the record earnings for 2004, our stockholders and creditors will be happy. Then I think our earnings for 2005 will be high enough so that the loss we expect to report in 2005 on the sale of the division will not look so bad." After the president leaves your office, you continue preparing the 2004 financial statements.

Required From financial reporting and ethical perspectives, what information, if any, will you include about the upcoming sale of the division in the 2004 financial statements?

RESEARCH

C4-12 Researching GAAP

During 2004, one of the customers of Klote Company declared bankruptcy. This customer had been a major purchaser of Klote's products and had owed $40,000 on account to Klote (a material portion of its receivables) at the time of bankruptcy. As a result of the bankruptcy, Klote had to write off the entire $40,000 account receivable of the customer as a loss. The president of Klote is concerned about how to report this loss on the company's 2004 income statement. The president says, "Since this company that went bankrupt was a major customer, surely that is an unusual and infrequent event, and the

$40,000 should be reported as an extraordinary loss. What do you think?"

Required Research the related generally accepted accounting principles and prepare a short memo to the president that summarizes how to report the $40,000 loss on Klote's 2004 income statement. Cite your reference and applicable paragraph numbers.

C4-13 Researching GAAP

The Kelly Company, a small corporation, is preparing its 2004 financial statements. At the end of 2004, the company purchased a building for $100,000, paying $20,000 as a down payment and signing an $80,000 mortgage. The president of Kelly is concerned about how to report this transaction on the company's statement of cash flows and has asked you to "look into this issue for me."

Required Research the related generally accepted accounting principles and prepare a short memo to the president that summarizes how to report this transaction on the 2004 statement of cash flows. Cite your reference and applicable paragraph numbers.

MULTIPLE CHOICE

Select the best answer for each of the following.

M4-1   The following information is available for Cooke Company for the current year:

Net sales	$1,800,000
Freight-in	45,000
Purchases discounts	25,000
Ending inventory	120,000

The gross margin is 40% of net sales. What is the cost of goods available for sale?

a. $840,000   c. $1,200,000
b. $960,000   d. $1,220,000

M4-2   A transaction that is material in amount, unusual in nature, and infrequent in occurrence is presented in the income statement separately as a component of income

a. Net of applicable income taxes
b. As a prior period adjustment
c. From continuing operations
d. From discontinued operations

M4-3   Effective January 1, 2004, Younger Company adopted the accounting principle of expensing as incurred advertising and promotion costs. Previously, advertising and promotion costs applicable to future periods were recorded in prepaid expenses. Younger can justify the change, which was made for both financial statement and income tax reporting purposes. Younger's prepaid advertising and promotion costs totaled $500,000 at December 31, 2003. Assume that the income tax rate is 30% for 2003 and 2004. The adjustment for the effect of this change in accounting principle should result in a net charge against income in the 2004 income statement of

a. $0   c. $350,000
b. $150,000   d. $500,000

M4-4   A company changes from the double-declining-balance method of depreciation for previously recorded assets to the straight-line method. The cumulative effect of the change on the amount of retained earnings at the beginning of the period in which the change is made is reported separately as a(n)

a. Extraordinary item
b. Component of income after extraordinary items
c. Component of income from continuing operations
d. Prior period adjustment

M4-5   Palo Corporation incurred the following losses, net of applicable income taxes, for the year ended December 31, 2004:

Loss on disposal of a component of Palo's business	$400,000
Loss on translation of foreign currency due to devaluation	500,000

How much should Palo report as extraordinary losses on its 2004 income statement?

a. $0   c. $500,000
b. $400,000   d. $900,000

M4-6   Which of the following is expensed under the principle of systematic and rational allocation?

a. Salespeople's monthly salaries
b. Insurance premiums
c. Transportation to customers
d. Electricity to light office building

M4-7   The following information is available for Wagner Corporation for the current year:

Sales	$500,000
Beginning inventory	180,000
Ending inventory	95,000
Freight-out	45,000
Purchases	215,000

How much is the cost of goods sold?

a. $200,000   c. $345,000
b. $300,000   d. $440,000

M4-8   Dobbin Corporation, a manufacturer of household paints, is preparing annual financial statements at December 31, 2004. Because of a recently proven health hazard in one of its paints, the government has clearly indicated its intention of having Dobbin recall all cans of this paint sold in the last six months. The management of Dobbin estimates that this recall would cost $1,000,000. What accounting recognition, if any, should be accorded this situation?

a. No recognition
b. Footnote disclosure
c. Operating expense of $1,000,000
d. Extraordinary loss of $1,000,000

M4-9   A loss from the sale of a component of a business enterprise is reported separately as a component of income

a. After cumulative effect of accounting changes and before extraordinary items
b. Before cumulative effect of accounting changes and after extraordinary items
c. After extraordinary items and cumulative effect of accounting changes

d. Before extraordinary items and cumulative effect of accounting changes

a. Investing activities
b. Selling activities
c. Operating activities
d. Financing activities

M4-10   In a statement of cash flows, receipts from sales of property, plant, and equipment generally are classified as

(AICPA adapted)

EXERCISES

E4-1   ***Simple Income Statement***   The following are selected account balances of the Albertson Company as of December 31, 2004:

Purchases (net)	$63,000	Sales (net)	$100,000
Merchandise inventory, January 1, 2004	20,000	Operating expenses	22,000
Gain on sale of equipment	5,000	Extraordinary loss (pretax)	8,000

The merchandise inventory on December 31, 2004 is $31,000. Ten thousand shares of common stock have been outstanding the entire year.

Required   Assuming a 30% income tax rate on all items of income, prepare a 2004 income statement for Albertson Company using (1) a multiple-step format, and (2) a single-step format.

E4-2   ***Simple Income Statement, Manufacturing***   The following are selected accounts taken from the adjusted trial balance of the Dibb Manufacturing Company on December 31, 2004:

Finished goods inventory, January 1, 2004	$ 70,000	Sales (net)	$198,000
Loss on sale of land	5,000	Operating expenses	45,000
Cost of goods manufactured	120,000	Extraordinary gain (pretax)	6,000

The finished goods inventory on December 31, 2004 is $60,000. Twelve thousand shares of common stock were outstanding the entire year.

Required   Assuming a 30% income tax rate on all items of income, prepare a 2004 income statement for Dibb Maufacturing using (1) a multiple-step format and (2) a single-step format.

E4-3   ***Classifications***   Where would each of the following 16 items most likely be reported in a company's financial statements? Assume the monetary amount of each item is material.

1. Purchases returns and allowances
2. Sales discounts taken
3. Depreciation expense on sales equipment
4. Loss from operations of discontinued Division B
5. Earnings per share
6. Gain on sale of land
7. Administrative salaries
8. Cash dividends on common stock
9. Correction of an error made in a prior period
10. Gain from sale of discontinued Division B
11. Cumulative effect on prior years' income of change in accounting principle
12. Advertising expense
13. Merchandise inventory (ending)
14. Loss from write-off of obsolete inventory
15. Net income
16. Unrealized increase in market value of available-for-sale securities

E4-4   ***Classifications***   Where would each of the following 15 items most likely be reported in a company's financial statements? Assume the monetary amount of each item is material.

1. Loss on sale of equipment
2. Office supplies used
3. Correction of miscount of last year's ending finished goods inventory
4. Raw materials used
5. Delivery expense
6. Dividend revenue
7. Gain from retirement of debt
8. Change in the estimated useful life of office equipment
9. Summary of accounting policies
10. Sales returns and allowances
11. Income tax expense on continuing income
12. Stock dividend
13. Loss resulting from tornado damage
14. Goods in process inventory (ending)
15. Unrealized decrease in market value of available-for-sale securities

E4-5   *Cost of Goods Sold and Income Statement*   The Fanta Company presents you with the following account balances taken from its December 31, 2004 adjusted trial balance:

Inventory, January 1, 2004	$ 43,000	Purchases returns	$3,500
Selling expenses	35,000	Interest expense	4,000
Extraordinary gain (pretax)	23,000	Sales discounts taken	2,000
Purchases	100,000	Gain on sale of property (pretax)	7,000
Sales	250,000	Freight-in	5,000
General and administrative expenses	22,000		

Additional data:

1. A physical count reveals an ending inventory of $22,500 on December 31, 2004.
2. Twenty-five thousand shares of common stock have been outstanding the entire year.
3. The income tax rate is 30% on all items of income.

Required

1. As a supporting document for Requirements 2 and 3, prepare a separate schedule for Fanta Company's cost of goods sold.
2. Prepare a 2004 multiple-step income statement.
3. Prepare a 2004 single-step income statement.

E4-6   *Cost of Goods Sold, Income Statement, and Statement of Comprehensive Income*   The Engle Company lists the following accounts on its adjusted trial balance as of December 31, 2004.

Sales	$147,100	Interest revenue	$ 3,300
Purchases returns	5,200	Purchases discounts taken	2,700
Gain on sale of equipment (pretax)	3,800	Inventory, January 1, 2004	12,100
Freight-in	3,400	Sales returns	8,100
Selling expenses	15,600	Purchases	89,700
Unrealized increase in value of available-		Administrative expenses	24,200
for-sale securities	2,400	Extraordinary loss (pretax)	6,500

The following additional information is also available. The December 31, 2004, ending inventory is $14,700. During 2004, 4,200 shares of common stock were outstanding the entire year. The income tax rate is 30% on all items of income.

Required

1. As a supporting document for Requirements 2 and 3, prepare a separate schedule for Engle Company's cost of goods sold.
2. Prepare a 2004 single-step income statement.
3. Prepare a 2004 multiple-step income statement.
4. Prepare a 2004 statement of comprehensive income.

E4-7   *Cost of Goods Manufactured and Income Statement*   Included in the December 31, 2004 adjusted trial balance of the Gold Company are the following accounts:

Goods in process, January 1, 2004	$ 24,000	Finished goods inventory, January 1, 2004	$34,000
Sales	200,000	Selling expenses	28,000
General and administrative expenses	20,000	Sales returns and allowances	5,000
Raw materials used	42,000	Interest revenue	4,000
Loss from strike (pretax)	9,000	Extraordinary loss (pretax)	17,000
Direct labor	30,000	Factory overhead	31,000

Additional data:

1. The December 31, 2004 ending inventories are (a) goods in process, $28,000, and (b) finished goods, $32,000.
2. Seven thousand shares of common stock have been outstanding the entire year.
3. The income tax rate is 30% on all items of income.

Required

1. As a supporting document for Requirements 2 and 3, prepare a separate schedule for Gold Company's cost of goods sold.

2. Prepare a 2004 single-step income statement.
3. Prepare a 2004 multiple-step income statement.

E4-8   *Cost of Goods Manufactured, Income Statement, and Statement of Comprehensive Income*   On December 31, 2004 the Adandt Company listed the following items in its adjusted trial balance:

Factory overhead	$ 28,000	Loss on sale of equipment (pretax)	$ 2,000
Extraordinary loss (pretax)	8,000	Raw materials used	39,000
Interest revenue	2,500	General and administrative expenses	17,000
Sales returns and allowances	3,000	Sales	163,000
Selling expenses	14,000	Goods in process inventory,	
Finished goods inventory,		January 1, 2004	21,000
January 1, 2004	35,000	Unrealized decrease in value of available-	
Direct labor	32,000	for-sale securities	1,800

Additional data:

1. The December 31, 2004 ending inventories are (a) goods in process, $18,000; and (b) finished goods, $42,000.
2. Seven thousand shares of common stock have been outstanding the entire year.
3. The income tax rate is 30% on all items of income.

Required

1. As a supporting document for Requirements 2 and 3, prepare a separate schedule for Adandt Company's cost of goods sold.
2. Prepare a 2004 multiple-step income statement.
3. Prepare a 2004 single-step income statement.
4. Prepare a 2004 statement of comprehensive income.

E4-9   *Income Statement and Retained Earnings*   The Senger Company presents the following partial list of account balances taken from its December 31, 2004 adjusted trial balance:

Retained earnings, January 1, 2004	$ 45,800	Operating expenses	$30,400
Sales (net)	124,000	Inventory, January 1, 2004	18,400
Interest expense	3,700	Common stock, $5 par	22,000
Purchases (net)	67,000		

The following information is also available for 2004 and is not reflected in the preceding accounts:

1. The ending inventory is $19,200.
2. The common stock has been outstanding all year. A cash dividend of $1.28 per share was declared and paid.
3. Land was sold at a pretax gain of $6,300.
4. Division X (a component of the company) was sold at a pretax gain of $4,700. It had incurred a $9,500 pretax operating loss during 2004.
5. A tornado, which is an unusual and infrequent event in the area, caused a $5,400 pretax loss.
6. The income tax rate on all items of income is 30%.
7. The average stockholders' equity is $90,000.

Required

1. Prepare a 2004 multiple-step income statement for Senger Company.
2. Prepare a 2004 retained earnings statement.
3. Compute the 2004 return on stockholders' equity (net income ÷ average stockholders' equity).

E4-10   *Income Statement and Retained Earnings*   The Cobler Manufacturing Company presents the following partial list of account balances taken from its December 31, 2004 adjusted trial balance:

Operating expenses	$ 35,800	Common stock, $15 par	$45,000
Dividend revenue	1,000	Finished goods inventory, January 1, 2004	24,000
Retained earnings, January 1, 2004	68,700	Cost of goods manufactured	79,200
Sales (net)	139,600		

The following information is also available for 2004 and is not reflected in the preceding accounts:

1. The common stock has been outstanding for the entire year. A cash dividend of $0.84 per share was declared and paid.
2. The income tax rate on all items of income is 30%.
3. The ending finished goods inventory is $27,300.
4. A pretax $4,000 loss was recognized on the sale of Division X (a component of the company). This division had earned a pretax operating income of $1,900 during 2004.
5. Obsolete raw materials were written off at a pretax loss of $6,600.
6. An earthquake, which is an unusual and infrequent event in the area, caused a $3,700 pretax loss.

Required

1. Prepare a cost of goods sold schedule for Cobler Manufacturing.
2. Prepare a 2004 single-step income statement.
3. Prepare a 2004 retained earnings statement.
4. Compute the 2004 profit margin (net income ÷ net sales).

E4-11   *Income Statement Calculations* The income statement information for 2004 and 2005 of the Connor Company (a sole proprietorship) is as follows:

	2004	2005
Beginning inventory	$ (a)	$ (d)
Sales	210,000	(e)
Purchases	130,000	140,000
Purchases returns and allowances	7,000	6,000
Ending inventory	62,000	(f)
Sales returns and allowances	4,000	9,000
Gross profit	(b)	100,000
Cost of goods sold	114,000	120,000
Selling expenses	35,000	36,000
Transportation-in	2,000	5,000
General and administrative expenses	20,000	(g)
Net income	(c)	43,000

Required Fill in the blanks labeled (a). through (g). All the necessary information is listed. (*Hint*: It is not necessary to calculate your answers in alphabetical order.)

E4-12   *Income Statement Calculations* The income statement information for 2004 and 2005 of the Thompson Company (a sole proprietorship) is as follows:

	2004	2005
Cost of goods manufactured	$68,000	$ 59,000
Raw materials used	20,000	18,000
Sales	(1)	130,000
Beginning finished goods inventory	42,000	26,000
Direct labor	30,000	(5)
Sales returns and allowances	5,000	4,000
Operating expenses	30,000	(6)
Factory overhead	(2)	13,000
Gross profit	56,000	(7)
Beginning goods in process inventory	24,000	(8)
Cost of goods sold	84,000	(9)
Ending finished goods inventory	(3)	20,000
Ending goods in process inventory	21,000	18,000
Sales discounts taken	3,000	2,600
Net income	(4)	30,000

Required Fill in the blanks numbered (1) through (9). All the necessary information is listed. (*Hint*: It is not necessary to calculate your answers in numerical order.)

E4-13   *Results of Discontinued Operations*   During December 2004, Smythe Company decides to sell Division F (a component of the company). On December 31, 2004, the company classifies Division F as held for sale. On that date, the book values of Division F's assets and liabilities are $950,000 and $600,000, respectively. Smythe expects to sell Division F in 2005 and estimates that the fair value of Division F is $250,000. During 2004, Division F earned revenues of $1,000,000 and incurred expenses of $1,300,000. Smythe Company is subject to a 30% income tax rate.

Required Prepare the results from discontinued operations section of Smythe Company's income statement for 2004. Show supporting calculations.

E4-14   *Results of Discontinued Operations*   On November 30, 2004, Feiner Company announced its plans to discontinue the operations of Division P (a component of the company) by selling the division. On December 31, 2004, Division, P had not yet been sold and was classified as held for sale. On this date, Division P had assets with a book value of $920,000 and liabilities with a book value of $610,000. Feiner Company estimates that the fair value of Division P on this date is $190,000. During 2004, Division P earned revenues of $920,000 and incurred expenses of $980,000. Feiner Company is subject to a 30% income tax rate.

Required Prepare the results from discontinued operations section of Feiner Company's income statement for 2004. Show supporting calculations.

E4-15   *Income Statement Deficiencies*   David Company's Statements of Income for the year ended December 31, 2005, and December 31, 2004, are presented here:

| | Year Ended December 31, | |
	2005	2004
Net sales	$900,000	$750,000
Costs and expenses:		
Cost of goods sold	$720,000	$600,000
Selling, general and administrative expenses	112,000	90,000
Other, net	11,000	9,000
Total costs and expenses	$843,000	$699,000
Income from continuing operations before income taxes	$ 57,000	$ 51,000
Income taxes	23,000	24,000
Income from continuing operations	$ 34,000	$ 27,000
Loss on sale of Dex Division, less applicable income taxes of $8,000	8,000	—
Cumulative effect on prior years of change in depreciation method, less applicable income taxes of $1,500	—	3,000
Net income	$ 26,000	$ 30,000
Earnings per share of common stock:		
Income before cumulative effect of change in depreciation method	$2.60	$2.70
Cumulative effect on prior years of change in depreciation method, less applicable income taxes	—	.30
Net income	$2.60	$3.00

Additional facts are as follows:

a. On January 1, 2004, David Company changed its depreciation method for previously recorded plant machinery from the double-declining-balance method to the straight-line method. The effect of applying the straight-line method for the year of and the year after the change is included in David Company's Statements of Income for the year ended December 31, 2005 and December 31, 2004 in "cost of goods sold."

b. The loss from operations of the discontinued Dex Division (a component of the company) from January 1, 2005, to September 30, 2005 (the portion of the year prior to the date of sale) and from January 1, 2004 to December 31, 2004 is included in David Company's Statements of Income for the year ended December 31, 2005 and December 31, 2004 respectively, in "other, net."

c. David Company has a simple capital structure with only common stock outstanding, and the net income per share of common stock was based on the weighted average number of common shares outstanding during each year.

d. David Company common stock is listed on the New York Stock Exchange and closed at $13 per share on December 31, 2005 and $15 per share on December 31, 2004.

Required Determine from the additional facts listed whether the presentation of those facts in David Company's Statements of Income is appropriate. If the presentation is appropriate, discuss the theoretical rationale for the presentation. If the presentation is not appropriate, specify the appropriate presentation and discuss its theoretical rationale. Do *not* discuss disclosure requirements for the Notes to the Financial Statements. (*AICPA adapted*)

E4-16   *Net Income and Comprehensive Income*   On December 31, 2004 TNT Company lists the following accounts in its adjusted trial balance:

Sales	$85,000
Unrealized increase in value of available-for-sale securities	4,000
Operating expenses	18,000
Cost of goods sold	47,000

The income tax rate is 30% on all items of income.

Required

1. Prepare a 2004 income statement, which includes comprehensive income (disregard earnings per share).
2. Prepare (a) a 2004 income statement (disregard earnings per share) and (b) a 2004 statement of comprehensive income.

E4-17   *Net Cash Flow From Operating Activities*   The following are accounting items taken from the records of the Tyrone Company for 2004:

a. Net income, $22,900

b. Payment for purchase of land, $4,000

c. Payment for retirement of bonds, $6,000

d. Depreciation expense, $7,800

e. Proceeds from issuance of common stock, $7,000

f. Patent amortization expense, $2,700

g. Bond discount amortization, $1,000

h. Increase in accounts receivable, $3,400

i. Payment of dividends, $5,000

j. Decrease in accounts payable, $2,600

Required Prepare the net cash flow from operating activities section of the Tyrone Company's 2004 statement of cash flows.

E4-18   *Operating Cash Flows: Direct Method*   The following are various cash flows and other information of the Lexie Company for 2004:

a. Payments of interest, $8,200

b. Proceeds from sale of land, $7,900

c. Interest collected, $10,000

d. Payment of dividends, $12,100

e. Depreciation expense, $24,700

f. Collections from customers, $101,600

g. Payments of income taxes, $15,400

h. Proceeds from issuance of stock, $18,900

i. Payments to suppliers and employees, $67,500

j. Increase in inventories, $4,600

Required Using the direct method, prepare the cash flows from operating activities section of the Lexie Company's 2004 statement of cash flows.

E4-19   *Statement of Cash Flows*   The following are several items involving the cash flow activities of the Rocky Company for 2004:

a. Net income, $41,000

b. Payment of dividends, $16,000

c. Ten-year, $28,000 bonds payable were issued at face value

d. Depreciation expense, $11,000

e. Building was acquired at a cost of $40,000

f. Accounts receivable decreased by $2,000

g. Accounts payable decreased by $4,000

h. Equipment was acquired at a cost of $8,000

i. Inventories increased by $7,000

j. Beginning cash balance, $13,000

Required Prepare the statement of cash flows of the Rocky Company for 2004.

E4-20 **Statement of Cash Flows** The following are several items involving the cash flow activities of the Jones Company for 2004:

a. Net income, $60,400

b. Proceeds from issuance of common stock, $32,000

c. Payment for purchase of equipment, $41,500

d. Payment for purchase of land, $19,600

e. Depreciation expense, $20,500

f. Patent amortization expense, $1,200

g. Payment of dividends, $21,000

h. Decrease in salaries payable, $2,600

i. Increase in accounts receivable, $10,300

j. Beginning cash balance, $30,700

Required Prepare the statement of cash flows of the Jones Company for 2004.

PROBLEMS

P4-1 **Comprehensive Income Framework** The following is an alphabetical list of accounts for the Mack Company:

Accounts payable
Accounts receivable
Accumulated depreciation, buildings and office equipment
Accumulated depreciation, store and delivery equipment
Administrative salaries
Advertising expense
Allowance for doubtful accounts
Bad debts expense
Bonds payable
Buildings
Cash
Cash dividends declared
Common stock, $10 par
Correction of previous years' error
Cumulative effect on prior years' income of change in accounting principle
Delivery expense
Depreciation expense, buildings and office equipment
Depreciation expense, store and delivery equipment
Dividend revenue
Dividends payable
Freight on purchases
Fund to retire long-term bonds
Gain on sale of equipment
Gain on sale of Division T
Income tax expense
Insurance expense
Interest expense
Interest payable
Interest revenue

Investment in securities (long-term)
Loss from expropriation
Loss from operations of discontinued Division T
Loss on sale of office equipment
Merchandise inventory, January 1, 2004
Merchandise inventory, December 31, 2004
Miscellaneous office expenses
Miscellaneous sales expenses
Mortgage payable
Office salaries
Office supplies used
Paid-in capital on common stock
Prepaid office supplies
Property tax expense
Purchases
Purchases discounts taken
Purchases returns and allowances
Rent revenue
Retained earnings, January 1, 2004
Salaries payable
Sales
Sales commissions
Sales discounts taken
Sales returns and allowances
Sales salaries
Service revenues
Stock dividends declared
Unearned rent
Unexpired insurance
Unrealized increase in value of available-for-sale securities
Utilities expense

Required Ignoring amounts, select the appropriate accounts of Mack Company and prepare for 2004:

1. A multiple-step income statement with proper subheadings
2. A statement of comprehensive income
3. A retained earnings statement

P4-2   *Account Classifications*   Given the following code letters and components of financial statements, indicate where each item would most likely be reported in the financial statements by inserting the corresponding code letters. Assume the monetary amount of each item is material.

Code Letter	Component
A	Sales revenues (net)
B	Cost of goods sold
C	Selling expenses
D	General and administrative expenses
E	Other items
F	Results from discontinued operations
G	Extraordinary items
H	Prior period adjustments
I	Additions to retained earnings (other than H)
J	Deductions from retained earnings (other than H)
K	Notes to financial statements
L	Ending balance sheet

_____   1. Purchases

_____   2. Loss on sale of equipment

_____   3. Utilities expense

_____   4. Cash dividends declared on common stock

_____   5. Bad debts expense

_____   6. Sales salaries

_____   7. Sales discounts taken

_____   8. Transportation-in

_____   9. Net income

_____   10. Gain on retirement of long-term debt

_____   11. Purchases returns and allowances

_____   12. Premium on bonds payable

_____   13. Gain on sale of land

_____   14. Interest expense

_____   15. Delivery expense

_____   16. Expenses incurred as a result of a strike

_____   17. Summary of accounting policies

_____   18. Gain on disposal of Division J

_____   19. Interest revenue

_____   20. Additional paid-in capital on common stock

_____   21. Loss from write-down of obsolete inventory

_____   22. Administrative salaries

_____   23. Stock dividends declared on common stock

_____   24. Correction of erroneous understatement of last year's ending inventory

_____   25. Operating loss related to discontinued Division J

_____   26. Additional depreciation on office equipment resulting from decrease in estimated useful life

_____   27. Loss from impairment of property

_____   28. Loss from frost in southern Arizona

_____   29. Sales returns

_____   30. Depreciation expense for office equipment

_____   31. Sales commissions

_____   32. Promotion expense

_____   33. Merchandise inventory (beginning)

P4-3   *Income Statement, Lower Portion*   At the beginning of 2004 the retained earnings of the Cole Company was $212,000. For 2004 the company has calculated its pretax income from continuing operations to be $120,000. During 2004 the following events also occurred:

1. During July the company sold Division M (a component of the company). It has determined that the pretax income from the operations of Division M during 2004 totals $39,000 and that a pretax loss of $40,500 was incurred on the sale of Division M.

2. The company had 21,000 shares of common stock outstanding during all of 2004. It declared and paid a $1 per share cash dividend on this stock.

3. The company experienced an extraordinary event. It recognized a material pretax gain of $26,000 on the event.

4. The company found and corrected a pretax $18,000 understatement of the 2003 ending inventory due to a mathematical error.

5. With the agreement of its auditors the company switched from straight-line to double-declining-balance depreciation on certain assets at the beginning of 2004. Had double-declining-balance depreciation been used prior to 2004, the cumulative effect would have been a pretax increase in depreciation expense for prior years of $11,000.

Required Assuming that all the "pretax" items are subject to a 30% income tax rate:

1. Complete the lower portion of Cole Company's 2004 income statement, beginning with "Pretax Income from Continuing Operations."
2. Prepare an accompanying retained earnings statement.

P4-4 ***Income Statement, Lower Portion*** Cunningham Company reports a retained earnings balance of $365,200 at the beginning of 2004. For the year ended December 31, 2004, the company reports pretax income from continuing operations of $150,500. The following information is also available pertaining to 2004:

1. The company declared and paid a $0.72 cash dividend per share on the 30,000 shares of common stock that were outstanding the entire year.
2. The company found and corrected a pretax $48,000 understatement of 2003 depreciation expense due to a mathematical error.
3. The company incurred a pretax $21,000 loss as a result of an earthquake, which is unusual and infrequent for the area.
4. The company sold Division P (a component of the company) in May. From January through May, Division P had incurred a pretax loss from operations of $33,000. A pretax gain of $15,000 was recognized on the sale of Division P.
5. Because of additional information, the company determined that the estimated useful life of certain depreciable assets had decreased. As a result, the current depreciation expense included in the 2004 pretax income from continuing operations is $7,000 higher than it would have been had the original estimated useful life been used in the calculations.

Required Assuming that all the "pretax" items are subject to a 30% income tax rate:

1. Complete the lower portion of Cunningham Company's 2004 income statement beginning with "Pretax Income from Continuing Operations."
2. Prepare an accompanying retained earnings statement.

P4-5 ***Comprehensive: Income Statement and Supporting Schedules*** The following selected accounts are taken from the Crandle Corporation's December 31, 2004 adjusted trial balance:

Retained earnings, January 1, 2004	$428,900	Transportation-out (deliveries)	$ 6,000
Interest expense	4,900	Purchases	187,700
Depreciation expense: sales fixtures	8,500	Sales discounts taken	5,200
Purchases discounts taken	3,000	Transportation-in	14,300
Sales returns and allowances	11,300	Bad debt expense	1,900
Advertising expense	14,100	Purchases returns and allowances	8,000
Common stock, $10 par	110,000	Sales supplies expense	4,600
Administrative and office salaries expense	29,500	Inventory, January 1, 2004	45,200
Dividend revenue	900	Sales salaries expense	16,500
Sales	378,000	Depreciation expense: buildings and	
Property tax expense	7,700	office equipment	10,000
Gain on sale of sales fixtures (pretax)	5,000	Income tax expense	15,870
Office supplies used	1,800		

In addition to the preceding account balances, you have available the following information:

1. The December 31, 2004 ending inventory is $45,000, as determined by a physical count.
2. In the middle of December 2004 the company incurred a material $5,500 pretax loss as a result of a freak flood of a river that had never flooded before.
3. While making its December 31, 2004 adjusting entries, the company discovered the following:
   a. In recording its December 31, 2003 adjusting entries, it had inadvertently recorded depreciation expense twice for the same asset. The amount of the error was $4,000 pretax and is considered material. The error did not have any effect upon the depreciation recorded for 2004.
   b. Based on an analysis of the company's recent favorable experience with uncollectible accounts receivable, the company decided to reduce the percentage used in computing bad debt expense. The use of the new percentage resulted in the $1,900 bad debt expense being $500 less than the amount that would have been calculated using the old percentage.
4. On April 1, 2004 the company sold Division M (a component of the company), which had been unprofitable for several years. For the first 3 months of 2004, Division M had incurred a pretax operating loss of $8,800. Division M was sold at a pretax loss of $7,500.

5. The company paid cash dividends of $0.90 per share on its common stock. All the stock was outstanding for the entire year.
6. The $15,870 Income Tax Expense account balance consists of $21,210 tax on continuing income and $1,200 tax on the depreciation correction, and tax credits of $2,640 on the operating loss of Division M, $2,250 on the loss from sale of Division M, and $1,650 on the loss due to the flood.

Required

1. As supporting documents for Requirement 2, prepare separate schedules for cost of goods sold, selling expenses, and general and administrative expenses (include each depreciation expense where applicable in these schedules).
2. Prepare a 2004 single-step income statement for the Crandle Corporation.
3. Prepare a 2004 retained earnings statement.
4. What was Crandle Corporation's profit margin for 2004? What is your evaluation of Crandle's 2004 profit margin if last year it was 8%?

P4-6 *Comprehensive: Income Statement and Supporting Schedules* The following is a partial list of the account balances, after adjustments, of the Silvoso Company on December 31, 2004:

Depreciation expense: buildings and office equipment	$ 14,500	Office supplies expense	$ 1,400
		Common stock, $10 par	80,000
Sales commissions and salaries	18,200	Loss on sale of office equipment (pretax)	5,000
Inventory, January 1, 2004	37,800	Insurance and property tax expense	8,500
Sales supplies used	5,600	Sales	340,700
Retained earnings, January 1, 2004	183,700	Rent revenue	6,900
Purchases returns and allowances	6,200	Office and administrative salaries expense	32,000
Bad debts expense	2,700	Promotion and advertising expense	17,000
Transportation-in	13,500	Sales returns and allowances	12,100
Sales discounts taken	4,900	Purchases discounts taken	4,100
Purchases	173,000	Depreciation expense: sales equipment	9,600
Delivery expense	7,700	Interest expense	3,700

The following information is also available:

1. The company declared and paid a $0.60 per share cash dividend on its common stock. The stock was outstanding the entire year.
2. A physical count determined that the December 31, 2004 ending inventory is $34,100.
3. A tornado destroyed a warehouse, resulting in a pretax loss of $12,000. The last tornado in this area had occurred 20 years earlier.
4. While making its December 31, 2004 adjusting entries, the company determined that:
   a. In 2003 it had inadvertently omitted $11,000 depreciation expense on its buildings and office equipment. The error did not have any effect upon the depreciation recorded in 2004.
   b. Due to recently increased obsolescence, its sales equipment should be depreciated over a shorter useful life. The resulting $2,500 of additional depreciation has been included in the 2004 depreciation expense.
5. On May 1, 2004, the company sold an unprofitable division (R). From January through April, Division R (a component of the company) had incurred a pretax operating loss of $8,700. Division R was sold at a pretax gain of $10,000.
6. The income tax expense for 2004 totals $930. The breakdown is as follows:

Income Tax Expense (Credit) Related to	Amount
Continuing income	$ 7,440
Operating loss of Division R	(2,610)
Gain on sale of Division R	3,000
Loss from tornado	(3,600)
Error in recording 2000 depreciation expense	(3,300)
	$ 930

7. The company had average stockholders' equity of $100,000 during 2004.

Required

1. As supporting documents for Requirement 2, prepare separate supporting schedules for cost of goods sold, selling expenses, general and administrative expenses, and depreciation expense.
2. Prepare a 2004 multiple-step income statement for the Silvoso Company.
3. Prepare a 2004 retained earnings statement.
4. What was Silvoso Company's return on stockholders' equity for 2004? What is your evaluation of Silvoso Company's return on stockholders' equity if last year it was 12%?

P4-7   *Comprehensive: Manufacturing Income Statement*   The Houston Manufacturing Company presents the following partial list of account balances, after adjustments, as of December 31, 2004:

Sales salaries expense	$ 27,400	Factory maintenance expense	$ 7,000
Miscellaneous administrative expenses	3,000	Sales personnel travel expenses	8,300
Raw materials used	63,300	Property taxes and insurance expense	9,000
Sales returns	5,000	Retained earnings, January 1, 2004	200,800
Factory superintendence salaries expense	25,000	Factory utilities expense	21,000
Finished goods inventory, January 1, 2004	32,000	Depreciation expense: sales equipment	9,000
Sales	468,200	Factory indirect labor expense	23,000
Direct labor	81,000	Advertising expense	15,700
Interest revenue	3,200	Depreciation expense: factory	18,000
Office and administrative salaries	30,000	Miscellaneous rent revenue	5,900
Delivery expenses	11,700	Common stock, $10 par	200,000
Goods in process inventory, January 1, 2004	19,900	Depreciation expense: buildings and	
Loss on sale of factory equipment (pretax)	4,100	office equipment	14,400

The following information is also available but is not reflected in the preceding accounts:

1. The company sold Division E (a component of the company) on August 1, 2004. During 2004 Division E had incurred a pretax loss from operations of $16,000. However, because the acquiring company could vertically integrate Division E into its facilities, the Houston Manufacturing Company was able to recognize a $42,000 pretax gain on the sale.
2. On January 2, 2004, without warning, a foreign country expropriated a factory of Houston Manufacturing Company, which had been operating in that country. As a result of that expropriation, the company has incurred a pretax loss of $30,000.
3. In preparing its 2004 adjusting entries at year-end, the company discovered that it had not recorded $10,100 of depreciation on its office building during 2003. This error did not affect the 2004 depreciation expense.
4. A December 31, 2004 physical inventory yielded the following ending inventories: goods in process, $22,000; finished goods, $36,000.
5. The common stock was outstanding for the entire year. A cash dividend of $1.20 per share was declared and paid in 2004.
6. The 2004 income tax expense totals $28,020 and consists of the following:

Tax expense on income from continuing operations	$32,250
Tax credit on Division E operating loss	(4,800)
Tax expense on gain from sale of Division E	12,600
Tax credit on loss from expropriation	(9,000)
Tax credit on 2003 depreciation error	(3,030)
	$28,020

*See WebTutor for annotated problem solution.

Required

1. As supporting documents for Requirement 2, prepare separate supporting schedules for cost of goods sold, selling expenses, and general and administrative expenses (include depreciation expense where applicable in these schedules).
2. Prepare a 2004 multiple-step income statement for the Houston Manufacturing Company.
3. Prepare a 2004 retained earnings statement.

4. What was Houston Manufacturing Company's return on stockholders' equity for 2004 if its average stockholders' equity during 2004 was $500,000? What is your evaluation of this return on stockholders' equity if its "target" for 2004 was 15%?

P4-8   *Misclassifications* The Rox Corporation's multiple-step income statement and retained earnings statement for the year ended December 31, 2004, as developed by its bookkeeper, are shown here:

ROX CORPORATION
Revenue Statement
December 31, 2004

Sales (net)		$179,000
Plus: Income from operations of discontinued Division P (net of $960 income taxes)		2,240
Less: Dividends declared ($1.50 per common share)		(7,500)
Net revenues		$173,740
Less: Selling expenses		(19,000)
Gross profit		$154,740
Less: Operating expenses		
Interest expense	$ 4,100	
Loss on sale of Division P (net of $1,200 income tax credit)	2,800	
Cost of goods sold	110,700	
Income tax expense on income from continuing operations	5,370	
Total operating expenses		(122,970)
Operating income		$ 31,770
Miscellaneous items		
Dividend revenue	$ 1,800	
General and administrative expenses	(24,300)	(22,500)
Income before extraordinary items		$ 9,270
Extraordinary items		
Loss on sale of land	$ (4,800)	
Correction of error in last year's income (net of $1,500 income taxes)	3,500	(1,300)
Net income		$ 7,970

ROX CORPORATION
Retained Earnings Statement
December 31, 2004

Beginning retained earnings	$62,850
Add: Net income	7,970
Adjusted retained earnings	$70,820
Less: Loss from expropriation (net of $2,760 income tax credit)	(6,440)
Ending retained earnings	$64,380

You determine that the account *balances* listed in the statements are correct but are incorrectly classified in certain cases. No shares of common stock were issued or retired during 2004.

Required

1. Review both statements and indicate where each incorrectly classified item should be classified.
2. Prepare a correct multiple-step 2004 income statement.
3. Prepare a correct 2004 retained earnings statement.

P4-9   *Misclassifications* The bookkeeper for the Olson Company prepared the following income statement and retained earnings statement for the year ended December 31, 2004:

OLSON COMPANY
December 31, 2004
Expense and Profits Statement

Sales (net)		$196,000
Less: Selling expenses		(19,600)
Net sales		$176,400
Add: Interest revenue		2,300
Add: Gain on sale of equipment		3,200
Gross sales revenues		$181,900
Less: Costs of operations		
Cost of goods sold	$120,100	
Correction of overstatement in last year's income due to error (net of $1,650 income tax credit)	3,850	
Dividend costs ($0.50 per share for 8,000 common shares)	4,000	
Extraordinary loss due to earthquake (net of $1,800 income tax credit)	4,200	(132,150)
Taxable revenues		$ 49,750
Less: Income tax on income from continuing operations		(12,480)
Net income		$37,270
Miscellaneous deductions		
Loss from operations of discontinued Division L (net of $900 income tax credit)	$ 2,100	
Administrative expenses	16,800	(18,900)
Net revenues		$ 18,370

OLSON COMPANY
Retained Revenues Statement
For Year Ended December 31, 2004

Beginning retained earnings	$59,300
Add: Gain on sale of Division L (net of $1,350 income taxes)	3,150
Recalculated retained earnings	$62,450
Add: Net revenues	18,370
	$80,820
Less: Interest expense	(3,400)
Ending retained earnings	$77,420

The preceding account *balances* are correct but have been incorrectly classified in certain instances.

Required Prepare a corrected 2000 multiple-step income statement and a 2004 retained earnings statement.

P4-10 *Classification of Unusual and/or Infrequent Items* The following are a number of unusual and/or infrequent gains or losses that might be disclosed on the income statement or retained earnings statement. All items are considered to be material in amount.

1. A loss from an earthquake that destroyed a chemical plant of a major chemical company. The region where the plant was destroyed had not had an earthquake in 15 years.
2. A gain resulting from the retirement of bonds payable. The bonds payable had been classified as current liabilities on last year's ending balance sheet because of their expected retirement during the current year.
3. A reduction in the current depletion expense as a result of the discovery of additional mineral deposits.
4. A gain from the sale of land. The land had been purchased for the construction of a new factory. The company has built several new factories over the past several years, and in each instance has acquired more land than necessary for the factory site. After completion of the factory, the excess land is sold at its appreciated value.

5. A loss incurred by a corporation on the sale of an investment in bonds of a publicly held company. The bonds constitute 5% of the net assets of the publicly held company. The corporation has been holding these bonds as an investment for several years. This is the only investment in securities the corporation has ever made.
6. A loss incurred as a result of an earthquake that destroyed a 2-year-old storage facility of a large retail chain. The storage facility is located in California. A major earthquake occurred in the same region 2 years ago, just prior to the construction of the facility.
7. A decrease in previous years' earnings as a result of a change from straight-line to sum-of-the-years'-digits depreciation on factory equipment at the beginning of the current year.
8. An increase in current depreciation expense as a result of the change in depreciation methods discussed in item 7.
9. A loss incurred in the spring by a retail store in a shopping center as a result of a flood of a nearby stream. Although the stream has overflowed several times in the past six years, only 3 stores (out of 38) in the shopping center had previously incurred a significant flood loss.
10. A gain recognized as the result of the sale by a food processing company of a 15% interest in a professional baseball team.
11. A reduction in last year's income as a result of the discovery in the current year of a miscount (overstatement) of last year's ending inventory.
12. A loss incurred by a diversified citrus grower due to frost damage in southern California. No frost damage has occurred in the region for seven years, although last year the citrus grower had incurred a loss due to frost damage to its Florida operations.

Required For each item, indicate in which section of the income statement or retained earnings statement it should be disclosed. Justify your disclosure.

P4-11   **Results of Discontinued Operations**   On November 1, 2004, Woods Company announced its plans to sell Division J (a component of the company). By December 31, 2004, Woods Company had not sold Division J and so it classifies the division as held for sale.

During 2004, Woods Company recorded the following revenues and expenses for Division J and the remainder of the company.

	Division J	Remainder of Company
Sales revenues	$170,000	$950,000
Cost of goods sold	119,000	560,000
Operating expenses	42,000	190,000

The company is subject to a 30% income tax rate.

On December 31, 2004, the net book value of Division J is $500,000, consisting of assets of $910,000 and liabilities of $410,000. On this date, Woods Company estimates that the fair value of Division J is $420,000. The company had 50,000 shares of common stock outstanding during all of 2004.

Required

1. Prepare the journal entry on December 31, 2004 to record the pretax loss on held-for-sale Division J. Show supporting calculations.
2. Prepare a 2004 multiple-step income statement for Woods Company.
3. Show how Division J would be reported on Woods Company's December 31, 2004 balance sheet.

P4-12   **Analyzing Coca-Cola's Income Statement and Cash Flow Statement Disclosures**   Review the financial statements, notes, and management's discussion and analysis of the Coca-Cola Company in Appendix A.

Required Answer the following questions. (*Note:* You do not need to make any calculations. All information may be found in the financial rep'ort.) Indicate on what page of the financial report you located the answer.

1. Does the company use a multiple-step or a single-step format on its income statement? Explain.
2. What was the net income for 2001? What was the basic net income (earnings) per common share for 2001?
3. What was the gross profit for 2001? Why did it increase compared to 2000?
4. How much interest expense was incurred in 2001? Why did it decrease compared to 2000?
5. What was the amount of the income taxes related to income before income taxes for 2001?
6. By what percent did net operating revenues on a consolidated basis increase in 2001? Why did they increase?
7. What was the amount of selling expenses in 2001? In 2000? What was the reason for the increase?

8. What amount of dividends on common stock were paid per share and in total in 2001?

9. What were the net operating revenues and gross profit, respectively, for the fourth quarter of 2001?

10. What was the company's return on common equity for 2001? How does this compare to 2000?

11. What method was used to determine the net cash provided by operating activities in 2001? What was the amount?

12. What was the net cash used in investing activities in 2001?

13. What was the cash provided by the issuances of debt in 2001?

P4-13 **Complex Income Statement** The following is the adjusted trial balance for the Woodbine Circle Corporation on December 31, 2004:

	Debit	Credit
Cash	$ 500,000	
Accounts receivable, net	1,500,000	
Inventory	2,500,000	
Property, plant, and equipment	15,100,000	
Accumulated depreciation		$ 4,900,000
Accounts payable		1,400,000
Income taxes payable		100,000
Notes payable		1,000,000
Common stock ($1 par value)		1,000,000
Additional paid-in capital		6,200,000
Retained earnings, Jan. 1, 2004		3,000,000
Sales—regular		10,100,000
Sales—AL Division		2,000,000
Cost of sales—regular	6,200,000	
Cost of sales—AL Division	900,000	
Administrative expenses—regular	2,000,000	
Administrative expenses—AL Division	300,000	
Interest expense—regular	210,000	
Interest expense—AL Division	140,000	
Loss on sale of AL Division	250,000	
Gain from extraordinary event		300,000
Income tax expense	400,000	
	$30,000,000	$30,000,000

Other financial data for the year ended December 31, 2004:

Federal Income Taxes

Paid on Federal Tax Deposit Form	$300,000
Accrued	100,000
Total charged to income tax expense (estimated)	$400,000
Tax rate on all types of taxable income	40%

Discontinued Operations

On September 30, 2004 Woodbine sold its Auto Leasing (AL) Division for $4,000,000. The book value of this division was $4,250,000 at that date. For financial statement purposes, this sale was considered as discontinued operation of a component of the company.

Liabilities

On June 30, 2004 Woodbine repurchased $1,000,000 carrying value of its long-term bonds for $700,000. All other liabilities mature in 2005.

Capital Structure

Common stock, par value $1 per share, traded on the New York Stock Exchange:
Number of shares outstanding during all of 2004   1,000,000

Required Using the multiple-step format, prepare a formal income statement for Woodbine for the year ended December 31, 2004, together with the appropriate supporting schedules. All income taxes should be appropriately shown. (*AICPA adapted*)

P4-14   *Complex Income Statement*   The following trial balance of Garr Corporation at December 31, 2004 has been adjusted except for income tax expense:

	Debit	Credit
Cash	$ 675,000	
Accounts receivable (net)	1,695,000	
Inventory	2,185,000	
Property, plant, and equipment (net)	8,660,000	
Accounts payable and accrued liabilities		$ 1,895,000
Income tax payable		360,000
Deferred income tax		285,000
Common stock		2,300,000
Additional paid-in capital		3,675,000
Retained earnings, 1/1/04		3,350,000
Net sales—Regular		10,750,000
—Plastics Division		2,200,000
Cost of sales—Regular	5,920,000	
—Plastics Division	1,650,000	
Selling and administrative expenses—Regular	2,600,000	
—Plastics Division	660,000	
Interest income—Regular		65,000
Gain on litigation settlement—Regular		200,000
Depreciation adjustment from accounting change—Regular	350,000	
Gain on sale of Plastics Division		150,000
Income tax expense	835,000	
	$25,230,000	$25,230,000

Other financial data for the year ended December 31, 2004:

Income Tax Expense

Estimated tax payments	$475,000
Accrued	360,000
Total charged to income tax expense (estimated)	$835,000
Tax rate on all types of income	40%

Gain from litigation settlement is a taxable gain and is not considered infrequent.

Discontinued Operations

On October 31, 2004 Garr sold its Plastics Division for $2,950,000 when the carrying amount was $2,800,000. For financial statement reporting, this sale was considered a sale of a component of the company.

Change in Depreciation Method

On January 1, 2004 Garr changed to the 150% declining-balance method from the straight-line method of depreciation for certain of its plant assets. The pretax cumulative effect of this accounting change was determined to be a charge of $350,000.

Capital Structure

Common stock, $10 par, traded on a national exchange: 230,000 shares outstanding during 2004.

Required Using the multiple-step format, prepare a formal income statement for Garr for the year ended December 31, 2004. All components of income tax expense should be appropriately shown. (*AICPA adapted*)

P4-15   *Comparative Income Statements*   The Century Company, a diversified manufacturing company, had four separate operating divisions engaged in the manufacture of products in each of the following areas: food products, health aids, textiles, and office equipment. Financial data for the 2 years ended December 31, 2005 and 2004 are presented here:

Net Sales	2005	2004
Food products	$3,500,000	$3,000,000
Health aids	2,000,000	1,270,000
Textiles	1,580,000	1,400,000
Office equipment	920,000	1,330,000
	$8,000,000	$7,000,000

Cost of Sales	2005	2004
Food products	$2,400,000	$1,800,000
Health aids	1,100,000	700,000
Textiles	500,000	900,000
Office equipment	800,000	1,000,000
	$4,800,000	$4,400,000

Operating Expenses	2005	2004
Food products	$ 550,000	$ 275,000
Health aids	300,000	125,000
Textiles	200,000	150,000
Office equipment	650,000	750,000
	$1,700,000	$1,300,000

On January 1, 2005, Century adopted a plan to sell the assets and product line of the office equipment division and considered it a component of the company. On September 1, 2005, the division's assets and product line were sold for $2,100,000 cash, resulting in a gain of $640,000.

The company's textiles division had six manufacturing plants that produced a variety of textile products. In April 2005 the company sold one of these plants and realized a gain of $130,000. After the sale the operations at the plant that was sold were transferred to the remaining five textile plants, which the company continued to operate.

In August 2005 the main warehouse of the food products division, located on the banks of the Bayer River, was flooded when the river overflowed. The resulting damage of $420,000 is not included in the financial data given previously. Historical records indicate that the Bayer River normally overflows every 4 to 5 years, causing flood damage to adjacent property.

For the 2 years ended December 31, 2005 and 2004 the company had interest revenue earned on investments of $70,000 and $40,000, respectively.

The provision for income tax expense for each of the 2 years should be computed at a rate of 40%.

Required Prepare in proper form a multiple-step comparative statement of income of the Century Company for the 2 years ended December 31, 2005 and December 31, 2004. Footnotes are not required. (*AICPA adapted*)

P4-16   *Financial Statement Deficiencies*   The following is the complete set of financial statements prepared by Oberlin Corporation:

OBERLIN CORPORATION
Statement of Earnings and Retained Earnings
For the Fiscal Year Ended August 31, 2004

Sales		$3,500,000
Less returns and allowances		(35,000)
Net sales		$3,465,000
Less cost of goods sold		(1,039,000)
Gross margin		$2,426,000
Less:		
Selling expenses	$1,000,000	
General and administrative expenses (Note 1)	1,079,000	(2,079,000)
Operating earnings		$ 347,000
Add other revenues		
Purchase discounts	$ 10,000	
Gain on increased value of investments in real estate	100,000	
Gain on sale of treasury stock	200,000	
Correction of error in last year's statement	90,000	400,000
Ordinary earnings		$ 747,000
Add extraordinary item—gain on sale of fixed asset		53,000
Earnings before income tax		$ 800,000
Less income tax expense		(320,000)
Net earnings		$ 480,000
Add beginning retained earnings		2,690,000
		$3,170,000
Less:		
Dividends (12% stock dividend declared but not yet issued)		(120,000)
Contingent liability (Note 3)		(300,000)
Ending retained earnings		$2,750,000

Statement of Financial Position
August 31, 2004

Assets

Current Assets		
Cash	$ 80,000	
Accounts receivable, net	110,000	
Inventory	130,000	
Total current assets		$ 320,000
Other Assets		
Land and building, net	$4,000,000	
Investments in real estate (current value)	1,668,000	
Goodwill (Note 2)	250,000	
Discount on bonds payable	42,000	
Total other assets		5,960,000
Total assets		$6,280,000

Liabilities and Stockholders' Equity

Current Liabilities		
Accounts payable	$ 160,000	
Income taxes payable	300,000	
Stock dividend payable	120,000	
Total current liabilities		$ 580,000

Other Liabilities

Due to Grant, Inc. (Note 3)	$ 300,000	
Accrued pension cost	450,000	
Bonds payable (including portion due within one year)	1,000,000	
Deferred taxes	58,000	
Total other liabilities		1,808,000
Total liabilities		$2,388,000

Stockholders' Equity

Common stock	$1,000,000	
Paid-in capital in excess of par	142,000	
Retained earnings	2,750,000	
Total stockholders' equity		3,892,000
Total liabilities and stockholders' equity		$6,280,000

Notes to Financial Statements

1. Depreciation expense is included in general and administrative expenses. During the fiscal year the Company changed from the straight-line method of depreciation to the sum-of-the-years'-digits method.
2. Goodwill is not being reviewed for impairment. The goodwill was "acquired" in 2004.
3. The amount due to Grant, Inc., is contingent upon the outcome of a lawsuit, which is currently pending. The amount of loss, if any, is not expected to exceed $300,000.

Required Identify and explain the deficiencies in the presentation of Oberlin's financial statements. There are no arithmetic errors in the statements. Organize your answer as follows:

1. Deficiencies in the statement of earnings and retained earnings
2. Deficiencies in the statement of financial position
3. General comments

If an item appears on both statements, identify the deficiencies for each statement separately. (*AICPA adapted*)

P4-17 *Financial Statement Violations of GAAP* The following are the financial statements issued by Allen Corporation for its fiscal year ended October 31, 2004:

ALLEN CORPORATION
Statement of Financial Position
October 31, 2004

Assets

Cash	$ 15,000	
Accounts receivable, net	150,000	
Inventory	120,000	
Total current assets	$285,000	
Patent (Note 3)	250,000	
Land	125,000	
Total assets	$660,000	

Liabilities

Accounts payable	$ 80,000	
Accrued expenses	20,000	
Total current liabilities	$100,000	
Deferred income tax payable (Note 4)	80,000	
Total liabilities	$180,000	

Stockholders' Equity

Common stock, par $1 (Note 5)	$100,000	
Additional paid-in capital	180,000	
Retained earnings	200,000	480,000
Total liabilities and stockholders' equity		$660,000

Earnings Statement
For the Fiscal Year Ended October 31, 2004

Sales		$1,000,000
Cost of goods sold		(750,000)
Gross margin		$ 250,000
Expenses		
Bad debt expense	$ 7,000	
Insurance	13,000	
Lease expenses (Note 1)	40,000	
Repairs and maintenance	30,000	
Pensions (Note 2)	12,000	
Salaries	60,000	(162,000)
Earnings before provision for income tax		$ 88,000
Provision for income tax		(28,740)
Net earnings		$ 59,260
Earnings per common share outstanding		$ 0.5926

Statement of Retained Earnings
For the Fiscal Year Ended October 31, 2004

Retained earnings, November 1, 2003	$150,000
Extraordinary gain, net of income tax	25,000
Net earnings for the fiscal year ended October 31, 2004	59,260
	$234,260
Dividends ($0.3426 per share)	(34,260)
Retained earnings, October 31, 2004	$200,000

Notes to Financial Statements:

1. *Long-Term Lease.* Under the terms of a 5-year noncancellable lease for buildings and equipment, the Company is obligated to make annual rental payments of $40,000 in each of the next four fiscal years. At the conclusion of the lease period, the Company has the option of purchasing the leased assets for $20,000 (a bargain purchase option) or entering into another 5-year lease of the same property at an annual rental of $5,000.

2. *Pension Plan.* Substantially all employees are covered by the Company's pension plan. Pension expense is equal to the total of pension benefits paid to retired employees during the year.

3. *Patent.* The patent had an estimated remaining life of 10 years at the time of purchase. The Company's patent was purchased from Apex Corporation on January 1, 2002, for $250,000.

4. *Deferred Income Tax Payable.* The entire balance in the deferred income tax payable account arose from tax-exempt municipal bonds that were held during the previous fiscal year, giving rise to a difference between taxable income and reported net earnings for the fiscal year ended October 31, 2004. The deferred liability amount was calculated on the basis of past tax rates.

5. *Warrants.* On January 1, 2003, one common stock warrant was issued to stockholders of record for each common share owned. An additional share of common stock is to be issued upon exercise of ten stock warrants and receipt of an amount equal to par value. For the six months ended October 31, 2004, the average market value for the Company's common stock was $5 per share and no warrants had yet been exercised.

6. *Contingent Liability.* On October 31, 2004, the Company was contingently liable for product warranties in an amount estimated to aggregate $75,000.

Required Review the preceding financial statements and related notes. Identify any inclusions or exclusions from them that would be in violation of generally accepted accounting principles, and indicate corrective action to be taken. Do *not* comment as to format or style. Respond in the following order:

1. Statement of Financial Position
2. Notes
3. Earnings Statement
4. Statement of Retained Earnings
5. General (*AICPA adapted*)

P4-18   *Comprehensive: Comparative Income Statements*   The accountant for the Tiger Company prepared comparative income statements for 2004 and 2005 as follows:

TIGER COMPANY
Comparative Statements of Income
For Years Ended December 31

	2005	2004
Sales	$3,500,000	$4,600,000
Cost of goods sold	(1,600,000)	(2,600,000)
Gross profit	$1,900,000	$2,000,000
Operating expenses	(1,300,000)	(1,500,000)
Operating income	$ 600,000	$ 500,000
Other items	(200,000)	100,000
Income before income taxes	$ 400,000	$ 600,000
Income tax expense (30%)	(120,000)	(180,000)
Net income	$ 0	$ 420,000

The auditor of Tiger Company reviewed the accounting records and income statements and discovered the facts described in items 1 and 2 below. All amounts incurred during 2004 and 2005 are included in the preceding statements.

1. Included in the category "Other Items" (along with other smaller miscellaneous items) were the following:
   a. A casualty loss of $60,000 in 2004 that was considered to be both unusual and infrequent
   b. A $150,000 loss in 2005 from an unusually large write-down of inventory due to obsolescence
   c. A $250,000 gain in 2004 that was considered to be both unusual and infrequent
2. On July 1, 2005, Tiger has announced its intention to sell its backscratcher division. This division is considered a component of the company. Operating results for this division are included in the company's overall operating results for 2004 and 2005, as shown previously, and are as follows:

	2005 (7/1–12/31)	2005 (1/1–6/30)	2004
Sales	$200,000	$400,000	$720,000
Cost of goods sold	300,000	320,000	290,000
Operating expenses	100,000	180,000	110,000

The division had not been sold by the end of 2005, so the company classified it as held for sale. The division consisted of the following items with book values and fair values on December 31, 2005:

Item	Book Value	Fair Value
Assets	$720,000	$620,000
Liabilities	450,000	510,000

Required Prepare corrected comparative statements of income for 2005 and 2004 for the Tiger Company. Ignore earnings per share.

P4-19   *Net Income and Comprehensive Income*   At the beginning of 2004, JR Company's stockholders' equity was as follows:

Common stock, $5 par	$35,000
Additional paid-in capital	49,000
Retained earnings	63,000

During 2004, the following events and transactions occurred:

1. The company earned sales revenues of $108,000. It incurred cost of goods sold of $62,000 and operating expenses of $12,000.

2. The company issued 1,000 shares of its $5 par common stock for $14 per share.

3. The company invested $30,000 in available-for-sale securities. At the end of the year, the securities had a market value of $35,000.

4. The company paid dividends of $6,000.

The income tax rate on all items of income is 30%.

Required

1. Prepare a 2004 income statement for JR Company which includes comprehensive income (ignore earnings per share).

2. Instead, prepare (a) a 2004 income statement (ignore earnings per share), and (b) a 2004 statement of comprehensive income.

3. Instead, prepare (a) a 2004 income statement (ignore earnings per share), and (b) a 2004 statement of changes in stockholders' equity that includes comprehensive income.

P4-20   *Statement of Cash Flows*   A list of selected items involving the cash flow activities of the Topps Company for 2004 is presented here:

a. Patent amortization expense, $3,500
b. Machinery was purchased for $39,500
c. At year-end, bonds payable with a face value of $20,000 were issued for $17,000
d. Net income, $47,200
e. Dividends paid, $16,000
f. Depreciation expense, $12,900
g. Preferred stock was issued for $13,600
h. Investments were acquired for $21,000
i. Accounts receivable increased by $4,300
j. Land was sold at cost, $11,000
k. Inventories increased by $15,400
l. Accounts payable increased by $2,700
m. Beginning cash balance, $19,400

Required Prepare the statement of cash flows of the Topps Company for 2004.

P4-21   *Statement of Cash Flows*   The following are several items involving the cash flow activities of the Mueller Company for 2004:

a. Net income, $68,000
b. Increase in accounts receivable, $4,400
c. Proceeds from sale of common stock, $12,300
d. Depreciation expense, $11,300
e. Dividends paid, $24,500
f. Payment for purchase of building, $65,000
g. Bond discount amortization, $2,700
h. Proceeds from sale of long-term investments at cost, $10,600
i. Payment for purchase of equipment, $8,000
j. Proceeds from sale of preferred stock, $20,000
k. Increase in income taxes payable, $3,500
l. Payment for purchase of land, $9,700
m. Decrease in accounts payable, $2,900
n. Increase in inventories, $10,300
o. Beginning cash balance, $18,000

Required Prepare the statement of cash flows of the Mueller Company for 2004.

P4-22   *Statement of Cash Flows: Direct Method*   The following are various cash flows and other information of the Trainer Company for 2004:

a. Payments of interest, $5,000
b. Depreciation expense, $22,700
c. Proceeds from sale of land, $3,100
d. Payments of income taxes, $6,200
e. Beginning cash balance, $16,500
f. Decrease in receivables, $7,400
g. Interest and dividends collected, $6,300
h. Payments of dividends, $5,200
i. Decrease in accounts payable, $8,600
j. Payments to suppliers and employees, $50,300
k. Proceeds from issuance of common stock, $11,000
l. Collections from customers, $61,700
m. Payment for purchase of investments, $17,800
n. Net income, $73,400

Required Using the direct method for operating cash flows, prepare the Trainer Company's 2004 statement of cash flows.

P4-23 *Comprehensive: Balance Sheet from Statement of Cash Flows* Gibb Company prepared the following balance sheet at the *beginning* of 2004:

GIBB COMPANY
Balance Sheet
January 1, 2004

Assets		Liabilities and Stockholders' Equity	
Cash	$ 1,000	Accounts payable	$ 4,000
Accounts receivable (net)	3,900	Salaries payable	1,100
Inventory	4,700	Total Liabilities	$ 5,100
Land	9,800	Common stock, $10 par	13,500
Buildings and equipment	68,900	Additional paid-in capital	11,200
Less: Accumulated depreciation	(14,100)	Retained earnings	44,400
Total Assets	$74,200	Total Liabilities and Stockholders' Equity	$74,200

At the *end* of 2004 Gibb prepared the following statement of cash flows:

GIBB COMPANY
Statement of Cash Flows
For Year Ended December 31, 2004

Net Cash Flow From Operating Activities

Net Income	$ 5,400	
Adjustments for differences between income flows and cash flows from operating activities:		
Add: Depreciation expense	1,900	
Decrease in inventory	500	
Increase in salaries payable	400	
Less: Increase in accounts receivable (net)	(1,100)	
Decrease in accounts payable	(1,000)	
Net cash provided by operating activities		$6,100

Cash Flows From Investing Activities

Payment for purchase of building	$(13,900)	
Proceeds from sale of land	3,000	
Net cash used for investing activities		(10,900)

Cash Flows From Financing Activities

Payment of dividends	$ (3,100)	
Proceeds from issuance of bonds	5,700	
Proceeds from issuance of common stock	4,500	
Net cash provided by financing activities		7,100
Net Increase in Cash		$ 2,300
Cash, January 1, 2004		1,000
Cash, December 31, 2004		$ 3,300

Additional information related to the statement of cash flows:

1. The long-term bonds have a face value of $6,000 and were issued on December 31, 2004.
2. The building was purchased on December 30, 2004.
3. The land was sold at its original cost.
4. The common stock which was sold totaled 300 shares and had a par value of $10 per share.

Required Prepare a classified balance sheet for the Gibb Company as of December 31, 2004. (*Hint:* Review the information on the statement of cash flows and the balances in the beginning balance sheet accounts to determine the impact on the ending balance sheet accounts.)

INTERNET ASSIGNMENTS

Go to the Nikolai and Bazley **Intermediate Accounting** web site (http://Nikolai.swcollege.com). Click on Student Resources and <u>internet</u> <u>homework</u> <u>assignments</u>. Then click on the appropriate hot link (icon) for each company's web site, find the relevant accounting information, and answer the following questions.

I4-1   Go to the Anheuser-Busch web site.

Required What format does the company use for its income statement? What were the company's net sales for each of the two most recent years? What did its "Other Income" consist of? What was its net income for each of the two most recent years? Compute the company's profit margin for each of these years. What do these results indicate to you?

I4-2   Go to the Brunswick web site.

Required What segment did Brunswick dispose of in 2000? How did it report the disposal on its income statement? What did management say about the disposal in the notes to the financial statements? Do you think this disposal will help or hinder Brunswick in its future operations? Why?

CHAPTER

Additional Aspects of Financial Reporting and Financial Analysis

5

objectives

1 Describe an auditor's report.

2 Explain the disclosures in management's discussion and analysis.

3 Understand the meaning of an operating segment.

4 Describe the disclosures in a segment report.

5 Explain interim reporting.

6 Prepare an interim report.

7 Understand intracompany and intercompany comparisons (Appendix).

8 Prepare horizontal and vertical percentage analyses (Appendix).

9 Perform ratio analysis (Appendix).

A company's financial statements summarize its various financial activities and operations. The information contained in the statements is examined, analyzed, and related to other information by external users for a variety of reasons. Current stockholders, for example, are concerned about their investment income, as well as about the company's overall profitability and stability. They also want assurance that the company's capital structure is sound and will support continued successful operations. Some potential investors are interested in "safe" companies, those whose financial statements indicate stable earnings and dividends with limited or moderate growth. Others prefer companies whose financial statements indicate a trend for financial flexibility, rapid growth, and diversification into different lines of business. Short-term creditors are interested in a company's short-run liquidity—its ability to pay current obligations as they mature. Long-term creditors are concerned about the long-term security of their interest income and the company's ability to maintain successful earnings and cash flows to meet continuing financial commitments. These are just a few of the users and uses of financial statements.

This book is designed for *preparers* of **general purpose** financial statements—statements that serve the needs of a diverse set of external users. The information contained in these statements should be understandable to users who have a reasonable understanding of business and economic activities and who are willing to examine the information with reasonable diligence.[1] These general purpose financial statements, which cover a fiscal year, are published in a corporation's **annual report** to its stockholders. In addition to the specific financial statements and accompanying notes, an annual report includes a variety of items. Items directly or indirectly related to the financial statements include the auditor's report, the report of management, and management's discussion and analysis. Companies also prepare *interim reports*, which include all or only parts of the general purpose financial statements for accounting periods of less than one year. Many companies include financial statements as well as additional financial information on their websites on the Internet. However, users should be careful because companies sometimes only provide summary information. Accountants must be familiar with these additional aspects of financial reporting.

Accountants, in the role of *preparers of financial statements*, do not themselves use the statements for investment and credit decisions.

---

1. "Objectives of Financial Reporting by Business Enterprises," *FASB Statement of Financial Accounting Concepts No. 1* (Stamford, Conn.: FASB, 1978), par. 34.

However, a better understanding of how external decision makers examine and analyze the data contained in the financial statements can lead to insights on how to improve that information. In some cases, companies may be required or may choose to present certain reports and analyses in conjunction with their annual reports as an aid to external users, and accountants must know how to prepare these documents. Finally, accountants often are called on by management, lending institutions, and other groups to provide additional analyses of the financial statements.

We include in this chapter a discussion of (1) market efficiency, (2) the auditor's report, (3) the report of management, (4) management's discussion and analysis, (5) segment reports, (6) interim reports, and (7) SEC reports. We also cover a discussion of various aspects of financial analysis, including an Appendix that covers financial analysis comparisons as well as a discussion of horizontal analysis, vertical analysis, and ratio analysis.

MARKET EFFICIENCY

Over the past two decades, research studies have been conducted based on an **efficient markets** hypothesis. Evidence from this research tends to show that (1) the prices of securities traded in the capital markets fully reflect all *publicly* available information, and (2) these prices are adjusted almost *immediately* based on new information and in an *unbiased* manner. That is, as soon as a new item of information becomes publicly available, it is interpreted, analyzed, and incorporated into the market prices. New items of information about companies may include, for instance, earnings amounts, cash flow and accrual components of earnings, and differences in accounting methods across companies. Information about companies becomes publicly available in a variety of ways, including news releases reported on the Internet and in newspapers such as *The Wall Street Journal*, and in published management forecasts, interim financial statements, and annual reports. The market prices adjust in an unbiased and immediate manner because of the market communication system and the sophistication of investors (professionals such as security analysts and stockbrokers) who continuously gather, interpret, analyze, and process information.

An efficient capital market means that an individual investor cannot use published information to earn an "abnormal" return on a security investment with a given amount of risk. That is, all securities with a similar amount of risk will yield approximately the same rate of return; only through the use of "insider information" can abnormal returns be obtained. On the other hand, some research appears to show that the market may not always be efficient. That is, the market may be mispricing the accrual component of earnings, thereby mispricing securities and enabling an astute investor to earn an abnormal return. If the efficient markets hypothesis is reasonably valid, how does the related research affect financial reporting and financial analysis, the topics of this chapter?

Since the market efficiently processes many types of public information, **full disclosure** of financial information is important for two reasons. First, full disclosure (so that the information becomes "public") helps to prevent the use of insider information by unscrupulous investors to earn abnormal returns. Second, full disclosure (at a reasonable cost) in the financial statements, the accompanying notes, or by other means that complement the information in the financial statements helps the market operate efficiently and in a cost-effective fashion.

The efficiency of the capital markets does not detract from the use of various financial analysis techniques. In fact, one of the reasons why the markets tend to be efficient is because professional analysts interpret and analyze the information. Furthermore, financial analysis techniques are useful in situations where an investor is considering the investment potential of a company whose securities are *not* traded in an organized capital market, where a financial institution is considering a lending arrangement with a company, or where a company must be monitored to make certain that it is adhering to any financial restrictions imposed by various lending agreements. Finally, not all investors believe in the efficient market hypothesis; some continue to use financial analysis techniques to try to earn abnormal returns.[2]

AUDITOR'S REPORT (OPINION)

Many investment and credit decisions are based on the information presented in a company's financial statements, which are prepared by and are the responsibility of its management. To provide an external perspective, most published financial statements are audited by an *independent* certified public accountant. In an **audit,** the certified public accountant conducts an examination of the accounting system, records, and financial statements in accordance with generally accepted auditing standards. Based on the examination, **the auditor expresses an opinion concerning the fairness of the financial statements in conformity with generally accepted accounting principles.** An auditor's standard report (opinion) includes the following statements:

1. The auditor is independent.
2. An audit was performed on specified financial statements.
3. The financial statements are the responsibility of the company's management; the opinion is the responsibility of the auditors.
4. The audit was conducted according to generally accepted auditing standards.
5. The audit was planned and performed to obtain reasonable assurance about whether the financial statements are free of material misstatement.
6. The audit included examination, assessment, and evaluation stages.
7. The audit provides a reasonable basis for an opinion.
8. An opinion is expressed concerning the fair presentation.[3]

1 Describe an auditor's report.

The report is also signed and dated by the auditing firm.

An audit report is *not* part of the financial statements because it is a report by the independent auditor. Nonetheless, it is considered an important item of information because external users place reliance on the report as to the fairness of the financial statements. The "standard" form of an auditor's report on *comparative* financial statements (often referred to as an *unqualified* opinion) is shown in Exhibit 5-1. (The audit report of The Coca-Cola Company is shown in Appendix A at the end of this book.)

An unqualified opinion contains three paragraphs. The first paragraph, known as the *introductory* paragraph, lists the financial statements that were audited, declares that management is responsible for those statements, and asserts that the auditor is responsible for expressing an opinion on them. Although the first paragraph of Exhibit 5-1 lists four financial statements, if a company reports comprehensive income, this paragraph must be modified either by adding a reference to a separate statement of comprehensive income (if presented) or by modifying a financial statement title.

The second paragraph, known as the *scope* paragraph, describes what the auditor has done. Specifically, it states that the auditor has examined the financial statements in accordance with generally accepted auditing standards and has performed appropriate tests. The auditor does *not* examine *all* of the information used to generate the financial statements, but performs tests to evaluate the reasonableness of the information. The auditor exercises skill and judgment in deciding what evidence to examine, when to examine it, and how much to examine. As we have seen throughout this book, financial statements include many estimates made by management. An auditor also designs tests to evaluate the reasonableness of the assumptions and other factors used in the

---

2. For a more complete discussion of efficient capital markets research and its implications, see R. L. Watts and J. L. Zimmerman, "Positive Accounting Theory: A Ten Year Perspective," *The Accounting Review* (January, 1990), pp. 131–156; T. R. Dyckman and D. Morse, *Efficient Capital Markets and Accounting: A Critical Analysis,* 2d ed. (Englewood Cliffs, N.J.: Prentice-Hall, 1986); and W. H. Beaven, *Financial Reporting: An Accounting Revolution,* 3rd ed. (Upper Saddle River, N.J.: Prentice Hall, 1998).
3. *AICPA Professional Standards,* Volume 1 (New York: AICPA, 2002), sec. 508.08.

EXHIBIT 5-1   Unqualified Audit Report

INDEPENDENT AUDITOR'S REPORT

We have audited the accompanying balance sheets of X Company as of December 31, 2005 and 2004, and the related statements of income, retained earnings, and cash flows for the years then ended. These financial statements are the responsibility of the Company's management. Our responsibility is to express an opinion on these financial statements based on our audits.

We conducted our audits in accordance with generally accepted auditing standards. Those standards require that we plan and perform the audit to obtain reasonable assurance about whether the financial statements are free of material misstatement. An audit includes examining, on a test basis, evidence supporting the amounts and disclosures in the financial statements. An audit also includes assessing the accounting principles used and significant estimates made by management, as well as evaluating the overall financial statement presentation. We believe that our audits provide a reasonable basis for our opinion.

In our opinion, the financial statements referred to above present fairly, in all material respects, the financial position of X Company as of [at] December 31, 2005 and 2004, and the results of its operations and its cash flows for the years then ended in conformity with generally accepted accounting principles.

[*Signature*]

[*Date*]

Q U E S T I O N S

Ⓠ Why do external users think an unqualified audit opinion is useful? Ⓠ What does an audit report *not* tell an external user?

---

estimates. Because estimates are inherently imprecise, the auditor's involvement supports their reasonableness but does not guarantee their accuracy.

The third paragraph, known as the *opinion* paragraph, gives the auditor's opinion. Like a doctor or lawyer, an auditor's opinion is based on professional judgment, not absolute certainty. When the opinion is unqualified, the auditor states that the financial statements present *fairly* in accordance with *generally accepted accounting principles* (GAAP). Thus the emphasis is not on presenting "fairly" in some general sense of the word but on presenting in accordance with GAAP. In other words, GAAP are defined as being fair. Therefore, the user of the financial statements must understand GAAP to be able to understand and interpret the statements. (In exceptional cases, the management of the company and the auditor may agree that a method other than GAAP provides more useful and "fairer" information about a transaction or event. In such a case, the non-GAAP method is fully disclosed.) The opinion also emphasizes that the statements comply with GAAP in all *material* respects; that is, the financial statements are free of material misstatements rather than precisely accurate. An audit enhances the confidence of users because the auditor is an objective, independent expert who is knowledgeable about the company's business and financial reporting requirements.

Note that there are three things that the audit report does *not* say. First, an unqualified opinion is not a "clean bill of health." The report does not, for example, endorse a company's policy decisions or its use of resources. Second, an unqualified opinion provides no assurance of the future success of the company. Generally accepted auditing standards include procedures to be followed to examine the financial viability of the company. However, a company may suffer financial difficulty, or even failure, within a relatively short time of receiving an unqualified opinion, a situation that does not necessarily indicate that the audit was negligent. In other words, there is a difference between a business failure and an audit failure. Third, an audit report does not provide an assurance that fraud has not been committed by a member, or members, of the company unless such fraud would cause a material misstatement in the financial statements. An audit is planned and performed with professional skepticism. The auditor assesses the risk of material misstatement and designs the audit to provide reasonable assurance of detection of significant errors or fraud. However, fraud that is concealed through forgery and collusion among the personnel of the company, especially management, may escape detection by the auditor. For large companies, such fraud would have to involve millions of dollars to be material.

In certain circumstances a modified report may be issued, or a qualified opinion, adverse opinion, or disclaimer of opinion may be expressed by the independent auditor. A *modified* report includes a fourth explanatory paragraph. The two most common types of modified reports are caused by material uncertainties and changes in accounting principles. A *qualified* opinion states that except for the effects of the qualified item, the financial statements present fairly the information in conformity with GAAP. An *adverse* opinion states that the financial statements do not present fairly the information in conformity with GAAP. A *disclaimer* of opinion states that the auditor does not express an opinion. These types of reports and opinions are discussed more fully in standard auditing books.

AUDIT COMMITTEE AND MANAGEMENT'S REPORT

Audit committees have existed in some companies for many years. Both the AICPA and the SEC have encouraged companies to establish audit committees; the New York Stock Exchange requires companies whose shares are traded on the Exchange to have such a committee. As a result, the number of companies using audit committees is increasing. An **audit committee is a group that has oversight over the financial reporting process of a company.** Since an auditor must keep in close communication with a company's management, the possibility exists that the auditor will not maintain independence from this management. A lack of independence would reduce the reliability that external users place on the company's financial statements. Consequently, a primary responsibility of an audit committee is to help maintain auditor independence. Therefore, most audit committee members usually are "outside directors" (not officers or employees of the company). The audit committee acts as the liaison between the auditor and management. Although the duties of an audit committee vary among companies, generally an audit committee of a company: (1) oversees the internal control structure, (2) helps in the selection of accounting policies, (3) helps select the auditor, (4) reviews the audit plan, (5) reviews suggestions by auditors concerning weaknesses in internal control, and (6) reviews the financial statements (both interim and annual) and audit report. Use of an audit committee enhances the credibility of a company's financial statements.

As we noted earlier, **the preparation and presentation of a company's financial statements are the responsibility of its management.** In the past, many external users have had the mistaken impression that because auditors reviewed the financial statements, the financial statements were the responsibility of the auditor. Then, if a company experienced financial difficulties that resulted in a "business failure," they erroneously thought this was an "audit failure." Consequently, officers of companies are encouraged to acknowledge their responsibilities regarding financial statements. Although not part of the financial statements, companies include a **"Management Report"** section in their annual report. In this report management acknowledges that it is responsible for preparing and presenting the financial statements. Furthermore, since sound internal control plays a vital role in these activities, this section frequently includes a discussion of internal control. Because the audit committee has oversight over internal control, reference to the audit committee's responsibilities often is made in this section. Finally, the report may identify the independent auditor's responsibilities. An example of the management report section of **Dow Chemical Company** is shown in Exhibit 5-2. Note the references to management's responsibility, the auditor's role, internal control, and the company's audit committee.

EXHIBIT 5-2 Management Responsibility Report

DOW CHEMICAL COMPANY

MANAGEMENT STATEMENT OF RESPONSIBILITY

The management of The Dow Chemical Company and its subsidiaries prepared the accompanying consolidated financial statements and has responsibility for their integrity, objectivity and freedom from material misstatement or error. These statements were prepared in accordance with accounting principles generally accepted in the United States of America. The financial statements include amounts that are based on management's best estimates and judgments. Management also prepared the other information in this annual report and is responsible for its accuracy and consistency with the financial statements. The Board of Directors, through its Audit Committee, assumes an oversight role with respect to the preparation of the financial statements.

Management recognizes its responsibility for fostering a strong ethical climate so that the Company's affairs are conducted according to the highest standards of personal and corporate conduct. Management has established and maintains internal controls that provide reasonable assurance as to the integrity and reliability of the financial statements, the protection of assets from unauthorized use or disposition, and the prevention and detection of fraudulent financial reporting.

Internal controls provide for appropriate division of responsibility and are documented by written policies and procedures that are communicated to employees with significant roles in the financial reporting process and updated as necessary. Management continually monitors internal controls for compliance. The Company maintains a strong internal auditing program that independently assesses the effectiveness of the internal controls and recommends possible improvements.

Deloitte & Touche LLP, independent auditors, with direct access to the Board of Directors through its Audit Committee, have audited the consolidated financial statements prepared by the Company, and their report follows.

Management has considered recommendations from the internal auditors and Deloitte & Touche LLP concerning internal controls and has taken actions that are cost-effective in the circumstances to respond appropriately to these recommendations. Management further believes the controls are adequate to accomplish the objectives discussed herein.

Q U E S T I O N S

 What does Dow say about its internal controls? What do you think "reasonable assurance" means?

MANAGEMENT'S DISCUSSION AND ANALYSIS

As we discuss later in this chapter, the Securities and Exchange Commission (SEC) requires certain information to be included in the *Form 10-K* annual report filed with it. One of these SEC reporting requirements involves a discussion and analysis *by management* of the company's financial condition, changes in financial condition, and results of operations. This discussion is called "management's discussion and analysis" or simply MD&A. The intent is to give investors the opportunity to look at the company "through the eyes of management" by providing both a short-term and a long-term analysis of the company's business. One focus of the MD&A is on "forward-looking" information. Thus, the MD&A provides a narrative explanation of the financial statements so that investors can judge the "quality" of earnings and the likelihood that past performance is indicative of future performance in regard to cash flows from operations and from outside sources. Although most companies are not under the jurisdiction of the SEC, its disclosure requirements have influenced accounting practice and many of these companies include the MD&A in their annual report.

In its MD&A, a company must provide information regarding liquidity, capital resources, and the results of operations, as well as other information necessary to understand its financial condition and changes in financial condition. This disclosure includes descriptions and amounts of items that may have an impact on future operations but that did not affect past operations, as well as amounts of items that affected past operations but are not expected to have an impact on future operations. Furthermore, where knowledge of segment information is useful to understanding a company's business, the discussion is to focus on each relevant, reportable operating segment, as well as on the whole company. The AICPA also requires companies to make disclosures about the risks and uncertainties existing as of the date of their financial statements in the following areas: nature of operations (e.g., products, markets), the use of estimates in preparing the financial statements, certain significant estimates (e.g., contingencies), and current vulnerability to certain concentrations (e.g., large volume of sales to a particular customer).[4]

Regulation S-K of the SEC provides instructions for preparing the nonfinancial statement information required in *Form 10-K*. It includes specific instructions concerning appropriate MD&A disclosures, as well as general instructions about overall MD&A disclosures. *Financial Reporting Release No. 36* provides additional guidance for MD&A disclosures, particularly those dealing with prospective information. The following is a brief discussion of the major disclosure issues that may involve intracompany and intercompany comparisons, and may include horizontal, vertical, and ratio analyses (discussed in the chapter Appendix). The discussion assumes that any items included in a company's MD&A are material.

1. *Liquidity.* A company is to identify any known trends or demands, commitments, events, or uncertainties that are likely to result in an increase or decrease in its short-term and long-term liquidity. If a significant deficiency in liquidity is identified, the company is to indicate the actions it expects to take to remedy the situation. The company also must identify and separately describe its internal and external sources of liquidity, and discuss any major unused sources of liquid assets.

2. *Capital Resources.* A company is to describe its commitments for capital expenditures at the end of the current period, as well as indicate the purpose of these commitments and the anticipated sources of funds needed to fulfill the commitments. In this regard, the company must describe any known favorable or unfavorable trends in its capital resources. This description is to include a discussion of any expected significant changes in the mix of its capital resources and the relative cost. The discussion also must explain any changes between debt and equity financing, and off-balance-sheet financing arrangements.

3. *Results of Operations.* A number of disclosures relate to income from continuing operations. First, a company is to describe any significant unusual or infrequent events or transactions and their effect on income from continuing operations. This description must include the impact on the various affected revenues and expenses. Second, a description of any known trends or uncertainties that are likely to favorably or unfavorably affect income from continuing operations must be included. Third, if a significant change in the relationship between costs and revenues is expected to occur, the change is to be described. Fourth, if there is a significant increase in net sales revenues, a discussion must be included to explain whether the increase was due to increased selling prices, increased volume, or the introduction of new products or services. Finally, a discussion must be included of the impact of inflation and changing prices on net sales revenues and income from continuing operations.

4. *General Instructions.* Lengthy general instructions for the presentation of a company's MD&A are included in *Regulation S-K* and various *Financial Reporting Releases*. The SEC distinguishes between "required" disclosures, that we briefly discussed earlier, and "voluntary" disclosures that are encouraged but not required in regard to prospective information. That is, *Required* disclosures involve *currently known* trends, events, and uncertainties that are *reasonably* expected to have significant effects on a company. In contrast, *voluntary* (optional) forward-looking disclosures involve *anticipated future* trends or events, or a less predictable impact of a known trend, event, or uncertainty.[5]

The AICPA Special Committee on Financial Reporting supports these disclosures and recommends that the focus be on the information that a company's "senior management"

2 Explain the disclosures in management's discussion and analysis.

---

4. "Disclosure of Certain Significant Risks and Uncertainties," *AICPA Statement of Position No. 94-6* (New York: AICPA, 1994).
5. "Regulation S-X," and "Codification of Financial Reporting Policies," *SEC Accounting Rules* (Chicago: Commerce Clearing House, 2002), reg. 229.303 and sec. 501.02.

uses to manage the business. The Committee acknowledges that high-level operating data and performance measures will vary by industry and company. Nonetheless, the Committee feels that management should identify and discuss those measures that it believes are significant and meaningful to its business, and that are the primary indicators of the company's future.[6] The Coca-Cola Company's financial review, incorporating its management discussion and analysis, is shown in Appendix A at the end of this book.

SEGMENT REPORTING

A company that has subsidiaries prepares its financial statements on a "consolidated" basis; that is, the accounting results of its various legal entities are *aggregated* into a set of financial statements for the entire economic entity (briefly discussed in Chapter 14). Although investors and creditors know the importance of consolidated statements in evaluating overall company performance, the *disaggregation* of total financial data also can be important in their financial analysis.

The evaluations of risk and return are significant factors in investment and credit decisions. Risk may result from a number of factors: (1) the way in which a company is organized and how its divisions are operated, (2) the nature and current status of the economy or economies in which the company operates, (3) the changing conditions in the geographic areas within which the company operates, and (4) the characteristics of its major customers. The profitability or return offered by a company also is affected by the same factors.

Financial analysis information on risk and return is improved through a company's presentation of disaggregated financial information about its operating segments. The AICPA Special Committee on Financial Reporting considers operating segment reporting to be very important. It suggests that a company should provide disaggregated information on segments if they are critical "drivers" of the company's risks and opportunities. The information reported should be based on the way in which the company uses the information for internal reporting to carry out its business activities.[7]

In light of the need for operating segment information, the FASB, in cooperation with its counterpart in Canada, issued **FASB Statement No. 131** which requires that a company's financial statements include certain disaggregated information about its operations.[8]

Reporting on Operating Segments

3 Understand the meaning of an operating segment.

A company's financial statements might be disaggregated in a number of ways, such as by products and services, geography, legal entity, or type of customer. The way a company identifies its operating segments for financial reporting is through the use of the "management approach." The management approach is based on the way a company's management organizes the company's segments for making operating decisions and for assessing performance. Thus, **an operating segment is a component of a company:**

1. **that engages in business activities to earn revenues and incur expenses,**
2. **whose operating results are regularly reviewed by the company's chief operating officer to make decisions about resources to be allocated to the segment and to assess its performance, and**
3. **for which financial information is available.**

Not all departments in a company are operating segments. For instance, a corporate headquarters normally does not earn revenues directly and is not an operating segment.

---

6. "Improving Business Reporting—A Customer Focus," *AICPA Special Committee on Financial Reporting* (New York: AICPA, 1994), App. II, p. 133.
7. *Ibid.*, pp. 10 and 140.
8. "Disclosures about Segments of an Enterprise and Related Information," *FASB Statement of Financial Accounting Standards No. 131* (Norwalk, Conn.: FASB, 1997), par. 1. Nonpublic companies, those whose securities are not traded publicly or that are not required to file financial statements with the SEC, are not required to report segment information.

Generally, an operating segment has a *segment manager* who is directly accountable for the segment's operating activities, and who maintains regular contact with the chief operating officer.

REPORTABLE SEGMENTS A company does not have to provide financial information about all its operating segments, however. Materiality determines whether or not a segment is a **reportable segment**—one whose operations are significant enough that its financial activities must be reported. **An operating segment is considered significant and is a reportable segment if it satisfies at least *one* of the three following tests:**

1. *Revenue Test.* Its reported revenues (including sales to external customers and intersegment sales) are 10% or more of the combined revenues of all the company's reported operating segments.
2. *Profit Test.* The absolute amount of its profit (loss) is 10% or more of the combined reported profits of all operating segments that did not report a loss.[9]
3. *Asset Test.* Its segment assets are 10% or more of the combined assets of all operating segments.

We discuss the terms "revenues," "profit (and loss)," and "segment assets" as applied in this *Statement* in the next section.

In addition to these tests, an overall materiality test states that the reportable segments must be a substantial portion of the company's total operations. That is, enough reportable segments must be disclosed so that their combined revenues are at least 75% of the entire company revenues. The remaining insignificant operating segments are combined and the segment information discussed in the next section is disclosed in an "all other" segment category. If a company has only one operating segment, it does not have disaggregated information to report, but it still must disclose the general information and company-wide information discussed in the next section.

INFORMATION REPORTED The disclosure requirements of *FASB Statement No. 131* are quite detailed. We summarize them as follows:

1. *General Information.* A company must (a) identify how it is organized (e.g., by product lines or geographic areas) and what factors were used to identify its operating segments, and (b) describe the types of products and services from which each reportable segment derives its revenues.

4 Describe the disclosures in a segment report.

2. *Information about Profit (or Loss).* A company must report a measure of the profit (or loss) for each reportable segment. It must also disclose certain amounts used in computing each segment's profit (or loss), as long as these amounts are included in the reports reviewed by the chief operating officer. These amounts are the segment's (a) revenues (separated into sales to external customers and intersegment sales), (b) interest revenue and interest expense, and (c) depreciation, depletion, and amortization expense.[10]
3. *Information about Assets.* A company must report a measure of the total assets of each reportable segment. Only segment assets that are included in the reports reviewed by the chief operating officer are included. For these assets, a company also must disclose the total capital expenditures for additions to long-lived assets for each reportable segment.
4. *Reconciliations.* A company must provide reconciliations of (a) the total of the reportable segments' revenues to the company's total revenues, (b) the total of the reportable segments' measures of profit (or loss) to the company's pretax

---

9. If the combined losses of all operating segments that reported a loss exceed the combined profits as calculated earlier, the combined loss amount is used for this 10% test.
10. These are the amounts for the most common items included in a company's pretax income from continuing operations. If an operating segment is evaluated using a more complex "income" measure (or on an after-tax basis), then the company must also disclose any unusual items, equity method income, other significant noncash items, and extraordinary items (and income tax expense or benefit) for each reportable segment.

income from continuing operations, and (c) the total of the reportable segments' assets to the company's total assets. The revenues, profit (or loss), and segment assets of the "all other" segment category must be included in these reconciliations.

5. *Company-Wide Disclosures.* A company (even one with only a single operating segment) must disclose (a) its revenue from external customers for each product and service, and (b) information about geographic areas including (1) revenues from external customers in the United States, and revenues from customers in individual foreign countries, and (2) total long-lived assets located in the United States, and total long-lived assets located in all foreign countries. If a company's revenues from transactions with a single external customer are 10% or more of the company's total revenues, then the company must disclose this fact and identify the segment(s) reporting the revenues.[11]

A company is not required to follow a specific format in making the preceding disclosures. The FASB encourages a company to use a format that provides the information in the most understandable manner for its specific circumstances.

ILLUSTRATION   Typically, a company will include its segment report and the related narrative discussion in the notes to the financial statements in its annual report. What a company includes in this segment report depends on the approach the company uses to evaluate its segment managers. This management approach will affect the *internal* reports the company uses in this evaluation process. These internal reports may be very detailed or broad in their information. Furthermore, they will vary from company to company. For instance, one company may require its segment managers to invest excess funds and earn interest revenue, as well as borrow funds and incur interest expense. These items would be included in the internal reports used by the chief operating officer to evaluate the segment managers. Another company may invest excess funds and borrow funds at the "corporate level" so that any interest revenue and interest expense are not attributable to segment activities. These items, frequently called "corporate interest revenue" and "corporate interest expense," are not assigned to each segment. Other types of corporate revenues, corporate expenses, and corporate assets related to operations in the company's headquarters also are not assigned to each segment.

Thus, a company frequently has to prepare a worksheet (based on information from internal reports) that appropriately assigns its total sales revenues, cost of goods sold, operating expenses, and assets to each operating segment. Based on these assignments, the company performs the revenue, profit, and asset tests to determine the *reportable segments*. The required financial information of the reportable segments (and the "all other" segments) then is reported separately in the company's segment report. Because companies vary in their management approaches, it is not practical to illustrate all possible types of segment reports. We do, however, illustrate the way one hypothetical company (the Teal Company) discloses its disaggregated financial information in its annual report. The Coca-Cola Company has more extensive disclosures, which are shown in Appendix A of this book.

Assume that on its 2004 income statement, the Teal Company reports sales of $3,800, cost of goods sold of $2,470, and operating expenses of $620, so that its pretax operating profit is $710 ($3,800 − $2,470 − $620). From this pretax operating profit, the company deducts interest expense of $80 to report pretax income from continuing operations of $630. The company also reports total assets of $19,000 on its December 31, 2004 balance sheet. The company's chief operating officer uses a segment's pretax operating profit to evaluate the segment manager; the company makes no intersegment sales, and interest expense is considered to be incurred at the corporate level. After preparing a worksheet to assign its segment revenues (sales), operating profits (sales minus cost of goods sold and operating expenses), and assets for segment reporting, Teal determines

---

11. *FASB Statement No. 131, op. cit.,* par. 18–39.

EXHIBIT 5-3   Segment Reporting

TEAL COMPANY

Operating Segment Financial Results
For Year Ended December 31, 2004

| | Reportable Operating Segments | | | All Other | Total |
	A	B	C	Segments	Results
Segment revenues (sales)	$ 300	$2,530	$ 370	$ 600	$ 3,800
Segment profit (pretax)	$ 70	$ 495	$ 105	$ 140	$ 810
General corporate expenses					(100)
Corporate interest expense					(80)
Pretax income from continuing operations					$ 630
Segment assets at December 31, 2004	$1,800	$9,400	$2,000	$2,800	$16,000
General corporate assets					3,000
Total assets at December 31, 2004					$19,000

NOTES: The company is organized into three major segments, A, B, and C (describe factors identifying segments). Operations in Segment A involve production and sales of (describe types of products and services). Operations in Segment B involve production and sales of (describe types of products and services). Operations in Segment C involve production and sales of (describe types of products and services). Total revenue by segment includes sales to external customers. The company makes no intersegment sales.

Segment profit is total revenue less operating expenses. In computing segment profit, none of the following items have been deducted: general corporate expenses, corporate interest expense, or income taxes.

Depreciation for Segments A, B, and C was $20, $300, and $40, respectively. Capital expenditures for the three segments were $100, $400, and $200, respectively. Segment assets are those assets that are used in the company's operations in each segment. General corporate assets are principally cash, temporary investments, and corporate headquarters.

The company only makes sales in the U.S. Contracts with a U.S. government agency account for $600 of the sales to external customers of Segment B.

---

that it has three reportable segments (A, B, and C) and several insignificant operating segments. Teal also determines that it has $100 of general corporate expenses and $3,000 of general corporate assets.

Exhibit 5-3 shows the schedule and narrative discussion that Teal Company includes in its annual report. Note that the revenues and profits of the segments are reconciled to the appropriate totals on the income statement. The segment revenues are reconciled to total sales. The segment profits are reconciled to the pretax income from continuing operations by deducting the general corporate expenses and corporate interest expense. Similarly, the segment assets are reconciled to the total corporate assets.

Conceptual Evaluation

FASB Statement No. 131 replaced *FASB Statement No. 14*, which was issued over 25 years ago. *FASB Statement No. 14* focused on reporting disaggregated information about a company's industry and geographic segments. When it was issued, some companies objected for several reasons. They felt that

1. Use of this disaggregated information would complicate the analysis of conditions, trends, and ratios;
2. Disaggregated information was too analytical or interpretive to be considered accounting information;

3. Unless a user had good knowledge of the company's business and economic environment, the disaggregated information would not be useful;

4. The flexibility that companies had in defining industry segments and the different ways they assigned common costs to segments and priced intersegment sales would result in noncomparable information;

5. The disaggregated information did not possess sufficient verifiability;

6. Disclosing disaggregated information would harm their competitive position because competitors would have access to this information; and

7. Disaggregated information was too costly to prepare.

Over the 25-year period, external users found that some of these criticisms were valid, but most were not. Thus, they argued for *more* and *better* disclosures. They argued that the disclosure of disaggregated information, along the lines that a company uses in its internal management decisions, is vital for investment and credit decision making. They felt that it is important for analysis and interpretation to be able to see the information "through the eyes of management." Furthermore, they argued that it is their job to learn about a company's business and economic environment. They were, however, critical of the existing standards. They felt that the focus of disaggregated information should be on a company's operating segments and not on arbitrary industry segments. They also felt that quarterly disaggregated information would be helpful in their decisions.

The FASB agreed and, hence, modified and expanded the disaggregated disclosure requirements by issuing *FASB Statement No. 131*. It stated that the intent of the disaggregated reporting requirements is to provide information about the different types of business activities in which a company operates and the different economic environments in which it operates to help users (1) better understand the company's current and past performance, (2) better assess its prospects for future net cash flows, and (3) make more informed judgments about the company as a whole. It also requires the disclosure of certain segment information in a company's interim reports (discussed in the next section). In other words, the FASB expects that this disaggregation will provide more *relevant* information that will improve the *feedback value*, *predictive value*, and *timeliness* of a company's financial reports.

The FASB adopted the "management approach" to disaggregated reporting to offset the criticism that the previously required disclosures did not provide a viewpoint of the way a company manages its operations. Furthermore, it felt that since segment managers have a vested interest in the "quality" of the information used to evaluate them, the information is more likely to be accurate. In other words, the FASB expects the new disclosures to be more *reliable* by having more *representational faithfulness* and a higher degree of *verifiability*.

In regard to the possibility of competitive harm, the Board did eliminate or reduce some disclosure requirements listed in the *Exposure Draft*. However, it felt that most competitors have other sources of more detailed information about a company than that disclosed in its disaggregated information. Furthermore, the Board felt that the possibility of competitive harm is the chance a company takes to have access to capital markets. The FASB also felt that by moving to a management approach, the cost of providing disaggregated information would be less than before, because a company is already preparing much of the information for internal purposes. Thus, the required disclosures meet the *benefits greater than costs* criterion.

There are still at least three *comparability* issues, however. First, not all companies are organized in the same way. Therefore, one company's operating segment information may not be comparable to another's. Second, companies vary as to what price a segment is charged when it "purchases" goods from another segment (this is called "transfer pricing"). So one company's intersegment sales revenue may be based on market prices, while other companies may use "full costing" or "variable costing" transfer pricing methods. Finally, if a company allocates expenses in determining each segment's profit, this must be done on a "reasonable" basis. But what is reasonable to one company may not be reasonable to another. While these issues may result in reduced comparability across companies, the *Statement* should result in increased *consistency* for each company. On balance, the FASB feels that the current requirements for disaggregated disclosures improve the financial reporting for external users by enhancing the *decision usefulness* of the information.

INTERIM FINANCIAL REPORTS

External users often want more frequent accounting information than that provided in the annual report. **Interim financial statements are reports for periods of less than a year.** Their purpose is to improve the *timeliness* of accounting information. These *interim reports* are issued by all publicly held companies on a quarterly basis (hence the term *quarterly financial statements*). One issue involving interim reports is the difficulty inherent in determining meaningful operating results for intervals of less than a year. Revenues of some businesses are seasonal and fluctuate widely across interim periods. Some companies incur heavy fixed costs in one interim period that benefit the operating activities in other periods. Other companies must estimate costs that will not be paid until subsequent interim periods but that benefit the current one. Estimates also must be made of such items as inventories and income taxes if the interim reports are to be relevant and reliable.

5 Explain interim reporting.

The APB studied these issues and established guidelines in **APB Opinion No. 28** for the presentation of interim financial information. The intent of this *Opinion* is to indicate which generally accepted accounting principles apply to interim financial statements and to specify the disclosures needed to present meaningful information for an interim period of less than a year. The Board was particularly concerned with reconciling two different views about interim periods. One view is that each interim period is a basic accounting period and the results of operations should be determined in essentially the same way as if the interim period were an annual accounting period. The other view is that each interim period is an integral part of the annual accounting period. Thus, deferrals, accruals, and estimates made at the end of each interim period should consider the impact on the results of operations for the rest of the annual period. The Board concurred with the second view and concluded that **each interim period is viewed primarily as an integral part of an annual period** and that a company must continue to use the generally accepted accounting principles that were used in the preparation of its latest annual report. However, certain principles are modified for interim reporting purposes so that the results are more informative and articulate better with the annual report results. The FASB has issued one *Statement* (No. 131) and an *Interpretation* (No. 18) to expand and clarify various aspects of *APB Opinion No. 28*. The current generally accepted accounting principles focus primarily on the income statement items and are summarized briefly in the following sections.

Revenues

A company must recognize revenues from products or services during an interim period in the same manner (when earned and realized) as during the annual accounting period. For example, when the percentage-of-completion method is used to recognize long-term construction contracts, revenues are recorded on the basis of the percent completed during that interim period. In cases where revenues are subject to seasonal variations, the company must disclose the seasonal nature of its activities and consider presenting supplemental information regarding revenues for previous periods.

Expenses

A company must match the expenses that are associated directly with product sales or the provision of services against interim revenues in the period the revenues are recognized. These include such items as inventory costs, wages, and warranties. With regard to inventories, a company generally must use the same inventory pricing methods (e.g., LIFO, FIFO, average) and make provisions for write-downs to market for interim reporting in the same way as it does for annual reporting, with the following exceptions:

1. A company that utilizes a periodic inventory system and uses estimated gross profit rates (or other estimation methods) to determine its cost of goods sold during interim periods must disclose the method used and any significant adjustments that result from reconciliation with the annual physical inventory.

2. If a company using the LIFO method encounters a temporary partial liquidation of its base-period inventory, but expects to replace that inventory by year-end, its cost of goods sold must include the expected cost to replace the liquidated inventory, and the inventory at the interim reporting date must *not* take the liquidation into account. Assuming rising prices, this requirement avoids the possibility of showing abnormally high interim period income due to LIFO "liquidation profits."

3. A company must recognize a permanent loss due to an inventory market decline in accordance with the lower of cost or market procedures in the interim period during which the decline occurred. It must recognize any recovery of such a loss in a subsequent interim period within the same year as a gain (not to exceed the previously recognized loss) in the later period. A temporary market decline need not be recognized in an interim period.

4. The accounting for all variances for a company using a standard cost accounting system must follow routine annual procedures. The company must disclose any significant unplanned or unanticipated purchase price or volume variances in the interim period.

The recognition of losses using lower of cost or market procedures is discussed in Chapter 8.

Expenses that are not directly associated with product sales (or services) are matched against revenues using a variety of bases. Expenses that can be identified as affecting the operating activities of more than one interim period are allocated among the interim periods based on an estimate of (1) time expired, (2) benefit received, or (3) activity associated with the periods. Such allocation procedures must be consistent with those used for annual reporting purposes. For example, accrued or deferred property taxes, advertising costs, depreciation charges, and uncollectible accounts (bad debts) expense are allocated among the interim periods. Expenses that cannot be identified with activities other than those of the current interim period are allocated to that period. No arbitrary allocations are allowed. Disclosure of the nature and amount of such costs must be made. For example, office utilities, rent expense, and interest costs are expensed as incurred in the interim period. Gains and losses that occur in an interim period and that would not be deferred at year-end are recognized in the interim period of occurrence. For example, a gain on the sale of land or a loss on the disposal of equipment is recognized in the interim period.[12]

Income Taxes

To present fairly the results of operations, at the end of *each* interim period a company must make its best estimate of the effective income tax rate expected to be applicable for the *entire* year. The effective rate includes the appropriate tax rate on *annual* income from continuing operations, after considering such items as foreign tax rates, percentage depletion, and other available tax planning techniques. In determining the rate, the company does not consider the income tax related to any items (such as extraordinary items) that are reported separately net of income taxes. Consequently, each quarter the company estimates its annual income from continuing operations and, based on this annual income, estimates its annual income taxes to derive an effective annual income tax rate. It then uses the effective rate to compute the income taxes related to income from continuing operations on a year-to-date basis. The amount of income taxes applicable to the current interim period is the difference between the income tax computed

---

12. "Interim Financial Statements," *APB Opinion No. 28* (New York: AICPA, 1973), par. 11–15.

EXHIBIT 5-4 Computation of Interim Income Taxes

1. Estimated Annual Income

First quarter	$ 20,000	actual income
Second quarter	26,000	actual income
Third quarter	25,000	estimated income
Fourth quarter	29,000	estimated income
	$100,000	estimated annual income

2. Estimated Effective Income Tax Rate

$$15\% \times \$20,000 = \$ 3,000$$
$$30\% \times (\$100,000 - \$20,000) = 24,000$$
$$\text{Estimated total tax} = \$27,000$$

$$27\% \text{ Effective income tax rate} = \frac{\$27,000 \text{ Estimated income tax}}{\$100,000 \text{ Estimated income}}$$

3. Estimated Income Tax for First Six Months

   $46,000 \times 27\% = \underline{\$12,420}$ estimated income tax on first six months' income

4. Estimated Income Tax for Second Quarter

$12,420	estimated income tax on first six months of income
(5,220)	estimated income tax on first-quarter income
$ 7,200	estimated income tax on second-quarter income

on year-to-date income from continuing operations and the related income taxes reported on previous interim reports of the accounting period.[13] This procedure must be completed for each of the four interim periods; it follows the general principle of intraperiod tax allocation.

To illustrate, assume a corporation reported pretax income from continuing operations of $20,000 at the end of the first quarter and estimated its income tax on this income to be $5,220. (This estimate was derived at the end of the first quarter, using the technique discussed previously.) For simplicity, this example ignores temporary differences and tax credits. The corporation now is preparing an interim income statement at the end of the second quarter for that quarter and the first six months. It determines that its pretax income from continuing operations for the second quarter is $26,000 and anticipates it will earn $25,000 and $29,000 in each of the next two quarters, respectively. The corporate income tax rates are 15% on the first $20,000 of earnings and 30% on earnings in excess of $20,000. As shown in Exhibit 5-4, based on an estimated effective income tax rate of 27%, the corporation lists income tax expense of $12,420 for the first six months and $7,200 for the second quarter of operations.

In the case of an *established* pattern of seasonal revenues resulting in an earlier interim period operating loss that is offset by income in later periods, the income tax effects (that is, the income tax credit) of the earlier loss are recognized in that interim period and offset against the income taxes incurred on the income of the later interim periods.

---

13. "Accounting for Income Taxes in Interim Periods," *FASB Interpretation No. 18* (Stamford, Conn.: FASB, 1977), par. 9.

Extraordinary Items, Discontinued Operations, and Cumulative Effects

Material extraordinary items and results of discontinued operations are reported (net of income taxes) in the usual manner in the interim period during which the events occurred. The cumulative effect of a change in accounting principle (net of income taxes) is reported in the first interim period, regardless of the interim period in which it occurs. None of these items is prorated over the entire annual accounting period. Materiality, however, is determined on the basis of a relationship of the item to the estimated income for the entire *year* and not to the interim period results.

Earnings per Share

The computation of earnings per share is discussed in Chapter 16.

Earnings per share is computed for each interim period presented. In its simplest form, earnings per share is computed by dividing the net income by the average number of common shares outstanding for the period. For computing the average number of common shares outstanding as well as for other earnings per share issues, the quarter (or year-to-date for longer periods) is considered the accounting "period." The resulting earnings per share is reported on the face of the interim income statement. A breakdown of earnings per share related to income from continuing operations, results of discontinued operations, extraordinary items, and the cumulative effect of a change in accounting principle is also disclosed.

Care should be taken in disclosing comparative interim earnings per share because of differences arising as a result of the short time periods. Shares issued in the second quarter result in a different number of outstanding shares than in the first quarter, making it difficult for a user to predict an annual earnings per share. Similarly, an extraordinary loss occurring in the fourth quarter affects earnings per share for that quarter and the year but does not affect the earnings per share listed in the first three quarters.

Preparation and Disclosure of Summarized Interim Financial Data

6 Prepare an interim report.

The accounting procedures a company uses in the preparation of its interim reports are similar to those for annual reports. Typically, a trial balance of the year-to-date account balances is taken. The trial balance is entered on a worksheet or other working paper. Year-to-date adjusting entries are prepared on the working paper, after which the year-to-date financial statements are prepared. However, the interim accounting procedures differ in several respects from those completed at year-end.

First, for a company using a periodic inventory system, the determination of the ending inventory for the interim reports is usually based on an estimation technique rather than on a physical inventory. Thus, the gross profit method, retail inventory method, or some other estimation technique is used to derive the ending interim inventory to be recorded on the working paper and reported in the financial statements. Second, the adjusting entries required at the end of the interim period to bring the accounts up to date usually are prepared only on the working paper and are not entered into the accounts. When this approach is used, only at the end of the year are the annual adjusting entries journalized and posted to the accounts.

Third, the accounts are not closed at the end of each interim period. Consequently, in an interim period subsequent to the first period, care must be taken not to include amounts applicable to previous interim periods in the revenue and expense accounts. To avoid this problem, as we mentioned previously, a company typically prepares the interim income statement on a year-to-date basis and then eliminates the income statement results from any previous interim periods. For example, at the end of six months, a company would prepare a half-year income statement and then "back out" (subtract) the first-quarter income statement results to determine the second-quarter income statement. Finally, interim reports typically are not audited (except for SEC reports) because of the time and cost involved. However, auditing procedures have been developed for cases where an accountant is engaged to make a review of the interim financial information.

While the APB recognized the advantages to users of more timely information in the form of interim reports, it also recognized that this advantage may be partially off-set by the lesser amount of detail in the interim reports. Thus, it has provided guidelines regarding *minimum* disclosure. When publicly held companies report interim summaries of financial information, the following data must be reported at a minimum: (1) sales or gross revenues, income taxes, extraordinary items (net of tax), the cumulative effect of a change in accounting principle, and net income; (2) earnings per share for each period presented; (3) seasonal revenues, costs, and expenses; (4) significant changes in estimates of income taxes; (5) results of discontinued operations and material unusual or infrequent items; (6) contingent items; (7) changes in accounting principles[14] or estimates; and (8) significant changes in financial position (i.e., cash flows).

When a company presents the preceding information on a quarterly basis, it also provides current year-to-date information, along with comparable data from the previous year. Companies are encouraged to provide condensed balance sheet and cash flow data for the interim periods to assist security holders in their analyses of *financial flexibility* and *liquidity*. When this information is not presented, a company must report any significant changes since the last reporting date in liquid assets, working capital, long-term liabilities, and stockholders' equity. A company also must disclose selected information about each of its reportable operating segments. This information includes items such as segment revenues from external customers, intersegment revenues, segment profit or loss, and segment assets.[15] The SEC requires more extensive interim disclosures, as we discuss later in the chapter. Although interim financial statements are too lengthy to illustrate here, the Coca-Cola Company includes quarterly data at the end of its annual report, as shown in Appendix A to this book.

SEC REPORTS

The Securities and Exchange Commission (SEC) was created to administer various securities acts under powers provided by Congress in the Securities Act of 1933 and the Securities Exchange Act of 1934. The intent of Congress was to regulate the disclosure of all significant financial information provided by companies issuing publicly traded securities (e.g., stocks and bonds). The SEC has the legal authority to prescribe accounting principles and reporting practices for these regulated companies.

The SEC is a large organization with headquarters in Washington, D.C. Among the administrative offices, the **Office of the Chief Accountant** is important to accountants because it is responsible for providing the SEC with advice concerning accounting and auditing. The *Chief Accountant* helps to establish administrative policies regarding accounting matters. This office is directly responsible for *Regulation S-X* (which establishes the form and content of financial statements filed with the SEC), and is primarily responsible for the *Financial Reporting Releases* (which prescribe accounting principles for regulated companies). Among the divisions, the **Division of Corporation Finance** is also important to accountants. This division is responsible for assisting in the establishment of reporting standards (except those directly related to financial statements, which are the responsibility of the Chief Accountant) and the requirements for adherence to these standards by regulated companies. The division is also responsible for reviewing the financial reports submitted to the SEC by regulated companies.

---

14. *APB Opinion No. 28* established certain guidelines for reporting accounting changes in interim reports. These guidelines were similar to those established in *APB Opinion No. 20* and are not discussed in this chapter. As a result of difficulties in interpretation, *FASB Statement of Financial Accounting Standards No. 3*, "Reporting Accounting Changes in Interim Financial Statements" (Stamford, Conn.: FASB, 1974), was issued to clarify the reporting of such changes, and is discussed in Chapter 22.
15. *FASB Statement No. 131, op. cit.*, par. 33.

Since all these reports generally must be certified by a certified public accountant, an understanding of its activities is useful to accountants responsible for filing them.[16]

Numerous forms are required to be filed with the SEC by regulated companies. Two forms that are important to accountants are:

- *Form 10-K.* An annual report.
- *Form 10-Q.* A quarterly report of operations.

Form 10-K is the most common SEC annual report form and is required to be filed with the SEC within 60 days of a company's fiscal year-end, effective in 2004. The current Form 10-K consists of four major parts. The SEC separates its required financial information into two types: (1) information that must be reported *both* in annual reports filed with the SEC and annual reports issued to stockholders, and (2) information required to be filed only with the SEC.

Information of the first type includes items such as the financial statements, notes, MD&A, and market information on the company's common stock. This information can be included in Form 10-K by *reference* to the company's annual report issued to stockholders. Note, however, that all the information *must* be included in the annual report. Thus, for instance, many companies include an MD&A as well as three years of comparative financial statements in their stockholders' annual reports. The second type of information (required to be filed only with the SEC) is considered to be important primarily to a limited and sophisticated group of users (e.g., security analysts). This type includes items such as directors and officers, executive compensation, legal proceedings, and voting matters.

Form 10-Q is used to report a company's quarterly financial information to the SEC and is required to be filed within 35 days of the end of each of the company's first three fiscal quarters, effective in 2004. It contains similar disclosures to that of Form 10-K, but includes only quarterly and year-to-date information. The accounting principles established in *APB Opinion No. 28*, "Interim Financial Reporting," discussed earlier in the chapter, are used to prepare the Form 10-Q disclosures, so that this financial information is very similar to that provided in a company's quarterly report to stockholders. However, it may be more extensive because the SEC *requires* the presentation of comparative interim financial statements. Form 10-K and Form 10-Q must be filed electronically by all companies according to the EDGAR requirements.

INTERNATIONAL ACCOUNTING DIFFERENCES

International accounting standards differ somewhat from U.S. accounting standards for both segment reporting and interim reporting. Segment reporting is required under international standards but reportable segments are identified differently than under U.S. standards. Under international standards, reportable segments include both business segments and geographic segments, with a business segment providing goods or services and being different from other business segments as to risks and returns. A geographic segment provides goods or services within a particular economic environment and is different from other geographic segments as to risks and returns. International and U.S. standards require a company to make similar segment disclosures (e.g., segment profit or loss, revenues, assets), but there are some differences in measurement and reporting requirements. For instance, a company (1) measures its segment profit (or loss) under international standards in the same way as it reports its consolidated income (as opposed to the management approach in the U.S.) and (2) includes in segment revenues and segment assets any reasonably allocated items (as opposed to the management approach). International standards also require a company to disclose each segment's liabilities and encourages segment cash flow disclosures.

---

16. For a more extensive discussion of the history and administrative responsibilities of the various segments of the SEC, see K. F. Skousen, *An Introduction to the SEC,* 5th ed. (Cincinnati, Ohio: South-Western Publishing Company, 1991).

International standards provide guidance for what to include in an interim report, but do not specify which companies must publish them or how frequently. Public companies, however, are encouraged to provide at least half-year reports. If a company issues an interim report, under international standards it is required to include a condensed balance sheet, income statement, cash flow statement, statement of changes in equity, and selected explanatory notes. However, international standards differ from U.S. standards in that they do not allow (1) the allocation of expenses between interim periods, (2) the deferral of manufacturing variances that are expected to be offset in a later interim period, or (3) the deferral of a temporary market decline in inventory that is expected to be recovered in a later interim period.

APPENDIX: FINANCIAL ANALYSIS COMPARISONS

This Appendix deals with various tools of financial analysis. The following diagram depicts financial analysis and its related tools that we discuss in later sections.

Before we discuss the preparation of these financial analyses, it is helpful to know how this information is used. The decision process of external users may be summarized as follows: (1) The external users examine the current financial reports for information important to them. (2) They look for criteria that will assist them in analyzing the reports and making decisions; usually, although not exclusively, they make comparisons with a particular company's past results as well as with similar companies within the same or related industries. (3) They make their decision. (4) They evaluate their decision based on feedback. Of importance here are the comparisons made in the financial analysis.

INTRACOMPANY COMPARISONS

One method of evaluating a company's current financial performance and condition is to compare them with the company's past results. This is called **intracompany comparison.** An important factor in this type of comparison is the evidence of **trends**—indications that a company's performance is stable, is improving, or is deteriorating, not only in the short run but also in the longer run. Most companies now present at least 2 years of comparable data in their financial statements, and many also include 5-, 10-, or 15-year summaries of key financial data.

A critical point to remember when preparing financial analysis information for use in intracompany comparisons is the need for **consistency** over time. Whether operating segment information, interim data, percentage analyses, ratios, or SEC reports are prepared, each year's information should be presented in a consistent fashion in terms of arrangement and content so that valid comparisons and reliable trend indications may be obtained.

7 Understand intracompany and intercompany comparisons.

INTERCOMPANY COMPARISONS

A second method of evaluation is to compare a company's performance with that of competitors, with the industry as a whole, or with the results in related industries. This is known as **intercompany comparison** and may be made for a single period or for several past periods. A competitor's financial information may be obtained from its respective financial statements. Information on the performance of the industry as a whole or of related industries may be based on compilations of financial information by such financial analysis companies as Moody's Investors Service, Standard and Poor's, Dun and Bradstreet, and Robert Morris and Associates. These companies not only provide information from annual reports but also publish periodic updates and supplements. Other organizations and trade associations supply similar information on a more selective basis. Much of this information is available on the Internet.

A user preparing financial analysis information for an intercompany comparison is concerned not only with consistency over time, but also with comparability of data across companies. A preparer of a company's financial information may not be able to exercise much control over the consistency of data across other companies. Nevertheless, the preparation of this data should take into consideration such factors as the use of comparable numbers in the numerator and denominator of financial ratios, the use of common industry classifications in the development of operating segment results, and the impact of different generally acceptable accounting practices (for example, LIFO versus FIFO for inventory costing or accelerated versus straight-line depreciation) on the results. When preparing financial analysis data, an accountant should be aware that this information may be used in both intracompany and intercompany comparisons.

PERCENTAGE ANALYSES

8 Prepare horizontal and vertical percentage analyses.

The interpretation of current results and the comparison of a company's operating results and financial position across several periods or with other companies may be enhanced by converting the monetary relationships in the financial statements to percentage relationships. The three types of analyses that use percentage relationships are called horizontal analysis, vertical analysis, and ratio analysis. We discuss the first two in this section and discuss ratio analysis in the following section.

Horizontal Analysis

In horizontal analysis, changes in a company's operating results and financial position *over time* are shown in percentages as well as in dollars. If this method is used, it usually is done in conjunction with the income statement. Horizontal analysis sometimes is used for balance sheet comparisons. It is used less frequently in the analysis of the statement of cash flows because many items do not recur consistently on this statement.

When only two years of comparative data are disclosed in percentages, the earlier year is used as the base year and the amount of change in each item is shown as a percentage of that item's base-year amount. When data are shown for more than two years, two alternative approaches may be used. In the first approach, the preceding year is used as the base year for each later year, and the percentage change from year to year is shown. Column (1) of Exhibit 5-5 illustrates this "year-to-year" approach for the Cooper Company. Although this approach identifies and highlights year-to-year changes, a user cannot easily analyze the relative changes over an extended period. Because different years are used as bases, it is not possible to add the changes from year to year to determine the total cumulative change. For this type of analysis, a second approach may be used. Here, the *initial* year is used as the base year, and the cumulative results from later years are compared with the initial year to determine the cumulative percentage changes. Column (2) of Exhibit 5-5 illustrates this "base-year-to-date" approach for the Cooper Company. With this approach, if a weak initial year is selected, the cumulative percentage changes appear stronger than may be warranted.

Whenever horizontal analysis is used, care must be taken in computing and interpreting percentage changes. If a base figure is zero or negative, although an *amount* of change may be shown, *no percentage* change may be validly expressed. Furthermore, in cases where changes are shown as percentages, no vertical addition or subtraction of the percentages (as we discuss in the next section) can be made because the percentage changes result from the use of different bases. Finally, for items with small base amounts, a relatively small dollar change may result in a very high percentage change, thus potentially making the item more significant than may be warranted.

EXHIBIT 5-5 Horizontal Analyses

COOPER COMPANY

Comparative Income Statements

| | For Years Ended December 31, | | | (1) Year-to-Year Increase (Decrease) | | | | | (2) Base-Year-to-Date Increase (Decrease) | |
| | | | | 2004 to 2005 | | 2003 to 2004 | | | 2003 to 2005 | |
	2005	2004	2003	Amount	Percent	Amount	Percent		Amount	Percent
Sales	$138,000	$130,000	$109,500	$ 8,000	6.2	$20,500	18.7		$28,500	26.0
Sales returns	(8,000)	(10,000)	(9,500)	(2,000)	(20.0)	500	5.3		(1,500)	(15.8)
Sales (net)	$130,000	$120,000	$100,000	$10,000	8.3	$20,000	20.0		$30,000	30.0
Cost of goods sold	(74,100)	(67,200)	(58,000)	6,900	10.3	9,200	15.9		16,100	27.8
Gross profit	$ 55,900	$ 52,800	$ 42,000	$ 3,100	5.9	$10,800	25.7		$13,900	33.1
Selling expenses	(14,900)	(14,300)	(10,800)	600	4.2	3,500	32.4		4,100	38.0
General expenses	(22,300)	(22,240)	(17,350)	60	0.3	4,890	28.2		4,950	28.5
Interest expense	(3,000)	(2,400)	(2,400)	600	25.0	0	0.0		600	25.0
Total expenses	$ (40,200)	$(38,940)	$(30,550)	$ 1,260	3.2	$ 8,390	27.5		$ 9,650	31.6
Pretax continuing income	$ 15,700	$ 13,860	$ 11,450	$ 1,840	13.3	$ 2,410	21.0		$ 4,250	37.1
Income tax expense	(4,700)	(4,160)	(3,450)	540	13.0	710	20.6		1,250	36.2
Net income	$ 11,000	$ 9,700	$ 8,000	$ 1,300	13.4	$ 1,700	21.3		$ 3,000	37.5
Number of common shares	5,400	4,800	4,000	600	12.5	800	20.0		1,400	35.0
Earnings per share*	$1.81	$1.77	$1.70	$.04	2.3	$.07	4.1		$.11	6.5

*Earnings per Share = $\dfrac{\text{Net Income} - \text{Preferred Dividends (\$1,200)}}{\text{Average Common Shares Outstanding}}$

Vertical Analysis

In vertical analysis, the monetary relationships between items on the financial statements of a company for a particular *period* are shown in percentages as well as in dollars. When vertical analysis is used for comparisons of financial statements from several periods, trends or changes in the relationships between items are more easily identified. Financial statements shown only in percentages are referred to as **common-size statements.**

Vertical analysis may be used in conjunction with the income statement, retained earnings statement, balance sheet, or the statement of cash flows. In the case of the income statement, net sales usually are expressed as 100% and all other components are expressed accordingly. On the balance sheet, total assets represent 100%; on the retained earnings statement, beginning retained earnings is 100%; and for the statement of cash flows, the increase in cash is usually expressed as 100%. Exhibits 5-6 and 5-7 illustrate vertical analyses for the Cooper Company.

EXHIBIT 5-6   Vertical Analysis (Income Statement)

COOPER COMPANY

Comparative Income Statements
For Years Ended December 31, 2004 and 2005

	2005 Amount	2005 Percent	2004 Amount	2004 Percent
Sales	$138,000	106.2	$130,000	108.3
Sales returns	(8,000)	(6.2)	(10,000)	(8.3)
Sales, net (70% on credit)	$130,000	100.0	$120,000	100.0
Cost of goods sold	(74,100)	(57.0)	(67,200)	(56.0)
Gross profit	$ 55,900	43.0	$ 52,800	44.0
Selling expenses	(14,900)	(11.5)	(14,300)	(11.9)
General expenses	(22,300)	(17.1)*	(22,240)	(18.5)
Interest expense	(3,000)	(2.3)	(2,400)	(2.0)
Total expenses	$(40,200)	(30.9)	$(38,940)	(32.4)
Pretax continuing income	$ 15,700	12.1	$ 13,860	11.6
Income tax expense	(4,700)	(3.6)	(4,160)	(3.5)
Net income	$ 11,000	8.5	$ 9,700	8.1
Number of common shares	5,400		4,800	
Earnings per share	$1.81		$1.77	

Comparative Retained Earnings Statements
For Years Ended December 31, 2004 and 2005

	2005 Amount	2005 Percent	2004 Amount	2004 Percent
Beginning retained earnings	$ 32,000	100.0	$ 28,300	100.0
Net income	11,000	34.4	9,700	34.3
	$ 43,000	134.4	$ 38,000	134.3
Preferred dividends, $8/share	(1,200)	(3.7)	(1,200)	(4.2)
Common dividends, $1/share	(5,400)	(16.9)	(4,800)	(17.0)
Ending retained earnings	$ 36,400	113.8	$ 32,000	113.1

*Rounded to balance.

EXHIBIT 5-7   Vertical Analysis (Balance Sheet)

COOPER COMPANY

Comparative Condensed Balance Sheets
December 31, 2004 and 2005

	2005 Amount	2005 Percent	2004 Amount	2004 Percent
Cash	$ 3,900	3.0	$ 4,800	4.3
Receivables (net)	7,600	5.9	8,600	7.7
Inventories	8,900	6.9	10,100	9.0
Prepaid items	1,000	.8	1,200	1.1
Total current assets	$ 21,400	16.6	$ 24,700	22.1
Noncurrent assets (net)	107,800	83.4	87,300	77.9
Total Assets	$129,200	100.0	$112,000	100.0
Accounts payable	$ 5,000	3.9	$ 6,600	5.9
Other current liabilities	6,200	4.8	6,400	5.7
Total current liabilities	$ 11,200	8.7	$ 13,000	11.6
Long-term liabilities (12%)	25,000	19.3	20,000	17.9
Total liabilities	$ 36,200	28.0	$ 33,000	29.5
Preferred stock, 8%, $100 par*	$ 15,000	11.6	$ 15,000	13.4
Common stock, $5 par†	27,000	20.9	24,000	21.4
Additional paid-in capital	14,600	11.3	8,000	7.1
Retained earnings	36,400	28.2	32,000	28.6
Total stockholders' equity	$ 93,000	72.0	$ 79,000	70.5
Total Liabilities and Stockholders' Equity	$129,200	100.0	$112,000	100.0

*The 150 shares of preferred stock are noncumulative and have a liquidation value of $140 per share.
†December 31, 2005 market price is $14.25 per share.

Both vertical and horizontal analysis may be used in conjunction with interim reports and reports of the results of operating segments. Vertical and horizontal analyses also are used in conjunction with ratio analysis.

RATIO ANALYSIS

Another form of percentage analysis involves the use of ratios. Ratios, which involve the division of one or more items on the financial statements by another related item or items, are frequently used to evaluate the financial aspects (i.e., return, risk, financial flexibility, liquidity, and operating capability) of a company. Many ratios have become standardized; they are recognized as useful indicators of financial performance and are computed routinely and published on a company and industry basis by financial analysis companies. These ratios become "benchmarks" against which to compare a company's results to evaluate its effectiveness. The ratios are used by different external users in intracompany and intercompany comparisons for a variety of economic decisions. Other ratios are developed by individual users or user groups for their own specific needs.

There are more than 30 different ratios or variations of ratios for financial analysis. However, we focus on the primary standard ratios, some of which we briefly discussed in earlier chapters. These may be classified into six groups: (1) stockholder profitability ratios, (2) company profitability ratios, (3) liquidity ratios, (4) activity ratios, (5) stability ratios, and (6) cash flow ratios. We briefly discuss how to compute

9 Perform ratio analysis.

and use each ratio in the following sections. The 2005 data for the computation of these ratios is included in Exhibits 5-6 and 5-7 for the Cooper Company. Since we do not discuss the numerical calculations of these ratios in the text, you should refer to these exhibits to identify the numbers used for each ratio.

Stockholder Profitability Ratios

Stockholder profitability ratios are used to evaluate how effective a company has been in meeting the profit (i.e., return) objectives of its owners. Exhibit 5-8 shows several stockholder profitability ratios, along with the calculations for the Cooper Company. We discuss each ratio in the following sections.

Earnings per share computations are discussed in Chapter 16.

EARNINGS PER SHARE   Earnings per share is probably the most frequently cited ratio in a financial analysis. It is considered important enough to be a required disclosure on the face of a company's income statement. As its name indicates, it shows the amount of earnings attributable to each share of common stock held by stockholders.

PRICE/EARNINGS   Although not precisely a stockholder profitability ratio, the price/earnings ratio is used by actual and potential stockholders to evaluate the attractiveness of an investment in the stock of a company. A higher price/earnings ratio compared to other similar companies may indicate that investors perceive expansion potential for the company. Care must be taken, however, that the comparison is made to other "similar" companies. The price/earnings ratios for companies in "growth" industries, such as the electronics industry, are likely to be higher than for, say, companies in the automobile or steel industries. Interpretation of the ratio also is affected by investors' perceptions of the company's quality and trend of earnings, relative risk, use of alternative accounting methods, and other factors. Earnings per share based on income from continuing operations usually is used as the denominator.

DIVIDEND YIELD   The market value of a company's stock represents the value a stockholder must forgo in order to continue holding the security. Stockholders are interested in their individual rates of return based on the actual dividends received as compared with the ending market price (or market price on another particular date) of the stock. The dividend yield provides this information. The dividend yield, combined with the percentage change in the market price of the stock held during the period, is the total annual return on the stockholders' investment.

Company Profitability Ratios

Company profitability ratios are used to evaluate how effective a company has been in meeting its overall profit (return) objectives, particularly in relation to the resources invested. Exhibit 5-9 shows several overall company profitability ratios, along with the calculations for the Cooper Company. We discuss each ratio in the following sections.

EXHIBIT 5-8   Stockholder Profitability Ratios

Ratio	Formula	Calculations (2005)
1. Earnings per Share	$\dfrac{\text{Net Income} - \text{Preferred Dividends}}{\text{Average Common Shares Outstanding}}$	$\dfrac{\$11,000 - \$1,200}{5,400} = \$1.81$
2. Price/Earnings	$\dfrac{\text{Market Price per Common Share}}{\text{Earnings per Share}}$	$\dfrac{\$14.25}{\$1.81} = 7.9 \text{ times}$
3. Dividend Yield	$\dfrac{\text{Dividends per Common Share}}{\text{Market Price per Common Share}}$	$\dfrac{\$1.00}{\$14.25} = 7.0\%$

EXHIBIT 5-9   **Company Profitability Ratios**

Ratio	Formula	Calculations (2005)	
1. Profit Margin	$\dfrac{\text{Net Income}}{\text{Net Sales}}$	$\dfrac{\$11,000}{\$130,000}$	$= 8.5\%$
2. Return on Total Assets	$\dfrac{\text{Net Income} + \begin{array}{c}\text{Interest Expense}\\\text{(net of tax)}\end{array}}{\text{Average Total Assets}}$	$\dfrac{\$11,000 + (\$3,000 \times 0.7)}{\dfrac{\$129,200 + \$112,000}{2}}$	$= 10.9\%$
3. Return on Stockholders' Equity	$\dfrac{\text{Net Income}}{\text{Average Stockholders' Equity}}$	$\dfrac{\$11,000}{\dfrac{\$93,000 + \$79,000}{2}}$	$= 12.8\%$

PROFIT MARGIN   The relationship of net income to net sales commonly is used to evaluate a company's efficiency in controlling costs and expenses in relation to sales. That is, the lower a company's expenses relative to sales, the higher the sales dollars remaining for other activities. If a company has nonrecurring items of income, income from continuing operations typically is used as the numerator. The reporting of segment information permits a variation of this ratio to be computed for the major operating segments of a company. For each reportable segment, the profit margin *before* income taxes can be computed by dividing the segment's profit by its revenues. A weakness of the ratio is that it does not consider the investment (the total assets or stockholders' equity) necessary to generate the sales and income. A "return on investment" ratio (either total assets or stockholders' equity) overcomes this weakness.

RETURN ON TOTAL ASSETS   The amount of net income earned in relation to total assets indicates how efficiently a company uses its economic resources. When a comparison is made of the return on total assets of one company to the return of another company, consideration should be given to the age of the assets of each company. That is, the return on a company's assets will get higher as the assets become older because the denominator will decrease each year due to the increase in accumulated depreciation. Furthermore, since prices tend to increase due to inflation, a company that uses recently purchased assets will tend to show a relatively lower return on these assets. Typically, extraordinary items, results of discontinued operations, and the effects of changes in accounting principles are excluded from the numerator because they are the result of infrequent events not directly related to a company's ongoing operations. Interest expense (after income taxes)[17] is added back to net income because it is a financial cost paid to creditors to acquire the assets as opposed to a cost of generating sales. Since net income is earned over the entire period, the *average* total assets (beginning plus ending assets divided by two) for the period are used as the denominator. Reporting the results of segments permits the computation of a variation of this ratio for the major operating segments of a company. For each reportable segment, the *pretax* return on the segment's assets can be computed by dividing the segment's profit by its total assets.

RETURN ON STOCKHOLDERS' EQUITY   Net income may be divided by stockholders' equity to show the residual return on the owners' equity. When this return is higher than the return on total assets, the company has favorable financial leverage (that is, it

---

17. After-tax interest expense is usually computed by multiplying the pretax interest expense by 1 minus the effective income tax rate. In the case of the Cooper Company, the effective tax rate approximates 30% ($4,700 ÷ $15,700), so that the $3,000 pretax interest expense is multiplied by 70% (1 − 0.30) to determine the after-tax results.

is trading on the equity, which we discuss later). A weakness of the return on stockholders' equity ratio (as well as the return on total assets ratio), however, is that it does not consider the current value of the capital invested, since financial statements are based primarily on historical cost. Extraordinary items and other nonrecurring items usually are excluded from the numerator, and *average* stockholders' equity typically is used for the denominator. Some companies deduct preferred dividends from net income and use only common stockholders' equity in this ratio; they argue that preferred stock is more similar in nature to long-term liabilities than it is to common stock.

Liquidity Ratios

Liquidity ratios are used to evaluate a company's ability to meet its currently maturing financial obligations. These ratios generally involve all or most of the components of a company's working capital, its current assets less its current liabilities. Current assets include cash, temporary investments, receivables, inventories, and prepaid items. Current liabilities include items such as accounts payable from the normal acquisition of goods or services; accruals for wages, taxes, and interest payable; short-term notes payable; advance collections of unearned revenues; and the currently maturing portion of long-term debt. Exhibit 5-10 shows the common liquidity ratios, along with the calculations for the Cooper Company. We discuss each ratio in the following sections.

EXHIBIT 5-10   Liquidity Ratios

Ratio	Formula	Calculations (2005)
1. Current Ratio	$\dfrac{\text{Current Assets}}{\text{Current Liabilities}}$	$\dfrac{\$21,400}{\$11,200} = 1.91$ times
2. Acid-Test Ratio	$\dfrac{\text{Quick Assets}}{\text{Current Liabilities}}$	$\dfrac{\$11,500}{\$11,200} = 1.03$ times

---

CURRENT RATIO   The current ratio probably is the most commonly used ratio to evaluate a company's short-run liquidity. Sometimes it is referred to as the *working capital ratio*. It is considered to be a better indicator of a company's current debt-paying ability than simply working capital. This is because working capital shows only the absolute difference between a company's current assets and its current liabilities. By computing the current ratio, the *relative* relationship between the current assets and current liabilities is known, so that comparisons of different-sized companies can be made. In the past, as a "rule of thumb," a 2.0 current ratio was considered satisfactory. Today, however, more attention is given to (1) industry practices, (2) the length of a company's operating cycle, and (3) the mix of the current assets. Too *high* a current ratio relative to similar companies within the same industry may indicate inefficient management of current assets. The shorter a company's operating cycle, the less likely it is to need a substantial amount of working capital, or as high a current ratio, to operate efficiently. A company's operating cycle is evaluated through the use of activity ratios, which we discuss in the next section. The proportion of different items that make up the total current assets is referred to as the "mix" of the current assets. This mix has an effect upon how quickly the current assets can be converted into cash. As an extreme, a high proportion of prepaid items in current assets may indicate a weak liquidity position, since prepaid assets are consumed within the operating cycle rather than converted back into cash. The mix of a company's current assets and the impact on its liquidity are considered in the acid-test ratio.

ACID-TEST RATIO   The acid-test or *quick* ratio is a more severe test of a company's short-term debt-paying abilities. In this ratio, only the current assets that may be easily converted into cash are used in the calculation. These items, referred to as **quick assets**, generally consist of cash, temporary investments, accounts receivable, and short-term notes receivable. Inventories are excluded because their salability is uncertain and they frequently are sold on credit; thus they may not be quickly converted into cash. Prepaid items are excluded because they are not convertible into cash. The acid-test ratio high-lights potential liquidity problems because of an inadequate mix of current assets. For instance, the use of this ratio usually reveals the lower liquidity of a company having a significant investment in inventories that would not be shown in the current ratio. However, care must be taken to consider which assets to include. Even though inventories usually are excluded from the acid-test ratio, sometimes these are, in fact, more liquid than certain receivables. A quick ratio of 1.0 used to be a general rule of thumb. Today, as with the current ratio, greater consideration is given to such factors as industry practices and the company's typical operations.

Activity Ratios

Activity ratios are used to evaluate the liquidity of certain current assets by estimating the length of various segments of a company's operating cycle. The ratios are indicators of the efficiency with which the company uses its short-term economic resources. Exhibit 5-11 shows the three common activity ratios, along with the calculations for the Cooper Company. We discuss each ratio in the following sections.

EXHIBIT 5-11   Activity Ratios

Ratio	Formula	Calculations (2005)
1. Inventory Turnover	$\dfrac{\text{Cost of Goods Sold}}{\text{Average Inventory}}$	$\dfrac{\$74,100}{\dfrac{\$8,900 + \$10,100}{2}} = 7.8$ times or 47 days*
2. Receivables Turnover	$\dfrac{\text{Net Credit Sales}}{\text{Average Net Receivables}}$	$\dfrac{\$130,000 \times 0.70}{\dfrac{\$7,600 + \$8,600}{2}} = 11.2$ times or 33 days*
3. Payables Turnover	$\dfrac{\text{Cost of Goods Sold}}{\text{Average Accounts Payable}}$	$\dfrac{\$74,100}{\dfrac{\$5,000 + \$6,600}{2}} = 12.8$ times or 29 days*

*365-day business year.

INVENTORY TURNOVER A company normally acquires, sells, and replenishes its inventory in its operations during its accounting period. The company's operating cycle is the length of time it takes to invest in inventory, make credit sales, and convert the receivables into cash. Dividing a company's cost of goods sold for the period by its average inventory indicates the number of times the inventory is "turned over" or sold during that period. As a general rule, the higher the inventory turnover, (1) the more effective the company is in its operations, (2) the lesser the amount of investment that must be tied up in inventory, and (3) the shorter the operating cycle necessary to replenish cash. A company with a higher inventory turnover is usually more efficient and is also minimizing the chance of having obsolete inventory. A smaller investment in inventory means the company either needs less capital or can invest its capital in other earnings activities. However, *too* high an inventory turnover may indicate lost sales as a result of insufficient inventory on hand.

The inventory turnover often is divided into the number of operating days in a "business" year (365, 300, or 250, depending on the industry) so that the inventory segment of the operating cycle may be shown in days. Care should be taken in developing the average inventory; seasonal factors can affect this average substantially. Furthermore, when a comparison is made of one company to another, both companies should be using similar inventory costing methods. In periods of rising prices, without an adjustment, no valid comparison of inventory turnovers can be made when one company is using FIFO and another company is using LIFO. This is because the company using LIFO will show a higher cost of goods sold and lower inventory than the FIFO company, even though their operations are similar. Therefore, the amounts for the company using LIFO must be adjusted to FIFO, as we discuss in Chapter 7.

RECEIVABLES TURNOVER   After a company has sold its inventory on credit, the company collects the receivables to complete its operating cycle. Dividing net credit sales by average net trade receivables indicates how many times receivables are "turned over" or collected each period. The receivables turnover is an indicator of the efficiency with which the company collects its receivables and converts them back into cash. As a general rule, the higher the turnover the better, because the company has fewer resources tied up in receivables, collects these resources at a faster pace, and usually has fewer uncollectible accounts. When net credit sales information is not available, net sales are used in the calculations. Care should be taken to consider seasonal factors and to exclude nontrade receivables in developing the average receivables.

The receivables turnover often is divided into the number of days in the business year to show the average collection period in days. A comparison of a company's average collection period to the days in its typical credit terms gives an indication of how aggressively the company's credit department collects overdue accounts.

PAYABLES TURNOVER   The payables turnover ratio measures the number of times accounts payable turn over during the year. The higher the turnover, the shorter the time between the purchase of inventory and the cash payment. However, too high a turnover may indicate that the company is making payments too quickly and losing the "free" credit provided by accounts payable. Alternatively, if a company's payables turn over slower than the average for its industry, it may indicate that the company is having financial difficulty. It may be preferable to compute the ratio by using purchases as the numerator. In this case purchases can be computed by adding the ending inventory to the cost of goods sold and subtracting the beginning inventory. The payables turnover ratio also may be divided into the number of days in the business year to show the average payment period in days.

The three turnover ratios may be analyzed together to estimate the total number of days in the company's operating cycle from the payment of cash to purchase inventory to the collection of cash from sales. This period is computed by adding the number of days in the receivables turnover to the number of days in the inventory turnover and subtracting the number of days in the payables turnover. For example, in Exhibit 5-11, the Cooper Company's operating cycle is 51 (47 + 33 − 29) days.

Stability Ratios

Stability ratios are used to evaluate the long-run solvency and stability of a company. They provide evidence of the safety (risk) of the investments in the company by long-term bondholders, preferred stockholders, and common stockholders. Exhibit 5-12 shows several stability ratios, along with the calculations for the Cooper Company. We discuss each ratio in the following sections.

DEBT RATIO   The debt ratio indicates the percentage of total assets contributed by creditors. Subtraction of this ratio from 100% shows the percentage of total assets (or *equity* ratio) contributed by stockholders.[18] Sometimes, when a company has issued a significant amount of preferred stock (which has some characteristics of both debt and common stock), the equity ratio is further divided into a preferred equity ratio and a

---

18. Sometimes total liabilities are divided by total stockholders' equity to determine the *debt/equity* ratio.

EXHIBIT 5-12 Stability Ratios

Ratio	Formula	Calculations (2005)	
1. Debt Ratio	$\dfrac{\text{Total Liabilities}}{\text{Total Assets}}$	$\dfrac{\$36,200}{\$129,200}$	$= 28\%$
2. Times Interest Earned	$\dfrac{\text{Pretax Operating Income}}{\text{Interest Expense}}$	$\dfrac{\$15,700 + \$3,000}{\$3,000}$	$= 6.2$ times
3. Book Value per Common Share	$\dfrac{\text{Common Stockholders' Equity}}{\text{Outstanding Common Shares}}$	$\dfrac{\$93,000 - (\$140 \times 150)}{5,400}$	$= \$13.33$ per common share

common equity ratio. The appropriate relationship (or "mix") between the debt and equity ratios depends on the industry. In general, creditors prefer to see a lower debt ratio because, in the event of business decline, their interests are better protected and there is less risk. Up to a point, stockholders prefer a higher debt ratio, particularly when the company is favorably "trading on the equity," or applying favorable "financial leverage." This occurs when the company borrows money from creditors at an interest rate (net of income taxes) that is lower than the return the company can earn in its operations. However, an extremely high debt ratio is likely to be a disadvantage when a company wishes to attract additional external capital. Investors in both long-term bonds and stocks usually consider a highly leveraged company to be a relatively unstable and more risky investment.

TIMES INTEREST EARNED   The times interest earned ratio (sometimes called the *interest coverage ratio*) is used to evaluate the ability of a company to cover its interest obligations through its annual earnings. It is a measure of the safety of creditors' (particularly long-term) investments in the company. As a general rule, the higher the ratio the better able the company is to meet its interest obligations. While interest obligations are legal commitments, it is also true that continued interest payments are endangered by low earnings over an extended period of time. Because both earnings and interest expense are based on accrual accounting, the times interest earned ratio is slightly inaccurate, since it should include only cash outflows for interest and cash inflows from earnings. Such refinements are rarely made to this ratio, however.

The numerator of the times interest earned ratio usually is a form of pretax *operating* income—that is, pretax continuing income to which interest expense is added back. If a company has preferred stock outstanding, a similar calculation may be made to evaluate the safety of preferred dividends. The *preferred dividends coverage ratio* is computed by dividing net income by the annual preferred dividends.

BOOK VALUE   The book value per common share shows the net assets per share of stock. It is sometimes erroneously referred to as the liquidation value per share. Although the book value per common share frequently is computed, for several reasons it is not very useful as an indicator of a company's financial stability. First, most companies are going concerns and a related liquidation value is not important. Second, even if a liquidation value were important, the book value per share is based on assets recorded primarily in terms of historical costs and thus has no relation to the liquidation value per share. Third, the market value per share of a company's common stock is important in evaluating its stability. Since book value is based on historical costs, it also has no direct relation to this market value. However, if the market price of a company's common stock falls below its book value per common share, some investors consider this to be unfavorable.

When the book value per share is computed and the company has both preferred and common stock outstanding, the equity relating to the common stock is determined first. To do so, stockholders' equity is separated into its preferred and common stock components on the basis of the legal claims of each class upon liquidation. Typically, preferred stock is allocated its par value unless the stock's characteristics include a liquidation value, in which case the latter value is used. When preferred dividends are cumulative and in arrears, an appropriate portion of retained earnings is also assigned as preferred stockholders' equity. The residual amount of stockholders' equity then is assigned as common stockholders' equity. The book value per common share is computed by dividing this residual stockholders' equity by the number of common shares outstanding. A book value per share of preferred stock also may be computed on the basis of the preferred stockholders' equity and the number of preferred shares outstanding.

Cash Flow Ratios

Cash flow ratios assist a user in understanding relationships and trends among a company's cash flows. Exhibit 5-13 summarizes four of these ratios. We do not compute these ratios for the Cooper Company, because they are not as generally accepted and the statement of cash flows is not provided.

EXHIBIT 5-13   Cash Flow Ratios

Ratio	Formula
1. Cash Flow From Operations to Sales	$\dfrac{\text{Cash Flow From Operations}}{\text{Sales}}$
2. Cash Flow From Operations to Net Income	$\dfrac{\text{Cash Flow From Operations}}{\text{Net Income}}$
3. Cash Flow From Operations Per Share	$\dfrac{\text{Cash Flow From Operations}}{\text{Average Shares of Common Stock Outstanding}}$
4. Cash Flow From Operations to Maturing Debt	$\dfrac{\text{Cash Flow From Operations}}{\text{Debt Maturing Next Year}}$

CASH FLOW FROM OPERATIONS (CFO) TO SALES   This ratio is used to evaluate the cash generated from sales, and the management of cash collections and payments. It enables users to understand the proportion of each sales dollar that is available for investing and financing activities. A comparison of the ratio with the profit margin may be useful. Generally, the CFO to sales ratio is higher than the profit margin, because noncash expenses such as depreciation are deducted in computing net income.

CASH FLOW FROM OPERATIONS TO NET INCOME   This ratio enables users to understand how the earning of net income relates to the receipt of CFO. While many users consider CFO as important as income, care should be exercised because income is computed on the accrual basis, whereas CFO may vary depending on when cash flows occur. Management may find it easier to influence the timing of cash flows than the measurement of income.

CASH FLOW FROM OPERATIONS PER SHARE   Disclosure of CFO per share is expressly prohibited by GAAP for the reasons we discussed above. However, users may wish to compute it, using the weighted average number of shares that the company discloses for its computation of earnings per share.

CASH FLOW FROM OPERATIONS DIVIDED BY THE AMOUNT OF DEBT MATURING IN THE NEXT YEAR   Since CFO is usually the primary source of cash, this ratio measures the ability of a company to make principal payments. It is an indicator of whether the company has the capacity to borrow additional debt.

Other cash flow ratios include CFO divided by cash operating expenses, total assets, or total liabilities, and CFO divided by the cash flows for investing activities that are needed to maintain the operating capacity of the company.

SUMMARY

At the beginning of the chapter, we identified several objectives you would accomplish after reading the chapter. The objectives are listed below, each followed by a brief summary of the key points in the chapter discussion.

1. **Describe an auditor's report.** In an audit report, the auditor expresses an opinion concerning the fairness of the financial statements in conformity with generally accepted accounting principles. An unqualified audit report includes an introductory paragraph, a scope paragraph, and the opinion paragraph.
2. **Explain the disclosures in management's discussion and analysis.** In the MD&A, the management of a company discusses its financial condition, changes in financial condition, and results of operations. Briefly, the major disclosure issues relate to the company's liquidity, capital resources, and results of operations.
3. **Understand the meaning of an operating segment.** An operating segment is a component of a company that engages in activities to earn revenues and incur expenses, whose operating results are regularly reviewed by the company's chief operating officer, and for which financial information is available.
4. **Describe the disclosures in a segment report.** In a segment report, a company provides general information (e.g., types of products); information about the profit (or loss) and total assets of each reportable segment; reconciliations to the company's total revenues, pretax income from continuing operations, and total assets; and various company-wide information.
5. **Explain interim reporting.** Interim financial statements are financial reports for periods of less than a year. Their purpose is to improve the timeliness of accounting information. In developing an interim report, each interim period is viewed primarily as an integral part of an annual period.
6. **Prepare an interim report.** To prepare an interim report, first a trial balance is prepared on a working paper. Next, year-to-date adjusting entries are prepared on the working paper. Then, the interim financial statements are prepared. In preparing the statements, inventory may have to be estimated, the adjusting entries are not entered into the accounts, and closing entries are not made.
7. **Understand intracompany and intercompany comparisons (Appendix).** Intracompany comparison involves comparing a company's current financial performance and condition to the company's past results. Intercompany comparison involves comparing a company's performance with that of competitors, with the industry as a whole, or with the results in related industries.
8. **Prepare horizontal and vertical percentage analyses (Appendix).** In horizontal analysis, changes in a company's operating results and financial position over time are shown in percentages as well as in dollars. In vertical analysis, the monetary relationships between items on a company's financial statements for a particular period are shown in percentages as well as in dollars.
9. **Perform ratio analysis (Appendix).** A ratio involves dividing one or more items on a company's financial statements by another related item or items. Ratio analysis involves computing ratios to evaluate a company's performance using intracompany and intercompany analysis. The six groups of ratios include (1) stockholder profitability, (2) company profitability, (3) liquidity, (4) activity, (5) stability, and (6) cash flow ratios.

QUESTIONS

Q5-1   In a standard auditor's report, what statements are included?

Q5-2   What is an *audit committee*? What is a *management report* and what is generally included in this report?

Q5-3   What is *management's discussion and analysis*? Why is it included in a company's annual report?

Q5-4   Why do investors and creditors desire financial information concerning the operating segments of a company?

Q5-5 Briefly describe the three alternative tests used to determine a "reportable segment."

Q5-6 Briefly describe the information that a company reports in regard to the profit (or loss) and assets of each reportable segment.

Q5-7 What company-wide disclosures must a company make related to its operating segments?

Q5-8 What are *interim financial statements* and why are they issued?

Q5-9 What specific principles must a company apply to the reporting of inventories in its interim financial reports?

Q5-10 What principles does a company apply to the accounting for expenses not directly associated with product sales during an interim period?

Q5-11 Briefly explain how the accounting procedures for preparing a company's interim reports are (a) similar and (b) dissimilar to those used in preparing annual reports.

Q5-12 List the minimum disclosures that must be made by a publicly held company in its interim financial report.

Q5-13 List the responsibilities of the Chief Accountant and the Division of Corporation Finance of the SEC.

Q5-14 What are the two SEC reports that are important to accountants?

Q5-15 (*Appendix*). What two types of comparisons may external users make in their financial decision making? Why is knowledge of these comparisons important to accountants?

Q5-16 (*Appendix*). What is *horizontal analysis* and how is it prepared?

Q5-17 (*Appendix*). What is *vertical analysis* and how does it differ from horizontal analysis?

Q5-18 (*Appendix*). What is *ratio analysis* and how is it used?

Q5-19 (*Appendix*). Briefly describe how each of the stockholder profitability ratios is computed.

Q5-20 (*Appendix*). Briefly describe how each of the company profitability ratios is computed.

Q5-21 (*Appendix*). Which financial ratios may be used to evaluate the effectiveness and efficiency of a company's reportable operating segments?

Q5-22 (*Appendix*). Briefly describe how each of the liquidity ratios is computed.

Q5-23 (*Appendix*). Briefly describe how each of the activity ratios is computed.

Q5-24 (*Appendix*). Briefly describe how each of the stability ratios is computed.

CASES

C O M M U N I C A T I O N

C5-1 Auditor's Report
Meyer Company is considering being audited for the first time. Mary Thomas, its president, has asked your advice. She says: "I understand that after an audit the accountant expresses an opinion, and that one type of opinion is 'unqualified.' What exactly is involved in an audit and what is included in an unqualified opinion?"

Required Prepare a written response to the president of Meyer Company.

C5-2 Management's Report
The subject of management reports has been prominent the past few years. A *management report* is a fairly new item included in the annual report to shareholders. This report should not be confused with management's discussion and analysis of operations and financial condition that also is relatively new to the annual report.

The management report is included in the annual report to shareholders as a result of the urging of a number of groups and organizations. Consequently, the form and content of the annual report to shareholders continues to

evolve as management attempts to present additional information that will be useful to the readers.

Required
1. Explain the general purposes of the management report.
2. Identify five subject areas or topics which have been recommended for inclusion in the management report.
3. Under what circumstances does the content of the management report influence the activities of the external auditor during the audit engagement? Explain your answer. (*CMA adapted*)

C5-3 Securities and Exchange Commission
The U.S. Securities and Exchange Commission (SEC) was created in 1934 and consists of five commissioners and a staff of approximately 1,900. The SEC professional staff is organized into four divisions and several principal offices. The primary objectives of the SEC are to support fair securities markets and to foster enlightened shareholder participation in major corporate decisions. The

SEC has a significant presence in financial markets and corporation-shareholder relations and has the authority to exert significant influence on entities whose actions lie within the scope of its authority. The SEC chairman has identified enforcement cases and full disclosure filings as major activities of the SEC.

Required

1. The SEC must have some "license" to exercise power. Explain where the SEC receives its authority.
2. Explain, in general, the major ways in which the SEC:
   a. Supports fair securities markets.
   b. Fosters enlightened shareholder participation in major corporate decisions.
3. The major responsibilities of the SEC's Division of Corporation Finance include full disclosure filings. Describe the means by which the SEC attempts to assure the material accuracy and completeness of registrants' financial disclosure filings. (*CMA adapted*)

C5-4 Segment Reporting

To understand current generally accepted accounting principles with respect to accounting for and reporting on the operating segments of a company, as stated in *FASB Statement No. 131*, it is necessary to be familiar with certain terminology. Furthermore, central issues in reporting on operating segments of a company are the determination of which segments are reportable, and what is to be reported.

Required

1. Explain what is meant by an operating segment of a company.
2. What are the tests to determine whether or not an operating segment is reportable?
3. Briefly identify the information that a company must disclose in regard to its reportable operating segments.

C5-5 Interim Reporting

Interim financial reporting has become an important topic in accounting. There has been considerable discussion as to the proper method of reflecting results of operations at interim dates. Accordingly, the Accounting Principles Board issued an opinion clarifying some aspects of interim financial reporting.

Required

1. Explain generally how revenue should be recognized at interim dates and specifically how revenue should be recognized for industries subject to large seasonal fluctuations in revenue and for long-term contracts using the percentage-of-completion method at annual reporting dates.
2. Explain generally how product and period costs should be recognized at interim dates. Also discuss how inventory and cost of goods sold may be afforded special accounting treatment at interim dates.
3. Explain how the provision for income taxes is computed and reflected in interim financial statements. (*AICPA adapted*)

C R E A T I V E   A N D   C R I T I C A L   T H I N K I N G

C5-6 Segment Reporting

Many accountants and financial analysts contend that a company should report financial data for operating segments of the enterprise.

Required

1. Explain what financial reporting for the operating segments of a business enterprise involves.
2. Identify the reasons for requiring financial data to be reported by operating segments.
3. Identify the possible disadvantages of requiring financial data to be reported by operating segments. (*AICPA adapted*)

C5-7 Interim Reporting

The unaudited quarterly statements of income issued by many corporations to their stockholders usually are prepared on the same basis as annual statements, the statement for each quarter reflecting the transactions of that quarter.

Required

1. Why do problems arise in using such quarterly statements to predict the income (before extraordinary items) for the year? Explain.

2. Discuss the ways in which quarterly income can be affected by the behavior of the costs recorded in a Repairs and Maintenance of Factory Machinery account.
3. Do such quarterly statements give management opportunities to manipulate the results of operations for a quarter? Explain your answer. (*AICPA adapted*)

C5-8 Analyzing Coca-Cola's MD&A Disclosures

Many companies must now include a management's discussion and analysis (MD&A) as a component part of their annual reports. The Coca-Cola Company includes an MD&A in the financial section of its annual report, as shown in Appendix A of this book.

Required

1. Explain the purpose of an MD&A and describe what it includes.
2. Review The Coca-Cola Company's MD&A and answer the following questions:
   a. In what lines of business does the company operate? How does it measure sales volume?
   b. By how much, and why, did net operating revenues increase in 2001?

c. What were selling expenses in 2001, and why did they increase over 2000?

d. In regard to liquidity, what does the company believe is one of its fundamental financial strengths?

e. What is the company's "free cash flow," and for what is it used?

f. What was the cash provided by operations in 2001, and why did it increase?

3. Briefly discuss management's outlook for Coca-Cola's future performance.

C5-9 Ethics and Quarterly Expenses

It is March 2005, and you have just been hired by the Tallas Company to be its accountant. Tallas is a small corporation that does a seasonal business of selling snow removal equipment, with most of its sales to retailers occurring in the last two quarters of the calendar year. Production is particularly heavy during the second quarter, in preparation for these sales. During the first quarter production is slowest, so this is when Tallas does the majority of its repairs and maintenance on its production equipment.

You are in the process of preparing Tallas Company's 2005 first quarter interim report. After preparing a pre-liminary income statement, which shows a modest $30,000 profit, you begin to prepare a preliminary balance sheet. In reviewing the asset accounts in the general ledger, you notice an account entitled Miscellaneous Factory Assets in the amount of $140,000. Since this is a large amount relative to the other assets and you are unclear how to classify this asset, you ask the controller for an explanation. The controller replies, "Oh that. Just include it under Property, Plant, and Equipment. That is the amount we spent on repairs and maintenance during the first quarter. If we expensed all of it now, we would show a loss for the first quarter. Instead, we record the amount as an asset, wait to see how the second quarter results are, and then expense some of it so we can show a reasonable profit. The remainder we expense during our busy season of the third and fourth quarters. We have been doing this for years. It makes all of our quarterly income statements look better. Besides, it makes no difference, since our total yearly income is the same regardless of when we report repairs and maintenance expense during the four quarters."

Required From financial reporting and ethical perspectives, when do you think Tallas Company should report its quarterly repairs and maintenance expense?

MULTIPLE CHOICE

Select the best answer for each of the following.

M5-1 The computation of a company's third quarter provision for income taxes should be based on earnings

a. For the quarter at an expected annual effective income tax rate

b. For the quarter at the statutory rate

c. To date at an expected annual effective income tax rate less prior quarters' provisions

d. To date at the statutory rate less prior quarters' provisions

M5-2 Which of the following ratios measures short-term solvency?

a. Current ratio

b. Age of receivables

c. Creditors' equity to total assets

d. Return on investment

M5-3 Kaycee Corporation's revenues for the current year were as follows:

Consolidated revenue per income statement	$1,200,000
Intersegment sales	180,000
Intersegment transfers	60,000
Combined revenues of all operating segments	$1,440,000

Kaycee has a reportable segment if that operating segment's revenues exceed

a. $6,000   c. $120,000

b. $24,000   d. $144,000

M5-4 An inventory loss from a market decline occurred in the first quarter that was not expected to be restored in the fiscal year. For interim financial reporting purposes, how would the dollar amount of inventory in the balance sheet be affected in the first and fourth quarters?

First Quarter	Fourth Quarter
a. Decrease	No effect
b. Decrease	Increase
c. No effect	Decrease
d. No effect	No effect

M5-5 Barr Corporation's capital stock at December 31, 2004 consisted of the following:

> Common stock, $2 par value; 100,000 shares authorized, issued, and outstanding
> 10% noncumulative, nonconvertible preferred stock, $100 par value; 1,000 shares authorized, issued, and outstanding

Barr's common stock, which is listed on a major stock exchange, was quoted at $4 per share on December 31, 2004. Barr's net income for the year ended December 31, 2004 was $50,000. The 2004 preferred dividend was declared. No capital stock transactions occurred during 2004. What was the price/earnings ratio on Barr's common stock at December 31, 2004?

a. 8 to 1   c. 16 to 1
b. 10 to 1   d. 20 to 1

M5-6 In August 2004, Ella Company spent $150,000 on an advertising campaign for subscriptions to the magazine it sells on getting ready for the skiing season. There are only two issues: one in October and one in November. The magazine is only sold on a subscription basis and the subscriptions started in October 2004. Assuming Ella's fiscal year ends on March 31, 2005, what amount of expense should be included in Ella's quarterly income statement for the three months ended December 31, 2004 as a result of this expenditure?

a. $37,500   c. $75,000
b. $50,000   d. $150,000

M5-7 When a company reports the profit (or loss) for a reportable operating segment, it also must disclose the segment's

a. Revenues
b. Interest revenue and interest expense
c. Depreciation, depletion, and amortization expense
d. All of the above

M5-8 Utica Company's net accounts receivable were $250,000 at December 31, 2003 and $300,000 at December 31, 2004. Net cash sales for 2004 were $100,000. The accounts receivable turnover for 2004 was 5.0. What were Utica's total net sales for 2004?

a. $1,475,000   c. $1,600,000
b. $1,500,000   d. $2,750,000

M5-9 During 2004, Red, Incorporated purchased $2,000,000 of inventory. The cost of goods sold for 2004 was $2,200,000, and the ending inventory at December 31, 2004 was $400,000. What was the inventory turnover for 2004?

a. 4.0   c. 5.5
b. 4.4   d. 11.0

M5-10 The following data pertain to Cowl, Inc. for the year ended December 31, 2004:

Net sales	$ 600,000
Net income	150,000
Total assets, January 1, 2004	2,000,000
Total assets, December 31, 2004	3,000,000

What was Cowl's rate of return on assets for 2004?

a. 5%
b. 6%
c. 20%
d. 24%   *(AICPA adapted)*

EXERCISES

E5-1 **_Segment Reporting_** York Drug Company has two reportable operating segments, A and B. The 2004 condensed income statement for the entire company is as follows:

YORK DRUG COMPANY
Income Statement
For Year Ended December 31, 2004

Sales	$90,000
Cost of goods sold	(50,000)
Gross profit	$40,000
Operating expenses	(18,000)
Income before income taxes	$22,000
Income tax expense	(8,800)
Net Income	$13,200

Additional Information:

1. Sales are made as follows: Segment A, $52,000; Segment B, $26,000; other segments, $12,000 of the total.
2. Cost of goods sold for each segment is as follows: Segment A, $30,000; Segment B, $12,500; other segments, $7,500.
3. Operating expenses are identified with the segments as follows: Segment A, $10,000; Segment B, $4,500; other segments, $3,500. There are no general corporate expenses.
4. The company has $110,000 total assets as of December 31, 2004. These assets are assigned to the segments as follows: Segment A, $49,500; Segment B, $38,500; other segments, $22,000. There are no general corporate assets.

Required Prepare a schedule that reports on the 2004 revenues, profit, and assets of Segments A and B and the other segments of the York Drug Company.

E5-2   **Segment Reporting** The Wilson Diversified Company has total assets of $130,000 at the end of 2004 and the following condensed income statement for 2004:

Sales	$90,000
Operating expenses	(66,600)
Income before income taxes	$23,400
Income tax expense	(7,020)
Net income	$16,380

The company has two reportable operating segments and has developed the following related information:

	Segments			
	1	2	Other	Totals
Sales	$51,700	$24,400	$13,900	$ 90,000
Operating expenses	36,780	15,400	10,420	66,600[a]
Segment assets	70,300	28,740	21,960	130,000[b]

a. Of the $66,600 total operating expenses, $4,000 are general corporate expenses.
b. Of the $130,000 total assets, $9,000 are general corporate assets.

Required Prepare a schedule that reports on the revenues, profit, and assets of Segments 1 and 2 and the other operating segments of the Wilson Diversified Company for 2004. Be sure to include the appropriate reconciliations.

E5-3   **Segment Reporting** Parks Conglomerate Company does business in several different industries. The following is a 2004 condensed income statement for the entire company:

Sales		$300,000
Less:		
Cost of goods sold	$140,000	
Depreciation expense	30,000	
Other operating expenses	60,000	
Total expenses		(230,000)
Pretax income		$ 70,000
Income tax expense		(21,000)
Net income		$ 49,000
Earnings per share (20,000 shares)		$2.45

Parks has two major operating segments, A and B. No other operating segment contributes 10% or more of the company's activities. Segments A and B make no sales to each other or to the other segments of the company. An analysis reveals that $2,000 of the total depreciation expense and $6,000 of the total other operating expenses are related to general corporate activities. The *remaining* expenses and total revenues are directly allocable to segment activities according to the following percentages:

	Percent Identified with		
	Segment A	Segment B	Other Segments
Sales	40%	46%	14%
Cost of goods sold	35	50	15
Depreciation expense	40	45	15
Other operating expenses	42	40	18

Required Prepare a schedule that reports on the revenues and profit of Segments A and B and the other operating segments of the Parks Conglomerate Company for 2004. Be sure to reconcile these amounts with the related totals on the preceding income statement. Include notes summarizing the depreciation related to each operating segment and the computation of segment profits.

E5-4   ***Determination of Reportable Segments***   Straub Diversified Company has five different operating segments. None of these segments makes sales to the other segments. The company has total assets of $155,000 at the end of 2004 and lists the following condensed income statement for 2004:

Sales	$100,000
Operating expenses	(72,000)
Pretax income	$ 28,000
Income taxes	(8,400)
Net income	$ 19,600

In preparing its segmental reporting schedule, the company determined that it has $7,000 of general corporate expenses and $10,000 of general corporate assets. It also developed the following information for each of its five segments:

	Segment				
	1	2	3	4	5
Sales	$ 9,200	$ 8,800	$ 9,000	$63,900	$ 9,100
Segment profit	3,300	3,200	3,400	21,500	3,600
Segment assets	15,100	13,900	14,300	87,900	13,800

Required On the basis of the preceding information:

1. Determine which segments are reportable operating segments (justify your conclusions).
2. Prepare a schedule that reports on the revenues, profit, and assets of the reportable operating segments and the remaining segments of the Straub Diversified Company for 2004. Reconcile these amounts to the related totals on the income statement and to total assets. Notes to the schedule are not necessary.

E5-5   ***Interim Reporting***   Jersey Company is in the process of developing its first-quarter interim report. It has developed the following condensed trial balance as of March 31, 2004:

	Debit	Credit
Cash	$ 900	
Accounts receivable (net)	4,000	
Inventory (1/1/04)	5,000	
Prepaid insurance	4,800	
Note receivable	6,000	
Land	3,000	
Buildings and equipment (net)	36,000	
Accounts payable		$ 9,100
Common stock, $1 par		6,000
Premium on common stock		12,400
Retained earnings (1/1/04)		23,080
Sales (net)		50,000
Purchases (net)	30,000	
Selling expenses	6,500	
General and administrative expenses	4,380	
	$100,580	$100,580

Additional information:

1. The company makes formal adjusting entries at year-end and enters the amounts in the appropriate accounts at that time.
2. The company uses control accounts for selling expenses and for general and administrative expenses.
3. The gross profit method is used to determine the interim inventory. Historical gross profit has averaged 47% of net sales.
4. Uncollectible accounts typically average 1% of net sales.
5. On January 1, 2004, buildings and equipment (net) have an average remaining life of 10 years. One-third of the account balance consists of assets related to selling activities. The company uses straight-line depreciation with no residual value.
6. The note receivable is dated January 1, 2004, matures on January 1, 2006, and carries an annual interest rate of 12% (interest will not be collected until the maturity date).

7. On January 1, 2004, the company had purchased a 3-year insurance policy, debiting Prepaid Insurance for the $4,800 payment.
8. The company expects its annual effective income tax rate to be 30%. Income taxes for 2004 will be paid at the beginning of 2005.
9. No common stock has been issued or retired in 2004.

Required On the basis of the preceding information, prepare the Jersey Company income statement for the first quarter of 2004 and a March 31, 2004 balance sheet. A worksheet is not required, but you should be prepared to document any adjustments you make to the preceding accounts.

E5-6   *Interim Reporting*   The Howard Corporation presented the following trial balance for the quarter ended March 31, 2004:

	Debit	Credit
Cash	$ 9,800	
Accounts receivable	13,000	
Inventory (1/1/04)	10,000	
Prepaid insurance	9,600	
Land	16,000	
Buildings and equipment	108,000	
Accumulated depreciation		$ 36,000
Accounts payable		28,200
Common stock, $1 par		13,200
Additional paid-in capital		24,800
Retained earnings (1/1/04)		44,900
Sales (net)		100,000
Purchases (net)	59,000	
Selling expenses	12,000	
General and administrative expenses	9,700	
Totals	$247,100	$247,100

Additional information:

1. The company uses control accounts for selling expenses and for general and administrative expenses.
2. The company makes formal adjusting entries at year-end and enters the amounts in the appropriate accounts at that time.
3. The company uses the gross profit method to determine interim inventory. Historical gross profit has averaged 43% of net sales.
4. On January 1, 2004, the company purchased a 4-year insurance policy for $9,600.
5. No common stock has been issued or retired in 2004.
6. The buildings and equipment have an estimated life of 15 years with no residual value. The company uses straight-line depreciation; it records one-fourth of the depreciation as a selling expense and the remainder as a general and administrative expense.
7. The company expects its annual effective income tax rate to be 30%; income taxes will be paid at the beginning of the next year.

Required On the basis of the preceding information, prepare the Howard Corporation income statement for the first quarter of 2004 and a March 31, 2004 balance sheet. A worksheet is not required, but you should be prepared to substantiate any adjustments you make to the preceding accounts.

E5-7   *Interim Reporting*   The Hill Company prepares quarterly and year-to-date interim reports. At the bottom of this page and top of the next page is its interim income statement for the quarter ended March 31, 2004:

Sales (net)		$150,000
Cost of goods sold		(90,000)
Gross profit		$ 60,000
Operating expenses		
Selling expenses	$18,000	
General expenses	10,600	
Depreciation expense	8,000	(36,600)
Pretax operating income		$ 23,400

Other items		
Dividend revenue	$ 600	
Interest expense	(1,000)	(400)
Income before income taxes		$ 23,000
Income tax expense		(7,000)
Net income		$ 16,000
Earnings per share (20,000 shares)		$.80

On June 30, 2004, the company accountant completed a worksheet in preparation for developing the year-to-date interim income statement. The following are the accounts and amounts listed in the income statement debit and credit columns of this worksheet:

	Debit	Credit
Sales (net)		$340,000
Interest revenue		500
Dividend revenue		1,000
Cost of goods sold	$190,000	
Selling expenses	50,000	
General expenses	20,000	
Depreciation expense	16,000	
Interest expense	2,100	
Income tax expense	19,200	

Required Based on the given information, and assuming 20,000 shares of common stock have been outstanding for the entire 6 months, for the Hill Company prepare:

1. A year-to-date interim income statement for the first 6 months of 2004.
2. An interim income statement for the second quarter of 2004.

E5-8 **Interim Taxes** Farris Company is subject to income taxes at a rate of 20% on its first $50,000 of income and 35% on any income in excess of $50,000. In the process of preparing its interim reports, each quarter Farris Company uses an estimated effective income tax rate based on its estimated annual income. The following is a schedule that shows the company's actual year-to-date pretax income and the estimate of the annual pretax income made at the end of each quarter. The company neither anticipates nor incurs any extraordinary items, and its pretax accounting income is the same as its taxable income.

	Pretax Income Amounts at End of			
	First Quarter	Second Quarter	Third Quarter	Fourth Quarter
Actual income (year-to-date)	$20,000	$42,000	$60,000	$82,000
Estimated remaining income	60,000	44,000	21,000	—
Estimated annual pretax income	$80,000	$86,000	$81,000	$82,000

Required Based on the preceding information, prepare a schedule for Farris Company to compute the income tax expense that would be listed on *each* quarterly income statement. (Carry your effective income tax rate computation to three decimal places.)

E5-9 **Horizontal Analyses (Appendix)** Slusher Company presents the following condensed comparative income statements for 2003, 2004, and 2005 at the bottom of this page and top of the next page:

	For Years Ended December 31,		
	2005	2004	2003
Sales (net)	$120,000	$100,000	$85,000
Cost of goods sold	(72,000)	(55,000)	(45,000)
Gross profit	$ 48,000	$ 45,000	$40,000
Operating expenses	(22,000)	(20,000)	(18,000)
Operating income	$ 26,000	$ 25,000	$22,000

	For Years Ended December 31,		
	2005	2004	2003
Other items			
Dividend revenue	400	500	200
Interest expense	(1,200)	(1,000)	(500)
Income before income taxes	$ 25,200	$ 24,500	$21,700
Income tax expense	(8,200)	(8,000)	(6,000)
Net income	$ 17,000	$ 16,500	$15,700
Number of common shares	6,000	6,000	5,000
Earnings per share	$2.83	$2.75	$3.14

Required Based on the preceding information for Slusher Company, prepare horizontal analyses for the years 2003, 2004, and 2005 using (1) a year-to-year approach and (2) a base-year-to-date approach. Do your analyses reveal any favorable or unfavorable trends?

E5-10   *Vertical Analyses (Appendix)*   The Samuels Company presents the following condensed income statement and balance sheet information for 2004 and 2005.

Income Statements

	For Years Ended December 31,	
	2005	2004
Sales (net)	$100,000	$90,000
Cost of goods sold	(60,000)	(51,000)
Gross profit	$ 40,000	$39,000
Operating expenses	(21,300)	(21,900)
Interest revenue	1,500	1,400
Interest expense	(3,700)	(2,500)
Income before income taxes	$ 16,500	$16,000
Income tax expense	(5,000)	(4,700)
Net income	$ 11,500	$11,300
Earnings per share	$1.92	$1.95

Balance Sheets

	December 31,	
	2005	2004
Cash	$ 3,000	$ 2,000
Receivables (net)	7,000	8,000
Inventories	11,000	12,000
Long-term investments (bonds)	20,000	15,000
Property and equipment (net)	79,000	63,000
Total Assets	$120,000	$100,000
Current liabilities	$ 10,000	$ 11,400
Bonds payable, 10%	37,000	25,000
Common stock, $2 par	12,000	11,600
Premium on common stock	21,000	19,500
Retained earnings	40,000	32,500
Total Liabilities and Stockholders' Equity	$120,000	$100,000

Required Based on the preceding information for Samuels Company, prepare vertical analyses of the income statements and balance sheets for the 2 years. Do your analyses reveal any trends in the company's operations and financial position?

E5-11   *Ratios (Appendix)*   The following are a condensed income statement for 2004 and a December 31, 2005 balance sheet for the Allen Company:

Income Statement

Sales (net)	$304,400
Cost of goods sold	(183,600)
Gross profit	$120,800
Operating expenses	(82,000)
Interest expense	(7,000)
Income before income taxes	$ 31,800
Income taxes	(10,000)
Net income	$ 21,800

Balance Sheet

Cash	$ 8,200	Accounts payable	$ 18,000
Receivables (net)	14,700	Other current liabilities	6,800
Inventory	19,300	Bonds payable, 10%	70,000
Property, plant, and equipment (net)	195,800	Common stock, $10 par	80,500
		Premium on common stock	24,000
		Retained earnings	38,700
Total Assets	$238,000	Total Liabilities and Stockholders' Equity	$238,000

Additional information: The corporate common stock was outstanding the entire year and is selling for $16 per share at year-end. On January 1, 2004, the inventory was $21,500, the total assets were $224,000, the accounts payable were $18,800, and the total stockholders' equity was $130,800. The company operates on a 300-day business year.

Required For the Allen Company, compute the following ratios:

1. Price/earnings
2. Profit margin
3. Return on total assets
4. Return on stockholders' equity
5. Current
6. Inventory turnover (in days)
7. Payables turnover (in days)
8. Debt

Is the company favorably "trading on its equity"? Explain.

E5-12 **Ratios (Appendix)** The Byers Company presents the following condensed income statement for 2004 and condensed December 31, 2004 balance sheet:

Income Statement

Sales (net)		$267,000
Less:		
Cost of goods sold	$160,000	
Operating expenses	62,000	
Interest expense	11,000	
Income taxes	10,000	
Total expenses		(243,000)
Net income		$ 24,000

Balance Sheet

Cash	$ 10,000	Current liabilities	$ 40,000
Receivables (net)	22,000	Bonds payable, 10%	110,000
Inventory	56,000	Preferred stock, $100 par	50,000
Long-term investments	30,000	Common stock, $10 par	100,000
Property and equipment (net)	282,000	Additional paid-in capital	45,000
		Retained earnings	55,000
Total Assets	$400,000	Total Liabilities and Stockholders' Equity	$400,000

Additional information:

1. The company's common stock and preferred stock were outstanding the entire year.
2. Dividends of $1.50 per share on the common stock and $6 per share on the preferred stock were declared in 2004.
3. On December 31, 2004, the common stock is selling for $20 per share.
4. The preferred stock has a liquidation value of $110 per share.
5. On January 1, 2004, the accounts receivable (net) balance was $24,000 and the total stockholders' equity was $246,000.
6. Of the company's net sales, 78% are on credit.
7. The company operates on a 365-day business year.

Required On the basis of the preceding information, compute the following ratios for the Byers Company:

1. Earnings per share
2. Dividend yield
3. Return on stockholders' equity
4. Current
5. Acid-test
6. Receivables turnover (in days)
7. Times interest earned
8. Book value per common share

On the basis of applicable "rules of thumb," what information is revealed by the acid-test ratio that is not disclosed by the current ratio?

E5-13   *Ratios (Appendix)*   Daley, Inc. is consistently profitable. Daley's normal financial statement relationships are as follows:

I. Current ratio:	3 to 1
II. Inventory turnover:	4 times
III. Total debt/total assets ratio:	0.5 to 1

In 2004 Daley was involved in the following transactions and events:

1. Daley issued a stock dividend.
2. Daley declared, but did not pay, a cash dividend.
3. Customers returned invoiced goods for which they had not paid.
4. Accounts payable were paid on December 31, 2004.
5. Daley recorded both a receivable from its insurance company and a loss from fire damage to a factory building.
6. Early in 2004, Daley increased the selling price of one of its products that had a demand in excess of capacity. The number of units sold in 2003 and 2004 was the same.

Required For items 1 through 6, determine whether each 2004 transaction or event increased (I), decreased (D), or had no effect (N) on each of the 2004 ratios. (*AICPA adapted*)

PROBLEMS

P5-1   *Income Statement and Segment Reporting*   Frahm Corporation presents the following account balances, after adjustments, on December 31, 2004:

Administrative and office salaries	$ 43,000	Sales salaries and commissions	$ 59,000
Interest expense	8,800	Property taxes	7,000
Bad debts expense	6,000	Depreciation expense: buildings,	
Sales (net)	600,000	sales equipment, and office equipment	31,000
Loss due to tornado (pretax)	12,000	Cost of goods sold	323,700
Advertising expense	40,000	Delivery expense	25,000
Miscellaneous office expenses	2,300	Interest revenue	3,000

The following information is also available:

1. The income tax rate on all items is 30%.
2. 10,000 shares of common stock have been outstanding the entire year.
3. Frahm Corporation operates several divisions, two of which, Divisions B and C, are considered reportable operating segments.

4. Sales (net) are made as follows: Division B, 60%; Division C, 25%; other divisions, 15% of the total. No intersegment sales are made.

5. The cost of goods sold as a *percentage of net sales* in each division is as follows: Division B, 55%; Division C, 52%; other divisions, 53%.

6. Operating expenses are traceable to divisions as follows:
   a. Sales salaries directly traceable to Division B total $27,000; Division C, $12,000; other divisions, $8,000.
   b. Sales commissions in each division are 2% of net sales.
   c. Bad debts average 1% of net sales in each division.
   d. Of the total delivery expense, 64% was spent in Division B, 20% was spent in Division C, and 16% was spent in the other divisions.
   e. Of the total advertising expense, $5,000 was spent on general advertising. Of the remainder, 52% was spent in Division B, 28% in Division C, and 20% in the other divisions.
   f. Administrative and office salaries are considered general corporate expenses, except for $17,000 allocated for the management of Division B, $12,000 for the management of Division C, and $10,000 for the management of the other divisions.
   g. Property taxes paid are $4,000 in Division B, $2,000 in Division C, and $1,000 in other divisions.
   h. Miscellaneous office expenses are not directly traced to divisions.

7. The depreciation expense is listed as a separate component on the corporate income statement. Of the total listed, $6,000 is due to depreciation on the corporate headquarters building and is not allocated. Of the remainder, $15,000 is traceable to Division B, $6,000 is traceable to Division C, and $4,000 is traceable to the other divisions.

8. Interest expense is for corporate bonds used to finance overall operating activities. Interest revenue is from corporate investments in marketable securities.

9. An infrequent and unusual tornado caused a warehouse used in Division B to be severely damaged, resulting in the material pretax loss shown earlier.

10. Of the $1,600,000 total company assets at year-end, $910,000 are assets of Division B, $420,000 are assets of Division C, $140,000 are assets of the remaining divisions, and $130,000 are assets related to corporate headquarters.

11. Capital expenditures of Divisions B and C amounted to $50,000 and $27,000, respectively, in 2004 and are included in the total company assets at year-end.

Required

1. Prepare a single-step 2004 income statement for the Frahm Corporation.
2. Prepare a separate schedule that shows the revenues, profit, and assets of Divisions B and C and the remaining operating divisions.
3. Prepare appropriate segment notes relating to depreciation, profits, and capital expenditures.
4. (*Appendix*) Compute the profit margin *before* income taxes for Divisions B and C, and for the other divisions. What do these ratios reveal?

P5-2   ***Income Statement and Segment Reporting***   The following accounts are taken from the December 31, 2004 adjusted trial balance of the Reed Company:

Cost of goods sold	$121,120	Loss due to flood (pretax)	$ 8,000
Interest expense	4,880	Sales (net)	200,000
Depreciation expense	7,000	Administrative expenses	16,000
Selling expenses	26,000	Interest revenue	1,000

Additional information:

1. The company had 5,000 shares of common stock outstanding the entire year.
2. The income tax rate is 30% on all items.
3. The Reed Company operates several divisions, two of which, Divisions 1 and 2, are reportable operating segments.
4. No intersegment sales are made by any division. Of the total sales (net), Division 1 made 49%; Division 2, 30%; and the remaining segments, 21%.
5. Cost of goods sold as a *percentage of net sales* in each division was: Division 1, 62%; Division 2, 60%; other segments, 58%.
6. Selling expenses consist of sales salaries, sales commissions, delivery costs, advertising, and miscellaneous expenses. These are traceable to the segments as follows:
   a. Sales salaries ($6,000): $3,000 to Division 1, $2,000 to Division 2, and $1,000 to the remaining segments.
   b. Sales commissions ($4,000): 2% of net sales in all segments.

c. Delivery costs ($5,000): 60% to Division 1, 30% to Division 2, and 10% to the remaining segments.

d. Advertising ($10,500): Of the total, $1,200 was spent on general advertising. The remainder was spent as follows: $4,600 in Division 1, $3,200 in Division 2, and $1,500 in the other segments.

e. The miscellaneous selling expenses of $500 are considered common costs and are not allocated to any segments.

7. Administrative expenses consist of bad debts, administrative salaries, property taxes, and miscellaneous expenses. These are allocable to the segments as follows:

a. Bad debts ($2,000): 1% of net sales in all segments.

b. Administrative salaries ($10,000): Of the total, $2,100 are considered general corporate salaries. The remainder is allocated $3,800 to Division 1, $2,500 to Division 2, and $1,600 to the other segments.

c. Property taxes ($3,000): Of the total, $1,600 are general corporate expenses. Of the remainder, 40% is allocable to Division 1, 35% to Division 2, and 25% to the remaining segments.

d. The miscellaneous administrative expenses of $1,000 are considered common costs and are not allocated to any segments.

8. Depreciation expense is listed as a separate item on the income statement. Of the total, $1,400 is a general corporate expense. Of the remainder, 40% is allocable to Division 1, 30% to Division 2, and 30% to the remaining segments.

9. Interest revenue is from corporate investments in marketable securities. Interest expense is related to corporate bonds used to finance general operating activities.

10. An unusual and infrequent flood causing the material pretax loss occurred in Division 1.

11. Of the $300,000 total assets on December 31, 2004, 45% are assets of Division 1, 29% are assets of Division 2, 18% are assets of the remaining segments, and 8% are assets related to corporate headquarters.

12. Capital expenditures amounted to $25,000 in Division 1 and $6,000 in Division 2 during 2004 and are included in the total assets on December 31, 2004.

Required

1. Prepare a 2004 multiple-step income statement for the Reed Company.

2. Prepare a separate schedule that discloses the revenues, profit, and assets of Divisions 1 and 2, and the remaining operating segments.

3. Prepare appropriate segment notes related to depreciation, profit, and capital expenditures.

4. (*Appendix*) Compute the *pretax* return on identifiable assets for Divisions 1 and 2, and for the other divisions. What do these ratios reveal?

P5-3   ***Interim Reporting*** The Schultz Company prepares interim financial statements at the end of each quarter. The income statement presented at the end of the first quarter of 2004 is as follows:

Sales (net)		$40,000
Cost of goods sold:		
Beginning inventory	$18,000	
Purchases (net)	27,000	
Cost of goods available for sale	$45,000	
Ending inventory	(22,000)	(23,000)
Gross profit		$17,000
Operating expenses:		
Selling expenses	$ 8,800	
Administrative expenses	4,210	
Total operating expenses		(13,010)
Pretax operating income		$ 3,990
Other items:		
Interest revenue	$ 40	
Rent revenue	300	
Interest expense	(330)	10
Income before income taxes		$ 4,000
Income tax expense		(700)
Net income		$ 3,300
Earnings per share (8,000 shares)		$.41

Shown next is the Schultz Company trial balance as of June 30, 2004:

	Debit	Credit
Cash	$ 7,200	
Accounts receivable (net)	10,300	
Note receivable (due 9/1/04)	4,000	
Inventory (1/1/04)	18,000	
Prepaid insurance	960	
Property and equipment	80,000	
Accumulated depreciation		$ 20,000
Accounts payable		8,000
Dividends payable		3,200
Unearned rent		1,800
Bonds payable, 10% (due 1/1/2009)		12,000
Discount on bonds payable	600	
Common stock, $1 par		8,000
Premium on common stock		34,580
Retained earnings		26,400
Sales (net)		90,000
Purchases (net)	55,000	
Selling expenses	19,750	
Administrative expenses	8,170	
	$203,980	$203,980

Additional information:

1. The company uses control accounts for selling and administrative expenses.
2. The company journalizes and posts its adjusting entries to its accounts *only at year-end*.
3. The gross profit method is used to estimate the interim inventory. Historical gross profit has averaged 46% of net sales.
4. Uncollectible accounts average 0.5% of net sales.
5. The $4,000 note receivable was received on March 1, 2004. The 6-month note carries an annual interest rate of 12%, the interest to be collected at the maturity date.
6. The balance in the Prepaid Insurance account represents payment made on January 1, 2004 for a one-year comprehensive insurance policy.
7. The Property and Equipment account consists of land, $5,000; buildings, $55,000; and equipment, $20,000. The buildings are being depreciated over a 25-year life; the equipment over an 8-year life. Straight-line depreciation is used; residual value is disregarded. No acquisitions have been made in 2004. The depreciation on the buildings is treated as an administrative expense; depreciation on the equipment as a selling expense.
8. On February 1, 2004, the company rented some floor space to another company, receiving one year's rent of $1,800 in advance.
9. The bonds pay interest semiannually on January 1 and July 1. Straight-line amortization of the discount is recorded at the end of each year.
10. The company estimates that its pretax income for the second half of 2004 will total $11,550. All items in income are subject to the same income tax rate schedule. The income tax rate schedule is 15% on the first $20,000 of taxable income and 30% on the excess. There is no difference between the company's pretax financial income and taxable income, and no tax credits are available. The company rounds its estimated effective income tax rate to the nearest tenth of a percent. Income taxes will be paid during the first quarter of 2005.
11. On June 29, 2004, the company had declared and recorded (directly in Retained Earnings) a semiannual dividend of 40¢ per share, payable on August 3, 2004.
12. The 8,000 shares of common stock have been outstanding the entire 6 months of 2004.

Required

1. Prepare a 10-column worksheet to develop the Schultz Company financial statements for the first 6 months of 2004 (refer to Appendix C for a worksheet illustration, if necessary).
2. Prepare the income statement for (a) the first 6 months of 2004 and (b) the second quarter of 2004.
3. Prepare a retained earnings statement for the first 6 months of 2004.
4. Prepare the June 30, 2004 balance sheet.

P5-4   *Interim Reporting*   The Sikyta Company prepares quarterly and year-to-date financial statements at the end of each quarter. The income statement presented at the end of the first quarter of 2004 is:

Sales (net)		$62,000
Cost of goods sold:		
Inventory, January 1, 2004	$23,000	
Purchases (net)	38,200	
Cost of goods available for sale	$61,200	
Inventory, March 31, 2004	(24,000)	
Cost of goods sold		(37,200)
Gross profit		$24,800
Operating expenses		(14,074)
Pretax operating income		$10,726
Other items		
Interest expense (bonds)		(726)
Income before income taxes		$10,000
Income tax expense		(2,000)
Net income		$ 8,000
Earnings per share (10,000 shares)		$.80

The following is the Sikyta Company trial balance as of June 30, 2004:

	Debit	Credit
Cash	$ 10,200	
Accounts receivable	14,700	
Allowance for doubtful accounts		$ 400
Note receivable (due April 2, 2005)	5,000	
Inventory (January 1, 2004)	23,000	
Prepaid rent (warehouse)	2,400	
Land	12,000	
Buildings	80,000	
Equipment	18,000	
Accumulated depreciation: buildings and equipment		23,000
Accounts payable		9,100
Dividends payable		3,000
Note payable (due October 1, 2004)		6,000
Bonds payable, 12% (due January 1, 2014)		25,000
Premium on bonds payable		960
Common stock, $0.50 par		5,000
Additional paid-in capital		52,000
Retained earnings		22,968
Sales (net)		120,000
Purchases (net)	77,920	
Operating expenses	24,208	
	$267,428	$267,428

Additional information:

1. The company journalizes and posts adjusting entries only at *the end of the year.*
2. The company uses a control account for operating expenses.
3. Bad debts average 0.5% of net sales.
4. The retail inventory method (average cost) is used to estimate the ending inventory at the end of each quarter. The ending inventories at cost and retail for each quarter are then used as the beginning inventories for the subsequent quarter, and the retail inventory method is applied based on the relevant information for *that quarter.* For the second quarter, the following information is available: 4/1/2004—inventory at retail, $40,000; sales (net), $58,000; purchases (net) at cost, $39,720, and at retail, $65,900; markups (net), $2,100; no markdowns.
5. On March 1, 2004, the company rented a small warehouse, paying a year's rent of $2,400 in advance.
6. The note receivable was received from a customer on April 1, 2004. The customer will pay the note plus interest of 14% on April 1, 2005.

7. The buildings are being depreciated over a 25-year life, the equipment over a 10-year life. No acquisitions have been made in 2004. The company uses straight-line depreciation. Residual value is expected to be nominal and is not considered for depreciation.

8. The note payable was issued on April 1, 2004. It carries an annual interest rate of 13%; interest is payable on the maturity date.

9. The bonds pay interest semiannually on January 1 and July 1. Straight-line amortization of the premium is recorded at the end of each year.

10. At the end of the second quarter, it estimated that the pretax income for the remaining 6 months would total $20,000. The income tax rate schedule is 15% on the first $20,000 of taxable income and 30% on the excess. The company rounds its estimated effective income tax rate to the nearest tenth of a percent. There is no difference between the company's pretax financial income and taxable income. Income taxes will be paid during the first quarter of 2005.

11. The company declared and recorded (directly in Retained Earnings) a 30¢ per share semiannual dividend (on 10,000 shares) on June 30, 2004, payable on July 31, 2004.

12. The 10,000 shares of common stock have been outstanding the entire 6 months of 2004.

Required

1. Prepare a 10-column worksheet to develop the Sikyta Company financial statements for the first 6 months of 2004 (refer to Appendix C for a worksheet illustration, if necessary).
2. Prepare the income statement for (a) the first 6 months of 2004 and (b) the second quarter of 2004.
3. Prepare a retained earnings statement for the first 6 months of 2004.
4. Prepare the June 30, 2004 balance sheet.

See WebTutor for annotated problem solution.

P5-5   **Interim Reporting**   The Anderson Manufacturing Company, a California corporation listed on the Pacific Coast Stock Exchange, budgeted activities for 2004 as follows:

	Amount	Units
Net sales	$6,000,000	1,000,000
Cost of goods sold	(3,600,000)	1,000,000
Gross margin	$2,400,000	
Selling, general, and administrative expenses	(1,400,000)	
Operating earnings	$1,000,000	
Nonoperating revenues and expenses	0	
Earnings before income taxes	$1,000,000	
Estimated income taxes (current and deferred)	(350,000)	
Net earnings	$ 650,000	
Earnings per share	$6.50	

Anderson has operated profitably for many years and has experienced a seasonal pattern of sales volume and production similar to the following forecasted for 2004. Sales volume is expected to follow a quarterly pattern of 10%, 20%, 35%, and 35%, respectively, because of the seasonality of the industry. Also, due to production and storage capacity limitations, it is expected that production will follow a pattern of 20%, 25%, 30%, and 25%, respectively.

At the conclusion of the first quarter of 2004, the controller of Anderson has prepared and issued the following interim report for public release:

	Amount	Units
Net sales	$ 600,000	100,000
Cost of goods sold	(360,000)	100,000
Gross margin	$ 240,000	
Selling, general, and administrative expenses	(275,000)	
Operating loss	$ (35,000)	
Loss from warehouse fire	(175,000)	
Loss before income taxes	$(210,000)	
Estimated income taxes	0	
Net loss	$(210,000)	
Loss per share of common stock	$(2.10)	

The following additional information is available for the first quarter just completed, but was not included in the public information released:

1. The company uses a standard cost system in which standards are set at currently attainable levels on an annual basis. At the end of the first quarter, there was underapplied fixed factory overhead (volume variance) of $50,000 that was treated as an asset at the end of the quarter. Production during the quarter was 200,000 units, of which 100,000 were sold.

2. The selling, general, and administrative expenses were budgeted on a basis of $900,000 fixed expenses for the year plus $0.50 variable expenses per unit of sales.

3. Assume that the warehouse fire loss met the conditions of an extraordinary loss. The warehouse had an undepreciated cost of $320,000; $145,000 was recovered from insurance on the warehouse. No other gains or losses are anticipated this year from similar events or transactions, nor has Anderson had any similar losses in preceding years; thus, the full loss will be deductible as an ordinary loss for income tax purposes.

4. The effective income tax rate, for federal and state taxes combined, is expected to average 35% of earnings before income taxes during 2004. There are no permanent differences between pretax financial income and taxable income.

5. Earnings per share were computed on the basis of 100,000 shares of capital stock outstanding. Anderson has only one class of stock issued, no long-term debt outstanding, and no stock option plan.

Required

1. Without reference to the specific situation described previously, what are the standards of disclosure for interim financial data (published interim financial reports) for publicly traded companies? Explain.

2. Identify the weaknesses in form and content of Anderson's interim report without reference to the additional information.

3. For each of the five items of additional information, indicate the preferable treatment for each item for interim reporting purposes and explain why that treatment is preferable. (*AICPA adapted*)

P5-6 *Financial Statement Presentation and Ratios* The Horizon Company is listed on the New York Stock Exchange. The market value of its common stock was quoted at $18 per share at both December 31, 2004 and December 31, 2003. Horizon's balance sheets at December 31, 2004 and December 31, 2003, and statements of income and retained earnings for the years then ended are as follows:

Balance Sheets

	December 31,	
	2004	2003
Assets		
Current assets		
Cash	$ 3,500	$ 3,600
Marketable securities, at market	13,000	11,000
Accounts receivable, net of allowance for doubtful accounts	105,000	95,000
Inventories at lower of cost or market	126,000	154,000
Prepaid expenses	2,500	2,400
Total current assets	$250,000	$266,000
Property, plant and equipment, net of accumulated depreciation	311,000	308,000
Other assets	29,000	34,000
Total Assets	$590,000	$608,000
Liabilities		
Current liabilities		
Notes payable	$ 5,000	$ 15,000
Accounts payable and accrued expenses	62,500	74,500
Income taxes payable	1,000	1,000
Payments due within one year on long-term debt	6,500	7,500
Total current liabilities	$ 75,000	$ 98,000
Long-term debt	169,000	180,000
Deferred income taxes	74,000	67,000
Other liabilities	9,000	8,000

Stockholders' Equity

Common stock, par value $1.00 per share; authorized 20,000 shares; issued and outstanding 10,000 shares	10,000	10,000
Additional paid-in capital	110,000	110,000
Retained earnings	142,000	134,000
Accumulated other comprehensive income		
Unrealized increase in value of marketable securities	1,000	1,000
Total stockholders' equity	263,000	255,000
Total Liabilities and Stockholders' Equity	$590,000	$608,000

Statement of Income and Retained Earnings

	Year Ended December 31,	
	2004	**2003**
Net sales	$600,000	$500,000
Costs and expenses		
Cost of goods sold	480,000	400,000
Selling, general and administrative expenses	74,200	68,000
Other, net	17,000	6,000
Total costs and expenses	571,200	474,000
Income before income taxes	$ 28,800	$ 26,000
Income taxes	8,600	7,800
Net income	$ 20,200	$ 18,200
Retained earnings at beginning of period, as previously reported	141,000	132,000
Adjustment required for correction of an error	(7,000)	(6,000)
Retained earnings at beginning of period, as restated	$134,000	$126,000
Dividends on common stock	12,200	10,200
Retained earnings at end of period	$142,000	$134,000

Additional facts are as follows:

(a) "Selling, general and administrative expenses" for 2004 included a usual but infrequently occurring charge of $9,000.

(b) "Other, net" for 2004 included an extraordinary item (charge) of $10,000. If the extraordinary item (charge) had not occurred, income taxes for 2004 would have been $11,600, instead of $8,600.

(c) "Adjustment required for correction of an error" was a result of a change from an accounting principle that is not generally accepted to one that is generally accepted.

(d) Horizon Company has a simple capital structure and has disclosed earnings per common share for net income in the Notes to the Financial Statements.

Required

1. Determine from the preceding additional facts whether or not the presentation of those facts in the Horizon Company statements of income and retained earnings is appropriate. If the presentation is appropriate, discuss the theoretical rationale for the presentation. If the presentation is not appropriate, describe the appropriate presentation and discuss its theoretical rationale. Do not discuss disclosure requirements for the notes to the financial statements.

2. Describe the general significance of the following financial analysis tools: (a) quick (acid-test) ratio, (b) inventory turnover, and (c) return on stockholders' equity.

3. Based on the Horizon Company balance sheets, statements of income and retained earnings, and additional facts, describe how to determine each of the above financial analysis tools (for the year 2004 only). (*AICPA adapted*)

P5-7 **Multiple-Step Income Statement** Before closing the books for the year ended December 31, 2004, Pitt Corp. prepared the following condensed trial balance:

	Debit	Credit
Total assets	$ 7,082,500	
Total liabilities		$ 1,700,000
Common stock		1,250,000
Additional paid-in capital		2,097,500
Donated capital		90,000
Retained earnings, 1/1/04		1,650,000
Net sales		6,250,000
Cost of sales	3,750,000	
Selling and administrative expenses	1,212,500	
Interest expense	122,500	
Gain on sale of long-term investments		130,000
Income tax expense	300,000	
Loss on disposition of plant assets	225,000	
Loss due to earthquake damage	475,000	
	$13,167,500	$13,167,500

Other financial data for the year ended December 31, 2004:
Federal income tax

Estimated tax payments	$200,000
Accrued	100,000

Total charged to income tax expense (Does not properly reflect current or deferred income tax expense or interperiod income tax allocation for income statement purposes.) $300,000

Pitt applied the provisions of FASB Statement No. 109, *Accounting for Income Taxes*, in its financial statements for the year ended December 31, 2004. The enacted tax rate on all types of taxable income for the current and future years is 30%. The alternative minimum tax is less than the regular income tax.

Temporary difference

Excess of book basis over tax basis in depreciable assets (arising from equipment donated as a capital contribution on December 31, 2004 and expected to be depreciated over five years beginning in 2005). There were no temporary differences prior to 2004. $ 90,000

Nondeductible expenditure
Officers' life insurance expense $ 70,000

Earthquake damage
This damage is considered unusual and infrequent.

Capital structure
Common stock, par value $5 per share, traded on a national exchange:
Number of shares:

Outstanding at 1/1/04	200,000
Issued on 3/30/04 as a 10% stock dividend	20,000
Sold for $25 per share on 6/30/04	30,000
Outstanding at 12/31/04	250,000

Required

1. Using the multiple-step format, prepare a formal income statement for Pitt for the year ended December 31, 2004.
2. Prepare a schedule to reconcile net income to taxable income reportable on Pitt's tax return for 2004. (*AICPA adapted*)

P5-8   *The Coca-Cola Company Disclosures*   Review the financial statements and related notes of The Coca-Cola Company in Appendix A.

Required Answer the following questions. (*Note:* All information is given in the financial report.) Indicate on what page of the financial report you located the answer.

1. What was the gross profit for 2001? The operating income?
2. What was the net income for 2001? What were the related earnings per share amounts?
3. What were the total assets on December 31, 2001? How much of this total were current assets?
4. What were the total liabilities on December 31, 2001?
5. What was the total share-owners' equity on December 31, 2001? How much was deducted from this share-owners' equity for treasury stock? What method does the company use to account for its treasury stock?
6. What was the net increase in cash and cash equivalents in 2001? How much of this was from net cash provided by operating activities?
7. Where does the company summarize its accounting policies? How are inventories valued and, generally, what costing methods are used? How are property, plant, and equipment depreciated?
8. What is the total of the lines of credit and other short-term credit facilities available, and how much was outstanding on December 31, 2001?
9. What was the percentage of total debt to total capital in 2001? How does this compare to 2000?
10. What was the return on capital in 2001? How does this compare to 2000?
11. What was the net cash used in financing activities in 2001? What was the net cash used in investing activities in 2001?
12. How many stock options were outstanding at December 31, 2001? What was the weighted-average price per share for exercised stock options in 2001?
13. What was the net periodic pension cost of the company's pension plan in 2001? What was the fair value of the company's benefit plan assets on December 31, 2001?
14. For the fourth quarter of 2001, what were the (a) net operating revenues, (b) gross profit, and (c) net income? What were the related earnings per share for (c)?
15. What were the net operating revenues in Africa for 2001? What were the identifiable operating assets held in Latin America at December 31, 2001?
16. Who are the auditors of the company? On what date was the audit report issued?
17. How is the internal accounting control system augmented to provide reasonable assurance that assets are safeguarded and that transactions are authorized, recorded, and reported properly?

P5-9   *Horizontal Analysis and Ratios (Appendix)*   The following are comparative financial statements of the Cohen Company for 2003, 2004, and 2005:

Comparative Income Statements

	For Years Ended December 31,		
	2005	2004	2003
Sales (net)	$102,200	$ 91,500	$ 81,700
Cost of goods sold	(61,100)	(52,800)	(47,150)
Gross profit	$ 41,100	$ 38,700	$ 34,550
Selling expenses	(11,400)	(10,000)	(8,900)
Administrative expenses	(8,700)	(7,843)	(6,950)
Interest expense	(3,000)	(4,000)	(4,000)
Total expenses	(23,100)	(21,843)	(19,850)
Income before income taxes	$ 18,000	$ 16,857	$ 14,700
Income tax expense	(5,400)	(5,057)	(4,410)
Net income	$ 12,600	$ 11,800	$ 10,290
Earnings per share	?	?	?

Comparative Retained Earnings Statements

	For Years Ended December 31,		
	2005	2004	2003
Beginning retained earnings	$ 28,800	$ 20,800	$ 14,310
Add: Net income	12,600	11,800	10,290
	$ 41,400	$ 32,600	$ 24,600
Less: Dividends distributed	(4,410)	(3,800)	(3,800)
Ending retained earnings	$ 36,990	$ 28,800	$ 20,800

Comparative Balance Sheets

	December 31,		
	2005	2004	2003
Cash	$ 4,200	$ 4,000	$ 4,100
Receivables (net)	7,600	7,000	6,200
Inventories	9,800	9,000	8,600
Noncurrent assets	119,390	112,000	107,100
Total Assets	$140,990	$132,000	$126,000
Current liabilities	$ 12,000	$ 10,000	$ 12,000
Bonds payable, 10%	30,000	40,000	40,000
Common stock, $2 par	8,400	7,600	7,600
Premium on common stock	53,600	45,600	45,600
Retained earnings	36,990	28,800	20,800
Total Liabilities and Stockholders' Equity	$140,990	$132,000	$126,000

Additional information: Credit sales were 65% of net sales in 2004 and 60% in 2005. At the beginning of 2005, 400 shares of common stock were issued, the first sale of stock in several years.

The Cohen Company is concerned. Although it increased the dividends paid per share by 5% in 2005 and its 2005 net income is higher than 2004 net income, the market price of its common stock dropped from $22 per share at the beginning of 2005 to $21 per share at year-end.

Required

1. For 2003, 2004, and 2005, prepare horizontal analyses for the Cohen Company using a year-to-year approach.
2. For 2004 and 2005, compute the following ratios:
   a. Current
   b. Acid-test
   c. Inventory turnover
   d. Receivables turnover
   e. Earnings per share
   f. Dividend yield
   g. Return on total assets
   h. Return on stockholders' equity
   i. Debt
3. Based on your results, discuss the possible reasons for the decrease in the market price per share in 2005.

P5-10 *Vertical Analysis, Ratios (Appendix)* The Pierce Company operates a high-volume retail outlet. The following are comparative financial statements for the company:
@

Comparative Income Statements

	For Years Ended December 31,	
	2005	2004
Sales (net)	$180,000	$150,000
Cost of goods sold	(108,000)	(85,500)
Gross profit	$ 72,000	$ 64,500
Selling expenses	(21,600)	(15,000)
Administrative expenses	(23,770)	(23,410)
Interest expense	(3,200)	(2,800)
Income before taxes	$ 23,430	$ 23,290
Income tax expense	(7,030)	(6,990)
Net income	$ 16,400	$ 16,300
Earnings per share (6,000 shares)	$2.73	$2.72

Comparative Balance Sheets

	December 31,	
	2005	2004
Cash	$ 4,200	$ 3,000
Investments (short-term)	2,000	2,100
Receivables (net)	8,600	6,400
Inventory	11,300	9,700
Noncurrent assets (net)	129,900	118,800
Total Assets	$156,000	$140,000

	December 31,	
	2005	2004
Accounts payable	$ 12,000	$ 10,000
Other current liabilities	1,000	2,400
Bonds payable	40,000	35,000
Common stock, $3 par	18,000	18,000
Additional paid-in capital	30,000	30,000
Retained earnings	54,100	43,600
Accumulated other comprehensive income	900	1,000
Total Liabilities and Stockholders' Equity	$156,000	$140,000

Additional data: The company has not issued any common stock for several years and the price of its common stock has remained relatively constant over that time. At the beginning of 2004, it had outstanding accounts receivable (net) of $7,600, an inventory of $11,000, accounts payable of $7,400, total liabilities of $44,600, and stockholders' equity of $85,400. The company typically makes 50% of its sales on credit.

Pierce Company management has become concerned. Although it feels that progress has been made in "tightening up" the company's operating cycle, this has caused only a modest increase in profits and no increase in the company's stock market price. Management has asked for your assistance in identifying problem areas as well as strong points.

Required

1. Prepare a vertical analysis for the 2004 and 2005 financial statements of Pierce.
2. Compute the following ratios for 2004 and 2005:
   a. Current
   b. Acid-test
   c. Inventory turnover
   d. Receivables turnover
   e. Payables turnover
   f. Return on total assets
   g. Return on stockholders' equity
   h. Debt
   i. Times interest earned
3. Briefly discuss any findings that your analyses reveal.

P5-11   *Horizontal and Vertical Analyses (Appendix)*   The following are comparative financial statements of the Perez Company for 2003, 2004, and 2005:

Comparative Income Statements

	For Years Ended December 31,		
	2005	2004	2003
Sales	$ 407,000	$361,500	$332,000
Sales returns	(7,000)	(11,500)	(12,000)
Net sales	$ 400,000	$350,000	$320,000
Cost of goods sold	(244,000)	(222,000)	(205,000)
Gross profit	$ 156,000	$128,000	$115,000
Selling expenses	(45,825)	(39,550)	(35,690)
Administrative expenses	(60,232)	(46,664)	(44,213)
Interest expense	(4,150)	(4,200)	(3,580)
Total expense	$(110,207)	$ (90,414)	$ (83,483)
Income before income taxes	$ 45,793	$ 37,586	$ 31,517
Income tax expense	(13,738)	(11,276)	(9,455)
Net income	$ 32,055	$ 26,310	$ 22,062
Number of common shares	10,000	9,000	8,000
Earnings per share	$3.21	$2.92	$2.76

Comparative Balance Sheets

	December 31,		
	2005	2004	2003
Cash	$ 15,500	$ 12,650	$ 9,300
Receivables (net)	11,000	9,350	6,600
Inventories	38,000	30,000	22,250
Noncurrent assets	286,500	250,000	220,350
Total Assets	$351,000	$302,000	$258,500
Accounts payable	$ 11,800	$ 9,500	$ 9,300
Notes payable	16,200	13,500	11,700
Bonds payable	38,000	39,000	36,500
Common stock, $5 par	50,000	45,000	40,000
Premium on common stock	90,000	72,000	56,000
Retained earnings	145,000	123,000	105,000
Total Liabilities and Stockholders' Equity	$351,000	$302,000	$258,500

Required On the basis of the given information:

1. Prepare horizontal analyses for Perez Company using a base-year-to-date approach for 2003 through 2004, and 2003 through 2005.
2. Prepare vertical analyses for the 2004 and 2005 financial statements.

P5-12   *Ratio Analysis (Appendix)*   Comparative financial statements of the Boeckman Company for 2003 and 2004 are as follows:

Comparative Balance Sheets

	December 31,	
	2004	2003
Assets		
Current assets		
Cash	$ 7,940	$ 5,760
Temporary investments (at market)	10,060	4,240
Accounts receivable	18,000	19,500
Inventories	32,000	27,000
Prepaid insurance	15,000	14,000
Total current assets	$ 83,000	$ 70,500
Property and plant (net)	64,000	46,000
Investments	36,000	32,000
Long-term receivables	38,600	31,000
Patents, net	13,000	9,000
Other assets	30,000	27,500
Total Assets	$264,600	$216,000
Liabilities		
Current liabilities		
Accounts payable	$ 17,800	$ 16,500
Income taxes payable	7,500	6,800
Accrued payables	1,500	1,400
Current portion of long-term debt	3,200	3,200
Total current liabilities	$ 30,000	$ 27,900
Long-term debt	$ 56,300	$ 48,000
Deferred income taxes	12,500	11,800
Total other liabilities	7,200	8,300
Total liabilities	$106,000	$ 96,000
Stockholders' Equity		
Common stock, $5 par	$ 35,000	$ 30,000
Premium on common stock	36,000	24,600
Retained earnings	86,600	64,800
Accumulated other comprehensive income	1,000	600
Total stockholders' equity	$158,600	$120,000
Total Liabilities and Stockholders' Equity	$264,600	$216,000

Comparative Income Statements

	For Years Ended December 31,	
	2004	2003
Sales	$278,000	$256,000
Sales returns	(8,000)	(6,000)
Net sales (68% on credit)	$270,000	$250,000
Cost of goods sold	(175,500)	(170,000)
Gross profit	$ 94,500	$ 80,000
Selling expenses	(21,500)	(18,200)
General expenses	(27,560)	(23,550)
Interest expense	(4,300)	(3,100)
Total expenses	$ (53,360)	$ (44,850)
Income before income taxes	$ 41,140	$ 35,150
Income tax expense	(12,340)	(10,550)
Net income	$ 28,800	$ 24,600
Beginning retained earnings	64,800	43,200
Common stock dividends	(7,000)	(3,000)
Ending retained earnings	$ 86,600	$ 64,800

Additional information: The Boeckman Company is listed on the New York Stock Exchange. It issued 1,000 additional shares of common stock at the beginning of 2004. The market value of its common stock was quoted at $17 per share at December 31, 2004. The company uses a 365-day business year in its ratio analysis.

Required

1. Based on the preceding information, compute (for the year 2004 only) the following ratios for Boeckman:
   a. Dividend yield
   b. Price/earnings
   c. Profit margin
   d. Return on total assets
   e. Return on stockholders' equity
   f. Current
   g. Acid-test
   h. Inventory turnover (in days)
   i. Receivables turnover (in days)
   j. Payables turnover (in days)
   k. Average operating cycle (in days)
   l. Debt
   m. Times interest earned
   n. Book value per common share
2. Briefly discuss what a potential investor might do to evaluate the results of these ratios.

P5-13   *Ratio Analysis (Appendix)*   The Printing Company is listed on the New York Stock Exchange. The market value of its common stock was quoted at $10 per share at December 31, 2004 and 2003. Printing's balance sheet at December 31, 2004 and 2003, and statement of income and retained earnings for the years then ended are as follows:

Balance Sheet

	December 31, 2004	December 31, 2003
Assets		
Current Assets		
Cash	$ 3,500,000	$ 3,600,000
Marketable securities, at market	13,000,000	11,000,000
Accounts receivable (net)	105,000,000	95,000,000
Inventories, lower of cost or market	126,000,000	154,000,000
Prepaid expenses	2,500,000	2,400,000
Total current assets	$250,000,000	$266,000,000
Property and plant (net)	311,000,000	308,000,000
Investments, at equity	2,000,000	3,000,000
Long-term receivables	14,000,000	16,000,000
Goodwill and patents (net)	6,000,000	6,500,000
Other assets	6,000,000	7,600,000
Total Assets	$589,000,000	$607,100,000
Liabilities		
Current Liabilities		
Notes payable	$ 5,000,000	$ 15,000,000
Accounts payable	38,000,000	48,000,000
Accrued expenses	24,500,000	27,000,000
Income taxes payable	1,000,000	1,000,000
Current portion of long-term debt	6,500,000	7,000,000
Total current liabilities	75,000,000	98,000,000
Long-term debt	169,000,000	180,000,000
Deferred income taxes	74,000,000	67,000,000
Other liabilities	9,000,000	8,000,000

Stockholders' Equity

Common stock, $1 par value	10,000,000	10,000,000
5% cumulative preferred stock, $100 par value; $100 liquidating value	4,000,000	4,000,000
Additional paid-in capital	107,000,000	107,000,000
Retained earnings	142,000,000	134,000,000
Accumulated other comprehensive loss		
Unrealized decrease in value of marketable securities	(1,000,000)	(900,000)
Total stockholders' equity	262,000,000	254,100,000
Total Liabilities and Stockholders' Equity	$589,000,000	$607,100,000

Statement of Income and Retained Earnings

	Year Ended December 31,	
	2004	**2003**
Net sales	$600,000,000	$500,000,000
Costs and expenses		
Cost of goods sold	$490,000,000	$400,000,000
Selling and general expenses	71,900,000	66,000,000
Other, net	7,000,000	6,000,000
Total costs and expenses	568,900,000	472,000,000
Income before taxes	$ 31,100,000	$ 28,000,000
Income tax expense	10,900,000	9,800,000
Net income	$ 20,200,000	$ 18,200,000
Beginning retained earnings	134,000,000	126,000,000
Dividends on common stock	12,000,000	10,000,000
Dividends on preferred stock	200,000	200,000
Ending retained earnings	$142,000,000	$134,000,000

Required Based on the preceding information, compute (for the year 2004 only) the following:
1. Current (working capital) ratio
2. Quick (acid-test) ratio
3. Number of days' sales in average receivables, assuming a business year consists of 300 days and all sales are on account
4. Inventory turnover
5. Book value per share of common stock
6. Earnings per share on common stock
7. Price/earnings ratio on common stock
8. Dividend yield ratio on common stock *(AICPA adapted)*

INTERNET ASSIGNMENTS

Go to the Nikolai and Bazley **Intermediate Accounting** web site (http://Nikolai.swcollege.com). Click on Student Resources and <u>internet homework assignments</u>. Then click on the appropriate hot link (icon) for each company's web site, find the relevant accounting information, and answer the following questions.

I5-1   Go to the Campbell Soup Company web site.

Required Refer to the Management's Discussion and Analysis section of the company's most recent annual report. In what three business segments does the company operate? By what percentage did sales increase or decrease in the current year for each of these segments? Why did it change? What was the company's gross margin as a percentage of sales in the current and previous year? Why did it change in each year?

I5-2   Go to the Avon web site.

Required Refer to the Management's Discussion and Analysis section of the company's most recent annual report. In regard to Liquidity and Capital Resources, what are the key points that management makes about its cash flows and working capital for the current year as compared to the previous year? About its inventories and capital expenditures? How much of its consolidated net sales for the current year did the company derive from its international subsidiaries? Does this surprise you? Why or why not?

PART 2

Financial Reporting: Asset Measurement and Income Determination

Chapter 6   Cash and Receivables

Chapter 7   Inventories: Cost Measurement and Flow
                   Assumptions

Chapter 8   Inventories: Special Valuation Issues

Chapter 9   Property, Plant, and Equipment: Acquisition
                   and Disposal

Chapter 10   Depreciation and Depletion

Chapter 11   Intangibles

objectives

1 Understand the importance of cash management.

2 Prepare a bank reconciliation.

3 Discuss revenue recognition when the right of return exists.

4 Understand the credit policies related to accounts receivable.

5 Explain the gross and net methods to account for cash discounts.

6 Estimate and record bad debts using a percentage of sales.

7 Estimate and record bad debts using an aging analysis.

8 Explain pledging, assignment, and factoring of accounts receivable.

9 Account for short-term notes receivable.

10 Prepare a proof of cash (Appendix).

CHAPTER

6

Cash and Receivables

Financial statement users focus upon a variety of information in making credit and investment decisions. Investors, long-term creditors, and short-term creditors are interested in a company's **financial flexibility**, the ability to use its financial resources to adapt to change. One part of a company's financial flexibility that external users are concerned about is liquidity. **Liquidity** is the availability of liquid assets (cash or assets that may be quickly converted into cash) to pay operating costs, dividends, and interest, and to repay short-term debts. The most common types of liquid assets are cash, temporary investments, accounts receivable, and notes receivable. In this chapter we discuss the measurement and valuation procedures associated with cash, accounts receivable, and notes receivable. Because the accounting principles for temporary investments are similar to those for most long-term investments, we defer discussion of temporary investments to Chapter 14.

CASH

Cash is the resource on hand to meet planned expenditures and emergency situations. **The amount a company reports as cash in the current assets section on its balance sheet must be available to pay current obligations.** It may not be subject to any contractual restrictions that prevent the company from using this money to pay current debts. For example, many companies establish sinking funds into which they deposit cash over an extended period. At the end of the period, the cash (plus accumulated interest) is to be used for a specific purpose (e.g., to retire long-term bonds). Amounts in sinking funds are not classified under the cash heading on the balance sheet; a company normally reports these amounts in the long-term investments category.

The measurement of **cash classified as a current asset includes coins, currency, unrestricted funds on deposit with a bank** (either checking accounts or savings accounts[1]), **negotiable checks,** and **bank drafts.** On the other hand, some items may be confused with cash but normally are listed under other balance sheet captions. Among these items are certificates of deposit, bank overdrafts, postdated checks, travel advances, and postage stamps. *Certificates of deposit (CDs)* are short-term investments issued by banks that allow a company to invest idle cash for short periods of time. CDs normally are classified as temporary investments. *Bank overdrafts* are overdrawn checking accounts. They are reported as current liabilities and should *not* be offset against positive balances in other bank accounts. *Postdated checks* from customers are checks dated in the future so they become payable on a date later than the issue date. Postdated checks are included as receivables

---

1. Although some banks place restrictions on the withdrawal of funds from savings accounts, they generally are included as a component of cash.

until the date they become negotiable. *Travel advances* are funds or checks given to company employees to cover out-of-pocket expenses while traveling on company business. Since travel advances are satisfied when the employee submits receipts for business expenses, they are classified as prepaid items. *Postage stamps* on hand are classified as prepaid items because they will be used rather than exchanged for cash. Below is a diagram that summarizes what is, and what is not, included in cash.

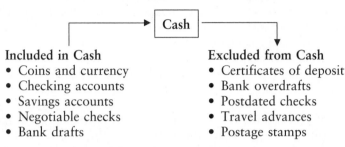

Included in Cash	Excluded from Cash
• Coins and currency	• Certificates of deposit
• Checking accounts	• Bank overdrafts
• Savings accounts	• Postdated checks
• Negotiable checks	• Travel advances
• Bank drafts	• Postage stamps

In summary, to be classified under the current asset—Cash—caption on the balance sheet, amounts must be available immediately to pay current debts and may not be bound by any contractual or legal restrictions. Items that do not meet these criteria are reported elsewhere within the assets (or liabilities) section on the balance sheet.

Cash and Cash Equivalents

Some companies use the title Cash on their balance sheets. An increasing number (approximately 85%)[2], however, use a title such as *Cash and Cash Equivalents*. In addition to cash, these companies include in this category items that are considered to be "cash equivalents" because of their liquidity and low risk. **Cash equivalents** are short-term, highly liquid investments that are readily convertible into known amounts of cash and so near their maturity that there is little risk of changes in value because of changes in interest rates. Generally, only investments with maturity dates of three months or less from the date acquired by the holder are cash equivalents.[3] Securities such as commercial paper, treasury bills, and money market funds are examples of cash equivalents. A clear understanding of what items a company includes in Cash and Cash Equivalents is important because when preparing its statement of cash flows, it must reconcile its cash inflows and outflows to the change in cash and cash equivalents. In this chapter for simplicity we focus our discussion on Cash.

The statement of cash flows is discussed in Chapter 21.

Cash Management

Efficient cash management is very important to every company. Each company must ensure that adequate cash resources are available to meet its current obligations. However, it must recognize the fact that idle cash is a nonproductive resource.

1 Understand the importance of cash management.

Although a company may wish to protect itself against business failure by amassing a large amount of cash to keep itself liquid, it can improve its performance by investing these funds and earning interest. Proper cash management requires the investment of idle funds and the estimation of the timing of cash inflows and outflows to ensure the availability of cash to meet the company's needs. Having too many liquid resources, however, may make a company the target of a takeover attempt.

Information on cash management is important in financial accounting because one objective of financial reporting is to communicate how well the managers of a company have discharged their stewardship responsibility to stockholders for the use of the company assets. In this regard, cash management includes planning and control aspects. **Cash planning** systems consist of those methods and procedures adopted to ensure that a company has adequate cash available to meet maturing obligations and that it invests

2. *Accounting Trends and Techniques* (New York: AICPA, 2001), p. 130.
3. "Statements of Cash Flows," *FASB Statement of Financial Accounting Standards No. 95* (Stamford, Conn.: FASB, 1987), par. 8.

any unused or excess cash. **Cash control** systems are the methods and procedures adopted to ensure the safeguarding of the company's funds.

The major component of a cash planning system is the cash budget. **The cash budget is a plan of cash activity that forecasts cash inflows and outflows, and identifies the timing of potential cash surpluses and shortages.** The cash budget is primarily a managerial accounting technique and is outside the scope of this book.

(A) Cash control systems require adequate internal control measures. **Internal control** is the process (policies and procedures) a company uses to enhance the reliability of its financial reports, promote the effectiveness and efficiency of its operations (including safeguarding its assets), and ensure its compliance with applicable laws and regulations.[4] The importance of this control is emphasized by a federal law requiring all publicly traded companies to maintain adequate internal control systems. Since cash cannot be traced easily, internal control over cash is enhanced by routine reviews of the accuracy of the recording of cash transactions and by the separation of employee duties. These procedures help to prevent theft unless there is collusion among employees. However, whenever a company adopts internal control measures, the cost associated with the use of the measures should not exceed the value of the derived benefits. Any measure that costs more than its benefits ultimately will result in lower profits for the company.

Cash control systems can be subdivided into two main functions: (1) control over receipts and (2) control over payments. The control procedures a company adopts for its cash receipts should be designed to safeguard all cash inflows from the time they arrive at the company until they are deposited in its bank account. Among the key elements in a cash receipts internal control system are (1) an immediate counting of receipts by the person opening the mail or the salesperson using the cash register, (2) a daily recording of all cash receipts in the accounting records, and (3) the daily deposit of all receipts in the company's bank account.

The control procedures for payments should ensure that only authorized payments for actual company expenditures are approved and made. The key elements in a cash payments internal control system include (1) making all payments by check so that a record exists for every company expenditure (for some payments a petty cash system may be used, as we discuss next), (2) authorizing and signing checks only after an expenditure is verified and approved, and (3) periodically reconciling the cash balance in the bank statement with the company's accounting records.

Two important elements of the internal control over cash are a petty cash system and a bank reconciliation. We discuss each of these elements in more detail in the following sections.

Petty Cash

A petty cash system involves a cash fund placed under the control of an employee to allow a company to pay for small amounts that might be impractical or impossible to pay by check. For example, a company requiring employees to work overtime may have a policy of sending late-working employees home by taxi. Since taxi drivers do not usually accept checks, the company may give these employees cash to pay the taxi fare. Small amounts of cash may also be needed to pay for postage, collect deliveries, the purchase of small amounts of office supplies, and other items. A company may use a petty cash system for these purposes. The design and operation of a petty cash system includes the following steps:

1. An employee is appointed petty cash custodian. The petty cash fund is established at an amount estimated to be enough to cover expenditures over a short period of time, and the fund is turned over to the employee. The journal entry to record the establishment of the fund is a debit to Petty Cash and a credit to Cash for $500 (amount assumed).

---

4. For auditing purposes, a company's internal control structure consists of its control environment, risk assessment procedures, control activities, information and communication system, and monitoring process. For more detail, see *AICPA Professional Standards* vol. 1 (New York: AICPA, 2002), sec. 319.

2. Petty cash vouchers are printed, prenumbered, and given to the custodian of the fund. The vouchers are used as evidence of expenditures. Therefore at all times the total of the cash in the fund plus the amounts of expenditure vouchers should be equal to the original amount of the fund, in this case $500. The custodian completes a petty cash voucher each time a payment from the fund is made, but journal entries are *not* recorded at this time.

3. When the amount of cash in the petty cash fund becomes low and/or at the end of an accounting period, the vouchers are sorted into expense categories and the remaining cash is counted. The expenses are then recorded and the fund is replenished. At this time, a Cash Short and Over account is used to record any "shortage" or "overage" between the original petty cash fund balance and the remaining cash in the fund plus the amounts of the petty cash vouchers. It helps to highlight errors and improve internal control. To illustrate, assume that a count at the end of the month shows $67.54 remaining in the petty cash fund, and the sorting of vouchers indicates the following costs were incurred during the month:

Office supplies	$ 34.16
Postage	178.00
Transportation	132.14
Miscellaneous	83.76
Total expenses	$428.06

Since these expenses total $428.06 and the amount needed to replenish the fund is $432.46 ($500 − $67.54), the fund is "short" by $4.40. The company records (debits) the actual expenses (along with Cash Short and Over), rather than petty cash, as follows when it replenishes the fund:

Office Supplies Expense	34.16	
Postage Expense	178.00	
Transportation Expense	132.14	
Miscellaneous Expense	83.76	
Cash Short and Over	4.40	
Cash		432.46

The $432.46 is given to the fund custodian, and the actual amount of cash in the petty cash fund is now equal to the original fund balance of $500. The company reports the expenses on its income statement. It reports a debit balance in the Cash Short and Over account at the end of the accounting period as a miscellaneous expense; it reports a credit balance as a miscellaneous revenue. The company includes the balance of the petty cash fund as part of the Cash amount reported on its balance sheet when it issues financial statements.

BANK RECONCILIATION

The Cash account is a company's only account that also is kept by an external independent party, the company's bank. Therefore it is possible, and desirable, to use one as a verification of the other. **A bank reconciliation is a schedule prepared by a company to analyze the difference between the ending cash balance in the company's accounting records and the ending cash balance reported by its bank in a bank statement in order to determine the correct ending cash balance.**

Banks send a monthly statement to each depositor summarizing the activities that have taken place in the depositor's account. These activities include deposits, checks cleared, miscellaneous items, and the ending balance in the checking account. Also included with the bank statement may be photos of the depositor's canceled checks. Every company has a checking account and maintains its own accounting records for its deposits and checks. The bank statement and the company's accounting records usually will not be in complete agreement. When the company receives the bank statement each month, it prepares a bank reconciliation to compare the bank statement balance and its cash balance to reconcile these records.

Causes of the Difference

The causes of the difference between the cash balance listed on a company's bank statement and the balance shown in the company's cash account include the following items:

1. *Outstanding Checks.* **An outstanding check is a check written by the company and deducted from its cash balance that the bank has not yet deducted from the balance reported on the bank statement.** On the date a company issues a check, it reduces its Cash account. A period of time is necessary for the check to be received by the payee (the recipient of the check), deposited in the payee's bank, and forwarded to the company's bank to be subtracted from the company's bank balance. Therefore a company has a certain number of outstanding checks at the end of each month that causes its Cash account balance to be less than the balance on the bank statement.

2. *Deposits in Transit.* **A deposit in transit is a cash receipt added to the company's cash balance but not yet added to the balance reported on the bank statement.** When a company receives a check, it increases its Cash account. A period of time may pass before the check is deposited by the company and recorded by the bank. At the end of each month the company may have deposits in transit (either cash or checks) that cause its Cash account balance to be greater than the balance on the bank statement.

3. *Charges Made Directly by the Bank.* A bank frequently imposes a service charge for a depositor's checking account and deducts this charge directly from the account. Banks also charge for the cost of printing checks and for stopping payment on checks. The bank reports these charges on the bank statement.

   When the company receives a customer's check, it deposits the check in its bank as a cash receipt even though the customer's bank has not yet transferred the cash from the customer's bank account to the company's bank account. Occasionally, the company's bank is unable to collect the amount of the customer's check. That is, the customer's check has "bounced." **NSF (not sufficient funds) is the term used for a customer's check that a company has deposited in its bank account but has not been paid by the customer's bank because there are insufficient funds in the customer's account.** Because the bank has not received payment from the customer, it deducts this amount from the company's bank account. Consequently, there may be some NSF checks included in the bank statement that the company has not recorded.

   At the end of the month the bank lists all of the previously mentioned charges as deductions from the company's cash balance on the bank statement even though the company may not have deducted them from its cash balance in its accounting records. Therefore the bank statement balance is less than the balance in the company's Cash account.

4. *Deposits Made Directly by the Bank.* A bank often acts as a collection agency for its customers on items such as notes receivable. In addition, most checking accounts earn interest. When the bank collects a note, it records the principal and interest as an increase in the company's bank account. Consequently, the bank statement may include notes received by the bank that the company has not yet recorded in its accounting records. The company may not know the amount of interest it has earned on its checking account until it receives the bank statement. In both these situations the bank statement balance is greater than the balance in the company's Cash account.

5. *Errors.* Despite the internal control procedures established by the bank and the company, the company may discover errors in either the bank's records or its records when it prepares the bank reconciliation. For example, a bank may include a deposit or a check from another customer's account or make an error in recording an amount. A company may similarly make an error in recording an amount. For example, a common error is to transpose two numbers, so that the correct amount of $426 is recorded as $462.

Procedures for Preparing a Bank Reconciliation

Given the items that might cause a difference between the ending balance in a company's Cash account and the ending cash balance from the bank statement, the company should follow a list of procedures in preparing its bank reconciliation:

2 Prepare a bank reconciliation.

1. **Compare the deposits listed on the company's records with the deposits shown on the bank statement.** Determine that the deposits in transit included in the *last* month's bank reconciliation are listed in this month's bank statement. These deposits do not need any adjustment in the bank reconciliation. If they are *not* shown on the bank statement, conduct an immediate investigation to determine if an error or theft has occurred. Identify any deposits for the current month that are not listed on the bank statement. Add the amounts of all the deposits in transit to the ending cash balance of the bank statement in the reconciliation.
2. **Compare the checks listed on the company's records with the checks shown on the bank statement.** Determine that the outstanding checks included in last month's bank reconciliation are listed in this month's bank statement. These checks do not need any adjustment in the bank reconciliation. If they are *not* shown on the bank statement, conduct an investigation to determine if the checks were received by the creditors so that the company's "credit rating" is not affected. Identify any checks for the current month not deducted in the bank statement. Subtract the amounts of all the outstanding checks from the ending cash balance of the bank statement in the reconciliation.
3. **Identify any deposits or charges made directly by the bank that are not included on the company's records.** These items include collections of notes receivable, interest earned on the checking account, service charges, NSF checks, and so on, which are listed on the bank statement. Add the collections to or subtract the charges from the company's ending cash balance in the bank reconciliation.
4. **Determine the effect of any errors.** If an error is found, the nature of the error determines whether to add the error to or subtract the error from the company's ending cash balance or from the ending cash balance of the bank statement.
5. **Complete the bank reconciliation.** Use the format we discuss below.

Generally accepted accounting principles require a company to report on its balance sheet the amount of cash over which it has control at the end of an accounting period. Our discussion focuses upon the form of reconciliation that arrives at an *adjusted*, or *corrected*, cash balance, indicating the amount of cash that a company reports on its balance sheet. We illustrate this form of bank reconciliation as follows (using assumed amounts):

Cash balance from bank statement		$7,218
Add:	Receipts recorded on the company's records but not reported on the bank statement. *Examples*: deposits in transit and cash received and recorded but not yet deposited	629
		$7,847
Deduct:	Payments recorded on the company's records but not reported on the bank statement. *Example*: outstanding checks	(516)
Adjusted Cash Balance		$7,331
Cash balance from company records		$6,925
Add:	Receipts reported on the bank statement but not recorded on the company's records. *Examples*: notes receivable and interest collected by the bank or interest earned on the funds on deposit	715
		$7,640
Deduct:	Payments reported on the bank statement but not recorded on the company's records. *Examples*: bank service charge and customers' checks returned for lack of funds (NSF checks)	(309)
Adjusted Cash Balance		$7,331

After the company completes the bank reconciliation, it makes journal entries to bring its accounts up to date. The company only makes journal entries for the adjustments it made to *its* records on the bank reconciliation. It does *not* make journal entries for the adjustments it made to the bank statement balance on the reconciliation; the bank will record these adjustments in its accounts at the appropriate time.

Illustration

The following example illustrates the preparation of a bank reconciliation and the required adjusting entries for the Craig Corporation for the month ended June 30, 2004. The unadjusted cash balances are as follows:

Cash balance from bank statement, June 30	$12,461.15
Cash balance from company records, June 30	12,437.94

The bank statement disclosed the following information:

1. A customer note for $1,200 plus $12 interest was collected on June 29.
2. A customer check for $138.14 was returned because of insufficient funds (NSF check).
3. The monthly service charge was $15.

A review of the company records disclosed the following:

1. A deposit for $1,142.87 at the end of the day on June 30 did not appear on the bank statement.
2. Customer checks totaling $327.40 were on hand at the end of June awaiting deposit.
3. The following company checks were outstanding at the end of June:
#862	$ 96.19
#864	147.18
#865	263.25
4. Check #843, written for $91.20 in payment of an account payable and included with the canceled checks in the bank statement, was erroneously recorded as $19.20 in the company's records.

Sometimes a "proof of cash" (four-column bank reconciliation) is prepared. This more comprehensive reconciliation is discussed in the Appendix at the end of the chapter.

The upper part of Exhibit 6-1 illustrates the preparation of a bank reconciliation based on this information. After completion of the reconciliation, the Craig Corporation prepares adjusting entries to record those items not previously included in its accounts, as we show in the bottom part of Exhibit 6-1 (with arrows to indicate which items are adjusted). These adjusting entries adjust the Cash account to $13,424.80, the amount that Craig Corporation reports as its cash balance (along with any petty cash) on its June 30, 2004 balance sheet.

SPECIAL TOPICS INVOLVING CASH

Two additional topics relate to the recording and reporting of cash. These items are electronic funds transfers and compensating balances.

Electronic Funds Transfer Systems

In the previous example of a bank reconciliation, for simplicity we dealt with only a few outstanding checks. In reality, a large company prepares and processes hundreds or even thousands of checks each month to pay its suppliers and employees. Furthermore, it receives and processes an equally large number of checks from its customers. Whether for payments or receipts, processing the paperwork for checks is expensive. In conjunction with the increased use of computer networks, banks offer **electronic funds transfers (EFT)** to their customers. Under EFT, funds are transferred between parties electronically without the need of a check. EFT systems are becoming more compatible, and their "networking" capabilities are increasing. As more and more parties are

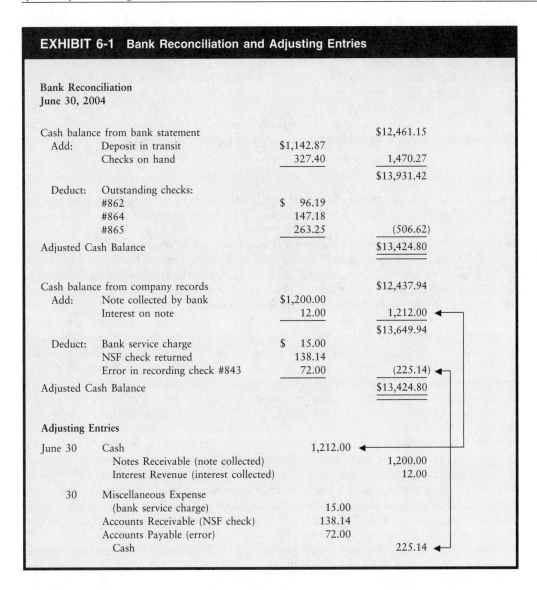

EXHIBIT 6-1 Bank Reconciliation and Adjusting Entries

Bank Reconciliation
June 30, 2004

Cash balance from bank statement			$12,461.15
Add:	Deposit in transit	$1,142.87	
	Checks on hand	327.40	1,470.27
			$13,931.42
Deduct:	Outstanding checks:		
	#862	$ 96.19	
	#864	147.18	
	#865	263.25	(506.62)
Adjusted Cash Balance			$13,424.80
Cash balance from company records			$12,437.94
Add:	Note collected by bank	$1,200.00	
	Interest on note	12.00	1,212.00
			$13,649.94
Deduct:	Bank service charge	$ 15.00	
	NSF check returned	138.14	
	Error in recording check #843	72.00	(225.14)
Adjusted Cash Balance			$13,424.80

Adjusting Entries

June 30	Cash	1,212.00	
	Notes Receivable (note collected)		1,200.00
	Interest Revenue (interest collected)		12.00
30	Miscellaneous Expense		
	(bank service charge)	15.00	
	Accounts Receivable (NSF check)	138.14	
	Accounts Payable (error)	72.00	
	Cash		225.14

using EFT systems, fewer physical documents (e.g., checks) are being processed. The need for a bank reconciliation is not reduced, however. In fact, even greater emphasis is being placed on internal control systems as they apply to computer technology because fewer physical source documents are available to substantiate cash inflows and outflows.

Compensating Balances

It is common for banks to require a portion of any amount loaned to a company to remain on deposit in the bank for the loan period. These required deposits are called **compensating balances.** For example, a bank loaning a company $100,000 may require that the company maintain a $10,000 deposit with the bank until the company repays the loan. Such arrangements have two main effects. First, they reduce the amount of cash available to the borrower, and second, they increase the effective interest rate the borrower pays for the use of the funds. For example, if the stated interest rate for the $100,000 loan is 12%, the effective rate for the actual funds used for a year is 13.33% ($12,000 ÷ $90,000), assuming the $10,000 compensating balance does not earn any interest.

The SEC studied funds subject to these withdrawal or usage restrictions. This study was partially in response to *liquidity* problems that were reported by companies with apparently adequate cash balances. The SEC found many cases in which a portion of the reported cash balance was legally restricted, and consequently required that compensating balances against short-term borrowings be separately reported in the current assets section of the balance sheet. Compensating balances for long-term borrowings are separately reported as noncurrent assets (as either investments or other assets). Compensating balance agreements that do not legally restrict the amount of funds shown on the balance sheet are disclosed in the notes to the financial statements. Since the SEC has the ultimate authority to issue accounting pronouncements, these procedures are generally accepted accounting principles for public companies.

RECEIVABLES

Receivables consist of various claims against customers and other parties arising from the operations of a company. Most receivables are canceled through the receipt of cash, although others may be canceled through the receipt of other assets or services. A company reports receivables on its balance sheet as either **current** or **noncurrent** items. **Those receivables expected to be collected or satisfied within one year or the current operating cycle, whichever is longer, are classified as current assets; the remainder are classified as noncurrent.** Furthermore, a company often groups receivables within its classified balance sheet as trade receivables and nontrade receivables.

Trade receivables arise from the sale of the company's products or services to customers. For instance, manufacturers may sell on credit to retailers (or other manufacturers), and retailers may sell on credit to consumers. Trade receivables generally comprise the majority of a company's total receivables balance. Trade receivables may be subclassified into **accounts receivable** (nonwritten promises by customers to pay for goods or services) and **notes receivable** (unconditional written agreements to receive a certain sum of money on a specific date). We discuss these subclassifications later in the chapter.

Nontrade receivables arise from transactions that are not directly related to the sale of the company's goods and services. Nontrade receivables are recorded in separate accounts and reported on the balance sheet in individual groups as current or noncurrent assets, depending upon the length of their collection period. Examples of nontrade receivables include deposits with utilities, advances to subsidiary companies, loans made by nonfinancial companies, deposits made to guarantee performance, and declared dividends and accrued interest on investments.

Utility companies often require a company to make a deposit to guarantee utility expense payments. This deposit normally is classified by the depositor as a noncurrent receivable because the timing of repayment by the utility company is indeterminate. An advance to a subsidiary typically is classified as long-term because repayment may be postponed indefinitely. A deposit made to guarantee contract performance is classified as either current or noncurrent, depending upon the expected completion date of the project guaranteed. Declared dividends to be received and accrued interest on investments are disclosed as current assets. In this chapter we focus upon the valuation issues associated with current trade receivables. We discuss nontrade receivables and noncurrent receivables in other chapters in this book.

Because accounting for trade receivables involves a number of issues, we include the following diagram to provide you with an overview.

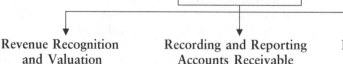

Trade Receivables		
Revenue Recognition and Valuation	**Recording and Reporting Accounts Receivable**	**Recording and Reporting Notes Receivable**
• Normal circumstances	• Cash discounts	• Interest-bearing
• Right of return	• Sales returns and allowances	• Non-interest-bearing
• Valuation	• Uncollectable accounts	• Discounted
	• Financing arrangements	

REVENUE RECOGNITION AND VALUATION OF TRADE RECEIVABLES

First, we look at several issues related to revenue recognition and receivables valuation.

Normal Revenue Recognition

A company usually makes sales of goods and services on "open accounts" that result in short-term extensions of credit by the seller. **A company records revenue from credit sales based on the revenue recognition criteria.** Revenue is recognized when **realization has occurred** (i.e., a noncash resource is exchanged for cash or a near cash resource) and the **revenue is earned** (i.e., the earning process is complete or virtually complete). Typically, the sale of goods and services on credit results in the creation of an asset called a trade receivable (account receivable or note receivable) and the recognition of revenue at the time of sale. This approach is used because the company expects to collect the asset (receivable), and very few activities remain in the earning process. However, in some cases a company may defer revenue recognition because the collectibility of the receivable is *not* reasonably assured (which we will discuss in Chapter 17). In other cases, a company may defer revenue because a right of return exists.

Revenue recognition criteria are discussed in Chapter 4 and Chapter 17.

Two methods of recognizing revenue on a deferred basis, the installment method and the cost recovery method, are discussed in Chapter 17.

Right of Return

In most industries sales returns and allowances are not material, so that companies typically record them at the time of the return or allowance even if they occur in a period later than the period of sale (as we discuss later in the chapter). In some industries, such as book publishing, the right of return is common and the amounts may be material. In these cases, credit "sales" in one period may be followed by substantial returns in another. These factors create a revenue recognition issue because sometimes (1) reliable estimates cannot be made of the collectibility of the receivable and (2) the risks and benefits of ownership are not transferred (the earning process is not complete). As a result, **FASB Statement No. 48** identifies criteria for recording sales revenue when the right of return exists. **Each of the following criteria must be satisfied when the right of return exists in order to recognize revenue at the time of sale**; if they are not, then revenue recognition must be deferred:

3 Discuss revenue recognition when the right of return exists.

1. The sales price is fixed or determinable at the date of sale.
2. The buyer has paid or will pay the seller, and the obligation is not contingent upon resale of the product.
3. The buyer's obligation to the seller would not be changed by theft or damage to the product.
4. The buyer has an economic substance apart from the seller.
5. The seller does not have significant obligations for future performance to directly bring about resale of the product by the buyer.
6. The seller can reasonably estimate the amount of future returns.[5]

In the event that a company defers the recognition of sales revenue and cost of goods sold because one or more of the preceding conditions are not met, it records the sales revenue and cost of goods sold either when the return privilege expires or when the conditions are met, whichever occurs first.

Valuation Issues

When the conditions in the previous section are met so that the company records a receivable and revenue at the time of sale, there still is an issue of valuing the trade receivable. As we discussed in Chapter 3, one purpose of reporting current assets is to

---

5. "Revenue Recognition When Right of Return Exists," *FASB Statement of Financial Accounting Standards No. 48* (Stamford, Conn.: FASB, 1981), par. 6.

disclose the **liquidity** of a company; that is, the "nearness to cash" of its economic resources. In this regard, the accounting issues associated with the valuation of current trade receivables are (1) the initial recording of the receivables based on the total future cash flows, and (2) the estimation of the probability of collection. Since there is a time value of money, there is a difference between the maturity value of a receivable and its present value. The longer the time period until maturity, the greater the difference. **APB Opinion No. 21** (discussed in Chapter 14) provides specific guidelines for recording and reporting receivables at their present values. However, the provisions do not apply to "receivables . . . arising from transactions with customers . . . in the normal course of business which are due in customary trade terms not exceeding approximately one year."[6] Consequently **most trade receivables are recorded initially at their maturity values** and not at their present values. Furthermore, since the collection period for most trade receivables is 60 days or less, the difference between their present value and maturity value is not material under normal circumstances.

The uncertainty of collection also affects the value of trade receivables. Whenever a company extends credit, the likelihood exists that it will not collect a few receivables. The company should consider this issue in the valuation of receivables on its balance sheet so as to report on their liquidity. We discuss the accounting procedures used to deal with the uncertainty of collecting receivables later in this chapter.

ACCOUNTS RECEIVABLE

As we discussed earlier, trade accounts receivable result from credit sales. A company sells on credit in order to increase sales, but credit sales create the need for a credit department to investigate credit ratings, approve the extension of credit, and attempt to collect delinquent accounts. Credit sales result in a certain amount of bad debts due to nonpayment by customers. When a company considers whether or not to sell on credit, it must evaluate the trade-off between the additional gross profit received from the expected credit sales and the additional expenses incurred due to these credit sales. In this regard, most companies establish a credit policy.

4 Understand the credit policies related to accounts receivable.

A credit policy reflects the degree of risk a company is willing to accept in order to increase sales. Credit policies are closely associated with customers' credit ratings. High credit ratings indicate low risk, whereas low credit ratings indicate high risk. A company should adopt a credit policy that results in the maximum increased profit consistent with maintaining customer satisfaction—that is, the combination of increased sales revenue and bad debt losses which results in the highest incremental profit and cash inflows. However, it should also consider other factors, such as the cost of additional sales and credit personnel necessary to handle these increased sales. A few companies have decided that this trade-off is negative. These companies believe that they can lower costs and increase profits by selling exclusively for cash. Note that retail "credit card" sales involving bank credit cards are treated as cash sales, as we discuss later in the chapter.

If a company decides to sell on credit and establishes a credit department, it must install an effective internal control system for processing sales on account and cash collections. We discussed the internal control procedures used for cash collections earlier in the chapter, but a company must also establish internal control procedures for the processing of accounts receivable. These control features include (1) prenumbered sales invoices so that all invoices are accounted for, and (2) the separation of the sales function from the cash collection responsibilities so that collusion is required for theft to take place.

Once management is satisfied that a reasonable trade-off exists between the incremental revenues and expenses of credit sales, and an adequate system of internal control for credit sales is established, other issues may arise in recording accounts receivable. These issues include cash discounts and sales returns and allowances. We discuss uncollectible accounts (bad debts) in a later section.

---

6.   "Interest on Receivables and Payables," *APB Opinion No. 21* (New York: AICPA, 1971), par. 3.

Cash (Sales) Discounts

Companies may offer a discount to induce prompt payment. This discount is called a **cash discount** (or **sales discount**) and frequently is expressed as 2/10, n/30 or perhaps 2/10, n/EOM (end of month). In both cases **the first component refers to the discount rate and period and the second to the invoice due date.** These terms are read in the first case as: A 2% discount may be subtracted from the invoice price[7] if payment is made by the purchaser within 10 days, and the total invoice price is due within 30 days. In the second example full payment is due by the end of the month. To illustrate, assume that Company S sells $5,000 of merchandise to Company B with terms of 2/10, n/30. If Company B pays for the merchandise within 10 days, it only has to pay $4,900. This $100 cash discount is a strong inducement to pay within the discount period because it represents a relatively high effective annual interest rate to Company B. By paying within the discount period, Company B is giving up the use of funds for 20 days (that is, the invoice is due 20 days after the discount period expires) to earn a discount of 2%. This is approximately equal to an annual effective interest rate of 36% ($0.02 \times 360/20$).

Cash discounts are an important consideration in the financial management of companies. Both sellers and purchasers should carefully analyze the potential effects of cash discounts. As we noted, the theory behind cash discounts is that they will induce prompt payment. A purchasing company should take advantage of any cash discounts that have a higher effective annual interest rate than the rate it must pay to borrow money. For a selling company, a cash discount has two main positive effects: (1) it stimulates a more rapid collection of cash for use in current operations, and (2) it tends to reduce the likelihood of losses resulting from uncollectible accounts. However, the seller should not overlook the negative effect of its reduced total cash inflow because of the discount. Sellers should attempt to set the cash discount rate at a level so that its positive effects exceed any negative effects.

Ⓐ

If a selling company extends cash discounts to its customers, it may use one of two methods (a "gross" method or a "net" method) to account for the discounts:[8]

5 Explain the gross and net methods to account for cash discounts.

1. *Accounts Receivable and Sales Recorded at Gross Price.* In using the gross price method, the selling company records the total invoice price in both the Accounts Receivable and Sales accounts at the time of sale as if no cash discount were involved. When the customer pays, if the allowable cash discount is taken, the company records the difference between the cash received and the original amount of Accounts Receivable as a debit to Sales Discounts Taken. If the cash discount is not taken, the amount of cash paid by the customer is equal to the original balance in the Accounts Receivable account, and no further adjustment is necessary. Sales discounts taken are deducted from sales on the income statement to determine net sales.

2. *Accounts Receivable and Sales Recorded at Net Price.* Under the net price method, the selling company records the net invoice price (after deducting the allowable cash discount) in both the Accounts Receivable and Sales accounts at the time of sale. When the customer pays, if the allowable cash discount is taken by the customer, no adjustment is necessary because the amount of cash received is equal to the recorded amount of the receivable. However, if the customer does *not* take advantage of the cash discount, the amount of cash received is greater than the recorded Accounts Receivable balance. The company credits this excess to an

---

7. Another type of discount is the **trade** (or *quantity*) discount, which is offered for purchases in excess of a certain quantity. For example, if a company offers a 10% trade discount and a customer purchases 100 units of an item with a list price of $80 per unit subject to the trade discount, the customer is billed $7,200 [$8,000 − (0.10 × $8,000)] as the invoice price. This $7,200 invoice price then is subject to the cash discount.

8. In a third method, accounts receivable are recorded at the gross price, sales are recorded at the net price, and the difference is recorded in an allowance account (a contra account to accounts receivable). The allowance account then is reduced by the difference between the cash collected from the customer and the accounts receivable balance. It also is adjusted for sales discounts not taken.

EXHIBIT 6-2   Alternative Methods of Accounting for Sales Discounts

	Gross Price Method			Net Price Method		
To record sale on December 4, 2004	Accounts Receivable Sales	8,000	8,000	Accounts Receivable [$8,000 − (0.02 × $8,000)] Sales	7,840	7,840
To record payment received on December 13, 2004	Cash [$5,500 − ($5,500 × 0.02)] Sales Discounts Taken Accounts Receivable	5,390 110	5,500	Cash Accounts Receivable	5,390	5,390
To record payment received on December 30, 2004	Cash Accounts Receivable	1,500	1,500	Cash Accounts Receivable [$1,500 − ($1,500 × 0.02)] Sales Discounts Not Taken	1,500	1,470 30
To adjust the accounts at the end of the period	No entry required			Accounts Receivable Sales Discounts Not Taken	20	20

account entitled Sales Discounts Not Taken, which is viewed as interest revenue and reported in the Other Items section of the income statement.[9]

To illustrate the application of these methods, assume that the Howe Corporation sold $8,000 of merchandise to various customers on December 4, 2004 with terms of 2/10, n/EOM. On December 13 Howe received payment on goods originally billed at $5,500. Howe received payment on goods billed at $1,500 on December 30. The remaining $1,000 was not collected by the end of the year. Exhibit 6-2 illustrates the journal entries to record these transactions and the year-end adjustments.

CONCEPTUAL EVALUATION   Theoretically the use of the net price method is sound because it values the accounts receivable at the net realizable value and also correctly reports the amount of sales revenue and financial revenue. The gross price method has the advantage over the net price method of reporting receivable accounts at gross amounts, which simplifies communications with customers (because discussions are based on the gross amount). The gross price method also has the advantage of enabling sales returns and allowances (discussed later) to be recorded at gross instead of net amounts. But since a company expects most customers to take advantage of the cash discount, the gross price method overstates its current sales and accounts receivable at the end of the period. However, because the gross price method requires less record keeping, most companies use this method. Furthermore, when the timing of collections does not vary significantly from period to period, no material difference is likely to result from using either method.

Sales Returns and Allowances

When a company sells merchandise, a few defective items may be returned by customers. In other cases existing practice or contractual agreements also may allow products that are not defective to be returned. **When goods are sold that are found to be defective, the customer may retain the goods and be allowed a reduction in the purchase price. This reduction is called a** *sales allowance*. **When goods are returned to the seller, the exchange is called a** *sales return*. Often a sales return or allowance occurs in an accounting period

---

9. At the end of the accounting period, an adjusting entry may be made for any cash discounts no longer available on the outstanding accounts receivable. This entry involves a debit to Accounts Receivable and a credit to Sales Discounts Not Taken. A reversing entry is usually made so that when these sales are ultimately collected, the collections may be recorded in the usual manner for when no discount is taken.

after the sale. From a theoretical standpoint, if a company can make reliable estimates, it should **record the estimated amount of future returns and allowances in the period of sale so as to correctly report net sales revenue and value ending accounts receivable.**

To illustrate the accounting for sales returns and allowances, assume that the Barclay Corporation sells $500,000 of goods during 2004 and the company estimates that returns and allowances will be 5% of sales. To anticipate the returns and allowances, the company records the following adjusting entry at the end of the period of sale (assuming it uses the gross price method of recording sales):

Sales Returns and Allowances ($500,000 × 0.05)	25,000	
Allowance for Sales Returns and Allowances		25,000

Consequently, when sales returns and allowances of $6,000 actually occur for goods sold on account, the company records this transaction as follows:

Allowance for Sales Returns and Allowances	6,000	
Accounts Receivable		6,000

If the company used the net price method to record sales, it would base the preceding entries on the net price after deducting the cash discounts.

When a company estimates its sales returns and allowances in the period of sale, it includes any balance in the Allowance for Sales Returns and Allowances account on the balance sheet as a valuation account offset against Accounts Receivable. In cases where returns and allowances are not material, most companies do not estimate these items. Instead they record the returns and allowances on account when they actually occur by debiting Sales Returns and Allowances and crediting Accounts Receivable (at the gross price or net price depending on which method they are using). Whether estimated or actual, a company reports sales returns and allowances on its income statement as a deduction from sales revenue.

VALUATION OF ACCOUNTS RECEIVABLE FOR UNCOLLECTIBLE ACCOUNTS

The preceding discussion focused on the issues involved in the initial recording of trade accounts receivable. Not all accounts receivable will be collected, however. Some will become bad debts. A company might record uncollectible accounts (bad debts) by either of two procedures:

1. In the year of sale, based upon an estimate of the amount of uncollectible accounts, or
2. When it determines that a specific customer account is uncollectible.

FASB Statement No. 5 requires that estimated losses from loss contingencies be accrued against income and recorded as reductions in assets (or as liabilities) when both of the following conditions are met:

1. Information available prior to the issuance of the financial statements indicates that it is probable that an asset has been impaired or a liability has been incurred at the date of the financial statements.
2. The amount of the loss can be reasonably estimated.[10]

Since both conditions normally are met in regard to uncollectible accounts, most companies estimate bad debts. For instance, over 90% of surveyed companies reported estimates of bad debts on their financial statements.[11] This approach enables these companies to **properly value their receivables and match expenses against revenues in the current period.**

---

10. "Accounting for Contingencies," *FASB Statement of Financial Accounting Standards No. 5* (Stamford, Conn.: FASB, 1975), par. 8.
11. *Accounting Trends and Techniques* (New York: AICPA, 2001), p. 152.

Estimated Bad Debts Method

Under the **estimated bad debts method** a company studies the historical data about the actual bad debts it has incurred as a result of a particular credit policy. It compares this information to its current sales or accounts receivable to determine relationships upon which to base estimates of current uncollectible accounts. **These relationships provide the information the company needs to prepare the adjusting entry to record the estimated bad debt expense for the period.**

When the company records the estimate of bad debts, the journal entry involves a debit to Bad Debt Expense and a credit to Allowance for Doubtful Accounts (or, alternatively, Allowance for Bad Debts or Allowance for Uncollectible Accounts). A company normally reports bad debt expense on its income statement as an operating expense. However, some companies offset the account against gross sales, or report it as a financial expense in the Other Items section. The authors advocate reporting bad debt expense as an operating expense because it is similar to other operating expenses. This disclosure has gained the most acceptance among accountants, and financial statement users normally expect companies to report bad debt expense in this manner.

The account Allowance for Doubtful Accounts is a valuation (contra) account that is offset against Accounts Receivable in the current assets section of the company's balance sheet. Although current credit sales create a likelihood of losses from bad debts, the company does not know at the time of sale which actual customer accounts that ultimately will not be collected (if they were known, the company would not have extended credit to these customers). **Offsetting Allowance for Doubtful Accounts against Accounts Receivable informs financial statement users of the net realizable value (the amount of cash expected to be collected) of the company's receivables.**[12]

It is possible to base the estimate of bad debt expense on historical relationships between the actual bad debts incurred and (1) sales or (2) accounts receivable. These relationships may be classified as follows:

1. Relationship to sales (income statement approach):
    a. Percentage of sales
    b. Percentage of net credit sales
2. Relationship to accounts receivable (balance sheet approach):
    a. Percentage of outstanding accounts receivable
    b. Aging of accounts receivable

Percentage of Sales (or Net Credit Sales)

6 Estimate and record bad debts using a percentage of sales.

Estimating bad debts based on the historical relationship to sales matches current expenses against current revenues. This method is income statement oriented because it is based on the matching principle and results in recording bad debt expense in the period during which credit sales occur. A percentage of total sales may be used for the estimate when there is a stable relationship between cash and credit sales. However, if the proportion of credit to total sales varies from period to period, it is not appropriate to use a percentage of total sales in any one period. For this reason most accountants favor the estimation of bad debts based on the historical relationship between bad debts and net *credit* sales. For example, if a company's net credit sales during the year were $525,000 and bad debts have historically amounted to 2% of net credit sales, the company makes the following year-end adjusting entry:

Bad Debt Expense ($525,000 × 0.02)	10,500	
Allowance for Doubtful Accounts		10,500

Since this method focuses on an expense account, any existing balance in the allowance account is ignored when determining the amount of the adjusting entry. Also, if a

---

12. If a company has other accounts, such as Allowance for Sales Returns and Allowances, Allowance for Sales Discounts, and Deferred Gross Profit, it also deducts these accounts from Accounts Receivable to determine the net realizable value.

company sells many products in different locations, it may choose to extend this analysis and estimate bad debts on the basis of historical credit sales of particular products or in specific locations. Although basing bad debt expense upon sales is a relatively straightforward income statement approach and adheres to the matching concept, it may not provide the best estimate of the net realizable value of accounts receivable because the balance in the allowance account is ignored when making the adjusting entry. Also, if deviations from the expected net realizable value of the accounts receivable balance are material, a change in the accounting estimate may be necessary. Furthermore it provides only limited information for the credit department to use in its collection activities. These disadvantages may be offset by the use of a balance sheet approach.

Percentage of Outstanding Accounts Receivable

Bad debts may be estimated based on the historical relationship between actual amounts not collected and accounts receivable. This approach is balance sheet oriented because the resulting accounts receivable is reported on the balance sheet at its estimated net realizable value. A relatively simple balance sheet approach is to base the estimated expense on the historical relationship between the actual bad debts and the outstanding accounts receivable balance at the end of the year.

In using this method, the goal is to determine the ending balance in Allowance for Doubtful Accounts. To determine the amount of its adjusting entry, a company must consider the existing balance (prior to adjustment) in the allowance account. The company records Bad Debt Expense at the amount necessary to adjust the existing allowance account balance to the required ending balance. For example, assume that a company has determined that historically there has been a 4% relationship between actual bad debts and the year-end accounts receivable balance. The company's accounts at the end of the year (prior to adjustment) are as follows:

Accounts Receivable	475,000
Allowance for Doubtful Accounts	4,500 (credit balance)

The expected net realizable value of Accounts Receivable is $456,000 [$475,000 − ($475,000 × 0.04)], and the required balance in Allowance for Doubtful Accounts is therefore $19,000 ($475,000 − $456,000, or simply $475,000 × 0.04). However, since the current credit balance in the allowance account is $4,500, only the amount necessary to increase the allowance account to its required ending balance is recorded as Bad Debt Expense. In this example the amount is $14,500 ($19,000 − $4,500), as we show in the following T-account:

Allowance for Doubtful Accounts

	4,500 (current balance)
	14,500 (required adjustment)
	19,000 (required ending balance)

Based on the preceding information, the company records the following year-end adjusting entry:

Bad Debt Expense	14,500	
Allowance for Doubtful Accounts		14,500

A potential weakness of basing bad debts on a percentage of total outstanding accounts receivable is its failure to consider the due date of the many individual accounts comprising the total balance. This deficiency is resolved by the aging of accounts receivable.

Aging of Accounts Receivable

The length of time an account is outstanding is an important factor in estimating the probability of its future collection. A company is much more likely to collect an account that is 20 days old than one that is 360 days old. For this reason a more sophisticated

7 Estimate and record bad debts using an aging analysis.

EXHIBIT 6-3 Aging Analysis

December 31, 2004

(a) Aging Schedule of Accounts Receivable

| | | Length of Time Outstanding | | | | |
Customer	Balance 12/31/04	Under 60 Days	60–120 Days	121–240 Days	241–360 Days	Over 1 Year
Goodwin Co.	$ 33,100	$21,000	$12,100			
Hobson Inc.	14,500					$14,500
Lomas Manufacturing	20,600	15,000	5,600			
McClendon Co.	15,700				$15,700	
Schauer Corporation	37,900	17,500	16,800	$3,600		
	$121,800	$53,500	$34,500	$3,600	$15,700	$14,500

(b) Estimated Uncollectibles

Age	Amount	Estimated Percentage Uncollectible	Estimated Amounts Uncollectible
Under 60 days	$ 53,500	2%	$ 1,070
60–120 days	34,500	8	2,760
121–240 days	3,600	15	540
241–360 days	15,700	30	4,710
Over 1 year	14,500	50	7,250
	$121,800		$16,330

method of estimating bad debts as a percentage of accounts receivable is used. **A company that "ages" its accounts receivable first classifies the individual accounts based upon the length of time they have been outstanding, and then applies an historically developed bad debts percentage to each age category.** The information in Exhibit 6-3 is taken from the records of the Rhorke Corporation and illustrates how bad debts are estimated with the use of an *aging schedule* (or aging analysis).[13]

In developing the aging schedule, the company reviewed the unpaid invoices in each customer's account, classified the invoice amounts according to the length of time the invoice has been outstanding, and totaled the amounts in each group. It then multiplied the total amount in each age group by the applicable estimated uncollectible percentage to determine the estimated amount uncollectible for that age group. It derived the total estimated uncollectible amount by summing the estimated uncollectible amounts related to each age group.

This analysis indicates that the ending balance of Allowance for Doubtful Accounts should be $16,330 on December 31, 2004. **Since the objective in an aging analysis is to determine the ending allowance account balance, a company also considers the previous balance of the allowance account in recording the amount of bad debt expense at the end of the period.** If Rhorke has a current $1,350 *debit* balance in its allowance account, the amount of recorded expense necessary to bring the allowance account up to its required balance is $17,680 ($16,330 + $1,350). Note that in this case the current *debit* balance in its allowance account is added. (We discuss the events that might cause the allowance account to have a debit balance in the next section.) A credit balance would be *subtracted* to determine the necessary adjustment amount. Based upon the preceding calculations, Rhorke makes the following year-end adjusting entry:

---

13. A company with few accounts receivable would probably not find an aging analysis to be a useful procedure, because each customer could be evaluated individually. Aging is appropriate when there are large numbers of customers who cannot reasonably be evaluated individually at the end of the period. In this example, for simplicity, only a few customers are used.

Bad Debt Expense	17,680	
Allowance for Doubtful Accounts		17,680

Use of the aging method, particularly when prepared in conjunction with interim financial reports, is very helpful to a company's credit department. As it prepares each new aging schedule, this method focuses attention on any accounts that have not been collected and that have shifted to an older age category. Frequently, a company will compute its "receivables turnover" (net credit sales ÷ average net accounts receivable) along with its aging schedule, to determine how efficient it is in collecting its accounts receivable. While the aging method has the advantage of properly reporting the net realizable value of accounts receivable on the balance sheet and of providing useful information to the credit department, it may not precisely match bad debt expense against revenue in the year of sale.

The receivables turnover is discussed in the Appendix to Chapter 5.

CONCEPTUAL EVALUATION In summary, a company should estimate and record bad debt expense in the period of sale rather than record bad debts as accounts are written off. There are two main approaches to estimating of bad debts. **The income statement approach, in which a percentage of sales (or net credit sales) is used, results in a matching of expenses with sales in the current period.** However, this approach does not necessarily result in reporting accounts receivable at their net realizable value, since it does not consider the characteristics of the individual accounts that comprise the total receivables balance. **The balance sheet approach, which uses a percentage of outstanding accounts receivable or an aging analysis as the basis for estimating bad debts, results in reporting accounts receivable at their expected net realizable value on the balance sheet.** Furthermore, the aging analysis provides useful credit information. With the FASB's concern for reporting on a company's *liquidity* and *future expected cash flows*, the balance sheet method may be more appropriate. Currently, both methods are used in practice, and both are allowed under generally accepted accounting principles.

Writing Off Uncollectible Accounts

If a company records bad debt expense based on an estimate, it writes off an individual account when it determines that the account is uncollectible. The journal entry is a debit to Allowance for Doubtful Accounts and a credit to Accounts Receivable. This write-off is simply an adjustment required because the company has confirmed a previously estimated expense. The write off does not affect the carrying value of the accounts receivable on the balance sheet. Consider the following information for a company:

Accounts Receivable	$175,000	
Allowance for Doubtful Accounts	8,750	(credit balance)
Customer account determined to be uncollectible	850	

At the time of the write-off, the company makes the following journal entry:

Allowance for Doubtful Accounts	850	
Accounts Receivable		850

This write-off has *no effect* on the net realizable value of the accounts receivable because the allowance account and the accounts receivable balance are reduced by the same amount. As shown in the following schedule, before the write-off the net realizable accounts receivable was $166,250 ($175,000 − $8,750). After the write-off the net carrying value of the accounts receivable is still $166,250, but it now consists of a $174,150 accounts receivable balance and a $7,900 allowance account balance. Similarly, there is no impact on the income statement as a result of this write-off because it did not involve a revenue or expense account.

	Before Write-off	Write-off	After Write-off
Accounts receivable	$175,000	$(850)	$174,150
Less: Allowance for doubtful accounts	(8,750)	850	(7,900)
Net realizable value	$166,250		$166,250

A company records its write-offs of accounts receivable as it determines the individual accounts that are uncollectible. Occasionally write-offs occur during the period of sale *prior to* recording the estimated bad debts at the end of the period. In these cases the journal entry for the write-off is the same as shown previously: a debit to Allowance for Doubtful Accounts and a credit to Accounts Receivable. The result may be a *debit* balance in Allowance for Doubtful Accounts prior to the year-end adjustment. When the company is using a balance sheet approach, the debit balance is considered in determining the amount of the adjusting entry. When the income statement approach is used, a debit (or credit) balance is ignored (unless it becomes significant). Additionally, estimates always involve future uncertainties, and the actual losses incurred from bad debts will not be the same as the amount of estimated expense. As new information becomes available, a company may need to change its estimated percentage of bad debts. If the company uses the balance sheet approach, it modifies the balance of the allowance account each year to reflect the most current information. When a company changes the estimated percentage of bad debts, it treats this change as an adjustment of bad debt expense in current and future periods. This change is considered to be a change in estimate as defined by *APB Opinion No. 20*.

Changes in estimates are discussed in Chapter 22.

Collection of an Account Previously Written Off

Occasionally a company will receive payment from a customer whose account it has already written off. Most accountants favor reestablishing the customer's account receivable on the books and then recording the payment. This procedure has the advantage of providing a complete credit history for each customer account and also eliminates the previous write-off entry. For example, if a company receives a $300 payment from a customer whose account it had previously written off, the company makes the following journal entries:

Accounts Receivable	300	
Allowance for Doubtful Accounts		300
Cash	300	
Accounts Receivable		300

Note that the first entry "reverses" the initial write-off and the second entry records the cash collection in the usual manner.

Direct Write-Off Method

The second method of recording uncollectible accounts is called the direct write-off method. This method has the advantages of simplicity and of reporting actual losses rather than estimates. **When a company uses the direct write-off method, it records bad debt expense when it determines that a specific customer account is uncollectible.** At that time it writes off the account by debiting Bad Debt Expense and crediting Accounts Receivable. However, this determination and write-off may not occur until a later period than the period of sale. The use of the direct write-off method has the disadvantage of matching the bad debt expenses associated with previous sales against revenues of the current period and of overstating accounts receivable associated with previous sales. Furthermore, it allows the manipulation of income because management selects the period of write-off (and expense). For these reasons the direct write-off method is not allowed under generally accepted accounting principles. However, some companies use it for financial reporting because they are required to use it for income tax purposes and the results do not differ materially from those obtained under the estimated methods we discussed earlier.

GENERATING IMMEDIATE CASH FROM ACCOUNTS RECEIVABLE

The net realizable value of the accounts receivable reported on a company's balance sheet is usually indicative of the amount of cash the company expects to collect in its normal operating cycle. However, in certain circumstances a company may find it necessary or desirable to accelerate the cash inflows from its accounts receivable.

In today's business environment there are many companies that specialize in "financing" other companies' accounts receivable. These finance companies include General Motors Acceptance Corporation (GMAC), General Electric Capital Services (GECS), and Sears Roebuck Acceptance Corporation (SRAC), as well as credit card companies such as VISA, MasterCard, American Express, and Diner's Club. There are many variations in financing arrangements, including which receivables are involved, which company collects the receivables, who has title, and who incurs bad debts.

In this section we discuss the accounting issues faced by a company that "transfers" its accounts receivable to a financing company in exchange for cash. For financial reporting, these issues involve revenue recognition and asset valuation. For **revenue recognition,** consideration is given to whether the risks of ownership of the receivables have been transferred (so revenue should be recognized). For **asset valuation,** consideration is given to who has control over the future benefits from the receivables (to determine who "owns" the asset). In addition, reporting on these types of arrangements is important in providing information about a company's **liquidity,** the nearness to cash of its receivables; and **financial flexibility,** its ability to use its receivables to adapt to changing financial conditions.

There are three basic forms of financing agreements to obtain cash from accounts receivable: (1) **pledging,** (2) **assigning,** and (3) **factoring (sale).** There may be variations in the conditions of each agreement so that the distinctions are not always clear-cut.[14] These agreements are evaluated on a "continuum," based on the transfer of risks of ownership and control over the benefits of the receivables, as shown in Exhibit 6-4.

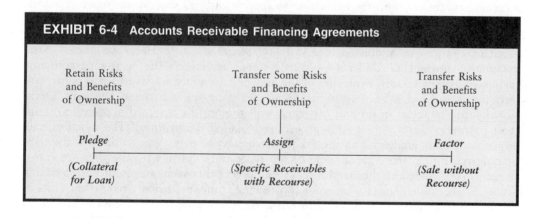

EXHIBIT 6-4 Accounts Receivable Financing Agreements

The FASB addressed these issues when it concluded in **FASB Statement No. 140** that a company (transferor) records the transfer of financial assets (e.g., accounts receivable) in which it surrenders control over the financial assets to another company (the transferee) as a sale when *all* the following conditions are met:

1. The transferred assets have been isolated from the transferor (i.e., put beyond the reach of the transferor).
2. The transferee obtains the right to exchange (e.g., sell) the transferred assets.
3. The transferor does not maintain effective control over the transferred assets through an agreement that entitles and obligates the transferor to repurchase the transferred assets before their maturity.

Upon completion of any transfer of financial assets, the transferor continues to report on its balance sheet any retained interest in the transferred assets. If the transfer meets the conditions for a sale, the transferor records the proceeds, eliminates the financial assets, and records a gain or loss. If the conditions for a sale are *not* met, the transferor

---

14. For a broad discussion, see "Asset Securitization: Economic Effects and Accounting Issues," *Accounting Horizons* (March 1992), pp. 5–16.

records the proceeds from the transfer of financial assets as a secured borrowing with a pledge of collateral.[15]

Of 600 surveyed companies nearly 25% reported pledging, assigning, or factoring their accounts receivable.[16] We discuss these three arrangements in the following sections.

Pledging of Accounts Receivable

When a company *pledges* **its accounts receivable, it is using these accounts only as collateral for a loan,** and the servicing activities remain its responsibility. (*Servicing activities* are the routine collection and administration functions.) The company records the loan as a liability in the usual manner and then when it collects the receivable, it uses the cash to repay the loan plus any interest charges. Upon full payment of the loan the pledge is canceled. In the event that the company defaults, the lender has the legal right to take title to the pledged receivables and sell them to recover the amount of the loan. Pledge agreements usually are not formally entered in a company's accounting records because there is no transfer of risk, and the company retains control over the receivables. A company generally discloses these agreements parenthetically or in the notes to its financial statements to indicate that a portion of the accounts receivable balance may not be available to general creditors.

8 Explain pledging, assignment, and factoring of accounts receivable.

Assignment of Accounts Receivable

When a company *assigns* **its accounts receivable to a financial institution, it enters into a lending agreement with the institution to receive cash on specific customer accounts.** Frequently, these agreements are long-term in nature. Assignment agreements can be very complex and involve issues such as interest rate swaps, call options, and unique servicing charges, as addressed in *FASB Statement No. 140*. Here, we discuss basic assignment agreements. Under a basic assignment agreement, the borrowing company (assignor) usually retains ownership of the assigned accounts, incurs any bad debts, collects the amounts due from customers, and uses these funds to repay the loan. Occasionally, the financial institution (assignee) will require the assigned accounts to remit their payments directly to it (this procedure is called *notification*). The assignee may impose collection guidelines on the assigned accounts or may agree to share in the risks of nonpayment. In these cases some of the risks and control of ownership are transferred to the assignee; this is the major difference between assigning and pledging accounts receivable. Since the assignor (borrowing company) usually retains the risks of ownership, accounts are assigned *with recourse*, which means that if the cash collected from the accounts is insufficient to repay the amount owed by the assignor, the assignee still can demand payment from (has recourse against) the assignor. This is the major difference between assignment agreements and factoring agreements, where the receivables are sold without recourse and the buyer assumes all the risks of ownership.

In assignment agreements the assignor company's relationship with the purchasers of its goods and services is not disrupted because the purchaser usually makes remittances directly to the company (*non-notification*) and is unaware of the financing arrangement. Usually, the amount of receivables assigned is somewhat greater than the amount of the advance; the excess amount serves to protect the assignee from sales returns and allowances. Under assignment arrangements the assignor pays a service charge and interest on the loan, makes periodic payments (including interest) to the assignee based on collections of assigned accounts receivable, and is required to absorb any reductions due to sales returns and allowances or losses from uncollectible accounts. On the assignor company's balance sheet, it reports assigned accounts receivable separately from unassigned accounts receivable because it must use cash receipts from these assigned receivables for a specific purpose. That is, some of the benefits of ownership of the asset are transferred

---

15. "Accounting for Transfers and Servicing of Financial Assets and Extinguishment of Liabilities," *FASB Statement of Financial Accounting Standards No. 140* (Norwalk, Conn.: FASB, 2000), par. 9–12.

16. *Accounting Trends and Techniques* (New York: AICPA, 2001), p. 147.

to the assignee. The assignor company reports the note payable as a current or noncurrent liability, depending on the due date.[17]

To illustrate, assume that on December 1, 2004 the Trussel Company assigns $60,000 of its accounts to a finance company. The finance company advances 80% of the accounts receivable assigned less a service charge of $500. It also charges an annual interest rate of 12% on any outstanding loan balance. The journal entries that Trussel makes to record this assignment are:

Cash [($60,000 × 0.80) − $500]	47,500	
Assignment Service Charge Expense	500	
Note Payable ($60,000 × 0.80)		48,000
Accounts Receivable Assigned	60,000	
Accounts Receivable		60,000

The first journal entry records the receipt of cash. The Assignment Service Charge Expense account is a cost of borrowed funds and most companies usually record it as an expense at the time of the advance due to the lack of materiality. The second journal entry reclassifies the receivables as assigned accounts receivable.

On December 31, 2004 Trussel collects $10,000 on assigned accounts. This amount along with the 12% interest for 1 month is paid to the finance company. Trussel records these transactions as follows:

Cash	10,000	
Accounts Receivable Assigned		10,000
Note Payable	10,000	
Interest Expense ($48,000 × 0.12 × 1/12)	480	
Cash		10,480

The interest expense on any future remittances is based upon the balance *remaining* in the Note Payable account (for example, the interest expense for the next payment in our example is based on the $38,000 note payable balance). During the period the note is outstanding, Trussel credits any bad debt losses and sales returns and allowances related to the assigned accounts receivable against the Accounts Receivable Assigned account. Upon full payment of the note, Trussel reclassifies any remaining balance in Accounts Receivable Assigned as Accounts Receivable.

On the December 31, 2004 balance sheet of the Trussel Company, it reports the assigned accounts and the remaining liability (assuming it is short-term) as follows:

Current Assets		*Current Liabilities*	
Accounts receivable assigned	$50,000	Note payable	$38,000

Trussel includes a description of the financing agreement in the notes to its financial statements.

Factoring (Sale) of Accounts Receivable

When a company factors its accounts receivable, it sells individual accounts to a financial institution (called a factor). Since the company *sells* the receivables, it transfers title to the factor who assumes all the risks of ownership. That is, the company sells the accounts receivable *without recourse*, which means that if the receivables are not collected, the factor cannot demand payment from it. Consequently, factoring agreements focus on control of the receivables and usually require (1) notification of the credit customers to remit the amounts owed directly to the factor, and (2) assumption by the factor of all collection activities, setting of credit policies, and losses from uncollectible accounts.

---

17. Prior to *FASB Statement No. 140*, some companies deducted the note payable from the assigned accounts receivable and reported the balance as an asset, equity in assigned accounts receivable. This "offsetting" is no longer allowed.

At the time of sale the factor (finance company) charges the selling company a commission. The commission usually is based on the amount of receivables transferred and is relatively high, although it varies depending on the perceived risk of noncollection. The way in which the selling company records the commission depends on its normal operating activities. A selling company records the commission as an *expense* if it normally factors its accounts receivable, or as a *loss* if it usually does not sell its accounts receivable. In addition to charging a commission, the factor usually will pay only 80% to 90% of the value of the accounts receivable transferred, as a protection against sales returns and allowances. The selling company records the amount withheld (i.e., the 20% to 10%) in a separate Receivable from Factor account to indicate the amount that may be returned by the factor. Since title is transferred, the selling company reduces (credits) Accounts Receivable for the amount of the receivables sold.

To illustrate, assume that the Farber Corporation sells $80,000 of accounts receivable to a factor, receives 90% of the value of the factored accounts, and is charged a 15% commission based on the gross amount of factored accounts receivable. Farber records the following journal entry (assuming that it normally factors its accounts receivable):

Cash [($80,000 × 0.90) − $12,000]	60,000	
Receivable from Factor ($80,000 × 0.10)	8,000	
Factoring Expense ($80,000 × 0.15)	12,000	
Accounts Receivable		80,000

If sales returns or allowances occur on factored accounts, the selling company debits Sales Returns and Allowances and credits Receivable from Factor. At the conclusion of the factoring agreement for a particular group of receivables, the selling company collects any balance remaining in the Receivable from Factor account from the factor and debits its Cash and credits Receivable from Factor. When a factoring agreement exists, the selling company discloses the agreement in a note to its financial statements. Factoring agreements are common in the furniture and textile industries; another common example is the sale of home mortgages from one financial institution to another. However, many companies are reluctant to use factoring agreements because of the cost of notifying their customers, and because their customers may dislike being required to make payments to a bank or finance company rather than to the seller.

CREDIT CARD SALES   Many retail companies make agreements with national credit card companies, which operate either independently or in affiliation with banks. Among the most popular are VISA, MasterCard, American Express, and Diner's Club. Under these arrangements, card holders establish a **line of credit** which may be used for retail purchases of goods and services. After a customer makes purchases, the bank or credit card company pays the retailer and the customer repays the bank or credit card company. These types of agreements are in essence factoring agreements.

The retailer accepting these credit cards charges its customers the selling price for goods and services, but is assessed a service charge on credit card sales by the bank or credit card company. This charge is usually a percentage of each sale, and the fee is for the use of a credit and collection department. Thus, the retailer usually records the fee as an operating expense. The individual retailer assumes little or no risk in accepting national credit cards, because most risk is borne by the bank or credit card company (except where there is fraud or negligence by the retailer) since the bank or credit card company originally granted the line of credit. The service charge assessed on credit card sales usually varies between 1 and 5% and is partially determined by the annual amount of sales or by exclusive arrangements. In an **exclusive arrangement** a retailer will accept only one national credit card, and in return the credit card company charges the retailer a lower service charge. For example, Sam's Club accepts only Discover cards in its stores.

To illustrate, assume that Kerns Shoes sold $1,500 of merchandise which was billed to an independent national credit card company. If the collection fee charged by the credit card company is 5%, Kerns makes the following journal entry when it forwards the credit card sales receipts for collection (assuming it is using the gross price method of recording sales):

Accounts Receivable	1,425	
Credit Card Expense ($1,500 × 0.05)	75	
Sales		1,500

Kerns records any sales returns or allowances in a similar manner. When Kerns receives cash from the credit card company, it eliminates the receivable. For credit cards affiliated with banks, any credit card sales receipts of a retailer may be deposited directly in its checking account. In this case the retailer treats the credit card sales as cash sales, and records the sales as a debit to Cash (instead of Accounts Receivable).

Disclosure of Financing Agreements of Accounts Receivable

As we noted in the previous discussion, the existence of pledge, assignment, or factor (sale) agreements should be disclosed parenthetically or in the notes to the financial statements. An example of this type of disclosure for a factoring agreement is shown in the first note of the UNIFI, Inc., 2001 financial statements shown in Exhibit 6-5.

EXHIBIT 6-5   **Disclosure of Factoring Agreement**

UNIFI, INC.

Notes to Consolidated Financial Statements (in part)

Accounting Policies and Financial Statement Information (in part)
    Receivables. Certain customer accounts receivable are factored without recourse with respect to credit risk. Factored accounts receivable at June 24, 2001, and June 25, 2000 were $34.7 million and $42.9 million, respectively. An allowance for losses is provided for known and potential losses rising from yarn quality claims and receivables from customers not factored based on a periodic review of these accounts. Reserves for such losses were $9.9 million at June 24, 2001, and $17.2 million at June 25, 2000.

Q U E S T I O N

Ⓠ Why didn't UNIFI provide an allowance for losses on the accounts receivable that it factored?

NOTES RECEIVABLE

A note receivable is an unconditional written agreement to collect a certain sum of money on a specific date. Notes receivable generally have two attributes that are not found in accounts receivable:

1. They are negotiable instruments, which means that they are legally and readily transferable among parties and may be used to satisfy debts by the holders of these instruments.
2. They usually involve interest, requiring the separation of the receivable into its principal and interest components.

Companies frequently require their customers to issue notes receivable when the customers wish to extend the repayment period on an account receivable. Sometimes notes receivable are required in the normal course of extending credit to new customers, and in some cases they may be required for all credit sales. Notes receivable also may result from long-term contracts.

A company may receive two types of short-term notes: (1) those bearing interest on the face amount of the note and (2) non-interest-bearing notes. We discuss these notes in the following sections.

Recording long-term notes at their fair (present) value is discussed in Chapter 13.

Short-Term Interest-Bearing Notes Receivable

9 Account for short-term notes receivable.

When an interest-bearing note is issued, the amount borrowed (the principal) is listed as the face value, and the interest charged is expressed as a specific rate applied to this face value. When a company receives a note, it debits the Note Receivable account for the face value. After issuance, it records interest revenue on the note in the usual fashion, including any necessary year-end adjustments for interest receivable. To illustrate, assume that on October 1, 2004 Trent Company made a $5,000 credit sale to Jaynik Company and required the company to sign a $5,000, 60-day, 12% note. The middle column of Exhibit 6-6 shows the journal entries on October 1, 2004 for the Trent Company to record the receipt of the interest-bearing note, and on December 1, 2004 to record the receipt of the principal and interest (assuming, for simplicity, a 360-day business year). If the note had extended past the end of the year, Trent Company would have made a year-end adjusting entry to record the interest receivable and recognize the interest revenue.

Bad debt losses may occur on transactions involving short-term notes receivable, particularly when it is common practice to require customers to sign notes for all credit sales. In these cases the company should assess the likelihood of these losses and establish an Allowance for Doubtful Notes. This procedure is the same as we discussed earlier for accounts receivable and results in an increase in expenses and a decrease in the net realizable value of notes receivable.

Short-Term Non-Interest-Bearing Notes Receivable

In the case of a non-interest-bearing note, the maturity value (the amount to be collected, which includes both principal and implicit interest) is listed as the face value. Actually the term non-interest-bearing is a misnomer because all notes implicitly contain interest. It is simply a case of the interest being included in the face value rather than being stated as a separate rate. A better term would be a note with no *stated interest rate*. *APB Opinion No. 21* does not *require* current trade receivables to be recorded at their present values because the difference between the present value and the maturity value is not likely to be significant. Consequently, many companies record short-term non-interest-bearing trade notes receivable at their maturity values. This approach, however, overstates sales revenue and understates interest revenue.

A conceptually better approach is to record the note receivable at its present value and to recognize interest revenue as it is earned. To illustrate, assume the same facts as in the earlier example except that Jaynik Company signs a $5,100 non-interest-bearing note, due on December 1, 2004. The top of the right column of Exhibit 6-6 shows the journal entry on October 1, 2004 for the Trent Company to record the receipt of the non-interest-bearing note. Observe in this entry that interest revenue is credited[18] for

---

EXHIBIT 6-6	**Accounting for Short-Term Notes Receivable**					
		Interest-Bearing			Non-interest-Bearing	
To record receipt of note on October 1, 2004	Notes Receivable Sales	5,000	5,000	Notes Receivable Interest Revenue Sales	5,100	100 5,000
To record receipt of maturity value on December 1, 2004	Cash Notes Receivable Interest Revenue*	5,100	5,000 100	Cash Notes Receivable	5,100	5,100

*$5,000 × 0.12 × 60/360

---

18. Alternatively, Discount on Notes Receivable could be credited (instead of Interest Revenue) at the time of issuance. Then, when the face value is collected (or at year-end if an adjustment is required), a journal entry must be made to reduce the discount account and increase interest revenue for the amount of interest earned.

$100. Although technically the company has not yet earned the interest, it will do so before the end of the accounting period. This procedure simplifies the accounting process. The journal entry on December 1, 2004 to record the receipt of the face value is shown at the bottom of the right column of Exhibit 6-6. If the note had extended past the end of the year, Trent Company would have made a year-end adjusting entry to *reduce* (debit) the interest revenue for the interest not yet earned and to adjust (credit) an account entitled Discount on Notes Receivable. This Discount account is a contra account and is deducted from the Notes Receivable account to report the net realizable value on the balance sheet.

Notes Receivable Discounted

Occasionally a company may find that it needs additional cash on a short-term basis, but the company does not wish to incur additional debt or sell or assign its accounts receivable. In these cases the company may discount a customer's note receivable at a bank in return for cash. **When a company discounts a customer's note receivable at the bank, it is transferring the note to the bank with recourse.** That is, the customer is notified to pay the bank directly at the maturity date, and the company guarantees payment of the note if the customer defaults. During the interim period between the discount date and the maturity date, the note is a contingent liability to the company. Under the provisions of **FASB Statement No. 5**, this type of *contingent liability* must be disclosed in the financial statements, even if the possibility of default by the customer is remote.[19] To make this disclosure, when a company transfers the note to the bank, it typically records the discounted note in a contra account entitled Notes Receivable Discounted. This account is offset against Notes Receivable on any balance sheet prepared prior to the note's maturity date. If the customer pays the note at maturity, the company removes the Notes Receivable and Notes Receivable Discounted accounts from its accounting records, and cancels the contingent liability.

When a customer's note receivable is discounted, the proceeds (cash received) are determined by multiplying the discount rate times the maturity value of the note (face value of the note plus total interest) for the discount period, and deducting the resulting discount from the maturity value. The *discount rate* is the interest rate charged by the bank. It has no relationship to the interest rate charged the customer on the note receivable. The *discount period* is the length of time from the date of discount to the maturity date. Any gain or loss from the discounting is computed by comparing the current book value of the note receivable (including accrued interest) to the proceeds. The company discounting the note makes journal entries on the date of the discount to accrue any interest revenue and to record the proceeds received, any gain or loss on the discounting of the note, and the contingent liability. It eliminates the discounted note on the maturity date.

To illustrate, assume that on August 31, 2004, the Kasper Corporation discounts a customer's note at its bank at a 14% discount rate. The note was received from the customer on August 1, is for 90 days, has a face value of $5,000, and carries an interest rate of 12%. The customer pays the note on the October 30, 2004 maturity date. The calculations on August 31 for the discounted note are as follows (assuming a 360-day business year for simplicity):

1. Face value of note	$5,000.00
2. Interest to maturity ($5,000 × 0.12 × 90/360)	150.00
3. Maturity value of note	$5,150.00
4. Discount ($5,150 × 0.14 × 60/360)	(120.17)
5. Proceeds	$5,029.83
6. Accrued interest revenue: $50 ($5,000 × 0.12 × 30/360)	
7. Book value of note ($5,000 + $50)	(5,050.00)
8. Loss from discounting of note	$ (20.17)

---

19. *FASB Statement No. 5, op. cit.,* par. 12.

Kasper Corporation makes the following journal entries to record the discounted note on August 31 and the payment by the customer on October 30:

August 31, 2004

Interest Receivable	50.00	
Interest Revenue		50.00
Cash	5,029.83	
Loss from Discounting of Note	20.17	
Notes Receivable Discounted		5,000.00
Interest Receivable		50.00

October 30, 2004

Notes Receivable Discounted	5,000.00	
Notes Receivable		5,000.00

When a note is discounted, the difference between the book value of the note and its proceeds is recorded as a gain or loss (as we did in this example) if a company usually does not discount its notes. Alternatively, if a company normally discounts its notes, the difference is reported as interest revenue or interest expense.

If the Kasper Corporation prepares an interim balance sheet on September 30, 2004 and has a $43,000 balance in notes receivable on that date, it reports the discounted note as follows:

Current Assets

Notes receivable	$43,000	
Less: Notes receivable discounted	(5,000)	$38,000

An alternative way of reporting the discounted note is to list the notes receivable at the net $38,000 on the interim balance sheet and to disclose the contingent liability in the notes to the financial statements. This note might read as follows: "The company is contingently liable for a discounted note receivable of $5,000. The company does not anticipate that this note will be defaulted on its maturity date."

In this illustration the contingent liability was eliminated on the maturity date when the customer paid the note. In the event that the customer does not pay this note at maturity, the bank would require Kasper to pay the maturity value of the note plus a service charge on the dishonored note. Kasper's only recourse is to attempt to collect these amounts from the customer. Consequently, upon default Kasper cancels the Notes Receivable and Notes Receivable Discounted accounts and establishes a Notes Receivable Dishonored account. For example, assume instead that on November 2, 2004 the bank notified Kasper that the note had not been paid and also charged Kasper a $10 fee. At that time Kasper would record the following journal entry:

Notes Receivable Dishonored	5,160	
Notes Receivable Discounted	5,000	
Notes Receivable		5,000
Cash [$5,000 + ($5,000 × 0.12 × 90/360) + $10]		5,160

If Kasper does not collect the dishonored note in the future, it recognizes a loss on the default.

FINANCIAL STATEMENT DISCLOSURES OF RECEIVABLES

Companies are required to disclose any accounting policies related to their receivables that might be helpful to external users. Furthermore, **FASB Statement No. 133** requires a company to *recognize* as assets any derivative financial instruments that involve rights of the company (e.g., a "hedge" of the exposure to changes in the fair value of receivables), based on their fair value. A company reports these items as current assets on its balance sheet if they meet the definition of a current asset. The *Statement* also requires a company to disclose information such as the types of derivative instruments it holds, its objectives in holding the instruments, and its strategies for achieving these objectives. The description must indicate the company's risk management policy in regard to each type of instrument. **FASB Statement No. 107** requires a company to *disclose* the fair value of all its financial instruments, whether recognized or not on the balance sheet. The *Statement* also requires a company to disclose all significant concentrations of credit risk due to its financial instruments. A company typically makes these disclosures in the notes to its financial statements. The intent of these disclosures is to improve the reporting of a company's *risk, liquidity, and financial flexibility.*[20] Exhibit 6-7 shows an excerpt from PepsiCo's 2001 year-end balance sheet and related Note 6 illustrating the presentation of receivables on corporate financial statements.

EXHIBIT 6-7 Disclosure of Accounts Receivable

PEPSICO, INC. AND SUBSIDIARIES

CONSOLIDATED BALANCE SHEET
December 29, 2001 and December 30, 2000

	2001	2000
(in millions)		
Current Assets: (in part)		
Accounts and notes receivable, net	$2,142	$2,129

Notes to Consolidated Financial Statements (in part)
Note 6   Accounts and Notes Receivable, net

	2001	2000
Trade receivables	$ 1,663	$ 1,613
Receivables from affiliates	171	190
Other receivables	429	452
	2,263	2,255
Allowance, beginning of year	126	109
Charged to expense	41	42
Other additions	2	8
Deductions	(48)	(33)
Allowance, end of year	121	126
Net receivables	$ 2,142	$ 2,129

Q U E S T I O N

Q For 2001 recreate the summary journal entries that PepsiCo must have made for its Allowance account (ignore the effects of the other additions).

---

20. "Accounting for Derivative Instruments and Hedging Activities," *FASB Statement of Financial Accounting Standards No. 133* (Norwalk, Conn.: FASB, 1998), par. 17 and 44; and "Disclosures about Fair Value of Financial Instruments," *FASB Statement of Financial Accounting Standards No. 107* (Norwalk, Conn.: FASB, 1991), par. 7 and 15A.

APPENDIX: PROOF OF CASH (FOUR-COLUMN RECONCILIATION)

10 Prepare a proof of cash.

The independent CPA (or internal auditor) responsible for auditing the company's records normally will prepare a more comprehensive bank reconciliation than the one we discussed in the chapter. This type of reconciliation, termed a *proof of cash*, incorporates **the monthly cash receipts and payments to test the internal control over cash and provides additional evidence of the accuracy of the cash balance.** Therefore the proof of cash identifies the sources of differences between the company records and the bank statement (such as receipts and payments). There are several forms of a proof of cash (sometimes called a **four-column reconciliation**); again, our discussion focuses on the form that arrives at adjusted balances. This form of the proof of cash begins with the reconciliation of the cash balance from the bank statement (bank balance) with the cash balance from the company's records (book balance) made the previous month. It then accounts, in summary form, for all of the receipts and payments that have occurred during the current month. In essence, the proof of cash provides four separate reconciliations:

1. The reconciliation of the bank balance and book balance for the previous month.
2. The reconciliation of the receipts recorded by the bank for the current month with the receipts recorded on the books.
3. The reconciliation of the payments recorded by the bank for the current month with the payments recorded on the books.
4. The reconciliation of the bank balance and book balance for the current month.

Exhibit 6-8 shows the proof of cash for the Craig Corporation. Note that the far right column contains the June 30, 2004 bank reconciliation that we presented in

EXHIBIT 6-8 Proof of Cash

Proof of Cash
June 30, 2004

	Reconciliation May 31, 2004	June Receipts	June Payments	Reconciliation June 30, 2004
Cash balance from bank	$13,617.42	$26,421.17	$27,577.44	$12,461.15
Deposit in transit:				
May 31	1,240.15 (1a)	(1,240.15) (1a)		
June 30		1,142.87 (1b)		1,142.87 (1b)
Undeposited cash		327.40 (1c)		327.40 (1c)
Outstanding checks:				
May 31				
#781	(163.15) (2a)		(163.15) (2a)	
#782	(212.90) (2a)		(212.90) (2a)	
June 30				
#862			96.19 (2b)	(96.19) (2b)
#864			147.18 (2b)	(147.18) (2b)
#865			263.25 (2b)	(263.25) (2b)
Adjusted Cash Balance	$14,481.52	$26,651.29	$27,708.01	$13,424.80
Cash balance from books	$14,481.52	$25,439.29	$27,482.87	$12,437.94
Note and interest collected		1,212.00 (1d)		1,212.00 (1d)
June service charge			15.00 (2c)	(15.00) (2c)
NSF check			138.14 (2d)	(138.14) (2d)
Error in recording check #843			72.00 (2e)	(72.00) (2e)
Adjusted Cash Balance	$14,481.52	$26,651.29	$27,708.01	$13,424.80

Exhibit 6-1. The May 31, 2004 reconciliation, shown in the first numerical column, was prepared the previous month using the same procedures as those for Exhibit 6-1. The June receipts and payments for the bank and company are obtained from the June 30, 2004 bank statement and company records, respectively.

We explain the reconciliation of the receipts and payments for the month of June below. The numbers and letters in parentheses after the amounts in Exhibit 6-8 reference the items in the following discussion.

1. *Reconciliation of June receipts*
    a. The May 31 deposit in transit of $1,240.15 was received and recorded by the bank on June 1. This amount was recorded as a May receipt by the company and was added to the bank balance on the May 31 reconciliation. Since it is a May receipt, it is deducted from the June receipts listed by the bank.
    b. The June 30 deposit in transit of $1,142.87 was properly recorded by the company as a June receipt and is added to the June receipts listed by the bank.
    c. Checks on hand (undeposited cash) of $327.40 are June receipts of the company and were recorded by the company. They are added to the June receipts listed by the bank.
    d. The $1,212.00 note and interest collected by the bank was included in the June receipts listed by the bank and properly is a part of the month's receipts for the company. The amount is added to June receipts of the company.

2. *Reconciliation of June payments*
    a. The outstanding checks of $163.15 and $212.90 at the end of May were deducted from the bank balance to determine the adjusted cash balance on May 31. The actual payment of these checks by the bank was included in the bank's June payments, but they must be excluded because they were May payments by the company. Therefore they are deducted from the June payments listed by the bank.
    b. The June 30 outstanding checks of $96.19, $147.18, and $263.25 were deducted from the company's records and must be included in the bank's June payments. Therefore they are added to the June payments listed by the bank.
    c. The service charge ($15.00) was included in the June payments by the bank and is a proper charge. This amount is added to the June payments by the company.
    d. The NSF check of $138.14 returned by the bank originally was included in the June receipts by the bank and by the company. When payment was refused, the bank recorded the NSF check as a June payment from the company's account. Consequently, the NSF check is added to the June payments by the company.
    e. The June payments listed by the bank reflect the correct $91.20 amount of check #843, erroneously recorded by the company at $19.20. The $72.00 difference is added to the June payments by the company.

Note that adding the adjusted June receipts ($26,651.29) to and deducting the adjusted June payments ($27,708.01) from the ending adjusted cash balance for May ($14,481.52) results in the ending adjusted cash balance for June ($13,424.80).

SUMMARY

At the beginning of the chapter, we identified several objectives you would accomplish after reading the chapter. The objectives are listed below, each followed by a brief summary of the key points in the chapter discussion.
1. **Understand the importance of cash management.** Cash management is important so that a company has enough cash available to pay its current obligations, but does not have idle cash as a nonproductive resource. To do so, a company must have sound cash planning systems (cash budget) and sound cash control systems (internal control).
2. **Prepare a bank reconciliation.** To prepare a bank reconciliation, add the amounts of any deposits in transit to, and subtract the amounts of any outstanding checks from, the ending bank statement balance. Next, add any collections or subtract any charges made directly by the bank to or from the company's ending cash balance. Then

adjust the ending bank statement balance or company's ending cash balance for any errors, and complete the bank reconciliation.

3. **Discuss revenue recognition when the right of return exists.** When the right of return exists, a company recognizes revenue at the time of the sale only when six conditions are met. Briefly, these are: (1) the sales price is known, (2) the buyer has paid or will pay, (3) the buyer's obligation is not affected by theft or damage, (4) the buyer is a separate entity from the seller, (5) the seller does not have to help resell the product, and (6) the seller can estimate the future returns.

4. **Understand the credit policies related to accounts receivable.** A company sells on credit to increase sales. Credit policies should be closely associated with customers' credit ratings. A company should adopt a credit policy that combines increased customer satisfaction with increased sales revenue, credit department costs, and bad debt losses in a way that results in the highest incremental profit and cash flows.

5. **Explain the gross and net methods to account for cash discounts.** Under the gross method, a company records accounts receivable and sales at the gross price. If the customer takes the cash discount, the company debits Sales Discounts Taken for the amount of the discount. Under the net method, a company records accounts receivable and sales at the net price. If the customer does not take the cash discount, the company credits Sales Discount Not Taken for the amount of the lost discount.

6. **Estimate and record bad debts using a percentage of sales.** Under the percentage of sales method, a company debits the bad debts expense account and credits the allowance account for an amount based on an estimate of the percentage of the current sales that will not be collected.

7. **Estimate and record bad debts using an aging analysis.** Under the aging method, a company first classifies its accounts receivable into categories based on their age. Then it multiplies the amount in each category by the percentage estimated to be uncollectible, and sums the expected uncollectible amounts. Finally, it deducts this sum from the balance in the allowance account to determine the amount to record as a debit to bad debts expense and a credit to the allowance account.

8. **Explain pledging, assignment, and factoring of accounts receivable.** When a company *pledges* accounts receivable, it uses these accounts as collateral for a loan. When a company *assigns* accounts receivable, it enters into a lending agreement with a financial institution to receive cash on specific customer accounts. When a company *factors* accounts receivable, it sells individual accounts to a financial institution.

9. **Account for short-term notes receivable.** When a company receives an interest-bearing note receivable, it records the note at its face value. It then records interest revenue when it collects the note. When a company receives a non-interest-bearing note, it records the note at its maturity value and, for simplicity, also records interest revenue at this time.

10. **Prepare a proof of cash (Appendix).** A proof of cash includes four separate reconciliations: (1) a reconciliation of the bank balance and book balance for the previous month, (2) a reconciliation of the receipts recorded by the bank and on the books for the current month, (3) a reconciliation of the payments recorded by the bank and on the books for the current month, and (4) a reconciliation of the bank balance and book balance for the current month.

QUESTIONS

Q6-1 What are the components of cash? What items may be confused with cash, but normally are categorized under other balance sheet captions? What are "cash equivalents"?

Q6-2 What is internal control? What are two important elements of internal control over cash?

Q6-3 What is the purpose of a petty cash system?

Q6-4 Why are actual expenses, rather than the account Petty Cash, debited when the fund is replenished?

Q6-5 What is a bank reconciliation? List the causes of the difference between the cash balance listed on a company's bank statement and the balance shown in the company's cash account.

Q6-6 Why are adjusting entries made after the bank reconciliation is completed? Give an example of an item on a bank reconciliation which requires an adjusting entry.

Q6-7 What are the two revenue recognition criteria and how do they relate to receivables in some industries?

Q6-8 Briefly discuss the two methods of recording accounts receivable when cash discounts are involved.

Q6-9 What is a sales return? A sales allowance? Conceptually, when should sales returns and allowances be recorded?

Q6-10 Discuss the differences between the estimation methods of recording bad debts and the direct write-off method.

Q6-11 Explain how a company estimates bad debts using (a) the sales or income statement approach, and (b) the accounts receivable or balance sheet approach.

Q6-12 Define the *net realizable value* of a company's accounts receivable. How is the net realizable value of accounts receivable reported on the company's balance sheet?

Q6-13 What method of bad debt estimation categorizes individual accounts receivable based on the length of time outstanding? Why is this length of time an important factor?

Q6-14 Why does the write-off of uncollectible accounts have no effect on the net realizable accounts receivable on the balance sheet if bad debts are estimated? What is the effect of this write-off on the income statement?

Q6-15 Define pledging, assigning, and factoring of accounts receivable.

Q6-16 When does a company record the transfer of accounts receivable as a sale? As a liability?

Q6-17 What is a note receivable? How do notes receivable differ from accounts receivable?

Q6-18 What is a non-interest-bearing note? How does the accounting treatment for a short-term non-interest-bearing note differ from a short-term interest-bearing note?

Q6-19 What are notes receivable discounted? How are discounted notes disclosed on the financial statements during the period between the discount date and maturity date?

Q6-20 How are the cash proceeds determined when a note receivable is discounted?

Q6-21 (*Appendix*). What four separate reconciliations are provided by the proof of cash?

CASES

C O M M U N I C A T I O N

C6-1 Cash Management

The president of Poor Corporation, who likes to have large balances of cash on hand, has recently been reading articles in highly respected financial magazines about very successful businesses. The president noticed that each company stressed the importance of cash management and internal control in making it a success. The president of Poor Corporation comes to you, the accountant, and asks you to explain the concept of cash management.

Required Explain the concept of cash management, including the two major subdivisions and their components.

C6-2 Bank Reconciliations (Appendix)

A discrepancy usually will exist between a company's bank statement balance and its cash records due to the time lag associated with the use of a checking account. The time lag results in many transactions being recorded on the company's records prior to their appearance on the bank statement. The bank statement balance and the cash records must be brought into agreement to determine their accuracy. This result can be achieved by using a two-column or a four-column reconciliation.

Required Prepare a written report that compares and contrasts the two-column and four-column reconciliations.

C6-3 Bad Debt Expense

When a company has a policy of making sales for which credit is extended, it is reasonable to expect a portion of those sales to be uncollectible. As a result of this, a company must recognize bad debt expense. There are basically two methods of recognizing bad debt expense: (1) direct write-off method, and (2) allowance method.

Required

1. Describe fully both the direct write-off method and the allowance method of recognizing bad debt expense.

2. Explain the reasons why one of these methods is preferable to the other and the reasons why the other method is not usually in accordance with generally accepted accounting principles. (*AICPA adapted*)

C6-4 Accounts Receivable

The Moore Company is undergoing a period of financial stress due to the depressed economy. The company is in desperate need of cash. The only liquid asset that the company holds is $500,000 of accounts receivable.

Required

1. Explain the various types of arrangements that may be used to obtain cash from outstanding accounts receivable.

2. Indicate how each method should be disclosed in the financial statements.

3. If Moore Company decides to sell its accounts receivable, should it account for the transfer as a pledge or a factoring agreement? Why?

C6-5 Receivables Issues

Magrath Company has an operating cycle of less than one year and provides credit terms for all of its customers. On April 3, 2004, the company factored, without recourse, some of its accounts receivable.

On August 1, 2004, Magrath sold special order merchandise and received an interest-bearing note due April 30, 2005.

Magrath uses the allowance method to account for uncollectible accounts. During 2004, some accounts were written off as uncollectible, and other accounts previously written off as uncollectible were collected.

Required

1. Explain how Magrath should account for and report the accounts receivable factored on April 3, 2004. Why is this accounting treatment appropriate?

2. Explain how Magrath should report the effects of the interest-bearing note on its income statement for the year ended December 31, 2004, and its December 31, 2004 balance sheet.
3. Explain how Magrath should account for the collection of the accounts previously written off as uncollectible.
4. What are the two basic approaches to estimating uncollectible accounts under the allowance method? What is the rationale for each approach? (*AICPA adapted*)

C6-6   Lockbox Account Bank Reconciliation

DGK Company maintains a lockbox account to facilitate the collection of its accounts receivable. All of the company's cash receipts from credit sales are sent directly to a post office box held in the company's name, which is accessed directly by bank personnel. Each day the bank processes the receipts, credits DGK's account, and provides the company with a hard copy package, which includes a detail and summary listing of all checks deposited, copies of actual checks, invoices, enclosures, and envelopes. The company usually receives its hard copy packages a day after the bank has processed the receipts.

In addition, DGK Company has authorized the bank to apply "collected balances" (balances for which the holding period allowed for collection and return of deposited items has elapsed) directly against the company's outstanding line of credit with the bank, unless instructed otherwise by the company. The company receives hard copy notices of amounts applied, generally within two business days.

The accounting records for DGK Company contain the following details for December, 2004:

1. Balance per bank for the lockbox account, 12/31/04	$55,000
2. Balance per books, 12/31/04	50,050
3. Deposit in transit from cash sales	5,000
4. Lockbox receipts, 12/31/04	30,000
5. Collected balances applied to line of credit on 12/31/04	20,000
6. Bank service charge for December	50
7. No checks are drawn on the lockbox account	

Required

1. Explain how a lockbox account might benefit a company.
2. Prepare a December 31, 2004 bank reconciliation of DGK Company's lockbox bank account.
3. Prepare any journal entries necessary to adjust DGK Company's books to reflect the results of the reconciliation performed in Requirement 2. (*Contributed by Daryl G. Krause.*)

C R E A T I V E   A N D   C R I T I C A L   T H I N K I N G

C6-7   Components of Cash

Cash is an important asset of a company.

1. What are the normal components of cash?
2. Under what circumstances, if any, do valuation problems arise in connection with cash? (*AICPA adapted*)

C6-8   Estimated Bad Debts

On December 31, 2004 Carme Company had significant amounts of accounts receivable as a result of credit sales to its customers. Carme Company uses the allowance method based on credit sales to estimate bad debts. Based on past experience, 1% of credit sales normally will not be collected. This pattern is expected to continue.

Required

1. Explain the rationale of using the allowance method based on credit sales to estimate bad debts. Contrast this method with the allowance method based on the balance in the trade receivables accounts.
2. Explain how Carme Company should report the allowance for bad debts account on its balance sheet at December 31, 2004. Also, describe the alternatives, if any, for presentation of bad debt expense in Carme Company's 2004 income statement. (*AICPA adapted*)

C6-9   Cash Discounts

In order to induce prompt payment, the Swope Company offers a cash discount of 2% to customers who make payment on their account within 10 days of the invoice date. The company's bookkeeper is not sure how these discounts should be recorded.

Required

1. Explain the methods of recording accounts receivable with cash discounts.
2. Discuss the theoretical soundness of each method.

C6-10   Assignment and Factoring

Marie Company has significant amounts of trade accounts receivable as a result of credit sales to its customers. On October 2, 2004 some trade accounts receivable were assigned to Daniel Finance Company on a with-recourse, nonnotification basis for an advance of 75% of their amount at an interest charge of 20% on the balance outstanding.

On November 3, 2004 other trade accounts receivable were factored on a without-recourse basis. The factor withheld 5% of the trade accounts receivable factored as protection against sales returns and allowances and charged a finance charge of 3%.

Required

1. How should Marie account for subsequent collections on the trade accounts receivable assigned on October 2, 2004 and the payments to Daniel Finance? Why?

2. How should Marie account for the trade accounts receivable factored on November 3, 2004? Why? (*AICPA adapted*)

C6-11 Receivables Issues

Hogan Company uses the net method of accounting for sales discounts. Hogan also offers trade discounts to various groups of buyers. On August 1, 2004 Hogan factored some accounts receivable on a without-recourse basis. Hogan incurred a finance charge.

Hogan also has some notes receivable bearing an appropriate rate of interest. The principal and total interest are due at maturity. The notes were received on October 2, 2004 and mature on October 1, 2005. Hogan's operating cycle is less than one year.

Required

1. Using the net method, how should Hogan account for the sales discounts at the date of sale? What is the rationale for the amount recorded as sales under the net method?
2. a. Using the net method, what is the effect on Hogan's sales revenues and net income when customers do not take the sales discounts?
   b. What is the effect of trade discounts on sales revenues and accounts receivable? Why?
   c. How should Hogan account for the accounts receivable factored on August 1, 2004? Why?
   d. How should Hogan report the effects of the interest-bearing notes receivable on its December 31, 2004 balance sheet and on its income statement for the year ended December 31, 2004? Why? (*AICPA adapted*)

C6-12 Assignment and Discounting

Tidal Company has significant amounts of trade accounts receivable. In March of this year, Tidal assigned specific trade accounts receivable to Herb Finance Company on a with-recourse, nonnotification basis as collateral for a loan. Tidal signed a note and received 70% of the amount assigned. Tidal was charged a 5% finance fee and agreed to pay interest at 12% on the unpaid balance. Some specific accounts of the assigned receivables were written off as uncollectible. The remainder of the trade accounts receivable assigned were collected by Tidal in March and April of this year. Tidal paid Herb Finance in full at the end of April of this year.

Tidal also sold some special order merchandise and received a 90-day, 15%, interest-bearing note receivable on July 1 of this year. After 30 days, the note receivable was discounted with recourse at 18% at a bank.

Required

1. Explain how Tidal should account for the transactions described here for the assignment of trade accounts receivable.
2. a. Explain how Tidal should determine the amount of the discount for the note receivable.
   b. Explain how the discounting transaction should be accounted for. (*AICPA adapted*)

C6-13 Analyzing Coca-Cola's Cash and Receivables Disclosures

Refer to the financial statements and related notes of the Coca-Cola Company in Appendix A of this book.

Required Answer the following questions. Indicate on what page of the annual report you found the answer.

1. What were the cash and cash equivalents at the end of 2001? What does the company classify as cash equivalents?
2. What were the trade accounts receivable (net) at the end of 2001? At the end of 2000?
3. Assuming that all net operating revenues were net credit sales and that the trade accounts receivable (net) at the end of 1999 were $1,798 million, compute the receivables turnover for 2001 and 2000. What is your evaluation of the difference?

C6-14 Ethics and Sales Returns

At the end of 2004, the accounting firm for which you work is auditing the books of Debitus Publishing Inc. for the first time. Debitus, a calendar year company, publishes textbooks that are used in colleges and universities across the country. These textbooks are purchased by students through their campus bookstores. Debitus normally makes its biggest sales at the beginning of the fall semester. In the past, Debitus has always recorded sales returns in the spring semester when the campus bookstores return any unsold textbooks. This has been satisfactory because the returns have been immaterial in amount.

In 2003, as a promotional strategy to stimulate sales, Debitus began offering bookstores a reduced price if they ordered more textbooks. There is no penalty for returns of these textbooks if the bookstores cannot sell them to customers. This strategy worked; sales increased by 10% during 2003. In early 2004, however, a substantial amount of unsold textbooks were returned by bookstores to Debitus. Continuing the promotional strategy, sales increased by 15% during 2004.

While reviewing the sales returns account for 2004, you notice that the only entry was for the textbooks returned earlier in the year. You note that these returns amounted to about 5% of the sales for the fall semester of 2003. Since this pattern of returns seems to you to be a trend that will continue, you raise the issue with the company controller as to whether all of the "sales" for the fall semester of 2004 are actually revenue. The controller responds, "Of course they are revenue; we sold the textbooks. Just because there will be some returns doesn't mean we haven't made sales. Besides, we don't know what percentage the returns will be; they might be as much as 5 percent, but definitely not more. Furthermore, we have already recorded all those returns at the beginning of 2004 that really applied to 2003. So we already have recorded our fair share of returns for 2004. As long as we record returns consistently, it will all work out. We don't want a drop in earnings for 2004 because of a change in customer returns; our shareholders wouldn't like that. Let's just leave this issue alone."

Required From financial reporting and ethical perspectives, what do you think about Debitus Publishing Inc.'s policy in regard to sales returns?

R E S E A R C H

C6-15   Researching GAAP

Hamilton Company operates in an industry with numerous competitors. It is experiencing a shortage of cash and decides to obtain money from a large bank by using some of its receivables as collateral. Hamilton pledges $100,000 of its receivables, is charged a 12% fee on this amount, and notifies these credit customers to make their payments directly to the bank. Hamilton transfers the receivables to the bank and the bank assumes the servicing activities, but Hamilton is responsible for all bad debts, which it reasonably estimates to be 2% of the receivables amount. When the balance of the receivables pledged is reduced to $3,000, Hamilton is required to "repurchase" the receivables, notify the remaining credit customers to make payments to it, and reassume the servicing activities. The bank has the right to sell the receivables, except to Hamilton's major competitor. Hamilton's president has asked you how to account for (and record) this transaction.

Required Research the related generally accepted accounting principles and prepare a short memo to the president that answers his question. Cite your reference and applicable paragraph numbers.

MULTIPLE CHOICE

Select the best answer for each of the following.

M6-1   Which of the following items should be classified under the heading of cash on the balance sheet?

	Postdated checks	Certificates of deposit
a.	Yes	Yes
b.	Yes	No
c.	No	No
d.	No	Yes

M6-2   The following bank reconciliation is presented for the Kingston Company for the month of November 2004:

Balance per bank statement, 11/30/04		$18,040
Add: Deposit in transit		4,150
		$22,190
Less: Outstanding checks	$ 6,300	
Bank credit recorded in error	20	(6,320)
Balance per books, 11/30/04		$15,870

Data for the month of December 2004 follow:

Per bank	
December deposits	$26,100
December disbursements	22,420
Balance, 12/31/04	21,720

All items that were outstanding as of November 30 cleared through the bank in December, including the bank credit. In addition, $2,500 in checks were outstanding as of December 31, 2004. What is the balance of cash per books at December 31, 2004?

a. $19,220
b. $19,240
c. $21,720
d. $24,220

M6-3   Greenfield Company had the following cash balances at December 31, 2004:

Cash in banks	$1,500,000
Petty cash funds (all funds were reimbursed on December 31, 2004)	20,000
Cash legally restricted for additions to plant (expected to be disbursed in 2006)	2,000,000

Cash in banks includes $500,000 of compensating balances against short-term borrowing arrangements at December 31, 2004. The compensating balances are not legally restricted as to withdrawal by Greenfield. In the current assets section of Greenfield's December 31, 2004 balance sheet, what total amount should be reported as cash?

a. $1,020,000
b. $1,520,000
c. $3,020,000
d. $3,520,000

M6-4   On January 1, 2004 King Company's Allowance for Doubtful Accounts had a credit balance of $15,000. During 2004 King, (1) charged $32,000 to bad debt expense, (2) wrote off $23,000 of uncollectible accounts receivable, and (3) unexpectedly recovered $6,000 of bad debts written off in the prior year. The Allowance for Doubtful Accounts balance at December 31, 2004 should be:

a. $47,000
b. $32,000
c. $30,000
d. $24,000

M6-5   A company is in its first year of operations and has never written off any accounts receivable as uncollectible. When the allowance method of recognizing bad debt expense is used, the entry to recognize that expense

a. Increases net income
b. Decreases current assets
c. Has no effect on current assets
d. Has no effect on net income

M6-6   Tallent Company received a $30,000, 6-month, 10% interest-bearing note from a customer. After holding the note for two months, Tallent was in need of cash and discounted the note at the United National Bank at a 12% discount rate. The amount of cash received by Tallent from the bank was

a. $31,260   c. $30,300
b. $30,870   d. $30,240

M6-7 When the accounts receivable of a company are sold outright to a company that normally buys accounts receivable of other companies without recourse, the accounts receivable have been

a. Factored   c. Pledged
b. Assigned   d. Collateralized

M6-8 A method of estimating bad debts that focuses on the income statement rather than the balance sheet is the allowance method based on

a. Direct write-off
b. Aging the trade receivable accounts
c. Credit sales
d. The balance in the trade receivable accounts

M6-9 Prior to adjustments, Barrett Company's account balances at December 31, 2004 for Accounts Receivable and the related Allowance for Doubtful Accounts were $1,200,000 and $60,000, respectively. An aging of accounts receivable indicated that $106,000 of the December 31, 2004 receivables may be uncollectible. The net realizable value of accounts receivable was

a. $1,034,000   c. $1,140,000
b. $1,094,000   d. $1,154,000

M6-10 Marmol Corporation uses the allowance method for bad debts. During 2004 Marmol charged $30,000 to bad debt expense and wrote off $25,200 of uncollectible accounts receivable. These transactions resulted in a decrease in working capital of

a. $0   c. $25,200
b. $4,800   d. $30,000

(AICPA adapted)

EXERCISES

E6-1 *Computing the Cash Balance* Indicate whether or not each of the following ten items should be included in the cash balance presented on the balance sheet. Also indicate the normal balance sheet treatment for those items not included as cash.

Item	Include in Cash Balance	Classification of Items Excluded
1. NSF checks		
2. Savings account		
3. Postage stamps		
4. Postdated checks		
5. IOUs		
6. Cash on hand		
7. Cash in sinking fund		
8. Travel advance		
9. Bank draft		
10. Traveler's checks		

E6-2 *Reporting Cash on the Balance Sheet* Your audit of the Watt Corporation discovers the following information:

1. Reconciled balance in First National Bank checking account	$ 2,360.75
2. Reconciled balance in City National Bank checking account	(40.20)
3. Balance in First Federal savings account	28,750.00
4. Certificate of deposit	30,000.00
5. Petty cash fund	500.00
6. Postage stamps	100.00
7. Employee's IOU	125.00
8. Employees' travel advances	1,640.00
9. Cash on hand (undeposited sales receipts)	3,109.40
10. Traveler's checks	600.00
11. Customer's postdated check	290.40

Required

1. What amount should be reported as cash on Watt's balance sheet?
2. Describe the balance sheet treatment of the items not included in the cash balance.

E6-3   ***Petty Cash Transactions***   The Crown Company established a petty cash fund of $600 for incidental expenditures on January 2, 2004. At the end of the month the count of cash on hand indicated that $57.35 remained in the fund. A sorting of petty cash vouchers disclosed that the following expenses had been incurred during the month, and the fund was replenished.

Postage expense	$250.40
Office supplies expense	165.90
Miscellaneous expense	119.05

Required   Prepare the journal entries necessary to record the Crown Company's petty cash transactions during the month of January 2004.

E6-4   ***Adjusting an Unknown Cash Balance***   The information that follows is available from the general ledger and the bank statement of the Gentry Corporation for the month of August 2004:

1. Bank statement balance, August 31	$1,342.50
2. Note collected by the bank not previously recorded by Gentry	600.00
3. Interest on the preceding note (not previously recorded)	25.00
4. NSF check returned with the bank statement (not previously recorded)	212.60
5. Outstanding checks at the end of August	684.70
6. Bank service charge for August	12.85
7. Deposit in transit, August 31	329.42

Required

1. Starting with the bank statement balance, prepare a schedule to determine Gentry's cash balance on August 31, 2004, prior to any required adjustments.
2. Prepare a bank reconciliation to determine Gentry's adjusted cash balance on August 31, 2004.
3. Prepare the journal entries necessary to bring Gentry's cash account balance up to date.

E6-5   ***Bank Reconciliation***   The following information is extracted from the bank statement and the accounting records of the Sun Corporation for the month of July 2004:

1. Cash balance from books, July 31	$1,967.35
2. Cash balance from bank, July 31	1,980.20
3. NSF check returned by bank with bank statement	81.00
4. Note collected by bank on July 31	190.00
5. Interest on preceding note	5.50
6. Bank service charge for July	4.40
7. Outstanding checks at end of July	150.00
8. Deposit in transit at end of July	247.25

Required

1. Prepare a bank reconciliation for the Sun Corporation for July 31, 2004.
2. Prepare the journal entries necessary to adjust Sun's books on July 31, 2004.

E6-6   ***Bank Reconciliation and Adjusting Entries***   The Odum Corporation's cash account showed a balance of $17,198 on March 31, 2004. The bank statement balance for the same date indicated a balance of $17,924.55. The following additional information is available concerning Odum's cash balance on March 31, 2004.

1. Undeposited cash on hand on March 31 amounted to $724.50.
2. A customer's NSF check for $173.80 was returned with the bank statement.
3. A note for $2,000 plus interest of $25 was collected for Odum by the bank during March. The bank notified Odum of this collection on the bank statement.
4. The bank service charge for March was $15.
5. A deposit of $951.75 mailed to the bank on March 31 did not appear on the bank statement.
6. The following checks mailed to creditors had not been processed by the bank on March 31:
#429	$ 57.40	#433	$214.80
#432	$147.50	#434	$191.90
7. A customer check for $149.50 in payment of his account and listed correctly for that amount on the bank statement had been incorrectly recorded on the accounting records as $194.50.

Required

1. Prepare a bank reconciliation for the Odum Corporation for March 31, 2004.
2. Prepare any adjusting journal entries necessary to record the information from Requirement 1.

E6-7   ***Computing the Bank Statement Balance***   Your cashier I. Amakrook has notified you that he has misplaced all the bank statements for the past year. You decide to review selected accounting records during the year and discover that the following journal entry was made to reconcile the June 30, 2004 bank statement and the accounting records:

Accounts Receivable	1,520.24	
Miscellaneous Expense	12.50	
Notes Receivable		200.00
Interest Revenue		10.00
Cash		1,322.74

Required

1. What events might have caused each of the preceding reconciling items to occur?
2. Compute the amount that would have appeared as the balance per bank statement on a bank reconciliation if the preadjustment cash balance in the accounting records was $7,683.70, outstanding checks were $207.50, and no other adjustments were required.
3. Assume that you contact the bank and are informed that a balance of $5,542.90 had been reported on the June 30, 2004 bank statement. What does this discrepancy indicate and how would you begin investigating it?

E6-8   ***Journal Entry to Separate Receivables***   An examination of the accounting records for the Hutton Corporation indicates that all receivables are being recorded in a single account entitled Receivables. An analysis of the account reveals the following:

Accounts receivable (trade)	$15,500
Accounts receivable (officers)	3,600
Common stock subscriptions receivable (current)	12,000
Advances to employees	1,800
Notes receivable (trade), due in 3 years	6,000
Deposit to guarantee contract performance	5,000
Utility deposit	500
Total	$44,400

Required

1. Prepare a journal entry to separate the preceding items into their proper accounts.
2. How would each of the preceding items normally be reflected on Hutton's balance sheet?

E6-9   ***Accounting for Sales Discounts***   On December 8, 2004 Lynch Incorporated sold $9,000 of merchandise with terms 2/10, n/EOM. On December 18, 2004 collections were made on sales originally billed for $5,000, and on December 31, 2004 additional collections on sales originally billed for $3,000 were received.

Required Prepare the journal entries to record the sale, collections, and any required year-end adjustments under (1) the gross price method, and (2) the net price method.

E6-10   ***Comparison of Discount Methods***   The Eastman Corporation sells merchandise with a list price of $13,000
@   on February 1, 2005, with terms of 1/10, n/30. On February 10, 2005, payment was received on merchandise originally billed for $7,500, and the balance due was received on February 28, 2005.

Required Prepare journal entries to record the preceding information using (1) the gross price method, and (2) the net price method.

E6-11   ***Returns and Allowances***   Towbin Products sells merchandise on credit for $7,000 on December 1, 2004. The company estimates that returns and allowances will amount to 4% of sales. On December 22, 2004 a customer returns for credit merchandise originally sold on December 1 for $200.

Required

1. Prepare journal entries to record the preceding sale and the return of merchandise if returns are recorded as they occur.
2. Prepare journal entries to record the preceding sale, the estimation of returns and allowances, and the actual return of goods, if returns and allowances are estimated at the end of the period of sale.

3. How would the preceding information be reflected on Towbin's December 31, 2004 financial statements if (a) returns are recorded as they occur, and (b) returns are estimated in the period of sale?

E6-12   *Estimation vs. Direct Write-Off of Bad Debts*   The Blunt Company sells products for $21,000 during the month of February 2004. During 2004 collections are received on February sales of $20,400, accounts representing $600 of these sales are written off as uncollectible, and a $100 account previously written off is collected.

Required   Prepare the journal entries necessary to record the preceding information if (1) bad debts are estimated as 3% of sales at the time of sale, and (2) the bad debts are recorded as they actually occur.

E6-13   *Estimating Bad Debts from Receivables Balances*   The following information is extracted from the accounting records of the Shelton Corporation at the beginning of 2004:

Accounts Receivable	$63,000
Allowance for Doubtful Accounts	1,400 (credit)

During 2004 sales on account amounted to $575,000, $557,400 was collected on outstanding receivables, and $2,600 of receivables were written off as uncollectible. On December 31, 2004 Shelton estimates its bad debts to be 4% of the outstanding gross accounts receivable balance.

Required

1. Prepare the journal entry necessary to record Shelton's estimate of bad debt expense for 2004.
2. Prepare the Accounts Receivable section of Shelton's December 31, 2004 balance sheet.
3. Compute Shelton's receivables turnover.

E6-14   *Aging Analysis of Accounts Receivable*   Cowen's, a large department store located in a metropolitan area, has been experiencing difficulty in estimating its bad debts. The company has decided to prepare an aging schedule for its outstanding accounts receivable and estimate bad debts by the due dates of its receivables. This analysis discloses the following information:

Balance	Age of Receivable	Estimated Percentage Uncollectible
$193,000	Under 30 days	0.8%
114,000	30–60 days	2.0%
73,000	61–120 days	5.0%
41,000	121–240 days	20.0%
25,000	241–360 days	35.0%
19,000	Over 360 days	60.0%
$465,000		

Required

1. Use the preceding analysis to compute the estimated amount of uncollectible receivables.
2. Prepare the journal entry to record Cowen's estimated uncollectibles, assuming the balance in the Allowance for Doubtful Accounts prior to adjustment is:
   a. 0
   b. $3,000 (debit)
   c. $2,800 (credit)

E6-15   *Comparison of Bad Debt Estimation Methods*   The following information (prior to adjustment) is available from the accounting records of the Bradford Company on December 31, 2004:

Cash sales	$ 93,100	
Net credit sales	262,900	
Total sales (net)		$356,000
Accounts receivable		126,300
Allowance for doubtful accounts		2,150 (credit)

Required   Prepare journal entries to record the estimate of Bradford's bad debt expense for 2004 assuming:

1. Bad debts are estimated to be 1.5% of total sales (net).
2. Bad debts are estimated to be 2% of net credit sales.
3. Bad debts are estimated to be 5% of gross accounts receivable.

E6-16 ***Receivables—Bad Debts*** At January 1, 2004 the credit balance in the Allowance for Doubtful Accounts of the Master Company was $400,000. For 2004 the provision for doubtful accounts is based on a percentage of net sales. Net sales for 2004 were $50,000,000. Based on the latest available facts, the 2004 provision for doubtful accounts is estimated to be 0.7% of net sales. During 2004 uncollectible receivables amounting to $410,000 were written off against the allowance for doubtful accounts.

Required Prepare a schedule computing the balance in Master's Allowance for Doubtful Accounts at December 31, 2004. Show supporting computations in good form. (*AICPA adapted*)

E6-17 ***Assigning Accounts Receivable*** White Corporation has entered into a long-term assignment agreement with a finance company. Under the terms of this agreement, White receives 80% of the value of all accounts assigned and is charged a 1% service charge which is based upon the actual dollar amount of cash received. Additionally, the finance company charges White 12% annual interest on the outstanding loan. The following selected transactions relate to this agreement:

December 1, 2004 Accounts receivable of $160,000 are assigned.
December 11, 2004 A sales return of $1,000 on an assigned account is allowed by White.
December 31, 2004 Collections are made on $86,000 of assigned accounts. This amount and 1 month's interest on the outstanding loan are remitted to the finance company. (For simplicity, compute interest to the nearest month.)
January 29, 2005 $50,000 of assigned accounts are collected and the remainder of the loan is repaid.

Required

1. Prepare journal entries on White's books to record the preceding transactions.
2. How would this assignment agreement be reported on White's December 31, 2004 balance sheet (assume the note payable is short-term)?

E6-18 ***Factoring Accounts Receivable*** The Inder Corporation is experiencing a temporary cash shortage and decides to factor a group of its accounts receivable. The factor accepts $80,000 of Inder's accounts receivable, remits 90% of the accounts receivable factored, and charges a 16% commission on the gross amount of the factored receivables. During the period, sales returns and allowances on factored accounts amounted to $1,500.

Required Prepare all the journal entries necessary by Inder to record the preceding information.

E6-19 ***Receivables from Credit Card Sales*** Dillon Shoes sold $2,100 of merchandise during the month of September, which was charged to a national credit card. On September 15, Dillon bills the independent national credit card company for these sales and is assessed a 5% service charge. On September 21, a customer returns merchandise originally sold for $200 and Dillon notifies the credit card company of the return. On September 29, the credit card company remitted the amount owed to Dillon.

Required Prepare the journal entries necessary to record this information on Dillon's books.

E6-20 ***Generating Cash from Receivables*** The Guide Company requires additional cash for its business. Guide has decided to use its accounts receivable to raise the additional cash as follows:

1. On June 30, 2004 Guide assigned $200,000 of accounts receivable to the Cell Finance Company. Guide received an advance from Cell of 85% of the assigned accounts receivable, less a commission on the advance of 3%. Prior to December 31, 2004 Guide collected $150,000 on the assigned accounts receivable and remitted $160,000 to Cell, $10,000 of which represented interest on the advance from Cell.
2. On December 1, 2004 Guide sold $300,000 of net accounts receivable to the Factoring Company for $260,000. The receivables were sold outright on a nonrecourse basis.
3. On December 29, 2004 Guide received an advance of $100,000 from the Domestic Bank by pledging $120,000 of Guide's accounts receivable. Guide's first payment to Domestic is due on January 29, 2005.

Required Prepare a schedule showing the income statement effect for the year ended December 31, 2004, as a result of the preceding facts. Show supporting computations in good form. (*AICPA adapted*)

E6-21 ***Interest-Bearing and Non-Interest-Bearing Notes*** On December 11, 2004 the Hooper Bank loans a customer $12,000 on a 60-day, 12% note.

Required Prepare the journal entries necessary to record the receipt of the note by Hooper, the accrual of interest on December 31, 2004, and the customer's repayment on February 9, 2005, assuming:

1. Interest was assessed in addition to the face value of the note.
2. The note was issued as a $12,000 non-interest-bearing note.

E6-22   *Computing the Proceeds from Discounted Notes*   Determine the proceeds from each of the following
@   discounted customer notes:

1. An $8,000, 60-day, non-interest-bearing note discounted after 15 days at 12%.
2. A $9,000, 12%, 60-day note discounted after 30 days at 14%.
3. A $6,000, 10%, 90-day note discounted after 30 days at 12%.
4. A $10,000, 12%, 120-day note discounted after 45 days at 15%.

E6-23   *Recording Notes Receivable Discounted*   The following are events of the Singer Corporation for the current
year:

June 30   Barney Manufacturing gives Singer a $5,000, 11%, 90-day note for merchandise purchased.
July 15   Dillon Construction Co. gives Singer a $6,000, 10%, 60-day note for merchandise originally
purchased on April 20 of the current year.
July 30   The Barney and Dillon notes are discounted by Singer at its bank at 12%.
Sept. 15   The bank notifies Singer that the Dillon note was paid.
Sept. 30   The bank notifies Singer that Barney defaulted on the note and charges the amount of
principal, interest, and a fee of $10 against Singer's bank account.

Required Prepare journal entries to record the preceding information on Singer's accounting records.
(Assume that the company does not normally discount its notes and uses a Notes Receivable Discounted
account.)

PROBLEMS

P6-1   *Cash and Other Items*   The following information has been extracted from the accounting records of the
Atwood Corporation:

1. Cash on hand (undeposited sales receipts)	$ 1,020
2. Certificates of deposit	25,000
3. Customer's note receivable	1,000
4. Reconciled balance in University National Bank checking account	(350)
5. Reconciled balance in Second National Bank checking account	9,350
6. Balance in City Federal savings account	8,560
7. Customer's postdated check	1,350
8. Employee travel advances	1,600
9. Cash in bond sinking fund	1,200
10. Bond sinking fund investments	8,090
11. Postage stamps	430

Required Determine the balance in Atwood's Cash account, and discuss the balance sheet treatment of any
items not included as cash.

P6-2   *Reconciliation of Bank and Company Cash Amounts*   The December 31, 2004 bank statement for Miller
Corporation showed a $2,049.25 balance. On this date the company's Cash account reflected a $325.60 over-
draft. In reconciling these amounts, the following information is discovered:

1. Cash on hand for undeposited sales receipts, December 31, 2004, $130.25.
2. Customer NSF check returned with bank statement, $420.40.
3. Cash sales of $640.25 for the week ended December 18, 2004 were recorded on the books. The cashier
reports this amount missing, and it was not deposited in the bank.
4. Note receivable of $2,500 and interest of $25 collected by the bank and not recorded on the books.
5. Deposit in transit December 31, 2004, $350.00.
6. A customer check for $290.40 in payment of its account was recorded on the books at $940.20.
7. Outstanding checks, $2,040.55. Includes a duplicate check of $70.85 to C. Brown, who notified Miller that
the original was lost. Miller stopped payment on the original check and has already adjusted the cash account in the accounting records for this amount.

Required

1. Prepare a December 31, 2004 bank reconciliation for Miller.
2. Prepare any journal entries necessary by Miller to record the information from Requirement 1.

P6-3   *Unknown Book Balance*   The following information pertains to the Cash account of the Nakamoto Corporation for the month of July 2004:

Bank statement

Balance July 31	$22,639.54
Service charge for July	15.00
NSF check returned with July bank statement	184.50
Note receivable collected by bank (not previously recorded on the books)	2,000.00
Interest on note collected by bank (not previously recorded on the books)	60.00

Books

Balance July 31	?
Cash on hand awaiting deposit	1,824.42
Outstanding checks:	
#257 $42.17	
#271 $120.19	
#272 $80.82	
Deposit in transit	2,420.98

Required

1. Prepare a bank reconciliation to determine Nakamoto's adjusted cash balance on July 31, 2004.
2. Determine Nakamoto's unadjusted cash balance (per books) on July 31, 2004.
3. Prepare the adjusting entries necessary to bring Nakamoto's cash account balance up to date on July 31, 2004.

P6-4   *Bank Reconciliation*   The Daisy Company received a bank statement for February 2005, as follows:

From: Central Bank, Denver, Co. 80222
To: Daisy Company, 1313 Williams St., Denver, Co. 80218

Date	Checks	Deposits	Balance
Feb. 1			$4,524.80
7	$2,700.33	$8,642.61	
9	3,484.81		
14	6.00 SC	460.00 CM	
16	274.09		
21	4,133.60	3,385.49	
23	69.69 NSF		
28			$6,344.38
	SC = Service Charge	NSF = Check Returned	
	CM = Credit Memo	DM = Debit Memo	

The receipt of $460 on February 14 was for a $445 note collected by the bank, plus $20 current interest, less a $5 service charge. The company's accounting records contained the following information:

Cash balance on February 28 from the books: $2,610.42

Cash Disbursements		Cash Receipts	
Check No. 155	$2,700.33	Feb. 7	$8,624.61
156	3,484.81	21	3,385.49
157	274.09	All receipts are verified and correct	
158	589.02		
159	4,133.60		
160	2,742.63		

Required

1. Prepare a bank reconciliation on February 28, 2005 for the Daisy Company.
2. Prepare the journal entries that the Daisy Company should record as a result of the reconciliation.

*See WebTutor for annotated problem solution.

P6-5   **Comprehensive Reconciliation**   In auditing the Train Company, you obtain directly from the bank Train's bank statement, canceled checks, and other memoranda which relate to the company's bank account for December 2004. In reconciling the bank balance on December 31, 2004 with that shown on the company's books, you observe the following facts:

1.	Balance per bank statement	$91,174.63
2.	Balance per books	59,088.46
3.	Outstanding checks, 12/31/04	33,378.82
4.	Receipts of 12/31/04 deposited on 1/1/05	5,317.20
5.	Service charge for December	22.50
6.	Proceeds of bank loan, 12/15/04 omitted from company records (discounted for 3 months at 12% per year)	11,640.00
7.	Deposit of 12/20/04 omitted from the bank statement	2,892.41
8.	Check of Rome Products Co. charged back on 12/22/04 for lack of countersignature. Redeposited 1/5/05. No entry was made for the chargeback or the redeposit.	873.74

9.	Error on bank statement in entering deposit of 12/18/04:
	  Correct amount $3,182.40
	  Entered in statement 3,181.40
		1.00

10.	Check No. 3917 of Trait Manufacturing Co. charged in error to company's account	2,690.00

11.	Proceeds of note of J. Somers & Co. collected by bank 12/11/04 not entered on books:
	  Principal $2,000.00
	  Interest 40.00
	      $2,040.00
	  Less: collection charge 5.00
		2,035.00

12.	Erroneous debit memo of 12/22/04 to charge company's account with settlement of bank loan, which was paid by check No. 8714 on same date	5,000.00

13.	Error on bank statement in entering deposit of 12/4/04
	  Entered as $4,817.10
	  Correct amount 4,807.10
		10.00

14.	Deposit of Trait Manufacturing Co. of 12/8/04 credited in error to the company	1,819.20

Required

1. Prepare a reconciliation of the Train Company's bank account.
2. Prepare journal entries to adjust the Train Company's books to reflect the correct bank balance on December 31, 2004. (*AICPA adapted*)

P6-6   **Analyzing Bad Debt Expense**   In 2005, 3 years after it began operations, the Pearce Corporation decided to
@   change from the direct write-off method of recording bad debts to estimating bad debts. The following information is available to you:

	Year			
	2002	**2003**	**2004**	**2005**
Sales	$125,000	$180,000	$250,000	$280,000
Credit sales	90,000	158,000	210,000	235,000
Collections on accounts receivable				
2002 sales	78,000	8,500	200	
2003 sales		137,000	15,000	300
2004 sales			178,800	19,500
2005 sales				200,000
Accounts receivable written off				
2002 accounts	2,500	500	300	0
2003 accounts		4,600	700	400
2004 accounts			6,200	1,000
2005 accounts				6,800

Required

1. Prepare an analysis to determine Pearce's estimated bad debt expense percentage based upon the average relationship of actual bad debts to credit sales.
2. Prepare an analysis to determine Pearce's estimated percentage of allowance for doubtful accounts based on year-end accounts receivable.
3. What amount should Pearce record as bad debts expense for 2005 if:
   a. Bad debts are estimated as a percentage of credit sales?
   b. Allowance for doubtful accounts is estimated as a percentage of outstanding year-end accounts receivable?

P6-7   *Analyzing Accounts Receivable*   The June 30, 2004 balance sheet of the Upham Company included the following information:

Notes receivable	$ 59,800	
Less: Notes receivable discounted	(38,000)	$ 21,800
Accounts receivable	$224,000	
Less: Allowance for doubtful accounts	(14,100)	209,900
Total receivables		$231,700

During the company's fiscal year ending June 30, 2005 the following transactions occurred:

1. Sales on account	$874,600
2. Collections on account	841,000
3. Accounts receivable written off as uncollectible	13,800
4. Notes receivable collected	29,000
5. Customer notes received in payment of accounts receivable	72,000
6. Notes receivable discounted paid at maturity	36,000
7. Notes receivable discounted defaulted, including interest of $20 and a $5 fee. This amount is expected to be collected during the 2006 fiscal year	2,025
8. Proceeds from customer notes discounted (face value $45,000, accrued interest revenue $200)	45,075
9. Collections on accounts previously written off	500
10. Sales returns and allowances (on credit sales)	2,000
11. Bad debts were estimated to be 1.5% of credit sales	

Required

1. Prepare journal entries necessary for Upham to record the preceding transactions.
2. Prepare an analysis that shows the amount of the notes receivable, notes receivable discounted, accounts receivable, and allowance for doubtful accounts balance that will be disclosed on Upham's June 30, 2005 balance sheet.

P6-8   *Recording Note Transactions*   The following information is extracted from the accounting records of the Tara Corporation:

May 1   Received a $6,000, 12%, 90-day note from V. Leigh, a customer.
May 6   Received a $9,000, 10%, 120-day note from C. Gable, a customer.
May 11   Discounted the Leigh and Gable notes at the bank at 13%. In addition, borrowed $10,000 from the bank for 90 days at 12%. The bank remits the face value less the interest.
July 31   The July bank statement indicated that the Leigh note had been paid.
Sept. 4   Received notice that Gable had defaulted on the May 6 note. The bank charged a fee of $10. Paid the amount due on the Gable note to the bank. Informed Gable to pay Tara the entire amount due plus 11% interest on the total of the face amount of the note, the accrued interest, and the fee from the maturity date until Gable remits the amount owed.
Sept. 23   Received the amount due from Gable.

Required Prepare journal entries to record the preceding information, assuming that Tara usually does not discount its notes.

P6-9   *Reconstructing Accounts Receivable and Expense Journal Entries*   The 2005 audit of the accounting records of the Lane Company discloses the following information:

	2004	2005
Accounts receivable (ending)	$186,000	$187,100
Allowance for doubtful accounts (ending)	7,400	7,000
Allowance for sales returns and allowances (ending)	4,700	3,916
Gross sales returns and allowances (estimated for the year)	4,900	5,200
Accounts receivable written off during the year	6,800	7,900
Estimated bad debts for the year	7,200	7,500
Actual gross sales returns and allowances for the year	4,700	6,000
Sales discounts not taken at end of year	0	400
Credit sales during the year (terms, 2/10, n/60)	375,000	380,000
Cash collected on accounts receivable during the year (net of discounts taken)	352,000	367,500

Required

1. Reconstruct the journal entries that were made by Lane during 2005 to record changes in the following accounts, assuming sales returns and allowances are estimated in the period of sale and the net price method is used to account for sales discounts.
    a. Allowance for doubtful accounts
    b. Allowance for sales returns and allowances
    c. Accounts receivable
2. What is the 2005 ending balance in each of the accounts in Requirement 1 and how will it be reported on Lane's 2005 financial statements?

P6-10   *Cash Discounts*   The Lambert Corporation sells merchandise at a list price of $70,000 with accompanying terms of 2/10, n/30 on December 8, 2004. By December 18, 2004 Lambert had collected from customers for merchandise originally billed at $46,000. By December 31, 2004 additional collections had been received on sales originally billed for $18,000, and sales returns and allowances of $1,500 had been granted by Lambert. By January 15, 2005 all the remaining balances due had been collected.

Required

1. Prepare the journal entries using (a) the gross price method and (b) the net price method to record each of the following items:
    a. The sale of the merchandise
    b. Collections received by December 18, 2004
    c. Collections received by December 31, 2004
    d. Sales returns and allowances (*not* estimated in the period of sale)
    e. Any required year-end adjustments
    f. Any January 1, 2005 reversing entries
    g. The collections received by January 15, 2005
2. Calculate the accounts receivable balance that would be reported under (a) the gross price method and (b) the net price method on the Lambert Corporation's December 31, 2004 balance sheet.

P6-11   *Aging Accounts Receivable*   On September 30, 2004 (the end of its fiscal year), the Lufkin Corporation reported accounts receivable of $331,750 and an allowance for doubtful accounts of $16,700. During fiscal 2005 the following transactions occurred:

Credit sales (terms, n/EOM)	$2,017,800
Collections on accounts receivable	1,956,000
Accounts receivable written off	16,200

On September 30, 2005 an aging of the accounts receivable balance indicated the following:

Age	Amount	Estimated Percentage Uncollectible
Under 30 days	$169,250	0.8%
30–90 days	100,000	1.6
91–180 days	55,900	5.0
181–360 days	38,200	15.0
Over 360 days	14,000	40.0
	$377,350	

Required

1. Prepare the journal entries necessary to record the credit sales, collections on account, write-off of accounts receivable, and the bad debts expense for Lufkin for fiscal 2005.
2. What are Lufkin's September 30, 2005 balances in Accounts Receivable and in its Allowance for Doubtful Accounts and how will they be disclosed on the September 30, 2005 balance sheet?
3. Compute Lufkin's receivables turnover in days, assuming a 360-day business year (as discussed earlier in the chapter and in the Appendix to Chapter 5). What is your evaluation of its collection policies?

P6-12 **Estimating Bad Debts** An examination of the accounting records of the Keegan Corporation disclosed the following information for 2004:

Cash sales	$680,000
Net credit sales	527,000
Accounts receivable (12/31/04)	190,000
Allowance for doubtful accounts (12/31/04, prior to adjustment)	1,500 (debit)

Keegan wishes to examine the effect of various alternative bad debt estimation policies.

Required

1. Prepare the adjusting entry that would be required under each of the following methods:
   a. Bad debts are estimated at 1.4% of total sales (net).
   b. Bad debts are estimated at 3% of net credit sales.
   c. Bad debts are estimated at 7.5% of gross accounts receivable.
   d. An aging of accounts receivable indicates that half of the outstanding accounts will incur a 3% loss, a quarter will incur a 6% loss, the remaining quarter will incur a 20% loss.
2. Discuss the difference between the income statement and balance sheet approaches to estimating bad debts.

P6-13 **Notes Receivable and Notes Receivable Discounted** The following notes receivable transactions occurred for the Harris Company during the last three months of the current year. (Assume all notes are dated the day the transaction occurred.)

Oct. 9	Received a $5,000, 12%, 60-day note from K. Weedon, a customer.
Oct. 12	Received a $6,000, 10%, 90-day note from M. Black, a customer.
Oct. 15	Discounted the Weedon note at the bank at 14%.
Nov. 11	Discounted the Black note at the bank at 15%.
Nov. 16	Received an $8,000, 12%, 60-day note from B. Butcher, a customer.
Nov. 20	Received a $6,000, 11%, 120-day note from D. Goldman, a customer.
Dec. 1	Received a $9,000, 13%, 60-day note from S. Lambert, a customer.
Dec. 8	Received notice that the Weedon note was paid at maturity.
Dec. 10	Discounted the Goldman note at the bank at 13%.

Required

1. Prepare journal entries to record the preceding note transactions and the necessary adjusting entries on December 31. (Assume that Harris does not normally discount its notes.)
2. Show how Harris Company's notes receivable would be disclosed on the December 31 balance sheet. (Assume these are the only note transactions encountered by Harris during the year.)

P6-14 **Assigning Accounts Receivable** The Furman Corporation entered into an assignment agreement with a finance company whereby Furman would be advanced 80% of all accounts assigned, less a $2,000 service charge. During the year, $300,000 of accounts receivable were assigned, $220,000 collections were made on outstanding assigned accounts, and $210,000 was remitted to the finance company. This remittance included interest charges of $2,100. Sales returns and allowances on assigned accounts amounted to $5,000.

Required

1. Prepare the journal entries necessary to record the preceding information.
2. Show how the preceding information would be reported on Furman's year-end balance sheet (assume the note payable is short-term).

P6-15   *Factoring Accounts Receivable*   Faeber Textile Company frequently factors its accounts receivable. During 2004 Faeber made credit sales of $100,000 to customers, under terms of 2/10, n/30. Faeber records its credit sales using the gross price method. From past experience, sales returns and allowances are expected to be minimal. In 2004 Faeber sold $70,000 of these receivables to a factor. The factor remitted 90% of the accounts receivable factored and charged a 12% commission on the gross amount of the factored receivables. The factoring agreement also requires Faeber to be responsible for any cash discounts taken by customers upon payment of the factored receivables. Faeber is charged for these cash discounts upon reimbursement by the factor. During 2004 sales returns and allowances were $3,000 on the factored accounts receivable and $1,300 on the unfactored accounts receivable. The factor collected the remaining amount of the factored receivables, less the 2% discount on 94% of the collected receivables, and returned the balance owed to Faeber. Faeber collected the remaining amount of the unfactored accounts receivable, less the 2% discount on 96% of the collected receivables.

Required Prepare all the journal entries necessary for Faeber to record the preceding information.

P6-16   *Factoring and Assignment of Accounts Receivable*   The Lazard Corporation has experienced cash flow problems and decides to improve its current cash position by factoring 30% of its receivables and assigning the remainder with the same finance company. The agreement with the finance company stipulates that a 10% commission will be assessed on factored accounts and 15% annual interest will be charged on the outstanding note payable balance related to the assigned accounts. Additionally, the finance company will advance only 80% of the factored and assigned accounts, and Lazard must continue the collection responsibilities on the assigned accounts. At the beginning of the last month of the company's fiscal year, the accounts receivable transferred to the finance company amounted to $187,000. During the month, collections on factored accounts were $46,000, and collections on assigned accounts amounted to $84,000. All collections on assigned accounts plus accrued interest were remitted to the finance company at the end of the month. The remaining amounts owed will be remitted within these months.

Required
1.   Prepare all journal entries to record the preceding information on Lazard's books.
2.   How would the accounts related to Lazard's factoring and assignment agreements be reported on Lazard's year-end financial statements?

P6-17   *Examination of Accounts Receivable*   You are engaged in the annual examination of Faulane Company, a wholesale office supply business, for the year ended June 30, 2004. You have been assigned to examine the accounts receivable. The following information is available at June 30, 2004.
1.   Your review of accounts receivable and discussions with the client disclose that the following items are included in the accounts receivable (of both the control and the subsidiary ledgers):
     a.   Accounts with credit balances total $1,746
     b.   Receivables from officers total $8,500
     c.   Advances to employees total $1,411
     d.   Accounts that are definitely uncollectible total $1,187
2.   Uncollectible accounts are estimated to be 0.50% of the year's net credit sales of $16,750,000.

Required Prepare any journal entry (entries) required:
1.   to reclassify items that are not trade accounts receivable,
2.   to write off uncollectible accounts, and
3.   to adjust the allowance for doubtful accounts. (*AICPA adapted*)

P6-18   *Allowance for Bad Accounts*   The Installment Jewelry Company has been in business for 5 years but has never had an audit made of its financial statements. Engaged to make an audit for 2004, you find that the company's balance sheet carries no allowance for bad accounts, bad accounts having been expensed as written off and recoveries credited to income as collected. The company's policy is to write off at December 31 of each year those accounts on which no collections have been received for 3 months. The installment contracts generally are for 2 years.

On your recommendation the company agrees to revise its accounts for 2004 to give effect to bad account treatment on the allowance basis. The allowance is to be based on a percentage of sales that is derived from the experience of prior years. Statistics for the past 5 years are shown in the following table:

	Charge Sales	Accounts Written Off and Year of Sale			Recoveries and Year of Sale
2000	$100,000	(2000) $ 550			
2001	250,000	(2000) 1,500	(2001) $1,000		(2000) $100
2002	300,000	(2000) 500	(2001) 4,000	(2002) $1,300	(2001) 400
2003	325,000	(2001) 1,200	(2002) 4,500	(2003) 1,500	(2002) 500
2004	275,000	(2002) 2,700	(2003) 5,000	(2004) 1,400	(2003) 600

Accounts receivable at December 31, 2004 were as follows:

2003 Sales	$ 15,000
2004 Sales	135,000
	$150,000

Required Prepare the adjusting journal entry or entries with appropriate explanations to set up the Allowance for Bad Accounts. (Support each item with organized computations; income tax implications should be ignored.) (*AICPA adapted*)

P6-19 **Allowance for Doubtful Accounts** From inception of operations to December 31, 2003 Harris Corporation provided for uncollectible accounts receivable under the allowance method: Provisions were made monthly at 2% of credit sales; bad debts written off were charged to the allowance account; recoveries of bad debts previously written off were credited to the allowance account; and no year-end adjustments to the allowance account were made. Harris's usual credit terms are net 30 days.

The balance in the Allowance for Doubtful Accounts was $130,000 at January 1, 2004. During 2004 credit sales totaled $9,000,000, interim provisions for doubtful accounts were made at 2% of credit sales, $90,000 of bad debts were written off, and recoveries of accounts previously written off amounted to $15,000. Harris upgraded its computer facility in November 2004 and an aging of accounts receivable was prepared for the first time as of December 31, 2004. A summary of the aging is as follows:

Classification by Month of Sale	Balance in Each Category	Estimated % Uncollectible
Nov.–Dec. 2004	$1,140,000	2%
July–Oct.	600,000	10
Jan.–June	400,000	25
Prior to 1/1/04	130,000	75
	$2,270,000	

Based on the review of collectibility of the account balances in the "prior to 1/1/04" aging category, additional receivables totaling $60,000 were written off as of December 31, 2004. Effective with the year ended December 31, 2004, Harris adopted a new accounting method for estimating the allowance for doubtful accounts at the amount indicated by the year-end aging analysis of accounts receivable.

Required

1. Prepare a schedule analyzing the changes in the allowance for doubtful accounts for the year ended December 31, 2004. Show supporting computations in good form.
2. Prepare the journal entry for the year-end adjustment to the Allowance for Doubtful Accounts balance as of December 31, 2004. (*AICPA adapted*)

P6-20 **Correction of Allowance Account** From inception of operations in 2001 Summit carried no allowance for doubtful accounts. Uncollectible receivables were expensed as written off, and recoveries were credited to income as collected. On March 1, 2005 (after the 2004 financial statements were issued), management recognized that Summit's accounting policy with respect to doubtful accounts was not correct, and determined that an allowance for doubtful accounts was necessary. A policy was established to maintain an allowance for doubtful accounts based on Summit's historical bad debt loss percentage applied to year-end accounts receivable. The historical bad debt loss percentage is to be recomputed each year based on the relationship of net write-offs to credit sales for all available past years up to a maximum of five years.

Information from Summit's records for five years is as follows:

Year	Credit Sales	Accounts Written Off	Recoveries
2001	$1,500,000	$15,000	$ 0
2002	2,250,000	38,000	2,700
2003	2,950,000	52,000	2,500
2004	3,300,000	65,000	4,800
2005	4,000,000	83,000	5,000

Accounts receivable balances were $1,250,000 and $1,460,000 at December 31, 2004 and December 31, 2005, respectively.

Required

1. Prepare the journal entry, with appropriate explanation, to set up the Allowance for Doubtful Accounts as of January 1, 2005. Disregard income taxes. Show supporting computations in good form.
2. Prepare a schedule analyzing the changes in the Allowance for Doubtful Accounts account for the year ended December 31, 2005. Show supporting computations in good form. (*AICPA adapted*)

P6-21   *Comprehensive Receivables Problem*   The December 31, 2003 balance sheet of the Blackmon Corporation disclosed the following information relating to its receivables:

Accounts receivable	$245,000	
Less: Allowance for doubtful accounts	(15,000)	
		$230,000
Notes receivable	$ 60,000	
Less: Notes receivable discounted	(10,000)	
		50,000
Total receivables		$280,000

During 2004, credit sales (terms, n/EOM) totaled $2,200,000 and collections on accounts receivable (unassigned) amounted to $1,900,000. Uncollectible accounts totaling $18,000 from several customers were written off, and a $1,350 accounts receivable previously written off was collected. Additionally, the following transactions relating to Blackmon's receivables occurred during the year:

Mar. 6	Received payment of $12,460 on a note from the Renko Company. The payment included interest revenue of $460.
Mar. 31	The March bank statement indicated that the discounted note had been paid at maturity.
May 1	Accepted a 120-day, 13% note from the Licata Company in exchange for its account receivable of $4,800.
May 18	Received a $6,900, 90-day, 12% note from the Eagle Manufacturing Corporation for a credit sale.
June 2	Discounted both the Licata and Eagle notes at the bank at 14% (assume that Blackmon normally does not discount its notes).
July 1	Assigned $140,000 of accounts receivable to a finance company. Under the terms of the agreement, Blackmon receives 85% of the value of the accounts assigned, less a service charge of $5,000, and is charged 1.5% per month on the outstanding loan balance.
July 6	A sales allowance of $2,500 on an assigned account is allowed by Blackmon.
July 13	A sales return of $800 on an assigned account is granted by Blackmon.
July 31	Collections of $50,000 are made on assigned accounts. This amount and 1 month's interest are remitted to the finance company.
Aug. 31	Assigned accounts of $60,000 are collected, and the remainder of the loan is repaid, including interest.
Aug. 31	The August bank statement indicated the Eagle note had been paid.
Sept. 1	The bank notifies Blackmon that Licata defaulted on its note and charges a fee of $25.
Sept. 4	Collected the amount due from the Licata Company.
Dec. 31	Collected interest of $5,000 on the outstanding notes receivable.

On December 31, 2004 an aging of the accounts receivable balance indicated the following:

Age	Amount	Estimated Percentage Uncollectible
Under 30 days	$240,487	0.5%
31–60 days	113,421	1.5
61–90 days	30,933	8.0
91–240 days	17,185	35.0
Over 240 days	6,874	70.0
	$408,900	

Required

1. Prepare the journal entries to record the preceding receivable transactions during 2004 and the necessary adjusting entry on December 31, 2004.
2. Prepare the receivables portion of Blackmon's December 31, 2004 balance sheet.
3. Compute Blackmon's accounts receivable turnover in days, assuming a 365-day business year (as discussed earlier in the chapter and in the Appendix to Chapter 5). What is your evaluation of its collection policies?

P6-22 *Proof of Cash (Appendix)* The following information is available concerning the cash balance of the Smith Corporation on July 31, 2004:

1. Cash balance from bank statement, June 30		$13,031.78
2. Cash balance from bank statement, July 31		17,756.43
3. Cash balance from company records, June 30 (adjusted)		12,057.16
4. Cash balance from company records, July 31		18,414.92
5. Deposit made by Smith on July 31 received by the bank August 2		1,098.51
6. NSF check returned by bank with the July bank statement		113.15
7. July 31 outstanding checks:		
#1345	$27.00	
#1353	$13.23	
#1354	$14.24	
8. A check written by Smith during July for $162.50 was erroneously recorded on the books as $126.50		
9. Note collected by the bank on July 31 (not previously recorded by Smith)		1,000.00
10. Interest on the preceding note (not previously recorded)		15.00
11. July bank service charge		7.80
12. June deposit in transit received by the bank July 1		146.73
13. Total receipts recorded by the bank during July		10,051.17
14. Total payments recorded by the bank during July		5,326.52
15. July 31 cash on hand (undeposited customer's checks)		472.50
16. June outstanding checks:		
#1082	$372.15 received by bank July 2	
#1086	$552.40 received by bank July 3	
#1087	$196.80 received by bank July 6	
17. Total July receipts per books		10,460.45
18. Total July payments per books		4,102.69

Required Prepare a four-column proof of cash for the Smith Corporation for the month ended July 31, 2004.

P6-23 *Proof of Cash (Appendix)* The following information is available concerning the cash balance of the Jones Corporation on August 31, 2004:

1. Cash balance from bank statement, July 31		$ 9,852.46
from bank statement, August 31		11,679.25
from company records, July 31 (adjusted)		10,206.76
from company records, August 31		11,306.74
2. Total receipts recorded by the bank during August		16,755.64
Total August receipts from books		15,913.93
3. Total payments recorded by the bank during August		14,928.85
Total August payments from books		14,813.95
4. Deposit made by Jones on August 31; received by the bank September 1		1,235.32
July 31 deposit in transit received by the bank August 2		953.71

5. July 31 outstanding checks:

#2150	$345.26 received by bank August 3
#2151	$156.72 received by bank August 4
#2152	$ 97.43 received by bank August 5

August 31 outstanding checks:

#2265	$ 56.89
#2269	$341.72
#2270	$185.75

6. NSF check returned by bank with the August bank statement	96.75
7. A check written by Jones during August for $112.51 was erroneously recorded on the books as $121.51	
8. Note collected by the bank on August 31 (not previously recorded by Jones)	1,500.00
Interest on the preceding note (not previously recorded)	45.00
9. August bank service charge	12.10
10. August 31 cash on hand (undeposited customer's checks)	421.68

Required Prepare a four-column proof of cash for the Jones Corporation for the month ended August 31, 2004.

INTERNET ASSIGNMENTS

Go to the Nikolai and Bazley **Intermediate Accounting** web site (http://Nikolai.swcollege.com). Click on Student Resources and <u>internet</u> <u>homework</u> <u>assignments</u>. Then click on the appropriate hot link (icon) for each company's web site, find the relevant accounting information, and answer the following questions.

I6-1   Go to the Sears web site.

Required How much are the company's "gross" and "net" credit card receivables at the end of the most current year? What do these receivables primarily arise from? How long does it usually take for the company to collect the full receivable balance? On what factors is the allowance for uncollectible accounts determined? When does the company write off uncollectible accounts? Do you think this is reasonable? How is finance charge revenue recorded?

I6-2   Go to the DuPont web site.

Required What was the total amount of the company's accounts and notes receivable at the end of the most current year? What was the net amount of trade receivables that the company held at the end of the most current year? How much was the company's allowance for doubtful accounts at the end of the most current year? At what approximate value are the company's accounts and notes receivable carried? What was the amount of accounts and notes receivable due from equity affiliates at the end of the most current year? What was the amount of the proceeds received from selling an interest in the company's revolving pool of its trade accounts receivable during the most current year, and how was this accounted for? What were the related expenses?

CHAPTER 7

Inventories: Cost Measurement and Flow Assumptions

objectives

1 Describe how inventory accounts are classified.

2 Explain the uses of the perpetual and periodic inventory systems.

3 Identify how inventory quantities are determined.

4 Determine the cost of inventory.

5 Compute ending inventory and cost of goods sold under specific identification, FIFO, average cost, and LIFO.

6 Explain the conceptual issues regarding alternative inventory cost flow assumptions.

7 Understand dollar-value LIFO.

8 Explain additional LIFO issues.

9 Understand inventory disclosures.

10 Record foreign currency transactions involving inventory (Appendix).

Inventories are assets of a company that are (1) held for sale in the ordinary course of business, (2) in the process of production for sale, or (3) held for use in the production of goods or services to be made available for sale. The category of inventory specifically *excludes* any assets that a company does not sell in the normal course of business, such as marketable securities, or property, plant, and equipment that the company intends to sell.

Accounting for inventories is especially significant because the acquisition, manufacture, and sale of products are important to the profitability of many companies. The cost (carrying value) of the inventory usually has a material impact on a company's balance sheet. Since the ending inventory of one period is the beginning inventory of the next period, the cost of the inventory on a company's balance sheet will have an impact on its cost of goods sold and net income of the next period. In addition, various accounting practices, such as alternative cost flow assumptions and valuation principles, are in widespread use and may have a significant impact on asset valuation and income determination. In this chapter we discuss the classifications of inventory, the perpetual and periodic inventory systems, the determination of inventory quantities and costs, and alternative inventory cost flow assumptions.

CLASSIFICATIONS OF INVENTORY

A company may use several different accounts to classify inventory, depending on the type of business. A merchandising company, whether wholesale or retail, acquires goods for resale and does not alter their physical form. Consequently it needs only one type of inventory account, usually entitled **merchandise inventory.** A manufacturing company *does* change the physical form of the goods and typically uses three inventory accounts in the financial statements; usually these are called **raw materials inventory, goods in process inventory,** and **finished goods inventory.** We illustrate the flow of inventory costs through these two types of companies in Exhibit 7-1. We discuss the three categories of inventory accounts used by a manufacturing company in the following sections. Both types of companies may use more accounts internally.

1 Describe how inventory accounts are classified.

Raw Materials Inventory

Raw materials inventory includes the tangible goods acquired for direct use in the production process. This inventory includes materials that a company acquired from natural sources, such as the iron ore used by a steel mill. Raw materials also may include products purchased from other companies, such as the steel or subassemblies used in the

EXHIBIT 7-1   Flow of Inventory Costs

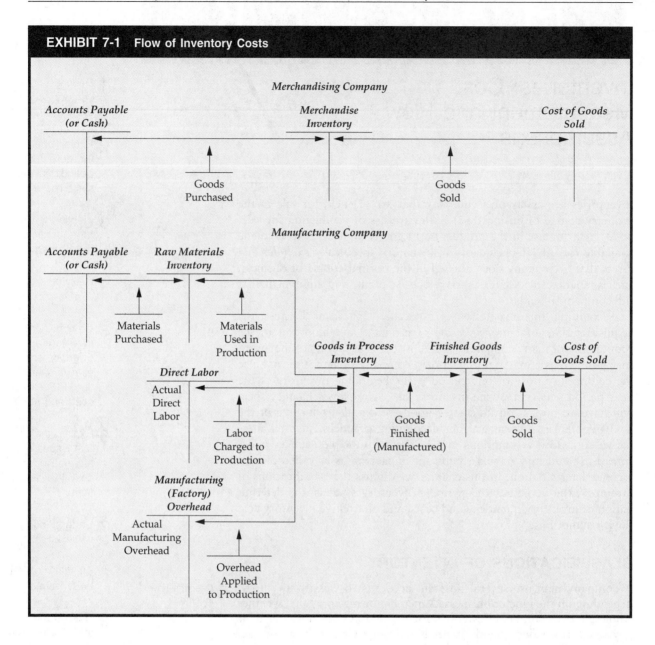

manufacture of appliances. Raw materials should be distinguished from **parts inventory,** which is the term often used for the inventory of replacement parts.

Sometimes, a company includes in raw materials inventory materials that are not directly a part of its manufacturing process but are necessary for its successful operation. However, the company often includes them in an account called **factory supplies, manufacturing supplies,** or **indirect materials.** Examples of materials in this category include lubricating oil and cleaning supplies.

Goods in Process Inventory

Goods (or work) in process inventory includes the products that are started in the manufacturing process but are not yet complete. This partially completed inventory includes three cost components: (1) raw materials, (2) direct labor, which is the cost of the labor used directly in the manufacture of the product, and (3) manufacturing (or factory) overhead, which includes the costs other than raw materials and direct labor that are associated with the manufacturing process. These latter costs include **variable**

manufacturing overhead, such as supplies and some indirect labor, and **fixed manufacturing overhead,** such as insurance, utilities, and depreciation on the assets used in the production activities.

Finished Goods Inventory

Finished goods inventory includes the completed manufactured products awaiting sale. The inventory includes the same three cost components as the goods in process inventory, but all the costs are combined into a single cost per unit for all the completed units.

The inventory cost that a company reports on its balance sheet is the final amount that results from a series of steps. First the company must decide what items to include in the inventory and count the physical inventory quantities. Then it must determine the costs of the units it purchased or produced during the accounting period, taking into consideration the costs for freight-in and the reductions for purchases discounts, returns, and allowances. The company uses a cost flow assumption to allocate the costs of the beginning inventory plus the units purchased or produced during the year between the ending inventory and the cost of goods sold. We discuss each of these steps in the following sections.

Inventories of Service Companies

A service company generally doesn't have a physical inventory that is material. However, it often has an "inventory" of services that it has provided but not yet billed. For example, a company that provides computer consulting services will pay its employees each period but may only bill its services when certain "contract milestones" are reached. The company has an inventory of "unbilled services provided" that it reports as an asset, and then recognizes as an expense when it recognizes the revenue.

ALTERNATIVE INVENTORY SYSTEMS

A company may account for inventory quantities and costs using either the **perpetual system** or the **periodic system.**

2 Explain the uses of the perpetual and periodic inventory systems.

Perpetual Inventory System

A company using a perpetual system maintains a continuous record of the physical quantities in its inventory. It records the purchase, or production, and use of each item of inventory in detailed subsidiary records, although often only in units without including costs. Such a perpetual physical system is essential if adequate management planning and control over inventory are to be maintained and stock-outs avoided. To facilitate management control and the preparation of periodic financial statements, many perpetual systems also include costs. Such systems are becoming much more common with the increased sophistication and lower cost of computer-based accounting systems. For example, most retail stores use "point of sale" cash register systems in which each product has a unique code, such as the UPC code, that is entered into the system as each unit is sold. This enables the retailer to immediately update its Inventory and Cost of Goods Sold accounts as each sale is made. A company maintains these accounts as summary accounts, thereby making it possible to know the inventory and the cost of goods sold at all times. The company usually records purchases returns and allowances, purchases discounts taken, and freight-in in separate accounts that it uses to compute the income for the period.

When a company uses a perpetual system, it should take a physical count at least once a year to confirm the balance in the inventory account. Variation between the physical count and the inventory account balance results from errors in recording, shrinkage, waste, breakage, theft, and other causes. The company adjusts its inventory account and also increases cost of goods sold (or recognizes a loss) for the cost of the difference in the two quantities so that the perpetual records are in agreement with the physical count.

The size of the difference provides useful information for management control purposes and is another advantage of the perpetual system.

Periodic Inventory System

A company using a periodic system does *not* maintain a continuous record of the physical quantities (or costs) of inventory on hand. It takes physical counts periodically, which should be at least once a year and generally at the end of the year. This is the only time(s) when it knows the physical quantities on hand, and therefore the quantities used or sold during the period. The company determines the cost of the ending inventory by attaching costs to the physical quantities on hand based on the cost flow assumption it is using. Then it calculates the cost of goods sold by subtracting the ending inventory from the cost of goods available for sale. The cost of goods available for sale is the sum of the beginning inventory and either the net purchases for a merchandising company or the costs of the units produced for the period for a manufacturing company. This system is adequate for relatively low cost inventory items, particularly when the costs of a perpetual inventory system are likely to be greater than its benefits.

In the periodic system a company typically does not record (debit) the costs of acquisitions of inventory in an inventory account. Such a procedure would lead to an overstatement of the permanent Inventory account, because the company does not reduce (credit) the account during the period for the cost of the inventory sold. Therefore, in a periodic system the company usually records (debits) costs of acquisitions of inventory in a temporary account, Purchases, while the beginning inventory cost remains in the Inventory account.

In both the perpetual and periodic systems, the company usually records purchases returns and allowances, purchases discounts taken, and freight-in in separate accounts. Each of these amounts is used in the computation of net purchases as follows:

$$\text{Net Purchases} = \text{Purchases} + \text{Freight-in} - \frac{\text{Purchases Returns}}{\text{and Allowances}} - \frac{\text{Purchases}}{\text{Discounts}}_{\text{Taken}}$$

In summary, the difference between a perpetual and a periodic inventory system may be illustrated by the following equations:

Perpetual Inventory System

Beginning Inventory + Purchases (net) − Goods Sold = Ending Inventory

Periodic Inventory System

Beginning Inventory + Purchases (net) − Ending Inventory = Goods Sold

Note that each equation can be thought of in terms of *units* or *costs*.

ITEMS TO BE INCLUDED IN INVENTORY QUANTITIES

3 Identify how inventory quantities are determined.

The basic criterion for including items in inventory is *economic control* rather than physical possession or legal ownership. In simple situations all three occur at the same time. However, because there may be differences in more complex situations, the *economic substance* of the transaction should always take precedence over its *legal form* to determine whether the buyer or the seller has economic control. While control is often easy to determine, it may be affected by the following issues.

Goods are often shipped under one of two alternatives: **FOB** (Free-on-Board) **shipping point** or **FOB destination.** When goods are in transit at the end of the accounting period, the terms of shipment determine whether the seller or the buyer includes them in its inventory. **If the goods are shipped FOB shipping point, control of (and legal title to) the goods is transferred at the shipping point when the seller delivers them to the buyer,** or to a transportation company that is acting as an agent for the buyer. The buyer has economic control and includes those goods in its inventory, and the seller excludes them. **If goods are shipped FOB destination, control of (and legal title to) the goods is not transferred until the goods are delivered to the buyer's destination.** The seller has economic control and includes those goods in its inventory, and the buyer excludes them. These situations may be illustrated as follows:

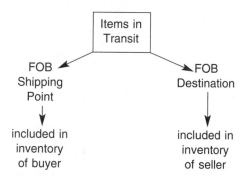

Economic control may also transfer before or after physical possession (and legal ownership) transfer. For example, if the sales contract specifies that the buyer will pick up the goods from the seller and the goods are segregated from the seller's other inventory so that the risk of ownership has passed to the buyer, control has passed and the seller should exclude the goods from inventory and the buyer should include them. Also, goods may be transferred on **consignment.** The company delivering the goods, the **consignor,** retains economic control (and ownership), while the company receiving the goods, the **consignee,** attempts to sell them. The goods are included in the inventory of the consignor until they are sold by the consignee. Transfer of control may also be affected by product financing arrangements (discussed in Chapter 8), and by sales made when there is a right of return (discussed in Chapter 5).

Accounting for consignments is discussed in Chapter 17.

Physical transfer of goods usually determines when the seller records the sale and the buyer records the inventory, respectively, in their accounting systems. However, both companies should adjust the recorded amounts in situations where physical possession is not consistent with economic control on the balance sheet date. However, companies may ignore these adjustments if the effects are not material.

As we discuss in Chapter 17, what a company includes in inventory is dependent on its revenue recognition decisions. A company first decides when it is appropriate to recognize revenue and then matches the cost of goods sold against that revenue. As it recognizes the cost of goods sold, it reduces its inventory.

DETERMINATION OF INVENTORY COSTS

There are two issues in the determination of inventory costs. We discuss the costs attached to each unit *available for sale* in this section. We discuss the costs attached to the *ending inventory* and *cost of goods sold* (the inventory cost flow assumption) later in this chapter.

4 Determine the cost of inventory.

The cost of inventory is the price paid or consideration given to acquire it.[1] Thus, **inventory cost includes costs directly or indirectly incurred in bringing an item to its existing condition and location.** For each item of inventory, purchased or manufactured, a company must make a decision as to whether or not each cost meets this definition. If it does, the company includes it in the cost of the inventory. If it does not, the company immediately recognizes it as an expense. The cost of purchased inventory should include the purchase price (net of purchases discounts, as we discuss later) plus payments directly associated with the inventory, such as freight-in, receiving, unpacking, inspecting, storage, insurance, personal property taxes, sales and other applicable taxes, and similar costs. When a company purchases more than one type of inventory for a single sum and

---

1. "Restatement and Revision of Accounting Research Bulletins," *Accounting Research and Terminology Bulletins, Final Edition, No. 43* (New York: AICPA, 1961), ch. 4, par. 4.

The relative fair value method is discussed in Chapter 9.

it cannot identify the costs of each type, it should use the relative fair value method to apportion the cost.

Some costs that should be attached to inventory normally are excluded on the grounds of the cost/benefit relationship. For example, the costs of operating a purchasing department are necessary to bring the item to its existing condition and location, but the practical difficulties involved in allocating such costs to the separate inventories often outweigh the significance of the differences (i.e., benefits) that result from not making an allocation.

Another cost that *could* be considered for inclusion in the cost of inventory is the interest cost associated with amounts a company borrowed to finance the purchase of the inventory. It can be argued that this interest cost is incurred indirectly in order to bring an item to its existing condition and location and, therefore, should be added to the inventory cost. Alternatively, it can be argued that borrowing costs are period costs associated with the general activities of the company, and none is related specifically to the acquisition of a particular inventory item. According to *FASB Statement No. 34*, interest costs are *not* included in the cost of inventory that is *routinely manufactured* (discussed in Chapter 9).

Additional issues in the determination of inventory costs are manufacturing overhead costs, standard costs, variable costs, and purchases discounts.

Manufacturing Overhead Costs

When a company manufactures inventory, it adds the costs that are directly and indirectly incurred in the production activity to the cost of inventory. The costs that it includes are acquisition and production costs (including manufacturing overhead). The company expenses general and administrative costs, except for the portion of such costs that are clearly related to production and thus are included in inventory costs.

> **Selling expenses constitute no part of inventory costs. It should also be recognized that the exclusion of all overhead from inventory costs does not constitute an accepted accounting practice.**[2]

Selling costs are not associated with bringing the item to its existing condition and location. Instead, they are a cost of the period and not an inventory cost because they apply to the units sold during the period and not to the units held in inventory.

Manufacturing costs that are related directly or indirectly to the production of inventory and thus are included in the cost of that inventory may be either variable or fixed manufacturing overhead. Including variable overhead costs in the cost of inventory should not present any difficulties. However, the allocation of fixed overhead costs is a difficult issue and the final allocation of costs usually involves somewhat arbitrary procedures. A discussion of these issues is beyond the scope of this book but may be found in a cost accounting book. An interpretation of "directly or indirectly incurred" presents some practical problems. One way in which this criterion can be applied is to ask whether the economic benefit to be derived from the asset in the future (i.e., sales revenue) has been increased by the expenditure in question. In other words, **the relationship between the costs incurred and the benefits produced has to be traceable.**

For example, a supervisor's salary may increase directly the economic benefit associated with the asset if the item would not have been produced or would not have been of the same quality *without* the supervisor. That is, there is a traceable relationship, and thus the supervisor's salary should be included in the cost of the inventory. In contrast, the company president's salary does not lead directly to an increase in the economic benefits to be derived from a particular unit of inventory. In this case there is no traceable relationship and the salary should be a period expense. Similarly, the cost of *normal* spoilage is considered an inventory cost, since some spoilage is a part of the production process. However, the cost of *abnormal* spoilage is an expense of the period, because it has not increased the economic benefits to be derived from the inventory.

2. *Ibid.*

In addition to traceability, **materiality is relevant to the decision to include overhead costs in the cost of inventory.** If the inclusion or exclusion of the cost will *not* have a material effect on the financial statements, the costs may be expensed in the period incurred.

Standard Costs

For internal reporting purposes most manufacturing companies use a standard-cost system in which unit costs are based on budgeted standards for the period. However, standard costs are acceptable for financial reporting only

> if adjusted at reasonable intervals to reflect current conditions, so that at the balance sheet date standard costs reasonably approximate costs computed under one of the recognized bases.[3]

In other words, a company must adjust the standard costs for the cost variances (direct materials, direct labor, and manufacturing overhead) that occur during the period. The usual practice is to close all the variances to cost of goods sold, although the preferred practice would be to allocate the variances, if material, between cost of goods sold and ending inventory on the basis of relative total costs.

Variable Costing

Under variable (or direct) costing, the cost of the inventory includes only the variable costs incurred in production, such as direct materials, direct labor, and variable manufacturing overhead. Fixed costs are treated as period expenses. In contrast, under absorption (or full) costing, the cost of the inventory includes allocated fixed manufacturing overhead in addition to the variable costs. We do not discuss the relative merits of variable and absorption costing, but if a company uses variable costing for internal purposes, it must adjust to absorption costing for financial reporting purposes. Thus, it must allocate a portion of the fixed manufacturing overhead to the units produced to convert to an absorption costing basis.

Purchases Discounts

Many sellers offer discounts to buyers in order to encourage prompt payment. These discounts, called purchases discounts, may be accounted for by the gross price method or the net price method. These methods raise questions about whether purchases discounts should directly affect a company's income or be treated as adjustments to inventory cost, and how management efficiency can best be identified.

Under the gross price method, a company records the purchase at the gross price, and records the amount of the discount in the accounting system only if the discount is *taken.* This discount should be deducted from the acquisition cost of the inventory. **Under the net price method, a company records the purchase at its net price, and records the amount of the discount in the accounting system only if the discount is** *not taken.* This discount lost should be treated as a period expense[4]. We illustrate these two alternatives in Exhibit 7-2 by an example in which a company purchases $1,000 of goods under terms of 1/10, n/30 (a 1% discount is allowed if payment is made within 10 days; otherwise, full payment is due within 30 days).

CONCEPTUAL EVALUATION OF THE TWO METHODS The correct inventory cost is the invoice price less all available discounts. Therefore, a company should treat the purchases discounts lost under the net price method as a financing expense for the period

---

3. *Ibid.*
4. In a third method, the allowance method, the purchase is recorded at the net price, the accounts payable at the gross price, and the difference is debited to an allowance account. The allowance account is reduced by the difference between the cash paid to the supplier and the accounts payable balance. It is also adjusted for purchases discounts not taken.

EXHIBIT 7-2 **Alternative Methods of Accounting for Purchases Discounts**

	Gross Price Method			Net Price Method		
To record the purchase	Inventory (or Purchases) Accounts Payable	1,000	1,000	Inventory (or Purchases) Accounts Payable	990	990
To record payment within the discount period	Accounts Payable Purchases Discounts Taken Cash	1,000	10 990	Accounts Payable Cash	990	990
To record payment outside the discount period	Accounts Payable Cash	1,000	1,000	Accounts Payable Purchases Discounts Lost Cash	990 10	1,000
Adjusting entry at end of period if discount has expired and invoice is unpaid	No entry required			Purchases Discounts Lost Accounts Payable	10	10

and should not include it in inventory cost, because **losing the discount does not increase the economic benefit to be derived from the inventory.** To be consistent, a company should treat the purchases discounts taken under the gross price method as a reduction in inventory cost. However, if some discounts were not taken, the inventory cost would include those discounts lost, even though they do not increase the economic benefits to be derived from the inventory. **Therefore, the correct inventory cost is always recorded under the net price method, but under the gross price method only if all discounts are taken** (or if an adjustment is made to remove the discounts lost from the cost of the inventory and the cost is recorded as a financing expense).

Sometimes it is argued that the discounts taken under the gross method should be treated as an increase in income. This is not correct because the matching principle would be violated, since the discounts may relate to goods that have not yet been sold. Furthermore a company does not earn income by buying goods and paying bills. **The revenue recognition principle requires that a sale of goods (or services) occur before a company recognizes income.** However, for practical reasons, a company may include purchases discounts in income; this is acceptable provided that the amount is not material. Retailing companies often follow this procedure.

Another advantage of the net price method is that it isolates the purchases discounts lost, thereby highlighting inefficiencies, which assists the management control process. For example, if a company purchases goods on terms of 2/10, n/30 and does not take the discount, it is paying 2% to delay payment by 20 days (the 30-day maximum less the 10 days allowed to take the discount), which is an approximate annual rate of 36% (2% × 360/20).

The net price method can be criticized, though, because Accounts Payable does not represent the maximum amount of the liability that the company may be required to pay, although it does reflect the most likely amount if the company generally takes the discounts. However, the adjusting entry illustrated in Exhibit 7-2 for expired discounts will ensure that the correct liability (the gross price) appears on the company's balance sheet. Despite the advantages of the net price method, the gross price method is more prevalent because it is simpler to use and the results produced usually are not materially different from the net price method.

Trade discounts are discussed in Chapter 6.

Purchases discounts are different from trade discounts. **Trade discounts are discounts deducted prior to arriving at the invoice price** and do not enter into the accounting system.

COST FLOW ASSUMPTIONS

A company typically starts an accounting period with some units in the beginning inventory and then purchases or produces additional units during the period. Together these constitute the *goods available for sale*, which the company then either sells or retains in its ending inventory.

For financial statement purposes, a company must attach *costs* to these units. The cost of the beginning inventory (the cost of the ending inventory of the preceding period) is the beginning balance in the Inventory account. The beginning balance in Inventory plus the cost of purchases or production (discussed earlier) is the *cost of the goods available for sale*. This total cost is allocated between the cost of goods sold and ending inventory by means of a *cost flow assumption*. The major cost flow assumptions currently used are specific identification; first-in, first-out (FIFO); average cost; and last-in, first-out (LIFO). We illustrate both the unit relationship and the cost flow relationship in Exhibit 7-3.

5 Compute ending inventory and cost of goods sold under specific identification, FIFO, average cost, and LIFO.

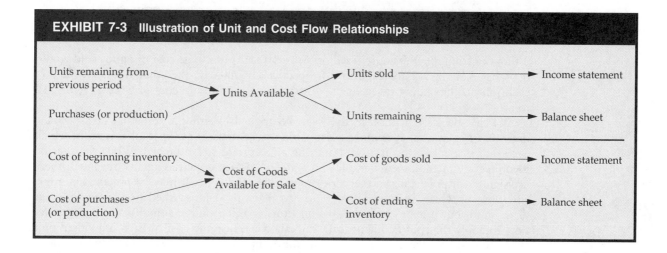

EXHIBIT 7-3 Illustration of Unit and Cost Flow Relationships

Cost flow assumptions are important for two reasons. First, a company has inventories at each year-end. If there were none, all the cost of goods available for sale would be transferred to cost of goods sold. Second, the costs of purchases and production change during the year. If these costs did not change, all units would have the same cost; therefore alternative cost flow assumptions would not affect the cost of goods sold or the ending inventory. Note that we are discussing *cost* flow assumptions here; there is no requirement that they be related to the *physical* flow (except for the specific identification method).

We discuss each cost flow assumption in the following sections and apply it to both the perpetual and the periodic inventory systems using the information for the Dalton Company shown in Exhibit 7-4. Recall that under the periodic system, the ending inventory is computed before the cost of goods sold, whereas under the perpetual system, the cost of goods sold is calculated first. To make the illustration less complicated, a merchandising company is used, although the cost flow assumptions are applied to manufacturing companies by following the same principles.

Specific Identification

Under the specific identification inventory cost flow assumption, a company identifies each unit sold and each unit remaining in the ending inventory and includes the actual costs of those units in cost of goods sold and ending inventory, respectively. For example, the company must specifically identify each unit sold on April 27. If all the units are from beginning inventory, the company's cost of goods sold is $10 for each unit, whereas

EXHIBIT 7-4 Inventory Inflows and Outflows for Dalton Company

Inventory, April 1	100	units @ $10 per unit	$1,000
Purchases, April 10	80	units @ $11 per unit	880
Purchases, April 20	70	units @ $12 per unit	840
Goods Available for Sale	250	units	$2,720
Sales, April 18	(90)	units ⎫ 140 units	
Sales, April 27	(50)	units ⎭	
Inventory, April 30	110	units	

Notes: (1) The beginning inventory is valued at $10 per unit for all the flow assumptions. However, if costs are changing, this value would be different for different flow assumptions, because the beginning inventory for the current period is the ending inventory of the preceding period. (2) The company uses a monthly accounting period.

if they are from the units purchased on April 10 or April 20, its cost of goods sold would be either $11 or $12 for each unit, respectively. Similarly, the company must identify each unit in the ending inventory and attach the appropriate cost of $10, $11, or $12 to it.

The specific identification method can be applied in either a perpetual or a periodic inventory system, but it is more reasonable to use it with a perpetual system in which each unit is identified as it is sold and the appropriate cost attached. While the specific identification method seems simple and matches costs as expenses against revenues, there are significant practical and theoretical objections to its use. It may be practical in a few situations in which units are costly and can be easily distinguished (for example, a car dealership), but in many complex manufacturing and retailing situations, it is not practical to apply the specific identification method because the cost of each individual unit is not identifiable (e.g., a single can of soup), and it is not known which specific units are sold. In addition, as volume increases, so does the cost of record keeping, and the method may become too expensive to use.

Another argument against the method is that the amount of profit varies even though the units of inventory are identical. Continuing the preceding example, if the units were sold on April 27 for $30, then the selection by the company's management of a $10 unit or a $12 unit for sale would make the gross profit either $20 per unit or $18 per unit, respectively. In summary, the specific identification method can produce ending inventory and cost of goods sold amounts at the two extremes of FIFO and LIFO, or at values in between. This ability of a company's management to select, or "manipulate," its profits is considered undesirable. However, the method is appropriate if each item is unique. No summary amounts are presented in this section because they are so dependent on the assumptions regarding the particular units selected for sale.

First-In, First-Out (FIFO)

Under the FIFO cost flow assumption, a company includes the earliest costs incurred in the cost of goods sold, and includes the most recent costs in the ending inventory. We illustrate these relationships as follows:

FIFO → Earliest Costs → Cost of Goods Sold → Income Statement
FIFO → Latest Costs → Ending Inventory → Balance Sheet

In other words, the first costs incurred are the first transferred to cost of goods sold (in a merchandising company) or to goods in process and then to finished goods and cost of goods sold (in a manufacturing company). Consequently the ending inventory consists of the most recent costs incurred. Therefore, in periods of rising costs, FIFO produces a lower cost of goods sold figure based on older and lower costs, whereas the ending inventory is based on the most recent and higher costs, as we discuss in the evaluation section later in this chapter.

If the Dalton Company uses the periodic method, it computes the ending inventory of $1,280 first, as we show in Exhibit 7-5. The ending inventory of 110 units is based on the most recent costs incurred. It includes 40 units purchased on April 10 for $11 each and 70 units purchased on April 20 for $12 each. The company calculates the cost of goods sold of $1,440 by subtracting the ending inventory from the cost of goods available for sale as we show in Exhibit 7-5. Therefore, it is based on the earliest costs incurred and includes the beginning inventory of 100 units at $10 each and 40 units from the April 10 purchase at $11 each.

EXHIBIT 7-5   FIFO Cost Flow Assumption (Periodic Inventory System)

Ending Inventory (110 units):

40 units @ $11	$ 440
70 units @ $12	840
	$1,280

Cost of Goods Sold (140 units):

Beginning Inventory	+	Purchases	−	Ending Inventory	=	Cost of Goods Sold
$1,000	+	$1,720	−	$1,280	=	$1,440

If the Dalton Company uses the perpetual inventory system (for costs as well as physical quantities), it calculates the cost of goods sold of $1,440 and the ending inventory of $1,280 as we show in Exhibit 7-6. The $1,440 cost of goods sold for 140 units is based on the earliest costs incurred. For the April 18 sale, the 90 units have a cost of $10 per unit (from the beginning inventory). For the April 27 sale of 50 units, 10 units have a cost of $10 per unit from the beginning inventory and 40 units have a cost of

EXHIBIT 7-6   FIFO Cost Flow Assumption (Perpetual Inventory System)

Cost of Goods Sold (140 units):

April 18	90 units @ $10	$ 900
April 27	50 units: 10 units @ $10	100
	40 units @ $11	440
Total		$1,440

Ending Inventory (110 units):

Beginning Inventory	+	Purchases	−	Cost of Goods Sold	=	Ending Inventory
$1,000	+	$1,720	−	$1,440	=	$1,280*

*40 units @ $11 =	$ 440
70 units @ $12 =	840
	$1,280

$11 per unit (from the April 10 purchase). The company determines the $1,280 ending inventory by deducting the $1,440 cost of goods sold from the $2,720 cost of goods available for sale. The ending inventory consists of 110 units and includes the most recent costs: the cost of the remaining 40 units from the first purchase on April 10 and the 70 units purchased on April 20.

Note that the ending inventory and the cost of goods sold under both the perpetual and the periodic systems are identical; this always is true for the FIFO cost flow assumption because the most recent costs incurred always are included in the ending inventory.

Average Cost

Under the average cost flow assumption, a company considers all the costs and units to be commingled so that no individual units or costs are identified. When a company uses the periodic inventory system, the average cost method is known as the **weighted average** method. The company calculates the cost of the units for the period on the basis of the cost of the beginning inventory and the average cost of the units purchased or manufactured, weighted according to the number of units at each cost. In other words, **under the weighted average method, the average cost per unit for the period is the cost of goods available for sale divided by the number of units available for sale.** The company uses this average cost for both its ending inventory and the cost of goods sold.

The weighted average unit cost for the Dalton Company in April is $10.88 (the cost of goods available for sale of $2,720 ÷ the number of units available for sale of 250), as we show in Exhibit 7-7. It records the ending inventory at this $10.88 cost per unit, resulting in a total cost of $1,197. The company computes the $1,523 cost of goods sold by deducting the ending inventory from the cost of goods available for sale of $2,720. It is also equal to the 140 units sold multiplied by the $10.88 weighted average cost.

EXHIBIT 7-7   Weighted Average Cost Flow Assumption (Periodic Inventory System)

Cost of goods available for sale ($1,000 + $1,720)	$2,720
Units available for sale	250
Average cost (Cost ÷ Number of units)	$10.88
Ending inventory (110 units @ $10.88)	$1,197

Beginning Inventory	+	Purchases	−	Ending Inventory	=	Cost of Goods Sold
$1,000	+	$1,720	−	$1,197	=	$1,523

When a company uses the average cost method under a perpetual inventory system (for costs as well as physical quantities), the same principles are applied, but it is known as a **moving average** method because a new weighted average cost must be calculated after *each* purchase as we show in Exhibit 7-8. The new weighted average is computed in the same way as in the weighted average method. That is, **under the moving average method, the average cost per unit is the cost of the units available for sale after the purchase divided by the number of units available for sale at that time.** This average cost is used to determine the cost of each sale made until the next purchase, at which time a new average cost is calculated. The average cost after the April 10 purchase is $10.44 (cost of goods available for sale of $1,880 ÷ the number of units available for sale of 180). Therefore the sales on April 18 have a cost of $10.44 per unit for a total cost of goods sold of $940. The purchase on April 20 increases the average cost to $11.125 per unit, and therefore the 50 units sold on April 27 have a total cost of $556. The total cost of goods sold for April is $1,496 ($940 + $556). The company records the ending

---

EXHIBIT 7-8   Moving Average Cost Flow Assumption (Perpetual Inventory System)

April 1, Beginning Inventory	100	units @ $10	$1,000
April 10, Purchases	80	units @ $11	880
April 10, Balance	180	units @ $10.44	$1,880
April 18, Sales	(90)	units @ $10.44	(940)
April 18, Balance	90	units @ $10.44	$ 940
April 20, Purchases	70	units @ $12	840
April 20, Balance	160	units @ $11.125	$1,780
April 27, Sales	(50)	units @ $11.125	(556)
April 30, Balance	110	units @ $11.125	$1,224
Cost of Goods Sold (140 units)		$940 + $556	$1,496
Ending Inventory (110 units @ $11.125)			$1,224

---

inventory at the final average cost for the period, which it calculates after the last purchase. The cost of $11.125 per unit for the 110 units results in a total ending inventory of $1,224 (see Exhibit 7-8).

Last-In, First-Out (LIFO)

Under the LIFO cost flow assumption, a company includes the most recent costs incurred in the cost of goods sold, and includes the earliest costs (part or all of which are costs incurred in previous periods) in the ending inventory. We illustrate these relationships as follows:

$$\text{LIFO} \begin{array}{l} \longrightarrow \text{Latest Costs} \longrightarrow \text{Cost of Goods Sold} \longrightarrow \text{Income Statement} \\ \longrightarrow \text{Earliest Costs} \longrightarrow \text{Ending Inventory} \longrightarrow \text{Balance Sheet} \end{array}$$

Therefore, in periods of rising costs, LIFO produces a higher cost of goods sold figure based on the most recent costs, whereas the ending inventory is based on the oldest and lowest costs. We discuss the logic behind this procedure later in this chapter.

If the Dalton Company uses the periodic inventory system, it gives no consideration to the timing of the individual sales. It calculates the ending inventory of $1,110 and the cost of goods sold of $1,610 as we show in Exhibit 7-9. The ending inventory includes

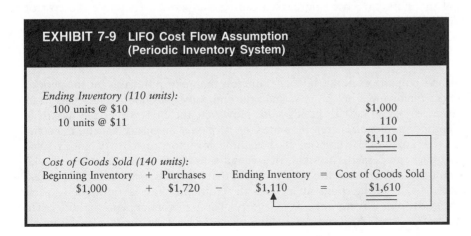

EXHIBIT 7-9   LIFO Cost Flow Assumption (Periodic Inventory System)

Ending Inventory (110 units):
100 units @ $10	$1,000
10 units @ $11	110
	$1,110

Cost of Goods Sold (140 units):

Beginning Inventory	+	Purchases	−	Ending Inventory	=	Cost of Goods Sold
$1,000	+	$1,720	−	$1,110	=	$1,610

the earliest costs, which consist of the beginning inventory and the cost of the 10 units from the first purchase on April 10. The company computes the cost of goods sold by subtracting the ending inventory from the cost of goods available for sale, and implicitly includes the cost of the 70 units purchased on April 20 ($840) and the cost of 70 units purchased on April 10 ($770).

If the Dalton Company uses the perpetual inventory system (for costs as well as physical quantities), it calculates the cost of goods sold for each sale at the cost(s) of the most recent purchase(s). The $1,580 cost of goods sold for 140 units includes the sale of 90 units on April 18 and 50 units on April 27, as we show in Exhibit 7-10. For the April 18 sale, 80 of the 90 units have a cost of $11 each from the April 10 purchase and 10 units have a cost of $10 each from the beginning inventory. The 50 units on April 27 have a cost of $12 from the April 20 purchase. The company computes the $1,140 ending inventory by deducting the $1,580 cost of goods sold from the $2,720 cost of goods available for sale. It consists of 110 units and includes the earliest costs: the cost of the 90 units left from the beginning inventory and the remaining 20 units from the April 20 purchase.

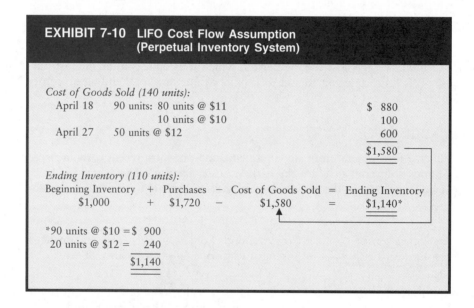

EXHIBIT 7-10   **LIFO Cost Flow Assumption (Perpetual Inventory System)**

Cost of Goods Sold (140 units):

April 18	90 units:	80 units @ $11	$ 880
		10 units @ $10	100
April 27	50 units @ $12		600
			$1,580

Ending Inventory (110 units):

Beginning Inventory	+	Purchases	−	Cost of Goods Sold	=	Ending Inventory
$1,000	+	$1,720	−	$1,580	=	$1,140*

*90 units @ $10 = $ 900
20 units @ $12 =   240
               $1,140

Note that the cost of goods sold and the ending inventory are not the same for the LIFO perpetual method and the LIFO periodic method due to differing assumptions about the timing of the sales. Under the periodic method, the whole accounting period (a month in this example) is treated as a single time period, and all the sales are assumed to take place after all the units have been purchased during the period. Therefore the cost of goods sold includes the costs of the *most recent purchases of the period.* Under the perpetual method, each event is recorded as it occurs. Therefore, the cost of goods sold is calculated when each sale is made and includes the costs of the *most recent purchase(s) at that time.*

In the Dalton Company example, unit sales are less than unit purchases for the period. Therefore, under the *periodic* inventory system, the company does *not* include costs from the beginning inventory in cost of goods sold. However, the first sale in the month is larger than the first purchase. Therefore, under the *perpetual* inventory system, the company includes the costs of 10 units of its beginning inventory in cost of goods sold. Furthermore, under the perpetual system, the second sale of 50 units has a cost of $12 per unit from the second purchase, leaving 20 units of that purchase in inventory. However, under the periodic system, the company includes the entire purchase of units at $12 each in its cost of goods sold, leaving none in inventory. These factors explain the difference of $30 in the cost of goods sold and the ending inventory between the two methods.

In each case the LIFO ending inventory of the Dalton Company consists of two layers. Each period in which the number of units in inventory *increases*, the company adds a layer of costs to its LIFO inventory. When the number of units in inventory *decreases*, the company removes costs from its beginning inventory of the period in the reverse order in which it added them—that is, it removes the most recent layers first and includes them in cost of goods sold.

Comparison of Inventory Cost Flow Assumptions

We summarize the cost of goods sold and the inventory amounts for the Dalton Company calculated in the preceding examples in Exhibit 7-11. However, we exclude the specific identification method because, as we discussed previously, the results are dependent on the assumptions regarding the particular units selected for sale.

EXHIBIT 7-11 Effects of Inventory Cost Flow Assumptions			
Cost Flow Assumption and Method	Cost of Goods Available for Sale	Cost of Goods Sold	Ending Inventory
FIFO, periodic	$2,720	$1,440	$1,280
FIFO, perpetual	2,720	1,440	1,280
Weighted average, periodic	2,720	1,523	1,197
Moving average, perpetual	2,720	1,496	1,224
LIFO, periodic	2,720	1,610	1,110
LIFO, perpetual	2,720	1,580	1,140

In this example, costs rose throughout the period. As a result, the FIFO method produces the lowest cost of goods sold because it includes the oldest and lowest costs. Since the cost of goods sold is lowest, the gross profit (and income) is highest. Correspondingly, the ending inventory using FIFO has the highest cost because it includes the most recent and highest costs. In contrast, the LIFO method produces the highest cost of goods sold and the lowest gross profit (and income) because it includes the most recent and highest costs. The LIFO ending inventory is lowest because it includes the earliest and lowest costs. The average cost amounts are between the FIFO and LIFO extremes because the ending inventory and the cost of goods sold include an average of both the lower and higher costs of the period. Note that this example is simplified because we assumed that the beginning inventory was $10 per unit for FIFO, average, and LIFO. When an inventory cost flow assumption is used in consecutive periods, the beginning inventory in each period is different under the alternative cost flow assumptions.

The Dalton Company was experiencing rising costs, but if costs were falling consistently, the opposite relationships would occur. The use of LIFO would produce a higher ending inventory, a lower cost of goods sold, and a higher gross profit (and income) than FIFO. When costs fluctuate, no general relationships can be described. The differences between the amounts under the periodic and the perpetual inventory systems for each cost flow assumption result from the different calculations and not from any differences in the logic underlying the cost flow assumptions.

CONCEPTUAL EVALUATION OF INVENTORY COST FLOW ASSUMPTIONS

Many arguments can be made in favor of each of the alternative cost flow assumptions. These arguments focus on a comparison of LIFO and FIFO, although the average cost method may be considered as similar to FIFO for this discussion. Sometimes, The FIFO

6 Explain the conceptual issues regarding alternative inventory cost flow assumptions.

and average cost methods are referred to as non-LIFO methods. Initially, our discussion assumes that inventory costs are rising. The advantages of LIFO are that it provides a better measure of income in times of rising costs, and it results in the payment of less income taxes. The disadvantages of LIFO are the impact of the liquidation of LIFO layers, the possibility of income manipulation, the inventory valuation on the balance sheet, and the lack of comparability between companies using LIFO. There also are several issues involved in management's selection of a method. We discuss and evaluate each of these issues in the following sections. In addition, we discuss specific arguments that relate solely to the average cost method. We discussed the arguments for and against the specific identification method earlier in the chapter.

Income Measurement

Income measurement adjusted for changing prices is discussed in Appendix E.

For financial reporting, the basic criterion a company uses to select a cost flow assumption is to achieve a "proper determination of income through the process of matching appropriate costs and revenues."[5] **There is no requirement that the assumed flow of costs be related to the actual physical flow of goods.** Most companies use a FIFO method for the physical management of inventory so as to reduce the likelihood of obsolescence. Such companies may use any of the alternative cost flow assumptions in their financial statements.

But what are "appropriate" costs? Unfortunately there is no simple answer as to whether income is better measured under LIFO or FIFO. Both methods match historical costs with revenues, but **the major argument in favor of LIFO is that it matches the most recent costs with revenue.** The most recent costs are closer to replacement costs. Therefore LIFO excludes from a company's income some (but not all) of the holding gains, so that the income reflects the earnings after capital has been maintained and is a better measure of the increase in wealth of the company. **A holding gain (or inventory profit) is the difference between the historical cost and the replacement cost of units sold.** In contrast, FIFO matches the earliest costs with revenue and *includes* all the holding gains in income.

In the Dalton Company example, when the company sells a unit on April 27 for $30, if the unit cost of the goods sold is $10 (FIFO) and the most recent acquisition cost was $12 per unit, the gross profit of $20 per unit (the selling price of $30 minus the cost of $10) includes a holding gain of $2 per unit (the most recent cost to replace the inventory of $12 less the cost of $10). The LIFO method records in cost of goods sold the cost of $12 per unit, resulting in a gross profit of $18 per unit, thereby *excluding* the holding gain of $2 from income. We illustrate these two alternatives in Exhibit 7-12. To continue this example, suppose that the company started with $10 cash, which it used to purchase a unit of inventory. When that unit is sold for $30, the profit (under FIFO) is recognized as $20. If the $20 income is distributed as a dividend, the company is left with $10 cash, which is not enough to purchase a unit of inventory at its higher price of $12. Thus the income of $20 includes a holding gain of $2, which is not real income since it cannot be distributed to the owners without leaving the company worse off in terms of its ability to maintain the same level of inventory.

In this example, the LIFO method excluded all the holding gains. However, in other situations, it may not exclude them all. Under LIFO the Dalton Company included units at $11 per unit in the cost of goods sold (for the periodic method), whereas the most recent purchase price was $12 per unit. Therefore the gross profit included holding gains of $1 on each of these units. We also illustrate this alternative in Exhibit 7-12.

Also note that if the replacement cost of the inventory was $13 at the end of the month, the Dalton Company has not achieved the matching of current costs with revenue, even on the $12 units, and would include even more holding gains in income. In summary, it can be seen that "matching appropriate costs and revenues" is interpreted very widely. FIFO, LIFO, average cost, and specific identification all match historical cost with revenue, and are generally accepted accounting principles.

---

5. *Accounting Research and Terminology Bulletins, Final Edition, op. cit.*

EXHIBIT 7-12   Alternative Cost Flow Assumptions and Holding Gains (per Unit)

	FIFO	LIFO ($12)	LIFO ($11)
Revenue	$30	$30	$30
Cost of goods sold	(10)	(12)	(11)
Gross profit	$20	$18	$19
Holding gains (excluded from income)		2	1
		$20	$20

Income Tax Effects

As we have seen, LIFO produces the highest cost of goods sold and the lowest income under conditions of rising costs. Although it might be thought that management would consider it undesirable to report low *accounting* income, it must be remembered that lower *taxable* income results in payment of lower income taxes. For example, three long-time LIFO users—Exxon, General Motors, and General Electric—have together saved more than $2 billion in taxes compared to what they would have paid using FIFO.

The use of LIFO for the computation of federal income taxes presents a special situation. The Internal Revenue Code permits a company to use LIFO for income tax purposes only if it also uses LIFO in its financial statements. This requirement is known as the **LIFO conformity rule.** The management of a company might prefer to report a higher income for accounting purposes when costs are rising by using FIFO even though, as discussed before, its income is overstated because it includes holding gains. The LIFO conformity rule prevents management from having "the best of both worlds" by using FIFO for financial reporting and LIFO for income taxes, in contrast to many situations in which a company can use different methods (e.g., when it uses straight-line depreciation for financial reporting and accelerated depreciation for income tax reporting). Management must decide whether it is willing to report a lower accounting income in order to achieve the advantages of the real economic benefits of reduced cash payments for income taxes.

Because of rulings by the Internal Revenue Service that allow a company using LIFO more latitude in the supplementary reporting of cost of goods sold and income on a FIFO basis, the Securities and Exchange Commission issued a ruling indicating how such disclosures should be made.[6] Also, since there was a lack of authoritative literature on the specifics of applying LIFO in complex situations, the tendency was to follow the income tax rules, which were much more specific. Since this did not always lead to appropriate financial reporting, the AICPA published an *Issues Paper* that was endorsed by the SEC, thereby giving it authoritative status.[7] The specific topics included in these two publications are beyond the scope of this book.

The Tax Reform Act of 1986 established "uniform capitalization rules" that require a company to include in inventory certain costs that previously it expensed as incurred for tax purposes. These costs include such items as purchasing, warehousing, and distribution costs, including related officer salaries and administrative costs. Because a cost must be capitalized for income tax purposes does not mean that capitalizing it for financial reporting is preferable, or even appropriate. Each situation must be analyzed

---

6. "Codification of Financial Reporting Policies," *SEC Accounting Rules* (Chicago: Commerce Clearing House, August 2001), sec. 205.

7. "Identification and Discussion of Certain Financial Accounting and Reporting Issues Concerning LIFO Inventories," *Issues Paper* (New York: AICPA, 1984), and "LIFO Inventory Accounting Practices for Financial Statement Purposes," *Staff Accounting Bulletin 58* (Washington, D.C.: SEC, 1985).

based on the particular circumstances. The likely result in many situations is that inventory cost is different between financial reporting and income tax reporting.

Liquidation of LIFO Layers

A company using the LIFO method may liquidate inventory during a period. This occurs when the number of units in ending inventory is less than the number in beginning inventory because unit sales have exceeded units acquired during the period. Therefore, some of the beginning inventory costs are included in cost of goods sold. In other words, the layers of LIFO inventory costs added in previous periods are removed in reverse order; the last costs added are the first expensed. Assuming rising costs, these units have lower costs attached to them; thus cost of goods sold is lower and gross profit (and income) is higher than if the liquidation did not occur. This increased amount of gross profit is referred to as a **LIFO liquidation profit.**

Many companies adopted LIFO in 1939 when the method was first allowed to be used by all companies for income tax purposes, and also in the higher inflation period between 1975 and 1985. Therefore, a company's LIFO liquidation profit may be significant because it includes some very old costs in cost of goods sold. An extreme example of LIFO liquidation profits arises if a company liquidates its inventory down to the base (the beginning inventory in the year it adopted LIFO). In summary, liquidations bring units with a cost from previous years into cost of goods sold and produce an unrealistically high gross profit (and income) figure.

To illustrate the concept of a LIFO liquidation profit, assume that a company was formed in 2000. Its 2004 beginning inventory of $644,000 is made up of four layers as follows:

2000:	10,000 units at $20 per unit =	$200,000
2001:	6,000 units at $22 per unit =	132,000
2002:	8,000 units at $24 per unit =	192,000
2003:	4,000 units at $30 per unit =	120,000
Inventory, January 1, 2004		$644,000

In 2004 the company purchases (or manufactures) 50,000 units at $35 per unit but sells 60,000 units. The company has experienced an inventory liquidation of 10,000 units. It includes these 10,000 units in cost of goods sold at the most recent beginning inventory costs; that is, the most recently added layers. Therefore, the company's cost of goods sold for 2004 includes costs from 2004, 2003, and 2002, as follows:

50,000 units at $35 per unit =	$1,750,000	(2004 costs)
4,000 units at $30 per unit =	120,000	(2003 costs)
6,000 units at $24 per unit =	144,000	(2002 costs)
60,000		$2,014,000	

If, instead, the company had purchased (or produced) 60,000 units at $35 each (thus avoiding the LIFO liquidation), the company would have had a cost of goods sold in 2004 of $2,100,000 (60,000 units $\times$ $35 per unit) consisting entirely of 2004 costs. The difference of $86,000 ($2,100,000 − $2,014,000) is the LIFO liquidation profit (before income taxes). If we assume an income tax rate of 30%, the effect of the LIFO liquidation is to increase gross profit by $86,000, income tax expense by $25,800 ($86,000 $\times$ 30%), and net income by $60,200 ($86,000 $\times$ 70%). Note that the company's income is higher (because cost of goods sold includes older and lower costs) even though there is **no economic substance to the higher income, and the company pays the additional income taxes** (because of the higher taxable income reported under the LIFO conformity rule). A company that reports to the SEC is required to disclose the amount of its LIFO liquidation profit so that users of the financial statements may obtain a better understanding of the profit earned by the company. For example, General Electric reported LIFO liquidation profits of $8 million, $6 million, and $4 million in 2001, 2000, and 1999, respectively.

Income Manipulation

As we have seen, a company's liquidation of inventory under LIFO, whether intentional or not, results in higher income (assuming rising costs). Such a liquidation may be caused by economic factors beyond the control of the company, such as a strike or a scarcity of raw materials, or as a result of a management decision such as the adoption of a "just-in-time" inventory system, which results in a permanent reduction in the size of the inventory. Also a liquidation may be deliberately created by delaying purchases. Intentional liquidation to artificially increase income is a significant concern. If a company is facing a period of lower profits, management can increase profits intentionally by liquidating inventory. This can be achieved by delaying purchases until after the end of the fiscal year.

Also a company may influence (manipulate) its income by increasing its purchases. To illustrate, refer back to the Dalton Company periodic LIFO example and assume that the company purchased an additional 40 units on April 29 at $12 per unit. Total purchases then would be $2,200 ($1,720 + $480). The ending inventory would then consist of 150 units (110 + 40) and have a cost of $1,550 (100 units at $10 each from the beginning inventory + 50 units at $11 each from the April 10 purchase). The cost of goods sold would be computed as follows:

$$\text{Beginning Inventory} + \text{Purchases} - \text{Ending Inventory} = \text{Cost of Goods Sold}$$
$$\$1,000 \quad + \quad \$2,200 \quad - \quad \$1,550 \quad = \quad \underline{\$1,650}$$

Thus purchasing additional units has increased cost of goods sold by $40 ($1,650 − $1,610) even though unit sales remain unchanged. **It is inconsistent with the revenue recognition principle for income to be affected by the purchasing activities of a company,** but it is an inevitable result of the LIFO method. The FIFO and average cost methods do not produce unusual results when inventory liquidation occurs, nor are they as susceptible to profit manipulation by management.

Management should make decisions about purchasing or manufacturing inventory on the basis of economic and operational factors. The use of LIFO, however, allows management to influence the company's income through the acceleration of, or delay in, acquiring inventory.

Inventory Valuation

The LIFO method produces a lower ending (and beginning) inventory value on a company's balance sheet (again assuming rising costs) because the oldest costs remain in this inventory. The recorded amount of this inventory often bears little or no relationship to the costs of the current period or to the costs that will be incurred to replace the inventory, and therefore is *not relevant*. This low valuation affects the computation and evaluation of current assets, working capital, total assets, and any financial ratios that include inventory, thereby *reducing comparability* between companies using LIFO and those using FIFO. Furthermore, comparability between two or more companies using LIFO is impaired, because each company's inventory valuation depends on the year in which it adopted LIFO. For example, if companies in the same industry adopted LIFO in different years, each company's LIFO base will include costs of different years. (The year of adoption is *not* a required disclosure.) In addition, if the companies increase their inventories by different amounts in subsequent years, the additional LIFO layers were added at different costs. Therefore, a user evaluating a company that uses LIFO should always convert the inventory to nonLIFO (FIFO or average) amounts. As we illustrate later, a company that uses LIFO and files with the SEC must disclose the nonLIFO value of its inventory.

The FIFO method produces a higher ending inventory value on the balance sheet (assuming rising costs) because it includes the most recent costs. This value tends to approximate the costs that will be incurred to replace the inventory, but how closely depends on when the purchases included in the ending inventory were made and how fast costs are rising. Therefore, the FIFO inventory value is more *relevant*.

Average Cost

The average cost method is based on the assumption that during the period a company commingles all the costs so that those included in cost of goods sold cannot be distinguished from those remaining in inventory. Thus the method produces the same cost in a particular period for identical units that have the same utility. The weighted average method treats the accounting period as a single time period and produces the same unit cost for cost of goods sold and ending inventory. The general principle underlying the moving average method is the same, except that the period used is the time between the respective purchases. The same unit cost is used for the sales made in that time period and for the inventory at the end of that period. However, over the total accounting period, the unit costs used for the cost of goods sold vary as each purchase is made, and the unit cost for the ending inventory is the average cost calculated after the last purchase of the period.

The disadvantage of the average cost method is that the average is continually affected by the costs incurred in previous periods. Although the influence from these past periods becomes minimal as time passes, it still means that the average cost does not reflect the actual costs paid, either for the units sold or for those held in inventory in the current period.

Management's Selection of an Inventory Cost Flow Assumption

The previous discussion has shown that there are many financial accounting and tax issues involved in the selection of an inventory cost flow assumption. In most cases, however, the decision should focus on the expectation of future cost changes.

If the management of a company expects that costs will *rise* for several years into the future, it should select LIFO because, as we discussed earlier, LIFO is a better measure of income. Also the LIFO conformity rule will allow the use of LIFO for income tax reporting and the company will save income taxes. Therefore the financial reporting rules and the income tax rules are consistent. However, most companies probably consider the tax savings to be more important than the financial reporting issues!

The additional cash that results from the tax savings is reduced because the LIFO method is more costly to use than the FIFO method. These costs result from the additional costs of record keeping and financial statement preparation, such as keeping track of the LIFO layers for each type of inventory and the requirements imposed by the Internal Revenue Service. For a small company these additional costs may be greater than the income tax savings that would result from the adoption of LIFO. For larger companies, however, the income tax savings are likely to exceed the additional costs (assuming rising prices), as is evidenced by the number of companies that use LIFO (see Exhibit 7-18).

Alternatively, if the expectation is that costs will *fall* for several years, the decision is not as simple. For financial reporting purposes it can be argued that LIFO is still preferable because the most recent (and lowest) costs should be included in cost of goods sold because the inventory can be replaced at those lower costs. However, for income tax purposes, the use of FIFO is preferable because the company pays less income taxes. Although a company could use LIFO internally and FIFO for income taxes, it is unlikely to do so because of the additional record keeping costs it would incur. Therefore, if a company expects falling costs, it will use FIFO. Unfortunately, this means that income tax considerations are determining the accounting principle used for financial reporting.

Arguments are made that a company should not adopt LIFO even when its costs are expected to rise because of the lower income that will result and a possible perception that the company is less successful and that its stock price will be lower. However, efficient capital markets research, discussed in Chapter 1, has indicated that stock market prices are *not* affected by the selection of an inventory cost flow assumption. That is, the stock market compensates for the lower reported income under LIFO.

In most situations the FIFO and weighted average *cost* flow assumptions approximate the *physical* flow of the items in inventory, whereas LIFO does not. For example, a retail store will try to impose a FIFO physical flow on its customers by selling the oldest items first, but the customers may impose more of an average flow on the store by the way they select items from the shelves. However, accounting principles do *not* require that the selected cost flow method approximate the physical flow of goods but only that the method be systematic, based on cost, and match costs and revenues appropriately, as we discussed earlier. Therefore a company's selection of a particular cost flow assumption should *not* depend on the perceived physical flow of goods.

Management also may be reluctant to adopt LIFO if the company pays them bonuses on the basis of accounting income. This tends to discourage management from using LIFO in periods of rising costs, since the lower reported income produces lower bonuses. In addition, a higher income results in higher earnings per share and a higher rate of return, factors that are considered important by many users of financial statements. Remember, however, that using a method other than LIFO in periods of rising costs causes the company to pay additional taxes.

There are several additional miscellaneous disadvantages of LIFO that a company should consider before adopting LIFO. First, the adoption of LIFO could increase its income taxes initially because the income tax rules require that the opening inventory in the year that LIFO is adopted must be stated at cost. Therefore, if the inventory previously had been written down to a market value lower than cost for income tax purposes (as we discuss in Chapter 8), it would be necessary to write the inventory back up and pay additional taxes on that amount. Second, the use of LIFO might also cause a company to be limited in its *financial flexibility*, because of covenants included in its bond indentures or other borrowing agreements. For example, the company might be required to maintain a certain current ratio or debt-to-equity ratio. Finally, the use of LIFO might cause a company to be less concerned about controlling the level of its inventories because of the company's lower *apparent* investment in those inventories.

Many manufacturing companies that expect falling costs use the average cost flow assumption in their financial statements. A company uses this method because (1) it operates a standard cost system (discussed in a cost accounting book) for its budgeting and control, and (2) it is unlikely to result in significantly more income taxes than FIFO.

DOLLAR-VALUE LIFO

The dollar-value LIFO method follows the same cost flow assumption as the LIFO method, but it overcomes three difficulties involved in the application of the simple LIFO approach.

7 Understand dollar-value LIFO.

First, the LIFO method requires a company to keep numerous detailed records. As with other methods, the company must record the physical quantities of each item in its inventory from either a physical count or the perpetual inventory records. Then, in addition, it must apply unit costs from the years since it adopted LIFO, in the LIFO order. Finally it must correctly account for the liquidations in LIFO inventory that occurred over the years.

Second, fluctuations in the physical quantities of similar inventory items may occur. For example, the quantity of one inventory item may significantly decline during a period causing a partial liquidation of its LIFO layers, whereas the quantity of a very similar inventory item may increase. As these fluctuations occur over time, the LIFO layers for each individual item would be reduced, thereby removing many of the advantages of LIFO.

Third, as technological changes take place, inventory made with one material is replaced by inventory made with substitute materials, or an outdated design is replaced by a newer design. Strict application of the LIFO method would require a company to start a new LIFO base for the new inventory item, and as the old item is phased out to reduce its inventory to zero. This would eliminate the advantages of LIFO built up in previous periods. With the rate of technological change in many industries, the advantages of LIFO would be lost.

Dollar-value LIFO overcomes part of the first problem by the use of *current costs* and *cost indexes*, and the second and third problems by the use of *inventory pools*. Under the dollar-value LIFO method, a company may group the inventory into pools that are similar as to types of material or use. Some companies may consider their entire inventory as one pool, but usually several pools are used. We discuss cost indexes and inventory pools in more detail later in the chapter.

The general principle underlying the dollar-value LIFO method is that a company initially values its ending inventory at current cost and "rolls back" this cost to the cost at the beginning of the base year (the year in which it adopted LIFO) to *eliminate the change in costs* from the physical quantity of the ending inventory. A comparison of the year's beginning and ending inventory at base-year costs indicates whether there has been a real increase (or decrease) in the physical quantity of the inventory. The company "rolls forward" the increase (or decrease) to the appropriate current cost level, and adds this layer of current cost (or subtracts it from) the beginning inventory to determine its ending inventory. The application of the dollar-value LIFO method requires the steps we show in Exhibit 7-13.

EXHIBIT 7-13   Dollar-Value LIFO Calculation Steps

1. Value the total ending inventory at current-year costs.
2. Convert (roll back) the ending inventory cost to base-year costs by applying the base-year conversion index:

$$\text{Ending Inventory at Base-Year Costs} = \text{Ending Inventory at Current-Year Costs} \times \frac{\text{Base-Year Cost Index}}{\text{Current Cost Index}}$$

3. Compute the change in the inventory level (physical quantity) for the year at base-year costs by comparing the ending inventory at base-year costs with the beginning inventory at base-year costs.
4. a. If there is an increase in the inventory level at base-year costs, there has been a real *increase* in the physical quantity of the inventory over the year. Convert (roll forward) this increase to current-year costs by applying the current-year conversion index:

$$\text{Layer Increase at Current-Year Costs} = \text{Increase at Base-Year Costs} \times \frac{\text{Current Cost Index}}{\text{Base-Year Cost Index}}$$

   The ending inventory cost is the dollar-value LIFO inventory cost at the beginning of the year *plus* the layer increase at current-year costs.

   b. If there is a decrease in the inventory level at base-year costs, there has been a real *decrease* in the physical quantity of the inventory over the period. This decrease reduces the inventory on a LIFO layer basis, and therefore it must be converted to the costs of the most recently added layer or layers:

$$\frac{\text{Decrease at Costs of}}{\text{Most Recently Added Layer}} = \text{Decrease at Base-Year Costs} \times \frac{\text{Cost Index of Most Recently Added Layer}}{\text{Base-Year Cost Index}}$$

   The ending inventory cost is the dollar-value LIFO cost at the beginning of the year *minus* the decrease at the costs of the most recently added layer. Note that the decrease may eliminate more than one layer of LIFO inventory, and therefore the decrease at base-year costs has to be converted to the costs of as many layers as is necessary to eliminate the total decrease.

It is necessary to convert the inventory to base-year costs in order to isolate the *quantity* increase from the *cost* increase. To illustrate that a comparison of base-year *costs* reflects changes in *quantity*, consider the following two simplified examples. First, assume a company has a beginning inventory of 100 units at $20 each, or $2,000, when it adopts dollar-value LIFO. At the end of the year, it has an ending inventory of 100 units at a current cost of $21 each, or $2,100. It might appear from a simple comparison of the two costs ($2,100 versus $2,000) that the *physical quantity* of the inventory has increased. However, this is not the case. The quantity has remained unchanged, and the cost change (from $20 to $21 per unit, or an increase of 5%) has accounted for the entire change in the cost of the inventory. Reducing the inventory of $2,100 to the base-year costs gives an amount of $2,000 [$2,100 × (100 ÷ 105) = $2,000]. Since the beginning and ending inventory amounts are $2,000 when they are both measured in terms of the same costs (base year), there has been no increase in quantity. The increase from $2,000 to $2,100 has resulted solely from the increase in costs.

In the second example, we can isolate the quantity increase from the cost increase without knowing the number and costs of the units. To illustrate, assume a company has a beginning inventory of $1,000 and a cost index (discussed later) of 100 when it adopted dollar-value LIFO. Assume further that the ending inventory at current cost is $1,430 and costs have increased 10%; that is, the cost index is 110 (100 × 1.10 = 110). The quantity increase in the inventory is not 43% ($1,430 ÷ $1,000 = 1.43). Rather, the ending inventory at base-year costs is $1,300 [$1,430 × (100 ÷ 110) = $1,300], and therefore inventory has increased in quantity by 30% ($1,300 ÷ $1,000 = 1.30). The total increase of 43% in the value of the inventory is made up of an increase in the quantity of 30% and a cost increase of 10% (1.30 × 1.10 = 1.43). To complete the example, the increase in inventory of $300 at base-year costs is converted to ending costs of $330 [$300 × (110 ÷ 100)], and therefore the LIFO ending inventory is valued at $1,330 ($1,000 + $330).

We illustrate the application of the four steps discussed in Exhibit 7-13 for the Wagner Company. The basic data are in Exhibit 7-14. The Wagner Company adopted LIFO at the beginning of 2003 and has taken an ending inventory at the *current costs* for each year as indicated. In addition, the company has experienced yearly changes in the level of its costs as indicated by its cost index for each year (we discuss the determination of a cost index later).

EXHIBIT 7-14 **Data for Wagner Company**

Date	Ending Inventory at Current Costs	Cost Index
January 1, 2003	$10,000	100
December 31, 2003	12,100	110
December 31, 2004	13,125	125
December 31, 2005	16,800	140
December 31, 2006	12,360	120

We show the calculation of the dollar-value LIFO ending inventory in Exhibit 7-15. The base year is 2003 and therefore the beginning inventory needs no adjustment. The 2003 ending inventory at the current cost of $12,100 is reduced to $11,000 at base-year costs. Therefore the real (quantity) increase in inventory is $1,000 ($11,000 − $10,000 at base-year costs), which is $1,100 [$1,000 × (110 ÷ 100)] in 2003 costs. The ending LIFO inventory cost for 2003 is $11,100, which is made up of two layers, the base layer of $10,000 plus the layer added in 2003 of $1,100.

In 2004 the company reduces its ending inventory of $13,125 at the current cost to $10,500 at base-year costs. This indicates a real (quantity) *decrease* in inventory of $500 (the $10,500 2004 ending inventory less the $11,000 2003 ending inventory, *both* at base-year costs). The company subtracts the decrease from the most recently added layer, which is the layer added in 2003. Therefore it converts the decrease of $500 in base-year costs to 2003 costs and *not* to 2004 costs. Consequently it applies the 110 cost index to the $500 decrease, resulting in a decrease of $550 in terms of 2003 costs and an ending inventory of $10,550.

In 2005 the company has an increase in inventory at base-year costs, and therefore adds another layer, so that its ending LIFO inventory of $12,650 consists of three layers.

In 2006 the company has a decrease in its cost index. It calculates the ending inventory at base-year costs in exactly the same manner as we discussed previously. In this case the $10,300 ending inventory at base-year costs is $1,700 lower than the $12,000

EXHIBIT 7-15   Dollar-Value LIFO Inventory Calculations

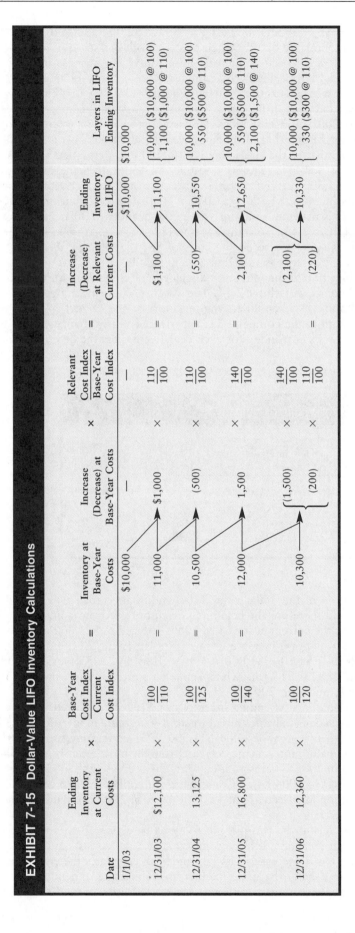

beginning inventory at base-year costs. This completely eliminates the layer of $1,500 (at base-year costs) added in 2005, and so the company must go back into the 2003 layer to account for the remaining decrease of $200 at base-year costs (no layer was added in 2004). The ending LIFO inventory of $10,330 consists of the base inventory plus the remainder of the layer added in 2003.

Determination of Cost Index

The preceding discussion refers to the use of a cost index rather than a price index. A **cost index** refers to an internally generated index that is specific to a company's particular inventory, whereas a **price index** is a more general index prepared by an external organization, such as a government or trade association. Although the concepts underlying the two are identical, we use the term *cost index* because IRS regulations require that in most situations a company use an internally developed index specific to the company's particular operations. However, the IRS has simplified the LIFO method by allowing the use of published price indexes in certain situations.

If a company uses an internally developed cost index, it must compute an index based on the particular cost per unit it has experienced in the current year as compared to the base year. Typically, the company prepares the index using a sample of its total inventory. Two methods to compute the cost index are used in practice, the double-extension method and the link-chain method.

Under the **double-extension** method, a sample of the ending inventory is priced at current-year costs and at base-year costs, and the cost index is computed as follows:

$$\text{Cost Index} = \frac{\text{Sample of Ending Inventory at Current-Year Costs}}{\text{Sample of Ending Inventory at Base-Year Costs}} \times 100$$

This is known as the double-extension method because the ending inventory is priced and "extended" twice—once at current costs and once at base-year costs. The double-extension method is appropriate for companies that have little change in the characteristics of their inventory items. When changes are frequent, determination of base-year costs for new items is difficult. For example, if a company adopted LIFO in 1990 and develops a new product in 2004, the double-extension method would require the computation of the cost in 1990 of the new product. Since the product, perhaps including the technology, did not exist in 1990, the difficulties of such a calculation are obvious. In such situations the link-chain method should be used.

Under the **link-chain** method, a company prices a sample of the ending inventory at current costs for the current year and for the previous year, and therefore the method avoids the problems of the double-extension method we just discussed. The ratio of the current-year current cost to the previous-year current cost is used to compute a cost index for the *year*. This index is multiplied by the cost index carried forward from the previous year to determine the current year cumulative index as follows:

$$\text{Cost Index} = \frac{\substack{\text{Sample of Ending Inventory} \\ \text{at Current-Year Costs}}}{\substack{\text{Sample of Ending Inventory} \\ \text{at Previous-Year Costs}}} \times \substack{\text{Previous-Year} \\ \text{Cost Index}}$$

Inventory Pools

As we discussed earlier in the chapter, a company may use inventory pools in conjunction with dollar-value LIFO. The purpose of the pools is to maintain the benefits from using LIFO when fluctuations in the physical quantities of similar inventory items occur and when technological change takes place.

To illustrate the concept of an inventory pool, consider the Herrmann Soup Company, which adopts dollar-value LIFO on January 1, 2004 using a single pool. The pool includes three types of soup that the company manufactures, and we show the calculation

EXHIBIT 7-16 Herrmann Soup Company Inventory, January 1, 2004

Type	Quantity	Cost per Unit	Total Cost
Mushroom	10,000	$0.25	$2,500
Vegetable	8,000	0.20	1,600
Tomato	22,000	0.16	3,520
	40,000		$7,620

of the total cost of the beginning inventory in Exhibit 7-16. The company assigns a cost index of 100 to the beginning inventory and uses it as the base for the calculation of the cost index in subsequent years.

During 2004, the transactions we show in Exhibit 7-17 occurred. The company purchased a total of 150,000 cans of soup and sold 139,000 cans, leaving 51,000 cans in ending inventory, including the quantities of each type as illustrated. Using the double-extension method, the company calculates a cost index of 107 for the ending inventory by dividing the ending inventory at current-year costs by the ending inventory at base-year

EXHIBIT 7-17 Inventory Pools

Purchases and Sales During 2004

Type	Beginning Quantity	Quantity Purchased	Cost per Unit	Quantity Sold	Inventory Quantity December 31, 2004
Mushroom	10,000	60,000	$0.30	54,000	16,000
Vegetable	8,000	40,000	0.24	38,000	10,000
Tomato	22,000	50,000	0.14	47,000	25,000
	40,000	150,000		139,000	51,000

$$
\begin{aligned}
\text{Cost Index} &= \frac{\text{Ending Inventory at Current-Year Costs}}{\text{Ending Inventory at Base-Year Costs}} \times 100 \\
&= \frac{(16{,}000 \times \$0.30) + (10{,}000 \times \$0.24) + (25{,}000 \times \$0.14)}{(16{,}000 \times \$0.25) + (10{,}000 \times \$0.20) + (25{,}000 \times \$0.16)} \times 100 \\
&= \frac{\$10{,}700}{\$10{,}000} \times 100 \\
&= 107
\end{aligned}
$$

LIFO Cost of Ending Inventory

$$
\begin{aligned}
\text{Ending Inventory at Base-Year Costs} &= \frac{\text{Ending Inventory}}{\text{at Current-Year Costs}} \times \frac{\text{Base-Year Cost Index}}{\text{Current Cost Index}} \\
&= \$10{,}700 \times \frac{100}{107} \\
&= \$10{,}000
\end{aligned}
$$

$$
\begin{aligned}
\text{Increase in Inventory at Base-Year Costs} &= \frac{\text{Ending Inventory at}}{\text{Base-Year Costs}} - \frac{\text{Beginning Inventory}}{\text{at Base-Year Costs}} \\
&= \$10{,}000 - \$7{,}620 \\
&= \$2{,}380
\end{aligned}
$$

$$
\begin{aligned}
\text{Layer Increase at Current-Year Costs} &= \frac{\text{Increase at}}{\text{Base-Year Costs}} \times \frac{\text{Current Cost Index}}{\text{Base-Year Cost Index}} \\
&= \$2{,}380 \times \frac{107}{100} \\
&= \$2{,}547 \text{ (rounded)}
\end{aligned}
$$

$$
\begin{aligned}
\text{Total LIFO Ending Inventory Cost} &= \$7{,}620 + \$2{,}547 \\
&= \$10{,}167
\end{aligned}
$$

costs. Completing the remaining steps in the dollar-value LIFO calculations results in an ending inventory at LIFO cost of $10,167, as we show in Exhibit 7-17.

The preceding discussion assumed that the entire ending inventory cost was considered to be a single inventory "pool." When a company uses the dollar-value LIFO method, however, it may include the inventory in one or several "inventory pools." IRS regulations do not specify what types of items are to be included in the same pool, other than to say they should be "substantially similar." If a company uses more than one pool, it must compute a separate cost index for each (or a representative sample of the pool). In general, the more items included in a pool, the more likely it is that increases in some items will offset decreases in other items in the pool, thereby avoiding the liquidation of LIFO layers and the loss of the tax benefits of LIFO. In other words, a company would typically prefer to have the fewest number of pools allowed. In a surprising decision several years ago, **Stauffer Chemical Company** increased its LIFO pools from 8 to 280 which increased its income by $16.5 million (and resulted in additional taxes being paid).

Note also that the current cost used in the dollar-value LIFO calculations can be the cost of the first acquisitions in a year, the last acquisitions in a year, or the average cost of all acquisitions during the year as assumed in the preceding example. Once a choice is made, however, it must be applied consistently.

ADDITIONAL LIFO CONSIDERATIONS

Several other items concerning LIFO are important, including the LIFO valuation adjustment, interim statements using LIFO, a change to or from LIFO, and international accounting differences. We discuss these topics in the following sections.

8 Explain additional LIFO issues.

LIFO Valuation Adjustment

Frequently, a company uses LIFO for external financial reporting and income tax purposes but uses another method for internal management. In this case, the company makes a valuation adjustment to convert its internally reported ending inventory to LIFO for external reporting. This adjustment increases (decreases) cost of goods sold for the period and decreases (increases) the ending inventory by the amount of the *change* in the difference between the beginning and ending inventories under the two methods. However, the company does not adjust the inventory account directly. Instead, it uses a valuation adjustment. This adjustment has a variety of names including *Valuation Allowance* or (inappropriately) *LIFO Reserve*. Typically, this adjustment is not part of the company's formal accounting system, but the company does report it in its balance sheet or its notes because the SEC requires the disclosure. When this occurs, the *cumulative* balance of the adjustment is subtracted to report the ending inventory at LIFO. We illustrate this situation with the disclosures of **General Mills**, **Wal-Mart**, and **Marathon Oil** in Exhibit 7-19 later in the chapter.

You should also note that the *change* in the adjustment for the year is the difference between the LIFO cost of goods sold and what the cost of goods sold would have been under the method used internally (FIFO or average). A user can use this change to adjust the cost of goods sold of a company using LIFO to the other method, thereby improving the comparability of the two companies. The *total* amount of the adjustment is the cumulative difference between the two cost of goods sold amounts since LIFO was adopted. Multiplying this amount by the income tax rate gives the cumulative savings in income tax expense, while multiplying the amount by the after-tax rate gives the cumulative effect on income.

Interim Statements Using LIFO

If a company uses LIFO for annual reporting purposes, it must, of course, use LIFO for interim (i.e., quarterly) reporting purposes. **APB Opinion No. 28** states that if a company using LIFO has an inventory liquidation at an interim date that it expects to replace by

Interim financial reporting is discussed in Chapter 5.

the end of the annual period, it does not include the LIFO liquidation in its inventory, and its cost of sales includes the expected cost of replacement of the liquidated LIFO inventory.[8]

Consequently, when a company has an inventory liquidation at the end of a quarter, it must make a forecast of its year-end physical quantities. If the forecast indicates that the company will not liquidate any inventory at the end of the year, it removes the impact of the LIFO liquidation from the interim financial statements. The company decreases the inventory value and increases the cost of goods sold by the difference between the replacement cost and the LIFO cost of the number of units that it has liquidated. If the forecast indicates that the liquidation will still exist at the end of the year, the company includes the impact of the LIFO liquidation in its interim financial statements.

Change to or from LIFO

Accounting changes are discussed in Chapter 22.

Although the adoption of an inventory cost flow assumption is a long-term decision, a company may occasionally change its method. When the company changes *to* LIFO from another method, usually the effect on the results of prior periods is not determinable. Thus, as prescribed by **APB Opinion No. 20**, the company only discloses the effect of the change on the results of current operations. If the company can determine the effect on prior periods, then it reports a cumulative effect change. A company that changes to another method *from* LIFO retroactively restates the results of prior periods.[9]

International Accounting Differences

International accounting standards for inventories are generally the same as U.S. standards. Both require a company to base its inventory values on cost with FIFO, weighted average, and LIFO being allowed methods. However, international standards specify FIFO and weighted average as "benchmark" methods with LIFO as an allowable alternative because LIFO is generally not allowed in most countries. This prohibition may exist because LIFO is not permitted to be used for income tax purposes in those countries and, therefore, there has been no incentive to allow its use for financial reporting. It also may be prohibited because it is clearly inconsistent with any presumed physical flow of the inventory, an issue that has not been considered relevant for U.S. accounting principles.

DISCLOSURE OF INVENTORY VALUES AND METHODS

9 Understand inventory disclosures.

Exhibit 7-18 shows the relative use of alternative inventory methods by 600 surveyed companies and the proportion of the inventory cost determined by LIFO. The trend to the use of LIFO between 1973 and 1982 is clearly indicated, although the trend has reversed a little with the lower inflation since then. There were more than 600 responses to the methods used, since many companies apply more than one method, as indicated by the categories listed in the second section.

Exhibit 7-19 shows examples of the way in which four companies disclose the methods used for inventory. Companies are required to disclose the inventory method, or methods, used. **Marathon Oil** reports a single inventory figure in the balance sheet and shows the breakdown in the notes to the financial statements. It categorizes its inventory by functional groups, while **General Mills** categorizes its inventory by type and product. **Hewlett-Packard** uses FIFO, while General Mills uses LIFO in the United States and FIFO elsewhere. **Wal-Mart Stores** discloses the "LIFO reserve" directly in the balance sheet and discloses that it uses the retail method for some inventories. Marathon Oil discloses the difference between LIFO costs and current costs.

The retail method is discussed in Chapter 8.

---

8. "Interim Financial Reporting," *APB Opinion No. 28* (New York: AICPA, 1973), par. 14(b).
9. "Accounting Changes," *APB Opinion No. 20* (New York: AICPA, 1971), par. 26.

EXHIBIT 7-18 Inventory Cost Determination

| | Number of Companies | | | | | | | | | |
Methods	2000	1997	1994	1991	1988	1985	1982	1979	1976	1973
First-in, first-out (FIFO)	386	415	417	421	396	381	373	390	389	394
Last-in, first-out (LIFO)	283	326	351	361	379	402	407	374	331	150
Average cost	180	188	192	200	213	223	238	241	232	235
Other	38	32	42	50	50	48	53	56	50	57
	887	961	1,002	1,032	1,038	1,054	1,071	1,061	1,002	836
Use of LIFO										
All inventories	23	17	17	23	20	26	28	20	9	8
50% or more inventories	148	170	186	186	207	231	206	194	167	49
Less than 50% of inventories	82	99	98	95	90	83	88	94	84	78
Not determinable	30	40	50	57	62	62	85	66	71	25

Source: Accounting Trends and Techniques (New York: AICPA, 1974, 1977, 1980, 1983, 1986, 1989, 1992, 1995, 1998, and 2001).

APPENDIX: FOREIGN CURRENCY TRANSACTIONS INVOLVING INVENTORY

Many U.S. companies conduct inventory transactions with customers and suppliers in foreign countries. Sometimes the transaction is expressed in U.S. dollars. For example, most purchases and sales of crude oil are expressed in terms of the U.S. dollar. In these situations there is no accounting issue. For example, if a U.S. oil company purchases 10,000 barrels of crude oil from Saudi Arabia, the price is quoted in dollars and not in the equivalent amount of riyals. If the price is $20 per barrel, the company records a purchase of inventory and the related payment of $200,000 ($20 × 10,000).

10 Record foreign currency transactions involving inventory.

In many situations, however, the transaction is expressed in terms of the foreign currency. In these cases the company must record the transaction in U.S. dollars. Therefore, it converts the foreign currency amount into dollars at the exchange rate on the day of the transaction. Exhibit 7-20 shows selected foreign exchange rates. For example, suppose a U.S. company purchases inventory of electronic components from a Japanese company for 50 million yen (¥) when the exchange rate is $0.008 (1 yen = $0.008). If the U.S. company pays cash of $400,000 (¥50,000,000 × $0.008) on the same day to purchase yen to settle the transaction, the U.S. company records the transaction as follows:

Inventory (or Purchases)	400,000	
Cash		400,000

More often, transactions between companies in different countries involve credit terms, if only to allow time for processing the order and payment across international borders. In addition, currency exchange rates change continuously. As a result, the exchange rate is likely to have changed between the date the U.S. company records a purchase transaction and the date it makes the payment. On the date of the payment, the company records an exchange gain or loss to account for the difference between the purchase price of the inventory and the amount of the payment. **An exchange gain or loss is caused by a change in the exchange rate between the date of a purchase or sale on credit and the date of the payment or receipt.** More specifically, when exchange rates are stated in terms of $ per unit of foreign currency, exchange gains and losses occur for purchases or sales on credit as follows:

1. An exchange *gain* occurs when the exchange rate *declines* between the date a company records a *payable* from a purchase of inventory and the date of the cash *payment*.

EXHIBIT 7-19   Examples of Disclosure of Inventory Values and Methods

HEWLETT-PACKARD COMPANY

(millions)
Balance Sheet

Assets (in part)	October 31, 2001	October 31, 2000
Inventory	$5,204	$5,699

Notes to Consolidated Financial Statements (in part)

Note a Summary of Significant Accounting Policies (in part)

Inventory—Inventory is valued at the lower of cost or market with cost computed on a first-in, first-out basis.

GENERAL MILLS, INC.

Notes to Consolidated Financial Statements (in part)

Note 1 Summary of Significant Accounting Policies (in part)

C. *Inventories.* Inventories are valued at the lower of cost or market. We generally use LIFO as the preferred method of valuing inventory because we believe that it is a better match with current revenues. However, FIFO is used for most foreign operations, where LIFO is not recognized for income tax purposes and the operations often lack the staff to accurately handle LIFO complexities.

Note 6 Inventories
The components of inventories are as follows:

In Millions	May 27, 2001	May 28, 2000
Raw materials, work in process and supplies	$ 128.7	$ 119.1
Finished goods	326.0	322.3
Grain	94.0	101.5
Reserve for LIFO valuation method	(29.8)	(32.4)
Total inventories	$518.9	$510.5

At May 27, 2001 and May 28, 2000, respectively, inventories of $282.3 million and $298.7 million were valued at LIFO. LIFO accounting had negligible impact on 2001 and 2000 earnings, and increased 1999 earnings by $0.01 per diluted share. Results of operations were not materially affected by a liquidation of LIFO inventory. The difference between replacement cost and the stated LIFO inventory value is not materially different from the reserve for the LIFO valuation method.

WAL-MART STORES, INC. AND SUBSIDIARIES

Balance Sheets
(Amounts in millions)

	January 31,	
	2002	2001
Assets		
Current assets:		
Cash and cash equivalents	$ 2,161	$ 2,054
Receivables	2,000	1,768
Inventories:		
At replacement cost	22,749	21,644
Less LIFO reserve	135	202
Inventories at LIFO cost	22,614	21,442
Prepaid expenses and other	1,471	1,291
Total Current Assets	28,246	26,555

EXHIBIT 7-19   Examples of Disclosure of Inventory Values and Methods Continued

Notes to Consolidated Financial Statements (in part)

Note 1 Summary of significant accounting policies (in part)
Inventories—The company uses the retail last-in, first-out (LIFO) method for the Wal-Mart segment, cost LIFO for the SAM's Club segment, and other cost methods including the retail first-in, first-out (FIFO) and average cost methods for the International segment. Inventories are not recorded in excess of market value.

MARATHON OIL

Notes to Financial Statements (in part)

Note 19. Inventories

(In millions) December 31	2001	2000
Crude oil and natural gas liquids	$ 693	$ 701
Refined products and merchandise	1,143	1,069
Supplies and sundry items	87	97
Total (at cost)	1,923	1,867
Less inventory market valuation reserve	72	–
Net inventory carrying value	$1,851	$1,867

Inventories of crude oil and refined products are valued by the LIFO method. The LIFO method accounted for 92% of total inventory value at December 31, 2001 and 2000. Current acquisition costs were estimated to exceed the above inventory values at December 31, 2000, by approximately $500 million. Cost of revenues was reduced and income from operations was increased by $17 million in 2001 and $14 million in 2000 as a result of liquidations of LIFO inventories.

The inventory market valuation reserve reflects the extent that the recorded LIFO cost basis of crude oil and refined products inventories exceeds net realizable value. The reserve is decreased to reflect increases in market prices and inventory turnover and increased to reflect decreases in market prices. Changes in the inventory market valuation reserve result in noncash charges or credits to costs and expenses. During 2000, there were no charges or credits to costs and expenses.

Q U E S T I O N S

1. Why do you think Hewlett-Packard uses FIFO while General Mills uses LIFO?
2. Why does General Mills use LIFO in the U.S. and FIFO elsewhere?
3. If the inventory costs of General Mills are rising throughout the world, what is the effect on the financial statements of its use of FIFO?
4. How much would General Mills' cost of goods sold and inventory be if it used FIFO exclusively?
5. How much income tax did Wal-Mart save in fiscal 2001, assuming a 35% tax rate?
6. How would you explain the meaning of General Mills's disclosure about the impact of LIFO accounting to a shareholder?
7. Compute the inventory turnover ratio (cost of goods sold of $2,841.2 divided by average inventory as discussed in Chapter 5) for General Mills in 2001.
8. For Marathon Oil, what percentage of the inventory was calculated using the LIFO method?

EXHIBIT 7-20 Selected Foreign Exchange Rates

Currency (Country)	Price in U.S. dollars*
Pound (Britain)	$1.44
Dollar (Canada)	0.63
Euro	0.88
Shekel (Israel)	0.21
Yen (Japan)	0.008
Peso (Mexico)	0.11
Riyal (Saudi Arabia)	0.27
Franc (Switzerland)	0.60

*Note that the exchange rates are stated in terms of $ per unit of foreign currency. Exchange rates are often stated in terms of units of foreign currency per $.

Source: *The Wall Street Journal* (April 10, 2002).

2. An exchange *gain* occurs when the exchange rate *increases* between the date a company records a *receivable* from a sale of inventory and the date of the cash *receipt*.
3. An exchange *loss* occurs when the exchange rate *increases* between the date a company records a *payable* from a purchase of inventory and the date of the cash *payment*.
4. An exchange *loss* occurs when the exchange rate *declines* between the date a company records a *receivable* from a sale of inventory and the date of the cash *receipt*.

To illustrate an exchange gain that occurs when the exchange rate declines between the date a company records a credit purchase of inventory and the date of the cash payment, suppose that in the preceding example the U.S. company made the purchase of the electronic components on account. Because the company purchased the inventory when the exchange rate was $0.008, it records the acquisition as follows:

Inventory	400,000	
Accounts Payable		400,000

The Japanese company has a right to receive 50 million yen, and the U.S. company is obligated to pay sufficient dollars that will convert to 50 million yen on the date that the payment is made. Now assume that the exchange rate on the date of payment is $0.0078 (1 yen = $0.0078). In this case, since only $0.0078 now is needed to buy 1 yen, the U.S. company will have to pay fewer dollars to buy 50 million yen. That is, the yen has become less expensive. More specifically, the U.S. company has to pay only $390,000 (¥50,000,000 × $0.0078). Therefore, the company has incurred an exchange *gain* of $10,000 ($400,000 − $390,000), which it records at the time of payment for the inventory as follows:

Accounts Payable	400,000	
Cash		390,000
Exchange Gain		10,000

The exchange gain occurs because the U.S. company has to pay only $390,000 to settle its credit purchase originally recorded at $400,000. The gain can also be computed by multiplying the amount owed by the change in the exchange rate [¥50,000,000 × ($0.008 − $0.0078) = $10,000]. Remember that the Japanese company still receives 50 million yen; it is the U.S. company that has the exchange gain.

To illustrate an exchange loss that occurs when the exchange rate declines between the date a company records a credit sale and the date of the cash receipt, suppose that a U.S. company sells computer equipment to a Swiss company on credit and agrees to a price of 300,000 francs rather than a price in dollars. On the date of the sale, the exchange rate is $0.60 (1 franc = $0.60), and therefore the U.S. company records the sale of $180,000 (300,000 francs × $0.60) as follows (assuming the inventory has a cost of $100,000):

Accounts Receivable	180,000	
Sales Revenue		180,000
Cost of Goods Sold	100,000	
Inventory		100,000

The Swiss company has an obligation to pay 300,000 francs regardless of the exchange rate on the date of payment. If the exchange rate is $0.58 when it pays the amount owed, the U.S. company can convert those francs into only $174,000 (300,000 francs × $0.58). As a result, it has incurred an exchange *loss* of $6,000 ($174,000 − $180,000), which it records at the time of the cash collection as follows:

Cash	174,000	
Exchange Loss	6,000	
Accounts Receivable		180,000

The exchange loss can also be computed by multiplying the amount receivable by the change in the exchange rate [300,000 francs × ($0.60 − $0.58) = $6,000]. For financial reporting purposes, the company reports the net amount of Exchange Gains and Losses in the Other Items section of its income statement. This amount is included in the income statement because the exchange gains and losses were caused by fluctuations in the exchange rates that resulted in increased or decreased dollar cash flows during the accounting period.

Note that the U.S. company experienced exchange gains and losses in the preceding situations because it agreed to transactions expressed in terms of foreign currencies. In such situations the U.S. company accepts the risks associated with exchange rate changes. When the transactions are expressed in U.S. dollars, the foreign company accepts, and the U.S. company avoids, the risks associated with exchange rate changes.

SUMMARY

At the beginning of the chapter, we identified several objectives you would accomplish after reading the chapter. the objectives are listed below, each followed by a brief summary of the key points in the chapter discussion.

1. **Describe how inventory accounts are classified?** A retailer needs only one type of inventory account, usually entitled merchandise inventory. A manufacturer typically uses three inventory accounts, usually called raw materials inventory, goods in process inventory, and finished goods inventory.

2. **Explain the uses of the perpetual and periodic inventory systems.** A company using a perpetual system maintains a continuous record of the physical quantities in its inventory. A company using a periodic system does not maintain a continuous record of the physical quantities (or costs) of inventory on hand.

3. **Identify how inventory quantities are determined.** The basic criterion for including items in inventory is economic control rather than physical possession. Issues include goods shipped FOB shipping point and FOB destination, and goods transferred on consignment.

4. **Determine the cost of inventory.** Inventory cost includes costs directly or indirectly incurred in bringing an item to its existing condition and location. Issues include manufacturing overhead costs, standard costs, variable costing, and purchases discounts.

5. **Compute ending inventory and cost of goods sold under specific identification, FIFO, average cost, and LIFO.** Under the specific identification cost flow assumption, a company identifies each unit sold and each unit remaining in the ending inventory, and includes the actual costs of those units in cost of goods sold and ending inventory. Under the FIFO cost flow assumption, a company includes the earliest costs incurred in the cost of goods sold and includes the most recent costs in the ending inventory. Under the average cost flow assumption, a company considers all the costs and units to be commingled so that no individual units or costs can be identified. Under the weighted average method, a company computes an average cost for the period. Under the moving average

method, a company computes an average cost after each acquisition of inventory. Under the LIFO cost flow assumption, a company includes the most recent costs incurred in the cost of goods sold and includes the earliest costs (including costs incurred in previous periods) in the ending inventory.

6. **Explain the conceptual issues regarding alternative inventory cost flow assumptions.** Conceptual issues include income measurement, income tax effects, liquidation of LIFO layers, income manipulation, inventory valuation, average cost, and management's selection of an inventory cost flow assumption.

7. **Understand dollar-value LIFO.** Exhibit 7-13 summarizes the dollar-value calculation steps.

8. **Explain additional LIFO issues.** Additional LIFO issues include the LIFO valuation adjustment, interim statements using LIFO, a change to or from LIFO, and international accounting differences.

9. **Understand inventory disclosures.** Exhibit 7-18 illustrates the proportion of companies using various methods. Companies must disclose the inventory method, or methods, used. A company using LIFO must disclose the difference between the LIFO and the nonLIFO inventory value.

10. **Record foreign currency transactions involving inventory (Appendix).** A U.S. company records a credit purchase from (or sale to) a company in a foreign country in the usual way. An exchange gain or loss is caused by a change in the exchange rate between the date of the credit purchase (sale) and the date of the payment (receipt), and is recorded as the difference between the accounts payable (receivable) and cash payment (receipt).

QUESTIONS

Q7-1   Distinguish between the types of inventory accounts used for merchandising and manufacturing companies.

Q7-2   What are the cost components of each of the three inventory accounts of a manufacturing company?

Q7-3   Explain the differences between the perpetual and periodic inventory systems in terms of inventory quantity and cost. Does the use of a perpetual system eliminate the need for taking a physical inventory count?

Q7-4   What is the general rule used to determine if a company includes an item in inventory? Apply the concept to the accounting for goods in transit and goods on consignment.

Q7-5   Which of the following items does a manufacturing company include in its inventory account? (a) Goods in transit purchased FOB shipping point, invoice received, (b) Raw materials, (c) Goods out on consignment, (d) Goods in transit sold to Breyer, Inc., shipped FOB destination, (e) Manufacturing supplies.

Q7-6   Which of these costs does a company include in its inventory cost? (a) Sales commissions, (b) Supervisor's salary, (c) Freight charges, (d) Indirect factory production labor, (e) Storage costs, (f) Corporate executive salaries.

Q7-7   Are standard costs of inventory acceptable for financial reporting? Describe two alternative methods of accounting for standard cost variances and discuss the advantages of each.

Q7-8   What is the difference between variable costing and absorption costing? Which of these two methods is considered acceptable for financial reporting?

Q7-9   Discuss the advantages and disadvantages of the two methods of accounting for purchases discounts taken in regard to management's needs, inventory cost, and the valuation of accounts payable.

Q7-10   What criteria should a company use to decide between alternative inventory cost flow assumptions? Evaluate the relevance of the LIFO cost flow assumption. Why is LIFO not allowed in most foreign countries?

Q7-11   During a period of rising costs, indicate whether the LIFO cost flow assumption results in a larger or a smaller net income as compared to the FIFO cost flow assumption and explain why. Explain how a company's net income would compare during a period of falling costs.

Q7-12   Discuss the cost flow assumptions of the LIFO inventory method. Under what conditions would a company's ending inventory differ under a perpetual and a periodic LIFO system?

Q7-13   Explain the issue of inventory liquidation when a company uses the LIFO cost flow assumption. Why is this an issue exclusive to LIFO?

Q7-14   Discuss the LIFO and FIFO cost flow assumptions relative to the issue of holding gains (inventory profits).

Q7-15   Explain the dollar-value LIFO method of inventory valuation. What are the advantages of dollar-value LIFO as compared to simple LIFO?

Q7-16   Describe the double-extension and link-chain methods used in dollar-value LIFO and when each should be used.

Q7-17   When a company changes from FIFO to LIFO, what effect does the change have on its net income and working capital of the current period?

Q7-18   What is the impact of LIFO inventory liquidation on a company's interim financial statements?

Q7-19   (Appendix) Explain what causes an exchange gain or loss and when each occurs.

CASES

C O M M U N I C A T I O N

C7-1 Dollar-Value LIFO

In January Broome, Inc., requested and secured permission from the Commissioner of Internal Revenue to compute inventories under the last-in, first-out (LIFO) method and elected to determine inventory cost under the dollar-value method. Broome, Inc., satisfied the Commissioner that cost could be accurately determined by use of an index number computed from a representative sample selected from the Company's single inventory pool.

Required

1. Why should a company include inventories in (a) its statement of financial position and (b) the computation of its net income?
2. The Internal Revenue Code allows some accountable events to be considered differently for income tax reporting purposes and financial accounting purposes, while other accountable events must be reported the same for both purposes. Discuss why it might be desirable to report some accountable events differently for financial accounting purposes than for income tax reporting purposes.
3. Discuss the ways and conditions under which the FIFO and LIFO inventory costing methods produce different inventory valuations. Do not discuss procedures for computing inventory cost.
4. Discuss the specific advantages and disadvantages of using the dollar-value LIFO application as compared to traditional LIFO methods. Ignore income tax considerations. (*AICPA adapted*)

C7-2 FIFO and LIFO

Part a. A company may compute inventory under one of various cost flow assumptions. Among these assumptions are first-in, first-out (FIFO) and last-in, first-out (LIFO). In the past, some companies have changed from FIFO to LIFO for computing portions or all of their inventory.

Required

1. Ignoring income tax, explain what effects a change from FIFO to LIFO has on a company's net earnings and working capital.
2. Explain the difference between the FIFO assumption of earnings and operating cycle and the LIFO assumption of earnings and operating cycle.

Part b. A company using LIFO inventory may establish a "Reserve for the Replacement of LIFO Inventory" account.

Required Explain why and how a company establishes this "reserve" account and where it should show the account on its statement of financial position. (*AICPA adapted*)

C7-3 Cash Discounts, FIFO, and LIFO

Taylor Company, a household appliances dealer, purchases its inventories from various suppliers. Taylor has consistently stated its inventories at the lower of cost (FIFO) or market.

Required

1. Taylor is considering alternate methods of accounting for the cash discounts it takes when paying its suppliers promptly. From a theoretical standpoint, discuss the acceptability of each of the following methods:
   a. Financial income when payments are made.
   b. Reduction of cost of goods sold for period when payments are made.
   c. Direct reduction of purchase cost.
2. Identify the effects on both the balance sheet and the income statement of a company using the LIFO inventory method instead of the FIFO method over a substantial time period when purchase prices of household appliances are rising. State why these effects take place. (*AICPA adapted*)

C7-4 Specific Identification

Happlia Co. imports expensive household appliances. Each model has many variations and each unit has an identification number. Happlia pays all costs for getting the goods from the port to its central warehouse in Des Moines. After repackaging, the goods are consigned to retailers. A retailer makes a sale, simultaneously buys the appliance from Happlia, and pays the balance due within one week.

To alleviate the overstocking of refrigerators at a Minneapolis retailer, some were reshipped to a Kansas City retailer where they were still held in inventory at December 31, 2004. Happlia paid the costs of this reshipment.

Happlia uses the specific identification inventory costing method.

Required

1. In regard to the specific identification inventory costing method
   a. Describe its key elements.
   b. Discuss why it is appropriate for Happlia to use this method.
2. a. What general criteria should Happlia use to determine inventory carrying amounts at December 31, 2004? Ignore lower of cost or market considerations.
   b. Give four examples of costs included in these inventory carrying amounts.
3. What costs should be reported in Happlia's 2004 income statement? Ignore lower of cost or market considerations. (*AICPA adapted*)

C R E A T I V E   A N D   C R I T I C A L   T H I N K I N G

C7-5 Cash Discounts

The Atgar Corporation records all purchases and the corresponding liabilities net of cash discounts. Whenever it pays after the discount period, it credits cash for the full amount of the invoice, and debits accounts payable for the net amount and an expense account for the discount lost.

Required Explain the arguments for and against this treatment of cash discounts. (*AICPA adapted*)

C7-6 Purchases Discounts

The Auge Company annually purchases 1,000 tons of raw material at a cost of $100,000 with terms of 2/10, n/30. Freight costs amount to $10,000 and storage and handling costs to $7,500.

Required

1. What is the correct inventory cost?
2. Explain whether your answer to Requirement 1 would change if the discount were not taken.
3. Would your answer to Requirement 1 change if the storage and handling costs were fixed costs and therefore not dependent on the volume of material stored?

C7-7 Cost Flow Assumptions

A company should determine cost for inventory purposes by the inventory cost flow method most clearly reflecting its periodic income.

Required

1. Explain the fundamental cost flow assumptions of the average cost, FIFO, and LIFO inventory cost flow methods.
2. Discuss the reasons a company uses LIFO in an inflationary economy.
3. Where there is evidence that the utility of goods, in their disposal in the ordinary course of business, will be less than cost, explain the proper accounting treatment and under what concept that treatment is justified. (*AICPA adapted*)

C7-8 LIFO

The 1970s were a period of historically high inflation. The 1976 financial statements of the Ford Motor Company included the following note:

Note 1 (in part): Inventory valuation. Inventories are stated at the lower of cost or market. In 1976 the company changed its method of accounting from first-in, first-out (FIFO) to last-in, first-out (LIFO) for most of its U.S. inventories.

The change to LIFO reduced net income in 1976 by $81 million or $0.86 a share. There is no effect on prior years' earnings resulting from the change to LIFO in 1976 and, accordingly, prior years' earnings have not been restated. If the FIFO method of inventory accounting had

been used by the company, inventories on December 31, 1976, would have been $166 million higher than reported.

Required

1. Explain the arguments that must have been used in favor of LIFO for the management of Ford to accept a reduction in net income of $81 million.
2. Explain the disadvantages that are likely to result from the adoption of LIFO.
3. Explain why prior years' earnings were not adjusted.
4. Explain why the effect on earnings is $81 million when the effect on the inventory valuation is $166 million.
5. Explain whether your answers to Requirements 1 and 2 would change if you were discussing a change to LIFO for a Ford dealer.

C7-9 Selection of an Inventory Method and Ethical Issues

The Kelly Company uses FIFO. It has experienced rising costs for the last 5 years and expects that trend to continue. The King Company increased the number of LIFO pools it uses to account for its inventory.

Required

1. Explain why you think each company follows its policy.
2. Does either practice create ethical issues?

C7-10 Interpretation of GAAP and Ethical Issues

Robin Smith is considering buying shares in the Mah Company. The company has reported an increase in net income this year. On careful reading of the notes to the financial statements, Robin learns that the company had a LIFO liquidation this year. Robin understands what caused the liquidation but has asked you for advice about how to interpret it.

Required

1. Prepare a short memo to Robin to answer the question.
2. Could a LIFO liquidation profit create ethical issues?

C7-11 Exchange Rates (Appendix)

The Gasper Company has transactions with companies in many countries. It purchases components from companies in Korea and several European countries and sells its products throughout the world. The CEO is concerned that the stock market does not like companies to have volatile earnings. However, she is more willing to accept volatility if earnings are higher than they otherwise would be.

Required Select a type of business with which you are familiar and that would be appropriate for Gasper Company's international activities. Write a memo to the CEO outlining how to eliminate her concerns.

C7-12 Analyzing Coca-Cola's Inventory Disclosures

Refer to the financial statements and related notes of the Coca-Cola Company in Appendix A of this book.

Required

1. Which inventory method(s) does the company use? Explain why you think the company selected this method(s).
2. Compute the inventory turnover ratio for 2001 and 2000 using the ending inventory instead of the average inventory. What is your evaluation of the difference?
3. Recreate summary journal entries to record the transactions that affected inventory during 2001.

C7-13 Ethics and Free Textbooks

Textbook publishers provide a copy of a particular book to each professor who is making a decision about adopting a book for the class. These books may be solicited by the professor or may be unsolicited. Some of the books are stamped "For Faculty Use Only." "Used book" companies send out reps who are reimbursed for their travel expenses and are paid a commission to buy these books from the professors at a low price. A lot of these books are purchased at the end of spring, held as inventory over the summer, and sold to university bookstores before the beginning of fall classes. The bookstores sell them to students or return them. Depending on the condition of the book, it is sold to students as either "new" or "used."

Required From financial reporting and ethical perspectives, discuss the issues raised by the above situation.

RESEARCH

C7-14 Researching GAAP

To pump up sales of all brands, Philip Morris is moving aggressively to ship extra cases of cigarettes into distributors' warehouses and record them as sales, a practice generally known as "trade loading." (Adapted from *Fortune*, April 6, 1992). Philip Morris' president has asked you whether these shipments may be recognized as revenue.

Required Research the related generally accepted accounting principles and prepare a short memo to the president. Cite your references and applicable paragraph numbers.

C7-15 Researching GAAP

The Fenimore Manufacturing Company uses the average cost method. It has followed a policy of expensing all its manufacturing cost variances. It is considering a change in its policy that will involve allocating them between cost of goods sold and inventory. Fenimore's president has asked you which of these alternative policies is consistent with GAAP.

Required Research the related generally accepted accounting principles and prepare a short memo to the president. Cite your references and applicable paragraph numbers.

MULTIPLE CHOICE

Select the best answer for each of the following.

M7-1 The moving average inventory cost flow method is applicable to which of the following inventory systems?

	Periodic	Perpetual
a.	Yes	Yes
b.	Yes	No
c.	No	No
d.	No	Yes

Questions M7-2 and M7-3 are based on the following data: City Stationers, Inc., had 200 calculators on hand at January 1, 2004, costing $18 each. Purchases and sales of calculators during the month of January were as follows:

Date	Purchases	Sales
Jan. 12		150 @ $28
15	100 @ $20	
27	100 @ $22	
30		100 @ $32

City does not maintain perpetual inventory records. According to a physical count, 150 calculators were on hand at January 31, 2004.

M7-2 The cost of the inventory at January 31, 2004 under the FIFO method is

a. $400   c. $3,100
b. $2,700   d. $3,200

M7-3 The cost of the inventory at January 31, 2004 under the LIFO method is

a. $400   c. $3,100
b. $2,700   d. $3,200

M7-4 Goods on consignment should be included in the inventory of

a. The consignor but not the consignee
b. Both the consignor and the consignee
c. The consignee but not the consignor
d. Neither the consignor nor the consignee

M7-5 On December 31, 2003 Kern Company adopted the dollar-value LIFO inventory method. All of Kern's inventories constitute a single pool. The inventory on December 31, 2003 using the dollar-value LIFO inventory method, was $600,000. Inventory data for 2004 are as follows:

Dec. 31, 2004 inventory at year-end prices $780,000
Relevant price index at year-end
    (base year 2003)   120

Under the dollar-value LIFO inventory method, Kern's inventory method, Kern's inventory at December 31, 2004 would be

a. $650,000   c. $660,000
b. $655,000   d. $720,000

M7-6 Assuming no beginning inventory, what can be said about the trend of inventory prices if cost of goods sold computed when inventory is valued using the FIFO method exceeds cost of goods sold when inventory is valued using the LIFO method?

a. Prices decreased.
b. Prices remained unchanged.
c. Prices increased.
d. Price trend *cannot* be determined from information given.

M7-7 Dixon Menswear Shop regularly buys shirts from Colt Company and is allowed trade discounts of 20% and 10% from the list price. Dixon purchased shirts from Colt on May 28, 2004, and received an invoice with a list price amount of $5,000, and payment terms of 2/10, n/30. Dixon uses the net method to record purchases. Dixon should record the purchase at

a. $3,600   c. $3,500
b. $3,528   d. $3,430

M7-8 The following items were included in Venicio Corporation's inventory account at December 31, 2004:

Merchandise out on consignment, at sales price,
    including 40% markup on selling price $14,000
Goods purchased, in transit, shipped F.O.B.
    shipping point   12,000
Goods held on consignment by Venicio   9,000

Venicio's inventory account at December 31, 2004 should be reduced by

a. $14,600   c. $23,000
b. $17,400   d. $35,000

M7-9 When the double-extension approach to the dollar-value LIFO inventory cost flow method is used, the inventory layer added in the current year is multiplied by an index number. How would the following be used in the calculation of this index number?

	Ending inventory at current-year cost	Ending inventory at base-year cost
a.	Numerator	Denominator
b.	Numerator	Not Used
c.	Denominator	Numerator
d.	Not Used	Denominator

M7-10 The LIFO inventory cost flow method may be applied to which of the following inventory systems?

	Periodic	Perpetual
a.	No	No
b.	No	Yes
c.	Yes	Yes
d.	Yes	No

(AICPA adapted)

EXERCISES

E7-1 **Inventory Accounts for a Manufacturing Company** The Fujita Company produces a single product. Costs accumulated at the end of the period are as follows:

Raw material purchases	$54,000	Production supervisor's salary	$ 20,000
Depreciation on manufacturing equipment	3,000	Shipping costs on units sold	43,500
Sales commissions	20,000	Materials used in production	81,400
Factory labor	36,000	Goods completed	115,000
Property tax on manufacturing equipment	3,500	Costs of units sold	150,000

Assume the beginning raw material inventory to be $67,400, the beginning finished goods inventory to be $123,500, and no beginning goods in process inventory.

Required Compute the closing account balances of each of the three inventory accounts: Raw Materials, Goods in Process, and Finished Goods.

E7-2 **Goods in Transit** The Gravais Company made two purchases on December 29, 2004. One purchase for $3,000 was shipped FOB destination, and the second for $4,000 was shipped FOB shipping point. Neither purchase had been received on December 31, 2004.

Required Which of these purchases, if either, does the Gravais Company include in inventory on December 31, 2004? What is the cost?

E7-3   *Items Included in Inventory*   The following are several items that the controller of the Golosow Company has questioned regarding their inclusion in Inventory:

1. An invoice has been received for goods ordered. The goods were shipped FOB destination but have not been received.
2. Purchases have been ordered and received, but no invoice has arrived.
3. Product was shipped to a customer today, FOB destination, and the invoice mailed.
4. Purchases are in the receiving department but they are damaged and will be returned.
5. Product is in the shipping department and the invoice has not been mailed to the customer.
6. Product is in the receiving department. It was returned by a customer without notification.

Required For each of the preceding items indicate whether Golosow should include them in Inventory.

E7-4   *Inventory Valuation*   A retailer of washing machines receives a rebate of $25 per machine purchased if total purchases exceed 1,000 units. On reviewing the inventory records in December, it discovers that it has purchased 1,100 units during the year. The company claims the rebate immediately but it is not received until January.

Required Prepare journal entries to record the claiming of the rebate and its receipt. What effect do these events have on the inventory valuation on December 31?

E7-5   *Discounts*   The Hirsch Company buys inventory for $20,000 on terms of 2/10, n/30. It pays within the discount period.

Required Prepare the journal entries to record the purchase and the payment under both the (1) gross price and (2) net price methods.

E7-6   *Discounts*   The Nelson Company bought inventory for $50,000 on terms of 2/15, n/60. It pays for the first $37,500 of inventory purchased within the discount period and pays for the remaining $12,500 two months later.

Required Prepare the journal entries to record the purchase and the payment under both the (1) gross price and (2) net price methods.

E7-7   *Alternative Inventory Methods*   The Nevens Company uses a periodic inventory system. During November
 the following transactions occurred:

Date		Transaction	Units	Cost/Unit
November	1	Balance	500	$3.50
	8	Sale	350	
	13	Purchase	300	4.00
	21	Purchase	200	5.00
	28	Sale	150	

Required Compute the cost of goods sold for November and the inventory at the end of November for each of the following cost flow assumptions:

1. FIFO
2. LIFO
3. Average cost

E7-8   *Alternative Inventory Methods*   The perpetual inventory records of the Park Company indicate the following transactions in the month of June:

	Units	Cost/Unit
Inventory, June 1	200	$3.20
Purchases		
June 3	200	3.50
June 17	250	3.60
June 24	300	3.65
Sales		
June 6	300	
June 21	200	
June 27	150	

Required Compute the cost of goods sold for June and the inventory at the end of June, using each of the following cost flow assumptions:

1. FIFO
2. LIFO
3. Average cost (round unit costs to 2 decimal places)

E7-9   ***Alternative Inventory Methods***   The Frate Company was formed on December 1, 2003. The following information is available from Frate's inventory records for Product Ply:

	Units	Unit Cost
January 1, 2004 (beginning inventory)	800	$ 9.00
Purchases:		
January 6, 2004	1,500	10.00
January 24, 2004	1,200	10.50
February 17, 2004	600	11.00
March 27, 2004	900	11.50

A physical inventory on March 31, 2004 shows 1,600 units on hand.

Required Prepare schedules to compute the ending inventory at March 31, 2004 under each of the following inventory methods:

1. FIFO
2. LIFO
3. Weighted average

Show supporting computations in good form. (*AICPA adapted*)

E7-10   ***LIFO, Perpetual and Periodic***   The inventory records of the Riedel Company showed the following transac-
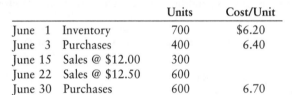
tions for the fiscal period ended June 30:

		Units	Cost/Unit
June 1	Inventory	700	$6.20
June 3	Purchases	400	6.40
June 15	Sales @ $12.00	300	
June 22	Sales @ $12.50	600	
June 30	Purchases	600	6.70

Required Compute the ending inventory and the cost of goods sold under the LIFO cost flow assumption, assuming both a perpetual and a periodic inventory system. Explain any difference in the final inventory valuations.

E7-11   ***Dollar-Value LIFO***   A company adopted the LIFO method when its inventory was $1,800. One year later its ending inventory was $2,100 and costs had increased 5% during the year.

Required What is the ending inventory using dollar-value LIFO?

E7-12   ***Dollar-Value LIFO***   On January 1, 2003 the Sato Company adopted the dollar-value LIFO method of inventory costing. The company's ending inventory records appear as follows:

Year	Current Cost	Index
2003	$40,000	100
2004	56,100	120
2005	58,500	130
2006	70,000	140

Required Compute the ending inventory for the years 2003, 2004, 2005, and 2006, using the dollar-value LIFO method (round to the nearest dollar).

E7-13   ***Dollar-Value LIFO***   The Belstock Company manufactures one product. On December 31, 2003 Belstock adopted the dollar-value LIFO inventory method. The inventory on that date, using the dollar-value LIFO inventory method, was $200,000. Inventory data for succeeding years are as follows:

Year	Inventory at Respective Year-End Prices	Price Index (Base Year 2003)
2004	$231,000	1.05
2005	299,000	1.15
2006	300,000	1.20

Required Compute the inventory for the following dates using the dollar-value LIFO method for each year:

1. December 31, 2004,
2. December 31, 2005, and
3. December 31, 2006. (*AICPA adapted*)

E7-14 **Dollar-Value LIFO** The Acute Company manufactures a single product. On December 31, 2003 Acute adopted the dollar-value LIFO inventory method. It computes the inventory on that date using the dollar-value LIFO inventory method as $300,000. Inventory data for succeeding years are as follows:

Year Ended December 31,	Inventory at Respective Year-End Prices	Relevant Price Index (Base Year 2003)
2004	$363,000	1.10
2005	420,000	1.20
2006	430,000	1.25

Required Compute the inventory amounts at December 31, 2004, 2005, and 2006, using the dollar-value LIFO inventory method for each year. (*AICPA adapted*)

E7-15 **Inventory Pools** The Stone Shoe Company adopted dollar-value LIFO on January 1, 2004. The company produces four products and uses a single inventory pool. The company's beginning inventory consists of the following:

Type	Quantity	Cost per Unit	Total Cost
Running	80,000	$16	$1,280,000
Tennis	30,000	15	450,000
Basketball	60,000	14	840,000
Soccer	40,000	17	680,000
	210,000		$3,250,000

During 2004 the company has the following purchases and sales:

Type	Quantity Purchased	Cost per Unit	Quantity Sold	Selling Price per Unit
Running	150,000	$19	140,000	$40
Tennis	130,000	16	100,000	38
Basketball	100,000	14	90,000	37
Soccer	120,000	18	140,000	42
	500,000		470,000	

Required

1. Compute the LIFO cost of the ending inventory. (Round the cost index to 4 decimal places.)
2. By how much would the company's gross profit be different if it had used four pools instead of a single pool?

E7-16 **FIFO Used Internally, LIFO Used Externally** The Grimstad Company uses FIFO for internal reporting purposes and LIFO for financial reporting and income tax purposes. At the end of 2004 the following information was obtained from the inventory records:

	2003	2004
Ending inventory, FIFO	$100,000	$140,000
Ending inventory, LIFO	80,000	115,000

Required

1. Prepare the necessary adjusting journal entry, assuming that the company converts the accounts to LIFO at the end of 2004.
2. Indicate how the company would disclose the inventory value on its comparative balance sheets prepared at the end of 2004.
3. By how much would the company's cost of goods sold be different in 2004 if it used FIFO for external reporting?

E7-17   *LIFO and Interim Financial Reports*   The following values were obtained from the inventory records of the Harris Company, which has a fiscal year ending on December 31:

Inventory, January 1, 2004, LIFO $80,000
Inventory, March 31, 2004, LIFO   70,000

Required

1. Under what conditions is the company's inventory liquidation not reflected in its first quarter interim financial statements?
2. Assuming that the liquidation is not to be reflected, what adjusting worksheet entry would the company make and how would you determine the amount?

E7-18   *Exchange Gains and Losses (Appendix)*   On January 15, 2004, the Searle Company, a U.S. company, acquired machinery on credit from a British company for £12,000. The company paid for the machine on January 30, 2004. The exchange rates on January 15 and 30 were $1.85 and $1.80, respectively.

Required   Record the journal entries for the acquisition and payment by the Searle Company.

E7-19   *Exchange Gains and Losses (Appendix)*   On June 21, 2004, the Livingston Company, a U.S. company, sold merchandise on credit to a Swiss company for 25,000 francs. The company received payment for the merchandise on July 10, 2004. The exchange rates on June 21 and July 10 were $0.69 and $0.68, respectively.

Required   Record the journal entries for the sale and collection by the Livingston Company.

PROBLEMS

P7-1   *Items to Be Included in Inventory*   As the auditor of the Hayes Company for the year ended December 31, 2004, you found the following transactions occurred near its closing date:

1. Merchandise received on January 8, 2005 and costing $800 was recorded on January 6, 2005. An invoice on hand showed the shipment was made FOB supplier's warehouse on December 31, 2004. Since the merchandise was not on hand at December 31, 2004, it was not included in the inventory.
2. A product costing $600 was in Hayes' shipping room when the physical inventory was taken. It was not included in the inventory because it was marked "Hold for customer's shipping instructions." Investigation revealed that the customer's order was dated December 18, 2004, but that the case was shipped and the customer billed on January 10, 2005.
3. A machine, made to order for a customer, was finished on December 31, 2004. The customer had inspected it and was satisfied with it. The customer was billed in full for $2,000 on that date. The machine was excluded from inventory although it was shipped on January 2, 2005.
4. Merchandise costing $800 was received on December 26, 2004, but a purchase was not recorded. The goods were "on consignment from Milliken Company."
5. Merchandise costing $4,000 was received on January 2, 2005, and the related purchase invoice recorded January 5. The invoice showed that the shipment was made on December 29, 2004, FOB destination.

Required   For each situation, state whether the Hayes Company should include the merchandise in its inventory. Give your reason for the decision on each item.

P7-2   *Valuation of Inventory*   The inventory on hand at the end of 2004 for the Reddall Company is valued at a cost of $87,450. The following items were not included in this inventory:

1. Purchased goods in transit, under terms FOB shipping point, invoice price $3,700, freight costs $170.
2. Goods out on consignment to Marlman Company, sales price $2,800, shipping costs of $210.
3. Goods sold to Grina Co. under terms FOB destination, invoiced for $1,700, including $251 freight charges to deliver the goods. Goods are in transit.
4. Goods held on consignment by the Reddall Company at a sales price of $2,700, including sales commission of 20% of sales price.
5. Purchased goods in transit, shipped FOB destination, invoice price $2,100 including freight charges of $190.

Required Determine the cost of the ending inventory that Reddall should report on its December 31, 2004 balance sheet, assuming that its selling price is 140% of the cost of the inventory.

P7-3   *Cost of Sales*   As an accountant for the Lee Company, your supervisor gave you the following calculations of the gross profit for the first quarter:

Alternative	Sales ($50 per unit)	Cost of Goods Sold	Gross Profit
A	$500,000	$200,000	$300,000
B	500,000	228,000	272,000
C	500,000	213,333	286,667

The three alternative cost flow assumptions are FIFO, Average, and LIFO (the alternatives are not necessarily presented in this sequence). The company uses the periodic inventory system. The computation of the cost of goods sold under each alternative is based on the following data:

	Units	Cost/Unit
Inventory, January 1	12,000	$20
Purchase, January 10	4,000	21
Purchase, February 15	6,000	22
Purchase, March 10	8,000	23

Required Prepare schedules computing the ending inventory (in units and dollars) and proving the cost of goods sold shown here under each of the three alternatives.

P7-4   *Discounts*   On April 11, Edwards Construction Company purchased inventory for $20,000 on terms of 2/10, n/30. It pays the account balance on April 21.

Required

1. Prepare the journal entries to record the purchase and payment using each of the following methods: (a) gross price, (b) net price.
2. If the company sold half the inventory during April for $12,000, how much income would it recognize under each method?
3. Assume that the invoice was misfiled and, as a result, the company did not pay until April 30. Prepare the journal entries to record the purchase and payment under each of the methods. If the company sold half the inventory during April for $12,000, how much income would it recognize under each method?

P7-5   *Alternative Inventory Methods*   The Garrett Company has the following transactions during the months of
@   April and May:

Date		Transaction	Units	Cost/Unit
April	1	Balance	400	
	17	Purchase	200	$5.50
	25	Sale	150	
	28	Purchase	100	5.75
May	5	Purchase	250	5.50
	18	Sale	300	
	22	Sale	50	

The cost of the inventory on April 1 is $5, $4, and $2 per unit, respectively, under the FIFO, average, and LIFO cost flow assumptions.

Required

1. Compute the costs of goods sold for each month and the inventories at the end of each month for the following alternatives:
   a. FIFO periodic
   b. FIFO perpetual
   c. LIFO periodic
   d. LIFO perpetual
   e. Weighted average (round unit costs to 2 decimal places)
   f. Moving average (round unit costs to 2 decimal places)
2. Reconcile the difference between the LIFO periodic and the LIFO perpetual results.

See WebTutor for annotated problem solution.

P7-6   ***Alternative Inventory Methods***   The Totman Company has the following transactions during the months of January and February:

Date		Transaction	Units	Cost/Unit
January	1	Balance	200	
	10	Purchase	50	$25
	22	Sale	40	
	28	Purchase	60	$27
February	4	Purchase	40	$28
	14	Sale	50	
	23	Sale	20	

The cost of the inventory at January 1 is $24, $23, and $15 per unit, respectively, under the FIFO, average, and LIFO cost flow assumptions.

Required

1. Compute the cost of goods sold for each month and the inventories at the end of each month for the following alternatives:
   a. FIFO periodic
   b. FIFO perpetual
   c. LIFO periodic
   d. LIFO perpetual
   e. Weighted average (round unit costs to 2 decimal places)
   f. Moving average (round unit costs to 2 decimal places)
2. Reconcile the difference between the LIFO periodic and the LIFO perpetual results.
3. If the company had purchased an additional 25 units for $30 each on February 27, compute the cost of goods sold for February under FIFO periodic and LIFO periodic.
4. For February, compute the company's inventory turnover under the FIFO and LIFO periodic methods. Use ending inventory instead of average inventory for convenience. Which measure would you use in your evaluation of the company? How would you convert a monthly inventory turnover into an annual measure to use for comparison with other companies? What assumptions are involved?

P7-7   ***Alternative Inventory Methods***   The Habicht Company was formed in 2003 to produce a single product. The production and sales for the next four years were as follows:

	Production		Sales		
	Units	Total Costs	Units	Sales Revenue	Units in Ending Inventory
2003	100,000	$200,000	80,000	$400,000	20,000
2004	120,000	234,000	110,000	550,000	30,000
2005	130,000	247,000	150,000	750,000	10,000
2006	130,000	240,500	120,000	600,000	20,000

Required

1. Determine the gross profit for each year under each of the following periodic inventory methods:
   (a) FIFO
   (b) LIFO
   (c) Average cost (round unit costs to 3 decimal places)
2. Explain whether the company's return on assets (net income divided by average total assets, as we discussed in Chapter 5) would be higher under FIFO or LIFO.

P7-8   *LIFO and Inventory Pools*   On January 1, 2001 Grover Company changed its inventory cost flow method to the LIFO cost method from the FIFO cost method for its raw materials inventory. It made the change for both financial statement and income tax reporting purposes. Grover uses the multiple-pools approach under which it groups substantially identical raw materials into LIFO inventory pools; it uses weighted average costs in valuing annual incremental layers. The composition of the December 31, 2003 inventory for the Class F inventory pool is as follows:

	Units	Weighted Average Unit Cost	Total Cost
Base year inventory—2001	9,000	$10.00	$ 90,000
Incremental layer—2002	3,000	11.00	33,000
Incremental layer—2003	2,000	12.50	25,000
Inventory, December 31, 2003	14,000		$148,000

Inventory transactions for the Class F inventory pool during 2004 were as follows:
- On March 2, 2004, 4,800 units were purchased at a unit cost of $13.50 for $64,800.
- On September 1, 2004, 7,200 units were purchased at a unit cost of $14.00 for $100,800.
- A total of 15,000 units were used for production during 2004.

The following transactions for the Class F inventory pool took place during 2005:
- On January 11, 2005, 7,500 units were purchased at a unit cost of $14.50 for $108,750.
- On May 14, 2005, 5,500 units were purchased at a unit cost of $15.50 for $85,250.
- On December 28, 2005, 7,000 units were purchased at a unit cost of $16.00 for $112,000.
- A total of 16,000 units were used for production during 2005.

Required
1. Prepare a schedule to compute the inventory (units and dollar amounts) of the Class F inventory pool at December 31, 2004. Show supporting computations in good form.
2. Prepare a schedule to compute the cost of Class F raw materials used in production for the year ended December 31, 2004.
3. Prepare a schedule to compute the inventory (units and dollar amounts) of the Class F inventory pool at December 31, 2005. Show supporting computations in good form. (*AICPA adapted*)

P7-9   *Dollar-Value LIFO*   The Olson Company adopted the dollar-value LIFO method for inventory valuation at the beginning of 2003. The following information about the inventory at the end of each year is available from the company records:

Year	Current Costs	Index
2002	$50,000	100
2003	60,000	108
2004	70,000	115
2005	73,000	125
2006	78,000	135

Required
1. Calculate the dollar-value LIFO inventory at the end of each year.
2. Prepare the appropriate disclosures for the year 2006 annual report if the company uses current cost internally and LIFO for financial reporting. Why would the company use current cost internally?

P7-10   *Dollar-Value LIFO*   The Kwestel Company adopted the dollar-value LIFO method for inventory valuation at the beginning of 2003. The following information about the inventory at the end of each year is available from the company records:

Year	Current Cost	Index
2002	$ 8,000	100
2003	10,800	120
2004	11,500	130
2005	14,000	145
2006	10,500	125

Required: Calculate the dollar-value LIFO inventory at the end of each year.

P7-11 *Dollar-Value LIFO and Inventory Pools* The Webster Company adopted dollar-value LIFO on January 1, 2004. The company produces three products: X, Y, and Z. The company's beginning inventory consisted of the following:

Type	Quantity	Cost per Unit	Total Cost
X	30,000	$4.25	$127,500
Y	10,000	3.50	35,000
Z	25,000	2.00	50,000
	65,000		$212,500

During 2004, the company had the following purchases and sales:

Type	Quantity Purchased	Cost per Unit	Quantity Sold	Selling Price per Unit
X	110,000	$4.75	90,000	$10.00
Y	100,000	3.75	85,000	7.50
Z	75,000	2.10	70,000	5.00
	285,000		245,000	

Required

1. Compute the LIFO cost of the ending inventory assuming Webster Company uses a single inventory pool. (Round cost index to 4 decimal places.)
2. Compute the LIFO cost of the ending inventory assuming Webster Company uses 3 inventory pools. (Round cost indexes to 4 decimal places.)

P7-12 *Comprehensive* The Kelly Company adopted dollar-value LIFO on January 1, 2003 using two inventory pools, each of which includes two types of inventory items. The following information about the inventory at the end of each year is available:

	Pool 1			Pool 2		
Year	Number of Units	Type	Average Cost per Unit	Number of Units	Type	Average Cost per Unit
2003	20,000	A	$10	40,000	C	$5
	10,000	B	20	20,000	D	8
2004	30,000	A	11	50,000	C	7
	12,000	B	24	22,000	D	9
2005	40,000	A	12	46,000	C	6
	14,000	B	22	20,000	D	8
2006	45,000	A	12	60,000	C	7
	13,000	B	25	25,000	D	8

Required

1. Compute the cost index for each year for each pool using a base of 100 for each index. (Round each cost index to 4 decimal places.)
2. Compute the dollar-value LIFO inventory at the end of each year.

P7-13 *Double-Extension: Dollar-Value LIFO* On January 1, 2004 Lucas Distributors, Inc., adopted the dollar-value LIFO inventory method for income tax and external financial reporting. However, Lucas continued to use the FIFO inventory method for internal accounting and management purposes. In applying the LIFO method, Lucas uses internal conversion cost indexes and the multiple-pools approach under which substantially identical inventory items are grouped into LIFO inventory pools. The following data were available for Inventory Pool No. 1, which is comprised of products A and B, for the 2 years following the adoption of LIFO:

	FIFO Basis per Records		
	Units	Unit Cost	Total Cost
Inventory, 1/1/04			
Product A	12,000	$30	$360,000
Product B	8,000	25	200,000
			$560,000
Inventory, 12/31/04			
Product A	17,000	$35	$595,000
Product B	9,000	28	252,000
			$847,000
Inventory, 12/31/05			
Product A	13,000	$40	$520,000
Product B	10,000	32	320,000
			$840,000

Required

1. Prepare a schedule to compute the internal conversion cost indexes for 2004 and 2005. Round indexes to two decimal places.
2. Prepare a schedule to compute the inventory amounts at December 31, 2004 and 2005, using the dollar-value LIFO inventory method. (*AICPA adapted*)

P7-14   *LIFO Liquidation Profit*   The Hammond Company adopted LIFO when it was formed on January 1, 2002. Since then, the company has had the following purchases and sales of its single inventory item:

Year	Units Purchased	Cost per Unit	Units Sold	Price per Unit
2002	10,000	$5	8,000	$12
2003	12,000	6	9,000	13
2004	15,000	8	14,000	16

In December 2005 the controller realized that because of an unexpected increase in demand, the company had sold 22,000 units but had purchased only 19,000 units during the year. In 2005 each unit had been sold for $19, and each unit purchased had cost $10. The income tax rate is 30%.

Required

1. If the company makes no additional purchases in 2005, how much LIFO liquidation profit will it report?
2. Prepare the appropriate annual report disclosures for 2005.
3. If the company purchases an additional 7,000 units in December 2005, how much income tax will the company save?
4. If the company purchases the additional 7,000 units, how much income tax has the company saved over the 4-year period by using LIFO instead of the FIFO cost flow assumption?

P7-15   *Comprehensive*   The following information for 2004 is available for the Marino Company:

1. The beginning inventory is $100,000.
2. Purchases of $300,000 were made on terms of 2/10, n/30. Eighty percent of the discounts were taken.
3. Purchases returns of $4,000 were made.
4. At December 31, purchases of $20,000 were in transit, FOB destination, on terms of 2/10, n/30.
5. The company made sales of $640,000. The gross selling price per unit is twice the net cost of each unit sold.
6. Sales allowances of $6,000 were made.
7. The company uses the LIFO periodic method and the gross method for purchases discounts.

Required

1. Compute the cost of the ending inventory before the physical inventory is taken.
2. Compute the amount of the cost of goods sold that came from the purchases of the period and the amount that came from the beginning inventory.

P7-16 ***Inventory Valuation***   You are engaged in an audit of the Roche Mfg. Company for the year ended December 31, 2004. To reduce the workload at year-end, the company took its annual physical inventory under your observation on November 30, 2004. The company's inventory account, which includes raw materials and work in process, is on a perpetual basis and it uses the first-in, first-out method of pricing. It has no finished goods inventory. The company's physical inventory revealed that the book inventory of $60,570 was understated by $3,000. To avoid distorting the interim financial statements, the company decided not to adjust the book inventory until year-end except for obsolete inventory items. Your audit revealed this information about the November 30th inventory:

  a. Pricing tests showed that the physical inventory was overpriced by $2,200.

  b. Footing and extension errors resulted in a $150 understatement of the physical inventory.

  c. Direct labor included in the physical inventory amounted to $10,000. Overhead was included at the rate of 200% of direct labor. You determined that the amount of direct labor was correct and the overhead rate was proper.

  d. The physical inventory included obsolete materials recorded at $250. During December, these materials were removed from the inventory account by a charge to cost of sales. Your audit also disclosed the following information about the December 31, 2004 inventory.

  e. Total debits to certain accounts during December are:

	December
Purchases	$24,700
Direct labor	12,100
Manufacturing overhead expense	25,200
Cost of sales	68,600

  f. The cost of sales of $68,600 included direct labor of $13,800.

  g. Normal scrap loss on established product lines is negligible. However, a special order started and completed during December had excessive scrap loss of $800, which was charged to Manufacturing Overhead Expense.

Required

  1. Compute the correct amount of the physical inventory at November 30, 2004.

  2. Without prejudice to your solution to Requirement 1, assume that the correct amount of the inventory at November 30, 2004 was $57,700. Compute the amount of the inventory at December 31, 2004. (*AICPA adapted*)

P7-17 ***Comprehensive***   The Allen Company is a wholesale distributor of automotive replacement parts. Initial amounts taken from Allen's accounting records are as follows:

Inventory at December 31, 2004 (based on physical
   count of goods in Allen's warehouse on December 31, 2004) $1,250,000

Sales in 2004 $9,000,000

Accounts payable at December 31, 2004:

Vendor	Terms	Amount
Baker Company	2% 10 days, net 30	$ 265,000
Charlie Company	Net 30	210,000
Dolly Company	Net 30	300,000
Eager Company	Net 30	225,000
Full Company	Net 30	—
Greg Company	Net 30	—
		$1,000,000

Additional information is as follows:

  1. Parts held on consignment from Charlie to Allen, the consignee, amounting to $155,000, were included in the physical count of goods in Allen's warehouse on December 31, 2004 and in accounts payable at December 31, 2004.

2. $22,000 of parts which were purchased from Full and paid for in December 2004 were sold in the last week of 2004 and appropriately recorded as sales of $28,000. The parts were included in the physical count of goods in Allen's warehouse on December 31, 2004 because the parts were on the loading dock waiting to be picked up by customers.

3. Parts in transit on December 31, 2004 to customers, shipped F.O.B. shipping point on December 28, 2004, amounted to $34,000. The customers received the parts on January 7, 2005. Sales of $40,000 to the customers for the parts were recorded by Allen on January 3, 2005.

4. Retailers were holding $210,000 at cost ($250,000 at retail) of goods on consignment from Allen, the consignor, at their stores on December 31, 2004.

5. Goods were in transit from Greg to Allen on December 31, 2004. The cost of the goods was $25,000, and they were shipped F.O.B. shipping point on December 29, 2004.

6. A quarterly freight bill in the amount of $2,000 specifically relating to merchandise purchases in December 2004, all of which was still in the inventory at December 31, 2004, was received on January 4, 2005. The freight bill was not included in either the inventory or in accounts payable at December 31, 2004.

7. All of the purchases from Baker occurred during the last seven days of the year. These items have been recorded in accounts payable and accounted for in the physical inventory at cost before discount. Allen's policy is to pay invoices in time to take advantage of all cash discounts, adjust inventory accordingly, and record accounts payable, net of cash discounts.

Required Prepare a schedule of adjustments to the initial amounts of inventory, accounts payable, and sales. Show the effect, if any, of each of the transactions separately and indicate if the transactions would have no effect on the amount. (*AICPA adapted*)

INTERNET ASSIGNMENTS

Go to the Nikolai and Bazley **Intermediate Accounting** web site (http://Nikolai.swcollege.com). Click on Student Resources and internet homework assignments. Then click on the appropriate hot link (icon) for each company's web site, find the relevant accounting information, and answer the following questions.

I7-1   Click on the **Colgate-Palmolive** web site and the **Procter & Gamble** web site.

  Required Which accounting method(s) does each company use for its inventories? Do you agree with the choices made by each company? Is the information provided by the two companies comparable? How can you make the information more comparable? What is the major disadvantage of the adjustment process you use to make the information comparable?

I7-2   Click on the **Wal-Mart** web site.

  Required Which accounting method does the company use for its inventories? How much is the company's ending inventory and cost of goods sold for each of the two most recent years? Compute the inventory turnover ratio for each of the two most recent years (use the ending inventory in your calculation). Compute the amount of cost of goods sold for the most recent year if the company used nonLIFO.

objectives

1 Understand the lower of cost or market method.

2 Explain the conceptual issues regarding the lower of cost or market method.

3 Understand purchase obligations and product financing arrangements.

4 Explain the valuation of inventory above cost.

5 Use the gross profit method.

6 Understand the retail inventory method.

7 Explain the conceptual issues regarding the retail inventory method.

8 Understand the dollar-value LIFO retail method.

9 Understand the effects of inventory errors on the financial statements.

CHAPTER

8

Inventories: Special Valuation Issues

In the preceding chapter we described the various methods of determining the historical cost of inventory. In certain situations a company does not report its inventory at the historical cost. The alternatives to historical cost are valuation at the lower of cost or market, valuation above cost, and estimation of cost by the gross profit or retail inventory methods, including the dollar-value LIFO retail inventory method. We discuss each of these topics in this chapter, as well as purchase obligations, product financing arrangements, and the effects of errors in inventory on a company's financial statements.

LOWER OF COST OR MARKET

1 Understand the lower of cost or market method.

The generally accepted accounting principle of valuation at historical cost, as determined by the cost flow assumption used, is modified in situations where the market value of a company's inventory has declined below its historical cost. This might occur for reasons such as declining costs, obsolescence, or physical deterioration. In these situations the lower of cost or market rule is applied. **The lower of cost or market rule requires that a company write down its inventory to market value when the inventory's utility has declined.** The writedown of the inventory is appropriate because the utility of the asset has declined, and to leave the inventory at its historical cost would overstate both its value and the expected future cash inflows. The lower of cost or market rule is consistent with the conservatism convention. Since the company writes down the asset, it reports a loss (or expense) in its income statement because the decline is an economic event of the period.

Accounting Research Bulletin No. 43 states:

A departure from the cost basis of pricing the inventory is required when the utility of the goods is no longer as great as its cost. Where there is evidence that the utility of goods, in their disposal in the ordinary course of business, will be less than cost, whether due to physical deterioration, obsolescence, changes in price levels or other causes, the difference should be recognized as a loss of the current period. This is generally accomplished by stating such goods at a lower level commonly designated as market.[1]

Since utility is difficult to measure except through a changed market value, the measurement of the decline in utility is, in practice, always made by valuing the inventory at the lower of cost or market (LCM). *Accounting Research Bulletin No. 43* defines **market value as the current replacement cost** (either by purchase or manufacture) and *not* as the selling price.

---

1. "Restatement and Revision of Accounting Research Bulletins," *Accounting Research Bulletins, Final Edition, No. 43* (New York: AICPA, 1961), ch. 4, par. 7.

Application of Lower of Cost or Market Method

When a company applies the lower of cost or market method, it compares the cost to the market value. It does not always use the current replacement cost as the market value, however. An upper (*ceiling*) and a lower (*floor*) constraint on the market value are imposed as follows:

1. **The upper constraint is that the market value should not exceed the net realizable value** (the estimated selling price in the ordinary course of business, less reasonably predictable costs of completion and disposal).
2. **The lower constraint is that the market value should not be below the net realizable value, reduced by an allowance for a normal profit margin** (normal markup).

These two constraints are used to determine which "market value" (current replacement cost, ceiling, or floor) is to be compared to cost. Note that the appropriate market value is determined before the comparison with the cost is made. **The purpose of the ceiling is to ensure that the write-down of the inventory is sufficient to cover all expected losses and therefore prevent the recognition of further losses in the future.** In contrast, **the purpose of the floor is to prevent an excessive loss from being recognized and therefore prevent the recognition of excessive profits in the future** (as we discuss later in this section).

Thus, to apply the lower of cost or market method a company completes three steps: (1) select the market value, (2) compare the market value to cost, and (3) report the results in its financial statements, as we illustrate in the following diagram:

Selection of Market Value	Comparison to Cost	Reporting the Results
Ceiling (NRV*) ↑ Replacement Cost ↓ Floor (NRV−NP**)	Use lower of (a) cost or (b) selected market value	Balance sheet: Inventory at LCM Income statement: Loss (if recognized)

*Net realizable value
**Normal profit

In the first step, the company calculates the current replacement cost, ceiling, and floor. It selects the middle value of the three. Then, it chooses the lower of the selected market value or the historical cost. Finally, the company reports the lower value on its balance sheet and, if it recognizes a loss, it reports the amount on the income statement, perhaps including it in cost of goods sold.

To illustrate the first step in the application of the lower of cost or market method, suppose that a company's unit of inventory has the following characteristics:

Selling price	$165
Packaging cost	10
Transportation cost	15
Profit margin	40

The company computes the ceiling and floor as follows:

Selling price	$165
Less: Costs of completion (i.e., packaging)	(10)
Costs of disposal (i.e., transportation)	(15)
Ceiling (net realizable value)	$140
Less: Normal profit margin	(40)
Floor (net realizable value less normal profit)	$100

EXHIBIT 8-1   Application of the Lower of Cost or Market Rule

Case	Current Replacement Cost	Net Realizable Value (Ceiling)	Net Realizable Value Less a Normal Markup (Floor)	Market (Constrained by Ceiling and Floor)	Cost	Lower of Cost or Market Inventory Value*	Loss
1	$120	$140	$100	$120	$110	$110	$ 0
2	150	140	100	140	110	110	0
3	75	140	120	120	110	110	0
4	105	140	100	105	110	105	5
5	105	90	80	90	110	90	20
6	80	140	100	100	110	100	10

*Cases 1, 2 and 3: Cost is used because it is lower than market.
Case 4: Replacement cost is used because it is between floor and ceiling and is less than cost.
Case 5: Net realizable value (ceiling) is used because replacement cost is higher than ceiling and net realizable value is less than cost.
Case 6: Net realizable value less a normal markup (floor) is used because replacement cost is less than floor and net realizable value less a normal markup is less than cost.

If the current replacement cost is between $100 and $140, it would be used as the market value. If the replacement cost is above $140, the ceiling would be used; if the replacement cost is below $100, the floor would be used.

We illustrate all three steps in the application of the lower of cost or market method in Exhibit 8-1 for a single unit of inventory. The logic behind the ceiling and floor can be explained by reference to Cases 5 and 6. If in Case 5 the ceiling constraint was ignored and the current replacement cost was used as market, the inventory would be written down only to $105 and a loss of $5 would be recognized. However, in a later period when the unit is sold for $90 (net), there would be an additional loss of $15. Therefore, the inventory would not have been written down to its expected utility, and the total loss associated with the decline in utility would not have been recognized in the period in which it occurred. Imposing an upper limit of net realizable value ensures that the full decline in utility is recognized in the period in which it occurred. At first it might be considered unusual that the net realizable value is below the replacement cost (of a new asset), but this can happen when there is physical deterioration to the inventory. If the volume of such items becomes significant, they should be transferred to a separate account.

If the floor constraint was ignored in Case 6 and the current replacement cost was used as market, the inventory would be written down to $80 and a loss of $30 would be recognized. However, in a later period when the unit is sold for $140 (net), there would be a profit of $60, which is higher than the normal profit of $40. Therefore, the inventory would have been written down below its expected utility, and an excessive loss followed by an excessive profit would have been recognized. Imposing a lower limit of net realizable value less normal profit prevents a write-down below the expected utility of the inventory and the arbitrary transfer of profit from one accounting period to another.

Conceptual Evaluation of the Ceiling and Floor

The implicit assumption underlying the lower of cost or market method is that selling (exit) prices move in parallel to replacement costs (entry prices) within the constraints of ceiling and floor. While the general trends of the two prices are likely to move together, there will be exceptions. Also, the lower of cost or market method may be criticized because it uses three different concepts for the loss recognized in the period. This loss recognition also affects the amount of profit a company will recognize in future periods. These differences create conceptual inconsistencies both within the lower of cost or market method and between that method and other applications of conservatism.

To illustrate these issues, assume the following facts for 1 unit of inventory of the Sahara Company, a retailer:

Cost: $19
Ceiling: 14 (Net realizable value)
Floor: 10 (Net realizable value − Normal profit)

SITUATION 1 If we also assume that the replacement cost is $15, the ceiling of $14 is used as the market value. Why would the Sahara Company sell an item for $14 when the replacement cost is $15? One explanation would be that the supplier of the inventory has introduced a lower price on a new product so that the inventory held by the Sahara Company has become obsolete.

The loss in the period of the *write-down* is equal to the net realizable value (ceiling) less the historical cost. The expected profit in the period of *sale* is equal to the net realizable value less the ceiling (the new carrying value of the inventory). The loss and expected profit are:

Loss in period of write-down = $14 − $19
$$= \underline{\underline{\$\,(5)}}$$

Expected profit in period of sale = $14 − $14
$$= \underline{\underline{\$\;0}}$$

The loss of $5 is a measure of the expected loss that *would* have been recognized at the time of sale if the lower of cost or market rule had *not* been used. The loss is recognized in the current period instead of in a future period and, therefore, the expected profit at the time of the sale is zero. This loss concept is the same as that applied in other areas where the conservatism principle is used (such as contingencies and construction contracts, which we discuss in Chapters 12 and 17, respectively) because no provision is made for the recognition of a profit when the sale occurs in a future period.

SITUATION 2 Assume now that the replacement cost is $12. In this situation the replacement cost is used as the market value. Why would the Sahara Company sell an item for $14 when the replacement cost is $12 and its normal profit (the difference between the ceiling and floor) is $4? One explanation would be that the supplier has reduced its price on the product, so that the Sahara Company has to reduce its selling price in order to remain competitive with other retailers who have reduced their prices.

The loss in the period of the *write-down* is equal to the replacement cost less the historical cost. The expected profit in the period of *sale* is the net realizable value less the replacement cost (the new carrying value of the inventory). The loss and expected profit are:

Loss in period of write-down = $12 − $19
$$= \underline{\underline{\$\,(7)}}$$

Expected profit in period of sale = $14 − $12
$$= \underline{\underline{\$\;2}}$$

The loss of $7 is the measure of the cost saving that was missed because the inventory was purchased before the price decline. This alternative allows the company to recognize a profit of $2 at the time of sale, although it is less than the normal profit of $4.

SITUATION 3 Assume now that the replacement cost is $9. In this situation the floor of $10 is used as the market value. Why would the Sahara Company be able to sell an item for $14 when the replacement cost is $9 and its normal profit is $4? One explanation would be that the supplier has reduced the price on the product and has so stimulated demand that the retail price has not fallen as much.

The loss in the period of the *write-down* is equal to the floor (net receivable value minus the normal profit) less the historical cost. The expected profit in the period of *sale* is equal to the net realizable value less the floor (the new carrying value of the inventory). The loss and expected profit are:

$$\text{Loss in period of write-down} = \$10 - \$19$$
$$= \underline{\$\,(9)}$$

$$\text{Expected profit in period of sale} = \$14 - \$10$$
$$= \underline{\$\,\,4}$$

The loss of $9 is measured as the amount needed to provide a normal profit in the future. The expected profit at the time of sale is the normal profit of $4.

The loss concept in Situations 2 and 3 is *not* consistent with the conservatism principle applied in other situations because it allows a company to recognize profits in future periods when the sale is made. Note also that the total loss in all three situations is $5 [$(5) + $0; $(7) + $2; $(9) + $4]. At issue is the inconsistent application of accounting principles which results in different amounts of loss and profit that a company may recognize in the period of write-down and the period of sale.[2]

Approaches to Implementing Lower of Cost or Market Rule

A company may apply the lower of cost or market rule:

> to each item or to the total of the inventory (or, in some cases, to the total of the components of each major category). The method should be that which most clearly reflects periodic income.[3]

Applying the rule to each individual item in inventory results in an inventory value less than (or equal to) the values obtained by the other two alternatives. Under these other two alternatives the price declines of some of the units in inventory are offset by price rises in other items. You can see this in Exhibit 8-2, which illustrates the three alternative methods of implementing the lower of cost or market rule for a company in the first year of its operations. To simplify the example, we assume that there was no beginning inventory. Similar results would be obtained if the cost of the beginning inventory was less than or equal to the market value. If the company applies the lower of cost or market rule to individual items, the inventory valuation is $6,100 and it recognizes a loss of $600 ($6,100 market − $6,700 cost). This method is the most conservative alternative. If the company applies the rule to each category, the inventory valuation is $6,500 and it recognizes a loss of $200. If the company applies the rule to the total inventory, the valuation is $6,600 and it recognizes a loss of $100.

EXHIBIT 8-2   Approaches to Implementing Lower of Cost or Market

Inventory	Cost	Market	Individual Items	Category	Total
Category A:					
Item 1	$1,000	$ 700	$ 700		
Item 2	1,200	1,300	1,200		
	$2,200	$2,000		$2,000	
Category B:					
Item 3	$2,000	$2,400	2,000		
Item 4	2,500	2,200	2,200		
	$4,500	$4,600		4,500	
Total	$6,700	$6,600			$6,600
Inventory valuation			$6,100	$6,500	$6,600
Loss recognition			$ 600	$ 200	$ 100

2. For additional discussion of these issues, see S.E. Warner and F.D. Whitehurst, "An Illustration of Inventory Loss Measurements Under the LCM Rule," *The Accounting Educators' Journal* (Fall 1988), pp. 32–7.
3. *Accounting Research Bulletin No. 43, op. cit.*, par. 10.

The use of three alternative methods to account for the *same economic events* is inappropriate, since the qualitative characteristic of *comparability* among companies is enhanced when only one method is allowed. However, it can be expected that in many situations there will be no material differences from the use of the alternative methods. The most common practice is to apply the lower of cost or market rule to each individual item since it is required for income tax purposes and is the most conservative alternative. Of course, the method chosen should be applied consistently each period.

Once the inventory is reduced to market, it is *not* written back up to cost even if the market value subsequently rises above cost. Effectively, the written-down value becomes the new "cost" for subsequent valuation purposes. If the company is using the FIFO or average cost flow assumptions this affects the cost of goods sold in the next period. Therefore, the company may *implicitly* recognize recoveries of losses because the amount of the loss it recognizes in a given year is a function of the relationship between cost and market value of both the beginning and ending inventory, as we show in the next section.

Recording the Reduction of Inventory to Market

Although it is acceptable for a company to record the write-down of inventory cost to market value directly in its inventory and cost of goods sold accounts (*direct* method), it is more desirable to use a separate inventory valuation account and a loss account (*allowance* method) so that the effects of the write-down can be clearly identified. We illustrate the journal entries for both methods in Exhibit 8-3 for a company using FIFO and the periodic inventory system that has the following inventory values:

	Cost	Market
December 31, 2003	$20,000	$20,000
December 31, 2004	25,000	22,000
December 31, 2005	30,000	28,000

EXHIBIT 8-3   Recording the Reduction of Inventory to Market

	Periodic Inventory System			
	Direct Method		Allowance Method	
December 31, 2004				
1. To close beginning inventory:				
Income Summary	20,000		20,000	
Inventory		20,000		20,000
2. To record ending inventory:				
Inventory	22,000		25,000	
Income Summary		22,000		25,000
3. To record inventory at market:				
Loss Due to Market Valuation	Not required		3,000	
Allowance to Reduce Inventory to Market				3,000
December 31, 2005				
1. To close beginning inventory:				
Income Summary	22,000		25,000	
Inventory		22,000		25,000
2. To record ending inventory:				
Inventory	28,000		30,000	
Income Summary		28,000		30,000
3. To record inventory at market:				
Allowance to Reduce Inventory to Market	Not required		1,000	
Loss Recovery Due to Market Valuation				1,000

In the *direct* method, the company includes the $3,000 decline in the value of the inventory at the end of 2004 in the year-end closing entry by recording the ending inventory at its lower *market* value of $22,000. Consequently the Inventory account balance is $3,000 *lower* and Cost of Goods Sold is $3,000 *higher* than they otherwise would be. This lower inventory value of $22,000 is the beginning inventory for 2005. At the end of 2005 the market value is $2,000 below the cost of $30,000, and so the market value of $28,000 is included in the closing entry. The effect of the value of the beginning and ending inventory on cost of goods sold in 2005 should be considered carefully. The market value of the beginning inventory is $3,000 below cost, and this causes the cost of goods sold to be $3,000 *lower* than it otherwise would be. The market value of the ending inventory is $2,000 below cost, and this causes the cost of goods sold to be $2,000 *higher* than it otherwise would be. Therefore the net effect is that the cost of goods sold is $1,000 lower and gross profit (and income) is $1,000 higher in 2005, because the lower of cost or market value method is used.

The same net results are obtained when the *allowance* method is used. However, the method reveals more information about the impact of the lower of cost or market method on a company's cost of goods sold. In the allowance method, a company records the amount by which the market value is below cost in an Allowance account, and shows the effect on the cost of goods sold explicitly in a Loss (or Loss Recovery) account. In the closing entry at the end of 2004, the company records the inventory at its cost of $25,000, and records the decline in value of $3,000 separately in the Loss account and the Allowance account. At the end of 2005 the company records the inventory in the closing entry at its cost of $30,000. As we discuss later, the net effect of recording the beginning inventory at a book value of $3,000 below cost and the ending inventory at a book value of $2,000 below cost is to make cost of goods sold $1,000 lower than it otherwise would be. Therefore the company reduces the Allowance account by $1,000 and recognizes a Loss Recovery of $1,000. These losses and recoveries are shown as adjustments to cost of goods sold (as in the example in Exhibit 8-4) and therefore disclose more information than the direct method. However, many companies may combine the two amounts in their published financial statements.

If the company was using a perpetual inventory system instead of a periodic system, the net results would again be the same. The journal entries to record the reductions to market would be as follows:

	Direct Method			Allowance Method	
	2004	2005		2004	2005
Cost of Goods Sold	3,000	2,000			
Inventory	3,000	2,000			
Loss (Loss Recovery)					
due to Market Valuation				3,000	1,000
Allowance to Reduce					
Inventory to Market				3,000	1,000

If the company was using the *direct* method, it would recognize the reduction of $3,000 in the 2004 ending inventory by increasing cost of goods sold and reducing inventory. In 2005 it recognizes the reduction of $2,000 in the ending inventory in exactly the same way. Again note that the net effect of the reduction of the beginning and ending inventory ($3,000 and $2,000, respectively) on cost of goods sold in 2005 is that it is $1,000 lower than it would otherwise be. If the company was using the *allowance* method, the amount it records in the Allowance and in the Loss (or Loss Recovery) accounts is the same as for the periodic method.

We show the financial statement reporting of the direct and allowance methods for the periodic inventory method in Exhibit 8-4, assuming purchases in each year are $100,000. The advantage of the allowance method is that it clearly discloses the loss and loss recovery in the company's income statements (but not as extraordinary items)

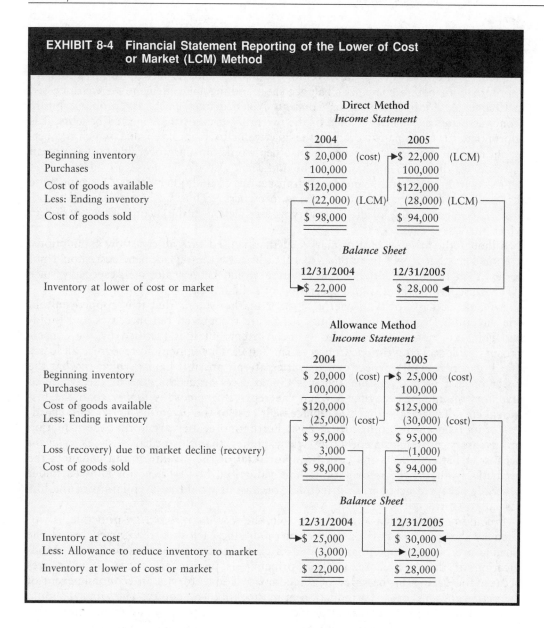

EXHIBIT 8-4   Financial Statement Reporting of the Lower of Cost or Market (LCM) Method

and the valuation adjustment in its respective balance sheets. Although this method is recommended and is used for many companies' internal financial statements, published financial statements generally do not disclose the size of the loss and the valuation allowance (unless one, or both, is material) but merely indicate that the lower of cost or market method is being used.

Lower of Cost or Market and Interim Financial Statements

APB Opinion No. 28 specifies that if a company experiences a market decline in an interim period and it considers the decline temporary, the company should ignore the decline in its interim financial statements. If the company is unlikely to recover the decline, it should recognize the amount. If the company recognizes a decline and then reverses it in a later *interim* period, it should recognize a loss recovery and increase the inventory value by the amount of the recovery, but only up to the original cost.[4]

---

4. "Interim Financial Reporting," *APB Opinion No. 28* (New York: AICPA, 1973), par. 14(c).

2 Explain the conceptual issues regarding the lower of cost or market method.

CONCEPTUAL EVALUATION OF LOWER OF COST OR MARKET

The reduction of the value of the inventory to market and the recognition of a loss are appropriate for both a company's balance sheet and income statement. As we discussed in Chapter 3, *FASB Statement of Concepts No. 6* defines *assets* as "probable future economic benefits." When the cost of the inventory exceeds the expected benefits, it is appropriate for a company to reduce the asset value to its market value, which is a better measure of the expected benefits. In other words, an unrecoverable cost is not an asset. As we discussed in Chapter 4, the *Statement* also defines *losses* as "decreases in net assets from peripheral or incidental transactions... and other events... except those that result from expenses or distributions to owners." Thus a company should recognize the decline in value of the inventory as a reduction in the income of the period in which the loss occurs.

Although the lower of cost or market method is used with all cost flow assumptions, it is unlikely that it will be applied to LIFO because the replacement cost should not be less than the LIFO cost. Such a situation would be very unusual, especially since LIFO is used when there is an expectation of rising costs.

A major criticism of the lower of cost or market rule is that it is applied only in one direction. Declines and (holding) losses are recognized but increases and (holding) gains are not. Obviously this is inconsistent but it is justified by the conservatism (prudence) convention. Conservatism requires a company to recognize all losses that it can reasonably expect and to anticipate no possible gains, which is what the lower of cost or market rule achieves. Some users argue that the market value of inventory should be recognized when the replacement cost is *higher* than the historical cost. They argue that the replacement cost of the inventory is *reliable* regardless of its relationship to historical cost. Furthermore, they argue that the valuation of inventory at replacement cost (when higher than historical cost) is *relevant* because it better reflects the **cash flow potential** of the inventory and enhances the predictive value of the information. This valuation, however, is not allowed under generally accepted accounting principles, because it would be a violation of the historical cost principle.

The valuation of assets at market value is discussed in Appendix E.

It could be argued that another principle, the *revenue recognition* principle, is violated by the lower of cost or market method, since a loss is recognized before the earning process is complete and before an exchange transaction has occurred. Modification of the revenue recognition principle is justified in these circumstances because the decline in the value of the company's inventory is an **economic event of the period** that has caused a reduction in its stockholders' equity. Therefore it should be included in the determination of income. However, the revenue recognition principle may be used to support the nonrecognition of increases in value, because the total difference between selling price and cost is usually recognized in the period of the sale. Also, recognition of an increase in the value of the inventory would require the recognition of income and would be a violation of the revenue recognition principle.

Since a company recognizes a loss in the period of the market decline, its income will be *higher* in the subsequent period when the inventory is sold than it would otherwise have been. In other words, the loss is transferred from the future period of the sale to the current period of the decline in market value. Total income over the two periods will be the same whether or not the lower of cost or market rule is used. This is shown by the earlier example in which recording the inventory at the lower of cost or market caused income to be lower by $3,000 in 2004 and higher by $1,000 in 2005. If the company recorded the inventory at cost in a subsequent year(s), its income will be higher by the $2,000 remaining in the Allowance account in that year(s). Therefore the company's total income over the years in which it recorded inventory at lower of cost or market will be the same as if it had recorded the inventory at cost for those years (because the beginning and ending inventory for the several years are both at cost).

International Accounting Differences

International accounting standards also require the use of the lower of cost or market method. However, market is defined as net realizable value and should typically be applied to individual items. International accounting standards also allow a reversal of a write-down and require disclosures about inventory that it written down, as well as any reversals.

PURCHASE OBLIGATIONS AND PRODUCT FINANCING ARRANGEMENTS

Accounting principles generally require that a company not record a purchase obligation in its accounts (except in governmental accounting), because neither an asset nor a liability is created by placing an order. **If a company has incurred an unconditional purchase obligation at a definite price, the company discloses this commitment in a note to its financial statements.**[5] This requirement is imposed because the commitment is important for the prediction of the cash outflows that the company will make in the future.

3 Understand purchase obligations and product financing arrangements.

If a company has an unconditional (noncancelable) purchase obligation to acquire inventory and the current market price (i.e., replacement cost) is less than the fixed purchase price, the company must recognize the loss in the period in which the decline occurs just as if it already owned the inventory. This procedure is consistent with the conservatism convention and also provides the users of the financial statements with information about the decision-making ability of the management. For example, if a company entered into a noncancelable commitment to purchase inventory at a fixed price of $500,000 and the market price (replacement cost) at the end of the year is $450,000, it would make the following year-end adjusting entry:

Loss on Purchase Commitments	50,000	
Accrued Loss on Purchase Commitments		50,000

The company reports the accrued loss as a liability on the balance sheet and writes it off when it purchases the goods as follows:

Inventory (or Purchases)	450,000	
Accrued Loss on Purchase Commitments	50,000	
Accounts Payable		500,000

If the market price rises by the time the company makes the purchase, it reduces the accrued loss and recognizes a loss recovery. It then records the purchases at the market price (cost) on the date of acquisition.

The company accrues the loss only when there is a loss on a *noncancelable* purchase commitment. Such a loss satisfies the criterion of a contingent loss contained in **FASB Statement No. 5,** namely, that the existence of the loss is probable and can be reasonably estimated. Losses on *cancelable* purchase commitments are not accrued because it is assumed that the purchase commitment can be canceled and the loss avoided.

Accounting for contingencies is discussed in Chapters 3 and 12.

Some companies have engaged in product financing arrangements as a way of financing the cost of inventory before the sale to the ultimate purchaser occurs. **In a product financing arrangement the company "sells" the inventory to another company and, in a related transaction, agrees to purchase the inventory (or a substantially identical item) back from the other company at specified prices over specified periods.** Typically the inventory is not delivered to the "buyer" and is repurchased at a higher price, the difference being an interest charge. When the "sale" under the product financing arrangement occurs, the transaction is similar to borrowing cash with the inventory being used as collateral, sometimes referred to as a "parking" transaction. Thus, according to **FASB Statement No. 49,** the company does *not* record sales revenue but instead records the proceeds received as a liability.[6] This procedure avoids the overstatement of revenues

---

5. "Disclosure of Long-Term Obligations," *FASB Statement of Financial Accounting Standards No. 47* (Stamford, Conn.: FASB, 1981), par. 7.

6. "Accounting for Product Financing Arrangements," *FASB Statement of Financial Accounting Standards No. 49* (Stamford, Conn.: FASB, 1981).

and stockholders' equity and the understatement of liabilities. As a result of not recording a sale, the inventory also remains in the accounts at cost. Note, however, that this *Statement* does *not* apply to agreements to repurchase at prices that are not specified.

VALUATION ABOVE COST

4 Explain the valuation of inven-tory above cost.

We stated earlier in this chapter that the lower of cost or market method does not result in a valuation of inventory above cost. However, generally accepted accounting principles do allow a company to value its inventory above cost in certain circumstances. **Accounting Research Bulletin No. 43** states:

> Only in exceptional cases may inventories properly be stated above cost. For example, precious metals having a fixed monetary value with no substantial cost of marketing may be stated at such monetary value; any other exceptions must be justifiable by inability to determine appropriate approximate costs, immediate marketability at quoted market price, and the characteristic of unit interchangeability. Where goods are stated above cost this fact should be fully disclosed.
>
> A similar treatment is not uncommon for inventories representing agricultural, mineral and other products, units of which are interchangeable and have an immediate marketability at quoted prices and for which appropriate costs may be difficult to obtain.[7]

Exhibit 8-5 shows an example of valuation at market prices for ConAgra. Justification for this method exists when it is highly certain that the inventory can be sold at the market price. Such a situation indicates that the income is earned by production rather than by sale. Therefore valuation at market, above cost, is considered to be appropriate. However, this practice violates the conservatism convention and the usual application of the revenue recognition principle, and is acceptable only in selected industries.

Revenue recognition is discussed in Chapter 17.

EXHIBIT 8-5   Inventory Valuation Above Cost

CONAGRA
NOTES (in part):

Inventories   Grain, flour, and major feed ingredient inventories are hedged to the extent practicable and are generally stated at market, including adjustment to market of open contracts for purchases and sales. Short-term interest expense incurred to finance hedged inventories is included in cost of sales in order to properly reflect gross margins on hedged transactions. Inventories not hedged are priced at the lower of average cost (first-in, first-out) or market.

GROSS PROFIT METHOD

5 Use the gross profit method.

Two commonly used methods of estimating inventory costs are (1) the gross profit method and (2) the retail inventory method, which companies in retail industries use and we discuss later in this chapter.

A company uses the gross profit method to estimate the cost of the inventory by applying a gross profit rate based on its income statements of previous periods to the net sales of the current period. It may be used in the following situations:

1. To determine the cost of the inventory at the end of an interim period without taking a physical count. Because of the cost of taking a physical inventory, a company using a periodic inventory system may use the gross profit method for its internal financial statements. It is also an acceptable method for interim financial

---

7. *Accounting Research Bulletin No. 43, op. cit.,* ch. 4, par. 15 and 16.

statements, provided that the company "disclose the method used at the interim date and any significant adjustments that result from reconciliations with the annual physical inventory."[8]

2. For the internal or external auditor to check the reasonableness of an inventory value developed from a physical inventory or perpetual inventory system. Also, the auditor can take a physical inventory count before the end of the year and then estimate the ending inventory.
3. To estimate the cost of inventory that is destroyed by a casualty, such as a fire.
4. To estimate the cost of the inventory from incomplete records. For example, if a company's inventory records are destroyed, the inventory can be estimated if the cost of goods available for sale and the sales are known or can be reconstructed.
5. To develop a budget of cost of goods sold and ending inventory from a sales budget.

The application of the gross profit method assumes that a company's gross profit rate (the rate of gross profit on net sales) in the current period is not materially different from that of the previous period(s). If there are any identifiable differences, adjustments should be made, as we discuss later. The steps that a company completes when using the gross profit method include:

1. The historical gross profit rate is calculated by dividing the gross profit of the prior period(s) by the net sales of the prior period(s).
2. The gross profit for the current period is estimated by multiplying the historical gross profit rate by the actual net sales for the period.
3. The estimated gross profit is subtracted from the actual net sales to determine the estimated cost of goods sold for the period.
4. The estimated cost of goods sold is subtracted from the actual cost of goods available for sale (the beginning inventory plus the net purchases) for the period to determine the estimated cost of the ending inventory.

We illustrate the application of this method for a company in Exhibit 8-6 and list each of the preceding steps in parentheses. The company uses the historical gross

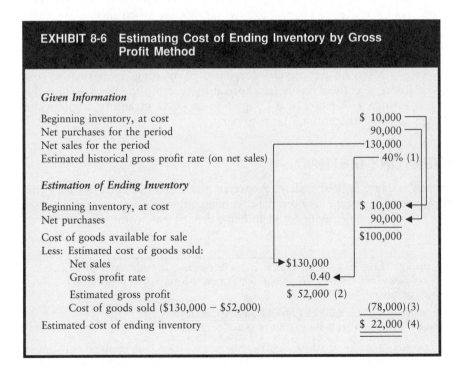

EXHIBIT 8-6 Estimating Cost of Ending Inventory by Gross Profit Method

Given Information

Beginning inventory, at cost	$ 10,000
Net purchases for the period	90,000
Net sales for the period	130,000
Estimated historical gross profit rate (on net sales)	40% (1)

Estimation of Ending Inventory

Beginning inventory, at cost		$ 10,000
Net purchases		90,000
Cost of goods available for sale		$100,000
Less: Estimated cost of goods sold:		
Net sales	$130,000	
Gross profit rate	0.40	
Estimated gross profit	$ 52,000 (2)	
Cost of goods sold ($130,000 − $52,000)		(78,000) (3)
Estimated cost of ending inventory		$ 22,000 (4)

8. *APB Opinion No. 28, op. cit.*, par. 14(a).

profit rate of 40% because it believes this rate represents the best estimate of conditions in the current year; that is, no material changes in conditions from previous years have occurred.[9]

One step may be removed from the calculation shown in Exhibit 8-6. Since the gross profit is 40% of net sales, the cost of goods sold is 60% of net sales. Therefore the cost of goods sold could be calculated directly as $78,000 (60% × $130,000).

Conceptual Evaluation of the Gross Profit Method

The gross profit method is useful in the situations outlined at the beginning of this section, but the relevance of the results depends on the accuracy of the gross profit percentage. Three modifications to the procedure outlined previously may enhance its accuracy.

First, a company should adjust the gross profit rate for known changes in the relationship between its gross profit and net sales. For example, if the company's costs of purchases have increased, but it has not passed on the increases to customers through increased sales prices, it should reduce the gross profit percentage accordingly. The company may also need to adjust the gross profit rate if it has experienced a change in productivity or a change in the amount of sales (and purchases) returns and allowances.

Second, a company may use a separate gross profit rate for each department or type of inventory that has a different markup percentage. It would then apply separate rates to each department's net sales, and sum the resulting amounts to compute the total inventory. Use of a single, overall gross profit rate assumes that all types of inventory are sold or held in inventory in equal proportions at all times. Since this is unlikely, use of separate gross profit rates enhances the accuracy of the cost of the ending inventory and the cost of goods sold.

Third, a company may use an average gross profit rate based on several past periods to average out period-to-period fluctuations. However, use of an average rate assumes that no significant changes occurred over the periods selected for the calculation of the average rate and that the company made no adjustments to account for such changes. The use of an average rate is particularly appropriate when there is an environment of relatively stable costs, selling prices, and operating methods.

The ending inventory estimated by the gross profit method is consistent with the cost flow assumption previously (and currently) used by the company. This occurs because the gross profit rate is based on past results developed from using the particular cost flow assumption. However, if there has been a special situation in the past, such as the reduction of the inventory to market, or a liquidation of LIFO inventory, appropriate adjustments to the gross profit rate will be required.

RETAIL INVENTORY METHOD

6 Understand the retail inventory method.

The retail inventory method is used widely to estimate the cost of inventory when there is a consistently observable pattern between the cost of a company's purchases and selling prices (either for the whole company or for identifiable departments within the company).

---

9. Sometimes a company will express gross profit as a percent of cost of goods sold instead of as a percent of net sales. In this case it must convert the gross profit percent to a percent of net sales before it can apply the gross profit method, as follows:

$$\frac{\text{Gross Profit to Net}}{\text{Sales Ratio}} = \frac{\text{Gross Profit to Cost of Goods Sold Ratio}}{1 + \text{Gross Profit to Cost of Goods Sold Ratio}}$$

Alternatively, if the gross profit to net sales ratio is known, and calculation of the gross profit to cost of goods sold ratio (often called the markup percentage) is required, the following formula can be used:

$$\frac{\text{Gross Profit to Cost of}}{\text{Goods Sold Ratio}} = \frac{\text{Gross Profit to Net Sales Ratio}}{1 - \text{Gross Profit to Net Sales Ratio}}$$

The method is particularly appropriate for retail stores where prices often are set on the basis of a consistent markup above cost and the accounting systems are based on retail values rather than costs. The retail inventory method can be applied on the basis of the average, FIFO, and LIFO cost flow assumptions, and the lower of cost or market method can be used in conjunction with each. The retail inventory method has gained wide acceptance because it is allowed under generally accepted accounting principles and for income tax purposes.

The retail inventory method requires a company to use the following information:

1. Beginning inventory at cost and retail
2. Goods purchased at cost and retail
3. Changes in selling price resulting from additional markups and markdowns
4. Sales

Assuming that a company uses the retail inventory method in conjunction with the *average* cost flow assumption, the following steps are necessary:

1. The total goods available for sale (beginning inventory plus purchases) is computed at both cost and retail value (selling price).
2. A cost-to-retail ratio is computed by dividing the cost of the goods available for sale by the retail value of the goods available for sale.
3. The ending inventory at retail is computed by subtracting the sales for the period from the retail value of the goods available for sale.
4. The ending inventory at cost is computed by multiplying the ending inventory at retail by the cost-to-retail ratio.

We illustrate the application of this method for a company using the following simplified data:

	Cost	Retail
Beginning inventory	$10,000	$17,000
Purchases	50,000	83,000
Sales		80,000

The ending inventory at cost is computed as follows (each of the preceding steps is referenced in the calculation):

	Cost	Retail	
Beginning inventory	$10,000	$ 17,000	
Purchases	50,000	83,000	
Goods available for sale	$60,000	$100,000	(1)

$$\text{Cost-to-retail ratio:} \frac{\$\,60,000}{\$100,000} = 0.60 \qquad (2)$$

Less: Sales	(80,000)	
Ending inventory at retail	$ 20,000	(3)

Ending inventory at cost (0.60 × $20,000) $12,000   (4)

The retail inventory method is similar to the gross profit method because it estimates inventory based on a profit percentage. It differs, however, and is more sensitive to price changes because it uses a current-period estimate of the profit percentage, whereas the gross profit method uses an estimate based on past periods. This similarity is summarized as follows:

Gross Profit Method	Retail Inventory Method
Beginning inventory at cost	Beginning inventory at retail
+ Purchases at cost	+ Purchases at retail
= Cost of goods available	= Retail value of goods available
− Cost of goods sold	− Retail value of goods sold (sales)
[sales × (1 − estimated gross profit rate)]	= Ending inventory at retail
	× actual cost-to-retail ratio
= Ending inventory at cost	= Ending inventory at cost

The major advantages of the retail inventory method are:

1. It permits a company to prepare interim reports without taking a physical inventory; but as with any inventory system, the company should take a physical count at least annually.
2. It simplifies a company's record-keeping procedures because the company does not need to maintain the costs of *individual* purchases and does not have to relate them to the particular units in inventory. In addition, retail stores typically price and display merchandise immediately, and base their record keeping on retail prices.
3. It expedites the verification of a company's ending inventory by physical count because the company records the inventory in the retail store at retail values and can therefore compare it directly with the accounting records, which are also based on retail prices. Thus, the company does not need to refer to the individual purchase invoices to determine the cost of each item.

Retail Inventory Method Terminology

In the preceding illustration we assumed that the retail value of the goods available for sale is the original sales price, and that the company made no subsequent changes in retail prices. However, the typical retail store makes many changes in selling prices after setting the original price. (For the average retail food store there are likely to be hundreds of changes each week.) The following seven terms are used to describe these changes:

1. *Markup.* The original markup from cost to the first selling price (also known as *mark-on*).
2. *Additional Markup.* An increase above the original sales price.
3. *Markup Cancellation.* A reduction in the selling price after there has been an additional markup. The markup cancellation cannot be greater than the additional markup.
4. *Net Markup.* The total additional markups less the total markup cancellations.
5. *Markdown.* A decrease below the original sales price.
6. *Markdown Cancellation.* An increase in the selling price after there has been a markdown. The markdown cancellation cannot be greater than the markdown.
7. *Net Markdown.* The total markdowns less the total markdown cancellations.

To illustrate the meaning of these terms, suppose that a company purchased an item for $6 and initially priced the item to sell for $10. The markup is $4. If the company subsequently increases the selling price to $12, there is an additional markup of $2. If it then lowers the selling price to $7, there is a markup cancellation of $2 and a markdown of $3. If the company then raises the selling price to $8, there is a markdown cancellation of $1. The net markup is zero ($2 − $2), and the net markdown is $2 ($3 − $1).

Application of the Retail Inventory Method

In the simplified example shown earlier, we used the average cost flow assumption. However, companies may use the retail inventory method to develop inventory valuations under four alternatives (we do not illustrate the lower of cost or market used with FIFO and LIFO):

1. *FIFO.* Exclude the cost and the retail value of the beginning inventory from the computation of the cost-to-retail ratio for the period. The ratio includes both net markups and net markdowns.
2. *Average Cost.* Include the cost and the retail value of the beginning inventory and net markups and markdowns in the cost-to-retail ratio.
3. *LIFO.* Compute separate ratios for each layer in the beginning inventory and for the purchases of the current period; include both net markups and net markdowns in the cost-to-retail ratio for the current period.
4. *Lower of Average Cost or Market.* Include the cost and retail value of the beginning inventory and net markups in the cost-to-retail ratio. Thus, the net markdowns are excluded from the computation of the cost-to-retail ratio. This method is also known as the *conventional retail* method.

The calculation of the cost-to-retail ratio of the current period for each of the alternative methods are summarized as follows:

	FIFO	Average Cost	LIFO*	Lower of Average Cost or Market
Beginning inventory	Exclude	Include	Exclude	Include
Purchases	Include	Include	Include	Include
Markups (net)	Include	Include	Include	Include
Markdowns (net)	Include	Include	Include	Exclude

*A separate cost-to-retail ratio is also computed for each layer in the beginning inventory.

Note that these alternative methods differ in the calculation of the cost-to-retail ratio, but that the net markups and markdowns *always* are added and subtracted in order to compute the retail value of the ending inventory. Also note that markups and markdowns are recorded only at *retail*. We illustrate each of these methods in the following sections, using the data for the Thompson Company given in Exhibit 8-7.

EXHIBIT 8-7   Thompson Company Inventory Cost and Retail Value

	Cost	Retail
Beginning inventory	$20	$ 35
Purchases	40	80
Net markups	—	5
Net markdowns	—	(10)
Goods available for sale	$60	$110
Sales		(66)
Ending inventory at retail		$ 44

Note: It is assumed that the beginning inventory is valued at a cost of $20 for all flow assumptions, although this value would be different for different cost flow assumptions because the beginning inventory for the current period is the ending inventory of the previous period.

FIFO   Under the FIFO cost flow assumption the beginning inventory is excluded from the computation of the cost-to-retail ratio for the period. The Thompson Company would compute the cost of its ending inventory at $23.45, as we show in Exhibit 8-8.

EXHIBIT 8-8   Retail Inventory Method—FIFO

	Cost	Retail
Purchases	$40	$ 80
Net markups		5
Net markdowns		(10)
	$40	$ 75
Cost-to-retail ratio: $\dfrac{\$40}{\$75} = 0.533$ (for purchases)		
Beginning inventory	20	35
Goods available for sale	$60	$110
Less: Sales		(66)
Ending inventory at retail		$ 44
Ending inventory at FIFO cost (0.533 × $44)	$23.45	

Excluding the beginning inventory from the computation of the cost-to-retail ratio produces the layering effect of FIFO for cost of goods sold. Since the ending inventory cost is based only on the activities of the current period, the entire beginning inventory is included in the cost of goods sold. Therefore the *cost of goods sold* is made up of two layers as follows:

	Cost	Retail
Beginning inventory	$20.00	$35
Purchases at retail		31
Purchases at cost ($31 × 0.533)	16.52	
	$36.52	$66

Thus the cost of goods available for sale of $60 is allocated (amounts rounded) between cost of goods sold ($36.52) and ending inventory ($23.45).[10]

AVERAGE COST   Under the average cost flow assumption the beginning inventory and the net markups and markdowns are included in the cost-to-retail ratio. The Thompson Company would estimate the cost of its ending inventory at $24, as we show in Exhibit 8-9.

There are similarities between this application of the average cost flow assumption and the more general average cost method we discussed in the preceding chapter. The beginning inventory and the purchases are commingled. Since the company sold at retail 60% ($66 ÷ $110) of the goods available for sale, 40% of the goods are left in ending inventory. The cost of the inventory is $24, which is 40% of the cost of the goods available for sale (40% × $60 = $24).

LIFO   Separate cost-to-retail ratios for the beginning inventory and the purchases must be calculated when the LIFO cost flow assumption is applied to the retail inventory method. The ratio for the purchases includes both markups and markdowns if the cost basis is used. (Remember that a company may use LIFO for income tax purposes only

---

10. Note that in this example we assumed that the units sold during the period exceed the units in the beginning inventory; therefore, under FIFO the company includes the cost of the entire beginning inventory in cost of goods sold during the current period. If some of the beginning inventory still remained at the end of the period, the ending inventory would include two layers, each with its own cost-to-retail ratio.

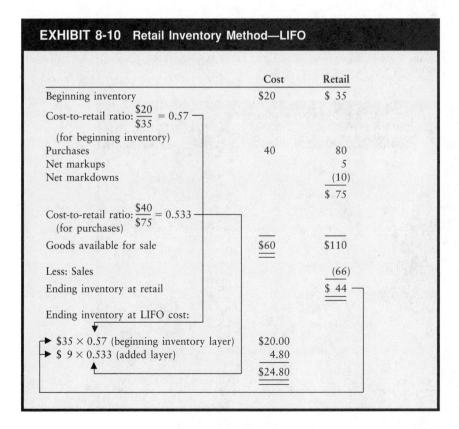

EXHIBIT 8-9   Retail Inventory Method—Average Cost

	Cost	Retail
Beginning inventory	$20	$ 35
Purchases	40	80
Net markups		5
Net markdowns		(10)
Goods available for sale	$60	$110

Cost-to-retail ratio: $\dfrac{\$60}{\$110} = 0.545$

| Less: Sales | | (66) |
| Ending inventory at retail | | $ 44 |

Ending inventory at average cost $(0.545 \times \$44)$ $24

if it also uses LIFO for financial reporting.) The layers of inventory are accounted for by using the same principles as those discussed in the preceding chapter. The Thompson Company would compute the cost of its ending inventory at $24.80, as we show in Exhibit 8-10.

The company had sales of $66, which left an inventory at retail of $44. This inventory consists of two layers, one of which is the base inventory at retail of $35, and the other an addition at retail of $9. Each layer is converted to cost at its own cost-to-retail ratio. Another way of looking at this example is to see that the Thompson Company sold 88% ($66 ÷ $75) of the goods purchased during the period. Therefore at cost the

EXHIBIT 8-10   Retail Inventory Method—LIFO

	Cost	Retail
Beginning inventory	$20	$ 35

Cost-to-retail ratio: $\dfrac{\$20}{\$35} = 0.57$
(for beginning inventory)

Purchases	40	80
Net markups		5
Net markdowns		(10)
		$ 75

Cost-to-retail ratio: $\dfrac{\$40}{\$75} = 0.533$
(for purchases)

Goods available for sale	$60	$110
Less: Sales		(66)
Ending inventory at retail		$ 44

Ending inventory at LIFO cost:

$35 × 0.57 (beginning inventory layer)	$20.00	
$ 9 × 0.533 (added layer)	4.80	
	$24.80	

company sold $35.20 (88% × $40) of the purchases, leaving $4.80 ($40 − $35.20) as an added layer in inventory.

Note that in the Thompson Company example, the LIFO method does not produce the lowest ending inventory cost (in comparison to FIFO or average). The reason is that the cost-to-retail ratio for the purchases is less than the cost-to-retail ratio for the beginning inventory. This situation was caused by the large markdowns during the period, indicating the existence of falling costs (which may be caused by a decline in the prices charged by the supplier or by obsolescence due to a change in tastes or the season of the year). When costs are rising, the retail method using LIFO will produce a lower inventory cost.

If there was a decrease in inventory over the period, the ending inventory would be composed only of a portion of the beginning inventory, and there would be no need to compute a cost-to-retail ratio for the purchases of the current period. In more complex situations the beginning inventory would be comprised of LIFO layers, each with its own cost-to-retail ratio, and the decrease would have to be removed according to the general LIFO principles discussed in the preceding chapter.

LOWER OF AVERAGE COST OR MARKET   The retail inventory method can be used with lower of cost or market under either the average, FIFO, or LIFO cost flow assumptions. In all three cases, net markdowns are excluded from the cost-to-retail ratio for the period to achieve the effects of the lower of cost or market method, and the appropriate flow assumption is used. Because the lower of average cost or market is commonly used, we will illustrate this alternative. The calculations follow the average cost example earlier, except that the net markdowns are *excluded* from the computation of the cost-to-retail ratio. The Thompson Company would compute the value of its ending inventory at $22, as we show in Exhibit 8-11.

Since the net markdowns are excluded from the computation of the cost-to-retail ratio, the denominator of the ratio is higher ($120 in Exhibit 8-11 as compared to $110 in Exhibit 8-9). Therefore, the ratio is lower (0.50 versus 0.545) and the cost of the ending inventory is lower ($22 versus $24). We discuss the assumptions underlying this calculation later in the chapter.

Additional Cost and Retail Adjustments

A company has to consider how to treat other costs and activities when it applies the retail inventory method. The cost of purchases includes the costs directly or indirectly

---

EXHIBIT 8-11   Retail Inventory Method—Lower of Average Cost or Market

	Cost	Retail
Beginning inventory	$20	$ 35
Purchases	40	80
Net markups		5
	$60	$120
Cost-to-retail ratio: $\frac{\$60}{\$120} = 0.50$		
Net markdowns		(10)
Goods available for sale	$60	$110
Less: Sales		(66)
Ending inventory at retail		$ 44
Ending inventory at lower of cost or market (0.50 × $44)	$22	

incurred in bringing the items to their existing condition and location (as we discussed in Chapter 7). Two items that affect net purchases are (1) freight charges, which are added to the cost of purchases, and (2) purchases discounts taken under the gross price method, which are subtracted from the cost of purchases. These two items affect only the *cost* of purchases and not the retail amount of purchases, because it is assumed that the original markup applied to the invoice cost by the company covers such incidental items. A third item that affects net purchases is purchases returns and allowances. Once the purchases are recorded by a company at retail, any subsequent purchases returns and allowances are subtracted from *both the cost and the retail value* of the purchases so as not to distort the computation of the cost-to-retail ratio.

Several items also affect the estimate of the ending inventory at retail. Sales returns and allowances are subtracted from sales at retail to determine net sales, which in turn are subtracted from goods available for sale at retail to compute ending inventory at retail. Sales discounts taken are *not* deducted to determine the ending inventory at retail, because they are considered to be financing items and not part of the original markup. Since inventory shrinkage, especially that due to breakage and theft, is a common problem in retail stores, whenever the retail inventory method is used for interim financial statements, an estimate should be made of normal shrinkage (such as 1% of sales) based on past experience. This estimate is then subtracted, in addition to the usual items, to determine the ending inventory at retail. An estimate is not necessary at year-end because a physical inventory is taken. Employee discounts—discounts from the normal sales price that are made available to employees—also are subtracted to compute ending inventory at retail (in the same way as sales). Both inventory shrinkage and employee discounts are subtracted because they are normal costs incurred by the company and therefore were reflected in the retail selling price determined by the original markup. Abnormal inventory spoilage would be subtracted at both cost and retail in the determination of goods available for sale so as not to distort the cost-to-retail ratio.

CONCEPTUAL EVALUATION OF THE RETAIL INVENTORY METHOD

7 Explain the conceptual issues regarding the retail inventory method.

Two general assumptions underlie the use of the retail inventory method. The first is that the items in a company's inventory are sufficiently homogeneous so that all have the same markup, or, if they have different markups, that the proportion of the different items in the ending inventory is the same as that in the goods available for sale. The company can reduce the limitations imposed by this assumption by using a separate cost-to-retail ratio for each category of inventory or for each department. The second general assumption is that the cost-to-retail ratio remains constant over the accounting period or that changes in the retail prices parallel the changes in the costs of purchases. The limitations imposed by this assumption can also be reduced by weighting the different cost-to-retail ratios used during the period according to the volume of activity that occurred for inventory items under each ratio.

Since the lower of average cost or market method is the most used version of the retail inventory method, it is important to consider whether this method actually does produce an inventory at lower of cost or market, or just a value that is lower than cost. We evaluate this in the three examples of Exhibit 8-12, which use the same basic information for the Thompson Company.

In all three examples we assume that the company sells 60% of the goods available for sale, but we use different assumptions regarding the markups and markdowns in each example. In the first example we assume that there are only markups and no markdowns. Thus, the cost-to-retail ratio is $60 \div $120 and the ending inventory $24. This cost is the same as the average cost figure computed in Exhibit 8-9. Since there were no markdowns, it can be assumed that the market value has not declined below cost, and therefore the inventory value is the lower of cost or market.

In the second example we assume that there are no markups but that there are markdowns. This produces a cost-to-retail ratio of $60 \div $115 and an ending inventory of $21.91. Since there are markdowns of $10, it can be assumed that prices have declined by

---

EXHIBIT 8-12   Assumptions Underlying the Use of the Retail Inventory Method: Lower of Average Cost or Market

	Example 1 (no markdowns)		Example 2 (no markups)		Example 3 (all markdowns sold)	
	Cost	Retail	Cost	Retail	Cost	Retail
Beginning inventory	$20	$ 35	$20	$ 35	$20	$ 35
Purchases	40	80	40	80	40	80
Net markups		5		—		5
	$60	$120	$60	$115	$60	$120
Cost-to-retail ratio:		0.50[1]		0.52[2]		0.50[3]
Net markdowns		—		(10)		(10)
Goods available for sale	$60	$120	$60	$105	$60	$110
Less: Sales		(72)[4]		(63)[5]		(62)[6]
Ending inventory at retail		$ 48		$ 42		$ 48
Ending inventory at lower of cost or market	$24[7]		$21.91[8]		$24[9]	

[1] $\frac{\$60}{\$120} = 0.50$ [2] $\frac{\$60}{\$115} = 0.52$ [3] $\frac{\$60}{\$120} = 0.50$ [4]($120 \times 60\%$)   [5]($105 \times 60\%$)

[6]($120 \times 60\% - \$10$)   [7]$\frac{\$60}{\$120} \times \$48$ [8]$\frac{\$60}{\$115} \times \$42$ [9]$\frac{\$60}{\$120} \times \$48$

---

a factor of 10 ÷ 115. To reflect this change, the ending inventory is valued at the lower of cost or market, which is $21.91 [$24 − ($24 × 10 ÷ 115)]. Therefore, in this situation the method again has produced an inventory amount equal to the lower of cost or market.

Now refer back to the original computation of the lower of cost or market in Exhibit 8-11. Since $22 is greater than $21.91, the $22 value is *not* the true lower of cost or market of the inventory, but simply a value that is lower than cost. This indicates that the lower of cost or market method is accurate only if the goods in the inventory are perfectly homogeneous. In other words, markups and markdowns for separate items within inventory cannot exist at the same time.

In the third example, again there are both markups and markdowns. The cost-to-retail ratio is $60 ÷ $120. But now we assume that all the goods that are marked down are sold. Since we also assumed that 60% of the goods available for sale are sold, sales would be equal to 60% of the goods available for sale, less the $10 markdowns [(60% × $120) − $10 = $62]. The ending inventory is $24, which is again the lower of cost or market, because we assumed that all goods marked down have been sold and thus the ending inventory contains items that have a retail value that is higher than their cost. Therefore, for the lower of cost or market method to be accurate, the goods in inventory do not have to be perfectly homogeneous if it can be assumed that all the units that have been marked down have been sold.

To summarize, **the lower of average cost or market method is accurate only if either markups and markdowns do not exist at the same time or if all the marked-down items have been sold.** Under other conditions the method produces an inventory value that is less than cost but only approximates the lower of cost or market.

DOLLAR-VALUE LIFO RETAIL METHOD

8 Understand the dollar-value LIFO retail method.

We discussed the advantages of the dollar-value LIFO method in the previous chapter, and we discussed the advantages of the retail method earlier in this chapter. Many retail companies take advantage of both these methods by using the dollar-value LIFO retail method, which combines the principles of the retail LIFO method with the dollar-value

---

EXHIBIT 8-13 Weston Company Cost and Retail Values and Price Indexes

| | 2004 | | 2005 | | 2006 | |
	Cost	Retail	Cost	Retail	Cost	Retail
Jan. 1, inventory	$ 8,000	$12,000				
Purchases	20,400	32,000	$25,600	$41,000	$26,040	$45,000
Net markups		3,000		2,000		1,000
Net markdowns		(1,000)		(3,000)		(4,000)
Sales		(29,800)		(32,240)		(42,990)

Price Index:
Jan. 1, 2004	100
Dec. 31, 2004	108
Dec. 31, 2005	115
Dec. 31, 2006	120

Note: It is assumed that LIFO is adopted on January 1, 2004.

LIFO method. Although no new principles are involved, we provide an illustration of the dollar-value retail LIFO inventory method for the Weston Company because of the complexity involved. We provide the basic information in Exhibit 8-13, and we show the calculation of the cost of the ending inventory in Exhibit 8-14.

The cost-to-retail ratio is computed in the same manner as we described earlier for the LIFO retail method; that is, the ratio includes both net markups and net markdowns but excludes the beginning inventory. The dollar-value LIFO concepts are applied to the retail values as follows (the numbers in parentheses are from Exhibit 8-14 for 2004):

1. The ending inventory at retail ($16,200) is computed by adding the beginning inventory, purchases, and the markups, and subtracting the markdowns and sales, or at year-end by taking a physical inventory in which the number of units in ending inventory is multiplied by the current-year retail prices.
2. The ending inventory at retail ($16,200) is converted to base-year retail prices ($15,000) by applying the base-year conversion index:

$$\frac{\text{Ending Inventory at}}{\text{Base-Year Retail Prices}} = \frac{\text{Ending Inventory}}{\text{at Retail}} \times \frac{\text{Base-Year Retail Price Index}}{\text{Current-Year Price Index}}$$

Note that the conversion index used here is based on a *price* index, while the conversion index used in Chapter 7 was based on a *cost* index. A price index is computed in the same way as a cost index, except that retail prices are used.
3. The increase (decrease) in the inventory at retail in base-year prices is computed by comparing the ending inventory with the beginning inventory when both are measured at retail in base-year prices (an increase of $3,000).
4. The increase (decrease) in the inventory at retail in base-year prices ($3,000) is converted to current-year retail prices ($3,240) by multiplying by the appropriate conversion index. If there is an *increase*, the current year conversion index is used as follows:

$$\frac{\text{Layer Increase at}}{\text{Current-Year Retail Prices}} = \frac{\text{Increase at Base-}}{\text{Year Retail Prices}} \times \frac{\text{Current-Year Price Index}}{\text{Base-Year Price Index}}$$

Alternatively, if there is a *decrease*, the conversion index for the appropriate LIFO layer is used as follows:

$$\frac{\text{Decrease at Retail Prices of}}{\text{Most Recently Added Layer}} = \frac{\text{Decrease at Base-}}{\text{Year Retail Prices}} \times \frac{\substack{\text{Price Index of Most} \\ \text{Recently Added Layer}}}{\text{Base-Year Price Index}}$$

EXHIBIT 8-14 Dollar-Value LIFO Retail Inventory Method

	2004 Cost	2004 Retail	2005 Cost	2005 Retail	2006 Cost	2006 Retail
Beginning inventory*	$ 8,000	$12,000	$ 9,944	$16,200	$14,238	$23,960
Purchases	20,400	$32,000	25,600	$41,000		$45,000
Net markups		3,000		2,000		1,000
Net markdowns		(1,000)		(3,000)		(4,000)
		34,000		40,000		42,000
Goods available for sale	$28,400	$46,000	$35,544	$56,200		$65,960
Sales		(29,800)		(32,240)		(42,990)
Ending inventory at retail		$16,200 (1)		$23,960		$22,970
Ending inventory at retail at base-year prices:						
$16,200 × (100 ÷ 108)	$15,000 (2)					
$23,960 × (100 ÷ 115)			$20,835			
$22,970 × (100 ÷ 120)						$19,142
Inventory change at retail base-year prices:						
$15,000 − $12,000	$ 3,000 (3)					
$20,835 − $15,000			$ 5,835			
$19,142 − $20,835						$ (1,693)
Change at retail at relevant current prices:*						
$3,000 × (108 ÷ 100)	$ 3,240 (4)					
$5,835 × (115 ÷ 100)			$ 6,710			
($1,693) × (115 ÷ 100)						$ (1,947)
Change at relevant current costs:*						
$3,240 × 0.60	$ 1,944 (5)					
$6,710 × 0.64			$ 4,294			
($1,947) × 0.64						$ (1,246)
Year-end LIFO inventory:						
Base-year layer	$ 8,000		$ 8,000			$ 8,000
Layer added in 2004	1,944		1,944			1,944
Layer added in 2005			4,294			4,294
Layer subtracted in 2006 at 2005 costs						(1,246)
Ending inventory	$ 9,944 (6)		$14,238			$12,992

*2004 cost-to-retail ratio for beginning inventory: $8,000 ÷ $12,000 = 0.667; 2004 cost-to-retail ratio for purchases: $20,400 ÷ $34,000 = 0.60; 2005 cost-to-retail ratio for purchases: $25,600 ÷ $40,000 = 0.64.

Note that for large decreases that affect more than one layer of inventory, the price index applicable to each layer must be used in the conversion index.

5. The increase (decrease) at current-year retail prices is converted to cost ($1,944) by multiplying by the cost-to-retail ratio for the appropriate year. If there is an increase, the cost-to-retail ratio for the current year is used (0.60). If there is a decrease, the cost-to-retail ratio(s) for the LIFO layer(s) being removed is used.

6. The ending inventory at cost ($9,944) is computed by adding (subtracting) the increase (decrease) at cost to the beginning inventory at cost ($1,944 + $8,000).

Continuing the example, in 2005 the ending inventory at retail of $23,960 is converted to base-year retail prices of $20,835 by multiplying by the base-year conversion index (100 ÷ 115). Comparing the $20,835 to the ending inventory at retail base-year prices in 2004 of $15,000 results in an increase in inventory at base-year retail prices of $5,835. This increase is multiplied by the current-year conversion index of 115 ÷ 100 to compute the increase at current retail prices of $6,710. The $6,710 is multiplied by the cost-to-retail ratio of 0.64 to compute the $4,294 increase at current-year costs, which is added to the $9,944 ending inventory cost from 2004 to determine the $14,238 cost of the ending inventory for 2005.

In 2006 there is a *decrease* in the inventory of $1,693 at base-year retail prices. This is converted into a $1,947 decrease by applying the conversion index for 2005, since part of the layer added in 2005 is being removed. This decrease of $1,947 at retail is converted to cost by applying the cost-to-retail ratio for 2005 of 0.64, resulting in a decrease at cost of $1,246. Note that the conversion index of 115 ÷ 100 and the cost ratio of 0.64 would be used only for a reduction in inventory at base-year retail prices of $5,835, because this is the amount of the increase from 2005. The next $3,000 reduction at base-year retail prices would be at the conversion index of 108 ÷ 100 and the cost ratio of 0.60 (for the layer added in 2004) and the remaining $12,000 at a conversion index of 100 ÷ 100 and the cost ratio of 0.667 (for the beginning inventory from 2004).

EFFECTS OF INVENTORY ERRORS

In addition to the special methods we described earlier in the chapter, errors made by a company may affect its ending inventory valuation. Errors in the valuation of inventory and the recording of purchases can result in inaccurate values on the company's balance sheet and income statement. Next we summarize the effects of some common errors (assuming a periodic inventory system and disregarding income taxes):

9 Understand the effects of inventory errors on the financial statements.

I. A purchase on credit is omitted from both the Purchases account and ending inventory and is *not* recorded in the succeeding year.
  A. **Current year**
    1. *Income Statement*. Income is correct because the errors in the purchases and ending inventory offset each other.
    2. *Balance Sheet*. Ending inventory and accounts payable are understated.
  B. **Succeeding year**
    1. *Income Statement*. Income is overstated because beginning inventory is understated and therefore cost of goods sold is understated.
    2. *Balance Sheet*. Accounts payable is understated and retained earnings is overstated. Note that if the purchase omitted from the current year was included in the succeeding year, the income would be correct in the second year because the errors would again offset each other. Accounts payable and retained earnings would also be correct.
II. A purchase on credit is omitted from the Purchases account but ending inventory is correct.
  A. **Current year**
    1. *Income Statement*. Income is overstated because purchases are understated and therefore cost of goods sold is understated.

  2. *Balance Sheet*. Accounts payable is understated because a purchase has been omitted. Retained earnings is overstated because income is overstated.

 B. **Succeeding year**

  1. *Income Statement*. No effect because the beginning inventory, purchases, and ending inventory are correct.

  2. *Balance Sheet*. Accounts payable is understated and retained earnings is overstated, due to the error in the previous period.

III. Ending inventory is over(under)stated due to quantity and/or costing errors, but purchases are correct.

 A. **Current year**

  1. *Income Statement*. Income is over(under)stated because cost of goods sold is under(over)stated.

  2. *Balance Sheet*. Ending inventory and retained earnings are over(under)stated.

 B. **Succeeding year**

  1. *Income Statement*. Income is under(over)stated because beginning inventory is over(under)stated, and therefore cost of goods sold is over(under)stated.

  2. *Balance Sheet*. Correct because the errors in inventory and retained earnings in the previous year were counterbalanced in this year.

Note that in this third situation the total income for the two years combined is correct, as is the ending inventory for the succeeding year. To illustrate, assume that a company's periodic inventory at December 31, 2004 is overstated by $5,000 but purchases are correct. The following errors occur (ignoring income taxes) in the company's financial statements:

 2004: *Income Statement*. Cost of goods sold is understated by $5,000 and income is overstated by $5,000.
   Balance Sheet. Ending inventory and retained earnings are overstated by $5,000.

 2005: *Income Statement*. Cost of goods sold is overstated by $5,000 and income is understated by $5,000.
   Balance Sheet. Ending inventory and retained earnings are correct because the errors have counterbalanced each other.

These errors are illustrated by the following equations:

	Beginning Inventory	**+ Purchases**	**= Cost of Goods Sold**	**+ Ending Inventory**
2004:	Correct	Correct	−$5,000	+$5,000
2005:	+$5,000	Correct	+$5,000	Correct

Note that if income taxes are considered, the effect of the error on income is reduced. For example, if the company has an income tax rate of 30%, the inventory is still is overstated by $5,000, but net income in 2004 is overstated by only $3,500 [$5,000 × (1 − 0.30)] and income taxes payable is increased by $1,500 ($5,000 × 0.30). Thus the errors affect more items on the company's balance sheet, but the balance sheet still balances because assets are overstated by $5,000, liabilities by $1,500, and stockholders' equity by $3,500.

  The discovery of inventory errors requires careful analysis and the preparation of adjusting entries to correct the company's accounts. If a company discovers a material error after it has closed the books, it treats the correction as a prior period adjustment. In this case it corrects the permanent (real) accounts. The company makes the corrections it would have made to temporary (nominal) accounts to Retained Earnings instead.

Accounting for errors is discussed in Chapter 22.

SUMMARY OF INVENTORY ISSUES

In Chapters 7 and 8, we discussed the inventory systems, methods, and adjustments that a company may use to account for its cost of goods sold and ending inventory. We summarize these issues in Exhibit 8-15 to help you understand their relationships.

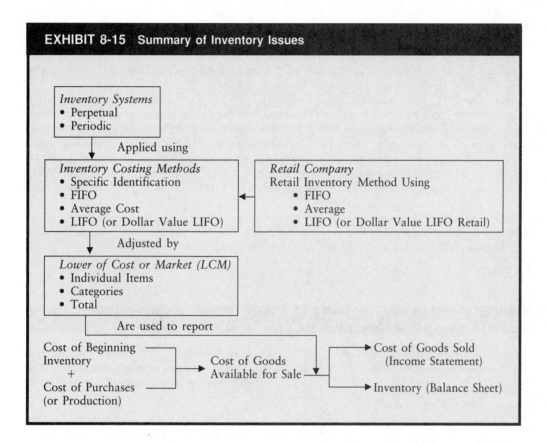

EXHIBIT 8-15 Summary of Inventory Issues

SUMMARY

At the beginning of the chapter, we identified several objectives you would accomplish after reading the chapter. The objectives are listed below, each followed by a brief summary of the key points in the chapter discussion.

1. **Understand the lower of cost or market method.** The lower of cost or market rule requires that a company write down its inventory to market value (replacement cost) when its utility has declined. The upper constraint on the market value is that the market value should not exceed the net realizable value. The lower constraint is that the market value should not be below the net realizable value reduced by an allowance for a normal profit margin. A company may apply the method to each item in inventory, to major categories, or to the inventory as a whole.

2. **Explain the conceptual issues regarding the lower of cost or market method.** The conceptual issues include the appropriateness of recognizing a loss and a reduction in the value of the inventory before a transaction occurs. Another issue is that a company only recognizes declines in value. The method also affects the amount of profit a company recognizes in future periods.

3. **Understand purchase obligations and product financing arrangements.** If a company has incurred an unconditional purchase obligation at a definite price, the company discloses this commitment in a note to its financial statements. In a product financing arrangement, the company does not recognize the transfer of the inventory as a sale, but records the proceeds received as a liability.

4. **Explain the valuation of inventory above cost.** Inventory may be valued above cost only in rare circumstances, such as for precious metals and certain agricultural and mineral products.

5. **Use the gross profit method.** A company uses the gross profit method to estimate the cost of the inventory by applying a gross profit rate based on its income statements of previous periods to the net sales of the current

period. It deducts the estimated gross profit from the actual net sales to determine the estimated cost of goods sold and deducts the latter amount from the cost of goods available for sale to determine the estimated ending inventory.

6. **Understand the retail inventory method.** Retail companies often use the retail inventory method in which they compute the ending inventory at cost by multiplying the ending inventory at retail by a cost-to-retail ratio. The computation of the cost-to-retail ratio varies depending on which cost flow assumption the company is using, and whether it is using the lower of cost or market method.

7. **Explain the conceptual issues regarding the retail inventory method.** The retail inventory method involves two assumptions. First, the items in inventory are assumed to be relatively homogeneous so that they have the same markup. Second, the cost-to-retail ratio is assumed to remain constant over the period. Furthermore, the lower of average cost or market retail method (the most widely used method) is accurate only if either markups and markdowns do not exist at the same time or if all the marked-down items have been sold.

8. **Understand the dollar-value LIFO retail method.** Under the dollar-value LIFO retail method, a company determines its ending inventory at retail and then converts this amount to the ending inventory at base-year retail prices by applying a base-year conversion index. It then determines the increase (decrease) in inventory at base-year retail prices and converts this amount to current-year retail prices using the appropriate conversion index. It converts the increase (decrease) to cost using the cost-to-retail ratio for the current year and then adds (subtracts) this amount to the beginning inventory at cost to determine the ending inventory at cost. The dollar-value LIFO retail method combines the advantages of the dollar-value LIFO method with those of the retail method.

9. **Understand the effects of inventory errors on the financial statements.** Errors in the valuation of inventory and the recording of purchases can result in inaccurate values on a company's balance sheet and income statement. The company must carefully examine each error to determine the appropriate correction.

QUESTIONS

Q8-1   Define the terms *cost* and *market* as used in the lower of cost or market inventory valuation rule.

Q8-2   Define the *upper* and *lower* constraints used in the lower of cost or market rule. What is the purpose of each constraint?

Q8-3   How may a company apply the lower of cost or market method to its inventory?

Q8-4   What arguments may be used against the lower of cost or market rule?

Q8-5   Under what conditions does a company anticipate price declines?

Q8-6   How, and under what conditions, does a company recognize a purchase obligation or a product financing arrangement in its financial statements?

Q8-7   What are the exceptions to historical cost valuation of inventory allowed under generally accepted accounting principles? Under what conditions is each allowed?

Q8-8   Describe four situations in which the gross profit method of estimating inventory would be useful.

Q8-9   What is the basic assumption underlying the gross profit method? How may the gross profit percentage for the prior year be modified to provide a better estimate of the inventory value?

Q8-10   What are the necessary conditions for the retail inventory method to provide valid results?

Q8-11   Explain the meaning of the following terms: *markup, additional markup, markup cancellation, net markup, markdown, markdown cancellation, net markdown.*

Q8-12   Describe how a company computes the cost-to-retail ratio for the following cost flow assumptions: FIFO, average cost, LIFO, lower of average cost or market. Why do the different methods approximate each cost flow assumption?

Q8-13   What assumptions are necessary for the lower of cost or market retail inventory method to actually produce an inventory value equal to the lower of average cost or market?

Q8-14   The retail inventory method indicated an inventory value of $80,000. A physical inventory indicated a value of $70,000. Suggest possible causes of this discrepancy.

Q8-15   Indicate the effect of each of the following errors on a company's balance sheet and income statement of the current and succeeding years:

a. The ending inventory is overstated.

b. Merchandise received was not recorded in the Purchases account until the succeeding year although the item was included in inventory of the current year.

c. Merchandise purchases shipped FOB shipping point were not recorded in either the Purchases account or the ending inventory.

d. The ending inventory was understated as a result of the exclusion of goods sent out on consignment.

CASES

C O M M U N I C A T I O N

C8-1 Retail Inventory Method

The Sandberg Paint Company, your client, manufactures paint. The company's president, Ms. Sandberg, has decided to open a retail store to sell Sandberg paint as well as wallpaper and other supplies that it would purchase from other suppliers. She has asked you for information about the retail method of pricing inventories at the retail store.

Required Prepare a report to the president explaining the retail method of pricing inventories. Your report should include these four points:

1. Description and accounting features of the method.
2. The conditions that may distort the results under the method.
3. A comparison of the advantages of using the retail method with those of using cost methods of inventory pricing.
4. The accounting theory underlying the treatment of net markdowns and net markups under the method. (*AICPA adapted*)

C8-2 Gross Profit

The Shelly Corporation is an importer and wholesaler. Its merchandise is purchased from several suppliers and is warehoused by Shelly Corporation until sold to consumers.

In conducting her audit for the year ended June 30, 2004 the corporation's CPA determined that the system of internal control was good. Accordingly, she observed the physical inventory at an interim date, May 31, 2004, instead of at year-end.

The CPA obtained the following information from the general ledger:

Inventory, July 1, 2003	$ 87,500
Physical inventory, May 31, 2004	95,000
Sales for 11 months ended May 31, 2004	840,000
Sales for year ended June 30, 2004	960,000
Purchases for 11 months ended May 31, 2004 (before audit adjustments)	675,000
Purchases for year ended June 30, 2004 (before audit adjustments)	800,000

The CPA's audit disclosed the following information:

Shipments received in May and included in the physical inventory but recorded as June purchases	$7,500
Shipments received in unsalable condition and excluded from physical inventory; credit memos had not been received nor had chargebacks to vendors been recorded:	
Total at May 31, 2004	$1,000
Total at June 30, 2004 (including the May unrecorded chargebacks)	$1,500
Deposit made with vendor and charged to purchases in April 2004. Product was shipped in July 2004.	$2,000
Deposit made with vendor and charged to purchases in May 2004. Product was shipped, FOB destination, on May 28, 2004, and was included in May 31, 2004 physical inventory as goods in transit.	$5,500
Through the carelessness of the receiving department, a June shipment was damaged by rain. This shipment was later sold in June at its cost of $10,000.	

Required In audit engagements in which interim physical inventories are observed, a frequently used auditing procedure is to test the reasonableness of the year-end inventory by the application of gross profit ratios. Prepare in good form the following schedules:

1. Computation of the gross profit ratio for 11 months ended May 31, 2004.
2. Computation by the gross profit ratio method of cost of goods sold during June 2004.
3. Computation by the gross profit ratio method of June 30, 2004 inventory. (*AICPA adapted*)

C R E A T I V E A N D C R I T I C A L T H I N K I N G

C8-3 Lower of Cost or Market Method

Blaedon Co. makes ongoing design refinements to lawnmowers that are produced for it by contractors. Blaedon stores the lawnmowers in its own warehouse and sells them at list price, directly to retailers. Blaedon uses the FIFO inventory method. Approximately two-thirds of

new lawnmower sales involve trade-ins. For each used lawnmower traded in and returned to Blaedon, retailers receive a $40 allowance regardless of whether the trade-in was associated with a sale of a 2004 or 2005 model. Blaedon's net realizable value on a used lawnmower averages $25.

At December 31, 2004, Blaedon's inventory of new lawnmowers includes both 2004 and 2005 models. When the 2005 model was introduced in September 2004, the list price of the remaining 2004 model lawnmowers was reduced below cost. Blaedon is experiencing rising costs.

Required

1. At December 31, 2004, how should Blaedon determine the carrying amounts assigned to its lawnmower inventory of
   a. 2005 models?
   b. 2004 models?
2. Considering only the 2005 model lawnmower, explain the impact of the FIFO cost flow assumptions on Blaedon's 2004
   a. Income statement amounts.
   b. Balance sheet amounts. (*AICPA adapted*)

C8-4   Retail Inventory Method

Retail, Inc., sells normal brand-name household products both from its own store and on consignment through The Mall Space Company.

Required

1. Explain whether Retail, Inc., should include in its inventory normal brand-name goods purchased from its suppliers but not yet received if the terms of purchase are FOB shipping point (manufacturer's plant).
2. Explain whether Retail, Inc., should include freight-in expenditures as an inventoriable cost.
3. Retail, Inc., purchased cooking utensils for sale in the ordinary course of business three times during the current year, each time at a higher price than the previous purchase. Explain the effect on ending inventory and cost of goods sold if Retail, Inc., used the weighted-average cost method instead of the FIFO method.
4. Explain how and why Retail, Inc., will treat net markdowns when it calculates the estimated cost of ending inventory using the conventional (lower of cost or market) retail inventory method.
5. Explain what products on consignment are and how they are presented on the balance sheets of Retail, Inc., and The Mall Space Company. (*AICPA adapted*)

C8-5   Various Inventory Issues

Diane Company, a retailer and wholesaler of national brand-name household lighting fixtures, purchases its inventories from various suppliers.

Required

1. a. What criteria are used to determine which of Diane's costs are inventoriable?
   b. Are Diane's administrative costs inventoriable? Defend your answer.
2. a. Diane uses the lower of cost or market rule for its wholesale inventories. Explain the theoretical arguments for that rule.
   b. The replacement cost of the inventories is below the net realizable value less a normal profit margin, which, in turn, is below the original cost. Explain the amount that is used to value the inventories.
3. Diane calculates the estimated cost of its ending inventories held for sale at retail using the conventional (lower of average cost or market) retail inventory method. Explain how Diane would treat the beginning inventories and net markdowns in calculating the cost ratio used to determine its ending inventories. (*AICPA adapted*)

C8-6   LCM, Dollar-Value LIFO, and Consignments

Caddell Company, a wholesaler, purchases its inventories from various suppliers FOB destination; it incurs substantial warehousing costs. Caddell uses the dollar-value LIFO inventory cost flow method. Caddell also consigns some of its inventories to Reed Company.

Reed also has items for sale that it purchases from other wholesalers. Reed uses the lower of FIFO cost or market inventory method.

Required

1. When are the purchases from various suppliers generally included in Caddell's inventory? Why?
2. Theoretically, how should Caddell account for the warehousing costs? Why?
3. a. Explain the advantages of using the dollar-value LIFO inventory cost flow method as opposed to the conventional quantity of goods LIFO method.
   b. How does the calculation of dollar-value LIFO differ from the conventional quantity of goods method?
4. Explain how Caddell should account for the inventories consigned to Reed Company.
5. When Reed applies the lower of cost or market method, what are the ceiling and floor limits? (*AICPA adapted*)

C8-7   Inventory Valuation Issues

Hanlon Company purchased a significant amount of raw materials inventory for a new product that it is manufacturing. Hanlon purchased insurance on these raw materials while they were in transit from the supplier.

Hanlon uses the lower of cost or market rule for these raw materials. The replacement cost of the raw materials is above the net realizable value and both are below the original cost.

Hanlon uses the average cost inventory method for these raw materials. In the last two years, each purchase has been at a lower price than the previous purchase, and the ending inventory quantity for each period has been higher than the beginning inventory quantity for that period.

Required

1. Explain the theoretically appropriate method that Hanlon should use to account for the insurance costs on the raw materials while they were in transit from the supplier.
2. a. Explain the amount at which Hanlon should report the raw materials inventory on its balance sheet.

b. In general, explain why the lower of cost or market rule is used to report inventory.

3. Explain what would have been the effect on ending inventory and cost of goods sold had Hanlon used the LIFO inventory method instead of the average cost inventory method for the raw materials. (*AICPA adapted*)

C8-8 Various Inventory Issues

Hudson Company, which is both a wholesaler and a retailer, purchases its inventories from various suppliers. Additional facts for Hudson's wholesale operations are as follows:

- Hudson incurs substantial warehousing costs.
- Hudson uses the lower of cost or market method.
- The replacement cost of the inventories is below the net realizable value and above the net realizable value less the normal profit margin. The original cost of the inventories is above the replacement cost and below the net realizable value.

Additional facts for Hudson's retail operations are as follows:

- Hudson determines the estimated cost of its ending inventories held for sale at retail using the conventional retail inventory method, which approximates lower of average cost or market.
- Hudson incurs substantial freight-in costs.
- Hudson has net markups and net markdowns.

Required

1. Theoretically, how should Hudson account for the warehousing costs related to its wholesale inventories? Why?
2. a. In general, explain why the lower of cost or market method is used to report inventory.
   b. At which amount should Hudson report the wholesale inventories on its balance sheet? Explain the

application of the lower of cost or market method in this situation.

3. In the calculation of the cost-to-retail percentage used to determine the estimated cost of its ending retail inventories, how should Hudson treat
   a. Freight-in costs?
   b. Net markups?
   c. Net markdowns?
4. Explain why Hudson's retail inventory method approximates lower of average cost or market. (*AICPA adapted*)

C8-9 Ethics and Retail Inventory

You are the accountant for the South-Western Division of HiValue Grocery Stores. Late in December, Kelly Cholak, the CEO of the Division stops by your office and says "I have a couple of questions. I recently received a report from the head office on the first 11 months of the year. We are not doing as well as we budgeted and they are not happy with the gross profit we have earned. But the good news is that I just got off the phone with a big supplier who has excess inventory and could sell us enough of their products to last us three months. They have offered us a great price—lower than we have paid in a couple of years. Then I remembered that you use that funny LIFO retail inventory method where you play with such confusing numbers. Will the purchase reduce our retail ratio, or whatever you call it, so that our inventory is lower and cost of goods sold higher, because that would only make us look worse? Alternatively, I thought that we could delay this purchase until after January 1 and we might be able to have one of those LIFO liquid profits and make ourselves look good for the year's results. Give these issues some thought and let's have a drink after work today to discuss them."

Required From financial reporting and ethical perspectives, how would you reply to Kelly?

MULTIPLE CHOICE

Select the best answer for each of the following.

M8-1 Moore Company carries product A in inventory on December 31, 2004 at its unit cost of $7.50. Because of a sharp decline in demand for the product, the selling price was reduced to $8.00 per unit. Moore's normal profit margin on product A is $1.60, disposal costs are $1.00 per unit, and the replacement cost is $5.30. Under the rule of cost or market, whichever is lower, Moore's December 31, 2004 inventory of product A should be valued at a unit cost of

a. $5.30   c. $7.00
b. $5.40   d. $7.50

M8-2 Under the retail inventory method, freight-in would be included in the calculation of the goods available for sale for which of the following?

	Cost	Retail
a.	No	No
b.	No	Yes
c.	Yes	No
d.	Yes	Yes

M8-3 The following information is available for the Silver Company for the three months ended March 31, 2004:

Merchandise inventory, January 1, 2004	$ 900,000
Purchases	3,400,000
Freight-in	200,000
Sales	4,800,000

The gross margin recorded was 25% of sales. What should be the merchandise inventory at March 31, 2004?

a. $700,000   c. $1,125,000
b. $900,000   d. $1,200,000

M8-4   The retail inventory method would include which of the following in the calculation of the goods available for sale at both cost and retail?

a. Freight-in
b. Purchases returns
c. Markups
d. Markdowns

M8-5   During 2004 R Corp., a manufacturer of chocolate candies, contracted to purchase 100,000 pounds of cocoa beans at $1.00 per pound, delivery to be made in the spring of 2005. Because a record harvest is predicted for 2005, the price per pound for cocoa beans had fallen to $.80 by December 31, 2004.

Of the following journal entries, the one that would properly reflect in 2004 the effect of the commitment of R Corp. to purchase the 100,000 pounds of cocoa is

		Debit	Credit
a.	Cocoa Inventory	100,000	
	Accounts Payable		100,000
b.	Cocoa Inventory	80,000	
	Loss on Purchase Commitments (an expense account)	20,000	
	Accounts Payable		100,000
c.	Loss on Purchase Commitments (an expense account)	20,000	
	Accrued Loss on Purchase Commitments (a liability account)		20,000
d.	No entry would be necessary in 2004		

M8-6   The replacement cost of an inventory item is below the net realizable value and above the net realizable value less the normal profit margin. The original cost of the inventory item is above the replacement cost and below the net realizable value. As a result, under the lower of cost or market method, the inventory item should be valued at the

a. Net realizable value
b. Original cost
c. Replacement cost
d. Net realizable value less the normal profit margin

M8-7   At December 31, 2004 the following information was available from Crisford Company's books:

	Cost	Retail
Inventory, 1/1/04	$14,700	$ 20,300
Purchases	83,300	115,500
Additional markups	—	4,200
Available for sale	$98,000	$140,000

Sales for the year totaled $110,600; markdowns amounted to $1,400. Under the approximate lower of average cost or market retail method, Crisford's inventory at December 31, 2004 was

a. $30,800
b. $28,000
c. $21,560
d. $19,600

M8-8   Hestor Company's records indicate the following information:

Merchandise inventory, January 1, 2004	$ 550,000
Purchases, January 1 through December 31, 2004	2,250,000
Sales, January 1 through December 31, 2004	3,000,000

On December 31, 2004 a physical inventory determined that ending inventory of $600,000 was in the warehouse. Hestors gross profit on sales has remained constant at 30%. Hestor suspects some of the inventory may have been taken by some new employees. At December 31, 2004 what is the estimated cost of missing inventory?

a. $100,000
b. $200,000
c. $300,000
d. $700,000

M8-9   Estimates of price-level changes for specific inventories are required for which of the following inventory methods?

a. Conventional retail
b. Weighted average cost
c. FIFO
d. Dollar-value retail LIFO

M8-10   A company forgets to record a purchase on credit in the Purchases account, but ending inventory is correct. The effect of this mistake in the current year is:

	Income	Cost of goods sold	Accounts payable	Retained earnings
a.	Overstated	Understated	Understated	Overstated
b.	Understated	Overstated	Overstated	Understated
c.	Overstated	Understated	Overstated	Understated
d.	Understated	Overstated	Understated	Overstated

(*AICPA adapted*)

EXERCISES

E8-1   *Lower of Cost or Market*   The Stiles Corporation uses the lower of cost or market method for each of two products in its ending inventory. A profit margin of 30% on the selling price is considered normal for each product. Specific data for each product are as follows:

	Product A	Product B
Historical cost	$ 68	$ 91
Replacement cost	60	93
Estimated cost of disposal	32	52
Estimated selling price	140	200

Required What is the correct inventory value for each product?

E8-2   *Lower of Cost or Market*   The following information for the Tuell Company is available:

	Case				
	1	**2**	**3**	**4**	**5**
Cost	$5.00	$5.00	$5.00	$5.00	$5.00
Net realizable value	5.10	5.50	4.80	4.20	4.70
Net realizable value less normal profit	4.80	5.30	4.70	4.00	4.60
Replacement cost	5.30	5.20	4.60	4.10	4.80

Required What is the correct inventory value in each of the preceding situations?

E8-3   *Lower of Cost or Market*   The following information is taken from the records of the Aden Company:

Product	Group	Units	Cost/Unit	Market/Unit
A	1	600	$ 1.00	$ 0.80
B	1	250	1.50	1.55
C	2	150	5.00	5.25
D	2	100	6.50	6.40
E	3	80	25.00	24.60

Required What is the correct inventory value if the company applies the lower of cost or market to each of the following?
1. Individual items
2. Groups of items
3. The inventory as a whole

E8-4   *Lower of Cost or Market*   The inventories of the Berry Company for the years 2004 and 2005 are as follows:

	Cost	Market
January 1, 2004	$10,000	$10,000
December 31, 2004	13,000	11,500
December 31, 2005	15,000	14,000

Required Prepare the necessary journal entries at the end of each year to record the correct inventory valuation. Use the allowance method and assume that a periodic inventory system is used.

E8-5   *Loss on Purchase Commitment*   During 2004 the Boge Corporation signed a noncancelable contract to purchase 10,000 bushels of soybeans at $5 per bushel with delivery to be made in 2005. On December 31, 2004, the price of soybeans had fallen to $4.50 per bushel. On May 1, 2005, the Boge Corporation takes delivery of the soybeans when the price is $4.75 per bushel.

Required Prepare the journal entries required on December 31, 2004 and May 1, 2005.

E8-6   *Estimation of Fire Loss*   On September 28, 2004 a fire destroyed the entire merchandise inventory of the Carroll Corporation. The following information is available:

Sales, January 1—September 28, 2004	$540,000
Inventory, January 1, 2004	$150,000
Merchandise purchases, January 1—September 28, 2004	
(including $60,000 of goods in transit on September 28,	
2004, shipped FOB shipping point)	$465,000
Markup percentage on cost	20%

Required What is the estimated inventory on September 28, 2004 immediately prior to the fire?

E8-7   **Gross Profit Method**   On November 21, 2004 a fire at Hodge Company's warehouse caused severe damage to its entire inventory of Product Tex. Hodge estimates that all usable damaged goods can be sold for $10,000. The following information was available from Hodge's accounting records for Product Tex:

Inventory at November 1, 2004 $100,000
Purchases from November 1, 2004 to date of fire   140,000
Net sales from November 1, 2004 to date of fire   220,000

Based on recent history, Hodge had a gross margin (profit) on Product Tex of 30% of net sales.

Required Prepare a schedule to calculate the estimated loss on the inventory in the fire, using the gross margin (profit) method. Show supporting computations in good form. (*AICPA adapted*)

E8-8   **Gross Profit**   The following gross profit data are taken from the financial records of the Eckhardt Company:

	2004	2005
Sales	$300,000	$296,000
Cost of goods sold	(200,000)	(203,300)
Gross profit	$100,000	$ 92,700

Required

1. If it is known that volume declined 5% from 2004 to 2005, by how much did selling prices change?
2. If it is known that volume declined 5% from 2004 to 2005, by how much did costs change?
3. If selling prices increased 4% from 2004 to 2005, what effect would this factor alone have on gross profit?
4. If costs increased by 7% from 2004 to 2005, what effect would this factor have on gross profit?

E8-9   **Gross Profit Percentage**   An accountant sometimes must convert gross profit percentages.

Required

1. Convert the following gross profit percentages based on net sales to gross profit as a percentage of the cost of goods sold: 20%, 25%, and 40%.
2. Convert the following gross profit percentages based on the cost of goods sold to gross profit as a percentage of net sales: 20%, 25%, and 40%.

E8-10   **Retail Inventory Method**   The Harmes Company is a clothing store that uses the retail inventory method. The following information relates to its operations during 2004:

	Cost	Retail
Inventory, January 1	$28,400	$ 40,200
Purchases	65,200	100,000
Markups (net)	—	1,900
Markdowns (net)	—	400
Sales	—	80,000

Required Compute the ending inventory by the retail inventory method for the following cost flow assumptions:

1. FIFO   3. LIFO
2. Average cost   4. Lower of cost or market (based on average cost)

E8-11   **Retail Inventory Method**   The following data were available from the records of the Hegge Department Store for the year ended December 31, 2004:

	At Cost	At Retail
Merchandise inventory, January 1, 2004:	$ 90,000	$130,000
Purchases	330,000	460,000
Markups	—	10,000
Markdowns	—	40,000
Sales	—	480,000

Required Using the retail method, what is the estimate of the merchandise inventory at December 31, 2004 valued at the lower of cost or market? (*AICPA adapted*)

E8-12 *Retail Inventory Method* The following information relates to the retail inventory method used by the Jeffress
@ Company:

	Cost	Retail
Beginning inventory	$11,160	$18,000
Purchases	54,600	92,400
Freight-in	840	—
Net markups	—	600
Net markdowns	—	1,144
Sales	—	94,056

Required Compute the ending inventory by the retail inventory method, using the following cost flow assumptions:

1. FIFO
2. Average cost
3. LIFO
4. Lower of cost or market (based on average cost)

E8-13 *Dollar-Value LIFO Retail* The Johns Company adopts the dollar-value LIFO retail inventory method on
January 1, 2004. The following information for 2004 is obtained from the company's records:

	Cost	Retail
Inventory, January 1, 2004	$20,000	$29,000
Purchases	60,000	92,000
Net markups	—	1,000
Net markdowns	—	3,000
Sales	—	75,000

The price index on January 1, 2004 was 100 and on December 31, 2004 it was 110.

Required Compute the cost of the inventory on December 31, 2004.

E8-14 *Dollar-Value LIFO Retail* The Wyatt Company adopts the dollar-value LIFO retail inventory method on
@ January 1, 2004. The company's records reveal that the inventory on January 1, 2004 had a cost of $75,000
and a retail value of $120,000. During 2004 the cost of purchases made was $110,000, and the retail value
was $165,000. In addition, net markdowns were $6,000, net markups were $8,000, and sales were $147,000.
The price index on January 1, 2004 was 100 and the index for 2004 was 110.

Required Compute the cost of inventory on December 31, 2004. (Round the cost-to-retail index to 3 decimal places.)

E8-15 *Dollar-Value LIFO Retail* On December 31, 2003 Davison Company adopted the dollar-value LIFO retail
inventory method. Inventory data for 2004 are as follows:

	LIFO Cost	Retail
Inventory, 12/31/03	$360,000	$500,000
Inventory, 12/31/04	?	660,000
Increase in price level for 2004		10%
Cost-to-retail ratio for 2004		70%

Required Compute the cost of Davison Company's inventory at December 31, 2004. (*AICPA adapted*)

E8-16 *Errors* A company that uses the periodic inventory system makes the following errors:

1. It omits a purchase on account from the Purchases account and the ending inventory.
2. It omits a purchase on account from the Purchases account, but the ending inventory is correct.
3. It overstates the ending inventory, but purchases are correct.

Required Indicate the effect of the preceding errors on the income statement and the balance sheet of the
current and succeeding years.

E8-17 *Errors* During the course of your examination of the financial statements of Burnett Co., a new client, for
the year ended December 31, 2004, you discover the following:

Inventory at January 1, 2004 was understated by $6,000.
Inventory at December 31, 2004 was overstated by $5,000.

During 2004 the company received a $1,000 cash advance from a customer for merchandise to be manufactured and shipped during 2005. It had credited the $1,000 to sales revenue. The company's gross profit on sales is 50%. Net income reported on the 2004 income statement (before reflecting any adjustments for the above items) is $20,000.

Required What is the correct net income for 2004? (*AICPA adapted*)

PROBLEMS

P8-1   *Lower of Cost or Market* The Palmquist Company has five different inventory items that it values by the lower of cost or market method. The normal markup on all items is 20% of cost. The following information is obtained from the company's records:

Item	Units	Cost	Replacement Cost	Net Realizable Value
1	500	$10.00	$ 9.10	$ 9.20
2	400	8.00	8.10	7.80
3	300	15.00	13.50	14.00
4	200	18.00	12.00	17.00
5	100	25.00	25.50	25.30

Required

1. Compute the lower of cost or market value for each item.
2. Compute the total inventory value if the lower of cost or market is applied to (a) each individual item and (b) the inventory as a whole. Explain the reason for the difference between the two values.

P8-2   *Lower of Cost or Market* The following are the inventories for the years 2004, 2005, and 2006 for the Parry Company:

	Cost	Market
January 1, 2004	$50,000	$50,000
December 31, 2004	64,000	60,000
December 31, 2005	71,000	70,000
December 31, 2006	75,000	78,000

Required Prepare journal entries to record the lower of cost or market for each of the following alternatives:

1. Allowance method, periodic inventory system
2. Allowance method, perpetual inventory system
3. Direct method, periodic inventory system
4. Direct method, perpetual inventory system

P8-3   *Lower of Cost or Market and Interim Financial Statements* The following values were obtained from the inventory records of the Robb Company, which has a fiscal year ending on December 31:

	Cost	Market
Inventory, January 1, 2004	$10,000	$10,500
Inventory, March 31, 2004	12,000	11,500

Required

1. Under what conditions does the company ignore the decline in inventory value below cost in its interim financial statements?
2. Assuming that the company records the market value, what is the journal entry to record the decline if the company uses the perpetual inventory system and the allowance method?

P8-4   *Lower of Cost or Market* The inventory records of the Frost Company for the years 2004 and 2005 reveal the cost and market of the January 1, 2004 inventory to be $125,000. On December 31, 2004 the cost of inventory was $130,000, while the market value was only $128,000. The December 31, 2005 market value of inventory was $140,000, and the cost was only $135,000. The Frost Company uses a periodic inventory system. Purchases for 2004 were $100,000 and for 2005 were $110,000.

Required

1. Prepare the journal entries at the end of 2004 and 2005 to record the lower of cost or market under the (a) allowance method, and (b) direct method.
2. Prepare the cost of goods sold section of the income statement and show how the company would record the inventory on its balance sheet for 2004 and 2005 under the (a) allowance method, and (b) direct method.

P8-5   *Gross Profit*   The following information relates to the activities of the Skeen Corporation for 2004:

Goods in process, January 1	$25,000	Finished goods, December 31	$ 30,000
Goods in process, December 31	40,000	Cost of production	70,000
Finished goods, January 1	37,000	Sales (net)	100,000

Required What is the gross profit as a percentage of net sales?

P8-6   *Estimation of Theft Loss*   You are requested by a client on September 28 to prepare an insurance claim for a theft loss which occurred on that day. You immediately take an inventory and obtain the following data:

Inventory, September 1	$38,000	Sales, September 1—September 28	$52,000
Purchases received, September 1—September 28	19,000	Sales returns	1,000

The inventory on September 28 indicates that an inventory of $15,000 remains after the theft. During the past year net sales were made at 50% above the cost of goods sold.

Required Compute the inventory lost during the theft.

P8-7   *Estimation of Fire Loss*   On January 20, 2005 the records of the Stewart Company revealed the following information:

Inventory, July 1, 2004	$ 53,600	Purchases discounts taken	$5,800
Purchases, July 1, 2004—January 20, 2005	368,000	Freight-in	3,800
Sales, July 1, 2004—January 20, 2005	583,000	Sales returns	6,600
Purchases returns	11,200		

A fire destroyed the entire inventory on January 20, 2005 except for purchases in transit, FOB shipping point, of $6,000 and goods having a selling price of $4,700 that were salvaged from the fire. The salvaged goods had an estimated salvage value of $2,900. The average gross profit on net sales in previous periods was 40%.

Required

1. Compute the cost of the inventory lost in the fire.
2. If a company discloses that it uses a periodic inventory system, what concerns might you have about its interim financial statements?

P8-8   *Estimation of Loss*   On February 17, 2004 a flood destroyed the goods in process inventory and half the raw
@   materials inventory of the LRT Company. There was no damage to the finished goods inventory. A physical inventory taken after the flood indicated the following values:

Raw materials	$35,000	Finished goods	$79,000

A review of the accounting records indicated the following:

Inventories, December 31, 2003			
Raw materials	$70,000	Raw materials purchases	$20,000
Goods in process	80,000	Direct labor cost	30,000
Finished goods	72,000	Manufacturing overhead cost	15,000
Sales (to February 17)	50,000	Gross profit rate (on sales)	40%

Required Compute the value of the inventory destroyed by the flood.

P8-9   ***Estimation of Flood Loss***   On June 30, 2004 a flash flood damaged the warehouse and factory of Padway Corporation, completely destroying the work-in-process inventory. There was no damage to either the raw materials or finished goods inventories. A physical inventory taken after the flood revealed the following valuations:

Raw materials	$ 62,000
Work in process	-0-
Finished goods	119,000

The inventory on January 1, 2004 consisted of the following:

Raw materials	$ 30,000
Work in process	100,000
Finished goods	140,000
	$270,000

A review of the books and records disclosed that the gross profit margin historically approximated 25% of sales. The sales for the first six months of 2004 were $340,000. Raw material purchases were $115,000. Direct labor costs for this period were $80,000, and manufacturing overhead was historically applied at 50% of direct labor.

Required Compute the value of the work-in-process inventory lost at June 30, 2004. Show supporting computations in good form. (*AICPA adapted*)

P8-10   ***Retail Inventory Method***   The Turner Corporation uses the retail inventory method. The following information relates to 2004:

	Cost	Retail		Cost	Retail
Inventory, January 1	$ 29,000	$ 45,000	Additional markups	—	$ 50,000
Purchases (gross price)	140,000	190,000	Markup cancellations	—	10,000
Purchases discounts taken	3,000	—	Markdowns	—	15,000
Purchases returns	5,000	8,000	Markdown cancellations	—	3,000
Freight-in	20,000	—	Sales	—	190,000
Employee discounts	—	3,000			

Required Compute the cost of the ending inventory under each of the following cost flow assumptions:
1. FIFO
2. Average cost
3. LIFO
4. Lower of cost or market (based on average cost)

P8-11   ***Comprehensive***   The EKC Company uses the retail inventory method. The following information for 2004 is
@   available:

	Cost	Retail		Cost	Retail
Inventory, January 1	$100,000	$180,000	Markdowns	—	$ 15,000
Purchases (gross price)	320,000	600,000	Markdown cancellations	—	4,000
Purchases discounts taken	6,000	—	Sales	—	610,000
Freight-in	16,000	—	Sales returns	—	30,000
Additional markups	—	60,000	Sales discounts	—	10,000
Markup cancellations	—	12,000			

Required Compute the cost of the ending inventory under each of the following cost flow assumptions:
1. FIFO
2. Average cost
3. LIFO
4. Lower of cost or market (based on average cost)

P8-12 **Retail Inventory Method** The Red Department Store uses the retail inventory method. Information relating to the computation of the inventory at December 31, 2004 is as follows:

	Cost	Retail		Cost	Retail
Inventory at January 1, 2004	$ 32,000	$ 80,000	Markups	—	$60,000
Sales	—	600,000	Markup cancellations	—	10,000
Purchases	270,000	590,000	Markdowns	—	25,000
Freight-in	7,600	—	Markdown cancellations	—	5,000

Estimated normal shrinkage is 2% of sales.

Required Prepare a schedule to calculate the estimated ending inventory at the lower of average cost or market at December 31, 2004, using the retail inventory method. Show supporting computations in good form. (*AICPA adapted*)

P8-13 **Retail Inventory Method** The Weber Corporation uses the retail inventory method to estimate its inventory balances. The following information is available on June 30:

	Cost	Retail		Cost	Retail
Inventory, January 1	$25,000	$ 60,000	Markdowns	—	$7,000
Purchases	75,000	180,000	Additional markups	—	3,000
Sales	—	210,000	Markdown cancellations	—	2,000
Purchases returns	2,000	5,000	Markup cancellations	—	1,000
Sales returns	—	5,000			

Required

1. Compute the inventory on June 30 using the "normal" retail inventory method (lower of average cost or market).
2. Independent of Requirement 1, assume that the June 30 inventory was $80,000 at retail and that the cost-to-retail ratio is 50%. If the price level of the inventory has risen by 5% during the period, compute the cost of the June 30 inventory under the dollar-value retail LIFO method, assuming that the company adopted the method at the beginning of the year.

P8-14 **Dollar-Value LIFO Retail** The following information is obtained from the records of the Burger Company, which uses the dollar-value LIFO retail method:

	2004		2005		2006	
	Cost	Retail	Cost	Retail	Cost	Retail
Purchases	$200,000	$420,000	$250,000	$550,000	$240,000	$500,000
Net markups	—	20,000	—	30,000	—	10,000
Net markdowns	—	10,000	—	40,000	—	20,000
Sales	—	400,000	—	600,000	—	450,000

The company adopted LIFO on January 1, 2004, when the cost and retail values of the inventory were $50,000 and $100,000, respectively. The following price indexes were experienced by the Burger Company:

January 1, 2004	100	December 31, 2005	115
December 31, 2004	108	December 31, 2006	120

Required Compute the cost of the ending inventory for 2004, 2005, and 2006.

*See WebTutor for annotated problem solution.

P8-15 **Dollar-Value LIFO Retail** Intella, Inc. adopted the dollar-value retail LIFO method on January 1, 2003. The following data apply to the 4 subsequent years:

		Cost	Retail			Cost	Retail
2003	Inventory, January 1	$40,000	$ 80,000	2005	Purchases	$117,600	$280,000
	Purchases	85,500	190,000		Sales	—	260,000
	Sales	—	200,000	2006	Purchases	147,200	320,000
2004	Purchases	92,000	230,000		Sales	—	300,000
	Sales	—	210,000				

In addition the following price indexes are available:

January 1, 2003	100	December 31, 2005	120
December 31, 2003	105	December 31, 2006	125
December 31, 2004	110		

Required Compute the inventory at the end of each of the 4 years.

P8-16   *Dollar-Value LIFO Retail and Fire Loss*   The Golden Company adopted the dollar-value retail LIFO method on January 1, 2004. The following information relates to the following 2 years:

	2004			**2005 (through September 7)**		
	Cost	Retail			Cost	Retail
Inventory, January 1	$ 40,000	$ 90,000	Purchases		$160,000	$350,000
Purchases	100,000	210,000	Sales		—	280,000
Sales	—	200,000	Net markups		—	40,000
Net markups	—	20,000	Net markdowns		—	70,000
Net markdowns	—	40,000				

In addition the following price indexes are available:

January 2004	100
December 2004	106
September 2005	110

On September 8, 2005 a fire destroyed the inventory except for goods in transit (properly recorded), FOB shipping point, at a cost of $8,000, and undamaged goods salvaged from the fire, which had a retail value of $10,000.

Required Compute the cost of the inventory destroyed in the fire.

P8-17   *Errors*   As controller of the Lerner Company, which uses a periodic inventory system, you discover the following errors in the current year:

1. Merchandise with a cost of $17,500 was properly included in the final inventory, but the purchase was not recorded until the following year.
2. Merchandise purchases are in transit under terms of FOB shipping point. They have been excluded from the inventory, but the purchase was recorded in the current year on the receipt of the invoice of $4,300.
3. Goods out on consignment have been excluded from inventory.
4. Merchandise purchases under terms FOB shipping point have been omitted from the Purchases account and the ending inventory. The purchases were recorded in the following year.
5. Goods held on consignment from Talbert Supply Co. were included in the inventory.

Required For each error indicate the effect on the ending inventory and the net income for the current year and on the net income for the following year.

P8-18   *Comprehensive*   Layne Corporation, a manufacturer of small tools, provided the following information from its accounting records for the year ended December 31, 2004:

Inventory at December 31, 2004 (based on physical count of goods in Layne's plant at cost on December 31, 2004)	$1,750,000
Accounts payable at December 31, 2004	1,200,000
Net sales (sales less sales returns)	8,500,000

Additional information is as follows:

1. Included in the physical count were tools billed to a customer FOB shipping point on December 31, 2004. These tools had a cost of $28,000 and had been billed at $35,000. The shipment was on Layne's loading dock waiting to be picked up by the common carrier.
2. Goods were in transit from a vendor to Layne on December 31, 2004. The invoice cost was $50,000, and the goods were shipped FOB shipping point on December 29, 2004.
3. Work-in-process inventory costing $20,000 was sent to an outside processor for plating on December 30, 2004.

4. Tools returned by customers and held pending inspection in the returned goods area on December 31, 2004 were not included in the physical count. On January 8, 2005 the tools costing $26,000 were inspected and returned to inventory. Credit memos totaling $40,000 were issued to the customers on the same date.

5. Tools shipped to a customer FOB destination on December 24, 2004 were in transit at December 31, 2004 and had a cost of $25,000. Upon notification of receipt by the customer on January 2, 2005, Layne issued a sales invoice for $42,000.

6. Goods, with an invoice cost of $30,000, received from a vendor at 5:00 p.m. on December 31, 2004, were recorded on a receiving report dated January 2, 2005. The goods were not included in the physical count, but the invoice was included in accounts payable at December 31, 2004.

7. Goods received from a vendor on December 24, 2004 were included in the physical count. However, the related $60,000 vendor invoice was not included in accounts payable at December 31, 2004 because the accounts payable copy of the receiving report was lost.

8. On January 4, 2005, a monthly freight bill in the amount of $4,000 was received. The bill specifically related to merchandise purchased in December 2004, one-half of which was still in the inventory at December 31, 2004. The freight charges were not included in either the inventory or in accounts payable at December 31, 2004.

Required Prepare a schedule of adjustments as of December 31, 2004 to the initial amounts in inventory, accounts payable, and sales. Show separately the effect, if any, of each of the eight transactions on the December 31, 2004 amounts. Indicate if the transactions would have no effect on the initial amount shown. (*AICPA adapted*)

INTERNET ASSIGNMENTS

Go to the Nikolai and Bazley **Intermediate Accounting** web site (http://Nikolai.swcollege.com). Click on Student Resources and <u>internet homework assignments</u>. Then click on the appropriate hot link (icon) for each company's web site, find the relevant accounting information, and answer the following questions.

I8-1   Click on the **Apple Computer** web site.

Required Which accounting method does the company use for its inventories? Do you agree with its choice? Does the company use the lower of cost or market method? Has the company had significant write-offs of its inventory? (You may have to access the Management's Discussion and Analysis [MD&A] for this information.)

I8-2   Click on the **Wal-Mart** web site.

Required Does the company use the retail inventory method for its inventories? Why did the company disclose the use of this method?

objectives

1 Identify the characteristics of property, plant, and equipment.

2 Record the acquisition of property, plant, and equipment.

3 Determine the cost of assets acquired by the exchange of other assets.

4 Compute the cost of a self-constructed asset, including interest capitalization.

5 Record costs subsequent to acquisition.

6 Record the disposal of property, plant, and equipment.

7 Understand the disclosures of property, plant, and equipment.

8 Explain the accounting for oil and gas properties (Appendix).

CHAPTER 9

Property, Plant, and Equipment: Acquisition and Disposal

Property, plant, and equipment are very important components of a company's assets. They include assets that a company needs to conduct its business, such as land, office buildings, factories, machinery, equipment, warehouses, retail stores, and delivery vehicles. They usually are a major portion of a company's total assets. In this chapter we include a discussion of the costs of acquisition, costs subsequent to acquisition, and disposal of property, plant, and equipment. We include additional issues related to oil and gas properties in an Appendix.

CHARACTERISTICS OF PROPERTY, PLANT, AND EQUIPMENT

1 Identify the characteristics of property, plant, and equipment.

Property, plant, and equipment is the title used to classify tangible noncurrent assets that a company uses in the normal operations of its business. Alternative terms are **plant assets, fixed assets, and operational assets.** To be included in this category, an asset must have three characteristics:

1. *The Asset Must Be Held for Use and Not for Investment.* Only assets used in the normal course of business should be included. However, the asset does not have to be used continuously; therefore machinery owned for standby purposes in case of breakdowns is included. In contrast, idle land or buildings should not be included and should be categorized separately as an investment. It is possible that a particular type of asset may be categorized as property, plant, and equipment by one company and as inventory by another. For example, trucks owned by a trucking company are included in its property, plant, and equipment, whereas trucks owned by a dealer are categorized as inventory.

2. *The Asset Must Have an Expected Life of More Than One Year.* The asset represents a bundle of future services that the company will receive over the life of the asset. To be included in property, plant, and equipment, the benefits must extend for more than one year or the operating cycle, whichever is longer; therefore the asset is distinguished from other assets, such as supplies, that are expected to be consumed within the current year. However, assets remain in the property, plant, and equipment category, even if the company intends to sell them in the next year.

3. *The Asset Must Be Tangible in Nature.* There must be a physical substance that can be seen and touched. In contrast, intangible assets such as goodwill or patents do not have a physical substance. Unlike raw materials, generally, property, plant, and equipment do not change their physical characteristics and are not incorporated into the product. Wasting assets are natural

Intangible assets are discussed in Chapter 11.

resources, such as minerals, oil and gas, and timber, that are used up by extraction. A company usually includes them under the category of property, plant, and equipment, even though it may incorporate them into the product. For example, an iron mine owned by a steel company produces iron ore which changes its characteristics as it is used in the manufacture of steel.

A company records an asset included in its property, plant, and equipment category initially at its acquisition cost. Since the asset provides benefits to the company over a period of more than one year, the matching principle requires that the company allocate the cost of the asset as an expense to each period in which it consumes the asset and receives benefits. We discuss this process of depreciation in the next chapter.

Evaluation of Use of Historical Cost

The use of acquisition (historical) cost as the basis for reporting property, plant, and equipment is consistent with the reporting of most other assets, liabilities, and stockholders' equity items. The advantages are that (1) the cost is equal to the fair value at the date of acquisition, (2) the cost is a *reliable* valuation, and (3) gains and losses from holding the asset are recognized only when realized through a sale transaction. However, the use of historical cost for reporting property, plant, and equipment on a company's financial statements raises more issues than for other assets because usually the time since acquisition is greater. For example, many users question the continued use of historical cost for reporting an asset such as land. How *relevant* is the cost of land purchased in the past, perhaps as much as 50 years ago? Similar issues arise with depreciable assets such as office buildings. Although depreciation is a process of cost allocation rather than of valuation, the book value of the assets (cost less accumulated depreciation) may become less relevant as it becomes much less than the asset's current value. In addition, as we discuss in the next chapter, a company writes down property, plant, and equipment to its fair value when its value is impaired.

Another factor to be considered is the manner in which a company uses the asset. The process of allocating the historical cost may be more relevant if the company holds the asset for use in its productive operations, because there is an appropriate matching of the cost of the asset against the revenues it produces. Alternatively, the current value may be more relevant if the company intends to sell the asset, or the entire company is for sale.

Since generally accepted accounting principles require that a company report its property, plant, and equipment at historical cost, their current cost generally is not available to users of financial statements. However, companies are encouraged to provide supplementary disclosures of the current cost of property, plant, and equipment.

The arguments for and against the use of current value are discussed in Appendix E.

ACQUISITION OF PROPERTY, PLANT, AND EQUIPMENT

The major types of assets that a company includes in the general category of property, plant, and equipment are land, buildings, equipment, machinery, furniture and fixtures, leasehold improvements, and wasting assets. The acquisition of an item of property, plant, and equipment raises many issues. These include the determination of the cost of an asset acquired singly or by a lump-sum purchase, with deferred payments, through the issuance of securities, or by donation. Furthermore, in more complex situations, assets may be acquired in exchange for other assets or by self-construction. We discuss each of these issues in the following sections.

2 Record the acquisition of property, plant, and equipment.

Determination of Cost

The cost of property, plant, and equipment is the cash outlay (not the "list" price) or its equivalent that is necessary to acquire the asset and put it in operating condition. In other words, **the acquisition costs that are necessary to obtain the benefits to be derived from the asset are capitalized** (recorded as an asset). These costs include the contract price, less discounts available, plus freight, assembly, installation, and testing costs. As for inventory, discounts *available* should be subtracted from the cost of the asset rather than recorded as discounts *taken*, because the benefits to be received from the asset are not increased by a discount not taken. To illustrate the acquisition of an asset, assume that the Devon Company purchases a machine with a contract price of $100,000 on terms of 2/10, n/30. The company does not take the cash discount of $2,000, and incurs transportation costs of $2,500, as well as installation and testing costs of $3,000. Sales tax is 5% of the invoice price, or $5,000. During the installation of the machine, uninsured damages of $500 are incurred and paid by the company. The company makes the following summary journal entry to record these costs:

Machine		
($100,000 − $2,000 + $2,500 + $3,000 + $5,000)	108,500	
Repair Expense	500	
Discounts Lost	2,000	
Cash		111,000

The company does not include the $500 of damages in the cost of the asset because it was not a "necessary" cost. We discuss the issues associated with the determination of the cost of various types of property, plant, and equipment in the following sections.

LAND The recorded cost of land includes (1) the contract price, (2) the costs of closing the transaction and obtaining title, including commissions, options, legal fees, title search, insurance, and past due taxes, (3) the costs of surveys, and (4) the costs of preparing the land for its particular use, such as clearing, grading, and razing old buildings (net of any proceeds from salvage) when such improvements have an indefinite life. A company should record the costs of improvements having a limited economic life, such as landscaping, streets, sidewalks, and sewers, in a Land Improvements account and depreciate these costs over their economic lives. Alternatively, if the local government authority is responsible for the continued upkeep of the improvements, then effectively the improvements have an indefinite economic life to the company and the company should add the costs of the improvements to the cost of the land. Since land is considered not to have a limited economic life and its residual value is unlikely to be less than its acquisition cost, land generally is not depreciated.

Land purchased for future use or as an investment should not be considered part of property, plant, and equipment. Questions arise about accounting for interest and property taxes on such land. **FASB Statement No. 34** (discussed later in the chapter) requires that a company capitalize interest only when an asset is undergoing the activities necessary to get it ready for its intended use. Therefore, if the company is involved in any planning activity, such as architectural design or the obtaining of permits, it capitalize interest. The *Statement* does not address the issue of property taxes (or other costs such as insurance).

FASB Statement No. 67 applies to real estate held for sale or rental and requires the costs incurred for property taxes and insurance to be capitalized only during periods in which activities necessary to get the property ready for its intended use are in progress. Costs incurred for such items after the property is substantially complete and ready for its intended use are expensed as incurred.[1] Thus the rules for interest, property taxes, and insurance are the same for real estate projects developed for sale or lease to others. However, the *Statement* does not apply to real estate developed by a company for use in its own operations and, therefore, the company could capitalize or expense the property taxes and insurance during the development period.

Arguments in favor of capitalizing property taxes are (1) the matching principle does not require expensing the costs since the asset is not being used in a revenue-producing activity, and (2) if the advance purchase of the land had been made at a lower price,

---

1. "Accounting for Costs and Initial Rental Operations of Real Estate Projects," *FASB Statement of Financial Accounting Standards No. 67* (Stamford, Conn.: FASB, 1982), par. 6.

capitalizing the costs would result in a cost nearer to that which the company would have paid later. Arguments in favor of expensing the property taxes are (1) property taxes are a maintenance cost that do not add value to the property, and (2) it is consistent with the conservatism convention. Once the land is used in the operating activities, both interest and property taxes must be expensed.

BUILDINGS The recorded cost of buildings includes (1) the contract price, (2) the costs of remodeling and reconditioning, (3) the costs of excavation for the specific building, (4) architectural costs and the costs of building permits, (5) capitalized interest costs in the particular circumstances discussed later in the chapter, and (6) unanticipated costs resulting from the condition of the land (such as blasting rock or channeling an underground stream). However, a company should expense unanticipated costs such as a strike or a fire associated with the construction of the building. The different treatment of such unanticipated events is justified because the avoidable costs of the fire or strike were not necessary to obtain the economic benefits of the building. The costs of property taxes and insurance during construction may be capitalized or expensed, as we discussed for land.

LEASEHOLD IMPROVEMENTS Improvements made by the lessee to leased property, unless specifically exempted in the lease agreement, revert to the lessor at the end of the lease. Therefore **a lessee capitalizes the cost of a leasehold improvement,** such as the interior design of a retail store, **and amortizes the cost over its economic life or the life of the lease, whichever is shorter.**

The preceding discussion has indicated the general rules to be followed but is not intended to provide solutions for all possible situations. A company's decision to expense a cost immediately, to capitalize it as an asset, such as a building that is subsequently depreciated, or to capitalize the cost as a nondepreciable asset, such as land, has an impact on both the company's income statement and balance sheet. **The general procedure is to determine whether incurring the cost has generated economic benefits for the company beyond the current period, and which asset is associated with the increase in benefits.** For example, when a company purchases land the cost of razing an old building on the land is properly capitalized to the land, because the benefits to be derived from the land are increased as a result of the old building no longer being there. Also, if the seller had razed the old building, the selling price presumably would have been higher. When a company razes an old building on land already owned so that a new building can be erected, the cost of razing is associated with the benefits previously realized from the old building and therefore is included in the calculation of the gain or loss on disposal. The new building does not have greater benefits because the old building is obsolete. Similarly if a company purchases an old building with the expectation of incurring some costs of renovation, but the actual costs exceed the planned costs because of unforeseen difficulties, the added cost should not be capitalized, since it resulted from an error of judgment and did not increase the economic benefits of the building above those benefits originally expected. However, given the difficulties of accurate budgeting, the total costs often are capitalized whether or not those total costs exceed the budgeted amount.

Lump-Sum Purchase

A company may acquire several dissimilar assets for a single lump-sum purchase price. The purchase price in such a situation is allocated to the individual assets purchased, because some of the assets may be depreciable and some not, and the depreciable assets may have different economic lives and be depreciated by different methods. **A company allocates the acquisition price in a lump-sum purchase based on the relative fair values of the individual assets.**

For example, suppose a company pays $120,000 for land and a building. If there is no evidence in the contract of separate prices agreed upon for the land and the building, the company allocates the $120,000 between the two assets based on their relative fair values. The company can obtain evidence of such values from several sources, such as an appraisal or the assessed values for property taxes, if it considers those values to be reasonably accurate indications of relative market values. Suppose that an appraisal of the land and building indicates values of $50,000 and $75,000, respectively. The company computes the cost of each as follows:

	Appraisal Value	Relative Fair Value	× Total Cost =	Allocated Cost
Land	$ 50,000	$50,000/$125,000 ×	$120,000 =	$ 48,000
Building	75,000	$75,000/$125,000 ×	$120,000 =	72,000
Total	$125,000			$120,000

The company records the land at a cost of $48,000 and the building at a cost of $72,000. If the cost of obtaining an appraisal is material, the company should add it to the purchase price so it is allocated to the respective assets. In some situations, it may be possible to determine only one of the market values. Then the remaining portion of the total cost is assigned to the other asset.

Deferred Payments

When a company acquires property, plant, and equipment on a deferred payment basis, such as by issuing notes or bonds or assuming a mortgage, it records the asset at its fair value or the fair value of the liability on the date of the transaction, whichever is more *reliable*. If neither is determinable, the company records the asset at the present value of the deferred payments at the stated interest rate, unless the stated rate is materially different from the market rate, in which case it uses the market rate.[2] For example, suppose that a company purchases equipment by issuing a $10,000 non-interest-bearing 5-year note, when the market rate for obligations of this type is 12%. The note will be paid off at the rate of $2,000 at the end of each year. Neither the fair value of the equipment nor the note is determinable directly. In this case the company values both the equipment and the note at the present value of the payments, which is $7,210 ($2,000 × 3.604776, the factor from Table 4 of Appendix D for 5 years and a 12% rate). The company records the acquisition of the equipment as follows:

Equipment	7,210	
Discount on Notes Payable	2,790	
Notes Payable		10,000

If the company purchased the equipment by issuing a $7,500 5-year note with a stated interest rate of 12%, the present value of the note is $7,500 (assuming that 12% is a fair rate), and it would record the acquisition as follows:

Equipment	7,500	
Notes Payable		7,500

Accounting for notes and bonds is discussed in Chapter 13.

Property, plant, and equipment may be purchased by issuing bonds. The same principles are followed, and the asset is recorded at the present value of the future payments.

Issuance of Securities

When a company acquires assets by issuing securities such as common stock or preferred stock, the company must determine the fair value of the transaction. In many cases two measures of fair value are available: the fair value of the asset acquired and the fair value of the securities issued. **The general rule is to record the exchange at the fair value of the asset acquired or of the stock issued, whichever is more reliable.**

---

2. "Interest on Receivables and Payables," *APB Opinion No. 21* (New York: AICPA, 1971), par. 11.

Normally the two values would be very similar, but if they are materially different, it is necessary to select one. In some situations, one of the values may be considered more reliable because it is quoted in an active market. For example, if the security is actively traded on a stock exchange and the asset being acquired is very specialized, the security value would be the preferred choice. Alternatively, if the security is not actively traded, but the asset is one that is commonly traded, the asset value would be the better choice. But what if neither of the two values can be readily determined?

For example, suppose that a company whose stock is not traded publicly issues stock to acquire a mining claim. Conceptually, the value of the asset is preferred to the value of the stock, because the value of the acquired asset is independent of the value of the stock; but the value of the stock is *not* independent of the asset being acquired, because the more valuable the asset is, the more valuable is the stock. In the absence of any other valuation approach, a final alternative is to allow the directors of the company to place a value on the transaction. State laws generally allow this procedure, provided the value is established in good faith.

Exchanges of stock for assets are discussed in Chapter 15.

Assets Acquired by Donation

When a company acquires property, plant, and equipment through donation (usually by a governmental unit or an individual), a strict interpretation of the cost concept would require that the asset be valued at zero. However, such transactions are defined by **APB Opinion No. 29** as nonreciprocal transfers of nonmonetary assets. A **nonreciprocal transfer** is a transfer of assets or services in one direction. An asset received in such an exchange must be recorded at its fair value. The justification is that when an asset is donated, cost provides an inadequate method of accounting for the asset and for subsequent income measurement. Therefore the cost principle is modified to produce more relevant asset and income values.

Generally accepted accounting principles require different treatment for recording an asset donated by a governmental unit and an asset donated by a nongovernmental unit (such as an individual stockholder). In both situations, the company records (debits) the asset at its fair value. In the case of a donation by a governmental unit, the credit is recorded in a donated capital account. The argument for this treatment is that the company should not increase earnings as a result of a donation by a governmental unit. In the case of a donation by a nongovernmental unit, the credit is recorded as a gain.[3] The argument for this treatment is that receiving something of value from a nongovernmental unit (e.g., a stockholder) represents earnings to the company. The company reports the gain in the other items section of its income statement.

To illustrate, suppose the City of Julesberg (a governmental unit) donates land worth $20,000 to the Klemme Company because the company relocates its production facilities to Julesberg. The company records this event as follows:

Land	20,000	
Donated Capital		20,000

Donations of this type often are accompanied by conditions. For example, the Klemme Company might be required to employ 100 people for 10 years. The company reports the condition in the notes to the financial statements, if material, but does not record it as a liability. The company includes the Donated Capital account in the Stockholders' Equity section of its balance sheet.

Start-up Costs

Many companies incur start-up costs as they expand their activities. For example, a retail company that opens a new store would incur start-up costs associated with hiring

---

3. "Accounting for Contributions Received and Contributions Made," *FASB Statement of Financial Accounting Standards No. 116* (Norwalk, Conn.: FASB, 1993), par. 8.

and training new employees and pre-opening advertising. Other examples are costs of opening new restaurants, new plants, new hotels, new casinos, and new golf courses. In the past, many companies capitalized those costs and expensed them over a relatively short time, such as 1 to 3 years.

AICPA Statement of Position No. 98-5 now requires that a company expense the costs of start-up activities as incurred.[4] The *SOP* defines start-up costs as "those one-time activities related to opening a new facility, introducing a new product or service, conducting business in a new territory, conducting business with a new class of customer or beneficiary, initiating a new process in an existing facility, or commencing some new operation." Costs associated with organizing a new entity, often referred to as organization costs, (e.g., costs of preparing a charter, bylaws, minutes of organizational meetings, and original stock certifications) are also included as start-up costs. Start-up activities do not include "activities related to routine, ongoing efforts to refine, enrich, or otherwise improve upon the qualities of an existing product, service, process or facility."

International Accounting Differences

The primary difference between U.S. and international accounting standards is that international standards allow a company to write the value of its property, plant, and equipment assets up to fair value. The increase is credited to stockholders' equity as a revaluation surplus. Such write-ups create significant differences that reduce international comparability among companies. There are some other minor differences between U.S. and international accounting standards that are beyond the scope of the book.

ASSETS ACQUIRED BY EXCHANGE OF OTHER ASSETS

3 Determine the cost of assets acquired by the exchange of other assets.

Accounting for assets acquired by the exchange of other assets (e.g., trade-in, swap) is covered by **APB Opinion No. 29.** This *Opinion* defines a **nonmonetary exchange** as a reciprocal transfer between a company and another entity, resulting in the company acquiring nonmonetary assets or services or satisfying liabilities by surrendering other nonmonetary assets or services or incurring other obligations. **The general principle is that the cost of a nonmonetary asset acquired in exchange for another nonmonetary asset is the fair value of the asset surrendered.** A gain or loss is recognized on the exchange as the difference between the fair value of the asset surrendered and its book value.[5] When **boot**[6] (monetary consideration) is given or received, the cost of the asset acquired and the gain or loss in a nonmonetary exchange generally is determined by these equations:

$$\text{Cost of Asset Acquired} = \frac{\text{Fair Value of}}{\text{Asset Surrendered}} + \text{Boot Paid or} - \text{Boot Received}$$

and

$$\text{Gain (Loss)} = \frac{\text{Fair Value of}}{\text{Asset Surrendered}} - \text{Book Value of Asset Surrendered}$$

If the fair value of the asset received is more reliable than the fair value of the asset surrendered, it is used to measure the cost of the asset acquired. Of course, the recorded

---

4. "Reporting on the Costs of Start-up Activities," *AICPA Statement of Position No 98-5* (New York: AICPA, 1998).

5. "Accounting for Nonmonetary Transactions," *APB Opinion No. 29* (New York: AICPA, 1973), par. 18.

6. *APB Opinion No. 29* refers to a *small* amount of boot. However, the intent was that the rules would apply no matter how much boot was involved. See James B. Hobbs and D. R. Bainbridge, "Nonmonetary Exchange Transactions: Clarification of APB Opinion No. 29," *The Accounting Review* (January, 1982), p. 171. This interpretation has been modified by the Emerging Issues Task Force as discussed later.

cost of the asset acquired cannot be greater than its fair value. Exchanges may involve similar or dissimilar assets and each type of exchange may involve a gain or loss.

Exchanges of Dissimilar Productive Assets

Productive assets are held for or used in the production of goods and services. *Dissimilar productive assets* are assets that are not of the same general type, do not perform the same function, *and* are not employed in the same line of business.[7] Accounting for dissimilar productive assets follows the principles in the equations just cited, and all gains and losses are recognized in full.

We illustrate an exchange of dissimilar productive assets between Company A and Company B, both with and without boot, in Exhibit 9-1. Company A exchanges a building for Company B's equipment. Before studying the exhibit, it is helpful to refer back to the equations for nonmonetary asset exchanges.

In example (a), boot is not involved. Each company gives up and receives an asset with a fair value of $40,000, which is, therefore, the fair value of the transaction. Since

---

EXHIBIT 9-1 **Exchange of Dissimilar Productive Assets**

(a) No Boot

	Company A (Building)	Company B (Equipment)
Cost of asset surrendered	$100,000	$60,000
Accumulated depreciation	54,000	32,000
Fair value of asset surrendered	40,000	40,000

Company A			Company B		
Equipment	40,000		Building	40,000	
Accumulated Depreciation	54,000		Accumulated Depreciation	32,000	
Loss [$40,000 −			Equipment		60,000
($100,000 − $54,000)]	6,000		Gain [$40,000 −		
Building		100,000	($60,000 − $32,000)]		12,000

(b) With Boot

	Company A (Building)	Company B (Equipment)
Cost of asset surrendered	$100,000	$60,000
Accumulated depreciation	54,000	32,000
Fair value of asset surrendered	40,000	35,000
Cash received (paid)	5,000	(5,000)

Company A			Company B		
Equipment			Building		
($40,000 − $5,000)	35,000		($35,000 + $5,000)	40,000	
Accumulated Depreciation	54,000		Accumulated Depreciation	32,000	
Cash	5,000		Equipment		60,000
Loss [$40,000 −			Cash		5,000
($100,000 − $54,000)]	6,000		Gain [$35,000 −		
Building		100,000	($60,000 − $32,000)]		7,000

---

7. "Accounting for Certain Nonmonetary Transactions," *FASB Emerging Issues Task Force Issue Summary 86–29* (FASB, Stamford, Conn., 1986). For an additional discussion, see D. Marcinko and E. Petri, "A Clarification of Certain Issues Arising out of Nonmonetary Exchanges," *Journal of Accounting Education* (Fall, 1991), pp. 365–372.

Company A gives up a building with a fair value of $40,000 and a book value of $46,000 (the cost of $100,000 less the accumulated depreciation of $54,000), it recognizes a loss of $6,000 ($40,000 − $46,000) and records the cost of the acquired equipment at the fair value of $40,000. Company B gives up equipment with a fair value of $40,000 and a book value of $28,000 ($60,000 − $32,000); therefore it recognizes a gain of $12,000 ($40,000 − $28,000) and records the cost of the building acquired at the fair value of $40,000.

In example (b), Company A receives boot of $5,000. Since Company A gives up a building with a fair value of $40,000 and a book value of $46,000, it recognizes a loss of $6,000. It records the acquired equipment at a cost of $35,000 (the $40,000 fair value of the building surrendered minus the $5,000 boot received). Company B gives up equipment with a fair value of $35,000 and a book value of $28,000. Therefore it records a gain of $7,000 and the acquired building at a cost of $40,000 (the $35,000 fair value of the equipment surrendered plus the $5,000 boot paid).

Exchanges of Similar Productive Assets

Similar productive assets are of the same general type, perform the same function, *and are used in the same line of business.* The intent of the APB was to have special rules for exchanges of similar productive assets only when the earning process is not complete for both parties. Thus, in order for the special rules of similar productive asset exchanges to be applied, an exchange must be between companies that are using the assets in the same line of business. We discuss these rules below. An exchange between two dealers or between two nondealers qualifies because they are both using the assets in the same line of business. However, an exchange between a dealer and a nondealer does not qualify because the dealer has completed its earning process in the normal course of business. Therefore, both the dealer and nondealer recognize all gains and losses in full.

When similar productive assets are exchanged, two modifications to the general rule are necessary. First, a company does not recognize revenue (gain), because the asset that originally was acquired has been exchanged for an asset with a similar purpose and the exchange is "not essentially the culmination of the earning process." Thus, the total revenue expected from the original asset has not yet been earned but will continue to be earned by the newly acquired asset. For example, suppose that two construction companies each purchase land for development. Before development occurs, but after the values of the two parcels of land have increased, the two companies agree to an exchange of the parcels. Considering that the purpose of the original acquisitions was development and that the revenue was to be generated by the sale of developed land, neither company's earning process is complete when the land is exchanged. Therefore both companies defer any gain on the exchange transaction. In contrast, if one of the companies exchanges the land for machinery (dissimilar assets), that company recognizes the revenue (gain). The company's earning process is complete because the original purpose of the land purchase has been superseded. Similarly, if two manufacturing companies (nondealers) or two truck dealers exchange delivery trucks, then both companies defer any gain. However, if a truck dealer and a manufacturing company exchange delivery trucks both companies recognize any gain. In situations in which no gain is recognized on the disposal of the original asset, the company records the newly acquired asset at the *book* value of the asset surrendered.

There is an opposing view that argues that a company should recognize the gain on the exchange of similar productive assets because a transaction has taken place. The transaction clearly has established a fair value for the asset disposed of, and the company should recognize this value in its financial statements. The newly acquired asset would be valued on a basis similar to that for dissimilar productive assets or assets acquired by means other than an exchange. However, this view is *not* supported by generally accepted accounting principles as defined in *APB Opinion No. 29.*

Note that our discussion only refers to *gains.* That is because the conservatism convention also is considered. So, if a company has a *loss* on the disposal of the original asset, it recognizes the loss.

The second modification arises when boot is involved in the exchange. When a company *receives* boot in the exchange of similar productive assets, it is considered that the company's earning process is complete *to the extent that boot is received*. Therefore the company recognizes a gain in proportion to the boot received. If the company *pays* boot, it does *not* recognize the gain. As before, a company recognizes a loss in full, irrespective of whether it receives or pays boot.

The FASB Emerging Issues Task Force (EITF) established that the exchange is *monetary* if the boot is equal to or exceeds 25% of the value of the exchange. Then the special rules discussed here do *not* apply and both the recipient and the payer of boot record the exchange at fair value. That is, deferral or partial recognition of a gain occurs only when the exchange is nonmonetary, which means that the boot must be less than 25% of the total value of the exchange.

The general principle modified by these two factors leads to six alternative situations for nonmonetary exchanges of *similar* productive assets. We discuss each of these alternatives in examples in the chapter, and summarize them in Exhibit 9-2. When boot is neither received nor paid by a company it recognizes a loss in full (alternative 1) but ignores any gain (alternative 2). When boot is *received*, a company recognizes a loss in full (alternative 5), but it recognizes a gain in proportion to the boot received (alternative 6). When the boot is *paid*, a company does not recognize a gain (alternative 4) but it recognizes a loss in full (alternative 3). Note that these same rules apply to exchanges of products or property held for sale in the ordinary course of business (primarily inventory). However, the discussion in this chapter concentrates on exchanges of productive assets.

Earlier we listed two general equations for computing the cost of the asset acquired when boot was paid or received in a nonmonetary exchange. These equations apply to dissimilar productive asset exchanges, and similar productive asset exchanges when the boot is equal to or exceeds 25% of the value of the exchange. The modifications that we have discussed provide alternative equations that can be used by a company to determine the cost of the asset acquired in a nonmonetary exchange of similar productive assets when the boot is less than 25%. When the fair value of the asset being surrendered is *less* than the book value, the following equation applies:

$$\text{Cost of Asset Acquired} = \begin{array}{c}\text{Fair Value of}\\\text{Asset Surrendered}\end{array} + \text{Boot Paid or} - \text{Boot Received}$$

When the fair value of the asset being surrendered is *greater* than the book value, the following equations apply:

$$\text{Cost of Asset Acquired} = \text{Book Value of Asset Surrendered} + \text{Boot Paid}$$

or

$$\text{Cost of Asset Acquired} = \begin{array}{c}\text{Book Value of}\\\text{Asset Surrendered}\end{array} - \text{Boot Received} + \text{Gain Recognized}$$

Note that the difference between the two sets of equations is the use of fair value when a loss is recognized and the use of book value when the gain is not recognized or when it is recognized partially. We illustrate each of these situations in Exhibits 9-3, 4, and 5.

No Boot. We illustrate the exchange of two similar productive assets (equipment) without boot in Exhibit 9-3. Since no boot is involved, Company B does not recognize the gain that is apparent in the transaction and records the cost of the acquired equipment at $28,000 ($60,000 − $32,000), which is the book value of the equipment surrendered. The reason for deferring the gain when these similar productive assets are exchanged is that Company B's earning process is not complete, so revenue (i.e., a gain) should not be recognized. Company A recognizes a loss of $6,000, which is the difference between the fair value of the equipment surrendered ($40,000) and the book value of the equipment surrendered ($100,000 − $54,000 = $46,000). Since Company A recognizes a loss, it records the acquired equipment at the fair value of $40,000. The treatment of Company A and Company B follows the conservatism convention and is

EXHIBIT 9-2 Nonmonetary Productive Asset Exchanges

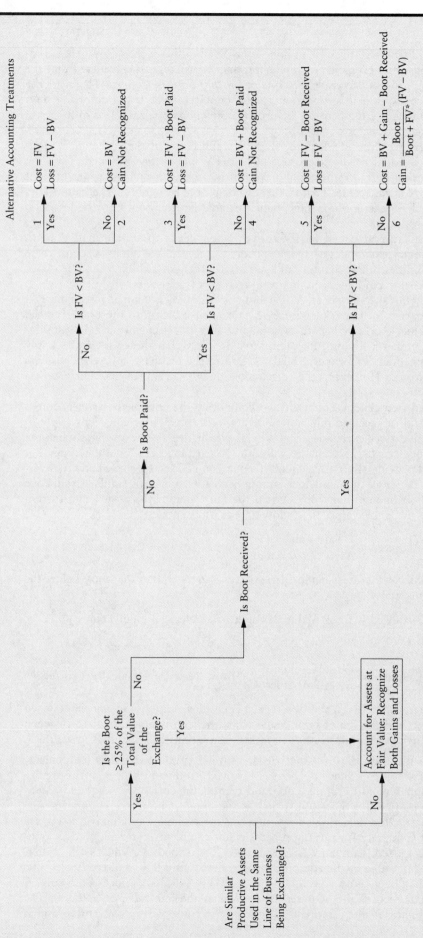

Key: FV = Fair value of nonmonetary productive asset surrendered
BV = Book value of nonmonetary productive asset surrendered
FV* = Fair value of nonmonetary productive asset received

EXHIBIT 9-3   Exchange of Similar Productive Assets: No Boot

	Company A	Company B
Cost of equipment surrendered	$100,000	$60,000
Accumulated depreciation	54,000	32,000
Fair value of equipment surrendered	40,000	40,000

Company A		Company B	
Equipment	40,000	Equipment	28,000
Accumulated Depreciation	54,000	Accumulated Depreciation	32,000
Loss ($40,000 − $46,000)	6,000	Equipment	60,000
Equipment	100,000		

---

consistent with alternatives 1 and 2 in Exhibit 9-2. It also results in the asset being valued at the lower of cost (or book value when the equipment has been depreciated) or market.

Boot Received by Company Incurring a Loss.   When similar productive assets are exchanged for a loss and boot is involved, the company *receiving* the boot recognizes the loss in full. We illustrate this situation for Company A in Exhibit 9-4. Company A incurs a loss of $6,000 ($40,000 − $46,000), recognizes it in full, and records the cost of the acquired equipment at its fair value of $35,000. This treatment is consistent with alternative 5 in Exhibit 9-2.

Boot Paid by Company Incurring a Gain.   When similar productive assets are exchanged for a gain and boot is involved, the company *paying* the boot does not recognize the gain if the boot is less than 25% of the value exchanged. We illustrate this situation for Company B in Exhibit 9-4. Company B records the equipment acquired at $33,000, which is the book value of the equipment surrendered ($28,000) plus the boot paid ($5,000, which is less than 25% of the value exchanged). This treatment is consistent with alternative 4 in Exhibit 9-2.

Boot Received by Company Incurring a Gain.   When similar productive assets are exchanged for a gain and boot is involved, the company *receiving* the boot recognizes the gain in proportion to the boot received if the boot is less than 25% of the value

---

EXHIBIT 9-4   Exchange of Similar Productive Assets: Boot Received by Company Incurring a Loss and Paid by Company Incurring a Gain

	Company A	Company B
Cost of equipment surrendered	$100,000	$60,000
Accumulated depreciation	54,000	32,000
Fair value of equipment surrendered	40,000	35,000
Cash received (paid)	5,000	(5,000)

Company A		Company B		
Equipment		Equipment		
($40,000 − $5,000)	35,000	($28,000 + $5,000)	33,000	
Accumulated Depreciation	54,000	Accumulated Depreciation	32,000	
Loss [$40,000 −		Equipment		60,000
($100,000 − $54,000)]	6,000	Cash		5,000
Cash	5,000			
Equipment	100,000			

EXHIBIT 9-5   Exchange of Similar Productive Assets: Boot Received by Company Incurring a Gain and Paid by Company Incurring a Loss

	Company A	Company B
Cost of equipment surrendered	$100,000	$60,000
Accumulated depreciation	80,000	32,000
Fair value of equipment surrendered	30,000	27,000
Cash received (paid)	3,000	(3,000)

Company A			Company B		
Equipment ($20,000 −			Equipment		
$3,000 + $1,000)	18,000		($27,000 + $3,000)	30,000	
Accumulated Depreciation	80,000		Accumulated Depreciation	32,000	
Cash	3,000		Loss [$27,000 −		
Equipment		100,000	($60,000 − $32,000)]	1,000	
Gain*		1,000	Equipment		60,000
			Cash		3,000

$$^*\text{Gain} = \frac{\text{Boot}}{\text{Boot} + \text{Fair Value of Asset Acquired}} \times \left(\begin{array}{c} \text{Fair Value of} \\ \text{Asset Surrendered} \end{array} - \begin{array}{c} \text{Book Value of} \\ \text{Asset Surrendered} \end{array} \right)$$

$$= \frac{\$3,000}{\$3,000 + \$27,000} \times (\$30,000 - \$20,000) = \$1,000$$

exchanged. This proportion of the gain has been realized through cash receipt, and therefore the earning process is complete for this portion. In this situation, the proportion is based on the ratio of the boot received to the total consideration received (i.e., boot plus the fair value of the asset *acquired*). The gain is computed as follows:

$$\text{Gain} = \frac{\text{Boot}}{\text{Boot} + \text{Fair Value of Asset Acquired}} \times \text{Gain on Asset Surrendered}$$

$$= \frac{\text{Boot}}{\text{Boot} + \begin{array}{c}\text{Fair Value}\\ \text{of Asset Acquired}\end{array}} \times \left(\begin{array}{c} \text{Fair Value of} \\ \text{Asset Surrendered} \end{array} - \begin{array}{c} \text{Book Value of} \\ \text{Asset Surrendered} \end{array} \right)$$

Typically the sum of the boot plus the fair value of the asset acquired is equal to the fair value of the asset surrendered. Since this may not be true when an advantageous exchange takes place, the gain should always be computed by the method we illustrate.

We illustrate this situation for Company A in Exhibit 9-5. Company A receives boot of $3,000, which is less than 25% of the value exchanged. The sum of the boot plus the fair value of the equipment acquired is $30,000. So the company receives 1/10 ($3,000 ÷ $30,000) of the value of the transaction as boot, and recognizes 1/10 of the gain on the equipment surrendered. Since the total gain on the equipment surrendered is $10,000 (the fair value of $30,000 less the book value of $20,000), Company A recognizes a gain of $1,000. Following the formula we developed previously, it computes the gain as follows:

$$\text{Gain} = \frac{\$3,000}{\$3,000 + \$27,000} (\$30,000 - \$20,000) = \$1,000$$

Company A records the equipment acquired at $18,000, the book value of the equipment surrendered less the cash received plus the gain recognized ($20,000 − $3,000 + $1,000). This treatment is consistent with alternative 6 in Exhibit 9-2.

Boot Paid by Company Incurring a Loss. When similar productive assets are exchanged for a loss and boot is involved, the company *paying* the boot recognizes the loss in full. We illustrate this situation for Company B in Exhibit 9-5. Company B incurs a loss of $1,000 ($27,000 fair value − $28,000 book value), recognizes it in full, and records the acquired equipment at $30,000 ($27,000 + $3,000). This treatment is consistent with alternative 3 in Exhibit 9-2.

Although these illustrations have used examples where one company incurs a loss and the other a gain, it is possible for both companies to have a loss, or for both companies to have a gain, depending on the relationship between each company's book value and fair value.

Summary of Productive Asset Exchanges

There are four issues involved in productive asset exchanges.

1. *Are dissimilar productive assets exchanged?* Gains and losses on dissimilar asset exchanges are recognized in full by both companies because the earning process is complete.
2. *Does the boot equal or exceed 25% of the value of a similar asset exchange?* If the boot equals or exceeds 25%, the exchange is recorded at fair value by both the recipient and the payer of boot.
3. *For exchanges of similar productive assets is there a loss?* A loss is recognized in full, following the conservatism principle.
4. *For exchanges of similar productive assets between two dealers or between two nondealers in which there is a gain, is cash received or paid?* If cash is paid, the "gain" is not recognized because the earning process is considered not to be complete. If cash is received, a partial gain is recognized because part of the earning process has been realized (completed).

To summarize, no gain (or a partial gain) is recognized when the exchange involves similar productive assets used in the same line of business (i.e., an exchange between two dealers or between two nondealers), the boot is less than 25% of the fair value of the transaction, and cash is received. In other situations the total gain is recognized. A loss is recognized in all situations.

SELF-CONSTRUCTION

Sometimes a company constructs an item of property, plant, and equipment that it intends to use in its production process. The costs directly related to the construction are added to the cost of the asset, including materials, labor, engineering, and variable manufacturing overhead. Three other components of the asset cost need additional consideration: (1) interest costs, (2) fixed manufacturing overhead costs, and (3) profit on the construction. We discuss each of these in the following sections.

4 Compute the cost of a self-constructed asset, including interest capitalization.

Interest During Construction

There has been a great deal of controversy as to whether a company should capitalize the interest on the funds borrowed to finance construction of an asset as part of the acquisition cost, or expense the interest. Furthermore, if the company uses internally generated funds to finance the acquisition, should it add imputed interest to the cost of the asset? Regulating authorities for public utilities usually allow a company to include both actual and imputed interest in the cost of the asset because the impact of the interest on the utility rates is deferred until the new plant is in operation. Therefore, the company assigns the cost of the plant (through depreciation expense) to the periods of use and to the customers who use the product. In the early 1970s the capitalization of interest by nonutility companies gained wider acceptance, but the SEC stopped this trend by preventing companies from adopting a policy of capitalization of interest cost. In 1979 **FASB Statement No. 34** was issued requiring the capitalization of interest in certain instances as we discuss later in this chapter.[8]

CONCEPTUAL ALTERNATIVES   The *Statement* outlines the three alternatives that were considered for the treatment of interest during construction.

(a) No Interest Is Capitalized During Construction.   Under this alternative a company would treat interest as a cost of borrowing funds, and would record the interest as an expense during the period incurred. This treatment would be consistent with all other interest costs, such as interest on funds borrowed to purchase inventory, or to purchase property, plant, and equipment. The principal argument in favor of this alternative is that interest is the price paid for borrowing funds for a period of time, and the benefit received is the availability of the funds. Therefore, the matching principle requires that the cost be expensed against the company's revenues in the period in which the funds are made available. Another argument is that expensing interest as incurred results in income flows that are more similar to cash flows.

(b) Capitalize an Amount of Interest for All Funds Used for Construction.   Under this alternative a company would assign an interest cost to all funds used in construction, whether borrowed or not. Therefore, the company would have to impute and capitalize an interest cost for the equity funds (common stock) used in construction in addition to the cost of borrowed funds. While it often is argued that this alternative provides the fairest economic cost of the asset, two major problems have prevented its adoption. First, there might be disagreement about the rate to be used for the imputed cost of the equity funds, and this amount would lack *reliability*. Second, since the computed interest cost of the equity funds would be debited to the asset, it would be necessary to record a credit. The credit could be to a revenue account, but that would violate the revenue recognition principle, since revenue should not be recognized as a result of acquiring assets. Another alternative would be to credit stockholders' equity directly, but there has been no contribution of capital by the owners, and the net worth of the company has not increased.

(c) Capitalize the Interest on Funds Borrowed for the Construction.   Under this alternative a company would treat the cost of borrowed funds as part of the cost of acquiring an asset and therefore as equivalent to the other costs of construction, such as materials and labor. The advantages are (1) the cost of the borrowed funds is necessary to obtain the benefits to be derived from the asset, and (2) since the asset is not yet generating revenue, the matching principle requires that the cost of interest (and depreciation) not be expensed during construction. The disadvantage is that the cost of the asset will differ depending on the type of financing (debt or equity) used for construction. There are two ways of interpreting this third alternative. The cost to be capitalized could be either the cost of funds *specifically* borrowed to finance the project or the *average* cost of all borrowed funds. Elements of both approaches are required by *FASB Statement No. 34.*

Three major factors must be considered in the application of the *Statement*: (1) Which assets qualify for interest capitalization? (2) What amount of interest is capitalized? (3) Over what period is the interest capitalized?

ASSETS QUALIFYING FOR INTEREST CAPITALIZATION   A company is required to capitalize interest on assets that are either constructed for its own use or constructed as discrete projects for sale or lease to others (for example, long-term construction projects such as ships or real estate developments, as discussed in Chapter 17). Interest *cannot* be capitalized for the following types of assets:

1. Inventories that are routinely manufactured or otherwise produced in large quantities on a repetitive basis. Inventories are not qualifying assets because, in the view of the FASB, "the informational benefit does not justify the cost"[9] of capitalization.

---

8.   "Capitalization of Interest Cost," *FASB Statement of Financial Accounting Standards No. 34* (Stamford, Conn.: FASB, 1979).
9.   *Ibid.*, par. 10.

2. Assets that are in use or ready for their intended use.
3. Assets that are not being used in the earning activities of the company and are not undergoing the activities necessary to get them ready for use.

AMOUNT OF INTEREST TO BE CAPITALIZED The amount of interest capitalized for a qualifying asset is based on the actual amounts borrowed and the cost of those borrowings. The amount is "intended to be that portion of the interest cost incurred during the asset's acquisition periods that theoretically could have been avoided."[10] **A company determines the amount of interest to capitalize by applying an interest rate to the average cumulative invested costs (expenditures) for the qualifying asset during the capitalization period.**

If a company incurs a specific borrowing for a qualifying asset, it applies the interest rate on that borrowing to the expenditures for the asset. If the expenditures on the asset exceed the cost of the specific borrowing or if no specific borrowing is made, the company applies the weighted average interest rate on all other borrowings. Because no imputed interest is allowed to be capitalized, **the total amount of interest cost that a company capitalizes each period may not exceed the interest cost incurred during the period.**

The expenditures to which this rate is applied are the cumulative capitalized expenditures (which include any capitalized interest on the qualifying asset from previous periods). It may be assumed for simplicity that the expenditures are incurred evenly throughout the period. Therefore, the average cumulative capitalized expenditures for a period are computed as follows: [(beginning cumulative costs + ending cumulative costs) ÷ 2]. If expenditures are not incurred evenly throughout the period, a weighted average calculation would be used. If the company receives any progress payments from the eventual purchaser of the asset, it deducts these amounts from its expenditures, so that it capitalizes interest on its net expenditures.

PERIOD OF INTEREST CAPITALIZATION The capitalization period begins when (a) expenditures for the asset have been made, (b) activities that are necessary to get the asset ready for its intended use are in progress, and (c) interest cost is being incurred. Interest capitalization continues as long as the three conditions are present. The term *activities* is construed broadly and should include all the steps necessary to prepare the asset for its intended use. For example, it includes administrative and technical activities during the preconstruction stage and activities undertaken to overcome technical difficulties after construction has begun, such as labor disputes or litigation. If a company suspends substantially *all* the activities related to the construction of the asset, however, it suspends interest capitalization until activities are resumed.

The capitalization period ends when the asset is (a) substantially complete and (b) ready for its intended use. If the asset is completed in parts and each part is capable of being used independently, interest capitalization stops for each part when that part satisfies the two criteria. In this case the interest to be capitalized is based on the average cost for that part. If the asset must be completed in its entirety before any part of the asset may be used, however, interest capitalization continues until the entire asset satisfies the two criteria.

ILLUSTRATION To illustrate these provisions of *FASB Statement No. 34*, consider the Cia Company, which started a building project on January 1, 2004 and completed it on December 31, 2005. Exhibit 9-6 shows the relevant facts.

The company incurred the costs (expenditures) evenly during each year. It computes the average cumulative capitalized costs in the project to date for each year using the equations discussed earlier as we show in Exhibit 9-6.

Since the company borrowed $1.5 million specifically for the project, it uses the 10% interest rate on this borrowing for each of the two years on the first $1.5 million of costs. It computes interest each year on costs greater than $1.5 million based on the weighted average of its remaining borrowings. It calculates the amount of interest to be capitalized in each of the two years as we show in Exhibit 9-6.

---

10. *Ibid.*, par. 12.

EXHIBIT 9-6   Capitalization of Interest Costs

Capitalization period: January 1, 2004 through December 31, 2005

Annual expenditures on the project (excluding capitalized interest):

2004 $1 million
2005 $2.9 million

Amounts borrowed and outstanding:

$1.5 million at 10% borrowed specifically for the project
$4 million at 12%
$6 million at 13%

Average cumulative costs: 2004, $500,000 [($0 + $1,000,000) ÷ 2]

Average cumulative costs: 2005, $2,500,000

$[(\$1,000,000 + \$50,000^a) + (\$1,050,000 + \$2,900,000)] \div 2$

Capitalized interest, 2004 = Average cumulative cost × Interest rate

$$= \$500,000 \times 10\%$$
$$= \$50,000$$

Capitalized interest, 2005 = Average cumulative cost × Interest rate

$$= (\$1,500,000^b \times 10\%) + (\$1,000,000^c \times 12.6\%^d)$$
$$= \$150,000 + \$126,000$$
$$= \$276,000$$

[a]$50,000 capitalized interest for 2004 as calculated below.
[b]$1.5 million specific borrowing
[c]$2,500,000 average cumulative cost for 2005 − $1,500,000 specific borrowing
[d]Weighted average interest rate $= \left(12\% \times \dfrac{\$4,000,000}{\$10,000,000}\right) + \left(13\% \times \dfrac{\$6,000,000}{\$10,000,000}\right)$
$$= 4.8\% + 7.8\%$$
$$= 12.6\%$$

The company calculates the $50,000 interest capitalized in 2004 by multiplying the $500,000 average cumulative cost by the 10% interest rate on the specific borrowing for the project. The interest capitalized in 2005 requires two calculations, since the $2,500,000 average cumulative cost exceeds the $1,500,000 specifically borrowed for the project. First, the company calculates the $150,000 ($1,500,000 × 10%) annual interest on the specific borrowing. Next, it multiples the $1,000,000 excess of average cost over specific borrowing ($2,500,000 − $1,500,000) by the 12.6% weighted average interest rate to determine the $126,000 additional interest to be capitalized. Thus it capitalizes a total of $276,000 ($150,000 + $126,000) interest in 2005.

As we mentioned earlier, the total amount of interest that is capitalized each period may not exceed the interest cost incurred during the period. Each year the company incurs interest costs of $1.41 million [($1.5 million × 10%) + ($4 million × 12%) + ($6 million × 13%)]. This amount is clearly more than the capitalized interest in either year. If it were less, however, it would be the maximum amount that the company could capitalize in any given year. Assuming the company has recorded interest expense for the $1.41 million interest cost each year, it would record the capitalized interest at the end of 2004 and 2005, respectively, as follows:

Building	50,000	
Interest Expense		50,000
Building	276,000	
Interest Expense		276,000

Note that these journal entries *reduce* the net interest expense for each year and *increase* the cost of the building because of the capitalized interest. The company reports the remaining net interest expense amounts of $1,360,000 ($1,410,000 − $50,000) and $1,134,000 ($1,410,000 − $276,000), respectively, on its 2004 and 2005 income statements and therefore pretax income is increased by $50,000 and $276,000. In addition, the company discloses the capitalized interest amounts of $50,000 and $276,000 in the notes to its financial statements. (Note that it also discloses the total interest paid each year, as we discuss in Chapter 21.)

The company reports a cost of $1,050,000 ($1 million construction cost + $50,000 interest cost) for the construction-in-process on its December 31, 2004 balance sheet, and a cost of $4,226,000 ($3.9 million total construction costs + $326,000 total interest cost) for the building on its December 31, 2005 balance sheet. The total interest capitalized over the two years is $326,000 ($50,000 + $276,000). Therefore, the cost of the asset is increased by this amount, which will reduce the gross profit on the sale if the asset is sold when completed, or increase the depreciation expense each year if the asset is held by the company.

In certain cases, a company may borrow a larger amount than it requires for its immediate construction needs. A question arises as to whether the company should offset the interest revenue earned by investing the excess funds against the interest cost to determine the amount of interest to be capitalized. Since *FASB Statement No. 34* states that the amount of interest to be capitalized is the portion of the interest that theoretically could have been avoided, the interest revenue should *not* be offset against the interest cost. The decision of a company to borrow greater amounts than needed and to invest the excess does not affect the avoidable interest and therefore does not affect the amount of interest to be capitalized.[11] Consequently, the interest earned is recognized and reported as interest revenue in the normal way.

International Accounting Differences

International accounting standards for the capitalization of interest may be different from U.S. standards. International standards state that the "benchmark" method is to expense all interest costs. However, the capitalization of interest during the acquisition, construction, or production of a qualifying asset is an allowable alternative. This allowed alternative approach is similar to the capitalization rules under U.S. GAAP. So the flexibility allowed under international standards may create a lack of comparability with companies following U.S. standards. (There are also some differences in the two sets of capitalization rules that are beyond the scope of the book.)

Fixed Overhead Costs

There are three alternatives for a company to include fixed overhead costs in the cost of a self-constructed asset. These alternatives are (1) to allocate a portion of the total fixed overhead, (2) to include only the incremental fixed overhead, and (3) not to include any fixed overhead in the cost of the asset. Each alternative should be considered in the context of two production situations. First, the company may be operating at full capacity, so that the construction activity reduces normal production activity. Second, the company may be operating at below-normal capacity, so that the construction activity does not affect normal production activity.

1. Allocate a Portion of Total Fixed Overhead to the Self-Constructed Asset. Under this alternative, the company allocates the fixed overhead to the construction in the same manner as to units of inventory produced. This is a "full costing" concept, because the total overhead costs of the period are allocated to the production of inventory and the construction of the asset. Arguments in favor of this alternative are (1) the

11. "Offsetting Interest Cost to Be Capitalized with Interest Income," *FASB Technical Bulletin No. 81–5* (Stamford, Conn.: FASB, 1981).

construction should be accounted for in the same way as regular products, even though this means that the regular products will be allocated less of the overhead, and (2) the cost of the constructed asset will tend to approximate more closely the cost of an equivalent purchased asset, since the seller normally would include fixed overhead in its selling price. The first argument is especially relevant if the company is operating at full capacity prior to the construction, so that the construction causes less regular production to take place. Then the lower total overhead allocated to production coupled with lower productive output results in more consistent unit costs. When the company is operating at below-normal capacity prior to construction, allocation of some fixed overhead to self-constructed assets reduces the costs allocated to regular production and therefore increases the income reported for these products when they are sold. Thus there is a transfer of overhead costs from regular production to the self-constructed asset.

2. Include Only Incremental Fixed Overhead in the Cost of the Self-Constructed Asset. Under this alternative, the company includes only the fixed overhead that increases as a result of the construction (but no allocated overhead) in the cost of the self-constructed asset. Arguments in favor of this alternative are (1) the cost of an asset is the additional cost incurred to produce it, (2) the normal operations should not receive different treatment by reducing the cost of the regular product and increasing income because of the construction, (3) the overhead would be incurred whether or not the construction takes place, and (4) the decision to construct the asset should be based on the total incremental cost and not include allocated fixed overhead. This method is particularly appropriate when the company has excess capacity available so that regular production and income are not affected by the construction. If this method is used in a full-capacity situation, the unit cost of the regular production is increased because the same total fixed overhead is allocated to the reduced production.

3. Include No Fixed Overhead in the Cost of the Self-Constructed Asset. The primary argument in favor of this alternative is that the company's fixed overhead does not change as a result of the construction. Therefore, if the company included some overhead, this would result in less overhead being expensed in the current period (or included in the cost of inventory) and an increase in income. Of course, this alternative is reasonable only if the fixed overhead does not increase as a result of the construction.

In summary, **the allocation of fixed overhead to a self-constructed asset is most appropriate when the company is operating at full capacity, the inclusion of only incremental fixed overhead is most appropriate in excess-capacity situations, and no allocation is appropriate if the overhead does not change.** Otherwise the self-construction activity affects income, an effect that many accountants consider undesirable. Income should be a measure of the success of selling goods and services, and it should not depend on the amount of construction undertaken.

However, the first alternative of allocating a portion of the total fixed overhead to the self-constructed asset is supported for both situations by the Cost Accounting Standards Board as follows:

> Tangible capital assets constructed for a contractor's own use must be capitalized at amounts which include general and administrative expenses when such expenses are identifiable with the constructed asset and are material in amount. When the constructed assets are identical with or similar to the contractor's regular product, such assets must be capitalized at amounts which include a full share of indirect costs.[12]

This method is the most commonly used and tends to produce an asset cost that is closer to the cost of a purchased asset, because an independent contractor would include an allowance to cover its overhead and income. However, it also tends to result in increased income during construction.

---

12. "Capitalization of Tangible Assets," *CASB Standard 404* (Washington, D.C.: CASB, 1973).

Income on Self-Construction

If a company constructs an asset for less than it would cost to purchase, should it recognize income for the difference between the two costs? An argument can be made in favor of recognizing income, since it would tend to produce an asset cost similar to the purchase price of the asset. However, generally accepted accounting principles do not allow recognition of income in this case. To do so would violate the revenue recognition principle that requires that income be recognized through asset use and disposal and not through acquisition. In addition, accounting is based on actions taken, not on what might have been. The saving through self-construction will be realized through reduced depreciation charges in the future. However, the conservatism convention requires that, if the construction cost materially exceeds the fair value of the asset, the capitalized construction costs of the asset be written down to the fair value and a loss recognized.

Development Stage Companies

Development stage companies devote substantially all their efforts to establishing a new business, and their planned principal operations have not yet started or no significant revenue has been generated. Some accountants argue that a new company should capitalize the costs of interest, taxes, and general overhead during its development stage—that is, before it makes significant sales. They argue that the costs incurred in the development stage will benefit future periods, and consequently the company should not report losses before it makes sales. In **FASB Statement No. 7** this argument was rejected. Instead normal capitalization criteria are applied to development stage companies. Therefore a company expenses such costs as interest (except for the provisions of *FASB Statement No. 34*), taxes, and general overhead in the period incurred. *FASB Statement No. 7* does impose some special disclosure requirements on development stage companies, but these are beyond the scope of the book.

COSTS SUBSEQUENT TO ACQUISITION

A company incurs costs over the life of its property, plant, and equipment for purposes ranging from routine repairs to major overhauls and improvements. The related accounting decision is whether these costs should be added (capitalized) to an asset account (a **capital expenditure**) or expensed (an **operating** or **revenue expenditure**). **A cost that increases the future economic benefits of the asset above those that originally were expected is a capital expenditure.** The future economic benefits can be increased by (1) extending the life of the asset, (2) improving productivity, (3) producing the same product at lower cost, or (4) increasing the quality of the product. **A cost that does not increase the economic benefits but is incurred to maintain the existing benefits is an operating expenditure.** We give special consideration to additions, improvements and replacements, rearrangement and moving, and repairs and maintenance in the following sections.

5 Record costs subsequent to acquisition.

Additions

The cost of an **addition** represents a new asset and therefore is capitalized. A new wing to a building and the installation of a pollution-control device are examples of additions. When the addition involves removing an old asset, an issue arises as to how to account for the cost of the removal. For example, when a company adds a new wing to a building, it frequently makes alterations to the old building. If these alterations increase the economic benefits originally anticipated for the old building, then the cost of alteration is capitalized. If the alterations do not increase the original benefits of the old building, the cost is expensed. In addition, the cost of any part of the asset that is demolished (for example, a connecting wall) should be removed from the accounts as the disposal of an asset, although this is rarely done because of immateriality or the difficulty of measurement.

Improvements and Replacements

Improvements (sometimes called **betterments**) and **replacements** (sometimes called **renewals**) involve the substitution of new parts for old ones, and increase the economic benefits to be derived from the asset. An improvement is the substitution of a better asset for the one currently used, such as the installation of a solar heating system in a building. A replacement is the substitution of an equivalent asset, such as a new engine in a truck. The related costs of improvements and replacements are capitalized. There are three alternative ways for a company to account for such capitalized expenditures, and the choice depends on the particular circumstances.

1. *Substitution Method.* When the book value of the old asset is known, it is removed from the accounts and the new asset recorded. For example, suppose that a company decides to replace its oil furnace with a gas furnace. The oil furnace is carried on the books at a cost of $50,000 with accumulated depreciation of $30,000. The scrap value of the old furnace is $5,000, and the new furnace costs $70,000. The company records these transactions as follows:

Furnace	70,000	
Accumulated Depreciation: Furnace	30,000	
Loss on Disposal of Furnace ($20,000 − $5,000)	15,000	
Furnace		50,000
Cash ($70,000 − $5,000)		65,000

Although this is the ideal method, it often is not practical because the company does not know the book value of the asset being replaced. For example, when the company replaces the engine on a truck, it may not know the book value of the engine. In these situations, it should use one of the following two alternative methods.

2. *Reduce Accumulated Depreciation.* The costs of improvements and replacements are often debited to Accumulated Depreciation on the grounds that some of the service potential that previously was written off has been restored. Therefore, it is appropriate to use this method for replacements when the service life of the asset has been extended. For example, suppose that a company incurs a capital expenditure of $50,000 to replace a roof on its factory. The company had not planned to replace the roof, but it has extended the life of the factory. The company records the cost as follows:

Accumulated Depreciation	50,000	
Cash		50,000

3. *Increase the Asset Account.* The costs of improvements and replacements may be capitalized directly to the asset account on the grounds that an addition to the service potential of the asset has been made. This method is particularly appropriate for improvements when the benefits are increased above those originally expected. For example, a company records a capital expenditure of $50,000 to enlarge a factory that increases its usefulness is recorded as follows:

Factory	50,000	
Cash		50,000

Note that alternatives 2 and 3 have exactly the same effect on the book value of the asset, although the gross amounts in the two accounts would be different. In both cases, a new depreciation rate would be computed, as we discuss in the next chapter.

Rearrangement and Moving

The costs of rearranging the facilities within a building or moving them to a new location are capitalized and expensed over the period expected to benefit. (This period is shorter than the economic life of the assets being moved if it is expected that the assets will be moved again before the end of their service lives.) However, many companies expense such costs immediately, which is an acceptable procedure if the difference is immaterial.

Repairs and Maintenance

When a company incurs routine repair and maintenance costs to maintain an asset in its operating condition and not to increase the economic benefits over those it originally intended, it expenses the costs in the period incurred. However, the classification of an expenditure as a repair may depend on how the company accounts for its assets. For example, if the company includes landscaping costs in a Land Improvements account, it would account for the replacement of some trees as repairs and maintenance. If the landscaping costs were included in a separate account, then the company would most likely account for the replacement of these trees as an improvement or replacement.

Since a company may incur repair and maintenance costs unevenly during the year (e.g., it may schedule repairs for slack production periods), its interim financial statements (such as quarterly reports) will absorb different amounts of repair costs that, in turn, may give a misleading picture of the company's income flows. The amount of repair costs recorded as an expense in each interim period may be equalized by using an allowance account. For example, suppose a company anticipates spending $60,000 on repair and maintenance during the year, but $45,000 will be spent in the third quarter, with the remainder spread equally over the remaining three quarters. The company records these events as follows:

First Quarter

Repair Expense ($60,000 ÷ 4)	15,000	
Allowance for Repairs		10,000
Cash, Accounts Payable, Inventory, etc.		5,000

Second Quarter

Repair Expense	15,000	
Allowance for Repairs		10,000
Cash, Accounts Payable, Inventory, etc.		5,000

Third Quarter

Repair Expense	15,000	
Allowance for Repairs	30,000	
Cash, Accounts Payable, Inventory, etc.		45,000

Fourth Quarter

Repair Expense	15,000	
Allowance for Repairs		10,000
Cash, Accounts Payable, Inventory, etc.		5,000

The repair expense for each quarter is $15,000 (one-fourth of the annual cost of $60,000), and Allowance for Repairs has a zero balance at the end of the year. This procedure is acceptable for *interim* reporting because it allows a company to record equal expenses in each interim period. The company reports the balance in Allowance for Repairs as an addition to or offset from the property, plant, and equipment and not as a liability because nothing is owed. However, a balance in Allowance for Repairs is not carried over from one *annual* fiscal period to another, because such smoothing of income is not allowed under generally accepted accounting principles. If a balance does remain in the Allowance for Repairs account at the end of the year, it is closed to the Repair Expense account.

DISPOSAL OF PROPERTY, PLANT, AND EQUIPMENT

A company may dispose of property, plant, and equipment by sale, involuntary conversion, abandonment, or exchange (which we discussed earlier in the chapter). Ideally, the depreciation, which is accumulated up to the time of disposal, will have reduced

6 Record the disposal of property, plant, and equipment.

the book value down to the disposal value. Usually, however, this does not occur, and the company must recognize a gain or a loss on the disposal. The gain or loss results from a transaction of the period, although it may also be considered a correction of the income that has been recorded in the years the asset has been owned, since it is an indication that the depreciation was not correct. The company usually includes the gain or loss in ordinary income, but it could also be reported as an extraordinary item or a disposal of a component of a business if it meets the appropriate criteria established in **FASB Statement No. 144,** as we discussed in Chapter 4.

To account for the disposal of property, plant, and equipment, the company first records the depreciation up to the date of the disposal (as we discuss in the next chapter). It then removes the cost of the asset and the related amount of accumulated depreciation from the respective accounts. For example, assume that a company has a machine that originally cost $10,000, has accumulated depreciation of $8,000 at the beginning of the current year, and is being depreciated at $1,000 per year. If the company sells the machine for $600 on December 30, it must first bring the depreciation up to date as follows:

Depreciation Expense	1,000	
Accumulated Depreciation		1,000

Once the book value is up to date, the company compares it to the proceeds to determine the gain or loss. Comparing the $1,000 [$10,000 − ($8,000 + $1,000)] book value of the asset on December 30 to the $600 proceeds yields a loss of $400, which the company records as follows:

Cash	600	
Accumulated Depreciation	9,000	
Loss on Disposal	400	
Machine		10,000

An involuntary disposal, such as condemnation of land by a governmental unit, is accounted for in the same manner.[13] An abandonment is handled in a similar way, except that there is no receipt of cash, so the loss is equal to the remaining book value.

Asset Retirement Obligations

The acquisition of some assets automatically creates a legal obligation related to the retirement of the asset. For example, companies owning power plants, mines, and industrial manufacturing sites frequently are legally required to incur significant costs related to their closure. **FASB Statement No. 143,** "Accounting for Asset Retirement Obligations," requires a company to record a legal liability for the obligation at its fair value when the obligation is incurred, which is usually when the asset is acquired. The most common method of measuring the fair value is likely to be the present value of the future cash flows that will be paid by the company. When the company acquires the asset (and records the liability) the presents value is less than the future cash flows, and therefore, it must increase the liability over time. So the company recognizes an interest expense (called accretion expense) each year it uses the asset by multiplying the book value of the liability by the discount rate it used to compute the original present value. On the date the company retires the asset and pays the retirement costs, it debits the obligation and credits cash. The company recognizes any difference between the estimated retirement costs (i.e., the liability) and the actual costs as a gain or loss.

When the company records (credits) the initial liability, it also records (debits) the same amount as an increase in the carrying value of the related asset. The company

---

13. "Accounting for Involuntary Conversions of Nonmonetary Assets to Monetary Assets," *FASB Interpretation No. 30* (Stamford, Conn.: FASB, 1979), requires that a gain or loss be recognized when a nonmonetary asset is involuntarily converted to monetary assets even though a company reinvests or is obligated to reinvest the monetary assets in replacement nonmonetary assets.

expenses (depreciates) this cost in the usual way by means of a systematic and rational allocation method over its useful life.[14]

DISCLOSURE OF PROPERTY, PLANT, AND EQUIPMENT

APB Opinion No. 12 requires a company to disclose the balances of its major classes of depreciable assets by nature or function.[15] We show an example of each of these methods in Exhibit 9-7. Johnson & Johnson illustrates disclosure by the nature of the assets, such as land, buildings, and machinery. Norfolk Southern discloses by function, such as road and equipment.

7 Understand the disclosures of property, plant, and equipment.

EXHIBIT 9-7 **Alternative Methods of Disclosure of Depreciable Assets**

JOHNSON & JOHNSON AND SUBSIDIARIES
Notes to Consolidated Financial Statements (in part)

1. Summary of Accounting Principles (in part):
Property, Plant, and Equipment and Depreciation
Property, plant, and equipment are stated at cost. The Company utilizes the straight-line method of depreciation over the estimated useful lives of the assets:

Building and building equipment	20-24 years
Land and leasehold improvements	10-20 years
Machinery and equipment	2-13 years

3 Property, Plant and Equipment
At the end of 2001 and 2000, property, plant and equipment at cost and accumulated depreciation were:

(*Dollars in Millions*)	2001	2000
Land and land improvements	$ 459	$ 427
Buildings and building equipment	3,911	3,659
Machinery and equipment	6,805	6,312
Construction in progress	1,283	1,468
	12,458	11,866
Less accumulated depreciation	4,739	4,457
	$ 7,719	7,409

The Company capitalizes interest expense as part of the cost of construction of facilities and equipment. Interest expense capitalized in 2001, 2000 and 1999 was $95 million, $97 million and $84 million, respectively.

Upon retirement or other disposal of fixed assets, the cost and related amount of accumulated depreciation or amortization are eliminated from the asset and accumulated depreciation accounts, respectively. The difference, if any, between the net asset value and the proceeds is adjusted to earnings.

NORFOLK SOUTHERN CORPORATION AND SUBSIDIARIES
Notes to Consolidated Financial Statements (in part)

1. Summary of Significant Accounting Policies (in part):
Properties: "Properties" are stated principally at cost and are depreciated using group depreciation. Rail is primarily depreciated on the basis of use measured by gross ton miles. Other properties are

---

14. "Accounting for Asset Retirement Obligations," *FASB Statement of Financial Accounting Standards No. 143* (Norwalk, Conn.: FASB, 2001), par. 3, 11, and 14.
15. "Omnibus Opinion—1967," *APB Opinion No. 12* (New York: AICPA, 1967), par. 5.

EXHIBIT 9-7   Alternative Methods of Disclosure of Depreciable Assets, Continued

depreciated generally using the straight-line method over the lesser of estimated service or lease lives. NS capitalizes interest on major capital projects during the period of their construction. Expenditures, including those on leased assets, that extend an asset's useful life or increase its utility, are capitalized. Maintenance expense is recognized when repairs are performed. When properties other than land and non-rail assets are sold or retired in the ordinary course of business, the cost of the assets, net of sale proceeds or salvage, is charged to accumulated depreciation rather than recognized through income. Gains and losses on disposal of land and non-rail assets are included in "Other income-net."

NS reviews the carrying amount of properties whenever events or changes in circumstances indicate that such carrying amount may not be recoverable based on future undiscounted cash flows or estimated net realizable value. Assets that are deemed impaired as a result of such review are recorded at the lower of carrying amount or fair value.

6. Properties

($ in millions)	December 31, 2001	December 31, 2000	Depreciation Rate for 2001
Railway property:			
Road	$10,452	$10,078	3.0%
Equipment	5,559	5,588	4.1%
Other property	632	653	3.2%
	16,643	16,319	
Less: Accumulated depreciation	5,435	5,214	
Net properties	$11,208	$11,105	

Included in properties are approximately $110 million in telecommunications assets consisting of fiber optic conduit. Because of the significant economic downturn in the telecommunications industry during the year, NS evaluated the recoverability of these assets at Dec. 31, 2001. Based on known facts and circumstances, management believes that its ultimate investment in these assets, which is expected to total approximately $130 million upon completion of the network, will be recovered.

Equipment includes $474 million at Dec. 31, 2001 and 2000, of assets recorded pursuant to capital leases. Other property includes the costs of obtaining rights to natural resources of $341 million at Dec. 31, 2001 and 2000.

Total interest cost incurred on debt in 2001, 2000 and 1999 was $570 million, $569 million and $546 million respectively, of which $17 million, $18 million and $15 million was capitalized.

Q U E S T I O N S

Q If Johnson & Johnson had not capitalized interest in 2001, how would its financial statements be different?   **Q** What are the effects on the financial statements of the method used by Norfolk Southern for the sale of properties? Is it different than the method used by Johnson & Johnson?   **Q** Why does Norfolk Southern account for the sale of land differently than the sale of other properties?

APPENDIX: OIL AND GAS PROPERTIES

8 Explain the accounting for oil and gas properties.

A company faces special issues when accounting for oil and gas properties that are included in its property, plant, and equipment. Two alternative methods of accounting for the cost of oil and gas properties are widely used. The principal difference between the two methods concerns the cost of dry wells—those that do not result in the production of oil or gas. Under the **successful-efforts** method, those costs are charged to expense; under the **full-cost** method, they are capitalized as part of the cost of oil and gas reserves, and subsequently amortized.

Proponents of the successful-efforts method argue that a direct relationship between costs incurred and specific reserves discovered is required before costs are recorded as assets. Costs of acquisition and development activities that are known not to have resulted in the discovery of reserves are charged to expense. In contrast, the full-cost method regards the costs of unsuccessful acquisition and exploration activities as necessary for the discovery of reserves. Thus, all costs incurred in oil and gas drilling are regarded as integral to the development of whatever reserves ultimately result from the efforts as a whole, and are thus associated with the company's reserves. Establishing a direct cause-and-effect relationship between drilling costs incurred and specific reserves discovered is not relevant to full costing. The basic difference between the two methods focuses on the nature of an asset. If the asset is viewed as an individual well, it is appropriate for a company to expense the costs incurred if no oil or gas is found, because no future cash flows will result. Alternatively, if the asset is viewed as the oil or gas that lies underground, it is appropriate for a company to capitalize the costs of drilling even if no oil or gas is found from a particular well, because the activity was necessary in the general activity of searching for oil or gas. It is the oil or gas that is discovered that will contribute to the future cash flows rather than the costs incurred to drill any particular well. A company that uses the full-cost method is required (by the SEC, as discussed later) to use a country as a cost center. Thus if costs are incurred in a new country and no oil or gas results, the costs are expensed.

Because both methods are widely used, difficulties are created for users of financial statements when making comparisons between companies that are each using different methods. Large oil and gas companies generally use the successful-efforts method, whereas small independent producers prefer the full-cost method because it enables them to defer more costs, thereby reducing current expenses and increasing current income.

In 1977 **FASB Statement No. 19** was issued, which required the use of the successful-efforts method. Two primary reasons justified the adoption of the successful-efforts method by the FASB. First, an asset is an economic resource that is expected to provide future benefits, so costs that are known not to have resulted in identifiable future benefits should be expensed. Second, financial statements should reflect risk and unsuccessful results, and the successful-efforts method highlights the cost of failures and the risks involved in the search for oil and gas reserves. In a politically motivated decision, the SEC decided not to support the FASB's position. Many of the owners and managers of oil and gas companies that were using full-cost accounting objected to its elimination and lobbied Congress. They argued that the use of successful efforts would cause reported income and assets to be lower, and would impair the ability of their companies to raise capital and search for oil and gas. This argument is inconsistent with efficient markets research, which indicates that users of financial statements would not be "fooled" by the different reporting of the same underlying economic facts. However, Congress accepted the argument and directed that the SEC must accept the use of the full-cost method in reports filed with it, thereby allowing both methods to continue to be used. Consequently, the FASB suspended *FASB Statement No. 19*.

It can be argued that neither method satisfies the needs of users of financial statements because they do not reflect the economic substance of oil and gas exploration; that is, neither one includes the current values of a company's oil and gas reserves in its financial statements. Thus, the SEC proposed a completely new method of accounting, Reserve Recognition Accounting (RRA), which would allow a company to report the current values of reserves on its balance sheet and changes in the values of those reserves to be included on its income statement. Effective in 1979 companies were required to present a supplementary income statement, based on RRA, while continuing to use successful-efforts or full-cost accounting. Subsequently, the SEC rescinded the requirement to use RRA, and therefore oil companies now either use the full-cost or the successful-efforts method. Once a company has selected one of the two alternative methods, it must follow specific SEC accounting rules.[16] If the successful-efforts method

---

16. "Codification of Financial Reporting Policies," *SEC Accounting Rules* (Chicago: Commerce Clearing House, October, 2002), sec. 406.

Current value accounting is discussed in Appendix E.

is chosen, the SEC requires that the rules of *FASB Statement No. 19* must be followed. In addition, *FASB Statement No. 69* requires that oil companies disclose the physical and dollar amounts of reserves at year-end and changes in these amounts. Since these accounting problems relate to a specific industry, we do not discuss them further.

SUMMARY

At the beginning of the chapter, we identified several objectives you would accomplish after reading the chapter. The objectives are listed below, each followed by a brief summary of the key points in the chapter discussion.

1. **Identify the characteristics of property, plant, and equipment.** Property, plant, and equipment is the title used to classify tangible noncurrent assets a company uses in the normal operations of its business. The asset must be held for use and not for investment, must have an expected life of more than one year, and must be tangible in nature.
2. **Record the acquisition of property, plant, and equipment.** Property, plant, and equipment is recorded at the total cost necessary to acquire the asset and put it in operating condition; that is, the costs that are necessary to obtain the benefits to be derived from the asset.
3. **Determine the costs of assets acquired by the exchange of other assets.** The cost of the asset acquired is the fair value of the asset surrendered plus any boot paid or minus any boot received. For a similar productive asset exchange, a loss is recognized in full, but a gain is recognized only if boot is received.
4. **Compute the cost of a self-constructed asset, including interest capitalization.** When a company constructs an item of property, plant, and equipment, the costs included in the asset cost are materials, labor, engineering, variable manufacturing overhead, interest, and perhaps allocated fixed manufacturing overhead. A company is required to capitalize interest on assets that are either constructed for its own use or constructed as discrete projects for sale or lease to others. The company determines the amount of interest to capitalize by applying an interest rate to the average cumulative invested costs for the qualifying asset during the capitalization period.
5. **Record costs subsequent to acquisition.** A subsequent cost that increases the future economic benefits of the asset above those that originally were expected is a capital expenditure. A subsequent cost that does not increase the economic benefits but is incurred to maintain existing benefits is an operating expenditure and is expensed.
6. **Record the disposal of property, plant, and equipment.** A company may dispose of property, plant, and equipment by sale, involuntary conversion, or abandonment. The company records depreciation up to the date of the sale and records a gain or loss for the difference between the book value of the asset and the proceeds received.
7. **Understand the disclosures of property, plant, and equipment.** A company is required to disclose the balances of its major classes of depreciable assets by nature or function.
8. **Explain the accounting for oil and gas properties** (Appendix). A company may account for oil and gas properties using either the full cost method, in which the cost of dry holes is capitalized, or the successful efforts method, in which the cost of dry holes is expensed.

QUESTIONS

Q9-1 What characteristics are necessary for a company to include an asset in the category of property, plant, and equipment?

Q9-2 What is the general criterion a company uses to decide whether to include an expenditure in the cost of property, plant, and equipment rather than expensing it?

Q9-3 How does a company categorize land held for investment on its balance sheet?

Q9-4 What is the book value of an asset?

Q9-5 What is the relationship between the book value and the market value of an asset during the life of the asset?

Q9-6 When a company purchases several assets for a single lump sum, what principle does it use for cost apportionment? Why is it necessary to apportion the cost?

Q9-7 How does a company determine the acquisition cost of an asset when it acquires the asset in exchange for securities?

Q9-8 What is the distinction between similar and dissimilar productive assets made by *APB Opinion No. 29*? What is the reason for the distinction?

Q9-9 Under what situations does a company recognize a gain or loss when it exchanges similar productive assets? When it exchanges dissimilar productive assets?

Q9-10 What is meant by the term *boot*? How is it relevant to accounting for a similar productive asset exchange?

Q9-11 What is the general principle underlying the accounting for dissimilar productive assets? For similar productive assets?

Q9-12 Under what conditions does a company capitalize the interest incurred during self-construction of an asset? Contrast your answer with accounting for interest on a note payable that is not associated with the construction of an asset.

Q9-13 Explain how a company determines the amount of interest to capitalize when it constructs an asset.

Q9-14 A company borrows some money which it uses to acquire a parcel of land for a real estate development project. Before construction begins, a period of time passes while the company obtains the necessary planning permission. May the company capitalize interest during this period? If so, should it capitalize the interest to the land or the building account?

Q9-15 What are the three common alternative treatments of overhead costs during self-construction of an asset? What are the arguments in favor of each?

Q9-16 May a company recognize profit during self-construction of an asset under generally accepted accounting principles? May it recognize a loss?

Q9-17 What is the distinction between a capital and an operating expenditure? Give two examples of each.

Q9-18 Distinguish between additions and improvements/replacements. How should a company account for each?

Q9-19 Distinguish between ordinary repairs and maintenance, and extraordinary repairs. How should a company account for each?

Q9-20 What are leasehold improvements? How should a company account for them?

Q9-21 Under what conditions would you expect to see Allowance for Repairs in a company's balance sheet?

Q9-22 How does a company account for the disposal of an asset? How does it report gains and losses on its financial statements?

Q9-23 (*Appendix*). Distinguish between successful efforts and full cost accounting for oil and gas properties.

CASES

COMMUNICATION

C9-1 Acquisition and Retirement

Among the principal topics related to the accounting for property, plant, and equipment of a company are acquisition and retirement.

Required

1. Explain the expenditures that a company capitalizes when it acquires equipment for cash.
2. Assume that a company cannot determine the market value of equipment acquired by reference to a similar purchase for cash. Explain how the company determines the capitalizable cost of equipment purchased by exchanging it for each of the following three items:
   a. Bonds having an established market price.
   b. Common stock not having an established market price.
   c. Similar equipment having a determinable market value.
3. Explain the factors that a company uses to determine whether it capitalizes expenditures relating to property, plant, and equipment already in use.
4. Explain how a company accounts for the gain or loss on the sale of property, plant, and equipment for cash. (*AICPA adapted*)

C9-2 Capitalization Issues

George Company purchased land for use as its corporate headquarters. A small factory that was on the land when it was purchased was torn down before construction of the office building began. Furthermore, a substantial amount of rock blasting and removal had to be done to the site before construction of the building foundation began. Because the office building was set back on the land, far from the public road, George Company had the contractor construct a paved road that led from the public road to the parking lot of the office building.

Three years after it occupied the office building, George Company added four stories to the office building. The four stories had an estimated useful life of 5 years more than the remaining estimated useful life of the original office building.

Ten years later George Company sold the land and building at an amount more than their book value and had a new office building constructed in another state for use as its new corporate headquarters.

Required

1. Which of the preceding expenditures does the company capitalize? How does it depreciate or amortize each? Explain the rationale for your answers.

2. How does a company account for the sale of the land and building? Include in your answer how to determine the book value at the date of sale. Explain the rationale for your answer. (*AICPA adapted*)

C9-3 Cost Issues

Deskin Company purchased a new machine to be used in its operations. The new machine was delivered by the supplier, installed by Deskin, and placed into operation. It was purchased under a long-term payment plan for which the interest charges approximated the prevailing market rates. The estimated useful life of the new machine is 10 years, and its estimated residual (salvage) value is significant. Normal maintenance was performed to keep the new machine in usable condition.

Deskin also added a wing to the manufacturing building that it owns. The addition is an integral part of the building. Furthermore, Deskin made significant leasehold improvements to office space used as corporate headquarters.

Required

1. What costs should Deskin capitalize for the new machine?
2. Explain how Deskin should account for the normal maintenance performed on the new machine.
3. Explain how Deskin should account for the wing added to the manufacturing building. Where should the added wing be reported on Deskin's financial statements?
4. Explain how Deskin should account for the leasehold improvements made to its office space. Where should the leasehold improvements be reported on Deskin's financial statements? (*AICPA adapted*)

C9-4 Acquisition Costs

A company may acquire plant assets (among other ways) for cash, on a deferred-payment plan, by exchanging other assets, or by a combination of these ways.

Required

1. Identify six costs that a company should capitalize as the cost of land. For your answer, assume that a company acquires land with an existing building for cash and that it removes the existing building immediately in order that it can construct a new building on that site.
2. At what amount should a company record a plant asset acquired on a deferred-payment plan?
3. In general, at what amount should a company record plant assets received in exchange for other nonmonetary assets? Specifically, at what amount should a company record a new machine acquired by exchanging an older, similar machine and paying cash? (*AICPA adapted*)

C9-5 Capital and Revenue Expenditures

Bristol Company purchased land as a site for construction of a factory. Outside contractors were engaged to:

1. Construct the factory
2. Grade and pave a parking lot adjacent to the factory for the exclusive use of the factory workers.

Operations at the new location began during the year and normal factory maintenance costs were incurred after production began.

Required

1. Distinguish between capital and revenue (operating) expenditures.
2. Indicate how the company should account for and report expenditures for each of the following at the time incurred and in subsequent accounting periods.
   a. Purchase of land
   b. Construction of factory
   c. Grading and paving parking lot
   d. Payment of normal factory maintenance costs

Do not discuss capitalization of interest during construction in your response. (*AICPA adapted*)

CREATIVE AND CRITICAL THINKING

C9-6 Lump-Sum Acquisition

In 1975 a trial was held to settle a tax dispute between the owners of the Atlanta Falcons, a National Football League franchise, and the Internal Revenue Service. In 1966 the owners had paid $8.5 million to purchase the franchise. They considered $50,000 to be the cost of the franchise (which is not depreciable for income tax reporting), $727,000 was deferred interest, and the remaining $7.7 million was claimed to be the cost of the players' contracts and options. The dispute centered on several variables:

1. How much of the purchase price was assignable to television rights?
2. Is the value assignable to television rights depreciable?

If so, what is the expected life?
3. How much of the purchase price was assignable to player contracts and options?
4. Over what life should the value assigned to the players be depreciated?
5. What is the value of the franchise?

Required

1. As an independent accountant, explain the approach you would take and the information you would need to provide advice to the court for the resolution of the points in dispute.
2. Do these valuation issues also create ethical issues?

C9-7 Interest Capitalization

The Gold Creek Company has borrowed large amounts of money to purchase 5,000 acres of land, which it will develop as a new ski area over the next 10 years. Development is currently under way on the first 2,000 acres, with trails being cut and ski lifts being built. When the company completes this initial development after four years, it will develop the remaining acreage at the rate of approximately 500 acres per year. The company also used some of the money it borrowed to purchase adjacent land, which it will use to expand the ski area if it is successful.

Since this is the first year of the company's existence, it has not developed a policy about interest capitalization. Specifically, it is uncertain about whether it is entitled to capitalize interest on the amounts borrowed to acquire the first 2,000 acres, the total 5,000 acres, the 5,000 acres plus the adjacent land, or the land and the development.

Required

1. Explain the interest capitalization that is appropriate under these circumstances.
2. How might the decision be influenced if the company were interested in earnings management?

C9-8 Purchase Options

The Morgan Company was planning to expand its production facilities. Therefore it acquired 1-year options to purchase two alternative sites. Each option cost $5,000 and could not be applied against the contract. One of the sites was bought for $100,000. The company was unsure whether to capitalize the land at $100,000, $105,000, or $110,000.

Required Write a short report that presents arguments in favor of each alternative.

C9-9 Donated Asset and Its Modification

The Birkby Company acquires a building as a donation from the City of Avalon. The controller argues that since there was no payment by the company, it is not necessary to record the asset and therefore no depreciation should be recorded.

The company has to spend $15,000 altering the building to suit its unique needs. The controller argues that the $15,000 should be expensed because if the building is sold or returned to the city, it cannot recover the $15,000. In addition, expensing the $15,000 results in a closer approximation of the apparent market value of the asset and reduces income taxes immediately.

Required Write a short memo to the controller that evaluates each of the arguments made by the controller.

C9-10 Natural Resource Assets

You have been engaged to examine the financial statements of Brahe Corporation for the year ending December 31, 2004. Brahe Corporation was organized in January 2004 by Messrs. Moses and Price, original owners of options to acquire oil leases on 5,000 acres of land for $350,000. They expected that first the oil leases would be acquired by the corporation and subsequently 180,000 shares of the corporation's common stock would be sold to the public at $6 per share. In February 2004 they exchanged their options, $150,000 cash, and $50,000 of other assets for 75,000 shares of common stock of the corporation. The corporation's board of directors appraised the leases at $600,000, basing its appraisal on the price of other acreage recently leased in the same area. The options were therefore recorded at $250,000 ($600,000 − $350,000 option price).

The options were exercised by the corporation in March 2004 prior to the sale of common stock to the public in April 2004. Leases on approximately 500 acres of land were abandoned as worthless during the year.

Required

1. Explain why the valuation of assets acquired by a corporation in exchange for its own common stock is sometimes difficult.
2. a. Explain the reasoning Brahe Corporation might use to support valuing the leases at $600,000, the amount of the appraisal by the board of directors.
   b. Assuming the board's appraisal was sincere, what steps might Brahe Corporation have taken to strengthen its position to use the $600,000 value and to provide additional information if questions were raised about possible overvaluation of the leases?
3. Discuss the propriety of charging one-tenth of the recorded value of the leases against income at December 31, 2004 because leases on 500 acres of land were abandoned during the year. (*AICPA adapted*)

C9-11 Ethics and Construction Costs

You are the accountant for a division of a company that is constructing a building for its own use. It is January 2005, and you are working on closing the books for 2004. The CEO of the division stops by your office and says, "I have some questions about our building. Although we started construction at the beginning of June this year, we started planning it at the beginning of the previous year. I believe that we can capitalize interest since then. Check to see if we did capitalize some in 2003. If not, we can take it out of this year's expense and get a double dose. Also, I want you to add lots of overhead to the cost of the building so we can increase our profit for this year. For example, you spent quite a bit of time on the project. So perhaps we could add 1/12 of your salary to the cost of the building. You get the idea?" When the CEO leaves, you check the files and find a letter to an architect dated January 2, 2003. There are numerous subsequent letters to and from the architect.

Required From financial reporting and ethical perspectives, how would you reply to the CEO?

R E S E A R C H

C9-12 Researching GAAP

The Tenth National Bank had taken possession of a shopping mall in foreclosure of a mortgage. When the mall was inspected prior to being sold by the bank to a real estate company, it was discovered that it had extensive asbestos problems. An estimate indicated that it would cost $1 million to remove the asbestos. The bank has also purchased an office building for its headquarters. The building was inspected before the purchase and a similar asbestos problem was discovered. An estimate indicated that it would cost $2 million to remove the asbestos, and the bank completed the purchase. The bank's president has asked you how to account for these transactions.

Required

1. Research the related generally accepted accounting principles and prepare a short memo to the president that answers her question. Cite your references and applicable paragraph numbers.
2. Does this situation create ethical issues?

C9-13 Researching GAAP

The Perry Park Company was searching for a way to expand its operating capacity even though it was short of cash. The president of the company was playing golf and mentioned his concern to his playing partner, who owned some land and a building and was interested in disposing of them. After some negotiation, the two agreed to swap the land and building for shares in the company. The president of the company has asked you how to account for this transaction, including whether the transaction qualifies as a nonmonetary exchange and the value to place on the transaction and its components.

Required

1. Research the related generally accepted accounting principles and prepare a short memo to the president. Cite your references and applicable paragraph numbers.
2. Does this situation create ethical issues?

MULTIPLE CHOICE

Select the best answer for each of the following.

M9-1 The Hickory Company made a lump-sum purchase of three pieces of machinery for $115,000 from an unaffiliated company. At the time of acquisition Hickory paid $5,000 to determine the appraised value of the machinery. The appraisal disclosed the following values:

Machine A $70,000   Machine B $42,000
Machine C $28,000

What cost should be assigned to machines A, B, and C, respectively?

	A	B	C
a.	$40,000	$40,000	$40,000
b.	$57,500	$34,500	$23,000
c.	$60,000	$36,000	$24,000
d.	$70,000	$42,000	$28,000

M9-2 A donated plant asset for which the fair value has been determined, and for which incidental costs were incurred in acceptance of the asset, should be recorded at an amount equal to its

a. Incidental costs incurred
b. Fair value and incidental costs incurred
c. Book value on books of donor and incidental costs incurred
d. Book value on books of donor

M9-3 The following expenditures were among those incurred by Jensen Corporation during the year ended December 31, 2004:

Replacement of tiles on portion of roof that had been leaking	$4,000
Overhaul of machinery that is expected to extend its useful life for another two years	6,000

How much should be charged to repairs and maintenance in 2004?

a. $0
b. $4,000
c. $6,000
d. $10,000

M9-4 The sale of a depreciable asset resulting in a loss indicates that the proceeds from the sale were

a. Less than current market value
b. Greater than cost
c. Greater than book value
d. Less than book value

M9-5 Electro Corporation bought a new machine and agreed to pay for it in equal annual installments of $5,000 at the end of each of the next 5 years. Assume a prevailing interest rate of 15%. The present value of an ordinary annuity of $1 at 15% for 5 periods is 3.35. The future amount of an ordinary annuity of $1 at 15% for 5 periods is 6.74. The present value of $1 at 15% for 5 periods is 0.5. How much should Electro record as the cost of the machine?

a. $12,500
b. $16,750
c. $25,000
d. $33,700

M9-6 When a company purchases land with a building on it and immediately tears down the building so that the land can be used for the construction of a plant, the costs incurred to tear down the building should be

a. Expensed as incurred
b. Added to the cost of the plant
c. Added to the cost of the land
d. Amortized over the estimated time period between the tearing down of the building and the completion of the plant

M9-7 When a company replaces an old asphalt roof on its plant with a new fiberglass insulated roof, which of the following types of expenditure occurs?

a. Ordinary repair and maintenance
b. Addition
c. Rearrangement
d. Betterment

M9-8 On January 2, 2004 Yuki Yogurt Company decided to replace its obsolete refrigeration system with a more efficient one. The old system had a book value of $9,000 and a fair value of $1,000. Yuki's new refrigeration system has a fair value of $190,000, for which Yuki paid $189,000 after permitting the contractor to keep the old refrigeration equipment. How much should Yuki capitalize as the cost of the new refrigeration system?

a. $189,000   c. $197,000
b. $190,000   d. $198,000

M9-9 During 2004 Belardo Corporation constructed and manufactured certain assets, and incurred the following interest costs in connection with those activities:

	Interest Costs Incurred
Warehouse constructed for Belardo's own use	$20,000
Special-order machine for sale to unrelated customer, produced according to customer's specifications	9,000
Inventories routinely manufactured, produced on a repetitive basis	7,000

All of these assets required an extended period of time for completion. Assuming that the effect of interest capitalization is material, what is the total amount of interest costs to be capitalized?

a. $0   c. $29,000
b. $20,000   d. $36,000

M9-10 Lyle, Inc., purchased certain plant assets under a deferred payment contract on December 31, 2004. The agreement was to pay $20,000 at the time of purchase and $20,000 at the end of each of the next 5 years. The plant assets should be valued at

a. The present value of a $20,000 ordinary annuity for five years
b. $120,000
c. $120,000 less imputed interest
d. $120,000 plus imputed interest

(*AICPA adapted*)

EXERCISES

E9-1 *Determination of Cost* Which of the following twenty-two items does a company include in the cost of property, plant, and equipment?

1. Contract price
2. List price
3. Freight costs
4. Discounts taken
5. Discounts not taken
6. Installation costs
7. Testing costs
8. Cost of overhaul before initial use
9. Costs of grading land prior to construction
10. Tax assessment for street improvements
11. Delinquent property taxes on acquired property
12. Cost of tearing down an old building (already owned) in preparation for new construction
13. Cost of insurance during construction
14. Excess of costs over revenues during the development stage of the company
15. Interest costs during construction
16. Landscaping costs
17. Severance pay for employees dismissed because of the acquisition of a new machine
18. Cost of tearing down a building on newly acquired land
19. Replacement of an electric motor in a machine
20. Expansion of the heating/cooling system to accommodate an expansion of a building and certain expected future needs
21. Service contract for 2 years on the acquired asset
22. Cost of training new employees

E9-2   *Inclusion in Property, Plant, and Equipment*   Which of the following does a company include in property, plant, and equipment on the balance sheet?

1. Idle equipment awaiting sale
2. Land held for future use as a plant site
3. Land held for investment
4. Deposits on machinery not yet received
5. Progress payments on building being constructed by a contractor
6. Fully depreciated assets still being used
7. Leasehold improvements
8. Assets leased to others

E9-3   *Acquisition Costs*   The Voiture Company manufactures compact, energy efficient cars. On April 1, it purchased a machine for its assembly line at a contract price of $200,000 with terms of 2/10, n/30. The company paid the contract price on April 8 and also incurred installation and transportation costs of $5,000, sales tax of $10,000, and testing costs of $2,000. During testing the machine was accidentally damaged, so the company had to pay $1,000 to repair it.

Required Prepare the journal entry to record the acquisition of the machine.

E9-4   *Determination of Acquisition Cost*   In January 2004 Cordova Company entered into a contract to acquire a new machine for its factory. The machine, which has a cash price of $215,000, was paid for as follows:

Down payment	$ 55,000
Note payable in four equal annual payments starting in January 2005	120,000
600 shares of Cordova preferred stock with a mutually agreed value of $100 per share (par value $100)	60,000
Fair rate of interest on the non-interest-bearing note	10%

Required

1. Prepare the journal entry to record the acquisition of the machine.
2. How would your answer change, if at all, if the $215,000 cash price were not available?

E9-5   *Determination of Acquisition Cost*   On August 1, 2004 Darmow Corporation purchased a new machine on a deferred payment basis. It made a down payment of $1,000 and will make four monthly installments of $2,500 each beginning on September 1, 2004. The cash equivalent price of the machine was $9,500. Darmow incurred and paid installation cost amounting to $300.

Required Prepare the journal entry to record the acquisition of the machine. (*AICPA adapted*)

E9-6   *Acquisition of Land and Building*   On February 1, 2004 Edwards Corporation purchased a parcel of land as
@   a factory site for $50,000. It demolished an old building on the property, and began construction on a new building that was completed on October 2, 2004. Costs incurred during this period are:

Demolition of old building	$ 4,000
Architect's fees	20,000
Legal fees for title investigation and purchase contract	2,000
Construction costs	500,000

The company sold salvaged materials resulting from the demolition for $3,000.

Required At what amount should Edwards record the cost of the land and the new building, respectively? (*AICPA adapted*)

E9-7   *Lump-Sum Purchase*   The Garrett Corporation paid $200,000 to acquire land, buildings, and equipment. At the time of acquisition, the company paid $20,000 for an appraisal, which revealed the following values: land, $100,000; buildings, $125,000; and equipment, $25,000.

Required What cost does the company assign to the land, buildings, and equipment, respectively?

E9-8   *Exchange of Assets*   Two independent companies, Denver and Bristol, each own a warehouse, and they agree to an exchange in which no cash changes hands. Neither company is a dealer. The following information for the two warehouses is available:

	Denver	Bristol
Cost	$90,000	$45,000
Accumulated depreciation	55,000	25,000
Fair value	30,000	30,000

Required Prepare journal entries for the Denver Company and the Bristol Company to record the exchange.

E9-9   **Exchange of Assets**   Use the same information as in E9-8, except that the warehouse owned by Denver Company has a fair value of $28,000, and therefore Denver agrees to pay Bristol $2,000 to complete the exchange.

Required Prepare journal entries for the Denver Company and the Bristol Company to record the exchange.

E9-10   **Exchange of Assets**   Use the same information as in E9-8, except that the warehouse owned by Denver Company has a fair value of $33,000, and therefore the Bristol Company agrees to pay the Denver Company $3,000 to complete the exchange.

Required Prepare journal entries for the Denver Company and the Bristol Company to record the exchange.

E9-11   **Exchange of Assets**   The Goodman Company acquired a truck from the Harmes Company in exchange for a machine. The machine cost $30,000, has a book value of $6,000, and has a market value of $9,000. The truck has a cost of $12,000 and a book value of $8,000 on Harmes' books. Neither company is a dealer.

Required Prepare journal entries for the Goodman Company and the Harmes Company to record the exchange.

E9-12   **Exchange of Assets**   Use the same information as in E9-11, except that the machine has a market value of $8,500, and therefore the Goodman Company agrees to pay $500 to complete the exchange.

Required Prepare journal entries for the Goodman Company and the Harmes Company to record the exchange.

E9-13   **Exchange of Assets**   Minor Baseball Company had a player contract with Doe that was recorded in its accounting records at $145,000. Better Baseball Company had a player contract with Smith that was recorded in its accounting records at $140,000. Minor traded Doe to Better for Smith by exchanging each player's contract. The fair value of each contract was $150,000.

Required What amount should each company show in its accounting records after the exchange of player contracts? (*AICPA adapted*)

E9-14   **Self-Construction**   The Harshman Company constructed a building for its own use. The company incurred costs of $20,000 for materials and supplies, $48,000 for direct labor, and $4,000 for a supervisor's overtime that was caused by the construction. The company uses a factory overhead rate of 50% of direct labor cost. Before construction, the company had received a bid of $100,000 from an outside contractor.

Required

1. At what value should the company capitalize the building? Justify your answer.
2. Would your answer change if the bid from the outside contractor had been $80,000? $60,000?

E9-15   **Asset Acquired by Donation**   The City of Littleton donated a building and land to the Hetting Co. without charge. The agreement provided that the company employ 350 people for 10 years. The land was appraised at $65,000 and the building at $44,000.

Required

1. Prepare the journal entry to record the acquisition of the land and building.
2. How should the 10-year agreement be reported in the financial statements?
3. If the title were not to pass until after 10 years, would your answer change?

E9-16   **Interest During Construction**   The Snowbird Company is constructing a building that qualifies for interest capitalization. It is built between January 1 and December 31, 2004. Expenditures, which occur evenly throughout the year, totaled $800,000. The company borrowed $500,000 at 12% to help finance the project. In addition, the Snowbird Company had outstanding borrowings of $2 million at 8%.

Required

1. Compute the amount of interest capitalized on the building.
2. What effect does the interest capitalization have on the company's financial statements after it completes the building?

E9-17 *Calculating Capitalized Interest* The Kit Company borrows $5 million at 12% on January 1, 2004 specifically for the purpose of financing a construction project. The company invests the total amount at 11% until it makes payments for the construction project. During the first year of construction, the company incurs construction costs of $4 million evenly over the year.

Required Compute the amount of interest that the company would capitalize and the amount of interest revenue it would recognize.

E9-18 *Capital and Operating Expenditures* Which of the following ten items does a company record as a capital expenditure and which as an operating expenditure?

1. Cost of installing machinery
2. Cost of moving machinery
3. Repairs as a result of an accident
4. Cost of major overhaul
5. Installation of safety device as a result of an OSHA inspection
6. Property taxes on land and buildings
7. Property taxes on land and buildings held for investment
8. Cost of rearranging offices
9. Cost of repainting offices
10. Ordinary repairs

E9-19 *Oil and Gas Accounting (Appendix)* The Lawrence Company spends $4 million in 2004 drilling oil wells. Sixty percent of the drilling is successful and results in commercial quantities of oil being found.

Required

1. How much drilling expense does the company recognize under
   a. The successful-efforts method?
   b. The full-cost method?
2. At what value does the company report the asset, Oil and Gas Properties, in its balance sheet under
   a. The successful-efforts method?
   b. The full-cost method?

PROBLEMS

P9-1 *Acquisition Costs* The Mawn Company bought land and built a warehouse during 2004. It debited the following related costs to an account titled Land and Buildings:

Land purchase	$22,000
Demolition of old building	3,000
Legal fees for land acquisition	1,500
Interest on loan for construction (based on average costs incurred)	2,900
Building construction	53,000
Assessment by city for sewer connection	1,200
Landscaping	3,500
Equipment purchased for excavation	18,800
Fixed overhead charged to building	15,000
Insurance on building during construction	1,000
Profit on construction	12,000
Compensation for injury to construction worker	3,000
Modifications to building ordered by building inspectors	7,500
Property taxes on land paid in 2004	2,500

The following credits were made to the account:	
Salvage from demolished old building	$ 700
Sale of excavation equipment	14,000

In addition, you discover that compensation for the worker's injury was necessary because it was not covered by the particular insurance policy purchased by the company. Accident insurance that would have covered the injury would have cost an additional $350. The modifications ordered by the building inspectors resulted from poor planning by the company.

Required Prepare adjusting entries on December 31, 2004 to properly reclassify the preceding items.

P9-2   *Costs Subsequent to Acquisition*   As the first auditor of the Newberg Company you discover that the following entries have been made in the property, plant, and equipment account:

Property, Plant, and Equipment

2003			2003	
Plant purchased	60,000		Depreciation	6,310
Legal fees	700			
Insurance	2,400			
2004			2004	
Repairs	2,000		Depreciation	6,879
Addition to building	10,000			
2005			2005	
Repairs	3,000		Machine sold	500
Insurance	2,800		Depreciation	7,421
Machine purchased	7,000			

You discover the following additional information:

1. The purchase of the plant included a building and machinery. When the plant was purchased, an appraisal showed that the building was valued at $39,000 and the machinery at $26,000.
2. Depreciation has been recorded each year at 10% of the balance in the account. The 10% was chosen because the property is being depreciated over 10 years for tax purposes. Subsequent investigation indicates that the expected lives at the time of acquisition were: building, 20 years; machinery, 8 years.
3. Each insurance payment was made on January 1 and was for a 2-year policy.
4. The machine that was sold in 2005 had an original cost of $800.
5. All purchases and sales of property, plant, and equipment items occurred at the beginning of the year indicated.

Required Prepare adjusting entries at December 31, 2005 to correct the books assuming they have not been closed for the year.

P9-3   *Classification of Costs Associated with Assets*   The following account balances were included in the balance sheet of the Bromley Company on December 31, 2003:

Land	$100,000
Land improvements	20,000
Buildings	300,000
Machinery and equipment	500,000

During 2004 the following transactions occurred:

1. Land was acquired for $70,000 for a future building site. Commissions of $4,000 were paid to a real estate agent.
2. A factory and land were acquired from the Kent Development Company by issuing 20,000 shares of $3 par common stock. At that time the stock was selling for $10 per share on the New York Stock Exchange. The independently appraised values of the land and the factory were $60,000 and $180,000, respectively.
3. Machinery and equipment was acquired at a cost of $120,000. In addition, sales tax, freight costs, and installation costs were $7,000, $10,000, and $16,000, respectively. During installation, the machinery was damaged and $2,000 was spent in repairs.
4. A new parking lot was installed at a cost of $30,000.
5. A machine that had cost $20,000 on January 1, 2000 and had a book value on December 31, 2004 of $4,000 was sold on that date for $6,000.
6. Half the land purchased in item 1 was prepared as a building site. Costs of $26,000 were incurred to clear the land, and the timber recovered was sold for $3,000. A new building was built for $60,000 plus architect's fees and imputed interest on equity funds used during construction of $18,000 and $15,000, respectively. No debt is outstanding.
7. Costs of $20,000 were incurred to improve some leased office space. The lease will terminate in 2006 and is not expected to be renewed.

8. A group of new machines was purchased under a royalty agreement that provides for payment of annual royalties based on units produced. The invoice price of the machines was $30,000, freight costs were $2,000, and royalty payments for 2004 were $12,000.

Required Prepare journal entries to record all the preceding events. Unless otherwise indicated, assume the company makes all payments in cash.

P9-4   *Self-Construction*   The Olson Machine Company manufactures small and large milling machines. Selling prices of these machines range from $35,000 to $200,000. During the 5-month period from August 1, 2004 through December 31, 2004, the company manufactured a milling machine for its own use. This machine was built as part of the regular production activities. The project required a large amount of time from planning and supervisory personnel, as well as that of some of the company's officers, because it was a more sophisticated type of machine than the regular production models.

Throughout the 5-month period, the company charged all costs directly associated with the construction of the machine to a special account entitled "Asset Construction Account." An analysis of the charges to this account as of December 31, 2004 follows:

ASSET CONSTRUCTION ACCOUNT

Item Description	Cost	
Raw Materials		
Iron castings:		
Main housing, 3 sections	$37,480	
Movable heads, 2 heads @ $3,900	7,800	
Machine bed	4,760	
Table, 2 sections @ $5,500	11,000	$ 61,040
Other raw materials:		
Electrical components and wiring	$28,000	
Worm screws and housing	8,600	
Cutter housings	2,700	
Conveyor system	8,400	
Other parts	2,500	50,200
Direct Labor Costs		
Layout 90 hr. @ $5.00	$ 450	
Electricians 380 hr. @ 9.00	3,420	
Machining 1,100 hr. @ 8.00	8,800	
Heat treatment 100 hr. @ 7.50	750	
Assembly 450 hr. @ 7.00	3,150	
Testing 180 hr. @ 8.00	1,440	18,010
Other Direct Charges		
Repairs and maintenance during testing period	$ 1,340	
Interest expense from 8/1/04 to 12/31/04 on funds borrowed for construction purposes	4,260	
Additional labor to assist during machine testing period, 180 hr. @ $5.00	900	6,500
Balance, December 31, 2004		$135,750

The company allocates factory overhead to normal production as a percent of direct labor dollars as follows:

Departments	Factory Overhead Rates (applied as a percent of direct labor dollars)		
	Variable	Fixed	Total
Layout and electricians	50%	20%	70%
Machining,* heat treatment, and assembly	50%	50%	100%

*All testing is conducted by employees in the machining department.

The company uses a flat rate of 40% of direct labor dollars to allocate general and administrative overhead.

During the machine testing period, a cutter head malfunctioned and did extensive damage to the machine table and one cutter housing. This damage was not anticipated and was the result of an error in the assembly operation. Although no additional raw materials were needed to make the machine operational after the accident, the following labor for rework was required:

	Direct Labor Hours
Electric	80
Machining	200
Assembly	100
Testing (conducted by machining department)	20

The company has included all these labor charges in the Asset Construction account. In addition, it included in the account the repairs and maintenance charges of $1,340 that it incurred as a result of the malfunction.

Required

1. Compute, in accordance with generally accepted accounting principles, the amount that Olson Machine Company should capitalize for the milling machine as of December 31, 2004 when it declares the machine operational.
2. Identify the costs you included in Requirement 1 for which there are acceptable alternative procedures. Describe the alternative procedure(s) in each case. (*CMA adapted*)

P9-5 *Acquisition Cost* The following transactions of the Weber Company occurred during 2004:

1. The company acquired a tract of land in exchange for 1,000 shares of $10 par value common stock. The stock was traded on the New York Stock Exchange at $24 on the date of exchange. The land had a book value on the selling company's records of $5,000, and it was believed to be worth "anything up to $30,000."
2. An engine on a truck was replaced. The truck originally cost $10,000 three years ago and was being depreciated at $2,000 per year. The engine cost $1,000 to replace.
3. The company acquired a tract of land that was believed to have mineral deposits by issuing 500 shares of preferred stock of $50 par value. The preferred stock was rarely traded. The last transaction was 2 months earlier, when 50 shares were sold at $75 per share. The owner of the land was willing to accept cash of $55,000, and an appraisal had shown a value of $60,000.
4. The company purchased a machine with a list price of $8,500 by issuing a 2-year $10,000 non-interest-bearing note when the market rate of interest was 10%.

Required Prepare journal entries to record the preceding events.

P9-6 *Comprehensive* At December 31, 2003 certain accounts included in the property, plant, and equipment section of the Townsand Company's balance sheet had the following balances:

Land	$100,000	Leasehold improvements	$500,000
Buildings	800,000	Machinery and equipment	700,000

During 2004 the following transactions occurred:

1. Land site number 621 was acquired for $1,000,000. Additionally, to acquire the land Townsand paid a $60,000 commission to a real estate agent. Costs of $15,000 were incurred to clear the land. During the course of clearing the land, timber and gravel were recovered and sold for $5,000.
2. A second tract of land (site number 622) with a building was acquired for $300,000. The closing statement indicated that the land value was $200,000 and the building value was $100,000. Shortly after acquisition, the building was demolished at a cost of $30,000. A new building was constructed for $150,000 plus the following costs:

Excavation fees	$11,000
Architectural design fees	8,000
Building permit fee	1,000

The building was completed and occupied on September 29, 2004.

3. A third tract of land (site number 623) was acquired for $600,000 and was put on the market for resale.
4. Extensive work was done to a building occupied by Townsand under a lease agreement that expires on December 31, 2013. The total cost of the work was $125,000, which consisted of the following:

Painting of ceilings	$ 10,000 (estimated useful life is one year)
Electrical work	35,000 (estimated useful life is ten years)
Construction of extension to current working area	80,000 (estimated useful life is thirty years)
	$125,000

The lessor paid one-half of the costs incurred in connection with the extension to the current working area.

5. During December 2004 costs of $65,000 were incurred to improve leased office space. The related lease will terminate on December 31, 2006, and is not expected to be renewed.
6. A group of new machines was purchased under a royalty agreement which provides for payment of royalties based on units of production for the machines. The invoice price of the machines was $75,000, freight costs were $2,000, unloading charges were $1,500, and royalty payments for 2004 were $13,000.

Required
1. Prepare a detailed analysis of the changes in each of the following balance sheet accounts for 2004:
   - Land
   - Buildings
   - Leasehold improvements
   - Machinery and equipment

   Disregard the related accumulated depreciation accounts.
2. List the items in the fact situation which were not used to determine the answer to Requirement 1, and indicate where, or if, these items should be included in Townsand's financial statements. (*AICPA adapted*)

P9-7 **Assets Acquired by Exchange**   The Bremer Company made the following exchanges of assets during 2004:

1. Acquired a machine worth $10,000 by paying $2,000 cash and giving a similar machine that had originally cost $40,000 and has a book value of $12,000.
2. Acquired a building worth $55,000 by paying $5,000 cash and giving a piece of land that had originally cost $35,000.
3. Acquired a machine worth $20,000 by paying $5,000 cash and giving a similar machine that had originally cost $13,000 and has a book value of $11,000.
4. Acquired a car by giving an old car that had originally cost $7,000, has a book value of $5,000, and has a "blue book" value of $6,800. In addition the company received $800 cash.

Required Prepare journal entries for the Bremer Company and for the other company involved in each exchange. Assume in each case that both Bremer Company and the other company are nondealers.

P9-8 **Assets Acquired by Exchange**   The Bussell Company exchanged the following assets during 2004:

1. **Acquired a machine worth $34,000 by paying $4,000 cash and giving a similar machine that originally cost $40,000, has a book value of $25,000, and is worth $30,000.**
2. **Same facts as in item 1, except that the asset being surrendered has a book value of $33,000.**
3. **Acquired a machine worth $27,000 by giving a similar machine that originally cost $45,000, has a book value of $20,000, and is worth $32,000. In addition $5,000 cash was received.**
4. **Same facts as in item 3, except that the asset being surrendered has a book value of $36,000.**
5. **Acquired a machine worth $90,000 by giving up a similar machine of equal value. The machine surrendered had originally cost $150,000 and has a book value of $80,000.**
6. **Same facts as in item 5, except that the asset being surrendered has a book value of $94,000.**
7. **Acquired a building worth $200,000 in exchange for land that had originally cost $130,000 and is now worth $200,000.**
8. **Same facts as in item 7, except that $30,000 was paid, because the land is worth $170,000.**
9. **Same facts as in item 7, except that $20,000 was received and the land is worth $220,000.**

Required Prepare journal entries to record each acquisition of the Bussell Company. Assume that neither the Bussel Company nor the other company is a dealer.

See WebTutor for annotated problem solution.

P9-9 **Interest During Construction**   The Alta Company is constructing a production complex which qualifies for interest capitalization. The following information is available:

Capitalization period: January 1, 2004 to June 30, 2006
Expenditures on project (incurred evenly during each period and excluding capitalized interest from previous years):
   - 2004 $2,000,000
   - 2005 $3,760,000
   - 2006 $4,324,000
Amounts borrowed and outstanding:
   - $3 million borrowed at 12%, specifically for the project
   - $6 million borrowed on July 1, 2000, at 14%
   - $14 million borrowed on January 1, 1996, at 8%

Required
1. Compute the amount of interest costs capitalized each year.
2. If it is assumed that the production complex has an estimated life of 20 years and a residual value of zero, compute the straight-line depreciation in 2007.

3. Explain the effects of the interest capitalization on the financial statements for all three years. Ignore income taxes.

P9-10   *Comprehensive*   The Foothills Power Company begins a 2-year construction project on a power plant on January 1, 2004. The following information is available:

1. The company borrows $10 million on January 1, 2004 at 12%, specifically for use on the project.
2. The company's other borrowings are:
     $20 million at 10%
     $60 million at 8%
3. The expenditures for the project, incurred evenly each year (excluding capitalized interest from previous years), are as follows:
     $6,000,000 in 2004
     $11,460,000 in 2005
     $1,800,000 in 2006
4. The project is completed on March 31, 2006. It took longer than originally planned because the company suspended construction for the last 3 months of 2004 because of a concern about the salability of the electricity produced by the plant.
5. Because of reduced demand for electricity, the plant does not begin operations until October 1, 2006.
6. The company invests at 11% the unused amounts of the $10 million borrowed in item 1.
7. Assume all transactions are in cash unless otherwise indicated.

Required

1. Prepare all the necessary journal entries for each of the 3 years. Record all construction costs in a Construction in Progress inventory account.
2. How would your answer to Requirement 1 change if the 3-month suspension in the construction activity was due to an environmental dispute with the federal government?

P9-11   *Events Subsequent to Acquisition*   The following selected events occurred during 2004:

Jan. 10   A motor breaks on a machine and is replaced for $800. This replacement was expected when the machine was purchased.

Jan. 24   A machine that was purchased for $10,000 and has a book value of $1,000 is sold for $600.

Feb. 3   A fully depreciated building that originally cost $25,000 is demolished so that a new building may be constructed. The demolition cost $2,200 and resulted in $700 of salvageable materials.

Feb. 14   A machine breaks down unexpectedly and requires repairs of $700.

Mar. 10   An accident damages some equipment. Repairs cost $2,000.

Mar. 19   A motor breaks on a machine and is replaced for $900. The new motor is of an improved design that increases the capacity of the machine.

Mar. 27   Office layout is rearranged at a cost of $700. At the same time, the walls are repainted for $500.

Required Prepare journal entries for the preceding transactions.

P9-12   *Comprehensive*   You are engaged in the examination of financial statements of the Dewoskin Company and are auditing the Machinery and Equipment account and the related depreciation accounts for the year ended December 31, 2004. Your permanent file contains the following schedules:

	Balance 12/31/02	2003 Retirements	2003 Addition	Balance 12/31/03
	Machinery and Equipment			
1993	$ 8,000	$2,100	—	$ 5,900
1994	400	—	—	400
1995	—	—	—	—
1996	—	—	—	—
1997	3,900	—	—	3,900
1998	—	—	—	—
1999	5,300	—	—	5,300
2000	—	—	—	—
2001	4,200	—	—	4,200
2002	—	—	—	—
2003	—	—	$5,700	5,700
	$21,800	$2,100	$5,700	$25,400

	Balance 12/31/02	2003 Retirements	2003 Addition	Balance 12/31/03
	Accumulated Depreciation			
1993	$ 7,840	$2,100	$ 160	$ 5,900
1994	340	—	40	380
1995	—	—	—	—
1996	—	—	—	—
1997	2,145	—	390	2,535
1998	—	—	—	—
1999	1,855	—	530	2,385
2000	—	—	—	—
2001	630	—	420	1,050
2002	—	—	—	—
2003	—	—	285	285
	$12,810	$2,100	$1,825	$12,535

Here is a transcript of the Machinery and Equipment account for 2004:

2004	Machinery and Equipment	Ref.	Debit	Credit
Jan. 1	Balance forward		$25,400	
Mar. 1	Burnham grinder	VR	1,200	
May 1	Air compressor	VR	4,500	
June 1	Power lawnmower	VR	600	
June 1	Lift-truck battery	VR	320	
Aug. 1	Rockwood saw	CR		$ 150
Nov. 1	Electric spot welder	VR	4,500	
Nov. 1	Baking oven	VR	2,800	
Dec. 1	Baking oven	VR	236	
			$39,556	150
Dec. 31	Balance			$39,406
			$39,556	$39,556

Your examination reveals the following eight items:

1. The company uses a 10-year life for all machinery and equipment for depreciation purposes. Depreciation is computed by the straight-line method. Six months' depreciation is recorded in the year of acquisition or retirement. For 2004 the company recorded depreciation of $2,800 on machinery and equipment.
2. The Burnham grinder was purchased for cash from a firm in financial distress. The chief engineer and a used machinery dealer agreed that the machine, which was practically new, was worth $2,100 in the open market.
3. For production reasons, the new air compressor was installed in a small building that was erected in 2004 to house the machine. The building will also be used for general storage. The cost of the building, which has a 25-year life, was $2,000 and is included in the $4,500 voucher for the air compressor.
4. The power lawnmower was delivered to the home of the company president for personal use.
5. On June 1, the battery in a battery-powered lift truck was accidentally damaged beyond repair. The damaged battery was included at a price of $600 in the $4,200 cost of the lift truck purchased on July 1, 2001. The company decided to rent a replacement battery instead of buying a new battery. The $320 expenditure is the annual rental for the battery paid in advance, net of a $40 allowance for the scrap value of the damaged battery that was returned to the battery company.
6. The Rockwood saw sold on August 1 had been purchased on August 1, 1991, for $1,500. The saw was in use until it was sold.
7. On September 1, the company determined that a production casting machine was no longer needed and advertised it for sale for $1,800 after having determined from a used machinery dealer that this was its market value. The casting machine had been purchased for $5,000 on September 1, 1999.
8. On November 1 a baking oven was purchased for $10,000. A $2,800 down payment was made, and the balance will be paid in monthly installments over a 3-year period. The December 1 payment includes interest charges of $36. Legal title to the oven will not pass to the company until the payments are completed.

Required

1. Prepare the auditor's adjusting journal entries required on December 31, 2004, for machinery and equipment and the related depreciation.

2. Prepare schedules for detailing the effect of additions and retirements on the assets and related accumulated depreciation balances. (*AICPA adapted*)

P9-13 *Adjusting Entries* In your examination of the financial statements of Ericson Corporation at December 31, 2004 you observe the contents of certain accounts and other pertinent information as follows:

		Building			
Date	Explanation	Post REF	Debit	Credit	Balance
12/31/03	Balance	X	$100,000	—	$100,000
7/1/04	New boiler	CD	16,480	$1,480	115,000
9/1/05	Insurance recovery	CR	—	2,000	113,000

	Accumulated Depreciation—Building				
Date	Explanation	LF	Debit	Credit	Balance
12/31/03	Balance: 15 years @ 4% of $100,000 (no salvage value)	X		$60,000	$60,000
12/31/04	Annual depreciation	GJ		4,440	64,440

You learn that on June 15 the company's old high-pressure boiler exploded and was partially damaged. Damage to the building was insignificant, but the boiler was replaced by a more efficient oil-burning boiler. The company received $2,000 as an insurance adjustment under terms of its policy for damage to the boiler. The disbursement voucher charged to the Building account on July 1, 2004 is reproduced here:

To: Leetsdale Heating Company	
Fair value—new oil-burning boiler (including fuel oil tank and 1,000 gallons fuel oil)	$16,000
Sales tax—3% of $16,000	480
Total	$16,480
Less: Allowance (fair value) for old coal-burning boiler in building—to be removed at the expense of the Leetsdale Heating Company	1,480
Total price	$15,000

In vouching the expenditure, you determine that the terms included a 2% cash discount that was properly computed and taken. Neither the sales tax nor the trade-in allowance on the old boiler is subject to discount. Your audit discloses that a voucher for $1,000 was paid to Monaco Company on July 3, 2004 and charged to the Repair Expense account. The voucher is adequately supported and is marked "installation costs for new oil-burning boiler."

The company's fuel oil supplier advises that fuel oil had a market price of 80¢ per gallon on July 1 and 85¢ per gallon on December 31. The fuel oil inventory at December 31 was 100 gallons.

A review of subsidiary property records discloses that the replaced coal-burning boiler was installed when the building was constructed and was recorded at a cost of $10,000. According to its manufacturers, the new boiler should be serviceable for the estimated useful life of the building.

In computing depreciation for retirements, Ericson Corporation consistently treats a fraction of a month as a full month.

Required Prepare the adjusting journal entries that you would suggest for entry on the books of the Ericson Corporation. The books have not been closed. Support your entries with computations in good form. Assume that the building has no salvage value. (*AICPA adapted*)

P9-14 *Oil and Gas Accounting Methods (Appendix)* The Iwata Oil Company incurred costs of $6 million during 2004 drilling for oil. Half the costs resulted in oil being found and half resulted in dry wells. The company expects the oil wells to produce 10% of their capacity each year from 2005 to 2014.

Required

1. What amounts appear in the financial statements for 2005 under
   a. The successful-efforts method?
   b. The full-cost method?
2. Why do small oil companies generally prefer the full-cost method?

INTERNET ASSIGNMENTS

Go to the Nikolai and Bazley **Intermediate Accounting** web site (http://Nikolai.swcollege.com). Click on Student Resources and internet homework assignments. Then click on the appropriate hot link (icon) for each company's web site, find the relevant accounting information, and answer the following questions.

I9-1   Go to the IBM web site.

Required How much interest did the company capitalize in each of the last three years? What effects did the interest capitalization have on the company's financial statements? Are the effects material?

I9-2   Go to the Marathon Oil web site and then the Forest Oil web site.

Required How does each company account for its oil and gas properties? How would you argue that each accounting principle is appropriate?

I9-3   Go to the CNF Transportation web site.

Required How does the company account for the maintenance on its aircraft? What method did it use before 2001? Explain why you agree or do not agree whether the change was to a better accounting principle.

CHAPTER 10

Depreciation and Depletion

objectives

1 Identify the factors involved in depreciation.

2 Explain the alternative methods of cost allocation, including activity- and time-based methods.

3 Record depreciation.

4 Explain the conceptual issues regarding depreciation methods.

5 Understand the disclosure of depreciation.

6 Understand additional depreciation methods, including group and composite methods.

7 Compute depreciation for partial periods.

8 Explain the impairment of noncurrent assets.

9 Understand depreciation for income tax purposes.

10 Explain changes and corrections of depreciation.

11 Understand and record depletion.

In the preceding chapter, we described property, plant, and equipment as a group of assets held by a company for use for a period of more than one year; that is, the company acquired the assets for their long-term revenue-generating ability. Since the company uses these assets to produce revenue, the matching principle requires that the company match the expenses connected with their use against the revenue. What is the expense? Over the life of the asset, the expense is the difference between the purchase price of the asset and its eventual residual value. **Depreciation is the process of allocating in a systematic and rational manner this total expense to each period benefited by the asset.** Land is not depreciated because it generally does not have a limited life and its expected residual value (that is, future selling price) usually is higher than its cost. Thus, there is no expense to be recognized over the life of the asset and, therefore, no periodic cost allocation.

Terms used to describe this allocation process depend on the type of asset:

1. **Depreciation** describes the allocation of the cost of *tangible assets*, such as property, plant, and equipment.
2. **Depletion** describes the allocation of the cost of *natural resource assets*, such as oil, gas, minerals, and timber.
3. **Amortization** describes the allocation of the cost of *intangible assets*, such as patents and copyrights. It may be used as a general term to describe the periodic allocation of costs; in that case, it is synonymous with depreciation and depletion.

The three terms all describe the same principle of a company allocating costs to match its expenses with revenue, but differ in their application to different types of assets. It is important to note that a company does *not* record depreciation, depletion, and amortization in an attempt to reflect a market value of the asset. We discuss depreciation and depletion in this chapter, and the amortization of intangible assets in the next chapter.

FACTORS INVOLVED IN DEPRECIATION

A company considers four factors in the computation of depreciation for a period: (1) asset cost, (2) service life, (3) residual value, and (4) method of cost allocation.[1]

1 Identify the factors involved in depreciation.

---

1. The service life, residual value, and method of cost allocation are different for income tax purposes under the Modified Accelerated Cost Recovery System (MACRS), as we discuss later in the chapter.

Asset Cost

The recording and reporting of asset cost is discussed in Chapter 9.

The cost of an asset includes all the acquisition costs necessary to obtain the benefits to be derived from the asset. These costs include the contract price plus freight, assembly, installation, and testing costs.

Service Life

The service life of an asset is the measure of the number of units of service expected from the asset before its disposal. Service life may be measured in *units of time*, such as years and months, or *units of activity or output*, such as hours of operation of a machine, tons produced for a steel mill, or miles driven for a truck.

The factors that limit the service life of an asset can be divided into two general categories: (1) physical causes and (2) functional causes. **Physical causes include wear and tear due to operational *use*, deterioration and decay that is independent of use but is a function of *time* (such as rust), and damage and destruction. Functional causes limit the service life of the asset through obsolescence and inadequacy, even though the physical life is not exhausted.** *Obsolescence* is a common occurrence in a technologically advanced economy when an asset becomes obsolete due to the introduction of new technology. *Inadequacy* refers to the situation in which an asset is no longer suitable for the size of the company's operations. For example, a warehouse may be physically sound and useful, but too small for the company's operations.

When a company estimates the service life, it should take all these factors into consideration because in many situations the service life is affected by a combination of factors. For example, the service life of a truck is likely to be affected by the passage of time (deterioration, decay, and possibly obsolescence) as well as by the amount of use. In addition, the company may be able to increase or decrease the service life by the amount it spends on repairs and maintenance and on improvements and replacements. The accountant will have to rely on others, such as engineers, for advice about such estimates, but will still have to make his or her judgement.

Residual Value

The residual (salvage) value is the net amount that is expected to be obtained from the disposition of an asset at the end of its service life. It is the difference between the expected value of the asset at the end of its service life and the costs of disposal, such as dismantling, removing, and selling the asset. The service life and the residual value are determined by company policy. If a company plans to hold an asset until it is physically exhausted or functionally obsolete and not useful to anyone else, the expected residual value is the expected scrap value, which is probably very low. Alternatively, if the company plans to dispose of the asset when it still has considerable economic usefulness to others (the service life to the company is less than the physical life), the expected residual value is the estimated net market value of the asset (the selling price less the disposal costs) at the time of the disposal, which may be relatively high. For example, many airlines sell their planes long before the end of their physical lives in order to replace them with technologically more advanced planes and to avoid passenger resistance to flying in old planes. In certain situations, such as a nuclear power plant, the acquisition of an asset automatically creates an obligation related to the retirement of the asset. As we discussed in Chapter 9, a company computes the present value of the obligation and adds the same amount to the cost of the asset.

In practice, because the residual value is difficult to estimate, it often is ignored in the computation of the depreciation amount, or else a standard rate, such as 10% of original cost, is used. This practice is acceptable if it does not have a material effect on the measurement of income and the book value of the asset.

METHODS OF COST ALLOCATION

Accounting principles require that a company use a method of cost allocation that is "systematic and rational."[2] *Systematic* **means that the calculation should follow a formula and not be determined in an arbitrary manner.** *Rational* **means that the amount of the depreciation should relate to the benefits that the asset produces in each period.** Although these criteria may appear to be very general and to allow numerous methods, only the following methods are used frequently in practice:

1. Activity (or use) methods
2. Time-based methods
   a. Straight line
   b. Accelerated (declining charge)
      (1) Sum of the years' digits
      (2) Declining balance

We discuss each of these methods in the following sections, using the data for the Troup Company shown in Exhibit 10-1. **The depreciation base (depreciable cost) of the asset is the cost less the estimated residual value,** or $100,000. The different depreciation methods all allocate the total of $100,000 over the expected service life of the asset, but differ in the pattern in which the cost is allocated to each year or each unit produced. We discuss additional special depreciation methods later in the chapter.

2 Explain the alternative methods of cost allocation, including activity- and time-based methods.

EXHIBIT 10-1   Asset Information

Asset cost	$120,000
Date of purchase	January 1, 2003
Estimated residual value	$20,000
Estimated service life	5 years; 10,000 hours; 20,000 units

Activity Methods

A company should use an activity method when the service life of the asset is affected primarily by the amount the asset is used and not by the passage of time. The activity usually is measured in terms of the number of hours worked or the output produced (such as miles driven or tons produced). In the case of the Troup Company, one measure of the life of the asset is estimated to be 10,000 hours of activity. We show the calculation of the depreciation per hour in Exhibit 10-2.

EXHIBIT 10-2   Depreciation Based on Activity

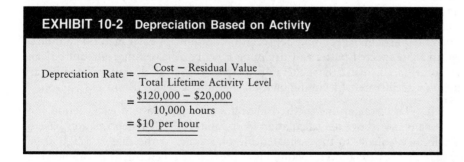

$$\text{Depreciation Rate} = \frac{\text{Cost} - \text{Residual Value}}{\text{Total Lifetime Activity Level}}$$
$$= \frac{\$120,000 - \$20,000}{10,000 \text{ hours}}$$
$$= \$10 \text{ per hour}$$

The depreciation base of $100,000 is divided by the life of 10,000 hours to derive a depreciation rate of $10 per hour. The total depreciation for the period is determined

---

2. *Accounting Terminology Bulletin No. 1* (New York: AICPA, 1953), par. 56.

by multiplying the depreciation rate by the number of hours the asset is used in the period. For example, if the Troup Company uses the asset for 2,100 hours during 2003, the depreciation for the year is $21,000 ($10 × 2,100).

It is important to note that this application of the activity method has produced a constant depreciation rate per *hour*, but one that varies per *unit* of production as the output per hour changes. For example, if the company produces 2 units per hour, the depreciation cost per unit is $5. If productivity increases so that the company produces 2.5 units per hour, the depreciation cost per unit is $4, although the depreciation per hour remains at $10. In contrast, if the activity method is based on the number of *units* expected to be produced over the life of the asset, then a depreciation rate is developed that is constant per *unit* produced but would vary per *hour* as productivity changes. For example, if the depreciation is based on the expected lifetime production of 20,000 units, the depreciation rate is $5 per unit produced ($100,000 ÷ 20,000). If productivity increases so that the company produces 2.5 units per hour, the depreciation cost per unit remains at $5, but the depreciation per hour increases to $12.50.

Although an activity method is appropriate for many assets because their lives are limited by physical causes, it often is not used because of the difficulty of estimating the lifetime units of activity. Also it would be a costly method to implement because of the need to measure and record the activity level of each asset each period. However, it is the method used for depletion, as we discuss later in the chapter.

Time-Based Methods

A company should use a time-based method when the service life of the asset is affected primarily by the passage of time and not by the usage of the asset. This situation includes the physical causes of deterioration and decay and the functional causes of obsolescence and inadequacy. Two general categories of time-based methods are the straight-line method and the accelerated methods. **The straight-line method is appropriate when a company estimates that the benefits it will derive from the asset will be approximately constant each period of its life.** Since straight-line depreciation is the same each period, the matching principle is satisfied because the company matches, as an expense, an equal cost each period against benefits that are approximately the same each period. Support for the straight-line method is enhanced further if maintenance costs are expected to be the same each period. Then the total costs of depreciation and maintenance each period are equal and matched against benefits that are approximately the same each period. It might be thought that the activity method based on hours is a time-based method, but the logic underlying that method is to compute depreciation from the activity of the asset.

The accelerated (or declining-charge) methods are appropriate when a company estimates that the benefits it will derive from the asset will decline each period. Thus, the accelerated methods match a depreciation cost that declines each period against revenues that also are declining each period. However, the benefits to be derived from the asset may be measured in physical terms or in dollars of revenue, as we discuss later. The choice of a particular accelerated method basically is arbitrary, because in most situations the particular declining depreciation amount of each method cannot be matched against the expected pattern of declining revenue. The estimates required cannot be that accurate. Instead, the general principle is that if declining benefits are expected, then an accelerated (declining-charge) method is selected.

STRAIGHT LINE   The straight-line method allocates an equal cost to each period. For the Troup Company, we show the calculation in Exhibit 10-3. The depreciation base of $100,000 is allocated equally to the estimated life of 5 years at the rate of $20,000 per year. The straight-line depreciation sometimes is expressed as a percentage of original cost ($20,000 ÷ $120,000 = 16.67%) or of depreciable cost ($20,000 ÷ $100,000 = 20%). Although widely adopted, the use of the straight-line method may be criticized because it often is used for convenience when an activity method would be more appropriate.

SUM OF THE YEARS' DIGITS   The sum-of-the-years'-digits method produces declining depreciation each period by applying a declining fraction each year to the depreciation

EXHIBIT 10-3 Straight-Line Depreciation

$$\text{Depreciation} = \frac{\text{Cost} - \text{Residual Value}}{\text{Service Life}}$$
$$= \frac{\$120,000 - \$20,000}{5}$$
$$= \$20,000 \text{ per year}$$

base. The denominator of the fraction is the sum of the years' digits. So, for an asset with a 5-year life, the sum is $5 + 4 + 3 + 2 + 1 = 15$.[3] The numerator of the fraction is the years' digits taken in reverse order—that is, 5 the first year, 4 the second year, etc. An alternative way of looking at the numerator is that it is the number of years remaining in the asset's life as of the *beginning* of the year. The fractions for the 5 years of the asset's life are 5/15, 4/15, 3/15, 2/15, and 1/15. We show the calculation of the depreciation for the Troup Company in Exhibit 10-4. Each year, the depreciation declines, and at the end of the fifth year, the book value of the asset is equal to the estimated residual value of $20,000. Note that in this method, the depreciation base remains constant, while the fraction decreases each year.

EXHIBIT 10-4 Sum-of-the-Years'-Digits Depreciation

Year	Depreciation Base	Fraction	Depreciation	Book Value at Year-End*
2003	$100,000	5/15	$ 33,333	$86,667
2004	100,000	4/15	26,667	60,000
2005	100,000	3/15	20,000	40,000
2006	100,000	2/15	13,333	26,667
2007	100,000	1/15	6,667	20,000
			$100,000	

*Cost minus accumulated depreciation

DECLINING BALANCE The declining-balance methods produce a declining depreciation amount each period by applying a *constant* rate to the book value of the asset at the beginning of the period. Note that the periodic depreciation declines because the book value is used and *not* the depreciation base. Also, the residual value is ignored in the calculation of the depreciation each period, although the asset is not depreciated below the estimated residual value. The constant rate is a function of the straight-line rate. The highest rate that can be used is double the straight-line rate. This rate was established as the highest rate by the income tax regulations and was also adopted as the highest rate for financial reporting. An asset that has a 5-year life is depreciated on a straight-line basis at the rate of 20% per year, so the double-declining rate is 40%. However, an alternative rate could be chosen, such as a 150% declining rate, which is 1-1/2 times the straight-line rate or, in this example, 30% per year. We show the application of both alternatives for the Troup Company in Exhibit 10-5.

Note the special situations that arise toward the end of the asset's life. Under the double-declining-balance method, the book value at the beginning of 2006 is $25,920.

---

3. The general formula to compute the sum of the years' digits is $n(n + 1)/2$. So, for an asset with a 50-year life, the sum is $50(50 + 1)/2 = 1,275$.

EXHIBIT 10-5 Declining-Balance Depreciation Methods

(a) *Double-Declining-Balance*

Year	Book Value of Asset at Beginning of Year	Rate	Depreciation	Book Value at End of Year
2003	$120,000	40%	$ 48,000	$72,000
2004	72,000	40%	28,800	43,200
2005	43,200	40%	17,280	25,920
2006	25,920	—	5,920	20,000
2007	20,000	—	—	20,000
			$100,000	

(b) *150%-Declining-Balance*

Year	Book Value of Asset at Beginning of Year	Rate	Depreciation	Book Value at End of Year
2003	$120,000	30%	$ 36,000	$84,000
2004	84,000	30%	25,200	58,800
2005	58,800	30%	17,640	41,160
2006	41,160	30%	12,348	28,812
2007	28,812	—	8,812	20,000
			$100,000	

A strict application of the 40% rate would result in depreciation of $10,368. However, this would reduce the book value below the estimated residual value. Therefore, the 2006 depreciation is only $5,920, which reduces the book value to the residual value, and there is no depreciation in 2007. A similar issue arises under the 150%-declining-balance method. Applying the 30% rate in 2007 would result in depreciation of $8,643.60, which would not be sufficient to reduce the book value down to the residual value. Consequently, the depreciation in 2007 is $8,812, which reduces the book value to the expected residual value of $20,000.

Many companies avoid these problems by switching from the declining-balance method to the straight-line method during the life of the asset. The change in the depreciation method might be made at the midpoint of the life of the asset or when the depreciation under the straight-line method exceeds the declining-balance depreciation. Either method is consistent with the requirement of being systematic and rational if the company decides on the policy at the time of purchase and applies it to all assets. In addition, this practice avoids the possible distortion in the depreciation in the last years of the asset's life. The procedure probably will not produce depreciation that is materially different from the continued application of the accelerated method.[4]

4. Another depreciation method also solves the issue of computing the correct amount of depreciation in the last year of an asset's life. It is the **fixed-percentage-of-declining-balance method,** in which a percentage depreciation rate is calculated that is multiplied by the book value to reduce it to the residual value at the end of the service life. The depreciation rate is calculated as follows:

$$\text{Depreciation Rate} = 1 - n\sqrt{\frac{\text{Residual Value}}{\text{Cost}}}$$

where n is the life of the asset. (The residual value cannot be zero because that makes the fraction zero and the depreciation rate 100%.) The Troup Company would compute the rate as follows:

$$\text{Depreciation Rate} = 1 - 5\sqrt{\frac{\$20,000}{\$120,000}} = 0.3012$$

This method is rarely used in practice because of its complexity.

RECORDING DEPRECIATION

It is important to note that a company may not expense all its depreciation cost in the period. **A company includes depreciation on manufacturing assets as a cost of the inventory produced and records the depreciation as an increase (debit) to the Goods in Process Inventory account.** In other words, the company capitalizes the depreciation to inventory rather than expensing it directly. Costs incurred during the period either remain in the inventory accounts, Goods in Process and Finished Goods Inventory, or they are included in Cost of Goods Sold. Only the portion of the total depreciation included in the units sold appears in the company's income statement as part of the cost of goods sold (and not separately as depreciation expense). Consequently, depreciation included in the cost of the units produced but not sold is part of the two inventory accounts on the company's balance sheet. Also note, when a company sells in the current period units produced in previous periods, its cost of goods sold includes an element of depreciation from previous periods.

A manufacturing company records depreciation on assets used for its selling, general, and administrative functions as an expense in the period, and includes the total Depreciation Expense each period on its income statement. Similarly, a merchandising company records depreciation on all its assets as an expense each period. Note, however, that many companies choose to disclose their expenses under functional classifications, such as selling, general, and administrative expenses, and therefore they would not separately report depreciation expense on their income statements.

The credit entry to record depreciation is to a contra-asset account usually called Accumulated Depreciation, or Allowance for Depreciation. In the past, sometimes companies credited an account entitled Reserve for Depreciation, but such terminology now is considered undesirable because of the uncertain meaning of the term *reserve*. A company maintains a separate contra-asset account for each class of assets and should deduct this amount on its balance sheet directly from the cost of that class. Alternatively, the company may report the book value on the balance sheet and disclose the cost and accumulated depreciation in the notes to its financial statements. However, many companies combine all the accumulated depreciation amounts and report only the total since this limited disclosure is allowed by GAAP.

3 Record depreciation.

CONCEPTUAL EVALUATION OF DEPRECIATION METHODS

A company may use any one of the previously discussed depreciation methods, provided the method relates the allocation of the depreciable cost of the asset to the expected pattern of benefits to be derived from the asset. The choice of a particular method can have a significant impact on a company's income and assets, as you can see by comparing the various depreciation amounts and the book value of the asset computed for the Troup Company. We illustrate these differences in Exhibit 10-6. Use of an inappropriate method has an adverse impact on the measurement of a company's income each year, although its total income over the life of the asset is unaffected because it expenses the same total depreciable cost. For example, if an asset produces equal (or increasing) benefits each year but a company uses an accelerated depreciation method, its income will increase each year of the asset's life (if other factors remain the same each period), even though there has been no change in the activity each period. The rising income may be misleading to users of the financial statements.

Three additional factors that should be considered when a company selects a depreciation method are repair and maintenance costs, changing prices, and the risk associated with the cash flows from the asset. Unfortunately, none have been addressed by generally accepted accounting principles. A company should consider the selection of the depreciation method together with the expected repair and maintenance costs, so that it evaluates the matching of the *total* costs associated with the asset and the benefits derived from the asset. For example, if a company expects that repair and maintenance costs and the total economic benefits of the asset all will remain similar each period, a similar total cost each period can be achieved through straight-line depreciation

4 Explain the conceptual issues regarding depreciation methods.

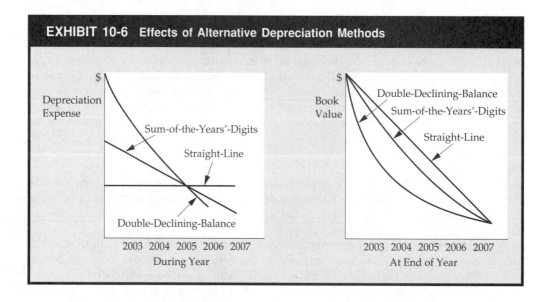

EXHIBIT 10-6   Effects of Alternative Depreciation Methods

and the similar repair and maintenance costs. Alternatively, if the company expects increasing repair and maintenance costs, accelerated (declining-charge) depreciation and the increasing repair and maintenance costs each period may produce similar total costs each period. However, repair and maintenance costs would have to increase significantly to offset the decreasing depreciation amounts. We illustrate these two situations in Exhibit 10-7. Alternatively, if the company expects that benefits will decline each year for the life of the asset, and that repair and maintenance costs are constant each period or are not rising as fast as the depreciation is declining, a declining total cost will be achieved by using accelerated (declining-charge) depreciation along with the expected repair and maintenance costs.

Accounting under conditions of changing prices is discussed in Appendix E.

Inflation is likely to have a significant effect on the measurement of the benefits, or revenue, over the life of the asset. In selecting a depreciation method, a company should consider whether its benefits are to be measured in terms of constant dollars or dollars realized in future periods. Since GAAP is silent on this issue, either alternative is acceptable.

In these periods of technological change, an asset may become obsolete before the end of its originally estimated useful life. Therefore, there is a greater risk associated with the estimated operating cash flows near the end of the life of the asset than for those at the beginning. Use of accelerated depreciation may be appropriate in such situations because the lower depreciation recorded late in the life of the asset reduces the amount of revenues that have to be earned for the asset to be profitable.

EXHIBIT 10-7   Selection of Depreciation Method According to Expected Maintenance Costs to Obtain Constant Total Cost

A ratio commonly used in financial analysis is the rate of return on total assets, which is defined as (net) income divided by the assets. An unfortunate impact of recording depreciation is that the rate of return on assets increases over time. Refer back to the Troup Company example using straight-line depreciation in Exhibit 10-3. Suppose, in addition, that net income after depreciation and income taxes is $12,000 per year and that the company owns only this one asset. The rate of return earned by the company increases each year as we show in Exhibit 10-8. (The calculation of the rate of return could also be based on the average of the beginning and ending book values of the asset.) The increase in the rate of return over the life of the asset would be even more dramatic if an accelerated depreciation method were used. As a result of this relationship, caution should always be exercised when the rate of return is calculated during financial statement analysis. Comparison between two companies can be distorted if one company has a newer asset base and hence a lower rate of return. Alternatively, if one company is analyzed over time, its rate of return will increase as its asset base gets older, other things being equal.

EXHIBIT 10-8 Effect of Depreciation on Rate of Return

Year	Net Income	Book Value of Asset at Beginning of Year	Rate of Return
2003	$12,000	$120,000	10%
2004	12,000	100,000	12
2005	12,000	80,000	15
2006	12,000	60,000	20
2007	12,000	40,000	30

Depreciation is intended only to allocate cost in a systematic and rational manner. It is *not* an attempt to measure the *value* of the asset. The only times that a company should expect to report the fair (market) value of a property, plant, and equipment asset is on the date of acquisition and the date of disposal. Therefore, accounting principles match the cost of the asset against the benefits it produces, rather than an alternative approach of valuing the asset at its market value. Many users consider the market value only to be relevant for assets that are held for sale rather than held for use. Also depreciation is *not* recorded in an attempt to provide funds for the replacement of the asset. Over the life of the asset, the total depreciation expense is equal to the depreciable cost. Since depreciation is a tax-deductible expense, there is an income tax savings over the life of the asset, but it is equal only to the tax rate multiplied by the total amount of tax depreciation. Therefore, there will not be sufficient cash saved over the life of the asset to replace it. Also, the purchase of an asset requires that cash be available at the time of the purchase, or that the company be able to obtain the necessary funds by borrowing or selling stock. However, the cash saved in income taxes may have been used to finance the company's operations and may not be available for asset acquisitions. Furthermore, in times of rising prices, the cost of replacing the asset will be higher than the original cost, so that additional funds will be required for the replacement.

Depreciation based on the current value of assets is discussed in Appendix E.

DISCLOSURE OF DEPRECIATION

APB Opinion No. 12 requires the following disclosure requirements for depreciation:

5 Understand the disclosure of depreciation.

   a. Depreciation expense for the period,

   b. Balances of major classes of depreciable assets, by nature or function, at the balance sheet date,

   c. Accumulated depreciation, either by major classes of depreciable assets or in total, at the balance sheet date, and

EXHIBIT 10-9   Consolidated Balance Sheet

ANHEUSER-BUSCH COMPANIES, INC. AND SUBSIDIARIES

NOTES TO CONSOLIDATED FINANCIAL STATEMENTS (in part)

Note 1. Summary of Significant Accounting Principles and Policies (in part):

FIXED ASSETS

Fixed assets are carried at cost less accumulated depreciation and include expenditures for new facilities as well as those that increase the useful lives of existing facilities. The cost of routine maintenance, repairs and minor renewals is expensed as incurred. When fixed assets are retired or otherwise disposed, the net carrying amount is eliminated, with any gain or loss on disposition recognized in earnings at that time.

Depreciation is recognized using the straight-line method based on the following weighted average useful lives: buildings, 25 years; production machinery and equipment, 15 years; furniture and fixtures, 10 years; computer equipment, 3 years.

Note 11. Supplemental Information (in part):

The components of plant and equipment as of December 31 are summarized below (in millions)

	December 31	
	2001	2000
Land	$ 272.4	$ 260.5
Buildings	4,033.9	3,863.0
Machinery and equipment	10,770.9	10,386.2
Construction in progress	401.1	642.1
	15,478.3	15,151.8
Accumulated depreciation	(7,088.3)	(6,908.0)
Net plant and equipment	8,390.0	8,243.8

Q U E S T I O N S

Q Why do you think the company selected its depreciation method? **Q** How can you estimate the average age of the property, plant, and equipment? **Q** Assuming the company estimates a residual value of 10% of the cost, compute the estimated average life of the property, plant, and equipment.

d. A general description of the method or methods used in computing depreciation with respect to major classes of depreciable assets.[5]

We show the disclosure of these items for Anheuser-Busch in Exhibit 10-9. The depreciation (and amortization) expense of $798.3 million in 2001 was disclosed (after adjusting for the amortization expense) in the company's statement of cash flows under the indirect method.

 We show the relative use of alternative depreciation methods by 600 surveyed companies in Exhibit 10-10. Note that the straight-line method is used by a large majority of the companies. There are more than 600 responses because many companies use more than one method of depreciation. Even with the current disclosure requirements, the reader of a company's financial statements is not able to evaluate whether the chosen depreciation method(s) is appropriate for the particular assets, but must accept that management and the company's auditors consider the method(s) to be systematic and rational. Nor is the reader able to estimate accurately the effect on income and assets

---

5. "Omnibus Opinion—1967," *APB Opinion No. 12* (New York: AICPA, 1971), par. 5.

EXHIBIT 10-10	Use of Alternative Depreciation Methods						
	Number of Companies						
	2000	1997	1994	1990	1986	1982	1978
Straight-line	576	578	573	560	561	562	560
Declining-balance	22	26	27	38	49	57	67
Sum-of-the-years'-digits	7	10	9	11	14	20	35
Accelerated method, not specified	53	50	49	69	77	69	67
Units-of-production	34	39	49	50	48	62	44

Source: Accounting Trends and Techniques (New York: AICPA, 2001, 1998, 1995, 1991, 1987, 1983 and 1979).

of the use of an alternative depreciation method, which might be useful when comparing the financial activities of two companies using different depreciation methods.

International Accounting Differences

International accounting standards for depreciation are essentially the same as those of the U.S. However, they only require that depreciation be "systematic," rather than "systematic and rational." International standards also require that the estimated useful lives of the assets, and the depreciation method, be reviewed periodically. They also require that companies disclose the accumulated depreciation for each class of asset, not just the total amount as allowed by U.S. standards. Also note that international standards allow a company to write up the value of its property, plant, and equipment assets to fair value, as we discussed in Chapter 9. Such a write-up would affect the amount of depreciation that the company records each period.[6]

ADDITIONAL DEPRECIATION METHODS

Some additional depreciation methods are **group-rate** and **composite-rate** methods, which are used frequently in conjunction with the straight-line or accelerated methods, and **retirement** and **replacement** methods, which are used in special industries.[7]

Group and composite depreciation are conceptually similar methods of applying depreciation to more than one asset. Group depreciation is applied to *homogeneous* assets that are expected to have similar service lives and residual values. Composite depreciation is applied to *heterogeneous* assets having some similar characteristics, but are expected to have varying service lives and residual values. Thus, group depreciation would be used for homogeneous assets such as PCs, whereas composite depreciation would be applied to heterogeneous assets such as office machines.

6 Understand additional depreciation methods, including group and composite methods.

Group Depreciation

A company uses group depreciation when it owns a group of homogeneous (similar) assets, it capitalizes the assets in a single asset account, and it treats the group as a single "asset" for purposes of depreciation. The group depreciation rate is based on the average life of the assets in the group, and the depreciation is accumulated in a single contra-asset account. Depreciation each period is calculated by multiplying this rate by

---

6. For additional discussion see Carrie Bloomer (editor), *The IASC–U.S. Comparison Project: A Report on the Similarities and Differences between IASC Standards and U.S. GAAP*, 2nd ed. (Norwalk, Conn: FASB, 1999).

7. Two other methods, the **compound-interest** and **sinking-fund** methods, are based on present value concepts. They result in an *increasing* depreciation amount and a constant rate of return on the asset each period. They are very rarely used because increasing depreciation each period generally is not considered to satisfy the matching principle.

the balance in the asset account. When an item in the group is retired, no gain or loss is recognized on that item because the entire "asset" is not retired. The individual retirement is recorded by a credit to the asset account for the original cost, and a debit to the accumulated depreciation account for the difference between the cost and the proceeds received. A total net gain or loss on the group as a whole is recognized when the final unit in the group is retired.

For example, suppose that a company purchases ten cars for $20,000 each, and the average expected service life is 3 years with a residual value of $5,000 each. Of those cars, three are sold after 2 years for $8,000 each, five after 3 years for $6,000 each, and two after 4 years for $4,800 each. The company computes the depreciation rate as follows:

$$\text{Depreciation} = \frac{\text{Cost} - \text{Residual Value}}{\text{Life}}$$
$$= \frac{\$200,000 - \$50,000}{3}$$
$$= \$50,000 \text{ (or 25\% of the cost of the assets)}$$

We show the journal entries used to record these events in Exhibit 10-11. Depreciation expense is based on the original estimates, and the rate is not changed by the

---

EXHIBIT 10-11   Journal Entries for Group Depreciation

1. To record the purchase:		
Cars	200,000	
Cash		200,000
2. To record the first year's depreciation expense:		
Depreciation Expense	50,000	
Accumulated Depreciation		50,000
3. To record the second year's depreciation expense:		
Depreciation Expense	50,000	
Accumulated Depreciation		50,000
4. To record the disposal of three cars at the end of the second year for $8,000 each:		
Cash	24,000	
Accumulated Depreciation	36,000	
Cars		60,000
5. To record the third year's depreciation expense:		
Depreciation Expense [25% × ($200,000 − $60,000)]	35,000	
Accumulated Depreciation		35,000
6. To record the disposal of five cars at the end of the third year for $6,000 each:		
Cash	30,000	
Accumulated Depreciation	70,000	
Cars		100,000
7. To record the depreciation expense for the fourth year, the disposal of two cars at the end of the fourth year for $4,800 each, and the *net* gain or loss of the *entire* group:		
Depreciation Expense	1,000[a]	
Accumulated Depreciation		1,000
Cash	9,600	
Accumulated Depreciation	30,000	
Loss on Disposal	400[b]	
Cars		40,000

[a] The depreciation expense is the amount needed to reduce the $11,000 book value ($40,000 remaining cost minus $29,000 remaining accumulated depreciation) of the group to the estimated residual value (2 × $5,000).
[b] The loss is equal to the proceeds of $9,600 (2 × $4,800) minus the remaining book value of $10,000 ($40,000 − $30,000).

particular experience of the early retirement of three cars after the second year. No gain or loss is recognized on the retirement at the end of the second and third years. The journal entries in the fourth year (the year of the final retirement) need further explanation. First, although the usual procedure in group depreciation is to multiply the asset cost by the group depreciation rate to determine the annual depreciation expense, it is a general rule that assets are not depreciated below their residual value. Since the book value of the group asset is $11,000 ($40,000 Cars − $29,000 Accumulated Depreciation) at the beginning of the year and the residual value of the two remaining cars is $10,000 (2 × $5,000), the depreciation expense must be $1,000 in this year. Second, the $400 loss on the *entire* group is determined by comparing the $9,600 (2 × $4,800) proceeds to the $10,000 book value at the end of the fourth year.

If the company purchases a new asset (i.e., more cars) before the group is retired, it computes a new depreciation rate by dividing the new depreciation base (book value at the beginning of the period plus the additional cost less the estimated residual value of the group) by the new weighted average of the remaining lives of the assets in the group.

Composite Depreciation

A company may apply composite depreciation to heterogeneous (dissimilar) assets that have somewhat similar characteristics or purposes. As with group depreciation, the company combines the assets in a single asset account and depreciates them accordingly. One accumulated depreciation account is used, no gain or loss is recognized on each item retired, and a net gain or loss is recognized when the final asset is retired.

For example, suppose that a company purchases three assets with the following characteristics:

Asset	Cost	Residual Value	Life	Annual Depreciation
A	$25,000	$5,000	10 years	$2,000
B	13,000	1,000	6	2,000
C	12,000	—	4	3,000
	$50,000	$6,000		$7,000

Assuming that the company uses straight-line depreciation, it computes the composite depreciation rate as follows:

$$\text{Depreciation Rate} = \frac{\$7,000}{\$50,000} = 14\%$$

The company computes the depreciation by multiplying 14% by the cost of the assets remaining in service until the book value equals the estimated residual value of $6,000. If the company purchases another asset, it may include the asset in the group by adding the cost to the asset account. Then it calculates a new composite depreciation rate.

The advantage of both the group and the composite methods is that they simplify a company's record keeping, especially when a large number of low-cost items are acquired. The methods also recognize that depreciation estimates are based on averages and that gains or losses on disposals of single assets are often immaterial. The major disadvantage of the two methods is that faulty estimates might be concealed for long periods and gains and losses deferred beyond the period in which they actually occurred. This is particularly true when heterogeneous assets are combined for the composite depreciation method and the average life is the result of combining varying individual lives.

Retirement and Replacement Methods

The retirement and replacement methods of expense recognition, instead of the depreciation methods discussed in the chapter, have been used by public utilities and railroads for such items as poles and tracks. In using these methods, a company recognizes an expense only when an asset is retired or replaced. Under the *retirement* method, the cost of the *old* asset (less its residual value) is expensed when it is retired. Under the *replacement* method, the cost of the *new* asset (less the residual value of the old asset) is expensed when it is acquired. If no retirement or replacement occurs, no expense is recognized. Neither method is desirable because neither matches expenses with revenues in each period of the asset's life. However, these methods did gain acceptance as special industry practices, particularly in cases where there are large numbers of low-cost interrelated items for which it is difficult to estimate the economic life and to distinguish between maintenance and replacement.[8] Furthermore, if a company has a policy of regular replacement, so that the amount expensed remains fairly stable, the difference in expense from straight-line depreciation may be immaterial.

Inventory Systems

The inventory (or appraisal) system typically is used in situations where there are large numbers of similar low-cost items, such as tools for a manufacturing company or dishes for a restaurant. The method is similar to a periodic inventory system, in that a cost is assigned to an expense by a physical count at the end of the year. That is, the cost that a company assigns to depreciation is determined by multiplying the physical number of units at the end of the year by the replacement cost. A key difference, however, is that the account debited is Depreciation Expense rather than Cost of Goods Sold. Also, the ending inventory usually is computed as the value (not the cost) of the assets, so that the depreciation becomes a measure of the change in the value of the assets. The method is criticized because it does not result in a systematic and rational allocation of cost, but rather is a measure of the value of the assets. Also, the value assigned to the inventory tends to be less reliable than cost.

DEPRECIATION FOR PARTIAL PERIODS

7 Compute depreciation for partial periods.

Our discussion so far has assumed that assets are purchased on the first day of the fiscal year and disposed of on the last day. Of course, transactions occur throughout the fiscal year and depreciation could be computed to the nearest day, but such precision is unnecessary, since the calculation of depreciation uses estimates. There are three common alternative policies that companies use to compute depreciation for partial periods.

Compute Depreciation to the Nearest Whole Month

Under this method, assets purchased on or before the 15th of the month are considered owned for the whole month; assets purchased after the 15th are considered *not* to be owned during the month. Similarly, assets sold on or before the 15th are considered not to be owned for the month; assets sold after the 15th are considered owned for the whole month. Depreciation is based on the fraction of the year the asset is used. For example, suppose a company purchases a $6,000 asset with a 3-year life and no residual value on August 18; thus 4 months remain in the year. The sum-of-the-years'-digits depreciation extends over 4 fiscal years and the company computes the amounts as follows:

---

8. In 1983, the Interstate Commerce Commission required the use of depreciation accounting in ICC filings. As a result, many railroads adopted depreciation accounting for financial reporting.

Fiscal Year	Annual Depreciation by Sum-of-the-Years'-Digits Method	Months	Computation	Annual Depreciation
1	$3,000	4	4/12 × $3,000	$1,000
2	2,000	12	8/12 × $3,000 + 4/12 × $2,000	2,667
3	1,000	12	8/12 × $2,000 + 4/12 × $1,000	1,667
4	—	8	8/12 × $1,000	666*
	$6,000			$6,000

*Adjusted for $1 rounding error

When double-declining depreciation is used for partial periods, two alternatives are available. In the first alternative, the double-declining-balance method can be used in the same manner as we just described for the sum-of-the-years'-digits method. That is, the depreciation on an annual basis is allocated to each fiscal year on the basis of the number of months. In the second alternative, after the computation of the depreciation for the first year as described for the first alternative, the double-declining-balance method can be applied by multiplying the book value by the appropriate percentage (66.7%). Using the same example of a $6,000 asset with a 3-year life and no residual value, the company computes the depreciation under the two alternatives as follows:

Fiscal Year	Annual Depreciation by the Double-Declining-Balance	Months	Computation	Reported Annual Depreciation
Alternative 1				
1	$4,000	4	4/12 × $4,000	$1,333
2	1,333	12	8/12 × $4,000 + 4/12 × $1,333	3,111
3	667	12	8/12 × $1,333 + 4/12 × $667	1,111
4	—	8	8/12 × $667	445
	$6,000			$6,000
Alternative 2				
Depreciation Year 1			4/12 × $4,000	$1,333
Depreciation Year 2			0.667* × ($6,000 − $1,333)	3,113
Depreciation Year 3			0.667 × ($4,667 − $3,113)	1,037
Depreciation Year 4			Remaining balance	517
				$6,000

*Two times straight-line rate = 2 × 1/3

When straight-line depreciation is used and it is necessary to calculate depreciation for months instead of years, the denominator of the depreciation calculation frequently is expressed in terms of the total months in the estimated service life, resulting in readily determinable depreciation per month.

Compute Depreciation to the Nearest Whole Year

For this partial depreciation method, exactly the same procedure is used as for the monthly situation, except that 6 months is used as the cutoff instead of the 15th of the month. That is, assets purchased during the first six months of the year are considered to be owned for the entire year, and assets purchased during the second six months are not depreciated for that year. Using the same example, there is no depreciation in the first fiscal year, since the asset was purchased in the second half of the year, but a full year's depreciation is recorded in the last year. Depreciation in the next three fiscal years is $3,000, $2,000, and $1,000, respectively, under the sum-of-the-years'-digits method.

Compute One-Half Year's Depreciation on All Assets Purchased or Sold During the Year

Under this method, all assets purchased or sold during the fiscal year are considered to have been purchased or sold at the midpoint of the year, so that one-half year's depreciation is recorded in all such situations. Using the same example, the depreciation for each fiscal year is computed as follows:

Fiscal Year	Annual Depreciation by Sum-of-the-Years'-Digits Method	Computation	Reported Annual Depreciation
1	$3,000	1/2 × $3,000	$1,500
2	2,000	1/2 × $3,000 + 1/2 × $2,000	2,500
3	1,000	1/2 × $2,000 + 1/2 × $1,000	1,500
4	—	1/2 × $1,000	500
	$6,000		$6,000

IMPAIRMENT OF NONCURRENT ASSETS

8 Explain the impairment of noncurrent assets.

Users have been concerned for a long-time about the values that a company assigns to its property, plant, and equipment. If the fair value of these noncurrent assets is less than their book value, then it may be argued that the company's past earnings are overstated (because it did not record sufficient depreciation in prior years). Conservatism would suggest that the company write down these assets and recognize a loss, but practice has varied considerably. Also, if a company writes down an asset by too much, then future profits will be overstated (because it would record too little depreciation in future years). In 2001, the FASB issued **FASB Statement No. 144,**[9] under which a company must review its property, plant, and equipment (and intangible assets with a finite life which we discuss in Chapter 11) for impairment whenever events or changes in circumstances indicate that the book value of a noncurrent asset may not be recoverable. Examples of such events or changes in circumstances include a significant decrease in the fair value of the asset, a significant change in the way the asset is used, a significant change in the business or regulatory environment, costs of constructing the asset that exceed the planned amount, a current period operating loss, a negative cash flow from operating activities, or an expectation that the asset will more-likely-than-not (i.e., more than 50%) be sold or otherwise disposed of before the end of its useful life. After the company identifies that an asset may be impaired, two steps are taken: (1) an impairment test, and (2) measurement of the loss.

To test for impairment, the company estimates the future net cash flows expected to result from the use of the asset and its eventual sale. If the total expected cash flows (undiscounted) are less than the book value of the asset, the company must recognize an impairment loss (we discuss the calculation of the *amount* of the loss later). One of the major issues faced by the FASB was asset grouping; that is, does the company test individual assets or large groups of assets? The FASB resolved this issue by requiring that assets be grouped at the lowest level at which identifiable cash flows are largely

---

9. "Accounting for the Impairment or Disposal of Long-Lived Assets," *FASB Statement of Financial Accounting Standards No. 144* (Norwalk, Conn.: FASB 2001). Certain assets are excluded from the scope of the *Statement*, including specialized assets in the record, music, broadcasting, and software industries. The *Statement* replaced, but made only minor changes to, *FASB Statement of Financial Accounting Standards No. 121* which was issued in 1995.

independent of the cash flows of other groups of assets. (We will use the singular term "asset" to describe the group of assets identified by a company.) If the future cash flows exceed the book value, an impairment loss is *not* recognized, but a review of the company's depreciation policies may be appropriate.

The *Statement* discusses the measurement of an impairment loss for an asset that the company intends to hold and use.[10] The impairment loss is the difference between the asset's book value and its lower fair value. The fair value is the amount at which the asset could be bought or sold in a current transaction between willing parties. However, quoted market prices will often not be available for the assets covered by *FASB Statement No. 144*. Therefore, fair value may be measured by using the present value method to determine the discounted cash flows (as we discuss in Appendix D). The discount rate is the rate of return that the company would require for a similar investment with similar risks. For example, this could be the rate used to evaluate capital budgeting projects. When a company recognizes an impairment loss (debit), it writes down the asset (credit) to reduce its book value to the lower fair value (as we illustrate in the example that follows). The company reports the impairment loss on its income statement as part of income from continuing operations and reports the new (reduced) book value on its ending balance sheet. The reduced book value (i.e., fair value) becomes the new "cost" of the asset and is used to compute the depreciation over the remaining life of the asset. Once an asset has been written down, if the fair value subsequently increases, the asset may not be written back up.

A company must include in its disclosures in the year of the write-down and the next two years (assuming the company provides two years of comparative income statements), a description of the impaired asset and the circumstances leading to the impairment, the amount of the loss, how the asset's fair value was determined, the income statement caption which includes the loss, and the operating segment affected (if applicable).

In summary, an impairment loss involves the following steps:

Event or Change in Circumstances Occurs

↓

Impairment Test
(Undiscounted Cash Flows < Book Value of Asset)

↓

Measurement of Loss
(Loss = Fair Value − Book Value)

To illustrate an impairment loss on an asset that is to be held for use, suppose that on January 1, 2001, the Hall Company purchased a factory for $1 million and machinery for $3 million. The company is depreciating the factory over 20 years and the machinery over 10 years, both by the straight-line method, to zero residual values. Late in 2004, because of technological changes in the industry and reduced selling prices for its products, the company believes that its asset(s) may be impaired and will have a remaining useful life of 5 years. The company combines the factory and machinery as a group because the cash flows from each are not separable and are independent of the company's other activities. To test for impairment, the company estimates that the asset will produce cash inflows of $700,000 and will incur cash outflows of $300,000 each year for the next 5 years. The company tests for impairment and measures the loss as follows:

---

10. The *Statement* also discusses the measurement of an impairment loss for an asset that the company *intends to sell*. The asset is reported at the lower of the (1) book value or (2) fair value less the costs to sell. The impairment loss is calculated in the same way as for an asset held for use, except that the estimated selling price less the costs to sell is used instead of the present value of the cash flows (or other measure of fair value). Thus, the GAAP related to an asset the company expects to sell is similar to that we discussed in Chapter 4 for the disposal of a component of a company and we do not discuss it further.

IMPAIRMENT TEST

December 31, 2004

Factory cost	$1,000,000	
Less: Accumulated depreciation (4 years × $50,000)	(200,000)	
Book value		$ 800,000
Machinery cost	$3,000,000	
Less: Accumulated depreciation (4 years × $300,000)	(1,200,000)	
Book value		1,800,000
Total Book Value		$2,600,000

$$
\begin{aligned}
\text{Undiscounted expected net cash flows} &= 5 \text{ years} \times (\$700,000 \text{ cash inflows} - \\
&\quad\quad \$300,000 \text{ cash outflows}) \\
&= 5 \times \$400,000 \\
&= \$2,000,000
\end{aligned}
$$

Because $2,000,000 is less than $2,600,000, the company must recognize an impairment loss.

Since the company is not able to determine the fair value based on the selling price of the factory and machinery, it uses the present value method instead. To apply this method, the company uses a discount rate of 16% (which is the rate of return it uses to evaluate capital budgeting projects). It calculates the impairment loss of $1,290,282 as follows:

MEASUREMENT OF THE LOSS

$$
\begin{aligned}
\text{Present value of the expected net cash flows (fair value)} &= \$400,000 \times 3.274294 \\
&\quad (n = 5, i = 0.16 \text{ from} \\
&\quad \text{Table 4 in Appendix D)} \\
&= \$1,309,718 \text{ (rounded)}
\end{aligned}
$$

$$
\begin{aligned}
\text{Impairment loss} &= \$1,309,718 \text{ fair value} - \$2,600,000 \text{ book value} \\
&= \$(1,290,282)
\end{aligned}
$$

Although the *Statement* does not specify how to record the write-down, it does indicate that the reduced book value of the asset is to be accounted for as the new cost. Therefore, we will treat the write-down as a "sale" with an acquisition at the new "cost." We also assume that the new cost is allocated among the individual assets based on their relative fair values at their original acquisition date. Then the Hall Company records the loss as follows:

Loss from Impairment	1,290,282	
Accumulated Depreciation: Factory	200,000	
Accumulated Depreciation: Machinery	1,200,000	
Factory (new cost)	327,429[a]	
Machinery (new cost)	982,289[b]	
Factory (old cost)		1,000,000
Machinery (old cost)		3,000,000

[a]$1,309,718 × [$1,000,000 ÷ ($3,000,000 + $1,000,000)]
[b]$1,309,718 × [$3,000,000 ÷ ($3,000,000 + $1,000,000)]

The company will depreciate the factory and machinery over their remaining useful life of 5 years. It reports the $1,290,282 loss in income from continuing operations on its 2004 income statement, and the property, plant, and equipment at a total of $1,309,718 on its 2004 ending balance sheet.

Conceptual Evaluation of Asset Impairment

FASB Statement No. 121 first established the impairment rules we just discussed. Although it has been replaced by *FASB Statement No. 144*, the principles it established have only changed slightly. *FASB Statement No. 121* was issued to enhance the usefulness of a company's financial statements by recognizing the loss when incurred and reflecting the fair value of productive assets. This should provide better financial reporting because the asset value reflects the value of the company's investment; thus, the information is expected to be more relevant and help users assess the return on investment, operating capability, and risk of the company. The information should also improve comparability across companies.

Although the *Statement* narrows GAAP, it still allows for significant management flexibility. For example, it does not require that assets be tested for impairment on a regular basis, because the FASB concluded that would be too costly. Management will also have some flexibility in deciding which assets to include in, and exclude from, each grouping. Also, estimating future cash flows is very subjective. For example, the company could use current or expected cost and volume information. Furthermore, the discount rate used to value the cash flows is a management choice.

The *Statement* was adopted by a 5-to-2 vote. The dissenters believed that the use of fair value is not appropriate if the asset will continue to be used, because there has not been an exchange transaction. They argued that such use of fair value is a precedent-setting departure from the transaction-based historical cost model (other than for investments in marketable securities that have a readily available fair value, as we discuss in Chapter 14). Therefore, the dissenters argued that the asset should be recorded at recoverable cost, either measured on a present value or undiscounted basis. One dissenter also argued that since fair value is not relevant and reliable information for property, plant, and equipment that is held and used in the normal course of business, then the fair value of an impaired asset is also not relevant and reliable. Also the write-down will "guarantee" future profits.

Two other concerns were also expressed. First, the cash flows expected by a company from using a specific asset are not necessarily the same as those used to determine the market value of the asset, since the company may use the asset differently from other companies. Therefore, the specific cash flows may not result in a measure of fair value. Second, the test for an impairment may differ for identical assets simply because of the depreciation method (or life) selected by the company. An asset depreciated by an accelerated method will have a lower book value than one depreciated by the straight-line method, and therefore be less likely to meet the impairment test. Even with these concerns, it is hoped that the *Statement* has improved financial reporting. For example, in 2001 Coca-Cola reported that it wrote down its noncurrent assets in India by $405 million in 2000, and its noncurrent assets in many different countries by $739 million.

International Accounting Differences

Although international accounting standards for the impairment of assets are similar to those of the U.S., there are some differences. International standards use the higher of the asset's net selling price or value in use to determine if an asset is impaired compared to the undiscounted cash flows used in U.S. principles. Typically, this should mean that international companies will recognize impairment losses earlier than U.S. companies. Under international standards, the impairment loss is the difference between the book value and the "trigger" value defined above. Therefore, it is likely that the impairment losses measured under the two sets of principles would be different. Also, international standards allow impairment losses to be reversed, which is not allowed under U.S. standards.

DEPRECIATION AND INCOME TAXES

9 Understand depreciation for income tax purposes.

Companies follow different depreciation rules for computing taxable income than for computing income for financial reporting purposes. The use of different methods is acceptable because the purpose of the depreciation methods required by the income tax laws is to stimulate capital investment through the rapid recovery of capital costs, whereas the purpose of accounting income is to present fairly the activities of the company over a particular period. However, companies that are not required to follow GAAP may use the tax method in their financial statements.

For assets acquired before 1981, depreciation for income tax purposes is based on use of the straight-line, sum-of-the-years'-digits, and declining-balance methods we discussed earlier. The asset may not be depreciated below the estimated residual value, and the IRS publishes tables that give a range of the estimated lives to use. For assets purchased in the years 1981 through 1986, the Accelerated Cost Recovery System (ACRS) is used. For assets purchased in 1987 and later, ACRS was modified and is known as MACRS.[11] The following discussion is based on these latest rules.

MACRS Principles

For an asset purchased in 1987 and later, a company's computations of depreciation for federal income tax purposes and financial reporting purposes differ in three major respects: (1) a mandated tax life, which is usually shorter than the economic life, (2) acceleration of the cost recovery (except for a building), and (3) elimination of the residual value. Each of these differences tends to cause depreciation early in the life of an asset to be higher for income tax purposes than for financial statement reporting, thereby lowering income taxes payable in those years. Over the life of an asset, the sum of the total depreciation and the gain or loss on disposal for both income tax reporting and financial reporting usually will be the same for both methods. Therefore, the total effect on a company's taxable income over the asset's life usually will be equal to the total effect on its income before income taxes reported in its financial statements. However, the transfer of income tax payments from early in the life of the asset to later in the life is desirable when present value concepts are taken into consideration. Since MACRS depreciation is so different from the depreciation used in a company's financial statements, we briefly discuss it. You should also note that for income tax reporting a company may use the straight-line method over the mandated tax life instead of MACRS. Refer to the Internal Revenue Code, or an income tax book, for a more detailed and technical discussion.

SHORTER LIFE   The MACRS establishes lives (recovery periods) of 3, 5, 7, 10, 15, 20, $27\frac{1}{2}$ (residential rental buildings), and 39 (commercial buildings) years. Each asset is defined to be in one of the categories, and a company uses that life no matter what economic life it uses for financial reporting purposes.

ACCELERATION OF COST RECOVERY   The depreciation is computed based on the *cost* of the asset. The method used depends on the life of the asset mandated by MACRS, as follows:

Method	MACRS Life (in years)
Double-declining-balance	3, 5, 7, 10
150%-declining-balance	15, 20
Straight-line	$27\frac{1}{2}$, 39

---

11. An asset other than a building had an ACRS life of 3, 5, 10, or 15 years. A building had an ACRS life of 18 or 19 years, depending on the year it was purchased. The depreciation was computed by multiplying the cost of the asset by a defined percentage. For example, an asset with a 3-year ACRS life was depreciated using 25% in the first year, 38% in the second year, and 37% in the third year. An asset with a 5-year ACRS life was depreciated using 15%, 22%, 21%, 21%, and 21% over the respective 5 years. Under MACRS, commercial buildings acquired before 1993 were depreciated over $27\frac{1}{2}$ years. Following the terrorist attacks of 9/11/01, Congress enacted a temporary change in the MACRS rules. For assets (other than buildings) placed in service between 9/10/01 and 9/11/04, a company receives a tax deduction of 30% of the cost of the asset and then applies MACRS procedures to the remaining 70%. We do not include the effects of this temporary rule in the examples and homework throughout the book.

EXHIBIT 10-12   MACRS Depreciation as a Percentage of the Cost of the Asset

Year of Life	Tax Life of Asset in Years					
	3	5	7	10	15	20
1	33.33%	20.00%	14.29%	10.00%	5.00%	3.750%
2	44.45	32.00	24.49	18.00	9.50	7.219
3	14.81	19.20	17.49	14.40	8.55	6.677
4	7.41	11.52	12.49	11.52	7.70	6.177
5		11.52	8.93	9.22	6.93	5.713
6		5.76	8.92	7.37	6.23	5.285
7			8.93	6.55	5.90	4.888
8			4.46	6.55	5.90	4.522
9				6.56	5.91	4.462
10				6.55	5.90	4.461
11				3.28	5.91	4.462
12					5.90	4.461
13					5.91	4.462
14					5.90	4.461
15					5.91	4.462
16					2.95	4.461
17						4.462
18						4.461
19						4.462
20						4.461
21						2.231

All the depreciation calculations for income tax purposes are based on the half-year convention; that is, a company records depreciation for half a year in the year of acquisition and in the last year of the MACRS life. Therefore, the depreciation for tax purposes is spread over one more tax year than the number of calendar years listed previously. Also, when one of the accelerated methods is used, a change is made to the straight-line method in the period in which the straight-line depreciation exceeds the amount calculated under the accelerated method. The IRS has published tables to simplify the application of these methods, as we illustrate in Exhibit 10-12.

RESIDUAL VALUE   The residual value is *not* considered when the MACRS system is used, and so the asset is depreciated to a zero value at the end of its MACRS life. However, the entire proceeds from the disposal of the asset will be taxable since the entire value received will represent a gain.

Illustration of MACRS

To illustrate the use of the MACRS system and the differences from the calculation of depreciation for financial reporting, consider the following facts for an asset purchased by the Melville Company on January 1, 2003:

Cost	$200,000
Estimated economic life	8 years
Estimated residual value	$20,000
Depreciation method for financial statements	Straight-line
MACRS life	5 years
MACRS method	200% declining balance
Disposal	$15,000 on January 3, 2011

The company computes the MACRS depreciation using the rates from Exhibit 10-12 as follows:

2003	$200,000 × 20%	=	$ 40,000
2004	$200,000 × 32%	=	$ 64,000
2005	$200,000 × 19.20%	=	$ 38,400
2006	$200,000 × 11.52%	=	$ 23,040
2007	$200,000 × 11.52%	=	$ 23,040
2008	$200,000 × 5.76%	=	$ 11,520
			$200,000

Note that the total depreciation deductions on the company's income tax returns for 2003 through 2008 are $200,000. Thus, the MACRS depreciation recovers the total cost of the asset on an accelerated basis and ignores any residual value. The taxable gain in 2008 when the asset is sold is $15,000, since the company has depreciated the asset to a zero residual value. Therefore, the total effect on its taxable income for the years 2003 through 2011 is $185,000 ($200,000 − $15,000).

The depreciation for financial reporting purposes is $22,500 [($200,000 − $20,000) ÷ 8] for each of the 8 years of the asset's economic life from 2003 through 2011. The loss on disposal in 2011 is $5,000 ($20,000 book value − $15,000 proceeds). The total effect on the company's income before income taxes for the years 2003 through 2011 in its income statement is $185,000 ($180,000 + $5,000), which is the same as the total effect on taxable income. The different amounts of depreciation for income tax reporting and financial reporting in each year result in temporary differences, which require interperiod tax allocation.

Interperiod tax allocation is discussed in Chapter 18.

CHANGES AND CORRECTIONS OF DEPRECIATION

10 Explain changes and corrections of depreciation.

APB Opinion No. 20, which we discuss more fully in Chapter 22, describes how a company may make each of the various changes in and corrections of depreciation for the following situations:

1. A change in the depreciation method for currently owned assets (change in accounting principle) is accounted for by a cumulative-effect change. The accumulated depreciation at the beginning of the year of the change is computed based on the old and the new methods, and the difference is reported on the company's income statement (net of income taxes) in the year of the change as a cumulative effect on prior years' income of a change in accounting principle (as we illustrated in Chapter 4).

2. Adoption of a new depreciation method for newly acquired assets does not require any adjustment to the accounts, but it does require disclosure in the notes to the company's financial statements of the nature of the change, its effects on income from continuing operations, and on net income, together with related earnings per share amounts.

3. A change in an estimate of the residual value or the service life of a currently owned asset is accounted for prospectively; that is, the company allocates the undepreciated cost of the asset at the beginning of the year of the change over the new remaining life, giving consideration to the new residual value. We include an illustration (using depletion) is in the next section of the chapter.

4. Correction of an error in depreciation is treated as a prior period adjustment; that is, the company's previous financial statements are corrected (restated). The effect on the current period's financial statements involves a correction to the amount in the accumulated depreciation account and an increase or decrease in retained earnings (net of income taxes) for the amount of the error in previously reported net income. We illustrate this reporting in Chapters 4 and 16, and it is consistent with the requirements of **FASB Statement No. 16.**

DEPLETION

Depletion is the allocation of the depletable cost for the consumption of a natural resource (wasting asset) to the periods in which benefits are received. It is the same concept as depreciation, but the different term is used for natural resources. Examples of such resources are oil, gas, minerals, timber, and gravel.

A company determines the recorded cost of natural resources by the same principles used for property, plant, and equipment. It is possible that there will be extensive reclamation costs. In this case the company would report a liability and add the same amount to the cost of the asset, as we discussed in Chapter 9.

A company normally records depletion using an activity method. The activity measure is the number of units of the resource that the company expects to extract over the life of the asset. A unit depletion rate is calculated as follows:

$$\text{Unit Depletion Rate} = \frac{\text{Cost} - \text{Residual Value}}{\text{Units}}$$

To determine the actual depletion for a period, the unit depletion rate is multiplied by the actual production for that period. Suppose that a company purchases land for $3,000,000 from which it expects to extract 1,000,000 tons of coal, the estimated residual value is $200,000, and it mines 80,000 tons of coal in the first year. It calculates the depletion for that year as follows:

$$\text{Unit Depletion Rate} = \frac{\$3,000,000 - \$200,000}{1,000,000 \text{ tons}}$$
$$= \$2.80 \text{ per ton}$$

$$\text{Depletion for Year} = \$2.80 \times 80,000 \text{ tons}$$
$$= \$224,000$$

The company typically makes the journal entry to record the depletion directly to an inventory account (so that the cost is included in Cost of Goods Sold for the units that are sold and in ending inventory for the units on hand at the end of the period). The credit is made either to Accumulated Depletion or directly to the asset account because disclosure of the accumulated depletion amount is not required by GAAP. However, this disclosure is required by the SEC.

The nature of natural resources is such that additional capital expenditures may be made in future periods. In addition, the estimation of the remaining number of units is often uncertain and therefore subject to revision based on new geological information. When additional capital expenditures are incurred or estimates are revised, a new depletion rate is calculated. The new depletion rate is based on the current book value of the asset (including the additional capital expenditures), the new estimate of the residual value, and the new estimate of the remaining units as of the beginning of the year. Continuing the preceding example, suppose that at the beginning of the second year of operation of the coal mine, a new estimate indicates that the mine has a capacity to produce another 1,600,000 tons (for a lifetime production of 1,680,000 tons). The company computes a new unit depletion rate as follows:

$$\text{Unit Depletion Rate} = \frac{\text{Book Value} - \text{Residual Value}}{\text{Remaining Units}}$$
$$= \frac{(\$3,000,000 - \$224,000) - \$200,000}{1,600,000}$$
$$= \$1.61 \text{ per ton}$$

The company uses the new unit depletion rate to compute each year's depletion until it makes new estimates and calculates another depletion rate.

The cost of a natural resource asset may include certain tangible assets, such as buildings and roads on the site of a mine. Since the useful life of the tangible assets is limited

11 Understand and record depletion.

by the life of the mine, a company depreciates their cost on the basis of the same activity method as it uses for the mine. Of course, if other improvements have a life shorter than the expected life of the mine, the company depreciates them over their expected economic lives.

Depletion for income tax purposes involves a different concept than for financial reporting. A company can deduct as depletion expense either the **cost depletion** just illustrated (based on the units sold) or **percentage depletion.** Under percentage (or **statutory**) depletion, the company deducts a stated percentage of gross income as depletion expense. This percentage varies, depending on the type of natural resource, from a minimum of 5% to a maximum of 22%. Furthermore, the total depletion over the life of the asset for income tax purposes may exceed the cost of the asset less the expected residual value. Consequently, most companies use percentage depletion for income tax purposes and cost depletion for financial reporting. The percentage depletion in excess of cost depletion results in a permanent tax difference.

Permanent tax differences are discussed in Chapter 18.

SUMMARY

At the beginning of the chapter, we identified several objectives you would accomplish after reading the chapter. The objectives are listed below, each followed by a brief summary of the key points in the chapter discussion.

1. **Identify the factors involved in depreciation.** To record depreciation, a company considers the asset cost, its service life, its residual value, and the method of cost allocation.

2. **Explain the alternative methods of cost allocation, including activity- and time-based methods.** Accounting principles require that the method of cost allocation be systematic and rational. The available methods include activity (or use) methods, and time-based methods, including straight-line, sum of the years' digits, and declining balance.

3. **Record depreciation.** A company includes depreciation on manufacturing assets as a cost of the inventory produced and records the depreciation as an increase to the Goods in Process Inventory account. Depreciation on the remaining assets is expensed in the period.

4. **Explain the conceptual issues regarding depreciation methods.** The choice of a depreciation method has an impact on a company's income measurement and asset valuation. The method should be chosen so that it matches the cost of the asset against the benefits the asset produces. Additional factors that should be considered are repair and maintenance costs, changing prices, and the risk associated with the cash flows from the asset. Also the rate of return on the asset increases as it ages.

5. **Understand the disclosure of depreciation.** A company is required to disclose depreciation expense for the period, balances of major classes depreciable assets by nature or function, accumulated depreciation either by major classes or in total, and a general description of the method or methods used in computing depreciation.

6. **Understand additional depreciation methods, including group and composite depreciation.** Group depreciation is applied to homogeneous assets whereas composite depreciation is applied to heterogeneous assets. In both cases the individual assets are capitalized in a single asset account and this asset is treated as a single asset for depreciation. A gain or loss on disposal is only recognized when the final individual asset is disposed of. Under the retirement method, the cost of the old asset less its residual value is expensed when it is retired. Under the replacement method, the cost of the new asset less the residual value of the old asset is expensed when the new asset is acquired.

7. **Compute depreciation for partial periods.** Depreciation may be computed to the nearest whole month or to the nearest whole year. Alternatively, one-half year's depreciation may be computed on all assets purchased or sold during the year.

8. **Explain the impairment of noncurrent assets.** A company must review its property, plant, and equipment for impairment whenever events or changes in circumstances indicate the book value of the asset may not be recoverable. If the total expected cash flows (undiscounted) are less than the book value of the asset, an impairment loss is recognized. The impairment loss is the difference between the asset's book value and its lower fair value.

9. **Understand depreciation for income tax purposes.** Depreciation for income tax purposes uses the Modified Accelerated Cost Recovery System (MACRS). MACRS usually involves a shorter life, an accelerated method (except for buildings), and does not recognize a residual value.

10. **Explain changes and corrections of depreciation.** A change in the depreciation method for currently owned assets is accounted for by the cumulative-effect method. Adoption of a new depreciation method for newly acquired assets must be disclosed in the notes to the financial statements. A change in an estimate of the residual value or the service life of a currently owned asset is accounted for prospectively. Correction of an error in depreciation is treated as a prior period adjustment.

11. **Understand and record depletion.** Depletion is the allocation of the depletable cost for the consumption of a natural resource asset to the periods in which the benefits are received. A company normally records depletion using an activity method.

QUESTIONS

Q10-1 Distinguish among the use of the terms *depreciation*, *depletion*, and *amortization*.

Q10-2 Briefly explain the meaning of the four factors that are involved in the computation of a company's periodic charge for depreciation.

Q10-3 What is the *depreciation base*?

Q10-4 What is the objective of accounting for depreciation?

Q10-5 Explain how recording depreciation affects a company's (a) income statement, (b) balance sheet, and (c) statement of cash flows.

Q10-6 Does recording depreciation generate funds for the replacement of the asset? Explain.

Q10-7 Under what circumstances is depreciation a fixed cost or a variable cost?

Q10-8 What are the primary causes of depreciation? For each cause, indicate which depreciation method may be most appropriate. Would it be desirable to require all companies to use the same method?

Q10-9 Under what circumstances are accelerated methods of depreciation most appropriate?

Q10-10 Compare the group and composite methods of depreciation.

Q10-11 Compare the retirement and replacement methods of expense recognition.

Q10-12 Under what circumstances is an asset's depreciation amount not included in total in a company's current income statement?

Q10-13 In a year in which the cost of replacing an asset rises, should a company record depreciation for that asset? Why?

Q10-14 A company should use an accelerated depreciation method because of the large decline in the value of an asset early in its life. Evaluate this statement.

Q10-15 The manager of a utility stated that since its transmission lines are kept in good condition by regular repairs and maintenance and their efficiency remains constant, the lines do not depreciate. Do you agree with this statement?

Q10-16 What disclosures of depreciation are required in a company's financial statements and the accompanying notes?

Q10-17 Why may depreciation on a company's financial statements be different from depreciation it computed for income tax purposes?

Q10-18 How does a company's depletion for income tax purposes vary from its depletion for financial reporting purposes?

CASES

C O M M U N I C A T I O N

C10-1 Depreciation

The certified public accountant is frequently called upon by management for advice regarding methods of computing depreciation. Although the question arises less frequently, of comparable importance is whether the depreciation method should be based on the consideration of the assets as units, as a group, or as having a composite life.

Required

1. Briefly describe the depreciation methods based on treating assets as:

   a. Units
   b. A group or as having a composite life
2. Explain the arguments for and against the use of each of the two methods.
3. Explain how retirements are recorded under each of the two methods. (*AICPA adapted*)

C10-2 Capitalization and Depreciation

Gehl Company purchased significant amounts of new equipment this year to be used in its operations. The equipment was delivered by the suppliers, installed by Gehl, and placed into operation. Gehl purchased some for cash with discounts available for prompt payments. It purchased some under long-term payment plans, for which the interest charges approximate prevailing rates. As a result, Gehl is studying its capitalization and depreciation policies.

Required

1. What costs should Gehl capitalize for the new equipment purchased this year?
2. What factors cause the equipment to lose its future economic benefit?
3. What factors should be considered in computing the equipment's depreciation expense?
4. What theoretical justifications are there for the use of accelerated depreciation methods? (*AICPA adapted*)

C10-3 Capitalization and Depreciation

At the beginning of the year, Patrick Company acquired a computer to be used in its operations. The computer was delivered by the supplier, installed by Patrick, and placed into operation. The estimated useful life of the computer is five years, and its estimated residual (salvage) value is significant.

During the year, Patrick received cash in exchange for an automobile that was purchased in a prior year.

Required

1. a. What costs should Patrick capitalize for the computer?
   b. Explain the objective of depreciation accounting. (Do not discuss specific methods of depreciation.)
2. Explain the rationale for using accelerated depreciation methods.
3. How should Patrick account for and report the disposal of the automobile? (*AICPA adapted*)

C10-4 Straight-Line and Composite Depreciation

Portland Co. uses the straight-line depreciation method for depreciable assets. All assets are depreciated individually,
except manufacturing machinery, which is depreciated by the composite method.

During the year, Portland exchanged a delivery truck with Maine Co. for a larger delivery truck. It paid cash equal to 10% of the larger truck's value.

Required

1. Explain the factors that should influence Portland's selection of the straight-line depreciation method.
2. Explain how Portland should account for and report the truck exchange transaction.
3. a. What benefits should Portland derive from using the composite method rather than the individual basis for manufacturing machinery?
   b. How should Portland calculate the manufacturing machinery's annual depreciation expense in its first year of operation? (*AICPA adapted*)

C10-5 Operating and Capital Expenditures

Property, plant, and equipment (plant assets) generally represent a material portion of the total assets of most companies. Accounting for the acquisition and usage of such assets is, therefore, an important part of the financial reporting process.

Required

1. Distinguish between operating (revenue) and capital expenditures and explain why this distinction is important.
2. Briefly define depreciation as used in accounting.
3. Identify the factors that are relevant in determining the annual depreciation and explain whether these factors are determined objectively or whether they are based on judgment.
4. Explain why depreciation is usually shown in the net cash flow from operating activities section of the statement of cash flows. (*AICPA adapted*)

C R E A T I V E   A N D   C R I T I C A L   T H I N K I N G

C10-6 Depreciation Concepts

Depreciation continues to be one of the most controversial, difficult, and important problem areas in accounting.

Required

1. a. Explain the conventional accounting concept of depreciation accounting, and
   b. Discuss its conceptual merit with respect to (1) the value of the asset, (2) the amount(s) expensed, and (3) the discretion of management in selecting the method.
2. a. Explain the factors that should be considered when applying the conventional concept of depreciation to the determination of how the value of a newly
acquired computer system should be assigned to expense for financial reporting purposes. (Ignore income tax considerations for this case.)
   b. What depreciation methods might be used for the computer system? (*AICPA adapted*)

C10-7 Depreciation Concepts

Prepare a short report that evaluates each of the following statements separately:

1. "Since our plant was shut down for part of the year, we will not depreciate it. Depreciating it for the full year would increase our costs and overstate our inventory."

2. "I think we should have increasing depreciation each period because it will increase the funds recovered near the end of the asset's life when maintenance costs are high and we will need to replace the asset. Also, I think tax rates will be higher toward the end of the asset's life, so we will be better off to have larger depreciation then."

C10-8 Depreciation

May Manufacturing Company was organized January 2, 2004. During 2004, it has used in its reports to management the straight-line method of depreciating its plant assets.

On November 9, you are having a conference with May's officers to discuss the depreciation method to be used for income tax and stockholder reporting. The president of May has suggested the use of a new method, which he feels is more suitable than the straight-line method for the needs of the company during the period of rapid expansion of production and capacity that he foresees. The following is a schedule in which the proposed method is applied to a fixed asset with an original cost of $32,000, an estimated useful life of 5 years, and a scrap value of approximately $2,000.

Year	Years of Life Used	Fraction Rate	Depreciation Expense	Accumulated Depreciation, Year-End	Book Value at Year-End
1	1	1/15	$ 2,000	$ 2,000	$30,000
2	2	2/15	4,000	6,000	26,000
3	3	3/15	6,000	12,000	20,000
4	4	4/15	8,000	20,000	12,000
5	5	5/15	10,000	30,000	2,000

The president favors the new method because he has heard that:

1. It will increase the funds recovered during the years near the end of the asset's useful life when maintenance and replacement disbursements are high.
2. It will result in increased write-offs in later years, thereby reducing taxes.

Required

1. Explain the purpose and, hence, the nature of accounting for depreciation.
2. Is the president's proposal within the scope of generally accepted accounting principles? In making your decision, explain the circumstances, if any, under which the method would be reasonable and those, if any, under which it would not be reasonable.
3. The president wants your advice.
   a. Explain whether depreciation recovers or creates funds.
   b. Assume that the Internal Revenue Service accepts the proposed depreciation method in this particular case. If the proposed method were used for stockholder and tax reporting purposes, explain how it would affect the availability of funds generated by operations. (*AICPA adapted*)

C10-9 Asset Writedowns

NBC paid $401 million for the rights to televise the 1992 Summer Olympic Games, and it was widely reported that it had a loss of over $60 million. CBS purchased the rights to the 1992 and 1994 Winter Olympic Games for a combined $543 million. CBS reported a $322 million pretax loss on its baseball and football contracts in 1991.

Required

1. Under what conditions, if any, should NBC and CBS have written-down the value of their assets?
2. Does this situation allow opportunities for earnings management?

C10-10 Analyzing Coca-Cola's Property, Plant, and Equipment Disclosures

Refer to the financial statements and related notes of the Coca-Cola Company in Appendix A of this book.

Required

1. Which depreciation method does the company use? Why do you think the company selected this method?
2. Compute the estimated average age of the property, plant, and equipment.
3. Assuming the company estimates a residual value of 10% of the cost, compute the estimated average life of the property, plant, and equipment.
4. Recreate summary journal entries to record the transactions and events that affected property, plant, and equipment during 2001.

C10-11 Ethics and Depreciation Issues

You are auditing the financial records of a company and are reviewing the depreciation computations. Included in the assets are two buildings and numerous machines in each building. One of the buildings is used to manufacture components of toys and the other for assembly and packing, using the manufactured components as well as others purchased from suppliers. You see that the company uses straight-line depreciation over 40 years for the buildings and 20 years for the machinery. You decide to ask the CFO about these calculations, and he replies, "We use 40 years for the buildings because it is close to the 39 we use for tax. And our best guess is that we will replace the machines twice while we use the building. And the method is easy to use and most companies use it, don't they? Or have things changed that much since I was in college?" You feel as if you have annoyed the CFO with your questions, so you decide to leave. As you walk back to your office, you recall from earlier in the audit that the company uses FIFO and LIFO for different segments of its inventory and that all top-level managers receive bonuses based on reported income.

Required From financial reporting and ethical perspectives, what depreciation methods and lives would you recommend?

R E S E A R C H

C10-12 Researching GAAP

The Magic Movie Company has been formed to produce films for showing in movie theaters. The president knows that there are some unusual accounting issues regarding asset valuation and income recognition and has asked for your advice.

Required

1. Research the related generally accepted accounting principles and prepare a short memo to the president. Cite your references and applicable paragraph numbers.
2. Does this situation allow opportunities for earnings management?

C10-13 Researching GAAP

Scientific Software sells software to the oil industry. Its policy is to recognize revenue when it signs a licensing agreement for the software. It uses a 13-year amortization period for the software products it capitalizes. The president has asked you to evaluate these revenue recognition and amortization policies.

Required

1. Research the related generally accepted accounting principles and prepare a short memo to the president. Cite your references and applicable paragraph numbers.
2. Why do you think the company might have selected a 13-year amortization period? (*Adapted from* The Wall Street Journal, *11/6/90*)

MULTIPLE CHOICE

Select the best answer for each of the following.

M10-1 A method that excludes residual value from the base for the depreciation calculation is
  a. Straight-line
  b. Sum-of-the-years'-digits
  c. Double-declining-balance
  d. Productive-output

Items 2 through 4 are based on the following information:

Vorst Corporation's schedule of depreciable assets at December 31, 2004 was as follows:

Asset	Cost	Accumulated Depreciation	Acquisition Date	Residual Value
A	$100,000	$ 64,000	2003	$20,000
B	55,000	36,000	2002	10,000
C	70,000	33,600	2002	14,000
	$225,000	$133,600		$44,000

Vorst takes a full year's depreciation expense in the year of an asset's acquisition, and no depreciation expense in the year of an asset's disposition. The estimated useful life of each depreciable asset is 5 years.

M10-2 Vorst depreciates asset A on the double-declining-balance method. How much depreciation expense should Vorst record in 2005 for asset A?
  a. $32,000
  b. $25,600
  c. $14,400
  d. $6,400

M10-3 Using the same depreciation method as used in 2002, 2003, and 2004, how much depreciation expense should Vorst record in 2005 for asset B?
  a. $6,000
  b. $9,000
  c. $11,000
  d. $12,000

M10-4 Vorst depreciates asset C by the straight-line method. On June 30, 2005, Vorst sold asset C for $28,000 cash. How much gain (loss) should Vorst record in 2005 on the disposal of asset C?
  a. $2,800
  b. ($2,800)
  c. ($5,600)
  d. ($8,400)

M10-5 The composite depreciation method
  a. Is applied to a group of homogeneous assets
  b. Is an accelerated method of depreciation
  c. Does not recognize gain or loss on the retirement of single assets in the group
  d. Excludes residual value from the base of the depreciation calculation

M10-6 On July 1, 2003, Mundo Corporation purchased factory equipment for $50,000. Residual value was estimated at $2,000. The equipment will be depreciated over 10 years using the double-declining-balance method. Counting the year of acquisition as one-half year, Mundo should record 2004 depreciation expense of
  a. $7,680
  b. $9,000
  c. $9,600
  d. $10,000

M10-7 A fixed asset with a 5-year estimated useful life is sold during the second year. How would the use of the straight-line method of depreciation instead of the double-declining-balance method of depreciation affect the amount of gain or loss on the sale of the fixed asset?

	Gain	Loss
a.	No effect	No effect
b.	No effect	Increase
c.	Decrease	Increase
d.	Increase	Decrease

M10-8 Crowder Company acquired a tract of land containing an extractable natural resource. Crowder is required by the purchase contract to restore the land to a condition suitable for recreational use after it has extracted the natural resource. Geological surveys estimate that the recoverable reserves will be 5,000,000 tons and that the land will have a value of $1,000,000 after restoration. Relevant cost information follows:

Land	$9,000,000
Estimated restoration costs	1,500,000

If Crowder maintains no inventories of extracted material, what should be the depletion expense per ton of extracted material?

a. $2.10
b. $1.90
c. $1.80
d. $1.60

M10-9 A machine with a 4-year estimated useful life and an estimated 15% residual value was acquired on January 1. Would depreciation expense using the sum-of-the-years'-digits method be higher or lower than depreciation expense using the double-declining-balance method in the first and second years?

	First year	Second year
a.	Higher	Higher
b.	Higher	Lower
c.	Lower	Higher
d.	Lower	Lower

M10-10 At the end of the expected useful life of a depreciable asset with an estimated 15% residual value, the accumulated depreciation would equal the original cost of the asset under which of the following depreciation methods?

	Straight-line	Sum-of-the-years'-digits
a.	Yes	Yes
b.	No	No
c.	Yes	No
d.	No	Yes

(*AICPA adapted*)

EXERCISES

E10-1 *Depreciation Methods* The Gruman Company purchased a machine for $220,000 on January 2, 2004. It made the following estimates:

Service life	5 years or 10,000 hours
Production	200,000 units
Residual value	$20,000

In 2004, the company uses the machine for 1,800 hours and produces 44,000 units.

Required Compute the depreciation for 2004 under each of the following methods:

1. Straight-line
2. Hours worked
3. Units of output

E10-2 *Depreciation Methods* The Sorter Company purchased equipment for $200,000 on January 2, 2004. The equipment has an estimated service life of 8 years and an estimated residual value of $20,000.

Required Compute the depreciation for 2004 under each of the following methods:

1. Straight-line
2. Sum-of-the-years'-digits
3. Double-declining-balance
4. Compute the company's return on assets (net income divided by average total assets, as we discussed in Chapter 5) for each method in 2004 if the income before depreciation is $100,000. For simplicity, use ending assets, and ignore interest, income taxes, and other assets.

E10-3 *Acquisition Cost and Depreciation* Reveille, Inc. purchased Machine #204 on April 1, 2004 and placed the machine into production on April 3, 2004. The following information is relevant to Machine #204:

Price	$60,000
Freight-in costs	2,500
Preparation and installation costs	3,900
Labor costs during regular production operation	10,200
Credit terms	2/10, n/30
Total productive output	138,500 units

The company expects that the machine could be used for 10 years, after which the salvage value would be zero. However, Reveille, Inc. intends to use the machine only 8 years, after which it expects to be able to sell it for $9,800. The invoice for Machine #204 was paid April 10, 2004. The number of units produced in 2004 and 2005 were 23,200 and 29,000, respectively. Reveille computes depreciation to the nearest whole month.

Required Compute the depreciation for the years indicated, using the following methods (round your answer to the nearest dollar):

1. 2004: Units of production
2. 2005: Sum-of-the-years'-digits method (*Contributed by Norma C. Powell*)

E10-4   *Depreciation Methods*   The Nickle Company purchased an asset for $17,000 on January 2, 2004. The asset has an expected residual value of $1,000. The depreciation expense for 2004 and 2005 is shown next for three alternative depreciation methods:

Year	Method A	Method B	Method C
2004	$4,000	$6,400	$6,375
2005	4,000	4,800	3,984

Required

1. Which depreciation method is the company using in each example?
2. Compute the depreciation expense for 2006 and 2007 under each method.

E10-5   *Depreciation and Rate of Return*   The Burrell Company purchased a machine for $20,000 on January 2, 2004. The machine has an estimated service life of 5 years and a zero estimated residual value. The asset earns income before depreciation and income taxes of $10,000 each year. The tax rate is 30%.

Required Compute the rate of return earned (on the average net asset value) by the company each year of the asset's life under the straight-line and the double-declining-balance depreciation methods. Assume that the machine is the company's only asset.

E10-6   *Determination of Acquisition Cost*   On January 1, 2003, the Emming Corporation purchased some machinery. The machinery has an estimated life of 10 years and an estimated residual value of $5,000. The depreciation on this machinery was $20,000 in 2005.

Required Compute the acquisition cost of the equipment under the following depreciation methods:

1. Straight-line
2. Sum-of-the-years'-digits
3. Double-declining-balance

E10-7   *Group Depreciation*   The Loban Company purchased four cars for $9,000 each, and expects that they would be sold in 3 years for $1,500 each. The company uses group depreciation on a straight-line basis.

Required

1. Prepare journal entries to record the acquisition and the first year's depreciation.
2. If one of the cars is sold at the beginning of the second year for $7,000, what journal entry is required?

E10-8   *Composite Depreciation*   The Wilcox Company acquires four machines that have the following characteristics:

Machine	Cost	Estimated Residual Value	Estimated Service Life
A	$26,000	$2,000	6 years
B	19,000	1,000	9
C	30,000	5,000	5
D	28,000	—	7

Required

1. Prepare journal entries to record the acquisition and the first year's depreciation, assuming that the composite method is used on a straight-line basis.
2. If the company sells machine B after 4 years for $10,000, prepare the journal entry.
3. What arguments may be used to support the composite depreciation method?

E10-9   *Retirement and Replacement Methods*   The Rifkin Company replaced 100 tools at a cost of $30 each. The old tools originally cost $20 each and have no residual value.

Required

1. Prepare the journal entries to record the replacement under the retirement method.
2. Prepare the journal entries to record the replacement under the replacement method.

E10-10 **Depreciation** On January 2, 2004, Lapar Corporation purchased a machine for $50,000. Lapar paid shipping expenses of $500, as well as installation costs of $1,200. The company estimated that the machine would have a useful life of 10 years and a salvage value of $3,000. In January 2005, the company made additions costing $3,600 to the machine in order to comply with pollution-control ordinances. These additions neither prolonged the life of the machine nor increased the salvage value.

Required If Lapar records depreciation under the straight-line method, how much is the depreciation expense for 2005? (*AICPA adapted*)

E10-11 **Partial Periods** On May 10, 2004, the Horan Company purchased equipment for $25,000. The equipment has an estimated service life of 5 years and zero residual value. Assume that straight-line depreciation is used.

Required Compute the depreciation for 2004 for each of the following four alternatives:

1. The company computes depreciation to the nearest day. (Use 12 months of 30 days each.)
2. The company computes depreciation to the nearest month. Assets purchased in the first half of the month are considered owned for the whole month.
3. The company computes depreciation to the nearest whole year. Assets purchased in the first half of the year are considered owned for the whole year.
4. The company records one-half year's depreciation on all assets purchased during the year.

E10-12 **Asset Impairment** On January 1, 2000, the Vallahara Company purchased machinery for $650,000 which it installed in a rented factory. It is depreciating the machinery over 12 years by the straight-line method to a residual value of $50,000. Late in 2004, because of increasing competition in the industry, the company believes that its asset may be impaired and will have a remaining useful life of 5 years, over which it estimates the asset will produce total cash inflows of $1,000,000 and will incur total cash outflows of $825,000. The cash flows are independent of the company's other activities and will occur evenly each year. The company is not able to determine the fair value based on a current selling price of the machinery. The company's discount rate is 10%.

Required

1. Prepare schedules to determine whether, at the end of 2004, the machinery is impaired and, if so, the impairment loss to be recognized.
2. If the machinery is impaired, prepare the journal entry to record the impairment.

E10-13 **Depreciation for Financial Statements and Income Tax Purposes** The Dinkle Company purchased equipment for $50,000. It has an estimated residual value of $5,000 and an expected useful life of 10 years. The company uses straight-line depreciation for its financial statements.

Required What is the difference between the company's income before taxes reported on its financial statements and the taxable income reported on its tax return in each of the first two years of the asset's life if the asset was purchased on January 2, 2004 and its MACRS life is 5 years?

E10-14 **Changes and Corrections of Depreciation** The Bailand Company purchased a building for $210,000 that had an estimated residual value of $10,000 and an estimated service life of 10 years. The company purchased the building 4 years ago, and has used straight-line depreciation. At the beginning of the fifth year (before it records depreciation for the year), the following *independent* situations occur:

1. The company changes to the sum-of-the-years'-digits method.
2. The company estimates that the asset has 8 years' life remaining (for a total of 12 years).
3. The company discovers that the estimated residual value has been ignored in the computation of the depreciation.

Required For each of the independent situations, prepare all the journal entries relating to the building for the fifth year. Ignore income taxes.

E10-15 **Change in Depreciation Method** The Wing Company purchased a machine on January 1, 2001 for $240,000. At the date of acquisition, the machine had an estimated useful life of 10 years with an estimated salvage value of $20,000. The company is depreciating the machine on a straight-line basis. On January 1, 2004, Wing appropriately adopted the sum-of-the-years'-digits method of depreciation for this machine.

Required

1. Prepare a schedule computing the book value of this machine, net of accumulated depreciation, that Wing would include in its balance sheet at December 31, 2004. Show supporting computations in good form.
2. Prepare a schedule computing the cumulative effect on prior years of changing to a different depreciation method for the year ended December 31, 2004. Assume that the income tax rate was 50% in all years. Show supporting computations in good form. (*AICPA adapted*)

E10-16 **Depletion** The Feller Company purchased a site for a limestone quarry for $100,000 on January 2, 2004. It estimates that the quarry will yield 400,000 tons of limestone. It expects to voluntarily incur restoration costs of $20,000, after which the land could be sold for $10,000. In 2004, 80,000 tons were quarried and 60,000 tons sold. Costs of production (excluding depletion) are $4 per ton.

Required

1. Compute the depletion cost per ton.
2. Compute the total cost of the inventory at December 31, 2004.
3. Compute the total cost of goods sold for 2004.

E10-17 **Depletion** The Lorton Company acquired land containing coal. Lorton will voluntarily restore the land to a condition suitable for recreational use after it has extracted the coal. Geological surveys estimate that the recoverable reserves will be 4,000,000 tons and that the land will have a value of $1 million after restoration. Relevant cost information follows:

Land	$12,000,000
Estimated restoration costs	1,200,000

Required If Lorton maintains no inventories of coal, what is the depletion expense per ton of coal? (*AICPA adapted*)

PROBLEMS

P10-1 **Depreciation Methods** The Winsey Company purchased equipment on January 2, 2004 for $700,000. The equipment has the following characteristics:

Estimated service life	20 years	Estimated residual value	$50,000
	100,000 hours		
	950,000 units of output		

During 2004 and 2005, the company used the machine for 4,500 and 5,500 hours, respectively, and produced 40,000 and 60,000 units, respectively.

Required Compute the depreciation for 2004 and 2005 under each of the following methods:

1. Straight-line
2. Hours worked
3. Units of output
4. Sum-of-the-years'-digits
5. Double-declining-balance
6. 150%-declining-balance
7. Compute the company's return on assets (net income divided by average total assets, as discussed in Chapter 5) for each method for 2004 and 2005, assuming that income before depreciation is $100,000. For simplicity, use ending assets, and ignore interest, income taxes, and other assets.

P10-2 **Depreciation Methods** The Lord Company purchased a machine on January 2, 2004 for $70,000. The machine had an expected residual value of $10,000, an expected life of 8 years or 24,000 hours, and a capacity to produce 100,000 units. During 2004, the company produced 12,000 units in 2,500 hours. In 2005, the company produced 15,000 units in 3,000 hours.

Required Prepare a schedule showing the depreciation for 2004 and 2005 and the book value of the asset at the end of 2004 and 2005 for each of the following methods:

1. Straight-line
2. Hours worked
3. Units of output

P10-3 *Depreciation Methods* The Sayers Company purchased a building for $250,000 on January 2, 2004. The building has an expected residual value of $20,000 at the end of its expected life of 20 years.

Required Prepare a schedule showing the depreciation for 2004 and 2005 and the book value on December 31, 2004 and December 31, 2005 for each of the following methods:

1. Straight-line
2. Sum-of-the-years'-digits
3. Double-declining-balance
4. 150%-declining-balance
5. Compute the company's return on assets (net income divided by average total assets, as discussed in Chapter 5) for each method in 2004 and 2005 assuming that income before depreciation is $50,000. For simplicity, use ending assets, and ignore interest, income taxes, and other assets. Why does the rate of return increase each year?

See WebTutor for annotated problem solution.

P10-4 *Fixed Percentage of Declining Balance* The Tubbs Company purchased a machine for $8,000 that has an estimated residual value of $1,000 and a life of 3 years.

Required

1. Compute the depreciation rate under the fixed-percentage-of-the-declining-balance method.
2. Compute the depreciation for each year of the asset's life.

P10-5 *Changing Depreciation* The Kam Company purchased a machine on January 2, 2004 for $20,000. The machine had an expected life of 8 years and a residual value of $300. The double-declining-balance method of depreciation is used.

Required

1. Compute the depreciation for each year of the asset's life.
2. Assuming that the company has a policy of always changing to the straight-line method at the midpoint of the asset's life, compute the depreciation for each year of the asset's life.
3. Assuming that the company always changes to the straight-line method at the beginning of the year when the annual straight-line amount exceeds the double-declining-balance amount, compute the depreciation for each year of the asset's life.

P10-6 *Cost of Asset and Depreciation Method* The Heist Company purchased a machine on January 2, 2004 and uses the 150%-declining-balance depreciation method. The machine has an expected life of 10 years and an expected residual value of $5,000. The following costs relate to the acquisition and use of the machine during the first year of its operations:

Invoice price	$50,000	Testing	$1,100
Discounts available and taken	1,000	Normal spoilage of materials during the year	750
Freight	700	Abnormal spoilage of materials during the year	250
Installation	900	Wages of machine operator	15,000

Required Compute the depreciation expense for 2004 and 2005.

P10-7 *Depreciation and Partial Periods* The following assets are owned by the Dinnell Company:

	Asset		
	A	B	C
Year purchased	2002	2003	2004
Cost	$20,000	$40,000	$100,000
Expected life	5 years	8 years	10 years
Residual value	$2,000	—	$10,000
Depreciation method	Straight-line	Sum-of-the-years'-digits	Double-declining-balance

In the year of acquisition and retirement of an asset, the company records depreciation for one-half year. During 2005, asset A was sold for $7,000.

Required Prepare the journal entries to record depreciation on each asset for 2002 through 2005 and the sale of asset A.

P10-8   *Group and Composite Depreciation*   The Cheadle Company purchased a fleet of 20 delivery trucks for $8,000 each on January 2, 2004. It decided to use composite depreciation on a straight-line basis, and calculated the depreciation from the following schedule:

Year	Number of Trucks to Be Retired at Year-End	Estimated Residual Value per Truck
2005	2	$4,000
2006	6	4,000
2007	8	2,000
2008	4	—

The company actually retired the trucks according to the following schedule (assume each truck was retired at the beginning of the year):

Year	Number of Trucks Retired	Total Proceeds from Retirements
2005	1	$ 4,000
2006	3	11,000
2007	6	19,000
2008	5	6,000
2009	3	4,000
2010	2	1,000

Required

1. Prepare the journal entries necessary to record the preceding events.
2. Assume that the company expected all the trucks to last 4 years and be retired for $1,600 each. Using group depreciation, prepare journal entries for all 6 years, assuming the company retired the trucks as shown by the latter schedule.

P10-9   *Composite Depreciation*   The Borrell Company purchased four delivery trucks on January 2, 2004 for $22,000 each. The company expected two of the trucks to last 5 years and have a residual value of $3,500 each. The other two trucks had an expected life of 8 years and no residual value. The company uses straight-line depreciation on a composite basis.

Required Prepare journal entries to record the following events:

1. January 1, 2006. One of the two trucks expected to last 5 years is destroyed in an accident. The truck was not insured and the scrap value is $400.
2. January 5, 2006. A new truck is acquired for $26,000. It has an expected life of 4 years and a residual value of $3,920.
3. Depreciation expense for 2006.

P10-10   *Asset Impairment*   On January 1, 1999, the Borstad Company purchased a factory for $180,000 and machinery for $1 million. It is depreciating the factory over 30 years and the machinery over 20 years, both by the straight-line method to zero residual values. Late in 2004, because of technological changes in the industry and reduced selling prices for its products, the company believes that its asset(s) may be impaired and will have a remaining useful life of 8 years. The cash flows from the factory and machinery are not separable, and are independent of the company's other activities. The company estimates that the asset will produce cash inflows of $400,000 and will incur cash outflows of $295,000 each year for the next 8 years. It is not able to determine the fair value of the asset based on a current selling price of the factory and machinery. The company's discount rate is 12%.

Required

1. Prepare schedules to determine whether, at the end of 2004, the machinery is impaired and, if so, the impairment loss to be recognized.
2. Prepare the journal entry to record the impairment.
3. How would your answer to Requirement 1 change if the discount rate was 16% and the cash flows were expected to continue for 6 years?
4. How would your answer change if management planned to implement efficiencies that would save $10,000 each year?

P10-11 ***Depreciation for Financial Statements and Income Tax Purposes*** The Hunter Company purchased a light truck on January 2, 2004 for $18,000. The truck, which will be used for deliveries, has the following characteristics:

Estimated life: 5 years
Estimated residual value: $3,000
Depreciation for financial statements: straight-line
Depreciation for income tax purposes: MACRS (3-year-life)

From 2004 through 2008, each year, the company had sales of $100,000, cost of goods sold of $60,000, and operating expenses (excluding depreciation) of $15,000. The truck was disposed of on December 31, 2008 for $2,000.

Required

1. Prepare an income statement for financial reporting through pretax accounting income for each of the 5 years, 2004 through 2008.
2. Prepare, instead, an income statement for income tax purposes through taxable income for each of the 5 years, 2004 through 2008.
3. Compare the total income for all 5 years under Requirement 1 and Requirement 2.

P10-12 ***Depletion*** On January 2, 2004, the Whistler Company purchased land for $450,000, from which it is estimated that 400,000 tons of ore could be extracted. It estimates that it will cost $80,000 to voluntarily restore the land, after which it could be sold for $30,000.

During 2004 the company mined 80,000 tons and sold 50,000 tons. During 2005, the company mined 100,000 tons and sold 120,000 tons. At the beginning of 2006, the company spent an additional $100,000, which increased the reserves by 60,000 tons. In 2006, the company mined 140,000 tons and sold 130,000 tons. The company uses a FIFO cost flow assumption.

Required

1. Calculate the depletion included in the income statement and ending inventory for 2004, 2005, and 2006.
2. Prepare the natural resources section of the balance sheet on December 31, 2004, 2005, and 2006, assuming that an accumulated depletion account is used.

P10-13 ***Depletion*** On July 1, 2004, the Amplex Company purchased a coal mine for $2 million. The estimated capacity of the mine was 800,000 tons. During 2004, the company mines 10,000 tons of coal per month and sells 9,000 tons per month. The selling price is $30 per ton and production costs (excluding depletion and depreciation) are $8 per ton. At the end of the mine's life, it is expected that it will cost $300,000 to voluntarily restore the land, after which it can be sold for $100,000. The company also purchased some temporary housing for the miners at a cost of $170,000. The housing has an expected life of 10 years but is expected to be sold for $10,000 at the end of the mine's life. The company uses the FIFO cost flow assumption.

Required

1. Compute the company's expenses included on the 2004 income statement.
2. Compute the cost of the company's inventory at December 31, 2004.
3. In January 2005 a new estimate indicated that the capacity of the mine was only 500,000 tons at that time. Compute the company's expenses included on the 2005 income statement if the company mines and sells 10,000 tons per month.

P10-14 ***Changes and Corrections of Depreciation*** During 2004, the controller of the Ryel Company asked you to prepare correcting journal entries for the following three situations:

1. Machine A was purchased for $40,000 on January 1, 2002. It had an estimated residual value of $5,000 and an estimated service life of 10 years. It has been depreciated under the double-declining-balance method for 2 years. Now, at the beginning of the third year, Ryel has decided to change to the straight-line method.
2. Machine B was purchased for $50,000 on January 1, 1999. Straight-line depreciation has been recorded for 5 years, and the Accumulated Depreciation account has a balance of $25,000. The estimated residual value remains at $5,000, but the service life is now estimated to be 1 year longer than estimated originally.
3. Machine C was purchased for $20,000 on January 1, 2003. Double-declining-balance depreciation has been recorded for 1 year. The estimated residual value of the machine is $2,000 and the estimated service life is 5 years. The computation of the depreciation erroneously included the estimated residual value.

Required Prepare any necessary correcting journal entries for each situation. Also prepare the journal entry necessary for each situation to record the depreciation for 2004. (Assume that the debit is to Depreciation Expense.)

P10-15 *Adjusting Entries* You are engaged in the examination of the financial statements of the Madle Corporation for the year ended December 31, 2004. The schedules for the property, plant, and equipment and the related accumulated depreciation accounts which follow have been prepared by the client. You have checked the opening balances to your prior year's audit workpapers. Your examination reveals the following information:

1. All equipment is depreciated on the straight-line basis (no salvage value taken into consideration) using the following estimated lives: buildings 25 years, all other items 10 years. The company's policy is to take one-half year's depreciation on all asset acquisitions and disposals during the year.
2. The company completed the construction of a wing on the plant building on June 30. The useful life of the building was not extended by this addition. The lowest construction bid received was $17,500, the amount recorded in the Buildings account. Company personnel were used to construct the addition at a cost of $16,000 (materials $7,500, labor $5,500, and overhead $3,000).
3. On August 18, $5,000 was paid for paving and fencing a portion of land owned by the company and used as a parking lot for employees. The expenditure was capitalized to the Land account.
4. The amount shown in the Machinery and Equipment asset retirement column represents cash received on September 4 upon disposal of a machine purchased 4 years ago in July for $48,000. The bookkeeper recorded depreciation expense of $3,500 on this machine in 2004.
5. Sydney City donated land and building appraised at $10,000 and $40,000, respectively, to the Madle Corporation for a plant. On September 1, the company began operating the plant. Because no costs were involved, the bookkeeper made no entry to record the transaction.

MADLE CORP.
Analysis of Property, Plant, and Equipment, and of
Related Accumulated Depreciation Accounts
Year Ended December 31, 2004

Description	Final 12/31/03	Additions	Retirements	Per Books 12/31/04
Assets:				
Land	$ 22,500	$ 5,000	—	$ 27,500
Buildings	120,000	17,500	—	137,500
Machinery and Equipment	385,000	40,400	$26,000	399,400
	$527,500	$62,900	$26,000	$564,400
Accumulated Depreciation:				
Buildings	$ 60,000	$ 5,150*		$ 65,150
Machinery and Equipment	173,250	39,220*		212,470
	$233,250	$44,370		$277,620

*Depreciation expenses for the year

Required Prepare the formal journal entries that you would suggest at December 31, 2004 to adjust the accounts for the transactions noted previously. Disregard income tax implications. The books have not been closed. Computations should be rounded off to the nearest dollar. (*AICPA adapted*)

P10-16 *Comprehensive* On December 31, 2004, the Vail Company owned the following assets:

Asset	Date of Purchase	Cost	Accumulated Depreciation	Life in Years	Residual Value
Building	1/1/2002	$50,000	$ 3,750[a]	40	$ 0
Office machinery	1/1/2002	20,000	9,760[b]	10	2,000
Office fixtures	1/1/2002	30,000	20,000[c]	5	5,000

a. Straight-line depreciation
b. Double-declining-balance depreciation
c. Sum-of-the-years'-digits depreciation

The company computes depreciation and amortization expense to the nearest whole year. During 2005, the company engaged in the following transactions:

Jan. 3 Extended the building at a cost of $30,000. The extension provided an addition to the service potential of the building.

Mar. 7 Sold a piece of office machinery that had originally cost $4,000 and that had accumulated depreciation of $1,952 on December 31, 2004. The machine was sold for $3,000.

Apr. 28 Obtained a patent on an invention by paying $7,000. The company expected that the patent would provide protection against competition for 10 years.

May 16 Purchased office fixtures and office machinery for $9,200. The supplier reduced the price because of the joint purchase. If purchased separately, the office fixtures would have cost $6,000 and the office machinery $4,000. Delivery costs paid by Vail were $200. The machinery was accidentally damaged during installation and cost $230 to repair. The office fixtures have an estimated life of 5 years and a residual value of $250. The office machinery has an estimated life of 10 years and a residual value of $500.

Aug. 10 Exchanged the president's desk (classified as office fixtures) for a desk belonging to a friend of the president. The desk had cost $600 and had accumulated depreciation on December 31, 2004 of $400 and an estimated residual value of $100. The new desk had a value of $900 and $700 cash was paid.

Oct. 20 Serviced and adjusted the office machinery at a cost of $125.

Required

1. Check the accuracy of the accumulated depreciation balances at December 31, 2004. (Round to the nearest whole dollar in all requirements.)
2. Prepare journal entries to record the preceding events in 2005, as well as the year-end recording of depreciation expense.
3. Prepare an Accumulated Depreciation account for each category of assets, enter the beginning balance, post the journal entries from Requirement 2, and compute the ending balance.

P10-17 **Comprehensive** On January 2, 2004, Brock Corporation purchased a tract of land (site number 101) with a building for $600,000. Additionally, Brock paid a real estate broker's commission of $36,000, legal fees of $6,000, and title guarantee insurance of $18,000. The closing statement indicated that the land value was $500,000 and the building value was $100,000. Shortly after acquisition, the building was razed at a cost of $75,000.

Brock entered into a $3,000,000 fixed-price contract with Barnett Builders, Inc. on March 2, 2004 for the construction of an office building on land site number 101. The building was completed and occupied on September 30, 2005. Additional construction costs were incurred as follows:

Plans, specifications, and blueprints	$12,000
Architects' fees for design and supervision	95,000

The company estimates that the building will have a 40-year life from date of completion and decides to use the 150%-declining-balance depreciation method.

To finance the construction cost, Brock borrowed $3,000,000 on March 2, 2004. The loan is payable in 10 annual installments of $300,000 plus interest at the rate of 14%. Brock's average amounts of accumulated building construction expenditures were as follows:

For the period March 2 to December 31, 2004	$ 900,000
For the period January 1 to September 30, 2005	2,300,000

Required

1. Prepare a schedule that discloses the individual costs making up the balance in the Land account with respect to land site number 101 as of September 30, 2005.
2. Prepare a schedule that discloses the individual costs that the company should capitalize in the Office Building account as of September 30, 2005. Show supporting computations in good form.
3. Prepare a schedule showing the depreciation expense computation of the office building for the year ended December 31, 2005. (*AICPA adapted*)

P10-18 **Comprehensive** Logan Corporation, a manufacturer of steel products, began operations on October 1, 2003. The accounting department of Logan has started the fixed asset and depreciation schedule shown as follows:

Assets	Acquisition Date	Cost	Salvage	Depreciation Method	Estimated Life in Years	Depreciation Expense Year Ended September 30 2004	2005
Land A	October 1, 2003	(1) ___	N/A*	N/A	N/A	N/A	N/A
Building A	October 1, 2003	(2) ___	$47,500	Straight line	(3) ___	$14,000	(4) ___
Land B	October 3, 2003	(5) ___	N/A	N/A	N/A	N/A	N/A
Building B	Under construction	$210,000 to date	—	Straight line	30	—	(6) ___
Donated equipment	October 3, 2003	(7) ___	2,000	150% declining balance	10	(8) ___	(9) ___
Machinery A	October 3, 2003	(10) ___	5,500	Sum of the years' digits	10	(11) ___	(12) ___
Machinery B	October 1, 2004	(13) ___	—	Straight line	15	—	(14) ___

* "N/A" means "not applicable"

You have been asked to assist in completing this schedule. In addition to ascertaining that the data already on the schedule are correct, you have obtained the following information from the company's records and personnel:

1. Depreciation is computed from the first of the month of acquisition to the first of the month of disposition.
2. Land A and building A were acquired from a predecessor corporation. Logan paid $812,500 for the land and building together. At the time of acquisition, the land had an appraised value of $72,000 and the building had an appraised value of $828,000.
3. Land B was acquired on October 3, 2003 in exchange for 3,000 newly issued shares of Logan's common stock. At the date of acquisition, the stock had a par value of $5 per share and a fair value of $25 per share. During October 2003, Logan paid $10,400 to demolish an existing building on this land so that it could construct a new building.
4. Construction of building B on the newly acquired land began on October 2, 2004. By September 30, 2005 Logan had paid $210,000 of the estimated total construction costs of $300,000. Estimated completion and occupancy are July 2006.
5. Certain equipment was donated to the corporation by a local university. An independent appraisal of the equipment when donated placed the fair value at $16,000 and the salvage at $2,000.
6. Machinery A's total cost of $110,000 includes installation expense of $550 and normal repairs and maintenance of $11,000. Salvage value is estimated at $5,500. Machinery A was sold on February 1, 2005.
7. On October 1, 2004, machinery B was acquired with a down payment of $4,000 and the remaining payments to be made in ten annual installments of $4,000 each beginning October 1, 2005. The prevailing interest rate was 10%. The data that follow were abstracted from present value tables:

Present Value of $1.00 at 10%		Present Value of Annuity of $1.00 in Arrears at 10%	
10 years	0.386	10 years	6.145
11 years	0.350	11 years	6.495
15 years	0.239	15 years	7.606

Required For each numbered item in the schedule, supply the correct amount next to the corresponding number. Round each answer to the nearest dollar. Show supporting computations in good form. (*AICPA adapted*)

P10-19 **Errors** Soon after December 31, 2004 the auditor requested a depreciation schedule for trucks of the Jarrett Trucking Company, showing the additions, retirements, depreciation, and other data affecting the income of the company in the 4-year period 2001 to 2004, inclusive. The following data were in the truck account as of January 1, 2001:

Truck no. 1	Purchased January 1, 1998	$12,000
Truck no. 2	Purchased July 1, 1998	10,400
Truck no. 3	Purchased January 1, 2000	12,800
Truck no. 4	Purchased July 1, 2000	15,000
Balance January 1, 2001		$50,200

The Accumulated Depreciation—Trucks account, previously adjusted to January 1, 2001 and duly entered in the ledger, had a balance on that date of $16,460. This amount represented the straight-line depreciation on the four trucks from the respective dates of purchase, based on a 5-year life and no residual value. No debits had been made to this account prior to January 1, 2001.

Transactions between January 1, 2001 and December 31, 2004 and their record in the ledger were as follows:

1. July 1, 2001: Truck no. 1 was sold for $1,000 cash. The entry was a debit to Cash and a credit to Trucks, $1,000.
2. January 1, 2002: Truck no. 3 was traded for a larger one (no. 5) with a 5-year life. The agreed purchase price was $12,000. The Jarrett Company paid the other company (which was also a trucking company) $1,780 cash on the transaction. The entry was a debit to Trucks, $1,780, and a credit to Cash, $1,780.
3. July 1, 2003: Truck no. 4 was damaged in a wreck to such an extent that it was sold as junk for $50 cash. Jarrett Company received $950 from the insurance company. The entry made by the bookkeeper was a debit to Cash, $1,000, and credits to Miscellaneous Revenue, $50, and Trucks, $950.
4. July 1, 2003: A new truck (no. 6) was acquired for $12,000 cash and debited at that amount to the Trucks account. The truck has a 5-year life.

Entries for depreciation had been made at the close of each year as follows: 2001, $8,840; 2002, $5,436; 2003, $4,146; 2004, $2,856.

Required

1. For each of the 4 years, calculate separately the increase or decrease in earnings arising from the company's errors in determining or entering depreciation or in recording transactions affecting trucks.
2. Prove your work by one compound journal entry as of December 31, 2004; the adjustment of the Trucks account is to reflect the correct balances, assuming that the books have not been closed for 2004.

P10-20 *Comprehensive* Information for Blake Corporation's property, plant, and equipment for 2004 is:

Account Balances at January 1, 2004

	Debit	Credit
Land	$ 150,000	
Building	1,200,000	
Accumulated depreciation		$263,100
Machinery and equipment	900,000	
Accumulated depreciation		250,000
Automotive equipment	115,000	
Accumulated depreciation		84,600

Depreciation Method and Useful Life

Building: 150%-declining-balance; 25 years.
Machinery and equipment: Straight-line; 10 years.
Automotive equipment: Sum-of-the-years'-digits; 4 years.
Leasehold improvements: Straight-line.
The residual value of the depreciable assets is immaterial.
Depreciation is computed to the nearest month.

Transactions during 2004 and other information were as follows:

1. On January 2, 2004, Blake purchased a new car for $10,000 cash and a trade-in of a 2-year-old car with a cost of $9,000 and a book value of $2,700. The new car has a cash price of $12,000; the market value of the trade-in is not known.
2. On April 1, 2004, a machine purchased for $23,000 on April 1, 1999 was destroyed by fire. Blake recovered $15,500 from its insurance company.
3. On May 1, 2004, costs of $168,000 were incurred to improve leased office premises. The leasehold improvements have a useful life of 8 years. The related lease, which terminates on December 31, 2010, is renewable for an additional 6-year term. The decision to renew will be made in 2010 based on office space needs at that time.
4. On July 1, 2004, machinery and equipment were purchased at a total invoice cost of $280,000; additional costs of $5,000 for freight and $25,000 for installation were incurred.
5. Blake determined that the automotive equipment comprising the $115,000 balance at January 1, 2004 would have been depreciated at a total amount of $18,000 for the year ended December 31, 2004.

Required

1. For each asset classification, prepare schedules showing depreciation and amortization expense, and accumulated depreciation and amortization that would appear on Blake's income statement for the year ended December 31, 2004 and on the balance sheet at December 31, 2004, respectively.
2. Prepare a schedule showing the gain or loss from disposal of assets that would appear in Blake's income statement for the year ended December 31, 2004.
3. Prepare the property, plant, and equipment section of Blake's December 31, 2004 balance sheet. (*AICPA adapted*)

P10-21 *Comprehensive* The Plant Asset and Accumulated Depreciation accounts of Pell Corporation had the following balances at December 31, 2003:

	Plant Asset	Accumulated Depreciation
Land	$ 350,000	$ —
Land improvements	180,000	45,000
Building	1,500,000	350,000
Machinery and equipment	1,158,000	405,000
Automobiles	150,000	112,000

Depreciation method and useful lives:

- Land improvements: Straight-line; 15 years.
- Building: 150%-declining-balance; 20 years.
- Machinery and equipment: Straight-line; 10 years.
- Automobiles: 150%-declining-balance; 3 years.
- Depreciation is computed to the nearest month. No salvage values are recognized.

Transactions during 2004:

1. On January 2, 2004, machinery and equipment were purchased at a total invoice cost of $260,000, which included a $5,500 charge for freight. Installation costs of $27,000 were incurred.
2. On March 31, 2004, a machine purchased for $58,000 on January 3, 2000 was sold for $36,500.
3. On May 1, 2004, expenditures of $50,000 were made to repave parking lots at Pell's plant location. The work was necessitated by damage caused by severe winter weather.
4. On November 2, 2004, Pell acquired a tract of land with an existing building in exchange for 10,000 shares of Pell's $20 par common stock, which had a market price of $38 a share on this date. Pell paid legal fees and title insurance totaling $23,000. The last property tax bill indicated assessed values of $240,000 for land and $60,000 for building. Shortly after acquisition, the building was razed at a cost of $35,000 in anticipation of new building construction in 2005.
5. On December 31, 2004, Pell purchased a new automobile for $15,250 cash and trade-in of an automobile purchased for $18,000 on January 1, 2003. The new automobile has a cash value of $19,000.

Required

1. Prepare a schedule analyzing the changes in each of the plant assets during 2004, with detailed supporting computations. Disregard the related accumulated depreciation accounts.
2. For each asset classification, prepare a schedule showing depreciation expense for the year ended December 31, 2004.
3. Prepare a schedule showing the gain or loss from each asset disposal that Pell would recognize in its income statement for the year ended December 31, 2004. (*AICPA adapted*)

P10-22 *Comprehensive* The Lurch Company's December 31, 2003 balance sheet follows:

Assets		
Cash		$ 540,000
Inventory		450,000
Prepaid rent		60,000
Machine	$500,000	
Less: Accumulated depreciation	(135,000)	365,000
		$1,415,000

Liabilities and Equities

Accounts payable	$ 400,000
Common stock, $10 par	300,000
Additional paid-in capital	515,000
Retained earnings	200,000
	$1,415,000

During 2004, the following transactions occurred:

1. To avoid paying monthly rent of $5,000 on existing plant facilities, the company decided to buy a tract of land and construct a building of its own on it. On January 2, 2004, Lurch exchanged 6,000 shares of its common stock to acquire the land; the stock was selling for $25 per share. Construction of the building also began on January 2, 2004. At the time, Lurch borrowed funds by issuing a one-year, $500,000 note at 12% to help finance the project. The principal and interest on the note are due January 3, 2005. Construction costs (paid in cash) that occurred evenly throughout the year totaled $700,000. The building was completed on December 30, 2004 and the move-in to the new building was to occur during the next week.

2. On January 2, 2004, Lurch exchanged its one existing machine plus $50,000 for a newer, similar machine with a fair value of $430,000. The exchange was with another company in the same industry. The new machine is to be depreciated using straight-line depreciation based on an economic life of 5 years and a residual value of $55,000.

3. Lurch uses a FIFO perpetual inventory system. Lurch sold $350,000 of its inventory for $700,000 cash, paid for its beginning accounts payable, and purchased $480,000 of inventory on account during the year.

4. On July 31, 2004, Lurch declared and paid a $2.50 per share cash dividend to its shareholders.

5. Lurch is subject to a 30% income tax rate, and income taxes are accrued at year-end.

Required Prepare Lurch's income statement and statement of retained earnings for the fiscal year ended December 31, 2004 and a balance sheet as of December 31, 2004. Show all supporting journal entries and computations made during 2004. (*Contributed by Scott I. Jerris*)

INTERNET ASSIGNMENTS

Go to the Nikolai and Bazley **Intermediate Accounting** web site (http://Nikolai.swcollege.com). Click on Student Resources and internet homework assignments. Then click on the appropriate hot link (icon) for each company's web site, find the relevant accounting information, and answer the following questions.

I10-1   Go to the **Vail Resorts** web site.

     Required Which method(s) and lives does the company use to depreciate its assets? Do you agree with these method(s) and lives? Why or why not?

I10-2   Go to the **Federal Express** web site.

     Required What lives does the company use for the depreciation of its property and equipment? Now go the **Airborne** web site. What lives does the company use for the depreciation of its property and equipment? Explain the effects of the differences. Are the differences significant? What does each company disclose about the residual values? Are the differences significant?

I10-3   Go to the **General Electric** web site.

     Required Which is the company's primary depreciation method for its property and equipment? Explain whether the effects of the method are likely to be significantly different than the straight-line method?

I10-4   Go to the **Walt Disney Corporation** web site.

     Required What method does the company use to amortize film costs? Evaluate this method in terms of its relevance and reliability.

objectives

1 Explain the accounting alternatives for intangibles.

2 Understand the amortization or impairment of intangibles.

3 Identify research and development costs.

4 Explain the conceptual issues for research and development costs.

5 Account for identifiable intangible assets including patents, copyrights, franchises, computer software costs, and trademarks and tradenames.

6 Account for unidentifiable intangibles including internally developed and purchased goodwill.

7 Understand the disclosure of intangibles.

8 Explain the conceptual issues regarding intangibles.

9 Estimate the value of goodwill. (Appendix)

CHAPTER

11

Intangibles

As we discussed in Chapter 9, tangible noncurrent assets have a physical substance that can be seen and touched. In contrast, **intangible assets, which generally result from legal or contractual rights, do not have a physical substance.** Intangible and tangible noncurrent assets do have characteristics in common, as both (1) are held for use and not for investment (although they are "used" in very different ways), (2) have an expected life of more than one year, (3) derive their value from their ability to generate revenue for their owners, and (4) are expensed by a company in the periods in which it receives their benefits, if the assets have finite lives.

Intangible assets have four additional characteristics that distinguish them from tangible assets:

1. There is generally a higher degree of uncertainty regarding the future benefits that may be derived.
2. Their value is subject to wider fluctuations because it may depend, to a considerable extent, on competitive conditions.
3. They may have value only to a particular company.
4. Goodwill and intangible assets with indefinite lives are not expensed.

Accounting terminology includes only noncurrent assets in intangible assets, whereas legal terminology includes as intangibles all assets without physical substance and therefore includes such current assets as accounts and notes receivable, and investments in securities. Accounting practice restricts the use of the term *intangible* to such items as patents, licenses, copyrights, franchises, computer software costs, trademarks and tradenames, and goodwill. We discuss each of these items later in the chapter.

ACCOUNTING FOR INTANGIBLES

1 Explain the accounting alternatives for intangibles.

Accounting for intangible assets follows some of the general principles used for tangible assets. They are both initially recorded at cost. As we discuss later, some intangibles are amortized and others are not amortized, but instead are reviewed for impairment. Those that are amortized are reported on a company's balance sheet at the book value, which is the cost less the accumulated amortization. The accumulated amortization results from a periodic allocation of the cost as amortization expense on the company's income statement. As we discussed in Chapter 10, amortization follows the same principle as depreciation, but is the term used specifically for intangible assets. We discuss the specific issues related to whether or not a company amortizes an intangible asset and the measurement of any amortization expense on its income statement in the following sections. The other accounting principles that we discussed in the previous two chapters also apply to intangible assets. Thus, the principles used for the determination of acquisition cost, capital and operating expenditures, impairment, and disposal apply to both tangible and intangible assets. However, the measurement of any impairment may be different, as we discuss later.

Cost of Intangibles

Intangibles may be classified by a company according to whether they are *purchased* from others (externally acquired) or *internally developed*. In addition they may be classified according to whether they are *identifiable* or *unidentifiable*. **Identifiable intangible assets** include such items as patents, franchises, and trademarks, whereas the primary **unidentifiable intangible asset** is goodwill. These classifications lead to the four alternatives, and the proper method of accounting for each, which we show in Exhibit 11-1.

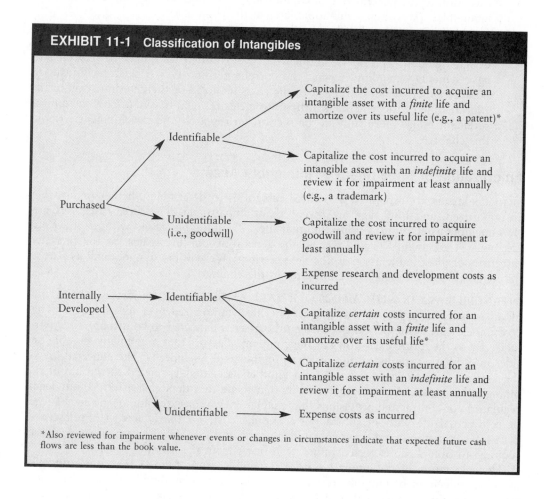

EXHIBIT 11-1   Classification of Intangibles

Purchased
- Identifiable
  - Capitalize the cost incurred to acquire an intangible asset with a *finite* life and amortize over its useful life (e.g., a patent)*
  - Capitalize the cost incurred to acquire an intangible asset with an *indefinite* life and review it for impairment at least annually (e.g., a trademark)
- Unidentifiable (i.e., goodwill)
  - Capitalize the cost incurred to acquire goodwill and review it for impairment at least annually

Internally Developed
- Identifiable
  - Expense research and development costs as incurred
  - Capitalize *certain* costs incurred for an intangible asset with a *finite* life and amortize over its useful life*
  - Capitalize *certain* costs incurred for an intangible asset with an *indefinite* life and review it for impairment at least annually
- Unidentifiable
  - Expense costs as incurred

*Also reviewed for impairment whenever events or changes in circumstances indicate that expected future cash flows are less than the book value.

Accounting for the cost of intangibles is discussed in **FASB Statement No. 142** as follows:[1]

1. *Purchased Identifiable Intangibles.* A company may purchase an intangible asset, such as a patent, from another company. The initial accounting for the acquisition of a purchased intangible presents no special issues and is handled in the

---

1. "Goodwill and Other Intangible Assets," *FASB Statement of Financial Accounting Standards No. 142* (Norwalk, Conn.: FASB, 2001).

same manner as we discussed in Chapter 9 for the acquisition of a single asset, in a group of assets, or in an exchange of similar or dissimilar assets.

2. *Purchased Unidentifiable Intangibles.* A company capitalizes the cost of a purchased unidentifiable intangible asset. The principal example of an unidentifiable intangible is goodwill, which can be acquired only through the purchase of another company or segment of a company. We discuss the nature of and accounting for goodwill in more detail later in this chapter.

3. *Internally Developed Identifiable Intangibles.* When a company internally develops an intangible asset, such as a patent, it can capitalize only certain costs. The costs of a patent include the legal and related costs of establishing the rights associated with a patent but not the costs of developing the product or process that is being patented. A company includes those latter costs in research and development costs and must expense them as incurred according to **FASB Statement No. 2.** Thus, the expensing of research and development costs represents an exception to the general rule of capitalization of internally developed identifiable intangibles. (We discuss this topic later in the chapter.)

4. *Internally Developed Unidentifiable Intangibles.* A company expenses the costs of internally developed unidentifiable intangibles, such as employee training and design of quality products, as incurred even though they may be expected to have benefits extending beyond the current period. This procedure is justified because either the measurement of the costs incurred or the determination of the expected life of the benefits is difficult to measure reliably. We discuss these measurement issues more fully in the section on research and development costs in this chapter.

Amortization or Impairment of Intangible Assets

2 Understand the amortization or impairment of intangibles.

Intangible assets are separated into three categories to determine whether or not they are amortized, and how they are reviewed for impairment. The three categories are: (1) intangible assets with a finite (limited) life, (2) intangible assets with an indefinite life, and (3) goodwill. We will discuss the general accounting issues for the first two categories of identifiable assets in the next sections. We will discuss goodwill as part of the unidentifiable intangibles section later in the chapter.

INTANGIBLE ASSETS WITH A FINITE LIFE ARE AMORTIZED   An identifiable intangible asset (such as a patent) that has a finite life is amortized over its useful life. That is, the useful life is the period over which the asset is expected to contribute directly or indirectly to the future cash flows of the company. Factors that a company should consider in estimating the useful life of an intangible asset include: (1) the expected life of the asset; (2) the expected useful life of another asset that is related to the life of the intangible asset, such as the mineral rights that relate to a depleting asset; (3) any legal, regulatory, or contractual provisions that enable renewal or extension of the asset's legal or contractual life without substantial economic cost; (4) the effects of obsolescence, demand, competition, and other economic factors; and (5) the level of maintenance costs required to obtain the expected future cash flows from the asset.[2]

The calculation of the amortization of intangible assets follows the same principles as the depreciation of tangible assets. The amount of an intangible asset to be amortized is the cost less the residual value, if any. As with depreciation, a company selects the amortization method based on the expected pattern of benefits the intangible asset will produce. If the company cannot reliably determine the pattern, then it must use the straight-line method. As for tangible assets, the amortization (debit entry) may be either a production cost and included in Goods in Process through fixed overhead (such as a patent on a manufacturing process) or an operating expense (such as a copyright). The credit entry is made to a contra account, Accumulated Amortization: Intangibles.

2. *Ibid.*, par. 11.

For example, suppose that a company purchases a patent for $85,000 and amortizes it using the straight-line method over 10 years (the estimated economic life) with no expected residual value. The journal entries to record the acquisition and the amortization for the first year are as follows:

Patent	85,000	
Cash		85,000
Amortization Expense (or Factory Overhead)	8,500	
Accumulated Amortization: Patent		8,500

The company reports the $76,500 book value ($85,000 cost − $8,500 accumulated amortization) of the patent in the intangible assets section of its balance sheet.

FASB Statement No. 142 requires a company to evaluate the estimated economic life every year to determine whether a revised estimate is warranted.[3] Such a change in estimate is accounted for by using the method we discussed in Chapter 10—that is, by computing a new periodic amortization amount based on the current book value and the new estimated remaining economic life.

If there is evidence that an intangible asset is impaired because its expected future net cash flows are less than its book value, a company must write down the asset to its fair value using the procedures of **FASB Statement No. 144,** as we discussed in Chapter 10.

INTANGIBLE ASSETS WITH AN INDEFINITE LIFE ARE REVIEWED FOR IMPAIRMENT
Some identifiable intangible assets, such as trademarks and tradenames, have a potentially indefinite life. For fiscal years beginning after December 15, 2001, an intangible asset with an indefinite life is not amortized (until its life is no longer considered to be indefinite), but is reviewed for impairment.[4] A company must review such intangible assets for impairment annually, *or* more frequently when events or circumstances occur that indicate the intangible may be impaired. A company tests an intangible asset for impairment by first estimating the fair value of the asset. The fair value of an intangible asset is the amount at which the asset could be bought or sold in a current transaction between willing parties. The quoted market price in an active market is the best measure of fair value. However, because a quoted market price is often unavailable for an intangible asset, a company may estimate the value by using the value of similar assets, or by using present value techniques.

An intangible asset is impaired when its fair value is less than its carrying value. The impairment loss is the amount by which the fair value of the intangible asset is less than its carrying value (i.e., the original cost, unless the asset was impaired in a previous period). The loss is recorded by debiting an impairment loss account and crediting the intangible asset account. For example, suppose a company purchased a trademark two years ago for $60,000. As the company considered the trademark to have an indefinite life, the trademark still has a carrying value of $60,000. At the end of the current year, the company determines that the fair value of the trademark is $20,000. The company records the $40,000 loss ($20,000 fair value − $60,000 cost) as follows:

Impairment Loss on Trademark	40,000	
Trademark		40,000

The company reports the loss as a component of income from continuing operations on its income statement. The company reports the $20,000 fair value of the trademark in the intangible asset section of its balance sheet. Every year the company must compare the fair value with the $20,000 carrying value to determine if the trademark is again impaired.

---

3. *Ibid.,* par. 14.
4. *Ibid.,* par. 16. Before the implementation of *FASB Statement No. 142,* all intangible assets were amortized over their economic lives, not to exceed 40 years (except those acquired before November 1, 1970, and for which there is no evidence of a decline in value or a limited economic life).

In the remaining sections of this chapter we discuss specific intangibles, starting with research and development costs. Although research and development costs are not capitalized, we discuss them first because of the impact they have on the capitalization of many other intangibles. We discuss specific identifiable intangible assets and unidentifiable assets (goodwill) in the remaining two sections.

RESEARCH AND DEVELOPMENT COSTS

Many companies spend large sums each year on research and development (R&D). Prior to 1974 some companies expensed their R&D costs, whereas other companies (even in the same industry) capitalized them. To prevent the use of alternative accounting principles in similar economic circumstances, *FASB Statement No. 2* requires that **all research and development costs must be expensed as incurred.**[5] Even though R&D costs often benefit future periods, the decision to require expensing in all circumstances was made primarily in the belief that uniformity would enhance *comparability* and would eliminate the possibility of income manipulation. It also avoids the *reliability* problems of how much to capitalize and over what period to amortize such capitalized costs. We evaluate the FASB's decision to require expensing of R&D costs at the end of this section.

Two issues in the expensing of R&D are the activities and costs that a company includes in each category. Research and development activities are defined by the FASB as follows:

3 Identify research and development costs.

(a) **Research** is the planned search or critical investigation aimed at discovery of new knowledge with the hope that such knowledge will be useful in developing a new product or service ("product") or a new process or technique ("process") or in bringing about a significant improvement to an existing product or process.

(b) **Development** is the translation of research findings or other knowledge into a plan or design for a new product or process or for a significant improvement to an existing product or process, whether intended for sale or use. It includes the conceptual formulation, design, and testing of product alternatives, construction of prototypes, and operation of pilot plants. It does not include routine or periodic alterations to existing products, production lines, manufacturing processes, and other ongoing operations, even though those alterations may represent improvements; it does not include market research or market testing activities.[6]

To assist in the implementation of these general definitions, we show examples of activities that are included as R&D and those that are excluded in Exhibit 11-2.

Capitalization criteria are discussed in Chapter 9.

Costs associated with activities *excluded* from R&D are either expensed or capitalized according to the normal capitalization criteria. Once it has been determined that an activity is included in R&D, a company must identify the costs so that it may record the correct amount of R&D expense. Expenditures for the following elements of R&D activities are *included* in R&D costs and thus expensed as incurred:

1. Materials, equipment, and facilities
2. Personnel
3. Intangibles purchased from others
4. Contract services—the costs of services performed by others in connection with the R&D activities of an enterprise
5. Indirect costs—R&D includes a reasonable allocation of indirect costs; however, general and administrative costs that are not clearly related to R&D activities are not included as R&D costs[7]

---

5. "Accounting for Research and Development Costs," *FASB Statement of Financial Accounting Standards No. 2* (Stamford, Conn.: FASB, 1974), par. 8.
6. *Ibid.*
7. *Ibid.*, par. 9–10.

EXHIBIT 11-2 Examples of Activities Included in and Excluded from R&D

Included in R&D

(a) Laboratory research aimed at discovery of new knowledge.
(b) Searching for applications of new research findings or of other knowledge.
(c) Conceptual formulation and design of possible product or process alternatives.
(d) Testing in search for or evaluation of product or process alternatives.
(e) Modification of the formulation or design of a product or process.
(f) Design, construction, and testing of preproduction prototypes and models.
(g) Design of tools, jigs, molds, and dies involving new technology.
(h) Design, construction, and operation of a pilot plant that is not of a scale economically feasible to the company for commercial production.
(i) Engineering activity required to advance the design of a product to the point that it meets specific functional and economic requirements and is ready for manufacture.

Excluded from R&D

(a) Engineering follow-through in an early phase of commercial production.
(b) Quality control during commercial production, including routine testing of products.
(c) Trouble-shooting in connection with breakdowns during commercial production.
(d) Routine, ongoing efforts to refine, enrich, or otherwise improve upon the qualities of an existing product.
(e) Adaptation of an existing capability to a particular requirement or customer's need as part of a continuing commercial activity.
(f) Seasonal or other periodic design changes to existing products.
(g) Routine design of tools, jigs, molds, and dies.
(h) Activity, including design and construction engineering, related to the construction, relocation, rearrangement, or start-up of facilities or equipment other than (1) pilot plants and (2) facilities or equipment whose sole use is for a particular research and development project.
(i) Legal work in connection with patent applications or litigation, and the sale or licensing of patents.

Source: FASB Statement No. 2, par. 9 and 10.

The inclusion in R&D expense of the cost of materials, equipment, facilities, and intangibles purchased from others requires further explanation. If the items have **alternative future uses**, then a company follows normal accrual procedures. For example, a company expenses the costs of personnel as payments are made and accrued at year-end, whereas it records the costs of materials in inventory and then includes them as R&D expense when the materials are used. Also, a company capitalizes the cost of a machine that has alternative future uses (even if only in other R&D projects) and *depreciates* the cost over the asset's estimated useful life. The company includes the depreciation in R&D expense. However, the company includes in R&D expense the costs of any materials, equipment, facilities, and intangibles purchased from others that have *no alternative future uses* in research and development or other activities. For example, if a company can use inventory or a machine only for one R&D project and so has no alternative future uses for it, the company includes the total acquisition costs in R&D expense in the period it incurs the cost.

To illustrate the accounting for R&D, assume that the Kent Company incurred the following costs for R&D activities:

Material used from inventory	$50,000
Wages and salaries	90,000
Allocation of general and administrative costs	20,000
Depreciation on building housing R&D activities	25,000
Machine purchased for R&D project that has no alternative future uses	30,000

The company includes all these costs in R&D expense and records them as follows:

Research and Development Expense	215,000	
Cash, Payables, etc.		140,000
Inventory		50,000
Accumulated Depreciation: Building		25,000

FASB Statement No. 2 does not cover the costs of R&D activities conducted for others (including the government) under a contractual arrangement. A company capitalizes these costs as incurred and expenses them when it recognizes the revenue from the contract.

Conceptual Evaluation of Accounting for Research and Development Costs

4 Explain the conceptual issues for research and development costs.

The FASB considered four methods for companies to account for R&D costs when *FASB Statement No. 2* was being prepared: (1) expense all costs when incurred, (2) capitalize all costs when incurred and amortize them over the periods expected to benefit, (3) capitalize costs when incurred if specified conditions are fulfilled and record all other costs as expenses, and (4) accumulate all costs in a special category until the existence of future benefits can be determined.

The first alternative is supported and the second alternative countered by the argument that there is a high degree of uncertainty about the future benefits of a company's individual R&D projects. The majority of projects do not result in any identifiable future benefits; therefore, it is desirable to expense all costs in the periods incurred. In addition, as it is difficult to demonstrate a direct relationship between R&D costs and specific future revenue generated, it is not possible to *reliably* estimate the expected life and the pattern of the benefits received, and thereby determine the appropriate amortization. Furthermore, if R&D costs are approximately the same each period, the amount of the expense each period will be similar, regardless of whether the cost was capitalized and then expensed by the straight-line method or simply expensed immediately. However, immediate expensing means that the company does not record an asset on its balance sheet. This omission may lead to a very significant understatement of assets for some companies, if it is agreed that the costs incurred on R&D projects often generate benefits for future periods.

The second alternative, capitalize all costs as incurred, is supported by the argument that a company undertakes R&D projects only to develop future benefits. Therefore, an asset is created and should be recognized by capitalizing the entire costs of R&D without regard to the certainty of future benefits from individual projects. However, such an approach is inconsistent with other areas of accounting where the cost of each asset is recorded and expensed over its individual life. In addition, capitalization of the entire costs of R&D would make it difficult to develop a meaningful amortization period.

The third alternative, selective capitalization, has desirable conceptual features. A company would accumulate the costs of each individual project and then capitalize and expense the costs over the life of the benefits to be received. If no such benefits were expected, the costs would be expensed immediately. Thus, R&D costs would be capitalized and expensed on the same basis as other costs. However, this alternative would be difficult to implement. What criteria for capitalization would be used? The FASB considered a number of criteria, such as definition of the product or process, technological feasibility, marketability and usefulness, economic feasibility, management action, and distortion of net income comparisons. Any set of criteria would have been very difficult to define and implement reliably, and in all likelihood would have led to a lack of comparability when implemented. In addition, it might be several periods after the costs have been incurred before the company could reasonably evaluate the likelihood of benefits being received.

The fourth alternative is to classify the costs in a special category on the company's balance sheet. The two alternative categories suggested were below the assets or as a reduction of stockholders' equity. Such a procedure is not appealing because it violates the basic concepts underlying the fundamental accounting equation. It was suggested as an alternative to draw attention to the basic uncertainty surrounding the nature of R&D costs, and to allow a decision regarding capitalizing or expensing to be delayed until sufficient information for a reliable decision becomes available.

The choice basically was between an alternative that has desirable conceptual features but significant implementation difficulties (capitalization) and an alternative that is less desirable conceptually but is much easier to implement and is likely to lead to greater *comparability* between companies (immediate expensing). As in so many situations, the choice was between *relevance* and *reliability*. It is not surprising that the FASB decided on the latter alternative. In addition, income tax regulations allow a company to immediately expense its R&D costs, so a major difference between financial income and taxable income was eliminated.

International Accounting Differences

Under International Accounting Standards, research costs are expensed but development costs may be capitalized. Also, the costs of items that are acquired for a particular research project and have no alternative future uses are expensed as the items are used in the project. In contrast, such costs are expensed when incurred under U.S. GAAP.

IDENTIFIABLE INTANGIBLE ASSETS

Identifiable intangible assets are those intangibles that can be purchased or sold separately from the other assets of the company. A company capitalizes the costs of identifiable intangibles (except for R&D costs). Remember that, because a company expenses R&D and operating costs, it capitalizes only certain costs of internally developed identifiable intangibles—not the total costs that might be related to the item. For example, it capitalizes only the direct legal costs of applying for and registering a tradename, and it expenses all indirect costs as incurred, such as advertising to promote the tradename. Also remember that, if a company *purchases* an identifiable intangible asset, it capitalizes the cost on the same basis as for a tangible asset by including all necessary costs. Exhibit 11-3 illustrates the differences between the amortization and impairment of intangible assets and the expensing of R&D costs in the period incurred. We discuss each of these identifiable intangible assets in the following sections.

5 Account for identifiable intangible assets including patents, copyrights, franchises, computer software costs, and trademarks and tradenames.

Patents

A patent is an exclusive right granted by the federal government giving the owner control of the manufacture, sale, or other use of an invention for 20 years from the date of filing. Patents cannot be renewed, but their effective life may be extended by obtaining new patents on modifications and improvements to the original invention.

A patent has value if it enables the company to obtain higher income by selling products at a higher price, producing products at a lower cost, or producing a product for which there is less competition. In many situations, the value of a patent is eliminated before the end of its legal life by the actions of other companies that produce a competing product without violating the patent, or through technological change or a change in demand for the product. Therefore, a company amortizes the patent over its expected *useful* life if that life is shorter than 20 years.[8]

Licenses often are granted to others to use the invention covered by a patent. A company accounts for amounts received under such agreements under the normal revenue recognition criteria by including them in income when earned and realizable rather than when received. A company should disclose license agreements in the notes to its financial statements if their effect on its income is material.

---

8. Prior to 1994, the legal life of a patent was 17 years from the date of grant.

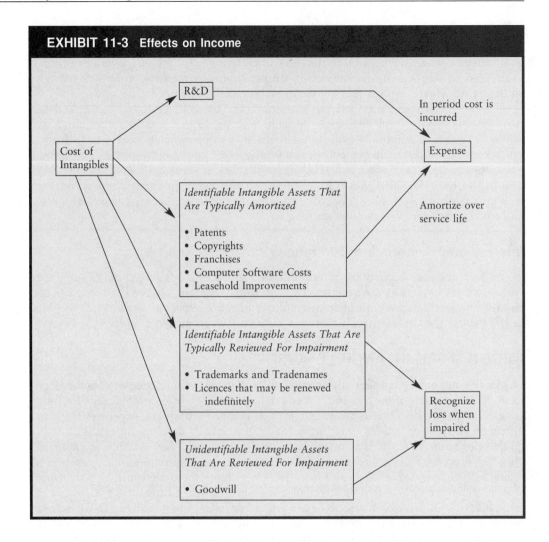

EXHIBIT 11-3 Effects on Income

It may be necessary for the owner of a patent to defend it against infringement by others. A company capitalizes the costs of successfully defending the legal validity of a patent because the benefits of the patent are maintained for its remaining economic life. However, given the length of time it may take to resolve a patent infringement suit, some companies may expense the legal costs when incurred because of the uncertainty of eventual success in the suit. If the company loses the suit, it immediately expenses all legal costs not previously expensed and the remaining book value of the patent because there is no remaining economic value. However, if a company expenses the legal costs and then wins the suit, it does *not* make a prior period adjustment.

Copyrights

A copyright is a grant by the federal government covering the right to publish, sell, or otherwise control literary or artistic products for the life of the author plus 70 years.[9] Copyrights cover such items as books, music, and films. Accounting for copyrights follows the same principles as those used for patents. The cost is amortized over the useful life either on a straight-line basis, or on an activity basis if that is a better measure of the pattern of benefits.

It is possible that a fully amortized copyright may develop a significant value, such as in the case of some old films or music. Under current generally accepted accounting principles, which require that assets are recorded at cost, such an increase in value is not recognized in the financial statements.

Franchises

Franchises are agreements entered into by two parties in which, for a fee, one party (the franchisor) gives the other party (the franchisee) rights to perform certain functions or sell certain products or services. In addition the franchisor may agree to provide certain services to the franchisee. Many franchises exist between governments and companies, such as a franchise to provide a monopoly service (e.g., utilities) or to use public property to provide a service (e.g., a ferry). A common example of a franchise between two companies is in the restaurant business, where many units of national chains such as **McDonald's** are locally owned and operated under the terms of a franchise agreement. Another example is the selling of name-brand items in the automotive parts market, such as **Midas Muffler**. A franchisee capitalizes the initial cost it pays to acquire the franchise, whereas it expenses the continuing franchise fees that it pays for services provided by the franchisor in subsequent years according to the normal matching criteria. If a franchise is granted in perpetuity, it would be considered to have an indefinite life and would be tested for impairment at least annually, as we discussed earlier. However, most franchises have a legal life that is specified in the franchise agreement. For these franchises, the franchisee amortizes the related initial franchise cost over its useful life.

Accounting for franchises by the franchisor is discussed in Chapter 17.

Computer Software Costs

Until the early 1980s most companies expensed the cost of software development. At that time, however, many companies started to adopt a policy of capitalizing software costs. In 1983, the SEC stopped such changes until the FASB adopted appropriate accounting principles. In 1985, the FASB issued **FASB Statement No. 86**, entitled "Accounting for the Costs of Computer Software to Be Sold, Leased, or Otherwise Marketed."[10]

There are three categories of costs associated with software that is to be sold, leased, or otherwise marketed directly or indirectly as part of a product, process, or service. First, **software production costs** are the costs of design, coding, testing, documentation, and preparation of training materials. A company includes these costs in research and development expense until technological feasibility of the product is established. Because companies use different development methods, **technological feasibility is established either on the date the company completes a detail program design or, in its absence, when it completes a working model of the product.** After this date, a company capitalizes all software production costs until the product is available for general release to customers. No software production costs may be capitalized after the product is ready for general release; they are expensed as incurred. The accounting for software production costs may be summarized as follows:

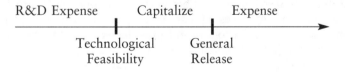

The company amortizes the capitalized software production costs incurred during the period between technological feasibility and general release over the expected life of the product, which typically will be a relatively short period, such as five years. The amount

---

10. "Accounting for the Costs of Computer Software to Be Sold, Leased, or Otherwise Marketed," *FASB Statement of Financial Accounting Standards No. 86* (Stamford, Conn.: FASB, 1985). For additional discussion, see N. Erikson and D. Herskovits, "Accounting for Software Costs: Cracking the Code," *Journal of Accountancy*, November 1985, pp. 81–96.

of the amortization expense is the greater of the amount calculated from either (1) the ratio of current gross revenues from the software to the total amount of current and anticipated future gross revenues from the software multiplied by the cost of the asset, or (2) the straight-line method. If the net realizable value of the software product is lower than the asset's book value, a company writes down the asset to this value and recognizes a loss. The lower value is then recognized as the new cost and the write-down may not be recovered. Note that two new concepts are involved. First, a new concept of amortization based on estimated revenues is introduced. Second, the lower of cost or market method is applied to this one intangible asset.

The second category of costs is the **unit cost of producing the software.** This would include amounts for the cost of the disks and duplication of the software, packaging, documentation, and training materials. A company records these unit costs as inventory and expenses them as cost of goods sold when the related revenue is recognized. The third category of costs is the **maintenance and customer support costs** incurred after the software is released. These costs are expensed as incurred.

CONCEPTUAL EVALUATION *FASB Statement No. 86* resulted in most computer software costs being expensed because, for many companies, the detail program design occurs after the detailed logic of the program is complete and after coding has already begun. For many companies, software may be a significant, or perhaps the only, revenue-generating asset. As the U.S. economy moves towards intangible outputs and creative processes, it may be argued that accounting should accommodate this transition by allowing the results of a company's creative processes to be recorded as an asset when they are likely to result in probable future cash flows. Another issue is that many costs incurred before the completion of the detail program design are not part of research and development but are incurred to perform an activity, just like other production processes. Therefore, *FASB Statement No. 86* expands the definitions of research and development established in *FASB Statement No. 2.* Finally, the amount of cost that a company may capitalize is dependent on the organization of its programming process and, in particular, the date on which technological feasibility is established. Because the capitalization criterion is based on a point in time rather than a function, the costs capitalized may vary significantly from company to company depending on whether the coding and testing parallels, or follows, the detail program design.

Internal-Use Software

AICPA Statement of Position No. 98-1 specifies the accounting for the costs of internal-use computer software.[11] Costs that are incurred in the preliminary stage of development are expensed as incurred. Capitalization of costs begins when (1) the preliminary stage is completed, and (2) management authorizes and commits to funding a computer software project and (a) it is probable that the project will be completed, and (b) the software will be used to perform the function intended. Once a company has met these capitalization criteria, it capitalizes the cost of (1) external direct costs of materials and services consumed in developing or obtaining internal-use software, (2) payroll and payroll-related costs for employees who are directly associated with the project based on the time spent directly on the project, and (3) interest costs incurred when developing the software. The company then amortizes the capitalized cost using the straight-line method over the estimated useful life of the software unless another method provides better matching.

Training costs for using the software are expensed as incurred. Costs incurred for upgrades and enhancements of the software are capitalized if they meet the capitalization criteria of the *SOP*, whereas costs incurred for maintaining the software are expensed as incurred. Impairment is measured and recognized according to *FASB Statement No. 144.*

---

11. "Accounting for the Costs of Computer Software Developed or Planned for Internal Use," *AICPA Statement of Position No. 98-1* (New York: AICPA, 1998).

Leases and Leasehold Improvements

Leases (or leaseholds) are intangible assets because a right to use the property is held by the lessee, but the property itself is still owned by the lessor. However, capital leases are normally included on the lessee's balance sheet within its property, plant, and equipment rather than under intangible assets. Leasehold improvements are also intangible assets of the lessee but normally are included as a separate item in its property, plant, and equipment.

Leases are discussed in Chapter 20, and leasehold improvements are discussed in Chapter 9.

Trademarks and Tradenames

Registration of a trademark or tradename with the U.S. Patent Office establishes a right to exclusive use of a name, symbol, or other device used for product identification (e.g., Coke™ or Scotch™ Tape). The right lasts for 20 years and is renewable indefinitely as long as the trademark or tradename is used continuously. Therefore, it typically is considered to have an indefinite life and is not amortized (unless the company decides its useful life is no longer indefinite). The company must review the asset for impairment at least annually, as we discussed earlier.

Deferred Charges

Deferred charges (or other "noncurrent assets") is a category often used on a company's balance sheet as a catchall category in which several individually immaterial items are accumulated. Examples of items included are intangibles from any of the categories previously discussed if the company does not include intangibles as a separate category in the balance sheet. In addition, long-term prepayments such as for insurance, rent, taxes, or moving and plant rearrangement costs may be included in deferred charges. All deferred charges are amortized over their expected economic lives. As we discussed in Chapter 3, most of these deferred charges can, and should, be included in other asset categories on the company's balance sheet.

Organization Costs

When a corporation is formed, it incurs organization costs such as legal fees, stock certificate costs, underwriting fees, accounting fees, and promotional fees. Because these costs are essential to the formation of a corporation and the life of the company is indefinite, it can be argued that these organization costs are an intangible asset with an indefinite life.

However, AICPA *Statement of Position No. 98-5* (which we discussed in Chapter 9) requires that the costs of start-up activities (including organization costs) be expensed as incurred.[12] An argument in favor of expensing the organization costs is that once the costs have been incurred and the company is formed, all the benefits associated with the costs have been realized. However, it can be argued that the matching principle is violated because the cost of forming the company is not matched against the revenue generated by the newly formed company. Also, income tax regulations allow organization costs to be amortized and deducted from taxable income over 60 months.

UNIDENTIFIABLE INTANGIBLES

We have discussed identifiable intangible assets in previous sections of this chapter. However, many additional intangibles of a company also contribute to its earning power. These unidentifiable intangibles are often called "goodwill." Accounting for such goodwill depends on whether it is internally developed or purchased through a transaction.

6 Account for unidentifiable tangibles, including internally developed and purchased goodwill.

---

12. "Reporting on the Costs of Start-Up Activities," *AICPA Statement of Position No. 98-5* (New York: AICPA, 1998).

Internally Developed Goodwill

All companies develop unidentifiable intangibles. For example, employees at all levels are an integral part of a company. They are an essential component in the utilization of the assets that are included in the company's balance sheet and that produce the products and services of the company. Superior employees may produce products with a higher quality and enable a company to earn a higher income. Also, service companies and companies that produce computer software rely almost entirely on their employees to generate revenue, yet record no asset related to their skills and talents. This unrecorded "asset" is often referred to as "intellectual capital." Another example of an unidentifiable intangible is a company that has an advantageous geographical location. Perhaps it is closer to its raw materials or suppliers or to its major customers. Such a geographical advantage may enable the company to earn a higher income. Yet a company's balance sheet does not include assets relating to such internally developed intangibles as quality, reputation, human resources, or geographical location.[13]

Two characteristics distinguish intangibles of this type. First, they are considered to be unidentifiable because they are not separable from the identified and recorded assets. For example, the employees of the company cannot be sold to another company, and the geographical location cannot be sold without selling the other assets of the company. Second, measuring the value of these unidentifiable intangibles would be very difficult and less *reliable* than measuring the value of identifiable intangibles. Because of these two characteristics, the costs associated with such *internally developed* intangibles (internally developed goodwill) are expensed as incurred.

Purchased Goodwill

Purchased goodwill (or simply goodwill) **arises when a company is acquired. It is the difference between the purchase price (market value) of the acquired company as a whole and the fair value of the reported identifiable net assets.** Goodwill is recorded only when a transaction occurs—that is, when a company (or a significant part of a company) is acquired by another company. The purchased goodwill is the price paid by the acquiring company for the unidentifiable intangibles that were internally developed by the acquired company. It is recorded as an asset by the acquiring company because a transaction has occurred that establishes a *reliable* valuation. From this perspective, goodwill can be considered a residual valuation account for the additional value associated with the unidentifiable intangible assets. In other words, it is the amount paid for the acquisition in excess of the cost of the identifiable net assets (assets less liabilities) acquired.

The capitalization of purchased goodwill is required by **FASB Statement No. 141,** which defines goodwill as the excess of the cost of an acquired entity over the net of the amounts assigned to assets acquired and liabilities assumed.[14]

Methods to value goodwill and set the purchase price are discussed in the chapter Appendix.

Recording the Acquisition

The acquisition of a company can be a very complex matter. To illustrate a simple alternative, suppose that after negotiation the Sara Company purchases all the assets of the Trevor Company for $790,000 cash and the Trevor Company is dissolved. If the Trevor Company has identifiable assets with a fair value of $920,000 and liabilities with a fair value of $530,000, Sara Company would record the acquisition as follows:

---

13. A few attempts have been made to value human resources and record them on the balance sheet. See, for instance, E. H. Caplan and S. Landkich, *Human Resource Accounting* (New York: National Association of Accountants, 1974).
14. "Business Combinations," *FASB Statement of Financial Accounting Standards No. 141* (Norwalk, Conn.: FASB, 2001), Appendix F.

Identifiable Assets	920,000	
Goodwill	400,000	
Liabilities		530,000
Cash		790,000

To record an actual acquisition, instead of debiting Identifiable Assets and crediting Liabilities as shown, the company would debit or credit each of the individual asset and liability accounts based on their current fair values. Also, if the Trevor Company had any "in-process" R&D, the Sara Company would expense that amount of the purchase price. Alternatively, if the Trevor Company is not dissolved, the Sara Company would record the entire acquisition cost in an Investments account. Subsequently, it would use the equity method (discussed in Chapter 14) and consolidated financial statements (discussed in advanced accounting books) to account for and report on the investment.

Impairment of Goodwill

For fiscal years beginning after December 15, 2001, a company must review its goodwill for impairment at least annually at the reporting unit level. (Goodwill is never amortized.) The reporting unit is the same as the operating segment that we discussed in Chapter 5 for segment reporting. A company must also review its goodwill for impairment whenever events or changes in circumstances occur that would more-likely-than-not reduce the fair value of the goodwill below its carrying value. Examples of events or changes in circumstances that indicate that goodwill may be impaired include: a significant adverse change in the business climate or market, a legal issue, an action by regulators, unanticipated competition, a loss of key personnel, and a more-likely-than-not expectation that a reporting unit may be sold.

A company reviews its purchased goodwill for impairment using a two-step approach. First, the company compares the fair value of the reporting unit with its book value (including goodwill).[15] The fair value of a reporting unit is the amount at which the unit as a whole could be bought or sold in a current transaction between willing parties. Sometimes this information is not available. In such a case, the company might determine the recording unit's fair value by multiplying the market price of its common stock by the number of shares outstanding (this is called the *market capitalization* of the reporting unit). However, this approach may not be representative of the fair value of the reporting unit, or the reporting unit may not have shares that trade in an active market. In such cases, estimates of the fair value may be based on valuation techniques, such as multiples of earnings or revenues, or measured as the present value of the estimated future cash flows of the reporting unit. Those cash flow estimates must be based on reasonable and supportable assumptions and should consider all available evidence.

If the fair value of the reporting unit is greater than the book value, goodwill is not considered to be impaired, and the second step is not necessary. If the fair value of the reporting unit is *less than* its book value, the second step of the impairment test must be performed to measure the *amount* of the impairment loss, if any. The second step is the recognition of an impairment loss for the amount by which the implied fair value of the goodwill is less than its carrying value.

To determine the implied fair value of the goodwill, the company first allocates the fair value of the reporting unit to all the identifiable assets and liabilities of the unit as if the unit had been acquired and the fair value was the purchase price. Then the implied fair value of the goodwill is the excess "purchase price" over the amounts assigned to the identifiable assets and liabilities. The impairment loss is the difference between the carrying value of the goodwill and the lower implied fair value of the goodwill. When the company records the impairment loss, it reduces the carrying value of the goodwill to the lower fair value.

---

15. Impairment tests must be performed on other assets of the reporting unit first, so that the resulting fair value of the reporting unit that is less than the book value must be from goodwill impairment.

To illustrate the impairment of goodwill, suppose that the Kent Company acquired the Devon Company as a subsidiary several years ago. The Devon Company has a book value (assets minus liabilities) of $3.6 million, including goodwill of $400,000. To test for the impairment of its goodwill, the Kent Company first estimates that the fair value of the Devon Company is $3 million. Because this $3 million fair value is less than its $3.6 million book value, the Kent Company must perform the second step. If Kent allocates $2.7 million of the fair value to Devon Company's identifiable assets and liabilities, this means that $300,000 ($3 million − $2.7 million) is the implied fair value of the goodwill. Because the $300,000 implied fair value of the goodwill is $100,000 less than the $400,000 carrying value, Kent Company records the $100,000 impairment loss as follows:

Impairment Loss on Goodwill	100,000	
Goodwill		100,000

Kent Company reports the impairment loss as a separate line item on its income statement as part of income from continuing operations and reports the new (reduced) $300,000 carrying value on its ending balance sheet. Every year, Kent Company must compare the fair value with the $300,000 carrying value to determine if the goodwill is again impaired.

Note also that the book value of the Devon Company's identifiable net assets is $3,200,000 ($3,600,000 − $400,000 goodwill). Because the fair value of the identifiable net assets is $2,700,000, the Kent Company should recognize additional impairment losses of $500,000 ($2,700,000 − $3,200,000) on the relevant assets. It is likely that other intangible assets recorded at the time of the acquisition of the Devon Company are impaired, but other assets that may be impaired include accounts receivable, inventory, property, plant and equipment, and investments (which we discuss in Chapter 14).

Negative Goodwill

The discussion and examples in this chapter have assumed that purchased goodwill is positive. That is, the price paid for the company is greater than the fair value of the net assets acquired. However, it is possible that the cash paid is less than the fair value of the net assets acquired. In such cases goodwill is a negative amount. This situation tends to raise questions about the rational behavior of the parties involved. The best course of action for the current owners of the company would be to liquidate it rather than to sell it. An exception is when the acquisition is made by buying common stock that is trading at less than the value of the net assets.

If such a purchase transaction does occur, *FASB Statement No. 141* requires that negative goodwill *not* be recorded. Instead, the acquiring company allocates the negative amount proportionately to reduce the amounts assigned to the noncurrent assets acquired. The exceptions to this allocation are: financial assets other than those accounted for by the equity method, assets to be sold, deferred tax assets (discussed in Chapter 18), prepaid assets relating to pension and other postretirement benefits (discussed in Chapter 19), and any other current assets. Any excess that remains after reducing those assets to zero is reported as an extraordinary gain (as we discussed in Chapter 4).

DISCLOSURES FOR INTANGIBLE ASSETS

7 Understand the disclosure of intangibles.

FASB Statement No. 142 requires a company to disclose certain information about its intangible assets, in either the financial statements or the notes, including:

1. In the period it acquires intangible assets:
    a. The cost of any intangible asset acquired, separated into assets subject to amortization, assets not subject to amortization, and goodwill
    b. For assets subject to amortization, the residual value and the weighted-average amortization period

    c. The cost of any research and development acquired and written off, and where it is included in the income statement

2. In each period for which it presents a balance sheet:
    a. For intangible assets that are amortized, the total cost, the accumulated amortization, the amortization expense, and the estimated amortization expense for the next five years
    b. For intangible assets that are not amortized, the total cost and the cost of each major intangible asset class
    c. For goodwill, the amount of goodwill acquired, the amount of any impairment losses recognized, and the amount of goodwill included in the disposal of a reporting unit
    d. For any intangible asset impairment, the facts and circumstances leading to the impairment, the amount of the impairment loss, and the method of determining the fair value

In addition, a company must report, as a minimum, the total of all identifiable intangible assets as a separate line item (asset) on the balance sheet. A company must include amortization expense and impairment losses in income from continuing operations. It must report goodwill impairment losses as a separate line item in income from continuing operations (unless the impairment is related to a discontinued operation).

CONCEPTUAL EVALUATION OF ACCOUNTING FOR INTANGIBLES

Generally accepted accounting principles for internally developed and purchased intangibles are complex and may have some apparent inconsistencies. For example, earlier in the chapter we discussed the arguments for and against expensing the R&D costs incurred by a company. Also, when one company acquires another company, it may acquire the R&D that is in-process in that other company. The acquiring company expenses, at the date of purchase, the cost of that in-process R&D. This is consistent with the principle of expensing R&D costs incurred by a company but is inconsistent with the general rule that items purchased are assets. It is possible that the purchasing company may have an incentive to reduce the amount of the purchase price it allocates to the acquired in-process R&D. This would increase the amount the company assigns to goodwill and reduce the total expenses it will recognize (unless the goodwill becomes impaired).

8 Explain the conceptual issues regarding intangibles.

    Another inconsistency may occur because only purchased goodwill is recorded as an asset, while internally developed goodwill is expensed. Suppose Company A internally develops goodwill, while Company B has purchased a company identical to A and records goodwill as an asset. Both companies expense the continuing costs of developing internal goodwill, but only Company B reports a goodwill asset. However, there are two different elements. One is the recognition of goodwill that was developed in the *past* and was purchased; the other is the expensing of the costs of internally generated goodwill in the *current period*.

    Two major arguments can be used to justify the expensing of internally generated goodwill and the capitalization of purchased goodwill. First, it would be very difficult to measure the cost of internally generated goodwill with a reasonable degree of *reliability*. We discuss the techniques and issues involved in estimating the value of *purchased* goodwill in the chapter Appendix to provide a better understanding of the process management goes through when considering the purchase of another company. However, this process does *not* result in the cost of the goodwill included on the acquiring company's balance sheet. That value results from the actual amount paid by the acquiring company, the recording of which is discussed in depth in advanced accounting books. While the estimation of goodwill is a valid component of the process, the agreed purchase price for a company is the result of negotiation. It is influenced by many factors such as the market price of any securities being exchanged and the synergy that is expected to result from the acquisition. However, to capitalize internally developed goodwill would raise issues similar to those for R&D, such as which costs should be capitalized and which should be expensed. For example, do some or all of a company's marketing costs provide benefits for just the current period, or do they also provide benefits for future periods?

The second argument for expensing internally developed intangibles is that capitalization would require amortization because any asset would have a finite life. However, it would be very difficult to identify the revenues generated and therefore to decide over which periods, and by which method, to match the amortization expense against the benefits.

The FASB argued that not amortizing certain intangible assets is appropriate because they have indefinite future lives, and amortizing those assets would not meet the criterion of being *representationally faithful*. The Board noted that most intangible assets have finite useful lives, and to classify an asset as having an indefinite life would require the asset to generate cash flows indefinitely. Examples of such intangible assets may include airport route authorities, certain trademarks, and taxicab medallions. There is little disagreement that these few intangible assets that have an indefinite life should not be amortized until there is evidence that they have a finite life.

The decision not to require amortization of goodwill was more controversial. The FASB argued that the life of goodwill cannot be predicted with a satisfactory level of *reliability,* nor can the pattern of benefits it generates. Therefore the amount that would be amortized would be only a rough estimate of the decrease in goodwill for the period. The FASB also argued that many financial analysts ignore goodwill amortization in their evaluation of a company's income.

In contrast, many people argue that goodwill is an asset with benefits that expire over time and therefore it should be amortized over a maximum life of, for example, 20 years. Supporters of this view argue that the goodwill recorded as a result of a transaction is an asset that is consumed over time and is replaced by internally generated goodwill, and therefore it should be amortized. Many of these people would also argue that internally generated goodwill should also be capitalized and amortized over its useful life.

Another alternative considered by the FASB was to require the immediate write off of goodwill. The Board rejected this alternative because the goodwill that is acquired and paid for meets the definition of an asset. It is also difficult to argue that the amount paid for goodwill suddenly has no value. However, this alternative was supported by **Accounting Research Study No. 10.**[16] Several major arguments can be made in favor of this position. First, purchased goodwill is different in nature than a company's other assets and cannot be sold or used independently of the other assets. Therefore, it is inappropriate to include it with the other assets on the company's balance sheet. Second, because internally developed goodwill is expensed immediately, this alternative creates a degree of consistency between internally developed and purchased goodwill. Third, as it is so difficult to estimate the life of the benefits, any choice of periods over which to amortize the goodwill is arbitrary, thus immediate write-off is justifiable.

Intangible assets are amortized over 15 years for computing taxable income. Therefore, there is a temporary difference between financial income and taxable income for intangible assets (unless those with a finite life are amortized for over 15 years for computing financial income). This temporary difference results in deferred income taxes. As we discuss in Chapter 18, some users would argue that for a growing company (which is increasing its tangible assets), there is no temporary difference because the company will never pay the deferred taxes. Some users would also argue that reporting deferred taxes for goodwill is not appropriate because there is no temporary difference due to the goodwill not being systematically amortized.

Once the FASB concluded that goodwill (and intangible assets with indefinite lives) would not be amortized, it had to develop an impairment test, as we discussed earlier in this chapter. Because the impairment test has to be applied annually, it may add a

---

16. G. R. Catlett and N. O. Olson, "Accounting for Goodwill," *Accounting Research Study No. 10* (New York: AICPA, 1968).

significant cost to companies. Many users are also concerned that the impairment loss will not be *reliable* due to the numerous estimates that a company has to make.

International Accounting Differences

International Accounting Standards require that goodwill is amortized over a maximum period of 20 years, unless there is evidence of a longer life. Thus, U.S. accounting principles are not consistent with those around the world because they require the recognition of an asset and do not allow amortization. Also, international accounting standards allow intangibles to be revalued upwards. For example, in the United Kingdom brand names such as Schweppes are accounted for this way. Also, International Accounting Standards allow some internally generated intangibles to be recorded as assets, as long as the cost can be measured reliably.

APPENDIX: ESTIMATING THE VALUE OF GOODWILL

We discussed purchased goodwill in the chapter and we assumed a purchase price, so that the goodwill was the difference between that price and the fair value of the identifiable net assets. We discuss methods of estimating the value of goodwill for negotiations or other reasons in this Appendix.

Goodwill can also be considered from an income perspective. In the chapter discussion we suggested that higher quality products, intellectual capital, and an advantageous geographical location would result in a higher income. But higher than what? A higher income than the company would earn otherwise, or more generally a higher income than is normal for companies in that industry? In this context, the rate of return earned by the company is more meaningful than the absolute value of the income. Therefore, goodwill can also be defined as **the value attached to the ability of a company to earn a higher than normal rate of return (an excess rate of return) on the market value of its identifiable net assets.**

Estimating the Value of Goodwill

When one company is negotiating to buy another company, the price offered is typically much greater than the book value of the net assets to be acquired. Three factors can account for the difference between the value of the company as a whole and the book value of the net assets (assets less liabilities). First, **identifiable net assets are generally listed on the balance sheet at their historical costs.** While some current assets and liabilities are listed at amounts that approximate their fair values, others (such as land and buildings) may have current fair values that are very different from the recorded historical costs. Second, **identifiable intangible assets may be unrecorded** (or undervalued). As we discussed in the chapter, R&D costs and operating costs are expensed as incurred. Therefore internally developed intangibles either are not recorded or are recorded at only the costs directly associated with the intangible after all R&D costs and operating costs have been expensed. Third, **unidentifiable intangibles may exist that are categorized as goodwill.** In the following sections, we discuss several methods that might be used to value the goodwill of a purchased company. However, it should be remembered that these methods are only guidelines. The price must be agreed upon by both the purchaser and the seller. Therefore the amount paid for goodwill in any purchase transaction is determined solely by the parties involved and is not defined by generally accepted accounting principles.

To illustrate the previously mentioned concepts, consider the potential purchase of the Kasper Company, which has a condensed balance sheet as we show in Exhibit 11-4. The book value of the company's net assets is $200,000 ($400,000 − $50,000 − $150,000). Since goodwill has been defined to include all the assets that cannot be identified, how can we determine the value of goodwill? We have discussed goodwill in terms of the ability to earn an above-normal return, and we can use this approach to develop a value

9 Estimate the value of goodwill.

EXHIBIT 11-4 Kasper Company

Balance Sheet, December 31, 2004

Current assets	$125,000	Current liabilities	$ 50,000
Noncurrent assets	275,000	Noncurrent liabilities	150,000
		Stockholders' equity	200,000
	$400,000		$400,000

---

for goodwill. To continue the example of the Kasper Company we must make two assumptions. First, suppose that the Kasper Company can be expected to earn $50,000 per year in perpetuity and that the normal return earned by companies in the industry is 10% of the identifiable net assets. In other words, 10% is the normal return required by investors (the acquiring company) for investments of this riskiness.

What is the value of the whole company? It is the amount that must be invested to earn $50,000 per year, when $50,000 is a return of 10% on the investment. Therefore, it is the present value of $50,000, in perpetuity, discounted at 10%, which is calculated as follows:

$$\text{Value of Company} = \frac{\text{Earnings}}{\text{Discount Rate}}$$
$$= \frac{\$50,000}{0.10}$$
$$= \$500,000$$

This valuation means that the Kasper Company is worth $300,000 more than the $200,000 book value of its identifiable net assets. Discounting expected cash flows would result in a more meaningful measure of value, but we use net income in this example as an approximation of net cash flows.

As we discussed previously, the difference of $300,000 may result from three causes. First, individual assets may be recorded at less than their fair values (or liabilities may be overvalued). Suppose that the $200,000 of Kasper Company's recorded net assets are estimated to have a fair value of $320,000. Land, for example, may be worth more than was originally paid. Also, because depreciation on plant and equipment is not related to fair value, it can be expected that the fair values of these assets will be different from their book values. Second, identifiable intangible assets may be unrecorded. Suppose that the Kasper Company owns an internally developed patent that has a fair value of $30,000. This provides a total fair value of identifiable net assets of $350,000. Third, the remaining difference between the value of the company as a whole and the value of its identifiable net assets is goodwill. For the Kasper Company, this is $150,000 ($500,000 – $350,000). We summarize the determination of the value of goodwill as follows:

Value of estimated annual earnings of $50,000, in perpetuity, discounted at 10% ($50,000 ÷ 0.10)		$500,000
Less: Book value of recorded net assets	$200,000	
Excess of fair value over book value of recorded net assets ($320,000 – $200,000)	120,000	
Fair value of unrecorded identifiable intangible asset	30,000	
Value of identifiable net assets		(350,000)
Value of goodwill		$150,000

Steps Used in Estimating the Value of Goodwill

Now that we have established the relationship between excess earnings and the valuation of goodwill, a company may use a series of six steps to compute a particular value for another company it is considering purchasing:

1. Estimate the average future annual earnings from the identifiable net assets.
2. Estimate the rate (or rates) of return that should be earned by the company on its identifiable net assets.
3. Estimate the current fair value of the identifiable net assets.
4. Compute the estimated excess annual earnings.
5. Estimate the expected life of the excess annual earnings.
6. Compute the present value of the estimated excess annual earnings.

Two additional steps may follow the calculation of the value of the goodwill:

7. Compute the total value of the company being considered for purchase.
8. Apply sensitivity analysis.

We discuss each of these steps in the following sections, although they may not actually be carried out in the sequence outlined. For example, the estimation in Step 1 may be a function of the values in Step 3. In addition, access to the records of the company being considered for purchase makes the estimation process easier.

STEP 1: ESTIMATE THE AVERAGE FUTURE EARNINGS   It is very difficult to develop an estimate of the average future annual earnings from a company's existing net assets. Many internal variables, such as management decisions and employee productivity, affect future earnings. There are also numerous external variables, such as the general state of the economy and the actions of competitors. Companies find it difficult enough to develop accurate budgets of earnings for a short time in the future, and it is usually impractical to consider using normal budgeting techniques to estimate annual earnings for sufficient years into the future that would be useful for the valuation of goodwill.

The alternative approach is to base estimated future annual earnings on the earnings of recent years. A single year is not likely to be reliable, and extending too many years into the past may be misleading because of changed conditions. The goal is to select a period that is relevant to the prediction of expected future earnings. The trend of earnings (or a simple average) over, say, the last 5 years may be extended into the future to provide the estimate of future annual earnings. Such estimates should be adjusted for any nonrecurring items and for changes in operating and competitive conditions that can be reliably predicted. Examples of adjustments are:

1. Eliminating unusual gains or losses, extraordinary items, the results of discontinued operations, and the effects of changes in accounting principles included in the income statement of the company being considered for purchase because they are not expected to recur in the future.
2. Adjusting for differences in accounting principles. For example, the company being considered for purchase may use FIFO and accelerated depreciation, whereas other companies in the same industry may use LIFO and straight-line depreciation. To permit better comparisons, the accounting methods (and related account balances) should be adjusted to conform to those of the other companies in the industry.

A more sophisticated way to estimate future earnings is to separate income into its revenue and expense components and to project each separately based on the past figures. It is also desirable to adjust these past figures so that they are based on the current values that are used to value the identifiable assets being purchased (as calculated in Step 3).

The Baley Company, which is considering acquiring the Greenfield Company, uses the data presented in Exhibit 11-5 for an analysis. We simplify this example because we

EXHIBIT 11-5 Greenfield Company

Estimate of the Average Future Annual Earnings

Average annual revenue for the past 5 years		$628,000
Average annual cost of goods sold for the past 5 years	$266,000	
Average annual operating expenses for the past 5 years	180,000	
Expected annual increase in wages not to be recovered by increased revenues	40,000	
Increase in annual depreciation on the current fair value of the assets	12,000	
Annual amortization of tangible assets with finite lives not previously recorded	10,000	
Expected expenses		(508,000)
Expected average annual earnings before income taxes		$120,000
Estimated income taxes (30%)		(36,000)
Expected average annual earnings		$ 84,000

calculate an average of past earnings rather than considering trends in each component. Three adjustments are made to the past earnings figures. First, expected increases in wages that will not be recovered by future price increases cause a reduction in future earnings. Second, depreciation is adjusted so that it is based on the fair value of the assets. Third, intangible assets with finite lives that were not previously recorded are amortized. The amounts of the depreciation ($12,000) and amortization ($10,000) are based on the additional values ($120,000 and $150,000, respectively) recorded in Step 3. These amounts are based on an assumed 10-year useful life for the property and plant and a 15-year life for the intangible asset. The Greenfield Company had an extraordinary loss in one of the past 5 years that we have excluded from the analysis because it is not expected to recur in the future.

STEP 2: ESTIMATE THE RATE OF RETURN The rate of return that should be earned by the acquired company on its identifiable net assets is based on the risk of the investment and the alternatives that are available. It is the rate necessary to attract investment capital to this kind of business under current conditions. Data on average rates of return are available in government publications and from various financial services. Such rates are usually based on the book value of the net assets of the company, and it may be necessary to adjust this rate to reflect the use of the fair value of the assets in the calculation. Care should be taken to consider the effects of particular accounting methods used by the company. For example, if the company being considered for purchase uses FIFO, but most comparable companies use LIFO, appropriate adjustments should be made. In the Greenfield Company example, it is assumed that the appropriate rate of return is 10% after income taxes.

STEP 3: ESTIMATE THE CURRENT FAIR VALUE OF THE IDENTIFIABLE NET ASSETS Because accounting records are based on the historical cost principle, it is unlikely that the book value of the net assets of the company being considered for purchase approximates the current fair value of its identifiable net assets.

The book value of the current assets and liabilities is usually a reasonable approximation of the fair value of these items. One major exception occurs when the LIFO inventory method is used, because the inventory book value will be less than the fair value if prices have risen since the adoption of LIFO. Other minor adjustments may be necessary, such as to update the allowance for uncollectible accounts. Property, plant, and equipment book values are likely to need significant adjustments and an appraisal may be required. Identifiable intangible assets must be adjusted to their fair values. Non-current liabilities may present some valuation problems. If interest rates have changed since bonds or notes were issued, these liabilities should be revalued using present value analysis based on current market rates. Also, there may be unrecorded liabilities in the form of future pension payments or contingencies.

The assets may be worth more to the Baley Company than to the Greenfield Company because a combination of the assets of the two companies may result in total earnings greater than the sum of the earnings of the two separate companies. Furthermore, since the Baley Company will record the purchased assets at their current fair values, higher depreciation will result if the fair values are greater than the book values.

Revaluation of the Greenfield Company's identifiable net assets is as follows:

Book value of identifiable net assets	$570,000
Revaluation of LIFO inventory to fair value	90,000
Increase in allowance for uncollectible accounts	(10,000)
Revaluation of property, plant, and equipment to fair value	120,000
Fair value of internally developed patent	150,000
Revaluation of bonds payable due to decline in interest rates	(60,000)
Unfunded projected benefit obligation of the pension plan	(140,000)
Current fair value of identifiable net assets	$720,000

STEP 4: COMPUTE THE ESTIMATED EXCESS ANNUAL EARNINGS The estimated excess annual earnings is the difference between the estimated average future annual earnings and the normal rate of return multiplied by the fair value of the net identifiable assets. For the Greenfield Company, this amount is computed as follows:

Average expected annual earnings (from Step 1)	$84,000
10% return on fair value of identifiable net assets	(72,000)
Estimated excess annual earnings	$12,000

Annual earnings of $72,000 are necessary for a normal return of 10% on identifiable net assets having a value of $720,000. Since the company expects to earn $84,000 annually, there must be additional unidentifiable assets in the form of goodwill. It should be noted that the 10% return was the normal rate based on the historical cost of the assets, but in this example we have used it as the normal return on the fair value of the net identifiable assets. In ordinary circumstances this is an acceptable approximation, but if there is a significant difference between the book value and the fair value, a downward adjustment of the normal rate may be appropriate.

STEP 5: ESTIMATE THE EXPECTED LIFE OF EXCESS ANNUAL EARNINGS It is sometimes argued that the excess annual earnings have an infinite life. This is not a realistic assumption, because competition or technological change can eventually eliminate the advantages that exist at the time of purchase. This does *not* mean that the company cannot earn a higher-than-normal return in the future, but it means that if the company does, it will be increasingly a result of the activities that occur *after* the purchase. In other words, it will be the result of continuing expenditures on such things as training employees, R&D, advertising, and production of high-quality products. If such continuing efforts are not made, the goodwill that existed at the time of purchase cannot be expected to continue and will become impaired. Therefore, it seems clear that the excess annual earnings have a limited life. For the Greenfield Company, we will assume that the excess annual earnings are expected to last for ten years.

STEP 6: COMPUTE THE PRESENT VALUE OF THE ESTIMATED EXCESS ANNUAL EARNINGS The usual approach to computing the present value of the estimated excess annual earnings (goodwill) is to discount these earnings at the normal rate of return for their estimated life. For the Greenfield Company, the excess annual earnings of $12,000 are discounted at 10% for 10 years as follows:

Estimated excess annual earnings	$ 12,000
Present value factor for an annuity of 10 periods at 10% (from Table 4 of Appendix D)	× 6.144567
Present value of estimated excess annual earnings (goodwill)	$ 73,735

An alternative is to use a discount rate higher than the normal rate of return. This has been suggested because the risk associated with higher-than-normal earnings is greater than the risk associated with normal earnings. For example, if we use a discount rate of 20% to capitalize the 10-year excess annual earnings of the Greenfield Company, goodwill is computed at $50,310 ($12,000 × 4.192472).

STEP 7: COMPUTE THE TOTAL VALUE OF THE COMPANY The ultimate purpose of estimating the value of goodwill is to determine the total value of the company being considered for purchase. In our example, the total *estimated* value of the Greenfield Company is $793,735, which consists of the $720,000 fair value of the identifiable net assets on which a 10% return is anticipated, and the $73,735 goodwill on which a 10% return is also anticipated.

STEP 8: APPLY SENSITIVITY ANALYSIS Estimates of the future earnings, the rate of return, the fair value of the assets, and the expected life of the excess annual earnings are used in the calculation of goodwill. A great deal of uncertainty and subjectivity are involved in these estimates. We emphasize that the calculation of goodwill does not produce a definitive valuation and is certainly not a final indication of the value of the company being considered for purchase. One additional step to improve the information that management has when it is involved in the negotiation process to purchase a company is to perform sensitivity analysis on the estimates used in the goodwill calculation. **Sensitivity analysis involves calculating the change in the estimated value of the company being considered for purchase as a result of changing the values of the items used in the calculation.** For example, a change in the discount rate used to value the excess earnings from 10% to 20% reduces the goodwill to $50,310, and therefore reduces the estimated value of the Greenfield Company to $770,310. By performing sensitivity analysis, management has both a value based on its best estimates and a range of values if those estimates are in error.

The valuation of the goodwill is an initial step toward the valuation of the company being considered for purchase, but the actual purchase price is the result of the negotiation process. Bargaining strength and skill are probably at least as important in determining the final price. Nevertheless, knowledge of the value of goodwill is an important element in improving this bargaining strength.

Other Methods of Estimating Goodwill

Because of the uncertainties involved in the estimation of goodwill, it is sometimes suggested that even simpler rules be used for its valuation. These include valuing goodwill by such arbitrary amounts as (1) 10 times annual earnings, (2) 4 times excess annual earnings (of course, numbers other than 10 and 4 could be used), and (3) determining the value of the company by capitalizing annual earnings at a normal rate (as we used in an illustration earlier in this chapter). Although these might be useful rules of thumb, it is difficult to argue that because of the difficulties of measurement it is better to attempt only a simple measurement. However, these alternative valuation methods might be used as a form of sensitivity analysis to complement the value of goodwill computed under the preferred method discussed earlier, even though they ignore the time value of money.

Another more rational way of reducing the uncertainties is to negotiate a price that involves contingent payments based on future excess income actually earned. If the company's shares are publicly traded on a stock market, the market value of the outstanding shares of the company may be a useful basis for estimating the value of that company. However, the price established by the stock market is based on the trading of a small number of the outstanding shares and probably does not give a valid indication of the value of all the shares. In addition, the prices of stocks tend to fluctuate as a result of many factors, some of which may not reflect changes in the underlying value of the company. However, it is likely that a company will have to pay more than the current market price of the shares of another company in order to purchase it.

SUMMARY

At the beginning of the chapter, we identified several objectives you would accomplish after reading the chapter. The objectives are listed below, each followed by a brief summary of the key points in the chapter discussion.

1. **Explain the accounting alternatives for intangibles.** The cost of a purchased identifiable intangible with a finite life is recorded as an asset and is amortized. The cost of a purchased identifiable intangible with an indefinite life and an unidentifiable intangible (goodwill) is recorded as an asset and is reviewed for impairment annually (but not amortized). The cost of an internally developed identifiable intangible is recorded as an asset and is amortized, except for research and development costs, which are expensed as incurred. The cost of an internally developed unidentifiable intangible is expensed as incurred.

2. **Understand the amortization or impairment of intangibles.** An intangible asset with a finite life must be amortized over its economic life. A company selects the amortization method based on the expected pattern of benefits that the intangible asset will produce, but if the company cannot reliably determine the pattern it uses the straight-line method. An intangible asset with an indefinite life is not amortized but is reviewed for impairment at least annually. A company tests an intangible asset for impairment by first estimating the fair value of the asset. An intangible asset is impaired when its fair value is less than its carrying value. The impairment loss is the amount by which the fair value is less than the carrying value.

3. **Identify research and development costs.** Research is the planned search or critical investigation aimed at discovery of new knowledge with the hope that such knowledge will be useful in developing a new product or service, or a new process or technique, or in bringing about a significant improvement to an existing product or process. Development is the translation of research findings or other knowledge into a plan or design for a new product or process, or for a significant improvement to an existing product or process, whether intended for sale or use. Research and development costs include materials, equipment, and facilities, personnel, intangibles purchased from others, contract services, and indirect costs. Research and development costs are expensed, including the costs of materials, equipment, facilities, and intangibles purchased from others that have no alternative future uses.

4. **Explain the conceptual issues for research and development costs.** The conceptual alternatives for research and development costs are to expense all costs as incurred, to capitalize all costs as incurred and amortize them over the periods expected to benefit, to capitalize costs when incurred if specified conditions are fulfilled and record all other costs as expenses, and to accumulate all costs in a special category until the existence of future benefits can be determined.

5. **Account for identifiable intangible assets including patents, copyrights, franchises, computer software costs, and trademarks and tradenames.** Each of these identifiable intangible assets is recorded at cost and amortized over its economic life, unless it has an indefinite life, such as trademarks and tradenames, in which case it is reviewed for impairment annually.

6. **Account for unidentifiable intangibles including internally developed and purchased goodwill.** The costs of internally developed goodwill are expensed as incurred. Purchased goodwill arises when a company is acquired and is the difference between the purchase price of the company as a whole and the fair value of the identifiable net assets. Purchased goodwill is recorded as an asset and is reviewed for impairment annually at the reporting unit level. A company uses a two-step approach. First, the company compares the fair value of the reporting unit with its book value. If the fair value is less than the book value, the second step must be performed. The company first allocates the fair value of the reporting unit to all the identifiable assets and liabilities of the unit as if the unit had been acquired. The implied fair value of the goodwill is the excess "purchase price" over the amount assigned to the identifiable assets and liabilities. The impairment loss is the difference between the carrying value of the goodwill and the lower implied fair value.

7. **Understand the disclosure of intangibles.** A company must disclose its total research and development expense. Intangible assets and goodwill are distinguished from tangible assets in the financial statements. A company must also disclose amortization expense, impairment losses, the method and period of amortization, as well as other disclosures.

8. **Explain the conceptual issues regarding intangibles.** The major conceptual issues are whether some internally developed intangibles, such as research and development, should be capitalized, and whether some intangible assets, such as purchased goodwill, should be amortized instead of being reviewed for impairment.

9. **Estimate the value of goodwill (Appendix).** To estimate the value of the goodwill of another company, a company may estimate the average future annual earnings from the identifiable net assets, estimate the rate(s) of return that should be earned by the company on its identifiable net assets, estimate the current fair value of the identifiable net assets, compute the estimated excess annual earnings, estimate the expected life of the excess annual earnings, and compute the present value of the estimated excess annual earnings.

QUESTIONS

Q11-1 How are intangible assets distinguished from tangible assets? What do they have in common?

Q11-2 How are identifiable intangibles distinguished from unidentifiable intangibles?

Q11-3 Explain how a company accounts for the cost of identifiable and unidentifiable intangibles.

Q11-4 Are all intangible assets amortized? If not, which ones are not? Why?

Q11-5 Which amortization method is required for intangibles? Are there any exceptions?

Q11-6 What factors should a company consider in estimating the useful life of an intangible?

Q11-7 What is meant by the terms *research* and *development*?

Q11-8 What activities are included in R&D? Which are excluded?

Q11-9 What expenditures for R&D does a company include in R&D costs?

Q11-10 What alternative methods of accounting for R&D were considered in *FASB Statement No. 2*? List an argument in favor and one against each alternative.

Q11-11 Over how many years are patents amortized? Copyrights? Goodwill?

Q11-12 How does a company record a patent worth $100,000 if: (a) It has just purchased it for $90,000? (b) The company has developed it?

Q11-13 List four possible causes of goodwill.

Q11-14 What is the definition of *goodwill* from an asset valuation perspective? From an income perspective?

Q11-15 What are the three factors that may account for the difference between the value of the company as a whole and the book value of the net assets?

Q11-16 Under what conditions is goodwill capitalized at acquisition? Expensed at acquisition? Explain the arguments used to justify this accounting.

Q11-17 Distinguish between internal and external goodwill. In which situations is each capitalized or expensed?

Q11-18 Under what conditions is purchased goodwill amortized? Explain how a company determines its goodwill impairment, if any.

Q11-19 It has been proposed that purchased goodwill should be written off immediately to stockholders' equity. Evaluate the arguments in favor of and against this proposal.

Q11-20 What is meant by the term *negative goodwill*? How is it recorded?

Q11-21 (Appendix) What are the eight steps in the valuation of goodwill?

Q11-22 (Appendix) What is meant by the following terms: *average future annual earnings; normal rate of return; excess annual earnings; expected life of excess annual earnings; current fair value of identifiable net assets?*

CASES

C O M M U N I C A T I O N

C11-1 Patents

In examining the books of Samson Manufacturing Company, you find on the December 31, 2004 balance sheet the item, "Costs of patents, $308,440." Referring to the ledger accounts, you note the following items regarding one patent acquired in 2001:

2001	Legal costs incurred in defending the validity of the patent	$3,500

2003	Legal costs in prosecuting an infringement suit	7,900
2003	Legal costs (additional expenses) in the infringement suit	1,500
2003	Cost of improvements (unpatented) on the patented device	4,800

There are no credits in the account, and the company has not recorded any amortization for any of the patents. There are three other patents issued in 1998, 2000, and 2001; all were developed by the staff of the client. The patented articles are presently very marketable, but are estimated to be in demand only for the next few years.

Required Discuss the items included in the Patent account from an accounting standpoint. (*AICPA adapted*)

C11-2 Patent and R&D

Clonal, Inc., a biotechnology company, developed and patented a diagnostic product called Trouver. Clonal purchased some research equipment to be used exclusively for Trouver and other research equipment to be used on Trouver and subsequent research projects. Clonal defeated a legal challenge to its Trouver patent and began production and marketing operations for the product.

Clonal allocated its corporate headquarters' costs to its research division as a percentage of the division's salaries.

Required

1. Explain how Clonal should report the equipment purchased for Trouver in its income statements and balance sheets.
2. a. Describe the matching principle.
   b. Describe the accounting treatment of research and development costs and consider whether this is consistent with the matching principle. What is the justification for the accounting treatment of research and development costs?
3. Explain how Clonal should classify its corporate headquarters' costs allocated to the research division in its income statement.
4. Explain how Clonal should report the legal costs incurred in defending Trouver's patent in its statement of cash flows. (*AICPA adapted*)

C11-3 Research and Development Costs

The Gratwick Company is in the process of developing a revolutionary new product. A new division of the company was formed to develop, manufacture, and market this new product. As of year-end (December 31, 2003), the new product has not been manufactured for resale; however, a prototype unit was built and is in operation.

Throughout 2004 the new division incurred certain costs. These costs include design and engineering studies, prototype manufacturing costs, administrative expenses (including salaries of administrative personnel), and market research costs. In addition, the company purchased approximately $500,000 in equipment (estimated useful life, 10 years) for use in developing and manufacturing the new product. The company built approximately $200,000 of this equipment specifically for the design and development of the new product; it used the remaining $300,000 of equipment to manufacture the preproduction prototype and will use it to manufacture the new product once it is in commercial production.

Required

1. What is the definition of *research* and of *development* as defined in *FASB Statement No. 2*?

2. Briefly indicate the practical and conceptual reasons for the conclusion reached by the FASB on accounting practices for research and development costs.
3. In accordance with *FASB Statement No. 2*, how should Gratwick record the various costs in the financial statements for the year ended December 31, 2004? (*AICPA adapted*)

C11-4 Goodwill

After extended negotiations, Rothman Corporation bought from Felzar Company most of the latter's assets on June 30, 2004. At the time of the sale, Felzar's accounts (adjusted to June 30, 2004) reflected the following descriptions and amounts for the assets transferred:

	Cost	Contra (Valuation) Account	Book Value
Receivables	$ 83,600	$ 3,000	$ 80,600
Inventory	107,000	5,200	101,800
Land	20,000	—	20,000
Buildings	207,500	73,000	134,500
Fixtures and equipment	205,000	41,700	163,300
Goodwill	50,000	—	50,000
	$673,100	$122,900	$550,200

You ascertain that the contra (valuation) accounts were allowance for doubtful accounts, allowance to reduce inventory to market, and accumulated depreciation. During the extended negotiations, Felzar held out for a consideration of approximately $600,000 (depending on the level of the receivables and inventory). As of June 30, 2004, however, Felzar agreed to accept Rothman's offer of $450,000 cash plus 1% of the net sales (as defined in the contract) of the next 5 years, with payments at the end of each year. Felzar expects that Rothman's total net sales during this period will exceed $15 million.

Required

1. Explain how Rothman Corporation should record this transaction.
2. Discuss the propriety of recording goodwill in the accounts of Rothman Corporation for this transaction. (*AICPA adapted*)

C11-5 Goodwill (Appendix)

Elson Corporation, a retail fuel oil distributor, has increased its annual sales volume to a level three times greater than the annual sales of a dealer it purchased in 2000 in order to begin operations.

The board of directors recently received an offer to negotiate the sale of Elson Corporation to a large competitor. As a result, the majority of the board wants to increase the stated value of goodwill on the balance sheet to reflect the larger sales volume developed through intensive promotion and the current market price of sales gallonage. A few of the board members, however, would prefer to eliminate goodwill altogether from the balance sheet in order to prevent "possible misinterpretations." Goodwill was recorded properly in 2000.

Required

1. Explain the meaning of the term *goodwill*.
2. List the techniques used to calculate the tentative value of goodwill in negotiations to purchase a going concern.

3. Explain why the book and fair values of the goodwill of Elson Corporation are different.
4. Discuss the propriety of (a) increasing the stated value of goodwill prior to the negotiations and (b) eliminating goodwill completely from the balance sheet prior to negotiations. (*AICPA adapted*)

C R E A T I V E   A N D   C R I T I C A L   T H I N K I N G

C11-6 Intangibles

Some intangibles that companies may report on their balance sheets include patents, copyrights, tradenames, computer software, and goodwill.

Required

1. Which of these intangibles would typically be amortized? How would they be amortized? Which of these intangibles would typically not be amortized? Why would they not be amortized? Which of these intangibles would never be amortized?
2. Which of these intangibles must be reviewed for impairment annually?

C11-7 Nature of Intangibles

The Johnson Company operates several plants at which it processes limestone into quicklime and hydrated lime. The Bland Plant, where most of the equipment was installed many years ago, continually deposits a dusty white substance over the surrounding countryside. Citing the unsanitary condition of the neighboring community of Adeltown, the pollution of the Adel River, and the high incidence of lung disease among workers at Bland, the state's Pollution Control Agency has ordered the installation of air pollution control equipment. Also, the Agency has assessed a substantial penalty, which will be used to clean up Adeltown. After considering the costs involved (which could not have been reasonably estimated prior to the Agency's action), Johnson decides to comply with the Agency's orders, the alternative being to cease operations at Bland at the end of the current fiscal year. The officers of Johnson agree that the air pollution control equipment should be capitalized and depreciated over its useful life, but they disagree over the period(s) to which the penalty should be expensed.

Required Explain the conceptual merits and reporting requirements of accounting for the penalty as a

1. Charge to the current period
2. Correction of prior periods
3. Capitalizable item to be amortized over future periods (*AICPA adapted*)

C11-8 Patents

On June 30, 2004 your client, Sprauge Corporation, was granted two patents covering plastic cartons that it has been producing and marketing profitably for the past 3 years. One patent covers the manufacturing process and the other covers the related products.

Sprauge executives tell you that these patents represent the most significant breakthrough in the industry in the past 30 years. The products have been marketed under the registered trademarks Safetainer, Duratainer, and Sealrite. Your client has already granted licenses under the patents to other manufacturers in the United States and abroad and they are producing substantial royalties.

On July 1 Sprauge commenced patent infringement actions against several companies whose names you recognize as those of substantial and prominent competitors. Sprauge management is optimistic that these suits will result in a permanent injunction against the manufacture and sale of the infringing products and collection of damages for loss of profits caused by the alleged infringement. The financial vice-president has suggested that the patents be recorded at the discounted value of expected net royalty receipts.

Required

1. Explain the meaning of *discounted value of expected net receipts*.
2. How would such a value be calculated for net royalty receipts?
3. Explain the basis of valuation of Sprauge's patents that would be generally accepted in accounting.
4. Assuming no practical problems of implementation and ignoring generally accepted accounting principles, explain the preferable basis of valuation for patents.
5. Explain what would be the preferable theoretical basis of amortization.
6. Explain what recognition, if any, the company should make of the infringement litigation in the financial statements for the year ending September 30, 2004. (*AICPA adapted*)

C11-9 Cost of Intangibles

After securing lease commitments from several major stores, Silver Springs Shopping Center, Inc., was organized and built a shopping center in a growing suburb. The shopping center would have opened on schedule on January 2, 2005 if it had not been struck by a severe tornado in December; it opened for business on October 2, 2005. All the additional construction costs incurred as a result of the tornado were covered by insurance.

In July 2004 in anticipation of the scheduled January opening, a permanent staff was hired to promote the shopping center, obtain tenants for the uncommitted space, and manage the property. A summary of some of the costs incurred in 2004 and the first 9 months of 2005 follows:

	2004	Jan. 1, to Sept. 30, 2005
Interest on mortgage bonds	$60,000	$90,000
Cost of obtaining tenants	28,000	58,000
Promotional advertising	34,000	34,000

The promotional advertising campaign was designed to familiarize shoppers with the center. Had the company known in time that the center would not open until October 2005, it would not have made the 2004 expenditure for promotional advertising. The company had to repeat the advertising in 2005.

All the tenants who had leased space in the shopping center at the time of the tornado accepted the October occupancy date on condition that the monthly rental charges for the first 9 months of 2005 be canceled.

Required Explain how the company should treat each of the costs for 2004 and the first 9 months of 2005. Give the reasons for each treatment. (*AICPA adapted*)

C11-10 Analyzing Coca-Cola's Intangibles Disclosures

Refer to the financial statements and related notes of the Coca-Cola Company in Appendix A of this book.

Required

1. Why did the company report "trademarks and other intangible assets"?
2. Do you think that the company has additional "intangibles" that are not recorded on the balance sheet? Why? How would this issue affect your understanding of the company's financial performance?
3. Recreate summary journal entries to record the transactions and events that affected the trademarks and other intangible assets in 2001, assuming there were no sales.
4. Compute the estimated average life of the trademarks and other intangible assets. Do you think that this life is appropriate? What will be the effect of adopting *FASB Statement No. 142*?

C11-11 Ethics and Intangibles

You are auditing the financial records of a company and you are aware that it has grown quickly in the last few years by acquiring other companies. You look up the disclosure in last year's annual report, which states, "The company amortizes its intangibles over periods ranging from 3 to 15 years." As you review the company's records, you find that the company made an acquisition of a "high-tech" company 3 years ago and has not recognized any impairment on the related goodwill. In the last 6 years, the company has made five other acquisitions and has not recognized any impairment related to them. Included in the acquisitions are several patents that are amortized over 9 years and some intangibles with indefinite lives.

Required From financial reporting and ethical perspectives, discuss the issues raised by this situation.

MULTIPLE CHOICE

Select the best answer for each of the following.

M11-1 The Plaza Company originated late in 2003 and began operations on January 2, 2004. Plaza is engaged in conducting market research studies on behalf of manufacturers. Prior to the start of operations, the following costs were incurred:

Attorney's fees in connection with organization of Plaza	$ 4,000
Improvements to leased offices prior to occupancy	7,000
Meetings of incorporators, state filing fees and other organization expenses	5,000
	$16,000

What is the amount of expense recognized for 2004?

a. $16,000
b. $9,000
c. $7,000
d. $4,000

M11-2 A purchased patent has a remaining legal life of 15 years. It should be

a. Expensed in the year of acquisition
b. Amortized over 15 years regardless of its useful life
c. Amortized over its useful life if less than 15 years
d. Not amortized

M11-3 Frye Company incurred research and development costs in 2004 as follows:

Equipment acquired for use in research and development projects	$1,000,000
Depreciation on the equipment	150,000
Materials used	200,000
Compensation costs of personnel	500,000
Outside consulting fees	100,000
Indirect costs appropriately allocated	250,000

The total research and development costs charged in Frye's 2004 income statement should be

a. $650,000   c. $1,200,000

b. $900,000   d. $1,800,000

M11-4 Which of the following assets typically are amortized?

	Patents	Trademarks
a.	No	No
b.	Yes	Yes
c.	No	Yes
d.	Yes	No

M11-5 What is the proper time or time period over which to match the cost of an intangible asset with revenues if it is likely that the benefit of the asset will last for an indefinite period?

a. Forty years

b. Fifty years

c. Immediately

d. At such time as a reduction in value can be quantitatively determined

M11-6 The general ledger of the Flint Corporation as of December 31, 2004 includes the following accounts:

Organization costs	$ 5,000
Deposits with advertising agency (will be used to promote goodwill)	8,000
Discounts on bonds payable	15,000
Excess of cost over book value of net assets of acquired subsidiary	70,000
Trademarks	12,000

In the preparation of Flint's balance sheet as of December 31, 2004, what should be reported as total intangible assets?

a. $82,000   c. $95,000

b. $87,000   d. $110,000

M11-7 Goodwill represents the excess of the cost of an acquired company over the

a. Sum of the fair values assigned to tangible assets acquired less liabilities assumed

b. Sum of the fair values assigned to identifiable assets acquired less liabilities assumed

c. Sum of the fair values assigned to intangible assets acquired less liabilities assumed

d. Book value of an acquired company

M11-8 During 2000 Traco Machine Company spent $176,000 on research and development costs for an invention. This invention was patented on January 2, 2001 at a nominal cost that was expensed in 2001. The patent had a legal life of 20 years and an estimated useful life of 8 years. In January 2005 Traco paid $16,000 for legal fees in a successful defense of the patent. Amortization for 2005 should be

a. $0   c. $4,000

b. $1,000   d. $26,000

M11-9 Which of the following amounts incurred in connection with a trademark should be capitalized?

	Cost of a Successful Defense	Registration Fees
a.	Yes	No
b.	Yes	Yes
c.	No	Yes
d.	No	No

M11-10 Sherwood Corporation incurred $68,000 of research and development costs in its laboratory to develop a patent that was granted on January 2, 2004. Legal fees and other costs associated with registration of the patent totaled $13,600. Sherwood estimates that the economic life of the patent will be 8 years. What amount should Sherwood charge to patent amortization expense for the year ended December 31, 2004?

a. $0   c. $1,700

b. $800   d. $10,200

(*AICPA adapted*)

EXERCISES

E11-1 *Cost of a Patent* The Befort Company filed for a patent on a new type of machine. The application costs totaled $12,000. R&D costs incurred to create the machine were $75,000. In the year in which the company filed for and received the patent, it spent $20,000 in the successful defense of a patent infringement suit.

Required

1. At what amount should the company capitalize the patent?
2. How would you determine the economic life of the patent?

E11-2 *Cost of a Patent* On January 3, 2004 the Franc Company purchased for $27,000 a patent that had been filed for 8 years earlier. The patent covers a manufacturing process that the company plans to use for 15 years. On January 2, 2005 the company paid its lawyers $10,000 for successfully defending the patent in a lawsuit.

Required Prepare all the journal entries associated with the patent in 2004 and 2005.

E11-3 *Cost of a Tradename* On January 10, 2004 the Hughes Company applied for a tradename. Legal costs associated with the application were $20,000. In January 2005 the company incurred $8,000 of legal fees in a successful defense of its tradename. The tradename was not impaired in 2004 and 2005.

Required Compute the ending carrying value of the tradename for 2004 and 2005. Should the company amortize the tradename?

E11-4   *Start-Up Costs*   Kling Company was organized in late 2004 and began operations on January 2, 2005. Prior to the start of operations, it incurred the following costs:

Costs of hiring new employees	$ 3,000
Attorney's fees in connection with the organization of the company	12,000
Improvements to leased offices prior to occupancy (10 year lease)	6,000
Costs of pre-opening advertising	5,000

Required What amount should the company expense in 2004? In 2005?

E11-5   *Research and Development Costs*   The KLK Clothing Company manufactures professional clothing for women. In order to keep costs low while still producing quality clothes, KLK conducts many research and development projects. On a current project, KLK researchers used $35,000 of cotton and $27,000 of wool from its inventory. KLK paid its researchers $30,000 in wages and purchased a special weaving machine for $60,000 cash. The machine was not suitable for use in production activities and was not expected to be used in other research projects. In addition, depreciation of the project's research lab amounted to $20,000.

Required Prepare the journal entry to record KLK's research and development costs.

E11-6   *Research and Development Costs*   In 2004 Lalli Corporation incurred R&D costs as follows:

Materials and equipment	$100,000
Personnel	100,000
Indirect costs	50,000
	$250,000

These costs relate to a product that will be marketed in 2005. The company estimates that these costs will be recouped by December 31, 2008.

Required What is the amount of R&D costs expensed in 2004? (*AICPA adapted*)

E11-7   *Research and Development Activities*   Which of the following activities are considered R&D? Justify your reasons for each answer.
1. Building an oil shale plant to test the feasibility of large-scale exploitation
2. Testing a new type of machine to evaluate its potential usefulness in production
3. Modifying a machine to make it suitable for filling a customer's order
4. Designing a new plant to produce the same products more efficiently
5. Testing in an attempt to find a more efficient production method

E11-8   *Research and Development Costs*   Which of the following are included in R&D costs of the current period? Justify each answer.
1. Current-period depreciation on the building housing the R&D activities
2. Cost of a market research study
3. Current-period depreciation on a machine used in R&D activities
4. Salary of the director of R&D
5. Salary of the vice-president who spends one-third of her time overseeing the R&D activities
6. Pension costs for the salaries in items 4 and 5

E11-9   *Intangibles*   The Barnum Company acquired several small companies at the end of 2003 and, based on the acquisitions, reported the following intangibles in its December 31, 2003 balance sheet:

Patent	$20,000
Copyright	40,000
Tradename	35,000
Computer software	10,000
Goodwill	90,000

The company's accountant determines the patent has an expected life of 10 years and no expected residual value, and that it will generate approximately equal benefits each year. The company expects to use the copyright and tradename for the foreseeable future. The accountant knows that the computer software is used in the company's 120 sales offices. The company has replaced the software in 60 offices in 2004, and expects to replace the software in 40 more offices in 2005 and the remainder in 2006.

Required How much amortization expense should the company recognize on each intangible asset in 2004?

E11-10   *Tradename*   Probst Company acquired a tradename several years ago at a cost of $60,000. The company has never considered the tradename to be impaired. However, at the end of 2004, the company has determined that the tradename is impaired because of a change in market conditions. It estimates that the tradename has a fair value of $40,000 at the end of 2004.

Required Prepare the journal entry (if any) for Probst Company to record the impairment of its trademark at the end of 2004.

E11-11   *Goodwill*   Several years ago, Blaha Company purchased Husker Company as a subsidiary. At that time, Blaha Company recorded goodwill of $100,000 related to the purchase. Since that time, the company has not considered the goodwill to be impaired. However, at the end of 2004, Blaha Company decides to evaluate the goodwill for impairment because of technological changes in the industry. The subsidiary has a book value (including the goodwill) of $900,000. Blaha Company estimates that the fair value of the subsidiary is $720,000, of which it allocates $660,000 to the subsidiary's identifiable assets and liabilities.

Required Prepare the journal entry (if any) for Blaha Company to record the impairment of its goodwill at the end of 2004.

E11-12   *Goodwill*   The Marino Company had the following balance sheet on January 1, 2004:

Current assets	$ 50,000	Current liabilities	$ 30,000
Property, plant, and equipment	200,000	Noncurrent liabilities	100,000
Intangible assets	20,000	Stockholders' equity	140,000
	$270,000		$270,000

On January 2, 2004 the Paul Company purchased the Marino Company by acquiring all its outstanding shares for $300,000 cash. On that date the fair value of the current assets was $40,000, and the fair value of the property, plant, and equipment was $240,000. In addition, the fair value of a previously unrecorded intangible asset was $25,000.

Required Compute the goodwill associated with the purchase of the Marino Company.

E11-13   *Normal Earnings and Goodwill (Appendix)*   The total earnings of the Jaeger Company for 2004 were $100,000 and included the following items:

Extraordinary gain	$10,000	Depreciation on building (straight-line)	$20,000
Liquidation of LIFO layer	7,000	Profit sharing payments to employees	25,000
Amortization of patents	12,000		

The profit sharing is based on a constant percent of total earnings *before* deducting the profit sharing amount. The building is worth 50% more than its recorded cost, and its economic life is double the current estimate.

Required Compute normal earnings for the year.

E11-14   *Goodwill (Appendix)*   For the past 5 years, the Satin Company has had average assets of $120,000, average liabilities of $35,000, and average annual earnings of $14,000. In the past 5 years, the company has had an extraordinary loss of $10,000 and a nonrecurring gain of $15,000. A 12% return on investment is considered normal for the industry. The expected life of any excess earnings is 10 years.

Required

1. Compute the implied goodwill of the Satin Company.
2. If excess annual earnings are capitalized at 14%, compute the implied goodwill.

E11-15 *Goodwill (Appendix)* The Hayes Company is considering acquiring the Ryan Company. The balance sheet of the Ryan Company is as follows:

Current assets	$ 50,000	Current liabilities	$ 30,000
Noncurrent assets	150,000	Noncurrent liabilities	50,000
		Stockholders' equity	120,000
	$200,000		$200,000

The Hayes Company believes that goodwill should be based on the book value of the assets and that excess earnings last only 5 years and should be capitalized at 14%. The Ryan Company believes that the assets are undervalued by 20%, that excess annual earnings will last forever, and that they should be capitalized at the normal rate of return. Both companies agree that the expected future annual earnings are $25,000 per year and the normal rate of return is 10%.

Required

1. Compute the implied goodwill under the proposal of each company.
2. Which of the two companies has the more reasonable approach to computing goodwill?

E11-16 *Goodwill (Appendix)* The owners of the Urwill Clothing Store are contemplating selling the business to new interests. The cumulative earnings for the past 5 years amounted to $550,000 including extraordinary gains of $40,000. The annual earnings based on an average rate of return on investment for this industry would have been $76,000. Excess earnings are to be capitalized at 10%.

Required Compute the value of the implied goodwill. (*AICPA adapted*)

E11-17 *Goodwill (Appendix)* The net assets of the Wiese Company were appraised at $100,000. Estimated future annual earnings are $15,000.

Required Compute the value of the goodwill under each of the following assumptions:

1. The future annual earnings will continue in perpetuity and are capitalized at 15%. The normal rate of return is 15%.
2. The excess annual earnings are expected to have a life of 5 years. The normal rate of return (and capitalization rate) is 12%.
3. The excess annual earnings are expected to have a life of 10 years. The normal rate of return is 11%, and excess annual earnings are capitalized at 12%.

E11-18 *Estimated Future Annual Earnings (Appendix)* The Stegman Company acquired the Band Company for $150,000. Excess annual earnings were capitalized at 20% in perpetuity. The normal rate of return is 11%. The goodwill was computed as $25,000.

Required What are the estimated future annual earnings of the Band Company?

PROBLEMS

P11-1 *Cost of Intangibles* The Brush Company engaged in the following transactions at the beginning of 2004:

1. Purchased a patent for $70,000 that had originally been filed for in January 1998. The purchase was made to protect another patent that the company had filed for in January 2000 and subsequently received.
2. Purchased the rights to a novel by a best-selling novelist in exchange for 10,000 shares of $10 par value common stock selling for $60 per share. The book sells 1 million copies in 2004 and is expected to sell a total of 500,000 copies in future years.
3. Purchased the franchise to operate a ferry service from the state government for $10,000. A bridge has been planned to replace the ferry, and it is expected that it will be completed in 5 years. Brush hopes that the ferry will continue as a tourist attraction, but profits are expected to be only 20% of those earned before the bridge is opened.
4. Paid $28,000 of legal costs to successfully defend the patent acquired in transaction 1.
5. Paid a race car driver $50,000 to have the Brush Company name prominently displayed on his car for 2 years.

Required Prepare journal entries to record the preceding transactions, including the first year's amortization of intangible assets where appropriate. Amortize over the legal life unless a better alternative is indicated.

P11-2   *Cost of Intangibles*   The Byrd Corporation engaged in the following transactions at the beginning of 2004:

1. Purchased a Hogburger franchise for a 5-year, $60,000, 10%-interest-bearing note. The franchise has an indefinite life providing the terms of the franchise are not violated.
2. Sold a tradename for $50,000. The tradename had a carrying value of $5,000.
3. Paid an advertising agency $60,000 to develop a 2-year advertising campaign to promote a new tradename.
4. Incurred legal fees of $5,000 to register a new tradename.
5. Purchased the copyright to a new movie for $500,000. The movie is made during 2004 at a cost of $15 million. It will begin showing in 2005 and is expected to gross $10 million during 2005, $20 million during 2006, and $10 million during 2007.

Required Prepare journal entries to record the preceding transactions, including any appropriate adjusting entries for 2004.

P11-3   *Correct Classification of Intangibles*   During the current year, the accountant for the Cartwright Corporation recorded numerous transactions in an account labeled Intangibles as follows:

Jan. 2	Incorporation fees	$17,500
Jan. 10	Legal fees for the organization of the company	7,500
Jan. 25	Paid for large-scale advertising campaign for the year	15,000
Apr. 1	Acquired land for $15,000 and a building for $20,000 to house the R&D activities. The building has a 20-year life.	35,000
May 15	Purchased materials exclusively for use in R&D activities. Of these materials, 20% are left at the end of the year and will be used in the same project next year. (They have no alternative use.)	15,000
June 30	Filed for a patent	10,000
July 1	Operating loss for first 6 months of the year	12,000
Dec. 11	Purchased an experimental machine from an inventor. The machine is expected to be used for a particular R&D activity for 2 years, after which it will have no residual value.	12,000
Dec. 31	Paid employees involved in R&D	30,000

Required Prepare adjusting journal entries to eliminate the Intangibles account and correctly record all the items. The company amortizes patents over 10 years.

P11-4   *Correcting Entries for Patents*   During the year-end audit of the Cressman Corporation's financial statements for 2004, you discover the following items:

1. The company had capitalized $57,000 to the Patent account at the beginning of 2003, for the cost of a patent. This amount included $50,000 of R&D costs. The patent was amortized over a 20-year life in 2003 and 2004.
2. At the beginning of 2003, the company had paid its lawyers $8,000 to successfully defend a patent infringement suit regarding the patent in Item 1. The company debited this cost to legal fees expense.
3. At the beginning of 2004, the company purchased a patent for $30,000 from the Baylor Company to prevent potential competition. It recorded the cost in the Patent account and amortized this cost over the remaining legal life of the patent obtained in Item 1. However, the company agreed to a suggestion by the auditors that the life of the company patent obtained in Item 1 was protected for only 7 more years as of the beginning of 2004.

Required Prepare adjusting journal entries on December 31, 2004.

P11-5   *Cost of Patents*   The Davis Research Company engaged in the following six transactions during 2004:

1. Purchased a patent for $35,000. Legal costs of $5,000 were also incurred.
2. Costs of improving patent:

Engineering costs	$20,000
Assembling and testing prototypes	10,000
Other R&D costs	25,000

3. Sold a prototype machine for $7,000. The research and development were performed in previous years.
4. Licensed a manufacturing process to another company and received $80,000 as an advance payment.

5. Successfully defended a patent infringement suit at a cost of $12,000.
6. Earned $5,000 of the advance payment on the licensed manufacturing process in Item 4.

Required Prepare journal entries to record the preceding transactions.

P11-6   *Research and Development Costs*   Cressman Company incurred research and development costs in 2004 as follows:

Materials used in research and development projects	$ 400,000
Equipment acquired that will have alternate future uses in future research and development projects for 4 years	2,000,000
Personnel costs of employees involved in research and development projects	1,000,000
Consulting fees paid to outsiders for research and development projects	100,000
Indirect costs reasonably allocable to research and development projects	200,000

Required What is the amount of research and development costs charged to Cressman's 2004 income? (*AICPA adapted*)

P11-7   *Intangibles*   The Jolis Company has provided information on the following items:
1. A patent was purchased from the Totley Company for $500,000 on January 1, 2003. At that time, Jolis estimated the remaining useful life to be 10 years. The patent was carried on Totley's books at $20,000 when it sold the patent.
2. On March 2, 2004 a franchise was purchased from the Unal Company for $240,000. In addition, 8% of the revenue from the franchise must be paid to Unal. Revenue earned during 2004 was $620,000. Jolis believes that the life of the franchise is indefinite and that the franchise is not impaired at the end of 2004.
3. Research and development costs were incurred as follows: (a) materials and equipment: $50,000; (b) personnel: $80,000; and (c) indirect costs: $40,000. The costs were incurred to develop a product that will go on sale in 2005 and will have an expected life of 5 years.
4. A tradename had been purchased for a sugar substitute at the beginning of 2000 for $80,000. In January 2004 it was suspected that the product caused cancer and so the tradename was abandoned.
5. The company purchased the net assets of Lansing Company on September 1, 2004 for $950,000, and the Lansing Company was liquidated. The Lansing Company had the following book (fair) values: current assets: $200,000 ($210,000); property, plant, equipment: $750,000 ($900,000); liabilities: $250,000 ($250,000). Any goodwill is not impaired at the end of 2004.

Required Prepare journal entries for the Jolis Company for 2004. The company uses the straight-line method of amortization computed to the nearest month over the maximum allowable life. Assume that the company pays all costs in cash, unless otherwise indicated.

P11-8   *Cost of a Copyright*   The Gansac Publishing Company signed a contract with an author to publish her book. The signing took place on January 1, 2004 and a payment of $20,000 was made. The agreement was that the author would receive 10% of the selling price of $10 per book. The company expects sales of the book to be 100,000 copies in 2004, 80,000 in 2005, and 20,000 in 2006. It incurred production costs of $800,000 for 200,000 copies during 2004.

Required
1. Prepare journal entries to record the preceding events during 2004 and 2005, assuming that sales were as projected.
2. How would your answer change if the projected sales were considered to be "probable"?

P11-9   *R&D Costs*   The controller of the Halpern Company prepared the following income statement and balance sheet at the end of the first year of the company's existence:

Income Statement	
Sales revenue	$40,000
Cost of sales	(20,000)
Operating expenses	(8,000)
Net income	$12,000

Balance Sheet

Cash	$ 33,000	Accounts payable	$ 5,000
Inventory	24,000	Notes payable	40,000
R&D costs	30,000	Common stock	50,000
Property, plant, and equipment (net)	20,000	Retained earnings	12,000
	$107,000		$107,000

Investigation shows that R&D costs include, among others, half the year's operating costs because "the company is not yet operating at capacity." In addition R&D costs include $5,000 of materials that were wasted during early production because "our employees made some unnecessary mistakes."

Required

1. Prepare the financial statements according to generally accepted accounting principles.
2. Compute the company's return on assets (net income divided by average total assets, as we discussed in Chapter 5) under both the original and revised financial statements.

See WebTutor for annotated problem solution.

P11-10   *Intangibles*   The Bailey Company was formed in January 2002 and is preparing its financial statements under GAAP for the first time at the end of 2004. Its general ledger at December 31, 2004 includes the following assets:

Patent	$120,000
Copyright	140,000
Tradename	150,000
Computer software	90,000
Organization costs	30,000
Research and development	250,000
Intellectual capital	150,000
Goodwill	90,000

As the recently hired accountant for the company, you have been asked to make sure that the company's accounting for intangibles follows GAAP. You know that, because the company has never issued financial statements according to GAAP, any adjustments that are made to correct violations of GAAP are recorded as an adjustment to its retained earnings. You determine that the patent has an expected life of 15 years at the end of 2004 and no residual value, and that it will generate approximately equal benefits each year. You also determine that the company will use the copyright and tradename for the foreseeable future. The computer software is used in the company's 20 offices around the country; it was replaced in 40% of the offices in 2004 and will be replaced in the remaining offices next year. On further examination, you find that the company had previously capitalized the expected value of its "human resources" as intellectual capital, with a corresponding increase in additional paid-in capital.

You also determine that the tradename and goodwill arose from an acquisition of a subsidiary company at the end of 2003. Because of a significant adverse change in the market, you decide that both assets are impaired. You estimate that the fair value of the tradename is $50,000. The subsidiary company has a book value of $500,000, including the goodwill of $90,000. You estimate that the subsidiary's fair value is $300,000, of which $250,000 is allocated to its identifiable assets and liabilities.

Required Prepare journal entries to provide the correct information under GAAP at the end of 2004.

P11-11   *Impairment*   Wember Company acquired a subsidiary company on December 31, 2000, and recorded the cost of the intangible assets it acquired as follows:

Patent	$100,000
Copyright	60,000
Tradename	80,000
Goodwill	150,000

The patent is being amortized by the straight-line method over an expected life of 10 years with no residual value. The copyright and tradename were considered to have indefinite lives.

Because of the continued success of the subsidiary, Wember has not considered any of the intangibles to be impaired. However, due to a recession and technological changes in the subsidiary's industry, Wember decides to review all its intangibles for impairment and record any adjustments at December 31, 2004.

Wember estimates that the fair value of the patent and copyright are $42,000 and $25,000, respectively. The company estimates the fair value of the tradename to be $90,000 but decides that it now has a limited life of 5 years. The subsidiary company has a book value of $700,000, including the goodwill of $150,000. Wember estimates that the fair value of the subsidiary company is $400,000, of which it allocates 80% to the identifiable assets and liabilities.

Required

1. Prepare journal entries for Wember Company to record the impairment of its intangible assets at December 31, 2004.
2. Prepare journal entries for Wember Company to record the amortization expense for its intangibles at December 31, 2005.

P11-12 *Goodwill* The Hamilton Company balance sheet on January 1, 2004 was as follows:

Cash	$ 30,000	Current liabilities	$ 20,000
Accounts receivable	80,000	Bonds payable	120,000
Marketable securities (short-term)	40,000	Pension liability	50,000
Inventory	100,000	Common stock	200,000
Property, plant, and equipment (net)	200,000	Retained earnings	60,000
	$450,000		$450,000

The Korbel Company is considering purchasing the Hamilton Company (a privately held company) and discovers the following about the Hamilton Company:

1. No allowance for uncollectibles has been established. A $10,000 allowance is considered appropriate.
2. Marketable securities are valued at cost. The current market value is $60,000.
3. The LIFO inventory method is used. The FIFO inventory of $140,000 would be used if the company is acquired.
4. Land, included in property, plant, and equipment, which is recorded at its cost of $50,000, is worth $120,000. The remaining property, plant, and equipment is worth 10% more than its depreciated cost.
5. The company has an unrecorded trademark that is worth $70,000.
6. The company's bonds are currently trading for $130,000 and the common stock for $300,000.
7. The pension liability is understated by $40,000.

Required

1. Compute the value of the implied goodwill if the Korbel Company agrees to pay $500,000 cash for the Hamilton Company.
2. Prepare the journal entry to record the acquisition on the books of the Korbel Company, assuming the Hamilton Company is liquidated.
3. If the Korbel Company agrees to pay only $400,000 cash, how much is the implied goodwill?
4. If the Korbel Company pays only $400,000 cash, prepare the journal entry to record the acquisition on its books assuming the Hamilton Company is liquidated.

P11-13 *Intangibles: Expense and Disclosure* Munn, Inc., had the following intangible account balances at December 31, 2003:

Patent	$192,000
Accumulated amortization	(24,000)

Transactions during 2004 and other information relating to Munn's intangible assets were as follows:

1. The patent was purchased from Grey Company for $192,000 on January 1, 2002, at which date the remaining legal life was 16 years. On January 1, 2004, Munn determined that the useful life of the patent was only 8 years from the date of acquisition.
2. On January 2, 2004, in connection with the purchase of a trademark from Cody Corporation, the parties entered into a noncompetition agreement and a consulting contract. Munn paid Cody $800,000, of which three-quarters was for the trademark and one-quarter was for Cody's agreement not to compete for a 5-year period in the line of business covered by the trademark. Munn considers the life of the trademark to be indefinite. Under the consulting contract, Munn agreed to pay Cody $50,000 annually on January 2 for 5 years. The first payment was made on January 2, 2004. The trademark is not impaired at the end of 2004.

Required

1. Prepare a schedule of the expenses for 2004 relating to Munn's intangible asset balances at December 31, 2003 and transactions during 2004.
2. Prepare the intangible assets section of Munn's balance sheet at December 31, 2004. (*AICPA adapted*)

P11-14 *Intangibles: Assets and Expenses* The Barb Company has provided information on intangible assets as follows:

1. A patent was purchased from the Lou Company for $1,500,000 on January 1, 2003. Barb estimated the remaining useful life of the patent to be 10 years. The patent was carried in Lou's accounting records at a net book value of $1,250,000 when Lou sold it to Barb.
2. During 2004 a franchise was purchased from the Rink Company for $500,000. In addition, 5% of revenue from the franchise must be paid to Rink. Revenue from the franchise for 2004 was $2,000,000. Barb estimates the useful life of the franchise to be 10 years and takes a full year's amortization in the year of purchase.
3. Barb incurred research and development costs in 2004 as follows:

Materials and equipment	$120,000
Personnel	140,000
Indirect costs	60,000
	$320,000

Barb estimates that these costs will be recouped by December 31, 2005.

4. On January 1, 2004 Barb, based on new events that have occurred in the field, estimates that the remaining life of the patent purchased on January 1, 2003 is only five years from January 1, 2004.

Required

1. Prepare a schedule showing the intangibles section of Barb's balance sheet at December 31, 2004. Show supporting computations in good form.
2. Prepare a schedule showing the income statement effect for the year ended December 31, 2004 as a result of the previously mentioned facts. Show supporting computations in good form. (*AICPA adapted*)

P11-15 *Comprehensive* Lee Manufacturing Corporation was incorporated on January 3, 2003. The corporation's financial statements for its first year's operations were not examined by a CPA. You have been engaged to examine the financial statements for the year ended December 31, 2004, and your examination is substantially completed. The corporation's trial balance at December 31, 2004 appears as follows:

	Debit	Credit
Cash	$ 61,000	
Accounts receivable	92,500	
Allowance for doubtful accounts		$ 500
Inventories	38,500	
Machinery	75,000	
Equipment	29,000	
Accumulated depreciation		10,000
Patents	85,000	
Leasehold improvements	26,000	
Prepaid expenses	10,500	
Organization costs	29,000	
Goodwill	24,000	
Licensing agreement No. 1	50,000	
Licensing agreement No. 2	49,000	
Accounts payable		147,500
Unearned revenue		12,500
Capital stock		300,000
Retained earnings, January 1, 2004	27,000	
Sales		768,500
Cost of goods sold	454,000	
Selling and general expenses	173,000	
Interest expense	3,500	
Extraordinary losses	12,000	
Total	$1,239,000	$1,239,000

The following information relates to accounts that may yet require adjustment:

1. Patents for Lee's manufacturing process were acquired January 2, 2004 at a cost of $68,000. An additional $17,000 was spent in December 2004 to improve machinery covered by the patents and charged to the Patents account. Depreciation on fixed assets has been properly recorded for 2004 in accordance with Lee's practice, which provides a full year's depreciation for property on hand June 30 and no depreciation otherwise. Lee uses the straight-line method for all depreciation and amortization and amortizes its patents over their legal life.

2. On January 3, 2003 Lee purchased Licensing Agreement No. 1, which was believed to have an indefinite useful life. The balance in the Licensing Agreement No. 1 account includes its purchase price of $48,000 and costs of $2,000 related to the acquisition. On January 1, 2004 Lee purchased Licensing Agreement No. 2, which has a life expectancy of 10 years. The balance in the Licensing Agreement No. 2 account includes its $48,000 purchase price and $2,000 in acquisition costs, but it has been reduced by a credit of $1,000 for the advance collection of 2005 revenue from the agreement. In late December 2003 an explosion caused a permanent 60% reduction in the expected revenue-producing value of Licensing Agreement No. 1, and in January 2005 a flood caused additional damage that rendered the agreement worthless.

3. The balance in the Goodwill account includes (a) $8,000 paid December 30, 2003 for newspaper advertising for the next 4 years following the disbursement, and (b) legal costs of $16,000 incurred for Lee's incorporation on January 3, 2003.

4. The Leasehold Improvements account includes (a) the $15,000 cost of improvements with a total estimated useful life of 12 years, which Lee, as tenant, made to leased premises in January 2003, (b) movable assembly line equipment costing $8,500 that was installed in the leased premises in December 2004, and (c) real estate taxes of $2,500 paid by Lee in 2004, which under the terms of the lease should have been paid by the landlord. Lee paid its rent in full during 2004. A 10-year nonrenewable lease was signed January 3, 2003 for the leased building that Lee used in manufacturing operations.

5. The balance in the Organization Costs account includes costs incurred during the organizational period.

Required Prepare a worksheet to adjust accounts that require adjustment and prepare financial statements. A separate account should be used for the accumulation of each type of amortization and for each prior period adjustment. Formal adjusting journal entries and financial statements are not required. No intangibles are impaired at the end of 2004. Ignore income taxes. (*AICPA adapted*)

P11-16 *Comprehensive* Information concerning Tully Corporation's intangible assets is as follows:

    a. On January 1, 2004 Tully signed an agreement to operate as a franchisee of Rapid Copy Service, Inc., for an initial franchise fee of $85,000. Of this amount, $25,000 was paid when the agreement was signed, and the balance is payable in four annual payments of $15,000 each beginning January 1, 2005. The agreement provides that the down payment is not refundable and no future services are required of the franchisor. The present value at January 2, 2004 of the four annual payments discounted at 14% (the implicit rate for a loan of this type) is $43,700. The agreement also provides that 5% of the revenue from the franchise must be paid to the franchisor annually. Tully's revenue from the franchise for 2004 was $900,000. Tully estimates the useful life of the franchise to be 10 years.

    b. Tully incurred $78,000 of experimental and development costs in its laboratory to develop a patent, which was granted on January 2, 2004. Legal fees and other costs associated with registration of the patent totaled $16,400. Tully estimates that the useful life of the patent will be 8 years.

    c. A trademark was purchased from Walton Company for $40,000 on July 1, 2001. Expenditures for successful litigation in defense of the trademark totaling $10,000 were paid on July 1, 2004. Tully estimates that the useful life of the trademark will be 20 years from the date of acquisition.

Required

1. Prepare a schedule showing the intangibles section of Tully's balance sheet at December 31, 2004. Show supporting computations in good form.

2. Prepare a schedule showing all expenses resulting from the transactions that would appear on Tully's income statement for the year ended December 31, 2004. Show supporting computations in good form. (*AICPA adapted*)

P11-17 *Comprehensive* Bryant Corporation was incorporated on December 1, 2003 and began operations 1 week later. Before closing the books for the fiscal year ended November 30, 2004, Bryant's controller prepared the following financial statements:

Balance Sheet
November 30, 2004

Assets			*Liabilities and Stockholders' Equity*	
Current assets			Current liabilities	
Cash	$ 180,000		Accounts payable and accrued expenses	$ 592,000
Accounts receivable	480,000		Income taxes payable	168,000
Less: Allowance for doubtful accounts	(59,000)		Total current liabilities	$ 760,000
Inventories	430,000		Stockholders' equity	
Prepaid insurance	15,000		Common stock, $10 par value	$ 400,000
Total current assets	$1,046,000		Retained earnings	392,000
Property, plant, and equipment	426,000		Total stockholders' equity	$ 792,000
Less: Accumulated depreciation	(40,000)		Total Liabilities and Stockholders' Equity	$1,552,000
Research and development costs	120,000			
Total Assets	$1,552,000			

Statement of Income
For Year Ended November 30, 2004

Net sales	$2,950,000
Operating expenses	
Cost of sales	$1,670,000
Selling and administrative	650,000
Depreciation	40,000
Research and development	30,000
Total expenses	$2,390,000
Income before income taxes	$ 560,000
Income tax expense	168,000
Net Income	$ 392,000

Bryant Corporation is in the process of negotiating a loan for expansion purposes, and the bank has requested audited financial statements. During the course of the audit, the following additional information was obtained:

1. Included in selling and administrative expenses were $5,000 of costs incurred on software being developed for sale to others. The technological feasibility of the software has been established.

2. Based on an aging of the accounts receivable as of November 30, 2004, it was estimated that $36,000 of the receivables will be uncollectible.

3. Inventories at November 30, 2004 did not include work-in-process inventory costing $12,000 sent to an outside processor on November 26, 2004.

4. A $3,000 insurance premium paid on November 30, 2004 on a policy expiring 1 year later was charged to insurance expense.

5. Bryant adopted a pension plan on June 1, 2004 for eligible employees to be administered by a trustee. Based upon actuarial computations, the first 12 month's accrued pension plan expense was estimated at $45,000.

6. On June 1, 2004 a production machine purchased for $24,000 was charged to repairs and maintenance. Bryant depreciates machines of this type on the straight-line method over a 5-year life, with no salvage value, for financial and tax purposes.

7. Research and development costs of $150,000 were incurred in the development of a patent that Bryant expects to be granted during the fiscal year ending November 30, 2005. Bryant initiated a 5-year amortization of the $150,000 total cost during the fiscal year ended November 30, 2004.

8. During December 2004 a competitor company filed suit against Bryant for patent infringement claiming $200,000 in damages. Bryant's legal counsel believes that an unfavorable outcome is probable. A reasonable accrual based on an estimate of the court's award to the plaintiff is $50,000.

9. The 30% effective tax rate was determined to be appropriate for calculating the provision for income taxes for the fiscal year ended November 30, 2004. Ignore computation of deferred portion of income taxes.

Required

1. Prepare the necessary correcting entries.
2. Prepare a corrected balance sheet of Bryant Corporation as of November 30, 2004 and a corrected statement of income for the year ended November 30, 2004. (*AICPA adapted*)

P11-18 *Goodwill (Appendix)*   The Humphries Company earned the following net income for the last 5 years:

2000 $100,000
2001   120,000
2002   140,000 (including an extraordinary loss of $4,000)
2003   150,000 (including an extraordinary loss of $22,800)
2004   215,000 (including an extraordinary gain of $7,640)

The fair value of the identifiable net assets is $1.4 million. The normal rate of return earned by a company in this industry is 10%. The excess annual earnings are expected to last 5 years and are to be capitalized at 14%.

Required

1. Compute the value of the implied goodwill if estimated future annual earnings are based on the average of the excess annual earnings for the past 5 years.
2. Compute the value of the implied goodwill if estimated future annual earnings are based on the trend apparent in the normal earnings of the past 5 years.

P11-19 *Goodwill (Appendix)*   The Elm Company is considering purchasing the EKC Company. The balance sheet of the EKC Company at December 31, 2004 is as follows:

Cash	$ 50,000	Current liabilities	$ 60,000
Accounts receivable	70,000	Bonds payable	200,000
Inventory	120,000	Common stock	300,000
Property, plant, and equipment (net)	600,000	Retained earnings	280,000
	$840,000		$840,000

The EKC Company earned the following net income for the last 5 years:

2000 $150,000
2001   162,000
2002   182,960 (including an extraordinary gain of $8,000)
2003   188,957
2004   200,073 (including an extraordinary loss of $4,000)

At December 31, 2004 the Elm Company discovered the following about the EKC Company:

1. No allowance for uncollectible accounts has been established. An allowance of $5,000 is considered appropriate.
2. The LIFO inventory method has been used. The FIFO inventory method would be used if EKC were purchased by Elm. The FIFO inventory valuation of the December 31, 2004 ending inventory would be $180,000.
3. The fair value of the property, plant, and equipment (net) is $730,000.
4. The company has an unrecorded patent that is worth $120,000.
5. The book values of the current liabilities and bonds payable are the same as their market values. The normal rate of return earned by a company in EKC's industry is 10%. Excess annual earnings are expected to last 7 years and should be capitalized at 14%.

Required

1. Compute the value of the implied goodwill if the Elm Company pays $1,350,000 for EKC.
2. Compute the value of the implied goodwill if estimated future annual earnings are based on the average of the excess annual earnings for the last 5 years.
3. Compute the value of the implied goodwill if estimated future annual earnings are based on the trend apparent in the normal annual earnings of the past 5 years.

INTERNET ASSIGNMENTS

Go to the Nikolai and Bazley **Intermediate Accounting** web site (http://Nikolai.swcollege.com). Click on Student Resources and <u>internet homework assignments</u>. Then click on the appropriate hot link (icon) for each company's web site, find the relevant accounting information, and answer the following questions.

I11-1   Go to the Johnson & Johnson web site.

Required What intangibles does the company have? Explain how each one would arise. Which intangibles is the company amortizing? How much was the company's R&D expense during each of the last three years?

I11-2   Go to the PepsiCo web site.

Required What intangibles does the company have? Explain how each one would arise. Which intangibles is the company amortizing? Did the company recognize any impairment in the last three years?

I11-3   Go to the AOL Time Warner web site.

Required How much was the goodwill impairment the company recognized in 2002?

PART 3

Financial Reporting: Valuation of Liabilities and Investments

Chapter 12   Current Liabilities and Contingencies

Chapter 13   Long-Term Liabilities and Receivables

Chapter 14   Investments

CHAPTER 12

Current Liabilities and Contingencies

objectives

1 Explain the characteristics of a liability.

2 Define current liabilities.

3 Account for compensated absences.

4 Understand and record payroll taxes and deductions.

5 Record property taxes.

6 Account for warranty costs.

7 Explain the terms "probable," "reasonably possible," and "remote" related to contingencies.

8 Record and report a loss contingency.

9 Disclose a gain contingency.

This is the first of two chapters on liabilities. In Chapter 12 we focus on current liabilities (including contingencies), while in Chapter 13 we address long-term (noncurrent) liabilities. Since the topics in both chapters depend on an understanding of the term *liabilities*, our initial discussion expands on the concept and definition of a liability we presented in the review of the balance sheet in Chapter 3. We address the nature, definition, and valuation of current liabilities, and explain the items comprising three major groups of current liabilities. Then we examine the important issue of contingencies, after which we discuss short-term debt expected to be refinanced and obligations that are callable by the creditor. Last, we discuss specific methods of reporting current liabilities on the balance sheet and in the notes to the financial statements, and we present examples of disclosures by actual companies.

CONCEPTUAL OVERVIEW OF LIABILITIES

In its *Conceptual Framework*, the FASB defines liabilities as follows:

> Liabilities are probable future sacrifices of economic benefits arising from present obligations of a company to transfer assets or provide services to other entities in the future as a result of past transactions or events.[1]

The FASB also explained two of the terms. The word *probable* refers to what can be expected or believed based on available evidence or logic, but is neither certain nor proved. The word *obligations* refers to duties imposed legally or socially which one is bound to do by contract, promise, moral responsibility, and so forth. In other words, liabilities include both legal and nonlegal (but not illegal) obligations. Legal liabilities are incurred in exchange transactions that are contractual in nature—based on written or oral agreements to pay cash or to provide goods or services to specified or determinable entities, on demand, at specified or determinable dates, on occurrence of specified events. Legal liabilities include such items as accounts payable, notes payable, and sales tax payable. **The nonlegal group (also called accounting liabilities) includes those obligations where there is *no legal requirement* for assets to be transferred, yet a transfer of assets typically occurs as a part of the normal operations of a business.**[2] Nonlegal liabilities include equitable and constructive obligations, such as the liability to employees for vacation pay or year-end bonuses, that a company accepts by paying them every year even

---

1. "Elements of Financial Reporting of Business Enterprises," *FASB Statement of Financial Accounting Concepts No. 6* (Stamford, Conn.: FASB, December 1985), par. 28.
2. *Ibid.*, fn. 21 and 22 and par. 38.

though it is not contractually bound to do so and has not announced a policy to do so. We discuss the accounting for both types of liabilities later in this chapter.

As we introduced in Chapter 3, there are **three essential characteristics of a liability** for a company:

1. It involves a present duty or responsibility of the company to one or more other entities that will be settled by the probable *future transfer* or *use of assets* at a specified or determinable date, on occurrence of a specific event, or on demand.
2. The duty or responsibility obligates the company, *leaving it little or no discretion to avoid* the future sacrifice.
3. The transaction or other event obligating the company *has already happened.*

1 Explain the characteristics of a liability.

The main features of these three characteristics are highlighted by italics: the requirement that a company transfer or use assets, that the obligation cannot be avoided, and that the liability transaction has already occurred.

There are two additional factors involving a liability. First, as long as payment or other transfer of assets to settle an existing obligation is probable, the company does not need to know the identity of the recipient before the time of settlement. Second, a legally enforceable claim is not a prerequisite for an obligation to qualify as a liability if, for other reasons, the company has a duty or responsibility to pay cash, transfer other assets, or provide services to another company.[3] You should note, however, that some liabilities are "liquidated" by conversion into common or preferred stock or by refinancing into other liabilities, as we discuss in Chapter 13.

The financial accounting issues related to liabilities are important in both income statement and balance sheet measurement. The primary issues discussed in the remainder of this chapter are:

1. *Identification* of liabilities—the detection of a company's obligations
2. *Measurement* or *valuation* of the liabilities and the related expense—the determination of an amount to attach to each obligation and to match as an expense against revenues
3. *Reporting* on the financial statements—the specific disclosures in both the company's financial statements and the related notes

Liabilities generally are classified as either current or long-term. We discuss the preceding issues in this chapter as they relate to obligations classified as current liabilities.

Long-term liabilities are discussed in Chapter 13 and in other chapters.

NATURE AND DEFINITION OF CURRENT LIABILITIES

The specific meaning, nature, and classification of current liabilities, which we discuss in the following sections, are important to users of financial statements.

Classification and the Operating Cycle or Year

Recall that **current liabilities are obligations whose liquidation is expected to require the use of existing current assets or the creation of other current liabilities within one year or an operating cycle, whichever is longer.** The usual criterion is one year. For certain companies, however, where the **operating cycle—from cash to inventory to receivables and back to cash**—extends beyond the year, the length of the operating cycle determines the classification of the liability. Many current liabilities, such as accounts payable, wages payable, warranty obligations, and notes payable, are incurred (and paid) during the operating cycle. For example, a current liability—Accounts Payable—is created when an inventory item is acquired. Also, a current liability, Salaries Payable, often arises as a result of accrued salaries for sales, as well as general and administrative, personnel.

2 Define current liabilities.

An example of a company's operating cycle was shown in Exhibit 3-3.

---

3. *Ibid.*, par. 36.

Some users question using different time periods for classifying liabilities as current—that is, the use of a year or an operating cycle, whichever is longer. They prefer to use the length of the operating cycle as the period for determining the classification of liabilities, regardless of whether it is longer or shorter than a year. Since this issue deals primarily with the question of liquidity, we discuss liquidity and the related issue of financial flexibility next.

Liquidity, Financial Flexibility, and Current Liabilities

One attribute of a liability (and also an asset) is its liquidity. **Liquidity refers to how quickly a liability can be paid, or its nearness to cash.** The FASB is concerned about reporting the liquidity of liabilities and assets because users evaluate future cash flows in their decision-making processes. In part, these *future cash flows are predicted based on the nearness to cash of liabilities and assets.* Therefore, the liquidity of liabilities and assets is important in these decision-making processes.

The FASB discussed various ways of reporting the liquidity of both liabilities and assets, including (1) continuing the current practice for classifying current liabilities and assets (mixture of operating-cycle and maturity-date approach), (2) classifying current liabilities and assets using the "pure" operating-cycle approach, (3) classifying current liabilities and assets under the maturity-date approach only, (4) adopting a different classification scheme, possibly using more classes, and (5) leaving the balance sheet unclassified but arranging items in order of liquidity.[4] Each method has certain advantages and disadvantages for disclosing a company's liquidity, but they are beyond the scope of this book.

The FASB also observed that the principal objective of financial reporting—that of providing information useful for assessing the amount, timing, and uncertainty of a company's future cash flows—depends on a knowledge of the liquidity of its liabilities and assets.[5] The Board studied ways of relating liabilities and assets to each other and of relating them to other financial statement data to obtain information about liquidity, and to determine what relationships might be the best predictors of failure. It listed five "liquidity" ratios as providing information to lending institutions, creditors, and other external users of financial information: (1) cash flows to total debt, (2) net income to total assets (return on total assets ratio), (3) total debt to total assets (debt ratio), (4) current assets to current liabilities (current ratio), and (5) cash to current liabilities. Four of the five require information about a company's liabilities; two require information about its current liabilities. Since we discussed ratio analysis in detail in Chapter 5, we do not discuss these ratios here.

The AICPA Special Committee on Financial Reporting reinforced the Board's view by observing that in a company's MD&A, its management should identify and describe internal and external sources of liquidity, and significant unused sources of liquid assets. It also believes that a company should disclose the impact of "illiquidity" on financial flexibility.[6] **Financial flexibility refers to a company's ability to use its financial resources to adapt to change.** This ability primarily involves the management of cash and other resources to achieve certain financial advantages from both an offensive and defensive point of view. In part, it also involves the potential to create new current and long-term liabilities, to restructure existing debt, and to manage debt in other ways. We discuss these features relating to financial flexibility later in this chapter and in other chapters.

Classification of Current Liabilities

Many current liabilities are easily identifiable and have a "contractual" amount. Others, though identifiable, have amounts that depend upon operations, while still others

4. "An Analysis of Issues Related to Reporting Funds Flows, Liquidity, and Financial Flexibility," *FASB Discussion Memorandum* (Stamford, Conn.: FASB, December 15, 1980), p. 87.

5. "Reporting Income, Cash Flows, and Financial Flexibility of Business Enterprises," *FASB Proposed Statement of Financial Accounting Concepts* (Stamford, Conn.: FASB, November 16, 1981), par. 28.

6. "Improving Business Reporting—A Customer Focus," *Report of the AICPA Committee on Financial Reporting* (New York: AICPA, 1994), Appendix II, p. 145.

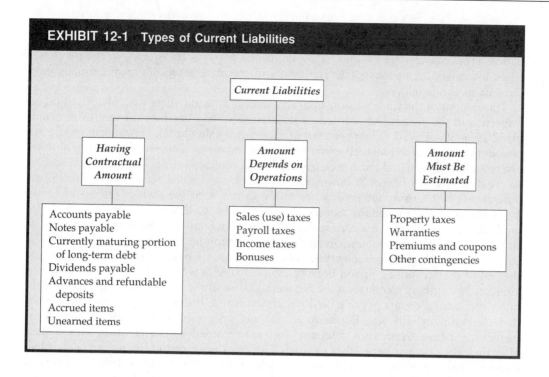

EXHIBIT 12-1 Types of Current Liabilities

Current Liabilities

Having Contractual Amount

Amount Depends on Operations

Amount Must Be Estimated

Accounts payable
Notes payable
Currently maturing portion
  of long-term debt
Dividends payable
Advances and refundable
  deposits
Accrued items
Unearned items

Sales (use) taxes
Payroll taxes
Income taxes
Bonuses

Property taxes
Warranties
Premiums and coupons
Other contingencies

require that amounts be estimated. We classify the primary types of current liabilities in three groups, as we show in Exhibit 12-1, although some types might fit in more than one category. We organize our discussion according to these three types.

VALUATION OF CURRENT LIABILITIES

Conceptually, a company should record (and report on its balance sheet) all its liabilities at the present value of the future outlays they will require, and should report them in a manner that will provide useful information about their liquidity. In practice, however, most current liabilities are measured, recorded, and reported at their maturity or face amount. The difference between the maturity amount and the present value of the maturity amount is usually not material because of the short time period involved (usually one year or less). While a slight overstatement of liabilities will result from the recording of these liabilities at their maturity amount, this overstatement is justified on the basis of cost/benefit and materiality constraints.

CURRENT LIABILITIES HAVING A CONTRACTUAL AMOUNT

The short-term liabilities in this group result from the terms of contracts or from the existence of laws. In these cases the debt and its maturity are known with reasonable certainty. The accounting issues we discuss in this section for each current liability are (1) identifying the item, (2) measuring it, and (3) recording it in the accounts.

Trade Accounts Payable

A company's trade accounts payable arise from the purchase of inventory, supplies, or services on an open charge-account basis. The credit time period generally varies from 30 to 120 days without any interest being charged. A company usually records the amount of the liability in the accounting system when it receives the invoice from the supplier. The accounting system is standardized so that efficient processing and payment are made.

Issues often arise when a company purchases inventory near the end of the accounting period. Goods may be shipped by the supplier and still be in transit at year-end as we discussed in Chapter 7. The purchaser should record both the purchase and the liability in the accounting period in which the economic control of the goods passes.

For goods shipped FOB shipping point, economic control of (and legal title to) the goods passes to the purchaser at the supplier's shipping point. For goods shipped FOB destination, economic control of (and legal title to) the goods is transferred to the purchaser when it receives the merchandise. The owner of the merchandise in transit usually pays the cost of the freight.

The amount of the trade accounts payable usually is readily determinable, based on an inspection of the invoice. An accounting issue arises when cash discount terms (for example, 2/10, n/30; or 3/10 EOM) are offered. A company should take advantage of all cash discounts because of the high effective interest rate involved. Theoretically, it should show inventory (purchases) and the associated liability (accounts payable) less the cash discount. As we discussed in Chapter 7, however, a company may record accounts payable in two different ways: (1) using the *gross price method*, that is, at the invoice price—the liability is stated at the maximum amount required to be paid, or (2) using the *net price method*, that is, at the invoice price less the cash discount—the liability is stated at its current cash equivalent amount. Assuming the company has a policy of taking cash discounts, use of the gross price method overstates accounts payable (a valuation issue) at the end of the accounting period because the company expects to pay less than the gross amount. The authors recommend the net method. Use of the net price method more accurately measures accounts payable (and liquidity) because it shows the most likely amount that the company will pay. Furthermore, the net price method highlights management inefficiency because purchases discounts lost are recorded whenever an invoice is paid after the cash discount period has expired. The gross price method is more widely used, however, because of its simplicity and the lack of materiality of the differences between the two methods. For an illustration of the two methods, refer to Chapter 7.

Notes Payable

A note payable is an unconditional written agreement to pay a sum of money to the bearer on a specific date. Notes payable may be either short term (discussed here) or long term (discussed in Chapter 13). Notes arise either out of a trade situation—the purchase of goods or services on credit—or the borrowing of money. The promissory note is the source document a company uses to determine the initial amount of the liability. However, interest is important in determining the subsequent value of the liability. The interest for a note payable may be stated or implied in different ways. One note may be *interest-bearing*, with the principal listed as the face value and the interest rate stated on the note, and with interest payable at maturity. Another note may be *non-interest-bearing* in which the note is stated at its maturity value that includes both the principal and interest to maturity. For a non-interest-bearing note, the note is discounted and the borrower receives less than the face value. The interest on this type of note is the amount of the discount.

ISSUANCE OF AN INTEREST-BEARING TRADE NOTE FOR MERCHANDISE For an interest-bearing note, the principal amount (face value) is the present value of the liability and is used to record the current liability. Interest expense then is recorded over the life of the note by applying the stated interest rate to the face value. To illustrate, assume that Trishan Corporation uses a perpetual inventory system and purchases merchandise for $7,000 on September 1, 2004 by issuing a $7,000, 12%, 30-day note to the supplier. The company records the issuance of the note and the payment of the principal and interest (assuming, for simplicity, a 360-day business year) on September 1, 2004 and October 1, 2004, respectively, as follows:

September 1, 2004

Inventory	7,000	
Notes Payable		7,000

October 1, 2004

Interest Expense ($7,000 × 0.12 × 30/360)	70	
Notes Payable	7,000	
Cash		7,070

If the note spans two fiscal periods, the company makes an adjusting entry at the end of the first fiscal period to accrue the interest expense and to record another current liability, Interest Payable.

ISSUE OF NON-INTEREST-BEARING NOTE TO BORROW MONEY For a non-interest-bearing note, the face value (which includes the interest to maturity) and the discount (the interest to maturity) of the note are used to record the current liability. Interest expense is then recorded over the life of the note as an adjustment of this discounted amount. To illustrate, assume that on December 1, 2004, the Trollingwood Corporation (which has a fiscal year ending December 31) borrows money at First National Bank by issuing a $10,000, 90-day, non-interest-bearing note that is discounted on a 12% basis. Trollingwood receives only $9,700 [$10,000 − ($10,000 × 0.12 × 3/12)]. It makes four journal entries to record the events related to this note. First, it records the proceeds of the note on December 1, 2004 as follows:

Cash	9,700	
Discount on Notes Payable	300	
Notes Payable		10,000

Observe that $10,000 is the maturity (face) value, but the company records the liability at its present value. The company debits the $300 amount of the discount (the interest expense applicable to the entire term of the note) to Discount on Notes Payable, and shows this account on its balance sheet as a contra account to Notes Payable in order to report the net amount of the current liquidation value.[7] Since the life of this note extends into 2005, the company makes a second journal entry on December 31, 2004 to record a portion of the discount (1/3 × $300) as interest expense[8] for 2004 as follows:

Interest Expense	100	
Discount on Notes Payable		100

Observe that the reduction in the Discount on Notes Payable account correspondingly increases the current liability amount shown on the company's balance sheet.[9] The company records the last two journal entries at maturity on March 1, 2005 as follows:

Interest Expense	200	
Discount on Notes Payable		200
Notes Payable	10,000	
Cash		10,000

After the company makes the first journal entry adjusting Interest Expense, Discount on Notes Payable has a zero balance so that the carrying value of the current liability equals the maturity value of the note. The second journal entry records the payment of the maturity value, which includes the $9,700 borrowed, plus the $300 total interest recognized (i.e., the amount of the discount).

In borrowing money, a manager must be aware of the effective interest rate, referred to in practice as the annual percentage rate (or APR), for each source of credit. In the preceding case, the approximate effective annual interest on the cash actually borrowed

---

7. Alternatively, the company could record the Notes Payable at the current value ($9,700), in which case it would show the maturity value parenthetically on the balance sheet. Subsequently, the company would make the Interest Expense adjusting entry credit directly to Notes Payable to increase it to the maturity value.

8. In this situation, for simplicity we use the "straight-line" method to allocate the interest expense. In Chapter 13, we use the more conceptually correct "effective interest" method to calculate interest expense for long-term notes.

9. An alternative approach involves debiting the original discount amount first to Interest Expense. Then, at the end of the period, an adjusting entry would be necessary to transfer the *unexpired* portion of the expense to the Discount on Notes Payable account. The Discount on Notes Payable account would be shown on the balance sheet as a contra account to Notes Payable, as we discussed earlier.

is higher than the discount rate of 12%. It is 12.37% [($300 ÷ $9,700) × 4 quarters]. Federal laws require lenders to disclose the APR to borrowers.

Currently Maturing Portion of Long-Term Debt

Serial bonds are discussed in an Appendix to Chapter 13.

As a general rule, although not directly related to the operating cycle, a company classifies the currently maturing portion of long-term debt as a current liability. Two different situations are involved here. First, any long-term debt requiring the use of current assets for its retirement will become a current liability on the balance sheet prepared immediately before the year of retirement. If a company has issued 20-year bonds and these are scheduled to become due on July 1, 2005, the company reports their total amount as a current liability on the balance sheet prepared as of December 31, 2004. The second situation involves the issuance of serial bonds—that is, bonds that are retired in periodic installments. For example, assume that on July 1, 2003, Rexlow Corporation issues 13% serial bonds with a face value of $1 million. These bonds are to be retired in installments of $100,000, beginning on July 1, 2005 and for each year thereafter until all bonds are retired. The company's balance sheet prepared as of December 31, 2004, would show the currently maturing installment of $100,000 as a current liability and the $900,000 (the installments due after December 31, 2005) as a long-term liability item. The current portion of other long-term debt (such as the current amount of lease obligations, which we discuss in Chapter 20, and certain deferred taxes, which we discuss in Chapter 18) is treated in the same manner. These items, however, are not included in current liabilities if it is expected that they will be refinanced on a long-term basis, as we discuss later in this chapter.

Dividends Payable

Dividends are discussed in Chapter 16.

A company may declare (on the dividend declaration date by the board of directors) a cash dividend, a property dividend (a dividend payable in property other than cash), or a scrip dividend (a dividend that creates a promissory note). When a company declares a dividend it reduces retained earnings and recognizes a current liability if there is an intention to distribute the dividend in the coming year or operating cycle. These dividends are recorded and reported at the amount to be paid. The liability is entitled Dividends Payable, Property Dividends Payable, or Dividends Payable in Scrip. Observe that for each dividend, accounting for the declaration results in a shift of a stockholders' equity element—retained earnings—to a current liability element. The company eliminates the liability on the date of payment.

There are two exceptions to the creation of current liabilities for dividends. First, a company does *not* report a stock dividend to be issued as a current liability. Since a stock dividend is liquidated by the issuance of the corporation's own stock, it is reported as an element of stockholders' equity. Second, a company does *not* report undeclared dividends in arrears on cumulative preferred stock (which we discuss in Chapter 15) as liabilities until they are formally declared by the corporation's board of directors, but it discloses them in the notes to the financial statements.

Advances and Refundable Deposits

Many utility and other companies require customers and employees to make deposits as guarantees to cover equipment used by the customer, to cover payments that may arise in the future, or to guarantee performance of a contract or service. Since these deposits either are refundable or are later offset against a trade accounts receivable, they are a special type of liability. The accounting for these deposits involves an increase in a liability account describing the nature of the refundable deposit. For example, the liability for a refundable deposit received by a utility company may be called Refundable Deposits Received from Customers. The law frequently requires that interest be paid on these deposits; therefore most utility companies refund the deposit as soon as a customer has established a good credit standing. The utility company must account for any related interest on a regular accrual basis and report the amount as a current liability, Interest Payable.

Accrued Liabilities

Accrued liabilities represent obligations that *accumulate* in a systematic way over time. Often a company waits until the end of the accounting period to record these liabilities and the related expenses as adjusting entries, because it is more convenient to do so. Most accrued liabilities are current liabilities; some are definite in amount, while the amounts of others are based on operations or estimates. Because of their special characteristics, we discuss several major accrued liabilities in separate sections of this chapter. Two additional issues also need special consideration: (1) the liability for compensated absences, and (2) the disclosure of "off-balance sheet" financing obligations.

ACCRUED LIABILITY FOR COMPENSATED ABSENCES   FASB Statement No. 43 defines the accounting for compensated absences. **Compensated absences include vacation, holiday, illness, or other personal activities for which the employee is paid.** They do not include items such as severance pay, stock options, or long-term fringe benefits. A company recognizes an expense and accrues a liability for employees' compensation for future absences if *all* the following conditions are met:

3 Account for compensated absences.

1. The company's obligation relating to the employee's rights to receive compensation for future absences is attributable to the employee's services already rendered;
2. The obligation relates to rights that vest or accumulate;
3. Payment of the compensation is probable; and
4. The amount can be reasonably estimated.[10]

If the company meets conditions (1), (2), and (3) and does not accrue a liability because the last condition is not met, it discloses the known facts about compensated absences in the notes to its financial statements.

Two of the terms used in the preceding conditions need more explanation. A **vested right** exists when an employer has an obligation to make payment to an employee that is not contingent upon the employee's future services. **Accumulated rights** are those that can be carried forward by the employee to future periods if not taken in the period in which they are earned. The most common type is vacation time that is allowed to accumulate and for which payment is probable. Even if these rights do not vest, they accumulate and the employer must recognize an expense and accrue a liability, allowing for those rights it does not expect to be exercised.

The second most frequent compensated absence is sick pay, which is treated by *FASB Statement No. 43* differently from vacation pay. If sick pay benefits *vest* and are not used by the end of the period, then the employer must recognize an expense and accrue a liability. If sick pay benefits *accumulate* but do *not* vest, recognition and accrual is optional. The reason for this exception to the general recognition rule is that employers administer sick pay in at least two different ways. Some companies permit employees to accumulate unused sick pay and take compensated time off from work even though they are not ill. A company must accrue a current liability for this type of sick pay because it is probable that it will be paid in the future, regardless of whether or not the employees are ill. Other companies require that employees receive accumulated sick pay only if they are absent from work because of illness. In this case, accrual is optional because payment is less likely and measurement of the amount is less reliable.

There is a **conceptual difference** between vacation pay and sick pay. *Vacation pay is earned as a result of past employment* (the services rendered by the employee), whereas

---

10. "Accounting for Compensated Absences," *FASB Statement of Financial Accounting Standards No. 43* (Stamford, Conn.: FASB, November, 1980), par. 6. These criteria also apply to postemployment benefits under *FASB Statement of Financial Accounting Standards No. 112*.

sick pay is earned only when the future event (sickness) *occurs.* In the latter case, the criteria for a liability have *not* been fulfilled during employment because the transaction or event obligating the company has not yet occurred.

When an accrual is made, the company records an expense and related current liability in the period in which the sick pay benefits are earned by the employees. In measuring the amount of the accrual, the rate of pay the company uses to record the liability is either: (1) the rate applicable to the current period, or (2) the rate applicable to the estimated time of absence. Since the current period's rate is more reliable than the future period's rate, and the difference is unlikely to be material, most companies use the current period's rate for the accrual. If the amount paid in the future for the compensated absence is larger than the amount of the previous accrual (because of a pay raise or promotion), the company records difference as an adjustment to the expense recorded in the period of the payment. In other words, the difference is treated as a change in estimate that is accounted for in the current (and future) period, as we discuss in Chapter 22.

COMPENSATED ABSENCE EXAMPLE To illustrate a compensated absence for vacations, assume that the Milton Company has 100 employees, who are each paid an average of $100 per day. The company has a policy (which meets the *FASB Statement No. 43* conditions) of allowing each employee 12 days of paid vacation per year. The total annual cost of the paid vacations—a form of compensated absence—is $120,000 (100 × 12 × $100). The company records the related liability on a quarterly basis for interim reporting purposes. Employees are paid monthly; half the employees are in the sales force and the remaining half are in the office staff. Assuming no vacation days were taken in the first quarter of 2005, the company records the expense and accrued liability on March 31, 2005 as follows:

Sales Salaries Expense: Compensated Absences	15,000	
Office Salaries Expense: Compensated Absences	15,000	
Liability for Employees' Compensation for		
Future Absences (3/12 × $120,000)		30,000

Some companies prefer to record the debit entry as Vacation Pay Expense. Generally, no payroll taxes are recorded at this time because companies wait until payment of the payroll to do so. Note that as a result of this journal entry **the salaries expense is recognized in the period during which the employees work and earn the vacation time and *not* during the vacation period,** thus adhering to the matching principle. The company's first-quarter interim financial statements include the expense and liability for compensated absences.

The liability for compensated absences will be satisfied when the employees take their vacations. The company will record the elimination of the liability, however, when it pays the regular payroll after the employees take their vacations. To illustrate, assume that the $200,000 April 30, 2005 payroll, including paid vacation time taken by the sales and office staff, is as follows:

	Payroll for	
	Time Worked	Vacation Taken
Sales staff	$97,000	$3,000
Office staff	96,500	3,500

The company records the payment of this payroll (ignoring payroll taxes) on April 30, 2005 as follows:

Sales Salaries Expense	97,000	
Office Salaries Expense	96,500	
Liability for Employees' Compensation		
for Future Absences	6,500	
Cash		200,000

As we discussed earlier, if the $6,500 payroll for vacation time were larger than the respective amount accrued earlier (because of a pay raise or promotion), the company would reduce the liability by the accrued amount, and would add the difference to the two expense accounts. In addition, payroll taxes would normally be recorded at this time. For simplicity however, since we discuss payroll taxes later in the chapter, we do not illustrate them here. If payroll taxes had been recorded, the withheld payroll taxes of the employees would apply to the entire $200,000 as of April 30, 2005 (the date of payment of the salaries and the vacation time) because the taxes are legally assessable. Furthermore, the payroll taxes applicable to the employer also would be recorded at this time.

Similar journal entries are made to record the expense for compensated absences and accrue (and eliminate) the liability during the remaining quarters for interim reporting purposes. At year-end, the Milton Company reports any remaining balance in the liability account as a current liability on its ending balance sheet.[11]

DISCLOSURE OF OFF-BALANCE-SHEET FINANCING OBLIGATIONS **FASB Statement No. 47**, though entitled "Disclosure of Long-Term Obligations," deals with current liability issues relating to *off-balance-sheet financing*. We discussed this topic in Chapter 8 as it relates to inventories; we also discuss it in Chapter 20 as it applies to leasing arrangements. Here we discuss it briefly as it relates to liabilities. This *Statement* focuses on accounting for an unconditional purchase obligation, which is one requiring transfer of funds in the future for fixed or minimum amounts or quantities of goods or services at fixed or minimum prices. Part of the obligation or contingent obligation created may be short term and part may be long term. If a company enters into an unconditional purchase obligation that (1) is noncancellable, (2) is negotiated as part of arranging financing for facilities to provide the contracted items, and (3) contains a term in excess of one year, the company is required to make certain disclosures in the notes to its financial statements, regardless of whether it reports the obligation and related asset on the balance sheet. These disclosures include, for example, information about required payments over the next five years.[12] The intent is to enhance the *prediction of future cash outflows*. Because of the complex nature of these disclosures, we do not discuss them further, but any part of the required payment falling within the year or operating cycle is similar to a current liability and is disclosed in the note.

The FASB continues to be concerned with "off-balance-sheet financing" because innovations in financial instruments involving such items as interest rate swaps, collateralized mortgages, and put and call options have arisen in recent years. Critics argue that these items have resulted in inadequate disclosures of potential liabilities, unjustifiable deferrals of losses, and premature recognitions of gains. In response, the FASB has issued **FASB Statements Nos. 107 and 133**. **FASB Statement No. 107** requires a company to *disclose* the fair value of all its financial instruments (both assets and liabilities), whether recognized or not on the balance sheet. The *Statement* also requires a company to disclose all significant concentrations of credit risk due to its financial instruments. A company typically makes these disclosures in the notes to its financial statements. **FASB Statement No. 133** requires a company to *recognize* as liabilities any "derivative" financial instruments that are obligations of the company, based on their fair value. Thus, the FASB has moved derivative financial instrument obligations from "off-balance-sheet financing" to "on-balance-sheet-financing" items. A company reports these items as current liabilities on its balance sheet if they meet the definition of a current liability. The *Statement* also requires a company to *disclose* information such as the types of derivative instruments it holds, its objectives in holding the instruments, and its strategies for achieving these objectives. The description must indicate the company's risk management

Accounting for derivatives is discussed in the Appendix to Chapter 14.

---

11. *FASB Statement No. 43* does not specifically address the allocation of the costs of compensated absences to interim periods. If a company did not make quarterly accruals for compensated absences because they were not material, it would need to determine its remaining liability for compensated absences at year-end and make the related accrual journal entry at that time.

12. "Disclosure of Long-Term Obligations," *FASB Statement of Financial Accounting Standards No. 47* (Stamford, Conn.: FASB, June, 1981), par. 10.

policy in regard to each type of instrument. The intent of these disclosures is to improve the reporting of a company's *risk*, *liquidity*, and *financial flexibility*.[13]

LIABILITIES FROM PRODUCT FINANCING ARRANGEMENTS In **FASB Statement No. 49**, "Accounting for Product Financing Arrangements," the FASB deals with off-balance-sheet financing transactions in which a company "sells" inventory and agrees to repurchase it (perhaps additionally processed) at a specified price. As we discussed in Chapter 8, the company does not record the transaction as a sale or remove the inventory from its balance sheet. Instead, the company records a liability for the proceeds received. *FASB Statement No. 49* also addresses transactions where a company has another entity purchase a product on its behalf. In this case the company records the asset (often an inventory item) and related liability when the product is purchased by the other entity.[14] A part, or all, of both of the preceding liabilities is likely to be current and the company reports the amounts as current liabilities on its balance sheet.

Unearned Items

A company's unearned items (sometimes called deferred revenues) include amounts that it has collected in advance but has not yet earned and has not recorded as revenues (i.e., it has not yet provided the product or service). Although companies often erroneously classify these under the balance sheet caption Deferred Credits, these unearned items should be more appropriately classified: some should be classified as current liabilities and some as long-term liabilities. In this chapter we discuss only the unearned items properly classified as current liabilities.

 Examples of unearned items that could be classified as either current or long-term liabilities are amounts collected in advance, such as interest, rent, magazine subscriptions, royalties, tickets, tokens, gift certificates, and service contracts. Most of these items are current liabilities. If more than one year (or one operating cycle, if longer) is required in the earning process and if noncurrent assets are primarily used to earn the revenue, then the unearned item is classified as a long-term liability. On the other hand, unearned interest included in the face value of notes receivable should be classified as a contra (Discount) account to Notes Receivable on the balance sheet as we discussed earlier.

The accounting by a company for these unearned items involves the recognition of a liability account (or possibly a revenue account). The company makes an adjusting entry at the end of the accounting period to correctly state the amount of revenue earned that it reports on the income statement, and the ending liability that it reports on the balance sheet.

CURRENT LIABILITIES WHOSE AMOUNTS DEPEND ON OPERATIONS

Several kinds of current liabilities relate to operations, and their amounts depend on these operations. Included are liabilities related to sales and use taxes, payrolls, a corporation's income taxes, and bonus agreements.

Sales and Use Taxes

A sales tax is a tax levied on the transfer of tangible personal property and on certain services. A seller must collect sales tax from the customer and remit the amount—usually on a monthly basis—to the proper governmental authority. **A use tax is a tax levied by a state or local governmental unit on goods bought from a nonsales-tax area**

---

13. "Disclosures about Fair Value of Financial Instruments," *FASB Statement of Financial Accounting Standards No. 107* (Norwalk, Conn.: FASB, 1991), par. 7, and 15A and "Accounting for Derivative Instruments and Hedging Activities," *FASB Statement of Financial Accounting Standards No. 133* (Norwalk, Conn.: FASB, 1998), par. 17 and 44.

14. "Accounting for Product Financing Arrangements," *FASB Statement of Financial Accounting Standards No. 49* (Stamford, Conn.: FASB, June, 1981), par. 8.

or sector. It is levied on the buyer of merchandise purchased for the buyer's own use or consumption. To illustrate, suppose that a company goes out of state to buy trucks because of an advantageous price. Upon registering the vehicles in its own state, the company has to file a use tax return and pay the tax. The sales taxes and use taxes are essentially the same, except for collection and remittance. In the following discussion, we only consider the sales tax.

We discuss two accounting situations. The first is a typical sale when the sales tax is added to the invoice price. For example, assume that Selleroy Company sells merchandise for cash with a retail sales price of $50,000 on which a sales tax of 6% is levied. The company collects $53,000 from its customers and records the collection as follows:

Cash	53,000	
Sales		50,000
Sales Taxes Payable		3,000

The $3,000 sales taxes collected by the Selleroy Company are owed to the state or local government levying the tax; hence the amount is *not* part of revenues (sales) and the company records it in a current liability account. Later, when Selleroy files the sales tax return and pays the tax to the governmental agency, it eliminates the current liability.

The second situation arises when a business includes the amount of the sales taxes directly in the price it charges for merchandise. In this case, it credits the Sales account for the sum of the sales taxes payable and the sales amount. When this procedure is followed, since sales taxes generally must be paid monthly, the company must make an adjusting entry at the end of each month to reduce the Sales account and to create the current liability, Sales Taxes Payable. To illustrate, suppose that the Smally Company collects sales taxes but records the combined amount of both the sales and the sales taxes in the Sales account. To calculate the sales, the amount in the Sales account must be divided by 1 plus the tax rate. The sales taxes owed are determined by subtracting the calculated sales from the amount in the Sales account. For instance, suppose that at the end of January, the Sales account shows a credit balance of $169,600. Assuming a 6% sales tax on all goods, the company makes an adjusting entry for $9,600 [$169,600 − ($169,600 ÷ 1.06)] at the end of January as follows:

Sales	9,600	
Sales Taxes Payable		9,600

In some cases the sales taxes payable computed by the company may differ slightly from the amount calculated as owed by the governmental authority (e.g., because of the use of graduated sales tax tables). In these cases the company makes an adjustment to Sales Taxes Payable and to Sales.

Liabilities Related to Payrolls

Companies are required by law to withhold from the pay of each employee a legal amount representing anticipated federal and state (and sometimes local governmental unit) taxes payable by employees. They also may voluntarily withhold amounts for union dues, group insurance, and various other amounts payable by the employees to third parties. In addition to these withheld items, federal and state (and sometimes local) laws levy on employers other taxes that are based on the payroll amount. These include social security taxes and unemployment insurance taxes. Since a company must remit these taxes and voluntary withholdings within a few months, it classifies them as current liabilities.

Exhibit 12-2 presents an overview of the withheld groups of items and related voluntary payroll deductions. We discuss each item briefly in the following sections.

PAYROLL TAX GROUP The federal income tax law, most state income tax laws, and some local governmental unit laws require employers to withhold from the pay of each employee an amount representing anticipated income taxes payable by the employee to the respective governmental units. (Since only a few local governmental units levy taxes based on the payroll, we ignore these taxes in the discussion that follows.) The amount

4 Understand and record payroll taxes and deductions.

EXHIBIT 12-2 Payroll Taxes and Voluntary Payroll Deductions

Payroll Tax Group	2002 Rate on		2002 Annual Salary per Employee Subject to Tax
	Employee	Employer	
Federal income tax	Graduated rates	—	100%
State income tax	Graduated rates	—	100%
F.I.C.A. taxes			
O.A.S.D.I.	6.20%	6.20%	$84,900
Medicare	1.45%	1.45%	100%
Federal unemployment tax	—	0.8%	$ 7,000
State unemployment tax	—	5.4%	$ 7,000

Voluntary Payroll Deductions Group

Union dues
Government bonds   } Amount withheld is stated in contract
Group insurance
Others

withheld depends upon the number of exemptions claimed and the amount of income earned by the employee. Employers determine the amount to be withheld from wages by using applicable legal rates or by referring to withholding tax tables. The employer must pay withheld amounts to the respective governmental unit at specified times and through specified channels. For example, the withheld federal income taxes must be paid to the Internal Revenue Service either electronically or through local depositories (e.g., banks).

Social security legislation requires that employers withhold Federal Insurance Contribution Act taxes (F.I.C.A.) from the wages of each employee under certain conditions. Also, employers must match the taxes of the employee and pay the sum of both taxes to the Internal Revenue Service along with the income taxes withheld. F.I.C.A. taxes have a dual purpose. The first is to pay federal old-age, survivor, and disability insurance (O.A.S.D.I.) benefits. The second is to pay federal hospital insurance (Medicare) benefits. Together, these taxes are referred to as *social security taxes*. As indicated in Exhibit 12-2, the 2002 F.I.C.A. taxes are 15.30% (6.20% + 1.45% + 6.20% + 1.45%) on the first $84,900 earned by each employee. One half of this amount—7.65% (6.20% + 1.45%)—is paid by the employee; the other half is paid by the employer. On income between $84,900 and the total income earned by the employee, additional F.I.C.A. taxes of 1.45% are paid by both the employee and employer. The actual tax rates and wage base for future years will be determined by Congress. Because Congress has changed (generally increased) these items virtually on an annual basis, for simplicity in the following examples and homework, we will use an assumed rate of 16%—8% on the employee and 8% on the employer—and a taxable wage base of $80,000 on *both* F.I.C.A taxes.

The fifth and sixth taxes indicated in Exhibit 12-2 are unemployment insurance taxes, another type of social security tax. These taxes are used by governmental units to make payments for a limited period of time to individuals who become unemployed. The Federal Unemployment Tax Act (F.U.T.A.) requires a tax with a maximum rate of 6.2% to be levied wholly on employers of one or more persons, but the rate applies to only the first $7,000 paid to each employee. The law provides, however, that 5.4% of the 6.2% is payable to the state, assuming that the state levies an approved unemployment insurance tax. Thus, in these cases, the net effective federal unemployment tax rate is 0.8%. Most state laws allow for a reduction of the 5.4% tax through merit-rating plans for those employers who maintain steady employment, because that reduces the amount drawn from the fund.

VOLUNTARY PAYROLL DEDUCTION GROUP Through a contractual arrangement between individual employees and their employer many kinds of payroll deductions can be authorized. Typical examples of these voluntary contractual deductions are for payment of group hospital insurance, accident insurance, life insurance, union dues, government bonds, tax-sheltered retirement annuities, and any other purchase of goods or services. These payroll deductions are made for the convenience of the employees of a company.

ACCOUNTING FOR PAYROLL TAXES AND DEDUCTIONS To illustrate the accounting for payroll taxes and voluntary payroll deductions, assume that the Wager Corporation summarizes the following weekly payroll from its payroll register during early February 2005:

Type of Salary	Gross Pay	Withheld Amounts				Net Pay
		F.I.C.A. Tax*	Federal Income Tax	State Income Tax	Union Dues	
Sales staff	$10,000	$ 800	$730	$300	$100	$ 8,070
Office staff	4,000	320	260	200	80	3,140
	$14,000	$1,120	$990	$500	$180	$11,210

*Assumed 8% rate.

Further assume that the effective federal and state unemployment tax rates are 0.8% and 5.4%, respectively, and *that all wages are subject to all payroll taxes*. The company makes the following two journal entries to record the payment of the payroll and the payroll taxes imposed on the employer:

1. To record salaries and employee withholding items:

Sales Salaries Expense	10,000	
Office Salaries Expense	4,000	
F.I.C.A. Taxes Payable		1,120
Employee Federal Income Taxes Withholding Payable		990
Employee State Income Taxes Withholding Payable		500
Employee Union Dues Withholding Payable		180
Cash		11,210

2. To record employer payroll taxes:

Payroll Taxes Expense	1,988	
F.I.C.A. Taxes Payable (8% × $14,000)		1,120
Federal Unemployment Taxes Payable (0.8% × $14,000)		112
State Unemployment Taxes Payable (5.4% × $14,000)		756

The company reports the various "payable" accounts as current liabilities. Instead of recording Payroll Taxes Expense in the second entry, the company may increase the respective Salaries Expense accounts for the appropriate amounts that are the additional cost of employing the sales and office staff. Regardless of approach, when Wager Corporation remits the payroll deductions, it eliminates the related current liability accounts.

Income Taxes Payable

The income of corporations is subject to a federal income tax separate from that of individuals. In addition, corporations may be subject to state and foreign income taxes. The separate federal corporate income tax imposes a rate schedule for 2003 that is an eight-step progressive structure, which ranges from a low of 15% on taxable income of less than $50,000 to 35% on taxable income over $18,333,333. Because Congress may change the income tax rates and because actual income tax computations are complex, for simplicity we generally assume an effective income tax rate (e.g., 30%) in our discussions and homework.

A corporation must file its Form 1120, Corporate Income Tax Return, $2\frac{1}{2}$ months after the end of the taxable fiscal year. Most corporations must pay estimated taxes throughout the fiscal year. Guidelines for the calculation of both estimated and actual income taxes are provided by the Internal Revenue Service. Since these guidelines are subject to change, we do not discuss them in this book.

We briefly consider accounting for the current liability for income taxes here. In accruing its applicable income taxes for either interim or end-of-period financial statement purposes, the corporation records a debit to Income Tax Expense and a credit to a current liability, Income Taxes Payable. If a prepayment of income taxes is required to be made, a debit to Prepaid Income Taxes is appropriate. Later, when the actual liability for taxes is determined, the corporation makes a journal entry to appropriately report the Income Tax Expense, to reduce the Prepaid Income Taxes, and to record a current liability for any excess of actual income taxes owed over the prepaid amount.

Income taxes for financial reporting is discussed in Chapter 18.

Bonus Obligations

As incentives to certain employees—particularly officers and managers—to increase company earnings, many companies establish an earnings-based bonus agreement. The bonus is usually payable shortly after the end of the year. The bonus, which is additional salary, is an operating expense of the company. The company records the bonus as an expense and as a current liability when it has been earned by the employees. Furthermore, the company deducts the bonus payments when computing its taxable income. Legal documents for bonus agreements may be written in a number of different ways. Two typical plans provide for the calculation of the bonus as follows:[15]

1. The bonus is based on the corporation's income after deducting income taxes, but before deducting the bonus.
2. The bonus is based on the corporation's net income after deducting both the bonus and the income taxes.

In either of these two approaches, the corporation cannot determine its income tax until it calculates the bonus. Thus, the computation requires solving two simple simultaneous equations. Exhibit 12-3 shows the computation of the bonus and income tax for each of these approaches.

The Bonex Corporation records the bonus and income taxes in Example 2 of Exhibit 12-3 as follows:

1. To record the bonus:

Salaries Expense (Officer's Bonus)	17,009	
Officer's Bonus Payable		17,009

2. To record the income tax expense:

Income Tax Expense	72,897	
Income Taxes Payable		72,897

The Bonex Corporation reports both the Officer's Bonus Payable and Income Taxes Payable as current liabilities on its balance sheet. Note that bonuses may have an undesirable impact on management's decisions in regard to accounting principles. That is, management might choose an accounting principle, method, or procedure only because it increases the company's income, thereby increasing management's bonuses.

---

15. Two other approaches are: (1) the bonus could be based on the corporation's income before income taxes and before bonus, or (2) the bonus could be based on the corporation's income before income taxes and after the bonus is deducted. The computations involved in these two approaches are similar to (but simpler than) the methods we discuss and we do not present them here.

EXHIBIT 12-3   Computation of Bonus and Income Tax

Basic Information

The two examples involve these assumptions: the Bonex Corporation reported income for the current year of $260,000 before deducting income taxes and before a bonus to the president; the effective tax rate is 30%, and the bonus rate is 10%. In the two examples, let: B = bonus and T = income tax.

Example 1

Bonus computed on income after deducting income taxes but before deducting the bonus.

The two equations for calculating the bonus are:

$B = 0.10 (\$260,000 - T)$ (1)
$T = 0.30 (\$260,000 - B)$ (2)

To solve the simultaneous equations, the value of T is substituted in Equation (2) for the element T in Equation (1) as follows:

$B = 0.10 [\$260,000 - 0.30 (\$260,000 - B)]$ (3)

Now Equation (3) has only one unknown and is solved as follows:

$$B = 0.10 [\$260,000 - \$78,000 + 0.30B]$$
$$B = \$26,000 - \$7,800 + 0.03B$$
$$B - 0.03B = \$18,200$$
$$0.97B = \$18,200$$
$$B = \$18,200 \div 0.97$$
$$B = \$18,763 \text{ (rounded to nearest dollar)}$$

To calculate the amount of the income tax, the amount of the bonus is substituted into Equation (2) as follows:

$T = 0.30 (\$260,000 - \$18,763)$
$T = \$72,371$ (rounded to nearest dollar)

Example 2

Bonus computed on net income after deducting both income taxes and the bonus.

The two equations for calculating the bonus are:

$B = 0.10 (\$260,000 - B - T)$ (4)
$T = 0.30 (\$260,000 - B)$ (5)

To solve the simultaneous equations, the value of T in Equation (5) is substituted for the element T in Equation (4) as follows:

$$B = 0.10 [\$260,000 - B - 0.30 (\$260,000 - B)]$$ (6)
$$B = 0.10 [\$260,000 - B - \$78,000 + 0.30B]$$
$$B = \$26,000 - 0.10B - \$7,800 + 0.03B$$
$$B + 0.10B - 0.03B = \$18,200$$
$$1.07B = \$18,200$$
$$B = \$18,200 \div 1.07$$
$$B = \$17,009 \text{ (rounded to nearest dollar)}$$

To calculate the amount of the income tax, the amount of the bonus is substituted into Equation (5) as follows:

$T = 0.30 (\$260,000 - \$17,009)$
$T = \$72,897$ (rounded to nearest dollar)

CURRENT LIABILITIES REQUIRING AMOUNTS TO BE ESTIMATED

A number of liabilities have amounts that a company must estimate as of the balance sheet date. We discuss the obligations that typically are current liabilities, namely property taxes, warranties, and premium obligations, in this section. Because these items are specific types of "contingent liabilities," we discuss the general issue of contingencies in the following section.

Property Taxes

Property taxes are assessed by municipal, county, and some state governments on the value of certain property as of a given date and become a lien against the property at a date specified by law. Legally a liability arises on this lien date. The lien date may precede the billing date by several months. For example, in Columbia, Missouri, the property tax is assessed on the value of the property as of January 1 of each year. The date that the tax becomes a lien against the property is July 1. The fiscal year of the city is July 1 to June 30. Property tax statements are mailed to property owners during November. Thus if a company records its property taxes before it receives the tax statement, it must estimate the amount. Also, when the accounting year of the company is different from the fiscal year of the municipality, the issue arises as to when the company should record the property tax liability and in which accounting period the property taxes should be expensed.

5 Record property taxes.

The Committee on Accounting Procedure concluded that, generally, a company is to accrue property taxes in equal monthly amounts during the fiscal periods of the taxing authority for which the taxes are levied. The accounting records then will show, at any closing date, the appropriate accruals or prepayment.[16] This method is preferred because the company recognizes the property tax expense in the same period it receives services from the governmental unit(s).

It is not difficult to estimate the amount of property taxes applicable to the fiscal year of the taxing authority. By law, the tax rate generally cannot vary too much from past rates, and the value of the property being taxed is generally determined by the municipality with a notification to the owner. Thus, the company can determine the total valuation subject to the tax. The company calculates the estimated property tax by applying the estimated rate to the assessed valuation amount. If a variation between the actual property taxes and the estimated property taxes occurs, *APB Opinion No. 20* requires the company to account for it prospectively.

To illustrate, assume that the Ezzell Company closes its books annually each December 31. The fiscal year for the town and county in which the Ezzell Company is located begins on July 1 and ends on the following June 30. The tax becomes a lien against the property on July 1 of each year. The estimated property taxes for the period July 1, 2004 to June 30, 2005 are $7,200. The tax bill is mailed in October with a requirement that the tax be paid before December 31, 2004. The tax bill for the Ezzell Company reported an actual tax of $7,290, and the company pays this amount on October 31, 2004. The company records monthly property tax adjustments for interim statements required by its management.

Assuming that the Ezzell Company did not recognize any property tax liability at the lien date and it records the property tax on a monthly accrual basis, it records the following series of journal entries:

<u>Three Monthly Entries: July 31–September 30, 2004</u>

Property Tax Expense ($7,200 ÷ 12)	600	
Property Taxes Payable		600

<u>October 31, 2004: Payment of Property Taxes</u>

Property Taxes Payable	1,800	
Prepaid Property Taxes	5,490	
Cash		7,290

<u>Three Monthly Entries: October 31–December 31, 2004</u>

Property Tax Expense	610	
Prepaid Property Taxes		610

The company reports a $600 current liability for property taxes on its September 30, 2004 interim balance sheet. Note that the $610 amount in the last journal entry is the result of the allocation of the $90 difference ($7,290 − $7,200) between the actual and

---

16. "Restatement and Revision of Accounting Research Bulletins," *Accounting Research Bulletin No. 43* (New York: AICPA, 1961), par. 14.

estimated property taxes to the remaining 9-month period ending June 30, 2005. That is, the $610 is computed by subtracting the previously estimated property tax expense to date ($600 × 3) from the total actual property tax ($7,290) and dividing the difference ($5,490) by the remaining months (9) in the year.

Assuming that Ezzell had recorded $598 each month from January 31 to June 30, 2004 (the portion of the tax authority's *previous* fiscal year occurring during the company's *current* accounting year), its property tax expense for 2004 is $7,218 [($598 × 6) + ($600 × 3) + ($610 × 3)].

Warranty Obligations

Product warranty agreements (whether oral or in writing) require the seller, over a specified period of time after the sale, to correct any deficiency in quality, quantity, or performance of the merchandise sold, to replace the item, or to refund the selling price. These promises are made by manufacturers and retailers to promote sales.

The period of the warranty may span two or more accounting periods. Adherence to **the matching principle requires that a company recognize the warranty expense in the period during which it makes the sale,** because the flaws in the merchandise are assumed to be present at the time of the sale. The actual use of cash and other resources to correct the defects in the merchandise, however, may occur partly in the period of sale and partly in a later period. Consequently, recognition of the warranty expense in the period of sale and the corresponding current liability requires an estimate of all costs that will be incurred after the sale to correct any defects and deficiencies. There are three methods of accounting for warranty costs: (1) expense warranty accrual method, (2) sales warranty accrual method, and (3) modified cash basis.

6 Account for warranty costs.

EXPENSE WARRANTY ACCRUAL METHOD Under the expense warranty accrual method, a company recognizes the estimated warranty expense and a liability for future performance under the warranty provision in the period of sale. This method assumes that the company makes the warranty offer to increase sales; hence, the estimated warranty expense is matched against these sales. The company classifies the estimated portion of the warranty liability applicable to the next accounting period (or operating cycle, if longer) as a current liability; it classifies the remainder as a long-term liability. During the period when cash and other resources are used to fulfill the warranty agreement, it debits the liability and credits the respective assets.

To illustrate, assume that Anglee Machinery Corporation begins production on a new machine in April 2004 and sells 200 of these machines at $6,000 each by December 31, 2004. Each machine carries a warranty for 1 year. Experience from the sale of similar machinery in the past has shown that the warranty costs will average $150 per unit or a total of $30,000 (200 × $150). The corporation spent $5,000 in 2004 and $25,150 in 2005 to fulfill the warranty agreements for the 200 machines sold in 2004. The company records this information under the expense warranty accrual method for the year 2004 in a series of journal entries as follows:

Sale of 200 Machines during April–December, 2004

Cash or Accounts Receivable ($6,000 × 200)	1,200,000	
Sales		1,200,000

Recognition of Warranty Expense for Period, April–December, 2004

Warranty Expense	30,000	
Estimated Liability under Warranties		30,000

Payment or Incurrence of Warranty Costs for Period, April–December, 2004

Estimated Liability under Warranties	5,000	
Cash (or other assets)		5,000

The company reports the Warranty Expense as an operating expense on its 2004 income statement. It reports the remaining $25,000 ($30,000 accrued − $5,000 paid) unpaid Estimated Liability under Warranties as a current liability on its December 31, 2004 balance sheet since the warranty period is a year in length.

The company records the transactions in 2005 relating to the 200 machines sold in 2004 as follows:

Payment or Incurrence of Warranty Costs during 2005

Estimated Liability under Warranties	25,000	
Warranty Expense	150	
Cash (or other assets)		25,150

Accounting for changes in estimates is discussed in Chapter 22.

In the preceding journal entry, the actual warranty costs are $150 more than were estimated. The company debited this amount to Warranty Expense for 2005 because it resulted from a change in accounting estimate.

The proportional performance method for separate service contracts is introduced in Chapter 4 and is also discussed in Chapter 17.

SALES WARRANTY ACCRUAL METHOD   Many companies encourage customers to buy a "service contract" when they buy merchandise. Service contracts require customers to make fixed payments for future services. In other cases, there is no explicit separate service contract but the sales price of each product includes the sale of two items: the product and an implied warranty contract. Use of the **sales warranty accrual method** separates the accounting for these two items *even when no separate service contract is involved.* Under this method, a company assumes that its revenue from the implied warranty contract is equal to the estimated warranty costs, and it defers and recognizes revenue in an amount equal to the warranty costs incurred. In essence, this is a *cost recovery approach to warranty revenue recognition.* To illustrate, in the case of the Anglee Machinery Corporation, the $6,000 selling price of each machine may be assumed to be both an implied service contract (sale of the warranty) of $150 and a sale of a machine with a selling price of $5,850 ($6,000 − $150). Under the sales warranty accrual method, the company records the transactions for 2004 as follows:

The cost recovery method of revenue recognition is discussed in Chapter 17.

Sale of 200 Machines during April–December, 2004

Cash or Accounts Receivable ($6,000 × 200)	1,200,000	
Sales ($5,850 × 200)		1,170,000
Unearned Warranty Revenue ($150 × 200)		30,000

Recognition of Warranty Expense for Period, April–December, 2004

Warranty Expense	5,000	
Cash (or other assets)		5,000

Recognition of Warranty Revenue for Period, April–December, 2004

Unearned Warranty Revenue	5,000	
Warranty Revenue		5,000

The company reports the $25,000 balance in Unearned Warranty Revenue as a current liability on its December 31, 2004 balance sheet. Note that on the company's 2004 income statement the Sales amount is $30,000 smaller than under the expense warranty accrual method. The 2004 income statement lists Warranty Revenue of $5,000 and also Warranty Expense of $5,000 (as compared to $30,000 under the expense warranty accrual approach). Thus, while the company's net income for 2004 is the same under each method, the amounts of revenue and expense and the classifications of revenues are different, reflecting the different nature of revenue earned.

The company records the transactions for 2005 related to the 200 machines sold in 2004 as follows:

Recognition of Warranty Expense during 2005

Warranty Expense	25,150	
Cash (or other assets)		25,150

Recognition of Warranty Revenue during 2005

Unearned Warranty Revenue	25,000	
Warranty Revenue		25,000

Note that it is assumed that, in general, no profit is realized from the sale of the implied warranty contract. As a matter of fact, in the Anglee Machinery Corporation example, there is a loss of $150; this loss results from the actual warranty costs exceeding the estimated costs by that amount. Thus, this method assumed the most conservative possible recognition of that part of the revenue applicable to the warranty.

MODIFIED CASH BASIS The modified cash basis is the only method accepted for federal income tax purposes, and for this reason companies often use it for financial reporting if the results are not materially different than those from either of the two previous methods. **Under the modified cash basis, a company records the warranty costs as an expense during the period in which it makes the repairs to merchandise under warranty.** Thus, it recognizes the expense in the period of the *repair*, and this period may be later than the period of the sale. The company records a current liability only if it incurs an obligation for the repair that it does not pay at the time of the repair. Since the company does not estimate and recognize the full warranty costs during the period of sale, it does not record a liability for these future warranty costs. This method is inappropriate for financial reporting because it violates the matching principle. In general, since an expenditure of cash or other resources in the future is expected to be made, a liability *does* in fact exist from the date of sale to the end of the warranty period. Therefore, despite its popularity, the modified cash basis is conceptually unsound. It is justified for accounting under two conditions: (1) from a cost/benefit standpoint, when the warranty period is relatively short, or (2) when it is not possible for the company to make a reliable estimate of the amount of the warranty obligation at the time of sale.

Premium and Coupon Obligations

Many companies offer premiums such as toys, dishes, CDs, and small appliances in exchange for labels, coupons, box tops, and wrappers from their products. Other companies offer coupons printed in newspapers and magazines that can be used to reduce the purchase price of their products. Still others offer a cash rebate upon the return of a cash register receipt for the purchase of their products. Many of these offers expire after a specified time, but some do not have an expiration date. All of these offers are intended to increase a company's sales. Accordingly, **a company matches the related costs as expenses against revenues in the period of sale.** Furthermore, at the end of the accounting period, the company reports any outstanding offers that it expects to be redeemed or claimed within the next year (or operating cycle, if longer) as a current liability.

For example, assume that on October 1, 2004, the American Meatball Corporation began offering to customers a serving dish in return for 30 meatball can labels. This offer expires on April 1, 2005. The cost of each premium serving dish is $2. Based on past experience, the company estimates that only 60% of the labels will be redeemed. During 2004, the company purchased 12,000 serving dishes. In 2004, it sold 300,000 cans of meatballs at $1.80 per can. From these sales 105,000 labels were returned for redemption in 2004. The company prepares the following series of journal entries in 2004 to match expenses against revenues and to record its current liabilities:

Purchase of 12,000 Serving Dishes

Inventory of Premium Serving Dishes	24,000	
Cash (or Accounts Payable)		24,000

Sale of 300,000 Cans of Meatballs

Cash (or Accounts Receivable)	540,000	
Sales		540,000

Redemption of 105,000 Labels

Premium Expense [(105,000 ÷ 30) × $2]	7,000	
Inventory of Premium Serving Dishes		7,000

End-of-Year Recording of Estimated Liability for
Outstanding Premium Offers

Premium Expense	5,000	
Estimated Premium Claims Outstanding		5,000

The company computes the year-end adjustment to premium expense as follows:

Total meatball cans (with labels) sold in 2004	300,000
Total labels estimated for redemption (60% × 300,000)	180,000
Deduct labels redeemed during 2004	(105,000)
Estimated number of labels for future redemption	75,000
Premium expense for estimated future redemptions [(75,000 ÷ 30) × $2]	$ 5,000

The company reports the Premium Expense as a selling expense on its 2004 income statement. The company reports the Inventory of Premium Serving Dishes as a current asset and the Estimated Premium Claims Outstanding as a current liability on its December 31, 2004 balance sheet since the offer expires in less than a year.

The future redemptions of these labels in 2005 will require a debit to the Estimated Premium Claims Outstanding liability account and a credit to Inventory of Premium Serving Dishes. The company treats any corrections necessary because actual redemptions differ from estimated redemptions as changes in accounting estimates and recognizes them as an adjustment to Premium Expense in the period of change.

Some companies prefer to record an estimate of the premium expense and current liability at the time of sale and reduce the liability each time a premium is claimed. Others prefer to record an estimate of the entire current liability at the end of the accounting period, but reduce the liability as premiums are claimed during the period. In either case, the effects on the financial statements are the same as those illustrated.

ADVERTISING COSTS   Most companies expense their advertising costs as incurred or at the first time the advertising takes place because it is difficult to measure the future economic benefits. This advertising can be very expensive. For instance, each company advertising for 30 seconds during the 2002 Super Bowl paid $1.9 million dollars. A company running such an ad would expense the cost of preparing the ad as well as the $1.9 million fee at the time the ad was first run (i.e., at the time of the Super Bowl). In the 6 case of "direct-response" advertising, however, the AICPA issued a *Statement of Position* that requires companies to record certain costs initially as assets. **Direct-response advertising** is advertising that is expected to result in a customer's decision to buy the company's product based on a specific response to the advertising. The specific response must be documented through, for instance, a coded coupon turned in by the customer or a coded order form included with an advertisement. In such a situation, the company capitalizes specific costs if it has evidence (e.g., historical patterns) that they will result in future revenues in excess of future costs.

The costs of direct-response advertising that a company capitalizes include (1) incremental direct costs incurred in transactions with independent third parties (e.g., costs of artwork, magazine space, mailing), and (2) payroll costs for activities (e.g., idea development, writing advertising copy) of employees directly related to the advertising. As we discussed in the previous section, also included as assets are premiums, contest prizes, gifts, and similar promotions directly related to the direct-response advertising activities. Costs for administration and occupancy (e.g., depreciation) are *not* included as assets. The costs of direct-response advertising that are reported as assets are amortized as advertising expense over the period during which the future benefits are expected to be received (e.g., up to the date a coupon expires).[17] A company generally reports any unpaid direct advertising costs as current liabilities because they will be paid in the near future.

CONTINGENCIES

External users are interested in information that helps them assess the amounts, timing, and uncertainty of the net cash inflows of a company. They need accounting information that has predictive value to help them forecast more accurately the future outcome of past or present events. The financial information that a company reports in its financial statements is based primarily on transactions that have affected it. However, there may be some information available at year-end about the company that is not yet recorded in its accounting system but may be useful in predicting what might happen to the company. These items commonly are referred to as "contingencies."

Specifically, **FASB Statement No. 5** defines the term **contingency** as:

> an *existing condition*, situation, or set of circumstances involving *uncertainty* as to possible gain (hereafter a "gain contingency") or loss (hereafter a "loss contingency") to [a company] that will ultimately be resolved when one or more future events occur or fail to occur. *Resolution* of the uncertainty may confirm the acquisition of an asset or the reduction of a liability or the loss or impairment of an asset or the incurrence of a liability.[18]

This definition includes the three primary characteristics of a contingency: **(1) an existing condition, (2) uncertainty as to the ultimate effect of this condition,** and **(3) resolution of the uncertainty based on one or more future events.** *FASB Statement No. 5* focuses primarily on *loss* contingencies and lists a number of examples. Some of these are familiar, such as the noncollectibility of receivables (accounting for bad debts) and the obligations relating to product warranties and premium offers we discussed earlier in this chapter. Less familiar loss contingencies include the risk of loss or damage of a company's property by fire, explosion, or other hazards, threat of expropriation of assets, pending or threatened litigation, actual or possible claims and assessments, guarantees of indebtedness of others, and agreement to repurchase receivables (or to repurchase the related property) that have been sold.

When a loss contingency exists for a company, the likelihood that the future event or events will confirm the loss and the impairment of an asset or the incurrence of a liability can vary over a wide range. *FASB Statement No. 5* uses the terms *probable, reasonably possible,* and *remote* to identify three areas within this range. These terms are defined as follows:

1. **Probable.** The future event (or events) is *likely* to occur.
2. **Reasonably possible.** The chance of the future event occurring is *more* than remote but *less* than likely.
3. **Remote.** The chance of the future event occurring is *slight*.[19]

7 Explain the terms "probable," "reasonably possible," and "remote" related to contingencies.

---

17. "Reporting on Advertising Costs," *AICPA Statement of Position 93-7* (New York: AICPA, 1993), par. 25–47.
18. "Accounting for Contingencies," *FASB Statement of Financial Accounting Standards No. 5* (Stamford, Conn.: FASB, 1975), par. 1. (Emphasis added.)
19. *Ibid.*, par. 3. (Emphasis added.)

A company's **accounting for loss contingencies** depends upon the likelihood of occurrence of the future event(s). Two separate methods of accounting are defined by *FASB Statement No. 5*.

1. *Accrual in Accounts*. An estimated loss from a loss contingency *is accrued* in the company's accounts and reported in its financial statements as a reduction of income and as a liability (or as a reduction in an asset) if *both* of the following conditions are met:
   a. Information available to the company prior to issuance of the financial statements indicates that it is *probable* that an asset has been impaired or a liability has been incurred at the date of the financial statements. It is implicit in this condition that it must be *probable* that one or more future events will occur to confirm the occurrence of the loss.
   b. The amount of loss can be *reasonably estimated* by the company. In certain situations a company's reasonable estimate of the loss may be a range of amounts. When some amount within the range is a better estimate than any other amount in the range, *the better estimate is accrued*. When no amount within the range is a better estimate, *the minimum amount in the range is accrued* because it is not likely that the loss will be less than this minimum.[20]

2. *Disclosure in Notes to Financial Statements*. If no loss accrual is made by the company because one or both of the preceding conditions are not met and when there is at least a reasonable possibility that a loss may have been incurred, then the company discloses the loss contingency in the notes to its financial statements. (Some remote loss contingencies are also disclosed in the notes, as we discuss later.)

To summarize, **a company recognizes a loss contingency in its financial statements if the future event is *probable* and if its amount can be *reasonably estimated*.** If a liability is recorded in this process, it is *not* necessary to know the exact payee or the exact date that it is to be paid. A company discloses a loss contingency in the notes to its financial statements if one of these criteria is not met and if there is a reasonable possibility that the company may have incurred a loss.

The following diagram is helpful in determining how to report a loss contingency.

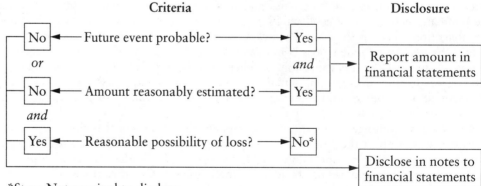

*Stop: Not required to disclose

The discussion that follows deals with accounting for the accrual of loss contingencies, disclosure of loss contingencies in the notes to the financial statements, and disclosure of gain contingencies in the notes to the financial statements.

Accrual of Loss Contingencies

Companies usually accrue certain loss contingencies because they are probable and can be reasonably estimated. They include the noncollectibility of receivables, sales returns

---

20. "Reasonable Estimation of the Amount of a Loss," *FASB Interpretation No. 14* (Stamford, Conn.: FASB, 1976), par. 3.

and allowances (which we discussed in Chapter 6), and the obligations related to property taxes, product warranties, and premium offers which we discussed earlier in this chapter. Several other loss contingencies *may be* accrued provided they meet the two stated conditions. These include the threat of expropriation of assets, pending or threatened litigation, actual or possible claims and assessments, guarantees of indebtedness of others, and agreements to repurchase receivables (or the related property) that were sold. On the other hand, at least three contingencies are *usually not* accrued. These include the uninsured risk of loss or damage of company property by fire, explosion, or other hazards, general or unspecified business risks, and risk of loss from catastrophes assumed by property and casualty insurance companies including reinsurance companies. For this latter group of items, a company's mere exposure to risk does not mean that an asset is impaired or that a liability has been incurred.

When a company recognizes a loss contingency, it records a debit to an *expense* (or *loss*) account and a credit to a *liability* account, *asset* account, or *contra-asset* account. To illustrate, assume a company estimates that its bad debt expense is $12,000 for 2004. The company records this loss contingency at the end of the year as follows:

8 Record and report a loss contingency.

Bad Debt Expense	12,000	
Allowance for Doubtful Accounts		12,000

Note that the debit is made to an expense account and the credit is made to a contra-asset account to accrue the loss contingency.

Accounting for damage lawsuits presents a very difficult problem. A company must analyze these pending lawsuits as possible loss contingencies. The company should consider the opinion of its legal counsel, the nature of the litigation, its precedent experience and that of other companies in similar cases, and management reaction to the lawsuit. If the cause of the litigation has occurred before the date of its financial statements, if the loss of the lawsuit is *probable*, and if the loss amount can be *reasonably estimated*, the company must recognize the loss. Management may decide only to disclose the pending lawsuit in the notes to the financial statements because the loss is not probable or because it is not possible to reasonably estimate the loss. However, this decision may be influenced by management's desire to maintain higher reported earnings and to minimize the amount of reported liabilities.

In regard to potential unfiled lawsuits and other possible assessments and unasserted claims, a company must determine the likelihood that the suit may be filed or the claim or assessment asserted, and the probability of an unfavorable outcome. For example, if Patterson Corporation is being investigated for a possible patent infringement suit, it must determine the probability that the suit will be filed and that the suit will be lost. If these future events are probable, if the loss is reasonably estimable, and if the cause for action has occurred on or before the date of the issuance of the financial statements, it accrues the loss and the liability in its accounts.

In practice, companies usually do *not* accrue the costs of actual or pending litigation. In the case where a company is being sued for a specific situation by a single complainant, it is unlikely that the company will have sufficient evidence to conclude that the likelihood of loss is probable. Or in a situation where there is a lack of precedence relating to the particular circumstances of a lawsuit, even if a company admits guilt it is unlikely to conclude that it can reasonably estimate the amount of the loss. However, a company may be sued by many complainants over the same, or similar, issue (a "class action" suit) in which case the thresholds of probable and reasonably estimable may be reached. In this relatively rare situation, the company typically will accrue the costs of the litigation. For instance, **Union Carbide Corporation** (a wholly owned subsidiary of Dow Chemical Company) has accrued losses of $233 million in regard to its potential liability for a class action lawsuit involving its manufacture of asbestos.

Disclosure of Loss Contingencies in the Notes to the Financial Statements

If a company does not accrue a loss for a loss contingency because one or both of the conditions listed are not met, or if an exposure to loss exists in excess of the amount that it actually accrues, it must disclose the contingency when there is at least a reasonable possibility that a loss or an additional loss may have been incurred. Recall that a loss contingency is reasonably possible when the chance is more than remote but less than likely that the future event or events will confirm the loss or impairment of an asset or the incurrence of a liability. Most of the examples of loss contingencies listed earlier could fall into this category, particularly the threat of expropriation of assets, pending or threatened litigation, and actual or possible claims and assessments. For this type of loss contingency, a company makes this disclosure in the notes to its financial statements. The disclosure must indicate the nature of the contingency and give an estimate of the possible loss or range of loss or state that such an estimate cannot be made.

Certain loss contingencies, where the possibility of loss is only remote, are also disclosed in the notes to a company's financial statements. Examples of these loss contingencies include direct and indirect guarantees of indebtedness of others, obligations of commercial banks under "standby letters of credit," and guarantees to repurchase receivables that have been sold or otherwise assigned. **Indirect guarantees are those arising out of an agreement requiring one company to transfer funds to another entity upon the occurrence of specified events, under conditions whereby (1) the funds are legally available to creditors of the other entity, and (2) those creditors may enforce that entity's claims against the company under the agreement.**[21] A common characteristic of these remote contingencies is a guarantee, normally with a right to proceed against an outside party in the event that the guarantor is called upon to satisfy the guarantee.[22] The disclosure of this group of guarantees must include the nature and amount of the guarantee and, if estimable, the value of any recovery that could be expected to result. This latter requirement would result from the guarantor's right to proceed against an outside party.

Disclosure of Gain Contingencies in the Notes to the Financial Statements

A gain contingency exists when the three characteristics of a contingency are present, and there is a potential increase in a company's assets or a potential decrease in its liabilities. Adhering to the convention of conservatism and to the revenue recognition criteria, **FASB Statement No. 5** requires that these gains usually are *not* accrued, but are disclosed in the notes to the company's financial statements. It states:

9 Disclose a gain contingency.

> (a) **Contingencies that might result in gains usually are not reflected in [a company's] accounts since to do so might be to recognize revenue prior to its realization.**
>
> (b) **Adequate disclosure shall be made of contingencies that might result in gains, but care shall be exercised to avoid misleading implications as to the likelihood of realization.**[23]

An example of a gain contingency is where a company is suing another company for patent infringement, and the probability of winning the suit is excellent. A second example is a probable expropriation of a company's property by a foreign government where probable reimbursement will exceed the book value of the property expected to be taken over by the foreign government.

Executory Contracts

An **executory contract** is a contract in which two parties agree to a future exchange of resources or services, but neither party has performed any of its responsibilities. Examples of executory contracts include an unused line of credit, a purchase commitment, an agreement to pay future compensation, and a contract for having a factory built. For instance, **Mariah Carey** and **Universal** agreed to a $20 million contract for future albums. Since in an executory contract (sometimes called an *unexecuted* contract) no exchange of resources or services has occurred, no liability (or asset reduction) or contingent liability

---

21. "Disclosure of Indirect Guarantees of Indebtedness of Others," *FASB Interpretation No. 34* (Stamford, Conn.: FASB, 1981), par. 2.
22. *FASB Statement No. 5, op. cit.*, par. 10 and 12.
23. *Ibid.*, par. 17.

exists. However, when an executory contract has a likely material impact on the future cash flows of a company, it discloses this information in the notes to the financial statements to enhance the predictive value of the information.

Illustrations of Contingency Disclosures

Exhibit 12-4 illustrates the loss contingency disclosures in the notes to the 2001 financial statements of several companies. These disclosures involve the potential violation of environmental regulations by Baker Hughes, a value-added tax dispute of Englehard, and financial guarantees of customers' lines of credit by Whirlpool.

EXHIBIT 12-4 Disclosure of Contingencies

BAKER HUGHES INCORPORATED

NOTES TO CONSOLIDATED FINANCIAL STATEMENTS (in part):
Note 13: Commitments and Contingencies (in part)
The company has been identified as a potentially responsible party ("PRP") in remedial activities related to various "Superfund" sites. Applicable United States federal law imposes joint and several liability on each PRP for the cleanup of these sites leaving the Company with the uncertainty that it may be responsible for the remediation cost attributable to other PRPs who are unable to pay their share of the remediation costs. Generally, the Company has estimated its share of such total cost based on the ratio that the estimated volume of waste contributed to the site by the Company bears to the total estimated volume of waste disposed at the site. The Company has accrued what it believes to have been its pro rata share of the total estimated cost of remediation of these Superfund sites based upon such a volumetric calculation.

At December 31, 2001 and 2000, the Company had accrued $17.6 million and $14.1 million, respectively, for remediation costs, including the Superfund sites referred to above. The measurement of the accruals for remediation costs is subject to uncertainty, including the evolving nature of environmental regulations and the difficulty in estimating the extent and type of remediation activity that will be utilized. The Company believes that the likelihood of material losses in excess of those amounts recorded is remote.

ENGELHARD CORPORATION

NOTES TO CONSOLIDATED FINANCIAL STATEMENTS (in part):
20. Litigation and Contingencies (in part)
The Company is involved in a value-added tax dispute in Peru. Management believes the Company was targeted by corrupt officials within the former Peruvian government.... In late October 2000, a criminal proceeding alleging tax fraud and forgery related to this value-added tax dispute was initiated against two Lima-based officials of Engelhard Peru, S.A. Although Engelhard Peru, S.A. is not a defendant, it may be civilly liable in Peru if its representatives are found responsible for criminal conduct. Accordingly, Engelhard Peru, S.A. is assisting in the vigorous defense of this proceeding. Management believes the maximum economic exposure is limited to the aggregate value of all assets of Engelhard Peru, S.A., including unpaid refunds, which is approximately $30 million.

WHIRLPOOL CORPORATION

NOTES TO CONSOLIDATED FINANCIAL STATEMENTS (in part):
14 Contingencies (in part)
The Company is a party to certain financial guarantees and standby letters of credit with risk not reflected on the balance sheet. The only significant arrangement in place at year-end is in its Brazilian subsidiary. As a standard business practice the subsidiary guarantees customer lines of credit at commercial banks following its normal credit policies. As of December 31, 2001 and 2000, these amounts totaled $124 million and $106 million, respectively. The company currently believes the risk of loss to be minimal.

Q U E S T I O N S

Q What journal entry did Baker Hughes make at the end of 2001 to record its estimated remediation costs? **Q** What is the maximum loss that Englehard could incur in regard to the alleged tax fraud? **Q** What is the only significant arrangement that Whirlpool has in regard to its guarantees of customers' lines of credit? Why do you think this is significant?

International Accounting Differences

International accounting standards and U.S. accounting standards are similar in regard to contingencies, but there are some critical differences. International standards deal with loss contingencies but refer to them as *provisions*. A company is required to recognize a provision when it has a present obligation as a result of a past event, it is probable that the company will have a future outflow of resources to settle the obligation, and it can make a reliable estimate of the amount. These provisions are similar to U.S. GAAP but international standards use probable to mean that the outcome is more likely than not to occur, while U.S. standards use probable to mean the outcome is likely to occur (a more stringent test). Furthermore, in a situation where a company cannot determine whether the obligating event has occurred, international standards require recognition of a liability if it is probable that the event has occurred. International standards also require a company to measure the provision at the *settlement price* on the balance sheet date using present value techniques whenever the effect on the measurement of the liability is material. A company is not allowed to recognize gain contingencies, but discloses a gain contingency in the notes to its financial statements if an inflow of economic benefits is probable.

OTHER LIABILITY CLASSIFICATION ISSUES

We discuss two additional liability classification issues addressed by the FASB in this section: (1) short-term debt expected to be refinanced, and (2) classification of obligations that are callable by the creditor.

Short-Term Debt Expected to Be Refinanced

Generally, a company classifies debt that is maturing within one year or the operating cycle, whichever is longer, as a current liability. This classification affects the company's liquidity ratios such as its current and acid test ratios. In certain situations, short-term debt that is expected to be refinanced on a long-term basis is *not* classified as a current liability. A company may refinance its short-term debt on a long-term basis by either: (1) replacing the short-term debt with long-term debt (such as bonds payable) or with ownership securities (such as common stock); or (2) extending, renewing, or replacing the short-term debt with other short-term obligations that, in turn, will be renewed or extended beyond one year or the operating cycle, whichever is longer.

FASB Statement No. 6 states that short-term obligations are *excluded* from a company's current liabilities if two conditions are met: (1) it intends to refinance the obligation on a *long-term basis*, and (2) it has an ability to refinance. The **intent to refinance** on a long-term basis means that the company intends to refinance the short-term obligations so that it will not have to use working capital during the subsequent year or operating cycle, whichever is longer. The **ability to refinance** on a long-term basis must be demonstrated by the fact that the company (1) has issued long-term obligations or equity securities after the date of its balance sheet but before it issues its balance sheet, or (2) has entered into a bona fide long-term financing agreement before it issues its balance sheet that clearly permits the company to refinance the short-term obligations on a long-term basis.

If a company actually has refinanced short-term debt after the year-end but before it issues its financial statements, it excludes an amount from the current liabilities shown on the year-end balance sheet. The amount excluded is only that portion of the short-term obligation that is equal to the proceeds from the new long-term obligations or equity securities issued to retire the short-term obligation. For example, assume that Rayvon Corporation, with $2,000,000 of short-term debt on December 31, 2004, issued 75,000 shares of common stock for $20 per share on January 9, 2005. The proceeds of $1,500,000 were scheduled to be used to retire the short-term obligation when it matured. On the December 31, 2004 balance sheet (issued on February 25, 2005), the company reports the short-term debt of $1,500,000 expected to be refinanced as a noncurrent liability. Note that the company reports the refinanced portion as a liability and *not* as stockholders' equity since, as of year-end, the item was debt and not equity. It reports the other $500,000 as a current liability.

When a company relies on a **financing agreement** to demonstrate the ability to refinance, the amount of the short-term debt that it excludes from current liabilities is reduced to an amount that is the *lesser* of

1. The amount available for refinancing under the agreement, or
2. The amount obtainable under the agreement after considering the restrictions included in other agreements, or
3. A reasonable estimate of the minimum amount expected to be available for future refinancing if the amount that could be obtained fluctuates (for example, in relation to the company's needs, in proportion to the value of the collateral, or in accordance with other terms of the agreement).[24]

If the company cannot make a reasonable estimate, it must include the entire outstanding short-term obligation as a current liability.

When a company excludes a short-term obligation to be refinanced from its current liabilities, the notes to the financial statements must include a general description of the financing agreement and the terms of any new obligations incurred or expected to be incurred, or equity securities issued or expected to be issued as a result of the refinancing. These obligations also may be shown in captions distinct from both the current liabilities and long-term debt, such as "Interim Debt" or "Short-Term Debt Expected to Be Refinanced."

REPAYMENT AND REPLACEMENT After the issuance of *FASB Statement No. 6*, an issue arose as to whether a company should exclude a short-term debt from its current liabilities if it repays the debt after the balance sheet date and then later issues long-term debt (or common stock) before the balance sheet actually is published. This action involves a reimbursement of the cash used to pay the short-term debt. **FASB Interpretation No. 8** concluded that a company must *not* exclude such short-term debt from its current liabilities at the balance sheet date.[25] Thus, since the repayment of a short-term debt required the use of an existing actual current asset (even though it is later replaced), the short-term debt is reported on the preceding year-end balance sheet as a current liability.

Classification of Obligations That Are Callable by the Creditor

As we noted earlier in the chapter, a company generally reports the *currently maturing portion* of its long-term debt as a current liability. Also, **FASB Statement No. 78** concluded that a company must report the *entire amount* of a long-term obligation as a current liability if (1) the company is in violation of a provision of a long-term debt agreement (a requirement in the debt indenture or contract) at the balance sheet date, and the violation makes the liability callable by the creditor within one year from the balance sheet date, or (2) the violation, if not resolved within a specified grace period, *will make* the liability callable within one year from the balance sheet date (or operating cycle, if longer, in both of the preceding situations).

An exception to this requirement is a callable obligation that meets the following conditions: (1) the creditor has waived or lost the right to request repayment for more than one year (or operating cycle, if longer) from the balance sheet date, or (2) it is probable that the company will resolve the violation of a debt agreement for a long-term obligation containing a grace period within that period, thus preventing it from becoming callable. In this case, the company reports the obligation as long-term debt;

---

24. "Classification of Short-Term Obligations Expected to Be Refinanced," *FASB Statement of Financial Accounting Standards No. 6* (Stamford, Conn.: FASB, 1975), par. 9–12.
25. "Classification of a Short-Term Obligation Repaid Prior to Being Replaced by a Long-Term Security," *FASB Interpretation No. 8* (Stamford, Conn.: FASB, 1976), par. 3.

furthermore, it discloses the circumstances involving an obligation under item (2) in the notes to its financial statements.[26]

The preceding GAAP indicate that the FASB concluded that a company's current liability classification is intended to include obligations that, by their terms, are due on demand or will be due on demand within one year (or the operating cycle, if longer) from the balance sheet date, *even though liquidation may not be expected within that period.* As indicated by the italicized phrase, this concept does not conform to the requirement that a current liability be "reasonably expected to require either the use of existing current assets or the creation of other current liabilities within one year or the operating cycle, whichever is longer." Rather, it substitutes a notion that obligations should be classified as current when they are legally callable within one year, whether or not they are likely to be called. In dissenting to *FASB Statement No. 78*, three Board members stated that:

> It is asserted that this amendment will improve comparability. It will, in fact, cause situations to appear the same even when underlying facts and circumstances are sufficiently different to justify different reasonable expectations. This is not comparability; it is substituting an arbitrary rule for judgment.[27]

FINANCIAL STATEMENT PRESENTATION OF CURRENT LIABILITIES

Conceptually, a company should report its three main balance sheet elements—assets, liabilities, and equity—in homogeneous classes because this disclosure is helpful to users in making decisions. One factor for deciding the number of classes and the content of each is that the result should help users assess the nature, amount, and liquidity of available resources, including management's intended use of the resources. Another factor is the amount and timing of obligations that require liquid resources for settlement. A company can report liabilities and assets as items in its balance sheet in various ways. The FASB has suggested broad guidelines as follows:

1. Assets and liabilities with different implications for the *financial flexibility* of the company should be reported as separate items.
2. Assets and liabilities with different general *liquidity* characteristics should be reported as separate items.
3. Assets and liabilities that differ regarding the attribute that is measured should be reported in separate categories.[28]

These broad (but not specific) guidelines suggest that a company should arrange the disclosure of its current liabilities in a manner that will **highlight their liquidity characteristics and their implications for financial flexibility.**

Most companies report current liabilities at the top of the Liabilities classification. Items within the current liability section typically are listed in the order of their average length of maturity, or according to amount (largest to smallest), or in the order of liquidation preference—that is, in the order of their legal claims against assets. Those liabilities having legal priority are shown first, secured obligations second, and unsecured third. A popular way of presenting these items is as follows:

- Accounts payable
- Notes payable
- Accrued liability items
- Unearned revenue items
- Other current liabilities

---

26. "Classification of Obligations That Are Callable by the Creditor," *FASB Statement of Financial Accounting Standards No. 78* (Stamford, Conn.: FASB, 1983), par. 5.
27. *Ibid.*, page 4.
28. "Reporting Income, Cash Flows, and Financial Flexibility of Business Enterprises," *FASB Proposed Statement of Financial Accounting Concepts, op. cit.,* par. 50 and 51. (Emphasis added.)

Since a company includes a description of all significant accounting policies in the notes to its financial statements, it presents any major issue affecting the measurement or disclosure of current liabilities in those notes. This presentation is made so that the notes and other supplemental information about current liabilities meet the requirement of full disclosure. For example, secured liabilities are identified clearly along with the related assets pledged as collateral. If the due date of any liability can be extended, that fact and any related details are disclosed. Current liabilities are *not* offset against the assets that are scheduled to be used for their liquidation, and currently maturing long-term debt is

---

EXHIBIT 12-5 **Disclosure of Current Liabilities**

GENERAL MILLS

	May 27, 2001	May 28, 2000
(millions of dollars)		
Liabilities (in part):		
Current Liabilities		
Accounts payable	$ 619.1	$ 641.5
Current portion of long-term debt	349.4	413.5
Notes payable	857.9	1,085.8
Accrued taxes	111.1	104.9
Accrued payroll	141.7	142.4
Other current liabilities	129.6	141.0
Total Current Liabilities	$2,208.8	$2,529.1

NOTES TO CONSOLIDATED FINANCIAL STATEMENTS (in part):

8. Notes Payable (in part):

The components of notes payable and their respective weighted average interest rates at the end of the periods are as follows:

	May 27, 2001		May 28, 2000	
Dollars in Millions	Notes Payable	Weighted Average Interest Rate	Notes Payable	Weighted Average Interest Rate
U.S. commercial paper	$ 733.1	4.4%	$1,043.2	6.3%
Canadian commercial paper	26.8	4.6	23.4	5.5
Euro commercial paper	768.0	4.9	43.0	4.2
Financial institutions	330.0	4.4	456.2	6.3
Amounts reclassified to long-term debt	(1,000.0)	–	(480.0)	–
Total notes payable	$ 857.9		$1,085.8	

See Note Seven for a description of related interest rate derivative instruments.

To ensure availability of funds, we maintain bank credit lines sufficient to cover our outstanding short-term borrowings. As of May 27, 2001, we had $2.0 billion fee-paid lines and $12.9 million uncommitted, no-fee lines available in the United States and Canada.

We have a revolving credit agreement expiring in January 2006 covering the fee-paid credit lines that provides us with the ability to refinance short-term borrowings on a long-term basis; accordingly, a portion of our notes payable has been reclassified to long-term debt.

Q U E S T I O N S

Q What must the revolving credit agreement include so that General Mills can reclassify a portion of its notes payable to long-term debt? **Q** If current assets were $1,408.2 million on May 27, 2001, compute the current ratio. **Q** If cost of goods sold was $2,841.2 million for the year ended May 27, 2001, compute the accounts payable turnover.

classified as a current liability (unless refinanced). Existing lines of credit and material commitments requiring obligations in subsequent periods are also disclosed.

Exhibit 12-5 is an excerpt of the **General Mills** balance sheets showing how it reports its current liabilities, along with the applicable note to the financial statements. This method of disclosure is representative of the reporting techniques used by most large companies.

SUMMARY

At the beginning of the chapter, we identified several objectives you would accomplish after reading the chapter. The objectives are listed below, each followed by a brief summary of the key points in the chapter discussion.

1. **Explain the characteristics of a liability.** The characteristics of a liability are: (1) a present responsibility for the probable future transfer or use of assets, (2) the obligation cannot be avoided, and (3) the liability transaction has already occurred.

2. **Define current liabilities.** Current liabilities are obligations that are expected to require the use of current assets or the creation of current liabilities within one year or an operating cycle, whichever is longer.

3. **Account for compensated absences.** Compensated absences include vacation, holiday, illness, or other personal activities for which an employee is paid. A company records an expense and a liability for an employee's compensation for future absences when: (1) its obligation relates to employee's services already rendered, (2) the obligation relates to rights that vest or accumulate, (3) payment is probable, and (4) it can estimate the amount.

4. **Understand and record payroll taxes and deductions.** Payroll taxes include social security taxes (F.I.C.A. taxes, including O.A.S.D.I and Medicare) levied on both the employee and employer, as well as unemployment taxes (F.U.T.A. and state) levied only on the employer. Payroll deductions include income tax withholdings and such items as union dues. A company records these items as liabilities at the time it records salaries expense and payroll tax expense.

5. **Record property taxes.** A company records property taxes in equal monthly amounts during the fiscal period of the taxing authority for which the taxes are levied. By doing so, at the end of the company's accounting period it reports the appropriate accrual or prepayment.

6. **Account for warranty costs.** Under the expense warranty accrual method, a company recognizes in the period of sale the estimated warranty expense and a liability for future performance. Under the sales warranty accrual method, a company separates the accounting for the product sale from the accounting for the (implied) warranty contract. Under the modified cash basis method, a company records the warranty cost as an expense during the period that repairs are made.

7. **Explain the terms "probable," "reasonably possible," and "remote" related to contingencies.** "Probable" means the future event is likely to occur. "Reasonably possible" means that the chance of the future event occurring is more than remote but less than likely. "Remote" means that the chance of the future event occurring is slight.

8. **Record and report a loss contingency.** A loss contingency is recognized if the future event is probable and if its amount can be reasonably estimated. If these two criteria are met, a company records a loss contingency by debiting an expense (or loss) and crediting a liability (or contra asset). Otherwise, it discloses a loss contingency in the notes to its financial statements.

9. **Disclose a gain contingency.** A gain contingency is usually not accrued; a company discloses a gain contingency in the notes to its financial statements.

QUESTIONS

Q12-1 Define *liabilities*. Explain the meanings of *probable* and *obligations* in the context of a liability.

Q12-2 Distinguish between a legal and a nonlegal (accounting) liability. Give an example of each.

Q12-3 List the three essential characteristics of a liability identified in *FASB Statement of Financial Accounting Concepts No. 6*. Discuss briefly.

Q12-4 Before a liability can be reported, a company must know the identity of the recipient. True or false? Justify your answer.

Q12-5 What are the primary issues in accounting for current liabilities?

Q12-6 Define a company's operating cycle.

Q12-7 Why is the liquidity of liabilities important in the accounting for liabilities?

Q12-8 How does the constraint of materiality affect the accounting for current liabilities?

Q12-9 Define a non-interest-bearing note that is discounted at a bank at a specific rate. How are the proceeds computed for a non-interest-bearing note?

Q12-10 What are compensated absences? How does a company account for them?

Q12-11 *FASB Statement No. 49* requires that a company selling inventory and agreeing to repurchase it later neither record the transaction as a sale nor remove the inventory from the balance sheet. If so, does a new current liability arise? How is its amount measured?

Q12-12 Identify how to account for warranty costs under the expense warranty accrual method, sales warranty accrual method, and modified cash basis.

Q12-13 Define *contingency*. What exactly is the company uncertain about—whether a future event will take place and give rise to a liability, or whether a future event will take place that will confirm that a liability exists from an event that has already taken place?

Q12-14 How do the matching principle and the conservatism convention enter into the accounting for contingencies?

Q12-15 What two criteria must be met before a loss contingency is accrued in a company's accounts?

Q12-16 With regard to a loss contingency, by what date must the event that gives rise to a probable loss have occurred before accrual is required? By what date must information be available for a company to assess the probability that a loss has been incurred?

Q12-17 What conditions would have to be met for a company to accrue the loss from an unfiled lawsuit?

Q12-18 Define *gain contingency*. Describe the accounting requirements for a gain contingency.

Q12-19 What two criteria must be met before a company can classify short-term debt that is expected to be refinanced as a noncurrent liability?

Q12-20 How does a company demonstrate the ability to refinance currently maturing short-term debt?

Q12-21 *FASB Statement No. 78* requires that a company report certain obligations due on demand within one year (or operating cycle, if longer) as current liabilities. Do you agree with this statement? Explain.

CASES

C O M M U N I C A T I O N

C12-1 Short-Term Debt Expected to Be Refinanced

The following is the current liability section of Hollo Hardware Company on December 31, 2004:

Accounts payable, trade	$ 50,000
Notes payable, 12%, due February 19, 2005	70,000
Unearned interest and revenue	12,000
Total current liabilities	$132,000

On January 15, 2005 Hollo enters into an agreement with the local bank to receive a line of credit for $60,000, available for the next 2 years with payment due 2 years after the date of the loan. Interest at 1% above the prime rate will be charged quarterly. On February 16, 2005 Hollo borrows the money to refinance the short-term note due in 3 days.

Required

1. Does the preceding agreement allow Hollo to exclude any of the short-term note from current liabilities on the December 31, 2004 balance sheet? If so, how much? Explain.
2. Would the result be the same if Hollo borrowed the money on February 26, 2005?

C12-2 Short-Term Debt Expected to Be Refinanced

While auditing the 2004 financial statements of Warder Corporation, you found evidence that the following were not included in its current liabilities on the December 31, 2004 balance sheet:

1. Convertible bonds maturing in 60 days that were never converted.
2. Note payable due 2 months after the balance sheet date, with refinancing agreement entered into 4 weeks after the balance sheet date.
3. Notes payable of Warder's completely owned subsidiary due its stockholders and payable upon demand.
4. Deposits from customers on equipment ordered by them from Warder.

Required Discuss the assumptions needed for Warder to correctly exclude the previously mentioned items from the December 31, 2004 current liabilities. The balance sheet was issued on March 2, 2005.

C12-3 Loss Contingencies

Part a. The two basic requirements for the accrual of a loss contingency are supported by several basic concepts of accounting. Three of these concepts are: periodicity (time periods), measurement, and objectivity.

Required Discuss how the two basic requirements for the accrual of a loss contingency relate to the three concepts listed previously.

Part b. The following three **independent** sets of facts relate to (1) the possible accrual or (2) the possible disclosure by other means of a loss contingency.

Situation I A company offers a one-year warranty for the product that it manufactures. A history of warranty claims has been compiled and the probable amount of claims related to sales for a given period can be determined.

Situation II Subsequent to the date of a set of financial statements, but prior to the issuance of the financial statements, a company enters into a contract that will probably result in a significant loss to the company. The amount of the loss can be reasonably estimated.

Situation III A company has adopted a policy of recording self-insurance for any possible losses resulting from injury to others by the company's vehicles. The premium for an insurance policy for the same risk from an independent insurance company would have an annual cost of $2,000. During the period covered by the financial statements, there were no accidents involving the company's vehicles that resulted in injury to others.

Required Explain the accrual and/or type of disclosure necessary (if any) and the reason(s) why such disclosure is appropriate for each of the three independent sets of facts in the situations described here. Complete your response to each situation before proceeding to the next situation. *(AICPA adapted)*

C12-4 Contingency Conditions and Disclosure

Loss contingencies may exist for companies. Write a short memo that answers the following questions.

Required

1. What conditions should be met for an estimated loss from a loss contingency to be accrued by a charge to income?

2. When is disclosure required, and what disclosure should be made for an estimated loss from a loss contingency that need not be accrued by a charge to income? *(AICPA adapted)*

C12-5 Contingency and Commitment

Supey Chemical Co. encountered the following two situations in 2004:

1. Supey must pay an indeterminate amount for toxic waste cleanup on its land. An adjoining land owner, Gap Toothpaste, sold its property because of possible toxic contamination by Supey of the water supply and resulting potential adverse public reaction towards its product. Gap sued Supey for damages. There is a reasonable possibility that Gap will prevail in the suit.

2. At December 31, 2004, Supey had a noncancellable purchase contract for 10,000 pounds of Chemical XZ, for delivery in June 2005. Supey does not hedge its contracts. Supey uses this chemical to make Product 2-Y. In December 2004, the U.S. Food and Drug Administration banned the sale of Product 2-Y in concentrated form. Supey will be allowed to sell Product 2-Y in a diluted form; however, it will take at least five years to use the 10,000 pounds of Chemical XZ. Supey believes the sales price of the diluted product will not be sufficient to recover the contract price of Chemical XZ.

Required

1. (a) In its 2004 financial statements, how should Supey report the toxic waste cleanup? Why is this reporting appropriate?

   (b) In its 2004 financial statements, how should Supey report Gap's claim against it? Why is this reporting appropriate?

2. In its 2004 financial statements, how should Supey report the effects of the contract to purchase Chemical XZ? Why is this reporting appropriate? *(AICPA adapted)*

C R E A T I V E   A N D   C R I T I C A L   T H I N K I N G

C12-6 Various Liability Issues

Angela Company is a manufacturer of toys. During the year, the following situations arose:

a. A safety hazard related to one of its toy products was discovered. It is considered probable that liabilities have been incurred. Based on past experience, a reasonable estimate of the amount of loss can be made.

b. One of its small warehouses is located on the bank of a river and could no longer be insured against flood losses. No flood losses have occurred after the date that the insurance became unavailable.

c. This year, Angela began promoting a new toy by including a coupon, redeemable for a movie ticket, in each toy's carton. The movie ticket, which costs Angela

$2, is purchased in advance and then mailed to the customer when the coupon is received by Angela. Angela estimated, based on past experience, that 60% of the coupons would be redeemed. Forty percent of the coupons were actually redeemed this year, and the remaining 20% of the coupons are expected to be redeemed next year.

Required

1. How should Angela report the safety hazard? Explain why. Do not discuss deferred income tax implications.

2. How should Angela report the noninsurable flood risk? Explain why.

3. How should Angela account for the toy promotion campaign in this year? *(AICPA adapted)*

C12-7 Pending Damage Suit Disclosure

On January 15, 2005 a truck driver for Cork Transfer Company negligently rounded a curve that was also a bridge covering several local merchant shops. The truck jumped the guardrail and fell 30 feet onto one of the shops, causing highly flammable chemicals in the truck to explode. Although by February 23, 2005 (the date on which Cork's financial statements for 2004 are issued), no claims had been filed against Cork, it fully expected that some will be filed in the future.

Required Explain the accounting treatment, if any, Cork should give the contingent loss occurring from the wreck in the December 31, 2004 financial statements.

C12-8 Estimate Liability Arising from Loss Contingency

Worldwide Motors has produced "Stallions" for 10 years as of December 31, 2004. In a civil judgment against it on July 20, 2004, it was found that for the period of January 1, 2001 until the present, Worldwide was negligent in the design of the cars because the gasoline tank was positioned in the rear in such a way that it would explode upon impact with another car. On December 31, 2004 Worldwide estimated that its ultimate liability on the Stallions would total $9 million.

Required Explain fully the accounting treatment Worldwide should give to the contingency on its financial statements as of December 31, 2004.

C12-9 Various Contingency Issues

Skinner Company has the following contingencies:

1. Potential costs due to the discovery of a possible defect related to one of its products. These costs are probable and can be reasonably estimated.
2. A potential claim for damages to be received from a lawsuit filed this year against another company. It is probable that proceeds from the claim will be received by Skinner next year.
3. Potential costs due to a promotion campaign whereby a cash refund is sent to customers when coupons are redeemed. Skinner estimated, based on past experience, that 70 percent of the coupons would be redeemed. Forty percent of the coupons were actually redeemed and the cash refunds sent this year. The remaining 30 percent of the coupons are expected to be redeemed next year.

Required

1. How should Skinner report the potential costs due to the discovery of a possible product defect? Explain why.
2. How should Skinner report this year the potential claim for damages that may be received next year? Explain why.
3. This year, how should Skinner account for the potential costs and obligations due to the promotion campaign? *(AICPA adapted)*

C12-10 Various Contingency Issues

At December 31, 2004, Niki Company reviewed the following situations to consider their impact on its 2004 financial statements:

1. In December 2004, Niki became aware of a safety hazard related to one of its products. Estimates of the probable costs resulting from the hazard include highest, most likely, and lowest amounts.
2. During 2004, Niki received a note for goods sold to a customer. The note was sold, with recourse, to a bank. The customer filed for bankruptcy in December 2004, before the note's 2005 due date.
3. In 2000, Niki moved and assigned the remaining 10 years of its old lease to Pro Company, an unrelated third party. Pro agreed to make all payments due on the assigned lease, but Niki has prime responsibility for the lease to the lessor. At December 31, 2004, it is reasonably possible that Pro will be unable to make all payments due on the assigned lease.

Required For each of the preceding situations, state how Niki should report the impact, if any, on its 2004 financial statements, and explain why the reporting is appropriate. *(AICPA adapted)*

C12-11 Product and Lawsuit Contingencies

Reese Company sells two types of merchandise, Type A and Type B. Each carries a 1-year warranty.

Type A merchandise: Product warranty costs, based on past experience, will normally be 1% of sales.

Type B merchandise: Product warranty costs cannot be reasonably estimated because this is a new product line. However, the chief engineer believes that product warranty costs are likely to be incurred.

Reese Company is also being sued for $2,000,000 for an injury caused to a child as a result of alleged negligence while the child was visiting the Reese Company plant in March 2004. The suit was filed in July 2004. Reese's lawyer states that it is probable that Reese will lose the suit and be found liable for a judgment costing anywhere from $200,000 to $900,000. However, the lawyer states that the most probable judgment is $400,000.

Required

1. How should Reese report the estimated product warranty costs for each of the two types of merchandise mentioned earlier? Explain the rationale for your answer. Do not discuss deferred income tax implications, or disclosures that should be made in Reese's 2004 financial statements or notes.
2. How should Reese report the suit in its 2004 financial statements? Explain the rationale for your answer. Include in your answer disclosures, if any, that should be made in Reese's financial statements or notes. *(AICPA adapted)*

C12-12 Analyzing Coca-Cola's Current Liabilities and Contingencies Disclosures

Refer to the financial statements and related notes of the Coca-Cola Company in Appendix A of this book.

Required

1. What were the total current liabilities at the end of 2001? What was the largest current liability?
2. What did accounts payable and accrued expenses consist of at the end of 2001?
3. What was the total loans and notes payable and what did they consist of at the end of 2001? What was the total of the lines of credit (and other short-term credit facilities) that were available to the company at the end of 2001? How much is outstanding? Why did the company disclose the lines-of-credit information?
4. How much was the company contingently liable for in regard to the guarantees of indebtedness owed by third parties at the end of 2001? What does this mean? How likely is it that the company will have to satisfy these guarantees?

C12-13 Ethics and Environmental Damage

Hart Corporation is a chemical company that produces cleaning fluids of different types; it is the main employer in a small town. Stan Hart has been the company president for 15 years and is paid a salary plus a 10% bonus based on pretax income; he is also the major stockholder. After treatment to remove pollutants, Hart Company has been draining the waste water from its production process into a nearby river for many years. Over the past year (2004) there have been several "fish kills" in the river and at the end of 2004 the Environmental Protection Agency (EPA) filed a $1 million lawsuit against Hart for violation of pollution control laws.

You are an accountant for the firm that is auditing Hart's 2004 financial statements. Preliminary calculations show that Hart earned a pretax income of $600,000 for 2004, before considering the effects of the lawsuit. In a discussion with Stan Hart and Bob Brandt, the company's attorney, you raise the issue of whether or not to report the lawsuit in the company's 2004 financial statements. Stan says "I've been president of this company for long enough to know that we didn't cause the fish kills; it must be something else. Furthermore, I don't want anything included in the income statement that would jeopardize the company's well being; the town depends on us. If we shut down, the town will die." Bob replies "I generally agree with you. But you need to be realistic. I don't expect the outcome of the lawsuit to be determined for a couple of years. However, there is a pretty good chance the company will lose. If that happens, then there is a 60 percent chance the loss will be $400,000 and a 40 percent chance the loss will be $1 million." Stan replies "Okay, then lets put it in a note to the financial statements."

Required From a financial reporting and ethical standpoint, prepare a written report that recommends how to account for the lawsuit.

RESEARCH

C12-14 Researching GAAP

Bogan Company is in need of cash to finance its operations. The company creates a new company, Hall Company, which is wholly owned by Bogan. On November 1, 2004 Bogan sells inventory on credit to Hall Company for $50,000, which in turn immediately uses the inventory for a $40,000, 12% loan (guaranteed by Bogan) from 8th National Bank. Hall then uses the proceeds from the loan to repay $40,000 of the $50,000 owed to Bogan. Bogan agrees to continue to extend credit for 9 months to Hall for the remaining $10,000. The inventory is Hall's only asset and is stored in a public warehouse. Bogan agrees to pay Hall the $200 monthly storage fee and $400 per month for a financing fee at the end of each month. Bogan also agrees to repurchase the inventory from Hall for $50,000 at the end of July, 2005. Bogan uses a perpetual inventory system; the cost of the inventory sold to Hall is $42,000. The president of Bogan has asked you how to account for this series of transactions in 2004.

Required Research the related generally accepted accounting principles and prepare a short memo to the president that explains how Bogan Company should record the sale of the inventory on November 1, 2004 and the payment of the fees at the end of November and December. Also explain how Bogan should report the recorded items in its 2004 financial statements. Cite your reference and applicable paragraph numbers.

C12-15 Researching GAAP

Gilmatt Company developed a new product that it planned to sell directly to customers and to promote heavily because of "stiff" competition in the market place. Its marketing department did extensive market surveys and developed a marketing plan for this product. The plan called for a series of television commercials and magazine advertisements. The television commercials aired for two months (September and October) in 2004 to (a) advertise the product and (b) indicate to viewers that "$5 off" coupons would be appearing in forthcoming magazine advertisements. The magazine advertisements appeared evenly over a 3-month period from November 2004 through January 2005 and further promoted the product, as well as included the coded $5-off coupons (which expired at the end of February 2005.) Gilmatt expected 20,000 coupons to be redeemed. During November and December 2004, Gilmatt sold 2,000 units of the new product at the $50 regular price and 8,000 units at the $45 coded-coupon price. In January 2005, the company sold another 3,000 units at $50 each and 7,000 units at $45 each. It expects customers to redeem another 5,000 coupons before the coupons expire.

It is now late January 2005 and the company is preparing its 2004 annual report.

The marketing department has prepared the following schedule of its 2004 costs related to the advertising and promotion of the new product: supervisor's salary, $10,000; payroll of employees working on magazine advertising copy, $40,000; depreciation, $7,500; cost of television commercials (independently produced), $180,000; cost of magazine space for advertisements, $100,000; cost of television airtime, $300,000.

Required Research the related generally accepted accounting principles and indicate how Gilmatt Company should report the costs of marketing the new product and the related sales revenues on its 2004 financial statements. Cite your reference and applicable paragraph numbers.

MULTIPLE CHOICE

Select the best answer for each of the following.

M12-1 Which of the following is classified as an accrued payroll liability?

	Federal Income Tax Withheld	Employee's Share of F.I.C.A. Taxes
a.	No	Yes
b.	No	No
c.	Yes	No
d.	Yes	Yes

M12-2 During 2004 Lawton Company introduced a new line of machines that carry a 3-year warranty against manufacturer's defects. Based on industry experience, warranty costs are estimated at 2% of sales in the year of sale, 4% in the year after sale, and 6% in the second year after sale. Sales and actual warranty expenditures for the first 3-year period were as follows:

	Sales	Actual Warranty Expenditures
2004	$ 200,000	$ 3,000
2005	500,000	15,000
2006	700,000	45,000
	$1,400,000	$63,000

What amount should Lawton report as a liability at December 31, 2006?

a. $0
b. $5,000
c. $68,000
d. $105,000

M12-3 How should a loss contingency that is reasonably possible and for which the amount can be reasonably estimated be reported?

	Accrued	Disclosed
a.	Yes	No
b.	No	Yes
c.	Yes	Yes
d.	No	No

M12-4 All of Rolf Co.'s employees are entitled to 2 weeks of paid vacation for each full year in Rolf's employ. Unused vacation time can be accumulated and carried forward to succeeding years and will be compensated at the salary in effect when the vacation is taken. Mary Beal started her employment with Rolf on January 1, 1998. As of December 31, 2004, when Beal's salary was $500 per week, Beal had used 10 weeks of her accumulated vacation time. In December 2004 Beal notified Rolf of her intention to use her accumulated vacation weeks in June 2005. Rolf regularly scheduled salary adjustments in July of each year. Rolf properly did not deduct compensation for unused vacations in Rolf's 2004 income tax return. How much should Rolf report as a liability at December 31, 2004 for Beal's accumulated vacation time?

a. $0
b. $500
c. $1,000
d. $2,000

M12-5 Bronson Apparel, Inc., operates a retail store and must determine the proper December 31, 2004 year-end accrual for the following expenses:

The store lease calls for fixed rent of $1,000 per month, payable at the beginning of the month, and additional rent equal to 6% of net sales over $200,000 per calendar year, payable on January 31 of the following year. Net sales for 2004 are $800,000.

Bronson has personal property subject to a city property tax. The city's fiscal year runs from July 1 to June 30 and the tax, assessed at 3% of personal property on hand at April 30, is payable on June 30. Bronson estimates that its personal property tax will amount to $6,000 for the city's fiscal year ending June 30, 2005.

In its December 31, 2004 balance sheet, Bronson should report accrued expenses of

a. $39,000
b. $39,600
c. $51,000
d. $51,600

M12-6 When a company receives a deposit from a customer to protect itself against nonpayment for future services, the deposit should be classified by the company as

a. Revenue
b. A liability
c. Part of the allowance for doubtful accounts
d. A deferred credit deducted from accounts receivable

M12-7 The balance in Ashwood Company's Accounts Payable account at December 31, 2004 was $900,000 before any necessary year-end adjustment relating to the following:

Goods were in transit from a vendor to Ashwood on December 31, 2004. The invoice cost was $50,000, and the goods were shipped F.O.B. shipping point on December 29, 2004. The goods were received on January 2, 2005.

Goods shipped F.O.B. shipping point on December 19, 2004 from a vendor to Ashwood were lost in transit. The invoice cost was $25,000. On January 5, 2005 Ashwood filed a $25,000 claim against the common carrier.

Goods shipped F.O.B. destination on December 22, 2004 from a vendor to Ashwood were received on January 6, 2005. The invoice cost was $15,000.

What amount should Ashwood report as accounts payable on its December 31, 2004 balance sheet?

a. $925,000   c. $950,000
b. $940,000   d. $975,000

M12-8 On September 1, 2004 a company borrowed cash and signed a 1-year, interest-bearing note on which both the principal and interest are payable on September 1, 2005. How will the note payable and the related interest be classified in the December 31, 2004 balance sheet?

	Note Payable	Accrued Interest
a.	Current liability	Noncurrent liability
b.	Noncurrent liability	Current liability
c.	Current liability	Current liability
d.	Noncurrent liability	No entry

M12-9 Morgan Company determined that (1) it has a material obligation relating to employees' rights to receive compensation for future absences attributable to employees' services already rendered, (2) the obligation relates to rights that vest, and (3) payment of the compensation is probable. The amount of Morgan's obligation as of December 31, 2004 is reasonably estimated for the following employee benefits:

Vacation pay $100,000
Holiday pay   25,000

What total amount should Morgan report as its liability for compensated absences in its December 31, 2004 balance sheet?

a. $0   c. $100,000
b. $25,000   d. $125,000

M12-10 Gain contingencies are usually recognized in the income statement when

a. Realized
b. Occurrence is reasonably possible and the amount can be reasonably estimated
c. Occurrence is probable and the amount can be reasonably estimated
d. The amount can be reasonably estimated

(AICPA adapted)

EXERCISES

E12-1   *Accounts Payable and Cash Discounts*   On January 5, 2004 Dunbar Company purchased, on account, 2,000 television sets at $500 each. Terms of the purchase were 2/10, n/30. Dunbar paid for one-fifth of these sets within 10 days and the remaining four-fifths by January 31.

Required Prepare the journal entries on Dunbar Company's books, assuming that it uses the net price method to record its merchandise. (Dunbar uses a perpetual inventory system.)

E12-2   *Notes Payable*   On December 1, 2004 Insto Photo Company purchased merchandise, invoice price $25,000, and issued a 12%, 120-day note to Ringo Chemicals Company. Insto uses the calendar year as its fiscal year and uses the periodic inventory system.

Required Prepare journal entries on Insto Photo's books to record the preceding information, including the adjusting entry at the end of the year and payment of the note at maturity.

E12-3   *Non-interest-bearing Notes Payable*   On November 16, 2004 the Clear Glass Company borrowed $20,000 from First American Bank by issuing a 90-day, non-interest-bearing note. The bank discounted this note at 14% and remitted to Clear Glass Company the difference.

Required
1. Prepare the journal entries of Clear Glass to record the preceding information, the related calendar year-end adjusting entry, and payment of the note at maturity.
2. Show how the preceding items would be reported on the December 31, 2004 balance sheet.
3. What is Clear Glass Company's effective interest rate?

E12-4   *Discounting of Notes Payable*   On October 30, 2004 the Sanchez Company acquired a piece of machinery and signed a 12-month note for $24,000. The face value of the note includes the price of the machinery and interest. The note is to be paid in four $6,000 quarterly installments. The value of the machinery is the present value of the four quarterly payments discounted at an annual interest rate of 16%.

Required

1. Prepare all the journal entries required to record the preceding information including the year-end adjusting entry and the installment payments. Present value techniques should be used.
2. Show how the preceding items would be reported on the December 31, 2004 balance sheet.

E12-5 *Compensated Absences* The Bettinghaus Corporation began business on January 2, 2004 with 5 employees. It created a sick leave and vacation policy stated as follows: Each employee is allowed 8 days of paid sick leave each year and 1 day of paid vacation leave for each month worked. The accrued vacation leave cannot be taken until the employee has been with the company 1 year. The sick leave, if not used, accumulates to an 18-day maximum. The vacation leave accumulates for 5 years, but at any time the employee may request additional compensation in lieu of taking paid vacation leave. The company considers that the requirements of *FASB Statement No. 43* have been met and desires to record the liability for both compensated absences on a quarterly basis. The daily gross wages for each employee are $96.

Required

1. Prepare journal entries to record the liability for compensated absences for the first quarter of 2004. Assume no sick leave had been taken by the employees.
2. Prepare a partial interim balance sheet showing how the liability created in Requirement 1 would be reported on March 31, 2004.

E12-6 *Sales Taxes* During August the Hill Sales Company had these summary transactions:

1. Cash sales of $210,000, subject to sales taxes of 6%
2. Sales on account of $260,000, subject to sales taxes of 6%
3. Paid the sales taxes to the state

Required Prepare journal entries to record the preceding transactions.

E12-7 *Payroll and Payroll Taxes* The payroll of the Rand Company on December 31 of the current year is as follows:

1. Total payroll, $500,000
2. Payroll in excess of $80,000 to each employee, $350,000
3. Payroll in excess of $7,000 to each employee, $400,000
4. Income taxes withheld, $85,000
5. Union dues withheld, $10,000
6. Tax rates: State unemployment tax, 5.4%; F.I.C.A. tax, 8% for both employees and employers; federal unemployment tax, 0.8%; 1% merit-rating reduction of state unemployment tax from normal rate of 5.4%

Required Prepare the journal entries for Rand's payroll and payroll taxes.

E12-8 *Bonus Obligation* Raymond Moss, vice-president of Moss Auto Parts, gets an annual bonus of 15% of net income after bonus and income taxes. Income before bonus and income taxes is $250,000. The effective income tax rate is 30%.

Required

1. Compute the amount of Raymond Moss's bonus.
2. Compute the income tax expense.

E12-9 *Property Taxes* Family Practice Associates has an estimated property tax liability of $7,200 assessed as of January 1, 2004 for the year May 1, 2004 to April 30, 2005. The property tax is paid on September 1, 2004. The property tax becomes a lien against the property on May 1.

Required Prepare the necessary monthly journal entries to record the preceding information for the period from May 1 to September 30, 2004 (assuming actual taxes are the same as estimated). What would be the amount of the liability on December 31, 2004?

E12-10 *Property Taxes* The Ames Company is located in a city and county that issue property tax statements in May of each year. The fiscal year for the two local governmental units is May 1 to April 30. Property taxes of $48,000 are assessed against the Ames Company property held on January 1, 2004. The taxes become a lien against Ames Company property on May 1, 2004. The actual amount of the property taxes of $48,000 is determinable on May 1, 2004; therefore no estimate of taxes is required. The tax bills are payable in two equal installments on July 10 and September 10.

Required Assuming that monthly accruals are recorded, prepare all property tax journal entries for the period May 1 to September 30, 2004.

E12-11 *Expense Warranty Accrual Method* On September 1, 2004 Carolina Calculator Company has ready for sale 1,000 calculators. On October 1, 2004, 900 are sold at $50 each with a 1-year warranty. Carolina estimates that the warranty cost on each calculator sold will probably average $4 per unit. During the final three months of 2004, Carolina incurred warranty costs of $1,500, and in 2005 warranty costs were $2,100.

Required

1. Prepare the journal entries for the preceding transactions, using the expense warranty accrual method.
2. Show how the preceding items would be reported on the December 31, 2004 balance sheet.

E12-12 *Sales Warranty Accrual Method* On August 1, 2004 Pereira Corporation has ready for sale 2,000 Wiglow instruments. During the next 5 months, 1,600 Wiglows are sold at $460 each with a 1-year warranty. Pereira estimates that the warranty cost on each Wiglow will probably average $10 per unit. In this period, Pereira incurred warranty costs of $9,200. Costs for 2005 were $7,000.

Required

1. Prepare the journal entries for the preceding transactions, using the sales warranty accrual method.
2. Show how the items would be reported on the December 31, 2004 balance sheet.

E12-13 *Premium Obligation* The Sweet Dates Company offers to its customers a premium—a glass bowl (cost to Sweet Dates, $0.90) upon return of 40 coupons. Two coupons are placed in each box of dates sold. The company estimates, on the basis of past experience, that only 70% of the coupons will ever be redeemed. During 2004, 10 million boxes of dates are sold at $0.30 each. Eight million coupons are redeemed during 2004. Sweet Dates purchased 360,000 glass bowls for the plan in 2004.

Required

1. Prepare the journal entries related to the sales of dates and the premium plan in 2004.
2. Show how the preceding items would be reported on the December 31, 2004 balance sheet.

E12-14 *Premium Obligation* On the back of its cereal boxes, the Tiger Cereal Company offers a premium to its customers. The premium, a toy truck, may be claimed by sending in $1 plus 10 coupons; one coupon is included in each box of cereal sold. The company estimates, based on past experience, that 60% of the coupons will be redeemed. During 2004, the company purchased 240,000 toy trucks at $1.25 each for the premium promotion and sold 5,000,000 boxes of cereal at $1.50 per box. In 2004, 2,200,000 coupons were redeemed.

Required

1. Prepare the journal entries related to the previous promotion (including sales) for 2004.
2. Show how the items related to the premium plan would be reported on the December 31, 2004 balance sheet.

E12-15 *Gift Certificates* On December 5, 2004 Super Circuit Store sold gift certificates totaling $4,000. By December 31, 2004 all but $750 worth of these certificates had been redeemed for merchandise. Outstanding certificates were then redeemed by January 15, 2005.

Required

1. Prepare journal entries on Super Circuit Store's books to reflect the preceding transactions.
2. How would the gift certificates be reported on Super Circuit's balance sheet on December 31, 2004?

E12-16 *Loss Contingency* On December 4, 2004 Dan Johnson, delivery truck driver for Farmers Products, Inc., ran a stop sign and collided with another vehicle. On January 8, 2005 the driver of the other vehicle filed suit against Farmers Products for damages to the vehicle. Estimated damages to this vehicle were $6,500. The dairy issued its 2004 financial statements on March 2, 2005.

Required Prepare the disclosures and/or journal entries Farmers Products should make in preparing its December 31, 2004 financial statements.

E12-17 *Gain Contingency* On December 31, 2004 Braino Tech., Inc. learned that its competitor had introduced a product making use of an accessory over which Braino Tech. has exclusive patent rights. Braino Tech. planned to file suit and in all likelihood, its attorneys felt, Braino should recover at least $500,000. Braino Tech.'s December 31, 2004 year-end financial statements were issued March 2, 2005. At that date Braino Tech. still planned to file suit, even though it had not yet done so.

Required Discuss the accounting treatment in regard to the 2004 financial statements of Braino Tech. called for by *FASB Statement No. 5* concerning the described circumstances.

E12-18 *Disclosure of Serial Bonds Payable*   On April 1, 2004 the Ramden Company issues 13% serial bonds with a face value of $2 million. The bond contract calls for retirement of the bonds in periodic installments of $200,000, starting on April 1, 2005 and continuing on each April 1 thereafter until all bonds are retired.

Required How would the preceding information appear in the Ramden Company's balance sheets on December 31, 2004 and 2005?

E12-19 *Short-Term Debt Expected to Be Refinanced*   On December 31, 2004 Excello Electric Company had $1 million of short-term notes payable due February 7, 2005. On January 15, 2005 the company issued bonds with a face value of $900,000 at 98; brokerage fees and other costs of issuance were $3,450. On January 22, 2005 the proceeds from the bond issue plus additional cash held by the company on December 31, 2004 were used to liquidate the $1 million of short-term notes. The December 31, 2004 balance sheet is issued on February 12, 2005.

Required Prepare a partial balance sheet as of December 31, 2004 showing how the $1 million of short-term notes payable should be disclosed. Include an appropriate footnote for proper disclosure.

E12-20 *Short-Term Debt Expected to Be Refinanced*   On December 31, 2004 Carrboro Textile Company had short-term debt in the form of notes payable totaling $600,000. These notes were due on June 1, 2005. On February 2, 2005 Carrboro entered into an agreement with Worldwide Life Insurance Company whereby Worldwide will lend Carrboro $450,000, payable in 5 years at 14%. The money will be available to Carrboro on May 20, 2005. Carrboro issues its December 31, 2004 year-end financial statements on March 2, 2005.

Required Show how the $600,000 notes payable will be classified on Carrboro Textile Company's balance sheet on December 31, 2004.

PROBLEMS

P12-1 *Accounts Payable and Cash Discounts*   The Byrd Company had the following transactions during 2004 and 2005:

1. On December 23, 2004 a computer was purchased on account from Computers International for $60,000. Terms of the sale were 2/10, n/30.
2. Byrd calculated that to forgo the discount for the computer would be the equivalent of paying 36% interest annually on the $58,800 for the extra 20 days. Therefore Byrd went to First Local Bank and signed a $60,000, 30-day note at 12% in order to take advantage of the discount terms. This transaction took place on December 29, 2004. (The account payable was paid on January 2, 2005 and the note was paid at maturity.)
3. On December 30, 2004, Byrd declared a $2.00 cash dividend to the common stockholders. Ten thousand shares were outstanding on this date. The dividend is to be paid on January 5, 2005.

Required

1. Prepare the journal entries for the Byrd Company for both 2004 and 2005. Assume that the net price method is used to account for the credit terms.
2. Show how the preceding items would be reported in the current liabilities section of Byrd's December 31, 2004 balance sheet.
3. Assuming Byrd's current assets were $1,200,000 and its current ratio was 2.4 at the end of 2003, compute the current ratio at the end of 2004 (based solely on the effects of the preceding transactions).

P12-2 *Notes Payable and Effective Interest*   On November 1, 2004 Edwin, Inc., borrowed cash and signed a $60,000, @   one-year note payable.

Required

1. Compute the following items assuming (i) an interest-bearing note at 12%, (ii) a non-interest-bearing note discounted at 12%:
   a. Cash received
   b. Effective interest rate
   c. Interest expense for 2004
2. Prepare the journal entries for Edwin, Inc. under each case for 2004 and 2005.

P12-3   *Trade Note Transactions*   The Adjusto Corporation (which is on a December 31 fiscal year-end) engaged in the following transactions during 2004 and 2005:

2004

Nov. 1   Issued a 120-day, 12% note, face value of $15,000, to Johnson Company to settle an open account of that amount

Dec. 1   Issued a 90-day, 12% note, face value of $22,000, to Winslow Corporation for the purchase of merchandise (the periodic inventory method is used)

2005

Mar. 1   Paid the principal and interest on both the Johnson and the Winslow notes

Required   Prepare journal entries to record the preceding transactions on Adjusto's books, including the adjusting entries at the end of 2004.

P12-4   *Compensated Absences*   The Rexallo Company begins business on January 2, 2005 with 15 employees. Its company policy is to permit each employee to take 6 days of paid sick leave each year and 1 1/2 days of paid vacation leave for each month worked. The accrued vacation leave cannot be taken until the employee has been with the company 9 months. The sick leave, if not used, accumulates to a 24-day maximum. The vacation leave accumulates for 2 years, but at any time after a 1-year period the employee may request additional compensation in lieu of taking paid vacation leave. The company desires to record the liability for compensated absences on a quarterly basis. Assume that the gross wages for each employee are $100 per day.

The following selected events take place during the first two quarters of 2005:

1. On March 31, 2005 the quarterly liability for compensated absences is to be recorded.
2. On April 30, 2005 the following $45,000 monthly payroll, including paid vacation and sick leave, is summarized from the records of Rexallo:

| | **Payroll for** | | |
	Time Worked	Vacation Taken	Sick Leave Taken
Salaries	$42,000	$1,800	$1,200

3. On June 30, 2005 the quarterly liability for compensated absences is to be recorded.

Required

1. Prepare journal entries to record the preceding events, ignoring payroll taxes and assuming that both sick leave and vacation time meet the requirements of *FASB Statement No. 43* for accrual.
2. Prepare a partial interim balance sheet as of March 31, 2005 to disclose the liability created in Requirement 1.

P12-5   *Sales Taxes*   The Mauldin Company makes sales on which a 5% sales tax is assessed. The following summary transactions were made during 2004:

1. Sales for cash of $1,665,400, excluding sales taxes
2. Sales on open charge account of $2,820,500, excluding sales taxes
3. Sales taxes of $168,220 were paid to the state government during 2004

Required

1. Prepare journal entries to record the preceding transactions.
2. Show how the unpaid sales taxes would be reported on the December 31, 2004 balance sheet of Mauldin.

P12-6   *Payroll and Payroll Taxes*   Bailey Dry Cleaners has six employees who were paid the following wages during 2004:

Frank Johnson	$ 27,000
Bill Long	18,000
Duff Morse	85,000
Laura Stewart	28,000
Cindy Sharpe	26,000
Melissa Ledbetter	30,000
Total	$214,000

The state allows the company a 1% unemployment compensation merit-rating reduction from the normal rate of 5.4%. The federal unemployment rate is 0.8%. The maximum unemployment wages per employee are $7,000 for both the state and the federal government. Income tax withholdings of 20% are applied to all employees. An 8% F.I.C.A. tax for both employees and employers is applied to the first $80,000 of each employee's wages.

Required

1. Calculate the amount of payroll taxes to be paid by Bailey.
2. Prepare the journal entries to record the payment of payroll and the payroll tax expense.

P12-7 **Bonus Obligation and Income Tax Expense**   James Kimberley, president of National Motors, receives a bonus of 10% of National's profits after his bonus and the corporation's income taxes are deducted. National's effective income tax rate is 30%. Profits before income taxes and his bonus are $5,000,000 for 2004.

Required

1. Compute the amount of Kimberley's bonus for 2004.
2. Compute National Motors' income tax expense for 2004.
3. Prepare journal entries at the end of 2004 to record the bonus and income taxes.
4. Show how the bonus and income taxes would be reported on National Motors' December 31, 2004 balance sheet.

See WebTutor for annotated problem solution.

P12-8 **Property Taxes**   The Rosen Corporation was formed on December 12, 2003. It plans to close its books annually each December 31. The corporation is located in Lanmark City and Apple County. The fiscal period of these two governmental units runs from July 1 to June 30. The property tax that they assess on property held on January 1 of each year becomes a lien against the property on July 1. The estimated property taxes for Rosen Corporation for the period July 1, 2004 to June 30, 2005 are $15,300. The tax bill is mailed in October with a requirement that the tax be paid before December 31. The tax bill received on October 30, 2004 for the Rosen Corporation revealed an actual tax of $15,680, and the corporation paid this amount on November 30, 2004. The corporation elects to record monthly property tax adjustments for interim statements required by management.

Required

1. Prepare all property-tax related entries for Rosen for the period July 1, 2004 to June 30, 2005.
2. Show how the preceding information would be reported on the December 31, 2004 balance sheet of Rosen Corporation.

P12-9 **Expense Warranty Accrual Method**   Clean-All, Inc., sells washing machines with a 3-year warranty. In the past Clean-All has found that in the year after sale, warranty costs have been 3% of sales; in the second year after sale, 5% of sales; and in the third year after sale, 7% of sales. The following data are also available:

Year	Sales	Warranty Expenditures
2004	$500,000	$62,000
2005	650,000	82,000
2006	700,000	85,000

Required

1. Prepare the journal entries for the preceding transactions for 2004–2006, using the expense warranty accrual method. Closing entries are not required.
2. What amount would Clean-All report as a liability on its December 31, 2006 balance sheet, assuming the liability had a balance of $88,200 on December 31, 2003?

P12-10 **Sales Warranty Accrual Method**   Wright Machinery Corporation manufactures automobile engines for major automobile producers. These engines have a warranty against any defects for a period of 5 years. Even though Wright Machinery does not have a separate warranty contract, it assumes that the $993 selling price of each engine includes an implied service contract of $73 per engine. During 2004 Wright Machinery sold 8,000 engines to National Motors. During 2004 Wright Machinery repaired defective motors at a cost of $94,400.

Required Prepare the journal entries for the preceding transactions, assuming that Wright Machinery uses the sales warranty accrual method to account for warranties.

P12-11 **Premium Obligation**   Yummy Cereal Company is offering one toy shovel set for 15 box tops of its cereal. Year-to-date sales have been off, and it is hoped that this offer will stimulate demand. Each shovel set costs the company $3. The following data are available for the last three months of 2004:

Month	Boxes of Cereal Sold	Shovel Sets Purchased by the Company	Box Tops Redeemed by Customers
October	21,000	880	12,000
November	24,000	1,083	16,005
December	33,000	1,697	20,745

It is estimated that only 70% of the box tops will be redeemed. The cereal sells for $2.80 per box.

Required

1. Prepare journal entries for each month to record sales, shovel set purchases, redemptions, and closing entries, assuming that the books are closed at the end of each month.
2. Assuming Yummy prepares monthly financial statements, indicate how the premiums and the estimated liability would be disclosed on Yummy's ending balance sheets for October, November, and December.

P12-12 **Contingencies** Fallon Company, a toy manufacturer that also operates several retail outlets, is preparing its December 31, 2004 financial statements. It has identified the following legal situations that may qualify as contingencies:

1. A customer is suing the company for $800,000 in damages because her child was injured in November 2004 while riding an escalator that stopped suddenly in one of its stores. The child was hurt when he tripped and fell while walking "down" an escalator that was going "up." Legal counsel feels that the child is partially at fault, but that it is probable that the lawsuit will be settled for between $50,000 and $100,000, with $80,000 being the most likely amount.
2. The company has discovered that a skateboard it began manufacturing and selling in 2004 has defective bearings, sometimes causing a wheel to fall off. The company has issued a "recall" notice in newspapers and magazines in which it offers to replace the bearings. It estimates a cost of $200,000 for these repairs. No lawsuits have been filed for injury claims, although the company feels that there is a reasonable possibility that claims may total as high as $2 million.
3. The company has an incinerator behind one of its retail outlets which is used to burn cardboard boxes received in shipments of inventory from suppliers. The state environmental protection agency filed suit against the company in August 2004 for air pollution. The company expects to stop using the incinerator and begin recycling. However, its lawyers believe that it is probable that a fine of between $40,000 and $60,000 will be levied against the company, although they cannot predict the exact amount.
4. In early 2004 the company signed a contract with a computer vendor to install "state of the art" cash registers in all of its retail outlets. Due to the vendor's inability to acquire sufficient cash registers, the vendor canceled the contract. The company has filed a breach of contract suit against the vendor, claiming $300,000 in damages. The company's lawyers expect that it will settle the suit "out of court" for $150,000.

Required For each situation, prepare the journal entry (if any) on December 31, 2004 to record the information for Fallon Company, and explain your reasoning. If no journal entry is recorded, explain how the information would be disclosed in Fallon Company's 2004 annual report.

P12-13 **Contingencies** Greenlaw, Inc., a publishing company, is preparing its December 31, 2004 financial statements and must determine the proper accounting treatment for each of the following situations:

1. Greenlaw sells subscriptions to several magazines for a one-year, two-year, or three-year period. Cash receipts from subscribers are credited to magazine subscriptions collected in advance, and this account had a balance of $2,500,000 at December 31, 2004. Outstanding subscriptions at December 31, 2004 expire as follows:

   During 2005 — $600,000
   During 2006 — 900,000
   During 2007 — 400,000

2. On January 3, 2004 Greenlaw discontinued collision, fire, and theft coverage on its delivery vehicles and became self-insured for these risks. Actual losses of $45,000 during 2004 were charged to delivery expense. The 2003 premium for the discontinued coverage amounted to $100,000, and the controller wants to set up a reserve for self-insurance by a debit to delivery expense of $55,000 and a credit to the reserve for self-insurance of $55,000.
3. A suit for breach of contract seeking damages of $1,000,000 was filed by an author against Greenlaw on July 3, 2004. The company's legal counsel believes that an unfavorable outcome is probable. A reasonable

estimate of the court's award to the plaintiff is in the range between $100,000 and $500,000. No amount within this range is a better estimate of potential damages than any other amount.

4. During December 2004 a competitor company filed suit against Greenlaw for industrial espionage claiming $2,000,000 in damages. In the opinion of management and company counsel, it is reasonably possible that damages will be awarded to the plaintiff. However, the amount of potential damages awarded to the plaintiff cannot be reasonably estimated.

Required For each of the preceding situations, prepare the journal entry that should be recorded as of December 31, 2004, or explain why an entry should not be recorded. Show supporting computations in good form. *(AICPA adapted)*

P12-14 ***Short-Term Debt Expected to Be Refinanced*** Several times during 2004, Palmer Company issued short-term commercial paper totaling $7 million. On December 31, 2004, the company's year-end, Palmer intends to refinance the commercial paper by issuing long-term debt. However, because of the temporary existence of excess cash, $3 million of the liability is liquidated in February 2005, as the commercial paper matures. On March 1, 2005 Palmer issues $9 million of long-term bonds, with $3 million of the proceeds going to replenish the working capital used to liquidate the $3 million of commercial paper, $4 million to pay the remaining balance of the commercial paper due after April, and the remaining $2 million to finance an equipment modernization program at Palmer's plant. Palmer's December 31, 2004 year-end financial statements are issued on March 13, 2005.

Required

1. How will the $3 million of commercial paper liquidated prior to the refinancing be classified on Palmer's December 31, 2004 balance sheet? Explain your reasoning.
2. How will the remaining $4 million of commercial paper be classified on Palmer's December 31, 2004 balance sheet? Explain your reasoning.

P12-15 ***Short-Term Debt Expected to Be Refinanced*** On December 31, 2004 Atwood Table Company has $8 million of short-term notes payable owed to City National Bank. On February 2, 2005 Atwood negotiates a revolving credit agreement providing for unrestricted borrowings up to $6 million. Borrowings will bear interest at 1% over the prevailing prime rate, will have stated maturities of 120 days, and will be continuously renewable for 120-day periods for 4 years. Atwood plans to refinance as much as possible of the notes outstanding with the proceeds available from this agreement. Assume that Atwood's December 31, 2004 year-end financial statements are issued on March 30, 2005.

Required Prepare a partial December 31, 2004 balance sheet for Atwood Table Company showing how the $8 million short-term debt should be reported.

P12-16 ***Non-interest-bearing Note Payable: Present Value*** On January 1, 2004 Northern Manufacturing Company
 bought a piece of equipment by signing a non-interest-bearing $80,000, 1-year note. The face value of the note includes the price of the equipment and the interest. The effective interest rate is an annual rate of 16%, and the note is to be paid in four $20,000 quarterly installments. The price of the equipment is the present value of the four payments discounted at the effective interest rate.

Required

1. Prepare all journal entries to record the preceding information. Present value techniques should be used.
2. If Northern's financial statements were issued on June 30, 2004, what amount would the company report as notes payable?

P12-17 ***Comprehensive*** Selected transactions of the Lizard Lick Corporation during 2004 are as follows:

Jan. 5 Purchased merchandise from Boston Company for $30,000; terms, 2/10, n/30. Purchases and accounts payable are recorded by Lizard Lick using the net price method.

Jan. 26 Paid the January 5 invoice.

Mar. 31 Purchased a van for $19,950 from the Hill Sales Company, paying $9,950 in cash and issuing a 12%, 1-year note for the balance of the purchase price.

May 1 Borrowed money from the Mebane National Bank by discounting its own 1-year, non-interest-bearing note made out for the maturity value of $50,000 at an interest rate of 12%.

Nov. 2 Received $500 from the Carr Mill Playhouse as a deposit to be refunded after certain rental furniture to be used in a play is returned on January 7, 2005.

Nov. 3 Made sales on account to Jones Company for $15,000. Sales taxes of $6\frac{1}{2}$% were added to the $15,000 price.

Nov. 6   Purchased another van at a cost of $18,000 from a company located in a state that does not levy a sales tax. The entire purchase price was paid in cash. Lizard Lick is located in a state that assesses a use tax of $6\frac{1}{2}\%$ on nonsalable equipment bought outside its sales tax authority. The van and the liability for the use tax are to be recorded.

Dec. 1   Estimated property taxes for the year December 1, 2004 to November 30, 2005 are $36,000 (ignore previous property taxes). The corporation follows the practice of recording its property tax by a monthly accrual starting one month following the lien date. The tax becomes a lien on December 1 and is payable in two installments on May 1 and October 1.

Dec. 31 Estimated quarterly income taxes for the last quarter of the year are $150,000.

Required Prepare journal entries to record the preceding transactions for 2004. Include year-end interest accruals. Assume the use of the periodic inventory system.

P12-18 *Comprehensive*   Selected transactions of the Shadrach Corporation during November and December of 2004 are as follows:

Nov. 1   Borrowed money from the bank by issuing a non-interest-bearing, $40,000, 90-day note. The note is discounted on a 12% basis.

9   Sold 100 computers with a 1-year warranty for $5,000 each. Past experience indicates that warranty costs average $125 per computer. The corporation uses the expense warranty accrual method for record keeping.

12 Sold 100 software packages at $300 each. With each software package the corporation offered a premium in the form of a package of disks for the return of one proof of purchase. The offer expires June 30, 2005. The cost of each package of disks is $5, and the company estimates that 80% of the premiums will be redeemed; therefore, 80 packages of disks were purchased.

20 Paid $2,900 in fulfillment of the warranty agreement on several of the computers sold on November 9.

30 Accrued monthly vacation pay. Shadrach Corporation has 90 employees, who are each paid an average of $80 per day. The corporation has a policy of allowing each employee 12 days' paid vacation per year; the related liability is recorded on a monthly basis. Employees are paid monthly; two-thirds of the employees work in the sales force and one-third work in the office.

30 Paid monthly payroll. Gross salaries for the sales force were $96,000 and for the office staff were $48,000. No vacations were taken during November. Income tax withholdings of 15% are applicable to the salaries of all employees. An 8% F.I.C.A. tax for both employees and employers is also applicable. These rates apply to all salaries because no employee's salary has exceeded the maximum wage limit. The state allows the corporation a 1% unemployment compensation merit-rating reduction from the normal rate of 5.4%. The federal unemployment rate is 0.8%. Prior to October, each individual employee had accumulated a gross salary in excess of $7,000 for 2004.

Dec. 14 Twenty proofs of purchase were returned from the November 12 sale.

29 An individual filed suit against Shadrach Corporation for damages caused in a November 5 accident that resulted when a member of the sales force hit the individual's car while on personal business. The amount of the suit filed was $1,500. Because the employee was on personal business, the company's insurance company will not pay the claim. In the opinion of the company's attorney, the amount of the suit is reasonable; furthermore, the company believes it is likely to lose the suit.

31 Accrued monthly vacation pay.

31 Paid monthly payroll. Gross salaries for the sales force were $97,200 and for the office staff were $48,600. The salaries included $3,400 of vacation pay in the sales force and $1,600 of vacation pay in the office staff. The F.I.C.A. tax rate still applies to all wages, because no employee's salary exceeded the maximum wage limit.

31 Recorded president's bonus. The president receives a 10% bonus computed on income after deducting income taxes but before deducting the bonus. The corporation's effective income tax rate is 30%, and income before income taxes and bonus for 2004 was $560,000. The bonus will be paid in January 2005.

Required Prepare journal entries to record the preceding transactions of the Shadrach Corporation for 2004. Include year-end accruals. Round all calculations to the nearest dollar.

INTERNET ASSIGNMENTS

Go to the Nikolai and Bazley **Intermediate Accounting** web site (http://Nikolai.swcollege.com). Click on Student Resources and <u>internet</u> <u>homework</u> <u>assignments</u>. Then click on the appropriate hot link (icon) for each company's web site, find the relevant accounting information, and answer the following questions.

I12-1   Go to the Deluxe Corporation web site.

Required What products and services does Deluxe Corporation provide its customers? What was the amount of the company's total current liabilities at the end of the current year? How does this compare to the previous year? What were the types of liabilities that the company had accrued at the end of the current year? What was the amount of the accrued rebates? How do these relate to the company's sales incentives? How does the company record these items?

I12-2   Go to the Hasbro, Inc. web site.

Required What products does Hasbro design, manufacture, and sell? What was the amount of the company's total current liabilities at the end of the current year? What was the amount of the company's short-term borrowings at the end of the current year? How does the company obtain cash under these borrowings, and to what restrictions does the company have to adhere? What was the total amount of the company's accrued liabilities at the end of the current year? How much of this was for royalties? Why does the company have an accrued liability for royalties? What amount did the company record as Accrued Expenses and Other Noncurrent Liability at the end of the current year to cover future environmental expenditures? Why did the company accrue this amount?

objectives

1 Explain the reasons for issuing long-term liabilities.

2 Understand the characteristics of bonds payable.

3 Record the issuance of bonds.

4 Amortize discounts and premiums under the straight-line method.

5 Compute the selling price of bonds.

6 Amortize discounts and premiums under the effective interest method.

7 Explain extinguishment of liabilities.

8 Understand bonds with equity characteristics.

9 Account for long-term notes payable.

10 Understand the disclosure of long-term liabilities.

11 Account for long-term notes receivable, including impairment of a loan.

12 Understand troubled debt restructurings. (Appendix)

13 Account for serial bonds. (Appendix)

CHAPTER 13

Long-Term Liabilities and Receivables

A company classifies an item as a long-term liability if it is *not* expected to be repaid within one year or the current operating cycle, whichever is longer. The most common examples of long-term liabilities are bonds payable, long-term notes payable, lease obligations, pension obligations, deferred income taxes and other long-term deferrals, and, occasionally, contingent liabilities. In this chapter we examine the recording and reporting requirements for bonds payable and long-term notes payable. We also discuss long-term notes receivable in this chapter, including accounting for an impairment in such notes. We discuss the other types of long-term liabilities listed above elsewhere in this book.

REASONS FOR ISSUANCE OF LONG-TERM LIABILITIES

1 Explain the reasons for issuing long-term liabilities.

Borrowing, which results in a long-term liability, is one of the choices available to companies seeking to obtain financial resources. There are five basic reasons why a company might issue long-term debt rather than offer other types of securities.

1. *Debt financing may be the only available source of funds.* Many small- and medium-sized companies may appear too risky to investors to attract equity (i.e., capital stock) investments. Debt securities issued by a company may be a less risky investment because by law interest is required to be paid on each interest payment date. Also, some types of debt are secured by a lien against specific company assets.

2. *Debt financing may have a lower cost.* Historically, since debt has a lesser investment risk than stock, it usually has offered a relatively lower rate of return. In general, investors in equity securities have earned a higher return. However, because market conditions change, the cost of debt financing varies, so that this advantage depends on the particular market conditions.

3. *Debt financing offers an income tax advantage.* Interest payments to debt holders are deductible by a corporation as interest expense for income tax purposes, whereas dividend payments on equity securities are not.

4. *The voting privilege is not shared.* Corporate stockholders may not wish to share ownership. Thus, by issuing debt, which does not provide voting rights, ownership interests are not diluted.

5. *Debt financing offers the opportunity for leverage.* The term **leverage** (or **trading on the equity**) refers to a company's use of borrowed funds. By investing these funds, the company expects to **earn a return greater than the interest it will pay for their use** and thereby benefit the stockholders. Earnings in excess of interest charges (net of the applicable income tax reduction)

increase earnings per share, but if the return falls below the effective interest rate, earnings per share will decline. Expectations of current and future earnings, inflation, and the debt/equity relationship influence the rate of interest needed to issue debt.

BONDS PAYABLE

One common method for a company to incur long-term liabilities is by issuing bonds. **A bond is a type of note in which a company agrees to pay the holder the face value at the maturity date and usually to pay interest periodically at a specified rate on the face value.** Thus the company that issues the bonds (the *issuer*) is borrowing money from the holder of the bonds (the *lender*). **The face (or par) value is the amount of money that the issuer agrees to pay at maturity.** It is the same concept as the principal of a note. **The maturity date is the date on which the issuer of the bond agrees to pay the face value to the holder.** The issuer also agrees to pay interest. **The contract rate is the rate at which the issuer of the bond agrees to pay interest each period until maturity.** The contract rate is also called the *stated*, *face*, or *nominal* rate. This information is printed on a bond certificate, which is the document that indicates ownership of the bond. **A bond certificate is a legal document that specifies the face value, the annual interest rate, the maturity date, and other characteristics of the bond issue.** Each bond usually has a bond indenture. **A bond indenture is a document (contract) that defines the rights of the bondholders.** Since bonds usually are issued to borrow large amounts of money, corporations (and government entities) are the most common issuers of bonds. Corporate bonds usually are issued so that each bond has a face value of $1,000. The entire bond issue may be sold to one purchaser or to numerous individual purchasers. Thus a $1 million bond issue includes 1,000 bonds, each with a $1,000 face value. In addition, interest usually is paid twice each year (semiannually) on dates stated on the bond certificate. Therefore the stated annual interest rate must be halved to obtain the interest rate per semiannual period. For example, a 10%, $1,000 bond will pay the annual interest of $100 (10% × $1,000) in two semiannual installments of $50 (10% × 1/2 × $1,000).

2 Understand the characteristics of bonds payable.

Characteristics of Bonds

Companies issue bonds that may have different characteristics, as we summarize in Exhibit 13-1. While some of these characteristics are mutually exclusive, several can be combined for a bond issue. The characteristics of a particular bond issue are listed on the bond certificates for that issue and spelled out in detail in the bond indenture. In addition to establishing these characteristics, a company may include in the bond indenture certain restrictions on its financial operations to protect the bondholders and improve the marketability of a bond issue. These restrictions may include limitations on dividends, adherence to certain minimum working capital amounts, or the maintenance of a certain debt/equity relationship. In this chapter, we focus primarily on the accounting for debenture bonds. We also discuss the accounting principles that apply when a bond issue includes a callable, convertible, or serial (Appendix 2) feature.

Bond Selling Prices

When a company issues bonds, it may offer them to the public or privately to an institution, such as an insurance company or a pension fund. When the bonds are offered to the public, the company usually deals with an underwriter (a stockbrokerage firm or an investment banker). The underwriter agrees on a price for the bonds, pays the company for them and then sells the bonds to its clients. Because the issuing company avoids having to find the purchasers and being involved in cash transactions with each purchaser, it pays the underwriter a fee for this service.

There are certain steps a company must follow when it issues bonds. The company must (1) receive approval from regulatory authorities such as the Securities and Exchange

EXHIBIT 13-1 Characteristics of Bonds

1. *Debenture Bonds.* Debenture bonds are bonds that are not secured by specific property. Their marketability is based on the general credit rating of the company. Generally, a company must have a long period of earnings and continued favorable predictions of future earnings and liquidity to sell debenture bonds. Debenture bondholders are considered to be general creditors, with the same rights as other creditors if the issuer fails to pay the interest or principal and declares bankruptcy.

2. *Mortgage Bonds.* Mortgage bonds are bonds that are secured by a lien against specific property of the company. If the company becomes bankrupt and is liquidated, the holders of these bonds have first claim against the proceeds of the sale of the assets that secured their debt. If the proceeds from the sale of pledged assets are not sufficient to repay the debt, mortgage bondholders become general creditors for the balance of the unpaid debt.

3. *Registered Bonds.* Registered bonds are bonds whose ownership is registered with the company. That is, the company maintains a record of the holder of each bond. Therefore, on each interest payment date, interest is paid to the individuals listed on the corporate records as owners of the bonds. When an owner sells registered bonds, the issuer or transfer agent must be notified so that interest will be paid to the proper person.

4. *Coupon Bonds.* Coupon bonds are unregistered bonds on which interest is claimed by the holder presenting a coupon to the company. These bonds can be transferred between individuals without the company or its agent being notified. Currently, coupon bonds are rarely issued because bonds issued after December 31, 1982 must be registered for the related interest expense to be deductible for income tax purposes.

5. *Zero-Coupon Bonds.* Zero-coupon bonds (also called *deep-discount* bonds) are bonds on which the interest is not paid until the maturity date. That is, the bonds are sold at a price considerably below their face value, interest accrues until maturity, and then the bondholders are paid the interest along with the principal at maturity.

6. *Callable Bonds.* Callable bonds are bonds that are callable by the company at a predetermined price for a specified period. That is, the company has the right to require the bondholders to return the bonds before the maturity date, with the company paying the predetermined price and interest to date.

7. *Convertible Bonds.* Convertible bonds are bonds that are convertible into a predetermined number of shares. That is, the owner of each bond has the right to exchange it for a predetermined number of shares of the company. Thus, upon conversion, the bondholder becomes a stockholder of the company.

8. *Serial Bonds.* Serial bonds are bonds issued at one time, but portions of the total face value mature in periodic installments at different future dates. For example, a serial bond issued in 2004 may have a face value of $50,000, and bonds with a face value of $10,000 mature each year for five years from 2010 through 2014.

Commission, (2) set the terms of the bond issue, such as the contract rate and the maturity date, and (3) make a public announcement of its intent to sell the bonds on a particular date and print the bond certificates. At the time of the sale, the underwriter negotiates with the company to determine an appropriate selling price. The selling price is based on the terms of the bond issue and such factors as the general bond market conditions, the relative risk of the bonds, and the expected state of the economy. The underwriter determines the rate (yield) that it believes best reflects the current market conditions for the particular bond issue. **The yield (effective rate) is the market rate at which the bonds are actually sold.**[1] The yield on the bonds may be different from the contract (stated) rate set by the company and printed on the bond certificates. Such a difference may result from a difference of opinion between the underwriter and the company about the correct yield, or from a change of economic conditions between the date the company set the terms of the bond issue and the date it was issued.

---

1. After a company has issued bonds, their yield will fluctuate in the bond market as changes occur in the risk premium and expected inflation rate. It is the yield at the time of *issuance*, however, that is relevant to the company in accounting for the bonds.

Once the company has set the terms of the bond issue, the selling price, and therefore the effective yield of the bonds, is determined. We illustrate the calculation later in the chapter. Three alternatives are possible for a company selling bonds.

1. If the yield is *equal* to the contract rate, the purchasers of the bonds pay the face value of the bonds—the bonds are sold at *par*.
2. If the yield is *more* than the contract rate, the purchasers of the bonds pay *less* than the face value of the bonds—the bonds are sold at a *discount*.
3. If the yield is *less* than the contract rate, the purchasers of the bonds pay *more* than the face value of the bonds—the bonds are sold at a *premium*.

The issuance price of bonds sold at a premium or discount is often quoted as a percentage of the face value. For example, bonds with a face value of $100,000 that are quoted at 103 (meaning 103% of the face value) are sold for $103,000—that is, at a premium of $3,000. Alternatively, bonds with a $200,000 face value quoted at 98 are sold for $196,000 ($200,000 × 0.98), a $4,000 discount.

It is important to understand why bonds sell at a price different from the face value when the yield is different from the contract rate. The difference between the price paid and the face value enables the purchaser to earn a return on the bonds equal to the yield at the time the bonds are purchased. For instance, bonds are sold at a discount when the yield is higher than the contract rate. The "savings" (i.e., the discount) between the lower selling price that the purchaser pays at acquisition and the face value that the purchaser collects at maturity, coupled with the contract interest received by the purchaser each interest period, results in a return equal to the higher yield. Alternatively, bonds are sold at a premium when the yield is lower than the contract rate. The "excess" (i.e., the premium) between the higher selling price and the face value, coupled with the contract interest received by the purchaser each interest period, results in a return equal to the lower yield. These relationships may be summarized as follows:

Bonds Sold at	Yield Compared to Contract Rate	Interest Over the Life of the Bonds
Premium ↑	Yield < Contract Rate	Interest Expense < Interest Paid
Par ↓	Yield = Contract Rate	Interest Expense = Interest Paid
Discount	Yield > Contract Rate	Interest Expense > Interest Paid

When the bonds yield a rate either lower (for bonds sold at a premium) or higher (for bonds sold at a discount) than the contract rate, the interest *expense* recorded by the issuing company each period is different from the interest *paid*. When bonds are sold at a *premium*, the interest expense is *less* than the interest paid. When bonds are sold at a *discount*, the interest expense is *more* than the interest paid. The difference between the interest expense and the interest payment is the amount of the premium or discount amortized by the issuing company in the period (which we discuss later).

RECORDING THE ISSUANCE OF BONDS

At the time of sale, the issuing company records the face value of bonds in a **Bonds Payable** account, and it records any premium or discount in a separate account entitled Premium on Bonds Payable or Discount on Bonds Payable. For example, assume the company sells bonds with a face value of $400,000 on the authorization date at 102. It records the sale as follows:

3 Record the issuance of bonds.

Cash ($400,000 × 1.02)	408,000	
Bonds Payable		400,000
Premium on Bonds Payable		8,000

A Premium account is an *adjunct* account and is added to the Bonds Payable account in the long-term liability section of the balance sheet. A Discount account is a *contra* account and is subtracted from the Bonds Payable account. **The book value (carrying value) of the bond issue at any time is the face value plus any unamortized premium or minus any unamortized discount.** In the preceding example, the book value on the issue date is $408,000.

Bonds Issued Between Interest Payment Dates

Recall that the interest on bonds usually is paid semiannually on the dates indicated on the bond certificates. Bonds often are sold after their authorization date and between interest payment dates. In such cases, the issuing company is obligated to pay interest only for the period of time the bonds are outstanding—that is, from the sale date to the next interest payment date. When a company sells bonds between interest dates, to reduce the record keeping for the first interest payment, the company normally will collect from the investors both the selling price and the interest accrued on the bonds from the interest payment date prior to the date of sale. This interest amount collected typically is *credited* to Interest Expense and is computed by multiplying the face value by the stated interest rate for the fraction of the year from the interest payment date prior to the sale date. On the next interest payment date, the company pays each bondholder 6 months of interest and records Interest Expense as usual. The following diagram illustrates this situation:

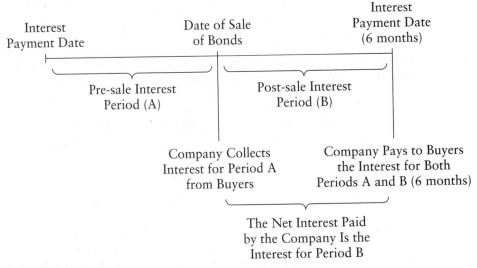

To illustrate, assume that on March 1, 2004, Grimes Corporation issues $800,000 of 10-year bonds dated January 1, 2004 at par. The bonds have a contract (stated) interest rate of 12% and pay interest semiannually on January 1 and July 1. On March 1, because two months have elapsed since the interest payment date prior to the sale, Grimes collects $16,000 ($800,000 × 0.12 × 2/12) accrued interest in addition to the face value. Grimes records the issue of the bonds on March 1, 2004 as follows:

Cash	816,000	
Interest Expense		16,000
Bonds Payable		800,000

On July 1, 2004, Grimes records the semiannual interest payment as follows:

Interest Expense ($800,000 × 0.12 × 6/12)	48,000	
Cash		48,000

As a result of the preceding journal entries, on July 1, 2004 the Interest Expense account has a debit balance of $32,000 ($48,000 − $16,000) representing the interest cost ($800,000 × 0.12 × 4/12) since the bonds were issued.

Alternatively, it is possible to record the previous transaction by using a liability account because part of the proceeds (i.e., the accrued interest) will be repaid in the future. Using this approach, Grimes would record the original transaction as follows:

Cash	816,000	
Interest Payable		16,000
Bonds Payable		800,000

On July 1, 2004, Grimes would record the first interest payment as follows:

Interest Expense ($800,000 × 0.12 × 4/12)	32,000	
Interest Payable	16,000	
Cash		48,000

Companies generally use the first method because it has less potential for errors in subsequent transactions. Also, this method enables a company to develop a single routine in its computerized accounting system for recording and distributing all interest payments.

AMORTIZING DISCOUNTS AND PREMIUMS

Recall that when a company sells bonds at a discount or premium, it is incurring an effective interest (yield) rate that is more, or less, than the stated rate of interest. When a company pays the interest on the bonds, this *payment* is an amount based upon the *stated* rate. However, in order to properly report the interest cost on the bonds, the Interest *Expense* on the company's income statement must reflect an amount based on the *effective* interest rate and the book value of the bonds. **The effective interest expense amount is computed by multiplying the effective interest rate (yield) times the book value of the bonds at the beginning of the period.** Consequently, a portion of the bond discount or premium is amortized, and **this amortization is the difference between the amount of interest expense and the cash payment.** This process is known as the effective interest method (sometimes called the *interest method*) of amortization. Another approach is the **straight-line method** of amortization. **APB Opinion No. 21** requires the use of the effective interest method unless the results produced by the straight-line method are *not materially different* from those obtained by using the effective interest method.[2] However, we discuss the straight-line method first as it is often used in practice if the amounts are not materially different from the preferred effective interest method amounts.

4 Amortize discounts and premiums under the straight-line method.

Straight-Line Method

When using the straight-line method, the discount or premium is amortized to interest expense in *equal amounts* each period during the life of the bonds. Therefore, the straight-line method amortizes the bond discount or premium so that the interest expense is an average cost for the period. For instance, assume that the Jet Company sells bonds for $92,976.39 on January 1, 2004. The bonds have a face value of $100,000 and a 12% stated annual interest rate. Interest is paid semiannually on June 30 and December 31, and the bonds mature on December 31, 2008. Thus, the bonds have a 5-year life, with 10 semiannual interest periods. Jet records the sale on January 1, 2004 as follows:

Cash	92,976.39	
Discount on Bonds Payable	7,023.61	
Bonds Payable		100,000.00

On the first interest payment date, Jet records both the cash payment and discount amortization. It computes the discount amortization of $702.36 per semiannual period

---

2. "Interest on Receivables and Payables," *APB Opinion No. 21* (New York: AICPA, 1971), par. 15.

by dividing the total discount ($7,023.61) by the number of semiannual periods (10) *until maturity*[3] (it may also use monthly or yearly amortization periods, whichever is more convenient). The interest expense is the sum of the cash payment and the discount amortization. Jet records the first interest payment on June 30, 2004 as follows:

Interest Expense ($6,000 + $702.36)	6,702.36	
Discount on Bonds Payable ($7,023.61 ÷ 10)		702.36
Cash ($100,000 × 0.12 × 1/2)		6,000.00

In this case, the interest expense is higher than the cash paid, indicating that the effective rate is higher than the stated rate. Jet makes a similar journal entry to record the second interest payment on December 31, 2004 and every 6 months after that. After this second entry, the long-term liabilities section of Jet's December 31, 2004 balance sheet includes the following:

Bonds Payable	$100,000.00
Less: Discount on Bonds Payable	(5,618.89)
	$ 94,381.11

Note that the $5,618.89 ($7,023.61 − $702.36 − $702.36) unamortized discount is subtracted from the $100,000 face value of the bonds to determine the $94,381.11 book value.

The straight-line amortization of a bond premium follows the same principles. Suppose the Jet Company sold the bonds on January 1, 2004 for $107,721.71. In this case, the premium amortization per semiannual period is $772.17 ($7,721.71 ÷ 10) and the interest expense is the cash payment less the premium amortization. Jet records the sale and first interest payment as follows:

January 1, 2004

Cash	107,721.71	
Bonds Payable		100,000.00
Premium on Bonds Payable		7,721.71

June 30, 2004

Interest Expense ($6,000 − $772.17)	5,227.83	
Premium on Bonds Payable ($7,721.71 ÷ 10)	772.17	
Cash ($100,000 × 0.12 × 1/2)		6,000.00

Here the interest expense is lower than the cash paid, indicating an effective rate lower than the stated rate. After a similar journal entry to record the second interest payment, Jet's December 31, 2004 balance sheet includes the following:

Bonds Payable	$100,000.00
Add: Premium on Bonds Payable	6,177.37
	$106,177.37

Note that the $6,177.37 ($7,721.71 − $772.17 − $772.17) unamortized premium is added to the $100,000 face value of the bonds to determine the $106,177.37 book value.

In both situations, the total discount or premium will be amortized by the maturity date, and the book value will equal the maturity value.

In summary, for both premiums and discounts, **the straight-line method results in a constant amount of interest expense each semiannual period** even though the book value of the liability changes each period. A schedule may be developed that summarizes the interest expense, discount or premium amortization, and book value of the bonds each

---

3. Note that the maturity date of bonds is established on the date they are authorized. When bonds are issued subsequent to the authorization date, any discount or premium is amortized over the *remaining* life until the maturity date.

EXHIBIT 13-2 Bond Interest Expense and *Discount* Amortization Schedule: *Straight-Line Method*

Date	Cash Credit[a]	Unamortized Discount Credit[b]	Interest Expense Debit[c]	Book Value of Bonds[d]
1/01/04				$ 92,976.39
6/30/04	$6,000.00	$702.36	$6,702.36	93,678.75
12/31/04	6,000.00	702.36	6,702.36	94,381.11
6/30/05	6,000.00	702.36	6,702.36	95,083.47
⋮	⋮	⋮	⋮	⋮
12/31/07	6,000.00	702.36	6,702.36	98,595.27
6/30/08	6,000.00	702.36	6,702.36	99,297.63
12/31/08	6,000.00	702.37[e]	6,702.37	100,000.00

a. $100,000 (face value) × 0.12 (stated annual interest rate) × 1/2 (year).
b. [$100,000 − $92,976.39 (issue price)] ÷ 10 (semiannual periods until maturity).
c. $6,000.00 + $702.36.
d. Previous book value + amount from footnote *b*.
e. Difference due to $0.01 rounding error.

EXHIBIT 13-3 Bond Interest Expense and *Premium* Amortization Schedule: *Straight-Line Method*

Date	Cash Credit[a]	Unamortized Premium Debit[b]	Interest Expense Debit[c]	Book Value of Bonds[d]
1/01/04				$107,721.71
6/30/04	$6,000.00	$772.17	$5,227.83	106,949.54
12/31/04	6,000.00	772.17	5,227.83	106,177.37
6/30/05	6,000.00	772.17	5,227.83	105,405.20
⋮	⋮	⋮	⋮	⋮
12/31/07	6,000.00	772.17	5,227.83	101,544.35
6/30/08	6,000.00	772.17	5,227.83	100,772.18
12/31/08	6,000.00	772.18[e]	5,227.82	100,000.00

a. $100,000 (face value) × 0.12 (stated annual interest rate) × 1/2 (year).
b. [$107,721.71 (issue price) − $100,000] ÷ 10 (semiannual periods until maturity).
c. $6,000.00 − $772.17.
d. Previous book value − amount from footnote *b*.
e. Difference due to $0.01 rounding error.

period. Exhibit 13-2 shows a partial schedule for the Jet Company bonds sold at a discount. Exhibit 13-3 presents a partial schedule for the same bonds sold at a premium. Again, remember that the straight-line method is acceptable only when it results in amounts of interest expense and book value that are not materially different from those computed by using the effective interest method.

Effective Interest Method

The basic assumption underlying the straight-line method that interest *expense* is the same every year is not realistic when a premium or discount is involved. Instead, the use of a stable interest *rate* per year (the *yield*) is appropriate. The yield is used to calculate

5 Compute the selling price of bonds.

the proceeds received when bonds are issued. The selling price of a bond issue is calculated by summing the present value of the principal and interest payments discounted at the effective interest (yield) rate. Recall the Jet Company discount example of $100,000 of 5-year bonds paying semiannual interest with a stated rate of 12%. Jet Company sold these bonds for $92,976.39, a price that yields an effective interest rate of 14%. **To determine this selling price and the related discount, the effective rate is applied to both the future principal and periodic interest payments,** as we show in the following computations. As we point out in Appendix D, in present value analyses when interest is paid semiannually, the effective rate (14%) is divided by the interest periods per year (two) to determine the effective rate (7%) per semiannual period. Similarly, the time to maturity is expressed in semiannual periods (10). The discount of $7,023.61 is computed[4] as follows:

Present value of principal: $100,000 × 0.508349[a]	$ 50,834.90
Present value of interest: $6,000[b] × 7.023582[c]	42,141.49
Selling price	$ 92,976.39
Face value	$100,000.00
Selling price	(92,976.39)
Discount	$ 7,023.61

a. From Present Value of 1 Table in Appendix D ($n = 10$; $i = 0.07$).
b. $100,000 × 0.12 × 1/2.
c. From Present Value of an Ordinary Annuity of 1 Table in Appendix D ($n = 10$; $i = 0.07$).

Similarly, in the second example, in which the Jet Company sold the bonds at a premium, they yielded 10%. The premium of $7,721.71 is computed as follows:

Present value of principal: $100,000 × 0.613913[a]	$ 61,391.30
Present value of interest: $6,000 × 7.721735[b]	46,330.41
Selling price	$107,721.71
Selling price	$107,721.71
Face value	(100,000.00)
Premium	$ 7,721.71

a. From Present Value of 1 Table in Appendix D ($n = 10$; $i = 0.05$).
b. From Present Value of an Ordinary Annuity of 1 Table in Appendix D ($n = 10$; $i = 0.05$).

---

4. The discount (or premium) and the selling price to yield a given interest rate can also be calculated by another method. The amount of the discount is the present value of the *deficiency* produced by the difference between the yield multiplied by the face value of the bonds and the stated rate multiplied by the face value of the bonds, discounted at the yield. The calculations of the discount and selling price for the Jet Company bonds are:

Face value		$100,000.00
Less: Discount on bonds payable		
Yield amount: 7% × $100,000	$7,000	
Stated amount: 6% × $100,000	(6,000)	
Deficiency	$1,000	
Discount [$1,000 × 7.023582 (Present Value		
of an Ordinary Annuity Table in Appendix D)]		(7,023.58)*
Selling Price		$ 92,976.42

* The difference between the $7,023.61 calculated in the text and the $7,023.58 calculated by this alternative method is due to a rounding error.

Again, to compute the present value, the effective rate is expressed on a semiannual basis, and the time to maturity is expressed in semiannual periods.

As we noted earlier, the book (carrying) value of the bond issue at any time is its face value plus any unamortized premium or minus any unamortized discount. Thus, this book value changes with each successive premium or discount amortization and is equal to **the present value of the remaining cash payments.** (Under the straight-line method, the book value is *not* equal to the present value of the remaining cash payments.) Since the bonds were issued to yield a particular interest rate, this interest rate (yield) should be reflected in interest expense over the life of the bond issue. Also, as we noted earlier, *APB Opinion No. 21* requires the use of the effective interest method, unless another method produces results that are *not materially* different. The effective interest method applies the semiannual yield to the book value of the bonds at the beginning of each successive semiannual period to determine the interest expense for that period. In this procedure, **the discount or premium amortization is the difference between the interest expense computed under the effective interest method and the cash payment.** This method is based on the compound interest techniques discussed in Appendix D.

6 Amortize discounts and premiums under the effective interest method.

To illustrate, after the Jet Company sold bonds for $92,976.39 (yielding an effective annual interest rate of 14%), it records the first two interest payments under the effective interest method as follows:

June 30, 2004

Interest Expense ($92,976.39 × 0.14 × 1/2)	6,508.35	
Discount on Bonds Payable		
($6,508.35 − $6,000.00)		508.35
Cash ($100,000 × 0.12 × 1/2)		6,000.00

December 31, 2004

Interest Expense		
[($92,976.39 + $508.35) × 0.14 × 1/2]	6,543.93	
Discount on Bonds Payable		
($6,543.93 − $6,000.00)		543.93
Cash		6,000.00

Alternatively, if the Jet Company sold the bonds for $107,721.71 (equivalent to an annual yield rate of 10%), it records the first two interest payments under the effective interest method as follows:

June 30, 2004

Interest Expense ($107,721.71 × 0.10 × 1/2)	5,386.09	
Premium on Bonds Payable		
($6,000.00 − $5,386.09)	613.91	
Cash ($100,000 × 0.12 × 1/2)		6,000.00

December 31, 2004

Interest Expense		
[($107,721.71 − $613.91) × 0.10 × 1/2]	5,355.39	
Premium on Bonds Payable		
($6,000.00 − $5,355.39)	644.61	
Cash		6,000.00

Schedules may be developed to show the interest expense, amortization of discounts and premiums, and book values using the effective interest method. Exhibit 13-4 illustrates a schedule for the Jet Company bonds issued at a discount. Exhibit 13-5 illustrates a schedule for these bonds issued at a premium. Note that **the amount of interest expense using the effective interest method reflects a constant *rate* based upon the remaining book value of the bonds.** (In contrast, in Exhibits 13-2 and 13-3 for the straight-line method, the *amount* of interest expense was constant.) The following

EXHIBIT 13-4 Bond Interest Expense and *Discount* Amortization Schedule: *Effective Interest Method*

12% Bonds Sold to Yield 14%

Date	Cash Credit[a]	Interest Expense Debit[b]	Unamortized Discount Credit[c]	Book Value of Bonds[d]
1/01/04				$ 92,976.39
6/30/04	$6,000.00	$6,508.35	$508.35	93,484.74
12/31/04	6,000.00	6,543.93	543.93	94,028.67
6/30/05	6,000.00	6,582.01	582.01	94,610.68
12/31/05	6,000.00	6,622.75	622.75	95,233.43
6/30/06	6,000.00	6,666.34	666.34	95,899.77
12/31/06	6,000.00	6,712.98	712.98	96,612.75
6/30/07	6,000.00	6,762.89	762.89	97,375.64
12/31/07	6,000.00	6,816.29	816.29	98,191.93
6/30/08	6,000.00	6,873.44	873.44	99,065.37
12/31/08	6,000.00	6,934.63[e]	934.63	100,000.00

a. $100,000 (face value) × 0.12 (stated annual interest rate) × 1/2 (year).
b. Previous book value × 0.14 (effective interest rate) × 1/2 (year).
c. Amount from footnote *b* − $6,000.00.
d. Previous book value + amount from footnote *c*.
e. Difference due to $0.05 rounding error.

EXHIBIT 13-5 Bond Interest Expense and *Premium* Amortization Schedule: *Effective Interest Method*

12% Bonds Sold to Yield 10%

Date	Cash Credit[a]	Interest Expense Debit[b]	Unamortized Premium Debit[c]	Book Value of Bonds[d]
1/01/04				$107,721.71
6/30/04	$6,000.00	$5,386.09	$613.91	107,107.80
12/31/04	6,000.00	5,355.39	644.61	106,463.19
6/30/05	6,000.00	5,323.16	676.84	105,786.35
12/31/05	6,000.00	5,289.32	710.68	105,075.67
6/30/06	6,000.00	5,253.78	746.22	104,329.45
12/31/06	6,000.00	5,216.47	783.53	103,545.92
6/30/07	6,000.00	5,177.30	822.70	102,723.22
12/31/07	6,000.00	5,136.16	863.84	101,859.38
6/30/08	6,000.00	5,092.97	907.03	100,952.35
12/31/08	6,000.00	5,047.65[e]	952.35	100,000.00

a. $100,000 (face value) × 0.12 (stated annual interest rate) × 1/2 (year).
b. Previous book value × 0.10 (effective interest rate) × 1/2 (year).
c. $6,000.00 − amount from footnote *b*.
d. Previous book value − amount from footnote *c*.
e. Difference due to $0.03 rounding error.

diagram shows how the book values of bonds are different between the straight-line and effective interest methods for both a premium and a discount:

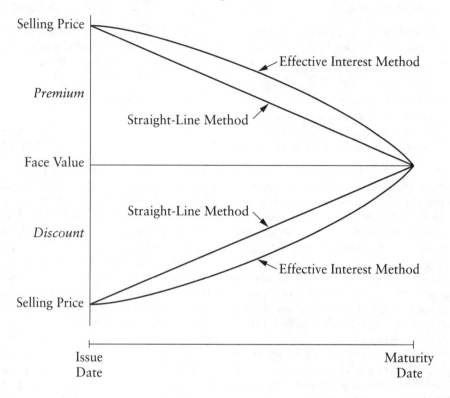

Bond Issue Costs

APB Opinion No. 21 requires that a company defer any expenditures connected with a bond issue (such as legal and accounting fees, printing costs, or registration fees). Conceptually a company with deferred bond issue costs should compute a new yield. However, because of a lack of materiality, generally these deferred bond issue costs are amortized over the life of the bond issue by the *straight-line* method. For example, assume that on January 1, 2004 Bergen Company issues 10-year bonds with a face value of $500,000 at 104, or $520,000. Expenditures connected with the issue totaled $8,000. Bergen records this issue as follows:

Cash ($520,000 − $8,000)	512,000	
Deferred Bond Issue Costs	8,000	
Premium on Bonds Payable (0.04 × $500,000)		20,000
Bonds Payable		500,000

Bergen amortizes deferred bond issue costs of $800 to bond interest expense (i.e., debit Bond Interest Expense and credit Deferred Bond Issue Costs) each year over the 10-year life of the bonds. The unamortized deferred bond issue costs typically are reported as other assets or deferred charges on any subsequent balance sheet.

Accruing Bond Interest

In the previous examples, the semiannual interest payments coincided with the company's fiscal year. However, frequently companies issue bonds with interest payment dates that differ from the fiscal year. In such cases, the matching principle requires that the company record an accrual of interest and a partial premium or discount amortization at the end of the fiscal year. For example, assume that McAdams Company issues $200,000 of 10%, 5-year bonds on October 1, 2004 for $185,279.87. Interest on these bonds is payable each October 1 and April 1. McAdams records this issue as follows:

Cash	185,279.87	
Discount on Bonds Payable	14,720.13	
Bonds Payable		200,000.00

At the end of the fiscal year, December 31, 2004, the company must accrue interest and amortize the discount for the months of October, November, and December. Thus, it must compute and record the amount of interest expense in 2004 for these 3 months. It records this adjusting entry (assuming straight-line amortization) as follows:

Interest Expense	5,736.01	
Discount on Bonds Payable		736.01
[($14,720.13 ÷ 5) × 3/12]		
Interest Payable ($200,000 × 0.10 × 3/12)		5,000.00

Typically, the company will record a reversing entry on January 1, 2005 so that it can make the April 1, 2005 entry to record interest expense as usual. If the company does not make a reversing entry, when it records interest expense it eliminates the Interest Payable account and records the 3 months of interest expense incurred in 2005.

If a company uses the effective interest method to amortize a premium or discount, it determines the amount of interest expense it accrues on December 31, 2004 by computing the semiannual effective interest cost for the next interest and amortization period, and using the straight-line approach to allocate this amount over the number of months of interest accrual. For example, the effective annual interest rate on the McAdams bonds is 12%; therefore, the amount of semiannual interest for the six-month period ending April 1, 2005 is $11,116.79 ($185,279.87 × 0.12 × 1/2).

There are 6 months in the interest period and the elapsed time since the date of issue (October 1) is 3 months; therefore the company expenses $5,558.40, or 3/6 of the $11,116.79 semiannual interest charge. It computes the amount of discount amortization as the difference between the effective interest expense, $5,558.40, and the $5,000.00 ($200,000 × 0.10 × 3/12) amount of interest owed, or $558.40. Using the effective interest method of discount amortization, McAdams records the accrued interest on December 31, 2004, as follows:

Interest Expense	5,558.40	
Discount on Bonds Payable		558.40
Interest Payable		5,000.00

Zero Coupon Bonds

Zero coupon bonds are bonds sold at a "deep" discount. As the name implies, zero coupon bonds *pay* no interest each period. The only cash outflow associated with the bonds is the payment of the face value on the maturity date. The calculation of the selling price follows the principles we discussed earlier; that is, it is the present value (based on the yield) of the face value. A company records the issuance of zero coupon bonds in the usual way; that is, it debits the discount account for the difference between the selling price and the face value.

Even though the bonds *pay* no interest each period, the company must still recognize an interest *expense* because it has incurred a cost each period on the amount borrowed. It computes the interest expense, as we discussed earlier, by multiplying the yield times the book value of the bonds at the beginning of the period. (Alternatively, the company may use the straight-line method.) Since the company makes no cash payment for interest each period, it recognizes the interest expense each period as a decrease (credit) in the discount account (and therefore raises the book value of the bonds).

International Accounting Differences

International accounting standards for long-term liabilities are generally similar to U.S. principles. One exception is that liabilities held for trading are measured at fair value, with the others being valued at amortized cost.

EXTINGUISHMENT OF LIABILITIES

The agreement between the bondholders and the issuing company always includes a specified maturity date. On this date the company agrees to repay the face value of the bonds to the bondholders. At this time any premium or discount associated with the issuance of the bonds will be completely amortized so that the book value of the bonds is equal to the face value. Occasionally, under certain circumstances, bonds may be retired (extinguished) prior to their scheduled maturity date.

7 Explain extinguishment of liabilities.

Over the past three decades, both the APB and the FASB have considered the various circumstances under which liabilities should be considered to be extinguished and what, if any, gain or loss should be recognized on that extinguishment. Under **FASB Statement No. 140,** a liability is derecognized (extinguished) for financial reporting purposes if either of the following occurs:[5]

1. The debtor pays the creditor and is relieved of its obligation for the liability.
2. The debtor is released legally from being the primary obligor under the liability, either judicially or by the creditor.

Bonds may be extinguished by retirement at maturity or prior to maturity. We discuss the accounting issues related to these retirements in the following sections.

Bonds Retired at Maturity

On the balance sheet issued immediately prior to the maturity date, a company reclassifies the face value (and any related premium or discount) of the bonds to be retired from a noncurrent (long-term) to a current liability if it will use current assets to repay the obligation. On the maturity date, after the last interest payment is recorded, any premium or discount on bonds payable is fully amortized. Therefore, the book value of the bonds is equal to the maturity value. The company records the retirement of bonds on the maturity date by a debit to Bonds Payable to eliminate the liability and a credit to Cash.

Bonds Retired Prior to Maturity

In order to be able to reduce their level of debt, eliminate any restrictions on operations included in the bond contract, or protect themselves from the inability to take advantage of future favorable changes in market conditions, many companies will include a **call provision** on long-term debt. **This provision allows the company to recall the debt issue at a prestated percentage of the face value prior to the maturity date.** Since the call price generally is above the issue price (if not, it is unlikely that the company would be able to sell the debt issue), a loss or, in unusual circumstances, a gain occurs when the company recalls the debt. An alternative method of retiring bonds prior to their maturity is for the company to purchase them on the open market. Then a gain or loss arises depending on the relationship between the book value and the market value of the bonds. This type of extinguishment of debt may take two forms: (1) the borrowed funds may no longer be needed, and the debt is not replaced (**debt retirement**), or (2) the existing debt may be replaced with another debt issue (**debt refunding**).

Conceptually, a company could recognize a gain or loss from a refunding either (1) over the remaining life of the old issue, (2) over the life of the new bond issue, or (3) in the current period. Recognizing the gain or loss over the remaining life of the old issue is favored by some because they view this as the period affected by the refunding. That is, a different interest cost would have been incurred if the old issue had been for a shorter period. Those who favor recognizing the gain or loss over the life of the

---

5. "Accounting for Transfers and Servicing of Financial Assets and Extinguishments of Liabilities," *FASB Statement of Financial Accounting Standards No. 140* (Norwalk, Conn.: FASB, 2000), par 16.

new issue base their arguments on the matching principle. That is, the different interest cost obtained for the life of the new issue should be adjusted to reflect any refunding gain or loss. Finally, those who favor an immediate write-off argue that this method is the most logical because the value of the debt has changed in prior periods and paying the call (or purchase) price recognizes this change in value through a transaction of the current period.

When **APB Opinion No. 26** was issued, the Board took the position that all extinguishments of debt securities prior to maturity were basically alike (whether retirements or refundings) and should be accounted for in the same way. Since a company reports gains or losses on retirements of liabilities in the period of recall, *APB Opinion No. 26* concluded that current income should reflect any gains or losses from refunding.[6] Thus, the gain or loss reported in a refunding transaction is computed in exactly the same way as a retirement.

After *APB Opinion No. 26* was issued, the FASB conducted a study of the reporting requirements for gains and losses from the extinguishment of liabilities. This review was partly in response to pressure from the SEC. The SEC was concerned because prevailing market conditions (i.e., high inflation and high interest rates) in 1973 and 1974 enabled many companies to reacquire their long-term liabilities at market prices well below face value, resulting in gains that were reported as ordinary income. For example, in 1973, **United Brands** recorded a $37.5 million gain by paying $12.5 million in cash and issuing $75 million in 9 1/8% debentures in exchange for $125 million of 5 1/2% convertible subordinated debentures. The company reported the total gain as ordinary income. After completing the study, the Board issued **FASB Statement No. 4,** which required that all material gains and losses from debt extinguishments (both retirements and refundings) were classified as extraordinary items[7] without regard to the criteria of "unusual nature" or "infrequency of occurrence," established in *APB Opinion No. 30.* **FASB Statement No 145** rescinded the provisions of *FASB Statement No. 4.*[8] Therefore, a company reports any gain or loss from the extinguishment of debt as a component of income from continuing operations. The reason for the change was that the extinguishment of debt has become a frequent event that many companies use as part of their risk management strategy. However a company may still report the gain or loss as extraordinary if it is considered to be unsual and infrequent according to the criteria in *APB Opinion No. 30.*

In summary, whether a company recalls, retires, or refunds bonds prior to maturity, **it reports any difference between the book value of the bonds (plus any unamortized bond issue costs) and the call price (or market price) as a gain or loss in income from continuing operations in the year the cancellation occurs.** As an example of the retirement of a liability prior to maturity, assume that Channing Corporation originally issued $100,000 of 12% bonds at 97 on January 1, 1999. The bonds have a 10-year life, pay interest on January 1 and July 1, and are callable at 105 plus accrued interest. Assume, for simplicity, that the company amortizes the discount by the straight-line method. On June 30, 2004 the company recalls the bonds. First, Channing records the current interest expense and liability, including the amortization of the discount that expired since the last interest payment, as follows:

Interest Expense	6,150	
Discount on Bonds Payable [($3,000 ÷ 10) × 1/2]		150
Interest Payable ($100,000 × 0.12 × 1/2)		6,000

6. "Early Extinguishment of Debt," *APB Opinion No. 26* (New York: AICPA, 1972).
7. "Reporting Gains and Losses from Extinguishment of Debt," *FASB Statement of Financial Accounting Standards No. 4* (Stamford, Conn.: FASB, 1975), par. 8.
8. "Rescission of FASB Statements No. 4, 44, and 64, Amendment of FASB Statement No. 13, and Technical Corrections," *FASB Statement of Financial Accounting Standards No. 145* (Norwalk, Conn.: FASB, 2002), par. 6. The *Statement* is effective for financial statements issued in fiscal years beginning after May 15, 2002, and must be applied retroactively to any comparative statements that the company presents.

Channing then records the reacquisition of the bonds as follows:

Bonds Payable	100,000	
Interest Payable	6,000	
Loss on Bond Redemption	6,350[b]	
Discount on Bonds Payable		1,350[a]
Cash [($100,000 × 1.05) + $6,000]		111,000

a.		
Original discount		$ 3,000
Amortization on straight-line basis for		
5 1/2 years = 5.5 × $300		(1,650)
Unamortized discount 6/30/04		$ 1,350

b.			
Call price (excluding interest)			$105,000
Less: Face value		$100,000	
Unamortized discount		(1,350)	(98,650)
Loss on bond redemption			$ 6,350

Channing reports the loss of $6,350 in income from continuing operations on its 2004 income statement.

Earlier we noted that the FASB has concluded that, in addition to retirement at maturity or prior to maturity, a liability can be extinguished if the debtor is legally released from being the primary obligor of the liability either judicially or by the creditor. This is sometimes referred to as *defeasance*. It might arise when an affiliated company agrees to become the primary obligor for the liability. The parent company removes the liability (e.g., bonds payable) from its balance sheet and reports a gain (or perhaps a reduction in an investment in affiliate account). The parent company may still be required to disclose a contingent liability. This situation would arise if the parent has been released from being the primary obligor because a third party has assumed the debt, but the creditor requires the parent to be a guarantor of the third party's debt.

Contingent liabilities are discussed in Chapter 12.

BONDS WITH EQUITY CHARACTERISTICS

A company may issue bonds that allow creditors to ultimately become stockholders either by attaching **stock warrants** to the bonds or including a **conversion feature** in the bond indenture. In either case, the investor has acquired a dual set of rights: (1) the right to receive interest on the bonds, and (2) the right to acquire common stock and to participate in the potential appreciation of the market value of the company's common stock. Conceptually, it can be argued that the economic substance of issuing bonds with either detachable warrants or a conversion feature is similar; for consistency therefore, a portion of the proceeds of a bond issue carrying either of these features could be assigned to stockholders' equity. However, generally accepted accounting principles differ in their treatment of these securities.

8 Understand bonds with equity characteristics.

Bonds Issued with Detachable Stock Warrants

When a company issues bonds with detachable stock warrants, these **warrants represent rights that enable the security holder to acquire a specified number of common shares at a given price within a certain time period.** Stock warrants are attached to bonds to increase their marketability and generally result in either a relatively lower interest rate or greater proceeds when compared with other bond issues with similar risk but without such rights. (The terms stock *warrants* and stock *rights* often are used interchangeably.) Because these warrants are detachable, they usually trade separately from the bonds on the open market.

APB Opinion No. 14 requires that a portion of the proceeds of bonds issued with detachable warrants be allocated to the stock warrants and accounted for as additional paid-in capital. This allocation is based on the relative fair values of the bonds and warrants as soon as both elements trade separately on the open market. The allocation is made as follows:

$$\text{Amount Assigned} \atop \text{to Bonds} = \frac{\text{Market Value of Bonds} \atop \text{Without Warrants}}{\text{Market Value of Bonds} + \text{Market Value} \atop \text{Without Warrants} \quad \text{of Warrants}} \times \text{Issuance} \atop \text{Price}$$

$$\text{Amount Assigned} \atop \text{to Warrants} = \frac{\text{Market Value of Warrants}}{\text{Market Value of Bonds} + \text{Market Value} \atop \text{Without Warrants} \quad \text{of Warrants}} \times \text{Issuance} \atop \text{Price}$$

For example, assume Paul Company sold $800,000 of 12% bonds at 101, or $808,000. Each $1,000 bond carried 10 warrants, and each warrant allows the holder to acquire one share of $5 par common stock for $25 per share. After issuance, the bonds are quoted at 99 *ex rights* (without the rights attached), and the warrants (rights) are quoted at $3 each. The company calculates the values assigned to each security as follows:

$$\text{Value Assigned to Bonds} = \frac{\$990 \times 800}{(\$990 \times 800) + (\$3 \times 800 \times 10)} \times \$808,000$$

$$= \frac{\$792,000}{\$792,000 + \$24,000} \times \$808,000 = \underline{\underline{\$784,235.29}}$$

$$\text{Value Assigned to Warrants} = \frac{\$3 \times 800 \times 10}{(\$990 \times 800) + (\$3 \times 800 \times 10)} \times \$808,000$$

$$= \frac{\$24,000}{\$792,000 + \$24,000} \times \$808,000 = \underline{\underline{\$23,764.71}}$$

In the denominator of each equation, note that the $792,000 fair value of the bonds without warrants is computed by multiplying the $990 (99 ex rights) quoted price times the 800 bonds. The fair value of the warrants is determined by multiplying the $3 quoted price times the 8,000 warrants (800 × 10). Paul records the transaction as follows:

Cash	808,000.00	
Discount on Bonds Payable		
($800,000 − $784,235.29)	15,764.71	
Bonds Payable		800,000.00
Common Stock Warrants		23,764.71

Each warrant is assigned a value of $2.971 ($23,764.71 ÷ 8,000), and if 500 of the warrants were later exercised at the $25 per share exercise price, Paul records the following journal entry:

Cash ($25 × 500)	12,500.00	
Common Stock Warrants ($2.971 × 500)	1,485.50	
Common Stock ($5 × 500)		2,500.00
Additional Paid-in Capital on Common Stock		11,485.50

If the remaining warrants expire, Paul would record the following journal entry:

Common Stock Warrants		
($23,764.71 − $1,485.50)	22,279.21	
Additional Paid-in Capital from Expired		
Warrants		22,279.21

This journal entry transfers the value assigned to the warrants to the existing stockholders.

Convertible Bonds

A company may also issue bonds that are convertible into common stock. **At conversion, the bondholder (creditor) exchanges the bonds for a specified number of common** shares (**and becomes a stockholder**). Debt securities that are convertible into common stock often have played a role in corporate financing, and this role appears to be growing. The use of these financial instruments gives rise to two questions. Why do companies issue such securities? Are the securities really bonds or are they a form of common stock?

Most financial analysts agree that a company sells convertible bonds for one of two primary reasons. Either the company wants to increase its equity capital at a later date and decides that the issuance of convertible bonds is the best way to do so, or it wants to increase its debt and finds the conversion feature necessary to make the security sufficiently marketable at a reasonable interest rate.

Several other factors have motivated companies to issue convertible bonds rather than common stock. For example, a company may wish to (1) avoid the downward price pressures on its stock that placing a large new issue of common stock on the market would cause, (2) avoid the direct sale of common stock when it believes its stock currently is undervalued in the market, (3) penetrate that segment of the capital market that is unwilling or unable to participate in a direct common stock issue, or (4) minimize the costs associated with selling securities.

For similar reasons, companies may issue convertible preferred stock (which we discuss in Chapter 16). In this chapter, we focus only on accounting for convertible bonds.

RECORDING THE ISSUANCE   When a company issues convertible debt, it must determine the proper valuation of these securities and their balance sheet presentation. Conceptually, there are two methods for recording the issuance of convertible debt. The company could either (1) attribute part of the proceeds from the sale of the security to the conversion privilege and allocate this to additional paid-in capital as part of stockholders' equity, or (2) treat the issue solely as debt. Both the conversion feature and the right to receive interest on the debt are valuable to an investor. Additionally, advocates of the first position argue that a lower interest rate or a higher selling price (or both) than might otherwise have been available usually accompanies the conversion feature. This indicates that investors are paying for the right to acquire common stock. Thus, an amount equal to the difference between the price at which the bonds might have been sold without the conversion privilege and the actual issue price should be allocated to additional paid-in capital. This position was taken in *APB Opinion No. 10* but soon was suspended in *APB Opinion No. 12*.[9] Companies had expressed widespread opposition to the convertible debt provisions of the earlier *Opinion*, and this viewpoint may have influenced the APB's suspension decision.

The decision was reversed in **APB Opinion No. 14**[10] and companies are required to treat the proceeds from the issuance of convertible debt solely as debt. The APB based its position on the inseparability of the debt and the conversion option, and on the lack of sufficiently reliable marketplace valuations. That is, the difficulty in assigning a *reliable* valuation to the conversion feature outweighed the arguments cited for the first method. Thus, treating the issue solely as debt is now the only generally accepted accounting principle. Thus, a company records the issuance of convertible debt in the same manner as the issuance of nonconvertible debt, without separately recording a value for the conversion feature.

RECORDING THE CONVERSION   When bonds are converted into common stock, a company must determine the amount to record as stockholders' equity. If the conversion takes place between interest dates, the company first must record interest expense and any discount or premium amortization to bring the book value of the bonds up to date. There are two generally accepted methods for a company to record the conversion:

9. "Omnibus Opinion—1966," *APB Opinion No. 10* (New York: AICPA, 1966), par. 8 and "Omnibus Opinion 1967," *APB Opinion No. 12* (New York: AICPA, 1967), par. 11.

10. "Accounting for Convertible Debt and Debt Issued with Stock Purchase Warrants," *APB Opinion No. 14* (New York: AICPA, 1969), par. 12.

1. *Book Value Method.* The stockholders' equity (common stock and additional paid-in capital) is recorded at the book value of the convertible bonds on the date of conversion, and no gain or loss is recorded upon conversion. (If the par value of the common stock is greater than the book value of the bonds, the difference is recorded as a reduction of retained earnings.)
2. *Market Value Method.* The stockholders' equity (common stock and additional paid-in capital) is recorded at the market value of the shares issued on the date of conversion, and a loss is recorded. The loss is computed by comparing the market value of the shares with the book value of the bonds at the time of conversion. (For a gain to be recognized, the market value of the shares would have to be less than the book value of the bonds—an unlikely event.) This loss is reported in income from continuing operations on the company's income statement.

To illustrate, assume that Shannon Corporation has outstanding convertible bonds with a face value of $10,000, it has just paid interest on these bonds, and the bonds have a book value of $10,500. Each $1,000 bond is convertible into 40 shares of common stock (par value $20 per share). If all the bonds are converted into common stock when the market value of Shannon's common stock is $26.50 per share, it may record the following alternative journal entries:

Book Value Method

Bonds Payable	10,000	
Premium on Bonds Payable	500	
Common Stock (40 × 10 × $20)		8,000
Additional Paid-in Capital from Bond Conversion ($10,500 − $8,000)		2,500

Market Value Method

Bonds Payable	10,000	
Premium on Bonds Payable	500	
Loss on Conversion ($10,600 − $10,500)	100	
Common Stock (40 × 10 × $20)		8,000
Additional Paid-in Capital from Bond Conversion (40 × 10 × $6.50)		2,600

Some users favor the market value method because they view the conversion as an economic event that should be recorded at fair value. Also, the company could have sold the stock at the market price and used the proceeds to retire the debt. Others criticize the market value method because it allows a company to manipulate its income by recording a loss (or gain) on transactions involving its own securities. They also argue that the book value method should be used because the conversion is not a new economic event, but rather a continuation of the contract terms established when the bonds were issued initially. For these reasons, most companies use the book value method, although both methods are acceptable under generally accepted accounting principles.

INDUCED CONVERSIONS   A company that has issued convertible bonds may desire to induce conversion of these bonds to common stock in order to reduce interest costs, improve its debt/equity ratio, or for other reasons. To induce conversion, the company may add a "sweetener" to the convertible bond issue so that the conversion privileges are changed or additional consideration is paid to the bondholder.

FASB Statement No. 84 applies in situations where the conversion privileges are changed after the initial issuance, are effective for a limited period of time, involve additional consideration, and are made to induce conversion. The changed terms (privileges) may involve a reduction of the original conversion price resulting in the issuance of additional shares of common stock, the issuance of warrants or other securities not included in the original conversion terms, or the payment of cash to bondholders who convert during the specified time period.

When convertible bonds are converted to common stock in such a situation, the debtor company recognizes an expense equal to the excess of the fair value of the common stock (and any other consideration) transferred in the transaction over the fair value of the common stock issuable under the original conversion terms. The fair values are measured on the date the inducement offer is accepted by the convertible bondholders.[11]

To illustrate, assume that the Harmon Company previously had issued convertible bonds with a face value of $10,000 at par. At the time of issuance, the conversion terms allowed each $1,000 bond to be converted into 40 shares of no-par common stock. To induce conversion, the company later changed the conversion terms so that each bond is convertible into 50 shares of no-par common stock if conversion is made in 60 days. All the bonds are converted within the time limit when the market price of the common stock is $30 per share. The bond conversion expense is $3,000 because the $15,000 ($10 \times 50 \times 30) fair value of the no-par common stock issued in the transaction is in excess of the $12,000 ($10 \times 40 \times 30) fair value of the shares that would have been issued under the original terms. Under the *book value method*, Harmon records the bond conversion expense at $3,000, eliminates the $10,000 par value of the bonds payable, and records the no-par common stock at $13,000 as follows:

Bonds Payable	10,000	
Bond Conversion Expense	3,000	
Common Stock, no par		13,000

Harmon reports the bond conversion expense in its income from continuing operations.

LONG-TERM NOTES PAYABLE

A long-term note is similar to a debenture bond because it represents a future obligation of the borrower to repay debt, and in many cases no collateral backs the note. Similarly, a long-term note generally includes a provision for interest on the borrowed funds, and the rate of interest charged will depend on such factors as the credit standing of the borrower, the amount of current debt, and other issues.

9 Account for long-term notes payable.

The APB reviewed procedures used by various companies to account for notes receivable and payable and found that some note transactions were conducted without an accompanying interest charge (i.e., these transactions involved *non-interest-bearing notes*). These transactions apparently were carried out to maintain favorable customer or supplier relations or to ensure future services. *APB Opinion No. 21* was issued to provide guidelines for cases in which a note does not stipulate a rate of interest or the stated interest rate is clearly not appropriate. The basic principle is that, regardless of how a note is structured legally, **the note is recorded at its present value and the effective interest method is used to record the subsequent interest.**[12] In essence, accounting for a note is based on its economic substance and not its legal form. The variety of transactions discussed in the *Opinion* did not allow the use of the same interest rate in all situations. In some situations, the borrower knows the present value so that it calculates the interest rate implicit in the transaction and uses this rate to apply the effective interest method. In other situations, where the present value is not known, the borrower uses its incremental interest rate to determine the present value and to apply the effective interest method. **The incremental interest rate is the rate that the borrower would be required to pay to obtain similar financing in the credit market at the time the note is issued.** Three major categories of notes were addressed: (1) notes exchanged for cash, (2) notes exchanged for cash and rights or privileges, and (3) notes exchanged for property, goods, or services.

Although *APB Opinion No. 21* addressed the accounting for most notes receivable and payable, it specifically exempted the following items: (1) normal trade transactions not exceeding one year, (2) amounts that will not be repaid but will be applied against

---

11. "Induced Conversions of Convertible Debt," *FASB Statement of Financial Accounting Standards No. 84* (Stamford, Conn.: FASB, 1985), par. 3 and 4.

12. The straight-line method may be used if the results obtained are not materially different from the effective interest method.

the purchase of property, goods, or services, (3) security deposits, (4) customary activities of financial institutions, (5) transactions where the rate is affected by the regulations of government agencies, and (6) transactions between parent and subsidiary companies (and subsidiaries of a common parent).[13]

Notes Payable Issued for Cash

When a company borrows cash and issues a long-term note payable bearing a stated (and fair) interest rate, it records the note initially at its face value (because it is equal to the present value). Subsequently, it records interest payments and accruals as debits to Interest Expense and credits to Cash or Interest Payable. Upon payment at maturity, it eliminates the Notes Payable account.

A more complex situation involves receiving cash in exchange for a long-term non-interest-bearing note. **When a long-term non-interest-bearing note is exchanged solely for cash, the note is assumed to have a present value equal to the cash proceeds. The difference between the cash proceeds and the face value of the note is recorded as a discount and amortized over the life of the note by the effective interest method.** To apply the effective interest method, a company must determine the implicit (effective) interest rate of the note. Since the cash received is the present value of the note and the face value is the future value of the note at maturity, **the effective (implicit) interest rate is the rate that equates the future value on the maturity date to the present value.** To illustrate, assume that on January 1 of the current year Johnson Company issues a 3-year, non-interest-bearing note with a face value of $8,000 and receives $5,694.24 in exchange. Johnson records the issuance of the note as follows:

Cash	5,694.24	
Discount on Notes Payable	2,305.76	
Notes Payable		8,000.00

The discount account is a contra account and is subtracted from the Notes Payable account on the company's balance sheet to report the carrying (book) value of the note.[14] From the Present Value of 1 Table (Appendix D), we find that the effective (implicit) interest rate that equates the present value of $5,694.24 to $8,000 at the end of 3 years is 12%.[15] The company computes the interest expense each year by multiplying the 12% effective interest rate by the carrying value at the beginning of the year. This amount also increases the carrying value of the note by reducing the discount. The company computes the interest each year as follows:

	Year 1	Year 2	Year 3
Note payable	$8,000.00	$8,000.00	$8,000.00
Less: Unamortized discount	(2,305.76)	(1,622.45)[a]	(857.14)[b]
Carrying value at beginning of year	$5,694.24	$6,377.55	$7,142.86
× Effective interest rate	0.12	0.12	0.12
Interest expense and discount amortization	$ 683.31	$ 765.31	$ 857.14

a. $2,305.76 − $683.31
b. $1,622.45 − $765.31

---

13. *APB Opinion No. 21, op. cit.*, par. 1, 3, and 15.
14. An alternative method is to record the Notes Payable account at its present value without the use of a Discount account. In this case, the adjusting entries for interest involve a debit to Interest Expense and a credit directly to the Notes Payable account. When a company uses this method, it discloses the difference between the maturity value and the carrying value parenthetically on its balance sheet as the amount of the discount.
15. Present Value = Future Value × Factor
    $5,694.24 = $8,000 × Factor
   Factor$_{n=3, i=?}$ = $5,694.24 ÷ $8,000 = 0.711780
        i = 12%

Johnson records the $683.31 interest expense for the first year as follows:

Interest Expense ($5,694.24 × 0.12)	683.31	
Discount on Notes Payable		683.31

The company records interest expense for the next two years in the same way so that the Discount account has a zero balance at the end of the third year. Therefore, the carrying value at the end of the third year is $8,000 (the face value of the note), and the repayment involves a debit to Notes Payable and credit to Cash for the $8,000 face value of the note.

Notes Payable Exchanged for Cash and Rights or Privileges

Long-term notes exchanged for cash may include special rights or privileges. A company must consider these rights or privileges when accounting for such long-term notes. For instance, a company might sign a contract with a customer in which the company borrows cash from the customer on a non-interest-bearing basis, with the understanding that the customer has the right to purchase certain goods from the company at less than prevailing prices over the period of the contract. In this situation the consideration received from the customer for the note is, in essence, a prepayment for future purchases. In such a case, for the company issuing the note, **the note is recorded at its present value at the time of issuance by discounting the maturity value using the incremental interest rate of the borrower.** Subsequently, **interest expense is recorded over the life of the note using the effective interest method.** In addition, **the difference between the cash proceeds and the present value of the note is recorded as unearned revenue, and revenue is recognized over the life of the contract using appropriate revenue recognition criteria.** For instance, revenue might be recognized on a per unit basis as goods are sold, or evenly throughout the contract on a straight-line basis.

To illustrate, assume that the Verna Company borrows $100,000 by issuing a 3-year, non-interest-bearing note to a customer. In addition, Verna Company agrees to sell inventory to the customer at reduced prices over a 5-year period. Verna's incremental borrowing rate is 12%, so the present value of $100,000 to be repaid at the end of 3 years is $71,178 ($100,000 × 0.711780, from the Present Value of 1 Table in Appendix D). The customer agrees to purchase an equal amount of inventory each year over the 5-year period so that a straight-line method of revenue recognition is appropriate. In this situation, Verna Company records the following journal entries during the first two years:

Issuing the Note

Cash	100,000.00	
Discount on Notes Payable		
($100,000 − $71,178)	28,822.00	
Notes Payable		100,000.00
Unearned Revenue		28,822.00

End of First Year

Interest Expense ($71,178 × 0.12)	8,541.36	
Discount on Notes Payable		8,541.36
Unearned Revenue ($28,822 ÷ 5 years)	5,764.40	
Sales Revenue		5,764.40

End of Second Year

Interest Expense [($71,178 + $8,541.36) × 0.12]	9,566.32	
Discount on Notes Payable		9,566.32
Unearned Revenue	5,764.40	
Sales Revenue		5,764.40

Recording the transactions according to these procedures results in the proper recognition of both the revenue and expense components. The company recognizes revenue as it earns it and recognizes the expense as it uses the proceeds from the loan.

Notes Payable Exchanged for Property, Goods, or Services

When a note is exchanged solely for property, goods, or services in an external transaction, *APB Opinion No. 21* states that the stipulated rate of interest should be presumed fair. This presumption can be overcome only if:

1. No interest is stated, or
2. The stated rate of interest is clearly unreasonable, or
3. The face value of the note is materially different from the cash sales price of the property, goods, or services, or the fair value of the note at the date of the transaction.[16]

In any of these cases, **the note is recorded at the fair value of the property, goods, or services, or the fair value of the note, whichever is more reliable.** The interest rate implicit in the transaction then is calculated and used to calculate the subsequent interest expense using the effective interest method. **If neither of these fair values is determinable, the note is recorded at its present value by discounting the future cash flow(s) using the incremental interest rate of the borrower.** The incremental interest rate then is used to apply the effective interest method to determine the subsequent interest expense.

In either situation, the carrying value of the note and the cost of the assets or services acquired are recorded at an amount that is less than the face value of the note. If the liability and asset had been erroneously recorded at the face value of the note, both would be overstated in the current period. Additionally, this would result in an overstatement of depreciation expense (or cost of goods sold) and an understatement of interest expense over the life of the asset and note, respectively. Recording the note at its fair (present) value results in correct asset and liability valuations and in the proper timing of expense recognition.

To illustrate, assume that on January 1, 2004 the Marsden Company purchases used equipment from the Joyce Company, issuing a non-interest-bearing $10,000, 5-year note in exchange. Neither the fair value of the equipment nor that of the note is determinable, so Marsden uses its incremental interest rate to compute the present value. If Marsden's incremental borrowing rate is 12%, the present value of $10,000 to be repaid at the end of 5 years at 12% is $5,674.27 ($10,000 × 0.567427, from Present Value of 1 Table in Appendix D). Assume the remaining asset life is 10 years (no residual value). Marsden records the issuance of the note, the first two interest payments, and annual straight-line depreciation as follows:

January 1, 2004

Equipment	5,674.27	
Discount on Notes Payable	4,325.73	
Notes Payable		10,000.00

December 31, 2004

Interest Expense [($10,000 − $4,325.73) × 0.12]	680.91	
Discount on Notes Payable		680.91
Depreciation Expense	567.43	
Accumulated Depreciation ($5,674.27 ÷ 10)		567.43

December 31, 2005

Interest Expense {[$10,000 − ($4,325.73 − $680.91)] × 0.12}	762.62	
Discount on Notes Payable		762.62
Depreciation Expense	567.43	
Accumulated Depreciation		567.43

---

16. *APB Opinion No. 21, op. cit.*, par. 12.

This example assumes that a 12% interest rate is appropriate for the transaction, but a borrower should attempt to determine the fair values of the property and of the note before applying its incremental interest rate. If either the fair value of the property or of the note is used, the note payable is recorded at the fair value, and it is necessary to find the implicit interest rate that equates the recorded (fair) value to the face value over the term of the loan. For example, assume in the previous example that Marsden determines that the fair value of the equipment is $6,209.21. From the Present Value of 1 Table (Appendix D), we find that the rate that equates $6,209.21 to $10,000 at the end of 5 years is 10%.[17] Marsden would record the note payable initially at $6,209.21, and then would record the interest expense of 10% on the carrying value of the note each year over the life of the note.

This example also assumes the issuance of a non-interest-bearing note. As discussed earlier, the same principles apply in the case where a note carries a stated interest rate that is unreasonable. For example, assume that on January 1, 2004 Fox Company issues a $30,000, 3-year note bearing interest of 6% for equipment when its incremental borrowing rate is 10%. If the fair value of the equipment or the note is not determinable, Fox records the transaction using the present value of the future cash flows with the 10% rate for the 3-year life. In this case, it records the equipment and note at $27,015.78 [($30,000 face value × 0.751315) + ($1,800 annual interest × 2.486852)]. It then applies the effective interest method using the 10% rate at the end of each year to determine the interest expense. For instance, at the end of 2004, it debits Interest Expense for $2,701.58 ($27,015.78 × 0.10), credits Cash for $1,800 ($30,000 × 0.06), and increases the book value of the note by $901.58.

Disclosure of Long-Term Liabilities

A company must disclose the various characteristics of its long-term debt. It normally does so in the notes to its financial statements. The disclosure by IBM Company of its long-term (and short-term) debt is shown in Exhibit 13-6. Also included are disclosures about scheduled repayments of long-term debt, interest payments, capitalized interest, and lines of credit.

10 Understand the disclosure of long-term liabilities.

LONG-TERM NOTES RECEIVABLE

Although this is a chapter on long-term liabilities, we discuss accounting for long-term notes receivable here because the generally accepted accounting principles that apply to notes receivable are very similar to those for notes payable. Companies may acquire long-term notes receivable as a result of lending cash to another entity or in return for the extension of certain rights or privileges. However, long-term notes receivable are acquired primarily as a result of an exchange for property, goods, or services. This type of exchange is the focus of this section.

11 Account for long-term notes receivable, including impairment of a loan.

As we discussed in the previous section, when a company receives a note in exchange for property, goods, or services, it should presume that the stipulated interest rate is fair unless no interest rate is stated, the stated interest rate is clearly unreasonable, or the face value of the note is materially different from the cash sales price of the property, goods, or services, or from the fair value of the note on the transaction date. In any of these situations, **the note receivable is recorded at the fair value of the property, goods, or services or the fair value of the note, whichever is more reliable. If neither of these values is reliable, the note is recorded at its present value by using the** *borrower's* **incremental interest rate.** The effective interest method is used to record the subsequent interest revenue. Recording the note at its fair value (present value) and using the effective interest method results in the correct asset valuation and in the proper timing of revenue recognition.

---

17. $6,209.21 ÷ $10,000 = 0.620921. In the *n* = 5 row, we find 0.620921 in the 10% column.

EXHIBIT 13-6 Disclosure of Long-Term Liabilities

**INTERNATIONAL BUSINESS MACHINES CORPORATION
AND SUBSIDIARY COMPANIES**

J Borrowings
Short-term debt
(Dollars in millions)

At December 31:	2001	2000
Commercial paper	$ 4,809	$ 3,521
Short-term loans	1,564	3,975
Long-term debt: Current maturities	4,815	2,709
Total	$11,188	$10,205

The weighted-average interest rates for commercial paper at December 31, 2001 and 2000, were approximately 1.9 percent and 6.7 percent, respectively. The weighted-average interest rates for short-term loans at December 31, 2001 and 2000 were approximately 4.0 percent and 2.9 percent, respectively.

Long-term debt
(Dollars in millions)

At December 31:	Maturities	2001	2000
U.S. Dollars:			
Debentures:			
6.22%	2027	$ 500	$ 500
6.5%	2028	700	700
7.0%	2025	600	600
7.0%	2045	150	150
7.125%	2096	850	850
7.5%	2013	550	550
8.375%	2019	750	750
Notes: 6.3% average	2002–2014	2,772	2,933
Medium-term note program: 5.4% average	2002–2014	3,620	4,305
Other: 4.5% average	2002–2009	828	1,092
		11,320	12,430
Other currencies (average interest rate at December 31, 2001, in parentheses):			
Euros (4.4%)	2002–2009	3,042	3,042
Japanese yen (1.1%)	2002–2014	4,749	4,845
Canadian dollars (5.8%)	2002–2011	441	302
Swiss francs (4.0%)	2002–2003	151	231
Other (6.1%)	2002–2014	726	275
		20,429	21,125
Less: Net unamortized discount		47	45
Add: SFAS No. 133 fair value adjustment*		396	—
		20,778	21,080
Less: Current maturities		4,815	2,709
Total		$15,963	$18,371

*In accordance with the requirements of SFAS No. 133, the portion of the company's fixed-rate debt obligations that is hedged is reflected in the consolidated statement of financial position as an amount equal to the sum of the debt's carrying value plus a SFAS No. 133 fair value adjustment representing changes recorded in the fair value of the hedged debt obligations attributable to movements in market interest rates.

EXHIBIT 13-6   Disclosure of Long-Term Liabilities, Continued

Annual maturities on long-term debt outstanding at December 31, 2001, are as follows:

2002	$5,186
2003	3,106
2004	1,501
2005	1,904
2006	2,216
2007 and beyond	6,471

Interest on debt
(Dollars in millions)

	2001	2000*	1999*
Cost of global financing	$964	$1,082	$1,100
Interest expense	238	347	352
Interest capitalized	33	20	23
Total interest paid and accrued	$1,235	$1,449	$1,475

*Reclassified to Conform with 2001 Presentation

Refer to the table and related discussion on page 104 in note v, "Segment Information," for the total interest expense of the Global Financing segment. See note k, "Derivatives and Hedging Transactions," on pages 85 through 87 for a discussion of the use of currency and interest rate swaps in the company's debt risk management program.

Lines of Credit
Effective May 31, 2001, the company replaced its $10 billion committed global credit facility, which was due to expire in February 2002, with two global credit facilities totaling $12.0 billion in committed credit lines, including an $8.0 billion five-year facility and a $4.0 billion 364-day facility. The company's other lines of credit, most of which were uncommitted, totaled $6,860 million and $7,646 million, respectively, at December 31, 2001 and 2000. Interest rates and other terms of borrowing under these lines of credit vary from country to country, depending on local market conditions.

(Dollars in millions)

At December 31	2001	2000
Unused lines		
From the committed global credit facility	$11,383	$9,103
From other committed and uncommitted lines	4,378	5,111
Total unused lines of credit	$16,121	$14,214

Q U E S T I O N S

Q Explain all the interest transactions and the changes that occurred in long-term debt (for example, by re-creating summary journal entries). **Q** What is the remaining life of the debt with the longest life? **Q** Did interest paid increase or decline in 2001? **Q** Explain whether the company has financial flexibility.

To illustrate, consider the previous example in which the Joyce Company accepted a $10,000, non-interest-bearing, 5-year note on January 1, 2004 in exchange for used equipment it sold to Marsden Company. Since a reliable fair value for the equipment or the note was not available, Joyce uses *Marsden's* 12% incremental borrowing rate to determine a present value of $5,674.27 for the note. Assume further that the equipment had originally cost the Joyce Company $8,000 and had a book value of $5,000 on the date of sale. The Joyce Company records the following journal entries for the exchange and the first two interest receipts:

January 1, 2004

Notes Receivable	10,000.00	
Accumulated Depreciation	3,000.00	
Discount on Notes Receivable		
($10,000 − $5,674.27)		4,325.73
Equipment		8,000.00
Gain on Sale of Equipment		674.27

December 31, 2004

Discount on Notes Receivable	680.91	
Interest Revenue		
[($10,000 − $4,325.73) × 0.12]		680.91

December 31, 2005

Discount on Notes Receivable	762.62	
Interest Revenue		
{[$10,000 − ($4,325.73 − $680.91)] × 0.12}		762.62

At the date of exchange, Joyce records the difference between the present value and face value of the note in a Discount on Notes Receivable account.[18] This account is a contra account and is subtracted from the Notes Receivable account to report the carrying (book) value of the note on the company's balance sheet. Joyce computes the $674.27 gain by comparing the book value ($5,000) of the equipment with the present value ($5,674.27) of the note. If the exchange takes place in the middle of the year, the company must make a depreciation adjusting entry to bring the book value of the equipment up to date. If the company receives cash in addition to the note, it computes the gain by comparing the book value of the equipment with the sum of the cash received plus the present value of the note.

At the end of each year the company records interest revenue using the effective interest method. By the maturity date, it will have amortized the entire discount to interest revenue, and the carrying value will equal the face value of the note. If a reliable value for the equipment or the note is available, the company records the note at this fair value and computes the implicit interest rate as we discussed in the previous section. The company then uses this interest rate to recognize periodic interest revenue under the effective interest method.

Loan Fees

The proper matching of revenues and expenses associated with the lending activities of financial services companies is defined by **FASB Statement No. 91**. Lending activities precede the disbursement of funds and generally include efforts to identify and attract potential borrowers and to originate a loan or loan commitment. The nonrefundable fees charged to borrowers for these activities are called *loan origination fees* and *commitment fees*. Generally, any loan origination fees or commitment fees are deferred and recognized over the life of the loan as an increase in the interest revenue related to the note receivable. Likewise, the direct loan origination costs are deferred and recognized over the life of the loan as a decrease in the interest revenue. In either case, a new, effective interest rate (yield) is computed. In other words, the revenues and expenses for these lending activities are matched over the life of the loan rather than recognized in the period in which the loan is originated.[19]

---

18. An alternative method is to record the Notes Receivable account at its present value without the use of a Discount account. The Notes Receivable account is then increased by each subsequent entry to record interest revenue and is equal to the maturity value on the due date.

19. "Accounting for Nonrefundable Fees and Costs Associated with Originating or Acquiring Loans and Initial Direct Costs of Leases," *FASB Statement of Financial Accounting Standards No. 91* (Stamford, Conn.: FASB, 1986), par. 5–9.

Impairment of a Loan

Since loans typically are made by financial institutions such as banks, it is helpful to understand how they estimate bad debts as compared to retailers or manufacturers which make sales on credit. The retailer or manufacturer estimates bad debts in the period of the sales because it is probable that a portion of the asset (accounts receivable) has been impaired and the amount of the loss can be reasonably estimated based on historical information (as we discussed in Chapter 6). Thus, the bad debt expense is matched against revenues in the period of sale, and the receivables are reported at their net realizable value at the end of the period. In a later period, a specific account receivable is written off when it is determined that the amount is not collectible.

There are several differences between the receivables of a financial institution and those of a retailer or manufacturer. In the case of the financial institution, (1) the notes receivable result primarily from loans made to customers, (2) the loans are made to more heterogeneous customers, (3) the repayment periods for the loans are frequently longer (i.e., several years), (4) there are fewer receivables because fewer loans are made, and (5) more thorough credit analyses are made before extending loans. These differences affect when and how bad debt expense is recognized by a financial institution.

A financial institution is likely to make a more thorough credit analysis before granting a loan and to analyze the noncollectibility of each individual loan. Therefore, it is likely to recognize bad debts in a later period than a retailer or manufacturer, both of which are likely to use historical percentages. In a later period, however, a financial institution will recognize bad debt expense when, for instance, there is evidence that a loan may not be collectible (e.g., when the customer misses a payment on a loan). Then, in an even later period, a specific note receivable is written off when it is determined that the amount is not collectible, perhaps after taking possession of, and selling, the collateral provided by the borrower. We illustrate the difference between bad debt recognition for a retailer or manufacturer and a financial institution in the following diagram of events occurring during several (perhaps nonconsecutive) accounting periods.

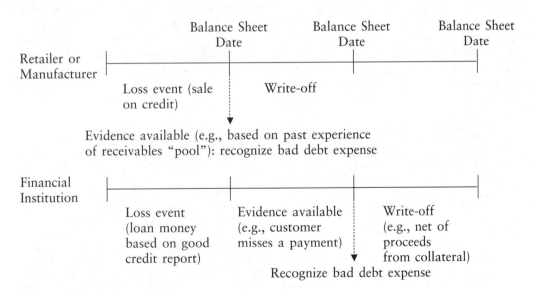

Note that because there is a delay in the recognition of bad debts by a financial institution, it does not recognize bad debt expense in the period in which the loan originates (and the financial institution does not recognize revenue from the loan origination), and it does not report its receivables at their net realizable value at the end of that period. However, *relevant* expense recognition and receivables valuation does occur when *reliable* information becomes available that a loan is impaired.

A loan (note receivable) is impaired if it is *probable* that the creditor will be unable to collect all amounts due according to the contractual terms of the loan agreement.[20] Impairment occurs when there is a delay in the payment or a shortfall in the amount of the principal or interest. The creditor company, often a financial institution, applies its normal loan review procedures in making this determination. A loan is *not* impaired even if there is a delay in making interest or principal payments provided the creditor expects to collect all amounts due, including interest accrued during the period of delay. When a loan is found to be impaired, the company computes the present value of the expected future cash flows of the impaired loan using the effective interest rate on the loan. **The effective interest rate is the original (contractual) interest rate on the loan** (adjusted for any loan fees, discount, or premium). The company recognizes the amount by which the present value is less than the recorded investment in the loan as Bad Debt Expense and Allowance for Doubtful Notes. Alternatively, the creditor may measure the impairment based on the loan's market price, or the fair value of the collateral if it expects repayment of the loan to be provided solely by the underlying collateral (net of the costs of selling the loan or the collateral).

Once the creditor has written down the loan, it computes the interest revenue each period by multiplying the carrying value of the loan by the effective interest rate. It recognizes the interest revenue as a reduction of the allowance account.[21] If there are additional changes in the amount or timing of an impaired loan's expected cash flows, or if actual cash flows are different than expected cash flows, the company recalculates the amount of the impairment. It recognizes the difference, whether an increase or decrease, as an adjustment to Bad Debt Expense and the Allowance account.

To illustrate the impairment of a loan using present value calculations, assume that the Snook Company has a $100,000 note receivable from the Ullman Company that it is carrying at face value. The original loan agreement specifies that interest of 8% is payable each December 31 and the principal is to be paid on December 31, 2009. The Ullman Company paid the interest due on December 31, 2004, but informed the Snook Company at that time that it probably would miss the next two year's interest payments because of its financial difficulties.[22] After that, it expects to resume the $8,000 annual interest payments, but the principal payment would be made one year late with interest paid for that additional year. On December 31, 2004 the Snook Company computes the present value of the impaired loan as we show on the next page. Note that the company discounts the principal for 6 years, the period from December 31, 2004 to December 31, 2010, but only discounts the interest for 4 years, deferred 2 years, because Ullman will not pay interest for 2 years.

---

20. "Accounting by Creditors for Impairment of a Loan," *FASB Statement No. 114* (Norwalk, Conn.: FASB, 1993). This *Statement* also applies to the impairment of accounts receivable of more than one year (which we do not discuss here). It does *not* apply to investments in debt securities, as defined in *FASB Statement No. 115* (which we discuss in Chapter 14).

21. This method is the conceptually preferred method for recognizing income. Alternatively, *FASB Statement No. 114* allows for the entire change in the present value (the bad debt expense *and* the interest revenue) to be recognized as a single amount and reported as an increase or decrease in bad debt expense. However, because the two alternatives were inconsistent with the accounting for impaired loans required by bank and thrift regulators, **FASB Statement No. 118** was issued in 1994. This amendment allows the use of any method of income recognition, such as cash basis or cost recovery, even though the current value of the impaired loan may be less than the present value of the expected cash flows discounted at the loan's effective interest rate. Thus, the Board decided to allow for a reduction of *comparability* in order to reduce implementation *costs* for companies. It also increased disclosure by requiring that companies must report their policy for recognizing interest income. Since illustrations of all the methods are beyond the scope of the book, we use the conceptually preferred effective interest method.

22. In a more complex situation, knowledge of the loan impairment would occur when a payment is missed. If the company has accrued interest revenue for the period, the bad debt expense would be the difference between the carrying value (including the accrued interest) and the present value of the expected cash flows (including any late interest payments).

$$\text{Present value of principal} = \$100,000 \times \text{present value of a single sum for}$$
$$\text{6 years at 8\% (from Appendix D)}$$
$$= \$100,000 \times 0.630170$$
$$= \$63,017.00$$
$$\text{Present value of interest} = \$8,000 \times \text{present value of an annuity for 4 years}$$
$$\text{at 8\% deferred 2 years (from Appendix D)}$$
$$= \$8,000 \times 3.312127 \times 0.857339$$
$$= \$22,716.93$$
$$\text{Value of the impaired loan} = \$63,017.00 + \$22,716.93$$
$$= \$85,733.93$$

At December 31, 2004, the Snook Company recognizes the impairment of $14,266.07 ($100,000 carrying value − $85,733.93 present value) as follows:

Bad Debt Expense	14,266.07	
Allowance for Doubtful Notes		14,266.07

At December 31, 2005, the Snook Company recognizes interest revenue of $6,858.71 [8% × $85,733.93 ($100,000 − $14,266.07)] as follows:

Allowance for Doubtful Notes	6,858.71	
Interest Revenue		6,858.71

At December 31, 2006 the Snook Company recognizes interest revenue of $7,407.36 [8% × $92,592.64 ($100,000 − $7,407.36), adjusted for $0.04 rounding error]. This eliminates the balance in the Allowance for Doubtful Notes account, and the carrying value of the receivable is now $100,000. Snook will recognize interest revenue of $8,000 each year for 2007 through 2010 as the cash payment is received. Snook will eliminate the $100,000 carrying value on December 31, 2010 when it receives the principal payment. If Snook's expectations of future cash flows decrease (increase) before December 31, 2006, it would debit (credit) Bad Debt Expense and credit (debit) the Allowance account for the decrease (increase) in the present value. In either situation, the company would recognize interest revenue each year, as we discussed earlier.

CONCEPTUAL EVALUATION *FASB Statement No. 114* was issued because companies were using a variety of practices when a loan was impaired. Some would make no adjustment to the value of the loan, some would value the loan based on undiscounted cash flows, and some would use discounted cash flows. Thus, one objective of issuing the *Statement* was to establish a consistent method for valuing impaired loans. Another objective was to require companies to measure the economic losses on impaired loans and to include them in income.

Perhaps the only controversial issue in the required principles is the use of the original (contractual) interest rate rather than a current market rate that would reflect the risk involved in the loan (which is now higher than at the origination of the loan). The FASB concluded that the loan impairment measurement should reflect only the deterioration in the borrower's credit quality (which is evidenced by the reduced future cash inflows), and should not reflect changes in interest rates.

The *Statement* was adopted by a 5-to-2 vote, however, with the two dissenters arguing that the *fair value* of the loan should be recognized. Such a fair value would be the market value of the loan or the present value of the expected cash flows discounted at the *market* rate of interest. The market rate reflects current economic events and conditions, and is commensurate with the risk involved. The dissenters argued that the fair value provides the most *relevant* information about the amount and riskiness of the expected future cash flows. The historical effective interest rate reflects the risk characteristics of the loan at the time it was originated or acquired, but not at the time it was impaired. Also they note that bad debt expense would be *overstated* if the historical rate is *higher* than the current market rate.

At first sight, it may seem surprising that interest revenue (based on the new carrying value) is recognized even though a loan is impaired. For example, the Snook Company recognizes interest revenue in 2005 when it receives no cash. However, it must be remembered that in 2004, it recognizes the economic loss of $14,266.07 associated with the receivable and values the loan at the present value of the future cash flows. It then recognizes interest revenue on that reduced value. As always, one of the major issues of income recognition is the period in which income (and losses) should be recognized. These principles for the impairment of a loan do recognize the true economic situation appropriately because a loss is recognized in the period of impairment and interest revenue is recognized in subsequent periods.

Future Developments

At the time of writing this book, the FASB has issued two *Exposure Drafts* that, if implemented, will have significant effects on how some companies account for liabilities. *Exposure Draft No. 213-B* "Accounting for Financial Instruments with Characteristics of Liabilities, Equity, or Both" will, if adopted, change the accounting for what the FASB has identified as **compound financial instruments**. These financial instruments have characteristics of both liabilities and equity. This *Exposure Draft* would require a company that issues a compound financial instrument to separately classify the liability component and the equity component. In measuring the amount to classify as each component, it must allocate the proceeds received to its liabilities and its stockholders' equity using the relative-fair-value-method.

This new GAAP would affect how a company accounts for the issuance of convertible bonds. When a company issues convertible bonds, it would allocate a portion of the proceeds to the conversion feature and account for this amount as additional paid-in capital. This allocation is based on the relative independent fair values of the liability (bonds) component and the equity (conversion rights) component.

When convertible bondholders exercise their rights to convert the bonds to common stock, the company must determine any gain or loss, as well as the amount to record as stockholders' equity. To determine these amounts, the company would complete a series of steps: (1) it would determine the total fair value of the convertible bonds on the conversion date; (2) it would determine the independent fair values of the liability (bonds) component and the stockholders' equity (conversion rights) component; (3) it would allocate the total fair value from step (1) to the liability component and the stockholders' equity component based on the relative independent fair values of each of these components; (4) it would subtract the fair value of the bonds component from the book value of the bonds to determine the gain or loss after conversion before and (5) it would assign the fair value of the bond component to the separate elements (i.e., common stock and additional paid-in capital) of the equity component. The company would then prepare a journal entry to eliminate the book value of the bonds, record the gain or loss on the conversion, and record the common stockholders' equity at the fair value of the bonds.

Another *Exposure Draft* "Guarantor's Accounting and Disclosure Requirements for Guarantees, Including Indirect Guarantees of Indebtedness of Others" will, if adopted, require some companies to recognize a new liability. When a company issues a guarantee, it will be required to record a liability for the fair value of the obligation it has incurred by issuing the guarantee, including its ongoing obligation to "stand ready" to perform over the term of the guarantee in the event that the specific triggering events or conditions occur. This rule would not apply to some guarantees, such as insurance and warranty contracts.

To illustrate the effect of the *Exposure Draft*, suppose the Probst Company sells a product to the Metcalf Company for $10 million. Since Metcalf does not have sufficient cash, it decides to take out a bank loan to finance the purchase. However, its financial status is such that the bank will not provide an unsecured loan. So the Probst Company guarantees Metcalf's loan from the bank, so that it can make the sale. Under current GAAP, Probst would not account for the guarantee (although it would disclose the guarantee in the notes to its financial statements). The *Exposure Draft* would require Probst to determine the value of the guarantee and record it as a liability, thereby reducing the profit it recognizes on the sale. Interestingly, the *Exposure Draft* does not specify how the liability is to be valued over the remaining term of the guarantee.

The *Exposure Draft* would also require the guarantor company to expand the disclosures it makes in the notes to its financial statements. These disclosures would include the nature of the guarantee, how it arose, the events or circumstances that would require it to perform under the guarantee, and the maximum potential amount of undiscounted future payments it could be required to make. The guarantor would also be required to disclose the carrying value of the liability.

APPENDIX 1: TROUBLED DEBT RESTRUCTURINGS

Some companies that experience difficulty in repaying long-term debt obligations enter into financial arrangements with their creditors to allow them to avoid bankruptcy. **FASB Statement No. 15** states that **a troubled debt restructuring occurs when a creditor for economic or legal reasons related to a debtor's financial difficulties grants a concession to the debtor that it would not otherwise consider.** A troubled debt restructuring may include, but is not limited to, one or any combination of the following:

12 Understand troubled debt restructurings.

1. **Modification of terms** of a debt, such as one or a combination of:
    a. Reduction of the stated interest rate for the remaining original life of the debt.
    b. Extension of the maturity date at a stated interest rate lower than the current market rate for new debt with similar risk.
    c. Reduction of the face amount or maturity amount of the debt.
    d. Reduction of accrued interest.
2. **Issuance or other granting of an equity interest** to the creditor by the debtor to satisfy a debt unless the equity interest is granted under existing terms for converting the debt into an equity interest.
3. **Transfer of receivables, real estate, or other assets** from the debtor to the creditor to satisfy a debt.[23]

ACCOUNTING BY THE DEBTOR

We first discuss the debtor's accounting for a troubled debt restructuring. Later we discuss the creditor's accounting.

Modification of Terms

When a restructuring agreement involves only a modification of terms, the carrying value of the *liability* (face value of the debt plus any unpaid accrued interest) is compared to the *undiscounted* future cash payments (principal plus interest) specified by the new terms. Then, two different situations may arise:

1. If the undiscounted total future cash payments are *greater* than (or equal to) the carrying value of the liability, the debtor does *not* recognize a gain, the carrying value of the liability is *not* reduced, and interest expense is recognized in future periods using an imputed interest rate.
2. If the future cash payments are *less* than the carrying value of the liability, the debtor recognizes a gain, the carrying value of the liability is reduced, and interest expense is *not* recognized in future periods.

NO GAIN RECOGNIZED BY THE DEBTOR When there is a modification of terms and the total cash to be repaid over the remaining life of the loan is greater than (or equal to) the carrying value of the liability, the debtor makes no adjustment to the carrying

23. "Accounting by Debtors and Creditors for Troubled Debt Restructurings," *FASB Statement of Financial Accounting Standards No. 15* (Stamford, Conn.: FASB, 1977), par. 2 and 5.

value. Subsequently, the debtor recognizes annual interest expense using the effective interest method. **The imputed interest rate used is the rate that equates the total amount of cash to be paid with the current carrying value of the debt.** In this situation, the debtor records a portion of each cash payment as interest expense and records the remainder as a reduction in the carrying value of the liability.

For example, assume that on December 31, 2004 Chapin Company restructures a $1,178,073 debt with its bank (a note payable of $1,100,000 plus accrued interest of $78,073). The bank (1) forgives the $78,073 of accrued interest and $100,000 of principal, (2) extends the maturity date from December 31, 2004 to December 31, 2009, and (3) reduces the interest rate from 10% to 8%. The total future cash payments under the new terms are $1,400,000 (principal of $1,000,000 at the end of 5 years and interest of $80,000 at the end of each year for 5 years). Since the *undiscounted* amount of the principal and interest to be paid ($1,400,000) exceeds the carrying value of the liability ($1,178,073), Chapin does not record a gain and therefore does not reduce the carrying value of the liability. It records the difference of $221,927 as interest expense over the next 5 years by using the effective interest method. It determines the interest expense each period by multiplying the effective interest rate times the carrying value at the beginning of the period.

The effective interest rate is that rate which discounts the principal of $1,000,000 and the interest payments of $80,000 to the $1,178,073 carrying value of the note. This discounting procedure involves two present value calculations, as we summarize in the following diagram:

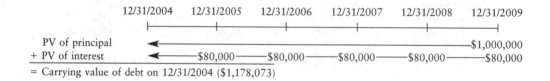

This rate is found to be 4%, as proven below:

Present value of interest payments:
(Present Value of an Ordinary Annuity Table
   in Appendix D, $n = 5$, $i = 0.04$) $\$80,000 \times 4.451822 = \$\ \ 356,146$
Present Value of Principal:
(Present Value of 1 Table in Appendix D,
   $n = 5$, $i = 0.04$) $\$1,000,000 \times 0.821927 = \underline{\ \ \ \ 821,927}$
Carrying Value of the Debt on 12/31/2004 $\underline{\underline{\$1,178,073}}$

On December 31, 2004 Chapin transfers the accrued Interest Payable balance to the Notes Payable account as follows:

Interest Payable	78,073	
Notes Payable		78,073

The Notes Payable account now contains the entire $1,178,073 carrying value of the note. Chapin computes the interest expense to be recorded in each period by applying the effective interest rate of 4% to the carrying value of the note each year. Exhibit 13-7 illustrates the computation of the interest expense and principal reduction for each year of the Chapin Company's restructuring agreement.

In reviewing Exhibit 13-7, note that each cash payment is separated into its principal and interest components by multiplying the carrying value of the note in each year by the imputed interest rate in the agreement (4% in this case). Chapin Company records the difference between the interest expense and each cash payment as a reduction

EXHIBIT 13-7   Debt Restructuring Agreement: Schedule to Compute Interest Expense

Date	Cash Credit[a]	Interest Expense Debit[b]	Notes Payable Debit[c]	Carrying Value of Note[d]
12/31/04				$1,178,073.00
12/31/05	$ 80,000	$47,122.92	$ 32,877.08	1,145,195.92
12/31/06	80,000	45,807.84	34,192.16	1,111,003.76
12/31/07	80,000	44,440.15	35,559.85	1,075,443.91
12/31/08	80,000	43,017.76	36,982.24	1,038,461.67
12/31/09	1,080,000	41,538.33[e]	1,038,461.67	-0-

a. From terms of restructuring agreement.
b. Previous carrying value × 0.04.
c. Amount from footnote *a* − amount from footnote *b*.
d. Previous carrying value − amount from footnote *c*.
e. Difference due to $0.14 rounding error.

in the carrying value of the note payable. For example, Chapin Company records the following journal entry on December 31, 2005:

Interest Expense	47,122.92	
Notes Payable	32,877.08	
Cash		80,000.00

GAIN RECOGNIZED BY THE DEBTOR An adjustment to the carrying value of the liability is required if the total cash to be repaid over the remaining life of the loan is less than that carrying value. In this case, the debtor recognizes a gain equal to the excess of the carrying value (face value plus accrued interest) over the sum of the future payments.

For example, assume that the Chapin Company was allowed the terms stated previously (reduction of principal by $100,000, forgiving of $78,073 of accrued interest, and extension of repayment period by 5 years), except that the stated interest rate was reduced to 3%. The aggregate future cash payments in this case total $1,150,000 ($1,000,000 principal and $30,000 interest per year for 5 years). This amount is $28,073 less than the carrying value of $1,178,073 ($1,100,000 face value + $78,073 accrued interest). Chapin Company reports this amount as a gain in its income from continuing operations for 2004, eliminates the accrued interest, and credits the difference between the gain and the accrued interest to the Notes Payable account so that the balance is now $1,150,000. Chapin records the restructuring on December 31, 2004 is as follows:

Interest Payable	78,073	
Notes Payable		50,000
Gain on Debt Restructure		28,073

Subsequently, each future cash payment reduces the carrying value of the payable and Chapin does *not* recognize interest expense, since the effective interest rate is 0%. That is, since the amount to be repaid is less than the original carrying value of the liability, the creditor is, in effect, accepting repayment without an accompanying interest charge. Chapin records the first cash payment on December 31, 2005 as follows:

Notes Payable	30,000	
Cash		30,000

The reduction of the Notes Payable account by $30,000 each year for five years will reduce this account to $1,000,000. This amount will then be eliminated at the time of the lump-sum principal payment at the end of the fifth year.

Equity or Asset Exchange

When a debtor satisfies a liability by exchanging an equity interest or an asset of lesser value, it records the transfer on the basis of the fair value of the equity interest or asset transferred and recognizes a gain on the debt restructuring. Furthermore, when an *asset* is exchanged, if the fair value is greater or less than its carrying value, the debtor also records a gain or loss on the disposal of the asset.

EQUITY EXCHANGE To illustrate an equity exchange, assume that on December 31, 2004 the Chapin Company repays the note payable and the accrued interest totaling $1,178,073 by issuing 35,000 shares of its own common stock to the bank. The shares have a par value of $10 per share and are selling currently for $25 per share on the open market. Chapin records the stock at the fair value of $875,000 (35,000 × $25), reduces the liability by $1,178,073, and recognizes a gain of $303,073. Chapin Company records the debt restructuring as follows:

Notes Payable	1,100,000	
Interest Payable	78,073	
Common Stock (35,000 × $10)		350,000
Additional Paid-in Capital on Common Stock		525,000
Gain on Debt Restructure		303,073

ASSET EXCHANGE To illustrate an asset exchange, assume the same information as the equity exchange except that the Chapin Company repays the liability by transferring land it owns to the bank. The land has a fair value of $800,000 and had cost the Chapin Company $600,000 five years ago. The Chapin Company recognizes a gain of $378,073 ($1,178,073 − $800,000) on the restructuring and a gain of $200,000 ($800,000 − $600,000) on the disposal of the land. Chapin Company records the debt restructuring as follows:

Notes Payable	1,100,000	
Interest Payable	78,073	
Gain on Debt Restructure		378,073
Gain on Disposal of Land		200,000
Land		600,000

Equity or Asset Exchange Combined with a Modification of Terms

In some situations, a troubled debt restructuring includes an equity or asset exchange as well as a modification of terms. In this case, the debtor records the equity or asset transfer first at the fair value as we discussed previously. It then compares the *remaining* carrying value of the liability, after deducting the fair value of the equity or assets transferred, to the total undiscounted future cash payments specified under the new terms. If the remaining carrying value is less than the total payments, the debtor does *not* recognize a gain, does *not* reduce the carrying value of the liability, and recognizes interest expense in future periods using an imputed interest rate. If the remaining carrying value is greater than the total payments, it recognizes a gain and reduces the carrying value of the liability, but does *not* record interest expense in future periods. The accounting procedures to be followed in these two situations are the same as those we discussed earlier.

Disclosure of Restructuring Agreements

The following disclosures are required for debtors who have entered into restructuring agreements: (1) A description of the principal changes in terms and/or the major features of settlement for each restructuring agreement; (2) the aggregate gain on debt restructures and the related income tax effect; (3) the per share amount of the aggregate gain on restructuring, net of the related income tax effect; (4) the aggregate gain or loss recognized during the period on transfers of assets; and (5) information on any contingent payments.[24]

---

24. *Ibid.*, par. 25 and 26.

The following is an example of the disclosure required for the Chapin Company's exchange of equity securities we discussed previously:

> During the year Chapin Company gave common stock with a fair value of $875,000 to the bank in exchange for full settlement of a 10% note in the amount of $1,100,000 and accrued interest of $78,073. As a result of this exchange, the company recognized a gain of $303,073 and increased earnings per share by $0.11.

ACCOUNTING BY THE CREDITOR

The accounting principles to be followed by the creditor are defined by *FASB Statement No. 15* and *FASB Statement No. 114*. Some of the principles are "mirror images" of those for the debtor, while others are not.

Equity or Asset Exchange

The accounting by the creditor (e.g., the bank) for a troubled debt restructuring that involves an equity or asset exchange is a "mirror image" of the accounting by the debtor. These principles are defined by *FASB Statement No. 15*. Thus, when a creditor receives an equity interest or asset to satisfy the receivable, **the creditor records the equity or asset investment at fair value, eliminates the carrying value of the receivable, and recognizes a loss.**

Exhibit 13-8 illustrates the journal entries by which the Tenth National Bank records the equity and asset exchanges for the troubled debt restructuring of the Chapin Company we discussed earlier. It is helpful to observe the mirror image by contrasting the bank's journal entries with those of the Chapin Company shown earlier.

EXHIBIT 13-8	Creditor Journal Entries for Troubled Debt Restructuring		
Equity Exchange			
12/31/04	Investment in Chapin	875,000	
	Loss on Restructured Loan	303,073	
	Notes Receivable		1,100,000
	Interest Receivable		78,073
Asset Exchange			
12/31/04	Land	800,000	
	Loss on Restructured Loan	378,073	
	Notes Receivable		1,100,000
	Interest Receivable		78,073

Modification of Terms

The accounting principles for a modification of terms are *not* a mirror image because the creditor must recognize a new value for the loan. **The investment in the restructured loan is valued by discounting the total future cash flows specified by the new contractual terms to their present value.** A loss is recognized as the difference between the present value of the future cash flows and the carrying value of the receivable. **The effective interest rate used in the present value calculation is the original (contractual) interest rate on the loan** (i.e., the same interest rate used for a loan impairment), and *not* the rate specified in the restructuring agreement.[25]

---

25. "Accounting by Creditors for Impairment of a Loan," *FASB Statement No. 114, op. cit.*

A loan whose terms are modified in a troubled debt restructuring usually will have been identified as impaired in a previous period. We discussed the accounting principles for an impaired loan earlier in the chapter.

To illustrate the accounting for a modification of terms in a troubled debt restructuring, consider the first Chapin Company example that we discussed earlier. Assume that the loan was from the Tenth National Bank and that the bank has *not* recognized a previous impairment. The bank's note receivable is $1,100,000 and the accrued interest is $78,073. On December 31, 2004, the bank restructures the note so that the new principal is $1,000,000, payable in 5 years, with an interest rate of 8% (i.e., the annual interest payment is $80,000). Since 10% is the original interest rate on the loan to the Chapin Company, the loan is valued as follows:

$$\text{Present value of principal} = \$1,000,000 \times \text{present value of a single sum for}$$
$$5 \text{ years at } 10\% \text{ (from Appendix D)}$$
$$= \$1,000,000 \times 0.620921$$
$$= \$620,921.00$$
$$\text{Present value of interest} = \$80,000 \times \text{present value of an annuity for}$$
$$5 \text{ years at } 10\% \text{ (from Appendix D)}$$
$$= \$80,000 \times 3.790787$$
$$= \$303,262.96$$
$$\text{Value of the restructured loan} = \$620,921.00 + \$303,262.96$$
$$= \$924,183.96$$

On December 31, 2004, the bank records a loss of $253,889.04 ($1,178,073 − $924,183.96) on the restructuring as follows:

Loss on Restructured Loan	253,889.04	
Interest Receivable		78,073.00
Notes Receivable		175,816.04

The carrying value of the Notes Receivable is now $924,183.96 ($1,100,000 − $175,816.04).

In subsequent periods, the bank earns interest at the original rate of 10% applied to the current carrying value. The bank recognizes interest revenue for 2005 of $92,418.40 (10% × $924,183.96) on December 31, 2005 as follows:

Cash	80,000.00	
Notes Receivable	12,418.40	
Interest Revenue		92,418.40

After five years of recording interest under the effective interest method, the Notes Receivable will grow to the principal amount of $1,000,000.

For another illustration, consider the second Chapin Company example, where the stated interest rate is reduced to 3% (i.e., the annual interest payment is $30,000) by the Tenth National Bank. Since the original interest rate for the loan is 10%, the bank computes the value of the loan as follows:

$$\text{Present value of principal} = \$1,000,000 \times \text{present value of a single sum for}$$
$$5 \text{ years at } 10\% \text{ (from Appendix D)}$$
$$= \$1,000,000 \times 0.620921$$
$$= \$620,921.00$$
$$\text{Present value of interest} = \$30,000 \times \text{present value of an annuity for}$$
$$5 \text{ years at } 10\% \text{ (from Appendix D)}$$
$$= \$30,000 \times 3.790787$$
$$= \$113,723.61$$
$$\text{Value of the restructured loan} = \$620,921.00 + \$113,723.61$$
$$= \$734,644.61$$

On December 31, 2004, the bank records a loss of $443,428.39 ($1,178,073 − $734,644.61) on the restructuring as follows:

Loss on Restructured Loan	443,428.39	
Interest Receivable		78,073.00
Notes Receivable		365,355.39

The carrying value of the Notes Receivable is now $734,644.61 ($1,100,000 − $365,355.39).

Since the bank earns interest at the original rate of 10%, it recognizes interest revenue for 2005 of $73,464.46 (10% × $734,644.61) on December 31, 2005 as follows:

Cash	30,000.00	
Notes Receivable	43,464.46	
Interest Revenue		73,464.46

After five years of recording interest under the effective interest method, Notes Receivable will grow to the principal amount of $1,000,000.

It is important to note the difference between the accounting by the debtor and creditor for a modification of terms. As we discussed earlier, the debtor does *not* record the liability at a present value and, therefore, either recognizes no interest expense at all or recognizes an interest expense that is based on a below-market rate that was never part of the contractual agreement. In contrast, the creditor records the receivable at a present value and, therefore, recognizes interest revenue at the original contractual rate. The FASB may eventually require that the debtor also use a present value.

Equity or Asset Exchange Combined with Modification of Terms

When an equity interest or asset is received and a modification of terms is made, the creditor records the equity or asset first at its fair value. It then discounts the future cash receipts to their present value at the effective (contractual) rate of interest. It records a loss as the difference between the carrying value of the receivable and the sum of the fair value of the equity interest or asset plus the present value of the future cash flows.

Following is a summary of the accounting principles we have discussed:

Modification of Terms		Equity or Asset Exchange	
Debtor	Creditor	Debtor	Creditor
(a) If undiscounted cash flows > carrying value, no gain and impute new interest rate	Compute present value using the original (contractual) rate	Record at fair value, recognize gain	Record at fair value, recognize loss
(b) If undiscounted cash flows < carrying value, recognize gain (no interest recognized)			

CONCEPTUAL EVALUATION OF ACCOUNTING FOR TROUBLED DEBT RESTRUCTURINGS

When *FASB Statement No. 15* was issued, many accountants and financial statement users criticized the accounting principles for the modification of terms for a troubled debt restructuring. With the issuance of *FASB Statement No. 114*, these criticisms apply only to the accounting by the debtor because there is no longer a mirror image between the debtor and creditor, as we discussed earlier. The critics argue that the procedures for the debtor (i.e., a limited or no gain) lead to inconsistencies in recording events that have similar economic substance (i.e., a modification of terms and an asset or equity exchange). They view a modification of terms as an economic event that should be recorded at a present value. In other words, they argue that the debtor should follow the procedures that are now required for the creditor. However, as we discussed earlier in the chapter for loan impairment, the *Statement* was adopted by a 5-to-2 vote with the two dissenters arguing that the fair value of the loan should be recognized.

At the time that *FASB Statement No. 15* was issued, it was widely believed that the rules to be followed by the creditor in a modification of terms were the result of lobbying by financial institutions. These institutions argued that the recognition of large losses under the fair value approach would undermine the public's confidence in the banking system and have an adverse effect on the economy. A counter-argument was that the nonrecognition of losses enabled banks to continue in business longer than they should have, resulting in larger payments by taxpayers to "bail out" failing banks.

Since these original rules for the creditor have now been superseded, it seems logical that the rules for the debtor should also be modified. However, some supporters of the original rules point out that the FASB was just being conservative in its approach so as to minimize the gain recognized by a financially distressed debtor in a restructuring. Therefore, the choice of the accounting principle for debtors is based on whether a person believes that conservatism or the recognition of fair value is more important to external decision makers.

APPENDIX 2: SERIAL BONDS

In the main part of this chapter, we focused on accounting for bonds in which the entire face value was due on one maturity date. Bonds also may contain provisions that require the issuer to **repay the face value in periodic installments over a number of years;** these bonds are termed **serial bonds.** Serial bonds may be especially attractive in cases where the bond issue is used to finance a particular project, because the issuer can use the yearly cash flow from that project to retire the bond issue.

RECORDING THE ISSUANCE AND INTEREST EXPENSE OF SERIAL BONDS

13 Account for serial bonds.

Serial bonds may sell at a premium or discount because of differences between the prevailing market rate and the stated rate of interest. Since the bonds mature over a number of periods and interest rates depend partly on the terms of the issue, some accountants have questioned the use of a single interest rate to record the initial issue of serial bonds. There are, however, no generally accepted principles for determining the different interest rates to assign to each individual installment, so it is assumed that they all yield the same rate of interest. Thus, a company records the initial issuance of serial bonds in the same manner as other bonds. That is, it records the entire face value in a Bonds Payable account and any discount or premium in a separate contra or adjunct account. After issuance, it computes interest expense and any premium or discount amortization on serial bonds by the **effective interest method.** Alternatively, it may use a method similar to the straight-line method, known as the **bonds outstanding method.** This method results in recording an amount of discount or premium amortization proportionate to the face value of the bonds outstanding. Under this method, if $400,000 of 13% serial bonds are to be repaid in four $100,000 installments, a proportionate (fractional) share of any premium or discount is amortized over the number of periods each installment is outstanding. The denominator of this fraction is derived by summing the face values of the bonds outstanding at the *beginning* of each period over the life of the entire issue. The numerator of this fraction is the face value of bonds outstanding at the *beginning* of each period.

To illustrate these two methods, assume that the Wallace Corporation issues $400,000 of serial bonds with a 13% stated rate of interest for $410,460.92 on January 1, 2002. The company is to repay the bonds in four semiannual $100,000 installments beginning June 30, 2004 and to pay interest semiannually. The $410,460.92 selling price of this serial bond issue reflects a yield of 12%, as we show in the following calculations using factors from Appendix D:

Present Value of Principal
Installment due 6/30/04
    Present value of $100,000 ($n = 5$, $i = 0.06$) × 0.747258 $74,725.80
Installment due 12/31/04
    Present value of $100,000 ($n = 6$, $i = 0.06$) × 0.704961   70,496.10
Installment due 6/30/05
    Present value of $100,000 ($n = 7$, $i = 0.06$) × 0.665057   66,505.70
Installment due 12/31/05
    Present value of $100,000 ($n = 8$, $i = 0.06$) × 0.627412   62,741.20
        Present Value of Principal $274,468.80

Present Value of Interest Payments
Installment due 6/30/04
    Present Value of an annuity of $6,500 ($n = 5$, $i = 0.06$) × 4.212364 $27,380.37
Installment due 12/31/04
    Present value of an annuity of $6,500 ($n = 6$, $i = 0.06$) × 4.917324   31,962.61
Installment due 6/30/05
    Present value of an annuity of $6,500 ($n = 7$, $i = 0.06$) × 5.582381   36,285.48
Installment due 12/31/05
    Present value of an annuity of $6,500 ($n = 8$, $i = 0.06$) × 6.209794   40,363.66
        Present value of Interest   135,992.12
Selling Price of Serial Bonds $410,460.92

The company records the issuance as follows:

Cash	**410,460.92**	
Bonds Payable		**400,000.00**
Premium on Bonds Payable		**10,460.92**

Exhibit 13-9 shows the use of the bonds outstanding (straight-line) method of amortization for these serial bonds. Exhibit 13-10 illustrates the use of the effective interest method for the same bonds.

In both Exhibits 13-9 and 13-10, the interest expense debit column reflects the interest that Wallace records for each period. The decreasing amounts of interest expense for the semiannual periods in 2004 and 2005 are attributable to the fact that the company makes partial repayments during these periods. The cash credit column during these periods also reflects these repayments. For example, on December 31, 2004, the company records the interest expense and partial retirement of the bonds (using straight-line amortization) as follows:

Bonds Payable	**100,000.00**	
Premium on Bonds Payable	**1,207.03**	
Interest Expense	**18,292.97**	
Cash		**119,500.00**

EARLY REDEMPTION OF SERIAL BONDS

If a company redeems bonds from any individual series prior to their maturity date, it eliminates the amount of unamortized discount or premium associated with these bonds. When the bonds outstanding method is used, this amount can be determined from the amortization table by applying the following formula:

$$\frac{\text{Number of Periods Before Maturity of Issue} \times \text{Par Value of Bonds Redeemed}}{\text{Total of Bonds Outstanding Column}} \times \text{Total Premium or Discount}$$

EXHIBIT 13-9   Interest Expense and Premium Amortization Schedule for Serial Bonds: *Straight-Line (Bonds Outstanding) Method*

Date	Fraction of Premium Amortized[a]	Cash Credit[b]	Premium Amortization Debit[c]	Interest Expense Debit[d]	Unamortized Premium[e]	Bonds Payable Debit[f]	Bonds Outstanding[g]	Book Value of Bonds[h]
1/01/02					$10,460.92		$ 400,000	$410,460.92
6/30/02	$4/26$	$ 26,000	$1,609.37	$24,390.63	8,851.55		400,000	408,851.55
12/31/02	$4/26$	26,000	1,609.37	24,390.63	7,242.18		400,000	407,242.18
6/30/03	$4/26$	26,000	1,609.37	24,390.63	5,632.81		400,000	405,632.81
12/31/03	$4/26$	26,000	1,609.37	24,390.63	4,023.44		400,000	404,023.44
6/30/04	$4/26$	126,000	1,609.37	24,390.63	2,414.07	$100,000	300,000	302,414.07
12/31/04	$3/26$	119,500	1,207.03	18,292.97	1,207.04	100,000	200,000	201,207.04
6/30/05	$2/26$	113,000	804.69	12,195.31	402.35	100,000	100,000	100,402.35
12/31/05	$1/26$	106,500	402.35[i]	6,097.65	-0-	100,000	-0-	-0-
	$26/26$						$2,600,000	

a. Bonds outstanding at beginning of each period ÷ sum of bonds outstanding, or $400,000 ÷ $2,600,000 in the first period.
b. Bonds outstanding ($400,000 in first period) × interest rate (0.13) × 6/12 + installment payment (amount from footnote *f*).
c. $10,460.92 × fraction from footnote *a*.
d. Amount from footnote *b* − amount from footnote *c* − installment payment.
e. Previous balance − amount from footnote *c*.
f. Installment payment.
g. Face value − amount from footnote *f*.
h. Amount from footnote *e* + amount from footnote *g*.
i. Difference due to $0.01 rounding error.

EXHIBIT 13-10 Interest Expense and Premium Amortization Schedule for Serial Bonds: *Effective Interest Method: 13% Bonds Sold to Yield 12%*

Date	Cash Credit[a]	Interest Expense Debit[b]	Premium Amortization Debit[c]	Unamortized Premium[d]	Bonds Payable Debit[e]	Book Value of Bonds[f]
1/01/02				$10,460.92		$410,460.92
6/30/02	$ 26,000	$24,627.66	$1,372.34	9,088.58		409,088.58
12/31/02	26,000	24,545.31	1,454.69	7,633.89		407,633.89
6/30/03	26,000	24,458.03	1,541.97	6,091.92		406,091.92
12/31/03	26,000	24,365.52	1,634.48	4,457.44		404,457.44
6/30/04	126,000	24,267.45	1,732.55	2,724.89	$100,000	302,724.89
12/31/04	119,500	18,163.49	1,336.51	1,388.38	100,000	201,388.38
6/30/05	113,000	12,083.30	916.70	471.68	100,000	100,471.68
12/31/05	106,500	6,028.32[g]	471.68	-0-	100,000	-0-

a. Bonds outstanding ($400,000 in first period) × interest rate (0.13) × 6/12 + installment payment (amount from footnote *e*).
b. Previous balance of footnote *f* × 0.12 × 6/12.
c. Amount from footnote *a* − amount from footnote *b* − installment payment.
d. Previous balance − amount from footnote *c*.
e. Installment payment.
f. Previous balance − amount from footnote *c* − amount from footnote *e*.
g. Difference due to $0.02 rounding error.

To illustrate, assume that on January 1, 2004 the $100,000 of the Wallace Corporation bonds due December 31, 2005 are redeemed. The unamortized premium associated with this redemption is calculated as:

$$\frac{4 \text{ periods} \times \$100,000}{\$2,600,000} \times \$10,460.92 = \$1,609.37$$

When the company records the redemption, it debits the Unamortized Premium account for $1,609.37, and calculates a gain or loss on the transaction by comparing the book value of the bonds redeemed with the redemption price. In addition, it reduces the amount of premium amortization shown in Exhibit 13-9 by $402.34 ($1,609.37 ÷ 4) for each semiannual period in 2004 and 2005.

When a company uses the effective interest method, the book value of the bonds being retired is the present value of the future cash payments required (principal and interest) on the bonds being retired at that time. The company calculates the book value by discounting the future principal and interest payments to the retirement date, using the effective interest rate. It computes and reports the gain or loss as we discussed in the preceding paragraph, and eliminates the book value of the retired bonds.

SUMMARY

At the beginning of the chapter, we identified several objectives you would accomplish after reading the chapter. The objectives are listed below, each followed by a brief summary of the key points in the chapter discussion.

1. **Explain the reasons for issuing long-term liabilities.** The five basic reasons why a company might issue long-term debt rather than offer other types of securities are as follows: (1) debt may be the only available source of funds, (2) debt financing may have a lower cost, (3) debt financing offers an income tax advantage, (4) the voting privilege is not shared and (5) debt financing offers the opportunity for leverage.
2. **Understand the characteristics of bonds payable.** A bond is a type of note in which a company agrees to pay the holder the face value at the maturity date and usually to pay interest periodically at a specified rate on the face value. The face (or par) value is the amount of money that the issuer agrees to pay at maturity. The maturity date is the date on which the issuer of the bond agrees to pay the face value to the holder. The contract rate is the rate at which the issuer of the bonds agrees to pay interest each period until maturity.

3. **Record the issuance of bonds.** At the time of sale, the company records the face value of the bonds in a Bonds Payable account and it records any premium or discount in a separate account entitled Premium on Bonds Payable or Discount on Bonds Payable. A premium account is an adjunct account and a discount account is a contra account.

4. **Amortize discounts and premiums under the straight-line method.** Any discount or premium is amortized to interest expense in equal amounts each period during the life of the bonds. The interest expense is the sum of the cash payment plus the discount amortization or minus the premium amortization.

5. **Compute the selling price of bonds.** The selling price of a bond issue is calculated by summing the present value of the principal and interest payments discounted at the effective interest (yield) rate.

6. **Amortize discounts and premiums under the effective interest method.** The effective interest method applies the semiannual yield to the book value of the bonds at the beginning of each successive semiannual period to determine the interest expense for that period. The discount or premium amortization is the difference between the interest expense and the cash payment.

7. **Explain extinguishment of liabilities.** A liability is extinguished for financial reporting purposes when either (1) the debtor pays the creditor and is relieved of its obligation for the liability, or (2) the debtor is released legally from being the primary obligor under the liability.

8. **Understand bonds with equity characteristics.** A company may issue bonds that allow creditors to ultimately become stockholders by attaching stock warrants to the bonds or including a conversion feature. In either case, the investor has acquired the right to receive interest on the bonds and the right to acquire common stock and to participate in the potential appreciation of the market value of the company's common stock.

9. **Account for long-term notes payable.** A note payable is recorded at its present value, and the effective interest method is used to record the subsequent interest. A note exchanged for property, goods, or services is recorded at the fair value of the property, goods, or services, or the fair value of the note, whichever is more reliable. If neither of these fair values is determinable, the note is recorded at its present value by discounting the future cash flow(s) using the incremental interest rate of the borrower.

10. **Understand the disclosure of long-term liabilities.** A company must disclose many characteristics of its long-term debt, including the book value, interest rates, maturity dates, scheduled repayments for each of the next five years, interest expense, interest paid, and capitalized interest. It normally makes these disclosures in the notes to its financial statements.

11. **Account for long-term notes receivable including impairment of a loan.** A note receivable is recorded at the fair value of the property, goods, or services or the fair value of the note, whichever is more reliable. If neither of these values is reliable, the note is recorded at its present value by using the borrower's incremental interest rate. A loan is impaired if it is probable that the creditor will be unable to collect all amounts due according to the contractual terms of the loan agreement. When a loan is impaired, the creditor company computes the present value of the expected future cash flows of the impaired loan using the effective interest rate, which is the original (contractual) interest rate on the loan. It records an expense for the difference between the carrying value and the present value, and recognizes future interest revenue based on the contractual rate applied to the new carrying (present) value.

12. **Understand troubled debt restructurings (Appendix).** A troubled debt restructuring occurs when a creditor for economic or legal reasons related to a debtor's financial difficulties grants a concession to the debtor that it would not otherwise consider. A troubled debt restructuring may include a modification of terms, the issuance or other granting of an equity interest, and the transfer of an asset.

13. **Account for serial bonds (Appendix).** Serial bonds require the issuer to repay the face value in periodic installments over a number of years. The initial issuance of the bonds is recorded in the same manner as other bonds. Subsequently, the company computes the interest expense and any premium or discount amortization by the effective interest method. Alternatively, it may use a method similar to the straight-line method known as the bonds outstanding method.

QUESTIONS

Q13-1 Why may a company that requires additional funds choose to issue long-term liabilities rather than equity securities?

Q13-2 What is a *bond*? Define *face value, maturity date, contract rate, bond certificate,* and *bond indenture.*

Q13-3 Distinguish between mortgage and debenture bonds.

Q13-4 Distinguish between registered and coupon bonds.

Q13-5 What are callable bonds? Convertible bonds?

Q13-6 Why does the stated (contract) rate and the effective rate (yield) of interest on bonds frequently differ?

Q13-7 Why do bond discounts and bond premiums arise at the time of sale?

Q13-8 Distinguish between bond premiums or discounts and bond issue costs.

Q13-9 Why does the recorded amount of interest expense for the first interest payment differ from the expense recorded for other interest payments when bonds are issued between interest payment dates?

Q13-10 What two methods may a company use to allocate a premium or discount over the life of a bond issue? Briefly describe each method.

Q13-11 How is the amount of interest expense a company records each period affected by the amortization of a bond discount using the straight-line method?

Q13-12 How is the amount of interest expense a company records each period affected by the amortization of a bond premium using the straight-line method?

Q13-13 How is the amount of proceeds from a bond issue determined once the market (yield) rate of interest is specified?

Q13-14 What is a call provision? Why do companies often include call provisions on bond issues?

Q13-15 Distinguish between bond retirements and bond refundings.

Q13-16 What are the three alternatives that could be used to account for gains or losses on bond refundings?

What reasons support each of these methods? Which method did the APB finally favor? Why?

Q13-17 Why does a company issue a bond with detachable warrants (rights)? At what value is each of these securities recorded at the time of the bond issuance?

Q13-18 What are convertible bonds? Why would a company issue convertible debt?

Q13-19 What two alternative methods are available to account for the issuance of convertible debt? What method did the APB finally require? Why?

Q13-20 When a company exchanges a long-term non-interest-bearing note for cash and no interest rate is stated, how does it determine the effective interest?

Q13-21 Describe the steps necessary for a company to determine the value at which to record a non-interest-bearing note payable exchanged for property, goods, or services.

Q13-22 What is the incremental interest rate of a borrower? When and for what calculations is this rate used if a company exchanges a note for property, goods, or services?

Q13-23 (*Appendix 1*) When does a troubled debt restructuring occur? What are three conditions a troubled debt restructuring may involve?

CASES

C O M M U N I C A T I O N

C13-1 Amortization of Bond Premium or Discount

The appropriate method of amortizing a premium or discount on issuance of bonds is the effective interest method.

Required

1. What is the effective interest method of amortization and how is it different from and similar to the straight-line method of amortization?
2. Explain how a company computes amortization using the effective interest method, and why and how do amounts obtained using the effective interest method differ from amounts computed under the straight-line method. (*AICPA adapted*)

C13-2 Various Bond Characteristics

One way for a corporation to accomplish long-term financing is through the issuance of long-term debt instruments in the form of bonds.

Required

1. Explain how to account for the proceeds from bonds issued with detachable stock purchase warrants.
2. Contrast a serial bond with a term (straight) bond.

3. For a 5-year term bond issued at a premium, why is the amortization in the first year of the life of the bond different using the interest method of amortization instead of the straight-line method? Include in your discussion whether the amount of amortization in the first year of the life of the bond is higher or lower using the interest method instead of the straight-line method.
4. When a company sells a bond issue between interest dates at a discount, what journal entry does it make and how is the subsequent amortization of bond discount affected? Include in your discussion an explanation of how the amounts of each debit and credit are determined.
5. Explain how to account for and classify the gain or loss from the reacquisition of a long-term bond prior to its maturity. (*AICPA adapted*)

C13-3 Convertible and Nonconvertible Bonds

On February 1, 2001 Aubrey Company sold its 5-year, $1,000 par value, 9% bonds, which were convertible at the option of the investor into Aubrey Company common stock at a ratio of 10 shares of common stock for each bond. Aubrey Company sold the convertible bonds at a discount. Interest is payable annually each February 1. On February 1, 2004 Mel Company, an investor in the Aubrey Company convertible bonds, tendered 1,000 bonds for conversion into 10,000 shares of Aubrey Company common stock, which had a market value of $110 per share at the date of the conversion.

On May 1, 2004 Aubrey Company sold its 10-year, $1,000 par value, 10% nonconvertible term bonds dated April 1, 2004. Interest is payable semiannually, and the first interest payment date is October 1, 2004. Due to market conditions, the company sold the bonds at an effective interest rate (yield) of 12%.

Required

1. Explain how Aubrey Company accounts for the conversion of the convertible bonds into common stock under both the book value and market value methods. Discuss the rationale for each method.
2. Were the nonconvertible term bonds sold at par, at a discount, or at a premium? Discuss the rationale for your answer.
3. Identify and discuss the effects on Aubrey Company's 2004 income statement associated with the nonconvertible term bonds. (*AICPA adapted*)

C13-4 Bond Refunding

A company's gains or losses from the early extinguishment of debt theoretically can be accounted for in three ways:

(a) Amortized over remaining life of old debt
(b) Amortized over the life of the new debt issue
(c) Recognized in the period of extinguishment

Required

1. Discuss the supporting arguments for each of the three theoretical methods of accounting for gains and losses from the early extinguishment of debt.
2. Which of the preceding methods is generally accepted? (*AICPA adapted*)

C13-5 Serial Bonds (Appendix 2)

On November 1, 2004 Janine Company sold directly to underwriters at a lump-sum price, $1,000 face value, 9% serial bonds dated November 1, 2004 at an effective annual interest rate (yield) of 11%. A total of 25% of these serial bonds are due on November 1, 2006, a total of 35% on November 1, 2007, and a total of 40% on November 1, 2008. Interest is payable semiannually and the first interest payment date is May 1, 2005. Janine uses the interest method of amortization and incurred bond issue costs in preparing and selling the bond issue.

Required

1. How does the company determine the market price of the serial bonds?
2. How does the company present all items related to the serial bonds, except for bond issue costs, in a balance sheet prepared immediately after it sold the serial bond issue?
3. How does the company determine the amount of interest expense for the serial bonds for 2004? (*AICPA adapted*)

CREATIVE AND CRITICAL THINKING

C13-6 Recording Convertible Debt

Zakin Co. recently issued $1,000,000 face value, 10%, 30-year subordinated debentures at 97. The debentures are redeemable at 103 upon demand by the issuer at any date upon 30 days notice 10 years after the issue. The debentures are convertible into $10 par value common stock of the Company at the conversion price of $12.50 per share for each $500 or multiple thereof of the principal amount of the debentures.

Required

1. Explain how the conversion feature of convertible debt has a value to the:
   a. Issuer
   b. Purchaser
2. Management of Zakin Co. has suggested that in recording the issuance of the debentures, it should assign a portion of the proceeds to the conversion feature.
   a. What are the arguments for according separate accounting recognition to the conversion feature of the debentures?
   b. What are the arguments supporting accounting for the convertible debentures as a single element?

3. Assume that the company assigns no value to the conversion feature upon issue of the debentures. Assume further that 5 years after issue, debentures with a face value of $100,000 and book value of $97,500 are tendered for conversion on an interest payment date when the market price of the debentures is 104 and the common stock is selling at $14 per share and that the Company records the conversion as follows:

Bonds Payable	100,000	
Bond Discount		2,500
Common Stock		80,000
Premium on		
Common Stock		17,500

Discuss the propriety of the preceding accounting treatment. (*AICPA adapted*)

C13-7 Debt with Detachable Stock Warrants

Incurring long-term debt with an arrangement whereby lenders receive an option to buy common stock during all or a portion of the time the debt is outstanding is a frequently used corporate financing practice. In some situations, the result is achieved through the issuance of convertible bonds; in others, the debt instruments and the warrants to buy stock are separate.

Required

1. a. Explain the differences that exist in current accounting for original proceeds of the issuance of convertible bonds, and of debt instruments with separate warrants to purchase common stock.
   b. Explain the underlying rationale for the differences described in Requirement 1a.
   c. Summarize the arguments that have been presented for the alternative accounting treatment.
2. At the start of the year, AB Company issued $6 million of 7% notes along with warrants to buy 400,000 shares of its $10 par value common stock at $18 per share. The notes mature over the next 10 years, starting one year from date of issuance, with annual maturities of $600,000. At the time, AB had 3,200,000 shares of common stock outstanding and the market price was $23 per share. The company received $6,680,000 for the notes and the warrants. For AB Company, 7% was a relatively low borrowing rate. If offered alone, at this time, the notes would have been issued at a 20 to 24% discount. Prepare journal entries for the issuance of the notes and warrants for the cash consideration received. (*AICPA adapted*)

C13-8 Long-Term Notes Payable

Business transactions often involve the exchange of property, goods, or services for notes or similar instruments that may stipulate no interest rate or an interest rate that varies from prevailing rates.

Required

1. When a company exchanges a note for property, goods, or services, what value does it place on the note:
   a. If it bears interest at a reasonable rate and is issued in a bargained transaction entered into at arm's length? Explain.
   b. If it bears no interest and/or is not issued in a bargained transaction entered into at arm's length? Explain.
2. If the recorded value of a note differs from the face value:
   a. Explain how the company should account for the difference.
   b. Explain how the company should present this difference in the financial statements. (*AICPA adapted*)

C13-9 Bonds: Sale, Interest, and Recall

On March 2, 2004 Wesley Company sold its 5-year, $1,000 face value, 8% bonds dated March 2, 2004 at an effective annual interest rate (yield) of 10%. Interest is payable semiannually and the first interest payment date is September 2, 2004. Wesley uses the interest method of amortization and incurred bond issue costs in preparing and selling the bond issue. Wesley can call the bonds at 101 at any time on or after March 2, 2005.

Required

1. a. How does the company determine the selling price of the bonds?
   b. Specify how the company presents all items related to the bonds in a balance sheet prepared immediately after the bond issue is sold.
2. What items related to the bond issue does Wesley include in its 2004 income statement, and how does it determine each?
3. Will the amount of bond discount amortization using the interest method of amortization be lower in the second or third year of the life of the bond issue? Why?
4. Assuming that the bonds are called in and retired on March 2, 2005, how does Wesley report the retirement of the bonds on the 2005 income statement? (*AICPA adapted*)

C13-10 Bonds: Issuance, Expense, and Conversion

On January 1, 2003 Brewster Company issued 2,000 of its 5-year, $1,000 face value, 11% bonds dated January 1 at an effective annual interest rate (yield) of 9%. Brewster uses the effective interest method of amortization. On December 31, 2004 Brewster extinguished the 2,000 bonds early through acquisition in the open market for $1,980,000.

On July 1, 2003 Brewster issued 5,000 of its 6-year, $1,000 face value, 10% convertible bonds dated July 1 at an effective annual interest rate (yield) of 12%. The bonds are convertible at the option of the investor into Brewster's common stock at a ratio of 10 shares of common stock for each bond. Brewster uses the effective interest method of amortization. On July 1, 2004 an investor in Brewster's convertible bonds tendered 1,500 bonds for conversion into 15,000 shares of Brewster's common stock, which had a market value of $105 per share at the date of the conversion.

Required

1. a. Were the 11% bonds issued at par, at a discount, or at a premium? Why?
   b. Is the amount of interest expense for the 11% bonds using the effective interest method of amortization higher in the first or second year of the life of the bond issue? Why?
2. a. How is a gain or loss on early extinguishment of debt determined? Does the early extinguishment of the 11% bonds result in a gain or loss? Why?
   b. How does Brewster report the early extinguishment of the 11% bonds on the 2004 income statement?
3. a. Does recording the conversion of the 10% convertible bonds into common stock under the book value method affect net income? What is the rationale for the book value method?
   b. Does recording the conversion of the 10% convertible bonds into common stock under the market value method affect net income? What is the rationale for the market value method? (*AICPA adapted*)

C13-11 Analyzing Coca-Cola's Long-Term Debt Disclosures

Refer to the financial statements and related notes of the Coca-Cola Company in Appendix A of this book.

Required

1. What was the difference between the interest expense and interest paid in 2001?
2. How much long-term debt will mature in 2003?
3. Assuming no long-term debt was issued or retired during 2001, which debt issues were issued at par? At a premium? At a discount?
4. Was the current yield at December 31, 2001 on the company's long-term debt the same as, greater, or less than the average yield at issuance? At December 31, 2000?

C13-12 Ethics and Long-Term Liabilities

You are an accountant for the Virden Company, which has two items of long-term convertible debt on its balance sheet. The president of the company calls you into his office and says, "We are too leveraged. So, you remember that convertible debt we issued at the beginning of the year? Let's figure out the value of the conversion feature and assign that to equity so that we can reduce the amount we report as debt. And I have also been thinking about that convertible debt we issued at par 5 years ago. If you remember, each $1,000 bond is convertible into 25 shares. Now that our shares are trading at $70, obviously that is no longer debt. So let's classify that debt as equity now."

Required From financial reporting and ethical perspectives, discuss the issues raised by this situation.

R E S E A R C H

C13-13 Researching GAAP

You are auditing the York Company when you come across a note receivable signed by the president of a company that is a major supplier. The note has a face value of $100,000, is payable to the York Company, is dated January 1, 2004, and is payable January 1, 2005. The interest rate on the note is 1%. You ask the president of the York Company about the note and she responds "That is fine. We lent him some money to help him through a difficult divorce. We wanted him to pay interest, but he couldn't afford the going rate of 8%. So how do you think we should account for the note?"

Required

1. Research the related generally accepted accounting principles and prepare a short memo to the president that answers her question. Cite your references and applicable paragraph numbers.
2. How would your answer change if the interest rate on the note was 16%?
3. Do these valuation issues also create ethical issues?

C13-14 Researching GAAP

The Wales Company has a $90,000, non-interest-bearing 4-year note receivable from the Spenser Company that was received on July 1, 2004 when Wales sold a used machine. The machine was custom made five years ago, cost the Wales Company $100,000, and was being depreciated over a 10-year life by the straight-line method to a zero residual value. As the accountant for the Wales Company you know that *APB Opinion No. 21* requires that the note be discounted using the borrower's interest rate. You phone the accountant for the Spenser Company and ask her what that company's incremental borrowing rate is. She responds cheerfully, "Sorry, I have no idea. We never borrow money because the owner provides all the capital we need." The president asks you to resolve this issue.

Required Research the related generally accepted accounting principles and prepare a short memo to the president that answers her question. Cite your references and applicable paragraph numbers.

MULTIPLE CHOICE

Select the best answer for each of the following.

M13-1 Should the following bond issue costs be expensed as incurred?

	Legal Fees	Underwriting Costs
a.	No	No
b.	No	Yes
c.	Yes	No
d.	Yes	Yes

M13-2 On December 31, 2003 Dumont Corporation had outstanding 8%, $2,000,000 face value convertible bonds maturing on December 31, 2007. Interest is payable annually on December 31. Each $1,000 bond is convertible into 60 shares of Dumont's $10 par value common stock. The unamortized balance on December 31, 2004 in the Premium on Bonds Payable account was $45,000. On December 31, 2004 an individual holding 200 of the bonds exercised the conversion privilege when the market value of Dumont's common stock was $18 per share. Using the book value method, Dumont's entry to record the conversion should include a credit to additional paid-in capital of

a. $80,000　　　c. $96,000
b. $84,500　　　d. $125,000

M13-3 On January 1, 2004 when the market rate for bond interest was 14%, Luba Corporation issued bonds in the face amount of $500,000, with interest at 12% payable semiannually. The bonds mature on December 31, 2014, and were issued at a discount of $53,180. How much of the discount should be amortized by the effective interest method at July 1, 2004?

    a. $1,277   c. $3,191
    b. $2,659   d. $3,723

M13-4 When the cash proceeds from a bond issued with detachable stock purchase warrants exceed the sum of the par value of the bonds and the fair value of the warrants, the excess should be credited to

    a. Additional paid-in capital
    b. Retained earnings
    c. Premium on bonds payable
    d. Detachable stock warrants outstanding

M13-5 When the issuer of bonds exercises the call provision to retire the bonds, the excess of the cash paid over the carrying amount of the bonds should be recognized separately as a(n)

    a. Extraordinary loss
    b. Extraordinary gain
    c. Loss from continuing operations
    d. Loss from discontinued operations

M13-6 Peterson Company has a $500,000, 15%, 3-year note dated January 1, 2003, payable to Forest National Bank. On December 31, 2004 the bank agreed to settle the note and unpaid interest of $75,000 for 2004 for $50,000 cash and marketable securities having a current market value of $375,000. Peterson's acquisition cost of the securities is $385,000. Ignoring income taxes, what amount should Peterson report as a gain from the debt restructuring in its 2004 income statement?

    a. $65,000   c. $140,000
    b. $75,000   d. $150,000

M13-7 When the interest payment dates of a bond are May 1 and November 1, and a bond issue is sold on June 1, the amount of cash received by the issuer will be

    a. Increased by accrued interest from June 1 to - November 1
    b. Increased by accrued interest from May 1 to June 1
    c. Decreased by accrued interest from June 1 to November 1
    d. Decreased by accrued interest from May 1 to June 1

M13-8 On January 1, 2004 Parke Company borrowed $360,000 from a major customer evidenced by a non-interest-bearing note due in 3 years. Parke agreed to supply the customer's inventory needs for the loan period at lower than market price. At the 12% imputed interest rate for this type of loan, the present value of the note is $255,000 at January 1, 2004. What amount of interest expense should be included in Parke's 2004 income statement?

    a. $43,200   c. $30,600
    b. $35,000   d. $0

M13-9 For the issuer of a 10-year term bond, the amount of amortization using the effective interest method would increase each year if the bond was sold at a

	Discount	Premium
a.	No	No
b.	Yes	Yes
c.	No	Yes
d.	Yes	No

M13-10 On April 1, 2004 Girard Corporation issued at 98 plus accrued interest, 200 of its 10%, $1,000 bonds. The bonds are dated January 1, 2004, and mature on January 1, 2014. Interest is payable semiannually on January 1 and July 1. From the bond issuance Girard would realize net cash receipts of

    a. $191,000   c. $198,500
    b. $196,000   d. $201,000

(AICPA adapted)

EXERCISES

E13-1   *Recording Bond Issue and Interest Payments*   The Kurten Corporation is authorized to issue $500,000 of 8% bonds. Interest on the bonds is payable semiannually; the bonds are dated January 1, 2004 and are due December 31, 2009.

    Required Prepare the journal entries to record the following:

    April 1, 2004   Sold the bonds at par plus accrued interest
    June 30, 2004   First interest payment
    Dec. 31, 2004   Second interest payment

E13-2   *Straight-Line Premium Amortization*   On April 30, 2004 Hackman Corporation issued $1 million face value 12% bonds dated January 1, 2004, for $1,023,000 plus accrued interest. The bonds pay interest semiannually on June 30 and December 31 and are due December 31, 2011. The company uses the straight-line amortization method.

    Required Record the issuance of the bonds and the first two interest payments.

E13-3   *Straight-Line Discount Amortization*   The Bryan Company issued $500,000 of 10% face value bonds on January 1, 2004 for $486,000. The bonds are due December 31, 2006, and pay interest semiannually on June 30 and December 31. The company uses the straight-line amortization method.

Required Prepare the journal entries to record the issuance of the bonds and the first two interest payments.

E13-4   *Effective Interest Discount Amortization*   The Cotton Corporation issued $100,000 of 10% bonds dated January 1, 2004 for $97,158.54 on July 1, 2004. The bonds are due December 31, 2007, were issued to yield 11%, and pay interest semiannually on June 30 and December 31. The company uses the effective interest method of amortization.

Required Record (1) the issuance of the bonds, and (2) the payment of interest and the discount amortization on December 31, 2004, June 30, 2005, and December 31, 2005.

E13-5   *Effective Interest Premium Amortization*   Addison Incorporated issued $200,000 of 13% bonds on July 1, 2004 for $206,801.60. The bonds were dated January 1, 2004, pay interest on each June 30 and December 31, are due December 31, 2008, and were issued to yield 12%. The company uses the effective interest method of amortization.

Required Prepare the journal entries to record the issue of the bonds on July 1, 2004, and the interest payments on December 31, 2004 and June 30, 2005.

E13-6   *Determining the Proceeds from Bond Issues*   The Madison Corporation is authorized to issue $800,000 of
@   5-year bonds dated June 30, 2004, with a face rate of interest of 11%. Interest on the bonds is payable semiannually and the bonds are sold on June 30, 2004.

Required Determine the proceeds that the company will receive if it sells (1) the bonds to yield 12%, and (2) the bonds to yield 10%.

E13-7   *Effective Interest Amortization of Premium or Discount*   The Taylor Company issued $100,000 of 13% bonds on January 1, 2004. The bonds pay interest semiannually on June 30 and December 31 and are due December 31, 2006.

Required

1. Assume the company sells the bonds for $102,458.71 to yield 12%. Prepare the journal entries to record:
   a. The sale of the bonds.
   b. Each 2004 semiannual interest payment and premium amortization, using the effective interest method.
2. Assume the company sells the bonds for $97,616.71 to yield 14%. Prepare the journal entries to record:
   a. The sale of the bonds.
   b. Each 2004 semiannual interest payment and discount amortization, using the effective interest method.

E13-8   *Bond Amortization Tables*   On January 1, 2004 the Calvert Company issues 12%, $100,000 face value bonds for $103,545.91, a price to yield 10%. The bonds mature on January 1, 2006. Interest is paid semiannually on June 30 and December 31.

Required

1. Prepare a bond interest expense and premium amortization schedule using the straight-line method.
2. Prepare a bond interest expense and premium amortization schedule using the effective interest method.
3. Prepare the journal entries to record the interest payments on June 30, 2004 and December 31, 2004, using both methods.

E13-9   *Premium Amortization and Partial Retirement*   Rockwood Company issued $100,000 of 10% bonds on November 1, 2004 at 103. Interest on the bonds is payable on November 1 and May 1 of each year, and the maturity date is November 1, 2014. Rockwood Company retired bonds with a face value of $20,000 on February 1, 2006, at 98 plus accrued interest. The company uses straight-line amortization and reverses any calendar year-end adjusting entries.

Required

1. Prepare the journal entry to record the issuance of the bonds on November 1, 2004.
2. Prepare all the journal entries to record the interest expense during 2005.
3. Prepare the journal entries to record the retirement of $20,000 of the bonds on February 1, 2006.

E13-10   *Effective Interest vs. Straight-Line Discount Amortization*   Burr Motor Company, a manufacturer of small-to medium-sized electric motors, needs additional funds to market a revolutionary new motor. Burr has arranged for private placement of a $50,000, 5-year, 11% bond issue. Interest on these bonds is paid annually each year on August 31. The issue was dated and sold on September 1, 2003, for proceeds of $48,197.62 to yield 12%. The company reverses any year-end adjusting entries.

Required

1. Prepare a bond interest expense and discount amortization schedule showing interest expense for each year, using the effective interest method.
2. Prepare journal entries to record the issuance of the bonds and the interest payments for 2004 and 2005, using (a) the effective interest method, and (b) the straight-line method.

E13-11 *Redemption of Bonds Prior to Maturity* The Hill Corporation issued $1,500,000 of 11% bonds at 98 on January 2, 2002. Interest is paid semiannually on June 30 and December 31. The bonds had a 10-year life from the date of issue, and the company uses the straight-line method of amortization. On March 31, 2005 the company recalls the bonds at the call price of 107 plus accrued interest.

Required Prepare the journal entries to record the reacquisition (recall) of the Hill Corporation bonds.

E13-12 *Extinguishment of Bonds Prior to Maturity* On December 1, 2002 the Cone Company issued its 10%, $2 million face value bonds for $2.3 million, plus accrued interest. Interest is payable on November 1 and May 1. On December 31, 2004 the book value of the bonds, inclusive of the unamortized premium, was $2.1 million. On July 1, 2005 Cone reacquired the bonds at 98, plus accrued interest. Cone appropriately uses the straight-line method for the amortization because the results do not materially differ from those of the interest method.

Required Prepare a schedule to compute the gain or loss on this extinguishment of debt. Show supporting computations in good form. (*AICPA adapted*)

E13-13 *Convertible Bond Entries* On July 2, 2003 the McGraw Corporation issued $500,000 of convertible bonds. Each $1,000 bond could be converted into 20 shares of the company's $5 par value stock. On July 3, 2005, when the bonds had an unamortized discount of $7,400, and the market value of the McGraw shares was $52 per share, all the bonds were converted into common stock.

Required

1. Prepare the journal entry to record the conversion of the bonds under (a) the book value method, and (b) the market value method.
2. Compute the company's debt-to-equity ratio (total liabilities divided by total stockholders' equity, as mentioned in Chapter 5) under each alternative. Assume the company's other liabilities are $2 million and stockholders' equity before the conversion is $3 million.

E13-14 *Convertible Bonds* On January 1, 2003, when its $30 par value common stock was selling for $80 per share, a corporation issued $10 million of 10% convertible debentures due in 10 years. The conversion option allowed the holder of each $1,000 bond to convert it into 6 shares of the corporation's $30 par value common stock. The debentures were issued for $11 million. At the time of issuance the present value of the bond payments was $8.5 million, and the corporation believes the difference between the present value and the amount paid is attributable to the conversion feature. On January 1, 2004 the corporation's $30 par value common stock was split 3 for 1. On January 1, 2005, when the corporation's $10 par value common stock was selling for $90 per share, holders of 40% of the convertible debentures exercised their conversion options. The corporation uses the straight-line method for amortizing any bond discounts or premiums.

Required

1. Prepare in general journal format the entry to record the original issuance of the convertible debentures.
2. Prepare in general journal format the entry to record the exercise of the conversion option, using the book value method. Show supporting computations in good form. (*AICPA adapted*)

E13-15 *Induced Conversion* On July 1, 2005 the Tuttle Company had bonds payable outstanding with a face value of $200,000 and a book value of $194,000. The interest on these bonds was paid on June 30. When these bonds were issued, each $1,000 bond was convertible into 20 shares of $10 par common stock. To induce conversion, on June 15, 2005 the terms were changed so that each bond was convertible into 22 shares of common stock if the conversion was made within 30 days. All the bonds were converted on July 1, 2005 when the market price of the common stock was $50 per share.

Required Using the book value method, record the conversion of the bonds on July 1, 2005.

E13-16 *Detachable Stock Warrants* Conroe Corporation sold $500,000 of 13% bonds at 107. Each $1,000 bond carried 20 warrants, and each warrant allowed the holder to acquire one share of $10 par value common stock for $20 per share. Subsequent to the issuance of the securities, the bonds were quoted at 102 ex rights, and the warrants were quoted at $4 each.

Required

1. Determine the value to be assigned to the bonds and the warrants, and prepare the journal entry to record the issuance of the convertible bonds.
2. Assume that 4,000 warrants are subsequently exercised. Prepare the journal entry for the issuance of the common stock.

E13-17 **Bonds with Detachable Warrants**   On July 1, 2004 Salem Corporation issued $3 million of 12% bonds payable in 10 years. The bonds pay interest semiannually. The bonds include detachable warrants giving the bondholder the right to purchase for $30, one share of $1 par value common stock at any time during the next 10 years. The company sold the bonds for $3 million. The value of the warrants at the time of issuance was $200,000.

Required Prepare in general journal format the entry to record the issuance of the bonds. (*AICPA adapted*)

E13-18 **Long-Term Notes Payable**   On January 1, 2004 the Johnson Corporation issued a 2-year note due December 31, 2005, with a face value of $10,000, receiving $7,694.68 in exchange.

Required Prepare the journal entries to account for the note:

1. On the date the note is issued
2. At the end of 2004
3. At the end of 2005

E13-19 **Note Payable Exchanged for Cash and Rights**   The Spath Company borrows $75,000 by issuing a 4-year, non-interest-bearing note to a customer on January 1, 2004. In addition, Spath Company agrees to sell inventory to the customer at reduced prices over a 5-year period. Spath's incremental borrowing rate is 12%. The customer agrees to purchase an equal amount of inventory each year over the 5-year period so that a straight-line method of revenue recognition is appropriate.

Required Prepare the journal entries on Spath Company's books for 2004 and 2005. (Round answers to two decimal places.)

E13-20 **Exchange of a Note Payable for an Asset**   The Webb Corporation purchased an asset from the Shaw Corporation on January 1, 2004. Shaw accepted a 3-year, non-interest-bearing note of $18,000 due December 31, 2006 in exchange for the asset. Neither the fair value of the asset nor that of the note is available. Webbs incremental borrowing rate is 12%.

Required Prepare the journal entries to record the issuance of the note, retirement, and any interest expense on the books of Webb on each of the following dates:

1. January 1, 2004   3. December 31, 2005
2. December 31, 2004   4. December 31, 2006

E13-21 **Note Payable Issued in Exchange for an Asset**   On January 1, 2004 the Sanders Corporation purchased equipment having a fair value of $68,301.30 by issuing a non-interest-bearing, $100,000, 4-year note due December 31, 2007.

Required Prepare the journal entries to record (1) the purchase of the equipment, (2) the annual interest charges over the life of the note, and (3) the repayment of the note.

E13-22 **Note Payable in Installments**   On January 1, 2004 the Billips Corporation purchased equipment having a fair value of $72,054.94 by issuing a $90,000 note, payable in three $30,000 annual installments beginning December 31, 2004.

Required Prepare (1) the journal entry to record the purchase of the equipment, (2) a schedule to compute the annual interest expense, and (3) the journal entries to record yearly interest expense and note repayments over the life of the note.

E13-23 **Notes Receivable**   On January 1, 2004 Crouser Company sold land to Chad Company, accepting a 2-year, $150,000 non-interest-bearing note due January 1, 2006. The fair value of the land was $123,966.90 on the date of sale. The company purchased the land for $120,000 on January 1, 1998.

Required Prepare all the journal entries on Crouser Company's books for January 1, 2004 through January 1, 2006 in regard to the Chad Company note.

E13-24 ***Notes Receivable*** On January 1, 2004 Worthylake Company sold used machinery to Brown Company, accepting a $25,000 non-interest-bearing note maturing on January 1, 2006. Worthylake Company carried the machinery on its books at a cost of $22,000 and a current book value of $15,000. Neither the fair value of the machinery nor the note was determinable at the time of sale; however, Brown's incremental borrowing rate was 12%.

Required Prepare the journal entries on Worthylake Company's books to record:
1. The sale of the machinery
2. The related adjusting entries on December 31, 2004 and 2005
3. The payment of the note by Brown Company on January 1, 2006

E13-25 ***Note Receivable in Installments*** On January 1, 2004 Tabor Company sold land with a book value of $50,000 to Wilson Company, accepting a $60,000 note, payable in three $20,000 annual installments beginning December 31, 2004. The note carried no stated interest rate and the fair values of the land and the note were not determinable. An appropriate interest rate for this note is 12%.

Required Prepare the journal entries on Tabor Company's books to record:
1. The sale
2. The annual interest revenue and receipt of each $20,000 installment

E13-26 ***Notes Receivable Discounted*** On January 1, 2004 Boiler Company received two notes for merchandise sold:

Note 1:   A $10,000, 10%, 60-day note from Wildcat, Inc.
Note 2:   A $20,000, 8%, 3-year interest-bearing note from Gopher, Inc.

On January 1, 2004 the fair rate of interest was 10%. Needing cash to meet the upcoming payroll, Boiler Company discounted the Wildcat, Inc. note at the local bank at 14% on January 12, 2004. On March 2, 2004 Wildcat, Inc. remitted the full amount owed to the bank.

Required Prepare journal entries on the books of Boiler Company to record the receipt of the two notes on January 1, 2004, the discounting of the Wildcat note on January 12, 2004, the payment by Wildcat to the bank on March 2, 2004, and the interest on the Gopher note on December 31, 2004. Round all calculations to the nearest dollar and use a 360-day year. (*Contributed by Scott I. Jerris*)

E13-27 ***Notes Receivable and Income*** On January 1, 2004 the Pitt Company sold a patent to Chatham, Inc., which had a carrying value on Pitt's books of $10,000. Chatham gave Pitt a $60,000 non-interest-bearing note payable in five equal annual installments of $12,000, with the first payment due and paid on January 1, 2005. There was no established price for the patent, and the note has no ready market value. The prevailing rate of interest for a note of this type at January 1, 2004 is 12%. Information on present value and future amount factors is as follows:

	Period				
	1	2	3	4	5
Present value of $1 at 12%	0.89	0.80	0.71	0.64	0.57
Present value of an annuity of $1 at 12%	0.89	1.69	2.40	3.04	3.60
Future amount of $1 at 12%	1.12	1.25	1.40	1.57	1.76
Future amount of an annuity of $1 at 12%	1.00	2.12	3.37	4.78	6.35

Required Prepare a schedule showing the income or loss before income taxes (rounded to the nearest dollar) that Pitt should record for the years ended December 31, 2004 and 2005 as a result of the preceding facts. Show supporting computations in good form. (*AICPA adapted*)

E13-28 ***Loan Impairment*** The Perry National Bank has a note receivable of $200,000 from the Mogren Company that it is carrying at face value and is due on December 31, 2008. Interest on the note is payable at 9% each December 31. The Mogren Company paid the interest due on December 31, 2004, but informed the bank that it would probably miss the next two years' interest payments because of its financial difficulties. After that, it expected to resume its annual interest payments, but it would make the principal payment one year late, with interest paid for that additional year at the time of the principal payment.

Required
1. Compute the value of the impaired loan on December 31, 2004.
2. Prepare the journal entries from 2004 to 2009 for the bank to record the above events.

E13-29 *Loan Impairment*   The Oaks National Bank has a note receivable of $500,000 from the Haldane Company that it is carrying at face value and is due on December 31, 2010. Interest on the note is payable at 6% each December 31. The Haldane Company paid the interest due on December 31, 2004, but informed the bank that it would probably miss the next three years' interest payments because of its financial difficulties. After that, it expected to resume its annual interest payments, but it would make the principal payment two years late, with interest paid for the additional years. On January 1, 2007 the bank received new information and now expected the Haldane Company to pay the interest for 2007 through 2012 on December 31st of each year.

Required

1. Compute the value of the impaired loan on December 31, 2004.
2. Prepare the journal entries from 2004 to 2012 for the bank to record the above loan impairment events.

E13-30 *Troubled Debt Restructuring (Debtor)—Modification of Terms (Appendix 1)*   On January 1, 2004 Northfield Corporation becomes delinquent on a $100,000, 14% note to the First National Bank, on which $16,651 of interest has accrued. On January 2, 2004 the bank agrees to restructure the note. It forgives the accrued interest, extends the repayment date to December 31, 2006, and reduces the interest rate to 10%.

Required Prepare a schedule for Northfield Corporation to compute the annual interest expense in regard to the preceding note for each year of the restructuring agreement.

E13-31 *Troubled Debt Restructuring (Debtor)—Equity and Asset Exchange (Appendix 1)*   On January 1, 2004 the Boonville Corporation is delinquent on a $300,000 note to the Great National Bank on which $66,000 of interest has accrued. On January 2, 2004 Boonville enters into a debt restructuring agreement with the bank.

Required Prepare the journal entries for Boonville to record the restructuring agreement assuming:

1. The bank accepts 10,000 shares of Boonville's $10 par common stock that is currently selling for $35 per share in full settlement of the debt.
2. The bank accepts land with a fair value of $342,000 in full settlement of the debt. The land is being carried on Boonville's books at a cost of $324,000.

E13-32 *Troubled Debt Restructuring (Creditor)—Modification of Terms (Appendix 1)*   On December 31, 2004 Central Bank agrees to a restructuring of a 12% note with a $200,000 face value and $60,000 of accrued interest owed to the bank by Carter Company. The bank agrees to forgive the accrued interest, extend the maturity date to December 31, 2007, and reduce the annual interest rate to 6%. Carter Company paid the interest due on December 31, 2005.

Required

1. Prepare the journal entry for Central Bank to record the restructuring of the note on December 31, 2004.
2. Prepare the journal entry for Central Bank to record the receipt of the interest on December 31, 2005.

E13-33 *Troubled Debt Restructuring (Creditor)—Equity and Asset Exchange (Appendix 1)*   Refer to the debt restructuring information in E13-31.

Required Prepare the journal entries for Great National Bank to record the restructuring agreement assuming:

1. The bank accepts the 10,000 shares of Boonville's stock.
2. The bank accepts the land.

E13-34 *Serial Bonds Entries (Appendix 2)*   On July 1, 2003 the Nicholsen Corporation issued $300,000 of bonds, with a 13% face rate of interest, for $318,000. The bonds pay interest semiannually on each January 1 and July 1 and are to be repaid in three equal semiannual installments beginning July 1, 2005. Assume the company's fiscal year ends May 31 and it makes reversing entries for year-end accruals.

Required Prepare the journal entries to account for this serial bond issue on each of the following dates, using the bonds outstanding method of amortization:

1. July 1, 2003   5. July 1, 2005
2. January 1, 2004   6. January 1, 2006
3. July 1, 2004   7. July 1, 2006
4. January 1, 2005

E13-35 *Serial Bond Issue Using the Effective Interest Method (Appendix 2)*   The Lewis Company sells $200,000 of 13% bonds dated January 1, 2003, on that date, for $204,650.74 to yield 12%. The bonds pay interest *annually* on December 31, and bonds of $40,000 mature on each December 31 for the next 5 years. The company uses the effective interest method of amortization.

Required

1. Prepare a serial bond premium amortization schedule for these bonds.
2. Prepare the journal entries necessary to record the yearly interest payments, premium amortization, and serial bond redemption.

E13-36　*Serial Bonds (Appendix 2):*　On January 1, 2003 Mykoo Corporation issued $1 million in 5-year, 10% serial bonds to be repaid in the amount of $200,000 on January 1, 2004, 2005, 2006, 2007, and 2008. Interest is payable at the end of each year. The bonds were sold to yield a rate of 12%. Information on present value and future amount factors is as follows:

	Present Value of an Ordinary Annuity of $1 for 5 Years		Future Amount of an Ordinary Annuity of $1 for 5 Years	
	10%	12%	10%	12%
	3.7908	3.6048	6.1051	6.3528

Number of Years	Present Value of $1		Future Amount of $1	
	10%	12%	10%	12%
1	.9091	.8929	1.1000	1.1200
2	.8264	.7972	1.2100	1.2544
3	.7513	.7118	1.3310	1.4049
4	.6830	.6355	1.4641	1.5735
5	.6209	.5674	1.6105	1.7623

Required

1. Prepare a schedule showing the computation of the total amount received from the issuance of the serial bonds. Show supporting computations in good form.
2. Assume the company originally sold the bonds at a discount of $46,498. Prepare a schedule of amortization of the bond discount for the first two years after issuance, using the interest (effective rate) method. Show supporting computations in good form. (*AICPA adapted*)

PROBLEMS

P13-1　*Amortizing Bond Issue Costs and Bond Premiums*　On January 1, 2003 the Baker Corporation issued $100,000 of 5-year bonds due December 31, 2007 for $103,604.79 less bond issue costs of $3,000. The bonds carry a face rate of interest of 13% payable annually on December 31 and were issued to yield 12%. The company uses the effective interest method of amortization.

Required Prepare the journal entries to record the issuance of the bonds, all the interest payments, premium amortizations, bond issue cost amortizations, and the repayment of the bonds.

P13-2　*Computation of Effective Interest Rate*　On June 30, 2004 the Watson Corporation sold $800,000 of 11% face value bonds for $761,150.96. On December 31, 2004 the Watson Corporation sold $700,000 of this same bond issue for $734,645.28. The bonds were dated January 1, 2004, pay interest semiannually on each December 31 and June 30, and are due December 31, 2011.

Required Compute the effective yield rate on each issuance of the Watson Corporation 11% bonds.

P13-3　*Premium Amortization Schedule with Retirement Before Maturity*　The Dorsett Corporation issued $600,000 of 13% bonds on January 1, 2003 for $614,752.24. The bonds are due December 31, 2005, were issued to yield 12%, and pay interest semiannually on June 30 and December 31. The company uses the effective interest method.

Required

1. Prepare a bond interest expense and premium amortization schedule.

2. Assume the company retired the bonds on September 30, 2005 for $630,000, which includes accrued interest. Prepare the journal entry to record the bond retirement.

P13-4   *Comprehensive*   The Batson Corporation issued $800,000 of 12% face value bonds for $851,705.70. The bonds were dated and issued on April 1, 2004, are due March 31, 2008, and pay interest semiannually on September 30 and March 31. The company sold the bonds to yield 10%.

Required

1. Prepare a bond interest expense and premium amortization schedule using the straight-line method.
2. Prepare a bond interest expense and premium amortization schedule using the effective interest method.
3. Prepare any adjusting entries for the end of the fiscal year, December 31, 2004, using:
   a. The straight-line method of amortization
   b. The effective interest method of amortization
4. Assume the company retires the bonds on June 30, 2005, at 103 plus accrued interest. Prepare the journal entries to record the bond retirement using:
   a. The straight-line method of amortization
   b. The effective interest method of amortization

P13-5   ***Discount Amortization Schedule and Retirement Before Maturity***   Donaldson Incorporated sold $500,000 of 12% bonds on January 1, 2003 for $470,143.47, a price that yields a 14% interest rate. The bonds pay interest semiannually on June 30 and December 31 and are due December 31, 2006. The company uses the effective interest method.

Required

1. Prepare an interest expense and discount amortization schedule.
2. Assume the company reacquired the bonds on July 1, 2005 at 104. Prepare journal entries to record the bond retirement.

P13-6   *Comprehensive*   The Wilkerson Corporation issued $1 million of 13.5% bonds for $985,071.68. The bonds are dated and issued October 1, 2004, are due September 30, 2008, and pay interest semiannually on March 31 and September 30. Assume an effective yield rate of 14%.

Required

1. Prepare a bond interest expense and discount amortization schedule using the straight-line method.
2. Prepare a bond interest expense and discount amortization schedule using the effective interest method.
3. Prepare adjusting entries for the end of the fiscal year December 31, 2004 using:
   a. The straight-line method of amortization
   b. The effective interest method of amortization
4. If income before interest and income taxes of 30% in 2005 is $500,000, compute net income under each alternative.
5. Assume the company retired the bonds on June 30, 2005 at 98 plus accrued interest. Prepare the journal entries to record the bond retirement using:
   a. The straight-line method of amortization
   b. The effective interest method of amortization
6. Compute the company's times interest earned (pretax operating income divided by interest expense) under each alternative.

See WebTutor for annotated problem solution.

P13-7   ***Bond Refunding***   The Baxter Corporation issued $400,000 of 11% bonds for $385,279.91 on January 1, 2003. The bonds pay interest semiannually on June 30 and December 31, were issued to yield 12%, and are due on December 31, 2007. Interest is amortized using the effective interest method, and the bonds are callable at 105. In 2005 Baxter wishes to take advantage of more favorable market interest rate conditions and issues $450,000 of 11%, 10-year bonds at 102 on June 1. Interest on these bonds is payable each May 31 and November 30. Sufficient proceeds from this issue are used to recall the original issue on July 1, 2005.

Required

1. Prepare the journal entries to record (a) the original issue, (b) the new issue, and (c) the recall of the old issue.
2. If the company were required to reflect the current yield each year, explain how it would account for the bonds. For simplicity, assume that the yield changes from 12% to 11% on January 1, 2005. No calculations are required.

P13-8 *Convertible Bonds* The Shank Corporation issued $1,500,000 of 10% convertible bonds for $1,620,000 on March 1, 2003. The bonds are dated March 1, 2003, pay interest semiannually on August 31 and February 28, and the premium is amortized using the straight-line method. The bonds are due on February 28, 2013, and each $1,000 bond is convertible into 25 shares of Shank Corporation $10 par common stock. On March 1, 2005, when the shares were selling for $28 per share, $300,000 of bonds were converted. On September 1, 2007, when the shares were selling for $30 per share, the remainder of the bonds were converted.

Required

1. Prepare the journal entries to record each bond conversion using (a) the book value method, and (b) the market value method.
2. If the company were required under GAAP to assign a value to the conversion feature, explain how the valuation would be determined (no calculations are required).
3. Compute the company's debt-to-equity ratio (total liabilities divided by total stockholders' equity, as mentioned in Chapter 5) under each alternative. Assume the company's other liabilities are $3 million, and that stockholders' equity before conversion is $3.5 million.

P13-9 *Bonds with Detachable Warrants* On January 1, 2004 the London Corporation issued $500,000 of 11.5% bonds due January 1, 2014 at 102. The bonds pay interest semiannually on June 30 and December 31. Each $1,000 bond carried 20 warrants, and the exchange of two warrants allowed the holder to acquire one share of $10 par common stock for $50. Shortly after the time of issue, the bonds were quoted at 98 ex rights and each individual warrant was quoted at $5. Subsequently, on March 31, 2004, 8,000 rights were exercised.

Required

1. Prepare the journal entry to record the bond issue.
2. Prepare the journal entries on March 31, 2004 to record the exchange of the warrants for common shares.

P13-10 *Notes Payable* The Houston Corporation acquires machinery from the South Company in exchange for a $20,000 non-interest-bearing, 5-year note on June 30, 2003. The note is due on June 30, 2008. The machinery has a fair value of $11,348.54, is subject to straight-line depreciation, and has an estimated life of 10 years (no residual value). Houston's fiscal year ends June 30.

Required Prepare the journal entries on each of the following dates to record the preceding information for Houston Corporation:

1. June 30, 2003
2. June 30, 2004
3. June 30, 2005
4. June 30, 2006
5. June 30, 2007
6. June 30, 2008

P13-11 *Notes Payable in Installments* Hamlet Corporation purchases computer equipment at a price of $100,000 on January 1, 2004, paying $40,000 down and agreeing to pay the balance in three $20,000 annual installments beginning December 31, 2004. It is not possible to value either the equipment or the $60,000 note directly; however, Hamlet's incremental borrowing rate is 12%.

Required

1. Prepare a schedule to compute the interest expense and discount amortization on the note.
2. Prepare all the journal entries for Hamlet to record the issuance of the note, each annual interest expense, and the three annual installment payments.

P13-12 *Notes Receivable* On January 1, 2004 the Somerville Corporation sold a used truck to the Cornelius Company and accepted a $28,000 non-interest-bearing note due January 1, 2007. Somerville carried the truck on its books at a cost of $30,000 and a current book value of $23,000. Neither the fair value of the truck nor the note was available at the time of the sale; however, Cornelius's incremental borrowing rate was 12%.

Required

1. Prepare the journal entries on Somerville's books to record:
   a. The sale of the truck
   b. The related adjusting entries on December 31, 2004, 2005, and 2006
   c. The collection of the note on January 1, 2007
2. Prepare the notes receivable portion of Somerville's December 31, 2004, 2005, and 2006 balance sheets.

P13-13 *Notes Receivable* On January 1, 2004 Lisa Company sold machinery with a book value of $118,000 to Mark Company. Mark Company signed a $180,000 non-interest-bearing note, payable in three $60,000 annual installments on December 31, 2004, 2005, and 2006. The fair value of the machinery was $149,211.12 on the date of sale. The machinery had been purchased by Lisa Company at a cost of $160,000.

Required

1. Prepare all the journal entries on Lisa Company's books for January 1, 2004 through December 31, 2006.
2. Prepare the notes receivable portion of the Lisa Company's balance sheet on December 31, 2004 and 2005.

P13-14   *Comprehensive*   On January 1, 2004 Seaver Company sold land with a book value of $23,000 to Bench Company. Bench Company paid $15,000 down and signed a $15,000 non-interest-bearing note, payable in two $7,500 annual installments on December 31, 2004 and 2005. Neither the fair value of the land nor of the note is determinable. Bench Company's incremental borrowing rate is 12%. Later in the year, on July 1, 2004, Seaver Company sold a building to Hane Company, accepting a 2-year, $100,000 non-interest-bearing note due July 1, 2006. The fair value of the building was $82,644.60 on the date of the sale. The building had been purchased at a cost of $90,000 on January 1, 1999, and had a book value of $67,500 on December 31, 2003. It was being depreciated on a straight-line basis (no residual value) over a 20-year life.

Required

1. Prepare all the journal entries on Seaver Company's books for January 1, 2004 through December 31, 2005 in regard to the Bench Company note.
2. Prepare all the journal entries on Seaver Company's books for July 1, 2004 through July 1, 2006 in regard to the Hane Company note.
3. Prepare the notes receivable portion of the Seaver Company's balance sheet on December 31, 2004 and 2005.

P13-15   *Comprehensive*   Linden, Inc., had the following long-term receivable account balances at December 31, 2003:

Note receivable from sale of division	$1,500,000
Note receivable from officer	400,000

Transactions during 2004 and other information relating to Linden's long-term receivables were as follows:

1. The $1,500,000 note receivable is dated May 1, 2003, bears interest at 9%, and represents the balance of the consideration received from the sale of Linden's electronics division to Pitt Company. Principal payments of $500,000 plus appropriate interest are due on May 1, 2004, 2005, and 2006. The first principal and interest payment was made on May 1, 2004. Collection of the note installments is reasonably assured.
2. The $400,000 note receivable is dated December 31, 2001, bears interest at 8%, and is due on December 31, 2006. The note is due from Robert Finley, president of Linden, Inc., and is collateralized by 10,000 shares of Linden's common stock. Interest is payable annually on December 31, and all interest payments were paid on their due dates through December 31, 2004. The quoted market price of Linden's common stock was $45 per share on December 31, 2004.
3. On April 1, 2004 Linden sold a patent to Bell Company in exchange for a $100,000 non-interest-bearing note due on April 1, 2006. There was no established exchange price for the patent, and the note had no ready market. The prevailing rate of interest for a note of this type at April 1, 2004 was 15%. The present value of $1 for two periods at 15% is 0.756. The patent had a carrying value of $40,000 at January 1, 2004, and the amortization for the year ended December 31, 2004 would have been $8,000. The collection of the note receivable from Bell is reasonably assured.
4. On July 1, 2004 Linden sold a parcel of land to Carr Company for $200,000 under an installment sale contract. Carr made a $60,000 cash down payment on July 1, 2004 and signed a 4-year, 16% note for the $140,000 balance. The equal annual payments of principal and interest on the note will be $50,000, payable on July 1, 2005 through July 1, 2008. The land could have been sold at an established cash price of $200,000. The cost of the land to Linden was $150,000. Circumstances are such that the collection of the installments on the note is reasonably assured.

Required

1. Prepare the long-term receivables section of Linden's balance sheet at December 31, 2004.
2. Prepare a schedule showing the current portion of the long-term receivables and accrued interest receivable that would appear in Linden's balance sheet at December 31, 2004.
3. Prepare a schedule showing interest income from the long-term receivables and gains recognized on sale of assets that would appear on Linden's income statement for the year ended December 31, 2004. (*AICPA adapted*)

P13-16 *Comprehensive* An examination of the accounting records of the Durham Corporation on January 1, 2005 (after reversing entries had been made for all accrued interest at the end of 2004) disclosed the following information regarding the company's long-term debt:

12.5% bonds, dated January 1, 2001, paying interest semiannually on June 30 and December 31, and due December 31, 2007.	$1,300,000
11% convertible bonds, dated April 1, 2003, paying interest semiannually on March 31 and September 30, and due March 31, 2008.	$ 500,000
Discount on convertible bonds payable	(17,500)
	$ 482,500
9% bonds, dated March 1, 2004, paying interest annually on February 28, and due February 28, 2009.	$ 100,000
Discount on bonds payable	(3,960)
	$ 96,040
4-year, non-interest-bearing note issued January 1, 2004. (Durham's incremental borrowing rate on the date the note was issued was 10%.)	$ 80,000
Discount on note payable	(19,895)
	$ 60,105

Additional information disclosed in the notes to Durham Corporation's 2004 financial statements:

1. The conversion option allows the holder of each $1,000 bond to exchange it for 30 shares of $10 par common stock. Durham uses the book value method to record conversions of bonds to common stock.
2. Each $1,000 bond of the 9% bonds dated March 1, 2004 carries 15 detachable warrants. The company had recorded the 1,500 warrants on the bonds at $4,800 in a Common Stock Warrants account. The exchange of three warrants allows the holder to acquire one share of $10 par common stock for $27.
3. The discount on the convertible bonds and the discount on the 9% bonds with detachable warrants are being amortized using the straight-line method.
4. The discount on the note payable is being amortized annually using the effective interest method.

During 2005, the Durham Corporation engaged in the following long-term debt transactions:

Jan.	1	Issued 11%, $800,000 face value bonds for $820,302, a price to yield 10%. Interest on these bonds is payable semiannually on June 30 and December 31, and they are due December 31, 2007. The effective interest method is to be used to amortize the premium. The bonds are callable at 107.
May	1	Six hundred warrants from the 9% bonds were exercised when the common stock was selling for $42 per share.
Sept.	29	Convertible bonds of $100,000 were exchanged when the common stock was selling for $45 per share.
Nov.	1	Retired $200,000 of the bonds issued on January 1, 2005, at the call price plus accrued interest.

Required

1. Prepare the journal entries for Durham Corporation to record all the transactions that occurred during 2005 relating to the preceding information.
2. Prepare the long-term debt section of the Durham Corporation's balance sheet on December 31, 2005.

P13-17 *Troubled Debt Restructuring (Debtor) (Appendix 1)* The Oakwood Corporation is delinquent on a $2,400,000, 10% note to the Second National Bank that was due January 1, 2004. At that time Oakwood owed the principal amount plus $34,031.82 of accrued interest. Oakwood enters into a debt restructuring agreement with the bank on January 2, 2004.

Required Prepare the journal entries for Oakwood to record the debt restructuring agreement and all subsequent interest payments assuming the following independent alternatives:

1. The bank extends the repayment date to December 31, 2007, forgives the accrued interest owed, reduces the principal by $200,000, and reduces the interest rate to 8%.
2. The bank extends the repayment date to December 31, 2007, forgives the accrued interest owed, reduces the principal by $200,000, and reduces the interest rate to 1%.

3. The bank accepts 160,000 shares of Oakwood's $5 par value common stock, which is currently selling for $14.50 per share, in full settlement of the debt.

4. The bank accepts land with a fair value of $2,300,000 in full settlement of the debt. The land is being carried on Oakwood's books at a cost of $2,200,000.

P13-18 ***Troubled Debt Restructuring (Creditor) (Appendix 1)***   Refer to the debt restructuring information listed in P13-17.

Required For each of the independent alternatives listed in Requirements 1 through 4 of P13-17, prepare the journal entries for Second National Bank to record the debt restructuring agreement and all subsequent interest receipts.

P13-19 ***Comprehensive—Loan Impairment and Troubled Debt Restructuring***   The 10th National Bank has a $200,000, 12% note receivable from the Priday Company that is due on December 31, 2007. On December 31, 2004 the company misses the interest payment due on that date. The bank expects that the company will also miss the next payment, but will pay the principal on the maturity date. On December 31, 2005 the company misses the interest payment due on that date. On December 31, 2006 the company pays half the interest payment due on that date and is not expected to pay the other half.

In early January 2007 the bank and the company agree to a loan restructuring because of the financial condition of the company. The bank forgives the unpaid interest, extends the loan to December 31, 2009, and reduces the interest rate to 6%. The market rate for the loan is estimated to be 10% at this time.

Required

1. Compute the value of the impaired loan on December 31, 2004.
2. Prepare the journal entries from 2004 to 2009 for the bank to record the above events.

P13-20 ***Serial Bond Amortization and Repayment Schedule (Appendix 2)***   On July 1, 2004 the Hubbard Corporation issued $600,000 of bonds with an 8% face rate of interest. The bonds were issued for $589,381.93, pay interest semiannually on June 30 and December 31, carry an effective yield rate of 9%, and are payable in three annual installments of $200,000 each, beginning June 30, 2005.

Required

1. Prepare a serial bond discount amortization schedule using the bonds outstanding method.
2. Prepare a serial bond discount amortization schedule using the effective interest method.
3. Prepare the journal entries necessary to record the payment of interest and the bond retirements on June 30, 2005, June 30, 2006, and June 30, 2007 using (a) the bonds outstanding method, and (b) the effective interest method.

P13-21 ***Call Provision of Serial Bonds (Appendix 2)***   The Case Corporation issued $600,000 of 13% bonds on January 1, 2003 for $636,000. The bonds are payable in three annual $200,000 installments beginning December 31, 2004, pay interest semiannually on June 30 and December 31, and are callable at 107. On January 1, 2005 the bonds due December 31, 2006 are recalled at the call price. The corporation uses the bonds outstanding method of amortization.

Required Prepare a serial bond premium amortization schedule and the journal entries to record the bond issue, payment of interest, and bond retirement on each of the following dates:

1. January 1, 2003
2. December 31, 2003
3. December 31, 2004
4. January 1, 2005
5. December 31, 2005

INTERNET ASSIGNMENTS

Go to the Nikolai and Bazley **Intermediate Accounting** web site (http://Nikolai.swcollege.com). Click on Student Resources and <u>internet</u> <u>homework</u> <u>assignments</u>. Then click on the appropriate hot link (icon) for each company's web site, find the relevant accounting information, and answer the following questions.

I13-1 Go to the General Motors web site.

Required How much are the notes and loans payable that the company owes at the end of the two most recent years? What are the components of the notes and loans payable—due dates and interest rates? Compute the company's debt ratio for each of the two most recent years. What is your evaluation of the change in the ratio?

I13-2   Go to the Raytheon Company web site.

Required How much is the long-term debt that the company owes at the end of the two most recent years? What are the components the notes and loans payable—due dates and interest rates? Compute the company's debt ratio for each of the two most recent years. What is your evaluation of the change in the ratio? How much must the company pay off in the next five years? Do you think the company can make the payments from internal cash flows or will it have to issue additional debt? Why or why not?

objectives

1 Explain the classification and valuation of investments.

2 Account for investments in debt and equity trading securities.

3 Account for investments in available-for-sale debt and equity securities.

4 Account for investments in held-to-maturity debt securities, including amortization of bond premiums and discounts.

5 Understand transfers and impairments.

6 Understand disclosures of investments.

7 Explain the conceptual issues regarding investments in marketable securities.

8 Account for investments using the equity method.

9 Describe additional issues for investments.

10 Account for derivatives of financial instruments. (Appendix)

CHAPTER

Investments

14

A corporation acquires securities of other corporations for many reasons. One reason is to obtain additional income. In Chapter 6 we emphasized that proper cash management requires the temporary investment of excess cash. Many companies have excess cash because the period of highest cash inflows does not coincide with the period of highest cash needs. Seasonal fluctuations in sales patterns frequently result in the period of greatest cash needs preceding the peak production or purchasing period when inventories are increasing. On the other hand, peak cash inflows follow the highest levels of sales activity. For efficient cash management, a company must invest excess cash from the time of peak inflows until the next period of cash outflows. For example, a department store must purchase large amounts of inventory for its peak Christmas selling season. Cash inflows from credit sales do not occur until the receivables are collected. The company may have excess cash until purchases are made for the next Christmas season. Companies may also have excess cash available to invest for longer periods of time.

As we discussed in Chapter 6, companies may invest excess cash in financial instruments called cash equivalents. Alternatively, to earn a higher return, companies may invest in other financial instruments, such as common stock, preferred stock, or bonds of other corporations, as well as municipal, state, or federal bonds. All these securities are classified as investments, and the entire group of securities is often referred to as a **portfolio of marketable securities**. Another reason why securities of other corporations are acquired is to establish long-term relationships with suppliers or to obtain significant influence or control over related companies. It is also common practice to include the cash surrender value of life insurance policies and sinking funds under the Investments category on the balance sheet. We discuss the recording and reporting issues associated with these types of investments in this chapter.

INVESTMENTS: CLASSIFICATION AND VALUATION

1 Explain the classification and valuation of investments.

FASB Statement No. 115 establishes generally accepted accounting principles for investments in debt securities and those equity securities that have readily determinable fair values.[1] A fair value is readily determinable if a sales price is currently available on a securities exchange registered with the SEC (e.g., the New York Stock Exchange)

---

1. "Accounting for Certain Investments in Debt and Equity Securities," *FASB Statement of Financial Accounting Standards No. 115* (Norwalk, Conn.: FASB, 1993), par. 3–13. This *Statement* applies, in the case of equity securities, to investments in equity securities when the investor does *not* have "significant influence." *Significant influence* generally occurs when the ownership percentage is more than 20%, as we discuss later in the chapter.

or in an over-the-counter market for which prices are publicly reported. A foreign market must be of a breadth and scope comparable to one of the U.S. markets. At acquisition, a company classifies each investment in debt and equity "marketable" securities into one of three categories. At each reporting date the company must assess the appropriateness of the classifications. The three categories are:

1. *Trading Securities.* Investments in debt and equity securities that are purchased and held principally for the purpose of selling them in the near term are classified as trading securities. Trading generally reflects active and frequent buying and selling, and the securities are held in the expectation of profiting on short-term differences in price. For example, a stockbrokerage firm that holds an "inventory" of securities for sale to its customers classifies them as trading securities. A bank that holds securities for active and frequent buying and selling in order to generate profits on short-term differences in price also classifies them as trading securities.

2. *Available-for-Sale Securities.* Investments in available-for-sale securities are (a) debt securities that are not classified as being held to maturity (see below), and (b) debt and equity securities that are not classified as trading securities.

3. *Held-to-Maturity Debt Securities.* Investments in held-to-maturity debt securities are debt securities for which the company has the "positive intent and ability to hold those securities to maturity."[2] Any sales of these securities prior to their maturity should be rare. A company does not classify a security as being held to maturity if it has the intent to hold the security only for an indefinite period. So the classification is *not* appropriate if the security will be sold for such reasons as a change in market interest rates or a need for liquid funds. However, sales of these securities are considered to be at maturity if (1) the security is sold near enough to its maturity (or its call date, if exercise of the call is probable) that interest rate risk is substantially eliminated (e.g., within three months of maturity or the call date), or (2) the sale occurs after the company has collected a substantial portion (e.g., 85%) of the principal. The sale of a debt security is *not* inconsistent with the original classification if there is a change of circumstances, such as a deterioration in the issuer's creditworthiness or a major acquisition or disposal that requires a restructuring of securities to maintain the company's existing credit risk policy; or a change in statutory or regulatory requirements, such as a change in a tax exempt status; or other events that are isolated, nonrecurring, and unusual for the company.

A company initially records each category of securities at cost, and reports dividend revenue, interest revenue, and realized gains or losses on sales in its income statement. However, the subsequent valuation of the securities on its balance sheet and the reporting of unrealized holding gains and losses (the changes in the fair value of the securities during the period) vary as follows:

1. *Trading Securities.* Investments in trading securities are reported at their fair values on the balance sheet date, and unrealized holding gains and losses are included in net income of the current period.

2. *Available-for-Sale Securities.* Investments in available-for-sale securities are reported at their fair values on the balance sheet date, the net unrealized holding gains or losses for the year are included in other comprehensive income for that year, and the cumulative net unrealized holding gains or losses are reported in the accumulated other comprehensive income section of stockholders' equity. Therefore, the unrealized holding gains and losses are *not* included in net income.

3. *Held-to-Maturity Debt Securities.* Investments in held-to-maturity debt securities are reported at their amortized cost[3] on the balance sheet date. Therefore, they are *not* reported at fair value.

---

2. *Ibid.*, par. 7.
3. "Amortized cost" is the term used by the FASB. It is the remaining amount (i.e., carrying value) of the cost (face value plus any premium or less any discount at acquisition) after any premium or discount has been amortized each period as interest revenue is recognized.

Some definitions are important for the application of these principles for investments in debt and equity securities:

1. **A debt security represents a creditor relationship with another entity.** Thus, *investments* in debt securities include U.S. treasury securities, municipal securities, corporate bonds, convertible debt, and commercial paper. Also included are investments in preferred stock that have a mandatory redemption feature or are redeemable at the option of the holder (discussed in Chapter 15). Trade accounts receivable are *not* investments in debt securities.

2. **An equity security represents an ownership interest in another company.** Thus, *investments* in equity securities include common stocks, preferred stocks, preferred stocks that are redeemable at the option of the company that issued the stock, stock warrants, stock rights, and put and call options. Investments in convertible debt or preferred stock with a mandatory redemption feature or that is redeemable at the option of the holder are *not* investments in equity securities.

3. **Fair value is the amount at which a security could be exchanged in a current transaction between willing parties.** Thus, the fair value is the number of units of the security times the quoted market price on a stock exchange. Note that there is no adjustment for any estimated change in the market price that might result from the attempted sale of a large number of a particular security.

There are two additional methods for reporting investments. However, these methods are *not* alternatives, but are applied depending on the level of ownership that the investor has in the investee. The **equity method** is used for investments in equity securities when the investor has *significant influence* over the investee. Significant influence generally occurs when the investor owns between 20% and 50% of the voting common stock of the investee, as we discuss later in the chapter. **Consolidation** occurs when the investor *controls* the investee through an investment in equity securities. Control generally occurs when the investor owns over 50% of the voting common stock of the investee. The FASB is considering a change so that consolidation will occur whenever a company controls another entity (unless control is temporary). Control will be defined as the power to use or direct the use of the individual assets of the other entity in essentially the same way as the company can use its own assets. This effective control can occur at a lower ownership level than legal control. The investor issues consolidated financial statements, which are the combined financial statements of both companies. The preparation of consolidated financial statements is discussed in an advanced accounting book and is beyond the scope of this chapter, although we briefly discuss the underlying concepts of consolidation accounting in a later section.

We summarize the various categories and methods for recording and reporting investments in securities in Exhibit 14-1.

EXHIBIT 14-1   Accounting for Investments

	Method	Reporting of Unrealized Holding Gains and Losses
Investments in Equity Securities		
1. No significant influence (less than 20% ownership)		
a. Trading	Fair value	Net income
b. Available for sale	Fair value	Other comprehensive income
2. Significant influence (20% to 50% ownership)	Equity method	Not recognized
3. Control (more than 50% ownership)	Consolidation	Not recognized
Investments in Debt Securities		
1. Trading	Fair value	Net income
2. Available for sale	Fair value	Other comprehensive income
3. Held to maturity	Amortized cost	Not recognized

INVESTMENTS IN DEBT AND EQUITY TRADING SECURITIES

The generally accepted accounting principles for investments in debt and equity securities classified as trading securities are: (1) the investment is initially recorded at cost, (2) it is subsequently reported at fair value, (3) unrealized holding gains and losses are included in net income of the current period, and (4) interest and dividend revenue, as well as realized gains and losses on sales, are included in net income of the current period. As we noted earlier, investments in debt and equity trading securities are held primarily by such institutions as banks and stockbrokers. Since the accounting principles for trading securities tend to apply to a relatively few companies, we do not illustrate them here. However, they are the same as those we discuss in the next section on available-for-sale securities, *except* that for investments in trading securities (1) unrealized holding gains and losses on changes in value are included in net income for the current period, and (2) any realized gains or losses on sales are computed by comparing the selling price to the *fair value* recorded on the most recent balance sheet date.

2 Account for investments in debt and equity trading securities.

INVESTMENTS IN AVAILABLE-FOR-SALE DEBT AND EQUITY SECURITIES

The accounting principles for investments classified as available-for-sale debt and equity securities are: (1) the investment is initially recorded at cost, (2) it is subsequently reported at fair value, (3) unrealized holding gains and losses are reported as a component of other comprehensive income, and (4) interest and dividend revenue, as well as realized gains and losses on sales, are included in net income for the current period. To illustrate each of these issues, assume that the Kent Company purchases the following securities on May 1, 2003 as an investment in available-for-sale securities:

3 Account for investments in available-for-sale debt and equity securities.

A Company common stock	100 shares at $50 per share
B Company common stock	300 shares at $80 per share
C Company preferred stock	200 shares at $120 per share
D Company 10% bonds	Face value of $15,000, acquired at par plus accrued interest. Interest is paid on May 31 and November 30 each year.

Recording Initial Cost

A company records all investments in securities initially at the acquisition price of the securities plus any other costs necessary for the transaction. Thus, the cost of equity securities is simply the quoted market price at the time of the transaction plus any brokerage fees and taxes. A special issue arises with debt securities because any accrued interest must be separated from the purchase price. Recall from Chapter 13 that bondholders receive 6 months' interest on each interest payment date. Since interest accrues over time, whenever bonds are purchased between interest payment dates, the purchaser pays the previous bondholder for the interest earned to date.

The accrued interest on the D Company bonds purchased by the Kent Company is the interest from November 30, 2002 to May 1, 2003, or 5 months, and is $625 ($15,000 × 0.10 × 5/12). Therefore, the payment for the bonds includes the $15,000 cost of the bonds plus the $625 accrued interest. Thus, the total cost of the securities purchased by the Kent Company is $68,000 [(100 × $50) + (300 × $80) + (200 × $120) + $15,000].[4] The total payment is $68,625 ($68,000 cost + $625 accrued interest) and the company records the purchase as follows:

Investment in Available-for-Sale Securities	68,000	
Interest Revenue	625	
Cash		68,625

---

4. Any costs necessary for the acquisition, such as brokerage fees and taxes, are included in the cost of the securities. However, those amounts then would be allocated among each security purchased to determine its cost. We do not discuss this procedure because the amounts would not be material.

Note that Kent debited Interest Revenue for the accrued interest. This procedure reduces the possibility of error in recording the next interest revenue transaction.[5]

Recording Interest and Dividend Revenue

A company records interest revenue as it is earned during the period. On May 31, 2003 the Kent Company receives the semiannual interest on the D Company bonds and records it as follows:

Cash	750	
Interest Revenue ($15,000 × 0.10 × 6/12)		750

Because the Kent Company initially debited interest revenue for 5 months of accrued interest on the date of acquisition, it credits interest revenue for the full 6 months of interest received. Therefore, by May 31 it has earned 1 month's interest and has that amount recorded in its accounting system. If the company purchased the D Company bonds at a premium or discount, it computes the interest revenue using the effective interest (or straight-line) method and amortizes a portion of the premium or discount, as we discuss later in the chapter.

On November 30, 2003 Kent Company receives the next interest payment and records it with the same journal entry. On December 31, 2003, it accrues 1 month's interest as follows:

Interest Receivable	125	
Interest Revenue ($15,000 × 0.10 × 1/12)		125

For the year, the Kent Company has earned interest revenue for 8 months, or $1,000 ($750 − $625 + $750 + $125, or $15,000 × 0.10 × 8/12).

Dividend revenue is recorded as it is received. So if the Kent Company receives dividends during 2003 of $3,000 on its investments in the stock of A, B, and C Companies, it records the following:

Cash	3,000	
Dividend Revenue		3,000

 It is conceptually more correct to record the Dividend Revenue when the dividends are declared by the investee company because that is the date on which the investor has the right to receive them. However, the date of receipt of the dividends is usually used for convenience. If the investee company has declared dividends at year-end but the investor company has not received them, it should record Dividends Receivable and Dividend Revenue to recognize the appropriate asset values and income, and also because the dividends receivable affect the calculation of any unrealized holding gain or loss, as we discuss later.

Note the different recognition of interest revenue and dividend revenue. Interest revenue accrues continuously over time, whereas dividend revenue is recognized only when dividends are received (or declared).

Recognition of Unrealized Holding Gains and Losses

On its ending balance sheet, a company reports any investments in available-for-sale securities at fair value. The fair values are determined by the year-end market prices on a securities exchange. *FASB Statement No. 115* uses the phrase "unrealized holding gains and losses" to describe the change in the value of investment securities. This may be confusing, since a company reports its *realized* gains and losses for the year from sales of securities in its net income on its income statement, but reports its *unrealized* gains and losses for the year in its other comprehensive income. Furthermore, a company reports its *cumulative* net unrealized gains and losses on investments in available-for-sale securities in its accumulated other comprehensive income section of stockholders' equity on its

---

5.   Alternatively, Kent Company could have debited Interest Receivable for $625, in which case it would eliminate the Interest Receivable account when it receives the interest on May 31, 2003.

balance sheet. We use the terms "unrealized holding gains and losses" in the text but prefer a more appropriate title for the account, Unrealized Increase/Decrease in Value of Available-for-Sale Securities, in recording journal entries and reporting in the financial statements. Note that this account is a permanent account whose value carries over to the next period.[6] A *credit balance* in the account represents the *cumulative* net unrealized holding *gains* and is reported as a positive element in the accumulated other comprehensive income section of stockholders' equity. A *debit balance* in the account represents the *cumulative* net unrealized holding *losses* and is reported as a negative element in the accumulated other comprehensive income section of stockholders' equity. Also note that a credit (debit) *change* in this account represents the net unrealized holding gains (losses) on the securities for the *year* and is included as a positive (negative) component of other comprehensive income for the year, as we discussed in Chapter 4.

To illustrate, assume that the total fair value of the available-for-sale securities held by the Kent Company is $71,000 on December 31, 2003 as follows:

Security	Cost	12/31/03 Fair Value	Cumulative Change in Fair Value
100 shares of A Company common stock	$ 5,000	$ 6,000	$1,000
300 shares of B Company common stock	24,000	23,500	(500)
200 shares of C Company preferred stock	24,000	26,000	2,000
$15,000 face value of D Company 10% bonds	15,000	15,500	500
Totals	$68,000	$71,000	$3,000

The Kent Company determined the fair value of the securities based on the December 31, 2003 ending quoted market prices, with one adjustment. The quoted market price of the 10% D Company bonds was $15,625, but this included the $125 of accrued interest that Kent Company previously recorded. To avoid double-counting, Kent eliminates this interest to determine the $15,500 ($15,625 − $125) fair value of the bonds. (If dividends had been declared but not paid on the equity securities, a similar adjustment would be made.) Furthermore, if the company had purchased bonds at a premium or discount, it would use the amortized cost (i.e., carrying value) in the "cost" column.

The Kent Company records the $3,000 increase (unrealized holding gain) in the value of the securities at the end of 2003 as follows:

Allowance for Change in Value of Investment	3,000	
Unrealized Increase/Decrease in Value of Available-for-Sale Securities		3,000

The Allowance account is an adjunct/contra account to the Investment in Available-for-Sale Securities account. On its December 31, 2003 balance sheet, Kent Company reports the investment as an asset at the $71,000 fair value of the securities ($68,000 cost *plus* the $3,000 increase in fair value recorded in the Allowance account). If some investments are current and some noncurrent, the asset account is separated between the current and noncurrent components, as we discuss later. We are assuming that the Kent Company uses an Allowance account to record the changes in the fair values of the securities so that information about the original cost of each security is retained in its accounts and can be used to compute the realized gain or loss on the sale of a security, as we discuss later.[7]

---

6. The term "unrealized holding gains and losses" for investments in trading securities is appropriate because the amounts are included in net income for the current period. Also the account is a temporary one which is closed to Income Summary each year.

7. Alternatively, a company may choose to record any changes in fair value directly in the Investment account. For example, companies investing in *trading securities* generally may *not* use an Allowance account because these securities "turn over" quickly. When this "direct" method is used for investments in available-for-sale securities, however, it is more difficult for a company to determine information needed for transactions in subsequent periods; therefore, we do not use this method for these securities.

Also, note that the fair value method is not allowed for federal income tax purposes so a company has to retain cost information to compute its taxable income.[8]

The Unrealized Increase/Decrease account is an adjunct/contra stockholders' equity account. Kent Company reports the $3,000 *change* (increase) in the Unrealized Increase/Decrease account as an unrealized holding gain in its other comprehensive income for 2003 (as we discussed in Chapter 4). It also reports the $3,000 credit *balance* in the Unrealized Increase/Decrease account as an addition to stockholders' equity on its balance sheet in the accumulated other comprehensive income section.[9] In other words, the change in this account is included in other comprehensive income for the year, and its total is included in accumulated other comprehensive income. In this first year that Kent owns securities, the two amounts are the same.

To illustrate subsequent increases or decreases in fair value, suppose that on December 31, 2004, the fair value of the available-for-sale securities held by Kent Company is $66,000 as follows:

Security	Cost	12/31/04 Fair Value	Cumulative Change in Fair Value
100 shares of A Company common stock	$ 5,000	$ 6,100	$1,100
300 shares of B Company common stock	24,000	22,700	(1,300)
200 shares of C Company preferred stock	24,000	23,200	(800)
$15,000 face value of D Company 10% bonds	15,000	14,000	(1,000)
Totals	$68,000	$66,000	$(2,000)

Once a company has established an Allowance account, it determines the amount of the year-end adjustment in a subsequent period by comparing the required amount of the Allowance account with the previous balance in the account. At December 31, 2004 the required amount of the Kent Company's Allowance account is a $2,000 *credit* balance, but the previous balance at December 31, 2003 was a $3,000 *debit* balance. Therefore, the Kent Company credits the Allowance account for $5,000 at the end of 2004 to record the decline in value (unrealized holding loss) as follows:

Unrealized Increase/Decrease in Value of Available-for-Sale Securities	5,000	
Allowance for Change in Value of Investment		5,000

On its December 31, 2004 balance sheet, the Kent Company reports the investment as an asset at the $66,000 fair value of the securities ($68,000 cost − $2,000 allowance).[10] It reports the $5,000 *change* (decrease) in the Unrealized Increase/Decrease account as an unrealized holding loss in its other comprehensive income for 2004. It also reports the $2,000 *debit balance* in the Unrealized Increase/Decrease account as a subtraction from stockholders' equity in the accumulated other comprehensive income section.

---

8. Since a company includes the unrealized holding gains and losses on investments in *trading securities* in its net income for the current period but may not include them in its taxable income, any difference is a temporary difference on which the company recognizes deferred income taxes, as we discuss in Chapter 18. A company also recognizes deferred income taxes on a change in the unrealized increase/decrease in the value of investments in available-for-sale securities. A change in the unrealized increase/decrease account is accompanied by a change in the deferred tax liability (or asset) account. In the journal entry to record the change in the deferred tax liability (or asset), the offsetting entry is a reduction of the unrealized increase/decrease account.

9. The amounts included in other comprehensive income for the year and accumulated other comprehensive income are reported net of tax. We do not include the tax effects in this discussion.

10. A company preparing interim (quarterly) financial statements would use the same accounting procedures, applied each quarter.

Realized Gains and Losses on Sales of Available-for-Sale Securities

A company reports realized gains and losses on sales of investments in available-for-sale securities in net income. They are measured as the difference between the selling price and the *cost* (of an equity security) or the *amortized cost* (of a debt security). Furthermore, since the security is no longer in the portfolio of available-for-sale securities, the portion of the balances in the Allowance and Unrealized Increase/Decrease accounts reported at the previous balance sheet date for the security sold must be "reversed" out of the accounts.

To illustrate, suppose that on March 1, 2005 the Kent Company sold the 100 shares of A Company common stock for $6,000. The cost of the securities was $5,000 and the fair value at the previous balance sheet was $6,100, as follows:

Security	Cost	12/31/04 Fair Value	Cumulative Change in Fair Value
100 shares of A Company common stock	$5,000	$6,100	$1,100

The company recognizes a gain of $1,000 ($6,000 selling price − $5,000 cost) and eliminates the $1,100 cumulative unrealized gain (and allowance) on the A Company stock. The company records the sale and the "reversal" on March 1, 2005 in two journal entries as follows:

Cash	6,000	
Investment in Available-for-Sale Securities		5,000
Gain on Sale of Available-for-Sale Securities		1,000
Unrealized Increase/Decrease in Value of		
Available-for-Sale Securities	1,100	
Allowance for Change in Value of Investment		1,100

The first journal entry records the sale and the $1,000 realized gain in 2005. The second journal entry reverses (eliminates) the $1,100 cumulative unrealized gain that had accumulated from May 1, 2003 (the date the company purchased the securities) until December 31, 2004 (the most recent balance sheet date). This is called a "reclassification adjustment," which we discuss in the next section. A sale of an investment in securities at a loss would be recorded in the same way. The company would record the sale and realized loss in the first journal entry and would reverse (eliminate) any cumulative unrealized loss (or gain) and allowance on that security.

At the end of 2005, Kent Company must adjust the Allowance and Unrealized Increase/Decrease accounts to report the fair values of the securities it still owns. To illustrate, assume that the total fair value of the remaining securities is $62,300 on December 31, 2005 as follows:

Security	Cost	12/31/05 Fair Value	Cumulative Change in Fair Value
300 shares of B company common stock	$24,000	$23,500	$(500)
200 shares of C Company preferred stock	24,000	24,100	100
$15,000 face value of D Company 10% bonds	15,000	14,700	(300)
Totals	$63,000	$62,300	$(700)

Before the 2005 year-end adjusting entry, the Allowance account has a credit balance of $3,100 ($2,000 12/31/04 credit balance + $1,100 from 3/1/05 reversal) and the Unrealized Increase/Decrease account has a $3,100 debit balance.[11] At December 31, 2005

---

11. The $3,100 debit balance (cumulative unrealized holding loss) in the Unrealized Increase/Decrease account is the difference between the $63,000 cost ($24,000 + $24,000 + $15,000) of the remaining securities held (in Company B, C, and D securities) and the 12/31/04 fair value of $59,900 ($22,700 + $23,200 + $14,000).

the required amount of the Allowance account is a $700 credit balance, so the Kent Company debits the Allowance account for $2,400 ($3,100 − $700) to record the increase in value (unrealized holding gain) as follows:

Allowance for Change in Value of Investment	2,400	
Unrealized Increase/Decrease in Value of		
Available-for-Sale Securities		2,400

The Kent Company reports the $1,000 gain on the sale of its investment in the A Company common stock in its 2005 net income because this amount is realized. The company reports the $2,400 unrealized holding gain (on the Company B, C, and D securities) in its 2005 other comprehensive income.

RECLASSIFICATION ADJUSTMENT   As we discussed in Chapter 4, a company's comprehensive income consists of two parts: net income and other comprehensive income. A reclassification adjustment is made to avoid "double counting" in the company's comprehensive income. Recall that the Kent Company reports the $1,000 gain on the sale of the Company A common stock in its income statement for 2005. So the company includes the $1,000 in the net income that it reports as the first part of its comprehensive income. Also recall that it computed the $1,000 gain by comparing the $6,000 selling price to the $5,000 *cost*. But the company had already reported a $1,100 cumulative unrealized gain ($6,100 fair value − $5,000 cost) on these securities in its other comprehensive income for 2003 and 2004. So to avoid double counting, this is why the Kent Company *reduced* its other comprehensive income for 2005 by the $1,100 adjustment of the Unrealized Increase/Decrease account that it made on March 1, 2003 (when it sold the Company A common stock). This offsets the $1,100 cumulative unrealized holding gain that it reported in the prior years. It reports the $1,100 reclassification adjustment as a *negative* component of other comprehensive income.

INVESTMENTS IN HELD-TO-MATURITY DEBT SECURITIES

4 Account for investments in held-to-maturity debt securities, including amortization of bond premiums and discounts.

The theoretical and practical issues related to the recording and reporting of bonds by the debtor are discussed in Chapter 13.

The generally accepted accounting principles for investments in held-to-maturity debt securities are (1) the investment is initially recorded at cost, (2) it is subsequently reported at amortized cost, (3) unrealized holding gains and losses are *not* recorded, and (4) interest revenue and realized gains and losses on sales (if any) are all included in net income. In Chapter 13 we pointed out that bonds carrying a stated interest rate above the prevailing yield for securities with a similar amount of risk sell at a premium. This premium lowers the stated interest rate to the market (yield) rate. Bonds carrying a stated interest rate below the prevailing market rate for securities with a similar amount of risk sell at a discount. The discount effectively increases the stated interest rate to the market rate. In contrast to accounting for premiums and discounts by debtor companies, investor companies generally do *not* use a separate valuation account for the premiums and discounts on investments in bonds. Instead, the acquisition price is recorded in the investment account, which is directly adjusted for any premium and discount amortization, even though *APB Opinion No. 21* recommended separate disclosure. The effect of not separately disclosing premiums or discounts is to report the Investment in Held-to-Maturity Bonds account directly at its carrying value (amortized cost) on each balance sheet date.

Recording Initial Cost

Investments in debt securities held to maturity are recorded in the same way as we discussed earlier. To illustrate, assume that a company purchases 9% bonds with a face value of $100,000 on August 1, 2003 at 99 plus accrued interest. Interest on these bonds is payable semiannually on May 31 and November 30. The company records this acquisition on August 1, 2003 as follows:

Investment in Held-to-Maturity Debt		
Securities ($100,000 × 0.99)	99,000	
Interest Revenue ($100,000 × 0.09 × 2/12)	1,500	
Cash		100,500

Note that the company debits the Investment account for $99,000. Therefore it includes the $1,000 discount directly in the Investment account and amortizes it as an adjustment to interest revenue, as we discuss later. Note also that, as we illustrated for investments in available-for-sale securities, the company debits the Interest Revenue account for the two months of accrued interest. It will credit the Interest Revenue account for $4,500 when it receives the November 30, 2003 semiannual interest, resulting in the recognition of $3,000 interest earned for the period August 1 through November 30, 2003.

Recognition and Amortization of Bond Premiums and Discounts

Investments in held-to-maturity debt securities that are purchased at a premium or discount result in an effective interest rate that is different than the stated rate. Consequently, for these investments in bonds, **the amount of interest revenue recognized each accounting period is based on the effective interest rate (yield) at the time of acquisition.** Therefore, **any premium or discount is amortized over the remaining life of the bonds in order to assign the proper amount of interest revenue to each accounting period.** The effective interest method and straight-line method are the alternative procedures that are used to record interest revenue and account for premiums and discounts. However, *APB Opinion No. 21* requires use of the effective interest method, unless the use of the straight-line method does not result in a material difference in the amount of interest revenue recognized in any year. Premium amortizations result in an effective interest rate lower than the stated rate, whereas discount amortizations result in an effective interest rate higher than the stated rate.

The effective interest and straight-line methods are explained in Chapter 13.

ACCOUNTING FOR PREMIUMS Assume that the Colburn Company invests in bonds that will be held to maturity, with a face value of $100,000, paying $102,458.71 on January 1, 2003. These bonds carry a stated interest rate of 13% payable semiannually on June 30 and December 31; they mature on December 31, 2005, and yield an effective interest rate of 12%. The Colburn Company records the acquisition on January 1, 2003 as follows:

> **Investment in Held-to-Maturity**
> **Debt Securities**   102,458.71
> **Cash**   102,458.71

Exhibits 14-2 and 14-3 show the schedules for computing interest revenue, the premium amortization, and the carrying value under the straight-line and effective interest methods for these bonds. We explained the preparation of similar schedules for bonds payable in Chapter 13, so our discussion here is limited. The Colburn Company records the first interest receipt on June 30, 2003 using the effective interest method for the bonds purchased at a premium, as follows:

EXHIBIT 14-2 **Bond Investment Interest Revenue and Premium Amortization Schedule: *Straight-Line Method***

Date	Cash Debit[a]	Investment in Debt Securities Credit[b]	Interest Revenue Credit[c]	Carrying Value of Investment in Debt Securities[d]
1/1/03				$102,458.71
6/30/03	$6,500.00	$409.79	$6,090.21	102,048.92
12/31/03	6,500.00	409.79	6,090.21	101,639.13
6/30/04	6,500.00	409.79	6,090.21	101,229.34
12/31/04	6,500.00	409.79	6,090.21	100,819.55
6/30/05	6,500.00	409.79	6,090.21	100,409.76
12/31/05	6,500.00	409.76[e]	6,090.24	100,000.00

a. $100,000 (face value) × 0.13 (stated rate of interest) × 1/2 (year).
b. ($102,458.71 − $100,000) = $2,458.71 ÷ 6 (remaining semiannual periods of bond life).
c. $6,500 − $409.79.
d. Previous investment carrying value − amount from footnote *b*.
e. Difference due to $0.03 rounding error.

EXHIBIT 14-3 Bond Investment Interest Revenue and Premium Amortization Schedule: *Effective Interest Method*

Date	Cash Debit[a]	Interest Revenue Credit[b]	Investment in Debt Securities Credit[c]	Carrying Value of Investment in Debt Securities[d]
1/1/03				$102,458.71
6/30/03	$6,500.00	$6,147.52	$352.48	102,106.23
12/31/03	6,500.00	6,126.37	373.63	101,732.60
6/30/04	6,500.00	6,103.96	396.04	101,336.56
12/31/04	6,500.00	6,080.19	419.81	100,916.75
6/30/05	6,500.00	6,055.01	444.99	100,471.76
12/31/05	6,500.00	6,028.24[e]	471.76	100,000.00

a. $100,000 (face value) × 0.13 (stated rate of interest) × 1/2 (year).
b. Previous investment carrying value × 0.12 (effective interest rate) × 1/2 (year).
c. Amount from footnote *a* − amount from footnote *b*.
d. Previous investment carrying value − amount from footnote *c*.
e. Difference due to $0.07 rounding error.

Cash	6,500.00	
Investment in Held-to-Maturity Debt Securities		352.48
Interest Revenue		6,147.52

Note that the company credits the premium amortization directly to the Investment account. If it uses the straight-line method, it makes a similar entry using the amounts from Exhibit 14-2.

ACCOUNTING FOR DISCOUNTS Now assume that Colburn acquired the bonds at a discount for $97,616.71. This discount indicates that the rate of interest desired by investors is greater than the stated rate of 13%. These bonds yield an effective interest rate of 14%. Exhibits 14-4 and 14-5 illustrate the schedules for computing interest revenue, the discount amortization, and the carrying value under the straight-line and effective interest methods for these bonds. On January 1, 2003 Colburn records the acquisition as follows:

Investment in Held-to-Maturity Debt Securities	97,616.71	
Cash		97,616.71

EXHIBIT 14-4 Bond Investment Interest Revenue and Discount Amortization Schedule: *Straight-Line Method*

Date	Cash Debit[a]	Investment in Debt Securities Debit[b]	Interest Revenue Credit[c]	Carrying Value of Investment in Debt Securities[d]
1/1/03				$ 97,616.71
6/30/03	$6,500.00	$397.22	$6,897.22	98,013.93
12/31/03	6,500.00	397.22	6,897.22	98,411.15
6/30/04	6,500.00	397.22	6,897.22	98,808.37
12/31/04	6,500.00	397.22	6,897.22	99,205.59
6/30/05	6,500.00	397.22	6,897.22	99,602.81
12/31/05	6,500.00	397.19[e]	6,897.19	100,000.00

a. $100,000 (face value) × 0.13 (stated rate of interest) × 1/2 (year).
b. ($100,000 − $97,616.71) = $2,383.29 ÷ 6 (remaining semiannual periods of bond life).
c. $6,500 + $397.22.
d. Previous investment carrying value + amount from footnote *b*.
e. Difference due to $0.03 rounding error.

EXHIBIT 14-5   Bond Investment Interest Revenue and Discount Amortization
Schedule: *Effective Interest Method*

Date	Cash Debit[a]	Interest Revenue Credit[b]	Investment in Debt Securities Debit[c]	Carrying Value of Investment in Debt Securities[d]
1/1/03				$ 97,616.71
6/30/03	$6,500.00	$6,833.17	$333.17	97,949.88
12/31/03	6,500.00	6,856.49	356.49	98,306.37
6/30/04	6,500.00	6,881.45	381.45	98,687.82
12/31/04	6,500.00	6,908.15	408.15	99,095.97
6/30/05	6,500.00	6,936.72	436.72	99,532.69
12/31/05	6,500.00	6,967.31[e]	467.31	100,000.00

a. $100,000 (face value) × 0.13 (stated rate of interest) × 1/2 (year).
b. Previous investment carrying value × 0.14 (effective interest rate) × 1/2 (year).
c. Amount from footnote *b* − amount from footnote *a*.
d. Previous investment carrying value + amount from footnote *c*.
e. Difference due to $0.02 rounding error.

Colburn records the first interest receipt on June 30, 2003, using the effective interest method for the bonds purchased at a discount, as follows:

Cash	6,500.00	
Investment in Held-to-Maturity Debt Securities	333.17	
Interest Revenue		6,833.17

Note that the company debits the discount amortization directly to the Investment account. If it uses the straight-line method, it makes a similar entry using the amounts from Exhibit 14-4.

Amortization for Bonds Acquired Between Interest Dates

As we illustrated earlier, held-to-maturity bonds may be acquired between interest dates. When these bonds are purchased at a premium or discount, the premium or discount is amortized over the remaining life of the bonds. To illustrate, assume that the Tallen Company purchased 13% bonds with a face value of $200,000 for $204,575.07 on April 3, 2003. Interest on these bonds is payable June 30 and December 31, and the bonds mature December 31, 2005 (33 months after the date of purchase). Tallen records the acquisition on April 3, 2003 as follows:

Investment in Held-to-Maturity		
Debt Securities	204,575.07	
Interest Revenue ($200,000 × 0.13 × 3/12)	6,500.00	
Cash		211,075.07

The company amortizes the $4,575.07 premium ($204,575.07 − $200,000) over the remaining 33-month life of the bond issue. If it uses straight-line amortization, it amortizes $138.64 ($4,575.07 ÷ 33) of the premium to reduce interest revenue for each month it holds the bonds.

When the effective interest method is used, the actual yield[12] is computed and then used to amortize the premium over the length of time the investment is to be held. The purchase of a $200,000 investment due in 33 months with a stated 13% interest rate, payable semiannually, for $204,575.07 results in an effective interest rate of 12%. Using the effective interest method of amortization, the company would record the first two interest receipts as follows:

---

12. See Chapter 13 for an illustration of the calculation of yields.

June 30, 2003

Cash	13,000.00	
Interest Revenue		
[($204,575.07 × 0.12 × 1/4) + $6,500*]		12,637.25
Investment in Held-to-Maturity		
Debt Securities ($13,000 − $12,637.25)		362.75

* Amount debited to interest revenue on the date the bonds were acquired.

December 31, 2003

Cash	13,000.00	
Interest Revenue		
[($204,575.07 − $362.75) × 0.12 × 1/2]		12,252.74
Investment in Held-to-Maturity		
Debt Securities ($13,000 − $12,252.74)		747.26

In calculating the premium amortization for the first interest payment, note that the actual amount of interest revenue is only $6,137.25 ($204,575.07 × 0.12 × 1/4)[13] even though Tallen credited the interest revenue account for $12,637.25. The additional $6,500 credit reflects the interest payment to the former owner. Subsequently, Tallen computes the amount of interest revenue by multiplying the carrying value of the investment (acquisition price less amortized premium) by the 6% semiannual yield (0.12 × 1/2). It records the difference between the amount of cash received and the amount of interest revenue as premium amortization in each successive period.

Sale of Investment in Bonds Before Maturity

Selling an investment in bonds being held to maturity before the maturity date should be rare because the sale may violate the original intent behind the acquisition and the valuation procedures underlying that intent. Alternatively, as we discussed earlier in the chapter, certain changes in circumstances are *not* inconsistent with the original intent. When such a sale occurs, a company must record any gain or loss from the transaction. Also, the company eliminates its Investment account, and collects any interest earned since the last interest date from the purchaser.

Before computing the gain or loss on the sale of an investment, the company amortizes any premium or discount on the bonds from the last interest date to the sale date. This procedure is necessary to ensure that the correct amount of interest revenue is recorded, and to determine the carrying value of the investment on the date of the sale. The carrying value of the bonds is then compared with the sales price (*excluding* any accrued interest) to determine the gain or loss. To illustrate, assume that the $100,000 of 13% bonds purchased by the Colburn Company for $97,616.71 that we discussed earlier were sold on March 31, 2004 for $102,000 plus accrued interest. Colburn records the following journal entries on March 31, 2004 (assuming it amortizes the bond discount by the straight-line method illustrated in Exhibit 14-4):

Investment in Held-to-Maturity Debt Securities		
[($2,383.29 ÷ 6) × 1/2]	198.61	
Interest Revenue		198.61
Cash ($102,000 + $3,250)	105,250.00	
Interest Revenue ($100,000 × 0.13 × 1/4)		3,250.00
Investment in Held-to-Maturity Debt		
Securities ($98,411.15 from Exhibit 14-4		
+ $198.61)		98,609.76
Gain on Sale of Debt Securities		3,390.24

---

13. This calculation assumes that the purchase price yields 12% interest for 33 months. Normally, it is necessary to find the present value of the bonds at the last interest payment date (December 31, 2002 in this case), subtract the present value of the bonds on the next interest payment date (June 30, 2003), and apply the straight-line method to amortize the premium for the interim period. See Chapter 13 (pp. 555–556) for an illustration of this procedure.

The first journal entry brings the investment carrying value up to date. In the second journal entry, the debit to Cash records the sales price plus the $3,250 interest earned in the 3 months since the last interest payment date, and the credit to the Investment account eliminates the current carrying value of the investment on the sale date. The Colburn Company computes the gain by comparing the $98,609.76 current carrying value of the Investment account on the sale date with the $102,000 selling price of the investment. Colburn reports this gain as ordinary income, unless considered unusual and infrequent, in which case it reports the gain as an extraordinary item.

The following diagram summarizes the accounting issues we have discussed for the three categories of investments in securities.

Event	Classify According to Management Intent as:	Initially Record at:	Classify Cash Flow as:	Subsequently Report on the Balance Sheet at:	
	Trading	Cost	Operating	Fair Value	
Company Purchases Securities	Available-for-Sale	Cost	Investing	Fair Value	(Continued below)
	Held-to-Maturity	Cost	Investing	Amortized Cost	

*Sales of held-to-maturity securities should be rare.

Classify According to Management Intent as:	Recognize Unrealized Holding Gains and Losses in:	Recognize Interest and Dividend Revenue in:	Recognize Realized Gain or Loss in:	Compute Realized Gain or Loss as:
Trading	Net Income	Net Income	Net Income	Selling Price minus Fair Value at Most Recent Balance Sheet Date
Available-for-Sale	Other Comprehensive Income	Net Income	Net Income	Selling Price minus (Amortized) Cost
Held-to-Maturity	—	Net Income	Net Income*	Selling Price* minus (Amortized) Cost

TRANSFERS AND IMPAIRMENTS

Two additional issues arise in accounting for investments. The first involves transfers between investment categories, while the second involves impairments of investments.

5 Understand transfers and impairments.

Transfers of Investments Between Categories

The transfer of a security between investment categories is accounted for at the fair value at the time of the transfer. However, transfers into or out of the trading category should be rare, as should transfers *from* the held-to-maturity category. In the journal entry to record the transfer, the fair value is used as the "new" investment carrying value, and the "old" investment carrying value is eliminated. However, the accounting for any related unrealized gain or loss varies, depending on the type of transfer.

1. A transfer *from the trading* category. No accounting for the unrealized holding gain or loss is necessary because it has already been recognized in net income.
2. A transfer *into the trading* category. The previous unrealized holding gain or loss is eliminated and a gain or loss is included in net income.
3. A transfer *into the available for sale* category *from the held-to-maturity* category. An unrealized holding gain or loss is established and included in other comprehensive income.
4. A transfer of a debt security *into the held-to-maturity* category *from the available-for-sale* category. The unrealized holding gain or loss on the available-for-sale security is eliminated and an unrealized holding gain or loss on the held-to-maturity security is created for the same amount and included in other comprehensive income. The amount is amortized over the remaining life of the security as an adjustment of interest revenue by computing a new yield to maturity for that security.

We will use three examples to illustrate transfers (we do not discuss a transfer *from* the trading category). To illustrate a transfer *into* the trading category *from* the available-for-sale category, assume the same facts as earlier for the Kent Company at December 31, 2004. Assume also that in 2005 Kent transfers the Company A securities into the trading category when their fair value is $6,300. Because Kent does not use an Allowance account for its investments in trading securities, it debits the asset account directly for the fair value of the securities. Since the available-for-sale securities had a cost of $5,000, it records a $1,300 realized holding gain. Furthermore, it debits the Unrealized Increase/Decrease account and credits the Allowance account related to the available-for-sale securities for $1,100, respectively, to eliminate the December 31, 2004 adjustment ($6,100 fair value − $5,000 cost) recorded on that date. It records the transfer as follows:

Investment in Trading Securities	6,300	
Investment in Available-for-Sale Securities		5,000
Gain on Transfer of Securities		1,300
Unrealized Increase/Decrease in Value of		
Available-for-Sale Securities	1,100	
Allowance for Change in Value of Investment		1,100

Kent includes the gain in its net income for 2005, and as we discussed earlier, includes the $1,100 as a reduction in its other comprehensive income for 2005.

To illustrate the transfer *into* the available-for-sale category *from* the held-to-maturity category, assume that the Devon Company has bonds included in the category of investments held to maturity. The bonds have a face value of $10,000 and the company purchased them at par. When the fair value of the bonds is $9,500, the company transfers the bonds into the available-for-sale category. Since an Investment in Available-for-Sale Securities is recorded at cost and an Allowance account is used to adjust the carrying value to fair value (with a corresponding adjustment to the Unrealized Increase/Decrease account), the company records the transfer as follows:

Investment in Available-for-Sale Securities	10,000	
Investment in Held-to-Maturity Debt Securities		10,000
Unrealized Increase/Decrease in Value of		
Available-for-Sale Securities	500	
Allowance for Change in Value of Investment		500

If the company purchased bonds being held to maturity at a premium or discount, it would record the investment in available-for-sale securities at the amortized cost, and it would compute the adjustment to the Allowance and Unrealized Increase/Decrease accounts by comparing the fair value to the amortized cost.

To illustrate the transfer *into* the held-to-maturity category *from* the available-for-sale category, assume the same facts for the Devon Company except that it currently classifies the bonds as available for sale and transfers them into the held-to-maturity category. Assume further that the available-for-sale bonds had a fair value of $9,700 on the previous balance sheet date. In this case, the company records the investment in debt securities at the current fair value of $9,500, and eliminates the previous $300 ($9,700 − $10,000) amounts in the Allowance and Unrealized Increase/Decrease accounts. It creates a new stockholders' equity account, Unrealized Increase/Decrease in Value of Held-to-Maturity Debt Securities for the $500 difference between the current fair value and the original cost. It records the transfer as follows:

Investment in Held-to-Maturity Debt Securities	9,500	
Unrealized Increase/Decrease from Transfer of Securities	500	
Investment in Available-for-Sale Securities		10,000
Allowance for Change in Value of Investment	300	
Unrealized Increase/Decrease in Value of Available-for-Sale Securities		300

In subsequent periods the company amortizes the $500 discount in the Investment account ($10,000 face value − $9,500 carrying value) using the effective interest method over the remaining life of the bonds. This requires the computation of a new effective interest rate. The new rate is computed by equating, on a present value basis, the future cash flows and the new "carrying value."[14] Interest revenue is then computed by multiplying the carrying value each period by the effective interest rate. We discussed this procedure in Chapter 13 in the section on troubled debt restructuring. The $500 unrealized amount is also amortized as an adjustment to interest revenue, using the effective interest method over the remaining life of the debt security (bonds), and this amount offsets the amortization of the discount.

Impairments

There may be an "other than temporary" decline below the amortized cost of an investment in a debt security classified as available for sale or held to maturity. A company uses such factors as the reason for the decline, the duration of the decline, the future potential of the investee, and the current state of the economy to determine whether a particular decrease in the value of a security should be considered other than temporary. Impairment occurs when it is probable that the company will be unable to collect all the amounts due. The company writes down the amortized cost of the security to the fair value and includes the amount of the write-down in net income as a realized loss. The fair value becomes the new "cost" and is not changed for subsequent recoveries in fair value, although increases and decreases in the fair value of available-for-sale securities are included in stockholders' equity as we discussed earlier.

To illustrate this situation, suppose that the Tracy Company has a bond investment categorized as held to maturity, which has a carrying value (amortized cost) of $21,500 and a fair value of $6,500. If it considers the decline in value to be other than temporary, the company records the decline of $15,000 ($21,500 − $6,500) as follows:

Realized Loss on Decline in Value	15,000	
Investment in Held-to-Maturity Debt Securities		15,000

The $6,500 becomes the new "cost" of the security. The company computes interest revenue using the effective interest method based on the new effective interest rate computed as we discussed earlier for bonds transferred into the held-to-maturity category.

A similar procedure is followed for an investment in a security classified as available for sale which experiences a decline in value that is considered to be other than temporary. Since a company is already reporting the security at fair value by using an allowance account, it establishes a new cost basis at the fair value. It eliminates the allowance and unrealized increase/decrease accounts, and records the loss from the write-down as a realized loss. It includes any subsequent changes in value (that are considered to be temporary) as unrealized holding gains and losses in other comprehensive income. The realized gain or loss on the eventual sale of the security is the difference between the selling price and the new "cost."

---

14. This procedure is used for investments in marketable debt securities. We discussed accounting for the impairment of a loan (which does not have a fair value available on a stock exchange) in Chapter 13.

DISCLOSURES

6 Understand disclosures of investments.

The following disclosures for investments in securities are required by *FASB Statement No. 115*:

1. *Trading Securities.* A company must disclose the change in the net unrealized holding gain or loss that is included in each income statement.
2. *Available-for-Sale Securities.* For each balance sheet date, a company must disclose the aggregate fair value, gross unrealized holding gains and gross unrealized holding losses, and (amortized) cost by major security types. Also, the contractual maturities of debt securities must be disclosed. For each income statement period, the company must disclose (1) the proceeds from sales and the gross realized gains and gross realized losses on those sales, (2) the basis on which cost was determined (e.g., the average cost method), (3) the gross gains and gross losses included in net income from transfers of securities from this category into the trading category, and (4) the change in the net unrealized holding gain or loss included as a separate component of other comprehensive income.
3. *Held-to-Maturity Debt Securities.* For each balance sheet date, a company must disclose the aggregate fair value, gross unrealized holding gains, gross unrealized holding losses, and amortized cost by major security types. Also, the contractual maturities of these securities must be disclosed. For any sales or transfers from this category, the disclosures must include the amortized cost, the related realized or unrealized gain or loss, and the circumstances leading to the decision to sell or transfer the security.

Exhibit 14-6 shows the disclosures of General Motors in its 2001 annual report. Financial institutions must make additional disclosures which we do not discuss here.

EXHIBIT 14-6   Disclosure of Marketable Securities

GENERAL MOTORS

Note 4. Marketable and Other Securities

Marketable securities held by GM are classified as available-for-sale, except for certain mortgage-related securities, which are classified as held to maturity or trading securities. Unrealized gains and losses, net of related income taxes, for available-for-sale and held to maturity securities are included as a separate component of stockholders' equity. Unrealized gains and losses for trading securities are included in income on a current basis. GM determines cost on the specific identification basis.

Automotive, Communications Services, and Other Operations
Investments in marketable securities were as follows (dollars in millions):

December 31, 2001	Cost	Book/Fair Value	Unrealized Gains	Unrealized Losses
Type of security				
Bonds, notes, and other securities				
Corporate debt securities and other	$ 777	$ 790	$13	$–
Total marketable securities 31/162	$ 777	$ 790	$13	$–

December 31, 2000	Cost	Book/Fair Value	Unrealized Gains	Unrealized Losses
Type of security				
Bonds, notes, and other securities				
United States government and agencies	$ 90	$ 91	$1	$–
States and municipalities	9	9	–	–
Corporate debt securities and other	1,063	1,061	–	2
Total marketable securities	$1,162	$1,161	$1	$2

EXHIBIT 14-6 Disclosure of Marketable Securities, Continued

Debt securities totaling $265 million mature within one year, $504 million mature after one through five years, and $21 million mature after ten years. Proceeds from sales of marketable securities totaled $373 million in 2001, $1.3 billion in 2000, and $2.0 billion in 1999. The gross gains related to sales of marketable securities were $6 million, $1 million, and $21 million in 2001, 2000, and 1999, respectively. The gross losses related to sales of marketable securities were $5 million, $12 million, and $6 million in 2001, 2000 and 1999, respectively.

Financing and Insurance Operations

Investments in securities were as follows (dollars in millions):

December 31, 2001	Cost	Book/Fair Value	Unrealized Gains	Unrealized Losses
Type of security				
Bonds, notes, and other securities				
United States government and agencies	$ 615	$ 626	$ 14	$ 3
States and municipalities	931	970	43	4
Mortgage-backed securities	924	913	17	28
Corporate debt securities and other	2,725	2,749	50	26
Total debt securities available-for-sale	5,195	5,258	124	61
Mortgage-backed securities held to maturity	371	371	–	–
Mortgage-backed securities held for trading purposes	4,305	3,722	–	583
Total debt securities	9,871	9,351	124	644
Equity securities	1,214	1,318	246	142
Total investment in securities	$11,085	$10,669	$370	$786

December 31, 2000	Cost	Book/Fair Value	Unrealized Gains	Unrealized Losses
Type of security				
Bonds, notes, and other securities				
United States government and agencies	$ 556	$ 565	$ 10	$ 1
States and municipalities	1,492	1,567	81	6
Mortgage-backed securities	387	384	14	17
Corporate debt securities and other	2,520	2,506	47	61
Total debt securities available-for-sale	4,955	5,022	152	85
Mortgage-backed securities held to maturity	218	218	–	–
Mortgage-backed securities held for trading purposes	3,445	3,298	–	147
Total debt securities	8,618	8,538	152	232
Equity securities	766	1,057	395	104
Total investment in securities	$9,384	$9,595	$547	$336

Debt securities abailable-for-sale totaling $896 million mature within one year, $2.3 billion mature after one through five years, $716 million mature after five years through 10 years, and $1.4 billion mature after 10 years. Proceeds from sales of marketable securities totaled $5.1 billion in 2001, $3.5 billion in 2000, and $2.9 billion in 1999. The gross gains related to sales of marketable securities were $228 million, $315 million, and $292 million in 2001, 2000, and 1999, respectively. The gross losses related to sales of marketable securities were $145 million, $147 million, and $126 million in 2001, 2000 and 1999, respectively.

Q U E S T I O N S

Q How much would General Motors include in other comprehensive income for 2001? **Q** In accumulated other comprehensive income at December 31, 2001? **Q** How much did the company include in its income statement and statement of cash flows for 2001 related to securities?

Financial Statement Classification

Investments in trading securities are always classified as current assets (if the company presents a classified balance sheet). Investments in available-for-sale securities are classified as current or noncurrent assets depending on whether or not they will be sold within one year or the operating cycle, whichever is longer.[15] For example, if the Kent Company investments in A and B are current and in C and D are noncurrent at December 31, 2003, it reports the $71,000 fair value (from our earlier example on page 609) as follows:

Assets

Current Assets

Temporary investment in available-for-sale securities (at cost)	$29,000
Plus: Allowance for change in value of investment	500
Temporary investment in available-for-sale securities (at fair value)	$29,500

Noncurrent Assets

Investment in available-for-sale securities (at cost)	$39,000
Plus: Allowance for change in value of investment	2,500
Investment in available-for-sale securities (at fair value)	$41,500

Investments in held-to-maturity debt securities are classified as noncurrent assets unless they mature within the next year.

Cash flows from purchases, sales, and maturities of available-for-sale securities and held-to-maturity securities are classified as cash flows from investing activities. The gross amounts of inflows and outflows are reported for each category. Cash flows from purchases, sales, and maturities of trading securities are classified as cash flows from operating activities.

FASB STATEMENT NO. 115: A CONCEPTUAL EVALUATION

7 Explain the conceptual issues regarding investments in marketable securities.

Prior to the issuance of *FASB Statement No. 115*, investments in marketable equity securities were accounted for by the lower of cost or market (LCM) method. There were no defined general principles for investments in debt securities. Most companies used the cost method, but financial institutions followed regulatory accounting principles which require that some securities be accounted for by the fair value method.

The use of the LCM method was widely criticized for two primary reasons. First, it was argued that it was not a *relevant* value because it did not reflect the *liquidity* of the securities when the fair value exceeded the cost. In that situation, more funds could be obtained through a sale in the current market than was indicated by the balance sheet. Secondly, the method allowed companies to engage in what was often referred to as "gains trading." Gains trading meant that companies would sell those securities that had a fair value above cost so that the realized gain on the sale would be included in income.

The major controversies involved in the new principles focus on four issues: (1) fair value is required in the balance sheet for trading securities and available-for-sale securities, whereas amortized cost is required for held-to-maturity securities, (2) fair value is *not* required for certain liabilities, (3) unrealized holding gains and losses are reported in net income for trading securities but in other comprehensive income for available-for-sale securities, and (4) the classification of securities is based on management intent. The *Statement* was adopted by a 5-to-2 majority and the dissenters raised some of the issues. They argued that a company should report all three categories at fair value, and include all unrealized holding gains and losses in net income.

---

15. *FASB Statement No. 115, op. cit.,* par. 17.

Fair Value Is Required for Certain Investments

It may be argued that the fair value of trading securities and available-for-sale securities is more *relevant* than the LCM value. In particular, reporting the fair value may assist users in evaluating the performance of a company's investment strategies and increase the *comparability* of balance sheets. Fair value is the market's estimate of the present value of the net future cash flows of those securities, discounted to reflect both the current interest rate and the market's estimate of the *risk* associated with those cash flows.

The fair value of investments also may provide a better indication of the *financial flexibility*, or *solvency*, of companies, particularly for financial institutions which have a large portion of their assets in such securities. In a *liquidity* shortage, the fair value of investments is the amount available to cover a company's obligations.

It also may be argued that the fair value of held-to-maturity debt securities is *not* relevant. Amortized cost may provide relevant information because it focuses on the decision to acquire the asset, the earnings effects of that decision that will be realized over time, and the ultimate future recoverable value of the asset. Fair value ignores those concepts and focuses instead on the effects of transactions and events that do not directly involve the company. If a debt security is held to maturity, the maturity value will be realized and any interim unrealized holding gains and losses will reverse. In summary, if a company has no intent to sell a security and has no need to, then the fair value may *not* be relevant because that cash flow will not occur. However, the two dissenters argued that fair value would be preferable for these securities also.

The FASB made the held-to-maturity category restrictive, so that the use of the amortized cost method must be justified by management for each investment in a debt security. At each acquisition, the company must establish the positive intent and ability to hold the security to maturity, which is *not* the same as the absence of an intent to sell. Thus the amortized cost method is appropriate if the security is actually held to maturity, but is not appropriate if management merely has no intent to sell it. Of course, the classification does involve judgment by management and that judgment may prove to be incorrect. Also, the judgment may be changed by unforeseen circumstances such as changes in tax laws or in the security's credit risk.

Note that the arguments in favor of reporting fair value for some securities do not necessarily apply to the reporting of inventories. Therefore the arguments do not invalidate the use of the LCM method for inventories.

Fair Value Is Not Required for Certain Liabilities

The FASB also considered the desirability of requiring certain liabilities to be reported at fair value because they are "mirror images" of the assets. This was supported particularly by financial institutions, which manage their interest rate risk by coordinating their holdings of financial assets and liabilities. Therefore they argued that financial statements would provide a more *relevant* view of a company's exposure to *risk* if some liabilities were also reported at fair value. In other words, they felt that recognizing fair value on only one side of their portfolios introduced an inappropriate bias into their financial statements.

The FASB rejected the fair value reporting of liabilities because of the difficulty of (1) determining which liabilities should be reported at fair value, and (2) obtaining a *reliable* value because many of the liabilities do not trade in an established market. Also nonfinancial companies do not manage risk in the same way and use the proceeds from borrowing to invest in physical and intangible assets that are not reported at fair value. Since liabilities are not reported at fair value, the FASB concluded that it would not require all investments (i.e., those held to maturity) to be valued at fair value. The FASB admitted that this conclusion represents a compromise, and one of the dissenters voted against adoption partly for this reason. However, the FASB has since announced an *intent* to change GAAP so that liabilities would be reported at fair value.

Reporting of Unrealized Gains and Losses

Since trading securities are actively managed, the FASB concluded that income measurement for those securities is more relevant if it includes the results of changes in fair value—the unrealized holding gains and losses. Therefore a company's net income includes the results of economic events that occur in the period and provides a better measure of the company's *return on investment*.

Partly in response to the issue of not reporting liabilities at fair value, the FASB concluded that including unrealized holding gains and losses in income for available-for-sale securities would create an unnecessary volatility into a company's reported net income. Such volatility does not represent the way that the company manages its business and the impact of economic events of the period. In addition, when the intent is to hold securities for a long period, it is more likely that any unrealized holding gains and losses will offset before the sale occurs. Therefore including those gains and losses in net income would also create unnecessary volatility in income. For these reasons, the FASB concluded that unrealized holding gains and losses on available-for-sale securities should not be included in net income, but instead should be reported as a component of other comprehensive income.

This reporting of unrealized holding gains and losses, however, does not eliminate the possibility of "gains trading," because the realized gain on a sale is the difference between the selling price and the cost of the security, and is included in net income. Note also that a company may tend to avoid selling a security classified as available for sale when its fair value is less than its cost. The sale would result in the recognition of a realized loss in net income, whereas if the company continues to hold the security, the decline in value is included in other comprehensive income. Therefore the decision not to sell avoids the recognition of the decline in value in net income. Thus, companies are able to "manage" the amount of net income they report by selecting which securities to sell. The two dissenters were concerned that the *Statement* does not prevent this practice.

Classification of Securities Is Based on Management Intent

Classifying securities into three categories, each of which has different accounting principles, and using management intent as a criterion to distinguish among the categories may result in an inconsistent application of the principles. Companies with three identical securities could account for those securities using three different accounting methods. Both issues may create a lack of *comparability*.

In addition, transfers between categories, which are also based partly on management intent and judgment, allow for management of earnings because the gain (or loss) is included in net income. Combined with the opportunities for gains trading, the new principles may not produce sufficient *relevance*.

International Accounting Differences

International accounting standards also use the trading, available-for-sale, and held-to-maturity categories but apply them to all financial assets, not just investments in securities. The valuation methods are the same for each category as U.S. principles, but for available-for-sale securities a company must make a one-time election to choose whether to record the changes in value in net income or equity (which would be similar to other comprehensive income).

EQUITY METHOD

8 Account for investments using the equity method.

When an investor corporation owns a sufficiently large percentage of common stock, it is able to exert significant influence over the operating and financial policies of the investee corporation. In particular, the investor may be able to influence the investee's dividend policy. The dividends paid may be affected by the investor's cash needs, desire to raise its income, or by tax considerations. The fair value methods, which recognize income when dividends are received (declared), are therefore inappropriate when significant influence exists because the investor could influence its income. Also, the fair value of the stock does not represent the cash that would be received if such a large number of shares were sold. The equity method of accounting is used to account for these investments.

The equity method (1) acknowledges the existence of a material economic relationship between the investor and the investee, (2) is based upon the requirements of accrual accounting, and (3) reflects the change in stockholders' equity of the investee company.

APB Opinion No. 18 requires that an investor use the equity method when it is able to exercise significant influence over the operating and financial policies of an investee. "Significant influence" is determined by such factors as representation on the board of directors, participation in policy-making processes, material intercompany transactions, interchange of managerial personnel, and technological dependency. In the absence of evidence to the contrary, however, an investment of *20% or more* in the outstanding common stock of the investee leads to the *presumption* of significant influence and the use of the equity method of accounting.[16] An investor also uses the equity method when significant influence exists even though the investor holds less than a 20% investment in the common stock of the investee. On the other hand, there are situations in which an investor holds 20% or more of the outstanding common stock of an investee and does not have the ability to exercise significant influence over the investee. In these cases, the investor does not use the equity method to account for the investment.

FASB Interpretation No. 35 suggests that the following facts and circumstances indicate that an investor holding an investment of 20% or more in the investee should *not* use the equity method: (1) opposition by the investee, such as litigation or complaints to governmental regulatory authorities, challenges the investor's ability to exercise significant influence; (2) the investor and investee sign an agreement under which the investor surrenders significant rights as a shareholder; (3) majority ownership of the investee is concentrated among a small group of shareholders who operate the investee without regard to the views of the investor; (4) the investor needs or wants more financial information to apply the equity method than is available to the investee's other shareholders, tries to obtain that information, and fails. (The application of the equity method requires information not typically included in published financial statements.); or (5) the investor tries and fails to obtain representation on the investee's board of directors.[17]

Accounting Procedures

When a company uses the equity method, it initially records an investment in common stock at its acquisition cost. However, in contrast to the fair value method, the investor records income when it is *reported* by the investee. The investor records income and an increase in the carrying value of the investment account at an amount that is based on the investor's percentage of ownership in the investee. The investor records dividends received (or receivable) as reductions in the carrying value of the investment account when they are paid (or declared) by the investee. Furthermore, (1) since a material relationship is presumed, the investor removes from its account the effects of all intercompany items of revenue and expense to avoid "double counting," and (2) if the acquisition cost is greater than the proportionate book value of the investee, the investor may recognize additional depreciation. Therefore, the investor must make certain adjustments to its investment income. The most frequent are to:

16. "The Equity Method of Accounting for Investments in Common Stock," *APB Opinion No. 18* (New York: AICPA, 1971), par. 17.

17. "Criteria for Applying the Equity Method of Accounting for Investments in Common Stock," *FASB Interpretation No. 35* (Stamford, Conn.: FASB, 1981), par. 4.

1. Eliminate intercompany transactions in the determination of investor income (e.g., a sale from the investor to the investee that results in revenue to the investor and an expense to the investee).
2. Depreciate the proportionate share of any difference between the fair values and book values of investee depreciable assets implied by the acquisition price of the investee shares. [In the event the investor cannot determine the fair value of the specific investee assets, the entire excess of cost (i.e., acquisition price) over the proportionate book value is treated as goodwill and is *not* amortized.]
3. Treat the proportionate share of investee extraordinary items as investor extraordinary items. The proportionate share of investee results of discontinued operations and cumulative effects of changes in accounting principles are treated similarly.[18]

In summary, the investor accounts for the investment and income under the equity method as follows:

$$\text{Investment} = \text{Acquisition Cost} + \frac{\text{Investor's Share of}}{\text{Investee Income}} - \text{Dividends Received}$$

where

$$\frac{\text{Investor's Share of}}{\text{Investee Income}} = (\text{Investee's Net Income} \times \text{Ownership \%}) - \text{Adjustments}$$

and

$$\text{Dividends Received} = \text{Total Dividends Paid by Investee} \times \text{Ownership \%}$$

The use of the equity method more closely fits the requirements of accrual accounting because the investor's share in investee income is reported by the investor during the period in which it is earned rather than as cash is received. The equity method, therefore, supplies more relevant information for decision makers who rely on financial statements.

To illustrate, assume Cliborn Company purchases 4,200 shares of the S Company's outstanding common stock on January 1, 2004. (On that date, S Company had 16,800 shares outstanding, so Cliborn's investment is 25% and significant influence is presumed to exist.) Cliborn paid $125,000 for the shares, and on the date of acquisition obtains the following information concerning S Company:

	Balance Sheet Book Value	Fair Value
Depreciable assets (remaining life, 10 years)	$400,000	$450,000
Other nondepreciable assets (e.g., land)	190,000	246,000
Total	$590,000	$696,000
Liabilities	$200,000	$220,000
Common stock	250,000	
Retained earnings	140,000	
Total	$590,000	

There were no intercompany transactions during the year. S Company paid a $20,000 dividend on August 27, 2004, and reported net income for 2004 of $81,000, consisting of ordinary income of $73,000 and an extraordinary gain of $8,000. Cliborn Company records these events as follows:

---

18. In addition, the investor recognizes deferred income taxes for any difference between income reported under the equity method for financial reporting purposes and dividend income reported for income tax purposes. We do not consider deferred income taxes further in this chapter; we discuss them in Chapter 18.

1. To record the original investment on January 1, 2004:

Investment in Stock: S Company	125,000	
Cash		125,000

2. To record the receipt of dividends on August 27, 2004:

Cash	5,000	
Investment in Stock: S Company		
(0.25 × $20,000)		5,000

The effect of this transaction is simply to exchange one asset (Investment in Stock: S Company) for another (Cash).

3. To record Cliborn Company's 25% share in the year's net income on December 31, 2004:

Investment in Stock: S Company		
(0.25 × $81,000)	20,250	
Investment Income: Ordinary		
(0.25 × $73,000)		18,250
Investment Income: Extraordinary		
(0.25 × $8,000)		2,000

Note that Cliborn increases the investment account by its share of the total net income, and separates the investment income into its share of the ordinary and extraordinary income.

4. To depreciate the increase in the recorded value of depreciable assets acquired:

Investment Income: Ordinary	1,250	
Investment in Stock: S Company		
($12,500 ÷ 10)		1,250

Recall that the depreciable assets acquired have a fair value that exceeds book value by $50,000 ($450,000 − $400,000) and that the remaining useful life of the assets is 10 years. Cliborn acquired 25% of this increase in asset value, so it depreciates $12,500 (0.25 × $50,000) of the additional depreciable asset value over the remaining useful life of the assets according to the matching principle. This $12,500 divided by the 10-year life results in $1,250 additional depreciation, which Cliborn records directly as a deduction from the ordinary investment income and the investment on December 31, 2004.

The proportionate excess of the cost of the investment over the underlying fair value of the assets acquired is goodwill (see Chapter 11). Cliborn calculates the $6,000 of goodwill as follows:

Purchase price		$125,000
Book value of net asset acquired		
[0.25 × ($590,000 − $200,000)]	$97,500	
Adjustments: Increase in depreciable assets acquired		
[($450,000 − $400,000) × 0.25]	12,500	
Increase in other nondepreciable assets acquired		
[($246,000 − $190,000) × 0.25]	14,000	
Increase in liabilities		
[($220,000 − $200,000) × 0.25]	(5,000)	
Fair value of identifiable net assets acquired		(119,000)
Purchased goodwill		$ 6,000

Prior to 2002, this goodwill was amortized over its economic life, not to exceed 40 years. The effect of the amortization was to reduce the investment income and the book value of the asset. However, beginning in 2002, the goodwill is no longer amortized.[19] Therefore, a company with an equity investment will report a higher investment income and a higher book value of the investment. Since the goodwill is no longer amortized, there is a greater possibility that the investment will be over valued. However, the investment must be reviewed for impairment. *APB Opinion No. 18* requires a company to recognize an impairment loss and reduce the investment to its fair value if there is an "other than temporary" decline in value, as we discuss later in the chapter.

Financial Statement Disclosures

Cliborn computes the carrying value of its Investment in Stock: S Company account by adding the reported income for the year and deducting the dividends, depreciation, and goodwill amortization. It reports the Investment in Stock: S Company account in the long-term investment section of its December 31, 2004 balance sheet. This account has a carrying value of $139,000, computed as follows:

Investment in S Company

Acquisition price January 1, 2004		$125,000
Add: Share of 2004 reported ordinary income	$18,250	
Share of 2004 reported extraordinary income	2,000	20,250
		$145,250
Less: Dividends received August 27, 2004	$ 5,000	
Depreciation on excess fair value of acquired assets		
($12,500 ÷ 10; see earlier computation)	1,250	(6,250)
Carrying value		$139,000

The total amount of investee income that Cliborn reports on its income statement for 2004 is $19,000. This amount consists of $17,000 that it reports as income from continuing operations and $2,000 that it reports as an extraordinary item. The accompanying notes to the financial statements include a supporting schedule reconciling these amounts. This schedule appears as follows:

Income from Investment

Share of 2004 ordinary income	$18,250
Less: Depreciation on excess fair value of acquired assets	(1,250)
Ordinary investment income	$17,000
Plus: Share of investee extraordinary income	2,000
Net investment income	$19,000

Special Issues

Sometimes an investor acquires enough additional common shares during a year to justify a change from the fair value method to the equity method, or an investor may dispose of a portion of its investment so that a change from the equity method to the fair value method is necessary. Additionally, an investment carried under the equity method may be acquired for a cost that is less than the fair value of the assets. Or investments carried under the equity method may suffer declines in value that are not temporary.

---

19. "Goodwill and Other Intangible Assets," *FASB Statement of Financial Accounting Standards No. 142* (Norwalk, Conn.: FASB, 2001), par. 18.

Finally, a company may acquire enough of an investee's outstanding common stock to issue consolidated financial statements.

CHANGE TO EQUITY METHOD When an investor currently using the fair value method acquires enough additional common shares during a year to exercise significant influence over the investee, the investor is required to adopt the equity method of accounting. It is most likely (and assumed in this discussion) that the shares were included in the category of available-for-sale securities. When the equity method is adopted, the investor restates its investment in the investee by debiting the Investment account and crediting Retained Earnings for its *previous* percentage of investee income (less dividends) for the period from the original date of acquisition to the date that significant influence was obtained. This is a prior period (retroactive) adjustment. The company also eliminates any amounts included in the allowance and unrealized increase/decrease accounts that recorded these shares at fair value. Thereafter, the equity method is applied in the usual manner based on the *current* percentage ownership.

For example, assume that on January 2, 2003, Short Company purchased as its only investment 15% of the outstanding common stock of J Corporation for $150,000 (when the book value of net assets was $1,000,000). At the end of 2003, the J Corporation reported net income of $300,000 and paid dividends of $60,000; at this time, the market value of the shares was $186,000 so the company wrote up the carrying value of the investment (using an allowance account) to fair value. On January 2, 2004, to exert significant influence on J Corporation, Short Company purchased an additional 25% of the outstanding common stock of the J Corporation for $310,000.

We show the journal entries that Short Company recorded in 2003 and 2004 related to this information in the upper portion of Exhibit 14-7. In 2003, Short Company used

---

EXHIBIT 14-7 Journal Entries to Illustrate a Change to the Equity Method

Fair Value Method

1/2/03	Investment in J	150,000	
	Cash		150,000
12/31/03	Cash	9,000[a]	
	Dividend Revenue[b]		9,000
12/31/03	Allowance for Change in Value of Investment	36,000	
	Unrealized Increase/Decrease in Value of Available-for-Sale Securities		36,000

Change to Equity Method

1/2/04	Investment in J	310,000	
	Cash		310,000
1/2/04	Investment in J	45,000[c]	
	Retained Earnings		45,000
1/2/04	Retained Earnings	9,000	
	Investment in J		9,000
1/2/04	Unrealized Increase/Decrease in Value of Available-for-Sale Securities	36,000	
	Allowance for Change in Value of Investment		36,000

Comparison of Book Values

	J Corporation Net Assets	Investment in J	
Book value, 1/2/03	$1,000,000	$150,000	
+ Net Income for 2003	300,000	45,000	
− Dividends for 2003	(60,000)	(9,000)	
Book value, 1/2/04	$1,240,000	$186,000	(15%[d])
Additional investment (25%)		310,000	(25%)
Book value, 1/2/04 (40%)		$496,000	

a. $60,000 × 0.15
b. Closed to Retained Earnings
c. $300,000 × 0.15
d. $186,000 ÷ $1,240,000

the fair value method to account for its investment. It recorded the dividends received as dividend revenue and made an adjustment to the Allowance and Increase/Decrease accounts to record the increase in the investment's carrying value to fair value. In 2004, the Short Company recorded the $310,000 additional investment that increased its ownership to 40%. The company also made two journal entries to account for its *previous* 15% ownership under the equity method. First, it recognized $45,000 ($300,000 × 0.15) of the 2003 net income of J Corporation as an increase in its Investment account and in Retained Earnings. Second, it reduced its Investment account and Retained Earnings by $9,000, its share of the 2003 dividends of J Corporation. (Note that Retained Earnings was adjusted directly for the share of net income and dividends because these are from the *prior* year.) Thus, the company recognized an increase in value of $36,000 ($45,000 − $9,000) in the Investment and Retained Earnings accounts. The company also "reversed" its December 31, 2003 adjustment to increase the carrying value of the investment. Because the purchase price (fair value) of the shares was equal to their underlying book value, no additional depreciation was recorded. Had this adjustment been necessary, it would have been recorded (based on the 15% ownership) as a reduction in the Investment and Retained Earnings accounts.

The lower portion of Exhibit 14-7 explains the rationale behind the adjustments. Note that the book value of the net assets of J Corporation was $1,240,000 on January 2, 2004. By increasing the $150,000 initial investment for the $45,000 share of 2003 net income and decreasing it for the $9,000 share of the 2003 dividends, the book value of the Investment account is $186,000 (prior to the additional investment), or 15% of the $1,240,000 net assets of J Corporation on January 2, 2004. Increasing the $186,000 for the $310,000 (25%) additional investment results in an Investment account balance of $496,000, or 40% of the net assets. From this point on, Short Company will apply the equity method using the 40% ownership interest.

CHANGE FROM EQUITY METHOD   Sometimes an investor using the equity method sells a portion of the investment so that its portion of ownership falls below 20%, or the investor may lose significant influence over the investee. Under these conditions, the use of the equity method is no longer appropriate and the investor no longer accrues its share of investee income. However, previously recorded income remains as a part of the book value of the Investment account. The company then accounts for the investment under the fair value method. The investor company deducts from the book value of its Investment account any dividends received in later periods that exceed its share of income for those periods.

ACQUISITION AT LESS THAN FAIR VALUE   When the purchase price of an investment in common stock accounted for by the equity method is less than the proportionate fair value of the net assets acquired, the investment initially is recorded at cost. However, the difference between the cost and proportionate fair value of the net assets acquired (i.e., "negative goodwill") is allocated to reduce the value assigned to noncurrent assets, as we discussed in Chapter 13.

DECLINES OTHER THAN TEMPORARY   The investor must recognize "other than temporary" declines in the value of investments accounted for under the equity method. Evidence of these declines may be provided by the bankruptcy of the investee, by lengthy declines in the market value of the stock, or by a number of years of operating losses, which bring into question the ability of the investee to sustain income sufficient to justify the carrying value of the investment. When a decline that is considered to be other than temporary occurs, the investor debits a Loss account and credits the Investment account for the difference between the carrying value of the investment and the fair value. If the market value of the investment later increases, the investor does not recognize the recovery in value.

CONSOLIDATED FINANCIAL STATEMENTS   When an investor using the equity method acquires *control* over the investee's operations, the entity concept is enhanced by preparing financial statements for the combined set of companies; however, the two (or more) companies continue to maintain separate accounting records. During the year, the investor accounts for its investment in the investee by the equity method, as we previously discussed. At the end of the year, the accounting results of the investor and investee are combined (and the Investment account is eliminated) and reported in consolidated financial statements.

The underlying philosophy of consolidation accounting is the presentation of financial statements for a single economic entity, even though there are separate legal entities. The two major principles that provide the guidelines for the preparation of consolidated financial statements are:

1. The entity cannot make a profit by selling to itself. That is, intercompany sales and profits must be eliminated from the consolidated financial statements.
2. The entity cannot own or owe itself. That is, intercompany receivables and payables are not reported in consolidated financial statements.

Discussion of the preparation of consolidated financial statements is included in an advanced accounting book.

International Accounting Differences

The application of the equity method is generally the same under both international and U.S. accounting standards. However, the U.S. standards require more detailed disclosures.

ADDITIONAL ISSUES FOR INVESTMENTS

Additional issues for investments include accounting for investments in nonmarketable securities, stock dividends and stock splits, stock warrants, convertible bonds, the cash surrender value of life insurance, and investments in funds. We discuss each of these in the following sections.

9 Describe additional issues for investments.

Nonmarketable Securities

Nonmarketable securities are those that are not traded in a "qualifying" market (e.g., New York Stock Exchange), as we discussed earlier in the chapter. For example, shares or bonds issued by a privately held company are considered nonmarketable (even though they may be traded between individual investors). Investments in nonmarketable securities are outside the scope of *FASB Statement No. 115*. Therefore there is no requirement to report them at fair value. It can be expected that companies typically report them at their historical cost and, therefore, ignore any unrealized holding gains and losses.

Stock Dividends and Splits

Corporations occasionally distribute additional shares of stock to current shareholders (as we discuss in Chapters 15 and 16). In such cases the investor retains the same relative percentage of ownership in the investee because it does not acquire an additional percentage of outstanding shares. Consequently, the investor records no income from the distribution when it receives the new shares. The fair value of each share typically falls. The fair value at year-end, however, is simply the new number of shares multiplied by the year-end fair value.

The investor does not make a formal journal entry in its accounts to record the receipt of shares of stock from either a stock dividend or a stock split. However, its cost is now spread over a larger number of shares, thereby lowering its average unit cost of the shares. It records a memorandum entry to assign the average unit cost to the old and new shares. It then uses this average cost when there is a sale transaction involving the shares.

To illustrate, assume that the Smith Corporation purchased 2,000 shares of Kell Company common stock for $30 per share, or a total of $60,000. Two months later

Kell issued a 50% stock dividend and Smith Corporation received another 1,000 shares. Smith records a memo entry for the receipt of the stock dividend as follows:

> **Memo: Received 1,000 shares of Kell Company common stock as a stock dividend. The cost of the shares is now $20 per share, computed as follows: $60,000 ÷ 3,000 (2,000 + 1,000) shares.**

Subsequently, Smith sold 500 of the shares for $25 per share, and the fair value at the most recent balance sheet date was $23 per share. Smith records the *sale* of the 500 shares as follows:

Cash (500 × $25)	12,500	
Investment in Available-for-Sale Securities		
(500 × $20)		10,000
Gain on Sale of Investment [500 × ($25 − $20)]		2,500
Unrealized Increase/Decrease in Value of Available-		
for-Sale Securities [500 × ($23 − $20)]	1,500	
Allowance for Change in Value of Investment		1,500

Note that the reduction of the Investment account and calculation of the Gain are based on the $20 per share cost and not the $30 original purchase price. Smith still owns a total of 2,500 shares and will report them on its balance sheet at fair value.

Stock Warrants

As we discussed in Chapter 13, stock warrants are certificates that enable their holders to purchase a specified number of shares of common stock at a predetermined price. They generally are issued to existing stockholders as evidence of preemptive rights (discussed in Chapter 15), or for other reasons. Each shareholder usually receives a warrant for each share owned, although it may take more than one warrant to purchase a share. Warrants are defined as equity securities under *FASB Statement No. 115*.

Stock warrants have value because they usually allow the holder the right to purchase additional shares at a fixed price, usually slightly less than their current market price. Thus, the warrants representing these rights will trade on the stock market soon after they are issued. Eventually, the right to purchase additional shares expires, so the shareholder (the investor corporation) who receives these warrants has three alternatives:

1. Purchase additional shares by exercising the warrants.
2. Sell the warrants.
3. Do nothing and allow the warrants to expire.

Option 3 obviously is not a suitable choice in most circumstances because by selling the warrants, the shareholder can convert them into cash and still retain the original number of shares held. The shareholder thus should choose either alternative 1 or 2, although either the exercise or the sale of the warrants creates a valuation issue. To determine the cost of the new investment shares, or the gain or loss on the sale of the warrants, a cost must be assigned to the warrants. Since no additional cost is incurred when the warrants are received by the corporation holding the investment in common stock, it is necessary to assign a portion of the cost of the stock to the warrants upon their receipt. This amount is determined by use of a weighted average based on the market value of the stock *ex rights* (without the rights attached) and the market value of the warrants (rights) as we discussed in Chapter 13.[20] The accounting for any subsequent purchase of additional shares by exercising the warrants (or the sale of the warrants) would use the amount assigned to the warrants.

---

20. If the market value is not available when the warrants are received, this process must be delayed until the market value becomes known.

Convertible Bonds

As we discussed in Chapter 13, some bonds (and preferred stock) carry a conversion privilege that allows investors to exchange them for common stock. Investments in convertible bonds are *not* included in the held-to-maturity category because the intent is that conversion will occur before the bonds mature. Since these investments in convertible bonds are included in the available-for-sale (or trading) category and valued at fair value, conversion requires only a memorandum entry which specifies the number of shares that are now owned instead of the bonds. Also, the cost per share is calculated to facilitate the accounting for future transactions, such as the sale of the shares.

Cash Surrender Value of Life Insurance

Since a company is dependent upon the skill and expertise of its officers, frequently it will purchase insurance policies on their lives. The rationale for this practice is that the company will be at least partly compensated for the loss of executive skill in the event of an unexpected death.

Many insurance policies allow a portion of accumulated premiums to build up as a savings plan; if the policy is canceled, this savings plan or **cash surrender value** of the policy is returned to the company buying the life insurance policy. When a company is guaranteed a return equal to the amount of the cash surrender value of the policy, part of each annual premium represents an investment. The company records the portion of the yearly premium that does not increase the cash surrender value of the policy as insurance expense. It includes the amount of the cash surrender value of life insurance policies as a long-term investment on the balance sheet. The investment increases from year to year and is stated in the policy. Typically, the company records the yearly increase in this investment at the end of the year. Additionally, some life insurance policies pay dividends. The company holding such a policy treats any dividends received as a reduction of insurance expense.

For example, suppose that at the beginning of the year the Mele Corporation pays an annual insurance premium of $5,500 to cover the lives of its officers. It records the payment as follows:

Prepaid Insurance	5,500	
Cash		5,500

According to the terms of the insurance contract, the cash surrender value of the policies increases from $7,200 to $8,300 during that year. The adjusting entry at the end of the year to record the Insurance Expense and the increase in the Cash Surrender Value of Life Insurance is as follows:

Insurance Expense	4,400	
Cash Surrender Value of Life Insurance		
($8,300 − $7,200)	1,100	
Prepaid Insurance		5,500

Upon the death of any of the insured officers, Mele would collect the face amount of the insurance policy and credit the cash surrender value account to close out the balance in the account related to this policy. The difference between the proceeds and the cash surrender value is reported as an ordinary gain, because the insuring of officers' lives is a usual operating procedure. For income tax purposes the premiums are not tax deductible and the gain is not taxable.

Investments in Funds

Companies may place assets in special funds for specific purposes, and some of these assets then become unavailable for normal operations because of indenture or other contractual arrangements. Special funds may be current, such as petty cash funds, or they may be long-term. The most common long-term funds are those used to accumulate cash to retire long-term liabilities (**sinking funds**), those used to retire preferred stock (**stock redemption funds**), and those used to purchase long-term assets (**plant expansion funds**). A company reports its long-term funds as investments on its balance sheet. It is important to understand the distinction between a fund and an appropriation of retained earnings. A fund actually sets aside cash and other assets to accomplish specific objectives, whereas an appropriation of retained earnings discloses managerial policy or legal or contractual restrictions (as we discuss in Chapter 16). An appropriation does not provide any cash.

Accounting for long-term funds requires separate accounts. In essence, the fund is accounted for as an individual set of books. For example, the accounts that a company might use in connection with a bond sinking fund are Sinking Fund Cash, Sinking Fund Securities, Sinking Fund Revenues, Sinking Fund Expenses, Allowance for Change in Value of Sinking Fund Securities, Unrealized Increase/Decrease in Value of Sinking Fund Securities, Gain on Sale of Sinking Fund Securities, and Loss on Sale of Sinking Fund Securities. This company makes journal entries to these accounts to record its (1) initial and/or periodic cash contributions to the sinking fund, (2) investments in various securities to earn dividends and interest, (3) expenses to administer the fund, (4) unrealized increases and decreases in value, and (5) sale of the securities to acquire cash to retire the bonds. The company reports any revenues, expenses, gains, and losses in the usual manner on its income statement.

APPENDIX: DERIVATIVES OF FINANCIAL INSTRUMENTS

10 Account for derivatives of financial instruments. (Appendix)

Companies have always held or issued financial instruments. However, derivatives of those financial instruments are relatively new and are becoming increasingly common. Companies often use derivatives to reduce the risk of adverse changes in interest rates, commodity prices, and foreign currency exchange rates. It is important for financial statements to reflect the effects of that risk management. In this Appendix, we discuss recording and reporting issues as they relate to selected derivative transactions.

A **financial instrument** is cash, evidence of an ownership interest in an entity, or a contract that both (1) imposes on one entity a contractual obligation (a) to deliver cash or another financial instrument to a second entity or (b) to exchange other financial instruments on potentially unfavorable terms with the second entity, and (2) conveys to that second entity a contractual right (a) to receive cash or another financial instrument from the first entity or (b) to exchange other financial instruments on potentially favorable terms with the first entity.[21] Thus, financial instruments include cash, accounts and notes receivable, accounts and notes payable, and investments in debt and equity securities, as well as bonds payable and common stock. We discuss accounting for these financial instruments throughout the book.

A **derivative financial instrument** (or simply **derivative**) derives its value from an underlying asset or index. Thus, derivatives include futures, forward, swap, and option contracts. Derivative contracts can be very complex, but involve the following concepts:[22]

1. A derivative's cash flows or fair value must fluctuate and vary based on the changes in one or more underlying variables.
2. The contract must be based on one or more notional (defined later) amounts or payment provisions or both, even though title to that amount never changes. The underlying and notional amounts determine the amount of the settlement.

---

21. "Accounting for Derivative Instruments and Hedging Activities," *FASB Statement of Financial Accounting Standards No. 133* (Norwalk, Conn.: FASB 1998), Appendix F and "Accounting for Certain Derivative Instruments and Certain Hedging Activities," *FASB Statement of Financial Accounting Standards No. 138* (Norwalk, Conn.: FASB 2000).

22. *FASB Statement of Financial Accounting Standards No. 133, ibid.*, par 6–9.

3. Many contracts require no initial net investment.
4. The contract can be readily settled by a net cash payment.

A recent study indicated that over $41 trillion of derivative contracts are outstanding worldwide. Derivatives contracts have been in the news in recent years, and include situations in which **Procter & Gamble** sustained significant losses, **Bankers Trust** has been sued by numerous clients, **Barings Bank** in London was bankrupted, and **Orange County, California**, lost millions of dollars.

A **hedge** is a means of protecting against a financial loss. For a derivative to be considered a hedge, it must be "highly effective" in offsetting risk exposure due to changes in fair values or cash flows of the hedged item. The three types of hedges are (1) fair value hedges, (2) cash flow hedges, and (3) hedges of foreign currency exposures of net investments in foreign operations. **FASB Statement No. 133** requires a different accounting treatment for each type of hedge. Accounting for derivatives can be very complex. To explain the basic issues, we illustrate the accounting for a fair value hedge using an interest-rate swap, and briefly discuss the accounting issues for a cash flow hedge (the third type is beyond the scope of this book). In our examples we use simplifying assumptions (such as a flat yield curve) and facts so that you can understand the basic accounting issues and avoid many real-world complexities regarding valuation.

An **interest-rate swap** is an agreement in which two companies agree to exchange the interest payments on debt over a specified period. The interest payments are based on a principal amount that often is referred to as a **notional** (i.e., imaginary) amount because the swap does not involve an exchange of principal at either inception or maturity. An example of a *fair value hedge* is an interest rate swap in which a company *receives* a fixed rate of interest and *pays* a variable rate. An example of a *cash flow hedge* is an interest rate swap in which a company *receives* a variable rate of interest and *pays* a fixed rate.

Although we discuss investments in this chapter, we focus on accounting for a derivative of a financial instrument that is a liability, because they are more common for nonfinancial companies. However, a derivative can result in either an "investment" asset or a liability being recognized by either party, as market conditions change. The other company involved in the original transaction, a bank in our example, has a financial instrument that is an asset.

FAIR VALUE HEDGE

A fair value hedge protects against the risk from changes in value caused by *fixed* terms, rates, or prices. For example, a company with debt that has a fixed interest rate that enters into an interest rate swap to receive a fixed rate of interest and pay a variable rate protects itself against paying a higher than market rate of interest if interest rates decline. Of course, it will pay a higher rate than the fixed rate if interest rates rise. Another example would be a company that purchases a commodity, such as oil, and agrees to a fixed price contract. It can enter into a futures contract so that if, for example, the purchase price of oil decreases, it pays an above market price for the oil that is offset by the value of the futures contract. In each case, the company has converted a fixed rate contract (for interest or oil) into a variable rate contract.

For a fair value hedge, *FASB Statement No. 133* requires a company to recognize in its current *net income* (1) any gain or loss from a change in the fair value of the derivative (fair value hedge), and (2) any gain or loss from the change in the fair value of the financial instrument being hedged, along with any interest revenue or expense. As a result the company reports both the derivative and the financial instrument on its balance sheet at their respective fair values. Hence, the FASB is using the *fair value method* in the valuation of derivatives and the related financial instruments.

To illustrate the accounting for an interest rate swap that is a fair value hedge, suppose that Laki Company has had a $1 million, 6% bank loan (the financial instrument) from MidAmerica Bank outstanding for several years. On January 1, 2004, when the $1 million loan (debt) has five years remaining, Laki contracts with Jordan Investment Bank (a swaps dealer) for a five-year interest-rate swap (the derivative) with a $1 million notional amount. The company agrees to *receive* from Jordan a fixed interest rate of 6% and to *pay* Jordan an interest rate each year that is variable. The variable rate is the LIBOR (London Interbank Offer Rate) interest rate at the beginning of each year. In other words, Laki has converted ("swapped") its fixed interest rate debt into the variable LIBOR interest rate debt. If the LIBOR interest rate debt is 5.3% at January 1, 2004, the company has converted 6% debt into 5.3% debt for that year. This type is called a "matched" swap because the notional amount is the same as the actual loan amount and the fixed interest rate on the derivative is equal to the fixed interest rate paid on the loan. Therefore the derivative is an effective hedge of the risk of interest rate changes. We summarize the facts for the loan and swap involving Laki Company, MidAmerica Bank, and Jordan Investment Bank in Exhibit 14-8.

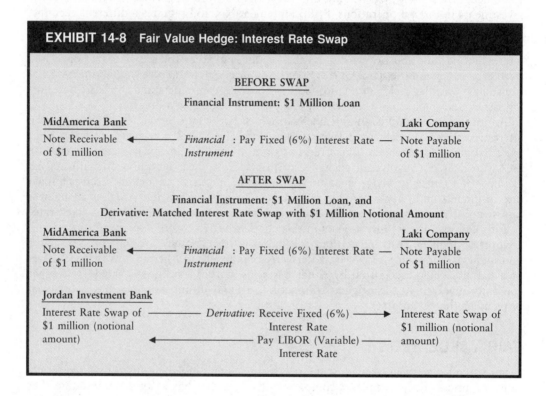

EXHIBIT 14-8   Fair Value Hedge: Interest Rate Swap

The Laki Company recorded the following journal entry for the financial instrument (the original loan):

<u>Original Bank Loan</u>

Cash	1,000,000	
Notes Payable		1,000,000

Laki accounts for the derivative (the fair value hedge) in 2004 and 2005, as follows:

<u>Interest Payment on Loan: December 31, 2004</u>

Laki pays MidAmerica the fixed rate of 6% on the $1 million loan and records this as interest expense, as follows:

Interest Expense	60,000	
Cash		60,000

<u>Interest Rate Swap Payment: December 31, 2004</u>

Since the LIBOR rate that was set at January 1, 2004 is 5.3%, there is a net payment (settlement) between Laki Company and Jordan Investment Bank. Since Laki owes to

Jordan the LIBOR 5.3% rate and receives from Jordan the fixed 6% rate, it receives from Jordan the *net* 0.7% on the notional amount of $1 million, or $7,000. Laki records the cash received as a *decrease* to interest expense, as follows:

Cash	7,000	
Interest Expense		7,000

Thus, Laki records a total interest expense of $53,000 ($60,000 − $7,000) in 2004, which is the equivalent of the variable rate of 5.3% on the $1 million loan.

Fair Values and Gains and Losses: December 31, 2003

The fair value method uses market values to recognize the value of derivatives if they are available, such as for futures contracts traded on exchanges. However, many derivatives are forward contracts that are custom designed for the two entities, and market values are not available for such distinctive contracts, as in this example. In these cases, discounted cash flows are used to value the derivative.

Laki determines the gain or loss for 2004 on the derivative (fair value hedge) by computing the net present value of the future cash flows over the remaining life of the derivative. It is based on the difference between the fixed interest rate contracted in the derivative and the current market fixed interest rate applied to the notional amount for the remaining life of the swap. Note that this rate is typically different than the LIBOR rate that is a short-term variable rate and has no inherent fair value because it can be obtained at any time. Thus, there are three interest rates:

1. The fixed interest rate (6%) on the loan and the derivative.
2. The variable LIBOR interest rate at the beginning of the year that is used to determine the swap payment at the end of the year (5.3% for 2004, and we assume it changes to 6.8% for 2005).
3. The fixed market rate of interest at the end of the year for the remaining life of the loan or derivative (7% for a four-year loan or derivative at December 31, 2004, and we assume it changes to 5.5% for a three-year loan or derivative at December 31, 2005).

We assume that, at December 31, 2004, the fixed market rate of interest for the four-year remaining life of the derivative is 7% (compared to the LIBOR rate of 6.8% that is set at January 1, 2005). Thus, the difference in the fixed interest rates at the end of 2004 is 1% (6% fixed rate − 7% four-year market rate). The $33,872 value of the derivative is $10,000 per year (the difference of 1% multiplied by the notional amount of $1,000,000) discounted at the current fixed market rate of 7% for the remaining four years, as follows:

$$\text{Present value of derivative} = \$10,000 \times 3.387211 \ (n = 4, i = 0.07)$$
$$= \$33,872$$

A swap derivative *liability* and *loss* exist because the 7% current market rate is higher than the 6% fixed interest rate that Laki receives on the derivative. Laki records the liability and loss as follows:

Loss in Value of Derivative	33,872	
Liability from Interest Rate Swap		33,872

Since interest rates have changed, the value of the Laki's debt (financial instrument) has also changed. The increase in interest rates decreases the value of the debt. The current value of the debt is computed based on the 7% market rate as follows:

Present value of principal $= \$1,000,000 \times 0.762895 \ (n = 4, i = 0.07)$
$= \$762,895$

Present value of interest $= \$60,000 \times 3.387211 \ (n = 4, i = 0.07)$
$= \$203,233$

Total present value of debt $= \$762,895 + \$203,233$
$= \$966,128$

Laki recognizes the $33,872 ($1,000,000 − $966,128) decrease in the value of the debt and the related *gain* as follows:

Notes Payable	33,872	
Gain in Value of Debt		33,872

The Laki Company reports both the $33,872 gain in the value of the debt and the $33,872 loss in value of the derivative in the other items section of its 2004 income statement. There is no net effect because it is an effective hedge. Laki reports the $33,872 derivative liability and the $966,128 ($1,000,000 − $33,872) value of the note payable on its December 31, 2004 balance sheet. Therefore, its total liability in regard to this debt is $1,000,000.

Interest Payment on Loan: December 31, 2005

Laki pays MidAmerica the fixed rate of 6% on the $1 million loan and records this as interest expense, as follows:

Interest Expense	60,000	
Cash		60,000

Interest Rate Swap Payment: December 31, 2005

We assume that at the beginning of 2005, the LIBOR interest rate is 6.8%. Since Laki pays Jordan the LIBOR 6.8% rate and receives from Jordan the fixed 6% rate, it pays to Jordan the *net* 0.8% on the notional amount of $1 million, or $8,000. Laki records the payment as an *increase* in interest expense, as follows:

Interest Expense	8,000	
Cash		8,000

Thus, Laki records a total interest expense of $68,000 ($60,000 + $8,000) in 2005, which is the equivalent of the variable rate of 6.8% on the $1 million loan.

Fair Values and Gains and Losses: December 31, 2005

Laki again determines the gain or loss for 2005 on the derivative (fair value hedge) by computing the net present value of the future cash flows over the remaining life of the derivative. It is again based on the difference between the fixed interest rate contracted in the derivative and the current market fixed interest rate, applied to the notional amount for the remaining life of the swap. We assume that at December 31, 2005 the three-year fixed interest rate is 5.5%. Thus, the difference in fixed interest rates at the end of 2005 is 0.5% (6% fixed rate − 5.5% three-year market rate). The $13,490 value of the derivative is $5,000 per year (the difference of 0.5% multiplied by the notional amount of $1,000,000) discounted at the current market rate of 5.5% for the remaining three years, computed as follows:

$$\text{Present value of derivative} = \$5,000 \times 2.697933 \ (n = 3, \ i = 0.055)$$
$$= \$13,490$$

A swap derivative *asset* and *gain* exist because the current 5.5% market rate is lower than the 6% fixed interest rate that Laki receives on the derivative. So Laki has moved from a $33,872 liability at the end of 2004 to a $13,490 asset position at the end of 2005, and has a $47,362 ($33,872 + $13,490) gain which it records as follows:

Liability from Interest Rate Swap	33,872	
Asset from Interest Rate Swap	13,490	
Gain in Value of Derivative		47,362

Again, since interest rates have changed, the value of Laki's debt (financial instrument) has also changed. The decrease in interest rates increases the value of the debt. The current value of the debt is computed based on the 5.5% current market rate as follows:

Present value of principal $= \$1,000,000 \times 0.851614$ ($n = 3$, $i = 0.055$)
$= \$851,614$

Present value of interest $= \$60,000 \times 2.697933$ ($n = 3$, $i = 0.055$)
$= \$161,876$

Total present value of debt $= \$851,614 + \$161,876$
$= \$1,013,490$

Laki recognizes the \$47,362 (\$1,013,490 current value − \$966,128 previous value) increase and the related loss as follows:

Loss in Value of Debt	47,362	
Notes Payable		47,362

The Laki Company reports the \$47,362 gain in value of the derivative and the \$47,362 loss in value of the debt in the other items section of its 2005 income statement. There is no net effect for this effective hedge. It reports the \$13,490 derivative asset as a long-term investment and the \$1,013,490 (\$966,128 + \$47,362) value of the note payable on its December 31, 2005 balance sheet. Note that Laki's *net* liability in regard to the debt is still \$1,000,000. Laki would account for the loan and the derivative (fair value hedge) in a similar manner for the years 2006 through 2009.

In summary, the Laki Company has converted a fixed interest rate bank loan into a variable interest rate loan with this interest rate swap. Laki pays a variable net interest rate on this loan and reports the amount each year as interest expense on its income statement. Laki reports the derivative asset or liability and the related financial instrument (note payable) on its balance sheet at their respective fair values. There is no effect from the change in the fair value of this derivative on the income statement because the change in the fair value of the derivative is offset by the change in the fair value of the financial instrument (i.e., an effective hedge of the fixed rate debt). Note that when a hedge is not perfect or is ineffective (e.g., the notional amount is not equal to the actual principal amount), then a net amount is reported on the income statement. The financial reporting reflects Laki's interest rate risk management strategy. Laki discloses the characteristics of its financial instrument and derivative in the notes to its financial statements.

CASH FLOW HEDGE

A cash flow hedge protects against the risk caused by *variable* prices, costs, rates, or terms that cause future cash flows to be uncertain. A cash flow hedge is a hedge of an anticipated or forecasted transaction that is probable of occurring in the future, but the amount of the transaction has not been fixed. This contrasts with a fair value hedge that protects against the risk from changes in value caused by *fixed* terms, rates, or prices.

For example, a company with a variable rate debt that enters into an interest rate swap to receive a variable rate of interest and pay a fixed rate protects itself against paying a higher rate of interest if interest rates increase. Of course, it will pay a higher rate than the variable rate if interest rates fall. The company has converted a variable rate contract into a fixed rate contract.

For a cash flow hedge, *FASB Statement No. 133* requires a company to recognize in its current *other comprehensive income* any gain or loss from a change in the fair value of the derivative (cash flow hedge). The company reports the derivative at its fair value and the related accumulated other comprehensive income in its stockholders' equity on its ending balance sheet. The company does *not* recognize in its financial statements any change in value of the financial instrument being hedged. When the hedged forecasted transaction occurs, the company transfers the accumulated other comprehensive income to its current net income.

To illustrate an interest rate swap that is a cash flow hedge, assume the same facts as for the fair value hedge, except that Laki has a 5.3% (for 2004) variable rate \$1 million loan (debt) with MidAmerica Bank that is based on the LIBOR rate. It enters into an interest rate swap with Jordan Investment Bank in which it will receive a variable (5.3%

for 2004) interest rate and pay a 6% fixed rate. Since this hedge protects against the risk caused by variable interest rates, it is a cash flow hedge. We summarize the facts for the loan and swap involving Laki Company, MidAmerica Bank, and Jordan Investment Bank in Exhibit 14-9.

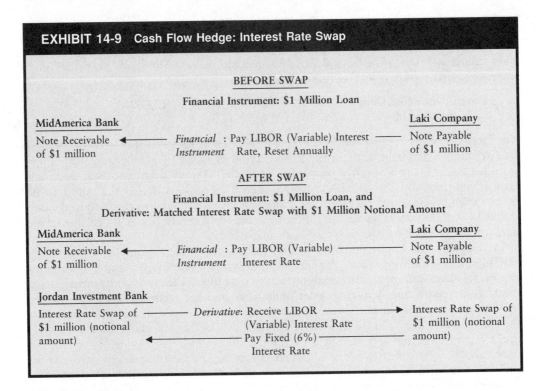

EXHIBIT 14-9   Cash Flow Hedge: Interest Rate Swap

Laki reports this swap at its fair (present) value on the balance sheet and reports any change in the fair value for the period in other comprehensive income. It reports the total change in fair value as accumulated other comprehensive income in the stockholders' equity section of its balance sheet. This type of interest rate swap does not hedge the liability. Instead, it hedges the interest payments. Thus, as Laki makes each interest payment, a hedged forecasted transaction occurs and Laki must transfer an amount from the accumulated other comprehensive income to its net income, based on the change in the present value. In this case, Laki must compute the present value of each interest payment separately. Because each payment occurs at a different point on the yield curve, Laki would use a different interest rate to determine its present value. These procedures are beyond the scope of this book.

SUMMARY

At the beginning of the chapter, we identified several objectives you would accomplish after reading the chapter. The objectives are listed below, each followed by a brief summary of the key points in the chapter discussion.

1. **Explain the classification and valuation of investments.** Trading securities are the investments in debt and equity securities that are purchased and held principally for the purpose of selling them in the near term. Trading securities are valued at their fair values on the balance sheet date. Available-for-sale securities are investments in (a) debt securities that are not classified as held-to-maturity, and (b) debt and equity securities that are not classified as trading securities. Available-for-sale securities are valued at their fair values on the balance sheet date. Held-to-maturity debt securities are investments in debt securities for which the company has the positive intent and ability to hold to maturity. Held-to-maturity securities are valued at their amortized cost on the balance sheet date.

2. **Account for investments in debt and equity trading securities.** Investments in debt and equity trading securities are initially recorded at cost and subsequently recorded at fair value. Unrealized holding gains and losses are included

in net income of the period, and interest and dividend revenue, as well as realized gains and losses on sales, are included in net income of the current period.

3. **Account for investments in available-for-sale debt and equity securities.** Investments in available-for-sale debt and equity securities are initially recorded at cost and subsequently recorded at fair value. Unrealized holding gains and losses are reported as a component of other comprehensive income of the period, and interest and dividend revenue, as well as realized gains and losses on sales, are included in net income of the current period. The cumulative net unrealized holding gains or losses are reported in the accumulated other comprehensive income section of stockholders' equity.

4. **Account for investments in held-to-maturity debt securities, including amortization of bond premiums and discounts.** Investments in held-to-maturity debt securities are initially recorded at cost and subsequently recorded at amortized cost. Unrealized holding gains and losses are not recorded, and interest and dividend revenue, as well as realized gains and losses on sales (if any), are included in net income of the current period.

5. **Understand transfers and impairments.** The transfer of a security between categories is accounted for at the fair value at the time of the transfer. Depending on the classification of the security transferred, the unrealized gain or loss is either eliminated or established. An impairment occurs when there is an other than temporary decline below the amortized cost of a debt security classified as available for sale or held to maturity. The company writes down the amortized cost of the security to the fair value and includes the amount of the write-down in net income as a realized loss.

6. **Understand disclosures of investments.** For trading securities, a company must disclose the change in the net unrealized holding gain or loss that is included in each income statement. For available-for-sale securities, a company must disclose for each balance sheet date the aggregate fair value, gross unrealized holding gains and gross unrealized holding losses, and amortized cost by major security types. The contractual maturities of debt securities must also be disclosed. For each income statement period, the company must disclose (1) the proceeds from the sales and the gross realized gains and losses on those sales as well as the basis on which cost was determined, (2) the gross gains and gross losses included in net income from transfers of securities from this category into the trading category, and (3) the change in the net unrealized holding gain or loss included as a separate component of other comprehensive income. For held-to-maturity securities a company must disclose for each balance sheet date the aggregate fair value, gross unrealized holding gains, gross unrealized holding losses, and amortized cost by major security types. The contractual maturities must also be disclosed. For any sales or transfers from this category, the disclosures must include the amortized cost, the related realized or unrealized gain or loss, and the circumstances leading to the decision to sell or transfer security.

7. **Explain the conceptual issues regarding investments in marketable securities.** The use of fair value creates a relevant value because it reflects the liquidity of the securities. The value is also reliable because the fair value is available on a securities exchange. The following points reflect the major controversies: (1) the fair value is required for trading and available-for-sale securities whereas amortized cost is required for held-to-maturity securities; (2) fair value is not required for certain liabilities; (3) unrealized holding gains and losses are reported in net income for trading securities but in other comprehensive income for available-for-sale securities; and (4) the classification of securities is based on management intent.

8. **Account for investments using the equity method.** An investor company uses the equity method when it is able to exercise significant influence over the operating and financial policies of an investee. The company initially records its investment at cost and records income and an increase in the carrying value of the asset at an amount based on its percentage ownership in the investee. The investor company records dividends received as reductions in the carrying value of the investment account. The investor must also eliminate any intercompany transactions and recognize any additional depreciation expense.

9. **Describe additional issues for investments.** Additional issues for investments include accounting for investments in nonmarketable securities, stock dividends and stock splits, stock warrants, convertible bonds, the cash surrender value of life insurance, and investments in funds.

10. **Account for derivatives of financial instruments (Appendix).** A derivative derives its value from an underlying financial instrument. A hedge is a means of protecting against a financial loss. The two types of hedges discussed in the Appendix are fair value hedges and cash flow hedges. A *fair value hedge* protects against the risk from changes in value caused by fixed terms, rates, or prices. A company recognizes in its current net income (1) any gain or loss from a change in the fair value of the derivative (fair value hedge), and (2) any gain or loss from the change in the fair value of the financial instrument being hedged, along with any interest revenue or expense. As a result the company reports both the derivative and the financial instrument on its balance sheet at their respective fair values.

A *cash flow hedge* protects against the risk caused by variable prices, costs, rates, or terms that cause future cash flows to be uncertain. A cash flow hedge is a hedge of an anticipated or forecasted transaction that is probable of occurring in the future, but the amount of the transaction has not been fixed. A company recognizes in its current other comprehensive income any gain or loss from a change in the fair value of the derivative (cash flow hedge). The company reports the derivative at its fair value and the related accumulated other comprehensive income in its stockholders' equity on its ending balance sheet.

QUESTIONS

Q14-1 Why do companies purchase securities of other corporations?

Q14-2 What are the three categories of investments in debt and equity securities when there is no significant influence?

Q14-3 Provide brief definitions for the following terms: (a) *debt security*, (b) *equity security*, and (c) *fair value*.

Q14-4 Identify the accounting methods a company uses for investments of 20 percent or more in the voting common stock of the investee.

Q14-5 Briefly summarize the accounting for an investment in trading securities.

Q14-6 Briefly summarize the accounting for an investment in available-for-sale securities.

Q14-7 Briefly summarize the accounting for an investment in debt securities held to maturity.

Q14-8 Briefly describe how to determine and record any subsequent increases or decreases in the fair value of an investment in available-for-sale securities.

Q14-9 Briefly describe how to determine and record the gain or loss on the sale of an investment in available-for-sale securities.

Q14-10 When are investments in bonds held to maturity purchased at a premium? How does the amortization of a premium under the effective interest method affect interest revenue?

Q14-11 When are investments in bonds held to maturity purchased at a discount? How does the amortization of a discount under the effective interest method affect interest revenue?

Q14-12 Briefly describe the two methods available to determine interest revenue and account for premiums and discounts on investments in bonds held to maturity.

Q14-13 Briefly describe how to record the transfer of an investment in a debt security (a) from the held-to-maturity category to the available-for-sale category, and (b) from the available-for-sale category to the held-to-maturity category.

Q14-14 Show the balance sheet disclosures of an investment in available-for-sale securities that a company classifies as current and has a fair value in excess of cost.

Q14-15 Discuss the rationale behind the use of the equity method for an investment in common stock.

Q14-16 Briefly describe the accounting for an investment in common stock under the equity method.

Q14-17 Identify the facts and circumstances that would preclude an investor from using the equity method, even if it owns more than a 20% investment in an investee.

Q14-18 Discuss the appropriate accounting treatment to use when (a) an investor acquires enough additional common stock during a year to change from using the fair value method to using the equity method, and (b) an investor using the equity method sells enough common stock so that its portion of ownership falls below 20%.

Q14-19 Why is the cash surrender value of a life insurance policy on which the company is the beneficiary carried as an investment? How does the company determine the increase in this amount and the amount of insurance expense determined each year?

Q14-20 What is a fund? Distinguish between a fund and an appropriation of retained earnings.

CASES

COMMUNICATION

C14-1 Realized and Unrealized Losses: Temporary Investments

FASB Statement No. 115 changed accounting principles with respect to certain marketable securities. An important part of this *Statement* is the distinction between investments categorized as trading, available for sale, or held to maturity.

Required

1. What types of securities are covered by this *Statement*?
2. Explain how the distinction between the three categories is made.

3. Discuss the distinction between realized and holding gains and losses on investments in debt and equity securities.
4. Explain how a company discloses realized and holding gains and losses on investments in equity securities on its financial statements.

C14-2 Investments in Securities

Cane Company has two portfolios of investments in marketable equity securities. It classifies one as trading securities and the other as available-for-sale securities. Cane does not have the ability to exercise significant influence over any of the companies in either portfolio. It sold some securities from each portfolio during the year. The company reclassified one of the securities in the available-for-sale category to the trading category when its fair value was less than cost. At the beginning and end of the year, the aggregate cost of each portfolio exceeded its aggregate market value by different amounts.

Required

1. Explain how Cane measures and reports the income statement effects of the securities sold during the year from each portfolio.
2. Explain how Cane accounts for the security which it reclassified.
3. Explain how Cane reports the effects of investments in each portfolio on its balance sheet as of the end of the year and on its income statement for the year. Do not discuss the securities sold.
4. Explain gains trading. Can Cane use gains trading on either portfolio? Does gains trading raise ethical issues?

C14-3 Investments in Securities

FASB Statement No. 115 was issued to change accounting methods and procedures with respect to investments in debt and equity securities. An important part of the *Statement* concerns the distinction between trading securities, available-for-sale securities, and held-to-maturity securities.

Required

1. Explain why a company invests in debt and equity securities.
2. Explain what factors a company should consider in determining which investments it should classify in each of the three categories, and how these factors affect the accounting treatment for unrealized gains and losses.

C14-4 Equity Method

The most common method of accounting for unconsolidated subsidiaries is the equity method.

Required Answer the following questions with respect to the *equity* method.

1. Under what circumstances does a company apply the equity method?
2. At what amount does a company record the initial investment and what events subsequent to the initial investment (if any) change this amount?
3. How does a company recognize investment earnings under the equity method, and how does it determine the amount? (*AICPA adapted*)

C14-5 Investments in Equity Securities

Walker Company has an investment portfolio of equity securities available for sale. Walker does not own more than 5% of the outstanding voting stock for any of the securities in the portfolio. At the beginning of the year, the aggregate market value of the portfolio exceeded its cost. It received cash dividends on these securities during the year. It sold none of the securities in the portfolio during the year. At the end of the year, the aggregate cost of the portfolio exceeded its market value. The decline in the market price of the securities in the portfolio is attributable to general market decline.

During this year, Walker purchased for cash 35% of the outstanding voting stock of Sipe Company. It received cash dividends on this investment from Sipe during the year, and Sipe reported its earnings after the acquisition date to Walker.

Required

1. Explain how Walker reports on its balance sheet and income statement the effects of its investment in the securities available for sale portfolio for the year.
2. Explain how Walker reports on its balance sheet and income statement the effects of its investment in Sipe for the year. (*AICPA adapted*)

C14-6 Various Investments

Houston Company has a portfolio of investments in available-for-sale securities that it classifies as a noncurrent asset. Houston owns less than 5% of the outstanding voting stock of each company's securities in the portfolio. At the beginning of the year, the aggregate market value of the portfolio exceeded its aggregate cost. Houston received cash dividends on these securities during the year. All cash dividends received represent distribution of earnings subsequent to Houston's acquisition of these securities. Houston sold some of the securities in the portfolio during the year. At the end of the year, the aggregate cost of the portfolio exceeded its aggregate market value.

Houston also owns 40% of the outstanding voting stock of Joy Company. The remainder of Joy's outstanding voting stock is widely dispersed among unrelated investors.

Required

1. a. Explain how Houston reports the income statement effects of the cash dividends received during the year on the securities in the available-for-sale portfolio.
   b. Explain how Houston reports the income statement effects of the securities sold during the year.
2. Explain how Houston reports the effect of ownership of the portfolio of securities available for sale in its balance sheet as of the end of the year and on its income statement for the year. Do *not* discuss the cash dividends or the securities sold.
3. Identify the method of accounting that Houston uses for its 40% investment in the outstanding voting stock of Joy. Why is this method appropriate? (*AICPA adapted*)

CREATIVE AND CRITICAL THINKING

C14-7 Available-for-Sale Securities

The following are four *unrelated* situations involving investments in available-for-sale securities:

Situation I

A portfolio of available-for-sale securities with an aggregate fair value in excess of cost includes one particular security whose fair value has declined to less than one-half of the original cost. The decline in value is considered to be other than temporary.

Situation II

The statement of financial position of a company does not classify assets and liabilities as current and noncurrent. The portfolio of available-for-sale securities includes securities normally considered current that have a net cost in excess of fair value of $2,000. The remainder of the portfolio has a net fair value in excess of cost of $5,000.

Situation III

An available-for-sale security, whose fair value is currently less than cost, is reclassified as a trading security.

Situation IV

A company's portfolio of available-for-sale securities consists of the common stock of one company. At the end of the prior year, the fair value of the security was 50% of original cost, and the effect was properly reflected in an allowance account. However, at the end of the current year, the fair value of the security had appreciated to twice the original cost.

Required Explain the effect upon classification, carrying value, and earnings for each of the preceding situations. (*AICPA* adapted)

C14-8 Change in Percent Ownership

For the past five years, Herbert has maintained an investment (properly accounted for and reported upon) in Broome amounting to a 10% interest in the voting common stock of Broome. The purchase price was $700,000 and the underlying net equity in Broome at the date of purchase was $620,000. On January 2 of the current year, Herbert purchased an additional 15% of the voting common stock of Broome for $1,200,000; the underlying net equity of additional investment at January 2 was $1,000,000. Broome has been profitable and has paid dividends annually since Herbert's initial acquisition.

Required Discuss how this increase in ownership affects the accounting for and reporting upon the investment in Broome. Include in your discussion adjustments, if any, to the amount shown prior to the increase in investment to bring the amount into conformity with generally accepted accounting principles. Also include how the company would report in current and subsequent periods. (*AICPA* adapted)

C14-9 Investments in Stocks and Bonds

Victoria Company has investments in equity securities classified as trading and available for sale. At the beginning of the year, the aggregate market value of each portfolio exceeded its cost. During the year, Victoria sold some securities from each portfolio. At the end of the year, the aggregate cost of each portfolio exceeded its market value.

Victoria also has investments in bonds classified as held to maturity, all of which were purchased for face value. During the year, some of these bonds held by Victoria were called prior to their maturity by the bond issuer. Three months before the end of the year, additional similar bonds were purchased for face value plus 2 months' accrued interest.

Required

1. a. Explain how Victoria accounts for the sale of securities from each portfolio.
   b. Explain how Victoria accounts for each equity securities portfolio at year-end.
2. Explain how Victoria accounts for the disposition prior to their maturity of the long-term bonds called by their issuer.
3. Explain how Victoria reports the purchase of the additional similar bonds at the date of the acquisition. (*AICPA* adapted)

C14-10 Analyzing Coca-Cola's Investments Disclosures

Refer to the financial statements and related notes of the Coca-Cola Company in Appendix A of this book.

Required

1. Did the fair value of the company's available-for-sale securities increase or decrease in 2001?
2. Is the fair value of the company's held-to-maturity securities different from their cost at December 31, 2001? At December 31, 2000?
3. Explain why the company has cost method investments.
4. If the company included the assets and liabilities of its equity investments in its December 31, 2001, balance sheet instead of using the equity method, determine whether the effects on the assets, liabilities, and debt ratio would be material.

C14-11 Ethics and Investments

You are an accountant for the Davanzo Company. The president of the company calls you into her office and says, "I want to ask you about two issues. First, we need to sell one of our investments to raise $1 million because I think I have found a better investment. We could sell the shares of Company X, which are currently worth $1 million even though they originally cost us $400,000. But I don't want to sell them, because the company seems to be getting better all the time. Or we could sell the shares in that dog, Company Z. These shares are also worth $1 million, but they cost us $1.5 million and I hate to admit we made such a big mistake. And then there's that loss. I don't want to report that. I am going to use the $1 million to buy about 20% of the shares of Company M, but I seem to remember that there is some accounting rule that might affect how much we buy. I was also wondering about buying some of Company M's convertible preferred stock so we can convert that into a large ownership position in the future. Let me know what you think." You are aware that

Company M is a new company that is not yet listed on the stock market, has been making losses, and is expected to continue making losses for a few more years.

Required From financial reporting and ethical perspectives, discuss the issues raised by this situation.

MULTIPLE CHOICE

Select the best answer for each of the following.

M14-1 On its December 31, 2003 balance sheet, Fay Company appropriately reported a $2,000 credit balance in its Allowance for Change in Value of Investment. There was no change during 2004 in the composition of Fay's portfolio of marketable equity securities held as available for sale. Pertinent data are as follows:

Security	Cost	Market Value at 12/31/04
A	$ 60,000	$ 63,000
B	45,000	40,000
C	80,000	78,500
Totals	$185,000	$181,500

What amount of loss on these securities should be included in Fay's income statement for the year ended December 31, 2004?

   a. $0   c. $3,500
   b. $1,500   d. $5,500

M14-2 A security in a portfolio of available-for-sale securities is transferred to the trading category. The security should be transferred between the corresponding portfolios at

   a. The book value at date of transfer if higher than the fair value at date of transfer
   b. The fair value at date of transfer, regardless of its cost
   c. Its cost, regardless of the fair value at date of transfer
   d. The lower of its cost or fair value at date of transfer

M14-3 On April 1, 2004, Aldrich Company purchased as an available-for-sale security $200,000 face value, 9% U.S. Treasury notes for $198,500, which included accrued interest of $4,500. The notes mature July 1, 2005, and pay interest semiannually on January 1 and July 1. The notes were sold on December 1, 2004 for $206,500, which included accrued interest of $7,500. Aldrich uses straight-line amortization. In its income statement for the year ended December 31, 2004, what amount should Aldrich report as a gain on the sale of the available-for-sale security?

   a. $1,800   c. $6,500
   b. $5,000   d. $8,000

M14-4 When the market value of a company's portfolio of available-for-sale securities is lower than its cost, the difference should be

   a. Accounted for as a liability
   b. Disclosed and described in a note to the financial statements but not accounted for
   c. Accounted for as a valuation allowance deducted from the asset to which it relates
   d. Accounted for as an addition in the shareholders' equity section of the balance sheet

M14-5 On January 2, 2004, Portela, Inc. bought 30% of the outstanding common stock of Bracero Corporation for $258,000 cash. Portela accounts for this investment by the equity method. At the date of acquisition of the stock, Bracero's property, plant, and equipment had a fair value in excess of its book value of $150,000. Bracero's property, plant, and equipment has a remaining life of 10 years. Bracero's net income for the year ended December 31, 2004 was $180,000. During 2004, Bracero declared and paid cash dividends of $20,000. On December 31, 2004, Portela should have carried its investment in Bracero in the amount of

   a. $258,000   c. $306,000
   b. $301,500   d. $312,000

M14-6 Cash dividends declared out of current earnings were distributed to an investor. How will the investor's investment account be affected by those dividends under each of the following accounting methods?

	Fair Value Method	Equity Method
a.	Decrease	No effect
b.	No effect	Decrease
c.	Decrease	Decrease
d.	No effect	No effect

M14-7 During 2004, Anthony Company purchased securities as a long-term investment and classified them as available for sale. Pertinent data are as follows:

Security	Cost	Market Value at 12/31/04
A	$ 20,000	$ 18,000
B	40,000	30,000
C	90,000	93,000
Totals	$150,000	$141,000

The amount of the holding gain or loss included in Anthony's year-end balance sheet should be

   a. $0   c. $9,000
   b. $3,000   d. $12,000

M14-8 For an available-for-sale securities portfolio included in noncurrent assets, which of the following should be included in net income of the period?

    a. Realized gains during the period

    b. Unrealized losses during the period

    c. Accumulated changes in the valuation allowance

    d. Increases in the valuation allowance during the period

M14-9 In 2003, Cromwell Corporation bought 30,000 shares of Fleming Corporation's listed stock for $300,000 and classified the investment as available for sale. In 2004, the market value declined to $200,000. In 2005, the market value of the Fleming stock rose to $230,000 and the stock was sold. How much should Cromwell record as a realized gain or loss in its determination of net income for 2005?

    a. $0   c. $70,000 loss

    b. $30,000 gain   d. $100,000 loss

M14-10 On January 1, 2004, Weaver Company purchased as held-to-maturity debt securities $500,000 face value of Park Corporation's 8% bonds for $456,200. The bonds were purchased to yield 10% interest and pay interest annually. The bonds mature on January 1, 2009. Weaver uses the effective interest method of amortization. What amount should Weaver report on its December 31, 2004 balance sheet as an investment in held-to-maturity debt securities?

    a. $450,580   c. $461,820

    b. $456,200   d. $466,200

(AICPA adapted)

EXERCISES

E14-1   *Trading Securities*   Midwest Bank invests in trading securities. At the beginning of December 2004, the bank held no trading securities. During December of 2004, it entered into the following trading securities transactions:

Dec. 10   Purchased 500 shares of C Company common stock for $76 per share

Dec. 21   Purchased 800 shares of D Company common stock for $34 per share

At the end of December, the C Company common stock had a quoted market price of $79 per share and the D Company common stock had a quoted market price of $33 per share.

Required

1. Prepare journal entries to record the preceding information.
2. What is the unrealized holding gain or loss and where is it reported in the 2004 financial statements?
3. Show how the bank reports the trading securities on its December 31, 2004 balance sheet.

E14-2   *Trading Securities*   Southeast Bank invests in trading securities and prepares quarterly financial statements. At the beginning of the fourth quarter of 2004, the bank held as trading securities 200 shares of Company E common stock which had originally cost $5,500. At that time, these securities had a fair value of $5,200. During the fourth quarter, the bank engaged in the following trading securities transactions:

Oct. 26 Purchased 300 shares of Company F common stock for $35 per share

Nov. 26   Sold 200 shares of Company E common stock for $25 per share

Dec. 10   Purchased 400 shares of Company G common stock for $41 per share

On December 31, 2004 the quoted market prices of the shares were as follows: E, $52 per share; F, $38 per share; and G, $40 per share.

Required

1. Prepare journal entries to record the preceding information for the fourth quarter.
2. Show what the bank reports on its fourth quarter 2004 income statement for these trading securities.
3. Show how the bank reports these trading securities on its balance sheet at the end of the fourth quarter of 2004.

E14-3   *Long-Term Investments*   On December 31, 2003 Marsh Company held 1,000 shares of X Company common stock in its portfolio of long-term investments in available-for-sale securities. The stock had cost $15 per share and has a current market value of $13 per share. The December 31, 2003 balance sheet showed the following:

Assets

Long-term investment in available-for-sale securities	$15,000
Less: Allowance for change in value of investment	(2,000)
	$13,000

Stockholders' Equity

Unrealized decrease in value of available-for-sale securities	$ (2,000)

During 2004 the company acquired as long-term investments 900 shares of Y Company common stock for $18 per share and 800 shares of Z Company common stock for $22 per share. At the end of 2004 the respective market values per share were: X—$14, Y—$17, and Z—$20.

Required Record the purchase of the investments in 2004 and the adjusting entry on December 31, 2004, and show the respective December 31, 2004 balance sheet accounts.

E14-4 *Available-for-Sale Securities* At the beginning of 2004 Ace Company had the following portfolio of investments in available-for-sale securities (common stock):

Security	Cost	12/31/03 Fair Value
A	$20,000	$25,000
B	30,000	29,000
Totals	$50,000	$54,000

During 2004 the following transactions occurred:

May   3 Purchased C securities (common stock) for $13,500
July 16 Sold all of the A securities for $25,000
Dec. 31 Received dividends of $800 on the B and C securities, for which the following information was available:

Security	12/31/04 Fair Value
B	$32,000
C	15,500

Required

1. Prepare journal entries to record the preceding information.
2. What is the balance in the Unrealized Increase/Decrease account on December 31, 2004?

E14-5 *Available-for-Sale Securities* At the end of 2003 Terry Company prepared the following schedule of investments in available-for-sale securities (common stock):

Security	Cost	12/31/03 Fair Value	Cumulative Change in Fair Value
M	$37,000	$34,200	$(2,800)
N	42,000	43,100	1,100
Totals	$79,000	$77,300	$(1,700)

During 2004, the following transactions occurred:

June   8 Purchased O securities (common stock) for $50,000
Oct. 11 Sold all of the M securities for $35,400
Dec. 31 Received dividends of $900 on the N and O securities, and the following year-end total market values were available: N common stock, $43,900; O common stock, $49,600

Required

1. Prepare journal entries to record the preceding information.
2. Show how the preceding items are reported on the December 31, 2004 balance sheet of the Terry Company. Assume all investments are noncurrent.

E14-6 *Purchase of Bonds Between Interest Dates* On March 31, 2004 the Brodie Corporation acquired bonds with a par value of $400,000 for $425,800. The bonds are due December 31, 2009, carry a 12% annual interest rate, pay interest on June 30 and December 31, and are being held to maturity. The accrued interest is included in the acquisition price of the bonds. The company uses straight-line amortization.

Required

1. Prepare journal entries for Brodie to record the purchase of the bonds and the first two interest receipts.
2. If the company failed to separately record the interest at acquisition, explain the errors that would occur in the company's financial statements (no calculations are required).

E14-7   *Amortizing a Discount on a Bond Investment*   On January 1, 2004 the Kelly Corporation acquired bonds with a face value of $500,000 for $483,841.79, a price that yields a 10% effective annual interest rate. The bonds carry a 9% stated rate of interest, pay interest semiannually on June 30 and December 31, are due December 31, 2007, and are being held to maturity.

Required Prepare journal entries to record the purchase of the bonds and the first two interest receipts using:
1. The straight-line method of amortization.
2. The effective interest method of amortization.

E14-8   *Purchase, Discount Amortization, and Sale of Bond Investment*   On November 1, 2003 the Reid Corporation acquired bonds with a face value of $700,000 for $673,618.61. The bonds carry a stated rate of interest of 10%, were purchased to yield 11%, pay interest semiannually on April 30 and October 31, were purchased to be held to maturity, and are due October 31, 2008. On November 1, 2004, in contemplation of a major acquisition, the bonds were sold for $700,000. Reid Corporation is on a fiscal year accounting period ending October 31. The company uses the effective interest method.

Required Prepare journal entries to record the purchase of the bonds, the interest receipts on April 30, 2004 and October 31, 2004, and the sale of the bonds.

E14-9   *Investment Discount Amortization Schedule*   On January 1, 2004 Rodgers Company purchased $200,000 face value, 10%, 3-year bonds for $190,165.35, a price that yields a 12% effective annual interest rate. The bonds pay interest semiannually on June 30 and December 31.

Required
1. Record the purchase of the bonds.
2. Prepare an investment interest revenue and discount amortization schedule, using the effective interest method.
3. Record the receipts of interest on June 30, 2004 and June 30, 2006.

E14-10   *Investment Premium Amortization Schedule*   On January 1, 2004 Lynch Company acquired 13% bonds with a face value of $50,000. The bonds pay interest on June 30 and December 31 and mature on December 31, 2006. Lynch Company paid $51,229.35, a price that yields a 12% effective annual interest rate.

Required
1. Record the purchase of the bonds.
2. Prepare an investment interest revenue and premium amortization schedule using the effective interest method.
3. Record the receipts of interest on June 30, 2004 and December 31, 2006.

E14-11   *Purchase, Premium Amortization, and Sale of Bond Investment*   The Glover Corporation purchased bonds with a face value of $300,000 for $307,493.34 on January 1, 2004. The bonds carry a face rate of interest of 12%, pay interest semiannually on June 30 and December 31, were purchased to be held to maturity, are due December 31, 2006, and were purchased to yield 11%. On January 1, 2005, in contemplation of a major acquisition, the bonds were sold for $300,000. The company uses the effective interest method.

Required Prepare journal entries to record the purchase of the bonds, the first two interest receipts, and the sale of the bonds.

E14-12   *Transfer Between Categories*   On December 31, 2003 the Leslie Company held an investment in bonds of Kaufmann Company which it categorized as being held to maturity. At that time, the 8%, $100,000 face value bonds had a carrying value of $107,023.56 and were being amortized using the effective interest method based on a yield of 7%. Interest on these bonds is paid annually each December 31.

On December 31, 2004, after recording the interest earned, the Leslie Company decided to reclassify the Kaufmann bonds to its available-for-sale category in anticipation of a major restructuring. At that time, the ending quoted market price for the bonds was 105.

Required Prepare the journal entries on December 31, 2004 to record the interest earned and the reclassification.

E14-13   *Equity Method*   The Miller Corporation acquired 30% of the outstanding common stock of the Crowell Corporation for $160,000 on January 1, 2004 and obtained significant influence. The purchase price of the shares was equal to their book value. During 2004, the following information is available for Crowell:

Mar. 31 Declared and paid a cash dividend of $50,000
June 30 Reported semiannual earnings of $120,000 for the first half of 2004
Sept. 30 Declared and paid a cash dividend of $50,000
Dec. 31 Reported semiannual earnings of $140,000 for the second half of 2004

Required

1. Prepare journal entries for Miller to reflect the preceding information.
2. What is the balance in Miller's investment account on December 31, 2004? (Show your computations.)

E14-14 *Equity Method* On January 1, 2004 the Field Company acquired 40% of the North Company by purchasing 8,000 shares for $144,000 and obtained significant influence. On the date of acquisition, Field calculated that its share of the excess of the fair value over the book value of North's depreciable assets was $15,000, and that the purchased goodwill was $12,000. At the end of 2004, North reported net income of $45,000 and paid dividends of $0.70 per share. Field Company depreciates its depreciable assets over a 12-year remaining life.

Required Prepare all the journal entries of Field Company to record the preceding information for 2004.

E14-15 *Equity Method* On January 1, 2004 Jones acquires a 30% interest in Fink Company by purchasing 3,000 of its 10,000 common shares for $16 per share and obtains significant influence. On the date of acquisition, the net assets of Fink Company were as shown here:

	Book Value	Fair Value
Nondepreciable assets (for example, land)	$ 15,000	$ 25,000
Depreciable assets (10-year remaining life)	90,000	115,000
	$105,000	$140,000
Liabilities	$ 10,000	$ 15,000

During 2004 Fink Company earned income of $22,000 and paid dividends of $6,000.

Required

1. Prepare all journal entries on Jones Company's books to record the acquisition, dividends, and income from the investment in Fink Company. Show supporting calculations.
2. Compute the amount of the purchased goodwill.

E14-16 *Convertible Bonds* On January 1, 2003 the Taylor Corporation purchased $20,000 of the Kalanda Corporation's 12% convertible bonds for $19,760. The bonds pay interest semiannually each December 31 and June 30 and are due December 31, 2007. Each $1,000 bond is convertible into 15 shares of the Kalanda Corporation's $10 par common stock. Taylor uses the straight-line method of discount amortization. At the end of 2003 and 2004, the quoted market price of the bonds was not materially different from the amortized cost. On July 1, 2005 Taylor exchanged all of the bonds for Kalanda common stock. At that time the market value of the common stock was $72 per share.

Required Prepare whatever entries are necessary to record the acquisition and conversion of the Kalanda bonds.

E14-17 *Receipt of Stock Dividends* On March 2, 2004 the Dawson Corporation acquired 5,000 common shares, representing a 1% interest in the Foreman Corporation, for $60,000. On May 1, 2004 Foreman issued a 20% stock dividend, and on December 31, 2004 the market value was $10 per share. On February 1, 2005 Dawson sold 1,500 shares for $12 per share.

Required Prepare journal entries for Dawson to record the acquisition, stock dividend, and sale of the shares.

E14-18 *Cash Surrender Value of Life Insurance* The Westford Corporation purchases life insurance policies on its officers, and these policies all carry a cash surrender value clause. At the beginning of 2004, Westford paid $13,300 in life insurance premiums for one year. During 2004 the cash surrender value of the policies increased from $98,450 to $103,900. At the beginning of 2005 the corporation's vice president lost his life in an automobile accident. The policy carried on this officer paid $50,000, and the cash surrender value of the policy was $6,480.

Required Prepare journal entries to record the preceding information on the Westford Corporation's books.

E14-19 *Sinking Funds Entries* The following information is available concerning the Nunan Corporation's sinking fund:

Jan.   1, 2004   Established a sinking fund to retire an outstanding bond issue by contributing $425,000

Feb.   3, 2004   Purchased securities for $400,000

July 30, 2004   Sold securities originally costing $48,000 for $45,000

Dec. 31, 2004   Collected dividends and interest on the remaining securities in the amount of $49,000; the securities had a market value of $355,000 at this time

Dec. 31, 2005   Collected dividends and interest on the remaining securities in the amount of $40,000

Dec. 31, 2005   Paid sinking fund expenses of $4,500

Dec. 31, 2005   Sold the remaining securities in the fund for $360,000

Dec. 31, 2005   Retired an outstanding bond issue of $500,000 with the cash from the fund and transferred the remaining fund balance back to the cash account

Required Prepare journal entries to record the preceding transactions for the Nunan Corporation.

E14-20 *Derivatives (Appendix)*   Anglar Company has a $3 million 7% bank loan from Castle Rock Bank. On January 1, 2004, when the $3 million loan has 3 years remaining, Anglar contracts with Susan Investment Bank to enter into a three-year interest-rate swap with a $3 million notional amount. Anglar agrees to receive from Susan a fixed interest rate of 7% and to pay Susan an interest amount each year that is variable based on the LIBOR interest rate at the beginning of the year. The interest payments are made at year-end. The applicable interest rate on the swap is reset each year after the annual interest payment is made. The LIBOR interest rate is 6.6% at the beginning of 2004. The three-year fixed interest rate is 8% at December 31, 2004.

Required

1. Prepare the journal entries of Anglar for the bank loan and derivative for 2004.
2. Prepare the appropriate disclosures in Anglar's financial statements for 2004.

PROBLEMS

P14-1 *Trading Securities*   The investment manager of 4th National Bank invests some of the bank's financial resources in trading securities. During the last quarter of 2004 the following transactions occurred in regard to these trading securities:

Nov.   5   Purchased 200 shares of M Company common stock at $86 per share

Nov. 19   Purchased 300 shares of P Company preferred stock at $63 per share

Nov. 29   Sold 100 shares of M Company common stock at $89 per share

Dec. 15   Purchased 400 shares of T Company common stock at $37 per share

Dec. 17   Sold 100 shares of P Company preferred stock at $62 per share

On December 31, 2004 the market values of the shares were as follows: M, $87 per share; P, $61 per share; and T, $37.25 per share. The bank held no trading securities at the beginning of the last quarter of 2004.

Required

1. Prepare journal entries to record the preceding information.
2. Show what the bank reports on its fourth quarter 2004 income statement for these trading securities.
3. Show how the bank reports these trading securities on its December 31, 2004 balance sheet.

P14-2 *Trading Securities*   The 8th State Bank prepares interim financial statements and follows an investment strategy of investing in trading securities. At the beginning of the third quarter of 2004, the bank held the following portfolio of trading securities:

Security	Cost	June 30, 2004 Fair Value
100 shares of G Company common stock	$ 2,900	$ 2,800
600 shares of O Company common stock	12,000	12,600
Totals	$14,900	$15,400

During the third quarter of 2004, the bank entered into the following trading securities transactions:

July 2 Received dividends of $1.50 per share on the G Company common stock
July 14 Sold 600 shares of O Company common stock for $20 per share
Aug. 9 Purchased 300 shares of P Company common stock for $36 per share
Aug. 24 Sold 100 shares of G Company common stock for $30 per share
Sept. 17 Purchased 500 shares of U Company common stock for $22 per share

On September 30, 2004 the P Company common stock had a quoted market price of $36.50 per share and the U Company common stock had a quoted market price of $21 per share.

Required

1. Prepare journal entries to record the preceding information.
2. Show what the bank reports on its third quarter 2004 income statement for these trading securities.
3. Show how the bank reports these trading securities on its September 30, 2004 balance sheet.

P14-3 *Available-for-Sale Securities* Holly Company invests its excess cash in marketable securities. At the beginning of 2004 it had the following portfolio of investments in available-for-sale securities:

Security	Cost	12/31/03 Fair Value
400 shares of I Company common stock	$ 8,400	$ 9,400
700 shares of O Company common stock	23,100	21,700
Totals	$31,500	$31,100

During 2004, the following transactions occurred:

Mar. 31 Purchased U Company 8% bonds with a face value of $10,000 for $10,000 plus accrued interest; interest is payable on the bonds each June 30 and December 31
May 17 Sold 200 shares of O Company common stock for $30 per share
June 30 Received the semiannual interest on the U Company bonds
Oct. 12 Sold 100 shares of I Company common stock for $24 per share
Dec. 31 Received the semiannual interest on the U Company bonds and dividends of $1 per share and $1.50 per share on the I and O Company common stock, respectively

The December 31 closing market prices were as follows: I Company common stock, $25 per share; O Company common stock, $31 per share; U Company 8% bonds, 101.

Required

1. Prepare journal entries to record the preceding information.
2. Show what is reported on the Holly Company's 2004 income statement.
3. Assuming the investment in I Company stock is considered to be a current asset and the remaining investments are noncurrent, show how all the items are reported on the December 31, 2004 balance sheet of the Holly Company.
4. If GAAP required that unrealized holding gains and losses on available-for-sale securities be included in income, how much would Holly recognize in 2004?

P14-4 *Investments in Equity Securities* The Noonan Corporation prepares quarterly financial statements and invests its excess funds in marketable securities. At the end of 2003 Noonan's portfolio of investments available for sale consisted of the following equity securities:

Security	Number of Shares	Cost Per Share	Fair Value Per Share
Keene Company	500	$60	$60
Sachs, Inc.	800	43	44
Bacon Company	400	70	72

During the first half of 2004, Noonan engaged in the following investment transactions:

Jan. 6 Sold one-half of the Sachs shares for $45 per share
Feb. 3 Purchased 700 shares of Jackson Corporation common stock for $45 per share
Mar. 31 Dividends of $2,500 were received on the investments, and the following information is available on market prices:

Security	Fair Value Per Share
Keene Company	$59
Sachs, Inc.	45
Bacon Company	70
Jackson Corporation	43

Apr. 14   Purchased 300 shares of Quinn Company preferred stock for $52 per share
May 11   Sold the remainder of the Sachs shares for $42 per share
June 30   Dividends of $2,800 were received on investments, and the following information is available:

Security	Fair Value Per Share
Keene Company	$62
Bacon Company	69
Jackson Corporation	46
Quinn Company	50

Required

1. Record Noonan's investment transactions for January 6 through June 30, 2004.
2. Show the items of income or loss from investment transactions that Noonan reports for each of the first and second quarters of 2004.
3. Show how the preceding items are reported on the first and second quarter 2004 ending balance sheets, assuming that management expects to dispose of the Keene and Sachs securities within the next year.

P14-5   *Temporary Available-for-Sale Investments*   Manson Incorporated reported the following current asset on its December 31, 2003 balance sheet:

Temporary investment in available-for-sale securities (at cost)	$63,475
Less: Allowance for change in value of investment	(2,980)
Temporary investment in available-for-sale securities (at fair value)	$60,495

An analysis of Manson's temporary investments on December 31, 2003 reveals the following:

Equity Security	Cost	Fair Value
400 shares of Turben Company, common	$14,275	$13,590
500 shares of Cook Corp., common	12,650	13,175
700 shares of Hill Corp., common	17,450	18,180
200 shares of Web Engines, preferred	19,100	15,550
Totals	$63,475	$60,495

During 2004 the following transactions related to Manson's temporary investments occurred:

Jan. 6   Received a $265 dividend on the Turben Company common
Mar. 31   Received the semiannual dividend of $500 on the Web Engines preferred

On March 31, 2004 the following information is available concerning Manson's temporary investments:

Equity Security	Fair Value
Turben Company	$13,470
Cook Corp.	13,765
Hill Corp.	18,940
Web Engines	15,500

June 30   Received a $375 dividend on the Cook Corp. common and a $700 dividend on the Hill Corp. common

On June 30, 2004 the following information is available concerning Manson's temporary investments:

Equity Security	Fair Value
Turben Company	$13,300
Cook Corp.	14,125
Hill Corp.	19,300
Web Engines	15,400

July 6 Sold the Turben Company common for $13,750
Sept. 29 Received the semiannual dividend of $500 on the Web Engines preferred

On September 30, 2004 the following information is available concerning Manson's temporary investments:

Equity Security	Fair Value
Cook Corp.	$14,230
Hill Corp.	19,500
Web Engines	15,900

Nov. 2 Sold the Hill Corp. common for $19,780
Dec. 30 Received a $375 dividend on the Cook Corp. common

On December 31, 2004, the following information is available:

Equity Security	Fair Value
Cook Investment Corp.	$14,280
Web Engines	16,400

Required

1. Assuming Manson prepares quarterly financial statements, prepare journal entries to record the preceding information.
2. Show the items of income or loss from temporary investment transactions that Manson reports for each quarter of 2004?
3. Show how Manson's temporary investments are reported on the balance sheet on March 31, 2004; June 30, 2004; September 30, 2004; and December 31, 2004.

See WebTutor for annotated problem solution.

P14-6 **Investment in Available-for-Sale Bonds** The following information relates to the Starr Company's Investment in Available-for-Sale Bonds account for 2004:

Jan. 1 Purchased $30,000 face value of Bradford Company 8% bonds at 97 to yield 10%; interest on the bonds is payable each June 30 and December 31
Jan. 1 Purchased $40,000 face value of Morris Company 10% bonds at 101 to yield 9.8%; interest on the bonds is payable each June 30 and December 31

On June 30, collected the interest and the following information is available:

Security	Fair Value
Bradford Company 8%	97.2
Morris Company 10%	102.0

July 1 Purchased $25,000 face value of Whipple Corporation 11% bonds at 92 to yield 12%; interest on the bonds is payable each June 30 and December 31
Nov. 30 Sold the Whipple bonds at 91 plus accrued interest

On December 31, collected the interest, sold the Morris bonds at 102, and the following information is also available:

Security	Fair Value
Bradford Company 8%	96

Required

1. Prepare journal entries to record the previous information for 2004. Use the effective interest method and round all amounts to the nearest *dollar*. Assume that Starr prepares semiannual financial statements.
2. Show the items of income or loss from investment transactions that Starr reports for each 2004 semiannual income statement.

3. Show how the investment items are reported on each of the 2004 semiannual balance sheets, assuming that management expects to dispose of all investments within one year of purchase.

P14-7   ***Temporary Investments in Available-for-Sale Bonds and Equity Securities***   During 2004 the Dana Company decided to begin investing its idle cash in marketable securities. The information contained below relates to Dana's 2004 marketable security transactions:

Feb.   3   Purchased 3,000 shares of Blair Company common stock for $12 per share

Apr.   1   Purchased $20,000 face value of Solomon Inc. 12% bonds at par plus accrued interest; interest on the bonds is payable each June 30 and December 31

June 30   Received the semiannual interest on the Solomon bonds and a $0.25 per share dividend on the Blair common

Sept.   1   Purchased 4,000 shares of Woodman Corporation common for $22 per share

Nov.   1   Purchased $30,000 face value of Edwards Company 11% bonds at par plus accrued interest; interest on the bonds is payable each June 1 and December 1

Dec.   1   Received the interest on the Edwards bonds and sold the bonds at 101

Dec. 30   Received a $0.25 dividend per share on the Blair common and sold all the shares for $35,300

Dec. 31   Received the interest on the Solomon bonds

On December 31, the following information is available concerning the year-end market prices:

Security	Quoted Market
Solomon 12% bonds	101
Woodman common	$23

Required

1. Record Dana's transactions in temporary investments for 2004.
2. Show the items of income or loss on temporary investments Dana reports on its 2004 income statement.
3. Show the carrying value of Dana's Temporary Investment account on its December 31, 2004 balance sheet.

P14-8   ***Investments, Petty Cash, Bank Reconciliation***   During the first quarter of 2004 the Payne Corporation entered into the following transactions:

Jan.   1   Acquired 150 shares of Block Corporation common stock for $20 per share, 200 shares of Bridle Corporation common stock for $30 per share, and 100 shares of Alpha Corporation common stock for $25 per share. These are the only shares the company owns and all are classified as securities available for sale.

Feb.   1   Purchased 12% A Company bonds with a face value of $20,000 at par, plus accrued interest. Interest on the bonds is payable February 28 and August 31 each year, and the bonds are due August 31, 2007. Also purchased 10% B Company bonds with a face value of $12,000 at par, plus accrued interest. Interest on the bonds is payable March 31 and September 30, and the bonds are due September 30, 2010. These are the only bonds the company owns and all are classified as securities available for sale.

Feb.   1   Established a petty cash fund for incidental expenditures at $500.

Feb. 28   Received the semiannual interest on the A Company bonds.

Feb. 28   A count of cash on hand indicated that $125.50 remained in the petty cash fund. A sorting of petty cash vouchers disclosed that $110.00 was spent for postage, $170.65 was spent for office supplies, $45.00 was spent for transportation, and $43.50 was spent for miscellaneous items. The fund was replenished.

Mar. 31   Received first quarter dividends of $1,500 and the semiannual interest on the B Company bonds. On this date, the aggregate fair value of Payne's securities available for sale is $42,600.

Mar. 31   A count of cash on hand indicated that $230.50 remained in the petty cash fund. A sorting of petty cash vouchers disclosed that $140.00 was spent for postage, $75.30 was spent for office supplies, and $54.20 was spent for miscellaneous items. The fund was replenished.

The bank statement and the accounting records of the Payne Corporation for the month of March 2004 indicated that the cash collected from the dividends and the B Company bond interest was deposited on March 31 but did not appear on the March bank statement. There were no other deposits in transit. The bank statement showed a balance on March 31 of $13,459.75, which included collection of a $1,500 note and $100 of interest by the bank for the Payne Corporation. Also listed was a $20 bank service charge and a $75.60 NSF check returned by the bank. The cash balance per the accounting records on March 31 was $11,689.95, which included checks totaling $2,365.40 that had not yet cleared the bank.

Required

1. Prepare journal entries to record the preceding transactions of the Payne Corporation for the first quarter of 2004.
2. Prepare a bank reconciliation for Payne for March 31, 2004.
3. Prepare any journal entries necessary to adjust Payne's books on March 31, 2004.

P14-9 *Premium Amortization on Bond Investment and Partial Sale of the Investment Using the Effective Interest Method* On January 1, 2004 the Hyde Corporation purchased bonds with a face value of $300,000 for $308,373.53. The bonds are due June 30, 2007, carry a 13% stated interest rate, and were purchased to yield 12%. Interest is payable semiannually on June 30 and December 31. On March 31, 2005, in contemplation of a major acquisition, the company sold one-half the bonds for $159,500 including accrued interest; the remainder were held until maturity.

Required Prepare the journal entries to record the purchase of the bonds, each interest payment, the partial sale of the investment on March 31, 2005, and the retirement of the bond issue on June 30, 2007.

P14-10 *Bond Investment Discount Amortization Schedule* The Tudor Company acquired $500,000 of Carr Cor-po-ration bonds for $487,706.69 on January 1, 2004. The bonds carry an 11% stated interest rate, pay interest semiannually on January 1 and July 1, were issued to yield 12%, and are due January 1, 2007.

Required

1. Prepare an investment interest revenue and discount amortization schedule using:
   a. The straight-line method
   b. The effective interest method
2. Prepare the July 1, 2006 journal entries to record the interest revenue under both methods.

P14-11 *Discount Amortization on Bonds Purchased Between Interest Dates* On October 1, 2003 the Jenkins Corporation bought bonds with a face value of $200,000 for $199,175, including accrued interest. The bonds are due December 31, 2005 and carry a face rate of interest of 10.5%. Interest on the bonds is payable semiannually on June 30 and December 31. The company uses the straight-line method to amortize the discount.

Required

1. Prepare journal entries to record the purchase of the bonds, each interest receipt, and the retirement of the issue on December 31, 2005.
2. If the company failed to separately record the interest at acquisition, explain the errors that would occur in the company's financial statements (no calculations are required).

P14-12 *Bond Investment Premium Amortization Schedule* The Mercer Corporation acquired $400,000 of the Park Company's bonds on June 30, 2003 for $409,991.12. The bonds carry a 12% stated interest rate, pay interest semiannually on June 30 and December 31, were issued to yield 11%, and are due June 30, 2006.

Required

1. Prepare an investment interest revenue and premium amortization schedule, using:
   a. The straight-line method
   b. The effective interest method
2. Prepare journal entries to record the December 31, 2003 and December 31, 2005 interest receipts using both methods.

P14-13 *Discount Amortization on Bond Investment and Partial Sale of Investment Using Effective Interest Method* On January 1, 2004 the Mark Corporation purchased bonds with a face value of $500,000 for $475,413.60. The bonds are due December 31, 2006, carry a 10% stated rate, and were purchased to yield 12%. Interest is payable semiannually on June 30 and December 31. On January 1, 2006, in contemplation of a major acquisition, one-fourth of the bonds were sold for $127,000. The remainder were held until maturity.

Required Prepare journal entries to record the purchase of the bonds, each interest payment, the partial sale of the investment on December 31, 2005, and the retirement of the bond issue on December 31, 2006.

P14-14 *Comparison of Fair Value and Equity Methods* On January 1, 2003 Snow Corporation purchased 20% of the 200,000 outstanding shares of common stock of Garvey Company for $4.00 per share as a long-term investment. The purchase price of the shares was equal to their book value. The following information is available about Garvey Company for 2003 and 2004:

End of 2003	Reported net income	$80,000
	Cash dividends declared and paid	$30,000
	Market value of shares	$3.80 per share
End of 2004	Reported net income	$90,000
	Cash dividends declared and paid	$35,000
	Market value of shares	$4.25 per share

Required

1. Prepare journal entries to record this information, assuming:
   a. The fair value method is used by Snow
   b. The equity method is used by Snow
2. Assume 10,000 of the Garvey shares are sold on January 4, 2005 by Snow for $4.25 per share. Prepare the journal entry for this sale, assuming:
   a. Snow is using the fair value method
   b. Snow is using the equity method

P14-15 *Application of Equity Method*   On January 1, 2004 Doe Company purchased 3,000 of the 10,000 common shares outstanding of the Ray Company for $15 per share and obtained significant influence. Doe amortizes its patents over 10 years. The December 31, 2003 condensed balance sheet of the Ray Company is shown here:

Current assets	$ 10,000	Liabilities	$ 50,000
Fixed assets (net)	100,000	Common stock, no par	30,000
Patents (net)	40,000	Retained earnings	70,000
	$150,000		$150,000

Doe Company was unable to determine the fair value of the Ray Company identifiable net assets shown on the preceding balance sheet. It did, however, determine that Ray Company uses the straight-line method (no residual value) to depreciate its fixed assets and to amortize its patents over 20 years and 10 years, respectively. At the end of 2004 Ray Company disclosed the following condensed income statement and retained earnings statement for 2004:

Revenues	$100,000	Beginning retained earnings	$ 70,000
Expenses	(60,000)	Add: Net income	32,000
Operating income	$ 40,000		$102,000
Extraordinary loss	(8,000)	Less: Cash dividends	(20,000)
Net income	$ 32,000	Ending retained earnings	$ 82,000

Required

1. Prepare all the 2004 journal entries that Doe should make related to this investment. Show and label all supporting calculations.
2. Compute the amount of the purchased goodwill.

P14-16 *Recording Investments Under the Equity Method*   The Harper Corporation acquired 80,000 of the 200,000 outstanding shares of the Moore Corporation on April 1, 2004 for $400,000 and obtained significant influence. The following information concerning the Moore Corporation is available on the date of acquisition:

	Book Value	Fair Value
Depreciable assets (remaining life, 15 years)	$ 600,000	$ 700,000
Other assets	500,000	450,000
Total	$1,100,000	$1,150,000
Liabilities	$ 300,000	$ 320,000
Common stock	250,000	
Retained earnings	550,000	
Total	$1,100,000	

Subsequently, Moore Corporation paid a cash dividend of $40,000 on August 31, 2004 and reported annual income from operations of $125,000 and extraordinary income (earned in the third quarter) of $30,000 on December 31, 2004.

Required

1. Prepare journal entries for Harper to record the preceding information.
2. Compute the amount of the purchased goodwill.
3. What is the balance in Harper's investment account on December 31, 2004? (Show all computations.)
4. Prepare Harper's net cash flow from operating activities section of its 2004 statement of cash flows under the indirect method, assuming the equity investment income is the only income Harper reports. Ignore income taxes.

P14-17 *Equity Method and Subsequent Sale* On January 1, 2004 the Easton Corporation acquired 30% of the outstanding common shares of Feeley Corporation for $140,000, and 25% of the outstanding common shares of Holmes Company for $82,500 and obtained significant influence in both situations. On this date the financial statements of Feeley and Holmes disclosed the following information:

	Feeley	Holmes
Current assets	$190,000	$140,000
Long-term assets	370,000	180,000
	$560,000	$320,000
Liabilities	$120,000	$ 90,000
Common stock (no par)	200,000	150,000
Retained earnings	240,000	80,000
	$560,000	$320,000

During 2004 Feeley reported income of $70,000 and paid dividends of $40,000; Holmes reported income of $45,000 and paid dividends of $28,000. On January 1, 2005 Feeley sold all the Holmes shares for $90,000. Assume the company records both investments under the equity method and considers that any difference between each purchase price and the respective book value of the net assets acquired is goodwill.

Required

1. Prepare journal entries to record (a) the purchase of the Feeley and Holmes shares, (b) the recognition of investment income, (c) the receipt of investee dividends, and (d) the sale of the Holmes shares.
2. Compute the amount of the purchased goodwill for each investment.

P14-18 *Change to Equity Method* On January 1, 2004 Lion Company paid $600,000 for 10,000 shares of Wolf Company's voting common stock, which was a 10% interest in Wolf. Lion does not have the ability to exercise significant influence over the operating and financial policies of Wolf. Lion received dividends of $1.00 per share from Wolf on October 2, 2004. Wolf reported net income of $400,000 for the year ended December 31, 2004 and the ending market price of its shares was $63.

On July 2, 2005 Lion paid $1,950,000 for 30,000 additional shares of Wolf Company's voting common stock, which represents a 30% investment in Wolf. The fair values of all of Wolf's assets, net of liabilities, were equal to their book values of $6,500,000. As a result of this transaction, Lion has the ability to exercise significant influence over the operating and financial policies of Wolf. Lion received dividends of $1.00 per share from Wolf on April 2, 2005 and $1.35 per share on October 1, 2005. Wolf reported net income of $500,000 for the year ended December 31, 2005, and $200,000 for the 6 months ended December 31, 2005.

Required

1. For the Lion Company show the dividend revenue for 2004, as well as the December 31, 2004 unrealized increase in value of available-for-sale securities and carrying value of the investment account.
2. Assuming that Lion Company issues comparative financial statements for 2004 and 2005, show the investment income for 2004 and 2005, as well as the December 31, 2004 and 2005 carrying value of the Investment account.

P14-19 *Cash Surrender Value of Life Insurance* On January 1, 2003 Kehoe Corporation insured the lives of its president, vice-president, controller, and treasurer for $100,000 each. The annual premium on each policy is $4,200, payable on January 1 of each year, and the cash surrender values for the policies increase by 4% of the annual premiums paid. Premium payments were made on the scheduled date by the Kehoe Corporation through 2005, and the following dividends were received at the end of the year on each policy: 2003, $450; 2004, $575; 2005, $550. On February 1, 2006 the treasurer died and Kehoe Corporation collected the face value of his policy plus eleven months' premium.

Required Prepare journal entries to record the preceding information for the years 2003 through 2006. (Round calculation to the nearest dollar.)

P14-20   *Derivatives (Appendix)*   Danburg Company has a $5 million 9% bank loan outstanding with its local bank. On January 1, 2004, when the loan has four years remaining, Danburg contracts with Bradford Investment Bank to enter into a four-year interest-rate swap with a $5 million notional amount. Danburg agrees to receive from Bradford a fixed interest rate of 9% and to pay Bradford an interest amount each year that is variable based on the LIBOR interest rate at the beginning of the year. The interest payments are made at year-end. The applicable interest rate on the swap is reset each year after the annual interest payment is made. The LIBOR interest rate is 8.6% and 9.5% at the beginning of 2004 and 2005, respectively. The three-year fixed interest rate is 10% at December 31, 2004, and the two-year rate is 8% at December 31, 2005.

Required
1. Prepare the journal entries of Danburg for the bank loan and derivative for 2004 and 2005.
2. Prepare the appropriate disclosures in Danburg's financial statements for 2004 and 2005.

INTERNET ASSIGNMENTS

Go to the Nikolai and Bazley **Intermediate Accounting** web site (http://Nikolai.swcollege.com). Click on Student Resources and internet homework assignments. Then click on the appropriate hot link (icon) for each company's web site, find the relevant accounting information, and answer the following questions.

I14-1   Go to the **Norwest** web site.

Required What are the balance sheet amounts of the company's trading, available-for-sale, and held-to-maturity securities at the end of the two most recent years? What is the cumulative change in the value of the available-for-sale securities at the end of the two most recent years. What is the change in the value of the available-for-sale securities in each of the two most recent years? If the change was included in income, would it have a material affect on your evaluation of the company's performance?

I14-2   Go to the **Coca-Cola Company** web site.

Required What are the company's equity investments? What are the balance sheet amounts of the company's equity investments at the end of the two most recent years? How much income did the company recognize on its equity investments in each of the two most recent years? How much cash dividends did it receive?

PART 4

Financial Reporting: Stockholders' Equity

Chapter 15   Contributed Capital

Chapter 16   Earnings Per Share and Retained Earnings

objectives

1 Explain the corporate form of organization.

2 Know the rights and terms that apply to capital stock.

3 Account for the issuance of capital stock.

4 Describe a compensatory stock option plan.

5 Recognize compensation expense for a compensatory stock option plan.

6 Account for a fixed compensatory stock option plan.

7 Account for a performance-based compensatory stock option plan.

8 Understand how to use the intrinsic value method to account for a compensatory stock option plan.

9 Describe the characteristics of preferred stock.

10 Know the components of contributed capital.

11 Understand the accounting for treasury stock.

CHAPTER 15

Contributed Capital

This chapter is the first of two on stockholders' equity. **FASB Statement of Concepts No. 6** defines **equity** as **the residual interest in the assets of a company that remains after deducting its liabilities.**[1] That is, the equity in a company is the ownership interest. Equity, which arises because of ownership rights, is created originally by owners' investments in the company. It may change because of several transactions or events, including cash dividends or other distributions of assets. Exhibit 15-1 summarizes these items.[2]

In the previous chapters we focused our discussion primarily on changes in assets and liabilities and their impact on net income (and equity). The main focus of Chapters 15 and 16, however, is on investments by owners, distributions to owners, and changes in equity not affecting assets or liabilities, as they apply to corporations.

In Chapter 15 we primarily address topics involving contributed capital. These issues include the formation of a corporation, the terminology relating to capital stock, the issuance of capital stock, compensatory stock option plans, the contributed capital section of stockholders' equity, and the reacquisition of capital (treasury) stock. In Chapter 16 we primarily address issues involving retained earnings.

CORPORATE FORM OF ORGANIZATION

The corporation is the dominant form of company in the U.S. economy today. The number of sole proprietorships and partnerships is much greater than the number of corporations, but corporations produce and sell many more goods and services. For example, according to recent government statistics, corporations comprised only 20% of companies in the U.S., but provided over 86% of the total revenues of all companies.

Types of Corporations

Corporations may be classified in several ways. These classifications include private versus public, open versus closed, and domestic versus foreign. We summarize each of these classifications briefly as follows:

1. **Private** corporations are privately owned. They include *nonstock* companies that do not issue stock and do not operate for profit (e.g., universities, hospitals, and churches), and *stock* companies that issue shares of stock to stockholders and operate for profit. Stock companies include open and closed corporations.

---

1. "Elements of Financial Statements of Business Enterprises," *FASB Statement of Concepts No. 6* (Stamford, Conn.: FASB, 1985), par. 49.
2. *Ibid.*, par. 60–63.

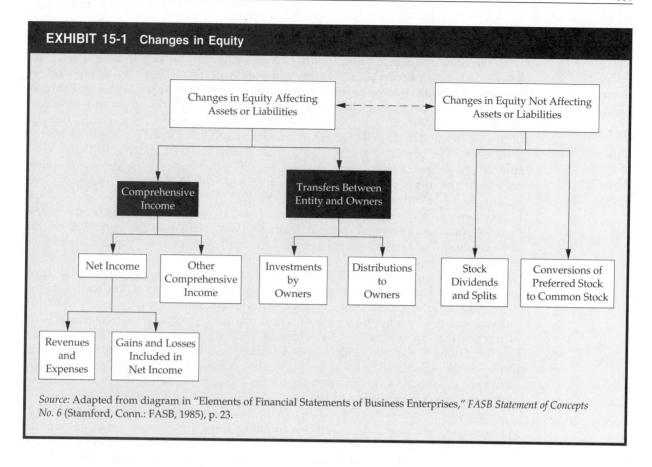

EXHIBIT 15-1 Changes in Equity

Source: Adapted from diagram in "Elements of Financial Statements of Business Enterprises," *FASB Statement of Concepts No. 6* (Stamford, Conn.: FASB, 1985), p. 23.

A. **Open** corporations are those whose stock is available for purchase by the public on a stock exchange or over-the-counter, and so is widely held. Open corporations often are called *publicly traded* corporations.

B. **Closed** corporations do not allow the sale of stock to the general public; such stock usually is held by a few stockholders. Closed corporations often are called *privately held* corporations.

2. **Public** corporations are owned or operated by governmental units, such as the Federal Deposit Insurance Corporation.

3. **Domestic** corporations, as viewed by a particular state, are companies that are incorporated in that state.

4. **Foreign** corporations, as viewed by a particular state, are companies that are operating in the state but are incorporated in another state.

The federal government applies a more global definition to domestic and foreign corporations. To the federal government a domestic corporation is one incorporated in the United States; a foreign corporation is one incorporated in another country.

In this book, we are concerned primarily with private corporations that issue shares of stock.

Formation of a Corporation

Although a corporation actually is a collection of individual owners, legally it is treated as an artificial entity, separate from and independent of these individuals. Thus, ownership is readily transferable. Owners (**stockholders**) have limited liability—that is, they ordinarily have no personal liability for the corporation's debts and risk only their capital investment. Furthermore, owners frequently play no active part in its management. As a result, the success of the corporation generally depends on its ability to attract large amounts of capital (from a diverse set of stockholders, each

1 Explain the corporate form of organization.

with limited liability), which is controlled by a professional management group for an indefinite period.

In the United States a corporation is a legal entity of a particular state. Each state has its own laws of incorporation; many are uniform throughout the country, others are not. Normally, one or more individuals may apply for approval to form a corporation. The application includes the names of the individual incorporators; the corporate name, address, and nature of business; the types, par value (if any), and number of shares of capital stock to be issued; and any other information required by the state's law. The application may also include the names and addresses of the initial subscribers to the capital stock, the number of subscribed shares, the subscription price, and the down payment (if any). If approved, the application is referred to as the **articles of incorporation** (or corporate *charter*). A stockholders' meeting then may be held, at which the initial issuance of capital stock is made to the incorporators, a board of directors is elected, a set of rules (bylaws) regulating the corporate operations is established, and the board appoints the executive officers ("top management") of the corporation.

In order for a corporation to perform its functions, the state gives it various rights and powers, including the right to enter into contracts, to hold, buy, and sell property, to sue and be sued, and to continue in perpetuity. In conjunction with these rights and powers, a corporation has a number of responsibilities. A corporation may engage only in the activities for which it was established, it must adhere to state laws concerning the distribution of income, and it must pay state and federal taxes. Because management has the responsibility to abide by state and federal laws and to safeguard and ensure the proper use of capital contributed by a diverse set of owners, accounting for corporate capital is important.

In this chapter we focus on capital stock transactions and their impact upon the corporate capital structure. Any statements we make about the characteristics of corporations, capital stock, and a corporation's capital structure are general statements. In any particular state, or for any particular corporation, these generalities may not hold.

CORPORATE CAPITAL STRUCTURE

Ownership in a corporation is evidenced by a **stock certificate**, a serially numbered document that indicates the number of shares owned and the par value (if any). Exhibit 15-2 shows a stock certificate for General Motors Corporation. Because stock certificates may be freely transferred from one individual to another, state laws require that each corporation keep appropriate records of its stockholders. The **stockholders' ledger** contains an account for each stockholder that shows the number of shares held. Whenever new shares are issued or shares are exchanged between stockholders, the ledger must be updated. Exchanges of stock are recorded initially in a **stock transfer journal**. This journal contains the names and addresses of the new and former stockholders involved in each stock transfer, the date of exchange, the stock certificate numbers, and the number of shares exchanged. Many corporations employ an independent **transfer agent** (such as a bank) to handle the issuance of stock certificates, as well as a **registrar** to maintain the stockholder records.

Capital Stock and Stockholders' Rights

2 Know the rights and terms that apply to capital stock.

The term **capital stock refers to the shares of stock issued by the corporation and owned by its stockholders.** Each stockholder has various rights. Generally, these include: (1) the right to share in the profits when a dividend is declared, (2) the right to elect directors and to establish corporate policies, (3) the right (called a **preemptive right**) to maintain a proportionate interest in the ownership of the corporation by purchasing a proportionate (pro rata) share of additional capital stock, if such stock is issued, and (4) the right to share in the distribution of the assets of the corporation if it is liquidated. These rights may be modified or waived for some types of capital stock or in specific circumstances. For instance, stockholders who own a certain class of stock may be entitled to

EXHIBIT 15-2   Illustration of Stock Certificate

vote only on particular issues. Another example is the case where the preemptive right is eliminated to allow a corporation to raise significant capital or acquire another company by issuing a large number of additional shares of stock.

A corporation may issue capital stock for cash, through installment sales, for nonmonetary assets, for compensatory stock option plans, and for other types of transactions. It may issue two basic classes of stock, generally designated as common stock and preferred stock. **Common stock** is capital stock that carries all of the preceding rights. Some corporations, however, issue more than one type of common stock such as Class A and Class B common stock. In this situation, usually one type of common stock has greater voting rights than the other to maintain control over the corporate activities. In exchange for certain other privileges, **preferred stock** usually is not granted all of the common stock's rights. We discuss the various stock transactions, as well as the characteristics and privileges of preferred stock, later in this chapter.

Basic Terminology

Several terms are often used in the discussion of capital stock and related transactions:

- **Authorized capital stock.** The number of shares of capital stock (both preferred and common) that a corporation may issue as stated in its corporate charter.
- **Issued capital stock.** The number of shares of capital stock that a corporation has issued to its stockholders as of a specific date.
- **Outstanding capital stock.** The number of shares of capital stock that a corporation has issued to stockholders and that are still being held by them as of a specific date.

- **Treasury stock.** The number of shares of capital stock that a corporation has issued to stockholders and has reacquired but not retired. The difference between issued shares and outstanding shares are treasury shares.
- **Subscribed capital stock.** The number of shares of capital stock that a corporation will issue upon the completion of an installment purchase contract with an investor.

These terms relate to each other as follows:

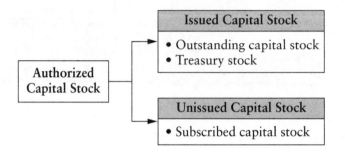

Legal Capital

As we indicated earlier, stockholders have *limited liability*. That is, generally they cannot be held legally responsible for the debts of the corporation unless it is determined that the corporation has been operated for the personal benefit of particular stockholders. In order to protect the corporation's creditors, state laws have established the concept of **legal capital** as the **amount of stockholders' equity that the corporation cannot distribute to stockholders.** A corporation may not pay dividends or reacquire capital stock if such a transaction would impair legal capital. The definition of legal capital varies among states. An investor must refer to the corporate laws of each state to determine the corporate legal capital in that state. However, in most states the par value or stated value of the issued capital stock is some or all of the legal capital.

PAR VALUE STOCK Historically, the primary way a corporation establishes its legal capital is by issuing par value stock. **The par value of a corporation's capital stock (either common or preferred) is a designated dollar amount per share that is established in the articles of incorporation and is printed on each stock certificate.** When a corporation issues par value stock, most states designate that the par value of all issued stock is the legal capital. The legal capital of the corporation is the par value per share multiplied by the number of shares issued. The par value of a share often is set very low—perhaps $5, $1, or even less per share. Note that the par value of the common stock listed on the stock certificate of General Motors in Exhibit 15-2 is $1⅔ per share. Since capital stock normally will sell at a price far in excess of the par value (e.g., General Motors' common stock was recently selling for $55 per share), the legal capital is usually only a small proportion of the total proceeds received. Stock rarely sells initially for less than its par value, because it is illegal to do so in most states. If such a sale occurs, the stock is said to have been sold at a *discount*, in which case the stockholder is contingently responsible to contribute sufficient additional capital to meet the corporation's legal capital requirements. In any event, par value has no direct relationship to the **market value,** the price at which the stock is issued. Generally, state regulations require only that a corporation make a separate accounting of its capital.

NO-PAR STOCK In order to avoid the contingent liability that would arise if stock were issued at less than par value, and to indicate to investors that the par and market value of stock are not directly related, many states now allow corporations to issue no-par capital stock. As the term implies, this stock does not carry a par value. When a corporation issues no-par stock, some states require that the corporation designate the entire proceeds received as legal capital. Many states, however, allow the corporate board of directors to establish a **stated value** per share of no-par stock. This stated value, when multiplied by the number of shares issued, generally determines the amount of the corporation's legal capital. The accounting for stated value, no-par stock parallels that of the accounting for par value stock.

The concept of legal capital has had a significant impact upon corporate reporting practices, particularly as they apply to the accounting for stockholders' equity. A corporation establishes capital stock accounts (for either common stock or preferred stock) to accumulate at least part of the legal capital, and it uses Additional Paid-in Capital accounts for the remainder of the capital contributed by stockholders (part of which also may be legal capital).

Additional Paid-in Capital

As we indicated earlier, a corporation may issue capital stock in a variety of transactions. Each of these transactions is likely to involve an exchange price (i.e., market value) significantly higher than the par or stated value of the stock. Adherence to state law requires the corporation to record the par or stated value. Sound accounting practice (as well as state law in certain states) also requires the corporation to identify, measure, and record the excess value received (the difference between the market value and the par value) in each type of stock transaction. The corporation records this excess in a specific **Additional Paid-in Capital** account. This account alternatively is entitled *Paid-in Capital in Excess of Par* (or *Stated*) *Value*, *Premium on Capital Stock*, or *Contributed Capital in Excess of Par* (or *Stated*) *Value*, or by an outdated term, *Capital Surplus*. Because this additional paid-in capital is likely to arise from a variety of transactions, a corporation may establish a single Additional Paid-in Capital *control* account and then have a subsidiary ledger containing separate additional paid-in capital accounts for each different source. When this occurs, it reports only the control account balance on its balance sheet. In this chapter we assume a control account is *not* used.

Stockholders' Equity

As we discussed earlier, total stockholders' equity is the residual interest of the owners in the net assets of the corporation—the equity or *capital* of the owners is the corporation's assets less its liabilities. In Chapter 3 we noted that the value of the assets and liabilities could be measured by several methods. The way in which a corporation measures its assets and liabilities will determine its measurement of total stockholders' equity, since the accounting equation: Assets = Liabilities + Stockholders' Equity must remain in balance. Total stockholders' equity, however, may be made up of several components.

A corporation reports the various components of its capital structure in the stockholders' equity section of its balance sheet. We noted earlier that a corporation records the results of all its stock transactions in capital stock accounts and additional paid-in capital accounts. To report the total amount invested by stockholders, a corporation lists and adds together these accounts in the **Contributed Capital** (or **Paid-in Capital**) section of its stockholders' equity.

In addition to disclosing total investments by stockholders, state laws and sound accounting practice require a corporation to disclose any net income that has been reinvested in the corporation and not paid out to stockholders in the form of dividends. A corporation reports this element of its corporate capital structure in the **Retained Earnings** section of stockholders' equity. Also, stockholders' equity may increase or decrease as a result of other comprehensive income. A corporation reports this element of its capital structure in an **Accumulated Other Comprehensive Income** section of stockholders' equity.

Retained earnings and accumulated other comprehensive income are discussed in Chapter 16.

The basic framework of a corporation's stockholders' equity is as follows:

Stockholders' Equity

Contributed Capital	
Capital stock	$ XX
Additional paid-in capital	XX
Retained earnings	XX
Accumulated other comprehensive income	XX
Total Stockholders' Equity	$XXXX

ISSUANCE OF CAPITAL STOCK

3 Account for the issuance of capital stock.

When a corporation issues only one class of capital stock, it is referred to as common stock. Common stockholders are the claimants to the residual interest in the corporation. Unless waived or modified, all the rights we discussed earlier in the chapter generally accrue to common stockholders. As we pointed out previously, corporations may engage in a variety of transactions related to the issuance of capital stock. We describe the proper accounting for each of these transactions next. Because most capital stock is common stock, our examples are in terms of common stock. However, the illustrated journal entries apply equally to preferred stock, with appropriate terminology changes.

Authorization

The corporate charter contains the authorization to issue capital stock. A corporation usually records this authorization in a memorandum journal entry. The entry identifies the number of authorized shares, the par or stated value per share, and, in the case of preferred stock, any preference provisions. Generally, the corporation establishes a separate account for each class of capital stock, and makes a similar memorandum entry in each account.

Issuance for Cash

A corporation may issue capital stock with a par value, as no-par stock with a stated value, or as true no-par stock. In the case of par value stock issued for cash, it records the difference between the proceeds and the total par value in an Additional Paid-in Capital account. To illustrate, assume a corporation issues 500 shares of its $10 par common stock for $18 per share. The corporation records the transaction as follows:

Cash ($18 × 500)	9,000	
Common Stock, $10 par ($10 × 500)		5,000
Additional Paid-in Capital on Common Stock		4,000

If, instead, the stock were no-par stock with a stated value of $10 per share, it would record the preceding transaction as follows:

Cash	9,000	
Common Stock, $10 stated value		5,000
Additional Paid-in Capital on Common Stock		4,000

Note that, with the exception of the terminology change, the accounting for the issuance of no-par stock with a stated value is identical to that of par value stock.

Alternatively, a corporation may be authorized to issue no-par stock without a stated value. In this case, unless otherwise stipulated, the entire amount of the proceeds is the legal capital and is recorded in the capital stock account. If the preceding transaction involved no-par, no-stated-value stock, the corporation would record it as follows:

Cash	9,000	
Common Stock, no-par (500 shares)		9,000

Note that in this journal entry the number of *shares* issued is included. This is necessary because the number of shares issued in this transaction cannot be determined by dividing the total increase in the Common Stock account by the par value per share. In the remaining examples of stock issuances we assume a par value for the stock.

As we discussed earlier, most states prohibit a corporation from issuing capital stock at a price below its par or stated value (at a discount). If such a transaction occurs, the original stockholder may be required to pay into the corporation the amount of the discount if the corporation is unable to meet its financial obligations. The corporation *debits* the difference between the proceeds and the par value to an account entitled Discount on Common Stock. It reports this account as a contra (negative) account in the Contributed Capital section of its stockholders' equity.

Stock Issuance Costs

A corporation may incur miscellaneous costs that are related directly to the issuance of capital stock. They include items such as legal fees, accounting fees, stock certificate costs, underwriter's fees, promotional costs, and postage. When related to the initial issuance of stock at incorporation, the corporation records these costs as an expense. On the other hand, the costs related to subsequent issuances of stock are considered to be normal financing expenditures and reduce the proceeds from the issuances. When a corporation incurs these costs, it reduces additional paid-in capital for the amount of the costs.

Stock Subscriptions

Investors sometimes agree to purchase capital stock on an "installment" basis. This means the corporation and the future stockholder enter into a legally binding subscription contract, which provides that the subscriber (investor) will buy a certain number of shares at an agreed-upon price, with payment spread over a specified time period. The contract often requires a down payment and may contain provisions for the handling of any defaults (nonpayments) by the subscriber. Usually, the corporation does not issue shares of capital stock to a subscriber until the subscriber has completed full payment of the subscription price.

To illustrate the accounting for a stock subscription, assume that a corporation enters into a subscription contract with several subscribers that calls for the subscribers to purchase 1,000 shares of $6 par common stock at a price of $13 per share. The contract further requires a down payment of $3 per share, with the remaining $10 per share collectible at the end of one month. The stock will be issued to each subscriber upon full payment. The corporation records the subscription as follows:

Cash ($3 × 1,000)	3,000	
Subscriptions Receivable: Common Stock ($10 × 1,000)	10,000	
Common Stock Subscribed ($6 × 1,000)		6,000
Additional Paid-in Capital on Common Stock		7,000

Note that the balance to be received is recorded in a Subscriptions Receivable account. There is disagreement among accountants as to how a corporation should report the subscriptions receivable on its balance sheet. Some accountants have argued that Subscriptions Receivable should be listed as a contra-stockholders' equity account because collection is uncertain and therefore the corporation is not assured of obtaining a future benefit. Consequently, they claim that the receivable does not meet the definition of an asset established in *FASB Statement of Concepts No. 6*. They also claim that receivables from subscriptions are different from normal trade receivables in that no goods or services were provided. The Securities and Exchange Commission supports this view by requiring a corporation to report its subscriptions receivable as a contra-stockholders' equity account in financial statements filed with it. The SEC was also concerned that a subscription contract could be a "sham" transaction used to inflate the corporation's assets and stockholders' equity. The only exception to reporting subscriptions receivable as a contra-stockholders' equity account is when the corporation collects the receivable after the balance sheet date but before its financial statements are issued.

Other accountants argue that the subscription contract is legally binding and most subscriptions actually are collected in full. Therefore, reporting subscriptions receivable as an asset on the balance sheet is more appropriate. In this case, a corporation reports the account as a current asset when the subscription contract calls for its collection within one year or the operating cycle, whichever is longer. Regardless of which disclosure method is used, when the subscription contract involves a number of different subscribers, Subscriptions Receivable is a control account. A *stock subscribers* subsidiary ledger is used to record the shares subscribed by each individual subscriber and the payments to date.

Note that a Common Stock Subscribed account is credited for the par value of the shares subscribed. This account is used because the shares have not yet been issued. Since the corporation expects the contract to be completed, the Common Stock Subscribed account is reported in the Contributed Capital section of its stockholders' equity. It indicates that the corporation has contracted to issue additional stock. Additional Paid-in Capital is credited for the entire difference between the subscription price (the proceeds) and the par value of the subscribed stock under the assumption that the contract will be completed and the stock fully paid for.

If no-par, no-stated-value common stock is used in a stock subscription, the entire subscription price is credited to the Common Stock Subscribed account. No-par stock with a stated value and preferred stock are accounted for as in the example, with suitable changes in terminology.

Subscribers may make their payments in the form of any assets stipulated in the contract and acceptable to the corporation. Usually, the subscribers pay cash. When the corporation receives payment, it debits Cash and credits the Subscriptions Receivable account. At the final payment by a subscriber, it makes a journal entry to transfer the balance in the Common Stock Subscribed account to the Common Stock account, and issues stock certificates for the number of subscribed shares fully paid for by that subscriber. To illustrate, assume in the previous example that the $10 per share final payment was received from subscribers to 950 shares at the end of the month. The corporation makes the following journal entries to record the final payment and the issuance of the 950 shares of stock:

Cash (950 × $10)	9,500	
Subscriptions Receivable: Common Stock		9,500
Common Stock Subscribed (950 × $6)	5,700	
Common Stock, $6 par		5,700

Subscription Defaults

Occasionally, a subscriber will not make the entire payment as required by the subscription contract. When a default occurs, the accounting is determined by the relevant contract provisions, such as: (1) return to the subscriber the entire amount paid in, (2) return to the subscriber the amount paid in, less any costs incurred by the corporation to reissue the stock, (3) issue to the subscriber a lesser number of shares based upon the total amount of payment received, or (4) require the forfeiture of all amounts paid in.

For example, assume the subscriber to the 50 remaining shares in the previous example defaults on the contract. If the contract requires forfeiture of the entire amount paid in, the corporation makes the following journal entry:

Common Stock Subscribed (50 × $6)	300	
Additional Paid-in Capital on Common Stock (50 × $7)	350	
Subscriptions Receivable: Common Stock (50 × $10)		500
Additional Paid-in Capital from Subscription Default		
(50 × $3)		150

If the subscription contract does not include a provision for subscription defaults, the laws of the state in which the corporation is incorporated usually will have provided for one of the preceding alternatives.

Combined Sales of Stock

Instead of issuing different classes of securities separately, a corporation may combine two or more classes and issue them in a single "package" transaction. When the securities are widely traded, to make the package attractive to investors, the corporation will set the selling price of the package at less than the amount it would receive if it sold each class of securities separately. These transactions may include combinations of common stock, preferred stock, and long-term bonds. When a corporation issues different classes of securities in a combined sale, to account for the different equity contributed by each type of security holder, it allocates the proceeds between the two (or more) securities. This allocation is based upon the **relative fair values of the separate securities.** If a fair (e.g., market) value is not known, the securities with the known fair values are assigned a portion of the proceeds equal to their fair values and the remaining proceeds are assigned to the security with the unknown fair value.

Suppose, for example, that a corporation issues 100 "packages" of securities for $82.80 per package, or a total of $8,280. Each package consists of two shares of $10 par common stock and one share of $50 par preferred stock. If the separate market values of $16 per share for the common stock and $60 per share for the preferred stock are both known, the corporation makes the following journal entry and supporting computations:

Cash	8,280	
Common Stock, $10 par (200 shares)		2,000
Additional Paid-in Capital on Common Stock		880
Preferred Stock, $50 par (100 shares)		5,000
Additional Paid-in Capital on Preferred Stock		400

Computations:

Aggregate Fair Value

Common Stock: $16 × 2 Shares × 100 Packages = $3,200
Preferred Stock: $60 × 1 Share × 100 Packages = 6,000
$9,200

Allocation

Common Stock: $\dfrac{\$3,200}{\$9,200} \times \$8,280 = \$2,880$

Preferred Stock: $\dfrac{\$6,000}{\$9,200} \times \$8,280 = \underline{\ \ 5,400\ }$
$8,280

Note that the corporation separates the fair value assigned to each class of stock into the par value and additional paid-in capital in the journal entry.

If only the separate market value of $16 per share for the common stock is known, the corporation assigns $3,200 ($16 × 2 shares × 100 packages) of the proceeds to the common stock, and allocates the remainder of $5,080 to the preferred stock, as follows:

Cash	8,280	
Common Stock, $10 par		2,000
Additional Paid-in Capital on Common Stock		1,200
Preferred Stock, $50 par		5,000
Additional Paid-in Capital on Preferred Stock		80

In the rare case when none of the securities has a market value, a corporation must estimate the fair values. Care must be exercised so that a reasonable allocation is made to the various elements of equity. If a fair value is established for one (or all) of the securities in the near future that makes this allocation unreasonable, it makes an adjustment of the allocation. If, in the preceding examples, the stock was issued in combination with bonds, then the corporation would record the bonds at a premium or discount based upon their relative fair value.

Nonmonetary Issuance of Stock

In certain instances a corporation may issue capital stock for assets other than cash, or for services performed. This type of transaction is called a *nonmonetary exchange*. The corporation must assign an appropriate value to the transaction so that it can record the exchange properly. This valuation is a particularly troublesome issue when it involves intangible assets such as patents, copyrights, or organization costs. The general rule is to **record the exchange at the fair value of the stock issued or the asset received, whichever is more *reliable*.** For instance, at the time of the exchange the stock may be selling on the stock market at a specified price but a verifiable value of the asset may be difficult to ascertain. In this case, the stock market price is used as the fair value at which to record the exchange transaction.

To illustrate, suppose a corporation issues 200 shares of $10 par common stock in exchange for a patent. The stock currently is selling for $22 per share on the open market, and no significant impact on the market price by the issuance of the additional shares is expected. The corporation assigns a value of $4,400 to the exchange, and records the transaction as follows:

Patent ($22 × 200)	4,400	
Common Stock, $10 par		2,000
Additional Paid-in Capital on Common Stock		2,400

The issuance of a large number of additional shares may significantly reduce the market price, however. In such a case, the corporation does not record the transaction until the reduced market price is known, and records the asset at that price.

Alternatively, the stock may be closely held and not actively traded. Here, using the fair value of the assets received may be more reliable for recording the exchange transaction. This determination may be based on a review of recent transactions involving similar assets or on an appraisal by an independent appraiser. To illustrate, assume a corporation issues 500 shares of $8 par common stock that is not widely traded in exchange for an acre of land. An independent appraiser indicates the land has a value of $20,000. The corporation uses the appraisal value of the land as the fair value and records the transaction as follows:

Land	20,000	
Common Stock, $8 par		4,000
Additional Paid-in Capital on Common Stock		16,000

When a corporation issues two or more securities for an asset, it uses the combination of the most reliable fair values to determine the total value at which to record the transaction. In the absence of reliable fair values for both the stock and the asset exchanged, the corporate board of directors is responsible for assigning the value used in recording the exchange. Such an assignment should be carefully made on the basis of available supporting evidence. Incorrect valuation of the exchange would lead either to an overstatement of the corporation's assets with a corresponding overstatement of its stockholders' equity (referred to as **watered stock**), or to an understatement of its assets and stockholders' equity (referred to as **secret reserves**). Furthermore, errors would arise in later financial statements if the asset is depreciated or amortized against future revenues, or sold.

Stock Splits

The market price of a corporation's common stock may increase to the point where it discourages investments by some stockholders. Many corporations believe that wide distribution of ownership improves their public image, increases the demand for their stock, and increases the likelihood of product sales to these stockholders. In order to reduce the market price so that it falls within the "trading range" of most investors, a corporation's board of directors—upon meeting state legal requirements—may authorize a stock split. **A stock split (or *stock split-up*) results in a decrease in the par value per share of stock accompanied by a proportional increase in the number of shares issued.** Generally, a stock split also results in a proportional increase in the number of shares authorized through an amendment to the articles of incorporation. For example, assume that a corporation has 250,000 authorized shares and has issued 60,000 shares of $10 par common stock. If the corporation declares a two-for-one stock split with a reduction to a $5 par value, after the split 500,000 shares are authorized and a total of 120,000 shares of $5 common stock are issued. Generally, the additional number of shares participating in the same amount of earnings will cause a corresponding decrease in the market price per share.

When a corporation has a stock split, it generally does not recall the existing shares. Instead, each stockholder is informed of the new par value per share and is issued an additional number of shares to compensate for the split. From an accounting standpoint, a stock split has no dollar impact upon any element of the corporation's stockholders' equity; consequently, it has no effect on total stockholders' equity. In the previous example, the total par value of the issued common stock is $600,000 prior to and after the stock split.

A corporation ordinarily records a stock split by a memorandum entry in its general journal that indicates the new par value, the total number of shares issued, and the impact (if any) on the number of authorized shares. For instance, in the previous example the memorandum entry might read as follows:

> **The board of directors split the common stock two for one, increasing the issued stock from 60,000 to 120,000 shares. The par value of the stock has been reduced from $10 per share to $5 per share and the authorized shares have been increased to 500,000 shares.**

Occasionally, a corporation will issue a **disproportionate stock split in which the reduction in par value is not proportionate to the increase in the number of shares.** In this case the corporation must make a journal entry to adjust the legal capital and additional paid-in capital. In the previous example, suppose instead that the par value were reduced to $4 per share. The corporation would record the disproportionate stock split as follows:

Common Stock, $10 par (60,000 × $10)	600,000	
Common Stock, $4 par (60,000 × 2 × $4)		480,000
Additional Paid-in Capital from Stock Split		120,000

Although a disproportionate stock split does not affect total stockholders' equity, it does have an impact on the components of Contributed Capital. Occasionally, a corporation may declare a reverse stock split to increase the market value of its stock. **A reverse stock split decreases the number of shares and increases the par value per share,** and is recorded in a manner opposite to that of a stock split.

Some corporations issue *stock dividends* instead of, or with, cash dividends. Certain large stock dividends are similar to stock splits.

Stock dividends are discussed in Chapter 16.

Stock Rights to Current Stockholders

As we discussed earlier, the preemptive right gives current stockholders the opportunity to maintain their proportionate share in the ownership of the corporation if additional shares of the same class of stock are issued. Thus, if a corporation's board of directors authorizes the issuance of additional shares, it must extend the preemptive right to the present stockholders, unless they have waived that right. The corporation fulfills the **right** by issuing stock **warrants** to each present stockholder who may then exchange them for additional shares of stock. Although one stock warrant (right) usually attaches to each share outstanding, usually a stockholder must exchange more than one warrant to acquire each additional share. Even if the corporation has satisfied the preemptive right (or the right has been waived), it may still issue stock rights to stockholders for a new issue of stock to encourage rapid sale of the stock. In either case, the rights usually allow stockholders to purchase the additional shares at a price slightly less than the current market price. The rights thus acquire a value themselves, and because the warrants are certificates that are readily transferable, they trade on the stock market in a manner similar to stocks. These stock warrants (rights) generally expire within a short period of time, usually a few weeks.

At the time a corporation issues the warrants, it makes a memorandum entry listing the number of additional shares that may be acquired through the exercise of the stock rights so that it will hold a sufficient number of unissued shares for this purpose. This entry also provides information for disclosure of the outstanding warrants in the notes to its financial statements. If the rights are exercised, the corporation makes the usual journal entry to record the issuance of the stock. If the rights expire, it makes another memorandum entry noting the expiration.

Many corporations also have programs that enable employees to acquire ownership by purchasing shares of stock, often at a price less than the current market price. These programs involve the issuance of warrants (rights) to the employees allowing them to purchase stock, and are commonly referred to as **stock option plans** or **stock purchase plans.** The degree of allowed participation in these plans varies. At one extreme, a plan is available only to one, or a few, key employees within the company; at the other extreme, all employees are eligible to participate. Also, the purchase price may be at a small discount from the current market price, or a price established when the options were granted. Such plans are established for various reasons: (1) the need to attract more equity capital, (2) the belief that employee ownership will lead to a greater commitment to corporate activities, and (3) the desire to provide further compensation for certain employees. **FASB Statement No. 123** addresses the accounting for the warrants involved in employee stock option plans. It is a complex *Statement*; we summarize only the primary elements here. The *Statement* differentiates between noncompensatory and compensatory stock option plans.

NONCOMPENSATORY STOCK OPTION PLANS

A noncompensatory stock option plan (sometimes called an *employee stock purchase plan*) is one that is designed by a corporation to raise capital or to obtain more widespread employee ownership of the corporate stock rather than to provide additional compensation for certain employees. Three criteria are essential in a plan of this type:

1. Substantially all full-time employees who meet limited employment qualifications may participate in the plan on an equitable basis.
2. The discount from the market price does not exceed the greater of (a) a per-share discount that would be reasonable in an offer of stock to stockholders or others, or (b) the per-share amount of stock issuance costs avoided by not issuing the stock to the public. A purchase discount of up to 15% automatically complies with this criterion.
3. The plan has no option features other than the following: (a) employees are allowed a short time (no longer than 31 days) from the date the purchase price is set to decide whether to enroll in the plan, and (b) the purchase price is based solely on the market price of the stock on the purchase date, and employees are permitted to cancel their participation before the purchase date and obtain a refund of any amounts previously paid.[3]

---

3. "Accounting for Stock-based Compensation," *FASB Statement of Financial Accounting Standards No. 123* (Norwalk, Conn.: FASB, 1995), par. 23 and "Accounting for Certain Transactions involving Stock Compensation," *FASB Interpretation No. 44* (Norwalk, Conn.: FASB, 2000), par. 24 and 25.

If **all** these criteria are met, the plan is defined as a **noncompensatory plan** because no compensation is considered to be paid to employees. The corporation makes a memorandum entry when it issues the stock warrants, indicating the number of additional shares that may be acquired upon exercise of the warrants. If the warrants are exercised, the corporation makes the usual journal entry to record the stock issuance. If not exercised, it makes a memorandum entry noting the expiration.

In some cases, employees of a corporation (with its assistance) will set up an employee stock ownership plan (called an ESOP) for investment purposes. The complexity of ESOPs varies from corporation to corporation. In one type of ESOP, a trustee borrows money from a financial institution and uses the funds to purchase shares in the corporation for the employees. Usually, the corporation guarantees the liability of the ESOP (using the shares as collateral). It also may agree to make contributions to the ESOP to pay the interest on the liability and to help the ESOP acquire more of the corporation's stock. If the corporation only assists in the initial financing of the ESOP, at the time of borrowing the corporation records an increase in cash (for the amount received from the trustee for the stock) and a liability. It also records the issuance of the stock and a contra-equity account for the unearned ESOP shares that are used as collateral on the loan. It reduces the liability and contra-equity accounts (and increases stockholders' equity) as the ESOP makes payments on the debt that it guaranteed. If the corporation also makes contributions to the ESOP, it treats these contributions as interest expense and "deferred compensation" (a "negative" component of stockholders' equity), which it allocates to compensation expense.[4]

COMPENSATORY STOCK OPTION PLANS

4 Describe a compensatory stock option plan.

In addition to cash salaries, many corporations establish stock-based compensation plans. A **stock-based compensation plan** is a compensation agreement established by a corporation under which its employees, in exchange for their services, receive shares of stock, stock options, or other equity instruments (or the corporation incurs liabilities to employees in amounts based on the price of its stock). In this chapter we focus primarily on stock options, because they are the most common type of plan.

A stock option plan that does *not* possess *all* three criteria we listed in the previous section is a compensatory plan. **A compensatory stock option plan is intended to provide additional compensation to selected employees within the corporation.** The terms of a compensatory stock option plan are often complex and relate to such items as the number of shares to which each employee is entitled and the option price (both of which may depend on some future event), whether cash may be received instead of shares, the period of service the employee must complete before becoming eligible, the date the option can first be exercised, and the date of expiration (if any).

Conceptual Overview and Historical Perspective

Before we look at the current generally accepted accounting principles for compensatory stock option plans, it is useful to review how these plans work, how corporations accounted for them in the past (and may still account for them), and related conceptual issues. Under a common type of plan, a corporation grants selected employees (e.g., top managers) the rights to purchase shares of stock at a set price (called the **exercise price** or **option price**; these terms are used interchangeably) some time in the future (usually several years) in exchange for their services. The corporation generally issues nontransferable warrants to the employees as evidence of the rights. Each warrant generally allows the employee to acquire one share of common stock. So, for instance, a corporation may grant an employee the right to purchase 1,000 shares of common stock at the end of three years at an exercise (option) price of $20 per share. If the market

---

4. For a more detailed discussion, see "Employer's Accounting for Employee Stock Ownership Plans," *AICPA Statement of Position 93-6* (AICPA: November 23, 1993).

price increases to $35 per share at the end of three years, the employee can exercise the option and acquire shares with a value of $35,000 ($35 × 1,000) by paying only $20,000 ($20 × 1,000). Clearly, this is a valuable stock option for the employee.

Until 1995, **APB Opinion No. 25** governed the accounting for compensatory stock option plans. It required the use of the "intrinsic value method" (which corporations still may elect to use, as we discuss later). **Under the intrinsic value method,** a corporation measures the total compensation cost for each employee as the excess of the market price of the stock over the exercise price for the specified number of shares on the measurement date. The **measurement date** is the date when the number of shares and the exercise price are known—usually the date on which the corporation grants the option. The corporation recognizes this total compensation cost as an expense on a "straight-line" basis over the **service period,** the years in which it receives the benefit of the employee's services under the terms of the contract.

In cases where the exercise price is *equal to or higher than* the market price on the measurement date, the corporation incurs *no* compensation cost and therefore recognizes *no* compensation expense. This situation frequently occurs because compensatory stock option plans usually are written to take advantage of Internal Revenue Service rules regarding the income taxes of the employees participating in the plans. These plans are called *qualified (incentive) stock option plans.* That is, according to the tax rules, if the exercise price is set at (or greater than) the market price of the stock on the grant date, then the plan qualifies for special tax treatment; the options are not considered to be taxable compensation of the employee on that date. Instead, the income taxes generally are deferred until the employee exercises the stock option (or in some cases even later when the stock is sold), at which time any gain is taxed at a lower, long-term capital gains rate.

From a conceptual standpoint, many accountants and external users are critical of the intrinsic value measurement method. They note that the value of a stock option may be a significant portion of the total compensation package of each employee. For instance, a study revealed that stock option grants averaged 81% of the total cash compensation of the top executives of the nation's 100 largest financial institutions.[5] External users feel that measuring a corporation's compensation cost as the difference between the market price of the stock and the exercise price on the grant date understates—in many cases, significantly—the fair value of the stock option and the corresponding compensation expense (and overstates the corporation's net income). They argue that while this measurement approach is *reliable,* it is *not relevant.* They are concerned that this approach overstates a corporation's *return on investment* (because of overstated net income) and misstates the *risk* associated with an investment (because of potential earnings dilution if the options are exercised) in the corporation. They are also concerned about the lack of *comparability* across corporations because of the inability to identify similarities and differences among different stock option plans.

Many views have been expressed about what should be the proper value (and compensation expense) of a compensatory stock option plan. We summarize these views under two alternatives. One alternative is that a corporation should measure the compensation based on the value of the *benefits received* (that is, the value of the employee's services) by the corporation at the time of grant. This might involve estimating the cash salary forgone in lieu of the stock option, perhaps adjusted to a present value basis, as a measurement of the stock option value. The second alternative is that the value of the option should be based on the *costs sacrificed* (the value of the stock given up) by the corporation. This might involve estimating the value of the option using an "option pricing model." With these conceptual issues as well as practical concerns in mind, amid considerable controversy the FASB studied compensatory stock option plans for several years before issuing *FASB Statement No. 123.*

Since accounting for a compensatory stock option plan may affect both a corporation's income statement and balance sheet, *FASB Statement No. 123* addresses several

---

5.   "Financial Institutions Newsletter," KPMG Peat Marwick, October 1990, p. 1.

related issues. These issues include (1) how to measure the value of stock options issued for employees' services, (2) how to recognize and report the related compensation expense, and (3) what additional disclosures should be made in regard to the plan.[6]

The following diagram of the recommended method of accounting will help you see the "big picture" before we discuss the detailed accounting issues.

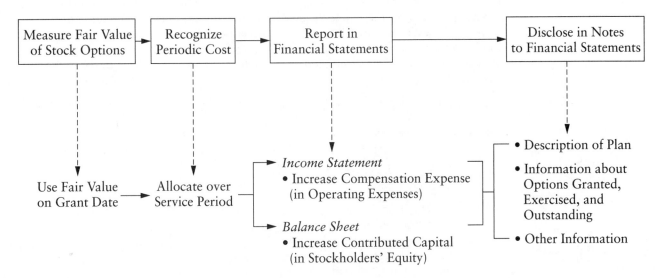

Measurement of Fair Value

FASB Statement No. 123 establishes a **fair value method of accounting for compensatory stock option plans.** This approach is consistent with the general principle we discussed earlier in the chapter that a nonmonetary exchange is recorded at the fair value of the stock issued or the asset received, whichever is more reliable. For a compensatory stock option plan, it is the fair value of the stock options or the services received. Usually it is very difficult for a corporation to determine the fair value of the services it received (in part, because the employees will provide these services in the future and also will receive a cash salary), so the focus is on determining the fair value of the stock options.

FASB Statement No. 123 recommends use of the fair value method, but allows corporations to elect to use the intrinsic value method established in *APB Opinion No. 25* (which we discussed earlier). However, **if a corporation uses the intrinsic value method, it must disclose its pro forma net income and earnings per share (in the notes to its financial statements) determined as if the fair value method had been used in measuring its compensation expense.** Hence, a corporation that elects to use the intrinsic value method in its financial statements still must compute the fair value of its compensatory stock options. Therefore, our discussion begins with the fair value method. Later in the chapter, we illustrate the intrinsic value method as it applies to stock appreciation rights and briefly discuss how it is used to account for compensatory stock option plans.

A corporation estimates the fair value of a stock option on the grant date using an option pricing model (e.g., the Black-Scholes model or a binomial model). The **grant date** is the date on which the corporation and an employee have an agreement concerning the terms of the stock-option-based compensation award. On this date, the corporation becomes contingently obligated to issue common stock to the employee who fulfills the service requirements of the plan (e.g., working for the corporation for a certain number of years). Once the fair value is estimated on the grant date, it is *not* subsequently adjusted for changes in the underlying variables (which we discuss below) of the option pricing model.

---

6. The discussion in the following three sections primarily is a summary of the generally accepted accounting principles established in *FASB Statement No. 123*, par. 6–48.

The option pricing model that a corporation uses must take into account, as of the grant date, the following variables: (1) exercise price, (2) expected life of the option, (3) current market price of the underlying common stock, (4) expected volatility of the stock, (5) expected dividends on the stock, and (6) risk-free interest rate for the expected term of the option. We do not illustrate complex option pricing models in this chapter because they involve the use of standard deviations and natural logarithms. Furthermore, computer programs of these models have been designed so that the fair value of a stock option can be estimated by providing the preceding variables as input. However, it is helpful to understand that a complex option pricing model is an expansion of the basic option pricing model. The basic model (for a stock option where it is known with certainty that the stock price at maturity will exceed the exercise price) is as follows:

Option value (fair value) = Current stock price − Present value* of exercise price

*See Appendix D for a discussion of present value

or

$$O = M - \frac{E}{(1 + i)^n}$$

where: O = option value on grant date
             M = market price of stock on grant date
             E = exercise price
             i   = risk-free interest rate
             n = number of years until option expires

Based on this basic equation, we can make the following observations: (1) the higher the market price of the stock (M) on the grant date, the more the option is worth; (2) the higher the exercise price (E), the less the option is worth; (3) the higher the risk-free interest rate (i), the more the option is worth; and (4) the longer the years (n) until the option expires, the more the option is worth. For instance, a higher market price of the stock on the grant date means that there is a greater difference between this price and the set exercise price; hence, the option is more valuable. The more complex option pricing models expand on this equation by including expected dividends and volatility variables in the equation.[7] For simplicity, in the examples that follow and the end-of-chapter exercises and problems we always assume a fair value (option value) for each option on the grant date.

Recognition of Compensation Expense

<table>
<tr>
<td>**5** Recognize compensation expense for a compensatory stock option plan.</td>
<td>**The total compensation cost is the total fair value of the stock options that actually become vested.** Stock options become **vested** on the date the employee's right to exercise the stock options is no longer contingent upon remaining in the service of the company. A corporation does not recognize immediately the total compensation cost in its financial statements. Instead, **it recognizes the total compensation cost as compensation expense over the service period using the straight-line method.** The **service period** is the years during which the employee must perform service (e.g., work for the company) in exchange for the stock options. Generally, the service period is the same as the vesting period.[8]</td>
</tr>
</table>

If the corporation expects that a significant number of employees will forfeit their nonvested stock options (because they will not fulfill the service requirements for vesting),

---

7.   For an explanation of more complex option pricing models, see, for instance, H. R. Stoll and R. E. Whaley, *Futures and Options*, (Cincinnati: South-Western Publishing Co., 1993).
8.   Typically, stock options that are vested are also immediately exercisable. However, if the exercise date (or exercise price) is affected by the service the employee must complete, the service period used to allocate the compensation expense must be consistent with the assumptions used to estimate the fair value of the stock options.

then it records the compensation expense each year based on an estimate. The estimated total compensation cost is determined at the grant date by multiplying the fair value per option times the estimate of the number of stock options expected to vest. If additional information becomes available after the grant date and estimated forfeitures change, the change is included in compensation expense in the year of the change (we will illustrate this in a later example).

The corporation records the compensation expense[9] each year as follows:

Compensation Expense	XXX
Common Stock Option Warrants	XXX

The corporation includes the compensation expense[10] as an operating expense on its income statement. It includes the Common Stock Option Warrants account balance in the contributed capital section of stockholders' equity on its ending balance sheet.

FASB Statement No. 123 deals with many different types of stock-based compensation plans. Appendix B of the *Statement* illustrates the accounting for stock option plans that are fixed (with cliff vesting and graded vesting) or performance-based (where the number of options to be earned or the exercise price varies); stock option plans with indexed exercise prices, with an exercise price that increases by a fixed amount, with stock appreciation rights, or with phantom shares; and stock option plans for which the terms are modified. We show examples of the measurement and recognition procedures for three of these plans.[11]

EXAMPLE 1: FIXED STOCK OPTION PLAN (WITH CLIFF VESTING) Assume that on January 1, 2004 Fox Corporation adopts a compensatory stock option plan and grants 9,000 stock options (to acquire 9,000 shares of common stock) with a maximum life of 10 years to 30 selected employees. The $50 exercise price is equal to the market price of the stock on this grant date. All the options vest at the end of 3 years (this is known as **cliff vesting**), so the service period is 3 years. This plan is called a **fixed plan** because all the terms (e.g., exercise price, number of shares) are set ("fixed") on the grant date.

6 Account for a fixed compensatory stock option plan.

Fox has had historical employee turnover rates of about 3 percent per year and it expects this rate to continue. Therefore, at the beginning of 2004 it uses a 3 percent annual forfeiture rate in its compensation cost (and expense) calculations. At the end of 2005, because of increased employee turnover rates in 2004 and 2005, Fox changes its estimated forfeiture rate to 6 percent per year for the entire service period. At the end of 2006, a total of 7,500 stock options for 25 employees actually vest and the other 1,500 are forfeited.

Using the Black-Scholes option pricing model in accordance with *FASB Statement No. 123*, Fox determines that the fair value of each option is $17.15 on the grant date. To determine the total estimated compensation cost on the grant date, Fox multiplies the fair value per stock option times the estimated stock options that will become vested. This amounts to $140,871 [$17.15 × (9,000 × 0.97 × 0.97 × 0.97), rounded]. On January 1, 2004 (the grant date), Fox makes a memorandum entry to summarize the terms of the compensatory stock option plan as follows:

---

9. In many cases the amount of compensation expense a corporation recognizes for financial reporting purposes in a given year will be more (less) than the amount of compensation expense the corporation reports on its income tax return. This difference is a temporary deductible difference and results in an increase (decrease) in a deferred tax asset. Thus, a corporation would make an additional journal entry to record the change in the deferred tax asset and the adjustment of income tax expense. Since we do not discuss deferred taxes until Chapter 18, we do not deal with deferred tax journal entries in this chapter.

10. For simplicity, we record and report the entire amount as compensation expense. Some companies might capitalize a portion of the amount as part of inventory or another asset.

11. The first two examples are adapted from Appendix B of *FASB Statement No. 123*, par. 288–297 and 306–308. The third example is adapted from *FASB Interpretation No. 28*, par. 20–22. For simplicity, in each of these examples we illustrate the adoption of a stock option plan in a single year. In reality, a company usually grants new stock options *every* year so that the impact on the company's net income (or pro forma net income, if it uses the intrinsic value method) is much greater than that shown.

Memorandum entry: On January 1, 2004 the company granted compensatory stock options to 30 employees. The plan allows each employee to exercise 300 stock options to acquire the same number of shares of the company's common stock at an exercise price of $50 per share. The options vest at the end of 3 years and expire at the end of 10 years. The estimated fair value of the stock options expected to be exercised is $140,871.

Exhibit 15-3 shows the compensation computations for Fox Corporation's fixed compensatory stock option plan over the 3-year service period. The 2004 compensation expense is $46,957, computed by multiplying the $140,871 total estimated compensation cost (fair value) times the fraction of the service period expired (1/3). On December 31, 2004, Fox records the compensation expense as follows:

Compensation Expense	46,957	
Common Stock Option Warrants		46,957

EXHIBIT 15-3   Fixed Compensatory Stock Option Plan

	2004	2005	2006
Estimated (actual) total compensation cost	$140,871[a]	$128,201[b]	$128,625[c]
Fraction of service period expired	× 1/3	× 2/3	× 3/3
Estimated compensation expense to date	$ 46,957	$ 85,467	$128,625
Previously recognized compensation expense	(0)	(46,957)	(85,467)[d]
Current compensation expense	$ 46,957	$ 38,510	$ 43,158

a. $17.15 fair value per option × (9,000 stock options × 0.97 × 0.97 × 0.97 retention rate), rounded
b. $17.15 × (9,000 × 0.94 × 0.94 × 0.94), rounded
c. $17.15 × 7,500 vested; actual total compensation cost
d. $46,957 (2004) + $38,510 (2005)

The computation of the 2005 compensation expense involves adjusting for the change in the estimated forfeitures. Based on the new estimate, at the end of 2005 the revised total compensation cost is $128,201 [$17.15 × (9,000 × 0.94 × 0.94 × 0.94), rounded]. Since two-thirds of the service period has expired, $85,467 ($128,201 × 2/3) of the cost is the compensation expense to date. Because Fox recorded $46,957 compensation expense in 2004, it recognizes $38,510 ($85,467 − $46,957) as compensation expense in 2005. By using this approach, it makes a "catch-up" correction for the previous measurement error regarding the estimated forfeitures. On December 31, 2005, Fox records the compensation expense as follows:

Compensation Expense	38,510	
Common Stock Option Warrants		38,510

The last year of the service period is 2006. Because the actual forfeitures were different from the estimated forfeitures, Fox includes another "catch up" correction in the computation of the compensation expense. The 2006 compensation expense is $43,158, computed as we show in Exhibit 15-3. The December 31, 2006 journal entry is the same as those shown earlier (except for the amount) so we do not repeat it here. After this journal entry, Fox has recorded the entire $128,625 actual compensation cost (fair value) as an expense over the 3-year service period. Also, the Common Stock Option Warrants account has a balance of $128,625 because each of the 7,500 vested stock options was recorded at its fair value of $17.15.[12]

---

12. In *graded vesting*, a certain percentage of the stock options vest each year (rather than in cliff vesting where all the options vest at the end of the service period). In the case of graded vesting, in addition to adjusting each year's computations for the estimated retention rate, the computations must also be adjusted for the percentage of options that vest in that year. See *FASB Statement No. 123* (par. 298–305) for an illustration.

When an employee exercises stock options, the employee pays the exercise price per share and turns in the stock option warrants to the corporation in exchange for the stock. The corporation records the issue of the common stock in the usual manner at **a price that is the sum of the cash received plus the previously recorded value of the warrants received.** For instance, suppose that on January 5, 2005 one employee exercises options to purchase 300 shares of Fox Corporation's $10 par common stock. On this date the stock is selling for $90 per share on the stock market. Fox records this transaction as follows:

Cash (300 × $50)	15,000	
Common Stock Option Warrants (300 × $17.15)	5,145	
Common Stock, $10 par		3,000
Additional Paid-in Capital on Common Stock		17,145

The common stock is recorded at a price of $67.15 ($50 exercise price + $17.15 option price). The current market price of $90 is *not* used because these shares were committed to the employee based on the terms (and values) set in the compensation agreement on the grant date. If an employee does not exercise stock options before they expire, the amount recorded in the Common Stock Option Warrants account for these options is transferred to Additional Paid-in Capital.

EXAMPLE 2: PERFORMANCE-BASED STOCK OPTION PLAN Now suppose that instead of the fixed stock option plan shown in Example 1, the Fox Corporation adopts a performance-based compensatory stock option plan. A **performance-based plan** has one or more terms that are *not* fixed at the grant date. These plans are set up so that the terms will vary depending on how well the selected employees perform during the service period (sometimes these plans are called *variable-term* plans). In other words, the better the employees manage the corporation, the better the terms in the stock option plan are for the employees. Performance may be based, for instance, on measures such as earnings or market share for the corporation's products. As earnings or market share increases, the terms of the plan may involve a decrease in the exercise price or an increase in the number of stock options awarded to the employees.

7 Account for a performance-based compensatory stock option plan.

Assume that the terms of Fox Corporation's performance-based plan adopted on January 1, 2004 are the same as in Example 1 (3-year vesting and service period, $50 exercise price, $17.15 fair value per option), except that Fox grants each of the 30 selected employees a *maximum* of 300 stock options. The stock options vest in differing numbers depending on the increase in market share of Fox's products over the 3-year service period. The terms are as follows: By December 31, 2006, (1) if the market share has increased by at least 5 percent, at least 100 stock options will vest for each employee on that date; (2) if the market share has increased by at least 10 percent, another 100 stock options will vest for each employee, for a total of 200; and (3) if the market share has increased by more than 20 percent, all 300 stock options will vest for each employee.

In a performance-based plan, the estimated total fair value depends on the number of options that are expected to be earned during the vesting period. For Fox Corporation's plan, on the grant date it bases the estimated total compensation cost on the estimate of market growth over the 3-year vesting period. This cost then is adjusted in later years for any changes in the expected or actual market share growth. On the grant date Fox Corporation estimates that its market share will increase between 10 and 20 percent, so it assumes 200 stock options will vest for each employee. However, at the end of 2006, Fox determines that its market share has increased over the 3-year period by more than 20 percent (so that 300 stock options actually vest for each employee). Furthermore, as in Example 1, on the grant date Fox estimates the forfeiture rate on the stock options to be 3 percent per year, but changes it to 6 percent at the end of 2005. At the end of 2006, 25 employees vest in 7,500 stock options.

Exhibit 15-4 shows the compensation computations for Fox Corporation's performance-based compensatory stock option plan over the 3-year service period. In 2004 the $93,914 estimated total compensation cost is based on the 200 stock options expected to vest and an expected annual forfeiture rate of 3 percent. At the end

EXHIBIT 15-4   Performance-Based Compensatory Stock Option Plan

	2004	2005	2006
Estimated (actual) total compensation cost	$93,914ª	$85,467ᵇ	$128,625ᶜ
Fraction of service period expired	× 1/3	× 2/3	× 3/3
Estimated compensation expense to date	$31,305	$56,978	$128,625
Previously recognized compensation expense	(0)	(31,305)	(56,978)
Current compensation expense	$31,305	$25,673	$ 71,647

a. 200 stock options × (30 employees × 0.97 × 0.97 × 0.97 retention rate) × $17.15 fair value per option, rounded.
b. 200 × (30 × 0.94 × 0.94 × 0.94) × $17.15, rounded
c. 300 × 25 × $17.15; actual total compensation cost

of 2005 the $85,467 estimated total compensation cost is based on the same expected stock options, but on an expected 6 percent annual forfeiture rate. At the end of 2006 the $128,625 actual total compensation cost is based on the 300 actual stock options that vest and the actual 25 employees who vest in the plan. Fox Corporation allocates the compensation cost to compensation expense each year using the same procedure as we illustrated in Example 1. The memorandum entry and journal entries to recognize the yearly compensation expense are the same as illustrated in Example 1 (except, of course, for the amounts), so we do not repeat them here.

EXAMPLE 3: STOCK APPRECIATION RIGHTS Although compensatory stock option plans provide selected employees with the opportunity to acquire shares of stock with a market value in excess of the option price, these plans have some disadvantages. At the time of exercise, the employee must have sufficient cash to pay the option price and any income taxes. In certain situations, this places a significant cash flow burden on the employee. To remedy at least part of this problem, corporations have developed compensatory stock option plans involving stock appreciation rights. **Stock appreciation rights (SARs)** are rights granted to selected employees that enable them to receive cash, stock, or a combination of both equal to the *excess* of the market value over a stated price of the corporation's stock on the date of exercise. SARs are advantageous to an employee because the employee can receive the market appreciation of the corporation's stock in cash on the date of exercise, thereby avoiding the cash outflow to actually acquire the stock. In **FASB Interpretation No. 28** (an interpretation of *APB Opinion No. 25*), the FASB concluded that plans involving stock appreciation rights are similar to other variable-term compensatory stock option plans and are accounted for using the *intrinsic value method*.[13] These principles were included in *FASB Statement No. 123*.

For SAR plans the compensation cost is measured on the measurement date, which is the date the rights are *exercised*.[14] Since the exercise date falls after the service period, (1) an estimate of the total compensation cost is made at the end of each year based on the difference between the market price of the stock at that time and the option price, (2) compensation expense is recorded over the service period on the basis of these estimates (and any corrections of previous estimation errors), and (3) because corrections of estimates are not made retroactively, additional adjustments to compensation expense are made at the end of each year *after* the service period has expired, up to the date of exercise, as illustrated in the following diagram:

---

13. "Accounting for Stock Appreciation Rights and Other Variable Stock Option or Award Plans," *FASB Interpretation No. 28* (Stamford, Conn.: FASB, 1978), par. 2.
14. A company may modify an existing *fixed* stock option price by reducing the exercise price. In this situation, if it is using the intrinsic value method, it accounts for the plan as a *variable* plan from the date of the modification until the date of exercise in a manner similar to an SAR plan. For more details, see *FASB Interpretation No. 44, op.cit.*, par. 38–48.

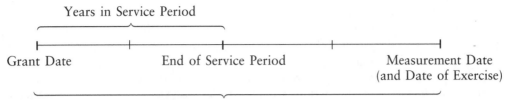

Years in Service Period

Grant Date   End of Service Period   Measurement Date
(and Date of Exercise)

Annual Compensation Expense
Based on *Estimated* Compensation Cost
(until date of exercise)

In addition to using the intrinsic value method instead of the fair value method, accounting for SAR plans differs from the accounting for compensatory stock option plans we discussed earlier in two ways. First, the adjustments (increases or decreases) that are made at the end of each year to compensation expense *after* the service period has expired (until the date of exercise) are based on the difference between 100% of the estimated total compensation cost and the accrued compensation expense recognized to date. Second, the credit entry to recognize the accrued compensation is made either to a liability or a stockholders' equity account depending on whether it is expected that the employees will elect to receive cash or stock on the date of exercise.

To illustrate, assume that on January 1, 2003, when the market price is $10 per share, a corporation grants stock appreciation rights to a selected employee. (For simplicity, in this example we show the calculations for one executive who is expected to remain in the employ of the company. If more employees were involved, estimates of turnover would be included in the calculations, as we illustrated in Examples 1 and 2.) Under the SAR plan, the executive is entitled to receive cash or stock for the difference between the quoted market price and a $10 option price for 1,000 shares of the company's stock on the date of exercise. The service period is 4 years and the rights must be exercised within 10 years from the grant date. We show the year-end market prices per share of the corporation's stock in Exhibit 15-5. The executive exercises the rights on December 31, 2007. The calculations of the annual compensation expense are shown in Exhibit 15-5. In each year, the corporation records the SAR compensation by debiting Compensation Expense and crediting SAR Compensation Payable (since the executive is expected to elect to receive cash upon exercise) for the amount calculated in the last column of Exhibit 15-5. For instance, on December 31, 2004, the corporation makes the journal entry on the next page:

EXHIBIT 15-5   SAR Annual Compensation Expense

Date	Market Price	Option Price	Estimated Total Compensation Cost[a]	Percent Accrued[b]	Total Compensation Expense to Date[c]	Accrued Compensation Expense to Date[d]	Yearly Compensation Expense[e]
12/31/03	$12.00	$10	$2,000	25%	$ 500	—	$ 500
12/31/04	13.00	10	3,000	50	1,500	$ 500	1,000
12/31/05	11.80	10	1,800	75	1,350	1,500	(150)
12/31/06[f]	12.60	10	2,600	100	2,600	1,350	1,250
12/31/07[g]	13.40	10	3,400	100	3,400	2,600	800
							$3,400

a. (Market price − Option price) × 1,000 shares; in 2003, ($12 − $10) × 1,000
b. Service years to date ÷ Total service period; in 2003, 1 ÷ 4 = 25%
c. Amount from footnote *a* × Percent from footnote *b*; in 2003, $2,000 × 0.25
d. Amount for previous year from footnote *c*
e. Amount from footnote *c* − Amount from footnote *d*
f. End of service period
g. Date of exercise (date of measurement)

| Compensation Expense | 1,000 | |
| SAR Compensation Payable | | 1,000 |

An exception to this procedure occurs in 2005. Because the market price at the end of 2005 decreased below that of 2003, the corporation makes an adjusting entry *debiting* SAR Compensation Payable and *crediting* Compensation Expense for $150 to reduce the total accrued liability. Of course, the SAR Compensation Payable account can never have a debit *balance* because the cumulative compensation expense can never be negative. On December 31, 2007 the corporation makes the following journal entry to recognize the SAR compensation expense for 2007 and to record the exercise of the rights:

Compensation Expense	800	
SAR Compensation Payable	2,600	
Cash		3,400

Note that by the end of 2007, the corporation has recognized total compensation expense of $3,400 for this SAR plan, the amount paid to the employee on the date of exercise.

Intrinsic Value Method for Compensatory Stock Option Plans

8 Understand how to use the intrinsic value method to account for a compensatory stock option plan.

Although *FASB Statement No. 123* recommends the use of the fair value method for fixed and performance-based stock option plans, it allows corporations to elect to use the intrinsic value method for these plans. Most have done so (although more companies are switching to the fair value method). As we stated earlier, under the intrinsic value method, the total compensation cost for a compensatory stock option plan is the excess of the quoted market price over the exercise (option) price on the measurement date for the number of shares expected to be issued under the plan. The *measurement date* is the date when both the number of shares an employee is entitled to receive and the exercise price are known. Usually the measurement date is the date of *grant*. The total compensation cost (if any) is recognized as compensation expense over the service period using the straight-line method.

To illustrate, refer back to Example 1. If Fox Corporation uses the intrinsic value method for its financial statements, it computes its total compensation cost on the date of grant (the measurement date) as follows:

$$\text{Total Compensation Cost} = (\text{Quoted market price} - \text{Exercise price}) \times \\ \text{Expected number of shares to be issued} \\ = (\$50 - \$50) \times (9,000 \times 0.97 \times 0.97 \times 0.97) \\ = \underline{\underline{\$0}}$$

Since the market price is equal to the exercise price on the measurement date, Fox Corporation's total compensation cost is *zero* and it records and reports *no* compensation expense in its financial statements for this compensatory stock option plan during the service period. This is typical of most compensatory stock option plans because the exercise price must be equal to (or greater than) the market price on the date of grant in order for the employee to defer income taxes on the "compensation."

In accordance with *FASB Statement No. 123*, since Fox Corporation is using the intrinsic value method, it must disclose its pro forma income and earnings per share (assuming it had used the fair value method) each year in the notes to its financial statements. Thus, Fox still has to compute its compensation expense for each year under the fair value method. For instance, in 2004 Fox would disclose its lower pro forma net income and lower earnings per share after taking into consideration the $46,957 compensation expense (as we calculated in Exhibit 15-3) that it would have recorded that year under the fair value method.

Occasionally, a company will grant compensatory stock options to executives at an option price that is *less* than the market price. In this case, under the intrinsic value method, the company does recognize some compensation expense. To illustrate, suppose that on January 1, 2004, the Conner Company grants 10,000 stock options (to acquire 10,000 shares of common stock at $27 per share) to selected employees. The market price on the date of grant is $29 per share, the service period is 4 years, and the stock options may not be exercised until the service period has expired. Conner Company chooses to use the intrinsic value method to record this compensatory stock option plan; it expects all executives to exercise their options.

Since for Conner Company's plan the measurement date is the date of grant, on January 1, 2004, Conner computes its total compensation cost to be $20,000 as follows:

$$\text{Total Compensation Cost} = (\text{Quoted market price} - \text{Exercise Price}) \times \\ \text{Expected number of shares to be issued} \\ = (\$29 - \$27) \times 10,000 \\ = \underline{\underline{\$20,000}}$$

To account for this plan, Conner Company makes a memorandum entry on January 1, 2004 describing the plan. It then recognizes $5,000 of compensation expense ($20,000 ÷ 4 years) at the end of each year over the 4-year service period using the straight line method. Conner Company must also disclose its pro forma income and earnings per share (assuming it had used the fair value method) each year in the notes to its financial statements.

Additional Disclosures

A corporation must disclose several items of information about its compensatory stock option plan. This information includes:

1. A description of the plan, including the accounting method used as well as the general terms, such as the vesting requirements, number of shares authorized for grants of options, and maximum term of options granted.
2. The number and weighted-average exercise prices for options granted, exercised, outstanding, forfeited, and expired during the year.
3. The weighted-average grant-date fair values of options granted during the year.
4. A description of the method and assumptions (e.g., risk-free interest rate, expected life, and volatility) used during the year to estimate the fair values of options.
5. The total compensation expense for the year related to its stock option plan.

If a corporation uses the intrinsic value method in its financial statements, it also must disclose the additional compensation expense that it would have recognized under the fair value method, and the pro forma net income and earnings per share determined as if the fair value method had been used.

ILLUSTRATION OF DISCLOSURE. Exhibit 15-6 shows Note 15 of the 2001 annual report of the International Multifoods Corporation relating to its stock option plans.

EXHIBIT 15-6 Disclosure of Stock Option Plan

INTERNATIONAL MULTIFOODS CORPORATION

Note 15: Stock Plans

The 1989 and 1997 stock-based plans of the Company permit awards of restricted stock, incentive units and stock options to directors and key employees subject to the provisions of the plans and as determined by the Compensation Committee of the Board of Directors. At March 3, 2001, a total of 186,261 common shares were available for grants.

In fiscal 2001, grants of 11,941 shares of restricted stock were awarded with varying performance criteria and vesting periods. At March 3, 2001, the total number of restricted shares outstanding was 81,185. The market value of shares issued under the plans, as of the date of grant, has been recorded as unearned compensation and is shown as a separate component of shareholders' equity. Unearned compensation is expensed over the period that restrictions lapse.

Stock options are granted to purchase shares of Company common stock at not less than fair market value at dates of grant. With the exception of certain options that become exercisable over a period of years based on varying performance criteria, options generally become exercisable one year after the date of grant. In addition, options generally expire 10 years after the date of grant.

The per share weighted average fair values of stock options granted were $3.46 in fiscal 2001, $5.35 in fiscal 2000 and $6.91 in fiscal 1999. The fair value of options at the date of grant was

EXHIBIT 15-6   Continued

estimated using the Black-Scholes option pricing model. The following weighted-average assumptions were used in the calculation:

Assumptions	2001	2000	1999
Expected dividend yield	4.4%	4.4%	3.8%
Expected volatility	31.6%	27.6%	24.0%
Risk-free interest rates	6.4%	5.7%	5.7%
Expected life (in years)	7.3	6.9	8.2

The Company applies APB Opinion No. 25 in accounting for the compensation costs of employee stock options in the financial statements. Had the Company determined compensation costs based on the fair value at the date of grant for its stock options, the Company's earnings from continuing operations would have been reduced to the pro forma amounts indicated below:

(in thousands, except per share data)	2001	2000	1999
Earnings from continuing operations:			
As reported	$21,175	$24,695	$6,832
Pro forma	19,805	23,968	5,944
Diluted earnings per share from continuing operations:			
As reported	$ 1.12	$ 1.31	$ 0.36
Pro forma	1.05	1.28	0.31

The following table contains information on stock options:

	Shares	Weighted Average Exercise Price per Share
Outstanding at February 28, 1998	1,336,496	$22.11
Granted	181,564	28.55
Exercised	(191,879)	21.52
Expired or canceled	(25,222)	25.75
Outstanding at February 28, 1999	1,300,959	$23.02
Granted	141,550	22.21
Exercised	(61,089)	20.21
Expired or canceled	(60,700)	25.38
Outstanding at February 29, 2000	1,320,720	$22.96
Granted	541,742	12.03
Exercised	(6,000)	16.00
Expired or canceled	(252,940)	22.37
Outstanding at March 3, 2001	**1,603,522**	**$19.38**

Options exercisable at:		
February 28, 1999	875,009	$21.74
February 29, 2000	934,670	$22.58
March 3, 2001	**924,152**	**$22.22**

For options outstanding at March 3, 2001, the range of exercise price per share was $11.84 to $28.91 and the average remaining contractual life was 7.3 years.

Q U E S T I O N

Q The market price at the end of fiscal 2001 was $19.21. Assuming that all stock options were exercised at fiscal year-end, what was the range of "profit" or "loss" per share made by employees who exercised their options in 2001? **Q** By how much would fiscal 2001 net income and EPS have decreased if the company had computed its compensation cost using the fair value method?

Conceptual Evaluation

From a conceptual standpoint, by establishing a fair value method of accounting for compensatory stock option plans, *FASB Statement No. 123* goes a long way toward remedying the criticisms raised about *APB Opinion No. 25*. Use of the fair value method increases the *relevance* of the accounting information because it shows the fair value of the stock options. Although the *reliability* of the accounting information is decreased because of the use of estimates, this is similar to using estimates for items such as depreciation and bad debts. Although the estimates involve complex issues, the issues are no more complex than those involving postemployment benefits (which we discuss in Chapter 19). Use of the fair value method provides a more relevant measure of a corporation's *return on investment* because compensation expense (based on fair value) is included in the corporation's net income. Similarly, a better assessment of *risk* is possible because external users are able to better evaluate the likelihood of the exercise of the stock options. Finally, *comparability* is improved because external users can better contrast the terms of different plans with the information provided in the notes to the financial statements.

On the other hand, there are several criticisms of the way the fair value method is applied in *FASB Statement No. 123*. First, the fair value of the stock options is established on the grant date using an option pricing model. This fair value is not further adjusted for changes in the variables of the model, even though some of these variables (e.g., volatility and risk-free interest rate) change with changes in the underlying economy. Not allowing adjustment of the fair value may distort reporting of the real value of the stock options. However, not adjusting is consistent with generally accepted accounting principles that are based on transactions.

Second, although the fair value method is the recommended and preferred approach, the *Statement* allows corporations to elect to use the intrinsic value method. As we illustrated earlier, most corporations have elected to do so because for a typical compensatory stock option plan where the exercise price is equal to (or greater than) the market price on the date of grant, the compensation expense under the intrinsic value method is zero. However, use of the fair value method always results in compensation expense, and therefore lower net income and earnings per share. Given the choice of recognizing an expense or no expense, these corporations have chosen the latter. For these corporations, the criticisms of the intrinsic value method apply, as we discussed earlier.

Finally, there may be even more of a lack of comparability than before because some corporations use the fair value method while others use the intrinsic value method to account for similar stock option plans. Even though corporations that use the intrinsic value method are required to disclose the fair values of compensatory stock option plans, external users must make intercompany comparisons in some cases based on information in the notes and in other cases based on information included in the financial statements.

The accounting standards (recommending use of the fair value method, but allowing use of the intrinsic value method) established in *FASB Statement No. 123* were the result of compromise, as evidenced by the 5 to 2 vote. In fact, the Exposure Draft preceding the *Statement* would have *required* all companies to use the fair value method, which was highly controversial. Various constituencies were strongly opposed to the fair value method. They lobbied the FASB (the Board received nearly 1,800 comment letters, mostly negative) to persuade it not to require use of the fair value method, and even had bills introduced in Congress to outlaw its use. However, many accountants and users believe the Board took a major step in the right direction and hope that as the fair value method is implemented over time, the intrinsic value method eventually will be unacceptable. In the meantime, the disclosures allow users to understand the impact of the fair value of options, and to adjust their decision models accordingly.

PREFERRED STOCK CHARACTERISTICS

Some investors consider certain stockholder rights to be more important than others and are willing to forgo the latter in exchange for preferences regarding these rights. To attract these investors, a corporation may issue a class of capital stock called

9 Describe the characteristics of preferred stock.

preferred stock. The preferred stock contract identifies the stockholders' rights as well as the rights of the corporation. Various preferred stock characteristics may be specified in the contract, including: (1) preference as to dividends, (2) accumulation of dividends, (3) participation in excess dividends, (4) convertibility into common stock, (5) attachment of stock warrants (rights), (6) callability by the corporation, (7) redemption at a future maturity date, (8) preference as to assets upon liquidation of the corporation, and (9) lack of voting rights.

Preference as to Dividends

Holders of preferred stock have a preference as to dividends because a corporation must pay any applicable dividends to preferred stockholders before a dividend may be paid to common stockholders. Since most preferred stock is issued with a par value, the preferred dividend may be expressed as a percentage of this par value. If no-par stock is issued, the preferred dividend is expressed as a dollar amount per share. For instance, assume a corporation has outstanding 2,000 shares of 8%, $100 par preferred stock. Each stockholder is entitled to an $8 ($100 × 0.08) annual dividend per share. The corporation must pay $16,000 of dividends (8% × $100 × 2,000 shares) to preferred stockholders before it may pay any dividends to common stockholders.

A preference as to dividends does not guarantee, however, that a corporation will pay preferred dividend in any given year, because dividend payments are at the discretion of the board of directors. To protect preferred stockholders further, a corporation may include a provision in the preferred stock contract that requires the accumulation of dividends. The preferred stock is then said to be cumulative.

Cumulative Preferred Stock

Stockholders are not legally entitled to share in dividends unless these dividends have been declared by the board of directors of the corporation. If dividends are "passed" (that is, *not* declared) in a particular year, a holder of **noncumulative** preferred stock will never be paid that dividend. For this reason, corporations seldom issue noncumulative preferred stock because investors perceive this feature to be a distinct disadvantage.

Dividend declarations are discussed in Chapter 16.

Most preferred stock is **cumulative.** If a corporation fails to declare a dividend on cumulative preferred stock at the stated rate on the usual dividend date, the amount of passed dividends becomes **dividends in arrears.** Dividends in arrears accumulate from period to period. A corporation cannot pay common stockholders any dividends until it has paid the preferred dividends in arrears. The dividends in arrears are *not* a liability to the corporation, because no liability exists until the dividend declaration. Nonetheless, such information is very important to investors and other interested parties in predicting future cash flows, and so a corporation discloses dividends in arrears in a note to its financial statements.

To illustrate dividends in arrears, assume a corporation has outstanding 1,000 shares of 10%, $100 par cumulative preferred stock. Each share of stock is entitled to a $10 annual dividend (computed by multiplying the 10% times the $100 par value). If the corporation does not pay dividends in 2004 and 2005, preferred stockholders would be entitled to dividends in arrears of $10,000 at the end of 2004 and $20,000 at the end of 2005. At the end of 2006, the corporation would have to pay $30,000 (for 3 years) to preferred stockholders before it could pay any dividends to common stockholders.

Participating Preferred Stock

When preferred stock is **participating,** preferred stockholders share with the common stockholders in any "extra" dividends. Extra dividends are paid only after preferred stockholders have been paid their stated dividend *amount* and common stockholders have been paid at a *rate* equal to that paid on the preferred stock. For example, if a corporation has 9%, $100 par participating preferred stock and $10 par common stock outstanding, it must pay preferred stockholders $9 per share (9% of the $100 par) and common stockholders 90 cents per share (9% of the $10 par). Then, if the total dividend to be paid is greater than the amount needed to meet these dividend requirements, an extra dividend arises.

Participating preferred stock may be either fully or partially participating. **Fully participating preferred stockholders share equally with the common stockholders in any extra dividends.** When a corporation pays extra dividends, they are distributed to the fully participating preferred stockholders and common stockholders on a proportionate basis relative to the respective total par values of each class of stock. **Partially participating preferred stockholders share in extra dividends, but this participation is limited to a fixed rate or amount per share.** In the preceding example, if the 9% preferred stockholders participated up to a maximum of 12% of the preferred stock par value, their share in any extra dividends would be limited to 3% of this par value. We present a numerical example of participating preferred stock dividends in Chapter 16 in the section dealing with cash dividends. Participating preferred stock, whether fully or partially participating, is rare. Corporations generally agree that preferred stockholders receive too much preference when they are given first preferences as to dividends and also are allowed to share in all dividends.

Convertible Preferred Stock

Convertible preferred stock allows stockholders, at their option and under specified conditions, to convert the shares of preferred stock into another security of the corporation. Usually this security is common stock, and the conversion provisions stipulate the conditions and a specific exchange ratio. This exchange ratio will be modified, however, if there is a stock split. Since most preferred stock is not participating, the conversion feature allows the holder to exchange the dividend preferences attached to preferred stock for the unlimited rights to corporate income held by common stockholders. This feature is attractive to investors because the exchange ratio tends to tie the market price of the preferred stock to the market price of the common stock when the latter is rising, thereby increasing the value of the preferred stock. Conversely, the preferred stock dividend rate tends to stabilize the market price of the preferred stock when common stock prices are falling.

Theoretically, both the preferred features and the potential for common stock equity are valuable to (and paid for by) an investor in convertible preferred stock. Conceptually, then, a corporation could separate the proceeds received when it issues the stock into preferred and common stockholders' equity. However, **APB Opinion No. 14** requires that when convertible preferred stock is issued, no value is assigned to the conversion provision, and any difference between par and market value is recorded as additional paid-in capital on preferred stock.[15] Thus, a corporation accounts for the *issuance* of convertible preferred stock in the same way as for the issuance of nonconvertible stock. This method of accounting is required because of the inseparability of the stock and conversion option, and the difficulty in reliably determining the fair value to attach to the conversion provision. Unfortunately, use of this method places more importance on the legal form of the security than the economic substance of the transaction. The FASB has issued an *Exposure Draft* which, if adopted, would treat convertible preferred stock as equity securities (in contrast to convertible bonds that would be treated as having a liability component and an equity component, as we discussed in Chapter 13). Therefore, the accounting principles for the issuance of convertible preferred stock would remain the same.

Accounting for the *conversion* of preferred to common stock is very straightforward because the *book value method* is used. The book value method is used (and the market

The book value method is discussed in Chapter 13.

---

15. "Accounting for Convertible Debt and Debt Issued with Stock Purchase Warrants," *APB Opinion No. 14* (New York: AICPA, 1969), par. 12.

value method is *not* allowed) because it does not result in a corporation recording gain or loss on a transaction involving its own capital stock. Under the book value method, the corporation eliminates the contributed capital (that is, the par value and additional paid-in capital) associated with the preferred stock and replaces it with the par (or stated) value of the common stock. If the total contributed capital eliminated in regard to the preferred stock is more than the common stock par value, the corporation records the excess as an increase in additional paid-in capital related to the conversion. If less, the corporation reduces retained earnings because it is considered to be a dividend distribution to the preferred stockholders.

To illustrate the accounting at conversion, assume that a corporation originally issued 500 shares of $100 par convertible preferred stock at $120 per share. If each preferred share may be converted into four shares of $20 par common stock and all the shares are converted, the corporation makes the following journal entry at conversion:

Preferred Stock, $100 par	50,000	
Additional Paid-in Capital on Preferred Stock	10,000	
Common Stock, $20 par (4 × 500 × $20)		40,000
Additional Paid-in Capital from Preferred Stock		
Conversion ($60,000 − $40,000)		20,000

Alternatively, if each preferred share may be converted into seven shares of common stock, upon conversion the corporation makes the following entry:

Preferred Stock, $100 par	50,000	
Additional Paid-in Capital on Preferred Stock	10,000	
Retained Earnings ($70,000 − $60,000)	10,000	
Common Stock, $20 par (7 × 500 × $20)		70,000

The conversion of preferred to common stock changes the components of, but does not affect the corporation's total, stockholders' equity.

Preferred Stock with Stock Warrants (Rights)

A corporation may also attach warrants to preferred stock to enhance their attractiveness. As we discussed earlier in the chapter and in Chapter 13 with regard to bonds payable, these **warrants** represent **rights** that allow the holder to purchase additional shares of common stock at a specified price over some future period. This period frequently involves a number of years, and in some cases no time limit is set. The longer the time period, the greater the attractiveness of such warrants, since stock prices over the long run have tended to increase. Because these warrants are separable (*detachable*) from the preferred stock, they usually begin trading on the stock market at some market price regardless of whether the specified purchase price of the common stock is greater than, less than, or the same as the current market price.

Theoretically, an investor in preferred stock with attached (detachable) warrants is investing in "dual" rights, each of which has a value. These rights include the right to dividends that will be paid on the preferred stock as well as the right to the market value appreciation of the common stock that may be purchased as a result of the warrants. Accounting theory suggests that, in recording the issuance of these securities, the economic substance of the event should take precedence over the legal form of the security. In accordance with this theory, *APB Opinion No. 14* states that **the proceeds from the issuance of preferred stock with attached warrants is allocated to preferred stockholders' equity and to common stockholders' equity, based on the relative independent fair values of the two securities at the time of issuance.**[16]

The relative fair value method is discussed in Chapter 13.

To illustrate, assume a corporation issues 1,000 shares of $100 par value preferred stock at a price of $121 per share. It attaches a warrant to each share of stock that allows the holder to purchase one share of $10 par common stock at $40 per share.

---

16. *Ibid.*, par. 16.

Immediately after the issuance, the preferred stock begins selling ex rights (without rights attached) on the market for $119 per share. The warrants begin selling for $6 each. Based on the $119,000 ($119 × 1,000) and $6,000 ($6 × 1,000) relative market values of the preferred stock (ex rights) and the warrants, respectively, the corporation makes the following journal entry to allocate the $121,000 ($121 × 1,000) issuance price:

Cash ($121 × 1,000)	121,000	
Preferred Stock, $100 par		100,000
Additional Paid-in Capital on Preferred Stock		15,192
Common Stock Warrants		5,808

Computations

Preferred Stock:
$$\frac{\$119,000}{\$119,000 + \$6,000} \times \$121,000 = \$115,192$$

Common Stock Warrants:
$$\frac{\$6,000}{\$119,000 + \$6,000} \times \$121,000 = \underline{\quad 5,808\quad}$$
$$\underline{\underline{\$121,000}}$$

If for some reason the warrants did not begin trading at some market price, the corporation must make the allocation based on an estimate of the value paid for the stock acquisition privilege.

Prior to exercise or expiration, the corporation lists the Common Stock Warrants account as an element of contributed capital in its stockholders' equity. Assuming all warrants are exercised, the corporation makes the following journal entry to record the issuance of the 1,000 shares of common stock in exchange for the warrants and $40 per share:

Cash ($40 × 1,000)	40,000	
Common Stock Warrants	5,808	
Common Stock, $10 par		10,000
Additional Paid-in Capital on Common Stock		35,808

If any warrants are not exercised, the corporation makes a journal entry debiting Common Stock Warrants and crediting Additional Paid-in Capital from Expired Warrants to transfer the value assigned to the warrants to the existing common stockholders.

Callable Preferred Stock

Preferred stock frequently has a *call* provision. **Callable preferred stock may be retired (recalled) under specified conditions by a corporation at *its* option.** The corporation includes the specified conditions and call price in the stock contract. The call price is usually several points (dollars) higher than the issuance price and usually establishes a ceiling on the market value of the stock. Typically, the stock contract requires the payment of dividends in arrears before the call is executed. Occasionally, callable preferred stock also will be convertible. In this case, the call price may be lower than the issuance price but usually will be higher than the par value. When a corporation recalls convertible preferred stock, the corporation will ordinarily allow the stockholder the choice of conversion or recall.

When a corporation *issues* callable preferred stock, no special accounting is required. The corporation credits the difference between the issuance price and par value to Additional Paid-in Capital. Upon *recall*, the difference between the call price and the original issuance price is *not* treated as a gain or loss. This prevents a corporation from influencing its earnings by recognizing a gain (or incurring a loss) in transactions involving its own equity securities. Instead, the corporation eliminates the original contributed capital—that is, the par value in the preferred stock account and the additional paid-in capital associated with the recalled preferred stock. If the call price exceeds the total of these amounts, the corporation debits the difference to retained earnings because it is treated like a dividend distribution. In the case in which the call price is less than the total of these amounts, the corporation records the difference as a credit to Additional Paid-in Capital because it is considered to be an additional contribution by the stockholder.

Assume, for example, that a corporation has outstanding 1,000 shares of $100 par callable preferred stock that were issued at $110 per share and that no dividends are in arrears. If the call price is $112 per share, the corporation makes the following journal entry to record the recall of these shares:

Preferred Stock, $100 par	100,000	
Additional Paid-in Capital on Preferred Stock	10,000	
Retained Earnings ($112,000 − $110,000)	2,000	
Cash ($112 × 1,000)		112,000

Although unlikely, if the call price had been $105 per share, the corporation makes the following journal entry:

Preferred Stock, $100 par	100,000	
Additional Paid-in Capital on Preferred Stock	10,000	
Cash ($105 × 1,000)		105,000
Additional Paid-in Capital from Recall of		
Preferred Stock ($110,000 − $105,000)		5,000

The recall and retirement of preferred stock causes a permanent reduction in the corporation's stockholders' equity. (This is not to be confused with *treasury stock*, which is reacquired but not retired, as we discuss later in the chapter.)

Redeemable Preferred Stock

In contrast to convertible preferred stock and callable preferred stock, some preferred stock is redeemable. **Redeemable preferred stock either may be subject to mandatory redemption at a specified future maturity date for a specified price, or redeemable at the option of the holder** (instead of being callable at the option of the issuer). Redeemable preferred stock has a key characteristic of a liability because of the likelihood of a cash outflow in the future that the company has no ability to prevent. Therefore, in reports filed with the SEC, it requires a corporation to report this stock as a separate component of its balance sheet (for instance, directly before stockholders' equity or within a classification such as "Stockholders' Equity and Redeemable Preferred Stock"). Furthermore, it requires separate disclosure of the redemption features, shares issued and redeemed, and other related issues in the notes to the financial statements.[17] The FASB does not currently require separate reporting (although it is considering requiring that a corporation report its mandatorily redeemable preferred stock as a *liability* on its balance sheet). However, it does require similar disclosures in the notes to the financial statements.[18] Note that, as we discussed in Chapter 14, if a company *invests* in redeemable preferred stock with a mandatory redemption feature or that is redeemable at the option of the holder, the company classifies the investment as a *debt* security.

Preference in Liquidation

If a corporation is liquidated, the preferred stock contract usually allows the preferred stockholders **preference** over the common stockholders (but secondary to the creditors) with respect to the corporate assets. The preference is typically expressed as a percentage of

---

17. "Codification of Financial Reporting Policies," *SEC Accounting Rules* (Chicago: Commerce Clearing House, 2002), sec. 211.01 and 211.04.

18. "Disclosure of Information about Capital Structure," *FASB Statement of Financial Accounting Standards No. 129* (Norwalk, Conn.: FASB, 1997) par. 4, 5, and 8.

(or equal to) the par value and frequently requires the payment of dividends in arrears. This liquidation preference is important to external users and is disclosed either parenthetically in the stockholders' equity section or in the notes accompanying the financial statements.[19]

Voting Rights

In exchange for the previously discussed provisions, the preferred stock contract often states that the holder has **no voting rights.** Otherwise, the preferred stockholder has full voting rights.

Disclosures

It is possible for preferred stock to have various combinations of the provisions we previously discussed. For instance, a preferred stock may be cumulative, nonparticipating, nonconvertible, and callable, with no voting rights. Some accountants and users have argued that this stock has more of the characteristics of a long-term liability than it does of capital stock (because there is a probable future cash outflow), and that a corporation should classify the "stock" as a long-term liability or in a separate section between its long-term liabilities and stockholders' equity. This view has not gained acceptance and preferred stock (except for redeemable preferred stock covered by the SEC rules) continues to be listed in the stockholders' equity section of the balance sheet. As we discuss in the next section, a corporation discloses the preferred stock characteristics either parenthetically or in a note to its financial statements.

CONTRIBUTED CAPITAL SECTION

A corporation includes the results of the various transactions involving the issuance of capital stock in the Contributed Capital (frequently called Paid-in Capital) section of stockholders' equity on its balance sheet. Contributed capital is usually separated into the par (or stated) value of the outstanding capital stock (or, in the case of no-par stock, the total proceeds received from the stock issue) and the additional paid-in capital arising from the different transactions. A corporation's contributed capital section includes:

10 Know the components of contributed capital.

1. Capital stock
   a. Par value of preferred stock
   b. Par value of common stock
   c. Common (or preferred) stock subscribed
   d. Stock warrants
   e. Stock dividends to be distributed (discussed in Chapter 16)
2. Additional paid-in capital
   a. On preferred stock
   b. On common stock
   c. From other sources (e.g., stock splits, preferred stock conversions, treasury stock)

In addition to reporting the specific amounts for the Capital Stock and Additional Paid-in Capital accounts, certain other information is necessary for adequate disclosure. For each class of stock this disclosure includes the par value and the number of shares authorized, issued, and outstanding. The FASB also requires certain disclosures.[20] These include the preferred stock dividend rate, preferred stock characteristics, any dividends in arrears, and any relevant details relating to the common stock. A corporation may present this information parenthetically adjacent to each capital stock account or in a note to its financial statements. As we discuss in the next chapter, a schedule summarizing the changes in these various components of contributed capital is also an integral part of a corporation's financial statements.

---

19. *Ibid.*, par. 6.
20. *Ibid.*, par. 4–7.

To illustrate the preceding contributed capital framework, Exhibit 15-7 presents the Contributed Capital section of a hypothetical company, Newsom Corporation. Exhibit 15-8 shows the contributed capital of Alcoa, Inc. on its comparative balance sheets dated December 31, 2001 and 2000, and the accompanying Note M (in part), which describes the capital stock.

This concludes the discussion of the major items affecting contributed capital. We now turn to a discussion of accounting for the reacquisition of capital (treasury) stock, which may or may not affect contributed capital.

TREASURY STOCK (CAPITAL STOCK REACQUISITION)

11 Understand the accounting for treasury stock.

In most states a corporation may reacquire its own previously issued capital stock, after which it may formally retire (cancel) the stock or hold the stock in its corporate treasury. **Treasury stock is a corporation's own capital stock that (1) has been fully paid for by stockholders, (2) has been legally issued, (3) is reacquired by the corporation, and (4) is being held by the corporation for future reissuance.** The reacquisition of previously issued shares may result from the exchange of corporate cash or other assets, the satisfaction of a debt owed *to* the corporation, or the donation of the treasury stock by the corporate stockholders.

A corporation may acquire treasury stock for various reasons: (1) to use for stock option, bonus, and employee purchase plans; (2) to use in the conversion of convertible preferred stock or bonds; (3) to use excess cash; (4) to use in the acquisition of other companies; (5) to reduce the number of shares outstanding and thereby increase the earnings per share and help maintain or increase the market price of its stock; (6) to reduce the number of shares held by hostile shareholders and thereby reduce the likelihood of being acquired by another company; and (7) to use for the issuance of a stock dividend. Each of these is subject to legal, governmental, and stock exchange regulations.

Treasury stock is clearly *not* an asset of a corporation; the corporation cannot own itself. A corporation cannot recognize a gain or loss when reacquiring its own stock; this restricts a corporation from influencing its net income by buying and selling its own stock. Consequently, a corporation treats treasury stock as a reduction of its stockholders' equity as we will discuss. To ensure that treasury stock is handled in the best interests of the stockholders, states have passed laws regulating corporate activities in this respect. Generally, a corporation must acquire treasury stock for some legitimate corporate purpose. Treasury stock carries no voting or preemptive rights, ordinarily cannot participate in any type of dividends, and has no rights at liquidation. However, it does participate in stock splits, since the par value must be reduced accordingly (the corporation makes a memorandum entry showing the increase in the number of treasury shares and the decrease in the par value). Although the acquisition of treasury stock does not formally reduce a corporation's legal capital, the amount that it may pay to acquire the stock is usually limited to the balance in its retained earnings (and perhaps additional paid-in capital) so that its legal capital is not impaired. Furthermore, a corporation ordinarily must restrict the amount of retained earnings available for dividends by the cost of the treasury stock held so that the payment of dividends does not reduce contributed capital.

Just as the original issuance of capital stock causes an increase in a corporation's stockholders' equity and the number of shares outstanding, its reacquisition has an opposite effect. The corporation's stockholders' equity (and the number of shares outstanding) is reduced. Reacquired capital stock may be formally retired, generally by filing the required documents in the state of incorporation. The shares then revert to authorized but unissued shares, and legal capital is appropriately reduced. If the shares are *not* retired, the corporation may reissue the treasury stock at a price above or below the acquisition price, or the par value. Ordinarily, the board of directors need not consider the par value when treasury stock is reissued because the legal capital requirements were met when the stock was originally issued. Upon reissuance, the corporation again increases its stockholders' equity and the number of shares outstanding.

A corporation may account for treasury stock transactions by either (1) the cost method or (2) the par (or stated) value method. Both are generally accepted accounting

EXHIBIT 15-7 Newsom Corporation

Contributed Capital
December 31, 2004

Stockholders' Equity
Contributed Capital

Preferred stock, $100 par (9%, cumulative, convertible, 10,000 shares authorized, 4,300 shares issued and outstanding)	$ 430,000
Common stock, $5 par (80,000 shares authorized, 32,800 shares issued and outstanding)	164,000
Common stock subscribed, $5 par (3,600 shares at a subscription price of $34 per share)	18,000
Common stock option warrants	23,000
Additional paid-in capital on preferred stock	107,500
Additional paid-in capital on common stock	590,400
Additional paid-in capital from conversion of preferred stock into common stock	10,100
Total Contributed Capital	$1,343,000

EXHIBIT 15-8 Contributed Capital

ALCOA AND SUBSIDIARIES

CONSOLIDATED BALANCE SHEET (in part):

Shareholders' Equity (in part):

	December 31	
(in millions)	2001	2000
Preferred stock (M)	$ 56	$ 56
Common stock (M)	925	925
Additional capital	6,114	5,927

NOTES TO CONSOLIDATED FINANCIAL STATEMENTS (in part):

M. Preferred and Common Stock
Preferred Stock. Alcoa has two classes of preferred stock. Serial preferred stock has 557,740 shares authorized and outstanding, with a par value of $100 per share and an annual $3.75 cumulative dividend preference per share. Class B serial preferred stock has 10 million shares authorized (none issued) and a par value of $1 per share.
Common Stock. There are 1.8 billion shares authorized at a par value of $1 per share. As of December 31, 2001, 94.5 million shares of common stock were reserved for issuance under the long-term stock incentive plans.
   In July 2001, the Alcoa Board of Directors authorized the repurchase of 50 million shares of Alcoa common stock. As of December 31, 2001, there were 37.5 million shares remaining on the stock repurchase authorization.

Q U E S T I O N S

Q How many classes of preferred stock does Alcoa have? **Q** What is the par value per share of each class? How many shares of each class are issued and outstanding?
Q What is the par value per share of common stock? **Q** How many shares of common stock were "reserved" on December 31, 2001, and for what purpose?

principles, although they affect the various components of stockholders' equity differently. Furthermore, the application of, and accounting procedures for, each method may differ according to the legal requirements of different states. Only the basic aspects of each method are presented here. Since the cost method is more widely used,[21] we discuss it first.

Cost Method

When a corporation uses the cost method, it treats the treasury stock "event" as though it consists of two elements: (1) the purchase (reacquisition) that initiates the event, and (2) the reissuance that completes the event. Under this method, it is assumed that the corporation reacquires its capital stock with the intent of reissuing rather than retiring it. When the corporation reacquires the stock, it debits a temporary account entitled Treasury Stock (and credits Cash, or other appropriate asset account) for the *cost* of the shares. A separate Treasury Stock account should be established for each class of stock (common and preferred). During the period between reacquisition and reissuance, the corporation treats the Treasury Stock account as a contra-stockholders' equity account representing a temporary reduction in its stockholders' equity. If it prepares a balance sheet during this period, it deducts the cost of the treasury stock from the total of contributed capital, retained earnings, and accumulated other comprehensive income (if any), as we illustrate later in the chapter.

When the corporation reissues the treasury shares, it reduces (credits) the Treasury Stock account for the *cost* of the shares reissued and treats the difference between the proceeds received and this cost as an adjustment of stockholders' equity. If the proceeds exceed the cost of the reissued treasury stock, the excess is treated as an increase in additional paid-in capital from the treasury stock transaction. If the proceeds are less than the cost, the deficit is treated as a reduction of additional paid-in capital related to previous issuances or retirements of treasury stock of the same class. If this additional paid-in capital is insufficient to absorb the deficit, the corporation records the remainder as a reduction in retained earnings.[22] Since a corporation may reacquire treasury stock at different dates and at different costs, it may maintain records to use the specific identification method when the stock is reissued. If the corporation does not keep such records, it may use either FIFO or average costing to record the reduction in the Treasury Stock account.

To illustrate the cost method, assume that Ball Corporation is authorized to issue 20,000 shares of $10 par common stock and enters into several treasury stock transactions. These transactions (1 through 5) are listed in the left column of Exhibit 15-9, followed by the journal entries Ball makes to record the transactions under the *cost method*. In journal entry 4, note that although the treasury stock was reissued at less than par, no consideration was given to this because the legal capital requirements were met in journal entry 1. Only the *cost* of the treasury stock is used to determine the impact on additional paid-in capital.[23]

---

21. *Accounting Trends and Techniques* (New York: AICPA, 2001, p. 265) reports that of the companies disclosing treasury stock holdings in common stock, 95% used the cost method and only 5% used the par or stated value method.

22. "Status of Accounting Research Bulletins", *APB Opinion No. 6* (New York: AICPA, 1965), par. 12.

23. Some corporations prepare a slightly different journal entry from that shown in transaction 4 when they reissue treasury stock at substantially less than cost. This involves reducing the additional paid-in capital from all the *original* issuances of the same class of stock by an average pro rata amount per share. Any further deficit below the average original issuance price is then debited to retained earnings. To illustrate, recall from transaction 1 that the original issuance price of $12 per share resulted in a $2 per share increase in additional paid-in capital (because this is the only issuance, the $2 excess per share is also the *average* excess per share). Since the reissuance price for $8 per share in transaction 4 is $5 below the per share cost of the treasury stock, a corporation might record transaction 4 as follows:

Cash	1,600	
Additional Paid-in Capital on Common Stock ($2 per share)	400	
Retained Earnings ($3 per share)	600	
Treasury Stock (200 shares at $13)		2,600

EXHIBIT 15-9 Comparison of Journal Entries for Treasury Stock

Cost Method		Par Value Method	

1. *Issuance of 6,000 shares of $10 par common stock for $12 per share:*

Cash	72,000	
Common Stock, $10 par		60,000
Additional Paid-in Capital on		
Common Stock		12,000

2. *Reacquisition of 1,000 shares of common stock at $13 per share:*

Treasury Stock	13,000	
Cash		13,000

3. *Reissuance of 600 shares of treasury stock at $15 per share:*

Cash	9,000	
Treasury Stock (600 shares at $13 per share)		7,800
Additional Paid-in Capital from Treasury Stock		1,200

4. *Reissuance of another 200 shares of treasury stock at $8 per share:*

Cash	1,600	
Additional Paid-in Capital from Treasury Stock	1,000	
Treasury Stock (200 shares at $13 per share)		2,600

5. *Reissuance of another 100 shares of treasury stock at $10 per share:*

Cash	1,000	
Additional Paid-in Capital from Treasury Stock	200	
Retained Earnings	100	
Treasury Stock (100 shares at $13 per share)		1,300

Par Value Method

1. *Issuance of 6,000 shares of $10 par common stock for $12 per share:*

Cash	72,000	
Common Stock, $10 par		60,000
Additional Paid-in Capital on		
Common Stock		12,000

2. *Reacquisition of 1,000 shares of common stock at $13 per share:*

Treasury Stock (1,000 shares at $10 par)	10,000	
Additional Paid-in Capital on Common Stock ($2 average excess × 1,000 shares)	2,000	
Retained Earnings	1,000	
Cash		13,000

3. *Reissuance of 600 shares of treasury stock at $15 per share:*

Cash	9,000	
Treasury Stock (600 shares at $10 par)		6,000
Additional Paid-In Capital on Common Stock		3,000

4. *Reissuance of another 200 shares of treasury stock at $8 per share:*

Cash	1,600	
Additional Paid-in Capital on Common Stock	400	
Treasury Stock (200 shares at $10 par)		2,000

5. *Reissuance of another 100 shares of treasury stock at $10 per share:*

Cash	1,000	
Treasury Stock (100 shares at $10 par)		1,000

Finally, it is possible that when a corporation reissues shares at a price below cost, any additional paid-in capital from the same class of treasury stock is insufficient to cover the deficit between the reissuance price and cost. In this case, the corporation debits the deficit to retained earnings. For example, after journal entry 4 the additional paid-in capital related to common treasury stock transactions amounts to $200. Suppose, in transaction 5, that Ball Corporation reissues 100 shares of treasury stock at $10 per share. When Ball records this transaction, it reduces the Additional Paid-in Capital from Treasury Stock account to zero and records the remaining deficit as a reduction of Retained Earnings (as a kind of dividend). The accounting for no-par treasury stock follows the same procedures.

Par Value Method

If a corporation uses the par value method to account for treasury stock, it treats the *reacquisition* of capital stock as an event entirely separate from the stock's *reissuance*.

That is, when the corporation reacquires its capital stock from a stockholder, it assumes that its financial relationship with that stockholder is ended. The corporation must reduce contributed capital in a manner that is essentially the reverse of what it recorded when it originally issued the stock.

A corporation may issue shares of capital stock at many different times during its life. At each issuance, it credits the Capital Stock account for the par value and credits the excess of the proceeds over the par to an Additional Paid-in Capital account. Consequently, when the corporation reacquires its capital stock, it debits the Treasury Stock (either common or preferred) account for the *par* value of the stock and debits the original Additional Paid-in Capital (on common or preferred) account for a pro rata amount based on the average price received from all the *original* issuances of the stock. If the reacquisition price is less than the original average issuance price, it credits the excess to a new Additional Paid-in Capital from Treasury Stock account. If the reacquisition price is more than the original average issuance price, it first records the deficit as a reduction of Additional Paid-in Capital from Treasury Stock (if any) and then as a reduction of Retained Earnings (as a kind of dividend paid upon reacquisition).

During the period between reacquisition and reissuance, the corporation treats the Treasury Stock account as a contra-capital stock account. Since fewer shares are outstanding, it deducts the Treasury Stock account from the Capital Stock (common or preferred) account to reduce the total par value (we illustrate this later in the chapter).

When the corporation reissues the treasury stock, it accounts for the proceeds as an investment by a new stockholder. The corporation increases its contributed capital (and the number of outstanding shares) by crediting the Treasury Stock account at *par* and crediting the existing Additional Paid-in Capital (on common or preferred) account for the excess of the proceeds over the par value. If the proceeds are less than par, it reduces the Additional Paid-in Capital account. If no additional paid-in capital exists related to this class of stock, it debits Retained Earnings. Note that a Discount on Capital Stock account is *not* debited because no contingent liability exists on the part of the new stockholders. The accounting for treasury stock with a stated value follows the same procedures as we just discussed for par value stock.

To illustrate the par (stated) value method, we list the same transactions for the Ball Corporation as shown in the cost method example in the right column of Exhibit 15-9, followed by the journal entries Ball makes to record the transactions. Note that because there was only one issuance of common stock in transaction 1, the average price received is the same as the original issuance price. Consequently, in the journal entry to record transaction 2, the $2 original excess per share is used to determine the total reduction in additional paid-in capital. Typically, the average additional paid-in capital originally received per share is computed by dividing the total additional paid-in capital from the various original issuances of common stock by the number of common shares issued.

Balance Sheet Presentation

If a corporation holds treasury stock on the balance sheet date, its stockholders' equity presentation will differ slightly depending upon the method it used to account for the stock. Under the cost method, it deducts the Treasury Stock account from the total of contributed capital, retained earnings, and accumulated other comprehensive income (if any). Under the par value method, it deducts the Treasury Stock account from the appropriate Capital Stock account (preferred stock or common stock). For example, assume that the Ball Corporation prepares its stockholders' equity section immediately after recording transactions 1–5 of the preceding example (assume further that retained earnings is $40,000 *prior to* recording any treasury stock transactions). The stockholders' equity, based on use of the two methods, is shown in Exhibits 15-10 and 15-11.

Note that total stockholders' equity is the *same* regardless of the method used; only the subtotals of the component parts are different. State laws generally require retained earnings to be restricted by the amount of the *cost* of the treasury stock, regardless of which accounting method is used.

Restrictions of retained earnings are discussed in Chapter 16.

EXHIBIT 15-10   Cost Method

Stockholders' Equity

Contributed Capital	
Common stock, $10 par (20,000 shares authorized, 6,000 shares issued, of which 100 are being held as treasury stock)	$ 60,000
Additional paid-in capital on common stock	12,000
Total contributed capital	$ 72,000
Retained earnings (see note)	39,900
Accumulated other comprehensive income	10,000
Total contributed capital, retained earnings, and accumulated other comprehensive income	$121,900
Less: Treasury stock (100 shares at cost)	(1,300)
Total Stockholders' Equity	$120,600

Note: Retained earnings are restricted regarding dividends in the amount of $1,300, the cost of the treasury stock.

EXHIBIT 15-11   Par Value Method

Stockholders' Equity

Contributed Capital:	
Common stock, $10 par (20,000 shares authorized, 6,000 shares issued)	$ 60,000
Less: Treasury stock (100 shares at par)	(1,000)
Common stock outstanding (5,900 shares)	$ 59,000
Additional paid-in capital on common stock	12,600
Total contributed capital	$ 71,600
Retained earnings (see note)	39,000
Accumulated other comprehensive income	10,000
Total Stockholders' Equity	$120,600

Note: Retained earnings are restricted regarding dividends in the amount of $1,300, the cost of the treasury stock.

Acquisition at Greater Than Market Value

Over the years, there have been numerous "takeover" attempts by hostile stockholders, in which their goal is to acquire a sufficient number of shares of a company's common stock to exercise control over its activities. To thwart these attempts, some companies have reacquired their common stock from these stockholders at prices in excess of the fair value of the stock. This excess is often referred to as "greenmail." In return for this greenmail, the selling stockholders may agree to abandon certain acquisition plans, to restrict purchases of additional shares, or to other limitations. When this occurs, a question arises as to how to account for the acquisition of this treasury stock and the related greenmail.

In a situation where a corporation pays more than the fair value to acquire treasury stock, *FASB Technical Bulletin 85-6* requires that the corporation record the treasury stock at its fair value. The difference between the price paid to acquire the treasury stock and the fair value is recorded as an expense. The corporation does *not* report this expense as an extraordinary item on its income statement.[24] The corporation records any subsequent reissuances in the usual manner under either the cost or par value method.

---

24. *FASB Technical Bulletin No. 85-6* (Stamford, Conn.: FASB, 1985), par. 3–7.

Donated Treasury Stock

Stockholders may donate treasury stock to the corporation, which then may be reissued. This relatively rare procedure usually occurs when the corporation needs to attract more working capital without increasing the number of outstanding shares. According to *FASB Statement No. 116*, a corporation records a donation from a nongovernmental unit as a gain in the period received, based on the fair value of the exchange.[25] If the corporation uses the cost method to account for treasury stock, on the date of the donation it debits the Treasury Stock account and credits a gain for the fair value of the stock. When the stock is reissued, it records the transaction in the usual manner for the cost method. If the corporation uses the par value method, on the date of the donation it debits the Treasury Stock account for the par value, credits a gain for the fair value, and debits (or credits) Additional Paid-in Capital for the difference between the fair value and the par value. When the stock is reissued, it records the transaction in the usual manner for the par value method. It reports the gain in the Other Items section of its income statement.

A corporation must adhere to state laws regarding donated treasury stock. Many of these laws were established to discourage what is referred to as *treasury stock subterfuge*, an activity that occurred in times of high par values and resulted in *watered stock* (discussed earlier). A corporation would issue an excess number of shares of par value stock in exchange for a nonmonetary asset. A limited number of shares then would be donated back to the corporation and reissued at a price less than par, thereby avoiding the contingent liability on the part of the stockholder. However, such subterfuges are unlikely in today's financial world with its legal restrictions.

Retirement of Treasury Stock

Occasionally, a corporation's board of directors may decide to retire treasury stock. As a result, the corporation's legal capital is reduced. Thus, the corporation must adhere to all legal requirements, because the reduction in legal capital can affect both creditor and stockholder financial security. After retirement, it accounts for the shares as authorized but unissued stock.

The journal entry a corporation makes to record the retirement of treasury stock will depend upon which method it uses for its treasury stock transactions. Under the *cost* method, the corporation offsets the cost of the retired shares in the Treasury Stock account against both the par value in the Capital Stock account and a pro rata share from the Additional Paid-in Capital (on common or preferred) account. Any difference between these latter amounts and the cost of the treasury stock either is debited to Retained Earnings or credited to an Additional Paid-in Capital from Treasury Stock account. Under the *par value* method, the corporation simply offsets the par value of the retired shares in the Treasury Stock account against the Capital Stock account. To illustrate, assume the Ball Corporation retires the remaining 100 shares of treasury stock from the previous example. The alternative journal entries are as follows:

1. *Cost Method Retirement*

Common Stock, $10 par	1,000	
Additional Paid-in Capital on Common Stock	200*	
Retained Earnings	100	
Treasury Stock (100 shares at $13 per share)		1,300

*$\dfrac{\$12,000}{6,000} \times 100 \text{ shares} = \$200$

Note that the pro rata reduction per share in additional paid-in capital on common stock was computed based on the current balance in Additional Paid-in Capital on Common Stock ($12,000) divided by the number of shares *issued* (6,000).

---

25. "Accounting for Contributions Received and Contributions Made," *FASB Statement of Financial Accounting Standards No. 116* (Norwalk, Conn.: FASB, 1993), par. 8.

2. *Par Value Method Retirement*

Common Stock, $10 par	1,000	
Treasury Stock (100 shares at $10 par)		1,000

Regardless of which method is used, when a corporation retires treasury stock, retained earnings is no longer restricted so the corporation eliminates the related note describing the restriction.

Conceptual Overview of Treasury Stock

The cost method of accounting for treasury stock is widely used because of its relative simplicity, but it is difficult to justify theoretically. Its use results in a mingling of the various components of corporate capital. Moreover, the application of this method falsely assumes that the same corporate body of stockholders exists after the reissuance as existed prior to the reacquisition. Although the par value method requires more analysis and record keeping, it is theoretically preferable because it properly identifies the separate sources and amounts of corporate capital. It is also more logical than the cost method because when a particular stockholder "disinvests" in the corporation, the associated contributed capital is eliminated and replaced by the contributed capital of the new stockholder.

Regardless of whether the cost or the par value method is used, the following items are important:

1. Treasury stock is not an asset; it is treated as a reduction in stockholders' equity.
2. Treasury stock does not vote, has no preemptive right, ordinarily does not share in dividends, and does not participate in assets at liquidation, but does participate in stock splits.
3. Treasury stock transactions do not result in gains or losses on the income statement, so that a corporation cannot influence its net income by buying and selling its own stock (which would be a violation of the concept of income).
4. Treasury stock transactions may reduce retained earnings but may never increase retained earnings.
5. Retained earnings usually must be restricted regarding dividends when treasury stock is held.
6. The total amount of a corporation's stockholders' equity is not affected by whether the cost or par value method is used, but the subtotals of the component elements (retained earnings, treasury stock, and additional paid-in capital) will be different.

SUMMARY

At the beginning of the chapter, we identified several objectives you would accomplish after reading the chapter. The objectives are listed below, each followed by a brief summary of the key points in the chapter discussion.

1. **Explain the corporate form of organization.** A corporation is a legal entity of a particular state. A corporation's articles of incorporation states the types, par value, and number of shares of capital stock to be issued. A corporation's owners (stockholders) have limited liability. A corporation may enter into contracts, hold property, sue and be sued, and continue in perpetuity.
2. **Know the rights and terms that apply to capital stock.** Each stockholder of a corporation has the right to: (1) share in the corporation's profits by receiving dividends, (2) elect directors and establish corporate policies, (3) maintain a proportionate interest in the ownership if additional shares are issued (preemptive right), and (4) share in the distribution of assets if the corporation is liquidated. The terms that apply to capital stock include authorized, issued, and outstanding capital stock, par (or stated) value, and additional paid-in capital.
3. **Account for the issuance of capital stock.** When a corporation issues capital stock for cash, it debits cash for the amount received, credits capital stock for the par value, and credits additional paid-in capital for the difference.

It modifies this entry accordingly for the issuance of stock subscriptions, for combined sales of stock, and for non-monetary issuances of stock.

4. **Describe a compensatory stock option plan.** A compensatory stock option plan is intended to provide additional compensation to selected employees within the corporation. The employees receive shares of stock, stock options, or other equity instruments in exchange for their services.

5. **Recognize compensation expense for a compensatory stock option plan.** Under the fair value method, the total compensation cost is the total fair value of the stock options that actually become vested. Under this method, a corporation recognizes the total compensation cost as compensation expense over the service period using the straight-line method, making adjustments each year for any changes in circumstances or changes in estimates.

6. **Account for a fixed compensatory stock option plan.** Under a fixed plan, a corporation estimates the total compensation cost by multiplying the fair value per option times the number of options granted times the estimated retention rate. It allocates the total compensation cost over the service period, adjusting for changes in the estimated turnover rate and for the number of options that actually vest.

7. **Account for a performance-based compensatory stock option plan.** Under a performance-based plan, a corporation estimates the total compensation cost by multiplying the fair value per option times the number of options expected to be granted times the estimated retention rate. It allocates the total compensation cost over the service period, adjusting for changes in estimates and for the number of options that actually vest.

8. **Understand how to use the intrinsic value method to account for a compensatory stock option plan.** Under the intrinsic value method, the total compensation cost is the excess (if any) of the quoted market price over the exercise price on the measurement date for the number of shares expected to be issued. Under this method, a corporation recognizes the total compensation cost (if any) over the service period using the straight line method. It also discloses its pro forma net income and earnings per share (assuming it had used the fair value method) each year in the notes to its financial statements.

9. **Describe the characteristics of preferred stock.** Preferred stock may have (1) a preference as to dividends, (2) accumulation of dividends, (3) participation in excess dividends, (4) convertibility into common stock, (5) attachment of stock warrants (rights), (6) callability by the corporation, (7) redemption at a future maturity date, (8) preference as to assets if the corporation is liquidated, and (9) lack of voting rights.

10. **Know the components of contributed capital.** Contributed capital usually includes capital stock (par value of preferred and common stock) and additional paid-in capital (on preferred and common stock).

11. **Understand the accounting for treasury stock.** Treasury stock is a corporation's own capital stock that it has reacquired. Treasury stock is not an asset; a corporation cannot recognize a gain or loss when reacquiring (or reissuing) its own stock. Under the cost method (the most common method), when a corporation acquires treasury stock, it debits the treasury stock account for the amount paid. When it reissues treasury stock, it debits cash for the proceeds received, credits the treasury stock account for the cost, and credits (or debits) additional paid-in capital from treasury stock for the difference.

QUESTIONS

Q15-1 What information is contained in a corporation's articles of incorporation?

Q15-2 What is the difference between (a) a public and private corporation, (b) an open and closed corporation, and (c) a domestic and foreign corporation (as viewed by a particular state)?

Q15-3 What is (a) a *stock certificate*, (b) a *stockholders' ledger*, (c) a *stock transfer journal*, and (d) a *transfer agent*?

Q15-4 List the basic rights of a stockholder. Which do you consider to be the most important?

Q15-5 What is the meaning of the following terms: (a) *authorized capital stock*, (b) *issued capital stock*, (c) *outstanding capital stock*, and (d) *treasury stock?* What is the difference between issued and outstanding capital stock?

Q15-6 What is a corporation's *legal capital* and why is it important?

Q15-7 How is a corporation's legal capital determined, assuming its capital stock has a par value, a stated value, or no par value?

Q15-8 What are the three components and the basic framework of stockholders' equity?

Q15-9 How does preferred stock differ from common stock?

Q15-10 What amount of the proceeds from the issuance of no-par, no-stated-value stock is recorded in the Capital Stock account?

Q15-11 What is a *stock subscription?* How does a corporation report the accounts Subscriptions Receivable and Preferred Stock Subscribed on its balance sheet? Why?

Q15-12 What alternatives are possible if a subscriber defaults on a stock subscription? How would you determine which alternative to use?

Q15-13 How would you record the proceeds received from the combined issuance by a corporation of shares of common stock with shares of preferred stock?

Q15-14 If a corporation issues capital stock for an asset other than cash, what amount would you use to record the transaction?

Q15-15 When do (a) watered stock or (b) secret reserves result from the recording of a nonmonetary issuance of stock? What impact does each have on a corporation's balance sheet?

Q15-16 What is a *stock split* and a *disproportionate stock split*? How do they affect each element of a corporation's stockholders' equity?

Q15-17 (a) What are the criteria for a noncompensatory stock option plan? (b) How does a compensatory stock option plan differ from a noncompensatory plan? (c) What is the intent of a noncompensatory plan? Of a compensatory plan?

Q15-18 Under the fair value method, how does a corporation determine the total compensation cost for a compensatory stock option plan? How does it recognize this amount as compensation expense?

Q15-19 What are stock appreciation rights? Why are they advantageous to an employee?

Q15-20 Define the following terms regarding preferred stock: (a) *dividend preference*, (b) *cumulative*, (c) *participating*, (d) *convertible*, (e) *warrants*, (f) *callable*, and (g) *redeemable*.

Q15-21 Why is a preferred stock similar to a long-term bond? Why is it similar to common stock?

Q15-22 What are the two segments of a corporation's contributed capital and what might be included in each segment?

Q15-23 (a) What is *treasury stock?* (b) Why might a corporation acquire treasury stock?

Q15-24 If a corporation uses the cost method to account for treasury stock, the treasury stock "event" is treated as though it consists of two elements; if it uses the par value method, the reacquisition and reissuance transactions are viewed as separate events. Explain the accounting differences resulting from these concepts.

Q15-25 How does a corporation report the Treasury Stock account under the cost method of accounting for treasury stock? Under the par value method?

Q15-26 What accounting procedures are involved under (a) the cost method, and (b) the par value method when a corporation retires treasury stock?

CASES

C O M M U N I C A T I O N

C15-1 Stockholder Rights and Preferences

A stockholder has several rights as an "owner" of a corporation. Furthermore, the rights of preferred stockholders are sometimes modified upon the issuance of preferred stock.

Required

1. List and briefly explain stockholders' rights as they pertain to common stockholders. Indicate the relative importance of each.
2. List and briefly explain what characteristics might be attached to preferred stock. Indicate the set of characteristics that makes preferred stock more like a long-term bond than a common stock.

C15-2 Exchange of Stock for Asset

As a general rule, when a corporation issues capital stock for assets other than cash, it is said that the exchange should be valued at the fair value of the stock or the asset, whichever is more reliable.

Required Write a short report that explains the reasoning behind this rule, including the concepts of *watered stock* and *secret reserves*. Give an example of a situation where

the fair value of (1) the stock or, alternatively, (2) the asset is used to record an exchange.

C15-3 Issuance of Security Packages

Occasionally, a corporation will combine securities into a "package" (for example, common stocks, preferred stocks, bonds) and issue these securities as a single unit.

Required Assuming that two securities (common stock and preferred stock) are issued as a unit, explain the alternative ways of valuing the separate stocks of the unit in an exchange for (1) cash, or (2) an asset(s) other than cash.

C15-4 Subscriptions

A corporation may enter into subscription contracts for the purchase of its stock.

Required What is a subscription contract and how does it work? What provisions are usually included in the contract? What are the arguments for reporting the Subscriptions Receivable account as a contra-stockholders' equity item and for reporting it as a current asset? Why is the Capital Stock account not credited at the time of the subscription instead of the Capital Stock Subscribed account? How is this latter account reported on the corporation's balance sheet? What are the alternative methods of handling subscription defaults?

C15-5 Stock Options

A corporation has a noncompensatory stock purchase plan for all its employees and a compensatory stock option plan for some of its corporate officers.

Required

1. Compare and contrast the accounting at the date the stock is issued for the noncompensatory stock purchase plan with that for the compensatory stock option plan.
2. What entry should be made for the compensatory stock option plan at the date of the grant? (*AICPA adapted*)

C15-6 Capital Stock

Capital stock is an important area of a corporation's equity section. Generally the term "capital stock" embraces common and preferred stock issued by a corporation.

Required

1. What are the basic rights inherent in ownership of common stock, and how are they exercised?

2. What is preferred stock? Discuss the various preferences afforded preferred stock. (*AICPA adapted*)

C15-7 Treasury Stock

A corporation sometimes engages in treasury stock transactions.

Required

1. Define *treasury stock*.
2. Why would a corporation acquire treasury stock?
3. Briefly explain the two alternative methods of accounting for the reacquisition and reissuance of treasury stock. Assume the treasury stock is common stock and has a par value.
4. Briefly explain the balance sheet presentation of treasury stock for each of the alternative methods.

C15-8 Definitions

In dealing with the various equity securities of a corporate entity, it is important to understand certain related terminology.

Required Define the following terms: (1) treasury stock, (2) legal capital, (3) stock right, and (4) stock warrant. (*AICPA adapted*)

C R E A T I V E   A N D   C R I T I C A L   T H I N K I N G

C15-9 Compensatory Stock Options

On November 5, 2003, Gunpowder Corp.'s board of directors approved a stock option plan for key executives. On January 2, 2004, a specific number of stock options were granted. These options were exercisable between January 2, 2006 and December 31, 2008 at 90% of the quoted market price on January 2, 2004. The service period is for 2004 and 2005. Some options were forfeited when an executive resigned in 2005. All other options were exercised during 2006.

Required

1. How should Gunpowder determine the compensation expense, if any, for the stock option plan in 2004?
2. What is the effect of forfeiture of the stock options on Gunpowder's financial statements for 2005?
3. What is the effect of the stock option plan on the balance sheet at December 31, 2006? Be specific as to the changes in balance sheet accounts between November 5, 2003 and December 31, 2006. (*AICPA adapted*)

C15-10 Stock Appreciation Rights

Instead of a fixed compensatory stock option plan, Wright Company is considering providing its key executives with a plan that involves stock appreciation rights (SAR).

Required

1. Explain what is meant by an SAR plan.
2. Identify the key differences between accounting for an SAR plan and a fixed compensatory stock option plan.

3. Briefly summarize the steps in accounting for an SAR plan (assume that the executive is expected to receive cash on the date of exercise).

C15-11 Compensatory Stock Option Plan

Tom Twitlet, president of Twitlet Corporation, is considering establishing a compensatory stock option plan for the company's 20 top executives. Tom desires to set the terms of the plan so that the number of stock options the executives can exercise increases based on a specified increase in the company's future earnings. Tom is concerned about how to specify and account for the terms of the plan, and has asked for your advice.

Required Prepare a memo to Tom that briefly explains the issues involved in specifying and accounting for the terms of this type of compensatory stock option plan.

C15-12 Convertible Preferred Stock and Warrants

The stockholders' equity of a corporation may include both preferred stock and common stock. Preferred stock may (1) be convertible into common stock, or (2) be issued with warrants attached enabling the acquisition of common stock.

Required

Discuss the following three items:

1. The similarities and differences between these types of preferred stock.

2. Theoretically, the appropriate accounting treatment for the proceeds from the issuance of both types of preferred stock.

3. Which accounting treatment is generally acceptable for each type and why?

C15-13 Treasury Stock

For numerous reasons a corporation may reacquire shares of its own capital stock. When a corporation purchases treasury stock, it has two options as to how to account for the shares: (1) cost method, and (2) par value method.

Required Write a short report that compares and contrasts the cost method with the par value method for each of the following:

1. Purchase of shares at a price less than par value.
2. Purchase of shares at a price greater than par value.
3. Subsequent resale of treasury shares at a price less than purchase price, but more than par value.
4. Subsequent resale of treasury shares at a price greater than both purchase price and par value.
5. Effect on net income. (*AICPA adapted*)

C15-14 Changes in Equity

FASB Statement of Concepts No. 6 defines a company's equity and discusses the various changes in equity.

Required Define and discuss the term equity. Identify the various changes in a company's equity in regard to their impact on assets and liabilities.

C15-15 Analyzing Coca-Cola's Contributed Capital

Refer to the financial statements and related notes of the Coca-Cola Company in Appendix A of this book.

Required

1. How many shares of preferred stock were authorized and issued at the end of 2001?
2. How many shares of common stock were authorized and issued at the end of 2001? What is the par value per share?
3. What does the company call its additional paid-in capital? What was the amount at the end of 2001?
4. How many shares of treasury stock did the company hold at the end of 2001? What was the average cost per share?
5. How many shares of treasury stock did the company reacquire during 2001? What was the average cost per share?

6. Briefly describe the company's 1999 Stock Option Plan. What was the weighted-average fair value of the stock options the company granted in 2001? What was the company's pro forma net income for 2001 if it had used the fair value method for its stock option plans? How does this compare to its reported 2001 net income? How many stock options were granted and exercised during 2001, and how many were outstanding at the end of 2001? At what weighted-average price per share were the options exercised in 2001? What were the closing market prices per share of the company's stock at the end of 2001 and 2000? Assuming the stock options were exercised in 2001 at the weighted-average price per share and that the average market price per share was $46, by how much did the officers "gain" from exercising the options?

C15-16 Ethics and Stock Options

Smaller Corporation has been in operation for several years and has reached the point where it is now making a reasonable return on its stockholders' equity. At the beginning of 2004, the board of directors established a compensatory stock option plan for Smaller's key executives. At that time the market price and the option (exercise) price were the same. The plan allocates a specified number of stock options to each executive based on the executive's level within the company and the company's meeting targeted income goals. The service period is 3 years, and the options must be exercised within 10 years.

You are the controller for Smaller and are one of the key executives who will participate in the plan; you also already own a substantial number of shares of Smaller common stock. The company president comes to you at the end of 2004 and says, "I see that preliminary calculations show that the company has just reached its targeted income for 2004, before considering the effects of this stock option plan. From my understanding, it looks like the plan is pretty valuable, since an option pricing model shows a high fair value for each stock option. How do you think the company should account for the plan? As I understand it, there are two methods. How do they work, and which method should the company use? What do you think?"

Required From financial reporting and ethical perspectives, how would you reply to the president?

R E S E A R C H

C15-17 Researching GAAP

Russell International, a publicly traded company, reacquired 500,000 shares of its common stock during July of 2005 at a cost of $25 per share. The current market price

of the stock was $20 per share when the 500,000 shares were reacquired.

The shares that were reacquired had been owned by a group of minority shareholders who had been dissatisfied with Russell International's earnings trend, stock price, and dividends paid. In fact, these minority shareholders had been so disgruntled that they had filed a suit against Russell's directors during 2004. The minority shareholders' suit claimed damages of $3.0 million because of the board's failure to fulfill its fiduciary responsibility to maximize shareholders' value.

In August 2005 the minority shareholders' suit was dropped, with neither Russell International nor its directors having to offer or pay a settlement. Russell International accounts for its treasury stock transactions using the cost method.

Required Research the related generally accepted accounting principles and explain how Russell International should account for the treasury stock transaction. Cite your reference and applicable paragraph numbers. (*Contributed by Daryl G. Krause*)

C15-18 Researching GAAP

Bowsher Company had 10% bonds payable outstanding with a total face value of $185,000. Each bond had an individual face value of $1,000 and paid interest semiannually on June 30 and December 31. On July 1, 2004 the 10% bonds had a total book value of $210,000. At that time, because of a financial restructuring, the company executed an "exchange agreement" in which all of these 10% bonds were extinguished. In exchange for their 10% bonds, the bondholders were given cash of $125 per 10% bond, 6 shares of 7%, $100 preferred stock per 10% bond, and 50 warrants per 10% bond allowing the holder to acquire 50 shares of $5 par common stock for $25 per share. On July 1, 2004 the 7% preferred stock was selling at $106 per share and the warrants were selling at $5 each on the open market. You are the assistant accountant for Bowsher Company and have been asked by the head accountant to recommend how to record this transaction.

Required Research the related generally accepted accounting principles and prepare a short memo that explains and justifies your recommended journal entry to record the transaction. Cite your reference and applicable paragraph numbers.

MULTIPLE CHOICE

Select the best answer for each of the following.

M15-1 On July 14, JX Corporation exchanged 1,000 shares of its $8 par value common stock for a plot of land. JX's common stock is listed on the NYSE and traded at an average price of $21 per share on July 14. The land was appraised by independent real estate appraisers on July 14 at $23,000. As a result of this exchange, JX's additional paid-in capital will increase by

  a. $0
  b. $8,000
  c. $13,000
  d. $15,000

M15-2 When treasury stock is purchased for cash at more than its par value, what is the effect on total stockholders' equity under each of the following methods?

	Cost Method	Par Value Method
a.	Increase	Increase
b.	Decrease	Decrease
c.	No effect	Decrease
d.	No effect	No effect

M15-3 On July 6, 2004 Metaro Corporation purchased for $108,000, 2,000 shares of Jean Corporation's newly issued 6% cumulative $20 par value preferred stock. Each share also had one stock warrant attached, which entitled the holder to acquire, at $19, one share of Jean $10 par value common stock for each two warrants held. On July 7, 2004 the market price of the preferred stock (without warrants) was $50 per share and the market price of the stock warrants was $10 per warrant. On September 1, 2004 Metaro sold all the stock warrants for $19,800. What should be the gain on the sale of the stock warrants?

  a. $0
  b. $800
  c. $1,800
  d. $9,800

M15-4 What is the most likely effect of a stock split on the par value per share and the number of shares outstanding?

	Par Value Per Share	Number of Shares Outstanding
a.	Decrease	Increase
b.	Decrease	No effect
c.	Increase	Increase
d.	No effect	No effect

M15-5 Landy Corporation was organized on January 2, 2004 with authorized capital of 100,000 shares of $10 par value common stock. During 2004 Landy had the following transactions:

Jan. 12	Issued 20,000 shares at $12 per share
Apr. 23	Issued 1,000 shares for legal services when the market price was $14 per share

What should be the amount of additional paid-in capital at December 31, 2004?

  a. $4,000
  b. $14,000
  c. $40,000
  d. $44,000

M15-6 During 2004 Bradley Corporation issued for $110 per share, 5,000 shares of $100 par value convertible preferred stock. One share of preferred stock can be converted into three shares of Bradley's $25 par value common stock at the option of the preferred shareholder. On December 31, 2005 all of the preferred stock was converted into common stock. The market value of the common stock at the conversion date was $40 per share. What amount should be credited to the common stock account on December 31, 2005?

    a. $375,000   c. $550,000
    b. $500,000   d. $600,000

M15-7 The Amlin Corporation was incorporated on January 1, 2004, with the following authorized capitalization:

- 20,000 shares of common stock, no par value, stated value $40 per share
- 5,000 shares of 5% cumulative preferred stock, par value $10 per share

During 2004 Amlin issued 12,000 shares of common stock for a total of $600,000 and 3,000 shares of preferred stock at $16 per share. In addition, on December 21, 2004 subscriptions for 1,000 shares of preferred stock were taken at a purchase price of $17. These subscribed shares were paid for on January 4, 2005. What should Amlin report as total contributed capital on its December 31, 2004 balance sheet issued on February 1, 2005?

    a. $520,000   c. $665,000
    b. $648,000   d. $850,000

M15-8 On January 1, 2004 Stoner Corporation granted compensatory stock options to key employees for the purchase of shares of the company's common stock at $25

per share. The options are intended to compensate employees for the next 2 years. The options are exercisable within a 4-year period beginning January 1, 2006 by grantees still in the employ of the company. The fair value of each option was $7 on the date of grant. Stoner expects to distribute 10,000 shares of treasury stock when options are exercised. The treasury stock was acquired by Stoner during 2003 at a cost of $28 per share and was recorded under the cost method. How much should Stoner charge to compensation expense for the year ended December 31, 2004?

    a. $70,000   c. $30,000
    b. $35,000   d. $15,000

M15-9 When treasury stock accounted for by the cost method is subsequently sold for more than its purchase price, the excess of the cash proceeds over the carrying value of the treasury stock should be recognized as

a. Extraordinary gain
b. Increase in additional paid-in capital
c. Income from continuing operations
d. Increase in retained earnings

M15-10 Preferred stock that may be retired by the corporation at its option is known as

a. Convertible   c. Cumulative
b. Redeemable   d. Callable

                                        (*AICPA adapted*)

EXERCISES

E15-1   *Par Value and No-Par Stock Issuance*   Cutler Corporation is authorized to issue 10,000 shares of common stock. It sells 6,000 shares at $19 per share.

Required Record the sale of the common stock, given the following independent assumptions:
1. The stock has a par value of $10 per share.
2. The stock is no-par stock, but the board of directors has assigned a stated value of $8 per share.
3. The stock has no par and no stated value.

E15-2   *Combined Sale of Stock*   Estes Company issues 300 shares of $50 par preferred stock and 1,000 shares of $10 par common stock in a "package" sale. Total proceeds received amount to $39,000.

Required Record the transaction for each independent assumption shown:
1. The common stock has a current market value of $19 per share; the current market value of preferred stock is not known.
2. The common stock and the preferred stock have a current market value per share of $22 and $60 respectively.

E15-3   *Sale of Stock with Bonds*   Kelly Company issues 12% bonds with a face value of $10,000 and 600 shares of $10 par common stock in a combined sale, receiving total proceeds of $23,000.

Required Record the transaction for each independent assumption shown:
1. The common stock has a current market value of $21 per share; the market value of the bonds is not known.
2. The common stock has a current market value of $24.50 per share; the bonds are selling at 98.

E15-4   *Issuance of Stock for Land*   The Putt Company issues 500 shares of $100 preferred stock for land. This land was carried on the seller's books for $40,000.

Required

1. Prepare the journal entry to record the acquisition of the land for each of the following independent situations:
    a. The preferred stock is currently selling for $120 per share. No appraisal is available on the land.
    b. The land is appraised at $65,000. There have been no recent sales of the preferred stock.
    c. The preferred stock is currently selling for $125 per share. The land is appraised at $64,000.
2. For Requirement 1(c), discuss why you chose the value used in the journal entry.

E15-5   *Stock Subscription*   On February 3 the Teel Corporation enters into a subscription contract with several subscribers for 5,000 shares of $10 par common stock at a price of $16 per share. The contract requires a down payment of 25%, with the remaining balance to be paid on May 3. The stock will be issued to each subscriber upon full payment.

Required Prepare journal entries to record the following:

1. The February 3 receipt of the down payment and signing of the contract.
2. The May 3 receipt of the remaining balance from subscribers to 4,000 shares. The market price is currently $17 per share.
3. The default of a subscriber to 1,000 shares. These shares are sold on the open market for $17 per share on May 4, and the down payment is returned to the subscriber.

E15-6   *Stock Split*   Holton Company currently has 9,000 shares of $12 par common stock outstanding that had been issued at an average price of $60 per share. It declares a three-for-one stock split.

Required Prepare whatever entry is necessary to record the stock split, assuming the following independent alternatives:

1. The par value is reduced to $4 per share.
2. The par value is reduced to $6 per share.
3. The par value is reduced to $3 per share.

E15-7   *Fixed Compensatory Stock Option Plan*   McEnroe Company has 20 executives to whom it grants compensatory stock options on January 1, 2004. At that time it grants each executive the right to purchase 100 shares of its $5 par common stock at $40 per share after a 3-year service period. The value of each option is estimated to be $10.25 on the grant date. Based on its average employee turnover rate each year, McEnroe expects that 2 executives will not vest in the plan. At the end of 2006 McEnroe confirms that the actual turnover was the same as expected. On January 5, 2007, 3 executives exercise their options. McEnroe uses the fair value method to account for this compensatory stock option plan.

Required Prepare the journal entries of McEnroe Company for 2004 through 2007 in regard to its compensatory stock option plan (round all calculations to the nearest whole number).

E15-8   *Fixed Compensatory Stock Option Plan*   On January 1, 2004 Sampress Company adopts a compensatory stock
@   option plan for its 50 executives. The plan allows each executive to purchase 200 shares of its $2 par common stock for $30 per share after completing a 3-year service period. Sampress estimates the value of each option to be $14.00 on the grant date. It has had a 4% employee turnover rate each year and uses this rate in its compensation cost calculations in 2004. Because of higher turnover, at the end of 2005 Sampress changes it estimated turnover rate to 5% per year for the entire service period. At the end of 2006, Sampress determined that the actual turnover was seven executives for the entire service period. On January 6, 2007, eight executives exercise their options. Sampress uses the fair value method to account for this plan.

Required

1. Prepare a schedule of the Sampress Company's compensation computations for its compensatory stock option plan for 2004 through 2006 (round all computations to the nearest dollar).
2. Prepare the journal entries of Sampress Company for 2004 through 2007 in regard to this plan.

E15-9   *Performance-Based Stock Option Plan*   On January 1, 2004 Seles Company adopts a performance-based stock option plan for its 80 key executives. Each executive is granted a maximum of 70 stock options, but the number of options that vest depends on the percentage increase in Seles Company's sales over a 3-year service period. If by December 31, 2006, sales have increased by at least 10%, 50 stock options will vest for each executive; if sales have increased by at least 15%, all 70 stock options will vest. On the grant date, Seles estimates that its sales will increase by 12% over the service period, and that its annual employee turnover rate will be 2%. It also determines that the fair value of an option expected to vest is $13.40. At the end of 2006, actual sales had increased by 16% for the service period and the actual turnover was six key executives for the service period. Seles uses the fair value method to account for this plan.

Required

1. Prepare a schedule of the Seles Company's computations for its compensatory stock option plan for 2004 through 2006 (round all computations to the nearest dollar).
2. Prepare the compensation expense journal entry for 2004.

E15-10 *Stock Appreciation Rights* On January 1, 2003, as a form of executive compensation, Wadlin Corporation grants stock appreciation rights to Robert Brandt. These rights entitle Brandt to receive cash equal to the excess of the quoted market price over a $20 option price for 4,000 shares of the company's common stock on the exercise date. The service period is 3 years (which Brandt is expected to complete) and the rights must be exercised within 5 years. Brandt exercises his rights on December 31, 2006. The quoted market price per share of common stock was $20 on January 1, 2003; $23 on December 31, 2003; $24.20 on December 31, 2004; $24 on December 31, 2005; and $25 on December 31, 2006.

Required

1. Prepare a schedule to compute the compensation expense related to this SAR plan for 2003 through 2006.
2. Prepare the December 31, 2006 journal entry related to this SAR plan.

E15-11 *Convertible Preferred Stock* On January 2, 2004 the Bray Corporation issues 900 shares of $100 par convertible preferred stock for $117 per share. On January 6, 2005, all the preferred stockholders convert their shares to common stock.

Required

1. Prepare the January 2, 2004 journal entry to record the issuance of the preferred stock.
2. Prepare the January 6, 2005 journal entry to record the conversion, assuming the preferred stock contract states that
   a. Each share of preferred stock is convertible into seven shares of $10 par common stock.
   b. Each share of preferred stock is convertible into twelve shares of $10 par common stock.

E15-12 *Callable Preferred Stock* On March 4, 2004 the Hein Corporation issues 1,000 shares of $100 par preferred stock for $125 per share. The stock is not callable by the corporation until 3 years have expired. On April 7, 2007, all the stock is called by the corporation.

Required

1. Prepare the journal entry to record the issuance of the stock.
2. Prepare the journal entry to record the recall
   a. At a price of $130 per share.
   b. At a price of $114 per share.

E15-13 *Stock Rights with Preferred Stock* The Nelson Corporation issues 6,000 shares of $100 par preferred stock at a price of $112 per share. A stock warrant is attached to each share of preferred stock that enables the holder to purchase one share of $10 par common stock for $25. Immediately after issuance, the preferred stock begins selling ex rights for $110 per share. The warrants (which expire in 30 days) also begin trading for $4 per warrant.

Required

1. Prepare the journal entry to record the sale of the preferred stock.
2. Prepare the journal entry to record the issuance of 5,000 shares of common stock in exchange for 5,000 warrants and $25 per share.
3. Prepare the journal entry to record the expiration of 1,000 warrants.

E15-14 *Various Journal Entries* Sapp Company is authorized to issue 20,000 shares of no-par, $5 stated-value common stock and 5,000 shares of 9%, $100 par preferred stock. It enters into the following transactions:

1. Accepts a subscription contract to 7,000 shares of common stock at $42 per share and receives a 30% down payment.
2. Collects the remaining balance of the subscription contract and issues the common stock.
3. Acquires a building by paying $23,000 cash and issuing 2,000 shares of common stock and 600 shares of preferred stock. Common stock is currently selling at $46 per share; preferred stock has no current market value. The building is appraised at $180,000.
4. Sells 1,000 shares of common stock at $45 per share.

5. Sells 900 shares of preferred stock at $112 per share.
6. Declares a two-for-one stock split on the common stock, reducing the stated value to $2.50 per share.

Required Prepare journal entries to record the preceding transactions.

E15-15   *Contributed Capital*   The following is a list of selected accounts and ending account balances taken from the books of the Adams Company on December 31, 2004:

Account Title	Amount
Premium on preferred stock	$ 17,000
Common stock	75,000
Premium on bonds payable	4,000
Preferred stock	80,000
Bonds payable	100,000
Preferred stock subscribed	20,000
Retained earnings	121,000
Premium on common stock	84,000

Additional information:

1. Common stock has a $5 par value, 50,000 shares are authorized, 15,000 shares have been issued and are outstanding.
2. Preferred stock has a $100 par value, 3,000 shares are authorized, 800 shares have been issued and are outstanding. Two hundred shares have been subscribed at $120 per share. The stock pays an 8% dividend, is cumulative and callable at $130 per share.
3. Bonds payable mature on January 1, 2008. They carry a 12% annual interest rate, payable semiannually.

Required Prepare the contributed capital section of the December 31, 2004 balance sheet for the Adams Company. Include appropriate parenthetical notes.

E15-16   *Treasury Stock, Cost Method*   On January 1 the Sanders Corporation had 1,000 shares of $10 par common stock authorized and outstanding. These shares were originally issued at a price of $26 per share. In addition, 500 shares of $50 par preferred stock were outstanding. These were issued at a price of $75 per share. During the year the following stock transactions occurred:

1. March 3: Sanders Corporation reacquired 100 shares of its own common stock at a cost of $24 per share.
2. April 27: It sold 25 shares of the stock acquired on March 3 for $30 per share.
3. July 10: It sold 25 shares of the stock acquired on March 3 for $22 per share.
4. October 12: It retired the remaining shares acquired on March 3.

Required Prepare journal entries to record the treasury stock transactions assuming the cost method is used.

E15-17   *Treasury Stock, Par Value Method*   The records of TMP Incorporated provide the following information on January 1, 2004:

Preferred stock, $50 par (5,000 shares authorized, issued, and outstanding)	$250,000
Common stock, $10 par (20,000 shares authorized, 10,000 shares issued and outstanding)	100,000
Additional paid-in capital on preferred stock	50,000
Additional paid-in capital on common stock	80,000
Retained earnings	95,000

During 2004 the following transactions were recorded by TMP:

1. Reacquired 250 shares of preferred stock for $53 per share.
2. Reacquired 500 shares of common stock for $20 per share.
3. Sold 200 shares of the common stock acquired in (2) for $27 per share.
4. Sold 250 shares of preferred stock acquired in (1) for $59 per share.
5. Sold 100 shares of the common stock acquired in (2) for $18 per share.

Required

1. Prepare journal entries to record the stock transactions of TMP Incorporated, assuming the par value method of accounting for treasury stock is used.
2. Prepare the stockholders' equity section of the TMP balance sheet at December 31, 2004 (assume 2004 net income was $30,000 and dividends distributed were $10,000).

E15-18 *Treasury Stock, Cost and Par Value Methods* On January 1 the West Company had outstanding 10,000 shares of $10 par common stock, which had been originally issued at an average price of $35 per share. During the year the company engaged in the following treasury stock transactions:

1. Reacquired 1,000 shares of its common stock for $33 per share.
2. Reissued 600 shares of the treasury stock for $35 per share.
3. Reissued 300 shares of the treasury stock for $32 per share.
4. Retired the remaining 100 shares of treasury stock.

Required Prepare journal entries to record the preceding treasury stock transactions assuming use of (1) the cost method and (2) the par value method.

E15-19 *Treasury Stock, No Par* The following information is taken from the accounting records of the Propst-Steele Production Corporation:

1. Issued 5,000 shares of no-par common stock at $15 per share.
2. Issued an additional 5,000 shares of no-par common stock at $17 per share.
3. Reacquired 500 shares of its no-par common stock at a cost of $12.50 per share.
4. Reissued 200 of its treasury shares at $14 per share.
5. Reissued the remaining treasury shares at $11 per share.

Required Prepare journal entries to account for the preceding stock transactions on the books of the Propst-Steele Production Corporation using the cost method for treasury stock.

PROBLEMS

P15-1 *Issuances of Stock* The Cada Corporation is authorized to issue 10,000 shares of $100 par, convertible, callable preferred stock and 80,000 shares of no-par, no-stated-value common stock. There are currently 7,000 shares of preferred and 30,000 shares of common stock outstanding. The following are several *alternative* transactions:

1. Purchased land by issuing 640 shares of preferred stock and 1,000 shares of common stock. Preferred and common are currently selling at $113 and $36 per share, respectively. No reliable appraisal of the land is available.
2. Same as transaction 1, except that land is appraised at $104,000 and the preferred stock has no current market value.
3. Issued, for $99,000 cash, a combination of 400 shares of preferred stock and bonds payable with a face value of $50,000. Currently, the preferred stock is selling for $120 per share and the bonds at 104.
4. Same as transaction 3, except that the bonds do not have a current market value.
5. Same as transaction 3, except that the preferred stock does not have a current market value.
6. Preferred stockholders (who had originally paid the corporation $110 per share for their stock) convert 6,500 preferred shares into 19,500 shares of common stock. The current market prices of the preferred stock and the common stock are $120 and $41 per share, respectively.
7. The corporation calls the 7,000 shares of preferred stock (originally issued at $110 per share) at $123 per share. Common stock is currently selling for $42 per share. Stockholders elect *not* to convert into common stock.
8. Same as transaction 7, except that stockholders owning 2,000 shares of preferred stock elect to convert each share into three shares of common stock. The remaining 5,000 preferred shares are retired.

Required Prepare the journal entry necessary to record each transaction. Below each entry, explain your reason for the values used.

P15-2 *Issuances of Stock* The Epple Corporation is authorized to issue 20,000 shares of $100 par, convertible, callable preferred stock and 100,000 shares of $10 stated value common stock. Currently, the company has outstanding 6,000 shares of preferred stock and 40,000 shares of common stock. The following are several *alternative* transactions:

1. Acquired a patent by issuing 2,500 shares of common stock and bonds with the face value of $100,000. The stock is currently selling for $27 per share and the bonds are selling at 98.
2. Sold, for $96,000 cash, a "package" consisting of 500 shares of preferred stock and 2,000 shares of common stock. Currently, the preferred and common stock are independently selling for $112 and $22 per share, respectively.

3. Purchased land by issuing 300 shares of preferred stock and 1,000 shares of common stock. The common stock is selling for $25 per share, but the preferred stock is not being actively traded. The value of the land is appraised at $57,000.
4. The corporation calls the 6,000 shares of preferred stock (originally issued at $108 per share) at a call price of $112 per share. Common stock is currently selling for $23 per share. The stockholders elect *not* to convert into common stock.
5. Same as transaction 4, except that stockholders owning 4,000 shares of preferred stock elect to convert each share into five shares of common stock. The remaining 2,000 shares of preferred stock are retired.
6. Upon approval by the state, the board of directors decides to split the common stock two for one, reducing the stated value to $5 per share and increasing the authorization to 200,000 shares (remember, only 40,000 shares are issued and outstanding).
7. Same as transaction 6, except that the stated value is reduced to $4 per share.

Required Prepare the journal entry necessary to record each transaction. Below each entry, explain your reason for the values used.

P15-3   *Subscriptions*   On August 3, 2004, the date of incorporation, the Quinn Company accepts separate subscriptions for 1,000 shares of $100 par preferred stock at $104 per share and 9,000 shares of no-par, no-stated-value common stock for $22 per share. The subscription contracts require a 10% down payment, with the balance due by November 1, 2004. Shares are issued to each subscriber upon full payment. Any defaulted shares will be sold on November 2, 2004, and the down payment returned to the defaulting subscribers.

   On November 1, the company received the remaining balances for 920 shares of preferred stock and 8,900 shares of common stock. The defaulted preferred shares and common shares were sold for $105 and $22.50 per share, respectively, on November 2, and the down payment was returned to the defaulting subscribers.

Required Prepare journal entries to record all the transactions related to
1. The preferred stock
2. The common stock

P15-4   *Subscriptions*   On July 3 the Wallace Company enters into a subscription contract with various investors. Terms of the contract are as follows:
1. Number of shares: 10,000 shares of no-par, $6 stated-value common stock.
2. Price and payment schedule: Subscription price is $13 per share. A $3 per share down payment is required, with a $5 per share payment due on both August 3 and October 3. Shares are issued to each subscriber upon full payment.
3. Default provisions: Defaulted shares are to be sold on October 4 at the then-current market price. If the proceeds from this sale are less than the total subscription price of the defaulted shares, an amount necessary to bring the proceeds up to the total subscription price is to be withheld from defaulted subscribers. Any remaining payments received from defaulted subscribers are to be returned to them.

Required Record the July 3, August 3, and the October 3 and 4 journal entries, assuming that a subscriber to 500 shares of stock defaulted after making the down payment. The 500 shares were sold on October 4 for $11 per share.

P15-5   *Stock Rights to Stockholders*   The Nichols Electronics Corporation has been experiencing a steadily growing demand for its products. In order to meet this demand, a major expansion of production facilities is necessary. The company plans to raise the money for this proposed expansion by issuing 10,000 shares of $50 par preferred stock and 50,000 shares of $10 par common stock. These shares were previously authorized but have not yet been issued.

   There are presently 200,000 shares of $10 par common stock issued and outstanding. In order that the preemptive right of the current stockholders be maintained, the board of directors authorizes the issuance of stock rights to the current common stockholders on March 2, 2004. The current market price of the common stock at this date is $24 per share. Each common stockholder is to receive one stock warrant for each share of common stock owned. One additional share of common stock may be purchased at any time prior to April 7, 2004 for $23 and four of the stock warrants.

   There are presently 20,000 shares of the $50 par preferred stock issued and outstanding. They were selling for $78 per share on March 4, 2004. No preemptive right applies to the preferred stock. In order to assure the sale of the additional 10,000 shares of the preferred stock, the board of directors also authorizes one stock warrant to be attached to each share of preferred stock in the new issue. One of these stock warrants allows the preferred stockholder to purchase one share of $10 par common stock for $18 per share at any time prior to April 7, 2004. The preferred shares with warrants attached are issued on March 5, 2004 at a price of $83 per share. The warrants begin trading in the market at $6 each.

Required

1. Prepare the entry to record the issuance of the common stock warrants on March 2, 2004.
2. Prepare journal entries to record the following transactions:
   a. The sale of the 10,000 shares of $50 par preferred stock with detachable warrants on March 5, 2004.
   b. The exercise on March 19, 2004 of 6,000 of the stock warrants that had been attached to the preferred stock (the common stock price is currently $24 per share and the preferred stock is selling ex rights for $79 per share).
   c. The exercise on April 2, 2004 of 120,000 stock warrants issued in conjunction with the preemptive right (the common stock is currently selling at $23.50 per share).
   d. 4,000 stock warrants related to the preferred stock and 80,000 stock warrants related to the preemptive right expire on April 6, 2004.

P15-6   *Fixed Compensatory Stock Option Plan*   On January 1, 2004 Roswall Corporation's common stock is selling for $55 per share. On this date, Roswall creates a compensatory stock option plan for its 60 key employees. The plan document states that each employee may purchase 500 shares of its $10 par common stock for $55 per share after working for the company for three years. On this date, based on the Black-Scholes option pricing model, Roswall estimates that each option has a value of $18. Historically, Roswall has experienced an employee turnover rate of 5% per year and, on the grant date, it expects this rate to continue over the next three years. Because of lower turnover, at the end of 2005 Roswall changes its estimated turnover rate to 4% for the entire service period. At the end of 2006, the stock options vest for 54 employees. On January 13, 2007, ten executives exercise their options when the stock is selling for $75 per share. Roswall uses the fair value method to account for this plan.

Required

1. Prepare a schedule of the Roswall Corporation's compensation computations for its compensatory stock option plan for 2004 through 2006 (round all computations to the nearest dollar).
2. Prepare the journal entries of Roswall Corporation for 2004 through 2007 in regard to this plan.
3. Show how the account(s) related to the plan is (are) reported in the stockholders' equity section of Roswall Corporation's balance sheet on December 31, 2005.
4. If Roswall Corporation uses the intrinsic value method *instead* of the fair value method to account for this plan, what would be its total compensation cost on the date of grant and how would it disclose its compensation expense for 2004?

P15-7   *Performance-Based Compensatory Stock Option Plan*   Connors Company has 70 executives to whom it grants
@   compensatory stock options on January 1, 2004. The plan grants each executive options to acquire a maximum of 100 shares of the company's $5 par common stock at $50 per share after completing three years of continuous service. However, the number of stock options that vest depends on the increase in the company's market share over the 3-year period. The following schedule shows the number of options granted to each executive based on the increase in market share by the end of the service period:

Increase in Market Share	Number of Stock Options Granted
0 to 4%	40
5 to 8%	60
More than 8%	100

Based on past trends, on the grant date Connors predicts that its market share will increase about 3% by the end of 2006. At the end of 2005, due to improved market position over the previous 2 years, Connors revises this estimate to 7%. At the end of 2006, Connors determines that its market share has increased 9% over the 3-year period.

On the grant date, Connors Company estimates that (1) the fair value of each option is $16.25, and (2) its employee turnover rate will be 3% per year over the service period. At the end of 2005; because of increased resignations, Connors changes its estimated turnover rate to 5% for each year in the service period. At the end of 2006, 59 executives vest in the plan. On January 17, 2007, thirty executives exercise their stock options when the stock is selling for $68 per share. Connors uses the fair value method to account for this plan.

Required

1. Prepare a schedule of the Connors Company's compensation computations for its compensatory stock option plan for 2004 through 2006 (round all computations to the nearest dollar).
2. Prepare the journal entries of Connors Company for 2004 through 2007 in regard to this plan.
3. Show how the account(s) related to the plan is (are) reported in the stockholders' equity section of Connors Company's balance sheet on December 31, 2005.

4. Do you see a problem with your answer to Requirement 3 and the eventual value of the vested stock options? How might this problem be avoided?

See WebTutor for annotated problem solution.

P15-8   *Performance-Based Compensatory Stock Option Plan*   On January 1, 2004 Pierce Company establishes a performance-based stock option plan for its 80 top executives. The terms of the plan are that each executive is granted a maximum of 200 options after completing a 3-year service period. The exact number of options granted, however, depends on the percentage increase in sales over the 3-year period. The terms are: (1) if sales increase between 0 and 3%, each executive is granted 90 options; (2) if, instead, sales increase between 4 and 6%, each executive is granted 140 options; and (3) if, instead, sales increase at least 7%, each executive is granted the maximum number of options. Each option entitles the executive to acquire one share of the company's $10 par common stock at a price of $45. The stock options expire at the end of 6 years.

On the grant date Pierce Company uses an option pricing model to estimate that the fair value of each stock option is $15.50. Pierce's employee turnover rate has averaged 6% per year and, on the grant date, it expects this rate to continue over the service period. At the end of 2005, because of lower turnover, Pierce revises its estimated annual turnover rate to 4% for the service period. At the end of 2006, stock options vest for 68 executives. On February 3, 2007, fifty executives exercise their stock options when the market price of the company's common stock is $62 per share. During the remainder of the year, the market price declines so that at the end of 2007 the other 18 executives allow their stock options to expire.

Based on a projection of past trends, on the grant date Pierce Company estimates that its sales will increase about 5% by the end of 2006. This estimate appears accurate through 2005. However, in the last half of 2006, sales increase so much that at the end of 2006 Pierce determines that its total sales have increased by 7% over the 3-year service period. All inventory is shipped by Pierce to its customers under FOB destination terms. Pierce uses the fair value method to account for this plan.

Required

1. Prepare a schedule of the Pierce Company's compensation computations for its compensatory stock option plan for 2004 through 2006 (round all computations to the nearest dollar).
2. Prepare the journal entries of Pierce Company for 2004 through 2007 in regard to this plan.
3. Show how the account(s) related to the plan is (are) reported in the stockholders' equity section of Pierce Company's December 31, 2005 balance sheet.
4. Do you see any problems with the way the terms of Pierce Company's compensatory stock option plan are structured? Explain.

P15-9   *Stock Appreciation Rights*   Smythe Company has a stock appreciation rights plan for its key executives. This SAR plan allows each qualifying executive to receive cash, stock, or a combination of both equal to the excess of the quoted market price over the option price of the company's $10 par common stock on the date of exercise. The key characteristics and requirements of this SAR plan are as follows:

Option price: Market price on date of grant
Service period: 4 years
Exercise limit: Within 6 years

On January 1, 2003 Sarah Mendelson was granted SARs to 3,000 shares of the company's common stock under the requirements of the SAR plan. On January 1, 2004 Donald Freeman was granted SARs to 4,000 shares under the requirements of the plan. Both executives are expected to complete the service period and receive cash on the date of exercise. On December 31, 2007 Mendelson exercised her rights to receive cash, while Freeman exercised his rights to receive $1,400 cash and the remainder in common stock. The quoted market prices per share of the company's common stock are as follows: 12/31/02, $16.00; 12/31/03, $20.00; 12/31/04, $21.00; 12/31/05, $20.80; 12/31/06, $21.50; and 12/31/07, $22.00.

Required

1. Prepare a schedule to compute the compensation expense related to this SAR plan for 2003 through 2007.
2. Prepare the journal entries related to the SAR plan on December 31, 2003 through December 31, 2007.

P15-10   *Comprehensive*   The Young Corporation has been operating successfully for several years. It is authorized to issue 24,000 shares of no-par common stock and 6,000 shares of 8%, $100 par preferred stock. The Contributed Capital section of its January 1, 2004 balance sheet is as follows:

8% preferred stock, $100 par	$190,000
Common stock, no par	184,000
Premium on preferred stock	15,200
	$389,200

Part a. A stockholder has raised the following questions:

1. What is the legal capital of the corporation?
2. At what average price per share has the preferred stock been issued?
3. How many shares of common stock have been issued (the common stock has been issued at an average price of $23 per share)?

Part b. The company engaged in the following transactions in 2004:

Mar. 2	Received a subscription to 400 shares of the 8% preferred stock. The total subscription price is $122 per share and the contract requires a $10 per share down payment. The remaining balance must be paid within 60 days or the stock subscription is defaulted. In the case of default, 20% of the down payment on the defaulted shares is forfeited, and the remainder is returned to the defaulting subscribers.
Apr. 5	Sold 900 shares of common stock for $34 per share.
Apr. 13	Issued 400 shares of common stock in exchange for land. The stock is currently selling at $33 per share.
Apr. 30	Received remaining subscription balance (from March 2) owed on 350 shares of preferred stock and issued the stock.
May 4	Returned 80% of their down payment to defaulting subscribers and canceled the related account balances.
June 1	Reacquired 500 shares of common stock at $36 per share. The company uses the cost method to account for treasury stock.
Oct. 19	Issued for $27,000 a combination of 500 shares of common stock and 100 shares of preferred stock. The common and preferred stock are currently selling for $35 and $125 per share, respectively.
Nov.16	Reissued the 500 shares of treasury stock at $38 per share.
Dec. 31	Distributed an $8 per share dividend on all preferred stock outstanding and a $2 per share dividend on all common stock outstanding on this date (debit Retained Earnings and credit Cash for each dividend).

Required

1. Answer the questions in part *a*.
2. Prepare journal entries to record the transactions in part *b*.
3. Prepare the contributed capital section of Young's December 31, 2004 balance sheet.

P15-11 *Comprehensive* The Byrd Company's Contributed Capital section of its January 1, 2004 balance sheet is as follows:

Preferred stock (6%, $50 par, 8,000 shares authorized, 3,400 shares issued and outstanding)	$170,000
Common stock ($10 stated value, 30,000 shares authorized, 12,000 shares issued and outstanding)	120,000
Preferred stock subscribed (800 shares subscribed at $54 per share)	40,000
Additional paid-in capital on preferred stock	12,800
Additional paid-in capital on common stock	72,000
Total contributed capital	$414,800

During 2004 the company entered into the following transactions:

Jan. 3	Established a compensatory stock option plan for its key executives. The options vest after a 3-year service period. The estimated fair value of the options expected to be exercised is $81,000.
Mar. 6	Received the remaining $40 per share on the subscribed preferred stock and issued the shares.
Apr. 24	Sold 300 shares of preferred stock at $55 per share.
May 5	Received a subscription down payment of $6 per share on 1,000 shares of common stock. The remaining $11 per share balance is due in 60 days.
June 7	Sold 600 shares of common stock at $17 per share.
July 3	Received the remaining balance on subscribed common stock and issued the shares.
Sept. 22	Purchased building by paying $9,000 cash and issuing 800 shares of common stock and 450 shares of preferred stock. Common and preferred stock are currently selling for $19 and $57 per share, respectively.

Oct. 13   Reacquired 900 shares of common stock at $19.50 per share. The company uses the cost method to account for treasury stock.

Nov. 15   Issued for $32,000 a combination of 700 shares of common stock and 12% bonds with a face value of $20,000. The common stock is currently selling for $18 per share. No market value exists for the bonds.

Dec. 15   Reissued the 900 shares of treasury stock at $20.50 per share.

Dec. 29   Distributed a $3.00 per share dividend to all outstanding preferred stock and a $1.50 per share dividend to all common stock outstanding on this date (debit Retained Earnings and credit Cash for each dividend).

Dec. 30   Declared a two-for-one stock split on the common stock, reducing the stated value to $4 per share and increasing the authorized shares to 60,000.

Required

1. Prepare journal entries to record the preceding transactions.
2. Prepare the contributed capital section of Byrd's December 31, 2004 balance sheet.

P15-12   **Contributed Capital**   A partial list of the accounts and ending account balances taken from the postclosing trial balance of the Jordan Corporation on December 31, 2004 is shown as follows:

Account Title	Amount
Retained earnings	$410,000
Bonds payable	220,000
Common stock subscribed	60,000
Long-term investments in stock	210,000
Additional paid-in capital on common stock	460,000
Premium on bonds payable	30,000
Common stock	500,000
Preferred stock subscribed	35,000
Additional paid-in capital on preferred stock	112,000
Preferred stock	300,000
Additional paid-in capital from treasury stock	4,000
Unrealized increase in value of securities available for sale	3,000
Common stock option warrants	20,000

Additional information:

1. Common stock is no-par, with a stated value of $10 per share, 90,000 shares are authorized, 50,000 shares are issued and outstanding, 6,000 shares have been subscribed at a price of $28 per share.
2. Preferred stock has a $50 par value, 8,000 shares are authorized, 6,000 shares are issued and outstanding, 700 shares have been subscribed at a price of $70 per share. Each share is cumulative, convertible into five shares of common stock, and pays a 7% annual dividend. Dividends are not in arrears.
3. Bonds payable mature on July 1, 2016. They carry a 12% annual interest rate, payable semiannually. The premium is being amortized using the straight-line method.

Required Prepare the contributed capital section of the December 31, 2004 balance sheet for the Jordan Corporation. Include appropriate parenthetical notes for the common and preferred stock.

P15-13   **Contributed Capital**   The following is a partial list of the accounts and ending account balances taken from the post-closing trial balance of the Clett Corporation on December 31, 2004:

Common stock subscribed	$ 10,000	Long-term investments in	
Premium on bonds payable	50,000	preferred stock	$ 90,000
Preferred stock	400,000	Preferred stock subscribed	100,000
Temporary investments in common stock	110,000	Retained earnings	610,000
Bonds payable	500,000	Premium on common stock	542,000
Common stock	150,000	Unrealized decrease in value of	
Premium on preferred stock	76,000	securities available for sale	6,000

Additional information:

1. Bonds payable mature on December 31, 2019. They carry a 12% interest rate, payable semiannually. The premium is being amortized using the straight-line method.

2. The 7.5% preferred stock is cumulative and convertible into 3 shares of common stock. It has a par value of $100 per share, 20,000 shares are authorized, 4,000 shares are issued and outstanding, 1,000 shares have been subscribed at $125 per share.

3. Common stock has a par value of $5 per share, 100,000 shares are authorized, 30,000 shares are issued and outstanding, 2,000 shares have been subscribed at $41 per share.

Required Prepare the contributed capital section of the December 31, 2004 balance sheet for the Clett Corporation. Include appropriate parenthetical notes for the common and preferred stock.

P15-14   *Reconstruct Journal Entries*   At the end of its first year of operations, the Leo Company lists the following accounts and ending account balances related to stock transactions and dividends:

| | Balance | |
Account	Debit	Credit
Cash (from stock and for dividends paid)	$250,000	
Subscriptions receivable: common stock	14,000	
Subscriptions receivable: preferred stock	33,600	
Equipment	69,000	
Preferred stock subscribed (for 300 shares)		$ 30,000
8% preferred stock, $100 par (2,300 shares)		230,000
Additional paid-in capital on preferred stock		33,000
Common stock subscribed (2,000 shares)		10,000
Common stock, $5 stated value (9,000 shares)		45,000
Additional paid-in capital on common stock		46,000
Retained earnings		2,600

During the first year the following events occurred:

1. Subscription contracts were entered into for common stock at $9 per share and preferred stock at $112 per share. Common stock subscriptions required a $2 per share down payment. Preferred stock subscriptions required no down payment. Shares (either common or preferred) were issued to subscribers upon full payment.

2. One thousand shares of common stock were sold for $11 per share, and the stock was issued to stockholders.

3. Equipment with an appraised value of $69,000 was acquired by issuing 600 shares of preferred stock. The appraised value of the equipment was used to record the transaction.

4. Net income of $30,000 was closed to Retained Earnings from Income Summary at the end of the year.

5. Dividends of $8 per share on all the preferred stock outstanding and $1 per share on all the common stock outstanding were distributed at the end of the year (the company debited Retained Earnings and credited Cash for each dividend).

Required On the basis of the preceding information, reconstruct all the journal entries that the company made to record the stock transactions, net income, and dividends.

P15-15   *Treasury Stock, Alternative Methods*   Bush-Caine Company reported the following data on its December 31, 2003 balance sheet:

Preferred stock, $50 par	$50,000	Common stock, $10 par	$100,000
Additional paid-in capital on		Additional paid-in capital on common stock	80,000
preferred stock	4,000	Retained earnings	95,000

The following transactions were reported by the company during 2004:

1. Reacquired 200 shares of its preferred stock at $57 per share.
2. Reacquired 500 shares of its common stock at $16 per share.
3. Sold 100 shares of preferred treasury stock at $58 per share.
4. Sold 200 shares of common treasury stock at $17 per share.
5. Sold 100 shares of common treasury stock at $9 per share.
6. Retired the shares of common stock remaining in the treasury.

The company maintains separate treasury stock accounts and related additional paid-in capital accounts for each class of stock.

Required

1. Prepare the journal entries required to record the treasury stock transactions using (a) the cost method, and (b) the par value method.
2. Assuming the company earned a net income in 2004 of $30,000 and declared and paid dividends of $10,000, prepare the stockholders' equity section of its balance sheet at December 31, 2004 (a) using the cost method to account for treasury stock, and (b) using the par value method to account for treasury stock.

P15-16   *Treasury Stock Analysis*   The Ray Holt Company has retained you as a consultant on accounting policies and procedure. During 2004 the company engaged in a number of treasury stock transactions, having foreseen an opportunity to realize a profit in trading its own stock. The transactions were as follows:

1. Reacquired 100 shares of its $10 par common stock at $20 per share. The shares had originally been issued at $23 per share.
2. Reacquired 150 shares of its $10 par common stock at $24 per share. The shares had originally been issued at $23 per share.
3. Reacquired 50 shares of its $100 par preferred stock at $140 per share. The shares had originally been issued at $170 per share.
4. Sold all common treasury shares held at $25 per share.
5. Reacquired 150 shares of its $100 par preferred stock at $130 per share. The shares had originally been issued at $170 per share.
6. Retired all preferred shares held in the treasury.

Required

1. Is the company correct in assuming a profit or gain is to be realized from treasury stock transactions? Explain.
2. Prepare an analysis of treasury stock accounting for Mr. Robert Richter, the controller. This analysis should contain proper journal entries for each of the treasury stock transactions occurring during 2004, prepared using (a) the cost method and (b) the par value method discussed in the chapter.
3. Conclude the analysis with your assessment of the strengths and weaknesses of each method of accounting for treasury stock.

P15-17   *Comprehensive*   Udall Corporation's post-closing trial balance at December 31, 2004 was as follows:

	Debit	Credit
Accounts payable		$ 290,000
Accounts receivable	$ 550,000	
Accumulated depreciation—building and equipment		200,000
Additional paid-in capital—common		
In excess of par value		1,560,000
From sale of treasury stock		250,000
Allowance for doubtful accounts		30,000
Bonds payable		400,000
Building and equipment	1,100,000	
Cash	220,000	
Common stock ($1 par value)		150,000
Dividends payable on preferred stock—cash		4,000
Inventories	620,000	
Land	380,000	
Long-term equity securities (at market)	285,000	
Marketable equity securities (at market)	215,000	
Preferred stock ($50 par value)		500,000
Prepaid expenses	40,000	
Retained earnings		231,000
Treasury stock—common (at cost)	180,000	
Unrealized decrease in value of available-for-sale securities	25,000	
Totals	$3,615,000	$3,615,000

At December 31, 2004 Udall had the following number of common and preferred shares:

	Common	Preferred
Authorized	500,000	50,000
Issued	150,000	10,000
Outstanding	140,000	10,000

The dividends on preferred stock are $4 cumulative. In addition, the preferred stock has a preference in liquidation of $50 per share.

Required Prepare the stockholders' equity section of Udall's balance sheet at December 31, 2004. (*AICPA adapted*)

INTERNET ASSIGNMENTS

Go to the Nikolai and Bazley **Intermediate Accounting** web site (http://Nikolai.swcollege.com). Click on Student Resources and <u>internet</u> <u>homework</u> <u>assignments</u>. Then click on the appropriate hot link (icon) for each company's web site, find the relevant accounting information, and answer the following questions.

I15-1   Go to the **3M** web site.

      Required What were the company's net income and earnings per share for the most current year? What method does the company use to account for its Management Stock Ownership Program (MSOP)? What would the company's net income and earnings per share have been if the company had been using the fair value method for its MSOP? Do you think these differences in net income and earnings per share are significant? Explain. What was the weighted-average exercise price per option exercised during the most current year for the MSOP? What was the price per share of the company's common stock at the end of the most current year? Do you think the options granted under the MSOP are valuable to the company's executives? Explain.

I15-2   Go to the **Citigroup** web site.

      Required What is the par value per share of the company's preferred stock? How many shares were authorized and outstanding at the end of the most current year? How many "series" of preferred stock were outstanding at the end of the most current year and what is the dividend rate on each series? How do these preferred stock series affect the company's risk and financial flexibility? How many shares of treasury stock did the company hold at the end of the most current year? How many shares of treasury stock were issued (and for what purpose) and acquired during the most current year?

objectives

1 Know the equation for computing basic earnings per share (EPS).

2 Understand how to compute the weighted average common shares for EPS.

3 Identify the potential common shares included in diluted EPS.

4 Apply the treasury stock method for including stock options and warrants in diluted EPS.

5 Calculate the impact of a convertible security on diluted EPS.

6 Compute diluted EPS.

7 Record the declaration and payment of cash dividends.

8 Account for a property dividend.

9 Explain the difference in accounting for small and large stock dividends.

10 Understand how to report accumulated other comprehensive income.

11 Prepare a statement of changes in stockholders' equity.

12 Account for a quasi-reorganization (Appendix).

CHAPTER

Earnings Per Share and Retained Earnings

16

In the previous chapter we introduced the topic of stockholders' equity by discussing the contributed capital that arises from the issuance of capital stock in a variety of exchange transactions. We also discussed the impact of the reacquisition of a corporation's capital stock (treasury stock) on stockholders' equity. In this chapter we continue the discussion of stockholders' equity by focusing primarily on retained earnings. The chapter begins with a discussion of earnings per share (EPS) because its computation involves items of contributed capital (common stock) and retained earnings (net income). The chapter then moves to a discussion of items affecting retained earnings, such as dividends, prior period adjustments, and appropriations. We conclude the chapter with a discussion of the statement of retained earnings, other changes in stockholders' equity, and the statement of changes in stockholders' equity. We include a discussion of quasi-reorganizations in the chapter Appendix.

EARNINGS AND EARNINGS PER SHARE

Net income (loss) is the amount of earnings resulting from a corporation's income-producing activities during its accounting period. A corporation summarizes the various components of its net income on its income statement. As we discussed in Chapter 4, the primary components are: (1) **income (loss) from continuing operations,** which combines ongoing operating revenues, offset by operating expenses, with nonoperating revenues and expenses, and the unusual *or* infrequent gains or losses resulting from nonextraordinary transactions; (2) **results from discontinued operations,** which includes the income (loss) from the operations of a discontinued component as well as the gain (loss) from the disposal of the discontinued component (3) **extraordinary gains or losses,** the results of unusual *and* infrequent events; and (4) the **cumulative effects of changes in accounting principles.** A corporation also includes its earnings per share on its income statement.

Corporations have been required to disclose earnings per share information for many years. **APB Opinion No. 15** originally contained the standards for calculating and reporting earnings per share. It required corporations to report "primary earnings per share" and "fully diluted earnings per share." Some of its standards, however, were very complex. To simplify the standards and to help make U.S. and international standards consistent, the FASB issued **FASB Statement No. 128** entitled "Earnings Per Share." We discuss the major issues involved in computing and reporting earnings per share in the following sections.

CONCEPTUAL OVERVIEW AND USES OF EARNINGS PER SHARE INFORMATION

All the information included in a corporation's financial statements and the related notes should be useful to external decision makers. Most users, however, focus on selected items that they consider to be of greatest *relevance*. Earnings per share is one measure that is very important to most users. It often is considered to be the measure that best summarizes the performance of a corporation, particularly for common shareholders. Earnings per share information is helpful to these users in evaluating the *return on investment* and *risk* of a corporation.

The amount of earnings per share, the change in earnings per share from the previous period, and the trend in earnings per share are all important indicators of the success, or failure, of the corporation. Many investors also are interested in the corporation's cash flow per share. Although corporations are prohibited from reporting cash flow per share, as we discuss in Chapter 21 earnings per share may be considered to be a long-run indicator of cash flow per share.

One ratio used to evaluate return and risk is the price/earnings ratio, which is often used in intercompany comparisons. To compute the price/earnings ratio, earnings per share is divided into the market price per share (of the common stock). For example, at the time of writing this book, two department stores, **Kohl's Corporation** and **Sears, Roebuck and Co.,** had price/earnings ratios of 45 and 20, respectively. Kohl's price/earnings ratio indicates that the stock is selling for a price of 45 times the most recent year's earnings per share. The difference in the ratios indicates that compared to Sears' price/earnings ratio, investors are more optimistic about the future of Kohl's and expect that it will experience a higher growth in earnings per share.

Investors often are interested in predicting earnings per share for future periods. While accountants generally do not provide information about the future, one required earnings per share computation is intended to indicate the potential impacts of possible future events. When a corporation has issued common stock options (discussed in Chapter 15), convertible debt (discussed in Chapter 13), or convertible preferred stock (discussed in Chapter 15), it will issue additional common shares when the options are exercised or the securities converted, thereby affecting earnings per share. Diluted earnings per share (which we define later) includes the potential effects of such conversions. Also, earnings per share may be computed on past reported earnings, or on future earnings as estimated by financial analysts. Given these possibilities, when using earnings per share information (e.g., price/earnings ratios) for intercompany comparisons, a user must be sure that the calculations are *comparable*. A corporation with common stock options, convertible debt, and/or convertible preferred stock is said to have a complex capital structure; we begin by discussing earnings per share for a corporation with a basic capital structure.

The price/earnings ratio is discussed in Chapter 5.

BASIC EARNINGS PER SHARE

For purposes of computing earnings per share, there are two types of corporate capital structures—simple and complex. **A simple capital structure is one that consists only of common stock outstanding.** A corporation with a simple capital structure is required to report basic earnings per share.[1] The **basic earnings per share** computation is as follows:

1 Know the equation for computing basic earnings per share (EPS).

$$\text{Basic Earnings Per Share} = \frac{\text{Net Income} - \text{Preferred Dividends}}{\text{Weighted Average Number of Common Shares Outstanding}}$$

---

1. "Earnings per Share," *FASB Statement of Financial Accounting Standards No. 128* (Norwalk, Conn.: FASB, 1997), par 36. A corporation also has a simple capital structure if it has nonconvertible preferred stock outstanding, in addition to its common stock.

A corporation reports the resulting basic earnings per share (or, in the case of a net loss, the basic loss per share) on its income statement, directly below net income. It also reports basic earnings per share for each comparative income statement presented.

Even in this relatively simple calculation, several complexities arise. Although we discuss these complexities within the basic earnings per share framework, they are also applicable to corporations that report diluted earnings per share (which we discuss in a later section).

Numerator Calculations

Only the amount of *earnings available to common stockholders* is used in the numerator of the earnings per share computation. If a corporation has outstanding *noncumulative* preferred stock, it deducts the dividends declared during the current period from the net income to determine the earnings available to common stockholders. If the corporation has *cumulative* preferred stock outstanding, it deducts the dividends for the *current* period, *whether declared or not*. It discloses the amount of the deduction in the notes to its financial statements.

Denominator Calculations

WEIGHTED AVERAGE SHARES Since a corporation earns its net income over the entire year, the earnings are related to the common shares outstanding during the year. Thus, the denominator of the equation is the weighted average number of common shares outstanding. The corporation discloses this number in the notes to its financial statements. If a corporation has not issued or reacquired any shares during the year, it uses the number of common shares outstanding at the end of the accounting period as the weighted average. If a corporation has issued or reacquired common shares during the period, it bases the denominator on the weighted average number of common shares outstanding during the period.

A corporation calculates the weighted average by starting with the actual number of common shares outstanding at the beginning of the period and multiplying this "layer" of shares by the fraction of the year it is outstanding until more common stock is issued (or shares are reacquired). These new shares are added to (or subtracted from) the actual beginning number of outstanding shares, and the new layer is multiplied by the fraction of the year it is outstanding. This process is continued for all the issuances of common stock during the year. The resulting "equivalent whole units" of stock for all the layers are summed to determine the weighted average number of common shares. To illustrate, assume a corporation had 12,000 shares of common stock outstanding at the beginning of the year. On March 2, it issued 2,700 shares; on July 3, it issued another 3,300 shares; and on December 1, it reacquired 480 shares as treasury stock. The weighted average number of common shares the corporation uses in computing its earnings per share is 15,860 shares, as we compute in Exhibit 16-1. Note that for simplicity, the nearest whole month is used to determine the fraction of the year each layer of shares was outstanding.

2 Understand how to compute the weighted average common shares for EPS.

EXHIBIT 16-1 Weighted Average Shares

Months Shares Are Outstanding	Shares Outstanding	×	Fraction of Year Outstanding	=	Equivalent Whole Units
January–February	12,000	×	2/12	=	2,000
March–June	14,700	×	4/12	=	4,900
July–November	18,000	×	5/12	=	7,500
December	17,520	×	1/12	=	1,460
		Total weighted average common shares			15,860

STOCK DIVIDENDS OR SPLITS When a corporation's common shares outstanding increase because of a stock dividend or stock split, it must give *retroactive* recognition to these events for all comparative income statements presented.[2] This retroactive adjustment results in comparable earnings per share amounts for all periods based on the most recent capital structure. The simplest way of giving retroactive recognition is to first assume (for earnings per share computations) that the stock dividend or split occurred at the *beginning* of the earliest comparative period. Then assume that all stock transactions between this beginning date and the *actual* date of the stock dividend or split included the additional shares resulting from the assumed dividend or split.

Suppose, for example, that a corporation begins operations in January 2004, and issues 5,000 shares of common stock that are outstanding during all of 2004. On December 31, 2004, it issues a two-for-one stock split. At the end of 2004, the weighted average number of shares that it uses in the earnings per share computation for 2004 is 10,000 (5,000 × 200% × 12/12) because the two-for-one stock split is *assumed* to have occurred on January 1, 2004. On May 28, 2005, the corporation issues 5,000 shares of common stock; on August 3, 2005, it issues a 20% stock dividend; and on October 5, 2005, it issues 2,000 shares of stock. At the end of 2005, when it reports comparative earnings per share for 2004 and 2005, the weighted average numbers of shares it uses in the computation are 12,000 shares for 2004 and 16,000 shares for 2005, as we show in Exhibit 16-2.

For comparative purposes at the end of 2005, the two-for-one stock split actually issued on December 31 *and* the 20% stock dividend actually issued on August 3, 2005 are both *assumed* to have been issued on January 1, 2004. Under this assumption, 12,000 shares of stock would have been outstanding during all of 2004. Similarly, during 2005, 12,000 shares initially would have been outstanding. The 5,000 shares issued on May 29 would have increased by 20% to 6,000 shares, resulting in 18,000 shares outstanding until October 5, 2005. The 2,000 shares issued on October 5, 2005 would *not* have increased because this issuance occurred *after* the actual stock dividend. The resulting weighted average number of shares is 16,000 at the end of 2005. Remember that the assumptions discussed earlier, although not reflecting the actual timing of the transactions, are necessary for a corporation to compute comparable earnings per share amounts for all its income statements presented.

EXHIBIT 16-2 Comparative Weighted Average Shares

Retroactive Recognition of Stock Split and Stock Dividend

Months Shares Are Outstanding	Actual Shares Outstanding	Assumed Shares Outstanding	×	Fraction of Year Outstanding	=	Equivalent Whole Units
2004						
January–December	5,000	5,000 × 200% × 120% = 12,000	×	12/12	=	12,000
2005						
January–May	10,000	10,000 × 120% = 12,000	×	5/12	=	5,000
June–July	15,000	15,000 × 120% = 18,000	×	2/12	=	3,000
August–September	18,000	15,000 × 120% = 18,000	×	2/12	=	3,000
October–December	20,000	15,000 × 120% + 2,000 = 20,000	×	3/12	=	5,000
						16,000

---

2. A corporation must also give retroactive recognition if the stock dividend or split occurs after the end of the accounting period but before it issues its financial statements.

Components of Earnings Per Share

Net income is the final earnings amount on a corporation's income statement. If the corporation includes any results from discontinued operations, extraordinary items, or the cumulative effects of changes in accounting principles in this amount, it is required to report separate earnings per share amounts for *both* income from continuing operations and net income on its income statement. It is also required to disclose the earnings per share related to any results from discontinued operations, extraordinary items, and the cumulative effects of changes in accounting principles. Each of these earnings per share component amounts is based upon the same weighted average number of shares. The corporation may report these component amounts on its income statement or in the notes to its financial statements.[3] When reported on the income statement, the components are summed to report the total earnings per share. The intent is to show the contribution of each income statement component to the total earnings per share. When a corporation has deducted preferred dividends in the computation of total earnings per share, it also deducts these dividends from the income related to continuing operations in order to reconcile the earnings per share amounts.

Example of Basic Earnings Per Share

Exhibit 16-3 shows the computation and disclosure of basic earnings per share (sometimes referred to as *earnings per common share*) for a corporation.

DILUTED EARNINGS PER SHARE

3 Identify the potential common shares included in diluted EPS.

Many corporations have a more complex capital structure, including securities such as stock options and warrants, convertible preferred stock and convertible bonds, participating securities and two-class stocks, and contingent shares. These securities are referred to as **potential common shares** because they can be used by the holder to acquire common stock. Since conversion of these securities into common stock would affect the earnings available to each common stockholder, they are considered in computing earnings per share.

Instead of a single earnings per share disclosure, **a corporation with a complex capital structure is required to report two earnings per share amounts on the face of its income statement.** The two amounts are basic earnings per share and diluted earnings per share. Basic earnings per share is computed as we discussed earlier for corporations with a basic capital structure. **Diluted earnings per share shows the earnings per share after including *all* potential common shares that would reduce earnings per share.** If a corporation has a *loss* from continuing operations, then it does **not** include potential common shares in diluted earnings per share (even if it reports net income). In this case, the corporation's basic and diluted earnings per share are the same.[4]

When a corporation with a complex capital structure computes diluted earnings per share, it must consider the impact of potential common shares in addition to the weighted average common shares calculation, stock dividends and stock split assumptions, and earnings presentations we discussed earlier. We discuss only the more common types of potential common shares—stock options and warrants, and convertible preferred stock and bonds—in this section.

To be included in the diluted earnings per share calculation, any potential common share must have a *dilutive* effect on (that is, decrease) earnings per share. Thus, a corporation may include a potential common share in the diluted earnings per share computation in one accounting period and not in another. Consequently, an

---

3. *FASB Statement of Financial Accounting Standards No. 128, op. cit.*, par. 37. These disclosures are also required for diluted earnings per share, as we discuss later.
4. *Ibid.*, par. 11 and 16.

EXHIBIT 16-3   **Computation and Disclosure of Basic Earnings Per Share**

1. Income statement information:
   a. Net income for 2004 is $14,000.
   b. An extraordinary gain (net of income taxes) of $3,600 is included in net income.
2. Stockholders' equity information (end of 2004):
   a. 8% Preferred stock, $100 par $30,000
   b. Common stock, $10 par $60,000
3. Additional information:
   a. No preferred stock was issued or reacquired during 2004.
   b. Preferred dividends were declared during 2004 at the stated rate.
   c. A review of the common stock account shows that on January 1, 2004, 2,000 shares of common stock were outstanding. On April 2, 500 shares of common stock were issued for cash. On June 1, a two-for-one stock split occurred, resulting in 5,000 total common shares. On November 2, 1,000 shares of common stock were issued for cash.
4. Basic earnings per share computations for 2004:

Explanation	Earnings (Adjustments)	÷	Shares (Adjustments)	=	Earnings Per Share
Net income	$14,000				
Preferred dividends[a]	(2,400)				
Common shares[b]			4,917		
Earnings and shares	$11,600	÷	4,917	=	$2.36

    a. Preferred dividends: $30,000 × 0.08 = $2,400
    b. Weighted average shares:

4,000 (2,000 × 200% stock split)	× 3/12 =	1,000
5,000 (2,500 × 200%)	× 7/12 =	2,917
6,000 (2,500 × 200% + 1,000)	× 2/12 =	1,000
Weighted average common shares		4,917

5. Condensed income statement presentation for 2004:

Income before extraordinary items	$10,400
Extraordinary gain (net of income taxes)	3,600
Net income	$14,000

Earnings per common share (see Note A):	
Income before extraordinary items	$1.63
Extraordinary gain	0.73
Net income	$2.36

6. Note A to financial statements: Preferred dividends of $2,400 are deducted from income before extraordinary items and net income to determine earnings available to common stock. The resulting amounts of $8,000 and $11,600 divided by the 4,917 weighted average number of common shares yield $1.63 and $2.36 earnings per common share, respectively. A total of 6,000 common shares were outstanding at the end of 2004.

---

accountant must be familiar with the types of potential common shares, the test to determine the dilution of each security, and the diluted earnings per share computations.

To evaluate the dilutive effect of each security, it is necessary to include potential common shares in the diluted earnings per share (DEPS) calculations in a certain order. Therefore, the following sequence of steps should be followed:

Step 1. Compute the basic earnings per share.
Step 2. Include dilutive stock options and warrants and compute a tentative DEPS.
Step 3. Develop a ranking of the impact of each convertible preferred stock and convertible bond on DEPS.

Step 4. Include each dilutive convertible security in DEPS in a sequential order based on the ranking and compute a new tentative DEPS.

Step 5. Select as the diluted earnings per share the lowest computed tentative DEPS.

Since we already have discussed the computation of basic earnings per share, the following discussion begins with stock options and proceeds through the steps necessary to compute diluted earnings per share. Exhibit 16-4 shows a flowchart summarizing these steps.

Stock Options and Warrants

A corporation always first considers stock options, warrants, and similar arrangements in its diluted earnings per share calculations. However, they are included in

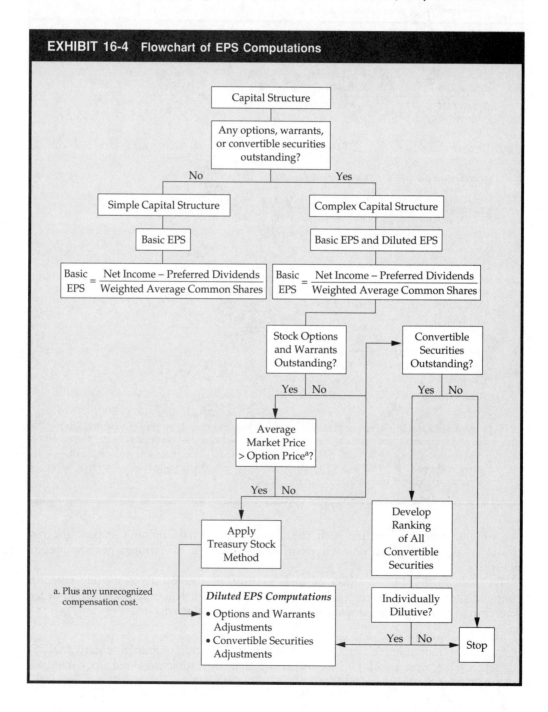

EXHIBIT 16-4   Flowchart of EPS Computations

diluted earnings per share only if they are *dilutive*. Since the exercise of stock options or warrants does not affect the corporation's net income, the focus is on the earnings per share denominator. **The treasury stock method is used to determine the change in the number of shares.** In this method, the impact upon common shares is computed under the assumption (for earnings per share computations) that the options were exercised at the beginning of the period (or at the time of the issuance of the options, if later) and that the assumed proceeds obtained from the exercise were used by the corporation to reacquire common stock at the *average* market price during the period. The intent is to approximate the impact upon the corporate capital structure if all stock options had been exercised. **Under the treasury stock method, the number of shares added to the earnings per share denominator is the difference between the assumed shares issued and the assumed shares reacquired.** We illustrate this relationship by the following diagram (we will discuss how to compute the proceeds shortly):

Whenever the shares issued exceed the shares reacquired, the effect is a dilution of earnings per share. **Dilution occurs whenever the average market price is greater than the option (exercise) price.**[5] In this case, it is assumed that fewer shares are reacquired than are issued via the exercise of the option. If the average market price is less than the option price, the assumed exercise would be antidilutive (i.e., would *increase* earnings per share) and the options are *excluded* from the diluted earnings per share computation (and the employees would not exercise their options under these circumstances). The steps to implement the treasury stock method are as follows:

4 Apply the treasury stock method for including stock options and warrants in diluted EPS.

Step 1. Determine the average market price of common shares during the period (if less than the option price, there is no need to continue; the assumed exercise of the options and warrants would be antidilutive).

Step 2. Compute the shares issued from the assumed exercise of all options and warrants.

Step 3. Compute the proceeds received from the assumed exercise by multiplying the shares issued by the option price [plus any unrecognized compensation cost (net of tax) per share, if the company uses the fair value method].

Step 4. Compute the assumed shares reacquired by dividing the proceeds (Step 3) by the average market price (Step 1).

Step 5. Compute the incremental common shares (the results of Step 2 minus Step 4).

Step 3 needs further explanation. Recall from Chapter 15 that a corporation may use the fair value method to account for its compensatory stock option plan. In this case it determines its total compensation cost on the grant date (based on the estimated fair value of the stock) and recognizes a portion of this cost as an expense over the service period. For earnings per share purposes, the portion of the compensation cost

---

5. The option price may have to be adjusted for any unrecognized compensation cost, as we discuss later.

(net of tax) that the corporation has *not* recognized as compensation expense is included in the proceeds received from the assumed exercise of compensatory stock options.[6] [This approach is used to determine an estimate of the fair value per share that the corporation would receive in regard to the stock options for the common stock assumed issued before the service period has expired. That is, if an employee exercised a stock option before the service period had expired, the corporation would require the employee to pay both the option price and a "premium" for the early exercise. The unrecognized compensation cost per share is an estimate of this premium. Hence, by adding this amount to the exercise price, the computation includes an estimate of the fair value per share of common stock that the corporation would receive at the point of early exercise.] The computation of the unrecognized compensation cost is complex; for simplicity, in the text and homework we always state the amount per share of any unrecognized compensation cost (net of tax) that should be included in the computation of the proceeds.

To illustrate, assume a corporation has compensatory stock options to purchase 1,000 common shares at $18 per share outstanding the entire year, and that the average market price for the common stock during the year was $25 per share. The unrecognized compensation cost (net of tax) related to the stock options is $2 per share. The net increase in the denominator is 200 shares, which has a dilutive effect on earnings per share. The share calculation is as follows:

Shares assumed issued from assumed exercise: 1,000

Shares assumed reacquired:

$$\frac{\text{Proceeds}}{\text{Average Market Price Per Share}} = \frac{1{,}000 \times (\$18 + \$2)}{\$25} = \frac{\$20{,}000}{\$25} = \underline{(800)}$$

Assumed increment in common shares for
computing diluted earnings per share   200

After the corporation has computed the number of incremental shares resulting from the assumed exercise of the options or warrants, it adds the increase to the denominator of the basic earnings per share. Then it divides the original numerator by the new denominator to determine the tentative diluted earnings per share. If no convertible securities are outstanding, this tentative figure is the final diluted earnings per share. We illustrate this procedure later in Exhibit 16-6.

Convertible Securities

Convertible bonds and convertible preferred stock are considered for inclusion in diluted earnings per share after stock options and warrants. A corporation includes convertible securities in its diluted earnings per share only if they are *dilutive*. It must be careful to include the individual convertible securities, one at a time, in the proper sequence, because a mistake in that sequence may lead to the inclusion of an antidilutive security in diluted earnings per share. That is, **a convertible security that may appear to be individually dilutive may, in fact, be antidilutive in combination with other convertible securities.**

To determine the sequence in which to include convertible securities in a corporation's diluted earnings per share, the securities are ranked. This ranking is determined by comparing the individual impacts on diluted earnings per share that result from the assumed conversion of each convertible security into common shares. To compute this impact, the *if-converted* method is used. Under this method, **each convertible**

---

6. "Accounting for Stock-Based Compensation," *FASB Statement of Financial Accounting Standards No. 123* (Norwalk, Conn.: FASB, 1995), par. 50.

stock or bond is *assumed* (for computing diluted earnings per share) to have been converted into common stock at the beginning of the earliest period reported (or at the date of issuance of the security, if later). This assumed conversion causes two changes in the earnings per share calculation: an increase in the denominator and an increase in the numerator. The denominator increases by the number of common shares issued in the assumed conversion. If bonds are assumed to be converted into common stock, the numerator increases because net income would be larger since the interest expense (net of income taxes) for the converted bonds would not be incurred.[7] If preferred stock is assumed to be converted into common stock, the preferred dividends would not be declared and the earnings available to common stockholders is increased.

The numerical value impact on the corporation's diluted earnings per share for each convertible security is computed by dividing the increase in the numerator by the increase in the denominator,[8] as we show in the following equation:

5 Calculate the impact of a convertible security on diluted EPS.

$$\text{Impact on DEPS} = \frac{\text{Increase in Earnings Per Share Numerator}}{\text{Increase in Earnings Per Share Denominator}}$$

After the corporation has computed the impact on its diluted earnings per share for each convertible security, it ranks the securities. The convertible security having the *lowest* impact on diluted earnings per share is listed at the *top* of the ranking, and the other convertible securities are ranked in sequential order so that the security with the *highest* impact is listed at the *bottom* of the ranking. Beginning with the convertible security listed at the top of the ranking, the corporation sequentially enters the dilutive securities into its diluted earnings per share computations.

It is important to understand that the convertible security with the lowest numerical value impact on diluted earnings per share causes the least increase in the numerator relative to the increase in the denominator from the assumed conversion. Consequently, **that security, which has the *lowest impact* and which *causes the greatest decrease* in diluted earnings per share, is the most dilutive convertible security and is the first (after options and warrants) to be considered for inclusion in diluted earnings per share.** The ranking enables the corporation to sequentially include dilutive convertible securities in its diluted earnings per share in the descending order of their individual dilutive effect on earnings per share.

Exhibit 16-5 illustrates the calculation of the impact of each convertible security on diluted earnings per share and the development of the ranking for a corporation that has four convertible securities outstanding the entire year. As you can see, security C has the lowest impact on diluted earnings per share and is the most dilutive. It is the first convertible security (after options and warrants) to be included in diluted earnings per share (assuming it is dilutive).

Computation of Tentative and Final Diluted Earnings Per Share

As we indicated earlier, a corporation begins the computation of its diluted earnings per share with the calculation of basic earnings per share. Then, it computes the increment in shares from the assumed exercise of stock options and warrants. It adds this increment to the denominator from basic earnings per share, and calculates an initial tentative diluted earnings per share. Next, it includes the dilutive convertible securities in diluted earnings per share in sequential order according to the ranking we discussed earlier. The convertible security listed at the top of the ranking is considered first. If its

---

7. The pretax savings in interest expense includes the interest paid or accrued, plus any bond discount amortization or less any bond premium amortization. The net-of-tax interest-expense savings is computed by multiplying the pretax interest-expense savings times one minus the effective income tax rate.

8. This and the subsequent discussion dealing with the computation of tentative diluted earnings per share is adapted from the presentation by S. Davidson and R. Weil in "A Shortcut in Computing Earnings Per Share," *Journal of Accountancy* (December, 1975), pp. 45–47.

EXHIBIT 16-5   Computation of Impact of Convertible Securities on Diluted Earnings Per Share

A. Summary of Convertible Securities

Security	Description
A	9% convertible preferred stock. Dividends of $5,400 were declared during the year. The preferred shares are convertible into 3,000 shares of common stock.
B	10% convertible bonds. Interest expense (net of income taxes) of $4,800 was recorded during the year. The bonds are convertible into 1,920 shares of common stock.
C	8% convertible preferred stock. Dividends of $8,000 were declared during the year. The preferred shares are convertible into 5,000 shares of common stock.
D	7% convertible bonds. Interest expense (net of income taxes) of $6,300 was recorded during the year. The bonds are convertible into 3,150 shares of common stock.

B. Computations and Rankings

Security	Impact	Order in Ranking
A	$\frac{\$5,400}{3,000} = \$1.80$	2
B	$\frac{\$4,800}{1,920} = \$2.50$	4
C	$\frac{\$8,000}{5,000} = \$1.60$	1
D	$\frac{\$6,300}{3,150} = \$2.00$	3

---

6 Compute diluted EPS.

impact is *less* than the initial tentative diluted earnings per share, it is dilutive and is included in diluted earnings per share. This involves computing a new numerator and denominator by adding the increase in the numerator and the increase in the denominator resulting from the assumed conversion to the amounts used to compute the initial tentative diluted earnings per share.[9] A second (and lower) tentative diluted earnings per share is computed based on the revised numerator and denominator.

We illustrate this procedure in the following diagram.

The second convertible security in the ranking is considered next. If its impact is *less* than the previously computed tentative diluted earnings per share, it is dilutive. The increase in the numerator and denominator from this convertible security is added to the revised numerator and denominator and a third (and still lower) tentative earnings per share is computed. This procedure is repeated for each security in the ranking until the impact of the next convertible security is *more* than the previously

---

9. If no stock options or warrants are outstanding, the corporation adds the increases in the numerator and denominator resulting from the assumed conversion of the top-ranked convertible security to the numerator and denominator used to compute its basic earnings per share.

computed tentative diluted earnings per share (or until the ranking is exhausted). The remaining securities in the ranking are antidilutive and are excluded from diluted earnings per share. The final diluted earnings per share is the last tentative figure and contains all the dilutive convertible securities included in the tentative diluted earnings per share computations.

If a corporation reports items such as extraordinary gains and losses, results of discontinued operations, and cumulative effects of changes in accounting principles in its net income, then the comparison of the impact of a convertible security on earnings per share to test for dilution is different. Instead of comparing the impact to the initial tentative *total* diluted earnings per share, it is compared to the initial tentative diluted earnings per share related to *income from continuing operations* to test for dilution.[10]

Exhibit 16-6 illustrates the computation of diluted earnings per share for a corporation, assuming (1) stock options are outstanding, (2) both convertible bonds and convertible preferred stock are outstanding, and (3) the convertible bonds are dilutive but the convertible preferred stock is antidilutive. The computations result in diluted earnings per share of $1.94. Note that the corporation reports *both* basic and diluted earnings per share on its income statement. Note, also, that if no ranking had been prepared, and if both the convertible preferred stock and bonds had been included in diluted earnings per share, the corporation would have reported an erroneous $1.96 [($2,000 + $800 + $224) ÷ (985 + 400 + 160)] diluted earnings per share.

ADDITIONAL CONSIDERATIONS

The previous sections focused on the primary issues related to computing earnings per share. Several other issues are relevant to basic and diluted earnings per share. These issues involve conversion ratios, contingent issuances, and disclosures in the notes to the financial statements.

Conversion Ratios

After issuing convertible securities or stock options, a corporation may declare a stock dividend or stock split. Typically, the "conversion ratio" for convertible securities and stock options is proportionally adjusted for the stock dividend or split. For instance, assume a share of preferred stock is convertible into 4 shares of common stock before a two-for-one stock split on the common stock. *After* the stock split, the preferred stock is convertible into 8 shares of common stock. The corporation uses the *current* conversion ratio for convertible securities and stock options in its diluted earnings per share computations.

Contingent Issuances

A corporation may be obligated to issue common shares in the future. Such stock is referred to as contingently issuable common stock, and its issuance may depend on the satisfaction of certain conditions, such as attaining or maintaining a certain level of earnings. When no further conditions must be met before issuance, the corporation considers these shares to be outstanding for basic and diluted earnings per share purposes. If the conditions have not been met, if dilutive, the corporation includes the shares in diluted earnings per share based on the number of shares that would be issuable if the end of the accounting period were the end of the contingency period.

Additional Disclosures

When a corporation reports its basic and diluted earnings per share on its income statement, it also is required to make additional disclosures in the notes to its financial

---

10. Unless we indicate otherwise, for simplicity we assume in the text and homework that the corporation does not report any of these items in its net income.

EXHIBIT 16-6 **Computation and Reporting of Diluted Earnings Per Share**

1. Income statement information:
   a. Net income for 2004 is $2,800.
   b. The income tax rate is 30%.
2. Balance sheet information:
   a. 900 shares of common stock were outstanding the entire year.
   b. Options were outstanding the entire year. The assumed exercise of these options results in an increment of 85 shares of common stock.
   c. 100 shares of 8%, $100 par (and issuance price) convertible preferred stock were outstanding the entire year. $800 dividends were declared on this stock in 2004. Each share of preferred stock is convertible into 4 shares of common stock.
   d. 6% convertible bonds, $5,000 face value were outstanding the entire year. These bonds were issued to yield 6.5%. Bond interest expense of $320 was recorded in 2004; the total discount is being amortized at the rate of $20 per year. Each $1,000 bond is convertible into 32 shares of common stock.
3. Impact on diluted earnings per share and resulting ranking:

Security	Impact	Ranking
Preferred	$\dfrac{\$800}{100 \times 4} = \dfrac{\$800}{400} = \$2.00$	2
Bonds	$\dfrac{[(\$5,000 \times 0.06) + \$20] \times (1 - 0.3)}{5 \times 32} = \dfrac{\$224}{160} = \$1.40$	1

4. Diluted earnings per share computations for 2004:

Explanation	Earnings (Adjustments)	÷	Shares (Adjustments)	=	Earnings Per Share
Basic earnings per share	$2,000[a]	÷	900		= $2.22 Basic
Increment in shares (options)			85		
DEPS$_1$ earnings and shares	$2,000	÷	985		= $2.03 DEPS$_1$[b]
Savings in interest expense (bonds)	224[c]				
Increment in shares (bonds)			160[d]		
Diluted earnings and shares	$2,224	÷	1,145		= $1.94 Diluted[e]

   a. $2,000 = $2,800 net income − $800 preferred dividends
   b. $1.40 is less than $2.03; therefore, the convertible bonds are individually dilutive and are included in diluted earnings per share.
   c. $224 = [($5,000 × 0.06) + $20] × (1 − 0.3)
   d. 160 = 5 bonds × 32 common shares
   e. The $2.00 impact on diluted earnings per share of the convertible preferred stock is more than $1.94; therefore, inclusion of the preferred stock in diluted earnings per share would be antidilutive.

5. Condensed income statement presentation for 2004:

Net income	$2,800
Earnings per share (see Note A):	
Basic earnings per share	$2.22
Diluted earnings per share	$1.94

6. Note A to financial statements: Basic earnings per share is based on 900 average common shares outstanding. Preferred dividends of $800 are deducted from income before extraordinary items and net income to determine earnings available to common stockholders. Diluted earnings per share is based on 900 average common shares outstanding plus 245 incremental shares from giving effect to the assumed exercise of stock options and the conversion of 6% convertible bonds. Earnings available to common stockholders are adjusted for the $224 savings in interest expense (net of taxes). The 8% convertible preferred stock is antidilutive and is not included in diluted earnings per share. A total of 900 common shares were outstanding at the end of 2004.

statements. These include a schedule or note identifying and reconciling the numerators and denominators on which it calculated both basic and diluted earnings per share. The schedule or note also includes information that:

1. Identifies the amount of preferred dividends deducted to determine the income available to common stockholders.
2. Describes the potential common shares that were *not* included in the diluted earnings per share computation because they were antidilutive.
3. Describes any material impact on the common shares outstanding of subsequent transactions after the close of the accounting period but before the issuance of the financial report.[11]

International Accounting Differences

International accounting standards and U.S. accounting standards are similar in regard to reporting earnings per share, but there are a few differences. International standards require a company to report both basic and diluted net income per ordinary share of the face of its income statement. However, a company is not required to disclose per-share amounts for the results from discontinued operations, extraordinary items, or the cumulative effects of accounting changes. Other differences include: (1) for stock options, in the treasury stock method a company is not required to include any unrecognized compensation cost in the assumed proceeds from issuing the stock as is required under U.S. GAAP for a company that uses the fair value method, (2) for unvested stock options, a company might treat them as contingently issuable shares, rather than including the options in diluted earnings per share as is required under U.S. GAAP, and (3) for convertible securities, a company is allowed to test for antidilution by using a different income amount than under U.S. GAAP.

EPS DISCLOSURE ILLUSTRATION

An illustration of the earnings per share disclosures of **Brunswick Corporation** in its 2001 annual report is shown in Exhibit 16-7.

CONTENT OF RETAINED EARNINGS

Now that we have completed the discussion of earnings per share as the last item that a corporation reports on its income statement, we turn to retained earnings. Retained earnings is the primary link between a corporation's balance sheet and income statement. The corporation's assets are financed by liabilities and stockholders' equity. The stockholders' share of assets results primarily from their investments and from net income (earnings) not distributed as dividends. A corporation uses the Retained Earnings account to summarize this latter component of stockholders' equity.

Most corporations (81%) prefer the account title **Retained Earnings,** with the terms *Earnings* or *Income* (with additional words) used by about 6%. A few (about 13%) have *negative* retained earnings and use the terms *Retained Earnings (Deficit)* or *Accumulated Deficit* (a **deficit,** or a negative retained earnings balance, is the result of a corporation's accumulated prior net losses or dividends in excess of its earnings).[12]

In addition to net income (or net loss), the primary factors that affect Retained Earnings include (1) dividends, (2) prior period adjustments, and (3) appropriations.

DIVIDENDS

Whereas a corporation's net income increases its assets (and capital) and the corporation records this increase in retained earnings, the distribution of dividends has the

---

11. *FASB Statement of Financial Accounting Standards No. 128*, par. 40 and 41.
12. *Accounting Trends and Techniques* (New York: AICPA, 2001), p. 275.

EXHIBIT 16-7   Earnings Per Share Disclosures

BRUNSWICK CORPORATION

Net Earnings and Earnings Per Share (in part)

In millions, except per share data

Years Ended December 31	2001	2000
Earnings from continuing operations	$84.7	$202.2
Cumulative effect of change in accounting principle, net of tax	(2.9)	—
Loss from discontinued operations, net of tax	—	(68.4)
Loss from disposal of discontinued operations, net of tax	—	(229.6)
Net earnings (loss)	$81.8	$ (95.8)
Basic earnings (loss) per common share:		
Earnings from continuing operations	$0.96	$ 2.28
Cumulative effect of change in accounting principle	(0.03)	—
Loss from discontinued operations	—	(0.77)
Loss from disposal of discontinued operations	—	(2.59)
Net earnings (loss)	$0.93	$ (1.08)
Diluted earnings (loss) per common share:		
Earnings from continuing operations	$0.96	$ 2.28
Cumulative effect of change in accounting principle	(0.03)	—
Loss from discontinued operations	—	(0.77)
Loss from disposal of discontinued operations	—	(2.59)
Net earnings (loss)	$0.93	$ (1.08)
Average shares used for computation of:		
Basic earnings per share	87.8	88.7
Diluted earnings per share	88.1	88.7
Cash dividends declared per common share	$0.50	$ 0.50

Q U E S T I O N S

Q What effect did the cumulative effect of change in accounting principle have on EPS in 2001? Is this important? Why or why not? **Q** What effect did the discountinued operations have on EPS in 2000? Is this important? Why or why not?

---

opposite effect. That is, the distribution of cash or property dividends decreases the assets (and capital) and is recorded as a reduction in retained earnings. Thus, the phrase "retained earnings paid out in dividends," or some similar phrase, often found in summaries of corporate financial activities is somewhat misleading. A corporation pays cash or property dividends out of *cash* or some other asset, and reduces its retained earnings (and capital) because the payment is a return *of* capital to the stockholders.

In order for a corporation to pay cash or property dividends, it must meet legal requirements and have assets available for distribution. The board of directors is responsible for the establishment of a dividend policy and determines the amount, timing, and type of dividends to be declared. In so doing, it must consider the articles of incorporation, applicable state regulations for dividends, the impact upon legal capital (established to protect corporate creditors), and compliance with contractual agreements, as well as the financial well-being of the corporation.

Legal requirements for dividends vary from state to state, but most states require a corporation to have a positive (credit) retained earnings balance before it may declare dividends. Furthermore, the amount of dividends it declares generally cannot exceed this retained earnings balance. Usually a corporation must restrict the amount of retained earnings available for dividends by the cost of treasury shares held. However, a few states allow a corporation to declare a dividend equal to the amount of current income even though it may have a prior deficit. In certain instances, some states allow dividends that reduce contributed capital, as long as legal capital is not impaired. Other states may allow a dividend from donated capital but not from other unrealized items in stockholders' equity. Furthermore, contractual agreements (such as long-term bond provisions) may restrict a corporation from declaring dividends. Corporate legal counsel is responsible for reviewing applicable state laws and corporate contracts to determine the legality of dividends. Nonetheless, accountants also should be aware of state regulations and contractual obligations, particularly as they affect restrictions of dividends.

In addition to meeting legal requirements, the board of directors must evaluate the financial desirability of a particular dividend. In this regard, the board may consult with the corporate accountants. Consideration should be given to the corporation's *financial flexibility* and *operating capability,* including such factors as the impact of a dividend upon the current assets and working capital, the ability to finance capital expansion projects, the effect upon the stock market price per share, and the maintenance of a liquidity "cushion" against possible future deteriorating economic conditions. The declaration of a dividend must be in the financial long- and short-term interests of the stockholders. A corporation's board of directors may consider several types of dividends, including: (1) cash, (2) property, (3) scrip, (4) stock, and (5) liquidating dividends.

The impact of each type of dividend upon a corporation's capital structure is as follows: (1) cash, property, and scrip dividends decrease retained earnings (and stockholders' equity); (2) liquidating dividends decrease contributed capital (and stockholders' equity); (3) stock dividends decrease retained earnings and increase contributed capital by the same amount (so there is no change in total stockholders' equity); and (4) stock splits do not affect the balance of any element of stockholders' equity.

Cash Dividends

The most common type of dividend is the cash dividend—the distribution of cash by the corporation to its stockholders. When used without a qualifying adjective, the term *dividends* refers to cash dividends.

Four dates are significant for a cash dividend (or any type of dividend): (1) the date of declaration, (2) the ex-dividend date, (3) the date of record, and (4) the date of payment. **On the date of declaration, the board of directors formally declares that a dividend will be paid to** *stockholders of record* **on a specific future date,** typically 4 to 6 weeks later. At this declaration date, the corporation becomes legally liable to pay the dividend. Prior to this date, stockholders ordinarily have no power to require that a dividend be paid; dividend policy has been legally entrusted to the board of directors. Since the corporation incurs a liability on the date of declaration, it makes a journal entry to reduce retained earnings and establish the current liability. After the date of declaration, the outstanding stock of the corporation trading in the open market normally sells "with dividends attached" (that is, at a higher market price that includes the amount of the future dividend payment). The ex-dividend date occurs several days before the date of record to enable the corporation to update its *stockholders' ledger* by the date of record. The ex-dividend date is important to investors because **on the ex-dividend date the stock stops selling with dividends attached.** Any purchaser of the stock on or after this date will not receive the current dividend. No accounting entry is required on the ex-dividend date. Normally, it takes a corporation some time to process the dividend checks. Thus, a "cut-off" date is needed—the date of record. **Only investors listed in the stockholders' ledger on the date of record can receive the dividend.** The date of record usually occurs several weeks after the declaration date and several weeks before the payment date, as specified in the dividend provisions. On the date of record, the corporation makes a memorandum entry indicating that the date of record has been reached and showing the future dividend payment date. **On the date of payment, the corporation distributes the dividend checks, and makes a journal entry to eliminate the liability and reduce the cash.**

On the date of declaration, the corporation determines and records the total amount of the dividend liability, as well as the portions applicable to preferred stock (if any) and to common stock. It usually reduces (debits) Retained Earnings directly. However, some corporations prefer to use a contra-retained earnings account entitled Dividends Declared for the dividends related to each class of stock. It either increases (credits) a current liability, Dividends Payable, or else increases separate liability accounts for the amounts owed to each class of stockholder.

The following diagram summarizes the accounting procedures for a cash dividend.

7 Record the declaration and payment of cash dividends.

For example, assume that on November 3, 2004, the board of directors of a corporation declares preferred dividends totaling $10,000 and common dividends totaling $20,000. These dividends are payable on December 15, 2004 to stockholders of record on November 24, 2004. The corporation makes the following journal entries to record the dividend:

November 3, 2004

Retained Earnings	30,000	
Dividends Payable: Preferred Stock		10,000
Dividends Payable: Common Stock		20,000

November 24, 2004

Memorandum entry: The company will pay dividends on December 15, 2004, to preferred and common stockholders of record as of today, the date of record.

December 15, 2004

Dividends Payable: Preferred Stock	10,000	
Dividends Payable: Common Stock	20,000	
Cash		30,000

If its accounting period ends before the dividend payment, the corporation reports the Dividends Payable account(s) as a current liability on its balance sheet. If it uses the contra account, Dividends Declared, it closes this account directly to Retained Earnings as part of the year-end closing process.

PARTICIPATING PREFERRED STOCK Usually the amounts of dividends payable to each class of stock are readily determinable. In certain cases, however, preferred stock may be either fully or partially participating. In these cases, a corporation must compute the dividends payable to preferred and common stockholders. Recall from Chapter 15 that *fully participating* preferred stock shares equally with the common stock in any extra dividends. These extra dividends are distributed proportionally, based on the respective *total* par values of each class of stock. *Partially participating* preferred stock is limited in its participation to a fixed rate (based on the respective par value) or amount per share.

To illustrate, assume that a corporation has issued 10%, participating, cumulative preferred stock with a total par value of $20,000 and common stock with a total par value of $30,000. Therefore, preferred stock constitutes 40% and common stock 60% of the total par value. The corporation intends to distribute cash dividends of $9,000, and there are no dividends in arrears. The dividend distribution is shown in Exhibit 16-8, assuming (a) the preferred stock is fully participating, and (b) the preferred stock participates up to 12% of its par value. If any preferred stock dividends had been in arrears, these would have been distributed *before* any participation calculations. In the participation calculations, common stock initially receives a rate equal to preferred *for the current year*. Common stock does *not* share in any dividends in arrears.

EXHIBIT 16-8   Dividend Distribution

		Preferred	Common
(a) Preferred Stock Is Fully Participating			
10% dividend to Preferred (on $20,000 par)		$2,000	
Common dividend (equal to 10% of $30,000 par)			$3,000
Extra dividend proportionate to par values:			
Total to allocate	$9,000		
Allocated ($2,000 + $3,000)	(5,000)		
Remainder (40% to preferred, 60% to common)	$4,000	1,600	2,400
Dividends to each class of stock		$3,600	$5,400
(b) Preferred Stock Participates up to 12%			
10% dividend to Preferred		$2,000	
Common dividend (equal to 10% of par)			$3,000
2% dividend on par of Preferred (2% × $20,000)		400	
2% dividend on par of Common (2% × $30,000)			600
Remainder to common ($9,000 − $6,000 allocated)			3,000
Dividends to each class of stock		$2,400	$6,600

Property Dividends

Occasionally, a corporation will declare a **property dividend that is payable in assets other than cash.** The corporation typically uses marketable securities of other companies that it owns for the property dividend because they are more easily distributable to the stockholders. However, it may pay the dividend with any assets designated by its board of directors.

A property dividend is classified as a *nonreciprocal, nonmonetary transfer to owners.* That is, the corporation enters into an exchange in which it gives up something of value (the asset) but for which it receives no asset or service in return. Furthermore, because no cash is involved, the exchange is a nonmonetary transfer. In accordance with **APB Opinion No. 29,** a corporation records a property dividend at the fair value of the asset transferred, and recognizes a gain or a loss.[13]

The logic behind using fair value for a property dividend is that the corporation could have sold the assets distributed in the dividend for cash and used the proceeds (fair value) to pay a cash dividend. The fair value is determined *on the date of declaration*

---

13. "Accounting for Nonmonetary Transactions," *APB Opinion No. 29* (New York: AICPA, 1973), par. 18.

(because this is the date the dividend becomes a legal liability) by referring to existing stock or bond market prices, recent cash exchanges of similar assets, or objective independent appraisals.

To illustrate, assume the board of directors of Corporation A declares a property dividend, payable in bonds of Company B being "held to maturity" (in accordance with paragraph 8 of *FASB Statement No. 115*). The bonds are carried on Corporation A's books at a book value of $40,000 but their current market (fair) value is $48,000. On the date of declaration, the corporation revalues the investment account to its fair value and records the dividend obligation at this value so that the amounts of both the gain and the dividend liability are properly reported. The corporation makes the following journal entries to record this property dividend:

Investments are discussed in Chapter 14.

8 Account for a property dividend.

Date of Declaration

Investment in Company B Bonds ($48,000 − $40,000)	8,000	
Gain on Disposal of Investments		8,000
Retained Earnings	48,000	
Property Dividends Payable		48,000

Date of Payment

Property Dividends Payable	48,000	
Investment in Company B Bonds		48,000

On the date of payment, the corporation does not adjust the gain or loss, even though the fair value may have changed since the date of declaration. It reports the gain or loss in the Other Items section of its income statement. If the corporation will not pay the dividend until next year, it reports the dividend liability as a current liability on its balance sheet.

In the case where a corporation distributes "available-for-sale" debt or equity securities (as defined in *FASB Statement No. 115*) as a property dividend, the computation of the gain or loss is more complex because it involves consideration of any previously recorded unrealized increase or decrease in value. The corporation is carrying its investment in available-for-sale securities (whether current or noncurrent) at the fair value (by use of an Allowance account) of the securities *on the last balance sheet date*, along with an "unrealized increase (or decrease) in value" amount (whose balance is the difference between the cost and the fair value) in its accumulated other comprehensive income section of its stockholders' equity. However, the realized gain or loss on this type of property dividend is computed as the difference between the fair value of the securities *on the date of declaration* and the original *cost* of the securities. The journal entry that the corporation makes on the date of declaration to revalue the investment (by adjusting the Allowance account) and to record the realized gain or loss also must eliminate the unrealized increase (decrease) in value for these securities.

To illustrate, assume Corporation C declares a property dividend on March 16, 2005, payable in Company D stock. The Company D stock was purchased early in 2004 for $24,000 and was reported as an asset at a fair value of $29,000 (i.e., at a cost of $24,000 plus an allowance for an increase in value of $5,000, along with an unrealized increase in value of $5,000 reported in its accumulated other comprehensive income) on the December 31, 2004 balance sheet. If the market value is $31,000 on March 16, 2005, the gain is $7,000, computed by comparing the current fair value ($31,000) to the original cost ($24,000). The corporation makes the following journal entries on the date of declaration to record this property dividend:

Allowance for Change in Value of Investment		
in Available-for-Sale Securities	2,000	
Unrealized Increase in Value of Available-for-Sale		
Securities	5,000	
Gain on Disposal of Investments		7,000
Retained Earnings	31,000	
Property Dividends Payable		31,000

The corporation makes the following journal entry on the date of payment to record the distribution of the securities to stockholders:

Property Dividends Payable	31,000	
Investment in Available-for-Sale Securities		24,000
Allowance for Change in Value of Investment		
in Available-for-Sale Securities		7,000

Scrip Dividends

As we discussed earlier, in establishing dividend policy, the board of directors must consider both the legal requirements and the corporate financial well-being. In certain instances, a corporation with adequate retained earnings to meet the legal dividend requirements but insufficient cash to justify a current cash dividend may declare a **scrip dividend**. Here, the corporation issues promissory notes (called "scrip") requiring it to pay dividends at some future date. It makes the usual journal entries on the date of declaration (although some companies may credit Notes Payable instead of Dividends Payable) and date of payment, except when the notes carry an interest rate. In this case, it also records interest expense on the date of payment. If the corporation will not make the scrip payment until next year, it must make a year-end adjusting entry to record accrued interest expense. A review of the maturity date is necessary to determine the proper classification of the dividend liability on the balance sheet. Scrip dividends are rare, however. If a corporation is having liquidity problems, it is usually unwise for the board of directors to commit it to cash outflows, even if these would be made in the future.

Stock Dividends

Another type of dividend that a corporation may declare and distribute is a stock dividend. **A stock dividend is a pro rata (proportional) distribution of additional shares of a corporation's own stock to its stockholders.** A stock dividend usually consists of the same class of shares; that is, a common stock dividend is declared on common stock outstanding. This type of distribution is called an *ordinary* stock dividend. The distribution of a different class of stock (common on preferred or preferred on common) sometimes is called a *special* stock dividend. Stock dividends are usually issued out of authorized but unissued shares, although treasury stock shares may be used. Unlike other dividends, a corporation may legally rescind the declaration of a stock dividend. A stock dividend also differs from other dividends in that *no corporate assets are distributed*. Each stockholder maintains the same percentage ownership in the corporation as was held prior to the distribution.

Stockholders often view stock dividends favorably even though (1) they receive no corporate assets, (2) their percentage ownership does not change, (3) theoretically the total market value of their investment will remain the same because the decrease in the stock market price per share will be offset by the increased number of shares each stockholder owns, and (4) future cash dividends may be limited because retained earnings is decreased by the amount of the stock dividend and most states set legal dividend restrictions based on positive retained earnings. However, the following factors may enhance the perceived attractiveness of stock dividends:

1. The stockholders may see the stock dividend as evidence of corporate growth.
2. The stockholders may see the stock dividend as evidence of sound financial policy.
3. Other investors may see the stock dividend in a similar light, and increased trading in the stock may cause the market price *not* to decrease proportionally.
4. The corporation may state that it will pay the same fixed cash dividend per share, in which case individual stockholders will receive higher total future cash dividends.
5. The stockholders may see the market price decreasing to a lower trading range, making the stock more attractive to additional investors so that the market price may eventually rise.

CONCEPTUAL ISSUES The **economic substance** of a stock dividend is that it is not really a "dividend" but instead is similar to a stock split. In both cases, even though the number of shares increases, a corporation does not distribute any assets to the stockholders and each stockholder's percentage ownership stays the same, so that the corporation's total assets and stockholders' equity remain unchanged. To depict the similar economic substance, then, in theory a corporation should record a stock dividend in a manner similar to a stock split. Recall from Chapter 15 that although a stock split usually is proportional and requires only a memorandum entry, in the case of a disproportionate stock split, the corporation must adjust capital stock and additional paid-in capital accounts by a formal journal entry. A similar entry could be made for a stock dividend. The corporation could increase (credit) the capital stock account for the par value (legal capital) of the additional shares issued. It would be logical, then, to decrease (debit) additional paid-in capital for the same amount, since the excess of the original issuance price over the current legal capital has now been reduced.

From an accounting standpoint, however, a corporation does *not* account for a stock dividend like a stock split, but instead records it in a manner similar to other dividends. When a stock dividend is recorded, total stockholders' equity is not changed. Retained earnings is decreased by the amount of the "dividend," and contributed capital is increased by the same amount because of the additional shares issued. This treatment is based on an **"opportunity cost"** argument. That is, the corporation should record the "dividend" at the fair value of the stock because this is the value it forgoes to issue the stock dividend.

Under this method, the fair value may be determined by assuming the stock is sold for cash at the current market price and the proceeds used to pay a cash dividend. In determining the "current market price," the corporation should consider the impact on this price of the additional shares outstanding as a result of the stock dividend. The appropriate fair value at which to record the stock dividend is the market price *after* the declaration of the dividend. The issuance of a very small number of shares in a stock dividend would cause only a small decrease in the market price, whereas larger stock dividends would cause greater decreases in the market price. To implement this fair value approach, an estimation technique for determining the decrease in fair value would need to be developed. However, no such technique has been implemented. Instead, a distinction is made between "small" and "large" stock dividends, and generally accepted accounting principles in accordance with state legal requirements have been developed for each.

GAAP In the case of a **small stock dividend** (presumably having no apparent effect upon the market price per share), the Committee on Accounting Procedure suggested that many recipients of the dividend consider it a distribution of corporate earnings in an amount equal to the fair value of the additional shares received. Even though a corporation does not distribute any corporate assets in a stock dividend (regardless of stockholder perceptions), the Committee apparently accepted the view that a stock dividend is a simultaneous sale of stock and payment of a dividend. **Therefore, a corporation accounts for a *small* stock dividend by transferring from retained earnings to contributed capital an amount equal to the fair value of the additional shares issued.**

9 Explain the difference in accounting for small and large stock dividends.

In distinguishing between a small and a large stock dividend, the Committee accepted the representations of a corporation as to the nature of the stock dividend as one of the principal considerations. However, it did say that **fair value is ordinarily the appropriate value to capitalize whenever the stock dividend (that is, small dividend) is less than 20 or 25% of the previously outstanding shares.**

State legal requirements govern the *minimum* amount that a corporation must capitalize (transfer from retained earnings to contributed capital as part of legal capital) in conjunction with stock dividends. Generally, this amount is the par or stated value of the additional shares distributed. In the case of no-par stock, the amount may be based on the average price at which all similar stock was previously issued, or it may be determined by the board of directors. The accounting for a **large stock dividend** relates to this legal capital. The Committee said that **a large stock dividend is similar in nature** to a stock split so that there is no need for a corporation to capitalize more than the amount necessary to satisfy legal requirements (that is, the par value). In such cases, it was also suggested that the use of the term *dividend* be avoided or, when this is not possible because of legal restrictions, the transaction should be described in terminology such as *a stock split effected in the form of a dividend*.[14]

Given the Committee's acceptance of the argument that a stock dividend is a distribution of earnings and should be based upon fair value, use of par value to record a large stock dividend seems inappropriate. Par value has no direct relationship to fair value. Furthermore, use of par value for large stock dividends and fair value for small stock dividends can lead to illogical accounting results. For instance, if a corporation with 2,000 shares of $10 par common stock outstanding issued a 15% (300 shares) small stock dividend when the market price per share is $40, it would reduce retained earnings and increase contributed capital by $12,000. If it issued a 50% (1,000 shares) large stock dividend, the corporation would reduce retained earnings and increase contributed capital by only $10,000. In this example, a small stock dividend has a greater effect on the components of the corporation's stockholders' equity than a large stock dividend! Nonetheless, use of fair value to record a small stock dividend and use of par value to record a large dividend are generally accepted accounting principles. The following diagram shows the effects on the various elements of stockholders' equity of a small and large stock dividend, respectively.

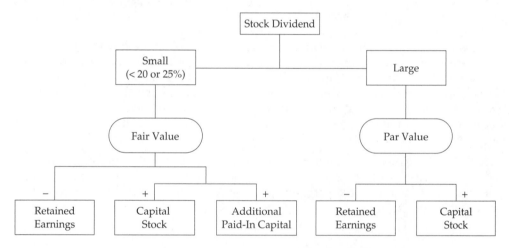

To illustrate the accounting for the two sizes of stock dividend, assume a corporation has the following stockholders' equity prior to the stock dividend:

Common stock, $10 par (20,000 shares issued and outstanding)	$200,000
Additional paid-in capital	180,000
Retained earnings	320,000
Total Stockholders' Equity	$700,000

Note, in this example there are 20,000 shares issued and outstanding; therefore, there is no treasury stock. Treasury stock normally does not participate in a small stock dividend because the dividend is based on the outstanding shares of stock. However, treasury stock may participate in a large stock dividend because the dividend is considered to be similar to a stock split.

EXAMPLE 1: SMALL STOCK DIVIDEND   Assume that the corporation declares and issues a 10% stock dividend. On the date of declaration, the stock is selling for $23 per share.

---

14. "Restatement and Revision of Accounting Research Bulletins," *Accounting Research Bulletin No. 43* (New York: AICPA, 1961), ch. 7, sec. B, par. 10 and 11.

The corporation records the 2,000-share stock dividend at the fair value of $46,000, as we show in the following journal entries:

Date of Declaration

Retained Earnings	46,000	
Common Stock To Be Distributed		20,000
Additional Paid-in Capital From Stock Dividend		26,000

Date of Issuance

Common Stock To Be Distributed	20,000	
Common Stock, $10 par		20,000

The resulting stockholders' equity is as follows:

Common stock, $10 par (22,000 shares issued and outstanding)	$220,000
Additional paid-in capital	206,000
Retained earnings	274,000
Total Stockholders' Equity	$700,000

Note that the amounts of the components of the corporation's stockholders' equity have changed, but its total stockholders' equity ($700,000) remains the same as before the small stock dividend.

If a corporation prepares a balance sheet after the declaration but before the issuance of the stock dividend, it reports the Common Stock To Be Distributed account as a component of Contributed Capital. The account is *not* a liability like the dividend payable accounts related to other types of dividends because it will not be satisfied by the distribution of assets. Instead, it is a temporary stockholders' equity item representing the legal capital related to the stock to be issued. As we illustrated, it is eliminated when the stock is issued.

EXAMPLE 2: LARGE STOCK DIVIDEND Assume, *instead*, that the corporation declares and issues a 40% stock dividend when the stock is selling for $23 per share. In this case, the corporation uses the par value of $80,000 for the 8,000 shares to record the stock dividend as follows:

Date of Declaration

Retained Earnings	80,000	
Common Stock To Be Distributed		80,000

Date of Issuance

Common Stock To Be Distributed	80,000	
Common Stock, $10 par		80,000

The resulting stockholders' equity is as follows:

Common stock, $10 par (28,000 shares issued and outstanding)	$280,000
Additional paid-in capital	180,000
Retained earnings	240,000
Total Stockholders' Equity	$700,000

Note again that the total stockholders' equity ($700,000) remains the same as before the large stock dividend.

FRACTIONAL SHARES In the case of a stock dividend, the number of shares that many stockholders own will not entitle them to receive additional whole shares from the dividend. For example, if a corporation declared a 10% stock dividend, a stockholder owning 43 shares would be entitled to 4.3 additional shares. Some corporations have a policy of not issuing fractional shares. These corporations usually offer stockholders two alternatives: (1) to receive cash equal to the market price of the fractional share, or (2) to pay in sufficient cash to receive a full share. In the first case, the corporation accounts for the cash it pays as a cash dividend and issues fewer shares. In the second case, it records the stock dividend in the usual manner and adjusts contributed capital for the cash it receives.

Liquidating Dividends

Liquidating dividends represent a return of contributed capital rather than a distribution of retained earnings. A corporation usually declares these dividends when it is ceasing or reducing operations. A liquidating dividend also may arise when a natural resources corporation pays a dividend based on earnings before depletion. That portion of the dividends equal to the amount of depletion is considered the liquidating dividend.

When a corporation pays a dividend that is in part (or in total) a liquidating dividend, it must adhere to state legal requirements in recording the dividend. It records the *normal* portion of the dividend as a reduction of retained earnings and the *liquidating* portion as a reduction of contributed capital. The latter may be recorded as a debit either to an additional paid-in capital account or to a special contra-contributed capital account entitled, for instance, Contributed Capital Distributed as a Liquidating Dividend. The corporation should disclose the liquidating dividend in a note to its financial statements to notify stockholders that a portion of contributed capital is being returned.

PRIOR PERIOD ADJUSTMENTS (RESTATEMENTS)

Corporations are required to report a few events as **prior period adjustments (restatements)** of retained earnings. These include certain changes in accounting principles, a change in accounting entity, and corrections of errors of prior periods.[15] We discuss the specific accounting treatment of these items in Chapter 22; the emphasis here is on the impact on retained earnings. The following discussion focuses on corrections of errors.

A corporation may make an error in the financial statements of one accounting period that is not discovered until a later period. These errors may be attributable to oversights, the incorrect use of existing facts, mistakes in mathematics, or errors in the application of accounting principles. Usually these errors affect an asset or liability and a revenue or expense of a prior year. Corporations are required to treat corrections of all material errors as prior period adjustments (restatements) of retained earnings. That is, in the year of correction, the asset or liability account balance is corrected (debited or credited) and the offsetting credit or debit (which involved a revenue or expense previously closed to retained earnings) is made directly to the Retained Earnings account or to an account such as Correction of Prior Years' Income Due to Material Error in. . . . If the latter account is used, it is closed directly to Retained Earnings in the year-end closing entries. Any related impact on income taxes is similarly recorded. For instance, assume that in 2005 Fox Corporation discovers that it inadvertently did not accrue $10,000 of interest expense for 2004. This material error overstated 2004 income before income taxes by a similar amount. Assuming a related income tax effect of $3,000, Fox makes the following correcting entries in 2005:

Retained Earnings (or Correction of Prior . . .)	10,000	
Interest Payable		10,000
Income Tax Refund Receivable	3,000	
Retained Earnings (or Correction of Prior . . .)		3,000

---

15. "Accounting Changes," *APB Opinion No. 20* (New York: AICPA, 1971), par. 27 and 34, and "Prior Period Adjustments," *FASB Statement of Financial Accounting Standards No. 16* (Stamford, Conn.: FASB, 1977), par. 10–12, as amended by "Accounting for Income Taxes," *FASB Statement of Financial Accounting Standards No. 109* (Norwalk, Conn.: FASB, 1992), par. 288(n).

When a corporation makes a prior period adjustment, it reports the item (net of the applicable income taxes) as an adjustment of the beginning balance of retained earnings on its statement of retained earnings. If the January 1, 2005 retained earnings balance of the Fox Corporation were $102,400, it reports the correction on its December 31, 2005 statement of retained earnings as a prior period adjustment as follows:

Retained earnings, as previously reported January 1, 2005	$102,400
Less: Correction of overstatement in 2004 net income due to interest expense understatement (net of $3,000 income taxes)	(7,000)
Adjusted retained earnings, January 1, 2005	$ 95,400

Fox then completes the remaining portion of the statement as we illustrate in Exhibit 16-9 later in the chapter. It discloses the effect of the error on the prior year's net income and earnings per share in the period in which the correction is made. With these disclosures, users can see the impact of the error on the company's financial statements. If Fox presents comparative financial statements, it makes corresponding adjustments to its net income (and components thereof), retained earnings, asset, or liability account balances for all the periods reported.[16]

APPROPRIATIONS (RESTRICTIONS) OF RETAINED EARNINGS

A corporation's board of directors is responsible for establishing dividend policy, while following legal requirements and sound financial practice. Stockholders sometimes consider only the legal requirements. As the corporation's Retained Earnings account balance increases, they may expect to be paid higher dividends. However, the corporation must use the *assets* represented by retained earnings for a variety of corporate activities, including financing on-going operations and long-term expansion projects, meeting principal and interest payments on debt securities, as well as making dividend payments.

To indicate that a certain portion of retained earnings is not available for dividends, a corporation may appropriate (restrict) retained earnings. An **appropriation** (or **restriction**) of retained earnings means that the board of directors establishes a formal policy that a portion of retained earnings is "earmarked" for a designated purpose and is unavailable for dividends. It is important to understand that such a policy does *not* directly earmark or restrict the use of any assets; it merely requires that the corporation not distribute any assets that would correspondingly reduce this restricted retained earnings. A board of directors may appropriate retained earnings for the following reasons: (1) to meet *legal* requirements, (2) to meet *contractual* restrictions, or (3) because of *discretionary* actions.

Corporations must adhere to the laws of the state in which they are incorporated. Certain states require restrictions of retained earnings when a corporation reacquires its own stock as treasury stock. Usually, the appropriation of retained earnings is in an amount equal to the cost of the treasury shares. The argument for this appropriation is that the acquisition of treasury stock reduces the amount of invested (permanent) capital, and by restricting retained earnings for an equal amount, the corporation's permanent capital is not impaired.

A corporation also may restrict retained earnings as a result of a contractual agreement. This type of agreement may be made when a corporation issues long-term bonds. In order to provide some assurance that sufficient assets will be maintained in the corporation to satisfy bondholders' claims, the bond provisions (sometimes called "debt covenants") may require the restriction of a certain amount of retained earnings.

A corporation's retained earnings also may be appropriated at the discretion of management. This type of restriction may be related to planning for future expansion or in anticipation of potential future losses. In the first case, a corporation may be planning to build a new plant or to add to existing facilities and wishes to finance this activity

---

16. "Reporting the Results of Operations," *APB Opinion No. 9* (New York: AICPA, 1966), par. 18 and 26.

through internally generated funds (funds that the corporation already holds or will soon receive from operations) rather than seek external funding (from creditors or through the issuance of more stock). To indicate that these internal funds are being held for this purpose and are not available for dividends, the board of directors may appropriate a portion of retained earnings.

A corporation may also restrict retained earnings when it anticipates future losses. For instance, a corporation may establish a policy of *self-insurance*. That is, it may elect to accept the risk of a future hazard (e.g., an earthquake, flood, or fire) and its accompanying losses rather than transfer this risk to an insurance company by paying insurance premiums. A corporation may self-insure because insurance companies will not insure the risk, or because insurance premiums are too high, or because it is widely dispersed geographically and large enough that the probability of a significant loss is relatively low. Actually, self-insurance is *no* insurance.

When a corporation decides to self-insure, it has no expense, but it may restrict retained earnings each year in an amount equal to the insurance premiums that would have been paid. When a hazard results in a loss, it must report that loss as a component of its income. Under *no* circumstances is the corporation allowed to close the amount directly to Retained Earnings. **FASB Statement No. 5** clearly states that "Costs or losses shall not be charged to an appropriation of retained earnings, and no part of the appropriation shall be transferred to income."[17] The corporation reports the loss as a negative component of its income from continuing operations on its income statement and simply cancels a portion (or all) of the appropriated retained earnings. This type of retained earnings restriction should be discouraged because it may mislead stockholders into thinking that the corporation has somehow "protected" itself against future losses, when, in fact, it carries no related insurance.

Most corporations disclose an appropriation of retained earnings in a note (or sometimes by parenthetical notations) to the financial statements.[18] When a note is used, a clear description of the legal, contractual, or discretionary provisions and the amount of the appropriation is required. To illustrate, suppose a corporation has a $300,000 retained earnings balance when it acquires treasury stock at a cost of $20,000. It would report the $300,000 retained earnings balance and disclose the restriction of retained earnings as follows:

Retained earnings (see *Note A*) $300,000

Notes to the Financial Statements

Note A: Retained earnings are restricted regarding dividends in the amount of $20,000, the cost of the treasury stock.

When a corporation cancels an appropriation (because, for instance, it no longer has treasury stock), it does not include the note in its financial statements.

STATEMENT OF RETAINED EARNINGS

Although not a required separate financial statement, some corporations include a statement of retained earnings in their financial statements. To disclose the earnings, dividends, prior period adjustments, and other reductions, we suggest the format shown in Exhibit 16-9.

A corporation may include the retained earnings statement as a separate statement within the financial statements, as a supporting schedule directly beneath the income statement, or, as is common, in the statement of changes in stockholders' equity which

---

17. "Accounting for Contingencies," *FASB Statement of Financial Accounting Standards No. 5* (Stamford, Conn.: FASB, 1975), par. 15.

18. A corporation may make a journal entry to separate its retained earnings into two components, appropriated and unappropriated retained earnings. This approach may be confusing and should be discouraged.

EXHIBIT 16-9   Statement of Retained Earnings for 2004

Retained earnings, as previously reported, January 1, 2004
   Plus (minus): Prior period adjustments (net of income tax effect)
Adjusted retained earnings, January 1, 2004
   Plus (minus): Net income (loss)
   Minus: Dividends (specifically identified, including per share amounts)
            Reductions due to retirement or reacquisition of capital stock
            Reductions due to conversion of bonds or preferred stock
Retained earnings, December 31, 2004

---

we discuss later in the chapter. Although the format in Exhibit 16-9 includes all items affecting retained earnings, items such as prior period adjustments, reductions due to conversions, or reductions due to the retirement of capital stock are relatively rare. Consequently, a retained earnings statement usually includes only adjustments to retained earnings for net income and dividends. Any restrictions (appropriations) of retained earnings are disclosed in a note to the financial statements.

Illustration of Retained Earnings Statement

The 2001 and 2000 consolidated statements of retained earnings for Merck & Co., Inc. are shown in Exhibit 16-10.

EXHIBIT 16-10   Retained Earnings Statement

MERCK & CO., INC. AND SUBSIDIARIES

Consolidated Statement of Retained Earnings

	Years Ended December 31	
($ in millions)	2001	2000
Balance, January 1	$27,363.9	$23,447.9
Net Income	7,281.8	6,821.7
Common Stock Dividends Declared	(3,156.1)	(2,905.7)
Balance, December 31	$31,489.6	$27,363.9

Q U E S T I O N S

Q Why does the company use the term "Common Stock Dividends Declared" in this statement? **Q** What is the common stock dividend as a percentage of net income for 2001? for 2000? **Q** What does this tell (or not tell) you?

Accumulated Other Comprehensive Income

10 Understand how to report accumulated other comprehensive income.

As we discussed in Chapters 3 and 4, a corporation is required to report its total comprehensive income for the accounting period. Comprehensive income includes both net income and "other comprehensive income." Other comprehensive income (loss) might include four items: (1) unrealized increases (gains) or decreases (losses) in the market (fair) value of investments in available-for-sale securities, (2) translation adjustments from converting the financial statements of a company's foreign operations into U.S. dollars, (3) certain gains and losses on "derivative" financial instruments, and (4) certain pension liability adjustments. A corporation may report its comprehensive income (net of income taxes) on the face of its income statement, in a separate statement of comprehensive income, or in its statement of changes in stockholders' equity. We illustrated these alternatives in Chapter 4.

A corporation includes its total net income *earned to date* in its retained earnings amount which it reports in its stockholders' equity. The corporation includes its other comprehensive income (or loss) *accumulated to date* in its **accumulated other comprehensive income** (or **loss**) amount[19] which it also reports in its stockholders' equity. If a corporation has more than one type of comprehensive income, it has a choice. It may report the amount of accumulated other comprehensive income for *each item* in its stockholders' equity. Or, it may report the *total amount* of accumulated other comprehensive income for *all the items* in its stockholders' equity. If the corporation uses this approach, it must disclose the amounts for each of the items in the notes to its financial statements.[20] Unless a corporation has miscellaneous items of stockholders' equity (which we discuss next), it adds the totals for contributed capital, retained earnings, and accumulated other comprehensive income (and subtracts the cost of any treasury stock) to determine its total stockholders' equity.

MISCELLANEOUS CHANGES IN STOCKHOLDERS' EQUITY

In rare instances, a corporation may increase stockholders' equity for events not related to the issuance of stock or to retained earnings. For example, as we discussed in Chapter 9, it is possible for a corporation to receive donated assets (e.g., a plant site) from a governmental unit to induce it to locate in a particular community. Since this is a nonreciprocal, nonmonetary transfer, the corporation records the asset at its fair value. It records the resulting credit in a Donated Capital account. The *discovery value* of natural resources is another example. Here, a corporation might record an increase in assets and stockholders' equity as a result of the discovery of previously unknown valuable natural resources. A corporation lists these items separately in its stockholders' equity.

STATEMENT OF CHANGES IN STOCKHOLDERS' EQUITY

As you learned from the discussion in this and the previous chapter, a corporation may engage in a variety of transactions that affect some component of its stockholders' equity. Conceptually, as we discussed in Chapter 3, **FASB Statement of Concepts No. 5** suggests that a full set of financial statements should show investments by and distributions to owners during the period. To inform external users of financial statements about corporate capital activities, **APB Opinion No. 12** states:

> ... disclosure of changes in the separate accounts comprising stockholders' equity (in addition to retained earnings) and of the changes in the number of shares of equity securities during at least the most recent annual fiscal period ... is required to make the financial statements sufficiently informative.[21]

Thus, a corporation must disclose the changes in the different classes of common stock, additional paid-in capital, retained earnings, accumulated other comprehensive income, and treasury stock in its annual report. The intent is to help report on the changes in the corporation's financial structure as an aid in assessing its *financial flexibility,*

11 Prepare a statement of changes in stockholders' equity.

---

19. This amount may create deferred taxes and is reported net of taxes. However, since we do not discuss deferred taxes until Chapter 18, for simplicity we ignore the tax effect in this chapter.
20. "Reporting Comprehensive Income," *FASB Statement of Financial Accounting Standards No. 130* (Norwalk, Conn.: FASB, 1997), par. 17 and 26.
21. "Omnibus Opinion—1967," *APB Opinion No. 12* (New York: AICPA, 1967), par. 10.

profitability, and *risk.* Although this disclosure may be made parenthetically or in a note to the financial statements, many corporations prepare a statement of changes in stockholders' equity that includes an analysis of the changes in these items. The ending amounts in this statement then tie to the stockholders' equity section of the year-end balance sheet. Furthermore, if a corporation chooses to report is comprehensive income on its statement of changes in stockholders' equity, it must display this statement as a *major* financial statement.

Exhibits 16-11 and 16-12 present a statement of changes in stockholders' equity and the ending stockholders' equity for the hypothetical Bardwell Corporation.[22] Colgate-Palmolive Company's ending 2001 and 2000 consolidated shareholders' equity and statements of retained earnings, comprehensive income, and changes in capital accounts are shown in Exhibits 16-13 and 16-14.

International Accounting Differences

Under *International Accounting Standards,* a corporation's shareholders' interests (the term used for stockholders' equity) consists of two sections: (a) share capital, and (b) other equity. Many of the disclosures required under *share capital* are the same as those required under U.S. GAAP; for example, the number of shares authorized, issued, and outstanding, par value, reacquired shares, and rights, preferences, and restriction regarding dividends. The differences from those required by U.S. GAAP include disclosure of any capital not yet paid in, any restrictions on the repayment of capital, and the shares reserved for future issuance under sales contracts.

Share premium (additional paid-in capital) is disclosed in the *other equity* section, along with revaluation surplus, reserves, and retained earnings. Revaluation surplus and reserves are equity items that are different from those allowed under U.S. GAAP. Although

---

EXHIBIT 16-11   Bardwell Corporation

Statement of Changes in Stockholders' Equity for 2004

Explanation	Common Stock		Additional Paid-in Capital		Common Stock Option	Retained	Accumulated Other Comprehensive	Treasury Stock
	Shares Issued	Par Value	Common Stock	Treasury Stock	Warrants	Earnings	Income	(Cost)
Balances, 1/1/2004	10,000	$50,000	$170,000	$2,300	$11,200	$322,000	$15,200	$(7,500)
Issued for cash	1,100	5,500	22,000					
Reissued treasury stock				2,700				4,500
Issued for exercise of stock options	300	1,500	5,400		(900)			
Compensation expense for stock options					3,300			
Unrealized increase in value of available-for-sale securities							$ 4,800	
Net income						97,000		
Cash dividends						(32,800)		
Balances, 12/31/2004	11,400	$57,000	$197,400	$5,000	$13,600	$386,200	$20,000	$(3,000)

---

22. Bardwell Corporation reports its comprehensive income in a separate financial statement.

EXHIBIT 16-12   Bardwell Corporation

Stockholders' Equity
December 31, 2004

Contributed capital	
Common stock, $5 par (30,000 shares authorized, 11,400 shares issued, of which 100 shares are being held as treasury stock)	$ 57,000
Additional paid-in capital on common stock	197,400
Additional paid-in capital from treasury stock	5,000
Common stock option warrants	13,600
Total contributed capital	$273,000
Retained earnings (see Note A)	386,200
Accumulated other comprehensive income	
Unrealized increase in value of available-for-sale securities	20,000
Total contributed capital, retained earnings, and accumulated other comprehensive income	$679,200
Less: Treasury stock (at cost)	(3,000)
Total Stockholders' Equity	$676,200

Notes to the Financial Statements

Note A: Retained earnings are restricted regarding dividends in the amount of $3,000, the cost of the treasury stock.

International Accounting Standards are based on historical cost, some countries allow companies to revalue (upward and downward) their property, plant, and equipment (and intangibles) based on professionally qualified appraisals. When a company increases its asset values due to a revaluation, it also credits a revaluation surplus account. (A decrease due to revaluation would reduce this revaluation account.) In some respects, reserves under international accounting standards are similar to appropriations of retained earnings under U.S. GAAP. They may differ, however, in that reserves may be required by foreign statutes or tax laws, whereas there are no such requirements in the United States.

EXHIBIT 16-13   Shareholders' Equity

COLGATE-PALMOLIVE COMPANY

Consolidated Balance Sheets (in part)

	December 31	
(In millions)	2001	2000
Shareholders' Equity		
Preferred stock	$ 341.3	$ 354.1
Common stock, $1 par value (1,000,000,000 shares authorized, 732,853,180 shares issued)	732.9	732.9
Additional paid-in capital	1,168.7	1,114.9
Retained earnings	5,643.6	4,893.7
Accumulated other comprehensive income	(1,491.2)	(1,269.7)
	$6,395.3	$5,855.9
Unearned compensation	(345.4)	(344.4)
Treasury stock, at cost	(5,203.5)	(4,043.4)
Total shareholders' equity	$ 846.4	$1,468.1

EXHIBIT 16-14 Consolidated Statements of Shareholders' Equity

COLGATE-PALMOLIVE COMPANY

Consolidated Statements of Retained Earnings, Comprehensive Income and Changes in Capital Accounts (in part)

(Dollars in Millions Except Per Share Amounts)	Common Shares		Additional Paid-in Capital	Treasury Shares		Retained Earnings	Accumulated Other Comprehensive Income	Comprehensive Income
	Shares	Amount		Shares	Amount			
Balance, December 31, 1999	578,863,046	$732.9	$1,063.2	153,999,624	$3,056.4	$4,212.3	$(1,136.2)	
Net income						1,063.8		$1,063.8
Other comprehensive Income:								
Cumulative translation adjustment							(133.5)	(133.5)
Total comprehensive income								$930.3
Dividends declared: Series B Convertible Preference Stock, net of income taxes						(20.3)		
Preferred stock						(.4)		
Common stock						(361.7)		
Shares issued for stock options	4,796,186		96.7	(4,796,186)	54.3			
Treasury stock acquired	(19,099,681)			19,099,681	1,040.6			
Other	2,096,323		(15.0)	(2,084,163)	(107.9)			
Balance, December 31, 2000	566,655,874	$732.9	$1,144.9	166,218,956	$4,043.4	$4,893.7	$(1,269.7)	
Net income						1,146.6		$1,146.6
Other comprehensive Income:								
Cumulative translation adjustment							(198.5)	(198.5)
Other							(23.0)	(23.0)
Total comprehensive income								$925.1
Dividends declared: Series B Convertible Preference Stock, net of income taxes						(21.3)		
Preferred stock						(.4)		
Common stock						(375.0)		
Shares issued for stock options	2,705,887		62.4	(2,705,887)	20.5			
Treasury stock acquired	(21,662,879)			21,662,879	1,230.2			
Other	-3,023,451		(38.6)	(3,023,261)	(90.6)			
Balance, December 31, 2001	550,722,333	$732.9	$1,168.7	182,152,687	$5,203.5	$5,643.6	$(1,491.2)	

QUESTIONS

Ⓠ How many shares of treasury stock were issued for stock options during 2001? Ⓠ At what average price per share were they issued? Ⓠ How many shares of treasury stock were acquired in 2001? Ⓠ At what average price per share were they acquired? Ⓠ What were the total dividends paid during 2001? Ⓠ What was the average dividend paid per share outstanding during 2001?

A company must disclose the "movement" in share capital accounts and in other equity for the period. In effect, these international disclosure requirements result in reporting the changes in shareholders' interests and are similar to the requirements of U.S. GAAP regarding the statement of changes in stockholders' equity, although the format of the disclosures may be different.

APPENDIX: QUASI-REORGANIZATION

A corporation that incurs net losses over an extended period may find itself in serious financial difficulty. Its assets may be overvalued and its liquidity position may be such that the corporation is, or shortly will be, unable to pay creditors. The long period of losses may have reduced its retained earnings to a very low amount or to a deficit (negative) figure, in which case most states restrict the payment of dividends. When this occurs, investors and creditors may feel that the current corporate management is unable to operate the corporation successfully. Nonetheless, the corporation may be entering different markets or developing new products that could lead to future profitability.

12 Account for a quasi-reorganization

Rather than enter into formal bankruptcy or other legal proceedings, the corporation may appoint a new management group capable of improving operating efficiency and effectiveness. At the same time, the corporation may engage in a process termed a quasi-reorganization. **A quasi-reorganization is primarily an accounting procedure, sanctioned by the applicable state laws, in which a corporation revalues its assets and liabilities, and realigns its capital structure to enable it to have a "fresh start" toward financial solvency and profitability.** These revaluations are referred to as *fresh-start measurements* that establish new carrying amounts unrelated to previous amounts.[23] Typically, the corporation writes down (or occasionally up) its individual net assets to their fair values and offsets the retained earnings deficit against existing additional paid-in capital. In so doing, the corporation must adhere to the state laws and to generally accepted accounting principles. The suggested readjustment procedures include the following steps:

1. The corporation reports to the stockholders about the restatements proposed and obtains the stockholders' formal consent.
2. Any amounts written off are first charged (debited) against retained earnings and then against additional paid-in capital.
3. The corporation begins its "fresh start" with a zero retained earnings balance.
4. The corporation presents a balance sheet as of the date of readjustment in which the assets and liabilities are reported at their fair values.

After the quasi-reorganization, several additional accounting procedures are suggested:

5. If losses or readjustments are identified that are determined to have occurred *before* the readjustment date, they are recorded as a reduction of additional paid-in capital and not current income or retained earnings.
6. Additional paid-in capital is *not* reduced for losses occurring *after* the readjustment.
7. Retained earnings is *dated* as of the readjustment date, and this dating is disclosed in a note to the financial statements until such dating loses its significance (usually 5 to 10 years).[24]

---

23. "Using Cash Flow Information and Present Value in Accounting Measurements," *FASB Statement of Concepts No. 7* (Norwalk, Conn.: FASB, 2000), p. 1.
24. *ARB No. 43, op. cit.*, ch. 7, sec. A, par. 3–11.

EXHIBIT 16-15   Blue Corporation: Before Quasi-Reorganization

Balance Sheet
December 31, 2004

Current assets	$ 30,000	Liabilities	$ 40,000
Property and equipment	200,000	Common stock, $10 par	150,000
Less: Accumulated depreciation	(60,000)	Additional paid-in capital	30,000
		Retained earnings (deficit)	(50,000)
Total Assets	$170,000	Total Liabilities and Stockholders' Equity	$170,000

The specific accounting procedures that a corporation completes in a quasi-reorganization generally include (1) a write-down of the assets to their fair values, with the loss being debited directly to retained earnings, (2) an increase in additional paid-in capital accomplished by a decrease in the par value of the capital stock, and (3) the elimination of the retained earnings deficit by a reduction of the additional paid-in capital.

Assume, for example, that the Blue Corporation reports the condensed December 31, 2004 balance sheet shown in Exhibit 16-15 prior to a quasi-reorganization on that date. In the quasi-reorganization process, the following information is relevant:

1. Property and equipment are determined to have a combined fair value of $92,000.
2. Contained within current assets are inventories that are overvalued by $8,000, and $4,000 of uncollectible accounts receivable.
3. The board of directors, with stockholder and state approval, has authorized a reduction in par value to $4 per share.

The journal entries that Blue makes for the reorganization are as follows:

1. To write down the fixed assets to fair value (typically accumulated depreciation is increased so that the new carrying value reflects the fair value):

Retained Earnings	48,000	
Accumulated Depreciation		48,000

2. To write down the current assets:

Retained Earnings	12,000	
Current Assets (inventories, $8,000,		
and accounts receivable, $4,000)		12,000

3. To reduce the par value of the common stock and increase additional paid-in capital (this procedure is similar to a disproportionate stock split, except no additional stock is issued):

Common Stock, $10 par	150,000	
Common Stock, $4 par		60,000
Additional Paid-in Capital		90,000

4. To eliminate the retained earnings deficit:

Additional Paid-in Capital	110,000	
Retained Earnings		
($50,000 + $48,000 + $12,000)		110,000

Exhibit 16-16 shows the Blue Corporation's balance sheet immediately following its quasi-reorganization, and reflects the preceding adjustments.

EXHIBIT 16-16   Blue Corporation: After Quasi-Reorganization

Balance Sheet
December 31, 2004

Current assets	$ 18,000	Liabilities	$ 40,000
Property and equipment	200,000	Common stock, $4 par	60,000
Less: Accumulated depreciation	(108,000)	Additional paid-in capital	10,000
		Retained earnings (see Note A)	0
Total Assets	$110,000	Total Liabilities and Stockholders' Equity	$110,000

Notes to Financial Statements
Note A: Retained earnings as of December 31, 2004 has a zero balance due to a quasi-reorganization on that date in which net assets were revalued, a deficit of $110,000 was charged against additional paid-in capital, and the par value of common stock was reduced from $10 to $4 per share.

SUMMARY

At the beginning of the chapter, we identified several objectives you would accomplish after reading the chapter. The objectives are listed below, each followed by a brief summary of the key points in the chapter discussion.

1. **Know the equation for computing basic earnings per share.** The numerator for computing basic earnings per share is net income minus preferred dividends. The denominator is the weighted average number of common shares outstanding.

2. **Understand how to compute the weighted average common shares for EPS.** The weighted average is computed by summing the "equivalent whole units" of shares for all the "layers" of stock. The equivalent whole units are computed by multiplying the number of shares for that layer times the fraction of the year the layer is outstanding.

3. **Identify the potential common shares included in diluted EPS.** The most common "potential common shares" that may be included in computing diluted EPS are stock options and warrants, as well as convertible preferred stock and convertible bonds. These securities are included in diluted EPS only if they decrease EPS.

4. **Apply the treasury stock method for including stock options and warrants in diluted EPS.** To apply the treasury stock method, compute the assumed shares issued and the proceeds received from the assumed exercise. Then compute the assumed shares reacquired by dividing the proceeds by the average market price. Finally, deduct the assumed shares reacquired from the assumed shares issued to determine the incremental shares.

5. **Calculate the impact of a convertible security on diluted EPS.** The impact is computed by dividing the increase in the EPS numerator by the increase in the EPS denominator, assuming the convertible security is converted into common stock. For a convertible bond, the numerator increases by the savings in interest expense (net of taxes). For a convertible bond, the numerator increases by the savings in preferred dividends.

6. **Compute diluted EPS.** Begin with the calculation of basic EPS. Then, increase the denominator for the increased shares from the assumed exercise of stock options and warrants. Then include the impact on the numerator and denominator of the assumed conversion of each dilutive convertible security in sequential order until the impact of the next security is antidilutive.

7. **Record the declaration and payment of cash dividends.** A corporation records the declaration by debiting retained earnings and crediting dividends payable. It records the payment by debiting dividends payable and crediting cash.

8. **Account for a property dividend.** A corporation accounts for a property dividend at the fair value of the asset transferred, and records a gain (or loss) on the date of declaration.

9. **Explain the difference in accounting for small and large stock dividends.** A corporation accounts for a small stock dividend by transferring from retained earnings to contributed capital an amount equal to the fair value of the additional shares issued. It accounts for a large stock dividend by transferring an amount equal to the par value.

10. **Understand how to report accumulated other comprehensive income.** A corporation reports its accumulated other comprehensive income in the stockholders' equity section of its balance sheet. It may report the amount of accumulated other comprehensive income for each item or it may report the total. If it reports the total, it must disclose the amounts for each of the items in the notes to its financial statements.

11. **Prepare a statement of changes in stockholders' equity.** Start with the beginning balance of each stockholders' equity account. Then add (or deduct) the change in each account resulting from the related transactions during the accounting period. Report the ending amounts on the stockholders' equity section of the balance sheet.

12. **Account for a quasi-organization (Appendix).** Write down (or up) the individual corporate net assets to their fair values and decrease (or increase) retained earnings. Increase additional paid-in capital by decreasing the par value of the capital stock. Eliminate the deficit in retained earnings by reducing additional paid-in capital.

QUESTIONS

Q16-1 What is a *simple capital structure*?

Q16-2 How is "basic earnings per share" computed for a corporation with a simple capital structure?

Q16-3 What is the "weighted average" number of shares for computing earnings per share and how is it calculated?

Q16-4 On what date are stock dividends and splits considered to be issued for computing earnings per share?

Q16-5 Identify several securities that might be found in the complex capital structure of a corporation.

Q16-6 What two earnings per share figures generally are reported by a corporation with a complex capital structure? Besides common shares outstanding, what additional securities are included in the second earnings per share calculation?

Q16-7 What is the *treasury stock method*? How is the increase in the diluted earnings per share denominator determined under the treasury stock method?

Q16-8 Discuss how to develop a ranking for determining in which order to include convertible securities in a corporation's diluted earnings per share calculations.

Q16-9 What additional disclosures does a corporation make concerning the basic and diluted earnings per share on its income statement?

Q16-10 What are the four important dates in regard to a cash dividend? What journal entry does the corporation make on each date?

Q16-11 What is fully participating preferred stock? Partially participating preferred stock?

Q16-12 Discuss how a corporation records the declaration of a property dividend.

Q16-13 Distinguish between an ordinary and special stock dividend.

Q16-14 Distinguish between a small and large stock dividend. What amounts does a corporation use to record the declaration of each dividend?

Q16-15 Distinguish between a stock split and a large stock dividend. How does each affect a corporation's stockholders' equity?

Q16-16 How does the accounting for a liquidating dividend differ from that for a normal cash dividend?

Q16-17 How does a corporation record and report a correction of a material error made in a previous year in its current year's financial statements?

Q16-18 For what reasons would a corporation appropriate (restrict) its retained earnings? How does it report an appropriation?

Q16-19 What is the suggested format for the statement of retained earnings? What are the two most common elements in this statement?

Q16-20 What items might a corporation include in the accumulated other comprehensive income section of its stockholders' equity?

Q16-21 What changes does a corporation include in its statement of changes in stockholders' equity?

Q16-22 *(Appendix)* (a) What is a quasi-reorganization? (b) Under what circumstances might it be advantageous for a corporation to engage in quasi-reorganization procedures?

Q16-23 *(Appendix)* What accounting procedures does a corporation generally include in a quasi-reorganization?

CASES

COMMUNICATION

C16-1 Earnings Per Share

"Earnings per share" (EPS) is the most featured single financial statistic about modern corporations. Daily published quotations of stock prices also include a "times earnings" figure for many securities that is based on EPS. Often, the focus of analysts' discussions will be on the EPS of the corporations receiving their attention.

Required

1. Explain how dividends or dividend requirements on any class of preferred stock that may be outstanding affect the computation of basic EPS.
2. One of the technical procedures applicable in diluted EPS computations is the "treasury stock method." Briefly describe the circumstances under which it might be appropriate to apply the treasury stock method.
3. In the case of convertible bonds that are assumed to be converted and are dilutive, explain how they are handled for purposes of diluted EPS computations. (*AICPA adapted*)

C16-2 Complex Capital Structure

The earnings per share data required of a company depend on the nature of its capital structure. A corporation may have a simple capital structure and compute only "basic earnings per share" or it may have a complex capital structure and have to compute basic earnings per share and "diluted earnings per share."

Required Define the term *complex capital structure* and discuss the disclosures (both financial and explanatory) necessary for earnings per share when a corporation has a complex capital structure. (*AICPA adapted*)

C16-3 Categories of Capital

A corporation's capital (stockholders' equity) is a very important part of its statement of financial position.

Required Identify and explain the general categories of capital (stockholders' equity) for a corporation. Be sure to enumerate specific sources included in each general category. (*AICPA adapted*)

C16-4 Dividends and Journal Entries

Problems may be encountered in accounting for transactions involving the stockholders' equity section of the balance sheet.

Required

1. Explain the significance of the three dates that are important in accounting for cash dividends to stockholders. State the journal entry, if any, needed at each date.
2. Assume retained earnings can be used for stock dividends distributable in shares. What is the effect of an ordinary 10% common stock dividend on retained earnings and total stockholders' equity? (*AICPA adapted*)

C16-5 Stock Dividends and Splits

Stock splits and stock dividends may be used by a corporation to change the number of shares of its stock outstanding.

Required

1. Explain what is meant by a stock split effected in the form of a dividend.
2. From an accounting viewpoint, explain how a stock split effected in the form of a dividend differs from an ordinary stock dividend.
3. How should a stock dividend that has been declared but not yet issued be classified in a statement of financial position? Why? (*AICPA adapted*)

C16-6 Quasi-Reorganization (Appendix)

A corporation may engage in a quasi-reorganization.

Required What is a corporate quasi-reorganization? Why is it undertaken? What accounting-related steps and procedures do you suggest during and after the quasi-reorganization process?

CREATIVE AND CRITICAL THINKING

C16-7 Convertible Securities

Public enterprises are required to present earnings per share data on the face of the income statement.

Required In regard to the computation of diluted earnings per share, discuss:

1. The effect of dilutive convertible securities.
2. The effect of antidilutive convertible securities. (*AICPA adapted*)

C16-8 Stock Options and EPS

Jones Company has adopted a traditional stock option plan for its officers and other employees. This plan is properly considered a compensatory plan.

Required Explain how this plan will affect diluted earnings per share. (*AICPA adapted*)

C16-9 Dividends and Treasury Stock

Brady Company has 30,000 shares of $10 par value common stock authorized and 20,000 shares issued and outstanding. On August 13, 2004 Brady purchased 1,000 shares of treasury stock for $12 per share. Brady uses the cost method to account for treasury stock. On September 14, 2004 Brady sold 500 shares of the treasury stock for $14 per share.

In October 2004 Brady declared and distributed 2,000 shares as a stock dividend from unissued shares when the market value of the common stock was $16 per share.

On December 21, 2004 Brady declared a $1 per share cash dividend, payable on January 11, 2005 to shareholders of record on December 31, 2004.

Required

1. How should Brady account for the cash dividend, and how would it affect Brady's balance sheet at December 31, 2004? Explain why.
2. How should Brady account for the stock dividend, and how would it affect Brady's stockholders' equity at December 31, 2004? Explain why.
3. How should Brady account for the purchase and sale of the treasury stock, and how should the treasury stock

be presented in Brady's balance sheet at December 31, 2004? (*AICPA adapted*)

C16-10 Analyzing Coca-Cola's Retained Earnings and EPS

Refer to the financial statements and related notes of the Coca-Cola Company in Appendix A to this book.

1. What does the company call its retained earnings? What was the amount at the end of 2001?
2. What was the balance of accumulated other comprehensive income on December 31, 2001? What caused it to change during 2001 and by what amounts?
3. What was the company's basic net income per share for 2001? How much preferred dividends were subtracted in the computation of this income per share? What was the average number of common shares outstanding used in the computation of this income per share? What was the company's diluted net income per share for 2001? How does this amount compare to 2000? What potential common shares were included in 2000 and why?
4. What were the dividends per share and in total for 2001?
5. Compute the return on share-owners' equity for 2001. How does this compare to 2000 (the share-owners' equity was $9,513 million at the end of 1999)?

C16-11 Ethics and EPS Adjustment

Ryan Company has as a goal that its earnings per share should increase by at least 3 percent each year; this goal has been attained every year over the past decade. As a result, the market price per share of Ryan's common stock also has increased each year. Last year (2003) Ryan's earnings per share was $3.00. This year, however, is a different story. Because of decreasing sales, preliminary computations at the end of 2004 show that earnings per share will be only $2.99 per share.

You are the accountant for Ryan Company. Ryan's controller, Jim Nastic, has come to you with some suggestions. He says, "I've noticed that the decrease in revenues has been primarily related to credit sales. Since we have fewer credit sales, I believe we are justified in reducing our bad debts expense from 4 to 2 percent of net sales. I also think that because of the decreased sales, we won't use our factory equipment as much, so we can extend its estimated remaining life from 10 to 15 years for computing our straight-line depreciation expense. Based on my calculations, if we make these changes, Ryan Company's 2004 earnings per share will be $3.06. This will sure make our stockholders happy, not to mention our CEO. You may even get a promotion. What do you think?"

Required From financial reporting and ethical perspectives, prepare a response to Jim Nastic regarding his suggestions.

RESEARCH

C16-12 Researching GAAP

In 2004, its first year of operations, Tara Corporation appropriately reported basic earnings per share of $1.05 on its income statement. During 2005 the company instituted a stock option plan and is required to report both basic and diluted earnings per share of $1.12 and $0.98, respectively, on its 2005 income statement. In its 2005 annual report, Tara Company presents comparative income statements for 2004 and 2005.

Required Research the related generally accepted accounting principles and prepare a short memo to Tara Corporation's president that explains how to report the 2004 and 2005 comparative earnings per share in its 2005 annual report. Cite your reference and applicable paragraph numbers.

MULTIPLE CHOICE

Select the best answer for each of the following.

M16-1 For purposes of computing the weighted average number of shares outstanding during the year, a midyear event that must be treated as occurring at the beginning of the year is the
  a. Issuance of stock warrants
  b. Purchase of treasury stock
  c. Sale of additional common stock
  d. Declaration and payment of stock dividend

M16-2 In determining basic earnings per share, dividends on nonconvertible cumulative preferred stock should be
  a. Deducted from net income only if declared
  b. Deducted from net income whether declared or not
  c. Added back to net income whether declared or not
  d. Disregarded

M16-3 Redford Corporation's capital structure at December 31, 2003 was as follows:

	Shares Issued and Outstanding
Common stock	100,000
Nonconvertible preferred stock	20,000

On July 2, 2004, Redford issued a 10% stock dividend on its common stock, and paid a cash dividend of $2.00 per share on its preferred stock. Net income for the year ended December 31, 2004 was $780,000. What should be Redford's 2004 basic earnings per share?

a. $7.80   c. $7.05
b. $7.09   d. $6.73

M16-4 Faucet Company has 2,500,000 shares of common stock outstanding on December 31, 2003. An additional 500,000 shares of common stock were issued on April 2, 2004, and 250,000 more on July 2, 2004. On October 1, 2004, Faucet issued 5,000, $1,000 face value, 7% convertible bonds. Each bond is dilutive and convertible into 40 shares of common stock. No bonds were converted into common stock in 2004. What is the number of shares to be used in computing basic earnings per share and diluted earnings per share, respectively, for the year ended December 31, 2004?

   a. 2,875,000 and 2,925,000
   b. 2,875,000 and 3,075,000
   c. 3,000,000 and 3,050,000
   d. 3,000,000 and 3,200,000

M16-5 At December 31, 2004, Gravin Corporation had 90,000 shares of common stock and 20,000 shares of convertible preferred stock outstanding, in addition to 9% convertible bonds payable in the face amount of $2,000,000. During 2004, Gravin paid dividends of $2.50 per share on the preferred stock. The preferred stock is convertible into 20,000 shares of common stock. The 9% convertible bonds are convertible into 30,000 shares of common stock. Net income for 2004 was $970,000. Assume an income tax rate of 30%. How much is the diluted earnings per share for the year ended December 31, 2004?

   a. $7.83
   b. $8.82
   c. $9.35
   d. $10.22

M16-6 A prior period adjustment should be reflected, net of applicable income taxes, in the financial statements of a business entity in the

   a. Retained earnings statement after net income but before dividends
   b. Retained earnings statement as an adjustment of the opening balance
   c. Income statement after income from continuing operations
   d. Income statement as part of income from continuing operations

M16-7 Cash dividends on the $10 par value common stock of Ray Company were as follows:

1st quarter of 2004	$ 800,000
2nd quarter of 2004	900,000
3rd quarter of 2004	1,000,000
4th quarter of 2004	1,100,000

The 4th quarter cash dividend was declared on December 21, 2004 to stockholders of record on December 31, 2004. Payment of the 4th quarter cash dividend was made on January 18, 2005.

In addition, Ray declared a 5% stock dividend on its $10 par value common stock on December 3, 2004 when there were 300,000 shares issued and outstanding and the market value of the common stock was $20 per share. The shares were issued on December 24, 2004.

What was the effect on the stockholders' equity accounts of Ray Company as a result of the preceding transactions?

	Common Stock	Additional Paid-in Capital	Retained Earnings
a.	$ 0	$ 0	$3,800,000 dr
b.	$150,000 cr	$ 0	$3,950,000 dr
c.	$150,000 cr	$150,000 cr	$4,100,000 dr
d.	$300,000 cr	$300,000 dr	$3,800,000 dr

M16-8 The following information was abstracted from the accounts of the Oar Corporation at December 31, 2004:

Total income since incorporation	$840,000
Total cash dividends paid	260,000
Proceeds from sale of donated stock	90,000
Total value of stock dividends distributed	60,000
Excess of proceeds over cost of treasury stock sold	140,000

What should be the current balance of retained earnings?

   a. $520,000   c. $610,000
   b. $580,000   d. $670,000

M16-9 Effective April 27, 2004 the stockholders of Bennett Corporation approved a two-for-one split of the company's common stock, and an increase in authorized common shares from 100,000 shares (par value $20 per share) to 200,000 shares (par value $10 per share). Bennett's stockholders' equity accounts immediately before issuance of the stock split shares were as follows:

Common stock, par value $20; 100,000 shares authorized; 50,000 shares outstanding	$1,000,000
Additional paid-in capital (premium of $3 per share on issuance of common stock)	150,000
Retained earnings	1,350,000

What should be the balances in Bennett's additional paid-in capital and retained earnings accounts immediately after the stock split is effected?

	Additional Paid-in Capital	Retained Earnings
a.	$ 0	$ 500,000
b.	$ 150,000	$ 350,000
c.	$ 150,000	$1,350,000
d.	$1,150,000	$ 350,000

M16-10 Newton Corporation was organized on January 1, 2002. On that date it issued 200,000 shares of $10 par value common stock at $15 per share (400,000 shares were authorized). During the period January 1, 2002 through December 31, 2004, Newton reported net income of $750,000 and paid cash dividends of $380,000. On January 5, 2004, Newton purchased 12,000 shares of its common stock at $12 per share. On December 28, 2004, 8,000 treasury shares were sold at $8 per share. Newton used the cost method of accounting for treasury shares.

What is the total stockholders' equity of Newton as of December 31, 2004?

a. $3,290,000
b. $3,306,000
c. $3,338,000
d. $3,370,000

EXERCISES

E16-1 **Weighted Average Shares** At the beginning of the current year, Heath Company had 20,000 shares of $10 par common stock outstanding. During the year, it engaged in the following transactions related to its common stock, so that at year-end it had 63,800 shares outstanding:

Apr.	2	Issued 5,000 shares of stock
June	4	Issued 4,000 shares of stock
July	1	Issued a 10% stock dividend
Sept.	28	Issued a two-for-one stock split, reducing the par value to $5 per share
Oct.	3	Reacquired 1,000 shares as treasury stock
Nov.	27	Reissued the 1,000 shares of treasury stock

Required Determine the weighted average number of shares outstanding for computing the current earnings per share.

E16-2 **Comparative Earnings Per Share** Ryan Company reports net income of $5,125 for the year ended December 31, 2004, its first year of operations. On January 3, 2004, the company issued 9,000 shares of common stock. On August 1, 2004 it issued an additional 3,000 shares of stock, resulting in 12,000 shares outstanding at year-end.

During 2005 Ryan Company earned net income of $16,400. It issued 2,000 additional shares of stock on March 2, 2005 and declared and issued a two-for-one stock split on November 2, 2005, resulting in 28,000 shares outstanding at year-end.

During 2006 Ryan Company earned net income of $23,520. The only common stock transaction during 2006 was a 20% stock dividend issued on July 2, 2006.

Required

1. Compute the basic earnings per share that would be disclosed in the 2004 annual report.
2. Compute the 2004 and 2005 comparative basic earnings per share that would be disclosed in the 2005 annual report.
3. Compute the 2004, 2005, and 2006 comparative basic earnings per share that would be disclosed in the 2006 annual report.

E16-3 **Basic Earnings Per Share** Sardel Company reported net income of $29,975 for 2004. During all of 2004 the company had 1,000 shares of 10%, $100 par, nonconvertible preferred stock outstanding, on which the year's dividends had been paid. At the beginning of 2004 the company had 7,000 shares of common stock outstanding. On April 2, 2004 the company issued another 2,000 shares of common stock, so that 9,000 common shares were outstanding at the end of 2004. Common dividends of $17,000 had been paid during 2004. At the end of 2004 the market price per share of common stock was $17.50.

Required

1. Compute the basic earnings per share of Sardel Company for 2004.
2. Compute the price/earnings ratio for 2004.

E16-4 **Basic Earnings Per Share** Burke Company shows the following condensed income statement information for the year ended December 31, 2004:

Income before extraordinary items	$29,936
Less: Extraordinary loss (net of income tax credit)	(2,176)
Net income	$27,760

The company declared dividends of $6,000 on preferred stock and $17,280 on common stock. At the beginning of 2004, 10,000 shares of common stock were outstanding. On May 4, 2004 the company issued 2,000 additional common shares, and on October 19, 2004 it issued a 20% stock dividend on its common stock. The preferred stock is not convertible.

Required

1. Compute the 2004 basic earnings per share.
2. Show the 2004 income statement disclosure of basic earnings per share.
3. Draft a related note to accompany the 2004 financial statements.

E16-5   *Impact on EPS and Rankings*   Matthews Company had five convertible securities outstanding during all of 2004. It paid the appropriate interest (and amortized any related premium or discount using the straight-line method) and dividends on each security during 2004. Each convertible security is described in the following table. The corporate income tax rate is 30%.

Security	Description
9.5% preferred stock	$200,000 par value. Issued at 112. Each $100 par preferred stock is convertible into 4.2 shares of common stock.
11.0% bonds	$220,000 face value. Issued at par. Each $1,000 bond is convertible into 44 shares of common stock.
8.0% preferred stock	$150,000 par value. Issued at par. Each $100 par preferred stock is convertible into 3.8 shares of common stock.
10.0% bonds	$100,000 face value. Issued at 94. Discount being amortized over 20-year life. Each $1,000 bond is convertible into 55 shares of common stock.
9.0% bonds	$200,000 face value. Issued at 108. Premium being amortized over 25-year life. Each $1,000 bond is convertible into 48 shares of common stock.

Required

1. Prepare a schedule that lists the impact of the assumed conversion of each convertible security on diluted earnings per share.
2. Prepare a ranking of the order in which the securities would be included in the diluted earnings per share computations.

E16-6   *Stock Options, EPS*   Butler Company has 30,000 shares of common stock outstanding during all of 2004. This common stock has been selling at an average market price of $45 per share. The company also has outstanding for the entire year compensatory stock options to purchase 4,000 shares of common stock at $32 per share. The unrecognized compensation cost (net of tax) relating to these stock options is $3 per share. During 2004 Butler Company earned income of $36,000 after income taxes of 30%.

Required Compute the 2004 diluted earnings per share.

E16-7   *Convertible Preferred Stock and EPS*   Jamieson Company earned net income of $43,800 during 2004. At the beginning of 2004 it had 10,000 shares of common stock outstanding; an additional 4,000 shares were issued on July 2. During 2004, 600 shares of 8%, $100 par, convertible preferred stock were outstanding the entire year. Dividends on this preferred stock were paid in 2004. Each share is convertible into 5 shares of common stock. The corporate income tax rate is 30%.

Required Compute the 2004 diluted earnings per share.

E16-8   *Convertible Bonds and EPS*   Clark Company's capital structure consists of common stock and convertible bonds. At the beginning of 2004 the company had 15,000 shares of common stock outstanding; an additional 4,500 shares were issued on May 4. The 7% convertible bonds have a face value of $80,000 and were issued in 2001 at par. Each $1,000 bond is convertible into 25 shares of common stock; to date, none of the bonds has been converted. During 2004, the company earned net income of $79,200 and was subject to an income tax rate of 30%.

Required Compute the 2004 diluted earnings per share.

E16-9   *Convertible Securities and Earnings Per Share*   Walker Company has 15,000 shares of common stock outstanding during all of 2004. It also has two convertible securities outstanding at the end of 2004. These are:

1. Convertible preferred stock: 1,000 shares of 9%, $100 par, preferred stock were issued in 2003 for $140 per share. Each share of preferred stock is convertible into 3.5 shares of common stock. The current dividends have been paid. To date, no preferred stock has been converted.

2. Convertible bonds: Bonds with a face value of $100,000 and an interest rate of 10% were issued at par on July 6, 2004. Each $1,000 bond is convertible into 35 shares of common stock. To date, no bonds have been converted.

The company earned net income of $54,000 during 2004. Its income tax rate is 30%.

Required Compute the 2004 diluted earnings per share. What earnings per share amount(s) would Walker report on its 2004 income statement?

E16-10 *Convertible Securities and Earnings Per Share*   Caldwell Company has 20,000 shares of common stock outstanding during all of 2004. It also has two convertible securities outstanding at the end of 2004. These are:

1. Convertible preferred stock: 2,000 shares of 9.5%, $50 par, preferred stock were issued on January 2, 2004 for $60 per share. Each share of preferred stock is convertible into 3 shares of common stock. Current dividends have been declared. To date, no preferred stock has been converted.
2. Convertible bonds: Bonds with a face value of $200,000 and an interest rate of 5.7% were issued at par in 2003. Each $1,000 bond is convertible into 22 shares of common stock. To date, no bonds have been converted.

The company earned net income of $61,500 during 2004. Its income tax rate is 30%.

Required Compute the 2004 diluted earnings per share. What earnings per share amount(s) would Caldwell report on its 2004 income statement?

E16-11 *Dividends*   Uhler Company has $80,000 available to pay dividends. It has 2,000 shares of 10%, $100 par, preferred stock and 30,000 shares of $10 par common stock outstanding. The preferred stock is selling for $125 per share and the common stock is selling for $20 per share.

Required

1. Determine the amount of dividends to be paid to each class of stockholder for each of the following independent assumptions:
   a. Preferred stock is nonparticipating and noncumulative.
   b. Preferred stock is nonparticipating and cumulative. Preferred dividends are two years in arrears at the beginning of the year.
   c. Preferred stock is fully participating and cumulative. Preferred dividends are one year in arrears at the beginning of the year.
   d. Preferred stock is participating up to a maximum of 15% of its par value and is noncumulative.
2. For 1(a), compute the dividend yield on the preferred stock and the common stock.

E16-12 *Various Dividends*   The Goodson Company listed the following account balances on December 31, 2003:

Investment in Xurk Company bonds	$ 25,000	Common stock, $10 par	$400,000
Dividends payable: preferred	4,000	Additional paid-in capital on preferred stock	20,000
Dividends payable: common	40,000	Additional paid-in capital on common stock	210,000
Preferred stock, 8%, $100 par	100,000	Retained earnings	270,000

During 2004, the following transactions occurred:

Feb. 2   Paid the semiannual dividends declared on December 15, 2003.
Mar. 5   Declared a property dividend, payable to common stockholders on April 5 in Xurk Company bonds being held to maturity. The bonds (which have a book value of $25,000) have a current market value of $31,000.
Apr. 5   Paid the property dividend.
July 6   Declared a $4 per share semiannual cash dividend on preferred stock and a $1.10 per share semiannual dividend on common stock, to be paid on August 17.
Aug. 17   Paid the cash dividends.
Oct. 15   Declared a 2% stock dividend on common stock to be issued on December 3. The current market price is $22 per share.
Dec. 3   Issued the stock dividend.
Dec. 28   Declared a $4 and $1.20 per share semiannual cash dividend on preferred and common stock, respectively, to be paid on February 15, 2005.

Required Prepare journal entries to record the preceding transactions.

E16-13 *Various Dividends* Mills Company lists the following condensed balance sheet as of the beginning of 2004:

Current assets	$ 60,000	Current liabilities	$ 30,000
Investment in M bonds	9,000	Common stock, no par	150,000
Fixed assets (net)	200,000	Retained earnings	89,000
	$269,000		$269,000

It is considering the impact of various types of dividends upon this balance sheet. Each dividend would be declared and paid in 2004. These include:

1. Cash dividend of $1.00 per share on the 10,000 shares outstanding.
2. Stock dividend of 5% on the 10,000 shares outstanding when the market price is $17 per share.
3. Property dividend consisting of the $9,000 (book value) investment in M bonds being held to maturity. This investment has a current market value of $13,000. (For Requirement 2 below, assume any gain or loss is to be reflected in retained earnings. Disregard income taxes.)
4. Scrip dividend of $0.80 per share on the 10,000 shares outstanding. The scrip earns interest at a 12% annual rate and is to be declared on January 30 and paid on December 30, 2004. (For Requirement 2 below, assume any interest expense is to be reflected in retained earnings. Disregard income taxes.)
5. Cash dividend consisting of a $0.70 per share normal dividend and a $0.30 per share liquidating dividend.

Required For each preceding *independent* dividend:

1. Prepare the appropriate journal entries for the declaration and payment of the dividend.
2. Prepare a condensed balance sheet after the dividend has been *paid*.

E16-14 *Stock Dividend* The stockholders' equity of the Sadler Company is as shown:

Common stock, $10 par	$250,000
Additional paid-in capital on common stock	150,000
Retained earnings	200,000
	$600,000

The company is considering the declaration and issuance of a stock dividend at a time when the market price is $30 per share.

Required

1. Assuming the board of directors recommends a 6% stock dividend, prepare:
   a. the journal entry at the date of declaration
   b. the journal entry at the date of issuance
   c. the stockholders' equity after the issuance
2. Assuming, instead, that a 40% stock dividend is recommended, repeat (a), (b), and (c) of Requirement 1.

E16-15 *Stock Dividend Comparison* Although Weaver Company has enough retained earnings legally to declare a dividend, its working capital is low. The board of directors is considering a stock dividend instead of a cash dividend. The common stock is currently selling at $34 per share. The following is Weaver's current stockholders' equity:

Common stock, $10 par	$ 400,000
Premium on common stock	800,000
Total contributed capital	$1,200,000
Retained earnings	1,300,000
Total stockholders' equity	$2,500,000

Required

1. Assuming a 15% stock dividend is declared and issued, prepare the stockholders' equity section immediately after the date of issuance.
2. Assuming, instead, that a 30% stock dividend is declared and issued, prepare the stockholders' equity section immediately after the date of issuance.
3. What unusual result do you notice when you compare your answers from (1) with (2)? From a theoretical standpoint, how might this have been avoided?

E16-16   *Prior Period Adjustments*   Miles Company began 2004 with a retained earnings balance of $142,400. During an examination of its accounting records on December 31, 2004, the company found it had made the following material errors, for both financial reporting and income tax reporting, during 2003.

1. Depreciation expense of $15,000 inadvertently had been recorded twice for the same machine.
2. No accrual had been made at year-end for interest; therefore, interest expense had been understated by $4,000.

The Miles Company's net income during 2004 was $60,000. The company has been subject to a 30% income tax rate for the past several years. It declared and paid dividends of $13,000 during 2004.

Required

1. Prepare whatever journal entries in 2004 are necessary to correct the Miles Company books for its previous errors. Make your corrections directly to the retained earnings account.
2. Prepare the statement of retained earnings for 2004.

E16-17   *Appropriations*   Perry Company has a retained earnings balance of $400,000 at the end of 2004. During 2004 it had issued $100,000 of 5-year, 12%, long-term bonds. The bond provisions require that each year over the 5-year period an additional $20,000 of retained earnings be unavailable for dividends. This restriction is in addition to any other retained earnings restrictions that the company might make. During 2004 the company also decided to "self-insure" against fire losses because of its previous safety record, and to avoid high insurance premiums. The board of directors decided to restrict retained earnings at the end of *each* year in an amount equal to the $8,000 annual premium that would have been paid.

During 2009 the Perry Company retired its bonds. On July 1, 2007, a building that had cost $90,000 and had a current book value of $60,000 was completely destroyed by fire. After this loss, the company reassessed its policy of self-insurance and acquired a comprehensive fire insurance policy.

Required

1. Show how Perry Company would report its retained earnings in its 2004 financial statements. Include a note to the financial statements fully describing the appropriations.
2. Prepare whatever journal entries are necessary to record the fire loss and indicate how the appropriations would be eliminated at the end of 2009.

E16-18   *Retained Earnings Statement*   Hernandez Company began 2004 with a $120,000 balance in retained earnings. During the year, the following events occurred:

1. The company earned net income of $80,000.
2. A material error in net income from a previous period was corrected. This error correction increased retained earnings by $9,800 after related income taxes of $4,200.
3. Cash dividends totaling $13,000 and stock dividends totaling $17,000 were declared.
4. One thousand shares of callable preferred stock that originally had been issued at $110 per share were recalled and retired at the beginning of 2004 for the call price of $120 per share.
5. Treasury stock (common) was acquired at a cost of $20,000. State law requires a restriction of retained earnings in an equal amount. The company reports its retained earnings restrictions in a note to the financial statements.

Required

1. Prepare a statement of retained earnings for the year ended December 31, 2004.
2. Prepare the note to disclose the restriction of retained earnings.

E16-19   *Retained Earnings Statement*   On January 1, 2004 Franklin Company had a retained earnings balance of $206,000. During 2004 the following events occurred:

1. Treasury stock (common) was acquired at a cost of $14,000. State law requires a restriction of retained earnings in an equal amount. The company reports its retained earnings restrictions in a note to the financial statements.
2. Cash dividends totaling $9,000 and stock dividends totaling $6,000 were declared and distributed.
3. Net income was $58,000.
4. Two thousand shares of callable preferred stock were recalled and retired at a price of $150 per share. This stock had originally been issued at $130 per share.
5. A material error in net income for a previous period was corrected. This error correction decreased retained earnings by $12,600 after a related income tax credit of $5,400.

Required

1. Prepare a statement of retained earnings for the year ended December 31, 2004.
2. Prepare a note to disclose the restriction of retained earnings.

E16-20 *Stockholders' Equity* Wilk Manufacturing Corporation completed the following transactions during its first year of operation, 2004:

1. The state authorized the issuance of 30,000 shares of $5 par common stock. 15,000 shares were issued at $22 per share.
2. The state authorized the issuance of 6,000 shares of $50 par preferred stock. All 6,000 shares were issued at $70 per share.
3. Wilk reacquired 1,000 shares of its outstanding common stock at $18 per share. The cost method is used to account for treasury stock.
4. Wilk invested $50,000 of excess cash, not needed to finance operations, in long-term available-for-sale equity securities. At year-end, the market value of these securities was $47,500.
5. Wilk sold 500 shares of treasury stock for $23 per share.
6. Net income for the first year of operations was $16,000. No dividends were declared.

Required Prepare the stockholders' equity section (and any related notes to the financial statements) of the Wilk Manufacturing Corporation balance sheet as of December 31, 2004.

E16-21 *Changes in Stockholders' Equity* The stockholders' equity section of Winslow Design Company's December 31, 2003 balance sheet appeared as follows:

Contributed capital

Preferred stock, $100 par (10,000 shares authorized, 1,250 shares issued)	$125,000
Additional paid-in capital on preferred stock	55,000
Common stock, $10 par (60,000 shares authorized, 15,000 shares issued)	150,000
Additional paid-in capital on common stock	105,000
Total contributed capital	$435,000
Retained earnings	78,000
Contributed capital and retained earnings	$513,000
Less: Treasury stock (300 shares of common at $14 per share)	(4,200)
Total Stockholders' Equity	$508,800

During 2004 the company entered into the following transactions affecting stockholders' equity:

1. Issued 250 shares of preferred stock at $164 per share.
2. Issued 3,000 shares of common stock at $17 per share.
3. Reacquired 200 of its own common shares as treasury stock for $15 per share.
4. Reissued 250 shares of treasury stock at $17 per share (FIFO basis).
5. Net income for 2004 was $46,500. Dividends of $25,000 were distributed.

Required

1. Prepare a statement of changes in stockholders' equity for the year ended December 31, 2004.
2. Compute the return on stockholders' equity for 2004.

E16-22 *Quasi-Reorganization (Appendix)* BMC Corporation has experienced a net loss for a number of years. On the advice of the board of directors, a new management team was appointed. Furthermore, the corporation has agreed to a quasi-reorganization and to the revaluation of certain balance sheet account balances, subject to stockholder approval. The BMC balance sheet on December 31, 2004 contained the following information prior to the reorganization:

Current assets	$ 20,000	Liabilities	$ 30,000
Property and equipment	110,000	Common stock, $10 par	100,000
Less: Accumulated depreciation	(30,000)	Additional paid-in capital on common stock	40,000
Total Assets	$100,000	Retained earnings (deficit)	(70,000)
		Total Liabilities and Stockholders' Equity	$100,000

The following information is relevant to the December 31,2004 quasi-reorganization as approved by the stockholders:

1. Property and equipment is determined to have a fair value of $45,000.
2. Current assets contain inventories overstated by $6,000.
3. Current assets contain uncollectible accounts receivable of $3,000.
4. Par value of common stock is to be reduced to $1 per share as approved by the state of incorporation.

Required

1. Prepare journal entries to record the quasi-reorganization.
2. Prepare the balance sheet of BMC Corporation immediately following the quasi-reorganization. Include a note to accompany retained earnings.

E16-23   *Quasi-Reorganization (Appendix)*   Current conditions warrant that the Austin Company have a quasi-reorganization (corporate readjustment) at December 31, 2004. Selected balance sheet items prior to the quasi-reorganization are as follows:

Inventory was recorded in the accounting records at December 31, 2004 at its market value of $3 million.
Property, plant, and equipment was recorded in the accounting records at December 31, 2004 at $6 million net of accumulated depreciation.
Stockholders' equity consisted of:

Common stock, par value $10 per share;	
authorized, issued, and outstanding 350,000 shares	$3,500,000
Additional paid-in capital	800,000
Retained earnings (deficit)	(450,000)
Total stockholders' equity	$3,850,000

Additional information is as follows:

Inventory cost at December 31, 2004 was $3,250,000.
Property, plant, and equipment had a fair value of $4 million.
The par value of the common stock is to be reduced from $10 per share to $5 per share.

Required Prepare the stockholders' equity section of the Austin Company's balance sheet at December 31, 2004 as it should appear after the quasi-reorganization (corporate readjustment) has been accomplished. Show supporting computations in good form. Ignore income tax and deferred tax considerations. (*AICPA adapted*)

PROBLEMS

P16-1   *Income Statement and Basic EPS*   Manty Company listed the following selected pretax items in its December
@   31, 2004 adjusted trial balance:

	Debit	Credit
Nonconvertible, 8% preferred stock, $100 par		$ 60,000
Common stock, $5 par		90,000
Sales		206,000
Cost of goods sold	$131,000	
Gain on disposal of discontinued Division B		8,000
Extraordinary gain from bond retirement		15,000
Operating expenses	19,250	
Loss from operations of discontinued Division B	20,000	

Additional information:

The preferred shares had been outstanding the entire year; annual dividends were declared and paid in 2004. During 2004, 2,000 common shares were issued on July 2, and 6,000 common shares were issued on November 3. Common dividends of $12,500 were declared and paid in 2004. The company is subject to a 30% income tax rate.

Required Prepare the Manty Company's 2004 income statement (multiple-step) and the related note.

P16-2   *Comparative Income Statements and Basic EPS*   Agocha Company reported the following selected items in
@   the stockholders' equity section of its balance sheet on December 31, 2004 and 2005:

	December 31,	
	2004	2005
7% preferred stock (nonconvertible), $100 par	$50,000	$50,000
Common stock, $10 par	70,000	84,000

In addition, it listed the following selected pretax items in its December 31, 2004 and 2005 adjusted trial balances:

	December 31, 2004		December 31, 2005	
	Debit	Credit	Debit	Credit
Sales		$124,300		$140,000
Extraordinary gain		6,000		—
Cost of goods sold	$75,000		$80,000	
Operating expenses	18,000		20,000	
Extraordinary loss	—		9,000	

The preferred shares were outstanding during all of 2004 and 2005; annual dividends were declared and paid
in each year. During 2004, 2,000 common shares were sold for cash on October 3. During 2005, a 20%
stock dividend was declared and issued in early May. At the end of 2004 and 2005, the common stock was
selling for $25.75 and $32.20, respectively. The company is subject to a 30% income tax rate.

Required

1. Prepare the comparative 2004 and 2005 income statements (multiple-step), and the related note that would
   appear in the Agocha Company's 2005 annual report.
2. Compute the price/earnings ratio for 2005. How does this compare to 2004? Why is it different?

P16-3   *Earnings Per Share*   Wheeler Company began 2004 with 10,000 shares of $10 par common stock and 2,000
shares of 9.4%, $100 par, convertible preferred stock outstanding. On April 2 and June 1, respectively, the
company issued 2,000 and 6,000 additional shares of common stock. On November 16 the company declared
a two-for-one stock split. Compensatory stock options that currently allow the purchase of 2,000 shares of
common stock at $16 per share were outstanding during 2004. To date, none of these options have been ex-
ercised. The unrecognized compensation cost (net of tax) related to these stock options is $2 per share. The
preferred stock was issued in 2003. Each share of preferred stock is currently convertible into 4 shares of common stock. To date, no preferred stock has been converted. Current dividends have been paid on both preferred and common stock. Net income for 2004 totaled $109,800. The company is subject to a 30% income
tax rate. The common stock sold at an average market price of $24 per share during 2004.

Required

1. Prepare supporting calculations and compute:
   a. Basic earnings per share
   b. Diluted earnings per share
2. Show how Wheeler Company would report the earnings per share on its 2004 income statement. Include
   an accompanying note to the financial statements.

P16-4   *Impact on EPS, Rankings, and Computations*   Madsen Company had five convertible securities outstanding
during all of 2004. It paid the appropriate interest (and amortized any related premium or discount using the
straight-line method) and dividends on each security during 2004. Each of the convertible securities is described
in the following table:

Security	Description
10.2% bonds	$200,000 face value. Issued at par. Each $1,000 bond is convertible into 28 shares of common stock.
12.0% bonds	$160,000 face value. Issued at 110. Premium being amortized over 20-year life. Each $1,000 bond is convertible into 47 shares of common stock.
9.0% bonds	$200,000 face value. Issued at 95. Discount being amortized over 10-year life. Each $1,000 bond is convertible into 44 shares of common stock.
8.3% preferred stock	$120,000 par value. Issued at 108. Each $100 par preferred stock is convertible into 3.9 shares of common stock.
7.5% preferred stock	$180,000 par value. Issued at par. Each $100 par preferred stock is convertible into 6 shares of common stock.

Additional data:

Net income for 2004 totaled $119,460. The weighted average number of common shares outstanding during 2004 was 40,000 shares. No stock options or warrants are outstanding. The effective corporate income tax rate is 30%.

Required

1. Prepare a schedule that lists the impact of the assumed conversion of each convertible security on diluted earnings per share.
2. Prepare a ranking of the order in which each of the convertible securities should be included in diluted earnings per share.
3. Compute basic earnings per share.
4. Compute diluted earnings per share.
5. Indicate the amount(s) of the earnings per share that Madsen Company would report on its 2004 income statement.

*See WebTutor for annotated problem solution.

P16-5 **Comprehensive: EPS**   Newton Company is preparing its annual earnings per share amounts to be disclosed on its 2004 income statement. It has collected the following information at the end of 2004:

1. Net income: $120,400. Included in the net income is income from continuing operations of $130,400 and an extraordinary loss (net of income taxes) of $10,000. Corporate income tax rate, 30%.
2. Common stock outstanding on January 1, 2004: 20,000 shares.
3. Common stock issuances during 2004: July 6, 4,000 shares; August 24, 3,000 shares.
4. Stock dividend: On October 19, 2004 the company declared a 10% stock dividend that resulted in 2,700 additional outstanding shares of common stock.
5. Common stock prices: 2004 average market price, $30 per share; 2004 ending market price, $27 per share.
6. 7% preferred stock outstanding on January 1, 2004: 1,000 shares. Terms: $100 par, nonconvertible. Current dividends have been paid. No preferred stock issued during 2004.
7. 8% convertible preferred stock outstanding on January 1, 2004: 800 shares. The stock was issued in 2003 at $130 per share. Each $100 par preferred stock is currently convertible into 1.7 shares of common stock. Current dividends have been paid. To date, no preferred stock has been converted.
8. Bonds payable outstanding on January 1, 2004: $100,000 face value. These bonds were issued several years ago at 97 and pay annual interest of 9.6%. The discount is being amortized in the amount of $300 per year. Each $1,000 bond is currently convertible into 22 shares of common stock. To date, no bonds have been converted.
9. Compensatory stock options outstanding: Key executives may currently acquire 3,000 shares of common stock at $20 per share. The options were granted in 2003. To date, none have been exercised. The unrecognized compensation cost (net of tax) related to the stock options is $4 per share.

Required

1. Compute the basic earnings per share. Show supporting calculations.
2. Compute the diluted earnings per share. Show supporting calculations.
3. Show how Newton Company would report these earnings per share figures on its 2004 income statement. Include an explanatory note to the financial statements.

P16-6 **Comprehensive: EPS**   The Frost Company has accumulated the following information relevant to its 2004 earnings per share.

1. Net income for 2004, $150,500.
2. Bonds payable: On January 1, 2004 the company had issued 10%, $200,000 bonds at 110. The premium is being amortized in the amount of $1,000 per year. Each $1,000 bond is currently convertible into 22 shares of common stock. To date, no bonds have been converted.
3. Bonds payable: On December 31, 2002, the company had issued $540,000 of 5.8% bonds at par. Each $1,000 bond is currently convertible into 11.6 shares of common stock. To date, no bonds have been converted.
4. Preferred stock: On July 3, 2003 the company had issued 3,800 shares of 7.5%, $100 par, preferred stock at $108 per share. Each share of preferred stock is currently convertible into 2.45 shares of common stock. To date, no preferred stock has been converted and no additional shares of preferred stock have been issued. The current dividends have been paid.
5. Common stock: At the beginning of 2004, 25,000 shares were outstanding. On August 4, 7,000 additional shares were issued. During September, a 20% stock dividend was declared and issued. On November 30, 2,000 shares were reacquired as treasury stock.

6. Compensatory stock options: Options to acquire common stock at a price of $33 per share were outstanding during all of 2004. Currently, 4,000 shares may be acquired. To date, no options have been exercised. The unrecognized compensation cost (net of tax) related to these stock options is $5 per share.

7. Miscellaneous: Stock market prices on common stock averaged $41 per share during 2004, and the 2004 ending stock market price was $40 per share. The corporate income tax rate is 30%.

Required

1. Compute the basic earnings per share. Show supporting calculations.
2. Compute the diluted earnings per share. Show supporting calculations.
3. Indicate which earnings per share figure(s) Frost Company would report on its 2004 income statement.

P16-7   *Earnings Per Share*   The controller of Lafayette Corporation has requested assistance in determining income, basic earnings per share, and diluted earnings per share for presentation in the Company's income statement for the year ended September 30, 2005. As currently calculated, the Company's net income is $540,000 for fiscal year 2004–2005.

Your working papers disclose the following opening balances and transactions in the Company's capital stock accounts during the year:

1. Common stock (at October 1, 2004, stated value $10, authorized 300,000 shares; effective December 1, 2004, stated value $5, authorized 600,000 shares):
   Balance, October 1, 2004—issued and outstanding 60,000 shares
   December 1, 2004—60,000 shares issued in a 2-for-1 stock split
   December 1, 2004—280,000 shares (stated value $5) issued at $39 per share
2. Treasury stock—common:
   March 2, 2005—purchased 40,000 shares at $38 per share
   April 1, 2005—sold 40,000 shares at $40 per share
3. Noncompensatory stock purchase warrants, Series A (initially, each warrant was exchangeable with $60 for one common share; effective December 1, 2004, each warrant became exchangeable for two common shares at $30 per share):
   October 1, 2004—25,000 warrants issued at $6 each
4. Noncompensatory stock purchase warrants, Series B (each warrant is exchangeable with $40 for one common share):
   April 1, 2005—20,000 warrants authorized and issued at $10 each.
5. First mortgage bonds, 5 1/2%, due 2017 (nonconvertible; priced to yield 5% when issued):
   Balance October 1, 2004—authorized, issued, and outstanding—the face value of $1,400,000
6. Convertible debentures, 7%, due 2024 (initially, each $1,000 bond was convertible at any time until maturity into 20 common shares; effective December 1, 2004, the conversion rate became 40 shares for each bond):
   October 1, 2004—authorized and issued at their face value (no premium or discount) of $2,400,000.

The following table shows the average market prices for the company's securities during 2004–2005:

	Average for Year Ended September 30, 2005
Common stock	$37\frac{1}{2}$*
First mortgage bonds	87
Convertible debentures	115
Series A Warrants	15
Series B Warrants	$9\frac{1}{2}$

*Adjusted for stock split.

Required Prepare a schedule computing:

1. The basic earnings per share.
2. The diluted earnings per share that should be presented in the Company's income statement for the year ended September 30, 2005.

A supporting schedule computing the numbers of shares to be used in these computations should also be prepared. Assume an income tax rate of 30%. (*AICPA adapted*)

P16-8   ***Earnings Per Share***   Mason Corporation's capital structure is as follows:

	December 31	
	2004	**2003**
Outstanding shares of:		
Common stock	336,000	300,000
Nonconvertible preferred stock	10,000	10,000
8% convertible bonds	$1,000,000	$1,000,000

The following additional information is available:

1. On September 1, 2004, Mason sold 36,000 additional shares of common stock.
2. Net income for the year ended December 31, 2004 was $750,000.
3. During 2004 Mason paid dividends of $3 per share on its nonconvertible preferred stock.
4. The 8% convertible bonds are convertible into 40 shares of common stock for each $1,000 bond.
5. Unexercised compensatory stock options to purchase 30,000 shares of common stock at $20.50 per share were outstanding at the beginning and end of 2004. The average market price of Mason's common stock was $36 per share during 2004. The market price was $33 per share at December 31, 2004. The unrecognized compensation cost (net of tax) related to the stock options is $2 per share.
6. Warrants to purchase 20,000 shares of common stock at $38 per share were attached to the preferred stock at the time of issuance. The warrants, which expire on December 31, 2009, were outstanding at December 31, 2004.
7. Mason's effective income tax rate was 30% for 2003 and 2004.

Required (Show supporting computations in good form, and round earnings per share to the nearest penny.)

1. Compute the number of shares that should be used for the computation of basic earnings per share for the year ended December 31, 2004.
2. Compute the basic earnings per share for the year ended December 31, 2004.
3. Compute the number of shares that should be used for the computation of diluted earnings per share for the year ended December 31, 2004.
4. Compute the diluted earnings per share for the year ended December 31, 2004. (*AICPA adapted*)

P16-9   ***Dividends***   The Keener Company has had 1,000 shares of 7%, $100 par-value preferred stock and 40,000 shares of $5 stated-value common stock outstanding for the last 3 years. During that period, dividends paid totaled $6,000, $28,000, and $30,000 for each year, respectively.

Required Compute the amount of dividends that Keener must have paid to preferred stockholders and common stockholders in each of the 3 years, given the following four independent assumptions:

1. Preferred stock is nonparticipating and noncumulative
2. Preferred stock is nonparticipating and cumulative
3. Preferred stock is fully participating and cumulative
4. Preferred stock participates up to a maximum of 9% of its par value and is cumulative

P16-10   ***Dividends***   Tomasco, Inc., began operations in January 2000 and had the following reported net income or loss for each of its 5 years of operations:

2000	$ 150,000 loss
2001	130,000 loss
2002	120,000 loss
2003	250,000 income
2004	1,000,000 income

At December 31, 2004, the Tomasco capital accounts were as follows:

Common stock, par value $10 per share; authorized 100,000 shares; issued and outstanding 50,000 shares	$ 500,000
4% nonparticipating noncumulative preferred stock, par value $100 per share; authorized, issued, and outstanding 1,000 shares	100,000
8% fully participating cumulative preferred stock, par value $100 per share; authorized, issued, and outstanding 10,000 shares	1,000,000

Tomasco has never paid a cash or stock dividend. There has been no change in the capital accounts since Tomasco began operations. The appropriate state law permits dividends only from retained earnings.

Required Prepare a work sheet showing the maximum amount available for cash dividends on December 31, 2004 and how it would be distributable to the holders of the common shares and each of the preferred shares. Show supporting computations in good form. (*AICPA adapted*)

P16-11 **Comprehensive** The Gray Company lists the following stockholders' equity items on its December 31, 2003 balance sheet:

Preferred stock, 8%, $100 par	$120,000
Common stock, $10 par	180,000
Additional paid-in capital on preferred stock	21,600
Additional paid-in capital on common stock	90,000
Total contributed capital	$411,600
Retained earnings	230,000
Accumulated other comprehensive income	
Unrealized increase in value of available-for-sale securities	6,000
Contributed capital, retained earnings, and accumulated other comprehensive income	$647,600
Less: Treasury stock (2,000 shares of common at $21 per share, acquired on March 3, 2003)	(42,000)
Total Stockholders' Equity	$605,600

The following stock transactions occurred during 2004:

Jan. 2	Issued 3,000 shares of common stock at $25 per share.
Jan. 30	Paid the annual 2003 per share dividend on preferred stock and the $2 per share dividend on common stock. These dividends had been declared on December 31, 2003.
Mar. 2	Issued 400 shares of preferred stock at $125 per share.
May 7	Reissued 600 shares of treasury stock at $24 per share.
June 15	Split the common stock two for one, reducing the par value to $6 per share.
July 2	Declared a 5% stock dividend on the outstanding common stock, to be issued on August 3. The stock is selling for $14 per share.
Aug. 3	Issued the stock dividend.
Oct. 1	Declared a property dividend payable to common stockholders on November 1. The dividend consists of 2,000 shares of an investment in Lamb Company available-for-sale common stock, which had been acquired at a cost of $12 per share and which have a carrying value of $15 per share. The stock is currently selling for $16 per share.
Nov. 1	Issued the property dividend to common stockholders.
Dec. 31	Declared the annual per share dividend on the outstanding preferred stock and a $1 per share dividend on the outstanding common stock, to be paid on January 30, 2005.

Required
1. Prepare journal entries to record the preceding transactions.
2. Prepare the December 31, 2004 stockholders' equity section (assume that 2004 net income was $225,000).

P16-12 **Comprehensive** Included in the December 31, 2003 Jacobi Company balance sheet was the following stockholders' equity section:

Preferred stock, 6%, $100 par	$200,000	
Premium on preferred stock	12,000	$ 212,000
Common stock, $5 par	$150,000	
Premium on common stock	240,000	390,000
Total contributed capital		$ 602,000
Retained earnings		627,000
Accumulated other comprehensive income (loss)		
Unrealized decrease in value of available-for-sale securities		(41,000)
Contributed capital, retained earnings, and accumulated other comprehensive income		$1,188,000
Less: Treasury stock (1,000 shares of common stock at cost, acquired on 2/3/2003)		(20,000)
Total Stockholders' Equity		$1,168,000

The company engaged in the following stock transactions during 2004:

Jan.   2   Paid the semiannual dividend on the outstanding preferred stock and a $1.60 per share annual dividend on the outstanding common stock. These dividends had been declared on December 1 of 2003.

Jan.   5   Issued 500 shares of preferred stock at $110 per share.

Jan. 23   Issued 4,000 shares of common stock at $23 per share.

Apr.   2   Reissued 700 shares of treasury stock at $24 per share.

May 14   Declared a 10% stock dividend on the outstanding common stock, payable on June 29. The common stock is currently selling for $25 per share.

June   1   Declared the semiannual cash dividend on the outstanding preferred stock, payable on July 1.

June 29   Issued the stock dividend declared on May 15.

July   1   Paid the cash dividend declared on June 1.

July 20   Split the common stock two for one and reduced the par value to $2.50 per share.

Aug.   3   Declared a property dividend, payable to common stockholders on September 14. The dividend consists of an investment in 5,000 shares of available-for-sale Drot Company common stock. The stock had been acquired at $9 per share, but has a carrying value of $6 per share. The stock is currently selling for $4 per share.

Sept. 14   Paid the property dividend declared on August 3.

Dec.   3   Declared the semiannual cash dividend on the outstanding preferred stock and a $0.90 per share annual dividend on the outstanding common stock.

Required

1. Prepare journal entries to record the preceding transactions.
2. Prepare the December 31, 2004 stockholders' equity section (assume that 2004 net income was $270,000).

P16-13   *Stock Dividends, Splits*   The stockholders' equity of the Nance Company prior to any of the following events is as follows:

Preferred stock, 8%, $100 par	$100,000
Common stock, $10 par	150,000
Premium on preferred stock	16,000
Premium on common stock	220,000
Retained earnings	264,000
	$750,000

The company is considering the following *alternative* items:

1. An 8% stock dividend on the common stock when it is selling for $30 per share.
2. A 30% stock dividend on the common stock when it is selling for $32 per share.
3. A *special* stock dividend to common stockholders consisting of one share of preferred stock for every 100 shares of common stock. The preferred stock and common stock are selling for $123 and $31 per share, respectively.
4. A two-for-one stock split on the common stock, reducing the par value to $4 per share (assume the same date for declaration and issuance). The market price is $30 per share on the common stock.
5. A property dividend to common stockholders consisting of 1,000 shares of West Company common stock. This stock is being carried on the Nance Company books at a cost of $48 per share; it has a current value of $54 per share.
6. A cash dividend, consisting of a normal dividend and a liquidating dividend, on both the preferred and the common stock. The 10% preferred dividend includes a 2% liquidating dividend, and the $2.30 per share common dividend includes a $0.30 per share liquidating dividend (separate liquidating dividend contra accounts should be used).

Required   For each of the preceding *alternative* items:

1. Record (a) the journal entry at the date of declaration, and (b) the journal entry at the date of issuance.
2. Compute the balances in the stockholders' equity accounts immediately after the issuance (any gains or losses are to be reflected in the retained earnings balance; ignore income taxes).

P16-14   *Retained Earnings Statement*   The Tate Company began 2004 with a Retained Earnings account balance of $180,000. During 2004 the following eight events occurred and were properly recorded by the company:

1. Bonds payable with a face value of $100,000 were issued on January 1 at 98. The bonds mature in 10 years. The bond provisions require the restriction of retained earnings (by means of a note to the

financial statements) equal to one-half the face value of the bonds during the period the bonds are outstanding.

2. On April 13 the company reissued 2,400 shares of treasury stock for $25 per share. The company had reacquired these shares in 2002 at a cost of $20 per share. At that time, it had appropriated retained earnings (by means of a note to the financial statements) in an amount equal to the cost of the treasury shares.

3. On January 5 the company recalled and retired 800 shares of $100 par preferred stock at the call price of $120 per share. The stock had originally been issued for $108 per share.

4. During June the company declared and issued a two-for-one stock split on its common stock, reducing the par value from $10 to $5 per share. Immediately prior to the split, 10,000 shares of common stock were outstanding. The stock market price on the date of the split was $25 per share.

5. In August the company declared and issued a 15% stock dividend when the common stock was selling at $13 per share.

6. During December the company declared and paid its annual $1.30 per share cash dividend on the outstanding common stock.

7. Net income amounted to $72,000.

8. During the year-end audit, it was found that in 2003 the company had recorded depreciation on a particular machine twice. The error resulted in a $13,000 overstatement of depreciation during 2003. It was also found that, due to an oversight, a $10,000 loss on the sale of land was omitted from the 2003 income statement. Both items are material. The company has been subject to a 30% income tax rate for several years.

Required Prepare Tate Company's statement of retained earnings and any related notes to its financial statements for the year ended December 31, 2004.

P16-15 *Corrections, Dividends, Retained Earnings Statement*   On January 1, 2004 the Fastor Company had a retained earnings balance of $218,600. It is subject to a 30% corporate income tax rate. During 2004 the company earned net income of $67,000, and the following events occurred:

1. Cash dividends of $3 per share on 4,000 shares of common stock were declared and paid.

2. A small stock dividend was declared and issued. The dividend consisted of 600 shares of $10 par common stock. On the date of declaration the market price of the company's common stock was $36 per share.

3. The company recalled and retired 500 shares of $100 par preferred stock. The call price was $125 per share; the stock had originally been issued for $110 per share.

4. The company discovered that it had erroneously recorded depreciation expense of $45,000 in 2003 for both financial reporting and income tax reporting. The correct depreciation for 2003 should have been $20,000. This is considered a material error.

Required

1. Prepare journal entries to record items 1 through 4.

2. Prepare Fastor Company's statement of retained earnings for the year ended December 31, 2004.

P16-16 *Comprehensive*   The stockholders' equity of the Cory Company on January 1, 2004 is as follows:

Preferred stock, 8%, $100 par, callable at $116	$100,000
Preferred stock, 7%, $100 par	150,000
Common stock, $10 par	220,000
Premium on capital stock	160,000
Retained earnings	182,200
	$812,200

In January 2004 the company recalled and retired the 8% preferred stock. This stock originally had been issued for $105 per share. In April it declared and issued a 10% stock dividend on the common stock; the stock was then selling for $16 per share. This was the only issuance of common or preferred stock during the year. During November the company reacquired as treasury stock 1,000 shares of its common stock at $18 per share (it uses the cost method for treasury stock). State law requires an appropriation of retained earnings equal to the cost of all treasury shares held. The company discloses this appropriation by means of a note to the financial statements. In December the annual cash dividends on the outstanding preferred stock and a $1 per share cash dividend on the outstanding common stock were declared and paid. At the end of December net income of $87,000 was closed from Income Summary to Retained Earnings. During the year-end audit it was found that two errors had been made during 2003 for both financial reporting and income tax reporting. First, depreciation on certain machinery in the amount of $10,000 was inadvertently omitted.

Second, a mathematical mistake was made in the calculation of the accumulated depreciation related to the sale of equipment. Consequently, the reduction in accumulated depreciation and the amount of the gain recognized were both understated by $8,000. Both errors are considered material. The company has been subject to a 30% income tax rate for the past several years.

Required

1. Prepare journal entries to record the preceding transactions.
2. Prepare Cory Company's statement of retained earnings and any related notes to its financial statements for the year ended December 31, 2004.

P16-17 *Corrections*   You are engaged to perform the first audit of the Marble Company for the year ended December 31, 2004. You find the following account balances related to stockholders' equity:

Preferred stock, $100 par	$ 30,000
Common stock, $10 par	65,000
Capital surplus	(16,400)
Retained earnings	150,000

Due to the antiquated terminology and negative balance, you examine the Capital Surplus account first and find in it the following entries:

	Credit (Debit)
Premium on common stock	$ 27,100
Capital from donated land	16,000
Treasury stock (500 common shares at cost)	(7,500)
Premium on preferred stock	3,000
Appropriation for self-insurance	25,000
Stock dividend (50%)	(20,000)
Prior period adjustment (net of income taxes)	(12,000)
Loss from fire (uninsured), 2003	(18,000)
Property dividend declared	(6,000)
Cash dividends declared	(24,000)
Balance	$(16,400)

Your examination of the Preferred Stock and Common Stock accounts reveals that the amounts shown correctly state the total par value of the issued capital stock. The Retained Earnings account contains the accumulated earnings of the company, with the exception of any items of retained earnings that were inappropriately debited or credited to the Capital Surplus account.

Required

1. Prepare whatever journal entries are necessary to eliminate the Capital Surplus account and to correct the Marble Company's stockholders' equity accounts.
2. Prepare a corrected stockholders' equity section of Marble Company's December 31, 2004 balance sheet. Include any related notes to its financial statements.

P16-18 *Comprehensive*   Ashwood, Inc. is a public enterprise whose shares are traded in the over-the-counter market. At December 31, 2003 Ashwood had 6,000,000 authorized shares of $10 par value common stock, of which 2,000,000 shares were issued and outstanding. The stockholders' equity accounts at December 31, 2003 had the following balances:

Common stock	$20,000,000
Additional paid-in capital	7,500,000
Retained earnings	6,470,000

Transactions during 2004 and other information relating to the stockholders' equity accounts were as follows:

1. On January 5, 2004, Ashwood issued at $54 per share, 100,000 shares of $50 par value, 9%, cumulative convertible preferred stock. Each share of preferred stock is convertible, at the option of the holder, into two shares of common stock. Ashwood had 600,000 authorized shares of preferred stock.
2. On February 2, 2004, Ashwood reacquired 20,000 shares of its common stock for $16 per share. Ashwood uses the cost method to account for treasury stock.

3. On April 27, 2004, Ashwood sold 500,000 shares (previously unissued) of $10 par value common stock to the public at $17 per share.

4. On June 18, 2004, Ashwood declared a cash dividend of $1 per share of common stock, payable on July 13, 2004 to stockholders of record on July 2, 2004.

5. On November 9, 2004, Ashwood sold 10,000 shares of treasury stock for $21 per share.

6. On December 14, 2004, Ashwood declared the yearly cash dividend on preferred stock, payable on January 14, 2005 to stockholders of record on December 31, 2004.

7. On January 18, 2005, before the books were closed for 2004, Ashwood became aware that the ending inventories at December 31, 2003 were understated by $300,000 (the after-tax effect on 2003 net income was $210,000). The appropriate correcting entry was recorded the same day.

8. After correcting the beginning inventory, net income for 2004 was $4,500,000.

Required

1. Prepare a statement of retained earnings for Ashwood for the year ended December 31, 2004. Assume that only single-period financial statements for 2004 are presented.

2. Prepare the stockholders' equity section of Ashwood's balance sheet at December 31, 2004. (*AICPA adapted*)

P16-19 *Comprehensive* Carr Corporation had the following stockholders' equity account balances at December 31, 2003:

Preferred stock	$1,800,000
Additional paid-in capital from preferred stock	90,000
Common stock	5,150,000
Additional paid-in capital from common stock	3,500,000
Retained earnings	4,000,000
Unrealized decrease in value of marketable equity securities	245,000
Treasury common stock	270,000

Transactions during 2004 and other information relating to the stockholders' equity accounts were as follows:

1. Carr's preferred and common shares are traded on the over-the-counter market. At December 31, 2003, Carr had 100,000 authorized shares of $100 par, 10%, cumulative preferred stock; and 3,000,000 authorized shares of no-par common stock with a stated value of $5 per share.

2. On January 9, 2004, Carr formally retired all 30,000 shares of its treasury common stock and had them revert to an unissued basis. The treasury stock had been acquired on January 21, 2003. The shares were originally issued at $10 per share.

3. Carr owned 10,000 shares of Bush, Inc. common stock purchased in 2001 for $750,000. The Bush stock was included in Carr's short-term marketable securities portfolio at the end of 2003 at a value of $650,000. On February 13, 2004, Carr declared a dividend-in-kind of one share of Bush for every hundred shares of Carr common stock held by stockholders of record on February 27, 2004. The market price of Bush common stock was $63 per share on February 13, 2004. The dividend-in-kind was distributed on March 12, 2004.

4. On April 2, 2004, 250,000 stock rights were issued to the common stockholders permitting the purchase of one new share of common stock in exchange for one right and $11 cash. On April 23, 2004, 210,000 stock rights were exercised when the market price of Carr's common stock was $13 per share. Carr issued new shares to settle the transaction. The remaining 40,000 rights were not exercised and expired.

5. On December 10, 2004, Carr declared the yearly cash dividend on preferred stock, payable on January 14, 2005 to stockholders of record on December 31, 2004.

6. After the year-end adjustment, the Unrealized Decrease in Value of Marketable Equity Securities account had a debit balance of $135,000 at December 31, 2004.

7. On January 14, 2005, before the accounting records were closed for 2004, Carr became aware that rent income for the year ended December 31, 2003 was overstated by $500,000. The after-tax effect on 2003 net income was $275,000. The appropriate correcting entry was recorded the same day.

8. After correcting the rent income, net income for 2004 was $2,600,000.

Required

1. Prepare Carr's statement of retained earnings for the year ended December 31, 2004. Assume that only single-period financial statements for 2004 are presented.

2. Prepare the stockholders' equity section of Carr's balance sheet at December 31, 2004. (*AICPA adapted*)

P16-20 *Comprehensive* Dana Company reported the following amounts in the stockholders' equity section of its December 31, 2003 balance sheet:

Preferred stock, 9%, $100 par (10,000 shares authorized, 1,000 shares issued)	$100,000
Common stock, $10 par (20,000 shares authorized, 9,000 shares issued)	90,000
Additional paid-in capital on preferred stock	20,000
Additional paid-in capital on common stock	99,000
Retained earnings	330,000

During 2004, the company's net income was $83,000 and its dividends on preferred and common stock were $9,900 and $17,600, respectively. In addition, the following transactions affected its stockholders' equity:

1. Purchased 750 shares of its outstanding common stock as treasury stock for $22 per share.
2. Sold 500 shares of treasury stock at $27 per share. The company uses the cost method to account for treasury stock.
3. Retired 200 of the common shares held in the treasury.
4. Issued 100 shares of preferred stock for $125 per share.
5. The aggregate market value of the company's long-term investments in available-for-sale equity securities dropped below the carrying value of these securities at year-end. The difference between the carrying value and the year-end market value totals $10,000 (net of taxes).

Required

1. Prepare Dana Company's statement of changes in stockholders' equity for 2004. (*Hint*: This statement will include more than 10 numerical columns.) Assume Dana Company reports its comprehensive income in this statement.
2. Prepare the stockholders' equity section of Dana Company's balance sheet as of December 31, 2004. Include any related notes to its financial statements.

P16-21 **Comprehensive** The stockholders' equity section of Gaines Industries' balance sheet appeared as follows at December 31, 2003:

Contributed capital		
Preferred stock, 8%, $100 par (5,000 shares authorized, 3,000 shares issued)		$ 300,000
Common stock, $10 par (25,000 shares authorized, 20,000 shares issued)	$200,000	
Less: Treasury stock (500 shares at $10 par)	(5,000)	195,000
Premium on preferred stock		120,000
Premium on common stock		280,000
Common stock option warrants		32,000
Total contributed capital		$ 927,000
Retained earnings		260,000
Total Stockholders' Equity		$1,187,000

During 2004, the following chronological transactions were recorded:

1. The company issued 1,000 shares of common stock for $40 per share.
2. The company has a stock option plan for key executives. In accordance with the plan, the shares under option and the option price per share for each executive are known on the grant date. During 2004 no new options were granted, and compensation expense of $3,000 was recorded in regard to the existing stock options.
3. Stock options to 500 common shares were exercised in 2004 at an option price of $30 per share. The stock option value originally recorded in the Common Stock Option Warrants account in regard to these shares amounted to $3 per share.
4. The company reissued 200 shares of its treasury stock for $41 per share.
5. The company accepted land in an industrial park for a factory building site from the Columbus Development Association. The fair value of the land is estimated by an independent appraiser to be $50,000.
6. The law firm of Crook, Rezich, and Romero agreed to accept 100 shares of preferred stock in lieu of legal fees. At the time the preferred stock was selling for $142 per share.
7. Net income for 2004 of $182,000 was transferred from Income Summary to Retained Earnings. Dividends on preferred and common were $24,800 and $43,000, respectively (debit Retained Earnings and credit Cash).

Required

1. Prepare journal entries to record the preceding 2004 transactions for Gaines Industries.
2. Prepare the statement of changes in stockholders' equity for 2004. (*Hint*: This statement will require 10 numerical columns.)

3. Prepare the stockholders' equity section of the December 31, 2004 balance sheet. Include appropriate notes to the financial statements (assume the treasury stock has a cost of $10,500 at year-end).
4. Compute the return on stockholders' equity for 2004.

P16-22 *Stockholders' Equity* Raun Company had the following account titles on its December 31, 2004 trial balance:

9% cumulative convertible preferred stock, $100 par value
Premium on preferred stock
Common stock, $1 stated value
Premium on common stock
Retained earnings

The following additional information about the Raun Company was available for the year ended December 31, 2004:

1. There were 2 million shares of preferred stock authorized, of which 1 million were outstanding. All 1 million shares outstanding were issued on January 2, 2001 for $120 a share. The preferred stock is convertible into common stock on a one-for-one basis until December 31, 2010; thereafter, the preferred stock ceases to be convertible and is callable at par value by the company. No preferred stock has been converted into common stock, and there were no dividends in arrears at December 31, 2004.
2. The common stock has been issued at amounts above stated value per share since incorporation in 1986. Of the 5 million shares authorized, 3,580,000 were outstanding at January 1, 2004. The market price of the outstanding common stock has increased slowly but consistently for the last 5 years.
3. The company has an employee stock option plan where certain key employees and officers may purchase shares of common stock at 100% of the market price at the date of the option grant. All options are exercisable in installments of one-third each year, commencing one year after the date of the grant, and expire if not exercised within 4 years of the grant date. On January 1, 2004, options for 70,000 shares were outstanding at prices ranging from $47 to $83 a share. Options for 20,000 shares were exercised at $47 to $79 a share during 2004. During 2004, no options expired and additional options for 15,000 shares were granted at $86 a share. The 65,000 options outstanding at December 31, 2004 were exercisable at $54 to $86 a share; of these, 30,000 were exercisable at that date at prices ranging from $54 to $79 a share.
4. The company also has an employee stock purchase plan whereby the company pays one-half and the employee pays one-half of the market price of the stock at the date of the subscription. During 2004, employees subscribed to 60,000 shares at an average price of $87 a share. All 60,000 shares were paid for and issued late in September 2004.
5. On December 31, 2004, there was a total of 355,000 shares of common stock set aside for the granting of future stock options and for future purchases under the employee stock purchase plan. The only changes in the stockholders' equity for 2004 were those described previously, 2004 net income, and cash dividends paid.

Required Prepare the stockholders' equity section of the balance sheet of Raun Company at December 31, 2004. Substitute, where appropriate, X's for unknown dollar amounts. Use good form and provide full disclosure. Write appropriate notes as they should appear in the published financial statements. (*AICPA adapted*)

P16-23 *Comprehensive* Fay, Inc. finances its capital needs approximately one-third from long-term debt and two-thirds from equity. At December 31, 2003, Fay had the following liability and equity account balances:

11% debenture bonds payable, face amount	$5,000,000	Additional paid-in capital	$2,295,000
Premium on bonds payable	352,400	Retained earnings	2,465,000
Common stock	8,000,000	Treasury stock, at cost	325,000

Transactions during 2004 and other information relating to Fay's liabilities and equity accounts were as follows:

1. The debenture bonds were issued on December 31, 2001 for $5,378,000 to yield 10%. The bonds mature on December 31, 2016. Interest is payable annually on December 31. Fay uses the interest method to amortize bond premium.
2. Fay's common stock shares are traded on the over-the-counter market. At December 31, 2003, Fay had 2,000,000 authorized shares of $10 par common stock.
3. On January 16, 2004, Fay reissued 15,000 of its 25,000 shares of treasury stock for $225,000. The treasury stock had been acquired on February 25, 2003.

4. On March 2, 2004, Fay issued a 5% stock dividend on all issued shares. The market price of Fay's common stock at the time of issuance was $14 per share.

5. On November 2, 2004, Fay borrowed $4,000,000 at 9%, evidenced by an unsecured note payable to United Bank. The note is payable in five equal annual principal installments of $800,000. The first principal and interest payment is due on November 2, 2005.

6. On December 31, 2004, Fay owned 10,000 shares of Ryan Corp.'s common stock, which represented a 1% ownership interest. Fay treats this marketable equity investment as a long-term investment in available-for-sale securities. The stock was purchased on November 2, 2004 at $20 per share. The market price was $18 per share on December 31, 2004.

7. Fay's net income for 2004 was $2,860,000.

Required

1. Prepare the long-term liabilities section of Fay's December 31, 2004 balance sheet, including all disclosures applicable to each obligation.
2. Prepare the stockholders' equity section of Fay's December 31, 2004 balance sheet.
3. Prepare a schedule showing interest expense for the year ended December 31, 2004. (*AICPA adapted*)

P16-24 *Comprehensive* Min Co. is a publicly held company whose shares are traded in the over-the-counter market. The stockholders' equity accounts at December 31, 2003 had the following balances:

Preferred stock, $100 par value, 6% cumulative; 5,000 shares	
authorized; 2,000 issued and outstanding	$ 200,000
Common stock, $1 par value, 150,000 shares authorized;	
100,000 issued and outstanding	100,000
Additional paid-in capital	800,000
Retained earnings	1,586,000
Total Stockholders' Equity	$2,686,000

Transactions during 2004 and other information relating to the stockholders' equity accounts were as follows:

- February 2, 2004—Issued 13,000 shares of common stock to Ram Co. in exchange for land. On the date issued, the stock had a market price of $11 per share. The land had a carrying value on Ram's books of $135,000, and an assessed value for property taxes of $90,000.
- March 2, 2004—Purchased 5,000 shares of its own common stock to be held as treasury stock for $14 per share. Min uses the cost method to account for treasury stock. Transactions in treasury stock are legal in Min's state of incorporation.
- May 11, 2004—Declared a property dividend of marketable securities held by Min to common shareholders. The securities had a carrying value of $600,000; fair value on relevant dates were:

Date of declaration (May 11, 2004)	$720,000
Date of record (May 28, 2004)	758,000
Date of distribution (June 4, 2004)	736,000

- October 1, 2004—Reissued 2,000 shares of treasury stock for $16 per share.
- November 2, 2004—Declared a cash dividend of $1.50 per share to all common shareholders of record November 16, 2004. The dividend was paid on November 26, 2004.
- December 21, 2004—Declared the required annual cash dividend on preferred stock for 2004. The dividend was paid on January 4, 2005.
- January 14, 2005—Before closing the accounting records for 2004, Min became aware that no amortization had been recorded for 2003 for a patent purchased on July 1, 2003. The patent was properly capitalized at $320,000 and had an estimated useful life of eight years when purchased. Min's income tax rate is 30%. The appropriate correcting entry was recorded on the same day.
- Adjusted net income for 2004 was $838,000.

Required Determine the amounts of each of the following items. Show supporting calculations.

1. Prior period adjustment.
2. Preferred dividends.
3. Common dividends—cash.
4. Common dividends—property.
5. Number of common shares issued at December 31, 2004.
6. Total legal capital of common stock issued.
7. Additional paid-in capital, including treasury stock transactions.

8. Total dollar amount of treasury stock.
9. Numerator used in calculation of 2004 earnings per share for the year. (*AICPA adapted*)

P16-25 **Quasi-Reorganization (Appendix)** The Moore Corporation experienced several years of operating losses and encountered serious financial difficulties, resulting in liquidity problems and a deficit in retained earnings. However, recent entry into several new markets has been encouraging. The board of directors, with its stockholders' consent, decides to complete a quasi-reorganization on December 31, 2004. The balance sheet, prior to any adjustments, is shown below:

Cash	$ 6,000	Accounts payable	$ 51,000
Accounts receivable	18,000	Accrued liabilities	7,000
Inventories	42,000	Bonds payable (due 1/1/2008)	84,000
Investments in M Company bonds	66,000	Common stock, $10 par	100,000
Property and equipment	193,000	Additional paid-in capital	82,000
Less: Accumulated depreciation	(71,000)	Retained earnings	(41,000)
Patents (net)	29,000		
Total Assets	$283,000	Total Liabilities and Stockholders' Equity	$283,000

On December 31, 2004, an examination of the company accounts discloses the following information:

1. Some $3,000 of the current accounts receivable are estimated to be uncollectible.
2. The inventories consist of several obsolete items. An analysis places the fair value of the inventory at $30,000.
3. The M Company bonds had been purchased in November 2004. They are being held to maturity and have a current market value of $60,000.
4. The appraisal value of the property and equipment is $100,000.
5. Several obsolete patents are being carried on the books at a carrying value of $8,000.

In addition, on December 31, 2004, approval is received to reduce the par value of the common stock to $5 per share.

During 2005, the company discovers additional obsolete inventory with no resale value. This inventory had been carried on the books since 2001 at a cost of $4,000. It is determined that the inventory had become obsolete during 2004.

Required

1. Prepare the journal entries to complete the quasi-reorganization.
2. Prepare the revised balance sheet on December 31, 2004, including an appropriate note to the financial statements.
3. Prepare the journal entry in 2005 to account for the obsolete inventory.

P16-26 **Quasi-Reorganization (Appendix)** FAHRS Corporation has experienced losses in each of the last three years. A reorganization of top management has taken place and the new chief executive officer is confident the company can be saved from bankruptcy. A quasi-reorganization has been proposed contingent upon stockholder approval. Prior to the reorganization, the December 31, 2004 balance sheet reflects the following amounts:

Cash	$ 10,000	Accounts payable	$ 90,000
Accounts receivable	70,000	Notes payable, long-term	43,000
Inventory	100,000	Preferred stock, $100 par	100,000
Fixed assets	220,000	Premium on preferred stock	20,000
Less: Accumulated depreciation	(80,000)	Common stock, $20 par	200,000
Other assets	15,000	Premium on common stock	60,000
		Retained earnings (deficit)	(178,000)
Total Assets	$335,000	Total Liabilities and Stockholders' Equity	$335,000

The following information relates to the quasi-reorganization as approved by the FAHRS Corporation stockholders:

1. Accounts receivable of $10,000 are estimated to be uncollectible.
2. Inventories have increased for several years but now have a fair value of only $80,000.
3. Fixed assets have a fair value of $100,000.
4. Other assets are composed of accumulated store fixtures that were replaced several years ago. It is estimated that proceeds from the sale of these fixtures will just cover the disposal costs involved.

5. Short-term creditors have agreed to a 10% reduction in the obligations owed to them.
6. The board of directors, with stockholder and state approval, has authorized:
    a. A reduction in par value of the common stock to $5 per share.
    b. A reduction in par value of the preferred stock to $50 per share.
    c. The retained earnings deficit to be charged against the premiums on preferred and common stock in proportion to their respective account balances.

Required
1. Prepare journal entries to record the quasi-reorganization.
2. Prepare the FAHRS Corporation balance sheet immediately after the reorganization. Include a retained earnings note to the financial statements.

INTERNET ASSIGNMENTS

Go to the Nikolai and Bazley **Intermediate Accounting** web site (http://Nikolai.swcollege.com). Click on Student Resources and <u>internet homework assignments</u>. Then click on the appropriate hot link (icon) for each company's web site, find the relevant accounting information, and answer the following questions.

I16-1   Go to the Colgate web site.

       Required What were the company's basic earnings per share and diluted earnings per share for the most recent year? What was the amount of preferred dividends that was deducted from net income for computing basic EPS? What items were added to the common shares for computing diluted EPS?

I16-2   Go to the Johnson & Johnson web site.

       Required What were the company's basic net earnings per share and diluted net earnings per share for the most recent year? What were the average shares outstanding used to compute the basic net earnings per share? How was this number adjusted to determine the adjusted average shares outstanding for computing diluted earnings per share? What was the company's retained earnings balance at the end of the most recent year? What items (and amounts) increased and decreased retained earnings during the most recent year?

PART 5

Financial Reporting: Special Topics

Chapter 17   Income Recognition and Measurement of Net Assets

Chapter 18   Accounting for Income Taxes

Chapter 19   Accounting for Postemployment Benefits

Chapter 20   Accounting for Leases

Chapter 21   The Statement of Cash Flows

Chapter 22   Accounting Changes and Errors

objectives

1 Understand the revenue recognition alternatives.

2 Explain revenue recognition at the time of sale, during production, and at the time of cash receipt.

3 Explain the conceptual issues regarding revenue recognition alternatives.

4 Describe the alternative revenue recognition methods.

5 Account for revenue recognition prior to the period of sale, including the percentage-of-completion and completed-contract methods.

6 Account for revenue recognition after the period of sale, including the installment and cost recovery methods.

7 Account for revenue recognition delayed until a future event occurs.

8 Understand software revenue recognition, franchises, real estate sales, retail land sales, and consignment sales.

CHAPTER 17

Income Recognition and Measurement of Net Assets

In Chapters 3 and 4 we discussed issues important to external users in evaluating the performance of a company. **Return on investment** is a measure of a company's overall performance, **risk** is the uncertainty or unpredictability of the future results of a company, **financial flexibility** is the ability of a company to use its financial resources to adapt to unexpected needs and opportunities, **operating capability** is a measure of a company's ability to maintain a given physical level of operations, and **liquidity** is a measure of the amount of time until an asset is converted into cash or a liability is paid. We also saw that revenues and expenses are defined in terms of changes in assets and liabilities, and that a company typically *recognizes* revenues in the period of sale even though they are earned gradually and continuously during the company's earning process. This recognition of revenue occurs if, at the time of sale, (1) realization has taken place, and (2) the revenues have been earned. We also noted that expenses are matched against revenues. In the discussion we observed the difference between recognition and realization. **Recognition** is the process of formally recording and reporting an item in the financial statements, whereas **realization** means the process of converting noncash resources into cash or rights to cash.

As we discussed in Chapter 4 revenue is recognized when *earned* and *realizable*. Generally, this recognition occurs at the time of sale. However, in today's business environment a company may advance and recognize revenues (and expenses) prior to the period of sale. In other situations, a company may defer and recognize revenues (and expenses) after the period of the sale. The purpose of advancing or deferring recognition is to increase the *usefulness* of a company's financial statements by a more *relevant* portrayal of the nature of its operations without a significant decrease in the *reliability* of the information. Note that in this discussion, we are referring to the "sale" as the transaction in which the product is transferred or the service is performed. It is also usually, but not necessarily, the point at which legal title is transferred. It is helpful to understand that the "sale," the transfer of legal title, and the recognition of revenue are three separate but related events. In this chapter we discuss the conceptual and practical issues of revenue recognition, the matching of expenses against the revenue, and the related issue of the measurement of the net assets (assets minus liabilities). Our discussion proceeds from an overview of revenue recognition alternatives, through a consideration of the conceptual issues, to an examination of the revenue recognition alternatives, and concludes with a discussion of consignment sales, franchises, and real estate sales. In our discussion we focus on asset valuation and revenue recognition, using historical cost accounting. In Appendix E at the end of this book, we discuss how different methods of asset valuation provide different information to users and affect income measurement.

OVERVIEW OF REVENUE RECOGNITION ALTERNATIVES

We illustrate the alternatives for recognizing revenue at various points in the earning process in Exhibit 17-1. In this simple example, a manufacturer purchases raw materials, converts them to finished goods in the production process, sells the finished goods on account, and later collects the cash. The usual point of revenue recognition at the time of sale is shown in the middle, preceded by the alternative of advancing revenue recognition by recording revenue during production, and followed by the alternative of deferring revenue recognition until the receipt of cash. (Note also that the cash receipt may be spread out over several time periods.)

1 Understand the revenue recognition alternatives.

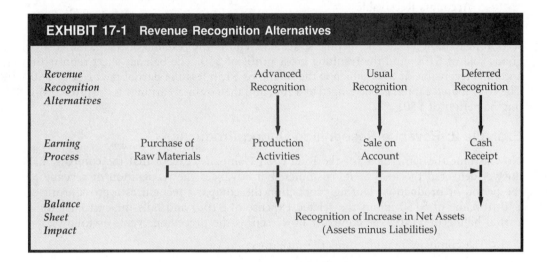

EXHIBIT 17-1 Revenue Recognition Alternatives

As we evaluate alternative revenue recognition methods, you must consider the related asset and liability recognition. The period in which a company recognizes revenue and expenses is also the period in which it recognizes an increase in the value of its net assets. We illustrate this relationship in the next section.

EXAMPLES OF REVENUE RECOGNITION ALTERNATIVES

The discussion of revenue recognition alternatives tends to focus on a company's income statement through the recognition of revenue and the matching of expenses. However, it is very important to understand the relationship between income (revenue and expense) recognition on a company's income statement and the measurement of the net assets (assets minus liabilities) on its balance sheet. In this section we illustrate the effects on the financial statements of the three basic revenue recognition alternatives using the following facts for the Ringwood Company, a small manufacturer of special order items in its first year of operations, which uses the perpetual inventory system:

1. The company begins the year with cash and contributed capital of $100.
2. The company contracts with a customer to produce and sell an item of inventory for $150. It costs $100 cash to manufacture the item.
3. The company sells the item on account.
4. The company collects $60 cash from the customer in partial payment.

Example 1: Revenue Recognition at Time of Sale

Assuming the company recognizes the revenue, expense, and increase in net assets at the time of sale, it records the preceding events as follows:

2 Explain revenue recognition at the time of sale, during production, and at the time of cash receipt.

1. The company manufactures the inventory:

Inventory	100	
Cash		100

2. The company sells the inventory, recognizes revenue of $150, the related expense of $100, and the increase in net assets of $50 ($150 − $100):

Accounts Receivable	150	
Revenue		150
Cost of Goods Sold	100	
Inventory		100

3. The company collects cash of $60:

Cash	60	
Accounts Receivable		60

Following these events, the company prepares the financial statements shown in the first section of Exhibit 17-2. The income statement reports the revenue of $150, the cost of goods sold of $100, and the resulting gross profit of $50. The balance sheet reports the accounts receivable at $90, which is the billing of $150 less the partial payment of $60. The contributed capital is unchanged at $100, and the retained earnings is the gross profit for the period of $50.

Example 2: Revenue Recognition During Production

Now assume the same facts for the Ringwood Company, except that the company has not yet delivered the item to its customer, but advances the recognition of revenue to the period of production. During production the company recognizes a gross profit of $50 (revenue of $150 minus the related expense of $100) and bills the customer for a partial billing of $130. The company now records the preceding events as follows:

1. The company manufactures the inventory:

Inventory	100	
Cash		100

2. The company recognizes revenue of $150, the related expense of $100, and the increase of $50 in the value of the inventory during production:

Production Expense	100	
Inventory	50	
Revenue		150

In this situation the company recognizes revenue of $150 and an expense of $100 during production even though it has not transferred the inventory to the customer. Since the company does not yet have a receivable (prior to the billing of $130), the value of the inventory is increased from its cost of $100 to its selling price of $150. In other words, since the company has recognized a gross profit, it must also increase the value of its net assets (inventory).

3. The company bills the customer for a partial billing of $130:

Accounts Receivable	130	
Partial Billings		130

When the company bills the customer, it credits Partial Billings, which is a contra account to the inventory. Thus, the net value of the inventory is reduced to the selling price less the amount billed, or $20 ($150 − $130). In other words, the $20 represents the net investment of the Ringwood Company in the inventory.

4. The company collects cash of $60:

Cash	60	
Accounts Receivable		60

Following these events, the company prepares the financial statements in the second section of Exhibit 17-2. The income statement reports the revenue of $150, the production

---

EXHIBIT 17-2 Ringwood Company: Revenue Recognition Alternatives

1. Revenue Recognition at Time of Sale

Income Statement

Revenue	$150
Cost of goods sold	(100)
Gross profit	$ 50

Balance Sheet

Assets		Stockholders' Equity	
Cash	$ 60	Contributed capital	$100
Accounts receivable	90	Retained earnings	50
Total Assets	$150	Total Stockholders' Equity	$150

2. Revenue Recognition During Production

Income Statement

Revenue	$150
Production expense	(100)
Gross profit	$ 50

Balance Sheet

Assets			Stockholders' Equity	
Cash		$ 60	Contributed capital	$100
Accounts receivable		70	Retained earnings	50
Inventory	$150			
Less: Partial billings	(130)	20		
Total Assets		$150	Total Stockholders' Equity	$150

3. Revenue Recognition at Time of Cash Receipt

Income Statement

Revenue	$ 60
Cost of goods sold	(40)
Gross profit	$ 20

Balance Sheet

Assets			Stockholders' Equity	
Cash		$ 60	Contributed capital	$100
Accounts receivable	$ 90		Retained earnings	20
Less: Deferred gross profit	(30)	60		
Total Assets		$120	Total Stockholders' Equity	$120

expense of $100, and the resulting gross profit of $50. The balance sheet reports the accounts receivable at $70 ($130 − $60), and the inventory at its net value of $20.

After the company bills the remaining $20 to its customer, the inventory and partial billings accounts have equal balances (of $150) and the company credits and debits them respectively, to eliminate their balances. Since the company recognized all the gross profit (revenue and expense) during production, it does not recognize any more income.

Example 3: Revenue Recognition at Time of Cash Receipt

Now assume the original facts for the Ringwood Company, except that the company defers the recognition of revenue to the period when the cash is received. The company now records the preceding events as follows:

1. The company manufactures the inventory:

Inventory	100	
Cash		100

2. The company "sells" (i.e., delivers) the inventory and defers the recognition of revenue:

Accounts Receivable	150	
Inventory		100
Deferred Gross Profit		50

    Since the company has transferred the item, it records the receivable of $150, removes the inventory of $100, and records the difference as Deferred Gross Profit, which is a contra account to accounts receivable. Thus, the net value of its accounts receivable is the *cost* of the item of $100 ($150 − $50).

3. The company collects cash of $60:

Cash	60	
Accounts Receivable		60

4. The company recognizes revenue on the basis of the cash received:

Cost of Goods Sold	40	
Deferred Gross Profit	20	
Revenue		60

    Since the company collects $60, it recognizes revenue of $60. This collection is 40% ($60 ÷ $150) of the total sale price of $150. Therefore, it recognizes 40% of the cost of the item as cost of goods sold of $40 (40% × $100). It reduces the deferred gross profit by $20 ($60 − $40), thereby increasing the value of the net receivable.

Following these events, the company prepares the financial statements shown in the third section of Exhibit 17-2. The income statement reports the revenue of $60, the cost of goods sold of $40, and the resulting gross profit of $20. The balance sheet reports the accounts receivable at a net value of $60, which represents the remaining $90 ($150 − $60) balance of the receivable, less the remaining $30 ($50 − $20) balance of the deferred gross profit. In other words, the $60 represents the *cost* of the receivable (60% of the cost of $100) to the Ringwood Company since it has not yet recognized revenue on that portion.

As the company collects the remaining $90 (60% of the total sale price of $150), it recognizes 60% of the total revenue (60% × $150 = $90) and cost of goods sold (60% × $100 = $60). This recognition eliminates the balance of $30 in the deferred gross profit account, thereby increasing the value of its net assets.

Summary of Revenue Recognition Alternatives

As we discuss in later sections of the chapter, a company advances or defers revenue recognition in certain situations because realization and the completion of the earning process occur in periods other than the period of sale (delivery). These alternative methods increase the relevance of the financial statements. For all three examples, note that when the company recognizes revenue, it also recognizes expenses, and increases its net assets from cost to selling price. In Example 1, the company recognizes revenue and expense at the time of sale, and records accounts receivable at the selling price and reduces inventory cost. At this point, realization has occurred, revenue and expense are recognized, and net assets are increased by the amount of the gross profit.

In Example 2, the company recognizes revenue and expense during production, and increases the inventory from cost to selling price. Therefore, it records the increase in net assets when it recognizes revenue and expense. Even though the "sale" has not occurred, realization has occurred and the earning process is complete. We discuss this situation later in the chapter as it relates to the percentage-of-completion method.

Alternatively, if revenue is not recognized at the time of "sale," the net assets remain at cost. In Example 3 the company recognizes revenue at the time of cash receipt; even though it records an account receivable at the selling price at the time of "sale," it reduces the receivable to cost through the subtraction of deferred gross profit. The increase to selling price only occurs as cash is received, revenue and expense are recognized, and deferred gross profit is reduced. In this situation realization occurs only as cash is received, as we discuss later in the chapter for the installment method.

Note also that the company starts the period with assets of $100. In Examples 1 and 2, it recognizes a gross profit of $50 and the net assets increase to $150. In Example 3, it recognizes a gross profit of $20 and the net assets increase to $120.

In the last two examples, the expenses are matched against the revenues so that they are either advanced or deferred in a consistent manner. It should be noted that this matching occurs only for certain expenses, usually those for which there is a direct "association of cause and effect" (as we discussed in Chapter 4). Other expenses recognized on the basis of "systematic and rational allocation" or "immediate recognition" are usually recognized in the normal manner, unless they can be directly associated with the product. For example, depreciation on a machine used by a company to make a product is included in its inventory cost, and the company advances or defers recognition of the expense in a manner consistent with its revenue recognition. A company expenses depreciation on an office building used by selling and administrative personnel in the normal manner, and therefore the recognition of that expense is *not* related to the revenue recognition alternative the company uses.

The selection of a revenue recognition alternative depends on the particular circumstances faced by each company. We discuss the conceptual issues that influence the decision in the next section.

CONCEPTUAL ISSUES

The decision as to when to recognize revenue focuses on three factors:

3 Explain the conceptual issues regarding revenue recognition alternatives.

1. **The economic substance of the event takes precedence over the legal form of the transaction.** Usually an exchange (sale) is considered to have taken place at the time of the legal transaction at which title to the property is transferred. However, if economic "reality" is substantially different from the legalities of a transaction, the recognition of revenues may be advanced to a period prior to the sale or deferred to a period after the sale; that is, the period in which the revenues are *earned* and *realizable*. For example, as we discuss in Chapter 20, a lessor recognizes the gross profit on a sales-type lease even though it retains legal title. As we discuss later in this chapter, a company may recognize the gross profit on a long-term construction contract each year during the contract, instead of when the construction is completed, even though title has not transferred. In each of these situations, the revenue is earned before title is transferred. Also, as we discussed in Chapter 8, a company does not recognize revenue on a product financing arrangement even though title has passed, because the exchange is, in an economic sense, a loan (borrowing) and not a sale.
2. **The risks and benefits of ownership have been transferred to the buyer.** For revenue to be *earned* (and recognized) by the seller, the risks and benefits of ownership must be substantially transferred from the seller to the buyer. The benefits are the expected net cash flows, while the risks are the likelihood of larger or smaller net cash flows actually being received. For example, a company may recognize revenue during a long-term construction contract because the risks and benefits are transferred to the buyer, as we discuss later in this chapter. Alternatively,

if the seller of a franchise has not substantially completed its obligations related to the exchange, then it has not transferred the benefits of ownership to the buyer, its earning process is not complete, and it defers revenue recognition, as we discuss later in this chapter. Also, if the seller of receivables can reacquire the benefits under a recourse provision, the exchange of benefits may not have occurred and the seller does not recognize revenue, as we discussed in Chapter 6. If the seller of real estate has substantial exposure to risk after the sale, a "full exchange" has not taken place and it defers revenue recognition, as we discuss later in this chapter. Finally, the lessor recognizes revenue on sales-type leases because the transfer of the risks and benefits of ownership has occurred, even though a legal sale has not taken place, as we discuss in Chapter 20.

3. **The collectibility of the receivable from the sale is reasonably assured.** If the collectibility is "*not* reasonably assured,"[1] then *realization* has not taken place and the earning process is not complete, so the company defers the recognition of revenue. This occurs when it is difficult to predict whether customers will pay their accounts or when significant collection efforts may be required, as for certain real estate situations and franchises discussed later in this chapter. Deferral of revenue recognition may also be appropriate when future refunds or returns cannot be reasonably estimated, as we discussed in Chapter 6.

In this chapter we discuss several revenue recognition methods. In some specialized situations the FASB has not issued *Statements of Standards*. In these situations generally accepted accounting principles are defined by alternative sources, such as *Statements of Position, Industry Accounting Guides,* and *Industry Audit Guides*, which cover particular industries and are issued by the AICPA, as we discussed in Chapter 1.

ALTERNATIVE REVENUE RECOGNITION METHODS

4 Describe the alternative revenue recognition methods.

Once a company has decided when to recognize revenues (during, before, or after the period of sale), then it selects a particular accounting method. We briefly summarize the revenue recognition alternatives and the methods used as follows:

1. *Revenue Recognition in the Period of Sale.* This method is generally used because realization has occurred and revenues are earned at the time of sale. The *accrual method* of accounting is used, in which revenues (accomplishments) are recognized at the time of the sales transaction and expenses (sacrifices) are matched against the revenues in the period of sale. The inventory is recorded at cost and the resulting accounts receivable are recorded at net realizable value. The completed-contract method is used for some long-term contracts and recognizes revenues and expenses in the period of sale.

2. *Revenue Recognition Prior to the Period of Sale.* This method is used to reflect economic substance instead of legal form, so that economic reality is not distorted. The *percentage-of-completion method* is used for most long-term construction contracts (or some real estate sales) or the *proportional performance method* is used for long-term service contracts to advance revenue recognition. These methods recognize revenues (and certain expenses) based on the percentage completed during the period. The inventory for a long-term construction project, for example, is recorded at cost until revenue is recognized, at which time it is raised to net realizable value.

3. *Revenue Recognition at the Completion of Production.* This method has been advocated for certain precious metals and farm products with immediate marketability at quoted prices, unit interchangeability, and an inability of the producer to determine unit acquisition costs. This method has become less appropriate over

---

1. "Omnibus Opinion—1966," *APB Opinion No. 10* (New York: AICPA, 1966), par. 12. In "Recognition and Measurement in Financial Statements of Business Enterprises," *FASB Statement of Concepts No. 5* (Stamford, Conn.: FASB, 1984), par. 84(g), the term "doubtful" is used. It is assumed that these two terms have the same meaning.

time as markets with fixed prices become less common. Also, since mining and agricultural companies generally recognize revenue in the period of the sale, we do not discuss this method in this chapter.[2] The inventory is recorded at replacement cost or net realizable value, and we presented a brief example in Chapter 8.

4. *Revenue Recognition After the Period of the Sale.* This method is appropriate when the collectibility of the receivable is not reasonably assured or there is no reliable basis for estimating the collectibility, so that revenue recognition is deferred. In the *installment method* a portion of the total gross profit on the sale is recognized in proportion to the cash received. In the cost *recovery method* no gross profit is recognized until the cost of the product is recovered; after the cost recovery, gross profit is recognized as an amount equal to the subsequent cash receipts. The accounts receivable, less the deferred gross profit, are recorded at their cost until the revenue is recognized.

5. *Revenue Recognition Delayed Until a Future Event Occurs.* This method is appropriate when there has been an insignificant transfer of the risks and benefits of ownership, so that revenue is not recognized either at the time of the sale or as cash is received. The *deposit method* is used and all cash receipts are recorded as deposits until an event occurs that transfers sufficient risks and benefits to the buyer so that revenue may be recognized. Related assets are recorded at their cost or book value until the revenue recognition occurs.

The following diagram summarizes many of the revenue recognition issues we have discussed:

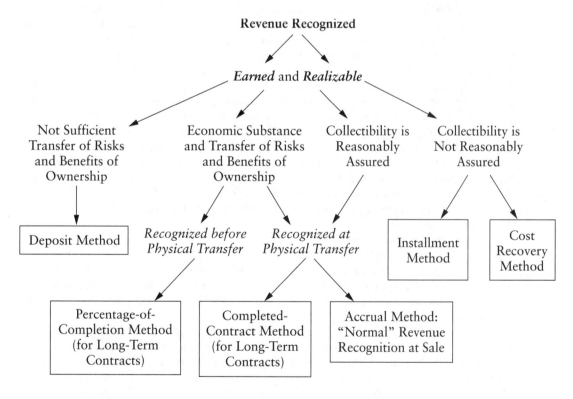

We discuss the accounting issues involved in the recognition of revenue (and expenses) in the period of sale in numerous places throughout this book and we will not discuss them further in this chapter. In the next section, we discuss revenue recognition prior to sale as it applies to construction contracts and service contracts. Following this section, we discuss revenue recognition after the period of sale.

---

2. H. J. Jaenicke, "Survey of Present Practices in Recognizing Revenues, Expenses, Gains, and Losses," *Research Report* (Stamford, Conn.: FASB, 1981), p. 75.

REVENUE RECOGNITION PRIOR TO THE PERIOD OF SALE

5 Account for revenue recognition prior to the period of sale, including the percentage-of-completion and completed-contract methods.

We discuss three methods of revenue recognition in this section. Each applies to long-term contracts where the production of a product or the provision of a service extends over several accounting periods. The percentage-of-completion method is widely used by construction companies for long-term contracts and we discuss it in considerable detail. The completed-contract method also may be used by construction companies for long-term contracts. Even though this method does *not* advance the recognition of revenue, we present it here for contrast with the percentage-of-completion method. We also discuss the proportional performance method that is used by companies for long-term service contracts.

Long-Term Construction Contracts

Some companies engage in long-term construction contracts in which they agree to construct an asset for another entity (e.g., company or governmental agency) over an extended period. Long-term construction contracts involve projects such as buildings, ships, roads, bridges, and dams, which can take several years to complete. Such a contract may involve advance payments by the buyer to help the seller finance the construction and to reflect the buyer's ownership interest in the asset under construction. The contract also may include specific responsibilities of the seller, such as the use of certain materials and the completion of production on a specific timetable. At completion, the buyer typically inspects and approves the finished asset before the legal "sale" takes place.

Because the construction process usually extends over more than one period, the question arises as to how the construction company should recognize revenue. The **percentage-of-completion method** is generally used. Under this method the company recognizes profit each period during the life of the contract in proportion to the amount of the contract completed during the period. As it recognizes the profit, it also increases the value of the inventory, so that it values the inventory at the costs incurred plus the profit recognized to date (less any partial billings). In certain situations, the **completed-contract method** is used. Under this method the company does *not* recognize profit during the life of the contract, but recognizes it only when the contract is completed. During the life of the contract, therefore, it records the inventory at cost (less any partial billings).

 Most long-term contracts are accounted for by the percentage-of-completion method, because it produces a *more relevant* measure of periodic income. When a company uses this method, **economic substance takes precedence over legal form;** i.e., the legal sale occurs at the completion of the contract, but revenue recognition is advanced to better depict economic reality.

The earning process is virtually complete because a "continuous sale" takes place. The arguments to support a continuous sale are that (1) the buyer and the seller obtain enforceable rights, including the right of the buyer to enforce specific performance, (2) the buyer usually makes progress payments to support its ownership investment and therefore realization is actually occurring, and (3) the buyer has the right to take over the work in progress.[3]

Thus, in accordance with the continuous sale concept, revenue is recognized continuously using the percentage-of-completion method. The method also has the following advantages: (1) It achieves the goal of accrual accounting to report the effects of transactions and other events in the periods in which they occur, (2) it is consistent with the argument that revenue is earned continuously over the entire earning process, and (3) it results in a more relevant measure of periodic income because income includes the results of the activities that occurred during the period.

Generally accepted accounting principles have supported the use of the percentage-of-completion method. **Accounting Research Bulletin No. 45** recommended its use when the total gross profit on the contract could be estimated with reasonable accuracy and

3. "Accounting for Performance of Construction-Type and Certain Production-Type Contracts," *AICPA Statement of Position No. 81–1* (New York: AICPA, 1981), par. 22.

ultimate realization is reasonably assured.[4] However *ARB No. 45* allowed the use of both the percentage-of-completion and completed-contract methods in all circumstances and did not specify the situations under which each method would be preferable. To clarify the use of the two methods, **AICPA Statement of Position No. 81-1** requires that a construction company use the percentage-of-completion method for long-term contracts when *all* the following conditions are met:

1. The company can make reasonably dependable estimates of the extent of progress toward the completion, contract revenues, and contract costs.
2. The contract clearly specifies the enforceable rights regarding goods or services to be provided and received by both the company and the buyer, the consideration to be exchanged, and the manner and terms of settlement.
3. The buyer can be expected to satisfy its obligations under the contract.
4. The company expects to perform its contractual obligations.[5]

The *Statement* also requires that a company use the completed-contract method only when at least one of the preceding conditions is *not* met, for short-term contracts, and when there are inherent hazards in the contract beyond the normal business risks for which reasonably dependable estimates cannot be made. *SOP No. 81-1* caused a considerable and desirable narrowing of generally accepted accounting principles. Instead of the two methods being allowed in all circumstances, each is acceptable only under specific and separate circumstances.

Percentage-of-Completion Method

When a company uses the percentage-of-completion method, it may determine the percentage completed by the use of either "input" or "output" measures.

INPUT MEASURES An input to the production activity may be used to measure the percentage of completion if a relationship is assumed to exist between the input and the production activity. Two input measures are the cost-to-cost method and the efforts-expended method. In the **cost-to-cost** method, the company measures the percentage of completion by comparing the costs incurred to date with the expected total costs for the contract. This percentage is multiplied by the total revenue on the contract to compute the total revenue recognized to date. This revenue to date, minus the revenue recognized in previous years, is the revenue recognized in the current year. The expense recognized is the costs incurred in the current year.

In the **efforts-expended** method, the company measures the percentage of completion by the work performed to date, such as labor hours, labor dollars, machine hours, or material quantities compared to the expected total work to be performed in the contract. The revenue recognized in the current year is computed by following the same procedures as for the cost-to-cost method. The expense recognized is computed using the same procedures as for the revenue.

OUTPUT MEASURES Output measures use the results achieved to date compared to the total expected results of the contract to measure the percentage of completion. Theoretically, output measures may be considered preferable to input measures, since they measure the results achieved (that is, the actual production completed). However, output measures often cannot be reliably measured. For example, it is difficult to measure output for a contract that involves research, engineering, and physical construction. Examples of output measures are units produced, units delivered, contract milestones, value added, or units of work completed (such as cubic yards of pavement laid on a highway contract). Once a company has determined the output percentage of completion, the revenue and expense recognized each period are computed in the same way as for the efforts-expended method.

---

4. "Long-Term Construction-Type Contracts," *Accounting Research Bulletin No. 45* (New York: AICPA, 1955), par. 4.
5. "Accounting for Performance of Construction-Type and Certain Production-Type Contracts," *op. cit.*, par. 23.

ACCOUNTING PROCEDURES In accounting for a long-term contract under the percentage-of-completion method, a company uses an inventory account entitled Construction in Progress to record all costs incurred on the project. In addition, it adds the gross profit that is recognized on the project to the account, so that at the end of the period the account is valued at cost plus gross profit recognized (i.e., net realizable value). Most long-term projects are financed by receipts from partial billings paid by the buyer, which are specified by the contract provisions and are usually less than the amount of revenue recognized. When these partial billings are made, the company debits a receivable account and credits a Partial Billings account. The company reports the balance in the Partial Billings account on its balance sheet as an offset (contra account) to the Construction in Progress account. Therefore the net balance sheet amount is an asset if Construction in Progress (which includes incurred costs plus gross profit recognized) exceeds Partial Billings, or a liability if Partial Billings exceeds Construction in Progress.

If the project's total estimated cost exceeds the contract price, then the company expects a loss on the project. The conservatism convention requires that the company recognize the total expected loss in the current year and reduce the carrying value of the inventory. We discuss the recognition of losses later in this chapter.

Completed-Contract Method

The completed-contract method requires that no revenue is recognized until the project is completed or substantially so (although anticipated losses are recognized immediately). In effect, this method is just like the production and sale of any unit of inventory. The recording and reporting of inventory costs and partial billings are handled in the same way as for the percentage-of-completion method. The principal advantage of the completed-contract method is that the revenue recognized is *more reliable* because it is based on final results rather than on estimates. The principal disadvantage is that it is *less relevant* because a company's net income does not reflect its current performance, but rather is a function of the date the contract is completed. Indeed, a company's net income may be negative if it completes no contracts in a period and expenses its selling and administrative costs.

Illustration of the Two Methods

To illustrate the two methods, assume that the Calder Company contracted to construct a dam that takes three years to complete. We show the contract price, costs incurred, estimated costs to complete, partial billings, and collections in Exhibit 17-3. The company estimates the percentage completed by the cost-to-cost method.

EXHIBIT 17-3 Calder Company: Dam Construction Contract Amounts			
	2004	2005	2006
Construction costs incurred during the year	$100,000	$186,000	$314,000
Estimated costs to complete the contract	400,000	264,000	—
Partial billings to customer	80,000	350,000	270,000
Collections from customer	50,000	330,000	320,000
Total contract price: $700,000			

COMPUTATIONS FOR THE PERCENTAGE-OF-COMPLETION METHOD We show the gross profit recognized each year under the percentage-of-completion method in Exhibit 17-4. In 2004 the Calder Company incurred $100,000 of construction costs and estimates that it will incur another $400,000 to complete the contract. Therefore, the company expects

EXHIBIT 17-4   Gross Profit Recognition: Percentage-of-Completion Method

	2004	2005	2006
Construction costs incurred to date	$100,000	$286,000	$600,000
Estimated costs to complete	400,000	264,000	—
Total estimated costs	$500,000	$550,000	$600,000
Percent complete (construction cost incurred to date ÷ total estimated costs)	20%	52%	100%
Revenue to date (% complete × $700,000 contract price)	$140,000	$364,000	$700,000
Revenue recognized for the year (revenue to date − revenue previously recognized)	$140,000	$224,000	$336,000
Construction cost (expense) incurred for the year	(100,000)	(186,000)	(314,000)
Gross profit recognized	$ 40,000	$ 38,000	$ 22,000

that the total cost of the contract will be $500,000. Since the contract price is $700,000, the company projects a gross profit of $200,000. The contract is 20% complete ($100,000 ÷ $500,000), and therefore the company recognizes 20% of the total revenue on the contract. This amounts to $140,000 (20% × $700,000). Since total estimated construction costs are $500,000, the construction expense recognized for 2004 is $100,000 (20% × $500,000)[6] and the gross profit is $40,000. Note that the contract is 20% complete, and the company recognizes 20% of the $200,000 projected gross profit.

In 2005 the company follows the same procedure. The costs incurred *to date* are $286,000 (the sum of the costs incurred in 2004 and 2005). Since estimated costs to complete the project are $264,000, the contract is 52% complete. Therefore the company's total revenue to *date* is $364,000 (52% × $700,000), and the revenue it recognizes for *the year* is $224,000 (the revenue to date of $364,000 less the revenue previously recognized of $140,000). Since total estimated construction costs are $550,000, the construction expense recognized for 2005 is $186,000 [(52% × $550,000) − $100,000], and there is a gross profit of $38,000. Note that the contract is 52% complete, the total profit expected on the contract is now $150,000 ($700,000 − $550,000), and therefore the total profit recognized to date is $78,000 (52% × $150,000). This is consistent with the $40,000 and $38,000 gross profit recognized in the two years.

In 2006 the company completes the contract at a total cost of $600,000. The revenue for *the year* is $336,000, which is the total revenue of $700,000 less the revenue *to date* of $364,000. Since construction costs for *the year* are $314,000, the gross profit for the year is $22,000. Note that the total gross profit for the three years is $100,000 ($40,000 + $38,000 + $22,000), which is consistent with the total revenue less the total actual costs ($700,000 − $600,000).

COMPUTATIONS FOR THE COMPLETED-CONTRACT METHOD Under the completed-contract method, the company does not recognize a gross profit until the contract is complete. The Calder Company recognizes the entire gross profit on the contract at the end of 2006. The total construction costs incurred over the three years (and recorded in Construction in Progress) are $600,000 ($100,000 + $186,000 + $314,000). The revenue recognized is the total contract price of $700,000, and therefore the company recognizes a gross profit of $100,000 ($700,000 − $600,000) in 2006.

---

6. Under the cost-to-cost method, construction expenses recognized for the year are equal to the construction costs incurred during the year (unless a loss is expected on the contract, as we discuss later), so that the construction expense computations are simplified as we show in Exhibit 17-4. If this method is not used, construction expenses recognized in a given year may differ from the actual yearly construction costs incurred.

JOURNAL ENTRIES FOR THE TWO METHODS   The journal entries to record the activities of the Calder Company for both the percentage-of-completion and the completed-contract methods are shown in Exhibit 17-5. Under both methods, in 2004 through 2006 the company debits the construction costs (from Exhibit 17-3) to the inventory account Construction in Progress. The accompanying credits are to various accounts such as Accounts Payable, Raw Materials Inventory, Cash, Prepaid Expenses, Accumulated Depreciation, etc. It debits the billings to the customer to Accounts Receivable and credits the

---

EXHIBIT 17-5   **Journal Entries to Record Dam Construction**

	Percentage-of- Completion Method		Completed- Contract Method	
2004				
1. *To record construction costs*:				
Construction in Progress	100,000		100,000	
Accounts Payable, Raw Materials Inventory, Cash, etc.		100,000		100,000
2. *To record partial billings*:				
Accounts Receivable	80,000		80,000	
Partial Billings		80,000		80,000
3. *To record collections*:				
Cash	50,000		50,000	
Accounts Receivable		50,000		50,000
4. *To record gross profit*:				
Construction Expense	100,000		No Entry	
Construction in Progress	40,000			
Construction Revenue		140,000		
2005				
1. *To record construction costs*:				
Construction in Progress	186,000		186,000	
Accounts Payable, Raw Materials Inventory, Cash, etc.		186,000		186,000
2. *To record partial billings*:				
Accounts Receivable	350,000		350,000	
Partial Billings		350,000		350,000
3. *To record collections*:				
Cash	330,000		330,000	
Accounts Receivable		330,000		330,000
4. *To record gross profit*:				
Construction Expense	186,000		No Entry	
Construction in Progress	38,000			
Construction Revenue		224,000		
2006				
1. *To record construction costs*:				
Construction in Progress	314,000		314,000	
Accounts Payable, Raw Materials Inventory, Cash, etc.		314,000		314,000
2. *To record partial billings*:				
Accounts Receivable	270,000		270,000	
Partial Billings		270,000		270,000
3. *To record collections*:				
Cash	320,000		320,000	
Accounts Receivable		320,000		320,000
4. *To record gross profit and to close out Construction in Progress and Partial Billings*:				
Construction Expense	314,000		No Entry	
Construction in Progress	22,000			
Construction Revenue		336,000		
Partial Billings	700,000		No Entry	
Construction in Progress		700,000		
Partial Billings	No Entry		700,000	
Construction Revenue				700,000
Construction Expense	No Entry		600,000	
Construction in Progress				600,000

Partial Billings, which is a contra account to Construction in Progress. It records the collection of cash from the customer in the normal manner. Under the percentage-of-completion method, the company recognizes the gross profit (calculated in Exhibit 17-4) each year by a journal entry to a revenue and an expense account. It debits the difference between these two amounts, the gross profit, to Construction in Progress, thereby raising the asset value from cost to net realizable value and eventually to the contract selling price. The increase in stockholders' equity (the gross profit) is accompanied by a corresponding increase in an asset value. Under the completed-contract method the company does not recognize a profit in 2004 or 2005, so no journal entry is required.

In 2006, when the contract is completed, closing entries for the contract are required. Under the percentage-of-completion method, the company closes Partial Billings against Construction in Progress. Note that both accounts include the selling price. Under the completed-contract method, the company recognizes the total gross profit on the contract at the completion date. It does this by closing Partial Billings against Construction Revenue because both accounts include the selling price, and Construction in Progress against Construction Expense because both accounts include the cost. At the end of the period, it closes the revenue and expense accounts to Income Summary.

We show how the Calder Company reports its activities for this contract under each method in Exhibit 17-6. To complete the income statement under each method, the company deducts its operating expenses from the gross profit to determine its income. On the balance sheet under each method, it offsets Partial Billings against Construction in Progress. At the end of 2004, Construction in Progress exceeds Partial Billings, so the company reports the net amount as inventory in the current asset section of its balance sheet. At the end of 2006, Partial Billings exceeds Construction in Progress, so the company reports the net amount as a current liability in its balance sheet. Note that the difference in the book values under the two methods is equal to the gross profit to date on the contract. Thus, at December 31, 2004, the book value under the percentage-of-completion method is $60,000 and under the completed-contract method it is $20,000; the difference of $40,000 is the gross profit for 2004 (which the company recognizes under the percentage-of-completion but not under the completed-contract method).

Losses on Long-Term Construction Contracts

A loss on a construction contract can be of two types. First, the estimate of future costs may indicate that there is a **loss in the current period,** but that there will still be a profit on the total contract. Second, the estimate may indicate that an **overall loss on the contract** is expected. In this case, *SOP 81-1* requires that the total estimated loss on the entire contract be recognized under both the percentage-of-completion and the completed-contract methods. This procedure is consistent with the *conservatism* convention of anticipating all foreseeable losses.

LOSS IN CURRENT PERIOD As an illustration of the computation of a loss for a period under the percentage-of-completion method, suppose that in 2005 the Calder Company estimates that the costs to complete are $364,000 *instead of* $264,000. Assuming that the data for 2004 are the same as in Exhibit 17-3, it recognizes an $18,000 loss in 2005, which it calculates as follows:

	2005
Construction costs incurred to date	$286,000
Estimated costs to complete	364,000
Total estimated costs	$650,000
Percent complete ($286,000 ÷ $650,000)	44%
Revenue to date (44% × $700,000)	$308,000
Revenue recognized for year ($308,000 − $140,000)	$168,000
Construction costs incurred for year	(186,000)
Loss recognized	$ (18,000)

EXHIBIT 17-6   Financial Statement Reporting

1. Percentage-of-Completion Method	2004	2005	2006
Income Statement (partial):			
Construction revenue	$140,000	$224,000	$336,000
Construction expense	(100,000)	(186,000)	(314,000)
Gross profit	$ 40,000	$ 38,000	$ 22,000
Balance Sheet (partial; end of year):			
Current Assets			
Accounts receivable	$ 30,000	$ 50,000	
Inventories			
Construction in progress	140,000		
Less: Partial billings	(80,000)		
Costs and recognized profit not yet billed	$ 60,000		
Current Liabilities			
Partial billings		$430,000	
Less: Construction in progress		(364,000)	
Billings in excess of costs and recognized profit		$ 66,000	

Notes to Financial Statements: Summary of Significant Accounting Policies (in part): The Company reports profits from long-term construction contracts in progress using the percentage-of-completion method of accounting. Profits are accrued based on the ratio of cost incurred to total estimated costs. Costs include direct material, direct labor, and job-related overhead. General and administrative expenses are charged to operations as incurred and are not allocated to contract costs.

2. Completed-Contract Method	2004	2005	2006
Income Statement (partial):			
Construction revenue	—	—	$700,000
Construction expense	—	—	(600,000)
Gross profit			$100,000
Balance Sheet (partial; end of year):			
Current Assets			
Accounts receivable	$ 30,000	$ 50,000	
Inventories			
Construction in progress	100,000		
Less: Partial billings	(80,000)		
Excess of costs over related billings	$ 20,000		
Current Liabilities			
Partial billings		$430,000	
Less: Construction in progress		(286,000)	
Excess of billings over related costs		$144,000	

Notes to Financial Statements: Summary of Significant Accounting Policies (in part): The Company reports profit from long-term construction contracts using the completed-contract method of accounting. Under this method, billings and costs are accumulated during the period of construction, but no profits are recorded before the contract is either completed or substantially completed. A contract is considered substantially completed if the costs to complete are not significant in amount. Costs include direct labor, direct materials, and job-related overhead. General and administrative expenses are charged to operations as incurred and are not allocated to contract costs.

If the costs in 2006 are $364,000 as expected, the Calder Company recognizes the remaining 56% of the revenue, or $392,000. Therefore the company reports a gross profit of $28,000 in 2006, with a total profit over the three years of the contract of $50,000 ($40,000 − $18,000 + $28,000). This is equal to the total revenue of $700,000 less the total cost of $650,000. Under the completed-contract method, no adjustment is needed in 2005 because the company expects an overall profit on the contract.

OVERALL LOSS ON CONTRACT   A more complicated situation arises if the estimated total costs exceed the contract price, so that an overall loss on the contract is anticipated.

To illustrate this situation for the percentage-of-completion method, suppose that at the end of 2005 the Calder Company estimates that its costs to complete are $429,000. Therefore, it expects that its total costs will be $715,000 ($286,000 + $429,000), indicating an overall loss of $15,000 by the end of the contract. Therefore, it has to remove the gross profit to date and recognize the loss of $15,000 in 2005. It recognizes the revenue for 2005 in the normal way, as we show in Exhibit 17-7. Because the project is 40% complete ($286,000 ÷ $715,000), the revenue to date is $280,000 (40% × $700,000). The revenue recognized in 2005 is $140,000 ($280,000 − $140,000). The total expense recognized includes two components: (1) the amount needed to create a cumulative profit of zero, and (2) the amount of the overall loss recognized. Since the revenue to date is $280,000 and the expense recognized in 2004 was $100,000, the company recognizes an expense of $180,000 in 2005 to make the cumulative profit equal to zero.[7] In addition, it recognizes the overall loss of $15,000, so the total expense for 2005 is $195,000. The company records the revenue and expense as follows:

Construction Expense	195,000	
Construction in Progress		40,000
Construction Revenue		140,000
Provision for Loss on Contract		15,000

The credit to the Construction in Progress account removes the increase in value resulting from the gross profit recognized in 2004, and therefore the account includes only the project costs incurred to date. The Provision for Loss on Contract is reported as a contra-account to Construction in Progress (less Partial Billings), or it may be reported as a liability.

If costs in 2006 are $429,000 as projected, the company recognizes a zero gross profit in 2006. The revenue recognized is the remaining amount of $420,000 ($700,000 − $140,000 − $140,000) left to be recognized on the contract, and the expense is also $420,000. Thus the company recognizes the total loss incurred on the contract in the year in which it was first estimated (2005).

The company debits the costs incurred on the contract in 2006 to the Construction in Progress account in the normal way up to a total of $700,000 ($414,000 in 2006). The balance in the account should not exceed the contract price, since the asset value cannot be greater than the total proceeds to be received on the contract. The company debits any additional costs incurred over $700,000 to the Provision for Loss on Contract account. Since the total costs incurred are $715,000, the excess of $15,000 eliminates the balance established in the account at the end of 2005.

Exhibit 17-7 summarizes the calculations we just discussed. The company records the construction costs and the revenue and expense in 2006 as follows:

Construction in Progress	414,000	
Provision for Loss on Contract	15,000	
Cash, Accounts Payable, etc.		429,000
Construction Expense	420,000	
Construction Revenue		420,000

Note that the amounts ($429,000 and $420,000) in these two journal entries are not equal. This difference occurs because each year the percent completed is computed on the basis of different expected total costs. In 2004 the percent completed of 20% is based on the expected total costs of $500,000, whereas in 2005 the 40% completion is based on the expected total cost of $715,000.

Under the completed-contract method, the company recognizes the loss in 2005 because there is an overall loss on the contract. It records this loss as follows:

Construction Expense	15,000	
Provision for Loss on Contract		15,000

---

7. "Accounting for Performance of Construction-Type and Certain Production-Type Contracts," *op. cit.*, par. 88, requires that the amount of the loss is added to the contract cost unless the amount is material, unusual, or infrequent, in which case the amount is reported separately.

EXHIBIT 17-7 Calculation of Revenues and Expenses When a Loss Is Expected on the Contract

	Current Year	Total to Date
2004		
Construction revenue	$140,000[a]	$140,000
Construction expense	(100,000)[b]	(100,000)
Gross profit	$ 40,000	$ 40,000
2005		
Construction revenue	$140,000	$280,000
Construction expense	(195,000)[d]	(295,000)[c]
Gross profit	$ (55,000)	$ (15,000)
2006		
Construction revenue	$420,000	$700,000
Construction expense	(420,000)	(715,000)
Gross profit	$ 0	$ (15,000)

a. (20% × $700,000)
b. (20% × $500,000)
c.

Contract price	$700,000
Percent complete	40%
Cost of earned revenue before loss provision	$280,000
Estimated total loss	15,000
Construction expense to date	$295,000

d.

Cumulative construction expense	$295,000
Less: Construction expense in previous year	(100,000)
Current construction expense	$195,000

The company debits an expense account to recognize the "loss" because the construction activity is *not* an incidental or peripheral activity. Note that there is no credit to the Construction in Progress account because under the completed-contract method the company did not add the gross profit to the account in previous years.

The company would recognize a gross profit or loss if the actual costs incurred in 2006 were less, or greater, than its estimated amount. This procedure is consistent with accounting for a change in estimate under *APB Opinion No. 20*.

Accounting for a change in estimate is discussed in Chapter 22.

Additional Considerations in Accounting for Long-Term Construction Contracts

We discuss several additional factors that affect the accounting for long-term construction contracts in this section.

OVERHEAD COSTS Contract costs include all direct costs, such as materials and direct labor, and indirect costs (overhead) identifiable with or allocable to the contract. This is consistent with generally accepted accounting principles for inventory and production costs. Therefore a company usually expenses general and administrative costs as incurred under the percentage-of-completion method. However, it may account for these costs as contract costs under the completed-contract method. Accounting for such costs theoretically provides a better matching of costs as expenses against revenues than would result from treating such costs as period expenses, particularly in years when no contracts are completed, and it is less likely to be misleading to users of financial statements.

OPERATING CYCLE *Accounting Research Bulletin No. 45* requires that the net amounts of Construction in Progress and Partial Billings be included as current assets or current liabilities. The operating-cycle concept is used to justify this classification.

OFFSETTING AMOUNTS It is a basic principle of accounting that the offsetting, or netting, of assets and liabilities is not acceptable, except when a right of offset exists. However, *Accounting Research Bulletin No. 45* does allow offsetting when contracts are closely related—for example, when separate contracts are parts of the same project. Therefore in these circumstances a contract that has a net liability (Partial Billings exceeds Construction in Progress) may be offset against one that has a net asset balance. A company should base its decision as to whether offsetting is appropriate in any situation on economic substance rather than legal form. For example, if separate legal contracts are economically one contract, then the right to offset exists in spite of the legal form of the separate contracts.

CAPITALIZED INTEREST When a company constructs an asset, it includes in the cost of the asset the interest cost associated with the funds used in the construction. Thus, if it incurs interest costs that are related to a long-term construction contract, it includes these costs in the Construction in Progress account rather than as interest expense.

The capitalization of interest is discussed in Chapter 9.

DISCLOSURE Exhibit 17-6 illustrates the disclosure of the method used to account for long-term construction contracts. Note that simply disclosing the use of an "accrual basis" is not sufficient, because both the percentage-of-completion and the completed-contract methods are accrual methods. The SEC requires additional long-term contract disclosures for financial statements filed with it. The overall effect is to require more detailed disclosure of accounts receivable and inventory components and the accounting policies and assumptions on which the amounts are based.

Long-Term Service Contracts

A company uses the percentage-of-completion method when it has a long-term contract for the construction and sale of a *product*. Other companies are in the business of providing a *service* instead of a product. **APB Statement No. 4** indicated that revenues from services rendered are recognized when these services have been performed and are billable.[8] Many service transactions involve a single service "act." In these cases a company recognizes revenues (and expenses) under the accrual method of accounting in the period when it performs the service. Some companies, however, have long-term contracts in which they agree to provide a service over an extended period. Generally, at the inception of the agreement, a service contract is signed at an agreed-on price and the seller agrees to perform certain service "acts" at a later date. The service contract may require performance of (1) a specified number of similar acts, (2) a specified number of defined but not similar acts, or (3) an unspecified number of similar acts. In these cases revenue should be based on performance, but when has the "performance" been completed and how should revenue be recognized? This is a difficult question to answer because long-term service contracts can be complex. Sometimes service contracts are sold in conjunction with products, and the performance activities can vary depending on the industry involved.

There are many companies in service industries such as advertising agencies, cable television companies, computer service firms, and companies engaged in research and development for the government. The accounting principles in some of these industries are underdeveloped; in others they are very specialized. The FASB issued an *Invitation to Comment* entitled "Accounting for Certain Service Transactions" as a prelude to its deliberations on setting general accounting standards of revenue (and expense) recognition for service transactions. The FASB deferred these deliberations because it decided to focus first on more conceptual revenue and expense recognition issues. However, the content of this *Invitation to Comment* does provide a good overview of revenue and expense recognition for long-term service contracts and forms the basis for the following general discussion.[9]

---

8. "Basic Concepts and Accounting Principles Underlying Financial Statements of Business Enterprises," *APB Statement No. 4* (New York: AICPA, 1970), par. 151.
9. The following discussion summarizes par. 10–19 of "Accounting for Certain Service Transactions," *FASB Invitation to Comment* (Stamford, Conn.: FASB, 1978), par. 5.

Proportional Performance Method

A company recognizes revenue for service transactions on the basis of performance because performance determines the extent to which its earnings process is complete. **When a long-term service contract requires services to be performed in more than one act, revenue is recognized by the proportional performance method—that is, based on the proportionate performance of each act.** In this regard, a company recognizes revenue depending on the type and number of service acts as follows:

1. *Specified Number of Similar Acts.* Recognize an equal amount of revenue for each act.
2. *Specified Number of Defined but Not Similar Acts.* Recognize revenue for each act based on the ratio of the direct costs (defined next) incurred to perform each act to the total estimated direct costs for the long-term contract.
3. *Unspecified Number of Similar Acts.* Recognize revenue on a straight-line method over the performance period.

Several types of service costs are involved in a long-term service contract. These include (1) **initial direct costs,** those costs that are directly associated with negotiating and signing a service contract (e.g., legal fees), (2) **direct costs,** those costs that have a clear causal relationship to the services performed (e.g., labor costs), and (3) **indirect costs,** those costs other than initial direct costs and direct costs (e.g., advertising and depreciation). Under the proportional performance method, a company recognizes these costs as expenses as follows:

1. *Initial Direct Costs.* Defer and allocate over the performance period in proportion to the recognition of service revenues, because initial direct costs are expensed when revenue is recognized.
2. *Direct Costs.* Expense as incurred, because there is a close relationship between the direct costs incurred and the extent of performance achieved.
3. *Indirect Costs.* Expense as incurred, because indirect costs provide no discernible future benefits.

To illustrate revenue recognition under the proportional performance method, assume the Health Spa Company sells memberships to use its facilities. For $500 in advance, a person signs a 2-year contract which allows use of area X (exercise room) 50 times and area Y (whirlpool and sauna) 100 times during the 2-year period. At the beginning of 2004, 120 people sign the service contract and the company collects $60,000 (120 × $500). Thus, the company is obligated to perform a total of 6,000 (120 × 50) and 12,000 (120 × 100) service acts in 2004 and 2005 involving areas X and Y, respectively. This service contract involves a specified number of defined but not similar acts, so the company recognizes revenue based on a ratio of direct costs per act to total estimated direct costs.

During 2004 members used area X 3,600 times and area Y 4,800 times. In 2005 members used area X 2,400 times and area Y 7,200 times.[10] The following is a summary of the relevant cost information regarding the 120 membership contracts:

Initial direct costs	$ 1,000
Annual indirect costs	2,000
Estimated (and actual) total direct costs (for 2-year period)	24,000
Direct cost per service act:	
Area X	$1.00
Area Y	1.50

---

10. In this example all members used the health spa facilities their entire allotted number of times. In reality this usage would probably not occur. In such a situation the company would have to make estimates of the expected usage, and make adjustments for the differences between actual and estimated usage. This topic is beyond the scope of this chapter. Also, in this example we assumed for simplicity that the company sold no new memberships in 2005.

Exhibit 17-8 illustrates the condensed income statements of the Health Spa Company for 2004 and 2005. The direct costs incurred in 2004 and 2005 are $10,800 and $13,200, or 45% and 55% of the total estimated (and actual) direct costs. Thus, the company recognizes revenues of $27,000 (45% × $60,000) and $33,000 (55% × $60,000) in each year. It allocates $450 of the $1,000 initial direct costs to 2004 and $550 to 2005 based upon the 45% and 55% recognition of revenues. Use of the proportional performance method is appropriate in this case because the company recognizes revenues neither too early (at the time of the signing), before the earning process is complete, nor too late (at the completion of the contract) and, therefore, the method helps to ensure that economic reality is not distorted.

EXHIBIT 17-8   Condensed Income Statements (Proportional Performance Method)

	For Year Ended December 31	
	2004	**2005**
Revenues	$27,000[b]	$33,000[e]
Expenses:		
Initial direct costs	$ 450[c]	$ 550[f]
Direct costs	10,800[a]	13,200[d]
Indirect costs	2,000	2,000
Total expenses	(13,250)	(15,750)
Net Income	$13,750	$17,250

a. ($1 × 3,600) + ($1.50 × 4,800) = $10,800

b. $\dfrac{(\$1 \times 3,600) + (\$1.50 \times 4,800)}{\$24,000 \text{ total direct costs}} = 45\%$; $60,000 receipts × 45% = $27,000

c. 45% × $1,000 = $450

d. ($1 × 2,400) + ($1.50 × 7,200) = $13,200

e. $\dfrac{(\$1 \times 2,400) + (\$1.50 \times 7,200)}{\$24,000} = 55\%$; $60,000 receipts × 55% = $33,000

f. 55% × $1,000 = $550

REVENUE RECOGNITION AFTER THE PERIOD OF SALE

As we discussed earlier in the chapter, the installment and cost recovery methods are the two principal ways of recognizing revenue after the sale. We discuss each method in this section.

6 Account for revenue recognition after the period of sale, including the installment and cost recovery methods.

Installment Method

Installment *sales* involve a financing agreement whereby the customer signs a contract, makes a small down payment, and agrees to make periodic payments over an extended period, often several years. The customer accepts possession of the item when the contract is signed (thereby enjoying its use during the payment period), while the seller retains legal title until the payments are complete. Before the establishment of "credit bureaus" and improved techniques for establishing, evaluating, and maintaining records of individuals' "credit ratings," companies often used installment sales contracts because they were uncertain about the collection of the installment payments. Today, companies may still use installment sales contracts for merchandise because of a customer's lower credit rating, and in certain real estate transactions. **APB Opinion No. 10** found the installment *method* of recognizing revenue for installment *sales* generally to be unacceptable. The Board, however, did agree that there are *exceptional* cases where receivables are collected over an extended period and the probability of collection is not reasonably assured. In these exceptional cases, the installment method is used.[11] In addition, the installment method is still acceptable for income tax purposes under certain circumstances.

---

11. "Omnibus Recognition—1966," *op. cit.*, par. 12 and fn. 8.

It is important to distinguish between an "installment sale" as a legal contract involving a buyer and a seller, and the "installment method" of revenue recognition. For example, for an installment *sale*, a company may recognize revenue in full at the time of the sale if collectibility is reasonably assured. In such a case the company must estimate the costs to be incurred in the future, such as costs of collection and bad debts, so that appropriate matching occurs. Alternatively, a company may use the installment *method* of revenue recognition for a sales transaction that is *not* an installment *sale*. In summary, a company selects the installment method of revenue recognition because the collectibility of the receivable from the sale is not reasonably assured, and this decision is independent of the legal form of the contract. Therefore, we discuss the installment method of revenue recognition in this chapter irrespective of the legal form of the contract.

A company completes the following steps when it uses the installment method:

1. Total sales, cost of goods sold, and collections are recorded in the normal manner during the year.
2. At the end of the year, sales for which the installment method is used are identified. The revenue and the related cost of goods sold that were recorded during the year are "reversed," and the deferred gross profit is recognized.
3. At the end of the year, the gross profit rate on the sales recognized under the installment method for that year is computed. The rate is calculated by dividing the deferred gross profit recognized in step 2 by the related installment sales for the year.
4. A portion of the deferred gross profit is recognized as gross profit for the year by multiplying the cash collected on the sales recognized under the installment method during the year times the gross profit rate calculated in step 3.
5. In future years the remaining deferred gross profit is reduced and the gross profit is recognized based on the cash collected each year from the previous sales recognized under the installment method times the gross profit rate for the year in which those sales were made.

Example of the Installment Method

To illustrate the installment method, consider the following information for the Lee Company in the first two years of its operations:

	2004	2005
Total credit sales	$500,000	$600,000
Total cost of goods sold	390,000	430,000
Installment method sales*	100,000	150,000
Installment method cost of goods sold*	75,000	105,000
Gross profit rate on installment method sales	25%	30%
Cash receipts on installment method sales		
2004 sales	20,000	30,000
2005 sales		40,000
Cash receipts on other credit sales	300,000	480,000

* Included in total credit sales and total cost of goods sold, respectively.

Assume that the company uses the perpetual inventory method and that, for simplicity, interest on the installment receivables is ignored. The Lee Company records the preceding events as follows:

During 2004

Accounts Receivable	500,000	
Sales		500,000
Cost of Goods Sold	390,000	
Inventory		390,000

The company records the total sales and cost of goods sold for the year in the normal manner. It does not separate the sales recognized under the installment method.

During 2004

Cash	320,000	
Accounts Receivable		320,000

The company recognizes cash collections in the normal manner. Of these collections, $20,000 is for installment sales and $300,000 for other credit sales.

December 31, 2004

Sales	100,000	
Cost of Goods Sold		75,000
Deferred Gross Profit, 2004		25,000

The company identifies the sales recognized under the installment method and the related cost of goods sold from the accounting records and "reverses" them, and recognizes the deferred gross profit. It computes a 25% gross profit rate for 2004 (deferred gross profit of $25,000 divided by the sales of $100,000).

December 31, 2004

Deferred Gross Profit, 2004	5,000	
Gross Profit Realized on Installment		
Method Sales		5,000

The company uses the gross profit rate of 25% to recognize the gross profit on the cash collected. Since the company collected $20,000 on these sales for 2004, it reduces the deferred gross profit and recognizes a gross profit of $5,000 ($20,000 × 25%). It closes the gross profit account to Income Summary along with the other sales, cost of goods sold, and expense accounts (not illustrated). The company reports the preceding events in its financial statements as we show in Exhibit 17-9.

EXHIBIT 17-9 Lee Company: Partial Financial Statements

Partial Income Statement
For Year Ended December 31, 2004

Sales	$400,000[a]	
Cost of goods sold	(315,000)[b]	
Gross profit	$ 85,000	
Gross profit realized on installment method sales	5,000	
Total gross profit	$ 90,000	

Partial Balance Sheet
December 31, 2004

Current Assets		
Accounts receivable		$100,000[c]
Installment accounts receivable	$ 80,000[d]	
Less: Deferred gross profit	(20,000)[e]	60,000

a. $500,000 − $100,000.
b. $390,000 − $75,000.
c. $500,000 − $320,000 − $80,000 (from footnote *d*).
d. $100,000 − $20,000.
e. $25,000 − $5,000.

You should understand three aspects of the financial statements. First, in the income statement a company should report the gross profit on the sales recognized under the installment method separately from the gross profit on the other sales. Some companies, however, might combine the two amounts and disclose the gross profit on these sales in the notes to the financial statements. Second, a company usually includes installment accounts receivable in current assets on the balance sheet under the operating cycle concept. Finally, a company usually deducts the deferred gross profit from the installment accounts receivable on the balance sheet. Some companies, however, include the deferred gross profit as a current liability rather than as a contra asset. Such reporting is inconsistent with the concept of a liability, because no future cash outflow will occur. We advocate the presentation as a contra asset because, as we discussed earlier in the chapter, accounts receivable is reduced from selling price to cost.

In 2005 the Lee Company records the following:

During 2005

Accounts Receivable	600,000	
Sales		600,000
Cost of Goods Sold	430,000	
Inventory		430,000
Cash	550,000	
Accounts Receivable		550,000

Of these collections, $70,000 is for installment sales and $480,000 for other credit sales. Note that the cash collections on the installment sales in 2005 include amounts from sales made in 2004 ($30,000) and 2005 ($40,000).

December 31, 2005

Sales	150,000	
Cost of Goods Sold		105,000
Deferred Gross Profit, 2005		45,000

The company "reverses" the sales recognized under the installment method and the related cost of goods sold for 2005, and recognizes the deferred gross profit for 2005. The gross profit rate in 2005 is 30% ($45,000 ÷ $150,000).

December 31, 2005

Deferred Gross Profit, 2004	7,500	
Deferred Gross Profit, 2005	12,000	
Gross Profit Realized on Installment Method Sales		19,500

During 2005 the company collected $30,000 on its 2004 installment method sales, for which its gross profit is 25%. As we show, the company reduces the deferred gross profit from 2004 and recognizes a gross profit of $7,500 ($30,000 × 25%). The company also collected $40,000 on its 2005 installment method sales, for which its gross profit is 30%. In the entry the company reduces the deferred gross profit for 2005 and recognizes a gross profit of $12,000 ($40,000 × 30%) on those collections. The combined gross profit for 2005 is $19,500, which the company closes to Income Summary.

The Lee Company includes the realized gross profit of $19,500 in its 2005 income statement, in addition to the sales and the cost of goods sold from those sales on which it recognized revenue at the time of sale. The company includes the installment accounts receivable of $160,000 ($100,000 − $20,000 + $150,000 − $30,000 − $40,000) and a deferred gross profit of $45,500 ($25,000 − $5,000 + $45,000 − $7,500 − $12,000) on its December 31, 2005 balance sheet. Note that the balance in the deferred gross profit account is the balance of the installment receivables multiplied by the gross profit percentage.

Additional Considerations for the Installment Method

We discuss several additional factors that affect the accounting under the installment method in this section.

ALTERNATIVE ACCOUNTING AND REPORTING   In the preceding example we assumed that it is acceptable to report only the gross profit amount in the income statement because the installment sales revenue is not material. If a company considered the installment sales to be material, then it should report separately both the installment sales and the cost of goods sold (a procedure that we used in the discussion of long-term construction contracts earlier in the chapter). In this situation the Lee Company would record an alternative journal entry as follows (using the amounts for 2004):

Deferred Gross Profit, 2004	5,000	
Installment Cost of Goods Sold	15,000	
Installment Sales		20,000

Under this alternative, when the company receives cash, it reduces the deferred gross profit as before. However, it records an amount equal to the cash collected as the sales revenue and recognizes an appropriate amount of cost of goods sold; in this case, 75% of the sales amount. Then the company would disclose the installment sales of $20,000 and deduct the installment cost of goods sold of $15,000 to report its gross profit of $5,000 for 2004.

OPERATING EXPENSES   As we have seen, a company matches the cost of goods sold against the installment sales in the same period as the sales. It does *not* defer operating expenses. Instead, it recognizes them in the normal way on an accrual basis. That is, the company recognizes them either in the period incurred, such as general and administrative salaries, or by systematic and rational allocation, such as depreciation on an office building.

INTEREST CHARGES   A company making an installment sale typically charges the buyer interest because of the extended collection period. The company usually includes the interest charge as a component of the periodic payment specified in the sales contract. The normal practice is to make the installment payment an equal amount each period, so that each succeeding payment includes a smaller interest component and a larger principal payment. In other words, the interest is treated in the same way as a loan.

When a company includes interest in an installment sale, it accounts for the interest revenue separately. It separates each installment payment received into two components, interest revenue and a reduction in the installment accounts receivable. It records the interest revenue on an accrual basis in the normal manner (in the period earned), and recognizes the gross profit as it receives cash, as we discussed earlier.

UNCOLLECTIBLE ACCOUNTS   Installment sales contracts usually provide for repossession of the item if the buyer defaults. If the experience of the company indicates that the price at which the repossessed item can be sold will be sufficient to cover the remaining payments on the original installment sale, then a provision for bad debts is not necessary. However, if past experience indicates that the expected resale price will be insufficient to cover the payments, the company should recognize bad debt expense and an allowance for doubtful installment accounts receivable.

DEFAULTS AND REPOSSESSIONS   When a company repossesses an item, it records the inventory and writes off the related receivable and deferred gross profit. To illustrate, assume that the Lee Company repossesses an item it sold in 2004 with a gross profit of 25%, and that the fair value of the repossessed item is $600. If $1,000 remained unpaid, it records the repossession as follows:

Repossessed Inventory	600	
Deferred Gross Profit	250	
Allowance for Doubtful Installment Accounts Receivable	150	
Accounts Receivable		1,000

The company eliminates the deferred gross profit ($1,000 × 25%) related to the remaining cash payments and debits the $150 "lost" on the recovery to Allowance for Doubtful Installment Accounts Receivable, which it established when it recognized the bad debt expense.

INCIDENTAL SALES   As we mentioned earlier, a company is most likely to use the installment method in special situations. In such cases, it is likely that the company recognizes a gain rather than a revenue and expense, because the transaction is incidental or peripheral to its normal operations. For example, suppose a company sold for $100,000 land that had originally cost $40,000. The company uses the installment method and collects $30,000 the first year. It make the following journal entries:

To Record the Sale

Accounts Receivable	100,000	
Land		40,000
Deferred Gain		60,000

To Record the Cash Collection and the Gain for the Year

Cash	30,000	
Accounts Receivable		30,000
Deferred Gain	18,000	
Gain on Sale of Land		18,000*

*$60,000 × ($30,000 ÷ $100,000)

In subsequent years, the company eliminates a proportion of the deferred gain and recognizes a gain when it collects each remaining cash receipt.

Cost Recovery Method

If a company makes a sale in which there is a very high degree of uncertainty about the collectibility of the sales price, it is appropriate to defer the recognition of any profit until the company has recovered the cost of the entire sale. As with the installment method, **APB Opinion No. 10** found the **cost recovery method** of recognizing revenue generally to be unacceptable. The Board, however, did agree that there are exceptional cases where receivables are collected over an extended period and where the terms of the transaction provide no reasonable basis for estimating the degree of collectibility. In such exceptional situations, the cost recovery method may be used. For example, a company may sell a distressed division, thereby transferring the risks and benefits of ownership, but agree that the purchaser will pay with the net operating cash inflows generated by the division.

Under the cost recovery method a company records sales, cost of goods sold, and collections during the year in the usual manner (as with the installment method). In contrast to the installment method, however, it does *not* recognize a gross profit under the cost recovery method until it has recovered all the cost of the item sold. Once it has recovered the cost, it records gross profit at an amount equal to the cash it receives in the period. To illustrate the cost recovery method, consider the following information for the Patken Company:

Sale of property under cost recovery method	$20,000
Cost of property sold (net)	12,000
Cash collections	
2004	5,000
2005	9,000
2006	6,000

The company records the preceding events using the cost recovery method as follows:

During 2004

Accounts Receivable	20,000	
Deferred Gross Profit		8,000
Property (net)		12,000
Cash	5,000	
Accounts Receivable		5,000

The company records the transaction and defers the profit. It does not recognize a gross profit when it collects the cash because it has not yet recovered the $12,000 cost of the property sold.

During 2005

Cash	9,000	
Accounts Receivable		9,000

December 31, 2005

Deferred Gross Profit	2,000	
Gross Profit Realized on Cost Recovery Transactions		2,000

In 2004, the company recovered $5,000 of the $12,000 cost of the property sold. Therefore, of the $9000 cash collected in 2005, the first $7,000 collected completes the recovery of the cost, and the remaining $2,000 collected results in the recognition of a gross profit of $2,000.

During 2006

Cash	6,000	
Accounts Receivable		6,000

December 31, 2006

Deferred Gross Profit	6,000	
Gross Profit Realized on Cost Recovery Transactions		6,000

Since the company recovered the total cost in 2005, the $6,000 cash collected in 2006 results in the recognition of an equal amount of gross profit. The Patken Company includes the gross profit in its income statement each year, and includes the Accounts Receivable, less the balance in the Deferred Gross Profit account, on its ending balance sheet.

Comparison of the Installment and Cost Recovery Methods

As we discussed earlier, *APB Opinion No. 10* allows the use of either the installment or cost recovery methods in certain exceptional circumstances and makes no distinction between the situations in which each should be applied. If collectibility is not reasonably assured, revenue should *not* be recognized at the time of sale. Instead, the installment method should be used. (Also, income tax rules allow the installment method to be used in certain situations for the computation of taxable income.) Since the cost recovery method is a more conservative revenue recognition method, it should be used only when such conservatism is appropriate. For example, **if the collectibility is *extremely* uncertain or there is *no* reliable basis for estimating the collectibility, then the cost recovery method is appropriate.** The method may also be used if there is significant uncertainty about the profitability of a new venture or product and for certain real estate transactions, as we discuss later in the chapter.

REVENUE RECOGNITION DELAYED UNTIL A FUTURE EVENT OCCURS

7 Account for revenue recognition delayed until a future event occurs.

In certain situations **there may not be a sufficient transfer of the risks and benefits of ownership for a company to recognize revenue.** For example, a company may "sell" a subsidiary and accept a long-term interest-bearing note receivable but maintain a continuing involvement in its management through representation on the board of directors, perhaps because the buyer made a very small down payment. In such situations, the company should not recognize either the receivable or the deferred gross profit. Instead, the company uses the deposit method.

Deposit Method

To illustrate the deposit method, assume that the Oscar Company sells a subsidiary to the Pet Company and accepts a $500,000 down payment and a 10% note for the balance of the sale price of $7 million. The net assets (i.e., book value) of the subsidiary are $5 million and the Pet Company uses the deposit method because it has the right to cancel the agreement for the next year. **The deposit method postpones the recognition of revenue until a company can determine whether it has made a sale for accounting purposes.** Until Oscar Company recognizes revenue (by any of the revenue recognition methods), it does not record a note receivable, and continues to report the property and any related debt (even if assumed by the Pet Company) on its balance sheet. However, it separately classifies the assets and liabilities under such headings as "assets of business transferred under contract" and "liabilities of business transferred." Furthermore, for depreciable assets the Oscar Company continues to record depreciation expense on the property. It records the down payment and all payments of principal and interest received from Pet Company as a deposit and reports them as a liability on its balance sheet if the interest will be returned should the terms of the contract not be fulfilled. For example, the Oscar Company records the receipt of the down payment as follows:

Cash	500,000	
Deposit from Purchaser		500,000

When the company eliminates the liability for the deposit because the circumstances have changed, it recognizes the revenue. To illustrate, suppose that the Oscar Company recognizes revenue (gain) one year after the original transaction. It records the note receivable and a gain, eliminates the net assets of the subsidiary and the deposit, and recognizes the interest revenue as follows:

Interest Receivable (10% × $6,500,000)	650,000	
Note Receivable	6,500,000	
Deposit from Purchaser	500,000	
Interest Revenue		650,000
Gain ($7,000,000 − $5,000,000)		2,000,000
Net Assets of Subsidiary		5,000,000

Alternatively, the company recognizes any interest that is *not* subject to refund as earned in the normal manner, and records only the principal portion of any payments as a deposit. If, instead, the contract is canceled without a refund, Oscar recognizes the deposits forfeited by Pet Company as income.

ADDITIONAL REVENUE RECOGNITION ISSUES

8 Understand software revenue recognition, franchises, real estate sales, retail land sales, and consignment sales.

The specific accounting principles used for software revenue recognition, sales of franchises, real estate sales, and retail land sales are important because of the significance of the industries and the relevance of their rules to a general understanding of revenue recognition. In certain industries, consignment sales also are used frequently and the recognition of revenue on such sales is an important issue. We also discuss the SEC's *Staff Accounting Bulletin No. 101* and international accounting differences in this section.

Software Revenue Recognition

The recognition of revenue by a company selling software can be complicated. *AICPA Statement of Position No. 97-2* provides the following guidance[12]:

1. If a company has an agreement to deliver software that requires significant production, modification, or customization of software, it uses contract accounting (e.g., percentage of completion) for the agreement in conformity with *Accounting Research Bulletin No. 45*, and *SOP 81-1*, which we discussed earlier in the chapter.

2. If a company has an agreement to deliver software that does *not* require significant production, modification, or customization of software, it recognizes revenue when (a) persuasive evidence of an agreement exists, (b) delivery has occurred, (c) its fee is fixed or determinable, and (d) collectibility is probable.

3. A company separately accounts for a service element if (a) the services are not essential to the functionality of any other element of the transaction, and (b) the services are stated separately in the contract such that the total price of the agreement would be expected to vary as the result of inclusion or exclusion of the services.

4. Software arrangements may consist of multiple elements such as additional software products, upgrades and/or enhancements, rights to exchange or return software, and customer support. If contract accounting does not apply, a company must allocate its fee to the various elements based on fair values. Fair value is determined by the price charged when the element is sold separately, or a price established by management for each element when the element is not sold separately. If sufficiently objective evidence of fair values does not exist, the company defers all revenue until it has sufficient evidence, or until it has delivered all the elements.

5. A company must allocate any discounts proportionately to all the elements, except that none can be allocated to upgrade rights.

Franchises

A **franchise agreement** involves the granting of business rights by the **franchisor** to a **franchisee** who will operate the franchised business. Franchises are common in several industries, such as fast foods (McDonald's), motels (Holiday Inn), and auto rentals (Hertz). Franchise agreements vary in complexity but usually involve an initial payment (called an **initial franchise fee**) by the franchisee and ongoing payments of **continuing franchise fees**. In return for the initial franchise fee, the franchisor may provide assistance in site selection and construction, equipment acquisitions, projections of franchisee's revenues and expenses, and other matters. For the continuing franchise fees, the franchisor may provide advertising, quality control, training of personnel, and budgeting and other accounting services.

Sometimes the franchisor collects the initial franchise fee far in advance of the performance of its services. At other times collection of part of the initial franchise fee is deferred until the franchise is operating successfully. Occasionally, the continuing franchise fee is not large enough to cover the franchisor's cost of the on-going services provided, but the initial franchise fee is unusually large (so, in effect, it involves a prepayment by the franchisee for the continuing services). Or the franchise agreement may involve the potential refund of the initial franchise fee if certain conditions or obligations are not met by the franchisor.

All these revenue recognition issues of the franchisor are addressed by **FASB Statement No. 45**.[13] The franchisor recognizes the initial franchise fee as revenue when it has substantially performed all material services. **Substantial performance** means that there is no

---

12. "Software Revenue Recognition," *AICPA Statement of Position No. 97–2* (New York: AICPA, 1997).
13. "Accounting for Franchise Fee Revenue," *FASB Statement of Financial Accounting Standards No. 45* (Stamford, Conn.: FASB, 1981), par. 3–7.

obligation or intent by the franchisor to refund any cash received or forgive any unpaid notes receivable, and the franchisor has performed substantially all the initial services required by the franchise agreement. The commencement of operations by the franchisee is presumed to be the earliest point at which substantial performance has occurred, unless the franchisor can demonstrate earlier performance. At this point it recognizes revenue under the accrual method. A franchisor uses installment or cost recovery methods for revenue recognition only in those exceptional cases when revenue is collectible over an extended period and no reasonable basis exists for estimating collectibility.

The franchisor recognizes continuing franchise fees as revenue as it earns the fees and they are receivable from the franchisee. The continuing fee may not cover the cost of continuing services provided by the franchisor because there is a large initial fee that is, in effect, a prepayment for continuing services. In such cases, the franchisor records a portion of the initial fee as a liability and amortizes the amount to franchise revenue over the life of the franchise.

ILLUSTRATION OF ACCOUNTING FOR INITIAL FRANCHISE FEES To illustrate the accounting for an initial franchise fee, assume that the Castle Company sells a franchise that requires an initial franchise fee of $70,000. A down payment of $20,000 cash is required, with the balance covered by the issuance of a $50,000, 10% note, payable by the franchisee in five equal annual installments. The following alternatives exist for accounting for this fee by the Castle Company (the franchisor):

1. Castle has substantially performed all material services, the refund period has expired, and the collectibility of the note is reasonably assured. Castle recognizes revenue as follows:

Cash	20,000	
Notes Receivable	50,000	
Franchise Revenue		70,000

2. The refund period has expired and the collectibility of the note is reasonably assured, but Castle has not substantially performed all material services. Castle does not recognize revenue, but instead recognizes a liability as follows:

Cash	20,000	
Notes Receivable	50,000	
Unearned Franchise Fees		70,000

Castle will recognize the unearned franchise fees as revenue when it has performed all material services.

3. Castle has substantially performed all material services and the collectibility of the note is reasonably assured, but the refund period has not expired. Castle does not recognize revenue, but instead recognizes a liability as follows:

Cash	20,000	
Notes Receivable	50,000	
Unearned Franchise Fees		70,000

Castle will recognize the unearned franchise fees as revenue when the refund period expires.

4. Castle has substantially performed all material services and the refund period has expired, but the collectibility of the note is not reasonably assured. Castle recognizes revenue by the installment or cost recovery method. If we assume that Castle uses the installment method, it recognizes revenue of $20,000 as follows:

Cash	20,000	
Notes Receivable	50,000	
Unearned Franchise Fees		50,000
Franchise Revenue		20,000

Since Castle is using the installment method, it recognizes the unearned franchise fees as revenue in the amount of $10,000 each year as it receives cash.

5. The refund period has expired, but Castle has not substantially performed all material services and there is no basis for estimating the collectibility of the note. Castle does *not* recognize the note as an asset. Instead, it uses a form of the deposit method. For example, suppose Castle has developed an entirely new product whose success is uncertain and the franchisee will pay the note from the cash flows generated by the sale of the product, if any. Castle records the initial transaction as follows:

Cash	20,000	
Unearned Franchise Fees		20,000

Castle recognizes the unearned franchise fees as revenue either under the accrual method in the normal manner at the completion of the services to be performed (if collectibility is reasonably assured) or under the installment method if it has no basis for estimating the collectibility of the note. Alternatively, if Castle has earned the franchise fees through the substantial performance of all material services, it would recognize franchise revenue of $20,000 instead of the liability.

6. Now assume that Castle has earned only $30,000 from providing initial services, with the balance being a down payment for continuing services. If the refund period has expired and the collectibility of the note is reasonably assured, Castle recognizes revenue of $30,000 as follows:

Cash	20,000	
Notes Receivable	50,000	
Franchise Revenue		30,000
Unearned Franchise Fees		40,000

Castle recognizes the unearned franchise fees of $40,000 as revenue when it performs the continuing services.

In all these cases except the fifth, Castle accounts for the collection of interest and principal on the note receivable in the usual manner. In the fifth situation, it does not recognize the note and revenue until a future event occurs. In addition, Castle accounts for its costs in a manner consistent with its revenue recognition. That is, if it defers revenue, then it defers the related cost of goods sold. Then, when it recognizes revenue, it matches the cost of goods sold against the revenues. The *franchisee* accounts for its payments as an intangible asset.

Intangible assets are discussed in Chapter 11.

ILLUSTRATION OF ACCOUNTING FOR CONTINUING FRANCHISE FEES To illustrate the accounting for continuing franchise fees, assume that the Castle Company also charges the franchisee a continuing franchise fee of $9,000 per year. The following alternatives exist for accounting for this fee by the Castle Company (the franchisor):

1. The fee is earned for providing continuing services:

Cash	9,000	
Continuing Franchise Fee Revenue		9,000

2. $1,000 of the fee is for national advertising:

Cash	9,000	
Continuing Franchise Fee Revenue		8,000
Unearned Franchise Fees		1,000

Castle recognizes the unearned franchise fees as revenue when it performs the advertising services and also records the costs as expenses.

In addition to providing services as part of the continuing franchise fee, a franchisor often sells supplies to the franchisee. These sales occur because the franchisor may be able to obtain quantity discounts from manufacturers or wholesalers, or to maintain uniform quality of the supplies. The franchisor records these sales and related expenses in the normal manner.

OPTION TO PURCHASE In some franchise situations, the franchise agreement will include a provision allowing the franchisor an option to purchase the franchisee's business. If, at the time the franchise agreement is signed and the option is granted, an understanding exists that the option will be exercised (or it is probable that the franchisor ultimately will acquire the franchise), the franchisor does not recognize the initial franchise fee as revenue. Instead it records the initial franchise fee as a liability. When the franchisor exercises its option and acquires the franchise, it records the liability as a reduction in its investment.

Real Estate Sales

In real estate sales, a company may sell land or a building or both. The land may be developed or undeveloped and the seller may be responsible for making improvements. The building may be completed or in the process of construction and may be for commercial use, such as a factory or office building, or residential use, such as a house or apartment building. Accounting for real estate sales is defined by **FASB Statement No. 66,** "Accounting for Sales of Real Estate." We discuss only the basic rules here because of their relevance to an understanding of revenue recognition alternatives.[14]

For real estate sales, **a selling company recognizes revenue and related expenses on the accrual basis in the normal manner in the period of the sale if** *all* **of the following conditions are met:** (1) a sale is consummated, (2) the buyer's initial and continuing investments are adequate to demonstrate a commitment to pay for the property, (3) the seller's receivable is not subject to future subordination (reduced in its liquidation rights), and (4) the seller has transferred to the buyer the usual risks and rewards of ownership in a transaction that is in substance a sale and does not have a continuing involvement with the property.

The evidence necessary to meet these criteria is discussed in the *Statement* but is beyond the scope of the text. It is important to understand that these criteria address the conceptual issues we discussed earlier in the chapter, namely the economic substance of the transaction, the transfer of the risks and benefits of ownership, and the collectibility (realizability) of the receivable. **When any of the criteria are** *not* **met, the selling company recognizes revenue under an alternative method as follows:**

1. If the sale is not consummated, the *deposit method* is used.
2. If the buyer's initial and continuing investment is not adequate, the *installment method* is used if the recovery of the cost of the property is reasonably assured, and the *cost recovery method* is used if recovery of the cost is not reasonably assured.
3. If the seller's receivable is subject to future subordination, the *cost recovery method* is used.
4. If the seller has continuing involvement with the property and does not transfer substantially all the risks and benefits of ownership, generally revenue and related expenses are recognized at the time of sale with a deduction for the maximum exposure to loss. Other methods may be appropriate depending on the circumstances.

Thus, various revenue recognition methods are appropriate depending on the circumstances. When a company has earned revenue and the related receivable is realized or realizable, the company recognizes revenue in full using the accrual method. When the

---

14. "Accounting for Sales of Real Estate," *FASB Statement of Financial Accounting Standards* No. 66 (Stamford, Conn.: FASB, 1982), par. 5–43.

earning process is not complete or realization has not occurred, the company uses an alternative method.

Retail Land Sales

In retail land sales, a company may acquire a large tract of unimproved land which it divides into lots. It then "sells" these lots to widely dispersed retail customers (individuals) through intensive marketing programs. Generally, part of the marketing program involves an agreement by the company to improve the lots by installing roads, utilities, and related amenities such as golf courses, lakes, and recreational centers. These improvements will require large future capital outlays on the part of the company. The company may agree to be continually involved in the operations of the recreational centers and to provide ongoing maintenance. The "sales contract" often has a low down payment, no (or limited) credit investigation of the buyer, periodic payments by the buyer that extend over several years, and the ability of the buyer to cancel the contract and obtain a refund within a specified period.

Several factors involved in retail land sales have a potential impact on the timing of revenue recognition by the company. These include the collectibility of the receivables, the financial ability of the company to fulfill its obligations, the length of the refund period, the accumulation of collections, and the ongoing completion of the project. For retail land sales, **the selling company recognizes revenue and the related expenses in the period of the sale on the accrual basis if** *all* **of the following conditions are met:** (1) the buyer has made the down payment and each required subsequent payment until the period of cancellation with refund has expired, (2) the cumulative payments of principal and interest equal or exceed 10% of the contract sales price, (3) collection experience for the project indicates that at least 90% of the contracts will be collected in full (a down payment of 20% is an acceptable indication of collectibility), (4) the receivable from the sale is not subject to subordination to new loans on the property, and (5) the seller is not obligated to complete improvements of lots sold or to construct amenities or other facilities applicable to lots sold.

As with real estate sales, the intent of these rules is to be consistent with the conceptual issues related to revenue recognition. **When at least one of the preceding criteria is** *not* **met, the selling company recognizes revenue under an alternative method as follows:**

1. The *percentage-of-completion method* is used if the first four criteria are met, there has been progress on the improvements, there are indications that the work will be completed according to plan, there is no indication of significant delaying factors, and development is practical.
2. The *installment method* of accounting is used if only the first two criteria are met and the seller is financially capable of honoring its obligations.
3. The *deposit method* is used if the first two criteria are not met.

Again, the selling company recognizes revenue in full using the accrual method if it is earned and the receivable is realized or realizable; it uses an alternative method if either criterion is not met.[15]

Consignment Sales

A manufacturer or wholesaler may transfer goods to a dealer for purposes of sale but retain the risks and benefits of ownership (as well as legal title). In these situations the dealer is acting as an *agent* for the manufacturer or wholesaler in the sale of the goods to a third party. The transfer of goods is a **consignment,** the manufacturer or wholesaler is the **consignor,** and the dealer is the **consignee.** The consignor is usually responsible for all costs associated with the goods and the consignee must exercise due care

---

15. *Ibid.*, par. 45–49.

in storing and selling the goods. When the sale to the third party takes place, legal title passes directly to the third party from the consignor.

Accounting for consignments may be summarized as follows:

1. Since title remains with the consignor, when the goods are transferred from the consignor to the consignee, the consignor does *not* record the sale of inventory, and the consignee does *not* record the acquisition of inventory.
2. The consignor recognizes revenue only when the sale to the third party occurs, because that is when it earns the revenue. The consignee must notify the consignor of the sale and must maintain detailed records of items held on consignment and various costs incurred.
3. The consignee uses a **Consignment-in** account. It credits the account for the proceeds received from the sale of the consigned goods and debits the same account for costs that will be reimbursed by the consignor and for commissions it earns. At the end of the period, if the account has a debit balance, the consignor has an obligation for that amount to the consignee; that is, it represents a receivable of the consignee. Alternatively, if the account has a credit balance, the consignee has an obligation to the consignor; that is, it represents a liability of the consignee. The consignee reports the Commissions Earned account as operating revenue on its income statement.
4. The consignor uses a **Consignment-out** account, which is a special inventory account. When it ships goods on consignment, it debits the account for the cost of the inventory shipped (and credits the normal inventory account). In addition, the consignor debits any consignment costs (e.g., transportation charges) it incurs to the account. On notification by the consignee, the consignor credits the account for the costs incurred for the sale of consigned goods and debits these costs to the respective expense accounts. The consignor reports any balance in the Consignment-out account as consignment inventory on its ending balance sheet.

SAB No. 101

In 1999, the Securities and Exchange Commission issued *Staff Accounting Bulletin No. 101*. While this did not change accounting principles, it did have some significant effects on the practice of revenue recognition, with many companies changing their policies. It also requires that all companies disclose their revenue recognition policies.

International Accounting Differences

The basic international accounting standards for revenue recognition are generally very similar to those of the U.S. However, there are some terminology differences. For example, international standards say that revenue is recognized when it is probable that future economic benefits will flow to the enterprise and these benefits can be measured reliably. Some of the specific criteria are that the significant risks and rewards of ownership are transferred, the company retains neither continuing managerial involvement nor effective control, and the costs can be measured reliably.

For construction contracts, international accounting standards also require the use of the percentage-of-completion method if the outcome can be estimated reliably, although they do not give as much guidance as U.S. principles on how to measure the estimated cost to complete. Otherwise, international standards require the use of the zero-profit method, which is a cost recovery method, in contrast to the completed contract method required by U.S. principles.

SUMMARY OF ALTERNATIVE REVENUE RECOGNITION METHODS

Exhibit 17-10 summarizes the various alternative revenue recognition methods. It includes the reasons for the use of each method and the primary impacts on the financial statements.

EXHIBIT 17-10 Summary of Alternative Revenue Recognition Methods

Method	Reasons for Use	Impact on Financial Statements
Accrual	Revenue is earned and realized or realizable in the period of sale.	Revenue and expenses are recognized in the period of sale, and net assets are increased.
Percentage-of-completion	Revenue is recognized during production because all four criteria are met (see p. 787).	Revenue and expenses are recognized in the period of production and inventory (net assets) is increased.
Completed-contract	Revenue is recognized at the completion of the contract because at least one of the four criteria is not met.	Revenue and expenses are recognized at the completion of production (sale) and net assets are increased.
Proportional performance	Same principles as percentage-of-completion, but applied to service contracts.	
Completion-of-production	Revenue is recognized at the completion of production because it is earned and the selling price is realizable due to the immediate marketability at quoted prices and unit interchangeability.	Revenue and expenses are recognized at the completion of production and inventory (net assets) is increased.
Installment	Revenue is recognized as cash is received because it is earned in the period of sale but is not realizable until the period of collection.	Gross profit is deferred in the period of sale and recognized as cash is received, at which time net assets are increased (deferred gross profit is reduced).
Cost recovery	Revenue is recognized after the cost has been recovered because it is earned in the period of sale but is not realizable due to the extreme uncertainty of collection.	Gross profit is deferred in the period of sale and recognized after the cost has been recovered, at which time net assets are increased (deferred gross profit is reduced).
Deposit	Revenue is not recognized until a future event occurs since it has not been earned because the risks and benefits of ownership have not been transferred.	All cash receipts are recorded as liabilities until a future event occurs, at which time revenue is recognized using one of the alternative methods.

SUMMARY

At the beginning of the chapter, we identified several objectives you would accomplish after reading the chapter. The objectives are listed below, each followed by a brief summary of the key points in the chapter discussion.

1. **Understand the revenue recognition alternatives.** The usual point of revenue recognition is the time of sale (delivery). Revenue recognition may also be advanced by recording revenue during production, or deferred until cash receipt.
2. **Explain revenue recognition at the time of sale, during production, and at the time of cash receipt.** If a company recognizes revenue at the time of sale, it recognizes revenue, the related expense, and the increase in net assets at the same time. If a company recognizes revenue during production, it recognizes the gross profit (revenue less the related expense) during production even though the inventory has not been transferred to the customer. It increases the value of the inventory from its cost to its selling price, and the increase in the value of the net assets occurs at the same time. If a company recognizes revenue as it receives cash, it records the receivable, removes the inventory, and records the deferred gross profit as a contra account to Accounts Receivable. It recognizes the gross profit (revenue less the related expense) as it collects the cash.
3. **Explain the conceptual issues regarding revenue recognition.** The decision to recognize revenue focuses on three factors: (1) the economic substance of the event takes precedence over the legal form of the transaction; (2) the

risks and benefits of ownership have been transferred to the buyer; and (3) the collectibility of the receivable from the sale is reasonably assured.

4. **Describe the alternative revenue recognition methods.** Revenue generally is recognized in the period of the sale. Revenue may also be recognized prior to the period of the sale under the percentage-of-completion method or the proportional performance method. Revenue may also be recognized at the completion of production. Revenue may also be recognized after the period of the sale under the installment method or the cost recovery method. Finally, revenue recognition may be delayed until a future event occurs, in which case the deposit method is used.

5. **Account for revenue recognition prior to the period of sale, including the percentage-of-completion and completed contract methods.** Under the percentage-of-completion method, the company recognizes profit each period during the life of the contract in proportion to the amount of the contract completed during the period. As it recognizes the profit, it also increases the value of the inventory, so that it values the inventory at the costs incurred plus the profit recognized to date, less any partial billings. Under the completed contract method, the company does not recognize profit during the life of the contract, but it recognizes the profit only when the contract is completed. During the life of the contract, the company records the inventory at cost, less any partial billings.

6. **Account for revenue recognition after the period of sale, including the installment and cost recovery methods.** Under the installment method, a company recognizes gross profit each period by multiplying the amount of cash it receives by the gross profit rate. Under the cost recovery method, a company does not recognize gross profit until it has recovered the cost of the item sold. Then it recognizes gross profit in an amount equal to the additional cash received during the period.

7. **Account for revenue recognition delayed until a future event occurs.** In certain situations, there may not be a sufficient transfer of the risks and benefits of ownership for a company to recognize revenue. In these situations, the company uses the deposit method and records all cash receipts as a liability, until it may recognize revenue.

8. **Understand software revenue recognition, franchises, real estate sales, retail land sales, and consignment sales.** If a company selling software has an agreement to deliver software that requires significant production, modifications, or customization, it uses contract accounting. If a company has an agreement to deliver software that does *not* require significant production, modification, or customization, it recognizes revenue when (a) persuasive evidence of an agreement exists, (b) delivery has occurred, (c) the seller's fee is fixed or determinable, and (d) collectibility is probable. A company separately accounts for a service element if (a) the services are not essential to the functionality of any other elements of the transaction, and (b) the services are stated separately in the contract such that the total price of the agreement would be expected to vary as the result of inclusion or exclusion of the services. Software arrangements may consist of multiple elements such as additional software products, upgrades and/or enhancements, rights to exchange or return software, and customer support. If contract accounting does not apply, a company must allocate its fee to the various elements based on fair values. If sufficiently objective evidence of fair values does not exist, the company defers all revenue until it has sufficient evidence, or until it has delivered all the elements.

   A franchisor recognizes the initial franchise fee as revenue when it has substantially performed all material services. It recognizes continuing franchise fees as revenue as it earns the fees. For real estate sales, a company recognizes revenue in the period of sale if all the following conditions are met: (1) a sale is consummated, (2) the buyer's initial and continuing investments are adequate to demonstrate a commitment to pay for the property, (3) the seller's receivable is not subject to future subordination, and (4) the seller has transferred to the buyer the usual risks and rewards of ownership. For retail land sales, a company recognizes revenue in the period of sale if all the following conditions are met: (1) the buyer has made the downpayment and each required payment until the refund period has expired, (2) the cumulative payments of principal and interest equal or exceed 10% of the contract sales price, (3) collection experience for the project indicates that at least 90% of the contracts will be collected in full, (4) the seller's receivable is not subject to future subordination, and (5) the seller is not obligated to complete improvements of lots sold or to construct amenities or other facilities applicable to lots sold. In a consignment, the consignor transfers goods to the consignee for sale to a third party. The consignor recognizes revenue when the goods are transferred to the third party.

QUESTIONS

Q17-1 Why is revenue sometimes recognized at a time other than the sale?

Q17-2 Distinguish between the terms *recognition* and *realization*.

Q17-3 Describe the effects on a company's financial statements of recognizing revenue at the time of sale, during production, and at the time of cash receipt.

Q17-4 What three factors affect the decision as to when to recognize revenue?

Q17-5 What are the five revenue recognition alternatives?

Q17-6 Under what circumstances does a company recognize revenue prior to the period of sale? What two methods may it use?

Q17-7 What are the differences between the two methods of accounting for long-term construction contracts?

Q17-8 Under what circumstances does a company use the percentage-of-completion method for long-term contracts?

Q17-9 How may the departure from the principle of recognizing revenue only at the time of the sale be justified when a company uses the percentage-of-completion method?

Q17-10 Describe input and output measures used in the percentage-of-completion method. Give an example of each.

Q17-11 How does a company account for losses under the two methods of accounting for long-term construction contracts?

Q17-12 How does a company classify the following accounts in its financial statements: Construction in Progress, Partial Billings, Construction Revenue, and Construction Expense?

Q17-13 How does a company recognize initial direct costs, direct costs, and indirect costs as expenses under the

proportional performance method? Explain the reason for each method.

Q17-14 Under what circumstances does a company recognize revenue after the period of the sale? What two methods are used?

Q17-15 Describe the steps involved in the installment method.

Q17-16 Describe the differences between the cost recovery method and the installment method.

Q17-17 Describe the basic characteristics of the deposit method.

Q17-18 Distinguish between the initial franchise fee and continuing franchise fee. When is each recognized as revenue?

Q17-19 How is revenue recognized for real estate sales?

Q17-20 How is revenue recognized for retail land sales?

Q17-21 In a consignment, does the consignee or consignor retain title to the property? When is revenue recognized by the consignor? The consignee?

CASES

COMMUNICATION

C17-1 Criteria for Revenue Recognition

The earning of revenue by a company is recognized for accounting purposes when the transaction is recorded. In some situations, revenue is recognized approximately as it is earned in the economic sense; in others, accountants have developed guidelines for recognizing revenue by other criteria, for example, at the point of sale.

Required (*ignore income taxes*)

1. Explain and justify why revenue is often recognized as earned at the time of sale.
2. Explain in what situations it would be appropriate to recognize revenue as the productive activity takes place.
3. Explain at what times it may be appropriate to recognize revenue other than those included in items (1) and (2). (*AICPA adapted*)

C17-2 Revenue Recognition Methods

In special cases, revenue is recognized by the use of several methods, including (a) percentage-of-completion method, (b) proportional performance method, and (c) installment method.

Required Briefly explain each of the methods and indicate the situations in which each is used.

C17-3 Construction Contracts

Village Company is accounting for a long-term construction contract using the percentage-of-completion method. It is a 3-year, fixed-fee contract that is presently in its first year. The latest reasonable estimates of total contract costs indicate that the contract will be completed at a profit. Village will submit progress billings to the customer and has reasonable assurance that collections on these billings will be received in each year of the contract.

Required

1. a. What is the justification for the percentage-of-completion method for long-term construction contracts?
   b. What facts in the preceding situation indicate that Village should account for this long-term construction contract using the percentage-of-completion method?
2. How would the income recognized in each year of this long-term construction contract be determined using the cost-to-cost method of determining percentage of completion?
3. What is the effect on income, if any, of the progress billings and the collections on these billings? (*AICPA adapted*)

C17-4 Long-Term Contracts

In accounting for long-term contracts (those taking longer than one year to complete), the two methods commonly followed are the percentage-of-completion method and the completed-contract method.

Required

1. Explain how earnings on long-term contracts are recognized and computed under these two methods.
2. Under what circumstances is it preferable to use one method over the other?
3. Why is earnings recognition as measured by interim billings not generally accepted for long-term contracts?
4. How are job costs and interim billings reflected on the balance sheet under the percentage-of-completion method and the completed-contract method? (*AICPA adapted*)

C17-5 Installment Method Sales

Installment sales usually are accounted for by one of the following methods: (1) the profit may be recognized as earned in the period of sale; (2) the profit may be recognized on a proportionate basis in the periods of collection (commonly called the "installment method").

Required

1. Discuss the propriety of the two methods, including in your discussion a list of the circumstances under which recognition of profit in the period of sale would be preferable to recognition of profit on the installment method.
2. The collection period of an installment sale contract is frequently 24 months or longer. Discuss, in terms of both methods, the presentation of the installment contracts receivable on the balance sheet.
3. Deferred gross profit arising from installment sales has been reported on the balance sheet variously as a contra or valuation account to installments receivable, an estimated liability, a part of stockholders' equity, or a deferred credit. Discuss the nature and, hence, the appropriate balance sheet classification(s) of "deferred gross profit" for an accrual-basis business that uses the installment sales method for financial reporting and income tax purposes. (*AICPA adapted*)

CREATIVE AND CRITICAL THINKING

C17-6 Revenue Recognition Methods

The following situations are independent.

1. Carlson Company is an international consulting firm that has received a 2-year engagement from a client for a fee of $2 million. The company will assign differing numbers of personnel to the project depending on the needs of the project and the availability of personnel. The company requires a down payment of 10% and makes periodic billings based on the hours worked by the personnel, plus 20% profit. At the end of the engagement, the company and the client will negotiate whether an adjustment to the fee is appropriate.
2. The Fast Loss Health Club has three types of memberships: 1-year, 3-year, and 10-year. Each type of membership requires an initial fee as well as monthly fees. To encourage memberships, the company offers numerous incentives, such as free dues for the first two months and drawings for free vacation trips. In addition, the company advertises heavily at certain times of the year, such as during the Christmas period. The company also offers special programs to its members for a fee and allows nonmembers to participate for a higher fee.
3. The New Encyclopedia Company ships five complete sets of its 12-volume encyclopedia to each of its new distributors. Each distributor has 6 months to sell all the encyclopedias and pay the company the selling price, less a 40% commission, within 5 days of each sale. During this period, the distributor may return the encyclopedias without obligation and at the company's expense. At the end of 6 months, the distributor must pay the selling price of the unsold encyclopedias, less a 60% commission.

Required Discuss the revenue recognition issues that exist in each independent situation. Discuss any issues that exist in matching the expenses against the revenues.

C17-7 Revenue Recognition

Bonanza Trading Stamps, Inc. was formed early this year to sell trading stamps throughout the Southwest to retailers who distribute them free to their customers. Books for accumulating the stamps and catalogs illustrating the merchandise for which the stamps may be exchanged are given free to retailers for distribution to stamp recipients. Centers with inventories of merchandise premiums have been established for redemption of the stamps. Retailers may not return unused stamps to Bonanza.

The following schedule expresses Bonanza's expectations of the percentages of a normal month's activity that will be attained. For this purpose, a normal month's activity is defined as the level of operations expected when expansion of activities ceases or tapers off to a stable rate. The company expects that this level will be attained in the third year, and that sales of stamps will average $2,000,000 per month throughout the third year.

Month	Actual Stamp Sales Percentage	Merchandise Premium Purchases Percentage	Stamp Redemptions Percentage
6	30%	40%	10%
12	60	60	45
18	80	80	70
24	90	90	80
30	100	100	95

Required

1. Explain the factors to be considered in determining when revenue should be recognized in measuring the income of a business enterprise.
2. Explain the accounting alternatives that Bonanza Trading Stamps, Inc. should consider for the recognition of its revenues and related expenses.
3. For each accounting alternative discussed in (2), give balance sheet accounts that Bonanza should use and indicate how it should classify each. (*AICPA adapted*)

C17-8 Exchanges and Revenue Recognition Issues

Certain business "exchanges" are very complex and may qualify as exceptional cases in which the related revenues and expenses are advanced or deferred. The following are four such cases:

1. Franchisor grants a franchise to a franchisee; it collects part of the initial franchise fee and agrees to perform related initial services over an extended period.
2. Land development company acquires land for future development into a "sports retirement community," subdivides the land into lots, and sells the lots on "credit" with payment to be made on a long-term basis.
3. Lessor leases equipment to a lessee on a long-term noncancelable lease; the fair value of the leased item is greater than the cost, and the ownership of the leased item is transferred to the lessee by the end of the lease life.
4. A construction company builds bridges; it enters into a contract to construct a bridge for Rice County over a 2-year period.

Required For each of the preceding exchanges, (a) explain the revenue recognition issues involved, and (b) discuss when the revenue is recognized and by what method.

C17-9 Construction Contracts

At December 31, 2004, Roko Co. has two fixed price construction contracts in progress. Both contracts have monthly billings supported by certified surveys of work completed. The contracts are:

(a) The Ski Park contract, begun in 2003, is 80% complete, is progressing according to bid estimates, and is expected to be profitable.

(b) The Nassu Village contract, a project to construct 100 condominium units, was begun in 2004. Thirty-five units have been completed. Work on the remaining units is delayed by conflicting recommendations on how to overcome unexpected subsoil problems. While the total cost of the project is uncertain, a loss is not anticipated.

Required

1. Identify the alternatives available to account for long-term construction contracts, and specify the criteria used to determine which method is applicable to a given contract.

2. Identify the appropriate accounting method for each of Roko's two contracts, and describe each contract's effect on net income for 2004.
3. Indicate how the accounts related to the Ski Park contract should be reported on the balance sheet at Decem-ber 31, 2004. (*AICPA adapted*)

C17-10 Franchise and Revenue Recognition

Southern Fried Shrimp sells franchises to independent operators throughout the southeastern part of the United States. The contract with the franchisee includes the following provisions:

1. The franchisee is charged an initial fee of $25,000. Of this amount, $5,000 is payable when the agreement is signed and a $4,000 non-interest-bearing note is payable at the end of each of the 5 subsequent years.
2. All of the initial franchise fee collected by Southern Fried Shrimp is to be refunded and the remaining obligation canceled if, for any reason, the franchisee fails to open the franchise.
3. In return for the initial franchise fee, Southern Fried Shrimp agrees to (1) assist the franchisee in selecting the location for the business, (2) negotiate the lease for the land, (3) obtain financing and assist with building design, (4) supervise construction, (5) establish accounting and tax records, and (6) provide expert advice over a 5-year period relating to such matters as employee and management training, quality control, and promotion.
4. In addition to the initial franchise fee, the franchisee is required to pay to Southern Fried Shrimp a monthly fee of 2% of sales for menu planning, recipe innovations, and the privilege of purchasing ingredients from Southern Fried Shrimp at or below prevailing market prices.

Management of Southern Fried Shrimp estimates that the value of the services rendered to the franchisee at the time the contract is signed amounts to at least $5,000. All franchisees to date have opened their locations at the scheduled time and none has defaulted on any of the notes receivable.

The credit ratings of all franchisees would entitle them to borrow at the current interest rate of 10%. The present value of an ordinary annuity of five annual receipts of $4,000 each, discounted at 10%, is $15,163.

Required

1. Explain the alternatives that Southern Fried Shrimp might use to account for the initial franchise fee, evaluate each by applying generally accepted accounting principles to this situation, and give illustrative entries for each alternative.
2. Given the nature of Southern Fried Shrimp's agreement with its franchisees, when should it recognize revenue? Discuss the question of revenue recognition for both the initial franchise fee and the additional monthly fee of 2% of sales and give illustrative entries for both types of revenue.

3. Assume that (a) Southern Fried Shrimp sells some franchises for $35,000 (which includes a charge of $10,000 for the rental of equipment for its useful life of 10 years); (b) $15,000 of the fee is payable immediately and the balance on non-interest-bearing notes at $4,000 per year; (c) no portion of the $10,000 rental payment is refundable in case the franchisee goes out of business; and (d) title to the equipment remains with the franchisor. What would be the preferable method of accounting for the rental portion of the initial franchise fee? Explain. (*AICPA adapted*)

C17-11 Publishing and Revenue Recognition

After the presentation of your report on the examination of the financial statements to the board of directors of the Savage Publishing Company, one of the new directors says he is surprised the income statement assumes that an equal proportion of the revenue is earned with the publication of every issue of the company's magazine. He feels that the "crucial event" in the process of earning revenue in the magazine business is the cash sale of the subscription. He says that he does not understand why—other than for the smoothing of income—most of the revenue cannot be "recognized" in the period of the sale.

Required Explain the propriety of timing the recognition of revenue in the Savage Publishing Company's accounts with

1. The cash sale of the magazine subscription.
2. The publication of the magazine every month.
3. Both events, by recognizing a portion of the revenue with the cash sale of the magazine subscription and a portion of the revenue with the publication of the magazine every month. (*AICPA adapted*)

C17-12 Recognition of Revenues and Expenses

On May 6, 2003, Sterling Corporation signed a contract with Stony Associates under which Stony agreed (1) to construct an office building on land owned by Sterling, (2) to accept responsibility for procuring financing for the project and finding tenants, and (3) to manage the property for 50 years. The annual profit from the project, after debt service, is to be divided equally between Sterling Corporation and Stony Associates. Stony is to accept its share of future profits as full payment for its services in construction, obtaining finances and tenants, and management of the project.

By April 30, 2004, the project was nearly completed and tenants had signed leases to occupy 90% of the available space at annual rentals aggregating $2,600,000. It is estimated that, after operating expenses and debt service, the annual profit will amount to $850,000. The management of Stony Associates believed that the economic benefit derived from the contract with Sterling should be reflected on its financial statements for the fiscal year ended April 30, 2004 and directed that revenue be accrued in an amount equal to the commercial value of the services Stony had rendered during the year, that this amount be carried in contracts receivable, and that all related expenditures be charged against the revenue.

Required Is the belief of Stony's management in accord with generally accepted accounting principles for the measurement of revenue and expense for the year ended April 30, 2004? Support your opinion by discussing the application to this case of the factors to be considered for asset measurement and revenue and expense recognition. (*AICPA adapted*)

C17-13 Recognition of Expenses

Kwik-Bild Corporation sells and erects shell houses. These are frame structures that are completely finished on the outside but are unfinished on the inside except for flooring, partition studding and ceiling joists. Shell houses are sold chiefly to customers who are handy with tools and who have time to do the interior wiring, plumbing, wall completion and finishing and other work necessary to make the shell houses livable dwellings.

Kwik-Bild buys shell houses from a manufacturer in unassembled packages consisting of all lumber, roofing, doors, windows and similar materials necessary to complete a shell house. Upon commencing operations in a new area, Kwik-Bild buys or leases land as a site for its local warehouse, field office and display houses. Sample display houses are erected at a total cost of from $10,000 to $30,000, including the cost of the unassembled packages. The chief element of cost of the display houses is the unassembled packages, since erection is a short, low-cost operation. Old sample models are torn down or altered into new models every three to seven years. Sample display houses have little salvage value because dismantling and moving costs amount to nearly as much as the cost of an unassembled package.

Required

1. A choice must be made between (a) expensing the costs of sample display houses in the period in which the expenditure is made, and (b) spreading the costs over more than one period. Discuss the advantages of each method.
2. Is it preferable to amortize the cost of display houses on the basis of (a) the passage of time, or (b) the number of shell houses sold? Explain. (*AICPA adapted*)

C17-14 Installment Method Sales

On October 2, 2004 the Television Company sold a set costing $400 to Jones for $600. Jones made a down payment of $150 and agreed to pay $25 the first of each month for 18 months thereafter.

Jones paid the first two installments due on November 1 and December 1, 2004. In 2005 Jones made five payments, but then defaulted on the balance of the payments. The set was repossessed on November 1, 2005. The company closes its books as of December 31.

Required

1. Give three different amounts that might be shown as realized income for 2004 and indicate the circumstances under which each of these amounts would be acceptable.
2. Assuming that the repossessed television set has a wholesale value of $50 and a retail value of $75,

prepare a journal entry to record the repossession under the "installment method" of accounting. Explain fully the reasoning applicable to your entry. (*AICPA adapted*)

C17-15 Analyzing Coca-Cola's Revenue Recognition and Advertising Costs Disclosures

Refer to the financial statements and related notes of the Coca-Cola Company in Appendix A of this book.

Required

1. What does the company disclose about its revenue recognition policies? Why?
2. Explain when you would expect the company to recognize revenue on its soft drinks.
3. When does the company expense the production cost of its advertisements? Does this result in appropriate matching?

C17-16 Ethics and Revenue and Expense Recognition

You are employed by a local CPA firm, and one of your clients is Tiger Manufacturing Company. Tiger has been very successful in recent years, averaging approximately 10% increase in earnings each year. The company is planning a public stock offering early next year, which would bring significant fees to your firm. It would also allow the company to finance a much needed expansion that would allow the company to hire additional employees.

The audit is nearing completion, and it appears that the company will again report a significant increase in earnings. However, two issues have arisen. First, the company has a large order from a purchaser to be shipped FOB shipping point in early January. The inventory was completed and warehoused late in December, but it was not segregated. Management has included the selling price (less the related expense) in the current year's net income. Second, the company has added capitalized interest to the cost of two large special orders that are nearing completion. If both these issues are resolved in a way that decreases net income, the company's net income will be lower than the amount reported last year.

Required From financial reporting and ethical perspectives, discuss the issues raised by this situation.

RESEARCH

C17-17 Researching GAAP

When asked about a $518 million "prepaid expense and deferred charge" on its balance sheet for 1990, Sears says that about $100 million of the figure—mainly for the catalog—consists of advertising costs whose impact on profit has been deferred. "These costs are paid but aren't charged against profits" yet, says a spokesman.

Procter and Gamble generally allocates advertising costs based on the number of cases of products it ships.

A spokesman for McDonald's says that a "small portion" of the $108 million in prepaid expenses and other current assets on its balance sheet for 1990 is deferred production costs for certain commercials and creative development.

Nike says that it deducts all advertising costs immediately, and calls advertising-cost deferral "a bogus exercise."

Philip Morris accrued $1.4 billion in marketing costs on the liability side of its balance sheet for 1990. This means that Philip Morris is deducting advertising costs it has not yet paid to help smooth out profits from year to year. An analyst says, "I call such amounts 'hidden earnings' for future years when financial results aren't as good as Philip Morris would like. Then, it could lower its advertising-cost deductions with this accrual." (*Adapted from* The Wall Street Journal, 1/8/92).

Required

1. Research the generally accepted accounting principles and prepare a short memo that summarizes how to report advertising costs. Cite your reference(s) and applicable paragraph numbers.

2. Are each of the companies complying with the policy? Assume that all the companies recognize revenue at the time of sale.

C17-18 Researching GAAP

Amre Inc. capitalized its marketing costs, such as the cost of purchasing mailing lists, instead of treating the costs as expenses.

Inspeech capitalized estimated selling, general, and administrative costs of various acquired companies' accounting and billing activities for a period of three months following the acquisition. Similarly, the company capitalized search costs to hire new management employees, salaries of individuals involved with the integration of newly acquired companies, and fees for studies by outside consultants. Management justified capitalizing these expenses because they were required to implement the company's expansion strategy and would benefit future periods.

Among the costs Chambers deferred were portions of executives' salaries for time spent on developing projects such as new landfills. In addition, the company delayed recognizing some public relations and legal costs, as well as executive travel expenses.

Required Research the generally accepted accounting principles and prepare a short memo that summarizes how to report advertising costs. Cite your reference(s) and applicable paragraph numbers.

MULTIPLE CHOICE

Select the best answer for each of the following.

M17-1 Real estate sales are recognized by the accrual method if all of the conditions defined by *FASB Statement No. 66* are met. Which of the following is *not* one of the conditions defined by the *Statement?*

a. The seller has transferred to the buyer the usual risks and rewards of ownership in a transaction that is in substance a sale and does not have a continuing involvement with property.

b. A sale is consummated.

c. The buyer's initial and continuing investments are adequate to demonstrate a commitment to pay for the property.

d. The seller's receivable is subject to future subordination.

M17-2 Green Company, which began operations on January 1, 2004, appropriately uses the installment method of accounting. The following information is available for 2004:

Gross profit on sales	40%
Deferred gross profit at 12/31/04	$240,000
Cash collected on installment sales	450,000

What is the total amount of Green's installment sales for 2004?

a. $600,000   c. $850,000
b. $690,000   d. $1,050,000

M17-3 When should an indicated loss on a long-term contract be recognized under the completed-contract method and the percentage-of-completion method, respectively?

	Completed-Contract	Percentage-of-Completion
a.	Immediately	Over life of project
b.	Immediately	Immediately
c.	Contract complete	Over life of project
d.	Contract complete	Immediately

M17-4 In accounting for a long-term construction contract for which there is a projected profit, the balance in the construction-in-progress asset account at the end of the first year of work using the completed-contract method would be

a. Zero

b. The same as the percentage-of-completion method

c. Lower than the percentage-of-completion method

d. Higher than the percentage-of-completion method

M17-5 Warren Construction Company has consistently used the percentage-of-completion method of recognizing income. In 2004 Warren started work on a $6,000,000 construction contract, which was completed in 2005. The accounting records disclosed the following data:

	2004	2005
Progress billings	$2,200,000	$3,800,000
Costs incurred	1,800,000	3,600,000
Collections	1,400,000	4,600,000
Estimated cost to complete	3,600,000	—

How much income should Warren have recognized in 2004?

a. $200,000   c. $300,000
b. $220,000   d. $400,000

M17-6 Kramer Manufacturing Company ships goods to Sikes Company on consignment. When the consigned goods are delivered to Sikes, Kramer should record

	Sale of Inventory	Revenue
a.	No	Yes
b.	No	No
c.	Yes	No
d.	Yes	Yes

M17-7 During 2004 Morgan Company recognized $30,000 of sales under the cost recovery method. This is the first time the Morgan Company has used the cost recovery method in recognizing sales. The cost of goods sold related to these sales was $21,000. Cash collections in 2004 were $15,000, in 2005 were $10,000, and in 2006 were $5,000. What amount of gross profit should be recognized in 2004, 2005, and 2006?

	2004	2005	2006
a.	$9,000	$ 0	$ 0
b.	$4,500	$3,000	$1,500
c.	$ 0	$ 0	$9,000
d.	$ 0	$4,000	$5,000

M17-8 On January 1, 2003, Bartell Company sold its idle plant facility to Cooper, Inc., for $1,050,000. On this date, the plant had a depreciated cost of $735,000. Cooper paid $150,000 cash on January 1, 2003, and signed a $900,000 note bearing interest at 10%. The note was payable in three annual installments of $300,000 beginning January 1, 2004. Bartell appropriately accounted for the sale under the installment method. Cooper made a timely payment of the first installment on January 1, 2004 of $390,000, which included interest of $90,000 to date of payment. At December 31, 2004, Bartell has deferred gross profit of

a. $153,000   c. $225,000
b. $180,000   d. $270,000

M17-9 The Schmidt Company sells a franchise that requires an initial franchise fee of $50,000. A $10,000 down payment is required, with the balance covered by the issuance of a 12% note, payable in 4 equal installments. All material services have been substantially performed by the Schmidt Company, the refund period has expired, and the collectibility of the note is reasonably assured. The journal entry recorded by Schmidt Company should be

a.
Cash	10,000	
Notes Receivable	40,000	
Franchise Revenue		10,000
Unearned Franchise Fees		40,000

b.
Cash	10,000	
Notes Receivable	40,000	
Franchise Revenue		50,000

c.
Cash	10,000	
Notes Receivable	40,000	
Unearned Franchise Fees		50,000

d.
Cash	10,000	
Franchise Revenue		10,000

M17-10 On April 1, 2003, Pine Construction Company entered into a fixed-price contract to construct an apartment building for $6,000,000. Pine appropriately accounts for this contract under the percentage-of-completion method. Information relating to the contract is as follows:

	At December 31, 2003	At December 31, 2004
Percentage of completion	20%	60%
Estimated costs at completion	$4,500,000	$4,800,000
Income recognized (cumulative)	$ 300,000	$ 720,000

What is the amount of contract costs incurred during the year ended December 31, 2004?

a. $1,200,000   c. $1,980,000
b. $1,920,000   d. $2,880,000

(*AICPA adapted*)

EXERCISES

E17-1   *Revenue Recognition Alternatives*   The Smith Construction Company received a contract on September 30, 2004 to build a warehouse over a period of 18 months. The contract price was $600,000 and the estimated cost to build was $400,000. The actual (and estimated) costs incurred and the payments made by the purchaser are as follows:

	Costs	Payments
September 30–December 31, 2004	$120,000	$ 90,000
January 1–December 31, 2005	240,000	210,000
January 1–March 31, 2006	40,000	300,000

Required

1. Compute the amount of revenue, expense, and gross profit each year for each of the following methods:
   a. Revenue recognition at the time of sale (completion)
   b. Revenue recognition during production
   c. Revenue recognition at the time of cash receipt
   d. Cost recovery (compute only the gross profit)
2. Which method provides the most useful information to users? Under what circumstances would the other methods provide more useful information?

E17-2   *Percentage-of-Completion Method*   In 2004 Tarlo Company agrees to construct a highway for Brice County over a 3-year period (2004 through 2006). The contract price is $1,200,000 and the construction costs (both actual and estimated) total $705,000 for the 3 years. The percentage completed at the end of each year is as follows: 2004, 20%; 2005, 75%; 2006, 100%.

Required

1. Prepare a schedule showing the amount of gross profit that Tarlo Company recognizes each year using the percentage-of-completion method.
2. Prepare a schedule showing the amount of gross profit that Tarlo Company recognizes each year using the completed-contract method.

E17-3   *Percentage of Completion*   The King Construction Company began work on a contract in 2004. The contract price is $4,000,000, and the company uses the percentage-of-completion method. Other information relating to the contract is as follows:

	2004
Costs incurred during the year	$ 800,000
Estimated costs to complete, December 31	2,400,000
Billings during the year	600,000
Collections during the year	400,000

Required

1. How much gross profit or loss does King recognize in 2004?
2. Prepare the appropriate sections of the 2004 income statement and ending balance sheet.

E17-4   ***Percentage of Completion***   The Koolman Construction Company began work on a contract in 2004. The contract price is $3,000,000, and the company uses the percentage-of-completion method. Other information relating to the contract is as follows:

	2004	2005
Costs incurred during the year	$ 600,000	$ 700,000
Estimated costs to complete, December 31	1,400,000	1,200,000
Billings during the year	500,000	850,000
Collections during the year	400,000	800,000

Required

1. Compute the gross profit or loss recognized in 2004 and 2005.
2. Prepare the appropriate sections of the income statement and ending balance sheet for each year.

E17-5   ***Percentage of Completion***   Newberg Construction Corporation contracted to construct a building for $400,000. Construction began in 2004 and was completed in 2005. Data relating to the contract are as follows:

| | Year Ended December 31, | |
	2004	2005
Costs incurred	$200,000	$110,000
Estimated costs to complete	100,000	—

Required Newberg uses the percentage-of-completion method as the basis for income recognition. For the years ended December 31, 2004 and 2005, respectively, how much income should Newberg report? (*AICPA adapted*)

E17-6   ***Long-Term Construction Contract***   The Osborn Construction Company began operations January 2, 2004.

During the year, Osborn entered into a contract with Redbeard Razor Corporation to construct a manufacturing facility. At that time, Osborn estimated that it would take 5 years to complete the facility at a total cost of $4,800,000. The total contract price for construction of the facility is $6,000,000. During the year, Osborn incurred $1,250,000 in construction costs related to the construction project. The estimated cost to complete the contract is $3,750,000. Redbeard was billed and paid 30% of the contract price.

Required Prepare schedules to compute the amount of gross profit to be recognized for the year ended December 31, 2004 and the amount to be shown as "cost of uncompleted contract in excess of related billings" or "billings on uncompleted contract in excess of related costs" on December 31, 2004, under each of the following methods:

1. Completed-contract method
2. Percentage-of-completion method

Show supporting computations in good form. (*AICPA adapted*)

E17-7   ***Proportional Performance Method***   The New Recreational Company sells 2-year memberships to its recreational facilities. For $2,200 in advance, each member receives the right to 30 nights at the company's campgrounds, 20 rounds on its golf courses, and 50 hours on its bowling lanes. In 2004 the company sold 400 memberships. Members used the campgrounds for 4,100 nights, played 3,000 rounds of golf, and bowled for 10,000 hours. The relevant cost information for the 400 contracts is as follows:

Initial direct costs	$ 40,000
Annual indirect costs	100,000
Estimated (and actual) total direct costs for 2-year period	340,000
Direct cost per	
Night at campground	10
Round of golf	15
Hour of bowling	5

Required Prepare the income statement for 2004.

E17-8   ***Revenue Recognition at Completion of Production***   In 2004 the Sterling Farm Company produced 100,000 bushels of wheat at a cost of $2.00 per bushel. The company has a contract to deliver 80,000 bushels at $2.15 per bushel in 2005. Delivery costs are estimated to be $0.02 per bushel. For guaranteed price contracts, the company recognizes revenue at the completion of production; otherwise, it recognizes revenue at the time of delivery.

Required

1. Prepare summary journal entries for 2004 and 2005.
2. At what value is the inventory of the company carried after the delivery of the 80,000 bushels? Why?

E17-9   *Sales Under the Installment Method*   Anibonita Company began operations in 2004. It sells goods on installment sales contracts; these transactions are considered to be exceptional, so it uses the installment method to recognize gross profit. The following is a summary of the installment sales, costs of installment sales, operating expenses, and collections for 2004 and 2005:

	2004	2005
Installment method sales	$80,000	$90,000
Costs of installment method sales	52,000	59,400
Operating expenses	13,000	15,000
Cash collections from		
2004 installment method sales	42,000	21,000
2005 installment method sales		41,000

Required Using the installment method to recognize gross profits, prepare 2004 and 2005 condensed income statements for the Anibonita Company.

E17-10   *Sales Under the Installment Method*   The following information is available for the Butler Company in 2004, its first year of operations:

Total credit sales (including installment method sales)	$205,000
Total cost of goods sold (including installment method cost of goods sold)	130,000
Installment method sales	65,000
Installment method cost of goods sold	39,000
Cash receipts on credit sales (including installment method sales of $20,000)	120,000

Required

1. Prepare the journal entries for 2004.
2. If the company collected $45,000 in 2005 on its 2004 installment method sales, prepare the appropriate journal entries in 2005.

E17-11   *Sales Under the Installment Method*   The following information is available for the Butler Company, which began operations in 2004:

	2004	2005
Total credit sales (including installment method sales)	$100,000	$160,000
Total cost of goods sold (including installment method cost of goods sold)	72,000	105,000
Installment method sales	60,000	80,000
Installment method cost of goods sold	42,000	52,000
Cash receipts on installment method sales		
2004 sales	25,000	26,000
2005 sales		30,000
Cash receipts on other credit sales	28,000	85,000

Required

1. Prepare the journal entries for 2004 and 2005.
2. Prepare a partial income statement and a partial balance sheet for 2004.

E17-12   *Analysis of Installment Sales*   The following partial information is available for the Cupp Company:

Installment method sales	$120,000	(3)
Installment method cost of goods sold	(1)	$63,000
Gross profit percentage	(2)	30%
Cash receipts on installment method sales		
2004 sales	25,000	(4)
2005 sales		(5)
Realized gross profit on installment method sales		
2004 sales	5,000	7,000
2005 sales		9,000

Required Compute the unknown amounts. (Note: It is not necessary to compute the amounts in the numerical sequence.)

E17-13   *Adjusting Entries for Installment Sales*   The Smookler Company uses the installment method for certain sales and experiences a constant gross profit rate of 20%. The following are the account balances at December 31, 2004 and 2005:

	Installment Receivables	Deferred Gross Profit	Installment Method Sales
2004	$50,000	$10,000	$100,000
2005	80,000	16,000	130,000

Required Prepare the journal entries for 2005.

E17-14   *Cost Recovery*   In 2004 the Huxley Company, a real estate company, purchased some raw land for $60,000 and resold it on credit for $90,000. Because of the speculative nature of the usefulness of the land, the company used the cost recovery method for the sale of the land. The cash collections in 2004, 2005, and 2006 were $25,000, $45,000, and $20,000, respectively.

Required Prepare the journal entries for each year.

E17-15   *Deposit Method*   On January 1, 2004, the Fritz Company sold a building in a depressed area for $200,000. The building had originally cost $500,000 and had a book value of $100,000. The sale agreement required the purchaser to pay $5,000 down and sign an 8% note for the balance. Interest on the note is payable at the end of each year; the interest is refundable if the following contingency is not met. The sale agreement is contingent on the commitment by the city government to support redevelopment of the area in which the building is located. Therefore, the company used the deposit method to record the sale.

Required

1. Prepare the journal entries for 2004.
2. On January 1, 2005 the city government made the necessary commitments. Prepare the appropriate journal entry.

E17-16   *Franchise*   The Chocomalt Company sells franchises. For each franchise, the company charges an initial franchise fee of $28,000. The franchise agreement requires a down payment of $8,000, with the balance covered by the issuance of a $20,000, 12% note, payable by the franchisee in 2 equal annual installments.

Required Prepare the journal entry required by the Chocomalt Company to record each initial franchise fee under each of the following independent situations:

1. All material services have been substantially performed, the refund period has expired, and the collectibility of the note is reasonably assured.
2. All material services have been substantially performed, the refund period has expired, and the collectibility of the note is not reasonably assured.
3. All material services have been substantially performed, the refund period has not expired, and the collectibility of the note is reasonably assured.
4. All material services have not been substantially performed, the refund period has expired, and there is no basis for estimating the collectibility of the note.
5. The refund period has expired and the collectibility of the note is reasonably assured, but all material services have not been substantially performed.

E17-17   *Consignee*   On April 16, 2004 the Winger Company shipped 10 tractors to the Yuma Farm Supply Company on consignment. Each tractor cost $30,000 and the Winger Company incurred cash shipment costs of $100 per tractor. The consignment agreement required payment to Winger at year-end. On December 31, 2004 the consignee reported that it had sold 6 tractors for $36,000 each. The consignee paid the Winger Company the amount required under the agreement, after deducting the commission of 5% and advertising costs of $2,000 incurred by the consignee.

Required Prepare the 2004 journal entries for the Yuma Farm Supply Company.

E17-18   *Consignor*   Refer to the information in E17-17.

Required

1. Prepare the 2004 journal entries for the Winger Company.
2. What amount related to the consignment activities, and in what category, would the company report on its balance sheet on December 31, 2004?

PROBLEMS

P17-1   *Revenue Recognition Alternatives*   Each of the following independent situations relates to the recognition of revenue:

- a. Interest on loans made by a bank
- b. Interest on loans made by a bank when the loans are in default
- c. Collection of fares by an airline when the passengers make the reservations
- d. Shipment of freight and mail by an airline before it receives payment
- e. Imposition of a penalty (service charge) by a retailer on overdue accounts
- f. Building a submarine for a foreign government
- g. Growing and harvesting soybeans
- h. Selling lots for vacation homes on long-term contracts with small down payments
- i. Building houses in a subdivision
- j. Growing timber over a 10-year period
- k. Payments received by a producer for films that are licensed to movie theaters for 2 years, after which the rights are licensed to television networks for 1 year, and finally the rights revert to the producer
- l. Rental of a building to another company for 5 years, with no payment of rent in the first year
- m. "One cent" sale in which the first item is sold at full price and the second identical item is sold for one cent
- n. Sale of a season pass by a ski resort

Required   For each situation indicate when a company should recognize revenue.

P17-2   *Revenue Recognition Alternatives*   The Slattery Company was formed on January 1, 2004 to build a single product. The company issued no-par common stock on that date for $300,000 cash. The product costs $20 to make, all of which is paid in cash at the time of production. The company sells each unit of the product for $35 on account and incurs sales commissions per unit of $5 cash. In 2004 the company produced 10,000 units, shipped 9,000 units, and received payment for 8,000 units.

Required

1. Prepare the 2004 income statement and ending balance sheet under each of the following methods:
   - a. Revenue recognition at the time of sale (shipment)
   - b. Revenue recognition during production
   - c. Revenue recognition at the time of cash receipt
2. Which method provides the most useful information to users? Under what circumstances would the other methods provide more useful information?
3. In 2005 the company produced 15,000 units, shipped 16,000 units, and received payment for 17,000 units. What conclusion can you make about the balance in Retained Earnings on December 31, 2005 for each method of revenue recognition?

P17-3   *Percentage of Completion*   In 2004 Dreyer Corporation began construction work under a 3-year contract. The contract price is $800,000. Dreyer uses the percentage-of-completion method. The financial statement presentations relating to this contract on December 31, 2004 follow:

Balance Sheet

Accounts receivable		$15,000
Construction in progress	$50,000	
Less contract billings	(47,000)	
Cost of uncompleted contract in excess of billings		3,000

Income Statement

Gross profit (before tax) on the contract	$10,000

Required

1. How much cash did Dreyer collect during 2004?
2. What was the initial estimated total income before tax on this contract? (*AICPA adapted*)

P17-4   *Long-Term Construction Contracts*   The Fender Construction Company receives a contract to build a building over a period of 3 years for a price of $700,000. Information relating to the performance of the contract is summarized as follows:

	2004	2005	2006
Construction costs incurred during the year	$150,000	$242,000	$168,000
Estimated costs to complete	350,000	168,000	—
Billings during the year	120,000	250,000	330,000
Collections during the year	100,000	260,000	340,000

Required Prepare journal entries for all three years under (1) the percentage-of-completion method, and (2) the completed-contract method.

P17-5   *Long-Term Construction Contracts*   The Forman Company has contracted to build a dam over a period of 4 years for $3,000,000. Information relating to the performance of the contract is summarized as follows:

	2004	2005	2006	2007
Construction costs incurred during the year	$ 300,000	$1,100,000	$ 863,000	$837,000
Estimated costs to complete	2,200,000	1,400,000	837,000	—
Billings during the year	280,000	870,000	1,030,000	820,000
Collections during the year	270,000	875,000	1,010,000	845,000

Required

1. Compute the profit or loss for each year of the contract under (a) the percentage-of-completion method, and (b) the completed-contract method.
2. Prepare the relevant sections of the income statement and ending balance sheet for each year under (a) the percentage-of-completion method, and (b) the completed-contract method.

See WebTutor for annotated problem solution.

P17-6   *Long-Term Construction Contracts*   The Rice Company signed a contract to build a dam over a period of 3 years for a price of $10,000,000. Information relating to the performance of the contract is summarized as follows:

	2004	2005	2006
Construction costs incurred during the year	$2,000,000	$4,000,000	$6,000,000
Estimated costs to complete	6,000,000	6,000,000	—
Billings during the year	1,500,000	3,500,000	5,000,000
Collections during the year	1,300,000	3,600,000	5,100,000

Required Prepare journal entries for all three years under (1) the percentage-of-completion method, and (2) the completed-contract method.

P17-7   *Proportional Performance Method*   The Hilt Company, a public relations company, signs 2-year contracts with its clients. For $80,000 in advance, the company agrees to ensure that the client's name is mentioned 5 times on a network national news program, 10 times in a national news magazine, and 15 times on a local news program. In 2004 the company signed 8 contracts; no additional contracts were signed in 2005.

In 2004 the company's clients were mentioned 10 times on network national news programs, 40 times in national news magazines, and 22 times on local news programs. In 2005 the company's clients were mentioned 30 times on national news programs, 40 times in national news magazines, and 98 times on local news programs. The relevant cost information for the 8 contracts is as follows:

Initial direct costs	$ 20,000
Annual indirect costs	80,000
Estimated (and actual) total direct costs for 2-year period	260,000
Direct cost per	
National news program	2,000
National news magazine	1,500
Local news program	500

Required

1. Prepare the income statements for 2004 and 2005.
2. From a theoretical viewpoint, how should the company compute the depreciation of its office building and office equipment that would be included in the preceding costs? Why?

P17-8   *Sales Under the Installment Method*   The following information is available for the Dassler Company, which began its operations in 2004:

1. Installment method sales
   2004 $520,000
   2005   600,000

2. Gross profit percentage
   2004   20%
   2005   24%
3. Cash collections on installment method sales
   2004   25% of 2004 sales
   2005   55% of 2004 sales
                30% of 2005 sales
4. Bad debt policy
   The company estimates its bad debts to be 2% of installment method sales.
5. Defaults and repossessions
   2004 $10,000 of 2004 installment method sales, of which $1,000 had been collected
   2005 $20,000 of 2004 installment method sales, of which $4,000 had been collected
                $15,000 of 2005 installment method sales, of which $2,000 had been collected

The policy of the company is to value repossessed items at 40% of their original selling price.

Required Prepare the journal entries for 2004 and 2005.

P17-9   *Sales Under the Installment Method*   The Dyson Company sells computer games to teenagers. Selected accounts included in the trial balance at December 31, 2003 and 2004 are as follows:

	2003	2004
Installment accounts receivable, 2003	$80,000	$ 20,000
Installment accounts receivable, 2004		112,500
Allowance for doubtful installment accounts receivable, 2003	(5,000)	(3,700)
Allowance for doubtful installment accounts receivable, 2004		(7,000)
Deferred gross profit, 2003	(16,000)	(3,500)
Deferred gross profit, 2004		(22,500)

During 2004 installment method sales and cost of goods sold were $200,000 and $160,000, respectively. In 2004 the company repossessed games that had been sold in 2003 for $6,000 and on which $2,500 had been collected. The games were believed to be worth $1,000. No repossessions occurred on 2004 sales.

Required Prepare summary journal entries for 2004.

P17-10 *Cost Recovery Method*   After a 2-year search for a buyer, Hobson, Inc. sold its idle plant facility to Jackson
@   Company for $700,000 on January 1, 2002. On this date the plant had a depreciated cost on Hobson's books of $500,000. Under the agreement Jackson paid $100,000 cash on January 1, 2002, and signed a $600,000 note bearing interest at 10%. The note was payable in installments of $100,000, $200,000, and $300,000 on January 1, 2003, 2004, and 2005, respectively. The note was secured by a mortgage on the property sold. Hobson appropriately accounted for the sale under the cost recovery method since there was no reasonable basis for estimating the degree of collectibility of the note receivable. Jackson repaid the note with three late installment payments, which were accepted by Hobson, as follows:

Date of Payment	Principal	Interest
July 1, 2003	$100,000	$90,000
December 31, 2004	200,000	75,000
February 1, 2006	300,000	32,500

Required Prepare a schedule (using the following format) to record the initial transaction for the sale of the idle plant facility, the application of subsequent cash collections on the note, and the necessary journal entry on the date the transaction is complete.

Date	Cash Received Debit	Note Receivable Dr. (Cr.)	Idle Plant (Net) (Credit)	Deferred Income Dr. (Cr.)	Income Recognized (Credit)
Jan. 1, 2002	$100,000				
July 1, 2003	190,000				
Dec. 31, 2004	275,000				
Feb. 1, 2006	332,500				
Feb. 1, 2006					

(*AICPA adapted*)

P17-11   *Franchise*   Year-Round Golf sells franchises for indoor golf driving ranges and putting greens. For each franchise, the company charges a nonrefundable initial franchise fee of $45,000. The franchise agreement requires a down payment of $10,000, with the balance covered by the issuance of a $35,000, 10% note, payable by the franchisee at the end of 5 years. Interest does not begin to accrue until the franchise opens, and the first interest payment is required 12 months after the franchise opens. The company sells only to qualified buyers so the collectibility of the note is always reasonably assured. The services required for the initial franchise fee are completed 6 months after the agreement is signed.

     The franchisee is also required to pay a continuing fee of $6,000 per year, plus 10% of its gross sales. Half the $6,000 is applied against purchases of supplies from the franchisor, which are paid for in cash at the time of purchase. The franchisor charges a sales price of 50% above its cost on these supplies.

     In the first six months of 2004, the company sold 4 franchises which began operating at the end of December. These franchisees had sales of $160,000 in 2005, and purchased the allowable amount of supplies. In the second six months of 2004, the company sold one franchise which began operating on April 1, 2005. The franchisee had sales of $25,000 in 2005 and purchased $1,500 of supplies.

Required Prepare the journal entries required by Year-Round Golf in 2004 and 2005 to record the preceding events.

P17-12   *Real Estate*   On January 1, 2004 the Hogback Company sold the Red Rocks Ranch, which constituted 20,000 acres of undeveloped land, to a limited partnership for $50 million. The land had originally cost Hogback $5 million. The terms of the sale included a cash payment of $9 million and a 10% note for $41 million to be paid in equal annual installments for 30 years. The note is secured by the land. Hogback paid a commission to a real estate company of 5% on the selling price.

Required

1. Should Hogback record the transaction as a sale? If so, prepare all the journal entries for 2004.
2. Assume, instead, that the company uses the installment method. Prepare all the journal entries for 2004.
3. Assume, instead, that the payments made to the Hogback Company were returnable at the option of the purchaser until June 30, 2005. Prepare all the journal entries for 2004. Ignore the sales commission.
4. Assume, instead, that the Hogback Company is obligated to make improvements costing $4 million over the next three years. In 2004 it made improvements costing $1 million. Prepare all the journal entries for 2004.
5. If the Hogback Company were the general partner of the limited partnership, would your answer to Requirement 1 change? If it were a limited partner?

P17-13   *Consignments*   On January 1, 2004 the Hadad Company entered into a consignment agreement with the Trinidad Company. The agreement specifies that the consignee (Trinidad) is to sell the merchandise at a price of 30% above cost. Trinidad is required to pay Hadad the net sales price within 15 days of each sale to a third party. The net sales price is defined as the sales price, less any advertising costs incurred by Trinidad, and less a commission of 10% deducted from the sales price less the advertising costs. Hadad pays any costs incurred in shipping the merchandise to Trinidad.

     In 2004 Hadad shipped merchandise costing $300,000 to Trinidad and incurred delivery costs of $8,000. During the year (through December 15), Trinidad made sales of $195,000 and incurred advertising costs of $15,000, and paid the required amount to Hadad. On December 31, 2004, Hadad phoned Trinidad and was told that since December 15 additional sales of $39,000 had been made and advertising costs of $3,000 incurred. (Record this information in separate journal entries.)

Required

1. Prepare the journal entries for the Hadad Company.
2. What amount, and in what category, would Hadad Company report on its balance sheet on December 31, 2004?
3. Prepare the journal entries for the Trinidad Company.
4. What amount related to the consignment activities, and in what category, would the Trinidad Company report on its balance sheet on December 31, 2004?

P17-14   *Revenue Recognition Alternatives*   The following are the operating activities of three different companies:

@   Company A: Engages in long-term construction contracts. Uses the percentage-of-completion method to recognize gross profits. Started contract X in 2003, contract Y in 2004, and contract Z in 2005. The total gross profit (estimated and actual) and the percentage completed for each contract during 2004 through 2006 are:

	Contract X	Contract Y	Contract Z
Gross profit	$600,000	$400,000	$500,000
% completed during			
2004	60%	40%	—
2005	25%	35%	30%
2006	—	25%	50%

Company B: Engages in long-term service contracts involving a specific number of defined but not similar service acts. Uses proportional performance method to recognize revenues. Sells 2-year service contracts for $400 in advance. Each service contract requires Company B to perform service act 1 a total of 50 times and service act 2 a total of 20 times during the 2-year period. At the beginning of 2004, 100 service contracts were sold. The following is a summary of the related cost information for the 100 service contracts:

Initial direct costs	$ 3,500
Annual indirect costs	4,500
Estimated (and actual) total direct costs (for 2-year period)	10,000
Direct cost per service act	
Service act 1	$1.20
Service act 2	2.00

During 2004, service act 1 was performed 2,700 times and service act 2 was performed 800 times. During 2005, service acts 1 and 2 were performed 2,300 and 1,200 times, respectively.

Company C: Sells goods on the installment basis. Uses the installment method (because these are exceptional cases) to recognize gross profits. The following is a summary of the installment sales, costs of installment sales, operating expenses, and collections for 2004 and 2005:

	2004	2005
Installment method sales	$80,000	$100,000
Costs of installment method sales	48,000	62,000
Operating expenses	17,000	20,000
Cash collections from		
2003 installment method sales (2003 gross profit is 39%)	58,000	—
2004 installment method sales	56,000	24,000
2005 installment method sales	—	68,000

Required

1. Prepare a schedule that shows Company A's gross profit for 2004, 2005, and 2006.
2. Prepare 2004 and 2005 condensed income statements for Company B.
3. Prepare 2004 and 2005 condensed income statements for Company C.

P17-15 *Revenue Recognition Alternatives* The following are the operating activities of three different companies.

Company X: Engages in long-term service contracts involving a specific number of defined but not similar service acts. Uses proportional performance method to recognize revenues. Sells 2-year service contracts for $600 in advance. Each service contract requires Company X to perform service act 1 a total of 30 times and service act 2 a total of 50 times during the 2-year period. At the beginning of 2004, 200 service contracts were sold. The following is a summary of the related cost information for the 200 service contracts:

Initial direct costs	$ 8,500
Annual indirect costs	9,300
Estimated (and actual) total direct costs (for 2-year period)	20,000
Direct cost per service act	
Service act 1	$1.60
Service act 2	1.04

During 2004, service act 1 was performed 5,000 times and service act 2 was performed 4,000 times. During 2005, service acts 1 and 2 were performed 1,000 and 6,000 times, respectively.

Company Y: Sells goods on the installment basis. Uses the installment method (because these are exceptional cases) to recognize gross profits. The following is a summary of the installment sales, gross profit, operating expenses, and collections for 2004 and 2005:

	2004	2005
Installment method sales	$90,000	$110,000
Gross profit	35,100	45,100
Operating expenses	18,000	21,000
Cash collections from:		
2003 installment method sales (2003 gross profit is 40%)	35,000	—
2004 installment method sales	67,000	23,000
2005 installment method sales	—	80,000

Company Z: Engages in long-term construction contracts. Uses the percentage-of-completion method to recognize gross profits. Started contract 1 in 2003, contract 2 in 2004, and contract 3 in 2005. The total gross profit (estimated and actual) and the percentage complete for each contract at the end of 2004 through 2006 are:

	Contract 1*	Contract 2	Contract 3
Gross profit	$800,000	$350,000	$600,000
% complete at the end of			
2004	75%	40%	—
2005	100%	70%	35%
2006	—	100%	80%

*30% was complete at the end of 2003.

Required

1. Prepare 2004 and 2005 condensed income statements for Company X.
2. Prepare 2004 and 2005 condensed income statements for Company Y.
3. Prepare a schedule that shows Company Z's gross profit for 2004, 2005, and 2006.

INTERNET ASSIGNMENTS

Go to the Nikolai and Bazley **Intermediate Accounting** web site (http://Nikolai.swcollege.com). Click on Student Resources and internet homework assignments. Then click on the appropriate hot link (icon) for each company's web site, find the relevant accounting information, and answer the following questions.

I17-1   Go to the **General Motors** web site.

Required How does the company recognize revenue? Why does the company use different methods? Explain whether you agree or disagree with the various methods described?

I17-2   Go to the **Raytheon Company** web site.

Required How does the company recognize revenue? How much are the contracts in process at the end of the two most recent years? How much of those amounts relate to U.S. government contracts? What proportion of the U.S. government contracts were unbilled? How much were the progress payments on those contracts?

I17-3   Go to the **Walt Disney** web site.

Required How does the company recognize revenue on movies? On advertising? On theme park ticket sales? How does the company expense film and television costs?

CHAPTER

Accounting for Income Taxes

18

objectives

1 Understand permanent and temporary differences.

2 Explain the conceptual issues regarding interperiod tax allocation.

3 Record and report deferred tax liabilities.

4 Record and report deferred tax assets.

5 Explain an operating loss carryback and carryforward.

6 Account for an operating loss carryback.

7 Account for an operating loss carryforward.

8 Apply intraperiod tax allocation.

9 Classify deferred tax liabilities and assets.

10 Discuss the additional conceptual issues concerning interperiod income tax allocation (Appendix).

The objectives of financial reporting and the Internal Revenue Code are different. The objective of generally accepted accounting principles for financial reporting is to provide useful information to decision makers about companies—information that will enable external users to make the investment and credit decisions we discussed in Chapter 1. The overall objective of the Internal Revenue Code, on the other hand, is to obtain funds, in an equitable manner, to operate the federal government. Additionally, tax laws frequently have been used to stimulate and regulate the economy (for example, the percentage depletion deduction attempts to stimulate new investment in natural resource productive capacity). In view of these different goals, most accountants favor the conformity of financial accounting and income tax reporting procedures only when the goals are equally applicable. For instance, when a company incurs an expense that represents both an expired cost and a tax deduction, it should deduct the expense from its revenues to determine both pretax financial income and taxable income.

Some people have argued that the accounting procedures adopted for financial reporting and income tax reporting should be the same. However, this conformity would result in the use of procedures that are chosen for their acceptability under the Internal Revenue Code, because reports filed for income taxation purposes must comply with the statutory provisions of the tax code. Moreover, since corporations legally try to avoid or postpone taxes, the conformity of financial accounting and income taxation reporting procedures would result in a tendency to select practices that minimize or delay income taxes (and income) without considering the usefulness of the practices for financial reporting.

Financial reporting practices may be influenced by the procedures adopted for income tax reporting. For example, under the provisions of the Internal Revenue Code, a corporation may use the LIFO method of inventory costing for income tax reporting only if it also uses LIFO for financial reporting. Because of such influences, and in an effort to save costs, some corporations attempt to minimize the effect of the Code on their accounting systems by using similar practices for both financial accounting and income tax purposes.

As a result of their differing objectives, financial reporting is governed by generally accepted accounting principles and income tax reporting is governed by the Internal Revenue Code.[1] If a corporation reports different revenues and/or expenses for financial reporting than it does for income tax reporting, it must determine (1) the current and noncurrent deferred income tax liabilities and/or assets to report on its balance sheet, and (2) the income tax expense to report in regard

---

1. Corporations may be subject to federal, state, and foreign income taxes. In this chapter we limit the discussion to the impact of federal income taxes on financial reporting.

to the pretax financial income[2] on its income statement. We discuss the procedures used to determine and report these items in the following sections.

OVERVIEW AND DEFINITIONS

Consider the condensed income statements and income tax returns for the Freese Corporation for 2004 and 2005 that we show in Exhibit 18-1.

EXHIBIT 18-1 Freese Corporation

Income Statement and Income Tax Return
Years Ended December 31, 2004 and 2005

	Income Statement		Income Tax Return	
	2004	2005	2004	2005
Revenues	$180,000	$200,000	$170,000	$210,000
Cost of goods sold	(75,000)	(85,000)	(70,000)	(90,000)
Gross profit	$105,000	$115,000	$100,000	$120,000
Other expenses	(60,000)	(50,000)	(60,000)	(60,000)
Pretax income from continuing operations	$ 45,000	$ 65,000	$ 40,000	$ 60,000
Income taxes	(11,000)	(16,000)	(9,200)	(15,300)
Income from continuing operations	$ 34,000	$ 49,000	$ 30,800	$ 44,700
Extraordinary item (net of income tax effect)	—	(10,000)	—	—
Net income	$ 34,000	$ 39,000	$ 30,800	$ 44,700

Causes of Differences

There are several differences between the Freese Corporation's income statements and income tax returns in Exhibit 18-1: (1) the amounts of revenues recognized in 2004 and 2005 are different, (2) the cost of goods sold subtracted from revenues differ in 2004 and 2005, (3) other expenses differ in 2005, and (4) an extraordinary item is separately reported on the income statement in 2005 but does not appear on the income tax return for that year. The causes of differences between a corporation's pretax financial income and taxable income (and potentially between its income tax expense and its income tax obligation) can be categorized into five groups:

1. *Permanent Differences.* Some items of revenue and expense that a corporation reports for financial accounting purposes are never reported for income tax purposes under the provisions of the Internal Revenue Code. Other items classified as allowable deductions for income tax reporting do not qualify as expenses under generally accepted accounting principles. These items result in permanent differences between the corporation's pretax financial income and taxable income.
2. *Temporary Differences.* A corporation reports some items of revenue and expense in one period for financial accounting purposes, but in an earlier or later period for income tax purposes. These items result in temporary differences between the corporation's pretax financial income and taxable income.
3. *Operating Loss Carrybacks and Carryforwards.* When a corporation reports an operating loss in a given year, the Internal Revenue Code allows the corporation to carry back or carry forward the loss to offset previous or future reported taxable income on its income tax return. The corporation reports its pretax financial income or loss in the year of occurrence on its income statement.

---

2. The terms *financial income, financial accounting income, book income,* and *accounting income* are synonymous and may be used interchangeably. Because the FASB uses the term *financial income* in its discussion of accounting for income taxes, we use that term throughout this chapter.

4. *Tax Credits.* To stimulate certain investments, or to provide tax relief in special circumstances, the Internal Revenue Code provides specific tax credits that a qualifying corporation may deduct from its income taxes owed to determine its current income taxes payable. Although use of a tax credit does not cause a difference between the corporation's pretax financial income and taxable income, it may cause a difference between the corporation's income tax expense and income tax obligation.

5. *Intraperiod Tax Allocation.* A corporation apportions its income tax for financial accounting purposes to (a) income from continuing operations, (b) results from discontinued operations, (c) extraordinary items, (d) the cumulative effects of changes in accounting principles, (e) prior period adjustments, and (f) other comprehensive income. No similar apportionment is made on its income tax return.

Definitions

The impact of using different accounting procedures for financial reporting and income tax reporting was studied by the FASB and resulted in the issuance of **FASB Statement No. 109,** entitled "Accounting for Income Taxes." The following sections include a discussion of the provisions of the *Statement* as they apply to the areas of difference between income reported for financial reporting purposes and income reported for taxation purposes. The discussion includes a number of definitions[3] related to a corporation's income taxes, which we list in Exhibit 18-2.

EXHIBIT 18-2   Key Terms Related to a Corporation's Income Taxes

Deductible temporary difference. Temporary difference that results in deductible amounts in future years when the related asset or liability is recovered or settled, respectively.

Deferred tax asset. The deferred tax consequences of deductible temporary differences and operating loss carryforwards. A deferred tax asset is measured using the applicable enacted tax rate and provisions of the enacted tax law. A deferred tax asset is reduced by a valuation allowance if, based on the weight of evidence available, it is more likely than not that some portion or all of a deferred tax asset will not be realized.

Deferred tax consequences. The future effects on income taxes, as measured by the applicable enacted tax rate and provisions of the enacted tax law, resulting from temporary differences and operating loss carryforwards at the end of the current year.

Deferred tax expense (or benefit). The change during the year in deferred tax liabilities and assets.

Deferred tax liability. The deferred tax consequences of taxable temporary differences. A deferred tax liability is measured using the applicable enacted tax rate and provisions of the enacted tax law.

Income tax expense (or benefit). The sum of income tax obligation and deferred tax expense (or benefit).

Income tax obligation (or refund). The amount of income taxes paid or payable (or refundable) for a year, as determined by applying the provisions of the enacted tax law to the taxable income or operating loss for that year. Sometimes called *current tax expense* (or *benefit*).

Operating loss carryback. An excess of tax deductible expenses over taxable revenues in a year that may be carried back to reduce taxable income in a prior year.

Operating loss carryforward. An excess of tax deductible expenses over taxable revenues in a year that may be carried forward to reduce taxable income in a future year.

Permanent difference. A difference between pretax financial income and taxable income in an accounting period, which will never reverse in a later accounting period.

Taxable income. The excess of taxable revenues over tax deductible expenses and exemptions for the year, as defined by the governmental taxing authority.

Taxable temporary difference. Temporary difference that results in taxable amounts in future years when the related asset or liability is recovered or settled, respectively.

Temporary difference. A difference between the tax basis of an asset or liability and its reported amount in the financial statements that will result in taxable or deductible amounts in future years when the reported amount of the asset is recovered or the liability is settled.

Valuation allowance. The portion of a deferred tax asset for which it is more likely than not that a tax benefit will not be realized.

---

3. These definitions are adapted from "Accounting for Income Taxes," *FASB Statement of Financial Accounting Standards No. 109* (Stamford, Conn.: FASB, 1992), par. 289.

INTERPERIOD INCOME TAX ALLOCATION: BASIC ISSUES

1 Understand
permanent and
temporary
differences.

Interperiod income tax allocation involves the allocation of a corporation's income tax obligation as an expense to various accounting periods. Differences between a corporation's pretax financial income and taxable income arise from both temporary and permanent differences. Temporary differences ultimately reverse and require interperiod tax allocation. Although permanent differences are *not* subject to interperiod tax allocation, we discussed them first in this section because an accountant must be able to classify differences as permanent or temporary for interperiod tax allocation purposes.

Permanent Differences

A **permanent difference** is a difference between a corporation's pretax financial income and taxable income in an accounting period that will *never* reverse in a later accounting period. These differences arise as a result of the U.S. Congress setting economic policy or partially offsetting a provision of the tax code that it believes may impose too heavy a tax burden on a particular segment of the economy. There are three types of permanent differences between a corporation's pretax financial income and taxable income. We show a diagram of these permanent differences in the upper part of Exhibit 18-3; we explain the examples in the lower part.

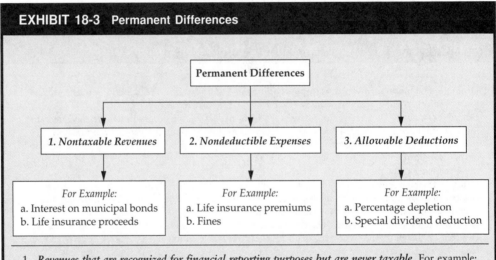

EXHIBIT 18-3   Permanent Differences

1. *Revenues that are recognized for financial reporting purposes but are never taxable.* For example:
    a. Interest on municipal bonds. For income tax purposes the interest received by a corporation on an investment in municipal bonds generally is never taxable. The provision enables municipalities to offer bonds that pay a relatively lower rate of interest than corporate bonds of a similar quality, thus reducing the cost of borrowing for these municipalities.
    b. Life insurance proceeds payable to a corporation upon the death of an insured employee. For income tax purposes the proceeds received as not taxable to the corporation but, rather, as partial compensation for the loss of the employee.
2. *Expenses that are recognized for financial reporting purposes but are never deductible for income tax purposes.* For example:
    a. Life insurance premiums on officers. For income tax purposes the periodic premiums for life insurance policies on officers are not deductible as expenses. This procedure is consistent with the treatment of the insurance proceeds discussed in 1(b).
    b. Fines. For income tax purposes, fines or other expenses related to the violation of a law are not deductible.
3. *Deductions that are allowed for income tax purposes but do not qualify as expenses under generally accepted accounting principles.* For example:
    a. Percentage depletion in excess of cost depletion. Certain corporations that own wasting assets are allowed to deduct a percentage depletion in excess of the cost depletion on a wasting asset from their revenues for income tax purposes. This provision of the tax code was designed to encourage exploration for natural resources.
    b. Special dividend deduction. For income tax purposes corporations are allowed a special deduction (usually 70% or 80%) for certain dividends from investments in equity securities.

Permanent differences affect *either* a corporation's reported pretax financial income *or* its taxable income, *but not both*. In other words, permanent differences do *not* have deferred tax consequences. They do not require interperiod income tax allocation because generally accepted accounting principles and the tax code differ on the items of revenue and expense that a corporation recognizes. A corporation that has nontaxable revenue or additional deductions for income tax reporting purposes will report a relatively lower taxable income (as compared to its pretax financial income) than it would have if these items were not present, whereas a corporation with expenses that are not tax deductible will report a relatively higher taxable income.

Temporary Differences

A **temporary difference** is a difference between the tax basis (i.e., book value) of a corporation's asset or liability for income tax purposes and the reported amount (i.e., book value) of the asset or liability in its financial statements that will result in taxable or deductible amounts in future years when the corporation recovers the reported amount of the asset (or settles the liability).[4] In other words, a temporary difference causes a difference between a corporation's pretax financial income and taxable income that "originates" in one or more years and "reverses" in later years. A corporation's temporary differences sometimes are called *timing* differences because of the different time periods in which they affect pretax financial income and taxable income. A corporation's temporary differences generally relate to its individual assets and liabilities and may be classified into four groups[5], which we show in Exhibit 18-4.

Temporary differences between pretax financial income and taxable income raise numerous conceptual issues regarding the measurement and reporting of the income tax liability (asset) and the income tax expense (benefit) in the accounting periods affected.

INTERPERIOD INCOME TAX ALLOCATION: CONCEPTUAL ISSUES

In 1992, after much debate over a 25-year period, the FASB issued *FASB Statement No. 109* which defines generally accepted accounting principles for income taxes. The accounting principles for income taxes initially were defined in *APB Opinion No. 11*, issued in 1967. This *Opinion* required the use of comprehensive income tax allocation applied under the deferred method. This approach meant that a corporation's annual income tax expense was based on all transactions and events included in pretax income on its income statement (i.e., comprehensive allocation), and the deferred tax amount reported on its ending balance sheet was based on the income tax rates in existence when the temporary differences originated (i.e., deferred method). *APB Opinion No. 11* was very controversial because of significant disagreements concerning its conclusions. Furthermore, the *FASB Statements of Concepts* issued after the *Opinion* contradicted these conclusions.

2 Explain the conceptual issues regarding interperiod tax allocation.

Consequently, *FASB Statement No. 96* was issued in 1987; it required the use of comprehensive income tax allocation applied under the asset/liability method. Under this approach a corporation's deferred tax asset or liability reported on its ending balance sheet was based on the enacted future income tax rates when the temporary differences were scheduled to reverse. The conclusions of the FASB in this *Statement* also were controversial because of scheduling complexities (sometimes involving schedules

Many arguments in favor of and against each of these approaches and the controversial conclusions of FASB Statement No. 96 are discussed in the Appendix to this chapter.

---

4. Temporary differences also include items that a corporation cannot identify with a particular asset or liability for financial reporting but which (a) result from events that it has recognized in the financial statements, and (b) will result in taxable or deductible amounts in future years based on provisions in the tax law.

5. *FASB Statement No. 109* identifies four other temporary differences: (1) a reduction in the tax basis of depreciable assets because of an investment tax credit accounted for by the deferred method, (2) a reduction in the tax basis of depreciable assets because of other tax credits, (3) an increase in the tax basis of assets because of indexing whenever the local currency is the functional currency, and (4) business combinations accounted for by the purchase method. We do not discuss these temporary differences in this chapter.

EXHIBIT 18-4   Temporary Differences

Future Taxable Income Will Be More Than Future Pretax Financial Income

1. *Revenues or gains are included in pretax financial income prior to the time they are included in taxable income.* For example, gross profit on installment sales normally is recognized at the point of sale for financial reporting purposes, but for income tax purposes, in certain situations it is recognized as cash is collected. Or, gross profit on long-term construction contracts may be recognized for financial reporting purposes under the percentage-of-completion method and for income tax purposes for certain corporations under the completed-contract method. Also, investment income may be recognized under the equity method for financial reporting purposes, but for income tax purposes it is recognized in subsequent periods as dividends are received.

2. *Expenses or losses are deducted to compute taxable income prior to the time they are subtracted to compute pretax financial income.* For example, a depreciable asset purchased after 1986 may be depreciated by the Modified Accelerated Cost Recovery System (MACRS) over the prescribed tax life (discussed in Chapter 10) for income tax purposes.[a] For financial reporting purposes, however, it may be depreciated by a financial accounting method (often straight-line) over a longer period. Also, interest and taxes on certain self-construction projects may be deducted as incurred in arriving at taxable income, but may be capitalized in certain instances as a part of the cost of the self-constructed assets for financial reporting.

Future Taxable Income Will Be Less Than Future Pretax Financial Income

3. *Revenues or gains are included in taxable income prior to the time they are included in pretax financial income.* For example, such items as rent, interest, and royalties received in advance are taxable when received but are not reported for financial reporting purposes until the service actually has been provided. Additionally, gains on "sales and leasebacks" are taxed at the date of sale, but are reported over the life of the lease contract for financial reporting purposes.

4. *Expenses or losses are subtracted to compute pretax financial income prior to the time they are deducted to compute taxable income.* For example, product warranty costs, bad debts, compensation expense for stock option plans, and losses on inventories in a later year may be estimated and recorded as expenses in the current year for financial reporting purposes but deducted, as actually incurred, for the determination of taxable income. Or, indirect costs of producing inventory may be recorded as expenses in the current year for financial reporting purposes, but capitalized in the cost of inventory and therefore deducted as part of cost of goods sold in a later year to determine taxable income. Also, a contingent liability may be expensed for financial reporting purposes if a loss is probable and is measurable, but is deducted in arriving at taxable income when it is actually paid.

[a]A depreciable asset purchased before 1981 may be depreciated by an accelerated method for income tax purposes and the straight-line method for financial accounting purposes. Or, a depreciable asset purchased between 1981 and 1986 may be depreciated by the Accelerated Cost Recovery System (ACRS).

for 20 to 30 years in the future) and restrictions imposed for recognizing deferred tax assets. It eventually was superseded by *FASB Statement No. 109*. In its deliberations, the FASB reexamined several conceptual questions (identified in Exhibit 18-5):

1. Should corporations be required to make interperiod income tax allocations for temporary differences, or should there be no interperiod tax allocation?
2. If interperiod tax allocation is required, should it be based on a comprehensive approach for all temporary differences or on a partial approach for certain temporary differences?
3. Should interperiod tax allocation be applied using the asset/liability method (based on enacted future tax rates), the deferred method (based on originating tax rates), or the net-of-tax method?

After considering the conceptual issues relating to the preceding questions and the criticisms raised regarding *FASB Statement No. 96*, in 1991 the FASB issued an *Exposure Draft* on accounting for income taxes. Based on responses from constituents and a limited-scope "field test" by participating corporations, in 1992 the Board (in a unanimous vote) issued *FASB Statement No. 109*, in which it identified two objectives of accounting for income taxes. The first is that a corporation should recognize the

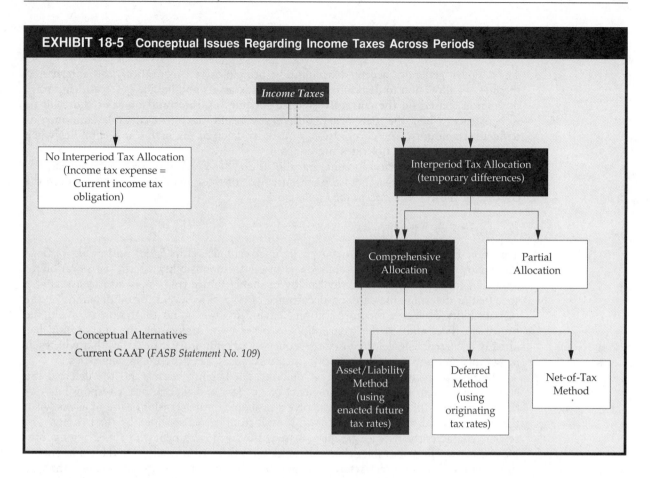

EXHIBIT 18-5   Conceptual Issues Regarding Income Taxes Across Periods

amount of its income tax obligation or refund for the current year. The second is that a corporation should recognize deferred tax liabilities and assets for the future tax consequences of all events that it has reported in its financial statements or income tax returns. Based on these objectives, the FASB concluded that:

1. Interperiod income tax allocation of temporary differences is appropriate.
2. The comprehensive allocation approach is to be applied.
3. The asset/liability method of income tax allocation is to be used.

Thus, nonallocation, partial allocation, and the deferred and net-of-tax methods listed in Exhibit 18-5 (and which we discuss in the Appendix) were rejected and are *not* generally accepted accounting principles. Furthermore, reporting deferred taxes by using a present value approach was not considered by the FASB, and is *not* acceptable.

To implement the objectives, the FASB established four basic principles that a corporation is to apply in accounting for its income taxes at the date of its financial statements:

1. A current tax liability or asset is recognized for the estimated income tax obligation or refund on its income tax return for the current year.[6]
2. A deferred tax liability or asset is recognized for the estimated future tax effects of each temporary difference.
3. The measurement of deferred tax liabilities and assets is based on provisions of the enacted tax law; the effects of future changes in tax laws or rates are not anticipated.

---

6. Since a corporation may make estimated tax payments during the year, the current tax liability or asset that it reports on its ending balance sheet may be different than its total tax obligation or refund.

4. The measurement of deferred tax assets is reduced, if necessary, by the amount of any tax benefits that, based on available evidence, are not expected to be realized.[7]

Thus, under generally accepted accounting principles, **a corporation uses interperiod income tax allocation to determine its deferred tax assets and liabilities for all temporary differences, based on the currently enacted income tax rates and on laws that will be in existence when the temporary differences result in future taxable amounts or deductible amounts. The corporation adjusts its deferred tax assets and liabilities when changes in the income tax rates are enacted.**

In regard to interperiod income tax allocation, the FASB discussed deferred tax liabilities, deferred tax assets, and the measurement of these items by a corporation in the context of the *FASB Conceptual Framework*.

Deferred Tax Liability

The three essential characteristics of a liability established in *FASB Statement of Concepts No. 6* are: (1) it must embody a present responsibility of the corporation to another entity that involves settlement by probable future transfer or use of assets at a specified or determinable date, on occurrence of a specified event, or on demand, (2) the responsibility obligates the corporation, leaving it little or no discretion to avoid the future sacrifice, and (3) the transaction or other event obligating the corporation has already occurred. The deferred tax consequences of temporary differences that will result in taxable amounts for a corporation in future years meet these characteristics.

The first characteristic is met by a deferred tax liability because (a) the deferred tax consequences stem from the requirements of tax law and, hence, are a responsibility to the government, (b) settlement will involve a probable future transfer or use of assets when the taxes are paid, and (c) settlement will result from events specified by the tax law. The second characteristic is met because, based on the government rules and regulations, income taxes will be payable when the temporary differences result in taxable amounts in future years. The third characteristic is met because the past events that created the taxable temporary differences are the same events that result in the deferred tax liability.

Deferred Tax Asset

The three essential characteristics of an asset are: (1) it must embody a probable future benefit that involves a capacity to contribute to the corporation's future net cash inflows, (2) the corporation must be able to obtain the benefit and control other entities' access to it, and (3) the transaction or other event resulting in the corporation's right to or control of the benefit must already have occurred.[8] The deferred tax consequences of temporary differences of a corporation that will result in deductible amounts in future years meet these characteristics.

The first characteristic is met because the deductible amounts in future years will result in reduced taxable income, therefore contributing to the corporation's future net cash inflows through reduced taxes paid. The second characteristic is met because the corporation will have an exclusive right to the reduced taxes paid. Finally, the third characteristic is met because the past events that created the deductible temporary differences are the same events that result in the deferred tax asset.

Measurement

After a corporation has identified a taxable or deductible temporary difference, it "measures" the difference before recording and reporting the amount as a deferred tax liability or deferred tax asset in its financial statements. The FASB addressed two issues

---

7. *FASB Statement No. 109, op. cit.,* par. 6 and 8. *FASB Statement No. 109* also addressed the accounting for operating loss carrybacks and carryforwards. For simplicity, we discuss these items in a later section.
8. "Elements of Financial Statements of Business Enterprises," *FASB Statement of Financial Accounting Concepts No. 6* (Stamford, Conn.: FASB, 1985), par. 26 and 36.

regarding the measurement of deferred tax liabilities and assets: (1) the applicable income tax rates, and (2) whether a valuation allowance should be established for deferred tax assets.

The U.S. federal corporate income taxes are assessed based on a "several step" rate schedule. However, if a corporation's taxable income exceeds a specified amount, its entire taxable income essentially is taxed at a "single flat rate." In regard to deferred taxes, the question arose as to what rate to use in measuring deferred tax liabilities and assets. For simplicity, the FASB decided to require a corporation to use the enacted income tax rate expected to apply to its *last* dollar of taxable income (i.e., its *marginal tax rate*) in the periods when the corporation expects the deferred tax liability or asset to be settled or realized. In other words, most corporations are required to use the single flat rate in their deferred tax calculations.[9]

The second issue—the possible use of a valuation allowance for deferred tax assets—was more controversial. A corporation will realize the tax benefits from a deferred tax asset only if it will have enough future taxable income from which to subtract the deductible temporary difference. If there is sufficient uncertainty about a corporation's future taxable income, the FASB decided that the corporation is to establish a valuation allowance to reduce its deferred tax asset(s) to the realizable amount. (This approach is similar to reporting accounts receivable at a gross amount and then reducing the amount by an allowance for doubtful accounts.)

But how much uncertainty is "sufficient" and how does a corporation make a judgment about the realizable amount? In regard to sufficiency, the FASB decided to apply a "more likely than not" (a likelihood of more than 50 percent) criterion to measure uncertainty. In other words, the FASB concluded that a corporation needs a valuation allowance if, based on available evidence, it is *more likely than not* that the deferred asset will *not* be realized.

In regard to making a judgment about the realizable amount, the FASB stated that a corporation should consider all available evidence, both positive and negative, in determining whether it needs a valuation allowance. The Board identified four possible sources of taxable income (positive evidence) that a corporation might use to realize the tax benefits from a deferred tax asset. These sources include:

1. Future reversals of existing taxable temporary differences.
2. Future taxable income, exclusive of reversing temporary differences.
3. Taxable income in prior carryback year(s) if carryback is permitted under the tax law.
4. Prudent and feasible tax-planning strategies.[10]

The FASB concluded that *at least one* of these sources is sufficient for a corporation to conclude that it does not need a valuation allowance.

The Board stated that it would be difficult for a corporation to conclude that a valuation allowance is *not* needed when there is negative evidence, such as cumulative losses in recent years. It also provided other examples of negative evidence, such as (1) a history of unused operating loss carryforwards, (2) losses expected in the near future years, and (3) unsettled circumstances that are potentially unfavorable. The Board noted, however, that other positive evidence may overcome negative evidence, making a valuation allowance unnecessary. Examples of positive evidence cited include (1) existing contracts or sales backlogs that will produce sufficient taxable income, (2) an excess of fair value over the tax basis (book value) sufficient to realize the deferred tax asset, and (3) a strong earnings history exclusive of the loss that created the future deductible amount, coupled with evidence that the loss was an aberration. A corporation must use good judgment in weighing the verifiable positive and negative evidence to determine if it needs a valuation allowance for some or all of a deferred tax asset.

---

9. Corporations for which graduated rates are a significant factor must use an "average graduated tax rate" approach for measuring their deferred tax liabilities and assets. We do not discuss this approach in this book.

10. A tax planning strategy is an action a corporation ordinarily would not take except to ensure that it can realize a deductible temporary difference (e.g., acceleration of taxable income).

If a corporation does establish a valuation allowance, there may be a change in circumstances at a later date that may cause a change in judgment about the realizability of the related deferred tax asset. There also may be a change in tax laws or rates that would affect the amount of previously recorded deferred tax assets and liabilities. In each case, the corporation includes the effect of the change as an adjustment to the income tax expense related to its income from continuing operations in the year of the change.[11]

INTERPERIOD INCOME TAX ALLOCATION: RECORDING AND REPORTING OF CURRENT AND DEFERRED TAXES

Recall that *FASB Statement No. 109* has as its objectives that a corporation recognize (record and report) the amount of its income tax obligation (refund), as well as the amount of its deferred tax liabilities and deferred tax assets. To measure and record the amount of a corporation's current and deferred income taxes, the following steps are completed:

Step 1.   Measure the income tax obligation for the year by applying the applicable tax rate to the current taxable income.

Step 2.   Identify the temporary differences and classify each as either "taxable" or "deductible."

Step 3.   Measure the year-end deferred tax liability for each taxable temporary difference using the applicable tax rate.

Step 4.   Measure the year-end deferred tax asset for each deductible temporary difference using the applicable tax rate.

Step 5.   Reduce deferred tax assets by a valuation allowance if, based on available evidence, it is *more likely than not* that some or all of the year-end deferred tax assets will not be realized.

Step 6.   Record the income tax expense (including the deferred tax expense or benefit), income tax obligation, change in deferred tax liabilities and/or deferred tax assets, and change in valuation allowance (if any).

A corporation reports its federal taxable income on *Form 1120,* "U.S. Corporation Income Tax Return." Included in this form is Schedule M-1, which identifies the differences between the corporation's pretax financial income and its taxable income. Because of its length, we do not include Form 1120 here. However, information about the taxable income and temporary differences discussed in the previous steps is obtained from this form.

We show the previous steps in the following diagram, after which we illustrate the related journal entries.

Item	Balance Sheet Impact	Change in Balance Sheet Accounts	Income Statement Impact
Taxable Income	➔ Current Tax Liability[a] ➔	Income Taxes Payable (+)	
Taxable Temporary Difference	➔ Deferred Tax Liability[b] ➔	Change in Deferred Tax Liability (−)	
Deductible Temporary Difference	➔ Deferred Tax Asset[c] ➔	Change in Deferred Tax Asset (+)	➔(=) Income Tax Expense[e]
Realization Concern	➔ Valuation Allowance[d] ➔	Change in Valuation Allowance	
Permanent Difference	————————————➔	No tax consequences	

[a]Taxable income for year × Tax rate
[b]Year-end taxable temporary difference × Tax rate
[c]Year-end deductible temporary difference × Tax rate
[d]Unrealizable amount of year-end deferred tax asset × Tax rate
[e]May affect other financial statements (as we discuss later)

---

11. *FASB Statement No. 109, op. cit.,* par. 18–27.

Basic Entries

A corporation's deferred tax expense or benefit is the change in its deferred tax liabilities or assets during the year. The amount of this change, then, combined with the amount of its income tax obligation (or refund) is the amount of the corporation's income tax expense (or benefit) for the year. Thus, in the case of a corporation that has one deferred tax liability at the beginning of the year, earns pretax income for the year, and incurs an increase in the liability, the corporation makes the following journal entry (amounts assumed):

Income Tax Expense	11,600	
Income Taxes Payable		10,000
Deferred Tax Liability		1,600

3 Record and report deferred tax liabilities.

For a similar situation involving one deferred tax asset (and *no* valuation allowance) instead of a deferred tax liability, the corporation makes the following journal entry (amounts assumed):

Income Tax Expense	12,800	
Deferred Tax Asset	1,300	
Income Taxes Payable		14,100

The corporation allocates the amount of income tax expense to the various components of its comprehensive income, as we discuss in a later section. It determines the amount of the income tax obligation by multiplying the current tax rate(s) by the taxable income for the year. For simplicity, we assume here (and in the later examples and homework) that the corporation does *not* make estimated income tax payments during the year; therefore, it records the entire obligation for the year as income taxes payable. The corporation calculates the amount of the adjustment to the deferred tax liability (asset) in the journal entry by determining the amount [based on the currently enacted future tax rate(s)] of the year-end deferred tax liability (asset) and then comparing this amount to the amount of the beginning deferred tax liability (asset). The corporation reports the amount of the year-end deferred tax liability (asset) on its ending balance sheet, classified as "current" or "noncurrent," as we discuss in a later section.

If, in the last example, the corporation previously had no valuation allowance but determined that one was necessary, it would make the following additional journal entry (amounts assumed):

Income Tax Expense	400	
Allowance to Reduced Deferred		
Tax Asset to Realizable Value		400

The corporation combines the $400 debit to income tax expense with the $12,800 amount of Income Tax Expense from the journal entry in the last example to determine its $13,200 *total* Income Tax Expense. If the amount of the Allowance is equal to the adjustment to the Deferred Tax Asset, then the Income Tax Expense is equal to the Income Taxes Payable. The corporation subtracts the Allowance account from the Deferred Tax Asset account on its ending balance sheet to report the expected net realizable value of the deferred tax asset.

When a corporation has more than one taxable or deductible temporary difference, permanent differences, and changes in enacted future tax rates, completion of the steps listed earlier becomes more complex.

Example 1: Deferred Tax Liability—Single Temporary Difference

Assume that in 2004, Track Company purchased an asset at a cost of $6,000. For financial reporting purposes, the asset has a 4-year life, no residual value, and is depreciated by the units-of-output method over 6,000 units (2004: 1,600 units; 2005: 2,800 units; 2006: 1,100 units; 2007: 500 units). For income tax purposes the asset is depreciated under MACRS using the 200% declining balance method over a 3-year life (no residual value), as we discussed in Chapter 10. Prior to 2004, the company had no deferred tax liability or asset. The difference between the company's depreciation for financial reporting purposes and income tax purposes is the only temporary difference between its pretax financial income and taxable income.[12] In 2004 the company has taxable income of $7,500 (after deducting the MACRS depreciation). The income tax rate for 2004 is 30% and no change in the tax rate has been enacted for future years.

Based on the preceding information, the depreciation expense for 2004 is $1,600 [1,600 × ($6,000 ÷ 6,000)] for financial reporting purposes and $2,000 [$6,000 × 33.33% (from Exhibit 10-12)] for income tax purposes. At the end of 2004 the asset has a book value of $4,400 for financial reporting purposes and a book value of $4,000 for income tax purposes, as we show in the top part of Exhibit 18-6. The $400 difference in book values is the result of a temporary difference in depreciation that originated in 2004 (and that caused taxable income to be lower than pretax financial income in that year). This difference will reverse in future years because tax depreciation will be *lower* than financial depreciation by $400 (to depreciate each book value to zero). Thus, the $400 is the ending *taxable temporary difference* for 2004 because future taxable income will be *higher* than future pretax financial income.

EXHIBIT 18-6   Asset Book Value and Deferred Tax Liability

	Financial Reporting (12/31/04)	Income Tax Reporting (12/31/04)
Cost of asset	$6,000	$6,000
Accumulation depreciation	(1,600)	(2,000)
Book value of asset	$4,400	$4,000
Ending taxable temporary difference		$400
Enacted future tax rate		0.30
Ending deferred tax liability		$120
Beginning deferred tax liability		(0)
Change (increase) in deferred tax liability		$120 (Deferred tax expense)

In applying the steps to determine the Track Company's current and deferred income taxes, the $2,250 income tax obligation for 2004 (Step 1) is calculated by multiplying the taxable income ($7,500) by the current tax rate (30%). The depreciation difference is identified as the only taxable temporary difference (Step 2). In Step 3, the $120 total deferred tax liability is calculated (measured) by multiplying the total taxable temporary difference ($400) times the enacted future tax rate (30%), as we show in the middle part of Exhibit 18-6. Steps 4 and 5 are not necessary because the company has no deferred tax asset. In Step 6, the company makes the following journal entry at the end of 2004:

Income Tax Expense ($2,250 + $120)	2,370	
Income Taxes Payable		2,250
Deferred Tax Liability		120

The income tax expense is the sum of the current income tax obligation and the deferred tax expense. Note that since the company has no deferred tax liability at the beginning of 2004, the deferred tax expense for 2004 is $120 as we show in the bottom part of

---

12. In reality, a corporation would have several depreciable assets of different ages and with varying lives, perhaps resulting in both originating (and deductible) and reversing (and taxable) depreciation differences in a given year. For simplicity, when dealing with depreciable assets in the text and homework, we generally focus on a single depreciable asset, with depreciation that results in a reversing (and taxable) difference in the future. The computations are best understood in this context.

Exhibit 18-6, and this is the amount of the credit (increase) to the deferred tax liability. [If a deferred tax liability had existed at the beginning of 2004, the change necessary to bring the balance up (or down) to the ending deferred tax liability is the deferred tax expense and would be recorded in the journal entry.] The company reports the income tax expense of $2,370 on its 2004 income statement, subject to intraperiod tax allocation (which we discuss in a later section of the chapter). The company reports the income taxes payable as a current liability on its 2004 ending balance sheet. As we discuss in a later section, the company reports the deferred tax liability on its ending balance sheet.

Example 2: Deferred Tax Liability—Single Temporary Difference and Multiple Rates

Now assume the same information as in Example 1, except that the income tax rate for 2004 is 40%, but Congress has enacted tax rates of 35% for 2005, 33% for 2006, and 30% for 2007 and beyond. In Example 1, the calculation of the deferred tax liability is straightforward because a 30% tax rate is applicable to all the future years in which the depreciation temporary difference reverses and results in higher taxable income. However, when different enacted tax rates apply to taxable income in different future years, the calculation of the amount of the ending deferred tax liability is more complicated. The calculation requires a corporation to prepare a schedule to determine the reversing difference (i.e., taxable amount) for each future year, multiply each yearly taxable amount by the applicable tax rate to determine the additional income tax obligation (deferred taxes) for that year, and sum the yearly deferred taxes to determine the total deferred tax liability.

In Example 2, before the Track Company can prepare a deferred tax liability schedule, it must first prepare a schedule to compute the 2005 through 2007 depreciation expense for financial reporting and income tax purposes. We show this schedule in the upper portion of Exhibit 18-7. Based on the differences in depreciation for financial reporting and income tax purposes, the company prepares a schedule to calculate its deferred tax liability. We show this schedule in the lower portion of Exhibit 18-7.

EXHIBIT 18-7 Depreciation and Deferred Tax Schedules

Depreciation Expense

Year	Financial Depreciation	Income Tax Depreciation
2005	$2,800[a]	$2,667[b]
2006	1,100	889[c]
2007	500	444[d]

Deferred Tax Liability

	2005	2006	2007	
Financial depreciation	$2,800	$1,100	$500	
Income tax depreciation	(2,667)	(889)	(444)	
Taxable amount[e]	$ 133	$ 211	$ 56	= $400
Income tax rate	0.35	0.33	0.30	
Deferred tax liability[f]	$ 47 +	$ 70 +	$ 17	= $134

a. Units produced × $1/unit.
b. $6,000 × 44.45% from Exhibit 10-12.
c. $6,000 × 14.81% from Exhibit 10-12.
d. $6,000 × 7.41% from Exhibit 10-12; $1 rounding error.
e. Lower income tax depreciation results in higher taxable income.
f. Amounts rounded to nearest dollar.

In Exhibit 18-7, for each year the income tax depreciation is deducted from the financial reporting depreciation to determine the taxable amount. Given the enacted tax rates for the respective years, the income taxes payable on the taxable amounts are $47 in 2005, $70 in 2006, and $17 in 2007. Thus, the total deferred tax liability is $134 at the end of 2004. Since the taxable income for 2004 is $7,500, the income tax obligation is $3,000 ($7,500 × 0.40) based on the 40% tax rate for 2004. The company makes the following journal entry at the end of 2004:

Income Tax Expense ($3,000 + $134)	3,134	
Income Taxes Payable		3,000
Deferred Tax Liability		134

The company reports the expense and liabilities in its financial statements as we discussed in Example 1.

Example 3: Deferred Tax Asset—Single Temporary Difference

4 Record and report deferred tax assets.

Assume that Klemper Company has been operating profitably for several years selling a product on which it provides a 3-year warranty. For financial reporting purposes, the company estimates its future warranty costs and records a warranty expense and liability at year-end. For income tax purposes the company deducts its warranty costs when paid. This difference in reporting warranty costs is the only temporary difference between the company's pretax financial income and taxable income. It is a *deductible temporary difference* (resulting in a deferred tax asset) because in future years the warranty costs that the company deducts for income tax purposes will exceed the warranty expense it deducts for financial reporting purposes, causing its future taxable income to be *lower* than its future pretax financial income. At the beginning of 2004, the company had a deferred tax asset of $330 related to the warranty liability on its balance sheet. At the end of 2004 the company estimates that its ending warranty liability is $1,400. In 2004 the company has taxable income of $5,000. The income tax rate for 2004 is 30% and no change in the tax rate has been enacted for future years.

In determining the Klemper Company's current and deferred income taxes, its 2004 year-end deferred tax asset is calculated to be $420 ($1,400 ending deductible temporary difference × 0.30), as we show in the top part of Exhibit 18-8. The $1,400 deductible difference arises because the book value of the ending warranty liability is $1,400 for financial reporting purposes, but $0 for income tax purposes. The company's 2004 income tax obligation is $1,500 ($5,000 × 0.30). The change (increase) in the deferred tax asset is $90, computed by deducting the beginning deferred tax asset ($330) from the required ending deferred tax asset ($420), as we show in the bottom part of Exhibit 18-8. This $90 is also the 2004 deferred tax benefit; it is subtracted from the

---

EXHIBIT 18-8   Liability Book Value and Deferred Tax Asset

	Financial Reporting (12/31/04)	Income Tax Reporting (12/31/04)
Book value of warranty liability	$1,400	$0
Ending deductible temporary difference	$1,400	
Enacted future tax rate	0.30	
Ending deferred tax asset	$ 420	
Beginning deferred tax asset	(330)	
Change (increase) in deferred tax asset	$ 90	(Deferred tax benefit)

$1,500 income taxes payable to determine the $1,410 income tax expense for 2004. The company makes the following journal entry at the end of 2004:

Income Tax Expense ($1,500 − $90)	1,410	
Deferred Tax Asset	90	
Income Taxes Payable		1,500

The company reports the deferred tax asset on its balance sheet, as we discuss in a later section. Since the company has a successful earnings history and expects to be profitable in the future, it does not need a valuation allowance.

Example 4: Deferred Tax Asset and Valuation Allowance

Now assume the same information as in Example 3, except that during the past few years the Klemper Company's sales and profits have been declining. At the end of 2004, due to uncertain future economic conditions, the company decides that it is "more likely than not" that $600 of the ending deductible temporary difference will not be realized. Therefore, in addition to the income tax entry made in Example 3, the company also records a valuation allowance of $180 ($600 × 0.30) at the end of 2004 as follows:

Income Tax Expense	180	
Allowance to Reduce Deferred		
Tax Asset to Realizable Value		180

The company subtracts the $180 ending balance in the allowance account from the $420 deferred tax asset ending balance to report the realizable value of $240 on its ending balance sheet as follows:

Deferred tax asset	$420
Less: Allowance to reduce deferred tax asset to realizable value	(180)
	$240

In 2005 and future years, the company must reexamine the available evidence to determine whether it needs to make an adjustment (increase or decrease) in the valuation allowance.

Example 5: Permanent and Temporary Differences

Assume that the Sand Company has been in operation for several years and has earned income in each of those years. At the end of 2004, the company reports pretax income of $75,500 for financial reporting purposes. Included in the calculation of this income are the following items: (1) interest revenue of $1,500 on investments in municipal bonds, (2) gross profit of $10,000 on installment sales recognized under the accrual method, and (3) rent revenue of $3,000 for the first year of a 3-year, $9,000 rental contract collected in advance.

For income tax purposes, the company reports gross profit on installment sales under the installment sales method as cash is collected. It also reports rent revenue for tax purposes as cash is collected. During 2004 the company reports gross profit of $2,000 on installment sales. The company had a deferred tax liability of $300 related to an installment sales temporary difference of $1,000 at the beginning of 2004. The income tax rate is 30% for 2004 and no change in the tax rate has been enacted for future years.

To determine the Sand Company's current and deferred income taxes, the company must first compute its 2004 taxable income. This amount is $72,000 as we show in Exhibit 18-9. This exhibit is similar to the schedule required to reconcile a corporation's pretax financial income to its taxable income on Form 1120, the federal corporate income tax return. In preparing the schedule in Exhibit 18-9, one permanent difference and two temporary differences are identified. The permanent difference ($1,500 tax-exempt interest revenue) is deducted from pretax financial income to determine taxable income; although it is included in pretax financial income, it is not

---

EXHIBIT 18-9   Computation of 2004 Taxable Income

Pretax financial income	$75,500
Less: Tax-exempt interest revenue on municipal bonds (permanent difference)	(1,500)
Excess of gross profit on installment sales over gross profit for taxes (temporary difference)	(8,000)[a]
Add: Excess of rent collected in advance over rent revenue (temporary difference)	6,000[b]
Taxable Income	$72,000

a. $10,000 gross profit on installment sales recognized under accrual method for financial reporting minus $2,000 gross profit recognized under installment sales method for income taxes.
b. $9,000 collected in advance and reported for income taxes minus $3,000 rent revenue recognized for financial reporting.

---

taxable. Thus, it is ignored for deferred tax calculations because it will *never* reverse and never be taxable.

The $8,000 *excess* of the gross profit on installment sales included in pretax financial income ($10,000) over the gross profit reported for taxes ($2,000) is subtracted to determine taxable income, because less cash is collected (and taxed). This difference is a *taxable temporary difference* because it will be included in future taxable income when the cash is collected. On the other hand, the $6,000 *excess* of rent collected in advance is added to pretax financial income to determine taxable income, because more cash ($9,000) is collected (and taxed) than reported as rent revenue ($3,000) in pretax financial income. This difference is a *deductible temporary difference* because future taxable income will be less than future pretax financial income when the rent is recognized as rent revenue for financial reporting purposes.

The Sand Company's 2004 income taxes payable are $21,600 ($72,000 taxable income from Exhibit 18-9 × 0.30). In computing its deferred taxes, the company determines that it has a total taxable temporary difference of $9,000 ($1,000 beginning + $8,000 increase during 2004) at the end of 2004 in regard to the installment sales. This amount is the difference between the book value of the installment accounts receivable that it reported under the accrual method for financial reporting purposes and the book value of the receivable that it reported under the installment sales method for income tax purposes. The Sand Company's 2004 year-end deferred tax liability for the installment sales taxable temporary difference is $2,700 ($9,000 × 0.30). Since the company had a $300 beginning deferred tax liability, it is increased by $2,400 ($2,700 − $300). The company's 2004 year-end deferred tax asset for the rent revenue deductible temporary difference is $1,800 ($6,000 × 0.30). The $6,000 deductible temporary difference is the difference between the book value of the $6,000 unearned rent reported for financial reporting purposes and the $0 book value reported for income tax purposes. The company makes the following journal entry at the end of 2004:

Income Tax Expense ($21,600 + $2,400 − $1,800)	22,200	
Deferred Tax Asset	1,800	
Income Taxes Payable		21,600
Deferred Tax Liability		2,400

Because the company's taxable temporary difference is greater than its deductible temporary difference, it does not need a valuation allowance for the deferred tax asset.

OPERATING LOSS CARRYBACKS AND CARRYFORWARDS

The previous section and examples dealt with the recognition of a deferred tax liability or asset when a corporation had taxable *income* in the current year. This section deals with the situation where a corporation has a taxable *loss* (and a pretax financial

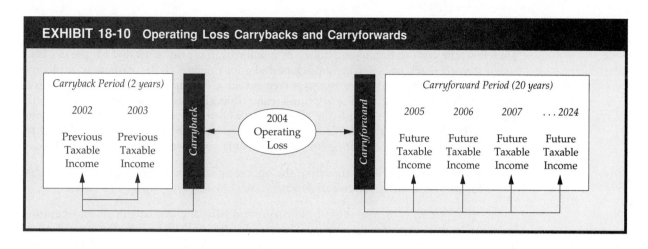

EXHIBIT 18-10 Operating Loss Carrybacks and Carryforwards

loss) in the current year, resulting in an operating loss carryback or carryforward for income tax purposes.

The Internal Revenue Code allows a corporation reporting an operating loss for income tax purposes in the current year to carry this loss back or carry it forward to offset previous or future taxable income. The corporation may first carry a reported operating loss back 2 years (in sequential order, starting with the *earliest* of the 2 years). This procedure is called an **operating loss carryback.** In such a case, the corporation files amended income tax returns showing lower taxable income for those years and receives a refund of income taxes previously paid. If the taxable income for the past 2 years is not enough to offset the amount of the currently reported operating loss, the loss is then sequentially carried forward 20 years and offset against future taxable income, if there is any.[13] This procedure is called an **operating loss carryforward.** The corporation then pays lower income taxes in the future based on lower future taxable income. Exhibit 18-10 shows a diagram of the operating loss carryback and carryforward sequence. A corporation also may elect to forgo the carryback and, instead, only carry forward an operating loss. Unless higher future income tax rates have been enacted, most corporations do not make this election because an operating loss carryback will result in a definite and immediate income tax refund, whereas a carryforward will reduce income taxes payable in future years only to the extent that taxable income is earned.

5 Explain an operating loss carryback and carryforward.

Conceptual Issues

When a corporation reports an operating loss for financial reporting purposes in a given year, several important accounting questions arise concerning the valuation of assets, the recognition of income tax expense, and the reporting of net income. These issues primarily involve operating loss carryforwards, but also relate to operating loss carrybacks.

OPERATING LOSS CARRYBACKS The FASB considered two conceptual issues related to an operating loss carryback in its deliberations on *FASB Statement No. 109.*

1. Should a corporation recognize the tax benefit of an operating loss carryback as a prior period adjustment or in the current period?

In the case of an operating loss carryback, the corporation obtains a tax benefit in the year of the operating loss. This benefit is a refund of income taxes paid in prior periods (which the corporation reported as income tax expense in those periods). An argument

---

13. Prior to 1998, a corporation could carryback an operating loss 3 years, but it was limited to a 15-year carryforward period.

in favor of the corporation reporting the tax benefit of a carryback as a prior period adjustment is that its prior income is what makes possible the realization of the benefit. Therefore, the corporation would adjust its income of that prior period(s) for the tax benefit of the carryback by reporting a prior period adjustment (i.e., decrease in prior income tax expense) on its retained earnings statement in the year of the loss. The counterargument is that the corporation's prior income that enables use of the carryback only gives value to the carryback. It is the corporation's current operating loss that creates the tax benefit. Thus, under the all-inclusive concept of income, the corporation would deduct the tax benefit from the operating loss on its income statement in the year of the loss.

2. Should the corporation incurring the operating loss recognize a current receivable for the tax benefit of the carryback?

The recognition of a receivable by a corporation for the tax benefit of an operating loss carryback is conceptually sound. The corporation will realize the tax benefit as an income tax refund when the refund is issued by the federal government. Thus, it represents an economic benefit obtained and controlled by the corporation as a result of a past transaction or event.

OPERATING LOSS CARRYFORWARDS The FASB considered two conceptual issues related to an operating loss carryforward that arises because a corporation either has no prior taxable income or its prior taxable income is insufficient to absorb the entire operating loss carryback.

1. Should a corporation recognize the tax effect of an operating loss carryforward in the current period or in the future when it is realized?

In the case of an operating loss carryforward, the tax effect is the result of the corporation's operating loss in the *current* year that it will realize in a *future* year(s) if it earns sufficient future taxable income. One alternative accounting treatment for the corporation is to recognize the tax effect (i.e., future tax savings) in the year of its operating loss. This approach is consistent with the concepts of interperiod tax allocation and matching. If this approach were taken, the corporation would recognize a deferred tax asset on its ending balance sheet and would deduct the tax effect from the operating loss on its income statement in the year of the loss, in a manner similar to an operating loss carryback. Arguments in favor of the corporation recognizing the tax effects of an operating loss carryforward in the year of the loss are: (1) the tax effects represent an economic resource that qualifies as an asset of the corporation because it has a right to and control over the future tax benefit, (2) there is better matching because the corporation offsets the tax benefit against the operating loss in the year the loss generated the benefit, (3) it enables better comparisons, because a corporation with an available operating loss carryforward is better off than one without it, and (4) it is consistent with the going-concern assumption.

Another alternative is for the corporation to defer recognition of an operating loss carryforward until it is realized. If this approach were taken, the corporation would not recognize an asset in the loss year. If and when realization occurs, it would recognize the tax benefit as a reduction in its income taxes payable for that future period. Arguments in favor of the corporation recognizing the tax effects of an operating loss carryforward in the year of realization are: (1) an operating loss carryforward is not a current economic resource of the corporation because it will provide a future tax benefit only if the corporation has sufficient future taxable income, (2) this approach is consistent with the consensus that the realization principle should take precedence over matching (that is, when collectibility is not reasonably assured, recognition should be deferred), and (3) the corporation's operating loss is the past event that created a right to the future benefit; however, it is the future event of earning taxable income that gives value to the carryforward.

2. How should the corporation report the tax effect of an operating loss carryforward on its financial statements?

If the corporation recognizes an operating loss carryforward in the year of the loss, it is generally agreed that the corporation should deduct the tax benefit from its operating loss. If the corporation recognizes the tax effect in the year of realization, it could (1) deduct the tax effect from that year's income tax expense, (2) report the tax effect as a prior period adjustment of the year in which the operating loss occurred, or (3) report the tax effect in a separate category on its income statement. An argument in favor of the first approach is that the earning of taxable income in that year enables the corporation to reduce its income taxes, so it should decrease its income tax expense accordingly. An argument in favor of the corporation reporting the tax benefit as a prior period adjustment is that the tax benefit arose in the year of the operating loss; it was just a matter of confirming the amount at the time of realization. An argument in favor of the corporation reporting the tax benefit in a separate section of the income statement is that, although it relates to the current period, the tax benefit is so significant that it warrants separate disclosure.[14]

Generally Accepted Accounting Principles

In its deliberations concerning *FASB Statement No. 109*, the FASB accepted parts of both alternatives. It concluded that the generally accepted accounting principles for the financial reporting of operating loss carrybacks and carryforwards are as follows:

1. A corporation must recognize the tax benefit of an operating loss **carryback** in the period of the loss as an asset (current receivable) on its balance sheet and as a reduction of the operating loss on its income statement.
2. A corporation must recognize the tax benefit of an operating loss **carryforward** in the period of the loss as a deferred tax asset. However, it must reduce the deferred tax asset by a valuation allowance if, based on the available evidence, it is *more likely than not* that the corporation will *not* realize some or all of the deferred tax asset.[15]

In other words, a corporation handles operating loss carryforwards in the same manner as the deductible temporary differences we discussed earlier in the chapter. That is, at year-end, the corporation measures a deferred tax asset for an operating loss carryforward using the enacted future tax rate. If necessary, it measures a valuation allowance and deducts the amount from the deferred tax asset to determine its net realizable value. In the year-end journal entry to record its current and deferred taxes, the corporation treats any increase (decrease) in the deferred tax asset and valuation allowance as an adjustment of its income tax expense (benefit). It is more likely that a corporation will need a valuation allowance for a deferred tax asset related to an operating loss carryforward, because the operating loss itself provides negative evidence as to the likelihood of having sufficient future taxable income to realize the tax benefits.

EXAMPLE 1: OPERATING LOSS CARRYBACK   Assume that Monk Company reports a pretax operating loss of $90,000 in 2004 for both financial reporting and income tax purposes, and that reported pretax financial income and taxable income for the previous 2 years had been: 2002 − $40,000 (tax rate 25%); and 2003 − $70,000 (tax rate 30%). Thus, the $110,000 total pretax income in the previous 2 years is more than sufficient to offset the $90,000 pretax operating loss. When the company carries back its 2004 operating loss, it is entitled to a tax refund of $25,000, calculated as we show in Exhibit 18-11.

Note in Exhibit 18-11 that all of the 2002 income of $40,000 is offset by the operating loss carryback, but only $50,000 of the $70,000 income in 2003 is offset because

6 Account for an operating loss carryback.

---

14. For a further discussion, see "Accounting for Income Taxes," *FASB Discussion Memorandum* (Stamford, Conn.: 1983), and D. Beresford, L. Best, P. Craig, and J. Weber, "Accounting for Income Taxes: A Review of Alternatives," *FASB Research Report* (Stamford, Conn.: FASB, 1983), par. 150–164 and pp. 95–106.
15. *FASB Statement No. 109, op. cit.*, par. 17.

EXHIBIT 18-11   Refund from Operating Loss Carryback

Year	Pretax Financial Income and Taxable Income Offset by Carryback	Income Tax Rate	Income Tax Refund
2002	$40,000	0.25	$10,000
2003	50,000	0.30	15,000
	$90,000		$25,000

the carryback is first applied to the earlier year. (Therefore, the remaining $20,000 of the 2003 income is available to offset any operating losses that might occur in 2005.) At the end of 2004, the company makes the following journal entry:

Income Tax Refund Receivable	25,000	
Income Tax Benefit from		
Operating Loss Carryback		25,000

The company reports the receivable on its balance sheet as a current asset until it collects the receivable. The company reports the operating loss carryback tax benefit in the lower portion of its 2004 income statement as follows:

Pretax operating loss	$(90,000)
Less: Income tax benefit from operating loss carryback	25,000
Net loss	$(65,000)

7 Account for an operating loss carryforward.

EXAMPLE 2: OPERATING LOSS CARRYFORWARD AND VALUATION ALLOWANCE
Assume that Lake Company reports a pretax operating loss of $60,000 in 2004 (its first year of operation) for both financial reporting and income tax purposes. The income tax rate is 30% and no change in the tax rate has been enacted for future years. Because the company had no income prior to 2004, it cannot carry back the operating loss. Since it carries forward the operating loss, the company reports a deferred tax asset at the end of 2004 for the deferred tax consequences (future tax benefit) of the carryforward. It calculates the deferred tax asset to be $18,000 ($60,000 × 0.30) and makes the following journal entry at the end of 2004:

Deferred Tax Asset	18,000	
Income Tax Benefit from		
Operating Loss Carryforward		18,000

Because the company has no history of taxable income and has insufficient positive evidence of future taxable income, it must also reduce the deferred tax asset by a valuation allowance. If we assume the company establishes a valuation allowance for the entire amount of the deferred tax asset, it also makes the following journal entry at the end of 2004:

Income Tax Benefit from		
Operating Loss Carryforward	18,000	
Allowance to Reduce Deferred Tax		
Asset to Realizable Value		18,000

Lake Company reports the $60,000 operating loss as a net loss on its 2004 income statement because it did not realize any tax benefit from the operating loss carryforward in 2004. The deferred tax asset, offset by the valuation allowance, normally is reported on a company's balance sheet, but the net amount is zero in this example. (Lake Company discloses both the deferred tax asset and the valuation allowance amounts in the notes to its 2004 financial statements, however.) Lake Company also discloses the operating loss carryforward as follows in a note to its 2004 financial statements: "The company has a $60,000 operating loss carryforward that can be used within 20 years to offset future taxable income and reduce income taxes."

Now assume that in 2005, Lake Company operates successfully and earns pretax operating income of $100,000 for both financial reporting and income tax purposes. The company realizes the tax benefit of the operating loss carryforward in 2005 as a reduction of its income tax obligation. It offsets the $60,000 carryforward from 2004 against the $100,000 pretax income in 2005, resulting in taxable income of $40,000. Based on the 30% income tax rate, its income taxes payable (and income tax expense) are $12,000 ($40,000 × 0.30). Since the company has used up the tax benefit of the operating loss carryforward, it eliminates the deferred asset and related valuation allowance. The company makes the following journal entry the end of 2005:

Income Tax Expense	12,000	
Allowance to Reduce Deferred Tax Asset		
to Realizable Value	18,000	
Income Taxes Payable		12,000
Deferred Tax Asset		18,000

The lower portion of the company's 2005 income statement is as follows:

Pretax operating income	$100,000
Less: Income tax expense	(12,000)
Net income	$ 88,000

The effect of the operating loss carryforward is to reduce the company's income tax expense for 2005 from $30,000 ($100,000 × 0.30)—the amount without the tax benefit of the carryforward—to $12,000, so that its 2005 net income (after tax) is increased by $18,000.

EXAMPLE 3: OPERATING LOSS CARRYFORWARD AND NO VALUATION ALLOWANCE
Now assume the same information as in Example 2, except that the Lake Company has signed a substantial number of contracts for the sales of its products in 2005. Based on this verifiable positive evidence, the company decides that the tax benefit of its operating loss carryforward will be realized in 2005 and that it does not need a valuation allowance at the end of 2004.

In this case, the company makes the same journal entry to record the $18,000 deferred tax asset as it did in Example 2. However, since it does not record a valuation allowance, the lower portion of the company's 2004 income statement is as follows:

Pretax operating loss	$(60,000)
Less: Income tax benefit from operating loss carryforward	18,000
Net loss	$(42,000)

The realizable tax benefit reduces the company's $60,000 pretax operating loss to a $42,000 net loss. This is in contrast to Example 2, where the company reported a $60,000 net loss on its 2004 income statement.

Continuing with the same assumptions as in Example 2, Lake Company earns pretax operating income of $100,000 in 2005. The $60,000 operating loss carryforward reduces the company's taxable income to $40,000, so that its income tax obligation is $12,000 as in Example 2. The company eliminates the deferred tax asset but since it does not have a valuation allowance, the 2005 income tax expense is $30,000, and the company makes the following 2005 year-end journal entry:

Income Tax Expense	30,000	
Income Taxes Payable		12,000
Deferred Tax Asset		18,000

The lower portion of the company's 2005 income statement is as follows:

Pretax operating income	$100,000
Income tax expense	(30,000)
Net income	$ 70,000

Note that Lake Company's total net income for 2004 and 2005 is $28,000 in both Examples 2 and 3. Its income is accelerated in Example 3, however (through a lower net loss in 2004), because the company had sufficient positive verifiable evidence in 2004 that it would realize the tax benefit from its operating loss carryforward in 2005.

In some cases a corporation's pretax operating income of a given year is not sufficient to offset the entire amount of an operating loss carryforward. In this situation, it offsets a portion of the operating loss against the income and continues to carry forward the remainder as a deferred tax asset (and discloses the amount in a note). For instance, if in the previous example, Lake Company had earned only $50,000 pretax operating (and taxable) income in 2005, then it would affect $50,000 of the $60,000 operating loss carryforward against this income and would pay no income taxes for 2005. The company would report income tax expense of $15,000 ($50,000 × 0.30) and would reduce its deferred tax asset by $15,000. It would eliminate the $3,000 ($18,000 − $15,000) deferred tax asset (30% of the $10,000 remaining operating loss carryforward) in a future year(s) when it realized the tax benefit.

COMPREHENSIVE ILLUSTRATION

The examples in the previous sections only illustrated the accounting for temporary differences separately from operating losses. In this comprehensive example, we illustrate a temporary difference and also an operating loss carryback and an operating loss carryforward. Assume that Branton Company begins operations in 2001 and is profitable through 2003. In 2004 the company reports a pretax financial loss of $8,000 and a taxable loss of $8,800. In 2005 and 2006, the company is again profitable, although at the end of 2004 the company felt that future profits were not likely. The income tax rate is 30%. Exhibit 18–12 shows the company's pretax financial income (loss) and taxable income (loss) for the years 2001 through 2006, as well as its income taxes payable (receivable). It is assumed that the only difference between pretax financial income (loss) and taxable income (loss) in any year results from additional (MACRS) depreciation reported for income tax purposes.

As we show in Exhibit 18-12, the company pays $360 of income taxes in 2001 and $840 in 2002 and 2003. In 2004, $2,800 of the $8,800 operating loss is carried back

EXHIBIT 18-12 Income Taxes Payable or Receivable				
Year	Pretax Financial Income (Loss)	Depreciation Difference	Taxable Income (Loss)	Income Taxes Payable (Receivable)
2001	$2,000	$ 800	$ 1,200	$ 360[a]
2002–2003	5,000	2,200	2,800	840[a]
2004	(8,000)	800	(8,800)	(840)[b]
2005	2,200	700	1,500	0[c]
2006	7,000	600	6,400	570[d]

a. Taxable income × 0.30 income tax rate.
b. $2,800 carryback to years 2002 and 2003, resulting in tax refund of $840; remaining carryforward of $6,000 ($8,800 − $2,800).
c. $1,500 taxable income offset by carryforward, therefore no income taxes owed; remaining carryforward of $4,500 ($6,000 − $1,500).
d. $6,400 taxable income offset by $4,500 carryforward; $1,900 × 0.30.

EXHIBIT 18-13 Deferred Tax Information

| Year | Depreciation Temporary Difference | | | Operating Loss Carryforward |
	Beginning	Addition	Ending[a]	
2001	$ 0	$ 800	$ 800	—
2002–2003	800	2,200	3,000	—
2004	3,000	800	3,800	(6,000)[b]
2005	3,800	700	4,500	(4,500)[c]
2006	4,500	600	5,100	—

a. Beginning depreciation temporary difference + additional difference for current year.
b. $8,800 taxable loss − $2,800 operating loss carryback (see Exhibit 18-12).
c. $6,000 operating loss carryforward from 2004 − $1,500 taxable income in 2005 (see Exhibit 18-12).

---

to offset the 2002 and 2003 taxable income, resulting in a tax refund of $840. Note that the 2004 operating loss is *not* carried back to 2001 because of the 2-year carry-back limitation. In 2005 and 2006, the $6,000 remaining operating loss is carried forward and (1) offsets the $1,500 taxable income in 2005 so that no income taxes are paid, and (2) offsets $4,500 of the $6,400 taxable income in 2006 so that $570 of income taxes are paid.

For financial reporting purposes, the company must determine its deferred tax liability (or asset) and income tax expense (or refund) for each year. Both the depreciation taxable temporary difference and the operating loss carryforward for each year affect the company's deferred taxes; Exhibit 18–13 shows these calculations. Note in Exhibit 18-13 that the depreciation taxable temporary difference increases each year by the difference in depreciation for financial reporting purposes and income tax purposes shown in Exhibit 18-12. The operating loss carryforward of $6,000 at the end of 2004 is the $8,800 operating loss in 2004 less the $2,800 operating loss carryback, as we discussed earlier. The operating loss carryforward at the end of 2005 is only $4,500, because $1,500 was used to offset the taxable income in 2005. The following "time-line" diagram further explains the relationships between the taxable incomes and the operating loss carrybacks and carryforwards for the various years:

	2001	2002	2003	2004	2005	2006
Taxable income before adjustments	$1,200		$2,800	$(8,800)	$1,500	$6,400
Loss carrybacks			(2,800) ◄————	2,800 $(6,000)		
Loss carryforward (to 2005)				1,500 →	(1,500)	
Loss carryforward (to 2006)				4,500 ————————►		(4,500)
Taxable income				$ 0	$ 0	$1,900

Exhibit 18-14 shows the computations of the company's deferred tax liability and asset (and valuation allowance) for each year, based on the information in Exhibit 18-13. As we show in Exhibit 18-13, the company has $800 additional depreciation for tax purposes at the end of 2001, which will result in taxable income of the same amount in future years. As we show in Exhibit 18-14, applying the 30% tax rate to the future taxable amount results in a deferred tax liability of $240 at the end of 2001. Since there was a $0 deferred tax liability at the beginning of 2001, the company makes a $240 adjustment (credit) to the deferred tax liability. The company makes similar computations for 2002 through 2006.

EXHIBIT 18-14 Annual Deferred Taxes

Year	Deferred Tax Liability			Deferred Tax Asset			Valuation Allowance		
	Beginning	Ending[a]	Adjustment	Beginning	Ending	Adjustment	Beginning	Ending	Adjustment
2001	$ 0	$ 240	$240	—	—	—	—	—	—
2002–2003	240	900	660	—	—	—	—	—	—
2004	900	1,140	240	—	$1,800[b]	$1,800	—	$660[c]	$660
2005	1,140	1,350	210	$1,800	1,350[d]	(450)	$660	0[e]	(660)
2006	1,350	1,530	180	1,350	0	(1,350)	—	—	—

a.   Ending depreciation taxable temporary difference (from Exhibit 18-13) × 0.30.
b. $6,000 operating loss carryforward (from Exhibit 18-13) × 0.30.
c.   [$6,000 carryforward − $3,800 ending depreciation temporary difference (from Exhibit 18-13)] × 0.30.
d. $4,500 operating loss carryforward × 0.30.
e.   ($4,500 carryforward − $4,500 ending depreciation temporary difference) × 0.30.

At the end of 2004, the $6,000 operating loss carryforward results in an ending deferred tax asset of $1,800 ($6,000 × 0.30). Since there was a $0 deferred tax asset at the beginning of 2004, the company makes an $1,800 adjustment (debit) to the deferred tax asset. A valuation allowance is required at the end of 2004 because the company does not expect to be profitable in future years. However, the valuation allowance does not have to be for the full amount of the deferred tax asset resulting from the operating loss carryforward. This is because the company has an existing depreciation temporary difference that will result in additional future taxable income against which to offset the operating loss carryforward. Since the operating loss carryforward is $6,000, but the total ending depreciation taxable temporary difference is $3,800 at the end of 2004 (see Exhibit 18-13), a valuation allowance of only $660 [($6,000 − $3,800) × 0.30] is required and the company makes an adjustment (credit) for that amount.

At the end of 2005 the company has a $1,350 deferred tax asset ($4,500 operating loss carryforward × 0.30), which requires a $450 adjustment (credit) to that account. Since the $4,500 total ending depreciation taxable temporary difference is the same as the $4,500 remaining operating loss carryforward, it does not need a valuation allowance. This requires an adjustment (debit) of $660 to the valuation allowance account. In 2006 the company uses the $4,500 remaining operating loss carryforward to offset an equal amount of taxable income, so it eliminates (credits) the $1,350 related deferred tax asset.

At the end of each year, the company prepares a journal entry to record its income taxes, based on the information in Exhibits 18-12 and 18-14. For instance, at the end of 2004, it makes the following journal entry:

Income Tax Refund Receivable	840	
Deferred Tax Asset	1,800	
Deferred Tax Liability		240
Allowance to Reduce Deferred Tax Asset to		
Realizable Value		660
Income Tax Benefit from Operating Loss Carryback		840
Income Tax Benefit from Operating Loss Carryforward		900

The $840 income tax benefit from the operating loss carryback relates to the income tax refund receivable. The $900 income tax benefit from the operating loss carryforward is the net amount that the company will realize in future years and that is related to the deferred tax asset, valuation allowance, and deferred tax liability.

The company reports operating loss carryback and carryforward tax benefits on its 2004 income statement as follows:

Pretax operating loss		$(8,000)
Less: Income tax benefit from operating loss carryback	$840	
Income tax benefit from operating loss carryforward	900	1,740
Net loss		$(6,260)

The company discloses the remaining operating loss carryforwards in 2004 and 2005 in a note accompanying the respective year's financial statements.

INTRAPERIOD INCOME TAX ALLOCATION

Intraperiod income tax allocation is the apportionment of a corporation's total income tax expense for a period to the various components of its income statement (and occasionally the statement of retained earnings, statement of comprehensive income, or statement of changes in stockholders' equity). Income tax allocation within a period is mandatory under generally accepted accounting principles. *APB Opinion No. 9* requires an allocation of the income tax effects to extraordinary items and to prior period adjustments, *APB Opinion No. 20* requires an allocation of the income tax consequences of the cumulative effects of changes in accounting principles, and *APB Opinion No. 30* requires an allocation of the income tax effects to a disposal of a segment of a business. *FASB Statement No. 109* and *FASB Statement No. 130* continue these required disclosures and extend the disclosures to the income tax effects of gains and losses included in other comprehensive income.[16] When a corporation has these types of income, it apportions income taxes between them and income from continuing operations. The rationale behind intraperiod tax allocation is based on the matching concept. A corporation *matches* its income tax expense against the major components of its pretax income to give a fair presentation of the after-tax impact of each of these items on net income.

8 Apply intraperiod tax allocation.

For intraperiod income tax allocation purposes, on its income statement a corporation reports the income tax expense applicable to its pretax income from continuing operations separately. The disclosure of the tax effect on its income from continuing operations is important because external users are very interested in the corporation's business activities that are expected to continue. The amount is based on the normal income tax rates applied to this income. However, the corporation reports any extraordinary items, cumulative effects of changes in accounting principles, the income or loss from the operations of a discontinued component, the gain or loss from the disposal of a discontinued component, prior period adjustments (reported on the statement of retained earnings), and any other comprehensive income items *net* of the related income tax effects. That is, for these items, the corporation deducts the income tax expense (or tax "savings" which is called a tax *credit* in the case of a loss) directly from each item and reports only the *after-tax* amount. (It discloses the amount of the income tax expense or tax credit applicable to each of these items either parenthetically or in a note to its financial statements.) Because these items are considered to be "incremental," the corporation determines the amount of the income tax expense or tax credit applicable to each item by applying the marginal (incremental) tax rate to each item.

To illustrate, assume the Kalloway Company reports the following items of *pretax* financial (and taxable) "income" for 2004:

Income from continuing operations	
(revenues of $270,000 less expenses of $190,000)	$80,000
Gain on disposal of discontinued Division X	18,000
Loss from operations of discontinued Division X	(5,000)
Extraordinary loss from tornado	(10,000)
Cumulative effect of change in accounting principle	
(accelerated depreciation to straight line)	15,000
Prior period adjustment	
(error in calculating bad debt expense for 2003)	(8,000)
Amount subject to income taxes	$90,000

The company is subject to income tax rates of 20% on the first $50,000 of income and 30% on all income in excess of $50,000. Exhibit 18-15 illustrates the schedule to allocate the total income tax expense, and Exhibit 18-16 illustrates Kalloway Company's 2004 income statement and statement of retained earnings as a result of applying intraperiod income tax allocation.

As we show in Exhibit 18-15, the total income taxes for the Kalloway Company on the $90,000 subject to income taxes in 2004 are $22,000. The company computes the

---

16. Currently, there are four items of other comprehensive income, as we discussed in Chapter 4. For instance, when a company records a change in the unrealized increase (decrease) stockholders' equity account for investments in available-for-sale securities, this causes a change in the deferred tax liability (or asset). In the journal entry to record the change in the deferred tax liability (or asset), the offsetting entry is a reduction of the unrealized increase (decrease) account.

EXHIBIT 18-15 Schedule of Income Tax Expense for 2004

Component (Pretax)	Pretax Amount	×	Income Tax Rate	=	Income Tax Expense (Credit)
Income from continuing operations	{ $50,000	×	0.20	=	$10,000
	30,000	×	0.30	=	9,000
Gain on disposal of discontinued Division X	18,000	×	0.30	=	5,400
Loss from operations of discontinued Division X	(5,000)	×	0.30	=	(1,500)
Extraordinary loss from tornado	(10,000)	×	0.30	=	(3,000)
Cumulative effect of change in accounting principle on prior years' income	15,000	×	0.30	=	4,500
Prior period adjustment	(8,000)	×	0.30	=	(2,400)
Total income tax expense					$22,000

$19,000 [(0.20 × $50,000) + (0.30 × $30,000)] income tax expense applicable to its pretax income from continuing operations by multiplying this $80,000 income by the normal income tax rates. This provision for income tax does *not* consider the tax consequences of any items not included in pretax income from continuing operations. The company reports the $19,000 income tax expense applicable to pretax income from continuing operations on its income statement in Exhibit 18-16 on a separate line directly below pretax income from continuing operations, and subtracts this amount to determine its income from continuing operations. The company reports the gain on the disposal of the discontinued Division X, the loss from the operations of the discontinued Division X, the extraordinary loss, and the cumulative effect of the change in accounting principle *net of income tax* on its income statement in Exhibit 18-16, and discloses each related income tax effect in parentheses. It reports the prior period adjustment net of its income tax effect on the statement of retained earnings in Exhibit 18-16. The company computed each of the related income tax effects in Exhibit 18-15 by multiplying the marginal tax rate (30%) by the pretax gain or loss.[17] Kalloway Company makes the following journal entry to record its 2004 intraperiod income tax allocation:

Income Tax Expense	19,000	
Gain on Disposal of Division X	5,400	
Cumulative Effect of Change in Accounting Principle	4,500	
Loss from Operations of Discontinued Division X		1,500
Extraordinary Loss from Tornado		3,000
Retained Earnings (prior period adjustment)		2,400
Income Taxes Payable		22,000

Note that the debit to Income Tax Expense of $19,000 relates *only* to the income taxes applicable to income from continuing operations. Since the company reports its results of discontinued operations, extraordinary items, cumulative effects of changes in accounting principles, and prior period adjustments on the financial statements *net* of their respective income tax effects, it debits or credits the income tax expense or credit related to each of these items directly to the applicable account (as we show in the journal entry)

---

17. In our example only two tax rates were in effect, and the income from continuing operations was sufficiently large that the gain and losses were taxed at a single marginal rate. It is possible for several tax rates to be in effect at the same time, and for the total income to be increased or decreased by other gains and losses, so that more than one marginal tax rate may be applicable. In these cases, a corporation uses a weighted averaging process to determine the appropriate tax effects on the gains and losses. This process is beyond the scope of this book.

EXHIBIT 18-16   Kalloway Company

Income Statement
For Year Ended December 31, 2004

Revenues (listed separately)		$270,000
Expenses (listed separately)		(190,000)
Pretax income from continuing operations		$ 80,000
Income tax expense		(19,000)
Income from continuing operations		$ 61,000
Results of discontinued operations:		
Gain on disposal of discontinued Division X		
(net of $5,400 income taxes)	$ 12,600	
Loss from operations of discontinued Division X		
(net of $1,500 income tax credit)	(3,500)	9,100
Income before extraordinary loss		$ 70,100
Extraordinary loss from tornado (net of $3,000 income tax credit)		(7,000)
Cumulative effect of change in accounting principle		
(net of $4,500 income taxes)		10,500
Net Income		$ 73,600

Statement of Retained Earnings
For Year Ended December 31, 2004

Retained earnings, January 1, 2004	$435,000
Less: Prior period adjustment, understatement of 2003 bad debt expense	
(net of $2,400 income tax credit)	(5,600)
Adjusted retained earnings, January 1, 2004	$429,400
Add: Net income	73,600
	$503,000
Less: Cash dividends	(23,500)
Retained Earnings, December 31, 2004	$479,500

to reduce the account balance to its after-tax amount, as it reports in Exhibit 18-16. Note also, in this example, we assume that taxable income and pretax financial income are the same. If a corporation's taxable income is not the same as its pretax financial income because of temporary differences, the total income tax expense is the sum of the income tax obligation and the adjustments to the deferred tax liabilities and assets. In this situation, the corporation must determine the impact of the adjustments on each component of pretax financial income before it can properly allocate the income tax expense. In the case of adjustments of (1) a valuation allowance because of changes in circumstances, and (2) deferred tax liabilities and assets because of changes in tax rates or laws, the corporation includes the amounts of the adjustments in its income tax expense related to continuing operations.[18]

FINANCIAL STATEMENT PRESENTATION AND DISCLOSURES

In addition to requiring the intraperiod allocation of income taxes on a corporation's income statement (and statement of retained earnings, statement of changes in stockholders' equity, or statement of comprehensive income), *FASB Statement No. 109* specifies

---

18. *FASB Statement No. 109, op. cit.*, par. 35.

what is required for (1) presentation of deferred tax liabilities and assets on the corporation's balance sheet, and (2) disclosures in the notes to the corporation's financial statements.

Balance Sheet Presentation

A corporation must report its deferred tax liabilities and assets in two classifications: a *net* current amount and a *net* noncurrent amount. It bases these classifications on the classifications of the related assets or liabilities for financial reporting. For instance, a corporation reports a deferred tax liability related to the excess of tax depreciation over financial depreciation as a noncurrent liability because the depreciable assets are noncurrent assets. It classifies a deferred tax liability or asset not directly related to an asset or liability (e.g., related to an operating loss carryforward) according to the expected reversal date of the temporary difference. A valuation allowance is allocated between current and noncurrent deferred assets on a proportional basis.[19]

9 Classify deferred tax liabilities and assets.

In other words, a corporation must (1) separate its deferred tax liabilities into current and noncurrent groups, (2) separate its deferred tax assets into current and noncurrent groups, (3) combine (*net*) the amounts in the current groups, and (4) combine (*net*) the amounts in the noncurrent groups.[20] If the net amount of the current groups is a debit balance, the corporation reports the amount as a current asset, whereas it reports a net credit amount as a current liability. The corporation reports a net debit balance for the noncurrent groups as a noncurrent asset, and reports a net credit balance as a noncurrent liability. This procedure is one of the few situations in which "offsetting" of assets and liabilities is allowed in financial reporting. The FASB requires this approach because of the close relationship between deferred tax assets and liabilities, and to avoid the detailed analyses necessary for more refined classification methods.

To illustrate, assume that the Anicar Company has the four deferred tax items we show in Exhibit 18-17. In this situation, the company combines the $6,000 credit balance of the current deferred tax liability (Item 1) with the $3,400 debit balance of the current deferred tax asset (Item 3), and reports a $2,600 net deferred tax liability as a *current liability* on its year-end balance sheet. Likewise, the company combines the $12,000 credit balance of the noncurrent deferred tax liability (Item 2) with the $2,500 debit balance of the noncurrent deferred tax asset (Item 4), and reports a $9,500 net deferred tax liability as a *noncurrent liability* on its year-end balance sheet.

EXHIBIT 18-17 **Schedule of Deferred Assets and Liabilities**

Deferred Tax Accounts	Account Balance	Related Balance Sheet Account	Deferred Income Tax Reporting Classification
Deferred Tax Liabilities			
1. Installment sales	$ 6,000 credit	Accounts receivable	Current
2. Depreciation	12,000 credit	Property, plant, and equipment	Noncurrent
Deferred Tax Assets			
3. Warranty costs	3,400 debit	Warranty liability	Current
4. Rent revenue (long-term)	2,500 debit	Unearned rent	Noncurrent

---

19. *Ibid.*, par. 41.
20. This "offsetting" applies to each tax jurisdiction. Furthermore, a corporation may have some assets and liabilities (e.g., warranty liability) for which it classifies the portion due to be collected or paid in the next year as current and classifies the remainder as noncurrent. In such a case, it must also proportionally classify the related deferred tax liability or asset into current and noncurrent amounts.

Financial Statement Disclosures

To help users evaluate a corporation's income taxes, *FASB Statement No. 109* also requires extensive income tax disclosures in the notes to the corporation's financial statements (or directly on the statements themselves). In regard to the net deferred tax liability or asset that a corporation reports on its balance sheet, it discloses the causes of the deferred tax assets and liabilities, the total of all deferred tax liabilities, the total of all deferred tax assets, the total valuation allowance, and the net change in the valuation allowance. In conjunction with a corporation's income statement (and statement of retained earnings, statement of changes in stockholders' equity, or statement of comprehensive income), it discloses the components of income tax expense. This disclosure includes the amount of income tax expense or benefit allocated to continuing operations, discontinued operations, extraordinary items, the cumulative effect of accounting changes, prior period adjustments, and gains and losses included in other comprehensive income. Furthermore, it discloses the significant components of income tax expense related to continuing operations for each year. These components include, for instance, (1) current tax expense or benefit (i.e., income tax obligation or refund), (2) deferred tax expense or benefit, (3) tax credits, (4) benefits of operating loss carryforwards, (5) adjustments of a deferred tax liability or asset for enacted changes in tax laws or rates, and (6) adjustments of the valuation allowance for changes in circumstances.

A corporation also is required to make other income statement related disclosures. These include (1) a reconciliation of the income tax expense related to continuing operations to the income tax expense that would result from applying federal tax rates to pretax income from continuing operations, (2) identification of the nature and amount of each significant item in the previous reconciliation, and (3) the amounts and expiration dates of any operating loss and tax credit carryforwards for income tax purposes.[21]

The intraperiod allocation of income taxes on the face of a corporation's income statement (and statement of retained earnings, statement of changes in stockholders' equity, or statement comprehensive income), as we previously illustrated, partially satisfies the preceding disclosure requirements. A corporation typically discloses the remaining information in a note to its financial statements. We illustrate these disclosures in Exhibit 18-18 later in the chapter for Emerson Radio Corp.

MISCELLANEOUS ISSUES

The previous discussion and examples focused on the major issues involved in accounting for income taxes. For simplicity, we omitted a number of miscellaneous topics.

Change in Income Tax Laws or Rates

As we discussed earlier, a corporation determines the balances of its deferred tax liabilities (or assets) at the end of a given year by applying the currently enacted income tax rate(s) and laws to its taxable (or deductible) temporary differences. Occasionally, Congress may change the income tax laws or rates so that they differ from the laws or rates previously used to calculate the corporation's deferred tax liabilities (or assets). A corporation must disclose the financial impact of this congressional action because such a change is an event that has economic consequences to the corporation. That is, a corporation's financial condition improves if it owes a smaller amount of future taxes (or would receive a larger refund) and its condition weakens if it owes more future taxes (or would receive a smaller refund).

When a change in the income tax laws or rates occurs, a corporation adjusts the deferred tax liabilities (and assets) for the effect of the change. It makes the adjustment to the balance of each deferred tax liability (and asset) as of the beginning of the year in which the change is made, and includes the resulting tax effect in the income tax expense related to its income from continuing operations.[22] The amount of the adjustment

---

21. *Ibid.*, par. 43–48.
22. *Ibid.*, par. 27.

is the difference between the deferred tax liability (or asset) balance at the beginning of the year, based on the newly enacted laws or rates, and the balance that was computed under the old law or rates.

For instance, refer back to Example 1 (page 839) for a deferred tax liability. If, in May 2005, Congress increases the income tax rate from 30% to 35%, then Track Company's deferred tax liability at the end of 2004 should be $140 ($400 × 0.35) instead of $120, as we previously computed. Therefore, the company increases the deferred tax liability and recognizes a tax effect in the amount of $20 ($140 − $120). In May 2005 the company records the increase and recognizes the expense as follows:

Income Tax Expense	20	
Deferred Tax Liability		20

The company increases the income tax expense related to income from continuing operations by $20 on its 2005 income statement, and reports the deferred tax liability at a credit balance of $140. At the end of 2005 the company computes its deferred taxes in the usual manner, except that it uses the newly enacted 35% income tax rate. A change in the balance of a valuation allowance—because of changes in circumstances concerning the future realization of a deferred tax asset—is recorded and reported in a similar fashion.

Investment Tax Credit

To encourage investment in productive facilities, Congress has permitted corporations to deduct a specified percentage of the cost of certain depreciable assets directly from their income taxes payable in the year in which the assets were acquired. This deduction, known as the **investment tax credit,** was first introduced in 1962 and has been suspended and reenacted at various times. The Tax Reform Act of 1986 suspended this credit, although there has been some discussion about its possible renewal on a permanent basis for small companies and on a temporary basis for large companies.

For financial reporting purposes, a corporation could account for the investment tax credit by either the deferred method or the flow-through method. **APB Opinion No. 2** required use of the deferred method. Under the **deferred method,** the investment tax credit was considered to be a reduction in the effective cost of the asset, and a corporation recognized the tax benefit by reducing its depreciation expense over the life of the asset. In response to political pressure, **APB Opinion No. 4,** allowing use of the flow-through method, was issued. Under the **flow-through method,** a corporation recognized the total tax benefit in the year of acquisition by reducing its income tax expense for the amount of the investment tax credit.

Although the flow-through method violated the matching principle, most corporations used this method because it resulted in an immediate increase in earnings. Corporations that use the deferred method show a reduced cost of their assets for financial reporting purposes, resulting in a temporary difference in regard to depreciation. This temporary difference is accounted for in the same manner as the other temporary differences we discussed earlier in the chapter.[23] Because few corporations still have investment tax credits, we do not discuss them further.

Alternative Minimum Tax and Other Tax Credits

The Tax Reform Act of 1986 imposed an *alternative minimum tax* (AMT) on corporations, designed to help ensure equity in income tax payments. A corporation pays the higher of its AMT (as computed according to the income tax laws) or its regular income tax liability. Thus, the AMT may affect the corporation's income tax obligation in a given year. The AMT also may affect the corporation's deferred tax liability or asset because calculation of the AMT depends, in part, on "adjusted current earnings (ACE)"

---

23. *Ibid.*, par. 117.

adjustments related to certain temporary differences. Furthermore, if a corporation pays the AMT, generally it can credit the amount paid against its future income taxes. The corporation uses this credit in a given future year when the regular tax liability exceeds the AMT. It may not carryback the minimum tax credit, but may carry it forward indefinitely.

The federal tax law also allows certain other "tax credits" that a corporation may deduct from its computed income taxes to determine the income taxes it owes. Among the tax credits that are, or have been, in the tax law are credits for certain research and experimental activities, for foreign taxes paid, for hiring certain employees, and for using certain fuels. To illustrate a foreign tax credit, assume the following situation for a corporation (amounts in millions):

	U.S.	Foreign
Taxable income	$100	$ 20
Tax rate (assumed)	0.35	0.40
Income taxes payable	$ 35	$ 8

On its U.S. income tax return, the corporation reports a total taxable income of $120 ($100 + $20), receiving a foreign tax credit based on the foreign taxes paid. However, the amount of the foreign tax credit cannot exceed an amount equal to the U.S. income tax imposed on the foreign-source income. Therefore, its foreign tax credit is the lesser of $8, the foreign tax imposed, or $7 ($20 × 35%), the U.S. tax imposed on foreign income. The corporation pays $35 [($120 × 35%) − $7] to the U.S. government. However, it pays total income tax of $43 ($35 + $8), which is also its income tax expense (assuming there are no temporary differences). In the notes to its financial statements, the corporation discloses that there is a difference between the statutory tax rate in the U.S. of 35% and its effective tax rate of 36% ($43 ÷ $120).

As we illustrated, specific restrictions apply to tax credits, and sometimes a corporation cannot use all of its tax credits in a given year. In certain circumstances, the corporation may carry forward these tax credits and apply them against future taxes owed in a manner similar to operating loss carryforwards. When this arises, the steps we outlined earlier in the chapter for computing a corporation's deferred taxes must be modified to include measurement of a deferred tax asset for each type of tax credit. Because the AMT and tax credits are complex and vary across corporations, we do not discuss them further.

International Accounting Differences

The international accounting principles for deferred income taxes differ in certain respects from those in the United States. Recall that *FASB Statement No. 109* requires comprehensive income tax allocation of temporary differences using the asset/liability method. International Accounting Standards require a company to use comprehensive allocation (in most cases) of temporary differences using the "balance sheet liability method" (which is very similar to the asset/liability method). However, there are differences between U.S. and International GAAP. For instance, in regard to deferred tax assets, International Accounting Standards allow a company to recognize a deferred tax asset only when it is *probable* that it will have sufficient future taxable income against which to utilize the deferred tax asset. In regard to deferred tax liabilities, a company recognizes a deferred tax liability if it revalues its assets. The measurement of a company's deferred tax assets and liabilities is based on future tax rates as well as how the tax laws of the country in which it is located allow it to recover or settle the deferred tax asset or liability.

International Accounting Standards require a company to report the income tax expense related to its pretax income from ordinary activities as a separate line item on its income statement and to show extraordinary items net of tax. It reports the tax effects of any equity adjustments (e.g., asset revaluations) directly in equity. A company is required to report its deferred tax balances as separate items on its balance sheet. However, in certain instances it may offset any debit and credit balances representing deferred tax items. It may *not* report deferred tax assets or liabilities as current items.

ILLUSTRATIVE DISCLOSURES

Exhibit 18-18 shows the 2001 income tax disclosures (in part) of Emerson Radio Corp. These disclosures are representative of the type necessary under the generally accepted accounting principles of *FASB Statement No. 109.*

EXHIBIT 18-18   Income Tax Disclosures

EMERSON RADIO CORP.
(in thousands)

Income Statement (in part):

	Years Ended March 31	
	2001	2000
Income before income taxes	$11,709	$3,043
Provision (benefit) for income taxes	(944)	(577)
Net income	$12,653	$3,620

Balance Sheet (in part):

	March 31	
	2001	2000
Assets		
Current Assets (in part):		
Deferred tax assets	$ 1,419	$ —
Noncurrent Assets (in part):		
Deferred tax assets	4,081	—
Current Liabilities (in part):		
Income taxes payable	481	135

Notes to Consolidated Financial Statements (in part):
Note 7--Income Taxes (in part)

The income tax (benefit) provision for the years ended March 31, 2001 [and] March 31, 2000 . . . consisted of the following:

	2001	2000
Current:		
Federal	$ 475	$ 47
Foreign, state and other	848	(624)
Deferred federal	(2,267)	—
	$ (944)	$ (577)

The Company, with the exception of SSG, files a consolidated federal and certain state and local income tax returns.

The difference between the effective rate reflected in the provision for income taxes and the amounts determined by applying the statutory U.S. rate of 34% to income before income taxes for the years ended March 31, 2001 [and] March 31, 2000 . . . are analyzed below:

	2001	2000
Statutory provision	$ 3,981	$1,035
Decrease in valuation allowance	(5,246)	(1,306)
Foreign income taxes	478	(642)
State taxes	723	183
Minority interest	(1,211)	—
Alternative minimum tax	305	47
Other, net	26	106
Total income tax (benefit) provision	$ (944)	$ (577)

(continued)

EXHIBIT 18-18,   Continued

Emerson Radio (Hong Kong) Ltd., was assessed $858,000 by the Hong Kong Inland Revenue Department (the "IRD") in May 1998. The assessment related to the fiscal 1993 through fiscal 1998 tax years and asserted that certain revenues reported as non-taxable by Emerson Radio (Hong Kong) Ltd. were subject to a profits tax. In fiscal 1999, the Company accrued $256,000 equaling its compromise offer, and in June 1999, the IRD accepted the offer in which the Company and the IRD settled, without prejudice, the assessment for $256,000.

Emerson Radio (Hong Kong) Ltd. was also in litigation with the IRD regarding the deductibility of certain expenses that related to the fiscal 1992 through fiscal 1999 tax years. In December 1999, the Company received a favorable ruling from the Hong Kong Court of Final Appeals regarding this matter and a tax credit of $619,000 was recorded in the Company's financial results for Fiscal 2000.

As of March 31, 2001 and 2000, the significant components of the Company's deferred tax assets and liabilities are as follows:

	2001	2000
Deferred tax assets:	(In thousands)	
Accounts receivable reserves	$ 5,345	$ 5,243
Inventory reserves	1,359	235
Net operating loss carryforwards	28,066	29,717
Other	1,311	491
Total deferred tax assets	36,081	35,686
Valuation allowance for deferred tax assets	(26,452)	(33,844)
Net deferred tax assets	9,629	1,842
Deferred tax liabilities:		
Intangible assets	(2,921)	—
Investment in affiliate	(969)	(1,479)
Other	(239)	(363)
Net deferred taxes	$ 5,500	$ —

Total deferred tax assets for the consumer electronics segment at March 31, 2001 and 2000 include the tax-effected net operating loss carryforwards subject to annual limitations (as discussed below) and tax-effected deductible temporary differences. A valuation reserve has been established for the consumer electronics segment against any expected future benefits as management believes it is not more likely than not that such benefit will be realized in the future.

The sporting goods segment has net operating loss carryforwards that can be used to offset future taxable income and can be carried forward for 15 to 20 years. No valuation allowance has been recorded for the deferred tax assets because management believes it is more likely than not such assets will be realized by future profitable operating results.

Income of foreign subsidiaries before taxes was $7,486,000, $1,578,000, and $1,492,000 for the years ended March 31, 2001 [and] March 31, 2000 respectively.

As of March 31, 2001, the Company had a federal net operating loss carryforward of approximately $115,500,000, which will expire in 2006 through 2019. The utilization of these net operating losses are subject to limitations under IRC section 382. In addition, SSG has federal net operating loss carryforwards of approximately $20,044,000, which will expire in the years 2011 through 2021.

Q U E S T I O N S

ⓠ What does the company call its income tax expense? ⓠ How much of the provision (benefit) for income taxes shown on the 2001 income statement is currently payable and how much is deferred? ⓠ Does the schedule of deferred tax assets (liabilities) shown in Note 7 reconcile to the deferred tax items shown on the balance sheet? ⓠ Does the company have an operating loss carryback or carry forward?

APPENDIX: ADDITIONAL CONCEPTUAL ISSUES CONCERNING INTERPERIOD INCOME TAX ALLOCATION

As we noted earlier in the chapter, there has been much debate about the various issues regarding interperiod income tax allocation. This Appendix discusses the primary arguments involved in each issue.

10 Discuss the additional conceptual issues concerning interperiod income tax allocation (Appendix).

ALLOCATION VERSUS NONALLOCATION

The first issue involves allocation versus nonallocation. Some people argue that the amount of income tax expense that a corporation reports on its income statement should be the same as its income tax obligation for the accounting period (as the corporation computed on its income tax return). Under this approach, there would be *no* interperiod allocation of income tax expense. This approach is not widely held, however, for the following reasons[24] in favor of interperiod income tax allocation: (1) income taxes are the result of a given transaction or event. As a result, a corporation's income tax expense should be based on the results of the transactions or events that it includes in its pretax financial income and should not be related to its taxable income; (2) income taxes are an expense of doing business and should involve the same accrual, deferral, and estimation concepts that a corporation applies to other expenses; (3) interperiod tax allocation makes a corporation's net income a more relevant measure of its long-term earning power and avoids periodic income distortions resulting from income tax regulations; (4) nonallocation of a corporation's income tax expense hinders the prediction of its future cash flows. For instance, a corporation's future cash outflows for warranty payments would usually be offset by reduced outflows for income taxes; and (5) a corporation is a going concern, and income taxes that are currently deferred will eventually have to be paid.

COMPREHENSIVE VERSUS PARTIAL ALLOCATION

The next issue involves whether this allocation should be applied on a comprehensive or partial allocation basis. **Under comprehensive allocation, the income tax expense that a corporation reports in an accounting period is affected by all the transactions and events that it includes in determining its pretax financial income for that period.** This approach is required by *FASB Statement No. 109* and considers the impact on income tax expense of *all* temporary differences, regardless of how significant or recurrent, during the period in which they may affect income taxes payable. A corporation recognizes the tax effect for *each individual* temporary difference when it originates, and defers and allocates the effect to the period or periods when the difference reverses. An originating temporary difference is analogous to an unpaid accounts receivable or accounts payable invoice; when the difference reverses, it is collected or paid.

In contrast, **under partial allocation, the income tax expense that a corporation reports in an accounting period is affected only by those temporary differences that it expects to reverse in the foreseeable future.** That is, in certain cases under partial allocation, groups of similar, recurring transactions or events continually may create originating differences in the future that will offset any reversing differences, resulting in an indefinite postponement of deferred tax payments. In effect, these types of temporary differences are more like permanent differences. Examples of these temporary differences include depreciation for manufacturing companies with large amounts of depreciable assets, and bad debts for financial institutions.

---

24. The discussion in this Appendix is primarily a summary of the discussion presented in "Accounting for Income Taxes," *FASB Discussion Memorandum* (Stamford, Conn.: FASB, 1983), and D. Beresford, L. Best, P. Craig, and J. Weber, "Accounting for Income Taxes: A Review of Alternatives," *FASB Research Report* (Stamford, Conn.: FASB, 1983).

For instance, consider depreciation. On a particular piece of equipment, assume a corporation uses MACRS depreciation for income tax purposes and straight-line depreciation for financial reporting purposes. In the early life of the equipment, MACRS depreciation is higher than straight-line, resulting in lower current income taxes payable for the corporation and a deferral of income taxes. In the equipment's later life, the difference in depreciation reverses and, *everything else held constant*, the corporation pays the income taxes deferred earlier. The point is that seldom is "everything else held constant." Most manufacturing companies have numerous pieces of equipment that they are continually replacing (generally at a higher price); most companies are expanding, requiring additional investments in depreciable assets. In these situations, the originating depreciation differences (that is, MACRS depreciation in excess of straight-line) on these newer assets offset the reversing depreciation differences for the older assets. Thus, when a corporation is maintaining or increasing its investment in depreciable assets, and these assets are *viewed as a group*, it will never pay taxes deferred from earlier periods in regard to this group.

Comprehensive income tax allocation is more widely accepted for the following reasons:

1. Individual temporary differences do reverse. By definition, a temporary difference cannot be permanent; the offsetting effect of future events should not be assumed. It is inappropriate to look at the effect of a group of temporary differences on a corporation's income taxes. Instead, the focus should be on the *individual* items comprising the group. Temporary differences should be viewed in the same manner as accounts payable. That is, although the total balance of accounts payable may not change, many individual credit and payment transactions affect the total.

2. Accounting is primarily historical. It is inappropriate for a corporation to offset the income tax effects of possible future transactions against the tax effects of transactions that have already occurred.

3. A corporation should report the income tax effects of temporary differences in the same period that it includes the related transactions and events in its pretax financial income.

4. Accounting results should not be subject to manipulation by management. That is, a corporation's management should not be able to alter the corporation's results of operations and ending financial position by arbitrarily deciding what temporary differences will and will not reverse in the future.[25]

ALTERNATIVE ALLOCATION METHODS

The third issue relates to the application of interperiod income tax allocation. Three methods have been advocated. These are: (1) the asset/liability method, (2) the deferred method, and (3) the net-of-tax method. They are closely linked to the income tax rates that a corporation uses to report its deferred taxes.

The asset/liability method is balance sheet-oriented and is required by *FASB Statement No. 109*. The intent is to require a corporation to accrue and report the total tax that it actually will be assessed on temporary differences when they reverse. A temporary difference is viewed as causing either a tax liability that the corporation will pay in the future or a tax asset that will result in a decrease in its future tax payments at the then current tax rates. **Under the asset/liability method, the deferred tax amount that a corporation reports on its balance sheet is the effect of temporary differences that will reverse in the future and that it measures using the currently enacted income tax rates and laws that will be in existence when the temporary differences reverse.** The corporation makes adjustments, however, to the deferred tax amount for any changes in the income tax rates or laws that are later enacted. In general, deferred taxes under the asset/liability method more closely meet

---

25. For counter arguments, see *Ibid.*, par. 124–144 and pp. 38–40.

the conceptual definitions of assets and liabilities established in *FASB Statement of Concepts No. 6*. Arguments in favor of the asset/liability method of interperiod tax allocation include the following:

1. A corporation's balance sheet is an important financial statement. Reporting deferred taxes based upon the enacted future tax rates when the temporary differences will reverse increases the predictive value of the corporation's future cash flows, liquidity, and financial flexibility.

2. As we discussed earlier, reporting deferred taxes based upon enacted future tax rates is conceptually more sound because the amount represents either a corporation's likely future economic sacrifice (future tax payments) or its economic benefit (future reduction in taxes).

3. A corporation's deferred taxes may be the result of historical transactions but, by definition, they are taxes that are postponed and will be paid (or will reduce taxes) in the future at the enacted future tax rates.

4. Estimates are used extensively in accounting. The use of enacted future tax rates for a corporation's deferred taxes creates information that is, perhaps, more reliable than depreciation based on estimated lives and residual values.[26]

The deferred method is income statement-oriented and was the method required under *APB Opinion No. 11*. The intent is to match a corporation's expenses against revenues in the determination of its current net income, and to spread the tax benefit (or cost) of originating temporary differences over the future periods in which the differences reverse. In applying the deferred method, a corporation's income tax expense in a period includes the income tax effects of all the revenues and expenses it recognized in pretax financial income. Essentially, the difference between its income tax expense and income taxes payable is called a deferred tax credit or deferred tax charge and the corporation reports this amount on the balance sheet. **Under the deferred method, the deferred tax amount that a corporation reports on its balance sheet is the effect of temporary differences that will reverse in the future and that it measures using the income tax rates and laws in effect when the differences originated.** The corporation makes no adjustments to deferred taxes for changes in the income tax rates or tax laws that occur after the period of origination. When the deferrals reverse, it records the reversal at the rates in existence *when the temporary differences originated.* Thus, under the deferred method, deferred taxes are not receivables or payables in a theoretical sense. They do not meet the conceptual definitions of assets or liabilities established in *FASB Statement of Concepts No. 6* because they are not measurements of probable future economic benefits or sacrifices. A corporation's deferred taxes simply represent the cumulative effects of temporary differences waiting to be adjusted in the matching process of some future accounting period. Thus, most people are not in favor of the deferred method of interperiod tax allocation.[27]

The net-of-tax method is more a method of disclosure than a different method of calculating deferred taxes. Under this method, a corporation computes the income tax effect of any temporary difference using either the enacted future tax rate for the period when the temporary difference reverses (asset/liability method) or the tax rate in effect when the temporary difference originated (deferred method). It does not separately disclose the resulting deferred taxes, however, on its balance sheet. Instead, **under the net-of-tax method a corporation treats the deferred tax assets (charges) or deferred tax liabilities (credits) as adjustments to the accounts to which the temporary differences**

---

26. A further refinement of reporting deferred taxes under the asset/liability method is to use a present value approach. That is, a corporation would report deferred taxes at their discounted amounts. Proponents of this approach argue that discounted amounts are considered to be the most appropriate indicators of future cash flows. Critics of discounting argue that discounting would conceal a corporation's actual tax burden by reporting as interest expense the discount factor that it would otherwise report as part of its income tax expense.

27. For arguments in favor of the deferred method, see *op. cit.*, par. 84–90 and pp. 54 and 59.

relate. Generally, the corporation adjusts the accounts through the use of valuation allowances rather than directly. For instance, if a temporary difference results from additional tax depreciation, it would subtract the related tax effect (by means of a valuation account) from the cost of the asset (along with accumulated depreciation) to determine the carrying value of the depreciable asset. Or it would reduce the carrying value of a warranty liability for the expected decrease in income taxes when the warranty is paid (and is a tax deduction). It would reduce the valuation allowance accounts for reversals of temporary differences. The net-of-tax method has very little support because it is very complex to use and distorts traditional concepts for measuring assets and liabilities.

SUMMARY

At the beginning of the chapter, we identified several objectives you would accomplish after reading the chapter. The objectives are listed below, each followed by a brief summary of the key points in the chapter discussion.

1. **Understand permanent and temporary differences.** A *permanent* difference is a difference between pretax financial income and taxable income in an accounting period, that will never reverse in a later accounting period. A *temporary* difference is a difference between the tax basis of an asset (or liability) and the financial statement reported amount of the asset (or liability) that will result in taxable or deductible amounts in future years when the reported amount of the asset is recovered (or the liability is settled).

2. **Explain the conceptual issues regarding interperiod tax allocation.** Conceptually, there are two objectives of income tax reporting. The first is that a corporation should recognize the amount of its income tax obligation (or refund) for the current year. The second is that the corporation should recognize deferred tax liabilities and assets for the future tax consequences of all events that it has recognized in its financial statements or income tax returns.

3. **Record and report deferred tax liabilities.** Measure the ending deferred tax liability for each taxable temporary difference using the applicable tax rate. Record the increase (or decrease) in the deferred tax liability. Report the ending deferred tax liability as a current or noncurrent liability on the ending balance sheet.

4. **Record and report deferred tax assets.** Measure the ending deferred tax asset for each deductible temporary difference using the applicable tax rate. Record the increase (or decrease) in the deferred tax asset. Report the ending deferred tax asset as a current or noncurrent asset on the ending balance sheet. Reduce the deferred tax asset by a valuation allowance when appropriate.

5. **Explain an operating loss carryback and carryforward.** An operating loss *carryback* occurs when a corporation carries back a current year operating loss to offset any taxable income in the previous 2 years. An operating loss *carryforward* occurs when a corporation's taxable income for the previous 2 years is not enough to offset the amount of the current year operating loss, so that it carries forward the loss to offset any future taxable income over the next 20 years.

6. **Account for an operating loss carryback.** Determine the amount of pretax financial (and taxable) income, as well as the income taxes paid in the previous 2 years. Carry back the pretax operating loss of the current year to the previous years and offset the previous pretax financial (and taxable) income. Report the resulting income tax refund of the income taxes previously paid as a receivable on the balance sheet and subtract the income tax benefit due to the carryback from the pretax operating loss on the income statement.

7. **Account for an operating loss carryforward.** Recognize the tax benefit of an operating loss carryforward in the current year as a deferred tax asset. Determine the amount by multiplying the current income tax rate times the pretax operating loss. Establish a valuation allowance for the amount of the deferred tax asset that the corporation is not likely to realize.

8. **Apply intraperiod tax allocation.** Report the income tax expense applicable to pretax income from continuing operations separately on the income statement, basing the expense on the normal income tax rates. Report any results of discontinued operations, extraordinary items, cumulative effects of changes in accounting principles, and prior period adjustments net of the income tax effects (with each related income tax effect reported in parentheses).

9. **Classify deferred tax liabilities and assets.** A corporation reports its deferred tax liabilities and assets in two classifications, a *net* current amount and a *net* noncurrent amount. To do so, it separates its deferred tax liabilities and deferred tax assets into current and noncurrent groups, and then combines (nets) the amounts in the current groups and the noncurrent groups.

10. **Discuss the additional conceptual issues concerning interperiod income tax allocation (Appendix).** Briefly, the additional conceptual issues include allocation versus nonallocation, comprehensive versus partial allocation, and alternative allocation methods (including the asset/liability method, deferred method, and net-of-tax method).

QUESTIONS

Q18-1 Distinguish between the objectives of financial reporting and the Internal Revenue Code.

Q18-2 Identify the five groups of possible differences between pretax financial income and taxable income (or between income tax expense and income taxes payable).

Q18-3 What is a permanent difference? Give two examples.

Q18-4 What is a temporary difference? Give two examples.

Q18-5 What did the FASB conclude in *FASB Statement No. 109* regarding interperiod income tax allocation?

Q18-6 What are the two objectives of accounting for income taxes identified in *FASB Statement No. 109?*

Q18-7 How does a corporation determine its deferred taxes under generally accepted accounting principles?

Q18-8 What are the three essential characteristics of a liability and why does a deferred tax liability of a corporation meet these characteristics?

Q18-9 What are the three essential characteristics of an asset and why does a deferred tax asset of a corporation meet these characteristics?

Q18-10 When does a corporation establish a valuation allowance? List the four sources of taxable income that might be used to justify that a valuation allowance is not needed.

Q18-11 List the steps necessary to measure and record a corporation's current and deferred income taxes.

Q18-12 Describe an operating loss carryback. List the two conceptual questions concerning accounting for a carryback.

Q18-13 Describe an operating loss carryforward. List the two conceptual questions concerning accounting for a carryforward.

Q18-14 Briefly summarize the generally accepted accounting principles for the financial reporting of operating loss carrybacks and carryforwards.

Q18-15 What is intraperiod income tax allocation? How is income tax expense reported on a corporation's income statement and retained earnings statement?

Q18-16 How are deferred tax liabilities and assets reported on a corporation's balance sheet?

Q18-17 Briefly describe the adjustment of a deferred tax liability (or asset) and the related income statement disclosure for a change in the income tax rate.

Q18-18 (Appendix). What is interperiod income tax allocation? List the reasons in favor of interperiod income tax allocation.

Q18-19 (Appendix). What is comprehensive interperiod tax allocation? List the reasons in favor of this allocation.

Q18-20 (Appendix). What are the three methods of interperiod tax allocation? *Briefly* describe each method.

CASES

C O M M U N I C A T I O N

C18-1 Asset/Liability Method and Temporary Differences

Interperiod tax allocation is necessary because there are differences in the timing of revenues and expenses between a corporation's financial statements and its federal income tax returns.

Required
1. Identify the two goals and four basic principles of accounting for income taxes.

2. Briefly explain interperiod income tax allocation under generally accepted accounting principles.
3. List the four groups of items that result in temporary differences and give examples for each group.

C18-2 Operating Losses

The Internal Revenue Code allows a corporation to carry back or carry forward an "operating loss" for a given year.

Required

1. Describe an operating loss carryback and a carryforward.
2. For a carryback, identify and briefly explain the two important conceptual questions.
3. For a carryforward, identify and briefly explain the two important conceptual questions.
4. Briefly summarize the generally accepted accounting principles for the financial reporting of (a) an operating loss carryback and (b) an operating loss carryforward.

C18-3 Intraperiod Tax Allocation

Income tax allocation is an integral part of generally accepted accounting principles. Income tax allocation consists of both intraperiod and interperiod tax allocation.

Required

1. Explain the difference between interperiod and intraperiod income tax allocation.
2. Explain how a corporation discloses its income tax expense (or credit) for the year under intraperiod allocation.
3. Provide an example of intraperiod tax allocation on a corporation's income statement that includes income from continuing operations, a loss from the sale of a discontinued component, a gain from the operations of the discontinued component, and an extraordinary gain. Assume a 30% tax rate.

C18-4 Interperiod Tax Allocation (Appendix)

A friend in a business policy class says, "I always thought the income taxes reported on a corporation's income statement were the same as the income taxes paid during that period. Now I am not so sure because some other students mentioned interperiod income tax allocation. Furthermore, I have heard about comprehensive and partial allocation. I am confused. Please explain this to me."

Required Prepare a written response for your friend. In your discussion be sure to compare interperiod income tax allocation with nonallocation, and comprehensive allocation with partial allocation. Include the reasons for interperiod allocation and comprehensive allocation.

C18-5 Methods of Interperiod Tax Allocation (Appendix)

Three methods of interperiod income tax allocation have been advocated. These include (1) the asset/liability method, (2) the deferred method, and (3) the net-of-tax method.

Required Define *interperiod income tax allocation* and briefly explain the three methods that have been advocated, including the reasons cited for the asset/liability method. Conclude by summarizing the generally accepted accounting principles for interperiod income tax allocation.

C R E A T I V E   A N D   C R I T I C A L   T H I N K I N G

C18-6 Permanent and Temporary Differences

To implement interperiod income tax allocation, an accountant must be able to distinguish between permanent and temporary differences. The following is a list of three differences between a corporation's pretax financial income and taxable income:

a. Estimated warranty costs (covering a 3-year warranty) are expensed for financial reporting purposes at the time of sale but are deducted for tax purposes when incurred.
b. MACRS depreciation for income tax purposes exceeds straight-line depreciation for financial reporting purposes.
c. Percentage depletion for tax purposes exceeds cost depletion for financial reporting purposes.

Required

1. Define (a) *permanent difference* and (b) *temporary difference*.
2. Define *interperiod income tax allocation* and briefly describe its application under generally accepted accounting principles.
3. Indicate and explain whether each of the three differences listed in this case should be treated as a temporary or permanent difference.

C18-7 Deferred Tax Assets and Liabilities

A friend says to you, "I don't understand how taxable temporary differences can be 'liabilities' and how deductible temporary differences can be 'assets.' It seems to me that these temporary differences relate only to the future, and that accounting is based on 'historical cost.' Furthermore, the government frequently changes the tax laws, so no one knows what the future tax laws will be."

Required Prepare a written response for your friend that explains why deferred tax assets and deferred tax liabilities are recognized and reported on a corporation's balance sheet. Include a discussion of a valuation allowance.

C18-8 Interperiod Tax Allocation

Chris Green, CPA, is auditing Rayne Co.'s 2004 financial statements. For the year ended December 31, 2004, Rayne is applying *Statement of Financial Accounting Standards No. 109*, "Accounting for Income Taxes." Rayne's controller, Dunn, has prepared a schedule of all differences between financial statement and income tax return income. Dunn believes that as a result of pending legislation, the enacted tax rate at December 31, 2004 will be increased for 2005. Dunn is uncertain which differences to include and which rates to apply in computing deferred taxes under *FASB 109*. Dunn has requested an overview of *FASB 109* from Green.

Required Prepare a brief memo to Dunn from Green that identifies the objectives of accounting for income taxes, defines temporary differences, explains how to measure deferred tax assets and liabilities, and explains how to measure deferred income tax expense or benefit. (*AICPA adapted*)

C18-9 Analyzing Coca-Cola's Income Tax Disclosures

Refer to the financial statements and related notes of the Coca-Cola Company in Appendix A of this book.

Required

1. What was the total income tax expense relating to income before income taxes for 2001? How much of this was current? How much was deferred?
2. What were the total deferred tax assets at the end of 2001? Total deferred tax liabilities? Net deferred tax liability?
3. How much was the noncurrent deferred tax asset at the end of 2001 and where was it reported? Noncurrent deferred tax liability?
4. How much were the operating loss carryforwards at the end of 2001? Over what time periods must these be utilized?

C18-10 Ethics and Deferred Taxes

It is the end of 2005, and the auditing firm for which you work is auditing the Weiss Company for the first time.

Prior to 2005, Weiss was audited by another firm. A substantial amount of Weiss Company's revenues for 2004 came from installment sales. Weiss has considerable property, plant, and equipment. It also has a large amount of debt outstanding, and one of the debt covenants is that the company maintain a 2.00 current ratio.

You have been reviewing the deferred taxes of Weiss at the end of 2005. On its preliminary ending balance sheet for 2005, Weiss has included a noncurrent deferred tax liability of $45,000. On its ending 2004 balance sheet, Weiss had also reported a noncurrent deferred tax liability. Upon examining the calculations supporting the $45,000, you find that 1/3 relates to the receivables from the installment sales and 2/3 relates to the depreciation on the property, plant, and equipment. Nearly all of the 2004 deferred tax liability related to the latter.

Based on your analysis, you raise the issue with Weiss Company's controller about the possibility of reclassifying $15,000 of the deferred taxes as a current liability. The controller responds, "We have always listed our deferred taxes as a noncurrent liability. This was okay with our previous auditor. It just isn't worth the hassle of splitting the amount into current and noncurrent portions. It is clearly not material, since our total equity is over $400,000. Besides, if we did that it would bring our current ratio down to 1.95 and we would have our creditors on our backs. Everyone knows that deferred taxes are never really paid, so that is a good reason for not including the amount in our current liabilities."

Required From financial reporting and ethical perspectives, prepare a response to Weiss Company's controller.

MULTIPLE CHOICE

Select the best answer for each of the following.

M18-1 A permanent difference is a difference between pretax financial income and taxable income in an accounting period that will never reverse in a later period. Which of the following is *not* an example of a permanent difference?

    a. Fine for air pollution
    b. Percentage depletion in excess of cost depletion on a wasting asset
    c. Interest on municipal bonds
    d. Rent received in advance

M18-2 Prior to and during 2004, the Shadrach Company reported tax depreciation at an amount higher than the amount of financial depreciation, resulting in a book value of the depreciable assets of $24,500 for financial reporting purposes and of $20,000 for tax purposes at the end of 2004. In addition, the company recognized a $3,500 estimated liability for legal expenses in the financial statements during 2004; it expects to pay this liability (and deduct it for tax purposes) in 2008. The current tax rate is 30%, no change in the tax rate has been enacted, and

the company expects to be profitable in future years. What is the amount of the net noncurrent deferred tax liability at the end of 2004?

    a. $300   c. $1,050
    b. $450   d. $1,350

M18-3 Which of the following is an argument in favor of the asset/liability method of interperiod income tax allocation?

    a. Deferred taxes are the result of historical transactions and should be reported in a similar manner.
    b. Tax effects should be recorded in the same manner as all other revenue and expense transactions that involve changes in specific asset and liability accounts.
    c. The predictive value of future cash flows, liquidity, and financial flexibility are increased when deferred taxes are reported based upon enacted tax rates that will be in effect when the temporary differences reverse.
    d. Historical tax rates are more verifiable and, therefore, the deferred tax amount is more reliable.

M18-4 At the beginning of 2004, Conley Company purchased an asset at a cost of $10,000. For financial reporting purposes, the asset has a 4-year life with no residual value, and is depreciated by the straight-line method beginning in 2004. For tax purposes, the asset is depreciated under MACRS using a 5-year recovery period. Prior to 2004, the company had no deferred tax liability or asset. The difference between depreciation for financial reporting purposes and income tax purposes is the only temporary difference between pretax financial income and taxable income. The current income tax rate is 30% and no change in the tax rate has been enacted for future years. In 2004 and 2005, taxable income will be higher or lower than financial income by what amount?

	2004	2005
a.	Higher by $150	Lower by $210
b.	Higher by $500	Lower by $700
c.	Lower by $500	Higher by $700
d.	Lower by $1,500	Higher by $100

M18-5 Brooks Company reported a prior period adjustment of $12,000 in pretax financial "income" and taxable income for 2005. The prior period adjustment was the result of an error in calculating bad debt expense for 2004. The current tax rate is 30% and no change in the tax rate has been enacted for future years. When the company applies intraperiod income tax allocation, the prior period adjustment will be

a. Shown on the income statement at $12,000
b. Shown on the income statement at $8,400 (net of $3,600 income taxes)
c. Shown on the retained earnings statement at $12,000
d. Shown on the retained earnings statement at $8,400 (net of $3,600 income taxes)

M18-6 In 2004 Swope Company reports a pretax operating loss of $70,000 for both financial reporting and income tax purposes. Pretax financial income and taxable income for the previous 3 years had been: 2001—$15,000 (tax rate 20%); 2002—$24,000 (tax rate 25%); and 2003—$49,000 (tax rate 30%). The current tax rate is 30% and no change in the tax rate has been enacted for future years. At the end of 2004 the journal entry recorded would contain an income tax benefit from an operating loss carryback of

a. $0   c. $19,800
b. $18,300   d. $19,950

M18-7 *FASB Statement No. 109* came to which of the following conclusions regarding interperiod income tax allocation?

a. The partial allocation approach should be applied.
b. The net-of-tax method of income tax allocation should be used.
c. Nonallocation of income tax expense is appropriate.
d. The asset/liability method of income tax allocation should be used.

M18-8 Which of the following is *not* a cause of difference between pretax financial income and taxable income in a given period?

a. Operating loss carrybacks and carryforwards
b. Permanent differences
c. Applicable tax rates
d. Temporary differences

M18-9 Which component of current income is not disclosed on the income statement net of tax effects?

a. Extraordinary loss from flood
b. Gain on disposal of milling machine
c. Cumulative effect of change in accounting principle
d. Loss from operations of discontinued component

M18-10 The Oliver Company earned taxable income of $7,500 during 2004, its first year of operations. A reconciliation of pretax financial income and taxable income indicated that an additional $2,500 of accelerated depreciation was deducted for tax purposes and that an estimated expense of $5,800 was deducted for financial reporting purposes. The estimated expense is not expected to be deductible for tax purposes until 2007, when the liability is paid. The current tax rate is 30% and no change in the tax rate has been enacted for future years. The resulting journal entry for 2004 would be:

a. Income Tax Expense	1,260	
Deferred Tax Asset	1,740	
Deferred Tax Liability		750
Income Taxes Payable		2,250
b. Income Tax Expense	1,260	
Deferred Tax Asset	990	
Income Taxes Payable		2,250
c. Income Tax Expense	3,240	
Deferred Tax Liability		990
Income Taxes Payable		2,250
d. Income Tax Expense	3,000	
Deferred Tax Liability		750
Income Taxes Payable		2,250

EXERCISES

E18-1   *Single Temporary Difference*   The Durn Company began operations at the beginning of 2004. At the end of 2004 the company reported taxable income of $9,800 and pretax financial income of $11,200, due to a single temporary difference. The income tax rate for the current year is 30%, but Congress has enacted a 40% tax rate for 2005 and beyond.

Required Prepare the income tax journal entry of the Durn Company at the end of 2004.

E18-2   *Temporary Difference*   At the end of 2004, its first year of operations, Slater Company reported a book value for its depreciable assets of $40,000 for financial reporting purposes and $33,000 for income tax purposes. The company earned taxable income of $97,000 during 2004. The company is subject to a 30% income tax rate and no change has been enacted for future years. The depreciation was the only temporary difference between taxable income and pretax financial income.

Required

1. Prepare the income tax journal entry of the Slater Company at the end of 2004.
2. Show how the deferred taxes would be reported on the Slater Company's December 31, 2004 balance sheet.

E18-3   *Single Temporary Difference: Multiple Rates*   At the end of 2004, Fulhage Company reported taxable income of $9,000 and pretax financial income of $10,600. The difference is due to depreciation for tax purposes in excess of depreciation for financial reporting purposes. The income tax rate for the current year is 40%, but Congress has enacted tax rates of 35% for 2005 and 30% for 2006 and beyond.

Fulhage Company has calculated the excess of its financial depreciation over its tax depreciation for future years as follows: 2005, $600; 2006, $700; and 2007, $300. Prior to 2004, the company had no deferred tax liability or asset.

Required   Prepare the income tax journal entry of the Fulhage Company at the end of 2004.

E18-4   *Single Temporary Difference*   Pito Company has been in operation for several years. During those years the company has been profitable, and it expects to continue to be profitable in the foreseeable future. At the beginning of 2004, the company has a deferred tax asset of $360 pertaining to one deductible temporary difference. During 2004, the company earned taxable income of $51,000, which was taxed at a rate of 30% (no change in the tax rate has been enacted for future years). At the end of 2004, the book value of the current liability to which the deferred tax asset relates for financial reporting purposes exceeded the book value for income tax purposes by $6,000.

Required

1. Prepare the income tax journal entry of the Pito Company at the end of 2004.
2. Show how the deferred tax asset is reported on the Pito Company's December 31, 2004 balance sheet.

E18-5   *Valuation Account*   At the end of 2004, its first year of operations, the Beattie Company reported taxable income of $38,000 and pretax financial income of $34,400. The difference is due to the way the company handles its warranty costs. For tax purposes, the company deducts the warranty costs as they are paid. For financial reporting purposes, the company provides for a year-end estimated warranty liability based on future expected costs. The company is subject to a 30% tax rate for 2004 and no change in the tax rate has been enacted for future years. Based on verifiable evidence, the company decides it should establish a valuation allowance of 60% of its ending deferred tax asset.

Required

1. Prepare the income tax journal entry of the Beattie Company at the end of 2004.
2. Prepare the lower portion of the Beattie Company's 2004 income statement.

E18-6   *Income Taxes*   Thun Company has been in operation for several years. It has both a deductible and a taxable temporary difference. At the beginning of 2004, its deferred tax asset was $690 and its deferred tax liability was $750. The company expects its deductible temporary difference to be "deductible" in 2005 and its taxable temporary difference to be "taxable" in 2006. In 2003 Congress enacted income tax rates for future years as follows: 2004, 30%; 2005, 34%; and 2006, 35%. At the end of 2004, the company reported income taxes payable of $12,600, an increase in its deferred tax liability of $300, and an ending balance in its deferred tax asset of $860. The company has prepared the following schedule of items related to its income taxes for 2004.

Item	Amount
Taxable income for 2004	_____
Taxable temporary difference, 12/31/04	_____
Increase in deductible temporary difference during 2004	_____
Income tax expense for 2004	_____

Required: Fill in the blanks in the preceding schedule. Show your calculations.

E18-7   *Originating and Reversing Difference*   The Tanner Corporation begins operations in 2003 and reports the following amounts of pretax financial income and taxable income for the years 2003 through 2007. The company has only one temporary difference, and only one originating or reversing difference occurs in any single year. The company is subject to a tax rate of 30% for all the years.

Year	Pretax Financial Income	Taxable Income
2003	$70,000	$ 50,000
2004	85,000	75,000
2005	90,000	90,000
2006	82,000	92,000
2007	93,000	113,000

Required
1. Prepare the income tax journal entry for each year.
2. What do you notice about the balance in the deferred taxes over the 5 years?

E18-8   *Multiple Temporary Differences*   Vickers Company reports taxable income of $4,500 for 2004. The company has two temporary differences between pretax financial income and taxable income at the end of 2004. The first difference is expected to result in taxable amounts totaling $2,470 in future years. The second difference is expected to result in deductible amounts totaling $1,360 in future years. The company has a deferred tax asset of $372 and a deferred tax liability of $690 at the beginning of 2004. The current tax rate is 30% and no change in the tax rate has been enacted for future years. The company has positive, verifiable evidence of future taxable income.

Required Prepare the income tax journal entry of the Vickers Company at the end of 2004.

E18-9   *Operating Loss*   At the end of 2004, Keil Company reports a pretax operating loss of $80,000 for both financial reporting and income tax purposes. Prior to 2004 the company had been successful and had reported and paid taxes on the following pretax financial income and taxable income: 2001, $37,000; 2002, $50,000; and 2003, $54,000. The company had been subject to tax rates of 20% in 2001, 25% in 2002, and 30% in 2003.

Required
1. Prepare the income tax journal entry of the Keil Company at the end of 2004.
2. Prepare the lower portion of Keil's 2004 income statement.

E18-10   *Operating Loss*   At the end of 2004, its first year of operations, the Swelland Company reported a pretax operating loss of $32,000 for both financial reporting and income tax purposes. At that time the company had no positive verifiable evidence that it would earn future taxable income. However, due to successful management, the company reported pretax operating income (and taxable income) of $70,000 in 2005. During both years, the income tax rate was 30% and no change had been enacted for future years.

Required
1. Prepare the income tax journal entries of the Swelland Company at the end of 2004.
2. Prepare the income tax journal entry of the Swelland Company at the end of 2005.
3. Prepare the lower portion of Swelland's 2005 income statement.

E18-11   *Operating Loss*   Baxter Company began operations in 2000 and was profitable through 2003, during which time the tax rate was 30%. At the end of 2004, the company reported a pretax operating loss of $135,000 for both financial reporting and income taxes. Because the tax rate was increased to 40% in 2004, the company elects to forgo any carryback of the operating loss. In 2005 the company reported pretax operating income of $150,000.

Required
1. Prepare the income tax journal entry of the Baxter Company at the end of 2004.
2. Prepare the lower portion of Baxter's 2004 income statement.
3. Explain why Baxter Company elected to forgo any carryback in 2004.
4. Prepare the income tax journal entry of the Baxter Company at the end of 2005.
5. Prepare the lower portion of Baxter's 2005 income statement.

E18-12 *Intraperiod Tax Allocation* The Wright Company reports the following information for the year ended December 31, 2004:

Pretax income from continuing operations	$160,000[a]
Pretax gain from sale of investment (extraordinary item)	30,000
Pretax income from operations of discontinued Division M	27,000
Pretax loss on disposal of Division M	(45,000)
Pretax cumulative effect of change in accounting principle	12,000
Pretax error in understating depreciation in 2003	(8,000)
Retained earnings, January 1, 2004	410,000
Cash dividends during 2004	48,000
Total income tax	39,000[b]

a. Of this amount, revenues are $400,000 and expenses are $240,000

b. Of this amount $7,500 relates to the extraordinary item; $6,750 relates to the pretax income from the operations of discontinued Division M; the pretax loss on the disposal of Division M resulted in an income tax savings of $11,250; $3,000 relates to the pretax cumulative effect of the change in accounting principle; and the pretax depreciation error resulted in an income tax savings of $2,000

Required

1. Prepare the year-end journal entry necessary to record the 2004 intraperiod income tax allocation in regard to the preceding information.
2. Prepare Wright's 2004 income statement and statement of retained earnings.

E18-13 *Calculating Intraperiod Income Taxes* The Stam Corporation reports the following *pretax* accounting (and taxable) income items during 2004:

Income from continuing operations	$90,000[a]
Loss from operations of a discontinued division	(10,000)
Gain from the disposal of the discontinued division	25,000
Extraordinary gain	20,000
Cumulative effect of change in accounting principle	(9,000)

a. Of this amount, revenues are $320,000 and expenses are $230,000.

Required

1. Prepare the journal entry necessary to record the 2004 intraperiod income tax allocation in regard to the preceding information. Assume a tax rate of 15% on the first $40,000 of income and a rate of 30% on income in excess of $40,000.
2. Prepare Stam's 2004 income statement.

E18-14 *Disclosure of Intraperiod Tax Allocation* The Lester Corporation reports $125,000 of both *pretax* accounting "income" and taxable income in 2004. In addition to income from continuing operations (of which revenues are $500,000), included in this income is a $25,000 extraordinary loss from a fire, a $17,000 loss from operations of discontinued Division W, a $15,000 gain on the disposal of Division W, a $6,000 gain from changing from double-declining-balance to straight-line depreciation, and a $14,000 correction of an error due to the understatement of bad debt expense in 2003. The company is subject to a 20% tax rate on the first $50,000 of income and a rate of 25% on income in excess of $50,000.

Required

1. Show how this information is disclosed on Lester's 2004 income statement.
2. Prepare Lester's 2004 statement of retained earnings. (Assume a beginning retained earnings balance of $191,000 and cash dividends during 2004 amounting to $65,000.)

E18-15 *Balance Sheet Presentation* The Thiel Company reports the following deferred tax items at the end of 2004:

Deferred Tax Item #	Account Balance	Related Asset or Liability
1	$ 7,200 credit	Current asset
2	6,700 debit	Current liability
3	15,500 credit	Noncurrent asset
4	10,600 debit	Noncurrent liability

Required Show how the preceding deferred tax items are reported on the Thiel Company's December 31, 2004 balance sheet.

E18-16   *Change in Tax Rates*   At the end of 2004, Rowet Company reported a deferred tax liability of $6,120 based on an income tax rate of 30%. On June 1, 2005 Congress changed the income tax rate to 35%.

Required

1. Calculate the amount of the adjustment to Rowet Company's 2004 year-end deferred tax liability.
2. Prepare the journal entry to correct Rowet Company's deferred tax liability.

PROBLEMS

P18-1   *Temporary and Permanent Differences*   In the current year you are calculating a diversified company's deferred taxes. Based on an analysis of the company's current taxable income and pretax financial income, you have identified the following items that create differences between the two amounts and that may result in differences between the company's future taxable income and its future pretax financial income:

_____   1. Percentage depletion deducted for taxes in excess of cost depletion for financial reporting
_____   2. Warranty costs to be deducted for taxes that were deducted as warranty expense for financial reporting
_____   3. Gross profit to be recognized for taxes under the completed-contract method that was recognized for financial reporting under the percentage-of-completion method
_____   4. Officers' life insurance premium expense deducted for financial reporting
_____   5. Rent revenue to be recognized for financial reporting that was reported for taxes when collected in advance
_____   6. Loss from writedown of inventory that was recognized for financial reporting but that will be deducted for taxes when the inventory is sold
_____   7. Interest revenue on municipal bonds recognized for financial reporting
_____   8. Loss due to contingent liability that was deducted for financial reporting that will be deducted for taxes when the liability is actually paid
_____   9. Gross profit to be recognized under installment method for tax purposes that was recognized on accrual basis for financial reporting
_____   10. Depreciation to be recognized for financial reporting in excess of MACRS depreciation to be deducted for tax purposes
_____   11. Investment income that has been recognized under the equity method for financial reporting that will be recognized as fully taxable for tax purposes when dividends are collected

Required For each difference, indicate whether it is a temporary difference (*T*) or a permanent difference (*P*) by placing the appropriate letter on the line provided. If the difference is a temporary difference, also indicate for the current year whether it will result in a future taxable amount (*T*) or a future deductible amount (*D*).

P18-2   *Definitions*   The FASB has defined several terms in regard to accounting for income taxes. Below are various code letters (for terms) followed by definitions.

Code Letter	Term	Code Letter	Term
A	Deductible temporary difference	H	Deferred tax consequences
B	Income tax obligation (or refund)	I	Taxable temporary difference
C	Operating loss carryback	J	Deferred tax liability
D	Valuation allowance	K	Temporary difference
E	Deferred tax asset	L	Income tax expense (or benefit)
F	Operating loss carryforward	M	Deferred tax expense (or benefit)
G	Taxable income		

_____   1. The deferred tax consequences of deductible temporary differences and operating loss carryforwards
_____   2. A difference between the tax basis of an asset or liability and its reported amount in the financial statements that will result in taxable or deductible amounts in future years when the reported amount of the asset or liability is recovered or settled, respectively

_____ 3. Temporary difference that results in taxable amounts in future years when the related asset or liability is recovered or settled, respectively

_____ 4. The future effects on income taxes, as measured by the applicable enacted tax rate and provisions of the enacted tax law, resulting from temporary differences and operating loss carryforwards at the end of the current year

_____ 5. The change during the year in a corporation's deferred tax liabilities and assets

_____ 6. The deferred tax consequences of taxable temporary differences

_____ 7. The portion of a deferred tax asset for which it is more likely than not that a tax benefit will not be realized

_____ 8. Temporary difference that results in deductible amounts in future years when the related asset or liability is recovered or settled, respectively

_____ 9. The sum of income tax obligation and deferred tax expense (or benefit)

_____ 10. The amount of income taxes paid or payable (or refundable) for the current year

_____ 11. An excess of tax deductible expenses over taxable revenues in a year that may be carried forward to reduce taxable income in a future year

_____ 12. The excess of taxable revenues over tax deductible expenses and exemptions for the year

_____ 13. An excess of tax deductible expenses over taxable revenues in a year that may be carried back to reduce taxable income in a prior year

Required Indicate which terms belongs with each definition by inserting the corresponding code letter on the line preceding the definition.

P18-3 **Multiple Temporary Differences** Wilcox Company has prepared the following reconciliation of its pretax financial income with its taxable income for 2004:

Pretax financial income	$3,000
Add: Estimated expense on 1-year warranties recognized for financial reporting in excess of actual warranty costs deducted for income taxes	100
Less: MACRS depreciation deducted for income taxes in excess of depreciation recognized for financial reporting	(150)
Taxable income	$2,950

At the beginning of 2004, Wilcox Company had a deferred tax liability of $495. The current tax rate is 30% and no change in the tax rate has been enacted for future years. At the end of 2004, the company anticipates that actual warranty costs will exceed estimated warranty expense by $100 next year and that financial depreciation will exceed tax depreciation by $1,800 in future years. The company has earned income in all past years and expects to earn income in the future.

Required

1. Prepare the income tax journal entry of the Wilcox Company at the end of 2004.
2. Prepare the lower portion of Wilcox's 2004 income statement.
3. Show how the income tax items are reported on Wilcox's December 31, 2004 balance sheet.

P18-4 **Interperiod Tax Allocation** Klerk Company had four temporary differences between its pretax financial income and its taxable income during 2004, as follows:

Number	Temporary Difference
1	Gross profit on certain installment sales is recognized under the accrual method for financial reporting and under the installment method for income taxes
2	MACRS depreciation is used for income taxes; a different depreciation method is used for financial reporting
3	Rent receipts are included in taxable income when collected in advance; rent revenue is recognized under the accrual method for financial reporting
4	Warranty expense is estimated for financial reporting; warranty costs are deducted as incurred for income taxes

At the beginning of 2004, the company had a deferred tax liability of $84,300 related to temporary difference #2 and a deferred tax asset of $21,090 related to temporary difference #4. Based on its tax records, the company earned taxable income of $270,000 for 2004. The company's accountant has prepared the following schedule showing the total future taxable and deductible amounts at the end of 2004 for its four temporary differences:

Taxable Amounts		Deductible Amounts	
#1	#2	#3	#4
$77,900	$241,000	$20,000	$55,300

The company has a history of earning income and expects to be profitable in the future. The income tax rate for 2004 is 40%, but in 2003 Congress enacted a 30% tax rate for 2005 and future years.

During 2004, for financial accounting purposes the company reported revenues of $750,000 and expenses of $447,100. The deferred tax related to temporary differences #1, #2, and #4 are considered to be noncurrent by the company; the deferred tax related to temporary difference #3 is considered to be current.

Required

1. Prepare the income tax journal entry of the Klerk Company for 2004.
2. Prepare a condensed 2004 income statement for the Klerk Company.
3. Show how the income tax items are reported on Klerk Company's December 31, 2004 balance sheet.

P18-5   *Interperiod Tax Allocation*   Peterson Company has computed its pretax financial income to be $66,000 in 2004 *after* including the effects of the appropriate items from the following information:

1. Depreciation taken for tax purposes	$40,000
2. Officers' life insurance premium expense recorded on accounting records	15,000
3. Interest revenue on investment in municipal bonds recorded on accounting records	25,000
4. Percentage depletion taken for tax purposes in excess of cost depletion taken for financial reporting purposes	10,000
5. Depreciation taken for financial reporting purposes	48,000
6. Actual product warranty costs deducted for tax purposes	20,000
7. Gross profit on installment sales recognized for tax purposes	80,000
8. Estimated product warranty expense recorded on accounting records	27,000
9. Gross profit on installment sales recognized for financial reporting purposes	91,000

The company's accountant has prepared the following schedule showing the future taxable and deductible amounts at the end of 2004 for its three temporary differences:

	Totals
Future Taxable Amounts	
Depreciation difference	$33,800
Installment sales: gross profit difference	26,700
Future Deductible Amounts	
Warranty difference	56,500

At the beginning of 2004 the company had a deferred tax liability of $12,540 related to the depreciation difference and $4,710 related to the installment sales difference. In addition, it had a deferred tax asset of $14,850 related to the warranty difference. The current tax rate is 30% and no change in the tax rate has been enacted for future years.

Required

1. Compute the Peterson Company's taxable income for 2004.
2. Prepare the income tax journal entry of the Peterson Company for 2004 (assume no valuation allowance is necessary).
3. Identify the permanent differences in Items 1–9 and explain why you did or did not account for them as deferred tax items in Requirement 2.

P18-6   *Interperiod Tax Allocation*   Quick Company reports the following revenues and expenses in its pretax financial income for the year ended December 31, 2004:

Revenues	$229,600
Expenses	(160,100)
Pretax financial income	$ 69,500

The revenues included in pretax financial income are the same amount as the revenues included in the company's taxable income. A reconciliation of the expenses reported for pretax financial income to the expenses reported for taxable income, however, reveals four differences:

1. Depreciation deducted for financial reporting exceeded depreciation deducted for income taxes by $11,000
2. Percentage depletion deducted for income taxes exceeded cost depletion deducted for financial reporting by $15,600
3. Warranty costs deducted for income taxes exceeded warranty expenses deducted for financial reporting by $8,900
4. Legal expense of $9,800 was deducted for financial reporting; it will be deducted for income taxes when paid in a future year

The company expects its percentage depletion to exceed its cost depletion in each of the next 5 years by the same amount as in 2004. At the end of 2004 the other three expenses are expected to result in total future taxable or deductible amounts as follows:

	Totals
Future Taxable Amounts	
Depreciation expense difference	$63,000
Future Deductible Amounts	
Warranty expense difference	48,400
Legal expense difference	9,800

At the beginning of 2004 the company had a deferred tax liability of $22,200 related to the depreciation difference and a deferred tax asset of $17,190 related to the warranty difference. The income tax rate for 2004 is 35%, but in 2003 Congress enacted a 30% rate for 2005 and future years.

Required

1. Compute the Quick Company's taxable income for 2004.
2. Prepare the income tax journal entry of the Quick Company for 2004. Assume no valuation allowance is necessary.
3. Prepare a condensed 2004 income statement for the Quick Company.

See WebTutor for annotated problem solution.

P18-7 **Deferred Tax Liability: Depreciation** At the beginning of 2004, its first year of operations, Cooke Company
@ purchased an asset for $100,000. This asset has an 8-year economic life with no residual value, and it is being depreciated by the straight-line method for financial reporting purposes. For tax purposes, however, the asset is being depreciated using the MACRS (200%, 5-year life) method.

During 2004, the company reported pretax financial income of $51,500 and taxable income of $44,000. The depreciation temporary difference caused the difference between the two income amounts. The tax rate in 2004 was 30% and no change in the tax rate had been enacted for future years.

Required

1. Prepare a schedule that shows for each year, 2004 through 2011, (a) MACRS depreciation, (b) straight-line depreciation, (c) the annual depreciation temporary difference, and (d) the accumulated temporary difference at the end of each year.
2. Prepare a schedule that computes for each year, 2004 through 2011, (a) the ending deferred tax liability, and (b) the change in the deferred tax liability.
3. Prepare the income tax journal entry at the end of 2004.
4. Explain what happens to the balance of the deferred tax liability at the end of 2004 through 2011.

P18-8 **Deferred Tax Liability: Depreciation** Gire Company began operations at the beginning of 2004, at which time it purchased a depreciable asset for $60,000. For 2004 through 2007, the asset was depreciated on the straight-line basis over a 4-year life (no residual value) for financial reporting. For income tax purposes the asset was depreciated using MACRS (200%, 3-year life).

For 2004 through 2007, the company reported pretax financial income and taxable income of the following amounts (the differences are due solely to the depreciation temporary differences):

Year	Pretax Financial Income	Taxable Income
2004	$24,998	$20,000
2005	38,670	27,000
2006	27,886	34,000
2007	29,446	40,000

Over the entire 4-year period, the company was subject to an income tax of 30% and no change in the tax rate had been enacted for future years.

Required

1. Prepare a schedule that shows for each year, 2004 through 2007, the (a) MACRS depreciation, (b) straight-line depreciation, (c) annual depreciation temporary difference, and (d) accumulated temporary difference at the end of each year.
2. Prepare the income tax journal entry at the end of (a) 2004, (b) 2005, (c) 2006, and (d) 2007. (Round to the nearest dollar.)
3. Prepare the lower portion of the income statement for (a) 2004, (b) 2005, (c) 2006, and (d) 2007.

P18-9   *Deferred Taxes: Multiple Rates*   Wicks Corporation began operations on January 1, 2004. At the end of 2004 the company reported pretax financial income of $60,000 and taxable income of $57,700, due to two temporary differences. The income tax rate is 30% for 2004, but Congress has enacted a tax rate of 35% for 2004 and beyond. To determine its deferred taxes, the company prepared the following schedule of expected future taxable and deductible amounts for the two temporary differences:

	2005	2006	2007	2008
Taxable amounts	$4,900	$4,200	$ 4,600	$4,100
Deductible amount			(15,500)	

Required

1. Prepare the income tax journal entry of the Wicks Corporation at the end of 2004. Assume a valuation allowance is not required.
2. Prepare the lower portion of the 2004 income statement for the Wicks Corporation.

P18-10   *Operating Loss*   Ross Company has been in business for several years, during which time it has been profitable. For each of those years, the company reported (and paid taxes on) taxable income in the same amount as pretax financial income based on the following revenues and expenses:

	Revenues	Expenses
2000	$182,000	$150,000
2001	220,000	170,000
2002	253,000	180,000
2003	241,000	196,000

The company was subject to the following income tax rates during this period: 2000, 20%; 2001, 25%; 2002, 30%; and 2003, 25%. During 2004 the company experienced a severe decrease in the demand for its products. The company tried to offset this decrease with an expensive marketing campaign, but was unsuccessful. Consequently, at the end of 2004 the company determined that its revenues were $60,000 and its expenses were $193,000 during 2004 for both income taxes and financial reporting.

The company decided to carry back its 2004 operating loss because it was not confident it could earn taxable income in the future carryforward period. The income tax rate was 30% in 2004 and no change in the tax rate had been enacted for future years.

In 2005 the company developed and introduced a new product that proved to be in high demand. On June 1, 2005 the company received a refund check from the government based on the tax information it filed at the end of 2004. For 2005 the company reported revenues of $181,000 and expenses of $155,000 for both income taxes and financial reporting. The applicable income tax rate was 30%.

Required

1. Prepare the income tax journal entries of the Ross Company at the end of 2004.
2. Prepare the Ross Company's 2004 income statement. Include a note for any operating loss carryforward.
3. Prepare the journal entry to record the receipt of the refund check on June 1, 2005.
4. Prepare the income tax journal entry at the end of 2005.
5. Prepare the Ross Company's 2005 income statement.

P18-11   *Operating Loss*   Refer to the information in Problem 18-10 and modify it as follows: The company decided to carry back its 2004 operating loss. Furthermore, since the company had already begun to develop the new product at the end of 2004 and had contracts for its sale in 2005, the company was confident at the end of 2004 that it would earn sufficient taxable income in the future carryforward period.

Required

1. Prepare the income tax journal entries of the Ross Company at the end of 2004.
2. Prepare the Ross Company's 2004 income statement. Include a note for any operating loss carryforward recognition.

3. Prepare the journal entry to record the receipt of the refund check on June 1, 2005.
4. Prepare the income tax journal entry at the end of 2005.
5. Prepare the Ross Company's 2005 income statement.

P18-12 *Balance Sheet Reporting and Tax Rate Change* At the end of 2003, Dolf Company prepared the following schedule of its deferred tax items (based on the currently enacted tax rate of 30%):

Deferred Tax Item #	Account Balance	Related Asset or Liability
1	$ 8,400 debit	Current asset
2	10,200 debit	Noncurrent asset
3	5,700 credit	Current liability
4	17,700 credit	Noncurrent liability

On April 30, 2004 Congress changed the income tax rate to 40% for 2004 and future years. At the end of 2004 the company reported taxable income of $62,500 for 2004. At that time, the company determined that its deferred tax items should have balances as follows at the end of 2004 (based on the 40% tax rate): #1, $10,700 debit; #2, $15,000 debit; #3, $7,000 credit; #4, $25,900 credit.

Required

1. Show how the deferred tax items are reported on the Dolf Company's December 31, 2003 balance sheet.
2. Prepare the April 30, 2004 journal entry to correct Dolf Company's deferred tax items.
3. Prepare the income tax journal entry of the Dolf Company at the end of 2004.
4. Show how the current and deferred tax items are reported on the Dolf Company's December 31, 2004 balance sheet.
5. Calculate the total income tax expense for 2004.

P18-13 *Comprehensive* Colt Company reports *pretax* financial "income" of $150,000 in 2004. In addition to pretax income from continuing operations (of which revenues are $295,000), the following items are included in this pretax "income":

Extraordinary gain	$30,000
Loss from disposal of Division B	(10,000)
Income from operations of discontinued Division B	16,000
Cumulative effect of change in accounting principle	7,000
Prior period adjustment	(8,000)

The taxable income of the company totals $130,000 in 2004. The difference between the pretax financial income and the taxable income is due to the excess of tax depreciation over financial depreciation on assets used in continuing operations.

At the beginning of 2004 the company had a retained earnings balance of $310,000 and a deferred tax liability of $8,100. During 2004 the company declared and paid dividends of $48,000. It is subject to tax rates of 15% on the first $50,000 of income and 30% on income in excess of $50,000. Based upon proper interperiod tax allocation procedures, the company has determined that its 2004 ending deferred tax liability is $14,100.

Required

1. Prepare a schedule for the Colt Company to allocate the total 2004 income tax expense to the various components of pretax income.
2. Prepare the income tax journal entry of the Colt Company at the end of 2004.
3. Prepare Colt Company's 2004 income statement.
4. Prepare Colt Company's 2004 statement of retained earnings.
5. Show the related income tax disclosures on the Colt Company's December 31, 2004 balance sheet.

P18-14 *Comprehensive* At the beginning of 2004 Norris Company had a deferred tax liability of $6,400, due to the use of MACRS depreciation for income tax purposes and units-of-production depreciation for financial reporting. The income tax rate is 30% for 2003 and 2004, but in 2003 Congress enacted a 40% tax rate for 2005 and future years.

The accounting records of the Norris Company show the following *pretax* items of financial income for 2004: income from continuing operations, $120,000 (revenues of $352,000 and expenses of $232,000); gain on disposal of Division F, $23,000; extraordinary loss, $18,000; loss from operations of discontinued Division F, $10,000; and prior period adjustment, $15,000, due to an error that understated revenue in 2003. All of these items are taxable; however, financial depreciation for 2004 on assets related to continuing operations exceeds tax depreciation by $5,000. The company had a retained earnings balance of $161,000 on January 1, 2004 and declared and paid cash dividends of $32,000 during 2004.

Required

1. Prepare the income tax journal entry of the Norris Company at the end of 2004.
2. Prepare Norris Company's 2004 income statement.
3. Prepare Norris Company's 2004 statement of retained earnings.
4. Show the related income tax disclosures on the Norris Company's December 31, 2004 balance sheet.

P18-15 *Comprehensive* Jayryan Company sells products in a volatile market. The company began operating in 2002 and reported (and paid taxes on) taxable income in 2002 and 2003. It has one taxable temporary difference, and reconciled its taxable income to its pretax financial income for 2002 and 2003 as follows:

	2002	2003
Taxable income	$25,000	$53,000
Temporary difference	2,500	4,800
Pretax financial income	$27,500	$57,800

In 2004, because of a downturn in the market, the company reported a taxable loss of $90,000 and it was uncertain as to future profits. A temporary difference of $2,700 resulted in an $87,300 pretax operating loss for financial reporting. In 2005 and 2006 the company was again profitable and reported the following items:

	2005	2006
Taxable income	$7,000	$19,000
Temporary difference	2,300	2,800
Pretax financial income	$9,300	$21,800

The income tax rate has been 30% since 2000 and no change in the tax rate has been enacted for future years.

Required

1. Prepare a schedule that shows the Jayryan Company's income taxes payable (or receivable) for each year, 2002 through 2006.
2. Prepare a schedule that shows the deferred tax information (change in temporary difference and operating loss carryforward) for each year, 2002 through 2006.
3. Prepare a schedule that shows the deferred taxes for each year, 2002 through 2006.
4. Based on the schedule prepared in Requirement 3, prepare the income tax journal entry at the end of 2004.
5. Prepare a partial income statement for 2004. Include a note for any operating loss carryforward.

INTERNET ASSIGNMENTS

Go to the Nikolai and Bazley **Intermediate Accounting** web site (http://Nikolai.swcollege.com). Click on Student Resources and internet homework assignments. Then click on the appropriate hot link (icon) for each company's web site, find the relevant accounting information, and answer the following questions.

I18-1   Go to the Dow web site.

Required What is the company's total deferred tax balance at the end of each of the two most recent years? What is the single largest component of the total deferred tax balance in each year? What is the amount of the company's valuation allowance in each year? How does the company report its deferred tax amounts on its consolidated balance sheet for each year? Do these amounts reconcile to the total deferred tax balance? Do you agree with how it reports its deferred tax amounts? Why or why not?

I18-2   Go to the Whirlpool web site.

Required What was the company's income tax expense that it reported on its income statement for the most current year? How much of this was current and how much was deferred? How much was (a) the total deferred tax asset balance and (b) the total deferred liability balance at the end of the most current year? What were the two largest deferred tax asset items at the end of the most current year? Does this seem reasonable to you? Why or why not? Did the company have a valuation allowance? If so, how much was it? To what does it relate?

CHAPTER 19

Accounting for Postemployment Benefits

objectives

1 Understand the characteristics of pension plans.

2 Explain the historical perspective of accounting for pension plans.

3 Explain the accounting principles for defined benefit plans, including computing pension expense and recognizing pension liabilities and assets.

4 Account for pensions.

5 Understand disclosures of pensions.

6 Explain the conceptual issues regarding pensions.

7 Understand several additional issues related to pensions.

8 Explain other postemployment benefits (OPEBs).

9 Account for OPEBs.

10 Explain the conceptual issues regarding OPEBs.

11 Understand present value calculations for pensions. (Appendix)

The average life expectancy of a male and female born in the U.S. in 1990 has increased to over 71 and 78 years respectively. Consequently, more people are living long enough to retire and to become dependent on other sources of income. Both the government and companies are concerned about providing income to these individuals, in response to which Congress passed the *Federal Insurance Contribution Act* (commonly called social security) in 1935. This Act requires most employers and employees to contribute to a federal retirement program. To supplement social security, many companies also have adopted private retirement plans. More than $4.9 trillion is invested in company pension funds.[1] Because these pension plans are important, Congress passed legislation affecting their operation. This legislation, the *Employee Retirement Income Security Act of 1974* (ERISA), often is referred to as the *Pension Reform Act of 1974*.

We discussed the accounting for the cost of social security taxes in Chapter 12. In this chapter we focus on the recording, reporting, and disclosure procedures applicable to company pension plans under generally accepted accounting principles and the provisions of the *Pension Reform Act of 1974*. In addition to pensions, many employers provide other postemployment benefits to their employees, and we discuss the accounting for these benefits later in the chapter.

CHARACTERISTICS OF PENSION PLANS

A pension plan requires that a company provide income to its retired employees in return for the services they provided during their employment. This retirement income, normally paid monthly, usually is determined on the basis of the employee's earnings and length of service with the company. For instance, under the retirement plan of one major company, employees who retire at age 65 receive annual retirement income according to the following formula: Average of last five years' salary × number of years of service × 0.0257. Thus, an individual who worked for this company for 30 years and had an average salary of $100,000 for the last five years of service receives annual pension benefits of $77,100 ($100,000 × 30 × 0.0257). A pension plan of this type is a **defined benefit plan** because the plan specifically states either the *benefits* to be received by employees after retirement or the method of determining such benefits. In contrast, a pension plan is a **defined contribution plan** when the employer's *contribution* is based on a formula, so that future benefits are limited to an amount that can be provided by the contributions and the returns earned on the investment of those contributions. The two types of plans involve

1 Understand the characteristics of pension plans.

---

1. Estimated for 1999. This amount does not include government pension funds.

different risks to the company and the employees. With a defined benefit plan, most of the risks lie with the company because the payments to the retired employees have been defined and the company has the responsibility of ensuring that those amounts are paid. In contrast, with a defined contribution plan, most of the risks lie with the employees because the company's responsibilities essentially end once the required contribution for the period has been made by the company. Defined benefit plans raise many complex accounting issues, and those issues are the primary focus of this chapter. We briefly discuss defined contribution plans later in the chapter.

Companies' pension plans are **funded.** Under a funded plan, the company makes periodic payments to a *funding agency* that assumes the responsibility for both safeguarding and investing the pension assets to earn a return on the investments for the pension plan, and for making payments to the recipients of the benefits. An **unfunded** plan, on the other hand, is one in which no periodic payments are made to an external agency; instead, the pension payments to retired employees are made from current resources. (Although the *Pension Reform Act of 1974* has eliminated *un*funded plans for companies, some plans are *under*funded. Also, many governmental plans are unfunded.) The amounts needed to fund a pension plan are determined (estimated) by **actuaries,** individuals trained in actuarial science who use compound interest techniques, projections of future events, and *actuarial funding methods* to calculate required current contributions by the company.

Companies' pension plans are usually **noncontributory.** With noncontributory plans, the entire pension cost is borne by the employer (company). Under a **contributory** plan, employees bear part of the cost of the plan and make contributions from their salaries into the pension fund. We discuss noncontributory plans in this chapter.

In addition, most companies design their pension plans to meet the Internal Revenue Code qualifications, which state that:

1. Employer contributions are deductible for income tax purposes
2. Pension fund earnings are exempt from income taxes
3. Employer contributions to the pension fund are not taxable to the employees until they receive their pension benefits

Exhibit 19-1 summarizes the relationships among the employees, the company, and the funding agency for a noncontributory defined benefit pension plan.

HISTORICAL PERSPECTIVE OF PENSION PLANS

2 Explain the historical perspective of accounting for pension plans.

Accounting for the cost of pension plans has been analyzed for many years. The first authoritative statement on the subject was published by the Committee on Accounting Procedure as **Accounting Research Bulletin No. 47,** which recommended the recognition of pension cost on the accrual basis instead of the cash basis. That is, it recommended that pension expense be recorded by an employer during the periods of employment as benefits are earned by employees, and *not* delayed until the periods when retirement benefits are actually paid. The pension expense is based on the present value of the future benefits earned by employees during the current accounting period. We use present value techniques (which we explain in Appendix D) in this chapter for the computation of amounts related to pension plans.

Since the pronouncements of the Committee on Accounting Procedure were not mandatory, most companies continued to use the cash basis of accounting for pension plans after the issuance of *ARB No. 47.* The use of the cash basis, however, violated the accrual concept and resulted in a lack of comparability among companies in reporting pension expense, sometimes causing wide year-to-year fluctuations in the pension expense for a single company. In an effort to solve such problems, the APB authorized **Accounting Research Study No. 8,** which ultimately resulted in the release of **APB Opinion No. 8,** "Accounting for the Cost of Pension Plans." This *Opinion* required the use of the accrual method for the recognition of the pension expense. However, considerable latitude was allowed in determining the amount of the pension expense through the use of various

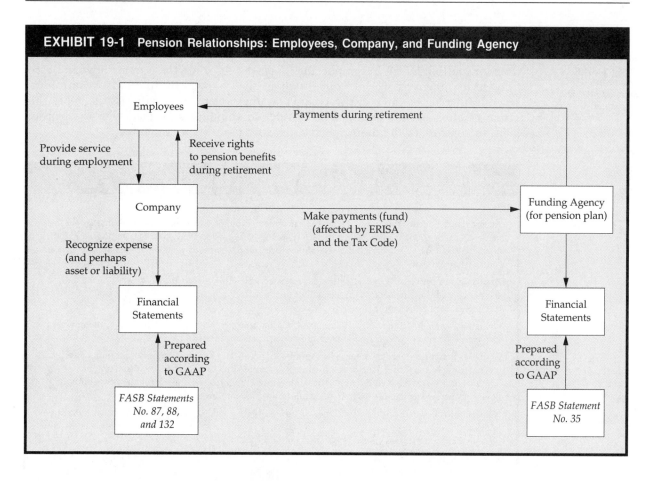

EXHIBIT 19-1 Pension Relationships: Employees, Company, and Funding Agency

actuarial methods. Criticism soon arose over the fact that companies with plans for which the obligation to pay benefits greatly exceeded the plan assets available did not record a liability. As a result, in 1974 the FASB added pension accounting to its agenda, and over a long period developed and refined the accounting for pensions. The FASB first issued a Discussion Memorandum in 1975 and then issued numerous Exposure Drafts in subsequent years. Then, in 1980 **FASB Statement No. 35,** "Accounting and Reporting by Defined Benefit Pension Plans," was issued. This *Statement* defined the principles to be used and the disclosures required by the funding agency administering a company's pension plan. This information, which we briefly discuss later in the chapter, is primarily for the benefit of the participants in the plan, but is also used by the employer company for its pension plan accounting calculations and disclosures. In 1985, the FASB issued **FASB Statement No. 87,** "Employers' Accounting for Pensions," which established the measurement, recognition, and disclosure principles for employers' pension plans. Also, in 1985, the FASB issued **FASB Statement No. 88,** "Employers' Accounting for Settlements and Curtailments of Defined Benefit Plans and for Termination Benefits," which we briefly discuss later in this chapter. Finally, in 1998, the FASB issued **FASB Statement No. 132,** which modified the disclosure requirements of *FASB Statement No. 87,* but did not change its measurement and recognition principles. In this chapter, we discuss the recording and reporting requirements of *FASB Statement No. 87* and the disclosure requirements of *FASB Statement No. 132.*

ACCOUNTING PRINCIPLES FOR DEFINED BENEFIT PENSION PLANS

The principles of *FASB Statement No. 87* are very complex and we include only the basic elements in the following discussion. Note that the minimum amount funded by the employer is defined by ERISA (which we discuss later).

Key Terms Related to Pension Plans

The conceptual issues related to pensions are discussed later in the chapter.

Before we discuss the accounting principles for pension plans, an understanding of the terms in Exhibit 19-2 is important.[2] You should study these terms now and carefully review them as we introduce each in the chapter. In addition, we introduce several other terms later in the chapter as they relate to specific issues. Note that actuaries often use the term *accrue* to refer to amounts associated with the pension plan, in contrast to the more specific meaning used by accountants.

EXHIBIT 19-2   Key Terms Related to Pension Plans

Accumulated Benefit Obligation. The actuarial present value of all the benefits attributed by the pension benefit formula to employee service rendered before a specified date. The amount is based on current and past compensation levels of employees and, therefore, includes no assumptions about future pay increases.

Actual Return on Plan Assets. The difference between the fair value of the plan assets at the end of the period and the fair value at the beginning of the period, adjusted for contributions and payments of benefits during the period.

Actuarial Funding Method. Any of several techniques that actuaries use in determining the amounts and timing of employer contributions to provide for pension benefits.

Actuarial Present Value. The value, on a specified date, of an amount or series of amounts payable or receivable in the future. The present value is determined by discounting the future amount or amounts at a predetermined discount rate. The future amounts are adjusted for the probability of payment (affected by factors such as death, disability, or withdrawal from the plan).

Assumptions. Estimates of the occurrence of future events affecting pension costs, such as mortality, withdrawal, disablement and retirement, changes in compensation and national pension benefits, and discount rates. Sometimes called *actuarial* assumptions.

Expected Return on Plan Assets. An amount calculated by applying the expected long-term rate of return on plan assets to the fair market value of the plan assets at the beginning of the period.

Discount Rate. The rate at which the pension benefits can be effectively settled, e.g., the rate implicit in current prices of annuity contracts that could be used to settle the pension obligation. The discount rate is used in the computation of the service cost, the projected benefit obligation, and the accumulated benefit obligation.

Gain or Loss. A change in the value of either the projected benefit obligation (or the plan assets) resulting from experience different from that assumed, or from a change in an actuarial assumption. Sometimes called *actuarial* or *experience* gain or loss.

Pension Benefit Formula. The basis for determining payments to which employees will be entitled during retirement.

Prior Service Cost. The cost of retroactive benefits granted in a plan amendment or at the initial adoption of the plan. The cost is the present value of the additional benefits attributed by the pension benefit formula.

Projected Benefit Obligation. The actuarial present value, at a specified date, of all the benefits attributed by the pension benefit formula to employee service rendered prior to that date. The amount includes future increases in compensation that the company projects it will pay to employees during the remainder of their employment, provided the pension benefit formula is based on those future compensation levels. The projected benefit obligation differs from the accumulated benefit obligation in that it includes anticipated future pay increases.

Service Cost. The actuarial present value of benefits attributed by the pension benefit formula to services rendered by employees during the current period. If the pension benefit formula is based on future compensation levels (e.g., average of last five years' salary), the service cost is based on those future compensation levels.

Vested Benefit Obligation. The actuarial present value of the vested benefits, which are those benefits for which the employee's right to receive a present or future pension benefit is no longer contingent on remaining in the service of the employer.

---

2. "Employers' Accounting for Pensions," *FASB Statement of Financial Accounting Standards* No. 87 (Stamford, Conn.: FASB, 1985), Appendix D and par. 44.

Pension Expense

In defining the annual pension cost, *FASB Statement No. 87* uses the term *net periodic pension cost* because a company may capitalize some of its annual pension cost as part of the cost of an asset, such as inventory. For simplicity, we will use the term *pension expense* and assume that none of the pension costs are capitalized. The pension expense that a company recognizes includes five components: service cost, interest cost, expected return on plan assets, amortization of unrecognized prior service cost, and gain or loss.[3]

1. *Service Cost.* **The service cost is the actuarial present value of the benefits attributed by the pension benefit formula to services rendered by the employees during the current period.** This amount is the present value of the deferred compensation to be paid to employees during their retirement in return for their current services. The service cost is computed using the *discount* rate selected by the company. Since the discount rate is defined as a settlement rate, it will vary as economic conditions change. If the rate increases (decreases), the present value decreases (increases). The nature of the service cost is illustrated by the following diagram:

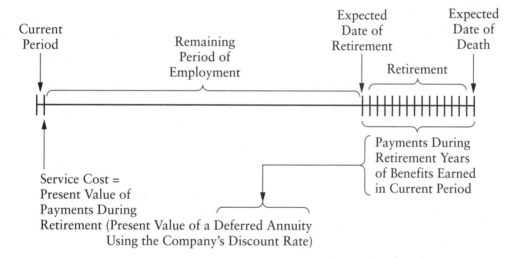

2. *Interest Cost.* **The interest cost is the increase in the projected benefit obligation due to the passage of time.** The projected benefit obligation is the present value of the deferred compensation earned by the employees to date (based on their expected future compensation levels). The interest cost is the projected benefit obligation at the beginning of the period multiplied by the *discount* rate used by the company. Since the pension plan is a deferred compensation agreement in which future payments are discounted to their present values, interest accrues due to the passage of time. The interest cost is added in the computation of pension expense.

3. *Expected Return on Plan Assets.* **The expected return on plan assets is the expected increase in the plan assets due to investing activities.**[4] Plan assets are held by the funding agency and consist of investments in securities such as stocks and bonds, as well as other investments. The expected return is calculated by multiplying the fair value of the plan assets at the beginning of the period by the expected long-term rate of return on plan assets. The rate of return reflects the average rate of earnings expected on the assets invested to provide for the benefits included in the

3. A sixth component is the amortization of any unrecognized liability or asset that existed at the initial application of *FASB Statement No. 87.* This item is a result of the transition from the requirements of *APB Opinion No. 8* and we briefly discuss it later.

4. Note that *FASB Statement No. 87* specifies that the third component of the pension expense is the actual return on plan assets. It then includes the difference between the actual and expected return in the computation of the fifth component (the gain or loss). Under the new disclosure requirements of *FASB Statement No. 132,* a company is only required to disclose the expected return in the computation of its pension expense. Therefore, in our discussion we combine the two amounts from *FASB Statement No. 87* into the expected return.

3 Explain the accounting principles for defined benefit plans, including computing pension expense and recognizing pension liabilities and assets.

projected benefit obligation. The expected return on plan assets is subtracted because the earnings "compensate" for the interest cost on the projected benefit obligation, as we illustrate in the following diagram:

4. *Amortization of Unrecognized Prior Service Cost.* Amendments to a pension plan often include provisions that grant increased retroactive benefits to employees based on services they rendered in prior periods, thereby increasing the projected benefit obligation. Similar retroactive benefits may also be granted at the initial adoption of a plan. The cost associated with these retroactive benefits is the **prior service cost.** The prior service cost is "unrecognized" because it is *not* recognized in the financial statements (i.e., is not recorded in the accounts) in total in the period granted. Instead, it is "recognized" by the actuaries as a relevant cost and the amortization is included in the computation of pension expense.

   The unrecognized prior service cost is amortized by assigning an equal amount to each future period of service of each active employee who, at the date of the amendment, is expected to receive future benefits under the plan. Alternatively, straight-line amortization over the average remaining service life of active employees may be used for simplicity. Employees hired after the date of the amendment or the plan adoption are not included in either calculation. The plan amendment usually increases the projected benefit obligation and, therefore, the amortization is added in the computation of pension expense. However, there have been several instances in recent years where companies in financial difficulty or under pressure from competitors have amended their pension plans to reduce the projected benefit obligation, in which case the amortization is subtracted in the computation. The unrecognized prior service cost and its amortization are illustrated in the following diagram:

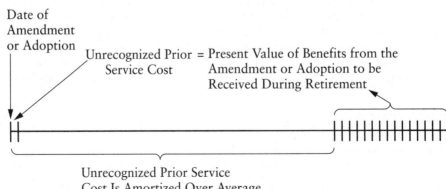

5. *Gain or Loss.* The gain or loss arises because actuaries make assumptions about many of the items included in the computation of pension costs and benefits, including future compensation levels, the interest (discount) rate, employee turnover, retirement rates, and mortality rates. Actual experience will not be the same as these assumptions. As a result, the *actual* projected benefit obligation at year-end will not be equal to the *expected* projected benefit obligation. Therefore, gains and losses result from (a) changes in the amount of the projected benefit obligation resulting from experience different from that assumed[5], and (b) changes in the assumptions.[6] Gains result when actual experience is more favorable than that assumed (e.g., the future compensation levels are lower than expected because of lower inflation), and losses result when the actual experience is unfavorable. It is important to distinguish between the impact on the company as compared to the impact on the employees. For example, a lower-than-expected mortality rate is obviously favorable to the employees, but it creates a loss to the company because it will have to make more pension payments than expected.

The entire gain or loss is *not* recognized in the period in which it occurs (so it is called an *unrecognized* net gain or loss) because it may include changes in estimates as well as real changes in economic values, and because gains in one period may be offset by losses in another period. Furthermore, immediate recognition in full might create significant fluctuations in the computation of pension expense. Therefore, the amount of any unrecognized net gain or loss is amortized over *future* periods. **Amortization of any unrecognized net gain or loss is included in the pension expense of a given year if, at the beginning of the year, the cumulative unrecognized net gain or loss from previous periods exceeds a "corridor" that is defined as 10% of the greater of the actual projected benefit obligation or the fair value of the plan assets.**[7] If amortization is required, the minimum amortization is the amount that the net gain or loss exceeds the corridor at the beginning of the year divided by the average remaining service period of the active employees expected to receive benefits under the plan. The amortization of an unrecognized net gain (loss) is subtracted (added) in the computation of pension expense.[8]

To summarize, the gain or loss component of pension expense generally consists of one of the following two items:

(1) Amortization of any unrecognized net loss from previous periods (added to compute pension expense), or

(2) Amortization of any unrecognized net gain from previous periods (deducted to compute pension expense).

Gains and losses that arise from a single occurrence not directly related to the pension plan are recognized in the period in which they occur. For example, a gain or loss that is directly related to the disposal of a component is included in the "gain or loss on disposal" and reported in accordance with the requirements of *FASB Statement No. 144.*

COMPONENTS OF PENSION EXPENSE In summary, the pension expense reported on a company's income statement generally consists of the following components:

---

5. In addition, gains and losses can occur because of the use of the market-related value of the plan assets, as we explain in footnote 7. These gains and losses are handled in a manner similar to those for changes in the projected benefit obligation, so for simplicity we do not discuss them further.

6. Although these gains and losses frequently are referred to as *experience* gains and losses or *actuarial* gains and losses, the FASB avoided using these terms.

7. In *FASB Statement No. 87*, the term **market-related value** is used. The market-related value of plan assets is either the fair value or a calculated value that recognizes changes in fair value in a systematic and rational manner over not more than five years. The use of the market-related value is allowed in order to reduce the volatility of the pension expense amount. For simplicity, we always use the fair value of the plan assets as the market-related value.

8. Alternatively, any systematic method of amortization may be used instead of the minimum just described, as long as it results in greater amortization. We use the minimum amount each period.

> Service cost = Present value of benefits earned during the year using the
>   discount rate
> + Interest cost = Projected benefit obligation at beginning of the year × Discount
>   rate
> − Expected return on plan assets = Fair value of plan assets at the beginning of
>   the year × Expected long-term rate of return
>   on plan assets
> + Amortization of prior service cost = Present value of additional benefits
>   granted at adoption or modification of the
>   plan amortized over the remaining service
>   lives of active employees
> ∓ Gain or loss = Amortization of the cumulative unrecognized net gain or loss
>   from previous periods in excess of the corridor.

Note that in unusual cases, the amortization of a reduction in unrecognized prior service cost would be deducted in the pension expense calculation.

Pension Liabilities and Assets

The amount of a company's pension expense may be different from the amount contributed by the company to the pension plan (the amount funded) because they are defined by different sets of rules. The expense is defined by *FASB Statement No. 87*, whereas the funding must be consistent with the rules of ERISA, as we discuss later. Therefore, the company records a liability if its pension expense is greater than the amount it funded. Alternatively, the company records an asset if its pension expense is less than the amount it funded. This asset or liability is similar to the numerous assets and liabilities that arise from the use of the accrual basis of accounting and it increases or decreases every year. Since either an asset or a liability can occur (but not both at the same time), we use a single title for the account, **prepaid/accrued pension cost.** If the account has a debit balance at the end of the year, the company reports the amount as an asset (prepaid pension cost) on its balance sheet; if the account has a credit balance at the end of the year, the company reports it as a liability (accrued pension cost). Typically, the amount is classified as noncurrent.

The minimum total pension liability that a company must recognize is the **unfunded accumulated benefit obligation,** which is the excess of the *accumulated* benefit obligation over the fair value of the plan assets at the end of the period. Therefore, a company may have to report an additional pension liability on its balance sheet. The accumulated benefit obligation is the present value of the deferred compensation earned by employees to date, based on *current* compensation levels. (Thus, the difference between the projected and accumulated benefit obligation is the inclusion of expected salary increases in the projected amount.) Therefore, the accumulated benefit obligation in excess of the fair value of the plan assets is a measure of the obligation of the company based on the legal concept of a liability. That is, it is based on historical events such as the actual service of the employees and their current pay levels. Therefore, the unfunded accumulated benefit obligation provides information about the liability a company would have if its pension plan were discontinued. Alternatively, if the plan is continued, the unfunded accumulated benefit obligation provides a minimum measure of the additional funds that a company will have to contribute in future periods. If a company has to report an Additional Pension Liability on its balance sheet, the amount is calculated as follows:

> Accumulated benefit obligation
> − Fair value of plan assets
> ─────────────────────────────
> = Unfunded Accumulated Benefit Obligation
> − Prepaid/accrued pension cost (credit balance)
> or + Prepaid/accrued pension cost (debit balance)
> ─────────────────────────────
> = Additional Pension Liability

So the additional pension liability "adjusts" the company's existing pension liability or asset to the amount of the unfunded accumulated benefit obligation.

Generally, the recognition of an additional liability is caused by two situations. First, a company may have an unrecognized prior service cost. In this case, the company also recognizes an intangible asset, **deferred pension cost,** of the same amount. The reason for recognizing an intangible asset is that the prior service cost has created an expectation of enhanced future performance by employees from such factors as reduced turnover and higher productivity. That is, the employer would take on an increased obligation only if future benefits of at least an equal amount were expected.

The second cause of an additional liability is that the company has earned low or negative returns on its plan assets. In this case the company also recognizes a negative component of other comprehensive income.

Note that a company might have both a prior service cost and poor returns on its plan assets. In this case, the amount of the intangible asset must not exceed the amount of any unrecognized prior service cost (plus any unrecognized transition liability or asset, as we noted in footnote 3). If the additional liability exceeds the unrecognized prior service cost, the company recognizes the intangible asset, and reports the excess (debit) as other comprehensive income.

The asset and accumulated other comprehensive income accounts related to the recognition of the additional pension liability are *not* amortized. Instead, the company recomputes the amount of the **additional liability at each balance sheet date and adjusts or eliminates the related intangible** asset or accumulated other comprehensive income as necessary.

In summary, a company may report the following pension asset, liability, and accumulated other comprehensive income items, depending on the circumstances, on its balance sheet:

Assets	**Liabilities**
1. Prepaid/accrued pension cost (debit balance)	1. Prepaid/accrued pension cost (credit balance)
2. Deferred pension cost (intangible asset)	2. Additional pension liability
	Stockholders' Equity
	1. Accumulated other comprehensive income: Excess of additional pension liability over unrecognized prior service cost (negative element)

Measurement Methods

The pension benefit formula usually is based on future compensation levels and defines benefits similarly for all years of service. Then, in computing the service cost, a constant amount of the total estimated pension benefit, based on an estimate of final salary, usually is **attributed** to each period (this method is known as the **benefit/years-of-service approach**). Using the pension benefit formula illustrated at the beginning of the chapter, the service cost would be based on the employee earning a benefit of $1/30 \times \$77,100$ each year for 30 years.

In computing the service cost, the projected benefit obligation, and the accumulated benefit obligation, the company uses a **discount rate that reflects the rates at which the pension benefits could be effectively settled.** For example, if the company could settle its obligation by purchasing an annuity from an insurance company for each employee, the rate on that annuity would be used as the appropriate discount rate. The rate of return on high-quality fixed-income investments currently available and expected to be available in the future could also be used. Companies are required by the SEC to evaluate the rate each year.

On the other hand, the expected (assumed) long-term rate of return on plan assets used to compute the expected return on assets is based on the average rate of earnings expected on the funds invested (or to be invested). Actual experience is considered along with the rates of return expected to be available in the future.

Disclosures

The disclosure requirements for defined benefit pension plans of employers are established in **FASB Statement No. 132.**[9] To provide users with relevant information, a company must disclose the following information about its defined benefit pension plan(s):

1. A reconciliation of the beginning and ending balances of the projected benefit obligation, including the amounts of the service cost, interest cost, actuarial gains and losses, benefits paid, and plan amendments.
2. A reconciliation of the beginning and ending balances of the fair value of the plan assets, including the actual return on plan assets, contributions by the company, and benefits paid.
3. The funded status of the plan, the amounts not recognized on the balance sheet, the amounts recognized on the balance sheet, including the amount of any unamortized prior service cost, the amount of any unrecognized net gain or loss, the amount of any remaining unamortized, unrecognized net obligation or net asset existing at the adoption of *FASB Statement No. 87*, the net pension prepaid asset or accrued liability; and any intangible asset and the related amount of accumulated other comprehensive income.
4. The amount of pension expense, including the service cost, the interest cost, the expected return on plan assets, the amortization of any unrecognized prior service cost, the amortization of any net gains or losses, and the amortization of any unrecognized transition obligation or asset.
5. The amount included in other comprehensive income from a change in the additional pension liability.
6. The discount rate, the rate of compensation increase, and the expected long-term rate of return on the plan assets.
7. The amounts and types of securities included in the plan assets.

A company generally discloses this information in a note to its financial statements.

EXAMPLES OF ACCOUNTING FOR PENSIONS

4 Account for pensions.

We illustrate various situations related to accounting for defined benefit pension plans in this section using *assumed* amounts. In the Appendix to the chapter, we illustrate the present value calculations for pension plans. In that example, we calculate the amounts of the service cost, the projected benefit obligation, the prior service cost, and the pension expense from basic information about a company's pension plan.

Example 1: Pension Expense Equal to Pension Funding

Assume the following facts for the Carlisle Company:

1. The company adopts a pension plan on January 1, 2004. No retroactive benefits were granted to employees.
2. The service cost each year is: 2004, $400,000; 2005, $420,000; and 2006, $432,000.
3. The projected benefit obligation at the beginning of each year is: 2005, $400,000; and 2006, $840,000.
4. The discount rate is 10%.
5. The expected long-term rate of return on plan assets is 10%, which is also equal to the actual rate of return.
6. The company adopts a policy of funding an amount equal to the pension expense and makes the payment to the funding agency at the end of each year.[10]
7. Plan assets are based on the amounts contributed each year, plus a return of 10% per year, less an assumed payment of $20,000 at the end of each year to retired employees (beginning in 2005).

---

9. "Employers' Disclosures about Pensions and Other Postemployment Benefits," *FASB Statement No. 132* (Norwalk, Conn.: FASB, 1998). There are additional disclosures beyond those we have listed.
10. Companies are required by law to make payments to funding agencies on a quarterly basis. For simplicity, in all examples and homework we assume a single annual payment is made at the end of each year.

Based on the preceding information, the service cost of $400,000 is the only component of the pension expense in 2004. This situation occurs because the company has (1) no interest cost because it has no projected benefit obligation at the beginning of the year since no employees had pension coverage before that time, (2) no expected return on plan assets because its expense recognition and funding were made at the end of the first year, (3) no prior service cost, and (4) no gain or loss. Since the company funds an amount equal to the pension expense, it records the following journal entry on December 31, 2004:

Pension Expense	400,000	
Cash		400,000

The calculation of the pension expense for 2005 is more complex because it now has three components: service cost, interest cost, and expected return on plan assets. The service cost is $420,000. Since the projected benefit obligation at January 1, 2005 is $400,000 (the service cost for 2004), the interest cost is $40,000 (the projected benefit obligation of $400,000 multiplied by the discount rate of 10%). The $40,000 expected return on the plan assets is the $400,000 invested by the funding agency for the pension fund at the end of 2004 multiplied by the 10% expected rate of return. Therefore, the company computes its pension expense for 2005 as follows:

Service cost (assumed)	$420,000
Interest cost ($400,000 × 10%)	40,000
Expected return on plan assets ($400,000 × 10%)	(40,000)
Pension expense	$420,000

Since the company funds an amount equal to the expense, it records the following journal entry on December 31, 2005:

Pension Expense	420,000	
Cash		420,000

For 2006 the service cost is $432,000. The projected benefit obligation at the beginning of 2006 is $840,000 ($400,000 beginning amount for 2005 + $420,000 service cost for 2005 + $40,000 interest cost − $20,000 payment to retired employees at end of 2005). The assets at the beginning of 2006 are $840,000 ($400,000 invested at the end of 2004 + $40,000 expected return in 2005 − $20,000 payment to retired employees at the end of 2005 + $420,000 invested at the end of 2005). Therefore, the company computes its pension expense for 2006 as follows:

Service cost (assumed)	$432,000
Interest cost ($840,000 × 10%)	84,000
Expected return on plan assets ($840,000 × 10%)	(84,000)
Pension expense	$432,000

Since the company funds an amount equal to the expense, it records the following journal entry on December 31, 2006:

Pension Expense	432,000	
Cash		432,000

Note that the interest cost and the expected return on the plan assets offset each other in this example. This situation occurs because the discount rate and the expected long-term rate of return on plan assets are both 10%, and because the company funds an amount equal to the expense.

Example 2: Pension Expense Greater Than Pension Funding

Assume the same facts for the Carlisle Company as in Example 1, except that instead of funding an amount equal to the pension expense, the company funds $385,000 in 2004, $400,000 in 2005, and $415,000 in 2006.[11] Since the company provides *fewer* assets to the pension fund, the expected return on those assets each period is less and, therefore, the pension expense must be larger to compensate for the lower expected return. The company's pension expense in 2004 is the $400,000 service cost, so the journal entry on December 31, 2004 is:

Pension Expense	400,000	
Cash		385,000
Prepaid/Accrued Pension Cost		15,000

Since the company funds only $385,000 in 2004 when the expense is $400,000, it recognizes a liability, Prepaid/Accrued Pension Cost, of $15,000.

In 2005 the only difference from the previous example in the computation of the pension expense is the reduced expected return on the plan assets. Since the company contributed only $385,000 on December 31, 2004, an expected return of only $38,500 was earned in 2005. The company computes its pension expense for 2005 as follows:

Service cost	$420,000
Interest cost ($400,000 × 10%)	40,000
Expected return on plan assets ($385,000 × 10%)	(38,500)
Pension expense	$421,500

Since the company funds $400,000 in 2005, it records the following journal entry on December 31, 2005:

Pension Expense	421,500	
Cash		400,000
Prepaid/Accrued Pension Cost		21,500

The balance in the liability account at the end of 2005 is $36,500 ($15,000 + $21,500).

In 2006 the computation of the pension expense is again affected by the reduced expected return on the plan assets. Since the company contributed only $400,000, the assets of the pension fund on January 1, 2006 are $803,500 ($385,000 invested at the end of 2004 + $38,500 actual return in 2005 − $20,000 payment to retired employees at the end of 2005 + $400,000 invested at the end of 2005), and an expected return of $80,350 on those assets was earned during 2006. Therefore, the company computes its pension expense for 2006 as follows:

Service cost	$432,000
Interest cost ($840,000 × 10%)	84,000
Expected return on plan assets ($803,500 × 10%)	(80,350)
Pension expense	$435,650

Since the company funds $415,000 in 2006, it records the following journal entry on December 31, 2006:

Pension Expense	435,650	
Cash		415,000
Prepaid/Accrued Pension Cost		20,650

---

11. For illustrative purposes, the amount funded is less than the service cost. In some circumstances this procedure might be a violation of the minimum funding requirements of ERISA. However, the amount funded may be less than the *total* pension expense.

The balance in the liability account at the end of 2006 is $57,150 ($36,500 + $20,650).

Example 3: Pension Expense Less Than Pension Funding, and Expected Return on Plan Assets Different from Both Actual Return and Discount Rate

Assume the same facts for the Carlisle Company as in Example 1, except that (a) instead of funding an amount equal to the pension expense, the company funds $415,000 in 2004, $425,000 in 2005, and $440,000 in 2006, and (b) the expected return is 11% in each year, whereas the actual return is 12% in 2005. Since the company provides *more* assets to the pension fund and expects to earn a higher return on those assets, the pension expense is less to compensate for the higher return. The company's pension expense in 2004 is the $400,000 service cost and the journal entry on December 31, 2004 is:

Pension Expense	400,000	
Prepaid/Accrued Pension Cost	15,000	
Cash		415,000

Since the company funds $415,000 in 2004 when the expense is $400,000, it recognizes an asset, Prepaid/Accrued Pension Cost, of $15,000.

In 2005 the only difference in the computation of the pension expense from Example 1 is the increased expected return on the plan assets. Since the company contributed $415,000 on December 31, 2004, its expected return on the plan assets is $45,650 in 2005. The company computes the pension expense for 2005 as follows:

Service cost	$420,000
Interest cost ($400,000 × 10%)	40,000
Expected return on plan assets ($415,000 × 11%)	(45,650)
Pension expense	$414,350

Since the company funds $425,000 in 2005, it records the following journal entry on December 31, 2005:

Pension Expense	414,350	
Prepaid/Accrued Pension Cost	10,650	
Cash		425,000

The balance in the Prepaid asset account at the end of 2005 is $25,650 ($15,000 + $10,650).

In 2006, the computation of the pension expense is slightly more complicated. This is because the company earned a higher actual return (12%) than its expected return (11%) on its plan assets in 2005, so it has more total plan assets. Its plan assets at the beginning of 2006 are $869,800 [$415,000 invested at the end of 2004 + $49,800 ($415,000 × 0.12) actual return on plan assets −$20,000 payment to retired employees + $425,000 invested at the end of 2005]. Assuming the company continues to expect to earn 11% on its plan assets, its expected return for 2006 is $95,678. Therefore, the company computes its pension expense for 2006 as follows:

Service cost	$432,000
Interest cost ($840,000 × 10%)	84,000
Expected return on plan assets ($869,800 × 11%)	(95,678)
Pension expense	$420,322

Since the company funds $440,000 in 2006, it records the following journal entry on December 31, 2006:

Pension Expense	420,322	
Prepaid/Accrued Pension Cost	19,678	
Cash		440,000

The balance in the Prepaid asset account at the end of 2006 is $45,328 ($25,650 + $19,678).

It is important that you understand the impact of the *expected* and *actual* rates of return on plan assets. As we have discussed, a company uses the expected return in the computation of its pension expense for the year. However, the actual return for the year increases the value of the plan assets at the end of the year. In the next year, the company multiplies those actual plan assets by the expected return to compute the amount that it subtracts to compute its the pension expense for that next year. In its pension plan disclosures, the company includes the actual return on its plan assets in the reconciliation of the beginning and ending balances of the fair value of its plan assets, as we show in Example 8.

Example 4: Pension Expense Including Amortization of Unrecognized Prior Service Cost

The previous three examples illustrated relatively simple computations of pension expense and the related pension liability or asset. The remaining examples deal with more complex issues. Recall that a company may grant increased retroactive benefits based on services performed by employees in prior periods. The cost of providing these benefits is called a prior service cost. A prior service cost also may arise when a company adopts a pension plan. A prior service cost causes an increase in the projected benefit obligation. However, the company does not recognize it (so it is called "unrecognized") in the balance sheet, but amortizes it as a component of pension expense.

To illustrate this amortization, assume the same facts for the Carlisle Company as in Example 3, except that the company awarded retroactive benefits to the employees when it adopted the pension plan on January 1, 2004. The company's actuary computed the unrecognized prior service cost to be $2 million, which is the amount added to the projected benefit obligation on January 1, 2004. To fund this projected benefit obligation, the company decided to increase its contribution by $260,000 per year. For simplicity, we also assume that the company amortizes the unrecognized prior service cost by the straight-line method over the remaining 20-year service life of its active employees. Thus, its amortization is $100,000 ($2,000,000 ÷ 20) per year.

The company's pension expense in 2004 now has three components. In addition to the service cost of $400,000, the company recognizes both the interest cost on the $2 million projected benefit obligation and the $100,000 amortization of the unrecognized prior service cost. Therefore, it computes the pension expense for 2004 as follows:

Service cost	$400,000
Interest cost ($2,000,000 × 10%)	200,000
Amortization of unrecognized prior service cost	100,000
Pension expense	$700,000

Since the company funds $675,000 ($415,000 + $260,000) in 2004, it records the following journal entry on December 31, 2004:

Pension Expense	700,000	
Cash		675,000
Prepaid/Accrued Pension Cost		25,000

Note that the company does *not* include the unrecognized prior service cost of $1.9 million ($2 million − $100,000 amortized) in its balance sheet, but includes it in the disclosures we discussed earlier.[12]

---

12. It is possible that the company might include an additional pension liability in its year-end balance sheet. We discuss this topic in Example 7.

On January 1, 2005 the projected benefit obligation is $2,600,000 ($2 million beginning amount + $400,000 service cost + $200,000 interest cost). Therefore, the company computes the pension expense for 2005 as follows:

Service cost	$420,000
Interest cost ($2,600,000 × 10%)	260,000
Expected return on plan assets ($675,000 × 11%)	(74,250)
Amortization of unrecognized prior service cost	100,000
Pension expense	$705,750

Since the company funds $685,000 ($425,000 + $260,000) in 2005, it records the following journal entry on December 31, 2005:

Pension Expense	705,750	
Cash		685,000
Prepaid/Accrued Pension Cost		20,750

On January 1, 2006 the projected benefit obligation is $3,260,000 ($2,600,000 beginning amount + $420,000 service cost + $260,000 interest cost − $20,000 paid to retired employees), the plan assets are $1,421,000 ($675,000 invested at the end of 2004 + $81,000 ($675,000 × 12%) actual return on plan assets + $685,000 invested at the end of 2005 − $20,000 paid to retired employees), and the company computes the pension expense for 2006 as follows:

Service cost	$432,000
Interest cost ($3,260,000 × 10%)	326,000
Expected return on plan assets ($1,421,000 × 11%)	(156,310)
Amortization of unrecognized prior service cost	100,000
Pension expense	$701,690

Since the company funds $700,000 ($440,000 + $260,000) in 2006, it records the following journal entry on December 31, 2006:

Pension Expense	701,690	
Cash		700,000
Prepaid/Accrued Pension Cost		1,690

Note that the plan assets at the end of 2006 are $2,271,520 [$1,421,000 + $170,520 ($1,421,000 × 12%) + $700,000 − $20,000].

Example 5: Calculation of Amortization of Unrecognized Prior Service Cost

In Example 4 the calculation of pension expense included the amortization of unrecognized prior service cost. In that example, we used an "average life" of 20 years to determine the amount of the amortization. We explain two methods of calculating the amount of the amortization in this example. The preferred method assigns an equal amount to each future period of service for each active participating employee at the date of the amendment who is expected to receive future benefits under the plan. Since the FASB did not give this method a title, we will refer to it as the "years-of-future-service" method. Alternatively, straight-line amortization over the average remaining service life of employees may be used for simplicity.

Exhibits 19-3 and 19-4 illustrate the preferred years-of-future-service method of amortization. We assume that at the beginning of 2004 the Watts Company has nine employees

EXHIBIT 19-3   Computation of Amortization Fraction

Employees	Expected Years of Future Service	Number of Service Years Rendered in Each Year						
		2004	2005	2006	2007	2008	2009	2010
A	3	1	1	1				
B	4	1	1	1	1			
C, D	5	2	2	2	2	2		
E, F	6	2	2	2	2	2	2	
G, H, I	7	3	3	3	3	3	3	3
Total		9	9	9	8	7	5	3	= 50
Amortization Fraction		9/50	9/50	9/50	8/50	7/50	5/50	3/50

participating in its pension plan who are expected to receive benefits. One employee (A) is expected to retire after 3 years, one (B) after 4, two (C and D) after 5, two (E and F) after 6, and three (G, H, and I) after 7 years. Exhibit 19-3 illustrates the computation of the amortization fraction. First, the company computes the number of service years rendered by the nine employees in each calendar year. Thus, in 2004 there are 9 service years rendered, while in 2008 there are only 7 service years rendered because employees A and B have retired. The total number of these service years is 50. Then, the company computes the amortization fraction for each year by dividing the total service years in each calendar year by the total of 50. Thus, in 2004, 9/50 is the amortization fraction, whereas in 2008, 7/50 is the fraction.

If we assume that the company's actuary computed the total unrecognized prior service cost at the beginning of 2004 to be $400,000, the company calculates the amount of the amortization each year as we show in Exhibit 19-4. For instance, the company amortizes $72,000 ($400,000 × 9/50) in 2004, while it amortizes $56,000 ($400,000 × 7/50) in 2008.[13] The company includes this amount in the total pension

EXHIBIT 19-4   Amortization of Unrecognized Prior Service Cost: Years-of-Future-Service Method

Year	Total Unrecognized Prior Service Cost[a]	Amortization Fraction[b]	Amortization to Increase Pension Expense[c]	Remaining Unrecognized Prior Service Cost[d]
2004	$400,000	9/50	$72,000	$328,000
2005	400,000	9/50	72,000	256,000
2006	400,000	9/50	72,000	184,000
2007	400,000	8/50	64,000	120,000
2008	400,000	7/50	56,000	64,000
2009	400,000	5/50	40,000	24,000
2010	400,000	3/50	24,000	—

a. Computed by actuary
b. From Exhibit 19-3
c. $400,000 × amortization fraction
d. Balance from end of previous year (or initial balance) − amortization for the current year

13. In *FASB Statement No. 87* (par. 85 and 86), a similar schedule and an amortization table are illustrated, but an assumption that an equal number of employees retire each year is made. This assumption provides a "pure" sum-of-the-years'-digits set of fractions that yield a constantly decreasing amortization amount each period. Since this may not be a realistic assumption, we assume a varying number of employees retiring each period, which results in a modified sum-of-the-years'-digits set of fractions.

expense on its income statement for each year. The remaining unrecognized prior service cost is the balance at the end of the previous year less the amount amortized for the year. Remember that the company does *not* include this amount in its balance sheet, but *does* include it in the required pension plan disclosures, as we discussed earlier.

To compute the alternative straight-line amortization, the company calculates the average remaining service life of the participating employees. We illustrate this method using the same employee group as we assumed earlier. The company computes the total number of service years rendered (50) by adding the expected years of service for all employees [i.e., $3(A) + 4(B) + 5(C) + 5(D) + 6(E) + 6(F) + 7(G) + 7(H) + 7(I)$] and dividing by the number of employees (9) to give an average service life of 5.56 years. Exhibit 19-5 illustrates the computation of the straight-line amortization. Under this method, the company amortizes $71,942 each year from 2004 through 2008 to increase the pension expense. In 2009 the amortization is only $40,290, the amount needed to reduce the remaining unrecognized prior service cost to zero. This straight-line method is also used for the amortization of the unrecognized net gain or loss we discuss in the next example. Note that if an amendment caused a decrease in future benefits, the resulting "negative" prior service cost is amortized in the same manner to *decrease* pension expense each period.

EXHIBIT 19-5   **Amortization of Unrecognized Prior Service Cost: Straight-Line Method**

Year	Total Unrecognized Prior Service Cost[a]	Amortization to Increase Pension Expense[b]	Remaining Unrecognized Prior Service Cost[c]
2004	$400,000	$71,942	$328,058
2005	400,000	71,942	256,116
2006	400,000	71,942	184,174
2007	400,000	71,942	112,232
2008	400,000	71,942	40,290
2009	400,000	40,290[d]	—

a. Computed by actuary
b. $400,000 total unrecognized prior service cost ÷ 5.56 (50 total service years ÷ 9 employees) average remaining service life
c. Balance from end of previous year (or initial balance) − amortization for the year
d. To reduce the remaining unrecognized prior service cost to zero

---

Example 6: Pension Expense Including Net Gain or Loss (to Extent Recognized)

An unrecognized gain or loss from previous periods arises from (a) changes in the amount of the projected benefit obligation resulting from experience different from that assumed, and (b) changes in actuarial assumptions. The excess of this unrecognized gain or loss over a "corridor" amount (discussed later) is amortized over the remaining service life of active employees expected to receive benefits under the plan. A company *adds* amortization of an unrecognized net loss to pension expense and *subtracts* any amortization of an unrecognized net gain from pension expense as part of the net gain or loss.

Exhibit 19-6 illustrates the computation of the net gain or loss included in pension expense for the years 2004 through 2007. This example is for the Bliss Company, which has had a defined benefit pension plan for its employees for several years. The amounts of the cumulative unrecognized net loss (gain), the projected benefit obligation (actual), and the fair value of the plan assets are based on information provided by the company's actuary and funding agency.

EXHIBIT 19-6   Computation of Net Gain or Loss

Year	Cumulative Unrecognized Net Loss (Gain)[a]	Projected Benefit Obligation: Actual[a]	Fair Value of Plan Assets[a]	Corridor[b]	Excess Unrecognized Net Loss (Gain)[c]	Recognized Net Loss (Gain)[d]
2004	$13,000	$110,000	$100,000	$11,000	$2,000	$200
2005	(2,300)	135,000	130,000	13,500	—[e]	—
2006	18,700	168,000	170,000	17,000	1,700	170
2007	27,500	230,000	215,000	23,000	4,500	450

a. At the beginning of the year
b. 10% of the greater of the actual projected benefit obligation or the fair value of the plan assets at the beginning of the year
c. Absolute value of the cumulative unrecognized net loss (gain) − corridor
d. Excess unrecognized net loss (gain) ÷ average remaining service life (10 years)
e. Since the absolute value of the cumulative unrecognized net loss (gain) is less than the corridor, there is no excess unrecognized net loss (gain)

To compute the amortization, the initial step is to determine the cumulative unrecognized net gain or loss at the beginning of the year. This amount reflects prior differences between the actual and expected projected benefit obligation and the related prior amortization. As we noted earlier, these differences may be due to experience different from that assumed or from changes in actuarial assumptions. Although the calculations to determine the cumulative unrecognized net gain or loss are too complex to make here, we briefly discuss the computational process. For instance, in a given year the company computes the expected projected benefit obligation at year-end by adjusting the beginning actual projected benefit obligation for the expected current service cost, interest cost, and benefits paid. The company (or its actuary) computes the actual projected benefit obligation at year-end based on current information. Any difference between the expected and actual projected benefit obligation is the unrecognized gain or loss for the year. This, in turn, is combined with any previously unamortized cumulative unrecognized net gain or loss to determine the cumulative unrecognized net gain or loss subject to potential amortization over future periods.

The company calculates the amounts in the Cumulative Unrecognized Net Loss (Gain) column of Exhibit 19-6 at the beginning of the year, based on previous periods. Thus, for instance, the $13,000 amount of cumulative unrecognized net loss at the beginning of 2004 is a result of experience different from that assumed and changes in actuarial assumptions in periods prior to 2004. Note in this example that we have assumed a high volatility to better explain the calculations. Also note that we show a cumulative unrecognized net *loss* without parentheses because the related amortization is *added* to pension expense, whereas we show a *gain* in parentheses because the amortization is *deducted*.

The company also calculates the amounts in the Projected Benefit Obligation and the Fair Value of Plan Assets columns at the beginning of the year. For instance, it calculates the $110,000 projected benefit obligation and the $100,000 fair value of the plan assets in 2004 at the beginning of 2004 based on information provided by its actuary and funding agency. These amounts are necessary to determine the **corridor** amount. **The corridor is 10% of the greater of the actual projected benefit obligation or the fair value of the plan assets at the beginning of the period.** As we discussed earlier, the corridor reduces the volatility of the pension expense.

The amortization of any cumulative unrecognized net gain or loss occurs in a given year only if, at the beginning of the year, the (absolute value of the) cumulative unrecognized net gain or loss exceeds the corridor. This 10% threshold (the corridor) is intended to reduce fluctuations in pension expense. In many cases the corridor will not be exceeded, so no amortization is recorded. Also, if a company had a large cumulative unrecognized net gain (loss) at the beginning of a given year, it would reduce (increase) its pension expense only by the amortization of the cumulative unrecognized net gain (loss) in excess of the corridor amount. It is unlikely that the company would have a cumulative unrecognized net loss (gain) at the beginning of the next year in excess of the corridor amount. Even in such an extreme situation, the pension expense would be increased (decreased) only by the amount of the amortization of the cumulative unrecognized net loss (gain) in excess of the corridor amount.

In Exhibit 19-6 the amount in the Corridor column for a given year is 10% of the higher of the actual projected benefit obligation or the fair value of the plan assets at the beginning of that year. Thus, in 2004 the company computes the $11,000 corridor as 10% of the $110,000 actual projected benefit obligation because it is the higher of the two amounts. In 2006, however, it computes the $17,000 corridor as 10% of the $170,000 fair value of the plan assets.

The amount in the Excess Unrecognized Net Loss (Gain) column for a given year is simply the excess of the (absolute value of the) cumulative unrecognized net loss (gain) over the corridor at the beginning of that year. Thus, in 2004 the $2,000 excess unrecognized net loss is the difference between the $13,000 cumulative unrecognized net loss and the $11,000 corridor. In 2005, however, the corridor exceeds the cumulative unrecognized net gain, so there is no excess.

The amount in the Recognized Net Loss (Gain) column for a given year is the adjustment to pension expense. The company computes each amortization amount by dividing the excess unrecognized net loss (gain) for that year by the average remaining service life of the active employees expected to receive benefits under the plan. In this example, we assume a 10-year average service life for all years. In reality, the company may have to recompute the average service life each year to reflect changes in its employee work force. For instance, in 2004 the $200 amortization that the company *adds* to pension expense as the recognized net loss is determined by dividing the $2,000 excess unrecognized net loss by the 10-year average service life.

Example 7: Recognition of Additional Pension Liability

The previous examples focused on the computation of a company's pension expense and the related pension liability or asset. This example deals with the recognition of an additional pension liability, which may arise when the company's accumulated benefit obligation is greater than the fair value of the plan assets. To illustrate the recognition of the additional liability, assume the following facts for the Devon Company at the end of 2004:

Projected benefit obligation	$2,000,000
Accumulated benefit obligation	1,200,000
Plan assets	1,000,000 fair value
Prepaid/accrued pension cost	50,000 liability
Unrecognized prior service cost	300,000

Remember that the difference between the two benefit obligations is that the *projected* benefit obligation includes assumed future pay increases, whereas the *accumulated* benefit obligation is based on current pay levels (see the definitions in Exhibit 19-2). The company computes the unfunded *accumulated* benefit obligation as the difference between the accumulated benefit obligation and the fair value of the plan assets as follows:

Accumulated benefit obligation	$1,200,000
Plan assets (fair value)	(1,000,000)
Unfunded accumulated benefit obligation	$ 200,000

This unfunded accumulated benefit obligation of $200,000 is the minimum liability that the company must recognize. Since the company already has recorded a liability (prepaid/accrued pension cost) of $50,000, it calculates the *additional* liability of $150,000 recognized at the end of 2004 as follows:

Unfunded accumulated benefit obligation	$200,000
Prepaid/accrued pension cost (liability)	(50,000)
Additional pension liability	$150,000

Besides recognizing the additional liability, the company also recognizes an intangible asset of an equal amount because the intangible asset is less than the unrecognized prior service cost of $300,000. Since the FASB did not suggest a title, we call it Deferred Pension Cost. Thus, the journal entry on December 31, 2004 to record the intangible asset and to increase the pension liability from $50,000 to $200,000 is as follows:

Deferred Pension Cost	150,000	
Additional Pension Liability		150,000

The Devon Company reports the Deferred Pension Cost account balance of $150,000 as an intangible asset on its 2004 year-end balance sheet. It combines the balances of the Additional Pension Liability and Prepaid/Accrued Pension Cost accounts to report a total pension liability of $200,000 on the balance sheet. The company also includes the additional liability ($150,000) in its pension plan disclosures.

The company makes a different journal entry if the preceding facts remained the same, except that the company had a prepaid/accrued pension cost *asset* of $40,000 instead of the liability of $50,000. In this case, the minimum liability must still be $200,000, but a $40,000 asset exists. Consequently, the company must record a liability and an intangible asset of $240,000 (the unfunded accumulated benefit obligation of $200,000 + the prepaid/accrued pension cost asset of $40,000). The journal entry is as follows:

Deferred Pension Cost	240,000	
Additional Pension Liability		240,000

The company combines (nets) the balances of the Additional Pension Liability and Prepaid/Accrued Pension Cost accounts to report a net pension liability of $200,000 on its balance sheet. The company also includes the additional liability in its pension plan disclosures.

In the previous situations we assumed that the intangible asset does not exceed the unrecognized prior service cost. In other words, the need for the recognition of the additional liability arose because of amendments to the plan that created prior service costs and increased the accumulated benefit obligation, but have not yet been funded by the company.

Another complexity in the recognition of the additional liability occurs if there is no unrecognized prior service cost, or if it exceeds the unrecognized prior service cost. Typically, this situation arises because there have been negative returns on the plan assets. Since it would be inappropriate for a company to record such declines in value of the plan assets as an intangible asset of the company, it includes the amount as a negative component of the year's other comprehensive income and also as a reduction in accumulated other comprehensive income. To illustrate this situation, we use the same facts as originally given for the Devon Company, but, in addition, the company has an unrecognized prior service cost of $120,000 instead of $300,000. The company recognizes the same additional liability of $150,000, but the intangible asset cannot exceed the unrecognized prior service cost of $120,000. Therefore, the company subtracts the $30,000 difference from accumulated other comprehensive income in its stockholders' equity. The journal entry by the Devon Company is as follows:

Deferred Pension Cost	120,000	
Excess of Additional Pension Liability Over		
Unrecognized Prior Service Cost	30,000	
Additional Pension Liability		150,000

In this case, the Devon Company reports on its 2004 year-end balance sheet the $120,000 balance in Deferred Pension Cost as an intangible asset. It combines the Prepaid/Accrued Pension Cost liability of $50,000 and the Additional Pension Liability of $150,000 in a single amount, and reports the $30,000 excess in the accumulated other comprehensive income component of its stockholders' equity section as follows (other amounts assumed):

Stockholders' Equity	
Common stock	$600,000
Additional paid-in capital	230,000
Retained earnings	170,000
Accumulated other comprehensive income (loss)	
Excess of additional pension liability over unrecognized prior service cost	(30,000)
Total stockholders' equity	$970,000

Note that the additional liability, the intangible asset, and the amount included in accumulated other comprehensive income (loss) are *not* amortized. The company computes the appropriate amounts each year and includes them in its balance sheet for that year. For example, refer back to the original facts for the Devon Company. In that situation, it recorded the additional liability of $150,000 at the end of 2004. Now suppose that at the end of 2005, the following information is available:

Accumulated benefit obligation	$1,300,000
Plan assets	1,220,000 fair value
Prepaid/accrued pension cost	60,000 liability
Unrecognized prior service cost	110,000

The unfunded accumulated benefit obligation is $80,000 ($1,300,000 − $1,220,000) and the required additional liability at the end of 2005 is $20,000 ($80,000 − $60,000). Since the additional liability is less than the unrecognized prior service cost of $110,000, the company does not include any reduction in its accumulated other comprehensive income for the year. The journal entry on December 31, 2005 to adjust the additional liability is as follows:

Additional Pension Liability	130,000	
Deferred Pension Cost		130,000

This entry reduces the existing account balances of $150,000 by $130,000 to $20,000. Note that the changes in the account balances have no effect on the income statement. Also note that when a company has recognized accumulated other comprehensive income at the end of one year, it must adjust that amount each year based on the new calculations. It reports the change in the accumulated other comprehensive income as a "reclassification adjustment" in its other comprehensive income for the year, as we discussed in Chapter 14.

Example 8: Disclosures

To improve the usefulness of a company's disclosures about its defined benefit pension plan, as we discussed earlier, the company must report certain information in the notes to its financial statements, in addition to the amounts contained in its financial statements. *FASB Statement No. 132* requires disclosure of, among other items, a reconciliation of the beginning and ending amounts of the projected benefit obligation, a reconciliation of the beginning and ending fair value of the plan assets, the components of the pension expense, and the discount rate used and the expected long-term rate of return on plan assets. We show these disclosures at the top of the next page for the

5 Understand disclosures of pensions.

Carlisle Company for 2006 using the facts from Example 3 that we illustrated earlier in the chapter.

Reconciliation of the beginning and ending amounts of the projected benefit obligation

Beginning projected benefit obligation	$ 840,000
Service cost	432,000
Interest cost	84,000
Actuarial gains and losses	0
Benefits paid	(20,000)
Plan amendments	0
Ending projected benefit obligation	$1,336,000

Reconciliation of the beginning and ending fair value of the plan assets

Beginning fair value of plan assets	$ 869,800
Actual return on plan assets	95,678
Contributions	440,000
Benefits paid	(20,000)
Ending fair value of plan assets	$1,385,478

Components of the pension expense

Service cost	$ 432,000
Interest cost	84,000
Expected return on plan assets	(95,678)
Amortization of prior service cost	0
Amortization of gains and losses	0
Amortization of any transition amount	0
Total pension expense	$ 420,332

Assumptions

Discount rate: 10%
Expected long-term rate of return on plan assets: 11%

It is important to note that in the reconciliation of the beginning and ending fair value of the plan assets, a company discloses the *actual* return on its pension plan assets. In the schedule listing the components of the pension expense, however, the company discloses the *expected* return on the pension plan assets. This aspect of the pension plan disclosures is important because it enables external users to compare the difference between the expected and actual returns to evaluate how well the pension funds are being managed.

Exhibit 19-7 illustrates these 2001 disclosures for **Yum! Brands** (owner of Pizza Hut, Taco Bell, and KFC) (these disclosures include information about postretirement benefit plans that we discuss later in the chapter). Note that Yum! Brands includes the information we have shown for the Carlisle Company, as well as the additional required disclosures.

Pension Worksheet

In Exhibit 19-8 we show a worksheet that you can use to help understand Examples 1 through 4 that we explained earlier in the chapter. We have completed the worksheet using the amounts in Example 4; it will be helpful for you to go back to this example and see how the amounts are included in the worksheet. Also, you should note three important aspects of this worksheet. First, the amounts at the bottom of the "pension expense" columns provide the information that Carlisle Company uses to determine the debit (dr) to the Pension Expense account, and the credits (cr) to the Cash and the Prepaid/Accrued Pension Cost accounts. Second, the ending projected benefit obligation and plan assets amounts for one year are the beginning amounts for the next year.

EXHIBIT 19-7 **Illustration of Pension Disclosures**

YUM! BRANDS

Note 15 Pension and Postretirement Medical Benefits

Pension Benefits

We sponsor noncontributory defined benefit pension plans covering substantially all full-time U.S. salaried employees, certain hourly employees and certain international employees. During 2001, the TRICON Retirement Plan (the "Plan") was amended such that any salaried employee hired or rehired by TRICON after September 30, 2001 will not be eligible to participate in the Plan. Benefits are based on years of service and earnings or stated amounts for each year of service.

Postretirement Medical Benefits

Our postretirement plan provides health care benefits, principally to U.S. salaried, retirees and their dependents. This plan includes retiree cost sharing provisions. During 2001, the plan was amended such that any salaried employee hired or rehired by TRICON after September 30, 2001 will not be eligible to participate in this plan. Employees hired prior to September 30, 2001 are eligible for benefits if they meet age and service requirements and qualify for retirement benefits.

   The components of net periodic benefit cost are set forth below:

	Pension Benefits		
	2001	2000	1999
Service cost	$ 20	$ 19	$ 20
Interest cost	28	24	22
Amortization of prior service cost	1	1	1
Expected return on plan assets	(29)	(25)	(24)
Recognized actuarial loss	1	—	—
Net periodic benefit cost	$ 21	$ 19	$ 19
Additional (gain) loss recognized due to:			
Curtailment	$ —	$ (4)	$ (4)
Special termination benefits	2	—	—

	Postretirement Medical Benefits		
	2001	2000	1999
Service cost	$ 2	$ 2	$ 2
Interest cost	4	3	3
Amortization of prior service cost	(1)	(1)	(2)
Net periodic benefit cost	$ 5	$ 4	$ 3
Additional (gain) recognized due to:			
Curtailment	$ —	$ (1)	$ (1)

Prior service costs are amortized on a straight-line basis over the average remaining service period of employees expected to receive benefits. Curtailment gains have generally been recognized in facility actions net gain as they have resulted primarily from refranchising and closure activities.

   The change in benefit obligation and plan assets and reconciliation of funded status is as follows:

	Pension Benefits		Postretirement Medical Benefits	
	2001	2000	2001	2000
Change in benefit obligation				
Benefit obligation at beginning of year	$ 351	$ 315	$ 48	$ 45
Service cost	20	19	2	2
Interest cost	28	24	4	3
Plan amendments	1	—	—	—
Special termination benefits	2	—	—	—
Curtailment (gain)	(3)	(5)	—	(2)
Benefits and expenses paid	(17)	(19)	(3)	(3)
Actuarial loss	38	17	7	3
Benefit obligation at end of year	$ 420	$ 351	$ 58	$ 48

continued

EXHIBIT 19-7, Continued

	Pension Benefits		Postretirement Medical Benefits	
	2001	2000	2001	2000
Change in plan assets				
Fair value of plan assets at beginning of year	$ 313	$ 290		
Actual return on plan assets	(51)	39		
Employer contributions	48	4		
Benefits paid	(17)	(19)		
Administrative expenses	(2)	(1)		
Fair value of plan assets at end of year	$ 291	$ 313		
Reconciliation of funded status				
Funded status	$(129)	$ (38)	$ (58)	$ (48)
Unrecognized actuarial loss (gain)	87	(30)	12	5
Unrecognized prior service cost	4	5	—	(1)
Net amount recognized at year-end	$ (38)	$ (63)	$ (46)	$ (44)
Amounts recognized in the statement of financial position consist of:				
Accrued benefit liability	$ (84)	$ (63)	$ (46)	$ (44)
Intangible asset	8	—	—	—
Accumulated other comprehensive loss	38	—	—	—
	$ (38)	$ (63)	$ (46)	$ (44)
Other comprehensive loss attributable to				
change in additional minimum liability recognition	$ 38	$ —		
Additional year-end information for pension plans with				
benefit obligations in excess of plan assets				
Benefit obligation	$ 420	$ 42		
Fair value of plan assets	291	—		
Additional year-end information for pension plans with				
accumulated benefit obligations in excess of plan assets				
Benefit obligation	$ 420	$ 42		
Accumulated benefit obligation	369	21		
Fair value of plan assets	291	—		

The assumptions used to compute the information above are set forth below:

	Pension Benefits			Postretirement Medical Benefits		
	2001	2000	1999	2001	2000	1999
Discount rate	7.6%	8.0%	7.8%	7.6%	8.3%	7.6%
Long-term rate of return on plan assets	10.0%	10.0%	10.0%	—	—	—
Rate of compensation increase	4.6%	5.0%	5.5%	4.6%	5.0%	5.5%

We have assumed the annual increase in cost of postretirement medical benefits was 8.0% for non-Medicare eligible retirees and 12.0% for Medicare eligible retirees in 2001 and will be 7.5% and 11.0%, respectively, in 2002. We are assuming the rates for non-Medicare and Medicare eligible retirees will decrease to an ultimate rate of 5.5% by 2008 and 2010, respectively, and remain at that level thereafter. There is a cap on our medical liability for certain retirees. The cap for Medicare eligible retirees was reached in 2000 and the cap for non-Medicare eligible retirees is expected to be reached between the years 2010–2012; once the cap is reached, our annual cost per retiree will not increase.

Assumed health care cost trend rates have a significant effect on the amounts reported for our postretirement health care plans. A one percent increase or decrease in the assumed health care cost trend rates would have increased or decreased our accumulated postretirement benefit obligation at December 29, 2001 by approximately $3 million. The impact on our 2001 benefit cost would not have been significant.

Q U E S T I O N S

Q Does the company have defined benefit plans or defined contribution plans? **Q** How much is the company's pension expense for 2001? **Q** Was the company's actual return on plan assets in 2001 greater or less than the expected return? **Q** How much are the accumulated and projected benefit obligations at the end of 2001? **Q** Why are the amounts different? **Q** Is the company in a net asset or liability position for its pension plans at the end of 2001? **Q** What would be the effect of a decrease in the discount rate on the amounts disclosed by the company for 2001? **Q** If the company decreased the expected return on pension plan assets, what would be the effect on the amounts disclosed by the company for 2001?

EXHIBIT 19-8   Pension Plan Worksheet (Using Amounts in Example 4)

Item	2004 Amount	2004 Pension Expense	2005 Amount	2005 Pension Expense	2006 Amount	2006 Pension Expense
Beginning projected benefit obligation	$2,000,000[a]		$2,600,000		$3,260,000	
× Discount rate	× 0.10		× 0.10		× 0.10	
= Interest cost	$ 200,000 →	$200,000	$ 260,000 →	$260,000	$ 326,000 →	$326,000
Beginning projected benefit obligation	2,000,000		2,600,000		3,260,000	
+ Service cost	400,000 →	400,000	420,000 →	420,000	432,000 →	432,000
− Benefits paid	(0)		(20,000)		(20,000)	
= Ending projected benefit obligation	$2,600,000		$3,260,000		$3,998,000	
Beginning plan assets	$ 0		$ 675,000		$1,421,000	
× Expected rate of return	× 0.11		× 0.11		× 0.11	
= Expected return	$ 0 →	(0)	$ 74,250 →	(74,250)	$ 156,310 →	(156,310)
Beginning plan assets	$ 0		$ 675,000		$1,421,000	
+ Actual return[b]	0		81,000		170,520	
+ Contributions	675,000		685,000		700,000	
− Benefits paid	(0)		(20,000)		(20,000)	
= Ending plan assets	$ 675,000		$1,421,000		$2,271,520	
Unrecognized prior service cost	$2,000,000		$2,000,000		$2,000,000	
÷ Average service life (years)[c]	÷ 20		÷ 20		÷ 20	
= Amortization of unrecognized prior service cost	$ 100,000 →	100,000	$ 100,000 →	100,000	$ 100,000 →	100,000
Net gain or loss[d]	$ 0 →	0	$ 0 →	0	$ 0 →	0
Total Pension Expense		$700,000 dr		$705,750 dr		$701,690 dr
Contribution (Cash)		675,000 cr		685,000 cr		700,000 cr
Adjustment to Prepaid/Accrued Pension Cost		$ 25,000 cr		$ 20,750 cr		$ 1,690 cr

[a] Unrecognized prior service cost at adoption of plan
[b] The actual return is assumed to be 12% each year × Beginning plan assets
[c] Or times amortization fraction
[d] Calculated using the corridor approach; see Exhibit 19-6

Third, the calculations for the projected benefit obligation and the plan assets provide much of the information that Carlisle would report in its notes to its financial statements that we illustrated in Example 8. Also, the worksheet is simplified because it does not include certain complexities, such as when the corridor needs to be used to determine the net gain or loss to be included in the pension expense, or the calculation of the minimum pension liability.

Summary of Issues Related to Pensions

In Exhibit 19-9, we summarize the major issues related to accounting for the defined benefit pension plan of a company in T-account form for 2004. While each "entry" balances, it is important to note that four of the "accounts" (plan assets, projected benefit obligation, unrecognized loss or gain, and unrecognized prior service cost) are *not* included

EXHIBIT 19-9 Summary of Issues Related to Defined Benefit Pension Plan for 2004

Not included in the company's financial statements:

Plan Assets

	Beginning balance	100*	(f)	Payments to retirees	14
(c)	Actual return on plan assets	9			
(g)	Funding	98			
	Ending balance	193			

Projected Benefit Obligation (Liability)

(f)	Payments to retirees	14		Beginning balance	90
			(a)	Service cost	95
			(b)	Interest	7
			(d)	Prior service cost	40
				Ending balance	218

Unrecognized Prior Service Cost

(d)	Prior service cost	40	(e)	Amortization	3
	Ending balance	37			

Included in the company's financial statements:

Pension Expense

(a)	Service cost	95	(c)	Expected return on plan assets	9
(b)	Interest	7			
(e)	Amortization of prior service cost	3			
(g)	Total expense	96			

Cash

			(g) Funding	98

Prepaid (Accrued) Pension Cost

	Beginning balance	10	
(g)	Funding exceeds expense	2	
	Ending balance	12	

*All amounts in thousands of dollars.

in the company's financial statements. The other three accounts [pension expense, cash, and prepaid (accrued) pension cost] are included in the financial statements. In this summary, the balance in the Prepaid (Accrued) Pension Cost is equal to the net balance of the Plan Assets, Projected Benefit Obligation, Unrealized Loss/Gain, and Unrecognized Prior Service Cost accounts. Thus, at the beginning of the year, $10,000 = $100,000 − $90,000. All amounts are assumed. We discuss each entry in the following sections.

We assume that the company started the plan in 2003, it had no prior service costs, and no employees retired during the year. Based on the actuarial computation of the service cost (the only component of pension expense for 2003), the company makes its first journal entry for the plan on December 31, 2003 as follows:

Pension Expense	90,000	
Prepaid (Accrued) Pension Cost	10,000	
Cash		100,000

Therefore, at the beginning of 2004 the plan assets are $100,000, the projected benefit obligation is $90,000, and the prepaid (accrued) pension cost is $10,000. The following information is for 2004.

(a) **Service Cost.** The service cost for 2004 of $95,000 is a component of the pension expense and increases the projected benefit obligation.

(b) **Interest Cost.** The interest cost for 2004 of $7,000 is a component of the pension expense and increases the projected benefit obligation.

(c) **Expected and Actual Return on Plan Assets.** The actual and expected return on plan assets for 2004 of $9,000 increases the plan assets and reduces the pension expense. Any difference between the actual and expected return on plan assets would be a component of the net gain or loss.

(d) **Unrecognized Prior Service Cost.** During 2004 the company provides retroactive benefits with a present value of $40,000. This creates an unrecognized prior service cost and increases the projected benefit obligation.

(e) **Amortization of the Unrecognized Prior Service Cost.** During 2004 the company amortizes the unrecognized prior service cost by $3,000. This increases the pension expense and decreases the unrecognized prior service cost.

(f) **Payments to Retired Employees.** Payments of $14,000 by the funding agency to retired employees in 2004 decrease the plan assets and the projected benefit obligation.

(g) **Pension Expense and Funding by the Company.** The $96,000 pension expense consists of the $95,000 service cost (a), plus the $7,000 interest cost (b), minus the $9,000 expected return on plan assets (c), plus the $3,000 amortization of the prior service cost (e). The payment of $98,000 by the company to the funding agency increases the plan assets. The prepaid (accrued) pension cost is also increased because the journal entry to record the payment of $98,000 involves a debit to pension expense for $96,000 and a debit to prepaid (accrued) pension cost for $2,000.

At the end of 2004, note that the balance in the Prepaid (Accrued) Pension cost account of $12,000 is equal to the balance in the Plan Assets of $193,000, minus the balance in the Projected Benefit Obligation of $218,000, plus the balance in the Unrecognized Prior Service Cost account of $37,000. In its disclosures the company reconciles the plan's funded status (the difference between the fair value of the assets and the projected benefit obligation) to the prepaid (accrued) pension cost as follows:

Fair value of plan assets	$ 193
Projected benefit obligation	(218)
Funded status	$ (25)
Unrecognized prior service cost	37
Prepaid (accrued) pension cost	$ 12

CONCEPTUAL ISSUES RELATED TO DEFINED BENEFIT PENSION PLANS

6 Explain the conceptual issues regarding pensions.

In their analyses of pension accounting, the APB and the FASB have considered several conceptual issues related to pension expense, pension liabilities, and pension assets. We briefly discuss each of these conceptual issues in the following sections.[14]

Pension Expense

The first conceptual issue in accounting for pension plans involves the proper amount of pension cost that the employer-company should recognize and when it should report that amount as pension expense on its income statement. *Expenses* are defined as "outflows or other using up of assets or incurrences of liabilities . . . (during a period) from delivering or producing goods, rendering services, or carrying out other activities that constitute an

---

14. This discussion is a brief summary of that presented in "Employers' Accounting for Pensions and Other Postemployment Benefits," *FASB Discussion Memorandum* (Stamford, Conn.: FASB, 1981).

entity's ongoing major or central operations."[15] Recall also that once a company has assigned revenues to a particular accounting period, it matches expenses against the revenues by association of cause and effect, systematic and rational allocation, or immediate recognition.

Pension cost may consist of several components. The primary component of pension cost is the deferred compensation (*service cost*) the employer will pay to employees in the future in return for their current services. However, since employees' compensation is deferred until retirement, the employees are, in effect, providing a "loan" to the employer. The *interest* on that loan may be a component of pension cost. In addition, an employer generally invests its pension contributions to a pension fund with the intent of earning a return on these assets. A possible *negative* component of pension cost is the *return* earned on the pension fund assets. An employer that begins a pension plan or makes modifications in its existing plan may provide additional benefits to employees as a result of *services they performed in previous years*. Part or all of the cost of these previously earned benefits may be a component of pension cost. Finally, unforeseen events related to a pension plan may result in (a) deviations in the current period between actual experience and the assumptions used, and (b) changes in the assumptions about the future. The resulting *gains* and *losses* may be a component of pension cost. Pension expense computed under *FASB Statement No. 87* includes all these components, although some are in a modified form.

Four alternative methods have been suggested for an employer to account for its prior service cost. The first is to account for it prospectively, which is the approach adopted by *FASB Statement No. 87*. This method requires that the cost be expensed in the current and future periods, and that no liability be recorded when the cost arises. It is often argued that this method violates the matching concept because all the services to be performed by the employees have been completed in previous periods. Also, it is often suggested that the lack of recognition of a pension obligation is a violation of the concept of a liability.

The second alternative is for an employer to recognize the total amount as an expense in the period in which it arises (i.e., the current period) and to record a liability. This procedure also violates the matching concept because the services were performed by the employees in previous periods and not in the current period. It might also tend to dissuade companies from adopting, or changing, pension plans because of the related effect (i.e., decrease) on net income of the current period.

The third alternative is for an employer to debit retained earnings (as a prior period adjustment) and to record a liability. This procedure violates the all-inclusive income concept because the total amounts are never included in the income statement. Also, many companies resist the recording of a liability because of the effect it has on their debt-to-equity ratios and on similar measures of financial performance.

The fourth alternative is for an employer to record an intangible asset and liability of equal amounts. Although it is difficult to see how an asset is created by the recognition of pension benefits earned by employees in previous periods, the argument is that the employer's decision to improve a pension plan is forward-looking and rational. That is, the employer would take on an increased obligation only if future benefits of at least an equal amount were expected to result. In this sense, the future economic benefits (intangible asset) should be recognized along with the liability and should be expensed over some future period. Similarly, gains and losses could be accounted for prospectively, currently, as a prior period adjustment, or as a deferred item.

Pension Liabilities

A second conceptual issue regarding accounting for pension plans involves the identification and recording of pension plan liabilities. *Liabilities* are probable future sacrifices of economic benefits arising from present obligations of a company to transfer assets or

---

15. "Elements of Financial Statements," *FASB Statement of Financial Accounting Concepts No. 6* (Stamford, Conn.: FASB, 1985), par. 80.

provide services to other entities in the future as a result of past transactions or events.[16] Furthermore, once a liability is identified, it must be measurable to be reported on a company's balance sheet.

Generally, it is agreed that a pension is a form of deferred compensation. An employer's pension obligation may be viewed as an obligation to make contributions to the plan, or as an obligation to employees for pensions promised. Since the exact amount of the pension obligation for each employee cannot be known until the employee (or related beneficiary) dies, actuaries can only estimate the amount of the obligation using assumptions about employee turnover, life expectancy, and other variables.

We briefly summarize the five alternatives for meeting the recognition-measurement criteria of a liability that have been identified, as follows:

1. *Amount Attributed to Employee Service to Date.* This alternative is based on the concept that the employer's pension obligation arises as the employees work and that the event or transaction resulting in the obligation is the employees' service. The pension transaction is viewed here as an exchange whereby employees render service in return for pension benefits (deferred compensation) in addition to current compensation. The resulting obligation for deferred compensation (the projected benefit obligation) is recorded in a manner similar to current compensation.

2. *Contributions Based on an Actuarial Funding Method.* Under this alternative, it is argued that the employer has an obligation to make contributions to the plan rather than directly to employees. In this situation, the employer's liability is based on the actuarial funding method used for funding the plan, in which case the only recorded pension liability would be for contributions due but not yet paid. This is the approach adopted by *FASB Statement No. 87.*

3. *Termination Liability.* This alternative is based on the argument that the employer's obligation should be limited to the amount that is payable on termination of the plan. Those disagreeing believe that a company is a going concern and that an assumption of plan termination is inappropriate unless there is clear evidence to the contrary.

4. *Amount of Vested Benefits.* Under this alternative the employer's obligation is based on the vested benefits earned by the employees. Nonvested benefits are contingent on and result from future services and, therefore, create a liability only as they become vested in future periods. Those disagreeing believe that vesting is a legal transaction, and that a portion of the nonvested benefits will become vested and, therefore, meet the definition of a liability.

5. *Amount Payable to Retirees.* This alternative is a form of "pay-as-you-go" accounting whereby the employer's liability arises only during the period in which pension benefits will be paid to employees. Under this alternative, the liability is readily measurable. Those disagreeing believe that this approach is a violation of the accrual concept of accounting.

If one of these alternatives meets the definition of a liability, the amount of the liability must be measurable in order for the employer to record and report the amount on its balance sheet. Most of the amounts are estimates. If uncertainty is considered to be so great that a reasonable estimate cannot be made because of the long-term nature of pension plans, then a liability cannot be recorded (although disclosure may be required).

Balance Sheet Presentation of Pension Plan Assets

A third conceptual issue involves the disclosure of assets used in the pension plan. *Assets* are probable future economic benefits obtained or controlled by a company as a result of past transactions or events.[17] As indicated earlier, a company having a pension plan

---

16. *Ibid.*, par. 35.
17. *Ibid.*, par. 25.

typically makes periodic payments to a funding agency. This agency, then, assumes the responsibility for safeguarding and investing the pension assets (to earn a return on the assets) held in trust, and for making benefit payments to retired employees. There are two alternative views for accounting by the employer-company for these pension assets.

The first view holds that funding is a discharge of the pension liability and that the assets of the pension plan held by the funding agency are not assets of the employer. The principal reasons are that: (1) the funding agency is a separate legal entity (e.g., a trust) with legal title to the plan assets; (2) the assets can be used only for the benefit of the employees and retirees, and ordinarily cannot be returned to the employer; (3) the employer's obligation is to make contributions to the funding agency, and the agency pays the actual pension benefits; and (4) the employer's obligation may be limited by termination of the plan. Accountants holding this view would exclude plan assets from the employer's balance sheet. This is the approach adopted by *FASB Statement No. 87*.

A second view is that the pension liability is not discharged until the retiree receives the pension payment, and that the pension plan assets are assets of the employer. Accountants holding this view argue that the employer remains obligated to provide benefits defined by the plan, and the trust is a legal device controlled by the employer for funding the pension obligation. Although the funding agency holds legal title to the assets, the employer is at risk with regard to the assets and ultimately reaps the rewards of economic ownership of them. If the assets grow, the employer's future contributions will be reduced. If the assets do not grow, or if losses are sustained, future contributions will be increased. These accountants would include plan assets on the employer's balance sheet. In doing so, however, it would still need to be decided whether the employer should show the plan assets separately on the asset side of the balance sheet or deduct them from the pension liability.

ADDITIONAL ASPECTS OF PENSION ACCOUNTING

7 Understand several additional issues related to pensions.

Several other issues have an impact on some aspects of pension accounting. These include the transition requirements from *APB Opinion No. 8* to *FASB Statement No. 87*, vested benefits, accounting for defined contribution plans, disclosures by funding agencies, the Employee Retirement Income Security Act of 1974, pension settlements and curtailments, termination benefits paid to employees, and multi-employer plans. We briefly discuss each of these topics, along with international accounting differences, in the following sections.

Transition Requirements

Although *FASB Statement No. 87* was issued in 1985, adoption was not required until 1987 because of the complexities of the requirements and a need to allow companies time to adjust their accounting systems. Furthermore, recognition of the minimum liability was not required until 1989, although early application of the entire *Statement* was encouraged.

In the period in which the *Statement* was adopted, an unrecognized net obligation or an unrecognized net asset may have existed. To make this determination, a company computed the projected benefit obligation at the beginning of the year of transition and compared it with the fair value of the plan assets plus (minus) any recognized prepaid/accrued pension cost liability (asset). If the projected benefit obligation was larger (smaller), the company had an unrecognized obligation (asset).

The company amortizes this obligation or asset on a straight-line basis over the remaining service life of employees expected to receive benefits under the plan. It includes the amount of this amortization as the sixth component of pension expense by adding it if an obligation exists and subtracting it if an asset exists. However, if the average remaining service period is less than 15 years, the company may use a 15-year amortization period. The purpose of this exception is to lessen the impact of the transition on companies with short average remaining service lives.

Vested Benefits

Vested benefits are pension benefits earned by employees that are not contingent on future service with the company. That is, the employees will receive retirement benefits based on service to date, even if they terminate employment. ERISA specifies the minimum vesting requirements that companies must follow. A company must disclose the vested portion of the accumulated benefit obligation. Also, the vesting provisions affect calculations made by the company's actuary because it is necessary to estimate the number of employees who will leave before vesting of their pension benefits occurs.

Accounting for Defined Contribution Plans

As we explained earlier, some pension plans are **defined contribution plans** because the employer-company determines its contribution based on a formula, and any future benefits paid to retired employees are limited to those that can be provided by the contributions and the earnings on those contributions. Accounting for defined contribution plans is very straightforward and is specified in *FASB Statement No. 87.*

A company records its pension expense at an amount equal to the contribution that it is required to make in that period. Thus, its journal entry is a debit to Pension Expense and a credit to Cash for the annual contribution. A company recognizes a liability only if the contribution for a given year has not been paid in full.

The company also is required to disclose the following two items:

1. A description of the plan, including employee groups covered, the basis for determining contributions, and the nature and effect of significant matters affecting the comparability of the information for all periods presented.
2. The amount of the pension expense recognized during the period.[18]

Disclosures by Funding Agencies

A company typically makes its periodic pension plan payments to a funding agency that administers the plan. A funding agency may be a specific corporate trustee or an insurance company. These agencies issue financial statements that summarize the financial aspects of a company's pension plan, aimed primarily toward providing financial information about the pension plan's ability to pay benefits when due. **FASB Statement No. 35** requires that the annual financial statements issued by a funding agency for a company's pension plan include: (1) a financial statement (on an accrual accounting basis) presenting information about the net assets (at fair value) available for benefits at the end of the plan year, (2) a financial statement presenting information about the changes during the year in the net assets available for benefits, (3) information regarding the actuarial present value of accumulated plan benefits as of either the beginning or the end of the plan year, and (4) information regarding the significant effects of factors affecting the year-to-year change in the actuarial present value of accumulated plan benefits.[19] Although these funding agency financial statements are beyond the scope of this book, the *company* sponsoring the pension plan discloses some of this information in the notes to its financial statements, as we discussed earlier.

Employee Retirement Income Security Act of 1974

The primary purpose of the **Employee Retirement Income Security Act of 1974** (ERISA), alternatively known as the *Pension Reform Act of 1974* (which we mentioned earlier in this chapter) is to create standards for the operation and maintenance of pension funds in an effort to prevent abuses in the handling of these funds. Also, it attempts to increase

---

18. *FASB Statement No. 87, op. cit.,* par. 65.
19. "Accounting and Reporting by Defined Benefit Pension Plans," *FASB Statement of Financial Accounting Standards No. 35* (Stamford, Conn.: FASB, 1980), par. 5 and 6.

the protection given to employees covered by such plans. For example, at the congressional hearings, it was revealed that some companies routinely followed a policy of terminating employees at ages 60 to 62, even though service until age 65 was a requirement for pension eligibility. This practice greatly minimized the company's pension liabilities and deprived these employees of pension income on their retirement.

The *Pension Reform Act of 1974* provides guidelines for employee participation in pension plans, vesting provisions, minimum funding requirements, financial statement disclosure, and the administration of the plan. In addition, the administrators of pension plans are required to file annual reports with the Department of Labor that include a description of the plan and copies of the relevant financial statements.

The Act also created the Pension Benefit Guaranty Corporation (PBGC), an organization that provides benefits to employees covered by plans that have been terminated (usually because of the bankruptcy of the sponsoring company). The PBGC receives an annual fee for every employee covered by a pension plan that is subject to the PBGC. The PBGC can also impose a lien against 30% of the net assets of the company. This lien has the status of a tax lien and, therefore, ranks above the claims of most other creditors. Since the company may be bankrupt, however, this lien may not result in the PBGC receiving many assets.

Pension Plan Settlements and Curtailments

In recent years many companies have either settled (terminated) or reduced (curtailed) their defined benefit pension plans. Some have settled their defined benefit pension plans and substituted defined contribution plans. Others have reduced the benefits to be paid to employees, while continuing the defined benefit pension plans. For example, a company may decide to terminate its pension plan and buy from an insurance company an annuity for each of its employees that provides the same expected benefits during retirement.

FASB Statement No. 88, "Employers' Accounting for Settlements and Curtailments of Defined Benefit Pension Plans and for Termination Benefits," requires that a company include the net gain or loss from a settlement or curtailment in its net income of the period. When a plan is *settled*, the net gain or loss is the unrecognized net gain or loss that has not been recognized as part of pension expense, as we discussed earlier, plus any remaining unrecognized net asset existing when *FASB Statement No. 87* was initially applied. When a plan is *curtailed*, the portion of the unrecognized prior service cost associated with the estimated reduced future benefits is a loss. The company combines this amount with any gain or loss from a change in the projected benefit obligation due to the curtailment in order to determine the net gain or loss.[20]

Termination Benefits Paid to Employees

When a company wishes to reduce the size of its work force without firing employees, it may provide special benefits for a period of time in the hope of encouraging some employees to terminate voluntarily. These benefits may include lump-sum cash payments, payments over future periods, or similar inducements. *FASB Statement No. 88* requires that a company record a loss and a liability for these *termination benefits* when the following two conditions are met:

1. The employee accepts the offer, and
2. The amount can be reasonably estimated.[21]

The amount of the loss includes the amount of any lump-sum payments and the present value of any expected future benefits.

---

20. "Employers' Accounting for Settlements and Curtailments of Defined Benefit Pension Plans and for Termination Benefits," *FASB Statement of Financial Accounting Standards No. 88* (Stamford, Conn.: FASB, 1985), par. 9–14.
21. *Ibid.*, par. 15.

Multi-Employer Plans

In the previous discussion we assumed that the pension plan is a single-employer plan. That is, the plan is maintained by one company for its employees. In contrast, **a multi-employer plan involves two or more unrelated companies in which assets contributed by each company are available to pay benefits to the employees of all the involved companies.** Generally, these plans result from collective-bargaining agreements with unions. Each company recognizes as pension expense the required contribution for the period. In other words, cash basis accounting is used for these plans. This difference in accounting principles results from the difference in the nature of the obligation of the company and the difficulty of obtaining *reliable* information for each separate company.

International Accounting Differences

The basic principles of accounting for defined benefit plans under international accounting standards are the same as U.S. principles. However, there are some differences, including the requirement under international standards to expense prior service costs immediately and no requirement to recognize a minimum liability. It is also important to understand that it is common for foreign governments to provide significantly higher state-funded benefits to retirees. Therefore, pension benefits provided by foreign companies are less likely to have a material effect on their financial statements.

OTHER POSTEMPLOYMENT BENEFITS

In addition to providing pensions to their employees, many companies also offer two types of additional benefits. *Postemployment* benefits are provided to former employees after employment but *before* retirement. Under **FASB Statement No. 112,**[22] a company must accrue the cost of these benefits during employment and recognize the amount as an expense and a liability if the four criteria for the recognition of compensated absences defined in *FASB Statement No. 43* are met. If any one of the criteria is not met, the company records the expense and liability when the liability is probable and the amount can be reasonably estimated, in accordance with the provision of *FASB Statement No. 5*.

In the rest of this section we discuss *postretirement* benefits, which include all forms of benefits provided to former employees *after* their retirement, other than pensions. For convenience, we use the widely-used acronym, OPEB, for these benefits. Healthcare benefits typically are the most significant of these OPEBs, but some companies also provide dental benefits, eye care, tuition assistance, life insurance, legal services, and financial advisory services. Our discussion focuses on accounting for healthcare benefits because they usually comprise the largest dollar amount, present the greatest measurement difficulties, and are the most controversial.

When Medicare was first created in the 1960s, many companies decided to offer an additional benefit by agreeing to pay for the medical costs of retirees who were not covered by the federal plan. At that time healthcare costs and the retiree population were relatively small, so management believed that it was providing a valuable benefit to employees at a low cost. Companies accounted for OPEBs by recording the costs as they were paid. This cash basis accounting was accepted because the liability was thought to be immaterial and because the benefits were considered to be revocable. However, the costs of the plans have increased significantly in recent years because (1) inflation in healthcare costs has significantly exceeded general inflation, (2) Medicare reimbursements have been decreasing, leaving a larger portion to be covered by companies, (3) the number of retired employees has increased both absolutely and relative to the number of current employees as companies have matured (and down-sized) and life expectancies have increased, and (4) many companies have encouraged early retirement and their healthcare programs cover the entire healthcare costs of the retired employees until age 65, when Medicare is available.

8 Explain other postemployment benefits (OPEBs).

Criteria for recognition of compensated absences are discussed in Chapter 12.

---

22. "Employers' Accounting for Postemployment Benefits," *FASB Statement No. 112* (Norwalk, Conn.: FASB, 1992).

In reaction to these changes, in 1990 the FASB issued **FASB Statement No. 106,** "Employers' Accounting for Postretirement Benefits Other Than Pensions."[23] The *Statement* requires that a company accrue the cost of OPEBs during the periods in which its employees earn the benefits. That is, accounting principles require the use of the accrual basis rather than the cash basis and are similar to those for pensions. (We discuss the principles later.) This accounting has had a dramatic impact on the financial statements of many companies, as we discuss later.

Many companies provided OPEBs without computing the long-term costs involved. It is interesting, for example, that companies generally have refused to index *pension* benefits because of the inflation risk involved. However, *healthcare* benefits essentially are indexed because companies have committed to benefits in terms of *services* rather than in terms of a specific dollar amount of those services. Also, healthcare benefits are more egalitarian, because they usually are *not* based on length of service or salary, but rather on some minimum length of service, after which the same benefits are provided equally to every employee. Since pensions and OPEBs are both postemployment benefits, it is helpful to understand their similarities and differences in considering GAAP for OPEBs.

Similarities to and Differences from Pensions

The basic argument that accounting for OPEBs should be similar to the principles used for pensions involves the concept of a liability. Recall that a liability of a company is a probable future sacrifice of economic benefits arising from present obligations of the company to transfer assets or provide services to other entities in the future as a result of past transactions or events. The term "obligations" includes not only legal duties defined in a contract, but also equitable and constructive obligations based on promises or moral responsibility.

Those who agree with the concepts underlying the accounting principles argue that a company offering OPEBs is essentially providing deferred compensation to employees because the benefits received during retirement were earned during the period of employment. Therefore, the company incurs an obligation as its employees provide services. *FASB Statement No. 106* follows this viewpoint.

Those who disagree with the concepts argue that many OPEBs do not have the same explicit legal contract as a pension agreement, and the obligation of the company to continue to provide benefits is not as clear. In other words, they argue that there is no liability because the company has the right to withdraw the benefits. That is, a company has no obligation for OPEBs until its employees retire, since they must retire to obtain the benefit. However, recent court decisions have not allowed companies to withdraw rights from retired employees, and there are indications that it may be difficult to withdraw rights already earned by current employees. Therefore, the concept of a liability appears to have been satisfied.

Also, if a liability does exist prior to the employees' retirement, it can be argued that it arises only when employees become eligible for the benefits. OPEB plans typically specify a minimum number of years of active service before the employees are eligible for the benefits. Vesting for these plans is "cliff" vesting, because vesting occurs when the requirements are met. A liability would be recorded then and not gradually over a period of years.

We summarize the major differences between OPEBs and pensions in Exhibit 19-10, which focuses on healthcare benefits. While the beneficiary of a pension plan is generally the retired employee, a company usually provides OPEBs to the retired employee, spouse, and dependents up to, say, age 21. The pension benefit is defined as a fixed dollar amount that is paid monthly. The OPEB, however, usually is not limited in amount because benefits are paid no matter how long or serious the illness, benefits are paid as

---

23. "Employers' Accounting for Postretirement Benefits Other Than Pensions," *FASB Statement of Financial Accounting Standards No. 106* (Norwalk, Conn.: FASB, 1990).

EXHIBIT 19-10	Major Differences Between Postretirement Healthcare Benefits and Pensions	
Item	Pensions	Healthcare
Beneficiary	Retired employee (some residual benefit to surviving spouse)	Retired employee, spouse, and dependents
Benefit	Defined, fixed dollar amount, paid monthly	Not limited, paid as used, varies geographically
Funding	Funding legally required and tax deductible	Usually not funded because not legally required and not tax deductible

used, and the amount of benefits varies geographically. Also, the amount is difficult to predict because of the incidence of new illnesses, such as AIDS, and the use of new treatments. Finally, companies fund pension plans because of ERISA requirements, and the contributions are tax deductible. On the other hand, companies generally do not fund OPEBs because there are no legal requirements and the contributions are *not* tax deductible.

Accounting Principles

FASB Statement No. 106 requires that companies follow accounting principles for OPEBs that closely parallel those for pensions. (Because we assume that you have studied the discussion of accounting for pensions, this section is simplified. However, it may be helpful to review those principles as the OPEB principles are discussed.)

Two concepts also need to be understood. The **expected postretirement benefit obligation** (*EPBO*) is the actuarial present value on a particular date of the benefits a company expects to pay under the terms of the postretirement benefit plan. The amount is measured based on the benefits that employees will receive after their expected retirement dates. In contrast, the **accumulated postretirement benefit obligation** (*APBO*) is the actuarial present value of the benefits attributed to employee service rendered to a specific date. Prior to an employee's full eligibility date, the APBO is the portion of the EPBO attributed to that employee's service rendered to that date; on or after the full eligibility date, the APBO and EPBO for an employee are the same. Thus, the difference between the EPBO and APBO is that the accumulated amount is based on benefits earned to date, whereas the expected amount is based on all benefits expected to be paid to employees. (In comparison, the difference between the projected and accumulated benefit obligation for pensions is the inclusion of expected salary increases in the projected amount.)

OPEB Expense

The net postretirement benefit expense[24] that a company recognizes includes the following components:

1. *Service Cost.* The service cost is the actuarial present value of the expected postretirement benefit obligation attributed to services rendered by the employees during the current period. Typically, a company provides OPEB benefits on an all-or-nothing basis; that is, benefits are generally not defined in terms of years of service. Therefore, an equal amount of the expected benefits is attributed to

---

24. The FASB prefers this term to the more commonly used term, OPEB, because other benefits such as layoff benefits may be paid after employment but before retirement.

each year of the attribution period (discussed later). The discount (interest) rate used to calculate the service cost is the rate of return on high-quality fixed-income investments currently available, whose maturities match the expected timing of benefit payments.

2. *Interest Cost.* **The interest cost is the increase in the accumulated postretirement benefit obligation due to the passage of time.** Since the OPEB is a deferred compensation plan in which future payments are discounted to their present values, interest accrues due to the passage of time. Thus, the interest cost is the accumulated postretirement benefit obligation at the beginning of the period multiplied by the discount rate. The interest rate used to calculate the accumulated postretirement benefit obligation is the same rate as that used for the service cost. The interest cost is added to the computation of the postretirement benefit expense.

3. *Expected Return on Plan Assets.* **The expected return on plan assets is the expected increase in the plan assets due to investing activities.** Plan assets are held by the funding agency and consist of investments in securities such as stocks and bonds, as well as other investments. The expected return is calculated by multiplying the fair value of the plan assets at the beginning of the period by the expected long-term rate of return on plan assets. The rate of return reflects the average rate of earnings expected on the assets invested to provide for the benefits included in the projected benefit obligation. Since OPEBs usually are *not* funded, we do not discuss this component further.

4. *Amortization of Unrecognized Prior Service Cost.* The prior service cost is the increase (decrease) in the accumulated postretirement benefit obligation that results from plan amendments (and at the initiation of the plan) and that is not recognized in total in the period granted. **The unrecognized prior service cost is amortized by assigning an equal amount to each remaining year of service until full eligibility for benefits is reached for each plan participant active at the date of amendment.** If all or almost all of a plan's participants are fully eligible for benefits, the prior service cost is amortized instead, based on the remaining life expectancy of the plan participants. Straight-line amortization over the average remaining years of service to full eligibility is also allowed for simplicity. The amortization amount is added (subtracted) in the computation of the postretirement benefit expense if the benefits are increased (decreased).

5. *Gain or Loss.* Gains and losses are changes in the amount of either the accumulated postretirement benefit obligation resulting from experience different from that assumed or from changes in assumptions. Gains and losses may be recognized in the periods in which they occur, or recognition may be delayed. If the company chooses to delay recognition, the amortization of any unrecognized net gain or loss is included in the postretirement benefit expense of a given year if, at the beginning of the year, the unrecognized net gain or loss exceeds 10% of the greater of the accumulated postretirement benefit obligation or the fair value of the plan assets. If amortization is required, the minimum amortization is the excess divided by the average remaining service period of active plan participants (or if most of the plan participants are retired, over their average remaining life expectancy). The total amount of any gain (loss) recognized is deducted (added) in the computation of the postretirement benefit expense.

6. *Recognition of the Obligation or Asset Existing at the Date of the Initial Adoption of the Statement.* The obligation is known as the **transition obligation.** The transition obligation is equal to the accumulated postretirement benefit obligation minus the fair value of the plan assets. (Since we assume the fair value of the plan assets to be zero, there would *not* be a transition *asset.*) A company either recognizes the transition obligation in full in the year in which it adopts the *Statement* as a cumulative effect adjustment due to a change in accounting principle, or it delays recognition and amortizes the unrecognized transition obligation on a straight-line basis over the average remaining service life of active plan participants or 20 years, whichever is greater. The company adds the amount of the

transition obligation amortized in any year in the computation of its postretirement benefit expense (this may also be affected by certain complexities that are beyond the scope of the book).

Changes in accounting principles are discussed in Chapter 22.

OPEB Liability or Asset

The *Statement* also addresses the calculation of the OPEB liability or asset because the amount of a company's net postretirement benefit expense to date may be different than the amount it has funded to date. Since a company usually does not fund the plan, it increases a liability, **accrued postretirement benefit cost**, each period by an amount equal to the expense. The company decreases this account by payments made to retired employees. However, in contrast to accounting for pensions, there is *no* provision for recognizing an **additional liability**.

Differences from Accounting for Pensions

You can see from the preceding discussion that the *Statement* requires accounting principles that closely parallel the accounting for pensions. The major differences are:

1. Although the attribution period is defined in the same way, the effect is different because the benefit formulas for most pension plans link benefits to years of service and salary levels. The result is that, for pension plans, the expected retirement date and date of full eligibility are the *same*. For many OPEBs, however, the benefit formula causes the two dates to be *different*. The attribution period for OPEBs generally begins with the date of hire (or the date on which credited service begins) and ends on the date the employee attains eligibility for full benefits. For example, for a plan which provides OPEBs to employees who render 15 years of service after age 35, the attribution (recognition) period is from 35 to 50 and, therefore, ceases prior to the retirement dates of the employees.
2. There is no provision for recognizing a minimum liability and the related intangible asset or component of accumulated other comprehensive income for OPEBs.
3. The interest component of the net postretirement benefit expense is based on the accumulated postretirement benefit obligation, whereas the interest component of the pension expense is based on the projected benefit obligation.

FASB Statement No. 132 requires disclosures for OPEBs that are similar to those we discussed earlier for pension plans. In addition, the *Statement* requires two disclosures not required for pensions: (a) the assumed healthcare cost trend rates, and (b) the effect of a 1% increase and a 1% decrease in the assumed healthcare cost trend rates on the aggregate of the service cost and the interest cost, as well as on the accumulated postretirement benefit obligation for healthcare benefits.

ILLUSTRATION OF ACCOUNTING FOR OPEBS

We illustrate the basic principles for OPEBs, using the following simplified example. Assume that the Livingston Company adopts a healthcare plan for retired employees on January 1, 2004. At that time the company has two employees and one retired employee, as shown in Exhibit 19-11. To determine eligibility for benefits, the company retroactively gives credit to the date of hire for each employee. Based on the information in the exhibit, the company makes the following two journal entries to record the OPEB items at December 31, 2004:

9 Account for OPEBs.

Postretirement Benefit Expense	31,100	
Accrued Postretirement Benefit Cost		31,100

The first entry records the expense for the year and, since the plan is not funded, the accompanying liability.

EXHIBIT 19-11   **Accrual of Postretirement Healthcare Benefits**

Basic Information

The plan is started on January 1, 2004, and is not funded.
The discount rate is 10%.
All employees were hired at age 25.
All employees become eligible for full benefits at age 55.
Employee C was paid $1,500 postretirement healthcare benefits in 2004.
The company elects to use straight-line amortization for any unrecognized
   prior service cost.
Additional information on January 1, 2004:

Employee	Status	Age	Expected Retirement Age	Accumulated Postretirement Benefit Obligation[a]
A	Employee	40	65	$ 15,000
B	Employee	60	65	60,000
C	Retired	70	—	25,000
				$100,000[b]

a. Actuarially determined at January 1, 2004.
b. This amount is the unrecognized prior service cost.

Computation of Postretirement Benefit Expense for 2004

1. Service cost	$ 1,100[a]
2. Interest cost	10,000[b]
3. Expected return on plan assets	0
4. Amortization of unrecognized prior service cost	20,000[c]
5. Gain or loss	0
6. Amortization of transition obligation	0
	$31,100

a. Actuarially determined based on expected postretirement benefit obligation. Note that there is no service cost
   for B and C because they have passed the date for full eligibility.
b. Accumulated postretirement benefit obligation at January 1, 2004 × Discount rate, or $100,000 × 10%.
c. $100,000 ÷ 5, or $20,000. Employees A, B, and C have 15, 0, and 0 years of remaining service to the full
   eligibility date (age 55), respectively. Therefore, the average remaining service period is 15 ÷ 3 = 5 years.
Note: If the company were changing from the cash to the accrual method, the accumulated postretirement benefit
obligation of $100,000 would be the transition amount. The company could choose to recognize the amount
immediately, or amortize it over 20 years.

Accrued Postretirement Benefit Cost	1,500	
Cash		1,500

The second entry records the payment of retirement benefits.

CONCEPTUAL EVALUATION OF ACCOUNTING FOR OPEBS

Since *FASB Statement No. 106* is based on accrual accounting, you might expect that it would not be controversial. Instead, several aspects have been questioned by critics.

Relevance and Reliability

10 Explain the conceptual issues regarding OPEBs.

It can easily be argued that accrual accounting is more *relevant* than cash basis accounting because costs are matched as expenses against revenues in the period in which the benefits are earned. For OPEBs, the benefits are earned while the employee is working, not when he or she is retired. Therefore, the *relevance* of a company's income statement is enhanced by inclusion of the OPEB expense. There is relatively little dispute about the nature of the obligation because of the similarity between the provisions of the *Statement* and the accounting for pensions.

Opposition did arise from companies that implemented the requirements of the *Statement*. In particular, the measurement problems created considerable controversy. The biggest argument is that OPEB costs cannot be measured with sufficient *reliability* to offset the increased relevance because of the numerous assumptions about future events that are required. The measurement of the various amounts used in accounting for OPEBs is even more difficult than for pensions. For example, healthcare plans agree to pay for some or all of a service, the amount and cost of which are unknown, whereas pension payments are tied to more predictable variables of length of service and pay levels. Also, healthcare plans require an estimate of such items as the medical-cost trend rate and marital and dependency status during retirement. Furthermore, because of the totally new information that is required, concern was expressed that the costs of implementation would be fairly high and might well exceed the benefits obtained. As a result of these concerns, the FASB included in the *Statement*, for the first time, an extensive discussion of the costs and benefits.

Those who favor the new principles argue that knowledge of these costs is essential for rational decision making by management and that accounting includes many estimates. Also, they argue that this OPEB cost information is useful for lending and investment decisions and that such decisions are never based on certainty. Therefore, they argued that it is better for a company to record the information based on the best estimates and provide disclosures of the subjectivity of the amounts rather than to report only cash payments.

Differences in Funding

As we discussed, there are few differences between pension and OPEB accounting. However, there are some differences in the practical impacts because the OPEB plans generally are not funded. Suppose, for example, that one company has an *unfunded* OPEB plan that is expected to provide exactly the same cash payments to retired employees as a *funded* pension plan of another company. The expense for the OPEB will be higher because the actual return on plan assets is not subtracted. This difference is appropriate because the company with the unfunded OPEB will have to pay more assets in the future, whereas the company with the pension plan has already paid the assets into a fund which is earning a return on those assets.

Transition Liability

As we discussed earlier, a company may recognize the transition liability either immediately or prospectively over 20 years (or the average remaining service period of active plan participants, if greater). Some accountants argued that a period longer than 20 years should be used in order to reduce the impact on its income statements.

The *Statement* allows the use of a cumulative-effect adjustment so that a company's future earnings are not "penalized" because of the past use of cash basis accounting, which was the accounting principle at that time. In this case the FASB decided that a company that could recognize the transition obligation immediately should be allowed to do so and should not be penalized because others cannot. These transition rules are inconsistent with the usual FASB policy of requiring retroactive adjustment when a new accounting principle has been mandated, as we discuss in Chapter 22. Also, they are inconsistent with the transition rules for pensions, which allowed only amortization, as we discussed earlier in this chapter. However, *FASB Statement No. 87* required the adoption of a new accrual method instead of the existing accrual method, whereas *FASB Statement No. 106* requires the adoption of a new accrual method instead of the cash method.

Many accountants and users of financial statements have criticized the FASB's decision to allow two alternative transition methods. Very simply, the choice means that

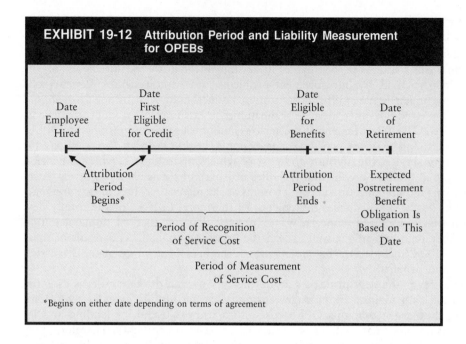

EXHIBIT 19-12   Attribution Period and Liability Measurement for OPEBs

there will be a lack of comparability for 20 years (from the date of adoption) between companies that chose different alternatives for recognizing the transition obligation.

Attribution Period

Attribution is the process of assigning the cost of postretirement benefits to periods of employee service. The attribution period begins with the date of hire or the date that credit for service begins, and ends on the date that the employee is eligible for full benefits, as we illustrate in Exhibit 19-12. Thus, the expected postretirement benefit obligation is attributed to the periods of employee service until the full eligibility date. However, the measurement of the accumulated postretirement benefit obligation at the full eligibility date is based on the benefits an employee is expected to receive and the expected retirement date (the expected postretirement benefit obligation). Thus, the attribution period (recognition) and the measurement period are different. Specifically, the period over which a company recognizes the service cost is based only on the period to full eligibility, whereas measurement of the service cost is based on the period beyond that date to the expected retirement date.

The decision that the attribution period ends on the date the employee attains full eligibility was adopted by the FASB because it more closely follows the implicit contract between the company and the employee. Since employee service after the date of eligibility does not earn additional OPEB benefits, the FASB reasoned that a company should have recognized the expenses in full by then. However, it can be argued that this alternative follows legal form rather than economic substance, because employers expect employees to render services up to the date of expected retirement rather than only up to the date of full eligibility for the benefits.

Others argue that the attribution period should end at the expected retirement date because the company should recognize the OPEB cost over the entire employment period rather than recognizing only the interest cost after the date of eligibility. This argument is consistent with the fundamental exchange of retirement benefits for employee service. It follows that the use of this period is more consistent with the measurement of the expected postretirement benefit obligation, which is based on the expected retirement date. This alternative would also lower the annual expense and liability that a company accrues, thereby reducing the impact on its financial statements.

Some accountants suggest that a company should also amortize the prior service costs over the period to the expected retirement date just like attribution.

Interaction with Deferred Income Taxes

As we discuss in Chapter 18, when a company recognizes a postretirement benefit expense for financial reporting without a related deduction for income tax reporting it creates a temporary deductible difference. Indeed, OPEBs are one of the primary causes of companies reporting deferred tax assets. The change in the deferred tax rules from *FASB Statement No. 96* to *FASB Statement No. 109*, which made it easier for a company to recognize deferred tax assets, enables it to recognize the full benefit of an asset (assuming realization is more likely than not).

Minimum Liability

As we discussed earlier, in contrast to the accounting for pensions, there is no requirement for a company to recognize a minimum liability for OPEBs. The FASB decided that a minimum liability is not required because users can obtain sufficient information from disclosures in the notes to its financial statements. Also, it may be argued that the only liability of the company is the difference between the expense and the funding if it has no legal obligation to pay postretirement benefits. Therefore, recognition of the minimum liability would be inappropriate. Also, the corresponding intangible asset is conceptually questionable and may not be understood by users. However, it may also be argued that the difference between accounting for pensions and OPEBs is undesirable because the same concept is accounted for in a company's financial statements for pensions and by disclosure in the notes to its financial statements for OPEBs.

The requirement that a company recognize the minimum liability for pensions was based on the belief that most pension plans were adequately funded. The purpose of the minimum liability provision is to identify those relatively rare situations in which the plan is significantly underfunded. In contrast, virtually all OPEB plans are significantly underfunded, and recognition of a minimum liability by companies would not serve to identify exceptions. Instead, a company provides information about the funded status in the notes to its financial statements.

Impacts of the Adoption of *FASB Statement No. 106*

Adoption of the *Statement* has had two basic effects. One is on the financial statements of companies, and the second *may* be on the retirement benefits offered by companies. As an indication of the effect on the financial statements of companies, IBM adopted the new principles in 1991 and reported a cost of $2.26 billion on its income statement and balance sheet. The loss reduced earnings per share by about $4 per share, and IBM recorded its first-ever quarterly loss. Note that there was no impact on its cash flows. The company's cash flow statement included only the cash payments to retired employees (unless funding of the plan occurs). The General Accounting Office has estimated that the total liabilities of all companies to their current and retired employees for retiree health benefits is over $400 billion.

Although the accounting issues and their impacts on the financial statements of companies are important, the effects of the *Statement* on benefit plans raise some difficult social issues. These effects are more difficult to evaluate because they involve management decisions that, in turn, may be affected by the financial reporting. According to one study, about 65% of companies cut back on their coverage of retirees' healthcare benefits.[25] About 47% are increasing premium payments, and 40% are making retirees bear a larger share of their medical bills. For example, retirees of Texas Instruments have lost free coverage, and Chrysler requires retirees to pay $100 or more yearly.

---

25. *Business Week*, August 24, 1992, p. 39.

It may appear to be undesirable for companies to reduce benefits. However, it must be remembered that the *Statement* does not change the benefits promised to the retirees or the cost of the healthcare involved. Most people would argue that it is desirable to force companies to realistically face the costs of their promises and to acknowledge how much they can afford and, if necessary, to reduce the benefits now rather than face financial difficulty in the future because of their inability to pay costs they have not recognized. However, any cost reductions by companies will raise the costs incurred by other entities, whether it be the individual retirees or the public through state and federal taxation.

Most companies would prefer that the funding of OPEB plans be tax deductible, but there do not appear to be any plans to lobby Congress for this. Some people may also argue that the principles place U.S. companies at a competitive disadvantage with foreign companies.

A qualitative characteristic of accounting information is *neutrality*. Accounting information is not intended to either encourage or discourage particular decisions, such as the offering of OPEBs, their funding, their tax deductibility, or their impact on foreign trade. Instead, its purpose is to provide useful information for those types of decisions. Accrual accounting does not change the nature, extent, or cost of the OPEB promise. However, it does require companies to report the effects of their commitments on their financial statements, and helps users understand the nature of the OPEB commitments and the ability of companies to fulfill their obligations.

There is a cost attached to implementing the accounting principles for OPEBs. Whether the benefits exceed the costs will, of course, never be known with certainty. However, the FASB, many accountants, many users of financial statements, and many company executives believe that they do.

APPENDIX: ILLUSTRATION OF PRESENT VALUE CALCULATIONS FOR DEFINED BENEFIT PENSION PLANS

11 Understand present value calculations for pensions.

In the chapter we illustrated various situations related to defined benefit pension plans in examples using assumed amounts. This illustration explains *how* a company computes the amounts of several key elements. The example involves the application of *FASB Statement No. 87* for the Lonetree Company, which adopted a defined benefit pension plan on January 1, 2004 The following are the relevant facts:

1. Number of employees	100
2. Years to retirement at December 31, 2004	30
3. Years of life expectancy after retirement	18
4. Discount rate	10%
5. Benefit formula	Average of last 5 years' salary $\times$ Number of years of service $\times$ 0.02
6. Average of last 5 years' salary (based on expected salary levels)	$90,000 per employee
7. Annual pension benefit earned each year of service by each employee	$90,000 $\times$ 0.02 = $1,800
8. Expected long-term (and actual) rate of return on plan assets	8%
9. Amount funded each year	Equal to the annual service cost
10. Date of computation of pension expense and pension funding	December 31 each year

Note that for simplicity we assume all employees are the same age, retire at the same time, and have the same life expectancy after retirement, and there are no gains or losses. The expected return on plan assets of 8% is less than the discount rate of 10% in order to create a liability at the time the company records the pension expense and makes the contribution. Exhibit 19-13 shows the computations of the components of

EXHIBIT 19-13   **Computation of Pension Expense**

Date	Service Cost[a]	Projected Benefit Obligation[b]	Interest Cost[c]	Cash Payment[d]	Plan Assets[e]	Expected (and Actual) Return on Plan Assets[f]	Amortization of Prior Service Cost[g]	Pension Expense[h]
12/31/04	$ 84,603	$ 84,603		$ 84,603	$ 84,603			$ 84,603
12/31/05	93,062	186,123	$ 8,460	93,062	184,433	$ 6,768		94,754
12/31/06	102,368	307,104	18,612	102,368	301,556	14,755		106,225
12/31/07	118,236	472,944	32,246	118,236	443,916	24,124	$548	126,906
12/31/08	130,058	650,292	47,294	130,058	609,487	35,513	548	142,387

a. For current year. Annual benefits earned × present value of annuity for period of retirement × present value of $1 for remaining period of employment. In 2004, $180,000 × present value of annuity for 18 years at 10% × present value of $1 for 30 years at 10%. In each subsequent year the present value of $1 factor is reduced by 1 year. In 2007 the annual benefits earned are increased to $189,000.

b. At end of year. Total benefits earned to date × present value of annuity for period of retirement × present value of $1 for remaining period of employment. In 2004, $180,000 × present value of annuity for 18 years at 10% × present value of $1 for 30 years at 10%. In each subsequent year the benefits are increased by the service cost for that year and the present value of $1 factor is reduced by 1 year. In 2004 the benefits earned to date are increased by the prior service cost.

c. Projected benefit obligation at end of previous year × discount rate, or 10%. In 2004 beginning projected benefit obligation is $307,104 + $15,355 adjustment due to amendment providing increased benefits to date.

d. Assumed equal to the service cost.

e. Balance at end of previous year + actual return on plan assets + contributions − payments ($0 in this example).

f. Plan assets at the end of previous year × expected long-term rate of return (8%), rounded.

g. Prior service cost ÷ average remaining service life of employees; $15,355 ÷ 28 years, rounded.

h. Service cost + interest cost − return on plan assets + amortization of prior service cost.

pension expense for the Lonetree Company (there is no gain or loss component). We discuss each component of the expense in the following sections.

Service Cost

The service cost per employee each year is the present value of the future pension benefits earned *that* year by each employee. Under *FASB Statement No. 87*, this cost is computed using the benefit/years-of-service method. We diagram the computation of the service cost for the current year as follows:

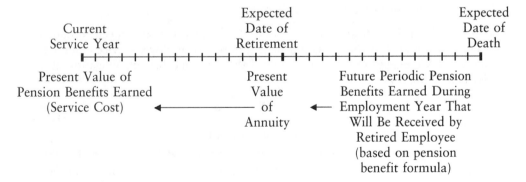

This diagram reads from right to left. Initially, the present value of the future periodic pension benefits earned during the current year is computed as of the expected date of retirement, based on the pension benefit formula, the discount rate, and the retirement period (from the expected date of retirement to the expected date of death).[26] Then, this present value as of the expected retirement date, is discounted back to the current year (based on the discount rate and the remaining years to the date of retirement) to determine the present

---

26. The present value calculations in this Appendix use factors from the tables in Appendix D.

value of the future pension benefits earned that year. This amount is the service cost for the current year. The equation for the calculation of the service cost is as follows:

$$\text{Service Cost} = \frac{\text{Present Value of Future Pension Benefits}}{\text{Earned by Employees in the Current Period}}$$

$$= \begin{matrix}\text{Annual}\\ \text{Benefits}\\ \text{Earned}\end{matrix} \times \begin{matrix}\text{Present Value of}\\ \text{Annuity for Period}\\ \text{of Retirement}\end{matrix} \times \begin{matrix}\text{Present Value of \$1}\\ \text{for Remaining Period}\\ \text{of Employment}\end{matrix}$$

In our example the future pension benefits earned for each year of service by each employee of the Lonetree Company under the benefit formula is $1,800 ($90,000 × 0.02), as we calculated earlier. These benefits are earned by each of the 100 employees and therefore the company's service cost is based on the $180,000 ($1,800 × 100) of future pension benefits earned each year by the employees. The company expects each employee to receive these amounts each year during the 18 years of retirement.

At the end of 2004 we assume the remaining period of employment to be 30 years. Therefore, the Lonetree Company calculates the service cost in 2004, based on the 10% discount rate, as follows:

$$2004 \text{ Service Cost} = \begin{matrix}\text{Annual}\\ \text{Benefits}\\ \text{Earned}\end{matrix} \times \begin{matrix}\text{Present Value of}\\ \text{Annuity for}\\ \text{18 Years at 10\%}\end{matrix} \times \begin{matrix}\text{Present Value of \$1}\\ \text{for 30 Years at 10\%}\end{matrix}$$

$$= \$180,000 \times 8.201412 \times 0.057309$$

$$= \$84,603 \text{ (rounded)}$$

Each year the company makes a similar calculation, but the remaining period of employment decreases. In 2005 the present value of $1 factor for 29 years is used, and in 2006, for 28 years, and so on.[27] The second column of Exhibit 19-12 summarizes the amount of the service cost for each year resulting from this calculation process. Note that the reason for the progression in amounts is that we have assumed, for simplicity, that there is no turnover of employees at the Lonetree Company. A typical company would have employees retiring each year and would be hiring new, younger employees. Thus, the service cost might increase or decrease depending on the characteristics of the particular employees. Note that if the Lonetree Company had selected a discount rate of 8%, the service cost in 2004 would be $167,643 ($180,000 × 9.371887 × 0.099377).

Interest on Projected Benefit Obligation

The projected benefit obligation is the actuarial present value, at a specified date, of all the benefits attributed by the pension benefit formula to employee service rendered prior to that date. We diagram the computation of the projected benefit obligation at a particular date as follows:

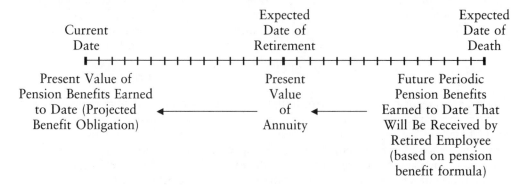

---

27. As we discuss later, however, note that a change in the pension benefit formula in 2007 increases the annual benefits earned from $180,000 to $189,000. This change causes a corresponding increase (on a present value basis) in the service cost for 2007 and 2008.

This diagram also reads from right to left. The present value of the future periodic pension benefits earned to date is computed as of the expected date of the retirement, based on the pension benefit formula, the discount rate, and the retirement period. Then, this present value as of the expected retirement date, is discounted back to the current date (based on the discount rate and the remaining years to the date of retirement) to determine the present value of the future pension benefits earned to date. This amount is the projected benefit obligation on the current date. Note that this diagram is similar to the one we illustrated for the service cost, except that it focuses on the projected pension benefits earned *to date*, while the service cost focuses on the future pension benefits earned *in a particular year*. There is a logical relationship between the two amounts, however, because the projected benefit obligation is the sum of the service costs to date (giving consideration to interest due to the passage of time and assuming there are no prior service costs and no employees have retired). The equation for the calculation of the projected benefit obligation is as follows:

$$\begin{matrix} \text{Projected Benefit} \\ \text{Obligation} \end{matrix} = \begin{matrix} \text{Present Value of Future Pension Benefits Earned by} \\ \text{Employees to Date (based on expected salary levels)} \end{matrix}$$

$$= \begin{matrix} \text{Total} \\ \text{Benefits} \\ \text{Earned} \end{matrix} \times \begin{matrix} \text{Present Value of} \\ \text{Annuity for Period} \\ \text{of Retirement} \end{matrix} \times \begin{matrix} \text{Present Value of \$1} \\ \text{for Remaining Period} \\ \text{of Employment} \end{matrix}$$

In our example, at December 31, 2004, the employees have earned pension benefits for *one* year ($90,000 × 1 × 0.02 × 100 employees, or $180,000), and therefore the company calculates the projected benefit obligation as follows:

$$\begin{matrix} \text{Projected Benefit} \\ \text{Obligation, 12/31/04} \end{matrix} = \begin{matrix} \text{Total} \\ \text{Benefits} \\ \text{Earned} \end{matrix} \times \begin{matrix} \text{Present Value of} \\ \text{Annuity for} \\ \text{18 Years at 10\%} \end{matrix} \times \begin{matrix} \text{Present Value of \$1} \\ \text{for 30 Years at 10\%} \end{matrix}$$

$$= \$180,000 \times 8.201412 \times 0.057309$$

$$= \$84,603 \text{ (rounded)}$$

At December 31, 2005 the employees have earned pension benefits for *two* years ($90,000 × 2 × 0.02 × 100 employees, or $360,000), and therefore the projected benefit obligation is:

$$\begin{matrix} \text{Projected Benefit} \\ \text{Obligation, 12/31/05} \end{matrix} = \$360,000 \times \begin{matrix} \text{Present Value of} \\ \text{Annuity for 18} \\ \text{Years at 10\%} \end{matrix} \times \begin{matrix} \text{Present Value of \$1} \\ \text{for 29 Years at 10\%} \end{matrix}$$

$$= \$360,000 \times 8.201412 \times 0.063039$$

$$= \$186,123 \text{ (rounded)}$$

The third column of Exhibit 19-13 shows the amount of the projected benefit obligation at the end of each year. To determine its pension expense for each year, the Lonetree Company includes the interest cost on the projected benefit obligation. It computes this interest cost by multiplying the projected benefit obligation at the *beginning* of the year by the 10% discount rate, as we illustrate in the fourth column of Exhibit 19-13. Thus, in 2004 there is no interest cost included in pension expense because there was no projected benefit obligation at the beginning of the year. In 2005 the interest cost is $8,460 ($84,603 × 0.10), and the company includes this amount in pension expense.[28] Note that if any retired employees had died during the year, the projected benefit obligation would be decreased by the total of the remaining benefits no longer due the deceased employees.

---

28. As we discuss later, however, note that an amendment to the pension benefit formula in 2007 causes an increase in the projected benefit obligation. This change causes a corresponding increase in interest cost.

Expected Return on Plan Assets

The funding of a pension plan must be within the guidelines of ERISA. Since those rules are beyond the scope of the book, in this example we assume that the company funds an amount each year that is equal to the service cost. We also assume that the company makes its annual contribution on December 31 of each year. Therefore, the company makes its first payment of $84,603 to the plan on December 31, 2004, and the funding agency invests this amount in plan assets, such as bonds, stocks, and real estate. The fifth column of Exhibit 19-13 shows the annual contribution.

To determine its pension expense for each year, the Lonetree Company *subtracts* the expected return on its plan assets for that year. In 2004 no return was earned on the plan assets because the company did not make the contribution until the end of the year. In 2005 the company earns an expected return based on the plan assets available at the beginning of the year and held during the year. Thus, if we assume that the plan assets are expected to earn earn 8% per year, the expected return in 2005 is $6,768 ($84,603 × 0.08, rounded). This amount *decreases* the 2005 pension expense. On December 31, 2005 (before the contribution for 2005), the total assets are $91,371 ($84,603 + the actual return of $6,768). The contribution of $93,062 on that date increases the plan assets to $184,433. During 2006 the expected return on the assets is $14,755 ($184,433 × 0.08), which is deducted from the 2006 pension expense. As a result, the total plan assets on December 31, 2006, after the contribution for 2006, are $301,556 ($184,433 + the actual return of $14,755 + the contribution for 2006 of $102,368). The sixth and seventh columns of Exhibit 19-13 show the plan assets and the expected and actual return on plan assets for each year, respectively. Note that if any employees had retired, the plan assets would be reduced each year by the payments made to the retired employees.

Amortization of Unrecognized Prior Service Cost

Prior service cost is the cost of retroactive additional benefits granted by a company in a plan amendment or at the initial adoption of the plan. The cost causes an increase in the company's projected benefit obligation, and the company amortizes the unrecognized prior service cost as a component of its pension expense in subsequent years. To illustrate the computation of the prior service cost, assume that on January 1, 2007, the Lonetree Company changes the factor in the benefit formula from 0.02 to 0.021, retroactive to the adoption of the plan. This action creates additional pension benefits for each employee that the company calculates as follows:

$$\begin{aligned} \text{Additional Benefits per Employee} &= \frac{\text{Average of Last}}{\text{5 Years' Salary}} \times \frac{\text{Number of Years}}{\text{of Service to Date}} \times \frac{\text{Change in}}{\text{Formula}} \\ &= \$90{,}000 \times 3 \times 0.001 \\ &= \$270 \end{aligned}$$

Since the Lonetree Company has 100 employees, the total additional benefits assigned to the employees is $27,000 ($270 × 100 employees). It calculates the prior service cost, which is the present value of those additional benefits, as follows:

$$\begin{aligned} \text{Prior Service Cost} &= \frac{\text{Present Value of Additional Pension}}{\text{Benefits Granted by Plan Amendment}} \\ &= \frac{\text{Additional}}{\text{Benefits}} \times \frac{\text{Present Value of}}{\text{Annuity for Period}} \times \frac{\text{Present Value of \$1}}{\text{for Remaining Period}} \\ &\qquad\qquad\quad \text{of Retirement} \qquad\qquad \text{of Employment} \end{aligned}$$

Recall that we assumed the life expectancy during retirement to be 18 years and, at the *beginning* of 2007, the remaining period of employment is 28 years. Therefore, the Lonetree Company calculates the prior service cost as follows:

$$\text{Prior Service Cost} = \frac{\text{Additional}}{\text{Benefits}} \times \frac{\text{Present Value of}}{\text{Annuity for}} \times \frac{\text{Present Value of \$1}}{\text{for 28 Years at 10\%}}$$
$$\frac{}{} \quad 18 \text{ Years at } 10\%$$

$$= \$27{,}000 \times 8.201412 \times 0.069343$$

$$= \$15{,}355 \text{ (rounded)}$$

The company amortizes the $15,355 unrecognized prior service cost as an element of pension expense in the current and future years. It amortizes its unrecognized prior service cost over the average remaining service life of its employees. Thus, the amortization in each year is $548 ($15,355 ÷ 28, rounded). The eighth column of Exhibit 19-13 shows this amount for each year.

ADJUSTMENTS OF SERVICE COST AND PROJECTED BENEFIT OBLIGATION The amendment of the pension benefit formula at the beginning of 2007 causes not only an unrecognized prior service cost, but also an increase in the projected benefit obligation and the service cost for the current and future years. The increase in the service cost causes an increase in pension expense. The increase in the projected benefit obligation also causes an increase in pension expense due to the additional interest cost. Since the company continues to fund an amount equal to the annual service cost, there is no change in the plan assets at the beginning of 2007.

The service cost in 2007 and 2008 that we show in Exhibit 19-13 is based on annual benefits earned of $189,000 ($90,000 × 0.021 × 100 employees), instead of $180,000. Thus, the company computes the 2007 service cost as follows:

$$\text{2007 Service Cost} = \frac{\text{Annual}}{\text{Benefits}} \times \frac{\text{Present Value of}}{\text{Annuity for}} \times \frac{\text{Present Value of \$1}}{\text{for 27 Years at 10\%}}$$
$$\text{Earned} \quad 18 \text{ Years at } 10\%$$

$$= \$189{,}000 \times 8.201412 \times 0.076278$$

$$= \$118{,}236 \text{ (rounded)}$$

The company makes a similar calculation in 2008 to determine the $130,058 service cost.

The company must include the present value of the additional benefits granted in the projected benefit obligation. Since the amendment occurred on January 1, 2007, the $307,104 projected benefit obligation on December 31, 2006 in Exhibit 19-13 is not adjusted because it is based upon the benefit formula at that time. The 2007 interest cost calculation, however, is based on the adjusted January 1, 2007 projected benefit obligation, which amounts to $322,459 ($307,104 + $15,355 prior service cost). Thus, the 2007 interest cost is $32,246 ($322,459 × 0.10).

The December 31, 2007 projected benefit obligation is based on the total benefits earned to date (after the amendment) and the company calculates it as follows:

$$\frac{\text{Total}}{\text{Benefits}} = \$90{,}000 \times \frac{\text{Number of Years}}{\text{of Service}} \times 0.021 \times 100 \text{ Employees}$$
$$\text{Earned}$$

$$= \$90{,}000 \times 4 \times 0.021 \times 100$$

$$= \$756{,}000$$

$$\frac{\text{Projected}}{\text{Benefit}} = \frac{\text{Total}}{\text{Benefits}} \times \frac{\text{Present Value of}}{\text{Annuity for Period}} \times \frac{\text{Present Value of \$1}}{\text{for Remaining Period}}$$
$$\text{Obligation} \quad \text{Earned} \quad \text{of Retirement} \quad \text{of Employment}$$

$$= \$756{,}000 \times \frac{\text{Present Value of Annuity}}{\text{for 18 Years at 10\%}} \times \frac{\text{Present Value of \$1}}{\text{for 27 Years at 10\%}}$$

$$= \$756{,}000 \times 8.201412 \times 0.076278$$

$$= \$472{,}944 \text{ (rounded)}$$

The company makes a similar calculation the next year to determine the projected benefit obligation on December 31, 2008 of $650,292.

Pension Expense and Liability

The pension expense each year for the Lonetree Company is the service cost, plus the interest on the projected benefit obligation, minus the expected return on plan assets, plus the amortization of the unrecognized prior service cost. (The gain or loss component does not arise in this example.) The company records any difference between the amount of the pension expense and the amount funded as a prepaid/accrued pension cost liability or asset. The ninth and fifth columns of Exhibit 19-13 show the pension expense and amounts funded for the Lonetree Company, respectively. The journal entry to record the pension expense on December 31, 2004 is as follows:

Pension Expense	84,603	
Cash		84,603

The journal entry to record the pension expense on December 31, 2005 is as follows:

Pension Expense	94,754	
Cash		93,062
Prepaid/Accrued Pension Cost		1,692

The company makes a similar journal entry at the end of each succeeding year, and each year the debit to Pension Expense is greater than the credit to Cash. As a result, the company's pension liability account balance at the end of each year increases as follows:

Prepaid/Accrued Pension Cost (Liability)	
12/31/04	$ 0, or ($84,603 − $84,603)
12/31/05	1,692, or ($0 + $94,754 − $93,062)
12/31/06	5,549, or ($1,692 + $106,225 − $102,368)
12/31/07	14,219, or ($5,549 + $126,906 − $118,236)
12/31/08	26,548, or ($14,219 + $142,387 − $130,058)

In addition to the Prepaid/Accrued Pension Cost, the Lonetree Company must determine whether it needs to record an additional liability at the end of each year. Generally, a company recognizes an additional liability only in situations where it has a large, unrecognized prior service cost or has experienced substantial losses in the investment of its plan assets.

SUMMARY

At the beginning of the chapter, we identified several objectives you would accomplish after reading the chapter. The objectives are listed below, each followed by a brief summary of the key points in the chapter discussion.

1. **Understand the characteristics of pension plans.** A pension plan requires that a company provide income to its retired employees in return for services they provided during their employment. A defined benefit plan states the benefits to be received by employees after retirement or the method of determining such benefits. A defined contribution plan states the employer's contribution, and the future benefits are limited to the amount that can be provided by the contributions and the returns earned on the investment of those contributions.

2. **Explain the historical perspective of accounting for pension plans.** The first authoritative statement on pensions was *Accounting Research Bulletin No. 45* that recommended that companies recognize pension cost on the accrual basis. These principles were superceded by *APB Opinion No. 8* that required the use of the accrual method. These principles were then superceded by *FASB Statement No. 87*, which contains the current measurement and recognition requirements for the pension plans of employers. Accounting and reporting by the funding agency administering the pension plan is defined by *FASB Statement No. 35*. Disclosure requirements for employers' pension plans were established by *FASB Statement No. 87*, but were replaced by *FASB Statement No. 132*.

3. **Explain the accounting principles for defined benefit plans, including computing pension expense and recognizing pension liabilities and assets.** Pension expense includes the service cost, plus the interest cost, minus the expected

return on plan assets, plus the amortization of the unrecognized prior service cost, minus or plus the gain or loss, which includes the effects of differences between actuarial assumptions and actual experience. The cumulative difference between the pension expense and funding is recognized as an asset or liability. The minimum total pension liability that a company must recognize is the unfunded accumulated benefit obligation. A company recognizing an additional pension liability may also recognize an intangible asset up to the amount of any unrecognized prior service cost. Any additional amount is recognized as a component of other comprehensive income.

4. **Account for pensions.** Compute the pension expense given the information about the components (e.g., service cost, interest cost). Record the pension expense and funding, and record any difference as an adjustment to prepaid/accrued pension cost. Compute and record any additional pension liability at an amount equal to the unfunded accumulated benefit obligation minus the accrued pension cost (or plus the prepaid pension cost).

5. **Understand disclosures of pensions.** A company must disclose the following information about its pension plan(s): a reconciliation of the beginning and ending balances of the projected benefit obligation, a reconciliation of the beginning and ending balances of the fair value of plan assets, the funded status of the plan, the amounts not recognized on the balance sheet, the amounts recognized on the balance sheet, the amount of pension expense, the amount included in other comprehensive income from a change in the additional pension liability, the discount rate, the rate of compensation increase, and the expected long-term rate of return on plan assets, and the amounts and types of securities included in plan assets.

6. **Explain the conceptual issues regarding pensions.** The conceptual issues include the proper amount to recognize as pension expense (and when to record it), the identification and measurement of pension liabilities, and the balance sheet presentation of pension plan assets by the company with the pension plan and by the funding agency.

7. **Understand several additional issues related to pensions.** Additional recording and reporting issues include transition requirements when *FASB Statement No. 87* was adopted, vested benefits, defined contribution plans, disclosures by funding agencies, the Employee Retirement Security Act of 1974, pension plan settlements and curtailments, termination benefits paid to employees, multi-employer plans, and international accounting differences.

8. **Explain other postemployment benefits (OPEBs).** Postemployment benefits are paid to employees after employment but before retirement. Postretirement benefits are benefits paid to employees after their retirement, other than pensions. The most important of the OPEBs is healthcare benefits.

9. **Account for OPEBs.** Compute the postretirement benefit expense given information about the components (e.g., service cost and interest cost). Record the postretirement benefit expense and the increase in the accrued postretirement benefit cost (liability) assuming no funding. Record the payment of retirement benefits by decreasing the accrued postretirement benefit cost.

10. **Explain the conceptual issues regarding OPEBs.** The conceptual issues involve the relevance and reliability of the information, differences in funding between pensions and OPEBs, the transition liability, the attribution period, the interaction with deferred income taxes, the lack of a minimum liability recognition, and the impacts on companies of the adoption of *FASB Statement No. 106*.

11. **Understand present value calculations for pensions (Appendix).** Compute the components of the pension expense based on information about the employee (e.g., expected pension benefits and years of retirement) and the funding assumptions (e.g., discount rate). Use present value of annuity and present value of $1 calculations to determine the present values of the pension expense components.

QUESTIONS

Q19-1 What is a pension plan? Explain how yearly income of retired employees is determined under a defined benefit pension plan.

Q19-2 Distinguish between a defined benefit pension plan and a defined contribution pension plan.

Q19-3 Distinguish between funded and unfunded pension plans; between contributory and noncontributory pension plans.

Q19-4 What is service cost? How does this differ from prior service cost?

Q19-5 Define *projected benefit obligation.* How does this differ from an accumulated benefit obligation?

Q19-6 In regard to pension plans, define *assumptions.* What is the relationship between a gain or loss and an assumption?

Q19-7 List and briefly define the five components of pension expense according to *FASB Statement No. 87.*

Q19-8 What is a company's accrued pension cost liability and when does it arise? What is a company's prepaid pension cost asset and when does it arise?

Q19-9 When does a company record an additional pension liability for a pension plan?

Q19-10 List the disclosures a company must make for its defined benefit pension plan in accordance with *FASB Statement No. 132.*

Q19-11 List the conceptual issues of importance in regard to pension expense.

Q19-12 List the conceptual issues of importance in regard to pension liabilities and pension assets.

Q19-13 List and define the potential components of pension expense.

Q19-14 Conceptually, what are the four possible alternative methods for accounting for the prior service cost that arises from pension plan modifications?

Q19-15 What are the five possible alternative methods of determining the extent of a company's pension plan liability?

Q19-16 What is a defined contribution pension plan and what are the related accounting principles?

Q19-17 What must be included in the annual financial statements issued by a funding agency?

Q19-18 Does *FASB Statement No. 87* specify the minimum amount that a company must pay into its pension fund each year? If not, how is the amount determined?

Q19-19 What is a pension plan settlement? Curtailment? How should the net gain or loss from a settlement or curtailment be accounted for by a company according to *FASB Statement No. 88*?

Q19-20 What are other postemployment benefits? How are they distinguished from postretirement benefits?

Q19-21 List and briefly define the six components of OPEB expense according to *FASB Statement No. 106*.

Q19-22 How does accounting for other postemployment benefits differ from accounting for defined benefit pension plans?

CASES

C O M M U N I C A T I O N

C19-1 Financial Reporting for a Defined Benefit Pension Plan

The Fink Company is considering establishing a defined benefit pension plan for its employees. The president of Fink Company is slightly familiar with *FASB Statement No. 87* and understands that accounting for a defined benefit pension plan may result in certain items being included in the financial statements of the sponsoring company. The president has come to you for help in better understanding these items.

Required List each item, summarize how it is calculated, and briefly explain its meaning.

C19-2 Pension Cost Components

Carson Company sponsors a single-employer defined benefit pension plan. The plan provides that pension benefits are determined by age, years of service, and compensation. Among the components that should be included in the net pension cost recognized for a period are service cost, interest cost, and expected return on plan assets.

Required
1. What two accounting issues result from the nature of the defined benefit pension plan? Why do these issues arise?
2. Explain how Carson should determine the service cost component of the net pension cost.
3. Explain how Carson should determine the interest cost component of the net pension cost.
4. Explain how Carson should determine the expected return on plan assets component of the net pension cost. (*AICPA adapted*)

C19-3 Pension and Future Vacation Costs

Essex Company has a single-employer defined benefit pension plan, and a compensation plan for future vacations for its employees.

Required
1. Define the interest cost component of net pension cost for a period. Explain how Essex should determine the interest cost component of its net pension cost for a period.
2. Define prior service cost. Explain how Essex should account for prior service cost.
3. What conditions must be met for Essex to accrue compensation for future vacations? Explain the theoretical rationale for accruing compensation for future vacations. (*AICPA adapted*)

C19-4 Conceptual Issues

In the chapter the conceptual issues related to pension expense, pension liabilities, and pension plan assets are discussed.

Required Explain how *FASB Statement No. 87* resolves each of these three conceptual issues.

C19-5 Other Postemployment Benefits

Companies often provide their employees with postemployment benefits other than pensions. These benefits may include health insurance, life insurance, and disability benefits.

Required Explain how the accounting for these other postemployment benefits is similar or dissimilar to accounting for pensions.

CREATIVE AND CRITICAL THINKING

C19-6 Additional Pension Liability

The development of *FASB Statement No. 87* took many years and included compromises among competing arguments. One of the areas of compromise was the additional pension liability.

Required Explain how the additional pension liability is calculated and describe any aspects that might be considered to be the result of compromises.

C19-7 Income Smoothing

Generally, accounting principles do not support the concept of income smoothing (the avoidance of year-to-year fluctuations in the amount of income). A friend of yours, however, after studying *FASB Statement No. 87*, claims, "Pension accounting includes income smoothing."

Required Describe the methods by which *FASB Statement No. 87* avoids year-to-year fluctuations in the amount of pension expense.

C19-8 Pension Issues

The MacAdams Company had engaged in large amounts of R&D to develop a new product that would put the company ahead of its Japanese competition. As a result, the company's profits were severely reduced and the president was concerned about the possibility of a takeover by a European competitor. The president was discussing the situation with the controller and said, "Your accounting principles make me so mad. Here we are working hard to develop a product to beat the rest of the world and you won't let me treat any of those costs as an asset."

The controller replied, "I understand your frustration. And please remember they are not 'my' principles."

"I know," responded the president. "Do you have any suggestions?"

"Well," the controller replied, "one easy way to increase our profits would be for the board of directors to vote to increase the discount rate used for computing the present values and to increase the expected rate of return on plan assets. Both of those would have the effect of reducing the pension expense."

"Great idea. I will have to remember that when it is time for the year-end bonuses."

Required Write a short report evaluating the controller's suggestion.

C19-9 OPEB Issues

"Will it cost your company your company? Ready for one of the most difficult challenges ever to confront corporate America? One that is estimated to cost up to $400 billion. New FASB regulations will force companies to measure and post as a debit their health expense obligation to current and *future* retirees. . . . We'll help you minimize the financial impact of these regulations and still enable you to remain responsive to the benefit needs of employees." (Excerpts from an advertisement by CIGNA, a large insurance company.)

"Forget about retiring with all-expenses-paid health care from your employer. About 65% of U.S. companies have reduced benefits. Some have asked retirees to pay more of the costs, while others have eliminated the plans altogether. Blame soaring medical expenses and a new accounting rule that requires companies to post long-term retiree medical benefits as liabilities on their balance sheets." (Adapted from *Business Week*, August 24, 1992, p. 39.)

Required

1. Critically evaluate the content of the advertisement.
2. Explain why companies may have reduced benefits when they adopted *FASB Statement No. 106*.

C19-10 OPEBs and Deferred Income Taxes

The following information is for the Dermer Company's OPEB plan, which it adopted on January 1, 2004:

Service cost, 2004	$100,000
Interest cost, 2004	20,000
Unrecognized prior service cost, 1/1/04	300,000
Benefits paid to employees, 2004	18,000
Pretax accounting income and taxable income for 2004 before any deductions for OPEB costs	500,000
Average remaining service period	12 years
Enacted tax rate for 2004	30%
Enacted tax rate for 2005 and beyond	35%
Any deferred tax assets are more likely than not to be realized	

Required

1. a. Prepare the journal entries to record the OPEB expense and payments for 2004.
   b. Prepare the income tax journal entry for 2004.
2. a. Assume instead that Dermer had an existing OPEB plan on January 1, 1996, and that the $300,000 was the accumulated postretirement benefit obligation at the date of adoption of *FASB Statement No. 106*, instead of the unrecognized prior service cost. Prepare the journal entries to record the OPEB expense and payments for 2004 if the company uses the maximum period for the amortization of the transition liability and adopted the *Statement* on January 1, 1996.
   b. Prepare the income tax journal entry for 2004.
   c. What is the balance of the deferred tax asset at December 31, 2004, if it is assumed that in each year since 1996 pretax accounting income and taxable income before any deductions for OPEB costs have been $500,000? Also assume that each year, the OPEB expense and payments were the same as in 2004.
3. a. Assume instead that the $300,000 accumulated postretirement benefit obligation was recognized as a cumulative effect. Prepare the journal entries

to record the activities related to the OPEB for 2004 if the *Statement* was adopted on January 1, 1996.

b. Prepare the income tax journal entry for 2004.

c. What is the balance of the deferred tax asset at December 31, 2004, if it is assumed that in each year since 1996 pretax accounting income and taxable income before any deductions for OPEB costs have been $500,000? Also assume that each year the OPEB expense (before including the cumulative effect adjustment) and payments were the same as in 2004.

C19-11 Analyzing Coca-Cola's Postemployment Benefit Disclosures

Refer to the financial statements and related notes of the Coca-Cola Company in Appendix A of this book. Answer each of the questions for (a) the company's pension benefits and (b) the company's other benefits.

Required

1. How much is the company's expense in 2001?
2. How much are the company's actual and expected return on plan assets?
3. How much is the benefit obligation at December 31, 2001?

4. Is the company in a net asset or liability position at December 31, 2001? Is this net amount greater or less than the net asset or liability reported on the balance sheet?

5. What were the effects of the decrease in the discount rate in 2001 on the amounts disclosed by the company (no calculations required)?

C19-12 Ethics and Pensions

You are an accountant for the Lanthier Company. The president of the company calls you into the office and says, "We have to find a way to reduce our pension costs. They are too high and they are making us uncompetitive against our foreign competitors whose employees have state-funded pensions. I think we might have to abandon our defined benefit plan, but I know the employees would not be happy about that. I was also thinking that perhaps we could raise the discount rate we use up to the high end of the acceptable range. I also think we need a trustee who will pursue a more aggressive investment strategy for the pension funds; that way we can raise our expected rate of return."

Required From financial reporting and ethical perspectives, discuss the issues raised by this situation.

MULTIPLE CHOICE

Select the best answer for each of the following.

M19-1 The actuarial present value of all the benefits attributed by the pension benefit formula to employee service rendered before a specified date based on expected future compensation levels is the

    a. Projected benefit obligation
    b. Prior service cost
    c. Service cost
    d. Accumulated benefit obligation

Items 2, 3, and 4 are based on the following information:

Spath Company adopted a noncontributory defined benefit pension plan on January 1, 2004. Spath Company uses the benefit/years-of-service method, which results in the following information:

	2004	2005
Service cost	$300,000	$450,000
Amount funded	240,000	390,000
Discount rate	10%	10%
Expected rate of return	10%	10%

The fair value of the plan assets at the end of each year exceeded the accumulated benefit obligation.

M19-2 What is the balance of the accrued pension cost as of December 31?

	2004	2005
a.	$ 0	$ 60,000
b.	$60,000	$ 60,000
c.	$60,000	$ 66,000
d.	$60,000	$126,000

M19-3 What is the pension expense for the year ended December 31, 2005?

    a. $390,000   c. $456,000
    b. $426,000   d. $480,000

M19-4 As of December 31, 2005, what is the balance in the pension plan asset fund?

    a. $456,000   c. $654,000
    b. $630,000   d. $840,000

M19-5 Which of the following is not a component of pension expense?

    a. Amount funded
    b. Service cost
    c. Expected return on plan assets
    d. Interest cost

M19-6 Davison Company has a noncontributory defined benefit pension plan for its employees. During 2004 the pension plan has a discount rate of 8%, service cost of $98,000, plan assets as of 1/1/04 of $432,000, and an expected return on plan assets of $34,560. On December 31, 2004 the company contributed $90,000 to the pension plan, resulting in a credit to Prepaid/Accrued Pension Cost of $6,300. What is the amount of the projected benefit obligation on January 1, 2004?

    a. $332,000   c. $410,750

    b. $345,600   d. $432,000

M19-7 On January 1, 2004 the Soloman Company changes the factor in the benefit formula from 0.02 to 0.022, retroactive to the adoption of the plan. The amendment will result in a(an)

    a. Decrease in projected benefit obligation

    b. Increase in service cost

    c. Decrease in pension expense

    d. Increase in plan assets

M19-8 The McCollum Company amended its noncontributory defined benefit pension plan at the beginning of 2001. The unrecognized prior service cost related to this amendment amounts to $240,000. Information regarding the four participating employees is as follows:

Employee	Expected to Retire After
A	Year 1
B	Year 2
C	Year 4
D	Year 5

Using the straight-line method, what is the amount of unrecognized prior service cost to be amortized in 2004?

    a. $0   c. $60,000

    b. $40,000   d. $80,000

M19-9 *FASB Statement No. 88* requires that a company record a loss and a liability for termination benefits paid to employees when

    a. The employee accepts the offer

    b. The amount can be reasonably estimated

    c. The employee accepts the offer or the amount can be reasonably estimated

    d. The employee accepts the offer and the amount can be reasonably estimated

M19-10 *FASB Statement No. 132* requires a company with a defined benefit pension plan to make all of the following disclosures except

    a. The amount of the pension expense, showing each of the components separately

    b. The estimates of future contributions

    c. The funded status of the plan

    d. The discount rate

EXERCISES

E19-1   *Pension Expense*   The Bailey Company has had a defined benefit pension plan for several years. At the end of 2004 the company's actuary provided the following information for 2004 regarding the pension plan: (1) service cost, $115,000; (2) expected return on plan assets, $14,000; (3) amortization of unrecognized net loss, $2,000; (4) interest cost on projected benefit obligation, $16,000; and (5) amortization of unrecognized prior service cost, $4,000. The company decides to fund an amount at the end of 2004 equal to its pension expense.

Required Compute the amount of Bailey Company's pension expense for 2004 and prepare the related journal entry.

E19-2   *Pension Expense*   On December 31, 2004 the Robey Company accumulated the following information for 2004 in regard to its defined benefit pension plan:

Service cost	$105,000
Interest cost on projected benefit obligation	12,000
Expected return on plan assets	11,000
Amortization of unrecognized prior service cost	3,000
Amortization of unrecognized net gain	1,000

On its December 31, 2003 balance sheet, the company had reported a prepaid/accrued pension cost liability of $14,000.

Required

1. Compute the amount of Robey Company's pension expense for 2004.
2. Prepare the journal entry to record Robey's 2004 pension expense if it funds the pension plan in the amount of: (a) $108,000, (b) $100,000, and (c) $112,000.

E19-3   *Interest Cost and Return on Assets*   On December 31, 2004 the Palmer Company determined that the 2004 service cost on its defined benefit pension plan was $120,000. At the beginning of 2004 Palmer Company had pension plan assets of $520,000 and a projected benefit obligation of $600,000. Its discount rate (and expected long-term rate of return on plan assets) for 2004 was 10%. There are no other components of Palmer Company's pension expense; the company had a prepaid/accrued pension cost liability at the end of 2003.

Required

1. Compute the amount of Palmer Company's pension expense for 2004.
2. Prepare the journal entry to record Palmer's 2004 pension expense if it funds the pension plan in the amount of: (a) $128,000, and (b) $120,000.

E19-4   ***Pension Expense Different Than Funding: One Year***   The Verna Company has had a defined benefit pension plan for several years. At the end of 2004 the company accumulated the following information: (1) service cost for 2004, $127,000; (2) projected benefit obligation, 1/1/2004, $634,000; (3) discount rate, 9%; (4) plan assets, 1/1/2004, $589,000; and (5) expected long-term rate of return on plan assets, 9%. There are no other components of Verna Company's pension expense; the company had a prepaid/accrued pension cost liability at the end of 2003. The company contributed $128,000 to the pension plan at the end of 2004.

Required Compute the amount of Verna Company's pension expense for 2004 and prepare the related journal entry.

E19-5   ***Pension Expense Different Than Funding: Multiple Years***   Baron Company adopted a defined benefit pension plan on January 1, 2003. The following information pertains to the pension plan for 2004 and 2005:

	2004	2005
Service cost	$160,000	$172,000
Projected benefit obligation (1/1)	120,000	289,600
Plan assets (1/1)	120,000	279,600
Company contribution (funded 12/31)	150,000	160,000
Discount rate	8%	8%
Expected long-term (and actual) rate of return on plan assets	8%	8%

There are no other components of Baron Company's pension expense.

Required

1. Compute the amount of Baron Company's pension expense for 2004 and 2005.
2. Prepare the journal entries to record the pension expense for 2004 and 2005.

E19-6   ***Determination of Projected Benefit Obligation***   Several years ago the Lewad Company established a defined benefit pension plan for its employees. The following information is available for 2004 in regard to its pension plan: (1) discount rate, 10%; (2) service cost, $142,000; (3) plan assets (1/1), $659,000; and (4) expected return on plan assets, $65,900. There is no amortization of unrecognized prior service cost and there is no gain or loss. On December 31, 2004, the company contributed $140,000 to the pension plan, resulting in a credit to Prepaid/Accrued Pension Cost of $8,200.

Required Compute the amount of Lewad Company's projected benefit obligation on January 1, 2004.

E19-7   ***Pension Expense Different Than Funding: Multiple Years***   Carli Company adopted a defined benefit pension plan on January 1, 2003, and funded the entire amount of its 2003 pension expense. The following information pertains to the pension plan for 2004 and 2005:

	2004	2005
Service cost	$200,000	$215,000
Projected benefit obligation (1/1)	180,000	396,200
Plan assets (1/1)	180,000	406,400
Company contribution (funded 12/31)	212,000	220,000
Discount rate	9%	9%
Expected long-term (and actual) rate of return on plan assets	8%	8%

There are no other components of Carli Company's pension expense.

Required

1. Compute the amount of Carli Company's pension expense for 2004 and 2005.
2. Prepare the journal entries to record the pension expense for 2004 and 2005.

E19-8   *Unrecognized Prior Service Cost*   On January 1, 2004 the Smith Company adopted a defined benefit pension plan. At that time the company awarded retroactive benefits to its employees, resulting in an unrecognized prior service cost that created a projected benefit obligation of $1,250,000 on that date. The company decided to amortize the unrecognized prior service cost by the straight-line method over the 20-year average remaining service life of its active participating employees. The company's actuary has also provided the following additional information for 2004 and 2005: (1) Service cost: 2004, $147,000; 2005, $153,000; (2) expected return on plan assets: 2005, $34,000; and (3) projected benefit obligation: 1/1/2005, $1,522,000. The discount rate was 10% in both 2004 and 2005. The company contributed $340,000 and $350,000 to the pension fund at the end of 2004 and 2005, respectively. There are no other components of Smith Company's pension expense; ignore any additional pension liability.

Required

1. Compute the amount of Smith Company's pension expense for 2004 and 2005.
2. Prepare the journal entries to record the pension expense for 2004 and 2005.

E19-9   *Straight-Line Amortization*   At the beginning of 2004 the Brent Company amended its defined benefit pension plan. The amendment entitled five active participating employees to receive increased future benefits based on their prior service. The company's actuary determined that the unrecognized prior service cost for this amendment amounts to $330,000. Employee A is expected to retire after 1 year, employee B after 2, employee C after 3, employee D after 4, and employee E after 5 years.

Required Using the straight-line method, (1) compute the average remaining service life, and (2) prepare a schedule to amortize the unrecognized prior service cost.

E19-10   *Years-of-Future-Service Amortization*   Refer to the information provided in E19-9.

Required Using the years-of-future-service method, prepare a set of schedules to determine (1) the amortization fraction for each year, and (2) the amortization of the unrecognized prior service cost.

E19-11   *Methods to Amortize Unrecognized Prior Service Cost*   Wolz Company, a small business, has had a defined benefit pension plan for its employees for several years. At the beginning of 2004 the company amended the pension plan; this amendment provides for increased benefits based on services rendered by certain employees in prior periods. The company's actuary has determined that the related unrecognized prior service cost amounts to $140,000. The company has four participating employees who are expected to receive the increased benefits. The following is a schedule identifying the employees and their expected years of future service:

Employee Numbers	Expected Years of Future Service
1	2
2	3
3	4
4	5

Required

1. Using the straight-line method, (a) compute the average remaining service life, and (b) prepare a schedule to amortize the unrecognized prior service cost.
2. Using the years-of-future-service method instead, prepare a set of schedules to determine (a) the amortization fraction for each year, and (b) the amortization of the unrecognized prior service cost.

E19-12   *Net Gain or Loss*   Lee Company has a defined benefit pension plan. During 2003, for the first time, the company experienced a difference between its expected and actual projected benefit obligation. At the beginning of 2004 the company's actuary accumulated the following information:

Unrecognized net loss (1/1/2004)	$ 44,000
Actual projected benefit obligation (1/1/2004)	228,000
Fair value of plan assets (1/1/2004)	260,000

On December 31, 2004, the company is in the process of computing the net gain or loss to include in its pension expense for 2004. The company has determined that the average remaining service life of its employees is 9 years. There was no difference between the company's expected and actual return on plan assets in 2004.

Required Compute the amount of the net gain or loss to include in the pension expense for 2004. Indicate whether it is an addition to or a subtraction from pension expense.

E19-13 *Net Gain or Loss*   The actuary of the Hudson Company has provided the following information concerning the company's defined benefit pension plan at the end of 2004:

Fair value of plan assets (1/1/2004)	$350,000
Actual projected benefit obligation (1/1/2004)	360,000
Expected projected benefit obligation (1/1/2004)	424,000
Average remaining service life of employees	10 years

The difference between the actual and expected projected benefit obligation first occurred in 2003.

Required

1. Compute the amount of the unrecognized gain or loss for the Hudson Company's pension plan at the beginning of 2004.
2. Compute the amount of the net gain or loss to include in the Hudson Company's pension expense for 2004. Indicate whether it is an addition to or a subtraction from pension expense.

E19-14 *Additional Pension Liability*   Derosa Company has a defined benefit pension plan for its employees. Prior to 2004 the company has not had an additional pension liability. At the end of 2004 the company's actuary developed the following information regarding its pension plan:

Projected benefit obligation	$1,429,000
Accumulated benefit obligation	987,000
Plan assets (fair value)	852,000
Unrecognized prior service cost	200,000

Required

1. Calculate the additional pension liability required at the end of 2004 and prepare the appropriate journal entry, assuming that the company had a prepaid/accrued pension cost (liability) of $73,000 before considering the preceding information.
2. Repeat Requirement 1 assuming, instead, that the company had a prepaid/accrued pension cost (asset) of $46,000.
3. Indicate how the liability and asset in Requirement 2 would be disclosed on the 2004 ending balance sheet.

E19-15 *Accounting for an OPEB Plan*   On January 1, 2004 Flash and Dash Company adopted a healthcare plan for its retired employees. To determine eligibility for benefits, the company retroactively gives credit to the date of hire for each employee. The following information is available about the plan:

Service cost	$ 30,000
Accumulated postretirement benefit obligation (1/1/04)	100,000
Accumulated postretirement benefit obligation for employees fully	
eligible to receive benefits (12/31/04)	40,000
Expected return on plan assets	0
Unrecognized prior service cost	12,000
Payments to retired employees during 2004	5,000
Interest rate	10%
Average remaining service period of active plan participants (1/1/04)	12 years

Required

1. Compute the OPEB expense for 2004 if the company uses the average remaining service life to amortize the unrecognized prior service cost.
2. Prepare all the required journal entries for 2004 if the plan is not funded.

E19-16 *Pension Plan Present Value Calculations (Appendix)*   The Ark Company adopted a defined benefit pension plan for its employees on January 1, 2004. All its employees are the same age, retire at the same time, and have the same life expectancy after retirement. The company decided to compute its pension expense on December 31 of each year; it also decided to fund an amount on that date equal to the year's service cost. The following is a listing of other relevant facts:

Annual pension benefits earned by all employees for each year of service	$100,000
Years to retirement (at end of 2004)	20
Years of life expectancy after date of retirement	15
Discount rate	9%
Expected long-term (and actual) rate of return on plan assets	8%

For the years 2004 through 2006 the company experienced no net gain or loss and did not have an additional pension liability in regard to the pension plan.

Required

1. Prepare a schedule to compute the Ark Company's pension expense for 2004 through 2006. Round to the nearest dollar.
2. Prepare the year-end journal entries to record the company's pension expense for 2004 through 2006.

PROBLEMS

P19-1 *Components of Pension Expense* The Nelson Company has a defined benefit pension plan for its employees. At the end of 2004 and 2005 the following information is available in regard to this pension plan:

	2004	2005
Expected return on plan assets	$ 27,000	$ 28,000
Amortization of unrecognized net gain	3,000	—
Amortization of unrecognized net loss	—	4,000
Amortization of unrecognized prior service cost	7,000	6,000
Company contribution (funded 12/31)	200,000	240,000
Interest cost on projected benefit obligation	32,000	35,000
Service cost	211,000	217,000

There are no other components of Nelson Company's pension expense in either year; ignore any additional pension liability.

Required

1. Compute the amount of Nelson Company's pension expense in 2004 and 2005.
2. Prepare the December 31 journal entry to record the pension expense in 2004 and 2005.
3. What is the total prepaid/accrued pension cost at the end of 2004, assuming no prepaid/accrued pension cost existed prior to 2004? Is it an asset or a liability?

P19-2 *Pension Expense Different Than Funding* On January 1, 2004 the Parkway Company adopted a defined benefit pension plan. At that time, the company awarded retroactive benefits to its employees, resulting in an unrecognized prior service cost of $2,180,000 on that date. The company decided to amortize these costs by the straight-line method over the 16-year average remaining service life of its active participating employees. The company's actuary and funding agency have also provided the following additional information for 2004 and 2005:

	2004	2005
Service cost	$ 340,000	$ 348,000
Projected benefit obligation (1/1)	2,180,000*	2,738,000
Plan assets (1/1)	-0-	670,000
Discount rate	10%	10%
Expected long-term (and actual) rate of return on plan assets	—	9%

*Due to the unrecognized prior service cost

The company contributed $670,000 and $700,000 to the pension fund at the end of 2004 and 2005, respectively. There are no other components of Parkway Company's pension expense; ignore any additional pension liability.

Required

1. Compute the amount of Parkway Company's pension expense for 2004 and 2005.
2. Prepare the December 31 journal entry to record the pension expense for 2004 and 2005.
3. What is the total prepaid/accrued pension cost at the end of 2005? Is it an asset or a liability?

P19-3 *Pension Expense Different Than Funding* When Turner Company adopted its defined benefit pension plan on January 1, 2004, it awarded retroactive benefits to its employees. These retroactive benefits resulted in an unrecognized prior service cost of $980,000 that created a projected benefit obligation of the same amount on that date. The company decided to amortize the unrecognized prior service cost using the years-of-future-service method. The company's actuary and funding agency have provided the following additional information for 2004 and 2005: (1) service cost: 2004, $187,000; 2005, $189,000; (2) plan assets: 1/1/2004, $0; 1/1/2005, $342,000; (3) expected long-term (and actual) rate of return on plan assets: 2005, 9%; (4) discount rate for both 2004 and 2005: 8%; and (5) amortization fraction for unrecognized prior service cost: 2004, 80/980; 2005, 79/980. The company contributed $342,000 and $336,000 to the pension fund at the end of 2004 and 2005, respectively. No retirement benefits were paid in either year. There are no other components of Turner Company's pension expense; ignore any additional pension liability. The company rounds its calculations to the nearest dollar.

Required

Prepare a pension plan worksheet that includes the calculation of the Turner Company's pension expense for 2004 and 2005, the reconciliation of the beginning and ending projected benefit obligation for 2004 and 2005, the reconciliation of the beginning and ending plan assets for 2004 and 2005, and the journal entry to record the pension expense at the end of 2004 and 2005, indicating whether each component is a debit or credit.

*See WebTutor for annotated problem solution.

P19-4   ***Pension Expense Different Than Funding***   The Lane Company was incorporated in 1995. Because it had become successful, the company established a defined benefit pension plan for its employees on January 1, 2004. Due to the loyalty of its employees, the company granted retroactive benefits to them. These retroactive benefits resulted in $1,240,000 of unrecognized prior service cost on that date. The company decided to amortize these costs using the years-of-future-service method. The company's actuary and funding agency have provided the following additional information for 2004 and 2005:

	2004	2005
Expected long-term (and actual) rate of return on plan assets	—	9%
Amortization fraction for unrecognized prior service cost	48/620	46/620
Discount rate	9%	9%
Plan assets (1/1)	$ -0-	$ 690,000
Projected benefit obligation (1/1)	1,240,000*	1,814,600
Service cost	463,000	475,000

*Due to the unrecognized prior service cost

The company contributed $690,000 and $650,000 to the pension fund at the end of 2004 and 2005, respectively. No retirement benefits were paid in 2004. There are no other components of Lane Company's pension expense; ignore any additional pension liability. The company rounds its calculations to the nearest dollar.

Required

1. Compute the amount of Lane Company's pension expense for 2004 and 2005.
2. Prepare the December 31 journal entry to record the pension expense for 2004 and 2005.
3. What is the total prepaid/accrued pension cost at the end of 2005? Is it an asset or a liability?
4. Prepare a schedule that reconciles the beginning and ending amounts of the projected benefit obligation for 2004.

P19-5   ***Pension Expense Different Than Funding***   The Carpenter Company adopted a defined benefit pension plan for its employees on January 1, 2004. At the time of adoption the pension contract provided for retroactive benefits for the company's active participating employees. These retroactive benefits resulted in an unrecognized prior service cost of $1,860,000 that created a projected benefit obligation of the same amount on that date. The company decided to amortize the unrecognized prior service cost by the straight-line method over the 20-year average remaining service life of the employees. The following additional information is also available for 2004 and 2005: (1) discount rate for both 2004 and 2005: 8%; (2) company contribution (funded 12/31): 2004, $550,000; 2005, $510,000; (3) expected long-term rate of return on plan assets: 9%; (4) actual rate of return on plan assets, 10%; (5) service cost: 2004, $257,000; 2005, $264,000; and (6) plan assets: 1/1/2004, $0. The company paid pension benefits of $30,000 each year. There are no other components of Carpenter Company's pension expense; ignore any additional pension liability.

Required

Prepare a pension plan worksheet that includes the calculaion of the Carpenter Company's pension expense for 2004 and 2005, the reconciliation of the beginning and ending projected benefit obligation for 2004 and 2005, the reconciliation of the beginning and ending plan assets for 2004 and 2005, and the journal entry to record the pension expense at the end of 2004 and 2005, indicating whether each component is a debit or credit.

P19-6   *Amortization of Unrecognized Prior Service Cost*   On January 1, 2004 the Baznik Company adopted a defined

@   benefit pension plan. At that time the company awarded retroactive benefits to certain employees. These retroactive benefits resulted in an unrecognized prior service cost of $1,200,000 on that date. The company has six participating employees who are expected to receive the retroactive benefits. Following is a schedule that identifies the participating employees and their expected years of future service as of January 1, 2004:

Employee	Expected Years of Future Service
A	1
B	3
C	4
D	5
E	5
F	6

The company decided to amortize the unrecognized prior service cost to pension expense using the years-of-future-service method. The following are the amounts of the components of Baznik Company's pension expense, in addition to the amortization of the unrecognized prior service cost for 2004 and 2005:

	2004	2005
Service cost	$469,000	$507,000
Interest cost on projected benefit obligation	108,000	159,930
Expected return on plan assets	—	85,000

The company contributed $850,000 and $830,000 to the pension fund at the end of 2004 and 2005, respectively. Ignore any additional pension liability.

Required

1. Prepare a set of schedules for the Baznik Company to determine (a) the amortization fraction for each year, and (b) the amortization of the unrecognized prior service cost.
2. Prepare the journal entries to record the pension expense for 2004 and 2005.

P19-7   *Net Gain or Loss*   For several years, Kent Company has had a defined benefit contribution plan for its employees. During those years the company experienced differences between its expected and actual projected benefit obligation. These differences resulted in a cumulative net gain or loss at the beginning of each subsequent year. The following schedule summarizes the amounts related to the preceding information for the years 2004 through 2006:

Year	Cumulative Unrecognized Net Loss (Gain)[a]
2004	$25,000
2005	26,000
2006	36,500

a. At beginning of year

The company's actuary and funding agency have also provided the following information about the company's actual projected benefit obligation and fair value of plan assets at the beginning of each year:

Year	Projected Benefit Obligation	Plan Assets
2004	$220,000	$200,000
2005	275,000	270,000
2006	320,000	325,000

The company amortizes any excess unrecognized gain or loss by the straight-line method over the average remaining service life of its active participating employees. Because of a consistent pattern of employee hirings and retirements, this average service life has remained at 20 years for 2004 through 2006.

Required Prepare a schedule to compute the amount of the net gain or loss to include in the Kent Company's pension expense for 2004 through 2006. Indicate whether the gain or loss is added to or subtracted from the pension expense.

P19-8 **Additional Pension Liability**   In the Fisk Company's negotiations with its employees' union on January 1, 2004, the company agreed to an amendment which substantially increased the employee benefits based on services rendered in prior periods. This resulted in an $80,000 unrecognized prior service cost that increased both the projected benefit obligation and the accumulated benefit obligation of the company. Due to financial constraints the company decided not to fund the total increase in its pension obligation at that time.

Prior to 2004 it had been the company's policy to fund enough of its pension expense each year so that the fair value of the plan assets at the end of the year was greater than the year-end accumulated benefit obligation. As a result the company reported a prepaid/accrued pension cost liability of $40,000 on its December 31, 2003 balance sheet.

The company appropriately amortized the unrecognized prior service cost as a component of pension expense in 2004 and 2005. The resulting pension and other information for 2004 and 2005 are as follows:

Year	Pension Expense	Company Contribution^a	Accumulated Benefit Obligation^b	Fair Value of Plan Assets^b
2004	$137,000	$125,000	$562,000	$500,000
2005	145,000	160,000	682,000	637,000

a. Funded December 31
b. At year-end

Required

1. Prepare the December 31, 2004 journal entries related to the Fisk Company's pension plan.
2. List the amounts of any assets and liabilities to be reported on the company's December 31, 2004 balance sheet.
3. Prepare the December 31, 2005 journal entries related to the Fisk Company's pension plan.
4. List the amounts of any assets and liabilities to be reported on the company's December 31, 2005 balance sheet.

P19-9 **Determination of Pension Plan Amounts**   Various pension plan information of the Kerem Company for 2004 and 2005 is as follows:

	2004	2005
Service cost	$100,000	(j)
Interest cost on projected benefit obligation	54,000	(g)
Accumulated benefit obligation, 12/31	(f)	(l)
Discount rate	9%	9%
Amortization of unrecognized prior service cost	4,000	4,000
Plan assets (fair value), 1/1*	500,000	615,000
Projected benefit obligation, 1/1	(a)	720,000
Deferred pension cost, 12/31	3,000	(k)
Expected long-term rate of return on plan assets	(b)	11%
Amortization of unrecognized net loss	(d)	700
Additional pension liability, 12/31	3,000	5,000
Accrued pension cost (liability), 12/31	17,000	26,000
Average service life of employees	10 years	10 years
Pension expense	(e)	110,850
Cumulative unrecognized net loss, 1/1	68,000	(i)
Expected return on plan assets	50,000	(h)
Corridor	(c)	72,000

* 1/1/2006: $740,000

Required   Fill in the blanks lettered (a) through (l). All the necessary information is listed. It is not necessary to calculate your answers in alphabetical order.

P19-10 **Comprehensive**   The Jay Company has had a defined benefit pension plan for several years. At the beginning of 2004 the company amended the plan; this amendment provided for increased benefits to employees based on services rendered in prior periods. The unrecognized prior service cost related to this amendment totaled $88,000; as a result, both the projected and accumulated benefit obligation increased.

The company decided not to fund the increased obligation at the time of the amendment, but rather to increase its periodic year-end contributions to the pension plan. In the past the company has never had an additional pension liability at year-end.

The following information for 2004 has been provided by the company's actuary and funding agency, and obtained from a review of its accounting records:

Accumulated benefit obligation (12/31)	$740,000
Service cost	183,000
Discount rate	9%
Cumulative unrecognized net loss (1/1)	64,500
Company contribution to pension plan (12/31)	200,000
Projected benefit obligation (1/1)*	513,000
Plan assets, fair value (12/31)	728,000
Prepaid pension cost (asset) (1/1)	31,500
Expected (and actual) return on plan assets	48,000
Plan assets, fair value (1/1)	480,000

*Before the increase of $88,000 due to the unrecognized prior service cost from the amendment

The company decided to amortize the unrecognized prior service cost and any excess cumulative unrecognized net loss by the straight-line method over the average remaining service life of the participating employees. It has developed the following schedule concerning these 50 employees:

Employee Numbers	Expected Years of Future Service*	Employee Numbers	Expected Years of Future Service*
1–5	2	26–30	12
6–10	4	31–35	14
11–15	6	36–40	16
16–20	8	41–45	18
21–25	10	46–50	20

*Per employee

Required

1. Compute the average remaining service life and prepare a schedule to determine the amortization of the unrecognized prior service cost of the Jay Company for 2004.
2. Prepare a schedule to compute the net gain or loss component of pension expense for 2004.
3. Prepare a schedule to compute the pension expense for 2004.
4. Prepare a schedule to determine the additional pension liability (if any) at the end of 2004.
5. Prepare all the December 31, 2004 journal entries related to the pension plan.

P19-11 *Comprehensive* The TAN Company has a defined benefit pension plan for its employees. The plan has been in existence for several years. During 2003, for the first time, the company experienced a difference between its expected and actual projected benefit obligation. This resulted in a cumulative unrecognized loss of $29,000 at the beginning of 2004, which did not change during 2004. The company amortizes any excess unrecognized loss by the straight-line method over the average remaining service life of its active participating employees. It has developed the following schedule concerning these 40 employees:

Employee Numbers	Expected Years of Future Service*	Employee Numbers	Expected Years of Future Service*
1–5	3	21–25	15
6–10	6	26–30	18
11–15	9	31–35	21
16–20	12	36–40	24

*Per employee

The company makes its contribution to the pension plan at the end of each year. However, it has not always funded the entire pension expense in a given year. As a result, it had an accrued pension cost liability of $36,000 on December 31, 2003. Furthermore, the company's accumulated benefit obligation exceeded the fair value of the plan assets at the end of 2003, so that the company also had an additional pension liability (and excess of additional pension liability over unrecognized prior service cost) of $2,300 on December 31, 2003.

In addition to the preceding information, the following set of facts for 2004 and 2005 has been assembled, based on information provided by the company's actuary and funding agency, and obtained from its accounting records:

	2004	2005
Plan assets, fair value (12/31)	$620,500	$859,550
Cumulative unrecognized net loss (1/1)	29,000	29,500
Expected (and actual) return on plan assets	40,500	62,050
Company contribution to pension plan (12/31)	175,000	177,000
Projected benefit obligation (1/1)	470,000	686,000
Discount rate	10%	10%
Accumulated benefit obligation (12/31)	660,000	903,000
Service cost	169,000	175,000
Plan assets, fair value (1/1)	405,000	620,500

Required

1. Calculate the average remaining service life of the TAN Company's employees. Compute to one decimal place.
2. Prepare a schedule to compute the net gain or loss component of pension expense for 2004 and 2005. For simplicity, assume the average remaining life calculated in Requirement 1 is applicable to both years.
3. Prepare a schedule to compute the pension expense for 2004 and 2005.
4. Prepare a schedule to determine the adjustment (if any) to additional pension liability required at the end of 2004 and 2005.
5. Prepare all the December 31, 2004 and December 31, 2005 journal entries related to the pension plan.

P19-12 *Accounting for an OPEB Plan* On January 1, 2004 the Vasby Software Company adopted a healthcare plan for its retired employees. To determine eligibility for benefits, the company retroactively gives credit to the date of hire for each employee. The service cost for 2004 is $8,000. The plan is not funded, and the discount rate is 10%. All employees were hired at age 28 and become eligible for full benefits at age 58. Employee C was paid $7,000 for postretirement healthcare benefits in 2004. On December 31, 2004 the accumulated postretirement benefit obligation for Employees B and C were $77,000 and $41,500, respectively. Additional information on January 1, 2004 is as follows:

Employee Status	Age	Expected Retirement Age	Accumulated Postretirement Benefit Obligation
A Employee	31	65	$ 14,000
B Employee	55	65	70,000
C Retired	67	—	45,000
			$129,000

Required

1. Compute the OPEB expense for 2004 if the company uses the average remaining service life to amortize the unrecognized prior service cost.
2. Prepare all the required journal entries for 2004 if the plan is not funded.

P19-13 *Pension Plan Present Value Computations (Appendix)* On January 1, 2004 the Cromwell Company adopted a defined benefit plan for its employees. All the employees are the same age, retire at the same time, and have the same life expectancy after retirement. The following are the relevant facts concerning the pension plan factors and the employee characteristics:

Pension Plan Factors

Benefit formula	Average of last 4 years' salary × Number of years of service × 0.025
Expected average of last 4 years' salary	$80,000 per employee
Annual pension benefit earned each year of service by each employee	$80,000 × 0.025 = $2,000
Date of computation of pension expense and pension funding	December 31
Amount funded each year	Equal to annual service cost
Discount rate	10%
Expected long-term (and actual) rate of return on plan assets	9%

Employee Characteristics

Number of employees	60
Age of employees	35
Years to retirement (at end of 2004)	25
Years of life expectancy after date of retirement	14

For the years 2004 through 2008 the company experienced no net gain or loss in regard to the pension plan. On January 1, 2007, however, the company agreed to an amendment of the pension plan. This amendment changed the factor in the pension benefit formula from 0.025 to 0.03. This amendment was made retroactive to the adoption of the plan. At the end of years 2005 through 2008 the company did not have an additional pension liability.

Required

1. Prepare a schedule to compute the Cromwell Company's pension expense for 2004 through 2008. Round to the nearest dollar.
2. Prepare the year-end journal entries to record the company's pension expense for 2004 through 2008.
3. Determine the balance in the Prepaid/Accrued Pension Cost account on December 31, 2008. Indicate whether it is an asset or liability.

INTERNET ASSIGNMENTS

Go to the Nikolai and Bazley **Intermediate Accounting** web site (http://Nikolai.swcollege.com). Click on Student Resources and <u>internet</u> <u>homework</u> <u>assignments</u>. Then click on the appropriate hot link (icon) for each company's web site, find the relevant accounting information, and answer the following questions.

I19-1   Go the the **General Motors** web site.

Required Does the company have a defined benefit pension plan(s)? Defined contribution plan(s)? OPEB plans? How much expense did it recognize for the two most recent years for each type of plan it has? How much did it recognize in the balance sheet for the two most recent years for each type of plan it has? Was its actual return on plan assets greater or less than its expected return? Did its discount rate, expected rate of return, or expected rate of compensation increase change in any of the periods disclosed?

I19-2   Go to **General Electric** web site.

Required Does the company have a defined benefit pension plan(s)? Defined contribution plan(s)? OPEB plans? How much expense did it recognize for the two most recent years for each type of plan it has? How much did it recognize in the balance sheet for the two most recent years for each type of plan it has? Was its actual return on plan assets greater or less than its expected return? Did its discount rate, expected rate of return, or expected rate of compensation increase change in any of the periods disclosed?

objectives

1 Explain the advantages of leasing.

2 Understand key terms related to leasing.

3 Explain how to classify leases of personal property.

4 Account for a lessee's operating and capital leases.

5 Understand disclosures by the lessee.

6 Account for a lessor's operating, direct financing, and sales-type leases.

7 Understand disclosures by the lessor.

8 Explain the conceptual issues regarding leases.

9 Understand lease issues related to real estate, sale-leaseback issues, leveraged leases, and changes in lease provisions. (Appendix)

CHAPTER 20

Accounting for Leases

Many companies choose to lease an asset rather than to purchase it. **FASB Statement No. 13 as Amended**, defines a lease as "an agreement conveying the right to use property, plant, or equipment (land or depreciable assets or both) usually for a stated period of time."[1] A lease involves a lessee and a lessor. **A lessee acquires the right to use the property, plant, and equipment; a lessor gives up the right.**

There are many kinds of leases: short-term, long-term, personal property, real property, cancelable, noncancelable, two-party, three-party, and others. Since it is a contractual agreement, the parties can include in the lease contract any provision that they desire. Today, all kinds of assets can be leased. Among the most popular are cars, photocopiers, computers, airplanes, railroad boxcars, and buildings.

This chapter focuses on long-term noncancelable leases involving depreciable personal property such as equipment, machinery, and trucks. We discuss the lease of real property (land, buildings, and other items attached to the land) and certain other specialized lease issues in the Appendix to this chapter.

ADVANTAGES OF LEASING

The lease arrangement has certain shortcomings—it is, for example, usually more expensive in the long run to lease than to buy. However, judging by its tremendous growth in popularity, for many companies the advantages of leasing must outweigh the disadvantages.

Advantages of Leasing from Lessee's Viewpoint

1 Explain the advantages of leasing.

From the lessee's point of view, the advantages may include:

1. *Financing benefits*
   a. The lease provides 100% financing, so that the lessee acquires the asset without having to make a down payment.
   b. The lease contract contains fewer restrictive provisions and is more flexible than other debt agreements.
   c. The leasing arrangement creates a claim that is against only the leased equipment and not against all assets.
2. *Risk benefit.* The lease may reduce the risk of obsolescence and inadequacy; in these cases, the risk is borne by the lessor.
3. *Tax benefit.* By deducting lease payments, the lessee can write off the full cost of the asset, including the part that relates to land. Also, the tax deduction may be accelerated, because it is

---

1. "Accounting for Leases," *FASB Statement No. 13 as Amended and Interpreted through January 1990* (Norwalk, Conn.: FASB, 1990), sec. L10.101.

often spread over the period of the lease rather than the actual economic life of the property.

4. *Financial reporting benefit.* In certain cases (for operating leases), the lease does not add a liability to the lessee's balance sheet and does not affect certain financial ratios, such as ratios using debt, and the rate of return. As a result, such ratios tend to be "better" because the leased asset and liability are omitted from the balance sheet. In particular, omitting the liability from the balance sheet may add to the perceived borrowing capacity of the lessee.

5. *Billing benefit.* For certain contract-type work, leasing may permit the contractor to charge more because the interest element contained in the rental payments is allowed as a contract charge, whereas interest on borrowed money to purchase assets usually is not.

Advantage number 4 is critical to some companies. In essence, certain leases (called "capital leases") enable lessees to acquire substantially all the risks and benefits associated with asset ownership. If a company can, in substance, acquire an asset without recording it or the liability in its accounts (an "operating" lease), it can substantially improve certain key ratios. The company would be practicing "off-balance-sheet financing."

Capital and operating leases will be defined more fully later.

To illustrate assume that in 2004, two identical companies, A and B, have the following financial data prior to any new acquisitions:

Current assets	$2,100,000
Noncurrent assets	2,900,000
Current liabilities	1,000,000
Noncurrent liabilities	1,600,000
Stockholders' equity	2,400,000

On December 31, 2004 Company A purchases equipment with a 10-year life, at a cost of $2,825,112, by signing a 10-year, 12% note requiring $500,000 to be paid at the end of each year, starting on December 31, 2005. The payments include interest at 12% on the beginning-of-year principal balance, the remainder of each annual payment reduces the principal. Since this transaction represents a purchase by the issuance of debt, Company A records the asset purchased and the note payable (part of which is a current liability). Company A's financial data show these changes: noncurrent assets increase to $5,725,112 ($2,900,000 + $2,825,112); current liabilities increase to $1,446,429 ($1,000,000 + the present value of $500,000 discounted for one year at 12%); and noncurrent liabilities increase to $3,978,683 ($1,600,000 + $2,825,112 less current amount of $446,429). The remaining items do not change. Considering these changes, note the effect on two balance sheet ratios of Company A:

	Before Acquisition	After Acquisition	
Current ratio (ratio of current assets to current liabilities)	2.10	1.45[a]	
Ratio of debt to stockholders' equity	1.08	2.26[b]	

a. Current assets of $2,100,000 divided by current liabilities of $1,446,429 ($1,000,000 + $446,429)
b. Debt of $5,425,112 ($1,446,429 + $3,978,683) divided by stockholders' equity of $2,400,000

The current ratio falls significantly, thus perhaps affecting the willingness of a bank to make a short-term loan. The ratio of debt to stockholders' equity more than doubles, thereby affecting the perceptions of long-term creditors or stockholders as to the risk of the company. These adverse changes, coupled with the impact that the purchase has on the rate of return on investment in 2005, might impair Company A's borrowing capacity or its ability to sell stock.

Next assume that at the end of 2004, Company B leases identical equipment, agreeing to pay $500,000 rent each year for the next 10 years (assume that the property has a 10-year life). If the interest rate is 12%, then the present value of 10 payments of

$500,000 discounted at 12% is $2,825,112 ($500,000 × 5.650223).[2] If Company B classifies the lease as a capital lease, it records an asset and a liability and the effects on its balance sheet are the same as the effects of the purchase on Company A's balance sheet. However, if the lease is classified as an operating lease, Company B does not record an asset or a liability. The current ratio after the lease remains at 2.10-to-1 and the ratio of debt to stockholders' equity, 1.08-to-1. Also, the rate of return on investment in 2005 (assuming that plant expansion was profitable) is significantly higher than for Company A, even though Company B acquires equipment identical to that acquired by Company A. In summary, two virtually identical economic events are reported very differently in the financial statements of the two companies. Today, many companies lease certain assets, but some object to capitalizing the lease payments (where required by *FASB Statement No. 13 as Amended*) because of the impact that reporting the asset and liability on the balance sheet has on key ratios.

The preceding discussion is based on the lessee's point of view. The opposite effect occurs in regard to the lessor. Thus, for an operating lease, the asset remains on the lessor's books, and the lessor recognizes rent revenue periodically, usually at an amount equal to the amount of the rent receipts. For a capital lease, the lessor treats the asset as "sold" and records the related receivable. These alternatives affect significant ratios of the lessor.

Advantages of Leasing from Lessor's Viewpoint

From the lessor's point of view, the chief advantages are that leasing provides (1) a way of indirectly making a sale, and (2) an alternative means of obtaining a profit opportunity by engaging in a transaction that enables the lessor company to transfer an asset by the lease agreement. This transfer also permits the lessor to earn a rate of return in the form of interest on the selling price of the leased asset.

KEY TERMS RELATED TO LEASING

2 Understand key terms related to leasing.

FASB Statement No. 13 as Amended defines a number of terms that are used in leasing arrangements. We list these terms in Exhibit 20-1 because they are necessary for an understanding of accounting for leases.[3] You should study the terms now and carefully review each one as we introduce it in the chapter.

CLASSIFICATION OF PERSONAL PROPERTY LEASES

3 Explain how to classify leases of personal property.

We discuss the classification and accounting for leasing of personal property (mostly for equipment) here; we summarize the variations involving real property (land, buildings, and other property attached to the land) in the Appendix to this chapter.

The basic premise of *FASB Statement No. 13 as Amended* is that **a lease that transfers substantially all the risks and benefits of ownership represents in substance a purchase by the lessee and a sale by the lessor.** Using the concept of economic substance over legal form (as we discussed in Chapters 4 and 17), such a transaction is an asset acquisition and a liability incurrence by the lessee, and for the lessor is either a sale of an asset and the creation of a financing instrument (a sales-type lease) or just the creation of a financing instrument (a direct financing lease). The *Statement* provides criteria for determining the classification of leases by both the lessee and the lessor, as we show in Exhibit 20-2. We list the criteria that relate to the transfer of the risks and benefits of ownership in Column A, whereas the criteria in Column B relate to revenue recognition.

By using the criteria we show in Exhibit 20-2, a **lessee** classifies a lease as one of two types: (1) capital lease, or (2) operating lease. A lease that meets any *one* of the four

---

2. The present value calculations in this chapter use factors from the tables in Appendix D.
3. Adapted from *FASB Statement No. 13 as Amended and Interpreted through January 1990, op. cit.,* sec. L10.401–.424.

EXHIBIT 20-1 Key Terms Related to Leasing

Bargain purchase option. A provision allowing the lessee to purchase the leased property at the end of the life of the lease at a price so favorable that the exercise of the option appears, at the inception of the lease, to be reasonably assured.

Bargain renewal option. A provision allowing the lessee to renew the lease for a rental that is so favorable that the exercise of the option by the lessee appears, at the inception of the lease, to be reasonably assured.

Estimated economic life of leased property. Regardless of the lease term, the estimated remaining period during which the property is expected to be usable for the purpose that was intended at the inception of the lease, with normal repairs and maintenance.

Estimated residual value of leased property. The estimated fair value of the leased property at the end of the lease term. (Note that this value is a different concept from the estimated residual value at the end of the *economic* life of the property.)

Executory costs. Ownership-type costs, such as insurance, maintenance, and property taxes. These costs may be paid either by the lessor or the lessee. Normally, it is expected that the cost should be borne by the party to the contract who controls the asset essentially in the manner of an owner.

Fair value of leased property. The price for which the property could be sold in an arm's length transaction between unrelated parties. If the lessor is a manufacturer or dealer, the fair value of the property at the inception of the lease is normally the selling price, adjusted for any unusual market conditions and less any trade discounts that may be applicable. If the lessor is not a manufacturer or dealer, the fair value is ordinarily the cost of the asset to the lessor.

Guaranteed residual value. The portion of the estimated residual value of the leased property that is guaranteed by the lessee or by a third party unrelated to the lessor.

Inception of the lease. The date of the lease agreement or written commitment, if earlier; or, if the leased property is being constructed or acquired in the future, the date that title passes to the lessor.

Initial direct costs. Costs incurred by the lessor to originate a lease that (1) result directly from and are essential to acquiring that lease, and (2) would not have been incurred had that leasing transaction not occurred. These costs also include certain costs directly related to specified activities performed by the lessor for that lease, such as evaluating the lessee's financial condition, negotiating lease terms, preparing and processing lease documents, and closing the transaction.

Interest rate implicit in the lease. The interest (discount) rate that, when applied on a present value basis to the sum of the minimum lease payments and any unguaranteed residual value accruing to the lessor, causes the resulting aggregate present value to be equal to the fair value of the leased property to the lessor.*

Lease term. The duration of the lease, which may be from a brief period to the full economic life of the leased property. More precisely, the lease term is the fixed, noncancelable term of the lease plus (1) any periods covered by bargain renewal options, (2) any periods for which failure to renew the lease imposes a significant penalty on the lessee, (3) any periods covered by ordinary renewal options during which a guarantee by the lessee of the lessor's debt related to the leased property is expected to be in effect, or a loan from the lessee to the lessor directly or indirectly related to the leased property is expected to be outstanding, (4) any periods covered by ordinary renewal options preceding the exercise date of a bargain purchase option, and (5) any periods during which the lessor has the option to renew or to extend the lease. The lease term, however, in no case extends beyond the date a bargain purchase option becomes exercisable.

Lessee's incremental borrowing rate. The rate that, at the inception of the lease, the lessee would have incurred to borrow, over a similar term, the funds necessary to purchase the leased property.

Manufacturer's or dealer's profit or loss. This profit or loss is the difference between the following two items: (1) the fair value of the property at the inception of the lease, and (2) the cost or carrying amount of the leased asset.

Minimum lease payments. These are the payments that are required or that may be required to be paid by the lessee to the lessor over the life of the lease. Specifically, for a lease that contains a *bargain purchase option*, the minimum lease payments include (1) the minimum periodic payments required by the lease over the lease term, and (2) the payment required by the bargain purchase option. Otherwise, the minimum lease payments include (1) the minimum periodic payments plus (2) any guaranteed residual value, and (3) any payments on failure to renew or extend the lease. Executory costs are *not* included in minimum lease payments.

Minimum lease payments receivable. The sum of (1) the undiscounted *minimum lease payments* plus (2) any unguaranteed residual value accruing to the benefit of the lessor at the end of the lease. Sometimes called *gross investment in the lease.*

Unguaranteed residual value. That portion of the estimated residual value of the leased property that is not guaranteed by the lessee or by a third party unrelated to the lessor.

Unreimbursable cost. These costs may include commitments by the lessor to guarantee performance of the leased property in a manner more extensive than the typical product warranty, or to effectively protect the lessee from obsolescence of the leased property. However, the necessity of estimating executory costs such as insurance, maintenance, and taxes to be paid by the lessor does not by itself constitute an important uncertainty.

* *FASB Statement No. 13 as Amended and Interpreted through January 1990* requires that the fair value of the leased property be reduced by any investment tax credit retained by the lessor. Since the Tax Reform Act of 1986 repealed the investment tax credit, it is not considered further in this chapter.

EXHIBIT 20-2   Classification of Leases Involving Personal Property

I. General criteria for classifying leases

Column A Criteria Applicable to Both Lessee and Lessor	Column B Criteria Applicable to Lessor Only
A. The lease transfers ownership of the property to the lessee by the end of the lease term.	A. The collectibility of the minimum lease payments is reasonably assured (i.e., predictable).
B. The lease contains a bargain purchase option.	B. No important uncertainties surround the amount of unreimbursable costs yet to be incurred by the lessor under the lease.
C. The lease term is equal to 75% or more of the estimated economic life of the leased property.[a]	
D. The present value of the minimum lease payments is equal to 90% or more of the fair value of the leased property to the lessor.[a,b]	

II. Classification by the lessee
   A. *Capital lease.* Lease that meets *one or more* of the criteria in Column A (Part I).
   B. *Operating lease.* Lease that does *not* meet any of the criteria in Column A (Part I). In other words, all leases other than capital leases are called operating leases.

III. Classification by the lessor[c]
   A. *Sales-type lease.* Lease that meets these three criteria:
       1. *One or more* of the four criteria listed in Column A (Part I), *and*
       2. *Both* of the criteria listed in Column B (Part I), *and*
       3. It must result in a manufacturer's or dealer's profit (or loss) to the lessor. A profit (loss) exists when the fair value of the leased property at the inception of the lease is greater (less) than its cost or carrying value.
   B. *Direct financing lease.* Lease that meets these three criteria:
       1. *One or more* of the four criteria listed in Column A (Part I), *and*
       2. *Both* of the criteria listed in Column B (Part I), *and*
       3. It must *not* result in a manufacturer's or dealer's profit (or loss) to the lessor.
   C. *Operating lease.* Lease that meets none of the criteria in Column A (Part I) or that does *not* meet both of the criteria in Column B. In other words, all leases other than sales-type or direct financing leases are called operating leases.

a. Items C and D do not apply if the beginning of the lease term falls within the last 25% of the total estimated economic life. This qualification was added by the FASB to prevent the possible manipulation of the kinds of leases that may result from renewal options. For example, without this qualification, for a tank car having an estimated useful life of 25 years and placed under five successive 5-year leases, the first four leases would be classified as operating leases and the last lease would be classified as a capital lease.
b. The fair value is reduced by an investment tax credit accruing to the lessor. (However, see footnote in Exhibit 20-1.)
c. A fourth type of lease, from the lessor's viewpoint, is the leveraged lease. This type of lease is a special three-party lease which we discuss in the Appendix to this chapter.

criteria listed in Column A of Exhibit 20-2 is a *capital lease* for the lessee. Since the transfer of substantially all the risks and benefits of ownership is considered to have occurred, the lessee treats the lease as, in substance, a purchase of an asset and the creation of an accompanying liability. If the lease meets *none* of the four criteria, a transfer of the risks and benefits is considered *not* to have occurred, making the lease an *operating lease*. In this case, the lessee does *not* recognize an asset or a liability.

By using the criteria listed in Exhibit 20-2, a **lessor** classifies a lease as one of three types: (1) sales-type lease, (2) direct financing lease, or (3) operating lease. A lease that meets any *one* of the four criteria listed in Column A and *both* criteria in Column B of Exhibit 20-2 is either a sales-type or a direct financing lease for the lessor. The lease is a *sales-type lease* if it results in a manufacturer's or dealer's profit (or loss); otherwise, it is a *direct financing lease*. Since the transfer of substantially all the risks and benefits of ownership is considered to have occurred and the revenue recognition criteria are met, the lessor treats the lease as, in substance, a sale of an asset and the creation of an accompanying receivable. Only if the lease meets *none* of the four criteria *or* fails *one* of the revenue recognition criteria is the lease an *operating lease*. In this case, the lessor does *not* recognize a sale or a receivable, and the leased asset remains on its books along with the related depreciation. We summarize the criteria and alternative classifications in Exhibit 20-3 using a flow chart. Exhibit 20-22 includes a summary of the accounting principles used by the lessee and lessor.

ACCOUNTING AND REPORTING BY A LESSEE

We include examples of accounting for leases by the lessee in this section, while we discuss accounting for leases by the lessor later in the chapter.

4 Account for a lessee's operating and capital leases.

Operating Lease (Lessee)

To illustrate an operating lease, assume that a lease agreement signed between the User Company and the Owner Company contains the terms and provisions we list in Exhibit 20-4. In this illustration the lease does not transfer ownership or provide a bargain purchase option, and the lease term is 50% of the economic life. In addition, the present value of the minimum lease payments is $201,867, as we show in Exhibit 20-4, which is only 67% of the fair value of the property. Therefore, this lease is an operating lease for the lessee because it does not meet any of the four criteria from Exhibit 20-2 (column A) (i.e., the risks and benefits are not transferred to the lessee), as we summarize in Exhibit 20-5.

The only journal entry recorded by the User Company is the following, which it makes each year on January 1, 2004 through 2008.

Rent Expense	50,000	
Cash		50,000

If the company prepares monthly or quarterly interim statements, it reports the unexpired portion of the expense as an asset, Prepaid Rent. A lessee does not report the rented equipment in its balance sheet; however, it discloses the future minimum rental payments and other information in the notes to its financial statements, as we discuss at the end of this section.

Capital Lease (Lessee)

When equipment is leased under a capital lease (i.e., the risks and benefits are transferred to the lessee), **the lessee records an asset and a liability equal to the sum of the present value, at the beginning of the lease term, of the minimum lease payments during the lease term.**[4] In accounting for the asset and liability, the lessee must consider the executory costs, the discount rate, amortization of the leased asset, and reduction of the lease obligation.

EXECUTORY COSTS Ownership-type costs such as insurance, maintenance, and property taxes, called **executory costs,** may be *paid* by either the lessee or the lessor, depending on how the lease contract is written. However, since the risks and benefits of ownership have been transferred in a capital lease, the *lessee* usually *incurs* these costs. Many capital leases provide for the *lessee* to pay the executory costs directly. In such cases, the lessee expenses the executory costs as incurred. The lessee computes the values of the asset and liability by discounting the minimum lease payments without an adjustment for executory costs. Each lease payment represents the interest cost and the reduction of the lease liability.

---

4. *Ibid.*, sec. L10.106. Note also that the lessee must not record the asset at an amount that exceeds its fair value.

EXHIBIT 20-3 Lease Criteria and Classifications

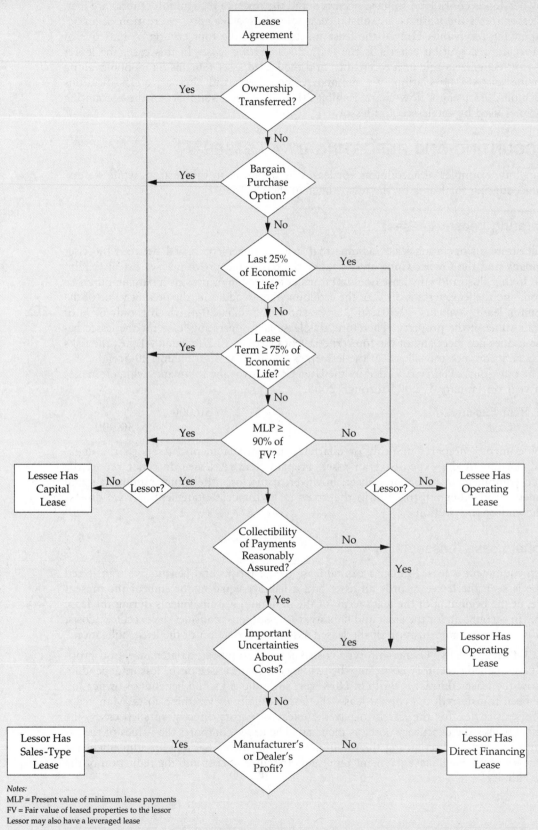

Notes:
MLP = Present value of minimum lease payments
FV = Fair value of leased properties to the lessor
Lessor may also have a leveraged lease

Source: Adapted from "Accounting for Leases: Decisions Flowcharts Supplement," *FASB Statement No. 13 as Amended and Interpreted through January 1990* (Norwalk, Conn.: FASB, 1990), pp. 5 and 15.

EXHIBIT 20-4 Terms and Provisions of Lease Agreement Between Owner Company (Lessor) and User Company (Lessee) Dated January 1, 2004

1. The lease term is 5 years. The lease is noncancelable and requires equal payments of $50,000 at the beginning of each year.
2. The cost, and also fair value, of the equipment to the Owner Company at the inception of the lease is $300,000. The equipment has an estimated economic life of 10 years and has a zero estimated residual value at the end of this time.
3. There is no guarantee of the residual value by the User Company.
4. The Owner Company agrees to pay all executory costs.
5. The equipment reverts to the Owner Company at the end of the 5 years; that is, the lease contains no bargain purchase option and no agreement to transfer ownership at the end of the lease.
6. The User Company's incremental borrowing rate is 12.5% per year.
7. For the Owner Company, the interest rate implicit in the lease is 12%.
8. The present value of an annuity due (in advance) of 5 payments of $50,000 each at 12% is $201,867 (4.037349 × $50,000 = $201,867.45).

EXHIBIT 20-5 Application of Lease Classification Criteria by User (Lessee)

Classification Criteria	Criteria Met?	Remarks
1. Transfer of ownership at end of lease	No	
2. Bargain purchase option	No	
3. Lease term is 75% or more of economic life	No	It is 50%
4. Present value of lease payments is 90% or more of fair value	No	The present value is $201,867.45, or 67% of fair value

Decision: A capital lease must meet one or more of the classification criteria; otherwise the lease is an operating lease.
Conclusion: The lease is an operating lease. It does not meet any of the criteria.

Alternatively, if the lessor pays the executory costs but adds the amount in determining the periodic lease amounts, the lessee *excludes* that portion of each lease payment that represents these executory costs from the minimum lease payments, and therefore from any present value calculations. That is, **the minimum lease payment is the lease payment minus the executory costs paid by the lessor.** The reason is that part of the lease payment represents a reimbursement by the lessee of the executory costs paid by the lessor. The remainder of the payment represents the interest cost and the reduction of the lease liability. If the executory costs are not specifically stated in the lease contract, the lessee estimates the amount of the executory costs included in each lease payment in order to determine the amount to subtract from each lease payment before computing the present value. The lessee expenses the portion of the total lease payment that represents the executory costs.

DISCOUNT RATE The lessee computes the present value of the minimum lease payments by using the *lower* of:

1. *The lessee's incremental borrowing rate*, or
2. *The lessor's interest rate implicit in the lease*, if known by the lessee (or if it is practicable for the lessee to learn).[5]

---

5. *Ibid.*, sec. L10.103.

Since the lessee is acquiring an asset, the rate it uses to borrow money to acquire an asset (the incremental borrowing rate) is appropriate. Alternatively, if it knows the rate in the contract (the implicit rate) and this rate is lower than the incremental borrowing rate, it is a more relevant rate to use. The lessor may disclose its implicit rate. If it does not and there is a guaranteed residual value, or a bargain purchase option, or if the lessee knows the lessor's estimate of the unguaranteed residual value, the lessee can compute the implicit rate. If the lessee does not know any of these amounts, it does not have sufficient information to compute the implicit rate. If the lessor does not disclose the implicit rate and the lessee cannot compute it, the lessee would use its incremental borrowing rate.

AMORTIZATION OF LEASED ASSET   Since the lessee records an asset, it must compute amortization. The FASB uses the term *amortization* more frequently than it does *depreciation*, because the leased asset technically is an intangible asset, although the lessee often includes the leased asset in the property, plant, and equipment section of its balance sheet. Either term could be appropriately used to name the expense. If the asset is written off over the estimated economic life of the property, the term that is usually used is *depreciation*. If the asset is written off over a shorter period of time (the term of the lease), the process is more often referred to as *amortization*.

Regardless of which term is used, if the capital lease agreement (1) transfers ownership of the asset to the lessee, or (2) contains a bargain purchase option, the lessee depreciates (or amortizes) the asset over its estimated *economic* life to its estimated residual value. The lessee uses the estimated economic life because it expects to acquire ownership of the asset. If the capital lease does not transfer ownership of the asset to the lessee, or if it does not contain a bargain purchase option, the lessee amortizes the leased asset over the lease life because its rights to the use of the asset cease at the end of the lease. It amortizes the leased asset down to its guaranteed residual value at the end of the lease term.[6] The lessee uses an amortization (depreciation) method that is consistent with its normal depreciation policy for similar, owned assets. We summarize the depreciation of leased property by the lessee (or the lessor if there is an operating lease) in Exhibit 20-6, using a flow chart.

The principles involved in the selection of an appropriate depreciation method are discussed in Chapter 10.

REDUCTION OF THE LEASE OBLIGATION   Since the lessee records a liability, it computes interest expense and the reduction of the principal for each lease payment using the effective interest method (also called the interest method). This method produces a constant rate of interest on the outstanding balance of the lease obligation at the beginning of each period. *FASB Statement No. 13 as Amended* permits other methods, provided the results obtained are not materially different from those that result from the use of the effective interest method. In this chapter we only use the effective interest method.

Illustrations of Lessee's Capital Lease Method

EXAMPLE 1: EQUIPMENT IS LEASED UNDER AN AGREEMENT WITHOUT A TRANSFER OF OWNERSHIP OR BARGAIN PURCHASE OPTION   The Martin Company, the lessee, and the Gardner Company, the lessor, sign a lease agreement dated January 1, 2004 that provides for the Martin Company to lease a piece of equipment from the Gardner Company beginning January 1, 2004. The lease contains the terms and provisions we show in Exhibit 20-7.

First, the lessee must determine whether the lease is a capital lease. The test we show in Exhibit 20-8 reveals that it is. Since it is a capital lease, the lessee records the leased asset at the present value of the minimum lease payments (the lessee pays the executory costs). This amount does not exceed the fair value. The discount rate is 12%, the interest rate implicit in the lease; we assume that the lessee knows this rate and the rate is lower than its incremental borrowing rate of 12.5%.

---

6. *Ibid.*, sec. L10.107.

EXHIBIT 20-6 Depreciation of Leased Property by the Lessee or the Lessor

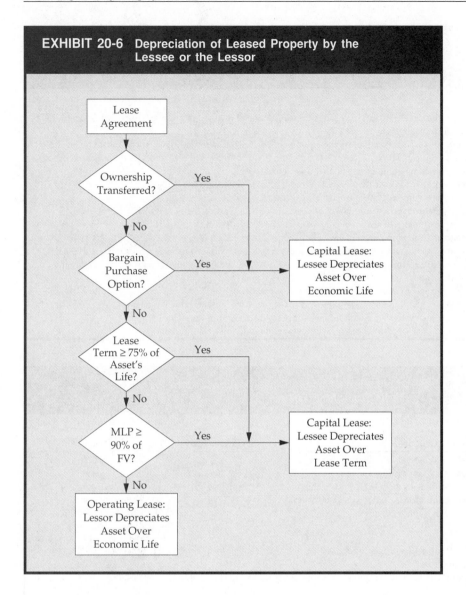

The Martin Company (the lessee) records the acquisition of the leased asset, the amortization (depreciation), and the minimum lease payments for two years as follows:

1. *Initial Recording of Capital Lease on January 1, 2004*

Leased Equipment Under Capital Leases	100,000.00	
Obligation Under Capital Leases		100,000.00

The accounting methods and account titles we use in this chapter are those recommended by *FASB Statement No. 13 as Amended*. The *Statement* uses the $100,000 "net" present value for both the asset and the liability rather than the "gross" value of $131,693.80 (4 × $32,923.45). It is acceptable, however, for the lessee to record the liability at the gross amount with an accompanying debit to a contra-liability account, Discount on Lease Obligation, for $31,693.80. This alternative procedure may be useful when the lessee prepares the required disclosures that we discuss later.

2. *First Annual Payment and Recognition of Interest Expense on Capital Lease on December 31, 2004*

Interest Expense	12,000.00	
Obligation Under Capital Leases	20,923.45	
Cash		32,923.45

EXHIBIT 20-7 Terms and Provisions of Lease Agreement Between Gardner Company (Lessor) and Martin Company (Lessee) Dated January 1, 2004

1. The lease term is 4 years. The lease is noncancelable and requires equal payments of $32,923.45 at the end of each year.
2. The cost, and also fair value, of the equipment to the Gardner Company at the inception of the lease is $100,000. The equipment has an estimated economic life of 4 years and has a zero estimated residual value at the end of this time.
3. There is no guarantee of the residual value by the Martin Company.
4. The Martin Company agrees to pay all executory costs.
5. The equipment reverts to the Gardner Company at the end of the 4 years; that is, the lease contains no transfer of ownership or bargain purchase option.
6. The Martin Company's incremental borrowing rate is 12.5% per year.
7. The Martin Company uses the straight-line method to record depreciation on similar equipment.
8. For the Gardner Company, the interest rate implicit in the lease is 12%. The Martin Company knows this rate.
9. The present value of an ordinary annuity of 4 payments of $32,923.45 each at 12% is $100,000 (3.037349 × $32,923.45 = $100,000). (This is the only present value calculation necessary, since there is no guaranteed residual value or bargain purchase option.)

EXHIBIT 20-8 Application of Lease Classification Criteria by Martin Company (Lessee)

Classification Criteria	Criteria Met?	Remarks
1. Transfer of ownership at end of lease	No	Title reverts to lessor
2. Bargain purchase option	No	
3. Lease term is 75% or more of economic life	Yes	100% of estimated life
4. Present value of lease payments is 90% or more of fair value	Yes	The present value is $100,000, or 100% of fair value

Decision: A capital lease must meet one or more of the classification criteria; otherwise, the lease is an operating lease.
Conclusion: The lease is a capital lease. It meets two of the four criteria.

The annual payment is $32,923.45. This amount represents (1) a payment of interest of $12,000 (12% × $100,000), and (2) a reduction of the lease obligation liability of $20,923.45 ($32,923.45 − $12,000). Note that this lease requires the payment to be made at the end of the year; thus, the annuity is an ordinary annuity. If the lease requires the payments to be made at the beginning of the year, the annuity is an annuity due (which we illustrate later in this chapter).

3. *Recognition of Annual Depreciation of Leased Equipment on December 31, 2004*

Depreciation Expense: Leased Equipment   25,000.00
  Accumulated Depreciation:
    Leased Equipment   25,000.00

The lessee depreciates (amortizes) the asset over the lease term because the lease does not include a transfer of ownership or a bargain purchase option. The lessee uses the straight-line method, and the annual depreciation is $25,000 ($100,000 ÷ 4). The lessee credits an Accumulated Depreciation account. It is acceptable (but less desirable) accounting to make the credit directly to the asset, Leased Equipment Under Capital Leases.

On the lessee's balance sheet for December 31, 2004, it includes the Leased Equipment Under Capital Leases less the Accumulated Depreciation (amortization) in the property, plant, and equipment section of its assets, and divides the Obligation Under Capital Leases between current liabilities and long-term liabilities, as we discuss in the next section.

4. *Second Annual Payment and Recognition of Interest Expense on December 31, 2005*

Interest Expense	9,489.19	
Obligation Under Capital Leases	23,434.26	
Cash		32,923.45

The amount of the second payment is the same as that for 2004, but the payment for interest is the effective rate of 12% multiplied by the balance of the lease obligation at the beginning of 2005. The interest is 12% × $79,076.55 ($100,000 − $20,923.45), or $9,489.19. The remainder of the annual payment is the reduction of the principal of $23,434.26 ($32,923.45 − $9,489.19). Exhibit 20-9 shows the interest expense and the reduction of the liability over the life of the lease.

5. *Recognition of Annual Depreciation on December 31, 2005*

Depreciation Expense: Leased Equipment	25,000.00	
Accumulated Depreciation:		
Leased Equipment		25,000.00

Under the straight-line method, the depreciation (amortization) entry for 2005 is the same as that for 2004.

The journal entries through 2007 follow a pattern similar to those presented for 2004 and 2005. For simplicity, we omitted from the preceding journal entries the entries to record the payment by Martin Company (the lessee) of executory costs such as insurance, maintenance, and property taxes. A lessee records these types of costs in regular operating expense accounts. For example, if the Martin Company pays $3,000 for repairs on the leased equipment during 2004, it would record the payment as a debit to Repair Expense.

CLASSIFICATION OF OBLIGATION UNDER CAPITAL LEASES When a lessee classifies its lease obligation on its balance sheet, it considers the usual criteria for classifying the lease as current or noncurrent.[7] Since the FASB provided no guidelines to measure the

---

EXHIBIT 20-9   Summary of Lease Payments in Arrears and Interest Expense of Martin Company (Lessee)

(1) Date	(2) Annual Lease Payment	(3) Interest at 12% on Unpaid Obligation[a]	(4) Reduction of Lease Obligation[b]	(5) Balance of Lease Obligation Liability[c]
January 1, 2004	—	—	—	$100,000.00
December 31, 2004	$32,923.45	$12,000.00	$20,923.45	79,076.55
December 31, 2005	32,923.45	9,489.19	23,434.26	55,642.29
December 31, 2006	32,923.45	6,677.07	26,246.38	29,395.91
December 31, 2007	32,923.45	3,527.54[d]	29,395.91	—

a. Column 5 at beginning of year × 12%
b. Column 2 − Column 3
c. Column 5 at beginning of year − Column 4
d. Adjusted for rounding error of $0.03

---

7. *Ibid.*, sec. L10.112.

respective amounts, a lessee may use two approaches to measure the amount of the current liability: (1) the present value of next year's payments, and (2) the change in the present value.[8]

PRESENT VALUE OF NEXT YEAR'S PAYMENTS   Under the present value of next year's payments approach, the amount of the lessee's current liability is the payment(s) the lessee will make in the next year discounted to the balance sheet date. For the Martin Company, the current liability each year is $29,395.93 (0.892857 × $32,923.45). The remaining portion of the obligation is classified as a noncurrent liability. This approach, which produces the same current liability each year for a given lease, is conceptually sound and consistent with the theoretical measurement of liabilities in general. In this chapter we use the present value of next year's payments to determine the current liability portion of the lease obligation.

CHANGE IN THE PRESENT VALUE   The change in present value approach often is used in practice by a lessee to measure the amount of its current liability. In this approach, the current liability is the amount by which the total balance of the lease liability will decrease in the next year. For the Martin Company the current portion of the liability on December 31, 2004 is $23,434.26 ($79,076.55 − $55,642.29); on December 31, 2005 it is $26,246.38 ($55,642.29 − $29,395.91). Note that the current liability on December 31, 2006 (the balance sheet preceding the final year's lease payment) is the same for each approach (with minor differences for rounding).

EXAMPLE 2: LEASE PAYMENTS ARE MADE AT THE BEGINNING OF THE YEAR   Suppose that all the lease provisions described in Exhibit 20-7 are the same *except* that the Martin Company (the lessee) is required to make the lease payments in advance, on January 1 of each year, and that the *cost* (and also fair value) of the equipment is $112,000. The annuity calculation is now the present value of an *annuity due* rather than that of an ordinary annuity. The value of the asset and the liability is different, as we show in the following calculation:

> **Present Value of Four Payments**
> of $32,923.45 in Advance at 12% = $32,923.45 × 3.401831
>   = $112,000 (rounded)

Exhibit 20-10 shows the information for the interest expense and the reduction of the lease obligation liability for each period. The journal entries through January 1, 2005 are as follows:

1. *Initial Recording of Capital Lease on January 1, 2004*

Leased Equipment Under Capital Leases	112,000.00	
Obligation Under Capital Leases		112,000.00

   Martin records both the asset and the obligation at the present value.

2. *First Annual Payment in Advance on January 1, 2004*

Obligation Under Capital Leases	32,923.45	
Cash		32,923.45

   The first payment is entirely a reduction of principal, since no interest has accrued. (The preceding two journal entries could be made as one compound entry.)

3. *Recognition of Annual Depreciation of Leased Equipment on December 31, 2004*

Depreciation Expense: Leased Equipment	28,000.00	
Accumulated Depreciation:		
Leased Equipment		28,000.00

   The straight-line depreciation (amortization) is $112,000 ÷ 4 years, or $28,000.

---

8. R. J. Swieringa, "When Current Is Noncurrent and Vice Versa!", *The Accounting Review* (January 1984), pp. 123–130.

EXHIBIT 20-10	Summary of Lease Payments in Advance and Interest Expense of Martin Company (Lessee)		
(1) Date	(2) Annual Lease Payment	(3) Interest at 12% on Unpaid Obligation[a]	(4) Balance of Lease Obligation Liability[b]
January 1, 2004	Before the initial lease payment		$112,000.00
January 1, 2004	$32,923.45		79,076.55
December 31, 2004		$9,489.19	88,565.74[d]
January 1, 2005	32,923.45[c]		55,642.29
December 31, 2005		6,677.07	62,319.36[d]
January 1, 2006	32,923.45		29,395.91
December 31, 2006		3,527.54[e]	32,923.45[d]
January 1, 2007	32,923.45		0

a. Column 4 at beginning of year × 12%.
b. Column 4 at beginning of year − Column 2 + Column 3.
c. Each lease payment, after the initial payment, includes the accrued interest for the previous year.
d. $32,923.45 of this amount is a current liability; it will be paid January 1 of the next year. The remaining amount is a noncurrent liability.
e. Adjusted for $0.03 rounding error.

4. *Recognition of Interest Expense on Capital Lease on December 31, 2004*

Interest Expense	9,489.19	
Accrued Interest on Obligation Under Capital Leases[9]		9,489.19

Even though Martin (the lessee) will not make the next payment until January 1, 2005, the accrual concept requires that the lessee recognize interest expense in the year that it is incurred. In 2004 the amount is $9,489.19, or 12% of $79,076.55 ($112,000 − $32,923.45), as we show in Exhibit 20-10. The lessee separates the Obligation Under Capital Leases into its current and noncurrent portions in its year-end balance sheet. In the December 31, 2004 balance sheet, it reports $32,923.45 as a current liability and the remaining part, $55,642.29, as a long-term liability.

5. *Second Annual Payment in Advance on January 1, 2005*

Accrued Interest on Obligation Under Capital Leases	9,489.19	
Obligation Under Capital Leases	23,434.26	
Cash		32,923.45

The interest applicable to 2005 is $9,489.19, as we show in Exhibit 20-10. The remaining entries follow the pattern of those for 2005.

Other Lessee Capitalization Issues

A lessee may also sign a lease agreement that includes: (1) a bargain purchase option, or (2) a guaranteed residual value.

IMPACT OF BARGAIN PURCHASE OPTION To illustrate the impact of a bargain purchase option, assume that Redd Company leases equipment for 4 years and agrees to a payment of $40,000 at the end of each year. The lease also includes an option to pay $2,000 at the end of the fourth year to purchase the asset. This amount is so much lower

---

9. If not material, the lessee may credit this amount to the liability account, Obligation Under Capital Leases.

than the expected fair value at the end of the fourth year that Redd (the lessee) is reasonably assured of exercising the option. Therefore, it is a bargain purchase option. Redd's incremental borrowing rate is 11%, and the lessor's implicit interest rate is 10%. The cost and fair value of the equipment is $128,160.63. This lease qualifies as a capital lease because there is a bargain purchase option. The lessee records the leased equipment at the present value of the minimum lease payments (which includes the bargain purchase option) based on the lower 10% rate, calculated as follows:

Present value of the annual payments discounted at 10% ($40,000 × 3.169865)	$126,794.60

Add: Present value of the single sum of $2,000
    (the bargain purchase option) discounted at 10%
    ($2,000 × 0.683013)
	1,366.03

Present value of the minimum lease payments	$128,160.63

The lessee records the leased asset as follows:

Leased Equipment Under Capital Leases	128,160.63	
Obligation Under Capital Leases		128,160.63

The subsequent accounting by the lessee follows the same principles as in the previous capital lease examples, except that the lessee depreciates the Leased Equipment Under Capital Leases asset amount of $128,160.63 over its estimated *economic life* (not over the term of the lease) to its estimated residual value (*not* the bargain purchase option of $2,000). The lessee reduces the liability account, Obligation Under Capital Leases, by the effective interest method, as we previously illustrated, but at the end of the fourth year, it has a balance of $2,000. When the lessee exercises the bargain purchase option, it debits Obligation Under Capital Leases and credits Cash for $2,000.

IMPACT OF GUARANTEED RESIDUAL VALUE The lessee may agree to guarantee part or all of the residual value; that is, it guarantees that the value of the leased asset at the end of the lease term will be at least the stated amount of the guarantee. If the asset is not worth this guaranteed value, the lessee must pay the lessor any difference between this smaller value and the guaranteed value. A lessor would generally prefer a guaranteed residual value because it transfers the risk associated with the future value of the asset to the lessee. The guaranteed residual value is included in the minimum lease payments and, therefore, the lessee capitalizes the present value of the amount guaranteed. To illustrate, assume that Karpas Company leases equipment for 4 years that cost the lessor $147,284.99 (its fair value) and agrees to pay an annual rent of $40,000 at the end of each year. The equipment has an estimated residual value of $30,000 at the end of the fourth year. The Karpas Company agrees to guarantee the entire amount of this residual value (and there is no transfer of ownership or bargain purchase option). Assume an appropriate interest rate of 10%. This lease is a capital lease because the present value of the minimum lease payments ($147,284.99), as we show in the following calculation, is equal to 90% or more of the fair value of the leased property ($147,284.99).

Present value of the annual lease payments discounted at 10% ($40,000 × 3.169865)	$126,794.60

Add: Present value of the single sum of $30,000
    (the guaranteed residual value) discounted at 10%
    ($30,000 × 0.683013)
	20,490.39

Present value of minimum lease payments	$147,284.99

The lessee records the leased equipment at the present value of the minimum lease payments (which includes the guaranteed residual value) as follows:

| Leased Equipment Under Capital Leases | 147,284.99 | |
| Obligation Under Capital Leases | | 147,284.99 |

The subsequent accounting for the lease follows the same principles as in the previous capital lease examples. The lessee amortizes the asset by an appropriate method over the *lease term* down to the guaranteed residual value. It reduces the liability using the effective interest method, and at the end of the fourth year the liability has a balance of $30,000. The elimination of this balance depends on the condition of the leased asset at the end of the lease term and the terms of the lease agreement.

ILLUSTRATION OF DISPOSAL WHERE LEASE HAS A GUARANTEED RESIDUAL VALUE Based on the previous information, at the beginning of the fifth year the records of the Karpas Company contain the following accounts with balances as indicated:

Account	Balance
Leased Equipment Under Capital Leases	$147,284.99 (debit)
Accumulated Depreciation: Leased Equipment	117,284.99 (credit)
Obligation Under Capital Leases	30,000.00 (credit)

If the fair value of the leased asset is less than $30,000, the lessee pays part of the liability by returning the asset to the lessor. It pays the remaining part in cash and recognizes a loss on disposal of the asset. To illustrate this situation, assume that the Karpas Company returns the leased equipment to the lessor. Both the Karpas Company and the lessor agree that the equipment is worth only $20,000. The Karpas Company pays the lessor $10,000 in cash, and records the disposal as follows:

Accumulated Depreciation: Leased		
Equipment	117,284.99	
Obligation Under Capital Leases	30,000.00	
Loss on Disposal of Leased Equipment	10,000.00	
Leased Equipment Under Capital Leases		147,284.99
Cash		10,000.00

If the fair value is more than $30,000, the lessee pays the liability in full by returning the asset to the lessor. In this case, the lessee does not recognize a gain or loss. Note that the lessee ignores any *unguaranteed* residual value.

Leases may be written with various provisions. For example, the lessee may be required to pay the lessor the full guaranteed residual value (in this case, $30,000) in cash. The lessee then may choose to sell the asset or keep it for continued use in its operating activities.

Disclosure Requirements of the Lessee

FASB Statement No. 13 as Amended requires certain disclosures by the lessee for both operating and capital leases. The lessee discloses the information presented in Exhibit 20-11 in its balance sheet or in the notes[10] to its financial statements. Wal-Mart Stores discloses its lease information in Note 7 of its 2002 financial statements, as we illustrate in Exhibit 20-12.

5 Understand disclosures by the lessee.

ACCOUNTING AND REPORTING BY A LESSOR

Recall that a lessor classifies a lease as follows:

1. *Operating Lease.* A lease that does not meet any of the criteria in Column A or does not meet both of the criteria in Column B of Exhibit 20-2.
2. *Sales-type Lease.* A sales-type lease results in a manufacturer's or dealer's profit (or loss) and meets one or more of the criteria in Column A and both the criteria in Column B of Exhibit 20-2.

6 Account for a lessor's operating, direct financing, and sales-type leases.

---

10. *FASB Statement No. 13 as Amended and Interpreted through January 1990, op. cit.,* sec. L10.112.

> **EXHIBIT 20-11** Disclosure Requirements for Lessee: Operating and Capital Leases
>
> A. For operating leases having initial or remaining noncancelable lease terms in excess of one year:
>   1. Future minimum rental payments required as of the date of the latest balance sheet presented, in the aggregate and for each of the 5 succeeding fiscal years.
>   2. The total of minimum rentals to be received in the future under noncancelable subleases as of the date of the latest balance sheet presented.
> B. For all operating leases, rental expense for each period, with separate amounts for minimum rentals, contingent rentals, and sublease rentals. Rental payments under leases with terms of a month or less that were not renewed need not be included.
> C. For capital leases:
>   1. The gross amount of assets recorded under capital leases as of the date of each balance sheet presented, by major classes according to nature or function. This information may be combined with comparable information for owned assets.
>   2. Future minimum lease payments as of the date of the latest balance sheet presented, in the aggregate and for each of the 5 succeeding fiscal years, with separate deductions from the total (1) for the amount representing executory costs, including any profit, included in the minimum lease payments, and (2) for the amount of the imputed interest necessary to reduce the net minimum lease payments to present value.
>   3. The total of minimum sublease rentals to be received in the future under noncancelable subleases as of the date of the latest balance sheet presented.
>   4. Total contingent rentals incurred for each period.
>   5. Assets, accumulated amortization, amortization expense, and liabilities.
> D. For all leases, a general description of the lessee's leasing arrangements including, but not limited to, the following:
>   1. The basis on which contingent rental payments are determined.
>   2. The existence and term of renewal or purchase options and escalation clauses.
>   3. Restrictions imposed by lease agreements, such as those concerning dividends, additional debt, and further leasing.

3. *Direct Financing Lease.* A direct financing lease does not result in a manufacturer's or dealer's profit (or loss) and meets one or more of the criteria in Column A and both the criteria in Column B of Exhibit 20-2.
4. *Leveraged Lease.* A leveraged lease is a special three-party lease that is always considered to be a direct financing lease. We discuss these leases briefly in the Appendix to this chapter.

We discuss the accounting method for each of the first three leases in the following sections.

Operating Lease (Lessor)

Under an operating lease, a lessor company leasing an asset to a lessee retains substantially all the risks and benefits of ownership. The lessor includes the leased asset, say equipment, on its balance sheet in a subsection of property, plant, and equipment entitled Plant and Equipment Leased to Others, and records depreciation on it. The lessor usually pays executory costs and records the rental receipts as revenue when they become receivable. If these rental receipts vary from a uniform straight-line basis, the lessor still recognizes the revenue on a straight-line basis unless another systematic and rational basis is more representative of the time pattern in which it earns the benefits from the leased property.[11]

For an illustration of an operating lease, assume that the Owner Company leases a piece of equipment to User Company for 5 years under the terms described in Exhibit 20-4. User Company agrees to pay $50,000 at the beginning of each year. In addition, the Owner

---

11. *Ibid.*, sec. L10.111.

EXHIBIT 20-12   Wal-Mart Stores: Long-Term Lease Obligations

Note 9 (in part)
The Company and certain of its subsidiaries have long-term leases for stores and equipment. Rentals (including, for certain leases, amounts applicable to taxes, insurance, maintenance, other operating expenses, and contingent rentals) under all operating leases were $1,043 million, $893 million, and $762 million in 2002, 2001, and 2000, respectively. Aggregate minimum annual rentals at January 31, 2002, under noncancelable leases are as follows (in millions):

Fiscal Year	Operating Leases	Capital Leases
2003	$ 623	$ 425
2004	602	424
2005	586	423
2006	565	419
2007	547	409
Thereafter	5,131	3,414
Total minimum rentals	$8,054	5,514
Less estimated executory costs		63
Net minimum lease payments		5,451
Less imputed interest at rates ranging from 6.1% to 14.0%		2,258
Present value of minimum lease payments		$3,193

Certain of the leases provide for contingent additional rentals based on percentage of sales. The additional rentals amounted to $63 million, $56 million, and $51 million in 2002, 2001, and 2000, respectively. Substantially all of the store leases have renewal options for additional terms from 5 to 80 years at comparable rentals.
   The Company has entered into lease commitments for land and buildings for 20 future locations. These lease commitments with real estate developers provide for minimum rentals for 10 to 20 years, excluding renewal options, which if consummated based on current cost estimates, will approximate $25 million annually over the lease terms.

Q U E S T I O N S

Ⓠ Why do you think Wal-Mart has operating leases that apparently have a life of 10 years or more? Ⓠ If Wal-Mart's operating leases were classified instead as capital leases, would the reclassification have a material effect on its debt ratio? On 1/31/02, Wal-Mart's total liabilities were $47,142 million and its total assets were $83,451 million.

Company purchased the equipment at a cost of $300,000. The equipment has an estimated life of 10 years and Owner Company uses the straight-line method of depreciation. On January 10, 2004 Owner pays the annual insurance premium of $2,000, and on December 15, 2004 it pays for repairs of $1,500. Assume that there are no initial direct costs involved in this lease. Owner records the preceding information as follows:

1. *Purchase of Equipment to Be Leased on January 1, 2004*

Equipment Leased to Others	300,000	
Cash (or Accounts Payable)		300,000

We show the acquisition of the equipment to reinforce your understanding of its classification. If the company already owned the equipment, in the preceding entry it would credit the Equipment account, and also would reclassify Accumulated Depreciation.

2. *Collection of Annual Payment on Operating Lease on January 1, 2004*

Cash	50,000	
Rental Revenue		50,000

Owner Company collects the annual rental payments at the beginning of each year and records them as revenue. If the amount is receivable at this date but not yet collected, Owner debits a Rent Receivable account. If Owner prepares monthly or quarterly interim statements, it reports the unearned portion of the preceding revenue as a liability, Unearned Rent.

3. *Payment of Annual Insurance Premium on January 10, 2004*

Insurance Expense	2,000	
Cash		2,000

Under operating leases, the lessor usually pays executory costs such as insurance; it records these costs as operating expenses and matches them against the gross rental revenue. The lessor makes an adjustment to the Prepaid Insurance account if it prepares interim financial statements.

4. *Payment of Repairs on December 15, 2004*

Repair Expense	1,500	
Cash		1,500

The repair expense is another example of an executory cost paid by the lessor.

5. *Recognition of Annual Depreciation Expense on December 31, 2004*

Depreciation Expense: Equipment Leased to Others	30,000	
Accumulated Depreciation: Equipment Leased to Others		30,000

The lessor records depreciation on the leased equipment over its 10-year economic life and reports the equipment with the accompanying accumulated depreciation on its balance sheet.

INITIAL DIRECT COSTS INVOLVED IN AN OPERATING LEASE In the preceding lease illustration, it was assumed that there were no initial direct costs. **Initial direct costs are costs that a lessor incurs directly from originating a lease that it would not have incurred if it had not entered into the lease contract.** For an operating lease, the lessor records these costs as an asset and allocates them as an operating expense in proportion to the rental receipts over the term of the operating lease. This procedure results in an appropriate matching of the initial direct costs as an expense against the rental revenue. If the rental receipts are of an equal amount, the amortization of the asset is by the straight-line method.

Direct Financing Leases (Lessor)

Under a direct financing lease, the lessor "sells" the asset at a fair value equal to its cost or carrying value and records an accompanying receivable. Since there is no manufacturer's or dealer's profit (or loss) in a direct financing lease, **the net amount at which the lessor records the receivable must be equal to the cost or carrying value of the property.** The *net* receivable is equal to the present value of the future lease payments to be received. There are, however, two components of the net receivable (net investment), the *gross receivable* (the total undiscounted cash flows) and the *unearned interest* (the interest to be earned over the life of the lease). The gross receivable of the lessor includes the sum of[12]

1. The *undiscounted* minimum lease payments to be received by the lessor (net of executory costs paid by the lessor) plus
2. Any unguaranteed residual value accruing to the benefit of the lessor.

---

12. *Ibid.*, sec. L10.114.

Note that the gross receivable includes the residual value, whether guaranteed or unguaranteed. If the residual value is guaranteed, it is included in the minimum lease payments. If it is unguaranteed, it is explicitly included as the second item. The lessor records the difference between the gross receivable (the Minimum Lease Payments Receivable[13] account) and the cost or carrying value of the leased property as unearned revenue, with a title such as Unearned Interest: Leases. This account is a contra account and the lessor deducts this account from the Minimum Lease Payments Receivable account to determine its net investment in the direct financing lease. The lessor reports this net investment on its balance sheet and divides the amount between the current and noncurrent asset sections. The current asset portion is determined by using the present value of next year's payments approach or by using the change in present value approach, as we explained earlier for the lessee's accounting. Note that the lessor's accounting according to *FASB Statement No. 13 as Amended* follows the "gross" method whereas, as we discussed earlier, the lessee's follows the "net" method. It is acceptable, however, for the lessor to record the asset at the "net" amount, provided it makes the appropriate disclosures, as we illustrate later. However, the main advantage of recording the receivable at the gross (undiscounted) amounts is that this accounting provides the information for the required disclosures, as we discuss later.

The lessor determines its interest revenue each period using the effective interest method to produce a constant periodic rate of return on the net investment of the lease. At the inception of the lease, the net investment is equal to the original cost of the asset, if it is new, or the carrying value, if it has been owned in previous periods. **The interest rate implicit in the lease is the rate that, when applied to the gross receivable, will discount that amount to a present value that is equal to the net receivable.** Thus, there are three variables: the present value (the net receivable), the implicit rate, and the future cash flows (the gross receivable). If the lessor knows two of these three variables, it can calculate the third. We illustrate three examples of accounting for a direct financing lease in the following sections.

EXAMPLE 1: DIRECT FINANCING LEASE WITH NO UNGUARANTEED RESIDUAL VALUE AND PAYMENTS MADE AT END OF YEAR For the first example, we illustrate the accounting by the Gardner Company that leases equipment to the Martin Company as shown earlier in Exhibit 20-7. In addition to the items in this exhibit, assume that:

1. The collectibility of the lease payments is reasonably assured, and there are no uncertainties involved in the lease.
2. There are no initial direct costs of negotiating and closing the lease transaction.

The cost, and fair value, of the equipment is $100,000. The interest rate implicit in the lease is 12% on the net investment. Though given in the data for the lessee, the lessor calculates the annual rental payments it charges the lessee as follows:

$$\text{Annual Payments} = \frac{\text{Present Value Equal to the Cost of Equipment}}{\text{Present Value of an Annuity for 4 Periods at 12\%}}$$

$$= \frac{\$100,000}{3.037349}$$

$$= \$32,923.45$$

As we show in Exhibit 20-13, based on the criteria from Exhibit 20-2 (columns A and B) the lease is a direct financing rather than a sales-type lease because the fair (present) value of the property is equal to its cost.

The lessor records the Minimum Lease Payments Receivable at the sum of the undiscounted annual payments to be collected from the lessee (less any executory costs paid by the lessor) plus the undiscounted unguaranteed residual value. Since there are no

---

13. The title "Minimum Lease Payments Receivable" is appropriate when there is a *guaranteed* residual value. The title "Gross Investment in the Lease" is most appropriate if there is an *unguaranteed* residual value, because then the probability of collection of the residual value is lower, thereby making the use of the term *Receivable* undesirable. For simplicity, we use the title "Minimum Lease Payments Receivable."

EXHIBIT 20-13   Application of Lease Classification Criteria by Gardner Company (Lessor)

Classification Criteria	Criteria Met?	Remarks
Column A		
1. Transfer of ownership	No	
2. Bargain purchase option	No	
3. Lease term is 75% or more of economic life	Yes	100% of economic life
4. Present value of lease payments is 90% or more of fair value	Yes	The present value is $100,000, or 100% of fair value
Column B		
1. Collectibility reasonably assured	Yes	
2. No uncertainties	Yes	

Decision: If the lease meets one or more of the Column A criteria and both of Column B criteria, it is either a direct financing or a sales-type lease. In addition, if there is a manufacturer's or dealer's profit or loss, it is a sales-type lease. If it meets the criteria and does not contain a profit or loss element, it is a direct financing lease.

Conclusion: The lease is a direct financing lease, since appropriate criteria are met and there is no manufacturer's or dealer's profit or loss. The present (fair) value of the lease payments equals the cost of the property.

executory costs or unguaranteed residual value, the Gardner Company records this asset at $131,693.80 {[4 × ($32,923.45 − $0)] + $0}. The beginning balance of the account, Unearned Interest: Leases, is the difference between the Minimum Lease Payments Receivable account and the cost or carrying value of the leased asset. For the Gardner Company lease, this difference is $31,693.80 ($131,693.80 − $100,000). The Gardner Company (the lessor) records the following for 2004 and 2005:

1. *Initial Recording of the Lease on January 1, 2004*

Minimum Lease Payments Receivable	131,693.80	
Equipment		100,000.00
Unearned Interest: Leases		31,693.80

The effect of this transaction is to replace the equipment asset with a monetary asset of an equal amount. Again, observe that Gardner records the receivable at the amount of the gross (undiscounted) rentals plus the estimated unguaranteed residual value of the leased asset (zero in this case). It credits the Equipment account for the cost of the item, because the transaction is interpreted from an *economic-substance-over-legal-form* point of view as the disposal of an asset, even though legal transfer of ownership has not occurred. Gardner records the Unearned Interest: Leases account as the difference between the cost of the equipment and the receivable; it is a contra account to the Minimum Lease Payments Receivable account.

2. *Collection of Annual Payment at End of First Year on December 31, 2004*

Cash	32,923.45	
Minimum Lease Payments Receivable		32,923.45

Gardner collects and records the payment of $32,923.45.

3. *Recognition of Interest Revenue for First Year on December 31, 2004*

Unearned Interest: Leases	12,000.00	
Interest Revenue: Leases		12,000.00

Gardner amortizes the Unearned Interest account using the effective interest method; that is, it recognizes the interest revenue as 12% of the net investment at the beginning of the period (the January 1, 2004 balance of the Minimum Lease Payments Receivable less the January 1, 2004 balance of the Unearned Interest: Leases) or $12,000.00 (12% × $100,000; that is, $131,693.80 − $31,693.80).

Gardner (the lessor) separates the receivable into its current and noncurrent portions for reporting the lease on its balance sheet. It calculates the current and noncurrent amounts of the Net Investment that it reports on its December 31, 2004 balance sheet as follows:

	Current	Noncurrent
Minimum lease payments receivable	$32,923.45	$65,846.90[a]
Unearned interest: leases	(3,527.52)	(16,166.27)[b]
Net investment	$29,395.93	$49,680.63

a. 2 × $32,923.45
b. [$32,923.45 − ($32,923.45 × 0.797194)] + [$32,923.45 − ($32,923.45 × 0.711780)]

Note that the $29,395.93 current portion plus the $49,680.63 noncurrent portion sum to the $79,076.55 (with a $0.01 rounding error) total Net Investment on December 31, 2004 shown in Exhibit 20-14.

4. *Collection of Annual Payment for Second Year on December 31, 2005*

Cash	**32,923.45**	
Minimum Lease Payments Receivable		**32,923.45**

Gardner records the receipt of the payment for the second period in the same way as during the first period.

5. *Recognition of Interest Revenue for Second Year on December 31, 2005*

Unearned Interest: Leases	**9,489.19**	
Interest Revenue: Leases		**9,489.19**

The calculation of the 2005 interest revenue by the effective interest method follows the same procedure as that for 2004. The only difference is that the net investment as of January 1, 2005 is less than that of January 1, 2004. The calculation for 2005 is 12% of the January 1, 2005 balance in the Minimum Lease Payments Receivable account less the January 1, 2005 balance of the Unearned Interest: Leases. For 2005 the interest revenue is $9,489.19 (12% × $79,076.55; that is, $100,000 − $20,923.45).

EXHIBIT 20-14 **Summary of Lease Payments Received in Arrears and Interest Revenue Earned by Gardner Company (Lessor)**

(1) Date	(2) Annual Lease Payment Received	(3) Interest Revenue at 12% on Net Investment[a]	(4) Amount of Net Investment Recovered[b]	(5) Minimum Lease Payments Receivable[c]	(6) Unearned Interest Leases[d]	(7) Net Investment[e]
January 1, 2004				$131,693.80	$31,693.80	$100,000.00
December 31, 2004	$32,923.45	$12,000.00	$20,923.45	98,770.35	19,693.80	79,076.55
December 31, 2005	32,923.45	9,489.19	23,434.26	65,846.90	10,204.61	55,642.29
December 31, 2006	32,923.45	6,677.07	26,246.38	32,923.45	3,527.54	29,395.91
December 31, 2007	32,923.45	3,527.54[f]	29,395.91	0	0	0

a. Column 7 at beginning of year × 12%
b. Column 2 − Column 3
c. Annual lease payment × Number of years remaining on lease, or Previous balance − Column 2
d. Previous balance − Column 3
e. Column 5 − Column 6
f. Adjusted for $0.03 rounding error

Exhibit 20-14 shows the interest revenue and the reductions in the receivable and the unearned interest over the life of the lease. The Gardner company would use the information we show in Exhibit 20-14 to record the journal entries for the remaining years of the lease. At the end of 2007 its net investment is zero.

EXAMPLE 2: DIRECT FINANCING LEASE WITH NO UNGUARANTEED RESIDUAL VALUE AND PAYMENTS RECEIVED IN ADVANCE To illustrate a direct financing lease with a different timing of the rent receipts, assume that on January 1, 2004 the Watkins Company leases equipment to the Hutton Company, with the terms and provisions of the lease we show in Exhibit 20-15. This lease is a direct financing lease because the provisions of the lease agreement we show in Exhibit 20-15 meet one or more of the Column A and both of the Column B classification criteria from Exhibit 20-2, do not include any manufacturer's or dealer's profit, and the fair (present) value of the property is equal to its cost.

EXHIBIT 20-15   Terms and Provisions of Lease Agreement Between Watkins Company (Lessor) and Hutton Company (Lessee) Dated January 1, 2004

1. The cost, and fair value, of the equipment is $391,371.20.
2. The initial direct costs incurred by Watkins Company are not material.
3. The term of the lease is 5 years, with annual payments of $100,000 received in advance at the beginning of each year.
4. The economic useful life of the equipment is 5 years and the estimated residual value to the lessor is zero.
5. The lease receipts are determined at an amount that will yield to the Watkins Company a 14% annual rate of return on net investment.
6. The Hutton Company pays all the executory costs.
7. The equipment reverts to the Watkins Company at the end of the fifth year; the lease contains no bargain purchase option.
8. The present value of the minimum lease payments receivable for the lessor is $391,371.20, calculated as follows:

$$\text{Present value of 5 amounts of } \$100,000 \text{ in advance at 14\%} = 3.913712 \times \$100,000$$
$$= \$391,371.20$$

9. The collectibility of the payments is reasonably assured, and there are no uncertainties involved in the lease.

The Watkins Company records the information for this lease in 2004 using the amounts from Exhibit 20-16, which summarizes the lease payments received and interest revenue earned by the Watkins Company for the 5 years of the lease.

1. *Initial Recording of Lease on January 1, 2004*

Minimum Lease Payments Receivable	500,000.00	
Equipment		**391,371.20**
Unearned Interest: Leases		**108,628.80**

Watkins (the lessor) records the Minimum Lease Payments Receivable at the undiscounted five annual rental payments totaling $500,000 (5 × $100,000) plus the unguaranteed residual value ($0 in this case). It records the Unearned Interest at $108,628.80; thus, the net receivable is the cost of the equipment of $391,371.20. Because the transaction is considered a disposal of an asset, Watkins also credits Equipment.

2. *Collection of Annual Payment for First Year on January 1, 2004*

Cash	100,000.00	
Minimum Lease Payments Receivable		**100,000.00**

EXHIBIT 20-16 Summary of Lease Payments Received in Advance and Interest Revenue Earned by Watkins Company (Lessor)

(1) Date	(2) Annual Lease Payment Received	(3) Interest Revenue at 14% on Net Investment[a]	(4) Minimum Lease Payments Receivable[b]	(5) Unearned Interest: Leases[c]	(6) Net Investment[d]
January 1, 2004			$500,000	$108,628.80	$391,371.20
January 1, 2004	$100,000		400,000		291,371.20
December 31, 2004		$40,791.97		67,836.83	332,163.17[e]
January 1, 2005	100,000		300,000		232,163.17
December 31, 2005		32,502.84		35,333.99	264,666.01[e]
January 1, 2006	100,000		200,000		164,666.01
December 31, 2006		23,053.24		12,280.75	187,719.25[e]
January 1, 2007	100,000		100,000		87,719.25
December 31, 2007		12,280.75[f]		0	100,000.00[e]
January 1, 2008	100,000		0		0

a. Column 6 at beginning of year × 14%
b. Annual lease payment × Number of years remaining on lease, or Previous balance − Column 2
c. Previous balance − Column 3
d. Column 4 − Column 5
e. $100,000 of this amount is a current asset; it will be received on January 1 of the next year. The remaining amount is a noncurrent asset.
f. Adjusted for $0.05 rounding error

The payments are collected in advance. The first payment collected consists entirely of principal since no interest has accrued. (The two preceding journal entries could be made as one compound entry.)

3. *Recognition of Interest Revenue for First Year on December 31, 2004*

Unearned Interest: Leases	40,791.97	
Interest Revenue: Leases		40,791.97

As we show in Exhibit 20-16, the interest earned in 2004 is $40,791.97 (14% × $291,371.20). Watkins would use the information we show in Exhibit 20-16 to record the journal entries for the remaining years of the lease. At the end of the lease term, there will be a zero balance in both the Minimum Lease Payments Receivable and Unearned Interest: Leases accounts.

EXAMPLE 3: DIRECT FINANCING LEASE WITH AN UNGUARANTEED RESIDUAL VALUE AT THE END OF THE LEASE AND PAYMENTS MADE IN ADVANCE To illustrate a direct financing lease with additional issues, assume that on January 1, 2004 the Carlson Company leases equipment to the Johnson Company, with the terms and provisions of the lease we show in Exhibit 20-17.

Since the provisions of the lease agreement in Exhibit 20-17 meet one or more of the Column A and both of the Column B lease classification criteria from Exhibit 20-2, and do not include any manufacturer's or dealer's profit, this lease is a direct financing lease.

The Carlson Company records the information relevant to this lease for the year 2004 using the amounts from Exhibit 20-18, which is a summary of the lease payments received and interest revenue earned by the Carlson Company for the 4-year life of the lease.

1. *Initial Recording of Lease on January 1, 2004*

Minimum Lease Payments Receivable	14,000.00	
Equipment		11,149.06
Unearned Interest: Leases		2,850.94

EXHIBIT 20-17   Terms and Provisions of Lease Agreement Between
Carlson Company (Lessor) and Johnson Company (Lessee)
Dated January 1, 2004

1. The cost, and fair value, of the equipment is $11,149.06.
2. The initial direct costs incurred by Carlson Company are not material.
3. The term of the lease is 4 years, with annual payments of $3,000 received at the beginning of each year.
4. The estimated economic life of the equipment is 5 years, the lease is for only 4 years and there is an estimated residual value of $2,000 at the end of the lease. The Johnson Company does not guarantee any of the estimated residual value.
5. The lease payments are determined at an amount that will yield to the Carlson Company a 14% annual rate of return on its net investment.
6. The Johnson Company pays all the executory costs.
7. The equipment reverts to the Carlson Company at the end of the fourth year. The lease contains no renewal or bargain purchase options.
8. The present value of the minimum lease payments receivable for the lessor, plus the unguaranteed residual value, is $11,149.06, calculated as follows:

Present value of 4 amounts of $3,000 in
advance at 14% (3.321632 × $3,000)   = $ 9,964.90

Add: Present value of a single sum of
$2,000 (the unguaranteed residual value)   =   1,184.16
at 14% for 4 periods (0.592080 × $2,000)
Total present value   = $11,149.06

9. The collectibility of the payments is reasonably assured, and there are no uncertainties involved in the lease.

Carlson (the lessor) records the Minimum Lease Payments Receivable at $14,000 (the undiscounted four annual rental payments totaling $12,000, plus the $2,000 unguaranteed residual value). Note that the discounted amount of the $2,000 unguaranteed residual value included in the receivable for purposes of determining the net investment must earn a return (14% in this case), as well as the remaining part of the net investment. Carlson records the Unearned Interest at $2,850.94; thus, the net receivable is the cost of the equipment of $11,149.06. Because the transaction is considered a disposal of an asset, Carlson also credits the Equipment account.

2. *Collection of Annual Payment for First Year on January 1, 2004*

Cash	**3,000.00**	
Minimum Lease Payments Receivable		3,000.00

The payments are collected in advance. This journal entry reduces the net investment that will earn interest.

3. *Recognition of Interest Revenue for First Year on December 31, 2004*

Unearned Interest: Leases	**1,140.87**	
Interest Revenue: Leases		1,140.87

As we show in Exhibit 20-18, the interest earned during 2004 is $1,140.87.

The Carlson Company would use the information we show in Exhibit 20-18 to record the entries for the remaining years. At the end of the lease, there will be $2,000 left in the Minimum Lease Payments Receivable account. When Carlson receives the asset, it records it at the lowest of the cost, carrying value, or fair value. Carlson records a loss if the asset value is less than $2,000.

EXHIBIT 20-18 Summary of Lease Payments Received in Advance and Interest Revenue Earned by Carlson Company (Lessor)

(1) Date	(2) Annual Lease Payment Received	(3) Interest Revenue at 14% on Net Investment[a]	(4) Minimum Lease Payments Receivable[b]	(5) Unearned Interest: Leases[c]	(6) Net Investment[d]
January 1, 2004			$14,000	$2,850.94	$11,149.06
January 1, 2004	$3,000		11,000		8,149.06[e]
December 31, 2004		$1,140.87		1,710.07	9,289.93
January 1, 2005	3,000		8,000		6,289.93
December 31, 2005		880.59		829.48	7,170.52[e]
January 1, 2006	3,000		5,000		4,170.52
December 31, 2006		583.87		245.61	4,754.39[e]
January 1, 2007	3,000		2,000[f]		1,754.39
December 31, 2007		245.61		0	2,000.00[f]

a. Column 6 at beginning of year × 14%
b. Annual lease payment × Number of years remaining on lease + $2,000 residual value, or Previous balance − Column 2
c. Previous balance − Column 3
d. Column 4 − Column 5
e. $3,000 of each of these December 31 balances is a current asset; the remaining amount is a noncurrent asset
f. The estimated unguaranteed residual value

Initial Direct Costs Involved in a Direct Financing Lease

The accounting for initial direct costs incurred by the lessor is different for each of the main types of leases. Recall that for an operating lease, the lessor records these initial direct costs as an asset, allocates them as an operating expense over the term of the operating lease, and matches them against the rental revenue. For a direct financing lease, **FASB Statement No. 91** has replaced the original requirements of *FASB Statement No. 13*.[14] The *initial direct costs* of a completed lease transaction include incremental direct costs and certain other direct costs. *Incremental direct costs* include those costs that result directly from and are essential to the leasing transaction and would not have been incurred by the lessor if the transaction had not occurred. The *other direct costs* that may be included are those costs of the lessor related to evaluating the lessee's financial condition, negotiating terms, preparing and processing lease documents, and closing the transaction. The costs directly related to these activities may include only the portion of employee compensation and fringe benefits directly associated with the time spent performing those activities and other costs that the lessor would not have incurred but for that lease.

Since the lessor does not recognize any revenue at the time a direct financing lease is signed, it does *not* expense the initial direct costs at that time, and thus there is no effect on net income at the time it records the direct financing lease. Instead, it defers the initial direct costs. This accounting procedure requires that the lessor determine a *new* (lower) implicit rate that will discount the remaining future minimum lease payments to the net investment at the inception of the lease.[15] It expenses all other lease-related costs, such as the costs of advertising, servicing existing leases, unsuccessful lease originations, supervision, and administration, as incurred.

To illustrate, if a lessor incurs initial direct costs of $5,000 on a direct financing lease, it records the costs as follows:

Unearned Interest: Leases	5,000	
Cash, etc.		5,000

---

14. "Accounting for Nonrefundable Fees and Costs Associated with Originating or Acquiring Loans and Initial Direct Costs of Leases," *FASB Statement No. 91* (Stamford, Conn.: FASB, 1987), par. 5–7. This *Statement* was clarified by *FASB Statement No. 98*.
15. *FASB Statement No. 13 as Amended and Interpreted through January 1990, op. cit.*, sec. L10.114.

This entry results in appropriate matching because the initial direct costs are deferred and recognized over the lease term. The reduction in the Unearned Interest: Leases account increases the net investment, but the future cash flows remain unchanged, thereby lowering the implicit rate. The lower rate results in less interest revenue being recognized each period, thereby achieving the goal of deferring the initial direct costs and including them as a reduction of income over the life of the lease.

The calculation of the new implicit rate requires the use of compound interest techniques, as we discuss in Appendix D. Since we do not illustrate the calculation, we assume a new implicit rate and list it in the related problems at the end of the chapter.

Sales-Type Leases (Lessor)

In a sales-type lease, like a direct financing lease, the lessor "sells" the asset and records an accompanying receivable.[16] In contrast, however, in a sales-type lease the fair value of the asset that is "sold" is greater (or less) than its cost or carrying value. Thus, **in distinguishing between a sales-type lease and a direct financing lease, the major differences are the presence of a manufacturer's or dealer's (gross) profit or loss in a sales-type lease and the accounting for initial direct costs.** The manufacturer's or dealer's profit or loss is measured as the difference between the following two items: (1) the present value of the minimum lease payments (net of executory costs) computed at the interest rate implicit in the lease (i.e., the sales price), and (2) the cost or carrying value of the asset plus any initial direct costs less the present value of the unguaranteed residual value accruing to the benefit of the lessor.[17]

To illustrate a sales-type lease, assume that on January 1, 2004 the York Company leases specialty equipment to the Lake Company with the terms and provisions of the lease we show in Exhibit 20-19. The test in Exhibit 20-20 shows that this lease qualifies as a sales-type lease.

EXHIBIT 20-19   Terms and Provisions of Lease Agreement Between York Company (Lessor) and Lake Company (Lessee) Dated January 1, 2004

1. The cost of the equipment is $120,000. The fair value is $190,008.49.
2. No initial direct costs are incurred by the York Company.
3. The term of the lease is 10 years, with annual payments of $30,000 received at the beginning of each year. The estimated economic life of the equipment is also 10 years.
4. The Lake Company agrees to pay all executory costs.
5. The Lake Company is given an option to buy the equipment for $500 at the end of the lease term, December 31, 2013. This is a bargain purchase option.
6. The interest rate implicit in the lease is 12%.
7. The present value of 10 payments of $30,000 at 12% on an annuity-due basis, plus the present value of the bargain purchase option is $190,008.49, calculated as follows:

Present value of 10 amounts in advance at 12% (6.328250 × $30,000) = $189,847.50

Plus: Present value of $500 discounted at 12% (0.321973 × $500) = $\underline{160.99}$

Total present value = $\underline{\underline{\$190,008.49}}$

8. The collectibility of the payments is reasonably assured, and there are no uncertainties involved in the lease.

---

16. A lessor may not classify a lease involving real estate as a sales-type lease unless the lease agreement provides for the transfer of title to the lessee at or shortly after the end of the lease term.
17. *FASB Statement No. 13 as Amended and Interpreted through January 1990, op. cit.*, sec. L10.113.

EXHIBIT 20-20 Application of Lease Classification Criteria by York Company (Lessor)

Classification Criteria	Criteria Met?	Remarks
Column A		
1. Transfer of ownership	No	
2. Bargain purchase option	Yes	
3. Lease term is 75% or more of economic life	Yes	100% of life
4. Present value of lease payments is 90% or more of fair value	Yes	The present value is $190,008.49, or 100% of estimated fair value
Column B		
1. Collectibility reasonably assured	Yes	
2. No uncertainties	Yes	

Decision: If the lease meets one or more of the Column A criteria and both of Column B criteria, it is either a direct financing or a sales-type lease. In addition, if there is a manufacturer's or dealer's profit or loss, it is a sales-type lease. If it meets the classification criteria but does not contain a profit or loss element, it is a direct financing lease.

Conclusion: The lease is a sales-type lease, since appropriate criteria are met and there is a manufacturer's or dealer's profit because the amount used as the selling price ($190,008.49) exceeds the cost ($120,000); that is, the present (fair) value of the lease payments is greater than the cost of the property.

Assuming that the York Company uses the perpetual inventory system and is a manufacturer or dealer in the specialty equipment being leased, it records the information relevant to the lease for 2004 as follows:

1. *Initial Recording of the Sales-Type Lease on January 1, 2004*

Minimum Lease Payments Receivable	300,500.00	
Sales Revenue		190,008.49
Unearned Interest: Leases		110,491.51
Cost of Goods Sold	120,000.00	
Merchandise Inventory (or Equipment Held for Lease)		120,000.00

The first journal entry records the "sale." Because this lease contains a bargain purchase option, York (the lessor) records the minimum lease payments receivable at the sum of the undiscounted annual rental payments ($300,000) plus the undiscounted amount of the bargain purchase option. It records the $190,008.49 sales revenue at the present value of the minimum lease payments, which is the present value of the annual payments of $189,847.50, plus the present value of the bargain purchase option of $160.99. The accounting treatment of the bargain purchase option is the same as that for a guaranteed residual value since each is included in the minimum lease payments. Thus, the present value of the bargain purchase option (or a guaranteed residual value) is included as a part of the sales price of the equipment. The Unearned Interest: Leases amount of $110,491.51 is the difference between the receivable of $300,500 (the gross investment) and the sales revenue of $190,008.49. In general, however, the Unearned Interest: Leases amount is the difference between the gross investment in the lease and the sum of the present value of the two components of the gross investment. That is, the present value of the minimum lease payments and the present value of the unguaranteed residual value accruing to the lessor (none in this example because of the bargain purchase option). The second journal entry records the cost of goods sold at the assigned inventory cost ($120,000) because there is no unguaranteed residual value. Thus the York Company reports a gross profit of $70,008.49 ($190,008.49 sales revenue − $120,000 cost of goods sold) on this sales-type lease at the time of the transfer of the property.

2. *Collection of Annual Payment for First Year on January 1, 2004*

Cash	30,000.00	
Minimum Lease Payments Receivable		30,000.00

The lease provisions require that payments are collected in advance at the beginning of each year. Also, remember that this collection reduces the net investment (the amount on which interest revenue is calculated) by $30,000.

3. *Recognition of Interest Revenue for First Year on December 31, 2004*

Unearned Interest: Leases	19,201.02	
Interest Revenue: Leases		19,201.02

York amortizes the Unearned Interest: Leases account using the effective interest method. It recognizes interest as 12% of the net investment *after* the collection of the first rent, or $19,201.02, calculated as follows:

$$12\% \times [(\$300,500 - \$30,000) - \$110,491.51] = \$19,201.02$$

As we discussed for a direct financing lease, York may prepare a schedule of the periodic interest revenue, similar to the one we show in Exhibit 20-18.

York's journal entries for the following nine years will show a pattern similar to the preceding ones. After it records the entries for the tenth year, its net investment on December 31, 2013 will be $500, the amount of the bargain purchase option. Also, as with a direct financing lease, since a sale is considered to have taken place, a lessor does not record any depreciation on the leased asset. The lessee typically would pay and record the executory costs. Other entries on the books of the lessee are not affected by the lessor's classification of the lease as sales-type or direct financing.

Initial Direct Costs Involved in a Sales-Type Lease

As we indicated previously, the accounting for the lessor's initial direct costs is different for each of the three main types of leases. In the preceding sales-type lease example, we assumed that there are no initial direct costs. If a lessor does incur initial direct costs on a sales-type lease, it expenses them in the same period.[18] The lessor could include them in cost of goods sold, but since the initial direct costs contain a large element of selling expense, it may report them as a selling expense entitled Initial Direct Sales-Type Lease Expense. Either procedure results in an appropriate matching of the costs against the revenue recognized.

Unguaranteed and Guaranteed Residual Values

As we discussed in the introduction to sales-type leases, the lessor deducts the present value of any *unguaranteed* residual value from the cost or carrying value of the asset when it recognizes the expenses associated with the signing of the lease. Note that the unguaranteed residual value is *not* included in sales revenue because it represents an item that is *not* sold.

The present value of any *guaranteed* residual value, on the other hand, is *not* subtracted from the expenses (e.g., cost of goods sold) and is included in sales. Since both the expense and the revenue items contain the present value of the guaranteed residual value, the gross profit element is the same as for an unguaranteed residual value of the same amount. The sales revenue and expenses for a sales-type lease with an unguaranteed

---

18. *Ibid.*

residual value are both reduced by the present value of the unguaranteed residual value. This method of accounting for the guaranteed residual value contained in a sales-type lease indicates that there has been a transfer of the risks and benefits to the lessee usually associated with ownership of an asset. Since the unguaranteed residual value accrues to the lessor, there has been a transfer of fewer ownership risks and benefits. Note, however, as we indicated earlier, this distinction does not prohibit a lease containing an unguaranteed residual value from qualifying as a sales-type lease.

Disclosure Requirements for the Lessor

FASB Statement No. 13 as Amended requires the lessor to make certain disclosures in its financial statements or the related notes. Exhibit 20-21 shows the disclosures for operating, direct financing, and sales-type leases for a lessor whose leasing activities represent a significant part of its business activities in terms of revenue, net income, or assets.[19]

7 Understand disclosures by the lessor.

EXHIBIT 20-21 **Disclosure Requirements for Lessor: Operating, Direct Financing, and Sales-Type Leases**

A. For operating leases:
   1. As of the date of the latest balance sheet presented, the cost and carrying amount, if different, of property on lease or held for leasing by major classes of property according to nature or function, and the amount of the total accumulated depreciation.
   2. Minimum future rentals on noncancelable leases as of the date of the latest balance sheet presented, in the aggregate and for each of the five succeeding fiscal years.
   3. Total contingent rentals included in income for each period for which an income statement is presented.
B. For direct financing and sales-type leases:
   1. The components of the net investment in direct financing and sales-type leases as of the date of each balance sheet presented:
      a. The future minimum lease payments to be received, with separate deductions for amounts representing executory costs, including any profit thereon, included in the minimum lease payments, and the accumulated allowance for uncollectible minimum lease payments receivable.
      b. The unguaranteed residual values accruing to the benefit of the lessor.
      c. For direct financing leases only, initial direct costs.
      d. Unearned income.
   2. Future minimum lease payments to be received for each of the five succeeding fiscal years as of the date of the latest balance sheet presented.
   3. Total contingent rentals included in revenue for each period for which an income statement is presented.
C. A general description of the lessor's leasing arrangements.

SUMMARY OF ACCOUNTING BY LESSEE AND LESSOR

The accounting issues involved in the various types of leases are numerous and sometimes complex. To assist in identifying the key issues involved, we include a summary of the accounting by the lessee and lessor in Exhibit 20-22.

ADDITIONAL LEASE ISSUES

Some aspects of lease accounting are controversial. In addition, international differences in accounting for leases exist.

---

19. *Ibid.*, sec. L10.119.

EXHIBIT 20-22   Summary of Accounting for Leases by the Lessee and the Lessor

LESSEE

Operating Lease

Rent expense is recognized each period.

Capital Lease

Leased property is recorded at the present value of the minimum lease payments.
Lease obligation is recorded at the present value of the minimum lease payments.
    The minimum lease payments are discounted at the lessee's incremental borrowing
       rate unless the lessor's implicit rate is both known and lower.
    The leased property cannot be recorded at an amount that exceeds its fair value.
Amortization (depreciation) of the leased property
    Over the economic life if the lease is capitalized under either of the following
       criteria:
         • the lease transfers ownership of the property to the lessee by the end of the lease term
           • the lease contains a bargain purchase option
    Over the lease life if the lease is capitalized but does not meet either of the
       preceding criteria
    Use the normal amortization (depreciation) policy
Interest expense is recognized by use of the effective interest method.

LESSOR

Operating Lease

Rent revenue is recognized each period.
Property leased to others is depreciated using the normal depreciation policy.

Direct Financing Lease

Minimum lease payments receivable (or gross investment in the lease) is recorded at the sum of the
    minimum lease payments plus the unguaranteed residual value (not discounted).
Unearned interest is recorded at an amount equal to the gross investment in the lease minus the cost
    or carrying value of the leased property.
Initial direct costs are deferred and amortized over the life of the lease.
Interest revenue is recognized by use of the effective interest method.

Sales-Type Lease

Minimum lease payments receivable (or gross investment in the lease) is recorded at the sum of the
    minimum lease payments plus the unguaranteed residual value (not discounted).
Unearned interest is recorded at an amount equal to the gross investment in the lease minus the sum
    of the present value of the two components of the gross investment.
Sales revenue is recorded at the present value of the minimum lease payments.
Expenses that are recognized include the cost or carrying amount of the leased property, plus the
    initial direct costs, minus the present value of the unguaranteed residual value.
Interest revenue is recognized by use of the effective interest method.

Conceptual Evaluation of Accounting for Leases

The four criteria used to determine if there is a capital lease are reasonable measures of whether the risks and benefits of ownership are transferred. Either of the first two criteria would be written into a lease agreement if both parties clearly wanted ownership of the leased property to transfer to the lessee. There is more controversy about the third and fourth criteria because they are fairly easy to avoid. For example, for the third criterion the economic life of the property may be "estimated" as a time period that ensures that the lease life is less than 75% of that period. Note that for the fourth criterion, the inclusion of a guaranteed residual value in the lease agreement will typically result in a present value of the minimum lease payments that is equal to the fair value of the property. Therefore, companies will often try to find a way to effectively protect the lessor's risk related to the residual value of the property without meeting the definition of a guaranteed residual value, and thereby make the present value of the minimum lease payments equal to less than 90% of the fair value of the property. For example, third-party guarantees of the residual value have been fairly widely used to ensure that the present value of the minimum lease payments is less than 90% of the fair value, while providing the lessor with an effective guarantee of the residual value.

 8 Explain the conceptual issues regarding leases.

These examples raise the issue of why the lessee and lessor may want to avoid a capital lease. The motivation usually comes from the lessee who wants to avoid reporting the liability on its balance sheet. The lessee apparently believes that a "stronger" balance sheet allows it either to borrow more money or to borrow money at a lower interest rate. However, the required disclosure in the notes to the lessee's financial statements of the future cash flows each year for the next five years and all years thereafter allows the user to perform a present value calculation that determines the approximate amount of the balance sheet liability (and asset) that the lessee has avoided. Therefore, it appears that the lessee must assume that users do not read (or understand) the notes.

Many users believe that both the relevance and reliability of lease accounting would be enhanced by having a simple rule that requires capitalization of all leases with, say, a life of more than one year. However, companies lobbied not to have such a rule included in *FASB Statement No. 13*. Instead, the FASB opted for the four capitalization criteria. However, the *Statement* also has been criticized for being very "mechanical." That is, the criteria used for capitalization are "absolutes" and are either met or not, thereby leaving no room for professional judgment.

International Accounting Differences

International accounting standards for leases are generally less detailed than U.S. standards. They focus more on the *substance* of the agreement rather than the *form* as defined by the four criteria in U.S. standards. They require capitalization when substantially all the risks and rewards of ownership are transferred, as measured by four criteria. While the first two criteria are very similar to those in the U.S. standards, the third criterion is less precise because it states that "the lease term is for a major part of the asset's useful life," as compared to the 75% used in the United States. The fourth criterion is different because it states that "the present value of the lease payments is equal to or greater than the fair value of the asset," as compared to the 90% used in the United States. These differences impair the comparability of financial statements prepared in different countries.

APPENDIX: SPECIALIZED LEASE ISSUES AND CHANGES IN LEASE PROVISIONS

Some companies engage in specialized leases. We discuss three specialized lease issues briefly in this Appendix: (1) real estate leases, (2) sales-leaseback transactions, and (3) leveraged leases. Other companies may be involved in lease agreements whose provisions are modified. We also briefly discuss changes in lease provisions.

9 Understand lease issues related to real estate, sale-leaseback issues, leveraged leases, and changes in lease provisions.

LEASE ISSUES RELATED TO REAL ESTATE

In the main portion of this chapter we considered only the leasing of personal property (the example we used was equipment). Special issues are involved in the classification of leases that include land, either alone or in combination with buildings or equipment.[20] We show the differences in the classification of leases involving real estate in Exhibit 20-23.

---

20. *FASB Statement No. 13 as Amended and Interpreted through January 1990, op. cit.*, sec. L10.120–.124.

EXHIBIT 20-23   Classification of Leases Involving Real Property

I. General Criteria for Classifying Leases
(Brief titles are given in this exhibit; see Exhibit 20-2 for fuller titles)

Column A
Criteria Applicable to Both Lessees and Lessors

1. Transfer of ownership
2. Contains bargain purchase option
3. Lease term is 75% or more of economic life
4. Present value of lease payments is
90% or more of fair value

Column B
Criteria Applicable to Lessors Only

1. Collectibility reasonably assured
2. No uncertainties

II. Lease of Land Only
   A. Lessee
      1. Capital lease. Lease must meet either
         criterion 1 or 2 in Column A (Part I).
         (Criteria 3 and 4 are *not* applicable.)
      2. Operating lease. Lease must not meet
         either criterion 1 or 2 in Column A
         (Part I).

   B. Lessor
      1. Sales-type lease. Lease must
         a. Meet either criterion 1 or 2
            in Column A (Part I), *and*
         b. Meet both criteria in
            Column B (Part I), *and*
         c. Results in a dealer's profit or loss.
      2. Direct financing lease. Lease must meet
         a. Either criterion 1 or 2 in Column A
            (Part I), *and*
         b. Both criteria in Column B (Part I).
      3. Operating lease. Lease that does *not*
         qualify as a sales-type or direct financing
         lease.

III. Lease of Both Land and Buildings
A. Lease of both land and buildings that transfers ownership or contains a bargain purchase option
   1. Lessee
      a. Capital lease. The lease is a
         capital lease since one or more of
         the criteria of Column A (Part I)
         are met. Land and buildings are
         separately capitalized.

   2. Lessor
      a. Sales-type lease. The two assets,
         land and buildings, are considered as
         a single unit and the lease must
         (1) Meet either criterion 1 or 2 in
             Column A (Part I), *and*
         (2) Meet both criteria in Column B
             (Part I), *and*
         (3) Results in a dealer's profit or loss.
      b. Direct financing lease. The lease of the
         two assets combined must meet
         (1) Either criterion 1 or 2 in Column A
             (Part I), *and*
         (2) Both criteria in Column B (Part I).

continued

Lease of Land Only

If land is the sole item of property leased, the lessee accounts for the lease as a capital lease only if the lease meets either criterion 1 of Column A (Part I) of Exhibit 20-23, the transfer of ownership at the end of the lease, or criterion 2, a bargain purchase option. Otherwise, the lessee accounts for the lease as an operating lease. Criterion 3 (dealing with the 75% of the estimated economic life) and criterion 4 (dealing with the 90% of the fair value of the leased property) do *not* apply because the asset would have to be depreciated over the lease life. Such a situation would be inappropriate for land. The lessee does *not* amortize the asset, Leased Land Under Capital Leases, because title to the land is expected to be transferred, and land as such is not subject to amortization. The lessor accounts for the lease of land as a sales-type lease if (1) the lease transfers ownership or contains a bargain purchase option, (2) the lease meets both the

---

EXHIBIT 20-23, Continued

B. If lease meets neither criterion 1 nor criterion 2 in Column A (Part I), and if fair value of land is less than 25% of fair value of both land and buildings. (The land portion is ignored and the classification is determined using the characteristics of building.)

1. Lessee
   a. Capital lease. Lease must meet either criterion 3 or 4 in Column A (Part I).
   b. Operating lease. Lease meets none of the criteria in Column A (Part I).

2. Lessor
   a. Sales-type lease. Lease must
      (1) Meet either criterion 3 or 4 in Column A (Part I), *and*
      (2) Meet both criteria in Column B (Part I), *and*
      (3) Results in a dealer's profit or loss.
   b. Direct financing lease. Lease must meet
      (1) Either criterion 3 or 4 in Column A (Part I), *and*
      (2) Both criteria in Column B (Part I).
   c. Operating Lease. Lease that does *not* qualify as a sales-type or direct financing lease.

C. If lease meets neither criterion 1 nor criterion 2 in Column A (Part I), and if fair value of land is more than 25% of fair value of both land and buildings. (The lease is separated into land and building portions.)

1. Lessee
   a. Land portion. Always an operating lease.
   b. Building portion. Classified by remaining criteria of Column A (Part I).

2. Lessor
   a. Land portion. Always an operating lease.
   b. Building portion. Classified by remaining criteria of Columns A and B (Part I).

---

collectibility and uncertainty criteria of Column B (Part I) of Exhibit 20-23, and (3) there is a dealer's profit or loss. If the criteria for a sales-type lease are met with the exception that there is no dealer's profit or loss, then the lease qualifies as a direct financing one. Otherwise, it is an operating lease.

Lease of Both Land and Buildings That Transfers Title or Contains a Bargain Purchase Option

When both land and buildings are leased, a new issue arises as to the classification of the lease because one portion involves a depreciable asset with an estimated economic life and the other involves a nondepreciable asset. The accounting treatment is considered in two parts: (1) a lease of both land and buildings that meets criteria 1 and 2 of Column A (Part I) of Exhibit 20-23, and (2) a lease of both land and buildings that does *not* meet either criterion 1 or 2.

LESSEE'S ACCOUNTING For a capital lease of land and buildings that transfers ownership or that contains a bargain purchase option, the lessee allocates the present value of the minimum lease payments between the two leased assets in proportion to their fair values at the inception of the lease (Exhibit 20-23, IIIA). It amortizes the amount assigned to Leased Buildings Under Capital Leases over the estimated economic life of the buildings; and it does *not* amortize the amount assigned to Leased Land Under Capital Leases.

LESSOR'S ACCOUNTING The lessor accounts for the lease as a single unit, either as a direct financing, a sales-type, or an operating lease. The term **single unit** means that for a sales-type or direct financing lease, the lessor uses one Minimum Lease Payments Receivable account to record the appropriate values for the lease of both land and buildings. In the original lease entry, however, the lessor credits both the land and the buildings accounts.

Lease of Land and Buildings That Does Not Transfer Title or Contain a Bargain Purchase Option

VALUE OF LAND IS LESS THAN 25%   If a lease of land and buildings does not transfer ownership or contain a bargain purchase option, it is a capital lease if it meets one of the other two criteria. If the fair value of the land is less than 25% of the total fair value of the leased property at the inception of the lease, the land is considered to be immaterial. Therefore, *both* the lessee and the lessor consider the land and buildings as a single unit. Note that for the purpose of applying criterion 3 of Column A (Part I) of Exhibit 20-23, the estimated economic life of the building is considered as the economic life of the unit.

1. *Lessee's Accounting.* If either criterion 3 or 4 of Column A (Part I) of Exhibit 20-23 is met, the lessee classifies the lease as a capital lease, recognizes the leased land and buildings as a single asset, and amortizes the total amount over the term of the lease, even though it is implicitly depreciating the land portion of the asset. If the lease does not meet any of the criteria in Column A (Part I), it is an operating lease.
2. *Lessor's Accounting.* If the lease meets either criterion 3 or 4 of Column A (Part I) of Exhibit 20-23 and both of the criteria of Column B (Part I), the lessor accounts for the lease as a single unit, as either a direct financing or a sales-type lease as appropriate; otherwise, the lease is an operating lease.

VALUE OF LAND IS MORE THAN 25%   On the other hand, if at the inception of the lease, the land represents 25% or more of the fair value of the leased property, the amount of the land is considered to be a material amount. Then, both the lessee and the lessor must consider the land and the buildings separately for purposes of applying the criteria listed in Exhibit 20-23. In this case, the lessee and lessor separate the minimum lease payments into amounts applicable to land and to buildings. Since the lease of the land results in an operating lease, the recommended way to make the preceding calculation is to determine the fair value of land, and then use the appropriate interest rate to determine the periodic minimum lease payments applicable to the land portion, as follows:

$$\frac{\text{Incremental}}{\text{Borrowing Rate}} \times \frac{\text{Fair Value}}{\text{of Land}} = \frac{\text{Periodic Minimum Lease}}{\text{Payment Applicable to Land}}$$

The periodic minimum lease payments applicable to both land and buildings, less the amount calculated, is the amount attributed to the buildings.

1. *Lessee's Accounting.* Once the amount assigned to the buildings is determined, if the lease of this portion meets either criterion 3 or 4 of Column A (Part I) of Exhibit 20-23, it is accounted for as a capital lease. The lessee amortizes the present value amount assigned to the asset, Leased Buildings Under Capital Leases, over the life of the lease. It accounts for the land portion of the lease separately as an operating lease. Therefore, if the buildings portion of the lease meets neither criterion 3 nor 4 of Column A (Part I) of Exhibit 20-23, the lessee accounts for both the buildings and the land as a single operating lease.
2. *Lessor's Accounting.* If the buildings portion of the lease meets either criterion 3 or 4 of Column A (Part I) and both criteria of Column B of Exhibit 20-23, the lessee accounts for the lease as a direct financing or sales-type lease, depending on whether a manufacturer's or dealer's profit or loss arises out of the transaction. It accounts for the land portion of the lease separately as an operating lease. If the buildings portion of the lease does not meet the relevant criteria, the lessor accounts for both the buildings and land as a single operating lease.

Lease Involving Equipment as Well as Real Estate

If a lease involves both equipment and real estate, the portion of the minimum lease payments applicable to the equipment portion of the lease is estimated by whatever means are appropriate under the circumstances. The equipment then is considered separately for the purposes of applying the criteria we list in Exhibit 20-23 and is accounted for separately according to its classification by both the lessee and lessor. The accounting for the remaining real estate portion follows the accounting standards described in the preceding section.

SALE-LEASEBACK ISSUES

If a company has limited cash resources or decides it does not want to be responsible for owning the property, it may sell an asset (often land and buildings, but not real property exclusively) and then immediately lease it back from the buyer. This kind of transaction may be advantageous to both the lessee and lessor: The lessee receives cash from the sale that is needed for its activities, and may derive a tax advantage; the lessor acquires a financial asset.

The sale of the asset and the leaseback are considered to be a single transaction, that essentially is like a secured loan, with the creditor obtaining legal title to the asset. The sales price of the asset, any profit earned, and the minimum lease payments must be considered together. If the lease meets one of the criteria for treatment as a capital lease (see Exhibit 20-2), the seller-lessee accounts for the lease as a capital lease[21]; otherwise, it accounts for the lease as an operating lease. It defers any profit on the sale. If the lease is a capital lease, the lessee amortizes the profit in proportion to the amortization of the leased asset. If the lease is an operating lease, the lessee amortizes the profit in proportion to the rental payments over the period of time it expects the asset to be used. However, when the fair value of the property at the time of the transaction is less than its undepreciated cost, it *recognizes a loss immediately* up to the amount of the difference between the undepreciated cost and fair value.[22]

Lessor's Accounting Issues

The purchaser-lessor follows the principles developed in the preceding sections to account for the purchase of the asset and the immediate lease of it back to the seller. From the lessor's point of view, no new issues are involved, so we do not illustrate its accounting entries here.

Lessee's Accounting Issues

If the lease meets at least one of the four criteria in Column A of Exhibit 20-2, the seller-lessee accounts for the lease as a capital lease. If none of the criteria are satisfied, the seller-lessee accounts for the lease as an operating lease. The accounting for the main provisions of the lease follows the procedures we already illustrated. The primary new issue from the lessee's viewpoint is the accounting for the profit or loss on the sale of the property by the seller-lessee. To illustrate, assume that on January 1, 2004 the High Point Railroad built ten boxcars, or rolling stock, costing $400,000. Because of a cash flow problem resulting from this new acquisition, High Point decided to sell these boxcars immediately to Landlord Company for $600,000, and then lease them back under the conditions we show in Exhibit 20-24.

Typical journal entries to record the information related to the preceding sale-leaseback for High Point Railroad (the seller-lessee) for 2004 are as follows:

1. *Sale of the Boxcars to Landlord Company on January 1, 2004*

Cash	600,000.00	
Rolling Stock		400,000.00
Unearned Profit on Sale-Leaseback		200,000.00

---

21. A sale-leaseback transaction involving real estate must qualify as a sale under the provisions of *FASB Statement No. 66,* "Accounting for Sales of Real Estate."

22. *FASB Statement No. 13 as Amended and Interpreted through January 1990, op. cit.,* sec. L10.129.

EXHIBIT 20-24   Terms and Provisions of Lease Agreement Between Landlord Company and High Point Railroad Dated January 1, 2004

1. The cost of the boxcars to High Point Railroad (the seller-lessee) is $400,000. The selling price to Landlord Company (the purchaser-lessor) is $600,000; thus, this amount becomes the new cost of the equipment to the seller-lessee.
2. The term of the lease is 15 years, with annual payments of $92,771.13 in advance at the beginning of each year. The estimated economic life of the equipment is 20 years, with no expected residual value at the end of this time. (The residual value at the end of 15 years is not considered because title passes at that time.)
3. The High Point Railroad agrees to pay all executory costs.
4. Title to the boxcars will be transferred to the seller-lessee at the end of lease term.
5. The interest rate implicit on the lease is 16%. High Point Railroad knows this rate, and the rate equals its incremental borrowing rate.
6. The present value of 15 payments of $92,771.13 at 16% on an annuity-due basis is $600,000, calculated as follows:

Present value of 15 amounts in advance at 16% = 6.467529 × $92,771.13
= $600,000 (rounded)

7. The lease qualifies as a capital lease to High Point Railroad, since it meets the criteria stated in Exhibit 20-2.

---

2. *Initial Recording of the Leaseback as a Capital Lease on January 1, 2004*

Leased Rolling Stock Under Capital Leases	600,000.00	
Obligation Under Capital Leases		600,000.00

3. *Annual Payment on January 1, 2004*

Obligation Under Capital Leases	92,771.13	
Cash		92,771.13

4. *Payment of Executory Costs on Various Dates in 2004 (amounts assumed)*

Insurance Expense	2,600.00	
Repairs and Maintenance Expense	2,300.00	
Property Tax Expense	9,700.00	
Cash		14,600.00

5. *Recording Depreciation of Rolling Stock on December 31, 2004*

Depreciation Expense: Leased Rolling Stock	30,000.00	
Accumulated Depreciation: Leased Rolling Stock		30,000.00

High Point uses the straight-line method and a life of 20 years because ownership is transferred at the end of the lease. Depreciation for 2004 is $30,000 ($600,000 ÷ 20).

6. *Amortization of Unearned Profit on Sale-Leaseback on December 31, 2004*

Unearned Profit on Sale-Leaseback	10,000.00	
Realized Profit on Sale-Leaseback (or Depreciation Expense: Leased Rolling Stock)		10,000.00

The amortization is $10,000 ($200,000 ÷ 20). Note that High Point amortizes the Unearned Profit on Sale-Leaseback and recognizes the profit over a 20-year period. For a capital lease, *FASB Statement No. 13 as Amended* requires that a seller-lessee recognize any realized profit using the same rate that it used to depreciate Leased Rolling Stock Under Capital Leases. For an operating lease, the seller-lessee defers such profit (or loss) and amortizes the amount in proportion to the lease payments over the period it expects to use the leased assets. A loss could be sustained by the seller-lessee if the book value or carrying amount were larger than the fair value of the asset. The seller-lessee recognizes the entire amount of this loss in the year of the sale-leaseback.

7. *Recognition of Interest Expense on December 31, 2004*

Interest Expense	81,156.62	
Obligation Under Capital Leases		81,156.62

This year-end adjusting entry is the same as that made for any capital lease for which the payment is made in advance. High Point calculates the amount the as $81,156.62 [16\% \times (\$600,000 - \$92,771.13)]$.

Leveraged Leases

A leveraged lease is a special arrangement involving three different participants to the agreement: (1) the equity participant (the owner-lessor); (2) the asset user (the lessee); and (3) the debt participant (the long-term creditor who provides nonrecourse financing for the leasing transaction between the lessee and lessor). Exhibit 20-25 shows the interrelated activities of the three parties to a leveraged lease. If the owner-lessor buys the equipment from a manufacturer, a fourth party to the transaction would be present.

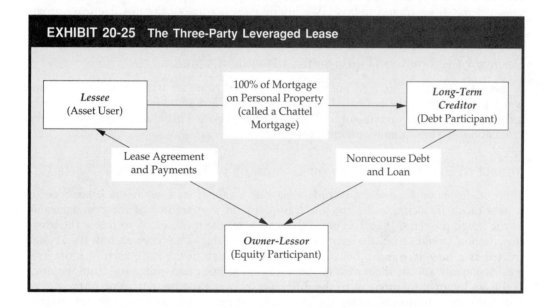

EXHIBIT 20-25 The Three-Party Leveraged Lease

Currently, over \$7 billion worth of capital equipment—such as aircraft, ships, and heavy machinery—is financed annually through the use of leveraged leases. This kind of leasing arrangement began in the late 1960s and has grown rapidly since then. The lease is designed to provide income tax benefits to the three parties involved in the transaction. The lessor may be able to retain various tax credits, and also can immediately recognize all the cost of the asset as an income tax deduction. The lessee receives the right to income tax deductions for the rent of land, buildings, and other personal property. The creditor receives the tax protection provided for the leveraged lease contract.

From the standpoint of the lessee, no new accounting issues arise. It classifies a leveraged lease and accounts for it in the same way as a nonleveraged lease. *FASB Statement No. 13 as Amended* requires that the lessor classify a leveraged lease as a direct financing lease, since no manufacturer's or dealer's profit can arise from the transaction and therefore it cannot be classified as a sales-type lease.[23]

---

23. *Ibid.*, sec. L10.144.

The lessor records its investment in a leveraged lease net of the nonrecourse debt, which usually consists of the (1) rental receivables, net of that portion applicable to the nonrecourse debt; (2) amount of any tax credits to be realized on the transaction; (3) estimated residual value of the leased asset; and (4) reduction for the unearned revenue items. Since leveraged leases are complex financial arrangements that vary in structure, the lessor's accounting for them is also complex and is beyond the scope of the book.[24]

CHANGES IN LEASE PROVISIONS

As we discussed earlier, lease contracts are written with many provisions, including renewal, extension, or purchase options, and penalties. Lessees and lessors may opt to change certain provisions that, in effect, change the classification of the lease. If at any time the lessee and lessor change the provisions of a lease (other than by renewing or extending its term) in such a way that the lease would have been classified differently *had the changed terms been in effect at the beginning of the lease term*, the revised agreement is considered a new agreement. The new agreement is reclassified as operating, direct financing, or sales-type, according to the criteria in Exhibit 20-2.

FASB Statement No. 13 as Amended also addresses the issue of renewals and extensions. A change in an operating lease to a direct financing or sales-type lease presents the fewest issues, since the accounting for the new lease would be similar to that described earlier in the chapter. The most complex issue involves a change in either a sales-type or direct financing lease. We briefly discuss some of the possible lease provision changes in the following sections.

Review of Estimated Unguaranteed Residual Value

A lessor reviews the estimated unguaranteed residual value annually. It *ignores* any upward adjustments in the estimated value, but must record any downward adjustment as a reduction in its net investment and a loss in the period. This recognition involves the calculation of a new implicit interest rate.

Impact of Renewal of Lease on Guarantee of Residual Value

Suppose, for example, a lessee records a lease as a capital lease while the lessor records it as a direct financing lease, and the lease contains a guarantee of the residual value of the leased property. If at the end of the lease term the lessee elects to renew the lease, this election would cancel the guarantee of residual value. The renewal, however, is *not* treated as a new agreement, because there is no change in the lease classification. The lessee company adjusts the remaining balances of the asset and obligation from the original lease by an amount equal to the difference between the present value of the future minimum lease payments under the new renewal agreement and the existing present balance of the obligation.

Changes to Sales-Type or Direct Financing Lease Prior to Lease Term Expiration That Change the Lease to an Operating Lease

If changes are made in either sales-type or direct financing lease provisions prior to the expiration of the lease term, and if these changes would have resulted in the original agreement at inception having been classified as an operating lease, the lessor removes the net investment remaining on its books from its accounts. It replaces the Minimum Lease Payments Receivable on its books with an asset at its original cost, fair value, or carrying amount, whichever is lowest, and reports any net adjustment as an operating loss in the period of change. It then accounts for the new lease as any other operating lease.

---

24. See Appendix E of *FASB Statement No. 13 as Amended and Interpreted through January 1990*, sec. L10.161, for an illustration of the accounting and financial statement presentation of leveraged leases.

An exception occurs when a guarantee or penalty is rendered inoperative. In this case, if the renewal or extension results in an operating lease, the lessor continues to account for the existing lease as either a sales-type or direct financing lease (depending on the original classification) to the end of its original term, and then accounts for the renewal or extension as any other operating lease. The accounting by the lessee follows a similar pattern.

Renewal or Extension of Sales-Type or Direct Financing Lease Resulting in a New Lease That Qualifies as a Sales-Type Lease

The accounting for a renewal or extension of sales-type and direct financing leases that results in a lease that qualifies again as a sales-type lease has been debated by the FASB since it originally issued *FASB Statement No. 13* in 1976. The original *FASB Statement No. 13* clearly indicated that upon renewal or extension of an existing sales-type or direct financing lease, the lessor could *not* classify the renewal lease as a sales-type lease even though it might otherwise meet the necessary criteria. This renewal lease had to be treated as a direct financing lease. *FASB Statement No. 13 as Amended* qualifies the prior position. If the renewal or extension takes place *during the term* of the lease, the position of the original *FASB Statement No. 13* will be followed. If the renewal or extension takes place *at the end* of the lease (or during the last few months of the existing lease), the lease change can qualify as a sales-type lease. We discuss these two renewal situations briefly.

RENEWAL OR EXTENSION OCCURRING DURING LEASE TERM The FASB concluded that if a lessor treated a renewal or extension of a sales-type or direct financing lease as a sales-type lease at the time of an interim renewal, a "second sale" would result in recognition of revenue before its realization. For this reason the FASB reiterates, in *FASB Statement No. 13 as Amended*, that a lessor classifies a renewal or extension of an existing sales-type or direct financing lease that *otherwise qualifies as a sales-type lease* as a direct financing lease if the lease change occurs *during the term* of the lease.

RENEWAL OR EXTENSION OCCURRING AT END OF LEASE TERM The FASB then altered its position regarding this type of lease change. It concluded that if the renewal or extension occurred at the end of the lease term, and if the new agreement qualified as a sales-type lease (according to criteria stated in Exhibit 20-2), the lessor accounts for the renewal or extension as a sales-type lease at the end of the original term of the existing lease.

Many other changes may be made in lease terms. These often involve complex changes in accounting and, thus, require careful consideration. The preceding discussion indicates the scope of the issues. An accountant faced with new changes should study carefully all current standards before taking action on a particular change.

SUMMARY

At the beginning of the chapter, we identified several objectives you would accomplish after reading the chapter. The objectives are listed below, each followed by a brief summary of the key points in the chapter discussion.

1. **Explain the advantages of leasing.** For the lessee, a lease may involve financing benefits, a risk benefit, a tax benefit, a financial reporting benefit, and a billing benefit. For the lessor, a lease may involve the benefits of indirectly making a sale, and an alternative means of obtaining a profit opportunity.
2. **Understand key terms related to leasing.** The key terms related to leasing are included in Exhibit 20-1.
3. **Explain how to classify leases of personal property.** A lessee classifies a lease as a capital lease if it meets any one of the four capitalization criteria (listed in Exhibit 20-2), and as an operating lease if it meets none of the four criteria. A lessor classifies a lease as a sales-type lease if it meets any one of the four capitalization criteria, both of the additional criteria, and involves a manufacturer's or dealer's profit or loss. A lessor classifies a lease as a direct financing lease if it meets any one of the four capitalization criteria, both of the additional criteria, and does not result in a manufacturer's or dealer's profit or loss. A lessor classifies a lease as an operating lease if it meets none of the four criteria.

4. **Account for a lessee's operating and capital leases.** A lessee accounts for an operating lease by expensing the periodic lease payments. For a capital lease, the lessee records an asset and a liability equal to the present value, at the beginning of the lease term, of the minimum lease payments during the lease term. The discount rate is the lower of the lessee's incremental borrowing rate or the lessor's implicit rate if known and lower. The lessee amortizes the asset over its economic life if the lease contained a transfer of ownership or a bargain purchase option. Otherwise, the lessee uses the lease life. The lessee computes interest expense using the effective interest rate, and reduces the lease obligation for the difference between the cash paid and the interest expense.

5. **Understand disclosures by lessees.** The disclosure requirements of the lessee are summarized in Exhibit 20-11. Among the most important are the future minimum lease payments in the aggregate and for each of the succeeding five years, separately reported for its operating and capital leases.

6. **Account for a lessor's operating, direct financing, and sales-type leases.** A lessor accounts for an operating lease by recording the amounts of the periodic lease receipts as revenue. It also reports the underlying asset on its balance sheet and records depreciation on the asset. For a direct financing lease, the lessor records a receivable at the undiscounted minimum lease payments plus any unguaranteed residual value. The difference between the receivable and the carrying value of the leased property is recorded as a contra-account to the receivable. The lessor computes interest revenue on a direct financing lease using its implicit interest rate. For a sales-type lease, the lessor records a receivable at the undiscounted minimum lease payments plus any unguaranteed residual value. It records a contra-account to the receivable as the difference between the gross receivable and the present value of the components of the receivable. The lessor also expenses the cost or carrying value of the property, plus any initial direct costs, minus the present value of any unguaranteed residual value. The lessor computes interest revenue on a sales-type lease using its implicit interest rate.

7. **Understand disclosures by lessors.** The disclosure requirements of the lessor are summarized in Exhibit 20-21. Among the most important are the future minimum lease payments in the aggregate and for each of the succeeding five years, separately for operating and capital leases.

8. **Explain the conceptual issues regarding leases.** The primary conceptual issue is whether the four capitalization criteria appropriately measure the transfer of the risks and benefits of ownership. A related issue is whether it is too easy for a lessee to avoid meeting any of the criteria and therefore not reporting the lease liability on its balance sheet.

9. **Understand lease issues related to real estate, sales-leaseback issues, leveraged leases, and changes in lease provisions (Appendix).** Leases of real estate follow special rules that are summarized in Exhibit 20-23. The primary issue in a sales-leaseback is that the seller-lessee recognizes a loss in the period of the transaction, but defers any gain and amortizes it over the remaining life of the lease. Leveraged leases involve three parties: the lessor, the lessee, and a long-term creditor who provides nonrecourse financing for the leasing transaction. When the lease provisions are changed in such a way that the lease would have been classified differently had the changed terms been in effect at the beginning of the lease term, the revised agreement is considered a new agreement.

QUESTIONS

Q20-1 What does *FASB Statement No. 13 as Amended* provide in reference to the measuring and reporting of leases?

Q20-2 List seven advantages to the lessee of leasing, as compared with purchasing, an asset.

Q20-3 Assume that a lessee leases equipment and insists on terms that qualify it as an operating lease, barely escaping the qualification as a capital lease. Discuss the impact that such an operating lease has on financial statements and related financial information as compared to the effect that a capital lease would have.

Q20-4 Define the following terms: (a) *lease*, (b) *sales-type lease*, (c) *direct financing lease*, (d) *sale-leaseback transaction*, (e) *operating lease*, (f) *leveraged lease*.

Q20-5 Define the following terms used in *FASB Statement No. 13 as Amended*: (a) *inception of lease*, (b) *bargain purchase option*, (c) *unguaranteed residual value*, (d) *implicit interest rate*, (e) *initial direct costs*.

Q20-6 What components make up the minimum lease payments of a typical capital lease?

Q20-7 List the four criteria used to determine if a lease is classified as a capital lease by the lessee.

Q20-8 Describe briefly the accounting procedures followed by the lessor and by the lessee for an operating lease.

Q20-9 Describe briefly the procedures followed by the lessee to account for a capital lease.

Q20-10 From the standpoint of the lessor, a sales-type lease must meet one or more of the criteria of a capital lease as well as two additional criteria. Name these two additional criteria.

Q20-11 What is the basic difference between the accounting procedures used by a lessor for a sales-type lease and those used for a direct financing lease?

Q20-12 Why are compound interest concepts appropriate and applicable in accounting for a direct financing lease?

Q20-13 The Owens Company leased equipment for 4 years at $50,000 a month, with an option to renew the lease for 6 years at $2,000 per month or to purchase the equipment for $25,000 (a price considerably less than the expected fair value) after the initial lease term of 4 years. How does Owens Company record this transaction?

Q20-14 McFarland Corporation leased equipment under a lease calling for the payment of $50,000 a year in rent. At the end of the current year, when the capital lease had a remaining term of 20 years, McFarland Company subleased the asset for a rental of $75,000 a year for 20 years. The new lease is acceptable to the lessor, who agrees that McFarland Company has completed its primary obliga-tion. When will McFarland Company report the gain from this transaction? Explain.

Q20-15 (a) What disclosures are lessees required to make? (b) What disclosures are lessors required to make for var-ious types of leases?

Q20-16 (Appendix). From the point of view of the seller-lessee, what is the primary accounting issue involved in accounting for a sale-leaseback transaction as compared to other lessee transactions? Discuss.

Q20-17 (Appendix). What distinguishes a leveraged lease from other leases? What, if any, is the major difference in the accounting of the lessee for a leveraged lease?

CASES

COMMUNICATION

C20-1 Initial Direct Costs

The Efland Company leases equipment to Orange Com-pany. Efland pays $3,000 initial direct costs in negotiat-ing the lease.

Required

1. Explain what initial direct costs are.
2. Indicate precisely how Efland should account for ini-tial direct costs if this lease is (a) an operating lease, (b) a sales-type lease, (c) a direct financing lease.
3. For a sales-type lease, *FASB Statement No. 13 as Amended* requires that: "The cost or carrying amount, if different, of the leased property, plus any initial direct costs . . . , less the present value of the unguaranteed residual value accruing to the benefit of the lessor, com-puted at the interest rate implicit in the lease, shall be charged against income in the same period." Does this provision require that initial direct costs for sales-type leases be charged to cost of goods sold? Discuss the rea-sons for or against this accounting treatment.

C20-2 Sales-Type Lease Issues

Jordan Industries manufactures and leases to its customers 5-ton construction dump trucks. The lease arrangements are usually as follows:

1. Payments on the lease are due for 5 years after its inception, but the present value is not greater than 90% of the fair value of the trucks at the time of sale.
2. The trucks revert to Jordan at the end of the lease. Esti-mated economic life of the trucks is 10 years.
3. No substantial uncertainties exist as to future payments Jordan must make, and potential customers are thor-oughly checked for creditworthiness before the trucks are leased to them.
4. Jordan's accountant has informed the company that there are advantages from a reporting standpoint in treating the leases as sales-type instead of operating leases.

Required

1. Discuss the reasons why Jordan would want to treat the leases as sales-type instead of operating leases.
2. Explain what Jordan should do, under the require-ments of *FASB Statement No. 13 as Amended*, to treat the leases properly as sales-type leases.

C20-3 Classification of Leases

Part a. Capital leases and operating leases are the two classifications of leases for the lessee.

Required

1. Explain how a capital lease is accounted for by the lessee, both at the inception of the lease and during the first year of the lease, assuming the lease transfers own-ership of the property to the lessee by the end of the lease.
2. Explain how an operating lease is accounted for by the lessee, both at the inception of the lease and during the first year of the lease, assuming equal monthly pay-ments are made by the lessee at the beginning of each month of the lease. Describe the change in accounting, if any, when rental payments are not made on a straight-line basis.

Do not discuss the criteria for distinguishing between cap-ital leases and operating leases.

Part b. Sales-type leases and direct financing leases are two of the classifications of leases for the lessor.

Required Write a short report that compares and con-trasts a sales-type lease with a direct financing lease as follows:

1. Gross investment in the lease.
2. Amortization of unearned interest income.
3. Manufacturer's or dealer's profit.

Do not discuss the criteria for distinguishing between the leases described above and operating leases. (*AICPA adapted*)

C20-4 Miscellaneous Lease Issues

On January 1, 2004 Von Company entered into two noncancelable leases for new machines to be used in its manufacturing operations. The first lease does not contain a bargain purchase option. The lease term is equal to 80% of the estimated economic life of the machine. The second lease contains a bargain purchase option. The lease term is equal to 50% of the estimated economic life of the machine.

Required

1. Explain the theoretical basis for requiring lessees to capitalize certain long-term leases. Do **not** discuss the specific criteria for classifying a lease as a capital lease.
2. Explain how a lessee should account for a capital lease at its inception.
3. Explain how a lessee should record each minimum lease payment for a capital lease.

4. Explain how Von should classify each of the two leases. (*AICPA adapted*)

C20-5 Sale-Leaseback

On January 1, 2004 Metcalf Company sold equipment for cash and leased it back. As seller-lessee, Metcalf retained the right to substantially all of the remaining use of the equipment.

The term of the lease is 8 years. There is a gain on the sale portion of the transaction. The lease portion of the transaction is classified appropriately as a capital lease.

Required

1. Explain the theoretical basis for requiring lessees to capitalize certain long-term leases. Do **not** discuss the specific criteria for classifying a lease as a capital lease.
2. a. Explain how Metcalf should account for the sale portion of the sale-leaseback transaction at January 1, 2004.
   b. Explain how Metcalf should account for the leaseback portion of the sale-leaseback transaction at January 1, 2004.
3. Explain how Metcalf should account for the gain on the sale portion of the sale-leaseback transaction during the first year of the lease. (*AICPA adapted*)

C R E A T I V E   A N D   C R I T I C A L   T H I N K I N G

C20-6 Capitalized and Operating Leases

On January 1 Borman Company, a lessee, entered into three noncancelable leases for brand-new equipment, Lease J, Lease K, and Lease L. None of the three leases transfer ownership of the equipment to Borman at the end of the lease term. For each of the three leases, the present value of the minimum lease payments at the beginning of the lease term, excluding that portion of the payments representing executory costs such as insurance, maintenance, and taxes to be paid by the lessor, including any profit thereon, is 75% of the fair value of the equipment to the lessor at the inception of the lease.

The following information is peculiar to each lease:

(a) Lease J does not contain a bargain purchase option. The lease term is equal to 80% of the estimated economic life of the equipment.
(b) Lease K contains a bargain purchase option. The lease term is equal to 50% of the estimated economic life of the equipment.
(c) Lease L does not contain a bargain purchase option. The lease term is equal to 50% of the estimated economic life of the equipment.

Required

1. Explain how Borman Company should classify each of the preceding three leases. Discuss the rationale for your answer.

2. What amount, if any, should Borman record as a liability at the inception of the lease for each of the preceding three leases?
3. Assuming that the minimum lease payments are made on a straight-line basis, how should Borman record the minimum lease payment for each of the preceding three leases? (*AICPA adapted*)

C20-7 Disclosure of Leases and Related Issues

United Manufacturing Company manufactures and leases computers to its customers. During 2004 the following lease transactions take place:

1. On January 1 a computer is leased to Superior Microelectronics Industries and is guaranteed by United against obsolescence. The present value of the lease payments is greater than 90% of the fair value of the computer to both United and Superior.
2. Also on January 1 a computer is leased to Pitt Steel Company. Because of Pitt's unstable financial condition, its incremental borrowing rate is substantially greater than United's rate implicit in the lease (which Pitt did not know and could not estimate).

Required

1. For the first transaction, explain on whose financial statements the leased computer is shown.
2. Explain under what conditions in the second transaction the computer could fail to be shown on either

United's or Pitt Steel's balance sheets at December 31, 2004.

C20-8 Types of Leases and Related Issues

Circuit Village Company entered into a lease arrangement with Thomas Leasing Company for a certain machine. Thomas's primary business is leasing, and it is not a manufacturer or dealer. Circuit Village will lease the machine for a period of 4 years, which is 50% of the machine's economic life. Thomas will take possession of the machine at the end of the initial 4-year lease and lease it to another smaller company that does not need the most current version of the machine. Circuit Village does not guarantee any residual value for the machine and will not purchase the machine at the end of the lease term. Circuit Village's incremental borrowing rate is 16% and the implicit rate on the lease is 14%. Circuit Village has no way of knowing or estimating the implicit rate used by Thomas. Using either rate, the present value of the minimum lease payments is between 90% and 100% of the fair value of the machine at the time of the lease agreement. Circuit Village has agreed to pay all executory costs directly, and no allowance for these costs is included in the lease payments. Thomas is reasonably certain that Circuit Village will pay all lease payments, and because it has agreed to pay all executory costs, there are no important uncertainties regarding costs to be incurred by Thomas.

Required

1. With respect to Circuit Village (the lessee), answer the following:
   a. What type of lease has been entered into? Explain the reason for your answer.
   b. How should Circuit Village compute the appropriate amount to record for the lease or asset acquired?
   c. What accounts will be created or affected by this transaction, and how will the lease or asset or other cost be matched with earnings?
2. With respect to Thomas (the lessor), answer the following:
   a. What type of leasing arrangement has been entered into? Explain the reason for your answer.
   b. How should this lease be recorded by Thomas, and how are the appropriate amounts determined?
   c. How should Thomas determine the appropriate amount of earnings to be recognized from each lease payment? (*AICPA adapted*)

C20-9 Capital Lease Issues

On January 1, 2004 Lani Company entered into a non-cancelable lease for a machine to be used in its manufacturing operations. The lease transfers ownership of the machine to Lani by the end of the lease term. The term of the lease is 8 years. The minimum lease payment made by Lani on January 1, 2004 was one of eight equal annual payments. At the inception of the lease, the criteria established for classification as a capital lease by the lessee were met.

Required

1. Explain the theoretical basis for the accounting standard that requires certain long-term leases to be capitalized by the lessee. Do not discuss the specific lease as a capital lease.
2. Explain how Lani should account for this lease at its inception and determine the amount to be recorded.
3. Explain what expenses related to this lease Lani will incur during the first year of the lease, and how they will be determined.
4. Explain how Lani should report the lease transaction on its December 31, 2004 balance sheet. (*AICPA adapted*)

C20-10 Sale-Leaseback (Appendix)

On December 31, 2003 Port Co. sold 6-month-old equipment at fair value and leased it back. There was a loss on the sale. Port pays all insurance, maintenance, and taxes on the equipment. The lease provides for 8 equal annual payments, beginning December 31, 2004, with a present value equal to 85% of the equipment's fair value and sales price. The lease's term is equal to 80% of the equipment's useful life. There is no provision for Port to reacquire ownership of the equipment at the end of the lease term.

Required

1. a. Explain why it is important to compare an equipment's fair value to its lease payments' present value, and its useful life to the lease term.
   b. Evaluate Port's leaseback of the equipment in terms of each of the four criteria for determination of a capital lease.
2. Explain how Port should account for the sale portion of the sale-leaseback transaction at December 31, 2003.
3. Explain how Port should report the leaseback portion of the sale-leaseback transaction on its December 31, 2004 balance sheet. (*AICPA adapted*)

C20-11 Ethics and Leasing

You are an accountant for the ABC Mining Company, and the CFO gives you a copy of a recent lease agreement to record. As you read the agreement you discover the company has leased 12 trucks from the XYZ Finance Co. The fair value of the trucks is $2.4 million. ABC has agreed to pay $250,000 semiannually, in advance. The lease term is 5 years, and the lessor's implicit rate is 8%. There is no option or requirement to purchase the trucks. This all seems straightforward, especially when you remember that the company recently borrowed from a bank and agreed to a 10% interest rate. Also, you recall that the company owns some similar trucks and depreciates them over 8 years. You are about to leave the office early to meet some friends when you notice that there is a contingent rental of $97,592, payable by ABC Mining and starting with the seventh semiannual payment if the Consumer Price Index prevailing at the beginning of the lease increases in any one of the first 3 years of the lease.

Required From financial reporting and ethical perspectives, discuss the issues raised by this situation.

RESEARCH

C20-12 Capital Lease Issues

The Cliborn Retail Company negotiated a lease for a retail store in a new shopping center that included 30 stores. The accountant for Cliborn, Gail Naugle, was given the lease agreement to analyze. She looked into whether the lease was a capital lease. The lease did not include a transfer of ownership or an option to purchase. The lease term was for 20 years and the present value of the minimum lease payments was $100,000. Unsure of the fair market value of the property or its life, she called the lessor's controller.

"That is easy," he replied. "There is no fair value because we would never sell a single store in a shopping center. And, let's see, 20 years divided by 75% is about 27 years, so the life of the property must be at least that much. Or do you want a capital lease?"

Required Assuming that you are Gail Naugle, research the generally accepted accounting principles and prepare a short memo to the controller of Cliborn that summarizes how to classify the lease. Cite your reference and applicable paragraph numbers.

C20-13 Capital Lease Issues

The Stirbis Company was negotiating a lease for a new building that would be used as a warehouse. Stirbis' accountant, Shannon Fenimore, had been invited to join Jim Stirbis (the president) in a meeting where the lease agreement

was settled. The president of the company that owned the building said, "I assume you want an operating lease."

"That is correct," replied Jim Stirbis.

The president responded, "So we will not include a transfer of ownership or an option to purchase. Anyway, I am sure you do not want to get into the real estate business."

"No, of course not."

"And we agree that the lease term is 30 years."

"Yes, but that seems to present some problems. We would have to argue that the life of the building is more than 40 years."

"You should not have any trouble persuading your auditors to agree to that."

"Maybe not. But the present value of the $53,040 annual lease payment is $500,000, which is the fair value of the building."

"That is a problem. But I think I have a solution. We will adjust the annual payment to $45,000, so that the present value is only 85% of the fair value. Then we will add a clause that you also pay 1% of your total sales, up to a maximum of $8,040 each year."

Required Assuming that you are Shannon Fenimore, research the generally accepted accounting principles and prepare a short memo to the controller of Stirbis that summarizes how to classify the lease. Cite your reference and applicable paragraph numbers.

MULTIPLE CHOICE

Select the best answer for each of the following.

M20-1 The present value of the minimum lease payments should be used by the lessee in the determination of a(an)

	Capital Lease Liability	Operating Lease Liability
a.	Yes	No
b.	Yes	Yes
c.	No	Yes
d.	No	No

M20-2 East Company leased a new machine from North Company on May 1, 2004 under a lease with the following information:

Lease term	10 years
Annual rental payable at beginning of each lease year	$40,000
Useful life of machine	12 years
Implicit interest rate	14%
Present value factor for an annuity of 1 in advance for 10 periods at 14%	5.95
Present value factor for 1 for 10 periods at 14%	0.27

East has the option to purchase the machine on May 1, 2014 by paying $50,000, which approximates the expected fair value of the machine on the option exercise date. On May 1, 2004 East should record a capitalized lease asset of

a. $251,500
b. $238,000
c. $224,500
d. $198,000

M20-3 For a lease that transfers ownership of the property to the lessee by the end of the lease term, the lessee should

a. Record the minimum lease payment as an expense
b. Amortize the capitalizable cost of the property using the interest method
c. Amortize the capitalizable cost of the property in a manner consistent with the lessee's normal depreciation policy for owned assets, except that the period of amortization should be the lease term
d. Amortize the capitalizable cost of the property in a manner consistent with the lessee's normal depreciation policy for owned assets

Items 4 and 5 are based on the following information:

Fox Company, a dealer in machinery and equipment, leased equipment to Tiger, Inc. on July 1, 2004. The lease is appropriately accounted for as a sale by Fox and as a purchase by Tiger. The lease is for a 10-year period (the useful life of the asset) expiring June 30, 2014. The first of 10 equal annual payments of $500,000 was made on July 1, 2004. Fox had purchased the equipment for $2,675,000 on January 1, 2004 and established a list selling price of $3,375,000 on the equipment. Assume that the present value at July 1, 2004 of the rent payments over the lease term, discounted at 12% (the appropriate interest rate), was $3,165,000.

M20-4 What is the amount of profit on the sale and the amount of interest income that Fox should record for the year ended December 31, 2004?

   a. $0 and $159,900
   b. $490,000 and $159,900
   c. $490,000 and $189,900
   d. $700,000 and $189,900

M20-5 Assuming that Tiger uses straight-line depreciation, what is the amount of depreciation and interest expense that Tiger should record for the year ended December 31, 2004?

   a. $158,250 and $159,900
   b. $158,250 and $189,900
   c. $168,750 and $159,900
   d. $168,750 and $189,900

M20-6 Rent received in advance by the lessor for an operating lease should be recognized as revenue

   a. When received
   b. At the lease's inception
   c. In the period specified by the lease
   d. At the lease's expiration

M20-7 For a 6-year capital lease, the portion of the minimum lease payment applicable in the third year to the reduction of the obligation should be

   a. Less than in the second year
   b. More than in the second year
   c. The same as in the fourth year
   d. More than in the fourth year

M20-8 On January 2, 2004, Lafayette Machine Shops, Inc. signed a 10-year noncancelable lease for a heavy-duty drill press, stipulating annual payments of $15,000 start-ing at the end of the first year, with title passing to Lafayette at the expiration of the lease. Lafayette treated this transaction as a capital lease. The drill press has an estimated useful life of 15 years, with no salvage value. Lafayette uses straight-line depreciation for all of its fixed assets. Aggregate lease payments were determined to have a present value of $92,170, based on implicit interest of 10%. For 2004 Lafayette should record

	Interest Expense	Depreciation Expense
a.	$0	$0
b.	$7,717	$6,145
c.	$9,217	$6,145
d.	$9,217	$9,217

M20-9 On August 1, 2004 Kern Company leased a machine to Day Company for a 6-year period requiring payments of $10,000 at the beginning of each year. The machine cost $48,000, which is the fair value at the lease date, and has a useful life of 8 years with no residual value. Kern's implicit interest rate is 10% and present value factors are as follows:

Present value for an annuity due of $1 at 10% for 6 periods	4.791
Present value for an annuity due of $1 at 10% for 8 periods	5.868

Kern appropriately recorded the lease as a direct financing lease. At the inception of the lease, the gross lease receivables account balance should be

   a. $60,000   c. $48,000
   b. $58,680   d. $47,910

M20-10 At its inception, the lease term of Lease G is 65% of the estimated remaining economic life of the leased property. This lease contains a bargain purchase option. The lessee should record Lease G as

   a. Neither an asset nor a liability
   b. An asset but not a liability
   c. An expense
   d. An asset and a liability

(AICPA adapted)

EXERCISES

E20-1   *Determining Type of Lease and Subsequent Accounting*   On January 1, 2004 the Caswell Company signs a 10-year cancelable (at the option of either party) agreement to lease a storage building from the Wake Company. The following information pertains to this lease agreement:

1. The agreement requires rental payments of $100,000 at the end of each year.
2. The cost and fair value of the building on January 1, 2004 is $2 million.
3. The building has an estimated economic life of 50 years, with no residual value. The Caswell Company depreciates similar buildings according to the straight-line method.
4. The lease does not contain a renewable option clause. At the termination of the lease, the building reverts to the lessor.
5. Caswell's incremental borrowing rate is 14% per year. The Wake Company set the annual rental to ensure a 16% rate of return (the loss in service value anticipated for the term of the lease).
6. Executory costs of $7,000 annually, related to taxes on the property, are paid by Wake Company.

Required

1. Determine what type of lease this is for the lessee.
2. Prepare appropriate journal entries on the lessee's books to reflect the signing of the lease agreement and to record the payments and expenses related to this lease for the years 2004 and 2005.

E20-2   *Lessee Accounting Issues*   The Sax Company signs a lease agreement dated January 1, 2004 that provides for it to lease computers from the Appleton Company beginning January 1, 2004. The lease terms, provisions, and related events are as follows:

1. The lease term is 5 years. The lease is noncancelable and requires equal rental payments to be made at the end of each year.
2. The computers have an estimated life of 5 years, a fair value of $300,000, and a zero estimated residual value.
3. Sax Company agrees to pay all executory costs.
4. The lease contains no renewal or bargain purchase option.
5. The annual rental is set by Appleton at $83,222.92 to earn a rate of return of 12% on its net investment. The Sax Company is aware of this rate, which is equal to its borrowing rate.
6. Sax Company uses the straight-line method to record depreciation on similar equipment.

Required

1. Determine what type of lease this is for Sax Company.
2. Calculate the amount of the asset and liability of the Sax Company at the inception of the lease (round to the nearest dollar).
3. Prepare a table summarizing the lease payments and interest expense.
4. Prepare journal entries for Sax Company for the years 2004 and 2005.

E20-3   *Lessee Accounting with Payments Made at Beginning of Year*   The Adden Company signs a lease agreement dated January 1, 2004 that provides for it to lease heavy equipment from the Scott Rental Company beginning January 1, 2004. The lease terms, provisions, and related events are as follows:

1. The lease term is 4 years. The lease is noncancelable and requires annual rental payments of $20,000 each to be paid in advance at the beginning of each year.
2. The cost, and also fair value, of the heavy equipment to Scott at the inception of the lease is $68,036.62. The equipment has an estimated life of 4 years and has a zero estimated residual value at the end of this time.
3. Adden Company agrees to pay all executory costs.
4. The lease contains no renewal or bargain purchase option.
5. Scott's interest rate implicit in the lease is 12%. Adden Company is aware of this rate, which is equal to its borrowing rate.
6. Adden Company uses the straight-line method to record depreciation on similar equipment.
7. Executory costs paid at the end of the year by Adden Company are:

2004	2005
Insurance, $1,500	Insurance, $1,300
Property taxes, $6,000	Property taxes, $5,500

Required

1. Determine what type of lease this is for Adden Company.
2. Prepare a table summarizing the lease payments and interest expense for Adden Company.
3. Prepare journal entries for Adden Company for the years 2004 and 2005.

E20-4   *Lessor Accounting Issues*   The Rexon Company leases equipment to Ten-Care Company beginning January 1, 2004. The lease terms, provisions, and related events are as follows:

1. The lease term is 8 years. The lease is noncancelable and requires equal rental payments to be made at the end of each year.
2. The cost, and also fair value, of the equipment is $500,000. The equipment has an estimated life of 8 years and has a zero estimated value at the end of that time.
3. Ten-Care Company agrees to pay all executory costs.
4. The lease contains no renewal or bargain purchase option.
5. The interest rate implicit in the lease is 14%.
6. The initial direct costs are insignificant and assumed to be zero.

7. The collectibility of the rentals is reasonably assured, and there are no important uncertainties surrounding the amount of unreimbursable costs yet to be incurred by the lessor.

Required

1. Assuming that the lease is a direct financing lease from Rexon's point of view, calculate the amount of the equal rental receipts.
2. Prepare a table summarizing the lease receipts and interest revenue earned by Rexon.
3. Prepare journal entries for Rexon for the years 2004 and 2005.

E20-5 **Lessor Accounting Issues** Ramallah Company leases heavy equipment to Terrell, Inc. on January 2, 2004 on the following terms:

1. Forty-eight lease rentals of $1,600 at the end of each month are to be paid by Terrell, Inc., and the lease is noncancelable.
2. The cost of the heavy equipment to Ramallah Company was $60,758.
3. Ramallah Company will account for this lease using the direct financing method. The difference between total rental receipts ($1,600 × 48 = $76,800) and the cost of the equipment ($60,758) was computed to yield a return of 1% per month over the lease term.

Required Prepare journal entries for Ramallah Company (the lessor) to record the lease contract and the receipt of the first lease rental on January 31, 2004. Record the part of the $16,042 Unearned Interest that was earned during the first month and carry calculations to the nearest dollar.

E20-6 **Lessee and Lessor Accounting Issues** Lessor Leasing Company agrees to provide Lessee Company with equipment under a noncancelable lease for 5 years. The equipment has a 5-year life, cost Lessor Company $30,000, and will have no residual value when the lease term ends. Lessee Company agrees to pay all executory costs ($500 per year) throughout the lease period. On January 1, 2004 the equipment is delivered. Lessor expects a 14% return. The five equal annual rents are payable in advance starting January 1, 2004.

Required

1. Assuming this is a direct financing lease for the lessor and a capital lease for the lessee, prepare a table summarizing the lease and interest payments suitable for use by either party.
2. On the assumption that both companies adjust and close books each December 31, prepare journal entries relating to the lease for both companies through December 31, 2004 based on data derived in the table. Assume that Lessee Company depreciates similar equipment by the straight-line method.

E20-7 **Lessor Accounting with Receipts at End of Year** The Berne Company, the lessor, enters into a lease with Fox Company to lease equipment to Fox beginning January 1, 2004. The lease terms, provisions, and related events are as follows:

1. The lease term is 4 years. The lease is noncancelable and requires annual rental payments of $50,000 to be made at the end of each year.
2. The cost of the equipment is $130,000. The equipment has an estimated life of 4 years and an estimated residual value at the end of the lease term of zero.
3. Fox agrees to pay all executory costs.
4. The interest rate implicit in the lease is 12%.
5. The initial direct costs are insignificant and assumed to be zero.
6. The collectibility of the rentals is reasonably assured, and there are no important uncertainties surrounding the amount of unreimbursable costs yet to be incurred by the lessor.

Required

1. Assuming that the lease is a sales-type lease from Berne's point of view, calculate the selling price and assume that this is also the fair value.
2. Prepare a table summarizing the lease receipts and interest revenue earned by the lessor.
3. Prepare journal entries for Berne Company, the lessor, for the years 2004 and 2005.

E20-8 **Lessor Accounting with Receipts at Beginning of Year** The Edom Company, the lessor, enters into a lease with Jebusite Company to lease equipment to Jebusite beginning January 1, 2004. The lease terms, provisions, and related events are as follows:

1. The lease term is 5 years. The lease is noncancelable and requires annual rental receipts of $100,000 to be made in advance at the beginning of each year.
2. The cost of the equipment is $313,000. The equipment has an estimated life of 6 years and, at the end of the lease term, has an unguaranteed residual value of $20,000 accruing to the benefit of Edom.

3. Jebusite agrees to pay all executory costs.
4. The interest rate implicit in the lease is 14%.
5. The initial direct costs are insignificant and assumed to be zero.
6. The collectibility of the rentals is reasonably assured, and there are no important uncertainties surrounding the amount of unreimbursable costs yet to be incurred by the lessor.

Required

1. Assuming that the lease is a sales-type lease from Edom's point of view, calculate the selling price and assume that this is also the fair value.
2. Prepare a table summarizing the lease receipts and interest revenue earned by the lessor.
3. Prepare journal entries for Edom Company, the lessor, for the years 2004 and 2005.

E20-9   ***Lessee and Lessor Accounting Issues***   The following information is available for a noncancelable lease of equipment that is classified as a sales-type lease by the lessor and as a capital lease by the lessee. Assume that the lease payments are made at the beginning of each month, interest and straight-line depreciation are recognized at the end of each month, and the residual value of the leased asset is zero at the end of a 3-year life.

Cost of equipment to lessor (Anson Company)	$50,000
Initial payment by lessee (Bullard Company) at inception of lease	2,000
Present value of remaining 35 payments of $2,000 each discounted at 1% per month	58,817

Required

1. Record the lease (including the initial receipt of $2,000) and the receipt of the second and third installments of $2,000 in the accounts of the Anson Company. Carry computations to the nearest dollar.
2. Record the lease (including the initial payment of $2,000), the payment of the second and third installments of $2,000, and monthly depreciation in the accounts of the Bullard Company. The lessee records the lease obligation at net present value. Carry computations to the nearest dollar.

E20-10   ***Comparisons of Operating and Sales-Type Leases***   On January 1, 2004 Nelson Company leases certain property to Queens Company at an annual rental of $60,000 payable in advance at the beginning of each year for 8 years. The first payment is received immediately. The leased property, which is new, cost $275,000 and has an estimated economic life of 8 years and no residual value. The interest rate implicit in the lease is 12% and the lease is noncancelable. Nelson Company had no other costs associated with this lease. It should have accounted for this lease as a sales-type lease but mistakenly treated it as an operating lease.

Required   Compute the effect on income before income taxes during the first year of the lease as a result of Nelson Company's classification of this lease as an operating rather than a sales-type lease.

E20-11   ***Lease Income and Expense***   Reuben Company retires a machine from active use on January 2, 2004 for the express purpose of leasing it. The machine had a carrying value of $900,000 after 12 years of use and is expected to have 10 more years of economic life. The machine is depreciated on a straight-line basis. On March 2, 2004 Reuben Company leases the machine to Owens Company for $180,000 a year for a 5-year period ending February 28, 2009. Under the provisions of the lease, Reuben Company incurs total maintenance and other related costs of $20,000 for the year ended December 31, 2004. Owens Company pays $180,000 to Reuben Company on March 2, 2004. The lease was properly classified as an operating lease.

Required

1. Compute the income before income taxes derived by Reuben Company from this lease for the calendar year ended December 31, 2004.
2. Compute the amount of rent expense incurred by Owens Company from this lease for the calendar year ended December 31, 2004.

E20-12   ***Determining Type of Lease and Subsequent Accounting***   The Ravis Rent-A-Car Company leases a car to Ira Reem, an employee, on January 1, 2004. The term of the noncancelable lease is 4 years. The following information about the lease is provided:

1. Title to the car passes to Ira Reem on the termination of the lease with no additional payment required by the lessee.
2. The cost and fair value of the car to the Ravis Rent-A-Car Company is $8,400. The car has an economic life of 5 years.
3. The lease payments are determined at an amount that will yield Ravis Rent-A-Car Company a rate of return of 10% on its net investment.

4. Collectibility of the lease payments is reasonably assured.
5. There are no important uncertainties surrounding the amount of unreimbursable costs yet to be incurred by the lessor.
6. Equal annual lease payments are due at the end of each year.

Required

1. What type of lease is this to Ravis Rent-A-Car Company? Why?
2. Prepare a table summarizing the lease receipts and interest revenue earned by the Ravis Rent-A-Car Company for the 4-year lease term.
3. Prepare the journal entries for 2004 and 2005 to record the lease agreement, the lease receipts, and the recognition of income on the books of Ravis Rent-A-Car Company.

E20-13 *Sale-Leaseback (Appendix)* On January 1, 2004 the Stimpson Company sells land to Barker Company for $2.5 million, then immediately leases it back. The relevant information is as follows:

1. The land was carried on Stimpson's books at a value of $2 million.
2. The term of the noncancelable lease is 25 years.
3. The lease agreement requires equal rental payments of $357,007 at the end of each year.
4. The incremental borrowing rate of Stimpson Company is 15%. Stimpson is aware that Barker Company set the annual rental to ensure a rate of return of 14%.
5. The land has a fair value of $2.5 million on January 1, 2004.
6. Stimpson Company has the option of purchasing the land for $150 at the end of 25 years.
7. Stimpson Company pays all executory costs. These costs consist of insurance and property taxes amounting to $12,000 per year.
8. There are no important uncertainties surrounding the amount of unreimbursable costs yet to be incurred by the lessor, and the collectibility of the rentals is reasonably assured.

Required

1. Prepare the journal entries for the seller-lessee, Stimpson, for 2004 to reflect the sale and leaseback agreement. In calculating the present value of the lease payments, ignore the $150 bargain purchase option as immaterial.
2. Describe briefly the accounting treatment of the gain by the seller-lessee.

PROBLEMS

P20-1 *Determining Type of Lease and Subsequent Accounting* On January 1, 2004 the Alice Company leases electronic equipment for 5 years, agreeing to pay $70,000 annually at the beginning of each year under the noncancelable lease. Superior Electronics Company, the lessor, agrees to pay all executory costs, estimated to be $3,450 per year. The cost and also fair value of the equipment is $500,000. Its estimated life is 10 years. The estimated residual value at the end of 5 years is $200,000; at the end of 10 years, it is $5,000. There is no bargain purchase option in the lease nor any agreement to transfer ownership at the end of the lease to the lessee. The lessee's incremental borrowing rate is 12%. During 2004 Superior Electronics pays property taxes of $650, maintenance costs of $1,600, and insurance of $1,200. There are no important uncertainties surrounding the amount of unreimbursable costs yet to be incurred by the lessor. Straight-line depreciation is considered the appropriate method by both companies.

Required

1. Identify the type of lease involved for Alice Company and Superior Electronics Company and give reasons for your classifications.
2. Prepare appropriate journal entries for 2004 for the lessee and lessor.

P20-2 *Determining Type of Lease and Subsequent Accounting* On January 1, 2004 the Ballieu Company leases specialty equipment with an economic life of 8 years to the Anderson Company. The lease contains the following terms and provisions:

The lease is noncancelable and has a term of 8 years. The annual rentals are $35,000, payable at the beginning of each year. The interest rate implicit in the lease is 14%. The Anderson Company agrees to pay all executory costs and is given an option to buy the equipment for $1 at the end of the lease term, December 31, 2011.

The cost of the equipment to the lessor is $150,000 and the fair retail value is approximately $185,100. The lessor incurs no material initial direct costs. The collectibility of the rentals is reasonably assured, and there are no important uncertainties surrounding the amount of unreimbursable costs yet to be incurred by the lessor. The lessor estimates that the fair value is expected to be significantly greater than $1 at the end of the lease term.

The lessor calculates that the present value on January 1, 2004 of 8 annual payments in advance of $35,000 discounted at 14% is $185,090.68 (the $1 purchase option is ignored as immaterial).

Required

1. Identify the classification of the lease transaction from the point of view of Ballieu Company. Give the reasons for your classification.
2. Prepare all the journal entries for Ballieu Company for the years 2004 and 2005.
3. Discuss the disclosure requirements for the lease transaction in the notes to the financial statements of the Ballieu Company.

P20-3   *Lessee Accounting Issues*   The Timmer Company signs a lease agreement dated January 1, 2004 that provides for it to lease equipment from Landau Company beginning January 1, 2004. The lease terms, provisions, and related events are as follows:

The lease is noncancelable and has a term of 5 years. The annual rentals are $83,222.92, payable at the end of each year, and provide Landau with a 12% annual rate of return on its net investment. The Timmer Company agrees to pay all executory costs at the end of each year. In 2004 these were: insurance $3,760; property taxes, $5,440. In 2005: insurance, $3,100; property taxes, $5,330. There is no renewal or bargain purchase option.

Timmer estimates that the equipment has an economic life of 5 years and a zero residual value. Timmer's incremental borrowing rate is 16%, it knows the rate implicit in the lease, and it uses the straight-line method to record depreciation on similar equipment.

Required

1. Calculate the amount of the asset and liability of the Timmer Company at the inception of the lease. (Round to the nearest dollar.)
2. Prepare a table summarizing the lease payments and interest expense.
3. Prepare journal entries on the books of Timmer for 2004 and 2005.
4. Prepare a partial balance sheet in regard to the lease for Timmer for December 31, 2004.

P20-4   *Direct Financing Lease*   Calder Company, the lessor, enters into a lease with Darwin Company, the lessee, to provide heavy equipment beginning January 1, 2004. The lease terms, provisions, and related events are as follows:

The lease is noncancelable, has a term of 8 years, and has no renewal or bargain purchase option. The annual rentals are $65,000, payable at the end of each year. The interest rate implicit in the lease is 15%. The Darwin Company agrees to pay all executory costs.

The cost and fair value of the equipment to the lessor is $308,021.03. The lessor incurs no material initial direct costs. The collectibility of the rentals is reasonably assured, and there are no important uncertainties surrounding the amount of unreimbursable costs yet to be incurred by the lessor. The lessor estimates that the fair value at the end of the lease term will be $50,000 and that the economic life of the equipment is 9 years.

The following present value factors are relevant:

$$PV_{n=8,i=15\%} = 4.487322; \; PV_{n=8,i=15\%} = 0.326902; \; PV_{n=1,i=15\%} = 0.869565$$

Required

1. Prepare a table summarizing the lease receipts and interest revenue earned by the lessor for this direct financing lease.
2. State why the lease is a direct financing lease.
3. Prepare journal entries for Calder Company for the years 2004, 2005, and 2006.
4. Prepare partial balance sheets for December 31, 2004 and December 31, 2005 showing how the accounts should be reported.

P20-5   *Comprehensive*   Landlord Company and Tenant Company enter into a noncancelable, direct financing lease on January 1, 2004 for new heavy equipment that cost the Landlord Company $300,000 (useful life is 6 years with no residual value). The fair value is also $300,000. Landlord Company expects a 14% return over the 6-year period of the lease. Lease provisions require 6 equal annual amounts payable each January 1, beginning with January 1, 2004. The Tenant Company pays all executory costs. The heavy equipment reverts to the lessor at the termination of the lease. Assume that there are no initial direct costs. The collectibility of the rentals is reasonably assured and there are no important uncertainties surrounding the amount of unreimbursable costs yet to be incurred by the lessor.

Required

1. (a) Show how the Landlord Company should compute the annual rental amounts. (b) Discuss how the Tenant Company should compute the present value of the lease rights. What additional information would be required to make this computation?
2. Prepare a table summarizing the lease and interest receipts that would be suitable for the Landlord Company. Under what conditions would this table be suitable for the Tenant Company?
3. Assuming that the table prepared in Requirement 2 is suitable for both the lessee and the lessor, prepare the journal entries for both firms for the years 2004 and 2005. Use the straight-line depreciation method for the leased equipment. The executory costs paid by the lessee in 2004 are: insurance, $700 and property taxes, $800; in 2005: insurance, $600 and property taxes, $750.
4. Show the items and amounts that would be reported on the comparative 2004 and 2005 income statements and ending balance sheets for both the lessor and the lessee. Include appropriate notes to the financial statements.

See WebTutor for annotated problem solution.

P20-6 *Direct Financing Lease with Unguaranteed Residual Value* Lessor Company and Lessee Company enter
@ into a 5-year, noncancelable, direct financing lease on January 1, 2004 for a new computer that cost the Lessor Company $400,000 (useful life is 5 years). The fair value is also $400,000. Lessor Company expects a 12% return over the 5-year period of the lease. The computer will have an estimated unguaranteed residual value of $20,000 at the end of the fifth year of the lease. The lease provisions require 5 equal annual amounts, payable each January 1, beginning with January 1, 2004. The Lessee Company pays all executory costs. The computer reverts to the lessor at the termination of the lease. Assume there are no initial direct costs, no important uncertainties surrounding the amount of unreimbursable costs yet to be incurred by the lessor, and that the collectibility of rentals is reasonably assured.

Required

1. Show how the Lessor Company should compute the annual rental amounts.
2. Prepare a table summarizing the lease and interest receipts that would be suitable for the Lessor Company.
3. Prepare the journal entries for Lessor Company for the years 2004, 2005, and 2006.

P20-7 *Sales-Type Lease with Receipts at End of Year* The Lamplighter Company, the lessor, agrees to lease equipment to Tilson Company, the lessee, beginning January 1, 2004. The lease terms, provisions, and related events are as follows:

The lease is noncancelable and has a term of 8 years. The annual rentals are $32,000, payable at the end of each year. The Tilson Company agrees to pay all executory costs. The interest rate implicit in the lease is 14%.

The cost of the equipment to the lessor is $110,000. The lessor incurs no material initial direct costs. The collectibility of the rentals is reasonably assured, and there are no important uncertainties surrounding the amount of unreimbursable costs yet to be incurred by the lessor. The lessor estimates that the fair value at the end of the lease term will be $20,000 and that the economic life of the equipment is 9 years.

Required

1. Calculate the selling price implied by the lease and prepare a table summarizing the lease receipts and interest revenue earned by the lessor for this sales-type lease.
2. State why this is a sales-type lease.
3. Prepare journal entries for Lamplighter Company for the years 2004, 2005, and 2007.
4. Prepare partial balance sheets for Lamplighter Company for December 31, 2004 and December 31, 2005, showing how the accounts should be disclosed.

P20-8 *Various Lease Issues for Lessor and Lessee* Lessee Company leases heavy equipment on January 1, 2004 under a capital lease from Lessor Company with the following lease provisions:

The lease is noncancelable and has a term of 10 years. The lease does not contain a renewal or bargain purchase option. The annual rentals are $27,653.77, payable at the beginning of each year. The Lessee Company agrees to pay all executory costs. The interest rate implicit in the lease is 12%, which is known by Lessee Company. The residual value of the property at the end of 10 years is estimated to be zero.

The cost and fair value of the equipment to the lessor is $175,000. The lessor incurs no material initial direct costs. The collectibility of the rentals is reasonably assured, and there are no important uncertainties surrounding the amount of unreimbursable costs yet to be incurred by the lessor.

Lessee's incremental borrowing rate is 15% and it uses the straight-line method to record depreciation on similar equipment. In 2004 the lessee pays insurance of $1,900, property taxes of $1,300, and maintenance of $600; and in 2005 the lessee pays insurance of $1,800, property taxes of $1,200, and maintenance of $500.

Required

1. Identify the type of lease involved for the lessee and the lessor, and give reasons for your classifications.
2. Prepare all the journal entries for both the lessee and the lessor for 2004 and 2005.

P20-9   *Various Lease Issues for Lessor and Lessee*   Benjamin Company has rented new equipment to Murrell Builders that cost $50,000. This equipment has a life of 4 years and no residual value at the end of that time. The lease is noncancelable and is signed on January 1, 2004. Murrell Builders assumes all normal risks and executory costs of ownership. The title to the property is transferred to Murrell Builders at the end of the 4 years. The Benjamin Company computes the rents on the basis of a 14% return. The lessee's incremental borrowing rate is also 14%. The collectibility of rentals is reasonably assured and there are no important uncertainties surrounding the amount of unreimbursable costs yet to be incurred by the lessor.

Required

1. Assuming the annual rentals are payable at the end of each year, complete the following:
   a. Lessor computation of periodic rental receipts.
   b. Lessee computation of the present value of the special property rights under the lease.
   c. A table summarizing lease and interest payments that would be suitable for both lessor and lessee.
2. Assuming the annual rentals are payable at the start of each year, compute the same three items listed in Requirement 1.
3. Prepare the journal entries for the lessor and lessee for Requirement 2 throughout 2004. Use the straight-line depreciation method.
4. Indicate the asset and liability amounts that the lessor and lessee would report on their balance sheets at December 31, 2004 under Requirement 2.

P20-10   *Initial Direct Costs and Related Issues*   On January 1, 2004 the Amity Company leases a crane to Baltimore Company. The lease contains the following terms and provisions:

The lease is noncancelable and has a term of 10 years. The lease does not contain a renewal or bargain purchase option. The annual rentals are $4,000, payable at the beginning of each year. The Baltimore Company agrees to pay all executory costs.

The cost and fair value of the equipment to the lessor is $24,913.94. The lessor incurs initial direct costs of $1,364.98. The interest rate implicit in the lease is 12.5%. After including the initial direct costs, the implicit rate is 12%. The collectibility of the rentals is reasonably assured, and there are no important uncertainties surrounding the amount of unreimbursable costs yet to be incurred by the lessor. The lessor estimates that the fair value at the end of the lease term will be $3,000 and that the economic life of the crane is 12 years.

Required

1. What are initial direct costs? Discuss the accounting treatment of these costs. Are they treated in the same manner for (a) an operating lease, (b) a sales-type lease, and (c) a direct financing lease?
2. From the lessor's viewpoint, is the preceding lease a sales-type or direct financing lease? Give reasons to support your conclusion.
3. Prepare the journal entries for Amity Company for 2004.

P20-11   *Various Lease Issues*   Farrington Company leases a computer from the Wilson Company. The lease includes the following provisions:

The lease is noncancelable and has a term of 8 years. The annual rentals are $60,000, payable at the end of each year. The Farrington Company agrees to pay all executory costs and has an option to purchase the computer for $1,000 at the end of the life of the lease. The interest rate implicit in the lease is 12%, which is known to Farrington.

Farrington estimates that the computer has an economic life of 12 years and a value of $70,000 at the end of 8 years. Farrington's incremental borrowing rate is 16% and it uses the straight-line method to record depreciation on similar equipment.

The computer cost Wilson $200,000 to manufacture. The lessor incurs initial direct costs of $10,000. The collectibility of the rentals is reasonably assured, and there are no important uncertainties surrounding the amount of unreimbursable costs yet to be incurred by the lessor.

Required

1. What is the correct classification of the lease for the lessee and lessor? Explain whether the lease meets *each* of the required criteria.

2. Assuming that the lease is signed on January 1, 2004, prepare all journal entries for 2004 for the lessor.
3. After 6 years, because of changes in the technology, the lessee and lessor independently conclude that the expected residual value of the computer at the end of the life of the lease is only $10,000. Discuss how the lessor should account for the change.

P20-12 **Accounting for Leases by Lessee and Lessor** Scuppermong Farms, the lessee, and Tyrrell Equipment, the lessor, sign a lease agreement on January 1, 2004 that provides for Scuppermong Farms to lease a cultivator from Tyrrell Equipment. The lease terms, provisions, and other related events are as follows: The lease is noncancelable and has a term of 6 years. The annual rentals are $56,100, payable at the beginning of each year. Tyrrell Equipment agrees to pay all executory costs, which are expected to be $1,100 annually, including property taxes of $500, insurance of $350, and maintenance of $250. Scuppermong Farms guarantees a residual value of $60,000 at the end of 6 years. The interest rate implicit in the lease is 14%, which is known by Scuppermong.

Scuppermong Farms' incremental borrowing rate is 15% and it uses the sum-of-the-years'-digits method to record depreciation on similar equipment.

The cost and fair value of the cultivator to Tyrrell Equipment is $271,154.68. The lessor incurs no material initial direct costs. The collectibility of the rentals is reasonably assured, and there are no important uncertainties surrounding the amount of unreimbursable costs yet to be incurred by the lessor.

Required
1. Identify the type of lease involved for both Scuppermong Farms and Tyrrell Equipment, and give reasons for your classifications.
2. Prepare the journal entries for both Scuppermong Farms and Tyrrell Equipment for 2004. (*Hint*: Scuppermong Farms should expense executory costs when annual payments are made to Tyrrell.)

P20-13 **Lessor's Income Statement** The Dahlia Company has two divisions, the Astor Division which started operating in 2002, and the Tulip Division which started operating in 2003. The Astor Division leases medical equipment to hospitals. All of its leases are appropriately recorded as operating leases for accounting purposes, except for a major lease entered into on January 1, 2004, which is appropriately recorded as a sale-type lease for accounting purposes.

Under long-term contracts, Tulip constructs wastewater treatment plants for small communities throughout the United States. All of its long-term contracts are appropriately recorded for accounting purposes under the percentage-of-completion method, except for two contracts which are appropriately recorded for accounting purposes under the completed-contract method because of a lack of dependable estimates at the time of entering into these contracts.

For the year ended December 31, 2004 the following information is available:

Astor Division:

Operating Leases. Revenues from operating leases were $800,000. The cost of the related leased equipment is $3,700,000, which is being depreciated on a straight-line basis over a 5-year period. The estimated residual value of the leased equipment at the end of the 5-year period is $200,000. No leased equipment was acquired or constructed in 2004. Maintenance and other related costs and the costs of any other services rendered under the provisions of the leases were $70,000 in 2004.

Lease Recorded as a Sale. The January 1, 2004 lease recorded as a sale is for a 6-year period expiring December 31, 2009. The cost of this leased equipment is $3,500,000. This leased equipment is estimated to have no residual value at the end of the lease. Maintenance and other related costs, and the costs of any other services rendered under the provisions of this lease, all of which were paid by the lessee, were $120,000 in 2004. Equal annual payments under the lease are $750,000 and are due on January 1. The first payment was made on January 1, 2004. The present value for an annuity of $1 in advance at 10% is as follows:

Number of Periods	Present Value
5	4.170
6	4.791
7	5.355

Tulip Division:

Long-Term Contracts: Percentage-of-Completion Method. Long-term contracts recorded under the percentage-of-completion method aggregate $6,000,000. Costs incurred on these contracts were $1,500,000 in 2003 and $3,000,000 in 2004. Estimated additional costs of $1,000,000 are required to complete these contracts. Revenues of $1,740,000 were recognized in 2003 and a total of $4,800,000 has been billed, of which $4,600,000 has been collected. No long-term contracts recorded under the percentage-of-completion method were completed in 2004.

Long-Term Contracts: Completed-Contract Method. The two long-term contracts recorded under the completed-contract method were started in 2003. One is a $5,000,000 contract. Costs incurred were $1,400,000 in 2003 and $1,600,000 in 2004. A total of $3,100,000 has been billed and $2,800,000 collected. Although it is difficult to estimate the additional costs required to complete this contract, indications are that this contract will prove to be profitable.

The second contract is for $4,000,000. Costs incurred were $1,200,000 in 2003 and $2,600,000 in 2004. A total of $3,300,000 has been billed and $2,900,000 collected. Although it is difficult to estimate the additional costs required to complete this contract, indications are that there will be a loss of approximately $550,000.

Dahlia Company:

Selling, general, and administrative expenses exclusive of amounts specified earlier were $600,000 in 2004. Other income exclusive of amounts specified earlier was $50,000 in 2004.

Required Prepare an income statement of the Dahlia Company for the year ended December 31, 2004, stopping at income (loss) before income taxes. Show supporting schedules and computations in good form. *Ignore income tax and deferred tax considerations.* Notes are *not* required. (*AICPA adapted*)

P20-14 **Determining Types of Leases (Appendix)**   Rigdon Company leases 50 acres of land to Christmas Tree International on January 1, 2004. The provisions of the lease are as follows:

The lease is noncancelable and has a term of 25 years. The annual rentals are $10,000, payable at the end of each year. The lease contains no bargain purchase option and the land reverts to Rigdon at the end of the lease. The incremental borrowing rate of Christmas Tree International is 12%.

The cost of the land to Rigdon Company is $60,000. The fair value is $78,431.39. The lessor incurs no material initial direct costs. The collectibility of the rentals is reasonably assured, and there are no important uncertainties surrounding the amount of unreimbursable costs yet to be incurred by the lessor.

Required
1. Determine the classification of this lease for both the lessor and the lessee.
2. Why are the final two criteria (lease term 75% of economic life and present value of lease payments 90% of fair value) not applicable when classifying a lease of land?

P20-15 *Sale-Leaseback (Appendix)*   On January 1, 2004 the Orr Company sells heavy equipment to Foible Company for $3 million, then immediately leases it back. The relevant information is as follows:

The lease is noncancelable and has a term of 8 years. The annual rentals are $603,908.50, payable at the end of each year. The seller-lessee agrees to pay all executory costs. The interest rate implicit in the lease is 12%.

The cost of the heavy equipment to Orr Company is $2,100,000. The purchaser-lessor incurs no material initial direct costs. The collectibility of the rentals is reasonably assured, and there are no important uncertainties surrounding the amount of unreimbursable costs yet to be incurred by the lessor.

Orr's incremental borrowing rate is 12% and the company estimates that the economic life of the equipment is 8 years. The present value on January 1, 2004 of 8 payments of $603,908.50, discounted at 12%, is $3 million ($603,908.50 × 4.967640). The executory costs for 2004 are:

Repairs and maintenance	$10,200
Property taxes	20,500
Insurance	18,000

Required
1. What type of lease is this to the seller-lessee? Discuss.
2. Prepare the journal entries for both the seller-lessee and the purchaser-lessor for 2004 to reflect the sale and leaseback agreement. Assume that the company uses the straight-line depreciation method.

INTERNET ASSIGNMENTS

Go to the Nikolai and Bazley **Intermediate Accounting** web site (http://Nikolai.swcollege.com). Click on Student Resources and <u>internet</u> <u>homework</u> <u>assignments</u>. Then click on the appropriate hot link (icon) for each company's web site, find the relevant accounting information, and answer the following questions.

I20-1   Go to the Delta Airlines web site.

Required Does the company have significant operating leases at the end of the most recent year? Capital leases? Do the operating leases affect your understanding of the financial risk of the company? Why do you think the company has many leases of aircraft that fail the four capitalization criteria?

I20-2   Go to the Wal-Mart web site.

Required Does the company have significant operating leases at the end of the most recent year? Capital leases? Have they changed significantly compared to the amounts disclosed in Exhibit 20-12? Do the operating leases affect your understanding of the financial risk of the company? Why do you think the company has many leases that fail the four capitalization criteria?

objectives

1 Define operating, investing, and financing activities.

2 Know the categories of inflows and outflows of cash.

3 Classify cash flows as operating, investing, or financing.

4 Explain the direct and indirect methods for reporting operating cash flows.

5 Prepare a simple statement of cash flows.

6 Use a worksheet for a statement of cash flows.

7 Compute and disclose interest paid and income taxes paid.

8 Identify the operating cash inflows and outflows under the direct method (Appendix).

9 Compute the operating cash flows under the direct method (Appendix).

CHAPTER 21

The Statement of Cash Flows

Users of financial statements are interested in the operating, investing, and financing activities of companies. For a particular company they pose such questions as (1) What is the relationship between net income and cash provided by operations? (2) Why are dividends not larger, especially in light of rising income? (3) What expansion activities took place and how were they financed? (4) Why did cash decrease even though a net income was reported? (5) What happened to the proceeds received from the issuance of capital stock? Each of these questions relates, either directly or indirectly, to the cash flows of the company. The FASB recognized the importance of providing answers to these questions by stating that financial reporting should provide information about how a company obtains and spends cash, about its borrowing and repayment of borrowing, about its capital transactions, including cash dividends and other distributions of resources to owners, and about other factors that may affect its liquidity or solvency.[1]

To satisfy these objectives, the FASB issued **FASB Statement No. 95,** "Statement of Cash Flows," which requires that a company present a *statement of cash flows* for the accounting period along with its income statement and balance sheet.[2] The cash flow statement evolved over the years. Traditionally, it was called a funds statement, where the term *funds* usually was defined as either cash or working capital (current assets less current liabilities). Initially, the statement was a simple "where got—where gone" schedule. This developed into the statement of sources and applications of funds, then into the statement of changes in financial position, and eventually into the statement of cash flows that is an integral part of a company's financial statements and the subject of this chapter.

CONCEPTUAL OVERVIEW AND REPORTING GUIDELINES

In Chapter 2 we noted that one of the specific objectives of financial reporting is to provide information about a company's cash flows. Consequently, the FASB is concerned that a company's financial statements include information useful to external users about its cash inflows and outflows, borrowings and repayments, and capital transactions (including dividends). A company's receivables, payables, and inventory (i.e., items of working capital) are the links between its

---

1. "Objectives of Financial Reporting by Business Enterprises," *FASB Statement of Financial Accounting Concepts No. 1* (Stamford, Conn.: FASB, 1978), par. 49.
2. "Statement of Cash Flows," *FASB Statement of Financial Accounting Standards No. 95* (Stamford, Conn.: FASB, 1987), par. 3.

operations and its cash inflows and outflows, and information about these relationships may be useful in understanding the operations of the company.

Information about a company's liquidity, financial flexibility, operating capability, and risk is related to these objectives as well. *Liquidity* is an indication of the company's ability to meet its obligations as they come due. *Financial flexibility* is a measure of the company's ability to take effective actions to change the amounts and timings of its cash flows in order to adapt to unexpected needs and opportunities. Financial flexibility arises primarily from a company's ability to modify operations so as to increase net operating cash inflows. It also comes from the company's ability to raise cash from the issuance of new debt or equity securities or to obtain cash by disposing of assets. *Operating capability* is the company's ability to maintain a given physical level of operations, measured in terms of either the quantity of goods (inventory) produced and sold or the physical capacity of the company's property, plant, and equipment. *Risk* is the uncertainty or unpredictability of the future results of a company. The wider the range within which future results are likely to fall, the greater the risk associated with an investment in or extension of credit to the company.

The primary purpose of a company's statement of cash flows is to provide relevant information about its cash receipts and cash payments during an accounting period that is useful in evaluating the preceding items. In this regard, the FASB states that the information in a statement of cash flows, if used with information in the other financial statements, helps external users assess (1) a company's ability to generate positive future net cash flows, (2) a company's ability to meet its obligations and pay dividends, (3) a company's need for external financing, (4) the reasons for differences between a company's net income and associated cash receipts and payments, and (5) both the cash and noncash aspects of a company's financing and investing transactions during the accounting period.[3]

Reporting Guidelines and Practices

To understand how to use and to prepare a statement of cash flows, it is important to have a definition of the statement and guidelines about the form and content of the statement. **A statement of cash flows is a financial statement of a company that shows the cash inflows, cash outflows, and net change in cash from its operating, investing, and financing activities during an accounting period, in a manner that reconciles the beginning and ending cash balances.**

1 Define operating, investing, and financing activities.

OPERATING ACTIVITIES   A company's operating activities include all its transactions and other events that are not investing and financing activities. These include transactions involving acquiring, selling, and delivering goods for sale, as well as providing services. Cash inflows from operating activities include cash receipts from the sale of goods or services and collections of accounts receivable, as well as returns on loans (i.e., collections of interest) and on investments in equity securities (i.e., receipts of dividends). Cash outflows for operating activities include cash payments to suppliers for inventory and on account, to employees, for taxes, to lenders for interest (unless capitalized), and to other suppliers for various expenses.

INVESTING ACTIVITIES   A company's investing activities include its transactions involving lending money and collecting on the loans, acquiring and selling investments (both current and noncurrent), and acquiring and selling property, plant, and equipment. Cash inflows from investing activities include cash receipts from principal repayments of loans by borrowers (i.e., collections of notes receivable), from sales of loans (i.e., discounting of notes receivable), from sales of investments in other companies (e.g., stocks and bonds), and from sales of property, plant, and equipment. Cash outflows for investing activities include cash payments for loans made to borrowers, for purchases of loans, for investments, and for acquisitions of property, plant, and equipment.

---

3. *Ibid.*, par. 5.

How a company classifies certain items depends on its operations. For instance, if a company regularly factors its accounts receivable, then it treats the cash receipts as cash inflows from operating activities. Similarly, if a company requires its customers to sign notes for credit sales, then it treats the cash receipts from collections of these notes receivable as cash inflows from operating activities.

FINANCING ACTIVITIES   A company's financing activities include its transactions involving obtaining resources from owners and providing them with a return on, and of, their investment, as well as obtaining money and other resources from creditors and repaying the amounts borrowed. Cash inflows from financing activities include cash receipts from the issuance of equity securities (i.e., common stock and preferred stock), from bonds, from mortgages, from notes, and from other short- or long-term borrowings. Cash outflows for financing activities include payments for dividends, for repurchase of the company's equity securities, and for repayments of amounts borrowed. Most borrowings and repayments of borrowings are financing activities. However, as we noted, the settlement of liabilities such as accounts payable incurred to acquire inventory and salaries payable are operating activities.

FORMAT   From a conceptual standpoint, **to predict the amounts, timing, and uncertainty of future cash flows external users need financial information that is segregated into reasonably homogeneous groups.**[4] To implement these guidelines and for consistent reporting, a company's statement of cash flows for the accounting period must clearly show (1) the cash provided by or used in its operating activities, (2) the cash provided by or used in its investing activities, (3) the cash provided by or used in its financing activities, (4) the company's net increase or decrease in cash, and (5) a reconciliation of the company's beginning cash balance to the ending cash balance reported on its year-end balance sheet.

 As we will see, most financing and investing activities of a company affect its cash; however, some transactions (such as the acquisition of land by the issuance of common stock) are "simultaneous" investing and financing activities that do not affect its cash. Because of their importance in providing an overall picture of a company's investing and financing activities and their impact on its prospective cash flows, the company is required to report these items either in a separate schedule or narrative explanation (in this chapter we will always use a schedule) that accompanies the statement of cash flows. Furthermore, if a company uses the indirect method (which we discuss later) of reporting operating cash flows, it must also disclose the amounts of interest paid and income taxes paid during the accounting period. (We discuss this disclosure later in this chapter.)

CASH AND CASH EQUIVALENTS   As we discussed in Chapter 6, as part of its cash management procedures, a company may invest its cash in short-term, highly liquid investments, such as treasury bills, commercial paper, and money market funds. These investments are called *cash equivalents*. Then, instead of reporting "Cash" as a current asset on its balance sheet, the company reports "Cash and Cash Equivalents." In this case, the purpose of the company's statement of cash flows is to explain the change during the accounting period in its *cash and cash equivalents*. In this chapter, for simplicity, we focus only on changes in *cash*.

Illustration

The statement of cash flows for The Coca-Cola Company is shown in Appendix A. Exhibit 21-1 illustrates a typical statement of cash flows for the Ryan Corporation. Note that the statement of cash flows is divided into three sections, entitled (1) Net Cash Flow From Operating Activities, (2) Cash Flows From Investing Activities, and (3) Cash Flows From Financing Activities. These are the titles a company generally uses in its statement of cash flows. Note also the schedule of investing and financing activities not affecting cash.

---

4. "Recognition and Measurement in Financial Statements of Business Enterprises," *FASB Statement of Financial Accounting Concepts No. 5* (Stamford, Conn.: FASB, 1984), par. 20.

EXHIBIT 21-1 Typical Statement of Cash Flows

RYAN CORPORATION

Statement of Cash Flows
For Year Ended December 31, 2004

Net Cash Flow From Operating Activities		
Net income	$ 14,000	
Adjustments for differences between income flows and cash flows from operating activities:		
Add: Depreciation expense	8,000	
Decrease in accounts receivable	2,600	
Increase in salaries payable	800	
Less: Increase in inventory	(2,000)	
Decrease in accounts payable	(7,000)	
Net cash provided by operating activities		$16,400
Cash Flows From Investing Activities		
Payment for purchase of building	$(28,000)	
Payment for purchase of equipment	(4,000)	
Proceeds from sale of land, at cost	10,000	
Net cash used for investing activities		(22,000)
Cash Flows From Financing Activities		
Proceeds from issuance of common stock	$ 18,000	
Proceeds from issuance of bonds	12,000	
Payment of dividends	(9,000)	
Payment of note payable	(13,000)	
Net cash provided by financing activities		8,000
Net Increase in Cash (see Schedule 1)		$ 2,400
Cash, January 1, 2004		10,900
Cash, December 31, 2004		$13,300
Schedule 1: Investing and Financing Activities Not Affecting Cash		
Investing Activities		
Acquisition of land by issuance of common stock		$ (6,000)
Financing Activities		
Issuance of common stock for land		6,000

CONTENT A company reports the net cash provided by or used in its operating activities in the first section of its statement of cash flows. Over the long run, it is likely that a company will be successful only if it is able to obtain most of its cash from its operations. This situation occurs when the cash received from selling goods or services exceeds the cash paid to provide the goods or services. Generating cash from operations generally is considered to be the most important cash flow activity of a company. The Ryan Corporation provided a net cash inflow of $16,400 from its operating activities during 2004, as we show in Exhibit 21-1. The company determined this $16,400 amount by adjusting the $14,000 net income for several differences between the income flows and cash flows from operating activities. This procedure is called the "indirect method" and we explain this method later in the chapter. External users can compare the company's net cash flow from operating activities with the same information from previous years in order to detect favorable or unfavorable *trends* in the company's liquidity, financial flexibility, operating capability, and risk. They can compare this information with the same information from other companies for the same purposes.

A company reports the cash inflows and outflows from its investing activities in the second section of the statement of cash flows. It lists each investing cash inflow and outflow and subtotals the amounts to determine the net cash used for (or provided by) investing activities. During 2004 the Ryan Corporation had a cash outflow of $28,000 to purchase a building and another cash outflow of $4,000 to purchase equipment. It received a cash inflow of $10,000 from the sale of land, at cost. The net result was that the company used $22,000 of cash for its investing activities.

A company reports the cash inflows and outflows from its financing activities in the third section of the statement of cash flows. It lists each financing cash inflow and outflow and subtotals the amounts to determine the net cash provided by (or used for) financing activities. During 2004 the Ryan Corporation had cash inflows of $18,000 and $12,000 from the issuance of common stock and bonds, respectively. It had a cash outflow of $9,000 for the payment of dividends, and a $13,000 cash outflow for the payment of a note. The net result was that $8,000 of cash was provided by its financing activities.

A company determines the net increase or decrease in cash by adding the amounts of the net cash flow from operating activities, the net cash flow from investing activities, and the net cash flow from financing activities. The $16,400 net cash provided by operating activities, combined with the $22,000 net cash used for investing activities, and the $8,000 net cash provided by financing activities resulted in a $2,400 net increase in cash for the Ryan Corporation in 2004. This $2,400 net increase in cash reconciles the $10,900 beginning cash balance to the $13,300 ending cash balance.

A company reports its investing and financing activities not affecting cash in a separate schedule accompanying the statement of cash flows. It lists each investing and/or financing activity and offsets the related amounts against each other. During 2004 the Ryan Corporation engaged in a simultaneous investing and financing transaction, the acquisition of land costing $6,000 by the issuance of common stock. The investing portion of the transaction was the acquisition of the land, while the financing portion was the issuance of common stock. Schedule 1 shows the investing activity as a $6,000 "outflow" which is offset by the $6,000 "inflow" from the financing activity. Although no cash was exchanged, both items are listed to show all of the Ryan Corporation's investing and financing activities during 2004.

USEFULNESS By reviewing the three sections of a company's statement of cash flows, external users can see how it obtained and used its cash. From the accompanying schedule, they can determine the types of investing and financing activities of the company that did not affect cash. They can examine the items in each section to see if important changes have occurred. For instance, the investing activities involving the acquisition of the building and equipment by the Ryan Corporation in 2004 may indicate an increase in its operating capability. In addition, the financing activities involving the issuance of both bonds and common stock by the Ryan Corporation in 2004 reveal a change in its capital structure and may indicate a change in its financial flexibility and risk.

A comparison with other companies can also reveal, for instance, whether the company is obtaining or using a greater proportion of its cash from financing or investing activities rather than operations. This may be important in assessing the relative risk of investing in the company. External users can evaluate the likelihood of future cash dividends, as well as the need for additional cash to finance existing operations or the expansion of operations. They also can evaluate the ability of the company to pay current obligations, make periodic interest payments, and pay off long-term debt when the debt reaches its maturity date. Thus, a company's statement of cash flows provides external users with information about its liquidity, financial flexibility, operating capability, and risk. In so doing, the statement enhances the predictive value and feedback value and, therefore, the *decision usefulness*, of a company's financial statements to help fulfill the objectives of financial reporting.

CASH INFLOWS AND OUTFLOWS

To classify a company's cash flows, the relationships between the changes in balance sheet accounts and the company's cash flows must be analyzed. A company's inflows of cash

EXHIBIT 21-2   Equations for Change in Cash

	Assets	= Liabilities	+ Stockholders' Equity	
	Changes in Assets	= Changes in Liabilities	+ Changes in Stockholders' Equity	
Changes in Cash +	Changes in Assets Other Than Cash	= Changes in Liabilities	+ Changes in Stockholders' Equity	
	Changes in Cash	= Changes in Liabilities	+ Changes in Stockholders' Equity	− Changes in Assets Other Than Cash
Where:	Increases in Cash	= Increases in Liabilities	+ Increases in Stockholders' Equity	+ Decreases in Assets Other Than Cash
And:	Decreases in Cash	= Decreases in Liabilities	+ Decreases in Stockholders' Equity	+ Increases in Assets Other Than Cash

are caused by decreases in its assets (other than cash) and by increases in liabilities and in stockholders' equity during an accounting period. A company's outflows of cash are caused by increases in its assets (other than cash) and by decreases in liabilities and in stockholders' equity during the accounting period. The difference between the inflows and outflows is the change in cash during the accounting period. This relationship is further illustrated by the equations we show in Exhibit 21-2, starting with the basic accounting equation. Each equation is a modification of the previous equation, to eventually show the increases and decreases in cash. With this background in mind, we can refine the relationships we show in the last two equations of Exhibit 21-2.

Inflows of Cash

There are three categories of a company's inflows (increases) of cash:

2 Know the categories of inflows and outflows of cash.

1. *Decreases in Assets Other Than Cash.* The sale or other disposal of assets (other than cash) causes an inflow (increase) of cash because cash is received in exchange for the assets.
2. *Increases in Liabilities.* The issuance or other incurrence of liabilities causes an inflow (increase) of cash because cash is received in exchange for the liabilities.[5]
3. *Increases in Stockholders' Equity.* Stockholders' equity increases mainly because of net income and additional investments by owners. Additional investments cause an inflow (increase) of cash because cash is received in exchange for the stock issued. Net income is slightly more complicated because the inflows and outflows of cash for operations are different than the revenues and expenses included in net income (we discuss this topic later).

Outflows of Cash

There are also three categories of a company's outflows (decreases) of cash:

1. *Increases in Assets Other Than Cash.* The acquisition of assets (other than cash) causes an outflow (decrease) of cash because cash is paid in exchange for the assets.[6]

---

5. Alternatively, as we discuss later, the increase in a liability such as accounts payable results, in effect, in a "savings" (i.e., increase) in cash because of a smaller cash outflow.
6. Alternatively, as we discuss later, the increase in an asset such as accounts receivable results, in effect, in a decrease in cash because of a smaller cash inflow.

2. *Decreases in Liabilities.* The payment of liabilities causes an outflow (decrease) of cash because cash is paid to satisfy the liabilities.
3. *Decreases in Stockholders' Equity.* Stockholders' equity may decrease as a result of several transactions. Two common transactions are the payment of dividends and the acquisition of treasury stock. In each case, a decrease in stockholders' equity is accompanied by an outflow (decrease) of cash.

Classifications of Cash Flows

We can further classify the cash inflows and outflows we just discussed into operating, investing, and financing cash flows.

3 Classify cash flows as operating, investing, or financing.

1. *Operating Cash Flows*
   A. *Inflows.* Increases in stockholders' equity (i.e., retained earnings) due to certain revenues, adjusted for changes in certain current assets (related to operating cycle) and for changes in certain current liabilities (related to operating cycle).
   B. *Outflows.* Decreases in stockholders' equity (i.e., retained earnings) due to certain expenses, adjusted for changes in certain current assets (related to operating cycle) and for changes in certain current liabilities (related to operating cycle).
2. *Investing Cash Flows*
   A. *Inflows.* Decreases in noncurrent assets and certain current assets (e.g., notes receivable and temporary investments related to investing activities).
   B. *Outflows.* Increases in noncurrent assets and certain current assets (e.g., notes receivable and temporary investments).
3. *Financing Cash Flows*
   A. *Inflows.* Increases in noncurrent liabilities, stockholders' equity, and certain current liabilities (e.g., notes payable related to financing activities).
   B. *Outflows.* Decreases in noncurrent liabilities, stockholders' equity, and certain current liabilities (e.g., notes payable and dividends payable).

Changes in assets (other than cash), liabilities, and stockholders' equity may be the result of investing and financing activities *not* affecting cash. Examples of these transactions include acquisitions of assets by issuing equity securities (noncash investing and financing activities), acquisitions of assets by assuming liabilities such as capital lease obligations (noncash investing and financing activities), exchanges of debt securities for equity securities such as the conversion of bonds to common stock (noncash financing activities), exchanges of assets for assets (noncash investing activities), exchanges of liabilities for liabilities (noncash financing activities), and exchanges of equity securities such as the conversion of preferred stock to common stock (noncash financing activities). Although these transactions are relatively rare, they do involve "simultaneous" investing activities and/or financing activities not affecting cash and generally have a significant effect on the prospective cash flows of a company, so that the company reports them in a schedule (or narrative explanation) that accompanies its statement of cash flows, as we discussed earlier.

The operating cash flows involve several adjustments for items relating to the operating cycle. We further explain the net cash flow from operating activities in the next section.

NET CASH FLOW FROM OPERATING ACTIVITIES

Operating cycles are discussed and illustrated in Chapter 3.

The calculation of a company's net cash flow from operating activities is usually the most detailed part of its statement of cash flows. To prepare this section, it is useful to understand the relationship between sales revenues, expenses, and cash flows within a company's operating cycle.

Recall that a company's operating cycle is the average time it takes to spend cash for inventory, process and sell the inventory, collect the accounts receivable, and convert them back into cash. To begin a company's operating cycle, the company purchases inventory for cash or on account. To make cash or credit sales, it incurs cost of goods sold and selling expenses and reduces inventory, and either pays cash, incurs current liabilities, or reduces prepaid items. In its operations, the company incurs general and administrative expenses and either pays cash, incurs current liabilities, or reduces prepaid items. Finally, the company collects its accounts receivable and converts them back into cash. This step completes the operating cycle.

Each phase of the operating cycle has an impact on both the company's net income and its net cash flow from operating activities. The impact is not the same for both items, however, because of differences in when the company records revenues and expenses and when it receives and pays cash. For instance, when the company purchases inventory for cash, an outflow of cash occurs but it does not record an expense. A purchase of inventory on credit increases accounts payable (a current liability) but involves no immediate expense or cash outflow. Later, when the company pays the accounts payable, it does not record an expense but a cash outflow occurs. The company records the expense (as cost of goods sold) when it sells the inventory even though no cash outflow occurs at that time. When the company makes a cash sale, it records revenue and there is a cash inflow. However, cash inflows may occur and be recorded as a current liability in the accounting period before the revenue is recognized (e.g., deferred revenues).

When the company makes a credit sale, it increases both revenue and accounts receivable (a current asset) but no inflow of cash occurs. Later, when the company collects the accounts receivable, it does not record revenue but a cash inflow occurs. Some accounts receivable are not collected so an expense (bad debts) is incurred even though no cash outflow occurs. In addition, throughout the accounting period, when the company pays selling expenses and general and administrative expenses in cash, it records expenses and cash outflows occur. However, when these expenses are accrued at the end of the period, the company records both the expenses and current payables but no cash outflows occur. The cash outflows are made in the next accounting period when the company pays the liabilities. Furthermore, cash outflows for some of these expenses may occur and be recorded as a current asset in the accounting period before the company records the expenses (e.g., prepaid insurance).

Exhibit 21-3 illustrates the basic differences between revenues and cash inflows from operating activities, and between expenses and cash outflows for operating activities that we discuss in this section. For example, assume for simplicity that the Smith Company made cash sales of $30,000 and credit sales of $42,000 during its first year of operations and collected $37,000 of the related accounts receivable. At the end of the year, the Sales Revenue account has a credit balance of $72,000 and the Accounts Receivable account has a debit balance of $5,000. As we show in Exhibit 21-4, an analysis of the related T-accounts shows an increase of $67,000 in the cash inflows from operating activities. (This $67,000 is equal to the cash sales of $30,000 plus the collections on accounts receivable of $37,000.)

Similarly, assume that Smith Company paid salaries of $13,000 and recorded salaries payable of $1,000 during its first year of operations. At the end of the year, the Salaries Expense account has a debit balance of $14,000 and the Salaries Payable account has a credit balance of $1,000. As we show in Exhibit 21-4, an analysis of the related T-account shows an increase of $13,000 in the cash outflows for operating activities. There are additional changes in a company's other current asset and current liability accounts that may affect its net cash flow from operating activities, and it analyzes each of these changes to determine the impact on its operating cash inflows and outflows.

There are also changes in certain noncurrent asset accounts that affect a company's net income but do not result in a cash inflow or outflow for operating activities. For instance, when a company records depreciation, the journal entry involves a debit to Depreciation Expense (a reduction of net income) and a credit to Accumulated Depreciation (a reduction of noncurrent assets). Although depreciation expense reduces net income (and noncurrent assets), there is no cash outflow for operating activities. The

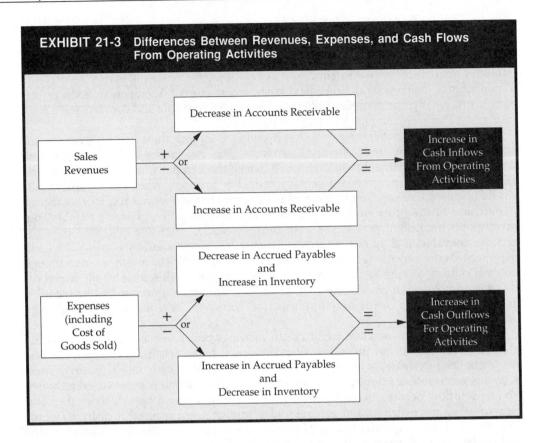

EXHIBIT 21-3   Differences Between Revenues, Expenses, and Cash Flows From Operating Activities

recording of amortization expense and depletion expense for intangible assets (such as a patent) and natural resource assets (such as a coal mine) have the same effect. That is, there is a reduction in net income (and noncurrent assets) but no operating cash outflow. A company analyzes each of the changes in these noncurrent asset accounts to determine the effect on its net cash flow from operating activities.

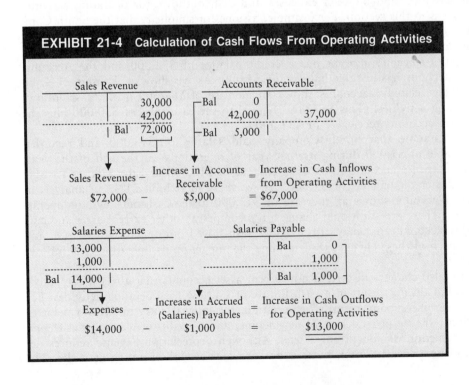

EXHIBIT 21-4   Calculation of Cash Flows From Operating Activities

Direct Method

FASB Statement No. 95 allows two ways for a company to calculate and report its net cash flow from operating activities on its statement of cash flows. The first is called the *direct* method. **Under the direct method, a company deducts its operating cash outflows from its operating cash inflows to determine its net cash flow from operating activities.** Using this method, the cash inflows from operating activities are computed first, based on an analysis like that we show in the upper portion of Exhibit 21-4. The cash outflows for operating activities are computed next, based on an analysis like that we show in the lower portion of Exhibit 21-4. To illustrate, suppose the Ryan Corporation presents the following income statement information for the year ended December 31, 2004:

Sales revenue (cash and accounts receivable)		$70,000
Less:		
Cost of goods sold (cash and accounts payable)	$(29,000)	
Salaries expense (cash and salaries payable)	(13,000)	
Depreciation expense	(8,000)	(50,000)
Income before income taxes		$20,000
Income tax expense (cash)		(6,000)
Net income		$14,000

A further analysis reveals the following changes in its current asset and current liability accounts for 2004: accounts receivable decreased by $2,600, inventory increased by $2,000, accounts payable decreased by $7,000, and salaries payable increased by $800. Under the direct method, Ryan Corporation reports the cash flows from operating activities on its statement of cash flows as follows:

Cash Flows From Operating Activities		
Cash Inflows:		
Cash received from customers	$ 72,600	
Cash inflows from operating activities		$72,600
Cash Outflows:		
Cash paid to suppliers	$(38,000)	
Cash paid to employees	(12,200)	
Cash paid for income taxes	(6,000)	
Cash outflows for operating activities		(56,200)
Net cash provided by operating activities		$16,400

The $72,600 cash received from customers is computed by adding the decrease in accounts receivable ($2,600) to the sales revenue ($70,000). This adjustment is made because the company's cash collections exceeded its sales during the year. This is the only cash receipt, so that cash inflows from operating activities are $72,600. The $38,000 cash paid to suppliers is computed by adding the increase in inventory ($2,000) and the decrease in accounts payable ($7,000) to the cost of goods sold ($29,000). These adjustments are made because on the one hand, the company's purchases exceeded its cost of goods sold but on the other hand, some of these purchases were on credit. The $12,200 cash paid to employees is computed by deducting the increase in salaries payable ($800) from the salaries expense ($13,000). This adjustment is made because the cash paid for salaries was less than its salaries expense. The entire amount of income tax expense ($6,000) was paid in cash. These cash outflows for operating activities total $56,200, so that the net cash provided by operating activities is $16,400. Note that the depreciation expense is *not* included in the net cash flows from operating activities because it did not result in an outflow of cash.

The direct method has the advantage of reporting a company's operating cash inflows separately from its operating cash outflows, which may be useful in estimating future cash flows. However, the direct method is criticized because it does not "tie" the net income reported on a company's income statement to the net cash provided by operating activities reported on the company's statement of cash flows. Furthermore, the direct method does not show how the changes in the elements (i.e., current assets and current liabilities) of a company's operating cycle affected its operating cash flows.

Indirect Method

Use of the *indirect* method to report a company's net cash flow from operating activities on its statement of cash flows resolves the two criticisms of the direct method. **Under the indirect method, a company's net income is adjusted to its net cash flow from operating activities** on the statement of cash flows. To do so, net income is listed first and then adjustments (additions or subtractions) are made to net income (1) to eliminate certain amounts (such as depreciation expense) that are included in its net income but do not involve a cash inflow or cash outflow for operating activities, and (2) to include any changes in the current assets (other than cash) and current liabilities involved in the company's operating cycle that affect its cash flows differently than they affect net income. In other words, under the indirect method, a company's income flows are converted from an *accrual* basis to a *cash flow* basis. In this manner, the indirect method shows the "quality" of a company's income by providing information about lead and lag intervals between its income flows and operating cash flows.

To illustrate, refer back to the Ryan Corporation's income statement and additional information presented earlier. Under the indirect method, Ryan Corporation reports the net cash flow from operating activities on its statement of cash flows as follows:

Net Cash Flow From Operating Activities

Net income		$14,000
Adjustments for differences between income flows and cash flows for operating activities:		
Add: Depreciation expense	8,000	
Decrease in accounts receivable	2,600	
Increase in salaries payable	800	
Less: Increase in inventory	(2,000)	
Decrease in accounts payable	(7,000)	
Net cash provided by operating activities		$16,400

It is important to understand the nature of each adjustment to convert the net income to the net cash provided by operating activities. First, the $8,000 depreciation expense is *added* to the $14,000 net income because it had been deducted to determine net income even though it did not involve an outflow of cash. The $2,600 decrease in the current asset, accounts receivable, is added to net income because it resulted in an additional inflow of cash from operations. The $800 increase in the current liability, salaries payable, resulted in an increase in expenses and a decrease in net income. It is added to net income because it did not result in a reduced cash outflow for operations. The $2,000 increase in the current asset, inventory, and the $7,000 decrease in the current liability, accounts payable, are both deducted from net income because they resulted in additional operating cash outflows. Note that by using either the direct method or the indirect method, net cash provided by operating activities is the same amount ($16,400). The indirect method is the method used by the Ryan Corporation in Exhibit 21-1 at the beginning of the chapter.

Prior to *FASB Statement No. 95*, nearly all companies reported the results of their operating activities using the indirect method on their statements of changes in financial position. *FASB Statement No. 95* expresses a preference for the direct method, but allows the use of either the direct method or the indirect method. However, if a company uses the direct method on its statement of cash flows, it must also include a separate schedule that reconciles its net income to its net cash flow provided by (or used in) operating activities (i.e., the indirect method). Because of the previous use of the indirect method and the extra schedule required under the direct method, most companies continue to use the indirect method. In a recent survey, over 98% of surveyed companies used the indirect method.[7] Therefore, we focus on the indirect method in the main part of the chapter, but fully discuss the direct method in the Appendix at the end of the chapter. (**You should use the** *indirect method* **for** *all homework,* **unless otherwise indicated.**)

In the previous example, under the indirect method we made only a few simple adjustments to convert the net income to the net cash flow from operating activities. In reality, a company may have many adjustments involving both increases and decreases in its current assets and current liabilities, as well as other noncurrent accounts. Exhibit 21-5 lists the major adjustments needed to convert a company's net income to its net cash flow from operating activities. We explain these adjustments in the examples that follow.

EXHIBIT 21-5   Adjustments to Convert Net Income to Net Cash Flow From Operating Activities

Net Income

Plus

Minus

Decreases in Current Assets
Decrease in accounts receivable
Decrease in interest receivable
Decrease in inventory
Decrease in prepaid expenses
Decreases in other current assets*

Increases in Current Liabilities
Increase in accounts payable
Increase in salaries payable
Increase in interest payable
Increase in income taxes payable
Increases in other current liabilities*

Other Adjustments
Depreciation, depletion, and amortization expense
Amortization of discount on bonds payable
Amortization of premium on investment in bonds
Increase in deferred tax liability
Decrease in deferred tax asset
Increase in accrued pension cost
Decrease in prepaid pension cost
Loss (net) on disposal (or write-down) of assets or liabilities
Loss under the equity method

Increases in Current Assets
Increase in accounts receivable
Increase in interest receivable
Increase in inventory
Increase in prepaid expenses
Increases in other current assets*

Decreases in Current Liabilities
Decrease in accounts payable
Decrease in salaries payable
Decrease in interest payable
Decrease in income taxes payable
Decreases in other current liabilities*

Other Adjustments
Amortization of premium on bonds payable
Amortization of discount on investment in bonds
Decrease in deferred tax liability
Increase in deferred tax asset
Decrease in accrued pension cost
Increase in prepaid pension cost
Gain (net) on disposal (or write-up) of assets or liabilities
Income under the equity method

Equals

Net Cash Flow From Operating Activities

* Related to operating activities.

---

7. *Accounting Trends and Techniques* (New York: AICPA, 2001), p. 505.

PROCEDURES FOR PREPARATION OF STATEMENT

When a company prepares its statement of cash flows, information for the accounting period from the following financial statements is required: (1) beginning and ending balance sheets, (2) income statement, and (3) retained earnings statement. In addition, other information is needed that explains the changes in the company's balance sheet accounts (other than cash). This additional information is obtained from its accounting records.

Visual Inspection Method of Analysis

There are two methods of analysis that a company may use to prepare its statement of cash flows, the visual inspection method and the worksheet method.[8] Under the **visual inspection method,** the company's financial statements are visually reviewed and its statement of cash flows is prepared without the use of a worksheet. This method may be used when a company's financial statements are not complex and when the relationships between changes in account balances can be easily observed and analyzed. There are seven steps in the visual inspection method, as we show in Exhibit 21-6.

Steps 5 and 6 do not have to be completed in sequential order; what is important is a complete analysis of the relevant information.[9] Companies rarely use the visual inspection method because of the lack of supporting documentation for the statement of cash flows.

EXHIBIT 21-6   Steps in Visual Inspection Method

1. Prepare the heading for the statement of cash flows and list the three major sections: (a) Net Cash Flow From Operating Activities, (b) Cash Flows From Investing Activities, and (c) Cash Flows From Financing Activities.
2. Calculate the net change in cash that occurred during the accounting period. This amount is a major subtotal, or "target figure," on the statement of cash flows.
3. Determine the company's net income and list this amount as the first item in the net cash flow from operating activities section.
4. Calculate the increase or decrease that occurred during the accounting period in each balance sheet account (except cash).
5. Determine whether the increase or decrease in each balance sheet account (except cash) caused an inflow or outflow of cash and, if so, whether the cash flow was related to an operating, investing, or financing activity.
6. If no cash flow occurred in Step 5, determine whether the increase or decrease in each balance sheet account (except cash) was the result of a noncash income statement item or a simultaneous investing and/or financing transaction. If the former, then determine the adjustment (addition or subtraction) to help convert net income to the net cash flow from operating activities. If the latter, then identify the components of the simultaneous investing and/or financing activity.
7. Complete the various sections of the statement of cash flows (based on the analysis in Steps 5 and 6), and check that the subtotals of the sections sum to the net change (increase or decrease) in cash (from Step 2) and that the sum of the net change in cash and the beginning cash balance is equal to the ending cash balance reported on the balance sheet.

---

8. A company sometimes uses a third method involving T-accounts to analyze and develop the information for its statement of cash flows. The T-account method, however, results in cumbersome working papers when the analysis becomes complex. Because the worksheet method uses the same general technique as the T-account method, but in a more efficient format, we discuss only the worksheet method in this chapter.
9. If the company engaged in any investing and financing transactions not affecting cash, then it also prepares the heading for a schedule of Investing and Financing Activities Not Affecting Cash in Step 1 of Exhibit 21-6.

Simple Example (Visual Inspection Method)

Knowledge of the visual inspection method is helpful in understanding the more complex worksheet method. To illustrate the visual inspection method, Exhibit 21-7 shows the condensed financial information of the Leyton Company for 2004. Exhibit 21-8 shows the statement of cash flows prepared from that information. After preparing the heading and listing the three sections of the statement, the $2,600 net increase in cash is determined. This increase is computed by comparing the $4,000 cash balance on the beginning balance sheet to the $6,600 cash balance on the ending balance sheet. Then, the $7,000 net income is obtained from the income statement and listed as the first item in the net cash flow from operating activities section. The following discussion explains the remaining steps in the visual inspection method by reviewing the items in each section of the statement.

5 Prepare a simple statement of cash flows.

NET CASH FLOW FROM OPERATING ACTIVITIES   In this section there are three adjustments to convert the net income to the net cash flow from operating activities. The first adjustment involves the $2,300 depreciation expense. This amount is obtained from the income statement in Exhibit 21-7. It is also the $2,300 increase (from $12,500 to $14,800) in the accumulated depreciation account on the balance sheets during the year (because there are no disposals of buildings and equipment during the year). Because depreciation is deducted in the computation of net income but does not cause a cash outflow, the $2,300 depreciation expense is added to net income. The second adjustment involves the $1,500 increase (from $7,500 to $9,000 in Exhibit 21-7) in accounts payable. Accounts payable increased because other operating expenses recorded during the year exceeded the cash payments for these items. Therefore, the expenses deducted to compute net income are greater than the related cash outflows. Consequently, the $1,500 increase in accounts payable is added to net income. The third adjustment involves the $2,700 increase (from $6,300 to $9,000) in accounts receivable. Accounts receivable increased during the year because sales on account exceeded the cash collections on account. Therefore, sales revenue and net income are greater

---

EXHIBIT 21-7   Leyton Company: Condensed Financial Information

Income Statement Information for 2004

Sales revenue		$31,800
Operating expenses		
Depreciation expense	$ 2,300	
Interest expense	1,400	
Other expenses	18,100	(21,800)
Income before income taxes		$10,000
Income tax expense		(3,000)
Net Income		$ 7,000

Retained Earnings Information for 2004

Beginning retained earnings	$11,300
Add: Net income	7,000
	$18,300
Less: Dividends	(3,500)
Ending retained earnings	$14,800

Balance Sheet Information

	Balances	
Accounts	12/31/03	12/31/04
Cash	$ 4,000	$ 6,600
Accounts receivable	6,300	9,000
Land	9,000	6,000
Buildings and equipment	48,000	60,000
Accumulated depreciation	(12,500)	(14,800)
Total Assets	$54,800	$66,800
Accounts payable	$ 7,500	$ 9,000
Bonds payable, 10%	14,000	21,000
Common stock, $10 par	22,000	22,000
Retained earnings	11,300	14,800
Total Liabilities and Stockholders' Equity	$54,800	$66,800

Supplemental Information for 2004

(a) A building was purchased for cash during the year.
(b) Land was sold (at cost) for cash during the year.

(c) No buildings or equipment were sold during the year.
(d) Bonds payable were issued at the end of the year.

EXHIBIT 21-8   Simple Statement of Cash Flows

LEYTON COMPANY

Statement of Cash Flows
For Year Ended December 31, 2004

Net Cash Flow From Operating Activities		
Net income	$ 7,000	
Adjustments for differences between income flows		
and cash flows from operating activities:		
Add: Depreciation expense	2,300	
Increase in accounts payable	1,500	
Less: Increase in accounts receivable	(2,700)	
Net cash provided by operating activities		$8,100
Cash Flows From Investing Activities		
Payment for purchase of building	$(12,000)	
Proceeds from sale of land, at cost	3,000	
Net cash used for investing activities		(9,000)
Cash Flows From Financing Activities		
Proceeds from issuance of bonds	$ 7,000	
Payment of dividends	(3,500)	
Net cash provided by financing activities		3,500
Net Increase in Cash		$2,600
Cash, January 1, 2004		4,000
Cash, December 31, 2004		$6,600

than the related cash inflows. Consequently, the $2,700 increase in accounts receivable is deducted from net income.

As a result of the preceding adjustments, the net cash flow from operating activities is $8,100 for the Leyton Company in 2004, as we show in Exhibit 21-8. Note that, with the exception of depreciation, the adjustments to net income involve changes in current assets (except cash) and current liabilities.

CASH FLOWS FROM INVESTING ACTIVITIES   There are only two cash flows from investing activities, one cash outflow and one cash inflow. During 2004 the Buildings and Equipment account increased by $12,000, from $48,000 to $60,000, as we show on the balance sheets in Exhibit 21-7. This increase is the result of the purchase of a building, an investing activity, which required a cash outflow of $12,000. This cash outflow is listed as the first item in this section. During 2004 the Land account decreased by $3,000, from $9,000 to $6,000. This is the result of the sale of land, an investing activity. Because the land was sold at cost, there is no gain or loss.[10] The $3,000 cash inflow is listed as the second item in this section. As a result of these two cash flows, net cash of $9,000 is used for investing activities by the Leyton Company in 2004, as we show in Exhibit 21-8.

CASH FLOWS FROM FINANCING ACTIVITIES   There are also two cash flows from financing activities, one cash inflow and one cash outflow. During 2004 the bonds payable account increased by $7,000, from $14,000 to $21,000, as we show in Exhibit 21-7. This increase is the result of the issuance of bonds, a financing activity, which provided a cash inflow of $7,000 that is listed as the first item in this section. There was no change in the common stock account during the year, so there is no cash inflow or outflow related to common stock. During 2004 the company declared and paid

---

10. We discuss the reporting of the sale of noncurrent assets at a gain or loss in a later example.

dividends of $3,500. The amount of the dividends is obtained from the retained earnings statement in Exhibit 21-7. [Note also that the $7,000 net income, offset by the $3,500 dividends, accounts for the $3,500 increase (from $11,300 to $14,800) in the retained earnings account shown on the balance sheets.] The payment of dividends, a financing activity, caused a cash outflow of $3,500 that is listed as the second item in this section. As a result of these two cash flows, net cash of $3,500 is provided by the financing activities of the Leyton Company during 2004.

SUMMARY Note that in the preparation of the three sections, we account for all the changes in the assets (except cash), liabilities, and stockholders' equity accounts during 2004, as we show in Exhibit 21-7. Note also that, with the exception of depreciation, the adjustments to net income in the net cash flow from operating activities section involve changes in current asset (except cash) and current liability accounts. On the other hand, all of the cash inflows and outflows listed in the cash flows from investing activities section and the cash flows from financing activities section involve changes in noncurrent asset, noncurrent liability, and stockholders' equity accounts. The statement of cash flows in Exhibit 21-8 is now complete. The $8,100 net cash provided by operating activities, less the $9,000 net cash used for investing activities, plus the $3,500 net cash provided by financing activities, equals the $2,600 net increase in cash. And, the $2,600 net increase in cash, added to the $4,000 beginning cash balance, is equal to the $6,600 ending cash balance (as reported on the company's December 31, 2004 balance sheet). With this background in mind, we now turn to the worksheet method of analysis.

Worksheet Method of Analysis

Companies usually use the **worksheet method** to prepare their statements of cash flows. Under this method a company's cash flow effects of its operating, investing, and financing activities during the accounting period are entered on the worksheet to (1) record the cash inflows and outflows according to the three sections of the statement of cash flows, (2) record the investing and financing activities not affecting cash, and (3) account for the change in each asset, liability, and stockholders' equity account. This method is most often used in practice because it allows a company to document the analysis of its complex transactions and events in a concise working paper. Because the worksheet method is used in more complex situations, it is helpful to follow a series of steps.

Steps in Preparation (Worksheet Method)

After gathering information from the financial statements and supplemental information from the accounting records, a company completes several steps to prepare the worksheet and its statement of cash flows. We list each step in Exhibit 21-9, followed by an explanation.

There are three issues related to the steps listed in Exhibit 21-9. First, other than usually starting with net income, there is no particular order in which the worksheet entries are reconstructed. You should develop a method to account for all the changes in the noncash accounts in an orderly way. Second, you may have to make more than one worksheet entry to reconcile the change in an account. For instance, the change in the Land account may be the result of both a sale and a purchase of land. In such cases, both the cash inflow and cash outflow are accounted for separately. Finally, remember that these worksheet entries are *not* posted to any accounts. They are recorded on the worksheet only to help in preparing the statement of cash flows.

Comprehensive Example (Worksheet Method)

To understand the process of preparing a worksheet and statement of cash flows we discuss a comprehensive example. The example is not intended to be all-inclusive but rather to provide a basis from which to develop a logical approach to using a worksheet for analyzing similar operating, investing, and financing transactions. The example includes a discussion of each step presented in Exhibit 21-9. As you study this example, it will be helpful to reread these steps. Exhibit 21-10 shows the condensed

6 Use a worksheet for a statement of cash flows.

EXHIBIT 21-9   Steps in Worksheet Method

Step 1. Prepare the column headings on a worksheet (see Exhibit 21-11). Then enter the account title Cash on the first line of the account titles column and list the beginning balance, ending balance, and change in cash in the respective columns.

Step 2. Enter the titles of all the remaining accounts from the balance sheets on the worksheet and list each beginning and ending account balance, and the change in the account balance directly below the cash information. (To simplify the worksheet, only the change in each account balance could be entered.) The accounts with debit balances are listed first, followed by the accounts with credit balances. Total the amount columns to verify that the debit totals equal the credit totals.

Step 3. Directly below these accounts, add the following headings:

A. Net Cash Flow From Operating Activities

B. Cash Flows From Investing Activities

C. Cash Flows From Financing Activities

D. Investing and Financing Activities Not Affecting Cash

Leave sufficient room below each heading so that each type of cash flow may be listed.

Step 4. Account for all the changes in the noncash accounts that occurred during the current period. *Reconstruct* the journal entries that caused the changes in the noncash accounts directly on the worksheet, making certain modifications to show the cash inflows and outflows for operating, investing, and financing activities. Remember that you are preparing this worksheet at the *end* of the accounting period. The actual journal entries that caused the changes have already been made and posted to the accounts. In this step you are reconstructing the entries on the worksheet to prepare the statement of cash flows. Use the following general rules:

A. *Start with net income.* The net income is a summary of all the journal entries from operating activities that affect current assets or current liabilities and retained earnings. The net income is adjusted on the worksheet to change it to the net cash flow from operating activities. Therefore, the entry on the worksheet to list net income and to explain the impact on retained earnings is a debit to the caption Net Income under the heading Net Cash Flow From Operating Activities and a credit to Retained Earnings.[a]

B. *Account for the changes in the current asset (except cash) and current liability accounts.* Because nearly all the changes in the current assets and current liabilities are part of the company's *operating cycle*, the impacts of these changes on cash are listed as *adjustments* (*additions* or *deductions*) to *net income* in the Net Cash Flow From Operating Activities section of the worksheet.[b] Review each current asset (except cash) and current liability account. Make an entry on the worksheet to record the change (debit or credit) in that account and the adjustment [credit (deduction) or debit (addition)] to net income.

C. *Account for the changes in the noncurrent accounts.* Review each noncurrent account and determine the journal entry responsible for its change. Identify whether the transaction involves an operating, investing, or financing activity. If the transaction involved an investing or financing activity, make the entry on the worksheet with the following changes:

   1. If the entry affects cash, replace a debit to cash with either an investing or financing cash inflow caption, and list the item as a debit (inflow) under the proper heading. Replace a credit to cash with a proper cash outflow caption, and list the item as a credit (outflow) under the proper heading.

   2. If the entry involves an operating activity and affects a noncash income statement item (e.g., depreciation, gain, or loss), replace the debit or credit to this noncash item with an adjustment to net income under the Net Cash Flow From Operating Activities heading.

   3. If the entry does not affect an operating activity or cash, it is a simultaneous financing and/or investing transaction. For this type of transaction, create expanded entries to record both the financing and/or investing activities.

Step 5. Make a final worksheet entry to record the net change in cash. The worksheet entries must account for all the changes in the noncash accounts recorded in Step 2. The difference between the total cash inflows and outflows must be equal to the change in the Cash account. The final worksheet entry to record a net increase in cash is a debit to Cash and a credit to Net Increase in Cash.[c] Total the debit and credit worksheet entries in the upper and lower portions to verify that the respective totals are equal.

Step 6. Prepare the statement of cash flows and accompanying schedule. Use the information developed in the lower part of the worksheet (and the beginning and ending cash balances). Under the major sections of the statement, list the various cash inflows and outflows. Subtotal the items under each major section and add or subtract the subtotals to determine the net change in cash. Add the net change in cash to the beginning cash balance to determine the ending cash balance. In an accompanying schedule, list the various investing and financing activities not affecting cash.

---

a. The entry to show a net loss involves a debit to Retained Earnings and a credit to Net Loss. Any adjustments for noncash items included in net income, such as in Step 4C(2), are made as usual.

b. The major exceptions to this adjustment are changes in short-term notes receivable and notes payable, changes in temporary investments (i.e., marketable securities), and changes in dividends payable. These changes are the results of investing or financing activities and are handled like the changes in the noncurrent accounts discussed in Step 4(C), except that changes in temporary investments may require additional analysis as discussed in a later section.

c. For a net decrease in cash, an opposite entry (a debit to Net Decrease in Cash and a credit to Cash) is made.

EXHIBIT 21-10 Jones Company: Condensed Financial Information

Income Statement Information for 2004

Sales		$ 88,020
Less: Cost of goods sold	$ (52,200)	
Other operating expenses	(15,800)	
Depreciation expense: equipment	(2,820) (b)	
Depreciation expense: building	(5,100) (c)	
Patent amortization expense	(600) (d)	
Bond interest expense	(1,100)	
Income tax expense	(3,630)	
Plus: Gain on sale of land	1,700	(79,550)
Income before extraordinary items		$ 8,470
Extraordinary loss (net of income taxes)		(2,100)
Net Income		$ 6,370 (a)

Balance Sheet Information

	Balances	
Accounts	12/31/03	12/31/04
Cash	$ 3,200	$ 5,900 (w)
Accounts receivable	5,600	7,600 (e)
Inventories	7,300	7,000 (f)
Prepaid expenses	1,200	1,400 (g)
Land	10,000	18,200
Equipment	35,000	35,000
Accumulated depreciation: equipment	(12,000)	(14,820)
Buildings	144,000	149,000
Accumulated depreciation: buildings	(39,300)	(39,600)
Leased equipment	0	5,300
Patents (net)	5,000	4,400
Total Assets	$160,000	$179,380
Accounts payable	$ 8,600	$ 7,300 (h)
Income taxes payable	1,500	2,130 (i)
Interest payable	0	500 (j)
Note payable	0	2,600
Obligation under capital lease	0	5,300
Bonds payable, 10%	0	10,000
Discount on bonds payable	0	(900)
Deferred tax liability	1,920	2,100
Preferred stock, $100 par	6,000	0
Premium on preferred stock	1,000	0
Common stock, $10 par	34,000	37,400
Premium on common stock	67,000	73,700
Retained earnings	39,980	39,250
Total Liabilities and Stockholders' Equity	$160,000	$179,380

Retained Earnings Information for 2004

Beginning retained earnings		$39,980
Add: Net income		6,370
		$46,350
Less: Stock dividends	$ 3,100	
Cash dividends	4,000 (v)	(7,100)
Ending Retained Earnings		$39,250

Supplemental Information for 2004

(k) On December 31, 2004 the company borrowed $2,600 from a bank by issuing a 12%, 90-day note payable.

(l) During the year additional land was acquired at a cost of $10,400.

(m) During the year land that cost $2,200 was sold for $3,900, resulting in a $1,700 gain.

(n) During the year a new building was acquired at a purchase price of $15,000.

(o) During the year an earthquake completely destroyed a building that cost $10,000 and had a book value of $5,200. Settlement with the insurance company, combined with the tax credit, resulted in after-tax cash proceeds of $3,100 and an extra-ordinary loss (net of income taxes) of $2,100.

(p) On December 31, 2004 the company leased equipment under a long-term capital lease, recording the lease at $5,300.

(q) On January 1, 2004 the company issued $10,000 of long-term bonds at 90. The bonds pay interest semiannually on July 1 and January 1 at a 10% annual rate and mature in 10 years on January 1, 2014.

(r) The company uses straight-line amortization for the bond discount in (q); consequently, bond discount amortization was $100 for the year.

(s) On January 1, 2004 sixty shares of preferred stock with a total par value of $6,000 and book value of $7,000 were converted into 240 shares of common stock. The book value method was used to record the conversion.

(t) Taxable income was less than pretax accounting income for the year, resulting in an increase in deferred taxes payable of $180.

(u) During the year, a small stock dividend was declared and issued. Involved were 100 shares of $10 par common stock. The market value of the stock on the declaration date was $31 per share.

EXHIBIT 21-11 Cash Flow Worksheet for 2004 (Jones Company)

Account Titles	Balances 12/31/03	Balances 12/31/04	Change Increase (Decrease)	Worksheet Entries Debit		Worksheet Entries Credit	
Debits							
Cash	3,200	5,900	2,700	(w)	2,700		
Noncash Accounts:							
Accounts receivable (net)	5,600	7,600	2,000	(e)	2,000		
Inventories	7,300	7,000	(300)			(f)	300
Prepaid expenses	1,200	1,400	200	(g)	200		
Land	10,000	18,200	8,200	(l)	10,400	(m)	2,200
Equipment	35,000	35,000	0				
Buildings	144,000	149,000	5,000	(n)	15,000	(o)	10,000
Leased equipment	0	5,300	5,300	(p-2)	5,300		
Patents (net)	5,000	4,400	(600)			(d)	600
Discount on bonds payable	0	900	900	(q)	1,000	(r)	100
Totals	211,300	234,700	23,400				
Credits							
Accumulated depreciation: equipment	12,000	14,820	2,820			(b)	2,820
Accumulated depreciation: buildings	39,300	39,600	300	(o)	4,800	(c)	5,100
Accounts payable	8,600	7,300	(1,300)	(h)	1,300		
Income taxes payable	1,500	2,130	630			(i)	630
Interest payable	0	500	500			(j)	500
Note payable	0	2,600	2,600			(k)	2,600
Obligation under capital lease	0	5,300	5,300			(p-1)	5,300
Bonds payable, 10%	0	10,000	10,000			(q)	10,000
Deferred tax liability	1,920	2,100	180			(t)	180
Preferred stock, $100 par	6,000	0	(6,000)	(s-2)	6,000		
Premium on preferred stock	1,000	0	(1,000)	(s-2)	1,000		
Common stock, $10 par	34,000	37,400	3,400			(s-1)	2,400
						(u)	1,000
Additional paid-in capital on common stock	67,000	73,700	6,700			(s-1)	4,600
						(u)	2,100
Retained earnings	39,980	39,250	(730)	(u)	3,100	(a)	6,370
				(v)	4,000		
Totals	211,300	234,700	23,400		56,800		56,800

(Lower portion shown on facing page.)

financial information of the Jones Company for 2004 that we use in the example. In Exhibit 21-10 we include letters of the alphabet in parentheses beside amounts or items of information. These letters correspond to the letters we use to explain the worksheet entries in Exhibit 21-11.

STEPS 1, 2, AND 3: SETTING UP THE WORKSHEET Steps 1 and 2 involve setting up the worksheet, entering the account titles and their beginning and ending balances, making changes in the appropriate columns of the worksheet, and totaling the columns to check your work. In Step 3 the major headings, Net Cash Flow From Operating Activities, Cash Flows From Investing Activities, Cash Flows From Financing Activities, and Investing and Financing Activities Not Affecting Cash, are then listed on the worksheet. Enough space is left under each heading so that the cash

EXHIBIT 21-11, Continued

Account Titles	Worksheet Entries			
	Debit		Credit	
Net Cash Flow From Operating Activities				
Net Income	(a)	6,370		
Add: Depreciation expense: equipment	(b)	2,820		
Depreciation expense: buildings	(c)	5,100		
Patent amortization expense	(d)	600		
Decrease in inventories	(f)	300		
Increase in income taxes payable	(i)	630		
Increase in interest payable	(j)	500		
Extraordinary loss	(o)	2,100		
Bond discount amortization	(r)	100		
Increase in deferred tax liability	(t)	180		
Less: Increase in accounts receivable			(e)	2,000
Increase in prepaid expenses			(g)	200
Decrease in accounts payable			(h)	1,300
Gain on sale of land			(m)	1,700
Cash Flows From Investing Activities				
Payment for purchase of land			(l)	10,400
Proceeds from sale of land	(m)	3,900		
Payment for purchase of building			(n)	15,000
Proceeds from building destroyed by earthquake	(o)	3,100		
Cash Flows From Financing Activities				
Proceeds from issuance of short-term note payable	(k)	2,600		
Proceeds from issuance of bonds	(q)	9,000		
Payment of dividends			(v)	4,000
Investing and Financing Activities Not Affecting Cash				
Incurrence of capital lease obligation for equipment	(p-1)	5,300		
Acquisition of equipment under capital lease			(p-2)	5,300
Issuance of common stock to convert preferred stock	(s-1)	7,000		
Conversion of preferred stock to common stock			(s-2)	7,000
Net Increase in Cash			(w)	2,700
Totals		49,600		49,600

flows may be listed accordingly. Exhibit 21-11 shows these accounts and their headings for the Jones Company.[11]

STEP 4: COMPLETION OF THE WORKSHEET   The worksheet entries to account for all the changes in the noncash accounts are entered directly on the worksheet in Step 4, as we show in Exhibit 21-11. We explain each entry in the following discussion. Entries (a) through (j) generally affect current assets and current liabilities and relate to operating activities. Entries (k) through (w) generally affect noncurrent assets, noncurrent liabilities, and stockholders' equity items and relate to investing and financing activities. As you study each entry, it will be helpful to review the discussion under Step 4 of Exhibit 21-9, as well as the financial information in Exhibit 21-10.

WORKSHEET ENTRIES FOR OPERATING ACTIVITIES   Entry (a) records net income as the first item on the worksheet under the heading Net Cash Flow From Operating Activities. A review of the expenses on the income statement in Exhibit 21-10 reveals three "noncash" expenses, depreciation expense on equipment, depreciation expense on

---

11. Normally, in Step 3 the major headings are listed *below* the account titles. However, because Exhibit 21-11 is so long, we show the lower portion of the worksheet on the facing page.

buildings, and patent amortization expense. Each of these is added back to net income to help reconcile it to the net cash flow from operating activities, as we show in entries (b), (c), and (d). Note that entries (b) and (d) account for the changes in Accumulated Depreciation: Equipment and Patents (net), respectively. Entry (o), which we discuss later, is also recorded to account for the change in the Accumulated Depreciation: Buildings account.

A review of the changes in the current assets (except cash) and the current liabilities reveals several additional adjustments that are made to help reconcile the net income to the net cash flow from operating activities. Accounts receivable increased by $2,000 during the year because the company collected less cash than the credit sales it made. To adjust net income for the lower operating cash inflow, entry (e) is made. Note that, for simplicity, we ignore bad debts here. If accounts receivable (net) are affected by a provision for bad debts, then both the change in accounts receivable due to the recognition of bad debts expense and the change due to cash collections in excess of (or less than) sales are treated as adjustments of net income.

In regard to the other current assets, inventories decreased by $300 during the year, indicating that the company purchased less inventory than it recorded as cost of goods sold. To adjust net income for the lower operating cash outflow, entry (f) is made. Prepaid expenses increased by $200 during the year, indicating that the company paid more cash for these items than the amount of expense it included in other operating expenses. To adjust net income for the higher operating cash outflow, entry (g) is made.

Turning to the current liabilities, accounts payable decreased by $1,300 during the year, indicating that the company's cash payments for operating activities exceeded expenses. To adjust net income for the higher cash outflow, entry (h) is made. Both income taxes payable and interest payable increased during the year, indicating that the company paid less cash than it reported as the respective expenses. To adjust net income for the lower cash outflows, entries (i) and (j) are made. A few entries which we record later also affect the net cash flow from operating activities.

WORKSHEET ENTRIES FOR INVESTING AND FINANCING ACTIVITIES Note that no adjustment is made to the net cash flow from operating activities for the $2,600 increase in the current liability, notes payable. This is because the increase was due to a *financing* activity, which we summarized in the supplemental information of Exhibit 21-10. To record the cash inflow from this financing activity, entry (k) is made.

At this point all the changes in the current assets (except cash) and current liabilities are accounted for. Turning to the noncurrent items, a review of the supplemental information is needed to identify the various investing and financing activities. During the year the company both purchased and sold land; both are investing activities. The acquisition of land resulted in a $10,400 cash outflow, which is recorded in entry (l). Land that cost $2,200 was sold for $3,900, which resulted in a $1,700 gain (not extraordinary) that increased net income. Because the entire $3,900 is reported as a cash inflow from an investing activity, the gain is excluded (*deducted*) from net income to avoid double counting, and because there was no cash inflow from *operating* activities. To do so, entry (m) is made.[12] Note that entries (l) and (m) account for the $8,200 increase in the Land account. The acquisition of a new building during the year resulted in a $15,000 cash outflow for an investing activity, which is recorded in entry (n).

FASB Statement No. 95 requires that a company report its cash flows from extraordinary items (as well as discontinued operations) as investing or financing activities and exclude them from its net cash flows from operating activities.[13] During the year, an earthquake (extraordinary event) occurred that destroyed a building owned by the company with a cost of $10,000 and a book value of $5,200. Because the company

---

12. If the land was sold at a loss, the loss would decrease net income even though there was no outflow of cash for operating activities. In this case, the worksheet entry would be modified so that the caption Loss on Sale of Land is *debited* under the heading Net Cash Flow From Operating Activities to *add back* the loss to net income in a manner similar to depreciation expense.

13. *FASB Statement No. 95, op. cit.,* par. 28.

received after-tax cash proceeds of $3,100 from its insurance company, it incurred an extraordinary loss (net of taxes) of $2,100, which it included in (and reduced) net income. The amount (proceeds) received is a cash inflow *from an investing activity*. To record the cash inflow, eliminate the book value, and exclude (i.e., *add back*) the extraordinary loss from net income, entry (o) is made. Because worksheet entry (o) is complex, we show it below in journal entry form to help you in your analysis:

(o)	Cash Flows From Investing Activities:		
	Proceeds From Building Destroyed by Earthquake	3,100	
	Accumulated Depreciation: Building	4,800	
	Net Cash Flow From Operating Activities:		
	Extraordinary Loss	2,100	
	Buildings		10,000

Note that entries (n) and (o) account for the $5,000 increase in the Building account, and that entries (c) and (o) account for the $300 increase in the Accumulated Depreciation account. Note also that the Extraordinary Loss is shown on the worksheet as an addition to net income in the usual manner, along with the other added items.

At the end of the year the company leased equipment under a capital lease, recording the asset and liability at $5,300. Although not affecting cash, this is a simultaneous investing and financing transaction, and the company reports both activities in a schedule accompanying the statement of cash flows. Entries (p-1) and (p-2) record these events.

On January 1 the company issued bonds payable with a face value of $10,000, at a discount, receiving proceeds of $9,000. This is a financing activity and is recorded in entry (q). Note that the $1,000 debit to Discount on Bonds Payable does not equal the net change ($900) in the account. This is because the company amortized part of the discount during the year. On the income statement in Exhibit 21-10, note that the bond interest expense is $1,100; however, the cash paid or owed on the bonds is 10% of $10,000, or $1,000. The additional $100 of interest expense is due to the discount amortization. This amortization increased interest expense and reduced net income but did not involve a cash outflow. To adjust for the lower operating cash outflow, entry (r) is made. The $900 increase in Discount on Bonds Payable is now accounted for. The adjustment for the amortization of a premium on bonds payable would be handled in a similar but opposite way. Bond premium amortization reduces interest expense to an amount *less* than the operating cash outflow. Therefore, the worksheet entry would involve a debit to Premium on Bonds Payable and a credit to Net Cash Flow From Operating Activities: Bond Premium Amortization for the amount of the premium amortization.

During the year, sixty shares of convertible preferred stock with a total par value of $6,000 and a book value of $7,000 were converted to 240 shares of $10 par common stock; the company accounted for the transaction by the book value method. Although not affecting cash, two simultaneous financing activities involving the exchange of equity securities occurred that the company reports in a schedule accompanying the statement of cash flows. Entries (s-1) and (s-2) record these events. Note that entry (s-1) did not account for all the changes in the Common Stock and Additional Paid-In Capital on Common Stock accounts. Entry (u) also affects these accounts.

The deferred tax liability increased by $180 because the company's income tax expense was higher than the actual income taxes it paid or owes (because of a temporary difference between pretax financial income and taxable income). To adjust net income for the lower operating cash outflow, entry (t) is made. The company declared and issued a small stock dividend during the year; it recorded the transaction at the market price of the stock. Recall that stock dividends affect only stockholders' equity accounts and do not involve the transfer of assets to stockholders or the exchange of equity securities. Consequently, the issuance of stock dividends is *not* considered to be a financing activity and is *not* reported on a company's statement of cash flows. However, in order to account for the $3,100 effect on the company's stockholders' equity accounts, entry (u) is made in the *upper* part of the worksheet. The $730 net decrease in retained earnings during the year has not yet been accounted for. Entry (a) increased retained earnings for the net income of $6,370, while entry (u) decreased it for the stock

Temporary differences are discussed in Chapter 18.

dividend of $3,100. The remaining decrease in retained earnings was due to the declaration and payment of $4,000 in cash dividends. This is a financing activity and is recorded in entry (v).

STEP 5: FINAL WORKSHEET ENTRY In Step 5 a check of the debit and credit entries in the upper portion of the worksheet reveals that all the changes in the noncash accounts have been accounted for. A final worksheet entry is made to record the increase in cash and to bring the debit and credit column totals into balance. This is entry (w). The debit and credit totals in the upper portion of Exhibit 21-11 are $56,800 and in the lower portion are $49,600. The worksheet for the Jones Company is now complete.

STEP 6: PREPARATION OF STATEMENT Exhibit 21-12 shows the statement of cash flows and the accompanying schedule of investing and financing activities not affecting cash for the Jones Company. They were prepared from the *lower* part of the worksheet in Exhibit 21-11, along with the beginning and ending cash balances. Note that in the Cash Flows From Investing Activities section, the company reports the payment for the purchase of land separately from the proceeds from the sale of land. Likewise, it reports the payment for the purchase of the building separately from the proceeds from the building destroyed by the earthquake. *FASB Statement No. 95* requires that a company report the cash inflows and cash outflows for related investing activities as well as for related financing activities separately and *not* "net" them against each other.[14] Note also that the reconciliation of the beginning and ending cash balances at the bottom of the statement of cash flows enables a user to trace the change in cash to related amounts on the company's successive balance sheets. Finally, note that the schedule of investing and financing activities not affecting cash discloses the $5,300 noncash transaction that had both an investing and financing element, and the $7,000 other transaction that involved two financing elements.

SPECIAL TOPICS

We designed the previous examples and discussion to illustrate the common issues involved in preparing the worksheet and statement of cash flows. For simplicity, we omitted several topics. We briefly discuss these topics in the following sections.

Sale of Depreciable Assets

A company computes the gain or loss on the sale of a depreciable asset by comparing the current book value of the asset to the selling price. When the company records the transaction it increases cash, eliminates the book value (cost and accumulated depreciation), and recognizes a gain or loss that it reports on its income statement. At the end of the year, when preparing the worksheet for the statement of cash flows, this journal entry must be properly reconstructed on the worksheet to account for the changes in the various accounts.

To illustrate, assume that during the year a company sold equipment with a cost of $2,200 and accumulated depreciation of $700 for $2,100. The company recorded an increase (debit) in Cash for $2,100, a decrease (debit) in Accumulated Depreciation for $700, and a decrease (credit) in Equipment for $2,200. Because the $2,100 selling price (proceeds) was more than the $1,500 ($2,200 − $700) book value, the company also recorded (credited) a Gain on the Sale of Equipment for $600. The proceeds of $2,100 are a cash inflow from an *investing* activity. The gain increased net income but there was no cash inflow from *operating* activities. In preparing the worksheet entry for this transaction, two modifications are made: (1) instead of debiting cash, the caption Proceeds From Sale of Equipment under the heading Cash Flows From Investing Activities is debited for the $2,100, and (2) the caption Gain on Sale of Equipment is *credited* under the heading Net Cash Flow From Operating Activities to *deduct* the gain from

---

14. *FASB Statement No. 95, op. cit.*, par. 31 and 75.

EXHIBIT 21-12 Comprehensive Statement of Cash Flows

JONES COMPANY

Statement of Cash Flows
For Year Ended December 31, 2004

Net Cash Flow From Operating Activities		
Net income		$ 6,370
Adjustments for differences between income		
flows and cash flows from operating activities:		
Add: Depreciation expense: equipment	2,820	
Depreciation expense: buildings	5,100	
Patent amortization expense	600	
Decrease in inventories	300	
Increase in income taxes payable	630	
Increase in interest payable	500	
Extraordinary loss (net) from earthquake	2,100	
Increase in deferred tax liability	180	
Bond discount amortization	100	
Less: Increase in accounts receivable	(2,000)	
Increase in prepaid expenses	(200)	
Decrease in accounts payable	(1,300)	
Gain on sale of land	(1,700)	
Net cash provided by operating activities		$13,500
Cash Flows From Investing Activities		
Payment for purchase of land	$(10,400)	
Proceeds from sale of land	3,900	
Payment for purchase of building	(15,000)	
Proceeds from building destroyed by earthquake	3,100	
Net cash used for investing activities		(18,400)
Cash Flows From Financing Activities		
Proceeds from issuance of short-term note payable	$ 2,600	
Proceeds from issuance of bonds	9,000	
Payment of dividends	(4,000)	
Net cash provided by financing activities		7,600
Net Increase in Cash (see Schedule 1)		$ 2,700
Cash, January 1, 2004		3,200
Cash, December 31, 2004		$ 5,900
Schedule 1: Investing and Financing Activities Not Affecting Cash		
Investing Activities		
Acquisition of equipment under capital lease		$ (5,300)
Financing Activities		
Issuance of capital lease obligation for equipment		5,300
Conversion of preferred stock to common stock		(7,000)
Issuance of common stock to convert preferred stock		7,000

net income to avoid double counting and to correctly show the cash provided by operating activities. The worksheet entry (in journal entry format) is as follows:

Cash Flows From Investing Activities:		
Proceeds From Sale of Equipment	2,100	
Accumulated Depreciation	700	
Equipment		2,200
Net Cash Flow From Operating Activities:		
Gain on Sale of Equipment		600

The sale of equipment (or other depreciable assets) at a loss is handled in a similar manner, except that the caption Loss on Sale of Equipment is *debited* under the heading Net Cash Flow From Operating Activities to *add back* the loss to net income because it did not involve an operating cash outflow.

Interest Paid and Income Taxes Paid

7 Compute and disclose interest paid and income taxes paid.

FASB Statement No. 95 requires that a company using the indirect method of reporting operating cash flows also disclose its interest *paid* and income taxes *paid*. This disclosure may be made in a separate schedule, narrative description, or the notes to the financial statements. Interest *expense* is affected by the cash paid, accruals, and any premium or discount amortizations on bonds (or notes) payable. Income tax *expense* is affected by the cash paid, accruals, and changes in deferred income taxes. To convert interest expense to interest paid, and to convert income tax expense to income taxes paid, the following adjustments[15] are necessary:

Interest	Income Taxes
Interest *expense*	Income tax *expense*
+ Decrease in interest payable	+ Decrease in income taxes payable
or	*or*
− Increase in interest payable	− Increase in income taxes payable
+ Amortization of premium on bonds payable	+ Decrease in deferred tax liability
or	*or*
− Amortization of discount on bonds payable	− Increase in deferred tax liability
= Interest *paid*	+ Increase in deferred tax asset
	or
	− Decrease in deferred tax asset
	= Income taxes *paid*

To illustrate, refer back to the Jones Company information shown in Exhibits 21-10 and 21-11. To determine its interest paid and income taxes paid for 2004, the Jones Company prepares the following schedules:

Bond interest expense	$1,100	Income tax expense		$3,630
− Increase in interest payable	(500)	− Increase in income taxes payable	(630)	
− Bond discount amortization	(100)			
Interest paid	$ 500	− Increase in deferred tax liability	(180)	
		Income taxes paid		$2,820

Based on these computations, Jones Company reports interest paid of $500 and income taxes paid of $2,820 in conjunction with its 2004 statement of cash flows shown in Exhibit 21-12. **Unless directed otherwise, you are *not* required to make these disclosures in the chapter homework.**

Flexibility in Reporting

FASB Statement No. 95 permits flexibility in reporting a company's net cash flow from operating activities under the indirect method. That is, the company may show the reconciliation of net income to the net cash provided by (or used in) operating activities in a separate schedule accompanying its statement of cash flows. Thus, for instance,

---

15. A company may have a valuation allowance related to its deferred tax asset. Since the valuation allowance is a contra account, it handles any changes in the account in a manner opposite to that of the deferred tax asset.

if the Jones Company used this approach, the first section of Exhibit 21-12 would appear as follows:

Net Cash Flow From Operating Activities
  Net cash provided by operating activities (Schedule 1) $13,500

Then the company would report the reconciliation of the $6,370 net income to the $13,500 net cash provided by operating activities in Schedule 1. The rest of the statement of cash flows would remain the same. (The schedule to report the investing and financing activities not affecting cash would be numbered as Schedule 2.) The advantage of reporting the reconciliation in a separate schedule is that it reduces the amount of detail that a company shows on its statement of cash flows. The disadvantage is that it removes from the statement a key factor in assessing the quality of the company's net income and its relationship to cash flows. By relegating the reconciliation to a separate schedule, this analysis may be overlooked by external users. For this reason, we advocate that a company include the reconciliation directly on its statement of cash flows.

Partial Cash Investing and Financing Activities

Throughout the previous examples and discussion, we assumed that no cash was exchanged in any "noncash" transactions involving investing and financing activities. In some transactions, however, a company may exchange a small amount of cash even though the majority of the transaction involves a noncash exchange. In other transactions, it may exchange a large amount of cash even though some of the transaction is a noncash exchange. In these cases, there are alternative ways the company may use to disclose simultaneous investing and financing activities involving an amount of cash. For instance, suppose a company acquired land for $10,000 by paying $1,000 down and signing a $9,000 note payable. One method it may use to disclose the effects of this transaction is to report the cash payment on its statement of cash flows and the noncash element on the accompanying schedule of investing and financing activities not affecting cash as follows:

Statement of Cash Flows
  Cash Flows From Investing Activities
    Payment for purchase of land $(1,000)
Schedule: Investing and Financing Activities Not Affecting Cash
  Investing Activities
    Purchase of land for $10,000 by issuance of note $(9,000)
  Financing Activities
    Issuance of note to acquire land   9,000

The advantage of this approach is that it keeps the significant noncash elements of the transaction separate from the cash elements. The disadvantage is that the external user cannot identify the relationships between the items.

When the amount of cash is large in such an exchange, it may be more appropriate to report the items in a cash flow section. Several alternative disclosure formats are acceptable. For instance, if a company acquired land for $18,000 by paying $15,000 down and signing a $3,000 note payable, it might report the effects on its statement of cash flows as follows:

Cash Flows From Investing Activities
  Purchase of land by issuance of note and cash $(18,000)
  Less: Issuance of note   3,000
  Cash payment for purchase of land $(15,000)

The advantage of this approach is that the related items are shown in close proximity. The disadvantage is that a financing element (issuance of note) is disclosed in an investing section. Each of the alternative disclosures has its advantages and disadvantages; you must use good judgment to determine the most informative disclosure for the given circumstances.

Temporary and Long-Term Investments

As we discussed in Chapter 14, a company reports its investments (whether temporary or long-term) in "available-for-sale" debt and equity securities as assets at their fair value (by using an allowance account) on its year-end balance sheet, and it includes any resulting unrealized increase or decrease in value as a component of its accumulated other comprehensive income[16] in its stockholders' equity. When the company sells this type of temporary or long-term investment, it eliminates the fair value (cost and allowance accounts) of the security, as well as any related unrealized increase or decrease in value, from its accounting records and records a realized gain or loss on the sale. It computes the realized gain or loss by comparing the proceeds to the *cost* of the security.

Because the company used an allowance account and an unrealized increase or decrease account to value the investment in available-for-sale securities, any changes in these accounts must be carefully analyzed to determine the impact (if any) on its statement of cash flows. The company reports an increase in the investment account due to the purchase of the securities on its statement of cash flows as a cash outflow for an investing activity. The entry on the worksheet to prepare the statement is also made in the usual manner. The company does *not* report any changes in the allowance and the unrealized increase or decrease accounts resulting from a revaluation to fair value at year-end on its statement of cash flows, but the changes must be accounted for on the worksheet. The company reports a decrease in the investment account due to the sale of the securities on its statement of cash flows as a cash inflow from an investing activity in the usual manner, but the worksheet entry must reconcile the changes in the investment, allowance, unrealized increase/decrease, and realized gain (or loss) accounts.

To illustrate, assume that on November 28, 2004, the Dougherty Company purchased 1,000 shares of Bear Company common stock for $40,000 as a temporary investment in available-for-sale securities. On December 31, 2004 the fair value of the stock has risen to $42 per share, so that the company reported the temporary investment as a current asset of $42,000 ($40,000 cost + $2,000 allowance), and reported a $2,000 unrealized increase in value of available-for-sale securities as a component of its accumulated other comprehensive income in its stockholders' equity on the December 31, 2004 balance sheet. For its cash flow analysis, Dougherty Company would make the following worksheet entries at the end of 2004 to reconcile the $42,000 change in the carrying value of the temporary investment:

Temporary Investment in Available-for-Sale Securities	40,000	
Cash Flows From Investing Activities:		
Payment for Purchase of Temporary Investments		40,000
Allowance for Change in Value of Investment	2,000	
Unrealized Increase in Value of Available-for-Sale		
Securities		2,000

The debit portion of the first entry is listed in the upper part of the worksheet and helps to reconcile the change in the temporary investment account. The credit portion of the first entry is listed in the lower part of the worksheet and accounts for the cash outflow for the purchase of the temporary investment, which the company reports in its 2004 statement of cash flows. Both the debit and credit portions of the second entry are listed in the upper portion of the worksheet and complete the reconciliation of the changes in the allowance and unrealized increase accounts. The company does *not* include this

---

16. The company would first include the periodic change in the unrealized increase or decrease in value in its other comprehensive income, as we discussed in Chapter 4.

portion of the increase in the carrying value of the temporary investment on its 2004 statement of cash flows because there was no cash outflow.

Now suppose that the Dougherty Company sold its investment in Bear Company stock for $45,000 on January 16, 2005. Dougherty Company would make the following worksheet entries at the end of 2005 to reconcile the changes in the various accounts:

Cash Flows From Investing Activities: Proceeds from Sale of Temporary Investment	45,000	
Temporary Investment in Available-for-Sale Securities		40,000
Net Cash Flow From Operating Activities: Gain on Sale of Temporary Investment		5,000
Unrealized Increase in Value of Available-for-Sale Securities	2,000	
Allowance for Change in Value of Investment		2,000

These two journal entries (1) record the $45,000 investing cash inflow from the sale of the securities, (2) treat the $5,000 gain on the sale as a deduction from net income to convert it from an accrual to a cash flow basis, and (3) reconcile the changes in the temporary investment, allowance, and unrealized increase accounts. The company reports the first two items on its 2005 statement of cash flows in the usual manner.

A company may also make a long-term investment in debt securities (e.g., bonds) that it expects to hold to maturity. It amortizes any premium or discount each year as an adjustment to interest revenue, and reports the investment at its book value on the year-end balance sheet. For cash flow reporting purposes, it reports the purchase as a cash outflow for investing activities. The company also adds any premium amortization on this type of investment to net income in the operating activities section of the statement of cash flows because the amortization reduced interest revenue to an amount lower than the cash received. The company subtracts any discount amortization from net income because the amortization increased interest revenue to an amount higher than the cash received. Each of these adjustments helps convert net income from an accrual to a cash basis. Although rare, if a company sells such an investment before maturity, it computes any gain or loss by comparing the proceeds to the unamortized cost. It reports the proceeds as a cash inflow from investing activities and deducts the gain from net income (or adds the loss to net income) in the usual manner on its statement of cash flows.

Cash Dividends Declared

In the previous examples, whenever we discussed cash dividends, we assumed that the dividends were declared *and* paid in the current year. The declaration and payment of cash dividends causes a decrease in both retained earnings and cash and a company reports this as a cash outflow from financing activities.

In some instances a company will declare a cash dividend in the *current* year and pay the cash dividend in the *next* year. In this situation the cash dividend is handled differently in preparing the worksheet for the statement of cash flows. The declaration of the cash dividend is recorded on the worksheet as a decrease (debit) in Retained Earnings and an increase (credit) in Dividends Payable. Because no cash outflow occurs in the current year, the company does not report dividends paid on its statement of cash flows. In the next year, the payment of the cash dividends is recorded on the worksheet as a decrease (debit) in Dividends Payable and a decrease (credit) in Cash. The company then reports the dividends paid as a cash outflow in the cash flows from financing activities section of its statement of cash flows.

When a company follows a policy of declaring a dividend in one year and paying the dividend in the next year, its Dividends Payable account balance will change during each year. A comparison of the change in the account balance to the dividends reported on the retained earnings statement will determine the worksheet entry necessary to account for the cash dividends.

Financial Institutions

When the FASB was deliberating on the requirements of *FASB Statement No. 95*, one issue that created controversy was the proper reporting of interest collected and interest paid, and collections and payments of notes receivable and notes payable. Most companies do not deal with notes receivable and notes payable as a primary part of their operating activities. On the other hand, notes are a major aspect of the operating activities of banks (and other financial institutions). Banks frequently buy and sell notes, mortgages, and similar securities. The question arose as to whether companies should be required to report the related cash inflows and outflows (i.e., interest and principal) as operating activities or as investing and financing activities. As we discussed in the chapter, after much deliberation, the FASB finally concluded that companies must report interest collected and interest paid as cash flows relating to operating activities to provide consistency with the reporting of the related interest revenue and interest expense on the income statement. However, the Board concluded that companies must report the collections and payments of the principal of notes receivable and notes payable as cash flows relating to investing and financing activities, respectively.

In *FASB Statement No. 102* the FASB reversed parts of its original requirements. For banks, brokers and dealers in securities, and other similar companies that hold loans for resale on a short-term basis or carry securities in a "trading account," other requirements now apply. (A trading account includes securities that are acquired specifically for resale and are turned over very quickly.) The Board concluded that financial institutions must report the cash flows from the purchases or sales of these trading securities in the operating activities section of the statement of cash flows.[17] In coming to this conclusion, the FASB reasoned that these types of assets for financial institutions are similar to inventory for other businesses and, as such, are part of the operating cycle.

Furthermore, in *FASB Statement No. 115* the FASB required that financial institutions report trading securities at fair value and report any resulting unrealized holding gain or loss in net income. Consequently, for reporting its operating cash flows under the indirect method, a financial institution adds (deducts) an unrealized holding loss (gain) on trading securities to net income to help adjust net income from an accrual to a cash flow basis.

As we discussed earlier in the chapter, in most situations *FASB Statement No. 95* does *not* allow a company to "net" its cash outflows against cash inflows for reporting the results of related investing or financing activities. An exception is made for certain activities of banks and other financial institutions. These institutions are allowed to report the net cash flows for (1) deposits and withdrawals with other financial institutions, (2) time deposits accepted and repaid, and (3) loans made to customers and principal collections of these loans.[18] This exception is allowed because showing these items on a "gross" basis provides information that is costly to accumulate and is of limited value to external users.

Effects of Exchange Rates

Many companies have operations in foreign countries. When a company with foreign operations prepares its statement of cash flows, the statement must disclose the "reporting currency equivalent" of the "foreign currency" cash flows using the exchange rates in effect at the time of the cash flows. It may use a weighted average exchange rate for the period if this yields similar results. On the statement, then, a company reports the

---

17. "Statement of Cash Flows—Exemption of Certain Enterprises and Classification of Cash Flows from Certain Securities Acquired for Resale," *FASB Statement of Financial Accounting Standards No. 102* (Norwalk, Conn.: FASB, 1989), par. 8 and 9.

18. "Statement of Cash Flows—Net Reporting of Certain Cash Receipts and Cash Payments and Classification of Cash Flows from Hedging Transactions," *FASB Statement of Financial Accounting Standards No. 104* (Norwalk, Conn.: FASB, 1989), par. 7.

effect of exchange rate changes on cash balances held in foreign currencies as a separate part of the reconciliation of the change in cash during the period.[19]

Cash Flow Per Share

In accordance with generally accepted accounting principles, a company must report the earnings per share on the face of its income statement. Although the cash flow information presented in a company's statement of cash flows is useful in evaluating the performance of the company, the FASB believes that cash flow (or any component) is not an alternative to income as an indicator of a company's performance. Consequently, in accordance with *FASB Statement No. 95*, a company is *not* allowed to report a cash flow per share amount in its financial statements.[20] Users often compute other cash flow ratios, however, as we discussed in Chapter 5.

International Accounting Differences

International accounting standards require a company to include a cash flow statement as one of its basic financial statements. These standards define operating, investing, and financing activities in a manner similar to U.S. standards. A company may present its operating cash flows under either the indirect or direct method. However, contrary to U.S. standards, international standards do not require a company using the direct method to reconcile its net income to its operating cash flows. There are also a few differences in the way a company presents certain items under international standards as compared to U.S. standards. For instance, under international standards a company is (1) allowed to report dividends paid as either an operating cash outflow or a financing cash outflow, (2) allowed to report payments of income taxes identified with financing and investing transactions as financing and investing activities, and (3) allowed to report cash flow per share. Finally, contrary to U.S. standards, international accounting standards encourage a company to disclose any undrawn borrowing facilities that may be available for future operating activities, the cash flows that represent increases in its operating capacity separately from the cash flows that are needed to maintain its operating capacity, and the operating, investing, and financing activities of each of its reported industry and geographic segments.

APPENDIX: DIRECT METHOD FOR REPORTING OPERATING CASH FLOWS

Throughout the main part of this chapter, we used the *indirect* method to report the net cash flow from operating activities on the statement of cash flows. Most companies (over 98%) use this method. Under this method, we started with net income and adjusted (reconciled) it for any noncash items and for changes in current assets (except cash) and current liabilities to convert net income to net cash provided by (or used in) operating activities. This approach has the advantage of providing information about lead and lag intervals between income and operating cash flows.

FASB Statement No. 95 allows a company to use either the indirect method or the direct method to report the cash flows from operating activities on its statement of cash flows, but encourages the use of the *direct method*. As we briefly discussed earlier in the chapter, **under the direct method a company deducts its operating cash outflows from its operating cash inflows to determine its net cash provided by (or used in) operating activities.** This approach has the advantage of separating the company's operating cash receipts from operating cash payments, and of directly showing the cash

19. *FASB Statement No. 95, op. cit.*, par. 25.
20. *Ibid.*, par. 33.

it paid for interest and income taxes. Each of these disclosures may be useful in estimating its future cash flows. Because of the FASB's support for the direct method, use of this method is likely to increase. Consequently, we explain the direct method in this Appendix.

The direct method is an alternative to the indirect method for a company to report its net cash flow from *operating* activities. However, the company reports its cash flows from *investing* activities and cash flows from *financing* activities on the statement of cash flows in exactly the same manner as we discussed earlier. Therefore, in this Appendix we focus on determining and reporting the cash flows from *operating* activities. However, because there are some slight differences in *preparing* information concerning investing and financing activities, we discuss these differences as well.

OPERATING CASH FLOWS

According to *FASB Statement No. 95*, under the direct method a company reports its operating cash inflows separately from its operating cash outflows. We discuss each of these classifications in the following sections.

Operating Cash Inflows

8 Identify the operating cash inflows and outflows under the direct method.

Under the direct method a company reports its cash inflows from operating activities in three categories: (1) collections from customers, (2) interest and dividends collected, and (3) other operating receipts, if any. Generally, these cash inflows from operating activities are calculated by an analysis of income statement and balance sheet items as follows:

1. *Collections from Customers.* Sales revenue, plus decrease in accounts receivable or minus increase in accounts receivable, and plus increase in deferred revenues or minus decrease in deferred revenues.
2. *Interest and Dividends Collected.* Interest revenue and dividend revenue, plus decrease in interest/dividends receivable or minus increase in interest/dividends receivable, and plus amortization of premium on investment in bonds or minus amortization of discount on investment in bonds.
3. *Other Operating Receipts.* Other operating revenues, minus gains on disposals of assets and liabilities, and minus investment income recognized under the equity method.

Most of the adjustments relate to the company's operating cycle. We illustrated one adjustment earlier in Exhibit 21-5. We discuss and illustrate these adjustments later in this Appendix.

Operating Cash Outflows

A company reports its cash outflows from operating activities in five categories: (1) payments to suppliers,[21] (2) payments to employees, (3) payments of interest, (4) other

---

21. *FASB Statement No. 95* (par. 27) combines payments to suppliers and payments to employees into one category. However, it encourages companies to provide further breakdowns of operating cash receipts and operating cash payments, when useful. The authors believe that separating payments to suppliers from payments to employees may be useful to different external users, and do so throughout this Appendix. In a manufacturing company, a separation of payments to suppliers and payments to employees may not be practical. This is because the company may record various manufacturing costs, including direct and indirect materials as well as direct and indirect labor, directly in the goods in process inventory and not show them as separate expenses. In such a case it would be difficult to separate the related cash flows, so that reporting the combined payments to suppliers and employees may be the only practical disclosure.

operating payments (if any), and (5) payments of income taxes. Generally, these cash outflows for operating activities are calculated by an analysis of income statement and balance sheet items as follows:

1. *Payments to Suppliers.* Cost of goods sold, plus increase in inventory or minus decrease in inventory, plus decrease in accounts payable or minus increase in accounts payable.
2. *Payments to Employees.* Salaries (wages) expense, plus decrease in salaries payable or minus increase in salaries payable.
3. *Payments of Interest.* Interest expense, plus decrease in interest payable or minus increase in interest payable, plus amortization of premium on bonds payable or minus amortization of discount on bonds payable.
4. *Other Operating Payments.* Other operating expenses, plus increase in prepaid items or minus decrease in prepaid items; minus depreciation, depletion, and amortization expense; minus losses on disposals of assets and liabilities; minus investment loss recognized under the equity method.
5. *Payments of Income Taxes.* Income tax expense, plus decrease in income taxes payable or minus increase in income taxes payable, plus decrease in deferred tax liability or minus increase in deferred tax liability.[22]

Most of the adjustments relate to the company's operating cycle. We illustrated one adjustment earlier in Exhibit 21-5. We discuss and illustrate these adjustments later in this Appendix.

Diagram of Operating Cash Flows

To summarize the discussion in the preceding sections, under the *direct* method a company computes the cash inflows from operating activities for its statement of cash flows by adjusting the various revenue accounts for changes in certain asset accounts (primarily current assets involved in the operating cycle) and to eliminate certain "noncash" revenues (gains). The company computes the cash outflows for operating activities by adjusting the various expense accounts for changes in certain liability (and asset) accounts (primarily current liabilities and current assets in the operating cycle) and to eliminate certain "noncash" expenses (losses). Exhibit 21-13 shows these adjustments. The adjustments may have to be modified depending on the manner in which the company reports and classifies the related items in its financial statements. For instance, an increase in deferred revenue of a retail company may be due to a collection of rent (for a sub-lease) in advance. In this case the adjustment is to other revenue instead of sales revenues. Under the direct method, then, the company's net cash provided by (or used in) operating activities is the difference between the cash inflows from operating activities and the cash outflows for operating activities, as computed according to Exhibit 21-13.

If a company uses the direct method of reporting its operating cash flows, *FASB Statement No. 95* requires the company to reconcile its net income to the net cash provided by (or used) in operating activities in a separate schedule accompanying its statement of cash flows. This reconciliation is intended to link the information on the income statement, prepared on an accrual basis, with the operating activities information on the statement of cash flows, prepared on a cash basis. This reconciliation is, in effect, prepared under the *indirect* method. Because we fully discussed the indirect method of reconciling net income to operating cash flows in the main part of the chapter, we do not repeat the discussion here.

---

22. For a company that has a deferred tax asset, it adds an increase in the deferred tax asset to income tax expense or subtracts a decrease. It handles a change in a related valuation allowance (contra account) in an opposite manner.

EXHIBIT 21-13   Major Adjustments to Convert Income Statement Amounts to Operating Cash Flows

Income Statement Amounts	Adjustments	Cash Flows From Operating Activities	Net Operating Cash Flows
Sales revenue	+Decrease in accounts receivable or −Increase in accounts receivable +Increase in deferred revenues or −Decrease in deferred revenues	= Collections from customers	Cash Inflows From Operating Activities
Interest revenue and dividend revenue	+Decrease in interest receivable or −Increase in interest receivable +Amortization of premium on investment in bonds or −Amortization of discount on investment in bonds	= Interest and dividends collected	
Other revenues	−Gains on disposals of assets and liabilities[a] −Investment income (equity method)[a]	= Other operating receipts	
Cost of goods sold	+Increase in inventory or −Decrease in inventory +Decrease in accounts payable or −Increase in accounts payable	= Payments to suppliers	Cash Outflows For Operating Activities
Salaries expense	+Decrease in salaries payable or −Increase in salaries payable	= Payments to employees	
Interest expense	+Decrease in interest payable or −Increase in interest payable +Amortization of premium on bonds payable or −Amortization of discount on bonds payable	= Payments of interest	
Other expenses	+Increase in prepaid items or −Decrease in prepaid items −Depreciation, depletion, and amortization expense[a] −Losses on disposals of assets and liabilities[a] −Investment loss (equity method)[a]	= Other operating payments	
Income tax expense	+Decrease in income taxes payable or −Increase in income taxes payable +Decrease in deferred tax liability[b] or −Increase in deferred tax liability	= Payments of income taxes	

a. Unless listed as separate items on income statement
b. A change in a deferred tax asset is handled in an opposite manner.

PROCEDURES FOR STATEMENT PREPARATION

When a company uses the direct method to prepare the information for its statement of cash flows, it may use either the visual inspection method or the worksheet method depending on the complexity of the accounting information. The information is obtained, however, in a slightly different manner. Normally, under the direct method, the information for the statement of cash flows is obtained from the following working papers:

1. **Post-closing trial balance (or balance sheet) from** *previous* **period.** Recall that a post-closing trial balance contains the debit and credit balances of all the *permanent* accounts in a company's general ledger. In other words, a post-closing trial balance of the previous period contains the same information as the *ending balance sheet* of the previous period.
2. **Adjusted trial balance of** *current* **period.** Recall that an adjusted trial balance contains the debit and credit balances (after adjustments but before closing) of all the temporary and permanent accounts in a company's general ledger. In other words, an adjusted trial balance of the current period contains the *balance sheet*, *income statement*, and *retained earnings statement* information for the current period.

In addition, other information is needed to explain the changes in the company's balance sheet (permanent) accounts (other than cash). This information is obtained from its accounting records. In complex situations, use of the post-closing trial balance of the prior period and the adjusted trial balance of the current period is the most efficient way to prepare the statement of cash flows. In simpler situations, however, the statement may be developed based on the information contained in the beginning and ending balance sheets, the income statement, and the retained earnings statement of the current year.

Visual Inspection Method

Under the visual inspection approach, the steps to complete the statement of cash flows using the direct method are virtually the same as those for the indirect method, except that the information for the cash flows from operating activities section is computed as follows:

9 Compute the operating cash flows under the direct method.

> Make adjustments to the applicable revenues for the period (e.g., to sales revenue for a change in accounts receivable) to determine the amounts of collections from customers, interest and dividend receipts, and other operating receipts, if any. Make adjustments to the applicable expenses for the period (e.g., to cost of goods sold for a change in accounts payable) to determine the amounts of payments to suppliers, payments to employees, payments of interest, other operating payments, if any, and payments of income taxes. Exhibit 21-13 is helpful for these adjustments.

Once the operating activities section is completed, the investing activities section and the financing activities section are completed by analyzing the changes in the other balance sheet accounts in the same way as we discussed for the indirect method.

To illustrate preparation of the operating activities section, assume that the following income statement items were taken from the adjusted trial balance of the Betha Company at the end of 2004:

	Debit	Credit
Sales		$94,000
Interest revenue		5,400
Cost of goods sold	$43,000	
Salaries expense	18,500	
Depreciation expense	11,000	
Interest expense	9,200	
Other expenses	4,700	
Income tax expense	3,900	

Also assume that a comparison of the post-closing trial balance for 2003 with the adjusted trial balance for 2004 shows the following *changes* in selected balance sheet accounts:

Accounts receivable	$ 8,200 credit
Interest receivable	1,200 debit
Inventory	6,300 debit
Prepaid expenses	600 debit
Accumulated depreciation	11,000 credit
Accounts payable	4,800 credit
Salaries payable	500 debit
Income taxes payable	300 credit
Discount on bonds payable	200 credit

Based on the preceding information, Exhibit 21-14 is prepared to determine each of the operating cash inflows and outflows. The $94,000 of sales revenue is increased by the $8,200 decrease (credit) in accounts receivable to determine the $102,200 collections from customers. This is because the company's cash collections exceeded its sales during the year. The $5,400 interest revenue is decreased by the $1,200 increase (debit) in interest receivable to determine the $4,200 interest collected because the company received less cash than it recorded as interest revenue. The total operating cash inflows were $106,400 in 2004.

The $43,000 cost of goods sold is adjusted for two items. It is increased for the $6,300 increase (debit) in inventory because the company's purchases exceeded its cost of goods sold by that amount. It is decreased by the $4,800 increase (credit) in accounts payable because the company's cash payments were less than its purchases. Thus, payments to suppliers totaled $44,500 in 2004. The $18,500 of salaries expense is increased by the $500 decrease (debit) in salaries payable to determine the $19,000 paid to employees, because salaries paid exceeded salaries expense. The decrease (credit) in the discount on bonds payable resulted from the amortization of the discount. Recall that the amortization of the discount on bonds payable increases interest expense to an amount greater than the cash the company paid for interest. Therefore, the $200 decrease (credit) to the discount on bonds payable is subtracted from the $9,200 interest expense to determine the $9,000 interest paid. The $4,700 of other expenses are increased by the $600 increase (debit) in prepaid expenses to determine the $5,300 other operating payments, because the company's cash payments for prepaid items exceeded its expenses. Note that the $11,000 depreciation expense (debit) is the same as the

---

EXHIBIT 21-14   Schedule to Compute Operating Cash Flows

Income Statement Amounts		Adjustments			Operating Cash Flows
Sales	$ 94,000	+ Decrease in accounts receivable of	$8,200	= $102,200	Collections from customers
Interest revenue	5,400	− Increase in interest receivable of	1,200	= 4,200	Interest collected
				$106,400	Operating cash inflows
Cost of goods sold	$(43,000)	{ + Increase in inventory of − Increase in accounts payable of	6,300 4,800 }	= $ (44,500)	Payments to suppliers
Salaries expense	(18,500)	+ Decrease in salaries payable of	500	= (19,000)	Payments to employees
Interest expense	(9,200)	− Decrease in discount on bonds payable (amortization) of	200	= (9,000)	Payments of interest
Other expenses	(4,700)	+ Increase in prepaid expenses of	600	= (5,300)	Other operating payments
Income tax expense	(3,900)	− Increase in income taxes payable of	300	= (3,600)	Payments of income taxes
				$(81,400)	Operating cash outflows
				$ 25,000	Net cash provided by operating activities

$11,000 credit to accumulated depreciation. Because this is a "noncash" income statement item and is listed separately from other operating expenses, no adjustment is made for operating cash flows. The $3,900 income tax expense is decreased by the $300 increase (credit) to income taxes payable to determine the $3,600 payments of income taxes, because the company paid less taxes than it recorded as expense. The total operating cash outflows were $81,400 in 2004, so that $25,000 net cash was provided by operating activities during 2004.

Exhibit 21-15 shows the cash flows from operating activities section of the Betha Company's statement of cash flows, under the direct method. The company includes cash flows from investing activities and the cash flows from financing activities in the usual manner to complete the statement of cash flows.

EXHIBIT 21-15 Operating Cash Flows (Direct Method)

BETHA COMPANY

Statement of Cash Flows (Partial)
For Year Ended December 31, 2004

Cash Flows From Operating Activities		
Cash Inflows:		
Collections from customers	$102,200	
Interest collected	4,200	
Cash inflows from operating activities		$106,400
Cash Outflows:		
Payments to suppliers	$ (44,500)	
Payments to employees	(19,000)	
Payments of interest	(9,000)	
Other operating payments	(5,300)	
Payments of income taxes	(3,600)	
Cash outflows for operating activities		(81,400)
Net cash provided by operating activities		$ 25,000

Worksheet Method

Under the worksheet approach, the steps completed using the direct method are very similar to those of the indirect method. There are enough slight differences, however, that we list all of the steps using the direct method in Exhibit 21-16, after which we present an example.

EXAMPLE: WORKSHEET AND DIRECT METHOD

To illustrate the use of a worksheet under the direct method, consider Exhibit 21-17. Assume that the post-closing trial balance and adjusted trial balance were obtained from the Copeland Company's accounting records. In addition, the following information was extracted from the accounting records for 2004:

1. Investments in nonmarketable securities costing $2,000 were sold for $2,800.
2. Equipment was purchased at a cost of $24,700.
3. Common stock was issued for $10,000.
4. Dividends of $3,500 were declared and paid.

After entering the accounts and amounts of the trial balances, the changes in the accounts are entered in the appropriate change column of the worksheet. Then, based

EXHIBIT 21-16   Steps in Worksheet Approach for Direct Method

Step 1. Prepare the column headings on a worksheet (see Exhibit 21-17). Then enter the account titles and the debit and credit amounts of the post-closing trial balance from the previous year and the adjusted trial balance for the current year in the respective columns. Total the amount columns to check the equality.

Step 2. Compare each account balance in the post-closing trial balance and adjusted trial balance, and record the debit or credit difference in the Change column. Note that each revenue and expense account listed on the adjusted trial balance will not have a beginning balance; in that case the ending balance is the change amount. (To simplify the worksheet, sometimes the debit and credit amounts of the accounts in the trial balances are omitted, and only the changes in the accounts are listed.) Total the amount columns to check the equality.

Step 3. Directly below the account titles, add the following headings:
A. Cash Flows From Operating Activities
B. Cash Flows From Investing Activities
C. Cash Flows From Financing Activities
D. Investing and Financing Activities Not Affecting Cash
Under the heading Cash Flows From Operating Activities, list the eight possible inflow and outflow captions (e.g., collections from customers). Leave sufficient room below each of the subheadings so that each cash flow can be listed where appropriate.

Step 4. Account for all the changes in the noncash accounts that occurred during the current period. *Reconstruct* the journal entries that caused the changes in the noncash accounts directly on the worksheet, making the necessary modifications to show the cash inflows and outflows related to operating, investing, and financing activities. Use the following general rules for the worksheet entries:

A. *Start with the routine, ongoing revenue and expense accounts.* The changes in these accounts during the year represent potential operating cash inflows or outflows. Therefore, the entry on the worksheet is to debit or credit the related operating cash inflow or outflow caption and to credit or debit the revenue or expense account. Observe that these changes represent potential cash flows. They may have to be adjusted later for changes in certain current assets (e.g., accounts receivable) and current liabilities (e.g., accounts payable), as well as other accounts, to reflect the actual cash flows.

   Note that there are two exceptions to the previous procedures. First, the worksheet entries for any noncash revenues and expenses (e.g., depreciation expense) are made in the usual manner, without any modifications.

   Second, worksheet entries are *not* prepared at this time to account for gains or losses (either ordinary or extraordinary). The changes in these accounts will be accounted for later when dealing with the investing or financing transactions to which they relate (e.g., retirement of bonds at a gain).

B. *Account for the changes in the current asset (except cash) and current liability accounts.* Because most of the changes in the current assets and current liabilities are part of the *operating cycle*, the impacts of these changes on cash are listed as adjustments to the related operating cash inflow or outflow. There are several exceptions to this procedure. These exceptions involve changes in short-term notes receivable and notes payable, changes in temporary investments (i.e., marketable securities), and changes in dividends payable. These changes are the results of investing or financing activities and are handled like the changes in the noncurrent accounts discussed in Step 4(C).

C. *Account for the changes in the remaining current assets (except cash) and current liabilities, as well as the changes in noncurrent accounts.* Review each account and determine the journal entry responsible for its change. Identify whether the transaction involves an operating,[a] investing, or financing activity. If the transaction involves an investing or financing activity, make the entry on the worksheet with the following changes:

   1. If the entry affects cash, replace a debit to cash with either an investing or financing cash inflow caption, and list the item as a debit (inflow) under the proper heading of the worksheet. Replace a credit to cash with a proper cash outflow caption, and list the item as a credit (outflow) under the proper heading of the worksheet. In the case of a transaction involving a gain or loss, record the gain or loss portion of the worksheet entry in the usual manner.

continued

EXHIBIT 21-16, Continued

2. If the entry does not affect an operating activity or cash, it is a "simultaneous" financing and/or investing transaction. For this type of transaction, create "expanded" entries on the worksheet to record both the financing and/or investing activities. The first entry shows the financing aspect of the exchange, while the second entry shows the investing aspect. These types of transactions are disclosed on a schedule accompanying the statement of cash flows.

Step 5. Make a final worksheet entry to record the net change in cash. The worksheet entries must account for all the changes in the noncash accounts recorded in Step 2. The difference between the total cash inflows and outflows must be equal to the change in the Cash account. Total the debit and credit worksheet entries in the upper and lower portions of the worksheet to verify that the respective totals are equal.

Step 6. Prepare the statement of cash flows and accompanying schedule. Use the information developed in the *lower* portion of the worksheet, along with the beginning and ending cash balances.

a. The primary examples of changes in noncurrent accounts that affect operating activities are the amortization of premiums or discounts on bonds payable or investments in bonds, changes in deferred taxes, and changes in prepaid/accrued pension costs. In these cases, the related income statement item (interest expense or interest revenue, income tax expense, and pension expense) has already been treated as an adjustment to an operating cash flow (payment of interest or receipt of interest, payment of income taxes, and payment of pensions) in Step 4A. Therefore, the worksheet entry involves a direct adjustment to the operating cash flow. For instance, a change (credit) in the discount on bonds payable due to amortization is accounted for as a debit to Cash Flows From Operating Activities: Payments of Interest and as a credit to Discount on Bonds Payable to adjust for the lesser cash outflow.

---

on the preceding information, entries (a) through (r) are entered on the worksheet to complete it. We briefly explain each of the worksheet entries next.

Entries (a) and (b) account for the sales and interest revenue and record the potential collections from customers and receipts of interest. (There are no other operating receipts.) Entries (c), (d), (e), (f), and (g) account for the cost of goods sold, salaries expense, interest expense, other expenses, and income tax expense, and record the potential payments to suppliers, payments to employees, payments of interest, other operating payments, and payments of income taxes. Entry (h) accounts for the depreciation expense and increase in accumulated depreciation. Note that it is made in the normal manner in the upper part of the worksheet and, therefore, has no impact on the operating cash flows. The entry is necessary, however, to help account for the changes in all the income statement and balance sheet accounts.

Entries (i) through (m) account for the effect of the changes in the current assets and current liabilities on the "potential" operating cash flows recorded earlier. Entry (i) reduces the collections from customers because of the increase in accounts receivable. Entries (j) and (k) reduce the payments to suppliers because of the decrease in inventory and the increase in accounts payable. Entry (l) increases the payments to employees because of the decrease in salaries payable. Finally, entry (m) reduces the interest payments because of the increase in interest payable. There are no adjustments to the other operating payments or to the payments of income taxes in this example.

Entries (n) through (q) record the investing and financing cash flows. Entry (n) records the $2,800 investing cash inflow from the sale of investments costing $2,000. Note that the $800 gain is recorded in the usual manner and accounts for that respective income statement item. Entry (o) records the investing cash outflow for the purchase of equipment. Entry (p) records the financing cash inflow from the sale of common stock. Entry (q) records the financing cash outflow for the payment of dividends.

Entry (r) is the final entry and records the increase in cash. The debit and credit columns in the upper and lower parts are totaled to check for equality and the worksheet is complete. Exhibit 21-18 shows the statement of cash flows of the Copeland Company, prepared from the worksheet in Exhibit 21-17. Note that the only difference

EXHIBIT 21-17   Cash Flow Worksheet for 2004 (Copeland Company)

Accounts	12/31/03 Post-Closing Trial Balance Debit	Credit	12/31/04 Adjusted Trial Balance Debit	Credit	Change Debit	Credit	Worksheet Entries Debit		Credit	
Cash	5,300		9,800		4,500		(r)	4,500		
Accounts receivable	9,600		10,900		1,300		(i)	1,300		
Inventory	12,500		11,000			1,500			(j)	1,500
Investments	22,000		20,000			2,000			(n)	2,000
Property and equipment	82,600		107,300		24,700		(o)	24,700		
Accumulated depreciation		32,800		41,900		9,100			(h)	9,100
Accounts payable		10,300		12,100		1,800			(k)	1,800
Salaries payable		1,100		800	300		(l)	300		
Interest payable		300		500		200			(m)	200
Notes payable		34,000		34,000		0				
Common stock, no par		30,000		40,000		10,000			(p)	10,000
Retained earnings		23,500		20,000	3,500		(q)	3,500		
Sales				98,700		98,700			(a)	98,700
Interest revenue				2,500		2,500			(b)	2,500
Gain on sale of investments				800		800			(n)	800
Cost of goods sold			51,000		51,000		(c)	51,000		
Salaries expense			23,000		23,000		(d)	23,000		
Depreciation expense			9,100		9,100		(h)	9,100		
Interest expense			4,000		4,000		(e)	4,000		
Other expenses			1,900		1,900		(f)	1,900		
Income tax expense			3,300		3,300		(g)	3,300		
Totals	132,000	132,000	251,300	251,300	126,600	126,600		126,600		126,600
Cash Flows From Operating Activities										
Collections from customers							(a)	98,700	(i)	1,300
Interest and dividends collected							(b)	2,500		
Other operating receipts										
Payments to suppliers							(j)	1,500	(c)	51,000
							(k)	1,800		
Payments to employees									(d)	23,000
									(l)	300
Payments of interest							(m)	200	(e)	4,000
Other operating payments									(f)	1,900
Payments of income taxes									(g)	3,300
Cash Flows From Investing Activities										
Proceeds from sale of investments							(n)	2,800		
Payment for purchase of equipment									(o)	24,700
Cash Flows From Financing Activities										
Proceeds from issuance of common stock							(p)	10,000		
Payment of dividends									(q)	3,500
Net Increase in Cash									(r)	4,500
Totals								117,500		117,500

between this statement, prepared under the direct method, and a statement of cash flows prepared under the indirect method is in the presentation of the cash flows from operating activities. (Remember, however, that a separate schedule reconciling net income to the net cash provided by operating activities would accompany the statement of cash flows under the direct method; we do not illustrate the schedule here.) The presentations of the cash flows from investing and financing activities are identical under both methods. Although most companies will continue to use the indirect method, with the encouragement of the FASB, more companies may begin using the direct method.

EXHIBIT 21-18 Statement of Cash Flows (Direct Method)

COPELAND COMPANY

Statement of Cash Flows
For Year Ended December 31, 2004

Cash Flows From Operating Activities		
Cash Inflows:		
Collections from customers	$ 97,400	
Interest and dividends collected	2,500	
Cash inflows from operating activities		$99,900
Cash Outflows:		
Payments to suppliers	$(47,700)	
Payments to employees	(23,300)	
Payments of interest	(3,800)	
Other operating payments	(1,900)	
Payments of income taxes	(3,300)	
Cash outflows for operating activities		(80,000)
Net cash provided by operating activities		$19,900
Cash Flows From Investing Activities		
Proceeds from sale of investments	$ 2,800	
Payment for purchase of equipment	(24,700)	
Net cash used for investing activities		(21,900)
Cash Flows From Financing Activities		
Proceeds from issuance of common stock	$ 10,000	
Payment of dividends	(3,500)	
Net cash provided by financing activities		6,500
Net Increase in Cash		$ 4,500
Cash, January 1, 2004		5,300
Cash, December 31, 2004		$ 9,800

SUMMARY

At the beginning of the chapter, we identified several objectives you would accomplish after reading the chapter. The objectives are listed below, followed by a brief summary of the key points in the chapter discussion.

1. **Define operating, investing, and financing activities.** A company's operating activities include all its transactions involving acquiring, selling, and delivering goods for sale, as well as providing services. Its investing activities include its transactions involving lending money and collecting on loans, acquiring and selling investments, and acquiring and selling property, plant, and equipment. Its financing activities include its transactions involving obtaining resources from owners and providing them with a return on, and of, their investment, as well as obtaining money and other resources from creditors and repaying the amounts borrowed.

2. **Know the categories of inflows and outflows of cash.** A company's inflows of cash come from decreases in assets other than cash, increases in liabilities, and increases in stockholders' equity. Its outflows of cash come from increases in assets other than cash, decreases in liabilities, and decreases in stockholders' equity.

3. **Classify cash flows as operating, investing, or financing.** Operating cash inflows (outflows) come from increases (decreases) in stockholders' equity due to revenues (expenses), adjusted for changes in certain current assets and current liabilities. Investing cash inflows (outflows) come from decreases (increases) in noncurrent assets and certain current assets. Financing cash inflows (outflows) come from increases (decreases) in noncurrent liabilities, stockholders' equity, and certain current liabilities.

4. **Explain the direct and indirect methods for reporting operating cash flows.** Under the direct method, a company deducts its operating cash outflows from its operating cash inflows to determine its net cash flow from operating activities. Under the indirect method, a company adjusts its net income for differences between income flows and cash flows for operating activities to determine its net cash flow from operating activities.

5. **Prepare a simple statement of cash flows.** To complete a simple statement of cash flows, prepare the heading and major sections, and list the net change in cash at the bottom. Next, list net income under the operating activities section. Then list the increase or decrease in each balance sheet account as a cash inflow or outflow (or adjustment) in the appropriate operating, investing, or financing section. Subtotal each section, add them together to calculate the net change in cash, then add the net change in cash to the beginning cash balance to determine the ending cash balance. Verify that this amount is the same as the ending cash balance reported on the balance sheet.

6. **Use a worksheet for a statement of cash flows.** Set up a worksheet that shows the change in the balance of each balance sheet account at the top and the sections of the statement of cash flows (and a section for noncash investing and financing activities) at the bottom. Make worksheet entries to account for the changes in all the noncash balance sheet accounts, making certain modifications to show the cash inflows and outflows for operating, investing, and financing activities. Make a final worksheet entry to record the net change in cash. Total the debit and credit worksheet entries in the upper and lower portions to verify that the respective totals are equal.

7. **Compute and disclose interest paid and income taxes paid.** To compute interest paid, start with interest expense and adjust this amount for any increase (decrease) in interest payable and any bond premium (discount) amortization. To compute income taxes paid, start with income tax expense and adjust this amount for any increase (decrease) in income taxes payable, deferred tax liability, and deferred tax asset. Disclose interest paid and income taxes paid in a separate schedule, narrative description, or notes to the company's financial statements.

8. **Identify the operating cash inflows and outflows under the direct method (Appendix).** The operating cash inflows are: (1) collections from customers, (2) interest and dividends collected, and (3) other operating receipts. The outflows are: (1) payments to suppliers, (2) payments to employees, (3) payments of interest, (4) other operating payments, and (5) payments of income taxes.

9. **Compute the operating cash flows under the direct method (Appendix).** To determine the operating cash inflows, make adjustments to the applicable revenues for changes in related balance sheet accounts to determine the collections from customers, interest and dividends collected, and other operating receipts. To determine the operating cash outflows, make adjustments to the applicable expenses for changes in related balance sheet accounts to determine the payments to suppliers, to employees, of interest, for other operating items, and for income taxes. Subtract the total operating cash outflows from the total operating cash inflows to determine the net cash flow from operating activities.

QUESTIONS

Q21-1 What is a *statement of cash flows*?

Q21-2 Briefly describe the three types of activities of a company reported in its statement of cash flows.

Q21-3 What does the information in a statement of cash flows help external users to assess?

Q21-4 Name the five items a company's statement of cash flows must clearly show. What items are reported in a separate schedule accompanying the statement?

Q21-5 What are "cash equivalents"? How does a company's reporting on its cash and cash equivalents affect the statement of cash flows?

Q21-6 What are the three categories of a company's inflows of cash? What are the three categories of a company's outflows of cash?

Q21-7 Starting with the basic accounting equation, derive a set of equations that illustrate the relationship between increases (decreases) in cash and increases (decreases) in assets other than cash, liabilities, and stockholders' equity.

Q21-8 Briefly describe a company's operating cycle and the relationship of its various stages to cash inflows and outflows.

Q21-9 What are the two ways to calculate and report a company's net cash flow from operating activities? Briefly describe each method.

Q21-10 Briefly describe the *indirect method* for reporting a company's net cash flow from operating activities. List several adjustments to net income and indicate whether they are additions or subtractions.

Q21-11 Give two examples of a company's (a) cash inflows from investing activities, and (b) cash outflows for investing activities.

Q21-12 Give two examples of a company's (a) cash inflows from financing activities, and (b) cash outflows for financing activities.

Q21-13 Give two examples of a company's investing and financing activities not affecting cash.

Q21-14 What is the *visual inspection method*? List the steps in this method.

Q21-15 Briefly describe the *worksheet method* of analyzing the information for a company's statement of cash flows. (Do *not* list the steps in preparation.)

Q21-16 Indicate how a company computes the amount of interest and income taxes that it paid during the year.

Q21-17 What two alternatives are allowed for *where* a company may disclose the net cash flow from operating activities prepared under the indirect method in regard to its statement of cash flows?

Q21-18 A company purchases equipment costing $12,500 by paying $5,000 down and signing a $7,500 note payable. Illustrate two ways of disclosing the effects of this transaction in regard to the statement of cash flows.

Q21-19 (*Appendix*) Define the *direct* method of reporting the cash flows from operating activities of a company.

Q21-20 (*Appendix*) List the three operating cash inflows that a company reports under the direct method.

Q21-21 (*Appendix*) List the five operating cash outflows that a company reports under the direct method.

Q21-22 (*Appendix*) Briefly describe how to determine each of the operating cash inflows and operating cash outflows under the direct method.

CASES

COMMUNICATION

C21-1 Financial Statement Interrelationships
Prepare an outline of the general format of the statement of cash flows (indirect method). Include examples of cash inflows and outflows that would be reported under each major section. Finally, discuss the information that is disclosed on the income statement, balance sheet, and statement of cash flows, respectively, that is not disclosed on the other statements.

C21-2 Statement of Cash Flows
A friend of yours is taking an elementary accounting course. He says, "I understand the income statement and balance sheet, but I am confused by the statement of cash flows (and accompanying schedule). What is this statement, what is it useful for, what are its major sections, and what items are reported in each section and the accompanying schedule? I need to understand this statement better so I can do well in my class."

Required Prepare a written response to your friend's questions.

C21-3 Cash Flow Activities
A company's statement of cash flows shows its cash inflows, cash outflows, and net change in cash from the operating, investing, and financing activities during an accounting period.

Required Prepare a short memo that defines a company's operating, investing, and financing activities, and identifies the cash inflows and cash outflows related to each activity.

C21-4 Worksheet Method
The worksheet method is commonly used to analyze the information for preparing a company's statement of cash flows. This method involves the completion of several steps.

Required Explain the worksheet method and list and briefly discuss the steps in this method.

C21-5 Operating Cash Flows
There are two methods to calculate and report a company's net cash provided by (or used in) operating activities.

Required Prepare a short memo that identifies the two methods and explains the calculations necessary for each method.

CREATIVE AND CRITICAL THINKING

C21-6 Financing and Investing Activities Not Involving Cash
The statement of cash flows is normally a required basic financial statement for each period for which an earnings statement is presented. The statement should include a separate schedule listing the financing and investing activities not involving cash.

Required
1. What are financing and investing activities not involving cash?
2. What are two types of financing and investing activities not involving cash?

3. Explain what effect, if any, each of the following seven items would have on the statement of cash flows.
   a. Accounts receivable
   b. Inventory
   c. Depreciation
   d. Deferred tax liability
   e. Issuance of long-term debt in payment for a building
   f. Payoff of current portion of debt
   g. Sale of a fixed asset resulting in a loss (*AICPA adapted*)

C21-7 Inflows and Outflows

Alfred Engineering Company is a young and growing producer of electronic measuring instruments and technical equipment. You have been retained by Alfred to advise it in the preparation of a statement of cash flows. For the fiscal year ended October 31, 2004, you have obtained the following information concerning certain events and transactions of Alfred:

1. The amount of reported earnings for the fiscal year was $800,000.
2. Depreciation expense of $240,000 was included in the earnings statement.
3. Uncollectible accounts receivable of $30,000 were written off against the allowance for uncollectible accounts. Also, $37,000 of bad debts expense was included in determining earnings for the fiscal year, and the same amount was added to the allowance for uncollectible accounts.
4. A gain of $4,700 was realized on the sale of a machine; it originally cost $75,000, of which $25,000 was undepreciated on the date of sale.
5. On July 2, 2004, a building and land were purchased for $600,000; Alfred gave in payment $100,000 cash, $200,000 market value of its unissued common stock, and a $300,000 mortgage.
6. On August 3, 2004, $700,000 of Alfred's convertible preferred stock was converted into $140,000 par value of its common stock. The preferred stock was originally issued at par.
7. The board of directors declared a $320,000 cash dividend on October 20, 2004, payable on November 16, 2004 to stockholders of record on November 5, 2004.

Required For each of the seven items, explain whether each is an inflow or outflow of cash and explain how it should be disclosed in Alfred's statement of cash flows (indirect method) for the fiscal year ended October 31, 2004. If any item is neither an inflow nor outflow of cash, explain why it is not and indicate the disclosure, if any, that should be made of the item in Alfred's statement of cash flows for the fiscal year ended October 31, 2004. (*AICPA adapted*)

C21-8 Analyzing Coca-Cola's Cash Flow Disclosures

Refer to the financial statements and related notes of the Coca-Cola Company in Appendix A of this book.

Required

1. What was the net cash provided by operating activities for 2001? What method was used to determine this amount? What was the largest positive adjustment to net income?

2. What was the net cash used in investing activities for 2001? What was the largest investing cash outflow? Investing cash inflow?
3. What was the net cash used in financing activities for 2001? What was the largest financing cash inflow? Financing cash outflow?
4. What was the interest paid in 2001? Income taxes paid?
5. Compute the "cash flow from operations to sales" ratio for 2001. How does this result compare to 2000? Why?
6. Compute the profit margin for 2001. How does this result compare to the cash flow from operations to sales ratio for 2001? Why?

C21-9 Ethics and Cash Flows

You are the accountant for Nello Company, which manufactures specialty equipment. Nello has been in financial difficulty, so its suppliers require purchases to be paid in cash. Furthermore, Nello has long-term debt with a debt covenant that requires it to maintain a 1:1 acid-test (quick) ratio. Nello's employees work a five-day week, Monday through Friday.

On Wednesday morning during the last week of the current year, Sam (the production supervisor) comes to you and says, "I don't understand it. We have this large special order from a customer that must be delivered at the end of the first week in January. Once we get the raw materials, it is going to take five solid days of work without overtime to produce the order. If Bob (the president) would let me order the raw materials this morning, we could have them by late today. This would give us two days this week and the four days after New Years Day (Monday) of next week to complete the order without incurring overtime costs. But Bob says we must wait until next Tuesday to order the materials. This means we will have to work doubletime that Wednesday through Friday to finish the order. That overtime cost is going to really increase next year's factory salary expense, so our profit and operating cash flows from that order will be very low. Please talk to him."

When you approach Bob about buying the raw materials this morning, he says, "If we purchase those materials today, we will have to write a check. And that means our cash flow from operating activities for this year will be much lower, which our stockholders won't like. Furthermore, our quick ratio will go down from 1.01:1 to .90:1, so our creditors may be upset. I know our profit and operating cash flows for next year will be lower if we delay the purchase, but that seems to be the best decision. Don't you agree?"

Required From financial reporting and ethical perspectives, how would you respond to Bob?

RESEARCH

C21-10 Researching GAAP

You are the new accountant for 12th National Bank and are preparing its 2004 statement of cash flows. The bank reports net income of $75,800 on its 2004 income statement. Included in this net income are the following items: $6,700 gain on sale of trading securities, $1,200 unrealized holding gain on trading securities, and $5,100 loss on sale of securities available for sale. Among its 2004 transactions, the bank sold trading securities with a carrying value of $22,900 for $29,600, and purchased trading securities for $65,200. The bank sold securities available for sale with a cost (and carrying value) of $58,700 for $53,600, and purchased securities available for sale for $39,400. It also made routine 90-day loans of $47,500 to customers and collected $20,000 principal on these customer loans. As a result of the preceding information, the bank's trading securities account increased by $43,500, the securities

available for sale account decreased by $19,300, and the loans receivable account increased by $27,500. The bank uses the indirect approach to report operating cash flows on its statement of cash flows.

Required Research the applicable generally accepted accounting principles and prepare a written memo to the 12th National Bank's auditors that explains how you plan to report the preceding items on the bank's 2004 statement of cash flows. Cite your reference and applicable paragraph numbers.

MULTIPLE CHOICE

Select the best answer for each of the following.

M21-1 If a company issues a balance sheet and an income statement with comparative figures from last year, a statement of cash flows

- a. Is no longer necessary, but may be issued at the company's option
- b. Should not be issued
- c. Should be issued for each period for which an income statement is presented
- d. Should be issued for the current year only

M21-2 Selected information from Brook Corporation's accounting records and financial statements for 2004 is as follows:

Net cash provided by operating activities	$1,500,000
Mortgage payable issued to acquire land and building	1,800,000
Common stock issued to retire preferred stock	500,000
Proceeds from sale of equipment	400,000
Cost of office equipment purchased	200,000

On the statement of cash flows for the year ended December 31, 2004, Brook should disclose a net increase in cash in the amount of

- a. $1,700,000
- b. $2,400,000
- c. $3,700,000
- d. $4,200,000

M21-3 In a statement of cash flows (indirect method), the amortization of patents of a company with substantial operating profits should be presented as a (an)

- a. Cash flow from investing activities
- b. Cash flow from financing activities
- c. Deduction from net income
- d. Addition to net income

M21-4 The net cash provided by operating activities in Seat's statement of cash flows for 2004 was $8,000,000. For 2004, depreciation on fixed assets was $3,800,000, amortization of patents was $100,000, and dividends on common stock were $2,000,000. Based on the preceding information, Seat's net income for 2004 was

- a. $2,100,000
- b. $4,100,000
- c. $8,000,000
- d. $11,900,000

M21-5 The retirement of long-term debt by the issuance of common stock should be presented in a statement of cash flows as a

	Cash Flow From Financing Activities	Cash Flow From Investing Activities
a.	No	No
b.	No	Yes
c.	Yes	No
d.	Yes	Yes

M21-6 The net income for Mountain Corporation was $4,000,000 for the year ended December 31, 2004. Additional information is as follows:

Depreciation on fixed assets	$2,000,000
Proceeds from sale of land	200,000
Increase in accounts payable	300,000
Dividends on preferred stock	400,000

The net cash provided by operating activities in the statement of cash flows for the year ended December 31, 2004 should be

- a. $6,000,000
- b. $6,100,000
- c. $6,300,000
- d. $6,500,000

M21-7 Which of the following need not be disclosed in a schedule accompanying the statement of cash flows as an investing and financing activity not affecting cash?

- a. Acquisition of fixed assets in exchange for capital stock
- b. Dividend paid in capital stock of the company (stock dividend)
- c. Retirement of a bond issue through the issuance of another bond issue
- d. Conversion of convertible debt to capital stock

M21-8 The following information on selected transactions for 2004 has been provided by the Smith Company:

Net income	$20,000,000
Proceeds from short-term borrowings	1,200,000
Proceeds from long-term borrowings	4,000,000
Purchases of fixed assets	3,200,000
Decrease in inventories	8,000,000
Proceeds from sale of Smith's common stock	2,000,000
Depreciation expense	500,000

What is the net increase in cash for the year ended December 31, 2004 as a result of the preceding information?

a. $32,500,000   c. $16,500,000

b. $25,700,000   d. $12,500,000

M21-9 The following information was taken from the accounting records of Oregon Corporation for 2004:

Proceeds from issuance of preferred stock	$4,000,000
Dividends paid on preferred stock	400,000
Bonds payable converted to common stock	2,000,000
Payment for purchase of machinery	500,000
Proceeds from sale of plant building	1,200,000

2% stock dividend on common stock	300,000
Gain on sale of plant building	200,000

Oregon's statement of cash flows for the year ended December 31, 2004 should show the following amounts for investing and financing activities, based on the preceding information:

	Net Cash Flows From Investing Activities	Net Cash Flows From Financing Activities
a.	$700,000	$3,600,000
b.	$700,000	$3,900,000
c.	$900,000	$3,900,000
d.	$900,000	$5,600,000

M21-10 (*Appendix*) A company reports sales of $200,000 and interest revenue of $17,000 for the current year. During the year accounts receivable increased by $21,000 and interest receivable decreased by $3,000. Under the direct method, the company would report cash inflows from operating activities of

a. $235,000   c. $241,000

b. $193,000   d. $199,000

EXERCISES

E21-1   *Classification of Cash Flows* The following are several transactions and events that might be disclosed on a company's statement of cash flows:

1. Issuance of common stock
2. Purchase of building
3. Net income
4. Increase in accounts receivable
5. Depreciation expense

6. Sale of land at cost
7. Conversion of bonds to common stock
8. Increase in accounts payable
9. Payment of cash dividends
10. Issuance of a stock dividend

Required Identify in which section (if any) of the statement of cash flows each of the preceding items would appear and indicate whether it would be an inflow (addition) or outflow (subtraction).

E21-2   *Net Cash Flow From Operating Activities* The following is accounting information taken from the Hyde

Company's records for 2004:

1. Amortization of premium on bonds payable, $600
2. Purchase of equipment, $6,000
3. Depreciation expense, $7,400
4. Decrease in accounts receivable, $800
5. Decrease in accounts payable, $2,800
6. Issuance of long-term note for cash, $4,200

7. Increase in inventories, $7,500
8. Gain on sale of land, $8,000
9. Increase in prepaid assets, $500
10. Declaration and payment of cash dividends, $1,800
11. Increase in wages payable, $300
12. Patent amortization expense, $1,000
13. Net income, $10,800

Required Prepare the net cash flow from operating activities section of the 2004 statement of cash flows for the Hyde Company.

E21-3   *Statement of Cash Flows* The following is a list of the items for the 2004 statement of cash flows of the Lombardo Company:

1. Depreciation expense, $4,200
2. Proceeds from sale of land, $5,600
3. Payment of dividends, $5,000
4. Net income, $7,900
5. Conversion of bonds to common stock, $7,000
6. Increase in accounts payable, $3,100

7. Proceeds from issuance of note, $6,200
8. Gain on sale of land, $1,800
9. Payment for purchase of building, $13,000
10. Increase in accounts receivable, $2,700
11. Ending cash balance, $13,900

Required Prepare the statement of cash flows.

E21-4 *Statement of Cash Flows* The following is a list of items for the 2004 statement of cash flows of the Witts Company:

1. Proceeds from sale of equipment, $2,700
2. Increase in inventory, $3,900
3. Net income, $13,500
4. Payment for purchase of building, $29,000
5. Depreciation expense, $8,700
6. Proceeds from issuance of bonds, $8,000

7. Increase in prepaid expenses, $800
8. Loss on sale of equipment, $2,200
9. Payment of dividends, $5,200
10. Decrease in accounts receivable, $1,700
11. Issuance of common stock for land, $6,900
12. Decrease in accounts payable, $1,500
13. Beginning cash balance, $10,200

Required Prepare the statement of cash flows.

E21-5 *Direct and Indirect Methods* The Dauve Company reported the following condensed income statement for 2004:

Sales		$100,000
Cost of goods sold		(58,000)
Gross profit		$ 42,000
Operating expenses		
Depreciation expense	$ 8,000	
Salaries expense	12,000	(20,000)
Income before income taxes		$ 22,000
Income tax expense		(6,600)
Net income		$ 15,400

During 2004, the following changes occurred in the company's current assets and current liabilities:

	Increase (Decrease)
Cash	$3,700
Accounts receivable	(5,500)
Inventories	8,900
Accounts payable (purchases)	(4,600)
Salaries payable	2,800

Required

1. By visual inspection, prepare the net cash flow from operating activities section of the Dauve Company's 2004 statement of cash flows using the indirect method.
2. By visual inspection, prepare the net cash flow from operating activities section of the Dauve Company's 2004 statement of cash flows using the direct method.

E21-6 *Fixed Asset Transactions* The following is an Equipment account and its associated Accumulated Depreciation account:

Equipment			
Beginning balance	$49,000	Machine A	8,100
Machine C	25,000	Machine B	5,200
Ending balance	$60,700		

Accumulated Depreciation			
Related to Machine A	6,300	Beginning balance	$29,000
Related to Machine B	4,600	Depreciation expense	12,000
		Ending balance	$30,100

Additional data:

1. Machine A was sold at a gain of $900
2. Machine B was sold for its scrap value of $200
3. Machine C was acquired during the year

Required Analyze the two accounts shown and illustrate, in journal entry form, the entries that would be made in preparation of the statement of cash flows to reflect all of the changes listed in the accounts.

E21-7 *Visual Inspection* The following changes in account balances and other information for 2004 were taken from the accounting records of the Gordon Company:

| | Net Changes for 2004 | |
	Debit	Credit
Cash	$ 1,000	
Accounts receivable		$ 1,100
Inventory	2,000	
Buildings and equipment	8,800	
Accumulated depreciation		2,900
Accounts payable	900	
Common stock, no par		5,500
Retained earnings		3,200
	$12,700	$12,700

Other information: Net income totaled $5,800. Dividends were declared and paid. Equipment was purchased for $8,800. No buildings and equipment were sold during the year. One hundred shares of common stock were sold for $55 per share. The ending cash balance was $4,200.

Required Using visual inspection, prepare a 2004 statement of cash flows for the Gordon Company.

E21-8 *Visual Inspection* The following changes in account balances and other information for 2004 were taken from the accounting records of the Noble Company:

| | Net Changes for 2004 | |
	Debit	Credit
Cash		$ 2,000
Accounts receivable	$ 1,900	
Inventory		2,400
Land		1,700
Buildings and equipment	23,000	
Accumulated depreciation		4,500
Accounts payable		1,600
Salaries payable	600	
Bonds payable		5,000
Common stock, no par		3,000
Retained earnings		5,300
	$25,500	$25,500

Other information: Net income was $9,900. Dividends were declared and paid. Land was sold for $1,700; a building was purchased for $23,000. No land was purchased and no buildings and equipment were sold. Bonds payable were issued at the end of the year. Two hundred shares of stock were issued for $15 per share. The beginning cash balance was $4,800.

Required Using visual inspection, prepare a 2004 statement of cash flows for the Noble Company.

E21-9 *Balance Sheet* The following beginning balance sheet and statement of cash flows for 2004 are available for Fazzi Company:

Balance Sheet
January 1, 2004

Cash		$ 900	Accounts payable	$ 1,600
Accounts receivable		2,300	Notes payable	3,900
Land		4,900	Common stock, $5 par	4,500
Equipment	$20,000		Additional paid-in capital	1,800
Less: Accumulated depreciation	(9,100)	10,900	Retained earnings	7,200
Total Assets		$19,000	Total Liabilities and Stockholders' Equity	$19,000

Statement of Cash Flows
For Year Ended December 31, 2004

Net Cash Flow From Operating Activities		
Net income		$3,900
Adjustments for differences between income flows		
and cash flows from operating activities:		
Add: Depreciation expense		900
Increase in accounts payable		100
Less: Increase in accounts receivable		(700)
Gain on sale of land		(200)
Net cash provided by operating activities		$4,000
Cash Flows From Investing Activities		
Payment for purchase of equipment	$(5,000)	
Proceeds from sale of land	1,200	
Net cash used for investing activities		(3,800)
Cash Flows From Financing Activities		
Proceeds from issuance of common stock (200 shares)	$ 2,600	
Payment of long-term note	(900)	
Payment of dividends	(1,300)	
Net cash provided by financing activities		400
Net Increase in Cash		$ 600
Cash, January 1, 2004		900
Cash, December 31, 2004		$1,500

Required On the basis of this information, prepare a balance sheet for the Fazzi Company as of December 31, 2004.

E21-10 *Erroneous Statement of Cash Flows* The 2004 statement of cash flows for the Andell Company, as developed by its bookkeeper, is shown here:

Cash Flows Statement
December 31, 2004

Inflows of Cash		
Operating Activities		
Net income	$10,600	
Add: Proceeds from sale of equipment	4,400	
Proceeds from issuance of stock	4,300	
Less: Payment for investment in bonds	(6,000)	
Payment of long-term note	(5,000)	
Net cash inflows from operations	$ 8,300	
Other Inflows		
Decrease in accounts receivable	$ 2,100	
Depreciation expense	4,800	
Total other inflows of cash		6,900
Total inflows of cash		$15,200
Outflows of Cash		
Payment for purchase of land	$(5,200)	
Decrease in accounts payable	(2,800)	
Payment of dividends	(3,000)	
Gain on sale of equipment	(700)	
Total outflows of cash		(11,700)
Net Increase in Cash		$ 3,500
Cash, December 31, 2004		11,700
Cash, January 1, 2004		$ 8,200

You determine that the *amounts* of the items listed on the statement are correct, but in certain circumstances, incorrectly classified.

Required Prepare a corrected 2004 statement of cash flows for the Andell Company.

E21-11 *Partially Completed Worksheet* The Hanks Company has prepared the following changes in account balances for the worksheet to support its 2004 statement of cash flows:

Account Title	Increase (Decrease)	Worksheet Entries Debit	Credit	Account Title	Increase (Decrease)	Worksheet Entries Debit	Credit
	Debits				*Credits*		
Cash	$ 830			Accumulated depreciation	$ 350		
Noncash Accounts				Accounts payable	120		
Accounts receivable	(290)			Bonds payable	2,000		
Inventory	1,280			Premium on bonds payable	300		
Investments	1,550			Common stock, $2 par	480		
Land	(700)			Premium on common stock	1,120		
Equipment	2,300			Retained earnings	500		
Patents (net)	(100)			Total	$4,870		
Total	$4,870						

Additional information: The net income was $1,300. Depreciation expense was $350 and patent amortization expense was $100. At the end of 2004, long-term investments were purchased at a cost of $1,550. Land that cost $700 was sold for $900. On December 31, 2004, bonds payable with a face value of $2,000 were issued for equipment valued at $2,300. Two hundred shares of common stock were issued at $7 per share. Forty shares of common stock were issued as a "small" stock dividend, the relevant market price being $5 per share. Cash dividends declared and paid totaled $600.

Required On the basis of the preceding information, align the accounts with credit changes below the accounts with debit changes and complete the worksheet.

E21-12 *Worksheet* The following 2004 information is available for the Payne Company:

	Comparative Balance Sheets	
	January 1, 2004	December 31, 2004
Cash	$ 400	$ 600
Accounts receivable	220	200
Inventory	370	610
Land	250	410
Equipment	2,070	2,200
Less: Accumulated depreciation	(310)	(400)
Total Assets	$3,000	$3,620
Accounts payable	$ 800	$ 500
Notes payable (long-term)	900	720
Common stock, no par	600	1,000
Retained earnings	700	1,400
Total Liabilities and Stockholders' Equity	$3,000	$3,620

Partial additional information: The net income for 2004 totaled $1,600. During 2004 the company sold for $390 equipment that cost $390 and had a book value of $300. The company sold land for $200, resulting in a loss of $40. The remaining change in the Land account resulted from the purchase of land through the issuance of common stock.

Required Making whatever additional assumptions that are necessary, prepare a worksheet to support the 2004 statement of cash flows for the Payne Company.

E21-13 *Worksheet and Statement* The following 2004 information is available for the Stewart Company:

Condensed Income Statement for 2004	
Sales	$9,000
Cost of goods sold	(6,000)
Other expenses	(2,000)
Loss on sale of equipment	(260)
Gain on sale of land	400
Net income	$1,140

	Comparative Balance Sheets	
	December 31, 2003	December 31, 2004
Cash	$ 700	$1,130
Accounts receivable	450	310
Inventory	350	400
Land	300	500
Equipment	1,600	1,800
Less: Accumulated depreciation	(200)	(150)
Total Assets	$3,200	$3,990
Accounts payable	$ 600	$ 750
Bonds payable (due 1/1/2009)	1,000	1,000
Common stock, $10 par	900	1,400
Retained earnings	700	840
Total Liabilities and Stockholders' Equity	$3,200	$3,990

Partial additional information:

1. The equipment that was sold for cash had cost $400 and had a book value of $300.
2. Land that was sold brought a cash price of $530.
3. Fifty shares of stock were issued at par.

Required Making whatever additional assumptions that are necessary,

1. Prepare a worksheet to support a statement of cash flows for the Stewart Company for 2004.
2. Prepare the statement of cash flows.

E21-14 *Interest and Income Taxes* The Staggs Company has prepared its 2004 statement of cash flows. In conjunction with this statement, it plans to disclose the interest and income taxes it paid during 2004. The following information is available from its 2004 income statement and beginning and ending balance sheet:

Income Statement	
Interest expense	$12,000
Income tax expense	35,000

	Balance Sheet	
	Cr. Bal. 01/01/04	Cr. Bal. 12/31/04
Interest payable	$ 600	$ 2,300
Income taxes payable	5,000	3,000
Bonds payable	80,000	80,000
Premium on bonds payable	9,000	8,100
Deferred taxes payable	3,300	4,400

Required Compute the amounts of interest paid and income taxes paid by the Staggs Company for 2004.

E21-15 *Investments* On October 6, 2004, Collins Company purchased 100 shares of Steph Company common stock for $64 per share as a temporary investment in securities available for sale. On December 31, 2004, the stock had a fair value of $63 per share, and on February 9, 2005, Collins sold the stock for $67 per share.

Required In journal entry form, prepare the worksheet entries to record these transactions for the Collins Company's 2004 and 2005 statement of cash flows.

E21-16 *Operating Cash Flows (Appendix)*   Use the information in E21-13.

Required Based only on the information presented and using the direct method, prepare the cash flows from operating activities section of the 2004 statement of cash flows for the Stewart Company.

E21-17 *Operating Cash Flows (Appendix)*   The following is accounting information taken from the adjusted trial balance of the Woodrail Company for 2004:

	Debit	Credit
Sales		$75,000
Interest revenue		4,300
Cost of goods sold	$43,600	
Salaries expense	13,600	
Interest expense	5,400	
Income tax expense	3,000	

In addition, the following changes occurred in selected accounts during 2004:

Accounts receivable	$5,700 credit
Inventory	9,800 debit
Accounts payable	7,000 credit
Salaries payable	900 debit
Interest payable	300 credit

Required Using the direct method, prepare the cash flows from operating activities section of the 2004 statement of cash flows for the Woodrail Company.

E21-18 *Statement of Cash Flows (Appendix)*   The following is a list of items to be included in the 2004 statement of cash flows of the Estes Company:

1. Payments to suppliers, $31,500
2. Other operating receipts, $1,200
3. Payments of dividends, $4,000
4. Payments of income taxes, $5,000
5. Collections from customers, $68,400
6. Payment for purchase of equipment, $18,500
7. Payments to employees, $19,300
8. Interest and dividends collected, $7,100
9. Other operating payments, $900
10. Proceeds from issuance of bonds, $11,300
11. Payments of interest, $8,400
12. Proceeds from sale of investments, $6,000
13. Beginning cash balance, $28,400

Required Prepare the statement of cash flows using the direct method for operating cash flows.

E21-19 *Visual Inspection (Appendix)*   The following changes in account balances were taken from the adjusted trial balance of the Walson Company at the end of 2004:

	Net Changes for 2004	
	Debit	Credit
Cash	$ 2,100	
Accounts receivable	8,700	
Inventory		$ 2,500
Land		1,900
Buildings and equipment	10,400	
Accumulated depreciation		6,800
Accounts payable	4,500	
Salaries payable		800
Income taxes payable		1,000
Common stock, no par		9,000
Retained earnings	4,000	
Sales		69,000
Cost of goods sold	34,000	
Salaries expense	17,200	
Depreciation expense	6,800	
Income tax expense	3,300	
Totals	$91,000	$91,000

In addition, the following information was obtained from the company's records:

1. Land was sold, at cost, for $1,900
2. Dividends of $4,000 were declared and paid
3. Equipment was purchased for $10,400
4. Common stock was issued for $9,000
5. Beginning cash balance was $17,000

Required Using visual inspection and the direct method, prepare a 2004 statement of cash flows for the Walson Company. (A separate schedule reconciling net income to cash provided by operating activities is not necessary.)

PROBLEMS

P21-1 *Classifications of Cash Flows* A company's statement of cash flows and the accompanying schedule of investing and financing activities not affecting cash may contain the following major sections:

A. Net Cash Flow From Operating Activities
B. Cash Flows From Investing Activities
C. Cash Flows From Financing Activities
D. Investing and Financing Activities Not Affecting Cash

The following is a list of items that might appear on a company's statement of cash flows or in the accompanying schedule.

_____ 1. Decrease in accounts payable
_____ 2. Payment of dividends
_____ 3. Increase in income taxes payable
_____ 4. Proceeds from issuance of note
_____ 5. Payment for purchase of available-for-sale temporary investments
_____ 6. Amortization of premium on investment in bonds
_____ 7. Increase in prepaid expenses
_____ 8. Payment of note
_____ 9. Gain on sale of equipment
_____ 10. Proceeds from sale of land
_____ 11. Net income
_____ 12. Payment for acquisition of building
_____ 13. Depreciation expense
_____ 14. Issuance of common stock for land
_____ 15. Proceeds (principal) from collection of note
_____ 16. Amortization of discount on bonds payable
_____ 17. Decrease in deferred taxes payable
_____ 18. Proceeds from issuance of bonds
_____ 19. Issuance of stock dividend
_____ 20. Payment for purchase of treasury stock
_____ 21. Depletion expense
_____ 22. Increase in inventory
_____ 23. Conversion of preferred stock to common stock
_____ 24. Proceeds from issuance of stock
_____ 25. Lease of equipment under capital lease
_____ 26. Proceeds from sale of patent

Required In the space provided and using the letters A through D, indicate in which section of the statement of cash flows (or the accompanying schedule) the preceding items would most likely be classified. After each letter indicate with a plus (+) or a minus (−) whether the items would be reported as an increase (inflow) or decrease (outflow). If an item would not be reported in the statement (or the accompanying schedule), put an X in the space provided.

P21-2 *Net Cash Flow From Operating Activities* The following is accounting information taken from the Verna Company's records for 2004:

1. Decrease in accounts payable, $4,600
2. Loss on sale of land, $1,900
3. Increase in inventory, $7,800
4. Increase in income taxes payable, $2,700
5. Net income, $68,400
6. Patent amortization expense, $1,600
7. Extraordinary loss (net), $6,200
8. Decrease in deferred taxes payable, $2,500
9. Amortization of discount on bonds payable, $1,300
10. Payment of cash dividends, $24,000
11. Depletion expense, $5,000
12. Decrease in salaries payable, $1,400
13. Decrease in accounts receivable, $3,500
14. Gain on sale of equipment, $6,100
15. Proceeds from issuance of stock, $57,000
16. Extraordinary gain (net), $3,700
17. Depreciation expense, $10,000
18. Amortization of discount on investment in bonds, $1,500

Required Prepare the net cash flow from operating activities section of the 2004 statement of cash flows for the Verna Company.

P21-3   *Statement of Cash Flows*   The following is a list of the items to be included in the preparation of the 2004 statement of cash flows for the Warrick Company:

1. Net income, $59,200
2. Payment for purchase of building, $98,000
3. Increase in accounts receivable, $7,400
4. Proceeds from issuance of common stock, $37,100
5. Increase in accounts payable, $4,500
6. Proceeds from sale of land, $7,000
7. Depreciation expense, $12,600
8. Payment of dividends, $36,000
9. Gain on sale of land, $5,300
10. Decrease in inventory, $3,700
11. Payment for purchase of long-term investments, $9,600
12. Amortization of discount on bonds payable, $1,900
13. Proceeds from issuance of note, $18,000
14. Increase in deferred taxes payable, $5,000
15. Equipment acquired by capital lease, $19,500
16. Decrease in salaries payable, $2,300
17. Beginning cash balance, $20,300

Required

1. Prepare the statement of cash flows.
2. Assume the company's preferred stock has been selling for $120 per share during 2004. How many shares would the company have had to issue to avoid having a decrease in cash during the year? Where would this issuance have been reported in the statement of cash flows?

P21-4   *Statement of Cash Flows*   The following is a list of the items to be included in the preparation of the 2004 statement of cash flows for the Trone Company:

1. Extraordinary gain (net), $9,200
2. Proceeds from issuance of note, $25,000
3. Decrease in accounts receivable, $5,000
4. Payment for purchase of patent, $19,800
5. Increase in inventory, $6,700
6. Payment of dividends, $30,000
7. Decrease in accounts payable, $4,000
8. Proceeds from sale of investments, $8,500
9. Amortization of premium on bonds payable, $2,100
10. Net income, $49,200
11. Common stock exchanged for land, $14,000
12. Payment for purchase of equipment, $39,400
13. Loss on sale of investments, $4,800
14. Decrease in deferred taxes payable, $3,600
15. Proceeds from issuance of preferred stock, $52,800
16. Payment to retire bonds, $37,800
17. Depreciation expense, $10,700
18. Ending cash balance, $22,100

Required

1. Prepare the statement of cash flows.
2. What would have happened if the company had not issued the note during 2004? How did the issuance of the note affect the company's debt ratio (discussed in Chapter 5) at the end of 2004?

P21-5   *Infrequent Transactions*   The following transactions were recorded on the books of the Baxter Company during the current year. The company:

1. Issued a "small" common stock dividend of 400 shares. The par value is $10 per share and the relevant market price was $20 per share.
2. Exchanged equipment with a cost of $10,000 and a book value of $3,800 for land valued at $12,000, paying an additional $8,500 in cash. The transaction was properly considered a dissimilar asset exchange.
3. Traded in equipment with a cost of $14,000 and a book value of $8,000 on a similar machine, paying an additional $1,000 in cash. The transaction was properly considered a similar asset exchange; the new asset was recorded at a cost of $9,000.
4. Created an Appropriation of Retained Earnings for Contingencies account in the amount of $5,000 as a result of a debit to Retained Earnings.
5. Converted preferred stock ($100 par) with a total par value of $20,000 and a book value of $22,800 to 1,500 shares of its $10 par common stock. The book value method was used to account for the conversion.
6. Recorded a loss of $4,200 as a result of retiring bonds payable with a face value of $30,000 and a related premium of $5,000 by paying $39,200.
7. Recorded an extraordinary gain (net of income taxes) of $6,000 as a result of a tornado that destroyed a building costing $100,000 and having an associated book value of $70,000. The insurance proceeds (net of income taxes) totaled $76,000.
8. Acquired equipment by entering into a capital lease. The lease required payments of $5,000 in advance; the present value of the lease payments (before the initial payment) was $34,000.

Required For each of the preceding items, discuss *if* and illustrate *how* the transaction would be recorded on the worksheet to support the statement of cash flows. Use a journal entry format for your illustrations.

P21-6 *Partially Completed Worksheet* The following partially completed worksheet has been prepared for the 2004 statement of cash flows of the Perrin Company:

Account Titles	Balances 12/31/03	Balances 12/31/04	Change Increase (Decrease)	Worksheet Entries Debit	Worksheet Entries Credit
Debits					
Cash	$ 800	$ 1,540			
Noncash Accounts:					
Accounts receivable	1,500	2,180			
Inventory	3,100	6,055			
Investments in stock	—	2,800			
Land	6,000	9,200			
Buildings	20,000	20,000			
Office equipment	4,000	6,100			
Delivery equipment	3,000	5,900			
Treasury stock	—	2,000			
Totals	$38,400	$55,775	$?		
Credits					
Accumulated depreciation	$ 7,000	$ 8,500			
Accounts payable	3,300	3,695			
Wages payable	600	500			
Bonds payable	—	5,000			
Premium on bonds payable	—	240			
Common stock, $10 par	6,000	8,200			
Additional paid-in capital	9,000	13,640			
Retained earnings	?	?	$3,500		
Totals	$38,400	$55,775	$?		

Other relevant information:

(a) Beginning retained earnings		$12,500
Plus: Net income		8,000
		$20,500
Less: Stock dividends	$ 840	
Cash dividends	3,660	(4,500)
Ending retained earnings		$16,000

(b) Accumulated depreciation is a contra account for all the depreciable assets. Depreciation on these assets totaled $2,200 for the year.

(c) On January 1, 2004 the company issued 10% bonds with a face value of $5,000 at 106. Interest was paid semiannually on June 30 and December 31. The bonds mature on January 1, 2006. Straight-line amortization is used for bond discount or premium. Bond interest expense was $440.

(d) Land was purchased for $3,200 during the year.

(e) Two hundred shares of common stock were issued for delivery equipment valued at $2,900 and office equipment valued at $3,100.

(f) Twenty shares of stock were issued as a stock dividend. The market price per share was $42.

(g) Office equipment with a cost of $1,000 and a book value of $300 was sold for $50.

(h) Fifty shares of its own common stock were reacquired by the company as treasury stock. The company purchased the shares for $40 per share.

(i) One hundred shares of Doe Company stock were purchased for $28 per share at year-end.

Required Complete the worksheet.

P21-7   *Worksheet and Statement of Cash Flows*   The following information was taken from the accounting records of the Lamberson Company:

	Account Balances	
	January 1, 2004	December 31, 2004
Debits		
Cash	$ 1,400	$ 2,400
Accounts receivable (net)	2,800	2,690
Marketable securities (at cost)	1,700	3,000
Allowance for change in value	500	800
Inventories	8,100	7,910
Prepaid items	1,300	1,710
Investments (long-term)	7,000	5,400
Land	15,000	15,000
Buildings and equipment	32,000	46,200
Discount on bonds payable	—	290
	$69,800	$85,400
Credits		
Accumulated depreciation	$16,000	$16,400
Accounts payable	3,800	4,150
Income taxes payable	2,400	2,504
Wages payable	1,100	650
Interest payable	—	400
Note payable (long-term)	3,500	—
12% bonds payable	—	10,000
Deferred taxes payable	800	1,196
Convertible preferred stock, $100 par	9,000	—
Common stock, $10 par	14,000	21,500
Additional paid-in capital	8,700	13,700
Unrealized increase in value of marketable securities	500	800
Retained earnings	10,000	14,100
	$69,800	$85,400

Additional information for the year:

(a) Sales	$39,930
Cost of goods sold	(19,890)
Depreciation expense	(2,100)
Wages expense	(11,000)
Other operating expenses	(1,000)
Bond interest expense	(410)
Dividend revenue	820
Gain on sale of investments	700
Loss on sale of equipment	(200)
Income tax expense	(2,050)
Net income	$ 4,800

(b) Dividends declared and paid totaled $700.

(c) On January 1, 2004, convertible preferred stock that had originally been issued at par value were converted into 500 shares of common stock. The book value method was used to account for the conversion.

(d) Long-term nonmarketable investments that cost $1,600 were sold for $2,300.

(e) The long-term note payable was paid by issuing 250 shares of common stock at the beginning of the year.

(f) Equipment with a cost of $2,000 and a book value of $300 was sold for $100. The company uses one Accumulated Depreciation account for all depreciable assets.

(g) Equipment was purchased at a cost of $16,200.

(h) The 12% bonds payable were issued on September 1, 2004 at 97. They mature on September 1, 2014. The company uses the straight-line method to amortize the discount.

(i) Taxable income was less than pretax accounting income, resulting in a $396 increase in deferred taxes payable.

(j) Short-term marketable securities were purchased at a cost of $1,300. The portfolio was increased by $300 to a $3,800 fair value at year-end by adjusting the related allowance account.

Required

1. Prepare a worksheet to support the Lamberson Company's statement of cash flows for 2004.
2. Prepare the statement of cash flows.
3. Compute the cash flow from operations to sales ratio and the profit margin ratio for 2004. What is the primary reason for the difference in the results of the ratios?

See WebTutor for annotated problem solution.

P21-8 **Worksheet and Statement of Cash Flows** The following information is available for the Bott Company:

	Account Balances	
	December 31, 2003	December 31, 2004
Debits		
Cash	$ 1,800	$ 2,000
Accounts receivable	4,600	4,720
Notes receivable (short-term)	0	1,000
Inventories	12,000	9,700
Prepaid items	1,700	1,380
Land	11,000	17,100
Buildings and equipment	78,000	110,000
Patent	4,400	4,000
Treasury stock (common, at cost, $25 per share)	2,500	1,000
Totals	$116,000	$150,900
Credits		
Accumulated depreciation	$ 24,000	$ 31,800
Accounts payable	6,000	8,210
Salaries payable	2,600	3,500
Miscellaneous current payables	1,400	1,200
Interest payable	0	140
12% bonds payable	0	7,000
Premium on bonds payable	0	650
Convertible preferred stock, $50 par	9,000	6,500
Premium on preferred stock	3,000	2,500
Common stock, $10 par	18,000	23,500
Premium on common stock	28,800	41,150
Retained earnings	23,200	24,750
Totals	$116,000	$150,900

Additional information for the year:

(a) Beginning retained earnings, unadjusted		$23,200
Less: Prior period adjustment—correction of understatement of depreciation (net of income taxes)		(1,300)
Adjusted beginning retained earnings		$21,900
Add: Net income		11,500
		$33,400
Less: Cash dividends	$(4,000)	
Stock dividends (150 shares at $31 per share)	(4,650)	(8,650)
Ending retained earnings		$24,750

(b) Last year depreciation expense was inadvertently understated in the amount of $1,800. The correction was made this year to Accumulated Depreciation and to Retained Earnings as a prior period adjustment. The company also received a related income tax refund of $500.

(c) Sixty shares of treasury stock (common) were reissued at $30 per share.

(d) Bonds payable with a face amount of $7,000 were issued for $7,750 on April 30, 2004. The bonds mature on April 30, 2009, and pay interest semiannually. The straight-line method is used to amortize the bond premium. Interest expense totaled $460 for 2004.

(e) Fifty shares of preferred stock (originally issued at $60 per share) were converted into 100 shares of common stock.

(f) Land costing $2,900 was sold for $3,800.

(g) Three hundred shares of common stock were sold for $33 per share.

(h) Equipment costing $32,000 was purchased during the year.

(i) Land was acquired at a cost of $9,000 during the year.

(j) Depreciation expense was $6,000.

(k) Patent amortization was $400.

(l) The company loaned money to one of its executives and received a $1,000 short-term note receivable on December 31, 2004. The note matures 90 days from the date of issuance.

Required

1. Prepare a worksheet to support a statement of cash flows for 2004.
2. Prepare the 2004 statement of cash flows for the Bott Company. Show the reconciliation of the net income to the net cash provided by operating activities in a separate schedule accompanying the statement.

P21-9   *Worksheet from Trial Balance*   The post-closing trial balance as of December 31, 2003 and the adjusted trial balance as of December 31, 2004 are shown here for the Heinz Company:

	December 31, 2003 Post-closing Trial Balance		December 31, 2004 Adjusted Trial Balance	
Cash	$ 2,700		$ 3,520	
Accounts receivable	5,900		6,215	
Inventories	15,300		15,530	
Prepaid items	1,400		1,000	
Investments in bonds (long-term)	8,300		7,300	
Land	16,300		19,000	
Buildings	68,700		60,700	
Accumulated depreciation: buildings		$ 35,000		$ 34,500
Equipment	29,600		25,600	
Accumulated depreciation: equipment		14,200		14,700
Patents (net)	8,700		9,185	
Accounts payable		8,900		9,195
Interest payable		630		300
Wages payable		2,500		2,600
Bonds payable		23,000		17,000
Discount on bonds payable	0		715	
Common stock, $10 par		22,000		22,650
Additional paid-in capital		15,320		15,970
Retained earnings		35,350		35,350
	$156,900	$156,900		
Sales (net)				49,550
Cost of goods sold			23,800	
Wages expense			16,510	
Other operating expenses			1,100	
Depreciation expense: buildings			2,700	
Depreciation expense: equipment			3,100	
Patent amortization			815	
Interest expense			1,715	
Loss (ordinary) on sale of investments			200	
Interest revenue				790
Gain (ordinary) on exchange of dissimilar assets				1,300
Income tax expense			500	
Extraordinary loss (net of income taxes)			2,600	
Dividends declared			2,100	
Totals			$203,905	$203,905

A review of the accounting records reveals the following additional information:

(a) Bonds payable with a face value, book value, and market value of $14,000 were retired on June 30, 2004.

(b) Bonds payable with a face value of $8,000 were issued at 90.25 on August 1, 2004. They mature on August 1, 2009. The company uses the straight-line method to amortize bond discount.

(c) A tornado completely destroyed a small building that had an original cost of $8,000 and a book value of $4,800. Settlement with the insurance company resulted in after-tax proceeds of $2,200 and an extraordinary loss (net of income taxes) of $2,600.

(d) Equipment with a cost of $4,000 and a book value of $1,400 was exchanged for an acre of land valued at $2,700. No cash was exchanged. The transaction was properly considered to be a dissimilar asset exchange.

(e) Long-term investments in bonds being held to maturity with a cost of $1,000 were sold for $800.

(f) Sixty-five shares of common stock were exchanged for a patent. The common stock was selling for $20 per share at the time of the exchange.

Required Prepare a worksheet to support a statement of cash flows for 2004.

P21-10 **Prepare Ending Balance Sheet** On December 31, 2004 a fire destroyed a significant portion of the Richey Company accounting records. Only the January 1, 2004 balance sheet, the statement of cash flows for 2004, and several additional documents were saved as follows:

Balance Sheet
January 1, 2004

Assets			
Current assets:			
Cash			$ 1,900
Accounts receivable			5,100
Inventories			13,900
Prepaid items			1,300
Total current assets			$22,200
Property, plant, and equipment:			
Land			$12,000
Buildings	$60,000		
Equipment	20,000	$80,000	
Less: Accumulated depreciation		(29,000)	51,000
Total fixed assets			$63,000
Patents (net)			7,100
Total assets			$92,300
Liabilities			
Current liabilities:			
Accounts payable			$ 5,500
Income taxes payable			4,100
Miscellaneous payables			1,200
Total current liabilities			$10,800
Long-term liabilities:			
10% bonds payable (due 12/31/2013)		$15,000	
Less: Discount on bonds payable		(1,000)	14,000
Total liabilities			$24,800
Stockholders' Equity			
Preferred stock, $100 par		$17,000	
Premium on preferred stock		1,500	$18,500
Common stock, $10 par		$14,000	
Premium on common stock		11,200	25,200
Retained earnings			23,800
Total stockholders' equity			$67,500
Total liabilities and stockholders' equity			$92,300

Statement of Cash Flows
For Year Ended December 31, 2004

Net Cash Flow From Operating Activities		
Net income	$ 10,000	
Adjustments for differences between income flows and cash flows from operating activities:		
Add: Depreciation expense	5,100	
Patent amortization expense	600	
Loss on sale of land	400	
Decrease in accounts receivable (net)	1,100	
Decrease in inventories	3,010	
Increase in income taxes payable	190	
Increase in miscellaneous payables	200	
Bond discount amortization	100	
Less: Gain on sale of equipment	(180)	
Gain on sale of patent	(1,100)	
Increase in prepaid items	(120)	
Decrease in accounts payable	(400)	
Net cash provided by operating activities		$18,900
Cash Flows From Investing Activities		
Purchase of building by issuance of mortgage and cash	$(43,000)	
Less: Issuance of mortgage	20,000	
Payment for purchase of building	$(23,000)	
Proceeds from sale of land	2,800	
Proceeds from sale of equipment	500	
Proceeds from sale of patent	2,100	
Net cash used for investing activities		(17,600)
Cash Flows From Financing Activities		
Proceeds from issuance of common stock (150 shares)	$ 3,000	
Payment of dividends	(5,000)	
Net cash used for financing activities		(2,000)
Net Decrease in Cash (see Schedule 1)		$ (700)
Cash, January 1, 2004		1,900
Cash, December 31, 2004		$ 1,200

Schedule 1: Investing and Financing Activities Not Affecting Cash

Investing Activities	
Acquisition of land by issuance of preferred stock (40 shares)	$ (4,800)
Financing Activities	
Issuance of preferred stock to acquire land	4,800

The remaining financial documents reveal the following additional data:

1. The new building was acquired on December 31, 2004. The related mortgage requires equal annual repayments of the principal over a 5-year period beginning December 31, 2006.
2. The company issued a stock dividend of 200 shares of common stock on December 15, 2004. On the date of declaration, the stock was selling for $18 per share.
3. The equipment that was sold had an original cost of $1,900.

Required Prepare a December 31, 2004 balance sheet for Richey Company. Include supporting calculations.

P21-11 *Erroneous Statement of Cash Flows* The bookkeeper of the Ryan Company prepared the following 2004 statement of cash flows:

Flows of Cash Statement
December 31, 2004

Sources (Inflows) of Cash		
Net Source from Operations		
Net income	$ 47,800	
Add: Cash receipt from sale of land	6,500	
Inflow from issuing 10% bonds payable	25,000	
Depreciation expense	13,200	
Reduction in inventory	1,900	
Less: Outflow to buy equipment	(16,400)	
Increase in prepaid expenses	(700)	
Cash (principal) paid on long-term note	(9,500)	
Extraordinary gain (net)	(2,000)	
Total source from operations		$ 65,800
Other Sources (Inflows) of Cash		
Loss on sale of land	$ 2,300	
Increase in accounts payable	1,000	
Cash from issuing preferred stock	38,700	
Patent amortization expense	2,100	
Total other sources of cash		44,100
Sources (Financing) Not Affecting Cash		
Issuance of common stock for patent		11,000
Total inflows of cash		$120,900
Uses (Outflows) of Cash		
To purchase building	$(62,000)	
Increase in accounts receivable	(7,800)	
For acquiring marketable securities	(7,100)	
Decrease in income taxes payable	(1,400)	
Total uses of cash		(78,300)
Uses (Investing) Not Affecting Cash		
Acquisition of patent by issuing common stock		(11,000)
Net inflow before dividends		$ 31,600
Less: Cash dividends		(24,000)
Net Increase in Cash		$ 7,600
Cash, January 1, 2004		15,300
Cash, December 31, 2004		$ 22,900

After a thorough investigation, you have determined that the *amounts* of the items listed on the statement are correct. However, you notice several items that are incorrectly classified and reported.

Required Prepare a corrected 2004 statement of cash flows for the Ryan Company.

P21-12 **Comprehensive** Angel Company has prepared its financial statements for the year ended December 31, 2004 and for the three months ended March 31, 2005. You have been asked to prepare a statement of cash flows for the three months ended March 31, 2005. The company's balance sheet data at December 31, 2004 and March 31, 2005, and its income statement data for the three months ended March 31, 2005, follow. You have previously satisfied yourself as to the correctness of the amounts presented.

	Balance Sheet Data	
	December 31, 2004	March 31, 2005
Cash	$ 25,300	$ 79,400
Marketable investments (at cost)	17,500	8,300
Allowance for decrease in value	(1,000)	(900)
Accounts receivable	24,320	49,320
Inventory	31,090	48,590
Total current assets	$ 97,210	$184,710
Land	40,000	18,700
Building	250,000	250,000
Equipment	—	81,500
Accumulated depreciation	(15,000)	(16,250)
Investment in 30% owned company	61,220	67,100
Other assets	15,100	15,100
Total	$448,530	$600,860
Accounts payable	$ 21,220	$ 38,081
Income taxes payable	—	13,865
Total current liabilities	$ 21,220	$ 51,946
Other liabilities	187,000	187,000
Bonds payable	50,000	115,000
Discount on bonds payable	(2,300)	(2,150)
Deferred taxes payable	510	846
Preferred stock	30,000	—
Common stock	80,000	110,000
Unrealized decrease in value of marketable investments	(1,000)	(900)
Dividends declared	—	(8,000)
Retained earnings	83,100	147,118
Total	$448,530	$600,860

	Income Statement Data For the Three Months Ended March 31, 2005
Sales	$242,807
Gain on sale of marketable investments	2,400
Equity in earnings of 30% owned company	5,880
Extraordinary gain on condemnation of land (net of tax)	8,560
Total revenues	$259,647
Cost of sales	$157,354
General and administrative expenses	22,010
Depreciation	1,250
Interest expense	1,150
Income taxes	13,865
Total expenses	$195,629
Net income	$ 64,018

Your discussion with the company's controller and a review of the financial records have revealed the following information:

(a) On January 6, 2005 the company sold marketable securities for cash. These securities had cost $9,200, and had a fair value of $8,600 at December 31, 2004. The remaining marketable securities were adjusted to their $7,400 fair value on March 31, 2005 by adjustment of the related allowance account. The dividend and interest revenue on these marketable securities is not material.

(b) The company's preferred stock was converted into common stock at a rate of 1 share of preferred for 2 shares of common. The preferred stock and common stock have par values of $2 and $1, respectively.

(c) On January 16, 2005, 3 acres of land were condemned. An award of $32,000 in cash was received on March 23, 2005. Purchase of additional land as a replacement is not contemplated by the company.

(d) On March 25, 2005 the company purchased equipment for cash.

(e) On March 26, 2005 bonds payable were issued by the company at par for cash.

(f) The investment in 30% owned company included an amount of $9,600 attributable to an increase in the recorded value of depreciable assets at December 31, 2004. This increase is being depreciated at a quarterly rate of $480.

Required

1. Prepare a worksheet to support the statement of cash flows for Angel Company for the 3 months ended March 31, 2005.
2. Prepare the statement of cash flows. (*AICPA adapted*)

P21-13 *Comprehensive* The following are the balance sheets of Farrell Corporation as of December 31, 2004 and 2000, and the statement of income and retained earnings for the year ended December 31, 2004:

	Balance Sheets		
	December 31		Increase
	2004	2003	(Decrease)
Assets			
Cash	$ 225,000	$ 180,000	$ 45,000
Accounts receivable, net	295,000	305,000	(10,000)
Inventories	549,000	431,000	118,000
Investment in Hall, Inc., at equity	73,000	60,000	13,000
Land	350,000	200,000	150,000
Plant and equipment	624,000	606,000	18,000
Less: Accumulated depreciation	(139,000)	(107,000)	(32,000)
Patent	16,000	20,000	(4,000)
Total assets	$1,993,000	$1,695,000	$298,000
Liabilities and Stockholders' Equity			
Accounts payable and accrued expenses	$ 604,000	$ 563,000	$ 41,000
Note payable, long-term	150,000	—	150,000
Bonds payable	160,000	210,000	(50,000)
Deferred taxes payable	41,000	30,000	11,000
Common stock, $10 par	410,000	400,000	10,000
Additional paid-in capital	196,000	175,000	21,000
Retained earnings	432,000	334,000	98,000
Treasury stock, at cost	—	(17,000)	17,000
Total liabilities and stockholders' equity	$1,993,000	$1,695,000	$298,000

Statement of Income and Retained Earnings
For the Year Ended December 31, 2004

Net sales	$1,950,000
Operating expenses:	
Cost of sales	1,150,000
Selling and administrative expenses	505,000
Depreciation	53,000
	1,708,000
Operating income	242,000
Other (income) expense:	
Interest expense	15,000
Equity in net income of Hall, Inc.	(13,000)
Loss on sale of equipment	5,000
Amortization of patent	4,000
	11,000
Income before income taxes	231,000
Income taxes:	
Current	79,000
Deferred	11,000
Provision for income taxes	90,000
Net income	$ 141,000
Retained earnings, January 1, 2004	334,000
	475,000
Cash dividends, paid August 13, 2004	43,000
Retained earnings, December 31, 2004	$ 432,000

Additional information:

1. On January 2, 2004 Farrell sold equipment costing $45,000, with a book value of $24,000, for $19,000 cash.
2. On April 2, 2004 Farrell issued 1,000 shares of common stock for $23,000 cash.
3. On May 14, 2004 Farrell sold all of its treasury stock for $25,000 cash.
4. On June 1, 2004 Farrell paid $50,000 to retire bonds with a face value (and book value) of $50,000.
5. On July 1, 2004 Farrell purchased equipment for $63,000 cash.
6. On December 31, 2004 land with a fair market value of $150,000 was purchased through the issuance of a long-term note in the amount of $150,000. The note bears interest at the rate of 15% and is due on December 31, 2009.
7. Deferred taxes payable represent temporary differences relating to the use of accelerated depreciation methods for income tax reporting and the straight-line method for financial statement reporting.

Required

1. Prepare a worksheet to support a statement of cash flows for the Farrell Corporation for the year ended December 31, 2004, based on the preceding information.
2. Prepare the statement of cash flows. (*AICPA adapted*)

P21-14   ***Operating Cash Flows (Appendix)***   Use the information presented in P21-7.

Required

1. Using the direct method, prepare the cash flows from operating activities section of the 2004 statement of cash flows for the Lamberson Company.
2. *(Optional).* If you completed P21-7 earlier, prepare the remaining portion of the statement of cash flows. (A separate schedule reconciling net income to cash provided by operating activities is not necessary.)

P21-15 *Statement of Cash Flows (Appendix)* The following is a list of the items to be included in the preparation of the 2004 statement of cash flows for the Yellow Company:

1. Proceeds from sale of land, $2,100
2. Payments of interest, $5,000
3. Equipment acquired by capital lease, $7,200
4. Proceeds from issuance of preferred stock, $11,000
5. Other operating payments, $1,300
6. Interest and dividends collected, $4,700
7. Payments to employees, $20,300
8. Payment for purchase of investments, $12,100
9. Collections from customers, $54,500
10. Payments of income taxes, $2,900
11. Payment of dividends, $5,200
12. Other operating receipts, $1,600
13. Payments to suppliers, $29,500
14. Beginning cash balance, $29,700

Required Prepare the statement of cash flows using the direct method for operating cash flows.

P21-16 *Worksheet and Statement (Appendix)* Use the information presented in P21-13 for the Farrell Corporation.

Required

1. Using the direct method for operating cash flows, prepare a worksheet to support a 2004 statement of cash flows. (*Hint*: Combine the income statement and December 31, 2004 balance sheet items for the adjusted trial balance. Use a retained earnings balance of $291,000 in this adjusted trial balance.)
2. Prepare the statement of cash flows. (A separate schedule reconciling net income to cash provided by operating activities is not necessary.)

P21-17 *Comprehensive (Appendix)* The following are the December 31, 2003 post-closing trial balance and the December 31, 2004 adjusted trial balance of the Adair Company:

	12/31/03 Post-Closing Trial Balance		12/31/04 Adjusted Trial Balance	
Accounts	Debit	Credit	Debit	Credit
Cash	2,700		3,300	
Accounts receivable	7,300		6,200	
Inventory	8,100		9,900	
Investments in bonds	10,000		18,600	
Property and equipment	105,300		133,300	
Accumulated depreciation		42,400		49,200
Accounts payable		8,100		8,500
Salaries payable		1,300		700
Interest payable		0		300
Notes payable		0		9,000
Common stock, no par		43,600		58,100
Retained earnings		38,000		31,500
Sales				89,000
Cost of goods sold			48,800	
Depreciation expense			6,800	
Salaries expense			12,000	
Other operating expenses			1,700	
Interest revenue				1,200
Interest expense			900	
Income tax expense			6,000	
Totals	133,400	133,400	247,500	247,500

A review of the accounting records reveals the following additional information for 2004:

(a) Investments in bonds to be held to maturity were purchased at year-end for $8,600.
(b) A building was purchased for $28,000.
(c) A note payable was issued for $9,000.
(d) Common stock was issued for $14,500.
(e) Dividends of $6,500 were declared and paid.

Required

1. Using the direct method for operating cash flows, prepare a worksheet to support the 2004 statement of cash flows for the Adair Company.
2. Prepare the statement of cash flows. (A separate schedule reconciling net income to cash provided by operating activities is not necessary.)

P21-18 *Complex Worksheet (Appendix)*   Use the information presented in P21-9 for the Heinz Company.

Required Using the direct method for operating cash flows, prepare a worksheet to support a 2004 statement of cash flows.

INTERNET ASSIGNMENTS

Go to the Nikolai and Bazley **Intermediate Accounting** web site (http://Nikolai.swcollege.com). Click on Student Resources and internet homework assignments. Then click on the appropriate hot link (icon) for each company's web site, find the relevant accounting information, and answer the following questions.

I21-1   Go to the Hewlett Packard web site.

Required What was the company's (a) net cash provided by (used in) operating activities, (b) net cash used in (provided by) investing activities, and (c) net cash used in (provided by) financing activities for the most current year ended October 31? How much was the company's depreciation and amortization for that year? Assuming the amortization amount was minimal, what was the approximate gain or loss on the sale of property, plant, and equipment for that year? What was the amount that the company paid to repurchase its common stock during that year? Reconstruct the summary journal entry the company made to record this repurchase.

I21-2   Go to the Tech Data Corporation web site.

Required What method does the company use to report its operating cash flows? What was the company's net cash provided by (used in) operating activities for each of the two most recent years? What were the two largest causes of the change from last year to the current year? What was the company's net cash used in (provided by) investing activities for each of the two most recent years? What were the major causes of the change from last year to this year? What was the company's net cash (used in) provided by financing activities for each of the two most recent years? What were the major causes of the change from last year to this year? What does this information tell you about the company's liquidity?

CHAPTER
22

Accounting Changes and Errors

objectives

1 Identify the types of accounting changes.

2 Explain the methods of disclosing an accounting change.

3 Account for a change in accounting principle using the cumulative effect method.

4 Account for a change in accounting principle using a prior period restatement.

5 Account for a change in estimate.

6 Explain the conceptual issues regarding a change in accounting principle and a change in estimate.

7 Identify a change in a reporting entity.

8 Account for a correction of an error.

9 Summarize the methods for making accounting changes and correcting errors.

One of the qualitative characteristics of accounting is consistency (which we discussed in Chapter 2)—the conformity of accounting principles, policies, and procedures from period to period. However, in some instances a company may improve its reporting by changing its accounting to adopt a preferable or newly mandated generally accepted accounting principle, or to reflect changing economic conditions. When a company changes an accounting principle, the consistency of its financial statements is impaired; therefore, it is important to report the effects of the change in its financial statements. Accounting for the effects of changes in accounting principles is the primary topic of this chapter. We also discuss the accounting for errors.

TYPES OF ACCOUNTING CHANGES

The generally accepted accounting principles a company uses when it makes an accounting change were established by **APB Opinion No. 20,** which defines three types of changes as follows:

1 Identify the types of accounting changes.

1. *Change in an Accounting Principle.* This type of change occurs when a company adopts a generally accepted accounting principle different from the one used previously for reporting purposes, such as changing from the FIFO to the LIFO inventory cost flow assumption or changing from straight-line to accelerated depreciation.
2. *Change in an Accounting Estimate.* This type of change is inherent in the periodic presentation of financial statements. Preparing financial statements requires the use of estimates to determine many revenues and expenses, and such estimates sometimes must be changed as new events occur, as more experience is acquired, or as additional information is obtained. For example, a company may change the estimated life of a depreciable asset to reflect newly available information.
3. *Change in a Reporting Entity.* This type of change is caused by a change in the entity being reported. For example, a change in which subsidiaries are included in a company's consolidated financial statements is a change in a reporting entity.

In addition to the preceding changes, *APB Opinion No. 20* specifies the accounting principles to be used when a company discovers an error in its published financial statements. *Errors* are not considered to be accounting changes, but are the results of mathematical mistakes or mistakes in the application of accounting principles.

METHODS OF DISCLOSING AN ACCOUNTING CHANGE

2 Explain the methods of disclosing an accounting change.

There are three possible methods for a company to disclose an accounting change in its financial statements: (1) **retroactively adjust its past financial statements** (restate its financial statements of prior periods, often referred to as a **prior period adjustment** or **restatement**), (2) include the **cumulative effect** of the change in its income of the current period, or (3) adjust for the change **prospectively**. The APB established rules stipulating that one particular method be used for each category of change and error listed above. To introduce the three methods, we present the following example of a change in depreciation. You should understand that *these methods are not alternative ways* to account for a change in a depreciation method under generally accepted accounting principles, but instead we present them here to illustrate the differences between the methods. Exhibit 22-8 shows a summary of the impacts of the various rules on the financial statements, and it may be helpful to use that exhibit to follow this discussion. For this example, assume that at the beginning of year 1, the Dowson Company purchased an asset for $20,000, which had an estimated life of 4 years and a zero residual value. The company was depreciating the asset using the sum-of-the-years'-digits method and decides to switch to the straight-line method at the beginning of year 3. Straight-line and sum-of-the-years'-digits methods produce the annual depreciation amounts we show in Exhibit 22-1. In this example, we ignore the effects of income taxes.

EXHIBIT 22-1   Alternative Depreciation Methods

DOWSON COMPANY

| Year | Method | | Reduced Depreciation Amount Under Straight-Line Method |
	Sum-of-the-Years'-Digits	Straight-Line	
1	$ 8,000	$ 5,000	$3,000
2	6,000	5,000	1,000
3	4,000	5,000	(1,000)
4	2,000	5,000	(3,000)
	$20,000	$20,000	$ 0

Recall that companies present *comparative* financial statements in their annual report. Thus, a company will include the previous year(s) financial statements in addition to the current year's financial statements so that users can make comparisons and analyze trends. We assume that the Dowson Company presents comparative financial statements for years 1 and 2 in its annual report for year 3. If the company accounts for the change in depreciation method by *retroactive adjustment* of its financial statements, it changes its prior years' statements to the amounts it *would have* reported if it had used the new method since the asset was first acquired. Therefore, it includes $5,000 of depreciation expense (computed under the straight-line method) each year in the restated comparative income statements of year 1 and year 2 *instead* of the $8,000 and $6,000 amounts it originally reported (computed under the sum-of-the-years'-digits method). This change increases the reported income of the two years by $3,000 and $1,000 (ignoring income taxes). The reduced depreciation expense in both years also results in corresponding decreases in accumulated depreciation and increases in the carrying value of the asset of $3,000 and $4,000 ($3,000 + $1,000) on the company's ending comparative balance sheets of year 1 and year 2, respectively. Similarly, since the company closes its income to retained earnings, it increases the ending retained earnings balances by the same amounts. For the beginning balance sheet of the year of the change (year 3), the company reports the asset at its increased carrying value, and the balance of retained earnings also is higher by $4,000. The depreciation expense in year 3 is $5,000.

Alternatively, if the company accounts for the change as a *cumulative effect change*, it includes the $4,000 difference between the two depreciation methods for years 1 and 2 in its income statement of the current period (i.e., year 3). It does *not* make adjustments to the comparative financial statements of prior periods (i.e., years 1 and 2) for a cumulative effect change. Therefore, it increases the carrying value of the asset at the beginning of year 3 by $4,000 in conjunction with the inclusion of the $4,000 of additional income in the period of the change in accounting principle (year 3). The depreciation expense in year 3 is $5,000.

Finally, if the change is accounted for *prospectively*, the company writes off the unadjusted carrying value of the asset at the beginning of year 3 over the remaining life of the asset. In this case, under the sum-of-the-years'-digits method, the asset has a carrying value at the beginning of year 3 of $6,000 ($20,000 − $8,000 − $6,000). The company writes off this amount by the straight-line method through a depreciation expense of $3,000 per year over the remaining life of 2 years. Thus, if the company accounts for the change prospectively, the only effect in the year of the change (year 3) is a depreciation expense of $3,000 instead of the $4,000 that the company would have reported under the sum-of-the-years'-digits method. No change is made in the financial statements for years 1 and 2. Once again, note that the three methods are **not** allowable alternatives to account for a change in depreciation, but we presented them for illustrative purposes.

The retroactive adjustment, cumulative effect, and prospective methods are all required under particular circumstances, according to the provisions of *APB Opinion No. 20*. The basic principles are that generally:

- A *change in an accounting principle* is accounted for by the *cumulative effect* method.
- A *change in an accounting estimate* is accounted for *prospectively*.
- A *change in a reporting entity* is accounted for by prior period restatement (*retroactively*).
- An *error* is accounted for by prior period restatement (*retroactively*).

We discuss each of these methods and rules in greater detail in the following sections of the chapter, along with the exceptions to the rules. We provide summaries in Exhibits 22-7 and 22-8. Note that a company reports an accounting change in its financial statements only if the amount is material.

ACCOUNTING FOR A CHANGE IN ACCOUNTING PRINCIPLE

APB Opinion No. 20 states that a change in accounting principle results from the adoption of a generally accepted accounting principle that is different from the one used previously for reporting purposes, and includes both principles and practices as well as the methods of applying them. A change in accounting principle can be a *voluntary* change from one generally accepted principle to another, or a *mandatory* change because the FASB has adopted a new principle. However, a change in an accounting principle does *not* include the initial adoption of a generally accepted accounting principle because of events or transactions occurring for the first time, nor the adoption or modification of an accounting principle for transactions or events that are clearly different in substance from those previously occurring.[1] Also, a change to a generally accepted accounting principle from one that is *not* generally accepted is a correction of an error and *not* a change in accounting principle.

---

1. "Accounting Changes," *APB Opinion No. 20* (New York: AICPA, 1971), par. 7 and 8.

Cumulative Effect Method

3 Account for a change in accounting principle using the cumulative effect method.

The general rule is that **a company accounts for a change in an accounting principle as a *cumulative effect change*** as follows:

1. The financial statements for prior periods included for comparative purposes are presented as previously reported.
2. The cumulative effect of changing to the new accounting principle (net of applicable income taxes) on the amount of retained earnings at the *beginning* of the period in which the change is made is reported immediately before the caption "net income" on the income statement of the period of the change.
3. Income before extraordinary items and net income computed on a **pro forma** basis (that is, *as if* the new principle had been in effect for all past periods) are shown on the face of the income statements (below earnings per share) for *all* periods presented.
4. A description of the change and the reason for it, as well as the effect of the change on income before extraordinary items and on net income (and on related earnings per share amounts) of the period of the change are disclosed in the notes to the financial statements.[2]

ILLUSTRATION OF CUMULATIVE EFFECT METHOD   To illustrate the cumulative effect method of accounting for a change in accounting principle, suppose that the Goddard Company has assets for which it has been using straight-line depreciation for its financial reporting, and modified accelerated cost recovery system (MACRS) depreciation for its income tax reporting. At the beginning of 2005 it adopts an accelerated depreciation method for its financial reporting instead of the straight-line method previously used. This change results in additional depreciation of $40,000 ($140,000 instead of $100,000) for the year 2005. The company has calculated the information in Exhibit 22-2 for the change (assuming a 30% income tax rate). It computes the cumulative effect reported on its income statement for the year of the change (2005) as the difference between (1) the amount of the retained earnings at the *beginning* of the year of the change, and (2) the amount of retained earnings that it *would have reported* at that date if it had applied the new accounting principle (accelerated depreciation) retroactively to all affected prior periods. For the Goddard Company, the difference in depreciation at the beginning of 2005 is $90,000 ($430,000 − $340,000) before income taxes. The after-tax difference of $63,000 is the effect on retained earnings at the beginning of 2005 and Goddard includes it as a *reduction* in income for 2005 because its change *to* an accelerated depreciation method results in additional depreciation expense for all affected prior periods.

Exhibit 22-3 illustrates the disclosure of the change in accounting principle, assuming the company presents both the current year's (2005) and the previous year's (2004) income statements for comparative purposes. The top portion of Exhibit 22-3 is condensed and includes only total revenues and total expenses for each year. The revenues and

---

EXHIBIT 22-2   **Effects of Different Depreciation Methods**

Year	Straight-Line Depreciation	Accelerated Depreciation	Difference	Difference Net of Tax
Prior to 2004	$240,000	$300,000	$60,000	$42,000
2004	100,000	130,000	30,000	21,000
Total at beginning of 2005	$340,000	$430,000	$90,000	$63,000
2005	$100,000	$140,000	$40,000	$28,000

---

2. *Ibid.*, par. 19.

EXHIBIT 22-3   Reporting the Cumulative Effect of a Change in Accounting Principle

Condensed Comparative Income Statements

	2005	2004
Revenues (amounts assumed)	$3,000,000	$2,600,000
Expenses (amounts assumed)	(1,800,000)*	(1,600,000)*
Income before income tax	$1,200,000	$1,000,000
Income tax expense (30%)	(360,000)	(300,000)
Income before cumulative effect of a change in accounting principle	$ 840,000	$ 700,000
Cumulative effect on prior years (to December 31, 2004) of changing to a different depreciation method (net of $27,000 income taxes)	(63,000)	—
Net income	$ 777,000	$ 700,000
Earnings per share (assuming 100,000 shares outstanding):		
Income before cumulative effect of a change in accounting principle	$8.40	$7.00
Cumulative effect on prior years (to December 31, 2004) of changing to a different depreciation method	(0.63)	—
Earnings per share	$7.77	$7.00
Pro forma amounts assuming the new depreciation method is applied retroactively:		
Net income	$ 840,000	$ 679,000
Earnings per share	$8.40	$6.79

Note: Depreciation of plant equipment is computed by the double-declining-balance method in 2005. Depreciation of plant equipment in prior years was computed by the straight-line method. The new method of depreciation was adopted to recognize . . . (state justification for change of depreciation method) . . . and has been applied retroactively to equipment acquisitions of prior years. The effect of the change in 2005 was to decrease income by $28,000 ($0.28 per share). The retroactive adjustment of $63,000 (after reduction for income taxes of $27,000) to apply the new method is included in 2005 income. The pro forma amounts shown on the income statement have been adjusted for the effect of retroactive application on depreciation and related income taxes.

*Includes depreciation of $140,000 (accelerated depreciation) in 2005 and $100,000 (straight-line depreciation) in 2004.

---

expenses are not restated, but the expenses for 2005 include depreciation of $140,000 based on the newly adopted accelerated method, while the expenses for 2004 include depreciation of $100,000 based on the straight-line method the company used at that time. The company reports the $63,000 after-tax cumulative effect on its 2005 income statement (it reports the $27,000 related income taxes parenthetically) in a special category between "extraordinary items" and "net income,"[3] as we discussed in Chapter 4. Additionally, the company discloses the effect of this change on the earnings per share amounts on the face of the income statement. The third section of Exhibit 22-3 shows the pro forma amounts for 2004 and 2005. These are the amounts that the company would have reported *if* it had applied the newly adopted depreciation method in past

---

3. Conceptually, the FASB has discussed the possibility of reporting the cumulative effect in "comprehensive income" but not in net income. See "Elements of Financial Statements," *FASB Statement of Financial Accounting Concepts No. 6* (Stamford, Conn.: FASB, 1985), fn. 1 and the related discussion in Chapter 4. However, *FASB Statement No. 130* does *not* require the cumulative effect to be reported separately in other comprehensive income, which we discussed in Chapter 4.

periods. There is no difference between the pro forma income for 2005 and the income *before* the cumulative effect of a change in accounting principle in 2005 because the new depreciation method is used in computing that income for the year. However, the pro forma income for 2004 is reduced by $21,000. This amount represents the after-tax effect of the increased depreciation (from $100,000 to $130,000) for 2004, *assuming* that the company had used the accelerated method (see Exhibit 22-3). The note to the Goddard Company's financial statements illustrates the required disclosure describing the change, the reasons for the change, and the effect of the change upon the current year's net income and earnings per share.

In addition to the $63,000 after-tax reduction in income due to the cumulative effect change, the company increases accumulated depreciation. Thus, it decreases the carrying value of the assets at the beginning of 2005 by $90,000. The difference between these amounts is a $27,000 adjustment of the company's deferred income tax liability. Goddard records the cumulative effect change as follows:

Loss on Cumulative Effect of a Change in Depreciation Method	63,000	
Deferred Tax Liability	27,000	
Accumulated Depreciation		90,000

Since the company has used MACRS depreciation for income tax purposes in previous years, its use of the straight-line method in the financial statements created a deferred tax liability, as we discussed in Chapters 4 and 18. The change to the accelerated method for financial reporting reduces the difference between the tax and financial statement depreciation. Therefore, the deferred tax liability is reduced because part of the past temporary difference is reversed in this period.

In other situations, however, there may be an effect on income taxes payable or receivable. Generally, if a company also adopts the new accounting principle for income tax reporting, it must file for permission with the Internal Revenue Service. Upon approval, the company either will have to pay the amount of prior income taxes saved (e.g., as in a change from LIFO), in which case it would record income taxes payable, or will receive a tax refund, in which case income taxes receivable would be recorded. Knowledge of how tax regulations affect the income taxes applicable to a change in accounting principle is essential to properly account for the change for financial reporting purposes.

DIRECT AND INDIRECT EFFECTS In the Goddard Company example, we assumed that the change in depreciation method was the only item affecting the previous year's income. In more complex situations, a change in accounting principle might have an "interactive" effect on other items that affect prior years' income. For instance, a company might have bonus arrangements with management, profit sharing plans for employees, or royalty payments, all of which are based on the company's income. In these cases, a change in an accounting principle has both a "direct" and an "indirect" effect on the company's income of prior years. The *direct effect* is the amount by which its prior years' income is increased or decreased specifically as a result of the change in accounting principle. The *indirect effect* is the amount by which the company's income of prior years is affected by how the change in principle affects other elements of income. For instance, suppose the Goddard Company also has a bonus arrangement with management based upon net income. If the company had used accelerated depreciation instead of straight-line depreciation in prior years, the direct effect is a decrease in income due to higher depreciation expense. However, this decrease in income would have been partially offset by the indirect effect on the bonus arrangement. That is, because income was reduced as a result of higher depreciation, the bonus expense also would have been lower, and this, in turn, would have offset some of the income reduction.

In situations in which a change in accounting principle has both a direct and indirect effect on prior years' income, *APB Opinion No. 20* states that **a company recognizes only the *direct effect* (net of applicable income taxes) in determining the amount of the cumulative effect change included in its net income.** However, the company **includes the combined result of both the direct effect and the indirect effect (net of taxes)**

in the pro forma amounts shown on its income statement.[4] This difference in reporting the direct and indirect effects is appropriate because the direct effect is based on events of past periods. For example, a bonus of a prior period that a company has already paid would not be changed because of a change in an accounting principle applicable to the current and future periods. The pro forma amounts are prepared to assist users in comparing past information with that of current and future periods in which the bonus is paid based on income computed under the new accounting principle. Therefore, the company computes the pro forma amount for prior periods using the new principle and the *assumption* that a bonus was paid based on that income, making the amounts more *comparable* and enhancing their *predictive ability*.

Returning to the Goddard Company example, suppose that the example remains the same except that management receives a bonus of 10% of income before taxes and the bonus. In this case, the cumulative effect change would remain at $63,000 on its income statement. However, the pro forma amount of its net income for 2004 would be different. The change in depreciation method reduced 2004 income before taxes by $30,000 (see Exhibit 22-2); therefore, the bonus expense is reduced by $3,000 (10% × $30,000). In this case, the net effect is a reduction in its pro forma net income for 2004 of only $18,900 [0.70 after-tax rate × ($30,000 − $3,000)] to $681,100 ($700,000 − $18,900), which the company would report (in Exhibit 22-3) instead of $679,000. Similarly, it would report pro forma earnings per share of $6.81 instead of $6.79.

EXCEPTIONS TO THE GENERAL RULE The previous example illustrates the general rule for reporting a change in an accounting principle. *APB Opinion No. 20* specifies **four exceptions to this rule:**[5]

1. *Adoption of New Principle for Future Events.* If a company adopts a new accounting principle for use in the future but does not change the method currently used, it does *not* make a cumulative effect change. For example, a company might use a new depreciation method for newly acquired assets, but continue to use the old method for currently owned assets. In this situation, the company describes the nature of the change and its effect on income before extraordinary items and net income of the period of the change, together with the earnings per share amounts, in the notes to its financial statements.

2. *Cumulative Effect Not Determinable.* In some situations, a company cannot determine the cumulative effect because its accounting system does not include sufficient information. The principal example of this type of change is a change *to* the LIFO cost flow method because records of the costs of the additions to and reductions in the LIFO layers that would have occurred in the past had LIFO been used are probably not available. In these situations, the company discloses the effect of the change on the results of operations of the period of change (including earnings per share data), and the reason for omitting the cumulative effect and the pro forma amounts for prior years, in the notes to its financial statements.

3. *Initial Public Sale of Common Stock.* If a company makes accounting changes when it makes an initial public distribution (the first sale of common stock made available to the general public), it restates retroactively the financial statements for all prior periods presented. This exemption from the normal rules is available only once for changes made at the time a company first uses its financial statements to (1) obtain additional equity capital from investors, (2) effect a business combination, or (3) register securities. This exemption is logical because the company's financial statements have never before been available to the public and therefore there is no need to explain the changes made to the statements.

---

4. *APB Opinion No. 20, op. cit.,* par. 19, 22, and fn. 6.
5. *Ibid.,* par. 24, 26, and 27; "Reporting a Change in Accounting for Railroad Track Structures," *FASB Statement of Financial Accounting Standards No. 73* (Stamford, Conn.: FASB, 1983); and "The Equity Method of Accounting for Investments in Common Stock," *APB Opinion No. 18* (New York: AICPA, 1971), par. 19(m).

4. *Prior Period Restatement (Retroactive Adjustment) More Useful.* For certain changes in accounting principles, the APB considered that the advantages of retroactive restatement of prior periods outweigh the disadvantages. Therefore, **a company is required to make a prior period restatement (retroactive adjustment) instead of a cumulative effect adjustment for the following changes in accounting principles: (1) a change *from* the LIFO inventory cost flow method to another method, (2) a change in the method of accounting for long-term construction-type contracts, (3) a change to or from the "full cost" method of accounting that is used in the extractive industries, (4) a change from retirement-replacement-betterment accounting to depreciation accounting for railroad track structures, and (5) a change from the fair value method to the equity method for investments in common stock.** The reason for these exceptions to the general rule is that the size of the cumulative effect change may be so much greater than operating income that including it in a company's income statement might appear to reduce the significance of its income from operations.

Prior Period Restatement Method

4 Account for a change in accounting principle using a prior period restatement.

A company accounts for a change in accounting principle by prior period restatement as follows:

1. The revenues and expenses (including applicable income taxes) affected by the change are restated in the income statements of previous years included for comparative purposes.
2. The aggregate change in income (net of applicable income taxes) at the beginning of each year is added to, or subtracted from, retained earnings as a prior period adjustment on the comparative statements of retained earnings.
3. The related assets and liabilities, including applicable income taxes, are restated in the comparative balance sheets of previous years.
4. A description of the change and the reason for it, as well as the effect of the change on income before extraordinary items and on net income (and on related earnings per amounts) for all periods, are disclosed in the notes to the financial statements.

ILLUSTRATION OF PRIOR PERIOD RESTATEMENT   As we noted previously, the prior period restatement method is used for exceptions to the general rule for a change in accounting principle, for a change in entity, and for the correction of errors. We discuss this method in more detail in this section as it applies to a change in accounting principle. Recall that prior period restatement requires that a company change the prior financial statements to what they would have been had it used the new method in previous periods. Exhibits 22-4 and 22-5 illustrate a prior period restatement. In this example, the Werner Company changes *from* the LIFO to the FIFO inventory method at the beginning of 2005, and it presents comparative financial statements for 2005

EXHIBIT 22-4   Change in Accounting for Inventory

Year	Pretax Income Under LIFO Inventory Method	Pretax Income Under FIFO Inventory Method	Difference	Difference Net of Tax
Prior to 2004	$ 550,000	$ 850,000	$300,000	$210,000
2004	650,000	600,000	(50,000)	(35,000)
Total at beginning of 2005	$1,200,000	$1,450,000	$250,000	$175,000
2005	500,000	700,000	200,000	140,000
Total	$1,700,000	$2,150,000	$450,000	$315,000

EXHIBIT 22-5 Reporting a Change in Accounting Principle by Prior Period Restatement

WERNER COMPANY

Condensed Comparative Income Statements

	2005	2004
Revenues (amounts assumed)	$3,000,000	$2,800,000
Expenses (amounts assumed)	(2,300,000)*	(2,200,000)*
Income before income taxes	$ 700,000	$ 600,000
Income tax expense (30%)	(210,000)	(180,000)
Net income	$ 490,000	$ 420,000
Earnings per share (assuming 100,000 shares)	$4.90	$4.20

Comparative Statements of Retained Earnings

	2005	2004
Balance at beginning of year, as previously reported (assumed)	$2,455,000	$2,000,000
Add: Adjustment for the cumulative effect on prior years of retroactively applying the new method of accounting for inventory (net of $75,000 income taxes in 2005 and $90,000 income taxes in 2004)	175,000	210,000
Balance at beginning of year, as adjusted	$2,630,000	$2,210,000
Net income	490,000	420,000
Balance at end of year	$3,120,000	$2,630,000

Note: In 2005 the company accounted for inventory and cost of goods sold under the FIFO cost flow assumption; in all prior years, inventory and cost of goods sold were determined under the LIFO cost flow assumption. The new method of accounting for inventory was adopted to recognize . . . (state justification for change in accounting principle) . . ., and financial statements of prior years have been restated to apply the new method retroactively. FIFO has also been adopted for income tax purposes. The effect of the accounting change on 2005 income and on income as previously reported in 2004 is:

	Increase	
	2005	**2004**
Net income	$140,000	$(35,000)
Earnings per share	$1.40	$(0.35)

The balance of retained earnings for 2004 and 2005 has been adjusted for the effect (net of income taxes) of applying retroactively the new method of accounting.

* Includes cost of goods sold under the FIFO method.

---

and 2004. Exhibit 22-4 includes information for the Werner Company under the two methods. In addition, assume the income tax rate is 30% and the retained earnings balance at the beginning of 2005 (before adjustment) is $2 million. For simplicity, Exhibit 22-5 shows condensed comparative income statements and complete retained earnings statements for 2005 and 2004. In actual practice, the company reports the cost of goods sold on the income statements at the proper amount, assuming use of FIFO. Likewise, the comparative balance sheets include the correct amounts, as if the company had always used FIFO. Therefore, the company changes the balances of the inventory, income taxes payable, and retained earnings accounts to their proper amounts in the respective 2005 and 2004 balance sheets. We assume that the company also changes the inventory method it uses for income tax reporting purposes because of the LIFO conformity rule.

In Exhibit 22-5, in 2005 the Werner Company reports its net income for both 2004 and 2005 on the basis of the FIFO method as $490,000 and $420,000, respectively. Note that when it reported its 2004 income in 2004, it was based on the LIFO method and was $455,000 [70% (the after-tax rate) × $650,000]. The company adjusts the beginning retained earnings balance for the cumulative effect to date for each year reported. The adjustment of $210,000 in 2004 is the difference in income, net of tax, for the two methods for all years prior to 2004. That is, the balance in retained earnings at the beginning of 2004 would have been $2,210,000 if the company had used FIFO in all previous years. The 2004 net income of $420,000 is based on FIFO; using FIFO the retained earnings balance at the beginning of 2005 (the end of 2004) would have been $2,630,000. However, it was only $2,455,000 under LIFO. The adjustment of $175,000 in 2005 changes the beginning retained earnings balance to the $2,630,000, which is the correct amount for FIFO. Of course, the $175,000 adjustment is also the difference, net of tax, between the two methods at the beginning of 2005, as we show in Exhibit 22-4. The company describes the change and the reasons for it in a note to its financial statements. In addition to this information, the company also discloses the effect of the change on income before extraordinary items, net income, and the related earnings per share amounts for each year reported.

At the beginning of 2005 Werner Company records the retroactive adjustment as follows:

Inventory	250,000	
Retained Earnings		175,000
Income Taxes Payable		75,000

The company adds the $250,000 difference in the inventory amounts at the beginning of 2005 to the inventory account. We explained the $175,000 credit to retained earnings earlier. The adoption of FIFO means that the company may no longer use LIFO for income tax reporting and is obligated under the Internal Revenue Code to repay the taxes saved by the use of LIFO.[6] Therefore, it records $75,000 (0.30 × $250,000) as income taxes payable.

Transition Methods Required by the FASB

As we discussed earlier, *APB Opinion No. 20* specifies the general rules to be applied for a change in an accounting principle. However, when issuing *FASB Statements of Financial Accounting Standards*, the Board specifies transition rules if appropriate. **Transition rules** define the accounting method a company uses when it changes an accounting principle to conform to a new principle required by the issuance of a *Statement*. In these situations, the accounting principle being used is no longer acceptable and a new principle is required. When a *Statement* specifies a method, the transition rule usually requires retroactive (prior period) restatement. However, you should carefully examine each *Statement* so that you follow the specific transition rules.

FASB Interpretation No. 20 specifies the transition method required for an accounting change made according to the provisions of an *AICPA Statement of Position*. The company conforms to the method required by the *Statement*, if specified, or to the provisions of *APB Opinion No. 20* if no transition method is specified.

In summary, the cumulative effect adjustment required by *APB Opinion No. 20* applies to a *voluntary* change by a company from one generally accepted accounting principle to another. The *mandatory* adoption of a new accounting principle as a result of an FASB *Statement* usually requires prior period restatement. These conflicting requirements may tend to confuse the reporting of a change in an accounting principle, and it might be more desirable if one method were required for all situations.

---

6. The repayment is required to be made over a maximum of six years.

ACCOUNTING FOR A CHANGE IN AN ESTIMATE

Generally accepted accounting principles frequently require a company to use estimates for items such as uncollectible accounts receivable, inventory obsolescence, service lives, residual values, recoverable mineral reserves, warranty costs, pension costs, and the periods that it expects to be benefited by a deferred cost. Since estimating future events is an inherently uncertain process, changes in estimates are inevitable as new events occur, as more experience is acquired, or as additional information is obtained.

5 Account for a change in estimate.

APB Opinion No. 20 requires that **a company accounts for a change in an accounting estimate in the period of the change if the change affects that period only, or the period of the change and future periods if the change affects both.**[7] In other words, a change in an accounting estimate does *not* result in a cumulative change or a prior period restatement, but is accounted for *prospectively*.

For example, if a company changes the estimated service life of an asset, it calculates a revised periodic depreciation expense based on the current book value, the estimated residual value, and the new estimated service life. Suppose that a company owns an asset with an original cost of $100,000, an estimated life of 20 years, an estimated residual value of zero, and that the company is using straight-line depreciation. The company has recorded depreciation of $5,000 each year, so the asset's book value at the end of eight years is $60,000 [$100,000 − (8 × $5,000)]. Now suppose that at the beginning of the ninth year of the asset's life, the company changes the estimate of its life to a total of 23 years, so that 15 years now remain in the asset's life. The company depreciates the remaining book value over the remaining service life so that the depreciation expense of current and subsequent years is $4,000 ($60,000 ÷ 15) per year.

In addition to including this new amount of depreciation in its financial statements, the company discloses the effect of the change on its income and on the related earnings per share amounts of the current period in the notes to its financial statements. (This disclosure is not required for estimates made each period in the ordinary course of accounting for items such as uncollectible accounts or inventory obsolescence, unless the change is material.) To continue the preceding example, assume that the income tax rate is 30% and the company has 10,000 shares outstanding. The after-tax effect of such a change is an increase in net income (due to lower depreciation expense) of $700 [($5,000 − $4,000) × 0.70], and the effect on earnings per share is an increase of $0.07 per share ($700 ÷ 10,000). The company discloses these amounts in the notes to its financial statements. We presented another example of a change in estimate in Chapter 10.

ADDITIONAL ISSUES

We discuss several additional issues related to accounting changes in the following sections.

A Change in Principle Distinguished from a Change in an Estimate

Sometimes it is difficult for a company to distinguish between a change in an accounting principle and a change in an estimate. For example, a company may change from capitalizing and amortizing a cost to recording it as an expense when incurred because future benefits associated with the cost have become doubtful. The company adopted the new accounting method because of the change in estimated benefits and therefore the change in method is *inseparable* from the change in estimate. *APB Opinion No. 20* specifies that a change in accounting estimate that is related in whole or in part to a change in accounting principle is reported by a company as a change in an estimate because the cumulative effect attributable to the change in accounting principle cannot be separated from the current or future effects of the change in estimate.[8]

---

7. *APB Opinion No. 20, op. cit.*, par. 31.
8. *Ibid.*, par. 32.

An additional complexity arises with respect to the amortization (including depreciation and depletion) of the cost of an asset over its useful life. It can be argued that a change in the method of amortization is in fact a change in estimate. That is, the criteria that a company uses to select a method of amortization are that it is systematic and rational, and results in an appropriate matching of costs and benefits. Therefore, if the estimate of the pattern of future benefits is changed, for example, from declining benefits to constant benefits, a change in the depreciation method is appropriate. Thus, a change in an accounting method (depreciation) results from a change in an estimate. Nevertheless, a change in the amortization or depreciation method is considered a change in an accounting principle under the provisions of *APB Opinion No. 20*, which specifies that the effect of a change in a method of amortization can be separated from the effect of a change in (an) estimate. A change in method of amortization for previously recorded assets is treated as a change in accounting principle, whereas a change in the estimated period of benefit or residual value is treated as a change in accounting estimate.[9]

Preferability of the New Accounting Principle

When a company changes an accounting principle, management must justify the change on the grounds that the new principle is preferable to the old. The issuance of an FASB *Statement* is sufficient support for a change in accounting principle and does not require special justification; that is, the newly mandated principle is automatically considered to be preferable.[10] When a company changes from one acceptable principle to another, it usually includes the justification in a note to its financial statements in which it discusses the effect of the change. For example, two companies justified changes to LIFO by stating that:

1. The change reflects earnings more realistically by matching current costs with current revenues (Ford Motor Company).
2. The change was implemented in order to match current costs with current revenues, and to partially offset the effect of inflation on earnings (General Motors Corporation).

Nike justified its change to FIFO by stating that "this change was predicated on the fact that the LIFO method no longer matches the realities of how we do business." None of these typical disclosures is extensive, and it is interesting to note that the two changes to LIFO are both technically incorrect, since LIFO does not match current costs with current revenues, but only the most recently incurred historical costs.

The SEC requires that when a company that files with it makes an accounting change, the auditor must submit a letter indicating whether or not the change is to an alternative principle that, in the auditor's judgment, is preferable under the circumstances. "Preferable" is defined to mean that the new method represents an improved method of measuring business operations in the particular circumstances. Some accountants object to the SEC's requirement because it relates only to a company making a change in an accounting principle. There is no requirement that the auditor make a statement about the preferability of the accounting principles the company is currently using.

Accounting Changes in Interim Financial Statements

The principles to be followed when accounting changes are reported in interim financial statements are established by **FASB Statement No. 3.**[11] If a company makes a

---

9. *Ibid.*
10. "The Meaning of 'Present Fairly in Conformity With Generally Accepted Accounting Principles' in the Independent Auditor's Report," *Statement on Auditing Standards No. 69* (New York: AICPA, 1992), specifies that companies must adopt principles specified in pronouncements included in Categories A through D, as we discussed in Chapter 1.
11. "Reporting Accounting Changes in Interim Statements," *FASB Statement of Financial Accounting Standards No. 3* (Stamford, Conn.: FASB, 1974).

cumulative effect accounting change during the *first* interim period of the fiscal year, it includes the cumulative effect of the change on retained earnings at the beginning of the year in the net income of the first interim period. However, if it makes a cumulative-type change in *other than the first interim period*, it does not include a cumulative effect change in the net income of the period of the change. Instead, it restates the prior interim periods by applying the newly adopted accounting principle to those prechange interim periods. It includes the cumulative effect of the change on retained earnings at the beginning of the fiscal year in the restated net income of the first interim period. In summary, **a company accounts for a cumulative effect change in the first interim period, regardless of the interim period in which it occurs.**

For the special situations in which sufficient information is not available for determining the amount of the cumulative effect adjustment, an alternative procedure is followed. (We discussed these types of changes earlier and the primary example is a change to LIFO.) If a company makes the change in the *first* interim period, disclosure of the change is necessary, but no adjustments are required. However, if the company makes the change in *other than the first interim period*, it restates the financial statements of the prechange interim periods by applying the newly adopted accounting principle to those periods. Again, the effect is to account for the change in the first interim period, no matter in which interim period the change is made.

CONCEPTUAL EVALUATION OF ACCOUNTING FOR A CHANGE IN ACCOUNTING PRINCIPLE AND A CHANGE IN ESTIMATE

As we discussed earlier, there are three possible alternatives that a company might use to account for a change in an accounting principle or in an accounting estimate. These alternatives are prior period (retroactive) restatement, cumulative effect adjustment, and prospective adjustment. We discuss the advantages and disadvantages of these alternatives, and selected additional issues, in the following sections.

6 Explain the conceptual issues regarding a change in accounting principle and a change in estimate.

Prior Period Restatement

The major argument in favor of prior period (retroactive) restatement is that all the financial statements that a company presents at a given date are prepared on the basis of *consistent* accounting principles. Thus, when a user of the financial statements evaluates the company's current financial results, it is possible to make a comparison with the previous year's financial statements without adjusting for a change in accounting principle. Prior period restatement is the usual method required for a change in accounting principle mandated by the FASB because it does not penalize (or increase) a company's current year's earnings for an event that is beyond the control of the company's management.

On the other hand, the prior period restatement method has several disadvantages. First, a company's financial statements issued in previous years are changed under this method. This creates the possibility that users may be confused by the change in the reported results, and that confidence in the information may be reduced because "the numbers changed." Second, the method is not consistent with the all-inclusive income concept, which is the basis of generally accepted accounting principles as we discussed in Chapter 4. Third, there may be an impact on a company's contractual arrangements (such as bonus agreements, borrowing indentures, royalties, or profit sharing) when its previously reported income is changed. Fourth, prior period restatement lends itself to income manipulation by a company's management because items are excluded from its current year's income statement. When a company makes a prior period restatement, it can decrease retained earnings without including the change as a reduction in its current year's income. Thus, the sum of the net incomes that it reports over the years would be more than the increase in its retained earnings (excluding consideration of dividends). Conversely, a prior period restatement that increases the balance in a company's retained earnings does so without being added to its current year's net income.

Cumulative Effect Adjustment

In contrast to prior period restatement, the use of the cumulative effect adjustment method *is* consistent with the all-inclusive income concept. The emphasis placed on a company's income statement by users of financial statements makes it desirable that changes in its stockholders' equity (excluding capital contributions and dividends) be included in its net income rather than directly in retained earnings. In addition, a company reports an event that occurs during the period of the change in accounting principle in its financial statements of that period, and does not adjust past financial statements. Cumulative effect adjustment is the basic method required for a voluntary change in accounting principle because the company reports the results of current decisions by its management in the current year's earnings.

The major argument against the cumulative effect adjustment method is that a company does not present comparative financial statements based on consistent application of accounting principles. Thus, its past financial statements are based on the old principle, its current financial statements include the cumulative effect of the change, and both current and future financial statements utilize the new principle. Users of financial statements may be confused by the lack of consistency between the years, and analyses of trends may be disrupted. However, the potential confusion can be mitigated by two factors. First, the auditor's report included with the company's financial statements is modified to indicate that there has been a change in accounting principle. This draws the reader's attention to the change. Second, the requirement that the company must report *pro forma* information is intended to enable the user of its financial statements to understand the impact of the change in accounting principle on the financial statements that are presented on the basis of the previously used principle.

Prospective Adjustment

Accounting estimates used for periodic reporting inevitably change over time. A company also adopts new accounting principles from time to time. It may be argued that it is better for a company to account for such changes by considering their effect on the future and to make no attempt to change what has already been reported.

Since a company makes an estimate with the best information available at that time, and changes this estimate only to reflect new information, accounting for a change in an estimate with a prospective adjustment is especially appropriate. In addition, the alternative of reporting the effect of a change of estimate cumulatively or retroactively might cause considerable confusion among users of financial statements because of the frequency of such changes.

In the case of a change in an accounting principle, the same arguments can be made about the desirability of a company not changing what it has already reported (that is, confusion and the all-inclusive income concept). Moreover, it may be argued that a change in an accounting principle, although it occurs in the current period, has little or no relation to the current period's economic events, or to the company's income generated from providing goods and services to its customers. Therefore, the change should be accounted for prospectively. Conversely, it can be argued that a change in an accounting principle is an event of the current period and a company should not account for it prospectively, but by a cumulative effect adjustment.

ACCOUNTING FOR A CHANGE IN A REPORTING ENTITY

7 Identify a change in a reporting entity.

The third type of change defined by *APB Opinion No. 20* is a change in a reporting entity. As we noted earlier, **a company accounts for a change in reporting entity as a prior period restatement (retroactively) so that all the financial statements it presents are for the same entity.**[12] This procedure improves consistency.

---

12. *APB Opinion No. 20, op. cit.,* par. 34.

A change in an accounting entity occurs mainly when (1) a company presents consolidated or combined statements in place of the statements of individual companies, (2) there is a change in the specific subsidiaries that make up the group of companies for which consolidated financial statements are presented, and (3) the companies included in combined financial statements change.

When a change in an accounting entity occurs, the company includes in the notes to its financial statements of the period in which it makes the change a description of the change as well as the reason for it, and the effect of the change on income before extraordinary items, net income, and related earnings per share amounts for all periods presented. However, financial statements of subsequent periods need not repeat the disclosures. We do not discuss the accounting for a change in an entity here, but it is included in advanced accounting books.

ACCOUNTING FOR A CORRECTION OF AN ERROR

The correction of an error is *not* an accounting change under the requirements of *APB Opinion No. 20.* However, after the issuance of the *Opinion*, it was still unclear whether a company should account for the results of a litigation settlement as a prior period adjustment. It could be argued that such a settlement is a prior period adjustment because it relates either to the period in which the event causing the litigation occurred or to the period in which the litigation was filed. Alternatively, it could be argued that the litigation settlement is an event of the period of settlement and should be included in the company's current period's income. This issue was resolved by **FASB Statement No. 16,** which specifies that corrections of errors are reported as prior period adjustments and therefore a litigation settlement is *not* a prior period adjustment.[13] **A company accounts for a material error of a past period that it discovers in the current period as a prior period adjustment (restatement)** and therefore excludes it from the determination of its net income for the period. A company reports an error of a past period (net of related income tax effects) as an adjustment to the beginning balance of retained earnings on its statement of retained earnings. As we illustrated in Exhibit 22-5, when a company presents comparative statements, it makes corresponding adjustments to the affected items on its income statements and to its retained earnings balances on its statement of retained earnings, as well as to the affected items on the balance sheets for *all* periods reported. In addition, it discloses the nature of the error in previously issued financial statements and the effect of its correction on income before extraordinary items, net income, and the related earnings per share amounts in the notes to the financial statements for each year reported. We discuss the journal entries required to correct errors later in the chapter.

Examples of errors that a company might make include:

1. The use of an accounting principle that is *not* generally accepted.
2. The use of an estimate that was *not* made in good faith.
3. Mathematical miscalculations, such as the incorrect computation of its inventory; or logical errors, such as the omission of residual value in the calculation of straight-line depreciation.
4. The omission of a deferral or accrual, such as the failure to accrue warranty costs.

Error Analysis

Because errors, by their very nature, happen in unpredictable and often illogical ways, it is difficult to generalize about the kinds of errors that a company might make and

8 Account for a correction of an error.

---

13. "Prior Period Adjustments," *FASB Statement of Financial Accounting Standards No. 16* (Stamford, Conn.: FASB, 1977).

the journal entries that may be required to correct them. Many errors are discovered automatically through proper use of the double-entry system; others are found by the company's internal or external auditors before being included in its financial statements. In this section we are concerned about errors that escape detection until after they are included in a company's published financial statements. We categorize them according to the effect they have on the financial statements.

ERRORS AFFECTING ONLY THE BALANCE SHEET Some errors affect only balance sheet accounts. For example, a company may include a long-term note receivable as a current note receivable. Reclassification of the note only affects its balance sheet. Therefore, if the error occurred in a prior period, the company does not make a correcting journal entry, but if it presents comparative financial statements in the current year, it corrects the financial statements of the prior period by reclassifying the item.

ERRORS AFFECTING ONLY THE INCOME STATEMENT Errors that affect only income statement accounts usually result from the misclassification of items. For example, a company may include interest revenue with sales revenue. Errors of this kind require reclassification but do not affect net income. Therefore, if the error occurred in a prior period, the company does not make a correcting journal entry, but if it presents comparative financial statements in the current year, it corrects the financial statements of the prior period by reclassifying the item.

ERRORS AFFECTING BOTH THE INCOME STATEMENT AND BALANCE SHEET An error may affect both an income statement account and a balance sheet account, such as the failure to accrue a liability at the end of the period. For example, if a company fails to accrue interest, it understates interest expense on its current income statement and omits interest payable from its ending balance sheet.

Errors that affect both the income statement and the balance sheet can be classified as counterbalancing or noncounterbalancing. **Counterbalancing** errors are those that are automatically corrected in the next accounting period, even if they are not discovered. Consider the effect of unrecorded interest in the previous paragraph, and assume that the amount of the interest is $2,000 and the income tax rate 30%. The effects of the error on the company's financial statements of the period in which it made the error are as follows:

1. Interest expense is understated by $2,000.
2. Income before income taxes is overstated by $2,000.
3. Income tax expense is overstated by $600.
4. Net income is overstated by $1,400.
5. Retained earnings is overstated by $1,400.
6. Interest payable is understated by $2,000.
7. Income taxes payable is overstated by $600.

In the next period, when the company pays the interest and records the entire payment as an expense, the following additional errors occur:

1. Interest expense is overstated by $2,000.
2. Income before income taxes is understated by $2,000.
3. Income tax expense is understated by $600.
4. Net income is understated by $1,400.

Since the amount of the interest expense overstatement in the second period is equal to the understatement of the previous period, the net income understatement in the second period offsets the overstatement in the first period. Therefore, no balance sheet accounts are in error at the end of the second period. That is, the total liabilities are no longer understated, and the retained earnings balance is now correct. The errors have automatically counterbalanced. Note also that even though the errors counterbalance, the need for a correcting journal entry and for correction of the financial statements depends upon *when* the error is discovered. If the company discovers the error *during* the second year, it must make a journal entry so that the interest expense and net income for the second year are reported correctly. If the company discovers the error *after* the second year, no correcting journal entry is needed. However, the financial statements for the two years are in error, so the company must correct (restate) the financial statements unless sufficient time has passed so that they are *not* being presented for comparative purposes.

Noncounterbalancing errors are those that are not offset in the next accounting period. For example, suppose that a company erroneously records the purchase of an asset costing $10,000 as supplies expense in the year of purchase, although it should capitalize and depreciate the asset by the straight-line method over 10 years with no residual value for both financial reporting and income tax purposes. Furthermore, the company records a full year's depreciation in the year of acquisition, the income tax rate is 30% and the MACRS depreciation is assumed to be $1,400. The effects of the error on the company's financial statements of the period in which it made the error are as follows:

1. Supplies expense is overstated by $10,000.
2. The asset is understated by $10,000.
3. Depreciation expense is understated by $1,000 ($10,000 ÷ 10).
4. Accumulated depreciation is understated by $1,000.
5. Income before income taxes is understated by $9,000 ($10,000 − $1,000).
6. Income tax expense is understated by $2,700 ($9,000 × 0.30).
7. Net income is understated by $6,300 ($9,000 − $2,700).
8. Retained earnings is understated by $6,300.
9. Deferred tax liability is understated by $120 [($1,400 − $1,000) × 30%]
10. Income taxes payable are understated by $2,580 ($2,700 − $120).

The understatement of the asset and the depreciation expense continues until the end of the asset's life, at which point the balance sheet accounts (asset, accumulated depreciation, income taxes payable, and retained earnings) are correct for the first time since the error was made. Consequently, if the company discovers the error before the end of the life of the asset, it must make a correcting journal entry.

Error Correction

The approach to correcting an error is difficult to generalize because of the variety of errors that may occur. Each error must be examined carefully to determine how the transaction *was* recorded and how it *should have been* recorded. The correction can then be made by (1) recording a single comprehensive journal entry (which is the preferred method in practice), or (2) reversing the original incorrect journal entry and then recording the original transaction or event as it should have been recorded initially. For example, consider a building improvement costing $20,000 that a company recorded as Repair Expense when it should have capitalized the item. A single comprehensive journal entry to correct the error when it is discovered *in the next period* is:

Building	20,000	
Retained Earnings		20,000

Note that in this entry, we are ignoring income taxes and depreciation, which we will discuss later. Note also that the correction is not made by a credit to Repair Expense because the company discovered the error in the period following the one in which it was made. At this point the company's revenue and expense accounts for the previous period have been closed to retained earnings, so the correction of the previous year's income is made directly to the Retained Earnings account (or to an account, Correction of Prior Years' Income Due to Error in Recording Building Improvement, which is closed to Retained Earnings). If the company presents comparative financial statements, it corrects them as we discussed earlier.

If the second approach is used, two separate journal entries are required. First, the company reverses the original entry (but it again credits the Retained Earnings account because the Repair Expense account has been closed), and then the company makes the journal entry that it should have made, as follows:

Cash	20,000	
Retained Earnings		20,000
Building	20,000	
Cash		20,000

In this simple situation, the second approach may seem unnecessary, but it can prove useful in more complex circumstances.

In the previous example, the company must also correct the recorded amount of depreciation. Since it discovered the error in the next period, it corrects Retained Earnings (for the previous period's depreciation expense understatement and income overstatement) and Accumulated Depreciation by the following journal entry (assuming a 10-year life, no residual value, straight-line depreciation, and that a full year's depreciation is recorded in the year of acquisition):

Retained Earnings	2,000	
Accumulated Depreciation		2,000

The company records depreciation expense for the second year in the normal way (because we assumed that it discovered the error during the second year).

A logical sequence of steps for the analysis and correction of an error is indicated by the preceding discussion:

Step 1. Analyze the original erroneous journal entry and determine all the debits and credits that were recorded.

Step 2. Determine the correct journal entry and the appropriate debits and credits.

Step 3. Evaluate whether the error has caused additional errors in other accounts.

Step 4. Prepare the correcting entry(ies), remembering to record any corrections of the revenues and expenses for prior years as adjustments to retained earnings.

We illustrate additional examples of some types of errors that can be expected to occur more frequently in the following sections for the Huggins Company. For simplicity, these corrections ignore the potential impact on taxable income, income tax expense, and deferred income taxes, although, in reality, correcting entries for these items may be required. Assume all errors are material.

OMISSION OF UNEARNED REVENUE In December 2004 the Huggins Company received $10,000 as a prepayment for renting a building to another company for all of 2005. The company recorded this transaction by a debit to Cash and a credit to Rent Revenue. The revenue should be reported in 2005, but the company erroneously included the revenue in its 2004 income. If the company discovers this error in 2005, it has overstated income for 2004 by including $10,000 rent revenue and therefore it has to decrease Retained Earnings by $10,000. Furthermore, it has to record the rent revenue in 2005. Therefore, the company makes the following correcting entry:

Retained Earnings	10,000	
Rent Revenue		10,000

If the company does not discover the error until 2006, it does not make a correcting entry because the error has counterbalanced. However, if the company presents 2004 and 2005 financial statements for comparative purposes, the company corrects (restates) them as we discussed earlier.

FAILURE TO ACCRUE REVENUE   On December 31, 2004 the Huggins Company failed to accrue interest revenue of $500 that it had earned but not received on an outstanding note receivable. If the company discovered the error in 2005, it has understated income for 2004 by omitting interest revenue of $500 and therefore it has to increase Retained Earnings by that amount. If we assume that the company credits any cash received in 2005 to Interest Revenue, it has overstated the revenue account by $500 in 2005, and so it makes the following correcting entry:

Interest Revenue	500	
Retained Earnings		500

If the company discovered the error in 2006, it does not make a correcting entry because the error has counterbalanced. However, if the company presents 2004 and 2005 financial statements for comparative purposes, it corrects them.

OMISSION OF PREPAID EXPENSE   In December 2004 the Huggins Company paid $1,000 for insurance coverage for the year 2005. It recorded the original entry as a debit to Insurance Expense and a credit to Cash, and did not record a year-end adjustment. If the company discovers this error at the end of 2005, it has understated its income for 2004 by the $1,000 overstatement of insurance expense and, therefore, it has to increase Retained Earnings by this amount. Since the company did not record prepaid insurance in 2004, it has understated Insurance Expense by $1,000 for 2005 and it makes the following correcting entry:

Insurance Expense	1,000	
Retained Earnings		1,000

Alternatively, if the payment of $1,000 in 2004 was for a two-year insurance policy, the correcting entry at the end of 2005 is:

Insurance Expense	500	
Prepaid Insurance	500	
Retained Earnings		1,000

If the company does not discover this error until 2006 and the payment in 2004 was for one year's insurance, it does not make a correcting entry because the error has counterbalanced. If the company discovered the error in 2006 and the payment was for two years' insurance, the correcting entry is:

Insurance Expense	500	
Retained Earnings		500

In this situation, $500 of the error has counterbalanced, leaving only $500 to be corrected. Once again, the company corrects the 2004 and 2005 financial statements if it presents them for comparative purposes.

ERROR IN ENDING INVENTORY   At December 31, 2004 the Huggins Company recorded its ending inventory at $50,000. During 2005 it discovered that the correct inventory value should have been $55,000 because it made an error in the inventory count. Since it understated the ending inventory for 2004 by $5,000, it overstated cost of goods sold for 2004, and understated income. Therefore, it has to increase Retained Earnings by this amount. Since the company has understated its beginning inventory in 2005, it has to increase it by $5,000, and so it makes the following correcting entry:

Inventory	5,000	
Retained Earnings		5,000

If the company does not discover this error until 2006, it does not make a correcting entry because the error has counterbalanced, but it corrects the 2004 and 2005 financial statements because the error in the inventory affects cost of goods sold in both years.

ERROR IN PURCHASES During December 2004 the Huggins Company made a purchase on credit that it had not paid at year's end. It recorded this transaction incorrectly at $17,000 although the invoice price of the inventory was $27,000. Since the company understated the purchases and accounts payable by $10,000, it understated cost of goods sold in 2004 (assuming it recorded the ending inventory correctly) and overstated income by $10,000. Therefore, it has to decrease Retained Earnings by this amount. The company understated Accounts Payable in 2005 by $10,000, and so it makes the following correcting entry:

Retained Earnings	10,000	
Accounts Payable		10,000

Because of the creditor's demand for payment, it is difficult to conceive of such an error remaining undetected until 2006, but if that did happen, the correcting entry is as shown. Since the ending inventory was correct, the error was not counterbalanced and the company has overstated its income for 2004 and retained earnings until it makes the correction. We illustrated more examples of the effects of errors in inventory and purchases in Chapter 7.

FAILURE TO ACCRUE ESTIMATED BAD DEBTS The Huggins Company failed to accrue an allowance for doubtful accounts of $7,000 in its 2004 financial statements. The result of this error was the understatement of bad debt expense by $7,000 and, therefore, the company has to decrease Retained Earnings by this amount. The discovery of the error in 2005 indicates that the company has overstated Accounts Receivable (net) by $7,000, and so it makes the following correcting entry:

Retained Earnings	7,000	
Allowance for Doubtful Accounts		7,000

Alternatively, if the company discovers the error after it makes the estimate of doubtful accounts and records it by the aging method at the end of 2005, it has overstated the bad debt expense because part of the charge relates to the 2004 error. Therefore, it makes the following correcting entry:

Retained Earnings	7,000	
Bad Debt Expense		7,000

It is obviously not possible to give examples of every possible error. In each situation the facts must be carefully examined, with particular consideration given to the time periods involved and the possibility of additional errors resulting from the initial error. For example, the effects of errors on the company's prior and current income tax expense and deferred income taxes must be assessed. Adjustments may have to be made to retained earnings if there were changes in income tax expense for prior periods. Furthermore, if taxable income is incorrect for prior periods, amended tax returns may be necessary.

Exhibit 22-6 shows a schedule which summarizes the effects of the multiple errors of the Huggins Company on its income before income taxes for the years affected. The schedule includes each of the errors. Note that the omission of the prepaid expense assumes a 2-year insurance policy (not a 1-year insurance policy). The net effect of the errors is to reduce its pretax income for 2004 by $20,500, increase pretax income for 2005 by $4,000, and reduce assets by $6,500 and increase liabilities by $10,000 on its 2005 balance sheet. If the income tax rate is 30% and the correction of each of these errors affects taxable income, the 2004 errors enable the company to obtain a tax refund of $6,150 (30% × $20,500), and it also makes the following journal entry:

Income Tax Refund Receivable	6,150	
Retained Earnings		6,150

EXHIBIT 22-6   Summary of Corrections of Errors Discovered in 2005

Error	Effect of Correction on Income		Increases on Balance Sheet
	2004	2005	December 31, 2005
Omission of unearned revenue	$(10,000)	$10,000	
Failure to accrue interest revenue	500	(500)	
Omission of prepaid expense (2-year insurance policy)	1,000	(500)	Prepaid insurance $500
Error in ending inventory	5,000	(5,000)	
Error in purchases	(10,000)		Accounts payable $10,000
Failure to accrue estimated bad debts	(7,000)		Allowance for doubtful accounts $7,000
Total pretax effect	$(20,500)	$ 4,000	
Less: Income tax effect	6,150		
After-tax effect	$(14,350)		

The 2005 corrections do not need a separate correction for income taxes in this example because we assume that the company has not closed its books for 2005.

International Accounting Differences

Considerable flexibility is allowed by international accounting standards in regard to accounting changes. The correction of an error may be accounted for by a prior period restatement or in the current period's net income. A change in accounting principle may be accounted for by a prior period restatement, a cumulative effect adjustment, or in the current and future periods. Accounting for a change in estimate is the same as U.S. standards, although a change in a depreciation method is treated as a change in estimate, and not as a change in accounting principle as required by U.S. standards.

EXHIBIT 22-7   Summary of Methods to Be Used for Changes in Accounting Principles and Corrections of Errors

1. Change in Accounting Principle — Cumulative effect adjustment

   Exceptions to this rule:
   Cumulative effect not determinable — Disclose effects of change
   Change *from* LIFO to another inventory cost flow method — Retroactive (prior period) restatement
   Change *to* LIFO from another inventory cost flow method (if cumulative effect not determinable) — Prospective adjustment
   Change for long-term construction-type contracts — Retroactive (prior period) restatement
   Change to or from the full-cost method for extractive industries — Retroactive (prior period) restatement
   Change from retirement-replacement-betterment accounting to depreciation accounting — Retroactive (prior period) restatement
   Change from fair value to equity method — Retroactive (prior period restatement)
   Change mandated by the FASB — Retroactive (prior period) restatement (usually)
2. Change in Accounting Estimate — Prospective adjustment
3. Change in Entity — Retroactive (prior period) restatement
4. Correction of Error — Retroactive (prior period) restatement

EXHIBIT 22-8 Summary of Impacts on Financial Statements of Methods Used for Accounting Changes and Errors

Retroactive (Prior Period) Restatement

Previous Years	Current Year
Income Statement Change revenue or expense amounts to reflect new accounting principle, correct information, or new accounting entity. *Ending Balance Sheet* Change asset, liability, and stockholders' equity account balances to reflect amounts that would have been computed if the principle had always been used, the error had not been made, or the new entity had always existed.	*Income Statement* Compute revenue or expense amounts using new accounting principle, corrected information, or new accounting entity. *Ending Balance Sheet* No additional changes. Asset, liability, and stockholders' equity account balances are amounts that would have been computed if the new principle had always been used, the error had not been made, or the new entity had always existed.

Cumulative Effect Adjustment

Previous Years	Current Year
Income Statement No change *Ending Balance Sheet* No change	*Income Statement* Include the cumulative effect of differences in revenues or expenses of previous years (net of tax) in net income. *Ending Balance Sheet* Change the asset, liability, and stockholders' equity account balances to amounts that would have been computed if the new principle had always been used.

Prospective Adjustment

Previous Years	Current Year
Income Statement No change *Ending Balance Sheet* No change	*Income Statement* Compute revenue and expense amounts using the new estimate or the newly adopted accounting principle for new events. *Ending Balance Sheet* Asset, liability, and stockholders' equity account balances include amounts based on the use of the old estimate or principle in past years and the new estimate or newly adopted principle for new events in the current (and future) year(s).

SUMMARY OF METHODS FOR ACCOUNTING CHANGES AND ERRORS

9 Summarize the methods for making accounting changes and correcting errors.

Exhibit 22-7 provides a summary of the methods to be used in the various situations we discussed in the chapter. Exhibit 22-8 presents the impacts of these methods on a company's financial statements.

SUMMARY

At the beginning of the chapter, we identified several objectives you would accomplish after reading the chapter. The objectives are listed below, each followed by a brief summary of the key points in the chapter discussion.

1. **Identify the types of accounting changes.** The three types of accounting changes are a change in accounting principle, a change in accounting estimate, and a change in a reporting entity.
2. **Explain the methods of disclosing an accounting change.** There are three possible methods for a company to disclose an accounting change: retroactively adjust its past financial statements, include the cumulative effect of the change in its income statement of the current period, or adjust for the change prospectively.
3. **Account for a change in accounting principle using the cumulative effect method.** Under the cumulative effect method, the financial statements of the company for prior periods are presented as previously reported, the cumulative effect of changing to the new accounting principle is included in net income in the period of the change, income before extraordinary items and net income is reported on a pro forma basis for all periods presented, and a description of the change and the reason for it are disclosed in the notes to the financial statements.
4. **Account for a change in accounting principle using a prior period restatement.** Under a prior period restatement, the revenues and expenses affected by the change are restated in the company's previous income statements, the aggregate change in income (net of taxes) at the beginning of each year is adjusted to retained earnings as a prior period adjustment, the related assets and liabilities are restated, and a description of the change and the reason for it are disclosed in the notes to the financial statements.
5. **Account for a change in estimate.** A company accounts for a change in estimate in the period of the change if the change affects that period only, or the period of the change and future periods if the change affects both.
6. **Explain the conceptual issues regarding a change in accounting principle and a change in estimate.** The conceptual issues include the consistency of the information presented, the changing of previously reported information, the all-inclusive income concept, income manipulation, and any impact on contractual arrangements.
7. **Identify a change in a reporting entity.** A change in a reporting entity occurs mainly when a company presents consolidated or combined statements in place of statements of individual companies, there is a change in the specific subsidiaries that make up the group of companies for which consolidated statements are presented, and the companies included in combined financial statements change.
8. **Account for a correction of an error.** A company accounts for a material error of a past period that it discovers in the current period as a prior period adjustment. That is, it includes the amount of the error (net of taxes) as an adjustment to its beginning balance of retained earnings on its statement of retained earnings, and restates its previous comparative financial statements.
9. **Summarize the methods for making accounting changes and correcting errors.** A summary of the methods for making accounting changes and correcting errors is included in Exhibit 22-7.

QUESTIONS

Q22-1 Describe the three types of accounting changes.

Q22-2 Describe the three possible methods that a company could use to report the effect of accounting changes. Give one reason in favor of, and one against, each alternative.

Q22-3 Describe two situations in which a company could justify a change in an accounting principle.

Q22-4 What distinguishes a change in an accounting principle from a change in an estimate? How should a company account for each?

Q22-5 What are the four exceptions to the normal method a company uses to account for a change in an accounting principle?

Q22-6 In which situations is it likely that a company may not be able to determine the cumulative effect? What is the correct accounting in such cases?

Q22-7 Which changes in accounting principles should a company account for retroactively? Why?

Q22-8 What is a *pro forma statement?* In which situations must a company report a pro forma statement?

Q22-9 How does a company report a change in an accounting principle in its interim financial statements?

Q22-10 Give three examples of a change in an estimate. How does a company account for such changes?

Q22-11 Describe a change in a reporting entity. How does a company account for such changes?

Q22-12 How does a company report an error of a prior period that it discovers in the current period?

Q22-13 Describe two errors that affect only a company's balance sheet.

Q22-14 Describe two errors that affect only a company's income statement.

Q22-15 Describe two errors that are counterbalanced in the following period.

Q22-16 Describe two errors that are not counterbalanced in the following period.

Q22-17 Why does a company correct errors even after they have counterbalanced?

CASES

C O M M U N I C A T I O N

C22-1 Accounting Changes

There are three types of accounting changes: changes in accounting principles, changes in accounting estimates, and changes in reporting entities.

Required Explain the differences and similarities between each of these types of changes, and explain the correct accounting for each. Include a discussion of the advantages and disadvantages of the required accounting method.

C22-2 Accounting Changes

There are four types of exceptions to the general rule that a company should account for a change in accounting principle by a cumulative effect change.

Required Explain each of the exceptions, and why cumulative effect accounting is not appropriate.

C22-3 Accounting Changes

The various types of accounting changes may significantly affect the presentation of a company's financial position and its results of operations for an accounting period, and also affect the trends shown in its comparative financial statements and historical summaries.

Required

1. Explain a change in accounting principle and how a company reports it in the income statement of the period of the change.
2. Explain a change in accounting estimate and how a company reports it in the income statement of the period of the change.

3. Explain a change in reporting entity and how a company reports it. Give an appropriate example of a change in reporting entity. (*AICPA adapted*)

C22-4 Accounting Changes

Berkeley Company, a manufacturer of many different products, changed its depreciation method for its production machinery from the double-declining-balance method to the straight-line method effective January 1, 2004. The straight-line method was determined to be preferable.

In addition, Berkeley changed the salvage values used in computing depreciation for its office equipment. It made this change on January 1, 2004 because it obtained additional information.

On December 31, 2004, Berkeley changed the specific subsidiaries comprising the group of companies for which consolidated financial statements are presented.

Required

1. What kind of accounting change is each of the preceding three situations? For each situation, indicate whether or not the company should show:
   a. The cumulative effect of a change in accounting principle in net income of the period of change.
   b. Pro forma effects of retroactive application.
   c. Restatement of the financial statements of all prior periods.
2. Why does the company have to disclose a change in accounting principle? (*AICPA adapted*)

C R E A T I V E   A N D   C R I T I C A L   T H I N K I N G

C22-5 Transition Methods for a Change in Accounting Principle

FASB Statement No. 5, "Accounting for Contingencies," required that a company make a cumulative effect adjustment at the time it adopted the *Statement*. Paragraph 104 states that the adoption of the prior period adjustment method was opposed because of ". . . significant difficulties involved in determining the degree of probability and estimability that had existed in prior periods."

FASB Statement No. 11, "Accounting for Contingencies—Transition Method," requires prior period adjustments instead of the previously required cumulative effect adjustment. Paragraph 6 states, "It is preferable for an enterprise adopting *FASB Statement No. 5* to restate its financial statements for as many immediately preceding periods as is practicable."

Required

1. Evaluate the reasonableness of the FASB change.
2. Why do you think that the FASB has generally required the use of prior period restatement rather than cumulative effect adjustments when a company adopts a newly required accounting principle?

C22-6 Accounting Changes

Sometimes a business entity may change its method of accounting for certain items. It may classify the change as a change in accounting principle, a change in accounting estimate, or a change in reporting entity.

The following are three independent, unrelated sets of facts relating to accounting changes.

Situation I A company determined that the depreciable lives of its fixed assets are presently too long to fairly match the cost of the fixed assets with the revenue produced. The company decided at the beginning of the current year to reduce the depreciable lives of all of its existing fixed assets by 5 years.

Situation II On December 31, 2003, Hyde Company owned 51% of Patten Company, at which time Hyde reported its investment using the cost method, owing to political uncertainties in the country in which Patten was located. On January 2, 2004, the management of Hyde Company was satisfied that the political uncertainties were resolved and the assets of the company were in no danger of nationalization. Accordingly, Hyde will prepare consolidated financial statements for Hyde and Patten for the year ended December 31, 2004.

Situation III A company decides in January 2004 to adopt the straight-line method of depreciation for plant equipment. The straight-line method will be used for new acquisitions, as well as for previously acquired plant equipment for which depreciation had been provided on an accelerated basis.

Required For each of the preceding situations, provide the following information. Complete your discussion of each situation before going on to the next situation.
1. Type of accounting change.
2. Manner of reporting the change under current generally accepted accounting principles, including a discussion, where applicable, of how amounts are computed.
3. Effect of the change on the statement of financial position and earnings statement.
4. Note disclosures that would be necessary. (*AICPA adapted*)

C22-7 Accounting Changes

It is important in accounting theory to be able to distinguish the types of accounting changes.

Required
1. If a public company desires to change from the sum-of-the-years'-digits depreciation method to the straight-line method for its fixed assets, what type of accounting change would this be? Discuss the permissibility of this change.
2. When pro forma disclosure is required for an accounting change, how are these pro forma amounts determined?
3. If a public company obtained additional information about the service lives of some of its fixed assets that showed that the service lives previously used should be shortened, what type of accounting change would this be? Include in your discussion how the change is reported in the income statement of the year of the change, and what disclosures are made in the financial statements or notes.
4. Changing specific subsidiaries comprising the group of companies for which consolidated financial statements are presented is an example of what type of accounting

change? What effect does it have on the consolidated income statements? (*AICPA adapted*)

C22-8 Enron, Arthur Andersen, and Accounting Changes

In 2001, Enron Corporation filed financial statements in which it did not consolidate various Special Purpose Entities, thereby keeping large amounts of debt off its balance sheet. The company has since declared bankruptcy and admitted that it violated GAAP. Enron's auditor, Arthur Andersen LLP, issued an unqualified audit opinion stating that Enron had followed GAAP. Instead Enron should have changed its accounting principles to conform to GAAP, and Andersen should not have issued an unqualified opinion.

The U.S. Department of Justice began an investigation of Enron and Arthur Andersen. Some employees of Arthur Andersen shredded certain documents related to the audit. As a result the firm was found guilty of obstruction of justice and therefore was no longer able to perform audits. Only a few of the Arthur Andersen partners and employees were involved in the audit and even fewer in the shredding. However, thousands of Arthur Andersen employees lost their jobs.

Required From an ethical perspective, discuss whether the actions of the Department of Justice were fair in regard to the employees of Arthur Andersen.

C22-9 Ethics and Accounting Changes and Errors

You are auditing the financial records of a company and reviewing the property, plant, and equipment records. Included in the assets are two buildings and numerous machines in each building. One of the buildings is used to manufacture components of toys; the other is used for assembly and packing, using the manufactured components as well as others purchased from suppliers. You see that the company has changed from the straight-line to the double-declining-balance depreciation method at the beginning of the year. You also discover that a $90,000 repair was added to the cost of the building in the previous year. You decide to ask the CFO about these calculations and she replies, "We decided to change the depreciation method because toys have such short lives and get obsolete so fast. You know how kids always want the latest fad. And that is partly why we are also going to recognize an asset impairment of $150,000 this year. And, as for that $90,000, those repairs should make the building last longer. But, anyway, the amount wasn't material to our depreciation calculations." As you walk back to your office, you recall from earlier in the audit that the company uses LIFO for its inventory and that income before income taxes has been around $1 million for each of the last several years.

Required From financial reporting and ethical perspectives, discuss the issues raised by this situation.

MULTIPLE CHOICE

Select the best answer for each of the following.

M22-1 During 2004 White Company determined that machinery previously depreciated over a 7-year life had a total estimated useful life of only 5 years. An accounting change was made in 2004 to reflect the change in estimate. If the change had been made in 2003, accumulated depreciation at December 31, 2003 would have been $1,600,000 instead of $1,200,000. As a result of this change the 2004 depreciation expense was $100,000 greater. The income tax rate was 30% in both years. What should be reported in White's income statement for the year ended December 31, 2004 as the cumulative effect on prior years of changing the estimated useful life of the machinery?

a. $0
b. $280,000
c. $300,000
d. $400,000

Items 2 and 3 are based on the following information:

The Shannon Corporation began operations on January 1, 2004. Financial statements for the years ended December 31, 2004 and 2005 contained the following errors:

	December 31	
	2004	2005
Ending inventory	$16,000 understated	$15,000 overstated
Depreciation expense	$6,000 understated	—
Insurance expense	$10,000 overstated	$10,000 understated
Prepaid insurance	$10,000 understated	—

In addition, on December 31, 2005 fully depreciated machinery was sold for $10,800 cash, but the sale was not recorded until 2006. There were no other errors during 2004 or 2005 and no corrections have been made for any of the errors.

M22-2 Ignoring income taxes, what is the total effect of the errors on 2005 net income?

a. Net income understated by $1,800
b. Net income overstated by $5,800
c. Net income overstated by $11,000
d. Net income overstated by $30,200

M22-3 Ignoring income taxes, what is the total effect of the errors on the amount of working capital at December 31, 2005?

a. Working capital overstated by $4,200
b. Working capital understated by $5,800
c. Working capital understated by $6,000
d. Working capital understated by $9,800

M22-4 A change in the expected service life of an asset arising because additional information has been obtained is

a. An accounting change that should be reported by restating the financial statements of all prior periods represented
b. An accounting change that should be reported in the period of change and future periods if the change affects both
c. A correction of an error
d. Not an accounting change

M22-5 The cumulative effect of an accounting change on the amount of retained earnings at the beginning of the period in which the change is made should generally be included in net income for the period of the change for a

	Change in Accounting Principle	Change in Accounting Entity
a.	Yes	Yes
b.	No	Yes
c.	Yes	No
d.	No	No

M22-6 On January 1, 2004 Belmont Company changed its inventory cost flow method to the FIFO cost method from the LIFO cost method. Belmont can justify the change, which was made for both financial statement and income tax reporting purposes. Belmont's inventories aggregated $4,000,000 on the LIFO basis at December 31, 2003. Supplementary records maintained by Belmont showed that the inventories would have totaled $4,800,000 at December 31, 2003 on the FIFO basis. Ignoring income taxes, the adjustment for the effect of changing to the FIFO method from the LIFO method should be reported by Belmont in the 2004

a. Income statement as an $800,000 debit
b. Retained earnings statement as an $800,000 debit adjustment to the beginning balance
c. Income statement as an $800,000 credit
d. Retained earnings statement as an $800,000 credit adjustment to the beginning balance

M22-7 When a cumulative effect type change in accounting principle is made during the year, the cumulative effect on retained earnings is determined

a. During the year using the weighted average method
b. As of the date of the change
c. As of the beginning of the year in which the change is made
d. As of the end of the year in which the change is made

M22-8 Generally, how should a change in accounting estimate that is recognized by a change in accounting principle be reported?

	Change in Accounting Estimate	Change in Accounting Principle
a.	No	No
b.	Yes	Yes
c.	No	Yes
d.	Yes	No

M22-9 On January 2, 2002 Garr Company acquired machinery at a cost of $320,000. This machinery was being depreciated by the double-declining-balance method over an estimated useful life of 8 years, with no residual value. At the beginning of 2004 it was decided to change to the straight-line method of depreciation. Ignoring income tax considerations, the cumulative effect of this accounting change is

a. $0   c. $65,000

b. $60,000   d. $140,000

M22-10 A company has included in its consolidated financial statements this year a subsidiary acquired several years ago that was appropriately excluded from consolidation last year. This results in

a. An accounting change that should be reported prospectively

b. An accounting change that should be reported by restating the financial statements of all prior periods presented

c. Neither an accounting change nor a correction of an error

d. A correction of an error

(AICPA adapted)

EXERCISES

E22-1 *Identification and Effects of Changes and Errors* The following are several independent events:

1. Change from the LIFO to the FIFO inventory cost flow assumption.
2. Reduction in remaining service life of machinery from 10 to 8 years.
3. A change from an accelerated method to the straight-line method of depreciating assets.
4. Write-down of inventories due to obsolescence.
5. Receipt of damages won in a court suit instigated 5 years ago.
6. Recording as an asset costs that were erroneously expensed in a previous period.
7. Write-down of property, plant, and equipment because of closure of inefficient plants.
8. A change from successful efforts to full cost accounting for oil exploration costs.

Required Indicate how a company reports the preceding items (specify whether increases or decreases can generally be expected) in its financial statements of the current year.

E22-2 *Identification and Effects of Changes and Errors* The following are several independent events:

1. Change from the FIFO to the LIFO inventory cost flow assumption.
2. Write-off of patent due to the introduction of a competing product.
3. Payment to the Internal Revenue Service in settlement of a dispute over previous year's taxes.
4. Increase in allowance for uncollectible accounts from 2% to 4% of credit sales.
5. Change from straight-line to double-declining-balance method.
6. Write-down of an asset to reflect probable future losses.
7. A change from full cost to successful efforts accounting for oil exploration costs.

Required Indicate how a company reports the preceding items (specify whether increases or decreases can generally be expected) in its financial statements of the current year.

E22-3 *Identification and Accounting for Changes and Errors* The following are several independent events:

1. A partnership is preparing to become a corporation and sell stock to the public. At this time, it is decided to switch from accelerated to straight-line depreciation.
2. A company has been debiting half its advertising costs to an intangible asset account and amortizing these costs over 3 years.
3. A company has been using accelerated depreciation. It now estimates that the pattern of benefits to be received in the future will be equal each period, so it decides to change to the straight-line depreciation method.
4. A company has been using straight-line depreciation in its property, plant, and equipment. It is now buying a new type of machine and elects to use accelerated depreciation on the new machines.
5. A company has been expensing all its manufacturing cost variances. It decides to allocate them between cost of goods sold and inventory in the future.

Required Describe the correct accounting treatment for the changes (if any) related to the preceding events.

E22-4 *Change in Depreciation Method* At the beginning of 2005 the Ardo Company decides to change from the double-declining-balance method to the straight-line depreciation method for all its assets. The following data are available for the Ardo Company:

Year	Reported Income Before Income Taxes	Excess of Double-Declining Over Straight-Line Depreciation
Prior to 2003	$800,000	$50,000
2003	500,000	70,000
2004	300,000	80,000
2005	400,000	60,000

The tax rate is 40%. The company has used, and will continue to use, the MACRS method for tax purposes. Assume that the company has a simple capital structure, with 100,000 shares of common stock outstanding. Ardo's 2004 and 2005 total revenues were $700,000 and $1,100,000, respectively.

Required

1. Prepare the journal entry for 2005 to reflect the change.
2. At the end of 2005 prepare comparative income statements for 2004 and 2005.

E22-5 *Change in Depreciation Method* The McCallum Company purchased a machine on January 3, 2000 for $190,000. It is depreciating the asset by the straight-line method over an 8-year life to a residual value of $10,000. At the beginning of 2004 the pattern of benefits generated by the asset indicated that a change to the sum-of-the-years'-digits method is appropriate. In 2004 and 2003 the company reported revenues of $250,000 and $220,000, and expenses (other than depreciation and income tax) of $120,000 and $100,000, respectively. The tax rate is 30% and the company uses the MACRS method. The company has a simple capital structure, with 20,000 shares of common stock outstanding during 2003 and 2004.

Required

1. Prepare the journal entry to reflect the change.
2. At the end of 2004 prepare the comparative income statements for 2004 and 2003.

E22-6 *Change in Inventory Cost Flow Assumption* At the beginning of 2005 the Brett Company decided to change from the FIFO to the average cost inventory cost flow assumption for financial reporting purposes. The following data are available in regard to reported pretax operating income and cost of goods sold:

Year	Reported Income Before Income Taxes	Excess of Average Cost of Goods Sold Over FIFO Cost of Goods Sold
Prior to 2003	$900,000	$85,000
2003	500,000	50,000
2004	600,000	45,000
2005	700,000	70,000

The tax rate is 30%, and the company received permission from the IRS to also make the change for income tax purposes. The company has a simple capital structure, with 100,000 shares of common stock outstanding. Assume that the company computed its reported income before income taxes in 2005 using the newly adopted inventory cost flow method. Brett's 2004 and 2005 revenues were $1,500,000 and $1,750,000, respectively.

Required

1. Prepare the journal entry for 2005 to reflect the change.
2. At the end of 2005 prepare comparative income statements for 2005 and 2004.

E22-7 *Change in Inventory Cost Flow Assumption* The Berg Company began operations on January 1, 2004 and uses the FIFO method in costing its raw material inventory. During 2005 management is contemplating a change to the LIFO method and is interested in determining what effect such a change will have on net income. Accordingly, the following information has been developed:

	2004	2005
FIFO—Ending inventory	$240,000	$270,000
LIFO—Ending inventory	200,000	210,000
Income before income taxes (computed under the FIFO method)	120,000	170,000

Required What is the effect on income before income taxes in 2005 of a change to the LIFO method? (*AICPA adapted*)

E22-8   *Change in Inventory Method*   The Fava Company began operations in 2003 and uses the LIFO inventory method for both financial reporting and income taxes. At the beginning of 2004 the anticipated cost trends in the industry had changed, so that it adopted the FIFO method for both financial reporting and income taxes. The company reported revenues of $300,000 and $270,000 in 2004 and 2003, respectively. The company reported expenses (excluding income tax expense) of $125,000 and $120,000 in 2004 and 2003, including cost of goods sold of $55,000 and $45,000, respectively. An analysis indicates that the FIFO cost of goods sold would have been lower by $8,000 in 2003. The tax rate is 30%. The company has a simple capital structure, with 15,000 shares of common stock outstanding during 2003 and 2004. It paid no dividends in either year.

Required

1. Prepare the journal entry to reflect the change.
2. At the end of 2004 prepare the comparative income statements for 2004 and 2003.
3. At the end of 2004 prepare the comparative retained earnings statements for 2004 and 2003.

E22-9   *Change in Accounting Principle*   The Delta Company uses the completed-contract method of accounting for long-term construction contracts. The company started business in 2002 and prepared the following income statements:

	2002	2003
Construction revenue	$100,000	$300,000
Construction expense	(40,000)	(130,000)
Other expenses	(50,000)	(70,000)
Income before income taxes	$ 10,000	$100,000
Income tax expense (30%)	(3,000)	(30,000)
Net income	$ 7,000	$ 70,000

The company changes to the percentage-of-completion method at the beginning of 2004. It determines the construction revenue and expense amounts under the percentage-of-completion method to be as follows:

	2002	2003	2004
Construction revenue	$200,000	$420,000	$900,000
Construction expense	80,000	182,000	420,000

The other expenses remain unchanged for 2002 and 2003, and are $80,000 in 2004. The company has not paid dividends on its 10,000 common shares outstanding. With the 2004 financial statements the company issues comparative statements for the previous two years. Under the completed-contract method, construction revenue and construction expense would be $600,000 and $280,000, respectively, in 2004. The company uses the percentage-of-completion method for income tax purposes.

Required Prepare the income statements and the statements of retained earnings for 2004.

E22-10   *Journal Entries to Correct Errors*   The following are several independent errors:

1. Goods in transit, purchased on account and shipped FOB destination, $10,000, were included in purchases but not in the ending inventory.
2. A purchase of a machine for $2,000 was expensed. The machine has a 4-year life, no residual value, and straight-line depreciation is used.
3. Wages payable of $2,000 were not accrued.
4. Payment of next year's rent, $4,000, was recorded as rent expense.
5. Allowance for doubtful accounts of $5,000 was not recorded. The company normally uses the aging method.
6. Equipment with a book value of $70,000 and a fair value of $100,000 was sold at the beginning of the year. A 2-year non-interest-bearing note for $129,960 was received and recorded at its face value. No interest revenue was recorded and 14% is a fair rate of interest.

Required Prepare the correcting journal entry or entries for each of the preceding errors, assuming the company discovers the error in the year after it was made. (Ignore income taxes.)

E22-11   *Journal Entries to Correct Errors*   Use the information in E22-10.

Required Prepare the correcting journal entries if the company discovers each error 2 years after it is made and it has closed the books for the second year. (Ignore income taxes.)

E22-12   *Effects of Errors*   The following are several independent errors:

1. Ending inventory is overstated.
2. Failure to record a purchase of inventory although the items are correctly recorded in the physical inventory.
3. Expensing the purchase of a machine.
4. Failure to accrue wages.
5. Failure to record an allowance for uncollectibles.
6. Including collections in advance as revenue.
7. Including payments in advance as expenses.
8. Failure to accrue warranty costs.
9. Discount on a note payable issued for purchase of a machine is ignored.
10. Failure to record depreciation expense on assets purchased during the year.

Required Indicate the effect of each of the preceding errors on (1) assets, (2) liabilities, (3) owners' equity, and (4) net income in the year in which the error occurs. State whether the error causes an overstatement (+), an understatement (−), or no effect (NE).

E22-13   *Correcting Journal Entries for Errors*   The following are several independent errors:

1. In January 2004 repair costs of $9,000 were debited to the Machinery account. At the beginning of 2004 the book value of the machinery was $100,000. No residual value is expected, the remaining estimated life is 10 years, and straight-line depreciation is used.
2. All purchases of materials for construction contracts still in progress have been immediately expensed. It is discovered that the use of such materials was $10,000 during 2003 and $12,000 during 2004.
3. Depreciation on manufacturing equipment has been excluded from manufacturing costs and treated as a period expense. During 2004, $40,000 of depreciation was accounted for in that manner. Production was 15,000 units during 2004, of which 3,000 remained in inventory at the end of the year. Assume there was no inventory at the beginning of 2004.

Required Prepare journal entries for the preceding errors discovered during 2005. (Ignore income taxes.)

E22-14   *Omission of Accruals and Prepayments*   The Dudley Company failed to recognize the following accruals. It also recorded the prepaid expenses and unearned revenues as expenses and revenues, respectively, in the year of payment or collection.

	2003	2004	2005
Prepaid expenses	$500	$ 900	$1,100
Accrued expenses	800	700	950
Revenue received in advance	300	400	1,300
Revenue earned but not received	600	1,000	1,200

The reported net income was $20,000 in 2003, $25,000 in 2004, and $23,000 in 2005.

Required

1. Compute the correct net income for 2003, 2004, and 2005.
2. Prepare the journal entries necessary in 2005 if the errors are discovered at the end of that year.
3. Prepare the journal entries necessary in 2006 if the errors are discovered at the end of that year.

PROBLEMS

P22-1   *Identification and Effects of Changes and Errors*   On January 2, 2004, Quo, Inc. hired Reed as its controller. During the year, Reed, working closely with Quo's president and outside accountants, made changes in accounting policies, corrected several errors dating from 2003 and before, and instituted new accounting policies. Quo's 2004 financial statements will be presented in comparative form with its 2003 financial statements. Items 1 through 10 represent Quo's transactions.

1. Quo manufactures heavy equipment to customer specifications on a contract basis. On the basis that it is preferable, it switched accounting for these long-term contracts from the completed-contact method to the percentage-of-completion method.
2. As a result of a production breakthrough, Quo determined that manufacturing equipment previously depreciated over 15 years should be depreciated over 20 years.

3. The equipment that Quo manufactures is sold with a five-year warranty. Because of a production breakthrough, Quo reduced its computation of warranty costs from 3% of sales to 1% of sales.

4. Quo changed from LIFO to FIFO to account for its finished goods inventory.

5. Quo changed from FIFO to average cost to account for its raw materials and work in process inventories.

6. Quo sells extended service contracts on its products. Because related services are performed over several years, in 2004 Quo changed from the cash method to the accrual method of recognizing income from these service contracts.

7. During 2004 Quo determined that an insurance premium paid and entirely expensed in 2003 was for the period January 1, 2003 through January 1, 2005.

8. Quo changed its method of depreciating office equipment from an accelerated method to the straight-line method to more closely reflect costs in later years.

9. Quo instituted a pension plan for all employees in 2004 and adopted Statement of Financial Accounting Standards No. 87, *Employers' Accounting for Pensions*. Quo had not previously had a pension plan.

10. During 2004, Quo increased its investment in Worth, Inc. from a 10% interest, purchased in 2003, to 30%, and acquired a seat on Worth's board of directors. As a result of its increased investment, Quo changed its method of accounting for investment in subsidiary from the fair value method to the equity method.

Required

1. Indicate whether Quo should classify each transaction as: (a) a change in accounting principle, (b) a change in accounting estimate, (c) a correction of an error in previously presented financial statements, or (d) neither an accounting change nor an accounting error.

2. Indicate the accounting treatment for each transaction as: (a) a cumulative effect approach, (b) a retroactive restatement approach, or (c) a prospective approach. *(AICPA adapted)*

P22-2   ***Changes in Inventory Cost Flow Assumption***   At the beginning of 2005 the Flynne Company decided to change from the average cost to the FIFO inventory cost flow assumption. The following data are available:

Year	Reported Income Before Income Taxes	Excess of Average Cost of Goods Sold Over FIFO Cost of Goods Sold
Prior to 2003	$200,000	$30,000
2003	40,000	12,000
2004	80,000	18,000
2005	70,000	6,000

The tax rate is 30%. The company has a simple capital structure and 10,000 shares of common stock outstanding. Assume that the balance in retained earnings is the sum of the company's reported income amounts (net of tax) and that the reported income before income taxes in 2005 uses the newly adopted method. Flynne's revenues for 2004 and 2005 were $225,000 and $200,000, respectively.

Required

1. At the end of 2005 prepare comparative income statements for 2005 and 2004.

2. If the change had been from LIFO to FIFO, prepare the comparative income statements and retained earnings statements that would be required. Indicate what items (if any) would be restated on the 2004 beginning and ending balance sheets. *Note:* In Requirements 2 and 3, assume that the "excess" figures represent the amount by which LIFO cost of goods sold exceeds FIFO cost of goods sold.

3. If the change had been from FIFO to LIFO, what disclosures would be required (assuming that only the excess cost of goods sold for 2005 was determinable)?

4. How would your answer to Requirement 1 change if the employees received a bonus of 10% of income before deducting the bonus and taxes?

P22-3   ***Change from FIFO to Average Cost***   Koopman Company began operations on January 1, 2003 and uses the FIFO inventory method for financial reporting and the average-cost inventory method for income taxes. At the beginning of 2005 the company decided to switch to the average-cost inventory method for financial reporting. The company had previously reported the following financial statements for 2004:

Income Statement

	2004
Revenues	$100,000
Cost of goods sold	(60,000)
Gross profit	$ 40,000
Operating expenses	(25,000)
Income before income taxes	$ 15,000
Income tax expense	(4,500)
Net income	$ 10,500
Earnings per share	$1.05

Retained Earnings Statement

	2004
Beginning retained earnings	$15,000
Add: Net income	10,500
	$25,500
Less: Dividends	(6,000)
Ending retained earnings	$19,500

Balance Sheet (12/31/04)

Cash	$ 9,000	Accounts payable	$ 3,000
Inventory	38,000	Income taxes payable	4,500
Other assets	66,800	Deferred tax liability	4,800
		Common stock, no par	82,000
		Retained earnings	19,500
	$113,800		$113,800

An analysis of the accounting records discloses the following cost of goods sold under the FIFO and average-cost inventory methods:

	FIFO Cost of Goods Sold	Average Cost of Goods Sold
2003	$50,000	$57,000
2004	60,000	69,000
2005	70,000	80,000

There are no indirect effects of the change in inventory method. Revenues for 2005 total $130,000; operating expenses for 2005 total $30,000. The company is subject to a 30% income tax rate in all years; it pays the income taxes payable of a current year in the first quarter of the next year. The company had 10,000 shares of common stock outstanding during all years; it paid dividends of $1 per share in 2005. At the end of 2005 the company had cash of $10,000, inventory of $24,000, and other assets of $82,000. The company desires to show financial statements for the current year and previous year in its 2005 annual report.

Required

1. Prepare the journal entry to reflect the change in methods at the beginning of 2005. Show supporting calculations.
2. Prepare the 2005 annual report. Notes to the financial statements are not necessary. Show supporting calculations.

P22-4   *Change from LIFO to Average Cost*   Schmidt Company began operations on January 1, 2003 and uses the LIFO inventory method for both financial reporting and income taxes, but at the beginning of 2005 decided to switch to the average-cost inventory method for financial and income tax reporting. The company had previously reported the following financial statements for 2004:

Income Statement

	2004
Revenues	$128,000
Cost of goods sold	(78,000)
Gross profit	$ 50,000
Operating expenses	(25,000)
Income before income taxes	$ 25,000
Income tax expense	(7,500)
Net income	$ 17,500
Earnings per share	$1.75

Retained Earnings Statement

	2004
Beginning retained earnings	$27,000
Add: Net income	17,500
	$44,500
Less: Dividends	(6,000)
Ending retained earnings	$38,500

Balance Sheet (12/31/04)

Cash	$ 8,000	Accounts payable	$ 4,000
Inventory	42,000	Income taxes payable	7,500
Other assets	60,000	Common stock, no par	60,000
		Retained earnings	38,500
	$110,000		$110,000

An analysis of the accounting records discloses the following cost of goods sold under the LIFO and average-cost inventory methods:

	LIFO Cost of Goods Sold	Average Cost of Goods Sold
2003	$62,000	$56,000
2004	78,000	69,000
2005	90,000	80,000

There are no indirect effects of the change in inventory method. Revenues for 2005 total $130,000; operating expenses for 2005 total $30,000. The company is subject to a 30% income tax rate in all years; it pays all income taxes payable in the next quarter. The company had 10,000 shares of common stock outstanding during all years; it paid dividends of $1 per share in 2005. At the end of 2005 the company had cash of $12,000, inventory of $34,000, other assets of $76,000, income taxes payable of $6,000, and accounts payable of ?. The company desires to show financial statements for the current year and previous year in its 2005 annual report.

Required

1. Prepare the journal entry to reflect the change in method at the beginning of 2005. Show supporting calculations.
2. Prepare the 2005 annual report. Notes to the financial statements are not necessary. Show supporting calculations.

P22-5 *Change in Depreciation Method* At the beginning of 2004 the Clarke Company decided to change from the straight-line method to the double-declining-balance method of depreciation because of a perceived change in the pattern of benefits. The following information is available:

Year	Income Before Income Taxes	Excess of Double-Declining over Straight-Line Depreciation
Prior to 2002	$400,000	$60,000
2002	200,000	50,000
2003	90,000	30,000
2004	150,000	70,000

The company's 2004 and 2003 revenues were $970,000 and $920,000, respectively. The company has been using MACRS depreciation for income taxes, and the income tax rate is 30%. Assume a simple capital structure, with 100,000 shares of common stock outstanding during 2003 and 2004.

Required

1. Prepare the journal entry to reflect the change.
2. At the end of 2004 prepare the comparative income statements for 2004 and 2003.
3. If the company paid a bonus to employees of 10% of pretax income, how would your answers to Requirements 1 and 2 change?
4. At the end of 2004 prepare the comparative retained earnings statements if the change was accounted for as a prior period adjustment. Assume the retained earnings balance at the beginning of 2003 was $500,000 and that the company paid no dividends in 2003 or 2004.

See WebTutor for annotated problem solution.

P22-6   ***Change in Method of Accounting for Long-Term Construction Contracts*** Since the Goode Construction Company was formed in 2003, it has used the completed-contract method for financial reporting, but at the beginning of 2005 it changes to the percentage-of-completion method. The company previously had reported the following pretax income:

	2003	2004
Sales of completed contracts	$300,000	$800,000
Less: Cost of completed contracts	(200,000)	(550,000)
Gross profit	$100,000	$250,000

Analysis of the accounting records discloses that the company earned the following gross profit on each of its projects based on the percentage-of-completion method:

	2003	2004	2005
Project A	$100,000	—	—
Project B	120,000	$125,000	—
Project C	—	75,000	$400,000

In 2005 the company would have reported sales and cost of completed contracts of $820,000 and $350,000, respectively, under the completed-contract method. The tax rate is 30%. The company has a simple capital structure, with 100,000 shares of common stock outstanding. It paid no dividends. Ignore other expenses (i.e., gross profit is income before income taxes). The company uses the percentage-of-completion method for income taxes.

Required

1. Prepare the journal entry to reflect the change in method at the beginning of 2005.
2. If the company also presents the 2003 and 2004 financial statements for comparative purposes, prepare the income statement disclosures (starting with income before income taxes) and retained earnings disclosures that are required in 2005. What items (if any) would be restated on the financial statements?

P22-7   ***Changes Related to Machinery*** At the beginning of 2005 the Freeman Company revised its estimate of the expected life of machinery. It purchased the machinery on January 1, 1995 for $100,000, at which time it estimated that the residual value would be $10,000 and the economic life 20 years. The revised estimate was that the total economic life was only 13 years. The company uses straight-line depreciation for financial accounting purposes, and sum-of-the-years'-digits depreciation for income tax purposes.

Required

1. Prepare the journal entry to record the depreciation on December 31, 2005.
2. Ignore the change in the estimated life. Assume, instead, that the company revised the estimated residual value to zero at the beginning of 2005. Prepare the journal entry to record the depreciation on December 31, 2005.
3. Ignore the change in the estimated life and the change in the estimated residual value. At the beginning of 2005 the company decided to change to sum-of-the-years'-digits depreciation for financial accounting purposes. Prepare the necessary journal entries assuming a tax rate of 30%. By how much would the pro forma net income for 2004 be different from the reported 2004 net income?

P22-8   ***Change in Accounting for Inventory*** The Kraft Manufacturing Company manufactures two products: Mult and Tran. At December 31, 2004 Kraft used the first-in, first-out (FIFO) inventory method. Effective January 1, 2005, Kraft changed to the last-in, first-out (LIFO) inventory method. The cumulative effect of this change is not determinable and, as a result, the ending inventory of 2004, for which the FIFO method was used, is also the beginning inventory for 2005 for the LIFO method. Any layers added during 2005 should be costed by reference to the first acquisitions of 2005, and any layers liquidated during 2005 should be considered a permanent liquidation.

The following information was available from Kraft's inventory records for the two most recent years:

	Mult		Tran	
	Units	Unit Cost	Units	Unit Cost
2004 purchases:				
January 7	5,000	$4.00	22,000	$2.00
April 17	12,000	4.50		
November 9	17,000	5.00	18,500	2.50
December 14	10,000	6.00		
2005 purchases:				
February 12	3,000	7.00	23,000	3.00
May 21	8,000	7.50		
October 15	20,000	8.00		
December 24			15,500	3.50
Units on hand:				
December 31, 2004	15,000		14,500	
December 31, 2005	16,000		13,000	

Required Compute the effect on income before income taxes for the year ended December 31, 2005, resulting from the change from the FIFO to the LIFO inventory method. (*AICPA adapted*)

P22-9 *Change in Accounting Principle and Estimate* Mitchell Corporation has decided that in the preparation of its 2005 financial statements, it will make two changes from the methods used in prior years:

1. *Depreciation.* Mitchell has always used the Modified Accelerated Cost Recovery System (MACRS) for tax and financial reporting purposes. This method was considered acceptable for financial reporting because the differences in the depreciation amounts were considered to be immaterial. The company has decided to change during 2005 to the straight-line method for financial reporting only, and to account for the change as a change in accounting principle. The effect of this change is shown as follows:

	Excess of MACRS Over Straight-Line Depreciation
Prior to 2004	$1,300,000
2004	101,000
2005	99,000
	$1,500,000

Depreciation is charged to cost of sales and to selling, general, and administrative expenses on the basis of 75% and 25%, respectively.

2. *Bad debt expense.* In the past, Mitchell has recognized bad debt expense equal to 1.5% of net sales. After careful review, it has been decided that a rate of 2% is more appropriate for 2005. Bad debt expense is charged to selling, general, and administrative expenses.

The following information is taken from the Mitchell Corporation's preliminary financial statements, prepared before giving effect to the two changes:

Condensed Comparative Balance Sheets

	December 31	
	2005	2004
Assets		
Current assets	$43,561,000	$43,900,000
Fixed assets, at cost	45,792,000	43,974,000
Less accumulated depreciation	(23,761,000)	(22,946,000)
	$65,592,000	$64,928,000
Liabilities and Stockholders' Equity		
Current liabilities	$19,091,620	$22,505,920
Long-term debt	15,154,000	14,097,000
Capital stock	11,620,000	11,620,000
Retained earnings	19,726,380	16,705,080
	$65,592,000	$64,928,000

Comparative Income Statements

	For the Year Ended December 31	
	2005	2004
Net sales	$80,520,000	$78,920,000
Cost of sales	(54,847,000)	(53,074,000)
	$25,673,000	$25,846,000
Selling, general, and administrative expenses	(19,540,000)	(18,411,000)
	$ 6,133,000	$ 7,435,000
Other income (expenses) net	(1,198,000)	(1,079,000)
Income before federal income taxes	$ 4,935,000	$ 6,356,000
Federal income taxes	(1,480,500)	(1,906,800)
Net income	$ 3,454,500	$ 4,449,200

There have been no temporary differences between any book and tax items prior to the preceding changes. The effective rate is 30%.

Required Based on *APB Opinion No. 20*, "Accounting Changes," compute for the following 7 items the amounts that would appear on the comparative (2005 and 2004) financial statements of Mitchell Corporation after adjustment for the two accounting changes. Show amounts for both 2005 and 2004 and prepare supporting schedules as necessary.

1. Accumulated depreciation.
2. Deferred tax liability.
3. Selling, general, and administrative expenses.
4. Current portion of federal income tax expense.
5. Deferred portion of federal income tax expense.
6. Retained earnings.
7. Pro forma net income. (*AICPA adapted*)

P22-10 *First Issuance of Financial Statements*   The Jackson Company has decided to issue common stock to the public in 2004. This will be the first public sale and therefore the company will issue its first publicly available financial statements since it was formed in 2001. The financial statements that it has prepared for its own use follow:

Income Statements

	For Years Ended December 31,		
	2001	2002	2003
Sales	$100,000	$130,000	$180,000
Cost of goods sold	(35,000)	(45,000)	(65,000)
Gross profit	$ 65,000	$ 85,000	$115,000
Other expenses	(62,500)	(75,000)	(83,200)
Income before income taxes	$ 2,500	$ 10,000	$ 31,800
Income tax expense	(750)	(3,000)	(9,540)
Net income	$ 1,750	$ 7,000	$ 22,260

Balance Sheets

	December 31		
	2001	**2002**	**2003**
Cash	$ 5,500	$ 12,500	$ 9,960
Accounts receivable	30,000	50,000	63,000
Inventory	40,000	60,000	65,000
Equipment	100,000	100,000	140,000
Less: Accumulated depreciation	(20,000)	(52,000)	(79,200)
	$155,500	$170,500	$198,760
Current liabilities	$ 19,250	$ 27,250	$ 33,250
Notes payable	50,000	50,000	50,000
Common stock	84,500	84,500	84,500
Retained earnings	1,750	8,750	31,010
	$155,500	$170,500	$198,760

These financial statements are audited for the first time at the beginning of 2004, and the following facts are discovered:

1. The company has not made any allowance for noncollection of accounts receivable. An allowance of 1% of total sales is considered appropriate. Uncollectible accounts of $630 should have been written off in 2003.
2. The notes payable are to officers of the company and have an interest rate of 12%. They were issued on January 1, 2001. No interest has been accrued or paid. (Assume simple interest and no compounding.)
3. The company has been using MACRS over a 5-year life for both financial reporting and income tax purposes. It has been decided that the straight-line method should have been used for financial reporting, based on an economic life of 10 years and a zero residual value, with a full year's depreciation being recorded in the year of acquisition. No disposals of property, plant, and equipment have occurred.
4. After adjustments, with the exception of depreciation, expenses deducted for financial accounting purposes are the same as those deducted for income tax purposes.
5. The company is subject to a 30% income tax rate and pays its taxes at the end of each year.

Required

1. Prepare the financial statements for 2001, 2002, and 2003 that the company would issue at the beginning of 2004.
2. Describe what method the company would use to account for each item if the financial statements for all 3 years had been publicly issued previously.

P22-11 *Error Correction* At the end of 2005 while auditing the books of the Sandlin Company, *before* the books have been closed, you find the following items:

a. A building with a 30-year life (no residual value, straight-line depreciation) was purchased on January 1, 2005 by issuing a $90,000 non-interest-bearing, 4-year note. The entry made to record the purchase was a debit to Building and a credit to Notes Payable for $90,000; 12% is a fair rate of interest on the note.
b. The inventory at the end of 2005 was found to be overstated by $15,000. At the same time it was discovered that the inventory at the end of 2004 had been overstated by $35,000. The company uses the perpetual inventory system.
c. For the last 3 years, the company has failed to accrue salaries and wages. The correct amounts at the end of each year were: 2003—$12,000; 2004—$18,000; 2005—$10,000.

Required

1. Prepare journal entries to correct the errors (ignore income taxes).
2. Assume, instead, that the company discovered the errors *after* it had closed the books. Prepare journal entries to correct the errors (ignore income taxes).

P22-12 *Error Correction* At the beginning of 2005 Tanham Company discovered the following errors made in the preceding two years:

	2003	2004
Overstatement of ending inventory	$5,000	$2,000
Omission of wages payable	700	800
Omission of allowance for doubtful accounts	1,300	1,700
Prepayment of insurance recorded as expense	500	200

Reported net income was $27,000 in 2003 and $35,000 in 2004. The allowance for doubtful accounts had a zero balance at the beginning of 2003. No accounts were written off during 2003 or 2004. Ignore income taxes.

Required

1. What is the correct net income for 2003 and 2004?
2. Prepare the adjusting journal entry in 2005 to correct the errors.

P22-13 *Error Correction* A review of the books of the Anderson Corporation indicates that the errors and omissions pertaining to the balance sheet accounts shown as follows had not been corrected during the applicable years.
The net income per the books is: 2002—$10,000; 2003—$12,000; 2004—$15,000; and 2005—$20,000. No dividends were declared during these years and no adjustments were made to retained earnings. The Retained Earnings balance on December 31, 2005, is $50,000.

December 31	Ending Inventory Overvalued	Ending Inventory Undervalued	Omissions			
			Prepaid Expense	Unearned Revenues	Accrued Expense	Accrued Revenues
2002	$ —	$4,000	$600	$ —	$300	$ —
2003	3,000	—	—	500	—	700
2004	2,000	—	400	—	100	—
2005	—	1,000	900	200	350	800

Required Prepare a worksheet to determine the correct net income for the years 2002, 2003, 2004, and 2005, and the adjusted balance sheet accounts as of December 31, 2005. (Ignore possible income tax effects.)

P22-14 *Error Correction* The bookkeeper of the Cask Company, who has maintained its accounting records since the company's formation in January 2002, has prepared the unaudited financial statements. In your examination of these statements at the end of 2004, you discover the following items:

1. Sales taxes collected from customers have been included in the sales account. The Sales Tax Expense account is debited when the sales taxes are remitted to the state in the month following the sale. All sales are subject to a 6% sales tax. Total sales (excluding sales tax) for the three years 2002 through 2004 were $200,000, $300,000, and $500,000, respectively. The Sales Tax Expense account balance for the three years was $10,000, $15,000, and $26,000, respectively.
2. An account payable of $15,000 for merchandise purchased in December 2002 was recorded in January 2003. The merchandise was not included in inventory at December 31, 2002.
3. Merchandise with a cost of $4,000 was included twice in the December 31, 2003 inventory.
4. The company has used the direct write-off method of accounting for bad debts. Accounts written off in the three years 2002 through 2004 were $2,000, $4,500, and $6,500, respectively. The appropriate balances of Allowance for Doubtful Accounts at the end of 2002 through 2004 are $5,000, $6,000, and $8,200, respectively.
5. On January 1, 2003, 12%, 10-year bonds with a face value of $600,000 were issued at 102. The premium was credited to Additional Paid-in Capital. The bonds pay interest on June 30 and December 31, and use of the straight-line amortization method is appropriate.
6. Travel advances to the sales personnel of $18,000 were included as selling expenses for 2003. The travel occurred in 2004.
7. Salaries payable at the end of each year have not been accrued. Appropriate amounts at the end of 2002 through 2004 are $10,000, $11,000, and $7,000, respectively.
8. Installation, freight, and testing costs of $25,000 on a machine purchased in January 2002 were expensed at that time. The machine has a life of 5 years and a residual value of $10,000.

Required Analyze the effects of the errors on income for 2002, 2003, and 2004, and the 2005 ending balance sheet (ignore income taxes), according to the following format:

Explanation	Income 2002		Income 2003		Income 2004		Balance Sheet December 31, 2004		
	Debit	Credit	Debit	Credit	Debit	Credit	Amount Debit	Credit	Account

P22-15 *Comprehensive* The financial statements of the Gray Company showed income before income taxes of $4,030,000 for the year ended December 31, 2005, and $3,330,000 for the year ended December 31, 2004. Additional information is as follows:

1. Capital expenditures were $2,800,000 in 2005 and $4,000,000 in 2004. Included in the 2005 capital expenditures is equipment purchased for $1,000,000 on January 1, 2005, with no salvage value. Gray used straight-line depreciation based on a 10-year estimated life in its financial statements. As a result of additional information now available, it is estimated that this equipment should have only an 8-year life.

2. Gray made an error in its financial statements that should be regarded as material. A payment of $180,000 was made in January 2005 and charged to expense in 2005 for insurance premiums applicable to policies commencing and expiring in 2004. No liability had been recorded for this item at December 31, 2004.

3. The allowance for doubtful accounts reflected in Gray's financial statements was $7,000 at December 31, 2005, and $97,000 at December 31, 2004. During 2005, $90,000 of uncollectible receivables were written off against the allowance for doubtful accounts. In 2004, the provision for doubtful accounts was based on a percentage of net sales. The 2005 provision has not yet been recorded. Net sales were $58,500,000 for the year ended December 31, 2005, and $49,230,000 for the year ended December 31, 2004. Based on the latest available facts, the 2005 provision for doubtful accounts is estimated to be 0.2% of net sales.

4. A review of the estimated warranty liability at December 31, 2005, which is included in "other liabilities" in Gray's financial statements, has disclosed that this estimated liability should be increased $170,000.

5. Gray has two large blast furnaces that it uses in its manufacturing process. These furnaces must be periodically relined. Furnace A was relined in January 1999 at a cost of $230,000 and in January 2004 at a cost of $280,000. Furnace B was relined for the first time in January 2005 at a cost of $300,000. In Gray's financial statements, these costs were expensed as incurred.

   Since a relining will last for 5 years, a more appropriate matching of revenues and costs would result if the cost of the relining were capitalized and depreciated over the productive life of the relining. Gray has decided to make a change in accounting principle from expensing relining costs as incurred to capitalizing them and depreciating them over their productive life on a straight-line basis with a full year's depreciation in the year of relining. This change meets the requirements for a change in accounting principle under *APB Opinion No. 20*, "Accounting Changes."

Required

1. For the years ended December 31, 2005 and 2004, prepare a worksheet reconciling income before income taxes as given previously with income before income taxes and cumulative effect of a change in accounting principle, as adjusted for the preceding additional information. Show supporting computations in good form. Ignore income taxes and deferred tax considerations in your answer. The worksheet should have the following format:

	Year Ended December 31	
	2005	2004
Income before income taxes, before adjustments	$4,030,000	$3,330,000
Adjustments		
Net adjustments		
Income before income taxes and cumulative effect of a change in accounting principle, after adjustments	$	$

2. For the year ended December 31, 2005, compute the cumulative effect before income taxes of the change in accounting principle from expensing to capitalizing relining costs. Ignore income taxes and deferred tax considerations in your answer. (*AICPA adapted*)

P22-16 *Comprehensive* The Ingalls Corporation is in the process of negotiating a loan for expansion purposes. The books and records have never been audited, and the bank has requested that an audit be performed. Ingalls has prepared the following comparative financial statements for the years ended December 31, 2005 and 2004:

Balance Sheet

| | As of December 31, | |
	2005	2004
Assets		
Current assets		
Cash	$163,000	$ 82,000
Accounts receivable	392,000	296,000
Allowance for uncollectible accounts	(37,000)	(18,000)
Available-for-sale securities	78,000	78,000
Merchandise inventory	207,000	202,000
Total current assets	803,000	640,000
Fixed assets		
Property, plant, and equipment	167,000	169,500
Accumulated depreciation	(121,600)	(106,400)
Total fixed assets	45,400	63,100
Total assets	$848,400	$703,100
Liabilities and Stockholders' Equity		
Liabilities		
Accounts payable	$121,400	$196,100
Stockholders' equity		
Common stock, par value $10, authorized 50,000 shares, issued and outstanding 20,000 shares	260,000	260,000
Retained earnings	467,000	247,000
Total stockholders' equity	727,000	507,000
Total liabilities and stockholders' equity	$848,400	$703,100

Statement of Income

| | For the Years Ended December 31, | |
	2005	2004
Sales	$1,000,000	$900,000
Cost of sales	(430,000)	(395,000)
Gross profit	570,000	505,000
Operating expenses	210,000	205,000
Administrative expenses	140,000	105,000
	(350,000)	(310,000)
Net income	$ 220,000	$195,000

During the course of the audit, the following additional facts were determined:

1. An analysis of collections and losses on accounts receivable during the past 2 years indicates a drop in anticipated losses due to bad debts. After consultation with management, it was agreed that the loss experience rate on sales should be reduced from the recorded 2% to 1%, beginning with the year ended December 31, 2005.

2. An analysis of the available-for-sale securities revealed that this portfolio consisted entirely of short-term investments in marketable equity securities that were acquired in 2004. The total market valuation for these investments as of the end of each year was as follows: December 31, 2004—$81,000; December 31, 2005—$62,000.

3. The merchandise inventory at December 31, 2004 was overstated by $4,000 and the merchandise inventory at December 31, 2005 was overstated by $6,100.

4. On January 2, 2004, equipment costing $12,000 (estimated useful life of 10 years and residual value of $1,000) was incorrectly charged to Operating Expenses. Ingalls records depreciation via the straight-line

method. In 2005, fully depreciated equipment (with no residual value) that originally cost $17,500 was sold as scrap for $2,500. Noble credited the proceeds of $2,500 to Property and Equipment.

5. An analysis of 2004 operating expenses revealed that Ingalls charged to expense a 3-year insurance premium of $2,700 on January 15, 2004.

Required

1. Prepare the journal entries to correct the books at December 31, 2005. The books for 2005 have not been closed. Ignore income taxes.

2. Prepare a schedule showing the computation of corrected net income for the years ended December 31, 2005 and 2004, assuming that any adjustments are to be reported on comparative statements for the 2 years. The first items on your schedule should be the net income for each year. Ignore income taxes. (Do not prepare financial statements.) (*AICPA adapted*)

INTERNET ASSIGNMENTS

Go to the Nikolai and Bazley **Intermediate Accounting** web site (http://Nikolai.swcollege.com). Click on Student Resources and <u>internet</u> <u>homework</u> <u>assignments</u>. Then click on the appropriate hot link (icon) for each company's web site, find the relevant accounting information, and answer the following questions.

I22-1   Go to the Xerox web site.

Required For which years did the company restate its results? What were the causes of the restatements? Which method(s) did the company use? What was the cumulative restatement amount? By how much was net income restated for 1997 to 2001?

I22-2   At the time of writing this book, several companies were considering restating their earnings. Among these companies were Adelphia Communications, Dynergy, K-Mart, Worldcom, and Qwest Communications. Select one of these companies.

Required For which years did the company restate its results? What were the causes of the restatements? What items and amounts were restated? Which method(s) did the company use? By how much was net income restated? By how much were total assets restated?

appendix A

The Coca-Cola Company 2001
Annual Report: Financial Section

37   Operations Review

57   Consolidated Statements of Income

58   Consolidated Balance Sheets

60   Consolidated Statements of Cash Flows

61   Consolidated Statements of Share-Owners' Equity

62   Notes to Consolidated Financial Statements

83   Report of Independent Auditors

84   Report of Management

85   Quarterly Data

86   Selected Financial Data

THE COCA-COLA COMPANY AND SUBSIDIARIES

Operations *Review*

2001 WORLDWIDE UNIT CASE VOLUME BY OPERATING SEGMENT

WORLDWIDE TOTAL:

17.8 billion

NORTH AMERICA	LATIN AMERICA	EUROPE, EURASIA & MIDDLE EAST	ASIA	AFRICA
30%	25%	22%	17%	6%

NORTH AMERICA OPERATING SEGMENT

POPULATION: AVERAGE CONSUMER:

321 million   enjoys at least one serving of our products every day.*

Our rate of volume growth increased in 2001 and was 2 percent for the year. Innovation was a key growth driver and new initiatives ranged from the launch of diet Coke with lemon to the debut of a reinvigorated and reformulated POWERADE brand. Dasani and POWERADE were the fastest-growing products in their respective categories.

In addition, the Company and our U.S. bottlers effectively teamed up to relaunch Fanta and introduce Minute Maid Lemonade and Minute Maid Fruit Punch. Connections between our brands and consumers were strengthened through marketing activities such as the Coca-Cola classic activation around Harry Potter and reading, the "Wellness" program with Dasani, and the Olympic Torch Relay promotion.

Coca-Cola Fountain continued to grow despite macroeconomic conditions that pressured the restaurant industry. Progress in 2001 included expansion of the Minute Maid juice product line, introduction of the industry's most sophisticated fountain equipment and the launch of "Good Answer," our hotline program for restaurants.

---

* Based on operating segment average per capita consumption.

LATIN AMERICA
OPERATING SEGMENT

TOAL UNIT CASE SALES

POPULATION:

522 million

AVERAGE CONSUMER:

enjoys nearly four servings of
our product per week.*

Other 21%

Chile 5%

Argentina 8%

Mexico 43%

Brazil 23%

Our core brands in Latin America continue to drive our growth and strengthen bonds with consumers. In this very challenging economic environment, we generated a 3 percent volume increase in 2001. We introduced value packages to meet consumer needs and economic realities. Our family of beverage brands broadened rapidly as we expanded our guaraná-based products: Kuat in Brazil and Senzao in Mexico. Our sports drink, POWERADE, is growing and entering new territories, as are our major water brands, Ciel and Bonaqua. Fanta, our primary flavor brand, is being offered in new flavors and packages, building on the brand's traditional leading position in its category.

While our business in Argentina has been impacted by an uncertain economic situation, we continue our commitment to our business and that market with a series of measures designed to strengthen our business there over the medium- and long-term.

EUROPE, EURASIA
& MIDDLE EAST
OPERATING SEGMENT

TOAL UNIT CASE SALES

POPULATION:

1.3 billion

AVERAGE CONSUMER:

enjoys nearly one-and-a-half
servings of our products each week.*

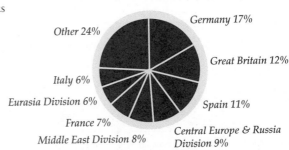

Other 24%

Germany 17%

Great Britain 12%

Italy 6%

Spain 11%

Eurasia Division 6%

France 7%

Central Europe & Russia
Division 9%

Middle East Division 8%

This year's volume increase of 2 percent was driven by growth across core brands and key markets, combined with successful product and package launches. Web-driven marketing in Great Britain and award-winning advertising in France grew sales of Coca-Cola in these key markets. Coca-Cola light expanded into five new markets, and innovative packaging continued its appeal to consumers in established markets. With the launch of POWERADE in 15 countries, we tapped into our distribution channels and expanded consumer choice in this beverage category. In addition, the introduction of new immediate consumption packages was well-received in Austria, Italy and Turkey.

Together with our bottling partners, the restructuring of our system in key markets created a foundation for the future. In Germany, our close cooperation with our bottling partners led to a strategy for renewed growth. And, the successful completion of the sale of Company-owned bottling operations in Russia to Coca-Cola HBC S.A. paved the way for future success.

* Based on operating segment average per capita consumption.

THE COCA-COLA COMPANY AND SUBSIDIARIES

ASIA OPERATING SEGMENT   TOAL UNIT CASE SALES

POPULATION:

3.2 billion

AVERAGE CONSUMER:

enjoys close to two servings of our
products each month.*

Through an intense focus on Coca-Cola, innovation and new beverages, we achieved volume growth of
10 percent in 2001. With developing economies and populations, this region has strong long-term potential, and we are building an exciting family of beverage brands in addition to expanding the popularity of
our core brands, led by Coca-Cola. In China, for example, sales of Coca-Cola increased 6 percent.

We are also profitably expanding our new beverage categories. We launched 27 products in 2001—a
record number for our system. Qoo became a successful regional brand, and water brands in India and
Indonesia are growing. Strong bottler relationships continue to drive momentum. In the Philippines, our
new partnership with San Miguel Corporation positions us for outstanding future opportunities. Across
the region, local insight continues to enrich our marketing and we are connecting with consumers as evidenced by the numerous awards we have received. In Japan, a campaign for GEORGIA coffee won the
country's most prestigious advertising award.

AFRICA OPERATING SEGMENT   TOAL UNIT CASE SALES

POPULATION:

706 million

AVERAGE CONSUMER:

enjoys close to three servings of
our products each month.*

*North & West
Africa Division 44%*

*Southern & East
Africa Division 56%*

Our ongoing commitment to investment in Africa and greater innovation there is creating immediate results,
and positioning us well to share in the long-term potential of the continent. The continued development
of a more stable and predictable economic and political environment in most markets, combined with
strong consumer preference for Coca-Cola, helped grow unit case volume by 10 percent last year, led by
Nigeria with total volume growth of 36 percent.

A world-class distribution system along with great marketing has given us the opportunity to expand
our range of products and introduce new beverages designed to appeal to local tastes. We are experiencing significant growth in markets with new product introductions across nonalcoholic beverage categories,
including brands such as Bibo, Bonaqua, Splash and Dr Pepper.

* Based on operating segment average per capita consumption.

THE COCA-COLA COMPANY AND SUBSIDIARIES

	Unit Case[1] Growth						Nonalcoholic Ready-to-Drink Beverages	All Commercial Beverages[2]	
	10-Year Compound Annual Growth		5-Year Compound Annual Growth		2001 Annual Growth		2001	2001	
	Company[3]	Industry[4]	Company[3]	Industry[4]	Company[3]	Industry[4]	Company Share	Company Share	Company Per Capita Consumption
Worldwide	6%	5%	5%	5%	4%	4%	18%	9%	70
North America[5]	4	5	3	3	2	2	22	15	398
United States	4	5	3	3	2	2	23	16	419
Latin America	6	7	6	6	3	4	24	15	205
Argentina	7	4	6	2	7	2	20	10	236
Brazil	5	5	3	6	3	5	23	13	144
Chile	9	6	5	3	(2)	3	56	23	336
Mexico	7	10	8	9	2	5	22	18	462
Europe, Eurasia & Middle East	6	3	5	3	2	4	12	6	72
Eurasia	17	8	6	5	(14)	1	14	5	39
France	8	3	9	3	7	3	9	5	110
Germany	1	2	(1)	1	(6)	1	14	7	193
Great Britain	8	2	11	2	8	3	17	6	193
Italy	1	3	4	3	2	2	9	6	104
Middle East	12	12	7	5	4	8	8	3	17
Spain	6	4	8	5	4	4	17	12	264
Asia	7	6	6	7	10	7	14	5	23
Australia	4	3	4	3	6	3	25	11	303
China	24	16	14	17	7	14	9	2	9
Japan	4	2	3	2	3	1	22	9	168
Korea	1	4	0	1	5	5	15	8	71
Philippines	8	12	9	12	32	5	49	24	159
Africa	7	6	8	3	10	6	34	11	34
North & West Africa	8	10	10	4	13	8	30	14	26
Southern & East Africa	5	3	6	3	7	4	38	10	44

[1] Unit case equals 24 eight-ounce servings.
[2] Consists of commercially sold beverages, as estimated by the Company based on available industry sources.
[3] Derived from the Company's unit case volume (see Glossary on inside back cover).
[4] Includes nonalcoholic ready-to-drink beverages only, as estimated by the Company based on available industry sources.
[5] Includes United States, Canada, Puerto Rico and The Minute Maid Company.

FINANCIAL REVIEW INCORPORATING MANAGEMENT'S DISCUSSION AND ANALYSIS

The Coca-Cola Company, together with its subsidiaries, (the Company or our Company) exists to benefit and refresh everyone who is touched by our business. We believe that our success ultimately depends on our ability to build and nurture relationships with constituents that are essential to our business: consumers, customers, bottlers, partners, government authorities, communities, employees and share owners. In order to serve and create value for these constituents, The Coca-Cola Company executes a business strategy to drive growth focused on the following priorities: (1) accelerate carbonated softdrink growth, led by Coca-Cola; (2) selectively broaden our family of beverage brands to drive profitable growth; (3) grow system profitability and capability together with our bottling partners; (4) serve customers with creativity and consistency to generate growth across all channels; (5) direct investments to highest potential areas across markets; and (6) drive efficiency and cost-effectiveness everywhere. Underlying these priorities are our objectives of increasing revenue by volume growth, expanding our share of worldwide nonalcoholic ready-to-drink beverage sales, maximizing our long-term cash flows and improving economic profit. We pursue these objectives by strategically investing in the high-return beverage business and by optimizing our cost of capital through appropriate financial strategies.

Investments

With a business system that operates locally in nearly 200 countries and generates superior cash flows, we consider our Company to be uniquely positioned to capitalize on profitable investment opportunities. Our criteria for investment are simple: New investments must directly enhance our existing operations and must be expected to provide cash returns that exceed our long-term, after-tax, weighted-average cost of capital, currently estimated at between 10 and 11 percent.

Because it has consistently generated high returns, we consider the beverage business to be a particularly attractive investment for us. In highly developed markets, our expenditures focus primarily on marketing our Company's brands. In emerging and developing markets, our objective is to increase the penetration of our products. In these markets, we allocate most of our investments to enhancing our brands and infrastructure such as production facilities, distribution networks, sales equipment and technology. We make these investments by forming strategic business alliances with local bottlers and by matching local expertise with our experience, resources and focus.

We pursue our strategic investment priorities in a way that capitalizes on the combination of our most fundamental and enduring attributes—our brands, our people and our bottling partners. There are over 6 billion people in the world who represent potential consumers of our Company's products. As we increase consumer demand for our family of brands, we produce growth throughout the Coca-Cola system.

Our Brands

We compete in the nonalcoholic ready-to-drink beverage business. Our offerings in this category include some of the world's most valuable brands—nearly 300 in all. These include carbonated softdrinks and noncarbonated beverages such as sports drinks, juice and juice drinks, water products, teas and coffees. Ultimately, consumer demand determines the Company's optimal brand offerings. Employing our localized business strategy with a special focus on brand Coca-Cola, the Company seeks to build its existing brands and, at the same time, to profitably broaden its historical family of brands. To meet our long-term growth objectives, we make significant investments to support our brands. This process involves investments to support existing brands, to develop new global or local brands, and to acquire global or local brands, when appropriate.

Our Company introduced a variety of new brands in 2001, including diet Coke with lemon, Simply Orange, Minute Maid Lemonade, Minute Maid Fruit Punch, Marocha Green Tea in Japan, Senzao in Mexico, and a reformulated POWERADE. Our Company acquired brands during 2001 such as Odwalla, Planet Java and Mad River. We also introduced existing brands in additional markets, such as the introduction of Qoo in Korea and Singapore.

We make significant investments in marketing to support our brands. Marketing investments enhance consumer awareness and increase consumer preference for our brands. This produces long-term growth in volume, per capita consumption and our share of worldwide nonalcoholic ready-to-drink beverage sales.

Our People

Our people—the employees of The Coca-Cola Company who work with our bottling partners and other key constituents—are essential to our success. To meet our long-term growth objectives, we recruit and actively cultivate a diverse workforce and establish a culture that fosters learning, innovation and value creation on a daily

FINANCIAL REVIEW INCORPORATING MANAGEMENT'S DISCUSSION AND ANALYSIS

basis. This means maintaining and refining a corporate culture that encourages our people to develop to their fullest potential, assuring enjoyment and satisfaction in the Company's work environment. Our Company values the uniqueness of all employees and the contributions they make, and we put the responsibility and accountability for ensuring local relevance and maximizing business performance in the hands of those closest to the market. Additionally, we have made innovation an explicit priority for all of our associates. Our associates work together with bottling partners to understand markets and what consumers want. Then we meet that need by delivering product through our unparalleled system.

Our Bottling Partners

The financial health and success of our bottling partners are critical components of the Company's ability to deliver leading brands. Our people work with our bottling partners to continuously look for ways to improve system economics. Our Company has business relationships with three types of bottlers: (1) independently owned bottlers, in which we have no ownership interest; (2) bottlers in which we have invested and have a non-controlling ownership interest; and (3) bottlers in which we have invested and have a controlling ownership interest.

The independently owned bottling operations and the bottlers in which we own a non-controlling interest generally have significant funding from majority owners and other financing sources that are otherwise unrelated to our Company. The terms of sales to these bottling partners are arms-length transactions.

During 2001, independently owned bottling operations produced and distributed approximately 23 percent of our worldwide unit case volume. Bottlers in which we own a non-controlling ownership interest produced and distributed approximately 61 percent of our 2001 worldwide unit case volume. Controlled bottling, fountain operations and The Minute Maid Company produced and distributed approximately 16 percent.

In July 2001, our Company and San Miguel Corporation (San Miguel) acquired Coca-Cola Bottlers Philippines, Inc. (CCBPI) from Coca-Cola Amatil Limited (Coca-Cola Amatil). Upon completion of this transaction, our Company owned 35 percent of the common shares and 100 percent of the Preferred B shares, and San Miguel owned 65 percent of the common shares of CCBPI.

Additionally, as a result of this transaction, our Company's interest in Coca-Cola Amatil was reduced from approximately 38 percent to approximately 35 percent.

During 2000, the Company entered into a joint venture in China with China National Oils and Foodstuffs Imports/Exports Corporation (COFCO), completion of which occurred in 2001. COFCO contributed to the joint venture its minority equity interests in 11 Chinese bottlers. Our Company contributed its equity interests in two Chinese bottlers plus cash in exchange for a 35 percent equity interest in the venture.

On December 31, 1999, we owned approximately 50.5 percent of Coca-Cola Beverages plc (Coca-Cola Beverages). In July 2000, a merger of Coca-Cola Beverages and Hellenic Bottling Company S.A. was completed to create Coca-Cola HBC S.A. (CCHBC). This merger resulted in a decrease of our Company's equity ownership interest from approximately 50.5 percent of Coca-Cola Beverages to approximately 24 percent of the combined entity, CCHBC. This change in ownership resulted in the Company recognizing a $118 million tax-free non-cash gain in the third quarter of 2000.

In 1999, two Japanese bottlers, Kita Kyushu Coca-Cola Bottling Company Ltd. and Sanyo Coca-Cola Bottling Company Ltd., merged to become a new, publicly traded bottling company, Coca-Cola West Japan Company Ltd. We own approximately 5 percent of this bottler.

In 1999, we increased our interest in Embotelladora Arica S.A. (since renamed Coca-Cola Embonor S.A.), a bottler headquartered in Chile, from approximately 17 percent to approximately 45 percent.

Bottlers in which we have a non-controlling ownership interest are accounted for under the cost or equity method as appropriate. Equity income or loss, included in our consolidated net income, represents our share of the net earnings or losses of our equity investee companies. In 2001, our Company's share of income from equity method investments totaled $152 million.

FINANCIAL REVIEW INCORPORATING MANAGEMENT'S DISCUSSION AND ANALYSIS

The following table illustrates the difference in calculated fair values, based on quoted closing prices of publicly traded shares, and our Company's carrying values for selected equity method investees (in millions):

December 31,	Fair Value	Carrying Value	Difference[1]
2001			
Coca-Cola Enterprises Inc.	$ 3,200	$ 788	$ 2,412
Coca-Cola Amatil Limited	748	432	316
Coca-Cola HBC S.A.	811	791	20
Coca-Cola FEMSA, S.A. de C.V.	858	316	542
Panamerican Beverages, Inc.	455	484	(29)
Grupo Continental, S.A.	231	160	71
Coca-Cola Bottling Company Consolidated	94	62	32
Coca-Cola Embonor S.A.	114	187	(73)
Embotelladoras Polar S.A.	33	51	(18)
			$ 3,273

[1] In instances where carrying value exceeds fair value, the decline in value is considered to be temporary.

Historically, in certain situations, we have viewed it to be advantageous for our Company to acquire a controlling interest in a bottling operation, often on a temporary basis. Owning such a controlling interest has allowed us to compensate for limited local resources and has enabled us to help focus the bottler's sales and marketing programs, assist in developing its business and information systems and establish appropriate capital structures.

In February 2001, our Company reached agreement with Carlsberg A/S (Carlsberg) for the dissolution of Coca-Cola Nordic Beverages (CCNB), a joint venture in which our Company had a 49 percent ownership. At that time, CCNB had bottling operations in Sweden, Norway, Denmark, Finland and Iceland. Under this agreement with Carlsberg, our Company acquired CCNB's Sweden and Norway bottling operations in June 2001, increasing our Company's ownership in those bottlers to 100 percent. Carlsberg acquired CCNB's Denmark and Finland bottling operations, increasing Carlsberg's ownership in those bottlers to 100 percent. Pursuant to the agreement, CCNB sold its Iceland bottling operations to a third-party group of investors in May 2001.

In 2001, our Company concluded negotiations regarding the terms of a Control and Profit and Loss (CPL) agreement with certain other share owners of Coca-Cola Erfrischungsgetraenke AG (CCEAG), the largest bottler in Germany, in which

the Company has an approximate 41 percent ownership interest. Under the terms of the CPL agreement, the Company obtained management control of CCEAG for a period of up to five years. In return for the management control of CCEAG, the Company guaranteed annual payments in lieu of dividends by CCEAG to all other CCEAG share owners. Additionally, all other CCEAG share owners entered into either a put or a put/call option agreement with the Company, exercisable at the end of the term of the CPL agreement at agreed prices. In early 2002, the Company assumed control of CCEAG. This transaction will be accounted for as a business combination. The present value of the total amount likely to be paid by our Company to all other CCEAG share owners, including the put or put/call payments and the guaranteed annual payments in lieu of dividends, is approximately $600 million. In 2001, CCEAG's revenues were approximately $1.7 billion. Additionally, our Company's debt will increase between $700 million and $800 million once this business combination is completed.

During the first half of 2001, in separate transactions, our Company purchased two bottlers in Brazil: Refrescos Guararapes Ltda. and Sucovalle Sucos e Concentrados do Vale S.A. In separate transactions during the first half of 2000, our Company purchased two other bottlers in Brazil: Companhia Mineira de Refrescos, S.A. and Refrigerantes Minas Gerais Ltda. In October 2000, the Company purchased a 58 percent interest in Paraguay Refrescos S.A. (Paresa), a bottler located in Paraguay. In December 2000, the Company made a tender offer for the remaining 42 percent of the shares in Paresa. In January 2001, following the completion of the tender offer, we owned approximately 95 percent of Paresa.

In July 1999, our Company acquired from Fraser and Neave Limited its 75 percent ownership interest in F&N Coca-Cola Pte Limited (F&N Coca-Cola). Prior to the acquisition, our Company held a 25 percent equity interest in F&N Coca-Cola. Acquisition of Fraser and Neave Limited's 75 percent stake gave our Company full ownership of F&N Coca-Cola. F&N Coca-Cola holds a majority ownership in bottling operations in Brunei, Cambodia, Nepal, Pakistan, SriLanka, Singapore and Vietnam.

In line with our long-term bottling strategy, we consider alternatives for reducing our ownership interest in a bottler. One alternative is to combine our bottling interests with the bottling interests of others to form

FINANCIAL REVIEW INCORPORATING MANAGEMENT'S DISCUSSION AND ANALYSIS

strategic business alliances. Another alternative is to sell our interest in a bottling operation to one of our equity investee bottlers. In both of these situations, we continue to participate in the bottler's results of operations through our share of the equity investee's earnings or losses.

In November 2001, our Company sold nearly all of its ownership interests in various Russian bottling operations to CCHBC for approximately $170 million in cash and notes receivable, of which $146 million in notes receivable remained outstanding as of December 31, 2001. These interests consisted of the Company's 40 percent ownership interest in a joint venture with CCHBC that operates bottling territories in Siberia and parts of Western Russia, together with our Company's nearly 100 percent interests in bottling operations with territories covering the remainder of Russia.

For additional information about transactions with our bottling partners, refer to Notes 2, 17 and 18 in our Consolidated Financial Statements.

Financial Strategies

The following strategies are intended to optimize our cost of capital, increasing our ability to maximize share-owner value.

Debt Financing

Our Company maintains debt levels we consider prudent based on our cash flow, interest coverage and percentage of debt to capital. We use debt financing to lower our overall cost of capital, which increases our return on share-owners' equity.

As of December 31, 2001, our long-term debt was rated "A+" by Standard & Poor's and "Aa3" by Moody's, and our commercial paper program was rated "A-1" and "P-1" by Standard & Poor's and Moody's, respectively. In assessing our credit strength, both Standard & Poor's and Moody's consider our capital structure and financial policies as well as aggregated balance sheet and other financial information for the Company and certain bottlers including Coca-Cola Enterprises Inc. (Coca-Cola Enterprises) and CCHBC. While the Company has no legal obligation for the debt of these bottlers, the rating agencies believe the strategic importance of the bottlers to the Company's business model provides the Company with an incentive to keep these bottlers viable. If the credit ratings were reduced by the rating agencies, our interest expense could increase.

Our global presence and strong capital position give us easy access to key financial markets around the world, enabling us to raise funds with a low effective cost. This posture, coupled with the active management of our mix of short-term and long-term debt, results in a lower overall cost of borrowing. Our debt management policies, in conjunction with our share repurchase programs and investment activity, typically result in current liabilities exceeding current assets.

In managing our use of debt capital, we consider the following financial measurements and ratios:

Year Ended December 31,	2001	2000	1999
Net debt (in billions)	$ 3.3	$ 3.9	$ 4.5
Net debt-to-net capital	23%	29%	32%
Free cash flow to net debt	95%	72%	52%
Interest coverage	20x	12x	14x
Ratio of earnings to fixed charges	18.1x	8.7x	11.6x

Share Repurchases

In October 1996, our Board of Directors authorized a plan to repurchase up to 206 million shares of our Company's common stock through the year 2006. In 2001, we repurchased approximately 5 million shares under the 1996 plan.

In 2000, we did not repurchase any shares under the 1996 plan. This was due to our utilization of cash for an organizational realignment (the Realignment), as discussed under the heading "Other Operating Charges," and the impact on cash from the reduction in concentrate inventory levels by certain bottlers, as discussed under the heading "Volume."

In 1999, we did not repurchase any shares under the 1996 plan due primarily to our utilization of cash for brand and bottler acquisitions. Since the inception of our initial share repurchase program in 1984 through our current program as of December 31, 2001, we have repurchased more than 1 billion shares. This represents 32 percent of the shares outstanding as of January 1, 1984, at an average price per share of $12.64.

We expect that the Company's share repurchases will be increased in 2002 and are currently estimating a range of $750 million to $1 billion of repurchases during the year.

Dividend Policy

At its February 2002 meeting, our Board of Directors again increased our quarterly dividend, raising it to

FINANCIAL REVIEW INCORPORATING MANAGEMENT'S DISCUSSION AND ANALYSIS

$.20 per share. This is equivalent to a full-year dividend of $.80 in 2002, our 40th consecutive annual increase. Our annual common stock dividend was $.72 per share, $.68 per share and $.64 per share in 2001, 2000 and 1999, respectively.

In 2001, our dividend payout ratio was approximately 45 percent of our net income. To free up additional cash for reinvestment in our high-return beverage business, our Board of Directors intends to gradually reduce our dividend payout ratio to 30 percent over time.

Financial Risk Management

Our Company uses derivative financial instruments primarily to reduce our exposure to adverse fluctuations in interest rates and foreign exchange rates and, to a lesser extent, adverse fluctuations in commodity prices and other market risks. We do not enter into derivative financial instruments for trading purposes. As a matter of policy, all our derivative positions are used to reduce risk by hedging an underlying economic exposure. Because of the high correlation between the hedging instrument and the underlying exposure, fluctuations in the value of the instruments are generally offset by reciprocal changes in the value of the underlying exposure. Virtually all of our derivatives are straightforward over-the-counter instruments with liquid markets.

Foreign Currency

We manage most of our foreign currency exposures on a consolidated basis, which allows us to net certain exposures and take advantage of any natural offsets. With approximately 77 percent of 2001 operating income generated outside the United States, weakness in one particular currency is often offset by strengths in others over time. We use derivative financial instruments to further reduce our net exposure to currency fluctuations.

Our Company enters into forward contracts and purchases currency options (principally euro and Japanese yen) to hedge certain portions of forecasted cash flows denominated in foreign currencies. Additionally, the Company enters into forward exchange contracts to offset the earnings impact relating to exchange rate fluctuations on certain monetary assets and liabilities. The Company enters into forward exchange contracts as hedges of net investments in international operations.

Interest Rates

Our Company maintains our percentage of fixed and variable rate debt within defined parameters. We enter into interest rate swap agreements that maintain the fixed-to-variable mix within these parameters.

Value at Risk

Our Company monitors our exposure to financial market risks using several objective measurement systems, including value-at-risk models. Our value-at-risk calculations use a historical simulation model to estimate potential future losses in the fair value of our derivatives and other financial instruments that could occur as a result of adverse movements in foreign currency and interest rates. We have not considered the potential impact of favorable movements in foreign currency and interest rates on our calculation. We examined historical weekly returns over the previous 10 years to calculate our value at risk. The average value at risk represents the simple average of quarterly amounts over the past year. As a result of our foreign currency value-at-risk calculation, we estimate with 95 percent confidence that the fair values of our foreign currency derivatives and other financial instruments, over a one-week period, would decline by less than $43 million using 2001 average fair values and by less than $37 million using December 31, 2001 fair values. On December 31, 2000, we estimated the fair value would decline by less than $37 million. According to our interest rate value-at-risk calculations, we estimate with 95 percent confidence that any increase in our net interest expense due to an adverse move in our 2001 average or in our December 31, 2001 interest rates over a one-week period would not have a material impact on our Consolidated Financial Statements. Our December 31, 2000 estimate also was not material to our Consolidated Financial Statements.

For additional discussion of financial risk management related to hedging transactions and derivative financial instruments, refer to Note 9 in our Consolidated Financial Statements.

Management's Discussion and Analysis

Our Business

We are the world's leading manufacturer, marketer and distributor of nonalcoholic beverage concentrates and syrups. Our Company manufactures beverage concentrates and syrups and, in certain instances, finished beverages, which we sell to bottling and canning operations,

FINANCIAL REVIEW INCORPORATING MANAGEMENT'S DISCUSSION AND ANALYSIS

authorized fountain wholesalers and some fountain retailers. We also market and distribute juice and juice-drink products. In addition, we have ownership interests in numerous bottling and canning operations.

Volume

We measure our sales volume in two ways: (1) gallons and (2) unit cases of finished products. Gallons represent our primary business and measure the volume of concentrates, syrups and other beverage products (expressed in equivalent gallons of syrup) included by the Company in unit case volume. Most of our revenues are based on this measure of "wholesale" activity.

We also measure volume in unit cases. As used in this report, "unit case" means a unit of measurement equal to 192 U.S. fluid ounces of finished beverage (24 eight-ounce servings); and "unit case volume" of the Company means the number of unit cases (or unit case equivalents) of Company trademark or licensed beverage products directly or indirectly sold by the Coca-Cola bottling system or by the Company to customers, including (i) beverage products bearing trademarks licensed to the Company and (ii) certain key products (which are not material) owned by our bottlers and for which the Company provides marketing support and derives profit from the sales.

Our worldwide unit case volume increased 4 percent in 2001, on top of a 4 percent increase in 2000. The increase in unit case volume reflects consistent performance across certain key operations despite difficult global economic conditions. Our business system sold 17.8 billion unit cases in 2001.

In 2000, certain bottlers reduced their concentrate inventory levels. This was based on a joint review performed by the Company and our bottlers around the world in order to determine the optimum level of bottler concentrate inventories. The joint review established that opportunities existed to reduce the level of concentrate inventory carried by bottlers in various regions of the world. During the first half of 2000, bottlers in these regions reduced concentrate inventory levels, the majority of which occurred during the first three months of 2000.

Critical Accounting Policies

Consolidation

Our Consolidated Financial Statements include the accounts of The Coca-Cola Company and all subsidiaries except where control is temporary or does not rest with our Company. All majority-owned entities in which our Company's control is considered other than temporary are consolidated. For investments in companies in which we have the ability to exercise significant influence over operating and financial policies, including certain investments where there is a temporary majority interest, such entities are accounted for by the equity method. Our judgments regarding the level of influence or control of each equity method investment include considering key factors such as our ownership interest, representation on the board of directors, participation in policy making decisions and material intercompany transactions. Our investments in other companies that we do not control and for which we do not have the ability to exercise significant influence as discussed above are carried at cost or fair value, as appropriate. All significant intercompany accounts and transactions, including transactions with equity method investees, are eliminated from our financial results.

Recoverability of Investments

Management periodically assesses the recoverability of our Company's investments. The significant judgment required in management's recoverability assessment is the determination of the fair value of the investment. For publicly traded investments, the fair value of our Company's investment is readily determinable based on quoted market prices. For non-publicly traded investments, management's assessment of fair value is based on our analysis of the investee's estimates of future operating results and the resulting cash flows. Management's ability to accurately predict future cash flows, especially in emerging and developing markets such as the Middle East and Latin America, may impact the determination of fair value.

In the event a decline in fair value of an investment occurs, management may be required to make a determination as to whether the decline in market value is other than temporary. Management's assessment as to the nature of a decline in fair value is largely based on our estimates of future operating results, the resulting cash flows and intent to hold the investment. If an investment is considered to be impaired and the decline in value is considered to be other than temporary, an appropriate write-down is recorded.

FINANCIAL REVIEW INCORPORATING MANAGEMENT'S DISCUSSION AND ANALYSIS

Other Assets

Our Company invests in infrastructure programs with our bottlers that are directed at strengthening our bottling system and increasing unit case sales. Additionally, our Company advances payments to certain customers for marketing to fund activities intended to generate volume. Advance payments are also made to certain customers for distribution rights. Payments under these programs are generally capitalized as other assets on the Consolidated Balance Sheets. Management periodically evaluates the recoverability of these assets by preparing estimates of sales volume, the resulting gross profit, cash flows and other factors. Accuracy of our recoverability assessments is based on management's ability to accurately predict certain key variables such as sales volume, prices, marketing spending and other economic factors. Predicting these key variables involves uncertainty about future events; however, the assumptions used are consistent with our internal planning. If the assets are assessed to be recoverable, they are amortized over the periods benefited. If the carrying value of these assets is considered to be not recoverable, such assets are written down as appropriate.

Trademarks and Other Intangible Assets

Trademarks and other intangible assets are stated on the basis of cost and are amortized, principally on a straight-line basis, over the estimated future periods to be benefited (not exceeding 40 years). Other intangible assets consist primarily of bottling and distribution rights in specific territories. Trademarks and other intangible assets are periodically reviewed for impairment whenever events or changes occur that indicate the carrying value may not be recoverable. When such events or changes occur, management estimates the future cash flows expected to result from the use and, if applicable, the eventual disposition of the assets. The key variables which management must estimate include sales volume, prices, marketing spending and other economic factors. Significant management judgment is involved in estimating these variables, and they include inherent uncertainties; however, the assumptions used are consistent with our internal planning. Therefore, management periodically evaluates and updates the estimates based on the conditions that influence these variables. If such assets are considered impaired, they are written down to fair value as appropriate.

The assumptions and conditions for "Recoverability of Investments," "Other Assets" and "Trademarks and Other Intangible Assets" reflect management's best assumptions and estimates, but these items involve inherent uncertainties as described above, which may or may not be controllable by management. As a result, the accounting for such items could result in different amounts if management used different assumptions or if different conditions occur in future periods.

Other Policies

The Company has adopted or will adopt the following new accounting standards: Statement of Financial Accounting Standards (SFAS) No. 133, "Accounting for Derivative Instruments and Hedging Activities," as amended by SFAS No. 137 and SFAS No. 138; SFAS No. 141, "Business Combinations"; and SFAS No. 142, "Goodwill and Other Intangible Assets." These standards are considered to be critical accounting policies and are explained under the heading "New Accounting Standards."

For further information concerning accounting policies, refer to Note 1 of our Consolidated Financial Statements.

Operations

Net Operating Revenues and Gross Margin

In 2001, on a consolidated basis, our net operating revenues and our gross profit grew 1 percent and 3 percent, respectively. The growth in net operating revenues was primarily due to an increase in gallon shipments, price increases in selected countries and the consolidation of the Nordic and Brazilian bottling operations. These gains were offset by the negative impact of a stronger U.S. dollar and the sale of our previously owned vending operations in Japan and canning operations in Germany. Our gross profit margin increased to 69.9 percent in 2001 from 68.8 percent in 2000, primarily due to the sale in 2001 of our Japan vending and German canning operations, partially offset by the consolidation in 2001 of the Nordic and Brazilian bottling operations. Generally, bottling and vending operations produce higher net revenues but lower gross margins compared to concentrate and syrup operations.

In 2000, on a consolidated basis, our net operating revenues and our gross profit each grew 3 percent. The growth in net operating revenues was primarily due to improved business conditions and price increases in selected countries. This growth was partially offset by the negative

FINANCIAL REVIEW INCORPORATING MANAGEMENT'S DISCUSSION AND ANALYSIS

impact of a stronger U.S. dollar and the inventory reduction by certain bottlers. Our gross profit margin of 68.8 percent remained unchanged in 2000 compared to 1999.

Selling, Administrative and General Expenses
Selling expenses totaled $6,930 million in 2001, $6,863 million in 2000 and $6,745 million in 1999.

During the first quarter of 2001, the Company announced plans to implement incremental strategic marketing initiatives in order to accelerate the Company's business strategies. During 2001, the Company invested $298 million of incremental marketing in the United States, Japan and Germany.

The increase in 2001 was primarily due to higher marketing in line with the Company's unit case volume growth, incremental marketing expenses discussed above and the consolidation in 2001 of the Nordic and Brazilian bottling operations. Such increases were partially offset by the sale in 2001 of our Japan vending and German canning operations and the impact of a stronger U.S. dollar. The increase in 2000 was primarily due to higher marketing expenditures in line with unit case volume growth and the consolidation in 2000 of F&N Coca-Cola. Additionally, as a result of the gain recognized in the third quarter of 2000 from the merger of Coca-Cola Beverages and Hellenic Bottling Company S.A., discussed in "Other Income-Net," the Company invested approximately $30 million in incremental marketing initiatives in CCHBC regions.

Administrative and general expenses totaled $1,766 million in 2001, $1,688 million in 2000 and $1,735 million in 1999. The increase in 2001 is due to the consolidation in 2001 of the Nordic and Brazilian bottling operations, partially offset by the sale in 2001 of our Japan vending and German canning operations and the impact of a stronger U.S. dollar. The decrease in 2000 was primarily a result of savings realized from the Realignment initiated in 2000, offset by the consolidation in 2000 of F&N Coca-Cola. See discussion under the heading "Other Operating Charges" for a more complete description of the Realignment.

Administrative and general expenses, as a percentage of net operating revenues, totaled approximately 9 percent in 2001, 8 percent in 2000 and 9 percent in 1999.

Other Operating Charges
During 2000, we recorded total nonrecurring charges of approximately $1,443 million. Of this $1,443 million, approximately $405 million related

to the impairment of certain bottling, manufacturing and intangible assets; approximately $850 million related to the Realignment; and approximately $188 million related to the settlement terms of a class action discrimination lawsuit and a donation to The Coca-Cola Foundation.

In the first quarter of 2000, we recorded charges of approximately $405 million related to the impairment of certain bottling, manufacturing and intangible assets, primarily within our Indian bottling operations. These impairment charges were recorded to reduce the carrying value of the identified assets to fair value. Fair value was derived using cash flow analysis. The assumptions used in the cash flow analysis were consistent with those used in our internal planning process. The assumptions included estimates of future growth in unit cases, estimates of gross margins, estimates of the impact of exchange rates and estimates of tax rates and tax incentives. The charge was primarily the result of our revised outlook for the Indian beverage market including the future expected tax environment. The remaining carrying value of long-lived assets within our Indian bottling operations, immediately after recording the impairment charge, was approximately $300 million.

In the first quarter of 2000, the Company initiated the Realignment, which reduced our workforce around the world and transferred responsibilities from our corporate headquarters to local revenue-generating operating units. The intent of the Realignment was to effectively align our corporate resources, support systems and business culture to fully leverage the local capabilities of our system.

Employees were separated from almost all functional areas of the Company's operations, and certain activities were outsourced to third parties. The total number of employees separated as of December 31, 2000, was approximately 5,200. Employees separated from the Company as a result of the Realignment were offered severance or early retirement packages, as appropriate, which included both financial and nonfinancial components. The Realignment expenses included costs associated with involuntary terminations, voluntary retirements and other direct costs associated with implementing the Realignment. Other direct costs included repatriating and relocating employees to local markets; asset write-downs; lease cancellation costs; and costs associated with the development, communication and administration of the Realignment. We recorded total charges of approximately $850 million related to the Realignment. During 2000, the Company achieved approximately $150 million in savings from the Realignment. For a more complete description of the costs related to the Realignment, refer to Note 16 in our Consolidated Financial Statements.

In the fourth quarter of 2000, we recorded charges of approximately $188 million related to the settlement terms of, and direct costs related to, a class action discrimination lawsuit. The monetary settlement included cash payments to fund back pay, compensatory damages, a promotional achievement fund and attorneys' fees. In addition, the Company introduced a wide range of training, monitoring and mentoring programs. Of the $188 million, $50 million was donated to The Coca-Cola Foundation to continue its broad range of community support programs. In 2001, our Company paid out substantially all of this settlement.

In the fourth quarter of 1999, we recorded charges of approximately $813 million. Of this $813 million, approximately $543 million related to the impairment of certain bottling, manufacturing and intangible assets, primarily within our Russian and Caribbean bottlers and in the Middle and Far East and in North America. These impairment charges were recorded to reduce the carrying value of the identified assets to fair value. Fair values were derived using a variety of methodologies, including cash flow analysis, estimates of sales proceeds and independent appraisals. Where cash flow analyses were used to estimate fair values, key assumptions employed, consistent with those used in our internal planning process, included our estimates of future growth in unit case sales, estimates of gross margins and estimates of the impact of inflation and foreign currency fluctuations. The charges were primarily the result of our revised outlook in certain markets due to the prolonged severe economic downturns. The remaining carrying value of these impaired long-lived assets, immediately after recording the impairment charge, was approximately $140 million.

Of the $813 million, approximately $196 million related to charges associated with the impairment of the distribution and bottling assets of our vending operations in Japan and our bottling operations in the Baltics. The charges reduced the carrying value of these assets to their fair value less the cost to sell. Consistent with our long-term bottling strategy, management intended to sell the assets of our vending operations in Japan and our bottling operations in the Baltics. On December 22, 2000, the Company signed a definitive agreement to sell the

assets of our vending operations in Japan, and this sale was completed in 2001. The proceeds from the sale of the assets were approximately equal to the carrying value of the long-lived assets less the cost to sell.

In December 2000, the Company announced it had intended to sell its bottling operations in the Baltics to one of our strategic business partners. However, that partner was in the process of an internal restructuring and no longer planned to purchase the Baltics bottling operations. At that time, another suitable buyer was not identified so the Company continued to operate the Baltics bottlers as consolidated operations until a new buyer was identified. Subsequently, in January 2002, our Company reached an agreement to sell our bottling operations in the Baltics to CCHBC in early 2002. The expected proceeds from the sale of the Baltics bottlers are approximately equal to the current carrying value of the investment.

The remainder of the $813 million charges, approximately $74 million, primarily related to the change in senior management and charges related to organizational changes within the Europe, Eurasia and Middle East, Latin America and Corporate segments. These charges were incurred during the fourth quarter of 1999.

Operating Income and Operating Margin
On a consolidated basis, our operating income increased 45 percent in 2001 to $5,352 million. This follows a decline of 7 percent in 2000 to $3,691 million. The 2001 results reflect an increase in gallon shipments, price increases in selected countries, the impact of nonrecurring charges in 2000 as previously discussed under the heading "Other Operating Charges" and the consolidation of the Nordic and Brazilian bottling operations. This is offset by the negative impact of a stronger U.S. dollar and the sale of our previously owned vending operations in Japan and canning operations in Germany. The 2000 results reflect the recording of nonrecurring charges, as previously discussed under the heading "Other Operating Charges," the impact of the stronger U.S. dollar, the consolidation of F&N Coca-Cola and the effect of the previously discussed reduction of concentrate inventory by certain bottlers within the Coca-Cola system, which was completed in the first half of 2000. Our consolidated operating margin was 26.6 percent in 2001, 18.6 percent in 2000 and 20.6 percent in 1999.

FINANCIAL REVIEW INCORPORATING MANAGEMENT'S DISCUSSION AND ANALYSIS

Margin Analysis

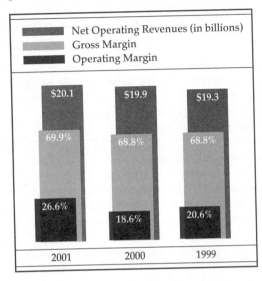

Interest Income and Interest Expense

In 2001, our interest income decreased 6 percent due primarily to lower interest rates. In 2000, our interest income increased 33 percent due primarily to higher average cash balances and higher interest rates. Interest expense decreased 35 percent in 2001 due to both a decrease in average commercial paper debt balances and lower interest rates. In 2001, the Company used free cash flow to reduce commercial paper debt balances. Interest expense increased 33 percent in 2000 due primarily to both an increase in average commercial paper debt balances and higher interest rates throughout the period. Average 2000 commercial paper debt balances increased from 1999 primarily due to our utilization of cash for the Realignment, as discussed under the heading "Other Operating Charges," and the impact on cash from the reduction in concentrate inventory levels by certain bottlers, as discussed under the heading "Volume."

In 2001, interest income exceeded interest expense. Interest income benefited from cash invested in locations outside the United States earning higher rates of interest than could be obtained within the United States. Our interest expense is primarily incurred on borrowings in the United States.

Equity Income (Loss)

In 2001, our Company's share of income from equity method investments totaled $152 million. The increase in our Company's share of income from equity method investments was due primarily to the continued improvement in operating performance by the majority of our equity investees and

the impact of impairment charges on equity investees in 2000 as discussed below.

As of January 1, 2001, Coca-Cola Enterprises changed its method of accounting for infrastructure development payments received from the Company. Prior to this change, Coca-Cola Enterprises recognized these payments as offsets to incremental expenses of the programs in the periods in which they were incurred. Coca-Cola Enterprises now recognizes the infrastructure development payments received from the Company as obligations under the contracts are performed. Because the Company eliminates the financial effect of significant intercompany transactions (including transactions with equity method investees), this change in accounting method has no impact on the Consolidated Financial Statements of our Company. For a more complete description of these transactions, refer to Note 2 in our Consolidated Financial Statements.

In 2000, our Company's share of losses from equity method investments totaled $289 million. This includes a nonrecurring charge of approximately $306 million, which represents the Company's portion of a charge recorded by Coca-Cola Amatil to reduce the carrying value of its investment in the Philippines. In addition, Panamerican Beverages, Inc. (Panamco) wrote down selected assets, including the impairment of the value of its Venezuelan operating unit. The Company's portion of this charge was approximately $124 million. Also contributing to the equity losses were nonrecurring charges recorded by investees in Eurasia and the Middle East. These nonrecurring charges were partially offset by an overall improvement in operating performance by our portfolio of bottlers and the positive impact of lower tax rates on current and deferred taxes at CCEAG.

Other Income-Net

In 2001, other income-net declined to $39 million from $99 million in 2000, primarily reflecting the impact of a gain related to the merger of Coca-Cola Beverages and Hellenic Bottling Company S.A. during the third quarter of 2000. This merger resulted in a decrease of our Company's equity ownership interest from approximately 50.5 percent of Coca-Cola Beverages to approximately 24 percent of the combined entity, CCHBC. As a result of our Company's decreased equity ownership, a tax-free non-cash gain of approximately $118 million was recognized. In 2000, this gain was partially offset by exchange losses recognized versus exchange gains in 1999 attributable to the hedging of our resources in Brazil.

FINANCIAL REVIEW INCORPORATING MANAGEMENT'S DISCUSSION AND ANALYSIS

Gains on Issuances of Stock by Equity Investees
At the time an equity investee issues its stock to third parties at a price in excess of our book value, our Company's equity in the underlying net assets of that investee increases. We generally record an increase to our investment account and a corresponding gain in these transactions. In July 2001, Coca-Cola Enterprises completed its acquisition of Hondo Incorporated and Herbco Enterprises, Inc., collectively known as Herb Coca-Cola. The transaction was valued at approximately $1.4 billion, with approximately 30 percent of the transaction funded with the issuance of approximately 25 million shares of Coca-Cola Enterprises common stock, and the remaining portion funded through debt and assumed debt. The issuance of shares resulted in a one-time non-cash pretax gain for our Company of approximately $91 million. This gain represents the increase in our Company's equity in the underlying net assets of the related investee. No gains on issuances of stock by equity investees were recorded to the Consolidated Statements of Income during 2000 or 1999. For a more complete description of these transactions, refer to Note 3 in our Consolidated Financial Statements.

Income Taxes
Our effective tax rates were 29.8 percent in 2001, 36.0 percent in 2000 and 36.3 percent in 1999. Our ongoing effective tax rates reflect tax benefits derived from significant operations outside the United States, which are taxed at rates lower than the U.S. statutory rate of 35 percent. The decrease in our effective tax rate in 2001 was primarily due to effective tax planning and the impact that the impairment charges recorded in 2000 had on the 2000 effective tax rate. The change in our effective tax rate in 2000 was primarily the result of our current inability to realize a tax benefit associated with the impairment charges recorded in 2000, as previously discussed under the headings "Other Operating Charges" and "Equity Income (Loss)," partially offset by the tax-free gain of approximately $118 million related to the merger of Coca-Cola Beverages and Coca-Cola Hellenic Bottling Company S.A., previously discussed under the heading "Other Income–Net." For a more complete description of our income taxes, refer to Note 14 in our Consolidated Financial Statements.

During the first quarter of 2000, the United States and Japan taxing authorities entered into an Advance Pricing Agreement (APA) whereby the level of royalties paid by Coca-Cola (Japan) Company, Ltd. (our Subsidiary) to our Company has been established for the years 1993 through 2001. Pursuant to the terms of the APA, our Subsidiary has filed amended returns for the applicable periods reflecting the negotiated royalty rate. These amended returns resulted in the payment during the first and second quarters of 2000 of additional Japanese taxes, the effect of which on both our financial performance and our effective tax rate was not material, due primarily to offsetting tax credits utilized on our U.S. income tax return. The majority of the offsetting tax credits will be realized by the end of the first quarter of 2002.

Management estimates that the effective tax rate for the year ending December 31, 2002 will be approximately 27.5 percent.

Income Per Share
Our basic net income per share increased by 82 percent in 2001, compared to a 10 percent decline in 2000. Diluted net income per share increased by 82 percent in 2001, compared to a 10 percent decline in 2000.

Recent Developments
In November 2001, our Company and CCBPI entered into a sale and purchase agreement with RFM Corp. to acquire its 83.2 percent interest in Cosmos Bottling Corporation (CBC), a publicly traded Philippine beverage company. As of the date of the agreement, the Company began supplying concentrate for this operation. The transaction valued CBC at 14 billion Philippine pesos, or approximately $270 million. The purchase of RFM's interest was finalized on January 3, 2002 with our Company receiving direct and indirect ownership totaling approximately 62.3 percent. A subsequent tender offer was made to the remaining minority share owners and is expected to close in March 2002. The Company and CCBPI have agreed to restructure the operations of CBC upon completion of the acquisition. The restructuring will result in the Company owning all acquired trademarks and CCBPI owning all the acquired bottling assets. No gain or loss is expected upon completion of this restructuring.

In early 2002, the Company entered into an agreement with Coca-Cola Enterprises designed to support profitable volume growth of Company brands within Coca-Cola Enterprises' territories. Under the terms of the agreement, Coca-Cola Enterprises will earn cash funding as they achieve mutually established unit

FINANCIAL REVIEW INCORPORATING MANAGEMENT'S DISCUSSION AND ANALYSIS

case volume growth targets. The total cash support expected to be paid to Coca-Cola Enterprises under this agreement is $150 million in 2002 and $250 million in 2003. Beginning in 2004, the expected annual cash support to be paid to Coca-Cola Enterprises under this agreement will be reduced each year through 2009 when the annual cash support expected to be paid to Coca-Cola Enterprises will be $80 million. Beginning in 2009 and for each year thereafter, the support expected to be paid is $80 million annually. The Company will expense the funding as it is earned by Coca-Cola Enterprises. The agreement can be cancelled by either party at the end of a fiscal year with at least six months notice. During 2001, the Company also entered into an agreement to provide financial support to Coca-Cola Enterprises for introducing certain Company brands within Coca-Cola Enterprises' recently acquired Herb Coca-Cola territories. Under the terms of this agreement, the Company expects to pay Coca-Cola Enterprises $14 million annually in the years 2002 through 2008 and $11 million in 2009.

Liquidity and Capital Resources

We believe our ability to generate cash from operations to reinvest in our business is one of our fundamental financial strengths. We anticipate that our operating activities in 2002 will continue to provide us with cash flows to assist in our business expansion and to meet our financial commitments.

Free Cash Flow

Free cash flow is the cash remaining from operations after we have satisfied our business reinvestment opportunities. We focus on increasing free cash flow to achieve our objective of maximizing share-owner value over time. We use free cash flow along with borrowings to pay dividends, make share repurchases and make acquisitions.

The consolidated statements of our cash flows are summarized as follows (in millions):

Year Ended December 31,	2001	2000	1999
Cash flows provided by (used in):			
Operations	$ 4,110	$ 3,585	$ 3,883
Business reinvestment	(963)	(779)	(1,551)
Free Cash Flow	3,147	2,806	2,332
Cash flows (used in) provided by:			
Acquisitions, net of disposals	(225)	(386)	(1,870)
Share repurchases	(277)	(133)	(15)
Dividends	(1,791)	(1,685)	(1,580)
Other financing activities	(762)	(254)	1,124
Exchange	(45)	(140)	(28)
Increase (decrease) in cash	$ 47	$ 208	$ (37)

In 2001, cash provided by operations amounted to $4,110 million, a 15 percent increase from 2000. The increase was primarily due to solid 2001 business results partially offset by a stronger U.S. dollar, 2000 being unfavorably impacted by the previously mentioned planned inventory reduction by certain bottlers as discussed under the heading "Volume," cash payments made to separated employees under the Realignment, as well as additional Japanese tax payments made pursuant to the terms of the APA entered into by the United States and Japan taxing authorities. Cash provided by operations in 2000 amounted to $3,585 million, an 8 percent decrease from 1999. The decrease was primarily due to 2000 being unfavorably impacted by the items mentioned above.

In 2001, net cash used in investing activities increased by $23 million compared to 2000. The increase was primarily the result of increased purchases of property, plant and equipment; the acquisition of the Nordic bottling operations and other investing activities such as the acquisitions of Odwalla, Inc. and Brazilian bottling operations. This was offset by proceeds received from the sale of our Japan Vending operations.

In 2000, net cash used in investing activities decreased by $2,256 million compared to 1999. The decrease was primarily the result of brand and bottler acquisitions during 1999.

FINANCIAL REVIEW INCORPORATING MANAGEMENT'S DISCUSSION AND ANALYSIS

Total capital expenditures for property, plant and equipment (including our investments in information technology) and the percentage distribution by operating segment for 2001, 2000 and 1999 are as follows (in millions):

Year Ended December 31,	2001	2000	1999
Capital expenditures	$ 769	$ 733	$ 1,069
North America[1]	44%	35%	25%
Africa	1%	1%	2%
Europe, Eurasia & Middle East	14%	27%	21%
Latin America	5%	2%	6%
Asia	14%	18%	30%
Corporate	22%	17%	16%

[1] Includes The Minute Maid Company

Financing Activities, Contractual Obligations and Commercial Commitments

Our financing activities include net borrowings, dividend payments and share issuances and repurchases. Net cash used in financing activities totaled $2,830 million in 2001, $2,072 million in 2000 and $471 million in 1999. The changes between 2001 and 2000 as well as between 2000 and 1999 were primarily due to the use of free cash flow to pay down outstanding debt.

Cash used to purchase common stock for treasury under the 1996 share repurchase plan and employee stock award programs totaled $277 million in 2001, $133 million in 2000 and $15 million in 1999. In 2000 and in 1999, we did not repurchase any shares under the 1996 share repurchase plan. As previously mentioned, we expect that the Company's share repurchases will be increased in 2002, and we are currently estimating a range of $750 million to $1 billion of repurchases during the year.

Commercial paper is our primary source of short-term financing. On December 31, 2001, we had $3,361 million outstanding in commercial paper borrowings compared to $4,549 million outstanding at the end of 2000, a $1,188 million decrease in borrowings. The 2001 decrease in commercial paper was due to the use of free cash flow to pay down outstanding debt. The Company's commercial paper borrowings normally mature less than three months from the date of issuance. In 1999, as part of our Year 2000 plan, we increased the amount of commercial paper borrowings with maturity dates greater than three months. The gross payments and receipts of borrowings greater than three months

from the date of issuance have been included in the Consolidated Statements of Cash Flows. On December 31, 2001, we had $2,468 million in lines of credit and other short-term credit facilities available, of which approximately $382 million was outstanding.

On December 31, 2001, we had $1,219 million outstanding in long-term debt, compared to $835 million outstanding at the end of 2000, a $384 million increase in borrowings. These increased borrowings were a result of the Company issuing $500 million in 10-year global notes in March 2001. This debt was incurred in order to obtain funds at attractive rates available in 2001. Current maturities of long-term debt were $156 million as of December 31, 2001 compared to $21 million as of December 31, 2000, an increase of $135 million.

The Company's contractual obligations and commercial commitments are as follows (in millions):

December 31,	2001
Short-term loans and notes payable:	
Commercial paper borrowings	$ 3,361
Lines of credit and other short-term borrowings	382
Current maturities of long-term debt	156
Long-term debt	1,219
Marketing commitments	1,326
Contractual obligations	$ 6,444
Contingent liability for guarantees of indebtedness owed to third parties	$ 436

For the year ended December 31, 2001, our Company generated cash flows provided by operating activities of $4,110 million. Management's expectations are that future cash flows provided by operating activities will be sufficient to meet the Company's contractual obligations. For further discussion of the above contractual obligations and commercial commitments, refer to Notes 5, 6 and 10 of the Consolidated Financial Statements.

Exchange

Our international operations are subject to certain opportunities and risks, including currency fluctuations and government actions. We closely monitor our operations in each country and seek to adopt appropriate strategies that are responsive to changing economic and political environments and to fluctuations in foreign currencies.

FINANCIAL REVIEW INCORPORATING MANAGEMENT'S DISCUSSION AND ANALYSIS

We use approximately 59 functional currencies. Due to our global operations, weaknesses in some of these currencies are often offset by strengths in others. In 2001, 2000 and 1999, the weighted-average exchange rates for foreign currencies in which the Company conducts operations (all operating currencies), and for certain individual currencies, strengthened (weakened) against the U.S. dollar as follows:

Year Ended December 31,	2001	2000	1999
All operating currencies	(8)%	(5)%	Even
Australian dollar	(13)%	(8)%	3%
British pound	(5)%	(7)%	(2)%
Canadian dollar	(4)%	Even	Even
French franc	(5)%	(14)%	(2)%
German mark	(5)%	(14)%	(2)%
Japanese yen	(11)%	4%	15%

These percentages do not include the effects of our hedging activities and, therefore, do not reflect the actual impact of fluctuations in exchange on our operating results. Our foreign currency management program is designed to mitigate over time a portion of the impact of exchange on net income and earnings per share. The impact of a stronger U.S. dollar reduced our operating income by approximately 5 percent in 2001 and approximately 4 percent in 2000. The negative trend from currencies on our 2002 operating income, including the recent devaluation in Argentina, is expected to continue.

Exchange gains (losses)-net amounted to $(9) million in 2001, $(12) million in 2000 and $87 million in 1999, and were recorded in other income-net in the Consolidated Statements of Income. Exchange gains (losses)-net includes the remeasurement of certain currencies into functional currencies and the costs of hedging certain exposures of our balance sheet.

Additional information concerning our hedging activities is presented in Note 9 in our Consolidated Financial Statements.

Off Balance Sheet Arrangements
The Company does not have transactions, arrangements or relationships with "special purpose" entities, and the Company does not have any off balance sheet debt.

Financial Position
Comparing 2001 to 2000, the increase in prepaid expenses and other assets was primarily due to the change in the carrying value of derivatives and hedging instruments and amounts due from CCHBC of $146 million related to the sale of the Russian bottling operations. For further discussion, refer to Note 2 of the Consolidated Financial Statements. The decrease in cost method investments was primarily due to the consolidation of our recently purchased Brazilian bottling operations that had been classified as temporary cost method investments. The increase in other assets was due to a higher cash surrender value of insurance due to the pay off of policy loans. The increase in trademarks and other intangible assets was due primarily to acquisitions of brands and bottling operations during 2001.

Comparing 2000 to 1999, the carrying value of our investment in Coca-Cola Amatil decreased, primarily as a result of a nonrecurring charge recorded by Coca-Cola Amatil to reduce the carrying value of its investment in the Philippines. The Company's portion of this charge was $306 million. The carrying value of our investment in CCHBC decreased due to the impact of foreign currency exchange partially offset by a gain of approximately $118 million related to the merger of Coca-Cola Beverages and Hellenic Bottling Company S.A. during the third quarter of 2000. The carrying value of other investments, principally bottling companies, decreased primarily due to a nonrecurring charge recorded by Panamco to write down selected assets, including the impairment of the value of the Venezuelan operating unit. The decrease in the carrying value of other equity investments was also impacted by the consolidation in 2000 of F&N Coca-Cola, which was previously recorded as an equity investment. The increase in other assets in 2000 is primarily due to an increase in marketing prepayments. The increase in accounts payable and accrued expenses in 2000 is due primarily to the accrual for the Realignment expenses.

Euro Conversion
In January 1999, certain member countries of the European Union established irrevocable, fixed conversion rates between their existing currencies and the European Union's common currency (the euro). The introduction of the euro was phased in over a period ended January 1, 2002, when euro notes and coins came into circulation. The replacement of other currencies with the euro did not have and is not expected to have a material impact on our operations or our Consolidated Financial Statements.

FINANCIAL REVIEW INCORPORATING MANAGEMENT'S DISCUSSION AND ANALYSIS

Impact of Inflation and Changing Prices

Inflation affects the way we operate in many markets around the world. In general, we are able to increase prices to counteract the majority of the inflationary effects of increasing costs and to generate sufficient cash flows to maintain our productive capability.

New Accounting Standards

Effective January 1, 2001, the Company adopted SFAS No. 133, "Accounting for Derivative Instruments and Hedging Activities," as amended by SFAS No. 137 and SFAS No. 138. As discussed further in Note 9, the 2001 Consolidated Financial Statements were prepared in accordance with the provisions of SFAS No. 133. Prior years' financial statements have not been restated. The 2000 and 1999 Consolidated Financial Statements were prepared in accordance with the applicable professional literature for derivatives and hedging instruments in effect at that time.

Effective January 1, 2001, our Company adopted the provisions of Emerging Issues Task Force (EITF) Issue No. 00-14, "Accounting for Certain Sales Incentives," and EITF Issue No. 00-22, "Accounting for 'Points' and Certain Other Time-Based or Volume-Based Sales Incentive Offers, and Offers for Free Products or Services to be Delivered in the Future." Both of these EITF Issues provide additional guidance relating to the income statement classification of certain sales incentives. The adoption of these EITF Issues resulted in the Company reducing both net operating revenues and selling, administrative and general expenses by approximately $580 million in 2001, $569 million in 2000 and $521 million in 1999. These reclassifications have no impact on operating income.

In April 2001, the EITF reached a consensus on EITF Issue No. 00-25, "Vendor Income Statement Characterization of Consideration Paid to a Reseller of the Vendor's Products." EITF Issue No. 00-25, which is effective for the Company beginning January 1, 2002, will require certain selling expenses incurred by the Company to be classified as deductions from revenue. With the adoption of this EITF Issue, we estimate that approximately $2.6 billion of our payments to bottlers and customers that are currently classified within selling, administrative and general expenses will be reclassified as deductions from revenue. In our 2002 Consolidated Financial Statements, all comparative periods will be reclassified.

In June 2001, the Financial Accounting Standards Board (FASB) issued SFAS No. 141, "Business Combinations," and SFAS No. 142, "Goodwill and Other Intangible Assets." SFAS No. 142 is effective for the Company as of January 1, 2002. Under the new rules, goodwill and indefinite lived intangible assets will no longer be amortized but will be reviewed annually for impairment. Intangible assets that are not deemed to have an indefinite life will continue to be amortized over their useful lives.

The adoption of SFAS No. 142 requires that an initial impairment assessment be performed on all goodwill and indefinite lived intangible assets. To complete this assessment, the Company will compare the fair value to the current carrying value of trademarks and other intangible assets. Fair values will be derived using cash flow analysis. The assumptions used in this cash flow analysis will be consistent with our internal planning. Any impairment charge resulting from this initial assessment will be recorded as a cumulative effect of an accounting change. The Company estimates the cumulative effect of adopting this standard will result in a non-cash charge in the first quarter of 2002 of approximately $1 billion on a pretax basis. This amount reflects intangible assets for both the Company and the Company's proportionate share of its equity method investees. The adoption of this new standard will also benefit earnings beginning in 2002 by approximately $60 million in reduced amortization from Company-owned intangible assets and approximately $150 million of increased equity income relating to the Company's share of amortization savings from equity method investees.

Outlook

While we cannot predict future performance, we believe considerable opportunities exist for sustained, profitable growth, not only in the developing population centers of the world, but also in our most established markets.

We firmly believe that the strength of our brands, our unparalleled distribution system, our global presence, our strong financial condition and the diversity and skills of our people give us the flexibility to capitalize on growth opportunities as we continue to pursue our goal of increasing share-owner value over time.

Forward-Looking Statements

Certain written and oral statements made by our Company and subsidiaries or with the approval of an

FINANCIAL REVIEW INCORPORATING MANAGEMENT'S DISCUSSION AND ANALYSIS

authorized executive officer of our Company may constitute "forward-looking statements" as defined under the Private Securities Litigation Reform Act of 1995, including statements made in this report and other filings with the Securities and Exchange Commission. Generally, the words "believe," "expect," "intend," "estimate," "anticipate," "project," "will" and similar expressions identify forward-looking statements, which generally are not historical in nature. All statements which address operating performance, events or developments that we expect or anticipate will occur in the future—including statements relating to volume growth, share of sales and earnings per share growth and statements expressing general optimism about future operating results—are forward-looking statements. Forward-looking statements are subject to certain risks and uncertainties that could cause actual results to differ materially from our Company's historical experience and our present expectations or projections. As and when made, management believes that these forward-looking statements are reasonable. However, caution should be taken not to place undue reliance on any such forward-looking statements since such statements speak only as of the date when made. The Company undertakes no obligation to publicly update or revise any forward-looking statements, whether as a result of new information, future events or otherwise.

The following are some of the factors that could cause our Company's actual results to differ materially from the expected results described in or underlying our Company's forward-looking statements:

- Foreign currency rate fluctuations, interest rate fluctuations and other capital market conditions. Most of our exposures to capital markets, including foreign currency and interest rates, are managed on a consolidated basis, which allows us to net certain exposures and, thus, take advantage of any natural offsets. We use derivative financial instruments to reduce our net exposure to financial risks. There can be no assurance, however, that our financial risk management program will be successful in reducing capital market exposures.
- Changes in the nonalcoholic beverages business environment. These include, without limitation, changes in consumer preferences, competitive product and pricing pressures and our ability to gain or maintain share of sales in the global market as a result of actions by competitors. While we believe our opportunities for sustained, profitable growth are considerable, factors such as

these could impact our earnings, share of sales and volume growth.

- Adverse weather conditions, which could reduce demand for Company products.
- Our ability to generate sufficient cash flows to support capital expansion plans, share repurchase programs and general operating activities.
- Changes in laws and regulations, including changes in accounting standards, taxation requirements (including tax rate changes, new tax laws and revised tax law interpretations) and environmental laws in domestic or foreign jurisdictions.
- The effectiveness of our advertising, marketing and promotional programs.
- Fluctuations in the cost and availability of raw materials and the ability to maintain favorable supplier arrangements and relationships.
- Our ability to achieve earnings forecasts, which are generated based on projected volumes and sales of many product types, some of which are more profitable than others. There can be no assurance that we will achieve the projected level or mix of product sales.
- Economic and political conditions, especially in international markets, including civil unrest, governmental changes and restrictions on the ability to transfer capital across borders.
- Our ability to penetrate developing and emerging markets, which also depends on economic and political conditions, and how well we are able to acquire or form strategic business alliances with local bottlers and make necessary infrastructure enhancements to production facilities, distribution networks, sales equipment and technology. Moreover, the supply of products in developing markets must match the customers' demand for those products, and due to product price and cultural differences, there can be no assurance of product acceptance in any particular market.
- The uncertainties of litigation, as well as other risks and uncertainties detailed from time to time in our Company's Securities and Exchange Commission filings.

The foregoing list of important factors is not exclusive.

Additional Information

For additional information about our operations, cash flows, liquidity and capital resources, please refer to the information on pages 57 through 84 of this report. Additional information concerning our operating segments is presented on pages 81 through 83.

Consolidated Statements of Income

Year Ended December 31, (In millions except per share data)	2001	2000	1999
Net Operating Revenues	$ 20,092	$ 19,889	$ 19,284
Cost of goods sold	6,044	6,204	6,009
Gross Profit	14,048	13,685	13,275
Selling, administrative and general expenses	8,696	8,551	8,480
Other operating charges	—	1,443	813
Operating Income	5,352	3,691	3,982
Interest income	325	345	260
Interest expense	289	447	337
Equity income (loss)	152	(289)	(184)
Other income-net	39	99	98
Gains on issuances of stock by equity investees	91	—	—
Income Before Income Taxes and Cumulative Effect of Accounting Change	5,670	3,399	3,819
Income taxes	1,691	1,222	1,388
Income Before Cumulative Effect of Accounting Change	3,979	2,177	2,431
Cumulative effect of accounting change, net of income taxes	(10)	—	—
Net Income	$ 3,969	$ 2,177	$ 2,431
Basic Net Income per Share			
Before accounting change	$ 1.60	$ .88	$ .98
Cumulative effect of accounting change	—	—	—
	$ 1.60	$ .88	$ .98
Diluted Net Income per Share			
Before accounting change	$ 1.60	$ .88	$ .98
Cumulative effect of accounting change	—	—	—
	$ 1.60	$ .88	$ .98
Average Shares Outstanding	2,487	2,477	2,469
Dilutive effect of stock options	—	10	18
Average Shares Outstanding Assuming Dilution	2,487	2,487	2,487

See Notes to Consolidated Financial Statements.

Consolidated Balance Sheets		THE COCA-COLA COMPANY AND SUBSIDIARIES

December 31,	2001	2000
(In millions except share data)		
Assets		
Current		
Cash and cash equivalents	$ 1,866	$ 1,819
Marketable securities	68	73
	1,934	1,892
Trade accounts receivable, less allowances of		
$59 in 2001 and $62 in 2000	1,882	1,757
Inventories	1,055	1,066
Prepaid expenses and other assets	2,300	1,905
Total Current Assets	7,171	6,620
Investments and Other Assets		
Equity method investments		
Coca-Cola Enterprises Inc.	788	707
Coca-Cola Amatil Limited	432	617
Coca-Cola HBC S.A.	791	758
Other, principally bottling companies	3,117	3,164
Cost method investments, principally bottling companies	294	519
Other assets	2,792	2,364
	8,214	8,129
Property, Plant and Equipment		
Land	217	225
Buildings and improvements	1,812	1,642
Machinery and equipment	4,881	4,547
Containers	195	200
	7,105	6,614
Less allowances for depreciation	2,652	2,446
	4,453	4,168
Trademarks and Other Intangible Assets	2,579	1,917
	$ 22,417	$ 20,834

Consolidated Balance Sheets   THE COCA-COLA COMPANY AND SUBSIDIARIES

December 31,	2001	2000
Liabilities and Share-Owners' Equity		
Current		
Accounts payable and accrued expenses	$ **3,679**	$ 3,905
Loans and notes payable	**3,743**	4,795
Current maturities of long-term debt	**156**	21
Accrued income taxes	**851**	600
Total Current Liabilities	**8,429**	9,321
Long-Term Debt	**1,219**	835
Other Liabilities	**961**	1,004
Deferred Income Taxes	**442**	358
Share-Owners' Equity		
Common stock, $.25 par value		
Authorized: 5,600,000,000 shares		
Issued: 3,491,465,016 shares in 2001; 3,481,882,834 shares in 2000	**873**	870
Capital surplus	**3,520**	3,196
Reinvested earnings	**23,443**	21,265
Accumulated other comprehensive income and unearned compensation on restricted stock	**(2,788)**	(2,722)
	25,048	22,609
Less treasury stock, at cost (1,005,237,693 shares in 2001; 997,121,427 shares in 2000)	**13,682**	13,293
	11,366	9,316
	$ **22,417**	$ 20,834

See Notes to Consolidated Financial Statements.

| Consolidated Statements of Cash Flows | THE COCA-COLA COMPANY AND SUBSIDIARIES |

Year Ended December 31,	2001	2000	1999
(In millions)			
Operating Activities			
Net income	$ 3,969	$ 2,177	$ 2,431
Depreciation and amortization	803	773	792
Deferred income taxes	56	3	97
Equity income or loss, net of dividends	(54)	380	292
Foreign currency adjustments	(60)	196	(41)
Gains on issuances of stock by equity investees	(91)	—	—
Gains on sales of assets, including bottling interests	(85)	(127)	(49)
Other operating charges	—	916	799
Other items	34	119	119
Net change in operating assets and liabilities	(462)	(852)	(557)
Net cash provided by operating activities	4,110	3,585	3,883
Investing Activities			
Acquisitions and investments, principally trademarks and bottling companies	(651)	(397)	(1,876)
Purchases of investments and other assets	(456)	(508)	(518)
Proceeds from disposals of investments and other assets	455	290	176
Purchases of property, plant and equipment	(769)	(733)	(1,069)
Proceeds from disposals of property, plant and equipment	91	45	45
Other investing activities	142	138	(179)
Net cash used in investing activities	(1,188)	(1,165)	(3,421)
Financing Activities			
Issuances of debt	3,011	3,671	3,411
Payments of debt	(3.937)	(4,256)	(2,455)
Issuances of stock	164	331	168
Purchases of stock for treasury	(277)	(133)	(15)
Dividends	(1,791)	(1,685)	(1,580)
Net cash used in financing activities	(2,830)	(2,072)	(471)
Effect of Exchange Rate Changes on Cash and Cash Equivalents	(45)	(140)	(28)
Cash and Cash Equivalents			
Net increase (decrease) during the year	47	208	(37)
Balance at beginning of year	1,819	1,611	1,648
Balance at end of year	$ 1,866	$ 1,819	$ 1,611

See Notes to Consolidated Financial Statements.

Consolidated Statements of Share-Owners' Equity

THE COCA-COLA COMPANY AND SUBSIDIARIES

Three Years Ended December 31, 2001	Number of Common Shares Outstanding	Common Stock	Capital Surplus	Reinvested Earnings	Outstanding Restricted Stock	Accumulated Other Comprehensive Income	Treasury Stock	Total
(In millions except per share data)								
Balance December 31, 1998	2,466	$ 865	$ 2,195	$ 19,922	$ (84)	$ (1,350)	$ (13,145)	$ 8,403
Comprehensive income:								
Net income	—	—	—	2,431	—	—	—	2,431
Translation adjustments	—	—	—	—	—	(190)	—	(190)
Net change in unrealized gain (loss) on securities	—	—	—	—	—	23	—	23
Minimum pension liability	—	—	—	—	—	25	—	25
Comprehensive income								2,289
Stock issued to employees exercising stock options	6	2	166	—	—	—	—	168
Tax benefit from employees' stock option and restricted stock plans	—	—	72	—	—	—	—	72
Restricted stock and other stock plans, less amortization of $27	—	—	5	—	25	—	—	30
Stock issued by an equity investee	—	—	146	—	—	—	—	146
Purchases of stock for treasury	—	—	—	—	—	—	(15)	(15)
Dividends (per share — $.64)	—	—	—	(1,580)	—	—	—	(1,580)
Balance December 31, 1999	2,472	867	2,584	20,773	(59)	(1,492)	(13,160)	9,513
Comprehensive income:								
Net income	—	—	—	2,177	—	—	—	2,177
Translation adjustments	—	—	—	—	—	(965)	—	(965)
Net change in unrealized gain (loss) on securities	—	—	—	—	—	(60)	—	(60)
Minimum pension liability	—	—	—	—	—	(10)	—	(10)
Comprehensive income								1,142
Stock issued to employees exercising stock options	12	2	329	—	—	—	—	331
Tax benefit from employees' stock option and restricted stock plans	—	—	116	—	—	—	—	116
Restricted stock and other stock plans, less amortization of $24	3	1	167	—	(136)	—	—	32
Purchases of stock for treasury	(2)[1]	—	—	—	—	—	(133)	(133)
Dividends (per share — $.68)	—	—	—	(1,685)	—	—	—	(1,685)
Balance December 31, 2000	2,485	870	3,196	21,265	(195)	(2,527)	(13,293)	9,316
Comprehensive income:								
Net income	—	—	—	3,969	—	—	—	3,969
Translation adjustments	—	—	—	—	—	(207)	—	(207)
Cumulative effect of SFAS No. 133	—	—	—	—	—	50	—	50
Net gain (loss) on derivatives	—	—	—	—	—	92	—	92
Net change in unrealized gain (loss) on securities	—	—	—	—	—	(29)	—	(29)
Minimum pension liability	—	—	—	—	—	(17)	—	(17)
Comprehensive income								3,858
Stock issued to employees exercising stock options	7	2	162	—	—	—	—	164
Tax benefit from employees' stock option and restricted stock plans	—	—	58	—	—	—	—	58
Restricted stock and other stock plans, less cancellations	—	1	132	—	(24)	—	(112)	(3)
Amortization of restricted stock	—	—	—	—	41	—	—	41
Unearned restricted stock adjustment	—	—	(28)	—	28	—	—	—
Purchases of stock for treasury	(6)[1]	—	—	—	—	—	(277)	(277)
Dividends (per share — $.72)	—	—	—	(1,791)	—	—	—	(1,791)
Balance December 31, 2001	2,486	$ 873	$ 3,520	$ 23,443	$ (150)	$ (2,638)	$ (13,682)	$ 11,366

[1] Common stock purchased from employees exercising stock options numbered .3 million, 2.2 million and .3 million shares for the years ended December 31, 2001, 2000 and 1999, respectively.

See Notes to Consolidated Financial Statements.

Notes to Consolidated Financial Statements

Note 1: Organization and Summary of Significant Accounting Policies

Organization

The Coca-Cola Company, together with its subsidiaries, (the Company or our Company) is predominantly a manufacturer, marketer and distributor of nonalcoholic beverage concentrates and syrups. Operating in nearly 200 countries worldwide, we primarily sell our concentrates and syrups to bottling and canning operations, fountain wholesalers and fountain retailers. We also market and distribute juice and juice-drink products. We have significant markets for our products in all the world's geographic regions. We record revenue when title passes to our bottling partners or our customers.

Basis of Presentation

Certain amounts in the prior years' financial statements have been reclassified to conform to the current year presentation.

Consolidation

Our Consolidated Financial Statements include the accounts of The Coca-Cola Company and all subsidiaries except where control is temporary or does not rest with our Company. Our investments in companies in which we have the ability to exercise significant influence over operating and financial policies, including certain investments where there is a temporary majority interest, are accounted for by the equity method. Accordingly, our Company's share of the net earnings of these companies is included in consolidated net income. Our investments in other companies are carried at cost or fair value, as appropriate. All significant intercompany accounts and transactions, including transactions with equity method investees, are eliminated from our financial results.

Recoverability of Investments

Management periodically assesses the recoverability of our Company's investments. For publicly traded investments, the fair value of our Company's investment is readily determinable based on quoted market prices. For non-publicly traded investments, management's assessment of fair value is based on our analysis of the investee's estimates of future operating results and the resulting cash flows. If an investment is considered to be impaired and the decline in value is other than temporary, an appropriate write-down is recorded.

Issuances of Stock by Equity Investees

When one of our equity investees issues additional shares to third parties, our percentage ownership interest in the investee decreases. In the event the issuance price per share is more or less than our average carrying amount per share, we recognize a non-cash gain or loss on the issuance. This non-cash gain or loss, net of any deferred taxes, is generally recognized in our net income in the period the change of ownership interest occurs.

If gains have been previously recognized on issuances of an equity investee's stock and shares of the equity investee are subsequently repurchased by the equity investee, gain recognition does not occur on issuances subsequent to the date of a repurchase until shares have been issued in an amount equivalent to the number of repurchased shares. This type of transaction is reflected as an equity transaction and the net effect is reflected in the accompanying Consolidated Balance Sheets. For specific transaction details, refer to Note 3.

Advertising Costs

Our Company expenses production costs of print, radio and television advertisements as of the first date the advertisements take place. Advertising expenses included in selling, administrative and general expenses were $1,970 million in 2001, $1,655 million in 2000 and $1,609 million in 1999. As of December 31, 2001 and 2000, advertising production costs of approximately $52 million and $69 million, respectively, were recorded primarily in prepaid expenses and other assets and noncurrent other assets in the accompanying Consolidated Balance Sheets.

Net Income Per Share

Basic net income per share is computed by dividing net income by the weighted-average number of shares outstanding. Diluted net income per share includes the dilutive effect of stock options.

Cash Equivalents

Marketable securities that are highly liquid and have maturities of three months or less at the date of purchase are classified as cash equivalents.

Inventories

Inventories consist primarily of raw materials and supplies and are valued at the lower of cost or market. In general, cost is determined on the basis of average cost or first-in, first-out methods.

Property, Plant and Equipment

Property, plant and equipment are stated at cost and are depreciated principally by the straight-line method over the estimated useful lives of the assets.

Other Assets

Our Company invests in infrastructure programs with our bottlers that are directed at strengthening our bottling system and increasing unit case sales. Additionally, our Company advances payments to certain customers for marketing to fund activities intended to generate volume. Advance payments are also made to certain customers for distribution rights. The costs of these programs are recorded in other assets and are subsequently amortized over the periods to be directly benefited. Management periodically evaluates the recoverability of these assets by preparing estimates of sales volume, the resulting gross profit, cash flows and other factors.

Trademarks and Other Intangible Assets

Trademarks and other intangible assets are stated on the basis of cost and are amortized, principally on a straight-line basis, over the estimated future periods to be benefited (not exceeding 40 years). Trademarks and other intangible assets are periodically reviewed for impairment to ensure they are appropriately valued. Conditions that may indicate an impairment issue exists include an economic downturn in a market or a change in the assessment of future operations. In the event that a condition is identified that may indicate an impairment issue exists, an assessment is performed using a variety of methodologies, including cash flow analysis, estimates of sales proceeds and independent appraisals. Where applicable, an appropriate interest rate is utilized, based on location-specific economic factors. Accumulated amortization was approximately $285 million and $192 million on December 31, 2001 and 2000, respectively.

Use of Estimates

In conformity with generally accepted accounting principles, the preparation of our financial statements requires our management to make estimates and assumptions that affect the amounts reported in our financial statements and accompanying notes including our assessment of the carrying value of our investments in bottling operations. Although these estimates are based on our knowledge of current events and actions we may undertake in the future, actual results may ultimately differ from estimates.

New Accounting Standards

Effective January 1, 2001, the Company adopted Statement of Financial Accounting Standards (SFAS) No. 133, "Accounting for Derivative Instruments and Hedging Activities," as amended by SFAS No. 137 and SFAS No. 138. As discussed further in Note 9, the 2001 Consolidated Financial Statements were prepared in accordance with the provisions of SFAS No. 133. Prior years' financial statements have not been restated. As required by SFAS No. 133, the 2000 and 1999 Consolidated Financial Statements were prepared in accordance with the applicable professional literature for derivatives and hedging instruments in effect at that time.

Effective January 1, 2001, our Company adopted the provisions of Emerging Issues Task Force (EITF) Issue No. 00-14, "Accounting for Certain Sales Incentives," and EITF Issue No. 00-22, "Accounting for 'Points' and Certain Other Time-Based or Volume-Based Sales Incentive Offers, and Offers for Free Products or Services to be Delivered in the Future." Both of these EITF Issues provide additional guidance relating to the income statement classification of certain sales incentives. The adoption of these EITF Issues resulted in the Company reducing both net operating revenues and selling, administrative and general expenses by approximately $580 million in 2001, $569 million in 2000 and $521 million in 1999. These reclassifications have no impact on operating income.

In April 2001, the EITF reached a consensus on EITF Issue No. 00-25, "Vendor Income Statement Characterization of Consideration Paid to a Reseller of the Vendor's Products." EITF Issue No. 00-25, which is effective for the Company beginning January 1, 2002, will require certain selling expenses incurred by the Company to be classified as deductions from revenue. With the adoption of this EITF Issue, we estimate that approximately $2.6 billion of our payments to bottlers and customers that are currently classified within selling, administrative and general expenses will be reclassified as deductions from revenue. In our 2002 Consolidated Financial Statements, all comparative periods will be reclassified.

In June 2001, the Financial Accounting Standards Board (FASB) issued SFAS No. 141, "Business Combinations," and SFAS No. 142, "Goodwill and Other Intangible Assets." SFAS No. 142 is effective for the Company as of January 1, 2002. Under the new rules, goodwill and indefinite lived intangible assets will no longer be amortized but will be reviewed annually for impairment. Intangible assets that are not deemed to have an indefinite life will continue to be amortized over their useful lives.

The adoption of SFAS No. 142 requires that an initial impairment assessment is performed on all goodwill and indefinite lived intangible assets. To complete this assessment, the Company will compare the fair value to the current carrying value of trademarks and other intangible assets. Fair values will be derived using cash flow analysis. The assumptions used in this cash flow analysis will be consistent with our internal planning. Any impairment charge resulting from this initial assessment will be recorded as a cumulative effect of an accounting change. The Company estimates the cumulative effect of adopting this standard will result in a non-cash charge in the first quarter of 2002 of approximately $1 billion on a pretax basis. This amount reflects intangible assets for both the Company and the Company's proportionate share of its equity method investees. The adoption of this new standard will also benefit earnings beginning in 2002 by approximately $60 million in reduced amortization from Company-owned intangible assets and approximately $150 million of increased equity income relating to the Company's share of amortization savings from equity method investees.

Note 2: Bottling Investments

Coca-Cola Enterprises Inc.

Coca-Cola Enterprises Inc. (Coca-Cola Enterprises) is the largest soft-drink bottler in the world, operating in eight countries. On December 31, 2001, our Company owned approximately 38 percent of the outstanding common stock of Coca-Cola Enterprises, and accordingly, we account for our investment by the equity method of accounting. As of December 31, 2001, our proportionate share of the net assets of Coca-Cola Enterprises exceeded our investment by approximately $283 million. This excess is amortized over a period consistent with the applicable useful life of the underlying transactions.

A summary of financial information for Coca-Cola Enterprises is as follows (in millions):

December 31,	2001	2000
Current assets	$ 2,876	$ 2,631
Noncurrent assets	20,843	19,531
Total assets	$ 23,719	$ 22,162
Current liabilities	$ 4,522	$ 3,094
Noncurrent liabilities	16,377	16,234
Total liabilities	$ 20,899	$ 19,328
Share-owners' equity	$ 2,820	$ 2,834
Company equity investment	$ 788	$ 707

Year Ended December 31,	2001	2000	1999
Net operating revenues	$ 15,700	$ 14,750	$ 14,406
Cost of goods sold	9,740	9,083	9,015
Gross profit	$ 5,960	$ 5,667	$ 5,391
Operating income	$ 601	$ 1,126	$ 839
Cash operating profit[1]	$ 1,954	$ 2,387	$ 2,187
Cumulative effect of accounting change	$ 302	$ —	$ —
Net income (loss)	$ (321)	$ 236	$ 59
Net income (loss) available to common share owners	$ (324)	$ 233	$ 56

[1] Cash operating profit is defined as operating income plus depreciation expense, amortization expense and other non-cash operating expenses.

Our net concentrate and syrup sales to Coca-Cola Enterprises were $3.9 billion in 2001, $3.5 billion in 2000 and $3.3 billion in 1999, or approximately 19 percent, 18 percent and 17 percent of our 2001, 2000 and 1999 net operating revenues, respectively. Coca-Cola Enterprises purchases sweeteners through our Company; however, related collections from Coca-Cola Enterprises and payments to suppliers are not included in our Consolidated Statements of Income. These transactions amounted to $295 million in 2001, $298 million in 2000 and $308 million in 1999. We also provide certain administrative and other services to Coca-Cola Enterprises under negotiated fee arrangements.

Cash payments made directly to Coca-Cola Enterprises for support of certain marketing activities and participation with them in cooperative advertising and other marketing programs amounted to approximately $606 million, $533 million and $525 million in 2001, 2000 and 1999, respectively. Cash payments made directly to Coca-Cola Enterprises' customers for support of certain marketing activities and programs amounted to approximately $282 million,

Notes to Consolidated Financial Statements   THE COCA-COLA COMPANY AND SUBSIDIARIES

$221 million and $242 million in 2001, 2000 and 1999, respectively. Pursuant to cooperative advertising and trade agreements with Coca-Cola Enterprises, we received approximately $252 million, $195 million and $243 million in 2001, 2000 and 1999, respectively, from Coca-Cola Enterprises for local media and marketing program expense reimbursements.

Our Company enters into programs with Coca-Cola Enterprises designed to assist their development of the cold drink infrastructure. Under these programs, our Company made payments to Coca-Cola Enterprises for a portion of the cost of developing the infrastructure necessary to support accelerated placements of cold drink equipment. These payments support a common objective of increased sales of Coca-Cola beverages from increased availability and consumption in the cold drink channel. In connection with these programs, Coca-Cola Enterprises agrees to: (1) purchase and place specified numbers of vendors/coolers or cold drink equipment each year through 2008; (2) maintain the equipment in service, with certain exceptions, for a period of at least 12 years after placement; (3) maintain and stock the equipment in accordance with specified standards; and (4) report to our Company minimum average annual unit case sales volume throughout the economic life of the equipment.

Coca-Cola Enterprises must achieve minimum average unit case sales volume for a 12-year period following the placement of equipment. These minimum average unit case sales volume levels ensure adequate gross profit from sales of concentrate to fully recover the capitalized costs plus a return on the Company's investment. Should Coca-Cola Enterprises fail to purchase the specified numbers of vendors/coolers or cold drink equipment for any calendar year through 2008, the parties agree to mutually develop a reasonable solution. Should no mutually agreeable solution be developed, or in the event that Coca-Cola Enterprises otherwise breaches any material obligation under the contracts and such breach is not remedied within a stated period, then Coca-Cola Enterprises would be required to repay a portion of the support funding as determined by our Company. No repayments by Coca-Cola Enterprises have ever been made under these programs. Our Company paid or committed to pay approximately $159 million, $223 million and $338 million in 2001, 2000 and 1999, respectively, to Coca-Cola Enterprises in connection with these infrastructure programs. These payments are recorded as other assets and amortized as a charge to earnings over the 12-year period following the placement of the equipment. Amounts recorded in other assets were approximately $931 million as of December 31, 2001. For 2002 and thereafter, the Company has no further commitments under these programs.

As of January 1, 2001, Coca-Cola Enterprises changed its method of accounting for infrastructure development payments received from the Company. Prior to this change, Coca-Cola Enterprises recognized these payments as offsets to incremental expenses of the programs in the periods in which they were incurred. Coca-Cola Enterprises now recognizes the infrastructure development payments received from the Company as obligations under the contracts are performed. Because the Company eliminates the financial effect of significant intercompany transactions (including transactions with equity method investees), this change in accounting method has no impact on the Consolidated Financial Statements of our Company.

Our Company and Coca-Cola Enterprises reached an agreement in 2000 to transfer all responsibilities and the associated staffing for major customer marketing (CMG) efforts to Coca-Cola Enterprises from our Company and for local media activities from Coca-Cola Enterprises to our Company. Under the agreement, our Company reimburses Coca-Cola Enterprises for the CMG staffing costs transferred to Coca-Cola Enterprises, and Coca-Cola Enterprises reimburses our Company for the local media staffing costs transferred to our Company. Amounts reimbursed to Coca-Cola Enterprises by our Company for CMG staffing expenses were $25 million and $3 million for 2001 and 2000, respectively. Amounts reimbursed to our Company for local media staffing expenses were $16 million for 2001.

The difference between our proportionate share of Coca-Cola Enterprises' income available to common share owners and the Company's equity income in Coca-Cola Enterprises is primarily related to the elimination of the financial effect of intercompany transactions between the two companies.

If valued at the December 31, 2001, quoted closing price of Coca-Cola Enterprises shares, the value of our investment in Coca-Cola Enterprises exceeded its carrying value by approximately $2.4 billion.

Other Equity Investments

Operating results include our proportionate share of income (loss) from our equity investments. A summary of financial information for our equity investments in the aggregate, other than Coca-Cola Enterprises, is as follows (in millions):

December 31,	2001	2000
Current assets	$ 6,013	$ 5,985
Noncurrent assets	17,879	19,030
Total assets	$ 23,892	$ 25,015
Current liabilities	$ 5,085	$ 5,419
Noncurrent liabilities	7,806	8,357
Total liabilities	$ 12,891	$ 13,776
Share-owners' equity	$ 11,001	$ 11,239
Company equity investment	$ 4,340	$ 4,539

Year Ended December 31,	2001	2000	1999
Net operating revenues[1]	$ 19,955	$ 21,423	$ 19,605
Cost of goods sold	11,413	13,014	12,085
Gross profit[1]	$ 8,542	$ 8,409	$ 7,520
Operating income (loss)	$ 1,770	$ (24)	$ 809
Cash operating profit[2]	$ 3,171	$ 2,796	$ 2,474
Net income (loss)	$ 735	$ (894)	$ (134)

Equity investments include non-bottling investees.

[1] 2000 and 1999 Net operating revenues and Gross profit have been reclassified for EITF Issue No. 00-14 and EITF Issue No. 00-22.

[2] Cash operating profit is defined as operating income plus depreciation expense, amortization expense and other non-cash operating expenses.

Net sales to equity investees other than Coca-Cola Enterprises were $3.7 billion in 2001, $3.5 billion in 2000 and $3.2 billion in 1999. Total support payments, primarily marketing, made to equity investees other than Coca-Cola Enterprises, the majority of which are located outside the United States, were approximately $636 million, $663 million and $685 million for 2001, 2000 and 1999, respectively.

In February 2001, the Company reached an agreement with Carlsberg A/S (Carlsberg) for the dissolution of Coca-Cola Nordic Beverages (CCNB), a joint venture bottler in which our Company had a 49 percent ownership. In July 2001, our Company and San Miguel Corporation (San Miguel) acquired Coca-Cola Bottlers Philippines (CCBPI) from Coca-Cola Amatil Limited (Coca-Cola Amatil).

In November 2001, our Company sold nearly all of its ownership interests in various Russian bottling operations to Coca-Cola HBC S.A. (CCHBC) for approximately $170 million in cash and notes receivable, of which $146 million in notes receivable remained outstanding as of December 31, 2001. These interests consisted of the Company's 40 percent ownership interest in a joint venture with CCHBC that operates bottling territories in Siberia and parts of Western Russia, together with our Company's nearly 100 percent interests in bottling operations with territories covering the remainder of Russia.

In July 2000, a merger of Coca-Cola Beverages plc (Coca-Cola Beverages) and Hellenic Bottling Company S.A. was completed to create CCHBC. This merger resulted in a decrease in our Company's equity ownership interest from approximately 50.5 percent of Coca-Cola Beverages to approximately 24 percent of the combined entity, CCHBC.

In July 1999, we acquired from Fraser and Neave Limited its ownership interest in F&N Coca-Cola Pte Limited.

If valued at the December 31, 2001, quoted closing prices of shares actively traded on stock markets, the value of our equity investments in publicly traded bottlers other than Coca-Cola Enterprises exceeded our carrying value by approximately $800 million.

Note 3: Issuances of Stock by Equity Investees

In July 2001, Coca-Cola Enterprises completed its acquisition of Hondo Incorporated and Herbco Enterprises, Inc., collectively known as Herb Coca-Cola. The transaction was valued at approximately $1.4 billion, with approximately 30 percent of the transaction funded with the issuance of approximately 25 million shares of Coca-Cola Enterprises common stock, and the remaining portion funded through debt and assumed debt. The Coca-Cola Enterprises common stock issued was valued in an amount greater than the book value per share of our investment in Coca-Cola Enterprises. The shares issued combined with other share issuances exceeded the amount of repurchased shares under Coca-Cola Enterprises' share repurchase plan. As a result, the issuance of these shares resulted in a one-time non-cash pretax gain for our Company of approximately $91 million. We provided deferred taxes of approximately $36 million on this gain. This transaction reduced our ownership in Coca-Cola Enterprises from approximately 40 percent to approximately 38 percent.

No gains on issuances of stock by equity investees were recorded during 2000. In the first quarter of 1999, Coca-Cola Enterprises completed its acquisition of various bottlers. These transactions were funded primarily

Notes to Consolidated Financial Statements   THE COCA-COLA COMPANY AND SUBSIDIARIES

with shares of Coca-Cola Enterprises common stock. The Coca-Cola Enterprises common stock issued was valued in an amount greater than the book value per share of our investment in Coca-Cola Enterprises. As a result of these transactions, our equity in the underlying net assets of Coca-Cola Enterprises increased, and we recorded a $241 million increase to our Company's investment basis in Coca-Cola Enterprises. Due to Coca-Cola Enterprises' share repurchase program, the increase in our investment in Coca-Cola Enterprises was recorded as an equity transaction, and no gain was recognized. We recorded a deferred tax liability of approximately $95 million on this increase to our investment in Coca-Cola Enterprises. These transactions reduced our ownership in Coca-Cola Enterprises from approximately 42 percent to approximately 40 percent.

Note 4: Accounts Payable and Accrued Expenses

Accounts payable and accrued expenses consist of the following (in millions):

December 31,	2001	2000
Accrued marketing	$ 1,160	$ 1,163
Container deposits	84	58
Accrued compensation	202	141
Sales, payroll and other taxes	148	166
Accrued realignment expenses	59	254
Accounts payable and other accrued expenses	2,026	2,123
	$ 3,679	$ 3,905

Note 5: Short-Term Borrowings and Credit Arrangements

Loans and notes payable consist primarily of commercial paper issued in the United States. On December 31, 2001, we had approximately $3,361 million outstanding in commercial paper borrowings. In addition, we had $2,468 million in lines of credit and other short-term credit facilities available, of which approximately $382 million was outstanding. Our weighted-average interest rates for commercial paper outstanding were approximately 1.9 percent and 6.7 percent at December 31, 2001 and 2000, respectively.

These facilities are subject to normal banking terms and conditions. Some of the financial arrangements require compensating balances, none of which is presently significant to our Company.

Note 6: Long-Term Debt

Long-term debt consists of the following (in millions):

December 31,	2001	2000
6⅝% U.S. dollar notes due 2002	$ 150	$ 150
6% U.S. dollar notes due 2003	150	150
5¾% U.S. dollar notes due 2009	399	399
5¾% U.S. dollar notes due 2011	498	—
7⅜% U.S. dollar notes due 2093	116	116
Other, due 2002 to 2013	62	41
	1,375	856
Less current portion	156	21
	$ 1,219	$ 835

After giving effect to interest rate management instruments, the principal amount of our long-term debt that had fixed and variable interest rates, respectively, was $1,262 million and $113 million on December 31, 2001, and $706 million and $150 million on December 31, 2000. The weighted-average interest rate on our Company's long-term debt was 5.8 percent and 5.9 percent for the years ended December 31, 2001 and 2000, respectively. Total interest paid was approximately $304 million, $458 million and $314 million in 2001, 2000 and 1999, respectively. For a more complete discussion of interest rate management, refer to Note 9.

Maturities of long-term debt for the five years succeeding December 31, 2001, are as follows (in millions):

2002	2003	2004	2005	2006
$ 156	$ 155	$ 2	$ 1	$ 1

The above notes include various restrictions, none of which is presently significant to our Company.

Note 7: Comprehensive Income

Accumulated other comprehensive income (AOCI) consists of the following (in millions):

December 31,	2001	2000
Foreign currency translation adjustment	$ (2,682)	$ (2,475)
Accumulated derivative net gains	142	—
Unrealized gain (loss) on available-for-sale securities	(55)	(26)
Minimum pension liability	(43)	(26)
	$ (2,638)	$ (2,527)

Notes to Consolidated Financial Statements

A summary of the components of other comprehensive income for the years ended December 31, 2001, 2000 and 1999, is as follows (in millions):

December 31,	Before-Tax Amount	Income Tax	After-Tax Amount
2001			
Net foreign currency translation	$ (285)	$ 78	$ (207)
Cumulative effect of adopting SFAS No. 133, net	83	(33)	50
Net gain (loss) on derivative financial instruments	151	(59)	92
Net change in unrealized gain (loss) on available-for-sale securities	(39)	10	(29)
Minimum pension liability	(27)	10	(17)
Other comprehensive income (loss)	$ (117)	$ 6	$ (111)

December 31,	Before-Tax Amount	Income Tax	After-Tax Amount
2000			
Net foreign currency translation	$ (1,074)	$ 109	$ (965)
Net change in unrealized gain (loss) on available-for-sale securities	(90)	30	(60)
Minimum pension liability	(17)	7	(10)
Other comprehensive income (loss)	$ (1,181)	$ 146	$ (1,035)

December 31,	Before-Tax Amount	Income Tax	After-Tax Amount
1999			
Net foreign currency translation	$ (249)	$ 59	$ (190)
Net change in unrealized gain (loss) on available-for-sale securities	37	(14)	23
Minimum pension liability	38	(13)	25
Other comprehensive income (loss)	$ (174)	$ 32	$ (142)

Note 8: Financial Instruments

Fair Value of Financial Instruments

The carrying amounts reflected in our Consolidated Balance Sheets for cash, cash equivalents, marketable equity securities, cost method investments, receivables, loans and notes payable and long-term debt approximate their respective fair values. Fair values are based primarily on quoted prices for those or similar instruments. Fair values for our derivative financial instruments are included in Note 9.

Certain Debt and Marketable Equity Securities

Investments in debt and marketable equity securities, other than investments accounted for by the equity method, are categorized as either trading, available-for-sale or held-to-maturity. On December 31, 2001 and 2000, we had no trading securities. Securities categorized as available-for-sale are stated at fair value, with unrealized gains and losses, net of deferred income taxes, reported as a component of AOCI. Debt securities categorized as held-to-maturity are stated at amortized cost.

On December 31, 2001 and 2000, available-for-sale and held-to-maturity securities consisted of the following (in millions):

December 31,	Cost	Gross Unrealized Gains	Gross Unrealized Losses	Estimated Fair Value
2001				
Available-for-sale securities				
Equity securities	$ 251	$ 43	$ (116)	$ 178
Collateralized mortgage obligations	13	—	(1)	12
Other debt securities	19	—	—	19
	$ 283	$ 43	$ (117)	$ 209
Held-to-maturity securities				
Bank and corporate debt	$ 978	$ —	$ —	$ 978
Other debt securities	8	—	—	8
	$ 986	$ —	$ —	$ 986

December 31,	Cost	Gross Unrealized Gains	Gross Unrealized Losses	Estimated Fair Value
2000				
Available-for-sale securities				
Equity securities	$ 248	$ 57	$ (90)	$ 215
Collateralized mortgage obligations	25	—	(2)	23
Other debt securities	15	—	—	15
	$ 288	$ 57	$ (92)	$ 253
Held-to-maturity securities				
Bank and corporate debt	$ 1,115	$ —	$ —	$ 1,115
	$ 1,115	$ —	$ —	$ 1,115

On December 31, 2001 and 2000, these investments were included in the following captions in our Consolidated Balance Sheets (in millions):

December 31,	Available-for-Sale Securities	Held-to-Maturity Securities
2001		
Cash and cash equivalents	$ —	$ 976
Current marketable securities	66	2
Cost method investments, principally bottling companies	127	—
Other assets	16	8
	$ 209	$ 986
2000		
Cash and cash equivalents	$ —	$ 1,113
Current marketable securities	71	2
Cost method investments, principally bottling companies	151	—
Other assets	31	—
	$ 253	$ 1,115

The contractual maturities of these investments as of December 31, 2001, were as follows (in millions):

	Available-for-Sale Securities		Held-to-Maturity Securities	
	Cost	Fair Value	Amortized Cost	Fair Value
2002	$ 16	$ 16	$ 978	$ 978
2003–2006	3	3	8	8
Collateralized mortgage obligations	13	12	—	—
Equity securities	251	178	—	—
	$ 283	$ 209	$ 986	$ 986

For the years ended December 31, 2001 and 2000, gross realized gains and losses on sales of available-for-sale securities were not material. The cost of securities sold is based on the specific identification method.

Note 9: Hedging Transactions and Derivative Financial Instruments

Our Company uses derivative financial instruments primarily to reduce our exposure to adverse fluctuations in interest rates and foreign exchange rates and, to a lesser extent, in commodity prices and other market risks. When entered into, the Company formally designates and documents the financial instrument as a hedge of a specific underlying exposure, as well as the risk management objectives and strategies for undertaking the hedge transactions. The Company formally assesses, both at the inception and at least quarterly thereafter, whether the financial instruments that are used in hedging transactions are effective at offsetting changes in either the fair value or cash flows of the related underlying exposure. Because of the high degree of effectiveness between the hedging instrument and the underlying exposure being hedged, fluctuations in the value of the derivative instruments are generally offset by changes in the fair value or cash flows of the underlying exposures being hedged. Any ineffective portion of a financial instrument's change in fair value is immediately recognized in earnings. Virtually all of our derivatives are straightforward over-the-counter instruments with liquid markets. Our Company does not enter into derivative financial instruments for trading purposes.

The fair values of derivatives used to hedge or modify our risks fluctuate over time. These fair value amounts should not be viewed in isolation, but rather in relation to the fair values or cash flows of the underlying hedged transactions or other exposures. The notional amounts of the derivative financial instruments do not necessarily represent amounts exchanged by the parties and, therefore, are not a direct measure of our exposure from our use of derivatives. The amounts exchanged are calculated by reference to the notional amounts and by other terms of the derivatives, such as interest rates, exchange rates or other financial indices.

As discussed in Note 1, the Company adopted SFAS No. 133, as amended by SFAS No. 137 and SFAS No. 138 on January 1, 2001. These statements require the Company to recognize all derivative instruments as either assets or liabilities in the Consolidated Balance Sheets at fair value. The accounting for changes in the fair value of a derivative instrument depends on whether it has been designated and qualifies as part of a hedging relationship and further, on the type of hedging relationship. At the inception of the hedge relationship, the Company must designate the derivative instrument as either a fair value hedge, a cash flow hedge or a hedge of a net investment in a foreign operation. This designation is based upon the exposure being hedged.

The adoption of SFAS No. 133 resulted in the Company recording transition adjustments to recognize its derivative instruments at fair value and to recognize the ineffective portion of the change in fair value of its derivatives. The cumulative effect of these transition adjustments was an after-tax reduction to net income of approximately $10 million and an after-tax net increase to AOCI of approximately $50 million. The reduction to net income is primarily related to the change in the time value and fair value of foreign currency options and interest rate agreements, respectively. The increase in AOCI is primarily related to net gains on foreign currency cash flow hedges. The Company reclassified into earnings during the year ended December 31, 2001 approximately $54 million of net gains relating to the transition adjustment recorded in AOCI as of January 1, 2001.

We have established strict counterparty credit guidelines and enter into transactions only with financial institutions of investment grade or better. We monitor counterparty exposures daily and review any downgrade in credit rating immediately. If a downgrade in the credit rating of a counterparty were to occur, we have provisions requiring collateral in the form of U.S. government securities for substantially all of our transactions. To mitigate presettlement risk, minimum credit standards become more stringent as the duration of the derivative financial instrument increases. To minimize the concentration of credit risk, we enter into derivative transactions with a portfolio of financial institutions. The Company has master netting agreements with most of the financial institutions that are counterparties to the derivative instruments. These agreements allow the net settlement of assets and liabilities arising from different transactions with the same counterparty. Based on these factors, we consider the risk of counterparty default to be minimal.

Interest Rate Management

Our Company maintains a percentage of fixed and variable rate debt within defined parameters. We enter into interest rate swap agreements that maintain the fixed-to-variable mix within these parameters. These contracts had maturities ranging from one to two years

Notes to Consolidated Financial Statements   THE COCA-COLA COMPANY AND SUBSIDIARIES

on December 31, 2001. Interest rate swap agreements, which meet certain conditions required under SFAS No. 133 for fair value hedges, are accounted for as such. Therefore, no ineffective portion was recorded in 2001. Accordingly, the changes in the fair value of these agreements are recorded in earnings immediately. The fair value of our Company's interest rate swap agreements was approximately $5 million at December 31, 2001. The Company estimates the fair value of its interest rate management derivatives based on quoted market prices.

Prior to January 1, 2001, our Company also used interest swaps and interest rate caps for hedging purposes. For interest rate swaps, any differences paid or received were recognized as adjustments to interest expense over the life of each swap, thereby adjusting the effective interest rate on the underlying obligation. Additionally, prior to January 1, 2001, our Company had entered into an interest rate cap agreement that entitled us to receive from a financial institution the amount, if any, by which our interest payments on our variable rate debt exceeded prespecified interest rates through 2004. This cap agreement was terminated during 2001, and the impact on the Consolidated Statements of Income was immaterial.

Foreign Currency Management
The purpose of our foreign currency hedging activities is to reduce the risk that our eventual U.S. dollar net cash inflows resulting from sales outside the U.S. will be adversely affected by changes in exchange rates.

We enter into forward exchange contracts and purchase currency options (principally euro and Japanese yen) to hedge certain portions of forecasted cash flows denominated in foreign currencies. The effective portion of the changes in fair value for these contracts, which have been designated as cash flow hedges, are reported in AOCI and reclassified into earnings in the same financial statement line item and in the same period or periods during which the hedged transaction affects earnings. Any ineffective portion (which was not significant in 2001) of the change in fair value of these instruments is immediately recognized in earnings. These contracts had maturities ranging from one to two years on December 31, 2001, the period in which all amounts included in AOCI will be reclassified into earnings.

Additionally, the Company enters into forward exchange contracts, which are not designated as hedging instruments under SFAS No. 133. These instruments are used to offset the earnings impact relating to the variability in exchange rates on certain monetary assets and liabilities denominated in non-functional currencies. Changes in the fair value of these instruments are recognized in earnings in the "Other income-net" line item of the Consolidated Statements of Income immediately to offset the effect of remeasurement of the monetary assets and liabilities.

The Company also enters into forward exchange contracts to hedge its net investment position in certain major currencies. Under SFAS No. 133, changes in the fair value of these instruments are recognized in foreign currency translation adjustment, a component of AOCI, immediately to offset the change in the value of the net investment being hedged. For the year ended December 31, 2001, approximately $43 million of losses relating to derivative financial instruments were recorded in foreign currency translation adjustment.

Prior to January 1, 2001, gains and losses on derivative financial instruments that were designated and effective as hedges of net investments in international operations were included in foreign currency translation adjustments, a component of AOCI.

For the year ended December 31, 2001, we recorded an increase to AOCI of approximately $92 million, net of both income taxes and reclassifications to earnings, primarily related to net gains on foreign currency cash flow hedges, which will generally offset cash flow losses relating to the underlying exposures being hedged in future periods. The Company estimates that it will reclassify into earnings during the next 12 months approximately $120 million of the net amount recorded in AOCI as of December 31, 2001 as the anticipated foreign currency cash flows occur. The Company recorded approximately $12 million in earnings classified within net operating revenues in the Consolidated Statements of Income, primarily related to the change in the time value of foreign currency options. During 2001, the FASB issued an interpretation to SFAS No. 133 allowing the entire change in fair value, including the time value, of certain purchased options to be recorded in AOCI until the related underlying exposure is recorded in earnings. The Company adopted this interpretation prospectively.

The Company did not discontinue any cash flow hedge relationships during the year ended December 31, 2001.

The following table summarizes activity in AOCI related to derivatives designated as cash flow hedges held by the Company during the period from January 1, 2001 through December 31, 2001 (in millions):

Year Ended December 31,	Before-Tax Amount	Income Tax	After-Tax Amount
2001			
Cumulative effect of adopting SFAS No. 133, net	$ 83	$ (33)	$ 50
Net changes in fair value of derivatives	311	(122)	189
Net gains reclassified from AOCI into earnings	(160)	63	(97)
Accumulated derivative net gains as of December 31, 2001	$ 234	$ (92)	$ 142

The following table presents the fair value, carrying value and maturities of the Company's foreign currency derivative instruments outstanding as of December 31, 2001 (in millions):

December 31,	Carrying Values	Fair Values	Maturity
2001			
Forward contracts	$ 37	$ 37	2002
Currency swap agreements	10	10	2002
Purchased options	219	219	2002–2003
	$ 266	$ 266	

The Company estimates the fair value of its foreign currency derivatives based on quoted market prices or pricing models using current market rates. This amount is primarily reflected in prepaid expenses and other assets within the Company's Consolidated Balance Sheets.

Prior to January 1, 2001, our Company also used foreign exchange contracts and purchased currency options for hedging purposes. Premiums paid and realized gains and losses, including those on any terminated contracts, were included in prepaid expenses and other assets. These were recognized in income, along with unrealized gains and losses, in the same period the hedging transactions were realized. Approximately $26 million of realized gains on settled contracts entered into as hedges of firmly committed transactions that had not yet occurred were deferred on December 31, 2000. Deferred gains and losses from hedging anticipated transactions were not material on December 31, 2000.

The following table presents the aggregate notional principal amounts, carrying values, fair values and maturities of our derivative financial instruments outstanding on December 31, 2000 (in millions):

December 31,	Notional Principal Amounts	Carrying Values	Fair Values	Maturity
2000				
Interest rate management				
Swap agreements				
Assets	$ 150	$ 1	$ 8	2003
Liabilities	25	(1)	(10)	2001–2003
Interest rate caps				
Assets	1,600	8	4	2004
Foreign currency management				
Forward contracts				
Assets	1,812	49	74	2001
Swap agreements				
Assets	48	2	(3)	2001
Liabilities	359	(2)	(19)	2001–2002
Purchased options				
Assets	706	18	53	2001–2002
Other				
Assets	87	2	3	2001
	$ 4,787	$ 77	$ 110	

Note 10: Commitments and Contingencies

On December 31, 2001, we were contingently liable for guarantees of indebtedness owed by third parties in the amount of $436 million, of which $10 million related to the Company's equity investee bottlers. We do not consider it probable that we will be required to satisfy these guarantees.

We believe our exposure to concentrations of credit risk is limited, due to the diverse geographic areas covered by our operations.

We have committed to make future marketing expenditures of $1,326 million, of which the majority is payable over the next 12 years.

The Company is involved in various legal proceedings. Management believes that any liability to the Company which may arise as a result of these proceedings will not have a material adverse effect on the financial condition of the Company taken as a whole.

Note 11: Net Change in Operating Assets and Liabilities

The changes in operating assets and liabilities, net of effects of acquisitions and divestitures of businesses and unrealized exchange gains/losses, are as follows (in millions):

	2001	2000	1999
Increase in trade accounts receivable	$ (73)	$ (39)	$ (96)
Increase in inventories	(17)	(2)	(163)
Increase in prepaid expenses and other assets	(349)	(618)	(547)
Increase (decrease) in accounts payable and accrued expenses	(179)	(84)	281
Increase (decrease) in accrued taxes	247	(96)	(36)
Increase (decrease) in other liabilities	(91)	(13)	4
	$ (462)	$ (852)	$ (557)

Note 12: Restricted Stock, Stock Options and Other Stock Plans

Our Company currently sponsors restricted stock award plans and stock option plans. Our Company applies Accounting Principles Board Opinion No. 25 and related Interpretations in accounting for our plans. Accordingly, no compensation cost has been recognized for our stock option plans. The compensation cost charged against income for our restricted stock award plans was $41 million in 2001, $6 million in 2000 and $39 million in 1999. In 2000, the Company recorded a charge of $37 million for special termination benefits as part of the Realignment (discussed in Note 16). Had compensation cost for the stock option plans been determined based on the fair value at the grant dates for awards under the plans, our Company's net income and net income per share (basic and diluted) would have been as presented in the following table.

The pro forma amounts are indicated below (in millions, except per share amounts):

Year Ended December 31,	2001	2000	1999
Net income			
As reported	$ 3,969	$ 2,177	$ 2,431
Pro forma	$ 3,767	$ 1,995	$ 2,271
Basic net income per share			
As reported	$ 1.60	$ .88	$ .98
Pro forma	$ 1.51	$ .81	$ .92
Diluted net income per share			
As reported	$ 1.60	$ .88	$ .98
Pro forma	$ 1.51	$ .80	$ .91

Under the amended 1989 Restricted Stock Award Plan and the amended 1983 Restricted Stock Award Plan (the Restricted Stock Award Plans), 40 million and 24 million shares of restricted common stock, respectively, may be granted to certain officers and key employees of our Company.

On December 31, 2001, 29 million shares were available for grant under the Restricted Stock Award Plans. In 2001, there were 116,300 shares of restricted stock granted at an average price of $48.95. In 2000, there were 546,585 shares of restricted stock granted at an average price of $58.20. In 1999, 32,100 shares of restricted stock were granted at an average price of $53.86. In 2001, 78,700 shares of restricted stock were cancelled at an average price of $48.49. In 2000, 80,500 shares of restricted stock were cancelled at an average price of $28.41. In 1999, 1,600 shares of restricted stock were cancelled at an average price of $86.75. Participants are entitled to vote and receive dividends on the shares and, under the 1983 Restricted Stock Award Plan, participants are reimbursed by our Company for income taxes imposed on the award, but not for taxes generated by the reimbursement payment. The shares are subject to certain transfer restrictions and may be forfeited if a participant leaves our Company for reasons other than retirement, disability or death, absent a change in control of our Company.

In addition, 270,000 shares of three-year performance-based and 2,025,000 shares of five-year performance-based restricted stock were granted in 2000. The release of these shares was contingent upon the Company achieving certain predefined performance targets over the three-year and five-year measurement

Notes to Consolidated Financial Statements   THE COCA-COLA COMPANY AND SUBSIDIARIES

periods, respectively. Participants were entitled to vote and receive dividends on these shares during the measurement period. The Company also promised to grant 180,000 shares of stock at the end of three years and 200,000 shares at the end of five years to certain employees if the Company achieved predefined performance targets over the respective measurement periods. In May 2001, these performance based restricted stock awards and promises made to grant shares in the future were cancelled. New awards, for the same number of shares, with the exception of the promise made in 2000 to grant 200,000 shares at the end of five years, were granted. The performance targets of these new awards are aligned with the Company's current long-term earnings per share growth target of 11 to 12 percent. In 2001, an additional 10,000 shares of three-year and 300,000 shares of five-year performance-based restricted stock were granted with performance targets aligned with the Company's current long-term earnings per share growth target of 11 to 12 percent.

Under our 1991 Stock Option Plan (the 1991 Option Plan), a maximum of 120 million shares of our common stock was approved to be issued or transferred to certain officers and employees pursuant to stock options and stock appreciation rights granted under the 1991 Option Plan. The stock appreciation rights permit the holder, upon surrendering all or part of the related stock option, to receive cash, common stock or a combination thereof, in an amount up to 100 percent of the difference between the market price and the option price. Options to purchase common stock under the 1991 Option Plan have been granted to Company employees at fair market value at the date of grant.

The 1999 Stock Option Plan (the 1999 Option Plan) was approved by share owners in April of 1999. Following the approval of the 1999 Option Plan, no grants were made from the 1991 Option Plan, and shares available under the 1991 Option Plan were no longer available to be granted. Under the 1999 Option Plan, a maximum of 120 million shares of our common stock was approved to be issued or transferred to certain officers and employees pursuant to stock options granted under the 1999 Option Plan. Options to purchase common stock under the 1999 Option Plan have been granted to Company employees at fair market value at the date of grant.

Generally, stock options become exercisable over a four-year vesting period and expire 15 years from the date of grant. Prior to 1999, stock options generally became exercisable over a three-year vesting period and expired 10 years from the date of grant.

The fair value of each option grant is estimated on the date of grant using the Black-Scholes option-pricing model with the following weighted-average assumptions used for grants in 2001, 2000 and 1999, respectively: dividend yields of 1.6, 1.2 and 1.2 percent; expected volatility of 31.9, 31.7 and 27.1 percent; risk-free interest rates of 5.1, 5.8 and 6.2 percent; and expected lives of five years for 2001 and 2000 and four years for 1999. The weighted-average fair value of options granted was $15.09, $19.85 and $15.77 for the years ended December 31, 2001, 2000 and 1999, respectively.

A summary of stock option activity under all plans is as follows (shares in millions):

	2001		2000		1999	
	Shares	Weighted-Average Exercise Price	Shares	Weighted-Average Exercise Price	Shares	Weighted-Average Exercise Price
Outstanding on January 1,	112	$ 51.23	101	$ 46.66	80	$ 42.77
Granted[1]	45	48.11	32	57.35	28	53.53
Exercised	(7)	24.30	(12)	26.00	(6)	26.12
Forfeited/Expired[2]	(9)	56.74	(9)	57.51	(1)	60.40
Outstanding on December 31,	141	$ 51.16	112	$ 51.23	101	$ 46.66
Exercisable on December 31,	65	$ 50.83	60	$ 46.57	59	$ 39.40
Shares available on December 31, for options that may be granted	25		65		92	

[1] No grants were made from the 1991 Option Plan during 2000 or 2001.
[2] Shares Forfeited/Expired relate to the 1991 and 1999 Option Plans.

The following table summarizes information about stock options at December 31, 2001 (shares in millions):

| Range of Exercise Prices | Outstanding Stock Options | | | Exercisable Stock Options | |
	Shares	Weighted-Average Remaining Contractual Life	Weighted-Average Exercise Price	Shares	Weighted-Average Exercise Price
$ 20.00 to $ 30.00	7	2.1 years	$ 23.44	7	$ 23.44
$ 30.01 to $ 40.00	9	3.8 years	$ 35.63	9	$ 35.63
$ 40.01 to $ 50.00	53	12.9 years	$ 48.22	9	$ 48.86
$ 50.01 to $ 60.00	59	12.2 years	$ 56.30	28	$ 56.54
$ 60.01 to $ 86.75	13	6.8 years	$ 65.87	12	$ 65.89
$ 20.00 to $ 86.75	141	10.9 years	$ 51.16	65	$ 50.83

Note 13: Pension and Other Postretirement Benefit Plans

Our Company sponsors and/or contributes to pension and postretirement health care and life insurance benefit plans covering substantially all U.S. employees and certain employees in international locations. We also sponsor nonqualified, unfunded defined benefit pension plans for certain officers and other employees. In addition, our Company and its subsidiaries have various pension plans and other forms of postretirement arrangements outside the United States.

Total expense for all benefit plans, including defined benefit pension plans, defined contribution pension plans, and postretirement health care and life insurance benefit plans, amounted to approximately $142 million in 2001, $116 million in 2000 and $108 million in 1999. In addition, in 2000 the Company recorded a charge of $124 million for special retirement benefits as part of the Realignment discussed in Note 16. Net periodic cost for our pension and other defined benefit plans consists of the following (in millions):

| Year Ended December 31, | Pension Benefits | | |
	2001	2000	1999
Service cost	$ 53	$ 54	$ 67
Interest cost	123	119	111
Expected return on plan assets	(125)	(132)	(119)
Amortization of prior service cost	8	4	6
Recognized net actuarial (gain) loss	3	(7)	7
Settlements and curtailments	—	1	—
Net periodic pension cost	$ 62	$ 39	$ 72

| Year Ended December 31, | Other Benefits | | |
	2001	2000	1999
Service cost	$ 13	$ 12	$ 14
Interest cost	34	29	22
Expected return on plan assets	(1)	(1)	(1)
Amortization of prior service cost	2	1	—
Recognized net actuarial gain	—	(1)	—
Net periodic cost	$ 48	$ 40	$ 35

The following table sets forth the change in benefit obligation for our benefit plans (in millions):

| December 31, | Pension Benefits | | Other Benefits | |
	2001	2000	2001	2000
Benefit obligation at beginning of year	$ 1,819	$ 1,670	$ 407	$ 303
Service cost	53	54	13	12
Interest cost	123	119	34	29
Foreign currency exchange rate changes	(23)	(55)	—	—
Amendments	—	57	3	21
Actuarial loss	62	77	96	25
Benefits paid	(126)	(146)	(23)	(17)
Business combinations	10	—	—	—
Divestitures	(12)	—	—	—
Settlements and curtailments	—	(67)	—	13
Special retirement benefits	—	104	—	20
Other	—	6	—	1
Benefit obligation at end of year	$ 1,906	$ 1,819	$ 530	$ 407

The following table sets forth the change in plan assets for our benefit plans (in millions):

December 31,	Pension Benefits		Other Benefits	
	2001	2000	**2001**	2000
Fair value of plan assets at beginning of year[1]	$ 1,555	$ 1,722	$ 17	$ 29
Actual return on plan assets	(96)	4	—	2
Employer contribution	130	31	—	—
Foreign currency exchange rate changes	(14)	(57)	—	—
Benefits paid	(91)	(120)	(17)	(14)
Business combinations	9	—	—	—
Divestitures	(4)	—	—	—
Settlements	—	(38)	—	—
Other	3	13	—	—
Fair value of plan assets at end of year[1]	$ 1,492	$ 1,555	$ —	$ 17

[1] Pension benefit plan assets primarily consist of listed stocks including 1,621,050 shares of common stock of our Company with a fair value of $76 million and $99 million as of December 31, 2001 and 2000, respectively.

The total projected benefit obligation and fair value of plan assets for the pension plans with projected benefit obligations in excess of plan assets were $687 million and $232 million, respectively, as of December 31, 2001 and $617 million and $194 million, respectively, as of December 31, 2000. The total accumulated benefit obligation and fair value of plan assets for the pension plans with accumulated benefit obligations in excess of plan assets were $583 million and $202 million, respectively, as of December 31, 2001 and $480 million and $152 million, respectively, as of December 31, 2000.

The accrued pension and other benefit costs recognized in our accompanying Consolidated Balance Sheets are computed as follows (in millions):

December 31,	Pension Benefits		Other Benefits	
	2001	2000	**2001**	2000
Funded status	$ (414)	$ (264)	$ (530)	$ (390)
Unrecognized net asset at transition	(5)	(6)	—	—
Unrecognized prior service cost	73	90	21	23
Unrecognized net actuarial (gain) loss	195	(89)	45	(51)
Net liability recognized	$ (151)	$ (269)	$ (464)	$ (418)
Prepaid benefit cost	$ 146	$ 39	$ —	$ —
Accrued benefit liability	(387)	(374)	(464)	(418)
Accumulated other comprehensive income	70	43	—	—
Intangible asset	20	23	—	—
Net liability recognized	$ (151)	$ (269)	$ (464)	$ (418)

The weighted-average assumptions used in computing the preceding information are as follows:

December 31,	Pension Benefits		
	2001	2000	1999
Discount rate	6½%	7%	7%
Rate of increase in compensation levels	4¼%	4½%	4½%
Expected long-term rate of return on plan assets	8½%	8½%	8½%

December 31,	Other Benefits		
	2001	2000	1999
Discount rate	7¼%	7½%	8%
Rate of increase in compensation levels	4½%	4¾%	5%
Expected long-term rate of return on plan assets	—	3%	3%

The rate of increase in per capita costs of covered health care benefits is assumed to be 9 percent in 2002, decreasing gradually to 5 1/4 percent by the year 2007.

A one percentage point change in the assumed health care cost trend rate would have the following effects (in millions):

	One Percentage Point Increase	One Percentage Point Decrease
Effect on accumulated postretirement benefit obligation as of December 31, 2001	$ 54	$ (45)
Effect on net periodic postretirement benefit cost in 2001	$ 7	$ (6)

Note 14: Income Taxes

Income before income taxes and cumulative effect of accounting change consists of the following (in millions):

Year Ended December 31,	2001	2000	1999
United States	$ 2,430	$ 1,497	$ 1,504
International	3,240	1,902	2,315
	$ 5,670	$ 3,399	$ 3,819

Income tax expense (benefit) consists of the following (in millions):

Year Ended December 31,	United States	State & Local	International	Total
2001				
Current	$ 552	$ 102	$ 981	$ 1,635
Deferred	70	(15)	1	56
2000				
Current	$ 48	$ 16	$ 1,155	$ 1,219
Deferred	(9)	46	(34)	3
1999				
Current	$ 395	$ 67	$ 829	$ 1,291
Deferred	182	11	(96)	97

We made income tax payments of approximately $1,351 million, $1,327 million and $1,404 million in 2001, 2000 and 1999, respectively. During the first quarter of 2000, the United States and Japan taxing authorities entered into an Advance Pricing Agreement (APA) whereby the level of royalties paid by Coca-Cola (Japan) Company, Ltd. (our

Subsidiary) to our Company has been established for the years 1993 through 2001. Pursuant to the terms of the APA, our Subsidiary has filed amended returns for the applicable periods reflecting the negotiated royalty rate. These amended returns resulted in the payment during the first and second quarters of 2000 of additional Japanese taxes, the effect of which on both our financial performance and our effective tax rate was not material, due primarily to offsetting tax credits utilized on our U.S. income tax return.

A reconciliation of the statutory U.S. federal rate and effective rates is as follows:

Year Ended December 31,	2001	2000	1999
Statutory U.S. federal rate	35.0%	35.0%	35.0%
State income taxes-net of federal benefit	1.0	.8	1.0
Earnings in jurisdictions taxed at rates different from the statutory U.S. federal rate	(4.9)	(4.0)	(6.0)
Equity income or loss[1]	(.9)	2.9	1.6
Other operating charges[2]	—	1.9	5.3
Other-net	(.4)	(.6)	(.6)
	29.8%	36.0%	36.3%

[1] Includes charges by equity investees for 2000 and 1999. See Note 15.

[2] Includes charges related to certain bottling, manufacturing and intangible assets for 2000 and 1999. See Note 15.

Our effective tax rate reflects the tax benefit derived from having significant operations outside the United States that are taxed at rates lower than the U.S. statutory rate of 35 percent.

In 2000, management concluded that it was more likely than not that local tax benefits would not be realized with respect to principally all of the items discussed in Note 15, with the exception of approximately $188 million of charges related to the settlement terms of a class action discrimination lawsuit. Accordingly, valuation allowances were recorded to offset the future tax benefit of these nonrecurring items resulting in an increase in our effective tax rate. Excluding the impact of these nonrecurring items, the effective tax rate on operations for 2000 was slightly more than 30 percent.

In 1999, the Company recorded a charge of $813 million, primarily reflecting the impairment of certain bottling, manufacturing and intangible assets. For some locations with impaired assets, management concluded that it was more likely than not that no local tax benefit would be realized. Accordingly, a valuation allowance was recorded offsetting the future tax benefits for such locations. This resulted in an increase in our effective tax rate for 1999. Excluding the impact, the Company's effective tax rate for 1999 would have been 31 percent.

Undistributed earnings of the Company's foreign subsidiaries amounted to approximately $5.9 billion at December 31, 2001. Those earnings are considered to be indefinitely reinvested and, accordingly, no U.S. federal and state income taxes have been provided thereon. Upon distribution of those earnings in the form of dividends or otherwise, the Company would be subject to both U.S. income taxes (subject to an adjustment for foreign tax credits) and withholding taxes payable to the various foreign countries. Determination of the amount of unrecognized deferred U.S. income tax liability is not practicable because of the complexities associated with its hypothetical calculation; however, unrecognized foreign tax credits would be available to reduce a substantial portion of the U.S. liability.

The tax effects of temporary differences and carryforwards that give rise to deferred tax assets and liabilities consist of the following (in millions):

December 31,	2001	2000
Deferred tax assets:		
Benefit plans	$ 377	$ 261
Liabilities and reserves	489	456
Net operating loss carryforwards	286	375
Other operating charges	169	321
Other	232	126
Gross deferred tax assets	1,553	1,539
Valuation allowance	(563)	(641)
	$ 990	$ 898
Deferred tax liabilities:		
Property, plant and equipment	$ 391	$ 425
Equity investments	196	228
Intangible assets	248	224
Other	185	129
	$ 1,020	$ 1,006
Net deferred tax asset (liability)[1]	$ (30)	$ (108)

[1] Deferred tax assets of $412 million and $250 million have been included in the consolidated balance sheet caption "Other assets" at December 31, 2001 and 2000, respectively.

On December 31, 2001 and 2000, we had approximately $240 million and $143 million, respectively, of net deferred tax assets, located in countries outside the United States.

On December 31, 2001, we had $1,229 million of tax operating loss carryforwards available to reduce future taxable income of certain international subsidiaries. Loss carryforwards of $440 million must be utilized within the next five years; $789 million can be utilized over an indefinite period. A valuation allowance has been provided for a portion of the deferred tax assets related to these loss carryforwards.

Note 15: Nonrecurring Items

In the first quarter of 2000, we recorded charges of approximately $405 million related to the impairment of certain bottling, manufacturing and intangible assets, primarily within our Indian bottling operations. These impairment charges were recorded to reduce the carrying value of the identified assets to fair value. Fair value was derived using cash flow analysis. The assumptions used in the cash flow analysis were consistent with those used in our internal planning process. The assumptions included estimates of future growth in unit cases, estimates of gross margins, estimates of the impact of exchange rates and estimates of tax rates and tax incentives. The charge was primarily the result of our revised outlook for the Indian beverage market including the future expected tax environment. The remaining carrying value of long-lived assets within our Indian bottling operations, immediately after recording the impairment charge, was approximately $300 million.

In July 2000, we recorded a tax-free non-cash gain of approximately $118 million related to the merger of Coca-Cola Beverages and Hellenic Bottling Company S.A. For specific transaction details refer to Note 2.

In the fourth quarter of 2000, we recorded charges of approximately $188 million related to the settlement terms of, and direct costs related to, a class action discrimination lawsuit. The monetary settlement includes cash payments to fund back pay, compensatory damages, a promotional achievement fund and attorneys' fees. In addition, the Company introduced a wide range of training, monitoring and mentoring programs. Of the $188 million, $50 million was donated to The Coca-Cola Foundation to continue its broad range of community support programs. In 2001, our Company paid out substantially all of this settlement.

In 2000, the Company also recorded a nonrecurring charge of approximately $306 million, which represents the Company's portion of a charge recorded by Coca-Cola Amatil to reduce the carrying value of its investment in the Philippines. In addition, Panamerican Beverages, Inc. wrote down selected assets, including the impairment of the value of its Venezuelan operating unit. The Company's portion of this charge was approximately $124 million. Also contributing to the equity losses were nonrecurring charges recorded by investees in Eurasia and the Middle East. These nonrecurring charges were partially offset by the impact of lower tax rates related to current and deferred taxes at Coca-Cola Erfrischungsgetraenke AG (CCEAG).

In the fourth quarter of 1999, we recorded charges of approximately $813 million. Of this $813 million, approximately $543 million related to the impairment of certain bottling, manufacturing and intangible assets, primarily within our Russian and Caribbean bottlers and in the Middle and Far East and in North America. These impairment charges were recorded to reduce the carrying value of the identified assets to fair value. Fair values were derived using a variety of methodologies, including cash flow analysis, estimates of sales proceeds and independent appraisals. Where cash flow analyses were used to estimate fair values, key assumptions employed, consistent with those used in our internal planning process, included our estimates of future growth in unit case sales, estimates of gross margins and estimates of the impact of inflation and foreign currency fluctuations. The charges were primarily the result of our revised outlook in certain markets due to the prolonged severe economic downturns. The remaining carrying value of these impaired long-lived assets, immediately after recording the impairment charge, was approximately $140 million.

Of the $813 million, approximately $196 million related to charges associated with the impairment of the distribution and bottling assets of our vending operations in Japan and our bottling operations in the Baltics. The charges reduced the carrying value of these assets to their fair value less the cost to sell. Consistent with our long-term bottling strategy, management intended to sell the assets of our vending operations in Japan and our bottling operations in the Baltics. The remaining carrying value of long-lived assets within these operations and the income from operations on an aftertax basis as of and for the 12-month period ending December 31, 2000, were approximately $143 million and $12 million, respectively. On December 22, 2000, the Company signed a definitive agreement to sell the assets of our vending operations in Japan and this sale was completed in 2001. The proceeds from the sale of the

assets were approximately equal to the carrying value of the long-lived assets less the cost to sell.

In December 2000, the Company announced that it had intended to sell its bottling operations in the Baltics to one of our strategic business partners. However, the partner was in the process of internal restructuring and no longer planned to purchase the Baltics bottling operations. At that time another suitable buyer was not identified so the Company continued to operate the Baltics bottlers as consolidated operations until a new buyer was identified. Subsequently, in January 2002, our Company reached an agreement to sell our bottling operations in the Baltics to CCHBC in early 2002. The expected proceeds from the sale of the Baltics bottlers are approximately equal to the current carrying value of the investment.

The remainder of the $813 million charges, approximately $74 million, primarily related to the change in senior management and charges related to organizational changes within the Europe, Eurasia and Middle East, Latin America and Corporate segments. These charges were incurred during the fourth quarter of 1999.

Note 16: Realignment Costs

In January 2000, our Company initiated a major organizational realignment (the Realignment) intended to put more responsibility, accountability and resources in the hands of local business units of the Company so as to fully leverage the local capabilities of our system.

Under the Realignment, employees were separated from almost all functional areas of the Company's operations, and certain activities were outsourced to third parties. The total number of employees separated as of December 31, 2000, was approximately 5,200. Employees separated from the Company as a result of the Realignment were offered severance or early retirement packages, as appropriate, which included both financial and nonfinancial components. The Realignment expenses included costs associated with involuntary terminations, voluntary retirements and other direct costs associated with implementing the Realignment. Other direct costs included repatriating and relocating employees to local markets; asset writedowns; lease cancellation costs; and costs associated with the development, communication and administration of the Realignment.

Notes to Consolidated Financial Statements   THE COCA-COLA COMPANY AND SUBSIDIARIES

The table below summarizes the balance of accured Realignment expenses and the movement in that accrual as of and for the year ended December 31, 2001 and 2000 (in millions):

Realignment Summary	2000 Expenses	2000 Payments	2000 Non-cash and Exchange	Accrued Balance December 31, 2000	2001 Payments	2001 Non-cash and Exchange	Accrued Balance December 31, 2001
Employees involuntarily separated							
Severance pay and benefits	$ 216	$ (123)	$ (2)	$ 91	$ (66)	$ (8)	$ 17
Outside services—legal, outplacement, consulting	33	(25)	—	8	(8)	—	—
Other—including asset write-downs	81	(37)	(7)	37	(33)	(4)	—
	$ 330	$ (185)	$ (9)	$ 136	$ (107)	$ (12)	$ 17
Employees voluntarily separated							
Special retirement pay and benefits	$ 353	$ (174)	$ —	$ 179	$ (26)	$ (12)	$ 141
Outside services—legal, outplacement, consulting	6	(3)	—	3	(3)	—	—
	$ 359	$ (177)	$ —	$ 182	$ (29)	$ (12)	$ 141
Other direct costs	$ 161	$ (92)	$ (9)	$ 60	$ (26)	$ (11)	$ 23
Total Realignment	$ 850	$ (454)	$ (18)	$ 378[1]	$ (162)	$ (35)	$ 181[1]

[1] As of December 31, 2001 and 2000, $59 million and $254 million, respectively, were included in the consolidated balance sheet caption "Accounts payable and accrued expenses." As of December 31, 2001 and 2000, $122 million and $124 million, respectively, were included in the consolidated balance sheet caption "Other liabilities."

Note 17: Acquisitions and Investments

During 2001, our Company's acquisition and investment activity totaled approximately $651 million. In February 2001, our Company reached an agreement with Carlsberg for the dissolution of CCNB, a joint venture bottler in which our Company had a 49 percent ownership. At that time, CCNB had bottling operations in Sweden, Norway, Denmark, Finland and Iceland. Under this agreement with Carlsberg, our Company acquired CCNB's Sweden and Norway bottling operations in June 2001, increasing our Company's ownership in those bottlers to 100 percent. Carlsberg acquired CCNB's Denmark and Finland bottling operations, increasing Carlsberg's ownership in those bottlers to 100 percent. Pursuant to the agreement, CCNB sold its Iceland bottling operations to a third-party group of investors in May 2001.

In March 2001, our Company signed a definitive agreement with La Tondena Distillers, Inc. (La Tondena) and San Miguel to acquire carbonated soft drink, water and juice brands for $84 million. CCBPI acquired the related manufacturing and distribution assets from La Tondena for $63 million.

In July 2001, our Company and San Miguel acquired CCBPI from Coca-Cola Amatil. Upon the completion of this transaction, our Company owned 35 percent of the common shares and 100 percent of the Preferred B shares, and San Miguel owned 65 percent of the common shares of CCBPI. Additionally, as a result of this transaction, our Company's interest in Coca-Cola Amatil was reduced from approximately 38 percent to approximately 35 percent.

In December 2001, our Company completed a cash tender offer for all outstanding shares of common stock of Odwalla, Inc. This acquisition was valued at approximately $190 million with our Company receiving an ownership interest of 100 percent.

During the first half of 2001, in separate transactions, our Company purchased two bottlers in Brazil: Refrescos Guararapes Ltda. and Sucovalle Sucos e Concentrados do Vale S.A. In separate transactions during the first half of 2000, our Company purchased two other bottlers in Brazil: Companhia Mineira de Refrescos, S.A. and Refrigerantes Minas Gerais Ltda. In October 2000, the Company purchased a 58 percent interest in Paraguay Refrescos S.A. (Paresa), a bottler located in Paraguay. In December 2000, the Company made a tender offer for the remaining 42 percent of the shares in Paresa. In January 2001, following the completion of the tender offer, we owned approximately 95 percent of Paresa.

The acquisitions and investments have been accounted for by either the purchase, equity or cost

Notes to Consolidated Financial Statements   THE COCA-COLA COMPANY AND SUBSIDIARIES

method of accounting, as appropriate. Their results have been included in the Consolidated Financial Statements from their respective dates of acquisition using the appropriate method of accounting. Had the results of these businesses been included in operations commencing with 1999, the reported results would not have been materially affected.

Note 18: Subsequent Events

In 2001, our Company concluded negotiations regarding the terms of a Control and Profit and Loss (CPL) agreement with certain other share owners of CCEAG, the largest bottler in Germany, in which the Company has an approximate 41 percent ownership interest. Under the terms of the CPL agreement, the Company obtained management control of CCEAG for a period of up to five years. In return for the management control of CCEAG, the Company guaranteed annual payments in lieu of dividends by CCEAG to all other CCEAG share owners. Additionally, all other CCEAG share owners entered into either a put or a put/call option agreement with the Company, exercisable at the end of the term of the CPL agreement at agreed prices. In early 2002, the Company assumed control of CCEAG. This transaction will be accounted for as a business combination. The present value of the total amount likely to be paid by our Company to all other CCEAG share owners, including the put or put/call payments and the guaranteed annual payment in lieu of dividends, is approximately $600 million. In 2001, CCEAG's revenues were approximately $1.7 billion. Additionally, our Company's debt will increase between $700 million and $800 million once this business combination is completed.

In November 2001, our Company and CCBPI entered into a sale and purchase agreement with RFM Corp. to acquire its 83.2 percent interest in Cosmos Bottling Corporation (CBC), a publicly traded Philippine beverage company. As of the date of the agreement, the Company began supplying concentrate for this operation. The transaction valued CBC at 14 billion Philippine pesos, or approximately $270 million. The purchase of RFM's interest was finalized on January 3, 2002 with our Company receiving direct and indirect ownership totaling approximately 62.3 percent. A subsequent tender offer was made to the remaining minority share owners and is expected to close in March 2002.

Note 19: Operating Segments

Our Company's operating structure includes the following operating segments: North America (including The Minute Maid Company); Africa; Europe, Eurasia and Middle East; Latin America; Asia; and Corporate. North America also includes the United States, Canada and Puerto Rico.

Effective January 1, 2001, our Company's operating segments were geographically reconfigured and renamed. Puerto Rico was added to North America from Latin America. The Middle East Division was added to Europe and Eurasia, which changed its name to Europe, Eurasia and Middle East. At the same time, Africa and Middle East, less the relocated Middle East Division, changed its name to Africa. During the first quarter of 2001, Asia Pacific was renamed Asia. Prior period amounts have been reclassified to conform to the current period presentation.

Segment Products and Services

The business of our Company is nonalcoholic ready-to-drink beverages, principally carbonated soft drinks, but also a variety of noncarbonated beverages. Our operating segments derive substantially all their revenues from the manufacture and sale of beverage concentrates and syrups with the exception of Corporate, which derives its revenues primarily from the licensing of our brands in connection with merchandise.

Method of Determining Segment Profit or Loss

Management evaluates the performance of its operating segments separately to individually monitor the different factors affecting financial performance. Segment profit or loss includes substantially all the segment's costs of production, distribution and administration. Our Company manages income taxes on a global basis. Thus, we evaluate segment performance based on profit or loss before income taxes. Our Company typically manages and evaluates equity investments and related income on a segment level. However, we manage certain significant investments, such as our equity interests in Coca-Cola Enterprises, at the Corporate segment. We manage financial costs, such as exchange gains and losses and interest income and expense, on a global basis at the Corporate segment.

Notes to Consolidated Financial Statements   THE COCA-COLA COMPANY AND SUBSIDIARIES

Information about our Company's operations by operating segment is as follows (in millions):

	North America	Africa	Europe, Eurasia & Middle East	Latin America	Asia	Corporate	Consolidated
2001							
Net operating revenues	$ 7,526	$ 621	$ 4,492	$ 2,273	$ 5,000[1]	$ 180	$ 20,092
Operating income	1,480	261	1,476	1,094	1,763	(722)	5,352
Interest income						325	325
Interest expense						289	289
Equity income (loss)	2	2	(63)	118	68	25	152
Identifiable operating assets	4,738	293	2,516	1,681	2,121	5,646[2]	16,995
Investments[3]	140	78	1,732	1,572	1,053	847	5,422
Capital expenditures	339	11	105	37	107	170	769
Depreciation and amortization	249	27	134	90	144	159	803
Income before income taxes and cumulative effect of accounting change	1,472	258	1,417	1,279	1,808	(564)[4]	5,670
2000							
Net operating revenues	$ 7,372	$ 608	$ 4,493	$ 2,140	$ 5,127[1]	$ 149	$ 19,889
Operating income[5]	1,409	174	1,300[6]	908	956	(1,056)[7]	3,691
Interest income						345	345
Interest expense						447	447
Equity income (loss)[8]	3	1	(39)	(75)	(290)	111	(289)
Identifiable operating assets	4,271	333	1,697	1,545	1,953	5,270[2]	15,069
Investments[3]	141	85	2,010	1,767	993	769	5,765
Capital expenditures	259	8	197	16	132	121	733
Depreciation and amortization	244	32	86	96	211	104	773
Income before income taxes	1,413	161	1,379[9]	859	651	(1,064)	3,399
1999							
Net operating revenues	$ 7,086	$ 662	$ 4,670	$ 1,932	$ 4,769[1]	$ 165	$ 19,284
Operating income[10]	1,447	212	912	829	1,194	(612)	3,982
Interest income						260	260
Interest expense						337	337
Equity income (loss)	(5)	1	(103)	(5)	(37)	(35)	(184)
Identifiable operating assets	3,591	361	1,935	1,653	2,439	4,852[2]	14,831
Investments[3]	139	75	2,128	1,833	1,837	780	6,792
Capital expenditures	269	18	222	67	317	176	1,069
Depreciation and amortization	263	27	100	96	184	122	792
Income before income taxes	1,443	199	797	836	1,143	(599)	3,819

Intercompany transfers between operating segments are not material. Certain prior year amounts have been reclassified to conform to the current year presentation.

[1] Japan revenues represent approximately 74 percent of total Asia operating segment revenues related to 2001, 75 percent related to 2000 and 79 percent related to 1999.

[2] Principally marketable securities, finance subsidiary receivables, trademarks and other intangible assets and fixed assets.

[3] Principally equity investments in bottling companies.

[4] Income before income taxes and cumulative effect of accounting change was increased by $91 million for Corporate due to a non-cash gain which was recognized on the issuance of stock by Coca-Cola Enterprises, one of our equity investees.

[5] Operating income was reduced by $3 million for North America, $397 million for Asia and $5 million for Corporate related to the other operating charges recorded for asset impairments in the first quarter of 2000. Operating income was also reduced by $132 million for North America, $33 million for Africa, $205 million for Europe, Eurasia & Middle East, $59 million for Latin America, $127 million for Asia and $294 million for Corporate

as a result of other operating charges associated with the Realignment.

[6] Operating income was reduced by $30 million for Europe, Eurasia & Middle East due to incremental marketing expenses in Central Europe.

[7] Operating income was reduced by $188 million for Corporate related to the settlement terms of a discrimination lawsuit and a donation to The Coca-Cola Foundation.

[8] Equity income (loss) was reduced by $35 million for Europe, Eurasia & Middle East, $124 million for Latin America and $306 million for Asia, as a result of our Company's portion of nonrecurring charges recorded by equity investees.

[9] Income before income taxes was increased by $118 million for Europe, Eurasia & Middle East as a result of a gain related to the merger of Coca-Cola Beverages plc and Hellenic Bottling Company S.A.

[10] Operating income was reduced by $34 million for North America, $3 million for Africa, $506 million for Europe, Eurasia & Middle East, $35 million for Latin America, $176 million for Asia and $59 million for Corporate related to the other operating charges recorded in the fourth quarter of 1999.

Compound Growth Rates Ending 2001	North America	Africa	Europe, Eurasia & Middle East	Latin America	Asia	Consolidated
Net operating revenues						
5 years	5.5%	4.2%	(5.7)%	2.4%	5.7%	1.9%
10 years	6.1%	10.9%	1.9%	7.6%	9.5%	6.0%
Operating income						
5 years	9.4%	14.1%	1.0%	4.9%	6.6%	6.5%
10 years	9.2%	8.2%	4.9%	10.4%	9.4%	8.8%

┌─────────────────────────────────┐
│ **Report of Independent Auditors** │
└─────────────────────────────────┘

THE COCA-COLA COMPANY AND SUBSIDIARIES

NET OPERATING REVENUES BY OPERATING SEGMENT[1]

OPERATING INCOME BY OPERATING SEGMENT[1]

[1] Charts and percentages are calculated excluding Corporate.

Board of Directors and Share Owners

The Coca-Cola Company

We have audited the accompanying consolidated balance sheets of The Coca-Cola Company and subsidiaries as of December 31, 2001 and 2000, and the related consolidated statements of income, share-owners' equity, and cash flows for flows for each of the three years in the period ended December 31, 2001. These financial statements are the responsibility of the Company's management. Our responsibility is to express an opinion on these financial statements based on our audits.

We conducted our audits in accordance with auditing standards generally accepted in the United States. Those standards require that we plan and perform the audit to obtain reasonable assurance about whether the financial statements are free of material misstatement. An audit includes examining, on a test basis, evidence supporting the amounts and disclosures in the financial statements. An audit also includes assessing the accounting principles used and significant estimates made by management, as well as evaluating the overall financial statement presentation. We believe that our audits provide a reasonable basis for our opinion.

In our opinion, the financial statements referred to above present fairly, in all material respects, the consolidated financial position of The Coca-Cola Company and subsidiaries at December 31, 2001 and 2000, and the consolidated results of their operations and their cash flows for each of the three years in the period ended December 31, 2001, in conformity with accounting principles generally accepted in the United States.

As discussed in Notes 1 and 9 to the Consolidated Financial Statements, in 2001 the Company changed its method of accounting for derivative instruments and hedging activities.

Ernst & Young LLP

Atlanta, Georgia
January 25, 2002

Report of Management

We are responsible for the preparation and integrity of the Consolidated Financial Statements appearing in our Annual Report. The financial statements were prepared in conformity with generally accepted accounting principles appropriate in the circumstances and, accordingly, include certain amounts based on our best judgments and estimates. Financial information in this Annual Report is consistent with that in the financial statements.

We are responsible for maintaining a system of internal accounting controls and procedures to provide reasonable assurance, at an appropriate cost/benefit relationship, that assets are safeguarded and that transactions are authorized, recorded and reported properly. The internal accounting control system is augmented by a program of internal audits and appropriate reviews by management, written policies and guidelines, careful selection and training of qualified personnel and a written Code of Business Conduct adopted by our Company's Board of Directors, applicable to all employees of our Company and our subsidiaries. In our opinion, our Company's internal accounting controls provide reasonable assurance that assets are safeguarded against material loss from unauthorized use or disposition and that the financial records are reliable for preparing financial statements and other data and for maintaining accountability of assets.

The Audit Committee of our Company's Board of Directors, composed solely of Directors who are not officers of our Company, meets with the independent auditors, management and internal auditors periodically to discuss internal accounting controls and auditing and financial reporting matters. The Committee reviews with the independent auditors the scope and results of the audit effort. The Committee also meets periodically with the independent auditors and the chief internal auditor without management present to ensure that the independent auditors and the chief internal auditor have free access to the Committee.

The independent auditors, Ernst & Young LLP, are recommended by the Audit Committee of the Board of Directors, selected by the Board of Directors and ratified by our Company's share owners. Ernst & Young LLP is engaged to audit the Consolidated Financial Statements of The Coca-Cola Company and subsidiaries and conducts such tests and related procedures as it deems necessary in conformity with generally accepted auditing standards. The opinion of the independent auditors, based upon their audits of the Consolidated Financial Statements, is contained in this Annual Report.

Douglas N. Daft
Chairman, Board of Directors,
and Chief Executive Officer

Gary P. Fayard
Senior Vice President
and Chief Financial Officer

Connie D. McDaniel
Vice President
and Controller

February 21, 2002

Quarterly Data (Unaudited)

(In millions except per share data)

Year Ended December 31,	First Quarter	Second Quarter	Third Quarter	Fourth Quarter	Full Year
2001					
Net operating revenues	$ 4,479	$ 5,293	$ 5,397	$ 4,923	$ 20,092
Gross profit	3,134	3,714	3,705	3,495	14,048
Net income	863	1,118	1,074	914	3,969
Basic net income per share	.35	.45	.43	.37	1.60
Diluted net income per share	.35	.45	.43	.37	1.60
2000					
Net operating revenues	$ 4,256	$ 5,487	$ 5,413	$ 4,733	$ 19,889
Gross profit	2,858	3,810	3,677	3,340	13,685
Net income (loss)	(58)	926	1,067	242	2,177
Basic net income (loss) per share	(.02)	.37	.43	.10	.88
Diluted net income (loss) per share	(.02)	.37	.43	.10	.88

The third quarter of 2001 includes a non-cash gain on the issuance of stock by one of our equity investees, Coca-Cola Enterprises, of approximately $91 million ($.02 per share after income taxes, basic and diluted).

The first quarter of 2000 includes other operating charges of approximately $405 million ($.16 per share after income taxes, basic and diluted) primarily related to the impairment of certain bottling, manufacturing and intangible assets. The first quarter of 2000 also includes other operating charges of approximately $275 million ($.08 per share after income taxes, basic and diluted) related to costs associated with the Realignment.

The second quarter of 2000 includes other operating charges of approximately $191 million ($.05 per share after income taxes, basic and diluted) related to costs associated with the Realignment.

The third quarter of 2000 includes a gain of $118 million ($.05 per share after income taxes, basic and diluted) related to the merger of Coca-Cola Beverages and Hellenic Bottling Company S.A. This gain was partially offset by other operating charges of approximately $94 million ($.03 per share after income taxes, basic and diluted) related to costs associated with the Realignment and $30 million ($.01 per share after income taxes, basic and diluted) for incremental marketing expense in Central Europe.

The fourth quarter of 2000 includes other operating charges of approximately $290 million ($.08 per share after income taxes, basic and diluted) related to costs associated with the Realignment. The fourth quarter of 2000 also includes other operating charges of approximately $188 million ($.05 per share after income taxes, basic and diluted) related to the settlement terms of a class action discrimination lawsuit and a donation to The Coca-Cola Foundation. The fourth quarter of 2000 also includes the Company's share of charges recorded by investees of approximately $463 million ($.19 per share after income taxes, basic and diluted).

Effective January 1, 2001, our Company adopted the provisions of EITF Issue No. 00-14, "Accounting for Certain Sales Incentives," and EITF Issue No. 00-22, "Accounting for 'Points' and Certain Other Time-Based or Volume-Based Sales Incentive Offers, and Offers for Free Products or Services to be Delivered in the Future." Both of these EITF Issues provide additional guidance relating to the income statement classification of certain sales incentives. The adoption of these EITF Issues resulted in the Company reducing both net operating revenues and gross profit by $135 million, $134 million, $130 million and $170 million for the first quarter, second quarter, third quarter and fourth quarter of 2000, respectively.

Stock Prices

Below is a summary of the New York Stock Exchange Composite high, low and closing prices of The Coca-Cola Company's stock for each quarter of 2001 and 2000.

	First Quarter	Second Quarter	Third Quarter	Fourth Quarter
2001				
High	$ 62.19	$ 49.35	$ 50.70	$ 50.45
Low	43.76	42.37	43.50	44.01
Close	45.16	45.00	46.85	47.15
2000				
High	$ 66.88	$ 60.88	$ 64.00	$ 63.38
Low	42.88	44.75	49.19	53.50
Close	46.94	57.44	55.13	60.94

Selected Financial Data

THE COCA-COLA COMPANY AND SUBSIDIARIES

	Compound Growth Rates		Year Ended December 31,	
(In millions except per share data, ratios and growth rates)	5 Years	10 Years	2001[2,3]	2000[3]
Summary of Operations				
Net operating revenues	1.9 %	6.0%	$ 20,092	$ 19,889
Cost of goods sold	(2.2)%	2.7%	6,044	6,204
Gross profit	4.0 %	7.8%	14,048	13,685
Selling, administrative and general expenses	3.7 %	7.3%	8,696	8,551
Other operating charges			—	1,443
Operating income	6.5 %	8.8%	5,352	3,691
Interest income			325	345
Interest expense			289	447
Equity income (loss)			152	(289)
Other income (deductions)-net			39	99
Gains on issuances of stock by equity investees			91	—
Income from continuing operations before income taxes and changes in accounting principles	4.3 %	9.1%	5,670	3,399
Income taxes	8.9 %	8.3%	1,691	1,222
Income from continuing operations before changes in accounting principles	2.6 %	9.4%	$ 3,979	$ 2,177
Net income	2.6 %	9.4%	$ 3,969	$ 2,177
Preferred stock dividends			—	—
Net income available to common share owners	2.6 %	9.4%	$ 3,969	$ 2,177
Average common shares outstanding			2,487	2,477
Average common shares outstanding assuming dilution			2,487	2,487
Per Common Share Data				
Income from continuing operations before changes in accounting principles—basic	2.7 %	10.1%	$ 1.60	$ .88
Income from continuing operations before changes in accounting principles—diluted	3.0 %	10.3%	1.60	.88
Basic net income	2.7 %	10.1%	1.60	.88
Diluted net income	3.0 %	10.3%	1.60	.88
Cash dividends	7.6 %	11.6%	.72	.68
Market price on December 31,	(2.2)%	8.9%	47.15	60.94
Total Market Value of Common Stock[1]	(2.1)%	8.2%	$ 117,226	$ 151,421
Balance Sheet and Other Data				
Cash, cash equivalents and current marketable securities			$ 1,934	$ 1,892
Property, plant and equipment-net			4,453	4,168
Depreciation			502	465
Capital expenditures			769	733
Total assets			22,417	20,834
Long-term debt			1,219	835
Total debt			5,118	5,651
Share-owners' equity			11,366	9,316
Total capital[1]			16,484	14,967
Other Key Financial Measures[1]				
Total debt-to-total capital			31.0%	37.8%
Net debt-to-net capital			22.6%	29.4%
Return on common equity			38.5%	23.1%
Return on capital			26.6%	16.2%
Dividend payout ratio			45.1%	77.4%
Free cash flow[9]			$ 3,147	$ 2,806
Economic profit			$ 2,466	$ 861

[1] See Glossary on inside back cover.

[2] In 2001, we adopted SFAS No. 133 "Accounting for Derivative Instruments and Hedging Activities."

[3] In 2001, we adopted EITF Issue No. 00-14 "Accounting for Certain Sales Incentives" and EITF Issue No. 00-22 "Accounting for 'Points' and Certain Other Time-Based or Volume-Based Sales Incentive Offers, and Offers for Free Products or Services to be Delivered in the Future." All prior years were reclassified to conform to the current year presentation.

[4] In 1998, we adopted SFAS No. 132 "Employers Disclosures about Pensions and Other Postretirement Benefits."

THE COCA-COLA COMPANY AND SUBSIDIARIES

1999[3]	1998[3,4]	1997[3,4]	1996[3,4]	1995[3,4]	1994[3,4,5]	1993[3,4,6]	1992[3,4,7,8]	1991[3,4,8]
$ 19,284	$ 18,357	$ 18,462	$ 18,290	$ 17,753	$ 15,845	$ 13,637	$ 12,769	$ 11,272
6,009	5,562	6,015	6,738	6,940	6,168	5,160	5,055	4,649
13,275	12,795	12,447	11,552	10,813	9,677	8,477	7,714	6,623
8,480	7,755	7,386	7,252	6,701	6,040	5,328	4,967	4,301
813	73	60	385	86	—	50	—	13
3,982	4,967	5,001	3,915	4,026	3,637	3,099	2,747	2,309
260	219	211	238	245	181	144	164	175
337	277	258	286	272	199	168	171	192
(184)	32	155	211	169	134	91	65	40
98	230	583	87	86	(25)	7	(59)	51
—	27	363	431	74	—	12	—	—
3,819	5,198	6,055	4,596	4,328	3,728	3,185	2,746	2,383
1,388	1,665	1,926	1,104	1,342	1,174	997	863	765
$ 2,431	$ 3,533	$ 4,129	$ 3,492	$ 2,986	$ 2,554	$ 2,188	$ 1,883	$ 1,618
$ 2,431	$ 3,533	$ 4,129	$ 3,492	$ 2,986	$ 2,554	$ 2,176	$ 1,664	$ 1,618
—	—	—	—	—	—	—	—	1
$ 2,431	$ 3,533	$ 4,129	$ 3,492	$ 2,986	$ 2,554	$ 2,176	$ 1,664	$ 1,617
2,469	2,467	2,477	2,494	2,525	2,580	2,603	2,634	2,666
2,487	2,496	2,515	2,523	2,549	2,599	2,626	2,668	2,695
$ .98	$ 1.43	$ 1.67	$ 1.40	$ 1.18	$ .99	$ .84	$ .72	$ .61
.98	1.42	1.64	1.38	1.17	.98	.83	.71	.60
.98	1.43	1.67	1.40	1.18	.99	.84	.63	.61
.98	1.42	1.64	1.38	1.17	.98	.83	.62	.60
.64	.60	.56	.50	.44	.39	.34	.28	.24
58.25	67.00	66.69	52.63	37.13	25.75	22.31	20.94	20.06
$ 143,969	$ 165,190	$ 164,766	$ 130,575	$ 92,983	$ 65,711	$ 57,905	$ 54,728	$ 53,325
$ 1,812	$ 1,807	$ 1,843	$ 1,658	$ 1,315	$ 1,531	$ 1,078	$ 1,063	$ 1,117
4,267	3,669	3,743	3,550	4,336	4,080	3,729	3,526	2,890
438	381	384	442	421	382	333	310	254
1,069	863	1,093	990	937	878	800	1,083	792
21,623	19,145	16,881	16,112	15,004	13,863	11,998	11,040	10,185
854	687	801	1,116	1,141	1,426	1,428	1,120	985
6,227	5,149	3,875	4,513	4,064	3,509	3,100	3,207	2,288
9,513	8,403	7,274	6,125	5,369	5,228	4,570	3,881	4,236
15,740	13,552	11,149	10,638	9,433	8,737	7,670	7,088	6,524
39.6%	38.0%	34.8%	42.4%	43.1%	40.2%	40.4%	45.2%	35.1%
32.2%	28.1%	22.0%	31.6%	32.3%	25.5%	29.0%	33.1%	24.2%
27.1%	45.1%	61.6%	60.8%	56.4%	52.1%	51.8%	46.4%	41.3%
18.2%	30.2%	39.5%	36.8%	34.9%	32.8%	31.2%	29.4%	27.5%
65.0%	41.9%	33.6%	35.7%	37.2%	39.4%	40.6%	44.3%	39.5%
$ 2,332	$ 1,876	$ 2,951	$ 2,215	$ 2,460	$ 2,356	$ 1,857	$ 875	$ 881
$ 1,128	$ 2,480	$ 3,325	$ 2,718	$ 2,291	$ 1,896	$ 1,549	$ 1,300	$ 1,073

[5] In 1994, we adopted SFAS No. 115 "Accounting for Certain Investments in Debt and Equity Securities."
[6] In 1993, we adopted SFAS No. 112 "Employers' Accounting for Postemployment Benefits."
[7] In 1992, we adopted SFAS No. 106 "Employers' Accounting for Postretirement Benefits Other Than Pensions."
[8] In 1992, we adopted SFAS No. 109 "Accounting for Income Taxes," by restating financial statements beginning in 1989.
[9] All years presented have been restated to exclude net cash flows related to acquisitions

appendix B

List of the Official Pronouncements
of the AICPA and FASB

Listed below are the major official pronouncements of the AICPA and the FASB which have established generally accepted accounting principles or which have had a significant impact upon the establishment of these principles.

Number	Title	Date of Issuance

Accounting Research Bulletins (ARBs), Accounting Procedures Committee, AICPA

43 Restatement and Revision of Accounting Research
Bulletin Nos. 1–42. . . . . June 1953
Chapter
  1 Prior Opinions
  2 Form of Statements
  3 Working Capital
  4 Inventory Pricing
  5 Intangible Assets
  6 Contingency Reserves
  7 Capital Accounts
  8 Income and Earned Surplus
  9 Depreciation
  10 Taxes
  11 Government Contracts
  12 Foreign Operations and Foreign Exchange
  13 Compensation
  14 Disclosure of Long-Term Leases in Financial Statements of Leases
  15 Unamortized Discount, Issue Cost, and Redemption Premium on Bonds Refunded
44 Declining-Balance Depreciation (Revised July 1958). . . . . October 1954
45 Long-Term Construction-Type Contracts . . . . October 1955
46 Discontinuance of Dating Earned Surplus. . . . . February 1956
47 Accounting for Costs of Pension Plans. . . . . September 1956
48 Business Combinations . . . . January 1957
49 Earnings per Share . . . . April 1958
50 Contingencies . . . . October 1958
51 Consolidated Financial Statements . . . . August 1959

Accounting Terminology Bulletins, Committee on Terminology, AICPA

1 Review and Résumé (of eight original terminology bulletins). . . . . August 1953
2 Proceeds, Revenue, Income, Profit, and Earnings . . . . March 1955
3 Book Value. . . . . August 1956
4 Cost, Expense, and Loss . . . . July 1957

Accounting Principles Board (APB) Statements, AICPA

1 Statement by the Accounting Principles Board . . . . April 1962
2 Disclosure of Supplemental Financial Information by Diversified Companies . . . . . . September 1967
3 Financial Statements Restated for General Price-Level Changes. . . . . June 1969
4 Basic Concepts and Accounting Principles Underlying Financial
Statements of Business Enterprises . . . . October 1970

Accounting Principles Board (APB) Opinions, AICPA

1 New Depreciation Guidelines and Rules . . . . November 1962
2 Accounting for the "Investment Credit". . . . . December 1962
3 The Statement of Source and Application of Funds . . . . October 1963
4 Accounting for the "Investment Credit" (Amending No. 2). March 1964
5 Reporting of Leases in Financial Statements of Lessee . . . . September 1964

Number	Title	Date of Issuance

Accounting Principles Board (APB) Opinions, AICPA, Continued

6   Status of Accounting Research Bulletins . . . . October 1965

7   Accounting for Leases in Financial Statements of Lessors . . . . May 1966

8   Accounting for the Cost of Pension Plans . . . . November 1966

9   Reporting the Results of Operations . . . . December 1966

10   Omnibus Opinion—1966 . . . . December 1966

11   Accounting for Income Taxes . . . . December 1967

12   Omnibus Opinion—1967 . . . . December 1967

13   Amending Paragraph 6 of the *APB Opinion No. 9*, Application to Commercial Banks . . March 1969

14   Accounting for Convertible Debt and Debt Issued with Stock Purchase Warrants . . . . . March 1969

15   Earnings per Share . . . . May 1969

16   Business Combinations . . . . August 1970

17   Intangible Assets . . . . August 1970

18   The Equity Method of Accounting for Investments in Common Stock . . . . March 1971

19   Reporting Changes in Financial Position . . . . March 1971

20   Accounting Changes . . . . July 1971

21   Interest on Receivables and Payables . . . . August 1971

22   Disclosure of Accounting Policies . . . . April 1972

23   Accounting for Income Taxes—Special Areas . . . . April 1972

24   Accounting for Income Taxes—Investments in Common Stock Accounted
for by the Equity Method . . . . April 1972

25   Accounting for Stock Issued to Employees . . . . October 1972

26   Early Extinguishment of Debt . . . . October 1972

27   Accounting for Lease Transactions by Manufacturer or Dealer Lessors . . . . November 1972

28   Interim Financial Reporting . . . . May 1973

29   Accounting for Nonmonetary Transactions . . . . May 1973

30   Reporting the Results of Operations—Reporting the Effects of Disposal of a Segment
of a Business, and Extraordinary, Unusual and Infrequently Occurring Events and
Transactions . . . . June 1973

31   Disclosure of Lease Commitments by Lessees . . . . June 1973

Financial Accounting Standards Board (FASB) Statements of Financial Accounting Standards

1   Disclosure of Foreign Currency Translation Information . . . . December 1973

2   Accounting for Research and Development Costs . . . . October 1974

3   Reporting Accounting Changes in Interim Financial Statements
(an amendment of *APB Opinion No. 28*) . . . . December 1974

4   Reporting Gains and Losses from Extinguishment of Debt
(an amendment of *APB Opinion No. 30*) . . . . March 1975

5   Accounting for Contingencies . . . . March 1975

6   Classification of Short-Term Obligations Expected to Be Refinanced
(an amendment of *ARB No. 43*, Chapter 3A) . . . . May 1975

7   Accounting and Reporting by Development Stage Enterprises . . . . June 1975

8   Accounting for the Translation of Foreign Currency Transactions and Foreign
Currency Financial Statements . . . . October 1975

9   Accounting for Income Taxes—Oil and Gas Producing Companies
(an amendment of *APB Opinion Nos. 11* and *23*) . . . . October 1975

10   Extension of "Grandfather" Provisions for Business Combinations
(an amendment of *APB Opinion No. 16*) . . . . October 1975

11   Accounting for Contingencies—Transition Method (an amendment of *FASB
Statement No. 5*) . . . . December 1975

12   Accounting for Certain Marketable Securities . . . . December 1975

13   Accounting for Leases . . . . November 1976

Number	Title	Date of Issuance

Financial Accounting Standards Board (FASB) Statements of Financial Accounting Standards, Continued

14   Financial Reporting for Segments of a Business Enterprise . . . . December 1976

15   Accounting by Debtors and Creditors for Troubled Debt Restructurings . . . . June 1977

16   Prior Period Adjustments . . . . June 1977

17   Accounting for Leases—Initial Direct Costs (an amendment of *FASB
Statement No. 13*) . . . . November 1977

18   Financial Reporting for Segments of a Business Enterprise Interim Financial
Statements (an amendment of *FASB Statement No. 14*) . . . . November 1977

19   Financial Accounting and Reporting by Oil and Gas Producing Companies . . . . . . December 1977

20   Accounting for Forward Exchange Contracts (an amendment of
FASB Statement No. 8) . . . . December 1977

21   Suspension of the Reporting of Earnings per Share and Segment Information by
Nonpublic Enterprises (an amendment of *APB Opinion No. 15* and *FASB Statement
No. 14*). . . . . April 1978

22   Accounting for Leases—Changes in the Provisions of Lease Agreements Resulting
from Refundings of Tax-Exempt Debt (an amendment of *FASB Statement No. 13*) . . . . June 1978

23   Inception of the Lease (an amendment of *FASB Statement No. 13*) . . . . August 1978

24   Reporting Segment Information in Financial Statements That Are Presented in
Another Enterprise's Financial Report (an amendment of
FASB Statement No. 14) . . . . December 1978

25   Suspension of Certain Accounting Requirements for Oil and Gas Companies
(an amendment of *FASB Statement No. 19*). . . . . February 1979

26   Profit Recognition on Sales-Type Leases of Real Estate
(an amendment of *FASB Statement No. 13*) . . . . April 1979

27   Classification of Renewals or Extensions of Existing Sales-Type or Direct
Financing Leases (an amendment of *FASB Statement No. 13*) . . . . May 1979

28   Accounting for Sales with Leasebacks (an amendment of *FASB Statement No. 13*) . . . . . May 1979

29   Determining Contingent Rentals (an amendment of *FASB Statement No. 13*). . . . . June 1979

30   Disclosure of Information About Major Customers (an amendment of *FASB
Statement No. 14*). . . . . August 1979

31   Accounting for Tax Benefits Related to U.K. Tax Legislation Concerning
Stock Relief . . . . September 1979

32   Specialized Accounting and Reporting Principles and Practices in AICPA
Statements of Position and Guides on Accounting and Auditing Matters
(an amendment of *APB Opinion No. 20*) . . . . September 1979

33   Financial Reporting and Changing Prices. . . . . September 1979

34   Capitalization of Interest Cost . . . . October 1979

35   Accounting and Reporting by Defined Benefit Pension Plans . . . . March 1980

36   Disclosure of Pension Information. . . . . May 1980

37   Balance Sheet Classification of Deferred Income Taxes (an amendment of *APB
Opinion No. 11*) . . . . July 1980

38   Accounting for Preacquisition Contingencies of Purchased Enterprises
(an amendment of *APB Opinion No. 16*) . . . . September 1980

39   Financial Reporting and Changing Prices: Specialized Assets—Mining and Oil
and Gas (a supplement to *FASB Statement No. 33*) . . . . October 1980

40   Financial Reporting and Changing Prices: Specialized Assets—Timberlands and
Growing Timber (a supplement to *FASB Statement No. 33*) . . . . November 1980

41   Financial Reporting and Changing Prices: Specialized Assets—Income-Producing
Real Estate (a supplement to *FASB Statement No. 33*) . . . . November 1980

42   Determining Materiality for Capitalization of Interest Cost
(an amendment of *FASB Statement No. 34*). . . . . November 1980

43   Accounting for Compensated Absences . . . . November 1980

Number	Title	Date of Issuance

Financial Accounting Standards Board (FASB) Statements of Financial Accounting Standards, Continued

44 Accounting for Intangible Assets of Motor Carriers (an amendment of Chapter 5
of *ARB No. 43* and an interpretation of *APB Opinion Nos. 17* and *30*) . . . . December 1980

45 Accounting for Franchise Fee Revenue . . . . March 1981

46 Financial Reporting and Changing Prices: Motion Picture Films. . . . . March 1981

47 Disclosure of Long-Term Obligations . . . . March 1981

48 Revenue Recognition When Right of Return Exists . . . . June 1981

49 Accounting for Product Financing Arrangements. . . . . June 1981

50 Financial Reporting in the Record and Music Industry . . . . November 1981

51 Financial Reporting by Cable Television Companies . . . . November 1981

52 Foreign Currency Translation . . . . December 1981

53 Financial Reporting by Producers and Distributors of Motion Picture Films . . . . . . December 1981

54 Financial Reporting and Changing Prices: Investment Companies (an amendment
of *FASB Statement No. 33*) . . . . January 1982

55 Determining Whether a Convertible Security Is a Common Stock Equivalent
(an amendment of *APB Opinion No. 15*) . . . . February 1982

56 Designation of AICPA Guide and Statement of Position (SOP) 81-1 on Contractor
Accounting and SOP 81-2 Concerning Hospital-Related Organizations as Preferable
for Purposes of Applying *APB Opinion 20* (an amendment of *FASB Statement No. 32*). February 1982

57 Related Party Disclosures . . . . March 1982

58 Capitalization of Interest Cost in Financial Statements That Include Investments
Accounted for by the Equity Method . . . . April 1982

59 Deferral of the Effective Date of Certain Accounting Requirements for Pension Plans
of State and Local Governmental Units (an amendment of *FASB Statement No. 35*) . . . April 1982

60 Accounting and Reporting by Insurance Enterprises . . . . June 1982

61 Accounting for Title Plant . . . . June 1982

62 Capitalization of Interest Cost in Situations Involving Certain Tax-Exempt Borrowings
and Certain Gifts and Grants . . . . June 1982

63 Financial Reporting by Broadcasters . . . . June 1982

64 Extinguishments of Debt Made to Satisfy Sinking-Fund Requirements
(an amendment of *FASB Statement No. 4*). . . . . September 1982

65 Accounting for Certain Mortgage Banking Activities. . . . . September 1982

66 Accounting for Sales of Real Estate . . . . October 1982

67 Accounting for Costs and Initial Rental Operations of Real Estate Projects. . . . . . . October 1982

68 Research and Development Arrangements. . . . . October 1982

69 Disclosures about Oil- and Gas-Producing Activities . . . . November 1982

70 Financial Reporting and Changing Prices: Foreign Currency Translation
(an amendment of *FASB Statement No. 33*) . . . . December 1982

71 Accounting for the Effects of Certain Types of Regulation . . . . December 1982

72 Accounting for Certain Acquisitions of Banking or Thrift Institutions
(an amendment of *APB Opinion No. 17*, an interpretation of *APB Opinion Nos. 16*
and *17*, and an amendment of *FASB Statement No. 9*) . . . . February 1983

73 Reporting a Change in Accounting for Railroad Track Structures
(an amendment of *APB Opinion No. 20*). . . . . August 1983

74 Accounting for Special Termination Benefits Paid to Employees . . . . August 1983

75 Deferral of the Effective Date of Certain Accounting Requirements for
Pension Plans of State and Local Governmental Units (an amendment of
FASB Statement No. 35) . . . . November 1983

76 Extinguishment of Debt (an amendment of *APB Opinion No. 26*) . . . . November 1983

77 Reporting by Transferors for Transfers of Receivables with Recourse . . . . December 1983

78 Classification of Obligations That Are Callable by the Creditor
(an amendment of *ARB No. 43*, Chapter 3A). . . . . December 1983

Number	Title	Date of Issuance

Financial Accounting Standards Board (FASB) Statements of Financial Accounting Standards, Continued

79 Elimination of Certain Disclosures for Business Combinations by Nonpublic
Enterprises (an amendment of *APB Opinion No. 16*) . . . . February 1984

80 Accounting for Futures Contracts . . . . August 1984

81 Disclosure of Postretirement Health Care and Life Insurance Benefits . . . . November 1984

82 Financial Reporting and Changing Prices: Elimination of Certain Disclosures
(an amendment of *FASB Statement No. 33*) . . . . December 1984

83 Designation of AICPA Guides and Statement of Position on Accounting by Brokers
and Dealers in Securities, by Employee Benefit Plans, and by Banks as Preferable
for Purposes of Applying *APB Opinion No. 20* . . . . March 1985

84 Induced Conversions of Convertible Debt (an amendment of *APB Opinion No. 26*) . . March 1985

85 Yield Test for Determining Whether a Convertible Security Is a Common Stock
Equivalent (an amendment of *APB Opinion No. 15*) . . . . March 1985

86 Accounting for the Costs of Computer Software to Be Sold, Leased, or Otherwise
Marketed . . . . August 1985

87 Employers' Accounting for Pensions. . . . . December 1985

88 Employers' Accounting for Settlements and Curtailments of Defined Benefit
Pension Plans and for Termination Benefits . . . . December 1985

89 Financial Reporting and Changing Prices . . . . December 1986

90 Regulated Enterprises—Accounting for Abandonments and Disallowances of
Plant Costs (an amendment of *FASB Statement No. 71*). December 1986

91 Accounting for Nonrefundable Fees and Costs Associated with Originating or
Acquiring Loans and Initial Direct Costs of Leases . . . . December 1986

92 Regulated Enterprises—Accounting for Phase-in Plans (an amendment of
FASB Statement No. 71) . . . . August 1987

93 Recognition of Depreciation by Not-for-Profit Organizations . . . . August 1987

94 Consolidation of All Majority-Owned Subsidiaries (an amendment of *ARB No. 51*,
with related amendments of *APB Opinion No. 18* and *ARB No. 43*, Chapter 12). . . October 1987

95 Statement of Cash Flows . . . . November 1987

96 Accounting for Income Taxes . . . . December 1987

97 Accounting and Reporting by Insurance Enterprises for Certain Long-Duration
Contracts and for Realized Gains and Losses from the Sale of Investments. . . . . . . December 1987

98 Accounting for Leases: Sale-Leaseback Transactions Involving Real Estate,
Sales-Type Leases of Real Estate, Definition of the Lease Term, and Initial
Direct Costs of Direct Financing Leases (an amendment of *FASB Statement
Nos. 13, 66, and 91* and a rescission of *FASB Statement No. 26* and
Technical Bulletin No. 79-11). . . . . May 1988

99 Deferral of the Effective Date of Recognition of Depreciation by Not-for-Profit
Organizations (an amendment of *FASB Statement No. 93*) . . . . September 1988

100 Accounting for Income Taxes—Deferral of the Effective Date of
FASB Statement No. 96 (an amendment of *FASB Statement No. 96*). . . . . December 1988

101 Regulated Enterprises—Accounting for the Discontinuation of Application of
FASB Statement No. 71 . . . . December 1988

102 Statement of Cash Flows—Exemption of Certain Enterprises and Classification of
Cash Flows from Certain Securities Acquired for Resale (an amendment of
FASB Statement No. 95) . . . . February 1989

103 Accounting for Income Taxes—Deferral of the Effective Date of
FASB Statement No. 96 (an amendment of *FASB Statement No. 96*). . . . . December 1989

104 Statement of Cash Flows—Net Reporting of Certain Cash Receipts and Cash
Payments and Classification of Cash Flows from Hedging Transactions
(an amendment of *FASB Statement No. 95*) . . . . December 1989

105 Disclosure of Information about Financial Instruments with Off-Balance-Sheet
Risk and Financial Instruments with Concentrations of Credit Risk . . . . March 1990

Number	Title	Date of Issuance

Financial Accounting Standards Board (FASB) Statements of Financial Accounting Standards, Continued

106 Employers' Accounting for Postretirement Benefits Other Than Pensions . . . . December 1990

107 Disclosure about Fair Value of Financial Instruments. . . . . December 1991

108 Accounting for Income Taxes—Deferral of the Effective Date of *FASB Statement No. 96* (an amendment of *FASB Statement No. 96*). . . . . December 1991

109 Accounting for Income Taxes. . . . . February 1992

110 Reporting by Defined Benefit Pension Plans of Investment Contracts (an amendment of *FASB Statement No. 35*). . . . . August 1992

111 Rescission of *FASB Statement No. 32* and Technical Corrections . . . . November 1992

112 Employers' Accounting for Postemployment Benefits (an amendment of *FASB Statement Nos. 5 and 43*). . . . . November 1992

113 Accounting and Reporting for Reinsurance of Short-Term and Long-Term Contracts . . . . December 1992

114 Accounting by Creditors for Impairment of a Loan (an amendment of *FASB Statement Nos. 5 and 15*). . . . . May 1993

115 Accounting for Certain Investments in Debt and Equity Securities. . . . . May 1993

116 Accounting for Contributions Received and Contributions Made . . . . June 1993

117 Financial Statements of Not-for-Profit Organizations. . . . . June 1993

118 Accounting by Creditors for Impairment of a Loan—Income Recognition and Disclosures (an amendment of *FASB Statement No. 114*). . . . . October 1994

119 Disclosure about Derivative Financial Instruments and Fair Value of Financial Instruments . . . . October 1994

120 Accounting and Reporting by Mutual Life Insurance Enterprises and by Insurance Enterprises for Certain Long-Duration Participating Contracts (an amendment of *FASB Statements No. 60, 97, and 113 and Interpretation No. 40*). . . . . January 1995

121 Accounting for the Impairment of Long-Lived Assets and for Long-Lived Assets to Be Disposed Of . . . . March 1995

122 Accounting for Mortgage Servicing Rights (an amendment of *FASB Statement No. 65*). . . . . May 1995

123 Accounting for Stock-Based Compensation . . . . October 1995

124 Accounting for Certain Investments Held by Not-for-Profit Organizations. . . . . . . November 1995

125 Accounting for Transfers and Servicing of Financial Assets and Extinguishments of Liabilities. . . . . June 1996

126 Exemption from Certain Required Disclosures about Financial Instruments for Certain Nonpublic Entities (an amendment of *FASB Statement No. 107*). . . . . December 1996

127 Deferral of the Effective Date of Certain Provisions of FASB Statement No. 125 (an amendment of *FASB Statement No. 125*). . . . . December 1996

128 Earnings per Share . . . . February 1997

129 Disclosure of Information about Capital Structure . . . . February 1997

130 Reporting Comprehensive Income . . . . June 1997

131 Disclosures about Segments of an Enterprise and Related Information. . . . . June 1997

132 Employers' Disclosures about Pensions and Other Postretirement Benefits (an amendment of *FASB Statements No. 87, 88, and 106*). . . . . February 1998

133 Accounting for Derivative Instruments and Hedging Activities . . . . June 1998

134 Accounting for Mortgage-Backed Securities Retained after the Securitization of Mortgage Loans Held for Sale by a Mortgage Banking Enterprise (an amendment of FASB Statement No. 65). . . . . October 1998

135 Rescission of FASB Statement No. 75 and Technical Corrections . . . . February 1999

136 Transfers of Asset to a Not-for-Profit Organization or Charitable Trust That Raises or Holds Contributions for Others . . . . June 1999

137 Accounting for Derivative Instruments and Hedging Activities–Deferral of the Effective Date of *FASB Statement No. 133* (an amendment of *FASB Statement No. 133*). . . . . June 1999

Number	Title	Date of Issuance

Financial Accounting Standards Board (FASB) Statements of Financial Accounting Standards, Continued

138 Accounting for Certain Derivative Instruments and Certain Hedging Activities
(an amendment of *FASB Statement No. 133*) . . . . June 2000

139 Rescission of *FASB Statement No. 53* and amendments to *FASB Statements
No. 63, 89, and 121* . . . . June 2000

140 Accounting for Transfers and Servicing of Financial Assets and Extinguishments
of Liabilities (a replacement of *FASB Statement No. 125*) . . . . September 2000

141 Business Combinations. . . . . June 2001

142 Goodwill and Other Intangible Assets . . . . June 2001

143 Accounting for Asset Retirement Obligations . . . . June 2001

144 Accounting for the Impairment or Disposal of Long-Lived Assets . . . . August 2001

145 Rescission of *FASB Statements No. 4, 44, and 64*, Amendment of *FASB Statement
No. 13*, and Technical Corrections. . . . . April 2002

146 Accounting for Costs Associated with Exit or Disposal Activities . . . . July 2002

147 Acquisitions of Certain Financial Institutions. . . . . October 2002

Financial Accounting Standards Board (FASB) Statements of Financial Accounting Concepts

1 Objectives of Financial Reporting by Business Enterprises . . . . November 1978

2 Qualitative Characteristics of Accounting Information. May 1980

3 Elements of Financial Statements of Business Enterprises . . . . December 1980

4 Objectives of Financial Reporting by Nonbusiness Organizations . . . . December 1980

5 Recognition and Measurement in Financial Statements of Business Enterprises . . . . . December 1984

6 Elements of Financial Statements (a replacement of *FASB Concepts Statement No. 3*,
incorporating an amendment of *FASB Concepts Statement No. 2*). . . . . December 1985

7 Using Cash Flow Information and Present Value in Accounting Measurements . . . . . February 2000

Financial Accounting Standards Board (FASB) Interpretations

1 Accounting Changes Related to the Cost of Inventory (an interpretation of *APB
Opinion No. 20*). . . . . June 1974

2 Imputing Interest on Debt Arrangements Made under the Federal Bankruptcy Act
(an interpretation of *APB Opinion No. 21*) . . . . June 1974

3 Accounting for the Cost of Pension Plans Subject to the Employee Retirement
Income Security Act of 1974 (an interpretation of *APB Opinion No. 8*). . . . . December 1974

4 Applicability of *FASB Statement No. 2* to Business Combinations Accounted for by
the Purchase Method. . . . . February 1975

5 Applicability of *FASB Statement No. 2* to Development Stage Enterprises . . . . February 1975

6 Applicability of *FASB Statement No. 2* to Computer Software . . . . February 1975

7 Applying *FASB Statement No. 7* in Financial Statements of Established
Operating Enterprises. . . . . October 1975

8 Classification of a Short-Term Obligation Repaid Prior to Being Replaced by a
Long-Term Security (an interpretation of *FASB Statement No. 6*). . . . . January 1976

9 Applying *APB Opinion Nos. 16 and 17* When a Savings and Loan Association
or a Similar Institution Is Acquired in a Business Combination Accounted for
by the Purchase Method . . . . February 1976

10 Application of *FASB Statement No. 12* to Personal Financial Statements. . . . . September 1976

11 Changes in Market Value after the Balance Sheet Date (an interpretation of
FASB Statement No. 12) . . . . September 1976

12 Accounting for Previously Established Allowance Accounts (an interpretation
of *FASB Statement No. 12*) . . . . September 1976

13 Consolidation of a Parent and Its Subsidiaries Having Different Balance Sheets
Dates (an interpretation of *FASB Statement No. 12*) . . . . September 1976

Number	Title	Date of Issuance

Financial Accounting Standards Board (FASB) Interpretations, Continued

14 Reasonable Estimation of the Amount of a Loss (an interpretation of *FASB Statement No. 5*) . . . . September 1976

15 Translation of Unamortized Policy Acquisition Costs by a Stock Life Insurance Company (an interpretation of *FASB Statement No. 8*) . . . . September 1976

16 Clarification of Definitions and Accounting for Marketable Equity Securities That Become Nonmarketable (an interpretation of *FASB Statement No. 12*) . . . . February 1977

17 Applying the Lower of Cost or Market Rule in Translated Financial Statements (an interpretation of *FASB Statement No. 8*) . . . . February 1977

18 Accounting for Income Taxes in Interim Periods (an interpretation of *APB Opinion No. 28*) . . . . March 1977

19 Lessee Guarantee of the Residual Value of Leased Property (an interpretation of *FASB Statement No. 13*) . . . . October 1977

20 Reporting Accounting Changes under AICPA Statements of Position (an interpretation of *APB Opinion No. 20*) . . . . November 1977

21 Accounting for Leases in a Business Combination (an interpretation of *FASB Statement No. 13*) . . . . April 1978

22 Applicability of Indefinite Reversal Criteria to Timing Differences (an interpretation of *APB Opinion Nos. 11 and 23*) . . . . April 1978

23 Leases & Certain Property Owned by a Governmental Unit or Authority (an interpretation of *FASB Statement No. 13*) . . . . August 1978

24 Lease Involving Only Part of a Building (an interpretation of *FASB Statement No. 13*) . . . . September 1978

25 Accounting for an Unused Investment Tax Credit (an interpretation of *APB Opinion Nos. 2, 4, 11, and 16*) . . . . September 1978

26 Accounting for Purchase of a Leased Asset by the Lessee during the Term of the Lease (an interpretation of *FASB Statement No. 13*) . . . . September 1978

27 Accounting for a Loss on a Sublease (an interpretation of *FASB Statement No. 13*) . . . . November 1978

28 Accounting for Stock Appreciation Rights and Other Variable Stock Option or Award Plans (an interpretation of *APB Opinion Nos. 15 and 25*) . . . . . . December 1978

29 Reporting Tax Benefits Realized on Disposition of Investments in Certain Subsidiaries and Other Investees (an interpretation of *APB Opinion Nos. 23 and 24*) . . . . February 1979

30 Accounting for Involuntary Conversions of Nonmonetary Assets to Monetary Assets (an interpretation of *APB Opinion No. 29*) . . . . September 1979

31 Treatment of Stock Compensation Plans in EPS Computations (an interpretation of *APB Opinion No. 15* and a modification of *FASB Interpretation No. 28*) . . . . February 1980

32 Application of Percentage Limitations in Recognizing Investment Tax Credit (an interpretation of *APB Opinion Nos. 2, 4, and 11*) . . . . March 1980

33 Applying *FASB Statement No. 34* to Oil and Gas Producing Operations Accounted for by the Full Cost Method (an interpretation of *FASB Statement No. 34*) . . . . August 1980

34 Disclosure of Indirect Guarantees of Indebtedness of Others (an interpretation of *FASB Statement No. 5*) . . . . March 1981

35 Criteria for Applying the Equity Method of Accounting for Investments in Common Stock (an interpretation of *APB Opinion No. 18*) . . . . May 1981

36 Accounting for Exploratory Wells in Progress at the End of a Period (an interpretation of *FASB Statement No. 19*) . . . . October 1981

37 Accounting for Translation Adjustments Upon Sale of Part of an Investment in a Foreign Entity (an interpretation of *FASB Statement No. 52*) . . . . July 1983

38 Determining the Measurement Date for Stock Option, Purchase, and Award Plans Involving Junior Stock (an interpretation of *APB Opinion No. 25*) . . . . August 1984

39 Offsetting of Amounts Related to Certain Contracts (an interpretation of *APB Opinion No. 10* and *FASB Statement No. 105*) . . . . March 1992

	Date of
Number	***Title***	***Issuance***

Financial Accounting Standards Board (FASB) Interpretations, Continued

40 Applicability of Generally Accepted Accounting Principles to Mutual Life
    Insurance and Other Enterprises (an interpretation of *FASB
    Statement Nos. 12, 60, 97, and 113*) . . . . April 1993

41 Offsetting of Amounts Related to Certain Repurchase and Reverse
    Repurchase Agreements (an interpretation of *APB Opinion No. 10*
    and a modification of *FASB Interpretation No. 39*) . . . . December 1994

42 Accounting for Transfers of Assets in Which a Not-for-Profit
    Organization Is Granted Variance Power (an interpretation of
    FASB Statement No. 116) . . . . September 1996

43 Real Estate Sales (an interpretation of *FASB Statement No. 66*) . . . . June 1999

44 Accounting for Certain Transactions involving Stock Compensation
    (an interpretation of *APB Opinion No. 25*). . . . . March 2000

45 Guarantor's Accounting and Disclosure Requirements for Guarantees, Including
    Indirect Guarantees of Indebtedness of Others . . . . November 2002

appendix C

Review of the Accounting Process

objectives

1   Understand the components of an accounting system.

2   Know the major steps in the accounting cycle.

3   Prepare journal entries in the general journal.

4   Post to the general ledger and prepare a trial balance.

5   Prepare adjusting entries.

6   Prepare financial statements.

7   Prepare closing entries.

8   Complete a worksheet.

9   Understand subsidiary ledgers.

10   Use special journals.

11   Convert cash-basis financial statements to accrual-basis.

A primary objective of financial reporting is to provide information that is useful to present and potential investors, and to creditors and other users in making rational investment, credit, and similar decisions.[1] A company provides this information in its financial statements and the accompanying notes. These statements are the result of a complex financial accounting process which we discuss throughout this book. To understand financial accounting, it is necessary to be familiar with the accounting system that a company uses to accumulate the information in its financial statements. This system is the topic of this Appendix.

THE ACCOUNTING SYSTEM

Although a major purpose of a company's accounting system is to provide useful information to external users, much accounting information is also useful to the company's managers for making operating decisions. Many transactions result in important financial and managerial accounting information. **An accounting system is the means by which a company records and stores the financial and managerial information from its transactions so that it can retrieve and report the information in an accounting statement.** All companies have accounting systems, ranging from the very simple, such as a checkbook, to the very complex, involving the use of networked computers.

1 Understand the components of an accounting system.

The intent in this Appendix is to present the basics of a *financial* accounting system that a company can use in either a manual or a computer accounting process. For convenience, our discussion is primarily in terms of a manual system. The components of an accounting system include (1) the framework for operation of the system, (2) the input source documents, (3) the records used to store accounting information, and (4) the output reports. We discuss each of these components in subsequent sections.

Accounting Equation

A company's financial accounting recording process involves (1) identifying the events occurring within its economic environment that are financial transactions, (2) gathering the documents related to these transactions, (3) analyzing the documents to determine the relevant financial information to be recorded, (4) recording the financial information, and (5) storing this information for future retrieval and use. A basic accounting model provides a framework for the accounting system and serves as the basis for recording transactions. This model for a corporation, called the **residual equity theory** model, is usually expressed in an equation as follows:

Assets = Liabilities + Stockholders' Equity

where **assets** are defined as the corporation's economic resources, **liabilities** are its obligations owed to creditors, and **stockholders' equity** is the owners' residual interest in its assets. This equation must remain in balance at all times because each side presents a different "picture" of the same information. That is, the left side summarizes the corporation's economic resources while the right side summarizes the sources of (or claims upon) the economic resources. There are several other interrelated equations pertaining to information desired by external users that evolve from this basic equation. We show these equations in Exhibit C-1.

Contributed capital includes the amounts of stockholder investments resulting from the sale of shares of stock by the corporation, while **retained earnings** is the lifetime amount of net income reinvested in the corporation and not distributed to stockholders.[2] **Dividends** (which are *not* expenses) are the amounts distributed to stockholders as a return on their investment. **Revenues** are charges to customers for goods or services

---

1. "Objectives of Financial Reporting by Business Enterprises," *FASB Statement of Financial Accounting Concepts No. 1* (Stamford, Conn.: FASB, 1978), par. 34.
2. A company may also have accumulated other comprehensive income which we discuss in Chapters 3 and 4.

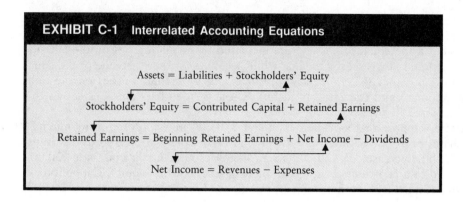

EXHIBIT C-1 Interrelated Accounting Equations

Assets = Liabilities + Stockholders' Equity

Stockholders' Equity = Contributed Capital + Retained Earnings

Retained Earnings = Beginning Retained Earnings + Net Income − Dividends

Net Income = Revenues − Expenses

provided and **expenses** are the costs incurred by the corporation to provide the goods or services.[3]

Transactions, Events, and Supporting Documents

For financial accounting purposes, a change in a company's economic resources (assets), obligations (liabilities), or residual interest (stockholders' equity) may be caused by a transaction or an event. A **transaction** involves the transfer of something valuable between the company and another party. An **event** is a happening of consequence to the company. The event may be *internal*, such as using equipment in operations, or *external*, such as a decline in price (fair value). The company records the transactions and events affecting its economic resources and obligations in its accounting system. The company uses business documents, or **source documents,** relating to these transactions and events as initial input information for the recording process. These documents (such as sales invoices, checks, and freight bills) normally contain information about the monetary amount to be recorded, the parties involved, the terms of the transactions, and other relevant information. After the company records a transaction or event, it stores the supporting source documents to verify and substantiate its accounting records.

Accounts

Within the accounting system, **a company uses accounts to store the recorded monetary information from its transactions and events.** It maintains a separate account for each asset, liability, revenue, expense, and other stockholders' equity item. Examples of these accounts include Cash, Accounts Receivable (amounts due from customers), Buildings, Accounts Payable (amounts owed to suppliers), Mortgage Payable, Sales Revenue, Salaries Expense, Purchases, Capital Stock, Retained Earnings, and Dividends Distributed. Each account is assigned a number in the company's **chart of accounts,** a numbering system designed to organize the accounts efficiently and to minimize errors in the recording process.

An account can be in several physical forms. It might be a location on a computer disk or a standardized business form in a manual system. A single logical format is used for all accounts. The format for the accounts in a manual system is called a *T-account*. Each T-account has a left (or *debit*) and a right (or *credit*) side for storing monetary information. Since each account accumulates information about both increases and decreases resulting from various transactions or events, there is a "double-entry" rule that standardizes the method of recording these changes. **In the double-entry system, for each transaction or event that a company records, the total dollar amount of the debits entered in all the related accounts must be equal to the total dollar amount of the credits.**

---

3. In this Appendix, for simplicity, we include *gains*, (those revenues from other than the sale of goods or services) in revenues and we include *losses* (those costs incurred that provide no revenues) in expenses. Throughout the book, we discuss and classify gains and losses separately from revenues and expenses.

The framework of an accounting system includes the accounts in the basic accounting equation as well as the double-entry system. In an accounting system, all accounts on the left side of the equation (assets) are increased by debits (entries on the left side of the accounts) and decreased by credits, while accounts on the right side of the equation (liabilities and stockholders' equity) are increased by credits (entries on the right side of the accounts) and decreased by debits. The left side of Exhibit C-2 shows this relationship.

To illustrate, suppose that stockholders invest $20,000 in a corporation by purchasing 2,000 shares of its no-par stock at $10 per share. The corporation records this transaction as a debit (increase) of $20,000 to an asset account, Cash, and as a $20,000 credit (increase) to a contributed capital account in stockholders' equity, Capital Stock. Note that the accounting equation remains in balance (both sides increase by $20,000) and that the total debits equal the total credits.

	Assets	=	Liabilities	+	Stockholders' Equity	

Cash		Capital Stock	
(debit)			(credit)
20,000			20,000

Accounts are classified as **permanent** (or real) accounts and **temporary** (or nominal) accounts. The permanent accounts are the asset, liability, and stockholders' equity accounts whose balances at the *end* of the accounting period are carried forward into the next accounting period. The accounts on the far right of Exhibit C-2, namely the revenue, expense, and dividend accounts, are temporary accounts. They are "temporarily" used to determine the changes in retained earnings that occur *during* an accounting period, and their account balances are *not* carried forward into the next period. Exhibit C-2 also shows the rules for recording transactions in temporary accounts. Because an increase in revenues causes an increase in retained earnings, the rules for recording transactions in revenue accounts are the same as those for retained earnings. However, because an increase in temporary accounts such as expenses and dividends causes a decrease in retained earnings, the rules for recording transactions in these accounts are the opposite of those for retained earnings.[4] For instance, since the

---

EXHIBIT C-2   **Accounting Equation and Double-Entry System**

Permanent Accounts					Temporary Accounts	

Assets	=	Liabilities	+	Stockholders' Equity	

Asset Accounts		Liability Accounts		Capital Stock Accounts		Revenue Accounts	
(debit)	(credit)	(debit)	(credit)	(debit)	(credit)	(debit)	(credit)
Increase	Decrease	Decrease	Increase	Decrease	Increase	Decrease	Increase

Retained Earnings		Expense Accounts	
(debit)	(credit)	(debit)	(credit)
Decrease	Increase	Increase	Decrease

Dividend Accounts	
(debit)	(credit)
Increase	Decrease

---

4.   Since *gains* are similar to revenues and *losses* are similar to expenses, the rules for increasing these accounts are the same as those for revenues and expenses, respectively.

payment of dividends reduces retained earnings, an increase in a Dividends account is recorded as a debit.

In certain instances a company will use a **contra** (or negative) account to emphasize a reduction in a related account. The rules for increasing or decreasing a contra account are also exactly the *opposite* of those for the related account. A contra account may be related to a permanent account or to a temporary account. For instance, a company uses a Sales Discounts Taken account to accumulate the cash discounts taken by customers on Sales Revenues, while it uses an Accumulated Depreciation account to accumulate the depreciation recorded for Buildings. We illustrate contra accounts in a later section.

The balance of an account on a particular date is the difference between the total debits and credits recorded in that account. A company uses these balances in the preparation of its financial statements.

Financial Statements

A company's financial statements are output summary reports of its accounting system. These statements are derived from the interrelated equations presented earlier. The major financial statements of a company include (1) the income statement, (2) the balance sheet (alternatively called the statement of financial position), and (3) the statement of cash flows.[5] A company prepares its financial statements at the end of each fiscal year, called the **accounting period**. The set of financial statements and accompanying supporting schedules and notes, along with other information distributed to the various external users, is called the company's **annual report**. Financial statements are often prepared for a shorter time period, such as three months; these are called **interim** (or quarterly) statements.

The income statement summarizes the results of a company's income-producing activities for the accounting period. In the income statement, the company's net income is determined by subtracting the total expenses from the total revenues. A supporting schedule (statement) is usually prepared to tie the income statement to the balance sheet. **The statement of retained earnings summarizes the amount of a company's net income retained in the business.** This procedure involves adding the current net income to the balance in the retained earnings account at the beginning of the period and subtracting the dividends distributed to stockholders.

The balance sheet summarizes the amounts of a company's assets, liabilities, and stockholders' equity on a particular date. The stockholders' equity section includes the ending retained earnings balance from the statement of retained earnings. The balance sheet is so named because it is an expansion of the basic accounting equation, which always remains in balance. Because of the "linkage" between the income statement, statement of retained earnings, and balance sheet due to net income and retained earnings, these financial statements are said to be **articulated.** We illustrate these statements later as part of a comprehensive example in Exhibits C-8, C-9, and C-10.

The third major statement, **the statement of cash flows, summarizes a company's cash receipts and cash payments during the accounting period.** It is not illustrated here but we briefly discuss it in Chapter 3 and more fully in Chapter 21. The statement of cash flows articulates with the balance sheet because it reconciles the beginning cash balance with the ending cash balance. We also discuss other supporting schedules, such as the schedule of changes in stockholders' equity and the schedule of investing and financing activities not involving cash receipts or cash payments, in Chapters 3 and 21.

THE ACCOUNTING CYCLE

A company completes a series of steps during each accounting period to record, store, and report the accounting information contained in its transactions. These steps are

2 Know the major steps in the accounting cycle.

---

5. Some companies also have a fourth major financial statement for reporting their "comprehensive income." We discuss this topic in Chapters 3 and 4.

referred to as the **accounting cycle**. The *major* steps include: (1) recording daily transactions in a journal, (2) posting the journal entries to the accounts in the ledger, (3) preparing and posting adjusting entries, (4) preparing the financial statements, and (5) preparing and posting closing entries for the revenue, expense, and dividend accounts.

Recording in the General Journal (Step 1)

A journal is called a "document of original entry" because a company initially records its transactions (and events) here. A company *could* record all its transactions in a single journal, called the **general** journal. However, many companies have a number of different **special** journals, each designed to record a particular type of transaction. We briefly discuss special journals in a later section of this Appendix.

The general journal consists of a date column, a column to list the accounts affected by each transaction, a column to list the account numbers (to save space, we do *not* use account numbers in the subsequent comprehensive illustration), and a debit column and a credit column to list the amounts recorded as a debit or credit to each account. Just below each journal entry is a written explanation of the transaction. **The process of recording the transaction in the journal is called journalizing. The resulting entry is referred to as a journal entry.** We show an example of a general journal in Exhibit C-4 later in this Appendix.

There are a number of advantages to using a general journal (and special journals). First, it helps prevent errors. Because the accounts and debit and credit amounts for each transaction are initially recorded on a single journal page, rather than directly in the numerous accounts, it is easier to verify the equality of the debits and credits. Second, all the transactional information (including the explanation) is recorded in one place, thereby providing a complete "picture" of the transaction. This is especially useful during the auditing process, or if an error is discovered later in the accounting cycle, because the general journal can be reviewed to determine the nature of the transaction. Finally, since the transactions are recorded as they occur, the journal provides a chronological record of the company's financial transactions.

To illustrate the entire accounting cycle, we present a comprehensive illustration throughout this section. Dapple Corporation incorporates on January 1, 2004 as a wholesaler. It purchases one type of product from suppliers and resells this inventory to commercial customers. It opens for business on April 1, 2004. The company uses a **periodic inventory system;** that is, it takes a physical inventory at the end of the accounting period. The company *derives* its **cost of goods sold** (a major operating expense) at the end of the period by computing the cost of goods available for sale (beginning inventory plus purchases of inventory during the period) and subtracting the amount of the ending inventory. Under this system the company does not know either the cost of inventory on hand or the cost of goods sold until the end of the accounting period.[6] During 2004 the company engages in several transactions. Exhibit C-3 lists these transactions and an analysis of the accounts and amounts to be debited and credited. Some of these transactions are partially condensed and overly simplified so that we may illustrate a variety of transactions.

Based on the transactional analysis listed in Exhibit C-3, the general journal entries shown in Exhibit C-4 are prepared. Traditionally, for each entry, the accounts to be

3 Prepare journal entries in the general journal.

---

6. Alternatively, a company could use a **perpetual inventory system.** Here the inventory records are continuously updated for the goods purchased and sold. When the company purchases merchandise, it records the increase (debit) directly in its Inventory account. At the time of each sale of merchandise, in addition to recording the sale the company also records an increase (debit) in a Cost of Goods Sold *expense* account and a decrease (credit) in the Inventory account. This inventory system is more expensive to operate than the periodic system, but it enables a company to plan more accurately and to control the amounts of its inventory and cost of goods sold on a continuous basis. We discuss both the perpetual and periodic inventory systems in Chapter 7.

EXHIBIT C-3 2004 Transactions and Analyses (Dapple Corporation)

Date	Transaction	Analysis
01/01	Various stockholders invest in Dapple by purchasing 2,000 shares of no-par stock at $10 per share.	Asset account Cash increased (debited) by $20,000; stockholders' equity account Capital Stock increased (credited) by $20,000.
01/16	Dapple purchases 2 acres of land as a building site, paying $1,500 an acre.	Asset account Land increased (debited) by $3,000; asset account Cash decreased (credited) by $3,000.
03/30	A building is built and equipment purchased for $15,320 and $2,120, respectively. Dapple pays $10,840 and signs a 12% note (interest and principal to be paid after 2 years) for the $6,600 balance.	Asset accounts Building and Equipment increased (debited) by $15,320 and $2,120, respectively; asset account Cash decreased (credited) by $10,840; liability account Notes Payable increased (credited) by $6,600.
03/30	Dapple purchases a 1-year comprehensive insurance policy for $360.	Asset account Prepaid Insurance increased (debited) by $360; asset account Cash decreased (credited) by $360.
03/31	Dapple purchases $7,400 of inventory on account. Supplier (Bark Company) allows a $100 cash discount if paid within 10 days.	Cost-of-goods-sold expense account* Purchases increased (debited) by $7,400; liability account Accounts Payable increased (credited) by $7,400.
04/02	Dapple sells inventory at total cash selling price of $8,000.	Asset account Cash increased (debited) by $8,000; revenue account Sales Revenue increased (credited) by $8,000.
04/08	Dapple pays $7,300 to Bark for inventory purchased on 03/31.	Liability account Accounts Payable decreased (debited) by $7,400; contra-purchases account Purchases Discounts Taken increased (credited) by $100; asset account Cash decreased (credited) by $7,300.
04/15	A customer returns defective items purchased on 02/02 and is given a $250 refund.	Contra-revenue account Sales Returns and Allowances increased (debited) by $250; asset account Cash decreased (credited) by $250.
04/20	Dapple returns defective inventory to its supplier and receives a $160 cash refund.	Asset account Cash increased (debited) by $160; contra-purchases account Purchases Returns and Allowances increased (credited) by $160.
07/15	Dapple makes $3,100 cash purchase of inventory and pays $200 of associated freight charges.	Cost-of-goods-sold expense accounts* Purchases and Freight-in increased (debited) by $3,100 and $200, respectively; asset account Cash decreased (credited) by $3,300.
09/01	Dapple sells one acre of land (original cost $1,500) for $1,320. It accepts a 6-month, 15% note from buyer.	Asset account Notes Receivable increased (debited) by $1,320; loss account Loss on Sale of Land increased (debited) by $180; asset account Land decreased (credited) by $1,500.
10/01	Dapple pays the first 6 months' salaries (April through September) totaling $1,800 to employees.	Expense account Salaries Expense increased (debited) by $1,800; asset account Cash decreased (credited) by $1,800.
11/23	Dapple makes sales on account of $5,000 to Frank Company and $4,000 to Knox Company. Terms of the sale are 2/10, n/60 (2% discount allowed if accounts paid within 10 days, total amount due in 60 days).	Asset account Accounts Receivable increased (debited) by $9,000; revenue account Sales Revenue increased (credited) by $9,000.
12/01	Dapple rents part of its building to Fritz Company, receiving 3 months' rent in advance at $150 per month.	Asset account Cash increased (debited) by $450; liability account Unearned Rent increased (credited) by $450.
12/02	Dapple collects $2,000 of accounts receivable from Frank Company. Frank takes a cash discount of $40, remitting the remaining $1,960.	Asset account Cash increased (debited) by $1,960; contra-revenue account Sales Discounts Taken increased (debited) by $40; asset account Accounts Receivable decreased (credited) by $2,000.
12/27	Dapple purchases $1,900 of inventory on account from the Ajax Company. Supplier pays the freight charges.	Cost-of-goods-sold expense account* Purchases increased (debited) by $1,900; liability account Accounts Payable increased (credited) by $1,900.
12/28	Dapple pays $428 of miscellaneous operating expenses.	Expense account Other Expenses increased (debited) by $428; asset account Cash decreased (credited) by $428.
12/29	Dapple distributes dividends of $500 ($0.25 per share for 2,000 shares) to stockholders.	Dividends Distributed account increased (debited) by $500; asset account Cash decreased (credited) by $500.

*Literally, the Purchases and Freight-in accounts include the cost of goods *available* for sale rather than the cost of goods *sold*. However, for convenience, we use the latter phrase to classify these accounts. We show the inclusion of the Purchases and Freight-in accounts in the computation of cost of goods sold in Exhibit C-8.

EXHIBIT C-4   General Journal Entries (Dapple Corporation)

Date	Account Titles and Explanations	Debit	Credit
2004			
Jan. 1	Cash	20,000	
	Capital Stock		20,000
	Issued 2,000 shares of no-par stock at $10 per share.		
16	Land	3,000	
	Cash		3,000
	Purchased 2 acres of land at $1,500 per acre.		
Mar. 30	Building	15,320	
	Equipment	2,120	
	Cash		10,840
	Notes Payable		6,600
	Purchased a building and equipment. The note bears annual interest of 12% and the principal and interest are due on March 30, 2003.		
30	Prepaid Insurance	360	
	Cash		360
	Purchased a 1-year comprehensive insurance policy.		
31	Purchases	7,400	
	Accounts Payable		7,400
	Purchased inventory for resale on account from Bark Company. Terms of sale include a $100 cash discount if paid within 10 days.		
Apr. 2	Cash	8,000	
	Sales Revenue		8,000
	To record cash sales.		
8	Accounts Payable	7,400	
	Purchases Discounts Taken		100
	Cash		7,300
	Paid Bark Company for purchases made on account on March 31, less the cash discount.		
15	Sales Returns and Allowances	250	
	Cash		250
	Customer returned defective inventory and cash refund was given.		
20	Cash	160	
	Purchases Returns and Allowances		160
	Returned defective inventory to Bark Company and received a cash refund.		

continued

debited are listed first. The accounts to be credited are listed next and indented. Finally, a brief explanation of the journal entry is made.

Posting to the Ledger (Step 2)

A general ledger is the entire group of accounts for a company. It might take several forms, such as a computer storage location on a disk, or in the case of our manual system, a loose-leaf binder with a page for each T-account. Once a company's transactions and events have been journalized in a general journal, each account in the general ledger is updated. This is accomplished through the process of **posting.** Posting involves transferring the date and debit and credit amounts from the journal entries in the general journal to the debit and credit sides of the accounts in the general ledger. Thus, **after posting, the general ledger accounts contain the same information as in the general journal, just in a different format.** Exhibit C-5 illustrates *all* the accounts in the general ledger of the Dapple Corporation. To conserve space, these accounts include the postings not only for the journal entries shown in Exhibit C-4, but also for the *adjusting*

4 Post to the general ledger and prepare a trial balance.

EXHIBIT C-4, Continued

Date	Account Titles and Explanations	Debit	Credit
July 15	Purchases	3,100	
	Freight-in	200	
	Cash		3,300
	Purchased inventory for resale and paid associated freight charges.		
Sept. 1	Notes Receivable	1,320	
	Loss on Sale of Land	180	
	Land		1,500
	Sold 1 acre of land at less than its cost, incurring a loss. Buyer issued a note due in 6 months and bearing 15% annual interest.		
Oct. 1	Salaries Expense	1,800	
	Cash		1,800
	Paid 6 months' of employees' salaries.		
Nov. 23	Accounts Receivable	9,000	
	Sales Revenue		9,000
	Made sales on account to Frank Company ($5,000) and Knox Company ($4,000). Terms of sale are 2/10, n/60.		
Dec. 1	Cash	450	
	Unearned Rent		450
	Received 3 months' rent in advance at $150 per month. Company owes use of portion of building to Fritz Company for the 3-month period.		
2	Cash	1,960	
	Sales Discounts Taken	40	
	Accounts Receivable		2,000
	Frank Company paid a portion of its accounts receivable, less applicable 2% discount.		
27	Purchases	1,900	
	Accounts Payable		1,900
	Purchased inventory on account from Ajax Company.		
28	Other Expenses	428	
	Cash		428
	Paid miscellaneous operating expenses.		
29	Dividends Distributed	500	
	Cash		500
	Distributed dividends of $0.25 per share to stockholders.		

entries (*Adj* is shown in the account) and the *closing* entries (*Cl*) discussed later in Exhibits C-6 and C-11.

TRIAL BALANCE After the journal entries are prepared and posted for the accounting period, the balance in each account is determined. Then a trial balance is often prepared. **A trial balance is a working paper that lists all the company's general ledger accounts and their account balances.** These account balances are listed in either the debit or the credit column. The trial balance is used to verify that the total of the debit balances is equal to the total of the credit balances. This working paper is not illustrated here but is shown on the worksheet in Exhibit C-13.

If a trial balance does not balance, there is an error. To find the error, the debit and credit columns of the trial balance should be added again. If the column totals do not agree, the amounts in the debit and credit columns should be checked to be sure that a debit or credit account balance was not mistakenly listed in the wrong column. If the error is still not found, the difference in the column totals should be computed and divided by 9. When the difference is evenly divisible by 9, there is a good chance that a *transposition* or a *slide* has occurred. A transposition occurs when two digits in a

EXHIBIT C-5   General Ledger (Dapple Corporation)

Cash

01/01	20,000	01/16	3,000
04/02	8,000	03/30	10,840
04/20	160	03/30	360
12/01	450	04/08	7,300
12/02	1,960	04/15	250
		07/15	3,300
		10/01	1,800
		12/28	428
		12/29	500
Balance	2,792		

Accounts Receivable

11/23	9,000	12/02	2,000
Balance	7,000		

Allowance for Doubtful Accounts

		12/31 Adj	170

Notes Receivable

09/01	1,320

Interest Receivable

12/31 Adj	66

Inventory

12/31 Cl	2,140	12/31 Cl	0
Balance	2,140		

Prepaid Insurance

03/30	360	12/31 Adj	270
Balance	90		

Land

01/16	3,000	09/01	1,500
Balance	1,500		

Building

03/30	15,320

Accumulated Depreciation: Building

		12/31 Adj	264

Equipment

03/30	2,120

Accumulated Depreciation: Equipment

		12/31 Adj	120

Accounts Payable

04/08	7,400	03/31	7,400
		12/27	1,900
		Balance	1,900

Notes Payable

		03/30	6,600

Salaries Payable

		12/31 Adj	900

Interest Payable

		12/31 Adj	594

Income Taxes Payable

		12/31 Adj	600

Unearned Rent

12/31 Adj	150	12/01	450
		Balance	300

Capital Stock

		01/01	20,000

Retained Earnings

12/31 Cl	500	12/31 Cl	1,400
		Balance	900

Dividends Distributed

12/29	500	12/31 Cl	500

Sales Revenue

12/31 Cl	17,000	04/02	8,000
		11/23	9,000

Sales Returns and Allowances

04/15	250	12/31 Cl	250

Sales Discounts Taken

12/02	40	12/31 Cl	40

Interest Revenue

12/31 Cl	66	12/31 Adj	66

Rent Revenue

12/31 Cl	150	12/31 Adj	150

Purchases

03/31	7,400	12/31 Cl	12,400
07/15	3,100		
12/27	1,900		

Purchases Returns and Allowances

12/31 Cl	160	04/20	160

Purchases Discounts Taken

12/31 Cl	100	04/08	100

Freight-in

07/15	200	12/31 Cl	200

Salaries Expense

10/01	1,800	12/31 Cl	2,700
12/31 Adj	900		

Other Expenses

12/28	428	12/31 Cl	428

Loss on Sale of Land

09/01	180	12/31 Cl	180

Depreciation Expense: Building

12/31 Adj	264	12/31 Cl	264

Depreciation Expense: Equipment

12/31 Adj	120	12/31 Cl	120

Bad Debts Expense

12/31 Adj	170	12/31 Cl	170

Insurance Expense

12/31 Adj	270	12/31 Cl	270

Interest Expense

12/31 Adj	594	12/31 Cl	594

Income Tax Expense

12/31 Adj	600	12/31 Cl	600

Income Summary

12/31 Cl	18,216	12/31 Cl	19,616
12/31 Cl	1,400		

number are mistakenly reversed. For instance, if the $1,500 Land balance is listed as $5,100 on the trial balance in Exhibit C-13, the debit column would total $49,810 instead of $46,210. The difference, $3,600, is evenly divisible by 9. A slide occurs when the digits are listed in the correct order but are mistakenly moved one decimal place to the left or right. For instance, in Exhibit C-13 if the $1,900 Accounts Payable balance is listed as $190, the credit column would total $44,500 instead of $46,210. The $1,710 difference is evenly divisible by 9.

If a transposition or slide has occurred, the error may have occurred when the account balances were transferred from the accounts to the trial balance or when the account balances were computed initially. Thus the account balances listed on the trial balance should be compared with the account balances listed in the ledger. Then the ledger account balances should be recomputed, and if no error is found, the postings should be double-checked. Finally, the journal entries should be reviewed for accuracy.

If the trial balance is in balance, it is likely that (1) equal debit entries and credit entries have been recorded for each transaction; (2) the debit and credit entries are posted to the accounts; and (3) the account balances are correctly computed. The equality of the debit and credit totals, however, does not necessarily mean that the information in the accounting system is error-free. A trial balance does not pick up several types of errors. First, an entire transaction may not have been journalized. Second, an entire transaction may not have been posted to the accounts. Third, equal debits and credits, but of the wrong amount, may have been recorded for a transaction. Fourth, a transaction may have been journalized to a wrong account. Finally, a journal entry may have been posted to the wrong account.

Preparation of Adjusting Entries (Step 3)

Most companies use generally accepted accounting principles which require the accrual method of accounting. Under *accrual accounting,* a company records revenues in the accounting period in which they are earned and realized (or realizable) and records (matches) expenses in the accounting period in which they are incurred, regardless of the inflow or outflow of cash. In many instances, not all accounts are up to date at the end of the accounting period. Certain amounts must be *adjusted* so that all revenues and expenses are recorded and the balance sheet accounts have correct ending balances. **Adjusting entries are journal entries made at the end of the accounting period so that a company's financial statements include the correct amounts for the current period.**

An adjusting entry ordinarily affects both a permanent (balance sheet) and a temporary (income statement) account. Adjusting entries may be classified into three categories. These categories and the types of balance sheet accounts involved in the adjusting entries are:

5 Prepare adjusting entries.

1. Apportionment of prepaid and deferred items
   a. Prepaid expenses
   b. Deferred revenues
2. Recording of accrued items
   a. Accrued expenses
   b. Accrued revenues
3. Recording estimated items

PREPAID EXPENSES   A prepaid expense (sometimes called a prepaid asset) is a good or service purchased by a company for its operations but not fully used up by the end of the accounting period. When the company initially purchases the good or service, it records the *cost* as an acquisition of an asset (prepaid expense). At the end of the accounting period, some of these goods or services were used in the process of generating revenues. The costs must be systematically *matched*, as expenses, against the current revenues, while the unused cost remains as an asset on the balance sheet. Examples of prepaid expenses include prepaid rent, office supplies, and prepaid insurance.

In the Dapple Corporation example, it purchased a 1-year comprehensive insurance policy on March 30, 2004. An asset, Prepaid Insurance, was recorded for $360. At the end of the year, 9 months of insurance coverage has expired while 3 months of coverage remains in force. The cost is apportioned as an expense on a straight-line basis (an equal amount each month). Insurance Expense is increased (debited) by $270 ($30 per month for 9 months) and Prepaid Insurance decreased (credited) by $270. The result is a $270 increase in expenses and a $90 remaining balance in the asset Prepaid Insurance. Exhibit C-6 shows this adjusting entry which is posted to the ledger accounts shown in Exhibit C-5. Since the December 31 date of the adjusting entries is the same as the December 31 date for the closing entries (which we discuss in Exhibit C-11), each adjusting entry date is followed by the abbreviation *Adj* to clarify the postings.

EXHIBIT C-6   Adjusting Entries for 2004 (Dapple Corporation)

Date	Account Titles and Explanations	Debit	Credit
	Adjusting Entries		
Dec. 31	Insurance Expense	270	
	Prepaid Insurance		270
	To record expiration of 9 months of insurance coverage purchased on March 30.		
31	Unearned Rent	150	
	Rent Revenue		150
	To record earning of 1 month of rent revenue from receipt collected in advance on December 1.		
31	Salaries Expense	900	
	Salaries Payable		900
	To record 3 months' salaries earned by employees but not yet paid.		
31	Interest Expense	594	
	Interest Payable		594
	To record interest accumulated on the note payable issued on March 30 and due March 30, 2006.		
31	Interest Receivable	66	
	Interest Revenue		66
	To record interest accumulated on the note receivable accepted on September 1.		
31	Depreciation Expense: Building	264	
	Accumulated Depreciation: Building		264
	To record 9 months' depreciation on building acquired March 30.		
31	Depreciation Expense: Equipment	120	
	Accumulated Depreciation: Equipment		120
	To record 9 months' depreciation on equipment acquired March 30.		
31	Bad Debts Expense	170	
	Allowance for Doubtful Accounts		170
	To record estimated uncollectible accounts receivable.		
31	Income Tax Expense	600	
	Income Taxes Payable		600
	To record income taxes for the period.		

DEFERRED REVENUES Deferred (or unearned) revenue is payment received by a company in advance for the future sale of inventory or performance of services. Initially the company usually records a liability because it has an obligation to provide the goods or services. When the company has provided the goods or services to the customer, it eliminates the liability and records the revenue in an adjusting entry. Although the adjusting entry may be made at the time the goods or services are provided, it may also be made at the end of the accounting period.

On December 1, Dapple Corporation received $450 for 3 months' rent in advance. It recorded the receipt as a liability, Unearned Rent. On December 31 an adjusting entry must be made because 1 month of rent is now earned. The adjusting entry is a debit (decrease) of $150 to Unearned Rent and a credit (increase) of $150 to Rent Revenue. The result is a $150 increase in revenues and a $300 remaining balance in the liability Unearned Rent. Exhibit C-6 shows this adjusting entry.

A company might *initially* record the entire prepayment of a cost as an expense (instead of as an asset) or the entire receipt in advance as a revenue (instead of a liability). In this case adjusting entries are still necessary at the end of the accounting period, but they are different in form and amount. For example, Dapple Corporation *could* have recorded the March 30 payment as a $360 debit to Insurance Expense (instead of Prepaid Insurance) and it *could* have recorded the December 1 receipt of

$450 as a credit to Rent Revenue (instead of Unearned Rent). In this case the adjusting entry procedure is to calculate the appropriate ending balances in the permanent accounts and adjust the accounts accordingly. For instance, Prepaid Insurance should have an ending balance of $90. The year-end adjusting entry must *reduce* the expense and *increase* the Prepaid Insurance account by this amount. The adjusting entry is a debit (increase) to Prepaid Insurance for $90 and a credit (decrease) to Insurance Expense for $90. Similarly, Unearned Rent should have an ending balance of $300. The year-end adjusting entry must *reduce* the revenue and *increase* the Unearned Rent account by this amount. The adjusting entry is a debit (decrease) to Rent Revenue for $300 and a credit (increase) to Unearned Rent for $300. The results of these adjusting entries are the *same* balances in the respective accounts as we show in the comprehensive illustration. Care must be taken to determine how advance payments and receipts were initially recorded before the adjusting entry is determined.

ACCRUED EXPENSES An accrued expense is an expense that a company has incurred during the accounting period but has neither paid nor recorded. In order to match expenses against revenues and to reflect the proper liabilities at the end of the period, an adjusting entry must be made for each accrued expense.

Dapple Corporation has three accrued expenses it has not yet recorded: employees' salaries, interest, and income taxes. For simplicity assume the company pays employees' salaries every six months, the last $1,800 payment having been made on October 1. At the end of December, its employees have earned salaries for 3 months (October through December) although they have not been paid. The adjusting entry is a debit (increase) to Salaries Expense for $900 and a credit (increase) to Salaries Payable for $900. The result is a $900 increase in expenses and a $900 ending balance in the liability, Salaries Payable. Exhibit C-6 shows this adjusting entry.

On March 30, Dapple Corporation issued a $6,600, 12% note payable due at the end of 2 years. Although the principal and interest will not be *paid* until 2006, 9 months of interest expense has accumulated and is a liability at the end of 2004. The interest is computed using the equation: Interest = Principal × Rate × Time, where time is expressed as a fraction of a year. The adjusting entry involves a debit (increase) to Interest Expense for $594 ($6,600 × 0.12 × 9/12) and a credit (increase) to Interest Payable for $594, as shown in Exhibit C-6.

Corporations are subject to a federal (and often state) income tax. Although a corporation may not pay its income taxes until the following period, they are an expense and year-end obligation of the period in which the corporation earned the income. The adjusting entry for income taxes is prepared *after* all the other adjusting entries because the amount is computed by multiplying the income tax rate times the current income before income taxes. Based on its current income before income taxes and on the current tax rate,[7] Dapple Corporation calculates that its 2004 income taxes are $600, with the entire amount payable in 2005. The adjusting entry is a debit (increase) to Income Tax Expense for $600 and a credit (increase) to Income Taxes Payable for $600, and is shown as the last item in Exhibit C-6.

ACCRUED REVENUES An accrued revenue is a revenue that a company has earned during the accounting period but has neither received nor recorded. An adjusting entry is necessary to increase the assets and revenues at the end of the period.

On September 1, Dapple Corporation accepted a $1,320, 15% note as payment when it sold an acre of land. Although the note and interest will not be collected until 2005, the company has earned 4 months of interest in 2004. The $66 of interest ($1,320 × 0.15 × 4/12) is recorded as a debit (increase) to Interest Receivable and a credit (increase) to Interest Revenue. The result is a $66 increase in revenues and a $66 increase in the asset Interest Receivable. Exhibit C-6 shows this adjusting entry.

---

7. As we show in Exhibit C-8, the Dapple Corporation's income before income taxes is $2,000. Multiplying this amount by an assumed tax rate of 30% yields income taxes of $600.

ESTIMATED ITEMS Certain other adjusting entries are based on estimated amounts because they are a function, at least in part, of expected future events. Adjustments involving (1) the depreciation on assets such as buildings and equipment, and (2) the uncollectibility of some accounts receivable are both based upon estimates.

When a company acquires an asset such as a machine, sales fixture, or building, for use in its operations, the company records the cost as an economic resource (asset). The company expects to use the asset for several periods after which it will dispose of the asset at a value significantly less than its original cost. The difference between the original cost and an estimate of this later value (alternatively called residual value, salvage value, scrap value, or trade-in value) is the asset's **depreciable cost.** This depreciable cost is systematically and rationally allocated as an expense to each accounting period in which the asset is used. This cost allocation process is referred to as **depreciation.** One systematic depreciation method is straight-line depreciation, which allocates a proportionate amount as an expense to each accounting period. Its computation is as follows:

$$\textbf{Annual Depreciation Expense} = \frac{\textbf{Cost} - \textbf{Estimated Residual Value}}{\textbf{Estimated Service Life}}$$

The company records depreciation at the end of the accounting period in an adjusting entry. The entry increases Depreciation Expense and decreases the remaining depreciable cost of the asset. However, this decrease is *not* recorded directly in the asset account. Instead a contra (negative) asset account entitled Accumulated Depreciation is *increased.* This contra account is subtracted from the asset account on the company's balance sheet. The resulting balance is referred to as the *book* value (or carrying value) of the asset.

Dapple Corporation has two depreciable assets, the building and equipment acquired on March 30, 2004. The company estimates that these assets will have lives of 35 years and 12 years, respectively. The company estimates that the building will have a residual value of $3,000 and the equipment will have a residual value of $200 at the end of these lives. Since the building and equipment were used for only 9 months during 2004, the depreciation expense is $264 {[($15,320 − $3,000) ÷ 35] × 9/12} on the building and $120 {[($2,120 − $200) ÷ 12] × 9/12} on the equipment. The adjusting entry for the building is a debit (increase) to Depreciation Expense: Building for $264 and a credit (increase) to the contra-asset Accumulated Depreciation: Building for $264. The adjusting entry for the equipment is a debit to Depreciation Expense: Equipment for $120 and a credit to the contra-asset Accumulated Depreciation: Equipment for $120. The result is an increase in expenses and a *decrease* in the book value that the company reports on its balance sheet for the building and the equipment. Exhibit C-6 shows these adjusting entries.

Many companies make a large amount of their sales on credit. Regardless of a company's collection efforts, it is likely to experience a certain amount of bad debts—customer accounts that will not be collected. Although a company may not know which particular customers will not pay their accounts until a later accounting period, it must match bad debt expense against revenues in the *period of the sale.* Furthermore, it must reduce its assets so that at the end of the period the accounting records reflect the amount of accounts receivable that it expects to collect. The adjusting entry to record the increase in expenses and the decrease in assets requires an estimate of future uncollectible accounts. However, since it is not known in the period of sale which specific customers will default on their accounts, Accounts Receivable is not directly reduced. Instead a contra-asset account, Allowance for Doubtful Accounts, is *increased.* This account is deducted from Accounts Receivable on the balance sheet to report the estimated collectible amount.

To illustrate, assume for simplicity that Dapple Corporation estimates its bad debts to be 1% of total sales. Since the balance in the Sales Revenue account totals $17,000, the adjusting entry is a debit (increase) to Bad Debts Expense for $170 and a credit (increase) to the contra-asset Allowance for Doubtful Accounts for $170. The result is an increase in expenses and a *decrease* in the collectible accounts receivable shown on the balance sheet. Exhibit C-6 shows this adjusting entry.

Preparation of the Financial Statements (Step 4)

After a company prepares and posts the adjusting entries to the general ledger accounts, it prepares the financial statements. This procedure involves several steps. First, the balance of each account in the ledger is recomputed if necessary. Next, an adjusted trial balance is frequently prepared; it is similar to a trial balance. **An adjusted trial balance lists all the accounts and the account balances of a company *after* adjustments (but *before* closing) in either a debit or a credit column.** The adjusted trial balance is used to verify that the total of the debit balances is equal to the total of the credit balances. This working paper also helps in the preparation of the company's financial statements because all the accounts and amounts included in the financial statements are listed on the adjusted trial balance. Exhibit C-7 shows the Dapple Corporation's adjusted trial balance. Finally,

EXHIBIT C-7   Adjusted Trial Balance (Dapple Corporation)

Adjusted Trial Balance
December 31, 2004

	Debit	Credit
Cash	$ 2,792	
Accounts receivable	7,000	
Allowance for doubtful accounts		$ 170
Notes receivable	1,320	
Interest receivable	66	
Inventory	0	
Prepaid insurance	90	
Land	1,500	
Building	15,320	
Accumulated depreciation: building		264
Equipment	2,120	
Accumulated depreciation: equipment		120
Accounts payable		1,900
Notes payable		6,600
Salaries payable		900
Interest payable		594
Income taxes payable		600
Unearned rent		300
Capital stock		20,000
Retained earnings		0
Dividends distributed	500	
Sales revenue		17,000
Sales returns and allowances	250	
Sales discounts taken	40	
Interest revenue		66
Rent revenue		150
Purchases	12,400	
Purchases returns and allowances		160
Purchases discounts taken		100
Freight-in	200	
Salaries expense	2,700	
Other expenses	428	
Loss on sale of land	180	
Depreciation expense: building	264	
Depreciation expense: equipment	120	
Bad debts expense	170	
Insurance expense	270	
Interest expense	594	
Income tax expense	600	
Totals	$48,924	$48,924

the company prepares its income statement, statement of retained earnings, and balance sheet in sequential order directly from the information in the adjusted trial balance.

6 Prepare financial statements.

INCOME STATEMENT   Exhibit C-8 shows Dapple Corporation's income statement for 2004. Net sales are computed first by subtracting sales returns and allowances and sales discounts taken from sales revenue. Because the cost of goods sold is directly related to net sales, it is shown next. Since the Dapple Corporation uses a periodic inventory system, it computes[8] the cost of goods sold. Cost of goods available for sale is computed first by adding purchases and freight-in to the beginning inventory, and deducting purchases returns and allowances and purchases discounts taken. Because 2004 is the company's first year of operations, it did not have a beginning inventory and the

---

EXHIBIT C-8   Income Statement

DAPPLE CORPORATION

Income Statement
For Year Ended December 31, 2004

Sales revenue		$17,000
Less: Sales returns and allowances	$ 250	
Sales discounts taken	40	(290)
Net sales		$16,710
Cost of goods sold		
Inventory, 1/1/2004	$ 0	
Purchases	12,400	
Purchases returns and allowances	(160)	
Purchases discounts taken	(100)	
Freight-in	200	
Cost of goods available for sale	$12,340	
Less: Inventory, 12/31/2004	(2,140)	
Cost of goods sold		(10,200)
Gross profit on sales		$ 6,510
Operating expenses		
Salaries expense	$ 2,700	
Other expenses	428	
Depreciation expense: building	264	
Depreciation expense: equipment	120	
Bad debts expense	170	
Insurance expense	270	
Total operating expenses		(3,952)
Income from operations		$ 2,558
Other items		
Loss on sale of land	$ (180)	
Interest revenue	66	
Rent revenue	150	
Interest expense	(594)	(558)
Income before income taxes		$ 2,000
Income tax expense		(600)
Net Income		$ 1,400
Earnings per share (2,000 shares)		$ 0.70

---

8. If the company used a perpetual inventory system, it would not have to make this computation because the Cost of Goods Sold expense account would contain the $10,200 amount.

cost of goods available for sale is $12,340. At the end of 2004 a physical count showed an ending inventory of $2,140. The ending inventory is deducted from the cost of goods available for sale to determine the cost of goods sold of $10,200. We discuss the way the company records the ending inventory in its *accounts* in the *Closing Entries* (Step 5) section. Cost of Goods Sold is deducted to determine the Gross Profit on Sales. Operating Expenses (often classified into two groups, Selling Expenses and Administrative Expenses) are next deducted to determine the Income from Operations. The total of the Other Items section (for recurring items that are not directly related to ongoing operations) is deducted to determine the Income Before Income Taxes. Finally the Income Tax Expense is deducted to determine the Net Income of $1,400. The $0.70 Earnings Per Share is computed by dividing the $1,400 net income by the 2,000 shares owned by the stockholders.

RETAINED EARNINGS STATEMENT Exhibit C-9 shows the retained earnings statement of the Dapple Corporation for 2004. Because 2004 is its first year of operations, the company did not have a beginning retained earnings balance. It did, however, earn net income of $1,400 and distributed dividends of $500, resulting in ending retained earnings (the excess of total earnings over total dividends) of $900.

EXHIBIT C-9   Retained Earnings Statement

DAPPLE CORPORATION

Statement of Retained Earnings
For Year Ended December 31, 2004

Retained earnings, January 1, 2004	$ 0
Add: Net income for 2004	1,400
	$1,400
Less: Dividends for 2004	(500)
Retained earnings, December 31, 2004	$ 900

BALANCE SHEET Exhibit C-10 shows the Dapple Corporation's balance sheet at the end of 2004. It includes three sections: assets, liabilities, and stockholders' equity. The assets are divided into current assets and property and equipment. The current assets are cash and those assets that are expected to be converted into cash or consumed within one year or the operating cycle, whichever is longer. Current assets generally include cash, receivables, temporary investments in marketable securities, inventories, and prepaid items such as insurance and office supplies. Property and equipment contains the longer-lived operational assets of the company. This section includes both nondepreciable assets and depreciable assets listed at their book values. The liabilities are divided into current liabilities and long-term liabilities. Current liabilities are those obligations that will become due within one year or the operating cycle, whichever is longer, and are expected to be paid with current assets or the creation of other current liabilities. Long-term liabilities are obligations that do not meet the current liability criteria. Stockholders' equity includes contributed capital (capital stock) and retained earnings. Total assets amount to $31,794, and equal the total of liabilities plus stockholders' equity.

Preparation of Closing Entries (Step 5)

The next step in the accounting process consists of preparing and posting closing entries. **Closing entries are journal entries of a company made at the end of the accounting**

7 Prepare closing entries.

EXHIBIT C-10   Balance Sheet

DAPPLE CORPORATION

Balance Sheet
December 31, 2004

Assets				*Liabilities*		
Current Assets				Current Liabilities		
Cash		$ 2,792		Accounts payable		$ 1,900
Accounts receivable	$ 7,000			Salaries payable		900
Less: Allowance for doubtful				Income taxes payable		600
accounts	(170)	6,830		Unearned rent		300
Notes receivable				Total current liabilities		$ 3,700
(due March 1, 2005)		1,320		Long-Term Liabilities		
Interest receivable		66		Notes payable (due March 30, 2006)		$ 6,600
Inventory		2,140		Interest payable (due March 30, 2006)		594
Prepaid insurance		90		Total long-term liabilities		$ 7,194
Total current assets		$13,238		Total Liabilities		$10,894
Property and Equipment						
Land		$ 1,500		*Stockholders' Equity*		
Building	$15,320					
Less: Accumulated depreciation	(264)	15,056		Contributed Capital		
Equipment	$ 2,120			Capital stock, no par		
Less: Accumulated depreciation	(120)	2,000		(2,000 shares)	$20,000	
Total property and equipment		$18,556		Retained Earnings	900	
				Total Stockholders' Equity		$20,900
				Total Liabilities and Stockholders'		
Total Assets		$31,794		Equity		$31,794

period (1) to reduce the balance in each temporary account to zero, and (2) to update the retained earnings and inventory accounts.

The temporary accounts (namely, all the revenue, expense, and dividend accounts) are used during each accounting period to accumulate and summarize information pertaining to a company's net income and dividends *for that period*. After the period is over and the company's financial statements are prepared, the balances in these accounts are no longer needed. Furthermore, these accounts must begin the *next* accounting period with a zero balance in order to summarize the company's net income and dividend information for the next period. Also, the company's permanent stockholders' equity account, Retained Earnings, must be updated for the net income and dividend information contained in the temporary accounts. Finally, if a company uses a periodic inventory system, its ending inventory must be updated, because this inventory affects its net income (as part of the cost of goods sold computation) and is also the beginning inventory of the next accounting period.

The revenue and expense accounts (including beginning and ending inventories used to compute cost of goods sold in a periodic system), are closed to a temporary closing account called Income Summary. The resulting balance in this account is the net income (or loss) for the period. This balance is then transferred to Retained Earnings.

The closing process is straightforward. Each temporary income statement account is debited or credited for the amount that will result in a zero balance in that account. The total of the credits to these accounts is recorded as a debit to the Income Summary account, and the total of the debits is recorded as a credit to Income Summary. A resulting *credit* balance in the Income Summary account is the net income for the period, and is the same amount as that shown on the income statement. This credit balance is closed to zero with a debit entry to Income Summary and a credit entry to Retained Earnings for the amount of the net income. If on the other hand, there is a *debit* balance in the Income Summary account, this means there is a net loss for the period. This debit balance is closed to zero with a debit entry to Retained Earnings and a credit entry to Income Summary for the amount of the net loss. Finally, the Dividends Distributed account is credited for the amount necessary to reduce its balance to zero; the corresponding debit to Retained Earnings reduces it for the amount of the dividends.

Exhibit C-11 shows the closing entries for the Dapple Corporation which are posted to the ledger accounts shown in Exhibit C-5. The abbreviation *Cl* is used to identify each December 31 closing entry. The temporary income statement accounts that have a credit balance are closed first. These include all the revenue accounts and the contra-purchases accounts, Purchases Returns and Allowances and Purchases Discounts Taken. The amount of the *ending* inventory (determined by the physical year-end count) is also recorded at this time. The total credit to Income Summary amounts to $19,616.

The temporary income statement accounts that have a debit balance are closed next. These include all the expense accounts and the contra-sales accounts. The amount of the *beginning* inventory is also eliminated at this time. Although Dapple Corporation

EXHIBIT C-11 Closing Entries for 2004 (Dapple Corporation)

Date	Account Titles and Explanations	Debit	Credit
	Closing Entries		
Dec. 31	Sales Revenue	17,000	
	Interest Revenue	66	
	Rent Revenue	150	
	Purchases Returns and Allowances	160	
	Purchases Discounts Taken	100	
	Inventory (12/31/2004)	2,140	
	Income Summary		19,616
	To close the temporary accounts with credit balances and to record the ending inventory.		
31	Income Summary	18,216	
	Sales Returns and Allowances		250
	Sales Discounts Taken		40
	Purchases		12,400
	Freight-in		200
	Salaries Expense		2,700
	Other Expenses		428
	Loss on Sale of Land		180
	Depreciation Expense: Building		264
	Depreciation Expense: Equipment		120
	Bad Debts Expense		170
	Insurance Expense		270
	Interest Expense		594
	Income Tax Expense		600
	Inventory (1/1/2004)		0
	To close the temporary accounts with debit balances and the beginning inventory.		
31	Income Summary	1,400	
	Retained Earnings		1,400
	To close the income summary balance (net income) to retained earnings.		
31	Retained Earnings	500	
	Dividends Distributed		500
	To close the dividends to retained earnings		

did not have a beginning inventory, we show the account for illustrative purposes. The total debit to Income Summary is $18,216.

The Income Summary account now has a credit balance of $1,400 ($19,616 credit less the $18,216 debit). This amount is the net income we computed on the income statement (Exhibit C-8). It is transferred to Retained Earnings by a debit to Income Summary for $1,400 (which creates a zero balance in this account) and a credit to Retained Earnings for $1,400 (which increases this account for the amount of the net income). Finally, the debit balance in the Dividends Distributed account is reduced to zero by a debit to Retained Earnings for $500 and a credit to Dividends Distributed for $500.

The result of the closing entries is that (1) all of the company's revenue, expense, and dividend accounts are closed (have zero balances) and are ready to accumulate the net income and dividend information for the next accounting period, (2) the ending balance in its Retained Earnings account is increased by $900 due to the excess of net income over dividends, (3) the ending inventory of $2,140 is the balance shown in its Inventory account, and (4) only the permanent balance sheet accounts are open (have nonzero account balances).

After the closing entries are prepared and posted, many companies will prepare a post-closing trial balance. **A post-closing trial balance is prepared to verify that the total of the debit balances is equal to the total of the credit balances in all of the company's permanent accounts.** We do not illustrate this working paper here. The accounting cycle is now complete and a new cycle for the next accounting period may begin.

Additionally, if a company uses a perpetual inventory system, only its Cost of Goods Sold expense account is closed with a credit to that account, because the Inventory account already contains the proper ending balance. Under this system the company has no purchases or purchases-related accounts.

We used a relatively simple accounting system to illustrate the accounting cycle. Certain additional complexities are common in companies today. These include the use of reversing entries, a worksheet, subsidiary ledgers, special journals, and voucher systems. We discuss each of these topics in the sections that follow.

REVERSING ENTRIES

After a company's accounts are adjusted and closed for the current period, a new accounting cycle is begun for the next accounting period. Prior to journalizing the daily transactions of the new accounting period in the general journal, most companies prepare reversing entries. **A reversing entry is the exact reverse (accounts and amounts) of an adjusting entry.** Reversing entries usually are made at the same time as closing entries but are dated the first day of the *next* accounting period. They are *optional* and have one purpose: to simplify the recording of a later transaction related to the adjusting entry. Reversing entries enable the later transaction to be routinely recorded, without having to consider the possible impact of the prior adjusting entry.

As a general guideline, reversing entries *should* be made for any adjusting entry that establishes a new balance sheet account, as follows:

1. Adjusting entries that establish accrued revenues or expenses to be collected or paid in the next accounting period
2. Adjusting entries related to prepayments of costs initially recorded as expenses or receipts-in-advance initially recorded as revenues

Reversing entries *should not* be made for:

1. Adjusting entries related to prepayments of costs initially recorded as assets or receipts-in-advance initially recorded as liabilities
2. Adjusting entries related to estimated items such as depreciation or bad debts

These guidelines are just that, *guidelines*. They are no substitute for good accounting judgment.

The Dapple Corporation should consider reversing two of the adjusting entries recorded in Exhibit C-6, namely, the entries to record accrued interest revenue and accrued salaries expense. Each of these is related to a transaction that will occur in the *next* accounting period. The entry to record income taxes is generally not reversed because complexities in the tax laws require careful analysis for each journal entry. Although the adjusting entry for interest expense established an accrued expense, Interest Payable, this entry is not reversed because the subsequent transaction will not occur until 2006. Exhibit C-12 illustrates reversing entries and how they simplify the recording of subsequent transactions for Interest Revenue and Salaries Expense.

Whether or not it makes reversing entries, the Dapple Corporation will collect $1,419 on March 1, 2005 for the 15%, 6-month note receivable accepted on September 1, 2004.

EXHIBIT C-12   Reversing Entries (Dapple Corporation)

Accrued Revenue

Adjusting Entry

12/31/04	Interest Receivable		66	
	Interest Revenue			66
12/31/04	Revenues and expenses are CLOSED.			

If reversing entry is not made:　　　　　　　　　　　If reversing entry is made:

Reversing Entry			*Reversing Entry*		
1/1/05　None			1/1/05　Interest Revenue	66	
			Interest Receivable		66

Subsequent Entry			*Subsequent Entry*		
3/1/05　Cash	1,419		3/1/05　Cash	1,419	
Notes Receivable		1,320	Notes Receivable		1,320
Interest Receivable		66	Interest Revenue		99
Interest Revenue		33			

Analysis of Subsequent Entry

Interest of $99 is collected, but $66 was recorded in Interest Receivable at end of last period. Consequently, Interest Receivable must be credited for $66 and Interest Revenue credited for $33.

Analysis of Subsequent Entry

Interest of $99 is collected and credited to Interest Revenue. Because reversing entry was made for $66, the net result in Interest Revenue is a $33 credit balance.

Accrued Expense

Adjusting Entry

12/31/04	Salaries Expense		900	
	Salaries Payable			900
12/31/04	Revenues and expenses are CLOSED.			

If reversing entry is not made:　　　　　　　　　　　If reversing entry is made:

Reversing Entry			*Reversing Entry*		
1/1/05　None			1/1/05　Salaries Payable	900	
			Salaries Expense		900

Subsequent Entry			*Subsequent Entry*		
4/1/05　Salaries Expense	900		4/1/05　Salaries Expense	1,800	
Salaries Payable	900		Cash		1,800
Cash		1,800			

Analysis of Subsequent Entry

Salaries of $1,800 for 6 months are paid, but $900 was recorded in Salaries Payable at end of last period. Consequently, Salaries Payable must be debited for $900 and Salaries Expense debited for $900.

Analysis of Subsequent Entry

Salaries of $1,800 for 6 months are paid and debited to Salaries Expense. Because reversing entry was made for $900, the net result in Salaries Expense is a $900 debit balance.

The $1,419 consists of the $1,320 note and $99 of interest ($1,320 × 0.15 × 6/12). If it does not make a reversing entry, when Dapple records this collection it must determine what portion of the interest relates to 2004 ($66 of Interest Receivable) and what portion represents Interest Revenue for 2005 ($33 for 2 months). Often this analysis is complex and impractical. The use of a reversing entry eliminates this analysis and promotes operational efficiency. The entire amount of the $99 received in excess of the face value of the note is credited to Interest Revenue. Since the reversing entry established a $66 *debit* balance in Interest Revenue, the $99 credit results in a $33 *credit* balance, the 2 months of interest for 2005, in the Interest Revenue account.

Similarly, on April 1, 2005 the Dapple Corporation will pay its employees another 6 months of salaries, or $1,800. If Dapple does not make a reversing entry, when it pays the salaries it must determine what portion of the salary payment relates to 2004 ($900 of Salaries Payable) and what portion is Salaries Expense for 2005 ($900 for 3 months). The use of a reversing entry eliminates this analysis. The entire $1,800 payment is debited to Salaries Expense. When combined with the $900 *credit* balance in Salaries Expense established by the reversing entry, the result is a $900 *debit* balance, the amount representing 3 months of salaries expense for 2005.

As we indicated in the discussion of the adjusting entry for deferred revenues, some companies initially record the receipt of revenues in advance of being earned as a revenue instead of a liability. We illustrated that Dapple Corporation *could* have recorded the December 1 receipt of 3 months' advance rent as a credit to Rent Revenue for $450. In this case the adjusting entry is a debit to Rent Revenue for $300 and a credit to Unearned Rent for $300. This adjusting entry establishes a balance sheet account and should be reversed. On January 1, 2005 a reversing entry should be made debiting Unearned Rent for $300 and crediting Rent Revenue for $300. This entry eliminates the Unearned Rent account balance and establishes a $300 balance in Rent Earned for the 2 months of 2005. No further adjusting entry is necessary in 2005.

THE WORKSHEET

8 Complete a worksheet.

At the end of an accounting period, a company prepares adjusting entries, closing entries, and its financial statements. **A worksheet is often prepared in conjunction with these activities to minimize errors, simplify the recording in the general journal of the adjusting and closing entries, and facilitate preparing the financial statements.** A worksheet is *not* a substitute for any accounting records or financial statements; it is merely a working paper designed for these purposes.

A worksheet in a manual system is a large sheet of multicolumn accounting paper. Exhibit C-13 shows a ten-column worksheet for the Dapple Corporation. It has a column for listing all the ledger accounts, plus debit and credit columns for the trial balance, adjustments, income statement, retained earnings statement, and balance sheet. The process of completing the worksheet begins with the preparation of the trial balance. All of the company's accounts and account balances (prior to adjustments) are listed and the debit and credit columns of the trial balance are totaled to verify the equality of the debits and credits. Note that since this is the first year of operations for the Dapple Corporation, the Inventory, Accumulated Depreciation: Building, Accumulated Depreciation: Equipment, and Retained Earnings accounts do not have balances (prior to adjustments). Normally these accounts *do* have balances so we include them in the illustrated trial balance.

Second, the accounts are analyzed to determine the necessary adjustments, which are initially entered in the adjustments columns on the worksheet. If an adjustment involves an account that does not currently have a balance, the account title is entered on the first available line below the other account titles. Each of the adjusting journal entries we show in Exhibit C-6 initially is prepared as shown on the worksheet. Note that the adjusting entry for income taxes is not made until after the income before income taxes is computed. Note also that the accounts in each adjusting entry are *keyed* with the same letter of the alphabet to reduce the likelihood of error. Explanations keyed to these entries are usually entered at the bottom of the worksheet. We do not illustrate these explanations in this example. The adjustments columns are subtotaled to prove the equality of the debits and credits. At this point, some companies prepare an adjusted trial balance in a next set of columns. For an adjusted trial balance, the adjustment amounts are combined with the trial balance amounts to determine the new account balances. This step may be omitted as we did in the Dapple Corporation worksheet.

Third, the trial balance amount of each account is combined with the adjustments to that account and carried over to the proper column of the financial statement in which the account is located. For instance, the $360 debit balance in Prepaid Insurance is combined with the $270 credit adjustment, and the new balance of $90 is carried over to the debit column of the balance sheet. It is important to understand how the Inventory account is handled in a periodic system. The *beginning* inventory ($0 in this case) is transferred to the debit column of the income statement because it eventually is added to purchases (which has a debit balance) to determine the cost of goods available for sale. The *ending* inventory (December 31, 2004) is listed near the bottom of the worksheet, and its amount is entered in *two* columns. The $2,140 is entered in the income statement *credit* column because it is a deduction from the cost of goods available for sale. It is also entered in the *debit* column of the balance sheet because it is an asset.[9]

Fourth, the income statement debit and credit columns are subtotaled. Ordinarily the debit column total differs from the credit column total, the difference being the income (or loss) before income taxes. For the Dapple Corporation the $19,616 credit total exceeds the $17,616 debit total, indicating income before income taxes of $2,000. At this point, the applicable tax rate (30% in this case) is multiplied by the income before income taxes to determine the income taxes ($600). The adjusting entry for income taxes is recorded, and the amounts are carried to the proper columns of the financial statements.

Finally, the financial statement debit and credit columns are totaled in sequential order. First the income statement columns are totaled. The difference between the debit and credit totals is the net income or loss for the period. For the Dapple Corporation the net income is $1,400. This amount is used to balance the income statement columns. It is also entered in the retained earnings statement credit column. We use the arrows in Exhibit C-13 for illustrative purposes; they ordinarily are not included on the worksheet. The beginning retained earnings balance ($0 in this case) is combined with the net income to determine the $1,400 credit total. The $500 debit total is the dividends distributed. The $900 difference is the ending retained earnings. It is used to balance the retained earnings statement columns and is also transferred to the balance sheet credit column. The balance sheet debit and credit columns are finally totaled. The $32,348 total of the debit and credit columns indicates that the system is in balance and the worksheet is complete.

The worksheet is prepared as a preliminary step, prior to the recording of the adjusting and closing entries in the general journal and the preparation of the financial statements. A brief review of the Dapple Corporation worksheet indicates how a worksheet facilitates the accounting process. All the adjusting entries are developed and shown on the worksheet in their basic format. They now must be recorded in the general journal. The closing entries are also simplified. The $19,616 total of the income statement credit column is credited to Income Summary, while the individual accounts with credit balances are debited. Similarly, the $18,216 debit subtotal is debited to Income Summary, while the individual accounts with debit balances are credited. The remaining closing entries involve closing both net income and dividends to Retained Earnings. Finally the preparation of the actual financial statements is facilitated. The amounts

---

9. There are other methods for eliminating the beginning inventory and establishing the ending inventory. One method includes eliminating and establishing the respective inventories in the adjustment columns by associated debits and credits to the Income Summary account.

EXHIBIT C-13 Worksheet (Dapple Corporation)

Worksheet
For Year Ended December 31, 2004

Account Titles	Trial Balance Debit	Trial Balance Credit	Adjustments Debit	Adjustments Credit	Income Statement Debit	Income Statement Credit	Retained Earnings Statement Debit	Retained Earnings Statement Credit	Balance Sheet Debit	Balance Sheet Credit
Cash	2,792								2,792	
Accounts receivable	7,000								7,000	
Notes receivable	1,320								1,320	
Inventory (1/1/04)	0				0					
Prepaid insurance	360			(a) 270					90	
Land	1,500								1,500	
Building	15,320								15,320	
Accumulated depreciation: building		0		(f) 264						264
Equipment	2,120								2,120	
Accumulated depreciation: equipment		0		(g) 120						120
Accounts payable		1,900								1,900
Notes payable		6,600								6,600
Unearned rent		450	(b) 150							300
Capital stock		20,000								20,000
Retained earnings (1/1/04)		0						0		
Dividends distributed	500						500			
Sales revenue		17,000				17,000				
Sales returns and allowances	250				250					
Sales discounts taken	40				40					
Purchases	12,400				12,400					

EXHIBIT C-13, Continued

Account Titles	Trial Balance Debit	Trial Balance Credit	Adjustments Debit	Adjustments Credit	Income Statement Debit	Income Statement Credit	Retained Earnings Statement Debit	Retained Earnings Statement Credit	Balance Sheet Debit	Balance Sheet Credit
Purchases returns and allowances		160				160				
Purchases discounts taken		100				100				
Freight-in	200				200					
Salaries expense	1,800		(c) 900		2,700					
Other expenses	428				428					
Loss on sale of land	180				180					
	46,210	46,210								
Insurance expense			(a) 270		270					
Rent revenue				(b) 150		150				
Salaries payable				(c) 900						900
Interest expense			(d) 594		594					
Interest payable				(d) 594						594
Interest receivable			(e) 66						66	
Interest revenue				(e) 66		66				
Depreciation expense: building			(f) 264		264					
Depreciation expense: equipment			(g) 120		120					
Bad debts expense			(h) 170		170					
Allowance for doubtful accounts				(h) 170						170
Inventory 12/31/04			2,534	2,534	17,616	2,140			2,140	
						19,616				
Income tax expense			(i) 600		600					
Income taxes payable				(i) 600						600
			3,134	3,134	18,216	19,616				
Net income					1,400		500	1,400		
					19,616	19,616	900	1,400		600
Retained earnings, 12/31/04							1,400	1,400	32,348	900
										32,348

from the worksheet columns for each financial statement are rearranged in the proper order on that financial statement. The worksheet is particularly useful in preparing *interim* (such as quarterly) financial statements when a company does not actually adjust or close its accounts. The adjusting entries necessary to update the financial statements may be made on the worksheet only, thereby enabling the company to maintain its accounts on an annual basis.

SUBSIDIARY LEDGERS

Even in the relatively simple Dapple Corporation example, the general ledger contains numerous accounts. For a larger company that sells to many customers and purchases from many suppliers, the general ledger is much larger because the company incurs additional types of expenses and earns other types of revenues. The company also must maintain adequate records of amounts owed by each customer and to each supplier.

In order to (1) reduce the size of the general ledger, (2) minimize errors, (3) divide the accounting task, and (4) keep up-to-date records of its dealings with charge customers and suppliers, a company establishes subsidiary ledgers that are *not* part of the double-entry system. **A subsidiary ledger is a group of accounts, all of which pertain to one specific company activity.** Most companies have separate subsidiary ledgers for accounts receivable and accounts payable. These ledgers enable the company to better focus its attention on the collection and payment process for the receivables and payables. Many companies also use subsidiary ledgers for major categories of accounts, such as property and equipment, selling expenses, and administrative expenses. The *accounts receivable* subsidiary ledger contains the individual accounts of all the company's charge customers. Since the individual customer accounts have debit balances, it follows that this subsidiary ledger has a *total* debit balance (computed by preparing a *schedule* of the individual customer account balances).

9 Understand subsidiary ledgers.

When a company uses this subsidiary ledger, it still maintains an Accounts Receivable account in the general ledger. This account is referred to as a **control account** because its debit balance must be equal to that of the subsidiary ledger on any balance sheet date. The postings to this control account are significantly reduced because only summary postings of customer account activities are necessary. Similarly, the *accounts payable* subsidiary ledger contains the individual accounts of all the company's charge suppliers. Since these accounts have credit balances, the credit total of this subsidiary ledger must agree with the credit total of the Accounts Payable control account in the general ledger on any balance sheet date. If the Dapple Corporation used a subsidiary ledger for the accounts receivable, the ledger and control account balances at the end of 2004 appear as we show in Exhibit C-14.

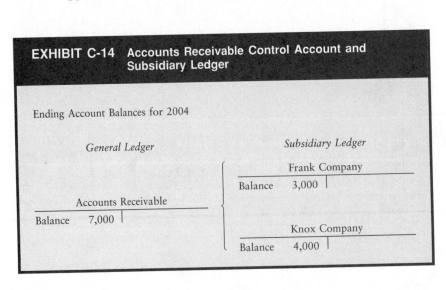

EXHIBIT C-14   Accounts Receivable Control Account and Subsidiary Ledger

Ending Account Balances for 2004

General Ledger

Accounts Receivable
Balance   7,000

Subsidiary Ledger

Frank Company
Balance   3,000

Knox Company
Balance   4,000

SPECIAL JOURNALS

A company's increasing size and complexity also create the need for efficiently record- ing and summarizing many daily transactions. Special journals are used for this pur- pose. **A special journal is a journal used by a company to record its business transactions with a similar characteristic.** Use of these journals (1) allows the accounting task to be divided, (2) reduces the time necessary to complete the various accounting activities, and (3) provides for a chronological listing of similar transactions. Because operating procedures and transactions vary across companies, each company organizes its special journals in a way best suited to its operations. However, there are four common types of transactions for which special journals are usually established: (1) sales of merchan- dise on account, (2) purchases of merchandise on account, (3) cash receipts, and (4) cash payments. A company still needs a general journal to record various other transactions or events not repetitive enough to require the use of special journals.

10 Use special journals.

The major journals and their uses are:

1. *Sales Journal.* Used to record all (and only) sales of merchandise on account.
2. *Purchases Journal.* Used to record all (and only) purchases of merchandise on account.
3. *Cash Receipts Journal.* Used to record all cash receipts.
4. *Cash Payments Journal.* Used to record all cash payments.
5. *General Journal.* Used to record adjusting, closing, and reversing entries and other transactions not recorded in the special journals.

Sometimes a company uses a voucher system, requiring modification of the special journals and the use of a different journal called a *voucher register*. We briefly discuss this system at the end of this section.

To illustrate the journalizing and posting activities for special journals in a manual system, we record the Dapple Corporation transactions for 2004 listed in Exhibit C-3 in the special journals shown in Exhibit C-15 *instead of* the general journal. The adjust- ing and closing entries, which are made in the general journal, are the same as we illustrated earlier so we do not repeat them here. We show these special journals in abbreviated form. Actual journals could include columns for explanations, account numbers, terms of sale and purchase, and other information.

Sales Journal

The sales journal is used to record all sales on account. (Cash sales are recorded in the cash receipts journal.) Each transaction is recorded by listing the customer account and the amount of the sale. After the daily sales are recorded, the amounts are posted as debits to the individual customer accounts in the accounts receivable subsidiary ledger. Use of this procedure ensures that customer account balances are always up-to-date. At the end of the period (or more frequently), the *total* of the sales journal is posted to two accounts—as a credit to the Sales Revenue account to record total sales on account and as a debit to the Accounts Receivable control account to bring its balance into agreement with the total of the accounts receivable subsidiary ledger.

Purchases Journal

The purchases journal is used to record all merchandise purchases on account. (Cash purchases are recorded in the cash payments journal.) Each transaction is recorded by listing the supplier's account and the amount of the purchase. After the daily purchases are recorded, the amounts are posted as credits to the individual supplier accounts in the accounts payable subsidiary ledger, thus maintaining up-to-date balances in these accounts. At the end of the period (or sooner) the *total* of the purchases journal is posted to two accounts—as a credit to the Accounts Payable control account to bring its balance into agreement with the subsidiary ledger total and as a debit to the Purchases account to record the total purchases on account.

EXHIBIT C-15   Special Journals (Dapple Corporation)

Sales Journal

Date	Customer Account	Amount
11/23	Frank Company	5,000
11/23	Knox Company	4,000
		9,000

Purchases Journal

Date	Supplier Account	Amount
3/31	Bark Company	7,400
12/27	Ajax Company	1,900
		9,300

Cash Receipts Journal

Date	Account Title	Cash Debit	Sales Discounts Taken Debit	Accounts Receivable Credit	Sales Revenue Credit	Miscellaneous Credit
1/1	Capital Stock	20,000				20,000
4/2		8,000			8,000	
4/20	Purchases Returns and Allowances	160				160
12/1	Unearned Rent	450				450
12/2	Frank Company	1,960	40	2,000		
		30,570	40	2,000	8,000	20,610

Cash Payments Journal

Date	Account Title	Cash Credit	Purchases Discounts Taken Credit	Miscellaneous Credit	Accounts Payable Debit	Purchases Debit	Miscellaneous Debit
1/16	Land	3,000					3,000
3/30	Building	10,840					15,320
	Equipment						2,120
	Notes Payable			6,600			
3/30	Prepaid Insurance	360					360
4/8	Bark Company	7,300	100		7,400		
4/15	Sales Returns and Allowances	250					250
7/15	Freight-in	3,300				3,100	200
10/1	Salaries Expense	1,800					1,800
12/28	Other Expenses	428					428
12/29	Dividends Distributed	500					500
		27,778	100	6,600	7,400	3,100	23,978

General Journal

Date	Account Title	Debit	Credit
9/1	Notes Receivable	1,320	
	Loss on Sale of Land	180	
	Land		1,500

Cash Receipts Journal

The cash receipts journal is used to record all transactions involving the receipt of cash. A cash debit column is established for this purpose. Since cash is received for a variety of transactions, each company determines which of its accounts are the most frequently credited and establishes column headings for these accounts. A miscellaneous column is used for recording infrequent transactions. Many cash receipts are for cash sales and collections of accounts receivable (less the sales discounts taken), so column headings usually are provided for these accounts.

To record a cash receipt transaction, it is necessary to list an account title only if the amount of the affected account is recorded in the miscellaneous column or if an individual customer account in the subsidiary ledger is involved. Account titles are *not* necessary for amounts listed in columns already identified as relating to a specific account in the general ledger. For instance, to record the April 2 cash sale in Exhibit C-15 it is necessary to enter the $8,000 only in the Cash debit and Sales Revenue credit columns. However, to record the January 1 issuance of stock, it is necessary to enter the $20,000 in the Cash debit and the Miscellaneous credit columns and to list the title of the account, Capital Stock, to be credited.

The cash receipts journal usually is posted on a daily and on an end-of-period basis. The entries to all the miscellaneous accounts are posted daily, as are any entries to individual customer accounts. At the end of the period, all the columns are totaled, and the total of the debit columns is compared to the total of the credit columns to verify equality. The totals of the Cash and Sales Discounts Taken columns are posted as debits to each of these accounts, respectively. The credit total of the Accounts Receivable column is posted to the control account to bring it into agreement with the subsidiary ledger. Finally the credit total of the Sales Revenue column is posted to the Sales Revenue account to record the total cash sales. The total of the miscellaneous column is *not* posted because the miscellaneous accounts already have been posted.

Cash Payments Journal

The cash payments journal is used to record all transactions involving the payment of cash. Its format and the journal entry and posting procedures are very similar to the cash receipts journal. A cash credit column is used to record each cash payment. Column headings are established for frequently debited accounts, and miscellaneous columns are used for recording amounts of infrequent transactions. Since cash payments frequently involve cash purchases and payments of accounts payable (less the purchases discounts taken), column headings are often provided for these accounts.

To record a cash payment transaction, an account title is listed only if its amount is recorded in the miscellaneous column or if it is an individual creditor account in the subsidiary ledger. Account titles are not necessary for entries in specific account columns. Posting usually is done on a daily and on an end-of-period basis. The miscellaneous accounts and the individual creditor subsidiary ledger accounts are posted daily. At the end of the period, the columns are totaled and the debit and credit equality is verified. The totals of the Cash and Purchases Discounts Taken columns are credited to these accounts, while the totals of the Accounts Payable and Purchases columns are debited to these accounts. The miscellaneous column totals are not posted.

General Journal

A company still needs a general journal even when it uses special journals. The general journal is used for recording adjusting, closing, and reversing entries, as well as certain other transactions that occur relatively infrequently, such as purchases returns and sales returns on credit and the purchase or sale of assets (other than merchandise) on credit. The journalizing and posting process is the same as described earlier, with one exception. If subsidiary ledgers are used, any debit or credit to accounts receivable or accounts payable is posted *twice*, once to the individual subsidiary account that is *not* part of the double-entry system and once to the appropriate control account.

Voucher System

To safeguard its cash payments, a company may establish a voucher system. When a company uses a **voucher system,** (1) it establishes a liability (Vouchers Payable, which replaces Accounts Payable) for each anticipated cash payment, (2) it supports each cash payment by a *voucher* (a written authorization) and substantiating documents to prove the validity of the payment, and (3) it makes all payments by check.

When a company uses a voucher system, the purchases journal is expanded to include a column for purchases on account as well as a column for vouchers payable, plus columns for other frequently used accounts as well as miscellaneous columns. This journal is called a **voucher register.** Each expenditure is recorded initially in this voucher register as a liability by a credit to Vouchers Payable and a debit to the related asset or expense account (such as Salaries Expense, Purchases, Equipment). Each expenditure is assigned a voucher number in sequential order and each voucher contains a file of supporting evidence (for example, purchase order, sales invoice, freight receipt).

When the company makes a payment, an authorization signature is required and a check is issued. The check number is entered in the voucher register beside the number of the paid voucher. In this manner all unpaid vouchers (which are liabilities) at the end of the period can be identified because they have no associated check number. Postings from the voucher register must be made daily and at the end of the period and are similar to those for the cash receipts and cash payments journals we discussed earlier.

Because all expenditures are initially recorded in the voucher register, the *check register* (the cash payments journal in a nonvoucher system) is substantially reduced. An account title column is needed only for identifying individual supplier subsidiary accounts. Columns are needed only for debits to Vouchers Payable and Purchases Discounts Taken and credits to Cash. A column is also usually included to record the number of the paid voucher. After each payment is recorded, the daily and end-of-period postings are similar to those we discussed earlier. Although the voucher system institutes greater control over cash payments, the related special journals involve relatively minor modifications from those we discussed earlier. Consequently we do not show an example of a voucher system.

COMPUTER SOFTWARE

In this Appendix (and throughout the book) we use a manual accounting system for convenience. In the business world, however, most companies use computers to process their accounting information. **Software** is the set of computer programs used to operate a computer. Software packages have been developed by software companies for the subsidiary ledgers and special journals we discussed earlier, as well as other financial accounting functions relating to accounts receivable, accounts payable, inventory, payroll, and the general ledger. In addition, "spreadsheet" packages have been developed to serve a variety of accounting needs. We briefly describe each of these software packages next.

ACCOUNTS RECEIVABLE   Because a company generates much of the cash needed for its operations from the collection of accounts receivable, the software program for accounts receivable is a very important aspect of a computer system. Accounts receivable software generally is designed to provide up-to-date balances in customers' accounts by immediately recording invoices and cash receipts from customers; print out monthly statements (bills) for customers; monitor sales returns and allowances as well as sales discounts taken by customers; generate a credit history of each customer to help avoid uncollectible accounts; and provide projections of future cash inflows.

ACCOUNTS PAYABLE   Accounts payable software monitors and controls the cash a company pays to suppliers. In the case of a retailer or wholesaler, payments for purchases of inventory for resale is the primary activity. The software for accounts payable generally is designed to provide up-to-date balances in suppliers' accounts by immediately recording purchase orders and cash payments to suppliers; generate a list to verify the quantity and unit price of an order when it is received from a supplier; monitor purchases returns and allowances and purchases discounts taken; write checks; and provide projections of future cash outflows.

INVENTORY Inventory is a very important asset for many companies. Most inventory software programs are linked to a company's accounts receivable and accounts payable software. Inventory software generally is designed to provide an up-to-date count of the number of units of each item of inventory by immediately recording all unit purchases and sales; highlight when a minimum or maximum stock level has been reached for each item of inventory; print price tags for newly acquired inventory; prepare reports on slow-moving or obsolete inventory items; and provide unit prices when a physical count of the inventory is taken.

PAYROLL Software for a company's payroll was one of the first to be developed. Payroll software can be very complex because of the various federal, state, and local tax laws. Payroll software may be designed to compute the salaries earned by each employee based on pay rates and overtime; allocate the salaries across departments in the company; calculate federal, state, and local withholding taxes; compute other voluntary withholdings such as for investments in U.S. savings bonds; print payroll checks; generate comparisons of actual with projected salaries; and prepare various tax-withholding reports.

GENERAL LEDGER A general ledger software package is broader than the name implies and includes many aspects of a company's accounting system. General ledger software usually includes all special journals and the general journal for recording transactions, a chart of accounts, and the ledger accounts on disks for storing the recorded information. Usually, the software is capable of preparing a trial balance and financial statements at any point in time. Frequently, supporting schedules (e.g., depreciation) and budgets also may be generated. The general ledger software of a company usually is linked to its accounts receivable, accounts payable, inventory, and payroll software.

SPREADSHEETS Spreadsheets are "electronic worksheets." They are laid out like a manual worksheet would appear on a large sheet of paper; the key difference is that they appear on a computer screen and the computer performs all the mathematical calculations defined by the user of the program. Spreadsheet software is "general purpose" because it is modified and programmed by a user for a particular purpose. Spreadsheets are, perhaps, more useful in managerial accounting. There they can be used, for example, to forecast sales, predict operating costs, and establish budgets for different levels of operations. A company also uses spreadsheet software in financial accounting for preparing its worksheets and financial statements, and for developing schedules involving such items as depreciation and interest computations.

CASH-BASIS ACCOUNTING

As we mentioned earlier in this Appendix, most companies use *accrual accounting,* whereby a company records revenues in the accounting period in which they are earned and records expenses in the accounting period they are incurred. A few companies such as small retail stores and professionals such as dentists, doctors, and architects use cash-basis accounting. Under *cash-basis accounting,* a company records revenues when it collects cash from sales and records expenses when it pays cash for its operations. On its income statement, then, the company computes its net income as the difference between its cash receipts and cash payments. In other words, net income is the same as the net operating cash flow for the period. The company may choose not to prepare a balance sheet. However, it frequently will keep track of certain assets such as amounts owed by customers (accounts receivable), amounts paid in advance (prepaid expenses), and any property and equipment it owns. It also frequently will keep track of certain liabilities such as amounts owed to suppliers (accounts payable) and amounts owed to employees (accrued expenses). Cash-basis accounting, however, is not allowed under generally accepted accounting principles.

11 Convert cash-basis financial statements to accrual-basis.

Sometimes a company that is using cash-basis accounting must prepare its financial statements based on accrual accounting. This might happen, for instance, if it applies for a bank loan and the bank requires financial statements in accordance with generally accepted accounting principles. In this case, the company must convert its cash-basis income statement to an accrual-basis income statement and must prepare a related balance sheet. This involves making adjustments to the cash receipts to convert them to sales revenues and making adjustments to the cash payments to convert them to cost of goods sold and operating expenses. It also involves combining the information it has about its assets and liabilities into a formal balance sheet.

Exhibit C-16 illustrates the basic adjustments that a company must make to convert its cash receipts and cash payments into accrual-based revenues, cost of goods sold, and operating expenses. In addition, the company must include depreciation expense on its property and equipment in the operating expenses.

EXHIBIT C-16   Adjustments to Convert Cash-Basis to Accrual-Basis Accounting

Cash Basis	Adjustments	Accrual Basis
Collections from customers	{ + Ending accounts receivable − Beginning accounts receivable }	= Sales revenue
Payments to suppliers	{ + Beginning inventory − Ending inventory + Ending accounts payable − Beginning accounts payable }	= Cost of goods sold
Payments for other operating costs	{ + Beginning prepaid expenses − Ending prepaid expenses + Ending accrued expenses − Beginning accrued expenses }	= Operating expenses (except depreciation)

To illustrate, assume that Gretta Gropples starts Gropples Company (a small retail store organized as a sole proprietorship) on January 1, 2004 by investing cash of $20,000. Gropples Company uses cash-basis accounting but wants to prepare its financial statements on an accrual basis. At the end of the year, the company's checkbook shows cash receipts from customers of $95,000, cash payments of $106,000, and an ending cash balance of $9,000. Based on a physical inventory, the company determined its inventory at the end of 2004 to be $7,200. It also determined that at the end of 2004 customers owed it $4,300, and that it owed suppliers $5,100 and employees $500. The company examined its checkbook and found that during 2004:

1. It paid suppliers $54,000 and paid other operating costs of $29,000. Included in the other operating costs was $6,000 that it paid on January 1 for 2 years of rent on store space.
2. It paid $8,000 for store equipment on January 1. It planned to use straight-line depreciation and expected to use the store equipment for 5 years, after which the store equipment would have a zero residual value.
3. Gretta withdrew $15,000 during the year.

Based on this information, using accrual accounting the company prepared its income statement for 2004 that we show in Exhibit C-17 and its balance sheet at the end of 2004 that we show in Exhibit C-18.

In Exhibit C-17, Gropples Company computed its $99,300 sales revenues by adding the $4,300 ending accounts receivable to the $95,000 it collected from customers. The company computed its $51,900 cost of goods sold by subtracting the $7,200 ending

---

EXHIBIT C-17 Income Statement (Gropples Company)

GROPPLES COMPANY

Income Statement
For Year Ended December 31, 2004

Sales revenue		$99,300[a]
Cost of goods sold		(51,900)[b]
Gross profit		$47,400
Operating expenses		
Depreciation expense	$ 1,600[d]	
Other operating expenses	26,500[c]	
Total expenses		(28,100)
Net Income		$19,300

[a]$95,000 collections from customers + $4,300 ending accounts receivable.

[b]$54,000 payments to suppliers − $7,200 ending inventory + $5,100 ending accounts payable.

[c]$29,000 payments for other operating costs − $3,000 ending prepaid rent ($6,000 × 1/2) + $500 ending salaries payable.

[d]$8,000 store equipment ÷ 5 years.

---

inventory and adding the $5,100 ending accounts payable to the $54,000 it paid to suppliers. It computed the $26,500 other operating expenses by subtracting the $3,000 prepaid rent (the cost of the remaining year of rent it had paid for in advance) and adding the $500 ending salaries payable to the $29,000 it paid for other operating costs. It computed the $1,600 depreciation expense by dividing the $8,000 cost of the store equipment by the 5-year estimated life.

In Exhibit C-18, most of the amounts come from the initial information we presented for the company. The $1,600 accumulated depreciation is the depreciation to date (one

---

EXHIBIT C-18 Balance Sheet (Gropples Company)

GROPPLES COMPANY

Balance Sheet
December 31, 2004

Assets			*Liabilities*		
Current Assets			Current Liabilities		
Cash	$ 9,000		Accounts payable	$ 5,100	
Accounts receivable	4,300		Salaries payable	500	
Inventory	7,200		Total liabilities	$ 5,600	
Prepaid rent	3,000				
Total current assets		$23,500	*Owner's Equity*		
Property and Equipment			G. Gropples, capital	$24,300[a]	
Store equipment	$ 8,000				
Less: Accumulated depreciation	(1,600)				
Total property and equipment		6,400			
Total Assets		$29,900	Total Liabilities	$29,900	

[a]$20,000 beginning investment + $19,300 net income (from Exhibit C-17) − $15,000 withdrawals.

year, in this example; in later years, this amount would increase each year by the amount of the annual depreciation expense). The company computed the $24,300 amount of the G. Gropples capital account by adding the $19,300 net income and subtracting the $15,000 withdrawals from the $20,000 initial investment.

In more complex situations, a company may have items such as deferred revenues and accrued revenues, sales returns and allowances, purchases returns and allowances, and interest revenue and expense, as well as gains or losses on sales of equipment. In these cases the company may make additional adjustments to determine its revenues and expenses, and may provide more detail in the revenues, cost of goods sold, and operating expenses sections of its income statement. For convenience, the company may prepare a worksheet to help it determine these amounts. Regardless of how simple or complex the adjustments are, the intent is to report the company's financial statements on an accrual basis, in accordance with generally accepted accounting principles.

SUMMARY

At the beginning of the Appendix, we identified several objectives you would accomplish after reading the Appendix. The objectives are listed below, each followed by a brief summary of the key points in the Appendix discussion.

1. **Understand the components of an accounting system.** The components of an accounting system include: (1) the framework for operating the system, (2) the input source documents, (3) the records used to store accounting information, and (4) the output reports.
2. **Know the major steps in the accounting cycle.** The major steps in the accounting cycle include: (1) recording (journalizing) daily transactions in a journal, (2) posting the journal entries to the accounts in the general ledger, (3) preparing and posting adjusting entries, (4) preparing the financial statements, and (5) preparing and posting closing entries for the revenue, expense, and dividend accounts.
3. **Prepare journal entries in the general journal.** To make a journal entry to record a transaction, enter the date in the date column. Next, enter the title of the account and amount to be debited in the account titles column and debit column, respectively. Then, enter the title of the account and amount to be credited in the account titles column and credit column, respectively. Finally, write a short explanation of the transaction in the account titles column.
4. **Post to the general ledger and prepare a trial balance.** To post to the general ledger, for each journal entry, first transfer from the general journal the date and the amount debited to the account in the general ledger. Next, transfer the date and the amount credited to the account in the general ledger. To prepare a trial balance at the end of the accounting period, first compute the balance in each account. Then, list each account and list its balance in the debit or credit column of the working paper (trial balance). Finally, total the debit and credit columns to verify that the totals are equal.
5. **Prepare adjusting entries.** Adjusting entries are journal entries made at the end of the accounting period so that a company's financial statements include the correct amounts for the current period. Adjusting entries are made to: (1) apportion prepaid and deferred items, (2) record accrued items, and (3) record estimated items. Adjusting entries are made in the usual manner in the general journal.
6. **Prepare financial statements.** To prepare a company's financial statements, first prepare an adjusted trial balance to verify that the total of the debit balances is equal to the total of the credit balances in the company's accounts. Then, prepare the income statement, which includes the company's revenues, expenses, and net income. Next, prepare the retained earnings statement, which shows the change in retained earnings due to the company's net income and dividends. Finally, prepare the balance sheet, which includes the company's assets, liabilities, and stockholders' equity.
7. **Prepare closing entries.** Closing entries are journal entries of a company made at the end of the accounting period (1) to reduce the balance in each temporary account (revenue, expense, and dividend accounts) to zero, and (2) to update the retained earnings and inventory accounts. Closing entries are made in the usual manner in the general journal.
8. **Complete a worksheet.** To complete a worksheet, first list each account and list its balance in the debit or credit column of the trial balance. Second, enter the adjusting entries as debits or credits in the adjustments columns. Third, combine the trial balance amount of each account with the adjustments to that account and carry over the resulting amount to the proper column of the financial statement in which the account is included. Fourth, subtotal the income statement debit and credit columns, make an adjusting entry for any income taxes on the difference between the columns (the pretax income), and carry the adjustment amounts to the appropriate financial statement columns. Finally, subtotal the income statement columns. List the difference as net income (or net loss), write the amount in the debit (credit) column and balance the income statement columns. Transfer the net income (net loss)

amount to the retained earnings columns and balance these columns. Then transfer the retained earnings balance to the balance sheet credit column and balance these columns.

9. **Understand subsidiary ledgers.** A subsidiary ledger is a group of accounts, all of which pertain to one specific company activity. Most companies have subsidiary ledgers for accounts receivable and accounts payable to better focus attention on collections from customers and payments for payables. When a company uses a subsidiary ledger it still maintains a *control account* in its general ledger. The balance of the control account must be equal to the total of the balances of all the individual accounts in the subsidiary ledger on any balance sheet date.

10. **Use special journals.** The major special journals are the: (1) sales journal (for sales on account), (2) purchases journal (for purchases on account), (3) cash receipts journal, (4) cash payments journal, and (5) general journal (for miscellaneous transactions).

11. **Convert cash-basis financial statements to accrual-basis.** First, start with the income statement. Make adjustments to the collections from customers for any changes in accounts receivable. Make adjustments to the payments to suppliers for any changes in inventory and accounts payable. Make adjustments to the payments for other operating costs for any changes in prepaid expenses or accrued expenses, and for depreciation expense. Complete the accrual-basis income statement using the resulting amounts. Use the cash balance from the company's checkbook and the information from the preceding adjustments (e.g., accounts receivable, accounts payable, etc.) to prepare the ending balance sheet.

QUESTIONS

QC-1 What is a primary objective of financial reporting?

QC-2 What is an *accounting system*?

QC-3 Illustrate how the basic accounting equation relates to the other equations pertaining to information useful to external investors.

QC-4 Discuss the relationship between the accounting equation and the double-entry system of recording transactions.

QC-5 What is the difference between a *permanent* and a *temporary* account? Give examples of each.

QC-6 What are the major financial statements of a company and what information does each summarize?

QC-7 Define the following:
a. *Account*
b. *Contra account*
c. *Ledger*
d. *Journal*
e. *Posting*

QC-8 Why is it advantageous to a company to initially record each of its transactions in a journal?

QC-9 Give examples of transactions that
a. Increase an asset and a liability.
b. Increase an asset and stockholders' equity.
c. Increase an asset and decrease an asset.
d. Decrease an asset and a liability.
e. Decrease an asset and stockholders' equity.

QC-10 Give examples of transactions that
a. Increase a cost of goods sold account and a liability.
b. Decrease a cost of goods sold account and a liability.
c. Increase a cost of goods sold account and decrease an asset.
d. Decrease a cost of goods sold account and increase an asset.

QC-11 What are the steps that a company completes in the accounting cycle? Briefly discuss each step.

QC-12 Why are adjusting entries necessary?

QC-13 What are *prepaid expenses* and *deferred revenues*? Give an example of an adjusting entry to update each of these items at year-end.

QC-14 What are *accrued expenses* and *accrued revenues*? Give an example of an adjusting entry to record each of these items.

QC-15 Give two examples of adjusting entries to record estimated items. Include in one example a discussion of how depreciation is computed.

QC-16 What is the difference between a *trial balance* and an *adjusted trial balance*? Why is the latter a useful accounting working paper?

QC-17 What is the difference between a *periodic* and a *perpetual* inventory system? How is this difference reflected in the accounts and financial statements?

QC-18 How is cost of goods sold computed when a company uses a periodic inventory system?

QC-19 What are the objectives of closing entries?

QC-20 Illustrate, without amounts, the form of the closing entries for a retail store using a periodic inventory system.

QC-21 What are *reversing entries* and why are they used? Give an illustration of an adjusting entry and a reversing entry for salaries payable, and the later entry to pay the salaries.

QC-22 What is a *worksheet*? How does the use of a worksheet facilitate the completion of the accounting cycle?

QC-23 What is a *subsidiary ledger* and a *control account*, and why are they used? Give an example of how they work.

QC-24 What are *special journals* and what advantages are achieved by using them?

QC-25 What are the major special journals? Give examples of transactions that would be recorded in each journal.

QC-26 Discuss the use of a voucher system.

QC-27 Identify the common software packages for the financial accounting functions.

QC-28 What is cash-basis accounting? What must a company do to convert its cash-basis accounting records to an accrual-based income statement?

EXERCISES

EC-1 **Financial Statement Interrelationship** Draw a diagram that shows the interrelationship between the beginning balance sheet, income statement, retained earnings statement, and ending balance sheet.

EC-2 **Journal Entries** The Mead Company uses a periodic inventory system and engaged in the following transactions during the month of May:

Date	Transaction
May 1	Made cash sales of $6,300.
5	Purchased $2,000 of merchandise on account, terms 2/10, n/30.
9	Made credit sales of $3,300.
13	Paid sales salaries of $900 and office salaries of $600.
14	Paid for the May 5 purchases less the applicable discount.
18	Purchased sales equipment costing $8,000; made a down payment of $2,000 and agreed to pay the balance in 60 days.
21	Purchased $600 of merchandise for cash and paid $20 for related freight.
24	Customer returned $400 of defective merchandise for credit to its account.
27	Sold land that had originally cost $1,900 for $2,600.

Required Record the preceding transactions in a general journal.

EC-3 **Journal Entries** The following are selected accounts and account balances of the Sawyer Company on May 31:

	Debit (Credit)
Cash	$12,523
Accounts receivable	23,052
Office equipment	35,860
Accumulated depreciation	(10,540)
Notes payable	(3,400)
Accounts payable	(3,500)
Sales revenue	(47,872)
Sales discounts taken	240
Gain on sale of office equipment	(400)
Purchases	22,354
Purchases discounts taken	(220)
Purchases returns and allowances	(420)
Utility expense	1,124

The Sawyer Company entered into the following transactions during June:

Date	Transaction
June 3	Sold for $700 office equipment that had cost $2,000 and has associated accumulated depreciation of $1,500.
7	Made sales of $2,000 on account, terms 2/10, n/30.
10	Purchased $1,000 of merchandise for cash.
15	Purchased new office equipment costing $4,000, paying $1,500 and signing a 90-day note for the balance.
16	Received $1,960 check for June 7 credit sale less the discount.
17	Made cash sales of $4,200.
20	Purchased $2,600 of merchandise on account, terms 2/10, n/30.
24	Returned $200 of defective merchandise from the June 20 purchase for a credit to its account.
29	Paid for the June 20 purchase less the return and the discount.
30	Paid the monthly utility bill, $210.

Required

1. Record the preceding transactions in a general journal.
2. Post to the accounts.

EC-4   *Partial Income Statement*   The following are selected account balances of the Rule Company:

	Debit	Credit		Debit	Credit
Cash	$3,900		Inventory, December 31, 2004	$4,100	
Sales returns and allowances	600		Purchases	8,300	
Inventory, January 1, 2004	5,300		Delivery expense	800	
Purchases discounts taken		$ 100	Purchases returns and allowances		$500
Sales salaries expense	1,200		Sales discounts taken	200	
Sales revenue		16,200	Freight-in	400	
Accounts payable		6,000			

Required Prepare a partial income statement through gross profit on sales.

EC-5   *Income Statement Calculations*   The following is partial information from the Ferdon Company income statements for 2004 and 2005:

	2004	2005
Beginning inventory	$ (2)	$ (4)
Sales	220,000	(6)
Purchases	118,000	140,000
Purchases returns	2,000	3,000
Ending inventory	48,000	74,000
Sales returns	1,000	3,000
Gross profit	(1)	77,000
Cost of goods sold	106,000	(5)
Expenses	65,000	62,000
Net income	(3)	15,000

Required Fill in the blanks numbered 1 through 6. (*Hint*: It probably is easiest to work through the blanks according to the sequential numbers.)

EC-6   *Financial Statements*   The Turtle Company has prepared the following adjusted trial balance for the year

ended December 31, 2004:

	Debit	Credit
Cash	$ 1,700	
Accounts receivable (net)	2,100	
Inventory, January 1, 2004	1,900	
Equipment	5,400	
Accumulated depreciation		$ 1,700
Accounts payable		2,300
Salaries payable		300
Income taxes payable		360
Capital stock (400 shares)		3,200
Retained earnings		2,500
Dividends distributed	200	
Sales revenue		7,900
Purchases	4,200	
Selling expenses	1,800	
Administrative expenses	600	
Income tax expense	360	
Totals	$18,260	$18,260

In addition, the company has determined that its ending inventory on December 31, 2004 is $1,800.

Required Prepare for 2004 in proper form: (1) an income statement, (2) a retained earnings statement, (3) an ending balance sheet, and (4) closing entries.

EC-7   **Adjusting Entries**   Your examination of the records of the Sullivan Company provides the following information for the December 31, 2004 year-end adjustments:

1. Bad debts are to be recognized at 2% of sales. Sales totaled $25,000 for the year.
2. Salaries at year-end that have accumulated but have not been paid total $1,400.
3. Annual straight-line depreciation for the company's equipment is based on a cost of $30,000, an estimated life of 8 years, and an estimated residual value of $2,000.
4. Prepaid insurance in the amount of $800 has expired.
5. Interest that has been earned but not collected totals $500.
6. Unearned rent in the amount of $1,000 has become earned.
7. Interest on a note payable that has accumulated but has not been paid totals $600.
8. The income tax rate is 30% on current income and is payable in the first quarter of 2005. The pretax income before the preceding adjusting entries is $6,800.

Required Prepare the adjusting entries to record the preceding information.

EC-8   **Adjusting Entries**   The following are several transactions of the Pruitt Company that occurred during the current year and were recorded in *real* (that is, balance sheet) accounts unless indicated otherwise:

Date	Transaction
Apr. 1	Purchased a delivery van for $10,000, paying $1,000 down, and issuing a 1-year, 12% note payable for the $9,000 balance. It is estimated that the van has a 4-year life and an $800 residual value; the company uses straight-line depreciation. The interest on the note will be paid on the maturity date.
May 15	Purchased $830 of office supplies.
June 2	Purchased a 2-year comprehensive insurance policy for $960.
Aug. 1	Received 6 months' rent in advance at $260 per month and recorded the $1,560 receipt as Rent Earned.
Sept. 15	Advanced $600 to sales personnel to cover their future travel costs.
Nov. 1	Accepted a $6,000, 6-month, 12% (annual rate) note receivable from a customer, the interest to be collected when the note is collected.

The following information also is available:

1. On January 1, the Office Supplies account had a $250 balance. On December 31, an inventory count showed $190 of office supplies on hand.
2. The weekly (5-day) payroll of Pruitt Company amounts to $2,000. All employees are paid at the close of business each Wednesday. A two-day accrual is required for the current year.
3. Sales personnel travel cost reports indicate that $490 of advances had been used to pay travel expenses.
4. The income tax rate is 30% on current income and is payable in the first quarter of next year. The pretax income before the adjusting entries is $8,655.

Required On the basis of the above information, prepare journal entries to record whatever *adjustments* are necessary to bring the accounts up to date on December 31. Each journal entry explanation should show any related computations.

EC-9   **Adjusting Entries**   The following partial list of accounts and account balances has been taken from the trial balance and the adjusted trial balance of the Barker Company:

	Trial Balance		Adjusted Trial Balance	
	Debit	Credit	Debit	Credit
Accumulated depreciation		$5,200		$6,600
Allowance for doubtful accounts		380		650
Income taxes payable		0		2,250
Interest payable		0		320
Prepaid insurance	$350		$90	
Salaries payable		0		720
Unearned rent		900		300

Required Prepare the adjusting entry that caused the change in each account balance.

EC-10 *Closing Entries* The Collins Corporation shows the following inventory, dividends, revenue, and expense account balances before closing:

Inventory (beginning)	$ 150		Purchases returns	$300
Dividends distributed	250		Salaries expense	$300
Sales revenue		$2,000	Utilities expense	130
Sales discounts taken	200		Miscellaneous expenses	120
Purchases	1,200		Income tax expense	180

At the end of the period, its ending inventory is $400.

Required Prepare closing entries.

EC-11 *Reversing Entries* On December 31, 2004 Adams Company made the following adjusting entries for its annual accounting period:

Depreciation Expense	2,400	
Accumulated Depreciation		2,400
To record depreciation on buildings.		
Interest Receivable	500	
Interest Revenue		500
To record interest on note receivable due January 28, 2005.		
Rent Expense	400	
Prepaid Rent		400
To record expired prepaid rent.		
Interest Expense	620	
Interest Payable		620
To record interest on note payable due March 16, 2005.		

Required Prepare whatever reversing entries are appropriate.

EC-12 *Special Journals* The following are several transactions of a company that uses special journals:

Transaction	Journal	Accounts
1. Purchase of merchandise for cash.		
2. Sale of merchandise on credit.		
3. Payment of sales salaries.		
4. Purchase of merchandise on credit.		
5. Sale of merchandise for cash.		
6. Purchase of land by issuing note payable.		
7. Collection of short-term note receivable and related interest.		
8. Return of defective merchandise to supplier for credit to account.		
9. Preparation of adjusting entries.		
10. Purchase of equipment for cash.		

Required In the space provided:

1. Indicate in which journal the transaction would be recorded using the codes: *G* for general journal, *S* for sales journal, *P* for purchases journal, *CR* for cash receipts journal, and *CP* for cash payments journal.
2. Indicate the accounts that would be debited or credited in the journal for each transaction.

EC-13 *Worksheet for Service Company* The Grant Consulting Company has prepared a trial balance on the following partially completed worksheet for the year ended December 31, 2004:

Accounts	Trial Balance		Adjustments		Income Statement		Retained Earnings Statement		Balance Sheet	
	Debit	Credit	Debit	Credit	Debit	Credit	Debit	Credit	Debit	Credit
Cash	3,800									
Prepaid rent	2,400									
Office equipment	7,000									
Accumulated depreciation		1,400								
Notes payable, due 7/1/05		2,000								
Capital stock (200 shares)		4,000								
Retained earnings, 1/1/04		3,200								
Dividends distributed	200									
Consulting revenues		6,100								
Salaries expense	2,500									
Miscellaneous expenses	800									
Totals	16,700	16,700								

Additional information: (a) On January 1, 2004 the company had paid 2 years' rent in advance at $100 a month on its office space, (b) the office equipment is being depreciated on a straight-line basis over a 10-year life, and no residual value is expected, (c) interest of $150 has accrued on the note payable but has not been paid, and (d) the income tax rate is 30% on current income and will be paid in the first quarter of 2005.

Required

1. Complete the worksheet.
2. Prepare financial statements for 2004.

EC-14   *Worksheet, Including Inventory*   The Murphy Company prepared a trial balance on the following partially completed worksheet for the year ended December 31, 2004:

Accounts	Trial Balance		Adjustments		Income Statement		Retained Earnings Statement		Balance Sheet	
	Debit	Credit	Debit	Credit	Debit	Credit	Debit	Credit	Debit	Credit
Cash	2,500									
Accounts receivable	4,000									
Allowance for doubtful accounts		300								
Inventory, 1/1/04	6,800									
Prepaid rent	3,600									
Equipment	30,000									
Accumulated depreciation		12,000								
Accounts payable		3,700								
Notes payable, due 7/1/05		5,000								
Capital stock (1,000 shares)		8,900								
Retained earnings, 1/1/04		10,200								
Dividends distributed	1,000									
Sales revenues		45,000								
Purchases	22,400									
Salaries expense	7,100									
Utilities expense	3,300									
Advertising expense	4,400									
Totals	85,100	85,100								

Additional information: (a) The equipment is being depreciated on a straight-line basis over a 10-year life, with no residual value; (b) salaries accrued but not recorded total $500; (c) on January 1, 2004 the company had paid 3 years' rent in advance at $100 per month; (d) bad debts are expected to be 1% of total sales; (e) interest of $400 has accrued on the note payable; (f) the December 31, 2004 inventory is $8,200; and (g) the income tax rate is 40% on current income and will be paid in the first quarter of 2005.

Required

1. Complete the worksheet.
2. Prepare financial statements for 2004.
3. Prepare closing entries in the general journal.

EC-15   *Cash-Basis Accounting*   Ellis Company keeps its accounting records on a cash basis during the year. At year-end, it adjusts its books to the accrual basis for preparing its financial statements. At the end of 2003, Ellis Company reported the following balance sheet items:

	Debit	Credit
Cash	$ 2,700	
Accounts receivable	4,200	
Inventory	5,600	
Equipment	12,000	
Accumulated depreciation		$ 4,800
Accounts payable		6,100
M. Ellis, capital		13,600
Totals	$24,500	$24,500

It is now the end of 2004. The company's checkbook shows a balance of $4,700, which includes cash receipts from customers of $51,300 and cash payments of $49,300.

An examination of the cash payments show that: (1) $30,600 was paid to suppliers, (2) $12,700 was paid for other operating costs (including $7,200 paid on January 1 for two years' annual rent), and (3) $6,000 was withdrawn by M. Ellis.

On December 31, 2004, (1) customers owed Ellis Company $5,900, (2) Ellis Company owed suppliers and employees $7,000 and $900, respectively, and (3) the ending inventory was $6,300. Ellis is depreciating the equipment using straight-line depreciation over a 10-year life (no residual value).

Required   Using accrual-based accounting, prepare (1) a 2004 income statement and (2) a December 31, 2004 balance sheet (show supporting calculations).

PROBLEMS

PC-1   *Journal Entries, Posting, and Trial Balance*   The account balances of the Antil Company on November 1, 2004 are as follows:

	Debit	Credit		Debit	Credit
Cash	$ 7,800		Common stock, no par		$165,000
Accounts receivable	12,530		Retained earnings, January 1,		
Allowance for doubtful			2004		24,958
accounts		$ 740	Sales revenue		38,400
Notes receivable	6,000		Sales discounts taken	$ 725	
Inventory, January 1, 2004	25,670		Sales returns and allowances	842	
Prepaid insurance	840		Purchases	32,000	
Office supplies	465		Purchases discounts taken		640
Land	74,350		Purchases returns and		
Buildings	66,580		allowances		1,042
Accumulated depreciation:			Freight-in	1,133	
buildings		21,400	Sales salaries expense	6,200	
Equipment	37,620		Office salaries expense	4,300	
Accumulated depreciation:			Advertising expense	1,250	
equipment		11,480	Utility expense	1,845	
Patents	25,000		Interest revenue		550
Accounts payable		38,750	Interest expense	210	
Notes payable		2,400			

During the month of November, the following transactions took place:

Date	Transaction
Nov. 2	Made cash sales of $3,400.
4	Purchased $900 of merchandise for cash.
5	Sold an unused 1/2 acre of land for $4,000; the land had originally cost $3,650.
8	Purchased a 2-year comprehensive insurance policy for $528.
9	Returned $100 of defective merchandise for a cash refund.
12	Leased an unused portion of its building to Charles Company, collecting 6 months' rent in advance at $220 per month.
13	Made $2,300 of sales on account to Grant Company, terms 2/10, n/30.
16	Collected the $200 monthly payment plus $30 interest on a customer's note receivable.
17	Purchased $1,600 of merchandise on account from Mason Company, terms 1/10, n/30. Paid $60 of associated freight charges.
19	Grant Company returned $200 of defective merchandise (from the November 13 transaction) for credit to its account.
20	Purchased land for a future building site. Made a $2,000 down payment and signed a 12%, 90-day $6,000 note payable for the balance.
23	Collected the Grant Company account for the November 13 sale less the return and the cash discount.
26	Paid for the November 17 purchase of merchandise less the cash discount.
27	Paid the city newspaper $420 for advertising that had appeared during November.
30	Paid $520 of sales salaries and $390 of office salaries.

Required

1. Prepare general journal entries to record the preceding transactions.
2. Post to the general ledger accounts.
3. Prepare a trial balance on November 30, 2004.

PC-2   *Financial Statements*   The Stern Company uses a periodic inventory system and has prepared the following *adjusted trial balance* on December 31, 2004:

	Debit	Credit
Cash	$ 2,000	
Accounts receivable	2,700	
Allowance for doubtful accounts		$ 250
Inventory, January 1, 2004	5,100	
Prepaid insurance	800	
Land	5,200	
Buildings and equipment	31,000	
Accumulated depreciation		15,000
Accounts payable		3,100
Salaries payable		420
Unearned rent		360
Income taxes payable		2,625
Note payable (due July 1, 2008)		5,000
Interest payable (due July 1, 2008)		750
Capital stock (1,500 shares)		9,000
Retained earnings, January 1, 2004		6,770
Dividends distributed	1,200	
Sales revenue		33,000
Sales returns	2,100	
Rent revenue		1,440
Purchases	15,900	
Purchases returns		1,240
Freight-in	1,780	
Selling expenses	4,800	
Administrative expenses	3,000	
Interest expense	750	
Income tax expense	2,625	
Totals	$78,955	$78,955

In addition, the company took its annual physical inventory on December 31, 2004. It determined that its ending inventory is $6,500.

Required Prepare in proper form for 2004 the company's: (1) income statement, (2) retained earnings statement, (3) ending balance sheet, and (4) closing entries in its general journal.

PC-3   *Financial Statements*   The Nealy Company uses a perpetual inventory system and has prepared the following alphabetical adjusted trial balance on December 31, 2004:

	Debit	Credit
Accounts payable		$ 6,400
Accounts receivable	$ 5,700	
Accumulated depreciation: buildings		19,000
Accumulated depreciation: equipment		11,000
Additional paid-in capital		15,000
Administrative expenses	6,500	
Allowance for doubtful accounts		600
Buildings	42,000	
Capital stock, $1 par (4,000 shares)		4,000
Cash	5,000	
Cost of goods sold	27,400	
Current income taxes payable		4,035
Dividends distributed	2,400	
Equipment	22,000	
Income tax expense	4,035	
Interest expense	650	
Interest payable (due July 1, 2005)		650
Inventory, December 31, 2004	10,800	
Land	6,800	
Notes payable (due July 1, 2008)		10,000
Rent revenue		2,800
Retained earnings, January 1, 2004		14,500
Sales discounts taken	1,200	
Sales returns and allowances	3,700	
Sales revenue		59,800
Selling expenses	9,700	
Unearned rent		700
Unexpired insurance	1,600	
Wages payable		1,000
	$149,485	$149,485

Required Prepare the following 2004 items in proper form for the Nealy Company: (1) the income statement, (2) the retained earnings statement, (3) the ending balance sheet, and (4) the closing entries in the general journal. (*Hint*: For the ending balance sheet, the Capital Stock, Additional Paid-in Capital, and Retained Earnings accounts are summed to determine the total stockholders' equity.)

PC-4   *Adjusting Entries*   The following 2004 information is available concerning the Drake Company, which adjusts
 and closes its accounts every December 31:
1. Salaries accrued but unpaid total $2,840 on December 31, 2004.
2. The $247 December utility bill arrived on December 31, 2004 and has not been paid or recorded.
3. Buildings with a cost of $78,000, 25-year life, and $9,000 residual value are to be depreciated; equipment with a cost of $44,000, 8-year life, and $2,000 residual value is also to be depreciated. The straight-line method is to be used.
4. A count of supplies indicates that the Store Supplies account should be reduced by $128 and the Office Supplies account reduced by $397 for supplies used during the year.
5. The company holds a $6,000, 12% (annual rate), 6-month note receivable dated September 30, 2004 from a customer. The interest is to be collected on the maturity date.

6. Bad debts expense is estimated to be 1% of annual sales. 2004 sales total $65,000.

7. An analysis of the company insurance policies indicates that the Prepaid Insurance account is to be reduced for the $528 of expired insurance.

8. A review of travel expense reports indicates that $310 advanced to sales personnel (and recorded as Travel Expenses) has not yet been used by these personnel.

9. The income tax rate is 30% on current income and will be paid in the first quarter of 2005. The pretax income of the company before adjustments is $18,270.

Required Journalize the necessary adjusting entries for the company at the end of 2004. Show supporting calculations in your journal entry explanations.

PC-5 *Adjusting Entries* The Franklin Retail Company entered into the following transactions during 2004. [The transactions were properly recorded in *real* (balance sheet) accounts unless otherwise indicated.]

Date	Transaction
Jan. 25	Purchased $480 of office supplies.
Feb. 1	Rented a warehouse from Tropple Company, paying 1 year's rent of $3,600 in advance. Recorded the $3,600 payment as rent expense.
Mar. 1	Borrowed $10,000 from the bank, signing a 1-year note at an annual interest rate of 12%. The interest was collected in advance by the bank. The company recorded the transaction as a debit to Cash $8,800, debit to Interest Expense $1,200, and credit to Notes Payable $10,000.
May 1	Purchased office equipment for $15,000, paying $3,000 down and signing a 2-year, 12% (annual rate) note payable for the balance. The office equipment is expected to have a useful life of 10 years and a residual value of $1,500. Straight-line depreciation is appropriate.
May 31	Purchased a 3-year comprehensive insurance policy for $720.
Aug. 1	Sold land for $9,000. The purchaser made a $2,000 down payment and signed a 1-year, 10% note for the balance. The interest and principal will be collected on the maturity date.
Sept. 30	Rented a portion of the retail floor space to a florist for $120 per month, collecting 8 months' rent in advance. Recorded the $960 receipt as rent revenue.
Nov. 13	Issued checks to sales personnel totaling $900. The checks are advances for expected travel costs during the remainder of the year.

On December 31, 2004 the following additional information is available:

1. Property taxes for 2004 are due to be paid by April 1, 2005. The company has not paid or recorded its $2,300 property taxes for 2004.

2. The $302 December utility bill has not been recorded or paid.

3. Salaries accrued but not paid total $927.

4. Travel cost reports indicate that $787 of travel advances have been used to pay travel expenses.

5. The Office Supplies account had a balance of $129 on January 1, 2004. A physical count on December 31, 2004 showed $174 of office supplies on hand.

6. On January 1, 2004 the Buildings account and the Store Equipment account had balances of $100,000 and $65,000, respectively. The buildings are expected to have an $8,000 residual value, while the store equipment is expected to have a $2,000 residual value at the end of their respective lives. They are being depreciated using the straight-line method over 20- and 10-year lives, respectively.

7. The income tax rate is 30% on current income and is payable in the first quarter of 2005. The pretax income of the company before adjustments is $27,749.

Required On the basis of the preceding information, prepare journal entries to adjust the company's books as of December 31, 2004. Each entry explanation should include supporting computations. (Round to the nearest dollar.)

PC-6 *Adjusting Entries* At the end of 2004 the Ritter Company prepared a trial balance, recorded and posted its adjusting entries, and then prepared an adjusted trial balance. Selected accounts and account balances from the trial balance and adjusted trial balance are as follows:

	Partial Trial Balance		Partial Adjusted Trial Balance	
	Debit	Credit	Debit	Credit
Depreciation expense	$ 0		$3,960	
Interest payable (due May 14, 2006)		$ 0		$ 810
Bad debts expense	0		410	
Utilities expense	1,480		1,682	
Rental revenue		1,650		2,635
Income tax expense	0		2,740	
Prepaid insurance	1,742		1,380	
Office salaries payable		0		540
Rent expense	0		800	
Accumulated depreciation		14,820		18,780
Interest receivable (due March 1, 2005)	0		320	
Prepaid rent	1,600		800	
Office salaries expense	5,600		6,140	
Income taxes payable		0		2,740
Insurance expense	300		662	
Allowance for doubtful accounts		130		540
Interest expense	0		810	
Unearned rent		600		0
Utilities payable		0		202
Interest revenue		620		940
Sales salaries expense	7,300		7,850	
Office supplies	1,150		700	
Rent receivable	0		385	
Advances to salespersons	770		220	
Office supplies expense	0		450	

Required

1. By comparing the partial trial balance to the partial adjusted trial balance, determine the adjusting entries that the company made on December 31, 2004. Prepare your answers in general journal form.
2. Assuming that the company uses reversing entries, indicate which adjusting entries should be reversed.

PC-7   ***Adjusting Entries***   The trial balance of the Trishia Company on December 31, 2004 (the end of its *annual* accounting period) included the following account balances *before* adjustments:

Notes receivable	$ 8,000 debit	Unearned rent	$4,320 credit
Insurance expense	6,000 debit	Notes payable	7,200 credit
Delivery equipment	14,000 debit	Office supplies expense	1,000 debit
Building	60,000 debit		

Reviewing the company's recorded transactions and accounting records for 2004, you find the following data pertaining to the December 31, 2004 adjustments:

1. On July 2, 2004 the company had accepted a $10,000, 9-month, 10% (annual rate) note receivable from a customer. The interest is to be collected when the note is collected.
2. On August 2, 2004 the company had paid $3,000 for a 2-year insurance policy.
3. The building was acquired in 1992 and is being depreciated using the straight-line method over a 25-year life. It has an estimated residual value of $8,000.
4. The delivery equipment was purchased on April 2, 2004. It is to be depreciated using the straight-line method over a 10-year life, with an estimated residual value of $2,000.
5. On September 1, 2004 the company had received 2 years' rent in advance ($4,320) for a portion of a building it is renting to Oscar Company.
6. On December 1, 2004 the company had issued a $7,200, 3-month, 12% (annual rate) note payable to a supplier. The interest is to be paid when the note is paid.
7. On January 2, 2004 the company purchased $1,000 of office supplies. A physical count on December 31, 2004 revealed that there are $400 of office supplies still on hand. No supplies were on hand at the beginning of the year.

Required Prepare the adjusting entries that are necessary to bring the Trishia Company accounts up to date on December 31, 2004. Each journal entry explanation should summarize your calculations.

PC-8   *Reversing Entries*   During 2004 the Garson Company entered into two transactions involving promissory notes and properly recorded each transaction. These are listed next:

1. On November 1, 2004 it purchased land at a cost of $8,000. It made a $2,000 down payment and signed a note payable agreeing to pay the $6,000 balance in 6 months plus interest at an *annual* rate of 10%.
2. On December 1, 2004 it accepted a $4,200, 3-month, 12% (*annual* interest rate) note receivable from a customer for the sale of merchandise. On December 31, 2004, the Garson Company made the following related adjustments:

Interest Expense	100	
Interest Payable		100
Interest Receivable	42	
Interest Revenue		42

Required

1. Assuming that the Garson Company uses reversing entries, prepare journal entries to record:
   a. The January 1, 2005 reversing entries
   b. The March 1, 2005 $4,326 collection of the note receivable
   c. The May 1, 2005 $6,300 payment of the note payable
2. Assuming instead that the Garson Company does *not* use reversing entries, prepare journal entries to record the collection of the note receivable and the payment of the note payable.

PC-9   *Effects of Errors*   During the current accounting period Page Company makes the following errors. The company uses a periodic inventory system.

Error	Net Income	Total Assets	Total Liabilities	Total Stockholders' Equity
Example: Failed to record a cash sale.	U	U	N	U
1. The purchase of equipment for cash is recorded as a debit to Equipment and a credit to Accounts Payable.				
2. Failed to record the purchase of merchandise on account.				
3. Cash received from a customer in payment of its account is recorded as if the receipt were for a current period sale.				
4. Failed to record a credit sale.				
5. At the end of the year the receipt of money from a 60-day, 12% bank loan is recorded as a debit to Cash and a credit to Sales Revenue.				
6. Failed to record depreciation at the end of the current period.				

Required Indicate the effect of the errors on the net income, total assets, total liabilities, and total stockholders' equity at the end of the accounting period by using the following code: O = overstated, U = understated, N = no effect. Disregard income taxes.

PC-10 *Errors in Financial Statements* At the end of the current year, the controller of the Jodi Corporation discovers the following items of information:

1. Salaries are paid every Friday for a 5-day work week. The normal weekly payroll is $40,000. The year-end falls on a Tuesday this year.
2. The company has a $20,000, 9-month, 12% (annual rate) note payable outstanding at the end of the year. The note was issued on October 1; the interest is to be paid when the note is paid.
3. Examining the Rent Expense account, the controller finds that it includes a $4,800 advance payment for 3 months' rent. The payment was made on November 1.
4. There are $500 of office supplies left in the storeroom. At the beginning of the year there were no office supplies. During a year the company purchased $3,500 of office supplies, which were debited to the Office Supplies account.
5. The company received a large order in May with a $13,000 advance payment. The advance payment was credited to Unearned Revenue. In November, the last of the order was received by the customer.

Required For each of the preceding items, indicate the effect on net income, assets, liabilities, and stockholders' equity in the financial statements of the company for the year if the controller fails to make an adjusting entry for the item (ignore income taxes). (*Contributed by Paula L. Koch*)

PC-11 *Reversing Entries* On December 31, 2004 the Cochran Company made the proper year-end adjusting entries shown here:

Dec. 31	Bad Debts Expense	530	
	Allowance for Doubtful Accounts		530
31	Salaries Expense	940	
	Salaries Payable		940
31	Unearned Rent	1,230	
	Rent Revenue		1,230
31	Interest Expense	220	
	Interest Payable (due July 1, 2005)		220
31	Rent Receivable	310	
	Rent Revenue		310
31	Depreciation Expense	5,100	
	Accumulated Depreciation		5,100
31	Insurance Expense	312	
	Prepaid Insurance		312
31	Interest Receivable (due February 1, 2006)	225	
	Interest Revenue		225
31	Office Supplies	100	
	Office Supplies Expense		100
31	Advances to Salespersons	300	
	Salaries Expense		300
31	Income Tax Expense	4,300	
	Income Taxes Payable		4,300

Required

1. Prepare journal entries to record whatever reversing entries you think are appropriate.
2. Explain your reasoning for each reversing entry.

PC-12   *Special Journals*   The Schnell Company uses a purchases, sales, cash receipts, cash payments, and general journal to record its transactions. The following are its transactions for May:

Date	Transaction
May 1	Made $5,500 sales on account to Gordon Company, terms 2/10, n/30.
3	Purchased office equipment from Myers Supply Company for $6,000, paying $2,000 down and agreeing to pay the remaining balance in 30 days.
6	Purchased merchandise from Ripley Company on account, $3,500. Terms 1/10, n/30.
10	Made cash sales of $3,000.
11	Collected the account receivable from May 1, less the discount.
12	Sold 1 acre of land for $4,500. The purchaser made a $600 down payment and signed a 90-day, 12% note for the balance. The land had originally cost $2,800.
16	Paid for the merchandise purchased on May 6, less the discount.
24	Made $8,300 sales on account to Altis Company, terms 2/10, n/30.
26	Purchased merchandise on account from Boon Company, $5,200. Terms 2/10, n/30.
29	Altis Company returned $1,000 of merchandise from the May 24 sale for credit to its account.
31	Paid the following expenses: salaries, $500; utilities, $220; advertising, $325.

Required Record each of the preceding transactions in the appropriate special journal.

PC-13   *Worksheet*   The Fiorillo Company has the following account balances on December 31, 2004 prior to any adjustments:

	Debit	Credit		Debit	Credit
Cash	$ 1,900		Mortgage payable (due		
Accounts receivable	4,700		January 1, 2009)		$ 7,300
Allowance for doubtful accounts		$ 60	Capital stock (2,000 shares)		10,000
Inventory, January 1, 2004	4,800		Retained earnings, January 1, 2004		18,075
Prepaid insurance	600		Dividends distributed	$ 1,300	
Land	4,100		Sales revenue		49,355
Buildings	38,000		Purchases	31,105	
Accumulated depreciation: buildings		11,500	Purchases returns		1,300
Equipment	10,700		Purchases discounts taken		760
Accumulated depreciation:			Freight-in	2,040	
equipment		3,100	Salaries expense	4,080	
Accounts payable		4,300	Utilities expense	2,000	
Note payable (due March 1, 2005)		1,400	Office supplies expense	770	
Unearned rent		1,200	Delivery expense	1,275	
			Other expenses	980	

Additional adjustment and inventory information: (a) depreciation on buildings, $1,100; on equipment, $600, (b) bad debts expense, $240, (c) interest accumulated but not paid: on note payable, $50; on mortgage payable, $530 (this interest is due during the next accounting period), (d) insurance expired, $175, (e) salaries accrued but not paid $370, (f) rent that was collected in advance and is now earned at year-end, $800, (g) office supplies on hand at year-end, $230 (expensed when originally purchased earlier in the year), (h) the December 31, 2004 ending inventory is $8,700, and (i) the income tax rate is 30% on current income and is payable in the first quarter of 2005.

Required

1. Transfer the account balances to a 10-column worksheet and prepare a trial balance.
2. Complete the worksheet.
3. Prepare the company's income statement, retained earnings statement, and balance sheet.
4. Prepare (a) adjusting, and (b) closing entries in the general journal.

PC-14 *Worksheet* The Langer Company has prepared the following partially completed worksheet for the year ended
@ December 31, 2004:

Accounts	Trial Balance Debit	Trial Balance Credit	Adjustments Debit	Adjustments Credit	Income Statement Debit	Income Statement Credit	Retained Earnings Statement Debit	Retained Earnings Statement Credit	Balance Sheet Debit	Balance Sheet Credit
Cash	1,000									
Accounts receivable	2,700									
Allowance for doubtful accounts		30								
Note receivable (due 5/1/05)	1,200									
Inventory, 1/1/04	3,300									
Land	4,500									
Buildings and equipment	20,600									
Accumulated depreciation		8,790								
Accounts payable		4,050								
Notes payable, due 4/1/2007		4,000								
Capital stock (2,000 shares)		5,000								
Retained earnings		6,120								
Dividends distributed	600									
Sales revenue		25,140								
Rent revenue		550								
Purchases	15,950									
Purchases returns		650								
Purchases discounts taken		350								
Salaries expense	2,750									
Delivery expense	720									
Heat and light expense	820									
Other expenses	540									
Totals	54,680	54,680								

The following additional information is available: (a) salaries accrued but unpaid total $250; (b) the $80 heat
and light bill for December has not been recorded or paid; (c) depreciation expense totals $810 on the build-
ings and equipment; (d) interest accrued on the note payable totals $380 (this will be paid when the note is
repaid); (e) the company leases a portion of its floor space to Brix Specialty Company for $50 per month, and
Brix has not yet paid its December rent; (f) interest accrued on the note receivable totals $80; (g) bad debts
expense is $70; (h) the December 31, 2004 ending inventory is $9,200; and (i) the income tax rate is 30% on
current income and is payable in the first quarter of 2005.

Required

1. Complete the worksheet. (Round to the nearest dollar.)
2. Prepare the company's financial statements.
3. Prepare (a) adjusting, and (b) closing entries in the general journal.

PC-15 *Special Journals and Posting* Refer to the transactions listed in PC-1.

Required

1. Journalize each of these transactions in the sales journal, purchases journal, cash receipts journal, cash
payments journal, or general journal as illustrated in the chapter.
2. Post to the general ledger accounts and to the subsidiary (Grant Company and Mason Company) accounts.

PC-16   *Comprehensive*   On November 30, 2004 the Zu Company had the following account balances:

	Debit	Credit		Debit	Credit
Cash	$ 3,200		Retained earnings (1/1/2004)		$42,400
Accounts receivable	9,900		Dividends distributed	$ 2,000	
Allowance for doubtful			Sales revenue		76,000
accounts		$ 100	Sales returns and allowances	6,300	
Inventory (1/1/2004)	12,600		Purchases	41,000	
Supplies	1,400		Purchases returns and		
Land	9,000		allowances		3,400
Building and equipment	42,000		Freight-in	4,300	
Accumulated depreciation		4,200	Salaries expense	12,500	
Accounts payable		10,700	Advertising expense	8,100	
Capital stock, no-par			Other expenses	4,500	
(2,000 shares)		20,000			

During the month of December the Zu Company entered into the following transactions:

Date	Transaction
Dec. 4	Made cash sales of $3,000.
7	Purchased $2,400 of merchandise on account. Paid $50 of related freight charges.
11	Customer returned $600 of defective merchandise for credit to its account.
14	Collected $900 of accounts receivable (no cash discount).
18	Sold land for $7,800; the land originally had cost $5,000.
20	Made credit sales of $4,000.
21	Returned $300 of defective merchandise to supplier for credit to the Zu Company's account.
27	Purchased $1,250 of merchandise for cash.
28	Paid $1,100 of accounts payable (no cash discount).
31	Purchased land at a cost of $6,000; made a $1,000 down payment and signed a 12%, 2-year note for the balance.

Required

1. Prepare general journal entries to record the preceding transactions.
2. Post to the general ledger accounts.
3. Prepare a year-end trial balance on a worksheet and complete the worksheet using the following information: (a) accrued salaries at year-end total $1,200; (b) for simplicity, the building and equipment are being depreciated using the straight-line method over an estimated life of 20 years with no residual value; (c) supplies on hand at the end of the year total $630; (d) bad debts expense for the year totals $830; (e) inventory on December 31, 2004 is $17,200; and (f) the income tax rate is 30%; income taxes are payable in the first quarter of 2005.
4. Prepare the company's financial statements for 2004.
5. Prepare the 2004 (a) adjusting and (b) closing entries in the general journal.

PC-17   *Comprehensive*   Tina Tunxis is the owner of Valley Sales, a distributor of horticulture supplies. The following is the balance sheet of the company as of December 31, 2003:

Cash	$ 2,300	Accounts payable	$ 6,400
Accounts receivable	10,400	Salaries payable	1,200
Inventory	12,500		
Equipment	8,000		
Less: Accumulated depreciation	(6,500)	T. Tunxis, Capital	$19,100
	$26,700		$26,700

Tina keeps very few records and has asked you to help her in the preparation of Valley Sales' 2004 financial statements. An analysis of the 2004 cash transactions recorded in the company's checkbook indicates deposits and checks as follows:

Total deposits: $173,200; all were collections from customers except for a long-term $10,000 bank loan.

Checks written: $169,800 summarized as follows:

Merchandise	$123,100	Note payments (including interest of $650)	$ 2,650
Salaries	4,250	Office expense	3,400
Rent	4,800	Auto expense	4,100
Equipment	4,000	Withdrawals	23,500

Other information about the company is as follows:

1. Accounts receivable at December 31, 2004, $9,200.
2. Accounts payable at December 31:

2003:	Merchandise	$6,100	2004:	Merchandise	$8,500
	Office expense	300		Auto expense	200
		$6,400			$8,700

3. Salaries payable at December 31, 2004, $1,800.
4. Equipment is depreciated by the straight-line method over a 10-year life. The equipment purchased in 2004 was acquired on July 1.
5. Interest payable at December 31, 2004, $140.
6. The company uses a periodic inventory system. Inventory at December 31, 2004, $17,400.

Required

1. Prepare a worksheet to summarize the transactions and adjustments of Valley Sales for 2004. (*Hint*: Include debit and credit columns for both transactions and adjustments.)
2. Prepare a 2004 income statement and a balance sheet as of December 31, 2004. (*Contributed by Walter A. Parker*)

PC-18   *Comprehensive*   Presented next is information pertaining to Ward Specialty Foods, a calendar-year sole proprietorship, maintaining its books on the cash basis during the year. At year-end, however, Mary Ward's accountant adjusts the books to the accrual basis only for sales, purchases, and cost of sales, and records depreciation to more clearly reflect the business income.

Trial Balance
December 31, 2004

	Debit	Credit
Cash	$ 18,500	
Accounts receivable, 12/31/03	4,500	
Inventory, 12/31/03	20,000	
Equipment	35,000	
Accumulated depreciation, 12/31/03		$ 9,000
Accounts payable, 12/31/03		4,800
Payroll taxes withheld		850
Mary Ward, withdrawals	24,000	
Mary Ward, capital, 12/31/03		33,650
Sales		187,000
Purchases	82,700	
Salaries	29,500	
Payroll taxes	2,900	
Rent	8,400	
Miscellaneous expense	3,900	
Insurance	2,400	
Utilities	3,500	
	$235,300	$235,300

During 2004, Ward signed a new 8-year lease for the store premises and is in the process of negotiating a loan for remodeling purposes. The bank requires Ward to present financial statements for 2004 prepared on the accrual basis. To do so, Ward's accountant obtained the following additional information:

1. Amounts due from customers totaled $7,900 at December 31, 2004.

2. A review of the receivables at December 31, 2004 disclosed that an allowance for doubtful accounts of $1,100 should be provided. Ward had no bad debt losses from the inception of the business through December 31, 2004.

3. The inventory amounted to $23,000 at December 31, 2004 based on a physical count of goods priced at cost. No reduction to market was required.

4. On signing the new lease on October 1, 2004, Ward paid $8,400 representing 1 year's rent in advance for the lease year ending October 1, 2005. The $7,500 annual rental under the old lease was paid on October 1, 2003 for the lease year ended October 1, 2004.

5. On April 1, 2004, Ward paid $2,400 to renew the comprehensive insurance coverage for one year. The premium was $2,160 on the old policy, which expired on April 1, 2004.

6. Depreciation on the equipment was computed at $5,800 for 2004.

7. Unpaid vendors' invoices for food purchases totaled $8,800 at December 31, 2004.

8. Accrued expenses at December 31, 2003 and December 31, 2004 were as follows:

	12/31/03	12/31/04
Payroll taxes	$250	$400
Salaries	375	510
Utilities	275	450

After obtaining the preceding information, Ward's accountant prepared the following partially completed worksheet:

	Cash Basis		Adjustments		Accrual Basis	
	Debit	Credit	Debit	Credit	Debit	Credit
Cash	$ 18,500					
Accounts receivable	4,500					
Allowance for doubtful accounts	—	—				
Inventory	20,000					
Equipment	35,000					
Accumulated depreciation		$ 9,000				
Prepaid rent	—					
Prepaid insurance	—	—				
Accounts payable		4,800				
Accrued expenses	—	—				
Payroll taxes withheld		850				
Ward, withdrawals	24,000					
Ward, capital		33,650				
Sales		187,000				
Purchases	82,700					
Income summary—inventory	—	—				
Salaries	29,500					
Payroll taxes	2,900					
Rent	8,400					
Miscellaneous expenses	3,900					
Insurance	2,400					
Utilities	3,500					
Depreciation	—	—				
Bad debts	—	—				
Totals	$235,300	$235,300				

Required

1. Complete the preceding worksheet to convert the trial balance of Ward Specialty Foods to the accrual basis for the year ended December 31, 2004.

2. Prepare the statement of changes in Mary Ward, Capital, for the year ended December 31, 2004. (*AICPA adapted*)

appendix D

Compound Interest

objectives

1 Understand simple interest and compound interest.

2 Compute and use the future value of a single sum.

3 Compute and use the present value of a single sum.

4 Compute and use the future value of an ordinary annuity.

5 Compute and use the future value of an annuity due.

6 Compute and use the present value of an ordinary annuity.

7 Compute and use the present value of an annuity due.

8 Compute and use the present value of a deferred ordinary annuity.

9 Explain the conceptual issues regarding the use of present value in financial reporting.

Suppose someone asked you, "Would you rather have $100 today or $100 next year?" Your answer should be, "I'd rather have $100 today." This reply involves considering the **time value of money**. The difference in worth between the two amounts, the time value of money, is interest. **Interest is the cost of the use of money over time.** It is an expense to the borrower and revenue to the lender. Therefore, it is a very important element in the decision making involved in the acquisition and disposal of many of the resources of a company.

Interest concepts are involved in the development of many values that a company reports on its financial statements. Also, managers need to understand the concept of interest when making decisions where cash paid or received *now* must be compared with amounts that will be received or paid in the *future*.

The cash flows at various dates, say some at 3 years from now, some at 2 years from now, and some at 1 year from now, cannot be added together to produce a relevant value. Future cash flows, before they can be added, must be converted to a common denominator by being restated to their present values as of a specific moment in time (often referred to as *time period zero*). The dollars to be received or paid 3 years from now have a *smaller* present value than those to be received or paid 2 years or 1 year from now. **The converting of these future value amounts to the present value common denominator is known as discounting** and involves the removal of the interest or discount—the time value of money—from those dollars that would be received or paid 3 years, 2 years, or 1 year from now.

Instead of restating some of the cash inflows and outflows to their present values at time period zero, a common denominator is also achieved by stating them at a future value by adding the time value of money (interest) to these inflows and outflows. The future value of any series of inflows or outflows is the sum of these periodic amounts plus the compound interest calculated on the amounts.

A company restates for the present value or the future value in many situations, such as (1) for measurement and reporting of some of its assets and liabilities, since many accounting pronouncements require the use of present value concepts in a number of measurement and reporting issues, and (2) when it accumulates information for decision making involving, for example, property, plant, and equipment acquisitions. We discuss these concepts in this Appendix and we apply them in various chapters when we discuss how a company records and reports (1) long-term notes payable and notes receivable when the interest rate is not specified or differs from the market rate at the time of the transaction, (2) assets acquired by the issuance of long-term debt securities that carry either no stated rate of interest, or a rate of interest that is different from the market rate at the time of the transaction, (3) bonds payable and investments in bonds and the amortization of bond premiums and discounts in each case, (4) long-term leases, (5) various aspects of employees' post-employment benefits, and (6) impairment of noncurrent assets.

Various compound interest techniques are used in the measurement of the values (costs) of these and other types of transactions. Most compound interest applications can be calculated by a longhand arithmetic process. However, quicker approaches and shortcuts to the solutions of the problems are available. In this Appendix we illustrate the basic principles of compound interest in a way that leads to the development of tables to resolving issues introduced throughout this book.

SIMPLE INTEREST AND COMPOUND INTEREST

Simple interest is interest on the original principal (amount originally received or paid) regardless of the number of time periods that have passed or the amount of interest that has been paid or accrued in the past. Interest rates are usually stated as an *annual* rate, which is adjusted for any other time period. Thus simple interest is calculated by the following equation:

1 Understand simple interest and compound interest.

$$\text{Interest} = \text{Principal} \times \text{Rate} \times \text{Time}$$

where time is either a fraction of a year or a multiple of years. If the term of a note is stated in days, say 90 days, the denominator of the time fraction in the preceding equation is usually stated in terms of a commercial year of 360 days rather than a full year of 365 days. In this practice the year is assumed to be a period of 12 months of 30 days each. To illustrate, the simple interest on a $10,000, 90-day, 12% note given to a company by Allen Sanders is $300 ($10,000 × 0.12 × 90/360). However, if the term of this note is 15 months, the simple interest is $1,500 ($10,000 × 0.12 × 15/12). Observe that simple interest for more than 1 year is still calculated on only the principal amount (in this case $10,000).

Compound interest is the interest that accrues on both the principal and the past unpaid accrued interest. Simple interest of 12% for 15 months on the Allen Sanders note is $1,500. If, on the other hand, the 12% interest is *compounded quarterly* for 15 months (5 quarters), the total compound interest is $1,592.74, as we show in Exhibit D-1. Observe that in the compound interest computation, the future accumulated amount (value) at the end of each quarter becomes the principal sum for purposes of computing the interest for the following period.

EXHIBIT D-1 Computation of Quarterly Compounded Interest

Period	Value at Beginning of Quarter*	× Rate × Time =	Compound Interest	Value at End of Quarter
1st quarter	$10,000.00	× 0.12 × 1/4	$ 300.00	$10,300.00
2nd quarter	10,300.00	× 0.12 × 1/4	309.00	10,609.00
3rd quarter	10,609.00	× 0.12 × 1/4	318.27	10,927.27
4th quarter	10,927.27	× 0.12 × 1/4	327.82	11,255.09
5th quarter	11,255.09	× 0.12 × 1/4	337.65	11,592.74
Compound interest on $10,000 at 12% compounded quarterly for 5 quarters			$1,592.74	

* This value is the amount on which interest is calculated.

To help solve the many business issues stated in the introductory section of this Appendix, accountants need to know the various types of compound interest computations. Although there are many variations, there are only four basic types:

1. **Future value (amount) of a single sum** at compound interest
2. **Present value of a single sum** due in the future
3. **Future value (amount) of an annuity,** a series of receipts or payments
4. **Present value of an annuity,** a series of receipts or payments

FUTURE VALUE OF A SINGLE SUM AT COMPOUND INTEREST

As we stated previously, the main objective of this Appendix is to explain shortcut methods to determine and apply the compound interest techniques. We will use the following step-by-step procedure, introducing the entire topic *only* with the future value of a single sum at compound interest: (1) we diagram the idea or concept; (2) we make the computation using a longhand calculation; (3) we make the computation using formulas; (4) we discuss the method of constructing and using tables; and (5) we illustrate the use of the tables to solve a compound interest problem.

The Idea

The future value of a single sum at compound interest is the original sum plus the compound interest, stated as of a specific future date. It is also often referred to as the

2 Compute and use the future value of a single sum.

future amount of a single sum. For example, suppose that a single amount of $1,000 is invested in a savings account on December 31, 2004. What will be the amount in the savings account on December 31, 2008 if interest at 14% is compounded annually each year? We show the issue graphically in Exhibit D-2. Most compound interest calculations can be made by applying longhand arithmetic. We follow this procedure here only to clarify the various shortcut devices used.

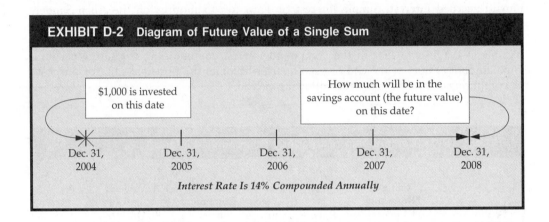

EXHIBIT D-2   Diagram of Future Value of a Single Sum

$1,000 is invested on this date

How much will be in the savings account (the future value) on this date?

Dec. 31, 2004   Dec. 31, 2005   Dec. 31, 2006   Dec. 31, 2007   Dec. 31, 2008

Interest Rate Is 14% Compounded Annually

The future value of $1,000 for 4 years at 14% a year can be calculated as we show in Exhibit D-3. The single sum of $1,000 invested on December 31, 2004 has grown to $1,688.96 by December 31, 2008. This is the **future value.** The total interest of $688.96 for the 4 years is referred to as **compound interest.**

EXHIBIT D-3   Calculation of Future Value of Single Sum at Compound Interest

(1) Year	(2) Value at Beginning of Year	(3) Annual Compound Interest (Col. 2 × 0.14)	(4) Future Value at End of Year (Col. 2 + Col. 3)
2005	$1,000.00	$140.00	$1,140.00
2006	1,140.00	159.60	1,299.60
2007	1,299.60	181.94	1,481.54
2008	1,481.54	207.42	1,688.96

A slight variation of the longhand arithmetic approach is to determine what $1 invested on December 31, 2004 will amount to by December 31, 2008 if interest at 14% is compounded annually. Then this amount is multiplied by the principal sum to find the future value. In this case, $1 amounts to $1.68896 in 4 years. Knowing this fact, the value of 1,000 different $1 investments (or $1,000) at the end of 4 years can be calculated by multiplying the $1,000 by 1.68896 as follows: $1,000 × 1.68896 = $1,688.96. To avoid a significant rounding error in the final results, when solving this problem, the intermediate figures must *not* be rounded to the nearest cent.

Formula Approach

Each amount in column 4 of Exhibit D-3 is 1.14 times the corresponding amount in column 2. The final future value is therefore $1,000 \times 1.14 \times 1.14 \times 1.14 \times 1.14 = \$1,688.96$. This means that 1.14 has been used as a multiplier four times; that is, 1.14 has been raised to the fourth power. The future value is therefore $1,000 multiplied by 1.14 to the fourth power:

Future Value = $1,000(1.14)^4 = \$1,688.96

Thus the formula to compute the future value of a single sum at compound interest is:

$$f = p(1 + i)^n$$

where f = future value of a single sum at compound interest i for n periods
p = principal sum (present value)
i = interest rate for each of the stated time periods
n = number of time periods

It is important to understand that the interest rate i is the rate of interest applicable for the particular time period for which interest is compounded. For example, a stated annual rate of interest of 12% is

- 12% per year if interest is compounded annually
- 6% per one-half year if interest is compounded semiannually
- 3% per quarter if interest is compounded quarterly
- 1% per month if interest is compounded monthly

In general **an interest rate per period (i) is the annual stated rate (sometimes called the nominal rate) divided by the number of compounding time periods in the year, and n is the number of time periods in the year multiplied by the number of years.**
The formula for the future value of 1 is:

$$f_{n,i} = (1 + i)^n$$

where $f_{n,i}$ is the future compound value of 1 ($1 or 1 of any other monetary unit) at interest rate i for n periods.

Using the preceding formula for the future value of 1, a short formula for the future compound value of any single amount at compound interest is:

$$f = p(f_{n,i})$$

The example of the future value of $1,000 invested at 14% with interest compounded annually can now be calculated in two steps:

Step 1 $f_{n=4, i=14\%} = (1.14)^4 = 1.688960$

Step 2 $f = \$1,000(1.688960) = \$1,688.96$

Recall that this is exactly the same as the *second* approach, which we used in the previous arithmetic method.

Table Approach

To develop additional shortcuts to the solution of the compound interest issue, tables for the future value of 1 have been constructed. These tables are simply a precalculation of the future values of 1 at different interest rates and for different time periods. They can be constructed by using the preceding formula with the desired interest rates and time periods. For example, suppose that you need tables of the future value of 1 at 2% and 14% for time periods 1 through 4 and for 40 years. The information for these can be calculated as follows:

$$f_{n=1, i=2\%} = (1.02)^1 = 1.020000 \qquad f_{n=1, i=14\%} = (1.14)^1 = 1.140000$$
$$f_{n=2, i=2\%} = (1.02)^2 = 1.040400 \qquad f_{n=2, i=14\%} = (1.14)^2 = 1.299600$$
$$f_{n=3, i=2\%} = (1.02)^3 = 1.061208 \qquad f_{n=3, i=14\%} = (1.14)^3 = 1.481544$$
$$f_{n=4, i=2\%} = (1.02)^4 = 1.082432 \qquad f_{n=4, i=14\%} = (1.14)^4 = 1.688960$$
$$f_{n=40, i=2\%} = (1.02)^{40} = 2.208040 \qquad f_{n=40, i=14\%} = (1.14)^{40} = 188.883514$$

This information can then be accumulated in a partial table as we show in Exhibit D-4. In this kind of table the factors are shown without the use of the dollar sign. Each factor is an amount for a certain time period and rate. We provide more complete tables at the end of this Appendix.

EXHIBIT D-4   Future Value of 1 Table $(1 + i)^n$

Periods	2%	14%
1	1.020000	1.140000
2	1.040400	1.299600
3	1.061208	1.481544
4	1.082432	1.688960
.	.	.
.	.	.
.	.	.
40	2.208040	188.883514

Since the factors in Exhibit D-4 and in Table 1 at the end of this Appendix are based on the formula $(1 + i)^n$, the table approach can be expressed as:

$$f = p(\text{Factor for } f_{n, i})$$

To calculate the future value that $1,000 will accumulate to in 4 years at 14% compounded annually, it is necessary to look up the table factor for $f_{n=4, i=14\%}$, namely, 1.688960; then, to arrive at the answer of $1,688.96, the calculation is: $f = \$1,000(1.688960) = \$1,688.96$.

Summary and Illustration

In addition to the straightforward situation of calculating the future value of a single sum at compound interest, you can solve other kinds of problems with the *future value of 1* table.

EXAMPLE: FINDING AN UNSTATED INTEREST RATE   If $1,000 is invested on December 31, 2004 to earn compound interest and if the future value on December 31, 2011 is $2,998.70, what is the quarterly interest rate on the investment?

We show the facts in Exhibit D-5. Using the table approach

$$f = p(\text{Factor for } f_{n, i})$$

and substituting in the formula the amounts shown in Exhibit D-5, the factor is determined as follows:

$$\$2,998.70 = \$1,000(\text{Factor for } f_{n=28, i=?})$$

$$\text{Factor for } f_{n=28, i=?} = \frac{\$2,998.70}{\$1,000.00} = 2.99870$$

The factor of 2.99870 is the future value of 1 for 28 time periods at an unknown interest rate. Using the future value of 1 table (Table 1) at the end of this Appendix,

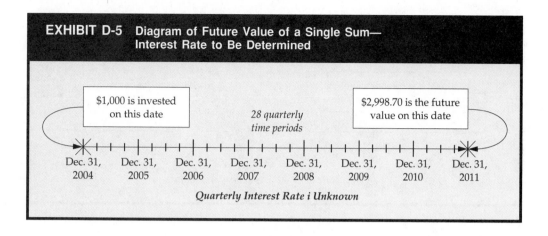

EXHIBIT D-5 Diagram of Future Value of a Single Sum—Interest Rate to Be Determined

you look down the periods (n) column until you get to 28. Then you move horizontally on the $n = 28$ line to the column factor closest to 2.99870. If the value appears in the table, you can determine the interest rate (shown at the top of the column) that produces this value. In this case, 2.99870 is equal to 2.998703 (rounded) located in the 4% column; thus the quarterly interest rate is 4%. This is often referred to as being a stated annual rate of 16%; you should understand, however, that a quarterly rate of 4% compounded four times yields an effective rate of more than 16%. If the factor of 2.99870 does not appear in the table, an interpolation procedure is required to approximate the quarterly interest rate.[1] Calculators and computer software that compute the interest rate are widely available.

You can solve other problems by using the future amount of 1 tables. Keep in mind, however, that most tables are incomplete. At times it will be necessary to construct tables for odd interest rates and time periods, or to use a calculator or computer software.

PRESENT VALUE OF A SINGLE SUM

For the remaining compound interest techniques, we focus on the shortcut approach. After we discuss the idea, we state the formula and use factors derived from the formula.

The Idea

The present value is the principal that must be invested at time period zero to produce the known future value. Also, **discounting is the process of converting the future value to the present value.** For example, if $1,000 is worth $1,688.96 when it earns 14% compound interest per year for 4 years, then it follows that $1,688.96 to be received 4 years from now is worth $1,000 now at time period zero; that is, $1,000 is the present value of $1,688.96 discounted at 14% for 4 years. Exhibit D-6 presents this information graphically.

---

1. You can use the following six steps to determine an interest rate by linear interpolation. (1) Calculate the compound interest factor as shown in the preceding example. (2) Look up in compound interest tables the two interest rates that yield the next largest and the next smallest factors from the calculated factor determined in step 1. (3) Determine (a) the difference between the two factors in step 2, and (b) the difference between the calculated factor from step 1 and the factor of the smaller interest rate from step 2. (4) Find the difference between the two interest rates found in step 2. (5) Apportion the difference in the interest rates in step 4 by multiplying it by a fraction: The numerator is the difference determined in step 3b and the denominator is the difference determined in step 3a. (6) The interest rate is then the lower rate found in step 2 *plus* the apportioned difference from step 5.

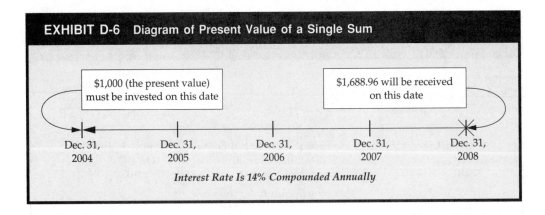

EXHIBIT D-6   Diagram of Present Value of a Single Sum

$1,000 (the present value) must be invested on this date

$1,688.96 will be received on this date

| Dec. 31, 2004 | Dec. 31, 2005 | Dec. 31, 2006 | Dec. 31, 2007 | Dec. 31, 2008 |

Interest Rate Is 14% Compounded Annually

Shortcut Approaches

3 Compute and use the present value of a single sum.

While it is possible to calculate the present value of $1,688.96 to be received at the end of 4 years discounted at 14% by a longhand approach by reversing the process described in the calculation of the future value, we do not illustrate this approach here. Instead we focus on the development of shortcut approaches to find the present value of a single sum. First we present the formula; then we consider how to create and use factors.

FORMULA APPROACH Since the present value of a single future amount is the reciprocal value of the future value of a single sum, the formula for this calculation is:

$$p = f\frac{1}{(1 + i)^n}$$

where p = present value of any given future value due in the future
   f = future value
   i = interest rate for each of the stated time periods
   n = number of time periods

In this example the present value of $1,688.96 received at the end of 4 years discounted at 14% is $1,000, calculated as follows:

$$p = \$1,688.96\,\frac{1}{(1.14)^4} = \$1,000$$

The formula for the present value of 1 is:

$$p_{n,i} = \frac{1}{(1 + i)^n}$$

where $p_{n,i}$ is the present value of 1 ($1 or 1 of any monetary unit) at interest rate i for n periods. It is now possible to express the formula for the present value of any given future amount as:

$$p = f(p_{n,i})$$

The example of the present value of $1,688.96 to be received 4 years from now with interest of 14% compounded annually can be calculated in two steps:

Step 1 $p_{n=4,\,i=14\%} = \dfrac{1}{(1.14)^4} = 0.592080$

Step 2 $p = \$1,688.96(0.592080) = \$1,000$

TABLE APPROACH Using the formula for $p_{n,i}$, tables have been constructed for any interest rate and for any number of periods by simply substituting in the formula the selected various interest rates for the various time periods desired. Table 3 at the end of this Appendix shows the factors for the present value of 1 ($p_{n,i}$).

Since the factors in Table 3 are based on the formula $p_{n,i} = 1/(1 + i)^n$, the generalized table approach can be stated as:

$$p = f(\text{Factor for } p_{n,i})$$

To calculate the present value of $1,688.96 to be received at the end of 4 years, discounted at 14%, look up the factor for $p_{n=4, i=14\%}$ in Table 3; it is 0.592080. Then the future value of $1,688.96 is multiplied by this present value of 1 factor to obtain the present value amount of $1,000, as follows: $p = \$1,688.96(0.592080) = \$1,000$.

Summary and Illustration

In addition to calculating the present value of a single sum using compound interest, you can solve other kinds of problems with the present value of 1 table.

EXAMPLE: FINDING AN UNSTATED INTEREST RATE   Assuming that the present value of $10,000 to be paid at the end of 10 years is $3,855.43, what interest rate compounded annually is used in the calculation of the present value?

Exhibit D-7 shows the known facts. Since both the present value and the future amount are known, this problem can be solved in two different ways: (1) by using the method we described in the future value section, or (2) by using the present value approach we describe here. Since we discussed the future value approach earlier in this Appendix, we use only the present value approach here to solve the problem. Using the table approach

$$p = f(\text{Factor for } p_{n,i})$$

and substituting in the formula the known amounts shown in Exhibit D-7, the factor is determined as follows:

$$\$3,855.43 = \$10,000.00 \, (\text{Factor for } p_{n=10, i=?})$$

$$\text{Factor for } p_{n=10, i=?} = \frac{\$3,855.43}{\$10,000.00} = 0.385543$$

The factor of 0.385543 is the present value of 1 for 10 periods at an unknown interest rate. Using the present value of 1 table (Table 3), you look down the periods (n) column until you get to 10. Then you move horizontally on the $n = 10$ line to the column factor closest to 0.385543. If the amount appears in the table, you can determine the interest rate (shown at the top of the column) that produces this amount. In this case, 0.385543 is in the 10% column. Thus the annual rate is 10%. If the factor of 0.385543 does not appear in the table, an interpolation procedure is required to approximate the annual interest rate (see footnote 1).

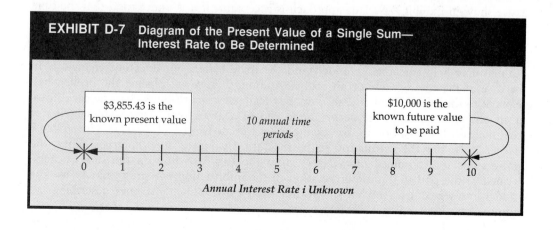

EXHIBIT D-7   **Diagram of the Present Value of a Single Sum— Interest Rate to Be Determined**

$3,855.43 is the known present value

10 annual time periods

$10,000 is the known future value to be paid

0   1   2   3   4   5   6   7   8   9   10

Annual Interest Rate i Unknown

MEASUREMENTS INVOLVING AN ANNUITY

An annuity is a series of equal cash flows (deposits, receipts, payments, or withdrawals) (sometimes referred to as *rents*) made at regular intervals with interest compounded at a certain rate. The regular intervals between the cash flows may be any time period—for example, a year, a 6-month period, a month, or even 1 day. In solving measurement problems involving the use of annuities, these four conditions must exist: (1) the periodic cash flows are equal in amount, (2) the time periods between the cash flows are the same length, (3) the interest rate is constant for each time period, and (4) the interest is compounded at the end of each time period.

FUTURE VALUE OF AN ORDINARY ANNUITY

The future value of an ordinary annuity is determined *immediately* after the last cash flow in the series is made. For the first example, assume that Debbi Whitten wants to calculate the future value of 4 cash flows of $1,000, each with interest compounded annually at 14%, where the first $1,000 cash flow occurs on December 31, 2004 and the last $1,000 occurs on December 31, 2007. Exhibit D-8 presents this information graphically.

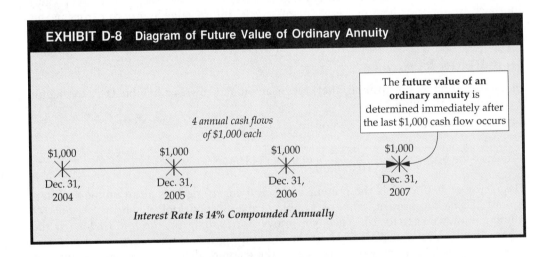

EXHIBIT D-8   Diagram of Future Value of Ordinary Annuity

4 annual cash flows of $1,000 each

The **future value of an ordinary annuity** is determined immediately after the last $1,000 cash flow occurs

$1,000 $1,000 $1,000 $1,000
Dec. 31,   Dec. 31,   Dec. 31,   Dec. 31,
2004   2005   2006   2007

Interest Rate Is 14% Compounded Annually

In drawing a **time line** such as that in Exhibit D-8, some accountants prefer to add a beginning time segment to the left of the time when the first cash flow occurs. For example, they would draw the time line for the future amount of an ordinary annuity, as we show in Exhibit D-9. This approach is acceptable if it is understood that the time from January 1, 2004 to December 31, 2004 (which is the period of time immediately *before* the first cash flow occurs) is not used to compute the future value of the ordinary annuity. It is similar to stating a decimal as .4 or 0.4. The zero in front of the decimal may help someone to understand the issue better, but does not change it. In the case of the future value of an ordinary annuity, however, placing the broken line segment to the left of the first cash flow may lead someone to think that the cash flows in an ordinary annuity *must occur* at the end of a given year. That statement is *not* true; the cash flows can occur, for example, on March 15 of each year, or November 5 of each year. For the calculation to be the future value of an *ordinary* annuity, the *future value* is determined *immediately after* the last cash flow in the series occurs. Because of the potential misinterpretation of the information, we prefer not to use the broken line segment to the left of the first cash flow in the time lines describing the future value of an ordinary annuity.

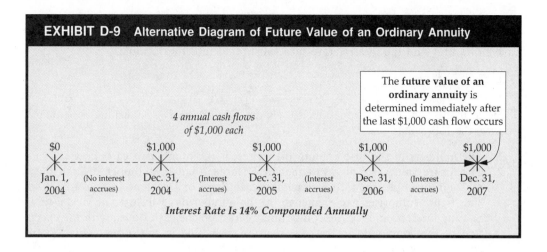

EXHIBIT D-9 Alternative Diagram of Future Value of an Ordinary Annuity

The **future value of an ordinary annuity** is determined immediately after the last $1,000 cash flow occurs

4 annual cash flows of $1,000 each

| $0 | $1,000 | $1,000 | $1,000 | $1,000 |

Jan. 1, 2004 (No interest accrues) Dec. 31, 2004 (Interest accrues) Dec. 31, 2005 (Interest accrues) Dec. 31, 2006 (Interest accrues) Dec. 31, 2007

Interest Rate Is 14% Compounded Annually

Shortcut Approaches

FORMULA APPROACH The formula for the future value of an ordinary annuity of any amount is:

$$F_0 = C \left[\frac{(1 + i)^n - 1}{i} \right]$$

where F_0 = future value of an ordinary annuity of a series of cash flows of any amount
  C = amount of each cash flow
  n = number of cash flows (not the number of time periods)
  i = interest rate for each of the stated time periods

In the example, the future value of an ordinary annuity of 4 cash flows of $1,000 each at 14% compounded annually is as follows:

$$F_0 = \$1,000 \left[\frac{(1.14)^4 - 1}{0.14} \right] = \$4,921.14$$

The formula for the future value of an ordinary annuity with cash flows of 1 each is as follows:

$$F_{0n, i} = \left[\frac{(1 + i)^n - 1}{i} \right]$$

where $F_{0n, i}$ is the future value of an *ordinary* annuity of n cash flows of 1 each at interest rate i.[2]

With the preceding formula for $F_{0n, i}$ it is possible to express another formula for the future value of an ordinary annuity of cash flows of any size in this manner:

$$F_0 = C(F_{0n, i})$$

In a two-step approach, the future value of an ordinary annuity of 4 cash flows of $1,000 each at 14% compounded annually is calculated as follows:

Step 1 $F_{0n=4, i=14\%} = \dfrac{(1.14)^4 - 1}{0.14} = 4.921144$

Step 2 $F_0 = \$1,000(4.921144) = \$4,921.14$

This two-step approach is used to solve the problem when factors are not available.

4 Compute and use the future value of an ordinary annuity.

---

2. F_{0n} is often expressed as $F_{0n, i}$, read as "large F sub-zero sub n at i."

TABLE APPROACH   The formula for $F_{0n,i}$ can be used to construct a table of the future value of any series of cash flows of 1 each for any interest rate. Here the number of cash flows of 1 and the interest rates are substituted into the formula

$$\frac{(1 + i)^n - 1}{i}$$

Table 2 at the end of this Appendix shows the factors for $F_{0n,i}$. Turning to Table 2, observe the following:

1. The numbers in the first column (n) represent the number of cash flows.
2. The future values are always equal to or larger than the number of cash flows of 1. For example, the future value of 4 cash flows of 1 each at 14% is 4.921144. This figure comprises two elements: (a) the number of cash flows of 1 each *without* any interest, and (b) the compound interest on the cash flows, with the exception of the compound interest on the last cash flow in the series, which in the case of an ordinary annuity *does not* earn any interest.

Since Table 2 shows the precalculation of $F_{0n,i}$ or

$$\frac{(1 + i)^n - 1}{i}$$

values, the generalized table approach is as follows:

$$F_0 = C(\text{Factor for } F_{0n,i})$$

To calculate the future value of an ordinary annuity of 4 cash flows of \$1,000 each at 14%, you must look up the $F_{0n=4,i=14\%}$ factor in the future value of an ordinary annuity of 1 table (Table 2); it is 4.921144. Then the amount of each cash flow, here \$1,000, is multiplied by the Table 2 factor to obtain the future value of \$4,921.14:

$$F_0 = \$1,000(4.921144) = \$4,921.14$$

Summary and Illustration

You can solve several kinds of problems using a future value of an ordinary annuity of 1 table, such as (1) calculating the future value when the cash flows and interest rate are known (the preceding problem), (2) calculating the value of each cash flow where the number of cash flows, interest rate, and future value are known, (3) calculating the number of cash flows when the amount of each cash flow, the interest rate, and the future value are known, and (4) calculating an unknown interest rate when the cash flows and the future value are known. To demonstrate the analysis used in the solution of all problems, we illustrate item (2) as follows.

EXAMPLE: DETERMINING THE AMOUNT OF EACH CASH FLOW NEEDED TO ACCUMULATE A FUND TO RETIRE DEBT   At the beginning of 2004 the Rexson Company issued 10-year bonds with a face value of \$1,000,000 due on December 31, 2013. The company will accumulate a fund to retire these bonds at maturity. It will make annual deposits to the fund beginning on December 31, 2004. How much must the company deposit each year, assuming that the fund will earn 12% interest compounded annually?

Exhibit D-10 shows the facts of the problem. The future value and the compound interest rate are known. The amount of each of the 10 deposits (cash flows) is the unknown factor. Starting with the formula

$$F_0 = C(\text{Factor for } F_0)$$

and then shifting the elements and substituting the known amount and applicable factor (from Table 2), the amount of each annual deposit is \$56,984.16, calculated as follows:

$$C = \frac{F_0}{\text{Factor for } F_{0n,\,i}}$$

$$= \frac{F_0}{\text{Factor for } F_{0n=10,\,i=12\%}}$$

$$= \frac{\$1,000,000}{17.548735}$$

$$= \$56,984.16$$

The 10 annual deposits of $56,984.16, plus the compound interest, will accumulate to $1,000,000 by December 31, 2013.

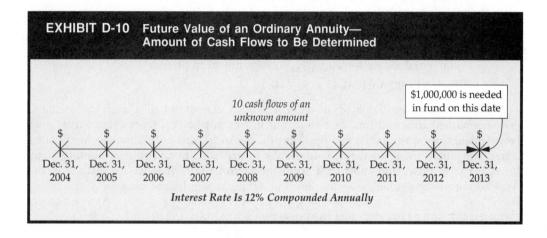

**EXHIBIT D-10   Future Value of an Ordinary Annuity—
Amount of Cash Flows to Be Determined**

$1,000,000 is needed in fund on this date

10 cash flows of an unknown amount

$ $ $ $ $ $ $ $ $ $
Dec. 31, 2004 Dec. 31, 2005 Dec. 31, 2006 Dec. 31, 2007 Dec. 31, 2008 Dec. 31, 2009 Dec. 31, 2010 Dec. 31, 2011 Dec. 31, 2012 Dec. 31, 2013

Interest Rate Is 12% Compounded Annually

FUTURE VALUE OF AN ANNUITY DUE

The future value of an annuity due (F_d) is determined 1 period after the last cash flow in the series. For example, assume that Ronald Jacobson deposits in a fund 4 payments of $1,000 each beginning December 31, 2004, with the last deposit being made on December 31, 2007. How much will be in the fund on December 31, 2007, 1 year after the final payment, if the fund earns interest at 14% compounded annually? Exhibit D-11 shows the facts of this problem.

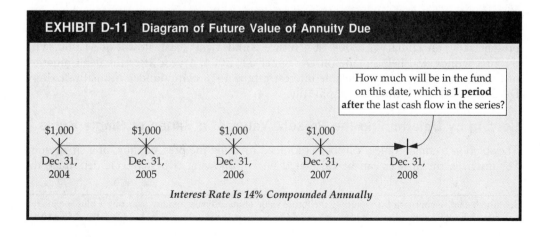

EXHIBIT D-11   Diagram of Future Value of Annuity Due

How much will be in the fund on this date, which is **1 period after** the last cash flow in the series?

$1,000 $1,000 $1,000 $1,000
Dec. 31, 2004   Dec. 31, 2005   Dec. 31, 2006   Dec. 31, 2007   Dec. 31, 2008

Interest Rate Is 14% Compounded Annually

Solution Approach

5 Compute and use the future value of an annuity due.

By observing the information contained in Exhibits D-11 and D-8, you can determine a quick way to compute the future value of an annuity due.[3] When only the future value of an *ordinary* annuity table is available, you can use the factors by completing the following steps:

Step 1	In the *ordinary* annuity table (Table 2), look up the value of $n + 1$ cash flows at 14% or the value of 5 cash flows at 14%.	6.610104
Step 2	Then subtract 1 without interest from the value obtained in Step 1.	(1.000000)
	This is the converted future value factor for $F_{d_{n=4, i=14\%}}$	5.610104

Step 3   Multiply the amount of each cash flow, here $1,000, by the converted factor for $F_{d_{n=4, i=14\%}}$ determined in Step 2:

$$F_d = \$1,000(5.610104) = \$5,610.10$$

Tables of the future value of an annuity due of cash flows of 1 each are available in some mathematics and finance books, but not in this book. Hence these values must be calculated using the tables for the future value of an *ordinary* annuity. As we illustrated previously, **the general rule is to use the future value of an ordinary annuity factor for $n + 1$ cash flows and subtract 1 from the factor.** (Note that we do include in this Appendix a present value of an annuity due table, as we discuss later.)

PRESENT VALUE OF AN ANNUITY

The present value of an annuity is the present value of a series of equal cash flows that occur in the future. In other words, it is the amount that must be invested now and, if left to earn compound interest, will provide for a receipt or payment of a series of equal cash flows at regular intervals. Over time, the present value balance is *increased* periodically for interest and is *decreased* periodically for each receipt or payment. Thus, the last cash flow in the series exhausts the balance on deposit.

A company frequently uses the present value of an annuity concept to report many items in its financial statements, as we stated in the introduction to this Appendix. Because of the importance of the present value of an annuity, we will discuss the (1) present value of an ordinary annuity, (2) present value of an annuity due, and (3) present value of a deferred annuity.

PRESENT VALUE OF AN ORDINARY ANNUITY

6 Compute and use the present value of an ordinary annuity.

The present value of an ordinary annuity is determined 1 period before the first cash flow in the series is made. For example, assume that Kyle Vasby wants to calculate the present value on January 1, 2004 of 4 future withdrawals (cash flows) of $1,000, with the first withdrawal being made on December 31, 2004, 1 year after the determination of the present value. The applicable interest rate is 14% compounded annually. Exhibit D-12 shows this information graphically.

Solving by Determining the Present Value of a Series of Single Sums

The solution to this problem can be determined by using the present value of a single sum. For instance, the answer can be calculated in the following two steps: (1) determine the

---

3. An alternative approach is to multiply the future value of an ordinary annuity factor by 1 plus the interest rate. Thus, the future value in this example would be computed as $1,000 × (4.921144 × 1.14) = $5,610.10.

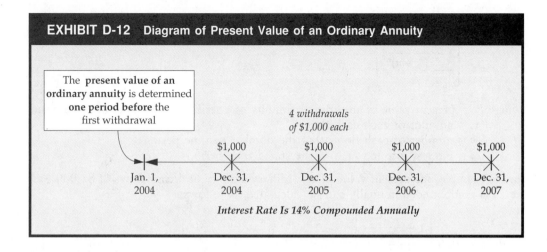

EXHIBIT D-12 Diagram of Present Value of an Ordinary Annuity

The **present value of an ordinary annuity** is determined **one period before** the first withdrawal

4 withdrawals of $1,000 each

$1,000 $1,000 $1,000 $1,000

Jan. 1, 2004   Dec. 31, 2004   Dec. 31, 2005   Dec. 31, 2006   Dec. 31, 2007

Interest Rate Is 14% Compounded Annually

present value of 4 individual cash flows of 1 each for 1, 2, 3, and 4 years, as we show in Exhibit D-13, and (2) then multiply the final results of the summation by $1,000.

Step 1 The present value of 4 cash flows of 1 for 1, 2, 3, and 4 years discounted at 14% is determined in Exhibit D-13.

Step 2 Now it is possible to determine the present value of the 4 cash flows of $1,000 each by multiplying the $1,000 by 2.913713:

$1,000 × 2.913713 = $2,913.71

The present value on January 1, 2004 is $2,913.71; or we can say that $2,913.71 must be invested on January 1, 2004 to provide for 4 withdrawals of $1,000 each starting on December 31, 2004, given an interest rate of 14%.

Shortcut Approaches

FORMULA APPROACH Even though the preceding approach can be used, it is time-consuming for calculations involving a large number of cash flows. The formula for the

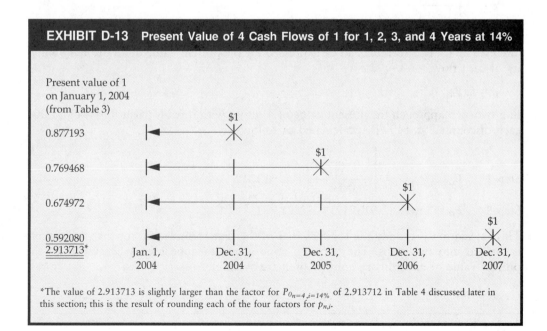

EXHIBIT D-13 Present Value of 4 Cash Flows of 1 for 1, 2, 3, and 4 Years at 14%

Present value of 1 on January 1, 2004 (from Table 3)

0.877193 $1

0.769468 $1

0.674972 $1

0.592080
2.913713*

Jan. 1, 2004   Dec. 31, 2004   Dec. 31, 2005   Dec. 31, 2006   Dec. 31, 2007

*The value of 2.913713 is slightly larger than the factor for $P_{0_{n=4, i=14\%}}$ of 2.913712 in Table 4 discussed later in this section; this is the result of rounding each of the four factors for $p_{n,i}$.

present value of an ordinary annuity of any amount is:

$$P_0 = C \left[\frac{1 - \dfrac{1}{(1 + i)^n}}{i} \right]$$

where P_0 = present value of an ordinary annuity of a series of cash flows of any amount
   C = amount of each cash flow
   n = number of cash flows (not the number of time periods)
   i = interest rate for each of the stated time periods

In the example, the present value of an ordinary annuity of 4 cash flows of $1,000 each at 14% compounded annually can be calculated as follows:

$$P_0 = \$1,000 \left[\frac{1 - \dfrac{1}{(1.14)^4}}{0.14} \right] = \$2,913.71$$

Based on these calculations and formula observe that:

1. The results are the same as those produced in the first approach, $2,913.71.
2. The formula is developed from the formulas for both the future value of $1(f)$ and the present value of $1(p)$:

$$(1 + i)^n = f$$

$$\frac{1}{(1 + i)^n} = p$$

3. Thus the formula can be restated as follows:

$$P_0 = C \left(\frac{1 - p}{i} \right)$$

   The formula for the present value of an ordinary annuity can be converted to that for a series of cash flows of 1 each as follows:

$$P_{0n,i} = \left[\frac{1 - \dfrac{1}{(1 + i)^n}}{i} \right]$$

where $P_{0n,i}$ is the present value of an ordinary annuity of n cash flows of 1 each at interest rate i.[4] This formula can be expressed for the present value of an ordinary annuity of cash flows of *any size* as:

$$P_0 = C(P_{0n,i})$$

In a two-step approach the present value of 4 future withdrawals (cash flows) of $1,000 each discounted at 14% is recalculated as follows:

Step 1 $\displaystyle P_{0n=4, i=14\%} = \left[\frac{1 - \dfrac{1}{1.14^4}}{0.14} \right] = 2.913712$

Step 2 $P_0 = \$1,000(2.913712) = \$2,913.71$

This calculation is exactly the same as that of the first formula, except that the process is divided into two steps. The two-step approach is the one used when tables of the present value of an ordinary annuity of 1 are available.

---

4. $P_{0n,i}$ is often stated as $P_{0n,i}$, read as "large P sub-zero sub n at i."

TABLE APPROACH The formula for $P_{0n,i}$ can be used to construct a table of the present value of any series of cash flows of 1 each for any interest rate. All that is necessary is to substitute in the formula the desired number of cash flows for the various required interest rates. Table 4 at the end of the Appendix shows the factors for $P_{0n,i}$. Turning to Table 4, observe the following:

1. The numbers in the first column (n) represent the number of cash flows of 1 each. In this calculation the number of cash flows and time periods are equal.
2. The present value amounts are always smaller than the number of cash flows of 1. For example, the present value of 3 cash flows of 1 at 2% is 2.883883.

Since Table 4 shows the precalculation of $P_{0n,i}$ or

$$\frac{1 - \frac{1}{(1 + i)^n}}{i}$$

the generalized table approach is as follows:

$$P_0 = C(\text{Factor for } P_{0n,i})$$

Thus, to calculate the present value on January 1, 2004 of 4 future withdrawals (cash flows) of $1,000 discounted at 14%, with the first cash flow being withdrawn on December 31, 2004, it is necessary to look up the $P_{0n=4,i=14\%}$ value in the present value of an ordinary annuity of 1 table (Table 4); it is 2.913712. This factor is then multiplied by $1,000 to determine the present value figure of $2,913.71:

$$P_0 = \$1,000(2.913712) = \$2,913.71$$

Over the 4 periods, the annuity yields interest each period as follows:

Period	Beginning Balance	Interest	Cash Flow	Ending Balance
1	$2,913.71	$407.92	$(1,000)	$2,321.63
2	2,321.63	325.03	(1,000)	1,646.66
3	1,646.66	230.53	(1,000)	877.19
4	877.19	122.81	(1,000)	0

Summary and Illustration

You can solve several kinds of problems by using the present value of an ordinary annuity of 1 table. We present one additional example: a problem involving the calculation of the periodic cash flows when the present value and interest rate are known.

EXAMPLE: DETERMINING THE VALUE OF PERIODIC CASH FLOWS WHEN THE PRESENT VALUE IS KNOWN Suppose that on January 1, 2004 Rex Company borrows $100,000 to finance a plant expansion project. It plans to pay this amount back with interest at 12% in equal annual payments over a 10-year period, with the first payment due on December 31, 2004. What is the amount of each payment?

Exhibit D-14 shows the facts of the problem. The present value and the compound interest rate are known. The amount of each of the 10 cash flows is the unknown item and is $17,698.42, calculated as follows:

$$C = \frac{P_0}{\text{Factor for } P_{0n,i}}$$

$$= \frac{P_0}{\text{Factor for } P_{0n=10,i=12\%}}$$

$$= \frac{\$100,000}{5.650223}$$

$$= \$17,698.42$$

Remember that each of these payments of $17,698.42 includes (1) a payment of annual interest, and (2) a retirement of debt principal. For example, the interest for 2004 is $12,000 (12% × $100,000). Thus the amount of the payment on principal is $5,698.42 ($17,698.42 − $12,000). For the year 2005 the interest is $11,316.19 [12% × ($100,000 − $5,698.42)], and the retirement of principal is $6,382.23 ($17,698.42 − $11,316.19). The *last* payment of $17,698.42 on December 31, 2013, will be sufficient to retire the remaining principal and to pay the interest for the tenth year.

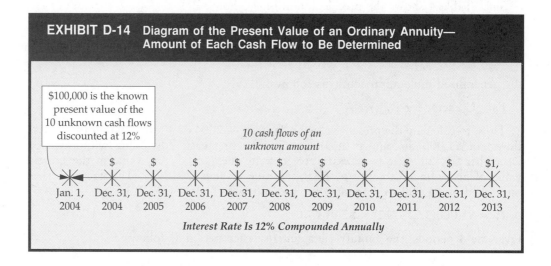

EXHIBIT D-14   Diagram of the Present Value of an Ordinary Annuity— Amount of Each Cash Flow to Be Determined

PRESENT VALUE OF AN ANNUITY DUE

7 Compute and use the present value of an annuity due.

The present value of an annuity due (P_d) is determined on the date of the first cash flow in the series. For example, assume that Barbara Livingston wants to calculate the present value of an annuity on December 31, 2004, which will permit 4 annual future receipts of $1,000 each, the first to be received on December 31, 2004. The interest rate is 14% compounded annually. Exhibit D-15 shows the facts of this problem.

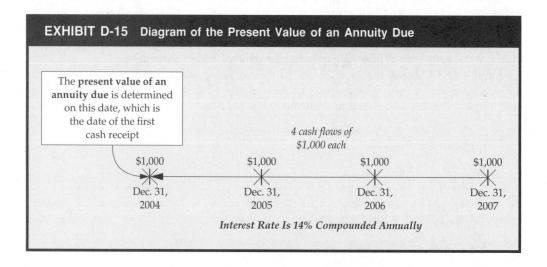

EXHIBIT D-15   Diagram of the Present Value of an Annuity Due

Shortcut Approaches

FORMULA APPROACH   The formula for the present value of an annuity due of any amount is:

$$P_d = C\left[\frac{1 - \dfrac{1}{(1 + i)^{n-1}}}{i} + 1\right]$$

where P_d = present value of an ordinary annuity of a series of cash flows of any amount
  C = amount of each cash flow
  n = number of cash flows (not the number of time periods)
  i = interest rate for each of the stated time periods

In the example, the present value of an annuity due of 4 cash flows of $1,000 each at 14% compounded annually is calculated as follows:

$$P_d = \$1,000\left[\frac{1 - \dfrac{1}{1.14^3}}{0.14} + 1\right] = \$3,321.63$$

The formula for the present value of an annuity due with cash flows of 1 each is:

$$P_{dn,i} = \left[\frac{1 - \dfrac{1}{(1 + i)^{n-1}}}{i} + 1\right]$$

where $P_{dn,i}$ is the present value of an annuity *due* of n cash flows of 1 each at interest rate i.

With the preceding formula for $P_{dn,i}$ it is possible to express another formula for the future value of an ordinary annuity of cash flows of any size as:

$$P_d = C(P_{dn,i})$$

In a two-step approach the present value of an annuity due of 4 cash flows of $1,000 each at 14% compounded annually is calculated as follows:

Step 1 $P_{dn=4, i=14\%} = \left[\dfrac{1 - \dfrac{1}{1.14^3}}{0.14} + 1\right] = 3.321632$

Step 2 $P_d = \$1,000(3.321632) = \$3,321.63$

This two-step approach is used to solve the problem when factors are not available.

TABLE APPROACH   The formula for $P_{dn,i}$ can be used to construct a table of the future value of any series of cash flows of 1 each for any interest rate. Table 5 at the end of this Appendix shows the factors for $P_{dn,i}$. Since the factors in Table 5 are based on the formula for $P_{dn,i}$ or

$$\frac{1 - \dfrac{1}{(1 + i)^{n-1}}}{i} + 1$$

values, the generalized table approach is as follows:

$$P_d = C(\text{Factor for } P_{dn,i})$$

To calculate the present value of an annuity due of 4 cash flows of $1,000 each at 14%, the $P_{dn=4, i=14\%}$ factor is found in the present value of an annuity due table (Table 5); it is 3.321632. Then the amount of each cash flow, here $1,000, is multiplied by the Table 5 factor to obtain the present value of $3,321.63:

$$P_d = \$1,000(3.321632) = \$3,321.63$$

ALTERNATIVE TABLE APPROACH   By observing the information contained in Exhibits D-15 and D-12, you can determine another way to compute the present value of an annuity due.[5] When only the present value of an *ordinary* annuity table is available, you can use the factors to determine the present value of an annuity due by completing the following steps:

Step 1	In the ordinary annuity table (Table 4), look up the present value of $n - 1$ cash flows at 14%, or the value of 3 cash flows at 14%.	2.321632
Step 2	Then add 1 without interest to the value obtained in Step 1.	1.000000
	This is the converted present value factor for $P_{d_{n=4, i=14\%}}$.	3.321632
Step 3	Multiply the amount of each cash flow, here $1,000, by the converted factor for $P_{d_{n=4, i=14\%}}$ determined in Step 2:	

$$P_d = \$1,000(3.321632) = \$3,321.63$$

Thus, if the present value of an annuity due is calculated using tables for the present value of an *ordinary* annuity, **the general rule is to use present value of an ordinary annuity factor for $n - 1$ cash flows and add 1 to the factor.**

Another Application

Besides determining the present value of an annuity due where the amount of each cash flow is known, you can solve other types of problems by using the preceding approaches. Suppose, for example, that Katherine Spruill purchases on January 1, 2004 an item that costs $10,000. She agrees to pay for this item in 10 equal annual installments, with the first installment on January 1, 2004 as a down payment. The equal installments include interest at 16% on the unpaid balance at the beginning of each year. After the interest is deducted, the balance of each payment reduces the principal of the debt. This problem involves the present value of an annuity due. It requires the determination of the amount of each of 10 cash flows that have a present value of $10,000 when discounted at an annual rate of 16%. Exhibit D-16 shows these facts graphically.

The solution to this problem requires the rearrangement of the present value of an annuity due formula:

$$C = \frac{P_0}{\text{Factor for } P_{d_{n,i}}}$$

$$= \frac{\$10,000}{5.606544} = \$1,783.63$$

The down payment of $1,783.63 plus 9 more payments of this same amount will retire the principal in 9 years, plus pay interest at 16% on the balance of the principal outstanding at the beginning of each year.

---

5. An alternative approach is to multiply the present value of an ordinary annuity factor by 1 plus the interest rate, which is consistent with the formula:

$$\frac{1 - \dfrac{1}{(1 + i)^n}}{i} \times (1 + i)$$

Thus, the present value in this example would be computed as $1,000 \times (2.913712 \times 1.14) = \$3,321.63$.

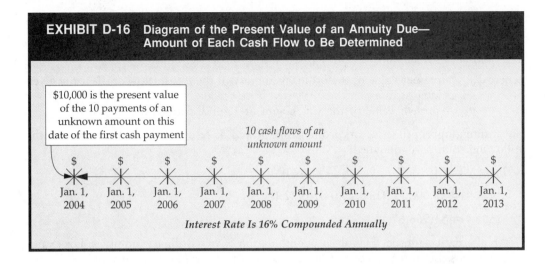

EXHIBIT D-16 Diagram of the Present Value of an Annuity Due—Amount of Each Cash Flow to Be Determined

$10,000 is the present value of the 10 payments of an unknown amount on this date of the first cash payment

10 cash flows of an unknown amount

Jan. 1, 2004 — Jan. 1, 2005 — Jan. 1, 2006 — Jan. 1, 2007 — Jan. 1, 2008 — Jan. 1, 2009 — Jan. 1, 2010 — Jan. 1, 2011 — Jan. 1, 2012 — Jan. 1, 2013

Interest Rate Is 16% Compounded Annually

PRESENT VALUE OF A DEFERRED ORDINARY ANNUITY

The present value of a deferred ordinary annuity ($P_{deferred}$) is determined on a date 2 or more periods before the first cash flow in the series. Suppose, for example, that Helen Swain buys an annuity on January 1, 2004 that yields her 4 annual receipts of $1,000 each, with the first receipt on January 1, 2008. The interest rate is 14% compounded annually. What is the cost of the annuity—that is, what is the present value on January 1, 2004 of the 4 cash flows of $1,000 each to be received on January 1, 2008, 2009, 2010, and 2011—discounted at 14%? Exhibit D-17 shows the facts of this problem diagrammatically.

8 Compute and use the present value of a deferred ordinary annuity.

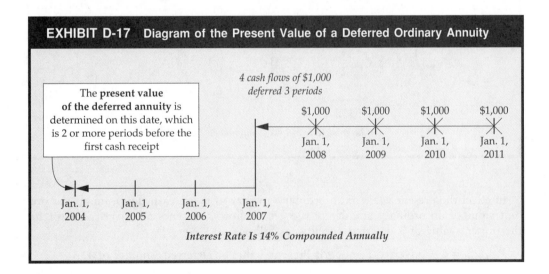

EXHIBIT D-17 Diagram of the Present Value of a Deferred Ordinary Annuity

The **present value of the deferred annuity** is determined on this date, which is 2 or more periods before the first cash receipt

4 cash flows of $1,000 deferred 3 periods

$1,000 — $1,000 — $1,000 — $1,000

Jan. 1, 2008 — Jan. 1, 2009 — Jan. 1, 2010 — Jan. 1, 2011

Jan. 1, 2004 — Jan. 1, 2005 — Jan. 1, 2006 — Jan. 1, 2007

Interest Rate Is 14% Compounded Annually

There are two ways to compute the present value of a deferred annuity. The first method involves a combination of the present value of an ordinary annuity (P_0) and the present value of a single sum due in the future (p). For the stated problem it is necessary to determine first the present value of an *ordinary* annuity of 4 cash flows of $1,000 each in order to find a single present value figure discounted to January 1, 2007. Note that because the present value of an ordinary annuity table is used, the present value of the 4 cash flows is computed on January 1, 2007, *not* January 1, 2008. That single sum is discounted for 3 more periods at 14% to arrive at the present value on January 1, 2004. Using the factors of $1 each, the present value is stated as follows:

$$P_{deferred} = C[(P_{0_{n,i}})(p_{k,i})]$$

where $P_{0_{n,i}}$ = present value of the ordinary annuity of the n cash flows of 1 at the given interest rate i

$p_{k,i}$ = present value of the single sum of 1 for k periods of deferment

Substituting appropriate factors from Tables 4 and 3, respectively, in this formula, the following solution is obtained:

$$P_{deferred} = C[(P_{0_{n=4, i=14\%}})(p_{k=3, i=14\%})]$$

$$= \$1,000[(2.913712)(0.674972)]$$

$$= \$1,966.67$$

An alternative approach involves a combination of two ordinary annuities. For example, it is possible to calculate the present value of an ordinary annuity of $n + k$ cash flows of 1. From this amount is subtracted the present value of the k (the period of deferment, which is 3 in this example) cash flows of 1. This procedure removes the cash flows that were not available to be received; yet the discount factor for the 3 periods of deferments on the 4 cash flows that are to be received remains in the calculated factor. This difference is multiplied by the value of each cash flow to determine the final present value of the deferred annuity. Exhibit D-18 illustrates this approach.

EXHIBIT D-18   Diagram of Converted Table Factor of Present Value of a Deferred Ordinary Annuity

Interest Rate Is 14% Compounded Annually

In effect the present value of an ordinary annuity of $n + k$ cash flows, minus the present value of an ordinary annuity of the k cash flows, becomes a converted factor for the present value of a deferred annuity, as follows:

$$P_{deferred} = C(\text{Converted Factor for Present Value of Deferred Annuity of 1})$$

Using the factors from Table 4, the converted factor for the deferred ordinary annuity stated in the preceding problem is determined as follows:

$$P_{0_{n+k=7, i=14\%}}(4.288305) - P_{0_{k=3, i=14\%}}(2.321632) = 1.966673$$

The present value of the 4 cash flows of $1,000 each, deferred 3 periods, is $1,966.67, calculated as follows:

$$P_{deferred} = \$1,000(1.966673) = \$1,966.67$$

Observe that the two methods produce the same present value figure. Also, observe that the period of deferment is *only* 3 periods and *not* 4 because the present value of an ordinary annuity table is used (see Exhibit D-18 in the second approach). This assumption *is* required if the problem is to be solved by the use of *ordinary* annuity factors rather than annuity due factors.

Another Application

Besides determining the present value of a deferred annuity, other types of problems can be solved by using the previous approaches. For example, suppose that David Jones wants to invest $50,000 on January 1, 2004 so that he may withdraw 10 annual cash flows of equal amounts beginning January 1, 2010. If the fund earns 12% annual interest over its life, what will be the amount of each of the 10 withdrawals?

Exhibit D-19 shows the facts of this problem. A simpler method that can be used to solve this problem is a variation of the second suggested solution. Here the value of C can be determined from the following expression of the present value of a deferred annuity formula:

$$C = \frac{P_{deferred}}{\text{Converted Factor for Present Value of Deferred Annuity of 1}}$$

Using Table 4, the converted factor for 10 cash flows of 1 each, deferred 5 periods at 12%, is as follows:

$$\text{Converted Factor} = P_{0n+k=15,\,i=12\%}(6.810864) - P_{0k=5,\,i=12\%}(3.604776)$$

$$= 3.206088$$

Then the amount of each cash flow is

$$C = \frac{\$50,000}{3.206088} = \$15,595.33$$

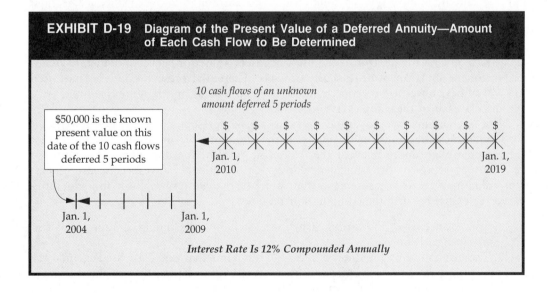

EXHIBIT D-19 Diagram of the Present Value of a Deferred Annuity—Amount of Each Cash Flow to Be Determined

The accuracy of the answer produced by the second approach can be tested using the amount of each cash flow and the solution from the first approach. The present value of 10 cash flows of $15,595.33 deferred 5 periods and discounted at 12% must be $50,000 if the first solution is correct. The proof can be calculated as follows:

$$P_{deferred} = \$15,595.33[(5.650223)(0.567427)]$$

$$= \$50,000$$

A slight rounding-error difference may occur with this method because the solution requires the multiplication of two factors, $P_{0n,\,i}$ and $p_{k,\,i}$, which are rounded.

SUMMARY OF PRESENT AND FUTURE VALUE CALCULATIONS

The present and future value calculations discussed in this Appendix may be summarized by the following diagrams:

	Present Value	Future Value
of a single sum for 3 periods		
of a 3-payment ordinary annuity		
of a 3-payment annuity due		

9 Explain the conceptual issues regarding the use of present value in financial reporting.

CONCEPTUAL EVALUATION OF PRESENT VALUE TECHNIQUES IN FINANCIAL REPORTING

Accounting principles have evolved without a unifying objective or rationale for determining when present value techniques should and should not be used. Among the issues are the use of present value for the initial valuation of assets and liabilities, the amortization of those assets and liabilities, and any subsequent revaluation when interest rates change.

Present values are used in generally accepted accounting principles for certain monetary items. A monetary item is money or a claim to money that is not affected by changes in the prices of specific goods or services. For example, a note payable is a monetary item, whereas a warranty payable is a nonmonetary item. Monetary items for which present values are used in generally accepted accounting principles include bonds payable and bond investments, long-term notes payable and receivable, leases, and postretirement benefits (e.g., pensions). Present value is not used for items such as deferred income taxes. Some accountants argue that present value should be used for nonmonetary items such as property, plant, and equipment. However, accounting principles have not been extended to the use of present value for such nonmonetary items, except for the impairment of noncurrent assets. Therefore, present values are not used for warranties, unearned revenue, compensated absences, or for nonmonetary assets. We discuss each of these topics in this book.

Most accountants would argue that the use of present value creates a *relevant* accounting measurement. For example, in the situations we discussed earlier, present value amounts are more relevant than, say, the total of the undiscounted cash flows because they represent the equivalent current cash amount. However, the use of present value may create measurements that are less *reliable* (especially if used for nonmonetary items) because the computation requires:

1. The estimation of the future cash flows, including the timing, amount, and risk of those cash flows.
2. The estimation of the interest rate. Interest rates that could be used include the historical rate, the current rate, the average expected rate, the weighted average cost of capital, or the incremental borrowing rate.[6]
3. The degree to which the cash flows from the individual assets may be added (and the liabilities subtracted) to give a measure of the value of the company.

In 1988 the FASB added the topic of "interest methods" to its agenda, and in 1990 it issued a related *Discussion Memorandum*.[7] In 1996, the FASB issued a *Special*

---

6. R. Aggarwal and C. H. Gibson, *Discounting in Financial Accounting and Reporting* (Morristown, N.J.: Financial Executives Research Foundation, 1989), p. 45.
7. "Present Value-Based Measurements in Accounting," *FASB Discussion Memorandum* (Norwalk, Conn.: FASB, 1990).

Report,[8] and in 2000, it issued **FASB Statement of Concepts No. 7**, "Using Cash Flow Information and Present Value in Accounting Measurements."[9] The *Statement* provides a framework for using future cash flows as the basis for an accounting measurement of both assets and liabilities. It provides general principles governing the use of present value as well as the objectives of present value accounting measurements. The *Statement* does not address recognition issues, and therefore does not address when fair value should be based on present value, or when assets or liabilities should be remeasured using present value. It describes five elements that together may be used to determine the value of various assets and liabilities:

1. An estimate of the future cash flow(s) and the timing of those cash flows;
2. Estimates about variations in the amount or timing of those cash flows;
3. The risk-free interest rate;
4. An increase in the interest for any expected risk;
5. Other factors, including a lack of liquidity and market imperfections.

The methodology introduced in the *Statement* permits development of a fair value using cash flow information even if uncertainties exist about the timing and/or amount of the cash flows. Present value calculations have typically been based on a single set of cash flows and a single discount rate. The *Statement* introduces the concept of "expected cash flows" when using present value techniques for accounting measurements.

Expected cash flows are a probability-weighted average of the range of possible estimated cash flow amounts and/or estimated timing of cash flows. For example, in regard to differing expected amounts a company may estimate that there is a 20% probability that the cash flow in a given year will be $1,000, a 50% probability that it will be $1,200, and a 30% probability that it will be $1,400. The company would use the expected cash flow of $1,220 [($1,000 × 0.20) + ($1,200 × 0.50) + ($1,400 × 0.30)] in its present value calculations. Or in regard to the timing of its cash flows, a company might determine that it has a 30% probability of receiving $1,000 in one year but a 70% probability of receiving $1,000 in two years. The present value would be calculated as [(30% × the present value of $1,000 in one year) + (70% × the present value of $1,000 in two years)].

The *Statement* also discusses the use of present value to estimate the fair value for a transaction between willing parties or to develop entity-specific measurements. The entity-specific value (or value in use) is the value of an asset or liability to a particular entity. In other words, the measurement substitutes the entity's assumptions for those of the market place. The FASB concluded that an entity-specific measurement might be appropriate in some situations. As with all *FASB Statements of Concepts,* the conclusions do not create specific GAAP, but will provide guidance for the development of future *FASB Statements of Financial Accounting Standards.*

SUMMARY

At the beginning of the appendix, we identified several objectives you would accomplish after reading the appendix. The objectives are listed below, each followed by a brief summary of the key points in the appendix discussion.

1. **Understand simple interest and compound interest.** Simple interest is interest on the original principal regardless of the number of time periods that have passed or the amount of interest that has been paid or accrued in the past. Compound interest is the interest that accrues on both the principal and the past unpaid accrued interest.
2. **Compute and use the future value of a single sum.** The future value of a single sum is the original sum plus the compound interest, stated as of a specific future date. The future value may be computed using a formula approach or a table approach (Table 1 at the end of this Appendix).

---

8. For a more complete discussion, see "FASB Report on Present Value Based Measurements—An Analysis of Deliberations and Techniques," *Special Report No. 158-A* (Norwalk, Conn.: FASB, February, 1996).
9. "Using Cash Flow Information and Present Value in Accounting Measurements," *FASB Statement of Financial Accounting Concepts No. 7* (Norwalk, Conn.: FASB, 2000).

3. **Compute and use the present value of a single sum.** The present value is the principal that must be invested at time period zero to produce the known future value. Discounting is the process of converting the future value to the present value. The present value may be computed using a formula approach or a table approach (Table 3).

4. **Compute and use the future value of an ordinary annuity.** An annuity is a series of equal cash flows made at regular intervals with interest compounded at a certain rate. The future value of an ordinary annuity is determined immediately after the last cash flow in the series is made. The future value may be computed using a formula approach or a table approach (Table 2).

5. **Compute and use the future value of annuity due.** The future value of an annuity due is determined one period after the last cash flow in the series. The general rule for determining the future value of an annuity due factor is to take the future value of an ordinary annuity factor (Table 2) for $n + 1$ cash flows and subtract 1 from the factor.

6. **Compute and use the present value of an ordinary annuity.** The present value of an ordinary annuity is determined one period before the first cash flow in the series is made. The present value may be computed using a formula approach or a table approach (Table 4).

7. **Compute and use the present value of annuity due.** The present value of an annuity due is determined on the date of the first cash flow in the series. The present value may be computed using a formula approach or a table approach (Table 5). The general rule for determining the present value of an annuity due factor is to take the present value of an ordinary annuity factor (Table 4) for $n - 1$ cash flows and add 1 to the factor.

8. **Compute and use the present value of a deferred ordinary annuity.** The present value of a deferred ordinary annuity is determined on a date two or more periods before the first cash flow in the series. The general rule for determining the present value of a deferred ordinary annuity factor is to take the factor for the present value of an ordinary annuity of $n + k$ cash flows and subtract the factor for the present value of an ordinary annuity of the k cash flows.

9. **Explain the conceptual issues regarding the use of present value in financial statements.** The conceptual issues include the lack of a unifying objective or rationale for determining when present value techniques should and should not be used. These include the use of present value for the initial valuation of assets and liabilities, the amortization of those assets and liabilities, and any subsequent revaluation when interest rates change. Another issue is that present value may create measurements that are less reliable. In 2000, the FASB issued *FASB Statement of Concepts No. 7,* "Using Cash Flow Information and Present Value in Accounting Measurements." The *Statement* identifies five elements that together may be used to determine the value of various assets and liabilities: (1) an estimate of the future cash flow(s) and the timing of those cash flows, (2) estimates about variations in the amount or timing of those cash flows, (3) the risk-free interest rate, (4) an increase in the interest for any expected risk, and (5) other factors, including a lack of liquidity and market imperfections.

QUESTIONS

QD-1 Define *interest*. Explain how the cost of interest is similar to the price of any merchandise item.

QD-2 Discuss the following concepts of interest: *simple interest, compound interest, time value of money, discount.*

QD-3 Distinguish between the *future value of 1* and the *future value of an ordinary annuity of 1.*

QD-4 What is the interest rate per period and the frequency of compounding per year in each of the following?
a. 18% compounded semiannually
b. 16% compounded quarterly
c. 15% compounded monthly

QD-5 Distinguish between the *future value of 1* and the *present value of 1* and between the *present value of 1* and the *present value of an ordinary annuity of 1.*

QD-6 Distinguish between the *future value of an ordinary annuity* and the *future value of an annuity due.* Draw a time line of each.

QD-7 Distinguish between the *present value of an annuity due* and the *present value of a deferred annuity.* Draw a time line of each.

QD-8 Explain how to solve each of the following without tables (in each case use the quickest approach possible):
a. The present value of $10,000 for 4 years at 10% compounded annually
b. The present value of $5,000 for 5 years at 10% [start with information developed in (a)]
c. The future value of 5 cash flows of an ordinary annuity of $3,000 each at 10% compound interest

QD-9 Potter wishes to deposit a sum that at 12% interest, compounded semiannually, will permit two withdrawals: $40,000 at the end of 4 years and $50,000 at the end of 10 years. Analyze the problem to determine the required deposit, stating the procedure to follow and the tables to use in developing the solution.

QD-10 The following factors are taken from the compound interest tables for the same number of time periods and/or cash flows for the same interest rate:
a. 8.137249
b. 50.980352
c. 6.265060
d. 7.142168
e. 0.122892

Identify each of the five compound interest table factors without reference to the tables. Discuss briefly.

QD-11 Explain how to determine the converted table factor for any deferred annuity by using the present value of an ordinary annuity table.

QD-12 Samuel Ames owes $20,000 to a friend. He wants to know how much he would have to pay if he paid the debt in 3 annual installments at the end of each year which would include interest at 14%. Draw a time line for the

problem. Indicate what table to use. Look up the table value and place in a brief formula, but do not solve.

QD-13 Starting with the given value for $(1.16)^{10} = 4.411435$, describe the fastest way to solve each of the following:

a. $p_{n=10, i=16\%}$
b. $f_{n=20, i=16\%}$
c. $F_{0 n=10, i=16\%}$
d. $P_{0 n=10, i=16\%}$
e. $F_{0 n=20, i=16\%}$

CASES

CD-1   Cost of Insurance Plans

The Johnson Company is considering three different time periods for an insurance policy on its main office building. The premiums on a fire insurance policy covering the building for the amount of $2,000,000 on a 1-year, 3-year, and 5-year basis are as follows:

One year	$ 4,480
Three years	11,200
Five years	17,920

In each case the entire premium for the full term of the policy is payable at the beginning of the year in which the policy is purchased.

Required Evaluate the annual cost of each insurance plan for the insured, assuming that money is worth 12% compounded annually. Which plan do you recommend? State the savings for the company.

CD-2   Acquisition of Equipment

The manager of the Taylor Company has consulted you, the controller, as to which of the following plans you would recommend in acquiring the use of a piece of heavy equipment:

1. Purchase the equipment and pay immediately a cash price of $36,800. The service life of the heavy equipment is estimated to be 5 years, with a resale value at the end of that time of $5,500.
2. Lease the equipment at the rate of $9,100 per year for 5 years, payable at the beginning of each year.

Required Assuming that the time value of money is 12%, evaluate the two alternatives and indicate which plan you would recommend to the manager, stating the value of savings to the company.

CD-3   Effective Interest in Various Situations

On March 1, 2004 the White Company purchased $400,000 worth of inventory on credit with terms of 1/20, n/60. In the past, White has always followed the policy of making payment 1 month (30 days) after the goods are purchased.

A new member of White's staff has indicated that the company he previously worked for never passed up its cash discounts, and he wonders if this is not a sound policy. It was pointed out, however, that if White were to pay the bill on March 20 rather than on March 30, it would have to borrow the necessary funds for the 10 extra days. White's borrowing terms with a local bank were estimated to be at 14% (annual rate), with a 15% compensating balance (a requirement by the bank that White maintain an amount in its account equal to 15% of the loan) for the term of the loan. Most members of White's staff felt that it made little sense to take out a 14% loan with a compensating balance of 15% in order to save 1% on $400,000 by paying the account 10 days earlier than planned.

Required

1. In terms of simple effective annual interest cost, explain whether it would be to White's advantage to borrow the amount necessary to take the 1% discount by paying the bill 10 days early.
2. It has also been pointed out to White that if it does not take advantage of the cash discount, it should wait the entire 60-day period to pay the full bill rather than pay within 30 days. Explain how your answer to Requirement 1 would change if White undertook this policy.
3. Your answer to Requirement 2 indicates that, in relation to Requirement 1, it has become either more desirable or less desirable to borrow in order to take advantage of the 1% cash discount.
   a. If you said *more desirable*, explain why.
   b. If you said *less desirable*, make a similar explanation.

CD-4   Future Value of Single Investment and Annuity

Jane Dough was a teller in a large northeastern bank. She was single and approaching age 30, and she considered herself an honest and upright citizen. After considering what she might do to build a retirement plan for the future, she decided to embezzle $1,500,000. Subsequently she gave herself up to the authorities but did not return the $1,500,000. She was tried, convicted, and sentenced to 20 years in prison. After completing her 20-year term, she returned the $1,500,000 that she had stolen. She then decided to take a world cruise. On board ship someone asked her how she had accumulated enough money to afford the trip. She replied, "Do you know how much *interest* $1,500,000 will earn in 20 years if invested at an annual rate of 16% compounded quarterly?"

Required

1. Determine the answer to Jane Dough's question. The table factor for $f_{n=40, i=4\%}$ is 4.801021.
2. Evaluate Jane's retirement decision, assuming that she could have earned $21,000 each year for each of the 20 years she was in prison. Assume that $11,000 is required each year to cover living expenses and that she could have invested the remaining $10,000 at the end of each year to earn interest at 16% compounded annually.

CD-5 Value of a Note

You have just been promoted to manager at a national CPA firm. On your first job a new accountant approaches you with the following situation: He has discovered that the president of the client company has a brother who is both the major stockholder and the president of a local bank. Your client has a $300,000, 5-year note payable to the bank at 4% interest compounded annually. Since the going interest rate is 16%, the accountant suggests that the note be recorded at its present value using this going rate. The president says that the effective liability is $300,000 and should be reported on the balance sheet at this figure. The note was issued on January 1, 2004 and is due on January 1, 2009.

Required

1. Explain who is correct.
2. At what amount should the company have valued the note on January 1, 2004, assuming that the accountant's assessment is correct?

CD-6 Future Value and Present Value Issues

Jean Perry has a $25,000 whole-life insurance policy that she began many years ago. She is presently 55 years old. One of the benefits of the policy is that Perry can borrow up to a given amount at 12% interest (2% below the current rate), with the principal due 2 years after the loan is made. The policy states that should Perry default on the principal payment, it will simply be deducted from the amount given her beneficiary when she dies. However, the interest will continue to accrue as long as the note is not paid. Perry has just borrowed $5,000 on this policy to take a vacation in Hawaii.

Required Assuming that a woman of Perry's health is expected to live to be 72, explain whether it would be financially advantageous for Perry to repay the principal on the loan in 2 years. (Calculations are not required.)

MULTIPLE CHOICE

Select the best answer for each of the following.

Items 1 through 4 require use of present value tables. The following are the present value factors of $1.00 discounted at 8% for 1 to 5 periods. Each item is based on 8% interest compounded annually from day of deposit to day of withdrawal.

Periods	Present Value of $1 Discounted at 8% per Period
1	0.926
2	0.857
3	0.794
4	0.735
5	0.681

MD-1 What amount should be deposited in a bank today to grow to $1,000 three years from today?
  a. $\dfrac{\$1,000}{0.794}$
  b. $\$1,000 \times 0.926 \times 3$
  c. $(\$1,000 \times 0.926) + (\$1,000 \times 0.857) + (\$1,000 \times 0.794)$
  d. $\$1,000 \times 0.794$

MD-2 What amount should an individual have in his bank account today, before withdrawal, if he needs $2,000 each year for 4 years, with the first withdrawal to be made today and each subsequent withdrawal at 1-year intervals? (He is to have exactly a zero balance in his bank account after the fourth withdrawal.)
  a. $\$2,000 + (\$2,000 \times 0.926) + (\$2,000 \times 0.857) + (\$2,000 \times 0.794)$
  b. $\dfrac{\$2,000}{0.735} \times 4$
  c. $(\$2,000 \times 0.926) + (\$2,000 \times 0.857) + (\$2,000 \times 0.794) + (\$2,000 \times 0.735)$
  d. $\dfrac{\$2,000}{0.926} \times 4$

MD-3 If an individual put $3,000 in a savings account today, what amount of cash will be available 2 years from today?
  a. $\$3,000 \times 0.857$ c. $\dfrac{\$3,000}{0.857}$
  b. $\$3,000 \times 0.857 \times 2$ d. $\dfrac{\$3,000}{0.926} \times 2$

MD-4 What is the present value today of $4,000 to be received 6 years from today?

a. $4,000 \times 0.926 \times 6$
b. $4,000 \times 0.794 \times 2$
c. $4,000 \times 0.681 \times 0.926$
d. Cannot be determined from the information given

MD-5 On January 1, 2004 Kern Company sold a machine to Burns Company. Burns signed a non-interest-bearing note requiring payment of $30,000 annually for 7 years. The first payment was made on January 1, 2004. The prevailing rate of interest for this type of note at the date of issuance was 10%. Information on present value factors is as follows:

Periods	Present Value of 1 at 10%	Present Value of Ordinary Annuity of 1 at 10%
6	0.56	4.36
7	0.51	4.87

Kern should record the sale in January 2004 at

a. $107,100
b. $130,800
c. $146,100
d. $160,800

MD-6 On May 1, 2004, a company purchased a new machine that it does not have to pay for until May 1, 2006. The total payment on May 1, 2006 will include both principal and interest. Assuming interest at a 10% rate, the cost of the machine would be the total payment multiplied by what time value of money concept?

a. Future value of annuity of 1
b. Future value of 1
c. Present value of annuity of 1
d. Present value of 1

MD-7 An office equipment representative has a machine for sale or lease. If you buy the machine, the cost is $7,596. If you lease the machine, you will have to sign a noncancellable lease and make 5 payments of $2,000 each. The first payment will be paid on the first day of the lease. At the time of the last payment you will receive title to the machine. The present value of an ordinary annuity of $1 is as follows:

Present Value Number of Periods	10%	12%	16%
1	0.909	0.893	0.862
2	1.736	1.690	1.605
3	2.487	2.402	2.246
4	3.170	3.037	2.798
5	3.791	3.605	3.274

The interest rate implicit in this lease is approximately

a. 10%
b. 12%
c. Between 10% and 12%
d. 16%

MD-8 An accountant wishes to find the present value of an annuity of $1 payable at the beginning of each period at 10% for 8 periods. He has only one present value table, which shows the present value of an annuity of $1 payable at the end of each period. To compute the present value factor he needs, the accountant would use the present value factor in the 10% column for

a. Seven periods
b. Seven periods and add 1
c. Eight periods
d. Nine periods and subtract 1

MD-9 On July 1, 2004, James Rago signed an agreement to operate as a franchisee of Fast Foods, Inc., for an initial franchise fee of $60,000. Of this amount, $20,000 was paid when the agreement was signed and the balance is payable in 4 equal annual payments of $10,000 beginning July 1, 2005. The agreement provides that the down payment is not refundable and no future services are required of the franchisor. Rago's credit rating indicates that he can borrow money at 14% for a loan of this type. Information on present and future value factors is as follows:

Present value of $1 at 14% for 4 periods	0.59
Future value of $1 at 14% for 4 periods	1.69
Present value of an ordinary annuity of $1 at 14% for 4 periods	2.91

Rago should record the acquisition cost of the franchise on July 1, 2004 at

a. $43,600
b. $49,100
c. $60,000
d. $67,600

MD-10 For which of the following transactions would the use of the present value of an annuity due concept be appropriate in calculating the present value of the asset obtained or liability owed at the date of incurrence?

a. A capital lease is entered into with the initial lease payment due one month subsequent to the signing of the lease agreement.
b. A capital lease is entered into with the initial lease payment due upon the signing of the lease agreement.
c. A 10-year, 8% bond is issued on January 2, with interest payable semiannually on July 1 and January 1 yielding 7%.
d. A 10-year, 8% bond is issued on January 2, with interest payable semiannually on July 1 and January 1 yielding 9%.

(AICPA adapted)

EXERCISES

ED-1 *Future Value of an Investment and Compound Interest* Using the future value tables, solve the following:

Required

1. What is the value on January 1, 2011 of $40,000 deposited on January 1, 2004 which accumulates interest at 12% compounded annually?

2. What is the value on January 1, 2010 of $10,000 deposited on July 1, 2004 which accumulates interest at 16% compounded quarterly?

3. What is the compound interest on an investment of $6,000 left on deposit for 5 years at 10% compounded annually?

ED-2   *Future Value of an Investment*   Hugh Colson deposited $20,000 in a special savings account that provides for interest at the annual rate of 12% compounded semiannually if the deposit is maintained for 4 years.

Required Calculate the balance of the savings account at the end of the 4-year period.

ED-3   *Present Value of a Sum and Compound Discount*   Using the present value tables, solve the following problems:

Required

1. What is the present value on January 1, 2004 of $30,000 due on January 1, 2009 and discounted at 12% compounded annually?

2. What is the present value on July 1, 2004 of $8,000 due January 1, 2009 and discounted at 16% compounded quarterly?

3. What is the compound discount on $8,000 due at the end of 5 years at 10% compounded annually?

ED-4   *Future Value of Annuity*   Using appropriate tables, solve the following future value of annuity problems:

Required

1. What is the future value on December 31, 2010 of 7 cash flows of $10,000, with the first cash payment being made on December 31, 2004 and interest at 12% being compounded annually?

2. What is the future value on December 31, 2011 of 7 cash flows of $10,000, with the first cash payment made on December 31, 2004 and interest at 12% being compounded annually?

ED-5   *Present Value of an Annuity*   Samuel David wants to make 5 equal annual withdrawals of $8,000 from a fund that will earn interest at 10% compounded annually.

Required How much would David have to invest on:

1. January 1, 2004 if the first withdrawal is made on January 1, 2005?

2. January 1, 2004 if the first withdrawal is made on January 1, 2004?

ED-6   *Amount of Each Cash Flow*   Six equal annual contributions are made to a fund, with the first deposit on December 31, 2004.

Required Using the future value tables, determine the equal contributions that, if invested at 10% compounded annually, will produce a fund of $30,000, assuming that this sum is desired on December 31, 2009.

ED-7   *Amount of an Annuity*   Beginning December 31, 2008, 5 equal annual withdrawals are to be made.

Required Using the appropriate tables, determine the equal annual withdrawals if $25,000 is invested at an interest of 12% compounded annually on

1. December 31, 2007
2. December 31, 2008
3. December 31, 2004

ED-8   *Amount of Each Cash Flow*   R. Lee Rouse borrows $10,000 that is to be repaid in 24 equal monthly installments payable at the end of each subsequent month with interest at the rate of $1\frac{1}{2}$% a month.

Required Using the appropriate table, calculate the equal installments.

ED-9   *Amount of Each Cash Flow*   On January 1, 2004 Charles Jamison borrows $40,000 from his father to open a business. The son is the beneficiary of a trust created by his favorite aunt from which he will receive $25,000 on January 1, 2014. He signs an agreement to make this amount payable to his father and, further, to pay his father equal annual amounts from January 1, 2005 to January 1, 2013, inclusive, in retirement of the debt. Interest is 12%.

Required What are the annual payments?

ED-10   *Amount of an Annuity*   Beginning with January 1, 2004, 5 equal deposits are to be made in a fund.

Required Using the appropriate tables, determine the equal deposits if interest at 10% is compounded annually and if $200,000 must be in the fund on

1. January 1, 2009
2. January 1, 2010

ED-11   *Series of Compound Interest Techniques*   The following are several situations involving compound interest.

Required Using the appropriate table, solve each of the following:

1. Hope Dearborn invests $40,000 on January 1, 2004 in a savings account that earns interest of 8% compounded semiannually. What will be the amount in the fund on December 31, 2009?
2. Ben Johnson receives a bonus of $5,000 each year on December 31. He starts depositing his bonus on December 31, 2004 in a savings account that earns interest of 12% compounded annually. What will be the amount in the fund on December 31, 2008 after he deposits his bonus received on that date?
3. Ron Sewert owes $30,000 on a non-interest-bearing note due January 1, 2014. He offers to pay the amount on January 1, 2004 provided that it is discounted at 10% on a compound annual discount basis. What would he have to pay on January 1, 2004 under this assumption?
4. June Stickney purchased an annuity on January 1, 2004 which, at a 12% annual rate, would yield $6,000 each June 30 and December 31 for the next 6 years. What was the cost of the annuity to Stickney?
5. Five equal annual contributions are to be made to a fund, the first deposit on December 31, 2004. Determine the equal contributions that, if invested at 10% compounded annually, will produce a fund of $30,000 on December 31, 2009.
6. Beginning on December 31, 2005, 6 equal annual withdrawals are to be made. Determine the equal annual withdrawals if $11,000 is invested at 10% interest compounded annually on December 31, 2004.

ED-12   *Amount of an Annuity*   John Goodheart wishes to provide for 6 annual withdrawals of $3,000 each beginning January 1, 2014. He wishes to make 10 annual deposits beginning January 1, 2004, with the last deposit to be made on January 1, 2013.

Required If the fund earns interest compounded annually at 10%, how much is each of the 10 deposits?

ED-13   *Present Value of Leased Asset*   On January 1, 2004 Ashly Farms leased a hay baler from Agrico Tractor Company. Ashly was having cash flow problems, so Agrico drew up the lease to allow Ashly to reestablish itself. The lease requires Ashly to make $3,000 payments on January 1 of each year for 5 years beginning in 2004. The interest rate is 12%.

Required Calculate the present value of the cost of the lease payments to Ashly on January 1, 2004.

ED-14   *Number of Cash Flows*   On July 1, 2004 Boston Company purchased a machine at a cost of $80,000. It paid $56,046.06 in cash and signed a 10% note for the difference. This note is to be paid off in annual installments of $5,000 each, payable each July 1, beginning immediately. The $5,000 includes a payment of interest on the balance of the principal at the beginning of each period and a payment on the principal.

Required Calculate the number of annual payments to be made by Boston Company.

PROBLEMS

PD-1   *Future Value of an Investment*   Several questions involving the future value of a single investment are presented as follows:

Required Using the appropriate tables, solve each of the following:

1. What is the future value on December 31, 2008 of a deposit of $35,000 made on December 31, 2004 assuming interest of 10% compounded annually?
2. What is the future value on December 31, 2008 of a deposit of $10,000 made on December 31, 2004 assuming interest of 16% compounded quarterly?
3. What is the future value on December 31, 2008 of a deposit of $25,000 made on December 31, 2004 assuming interest of 12% compounded semiannually?

PD-2   *Present Value Issues*   Several questions involving the present value of a single sum are presented next.

Required Using the appropriate tables, solve each of the following:

1. What is the present value on January 1, 2004 of $30,000 due on January 1, 2008 and discounted at 10% compounded annually?
2. What is the present value on January 1, 2004 of $40,000 due on January 1, 2008 and discounted at 11% compounded semiannually?

3. What is the present value on January 1, 2004 of $50,000 due on January 1, 2008 and discounted at 16% compounded quarterly?

PD-3   ***Future Value Issues***   Several questions involving future values are presented next.

Required Using the appropriate tables, solve each of the following:

1. What is the future value on December 31, 2013 of 10 cash flows of $20,000 with the first cash payment made on December 31, 2004 and interest at 10% being compounded annually?
2. What is the future value on June 30, 2014 of 20 cash flows of $15,000 with the first cash payment made on December 31, 2004 and the annual interest rate of 10% being compounded semiannually?
3. What is the future value on December 31, 2014 of 20 cash flows of $15,000 with the first cash payment made on December 31, 2004 and the annual interest rate of 10% being compounded semiannually?

PD-4   ***Amount of Each Cash Flow***   On December 31, 2011 Michael McDowell desires to have $60,000. He plans to make 6 deposits in a fund to provide this amount. Interest is compounded annually at 12%.

Required Compute the equal annual amounts that McDowell must deposit assuming that he makes the first deposit on

1. December 31, 2006
2. December 31, 2005

PD-5   ***Value of an Annuity***   John Joshua wants to make 5 equal annual withdrawals of $20,000 from a fund that will earn interest at 12% compounded annually.

Required How much would Joshua have to invest on January 1, 2004 if he makes the first withdrawal on

1. January 1, 2005?
2. January 1, 2004?
3. January 1, 2009?

PD-6   ***Value of an Annuity***   Ralph Benke wants to make 8 equal semiannual withdrawals of $8,000 from a fund that will earn interest at 11% compounded semiannually.

Required How much would Benke have to invest on:

1. January 1, 2004 if the first withdrawal is made on July 1, 2004?
2. July 1, 2004 if the first withdrawal is made on July 1, 2004?
3. January 1, 2004 if the first withdrawal is made on January 1, 2007?

PD-7   ***Various Compound Interest Issues***   You are given the following situations:

1. Thomas Petry owes a debt of $7,000 from the purchase of a boat. The debt bears interest of 12% payable annually. Petry will pay the debt and interest in 5 annual installments beginning in one year. Calculate the equal annual installments that will pay off the debt and interest at 12% on the unpaid balance.
2. On January 1, 2004 John Cothran offers to buy Ruth House's used tractor and equipment for $4,000 payable in 12 equal semiannual installments, which are to include payment of 10% interest on the unpaid balance and payment of a portion of the principal, with the first installment to be made on January 1, 2004. Calculate the amount of each of these installments.
3. Nadine Love invests in a $60,000 annuity at 12% compounded annually on March 1, 2004. The first of 15 receipts from the annuity is payable to Love on March 1, 2014, 10 years after the annuity is purchased and on the date Love expects to retire. Calculate the amount of each of the 15 equal annual receipts.

Required Using the appropriate tables, solve each of the preceding situations.

PD-8   ***Value of an Annuity***   Several questions involving the value of an annuity are presented next.

Required Using the appropriate tables, solve each of the following:

1. Beginning December 31, 2005, 5 equal withdrawals are to be made. Determine the equal annual withdrawals if $30,000 is invested at 10% interest compounded annually on December 31, 2004.
2. Ten payments of $3,000 are due at annual intervals beginning June 30, 2005. What amount will be accepted in cancellation of this series of payments on June 30, 2004 assuming a discount rate of 14% compounded annually?
3. Ten payments of $2,000 are due at annual intervals beginning December 31, 2004. What amount will be accepted in cancellation of this series of payments on January 1, 2004 assuming a discount rate of 12% compounded annually?

PD-9   *Amount of Each Cash Flow*   On January 1, 2004 Philip Holding invests $40,000 in an annuity to provide 8 equal semiannual payments. Interest is 10%, compounded semiannually.

> **Required** Compute the equal semiannual amounts that Holding will receive, assuming that the first withdrawal is to be received on
>
> 1. July 1, 2004
> 2. January 1, 2004
> 3. July 1, 2007
> 4. January 1, 2009

PD-10   *Number of Cash Flows*   The following are two independent situations.

> 1. Houser wishes to accumulate a fund of $40,000 for the purchase of a house and lot. He plans to deposit $4,000 semiannually at the end of each 6 months. Assuming interest at 14% a year compounded semiannually, how many deposits of $4,000 each will be required and what is the amount of the last deposit?
> 2. On January 1, 2004 Joan Campbell borrows $20,000 from Susan Rone and agrees to repay this amount in payments of $4,000 a year until the debt is paid in full. Payments are to be of an equal amount and are to include interest at 12% on the unpaid balance of principal at the beginning of each period. Assuming that the first payment is to be made on January 1, 2005, determine the number of payments of $4,000 each to be made and the amount of the final payment.

> **Required** Using the appropriate tables, solve each of the preceding situations.

PD-11   *Serial Installments; Amounts Applicable to Interest and Principal*   Ronald McDuffie purchases a new car
@   at a cost of $14,400. He pays $3,000 down and issues an installment note payable by which he promises to pay the balance in 18 equal monthly installments, which include interest at an annual rate of 18% on the remaining unpaid balance at the beginning of each month, starting with the first month after the purchase.

> **Required**
>
> 1. Compute the equal installment payments.
> 2. Compute the interest that will be paid for each of the first 2 periods. Indicate the amount of each payment that will be a reduction of principal.

PD-12   *Determining Loan Repayments*   Rockness needs $40,000 to pay off a loan due on December 31, 2013. His plans included the making of 10 annual deposits beginning on December 31, 2004 in accumulating a fund to pay off the loan. Without making a precise calculation, Rockness made 3 annual deposits of $4,000 each on December 31, 2004, 2005, and 2006, which have been earning interest at 10% compounded annually.

> **Required** What is the equal amount of each of the next 7 deposits for the period December 31, 2007 to December 31, 2013 to reach the fund objective, assuming that the fund will continue to earn interest at 10% compounded annually?

PD-13   *Purchase of Asset*   William Thomas intends to purchase a tractor on credit. Two local implement dealers have
@   offered him the following payment plans for identical tractors:

> 1. Redd Truck & Tractor's plan calls for 5 annual payments of $10,350, with the first payment now and the remaining payments at the beginning of each of the next 4 years.
> 2. Greene Farm Implements requires semiannual payments of $5,750 at the end of each of the next 10 semiannual periods, with the first payment to be in 6 months.

> **Required** Determine which of the preceding plans offers Thomas the lower present value. The applicable annual interest rate is 10% for both alternatives.

PD-14   *Fund to Retire Bonds*   At the beginning of 2004 Shanklin Company issued 10-year bonds with a face value of $1,000,000 due on December 31, 2013. The company wants to accumulate a fund to retire these bonds at maturity by making annual deposits beginning on December 31, 2004.

> **Required** How much must the company deposit each year, assuming that the fund will earn 12% interest a year compounded annually?

PD-15 *Asset Purchase Price* BWP, Inc., is considering the purchase of an asset. BWP's required rate of return on new assets is 12%. The expected net cash inflows generated by the new asset are as follows:

Years	Amount	Nature of the Cash Inflows
1–4	$3,000	Net operating revenues
5–9	2,500	Net operating revenues
10	2,000	Net operating revenues
10	1,000	Sale of asset

Required Given that the net cash inflows can be realized, what is the maximum amount BWP should be willing to pay for the new asset? Assume that each cash inflow occurs at the end of the year. (*Contributed by Norma C. Powell*)

PD-16 *Acquisition of Asset* SuMar Company purchased a new piece of machinery by paying $2,000 down and agreeing to pay $1,000 at the end of each year for 5 years. The appropriate interest rate is 8%.

Required

1. What is the cost of the machinery?
2. Prepare the journal entry to record the purchase of the machinery.
3. Prepare a table that shows the interest and ending balance of the liability each year. (*Contributed by Norma C. Powell*)

PD-17 *Present Value Issues* Nello Construction Company has just purchased several major pieces of road-building equipment. Since the purchase price is so large, the equipment company is giving Nello an option of choosing one of four different payment plans:

1. $600,000 immediately in cash.
2. $200,000 down payment now; $65,000 per year for 12 years, beginning at the end of the current year.
3. $200,000 down payment now; $25,000 per year for 3 years beginning at the end of the current year; $75,000 per year for 11 years beginning at the end of the fourth year after the purchase.
4. $80,000 now and at the beginning of each of the next 13 years.

Required You have been asked by the Nello Construction Company to decide which payment plan will provide the smallest present value. The expected effective interest rate during the future periods stated above is 12%.

PD-18 *Comprehensive*

Part a. Reproduced in the following table are the first three lines from the 2% columns of each of several tables of mathematical values. For each of the following items, you are to select from among these fragmentary tables the one from which the amount required can be obtained *most directly* (assuming that the complete table was available in each instance):

Periods	Table A	Table B	Table C	Table D	Table E	Table F
0	1.0000		1.0000			
1	0.9804	1.0200	1.0200	1.0000	0.9804	1.0200
2	0.9612	2.0604	1.0404	0.4950	1.9416	0.5150
3		3.1216		0.3268	2.8839	0.3468

1. The amount to which a single sum would accumulate at compound interest by the end of a specified period (interest compounded annually).
2. The amount that must be appropriated at the end of each of a specific number of years to provide for the accumulation, at annually compounded interest, of a certain sum.
3. The amount that must be deposited in a fund that will earn interest at a specified rate, compounded annually, in order to make possible the withdrawal of certain equal sums annually over a specified period starting 1 year from date of deposit.
4. The amount of interest that will accumulate on a single deposit by the end of a specified period (interest compounded semiannually).
5. The amount, net of compound discount, that if paid now would settle a debt of larger amount due at a specified future date.

Part b. The following tables of values at 10% interest may be used as needed to answer the questions in this part of the problem.

Periods	Future Value of 1 at Compound Interest	Present Value of 1 at Compound Interest	Future Value of Annuity of 1 at End of Each Period	Present Value of Annuity of 1 at End of Each Period
1	1.100	0.9091	1.0000	0.9091
.	.	.	.	.
.	.	.	.	.
.	.	.	.	.
6	1.7716	0.5645	7.7156	4.3553
7	1.9487	0.5132	9.4872	4.8684
8	2.1436	0.4665	11.4359	5.3349
9	2.3579	0.4241	13.5795	5.7590
10	2.5937	0.3855	15.9374	6.1446
11	2.8531	0.3505	18.5312	6.4951
12	3.1384	0.3186	21.3843	6.8137
13	3.4523	0.2897	24.5227	7.1034
14	3.7975	0.2633	27.9750	7.3667
15	4.1772	0.2394	31.7725	7.6061
16	4.5950	0.2176	35.9497	7.8237

1. Your client has made annual payments of $2,500 into a fund at the close of each year for the past 3 years. The fund balance immediately after the third payment totaled $8,275. He has asked you how many more $2,500 annual payments will be required to bring the fund to $22,500, assuming that the fund continues to earn interest at 10% compounded annually. Compute the number of full payments required and the amount of the final payment if it does not require the entire $2,500. Carefully label all computations supporting your answer.

2. Your client wishes to provide for the payment of an obligation of $200,000 due on July 1, 2011. He plans to deposit $20,000 in a special fund each July 1 for 7 years, starting July 1, 2005. He wishes to make an initial deposit on July 1, 2004 of an amount that, with its accumulated interest, will bring the fund up to $200,000 at the maturity of the obligation. He expects that the fund will earn interest at the rate of 10% compounded annually. Compute the amount to be deposited July 1, 2004. Carefully label all computations supporting your answer. (*AICPA adapted*)

PD-19 *Comprehensive* The following are three independent situations:

1. M. Herman has decided to set up a scholarship fund for students. She is willing to deposit $5,000 in a trust fund at the end of each year for 10 years. She wants the trust fund to then pay annual scholarships at the end of each year for 30 years.

2. Charles Jordy is planning to save for his retirement. He has decided that he can save $3,000 at the end of each year for the next 10 years, $5,000 at the end of each year for years 11 through 20, and $10,000 at the end of each year for years 21 through 30.

3. Patricia Karpas has $200,000 in savings on the day she retires. She intends to spend $2,000 per month traveling around the world for the next two years, during which time her savings will earn 18%, compounded monthly. For the next 5 years, she intends to spend $6,000 every six months, during which time her savings will earn 12%, compounded semiannually. For the rest of her life expectancy of 15 years, she wants an annuity to cover her living costs. During this period her savings will earn 10% compounded annually. Assume that all payments occur at the end of each period.

Required

1. In Situation 1, how much will the annual scholarships be if the fund can earn 6%? 10%?
2. In Situation 2,
   (a) How much will Jordy have at the end of 30 years if his savings can earn 10%? 6%?
   (b) If Jordy expects to live for 20 years in retirement, how much can he spend each year if his savings earn 10%? 6%?
   (c) How much would Jordy need to invest today to have the same amount available at the time he retires as calculated in 2(a) at 10%? 6%?
3. In Situation 3, how much will Karpas's annuity be?

COMPOUND INTEREST TABLES

TABLE 1 FUTURE VALUE OF 1: $f = (1 + i)^n$

TABLE 2 FUTURE VALUE OF AN ORDINARY ANNUITY OF 1:

$$F_0 = \frac{(1 + i)^n - 1}{i}$$

TABLE 3 PRESENT VALUE OF 1: $p = \dfrac{1}{(1 + i)^n}$

TABLE 4 PRESENT VALUE OF AN ORDINARY ANNUITY OF 1:

$$P_0 = \frac{1 - \dfrac{1}{(1 + i)^n}}{i}$$

TABLE 5 PRESENT VALUE OF ANNUITY DUE: $P_d = \dfrac{1 - \dfrac{1}{(1 + i)^{n-1}}}{i} + 1$

Table 1 FUTURE VALUE OF 1: $f = (1 + i)^n$

n	1.5%	4.0%	4.5%	5.0%	5.5%	6.0%	7.0%
1	1.015000	1.040000	1.045000	1.050000	1.055000	1.060000	1.070000
2	1.030225	1.081600	1.092025	1.102500	1.113025	1.123600	1.144900
3	1.045678	1.124864	1.141166	1.157625	1.174241	1.191016	1.225043
4	1.061364	1.169859	1.192519	1.215506	1.238825	1.262477	1.310796
5	1.077284	1.216653	1.246182	1.276282	1.306960	1.338226	1.402552
6	1.093443	1.265319	1.302260	1.340096	1.378843	1.418519	1.500730
7	1.109845	1.315932	1.360862	1.407100	1.454679	1.503630	1.605781
8	1.126493	1.368569	1.422101	1.477455	1.534687	1.593848	1.718186
9	1.143390	1.423312	1.486095	1.551328	1.619094	1.689479	1.838459
10	1.160541	1.480244	1.552969	1.628895	1.708144	1.790848	1.967151
11	1.177949	1.539454	1.622853	1.710339	1.802092	1.898299	2.104852
12	1.195618	1.601032	1.695881	1.795856	1.901207	2.012196	2.252192
13	1.213552	1.665074	1.772196	1.885649	2.005774	2.132928	2.409845
14	1.231756	1.731676	1.851945	1.979932	2.116091	2.260904	2.578534
15	1.250232	1.800944	1.935282	2.078928	2.232476	2.396558	2.759032
16	1.268986	1.872981	2.022370	2.182875	2.355263	2.540352	2.952164
17	1.288020	1.947900	2.113377	2.292018	2.484802	2.692773	3.158815
18	1.307341	2.025817	2.208479	2.406619	2.621466	2.854339	3.379932
19	1.326951	2.106849	2.307860	2.526950	2.765647	3.025600	3.616528
20	1.346855	2.191123	2.411714	2.653298	2.917757	3.207135	3.869684
21	1.367058	2.278768	2.520241	2.785963	3.078234	3.399564	4.140562
22	1.387564	2.369919	2.633652	2.925261	3.247537	3.603537	4.430402
23	1.408377	2.464716	2.752166	3.071524	3.426152	3.819750	4.740530
24	1.429503	2.563304	2.876014	3.225100	3.614590	4.048935	5.072367
25	1.450945	2.665836	3.005434	3.386355	3.813392	4.291871	5.427433
26	1.472710	2.772470	3.140679	3.555673	4.023129	4.549383	5.807353
27	1.494800	2.883369	3.282010	3.733456	4.244401	4.822346	6.213868
28	1.517222	2.998703	3.429700	3.920129	4.477843	5.111687	6.648838
29	1.539981	3.118651	3.584036	4.116136	4.724124	5.418388	7.114257
30	1.563080	3.243398	3.745318	4.321942	4.983951	5.743491	7.612255

n	8.0%	9.0%	10.0%	12.0%	14.0%	16.0%	18.0%
1	1.080000	1.090000	1.100000	1.120000	1.140000	1.160000	1.180000
2	1.166400	1.188100	1.210000	1.254400	1.299600	1.345600	1.392400
3	1.259712	1.295029	1.331000	1.404928	1.481544	1.560896	1.643032
4	1.360489	1.411582	1.464100	1.573519	1.688960	1.810639	1.938778
5	1.469328	1.538624	1.610510	1.762342	1.925415	2.100342	2.287758
6	1.586874	1.677100	1.771561	1.973823	2.194973	2.436396	2.699554
7	1.713824	1.828039	1.948717	2.210681	2.502269	2.826220	3.185474
8	1.850930	1.992563	2.143589	2.475963	2.852586	3.278415	3.758859
9	1.999005	2.171893	2.357948	2.773079	3.251949	3.802961	4.435454
10	2.158925	2.367364	2.593742	3.105848	3.707221	4.411435	5.233836
11	2.331639	2.580426	2.853117	3.478550	4.226232	5.117265	6.175926
12	2.518170	2.812665	3.138428	3.895976	4.817905	5.936027	7.287593
13	2.719624	3.065805	3.452271	4.363493	5.492411	6.885791	8.599359
14	2.937194	3.341727	3.797498	4.887112	6.261349	7.987518	10.147244
15	3.172169	3.642482	4.177248	5.473566	7.137938	9.265521	11.973748
16	3.425943	3.970306	4.594973	6.130394	8.137249	10.748004	14.129023
17	3.700018	4.327633	5.054470	6.866041	9.276464	12.467685	16.672247
18	3.996019	4.717120	5.559917	7.689966	10.575169	14.462514	19.673251
19	4.315701	5.141661	6.115909	8.612762	12.055693	16.776517	23.214436
20	4.660957	5.604411	6.727500	9.646293	13.743490	19.460759	27.393035
21	5.033834	6.108808	7.400250	10.803848	15.667578	22.574481	32.323781
22	5.436540	6.658600	8.140275	12.100310	17.861039	26.186398	38.142061
23	5.871464	7.257874	8.954302	13.552347	20.361585	30.376222	45.007632
24	6.341181	7.911083	9.849733	15.178629	23.212207	35.236417	53.109006
25	6.848475	8.623081	10.834706	17.000064	26.461916	40.874244	62.668627
26	7.396353	9.399158	11.918177	19.040072	30.166584	47.414123	73.948980
27	7.988061	10.245082	13.109994	21.324881	34.389906	55.000382	87.259797
28	8.627106	11.167140	14.420994	23.883866	39.204493	63.800444	102.966560
29	9.317275	12.172182	15.863093	26.749930	44.693122	74.008515	121.500541
30	10.062657	13.267678	17.449402	29.959922	50.950159	85.849877	143.370638

Table 2 FUTURE VALUE OF AN ORDINARY ANNUITY OF 1: $F_0 = \dfrac{(1 + i)^n - 1}{i}$

n	1.5%	4.0%	4.5%	5.0%	5.5%	6.0%	7.0%
1	1.000000	1.000000	1.000000	1.000000	1.000000	1.000000	1.000000
2	2.015000	2.040000	2.045000	2.050000	2.055000	2.060000	2.070000
3	3.045225	3.121600	3.137025	3.152500	3.168025	3.183600	3.214900
4	4.090903	4.246464	4.278191	4.310125	4.342266	4.374616	4.439943
5	5.152267	5.416323	5.470710	5.525631	5.581091	5.637093	5.750739
6	6.229551	6.632975	6.716892	6.801913	6.888051	6.975319	7.153291
7	7.322994	7.898294	8.019152	8.142008	8.266894	8.393838	8.654021
8	8.432839	9.214226	9.380014	9.549109	9.721573	9.897468	10.259803
9	9.559332	10.582795	10.802114	11.026564	11.256260	11.491316	11.977989
10	10.702722	12.006107	12.288209	12.577893	12.875354	13.180795	13.816448
11	11.863262	13.486351	13.841179	14.206787	14.583498	14.971643	15.783599
12	13.041211	15.025805	15.464032	15.917127	16.385591	16.869941	17.888451
13	14.236830	16.626838	17.159913	17.712983	18.286798	18.882138	20.140643
14	15.450382	18.291911	18.932109	19.598632	20.292572	21.015066	22.550488
15	16.682138	20.023588	20.784054	21.578564	22.408663	23.275970	25.129022
16	17.932370	21.824531	22.719337	23.657492	24.641140	25.672528	27.888054
17	19.201355	23.697512	24.741707	25.840366	26.996403	28.212880	30.840217
18	20.489376	25.645413	26.855084	28.132385	29.481205	30.905653	33.999033
19	21.796716	27.671229	29.063562	30.539004	32.102671	33.759992	37.378965
20	23.123667	29.778079	31.371423	33.065954	34.868318	36.785591	40.995492
21	24.470522	31.969202	33.783137	35.719252	37.786076	39.992727	44.865177
22	25.837580	34.247970	36.303378	38.505214	40.864310	43.392290	49.005739
23	27.225144	36.617889	38.937030	41.430475	44.111847	46.995828	53.436141
24	28.633521	39.082604	41.689196	44.501999	47.537998	50.815577	58.176671
25	30.063024	41.645908	44.565210	47.727099	51.152588	54.864512	63.249038
26	31.513969	44.311745	47.570645	51.113454	54.965981	59.156383	68.676470
27	32.986678	47.084214	50.711324	54.669126	58.989109	63.705766	74.483823
28	34.481479	49.967583	53.993333	58.402583	63.233510	68.528112	80.697691
29	35.998701	52.966286	57.423033	62.322712	67.711354	73.639798	87.346529
30	37.538681	56.084938	61.007070	66.438848	72.435478	79.058186	94.460786

n	8.0%	9.0%	10.0%	12.0%	14.0%	16.0%	18.0%
1	1.000000	1.000000	1.000000	1.000000	1.000000	1.000000	1.000000
2	2.080000	2.090000	2.100000	2.120000	2.140000	2.160000	2.180000
3	3.246400	3.278100	3.310000	3.374400	3.439600	3.505600	3.572400
4	4.506112	4.573129	4.641000	4.779328	4.921144	5.066496	5.215432
5	5.866601	5.984711	6.105100	6.352847	6.610104	6.877135	7.154210
6	7.335929	7.523335	7.715610	8.115189	8.535519	8.977477	9.441968
7	8.922803	9.200435	9.487171	10.089012	10.730491	11.413873	12.141522
8	10.636628	11.028474	11.435888	12.299693	13.232760	14.240093	15.326996
9	12.487558	13.021036	13.579477	14.775656	16.085347	17.518508	19.085855
10	14.486562	15.192930	15.937425	17.548735	19.337295	21.321309	23.521309
11	16.645487	17.560293	18.531167	20.654583	23.044516	25.732904	28.755144
12	18.977126	20.140720	21.384284	24.133133	27.270749	30.850169	34.931070
13	21.495297	22.953385	24.522712	28.029109	32.088654	36.786196	42.218663
14	24.214920	26.019189	27.974983	32.392602	37.581065	43.671987	50.818022
15	27.152114	29.360916	31.772482	37.279715	43.842414	51.659505	60.965266
16	30.324283	33.003399	35.949730	42.753280	50.980352	60.925026	72.939014
17	33.750226	36.973705	40.544703	48.883674	59.117601	71.673030	87.068036
18	37.450244	41.301338	45.599173	55.749715	68.394066	84.140715	103.740283
19	41.446263	46.018458	51.159090	63.439681	78.969235	98.603230	123.413534
20	45.761964	51.160120	57.274999	72.052442	91.024928	115.379747	146.627970
21	50.422921	56.764530	64.002499	81.698736	104.768418	134.840506	174.021005
22	55.456755	62.873338	71.402749	92.502584	120.435996	157.414987	206.344785
23	60.893296	69.531939	79.543024	104.602894	138.297035	183.601385	244.486847
24	66.764759	76.789813	88.497327	118.155241	158.658620	213.977607	289.494479
25	73.105940	84.700896	98.347059	133.333870	181.870827	249.214024	342.603486
26	79.954415	93.323977	109.181765	150.333934	208.332743	290.088267	405.272113
27	87.350768	102.723135	121.099942	169.374007	238.499327	337.502390	479.221093
28	95.338830	112.968217	134.209936	190.698887	272.889233	392.502773	566.480890
29	103.965936	124.135356	148.630930	214.582754	312.093725	456.303216	669.447450
30	113.283211	136.307539	164.494023	241.332684	356.786847	530.311731	790.947991

Table 3 PRESENT VALUE OF 1: $p = \dfrac{1}{(1 + i)^n}$

n	1.5%	4.0%	4.5%	5.0%	5.5%	6.0%	7.0%
1	0.985222	0.961538	0.956938	0.952381	0.947867	0.943396	0.934579
2	0.970662	0.924556	0.915730	0.907029	0.898452	0.889996	0.873439
3	0.956317	0.888996	0.876297	0.863838	0.851614	0.839619	0.816298
4	0.942184	0.854804	0.838561	0.822702	0.807217	0.792094	0.762895
5	0.928260	0.821927	0.802451	0.783526	0.765134	0.747258	0.712986
6	0.914542	0.790315	0.767896	0.746215	0.725246	0.704961	0.666342
7	0.901027	0.759918	0.734828	0.710681	0.687437	0.665057	0.622750
8	0.887711	0.730690	0.703185	0.676839	0.651599	0.627412	0.582009
9	0.874592	0.702587	0.672904	0.644609	0.617629	0.591898	0.543934
10	0.861667	0.675564	0.643928	0.613913	0.585431	0.558395	0.508349
11	0.848933	0.649581	0.616199	0.584679	0.554911	0.526788	0.475093
12	0.836387	0.624597	0.589664	0.556837	0.525982	0.496969	0.444012
13	0.824027	0.600574	0.564272	0.530321	0.498561	0.468839	0.414964
14	0.811849	0.577475	0.539973	0.505068	0.472569	0.442301	0.387817
15	0.799852	0.555265	0.516720	0.481017	0.447933	0.417265	0.362446
16	0.788031	0.533908	0.494469	0.458112	0.424581	0.393646	0.338735
17	0.776385	0.513373	0.473176	0.436297	0.402447	0.371364	0.316574
18	0.764912	0.493628	0.452800	0.415521	0.381466	0.350344	0.295864
19	0.753607	0.474642	0.433302	0.395734	0.361579	0.330513	0.276508
20	0.742470	0.456387	0.414643	0.376889	0.342729	0.311805	0.258419
21	0.731498	0.438834	0.396787	0.358942	0.324862	0.294155	0.241513
22	0.720688	0.421955	0.379701	0.341850	0.307926	0.277505	0.225713
23	0.710037	0.405726	0.363350	0.325571	0.291873	0.261797	0.210947
24	0.699544	0.390121	0.347703	0.310068	0.276657	0.246979	0.197147
25	0.689206	0.375117	0.332731	0.295303	0.262234	0.232999	0.184249
26	0.679021	0.360689	0.318402	0.281241	0.248563	0.219810	0.172195
27	0.668986	0.346817	0.304691	0.267848	0.235605	0.207368	0.160930
28	0.659099	0.333477	0.291571	0.255094	0.223322	0.195630	0.150402
29	0.649359	0.320651	0.279015	0.242946	0.211679	0.184557	0.140563
30	0.639762	0.308319	0.267000	0.231377	0.200644	0.174110	0.131367

n	8.0%	9.0%	10.0%	12.0%	14.0%	16.0%	18.0%
1	0.925926	0.917431	0.909091	0.892857	0.877193	0.862069	0.847458
2	0.857339	0.841680	0.826446	0.797194	0.769468	0.743163	0.718184
3	0.793832	0.772183	0.751315	0.711780	0.674972	0.640658	0.608631
4	0.735030	0.708425	0.683013	0.635518	0.592080	0.552291	0.515789
5	0.680583	0.649931	0.620921	0.567427	0.519369	0.476113	0.437109
6	0.630170	0.596267	0.564474	0.506631	0.455587	0.410442	0.370432
7	0.583490	0.547034	0.513158	0.452349	0.399637	0.353830	0.313925
8	0.540269	0.501866	0.466507	0.403883	0.350559	0.305025	0.266038
9	0.500249	0.460428	0.424098	0.360610	0.307508	0.262953	0.225456
10	0.463193	0.422411	0.385543	0.321973	0.269744	0.226684	0.191064
11	0.428883	0.387533	0.350494	0.287476	0.236617	0.195417	0.161919
12	0.397114	0.355535	0.318631	0.256675	0.207559	0.168463	0.137220
13	0.367698	0.326179	0.289664	0.229174	0.182069	0.145227	0.116288
14	0.340461	0.299246	0.263331	0.204620	0.159710	0.125195	0.098549
15	0.315242	0.274538	0.239392	0.182696	0.140096	0.107927	0.083516
16	0.291890	0.251870	0.217629	0.163122	0.122892	0.093041	0.070776
17	0.270269	0.231073	0.197845	0.145644	0.107800	0.080207	0.059980
18	0.250249	0.211994	0.179859	0.130040	0.094561	0.069144	0.050830
19	0.231712	0.194490	0.163508	0.116107	0.082948	0.059607	0.043077
20	0.214548	0.178431	0.148644	0.103667	0.072762	0.051385	0.036506
21	0.198656	0.163698	0.135131	0.092560	0.063826	0.044298	0.030937
22	0.183941	0.150182	0.122846	0.082643	0.055988	0.038188	0.026218
23	0.170315	0.137781	0.111678	0.073788	0.049112	0.032920	0.022218
24	0.157699	0.126405	0.101526	0.065882	0.043081	0.028380	0.018829
25	0.146018	0.115968	0.092296	0.058823	0.037790	0.024465	0.015957
26	0.135202	0.106393	0.083905	0.052521	0.033149	0.021091	0.013523
27	0.125187	0.097608	0.076278	0.046894	0.029078	0.018182	0.011460
28	0.115914	0.089548	0.069343	0.041869	0.025507	0.015674	0.009712
29	0.107328	0.082155	0.063039	0.037383	0.022375	0.013512	0.008230
30	0.099377	0.075371	0.057309	0.033378	0.019627	0.011648	0.006975

Table 4 PRESENT VALUE OF AN ORDINARY ANNUITY OF 1: $P_0 = \dfrac{1 - \dfrac{1}{(1+i)^n}}{i}$

n	1.5%	4.0%	4.5%	5.0%	5.5%	6.0%	7.0%
1	0.985222	0.961538	0.956938	0.952381	0.947867	0.943396	0.934579
2	1.955883	1.886095	1.872668	1.859410	1.846320	1.833393	1.808018
3	2.912200	2.775091	2.748964	2.723248	2.697933	2.673012	2.624316
4	3.854385	3.629895	3.587526	3.545951	3.505150	3.465106	3.387211
5	4.782645	4.451822	4.389977	4.329477	4.270284	4.212364	4.100197
6	5.697187	5.242137	5.157872	5.075692	4.995530	4.917324	4.766540
7	6.598214	6.002055	5.892701	5.786373	5.682967	5.582381	5.389289
8	7.485925	6.732745	6.595886	6.463213	6.334566	6.209794	5.971299
9	8.360517	7.435332	7.268790	7.107822	6.952195	6.801692	6.515232
10	9.222185	8.110896	7.912718	7.721735	7.537626	7.360087	7.023582
11	10.071118	8.760477	8.528917	8.306414	8.092536	7.886875	7.498674
12	10.907505	9.385074	9.118581	8.863252	8.618518	8.383844	7.942686
13	11.731532	9.985648	9.682852	9.393573	9.117079	8.852683	8.357651
14	12.543382	10.563123	10.222825	9.898641	9.589648	9.294984	8.745468
15	13.343233	11.118387	10.739546	10.379658	10.037581	9.712249	9.107914
16	14.131264	11.652296	11.234015	10.837770	10.462162	10.105895	9.446649
17	14.907649	12.165669	11.707191	11.274066	10.864609	10.477260	9.763223
18	15.672561	12.659297	12.159992	11.689587	11.246074	10.827603	10.059087
19	16.426168	13.133939	12.593294	12.085321	11.607654	11.158116	10.335595
20	17.168639	13.590326	13.007936	12.462210	11.950382	11.469921	10.594014
21	17.900137	14.029160	13.404724	12.821153	12.275244	11.764077	10.835527
22	18.620824	14.451115	13.784425	13.163003	12.583170	12.041582	11.061240
23	19.330861	14.856842	14.147775	13.488574	12.875042	12.303379	11.272187
24	20.030405	15.246963	14.495478	13.798642	13.151699	12.550358	11.469334
25	20.719611	15.622080	14.828209	14.093945	13.413933	12.783356	11.653583
26	21.398632	15.982769	15.146611	14.375185	13.662495	13.003166	11.825779
27	22.067617	16.329586	15.451303	14.643034	13.898100	13.210534	11.986709
28	22.726717	16.663063	15.742874	14.898127	14.121422	13.406164	12.137111
29	23.376076	16.983715	16.021889	15.141074	14.333101	13.590721	12.277674
30	24.015838	17.292033	16.288889	15.372451	14.533745	13.764831	12.409041

n	8.0%	9.0%	10.0%	12.0%	14.0%	16.0%	18.0%
1	0.925926	0.917431	0.909091	0.892857	0.877193	0.862069	0.847458
2	1.783265	1.759111	1.735537	1.690051	1.646661	1.605232	1.565642
3	2.577097	2.531295	2.486852	2.401831	2.321632	2.245890	2.174273
4	3.312127	3.239720	3.169865	3.037349	2.913712	2.798181	2.690062
5	3.992710	3.889651	3.790787	3.604776	3.433081	3.274294	3.127171
6	4.622880	4.485919	4.355261	4.111407	3.888668	3.684736	3.497603
7	5.206370	5.032953	4.868419	4.563757	4.288305	4.038565	3.811528
8	5.746639	5.534819	5.334926	4.967640	4.638864	4.343591	4.077566
9	6.246888	5.995247	5.759024	5.328250	4.946372	4.606544	4.303022
10	6.710081	6.417658	6.144567	5.650223	5.216116	4.833227	4.494086
11	7.138964	6.805191	6.495061	5.937699	5.452733	5.028644	4.656005
12	7.536078	7.160725	6.813692	6.194374	5.660292	5.197107	4.793225
13	7.903776	7.486904	7.103356	6.423548	5.842362	5.342334	4.909513
14	8.244237	7.786150	7.366687	6.628168	6.002072	5.467529	5.008062
15	8.559479	8.060688	7.606080	6.810864	6.142168	5.575456	5.091578
16	8.851369	8.312558	7.823709	6.973986	6.265060	5.668497	5.162354
17	9.121638	8.543631	8.021553	7.119630	6.372859	5.748704	5.222334
18	9.371887	8.755625	8.201412	7.249670	6.467420	5.817848	5.273164
19	9.603599	8.950115	8.364920	7.365777	6.550369	5.877455	5.316241
20	9.818147	9.128546	8.513564	7.469444	6.623131	5.928841	5.352746
21	10.016803	9.292244	8.648694	7.562003	6.686957	5.973139	5.383683
22	10.200744	9.442425	8.771540	7.644646	6.742944	6.011326	5.409901
23	10.371059	9.580207	8.883218	7.718434	6.792056	6.044247	5.432120
24	10.528758	9.706612	8.984744	7.784316	6.835137	6.072627	5.450949
25	10.674776	9.822580	9.077040	7.843139	6.872927	6.097092	5.466906
26	10.809978	9.928972	9.160945	7.895660	6.906077	6.118183	5.480429
27	10.935165	10.026580	9.237223	7.942554	6.935155	6.136364	5.491889
28	11.051078	10.116128	9.306567	7.984423	6.960662	6.152038	5.501601
29	11.158406	10.198283	9.369606	8.021806	6.983037	6.165550	5.509831
30	11.257783	10.273654	9.426914	8.055184	7.002664	6.177198	5.516806

Table 5 PRESENT VALUE OF ANNUITY DUE: $P_d = \dfrac{1 - \dfrac{1}{(1+i)^{n-1}}}{i} + 1$

n	1.5%	4.0%	4.5%	5.0%	5.5%	6.0%	7.0%
1	1.000000	1.000000	1.000000	1.000000	1.000000	1.000000	1.000000
2	1.985222	1.961538	1.956938	1.952381	1.947867	1.943396	1.934579
3	2.955883	2.886095	2.872668	2.859410	2.846320	2.833393	2.808018
4	3.912200	3.775091	3.748964	3.723248	3.697933	3.673012	3.624316
5	4.854385	4.629895	4.587526	4.545951	4.505150	4.465106	4.387211
6	5.782645	5.451822	5.389977	5.329477	5.270284	5.212364	5.100197
7	6.697187	6.242137	6.157872	6.075692	5.995530	5.917324	5.766540
8	7.598214	7.002055	6.892701	6.786373	6.682967	6.582381	6.389289
9	8.485925	7.732745	7.595886	7.463213	7.334566	7.209794	6.971299
10	9.360517	8.435332	8.268790	8.107822	7.952195	7.801692	7.515232
11	10.222185	9.110896	8.912718	8.721735	8.537626	8.360087	8.023582
12	11.071118	9.760477	9.528917	9.306414	9.092536	8.886875	8.498674
13	11.907505	10.385074	10.118581	9.863252	9.618518	9.383844	8.942686
14	12.731532	10.985648	10.682852	10.393573	10.117079	9.852683	9.357651
15	13.543382	11.563123	11.222825	10.898641	10.589648	10.294984	9.745468
16	14.343233	12.118387	11.739546	11.379658	11.037581	10.712249	10.107914
17	15.131264	12.652296	12.234015	11.837770	11.462162	11.105895	10.446649
18	15.907649	13.165669	12.707191	12.274066	11.864609	11.477260	10.763223
19	16.672561	13.659297	13.159992	12.689587	12.246074	11.827603	11.059087
20	17.426168	14.133939	13.593294	13.085321	12.607654	12.158116	11.335595
21	18.168639	14.590326	14.007936	13.462210	12.950382	12.469921	11.594014
22	18.900137	15.029160	14.404724	13.821153	13.275244	12.764077	11.835527
23	19.620824	15.451115	14.784425	14.163003	13.583170	13.041582	12.061240
24	20.330861	15.856842	15.147775	14.488574	13.875042	13.303379	12.272187
25	21.030405	16.246963	15.495478	14.798642	14.151699	13.550358	12.469334
26	21.719611	16.622080	15.828209	15.093945	14.413933	13.783356	12.653583
27	22.398632	16.982769	16.146611	15.375185	14.662495	14.003166	12.825779
28	23.067617	17.329586	16.451303	15.643034	14.898100	14.210534	12.986709
29	23.726717	17.663063	16.742874	15.898127	15.121422	14.406164	13.137111
30	24.376076	17.983715	17.021889	16.141074	15.333101	14.590721	13.277674

n	8.0%	9.0%	10.0%	12.0%	14.0%	16.0%	18.0%
1	1.000000	1.000000	1.000000	1.000000	1.000000	1.000000	1.000000
2	1.925926	1.917431	1.909091	1.892857	1.877193	1.862069	1.847458
3	2.783265	2.759111	2.735537	2.690051	2.646661	2.605232	2.565642
4	3.577097	3.531295	3.486852	3.401831	3.321632	3.245890	3.174273
5	4.312127	4.239720	4.169865	4.037349	3.913712	3.798181	3.690062
6	4.992710	4.889651	4.790787	4.604776	4.433081	4.274294	4.127171
7	5.622880	5.485919	5.355261	5.111407	4.888668	4.684736	4.497603
8	6.206370	6.032953	5.868419	5.563757	5.288305	5.038565	4.811528
9	6.746639	6.534819	6.334926	5.967640	5.638864	5.343591	5.077566
10	7.246888	6.995247	6.759024	6.328250	5.946372	5.606544	5.303022
11	7.710081	7.417658	7.144567	6.650223	6.216116	5.833227	5.494086
12	8.138964	7.805191	7.495061	6.937699	6.452733	6.028644	5.656005
13	8.536078	8.160725	7.813692	7.194374	6.660292	6.197107	5.793225
14	8.903776	8.486904	8.103356	7.423548	6.842362	6.342334	5.909513
15	9.244237	8.786150	8.366687	7.628168	7.002072	6.467529	6.008062
16	9.559479	9.060688	8.606080	7.810864	7.142168	6.575456	6.091578
17	9.851369	9.312558	8.823709	7.973986	7.265060	6.668497	6.162354
18	10.121638	9.543631	9.021553	8.119630	7.372859	6.748704	6.222334
19	10.371887	9.755625	9.201412	8.249670	7.467420	6.817848	6.273164
20	10.603599	9.950115	9.364920	8.365777	7.550369	6.877455	6.316241
21	10.818147	10.128546	9.513564	8.469444	7.623131	6.928841	6.352746
22	11.016803	10.292244	9.648694	8.562003	7.686957	6.973139	6.383683
23	11.200744	10.442425	9.771540	8.644646	7.742944	7.011326	6.409901
24	11.371059	10.580207	9.883218	8.718434	7.792056	7.044247	6.432120
25	11.528758	10.706612	9.984744	8.784316	7.835137	7.072627	6.450949
26	11.674776	10.822580	10.077040	8.843139	7.872927	7.097092	6.466906
27	11.809978	10.928972	10.160945	8.895660	7.906077	7.118183	6.480429
28	11.935165	11.026580	10.237223	8.942554	7.935155	7.136364	6.491889
29	12.051078	11.116128	10.306567	8.984423	7.960662	7.152038	6.501601
30	12.158406	11.198283	10.369606	9.021806	7.983037	7.165550	6.509831

appendix E

Accounting for Changes in Prices

objectives

1. Understand the difference between current value and general price level adjustments.

2. Explain the three alternatives to historical cost.

3. Understand issues related to the measurement of current cost, the adjustment of historical dollars for general price-level changes, and the purchasing power gain or loss on net monetary items.

4. Explain the conceptual issues relating to the alternatives to historical cost.

5. Be aware of the disclosure requirements that have existed for alternative disclosures, including the reasons for the elimination of the required disclosures.

In Chapter 17, we focused on asset valuation and revenue recognition issues using historical cost accounting. However, different methods of asset valuation provide different information to users if the prices of individual assets owned by companies change with time. Suppose a company purchases a parcel of land for $100,000. A year later the value of the land is $120,000, but there has been inflation of 5%. Theoretically, the company could value the land on its balance sheet either at its current value of $120,000 or at $105,000—the historical cost of $100,000 adjusted for the 5% inflation. However, under generally accepted accounting principles, the company values the land on its balance sheet at $100,000. In other words, the change in the value of the land is ignored, as is the change in the value of the dollar due to inflation.

Furthermore, under historical cost accounting the effect of a change in value is generally recognized only when a transaction takes place, such as when the land is sold. Suppose that the company sells the land for $120,000. At this time, it recognizes a gain of $20,000 (the $120,000 selling price less the $100,000 original cost). However, should it recognize a gain of zero ($120,000 less the $120,000 current value) or of $15,000 ($120,000 less the $105,000 historical cost adjusted for the 5% inflation rate) instead? Which information is more useful to users of financial statements?

This Appendix briefly explains the concepts and procedures underlying the alternative methods of accounting for changing prices. We also discuss the *voluntary* supplementary disclosures encouraged by *FASB Statement No. 89.*

CURRENT VALUE AND THE GENERAL PRICE LEVEL

Two types of price changes are relevant for accounting purposes. First, the price of an individual asset or liability, such as inventory, buildings, or bonds payable, changes in response to the dynamics of the market for that particular item. This is known as a **specific price change** or a **current value change**. Second, there may be a change in the value, or purchasing power, of the dollar. Such a change is caused by the overall change in the prices of all goods and services in the economy and is known as a **general price-level change**. Changes in the general purchasing power of money are known as *inflation* or *deflation*. During inflation (deflation), the general purchasing power of money declines (increases) as the general level of prices of goods and services rises (falls). The general purchasing power of money and the general price level are reciprocals.

For a company's specific assets and liabilities, the price changes may be very different from the change in the general price level. For example, if the general price level rises, the specific price of an inventory item (its current value) may increase faster or slower, or even decline, in comparison with the general price level.

So the two types of price changes are related, but it is important to understand that accounting for the current value of assets and accounting for changes in the general price level are *not* alternatives or substitutes for each other. Each method represents the use of a different concept and, therefore, has a different purpose. Although neither method is required under generally accepted accounting principles, selected current cost and general price-level adjusted *supplementary* disclosures are encouraged (but not required) under *FASB Statement No. 89*, as we discuss later in this Appendix.

1 Understand the difference between current value and general price level adjustments.

Current Value

Current value adjustments account for changes in the values of individual assets and liabilities and *not* for the change in the value of the dollar. As the specific current values change, they are recognized in the financial statements by recording assets and liabilities on the balance sheet at their current values. In the income statement, expenses are matched against revenues at the current value of the assets used up or the liabilities created. Therefore, this method significantly changes the basic concepts of asset valuation and income measurement. Current value is a general concept and may be measured in several ways, including (1) an *exit value*, such as net realizable value (the net amount that can be realized from sale), (2) the present value of future cash flows, and (3) an *input value*, such as current cost. Our discussion concentrates on **current cost** as the measure of current value because this method is the basis for the current value disclosures encouraged by *FASB Statement No. 89*. **Current cost is the cost in the current period of replacing (i.e., acquiring or producing) the items concerned,** as we discuss later. Generally accepted accounting principles do allow occasional uses of current value, such as when there is a decline in the price of inventory and the lower of cost or market rule is used, and for certain investments and financial instruments.

General Price Level

General price-level adjustments account for the change in the value of the *dollar* and *not* for changes in the values of individual assets and liabilities. As the general price level increases, the goods and services that can be purchased with a given number of dollars decreases. Therefore, financial statements that include dollars measured at different times are potentially misleading, because the dollars vary in purchasing power. The adjustments for changes in the general price level convert these dollars of different purchasing power into dollars of constant purchasing power. In essence, the adjustments account for changes in the size of the measuring unit used in accounting. In contrast to a physical measuring unit such as a foot or a meter which remains constant, the dollar is not a constant measure because its purchasing power changes. Just as no one advocates adding and subtracting U.S. and Canadian dollars, for example, it can be argued that it is equally inappropriate to add and subtract dollars of different purchasing power, even though they are always called U.S. dollars.

Four Alternative Concepts

Just as with historical costs, current costs may be measured in different time periods. Since the general price-level adjustments account only for the change in the value of the dollar over time, these adjustments are equally applicable to historical cost and current cost financial statements. In both cases, amounts are included in the adjusted financial statements (or selected supplemental disclosures) that are measured in dollars of different dates, and so of different values. Thus, there are four alternative accounting methods to be considered (the common terminology used to differentiate the alternatives is in parentheses):

1. Historical cost
2. Historical cost adjusted for changes in the general price level (historical cost/ constant purchasing power)
3. Current value (current cost)
4. Current value adjusted for changes in the general price level (current cost/ constant purchasing power)

Constant purchasing power amounts also are known as **constant dollar** amounts. The historical cost concept, which is the basis of generally accepted accounting principles, is covered throughout this book. We discuss the other three alternatives in the following section.

THREE ALTERNATIVES TO HISTORICAL COST

2 Explain the three alternatives to historical cost.

To briefly illustrate the differences between constant purchasing power and current cost financial statements, consider the following sequence of events for the Hallas Company:

1. The company begins operations with $3,000 cash from issuing capital stock.
2. The company purchases one unit of inventory for $1,000 cash.
3. The current (replacement) cost of the inventory increases to $1,250 and the general price-level index increases from 100 to 110, an increase of 10%.
4. The company sells the inventory for $2,000 cash.
5. The company purchases another unit of inventory for $1,250.

The events are reflected in the historical cost financial statements in Exhibit E-1 (ignoring operating expenses and income taxes). The company prepares a set of financial statements after each event, labeled Steps 1 through 5. It recognizes income only in Step 4, when it sells the inventory; consequently, it recognizes the increase in asset values at the same time.

EXHIBIT E-1   Historical Cost Financial Statements

	Step 1	Step 2	Step 3	Step 4	Step 5
Income Statements					
Revenue	—	—	—	$2,000	—
Cost of goods sold	—	—	—	(1,000)	—
Net income	—	—	—	$1,000	—
Balance Sheets					
Cash	$3,000	$2,000	$2,000	$4,000	$2,750
Inventory	—	1,000	1,000	—	1,250
Total Assets	$3,000	$3,000	$3,000	$4,000	$4,000
Capital	$3,000	$3,000	$3,000	$4,000	$4,000

Current Cost Financial Statements

Exhibit E-2 illustrates the current cost financial statements for the Hallas Company. The financial statements at Steps 1 and 2 are the same as the historical cost statements because no changes in current costs have occurred. However, in Step 3, when the current cost of the inventory rises to $1,250, the company recognizes the $250 increase. Since this gain results from holding the asset and is not realized through a sale, it is known as an **unrealized holding gain.** In Step 4, when the inventory is sold for $2,000, the company recognizes the cost of goods sold at the current cost of the inventory, or $1,250. Therefore, operating income is $750 as compared with the historical cost income of $1,000. The unrealized holding gain is now realized through a sale, so it recognizes a **realized holding gain** and removes the unrealized holding gain.

The basic argument in favor of current cost financial statements can be seen by comparing the balance sheets in Steps 2 and 5. At both steps, the company has only two assets—cash and one unit of inventory. Since the inventory is identical at both steps in terms of its physical characteristics, the company is better off at Step 5 by the increase in its cash balance, or $750. The current cost financial statements recognize an *operating income* of only $750. Therefore, this measure of income is consistent with the increase in the wealth of the company (the amount the company can distribute to the owners and remain as well off). In contrast, the historical cost financial statements recognize an operating income of $1,000. However, this income includes $250 that is not really income, because the company is required to replace the inventory to remain in business. For example, suppose that after Step 4 the company decides to distribute the historical cost income of $1,000 as dividends. This would leave the company with $3,000 cash. After purchasing a unit of inventory of $1,250, the company would have $1,750 cash left, and thus would have suffered a decrease in wealth of $250 since Step 2, when it held $2,000 cash and one unit of inventory.

EXHIBIT E-2   Current Cost Financial Statements

	Step 1	Step 2	Step 3	Step 4	Step 5
Income Statements					
Revenue	—	—	—	$2,000	—
Cost of goods sold	—	—	—	(1,250)	—
Operating income	—	—	—	$ 750	—
Unrealized holding gain	—	—	$ 250	(250)	—
Realized holding gain	—	—	—	250	—
Net income	—	—	$ 250	$ 750	—
Balance Sheets					
Cash	$3,000	$2,000	$2,000	$4,000	$2,750
Inventory	—	1,000	1,250	—	1,250
Total Assets	$3,000	$3,000	$3,250	$4,000	$4,000
Capital	$3,000	$3,000	$3,250	$4,000	$4,000

Note that the company includes the unrealized and realized holding gains in income in this example. Many accountants, however, argue that these gains are not really income, as we illustrated in the previous paragraph. Therefore, they argue, the gains should be excluded from the income statement and reported directly in stockholders' equity, or in other comprehensive income. Whichever way the gains (or losses) are classified, it is very important to understand the nature of these gains in contrast to income that represents real profit obtained through a sale.

Historical Cost/Constant Purchasing Power Financial Statements

Exhibit E-3 illustrates the historical cost/constant purchasing power financial statements of the Hallas Company. Remember that this adjustment process is completely separate from the current cost financial statements we just discussed. The only change in the general price level is in Step 3, when the price-level index rises from 100 to 110, an increase of 10%. When the company *originally* prepared the financial statements for Steps 1 and 2, they were identical to the historical cost financial statements in Exhibit E-1 because no change in the general price level had occurred. However, *all* the financial statements in Exhibit E-3 are presented in terms of the value of the dollar *after* the 10% increase in the price level (that is, in Step 3 prices). Therefore, the cash and capital in Step 1, and the cash, inventory, and capital in Step 2 are all increased by 10% to reflect the increase in the general price level that has occurred since these amounts were measured originally. For example, the $3,000 in the historical cost balance sheet in Step 1 of Exhibit E-1 is measured in dollars *before* the rise in the general price level. This amount has a purchasing power that is equivalent to $3,300 after the price rise (an increase of 10%). The $3,000 measured in dollars before the price rise is adjusted to $3,300 measured in dollars after the price rise, so that the statements in Steps 1 and 3 reflect dollars of the same purchasing power.

The rise in the general price level takes place in Step 3. Thus, the $2,000 cash in the historical cost balance sheet is measured in dollars after the price-level increase. As a result, the company has lost $200 ($2,200 − $2,000) of purchasing power because it held the cash while the price level rose. This $200 loss is included in income, and it also reduces the purchasing power of the capital to $3,100. The inventory is measured at the historical cost of $1,000 adjusted for the 10% increase in the general price level.

EXHIBIT E-3 Historical Cost/Constant Purchasing Power
Financial Statements

	Step				
	1	2	3	4	5
Income Statements					
Revenue	—	—	—	$2,000	—
Cost of goods sold	—	—	—	(1,100)	—
Purchasing power loss	—	—	$ (200)	—	—
Net income	—	—	$ (200)	$ 900	—
Balance Sheets					
Cash	$3,300	$2,200	$2,000	$4,000	$2,750
Inventory	—	1,100	1,100	—	1,250
Total Assets	$3,300	$3,300	$3,100	$4,000	$4,000
Capital	$3,300	$3,300	$3,100	$4,000	$4,000

General price-level index: Step 1, 100; Step 2, 100; Step 3, 110; Step 4, 110; and Step 5, 110.

The $1,100 is the current purchasing-power equivalent of the original $1,000. No purchasing-power gain or loss results from holding a nonmonetary asset such as inventory, as we discuss later in the appendix. In Step 4 the inventory is sold for $2,000. The cost of goods sold is recorded at the constant purchasing power of the inventory, $1,100, and therefore the net income is $900.

The major argument in favor of historical cost/constant purchasing power financial statements can be illustrated by considering the income statement in Step 4 and the balance sheets in Steps 1 and 4. In the historical cost income statement in Exhibit E-1, dollars of one price level (the cost of goods sold) are subtracted from dollars of another price level (the revenue). Since these dollars do not have the same purchasing power, subtracting one from the other may not be very relevant. In contrast, the constant purchasing power income is measured by comparing two amounts measured in dollars of the same purchasing power.

Comparing Steps 1 and 4 in the historical cost balance sheets in Exhibit E-1 raises similar issues. The capital in Step 4 includes $3,000 original capital (and $1,000 retained earnings). However, Step 1 also shows original capital of $3,000. Does this reflect reality? If it is agreed that the purpose of dollars is to purchase goods and services, then to show the contributed capital as $3,000 in both balance sheets may be misleading. The owners of the company contributed $3,000 of purchasing power in Step 1 when the company was formed. However, in Step 4 an appropriate measure of the capital contributed is in terms of the dollars existing at the time the financial statements are prepared. In these terms, the owners have contributed $3,300 of purchasing power. The same argument may be applied to inventory. Although the inventory cost $1,000, that $1,000 is equivalent to $1,100 of purchasing power after the price-level increase. Thus, the historical cost/constant purchasing power financial statements do not reflect current value. They simply adjust the historical costs for changes in the purchasing power, or value, of the dollar that have occurred since the historical cost was recorded.

Current Cost/Constant Purchasing Power Financial Statements

The arguments in favor of current cost financial statements and of historical cost/constant purchasing power statements are entirely separate. Current cost financial statements do *not* reflect the changing value of the dollar, and historical cost/constant purchasing power statements do *not* recognize the current cost of assets. However, the two concepts may be combined so that financial statements prepared on the current cost basis are adjusted for changes in the general price level. Exhibit E-4 illustrates financial statements prepared on this basis.

EXHIBIT E-4   Current Cost/Constant Purchasing Power Financial Statements

	Step 1	Step 2	Step 3	Step 4	Step 5
Income Statements					
Revenue	—	—	—	$2,000	—
Cost of goods sold	—	—	—	(1,250)	—
Operating income	—	—	—	$ 750	—
Unrealized holding gain	—	—	$ 150	(150)	—
Realized holding gain	—	—	—	150	—
Purchasing-power loss	—	—	(200)	—	—
Net income	—	—	$ (50)	$ 750	—
Balance Sheets					
Cash	$3,300	$2,200	$2,000	$4,000	$2,750
Inventory	—	1,100	1,250	—	1,250
Total Assets	$3,300	$3,300	$3,250	$4,000	$4,000
Capital	$3,300	$3,300	$3,250	$4,000	$4,000

The financial statements in Steps 1 and 2 are prepared on a current cost/constant purchasing power basis in terms of the price level existing *after* the rise in the general price level. That is, they are adjusted to reflect the 10% rise in the price level in the same manner as the historical cost/constant purchasing power statements in Exhibit E-3. In Step 3 the rise in the general price level is recognized through the purchasing-power loss from holding cash. In addition, the unrealized holding gain on the inventory is recognized, but in this situation it is $150. This is the difference between the current cost of the inventory ($1,250) and the constant purchasing power cost of the inventory ($1,100). In Step 4 the inventory is sold and the cost of goods sold is recorded at the current cost of $1,250.

The advantages of this method may be understood by considering the income statement in Step 4 and by comparing the balance sheets in Steps 2 and 5. The $750 operating income recognized in Step 4 is the real increase in value for the company, for exactly the same reasons as we discussed earlier for the unadjusted current cost financial statements in Exhibit E-2. A comparison of the balance sheets in Steps 2 and 5 shows an increase in value of $550 since the cash has increased by $550 and one unit of inventory is held in each case. The $550 increase is the operating income of $750 in Step 4 less the purchasing power loss of $200 in Step 3. The relationship between the increase in wealth and the income statement is clearer if the holding gains are omitted from the income statement, which lends support to those accountants who advocate such exclusion.

ADDITIONAL MEASUREMENT ISSUES

The previous section dealt with a simple example involving current cost and constant purchasing power financial statements. We discuss several additional issues related to measuring current costs and constant purchasing power amounts in this section.

Measurement of Current Cost

In the previous examples we focused on a few simple transactions. The two most significant differences between current cost and historical cost usually occur for inventory and property, plant, and equipment. The FASB defines the current cost of *inventory* as the current cost of purchasing or producing the goods concerned. It defines the current cost of *property, plant*, or *equipment* as the current cost of acquiring the same service potential (indicated by operating costs and physical output capacity) provided by the asset owned.[1]

Three alternative methods of measuring the current costs of inventory and property, plant, and equipment are:

1. *Direct Pricing*. Current invoice prices, vendors' price lists, other quotations or estimates (e.g., appraisals), or standard manufacturing costs.
2. *Functional or Unit Pricing*. The estimation of construction (or acquisition) costs per unit (such as per square foot of building space) and multiplication by the number of units in the asset being measured.
3. *Revision of Historical Acquisition Cost (Indexation)*. Using (a) externally (independently) generated specific price indexes[2] for the class of goods or services being measured, or (b) internally generated indexes of cost changes for the class of goods or services being measured.[3]

A company might choose any one of the methods for any asset or liability. Generally direct pricing would be used for inventory and readily available property, plant, and equipment such as office equipment. Functional, or unit, pricing would be used to estimate the current cost of a complete productive asset such as a building or a chemical plant. A specific price index could be used for any asset, and often it is the simplest to use because once the index for the asset is selected, the adjustment process is arithmetically simple.

Because technology changes, the property, plant, and equipment (and perhaps some inventory) that would be purchased today do not have the same service potential as the assets the company owns. Therefore, the current cost of property, plant, and equipment may be determined by either (1) the current cost of a used asset of the same age and in the same condition as the asset owned, (2) the current cost of a new asset with the same service potential as the used asset had when new, less a deduction for depreciation, or (3) the current cost of a new asset with a different service potential, less a deduction for depreciation, and adjusted for the cost of the difference in service potential due to differences in life, output capacity, and nature of service, including any operating cost savings.

Inventory is valued on the balance sheet at its current cost at the end of the period. The cost of goods sold is valued on the income statement at the average current cost, which is measured as the units sold $\times$ [(beginning current cost per unit + ending current cost per unit) $\div$ 2]. Alternatively, the actual current costs incurred during the period could be used if the company recorded the current cost when each sale was made.

3 Understand issues related to the measurement of current cost, the adjustment of historical dollars for general price-level changes, and the purchasing power gain or loss on net monetary items.

---

1. "Financial Reporting and Changing Prices," *FASB Statement of Financial Accounting Standards No. 89* (Stamford, Conn.: FASB, 1986), par. 44.
2. The federal government publishes numerous specific price indexes.
3. These are examples of a **reproduction cost,** which is the current cost of acquiring an asset identical to that currently owned. An alternative concept is a **replacement cost,** which is the current cost of acquiring the best asset available to undertake the function of the asset owned.

Property, plant, and equipment are valued on the balance sheet at their current costs at the end of the period, less a proportional amount of accumulated depreciation. The depreciation expense on the income statement is based on the average current cost of the depreciable assets, which is measured as [(beginning current cost + ending current cost) ÷ 2] ÷ estimated life. For both costs of goods sold and depreciation expense, an average is used because sales are made at prices current throughout the period, and it is appropriate to match the average current cost of the assets used during the period against those sales.

Adjustment of Historical Dollars

The conversion of historical dollars to the purchasing power of the current period by means of a price-level index is a simple mathematical procedure. Dividing the index of the current period by the index of the period in which the historical dollar was originally recorded provides a measure of the relative price change. Multiplying the historical dollar amount by this relative price change gives the constant purchasing power dollar amount. This computation is as follows:

$$\text{Constant Purchasing Power Dollars} = \text{Historical Dollars} \times \frac{\text{Current Period Price-Level Index}}{\text{Historical Price-Level Index}}$$

For example, suppose a company purchased land for $24,000 when the price index was 120 and that the index is now 150. The cost of the land in constant purchasing power dollars is $30,000 [$24,000 × (150 ÷ 120)].

The current period index depends on the financial statement. The use of the average index for the year is the most appropriate for the income statement and the cash flow statement, which measure flows over a period of time. The use of the index at the end of the year is the most appropriate for the balance sheet, which measures amounts at the end of the year. The average Consumer Price Index for All Urban Consumers (CPI-U) is used for the disclosures encouraged by *FASB Statement No. 89*.

Purchasing-Power Gain or Loss on Net Monetary Items

Holding cash during periods of *inflation* results in a purchasing-power *loss*. If $100 can buy a certain quantity of goods and services, and prices later rise, the $100 can then buy fewer goods and services, and purchasing power has been lost. The same principle applies to all **monetary assets**. A monetary asset is defined as "money or a claim to receive a sum of money, the amount of which is fixed or determinable without reference to future prices of specific goods or services."[4] In addition to cash, principal monetary assets are accounts receivable and notes receivable.

The reverse effect occurs with **monetary liabilities**. Since an obligation exists to *repay* a fixed amount of dollars in the future, inflation reduces the purchasing power of the dollars necessary to repay these liabilities, thus resulting in a purchasing-power *gain*. Principal monetary liabilities include accounts payable, notes payable, and bonds payable.[5]

Suppose Peter Cameron borrows $1,000 from a bank when the price index is 120. He has a monetary liability of $1,000 and the bank has a monetary asset of $1,000. Disregarding interest, if the money is repaid when the price index is 150, Peter Cameron has a general purchasing-power gain. The equivalent purchasing power of the $1,000 when it is repaid is $1,250 [$1,000 × (150 ÷ 120)], and since he only has to repay the $1,000, he has a gain of $250. Conversely, the bank has a general purchasing-power loss because it has received $1,000 in full payment of a historical debt that now has a current purchasing-power equivalent of $1,250. Since the bank knows that inflation will occur, it includes the expected level of inflation when it sets the interest rate.

---

4. *FASB Statement No. 89, op. cit.*, par. 44.

5. For a classification of items as monetary or nonmonetary, see *FASB Statement of Financial Accounting Standards No. 89*, par. 96.

Monetary assets and liabilities are combined to derive **net monetary items** on which gains or losses from inflation are computed. The FASB calls these gains and losses purchasing-power gains and losses. (They are also known as *monetary gains and losses*, or *general price-level gains and losses*.) **Purchasing-power gains result from holding negative net monetary items** (liabilities exceed assets) and **purchasing-power losses result from holding positive net monetary items** (assets exceed liabilities) **during periods of rising general prices.**

In contrast to monetary items, holders of **nonmonetary assets and liabilities** do not gain or lose general purchasing power simply as a result of general price-level changes. If the price of a nonmonetary item changes at the same rate as the general price level, no gain or loss of general purchasing power results. Holders of nonmonetary assets and liabilities gain or lose general purchasing power if the specific price of the item owned or owed rises or falls faster or slower than the change in the general price level.[6] Historical cost financial statements usually report gains and losses on nonmonetary items only when the items are *sold*. Gains and losses from *holding* nonmonetary items are recognized in the period of the sale by inclusion in the profit or loss from the sale.[7]

CONCEPTUAL ISSUES RELATING TO ALTERNATIVES TO HISTORICAL COST

The simple examples of the current cost, historical cost/constant purchasing power, and current cost/constant purchasing power concepts discussed in this Appendix focus on the logic underlying the adjustment processes and deliberately avoid the many complexities that would be involved in preparing comprehensive financial statements for a company.[8] In this section we evaluate the three methods in greater detail with respect to selected criteria and compare them with historical cost financial statements. Also, we discuss the concept of using an exit value as a measure of current value.

4 Explain the conceptual issues relating to the alternatives to historical cost.

Capital Maintenance Concept (Income Statement)

One of the major purposes of financial accounting is to measure a company's income. But what is income? A common definition is that income for a year is

> the amount the corporation can distribute to the owners of equity in the corporation and be as well off at the end of the year as at the beginning.[9]

This is a useful definition of income, but it does raise the question of what is meant by being "as well off." In other words, what is the capital that is to be maintained during the year so that income may be measured as the excess above the capital maintained? Another way of looking at this issue is to consider the distinction between the maintenance *of* capital and the return *on* capital. During each period, a company first should earn enough to maintain the capital invested in the business. Then, any excess, or return on capital, is considered income.

---

6. "Financial Statements Restated for General Price-Level Changes," *APB Statement No. 3* (New York: AICPA, 1969), par. 19.

7. Current cost financial statements report (holding) gains and losses on nonmonetary items in the period in which the gain or loss occurs. When current cost financial statements are adjusted for general price-level changes, the holding gain or loss is adjusted for the purchasing-power gain or loss from holding the nonmonetary items. For example, in Exhibit E-4, the unrealized holding gain on the inventory in Step 3 is $150. This is the increase in the current cost of $250, less the increase that results from inflation of $100 (10% × $1,000).

8. See *APB Statement No. 3, op. cit.*, Appendix C, for an example of general price-level adjustments, and "Conceptual Framework for Financial Accounting and Reporting: Elements of Financial Statements and Their Measurement," *FASB Discussion Memorandum* (Stamford, Conn.: FASB, 1976), Appendix B, for examples of general price-level, replacement cost, and general price-level adjusted replacement cost financial statements.

9. Sydney S. Alexander, "Income Measurement in a Dynamic Economy," *Five Monographs on Business Income* (New York: Study Group on Business Income, AICPA, 1950), p. 15.

The capital maintenance concepts underlying each type of financial statement that we illustrated in Exhibits E-1 through E-4 are as follows:

Financial Statements	Capital Maintenance Concept
Historical cost	Historical dollars of capital at the beginning of the year
Historical cost/constant purchasing power	Purchasing power of the capital at the beginning of the year
Current cost	Operating capacity (the ability to provide goods and services) at the beginning of the year, measured in dollars
Current cost/constant purchasing power	Operating capacity (the ability to provide goods and services), measured in units of constant purchasing power

Although it may not be reasonable to make a categorical statement that one of the alternative capital maintenance concepts is the best, it should be clear that they are different, and that each has advantages and disadvantages. The historical cost concept has the advantage of being the most *verifiable* and widely understood of the different methods, but it may *not* be the most *relevant* to the needs of the user of financial statements. The user has no assurance that the purchasing power of a company's capital is maintained, or that the company can continue to operate at the same level. In other words, income may be overstated since it is likely to include a return *of* some of the capital as well as a return *on* the capital.

To ensure that the company maintains the purchasing power of its capital probably would be considered desirable by most stockholders. They did contribute a certain number of dollars to the company, but they are more concerned about the purchasing power of those dollars than about the number of their dollars originally contributed. Stockholders would not be satisfied to get back the same number of dollars as they contributed if these dollars represent less purchasing power. Therefore, the stockholders are likely to be interested in knowing that the purchasing power represented by the capital of the company is maintained before income is reported as a return on capital. Historical cost/constant purchasing power income statements disclose this information.

A company needs specific assets to conduct its operations, and it is possible that the company could be maintaining the general purchasing power of its capital but not its ability to replace the assets. Use of the current cost concept ensures that the operating capability of the company is maintained before it reports earnings as a return on capital. However, when these results are reported in unadjusted dollars, a flexible measuring unit is being used. For example, cost of goods sold at its current cost is subtracted from sales. Both measures are in terms of current dollars, so no problem exists. But any holding gain or loss is computed as the difference between the current cost and the historical cost of the inventory, and these two values are measured in terms of different dollar values. Consequently, it is difficult to evaluate the meaning of the holding gain, and also to compare the holding gain with operating income; in each case the two amounts being compared are measured in different dollar values. Use of current cost/constant purchasing power income statements resolves these issues.

In summary, the historical dollar/constant purchasing power income statements resolve one issue with the historical dollar measurement concept, and current cost income statements resolve a different issue. Only current cost/constant purchasing power income statements resolve both issues and ensure that income is the excess after the capital is maintained in terms of operating capacity measured in units of constant purchasing power.

The primary conceptual argument against the use of current costs is that those costs are not relevant if the intent of the company is to hold and use the asset rather than to sell it. For example, a company purchases property, plant, and equipment to use it in its operations and not for sale. Therefore it may be argued that the current cost is not relevant. Also the use of current costs would substantially change the revenue recognition and matching principles.

Balance Sheet

The values attached to items on the balance sheet are closely related to the capital maintenance concept and the resulting rules of valuation and income realization. Historical cost balance sheets disclose items at the historical dollars exchanged (except for securities reported at fair value). The difficulty of interpreting the information on the balance sheet arises because the dollar figures represent different purchasing powers, and adding and subtracting them is as inappropriate as relating U.S. and Canadian dollars, as we discussed earlier. Use of historical cost/constant purchasing power amounts does ensure that all the values on the balance sheet represent equivalent purchasing power.

Current cost balance sheets present assets and liabilities at their current replacement cost or, in other words, at a measure of their current value at the balance sheet date. It is difficult to compare them over time (for example, on the balance sheets for two years), however, because of the changing value of the dollar. Only current cost/constant purchasing power balance sheets value the assets at their current cost and also enhance comparability over time by measuring current costs in dollars of constant purchasing power.

Reliability

Historical cost financial statements clearly are the most reliable, and adjusting historical dollars for changes in the general price level affects that reliability very little, if at all. Under *FASB Statement No. 89*, the historical dollars are adjusted by an index published by the federal government, and all companies would use the same index and follow established procedures.

Current cost financial statements are considerably less reliable than historical cost financial statements. Several general approaches (discussed earlier in this Appendix) to the determination of current cost are available. Although each approach is more suitable for certain types of assets, there are no requirements that a particular method be used in any given situation. For example, Shell Oil Company tested four indexes for estimating the current cost of refineries and found that the current cost varied by 25%.

Understandability

An argument frequently made in favor of historical cost financial statements is that they are more understandable than financial statements prepared under other concepts. This is difficult to disagree with, because historical costs have been used for so many years. This argument suggests, however, that no change should ever take place, because initially users would be less familiar with the new method than with the old.

There also is a trend toward giving greater consideration to the needs of sophisticated users of financial statements who presumably have, or would soon develop, the ability to understand financial statements prepared on a different basis. Many supporters of the use of a changed concept have argued that the historical cost financial statements should be continued and the new data supplied in supplementary form. This would enable users to gain experience with the new methods and concepts and limit the potential for misunderstandings from the adoption of alternative concepts. This is the approach used by the FASB, as we discuss later.

Costs and Benefits

The implementation of each of the different concepts discussed in this appendix would involve additional costs for the company in preparing the data, and for audit fees if the financial statements are to be audited. For example, in a survey of companies, 62% of the respondents estimated that up to 800 hours of employee time would be necessary to compute the supplementary disclosure requirements of *FASB Statement No. 33.*[10] Although it may be expected that such costs would decline as experience increased, it was still a significant cost, and the FASB requirements did not involve complete implementation of current costs.

Historical cost/constant purchasing power financial statements would also involve additional costs, but these would be much less than with current cost financial statements. Since the adjustment process involves the use of generally accepted accounting principles and a publicly available price-level index, the costs mainly result from modifying accounting systems.

Current Cost and Operating Savings

Current cost net income includes depreciation expense based on the current cost of the property, plant, and equipment. If the current cost were based on the current productive capacity of the assets, which incorporates technological changes, it is argued that the *savings*, as well as the higher depreciation charges, that would result from the technological changes should be included. For example, suppose a company owns a fleet of trucks. The current cost depreciation expense would be based on the higher purchase price of trucks. But if new trucks get better gas mileage and have lower repair and maintenance costs, other operating expenses would be lower. Since the new trucks have not been acquired, the operating savings have not been realized and would have to be estimated. Complete implementation of this current cost framework would require that these lower costs, as well as the higher depreciation, be reflected in the income statement. However, it is difficult to estimate operating savings objectively. The SEC's rescinded requirements (which we discuss later) allowed estimation of such operating savings. **Bethlehem Steel** reported that its estimated cost savings were 167% of the excess of current cost depreciation over historical cost depreciation. **Sears** reported savings of 86% and the **Ford Motor Company** savings of 72%. You should also note that the operating savings might be offset to some extent by the increased interest costs on the money that would have to be borrowed to finance the acquisition of the new property, plant, and equipment.

The FASB avoided this issue by requiring that a company measure current cost in terms of the reproduction cost of currently owned assets, thereby ignoring any changes in technology and the operating savings that might result. This advantage is offset by the fact that the current cost is measuring replacements that the company may not make.

Current Cost versus Partial Adjustments

Generally accepted accounting principles require several current cost methods that tend to modify the historical dollar concept, so that historical cost financial statements achieve some of the objectives of current cost accounting. The LIFO inventory costing method matches approximately the current cost of the inventory (or a value close to the current cost) as cost of goods sold against revenue. Accelerated depreciation methods expense a high percentage of the historical cost of the asset against revenue early in the life of the asset, thus partially offsetting the effects of price changes on those assets. However, the extra amount of the expense may not be related in any rational way to the change in the asset's current cost. Also, the total depreciation expense over the life of the asset is limited by the historical dollars paid for it. Furthermore, neither LIFO nor accelerated depreciation methods reflect current costs in the balance sheet. The use of LIFO and accelerated depreciation do reduce income, so that it is likely to be closer numerically to current cost income, but they should *not* be considered as substitutes for current cost financial statements.

---

10. K. Evans and R. Freeman, "Statement 33 Disclosures Confirm Profit Illusion in Primary Statements," *FASB Viewpoints* (Stamford, Conn.: June 24, 1983), p. 13. *FASB Statement No. 33* required certain supplementary disclosures, but was rescinded by *FASB Statement No. 89,* as discussed later.

Generally accepted accounting principles also require the use of the lower of cost or market method for inventory (as we discussed in Chapter 8), fair value for impaired noncurrent assets (as we discussed in Chapters 10 and 11), fair value for investments in trading and available-for-sale securities (as we discussed in Chapter 14), and for some financial instruments and derivatives (as we discussed in Chapters 6 and 14). Both the market value and fair value typically approximate current costs. A company is required to report the gains and losses on these items in its comprehensive income (either in net income or other comprehensive income). So a company's comprehensive income has a few similarities to current cost income.

Current Exit Values

The three alternative measurement methods that we have discussed use *entry*, or input, values. An historical cost is, of course, the cost measured at the time of the acquisition of the item. A constant purchasing power amount is an adjusted historical cost amount. A current cost is the amount that would have to be paid to purchase an item. In contrast, some users of financial statements argue that it would be more appropriate to use exit values. **A current exit value is the net cash amount that a company would receive if it sold the item.** An exit value often is referred to as the *net realizable value* because it is the net amount to be received from the sale after deducting any costs associated with the sale, such as transportation costs and sales commissions. The basic argument in favor of the use of exit values in a company's financial statements is that the company will have to dispose of each item at some point in the future, and therefore the current measure of the cash to be received from such sales is relevant to users of financial statements. It is argued that exit values provide a better measure of the return on investment, liquidity, and financial flexibility.

Exhibit E-5 illustrates the use of exit values using the facts for the Hallas Company earlier in the Appendix. In addition, it is assumed that at Steps 2 and 5, the exit values of the inventory are $1,800 and $2,200, respectively. There are two components of income. The first is the **purchasing margin,** which is the difference between the exit value and the acquisition cost of the assets on the date of acquisition. The second is the **holding gain or loss,** which is the change in the exit values of the assets. In the Hallas Company example, inventory is acquired at Step 2 for $1,000 when its exit value is $1,800, so that the company recognizes a purchasing margin of $800 and includes it in net income. At Step 4, when the inventory is sold, the exit value is $2,000 and the

---

EXHIBIT E-5   Exit Value Financial Statements

	Step				
	1	2	3	4	5
Income Statements					
Purchasing margin	—	$ 800	—	—	$ 950
Holding gain	—	—	—	$ 200	—
Net Income	—	$ 800	—	$ 200	$ 950
Balance Sheets					
Cash	$3,000	$2,000	$2,000	$4,000	$2,750
Inventory	—	1,800	1,800	—	2,200
	$3,000	$3,800	$3,800	$4,000	$4,950
Capital	$3,000	$3,800	$3,800	$4,000	$4,950

company recognizes the holding gain of $200 (the increase in the exit value from $1,800). At Step 5 the company acquires inventory for $1,250 when its exit value is $2,200, so that it recognizes a purchasing margin of $950 and includes it in net income. At all times, the company includes the exit value of the inventory in its balance sheet.

Generally accepted accounting principles require the use of exit values in the financial statements of a company for reporting certain investments (as we discussed in Chapter 14) because the securities are readily saleable. In this case, the exit value and the current cost are the same, except for transaction costs. Many people argue that the use of exit values for other items would not provide relevant information, however. Consider two examples. If a company used an exit value for its inventory, it would record that inventory at its selling price (less costs of disposal) before any sale transaction occurred and therefore would recognize income simply by acquiring inventory. Second, suppose that a company acquired a specialized machine for use in its activities. If the machine has no value to another company, its value would immediately be recorded as zero and its entire purchase price expensed in the period of acquisition, even though the company intends to use the machine for several years.

Alternatively, it can be argued that in certain situations (in addition to certain investments) exit values have more relevance than input values. For example, if a company is to be liquidated, then exit values are more relevant. Of course, in this case the going concern (continuity) assumption is no longer valid. Furthermore, when a company is being sold in its entirety, many purchasers are interested in exit values because they may intend to sell some of the assets. Regardless of their position on the relevance of exit values, few accountants argue that exit values should be the basis of the accounting principles for financial statements used in most investment and lending decisions.

DISCLOSURES

5 Be aware of the disclosure requirements that have existed for alternative disclosures, including the reasons for the elimination of the required disclosures.

The APB, FASB, and SEC have recommended or required various disclosures of the effects of changing prices. In 1969 the APB issued **APB Statement No. 3,** which stated that general price-level adjusted historical cost financial statements present useful information not available from historical cost financial statements and concluded that:

> General price-level information may be presented in addition to the basic historical dollar financial statements, but general price-level financial statements should not be presented as the basic statements.[11]

In 1977 the Securities and Exchange Commission adopted a requirement for supplementary disclosure on the annual 10-K report of the current replacement cost of the inventories, cost of goods sold, net productive assets, and depreciation. Companies with inventories and gross property, plant, and equipment of more than $100 million that represented more than 10% of their total assets were required to make these disclosures. These requirements were rescinded when *FASB Statement No. 33* was issued.

In 1979 the FASB issued **FASB Statement No. 33,** "Financial Reporting and Changing Prices," which required disclosure of the effects of changing prices as a supplement to the basic historical cost financial statements.[12] Public companies having $1 billion of assets (after deducting accumulated depreciation) or $125 million of inventories and property, plant, and equipment (before deducting accumulated depreciation) were required to make such disclosures, although all companies were encouraged to do so. Then, in 1986 **FASB Statement No. 89** rescinded the *requirement* that qualifying companies disclose the information specified in *FASB Statement No. 33* as amended. However, *FASB Statement No. 89* encourages the continued disclosure of information about the effects of changing prices and includes guidelines for measurement and disclosure. We discuss the reasons for making the disclosures voluntary in the next section.

---

11. *APB Statement No. 3, op. cit.,* par. 25.
12. "Financial Reporting and Changing Prices," *FASB Statement of Financial Accounting Standards No. 33* (Stamford, Conn.: FASB, 1979).

If a company decides to voluntarily report supplementary information on the effects of changing prices, the FASB disclosure guidelines for the current year and for a 5-year summary are as follows:

The selected disclosures for the current year are (1) income from continuing operations under the current cost basis, including disclosure of the current cost amounts of cost of goods sold, and depreciation, depletion, and amortization expense, (2) purchasing power gain or loss on net monetary items (excluded from income from continuing operations), (3) current cost (or lower recoverable) amount of inventory and of property, plant, and equipment at the end of the current year, (4) increase or decrease in the current cost (or lower recoverable) amount of inventory and of property, plant, and equipment, before and after eliminating the effects of inflation (excluded from income from continuing operations), and (5) aggregate foreign currency translation adjustment on a current cost basis, if applicable.

The selected disclosures included in a 5-year summary, adjusted to average-for-the-year, end-of-year, or base-period constant purchasing power are (1) net sales and other operating revenues, (2) income from continuing operations (and related earnings per share) under the current cost basis, (3) purchasing power gain or loss on net monetary items, (4) increase or decrease in the current cost (or lower recoverable) amount of inventory and of property, plant, and equipment, net of inflation, (5) aggregate foreign currency translation adjustment on a current cost basis, if applicable, (6) net assets at year-end on a current cost basis, (7) cash dividends declared per common share, and (8) market price per common share at year-end.[13]

Additional disclosures include (1) the principal types of information used to calculate the current costs, and (2) differences between the depreciation methods, estimates of useful lives, and residual values used for calculations of current cost depreciation and the methods and estimates used in the primary financial statements (there is a presumption that the methods and estimates should be the same).

The FASB states that the objective of the calculations is "to obtain a *reasonable degree* of accuracy" and that "preparers are encouraged to devise short-cut methods."[14] **The *Statement* requires that the constant purchasing power adjustments use the average Consumer Price Index for All Urban Consumers (CPI-U) for the year.**

Conceptual Evaluation of the Elimination of the Required Disclosures

When *FASB Statement No. 33* was adopted in 1979, it was intended that its provisions would be reviewed after a period of not more than five years. Consequently, the FASB sponsored and monitored research to help assess the usefulness of information about the effects of changing prices. In 1983 the FASB issued an *Invitation to Comment* on the need for disclosures of information on the effects of changing prices and the best way to meet that need. In 1984 the FASB responded to the related comments and research results by issuing *FASB Statement No. 82,* which eliminated certain disclosure requirements. Then, in 1986 *FASB Statement No. 89* eliminated the requirement for the remaining disclosures. This *Statement* was adopted by a 4-to-3 majority.

There were several arguments in favor of eliminating the required disclosures. First, there was evidence that the disclosures were not widely used. Among the reasons for the lack of use were concerns that the information was not *relevant*. It was argued that the concept of current cost (the cost of replacing existing service potential) was not relevant because many companies intended to replace their assets with others that had a different service potential. It was also argued that applying a specific price index to the historical cost did not provide a relevant value because technological change may not be appropriately reflected in the index. The lack of use also resulted from concerns about the *reliability* of the information. For example, the determination of the current cost

---

13. *FASB Statement No. 89, op. cit.,* par. 7, 8, 11–13.
14. *Ibid.,* par. 48.

when an asset with equivalent service potential was not available required considerable judgment and therefore could be viewed as unreliable. Also, the determination of the recoverable amount required substantial judgment. Furthermore, since the disclosures were labeled "unaudited" and "supplementary," they were considered to lack reliability.

Second, responses to the *Invitation to Comment* expressed the concern that the *costs of providing the information exceeded the benefits.* Because neither the costs nor the benefits could be accurately measured, it was appropriate for the FASB to suspend disclosure requirements if preparers and users perceive an unfavorable cost/benefit relationship. Third, it was argued that the disclosures lacked *comparability*. This situation resulted from the degree of flexibility in methods of application, from differences in the quality of the raw data used to prepare the disclosures, and from failure to disclose the assumptions used. Fourth, concern was expressed that the disclosures lacked *understandability* because they were overly complex. Also, it was argued that the disclosures were difficult to understand because they were not adequately explained and did not include comprehensive financial statements. Fifth, many users of financial statements indicated that they used information about changing prices in their decisions but had developed their own methods for making the adjustments. Therefore, additional disclosures might not be useful because users had information that was better or different from that required by *FASB Statement No. 33.*

The final argument against continuing the required disclosures was that the significance of the disclosures had decreased because prices were changing much less than in previous years. Therefore, other concerns were more important to users, such as the ability of the company to finance replacements of productive capacity or the effects of changing interest rates on monetary assets and liabilities.

There were several arguments in favor of continuing the required disclosures. First, it was argued that the basic concept underlying *FASB Statement No. 33* (inflation causes historical cost financial statements to show illusory profits and to mask the erosion of capital) is virtually undisputed. Second, although there was evidence of limited use of the disclosures, five years is an insufficient time to assess the usefulness of the information. Therefore, an effort should be made to improve any shortcomings of the information. Third, suspension of the required disclosures will encourage companies to remove the systems used to develop the information. Therefore, information will no longer be available for research on the relevance and reliability of the information.

The final argument against the elimination of the required disclosures was that when inflation rates increase at some time in the future, the FASB will again be asked to require supplementary disclosures of the effects of changing prices. The effort required at that time will be as difficult, time-consuming, and costly as the implementation of *FASB Statement No. 33* disclosures.

International Accounting Differences

International accounting standards require that the *primary* financial statements of a company that reports in the currency of a hyperinflationary economy are prepared in terms of the currency at the balance sheet date; that is, the statements are adjusted in a way similar to the constant dollar process we discussed in this Appendix. The standards also require that the company include the purchasing power gain or loss on net monetary items in its net income.

SUMMARY

At the beginning of the chapter, we identified several objectives you would accomplish after reading the chapter. The objectives are listed below, each followed by a brief summary of the key points in the appendix discussion.

1. **Understand the difference between current value and general price level adjustments.** A current value (or specific price change) is the change in the price of an individual asset or liability caused by changes in the dynamics of the market for that particular item. A general price-level change is the change in the value, or purchasing power, of the dollar.

2. **Explain the three alternatives to historical cost.** The three alternatives to historical cost are (1) current cost financial statements, (2) historical cost/constant purchasing power financial statements, and (3) current cost/constant purchasing power financial statements.

3. **Understand issues related to the measurement of current cost, the adjustment of historical dollars for general price-level changes, and the purchasing power gain or loss on net monetary items.** Current cost may be measured by direct pricing, functional or unit pricing, or a specific-price index. Historical dollars are adjusted to constant purchasing power amounts by multiplying by the ratio of the current period price-level index to the historical price-level index. A purchasing power gain (loss) results from holding net monetary liabilities (assets) during a period of inflation.

4. **Explain the conceptual issues relating to the alternatives to historical cost.** The conceptual issues include the capital maintenance concept for each of the three alternatives, the related values on the balance sheet, reliability, understandability, costs and benefits, current cost and operating savings, current cost versus partial adjustments, and current exit values.

5. **Be aware of the disclosure requirements that have existed for alternative disclosures, including the reasons for the elimination of the required disclosures.** The supplementary disclosures required by *FASB Statement No. 33* were suspended by *FASB Statement No. 89*. Among the reasons were concerns that the information was not relevant or reliable, the costs exceeded the benefits, the disclosures lacked comparability and understandability, users made their own adjustments, and the significance of the disclosures had decreased because price changes were small.

QUESTIONS

QE-1 Distinguish between a *general price-level change* and a *specific price change*. What, if any, is the relationship between them?

QE-2 List the four alternative accounting methods discussed in the appendix. What is the appropriate capital maintenance concept for each?

QE-3 What is a *realized holding gain?* How is it measured? Where should it appear in current cost financial statements?

QE-4 What is an *unrealized holding gain* for an accounting period? How is it measured? Where should it appear in current cost financial statements?

QE-5 What is the major argument in favor of historical cost/constant purchasing power financial statements? Of current cost financial statements?

QE-6 How may historical cost net income include a return of capital in income?

QE-7 What causes a purchasing-power gain or loss?

QE-8 Distinguish between *monetary* and *nonmonetary* items.

QE-9 Consider the major items included in the income statement. Which are most nearly measured on a current cost basis on historical cost financial statements? Which are least?

QE-10 Are historical cost constant/purchasing power financial statements allowed under generally accepted accounting principles? Explain.

QE-11 What is an *exit value?* What are the two components of income when exit value financial statements are prepared?

CASES

CE-1 Four Alternative Accounting Methods

Part a. Advocates of current value accounting propose several methods for determining the valuation of assets to approximate current values. Two of the methods proposed are replacement cost and present value of future cash flows.

Required Describe each of the two previously cited methods and discuss the pros and cons of the various procedures used to arrive at the valuation for each method.

Part b. The financial statements of a business entity could be prepared by using historical cost or current value as a basis. In addition, the basis could be stated in terms of unadjusted dollars or dollars restated for changes in

purchasing power. The various permutations of these two separate and distinct areas are shown in the following matrix:

	Unadjusted Dollars	Dollars Restated for Changes in Purchasing Power
Historical cost	1	2
Current value	3	4

Block number 1 of the matrix represents the traditional method of accounting for transactions in accounting today, wherein the absolute (unadjusted) amount of dollars given up or received is recorded for the asset or liability obtained (relationship between resources). Amounts recorded in the method described in block 1 reflect the original cost of the asset or liability and do not give effect to any change in value of the unit of measure (standard of comparison). This method assumes the validity of the accounting concepts of going concern and stable monetary unit. Any gain or loss (including holding and purchasing-power gains or losses) resulting from the sale or satisfaction of amounts recorded under this method is deferred in its entirety until sale or satisfaction.

Required For each of the remaining matrix blocks (2, 3, and 4), respond to the following questions. Limit your discussion to nonmonetary assets only.

1. Explain how this method of recording assets will affect the relationship between resources and the standard of comparison.
2. Explain the conceptual justification for using each method.
3. Explain how each method of asset valuation will affect the recognition of gain or loss during the life of the asset and ultimately from the sale or abandonment of the asset. Your response should include a discussion of the timing and magnitude of the gain or loss and conceptual reasons for any difference from the gain or loss computed using the traditional method. (*AICPA adapted*)

CE-2 Current Value and Fair Presentation of Financial Statements

The total assets of the Sunset Land Company were $2\frac{1}{2}$ million on December 31, 2004, including land of $150,000. Net income was negligible because no land sales took place and none were planned.

The land consisted of 50,000 acres valued at its acquisition cost in the early part of the century of $3 per acre. The market value of the land is now believed to exceed $15 million.

The auditor's opinion attached to the financial statements states, in part, "The financial statements present fairly the financial position of the Sunset Land Company . . . in conformity with generally accepted accounting principles."

Required Explain whether the use of generally accepted accounting principles enables the financial position of the Sunset Land Company to be presented fairly.

CE-3 Constant Purchasing Power Adjustments

Barden Corp., a manufacturer with large investments in plant and equipment, began operations in 1941. The company's history has been one of expansion in sales, production, and physical facilities. Recently, some concern has been expressed that the conventional financial statements do not provide sufficient information for decisions by investors. After consideration of proposals for various types of supplementary financial statements to be included in the 2004 annual report, management has decided to present a

balance sheet as of December 31, 2004 and a statement of income and retained earnings for 2004, both restated for changes in the general price level.

Required

1. On what basis can it be contended that Barden's conventional statements should be restated for changes in the general price level?
2. Distinguish between historical cost/constant purchasing power financial statements and current value financial statements.
3. Distinguish between monetary and nonmonetary assets and liabilities, as the terms are used in general price-level accounting. Give examples of each.
4. Outline the procedures the Barden Corp. should follow in preparing the proposed supplementary statements.
5. Indicate the major similarities and differences between the proposed supplementary statements and the corresponding conventional statements.
6. Assuming that in the future Barden will want to present comparative supplementary statements, can the 2004 supplementary statements be presented in 2005 without adjustment? Explain. (*AICPA adapted*)

CE-4 Current Costs

The controller of the Robinson Company is discussing a comment you made in the course of presenting your audit report.

". . . and frankly," Mr. Fisher continued, "I agree that we, too, are responsible for finding ways to produce more relevant financial statements which are as reliable as the ones we now produce.

"For example, suppose the company acquired a finished item for inventory for $40 when the general price-level index was 110. And, later, the item was sold for $75 when the general price-level index was 121 and the current replacement cost was $54. We could calculate a 'holding gain.'"

Required

1. Explain to what extent and how current replacement costs already are used within generally accepted accounting principles to value inventories.
2. Calculate in good form the amount of the holding gain in Fisher's example.
3. Explain why the use of current replacement cost for both inventories and cost of goods sold is preferred by some accounting authorities to the generally accepted use of FIFO or LIFO. (*AICPA adapted*)

CE-5 Constant Purchasing Power Adjustments

Published financial statements of United States companies are currently prepared on a stable dollar assumption, even though the general purchasing power of the dollar has declined because of inflation in recent years. To account for this changing value of the dollar, many accountants suggest that financial statements should be adjusted for general price-level changes. Three independent, unrelated statements regarding constant purchasing power financial statements follow. Each statement contains some fallacious reasoning.

Statement I

The accounting profession has not seriously considered constant purchasing power financial statements before, because the rate of inflation usually has been so small from year to year that the adjustments would have been immaterial in amount. Constant purchasing power financial statements represent a departure from the historical cost basis of accounting. Financial statements should be prepared from facts, not estimates.

Statement II

If financial statements were adjusted for general price-level changes, depreciation charges in the earnings statement would permit the recovery of dollars of current purchasing power and, thereby, equal the cost of new assets to replace the old ones. General price-level adjusted data would yield statement-of-financial-position amounts closely approximating current values. Furthermore, management can make better decisions if constant purchasing power financial statements are published.

Statement III

When adjusting financial data for general price-level changes, a distinction must be made between monetary and nonmonetary assets and liabilities, which, under the historical cost basis of accounting, have been identified as "current" and "noncurrent." When using the historical cost basis of accounting, no purchasing power gain or loss is recognized in the accounting process, but when financial statements are adjusted for general price-level changes, a purchasing-power gain or loss will be recognized on monetary and nonmonetary items.

Required Evaluate each of the independent statements and identify the areas of fallacious reasoning in each and explain why the reasoning is incorrect. Complete your discussion of each statement before proceeding to the next statement. (*AICPA adapted*)

CE-6 Constant Dollar and Current Cost

Financial reporting should provide information to help investors, creditors, and other users of financial statements. *Statement of Financial Accounting Standards No. 89* encourages companies to disclose certain supplementary information.

Required

1. Describe the historical cost/constant purchasing power method of accounting. Include in your discussion how historical cost amounts are used to make historical cost/constant purchasing power measurements.
2. Describe the principal advantage of the historical cost/constant purchasing power method of accounting over the historical cost method of accounting.
3. Describe the current cost method of accounting.
4. Why would depreciation expense for a given year differ using the current cost method of accounting instead of the historical cost method of accounting? Include in your discussion whether depreciation expense is likely to be higher or lower using the current cost method of accounting instead of the historical cost method of accounting in a period of rising prices, and why. (*AICPA adapted*)

EXERCISES

EE-1   *Four Alternative Accounting Methods* A company purchased inventory for $10,000 at the beginning of the year when the CPI-U was 100. It sold the inventory in the middle of the year for $15,000 at which time the index was 110 and the current cost was $13,000.

      Required Compute the gross profit on the sale of the inventory under each of the following methods (compute the constant purchasing power amounts in terms of the average CPI-U of 110): (1) historical cost, (2) historical cost/constant purchasing power, (3) current cost, and (4) current cost/constant purchasing power.

EE-2   *Constant Purchasing Power Adjustments to Balance Sheet Items* The Desmond Company is preparing a constant purchasing power balance sheet at the average CPI-U for the year of 150. The CPI-U at the end of the year is 155. The following are the amounts in selected accounts and the index when the amount was recorded:

	Amount	Index
Accounts receivable (net)	$10,000	155
Machinery	50,000	130
Accumulated depreciation on machinery	10,000	130
Patent (net)	5,000	125
Accounts payable	20,000	155
Bonds payable	50,000	120
Common stock	40,000	80

      Required Compute the amounts that would appear in the constant purchasing power year-end balance sheet.

EE-3   *Constant Purchasing Power Adjustments to Property, Plant, and Equipment* The Grembar Company purchased a building on January 1, 2004 for $100,000 when the CPI-U was 125. The building has an expected residual value of zero and a life of 10 years, and straight-line depreciation is used. The December 2004 price index is 135 and the December 2005 index is 145, and the price index rose evenly during each year.

Required

1. What is the depreciation expense for 2004 and 2005 if the company prepares a constant purchasing power income statement adjusted to the average index for each year?
2. What is the carrying value of the asset at December 31, 2004 and December 31, 2005, if the company prepares a constant purchasing power balance sheet each year at the average index for the year?
3. How will the company adjust the amounts in its 2004 constant purchasing power financial statements when those statements are published in 2005 for comparison with the constant purchasing power financial statements of 2005?

EE-4   *Current Costs—Inventory*   The following is the cost of goods sold section of the 2004 income statement for the Higgins Company:

Inventory, 12/31/2003	$ 39,000
Purchases	138,000
Cost of goods available for sale	$177,000
Less: Inventory, 12/31/2004	(60,000)
Cost of goods sold	$117,000

Additional information:

1. The December 31, 2003 inventory consisted of 11,000 units purchased in August 2003.
2. The December 31, 2004 inventory consisted of 13,000 units purchased in October 2004.
3. Purchases of 30,000 units were made during the year.
4. The current cost of the inventory was $4.10 per unit in December 2003 and $5.10 per unit in December 2004.

Required Prepare the following 2004 disclosures for the Higgins Company:

1. Cost of goods sold on an average current cost basis.
2. Current cost of ending inventory.

EE-5   *Current Costs—Property and Plant*   The Turner Company has the following fixed assets at the end of 2004:

Land: Purchased for $15,000 in January 1998
         Current cost, December 2003: $25,000
         Current cost, December 2004: $30,000
Building: Purchased for $100,000 in January 1998
         Estimated life: 25 years
         Depreciation method: Straight-line (no residual value)
         Current cost, December 2003: $180,000
         Current cost, December 2004: $200,000

No land or buildings were acquired or sold in 2004.

Required Prepare the following 2004 disclosures for the Turner Company:

1. Depreciation expense on an average current cost basis.
2. Current cost (net) of property and plant.

EE-6   *Current Cost and Sale of an Asset*   The Marino Company purchased some land for $100,000 on January 1, 2004. In December 2004 and December 2005, the current cost of the land was $110,000 and $130,000, respectively. The land was sold on January 5, 2006 for $140,000.

Required If the company prepares current cost financial statements,

1. What is the realized holding gain on the land in 2004 and 2005?
2. What is the unrealized holding gain on the land in 2004 and 2005?
3. What is the gain on the sale of the land in 2006?

PROBLEMS

PE-1   *Inventory and the Four Alternative Accounting Methods*   The Turner Company, a retail company, began operations on January 1, 2004 and engaged in the following transactions:

January 1, 2004	Purchased 100 units of inventory for $200 per unit. The general price-level index was 110.
First quarter 2004	Sold 50 units for $400 per unit. The average replacement cost of the inventory was $220 per unit and the general price-level index was 115.
Second quarter 2004	Purchased 200 units for $250 per unit. The general price-level index was 118.
Third quarter 2004	Sold 100 units for $450 per unit. The average replacement cost of the inventory was $260 per unit and the general price-level index was 120.
Fourth quarter 2004	No purchases or sales were made. The average replacement cost of the inventory was $275 per unit and the general price-level index was 120.

Required If the company uses a FIFO inventory flow assumption, compute the value of the inventory at December 31, 2004, the gross profit, and the holding gains for 2004 under each of the following four alternatives:

1. Historical cost
2. Constant purchasing power (at the average index of 115)
3. Current cost
4. Constant purchasing power adjusted current cost (at the average index of 115)

PE-2   *Land and the Four Alternative Accounting Methods*   Several transactions concerning one asset (land) of a company are summarized as follows:

2003	Purchased land for $40,000 cash on December 31.
2004	Held the land all year; replacement cost at year-end was $52,000.
2005	Sold the land for $68,000 on December 31.

General price-level index (CPI-U): December 2002, 90; December 2003, 100; December 2004, 110; December 2005, 120

Required Compute the value of the land on the ending balance sheets and the gain recognized (including holding gains) on the income statements for 2003, 2004, and 2005 under each of the following alternatives:

1. Historical cost
2. Constant purchasing power (at the average index for each year)
3. Current cost
4. Constant purchasing power adjusted current cost (at the average index for each year)

PE-3   *Constant Purchasing Power Adjustments to Income Statement Items*   The Fishburn Company is preparing a
@   constant purchasing power income statement for the year at the average CPI-U of 150. The following are the amounts in selected accounts and the index when the amount was recorded:

	Amount	Index
Sales revenue	$150,000	150
Cost of goods sold	60,000	145
Depreciation expense	20,000	—
Wages expense	30,000	150
Interest expense	10,000	—

The depreciation expense was for assets purchased when the index was 130 and the interest expense is on bonds issued (at par) when the index was 120. The tax rate is 30%. Taxes and interest are paid evenly throughout the year.

Required

1. Prepare an historical cost income statement.
2. Prepare a constant purchasing power income statement.

PE-4   *Current Cost*   The Jaeger Company is preparing a comprehensively adjusted current cost balance sheet. The following are the amounts in selected accounts:

Inventory (materials)	$30,000
Debt securities held to maturity	21,000
Machinery	50,000
Accumulated depreciation on machinery	10,000
Patent (net)	5,000

The following additional information is available:

1. The average cost inventory method is used. The acquisition cost of the units in inventory rose from $1.40 to $1.60 per unit during the year. The weighted average current cost is $1.55 per unit.
2. Debt securities held to maturity:

Security	Cost	Market Value
Company A	$10,000	$12,000
Company B	8,000	6,000
Company C	3,000	2,000

3. The machinery was purchased at the beginning of the year. Double-declining-balance depreciation is used. The current cost of the machinery fell by 10% during the year.
4. The patent was purchased 5 years ago for $10,000. It is estimated that an equivalent patent would cost $25,000 now.

Required

1. At what amount should the company include each item in its current cost balance sheet?
2. Cost of goods sold on the historical cost basis is $100,000. This includes wages of $30,000, the depreciation on the machinery, and cost of materials. What is the cost of goods sold on a current cost basis?

INDEX

Note: The letter *n* following a page number indicates a footnote; the letter *f*, an exhibit; the letter *d*, a definition.

A

AAA. *See* American Accounting Association (AAA)
Absentee ownership, 73
Accelerated Cost Recovery System (ACRS), 434–436, 434*n*
Accelerated depreciation methods, 418–420, 420*f*
Account form, 82
Accounting, 2*d*; assumptions and conventions in, 26–28, 38–43, 39*f*; for a change in entity, 1078–1079; creative thinking in, 20–22, 20*d*, 21*f*; critical thinking in, 20–22, 21*d*, 21*f*; entity, 38; equations, 665, C2–C3, C3*f*; for error correction, 1079–1085, 1085*f*, 1086*f*; ethics in, 18–20, 19*f*; financial *vs.* managerial, 5–6, 5*f*; income tax *vs.* financial, 16; for loss contingencies, 520; models, C2–C3, C3*f*; for payroll and deductions, 511; period, 40, C5; procedures for investments, 625–628; research and development (R&D) in, 462–463; stewardship function of, 102
Accounting changes: in accounting estimate, 130, 130*d*, 1075; in accounting principle, 129, 129*d*, 129*n*, 1067, 1075–1076; conceptual evaluation of, 1077–1078; cumulative effect method and, 1068–1072, 1068*f*, 1069*f*, 1078; disclosure methods of, 1066–1067; in interim financial statements, 1076–1077; prior period restatement method and, 1072–1074, 1073*f*, 1077; prospective adjustment and, 1078; transitions method and, 1074; types of, 1065
Accounting cycle, C5–C20; adjusting entries in, C11–C14, C12*f*; closing entries in, C17–C20, C19*f*; financial statements in, C14–C17, C15*f*, C16*f*, C17*f*, C18*f*; journal entries in, C6–C8, C8*f*–C9*f*; ledger in, C8–C11, C10*f*
Accounting information: benefit/cost constraint on, 37; comparability of, 36; consistency of, 36; external users of, 3–4, 3*d*, 4*f*, 4*n*; internal users of, 3–4, 4*d*, 4*f*; materiality in, 37–38, 39*f*; measurement bias in, 36; neutrality in, 36; relevance and reliability of, 35–36; SEC integrated disclosure requirements for, 80–81; types of, 32–33, 32*f*; understandability of, 35; uses of, 2–4, 30–37, 32*f*, 34*f*
Accounting Interpretations, AICPA, 7*f*, 15, 127*n*

Accounting Principles Board (APB), 8–9; Statement No. 4, 26; *vs.* other sources of GAAP, 6–7, 7*f*
Accounting Research and Terminology Bulletins, Final Edition, AICPA, 298*n*; No. 1, 417*n*; No. 43, 64*n*, 287*n*
Accounting Research Bulletin , AICPA, 8; No. 43, 332, 336*n*, 342; No. 45, 786–787, 794; No. 47, 882
Accounting Research Study: No. 8, 882; No. 10, 472
Accounting system, C2–C5, C2*d*
Accounting Trends and Techniques, AICPA, 7*f*, 15, 82*n*, 118*n*, 121*n*, 139*n*, 233*n*, 245*n*, 252*n*
Accounts, C3–C5
Accounts payable: as current liabilities, 501–502; software for, C30
Accounts receivable(s): aging of, 247–249, 247*d*, 248*f*, 248*n*; Allowance for Doubtful Accounts against, 246–250; assignment of, 252–253; bad debts estimate as percentage of, 247; collection of a previously written off, 250; factoring of, 253–254, 255*f*; financing agreements' disclosure of, 255, 255*f*; generating immediate cash from, 250–252, 251*f*; pledging of, 252; recording and reporting, 240–245; software for, C30; as trade receivables, 240, 242–245; uncollectible accounts' valuation of, 245–250
Accrual accounting, 104, C13; conversion from cash-basis to, C31–C34, C32*f*, C33*f*; matching principle and, 42–43; in measuring comprehensive income, 31
Accumulated Benefit Obligations, 884
Accumulated rights, 505
Acid-test ratio, 198–199
Activity methods, of depreciation, 417–423, 417*d*, 417*f*
Activity ratios, 195, 199–200, 199*f*
Actual Return on Plan Assets, 884
Actuarial Funding Method, 884
Actuarial Present Value, 884
Additional paid-in capital, 665
Adjusted current earnings (ACE), 859–860
Adjusted trial balance, C15–C16, C15*f*
Adjusting entries: accrued expenses in, C13; accrued revenues in, C13; deferred revenues in, C12–C13; estimated items in, C13
Advertising: costs, 518–519; direct response in, 518
Agency theory, 5–6
Aging analysis, 248–249

AICPA Committee on Financial Reporting, 500*n*
AICPA *Professional Standards,* 7*n*, 79*n*, 175*n*
AICPA. *See* American Institute of Certified Public Accountants (AICPA)
AICPA *Statements of Position,* 7*f*, 15, 784; No. 81-1, 805; No. 93-6, 673*n*; No. 94-6, 179*n*; No. 97-2, 805; No. 98-1, 466; No. 98-5, 378, 378*n*
AIMR. *See* Association for Investment Management and Research (AIMR)
Alcoa, Inc., 692, 693*n*
All-inclusive concept, 111–113
Allowance: for Bad Debts, 246; for Doubtful Accounts, 246–251, 256; method, 289*n*, 337–339, 337*f*, 339*f*; for Sales Discounts, 246*n*; for Sales Returns and Allowances, 246*n*; for Uncollectible Accounts, 246
Allowance account, in cash discounts, 243, 243*n*
Alternative minimum tax (AMT), 859
American Accounting Association (AAA), 16, 18*f*
American Express, 251, 254–255
American Institute of Certified Public Accountants (AICPA), 8, 15; Code of Professional Conduct (CPC), 19–20, 19*f*; *Industry Accounting Guides,* 7*f*, 15, 784; *Industry Audit Guides,* 7*f*, 15, 784; *Issues Papers,* 7*f*, 15; Special Committee on Financial Reporting, 47*n*, 71–72, 72*n*, 115, 179–180, 180*n*; *vs.* others sources of GAAP, 6–7, 7*f*, 18, 18*f*
Amortization, 415*d*
Amortized cost, 605*n*
Anheuser-Busch Companies, Inc., 424*f*
Annual report(s), C5; contents of, 6, 55, 173; management's, 177, 178*f*; MD&A as, 178–180; period, 40
APB *Opinions,* 8–9, 14; No. 2, 859; No. 4, 859; No. 6, 76*n*; No. 8, 882; No. 9, 125–126, 143*f*, 742*n*, 853–854; No. 10, 561, 784, 802–803; No. 11, 833, 865; No. 12, 75*n*, 395*n*, 424*n*, 561, 745; No. 14, 559, 561, 687–688; No. 15, 718; No. 18, 625, 628; No. 19, 138; No. 20, 129*n*, 130*n*, 143*f*, 189*n*, 310, 436, 514, 741*n*, 794, 853, 1065, 1074–1075, 1078; No. 21, 242*n*, 256, 376*n*, 553, 563, 564*n*, 566*n*, 612–613; No. 22, 77*n*; No. 25, 674–675, 685; No. 26, 558; No. 28, 185, 186*n*, 189*n*, 190, 309–310, 339, 343*f*; No. 29, 278*n*, 378; No. 30, 112*n*, 126–128, 126*n*–127*n*, 142*f*–143*f*, 558, 854

APB Statement No. 4, 26, 795
Appraisal value, 41
Asset(s), 45*d*, 59*d*. *See also* Property, & Equipment (PP&E): account for contra, 67; additions as, 391; classifications on balance sheet, 59, 63, 64*f*; contingent, 78, 79*f*; costs, 416*d*; current, 64–65, 64*d*, 64*f*; exchange in troubled debt restructuring, 578–581; exchange to acquire PP&E, 378–379; identifiable intangible, 457–458, 457*f*, 463–470; impairment and depreciation, 430–433; improvements and replacements as, 392; intangible, 66*f*, 70, 415, 457–471, 457*d*; interest capitalization on, 386–389, 386*d*; inventories as, 283–285, 283*d*; liquid, 66–67; long-term investments as, 67–68, 67*f*; MACRS depreciation and cost of, 434–436, 435*f*; natural resources as, 415; net, 57; PP&E and exchange for dissimilar productive, 379–380, 379*d*, 379*f*; PP&E and exchange for similar productive, 380–385, 382*f*, 383*f*, 384*f*; property, plant and equipment as, 68–70, 69*f*; quick, 199; rearrangement and moving costs in, 392–393; relationship of cost and expense, 59, 63, 64*f*; repairs and maintenance cost on, 393; reporting of, 71–72; residual value of, 416*d*; return on total, 197; separable, 67; service life of, 416*d*; tangible, 415; test, 181; unidentifiable intangible, 457–458, 457*f*, 467–471; valuations of, 61–62, 61*f*, 251–252; working capital and, 66–67
Association for Investment Management and Research (AIMR), 17, 18*f*
Assumptions, 884
Attest function, of the CPA, 36
Audit committee, 178*d*; management's report and, 177–178, 178*f*
Auditing: market values in, use of, 14; verification in, 36
Auditor's report: adverse opinion in, 177; description of, 175; GAAP and, 176–177; modified, 177; qualified or unqualified, 175–177; standard form of, 175, 176*f*
Available-for-sale securities, 605
Average cost flow assumptions, 291; in inventory measurement, 294–295, 294*d*, 294*f*, 295*f*, 302–303; in retail inventory, 346–350, 349*f*

B

Bad debts: Allowance for, 246; conceptual evaluation of, 249; direct write-off method for, 250; estimate using percentage of accounts receivable, 247; estimate using percentage of sales, 246–247; estimated method for, 246; expense, 246–247; recording, 246
Baker Hughes Inc., 523*f*
Balance sheet(s), 6, C5, C17, C18*f*; assets on, 57, 59–70, 61*f*, 66*f*–67*f*, 69*f*; bad

debts' estimation and, 249; cash equivalents and, 64–65; classifications/elements of, 44–45, 44*f*, 63–70; contributed capital on, 66*f*, 73–74; deferred charges and, 70; disclosures, 76–82, 77*f*; GAAP and, 44–45, 44*f*; liabilities on, 59–60, 65, 66*f*–67*f*, 70–72; limitations of, 62–63; purposes of, 56–58; recognition in, 58; securities' valuation on, 605; statement format of, 82–83; treasury stock and, 696; valuation methods for, 61–63; vertical analysis on, 194–195, 195*f*
Bank overdrafts, 233
Bank reconciliation, 235*d*
Bankers Trust, 635
Banner Corporation, 114, 114*f*–115*f*, 116*f*, 117, 117*f*, 119*f*, 134*f*
Barings Bank, 635
Black & Decker Corporation, 77, 77*f*
Boise Corporation, 78, 79*f*
Bond(s), 70*d*, 546, 546*n*; acquired between interest dates, 615–616; amortizing discounts and premiums of, 549–555, 551*f*, 554*f*, 613–615; certificate, 545; characteristics of, 545, 546*f*; convertible, 560–563, 560*d*, 633; effective interest method and, 549, 551–555, 554*f*, 564, 614*f*; effective yield of, 546–547, 546*n*; with equity characteristics, 559–563; indenture, 545; interest accrual of, 555–556; international accounting differences of, 556; issue costs, 555; issued between interest payment dates, 548–549; issued with detachable stock warrants, 559–560; liabilities extinguishment of, 557–559; as long-term liability, 70–71; payable, 545, 547–548; retired at maturity, 557; retired prior to maturity, 557–559; sale before maturity, 616–617; serial, 582–585, 584*f*, 585*f*; zero coupon, 556
Book value, 124; of method and convertible bonds, 562; per common share, 201–202, 201*f*
Boot: in dissimilar productive asset exchanges, 379–380, 379*f*; in similar productive asset exchanges, 380–385, 382*f*, 383*f*, 384*f*
Brunswick Corporation, 731, 732*f*
Buildings, cost of, 375
Business cycle, 40, 40*f*
Business reporting, model of, 46–47

C

Call provisions, 557, 669
Campbell Soup Company, 69, 69*f*
CAP. *See* Committee on Accounting Procedure (CAP)
Capital, 57–58, 57*d*; account, 73; additional paid-in, 74; contributed, 73; legal, 73–74; markets' efficiency, 174–175; resources, 179; working, 66–67
Capital leases: on balance sheet, 69
Capital maintenance, 57–58; concept, 103–104

Capital markets, 2, 3*f*; decision making in, 3–4, 4*f*, 4*n*; market efficiency in, 174–175
Capital stock: additional paid-in, 665; authorization, 666; basic terminology of, 663–664; issuance and costs of, 666–667; nonmonetary issuance of stock and, 670; preferred stock and, 685–686; stockholders' rights and, 662–663; subscriptions and defaults, 667–669; value of, 73–74, 73*n*
Capital structure: complex, 719, 722–731; simple, 719, 719*d*
Carey, Mariah, 522
Caron Manufacturing Company, 65, 66*f*–67*f*, 68, 74–75
CASB. *See* Cost Accounting Standards Board (CASB)
Cash, 233*d*, 1002; classifications of, 233, 233*n*; compensating, 239–240; differences, 236; electronic funds transfers (EFT), 238–239; inflows, 1004–1006; management and systems, 233–234; outflows, 1004–1006; petty, 234–235, 234*d*; proof of, 260–261, 260*f*; sales discounts, 243–244, 243*d*, 244*f*; surrender value of life insurance, 633
Cash basis accounting, 43, C31–C33
Cash equivalents, 64*d*, 140*n*, 233, 1002
Cash flows. *See also* Statement of Cash Flows
Cash receipts, 30
Certificates of Deposit (CDs), 233
Certified public accountant (CPA), 36*d*; attest function of, 36; as auditor, 175–177, 260
Checks, outstanding, 236, 236*d*
Chrysler, 921–922
Cliff vesting, 678*n*
Closing entries, C17–C20, C17*d*, C19*f*
Coca-Cola Company, 63, 80, 83–84, 131, 140, 175
Coca-Cola Company: Annual Report of, A3–A53
Colgate-Palmolive Company, 746, 747*f*, 748*f*
Commitment fees, 570
Committee on Accounting Procedure (CAP), 8
Common stock, 73–74, 663*d*; issuance of, 666–667; potential, 722; splits, 671
Company profitability ratios, 195–198, 197*f*
Comparability, of accounting information, 36–37
Compensated absences, 505–507
Compensation expenses, 676–682, 677*n*
Completed-contract method, 786; illustration of, 788, 790*fi*
Composite-rate depreciation method, 425–427
Compound-interest depreciation method, 425*n*
Comprehensive income, 104*d*, 135*d*; accumulated other, 74–75, 665, 744–745; conceptual evaluation of, 137–138; financial reporting and, 31,

31*n*; four items of, 854*n*; GAAP summary for, 142*f*–143*f*; income statement and, 135–137; reclassification adjustment and, 136*n*; statement of, 6*n*

Computer software, C30–C31; costs, 465–466, 465*d*

Con-Agra, 342*f*

Conservatism, 43

Consignments, 287

Consolidations, 606

Construction contracts, long-term; additional accounting considerations for, 794–795; disclosure of, 795; losses on, 791–794, 792*f*, 794*f*; offsetting amounts of, 795; overhead costs of, 794; revenue recognition in, 786–787

Contingencies, 519–520, 523–524

Contingencies, gain, 78, 79*f*; disclosure in financial statements, 521–522

Contingencies, loss, 78, 79*f*; accounting for, 520; accrual for, 520–521; disclosure in financial statements, 521–522

Contingent liabilities, 78, 79*f*, 257

Continuing franchise fees, 805, 807–808

Continuity assumption, 38–40, 39*f*

Contra-asset account, 69, C5

Contract rate, of bonds, 545

Contributed capital: on balance sheet, 67*f*, 73–74; of corporations, 665, 691–692, 693*n*

Convertible bonds, 560–563, 560*d*

Copyrights, 464–465, 464*d*, 464*n*

Corporation(s): accrual-based transactional approach and, 104–105; capital structure of, 662; capital structures of, 719–731; combined stock sales of, 669–670; compensatory stock option plans and, 682–683, 683*f*–684*f*, 685; contributed capital and, 665; Employee stock ownership plan (ESOP) in, 673; Form 1120 for, 512; formation of, 661–662; issuance for cash and, 666–667; nonmonetary issuance of stock and, 670; operating, investing and financing activities of, 139–142; primary consideration of, 126; recognition of compensation expense by, 676–682, 677*n*; stock appreciation rights (SAR) of, 680–682, 681*f*; stock issuance costs of, 667; stocks' conceptual and historical overview of, 673–675; total income of, 104; treasury stock and, 692–694, 697; types of, 660–661

Cost(s), 109–110, 110*n*; acquisition of PP&E and, 373–375; allocation methods, 417–423, 417*f*; amortized, 605*n*; computer software, 465–466, 465*d*; depletion, 438; depreciable, 417*d*; index, 307; method, 694–695, 695*n*, 697*f*; overhead, 794; research and development (R&D), 460–462, 461*f*; start-up, 377–378; to-cost method, 787

Cost Accounting Standards Board (CASB), 15–16, 18*f*; Standard 404, 390

Cost Flow Assumptions, 291*f*, 292*f*; average cost in, 291; first-in, first-out (FIFO) in, 291, 292–294, 292*d*, 293*f*, 297; last-in, first-out (LIFO) in, 291, 295–298, 295*d*, 295*f*, 296*f*; specific identification, 291–292

Cost of Goods: Available for Sale, 114, 291; Manufactured, 114

Cost of Goods Sold, 113–114, 114*f*

Cost recovery method, in revenue recognition, 42, 108–109

Coupon obligations, 517–519

CPA. *See* Certified public accountant (CPA)

Creative thinking, in accounting, 20–22, 20*d*, 21*f*

Credit balance, 609

Critical thinking, in accounting, 20–22, 21*d*, 21*f*

Cumulative effect, 129, 129*d*; interim financial reports and, 188

Current assets, 64–65, 64*d*, 64*f*; prepaid items in, 65; receivables as, 63

Current costs, 60–61, 60*d*, 60*f*

Current exit value. *See* Current market value

Current liabilities: accrued liabilities and, 505–508; advances and refundable deposits as, 504–505; bonus obligations as, 512, 512*n*, 513*f*; classification of, 500–501, 501*f*; conceptual overview of, 498–499; with contractual amount, 501–508; dependent on operations, 508–512; dividends payable as, 504; estimated amounts and, 513–519; financial statement presentation of, 526–528, 527*f*; income taxes payable as, 511–512, 513*f*; liquidity, financial flexibility and, 500; long-term debt's maturing portion and, 504; nature of, 499–500, 499*d*; notes payable, 502–504, 503*n*; payroll liabilities as, 509–511; premium and coupon obligations as, 517–519; property taxes and, 513–515, 514*n*; sales and use tax, 508–509, 508*d*; trade accounts payable, 501–502; valuation of, 501; warranty obligations as, 515–517

Current market value, 61, 61*d*, 61*f*; *vs.* historical cost, 41

Current operating performance concept, 111–113

Current ratios, 66, 198

D

Debentures, 69

Debit balance, 609

Debt. *See also* Bad debts; Long-term liabilities: financing, 544–545; ratio, 90, 198–199, 198*f*; refunding, 557; retirement, 557

Debt and equity securities, 606*d*; available-for-sale, 607, 611–612; categories of, 605; classification of, 624; fair value of, 623; Generally Accepted Accounting Principles (GAAP) and, 607; held-to-maturity debt, 605, 612–615, 613*f*, 614*f*; impairments of, 617, 619; investments and, 607; recording initial cost in, 607–608, 607*n*; recording interest and dividend revenue in, 608; transfers of, 617–619

Decision making, in financial reporting, 29*f*, 30–32, 32*f*

Declining-balance depreciation method, 418–420, 420*f*

Deductible temporary difference, 831

Deferred charges, 70; identifiable intangible assets and, 467

Deferred payments, 376

Deferred revenues, 508

Deferred tax asset, 831; balanced sheet presentation of, 857, 857*f*; characteristics of, 836; financial statement disclosures of, 858; net-of-tax method and, 865; permanent and temporary differences, 843–844; single temporary difference and, 842–843, 842*f*; valuation allowance and, 843

Deferred tax liability, 831; annual, 852*f*; on balance sheet, 857, 857*f*, 865; characteristics of, 836; financial statement disclosures of, 858; measurement of, 836–838; net-of-tax method and, 865; simple temporary difference and, 839–842, 840*f*, 841*f*

Defined contribution pension plans, 911

Depletion, 415*d*, 437–438, 437*d*

Deposit method, 804

Deposits in Transit, 236, 236*d*

Depreciation, 415*d*, C14; accelerated methods of, 418–420, 420*f*; activity methods of, 417–418, 417*d*, 417*f*; additional methods for, 425–428, 426*f*; asset impairment and, 430–433; base, 417*d*; changes and corrections of, 436; conceptual methods evaluation of, 421–423, 422*f*, 423*f*; cost allocation methods of, 417–423, 417*f*; declining-balance methods of, 418–420, 420*f*; disclosure of, 423–425, 424*f*, 425*f*; factors, 415; fixed-percentage-of-declining balance method of, 420*n*; income taxes and, 433–436; international accounting differences for, 425; for partial periods, 428–430; recording, 421, 421*d*; straight-line methods of, 418, 419*f*; sum-of-the-years'-digits method of, 418–420, 419*f*; time-based methods of, 418–420, 418*d*

Depreciation; income tax. *See* Interperiod income tax allocation; Intraperiod income tax allocation

Development stage companies, 391

Diner's Club, 251, 254–255

Direct financing leases: classification criteria for, 948–949, 948*f*; initial direct costs in, 969–970; with no guaranteed residual value, 963–966, 964*f*, 965*f*, 966*f*; with no unguaranteed residual value, 966–967, 966*f*,

967–968, 967*f*, 968*f*; payments made at end of year and, 963–966, 964*f*, 965*f*, 966*f*; payments made in advance and, 967–968, 967*f*, 968*f*, 969*f*; payments received in advance and, 966–967, 966*f*, 967*f*

Direct write-off method, 250

Disclosure(s): accounting policies and, 76–77, 77*f*; of accounts receivables' financing agreements, 255, 255*f*; auditor's report and, 80; on balance sheet, 76–82, 77*f*; for basic computation of EPS, 719–720, 723*f*; constraints on, 37–38; of contingent liabilities or assets, 78, 79*f*, 257; on depreciation, 423–425, 424*f*, 425*f*; of discontinued operations' sale, 125; Electronic Data Gathering Analysis and Retrieval System (EDGAR) and, 80; financial instruments and, 77–78, 174–175; of gain contingencies' financial statements, 521–522; of historical inventory costs, 310, 311*f*, 312*f*, 313*f*; for intangible assets, 470–471; on interim financial reports, 188–189; International Accounting Standards Board (IASB) and, 82–83; for investments in securities, 620, 620*f*–621*f*; issues, 76–82; of long-term liabilities, 567, 568*f*–569*f*; in loss contingencies, 521–522; Management's discussion and analysis (MD&A) and, 81; miscellaneous, 80; of Property, plant, and equipment (PP&E), 395–396, 395*f*–396*f*, 396*n*; on receivables' financial statements, 258–259, 259*f*; of related party transactions, 79–80; SEC integrated, 80–81; of stockholders' equity, 75–76, 76*f*; of subsequent events, 78–79; through comparative statements, 80

Discontinued operations: disclosures on, 125; gains and, 120–125, 120*d*, 120*n*, 121*f*; income statements and, 120–125, 120*d*, 121*f*; interim financial reports and, 188; losses and, 120–125, 120*d*, 120*n*, 121*f*; results from, 716

Discount(s): amortizing, 549–555, 551*f*, 554*f*; of bonds, 547; cash sales, 243–244, 243*d*, 244*f*; conceptual evaluation of, 244; rate or period, 257

Discount rate, 884

Dividends: cash, 733–735; debt and equity securities' recording of, 608; liquidating, 741; payable, 504; preferred stock, 686; property, 504, 735–737; retained earnings and, 731–733; scrip, 737; stock, 737; stock splits and, 631–632

Double-entry system, C3–C4, C4*f*

Double-extension method, 307

Dow Chemical Company, 177, 178*f*

E

Earning process, 107–108, 107*d*

Earnings per common share. *See* Earnings per share (EPS)

Earnings per share (EPS), 130–131, 130*d*, 130*n*, 132*f*; additional considerations in, 729–731; basic computation for, 719–720, 723*f*, 724*f*; components of, 722; computation of tentative and diluted, 727–729, 727*n*, 728*f*, 730*f*; conceptual overview of, 718–719; contingent issuances in, 729; conversion ratios in, 729; convertible securities in, 726–727; denominator calculations of, 720, 720*f*; diluted (DEPS), 722–731, 722*d*; interim financial reports and, 188; international accounting differences in, 731; numerator calculations of, 720; stock options and warrants in, 724–726; weighted average shares for, 720, 720*f*

Economic entities, in financial accounting, 38–40, 39*f*

Economic resources, in financial reporting, 45*d*. *See also* Assets

EDGAR. *See* Electronic Data Gathering Analysis and Retrieval System (EDGAR)

Effective interest method, 549, 551–555, 554*f*, 564, 614*f*

Effective rate, of bonds, 546, 546*n*

Efficient markets hypothesis, 174–175

Efforts-expended method, 787

Electronic Data Gathering Analysis and Retrieval System (EDGAR), 14; disclosures and, 80; Form 10-K and Form 10-Q filing requirements by, 190

Electronic funds transfers (EFT), 238–239

Emerging Issues Task Force (EITF), 15; *Abstracts*, 15; *Consensus Positions*, 7*f*, 15

Emerson Radio Corp., 861, 861*f*–862*f*

Employee Retirement Income Security Act of 1974 (ERISA), 881–883, 911–912

Employee stock ownership plan (ESOP)

Engelhard Corporation, 523*f*

EPS. *See* Earnings per share (EPS)

Equipment, 66*f*, 68–70. *See also* Property, Plant & Equipment (PP&E)

Equity, 45*d*, 60, 660*d*. *See also* Stockholders' equity; exchange in troubled debt restructuring, 578–581; statement of changes in, 44, 46; trading on the, 544; trading securities and debt, 607

Equity method, 606; for investments, 624–625; special issues of, 628–631, 629*f*

Equity securities. *See* Debt and equity securities

Estimated economic life of leased property, 947

Estimated residual value of leased property, 947

Events, 126–127, C3*d*

Exchange gain, 311–315

Exchange loss, 311–315

Executory contracts, 522–523

Expected exit value, 61–62, 61*f*

Expected Return on Plan Assets, 884

Expense(s), 45*d*, 109*n*; Bad Debt, 246–247; capital, 391–395, 391*d*; fixed *vs.* variable, 115; general and administrative, 114–115; on income statement, 104, 109–110; in interim financial reports, 185–186; operating or revenue, 114–115, 116*f*, 391–395, 391*d*; research and development (R&D), 114–115, 114*ni*; salaries, 506–507, 506*d*; selling, 114–115, 288

Expense recognition, 43, 109*n*; principles, 109–110

Expense warranty accrual method, 515–516

External users, 3–4, 3*d*, 4*f*, 4*n*; balance sheet and, 56

Extraordinary items: on income statements, 126–128, 126*d*, 128*f*; on interim financial statements, 188

ExxonMobil Corporation, 38, 128, 128*f*, 299

F

Face value, 545

Factoring, 253–254

Factory overhead, 114

Fair value: financial instuments and, 77–78; hedge, 635–639, 636*f*; measurement of, 675–676; of securities, 606*d*

Fair value of leased property, 947

FASB. See Financial Accounting Standards Board (FSAB)

FASB *Discussion Memorandum*, 57*n*, 61*f*, 62*n*, 67*n*, 500*n*

FASB Emerging Issues Task Force (EITF); *Issue 01-10*, 126*n*; *Summary 86-29*, 379*n*

FASB *Exposure Draft*, 184, 687, 834; *No. 213-B*, 574–575

FASB *Financial Accounting Research System (FARS)*, 6

FASB *Interpretations*, 7*f*, 10, 14; No. 8, 525; No. 18, 185, 187*n*; No. 20, 1074; No. 28, 677*n*; No. 30, 394*n*; No. 35, 625; No. 39, 83*n*; No. 41, 83*n*; No. 44, 680*n*

FASB *Invitation to Comment*, 795

FASB *Statements of Financial Accounting Concepts*, 10, 10*n*, 27*f*; No. 1, 27, 27*f*, 29*n*, 31*n*, 104*n*, 173in; No. 2, 27, 31, 33, 33*n*, 34*f*, 43*n*, 458, 460–462, 466; No. 3, 28, 189*n*; No. 4, 28*n*, 143*f*, 558; No. 5, 28, 31*n*, 42*n*, 44*f*, 55, 55*n*, 58*n*, 61*f*, 62*n*, 63*n*, 78*n*, 113*n*, 245*n*, 257, 341, 519, 522, 784*n*; No. 6, 28, 31, 43*n*, 44*n*, 59–60, 59*f*, 104*n*, 107, 107*n*, 498, 524–525, 660, 667, 836, 865; No. 7, 28, 62*n*, 391; Proposed, 33*n*, 57*n*, 72*n*, 106*n*, 500*n*

FASB *Statements of Financial Accounting Standards*, 10, 10*n*, 14, 1074; No. 13, 944–947, 981; No. 14, 183, 520*n*; No. 15, 575, 575*n*, 579; No. 16, 113, 133–134, 134*n*, 143*f*,

436, 741*n*; No. 19, 14, 397–398; No. 34, 374, 385–389, 391, 522; No. 35, 883; No. 43, 505–507, 913; No. 45, 805; No. 47, 341*n*, 507*n*; No. 48, 241, 241*n*; No. 49, 341, 508; No. 57, 80*n*; No. 66, 808; No. 67, 374, 374*n*; No. 68, 398; No. 78, 525–526; No. 84, 562, 563*n*; No. 86, 465–466; No. 87, 883–884, 911–912; No. 88, 883, 912; No. 91, 570; No. 95, 12, 44*n*, 138, 139–141, 143*f*, 233*f*, 1000, 1024; No. 96, 833–834; No. 102, 12; No. 106, 914; No. 107, 12, 259, 507; No. 109, 117*n*, 134*n*, 143*f*, 833–838, 854; No. 112, 913; No. 114, 572*n*, 573, 579; No. 115, 14, 604–605, 608, 622, 632; No. 116, 377*n*, 698; No. 118, 572*n*; No. 121, 430*n*; No. 123, 672*n*, 674–682, 685; No. 128, 130*n*, 143*f*, 718–719*n*; No. 129, 690*n*; No. 130, 75*n*, 136*n*, 137–138, 745*n*, 854; No. 131, 180–185, 180*n*, 182*n*, 189*n*; No. 132, 883, 901–902; No. 133, 77, 258, 259*n*, 507–508, 634*n*, 635; No. 138, 634*n*; No. 140, 251–252, 253*n*, 557*n*; No. 141, 126, 468*n*, 470; No. 142, 457*n*, 459*n*, 470–471, 628*n*; No. 143, 394, 395*n*; No. 144, 112, 120, 122–125, 126*n*, 142*f*–143*f*, 394, 430–433, 459, 466; No. 145, 128*n*, 143*f*, 558; No. 146, 122

FASB *Technical Bulletins,* 10; 85-6, 697

Federal Insurance Contribution Act, 881

FIFO. *See* First-In, first-out (FIFO) cost flow assumption

Financial accounting, 5–6. *See also* Financial reporting, 5*d,* 5*f*; theory and practice of, 39*f*; *vs.* income tax accounting, 16

Financial Accounting Foundation: FASB and, 9–10, 9*f*; GASB and, 10*n,* 17

Financial Accounting Research System (FARS), 6

Financial Accounting Standards Board (FASB): auditing standards of, 14–15; conceptual framework of, 26–28, 27*f,* 28*f*; and Emerging Issues Task Force. *See* Emerging Issues Task Force (EITF); and Financial Accounting Foundation, 9–10, 9*f*; International Accounting Standards Committee, 12–13, 16; operating procedures of, 11–12, 11*f*; organization of, 9–11, 9*f*; problem solving and, 21–22; pronouncements of, 10; sociopolitical environment of, 12–13; *vs.* other sources of GAAP, 6–7, 7*f,* 14–18, 18*f*

Financial analysis: audit committee and management report in, 177, 178if; auditor's report in, 175–177, 176if; conceptual evaluation in, 183–185; intercompany comparisons in, 191–192; interim financial reports and, 185–189, 187*f*; intracompany comparisons in, 191; market efficiency in, 174–175; MD&A in,

178–180; percentage analyses in, 192–203; SEC reports in, 189–190; segment reporting and, 180–183, 183*f*

Financial Analysts Journal, 17

Financial Executive International (FEI), 17

Financial Executives Institute (FEI), 17

Financial flexibility, 57, 778; accounts receivables and, 251–252; current liabilities and, 500, 500*d*; fair value and, 623; financial reporting and, 33, 138–139; financial resources and, 133; working capital and, 66–67

Financial instruments, 634*d*; derivatives of, 634–640; disclosure of, 77–78

Financial Loss, pretax. *See* Operating loss carrybacks; Operating loss carryforwards

Financial position form, 82

Financial reporting, 6, 6*d*; additional aspects of, 173–203; conceptual framework for, 26–47, 27*f,* 28*f*; decision making and, 30, 32; environment of, 2–20, 48, 48*f*; financial flexibility and, 33; financial statements and, 44–47, 44*f*; income tax and, 16–17, 831; international standards in, 16–17; by management, 31; model, 46–47; objectives of, 29–32, 29*f,* 104; useful information in, 32–38, 32*f*

Financial statement(s), C5; classification, 622; comparative, 80; current liabilities in, 65; disclosure of gain contingencies in, 521–522; disclosure of loss contingencies in, 521–522; disclosures for investments, 628; effects of inventory errors on, 355–357; elements of, 44–47, 44*f*; interrelationship of, 56, 56*f*; investments on, 65, 67–68; notes, schedules and notations on, 83; preparation of, 173–203, C15–C20; receivables' disclosure, 258–259, 259*f*; reporting techniques in, 82–83

Financing agreements, 251–252, 525

First-in, first-out (FIFO) cost flow assumptions, 200, 291; inventory valuation in, 301–302; management's selection of, 302–303; periodic inventory system and, 292–294, 292*d,* 293*f*; perpetual inventory system and, 292–294, 292*d,* 293*f*; retail inventory and, 346–350, 348*f*

Fiscal year, 40

Fixed assets, 68–70. *See also* Property, and equipment (PP&E), plant

Fixed-percentage-of-declining balance depreciation method, 420*n*

Foreign currency: exchange rates in, 314*f,* 1028–1029; transactions involving, 311–315, 314*f*

Form 8-K, 14

Form 10-K, 14, 35, 80, 178–179, 190

Form 10-Q, 14, 35, 80, 190

Form S-1, 14

Franchises, 805–808

Freight, 286; FOB destination, 286–287, 287*d*; FOB (Free-on-Board)

shipping point, 286–287, 286*d*

Full-cost accounting methods, 396–398

G

GAAP. *See* Generally Accepted Accounting Principles (GAAP)

Gain(s), 45*d,* 110*d,* 884; cumulative net unrealized holding, 609, 609*n,* 610*n*; exchange, 311–315; holding, 298, 298*d,* 299*f*; on income statement, 104–105, 110–111; material extraordinary, 126–128, 128*f*; realized and unrealized, 608; results from discontinued operations and, 120–125, 120*d,* 120*n,* 121*f*

GASB. *See* Governmental Accounting Standards Board (GASB)

General Electric, 299

General Electric Capital Services (GECS), 251

General journal, C6–C8, C7*f*–C8*f,* C29

General ledger, C8–C11, C10*f*

General Mills, 309–310, 312*f,* 527*f*

General Motors Acceptance Corporation (GMAC), 251

General Motors Corporation, 75, 137, 299, 620, 620*f*–621*f,* 663*f*

Generally Accepted Accounting Principles (GAAP), 5*f,* 6*d*; accounting assumptions and conventions in, 38–43, 39*f*; on asset impairment, 431*n, 433*; auditor's report and, 176–177; for Comprehensive Income and Cash Flows, 142*f*–143*f*; financial statements and, 44–47, 44*f*; history of, 7–18, 7*f,* 8*f,* 18*f*; for investments in debt and equity securities, 607; SEC and, 14–15; sources of, 6–7, 8*f*; stock dividends, 738–741; *vs.* international standards, 16–17

Going-concern assumption, 38–40, 39*f*

Goods available for sale, 291

Goodwill: estimating the value of, 473–474, 473–479, 474*f,* 476*f*; impairment of, 469–470, 469*n*; internally developed, 468; purchased, 468

Governmental Accounting Standards Board (GASB), 6*n,* 17, 18*f*

Graded vesting, 678*n*

Greenmail, 697

Gross margin, 118

Gross price method: for cash discounts, 243–244, 244*f*; of inventory valuation, 289–290, 290*f*; trade accounts payable and, 501–502

Gross profit, 118; deferred, 246*n*; method, 342–344, 343*f,* 344*n*

Group-rate depreciation method, 425–427, 426*f*

H

Held-to-maturity debt securities, 605, 612–615, 613*f,* 614*f*

Hertz, 805

Hewlett-Packard Company, 310, 312*f*

Historical cost, 41, 60, 60*d*; transactional approach to, 104

Holding gain, 298, 298*d*, 299*f*
Holiday Inn, 805
Horizontal analysis, 192–193, 193*d*, 193*f*

I

IASC. *See* International Accounting Standards Committee (IASC)
Identifiable intangible assets, 457–458, 457*f*, 467, 473; computer software costs as, 465–466, 465*d*; copyrights as, 464–465, 464*d*, 464*n*; deferred charges and, 467; franchises as, 465, 465*d*; internal-use software and, 466; leases and leasehold improvements, 467, 467*d*; organization costs as, 467, 467*d*; patents as, 463–464, 463*d*, 464*f*; trademarks and tradenames as, 467, 467*d*
IMA. *See* Institute of Management Accountants (IMA)
Impairment: of assets, 430–433; of debt and equity securities, 617, 619; of goodwill, 469–470, 469*n*; of intangible assets, 458–460; of investments, 617, 619
Income. *See also* Comprehensive income; concepts of, 102–107; conceptual reporting guidelines for, 105–107, 118; continuing operations and, 116–118, 119*f*, 718; information, 103–104; operating, 115, 115*f*, 118; pretax financial, 116; taxable, 116, 831
Income measurement, 6; accrual accounting and, 31; cost flow assumptions in, 298
Income statement(s), 6, 44–45, C16–C17, C16*f*; alternative income captions on, 118–119; bad debts estimation and, 249; concepts of income and, 102–103; condensed, 113; content, 111–113, 112*f*; continuing operations' income and, 113–116, 114*f*; Cost of Goods Sold and, 113–114, 114*f*; cumulative effect on, 129, 129*d*; earnings per share, 130–131, 130*d*, 130*n*; elements of, 107–111; extraordinary item on, 125–128, 128*f*; income tax returns and, 830–831, 830*f*; multiple-step, 118; profit margin and, 131; raw materials on, 114, 115*n*; related issues of, 131–133; results from discontinued operations on, 120–125, 120*d*, 121*f*; single-step, 118, 119*f*; statement of retained earnings and, 133–135, 134*f*
Income tax(es): alternative credits and, 859–860; change in, 858–859; conceptual issues regarding, 834–836, 835*f*; continuing operations and, 116–118; disclosures, 861, 861*f*–862*f*; expense, 117–118, 831, 855*f*; financial reporting and, 16–17, 831; interim financial reports and, 186–187, 187*f*; international accounting differences on deferred, 860;

interperiod tax allocation and, 116–117, 116*d*, 832–844; intraperiod tax allocation, 117–118, 117*d*, 117*f*, 853–856; investment tax credit and, 859; objectives, 829–830; obligations, 831; payable, 511–512, 513*f*, 850*f*; reported net of, 120, 127; returns and income statement, 830–831, 830*f*
Income tax accounting, 16
Indirect guarantees, 522
Industry Accounting Guides, AICPA, 7*f*, 15
Industry Audit Guides, AICPA, 7*f*, 15
Initial franchise fees, 805–807
Installment method: defaults and repossessions with, 801; incidental sales with, 802; of revenue recognition, 42, 108–109; revenue recognition and, 797–800, 799*f*; revenue recognition and additional considerations for, 801–802
Institute of Management Accountants (IMA), 17–18, 18*f*
Intangible assets, 66*f*, 70, 457*d*; accounting for, 457–458; amortization or impairment of, 458–460; characteristics of, 457; conceptual accounting evaluation of, 471–473; costs of, 457–458, 457*f*; disclosures for, 470–471; international accounting differences with, 463, 473
Intercompany comparisons, in financial analysis, 191–192
Interest(s): capitalization during construction, 386–389, 387*d*, 388*f*, 795; coverage ratio, 201; debt and equity securities' recording of, 608; international accounting differences for capitalization of, 389; method, 549, 551–555, 554*f*; rate swap, 635; Revenue, 256*n*
Interim financial reports, 185*d*; contents of, 185; cumulative effects in, 188; discontinued operations in, 188; earnings per share in, 188; expenses in, 185–186; extraordinary items in, 188; income taxes in, 186–187, 187*f*; lower of cost or market (LCM) method and, 339; revenues in, 185; using LIFO, 309–310
Internal cash control systems, 234
Internal Revenue Code, 16, 18*f*; Form 1120, 512; income tax expense and, 116–117, 299, 829; Tax Reform Act of 1986, 299, 859–860
Internal Revenue Service, 16
Internal users, 3–4, 4*d*, 4*f*
International accounting differences: with asset impairment, 433; with bonds, 556; contingencies and, 524; on deferred income taxes, 860; in depreciation, 425; in Earnings per share (EPS), 731; on equity method, 631; on financial statements, 81–82; on income statements, 132–133; with intangible assets, 463, 473; on interest capitalization, 389; in inventories, 310; for investments and securities, 624; lower of cost or market (LCM)

method and, 341; in revenue recognition, 809; on segment and interim reporting, 190–191
International Accounting Standards Board (IASB), 16; disclosures on, 82–83; Framework for the Preparation and Presentation of Financial Statements, 47; on income statements, 132–133
International Accounting Standards Committee (IASC), 16; FASB and, 12–13
International Business Machines Corporation (IBM), 567, 568*f*–569*f*, 921
International Multifoods Corporation, 683*f*–684*f*
Interperiod income tax allocation, 116–118, 116*d*; allocation *vs.* nonallocation in, 863; alternative allocation methods in, 864–866; basic entries in, 839; comprehensive *vs.* partial allocation in, 863–864; conceptual issues concerning, 863–866; income taxes and, 832–838; recording and reporting steps in, 838–844
Interstate Commerce Commission, 428*n*
Intracompany comparisons, in financial analysis, 191
Intraperiod income tax allocation, 117–118, 117*d*, 117*f*; on income statement, 853–856, 855*f*, 856*f*
Intrinsic value method, 674, 682–683
Inventory(ies), 283*d*; alternative systems of, 285–286; classifications of, 283–285; depreciation systems and, 428; ending, 286; error effects on financial statements, 355–357; finished goods as, 284*f*, 285, 285*d*; foreign currency transactions involving, 311–315, 314*f*; goods in process as, 284–285, 284*d*, 284*f*; international accounting differences in, 310; merchandise as, 283; periodic system of, 113–114, 286, 286*d*; perpetual system, 113–114, 285–286, 285*d*; profit, 298, 298*d*, 299*f*; raw materials as, 283–284, 283*d*, 284*f*; of service companies, 285; summary issues of, 357, 357*f*; turnover, 199–200
Inventory cost(s), historical, 287–288, 287*d*. *See also* First–in, first–out (FIFO) cost flow assumptions; Average cost flow assumptions; Last–in, first–out (LIFO) cost flow assumptions; conceptual evaluation of, 289–290, 290*f*, 297–298; cost index determination in, 307; determination of, 284–290, 284*d*; disclosure of, 310, 311*f*, 312*f*, 313*f*; flow comparisons, 297; flow of, 284*f*; link-chain method in, 307; management's selection of, 302–303; manufacturing overhead costs in, 288–289, 288*d*; pools, 307–309, 308*f*; purchases discounts in, 289–290, 290*f*; standard costs in, 289, 289*d*; variable costing in, 289
Inventory cost(s), special valuation issues of: gross profit method and,

342–344, 343*f*, 344*n*; lower of cost or market (LCM) method and, 332–340; recording reduction of, 337–339, 337*f*, 339*f*; retail inventory method and, 344–355; valuation above cost of, 342, 342*f*

Investment(s): additional issues for, 631–634; in available-for-sale debt and equity trading securities, 607; classification of, 624; in debt and equity trading securities, 607; disclosures for securities, 620, 620*f*–621*f*; equity method for, 624–625; equity method's accounting procedures for, 625–628; fair value of, 623; financial statement disclosures for, 628; financial statements' classifications for, 63–65, 66*f*, 67–70; in funds, 633–634; impairments of, 617, 619; international accounting differences for, 624; long-term, 67–68; nonmarketable securities in, 631; reporting methods for, 606, 606*f*; return on, 32; securities as, 604; special issues in, 628–631, 629*f*; stock dividends and splits in, 631–632; stock warrants in, 631–632; tax credits, 859; temporary, 65; transfers of, 617–619; unrealized holding gains and losses in, 608–610, 609*n*, 624

J

Johnson & Johnson, 68*f*, 395*f*
Journals, C6–8, C8*f*–C9*f*; cash payments, C29; cash receipts, C29; general, C29; purchase, C27; sales, C27; special, C27–C30, C28*f*

K

Kimberly-Clark Corporation, 72*f*
Kohl's Corporation, 719

L

Land, 374–375
Last-in, first-out (LIFO) cost flow assumptions, 200, 291; additional considerations in, 309–310; conformity rule, 299; dollar-value, 303–305, 304*f*, 305*f*, 306*f*; income manipulation under, 301; income tax effects on, 299–301; inventory valuation in, 301–302; liquidation layers of, 300–301; management's selection of, 302–303; periodic inventory system in, 291, 295–297, 295*d*, 295*f*; perpetual inventory system in, 291, 295–297, 295*d*, 296*f*; retail inventory and, 346–350, 349*f*, 352–355, 353*f*, 354*f*
LCM. *See* Lower of cost or market (LCM) method
Lease(s), 375, 944*d*; accounting, 949–959, 973, 974–975, 974*f*; advantages, 944–946; bargain purchase option of, 947; capital, 949, 952–957; classification of

personal property and, 946–949, 948*f*; classifications of real property and, 976*f*, 977–978; criteria and classifications of, 950*f*; direct financing, 960, 962–970, 982–983; equipment and real estate in, 978–979; executory costs of, 947, 949–951; guaranteed/unguaranteed residual value of, 947, 958, 972–973, 982; inception of the, 947; initial direct costs of, 947; interest rate implicit in the, 947, 957*f*; international accounting differences for, 975; key terms for, 946, 947*f*; of land, 976–977; leveraged, 960, 981–982, 981*f*; manufacturer's or dealer's profit or loss on, 947; minimum payments receivable, 947; operating lease, 949, 959, 962, 982–983; property depreciation of, 953*f*; provision changes in, 982; real estate and, 975–976; sale leaseback issues of, 979, 979*n*; sales-type, 959, 970–972, 982–983; term, 947; unguaranteed residual value of, 947; unreimbursable cost of, 947

Leasehold improvements, 375; as identifiable intangible assets, 467, 467*d*
Legal capital, 73, 664–665
Lessee: accounting of, 949–959, 973, 974*f*, 979–981; bargain purchase option impact of, 957–958; capital lease by, 949, 952–957; capitalization issues of, 957–958; classification criteria by, 951*f*, 954; depreciation of leased property by, 953*f*; guaranteed residual value and, 958–959; lease agreement terms and provisions for, 952–955, 954*f*; lease payment summary of, 957*f*, 974*f*
Lessor: accounting for, 973, 974*f*, 979–981; direct financing leases of, 951*f*, 962–970, 967*f*; disclosure requirements of, 973, 973*f*; incremental borrowing rate and, 947; lease agreement and, 951*f*, 954*f*, 968*f*, 970*f*; lease payment summary of, 969*f*; leasing advantages of, 944–946; operating lease by, 948–949, 959–962, 960*f*; residual value and, 972–973; sales-type leases of, 970–972, 970*f*, 971*f*
Leverage, 544
Liabilities, 45*d*, 59–60, 498*d*. *See also* Contingent Liabilities; Current liabilities; accounting or nonlegal, 498; accrued, 505–508; characteristics of, 499; legal, 498; long-term, 70–71, 70*d*; obligations callable by creditor, 5–52, 625; reporting guidelines for, 71; short-term, 524–525
LIFO. *See* Last-in, first-out (LIFO) cost flow assumptions
Link-chain method, 307
Liquid assets, 66–67
Liquidity: bad debts and, 249; current liabilities and, 500, 500*d*; fair value and, 623; financial reporting and, 33, 138–139, 179; liquid assets and, 233–235, 251–252; ratios, 195,

198–199, 198*f*; working capital and, 66–67
Loan(s): commitment fees, 570; conceptual evaluation, 573–574; effective interest rate of, 572; impairment of, 571–574, 572*n*; as long-term liabilities, 570–574; origination fees, 570
Loan origination fees, 570
Long-term construction contracts. *See* Construction contracts, long-term
Long-term investments, 67–68
Long-term liabilities, 70–71, 70*d*; amortizing discounts and premiums bonds, 549–555, 551*f*, 554*f*; bond characteristics and, 545, 546*f*; bonds with equity characteristics as, 559–563; current liabilities and maturing portion of, 504; disclosure of, 567, 568*f*–569*f*; extinguishment of, 557–559; future developments for, 574–575; international accounting differences for, 556; loans as, 570–574; notes payable as, 563–564; notes receivables and, 567–575; reasons for issuance of, 544–545.; serial bonds as, 582–585, 584*f*, 585*f*; troubled debt restructuring and, 575–582, 577*f*
Long-term service contracts, 795, 795*n*
Loss(es), 45*d*, 110*d*, 884; exchange, 311–315; on income statement, 104–105, 110–111; material extraordinary, 126–128, 128*f*; on purchase commitments, 341–342; results from discontinued operations and, 120–125, 120*d*, 120*n*, 121*f*
Lower of cost or market (LCM) method, 332*d*; application of, 333–334, 334*f*; approaches to implementing, 336–337, 336i*f*; ceiling and floor evaluation of, 334–336; conceptual evaluation of, 340; interim financial statements and, 339; international accounting differences in, 341; in retail inventory, 346–350, 350*f*
Lump-sum purchase, 375–376

M

MACRS. *See* Modified Accelerated Cost Recovery System (MACRS)
Management: financial reporting and, 31; report, 177–178, 177*d*, 178*f*; selection of cost flow assumption, 302–303
Management's discussion and analysis (MD&A): contents of, 177, 178*f*; disclosure requirements of, 81; in financial analysis, 178–180
Managerial accounting, 5–6, 5*d*, 5*f*
Marathon Oil Company, 121, 121*f*, 309–310, 313*f*
Markdown, 346
Market: efficiency, 174–175; method; value, 332*d*, 333, 562, 632*n*
Markup, 346
Mastercard, 251, 254–255
Matching principle, in accrual accounting, 42–43

Materiality, of accounting information, 37–38, 39*f*

Maturity date, of bonds, 545, 550*n*

McDonald's, 465, 805

MD&A. *See* Management's discussion and analysis (MD&A)

Measurement: bias, 36; date, 674, 682; of fair value, 675–676

Medicare, 913

Merck & Co., Inc., 744*f*

Midas Muffler, 465

Modified Accelerated Cost Recovery System (MACRS), 434–436, 434*n*, 435*f*

Modified cash basis method, 517

Monetary unit, in financial statements, 41–42

N

Negative goodwill, 126

Net: assets, 57, 473; Cash Flow from Operating Activities, 139–140; markdown, 346; markup, 346; of-tax, 865

Net income: accrual-based transactional approach and, 104–105; components of, 105–106, 718; on income statement, 118–119, 119*f*; statement of retained earnings and, 134–135, 134*f*

Net price method: for cash discounts, 243–244, 244*f*; of inventory valuation, 289–290, 290*f*; trade accounts payable and, 501–502

Net realizable value (NRV), 61–62, 61*f*, 333

Net sales revenue, 113

Neutrality, in accounting information, 36

Nonmonetary exchange, 378, 378*n*

Nontrade receivables, 240

No-par stock, 73, 664–665

Norfolk Southern Corporation, 395*f*–396*f*

Normal profit (NP), 333

Not Sufficient Funds (NSF), 236, 236*d*

Notes payable: for cash and rights or privileges, 565; current liabilities and, 502–504, 503*n*; exchanged for property, goods and services, 566–567; issued for cash, 564–565, 564*n*; long-term, 563–564; straight-line method and, 563*n*

Notes receivables, 255, 255*d*, 567*d*; Discount on, 256*n*, 257–258, 257*d*; loan fees as, 570, 570*n*; long-term, 567–575; recording and reporting, 240–241; short-term interest-bearing, 256, 256*f*; short-term non-interest-bearing, 256–257, 256*f*

Notional, 635

O

Off-balance-sheet financing, 507–508

Offsetting amounts, 253*n*, 795

Operating capability, 33, 57, 105*d*, 138–139, 778

Operating cash flows, 46*d*, 64*f*

Operating cycle, 64–65, 64*f*; of current liabilities, 499–500

Operating income, 123

Operating loss carrybacks, 830–831, 844–845; comprehensive illustration of, 850–853, 850*f*, 851*f*; conceptual issues of, 845–846; GAAP and, 847–848, 848*f*

Operating loss carryforwards, 830–831, 844–845; comprehensive illustration of, 850–853, 850*f*, 851*f*, 852*f*; conceptual issues of, 846–847; GAAP and, 847–850

Operating segments, 180–183, 180*d*, 183*f*

Orange County, California, 635

Other Postemployment Benefits (OPEB), 913–914; accounting differences of, 917; accounting principles for, 915; attribution period of, 920, 920*f*; conceptual evaluation of, 918–922; deferred income taxes and, 921; expense components of, 915–917; FASB Statement No. 16 impact on, 921–922; funding differences of, 919; illustration of, 917–918; liability or asset, 917, 921; relevance and reliability of, 918–919; similarities and differences of, 914–915, 915*f*; transition liability of, 919–920, 920*f*

Ownership, absentee, 73

P

Paid-in capital. *See* Contributed capital

Par value, 73*n*, 545*d*; method, 695–696, 697*f*; stock, 73, 664

Partnerships, 73

Patents, 463–464, 463*d*, 464*f*

Payables turnover ratio, 199*f*, 200

Payroll: accounting for deductions and, 511; tax group, 509–510, 510*f*; voluntary group, 510–511, 510*f*

Pension(s): accounting aspects of, 910–913; assets, 888–889, 926; benefit formula, 884, 889; benefit/years-of-service approach to, 889, 896*f*; defined contribution plans in, 911; discount rates, 889; liabilities, 888–889, 908–909, 928; measurement methods for, 889; transition requirements of, 910; vested benefits of, 911; worksheet, 902–905, 905*f*

Pension Benefit Guaranty Corporation (PBGC), 912

Pension expense: components of, 885–888; deferred costs as, 888; Expected Return on Plan Assets of, 885; gain or loss of, 886, 898*f*; interest costs of, 885; service costs of, 885, 923–924; unrecognized prior service costs' amortization, 886, 897*f*, 926–928

Pension plan(s): accounting principles for benefit, 883; assets on balance sheet, 909–910; characteristics of, 881–882; defined benefit plan for, 881–882, 907–910, 922–928; defined contribution plan as, 881–882; disclosures of, 890, 901–902,

903*f*–904*f*; examples of accounting for, 890–905, 896*fi*; funding agencies' disclosures of, 911; historical perspective of, 882–883; international accounting differences of, 913; issues' summary related to, 905–907, 906*f*; key items related to, 884; multi-employer, 913; noncontributory, 882; prepaid/accrued pension cost of, 888; relationships, 883; settlements and curtailments in, 912; termination benefits and, 912; unfunded accumulated benefit obligations of, 888

Pension Reform Act of 1974, 881–882, 912. *See also* Employee Retirement Income Security Act of 1974 (ERISA)

PepsiCo's, 259, 259*fi*

Percentage analyses, 192–195, 193*f*, 194*f*, 195*f*

Percentage depletion, 438

Percentage-of-completion method, 42, 108–109, 786; accounting procedures in, 788; illustration of, 788, 788*f*, 789*f*, 790*f*; input measures in, 787; output measures in, 787

Period costs, 43

Periodic inventory system, 113–114; FIFO and, 293–294, 293*f*; last-in, first-out (LIFO) in, 291, 295–297, 295*d*, 295*f*; weighted average cost flow assumption in, 291, 294–294, 294*d*, 294*f*

Period-of-time assumption, 40

Permanent difference, 831–833, 832*f*

Perpetual inventory system, 113–114; FIFO and, 293–294, 293*f*; last-in, first-out (LIFO) in, 291, 295–297, 295*d*, 296*f*; moving average cost flow assumption in, 291, 294–294, 294*d*, 295*f*

Plant expansion funds, 634

PP&E. *See* Property, plant and equipment (PP&E)

Practice Bulletins, AICPA, 7*f*, 15

Preemptive right, 662

Preferred stock, 73–74, 663*d*; callable, 689–690; characteristics, 685–686; convertible, 687–688, 726–727; cumulative, 686; dividends, 686; liquidation preference of, 690–691; participating, 686–687; redeemable, 690, 690*d*; retained earnings and, 734–735; with stock warrants, 688–689; voting rights of, 691

Premium obligations, 517–518

Premium, of bonds, 547; amortizing, 549–555, 551*f*, 554*f*

Prepaid expenses, C11

Present value, 62, 564–565

Price: earnings ratio, 719; index, 307

Prior service cost, 884

Procter & Gamble, 635

Product: costs, 43; financing arrangements, 341–342

Product obligations, 515–517

Profit: margin, 131; Normal (NP), 333; test, 181

Projected Benefit Obligations, 884, 924–926

Property, plant, and equipment (PP&E), 372*d*; acquisition of, 373–378; assets' exchange to acquire, 378–379; on balance sheet, 68–70; characteristics of, 372–373; cost determination in acquiring, 373–375; costs subsequent to acquisition and, 391–393, 391*d*; deferred payments on, 376; disclosure of, 395–396, 395*f*–396*f*, 396*n*; disposal of, 393–394; dissimilar productive assets' exchange for, 379–380, 379*d*, 379*f*; historical cost basis for reporting, 373; issuance of securities for, 376–377; lump-sum purchase of, 375–376; oil and gas properties' appendix as, 396–398; retirement of, 394–395, 395*n*; self-construction and, 385–391, 388*f*; similar productive assets' exchange for, 380–385, 382*f*, 383*f*, 384*f*; start-up costs and, 377–378; summary of productive asset exchange for, 385; through donation, 377

Property taxes, 513–515, 514*n*

Proportional performance method of revenue recognition, 42, 108–109

Proxy Statement, 14

Prudence, 43

Purchases, 285–286; discounts on, 289–290, 290*f*; Net, 286; obligations, 341–342, 341*d*; Returns and Allowances, 286

Q

Quarterly report. *See Form 10-Q*

Quasi-reorganization, 749–751, 749*d*, 750*f*, 751*f*

Quick ratio, 198–199

R

Rate of return, in depreciation, 421–423, 423*f*

Ratio analysis: activity ratios in, 195, 199–200, 199*f*; cash flow ratios in, 195, 202–203, 202*f*; company profitability ratios in, 195–198, 197*f*; liquidity ratios in, 195, 198–199, 198*f*; stability ratios in, 195, 200–202, 201*f*; stockholder profitability ratios in, 195–196, 196*f*

Raw materials, 114, 115*n*

R&D. *See Research and Development (R&D)*

Realization, 42, 42*d*, 108*d*, 778

Receivables, 240*d*; current asset and, 64–65, 64*f*, 240; as noncurrent assets, 240; nontrade, 240; trade, 240, 242–24; turnover ratio, 200

Reclassification adjustment, 136*n*

Recognition, 42, 42*d*, 778; in the balance sheet, 58

Refinance, 524

Registrar, 662

Regulation S-K, 179

Regulation S-X, 14, 80, 189

Related party transactions, 79–80

Reportable segments, 181

Reporting techniques: balance sheet format and, 82; combined amounts in, 82–83; notes, schedules and notations as, 83; rounding in, 83

Research and development (R&D), 114–115, 114*n*; conceptual evaluation of accounting for, 462–463, 471; costs, 460–462, 461*f*

Reserve Recognition Accounting (RRA), 397

Reserve stock split, 671

Residual value: of assets, 416*d*; depletion and, 437–438

Retail inventory method, 344–346; additional adjustments in, 350–351; application of, 346–350, 347*f*, 348*f*, 349*f*, 350*f*; conceptual evaluation of, 351–352; dollar-value LIFO, 352–355, 353*f*, 354*f*; terminology, 346

Retained earnings, 74*d*, C2*d*, C3*f*; appropriations of, 742–743; cash dividends and, 733–735; conceptual issues of, 738; content of, 731; dividends and, 731–733, 734*f*; liquidating dividends and, 741; preferred stock, 734–735; prior period adjustments of, 741–742; property dividends and, 735–737; scrip dividends and, 737; statement of, 743–745, 743*n*, 744*f*, C17, C17*f*; stock dividends and, 737; stockholders' equity and, 74, 665

Retirement and replacement depreciation method, 425–428

Retirement benefits. *See Pension plans*

Return on investment, 32, 105*d*, 778

Return on total assets, 197

Revenue(s), 107*d*; deferred, 508; earned, 107–109, 108*d*; on income statement, 104–105, 107–109; interest, 256*n*; in interim financial reports, 185; test, 181

Revenue realization, 42

Revenue recognition, 42, 42*d*; accounts receivable financing agreements and, 251–252; additional issues of, 804–810; additional long-term construction contract considerations, 794–795; after period of sale of, 797–803; alternatives, 779–783, 779*f*, 781*f*, 784–785; conceptual issues of, 783–784; consignment sales and, 809–810; delayed until future event occurs, 804; earning process and, 107–109; franchises and, 805–808; international accounting differences in, 809; long-term construction contracts, 786–787, 791–794, 792*f*, 794*f*; lower of cost or market (LCM) method and, 340; real estate sales and, 808–809; retail land sales and, 809; right of return in, 241; sale of goods or services and, 290; software, 805; trade receivables and, 240–245

Revenue recognition methods: additional installment method considerations in, 801–802; cost recovery method of, 42, 516, 802–803; deposit method in, 804; installment

and, 42, 797–800, 799*f*; proportional performance and, 42; summary of alternative, 810–811, 811*f*

Right of offset, 81

Risk, 32–33, 32*f*, 105*d*, 778; evaluations of, 180; of financial instruments, 77–78

Rounding in, 83

S

Sale(s): of a component, 120–125, 120*d*, 122*f*; consignment, 809–810; credit card, 254–255; Discounts Allowance, 246*n*; of goods or services and, 290; gross profit or margin on, 118; real estate, 808–809; retail land, 809; Returns and Allowances, 244–245, 244*d*

Sales taxes, 508–509, 508*d*

Sales warranty accrual method, 515–516

Sam's Club, 254

Sara Company, 136–137

Schweppes, 473

Sears Roebuck Acceptance Corporation (SRAC), 251

Sears, Roebuck and Co., 719

SEC *Accounting Bulletins,* 14; *No. 101,* 810

SEC *Accounting Rules,* 14*n*, 179*n*, 690*n*

SEC *Accounting Series Releases,* 14*n*

SEC *Financial Reporting Releases,* 14, 14*n*, 189

SEC *Form 8-K,* 14

SEC *Form 10-K,* 14, 35, 80, 90, 178–179

SEC *Form 10-Q,* 14, 35, 80, 190

SEC *Form S-1,* 14

SEC *Proxy Statement,* 14

SEC. *See Securities and Exchange Commission (SEC)*

SEC *Staff Accounting Bulletin No. 101,* 109, 109*n*

Secret reserves, 670

Securities: additional issues for, 631–634; available-for-sale, 605, 611–612; classification of, 624; fair value of, 623; held-to-maturity debt, 605, 612–615, 613*f*, 614*f*; impairments of, 617, 619; international accounting differences for, 624; as investments, 604; nonmarketable, 631; portfolio of marketable, 604; stock dividends and splits in, 631–632; stock warrants in, 631–632; trading, 605; transfers of, 617–619; unrealized gains and losses, 608–610, 609*n*, 624

Securities and Exchange Commission (SEC), 189–190; auditing standards of, 15; on compensating balances, 239–240; financial analysis and, 179–190; integrated disclosures, 80–81; on LIFO, 299; MD&A disclosure guidelines of, 179–180; redeemable preferred stock requirement of, 690; reporting requirements of, 14; Reserve Recognition

Accounting (RRA), 397; *vs.* other sources of, 6–7, 7*f*, 18, 18*f*
Securities Exchange Act of 1933, 14, 189
Securities Exchange Act of 1934, 14, 189
Segment reporting, 180–183, 183*f*
Self-construction: fixed overhead costs during, 389–390, 390*d*; income on, 391; interest during, 385–389
Selling prices, 545–547
Sensitivity analysis, 478, 478*d*
Serial bonds, 582–585, 584*f*, 585*f*
Service cost, 884
Service period, 674
Shareholders' interests. *See* Stockholders' equity
Sick pay, 505–507
Significant influence, 604*n*
Sinking funds, 634
Sinking-fund depreciation method, 425*n*
Software revenue recognition, 805
Sole proprietorship, 73
Stability ratios, 195, 200–202, 201*f*
Statement of cash flows, 6, 44–46, 44*f*, 102, C5; cash dividends declared on, 1027; Cash Flows from Financing Activities, 140; conceptual overview and uses of, 138–139, 1000–1001; depreciable assets' sale and, 1022–1024; exchange rates' effects on, 1028–1029; financing activities and, 1002, 1025–1026; format, 1002; illustration of, 1002–1004; income taxes paid and, 1024; interest paid and, 1024; international accounting differences and, 1029; interrelationship to other statements and, 56*f*, 138; investing activities and, 1001; Net Cash Flow from Operating Activities, 139–140; operating activities and, 1001; partial cash investing, 1025–1026; preparation procedures of, 1012, 1033–1039; reporting guidelines and practices on, 139–142, 140*n*, 141*f*, 1001–1002; temporary and long-term investments on, 1026–1027; visual inspection method and, 1012–1015, 1012*f*, 1013*f*, 1014*f*, 1033–1035; worksheet method and, 1015–1022, 1016*f*, 1017*f*, 1018*f*–1019*f*, 1035–1039, 1036*f*–1037*f*, 1038*f*
Statement of comprehensive income, 6*n.* *See also* Comprehensive income; income statement and, 135–137
Statement of earnings, 102. *See also* Income statements
Statement of financial position, 6, 44, 44*f*. *See also* Balance sheets
Statement of income. *See* Income statements
Statement of operations, 102
Statement of retained earnings, 102, 133–35, 134*f*. *See also* Income statements
Statutory depletion, 438
Stauffer Chemical Company, 309
Stock(s): appreciation rights (SAR), 680–682, 681*f*; certificate, 662;

combined sales of, 669–670; dividends or splits, 721, 721*f*; issuance costs, 667; noncompensatory option plan and, 672–673; nonmonetary issuance of stock, 670; purchase plans, 672; redemption funds, 634; rights, 559–560; rights to stockholders, 671–672; splits, 671; subscribers subsidiary, 668; subscriptions and defaults, 667–669; transfer journal, 662; watered, 670
Stock option plans, 672, 676*n*, 724–726; compensatory, 682–683, 683*f*–684*f*, 685; fixed, 677–679, 678*f*; performance-based, 679–680, 680*f*; recognition of, 676–682, 676*n*
Stock warrants, 671–672, 724–726; bonds and, 559–560; in investments, 631–632; preferred stock with, 688–689; in securities, 631–632
Stockholder(s), 661; ledger, 662; legal capital concept and, 664–665; profitability ratios, 195–196, 196*f*; rights and capital stock, 662–663
Stockholders' equity: balance sheet and, 60, 63, 67*f*, 73–75; contributed capital and, 73; disclosure of, 75–76, 76*f*; retained earnings and, 74, 665; return on, 131, 197–198; statement of changes in, 6, 44–46, 75–76, 76*f*, 745–746, 747*f*, 748*f*
Straight-line method: for amortizing bond discounts and premiums, 549–551, 551*f*, 613–615, 615*f*; of depreciation, 418, 419*f*; notes payable and, 563*n*
Subsidiary ledgers, C26, C26*f*
Substantial performance, 805–806
Successful-efforts accounting methods, 396–398
Sum-of-the-years'-digits depreciation method, 418–420, 419*f*

T

Tax credit, 117–118; investment, 859; other, 859–860
Taxable loss. *See* Operating loss carrybacks; Operating loss carryforwards
Taxable temporary difference, 831
Temporary differences, 831, 833, 833*n*, 834*f*
Texas Instruments, 921–922
Time-based depreciation method, 418–420, 418*d*
Times interest earned ratios, 201, 201*f*
Timing differences. *See* Temporary differences
Trade accounts payable, 501–502
Trade discounts, 243–244, 243*n*, 290*d*
Trade receivables: normal revenue recognition and, 240–241; right of return in, 241; valuation of, 241–242
Trademarks and tradenames, 467, 467*d*
Trading on the equity, 544
Trading securities, 605
Transactional approach, 104*d*, 105; comprehensive income and, 104

Transfer agent, 663
Travel advances, 233
Treasury stock, 663, 725–726; conceptual overview of, 699; corporations and, 692–694, 697; cost method and, 694–695, 695*n*, 697*f*; donated, 698; par value method and, 695–696, 697*f*; retirement of, 698–699
Trevor Corporation, 140–141, 141*f*
Trial balance, C9–C11, C9*d*, C15*f*

U

Uncollectible accounts. *See* Bad debts
Unearned items, 508
Unidentifiable intangible assets, 457–458, 457*f*, 467; impairment of goodwill as, 469–470, 469*n*; internally developed goodwill as, 468; negative goodwill and, 470; purchased goodwill as, 468; recording of acquisition as, 468–469
Uniform capitalization rules, 299
United Kingdom, 473
Universal, 522
Use tax, 508–509, 508*d*

V

Valuation(s), 62; Allowance, 309, 831; of assets, 61–62, 61*f*; on balance sheet, 62; conservatism in, 43; methods for balance sheet, 61–63; of trade receivables, 241–242; of uncollectible accounts receivables, 245–250
Vertical analysis, 194–195, 194*f*, 195*f*
Vested Benefit Obligations, 884
Vested rights, 505
Visa, 251, 254–255
Voluntary payroll deduction group, 510–511, 510*f*
Voucher system, C30

W

Wall Street Journal The, 174
Wal-Mart Stores, 40, 309–310, 312*f*, 961*f*
Warranties. *See* Product warranties
Wheat Committee, 9
Whirlpool Corporation, 131, 132*f*, 523*f*
Working capital ratio, 66–67
Worksheet, C22–C26, C24*f*–C25*f*

Y

Years-of-future-service method, unrecognized prior service costs, 884, 895–897, 896*f*, 897*f*
Yield, of bonds, 546–547, 546*n*
Yum! Brands, 902, 903*f*–904*f*

Z

Zero coupon bonds, 556